CONCISE DICTIONARY OF AMERICAN HISTORY

CONCISE DICTIONARY OF AMERICAN HISTORY

CHARLES SCRIBNER'S SONS / *NEW YORK*

Library of Congress Cataloging in Publication Data

Dictionary of American history.
Concise dictionary of American history.

"An abridgement of the eight-volume Dictionary of American history, published in 1976"—Foreword.
1. United States—History—Dictionaries. I. Title.
E174.D522 1983 973'.03'21 82–42731
ISBN 0–684–17321–2

This book published simultaneously in the United States of America and in Canada - Copyright under the Berne Convention.

1 3 5 7 9 11 13 15 17 19 V/C 20 18 16 14 12 10 8 6 4 2

PRINTED IN THE UNITED STATES OF AMERICA

The paper in this book meets the guidelines for permanence and durability of the Committee on Production Guidelines for Book Longevity of the Council on Library Resources.

Foreword

The *Concise Dictionary of American History* presents in one volume an abridgment of the eight-volume *Dictionary of American History,* published in 1976 and itself a revision of the *Dictionary of American History* begun by James Truslow Adams in 1936. The goal of the multi-volume *Dictionary of American History* is to present in one readily available source scholarly accounts of all the major movements and ideas in American history. The intention of the *Concise Dictionary of American History* is to make accessible as much of this information as possible within the confines of a single volume.

Arranged in alphabetical order, the *Concise Dictionary of American History* contains condensed versions of the over six thousand articles found in the parent set—battles, terms, acts of Congress, Supreme Court decisions, and all of the events that have played an important part in the development of the United States. Each entry provides the essential information on the topic, including dates and a basic description of the event or concept. Topical entries give brief overviews of such aspects of American life as banking, immigration, labor, literature, medicine, painting, philosophy, and religion. As in the 1976 edition, major entries have been devoted to American Indian cultures and Afro-Americans. Entries are also devoted to scientific and technological developments. Complete renderings of the Declaration of Independence and the Constitution, as well as a complete list of presidents and vice-presidents, are provided. New topics and additional information have been added as necessary to bring the work up to date.

This new edition of the *Concise Dictionary of American History* is designed above all to give the reader quick access to all of American history in one convenient volume. Librarians, students, and the layman will find this work indispensable as a source of ready reference. In preparing the *Concise Dictionary of American History,* every effort has been made to maintain the high standards established by the parent *Dictionary of American History.*

—DAVID WILLIAM VOORHEES

CONCISE DICTIONARY OF AMERICAN HISTORY

CONCISE DICTIONARY OF AMERICAN HISTORY

AACHEN (1944). First major German city to fall to American troops in World War II. The American First Army crossed the German frontier near Aachen on Sept. 11. The U.S. XIX Corps and VII Corps circled the city on Oct. 16, and the Germans surrendered on Oct. 21.

ABC CONFERENCE (Niagara Falls, May 18–July 2, 1914). Argentina, Brazil, and Chile tendered mediation to prevent a conflict between the United States and Mexico (*see* Veracruz Incident). The conference failed when Venustiano Carranza rejected the proposal for a provisional government.

ABILENE (Kans.). Settled in 1858, it was selected by Joseph G. McCoy (1867) as a depot to which Texas cattle might be driven for shipment by rail to Kansas City (*see* Abilene Trail; Chisholm Trail). Boyhood home of Dwight D. Eisenhower, it is the site of the Eisenhower Museum (1954). A major cattle, grain, and dairy center, the 1980 population was 6,572.

ABILENE TRAIL. A cattle trail from Texas to Abilene, Kans. Its exact route is disputed, but it crossed the Red River a little east of Henrietta, Tex., and continued north across Indian Territory to Caldwell, Kans., and on to Abilene. The first herds were driven over it in 1866.

AB-INITIO MOVEMENT. A controversy during Reconstruction in Texas (1866) over the question, Was secession null and void from the beginning *(ab initio)* or as a result of the Civil War? The anti-Ab-Initios emerged victorious.

***ABLEMAN* V. *BOOTH*,** 21 Howard 506 (1859). Sherman Booth, sentenced to jail for assisting in the rescue of a fugitive slave at Milwaukee, was released on a writ of habeas corpus issued by the Wisconsin Supreme Court on the ground that the Fugitive Slave Act was unconstitutional. The U.S. Supreme Court rendered a unanimous opinion pronouncing the act valid and forbidding a state to interfere with federal prisoners by habeas corpus writs.

ABNAKI (from *Wabnaki,* "those of the sunrise"). A tribe of Algonkin-speaking Indians resident in western and central Maine. A population of 3,000 is estimated for 1600. Hunting was the primary basis of subsistence. The localized patrilineal family was identified with a specific hunting area that it owned and guarded, and social units were thus made up of kindred people identified with a particular region. Birch bark canoes; wigwams and bark-covered houses; birch bark containers; snowshoes of rawhide; and a variety of traps and snares characterized the culture. Missionized by the French in the 18th century, the Abnaki identified with French interests. They were unsuccessful in hindering British expansion in 1724–25, and severe defeats (*see* Norridgewock Fight) forced their movement to the St. Francis River, in Quebec. They are best known through a dictionary compiled by the missionary Sebastian Rasles.

ABOLITION. *See* **Antislavery.**

ABOMINATIONS, TARIFF OF. *See* **Tariff.**

A. B. PLOT. William H. Crawford, secretary of the treasury, employed western banks to collect public land revenues in fluctuating banknote currencies; this justifiable policy resulted in losses to the government. In 1823 the *Washington Republican* published a series of articles, signed "A. B.," attacking Crawford for malfeasance. These articles were written by Sen. Ninian Edwards (Ill.), who brought formal charges against Crawford, perhaps to damage him in the 1824 presidential campaign. The committee report exonerated Crawford but severely damaged Edwards.

ABRAHAM, PLAINS OF. On the west side of the city of Quebec; named after Abraham Martin, a pilot, who once owned part of the land. The scene of the 1759 battle (*see* Quebec, Capture of) that brought an end to the French empire in North America.

ABRAHAM LINCOLN, FORT (N.Dak.). Built by Gen. George A. Custer (1873) on the Missouri River, just below Heart River; abandoned in 1895. Fort McKean, an infantry post on a hill above this fort, was usually considered part of Fort Abraham Lincoln.

ABSENTEE OWNERSHIP. A situation in which the actual ownership of an asset is divorced from day-to-day management and control; historically, the asset consisted of land, but in modern times it may also include urban rental dwellings and mineral lands. Absentee property owners typically employ real estate or rental agencies to supervise their property.

ACADEMIC FREEDOM. A group of rights claimed by teachers: to study, to communicate ideas, and to publish the results of reflection and research without external restraints; usually asserted in terms of the individual teacher's freedom from interference with the free play of the intellect. Academic freedom is well established in the jurisprudence of the U.S. Supreme Court. The first case in which the Court ruled that academic freedom is protected by the due process clauses of the Constitution was in 1957. In 1967, the Court held invalid a statute requiring the dismissal of "subversive" professors.

ACADEMIES. A type of secondary school popular 1750–1850, it was largely displaced by the public high school. Many academies were denominational and most were private, although some states undertook to provide for county systems of academies. Tuition fees were usually charged, but occasionally the legislature would charter an academy or grant it other privileges with the provision that poor children should be taught free. By 1830 there were 1,000 such institutions and by 1850 about 6,000, instructing more than 260,000 pupils. The academies stimulated interest in the training of teachers and may be considered the forerunners of the normal schools; they served also to encourage the education of girls and women. Variants of the academy are vocational and military schools.

ACADIA. A former French colony in Canada (now Nova Scotia). The name (of European origin or a derivative of the Indian word *aquoddiake*) was first applied in letters-patent to the grant obtained by Pierre de Guast in 1603. The boundaries roughly embraced the North American coast from Cape Breton to below the Hudson River and overlapped considerably the land claimed by England, which resulted in a hundred and fifty years of warfare, during which Acadia was traded back and forth between the two powers.

The Treaty of Utrecht (1713) ceded "all Nova Scotia with its ancient boundaries" to England. The French tacitly narrowed the indefinite limits of Nova Scotia to what is now the peninsula bearing that name. England came to view the French inhabitants of the peninsula, the Acadians, with alarm, and starting in 1755, over 4,000 of these Acadians were deported to other English colonies.

ACADIANS. Acadians came in directly from Nova Scotia to Louisiana (1755–76) by ship, by land, or by flatboat. They were settled in what is now Saint James parish (the Acadian Coast), upriver as far as Pointe Coupée, and westward 70 to 100 miles from New Orleans. They founded the town of Saint Martinville, which has remained the center of Acadian life in Louisiana, and spread westward into the parish named for them, Acadia, and the surrounding territory. They and their descendants (called "Cajuns") have been largely farmers. French, the language of the Acadians, has given way to English as the first language.

ACKIA, BATTLE OF (May 26, 1736). The Chickasaw, with aid from British traders, decisively defeated the French at Ackia, near present Tupelo, Miss. This defeat reduced French prestige in the contest between French and English traders for control of Indian trade. (*See also* Chickasaw-French War.)

ACOMA (N.Mex.). One of seven Keresan-speaking towns in the center of the present-day Pueblo area. It is located on a rock mesa 357 feet in height, about sixty miles west of the Rio Grande. Intensive maize cultivation, a ritual calendar, and priestly cults reflect the retention of a pre-Columbian cultural system.

Acoma was visited by Spanish explorers and subjected to Franciscan missionization. In December 1598 the Indians killed fifteen Spaniards. The following month a spanish force of seventy scaled the mesa and killed nearly 1,500 Acoma. The Acoma also participated in the Pueblo Revolt of 1680.

ACRE RIGHT. *See* **Cabin Rights.**

ACT FOR THE IMPARTIAL ADMINISTRATION OF JUSTICE (May 1774, one of the Coercion Acts). This act provided that whenever the governor of Massachusetts doubted whether a person accused of misconduct in suppressing a riot or executing the law could secure a fair trial in Massachusetts, he might, with consent of the council, transfer the trial to another colony or to Great Britain. Known in America as the "Murder Act."

ACTION. A federal agency created by executive order on July 1, 1971, to help solve social and economic problems at home and abroad through the cooperative efforts of a number of different volunteer programs. It originally included six volunteer programs formerly administered by several federal agencies: Peace Corps, Volunteers in Service to America (VISTA), Foster Grandparent Program, Retired Senior Volunteer Program (RSVP), Service Corps of Retired Executives (SCORE), and Active Corps of Executives (ACE). By 1974 ACTION had developed three additional programs—the Senior Companion Program, University Year for ACTION (UYA), and ACTION Cooperative Volunteers (ACV).

***ACTIVE* CASE** *(Olmstead et al.* v. *Rittenhouse's Executives).* Gideon Olmstead of Connecticut and others seized the British sloop *Active* (1777), which was later captured by the Pennsylvania armed brig *Convention.* Award of prize money to the *Convention* crew by state courts of Pennsylvania was set aside by the Supreme Court (1809) after a bitter dispute regarding jurisdiction.

ACTS OF TRADE. *See* **Navigation Acts.**

ADAIR V. UNITED STATES, 208 U.S. 161 (1908). In violation of a federal law of 1898, William Adair, acting for the Louisville & Nashville Railroad, dismissed O. B. Coppage because he was a member of a labor union. The Supreme Court declared this law unconstitutional because it violated the due process clause of the Fifth Amendment.

ADAMS, FORT (Miss.). Built 1798–99 eight miles above the thirty-first parallel on the east bank of the Mississippi River for boundary defense against the Spanish. It was the U.S. port of entry on the Mississippi. After acquisition of Louisiana and Florida, Fort Adams was abandoned.

ADAMS EXPRESS COMPANY. In 1839 Alvin Adams began carrying letters, small packages, and valuables for patrons between Boston and Worcester. Adams and Company extended its territory to other eastern cities, the South, and, by 1850 to Saint Louis. In 1854 it was reorganized as the Adams Express Company, having merged with several rival firms. A subsidiary concern, Adams and Company of California, organized in 1850, failed in 1854. The Civil War necessitated the splitting off of another company, the Southern. With other expresses, in 1918 Adams merged its shipping interests into the American Railway Express Company, but continued its corporate existence as an investment trust.

ADAMSON ACT (Sept. 2, 1916). Enacted under administration pressure backed by a strike threat, it established an eight-hour day in place of a ten-hour day for trainmen. The railroads claimed the law raised wages rather than regulated hours, as normal operation required over eight hours' work. The law was upheld, in *Wilson* v. *New,* 243 U.S. 332 (1917), as hour legislation in the interests of interstate commerce.

ADAMS-ONÍS TREATY (Feb. 22, 1819). Signed at Washington by John Quincy Adams, secretary of state, and Luis de Onís, Spanish minister. It provided for the cession of East Florida, the abandonment of the controversy over West Florida, and a boundary delineation to the Pacific Ocean. The United States assumed claims of its own citizens against Spain. Ratifications were exchanged at Washington on Feb. 22, 1821.

"ADDRESS OF THE SOUTHERN DELEGATES." Southern delegates in Congress, aroused by hostile resolutions on slavery, called a caucus for Dec. 23, 1848. John C. Calhoun submitted an address calculated to unite the South. It was adopted, but fewer than half the southern delegates signed it. (*See also* Tarpley Letter.)

***ADDYSTON PIPE COMPANY* CASE,** 175 U.S. 211 (1899). The Supreme Court, by a unanimous decision based on the Sherman Antitrust Act, permanently enjoined six producers of cast-iron pipe from continuing an agreement eliminating competition among themselves.

ADENA. First of a series of Early and Middle Woodland cultures in eastern North America. Dating from about 1000 B.C. to A.D. 200, Adena sites are mainly in the central Ohio valley within 150 miles of Chillicothe, Ohio. The culture is characterized by ceremonial centers with conical earthen burial mounds and large earthworks, with occasional wooden palisades and round houses 20 to 80 feet in diameter. The Adena people lived in hamlets nearby. Among the more unusual artifacts are bowls made from human crania, rectangular stone tablets engraved with zoomorphic figures, stone chest ornaments in a variety of geometric shapes, shell beads, tubular pipes, and stone atlatl weights. Woodland cord-marked pottery and some southern check-stamped wares were used as containers. Pumpkin, gourd, sunflower, corn, and goosefoot may have been domesticated. The basic subsistence pattern seems to have continued the broadly exploitive collecting emphasis characteristic of the Archaic. It seems likely that the roots of the Adena florescence were an increased sedentism, population growth, and other indigenous Eastern Woodland processes. The Middle Woodland Hopewell cultures were in part a later elaboration of classic Adena.

ADKINS* V. *CHILDREN'S HOSPITAL, 261 U.S. 525 (1923). A Supreme Court decision holding invalid an act of Congress that created a minimum wage board for women employees in the District of Columbia. The Court held by a vote of five to three that the act was an unjustified interference by Congress with the freedom of employer and employee to contract as they pleased. (*See also West Coast Hotel Company* v. *Parrish.*)

ADMINISTRATIVE DISCRETION, DELEGATION OF. The U.S. Constitution was a deliberate attempt to limit the use and abuse of executive discretion in government by a formal differentiation and separation of governmental functions. Delegations of discretionary powers to the president or subordinate executive officers have occurred so frequently as to be commonplace. Discretionary powers pervade the executive branch. A great acceleration in delegation of powers to specialized administrative agencies has been the response of all levels of government.

The hallmark of delegation of administrative powers, particularly in the regulatory agencies, has been the merging of governmental functions ostensibly separated constitutionally. Thus, discretion is conferred not only in executive powers (investigation, supervision, prosecution), but also in the legislative (rulemaking) and judicial spheres. Criticism of this merger led Congress in the Administrative Procedure Act of 1946 to require separate performance of adjudicatory functions by special personnel.

Substantial constitutional limitations on discretion exist, especially the requirement of due process of law. For delegations to be effective, Congress must by statute provide standards for the exercise of the delegated power. Substantive legislation establishing agencies frequently contains specific limitations on the scope of their authority, and specific procedural requirements for its exercise. Agency acts, as well as adjudication, are subject to judicial review within limits.

ADMINISTRATIVE JUSTICE (or administrative adjudication). The exercise by an administrative agency of judicial powers delegated to the agency by a legislative body. Agencies that have these judicial powers are often termed "administrative tribunals"; this usage derives from the separation of powers in the Constitution and from the limitation therein of the judicial power of the United States to certain types of cases and controversies.

Administrative tribunals ordinarily deal with individuals in relation to government, in terms of benefits sought or disabilities incurred from government action. In contrast to the criminal courts, most administrative tribunals are empowered to assess various penalties, such as forfeiture of licenses, for violation of statutory or administrative regulation. The subject matter of administrative regulation and adjudication by an agency is normally a single economic activity, a set of closely related economic activities, or specific benefits conferred by government. The concern of the National Labor Relations Board with labor relations is an example of the first; the jurisdiction of the Federal Communications Commission over radio, television, and telephone, of the second; and adjudication of the validity of claims to benefits by such agencies as the Veterans Administration, of the third.

Administrative regulation and adjudication has become widespread in the states and municipalities, embracing such subjects as public utilities, natural resources, banking, securities, workmen's compensation, insurance, employment discrimination, rents, automobile operation and inspection, corporations, elections, welfare, land use, and environmental and consumer protection. Some states have administrative procedure acts comparable to the federal act of 1946, but their judicial review is characteristically broader.

ADMINISTRATIVE OFFICE OF U.S. COURTS. *See* **Federal Agencies.**

ADMINISTRATIVE PROCEDURE ACT OF 1946. Applicable to most U.S. administrative tribunals, the act imposes uniform procedural requirements on the agencies, and requires the judicial function to be separated from the legislative and executive aspects. The act specifies requirements as to notice and hearing for covered agencies. It provides that decision must be made upon a record established in the hearing, and that an initial decision be made by the officer who hears the evidence. The initial decision is frequently subject to appeal to intraagency boards or to the highest administrative authority of the agency. The act provides for a broad right of review of agency adjudication by the courts.

ADMIRALS AND COMMODORES. Prior to the Civil War the highest naval rank was that of captain, equal to an army colonel. On July 16, 1862, Congress established the ranks of rear admiral (two-star flag and insignia) and commodore (one star). In 1864 David Farragut was made the first vice admiral (three stars) and, a year later, the first "full" admiral (four stars). In 1899 George Dewey was given the four-star rank Admiral of the Navy. The eighteen rear admirals he headed displaced the need for commodores, and the grade was abolished in 1912.

The navy entered World War I with thirty rear admirals. Three billets had the temporary rank of admiral—Chief of Naval Operations, or CNO; Commander-in-Chief, Atlantic Fleet; and Commander of Naval Forces Operating in European Waters. After the war the temporary admiral rank continued with the billets of CNO or fleet command, and vice admiral for seconds-in-command. World War II opened the purse for permanent higher ranks and even created the five-star rank of fleet admiral for the remaining lifetimes of Ernest J. King, Chester W. Nimitz, William D. Leahy, and William F. Halsey. Commodore was reinstituted for command of wartime convoys. The Korean War had some 200 line and 60 staff admirals, and in 1972, the navy had 9 four-star, 40 three-star, and 313 two-star admirals. There was some newspaper criticism that 362 flag officers were too many, and in 1973 a 10 percent reduction took place.

ADMIRALTY LAW AND COURTS. Admiralty law governs traffic by water. In America its sources were British admiralty law, the less restricted colonial vice-admiralty jurisdiction of the crown, and the broad and ancient European maritime legal traditions. Most American colonial admiralty tribunals enjoyed a jurisdiction less restricted than in England. Immediately following American independence, most admiralty concerns were placed under state authority; the Articles of Confederation did provide for courts governing piracy, sea felonies, and prize, but national jurisdiction was implemented only in prize cases.

Under the Constitution, federal authority "extends to all cases of admiralty and maritime jurisdiction" (including inland waterways), and the district courts have original jurisdiction by law. Admiralty jurisdiction includes insurance, bills of lading, charters, general average, seamen's rights, collision, salvage, maritime liens, ships' mortgages, liability limitations, piracy, and the laws of sea warfare.

ADMISSION OF STATES. *See* **State-making Process.**

ADOBE. A type of construction introduced by the Spanish into the Southwest in the 16th century. Wet clay and chopped hay or other fibrous material are mixed and molded into bricks and sun-dried or molded directly into the wall.

ADOBE WALLS, BATTLE OF (June 27, 1874). In retaliation against hunters who were killing buffalo, Comanche, Cheyenne, and Kiowa Indians attacked Adobe Walls, a trading post on the north side of the Canadian River in the Texas Panhandle.

ADVENTIST CHURCHES. The adventist movement was a response to the prophecies of William Miller in the 1830's that maintained the Second Coming of Christ would occur in 1843. After the failure of his predictions his disciples, known also as Millerites, divided over such issues as the name of the denomination, the dating of the end, and whether Saturday or Sunday should be observed as the day of rest. The two largest Adventist groups are the Advent Christian Church and the Seventh-Day Adventists.

The Advent Christian Church, organized in 1860 by Jonathan Cummings, holds that the soul sleeps until the end of the age, when it is reunited with the body for the Last Judgment. The church had 31,324 members in 1980. The Seventh-Day Adventists were organized in 1863. They adopted the seventh-day pattern of worship after a study of the Decalogue and in deference to Mrs. Rachael D. Preston, a former Seventh-Day Baptist. They believe that the Scriptures are an infallible guide to faith, and they abstain from tobacco, liquor, and sometimes tea and coffee. Each member is expected to contribute a full tithe to the work of the church. The group had 556,567 members in 1980. Other adventist denominations are the Church of God (Abrahamic Faith) with 8,000 members and the Primitive Advent Christian Church with 550 members in 1980.

***ADVENTURE*.** Built in the winter of 1791–92, in British Columbia, it was the first American sailing vessel built on the Pacific coast.

ADVENTURERS. A term sometimes applied to English merchants who supplied the capital for colonization in the New World (*see also* Trading Companies; Virginia Company of London).

ADVERTISING. Before 1700, signboards constituted the only advertising medium. The *Boston News-Letter* contained in its third issue (1704) the first advertisements, an offer for the sale of real estate and two notices of lost articles. Benjamin Franklin's *Pennsylvania Gazette* (1728) introduced the use of 14-point headings; the separation of advertisements with space; and, after 1750, the use of small woodcut illustrations. Amusement notices and "wanted" advertisements were featured first in separate sections in the 1830's by the *New York Sun,* which also started the practice of printing marriage and death announcements for revenue.

The Revolution provoked a severe paper shortage, which continued until about 1830. The necessity of conserving space led to the use of single-column agate advertisements, which remained the standard until the 1860's, when large display advertisements began to appear. P. T. Barnum's promotional successes were largely responsible for a sizable increase in outdoor advertising in the form of posters and handbills. The mail-order catalog was introduced in 1870 by E. C. Allen of Augusta, Maine, a manufacturer of a washing powder recipe.

In the 1830's the *New York Herald* initiated the modern line rate—establishing a minimum advertising unit and rates. Advertising agents, who appeared before 1850, negotiated with newspapers for space, and then sold the space to advertisers at a profit, thus acting in effect as rate makers.

Manufacturers sought to create widespread consumer demand through national advertising, obliging retailers to order goods from wholesalers rather than deal with jobbers. George Eastman spent $25,000 to advertise the Kodak in 1888. The Royal Baking Powder Company expended $500,000 for advertising in 1893 alone.

Montgomery Ward's first mail-order catalog was issued in 1874. Carleton and Kissam of New York City was the agency leader in systematic streetcar advertising, and by 1905 it controlled this medium in fifty-four cities. Outdoor advertising also prospered, the increased number of billboards paralleling the growth of automobile use.

Reliable systems for checking circulation were established; a complete modification of the role of the advertising agency occurred; more attention was paid to the design and message of advertisements; and critical appraisal of the advertised products and advertising practices began. To gain a more professional status a few agencies, notably N. W. Ayer and Son of Philadelphia, about 1880 began to offer advertisers an "open contract," in which the advertiser contracted to allow the agent to handle his entire advertising budget for an unspecified period of time. On his part the agent agreed to purchase the most valuable space in the advertiser's behalf, invoicing him for his cost plus a certain percentage as a commission. The cost-plus-commission basis for the agency was accepted industrywide in 1919, and the commission was standardized at 15 percent. In order to justify the commission and to retain the loyalty of the client, the agent began to perform services that had previously been the responsibility of the advertiser. One of the first was the coining of slogans and brand names. Ivory soap's slogan "99 44/100ths percent pure" appeared in 1885; Prudential's "Rock of Gibraltar" originated in 1896; and N. W. Ayer and Son suggested the brand name "Uneeda" to the National Biscuit Company in 1900. In 1905 federal legislation provided for the registration of trademarks for a period of twenty years with provision for renewal.

Beginning in 1888, *Printer's Ink* undertook to train readers on the design of advertisements, besides disseminating information on every phase of the profession. About 1900, psychologists entered the field and convinced the industry that there was great value in their studies. One consequence of these studies was the establishment of courses in the techniques and practices of advertising.

The Food and Drug Act of 1906 aided "truth in advertising." Several states acted to make false advertising a misdemeanor; Better Business Bureaus were established in many cities; and the Post Office Department, the Department of Agriculture, and the Federal Trade Commission also sought to prevent fraudulent and deceptive advertising. Further excesses during the depression of the 1930's led to the passage in 1938 of the Wheeler-Lea amendments to the Federal Trade Commission Act.

Radio became an additional advertising medium in 1922. Rather than employing radio to compete with other media, agencies used it as an integral part of an advertising campaign.

After 1946 television became the fastest-growing medium. With the introduction of computerized mailing lists and autotypewriters, direct mail advertising increased substantially after 1955. The circulation of newspapers and periodicals, as well as their advertising revenues, mounted, even though the number of publications declined. Only network radio advertising showed a substantial decrease, although advertising through the independent radio stations established after 1950 more than compensated for this reduction.

Consumer surveys became common in the 1930's. After 1950, increased costs of advertising led to the establishment of additional consumer research organizations. Congress passed the Highway Beautification Act (1965), which regulated placement of billboards near interstate highways. The practice of appealing to the authority of scientists and physicians practically ceased after the Television Code in 1967 forbade actors from assuming these roles in food and drug commercials. The ruling of the Federal Trade Commission in 1965 requiring cigarette companies to include the notice that smoking might be dangerous to health was followed in 1971 by the agreement of these companies to cease television advertising altogether. Political advertising came particularly under fire—both the carefully prepared and produced question-and-answer session, and the twenty-second spot announcements, first used in the 1952 Dwight D. Eisenhower presidential campaign, that presented simplistic views of complicated political questions. In the 1980's the development of cable TV networks and complicated home video units opened new avenues for the advertiser.

AEF. *See* **American Expeditionary Forces.**

AEOLUS. An early experiment in railroad cars, the yachtlike *Aeolus* was designed to sail before the wind. It was tried on the Baltimore and Ohio Railroad in 1830.

AERONAUTICS. *See* **Air Transportation.**

AERONAUTICS AND SPACE ADMINISTRATION, NATIONAL. *See* **National Aeronautics and Space Administration.**

AERONAUTICS BOARD, CIVIL. *See* **Federal Agencies.**

AFL. *See* **American Federation of Labor-Congress of Industrial Organizations.**

AFRICAN-AMERICAN RELATIONS. Although sustained interaction between Africa and America dates from 1619, when nineteen Africans were brought to Virginia, it was not until the antebellum period that there was some diversification of African-American relations resulting from legitimate trade, the founding of Liberia, and the beginning of American missionary activities. The idea of settling free black Americans in West Africa, advocated by certain Afro-American spokesmen, won support among whites and led to the formation of the American Colonization Society in 1817 and the founding of Liberia in 1822. By 1861, some 12,000 Afro-Americans had emigrated to Liberia through the society. In 1847 Liberia declared itself an independent republic, and in 1862 the United States recognized Liberia.

Between the end of the Civil War and World War I, the United States showed little interest in Africa. Trade was desultory, but spurted somewhat during World War I. Some Afro-American leaders, notably Bishop Henry McNeal Turner, advocated emigration to Africa, even after its partition by the major European powers in the late 19th century; some 3,000 went to Liberia in the late 19th century, and a few to other parts of the continent. But the major impact of Americans on Africa came through missionaries, particularly in West Africa and southern Africa. These missionaries arranged for dozens of African students to study in the United States.

African-American relations remained essentially unchanged between the two world wars. Commercially, the most important development was the grant by the Liberian government of a million acres to the U.S. Firestone Company in 1926 for plantations to grow rubber. Politically, Marcus Garvey's American-based Universal Negro Improvement Association (UNIA), founded in 1914, with its bold cry of "Africa for the Africans," served to stimulate African nationalism—particularly in the urban areas of West and South Africa. Branches of the UNIA were formed, and Garvey's militant weekly newspaper, *The Negro World* (1918–23), was read. Additionally, a few African leaders participated in the four Pan-African conferences organized between 1919 and 1927 by Dr. W. E. B. Du Bois. Italy's conquest of Ethiopia in 1935–36 called forth widespread expressions of Pan-African solidarity and served to stimulate greater American interest in Africa. In 1937 the Council on African Affairs was founded under the leadership of Paul Robeson and Max Yergan, with the goal of influencing U. S. policy; it remained active until 1955.

American interest in Africa grew enormously during and after World War II, because of the strategic importance of Africa and the value of Africa as a major source of strategic raw materials. This new interest expressed itself in vastly increased investments; in the establishment of a military base in Ethiopia; in the founding of such educational and cultural organizations as the African-American Institute, the African Studies Association, the American Society for African Culture, and Cross Roads Africa; in the increased activities of American labor organizations in Africa; and in the operation of Peace Corps Africa. By 1970 U.S. investments in sub-Saharan Africa had grown to a substantial $2.25 billion, about 40 percent of which was invested in the white-dominated territories of southern Africa, particularly South Africa and Angola. As a result the United States was charged with supporting the minority white ruling elements against the aspirations of Africans for freedom. However, as African countries started to achieve independence, beginning with Ghana in 1957, the U.S. government quickly recognized the new regimes.

The 1970's saw a relative diminution of U.S. governmental and public interest in Africa, but growing U.S. investments, the concern of Afro-Americans, and the potentially explosive struggle in southern Africa ensure a continuing major American interest in, and interaction with, Africa.

AFRICAN COMPANY, ROYAL. One of a series of English trading companies granted a monopoly of the African slave trade. In 1672 it took over the charter and African trading posts of the Company of Royal Adventurers to Africa, established in 1662. In 1697 its monopoly was destroyed, when independent merchants were permitted to engage in the trade upon payment for fourteen years of export duties which were turned over to the company to maintain its posts. The company endeavored to prevent independent traders from bargaining directly with the dealers in Africa. Most of the slaves it secured were sold to the independents, to the English South Sea Company after it was granted the Asiento (1713), or even to foreign traders. Competition, the expense of maintaining its posts, and the imposition of duties by the colonies proved disastrous to the company, and its affairs were ended in 1750.

AFRICAN METHODIST EPISCOPAL CHURCH. Oldest and largest denomination of Afro-American Methodists, organized in 1816 in Philadelphia with Richard Allen as its first bishop. Allen had tried to set up a separate place of worship for blacks soon after his arrival in Philadelphia in 1786, but was opposed by blacks and whites. When friction developed around efforts to segregate blacks attending St. George's Methodist Episcopal Church, Allen, Absolom James, William White, and other blacks withdrew. Under Allen's leadership they organized the Free African Society, which developed into the Bethel African Methodist Episcopal church in 1794. Branches of the church were established and by 1816 a formal denominational organization was possible. In 1980 there were 2 million members. In doctrine the church is similar to the Methodist Episcopal.

AFRO-AMERICAN CHURCHES. Black congregations date back to the federal period, when separatist black churches were constituted among free black Baptists, Presbyterians, Methodists, and Episcopalians who adopted the descriptive adjective "African."

After emancipation, religious organizations provided opportunities for leadership by Afro-Americans and served as a refuge and center of hope for those who were discriminated against in their day-to-day activities, giving rise to separate Afro-American denominations among the former slaves. Whereas the Methodist Episcopal Church South had had 207,000 Afro-American members in 1860, the number had dropped to 78,000 by 1866, as the membership of the African Methodist church had grown; the remaining group withdrew in 1870 to form the Colored Methodist Episcopal church. By 1880 black and white Baptists had split. Where denominational separation did not take place, as with the Presbyterians and Catholics, Afro-American communicants usually worshipped in separate churches.

Churches were in the forefront of the Afro-American self-help programs of the post-Reconstruction period and were instrumental in the establishment of schools and colleges. (Black Methodists established eleven colleges between 1870 and 1902.)

As Afro-Americans migrated to the North, their religious institutions changed. In the ghettos of large cities numerous "storefront" churches were created and a number of non-Christian sects appeared, including the Black Muslims, the peace movement of Father Divine, and the United House of Prayer of Daddy Grace.

In the post–World War II period much of the leadership in civil rights activity came from the clergy, most notably Martin Luther King, Jr., Adam Clayton Powell, Jr., Ralph D. Abernathy, Nathan Wright, Jesse L. Jackson, and Leon Sullivan. Black churches in the South served as rallying points and often bore the brunt of hostile reactions.

In the 1970's Baptists formed the largest of the Afro-American church groups, with a membership of 7,253,000. Afro-American membership in other Christian churches was distributed as follows: Methodist, 2,067,000; Catholic, 774,000; Presbyterian, 107,000; other groups, 1,050,000. The rest of the religious membership among Afro-Americans consisted of 190,000 non-Christians, of whom 9,000 were Jewish.

AFRO-AMERICANS. People of African descent first arrived in the New World with the Spanish in the 16th century. One of them, Estevanico, led an expedition into what is now Arizona and New Mexico and planted the first wheat crops ever harvested in the American Southwest. Other blacks were members of French expeditions that opened up the Mississippi valley; for example, Jean Baptiste Point du Sable established the trading post on Lake Michigan that in time became the city of Chicago. But the African peoples had relatively little contact with the French, and Spanish interests were quickly displaced by those of the English. As the English and their Anglo-American successors came to be the chief colonizers of what is now the United States, the introduction of Africans to fill the labor needs of the colonies linked the black experience in America to that of Anglo-Americans.

In 1619 the captain of a Dutch man-of-war sold nineteen blacks as indentured servants to Englishmen at Jamestown, Va. Between 5 million and 10 million Africans were transported to the Americas and the West Indies between 1619 and 1865. The vast majority of these people came from that stretch of the West African coast extending from present-day Senegal to Angola; a small percentage came from Madagascar and East Africa. The 1980 census identified 26,488,218 Afro-Americans, or black Americans, in the United States, constituting slightly more than 11 percent of the total population.

The first Africans introduced at Jamestown competed with, and were outnumbered by, indentured servants from Europe. But it was difficult to work white servants beyond the time of their indenture, while for Africans the situation was different. Their presence as servants was not voluntary: they had been captured and sold; moreover, the areas from which they came could not influence the English North American colonies to provide protection for Africans equal to that provided various Europeans. As the relative number of black servants continuously increased, their status changed. By 1670 servants of African descent were generally viewed as slaves and the evolution of the institution of slavery had reduced Africans to the status of personal property (*see* Slavery).

The American Revolution and a declining profit from slaves led to the end of slavery in the North. Movements to curb slavery took place in the South but came to a halt with the invention of the cotton gin by Eli Whitney (1793). His invention led to an increase in the amount of land planted in cotton and in the demand for slaves; thus, despite the ideals of the Declaration of Independence, slaveholding interests increased in influence well into the 19th century. The Constitution recognized the existence of slavery, and federal legislation protected property in slaves, as did the constitutions of the new states of Mississippi and Alabama in 1817 and 1819; free blacks were discriminated against in both North and South. The position of the Afro-American in the United States at midcentury was articulated in 1857 in the Supreme Court decision of *Dred Scott* v. *Sandford:* the Court held that people of African descent "were not intended to be included under the word 'citizen' in the Constitution and can, therefore, claim none of the rights and privileges which that instrument provides for and secures to citizens of the United States whether emancipated or not."

Blacks sought a variety of means to counter physical and psychological bondage. Conspiracies and revolts continued as long as the institution of slavery existed, among them those of Denmark Vesey (1822) and Nat Turner (1831). No firm statistics exist on the number of escapees, but a variety of evidence shows it to be high. Notable among escaped slaves is Frederick Douglass, who fled from slavery in Maryland (1838).

Opposition to slavery among free persons also existed and in the 19th century abolition became an influential force, largely through the activities of Douglass, Benjamin Lundy, David Walker, William Lloyd Garrison, and Theodore D. Weld (*see* Antislavery).

The effect the Civil War would have on slavery was not clear at the start of the conflict. Southern states went to war determined to maintain slavery, and President Abraham Lincoln announced that he had no intention to interfere with slavery in the states. Not until military conditions made it seem beneficial did the Lincoln administration issue the Emancipation Proclamation (January 1863) and allow the enlistment of blacks in the military. Some 140,000 blacks served in the Union army and navy during the remaining years of the conflict.

The Emancipation Proclamation and the Thirteenth, Fourteenth, and Fifteenth amendments to the Constitution provided the legal basis for full citizenship for blacks, and for a brief period they enjoyed these benefits under federal protection, but several factors combined to prevent their new status from becoming effectively established. First, blacks lacked political experience, education, and independent economic activity. Second, the opposition of southern whites to citizenship rights for blacks was almost unanimous, and no broad base of support existed in the North. When the war ended, the federal retreat from the civil rights field placed protection of the rights of blacks in the hands of the southern states. Also, the frailty of the mutual support that supposedly existed between Republicans and blacks became clear with the compromise of 1876: this bargain between Republican and Southern Democratic conservatives put Rutherford B. Hayes in the presidency in return for the withdrawal of federal troops from the South and a federal hands-off policy with regard to the rights of blacks.

Nevertheless, blacks made impressive steps in the areas of education and politics. Blacks and their white supporters established a number of institutions of higher education, among them Fisk University, Talladega College, Morehouse College, Atlanta University, Johnson C. Smith University, and Shaw University. A number of blacks held political office and voting was widespread. Economic success was far more limited. Blacks sought to secure land for farming, but were unsuccessful; they had to turn to former slaveowners for employment, land rentals, or sharecropping arrangements. Economic dependency in turn weakened chances for effective use of politics and education.

In the 1890's, after southern Populists threatened and sometimes overthrew the political control of the old southern elite. Legislative and judicial action reduced the political influence and civil rights of blacks in every state in the Old South. At the same time, school funds for black education came under serious attack. Laws requiring segregation became commonplace. Court tests of Jim Crow laws produced no relief. In the case of *Plessy* v. *Ferguson* (1896) the Supreme Court put its stamp of approval on racial separation in public accommodations.

World War I represents a watershed in the experience of black Americans. Most significant was the impetus given to the urbanization of blacks by the labor needs of northern industries. This movement had begun in the years immediately after emancipation in a large migration to southern cities; by 1900 blacks outnumbered whites in many cities. When Southern Democrats regained political control of state governments in the 1870's, a similar move to northern cities began. Besides relief from the low wages and hardships of farming, the North offered less overt discrimination, better schools, suffrage, possibilities for justice in the courts, and access to public places. When war in Europe stopped the flow of immigrants for industrial labor, job opportunities for blacks increased and the trickle of blacks to the cities of the Northeast and West became a flood. By 1920 half a million southern blacks had relocated. At the outbreak of the Civil War 92 percent of the black population lived in the South, and 95 percent on farms. At the turn of the century the South still claimed almost 90 percent of all blacks. By 1970 blacks in the South had declined to 52 percent with less than 12 percent living on farms. Blacks had come to be more urbanized than the general population. The 1970 census reported 72 percent of all blacks lived in cities, compared with 70 percent for the total population.

The presence of blacks in large numbers in major population centers had both benefits and drawbacks. Some black officials were elected to municipal, state, and federal governments. But increased numbers meant greater pressure on the limited housing available to blacks and greater antiblack feeling as Afro-Americans tried to move out of traditionally black areas. Blacks were employed mainly in unskilled positions, were the last hired and first fired, and were, for the most part, refused membership in the established labor unions. There were also race riots. A series of riots spread across the country in the first two decades of the 20th century.

When World War I began in 1914, there were 20,000 blacks among the 750,000 men in the regular army and National Guard. Before November 1918 there were 2,290,000 registered blacks and 367,000 of them were called into service; they served in segregated units in the army and were excluded from the navy except for menial jobs. None were admitted to the Marine Corps. The all-black 369th, 371st, and 372nd regiments received the Croix de Guerre for valor. Any hopes that the demonstration of loyalty and support for the war effort would convince Americans that blacks were entitled to equal rights disappeared in the years immediately after the war. The Ku Klux Klan was revived as early as 1915, and the number of lynchings, which had dropped considerably after reaching a peak of 235 in 1892, turned upward again. Among the 70 blacks lynched in 1919 were ten veterans, some still in uniform. Another series of race riots spread across the country.

Despite the absence of appreciable progress in the area of civil rights, there were significant cultural developments. A growing sense of racial pride, of which the Universal Negro Improvement Association (1920) was the prime example, resulted in important works of literature and art. The Harlem Renaissance, as the post–World War I movement came to be called, centered in New York City (*see* Harlem Renaissance).

The Great Depression temporarily set back race pride and dissent; for many, the hard times were only more of the same. No New Deal legislation was specifically concerned with the civil rights of Afro-Americans. Some measures actually increased the economic hardship of rural blacks (tenant farmers and sharecroppers) who were forced off the land as a result of legislation aimed at assistance to agriculture (subsidies withdrawing land from cultivation).

When World War II began, there were 10,000 blacks in the regular army and National Guard. An amendment to the Selective Service Act of 1940 forbade discrimination in the drafting or training of men. The War Department interpreted this to mean that blacks should be received into the army in proportion to their percentage of the population but should be organized in separate units. The number of black officers reached 7,768, as against only 1,400 in World War I. In all, 750,000 blacks served in the army, 165,000 in the navy, and between 20,000 and 25,000 in the Coast Guard and Marine Corps. Approximately 500,000 saw service overseas. Blacks expressed hopes that participation in the war against the racist policies of Nazism would aid America to see the brutality of its own racial patterns and to move to change them. The result was a stepping-up of the activity of the National Association for the Advancement of Colored People (NAACP), the National Urban League, and other organizations long in existence, and the creation of new organizations and approaches. Judicial process continued to be considered a means toward racial justice, but direct protest characterized the actions of blacks on these matters in the 1950's, 1960's, and 1970's.

The chief characteristics of protest by blacks between World War II and 1960 were a moderate, nonviolent approach, opposition to physical confrontation, a willingness of protesters to suffer physically to make their point, and an implied and expressed desire to find for blacks a place in the mainstream of American life. A series of court cases instituted by the NAACP led eventually to the 1954 and 1955 Supreme Court decisions in *Brown* v. *Board of Education of Topeka, Kansas,* stating that separate but equal education was unconstitutional and ordering the desegregation of educational facilities "with all deliberate speed." The 386-day Montgomery bus boycott (1955–56) spawned the Southern Christian Leadership Conference (SCLC) and produced the foremost civil rights leader, the Rev. Dr. Martin Luther King, Jr. The SCLC joined the Congress of Racial Equality (CORE), in existence since 1942, and the Student Nonviolent Coordinating Committee (SNCC), organized in 1960.

Black protest after 1960 fostered confrontation, expressed objection to much in the existing political and economic structure, and placed less emphasis on integration and more on self-help and work through all-black organizations. This new wave of "creative disorder" was introduced by the sit-in of four black college students in Greensboro, N.C., in 1960. Sit-ins became stand-ins at segregated theater box offices, kneel-ins at segregated churches, and wade-ins at segregated beaches. A series of "freedom rides" was organized by CORE to protest segregation in interstate travel, and voter registration drives and demonstrations were organized against discriminatory practices in voting. Many among the white majority reacted with hostility and violence to both phases of the movement. In 1955, Emmet Till, a fourteen-year-old black boy, was kidnapped and lynched in Mississippi. The National Guard had to be used to quell mobs attempting to prevent the implementation of court orders to desegregate educational facilities in Tennessee and Kentucky (1956), Arkansas (1957), Mississippi (1962), and Alabama (1963). Dozens of churches and homes were bombed and burned, and peaceful demonstrators were beaten and gassed. Both black and white civil rights workers were killed.

One expression of the frustration of blacks and their hostility to white reaction to their movement was a series of riots beginning in 1963: Birmingham, Ala.; New York City; the Watts section of Los Angeles; Detroit; Newark; Cambridge, Md.; Chicago; Philadelphia; Rochester; Atlanta; Plainfield, N.J.; Nashville; and Boston.

Race riots before 1963 had been characterized by attacks of whites on blacks; the conflicts after 1963 represented the lashing out of blacks at examples and symbols of discrimination and segregation. Attacks on whites were rare. The majority of those killed were black. Another round of riots occurred in 1968 after the assassination of Martin Luther King. Racial violence erupted in more than 110 cities: the most serious conflicts took place in Washington; Chicago; Detroit; Newark; Baltimore; Pittsburgh; Kansas City, Mo.; New York; Saint Louis; and Philadelphia.

During the post–World War II period the major accomplishments at the national level were the Civil Rights Act of 1964 and the Voting Rights Act of 1965. Also, a series of Supreme Court decisions had been made supporting the rights of blacks to equality of treatment and protecting the right to protest in an effort to secure that equality. One positive result was the election of black mayors in Los Angeles, Newark, Atlanta, and Cleveland. On the local level, white-collar job opportunities, housing, and higher education improved. But by 1980, some school districts were more segregated than they had been at the time of *Brown* v. *Board of Education,* and although the average income of blacks had increased, the difference in the average for the two races was greater than it had been in the 1960's.

Since World War II the cultural image of the black American has been under continuous restructuralization. The traditional self-concept of most blacks from the Civil War until the mid-20th century was one closely identified with the American mainstream and its values. A sharp reversal toward ethnocentricity emerged with the civil rights struggles. And this revived sense of "Africanness" expressed itself in such slogans as "Black Is Beautiful" and in demands for "black power" in political and economic affairs. A serious school of black theologians emerged. "Black religion" as a corrective approach to traditional American interpretations of Christianity became popular, especially among the younger and better-educated black Americans. The music of black Americans has always been distinctive and remains so in spite of heavy borrowings by other groups. In dance, Katherine Dunham, Alvin Ailey, and Arthur Mitchell provided classical training and careers for blacks. Black arts centers grew up around the country, a notable example being the center founded by Alma Lewis in Boston. The Negro Ensemble Company in New York fostered black playwrights and delineated the black experience for playgoers.

AGAMENTICUS (Maine). Settled about 1624 and successively known as Bristol (1632), Agamenticus (1641), Gorgeana (1642), and York (1652). The first municipal corporation in America (1642), created so by Sir Ferdinando Gorges.

AGENCIES, FEDERAL. *See* **Federal Agencies.**

AGENCY SHOP. A nonunion worker may be represented by a labor union for collective bargaining if the union has an "agency shop" arrangement. The worker must pay the union a fee equal to what union dues would be.

AGENT, COLONIAL. *See* **Colonial Agent.**

AGRARIAN MOVEMENT. A mixture of philosophic idealism, rooted in the 18th-century Enlightenment, and the hard, practical demands of colonial farmers; agrarianism became a tradition of independence and self-reliance, of progress and scientific improvement, tinged with a sentimental romanticism that reached its height in the 19th century.

From the beginning the agrarian movement was closely involved with politics. The rivalry between agricultural and commercial interests was an important factor in the development of the two-party political system.

Agrarianism was also a major force in the national expansionist movement. The expanding frontier was regarded as a natural right, and the image of the farmer-settler became the national ideal.

As an intellectual movement agrarianism again flowered briefly in the 1930's through a group of southern writers known as the Fugitives.

AGRICULTURAL ADJUSTMENT ADMINISTRATION (AAA). The AAA was created in 1933 to stabilize farm prices by restricting production of certain farm products. It was declared unconstitutional by the U.S. Supreme Court in 1936, but a new act was passed in 1938, which was found constitutional. The new act attempted to set a policy for a "normal" grain supply in the United States. The AAA was ended as a separate agency of the government in 1942.

AGRICULTURAL EDUCATION. As early as 1754, King's College in New York (now Columbia University) was offering a course in husbandry, and during the first half of the 19th century Rensselaer Polytechnic Institute and Amherst College provided instruction in scientific courses relating to agriculture. The Agricultural Land Grant College Act of 1862 helped establish colleges for the teaching of "such branches of learning as are related to agriculture and the mechanic arts."

Between 1880 and 1900, farmers' institutes in many states attempted to bring new discoveries directly to farmers by cooperating with agricultural colleges; out of this specialized model for adult education came the federal agricultural extension movement.

The teaching of agriculture at the secondary school level was given federal support under the Smith-Hughes Act of 1917. The vocational education acts of 1946 and 1963 considerably broadened the original act.

AGRICULTURAL EXPERIMENT STATIONS. The Hatch Act of 1887 allotted funds to land-grant colleges to conduct experiments in agriculture and publish results of the research. Wesleyan University established the first state agricultural station and during the early 1880's several states organized similar stations. The Office of Experiment Stations acted as a center for exchange of information; in 1961, its functions were assigned to the Cooperative State Experiment Station Service.

AGRICULTURAL MACHINERY. The Industrial Revolution dramatically affected the raising of food and fiber. Eli Whitney's cotton gin, patented in 1794, was the last link in the industrialization of the cotton textile industry. Cotton farming boomed, and the dying institution of slavery acquired a brief new lease on life. The Civil War, by creating a shortage of labor, brought on a mechanical revolution in farming, followed by the introduction of power machinery near the turn of the century.

The invention of the steel plow by John Deere in 1837 solved the problem of how to plow the rich earth of the primeval American prairie. In 1864 a two-wheeled sulky plow was invented. A disk plow was patented as early as 1847. The harrow became a family of specialized tools during the middle of the 19th century. At the same time, the lister, or double moldboard plow, was developed, making it possible to plant row crops in furrows.

Though most of the elements of the modern drill were present in a machine developed in Italy about 1600 and in a more advanced machine developed by the British agronomist Jethro Tull in 1733, lack of an effective metering device hindered the machine's acceptance. Several such devices were patented in the United States in the early 1840's, and in 1851 a force-feed device utilizing a rotating fluted cylinder was developed. By the time of the Civil War, mechanized seeding had increased the number of acres a farmer might cultivate. It was not until 1971 that the International Harvester Company introduced a new approach with a machine that utilizes a flow of air to select and transport the seed.

As the plow is the basic tool of soil preparation, the hoe is that of cultivation. A horse hoe, designed to be drawn between rows by a single horse, was developed about 1820. A second hoe blade was added about 1850, and a two-horse straddle-row cultivator, which doubled productivity, was patented in 1856.

Harvesting. The sickle, later improved as the scythe and the cradle, remained the tool of the grain harvest throughout the preindustrial period. All crops except small grains were harvested completely by hand. Cyrus McCormick developed his famous reaper in 1831, and although far from a perfected harvesting machine, it cut harvest time in half.

H. Moore and J. Hascall developed a horse-drawn combine in 1836. Improved combines drawn by teams of more than thirty mules were harvesting two-thirds of the California wheat crop by 1900. Wide acceptance of the combine principle had to wait for the mechanically powered, self-propelled machine developed by Thomas Carroll in 1938.

The basic hay harvesting tool is a mower with a serrated, reciprocating knife much like a barber's clippers. By 1865 nearly all haymowing was done mechanically. A baling press was developed in 1853. The advent of powered machinery, particularly the development of the automatic pickup baler by the New Holland Company in 1940, made possible a much more efficient use of hay. Hay use varies, and a wide variety of machines has been developed to swath, windrow, condition, chop, and otherwise prepare the forage for storage or immediate use.

Cotton resisted mechanical harvesting longer than any other major crop. The modern cotton picker is based upon the use of a rotating spindle, patented in 1895. Commercial success did not come until 1942.

Harvesters for root crops such as potatoes were developed only when more powerful and versatile tractors became available in the 1930's. A notable effort was the development simultaneously of a mechanized tomato harvester and a tomato amenable to such harvesting.

Mechanical Power. The first major application of mechanical power to farm machinery was in the operation of threshers, as early as 1849. It was not until the 1880's that steam traction engines attained widespread success and use.

In 1892 was introduced the first true gasoline traction engine. The first commercially successful machine (1906) was the Hart-Parr Company's "Old No. 1," for which the name "tractor" was coined. The tractor remained chiefly a pulling vehicle until the development of the power takeoff device which made it possible to power by the tractor's engine many implements that had formerly been ground-propelled. A tricycle-type all-purpose tractor in 1924 widened the application of the principle to cultivation. In 1936 the three-point hitch made it possible to tractor-mount many other implements. After World War II advances in the use of hydrostatics and hydraulics broadened the tractor's versatility and development occurred in the self-propulsion of many specialized machines.

AGRICULTURAL POLICIES, FEDERAL. Although at first influenced by the feudal systems of western Europe, American land policy gradually came to favor settlers. After the cession of the western lands to the Union, the federal government transferred these holdings as soon as possible to farmer-settlers. Land-grant policy was closely linked with the slavery question, and no effective act was passed until the Homestead Act of 1862, which provided a free title grant for 160 acres of land to a settler who maintained residence for five years. After 1900 this act was modified to grant larger tracts in arid western regions. Twentieth-century land policies have involved efforts to conserve and reconstruct soils and to exercise more public control over forest lands, waters, and mineral resources.

During World War I American agriculture fell into a severe economic depression. Several proposals for farm relief legislation—notably the McNary-Haugen bills—were actively discussed and promoted during the 1920's. "Orderly marketing" of farm products was encouraged by the Cooperative Marketing Act of 1922; other laws provided special credit facilities for farmers. The Agricultural Marketing Act of 1929 created the Federal Farm Board, designed to stabilize prices of commodities; it failed but it led to more successful legislation during the 1930's (*see* Agricultural Adjustment Administration). From the 1940's into the 1960's the Agricultural Adjustment Act was amended several times, the basic aim being formation of a price-support program to bring farm income into balance with the national income. The original "parity" formula underlying the program was based on market statistics for the years 1910–14, a period during which farm and nonfarm prices were considered to be in reasonable balance. In 1950 the formula was changed to permit use of average prices paid and received during the ten-year period immediately preceding any current year.

The 1956 act established the Soil Bank program. The acreage reserve section of the Soil Bank was terminated in 1959, leaving the conservation reserve program in effect; the entire act was repealed by passage of the Food and Agriculture Act of 1965. This latter act established a long-term land-retirement policy, the Cropland Adjustment program; it also established a new four-year price-adjustment program. The Agriculture Act of 1970 included a payment limitation of $55,000 for price supports to any one person or company. Other legislation of the 1960's and early 1970's indicated a shift away from price supports and toward government subsidies for producing food for export to underdeveloped countries. The Commodity Credit Corporation (CCC), formed in 1933, was the principal agency through which price-support activities were carried out. When it was not possible to support prices through loans or purchase agreements, the CCC bought farm commodities outright.

To increase exports of surplus products, Congress in 1954 passed the Agricultural Trade Development Act, authorizing the secretary of agriculture to accept foreign currencies for commodities shipped abroad to friendly nations. In 1972, after more than 400 million bushels of wheat were sold to the Soviet Union, surplus stocks of American grains were depleted for the first time in a generation.

In 1973 the Department of Agriculture established "target prices" for certain commodities; if a farmer's average sale prices fell below the targets, the government paid the difference to the farmer. The objective was increased production to meet worldwide demands for American food crops.

Scientific Aid to Agriculture. When the Department of Agriculture was established in 1862, the commissioner was directed "to acquire and preserve . . . all information concerning agriculture which he [could] obtain by means of books and correspondence, and by practical and scientific experiments." The first experiments backed by federal funds were chemical analyses of soils and plants and entomological research and studies of animal and plant diseases. In 1887 the Hatch Act provided for the establishment of experiment stations in connection with land-grant colleges.

Some results of federally financed research were the discovery that hog cholera was viral in origin; research showing that ticks transmitted cattle fever; the demonstration that bacteria could cause diseases in plants and that some of these diseases were spread by insects; the breeding of plants resistant to disease and work on plants resistant to disease-spreading insects; the demonstration that harmless insects could be used to destroy harmful insects; the development of soil classification; and the early work on hybrid corn.

In the 1930's the Department of Agriculture established several regional laboratories and field stations; the Agricultural Research Center at Beltsville, Md., became the national experimental station for basic research.

Between the 1940's and the 1970's the extensive application of chemicals brought about a great increase in agricultural production, but their effects upon the environment created such concern that controls were put upon them. Agriculture also adopted ultrasonics for research on plants, livestock, and insects; hormones to increase both the number of multiple births and the size of livestock; brain stimulation devices to increase milk production; infrared photography for identification of crops, forests, and soils; and earth satellites to monitor disease, insect infestations, and drought.

AGRICULTURAL SOCIETIES AND FARM ORGANIZATIONS. Shays's Rebellion, the Whiskey Rebellion, and Fries's Rebellion (1799) were farmers' uprisings against taxes. Such violent rural protest then declined and a more calm type of organization arose—the agricultural society. During the following half century almost every state, region, and county organized a society or farmers' club to promote agriculture. In 1852 representatives from local organizations met in Washington, D.C., to form the U.S. Agricultural Society, which was largely responsible for passage of the law creating the U.S. Department of Agriculture.

In 1867 Oliver Hudson Kelley and six associates founded the National Grange of the Patrons of Husbandry, or simply the Grange. Within ten years it attracted a membership of nearly a million and gave its name to the Granger movement of the 1870's. The organization's membership greatly decreased during the rise of the more radical Farmers' Alliance of the late 1880's, but after the latter became part of the Populist movement, the Grange came back into influence. In 1974 it had about 600,000 members.

The National Farmers Union (1902) was considered the natural successor to the Farmers' Alliance. Its national membership in 1974 included about 250,000 farm families.

The national American Farm Bureau Federation was formally organized in Chicago, Mar. 1, 1920. In 1921 the Farm Bureau organized the first farm bloc in Congress, and by 1923 was urging action to solve the problems of farmers. In the 1970's the Farm Bureau was the largest farmers' organization, with a membership of more than 2 million families.

The National Farmers Organization was founded in 1955 to protest low farm prices; within a few months it had 71,000 members. Its goal was a system whereby farmers would set prices for their produce, and it initiated a system of withholding products from market until prices were met. Membership estimates vary from 115,000 to 270,000. The United Farm Workers Union developed out of the California farm labor movements of the 1960's, and in 1980 claimed a membership of 100,000.

AGRICULTURE.

American Indian. In pre-Columbian America a basic triad of food plants was developed: Indian corn, beans, and pumpkins and squashes. Associated with the maize complex was tobacco.

The elaborate urbanized and religiopolitical structures of the Maya, Aztec, and Inca and their precursors depended on the essentially predictable food supply provided by well-regulated agricultural patterns. These regions also showed the greatest diversity of food plants: pineapples, tomatoes, bananas, guavas, peanuts, chile peppers, and cacao were included in the inventory of pre-Columbian products, and potatoes of many varieties originated in the South American highlands. Other areas were only marginally agricultural.

The maize complex moved slowly northward from Mexico. Among Algonkin-speaking peoples of New England and the St. Lawrence River valley, maize, beans, squash, and tobacco constituted the entire farming array. Tobacco farming spread quickly, many nonfarming groups planting and cultivating it as their sole agricultural endeavor.

Lacking domesticated animals, the wheel, and the plow, farming depended entirely on human labor. Irrigation was limited to the areas of intensive cultivation in the American Southwest. The principal tool was the digging stick; the general practice was to drop in a few seed kernels, thin the growing corn, and follow it with bean and squash vines trained against the stalk.

Colonial. The first settlers were unable to produce adequate food supplies until they combined their skills with the American Indians' ways. Faced with a shortage of metal tools, the pioneer farmers adopted the Indians' digging stick, flint or bone hoe, winnowing basket, and cornhusking peg, and the design of the corncrib set on posts to dry the grain. They followed the native custom of planting, and learned the art of maple sugaring, the use of dye plants, and the making of pemmican.

The soil was seldom good, and soon the colonists were moving into the interior, resorting to primitive slash-and-burn methods to clear forests for farming.

From the beginning labor scarcities influenced American agricultural practices, often acting as an incentive for the development of labor-saving tools, equipment, and machinery. Because of the abundance and accessibility of cheap land, almost all farmers worked their own fields. In the northern colonies the labor shortage was compensated for in some measure by community cooperation. During the 17th and 18th centuries apprenticeship systems brought thousands of indentured servants and redemptioners into the middle colonies as farm laborers, but since most of these immigrants soon gained their independence and acquired farms of their own, the labor shortage persisted. Eventually slave labor drove out most of the free labor in the South, although only one-fourth of the population there owned slaves.

Agriculture during the colonial period was characterized by the misuse of soil, forests, and water. The New World appeared an inexhaustible continent. Before the end of the 18th century the best of the farmlands east of the Alleghenies were under cultivation, and agricultural experimenters were beginning to advocate rotation and fertilization practices. As the colonists moved inland, clearing forests, maize was usually the first crop; wheat and rye followed when the ground had been worked sufficiently. In the North, wheat, flax and livestock began to be grown commercially for the West Indian trade. The South was exporting great quantities of tobacco, sugar, rice, and indigo before the revolutionary war. Cotton, grown for home use from early times, did not become a commercial crop until after the war.

The typical northern farm was equipped with a few cattle, swine, and sheep. In the South the livestock industry was slow to develop, partly due to the desire of land-grant owners to concentrate on production of staple crops. The open-range system was generally used, thus establishing the pattern of later far-western ranching—with brands and marks to denote ownership, annual roundups, and overland drives to markets.

19th Century. Agriculture expanded rapidly westward, in ever sharper competition for labor with the Industrial Revolution. The period from 1840 to the Civil War saw hundreds of new patents being registered (*see* Agricultural Machinery). One side result of the emergence of improved agricultural machinery was the gradual disappearance of the ox. In 1840 oxen outnumbered horses by three to two on American farms; soon after the Civil War the ox had nearly vanished. The horse became the primary power source.

Between 1840 and 1860, a large-scale beef cattle industry flourished in Ohio and in the Kentucky Bluegrass regions, the animals being trailed overland to markets in the East. Sheep and swine production also shifted westward, whereas dairying remained concentrated in the East, closer to markets. By midcentury the South was taking the lead in animal husbandry; the best types of animals were imported. During the 1850's Texans were beginning to drive cattle into the Midwest for fattening.

At the outbreak of the Civil War, the center of agriculture was shifting to the vast prairie lands. Invention of the steel plow opened the richest grain-growing region in the world. In the South, also, the plantation system was exploding westward on the basis of cotton production. In addition to cotton, the South produced more than half the nation's corn, almost all of the tobacco, and all of the rice and sugar. As the Civil War approached, the self-sufficient northern farmers were also struggling toward commercial agriculture, but were hindered by habits and by lack of working capital.

The war's outbreak had little effect on the agricultural labor supply in the South; the major change was a switch from large cotton crops to corn and other food crops. In the North, however, the army drew men from the farms at a time when produce was bringing high prices because of increased demands. Output of farm machines was thus increased sharply. The farm frontier moved across the western plains ten times as fast as it had moved across the wooded regions of the East. The Homestead Act of 1862 was an accelerating force. Specialization of crops became more important. Wheat was the principal crop in the West, but land abuse was repeated. In the wake of crop failures resulting from drought or pests, overextended debts were claimed and mortgages foreclosed. Prices of commodities began falling, and the postwar boom ended.

The late 19th century saw a major shift of livestock production from East to West, the corn-hog pattern of farming developing in the Middle West; the cattle kingdom, in the Southwest and on the Great Plains. Shorthorns and Herefords gradually replaced the Texas longhorns; the open range was closed; and in the mountain states sheep outnumbered cattle.

In 1867 agricultural leaders organized the Patrons of Husbandry, or National Grange, to fight for lower railroad rates, more favorable banking practices, and the elimination of middlemen. During the 1880's an outbreak of farm unrest resulted in the organization of the militant Farmers' Alliance. The power of these movements was concentrated in the central plains. By 1894 this Populist movement loomed as a national third party.

20th Century. After the turn of the century, demand for commodities caught up with supply, and prices rose. The first half of the 20th century brought an agricultural revolution comparable in scope to the Industrial Revolution of the 19th century. At the time of the Civil War 60 percent of the population was engaged in agriculture; in 1900 it was only 37 percent; by 1930 it was 24.9 percent; and in 1972 it was 4.6 percent. The total farm population declined by more than 10 million during the first half of the 20th century. Although considerably more land was converted to farming acreage, the total number of farms declined from 6.4 million in 1910 to 2.8 million in 1973. During this period the average size of farms increased from 138 to 385 acres. Production increased significantly for many of the staple crops: in 1940 one farm worker could supply only eleven persons with food; in 1970 one worker could supply forty-seven persons. Except in the harvesting of some perishable fruit and vegetable crops, mechanization and automation replaced hand labor. Tractors increased from fewer than 1,000 in 1910 to 5.5 million in 1970. During the same period the number of horses and mules on farms decreased from 25 million to about 2.4 million. More than 98 percent of the nation's farms were electrified.

At the same time, federal controls eliminated many economic risks. Price and income supports and soil conservation programs acted as stabilizing forces. In a half century farm assets rose from $40 billion to more than $300 billion. Corporation farming was on the increase, and fear was expressed for the future of the traditional family farm. Orbiting satellites monitored crops through the growing seasons, estimating yields, detecting insect and disease outbreaks, observing soil nutrient and moisture conditions, and warning of pollution patterns. (*See also* farm related articles; and specific crops.)

AGRICULTURE, DEPARTMENT OF. Although recommended by George Washington as a separate federal body, an agriculture department was not established until 1862. In 1884 the Bureau of Animal Industry was created, and in 1890 the Weather Bureau was transferred from the War Department. In 1887 an Office of Experiment Stations was formed. The head of the department achieved cabinet status in 1889.

The department's present activities include the Forest Service, Soil Conservation Service, Rural Electrification Administration, Farmers Home Administration, the food stamp and other nutritional programs, the standardization of farm products, and the regulation of packers and stockyards. The department conducts scientific research in all areas of agriculture and transmits its findings through the state extension services. It gathers and publishes agricultural statistics, administers price-support programs, and promotes exports through its Foreign Agricultural Service. The national agricultural library has 1.3 million volumes.

AGUAYO EXPEDITION (1720–22). Marquis San Miguel de Aguayo, governor of Coahuila and Texas, left Monclova in 1720 with 500 soldiers to reestablish the Spanish missions and presidios in East Texas which had been abandoned in 1719 because of trouble with the French at Natchitoches. Joined by eighty refugees at San Antonio, Aguayo continued northeast, reestablished six missions, and fortified Adaes (now Robeline, La.) near the French; on his return in 1722, he erected a mission near the site of Fort Saint Louis, in Texas. He thus effectively put an end to French claims in Texas.

AIR COMMERCE ACT OF 1926. *See* **Civil Aeronautics Act.**

AIR CONDITIONING. *See* **Heating and Air Conditioning.**

AIRCRAFT, COMMERICIAL. *See* **Air Transportation.**

AIRCRAFT, MILITARY.

Armament. The fighter aircraft of World War I carried a single drum-fed Lewis gun, difficult for the pilot to reload. With more powerful engines and synchronized guns, planes were armed with twin belt-fed machine guns. Between the world wars, American fighters carried either two Browning air-cooled .30-caliber machine guns, or one .30- and one .50-caliber machine gun. The first practical aerial cannon appeared only in World War II. The P-39 Airacobra carried a 37mm coaxial cannon, but the most widely used was the Swiss 20mm Oerlikon. The largest was the 75mm M-4 cannon mounted on some B-25 bombers for attacking ground targets.

Flexible guns remained small and light until the development of a mount that allowed a gunner to overcome slipstream interference. During and immediately following World War I, one or two Lewis guns mounted on a Scarff ring were standard. Enclosed turrets first appeared in 1930 on the B-10 bomber, followed by American adoption of the British power turret, usually mounting twin .50-caliber guns. Remote-controlled turrets came in 1942 and were standard after World War II, as in the retractable twin turrets with 20mm cannon on the B-36.

The B-52 was equipped with radar-aimed 20mm cannon, while fighters carried radar-guided and computer-fired air-to-air rockets—the earliest being the Folding Fin Aircraft Rocket (Mighty Mouse) carried by a modified F-86. Rockets have generally replaced guns as the primary fighter weapon, although most fighters continue to carry at least one gun. The F-14 carries only the Phoenix missile. Further developments in air-to-air ordnance include the infrared-homing Sidewinder; the beam-riding Sparrow I; the radar-homing Sparrow III; the Falcon GAR-3 or GAR-4 heat-seeking missiles; and the MB-1 Genie, with a nuclear warhead capable of destroying any aircraft within 1,000 feet of detonation. Gunnery developments include the 20mm T-171 Vulcan multibarreled cannon firing 6,000 rounds per minute and a similar 37mm cannon.

Bombers. America's first bomber, the Martin MB-1, was developed late for World War I. In the 1920's the United States had only a few British DH-4's and Martin NBS-1's; these were replaced by the twin-engine Keystone biplane, which was standard until 1932, and a few Curtiss B-2 Condors. The Boeing Y1B-9 twin-engine monoplane replaced the Keystone but was eclipsed by the Martin B-10. Its replacements were the Douglas twin-engine 218-mph B-18 and the Boeing four-engine B-17.

In World War II the main strategic bombers were the Boeing B-17 Flying Fortress and Consolidated twin-tailed B-24 Liberator. The Boeing B-29 Superfortress was the war's largest bomber.

Tactical and supplemental strategic tasks were carried out by medium and attack bombers. The medium bombers were the North American B-25 Mitchell and the Martin B-26

Marauder. Attack bombers operated at low altitudes and were noted for speed and maneuverability. The Douglas A-20 Havoc was a twin-engine monoplane the Douglas A-26 Invader, appearing in 1944, though classed as an attack bomber, was the war's most advanced medium.

The first intercontinental bomber (1946) was the Consolidated-Vultee B-36. The first jet bomber (1948) was the North American B-45 Tornado. The second fully jet-powered bomber was the Boeing B-47 Stratojet. The B-47 replaced the B-29 and B-50 (an improved B-29) as a medium bomber until the 1960's. The Korean War had demonstrated the need for an attack jet to replace the B-26: the Martin B-57 and the Douglas B-66 Destroyer were chosen.

In 1954 the B-52 Stratofortress began replacing the B-36 as the mainstay of the Strategic Air Command. The General Dynamics B-58 Hustler also served the Strategic Air Command until it was retired in 1970. It carried four nuclear weapons underwing. The U.S. Air Force 1980 bomber force comprised the B-52D, B-52H, B-52G, and a few FB-111A's.

Fighters. The first American-built fighter, the Thomas-Morse MB-1 Scout, appeared in 1919. The U.S. Army relied on the Curtiss Hawk series until 1930 when, to gain higher speeds, they switched to monoplanes: the Boeing P-26 was the first. In 1935 the Republic P-35 and the Curtiss P-36 (Hawk 75) replaced the P-26.

The Army Air Corps's standard fighters—the Curtiss P-40 Warhawk (1940) and the Bell P-39 Airacobra (February 1941)—were obsolescent in 1941. The first advanced U.S. fighter (ordered August 1939) was the Lockheed P-38 Lightning. The Republic P-47 Thunderbolt (1943), the Army Air Force's (AAF) only radial-engined fighter, was widely used in the ground-support role. Perhaps the war's best fighter, the North American P-51 Mustang (1943) was the AAF's fastest operational plane. The Northrop P-61 Black Widow (1943) was the first American plane specifically designed as a night fighter. Ground-support duties required single-engine types. The army modified 500 P-51's into A-36 fighter-bombers, which performed so well that unmodified P-51's and P-47's were also pressed into that role.

The United States used no jet aircraft operationally during World War II. The first U.S. jet, the Bell XP-59 Airacomet (1943), copied a British engine and was capable of only 418 mph. It was soon relegated to a transition training role. The Lockheed P-80 (553 mph) was the AAF's fastest World War II fighter; in production as the Shooting Star, it arrived too late for combat. The last AAF propeller fighter was the P-82 Twin Mustang, which saw service in Korea. The first postwar fighter was the Republic F-84 Thunderjet, which began in 1947 as a 587-mph fighter and evolved into the 693-mph F-84F Thunderstreak. The Strategic Air Command (SAC) used the latter for its escort groups until 1957, when escorts were deemed unnecessary. It then became Tactical Air Command's (TAC) main fighter-bomber until the F-100C. The North American F-86 Sabre was the first American-built jet with swept wings and tail surfaces (which overcame the effects of compressibility); it participated in the first jet-versus-jet battles over Korea. The first jet night fighter and the first fighter with an afterburner was the Lockheed F-94. The Northrop F-89 Scorpion was the first successful all-weather jet.

The Soviet 1949 nuclear tests spurred interceptor development. The first automatic interceptor was the YF-86; its twenty-four 2.75-inch rockets were fired by ground command. Next was the Lockheed F-94C Starfire with 48 rockets, followed by the Scorpion with 104.

The U.S. Air Force ordered its first supersonic aircraft in the early 1950's. The Century series consisted of the North American F-100 Super Sabre, McDonnell Douglas F-101A Voodoo, Convair F-102 Delta Dagger (first with area-rule or "Coke bottle" configuration), and the Lockheed F-104 Starfighter. The TAC's first specially designed aircraft—the Republic F-105 Thunderchief—was delivered in 1956; it was the first fighter with a bomb bay. Other attack aircraft include the Vought A-7D Corsair II, which replaced the A-1E Skyraider, a World War II vintage propeller plane recycled for Vietnam; the Northrop F-5 series; and the Cessna A-37, an interim support plane. Three cargo planes, the AC-47 Spooky, the AC-119 Shadow, and the AC-130 Super Spooky —all with side-mounted, rapid-fire, multibarreled weapons— are also in the attack category. The Convair Delta Dart, an almost fully automatic fighter, appeared in 1956.

A new generation of aircraft began to appear in the 1960's. The first was the McDonnell Douglas F-4 Phantom II series, a twin-engine jet carrying a 20mm rapid-fire cannon and performing as both interceptor and attack plane. In 1981, new fighters included F-14 Tomcat (Grumman); F-15 Eagle (McDonnell Douglas); F-16 Fighting Falcon, a supersonic, daytime fighter (General Dynamics); and F-18 Hornet (McDonnell Douglas; Northrop).

AIRCRAFT CARRIERS AND NAVAL AIRCRAFT. The first airplane ever launched from a ship flew from the light cruiser *Birmingham,* Nov. 10, 1910. A civilian pilot, Eugene B. Ely, made the first shipboard landing (Jan. 18, 1911) on a platform over the stern guns of the cruiser *Pennsylvania.* The first U.S. carrier (1922) was *Langley,* converted from the collier *Jupiter.*

The Washington Naval Conference of 1922 limited construction of capital warships. Two U.S. battle cruisers were completed as aircraft carriers: *Lexington* and *Saratoga.* They not only provided a training base for carrier pilots but also enabled strategists to develop the doctrine and tactics that could project air power across oceans. *Lexington* and *Saratoga* were classic attack carriers (CV's). Additional CV's were added to the fleet, beginning with *Ranger* (1934), *Yorktown* (1937), *Enterprise* (1938), *Wasp* (1940), and *Hornet* (1941).

Essex defined a class of twenty-four 27,000-ton vessels (1942–46), almost all of which saw service in the Pacific. None was ever sunk. The last on active duty, *Ticonderoga,* was retired in 1973.

Wartime conversions from light cruiser hulls added nine light carriers (CVL's) to the fleet in one year (1943). These 15,000-ton ships operated at 31 knots or more with the fast carrier task force but had a complement of only some forty-five airplanes. Concurrently a class of escort carriers (CVE's) sprang from conversions of merchant hulls. Some 112 of these were built; they made less than 20 knots and carried fewer than thirty planes.

The three major carrier battles of World War II were the Coral Sea, Midway, and the Philippine Sea (*see* individual articles). The three-month campaign for Okinawa resulted in major damage to nine CV's, one CVL, and three CVE's, but the destruction of more than 2,000 enemy aircraft by carrier-based planes. Carrier raids against Japanese positions commenced early in 1942, the most notable being the "Shangri-La" raid on Tokyo itself, on Apr. 18, 1942. Air strikes from carriers spearheaded the North African landings in 1942 and every Pacific assault.

Five larger classes of carrier have evolved since the war: *Midway,* 53,000 tons (1945); *Forrestal,* 80,000 tons (1955); the nuclear-powered *Enterprise,* 91,000 tons (1961); *Kitty Hawk*, 85,000 tons; and the world's largest warship, the nuclear-powered *Nimitz*, 95,000 tons. With them have come jet aircraft (1948), nuclear-bomb delivery capability (1951), and true all-weather operational capability. Further technological progress came in the 1950's with the adoption of the angled deck (which permits simultaneous launch and recovery and power-on landings) and the steam catapult. At the same time, optical landing systems were introduced, advancing toward an automatic landing system.

Antisubmarine warfare carriers (CVS's) replaced CVE's in the postwar fleet. The CVS became the nucleus of a carrier-destroyer force utilized to sanitize an operating area, to search out and destroy enemy submarines, or to close off a route for enemy submarines. Aircraft complements aboard CVS's have stabilized with S2F Grumman Tracker twin-engine aircraft, helicopters, and an early-warning detachment of specially configured electronic S2F's. Helicopters became operational aboard carriers with the first helicopter ASW (HS) squadron in 1952, although the XOP-1 autogiro was tested on *Langley* in 1931. The first ASW squadron was equipped with the Piasecki HUP-1, to be replaced by the Sikorsky HSS-1 piston engine Seabat and then the HSS-2 turbine-powered Sea King.

In the 1950's carrier attack planes became available for nuclear missions; the carriers could cover Europe, including the Ukraine and Caucasus; most of China; and eastern Siberia. Naval aircraft shared the national nuclear deterrent responsibility with the Strategic Air Command through the 1950's and into the 1960's, when the Polaris fleet and ICBM's took over the major burden.

Aircraft. The development of naval carrier aircraft before World War II produced three basic types of planes: the fighter (VF), the scout bomber (VSB), and the torpedo plane (VT). Fighters tended to become fighter-bombers (VBF's) near the end of the war.

By 1929 a typical carrier complement included either F2B-1 or F3B-1 fighters, T4M-1 torpedo planes, and O2U-1 scout bombers. All were fabric-covered biplanes. The early 1930's produced the first of the Grumman fighter series—FF-1, F2F, and F3F. The Douglas TBD torpedo plane began the trend to low-wing monoplanes (1935). Scout divebombers of the 1930's included the SBU biplane and the SB2U low-wing.

During World War II fighters evolved from the prewar F2A Brewster Buffalo and the F4F Grumman Wildcat to the F6F Grumman Hellcat and the F4U Chance Vought Corsair.

Scout bombers progressed from the fabric-covered SB2U Vought Vindicator, through the SBD Douglas Dauntless, to the SB2C Curtiss Helldiver.

Torpedo planes entered the war with the inadequate TBD Douglas Devastator, which carried Torpedo Squadron 8 to extinction at Midway. Its replacement, the TBF Grumman Avenger, saw postwar service as an interim antisubmarine warfare (ASW) platform.

Patrol planes (VP's), operating from land or water, supplemented carrier aircraft chiefly for search, ASW patrols, and antishipping attacks. The PBY Consolidated Catalinas—the famed Black Cats—performed well all over the world throughout the war. The PBM Martin Mariner provided better performance after 1943, and the PB4Y Consolidated Privateer, a navy version of the Liberator, gave improved radar periscope detection.

Scout observation aircraft (VSO-VOS) played a unique role until the advent of helicopters after World War II—the biplane SOC Curtiss Seagull and the OS2U Vought Kingfisher.

Naval aircraft since World War II have been predominantly jet-powered, but the single-engine propeller dive-bomber AD Douglas Skyraider persisted as the world's best attack airplane from the late 1940's into the 1970's. During the 1950's, three attack planes and two outstanding fighters emerged. The A4 McDonnell Douglas Skyhawk, designed originally as an atomic-delivery vehicle, was modified for conventional weapons. The twin-engine A-6 Grumman Intruder was introduced in 1963. The A-7 Vought Corsair II, a single-engine jet designed to carry either nuclear or conventional weapons, first saw combat in 1967 in the Tonkin Gulf. The F8U-1 Vought Crusader, a day fighter with missile capability, became operational in 1957. The F4 McDonnell Douglas Phantom II, an all-weather missile fighter, was first produced in 1961.

AIR DEFENSE. Although American cities were not in danger of attack by air during World War I, American military planners began to contemplate the use of fighter aircraft, antiaircraft artillery (AAA), and ground observers against that possibility. In the 1920's and 1930's studies were made of electronic aircraft warning; in 1935 the War Department ordered the establishment of regional air defense systems, to which radar was added at the end of the decade. By Dec. 7, 1941, air defense systems—including radar, fighters, AAA, ground observers, and control centers—had been established along both continental coasts, in Panama, and in Hawaii. After Pearl Harbor, these defenses were greatly expanded, resulting in a total of more than 100 radar stations, about a million volunteer civilian ground observers and control center operators, and substantial numbers of fighters and AAA batteries.

The Air Defense Command (renamed the Aerospace Defense Command in 1968) was established in 1946. By 1960 several hundred radar stations blanketed the country (*see* Radar). Until the electronic network came into full operation, about 500,000 civilian volunteers constituted a Ground Observer Corps (GOC), providing backup warning capability. Jet fighters were similarly deployed. The Distant Early Warning (DEW) radars along the Arctic Circle were completed in 1957. The combined North American Air Defense Command (NORAD) was created in 1957. Navy radar picket ships patrolled the coasts, and radar-bearing platforms (Texas Towers) were embedded in shoals off the East Coast. By the end of the 1950's, antiaircraft guns had been replaced by surface-to-air missiles (Nike and Bomarc) to defend cities and military installations. In the early 1950's intensive research in the application of electronic computers to air defense was undertaken, culminating in the early 1960's in the deployment of about twenty Semi-Automatic Ground Environment (SAGE) combat operation centers, integrating all air defense operations both regionally and nationally.

The coming of the space age brought the new threat of intercontinental ballistic missiles (ICBM's). A Ballistic Missile Early Warning System (BMEWS) was erected, with special radar stations in Alaska, Greenland, and the United Kingdom. Attention was also given to the possibility of attack by earth-orbiting satellites, and an elaborate network of space sensors, the Space Detection and Tracking System (SPADATS), was deployed worldwide.

In 1969 Congress approved a decision to construct a Ballistic Missile Defense System (BMDS), with the code name Safeguard; it included radars, short- and long-range missiles, and supporting automatic data processing equipment. Plans called for large-scale deployment; but the Strategic Arms Limitation Treaty (SALT I) with the Soviet Union (ratified July 1972) limited each country to two antiballistic missile (ABM) defenses, one to protect each nation's capital and the other to defend one ICBM complex. The United States constructed its Safeguard missile site in North Dakota (1974), but Congress did not authorize construction of the Washington, D.C., site. The control facility for the Safeguard system was the Missile Defense Center near Colorado Springs, Colo. The entire system began operations in 1975.

Because all three services were operating air defense equipment, the Continental Air Defense Command (CONAD) was established in 1954 to coordinate their efforts. CONAD was integrated into NORAD, whose headquarters was established in a cavern under Cheyenne Mountain near Colorado Springs. By 1974 CONAD was inactivated, leaving the USAF's Aerospace Defense Command the only U.S. component of NORAD.

AIR FORCE, UNITED STATES. The history of U.S. military aviation reaches back to the Civil War, when civilian aeronauts and enlisted ground crews operated observation balloons for Union forces. On Aug. 1, 1907, the U.S. Army created an aeronautical division within the Signal Corps, and in 1909 it purchased its first airplane from the Wright brothers. The First Aero Squadron (1913) was the only tactical air unit in the army prior to 1917.

When the United States entered World War I, its aviation arm possessed only thirty-five pilots and fifty-five mechanics. The wartime Congress voted large sums for aviation, but fewer than 200 planes of 740 in use by American squadrons were American-built. In August 1918 all American frontline air units were placed under a single commander, Brig. Gen. William (Billy) Mitchell.

The air arm was separated from the Signal Corps in May 1918 and by legislation in 1920 became the Air Service. Mitchell promoted projects to increase awareness of the potential of aviation: a mass transcontinental flight in 1919, tests against battleships in 1921 and 1923, and a global circumnavigation advanced aviation, but failed to win further reform. The Air Corps Act of 1926 changed the Air Service to the Air Corps, increased air representation on the General Staff, and authorized expansion. Funding remained tight, and when in 1934 the Air Corps undertook to fly the nation's airmail, the arm's poor condition was revealed. Partial reorganization followed, establishing a single headquarters for control of most combat units. In the 1930's aircraft and doctrine for "strategic" (or independent) air warfare emerged. The Army Air Forces (AAF) was created in June 1941, becoming coequal the following year with the army ground forces and the services of supply.

The basic USAF tactical unit has been the squadron, consisting of aircrews and ground crewmen for twelve to twenty-four assigned aircraft. During World War II, tactical squadrons were combined into groups; later, they were placed under a wing headquarters. A wing could occupy a single base, or its units could be dispersed. Several wings could be organized into an air division or be placed directly under the next echelon, the numbered air force. The B-29 units in the Marianas were organized as XXI Bomber Command.

The National Security Act of 1947 established a single Department of Defense, with three departments—the army, the navy (which retained naval and marine aviation), and the air force.

Reorganizations also brought into being the major air commands: SAC, the Air Defense Command, and the Tactical Air Command. The Air Materiel Command and the Air Research and Development Command were reorganized in 1961 as the Air Force Logistics Command (responsible for maintenance, supply, and procurement) and the Air Force Systems Command (applied research and development). Overseas, air force component commands served in unified theater commands. Headquarters, USAF, headed by the chief of staff, under the office of the secretary of the air force, is located in Washington, D.C.

Research and Space Activities. The air force has focused much effort toward future air weaponry. Meteorological research, aerial geodetic surveys, and various aeromedical research efforts have had wide application. Air force transports have provided essential airlift for scientific projects in the Arctic and Antarctic.

Air force space activities have included unmanned research, weather, detection, and communications satellite projects, as well as systematic tracking of space objects. Upon cancellation of air force manned projects—a piloted space glider in 1963 and the Manned Orbital Laboratory in 1969—the USAF supported the manned ventures of the National Aeronautics and Space Administration, contributing technical personnel and astronauts for projects Mercury, Gemini, Apollo, and Skylab. Air force ballistic missiles (Atlas, Titan, and Thor) were transformed into reliable space-launch systems.

Air University. Formal professional education for air officers evolved from the Air Service Field Officers' School, created in 1920 at Langley Field, Va. The school was renamed Air Service Tactical School in 1922, and Air Corps Tactical School in 1926, moving to Maxwell Field, Ala., in 1931.

The Air University was established in September 1946 at Maxwell, with three main components: the Air Tactical School (later renamed Squadron Officer School), designed for regular officers in their first five years; the Air Command and Staff School (later College), designed for selected officers prior to their twelfth year; and the ten-month Air War College, with annual classes selected from the best-qualified officers prior to their twentieth year of service.

Air Reserve Forces. The Air National Guard and the Air Force Reserve constitute the air reserve forces of the United States. The first National Guard aviation unit was organized in New York in 1915; no such units were mustered into federal service in World War I, but postwar National Guard regulations established air observation, balloon, and photo units. All twenty-nine observation squadrons were ordered to federal duty in September 1940. The Air National Guard separated from the National Guard upon USAF independence in 1947. Guard squadrons began participating in the continental air defense system in 1954, and guard fighter squadrons mobilized and were deployed overseas during the Berlin crisis (1961) and after the *Pueblo* affair (1968). The Air National Guard in 1974 included over 90,000 personnel and was principally equipped with Vietnam-vintage aircraft, including the F-100, F-102, F-105, and C-130.

The Air Force Reserve includes individuals assigned as augmentees for active duty units and members of reserve squadrons equipped with transport and other aircraft. Organized reservists in 1949 numbered 42,000; another 60,000 were unpaid Volunteer Air Reservists. During the Korean War, all twenty-five reserve troop carrier and light bomber wings were recalled; four squadrons were recalled in 1961, and eight during the Cuban missile crisis. C-124's with Air Force Reserve crews proved vital during the 1965 Dominican intervention and flew trans-Pacific hauls during the war in Southeast Asia. An "associate unit" system was begun in 1968, whereby reserve unit members helped fly and maintain aircraft belonging to an active unit. In 1974, the Air Force Reserve numbered thirty-eight squadrons, mostly equipped with C-130's, as well as eighteen associate squadrons affiliated with active units of Military Airlift Command.

AIR FORCE ACADEMY, UNITED STATES. The academy was conceived as a four-year undergraduate institution, leading to the B.S. degree and a regular air force commission. The first class (numbering 207) entered in summer 1955, using facilities at Denver, Colo., prior to occupation of the permanent site at Colorado Springs three years later. The full authorized enrollment of 2,500 was reached in 1962; in 1964 legislation set the authorization at 4,417. Each congressman was authorized five appointments and could nominate several individuals to compete for each vacancy. The period of obligatory service was also increased from three to five years, beginning with the class of 1968.

The Air Force Academy provides advanced and accelerated studies beyond the prescribed curriculum; in 1964 a system of specialized majors programs was instituted. The academy has retained an all-military faculty, subsidizing graduate work for line officers at civilian institutions prior to faculty tours of about four years. A cheating incident in 1965 received national attention and resulted in over 100 cadets leaving the academy; reassessment left the traditional honor code unchanged, although certain rigidities in cadet life were reduced.

AIRMAIL. The first test of airmail service was made in May 1918, when the U.S. Army and the Post Office Department set up an experimental line between New York and Washington, D.C., using army pilots. After three months, the Post Office assumed control of the line and employed civilian aviators. This route was too short to give planes much advantage over trains. Other routes were tried, but all were too short to attract mail at high rates. In 1920 the Post Office began service between New York and San Francisco: the planes flew only by daylight, the mail being transferred at dusk to trains. This was replaced in 1924 by a continuous, day-and-night service across the continent. In 1926–27 the department turned over the handling of airmail to private contractors; branch lines and north-and-south lines were rapidly added. After what appeared to be collusion among airline owners, the postmaster general in 1934 canceled all airmail contracts, and for four months army planes carried the mail. New contracts were signed and the service was returned to private planes. In 1935 regular mail service was established between San Francisco and Manila, and in 1939 between New York and London.

AIR NAVIGATION AGREEMENTS. *See* **Air Transportation.**

AIRPLANE. See **Air Transportation.**

AIRPLANE DISASTERS. *See* **Disasters.**

AIRPLANE RACES. *See* **Air Transportation.**

AIRPORTS. *See* **Air Transportation.**

AIR POWER, STRATEGIC. The concept of strategic air power involves the employment of aerial weapons to bypass the surface battlefield and strike at the key industries that permit a country to carry on its war effort. Because the industrial strength of a nation lies principally in its cities, cities themselves are targets in an all-out strategic bombardment campaign.

In the 1930's a small group at the Air Corps Tactical School, Maxwell Field, Ala., discovered a prophetic book, *Command of the Air* (1921), by Italian artillery officer Giulio Douhet. The school made a translation and this theoretical work was argued and refined by the officers who were to become the American air leaders of World War II.

By the time the United States entered the war in 1941, the concept of strategic air power had found its way into war plans.

With the advent of nuclear weapons and the development of rockets, the United States organized the Strategic Air Command (SAC). By 1973 SAC was composed primarily of B-52 jet bombers and Minuteman intercontinental ballistic missiles (ICBM's). (*See also* Air Defense.)

AIR TRANSPORTATION. Balloon experiments were made in the United States during the 19th century, the most spectacular being the use of observation balloons by the Union army. Of more significance were glider experiments conducted in the late 19th century, which provided the basic body of aerodynamic data necessary for the development of powered flight.

Heavier-than-air flight was definitely an American achievement. Samuel P. Langley experimented with such flight from 1887 to 1903. Langley tried twice, in 1903, to launch his "aerodrome," but on both occasions the launch gear failed to function properly and Langley abandoned his efforts.

On Dec. 17, 1903, Orville and Wilbur Wright flew a biplane that achieved sustained, powered, and controlled flight.

In 1907 Alexander Graham Bell established the Aerial Experiment Association, located in Nova Scotia. The association's principal contribution was to introduce Glenn Curtiss to aviation. Curtiss conceived the seaplane, putting a "step" in its float, thus breaking the surface tension of the water and enabling it to take off without excessive power.

Before the outbreak of World War I, tests showed the military potential of airplanes. Glenn Curtiss experimented with aerial bombing as early as 1910; Eugene Ely performed shipboard takeoffs and landings (1910–11); James McCurdy demonstrated the feasibility of two-way radio contact between air and ground (1911); and Riley Scott invented a bombsight (1914).

America's principal technological accomplishment of World War I was the liquid-cooled, mass-produced Liberty engine. The National Advisory Committee for Aeronautics (NACA), founded in 1915, opened a modern laboratory in 1920 and over the years made numerous discoveries, among them a cowling to streamline radial engines and a variety of airfoils.

Wright engines powered the Ryan Aeronautical *Spirit of St. Louis* for Charles Lindbergh's May 1927 nonstop flight from New York to Paris, and the Wright-Bellanca in which Clarence Chamberlain, accompanied by Charles Levine, flew nonstop from the United States to Germany. These two planes overshadowed such single-engine, Liberty-powered craft as the 1924 Douglas World Cruisers, in which army aviators circled the earth, and Grover Loening's amphibian.

The Lockheed Vega, a single-engine monoplane designed by Allan Loughhead and John Northrop, was first flown in 1927 and later used by Wiley Post on two around-the-world flights. Of wooden monocoque construction, it marked the successful revival of a building technique introduced in France before World War I. Post's second around-the-world flight (1933) was made possible by an automatic pilot built by Sperry Gyroscope Company.

A major contribution to the development of the dirigible was the introduction of helium, a nonflammable lifting gas. A metalclad airship flew successfully, but loss of the navy's *Shenandoah, Akron,* and *Macon*—followed by the destruction in 1937 of Germany's hydrogen-filled *Hindenburg*—brought to an end the era of the great dirigibles (*see also* Dirigibles).

The most striking American achievement of the 1930's was the development of transport aircraft synthesizing in their design all-metal monocoque construction; retractable landing gear; controllable pitch propellers; wing flaps and wing slots; and, for the most part, radial air-cooled engines with the cowling introduced by the NACA in 1928, which permitted effective cooling with reduced drag. The all-metal, monocoque, low-wing monoplane, with retractable landing gear, controllable pitch propeller, wing flaps, and wing slots, became the virtually universal design for military and commercial transport planes. The first planes to incorporate these features in the early 1930's were the Martin B-10 and the Boeing B-9 bombers and the Boeing 247 transport; what gave the American industry a commanding lead in developing and producing such planes was the rivalry between airlines and between manufacturers. The desire for a competitor to the 247 led to the development of the Douglas DC series, with the result that by 1939 the DC-3, introduced in 1935, dominated the world's airways. The introduction of long-range flying boats—the Sikorsky, Boeing, and Martin clippers—made possible regular transoceanic service. As the decade ended, Boeing, Douglas, and Lockheed were all working on four-engined landplanes with pressurized cabins for high-altitude flight, but these did not go into regular commercial operation until after World War II. Simultaneously the American aviation industry became the leading producer of large bombers, beginning with the Boeing B-17 Flying Fortress in 1935.

In World War II the aircraft carrier replaced the battleship as the basis of seapower. Oxygen masks, pressure suits, and airborne radar were also introduced. Ground Control Approach (GCA) and Instrument Landing Systems (ILS) were developed, and extensive use was made of transport aircraft, especially landplanes, on intercontinental flights.

The first practical helicopter appeared during World War II, but too late to see much service.

German data on jet propulsion became available to American engineers after the war. In the postwar advance of aviation technology several experimental craft were trailblazers, such as the rocket-powered Bell X-1, in which Charles Yeager exceeded the speed of sound in level flight (Oct. 14, 1947).

Most famous of the series was the North American X-15 rocket plane, which exceeded 4,000 mph and climbed above 300,000 feet.

American-designed transports continued to dominate the world's commercial airlines. The long-range, piston-powered types culminated in the Lockheed Super Constellation and the Douglas DC-7C, a descendant of the wartime Skymaster. Boeing built a prototype jet transport in 1954. When the U.S. Air Force purchased a tanker model, the KC-135, Boeing arranged to lease government-owned tools to build a commercial type, the successful 707.

In 1961 three U.S. Air Force B-52 bombers made a nonstop flight around the world, refueling in the air en route; and ten years later (Apr. 26, 1971) an air force SR-71 reconnaissance jet established a new record—combining duration, total distance covered, and altitude—for a flight of 10.5 hours, a distance of 15,000 miles at speeds in excess of Mach 3 (more than 2,000 mph), and altitudes over 80,000 feet.

Progress in general aviation culminated in the production of William P. Lear's Learjet (1964), a jet-powered executive transport designed exclusively for the civilian market. Other milestones in general aviation included the twin-engine Beechcraft Model 18 (1937), the Stinson Reliant (1936), and Cessna Airmaster (1934) single-engine monoplanes, and the Beechcraft Model 17 Staggerwing single-engine biplane (1932). The most popular of American light planes was the two-place, single-engine Cub, designed in 1932 by C. Gilbert Taylor. Piper Aircraft later took over Taylor's design, which remained in production for two decades.

In the early 1970's, the American aircraft industry concentrated on big transports such as the Boeing 747, McDonnell Douglas DC-10, and Lockheed L-1011 TriStar. Boeing began preliminary work on a supersonic transport (SST), but the government in March 1971 ended its subsidy. France and England started passenger service with the SST Concorde in 1976.

Aviation Industry. The American aviation industry began in 1909, when the Wright brothers formed a company to build airplanes and conduct flying schools. They were followed by Glenn Curtiss (1909), W. Starling Burgess (1910), Glenn L. Martin (1912), William E. Boeing (1915), and Allan and Martin Loughead (1915). Growth was slow because of minimal support from the government. Total output in 1914 was forty-nine planes.

Governmental pressure brought about the creation of the Aircraft Manufacturers' Association in 1917. The wartime program produced some 14,000 planes. When the armistice came, the aviation industry virtually collapsed. The principal holdovers were the Wright Aeronautical Company, Curtiss Aeroplane and Motor, Boeing, and the Glenn L. Martin Company. Two important new arrivals appeared in the early 1920's: Douglas and Consolidated.

The 1920's witnessed a steady growth of the industry, stimulated by the Kelly Air Mail Act of 1925 and the Morrow Board in 1926, which provided a systematic five-year program of military and naval procurement. A number of new American airframe firms appeared, including Lockheed, Fairchild, Sikorsky, and Fokker. An outstanding entrant was William B. Stout's company, one of the first in the world to build all-metal aircraft; it was taken over by the Ford Motor Company in 1924 and produced the well-known Ford trimotor transport, the "tin goose." Wichita, Kans., emerged as the country's principal center for the manufacture of planes for general aviation.

By the end of the decade the United States had attained a clear leadership in radial air-cooled engines. There was also an American effort to enter the lighter-than-air field, because of naval interest. The dirigible *Shenandoah* was completed in 1923. In 1924 the Goodyear Zeppelin Corporation was formed, with both German designs and German technicians. This company built the *Akron* (1931) and the *Macon* (1933).

The enthusiasm generated by Charles A. Lindbergh's New York to Paris flight in 1927 led to several efforts at large-scale combinations of aircraft manufacturers and air-transport companies, the most important being United Aircraft and Transport, started in 1928 by William E. Boeing, North American Aviation, and the Aviation Corporation. However, in 1934 a political controversy over the award of airmail contracts resulted in legislation requiring the separation of manufacturing and transport companies.

In the mid-1930's the Pacific Coast acquired the bulk of the country's airframe production. Engine production was heavily concentrated in the Northeast. Total output as late as 1939 was fewer than 6,000 planes for the year, and it ranked forty-first among American industries.

World War II brought drastic changes; by 1943 the aviation industry was the country's largest producer and employer. Total output between 1939 and 1945 was approximately 300,000 aircraft. Peak employment in the aviation industry was 1,345,600 in 1943.

When the war ended, the aviation industry faced major readjustments. A substantial growth in helicopter manufacture took place. Jet airplanes developed much faster than had been anticipated, largely because of intensive research and development by the military (*see* Aircraft, Bomber; Aircraft, Fighter). The prototype 707 flew in 1954, based on the design of the KC-135 air force tanker; it went into regular airline service in 1958. Douglas followed a year later with the DC-8. The only other serious competitors in the field of large jet planes were Convair and Lockheed.

Airframe manufacturers became the prime producers of missiles and, after 1957, of space vehicles. The industry continued to be acutely dependent on the government, to which it made 80 percent of its sales. Research and development became the largest single item of cost, and there were more managerial and technical personnel than production workers.

In the 1970's the American aerospace industry led the world in the design and manufacture of transport aircraft, with the exception of a supersonic transport (SST), which was abandoned. Declining military demand and curtailment of the space program caused distress, reflecting again the industry's acute dependence on government.

Commercial Aviation. Passenger service was first launched Jan. 1, 1914, between Saint Petersburg and Tampa, on a seasonal basis, but World War I halted development of commercial air transportation. During 1919–23, Aeromarine Airways made the only impressive record among commercial air companies, carrying mail and passengers between Miami and the Bahama Islands and between Key West and Havana during the winter, and passengers between New York and Cleveland during the summer.

The Kelly Air Mail Act of 1925 stimulated the rise of commercial airlines; twenty companies contracted to carry the mail (*see* Airmail). Only two carriers showed much interest in transporting passengers.

The public became enthusiastic about the potential of aviation following Lindbergh's flight from New York to Paris. Within two years Pan American World Airways and the "big four" domestic air transportation companies were formed: United Airlines, Eastern Airlines, Transcontinental Air Transport (later Trans World Airlines), and American Airlines. The expansion of air passenger traffic, the reliability of the DC-3 and other aircraft, and discontent with Post Office contracts led to the Civil Aeronautics Act of 1938. The sixteen domestic airlines and Pan American were placed under the economic regulation of the Civil Aeronautics Authority, soon renamed the Civil Aeronautics Board (CAB).

Feeder lines were authorized by the CAB, first as an experiment to supplement the trunk lines, then by 1947 as the components of a national network constituting a second level of scheduled services. These feeder lines were aided by such subsidy payments. When the war ended, both Pan American and Trans World Airlines (TWA) were authorized to expand as round-the-world carriers; Northwest Orient Airlines obtained a route across the northern Pacific; American Airlines into the southern Pacific; and Braniff Airways into South America. Beginning in 1946 several domestic carriers were permitted to operate scheduled flights into the Caribbean. The Chicago and Southern Air Lines, which has since merged with Delta Airlines, obtained the longest routes. In 1974, Pan American, Eastern, American, and Delta were the American-flag carriers in that area.

During 1945–46, about 3,000 small nonscheduled carriers were formed, usually using inexpensive war surplus aircraft. The CAB authorized 142 to be large irregular carriers. Since 1959 this group has been relabeled supplemental air carriers, and the number has dwindled to eight; they may also engage in irregular service to specified foreign areas. Some of the early nonscheduled companies became all-cargo carriers. Air taxis have developed since 1962 as the third level of scheduled air carriers. Within seven years there were some 3,500 such operators; by mid-1973 the number had declined to less than 2,000, which included 124 commuter air carriers transporting passengers on an individually ticketed basis.

Routes have been modified, with many new nonstop schedules and more one-carrier service, thus increasing competition. Additional competition resulted from the rapid introduction of jet aircraft. Air cargo has become an increasing proportion of the airline business. The rapid expansion of both passenger and freight traffic led airline management to begin its big swing to wide-bodied aircraft, such as Boeing 747 (introduced in 1970), which can carry as many as 490 passengers. Jumbo jets disrupted the patterns of flight frequencies and the balances between the larger capacity of the new planes and the limitations of the market. The consequent decrease of net revenues was sufficient in 1972 to cause managements to ground various aircraft, including some wide-bodies, and offer them for sale. The fuel crisis during the winter of 1973–74 brought deficits and accelerated the trend of grounding planes. Another cost-cutting effort in 1974 was the exchange of routes between carriers, with CAB permission, and proposals for more route revisions to reduce expensive competition.

On Dec. 31, 1958, all aspects of federal regulation of aviation were gathered under the Federal Aviation Agency (Federal Aviation Administration since 1966), except that the CAB has retained authority over its basic transport regulations and over determination of probable causes of aircraft accidents. Air safety always has commanded major attention and the carriers and aircraft manufacturers have logged a remarkable safety record, due in part to the increase in sophistication of the airspace system since the development of radar in the early 1940's. The number of flights under instrument flight rules and the use of advanced types of communications, navigation, and radar facilities have increased greatly.

Many of the new airports constructed near the major cities under the Federal Airport Act of 1946 are becoming inadequate. Consequently, a few mammoth regional airports are now planned or under construction. The first one, between Dallas and Fort Worth, is already completed. By 1978 there were 14,574 airports in the United States, of which about 500 were used for scheduled airline service.

In the late 1970s commercial airlines experienced increasing financial difficulties and engaged in fierce price competition to attract passengers, offering various bargain fares on standby basis and "no frills" tickets. The Airline Deregulation Act, passed in 1978, provided for dissolution of the CAB by 1985. In August 1981, a strike by air traffic controllers and the subsequent firing of strikers by President Ronald Reagan resulted in massive chaos and showed the need for industry revision.

AISNE DEFENSIVE (May 27–June 5, 1918). The Germans attacked southward between Soissons and Reims and reached the Marne near Château-Thierry, only forty miles from Paris. They then vainly attempted to establish a bridgehead on the Marne and to push westward toward Paris.

AISNE-MARNE OPERATION (July 18–Aug. 6, 1918). The Franco-American counteroffensive following the German offensive of July 15 in the Marne salient.

From July 21 on, the armies farther east joined in the advance—the Sixth (Degoutte) and the Fifth (Berthelot), along both faces of the salient. The Germans conducted their retreat skillfully, making an especially strong stand on the Ourcq on July 28; but early in August they were back behind the Vesle. The Marne salient had ceased to exist, and the Germans were never again able to undertake a serious offensive.

AIX-LA-CHAPELLE, TREATY OF (Oct. 18, 1748). This treaty ended the War of the Austrian Succession (*see* King George's War). The restoration of Louisburg, Nova Scotia, to France irritated the New Englanders who had been active in the capture. The peace was merely an intermission in the protracted struggle for control of the Saint Lawrence and Mississippi basins.

AKRON (Ohio). Founded in 1825 as a stopping point on the Ohio and Erie Canal: its name comes from the Greek word *akros* ("high"), for it was the highest point reached on the canal. During the late 19th century it was known as a center for milling cereals. Benjamin F. Goodrich located his rubber plant there as a result of a town publicity campaign. Half a dozen other rubber companies located there early in the 20th century. The rubber industry grew rapidly and Akron, the "Rubber Capital" of the world, became the center for the production of rubber-based items. Other industries located in and around the city include salt-processing and chemical plants, and the production of earth-moving equipment and tools.

Akron's population reached a high of 290,351 in 1960 but began to drop off as some of its residents moved out of the central city into suburban areas. The population in 1980 was 275,425. Among the annual events held in Akron is the "International Soap Box Derby" in August.

AKRON. *See* **Dirigibles.**

AKRON LAW (Feb. 8, 1847). To improve the public school system in Akron, the Ohio General Assembly passed a law providing for an elected board of education, the organization of the city as a single school district, free admission of all children to the public schools, the adoption of a system for the classification and promotion of pupils, and local taxation for financing the schools. The law, with some modifications, came to be applied generally throughout the state.

ALABAMA. The first Europeans to reach Alabama were the Spanish explorers Alonzo Alvares de Piñeda (1519) and Pánfilo de Narváez (1528). In the 1540's Hernando de Soto crossed through the region (*see* Mauvilla, Battle of). The first permanent settlement was established by the French under Jean Baptiste Le Moyne, Sieur de Bienville, at Mobile Bay (1702), which was then a part of Louisiana. In 1763 France ceded the territory to Great Britain, and in 1783 the southern portion was ceded to Spain and the remainder to the United States. Mobile, the seat of Spanish power, was taken by the United States in 1813. In 1817 the Alabama Territory was organized out of the Mississippi Territory, of which it had been a part since 1798, and was admitted to the Union on Dec. 14, 1819.

Alabama was settled by farmers, planters, and professional men, mostly from Georgia and the Carolinas; cotton farming and the plantation system prevailed. The predominance of agriculture expressed itself in politics before 1860. The Democrats were dominant, with a Jeffersonian and proslavery philosophy. States' rights sentiment grew rapidly, and defense of southern rights became a dominant issue under the leadership of William L. Yancey; on Jan. 11, 1861, Alabama seceded.

The Confederate government was organized at Montgomery (Feb. 4, 1861), its first capital (the "Cradle of the Confederacy"). Estimates of Alabama's property losses during the Civil War run as high as $500 million; losses among the white male population, which was heavily enrolled in the Confederate army, were one in ten. The state attempted to reenter the Union under President Andrew Johnson's plan of reconstruction, but the provisional government, which had been functioning under its new constitution (drafted September 1865), was repudiated by Congress. Reconstruction brought the state under federal military control on Mar. 2, 1867. A new constitution was drafted in November 1867, and the state was readmitted to the Union in June 1868. The decade following the Civil War saw Alabama torn by party dissension and its government characterized by extravagance and dishonesty.

From 1876 through 1944 Alabama was controlled politically by Democrats. In 1948 the state joined other southern states in leaving the Democratic National Convention, owing to the stand on civil rights taken by the national party. Later, in Birmingham, the southern states organized the States' Rights Democratic party. In 1952 the state returned to the Democratic party to remain until 1968, when it supported the American Independent party, organized and led by George C. Wallace (governor 1962–66). In 1972 Wallace attempted to capture the presidential nomination of the national Democratic party. In the 1970's the Democratic structure of the state was broken.

Disturbances in Alabama's allegiance to the Democratic party reflect the controversy over civil rights. In 1956 the state was a focus of national attention as black residents of Birmingham, under the leadership of Martin Luther King, carried through a successful boycott of local buses, prompted by discriminatory practices. In 1961 a confrontation of busloads of representatives of the Congress of Racial Equality and local mobs necessitated the imposition of martial law. In 1963 Alabama was forced by federal court order to grant admission to blacks at the University of Alabama and various public schools in Birmingham, Mobile, and Tuskegee.

Cotton has remained the chief money crop of Alabama, but since World War II more farmland has been turned over to the raising of livestock, especially chickens. Two-thirds of the state's land area has come to be devoted to timber, leading to the development of related industries. Iron and steel manufacture, begun in the late 19th century, have expanded rapidly, especially in Birmingham, but more than 50 percent of the state's mineral production is constituted of bituminous coal. Mobile, a major cotton port before the Civil War, has regained a prominent rank, principally in the handling of coal. A major aerospace industry has developed around Huntsville.

Alabama has followed the national trend toward urbanization: in 1900, the state had an urban population of only 12 percent; in 1950, 40 percent; and in 1975, 58 percent. The overall population has increased to 3.9 million in 1980.

***ALABAMA*.** In June 1861, Capt. J. D. Bulloch reached England as Confederate agent to contract with private builders for warships; he obtained the *Florida* and a second more powerful ship, the *Alabama,* launched at Liverpool, May 15, 1862. U.S. Minister C. F. Adams attempted to detain the *Alabama,* but it had already sailed. It became the terror of Union vessels. Under Capt. Raphael Semmes, before its destruction in 1864 (*see Kearsarge-Alabama* Fight), it sank, burned, or captured more than sixty ships.

ALABAMA CLAIMS. U.S. grievances against Great Britain during and just after the Civil War clustered about this generic phrase. The queen's proclamation of neutrality, giving the South belligerent rights, and Confederate cruisers, built or armed by Britons, led Secretary of State William H. Seward to lay before the British government a demand for redress. Ultimately, the United States entered claims against Great Britain for damage wrought by eleven vessels, totaling $19,021,000.

The claims met no response until 1868, when the Johnson-Clarendon Convention, signed under Seward's close supervision, made no mention of the Alabama Claims but provided for a settlement of all Anglo-American claims since 1853; it was overwhelmingly defeated by the Senate (Apr. 13, 1869). Hamilton Fish, becoming secretary of state in 1869, adopted the view that the whole set of Alabama Claims could be met by the payment of a lump sum, an apology, and a definition of maritime international law meeting U.S. wishes. With Sir John Rose acting as intermediary, Fish and Lord Granville decided that a joint commission should settle the whole nexus of disputes—Canadian fisheries, northwestern boundary, and Alabama Claims. The commission, meeting under Fish and Earl DeGrey, drew up the Treaty of Washington (signed May 8, 1871), which expressed British regret for the escape of the *Alabama* and other cruisers, laid down three rules of maritime neutrality, and provided for submission of the Alabama Claims to a board of five arbitrators, American, British, Italian, Swiss, and Brazilian. This tribunal decided, Sept. 14, 1872, that Great Britain had failed in its duties as a neutral and awarded the United States $15.5 million in gold. (*See* Washington, Treaty of.)

ALABAMA PLATFORM. Adopted by the Democratic state convention in 1848 and approved by other southern groups, it demanded congressional protection of slavery in the Mexican cession. Rejected by the Democrats in 1848, the principle was adopted by a majority of the Democratic convention at Charleston in 1860.

ALAMANCE, BATTLE OF (May 16, 1771). To suppress the Regulators of North Carolina, Gov. William Tryon ordered Gen. Hugh Waddell to Hillsboro with a force of about 1,000 militia. Two thousand Regulators had assembled on the Alamance River, about one-half without arms and with no officer higher than captain. The provincial army had artillery and was adequately equipped. The battle lasted two hours and ended in disaster for the Regulators. (*See also* Regulators of North Carolina.)

ALAMO, SIEGE OF THE (Feb. 23–Mar. 6, 1836). A battle during the Texas Revolution. Lt. Col. William Barret Travis found himself in joint command with James Bowie of about 145 men at San Antonio when on Feb. 23 Antonio López de Santa Anna appeared with between 3,000 and 4,000 Mexican troops. Travis and Bowie moved into the stout-walled Alamo mission, refused to surrender, and sent couriers for reinforcements. On the eighth day of battle 32 recruits crept through the Mexican lines, bringing the strength of the garrison to about 187.

On the thirteenth day of battle, Santa Anna stormed the Alamo on all sides and the walls were breached. The defenders fought throughout the mission compound, clubbing rifles and drawing knives. The last point taken was the church, where David Crockett fell. All 187 defenders were killed, though the Mexicans spared about 30 noncombatants. Mexican losses were about 1,500.

ALASKA. The northwestern extension of the North American continent, 586,000 square miles in extent, acquired by purchase from Russia in 1867, became the forty-ninth state of the Union in 1958. In 1980, it had a population of 400,481. At the beginning of the 18th century Peter the Great and Empress Catherine I sent exploratory expeditions under naval captain Vitus Bering, leading to exploration of Alaska in 1741. The Russians established the Russian-American Company in Alaska and under the management of Aleksandr Baranov extended the czar's dominions far eastward. On an island in the Alexander Archipelago—the Panhandle—Baranov founded a military and trading post named New Archangel, later Sitka, which became the capital of Russian America. While a rival British concessionaire, the Hudson's Bay Company, was advancing westward with the similar objective of exploiting the region's resources, clashes between the two companies were averted by a convention signed by Britain and Russia in 1828.

The Russian-American Company did not fare well; its deficits could be more than wiped out by a sale of Russian America, and Russia's expansion more profitably diverted. On Mar. 29, 1867, after some weeks of negotiation, U. S. Secretary of State William H. Seward and Baron Eduard Stoeckl, Russia's minister to the United States, completed the draft of a treaty of cession of Russian North America. The price was $7.2 million, less than two cents an acre. Charles Sumner of Massachusetts, chairman of the Senate's Foreign Relations Committee, in a speech spelled out all the advantages of the acquisition and gave the area its name, Alaska, from an Aleut word meaning "the great land." The ceremonies of transfer took place on Oct. 18, 1867.

In the seventeen years following the purchase, Congress enacted only two bills dealing with Alaska. One extended to it the commerce and navigation laws and provided a collector of customs, who at that period was its principal government official. The other act turned over administration of the fur seal fisheries of the Pribilof Islands to the secretary of the treasury, who leased them to a private enterprise in San Francisco. During those seventeen years such authority as there was in Alaska was exercised without legal proviso by the general commanding the U.S. forces stationed at Sitka.

The Organic Act of 1884, which gave Alaska its first vestige of government and law, provided a governor, a federal district judge, and five commissioners. The act extended to this newly established civil and judicial district the nation's mining laws and appropriated $25,000 for education. It extended the laws of the state of Oregon to Alaska. But it specifically forbade the application of U.S. land laws, the establishment of a legislature and of an office of delegate to Congress, and the creation of counties.

For the next twenty years successive governors voiced condemnation of the omissions and restrictions in the Organic Act, but no attention was paid to these complaints until the discovery of gold in the Klondike in the 1890's brought a rush of prospectors. These prospectors were voters in their own states, and their complaints consequently registered with their senators and representatives. A bill to provide a delegate in Congress for Alaska was finally enacted on May 7, 1905; the law also established voting—for the office of delegate to Congress only—limited to males who had resided in Alaska for one year.

The Organic Act of 1912 permitted Alaska to have a legislature, but denied Alaska the control and management of its fisheries and wildlife; forbade the enacting of any basic land laws; kept the judiciary in federal control; and forbade the creation of counties without the prior consent of Congress. Despite the self-serving precautions of outside interests, local self-government began promisingly. The first legislature in 1913 enfranchised women. The second legislature in 1915 enacted the first old-age pension system in the United States. The two legislatures established a modest revenue system by a series of license and poll taxes. Having found vast fields requiring legislation in which they were forbidden to act, the legislatures pleaded with Congress to revise the land laws to promote homesteading; to transfer to Alaska the management of the fisheries, which were inadequately protected against depletion under federal management; to make appropriations for highway construction; and to pay the federal lower court judges a salary. Not one of these requests was honored by the Congress during the next forty years.

Alaska's congressional delegate, James Wickersham, introduced the first legislation to achieve Alaskan statehood as early as 1916. Wickersham secured the establishment of a land-grant college, which became the University of Alaska, and legislation to provide a railroad from Seward on the Pacific coast to Fairbanks, a new community born of the gold discoveries in the Tanana Valley. Also, a low-grade wagon road named the Richardson Highway, 371 miles long, was completed in 1913 from Valdez to Fairbanks. During the 1940's the struggle between the absentee interests and those who wanted to develop Alaska as a place of permanent abode intensified, but the 1948 election broke the blockade; the resulting 1949 session enacted a comprehensive tax program and prepared the way for statehood. Statehood legislation sponsored by Alaska's delegates, Anthony J. Dimond and his successor, E. L. (Bob) Bartlett, was supported by President Harry S. Truman. President Dwight D. Eisenhower opposed Alaskan, but not Hawaiian, statehood, on the assumption that Alaska would elect Democrats to Congress. Bills to achieve statehood for both were unable to secure approval of both houses for a decade, but public sentiment for both was increasing.

The 1955 Alaska legislature had passed an act calling for a constitutional convention to formulate a plan for statehood. This convention adopted a plan proposed by George Lehleitner, known as the Tennessee Plan, to send a special elected delegation to Washington as members of Congress. Elected as senators were William Egan, president of the convention, and former Gov. Ernest Gruening, and as representative, Ralph J. Rivers, also a state legislator. When they arrived in Washington in 1957, they were not seated, and were informed that if statehood was to be secured, they would have to run again. For the next two sessions of the Eighty-fifth Congress, the three lobbied the Senate and House. The House passed the statehood bill by a vote of 217 to 172; the Senate passed it on June 30, 1958, by 64 to 20. The following January President Eisenhower signed the bill. A constitution was written by the constitutional convention of 1956.

The conflict of developers versus conservationists arose in the late 1950's with the discovery of oil and gas deposits in the Kenai Peninsula. Some years earlier Secretary of the Interior Harold Ickes had withdrawn 200,000 acres there as a moose range. Secretary of the Interior Fred Seaton was confronted with the opposition of all but one conservation organization (the Izaak Walton League); Seaton decided to open half the moose range for drilling. The issue recurred in the 1960's concerning the oil discoveries at Prudhoe Bay on the Arctic coast. To get the oil to market, a pipeline to Alaska's gulf coast was planned, but conservation societies argued that the pipeline would pass through earthquake-prone terrain, that it would impede migration of animals, and that oil spills from tankers would be perilous to the fisheries. The efforts to block the pipeline were defeated in successive court actions; Congress approved legislation authorizing its construction, and the legislation became law on Nov. 16, 1973.

Similar fights occurred in the mid-1970's to prevent establishment of a pulp mill in the northern end of the Tongass National Forest; the Alaska district court allowed the project, but opponents vowed to continue their fight in the courts. A project to extract iron ore from a large deposit near Haines also was opposed. An even more intense conflict arose in 1973 with the withdrawal by Secretary of the Interior Rogers Morton of 83 million acres of public domain for national parks and wildlife refuges, to be managed by federal agencies; this acreage was subsequently increased to about one-third of the state's area. During the ensuing battle between the conservationists and developers, Alaska Gov. William Egan and former Gov. Walter Hickel strongly opposed the new legislation, but after delays the Congress approved the bill designating more than 104 million acres in Alaska as national parks, wildlife refuges and wilderness areas. President Carter signed the bill on Dec. 2, 1980.

ALASKA-PACIFIC-YUKON EXPOSITION (Seattle, 1909). The federal government spent $600,000 for exhibits on the Philippines, Hawaii, and Alaska to reveal to the American people, the peoples, arts, and industries of these possessions. Japan presented the largest foreign exhibit it had ever attempted; China and Oceania were well represented. The enterprise was highly successful.

ALBANY (N.Y.). In September 1609, Henry Hudson moored the *Half Moon* near the site of Albany, but no serious attempt at settlement was made until 1624, when eighteen Walloon families built Fort Orange on the site of the present capitol. In 1652 the village became known as Beverwyck. Shortly afterward, the fur trade rapidly increased.

On Sept. 24, 1664, Fort Orange surrendered to the English and Beverwyck became Albany. Chartered in 1686, for many years Albany was the key in the regulation of Indian affairs. During the colonial wars many conferences, including the Albany Congress of 1754, were held there. On the eve of the Revolution, Albany was a city of 3,000 inhabitants. In 1777 Gen. John Burgoyne and Col. Barry St. Leger advanced toward the city (*see* British Campaign of 1777), but the former surrendered at Saratoga and the latter retreated from Fort Stanwix. By a law enacted on Mar. 10, 1797, Albany became the capital of the state of New York.

Because of its strategic location, Albany has been a crossroads since colonial times. The completion (1825) of the Erie Canal made Albany the junction of the water route from the East to the Great Lakes, and also a point of departure for the Northwest; completion of the Albany-Schenectady Railroad (1831) began the city's role as a rail center. The first municipal airport in the United States was opened in Albany in 1919.

In the late 1970s about one-tenth of Albany's work force worked in manufacturing; the federal, state, and local government agencies employed approximately 50,000. The population in 1980 was 101,727.

ALBANY CONGRESS (1754). Called by the British in order to conciliate the Iroquois and secure their support in the war against France. In June commissioners from New York, Massachusetts, Rhode Island, Connecticut, Pennsylvania, New Hampshire, and Maryland met with the chiefs of the Six Nations, who had been disaffected by encroachment on their lands, the trading of Albany with Canada, and the removal of William Johnson from the management of their affairs. Although the alliance was renewed, the Iroquois went away only half satisfied.

Discussion of a closer union among colonies became one of the principal subjects of the congress. The adopted plan, proposed by Benjamin Franklin, was referred to as the Albany Plan: it provided for a voluntary union of the colonies with "one general government," each colony to retain its own separate existence and government. The new government was to be administered by a president general appointed by the crown and a council of delegates from colonial assemblies, and was given exclusive control of Indian affairs. The home government rejected the plan.

ALBANY CONVENTION (1689–90). A convention of the civil and military officers of Albany (Aug. 1, 1689), which set itself up as an emergency government until the intentions of William and Mary were made known. Badly frightened by a French attack on Schenectady, the convention sought aid from New England and in the spring yielded to renewed demands from Jacob Leisler, who had seized control of southern New York, that he be recognized as commander in chief.

ALBANY REGENCY. The first American political machine. Organized in 1820 under Martin Van Buren, it acquired its name because his aides, residing in Albany, managed the machine during his absence in the U.S. Senate. The regency developed party discipline and originated the control of party conventions through officeholders and others subservient to it; the spoils system was the core of its philosophy. The regency waned following Van Buren's unsuccessful bid for the presidency in 1848.

***ALBATROSS*.** The Yankee-owned ship that brought news of the outbreak of the War of 1812 to W. P. Hunt, partner of the Pacific Fur Company at Astoria. Hunt chartered the ship and removed the furs from Astoria, thus abandoning the first American fur post on the Columbia River.

***ALBEMARLE*.** Confederate ram, built in 1853. In April 1864, it sank the gunboat *Southfield*, put the *Miami* to flight, and captured Plymouth, N.C. On May 5 it fought Capt. Melancton Smith's seven blockaders at the mouth of the Roanoke. It was sunk on Oct. 27.

ALBEMARLE AND CHESAPEAKE CANAL. Built in 1856–60 to afford inland navigation between Chesapeake Bay and Albemarle Sound. It consists of two canals, one connecting the Elizabeth River with North Landing River in Virginia, and the other connecting Currituck Sound with the North River in North Carolina.

ALBEMARLE SETTLEMENTS. The first permanent settlement in North Carolina, made by Virginians (1655). When it was learned in 1665 that the Albemarle settlements were not included in the Carolina proprietary grant of 1663, a new charter was granted. Government was instituted in 1664 with the appointment of William Drummond as governor of the county of Albemarle, and an assembly met the following year. Land grants were issued and settlers in large numbers began to move into the region in 1665. In 1689 the county of Albemarle was abolished as a unit of government.

ALBUQUERQUE (N. Mex.). The largest city in New Mexico, with a population of 331,767 (1980), it originated in 1706 as the Spanish villa San Felipe de Albuquerque. It was on the Chihuahua Trail and dominated the Rio Abajo (downriver) part of the province. Exposed to Apache and Navajo inroads, the settlers were "reduced" (1779) to the plaza arrangement which survives in Old Town. New Albuquerque started a century later (1880) a mile to the east, as a railroad center (*see* Railroads, Sketches). The automobile and airplane have made Albuquerque an important crossroads of transcontinental routes.

ALCALDES. Mayors of Mexican towns. Under the American provisional government in California these officers were recognized by military governors and continued in office until 1850.

ALDER GULCH (Mont.). Gold was discovered at Alder Gulch, and the first stampede reached there June 6, 1863; later in the year a town, named Virginia City, sprang up nearby. The diggings were the richest gold placer deposits ever discovered; in three years $30 million was taken from them.

ALDRICH COMMISSION. *See* **National Monetary Commission.**

ALDRICH-VREELAND ACT. An emergency currency law enacted May 30, 1908, as a result of the panic of 1907. Its aim was to give elasticity to the currency through the next six years by permitting national banks to issue, under strict supervision, additional currency. The act also created the National Monetary Commission.

ALEUT. Together with the Eskimo, the Aleut, native inhabitants of southwestern Alaska, the Shumagin Islands, and the long Aleutian archipelago, form the single language family of Eskaleut, but with no mutual intelligibility. The population estimate for 1740 of 16,000 Aleut points to a dispersal of maritime hunters over a wide and insular geographic area. Living in sod houses, often semisubterranean, the Aleut made capital of seal, sea otter, walrus, and occasional whales; they also depended on wildfowl and fishing. Local groups of Aleut developed semipermanent villages. Kinship relationships rather than political organization were the rule.

ALEUTIAN ISLANDS. Extending westward in a curve 1,200 miles from the tip of the Alaska Peninsula, they are largely volcanic and unsuitable for agriculture. Although they appear to provide a natural bridge between North America and Asia, population migration from Siberia to Alaska probably took place to the north. Before the Russian exploration in 1741, the islands were peopled exclusively by Aleut. The Russian-American Fur Company exploited the region and massacred and enslaved the Aleut. Added to the Russian incursions were British and American slaughtering of seals. After the U.S. purchase of Alaska in 1867, controversies over sealing rights in the Bering Sea proliferated; a settlement by a court of arbitration in Paris in 1893 left the sea open (*see* Pelagic Sealing Dispute).

In June 1942 a Japanese task force moved into the Aleutians to destroy military bases at Dutch Harbor and to occupy the undefended islands of Attu and Kiska. In May 1943 the U.S. Seventh Infantry Division captured Attu. Under cover of fog and darkness late in July, the Japanese evacuated Kiska; unaware of this, U.S. forces bombarded the island on Aug. 15, and a combined American-Canadian force landed unopposed.

After World War II a U.S. Coast Guard fleet was stationed at Unalaska Island to patrol the sealing grounds and, after 1956, to supervise the effectuation of a convention signed by the United States, Canada, Japan, and the Soviet Union for the protection of the seals. (*See also* Alaska.)

ALEXANDRIA (Va.). Located on the Potomac River, it was an important tobacco shipping port until early in the 19th century. First settled in 1695, it was established as a town in 1749 on an original grant of 6,000 acres awarded in 1669 to the Alexander family. The Fairfax Resolves were signed there on July 18, 1774. Alexandria was incorporated in 1779; from 1791 to 1847 it was part of the District of Columbia. The city's population greatly increased in the 20th century (103,217 in 1980); it has become a residential city noted for its colonial architecture.

ALEXANDRIA CONFERENCE (March 28, 1785). Dealing with navigation and commerce in Chesapeake Bay and the Potomac and Pocomoke rivers and scheduled to be held at Alexandria, it actually met at Mount Vernon. In ratifying the agreement, Maryland urged the inclusion of Pennsylvania and Delaware, while Virginia urged a meeting of all the states to adopt uniform commercial regulations. This produced the Annapolis Convention, the origin of the Convention of 1787.

ALGECIRAS CONFERENCE. In 1904 France made agreements with England and Spain which allowed it to increase its influence in Morocco. Germany, angered because it was not consulted, demanded a conference of the signatories of the Morocco agreement (1880) and appealed to the United States. President Theodore Roosevelt persuaded England and France to attend a conference at Algeciras, Spain, in 1906. In the conference the Germans appeared so uncompromising that Roosevelt supported France, which in the end obtained a privileged position in Morocco. The U.S. Senate ratified the treaty but declared that this action was taken solely to protect American interests and was not an abandonment of a nonintervention policy toward Europe.

ALGIERS, WAR WITH. *See* **Barbary Wars.**

ALGONQUIN. The Algonquin tribe, located on the northern tributaries of the Ottawa River in southwestern Quebec, is to be contrasted with the extensive North American speech family, Algonkin (or Algonquian, or Algonquin), to which it has lent its name. The tribe was small (perhaps 6,000 in 1600) and consisted of nonagricultural hunters. Extensive use of birch bark for housing, canoes, and containers characterized their culture. The Algonquin, along with the neighboring Ottawa, appear to be a remnant of various Ojibwa bands that gradually shifted westward as a result of the pressures of European settlement. The group suffered decimation at the hands of the hostile Iroquois, and modern survivors are identified only with difficulty.

The language phylum to which the Algonquin lent their name is one of the most widely spread of the Native American, extending to the Arapaho, Cheyenne, and Blackfoot in the Plains and the Yurok and Wiyot in California. Certain Gulf languages and some languages of Central America may also have remote connections with the major Algonkin grouping. The source of the name of both the tribe and the language family is uncertain.

ALGONQUIN ROUND TABLE. A literary-luncheon group that gathered at the Algonquin Hotel in New York City during the 1920's and 1930's. Its members included Alexander Woollcott, Dorothy Parker, George Kaufman, F.P. Adams, Robert Benchley, and Harold Ross.

ALIEN AND SEDITION LAWS. In 1798, the Federalists, fearful of French invasion, introduced four bills designed to impede political opposition.The Naturalization Act (June 18, 1798) extended the residency requirement to fourteen years, five of which were to be spent in the state or territory in which the individual was being naturalized; the alien was required to declare an intention of becoming a citizen five years before the ultimate application (repealed 1802). The Alien Friends Act (June 25, 1798) gave the president the power to deport aliens "dangerous to the peace and safety of the United States"; its terms were sweeping, but it was limited to two years and it was never enforced. The Alien Enemies Act (July 6, 1798) gathered strong Republican support as a clearly defensive measure in time of declared war; it gave the president the power to restrain, arrest, and deport male citizens or subjects of a hostile nation. The Act for the Punishment of Certain Crimes (July 14, 1798) was the nation's first sedition act. It made it a high misdemeanor "unlawfully to combine and conspire" in order to oppose legal measures of the government, to interfere with an officer in the discharge of his duty, to engage in or abet "insurrection, riot, or unlawful assembly or combination." The writing or printing of "any false, scandalous and malicious writing" with intent to bring the government, Congress, or the president "into contempt or disrepute" was also punishable. The Sedition Act carefully specified, however, that truth might be admitted as a defense, that malicious intent had to be proved, and that the jury had the right to judge whether the matter was libelous. Because the Sedition Act failed to distinguish between malicious libel and the expression of political opinion, the law prompted a broader definition of freedom of the press.

The protest against these laws received its most significant formulation in the Kentucky and Virginia resolutions (*see* Virginia and Kentucky Resolutions).

ALIEN CONTRACT LABOR LAW. *See* **Contract Labor, Foreign.**

ALIEN LANDHOLDING. The common-law disability of aliens to inherit lands in the United States has always been removable by statute and by treaty. Alienage occasioned by the Revolution was excepted by the Definitive Treaty of Peace, which also recommended restitution of confiscated estates. The Jay Treaty guaranteed existing titles wherever held and treated British subjects with respect thereto as equal to citizens. The Convention of 1800 removed the disability of alienage for French citizens in all the states. A treaty with Switzerland (1850) similarly affected Swiss citizens. In the absence of such a treaty, state laws applied: in Kansas, the disability was expressed in the state constitution; in California, aliens were authorized to acquire, transmit, and inherit property equally with citizens. Illinois led in 1887 in denying aliens the right to acquire land. Nine other states rapidly followed suit, and Congress banned further acquisition of land by aliens in the territories.

ALIENS. *See* **Naturalization.**

ALIENS, RIGHTS OF. For the first hundred years the U.S. government imposed no restrictions on the entry of aliens. The first controls appeared in an 1875 statute that barred convicts and prostitutes; the first general immigration statute was passed in 1882. Thereafter, the classes of aliens barred from entry were steadily enlarged, and these qualitative controls remain an important feature of U.S. immigration laws. In 1882 Congress also passed the Chinese Exclusion Act, which remained effective until 1943. A substantial increase in the volume of immigration early in the 20th century led to increasing sentiment for restriction of the number of immigrants. (*See* Immigration; Immigration Restriction.)

Aliens who are lawfully in the United States can become American citizens after a prescribed period of residence, usually five years, and the establishment of good moral character and attachment to the principles of the Constitution (*see* Naturalization). The status of aliens residing in the United States in regard to judicial proceedings is virtually the same as that of U.S. citizens. The protections of the Fifth and Fourteenth amendments relate to "persons"; therefore, in 1973 the Supreme Court declared unconstitutional state laws that sought to limit the employment opportunities available to aliens. *Graham* v. *Richardson* (1971) declared unconstitutional various state statutes that denied welfare benefits to resident aliens.

ALLATOONA PASS, BATTLE AT (Oct. 5, 1864). After the fall of Atlanta, Confederate commander J. B. Hood moved his army north to destroy Gen. William T. Sherman's communications. Sherman followed. Hood detached S. G. French's division to destroy a railroad bridge; on his march French destroyed stores at Allatoona and attacked federal troops stationed there under J. M. Corse. The popular song "Hold the Fort" was based on messages exchanged between Corse and Sherman.

ALLEGHENY MOUNTAINS, ROUTES ACROSS. The steep eastern escarpment of the Allegheny Mountains (3,000–5,000 feet high, extending from the Mohawk Valley to the Tennessee River) was an impediment to the westward movement. The West Branch of the Susquehanna furnished a route used by the Indians, though only fur traders made use of it during the early period. The branches of the Juniata River provided the Frankstown Path, much used by Pennsylvania fur traders, and the Traders Path, followed by the Pennsylvania Road and Gen. John Forbes's expedition (Forbes's Road). The route used by Christopher Gist, George

Washington, and Edward Braddock ran from the Potomac River at Wills Creek. From the headwaters of the Potomac also ran a route, later known as the Northwestern Pike. The headwaters of the James River determined a route to branches of the Great Kanawha; one branch, the New River, also provided a route from the headwaters of the Roanoke River. Farthest south, Cumberland Gap offered easy passage from eastern Tennessee to central Kentucky, making possible the Wilderness Road.

ALLEGHENY PORTAGE RAILWAY. A thirty-six-mile span between Hollidaysburg and Johnstown that linked the eastern and western canals of the Pennsylvania System. Constructed in 1831–35, when the ascent of 1,400 feet within 10.1 miles seemed a prohibitive gradient for a continuous roadbed, the railway consisted of eleven level stretches and ten inclined planes. Locomotives quickly replaced horses as motive power. In 1856 the planes were superseded by a continuous railway. The railway was sold to the Pennsylvania Railroad in 1857 and abandoned shortly thereafter.

ALLEGHENY RIVER. Rising in Potter County, Pa., the Allegheny flows in an arc through New York and back into Pennsylvania, where it unites with the Monongahela to form the Ohio River. The Delaware and Shawnee settled along its course soon after 1720; white settlement followed after 1790. It was an important highway for settlers and freight. Its name is probably a corruption of *Alligewi-hanna,* "stream of the Alligewi," a tribe that tradition says once inhabited the region.

ALLENTOWN (Pa.). An industrial city on the Lehigh River, Allentown had a population of 103,758 in 1980; together with the neighboring cities of Bethlehem and Easton, it was the center of a metropolitan area of 599,734 people. Laid out in 1762, the town was settled largely by German immigrants. During the American Revolution, it was a refuge for people fleeing from Philadelphia; in 1777 the Liberty Bell was moved there until the British left Philadelphia.

ALLIANCE. A Continental frigate built in 1778, it carried the Marquis de Lafayette and Thomas Paine to France. Its first commander, Pierre Landais, showed doubtful loyalty in the *Bonhomme Richard–Serapis* engagement (1779) and was relieved of his command. Defiant, he sailed the *Alliance* from France to America; the crew mutinied twice during the voyage. Capt. John Barry cruised in the *Alliance* from 1780 through the last sea fight of the Revolution with the *Sybil,* Mar. 10, 1783.

ALLIANCE FOR PROGRESS. A policy statement calling for a joint effort to accelerate the economic and social development of Latin America within a democratic political framework. The ten-year plan was proposed by President John F. Kennedy to the Latin-American diplomatic corps at a White House reception on Mar. 13, 1961; it included economic and social planning, land and tax reform, education and health services, commodity stabilization arrangements, training of technical and scientific personnel, economic integration, and hemispheric defense arrangements. Its immediate effect was to improve dramatically the political relations between the United States and Latin America, but a major shift in U.S. energies and resources associated with the Vietnam War drained the alliance effort of its vitality.

ALLISON COMMISSION. A joint, bipartisan congressional committee chaired by Sen. William B. Allison that investigated four federal scientific agencies from 1884 to 1886. In addition to examining a jurisdictional dispute between the Navy Hydrographic Office and the Coast and Geodetic Survey over the charting of offshore waters, the commission inquired into the charge that the Geological Survey, the Coast Survey, and the Weather Service were doing research for abstract, not strictly practical, purposes. The majority of the commission favored retaining the status quo in federal science, and the Congress upheld the majority report.

"ALL QUIET ALONG THE POTOMAC." The opening words of a poem published as "The Picket Guard," by Mrs. Ethel Lynn Beers, in *Harper's Weekly,* Nov. 30, 1861. It refers to telegrams reporting "all is quiet tonight" to the secretary of war by Maj. Gen. George B. McClellan.

ALMANACS. In colonial days the almanac was second in importance only to the Bible. The first almanac printed in America was the *Almanacke for New England for the Year 1639,* printed at Cambridge; in 1676 an almanac was published in Boston; and in 1686 the *America's Messenger* was compiled in Philadelphia. Almanacs were published in New York in 1697, in Rhode Island in 1728, and in Virginia in 1731. The most famous of the early almanacs were *The Astronomical Diary and Almanack* published by Nathaniel Ames in Boston (1726–75); and *Poor Richard's Almanac* by Benjamin Franklin in Philadelphia (1732–57). The former was more versatile than any other almanac of the century: it included tide charts, solar table calculations and eclipses, and changes of the moon. The most enduring American almanac is *The Farmer's Almanac,* begun in 1793.

The 19th-century almanacs included the *Sun Anti-Masonic Almanac* (1831); *Henry Clay Almanac* (1844); *General Taylor's Rough and Ready Almanac* (1848); *Common School Almanac* (1842); and *Temperance Almanac* (1834). *The Confederate Almanac and Register* (1862) and *Uncle Sam's Union Almanac* (1863) gave military statistics. The first comic almanac appeared in Boston in 1831 and was quickly imitated, one example being *Davy Crockett's Almanack of Wild Sports of the West.*

All the major religious denominations have published almanacs; medical almanacs of all types have also been widely distributed. Astronomical almanacs for use in sea and air navigation are prepared by official organizations of the United States (beginning in 1849 by an act of Congress). Encyclopedic information appeared in the *Tribune Almanac and Political Register* (1846); and *The World Almanac* (1868) continues to cover a wide range of statistical and historical information.

ALPHADELPHIA ASSOCIATION. A Fourierist community established in Comstock township, Kalamazoo County, Mich., in 1844, led by a German, Dr. H. R. Schetterly. It was disbanded in 1848.

ALTA CALIFORNIA. Under Spain (1533–1822), California embraced the whole Pacific coast of North America from Cape San Lucas to Oregon; it was frequently represented on maps as an island some 3,000 miles long. Early in the 18th century the Jesuit Eusebio Kino proved that the southern portion was a peninsula and the rest mainland; the peninsula came to be called Baja (Lower) and the rest Alta (Upper) California.

ALTA VELA CLAIM. A flimsy claim against the Dominican government by American adventurers ejected on the eve of the unsuccessful Spanish reoccupation (1861–65) of the guano island by that name located fifteen miles south of the Dominican Republic. Former Secretary of State Jeremiah S. Black resigned as defending counsel in the impeachment trial of President Andrew Johnson in 1868 when the latter would not order Secretary of State William H. Seward to approve the claim.

ALTON PETROGLYPHS. Near the present town of Alton, Ill., the Jesuit Jacques Marquette in 1673 saw painted upon a rocky bluff a "monster," which terrified him and interested later travelers until its destruction about 1856. Called "Piasa" by the Indians, the figure was that of an imaginary bird legendary with many tribes.

ALUMINUM INDUSTRY. Aluminum was first isolated in metallic form in 1825 in Denmark; it remained a laboratory curiosity until 1854, when Henri Sainte-Claire Deville discovered a process using metallic sodium as a reductant that led to the first commercial production of aluminum. In 1886, an American, Charles Martin Hall, and a Frenchman, Paul Heroult, independently discovered that aluminum could be produced by electrolyzing a solution of aluminum oxide in molten cryolite (sodium aluminum fluoride). The electrolytic process remains the sole commercial method used throughout the world for making aluminum.

Hall's invention led to the formation of the Pittsburgh Reduction Company in 1888. This company, now known as the Aluminum Company of America (ALCOA), produced 50 pounds of aluminum per day at first; it became the world's largest producer of aluminum. By 1900 total world production was about 7,500 short tons; American production was 2,500 tons. With the advent of the airplane in World War I, quantities of aluminum were needed. In 1918 the primary capacity in the United States had grown to 62,500 short tons; world production amounted to 143,900 tons. In 1978 total world production of aluminum came to 14,052,000 tons, and the American share was 31 percent, or 4,804,000 tons.

Aluminum, the most abundant metallic element in the earth's crust, is made from the mineral bauxite. Australia, Jamaica, Guinea, Surinam, the Soviet Union, Guyana, and Greece are the leading bauxite-producing countries. The United States produces less than 13 percent of its bauxite needs and relies upon imports. Aluminum is extensively employed in building and construction, in automobile production, and in packaging industry.

AMANA COMMUNITY. Founded in Germany in 1714 as the Community of True Inspiration in protest against the arbitrary rule of church and state. Its members crossed the Atlantic in the early 1840's and settled near Buffalo, N.Y. Here they laid out six villages, called the settlement Ebenezer, and formally adopted communism as a way of life. The rapid expansion of nearby Buffalo threatened their isolation, and in 1855 they moved to Iowa, and incorporated as the Amana Society, consisting of seven villages and 26,000 acres of land. In 1932 by unanimous vote the community reorganized as a joint stock company where stockholders are both owners and employees.

AMARILLO (Tex.). The largest city in the Texas panhandle, with a population of 149,230 in 1980. It is one of the most important world centers for the production of helium gas, which is found with other natural gases and oils in the vicinity. Amarillo is also a leading center for gathering and shipping beef raised on the panhandle ranches, and for processing the cotton seed and cotton.

Founded in 1887 by a land speculator, Amarillo became a resort for cowboys, with shops, hotels, and saloons. Farmers moved into the area late in the 19th century, and the city was well established before the first oil and gas discoveries provided it with a major local industry in the early 1900's.

AMBASSADORS. Through the great-power Congress of Vienna (1815) and the Congress of Aix-la-Chapelle (1818), four standardized diplomatic grades were established: ambassadors; ministers plenipotentiary and envoys extraordinary; ministers resident; and chargés d'affaires. The revised rules of the Vienna Convention on Diplomatic Relations of 1961 eliminated ministers resident. Ambassadors, accredited directly to the sovereign or the head of state, represent the highest authority of their own governments. The ambassador longest accredited in a foreign capital is known as the dean, or doyen, of the international diplomatic corps, and as such represents it for certain purposes. U.S. ambassadors rarely attain this distinction because of frequent rotation.

Until well into the 19th century only great powers exchanged ambassadors; other nations exchanged ministers (plenipotentiary). The first U.S. ambassador was commissioned to Great Britain in 1893. By 1939 the United States was exchanging ambassadors with twenty nations. After World War II the number increased steadily, and in 1980 the United States exchanged ambassadors with 146 nations, sending ministers to none. Also, nine ambassadors were accredited to international organizations, such as the United Nations and North Atlantic Treaty Organization.

AMBRISTER. *See* **Arbuthnot and Ambrister, Case of.**

AMELIA ISLAND AFFAIR. The Embargo Act (1807) and the abolition of the American slave trade (1808) made Amelia Island, off the coast of Spanish Florida, a resort for smugglers. Luis Aury, formerly a leader of a piratical band on Galveston Island, Tex., assumed control of Amelia in the fall of 1817 and invited all Florida to unite in throwing off the Spanish yoke. The United States sent a naval force that captured Amelia on Dec. 23, 1817, and put an end to the miniature republic. The island was returned to the Spaniards.

AMEN CORNER. Celebrated niche in the corridor of the old Fifth Avenue Hotel (1859–90), New York City, where politicans and reporters discussed coming political events. Sen. Thomas C. Platt's "Sunday school class" was held there in the late 1890's; when the senator announced his decisions his associates would say, "Amen."

AMENDMENT. Amendments to the U.S. Constitution are discussed in individual articles listed under the number of the amendment, such as **Fourteenth Amendment.** *See also* **Constitution of the United States.**

"AMERICA." *See* **"My Country, 'tis of Thee."**

***AMERICA*.** An American yacht that in 1851 won the trophy cup presented by the Royal Yacht Squadron; since 1857 the trophy has been the *America's* Cup. The *America* served later as a Confederate dispatch boat, was captured, and served as practice ship at the Naval Academy. It was permanently docked at the Naval Academy in 1921, and was broken up in 1946.

AMERICA, EARLY EXPLORATION OF.

Norse Exploration. About the year A.D. 1000 Norsemen, starting from Greenland, reached the coast of North America between Labrador and the Chesapeake. The legends of the voyages of Leif Ericson (who called the new land Vinland the Good) and Thorfinn Karlsefni depend upon three manuscripts of sagas.

Spanish Exploration. On Aug. 3, 1492, the Genoese Christopher Columbus sailed from Palos, Spain, under the authority of the Spanish king and queen. On Oct. 12, 1492, Columbus set foot on an island in the Bahamas, which he named San Salvador; it was probably Watling Island. Columbus made three other voyages to the New World (1493, 1498, and 1502), and touched the coasts of South and Central America. Most likely he met with, or knew of, a Spanish pilot who had been wrecked on an island far west of the Madeiras in 1484. In 1499, Alonso de Ojeda and Juan de la Cosa visited South America, and with them went Amerigo Vespucci who wrote such popular accounts of his own deeds that German geographers coined the word "America" in 1507 (*see* America, Naming of).

The island of Española (now Hispaniola) became the Spanish outpost from which Vasco Núñez de Balboa went to Central America, crossed the Isthmus of Panama, and discovered the Pacific Ocean (Sept. 25, 1513). The eastern coast of the mainland of North America had been cartographically traced by 1502. On Easter Sunday, 1513, Juan Ponce de León found his way to the site of the present city of St. Augustine, Fla. Francisco Gordillo coasted as far north as Cape Fear (1521) and Lucas Vásquez de Ayllón got as far as the James River in Virginia (1526). Meantime Hernando Cortés had landed in Mexico and conquered it (1519). Pánfilo de Narváez explored western Florida and possibly Georgia (1528) while Álvar Núñez Cabeza de Vaca walked overland from Pensacola Bay, Fla., to the Gulf of California. In 1539 Hernando de Soto took an expedition from Tampa Bay, Fla., marched north to the Savannah River, and then proceeded west to the Mississippi River in 1541.

By this time Franciscan friars were pushing up into what is now the Southwest of the United States. Fray Marcos de Niza (1539) brought back such reports of wealth that Francisco Vásquez de Coronado started out in April 1540 on an expedition that took him as far north as central Kansas (1541).

French Exploration. Giovanni da Verrazano, acting under the favor of Francis I, came to North America in 1524 and possibly saw the Lower Bay of New York. Jacques Cartier coasted Labrador in 1534 and in the next year explored the St. Lawrence River to the Lachine Rapids above Quebec. Samuel de Champlain found Maine in 1603–04, and Cape Cod in 1605, and got as far as central New York State in 1615.

English Exploration. In May 1497 John Cabot sailed from Bristol, England, under a patent from Henry VII, and in June probably discovered the continent of North America. The Hawkinses—William, John, and James—explored the West Indies in the late 16th century. Sir Francis Drake doubled Cape Horn and reached the coast of California in June 1579. In 1602 Bartholomew Gosnold reached the coast of Maine, skirted Cape Cod (which he named), and found Narragansett Bay. George Weymouth in 1605 sighted Nantucket and then headed north.

Other Exploration. Swedes and Norwegians allegedly discovered America from Greenland in the 13th century, through Hudson Bay and the Red River of the North into the present state of Minnesota. This theory rests on an inscribed stone and certain artifacts (*see* Kensington Stone). There are also legends of pre-Columbian discoveries of America by the Chinese, Welsh, Irish, Phoenicians, and others.

AMERICA, NAMING OF. The earliest explorers and historians designated America as the Indies, the West Indies, or the New World. Beyond the Pyrenees the chief source of information on the discoveries was Amerigo Vespucci's account of his voyages. A coterie of scholars at Saint-Dié, in Lorraine, chiefly Martin Waldseemüller and Mathias Ringmann, printed this in 1507 in *Cosmographiae Introductio,* a small work designed to accompany a wall map and globe by Waldseemüller. Two names were suggested for the new "fourth part" of the world: *Amerige* (pronounced A-mer-i-gay, with the *-ge* from the Greek, meaning "earth"), and *America* (parallel to *Europa* and *Asia*). The latter form was placed on Waldseemüller's maps of 1507, and their wide circulation brought about the adoption of the name. Waldseemüller was aware of only South America, but the designation was extended in 1538 to both continents. The injustice to Columbus has aroused a series of protests since 1535.

AMERICA FIRST COMMITTEE. Founded in 1940 to fight against U.S. participation in World War II, it was endorsed by Henry Ford and the historian Charles A. Beard. The committee was especially active in Chicago, but by October 1941 it began to disintegrate.

AMERICAN ACADEMY OF ARTS AND SCIENCES. The second oldest learned society in the United States: plans were initiated by John Adams in 1779, and a charter was granted to the academy by the Massachusetts House of Representatives in 1780. Its avowed purpose was "to cultivate every art and science which may tend to advance the interest, honor, dignity, and happiness of a free, independent, and virtuous people." The present headquarters are at Norton's Woods, 136 Irving Road, Cambridge. There is also a Western Center branch, located at the Center of Advanced Study and Behavioral Sciences at Stanford, Calif.; monthly meetings are held during the academic year at both locations.

Publications of the academy began with a quarto series of *Memoirs* (four volumes appeared during 1785-1821). In 1833 a new series was begun, and nineteen volumes were issued in the next 113 years. In 1848 a series of octavo *Proceedings* was added. In 1955 the academy initiated the quarterly *Daedalus,* intended to serve as a medium of publication for special studies and commissions sponsored by the academy; many of the issues have been republished in book form.

The academy gives three prizes: the Rumford Premium, set up by Benjamin Thompson, Count Rumford, to honor "the author of the most important discovery or useful improvement . . . in heat and light"; the Emerson-Thoreau medal in the humanities; and the Social Science Prize. In 1980 the academy had 2,300 members.

AMERICAN ASSOCIATION FOR THE ADVANCEMENT OF SCIENCE. (AAAS). Several geologists founded the AAAS in 1840, with the intention of gradually broadening the scope of their organization; after seven years the geologists determined to move directly to an organization "for the advancement of science." The AAAS was voted into existence in 1847 and held its first meeting in Philadelphia in 1848.

From 1848 to 1860 the AAAS was the preeminent scientific organization in the United States. Nearly all practicing scientists were members and most attended the annual meetings. The organization had two goals—to promote (popularize) and to advance (sponsor research in) science. However, tensions between amateurs and professionals, between some natural and physical scientists, and between regions resulted in decreased attendance and membership. When the organization regrouped after the Civil War, it faced competition from the new National Academy of Sciences and from a movement toward scientific societies organized in specialized fields.

In 1873 the AAAS adopted a revised constitution that established new possibilities for more diversified sections. Incorporation in 1874 by the Commonwealth of Massachusetts meant that a research fund could be accumulated. Membership gradually increased as more Americans took graduate degrees in science. In 1900 the AAAS took *Science* as its official journal, supplementing the annual volumes of *Proceedings.*

In 1907 the Smithsonian Institution gave the AAAS free office space; not until 1945 was land purchased in Washington, D.C., where the permanent headquarters are now. In 1915 the association organized *The Scientific Monthly,* an illustrated nontechnical magazine (it was merged with *Science* in 1957). The 1920 constitution of the AAAS gave more influence to specialized societies in the hope of better coordination of scientific efforts. From World War II on, the association concentrated its efforts both to provide a common ground on which scientists from different disciplines could share related knowledge and to make science more available to the public, and maintained its tradition as the most broad-based spokesman for science in America.

AMERICAN AUTOMOBILE ASSOCIATION. (AAA). A federation of state and local automobile clubs, it has been the principal spokesman for American motorists since its formation in 1902. Until that time, the automobile club movement in the United States was dominated by the Automobile Club of America (ACA)—an elite group of New York City automobilists who organized in 1899. The AAA was the outcome of nine local clubs recognizing the need for a national federation. By its 1909 annual meeting the AAA represented 30 state associations with 225 affiliated clubs and had 25,759 members.

Emergency road service for its members was inaugurated in 1915. The AAA issued its first domestic tour book in 1917 and in 1926 published its first series of tour books, issued the first modern-style road maps, and began rating tourist accommodations. The AAA has lobbied for toll-free improved highways, for highway beautification programs, and against the diversion of motor vehicle use taxes into nonhighway expenditures. Over the years the AAA has been the leading advocate of highway safety; in 1955 it discontinued its supervision of all automobile racing. In 1980 the association had 975 clubs and branches throughout the United States and Canada, and membership was 21 million.

AMERICAN BAR ASSOCIATION. (ABA). With approximately 270,000 members in 1980, the ABA is the largest and most influential association of lawyers in the United States. It directly or indirectly publishes some 150 periodicals. Founded in 1878, the ABA originated as an instrument of social intercourse for lawyers and as a means of improving American jurisprudence. In 1936 the present constitution was adopted; it provides for a house of delegates, elected at the state and local levels, which is the association's principal governing body; between sessions the house acts through a board of governors. The ABA's principal publication, the monthly *American Bar Association Journal,* contains news of general interest to the legal profession. Many sections of the ABA issue publications in their respective fields. The association judges the qualifications of prospective nominees to the federal bench, and has had enough influence to prevent some appointments.

AMERICAN BATTLE MONUMENTS COMMISSION. *See* **Federal Agencies.**

AMERICAN BIBLE SOCIETY. Organized in 1816 by Elias Boudinot to promote the distribution of the Holy Scriptures without doctrinal comment and without profit. In its first year forty-three state, county, regional, and local Bible societies became associated with it as auxiliaries, to help supply the needs of the westward-expanding nation for the Scriptures in English and other European languages and to prepare translations for Indians. The program's emphasis gradually shifted from national to worldwide distribution, until today the society cooperates with the United Bible Societies in a coordination of Scripture translation, production, and distribution on every continent.

Through the coordination of the labors of individual scholars the entire Bible has been translated and published in 255 languages, the complete New Testament in 359 more, and at least one book in another 912 languages and dialects, to make a total of 1,526 languages, representing over 97 percent of the world's population. Translators are now preparing new popular-language translations, to be published in more than 230 languages. The Scriptures have been reproduced on tapes, records, and cassettes, as well as in braille. In 1980, Bible distribution in the United States totaled more than 77 million copies; the total number of Bibles distributed by the society since its founding was almost 3.2 billion by 1980.

AMERICAN BOTTOM. A narrow Mississippi River flood plain extending roughly 100 miles between Chester and Alton, Ill.. Its name comes perhaps from the first American settlers in the Old Northwest and from serving as part of the territorial boundary before the Louisiana Purchase.

AMERICAN CIVIL LIBERTIES UNION (ACLU). Founded in 1920 to defend constitutional freedoms, especially freedom of expression, due process, the right to privacy, and equal protection under the law. The ACLU's main activity consists of court litigation of test cases selected on the basis of constitutional principles involved. Counsel is provided without charge from a staff of about 5,000 volunteer lawyers, with expenses paid by contributions from the organization's 200,000 (1980) members. The ACLU defended the right to teach evolution in public schools and the right of labor unions to organize; was defense counsel in the controversial Sacco-Vanzetti case; and won major Supreme Court cases in the 1930's protecting the right of public protest. More recently it has focused on amnesty for Vietnam War resisters, abortion and birth control, equal rights for women and children, sexual privacy, humane treatment of mental patients, and prison reform. (*See also* Civil Rights and Liberties.)

AMERICAN COLONIZATION SOCIETY. Formed in 1817 to alleviate the plight of free Afro-Americans by removing them from the United States to Africa, the society also worked to aid the manumission of slaves and to suppress the African slave trade.

Various colonization schemes had appeared in the late 18th century. The idea received impetus when in 1815 a black shipowner transported thirty-eight American blacks to Africa at his own expense. In 1816 a New Jersey Presbyterian minister, Robert Finley, convened a series of meetings that led to the formation of the society the following year. The society gained the support of Congregational and Presbyterian clergy and of prominent politicians. In 1822 it established the colony of Liberia on the west coast of Africa. In the following decade the number of auxiliary societies increased yearly and receipts grew; but a total of only 2,638 blacks migrated to Liberia. During the 1830's, opposition to the society from both abolitionists and proslavery forces combined with mounting debts and internal strife to undermine it.

The independence of Liberia after 1846 lifted a great financial burden, and in the 1850's the fortunes of the society revived. After the Civil War, however, Republicans reviled the society and most blacks rejected it. The society subsequently stressed its educational and missionary activities, sending fewer than 2,000 blacks to Liberia after 1870. In the 1890's the organization languished; by 1910, it had all but ceased to exist.

AMERICAN EXPEDITIONARY FORCES (AEF). American troops serving in Europe during World War I. On May 26, 1917, Maj. Gen. John J. Pershing was directed to proceed to France to command American land forces abroad. When the armistice came, approximately 2 million men had been transported to Europe.

In the spring and early summer of 1918 powerful German offensives threatened the Allies, and Pershing placed the AEF at the disposal of the Allied High Command, postponing until July 24, 1918, the formation of the American First Army. The first independent American offensive operation of the war was the capture of Cantigny in May. Early in June two divisions stopped the German advance on Paris. In July two American divisions, with one Moroccan division, formed the spearhead of the counterattack against the Château-Thierry salient, the turning point of the war. In the middle of September the American First Army of 550,000 men reduced the Saint-Mihiel salient. More than 1.2 million American soldiers participated in the Meuse-Argonne offensive, beginning in the latter part of September. By the end of August 1919 the last American division had been repatriated.

AMERICAN EXPEDITIONARY FORCES IN ITALY. As tangible proof of American cooperation in World War I, the Italian minister of war urged that American units be sent to Italy. The 332nd Infantry Regiment, the 331st Field Hospital, and the 102nd Base Hospital were so dispatched. With headquarters at Treviso, the 332nd Infantry made numerous marches to the front line, and participated in the attack to force a crossing of the Piave River (Oct. 26, 1918) and in the Battle of the Tagliamento River (Nov. 4).

AMERICAN EXPRESS COMPANY. In 1850 two express companies—Wells, Butterfield and Company and Livingston, Fargo and Company—were united to form a joint stock association, It operated in New England, the Midwest and Northwest, and even thrust into Canada. Its incorporators organized Wells, Fargo and Company in 1852 for the western half of the country; the United States Express Company was organized in 1854 as a subsidiary, but within two decades it became a sharp competitor. In 1918 all the companies merged their shipping interests in the American Railway Express Company, which was taken over in 1929 by the Railway Express Agency. The American Express Company, which had begun selling money orders in 1882 and traveler's checks in 1891, continued as a banking and tourist bureau; in 1958 it introduced the American Express credit card.

AMERICAN FEDERATION OF LABOR–CONGRESS OF INDUSTRIAL ORGANIZATIONS (AFL-CIO). The AFL and CIO were united in 1955 after almost twenty years of rivalry; one force leading to the merger was a hostile political environment (evident from passage of the Taft-Hartley Act in 1947 and election of a Republican president in 1952). The merger did not change the decentralized and essentially economic nature of the labor movement. The AFL-CIO does not itself engage in collective bargaining or issue strike calls (with minor exceptions), this power residing with the autonomous national and international affiliates. The AFL-CIO, however, has explicit constitutional authority to expel unions for corruption or domination by Communist, Fascist, or other totalitarian forces. The AFL-CIO also adopted a vigorous antidiscrimination vow, created a single political arm (the Committee on Political Education), and moved into electioneering politics—officially on a nonpartisan basis but in reality in close alliance with the Democratic party.

In the late 1950's, the AFL-CIO focused on corruption and racketeering. Although President George Meany expelled several unions, including the International Brotherhood of Teamsters, the AFL-CIO could not prevent the passage of the Landrum-Griffin Act (1959), which regulated internal union affairs and guaranteed democratic rights to union members. In the 1960's, the AFL-CIO identified with the New Frontier and Great Society domestic programs of presidents John F. Kennedy and Lyndon Johnson. The organization cpposed many of the domestic policies of President Richard Nixon, particularly his anti-inflationary wage- and price-control program. Nevertheless, labor remained neutral in the 1972 presidential race for the first time in years; after the election and the Watergate scandal, the AFL-CIO reasserted its influence in the Democratic party and called for the impeachment of President Nixon.

The AFL-CIO had about 13.6 million members in 1980. Some unions have always remained independent or have been expelled or suspended from the AFL-CIO; two of its biggest independent unions in 1980 were the International Brotherhood of Teamsters and the National Education Association. The AFL-CIO has made some progress in organizing white-collar, public, and professional workers, but these groups are still among the largest potential sources for new union recruits.

American Federation of Labor. Launched in 1886, the AFL was a trade union center, a "roof organization" under whose banner a large number and variety of unions rallied in order to achieve greater economic and political strength and to pursue common objectives. The most powerful affiliates were the national and international unions (so called because they enrolled Canadian, as well as U.S., workers), such as the United Brotherhood of Carpenters and Joiners and the United Mine Workers. Initially their jurisdictions covered a single trade or craft of skilled workers, but under pressures of technological change they came to exercise jurisdiction over entire industries, and even related industries. Eventually well over a hundred such unions became affiliated with the AFL. They in turn were composed of local unions, which frequently formed city centrals to pursue common local goals. State federations of labor were also erected, largely for political interaction with state governments.

The unions carried primary responsibility for the achievement of higher wages, shorter hours, and improved conditions of work. Their strategy was to organize enough of the trade or industry to gain control over the supply of labor, use that power position to force employers (via the strike or threat of it) to bargain collectively over the terms of their workers' employment, and sign a trade agreement embodying such terms. Unionism of this type has been called "business" unionism, "job control" unionism, or "pure and simple" unionism. Within this decentralized, essentially economic structure, the AFL itself carried out limited functions of a service, political, and representative nature.

Congress of Industrial Organizations. An effort to reform the AFL from within began in 1933 and the labor progressives set up the Committee for Industrial Organization in 1935. Unions supporting the committee were suspended from the AFL the following year, and after spectacular organizing successes in the steel, automobile, rubber, and other industries, the committee became the Congress of Industrial Organizations in November 1938. The CIO emerged as a strong rival of the AFL. It did not challenge the AFL on ideological or philosophical grounds; the major quarrel concerned structure, organizing, and power. CIO leaders wanted to organize the workers in the mass-production industries (auto, rubber, steel, glass, aluminum, chemical), which had grown explosively since the turn of the century; moreover, they wanted to organize all of them, regardless of skills, into industrial unions rather than into the traditional craft unions of skilled workers. That the CIO was successful is traceable both to the procapitalist philosophy it shared with the AFL and to the accuracy of its views on structure and organizing. As the CIO began to leap forward in membership in the late 1930's, the AFL had to abandon antiquated policies and compete vigorously for members in the mass-production industries.

AMERICAN FORCES IN GERMANY. *See* **Army of Occupation; Germany, American Occupation of.**

AMERICAN FUR COMPANY. Incorporated by John Jacob Astor (the sole stockholder) in 1808. Its capital stock was not to exceed $1 million for two years; thereafter it might not exceed $2 million. Astor challenged unaided the two great fur-trading companies of Canada that were securing a large part of their furs within the limits of the United States—the North West Company, with a capital of 1.2 million, and the Michilimackinac Company, capitalized at about $800,000. To get control of the fur trade of the Great Lakes, the American Fur Company first came to an agreement with the other two companies, whereby the Southwest Fur Company, representing all three, was constituted in 1811. By 1817 Astor bought out his partners at a very low price; thereupon the Northern Department of the American Fur Company was established, with headquarters at Mackinac. In 1822 the company established a branch in St. Louis that became known as the Western Department of the American Fur Company.

An obstacle in securing monopoly of the fur trade was the federal government's Indian factory system; because the Indians could compete successfully with Astor for the trade, he determined to get rid of the system and succeeded in 1822. Private traders and other companies were treated in the same high-handed manner. An act excluding foreigners from the trade was passed by Congress in 1816, probably at the instigation of the American Fur Company; another act favoring the company was passed in 1824.

In 1827 the greatest rival of the company—the Columbia Fur Company—united with it and was known thenceforth as the Upper Missouri Outfit of the American Fur Company. By 1828 the company had a virtual monopoly. In 1834 it became politic for the company to withdraw from the Rocky Mountain area. In that year, too, Astor withdrew from the company, whose charter had lapsed in April 1833. His interests in the Western Department were sold to Pratte, Chouteau and Company, and those in the Northern Department, to a group of some ten stockholders, which now became the American Fur Company. The latter's operations were confined roughly to the area between Detroit, the Ohio River, and the Red River of the North. After its failure in 1842 it seems to have been reconstituted once more in 1846 as a commission house. Its papers end in 1847. (*See also* Astoria; Pacific Fur Company.)

AMERICAN HISTORICAL ASSOCIATION. (AHA). The AHA was founded Sept. 9, 1884, in Saratoga Springs, N.Y., at an annual meeting of the American Social Science Association. Of the forty original members, only thirteen were trained in history. The AHA began to hold annual meetings and publish *The Papers of the American Historical Association.* Herbert Baxter Adams of Johns Hopkins University, secretary during 1884–1900, was the leading figure. In 1889 he obtained a charter of incorporation from Congress, thus securing the AHA a permanent home in Washington, D.C., as well as its claim to being a national organization. In 1895 the association established the Historical Manuscripts Commission to edit, index, and collect information about unprinted documents relating to American history. In 1899 it formed the Public Archives Commission, which stimulated twenty-four states to establish archives and led the movement to establish the National Archives and Records Service. In 1895 the *American Historical Review* began publication, and in 1915 it became the association's official organ. Through the report of its Committee of Seven on the Teaching of History in the Secondary Schools (1899), the AHA established the long-enduring four-year curriculum. The association publishes reports and guides, an annual report, and an annual bibliography of writings on American history, as well as a variety of other bibliographies.

AMERICAN INDEPENDENT PARTY. Organized in 1968 by George C. Wallace, governor of Alabama (1963–66; 1971–79), in support of his presidential candidacy. Wallace opposed forced racial integration and the enhancement of federal power. The party won 13.53 percent of the popular vote and forty-six electoral votes, all save one from the five states of the Deep South. It was renamed the American party in 1969 and then split into two groups in 1976 (one calling itself the American Independent party and the other the American party).

AMERICAN INDIAN DEFENSE ASSOCIATION. Organized in 1923 with John Collier as executive secretary, it was the forerunner of the Association on American Indian Affairs. It emphasized the rights of Indians to religious freedom and opposed bills proposing to take Indian lands. It promoted the Act of June 2, 1924 (the Curtis Act), granting citizenship to all Indians. Collier became U.S. commissioner of Indian affairs in 1933 and administered the Indian New Deal policies of the Indian Reorganization Act of 1934 (*see* Wheeler-Howard Act) until 1946.

AMERICAN INDIAN MOVEMENT (AIM). A militant movement using tactics of direct confrontation in seeking full rights and redress for Indians. Organized in Minneapolis in 1968 to protest alleged police brutality to Indians. AIM has played a leading role in a number of protests, including the forceful occupation of the Washington, D.C., headquarters of the Bureau of Indian Affairs in November 1972. Three months later members of AIM seized the village of Wounded Knee, S.Dak., scene of a massacre of Sioux Indians by U.S. troops in 1890, and occupied it for seventy-one days. In 1980, the organization had five thousand members. It offered charitable and educational services, conducted research, and compiled statistics.

AMERICANISM. By an apostolic letter entitled *Testem benevolentiae* (Jan. 22, 1899), Leo XIII, while expressing praise for the progress Catholicism had made in the United

States, singled out some dogmatic and moral tendencies for correction. Principal among these was the alleged effort to have the church adapt its teaching to contemporary religious thought. The term "Americanism" was defined at the time as "a spirit that is democratic, tolerant, anti-medieval, up-to-date, individualistic, believing chiefly in good works, and lastly, very ultramontane."

AMERICAN JOINT COMMISSION TO FRANCE. *See* **France, American Joint Commission to.**

AMERICAN LABOR PARTY (ALP). The ALP was formed in 1936 as the New York State unit of the Nonpartisan League. Circumstances specific to New York dictated the creation of a separate party: a Tammany machine unsympathetic to President Franklin D. Roosevelt and the New Deal; a large, traditionally socialistic ethnic block; and a state law permitting dual nominations. The successful campaigns of Fiorello H. La Guardia for New York City mayor in 1937 and Herbert H. Lehman for governor in 1938 demonstrated that the ALP held the balance of power between the two major parties. Nevertheless, this potent position eroded because of factional disputes and Communist influence in the ALP. In 1944 the right wing split off to form the Liberal party. Although the ALP recorded its highest vote in the national election in 1948, it declined rapidly thereafter and disbanded in 1954. Its legacy of third-party pressure politics in New York continued, however.

AMERICAN LAND COMPANY. One of large land companies speculating in public lands in the 1830's. Capitalized at $1 million, the company purchased some 322,000 acres of public land in Mississippi, Arkansas, Michigan, Wisconsin, and Illinois and town lots in Chicago and Toledo during the frenzy of speculation in 1835–36. The company fell into financial difficulty following the issue of the Specie Circular in 1836 and the panic of 1837, but the partial record of its dividends suggests that stockholders who held on to their investment may not have done badly. Almost from its inception the company was criticized as a "gigantic monopoly" that was corrupting public officials, cheating Indians, preventing competitive bidding at public-land sales, and charging outrageous prices up to $10 an acre for lands that it had bought less than a year before for $1.25 an acre.

AMERICAN LEGION. The largest U.S. veterans' organization, with membership open to any man or woman who has served in the U.S. armed forces in wartime. It was founded in February 1919 by a group of Allied Expeditionary Forces staff officers at Paris to bolster soldier morale during the postarmistice period and to provide an alternative to other veterans' groups. The organization's purposes were reaffirmed at the Continental Caucus, held three months later at St. Louis, Mo.: the Legionnaires promised to perpetuate the principles for which they had fought, to inculcate civic responsibility to the nation, and to preserve the history of their participation in the war. The Legion soon became the spokesman for all veterans, although its 1920 membership of 840,000 represented only about 18.5 percent of those eligible. Over the next half-century membership fluctuated from a low of 610,000 in 1925 to a high of 3,325,000 in 1946, leveling off by 1980 to about 2,630,000.

Pursuit of Americanism and military preparedness has led the Legion into many controversies. It has striven to rid school textbooks and public libraries of Communist, syndicalist, or anarchist influences. During the "Red scare" of 1919–20, four Legionnaires were killed in a shootout with Industrial Workers of the World organizers at Centralia, Wash. Advocacy of preparedness during the late 1930's made the organization unpopular with many, as did its support of universal military training in the 1950's and its call for a total blockade of Communist Cuba during the 1960's.

By the late 1930's the Legion was one of the nation's most effective interest groups. Its promotion of the GI Bill of Rights for World War II veterans, achieved in 1944, testified to its dedication to all veterans—not just its members.

The Legion has some 16,100 local posts throughout the world. The annual national convention sets policy and elects the national commander and national executive committee. The Legion's charter forbids formal political activity by the organization or its elective officers, but the Legion does maintain a liaison office in Washington, D.C., and publishes the monthly *American Legion Magazine*.

AMERICAN LIBERTY LEAGUE. Organized in August 1934 with the express purpose of fighting radicalism and defending property rights and the Constitution. Among its organizers were many wealthy, conservative Democrats, inimical to the New Deal. Denounced by the Franklin D. Roosevelt administration as reactionary, the league dissolved in 1940.

AMERICAN MATHEMATICAL SOCIETY. On Nov. 24, 1888, Thomas Scott Fiske and a handful of Columbia College faculty and students met to organize the New York Mathematical Society. In 1892 the society published the first volume of its *Bulletin.* Its name was changed to the American Mathematical Society in 1894, and in 1923 it was incorporated under the laws of the District of Columbia. In 1893 lecture series were initiated, which resulted in the publication of *Colloquium Publications.* In 1900 the society established the *Transactions,* for longer research papers; in 1950, the *Proceedings,* for papers of moderate length, and the *Memoirs,* for monographs or groups of cognate papers. In 1940 it undertook the publication of *Mathematical Reviews,* a monthly abstracting journal; it has also initiated series of translations, including *Soviet Mathematics—Doklady* (from 1960) and *Chinese Mathematics—Acta* (from 1962), and in 1962 it took over the publication of *Mathematics of Computing.*

In 1915 members of the Chicago section founded the Mathematical Association of America. The society represents the research interests of mathematicians, while the association—especially through the publication of the *American Mathematical Monthly*—meets the interests of teachers and students on the college level.

AMERICAN MEDICAL ASSOCIATION (AMA). A national organization of physicians and surgeons, established in 1847 in Philadelphia. The AMA publishes an influential magazine to bring new medical developments to the attention of doctors and acts as a lobbying organization representing the interests of medical professionals.

AMERICAN-MEXICAN MIXED CLAIMS COMMISSIONS. For over a century after the United States recognized Mexico's independence in 1822, there were claims by citizens of each nation for losses attributed to the actions of the other. A joint commission established in 1839 had awarded $2,026,139 to Americans by 1842. Mexico's failure to honor the adjudication contributed to President James K. Polk's decision to ask Congress for a declaration of war in 1846. By the terms of the Treaty of Guadalupe Hidalgo (1848) the U.S. government assumed liability for American claims to the amount of $3,250,000. Claims accruing during the next twenty years were examined by a second mixed commission (1869–76), which granted $4,125,633 to Americans and $150,498 to Mexicans. The decade following the 1910 revolution generated more claims; the Bucareli accords of 1923 instituted the Special Commission on Revolutionary Claims and the Mexican-United States General Claims Commission, but neither body accomplished its task and both were suspended in 1931. In 1934 the United States accepted a settlement of most revolutionary claims for a lump payment equivalent to 2.64 percent of their value. By another agreement in 1941, Mexico paid remaining American claims to the amount of $40 million and agreed to the appointment of a joint commission to determine the value of U.S. oil holdings expropriated in 1938.

AMERICAN PARTY (Know-Nothing party). Founded in New York in 1849 as a secret patriotic society known as the Order of the Star Spangled Banner, it expanded rapidly and by 1854 was a national organization. Its phenomenal growth was due partly to the charm of secrecy. Members were sworn not to reveal its mysteries; their universal answer to questions was "I know nothing about it," thus giving their organization its popular name. All who joined were pledged to vote only for native Americans, to work for a twenty-one-year probationary period preceding naturalization, and to combat the Catholic church.

In the elections of 1854 and 1855 the party was successful in a number of New England and border states, and its supporters expected to carry the country in 1856 but the slavery issue caused a split in ranks. A proslavery resolution, pushed through the 1855 convention by southern delegates, caused a lasting breach, and the American party entered the election of 1856 so divided that its presidential candidate, Millard Fillmore, carried only Maryland. This defeat brought about the party's end.

AMERICAN PHILOSOPHICAL SOCIETY. The oldest learned society in America. Benjamin Franklin issued a public call to found a society of "Virtuosi or ingenious Men," and several meetings were held in 1743; but the society languished and by 1746 it was dead. In 1766 some younger Philadelphians formed the American Society for Promoting Useful Knowledge. Survivors of the 1743 group and some others, Anglican and proprietary in sentiment, then revived the "dormant" American Philosophical Society. The rival societies merged in 1769 as the American Philosophical Society, Held at Philadelphia, for Promoting Useful Knowledge; Franklin was chosen president.

The society's first scientific undertaking was to observe the transit of Venus (June 3, 1769). Its reports were first published in the *Philosophical Transactions* of the Royal Society and then, in full, in its own *Transactions* (1771), which quickly established the society's reputation. Reorganized in 1784–85, the society expanded its membership, erected a hall (still in use), and resumed publication of the *Transactions.* Its tone was Jeffersonian, republican, deistic, and pro-French. Thomas Jefferson, president of the United States and the society simultaneously, used the society as a national library, museum, and academy of sciences. The explorers Meriwether Lewis and William Clark deposited their specimens in its museum and library. Materials on American Indian languages also went into the library. Joel R. Poinsett donated a collection of ancient Mexican artifacts. During the 19th century, the *Transactions* carried many descriptive articles on American natural history; Joseph Henry's experiments on electromagnetism were reported in the society's *Proceedings.*

The society lost preeminence during the second third of the century, when the specialized learned societies arose; but the bicentennial of Franklin's birth in 1906 brought a renewal of activity. In 1927–29 plans were drafted to reorganize the society as a clearinghouse for scientific knowledge, but these plans collapsed with the economic depression. After 1940 the society expanded its scholarly publications program, inaugurated a program of research grants to individuals (345 grants amounting to $320,000 were made in 1979), and developed its library into one of the principal collections on the history of science in America.

AMERICAN PROTECTIVE ASSOCIATION. A secret anti-Catholic society, founded at Clinton, Iowa, in 1887 by Henry F. Bowers. It attracted a million members by 1896. The association gained control of local Republican organizations and carried elections throughout the Midwest, but in 1896 it split over the question of supporting William McKinley. It lingered on until 1911.

AMERICAN RAILWAY ASSOCIATION. Originated in meetings of managers and ranking railway operating officials known as Time Table Conventions, first held on Oct. 1, 1872 (Louisville, Ky.). A major achievement was the decision to establish the four zones of standard time in the United States. In 1875 the group changed its name to General Time Convention and in October 1891 to American Railway Association. In 1934 it was included in the Association of American Railroads.

AMERICAN RAILWAY UNION. Started by Eugene V. Debs in June 1893 in an attempt to unite all railroad workers.

In June 1894 it ordered its members not to handle Pullman cars, in sympathy with the Pullman shop strikers. Violence resulting, President Grover Cleveland sent troops to stop interference with the mails. The union officers were jailed under the Sherman Antitrust Act; the strike was lost, and the union collapsed.

AMERICAN REPUBLICAN PARTY. A nativistic political organization, launched in New York in June 1843 as a protest against immigrants. In 1844 it carried municipal elections in New York City and Philadelphia; in July 1845 a national convention changed the name to the Native American party and drafted a legislative program of sweeping reforms in the naturalization machinery. Failure to force congressional action on these proposals led to the party's rapid decline.

AMERICAN REPUBLICS, BUREAU OF. *See* **Pan-American Union.**

AMERICAN REVOLUTION. *See* **Revolution, American.**

AMERICAN SAMOA. *See* **Samoa, American.**

AMERICAN STUDIES. An approach to the study of American civilization that achieved grudging institutional acceptance in American universities in the 1930's and growing popularity in the period following World War II. The American studies movement seeks to approach American culture in a comprehensive fashion, primarily through its history and literature, but also through its fine arts, religion, and philosophy. American studies programs were at first under the control of interdepartmental committees from such departments as English, history, fine arts, philosophy, and government. More recently, some institutions have created separate American studies departments. The movement acquired a journal in 1949, when the first issue of *American Quarterly* appeared; in 1952 it became the official journal of the newly organized American Studies Association.

Despite the rapid growth of the American studies movement (243 colleges and universities in 1980, 17 with Ph.D. programs), its supporters have usually been ill at ease with themselves and with the movement. Henry Nash Smith concluded in 1957 that no existing method, including that of cultural anthropology, provided a ready-made method of American studies. As American studies programs expanded, criticism increased. In the 1950's the charge was that American studies reflected a jingoistic exaltation of American virtues and a concealment of American vices. Another criticism has been that American studies members are distinguished less by their knowledge of America than by their ignorance of Europe; most doctoral programs in American studies now require that competence in at least one non-American field. Perhaps the most serious criticism has been that writers in the field do not deal with social, economic, or literary history, but play fast and loose with symbols and myths, with notions of national character, and with a few literary works thought by literary critics, but not the public, to be particularly representative of American thought.

American studies in the 1960's and 1970's extended its grasp to anthropology, sociology, historical archaeology, industrial archaeology, folk culture, material culture, museum studies, and popular culture, as well as urban, minority, and women's studies.

AMERICAN SYSTEM. A term applied by Henry Clay, in his tariff speech of Mar. 30–31, 1824. His object was to create a home market and to check the decline of American industry through internal improvement, and to protect American interests, labor interests, labor, industry and arts. Implicit in the arrangement was the availability of more revenue for internal improvements. Since Clay became known as the father of the American system, the practice soon developed of applying this label to collateral measures for which he stood, such as his proposal to have the national government distribute among the states the proceeds of the sale of public lands.

***AMERICAN TOBACCO* CASE,** 221 U.S. 106 (1911). In this decision the Supreme Court, following the same line of reasoning as in the Standard Oil decision of the same year, found that the American Tobacco Company had attempted to restrain commerce and monopolize the tobacco business in violation of the Sherman Antitrust Act.

***AMERICA'S* CUP RACES.** *See* **Yacht Racing.**

AMISH MENNONITES. *See* **Mennonites.**

***AMISTAD* CASE.** In 1839 fifty-four slaves on the Spanish schooner *Amistad* mutinied near Cuba, murdered part of the crew, and attempted to cause the remainder to sail to Africa; but they landed in Connecticut. Salvage claims, initially awarded by legal proceedings in Connecticut, were overturned by the Supreme Court in 1841 and the Africans were freed. Private charity provided their transportation back to Africa, and the organized support on their behalf played a part in the later establishment of the American Missionary Association. (*See also Creole* Slave Case.)

AMITE, BATTLE OF (August 1808). A skirmish fought on the Amite River in Mississippi Territory between nineteen frontier settlers and thirty Choctaw Indians. Regular troops and militia were called out, but the Indians disappeared.

AMNESTY. The decision of a government not to punish certain offenses, typically of a political nature. Amnesty is usually general, applies to certain groups or communities of people, and relates to a particular historical event. The U.S. Constitution gives the president the authority to grant pardon and, by interpretation, amnesty.

Amnesty was used by President George Washington to quell the Whiskey Rebellion of 1794. In 1807, President Thomas Jefferson pardoned army deserters outside the country if they turned themselves in within four months and resumed their duties. President James Madison issued three amnesty proclamations for deserters after the War of 1812, and President Andrew Jackson issued an amnesty proclamation in 1830.

President Abraham Lincoln granted amnesty to all Union deserters; they were to return to their units within sixty days and serve out their enlistment or lose their citizenship. He attempted—unsuccessfully—to establish a parole system for political prisoners and offered a pardon to southerners who would take an oath of allegiance to the federal government. Andrew Johnson proclaimed three executive amnesties, each more liberal than the previous one. His final proclamation, on Christmas of 1868, was a universal amnesty. It was not until May 22, 1872, however, that the Congress passed a limited amnesty law.

After World War I, there was no general amnesty for deserters, although President Woodrow Wilson did grant full amnesty to nearly 5,000 persons serving sentences for conscription violations. In 1924, President Calvin Coolidge restored citizenship to those who had deserted after the fighting in Europe stopped and before a final peace treaty was signed. Following World War II, President Harry S. Truman established an amnesty board, which recommended individual consideration of each amnesty request. Only 1,523 out of 15,000 persons were pardoned. No amnesty was granted to draft evaders or deserters following the Korean War.

During the Vietnam War over 500,000 men deserted the armed services; an additional 8,000 men were convicted of draft violations. On Sept. 16, 1974, President Gerald R. Ford proclaimed a conditional clemency, by which draft dodgers and military deserters would be forgiven following a prescribed time of public service. On Jan. 27, 1977, President Jimmy Carter pardoned most Vietnam War evaders.

***AMY WARWICK* ADMIRALTY CASE,** 2 Black 635 (1863). One of the prize cases in which the Supreme Court upheld the power of the president to recognize the existence of a civil war and thereupon to establish a blockade, without awaiting congressional action.

ANACONDA COPPER. One of the largest copper mining companies of the world, and the principal producer of the Butte district of Montana. It was organized in 1881 as the Anaconda Silver Mining Company, but it soon became evident that the small Anaconda silver mine (purchased for $30,000) contained mainly copper; a smelter was erected in 1884 and 3,000 tons of ore were being treated daily by 1889. The company expanded and was reorganized as the Anaconda Mining Company in 1891, with a capital of $25,000,000. In 1895 it became the Anaconda Copper Mining Company.

ANAHUAC, ATTACK ON (June 1832). Anahuac was a Mexican military post on the northeast shore of Galveston Bay. To effect the release of William B. Travis and other Americans held there, a group of American settlers in Texas attacked the post. The resulting negotiations led the Texans to declare for the Santa Anna party in Mexico. The incident was an important preliminary to the Texas Revolution.

ANANIAS CLUB. An expression employed by the press in 1906–07 and referring to the biblical story of Ananias, who was struck dead for lying. Persons were eligible for membership in the "club" once they had been called a liar by President Theodore Roosevelt. Membership included opponents of Roosevelt's policies.

ANARCHISTS. Anarchism is a political philosophy that rejects the rule of the state. In the United States, anarchist views began to be expressed very early. The statement "That government is best which governs least," associated with Thomas Jefferson, while not anarchist, moves strongly in an anarchist direction. Josiah Warren (1798–1874), with his philosophy of the "sovereignty of the individual," was a good representative of early 19th-century anarchism.

American anarchism between the Civil War and World War I developed two schools of thought about its goals and two about means. In terms of goals, some anarchists, like Benjamin E. Tucker (1854–1939), were "individualists," while others, like Emma Goldman (1869–1940) and Alexander Berkman (1870–1936), were "communist." Goldman did much to advance the cause of freedom of expression through her journal *Mother Earth* (1906–17). Berkman was an advocate of communist anarchism in such books as *Now and After: The ABC of Communist Anarchism* (1929). In terms of means, there were "anarchists of the deed," who thought physical violence was permissible, and others who stressed the importance of nonviolent methods. Leon Czolgosz, the assassin of President William McKinley, was an anarchist of the deed; and Berkman, in his 1892 attempt on the life of steel magnate Henry Clay Frick, seemed to espouse the same position. Tucker, in his magazine *Liberty* (1881–1908) and in books like *Instead of a Book* (1893), argued that the state must be abolished by education and nonviolent resistance; and in the latter part of his life Berkman emphasized nonviolent approaches. American anarchist followers of Leo Tolstoy were radical pacifists. The Industrial Workers of the World, founded in 1905, was said to be anarchosyndicalist in its outlook: it hoped to reorganize society along syndicalist (industrial union) lines.

Anarchism left its imprint on American legislation and administrative practice; immigration legislation excluded anarchists, and in 1919 Goldman and Berkman were deported to the Soviet Union. Anarchist influence declined after World War I. However, many in the New Left movement of the 1960's, during their attacks on the largely Marxist Old Left, developed an outlook that resembled anarchist positions.

ANASAZI. A prehistoric culture developed on the high mesas and in the deep canyons surrounding the juncture of Arizona, New Mexico, Utah, and Colorado, the cliff-dwelling ruins of which have made this the best-known prehistoric culture in the Southwest. A distinctive way of life began to emerge by the Basketmaker II period (A.D. 1–500) with the addition of cultigens (corn and squash) and pithouses to the Desert culture base. During the Pueblo I and II periods (A.D. 750–1100) domesticated plant foods became the staple of the economy and large settlements of contiguous rooms began to replace pithouses, which survived as ceremonial structures or "kivas." During the Classic period (A.D. 1100–1300) most of the population lived in towns. Pueblo Bonito in Chaco Canyon, N.Mex., the largest of these, was a D-shaped, semicircular apartment with about 800 rooms. Advanced agricultural techniques, including irrigation canals, were known; high-quality ceramics, textiles, and ornaments of turquoise demonstrate the artistry of the Classic Anasazi. After A.D. 1300 climatic and social factors resulted in the abandonment of these flourishing towns.

ANCHORAGE (Alaska). The largest city in Alaska, with a population of 173,017 in 1980. It was founded in 1915 and named because it stands in a protected portion of Cook Inlet, with easy access to the sea. During World War II, Anchorage became an important headquarters for U.S. ground, sea, and air forces. It is the center for the farming region of the Matanuska River Valley, and a major shipping and air terminal between Asiatic and North American cities.

***ANDERSON* V. *DUNN*.** 6 Wheaton 204 (1821). The right of the House of Representatives to charge, hear, and punish contempt and to detain, arrest, and imprison those so charged was unanimously upheld on the analogy of the right of the judiciary to punish contempt.

ANDERSONVILLE PRISON (Ga.). Confederate military prison established in February 1864; the prison consisted of a log stockade of sixteen and one-half acres (later enlarged to twenty-six acres) through which ran a stream of water. Bad sanitary conditions, poor food, crowding, and exposure soon produced respiratory diseases, diarrhea, and scurvy. The inadequate medical staff could not cope with the situation. During the summer the number of prisoners increased to 31,678; there are 12,912 graves in the national cemetery at Andersonville, but the number of deaths was higher. In September, the approach of Gen. W. T. Sherman's army caused the removal of all well prisoners to Charleston, S.C. It appeared that the Confederates were deliberately murdering the captives, and Capt. Henry Wirz, commander of the prison, was tried in August 1865 on charges of murder and conspiring to murder. Although found guilty and hanged, subsequent investigation has revealed much in his favor. For many years Andersonville prison was a vital element in the "bloody shirt" issue in politics.

ANDRÉ, CAPTURE OF. Maj. John André, adjutant-general of the British Army in North America during the Revolution, was entrusted by Sir Henry Clinton with the correspondence between the British headquarters and the American traitor Brig. Gen. Benedict Arnold (1779–80). On Sept. 21, 1780, he met Arnold on the Hudson River to complete arrangements for the betrayal of West Point to the British. He had arrived on the *Vulture,* but while he and Arnold were in conference, American artillery fire compelled the ship to fall downstream. André changed into a disguise and carried the treasonable papers back overland by horseback. He was captured (September 23) by three American irregulars, who turned him over to the American army. Clinton demanded his release on the ground that he had gone to consult with Arnold under a flag of truce, which was true; but, in fact, his conduct had made him a spy. André was tried before a court-martial (September 29), convicted, and hanged on Oct. 2, 1780, at Tappan, N.Y.

ANDREWS' RAID (Apr. 12, 1862). Twenty-two Union spies attempted to destroy the strategic railroad between Atlanta, Ga., and Chattanooga, Tenn. After a race in the engine *General* they were captured by men from the pursuing engine *Texas;* eight were subsequently hanged.

ANDROS REGIME. *See* **New England, Dominion of.**

ANESTHESIA, DISCOVERY OF. Late in the 18th century, physicians discovered the exhilarating properties of nitrous oxide. William E. Clarke of Rochester, N.Y., is said to have administered ether successfully for a tooth extraction in January 1842. In March 1842, Crawford W. Long, a Georgia surgeon, began to perform operations with ether anesthesia. In December 1844, after witnessing a nitrous oxide entertainment in which a young man injured himself but felt no pain, the Hartford, Conn., dentist Horace Wells had the gas administered to himself and had a tooth extracted while under its influence. After experimenting on several patients, Wells then attempted the technique publicly in Boston, but the demonstration failed. Following this, his former student and partner, William T. G. Morton, began experimenting with sulfuric ether. After succeeding with a dental patient, Morton received permission to demonstrate his procedure at the Massachusetts General Hospital; and on Oct. 16, 1846, Dr. John C. Warren operated on a patient after Morton had anesthetized him. The demonstration was an unqualified success.

ANGLICAN CHURCH. *See* **Church of England in the Colonies.**

ANGLO-AMERICAN RELATIONS. Prior to the American Revolution, America had been an intimate, if dependent, part of Great Britain. Although the Revolution snapped the political ties, the United States found it impossible to lessen its economic dependence on Britain immediately after the Revolution: British merchants were the only source of credit, and long-standing commercial relationships were difficult to replace. In the first few years after the Revolution, Britain supplied 90 percent of America's imports; by 1795, this had declined to 30–40 percent, where it remained until 1850. During this same period, the United States sent 30–50 percent of its exports to Great Britain, most importantly cotton and, after the Corn Laws and other navigation acts were repealed in the late 1840's, foodstuffs. After 1850, American exports to Britain maintained their high level, but British exports to America steadily dwindled.

During the peace negotiations following the Revolution, the British felt that the United States was more a rival than a potential ally, and refused to send a diplomatic representative to the United States in response to America's dispatch of John Adams as minister to St. James's. Adams tried to settle diplomatic problems and conclude a trade treaty, but the British closed Canada and the West Indies to American ships and to most American products; they also refused to turn over the military posts that the Peace of 1783 had placed on the American side of the Canadian-American border. Under the Articles of Confederation, the United States found itself impotent in the face of British power and intransigence, and Congress debated the restriction of British commerce as a means of forcing Britain toward a more friendly policy. In response, Britain dispatched a diplomatic representative to the United States in 1791 but still refused to give up the Canadian border posts or open its empire to American ships.

War between France and Britain in 1793 brought the United States and Britain to the brink of war. American ships and goods intended for France were captured by the British in defiance of U.S. rights as a neutral. In 1794, George Washington sent John Jay to England on an emergency peace mission. Jay got the British to give up the border posts; he did not get agreement to America's conception of its proper neutral rights, nor did he succeed in opening much of the British empire to American trade (*see* Jay's Treaty). France retaliated by capturing American ships, and America was driven into waiting British arms; British warships even convoyed American merchant vessels to protect them during this undeclared Franco-American naval war (1797–1800). By 1805 the British once again began captures of U.S. merchant ships. President Thomas Jefferson embargoed all U.S. exports, but when these measures failed, the United States declared war on England in 1812. (*See* War of 1812.)

The Treaty of Ghent (1815) marked the beginning of a new era. Ill feelings and conflicts were slowly overcome as the two governments came to one agreement after another. In 1817, they restricted naval armaments on the Great Lakes; the following year, they settled the location of the Canadian border and agreed to joint occupation of the Oregon Territory. Also in 1818, the British showed restraint in their response to Andrew Jackson's arbitrary hanging of two British citizens in Spanish Florida (*see* Arbuthnot and Ambrister, Case of).

By 1823, British Foreign Secretary George Canning offered to ally with the United States against a possible European invasion of Latin America, but President James Monroe and Secretary of State John Quincy Adams decided to issue a unilateral declaration, the Monroe Doctrine, aimed at England as well as the rest of Europe. This stopped the movement toward any formal intimate Anglo-American connection, but amicable settlement of particular points of conflict continued. In 1830, the British opened the West Indies to American ships; long-simmering border disputes were settled by the Webster-Ashburton Treaty of 1842 and the Oregon Treaty of 1846.

At the same time, the British were forced to abandon any hopes of forming independent buffer states in Texas and California. The Texas Republic accepted annexation to the United States rather than ratify a treaty calling for British mediation with Mexico to guarantee the independence of Texas. The resulting Mexican War saw the United States invade California, ending British hopes there. In Latin America, both nations had an interest in any projected canal across the isthmus of Central America, and the two came close to blows before the Clayton-Bulwer Treaty of 1850 reached a compromise on the issue.

The Civil War imposed new strains on relations. Americans forcibly removed two Confederate diplomats from the British ship *Trent* (see *Trent* Affair). Then the British failed to stop the *Alabama,* a ship built and outfitted by the Confederates in England, from leaving port; Union protests were finally settled by the Geneva Arbitration of 1871 (*see* Alabama Claims). Yet the British did not try to break the Union blockade of the South, despite Britain's need for southern cotton. In addition, the secession of the South allowed the British and the Union to agree to searches of one another's ships in African waters to destroy the slave trade.

After the Civil War, disputes over the Newfoundland cod fisheries and the Bering Strait seal fisheries were arbitrated; economic relations were good; and the only potential area of rivalry, Latin America, was quiescent. A serious crisis came in 1895, when President Grover Cleveland and Secretary of State Richard Olney demanded that a boundary dispute between Venezuela and British Guiana be submitted to American arbitration, threatening to draw the boundary unilaterally and fight if the British crossed it. Britain, apprehensive about the rise of German power in Europe and wishing to avoid war with America, gave in. Thereafter, Britain avoided any challenge to America in the Western Hemisphere. It also agreed to the abrogation of the Clayton-Bulwer Treaty and permitted the United States sole control of the projected Panama Canal (the Hay-Pauncefote Treaty of 1901).

Americans found points of agreement with the British in Asia. In 1899 Secretary of State John Hay proclaimed the Open Door policy in China, partially in response to the requests of English friends. But in 1902 Britain allied with Japan to fight together if either were challenged by more than one enemy in China. This was an embarrassment to the growing amity between Britain and the United States, as Japan and the latter were becoming increasingly estranged. But the British let it be known that the alliance would never commit the British to fight the Americans. America's benevolent neutrality toward England during the Boer War further solidified Anglo-American friendship. Even President Theodore Roosevelt's uncompromising stand and sharp tactics in the arbitration of the Canada-Alaska border dispute in 1902 did not interrupt it.

By the time World War I broke out, American public opinion was thoroughly ready to favor the British. Although Americans resented the British blockade of Germany and the interruption of America's trade with the Continent, they resented Germany's submarine warfare even more; supplies, arms, and loans to the British flowed in ever-increasing amounts. When the Germans resumed submarine warfare in 1917, sinking American ships, the United States entered the war, but as an "associated" rather than an "allied" power.

During the peace conference after the war, President Woodrow Wilson tried to resist Allied demands for new colonies and large-scale reparations, but ultimately he had to compromise with these demands; the Americans, disillusioned, rejected the Treaty of Versailles and association with Great Britain in the League of Nations. World War I also marked a turning point in the Anglo-American economic relationship. The war had forced the British to spend most of their U.S. assets and to borrow a great deal of money from the United States; in a startling reversal, England became the debtor and America the creditor. In addition, American need for British imports was declining, and England found it difficult to afford American goods; nonetheless, America refused to scale down British debts, and so Britain refused to scale down the reparations owed it by Germany. Despite the dwindling economic relationship and America's refusal to join the League of Nations, Anglo-American political relations remained good. At the Washington Naval Conference of 1922, the two countries agreed to accept naval parity with one another, and the Anglo-Japanese Treaty was abrogated. A far-reaching Anglo-American trade treaty was signed in 1938.

President Franklin Roosevelt, fearing public opinion, was at first wary of concrete measures to aid Britain; but in late 1939, by executive agreement, he traded fifty destroyers for permission to build U.S. bases on various British possessions in the Western Hemisphere. In 1941, America began lend-lease aid to the British, making America Britain's arsenal, and British and American military representatives began joint planning for war if America should come in. Once in the war, the United States fought in close collaboration with England. Command of the European theater was united under Gen. Dwight D. Eisenhower, and American arms poured into England. There were problems: Winston Churchill had to be thwarted in his desire to invade southern Europe rather than Normandy; the United States used the economic leverage of lend-lease to force open some of Britain's colonial markets; Roosevelt and Churchill clashed repeatedly over the disposition of the British and other European empires in Asia and the Middle East and over support for the return of the monarchies in Italy and Greece. Nevertheless, the wartime Anglo-American alliance operated with remarkable smoothness and good feeling.

The end of the war placed great strains on the Anglo-American relationship. Expecting a much faster recovery than the British could possibly achieve, the United States continued to drive hard bargains in its economic dealings. The British, increasingly reliant on American economic aid and loans, sought new markets anywhere, even in areas politically unpopular with the United States. Another strain was the issue of sharing atomic information. In 1940, the British and Americans had begun pooling their knowledge of nuclear physics, and Churchill had agreed that production of actual weapons should be concentrated in the United States (*see* Quebec Conferences). But after the war, the Americans insisted on keeping the "secret" of the atomic bomb; Congress responded with the McMahon Act, prohibiting dissemination of most atomic information. Only when the British produced an atomic bomb and later a hydrogen bomb was the sharing of atomic information gradually resumed, with full nuclear partnership established by revisions to the Atomic Energy Act in 1958. Another bitter quarrel arose over Palestine: President Harry Truman intervened to push the Jewish case while refusing any responsibility for making a settlement work; with both Arabs and Jews now refusing to compromise, the British abandoned the question to the United Nations and pulled out in 1947, with bitter feelings about the role of the United States in the affair.

Despite these quarrels, the mutual fear of the Soviet Union helped to maintain the special Anglo-American relationship. In 1947 the British notified the Americans that they could no longer assume responsibility for the defense of Greece; the United States responded with the Truman Doctrine, extending military and economic aid to Greece and Turkey. This was soon followed by the Marshall Plan, giving economic aid to England and the rest of Europe. In 1948, Britain agreed to permit American atomic air bases on British soil. Finally, England and America joined other Western European nations to form the North Atlantic Treaty Organization (NATO).

Cooperation was not so close in Asia and the Middle East. The United States wanted a strong line against Communism in Asia and a more moderate stance toward the Arab states in the Middle East; Great Britain wanted the priorities reversed. Britain recognized Mao Tse-tung's regime in China on Jan. 6, 1950, and refused to honor the American economic boycott, giving rise to much bitterness in America. When the French empire in Indochina was crumbling and particularly after the siege of Dien Bien Phu, Secretary of State John Foster Dulles publicly chastised the British for refusing a joint intervention there and refused a full commitment to the Geneva Settlement. In the Middle East, Egypt reacted to the withdrawal of U.S. financial aid for the Aswan High Dam by seizing the Suez Canal in 1956. Britain joined France and Israel in an attempt to regain the canal, but the United States publicly rebuked them and forced an abandonment of the invasion.

Relations were soon mended. The United States encouraged England toward association with the European Common Market. The British allowed the stationing of U.S. Intermediate Range Ballistic Missiles and Polaris submarines in Britain, while the United States supplied atomic plants and delivery systems for British nuclear weapons. In the Middle East, the British and Americans intervened in Lebanon and Jordan to prevent the spread of the Iraqi revolution of 1958, and together they suffered the steady erosion of Anglo-American influence in that area. In Asia, the British were reluctant supporters of American policy in Vietnam, although even that reluctant support was endangered by American resumption of bombing in North Vietnam in 1967 during delicate discussions between the British and the Soviets. In Europe, Anglo-American cooperation remained close, in spite of some dispute over the proper rate of disarmament there.

During the 1970's the United States cooperated with Great Britain in efforts to settle the racial strife in Rhodesia, which achieved independence in 1980 as Zimbabwe. After the election of Margaret Thatcher, a Conservative, as prime minister in 1979, Anglo-American relations were especially warm.

ANGLO-CHINESE WAR (1839–42). Commodore Lawrence Kearny, arriving off Canton with the *Constellation* and *Boston* in March 1842, found this war, precipitated by the opium dispute, nearly ended. He cultivated friendly relations with both sides, and when the victorious British demanded special trade privileges, he pleaded with the Chinese that equal privileges be granted Americans. This principle formed the basis of the first U.S. treaty with China (1844).

ANIÁN, STRAIT OF. A mythical strait, supposed to connect the Atlantic and Pacific, sought by the Spaniards in the 16th and 17th centuries.

ANIMAL PROTECTIVE SOCIETIES. Incorporated as humane societies, anticruelty societies, animal rescue leagues, or societies for the prevention of cruelty to animals, they operate animal shelters either independently or in conjunction with local city governments. These societies work to secure and enforce laws that prevent cruelty to animals and to promote humane education.

The American Society for the Prevention of Cruelty to Animals, the first of its kind in the United States, was organized by Henry Bergh in New York City in 1866; he also secured the first effective animal protective legislation that same year. In 1877 the American Humane Association was organized in Cleveland as a federation of animal protective societies. The following year the organization's declaration of organization was revised to include children. The movement has continued to grow, and the American Humane Association (incorporated 1903), headquartered in Denver, Colo., provides printed materials and services to more than 1,100 local humane groups.

ANIMAL HUSBANDRY. Animals have been raised extensively for meat, leather, and wool. The cattle industry is one of the largest in the country, and the United States has been a leader in beef and leather production. Hogs, a key element in the farm economy, supply pork, ham, bacon, lard, and leather. Sheep raising, an important industry for both wool and meat, utilizes cooler lands with less plentiful grasses than cattle-ranching. The dairy farm and manufacturing business is also based on animal raising and care.

Until the 20th century, Americans used animal power for transportation and farming. Oxen imported from Europe were important in colonial farming and in the heavy construction work done on roads and canals in the early 19th century; ox-drawn wagons were used by settlers pushing westward. Horses were bred both for riding and for drawing carriages and stagecoaches. Mules became popular in the early 19th century, providing power for plows, ore-carts in mines, and pack-carrying. (*See also* Agriculture.)

ANNAPOLIS (Md.). Capital city of Maryland, with a population of 31,740 in 1980. Located on the south shore of the Severn River, close to where that river empties into Chesapeake Bay, it is the home of two important American colleges: St. John's College (which grew from a small academy known in 1696 as King William School) and the United States Naval Academy, established in 1845. (*See also* Naval Academy, United States.)

Annapolis traces its origins to Anne Arundel Town, founded 1655 and named for the second wife of Lord Baltimore. Settlers had been on the north bank of the Severn since 1648, when Puritan refugees from Virginia were permitted to establish there a town they named Providence. Annapolis became the state capital in 1694 and received its present name in 1695, in honor of Princess Anne, later Queen Anne of England.

Colonial Annapolis was an important cultural and commercial city. It was one of the first "zoned" and "planned" cities in America. Its dock facilities were the most important in Maryland until the late 18th century, when superseded by Baltimore.

ANNAPOLIS. *See* **Naval Academy, United States.**

ANNAPOLIS CONVENTION (1786). Precursor of the Constitutional Convention of 1787. On Sept. 11, 1786, twelve commissioners from New York, New Jersey, Pennsylvania, Delaware, and Virginia met in the State House at Annapolis, Md., to discuss reform of the restrictions placed on interstate commerce by the various states. They took no action except to recommend that a larger convention be held in Philadelphia the following May.

ANNAPOLIS ROYAL. *See* **Port Royal.**

ANN ARBOR (Mich.). Home of the University of Michigan, one of the largest U.S. universities. Ann Arbor is an important marketing and wholesaling center for the Michigan fruit-raising district. Several industries employ the technical knowledge of university people in the manufacture of products such as ball bearings, cameras, and automobile parts. According to the 1980 census, Ann Arbor had a population of 107,316, and its metropolitan area, 264,748.

ANNEXATION OF TERRITORY. No specific provision was made in the Constitution for the annexation of territory. The wars that followed the French Revolution (1793–1815) exhausted the energies of Great Britain, Spain, and France, and enabled the United States to clear its own territory of foreign troops and to expand. In 1803 President Thomas Jefferson unexpectedly purchased by treaty the vast territory of Louisiana. After 1815 England was so exhausted that it made a boundary treaty in 1818 (*see* Convention of 1818) that accepted the line of forty-nine degrees north latitude to the Rocky Mountains and the claim of the United States to the Pacific Northwest. Spain, harassed by South American revolutions, in 1819 gave up Florida to the United States in a treaty that established a frontier line from Texas to California (*see* Adams-Onís Treaty).

The new boundaries were soon expanded in both directions: to the southwest, by the annexation of Texas and by the purchase of Mexican territory in the Treaty of Guadalupe Hidalgo, 1848; to the northwest, by the Oregon Treaty, in which England recognized U.S. sovereignty south of forty-nine degrees north latitude to the Pacific Ocean. In 1853 the United States bought from Mexico a small strip of territory, the Gadsden Purchase.

Two treaties of purchase vastly expanded American territory: Alaska, from Russia in 1867; and the Philippines from Spain in 1899, as a result of the war of 1898. In the same treaty of peace, Puerto Rico and Guam were ceded as outright conquests. The Hawaiian Islands were annexed by joint resolution of Congress, which was reciprocally voted by the Hawaiian legislature, as in the case of Texas. The Danish West Indies were acquired by a treaty of purchase in 1917. A number of small islands in the Atlantic and Pacific were annexed by presidential proclamation.

ANTARCTIC EXPLORATION. *See* **Byrd's Polar Flights; Polar Exploration; Wilkes Exploring Expedition.**

ANTELOPE. A Spanish vessel taken March 1820 by an American privateer. The privateer, with a cargo of slaves captured from Spanish and Portuguese ships, was seized by a U.S. revenue cutter. The vessel and Africans were claimed by Spanish and Portuguese vice-consuls on behalf of their citizens. Chief Justice John Marshall, declaring for the U.S. Supreme Court (10 Wheaton 66), directed that the slaves be restored to the foreigner in possession at the time of the capture.

ANTHRACITE STRIKE. In May 1902, 150,000 anthracite miners, members of the United Mine Workers, went on strike for higher wages, shorter hours, and recognition of the union. The owners refused any dealings with the striking miners. As winter approached, an acute coal shortage developed. President Theodore Roosevelt was ready to send federal troops, even to take over and operate the mines. The owners and operators yielded and agreed to a committee of arbitration to be appointed by the president. The miners returned to work and, in March 1903, the commission awarded them a 10 percent increase in wages and other concessions, but refused to recognize the union.

ANTHRACITE-TIDEWATER CANALS. Anthracite was discovered in northeastern Pennsylvania in the late 18th century, but it could be gotten to market only by floating it down turbulent streams. Josiah White in 1818 built the Lehigh Canal, completing it to the Delaware River at Easton in 1829. The Delaware Division of the Pennsylvania Canals continued the haul to tidewater at Bristol. Later, some of the coal crossed New Jersey to New York Harbor through the Morris Canal, built 1824–32. The Schuylkill Canal was completed in 1825. The Delaware and Hudson Canal, built 1825–29, hauled coal out of the Lackawanna region, also served by the Pennsylvania State Canals, following down the Susquehanna, transferring some of its coal at Middletown to the Union Canal, whence it passed via the Schuylkill to Philadelphia and New York; or it carried on to Columbia, where the Susquehanna and Tidewater, built 1835–38, took over and hauled the coal to Baltimore, sometimes through the Chesapeake and Delaware Canal, Delaware River, and Delaware and Raritan Canal to New York.

ANTHROPOLOGY AND ETHNOLOGY. The distinctive character of American anthropological inquiry was determined largely by the presence of the Indians on the North American continent. Systematic inquiry emerged contemporaneously with the Republic in the work of men associated with the American Philosophical Society. The focal issues of their inquiry were inherited from biblical assumption, the Age of Discovery, and the philosophical speculation of the Enlightenment. In 1797 the Standing Committee on Antiquities was formed in the American Philosophical Society, and in 1805 a precedent-setting questionnaire on Indians was sent with Lewis and Clark. The society played a major role in what came to be called ethnology—a study exemplified by the linguistic scholar Albert Gallatin, who in 1842 founded the American Ethnological Society in New York City. During this same period, impressive Indian mounds were used to buttress both the degenerationist view of Henry Schoolcraft and the polygenetic arguments of Samuel G. Morton.

Although large amounts of anthropometric data were collected on Union soldiers, physical anthropology lagged somewhat after the Civil War. In the context of the Darwinian revolution, the evolutionary viewpoint continued to dominate American anthropological thought. Lewis Henry Morgan's *Systems of Consanguinity* (1871) provided the basis for much modern social anthropology. When the Bureau of (American) Ethnology was founded under John Wesley Powell in 1879, Morgan's *Ancient Society* (1877) became the intellectual manual for government researchers. Work was also carried on in Cambridge, Mass., under F. W. Putnam at the Peabody Museum and in Philadelphia by Daniel G. Brinton. The work of Franz Boas at the American Museum of Natural History and at Columbia University culminated in 1911 with three landmark works: *Changes in Bodily Form of the Descendants of Immigrants,* the "Introduction" to the *Handbook of American Indian Languages,* and *The Mind of Primitive Man.*

The American Anthropological Association was founded in 1902. During the first decades of the century the characteristic focus of Boas's students' research was the geographical distribution and historical diffusion of culture elements. In the late 1920's, other lines of inquiry began to develop. On the one hand, there was the study of the integration of whole cultures, most notably in Ruth Benedict's *Patterns of Culture* (1934), and the related development of the culture and personality school, to which Edward Sapir and Margaret Mead made important contributions. On the other hand, as aboriginal ethnic identities receded more and more into the past, there was increasing emphasis on "acculturation" studies, exemplified by Melville Herskovits.

In the immediate pre– and post–World War II period, important new influences of a more sociological and scientistic character began to be asserted: at Yale, George Murdock worked on the statistical study of *Social Structure* (1949); at Michigan, Leslie White contributed to a minor revival of cultural evolutionary theory; and at Columbia, cultural ecological viewpoints were introduced by Julian Steward. Major new intellectual influences continued to be felt, most notably the structuralism of Claude Levi-Strauss. The broadening of the areal range of research, which had really begun in the 1920's with the work of Mead and Herskovits in Oceania and Africa, was given great impetus by World War II. In the postwar decades of American global commitment, American anthropologists carried on fieldwork on every continent.

ANTIBANK MOVEMENT OF THE WEST. Opposition to banks of issue existed from their beginning in America in the late 18th century. After the panic of 1837 sentiment reached the stage of a movement to abolish banks, centered in the new Jacksonian states of the Mississippi Valley. Between 1845 and 1863, banks were abolished in seven states and on the Pacific Coast.

ANTIETAM, BATTLE OF (Sept. 17, 1862). Early in September 1862, Gen. Robert E. Lee's Army of Northern Virginia crossed the Potomac into Maryland. He concentrated at Frederick and then sent T. J. (Stonewall) Jackson's corps south to take Harpers Ferry, and Gen. James Longstreet's corps westward across the South Mountain. On the 14th Union Gen. G. B. McClellan's Army of the Potomac forced the mountain passes. Lee took position at Sharpsburg, on the Antietam Creek, heard that Jackson had captured Harpers Ferry, and decided to stand and fight behind the creek, with the Potomac at his back. Longstreet took the right of the line; Jackson's troops, as they arrived, the left. McClellan's uncoordinated attacks mauled Lee's army but did not rout it. On the 18th Lee stood fast and McClellan did not renew his attack. On the 19th Lee effected his withdrawal across the Potomac.

ANTIFEDERALISTS. The name Antifederalists was fixed upon the opponents of the adoption of the Constitution of the United States (1787–88) by the supporters of the Constitution, the Federalists. Antifederalism originated as a political force during the American Revolution and represented those who favored the retention of power by state governments, in opposition to those who wanted a strong central government.

ANTI–HORSE THIEF ASSOCIATION. Organized at Fort Scott, Kans., in 1859 to provide protection against marauders thriving on border warfare. From 1869 to 1875 officers were unable to cope with the bandits. The organization spread as necessity arose, but eventually turned into a social organization.

ANTI-IMPERIALISTS. A term given to Americans who opposed U.S. colonial expansion after the Spanish-American War. Anti-imperialism as a movement of political significance is limited to 1898–1900. A majority claimed membership in one of the branches of the Anti-Imperialist League founded in Boston in 1898. By 1900 the league claimed to have 30,000 members and over half a million contributors.

ANTI-MASONIC MOVEMENTS. In 1826, William Morgan, a Freemason and author of a book revealing secrets of the order, disappeared, causing a widespread reaction in western New York, which assumed national importance with the organization of the Anti-Masonic party. Many Masons renounced their vows, membership in New York dwindling from 20,000 to 3,000 between 1826 and 1836. In 1832 there were forty-six Anti-Masonic papers in New York and fifty-five in Pennsylvania. In September 1831 a national Anti-Masonic convention was held at Baltimore, the first national nominating convention of any party, naming William Wirt of Maryland for president. This, the first third party, only drew support away from Henry Clay, and helped the sweep for Andrew Jackson in 1832. In the late 1830's the excitement subsided or was replaced by the antislavery agitation. By 1838 the party had merged with the Whigs.

ANTIMONOPOLY PARTIES (1873–76). Sometimes called Independent or Reform parties; political parties organized by farmers, especially Grange members. Their platforms demanded government reform, economy, and reduced taxation; all but two also demanded state regulation of corporations, particularly railroads. In some states they fused with the Democrats; in other states they remained independent.

ANTINOMIAN CONTROVERSY (1636–38). Anne Hutchinson, a devout admirer of John Cotton, began innocently to repeat to small gatherings in Boston the substance of Cotton's sermons. She caused turmoil by putting a different conclusion from that maintained by the clergy upon the doctrine of the covenant of grace. The standard view held that the elect entered a covenant with God on the condition of their believing in Christ, in return for which God contracted to give them salvation, but that thereafter the justified saints devoted themselves to good works, not in order to merit redemption, but as evidence of their having been called. Mrs. Hutchinson declared that this denied the fundamental Protestant tenet of salvation by faith alone.

The New England clergy, recognizing in her teachings a form of "Antinomianism," a discarding of the moral law, could not possibly tolerate her. Her teachings threatened to split the colony into factions, and in May 1637, Gov. John Winthrop proceeded to disarm Anne's partisans and suppress the movement. Anne was found guilty of eighty erroneous opinions. She was excommunicated from the First Church in March 1638 and banished from the colony by the court, whereupon she fled to Rhode Island.

ANTIRENT WAR (1839–46). A culmination of the resentment of farmers in upstate New York against the leasehold system, whereby the great landlords and land companies collected yearly tribute in produce, labor, or money and exacted a share from the sale of a leasehold. In 1839 the militia sobered rioters and ended the so-called Helderberg War. Antirent secret societies spread rapidly and elected John Young governor. The amended constitution of 1846 prohibited new feudal tenures. Old leases became fee simple ownership.

ANTI-SALOON LEAGUE. Founded at Oberlin, Ohio, May 24, 1893. In 1895 the Anti-Saloon League of America was established in Washington, D.C. Prior to the Eighteenth Amendment the league centered upon destroying liquor traffic by legislation. When in 1933 the Eighteenth Amendment was repealed, the league campaigned again for local option. In 1948 the league changed its name to the Temperance League of America; in 1950 it merged with the National Temperance Movement, forming the National Temperance League.

ANTISLAVERY. Antislavery in the United States took several forms during its evolution from the quiet protest of the Germantown Quakers in 1688 through the tragic and violent Civil War, which spawned the Thirteenth Amendment in December 1865.

Gradualism. Early antislavery in America consisted primarily of the agitation of certain English and American Quakers. But even among the Friends, antislavery sentiments grew slowly. By the 1780's the opposition to slavery had spread. Because of its underlying republican ideology, emphasizing liberty and the rights of man, the American Revolution encouraged antislavery sentiments. During these years all the states abolished the African slave trade and most moved toward the ultimate eradication of slavery. With the enactment of the Northwest Ordinance in 1787, slavery was confined to the area that increasingly became known as the South. Gradual emancipation in the northern states was not achieved without opposition; and the newly formed antislavery societies played a crucial role in these early achievements. Pennsylvania Quakers established the first such society in 1775. In 1794 the American Convention for Promoting the Abolition of Slavery and Improving the Condition of the African Race held its first meeting.

Colonization. During the three decades following 1800, efforts at gradual emancipation gave way to proposals for the colonization of free blacks, and the center of antislavery activity shifted to the upper South. True abolitionism never gained a foothold anywhere in the South. All the southern states except Georgia and South Carolina moved toward emancipation by easing the process of private manumission. After 1800 the tide turned and flowed in the opposite direction. By 1830 nearly all the vocal abolitionists were forced to leave the South. In 1832 the only antislavery advocates remaining in the South were the rapidly dwindling supporters of the American Colonization Society (ACS), which had originated in response to fears that free blacks could not be successfully incorporated into American society. As the ACS became increasingly dominated by those whose main purpose was the deportation of free blacks and shed its antislavery character, the abolitionists turned against the organization.

Immediatism. One can trace the roots of the doctrine of immediatism to the basic elements of 18th-century antislavery thought and relate its appearance in the United States in the 1830's to such causes as English influence, increasing black militancy, and the failure of gradual emancipation in the South. In the 1830's, antislavery sentiments spread throughout the northern states. The New England Anti-Slavery Society was formed in 1831; two years later delegates from Massachusetts, New York, and Pennsylvania established the American Anti-Slavery Society (AAS). By 1835 there were 225 auxiliaries of the AAS, and by 1840 there were 1,650. A distinctive group within the movement was made up of the free blacks who were prominent in the activities of the underground railroad and who provided a crucial element of abolitionist leadership. However, blacks were generally denied positions of power. During the 1830's and 1840's a series of all-black National Negro Conventions acted to focus the efforts of black abolitionists. The major activity of abolitionists in the 1830's consisted of sentimental appeals through newspapers, magazines, and pamphlets. Theodore Dwight Weld's *Slavery As It Is* made the most powerful appeal. When the AAS's postal campaign to inundate the South with antislavery publications failed, they attempted an unsuccessful petition campaign in Congress.

Political Antislavery. Although it had grown rapidly during the 1830's, at the end of the decade the abolition movement remained unpopular and generally weak. In 1839 the majority of American abolitionists decided to establish a political party. Alvan Stewart, Gerrit Smith, and Myron Holley moved to form the Liberty, or Human Rights, party, which nominated James G. Birney for president in 1840 and in 1844. After 1844 the Liberty party split over the question of broadening the party's appeal, and the majority of its members drifted into the Free Soil party, which appeared in 1848.

The failure of both moral suasion and political activity led many blacks and a few whites to greater militancy. In 1859 John Brown, with financial aid from white abolitionists and accompanied by sixteen whites and five blacks, launched his unsuccessful raid on Harpers Ferry. Although individual abolitionists continued to agitate throughout the 1850's, organized abolitionism passed from the scene. The final phase of antislavery activity in the United States was based primarily on hostility toward the slaveholder and the values of the society in which he lived, a hostility encouraged by Harriet Beecher Stowe's *Uncle Tom's Cabin* (1851). Antisouthernism provided a vehicle through which the Republican party could unite all forms of northern antislavery feeling by 1860. (See also Emancipation, Compensated; Emancipation Movement; Emancipation Proclamation.)

ANTITRUST LAWS. The broad purpose of the federal antitrust laws is the maintenance of competitive conditions in the American private enterprise economy.

The Sherman Antitrust Act (1890) declared illegal every combination in restraint of interstate or foreign commerce and prohibited monopolization of any part of such trade. The U.S. attorney general was authorized to institute civil or criminal proceedings in the federal circuit courts, and injured private parties were allowed to bring civil suits for recovery of triple damages. For the first decade or more its enforcement was generally feeble. A landmark in its judicial interpretation was the "rule of reason" applied in the Standard Oil and American Tobacco cases in 1911, when the Supreme Court drew a distinction between reasonable and unreasonable restraints of trade that influenced subsequent decisions.

The Sherman Act has been amended by the Webb-Pomerene Export Trade Act of 1918, which allows American exporters to enter into certain agreements in foreign commerce, and by the Miller-Tydings Act of 1937 and the McGuire-Keogh Act of 1952, both of which give federal sanction to resale price maintenance.

Trust regulation was still a national issue in the election of 1912. Progressive reformers pressed for legislation prohibiting specific trade practices. The result was the Clayton Act of 1914, which forbade price discrimination, exclusive dealing and tying contracts, stock acquisitions of other companies, and interlocking directorates in industry and banking. The Clayton Act was amended by the Robinson-Patman Act of 1936, which outlawed unreasonably low prices, and the Celler-Kefauver Act of 1950, which strengthened the provision against anticompetitive mergers.

The Federal Trade Commission Act of 1914 established a five-member independent regulatory agency, the Federal Trade Commission (FTC), empowered to investigate unfair methods of competition. The Wheeler-Lea Act of 1938 banned "unfair or deceptive acts or practices in commerce."

In December 1974 President Gerald R. Ford signed into law the Antitrust Procedures and Penalties Act, the most significant reform of the federal antitrust laws in a quarter-century. It changed some criminal violations, notably price-fixing, from misdemeanors to felonies; raised maximum allowable fines; and increased the maximum prison sentence.

ANZA EXPEDITION (Oct. 23, 1775–Jan. 4, 1776). Sent by New Spain to occupy Alta California in the face of English and Russian threats. Led by Juan Bautista de Anza, 244 persons crossed the Colorado desert and reached San Gabriel. Local jealousies prevented Anza from founding a city, but his lieutenant dedicated a presidio on the site of modern San Francisco, and on Oct. 9, 1776, the mission San Francisco de Asís was started.

ANZIO. A town on the west coast of Italy which became a battleground in the spring of 1944 during World War II. By sending a seaborne invasion force northward from Naples around the German defensive line to land at Anzio, the Allies hoped to loosen the German grip on the mountainous terrain around Cassino, precipitate a battle for Rome, and compel the Germans to retreat to positions north of Rome. The Sixth Corps under Gen. John Lucas landed British and American troops at Anzio and Nettuno on Jan. 22. The Germans rallied quickly, penned the invaders into a small beachhead, brought reinforcements, and almost drove the Anglo-American force into the sea. The Allies held their precarious positions for four months. Sir Harold Alexander's spring offensive of May 11 broke the German Gustav Line, and Gen. Mark Clark's units linked up with the beachhead fourteen days later.

APACHE. The Athapascan-speaking Apache pushed into New Mexico in prehistoric times, later fanning out into Arizona, western Texas, and northern Mexico. The Apache became noted for the depredations they carried on against Indian neighbors and Spanish, Mexican, and U.S. settlers. Their war orientation reached a climax under Cochise and Geronimo (*see* Apache Wars).

Some Apache adapted to a modified agriculture and others to hunting and gathering. In the north of New Mexico the Jicarilla Apache took on Plains traits—the tipi and bison hunting. In central Arizona and New Mexico the San Carlos, White Mountain, Tonto, Mescalero, Chiricahua, and other groups, all divided in several bands. The Lipan Apache are a Mexican remnant. It has been suggested that the harsh desert environment led to the Apache "raiding economy."

APACHE, FORT, INCIDENT AT (Sept. 13, 1886). After Geronimo surrendered on Sept. 4, 1886, Chiricahua and Mimbreño Apache who were believed to be aiding hostiles under Geronimo were summoned to Fort Apache and with Geronimo's band were shipped to Fort Marion, Fla., for internment.

APACHE PASS EXPEDITION (Feb. 4–23, 1861). Led by Lt. George N. Bascom of the Seventh Infantry against Cochise, a chief of the Chiricahua Apache, who was falsely accused of having kidnapped a boy from a ranch. Cochise went voluntarily under a flag of truce to deny the charge, but Bascom ordered Cochise and those with him seized. Cochise escaped and led attacks on the nearby stage station and a wagon train. Bascom ordered the hanging of the six Apache hostages, turning Cochise into an implacable foe.

APACHE WARS (1871–86). With the announcement of President Ulysses S. Grant's peace policy toward the Indians, some 5,000 Apache had been concentrated on the San Carlos Reservation in Arizona. A massacre of over 100 Apaches at Camp Grant, Ariz., on Apr. 30, 1871, began a series of repeated raids under such leaders as Victorio and Geronimo. Victorio was killed in a fight with Mexican troops in 1880. The Apache wars were finally ended with Geronimo's surrender in 1886. (*See also* Camp Grant Massacre.)

APALACHE MASSACRE (1704). An episode in Queen Anne's War. Former Gov. James Moore of Carolina with 50 Englishmen and 1,000 Creek Indians invaded the Apalache district in western Florida, defeating Captain Mexia's force of 30 Spaniards and 400 Apalache, destroying all but one of the fourteen Franciscan mission settlements and carrying off considerable loot, including about 1,400 Christian Indians.

APIA, DISASTER OF. On Mar. 16, 1889, warships were in Apia Harbor in Samoa, ready for hostilities because of the German attempt to set up a protectorate. A hurricane destroyed the German *Eber, Adler,* and *Olga* and the U.S. *Trenton* and the *Vandalia.* The U.S. *Nipsic* was run ashore. The British *Calliope* escaped out to sea. The Berlin Conference followed, establishing a tripartite government.

APOSTOLIC DELEGATION. Established in Washington, D.C., by Pope Leo XIII, Jan. 14, 1893. Archibishop Francesco Satolli, representative of the Holy See at the World's Columbian Exposition, was appointed as the first apostolic delegate.

APPALACHIA. A largely mountainous region in the eastern United States, extending generally from southwestern Pennsylvania southward through West Virginia and eastern Kentucky, and including western portions of Virginia, North Carolina, and South Carolina, eastern portions of Tennessee, and northern portions of Georgia and Alabama. In the 1790's and early 1800's the settlers built their log cabins and clapboard houses on land lying generally between the Blue Ridge Mountains and the southern extension of the Allegheny Mountains. Many of the original settlers and their descendants remained in the area, engaging in logging, coal mining, small local industries, handicraft operations, and agricultural pursuits. After many years of comparative isolation and neglect, Appalachia (since the 1930's) has come to the attention of the public and has gained government support for its efforts to improve its economy, living conditions, and quality of education. During the 1960's Appalachia became a *cause célèbre* for many former members of the Peace Corps, VISTA, and similar organizations.

APPALACHIAN MOUNTAINS BOUNDARY. *See* **Indian Barrier State; Proclamation of 1763; Quebec Act.**

***APPAM* CASE**, 243 U.S. 124 (1917). On Jan. 15, 1916, a German cruiser captured the *Appam,* a British merchantman, and took it into Hampton Roads, Va. There its British crew was released by order of the American government, and the shipowner filed a libel suit; the court decreed restitution of ship and cargo. On appeal by the German government to the Supreme Court the decree was affirmed.

APPEAL OF THE INDEPENDENT DEMOCRATS. A manifesto issued in January 1854, inspired by the Kansas-Nebraska Act, then pending. The signers, led by Sen. Salmon P. Chase, helped to create the Republican party. The "appeal" was sincere and effective, though it contained exaggerated statements and unsound prophecies relative to the possible influence of the measure, introduced by Sen. Stephen A. Douglas, on the spread of slavery.

APPEALS FROM COLONIAL COURTS. In the latter part of the 17th century the new colonial charters, proprietary and royal, reserved for the king-in-council the right to hear cases on appeal from provincial courts where the sum litigated exceeded £300 sterling. In the New England colonies particularly, the appellate authority was at best grudgingly conceded. At times an order of the privy council was deliberately ignored. Pending appeals, executions of the colonial courts were suspended. Through this appellate procedure the privy council sought to bring the legal systems of the colonies into conformity with that of England.

APPLESEED, JOHNNY. As the frontier moved into Ohio, Indiana, and Illinois, the settlers were deprived of fruit until orchards could be grown. John Chapman ("Johnny Appleseed") consecrated himself from 1801 to 1847 to bringing seed from Pennsylvania and planting flowers and fruits, especially apple seed, in the forests to be ready for the settlers when they arrived.

APPLIANCES, ELECTRICAL HOME. *See* **Electrification, Household.**

APPOINTMENT, COUNCIL OF. *See* **Council of Appointment, New York.**

APPOINTMENTS TO GOVERNMENT OFFICE AND APPOINTING POWER. Whether appointment to government positions should be used mainly to reward party service and assist in executing party policies or to obtain the "best qualified man" has been an issue for continuing debate in American history. In his early appointments President George Washington emphasized "fitness of character," selecting men of high reputation. As the party system developed, however, Washington and his successors sought men of their own political persuasion. Within the states vigorous political battles occurred over patronage, marked by the wholesale replacement of administrative officials by the victorious faction at each turn of the political wheel.

President Andrew Jackson argued that "rotation" in office every few years was needed to keep officials sensitive to popular needs. Responding to widespread criticism of his predecessors' tendency to make appointments from the social elite, Jackson replaced hundreds of officials with men of his own party of working-class origins.

During the next fifty years federal and state appointments were largely based upon party service and personal connections. By the 1870's this "spoils system" was widely condemned as having caused a sharp decline in competence and honesty in government service. After President James A. Garfield was killed by a disappointed office-seeker (1881), Congress yielded to public pressure and approved the Pendleton Civil Service Act (1883). (*See* Civil Service.)

APPOMATTOX (Va.). Village 20 miles east southeast of Lynchburg; scene of the surrender of the Confederate Army of Northern Virginia to the Union Army of the Potomac, Apr. 9, 1865. Gen. Robert E. Lee, commanding the Confederate forces which evacuated Petersburg and Richmond on Apr. 2–3, planned to move westward to Lynchburg. Long marches without food had so depleted the Confederate ranks that Gen. Ulysses S. Grant addressed Lee a proposal for the surrender of the army. Lee pushed on toward Lynchburg by the Richmond Stage Road. When the army bivouacked around Appomattox Courthouse on Apr. 8, the surviving Confederates were surrounded on three sides. Lee closed his column and prepared to cut his way out, but when he found the next morning that they faced impossible odds, he sent a flag of truce to Grant. After some delay in communicating with Grant, Lee rode into the village and, at the house of Maj. Wilmer McLean, formally arranged the surrender of all forces then under arms in Virginia.

APPORTIONMENT.

Congressional Apportionment. The U.S. Constitution as amended by the Fourteenth Amendment provides for the apportionment of seats in the U.S. House of Representatives every ten years on the basis of population, except for the rule that each state shall have at least one representative. The Apportionment Act of 1842 required single-member congressional districts composed of "contiguous" or adjoining territory. In 1872 Congress legislated that all districts should contain "as nearly as practicable an equal number of inhabitants," and in 1901 it passed a law requiring that districts should be of "compact territory."

After the 1920 census, which showed for the first time that urban Americans outnumbered rural Americans, Congress in 1929 provided for a so-called permanent system of reapportionment. As amended in 1941, the 1929 act required that (1) the size of the House be fixed at 435; (2) the Bureau of Census prepare for the president a table showing the number of inhabitants of each state and the number of representatives to which each state is entitled; and (3) the president transmit the information to Congress, with the proposed distribution becoming effective in fifteen days unless Congress enacts a different distribution. If a state fails to redraw district lines after gaining or losing seats, the expediency of using at-large elections is authorized. Unfortunately, the 1929 reapportionment act did not specify that districts were to be contiguous, compact, and of equal size. Thus, voters complained of districts of grossly unequal population and of gerrymandering. Not until *Baker* v. *Carr* in 1962 did the Court rule that federal courts could review apportionment cases. In 1964, the Supreme Court ruled that congressional districts must be substantially equal in population.

Apportionment of State Legislatures. Until *Baker* v. *Carr,* constitutional standards by which apportionment should be measured were not established. In a group of six state legislative reapportionment cases, *Reynolds* v. *Sims* (1964), the Supreme Court made these major points: the Fourteenth Amendment's equal protection clause "requires that the seats in both houses of a bicameral state legislature must be apportioned on a population basis"; apportionments must be "based substantially on population"; "the so-called federal analogy is inapplicable as a sustaining precedent for state legislative apportionments"; and deviation from the one-man, one-vote rule for both houses is unconstitutional.

APPRENTICESHIP. A system of occupational training for a specific period and under written contract whereby a young person learns a skill on the job, in a classroom, or in a combination of both. In 1642, the Virginia legislature ordered that children of poor parents be apprenticed to learn "carding, knitting and spinning," while Massachusetts passed a similar law that became the prototype of legislation in the North. The voluntary contracts or indentures often included basic education. The system even prevailed in the professions of law and journalism.

With the Industrial Revolution and expansion of educational opportunity, industrialists and educators felt increasingly that vocational and industrial training could do a better job of preparing skilled workers. During the 20th century, apprenticeship was revived and refined, especially after the National Apprenticeship Act (1937), which established a Bureau of Apprenticeship and Training in the U.S. Department of Labor.

APPROPRIATIONS BY CONGRESS. Congressional appropriations provide much of the money laid out by the federal government. The appropriations process begins each year with the president's budget requests. Currently about twelve separate appropriations bills are considered each year: customarily first by the subcommittees of the House Appropriations Committee, then by the full committee, and then by the full House. Similar units act in the Senate, and conference committees attempt to resolve House-Senate differences. Their recommendations return to each house for approval. The president then accepts or rejects each bill. Initially Congress acts in the context of the executive budget: it is free to accept, amend, or reject the president's proposals. Normally, Congress accepts them or amends them only incrementally.

AQUIDNECK ISLAND. An Indian name for Rhode Island, largest island in Narragansett Bay. The island's purchase from the Narragansett sachems was witnessed by Roger Williams on Mar. 24, 1638. Portsmouth was founded at the northern end, and in 1639 Newport was established on the southern end.

ARAB-AMERICAN RELATIONS. Before World War I the United States had no important political connection with the Arab world. However, during the 19th century, American missionaries established enduring religious and educational ties with the Arabs. Following the Ottoman Empire's dismemberment after World War I, Egypt, Yemen, and Saudi Arabia achieved independence, and other Arab areas became French and British mandates.

Political interest in the Arabs was awakened by World War II. Recognizing the Arab world's strategic location and vast oil reserves, the United States strengthened its political ties with Arab countries; obtained air bases in Saudi Arabia, Morocco, and Libya; and backed American oil companies' efforts in Arab areas. Yet for several years after the war, the United States avoided deep involvement in Arab affairs. While extending major commitments to Turkey and Iran, the United States preferred working through Britain and France to protect its interests in the Arab world. Meanwhile, deepening American association with the European colonial powers and President Harry Truman's strong support for Israel produced the first serious strains between the United States and the Arabs. Nevertheless, overall Arab-American relations remained reasonably good.

These relations deteriorated during 1955 and 1956 after Secretary of State John Foster Dulles encouraged the pro-Western Iraqi monarchy to help form the Baghdad Pact, despite Arab nationalist opposition; condemned Nasser's espousal of nonalignment; refused to sell Egypt arms; and abruptly withdrew an American offer to assist in financing the High Dam at Aswan, which led to the nationalization of the Suez Canal Company by Egypt. The Soviet Union, switching support from Israel to the Arabs and taking advantage of Dulles's actions, made its first major penetration into the Arab world by providing weapons to Egypt and financing the Aswan High Dam.

American opposition to the British-French-Israeli invasion of Egypt in late 1956 brought about some improvement in Arab-American relations. But during 1957 and 1958 tensions developed between the United States and Egypt, Syria, and Iraq. The primary causes of tension were Nasser's move toward socialism; influence of anti-Western elements in Syria; overthrow of the Iraqi monarchy; American efforts to strengthen the conservative, pro-Western regimes by providing them with economic and arms aid and promising them military support against any "Communist" threat under the Eisenhower Doctrine; and the landing of U.S. Marines in Lebanon to back the anti-Nasser government during the 1958 civil war.

After Dulles resigned in 1959, American officials believed that Arab nationalism and nonalignment could be exploited against the Soviet Union. In 1961 President John F. Kennedy recognized the new republican regime in Yemen, provided wheat to Egypt, and took a more neutral position in the conflict between Israel and the Arabs and in the contention between conservative and socialist Arab leaders.

After Lyndon B. Johnson became president in 1963, he revived partisan backing for the conservative Arabs and withheld badly needed economic aid to Egypt. American relations with all Arabs worsened when Johnson gave strong support to Israel during the June 1967 war, which led to an Arab defeat and Israeli occupation of Egyptian, Syrian, and Jordanian territories.

Initially the administration of Richard M. Nixon assumed a more balanced position on the Arab-Israeli question. Because of their military weakness and the Soviet unwillingness to supply offensive weapons on a large scale, the more moderate leaders, including President Nasser and his successor Anwar el-Sadat, sought closer ties with, and the aid of, the United States—despite protests from the Palestinian commandos and other militant Arabs. But the U.S. failure to promote the return of Arab lands, the resumption of large-scale American arms and economic aid to Israel in 1971, and continued U.S. support of Israel at the United Nations caused relations to deteriorate again. These developments also encouraged Egypt and Syria to resort to war with Israel in October 1973 in a desperate attempt to compel the superpowers to make more determined efforts to break the Arab-Israeli impasse.

The Arabs were so aroused when the Nixon administration airlifted arms to Israel during the October war and decided to grant it up to $2.2 billion in military aid that they initiated an oil embargo against the United States. However, by early 1974 Secretary of State Henry Kissinger was able to obtain the lifting of the oil embargo and to enhance significantly America's position in much of the Arab world. Kissinger succeeded in arranging two disengagement agreements that enabled Egypt and Syria to regain for the first time some of their occupied lands. However, on Mar. 25, 1975, one of the staunchest and most influential friends of the United States in the Middle East, King Faisal of Saudi Arabia, was assassinated. Arab-American relations entered a period of uncertainty as a result of the failure of Kissinger's step-by-step diplomacy to bring about further Israeli withdrawals from Arab territories and to provide for the nationalist aspirations of the Palestinians.

Shortly after Jimmy Carter became president in January 1977, he began a series of meetings with Arab and Israeli statesmen to bring about a settlement in the Middle East. In September 1978 Carter, Prime Minister Menachem Begin of Israel, and Egyptian President Anwar el-Sadat reached a general agreement at Camp David, and subsequently Israel and Egypt concluded a peace treaty in March 1979. The treaty provoked harsh criticism from other Arab countries and suspension of Egypt's membership in the Arab League. At the same time Israel (despite American disapproval) continued to found new settlements in the occupied territories. When Sadat was assassinated in October 1981, the United States lost an important friend in the Middle East, but his successor promised to continue Sadat's foreign policy course. Shortly after the assassination, President Ronald Reagan won an important victory when Congress approved the sale of AWAC planes to Saudi Arabia. The sale was severely criticized as a threat to Israel's security, but Saudi Arabia claimed that the planes would only serve for defense.

ARABIAN GOLD. Gold coins captured by colonial pirates from Arabian or Indian ships in the Arabian Sea after 1685. These coins were common in New York, Philadelphia, and Rhode Island, having been brought to the West Indies, where the colonies got their supply of specie.

***ARABIC* CASE.** On Aug. 19, 1915, a German submarine torpedoed without warning the British White Star passenger liner *Arabic,* with the loss of two U.S. citizens. After seeking to justify the attack on the ground that the *Arabic* was attempting to ram the submarine, the German government disavowed the act and offered indemnity.

ARANDA MEMORIAL. Statements of regret that Spain and France entered the Revolution in behalf of the American colonies, said to have been presented by Pedro Pablo Abarca y Bolea, Count of Aranda, to Charles III of Spain in 1783 or 1784.

ARANJUEZ, CONVENTION OF (Apr. 12, 1779). Provided for the entrance of Spain into the revolutionary war, as an ally of France, in case Great Britain should reject (which it did) Spain's intrusive offer of mediation.

ARAPAHO. A Plains tribe, the Arapaho spoke an Algonkin language and appear to have lived in the Red River Valley in early historic times. With the Atsina and followed by the Cheyenne, they pushed into the Dakotas and northeastern Wyoming. They adapted to bison hunting and assimilated the Plains war pattern, intermittently warring with the Ute, Shoshone, Pawnee, Dakota, and Comanche. Peace was maintained with the Cheyenne. The tribe was dispersed following U.S. treaty and reservation allocation.

***ARBELLA*.** Flagship of the "Winthrop Fleet" on which, between Apr. 8 and June 12, 1630, Gov. John Winthrop, other members of the Massachusetts Bay Company, and Puritan emigrants sailed with the charter of the company from England to Salem.

ARBITRATION. Arbitration is a judicial, if somewhat informal, process: the disputants agree to forgo other methods of resolving an issue—for example, by strikes in labor conflicts or by courtroom litigation in business controversies—in favor of the decision of an impartial person or board, whose judgment they have agreed in advance to accept as final and binding.

Labor arbitration is concerned principally with employee grievances. There is also a small, but growing, practice of "interest" arbitration—impartial determination of new contract terms after union and management negotiators have reached an impasse. Labor-grievance arbitration is a creature of the collective-bargaining era. Its history in the United States dates back at least 100 years. But the modern era of collective bargaining began in 1933 with the passage by Congress of section 7a of the National Industrial Recovery Act and, two years later, of the National Labor Relations Act. By means of these and subsequent laws collective bargaining became not merely a permissible activity but rather a practice that was advocated as national policy.

Commercial arbitration takes many forms: it ranges from the small-claims procedures to international-trade arbitration cases, which may involve many millions of dollars. The largest single group of commercial arbitration cases in the United States grows out of automobile accidents. Commercial arbitration is a much older practice than labor arbitration. One of the earliest tribunals in the New World was that of the New York Chamber of Commerce (1768), an organization that had much to do with the founding of the American Arbitration Association in 1926.

ARBOR DAY. On the motion of agriculturist J. Sterling Morton, the Nebraska State Board of Agriculture designated Apr. 10, 1872, as a day to plant trees, naming it Arbor Day. In 1875 the state legislature changed the day to April 22, Morton's birthday, and made it a legal holiday. It is now observed in every state except Alaska, usually on the last Friday in April.

ARBUTHNOT AND AMBRISTER, CASE OF. An incident of Gen. Andrew Jackson's raid into East Florida in 1818. Believing himself tacitly authorized to seize the Floridas in view of Spain's delay in diplomacy, Jackson attacked the Seminole in Spanish territory. He captured Indian collaborators Alexander Arbuthnot, a Scottish trader, and Robert Ambrister, an English trader. After courts-martial, Ambrister was shot and Arbuthnot hanged.

ARCHAEOLOGY AND PREHISTORY, NORTH AMERICAN. Man is not indigenous to the New World. His biologic and cultural evolution began in the Old World millions of years before he first entered the Western Hemisphere. Nearly all archaeologists recognize three major stages or fundamental lifeways among North America's prehistoric cultures. These stages, which are not time-dependent or limited to any one ecosystem, are called the Lithic, the Archaic, and the Formative.

The Lithic was characterized by small bands of hunters and gatherers with game-focused subsistence patterns. The hunters in part exploited now-extinct fauna in Pleistocene environments 10,000 years ago and earlier. Their comparatively simple tools consisted primarily of chipped stone artifacts. For convenience this stage can be divided into three hypothetical time periods: early (more than 28,000 years ago), middle (from 28,000 to 11,800 years ago), and late (from 11,800 to about 10,000 years ago).

The existence of widespread early Lithic cultures characterized by the absence of projectile points and by rough, percussion-flaked stone choppers, scrapers, and knives has been both vigorously proposed and denied. In the mid-1970's not one site was agreed upon by prehistorians as dating from this period, but several are intriguing possibilities.

In contrast to the diminishing evidence of early Lithic man, the middle Lithic witnessed an upsurge in both number of sites and dating control after 1960. For example, at Old Crow Flats, Yukon, a toothed skin flesher made on a caribou tibia, mammoth- and horse-bone artifacts, a few possible stone artifacts, and hundreds of allegedly artificially broken bones were found among several tons of vertebrate fossils. A series of human skulls also has been dated to this period.

The late Lithic was a time of big-game hunting in the High Plains and in the Southwest. The Clovis culture, characterized by the use of fluted lanceolate projectile points and the exploitation of mammoth, was the earliest and most widespread of the late Lithic cultures, dating about 11,250 years ago.

From this often inconclusive and fragmentary evidence nearly all archaeologists agree that man's major early movement into the Americas was across a dry land bridge that periodically stretched between Siberia and Alaska. Accumulating evidence indicates that man was in the Americas as a generalized Mongoloid physical type by at least 25,000 years ago.

In contrast to the game-focused economy of the Lithic, the Archaic emphasized exploitation of seasonally available resources. In the East the progressive adaptations to forest, riverine, and coastal conditions begun at the end of the Pleistocene culminated in developed broad-spectrum hunter-gatherer lifeways some 5,000 years ago. This Eastern Archaic was characterized by polished and chipped stone artifacts and a semisedentary, or even sedentary, existence in some localities. West of the Rockies the Western Archaic, or Desert, culture was essentially an adaptation to arid land with sparse vegetation, although semisedentary societies based on fishing and acorn-gathering emerged along the Pacific coast. Typical artifacts were baskets and milling stones.

The Formative lifeway was molded by intensive plant cultivation. Unlike the Lithic and the Archaic, the Formative was not a continentwide stage, for the adoption of this lifeway was limited by climatic and, in some areas, cultural factors. The incipient domestication of native North American plants began about 3,000 years ago in the Mississippi Valley and other midcontinent riverine areas. This innovation was either an indigenous development or the result of stimulus from Middle America, where Desert Archaic people had begun cultivating corn 6,000 years earlier. The eastern North American cultigens (sunflower, goosefoot, sumpweed, and pumpkin) were soon supplemented by Middle American domesticates that had already reached the Southwest between 3000 and 2000 B.C. Primitive corncobs appear in the Southwest at Bat Cave, N.Mex., in a Desert culture context by this early period. Squash and gourd were apparently introduced into the East from the Southwest by about 1000 B.C.

The earliest pottery vessels north of Mexico—fiber-tempered, soft-paste wares found in southeastern sites, dated as early as 2500 B.C.—have counterparts in Middle America that date at least 500 years earlier. A second eastern ceramic tradition became well established in more northerly states between 1000 and 500 B.C. The origins of this Woodland tradition remain undemonstrated. The source of the earliest pottery vessels in the Southwest that appear by 300 B.C. is generally believed to be Middle America.

A cultural florescence was experienced by the Adena and Hopewell peoples in the Eastern Woodlands between about 600 B.C. and A.D. 250. They made pottery, planted some domesticates, and constructed impressive mounds and earthworks. In other areas of native America cultivation of food plants was not practiced. For example, settled villages and dense populations on the Northwest Coast and in California focused on the harvesting of acorns and the exploitation of marine animals.

In general, Formative settlements can be distinguished from earlier Archaic settlements by their greater size, complexity, and permanence, by expanded food storage capacities, and by new, more complex patterns of social organization.

Formative developments can be traced in the three major cultural traditions of the Southwest—the Anasazi, the Mogollon, and the Hohokam. Towns reached their apogee of construction in the Anasazi Pueblo III and IV periods and in the Classic Hohokam phases. Strong and direct influence from Mexico is clearly evident in the presence of exotic artifacts, stepped pyramids, and ball courts. The town-and-temple, mound-and-plaza complex developed in the bottom lands of the major rivers of the lower Mississippi drainage system sometime between A.D. 500 and 800; the complex climaxed with the appearance of Mississippian cultures shortly afterward. The spectacular site of Cahokia in East Saint Louis, Ill. covered six square miles. Both Woodland- and Mississippian-influenced village-farming communities had become widespread throughout the East to the Plains periphery by A.D. 1000–1200. By about A.D. 1300, the cultural climaxes in the East and Southwest had waned under the impact of changing climatic and social conditions, although a village-farming lifeway continued to dominate both areas to the historic period.

ARCHANGEL, U.S. TROOPS AT. On Mar. 16, 1918, revolution-shattered Russia was compelled by Germany to ratify the Treaty of Brest-Litovsk. The Allies were concerned because the treaty gave the German army entry into Finland, thus positioning it for marches upon the Russian ports of Murmansk and Archangel, where military supplies had been stockpiled from Allied ships. The unstable Bolshevik government welcomed Allied troop landings at Murmansk in March 1918. By Aug. 3 the Allied posture had become anti-Bolshevik, and Archangel was seized. Americans ultimately constituted 40 percent of the Allied troops under the command of the British. By September civil war was raging in Russia. Britain and France favored the Whites, and President Woodrow Wilson's urge toward strict neutrality was compromised. In the summer the Bolshevik army had been too feeble to prevent the Allied seizure of Archangel, but by October the U.S. 339th was responsible for a front of nearly 450 miles. The armistice on Nov. 11, 1918, removed the anti-German rationale for the campaign. Continuation would be clearly an intervention in the Russian domestic struggle. The 339th held place through a more or less peaceful winter and spring, and began sailing for home on June 2, 1919.

ARCHITECTURE.

American Indian. The public and ceremonial structures of native America consist mainly of Maya and Aztec temples, pyramids, palaces, and ball courts in Mexico and Inca citadels in Peru. A North American exception is the mounds and earthworks of the Mississippi Valley. There is prehistoric evidence of ceremonial buildings, not so elaborate as in Mexico, of wood rather than stone, set on mounds.

The Indians of North America north of Mexico varied so greatly that a general statement on house types is impossible. Hunting peoples favored the transportable skin tent, which gave rise to the hide-covered conical tipi of the bison-hunting Plains Indians. With seasonal movement, a domed brush shelter, the wickiup, was developed. Permanently settled gatherers depended basically on brush, straw, or matting. Thatched, round houses in central California contrast with multiple-family elongated tents of matting, each family possessing a single segment, or with semisubterranean earth lodges in the Plateau and sporadically in California.

The central Eskimo's igloo constituted the one native American instance of the use of the keystone arch. The western Eskimo made sod houses, usually circular, over an excavation, with a central firepit. The beautifully elaborate plank houses of the Northwest Coast appear to be variants of this pattern. The same semisubterranean style appears among the Pueblo in the ceremonial underground chamber, the kiva, center of all ritual. Pueblo dwellings were originally made of adobe and stone; adobe bricks are post-Spanish. The birch bark lozenge-shaped tent, the wigwam, generally appeared among the Algonkin-speaking peoples of the Northeast. The Iroquois offer a variation with elm bark covering. Wattle-and-daub houses appear in the round, rectangular, or L-shaped cabins of the Gulf peoples.

Although European settlers used Indian buildings and building techniques, there are only a few remnants of 16th-century Spanish-Indian pueblos in the Southwest.

Spanish Colonial Styles. The first major European buildings of which there is evidence were those of the Spanish in the Southwest, Florida, and on the Texas Gulf coast. From the 1540's the Spaniards, employing Indian labor, built religious, civil, and military buildings in which Indian adobe techniques were combined with baroque decorative forms from Spain and Mexico. Forts and mission churches were built mainly of wood, but the greatest work was the stone fort at St. Augustine, the Castillo de San Marcos, derived from the international Renaissance fortification style.

The last phase of Spanish colonial architecture produced mission settlements in Texas (18th century) and Arizona and California (late 18th and early 19th centuries), incorporating the arch, the vault, and the dome, as well as rich Spanish baroque stone carving.

French Colonial Styles. Of the forts, trading posts, and towns established by the French in the late 17th and early 18th centuries, New Orleans became the greatest center and retains the strongest French traditions. Many churches and houses in the Great Lakes and Mississippi areas were probably built in the French colonial version of log construction, with squared logs set upright and chinked with stone.

Other buildings reflect late medieval French (principally Norman) traditions in form and construction: massive framing; well-developed support systems for high, sloping roofs, flared at the eaves and often heavy with tile coverings; and stucco or boarding over stone-chinked or brick-filled frames. The *galerie* is a prominent feature of these houses, on from one to four sides, usually covered by a second pitch from the eave flare. In the wet and often flooded Mississippi lands, houses were frequently raised on an exposed basement, and thus the two-story galleried form of raised cottage or plantation house was developed.

Late Medieval and Early Renaissance Traditions. The first settlers' primary shelters provided quickly built protections against the weather: dugouts roofed with sod; cabins of poles woven with willow withes and daubed with clay; Indian-style wigwams; and, probably, houses of squared timbers or hewn planks. By the mid–18th century squared-log construction may have accounted for as many as half the buildings on the East Coast.

As soon as they could, the settlers built houses as much like their former homes as possible: in New England, English-style half-timbered frames covered with clapboards or shingles; in New Netherlands, Dutch, Flemish, and Huguenot houses of brick, stone, and wood; in New Sweden, log, frame, and stone buildings; and in Maryland, Virginia, and Carolina, brick and frame English houses. These houses contained a few Renaissance technical advances (developed flues and chimneys, plastered walls, glass windows), but they followed late-medieval national traditions in the basic shape and technique of framing and covering. The influence of Renaissance classicism did show itself in ornament, in gradual style changes, and in technique by the end of the 17th century.

Jones-Wren English Classical Style. A pure Italian Renaissance style, developed by Inigo Jones, John Webb, Roger Pratt, Hugh May, and Sir Christopher Wren, was influential in a number of buildings in the growing ports and governmental centers of the seaboard colonies. The facade of the long-demolished Foster-Hutchinson House, built about 1688 in Boston, was decorated with a giant order of Ionic pilasters and, probably, an eaveline balustrade to hide the roof and make the house look as much as possible like a rectangular Italian palace. At Williamsburg, Va., the town plan and capitol, the college, and the governor's palace form the greatest single American monument to Italian Renaissance style.

Later Anglo-Palladianism. The revival of the designs of the Italian architect Andrea Palladio in the 18th century by the group around Richard Boyle, Lord Burlington, left the greatest mark on the colonies. The two-story portico of Drayton Hall (1738–42), near Charleston, S.C., is the earliest American example of the pedimented projecting pavilion typical of gentlemanly architecture in the 1750's and 1760's. The most noted other Palladianism, the five-part plan (two blocks on each side of a central block, connected with narrow "hyphens"), appeared during the same period.

Knowledgeable Americans were changing, under the English Palladian influence, from the use of classical details to the use of entire classical forms, particularly the temple form. In this period the change toward forms with sophisticated proportions and integrated decorations led to the appearance of the architect along more or less modern lines. Peter Harrison was the first American architect in this sense.

Many of the Anglo-Palladian ideas came to the English colonies in design books by various architects. James Gibb's *Book of Architecture* (1728) was one of the most influential of these for all sorts of buildings, but particularly churches.

Neoclassicism and the Federal Style. Drawing anew on the severest architecture of republican Rome, democratic Greece, and other historic styles (Egyptian, Oriental, Gothic), romantic classicism provided the framework for the first great American national style.

The plan for the new capital city of Washington provided

a single American focus for architectural ideas and for architects, including Thomas Jefferson, who had shown himself a master of the use of the neoclassical style in his design of the Virginia state capitol (1785). Washington was a magnet for designers and builders. The greatest of these was Benjamin Henry Latrobe, an imaginative young English architect who had been working in Virginia and Philadelphia in the late 1790's, in the latter city introducing the severest neoclassical and Gothic styles. Latrobe was appointed by Jefferson as both architect of the Capitol and surveyor of the public buildings. His designs included three new "classical orders" based on the corn plant, the tobacco plant, and the cotton plant. Charles Bulfinch, whose first great work was the Massachusetts State House (1795), in Adamesque style, succeeded Latrobe as architect of the Capitol (1817). Jefferson's own architecture continued to develop, in his rebuilding of Monticello as a Franco-Palladian villa (1793–1809) and his brilliant designs for the University of Virginia (1817–26).

Growing Eclecticism. The period 1825–50 was dominated by the Greek revival, the first continentwide style: Robert Mills's Washington Monument (1836–78) and U.S. Treasury Building (1836–79) in Washington, D.C.; Thomas U. Walter's Girard College (1833–47) and Andalusia (1834–47) in Philadelphia; and many southern plantation houses.

There was also an ever-stronger Gothic revival, with such milestones as Alexander J. Davis's Lyndhurst (1838–41, 1864–66) at Tarrytown, N.Y., and the beginning of the use of "correct" Gothic styles for churches. The great engineer-architect Ithiel Town and his partner Alexander J. Davis helped popularize the Egyptian and Italian-villa styles, and Davis's designs were principal parts of Andrew J. Downing's popularization of the Gothic cottage as an inexpensive house style. The Romanesque revival was introduced by James Renwick in the Smithsonian Institution building (1846–55) at Washington, D.C., and John Notman, introduced a new phase of the Renaissance revival, notably in the Atheneum (1845–57), in Philadelphia. Technical change accelerated stylistic change. Most important was the invention of the "balloon" frame at Chicago in the 1830's, in which lightweight prefabricated members were nailed together, rather than heavy frame timbers dressed, jointed, and fitted by hand.

Beaux Arts and the Rise of Modern Architecture. Academic architectural training and illustrated professional periodicals were new factors after 1850. The École des Beaux Arts in Paris was the leading training ground from the 1850's to the 1920's. Richard Morris Hunt, the first American architect trained there, created trend-setting designs in academic French and English Gothic and Renaissance styles.

Henry Hobson Richardson, who returned from the École des Beaux Arts just after the Civil War, was, by the 1870's, the major source of new American styles. Richardsonian Romanesque was the first American-created style that had a strong influence elsewhere in North America and in Europe. Trinity Church in Boston (1873–77) was the first great success in the style. In the 1870's he followed the English Queen Anne style in the revival of vernacular details, notably in the Watts Sherman House (1874), at Newport. His design for a Marshall Field wholesale store in Chicago was the beginning of a new American business-building style.

Trained at the École, Louis H. Sullivan also studied at M.I.T., where the first American architectural school was established. Sullivan went to Chicago and developed Richardsonian themes into his own business-building style.

Apartment Houses. Horizontal dwelling was a new concept in the United States—except for the lowly tenement—when Arthur Gilman, in 1858, designed the Hotel Pelham in Boston for Dr. John D. Dix. This was the prototype of apartment houses, borrowed from the French, complete with mansard roof. New York followed suit in 1869, when Richard Morris Hunt designed the five-story Stuyvesant Apartments on East 18th Street. The apartment hotel was the forerunner of the apartment house; however, it rarely had cooking facilities in the apartments; residents ate in the main dining room or were served in their apartment. By the early 1880's apartments had been built in all the major cities.

By the end of the 19th century, with the cost of building, furnishing, and staffing the average private home becoming prohibitive, middle-class families came to see apartment living as a desirable solution. It had at first been thought immoral for several families to live under one roof, and it took the well-to-do to render them fully respectable.

The cooperative apartment was introduced as a "home club" in 1879 with Rembrandt House at 152 West 57th Street, designed by Hubert, Pirsson and Company. A New York State law (Jan. 23, 1881) made it possible for tenants to purchase their apartments.

Variety and a Changing Future. In the late 19th and 20th centuries, following the vernacular forms and details brought together in the Queen Anne and colonial styles, American architects developed many important changes in the plan, form, and decoration of the detached house—the suburban house. Two variations were the Stick style and the Shingle style. Charles McKim and Stanford White, both of whom had worked for Richardson, introduced specific American colonial revival details into such houses in the 1880's. In such works as the New York Herald Building (1878, since demolished) and the Boston Public Library (1887), they turned to the Italian Renaissance for inspiration. They took their version of Renaissance classicism to the planning sessions of the World's Columbian Exposition to be held in Chicago in 1893, and the design committee chose it for the fair.

From the mid-19th century, technical developments permitted designing of cast-iron buildings, notably by James Bogardus. In Chicago and New York a new business-building architecture was created, using steel frame, pipes in floor slabs, elevators, and prefabricated window walls. From the Chicago system of the late 19th century, a straight-line development carried to the great skyscrapers of the 20th century. The most important of these are in New York.

Chicago was the center for the most significant developments in the detached house around 1900, the year in which Frank Lloyd Wright designed "A House in a Prairie Town" for the *Ladies' Home Journal.* For six decades Wright created buildings whose influences permeated American and international architecture.

In the early 20th century, important experiments in the detached house were made on the West Coast, fusing Queen Anne, Wrightian, Oriental, and Mission ideas, in the work of the firm of Greene and Greene, Bernard Ralph Maybeck, and Irving Gill. In California the early 20th-century expositions were the sources of a Spanish colonial revival.

International Style. The ideas of Wright and of the European avant-garde architects culminated in the style named International by Henry-Russell Hitchcock and Philip Johnson, in their important 1931 exhibition for the Museum of Modern Art in New York City. This crisp, plain style was slowly accepted, and what shocked many in the 1920's was widely admired by the 1950's. Philip Johnson's house (1949), New Canaan, Conn., exhibits the startling and beautiful innate classicism of the International style: a steel-framed glass box, architecturally decorated with only elegant proportions, a beautiful setting, and a small group of carefully chosen art objects.

In the 1960's and 1970's virtually every city had at least one tall building built in the International style. The Empire State Building was the world's tallest building until the opening in 1970 of the twin-towered World Trade Center in New York City. That, in turn, was soon superseded as the tallest building by the Sears Tower in Chicago.

Major architectural changes of the 1950's, 1960's, and 1970's occurred through experiments in the sculptural forming of space, in structural techniques, and in the pursuit of ornamentation through textured materials. Examples are Buckminster Fuller's tetrahedron domes. A complete freedom with steel-supported concrete was demonstrated by Wright and Eero Saarinen in the Trans World Airlines Terminal (1962) at Kennedy Airport, New York City, and the brilliant Dulles Airport (1958–62) for Washington, D.C., at Chantilly, Va. The boldest architecture of the period was that of the "new brutalism"—experiments in tough and overpowering forms and textured finished—epitomized by Paul Rudolph's Temple Street Parking Garage (1962), New Haven, Conn., and his Art and Architecture Building (1963) for Yale University, the Everson Gallery of Art (1968) by I. M. Pei, in Syracuse, N.Y.; and the East Building for the National Gallery of Art (1973–75), by Pei, in Washington, D.C. Post-modernism, a controversial movement of the 1970s, revived some historical styles such as Renaissance.

ARCHIVES. The body of records and papers officially produced or received by a government, and filed and preserved by it for future reference. In the United States, government archives (public records) are accumulated by federal, state, and local governments. The term may be applied also to records of semipublic and private organizations.

The National Archives. The National Archives of the United States consists of the records of all agencies of the federal government. In 1926 Congress made provision for the construction of the National Archives building in Washington, D.C., which was occupied in 1935. The National Archives was created by law in 1934 as an independent agency of the executive branch, to have the custody and administration of the records transferred to this building. The Federal Register Act of 1935 provided that all regulations intended to have the force of law must be filed at the National Archives and published in the daily *Federal Register* before being put into effect. Those of continuing effect are also printed in a cumulative *Code of Federal Regulations.*

Under the direction of Robert D. W. Connor, the first Archivist of the United States (1934–41) a comprehensive survey was made of federal records both at the capital and in offices throughout the states. All but a few of the 19th-century records and, in bulk, even greater quantities of 20th-century records were in the building by the end of World War II. The *Guide to the Records in the National Archives,* published in 1948, described the more than 800,000 cubic feet of records accessioned by June 30, 1947.

Connor was succeeded by Solon J. Buck (1941–48) and Wayne C. Grover (1948–65). The National Archives lost its independent status in 1949, when it was made a bureau of the newly created General Services Administration and renamed the National Archives and Records Service. Responsibility for receiving the original laws and publishing the *Statutes at Large* was transferred from the Department of State to the National Archives in 1950. Still greater expansion of the Archivist's responsibilities came with the Federal Records Act of 1950. The Archivist was directed to assist agencies in the control and maintenance of their current records. Authority was also granted for the establishment of intermediate records centers to house records not needed at hand. Another area of responsibility has been that of presidential libraries. A resolution of 1955 provided for the acceptance, maintenance, and administration of such presidential libraries.

Outside the National Archives building, national and regional intermediate centers now hold nearly 12 million cubic feet of records in custody. Probably more than 90 percent can be destroyed in time.

State and Local Archives. Many states preceded the federal government in making some provision for the centralized custody and administration of noncurrent records, but the provisions were extremely diverse and frequently inadequate. Usually the archival functions have been assigned to a state historical society or commission, a state department of archives and history, a state library, or the secretary of state. Some states have modern, especially constructed, buildings to house the archives. Most state archival agencies have some authority over the records of counties, municipalities, and other state-created local governing bodies. Municipal archival programs exist in some of the larger cities.

Archives of Private Organizations. Greatly increased interest in business, social, and cultural history in recent years has led to more widespread concern for the archives of all influential organizations of the past. *A Directory of Business Archives in the United States and Canada,* published in 1969 by the Society of American Archivists, contained entries for 135 companies, nearly one-half of them manufacturing firms.

College and university archives have expanded significantly. A directory of these, published by the Society of American Archivists in 1966, showed that 558 educational institutions in the United States had archival programs.

A third important group of private archives is the archives of religious organizations; the Society of American Archivists issued a directory of these in 1963. They ranged from the archives of denominational headquarters organizations to those of individual churches. Of special interest are the records of home and foreign missionary societies.

ARCHIVE WAR (1842). A contest between Austin and Houston, Tex., over the Texas archives. President Sam Houston, after a Mexican raid on San Antonio in 1842, fearing the archives at the capital, Austin, might be lost, undertook to remove them to Houston. The citizens of Austin overtook the wagons and forced them to be returned to Austin.

ARCTIC EXPLORATION. *See* **Byrd's Polar Flights; Polar Expeditions.**

d'ARGES COLONY. In 1787 Pierre Wouves d'Arges acted as agent of the Spanish minister to the United States in forwarding a plan to protect Florida and Louisiana from American encroachment by inducing Kentucky families to settle within those Spanish domains. Liberal grants of land; freedom of religion; and free importation of slaves, stock, farming implements, and provisions for two years were promised. A considerable number of Americans took advantage of the offer and became Spanish subjects.

ARGONAUTS OF CALIFORNIA. *See* **Forty-niners.**

***ARGUS-PELICAN* ENGAGEMENT** (Aug. 14, 1813). Off Saint David's Head, Wales, the British brig *Pelican* captured the American brig *Argus,* which had sunk more than twenty ships in the English Channel in one month.

ARIKARA. A tribe in the northern Plains, the Arikara were river-bottom farmers in an area otherwise devoted to bison hunting; they represent the northernmost movement of Caddoan speech. In the course of their migration northward from the Caddoan focus of the lower Mississippi, the Arikara adopted characteristic Plains traits, although retaining their agricultural inclination. They were assigned the North Dakota Fort Berthold Reservation in the 1880's.

ARIZONA. The forty-eighth state; it contains a northern plateau, central mountain belt, and dry, southern desert. In each of these regions ancient cultures flourished from ca. 500 B.C. to ca. A.D. 1350 and then mysteriously decayed. The inhabitants that emerged later were the Pima, Papago, Apache, and Navajo. Fray Marcos de Niza ventured into the eastern mountains in 1539, followed a year later by Francisco Vásquez de Coronado, whose captains discovered the Grand Canyon and ascended the Colorado River to Yuma. Antonio de Espejo in 1583 discovered copper and silver deposits in central Arizona. Missionaries were in the area by the 1630's.

Rich silver discoveries in 1736 at Arizonac ("Small Spring"), a Pima village near present Nogales, drew the first settlers and gave the region a name. Spain established its first presidio-town in Arizona at Tubac in 1752 but moved the garrison north to Tucson in 1775. In 1821 Arizona became a part of Mexico and entered a period of extended neglect.

By the Treaty of Guadalupe Hidalgo of 1848, Arizona north of the Gila passed to the United States; on Sept. 9, 1850, it became a part of New Mexico Territory; and by the Gadsden Purchase of Dec. 30, 1853, southern Arizona was added to New Mexico. American troops reached Tucson in November of 1856. Influenced by mining interests, Congress on Feb. 24, 1863, established Arizona Territory. Gold discoveries and silver bonanzas spurred population growth. The army forced hostile Indians onto reservations; a cattle industry arose; and transcontinental railroads were built. Arizona entered the Union on Feb. 14, 1912.

Arizona mirrored the impact of two world wars. In 1917–18 copper, cotton, and beef found ready markets, while mining labor unrest resulted in deportations from Jerome and Bisbee. Although the 1920's brought depression, a thriving tourist industry took root. World War II ushered in a new age. The military services established training camps and subsidiary industries, which stimulated a surge in manufacturing. During the 1960's Arizona enjoyed an unprecedented prosperity from mining (producing nearly 50 percent of the nation's copper), agriculture, manufacturing, and tourism. In 1980 the population was 2,717,866; 50 percent of the inhabitants were concentrated around Phoenix, the state capital.

***ARK* AND *DOVE*.** The two vessels that brought the first colonists, about 200 in number, to Maryland. Sailing from the Isle of Wight, Nov. 22, 1633, the *Ark* and the *Dove* entered the Potomac during the first week in March 1634; they explored until, on March 25, it was decided to make the first permanent settlement, still known as St. Marys.

ARKANSAS. First explored by Hernando de Soto in 1541, and claimed for France by Robert Cavelier, Sieur de La Salle, and Henry de Tonti in 1682; the first permanent settlement, Arkansas Post, was founded in 1686 by Tonti. As a part of Louisiana, Arkansas was a French possession until 1762 and a Spanish possession from 1762 to 1800, when France again acquired it. The region became American territory with the Louisiana Purchase in 1803. A part of Missouri Territory, Arkansas became a separate territory in 1819, after Missouri applied for statehood. The first capital was Arkansas Post, but in 1821 Little Rock became the permanent capital. In 1836 citizens prepared a constitution and successfully petitioned for statehood.

A Unionist-controlled convention in March 1861 defeated a movement for secession but resolved against coercion of the Confederate states. When Abraham Lincoln asked Arkansas for troops, the convention reassembled, voted secession, and put Arkansas into the Confederacy. By September 1863, the northern half of the state was in Union hands, and early in 1864 a loyal state government was organized at Little Rock. Congress refused to recognize it and in 1868 set up a new state government that extended full citizenship to blacks.

The railroad age of the late 19th century opened the rich coal, bauxite, and timber resources of Arkansas to northern industrial exploitation. An extensive, disorganized road-building program between 1900 and 1930 left the state with a heavy bonded indebtedness.

An agriculture based on cotton farming, sharecropping, and mule-drawn implements has given way to a highly diversified, mechanized agriculture. The state government is mainly concerned with financing public schools, higher education, public welfare programs, and highways, attracting new industry, and encouraging tourism. The loss of population that accompanied the agricultural revolution during the 1930's and World War II has been followed by a steady increase. In 1980 Arkansas had 2.3 million inhabitants.

***ARKANSAS*, DESTRUCTION OF THE** (Aug. 5, 1862). After the Confederate ironclad *Arkansas* passed through the federal fleet before Vicksburg to cooperate in Gen. John C. Breckinridge's attempt to recapture Baton Rouge, its machinery became disabled within five miles of its destination. The ship was run ashore and blown up to escape capture.

ARKANSAS POST. When Robert Cavelier, Sieur de La Salle, laid claim to the Mississippi Valley for France in 1682, he granted to Henry de Tonti a large concession on the Arkansas River, and in 1686 Tonti established the Arkansas Post as the earliest French settlement in the lower Mississippi Valley. When French Louisiana was divided in 1721, Arkansas Post became the administrative center for the Arkansas District. Until the end of the French regime in 1762 Arkansas Post remained important as an administrative and commercial center and as the site of a Jesuit mission. Following the Civil War, the village declined.

ARKANSAS POST, BATTLE OF (1863). Arkansas Post (Fort Hindman) was fortified by the Confederates for the protection of Little Rock. After the repulse of Union Gen. W. T. Sherman's attack upon Vicksburg it was considered essential to capture the post. Union Gen. John A. McClernand, backed by Adm. David D. Porter's fleet of ironclads, forced Gen. Thomas J. Churchill to surrender Jan. 11.

ARKANSAS RIVER. Known to the early French as Rivière des Ark or d'Ozark, the 1,450-mile river was discovered and explored by Hernando de Soto in 1541. The French explorers, Louis Jolliet and Jacques Marquette, reached its mouth in 1673. The early history of the river centered around the Arkansas Post, the first permanent settlement in the region.

The headwaters of the Arkansas were in Spanish territory. The treaty with Spain in 1819 made the Arkansas River west of the 100th meridian a part of the western boundary of the United States. The river was navigable with keelboats as far west as Grand River.

ARKANSAS RIVER, GREAT BEND OF THE. An important landmark on the Santa Fe Trail, marking the first point at which the river was encountered, 278 miles from the start of the trail at Independence, Mo., and roughly halfway to Bent's Fort in Colorado.

ARKANSAS RIVER ROUTE. The mountain or Pikes Peak division of the Santa Fe Trail, which avoided the dangerous Jornada del Muerto desert of the Cimarron cutoff. This route followed up the Arkansas River to old Bent's Fort near present-day La Junta and there turned southwesterly to the mountains and crossed the difficult Raton Pass. The Arkansas River route, though longer, was extensively used because of the importance of Bent's Fort; the presence of water; and the demand for freight at the settlements along the way. Also it was the route to the Colorado goldfields.

"ARKANSAS TRAVELER." Arkansas's best-known piece of folklore as well as the favorite of all old-time breakdown fiddle tunes in America. First published in 1847, but neither the author of the dialogue nor the composer of the tune has been determined. Newspapers, books, and articles of commerce have taken the title.

ARKS (flatboats, broadhorns, Kentucky or Orleans boats). Until 1860 arks carried a large part of downstream traffic on rivers of the West. Cheaply constructed of green wood, shaped like boxes with raked bows, and roofed over in whole or in part, they were steered by a long oar and were sold for lumber or firewood at their destinations.

ARKWRIGHT MACHINERY. A spinning machine developed by Richard Arkwright in England about 1770. Samuel Slater carried the idea to Providence, R.I., and constructed a set of Arkwright machines carrying seventy-two spindles. These were installed in 1790 at Pawtucket, introducing the modern factory to the United States.

ARLINGTON NATIONAL CEMETERY. On the Virginia bank of the Potomac River, directly opposite Washington, D.C. Originally part of the estate of George Washington. The cemetery has become one of the most important shrines maintained by the United States. Buried therein are the dead of every war since the Revolution, and distinguished statesmen, including President John F. Kennedy. The Tomb of the Unknowns commemorates the dead of the two world wars and the Korean War.

ARMAMENTS. *See* **Defense, National.**

ARMED MERCHANTMAN. *See* **Merchantmen, Armed.**

ARMED NEUTRALITY OF 1780. A declaration by Catherine II, empress of Russia, who desired to free neutral trade from the interference of belligerents. It restricted the category of contraband to munitions and the essential instruments of war; it asserted as an established rule of international law the principle that free ships make free goods; and it set forth a new theory of blockade. The declaration was followed by the arming of the neutrals of northern Europe to protect their commerce.

The United States, on Oct. 5, 1780, accepted unreservedly the rules of the armed neutrality declaration, but could not, while a belligerent, become a party to the armed neutrality; the Definitive Treaty of Peace in 1783 altered the situation. James Madison pointed out that it would be "unwise" to become a party to a confederacy which might thereafter complicate the interests of the United States with the politics of Europe." That the United States should have escaped from participation in this confederacy was fortunate, for all the members of the armed neutrality abandoned the creed at the very next opportunity of their becoming belligerents.

ARMIES, DISBANDING OF THE. *See* **Demobilization.**

"ARM IN ARM" CONVENTION. *See* **National Union ("Arm in Arm") Convention.**

ARMINIANISM. The Reformed theology that arose in opposition to the prevailing Calvinism, and received its name from Jacobus Arminius (1560–1609), a Dutch theologian. It places chief emphasis upon man's freedom and holds that God's sovereignty is so exercised as to be cooperable with the freedom of man. Introduced into America in the early 18th century, its influence spread rapidly.

ARMISTICE DAY. On Oct. 4, 1918, the German government appealed to President Woodrow Wilson for an armistice on the basis of the Fourteen Points. On Nov. 5, the United States notified Germany that the Fourteen Points were accepted subject to two reservations: (1) the freedom of the seas was not to be discussed at that time; (2) Germany must make reparation for the damage done to the property of Allied nationals. The terms were communicated to Germany on Nov. 8 and signed on Nov. 11. The armistice was for one month and was renewed from time to time until peace was signed in 1919. (*See* Fourteen Points.)

Until 1954, November 11 was observed as a legal holiday in the United States under the title "Armistice Day." Congress then officially declared the day "Veterans Day," to recognize veterans of all U.S. military activities. Veterans Day was shifted in 1971 to the fourth Monday of October.

ARMORY ART SHOW. One of the turning points in the acceptance of "modern" art by Americans, conducted from Feb. 15 to Mar. 15, 1913, in the 69th Regiment Armory, New York City. The exhibition was officially known as the International Exhibition of Modern Art. It was the largest American display of contemporary art styles up to that time.

ARMS MANUFACTURING. The manufacture of arms has been an important industry in the United States since colonial times. The key to modern machine making—the use of interchangeable parts—was demonstrated first in the arms industry, by Eli Whitney and Samuel Colt, early in the 19th century. Arms making requires precise workmanship and design, to insure that weapons can be fired accurately and safely. One of the key elements in the success of the American revolutionary armies was the presence of many gunsmiths in the colonies who beat the British blockade by producing guns locally. Some of the more famous American-made weapons were the "Kentucky long rifle," the Colt automatic revolver, and the Winchester repeating rifle. During the 20th century, weapons became very complex and sophisticated, and weapon equipment began to include such devices as radar sights, heat-sensing projectiles, and proximity fuses.

ARMS RACE WITH THE SOVIET UNION. The United States began a rapid postwar demobilization at the end of World War II. Although some U.S. leaders saw that Soviet-style totalitarianism was flourishing wherever Joseph Stalin's troops had advanced into Europe, the new threat was only slowly recognized by an American public sated with war. To many, President Harry Truman seemed alarmist in obtaining, in March 1947, legislation for aid to Greece and Turkey, which effectively stopped Communist takeovers. However, apologists for Stalin were largely silenced by his June 1948 attempt to squeeze the United States, Britain, and France out of Berlin, foiled by the Berlin airlift. An anti-Communist reaction began, intensified by the 1949 Communist victory in China and explosion of the Soviet Union's first atomic bomb.

In January 1950 Truman funded research to develop hydrogen bombs, meeting success in November 1952, a bare nine months before the Russians. Truman in February 1952 welcomed the foundation of the North Atlantic Treaty Organization, establishing a European army of fifty divisions.

During the period immediately after the Korean conflict U.S. defense rested on improving the strategic bomber force and aircraft-carrier navy, neither seriously rivaled by the Soviet Union, whose strength was in a huge, tank-centered army. The U.S. Navy made a quantum jump in submarines by the harnessing of atomic energy. But the Soviet Union astonished the world in August 1957 by demonstrating a 4,000-mile intercontinental ballistic missile (ICBM).

A contest then began to perfect rockets for lifting nuclear warheads from one continent to another at supersonic speeds. In sheer size and payload of missiles, the Soviets maintained their early lead, while U.S. engineers used superior miniaturization to obtain greater sophistication and accuracy. For the United States the first advantage stemmed from the July 1960 launch of a missile from the submerged *George Washington,* the original Polaris nuclear-powered submarine.

In October 1962 the world teetered toward holocaust after U.S. aerial surveillance of Cuba uncovered the presence of Russian medium-range weapons. President John F. Kennedy's firm stand and his naval quarantine of Cuba compelled the withdrawal of the missiles. This triumph vanished as the Soviets developed their own Polaris submarines and the requisite covering ships.

American presidents repeatedly tried to control the burgeoning atomic arms race. Eisenhower was apparently successful in October 1958, when the Soviet Union was persuaded to sit with the United States and Britain at Geneva to work out a treaty to outlaw nuclear testing. Eisenhower suspended U.S. testing and Soviet Premier Nikita Khrushchev ostentatiously agreed to a moratorium. The talks, however, were futile because of Soviet intransigence over inspection methods to ensure future compliance. Khrushchev was buying time to gain secret momentum for a series of tests, in September 1961, of more than forty bombs, climaxed by the detonation in the polar sky of an unprecedented 50-megaton hydrogen bomb. Khrushchev gloated that a 100-megaton bomb was in the Soviet arsenal. Kennedy persisted in trying to reach an agreement upon effective controls, and in July 1963, brought about an agreement with the Soviet Union and Britain banning every type of test except underground tests.

This vital, if partial, success owed much to enormous advances in reconnaissance by orbiting satellites. For the Soviet Union, perhaps the dominant motive was to take a giant step toward nonproliferation of nuclear weapons, inasmuch as a hundred nations accepted the invitation to subscribe to the treaty. Communist China did not, however. In October 1964 China also had "the bomb," and the Sino-Soviet dispute suddenly had genocidal teeth. The U.S.–Soviet SALT I treaty of May 26, 1972, found the United States agreeing to a five-year freeze on production of weapons, which superficially gave the Soviet Union some superiority—enough, it was hoped, to deter China while keeping a stand-off mutual deterrence with the United States. Then, in November 1974, President Gerald R. Ford and Leonid Brezhnev in furtherance of "détente" signed an agreement at Vladivostok. Ostensibly defining "nuclear parity," the agreement raised weapons levels. Some critics thought that the terms heavily favored the USSR, and alarm about the Soviet threat persisted. In June 1979 President Jimmy Carter and Brezhnev signed the SALT II treaty in Vienna. It encountered heavy opposition in the United States, especially after the Soviet invasion of Afghanistan in December 1979, and was never ratified. Despite worsening of U.S.-Soviet relations during the first year of President Ronald Reagan's administration, talks on medium-range nuclear weapons in Europe opened on Nov. 30, 1981.

ARMSTRONG, FORT. One of a chain of frontier defenses erected after the War of 1812. It was located at the foot of Rock Island, in the Mississippi River, five miles from the principal Sauk and Fox village on Rock River, Ill.

ARMY, CONFEDERATE. Officially, the Army of the Confederate States of America was the small regular force established by the Confederate Provisional Congress on Mar. 6, 1861, to consist of one corps of engineers, one of artillery, six regiments of infantry, one of cavalry, and four staff departments. This was soon overshadowed by the volunteer forces (provisional army). Other acts authorized the president to assume control over military operations, to accept state forces and 100,000 volunteers for twelve months. By the end of April, President Jefferson Davis had called for 82,000 men. On May 8 the Confederate congress authorized enlistments for the war and on Aug. 8, four more states having joined the Confederacy, 400,000 volunteers for one or three years' service. After the passage of the first conscription act in April 1862, men were taken into the provisional army directly.

Serious difficulties were encountered in arming, clothing, and feeding the troops. Most arms available in May 1861 were obsolete or inferior. Only one foundry could cast cannon, and only one small powder mill was in operation. The chief reliance for improved arms was in purchases abroad, but getting them through the Union blockade was slow, risky, and expensive. The Confederacy made contracts with private firms for arms and set up its own arsenals and powder mills. Shoes, clothing, and blankets were hard to procure. Food supplies were often reduced by weak transportation facilities. By 1863 horses and mules were scarce, reducing the mobility of cavalry, artillery, and baggage trains.

The Confederacy was divided into military departments under commanders responsible only to the war department and the president. Other than President Davis himself, there was no commander in chief until Robert E. Lee was appointed on Feb. 6, 1865.

The number of enlistments in the Confederate armies has long been in dispute. Probably between 800,000 and 900,000 actually enrolled, but so many were never in service at any given date. Liberal allowances for scattered commands not reported and for irregular organizations would not bring the total enrolled to more than 600,000 at any one time.

ARMY, UNION. When Fort Sumter was fired on, the United States had an army barely exceeding 16,000, and its effectiveness was soon lessened by the resignations of Robert E. Lee and other southern officers. Northern states were feverishly raising and training volunteers. By April 1861, the governors had offered some 300,000 such troops to the federal government. Although determined to restore the Union by force, President Abraham Lincoln would not assemble Congress before July 4. Without new legislation there was no authority for an increase in the army, so all the recruiting fervor of the early spring was wasted.

Starting July 22, 1861, Congress authorized a volunteer army of 500,000 men and legalized the president's call of May 3 for 42,000 three-year volunteers and 22,700 regulars. The regular army was used in the war for border defense against Indians. The volunteer army, with which the war was fought, was officered mainly by political generals chosen by the governors and by regimental officers elected by the enlisted men. Thus, development of discipline and efficiency was slow. Competition of state governments with the War Department for uniforms, munitions, food, and supplies led to contract grafts, high prices, and shoddy products.

By the middle of 1862 the first army had been so badly depleted by disease and battle that on July 2 an additional 300,000 volunteers were called for. On Aug. 4, when volunteering proved sluggish, a draft of a 300,000-man nine months' militia was ordered. This draft proved a failure, only about 65,000 men being provided.

By 1863, heavy casualties, desertions, the expiration of short-term enlistments, and scanty volunteering seemed likely to cause a collapse of the army. Consequently, the Enrollment Act of Mar. 3, 1863, was passed to stimulate volunteering by threat of conscription, thus encouraging the states and localities to avoid this by offering bounties. Men of means were given an escape from the draft by the payment of a $300 commutation fee or the hiring of substitutes. Later the fee was limited to conscientious objectors. Two years of repeated drafting yielded about 50,000 conscripts and 120,000 substitutes. The total effective strength of the army on Jan. 1, 1863, before federal conscription, was just under 700,000. On May 1, 1865, at its highest point, the number was nearly 1 million.

ARMY, UNITED STATES. The United States Army has traditionally consisted of a small professional force, the regular army, augmented in wartime by citizen soldiers—militia, National Guard, Organized Reserve, volunteers, or draftees. The army of today is the lineal descendant of the Continental army of the American Revolution.

Revolutionary War (1775–82). The accepted birthdate of the U.S. Army is June 14, 1775, the day the Second Continental Congress appointed a committee to draw up rules and regulations to govern the New England army that had gathered near Boston and also voted to enlist ten rifle companies. Congress selected George Washington to be commander in chief. The 26 battalions authorized by Congress had grown to 110 by 1781, when Congress, recognizing its inability to raise or support this number, reduced it to 59. It seems doubtful that there were ever more than 30,000 men in the Continental service at any one time, despite bounties for enlistment and the limited application of a draft.

The Continental army was composed mainly of infantry and artillery, with a small contingent of cavalry, a small corps of engineers, and an even smaller contingent of artificers to service and repair ordnance.

At the end of the Revolution the army was almost entirely disbanded, reaching its nadir of eighty men guarding stores in 1784. The need for protection of the frontiers led to some modest augmentation. The new Constitution gave Congress power to raise an army and to levy taxes to support it and designated the president as commander in chief.

War of 1812. During the troubled years leading to the War of 1812, the regular army was expanded to about 6,000–7,000 officers and men, and during the war the authorization was increased to 62,274. But recruitment fell short, and the regulars numbered only about 38,000 in 1814. Perhaps an equal number was recruited in volunteer units raised by the states, and larger numbers yet served as short-term militia.

Establishment of a Peacetime Army (1815–45). In the wake of the War of 1812 the regular army developed the professionalism and efficient administration it had largely lacked during the war, under the guidance of John C. Calhoun, secretary of war between 1817 and 1825. Sylvanus Thayer made the U.S. Military Academy at West Point a vital force in creating professionally trained officers.

The regular army was, nevertheless, kept quite small for its tasks: policing the frontiers, a long war with the Seminole in Florida, and establishment and manning of coastal fortifications. In 1820, it was reduced by almost half and maintained until 1835 at about 5,000–7,000. On the eve of the Mexican War the army's strength stood at about 8,500.

Mexican War (1846–48). The regular army underwent only limited expansion during the Mexican War. Most new troops were recruited as volunteers by the various states and were organized in accordance with their militia laws. The army expanded to a peak of around 50,000 and showed a remarkable proficiency, particularly in the artillery.

The immense new territories acquired increased the army's responsibilities, and its peacetime strength reached 17,678 officers and men by 1858. In protecting emigrants to California and Oregon, the army encountered mounted Indians and the cavalry came into its own.

Civil War (1861–65). The U.S. Army expanded more than sixtyfold during the Civil War, reaching a peak strength of more than 1 million. The regular army was increased only slightly and most of its regiments remained in the West providing defense against the Indians. The Union army was mostly an army of state volunteer regiments, and some regiments, notably those composed of former slaves, were raised directly as U.S. Volunteers. The federal government resorted to conscription to keep the ranks of volunteer regiments filled. Sixteen armies were organized during the war—most of them taking their names from the rivers along which they operated. (*See* Army, Confederate; Army, Union.)

Post–Civil War Period (1866–98). With Gen. Robert E. Lee's surrender, the great volunteer army was hastily demobilized; by mid-1866 only a regular force of 57,000 remained. In 1869 Congress cut the authorized strength to 45,000, and in 1876 to 27,442, a limit that was to remain virtually stationary down to the Spanish-American War. The army played a major role in the occupation of the South, and the last troops were not removed until 1877. The army's major strength was again scattered at posts in the West, battling with the Indians. Another major activity was the maintenance of order in strikes and other civil disorders.

Spanish-American War (1898) and Subsequent Reforms. The army of the Spanish-American War was poorly prepared for an overseas venture. Its units were scattered across the country in company- and battalion-size organizations and had no training or experience in operations larger than those of a regiment. The army was composed of an expanded regular army and state and federal volunteer units, the former almost entirely National Guard. At war's end the total force consisted of 274,717 men, most of whom never left training camps. In Cuba and the Philippines, sickness and disease took a far higher toll than enemy bullets.

A series of reforms was initiated by Secretary of War Elihu Root. The commanding general was replaced by a chief of staff heading up a general staff and responsible for both management of the army and central planning. The Army War College was established and the whole school system modernized. The Dick Act of 1903 and later legislation recognized the National Guard as the Organized Militia.

The army between 1900 and 1916 ranged between 65,000 and 108,000. By the later date it was equipped with new and destructive weapons, such as the machine gun, and was beginning to experiment with motor transport and the airplane. It assumed new responsibilities: suppressing the Philippine Insurrection (1899–1902), participating in the relief expedition to China during the Boxer Rebellion (1899), occupying Cuba (1899–1902), building the Panama Canal (1907–14), and conducting a punitive expedition to Mexico (1916).

The National Defense Act of 1916 enlarged the army and National Guard and added the Reserve Corps and the Reserve Officers' Training Corps (ROTC) in the colleges.

World War I (1917–18) and Postwar Years. Despite these forward steps, the army entered World War I unprepared. The World War I army was raised by a national selective service system, not by volunteers; even National Guard units were drafted. The army was expanded from 210,000 to 3,685,000. Nearly 2 million men were shipped to France to form the American Expeditionary Forces under Gen. John J. Pershing. Sixty-two square infantry divisions were organized and forty-three shipped to France. At home the massive effort in training troops was directed by a reorganized War Department and general staff.

The national army of World War I was demobilized rapidly and by 1920 the army stood at 202,394. The National Defense Act of 1920 defined the army as an organization composed of three components—the regular army, the National Guard, and the Organized Reserve.

World War II (1940–45). After the Germans overran France in 1940 the entire National Guard was called to federal service, a one-year draft authorized, and most of the officers from the Organized Reserve called to active duty. At the time of Pearl Harbor the army numbered 1,643,500; but many of its units were still semitrained, and the whole army was woefully short of modern equipment.

The national army of World War II reached a peak strength of about 8.3 million, more than 5 million deployed overseas. In this war the U.S. Army, under leaders who had been trained in its schools in the interwar period, truly came of age. Within the United States, the army was reorganized into Army Air Forces, Army Ground Forces, and Army Service Forces.

Since 1945. Rapid demobilization again followed the end of the war, and by 1949 the active establishment had been reduced to 591,000. In 1947 the Air Force became a separate service in the new Department of Defense. Except for a brief period in 1946–47 the postwar army was for twenty-eight years a mixed force of volunteers and draftees. It also became, during the Korean War, an integrated army—a reversal of the policy, inaugurated during the Civil War, of admitting blacks into the army but placing them in segregated units.

The outbreak of the Korean War in June 1950 reversed the trend toward demobilization. By July 1951 the army had been increased to a total of 1.5 million. Expansion was achieved by calling up National Guard and reserve units and individuals and by expanded draft calls.

Demobilization after the Korean War was far more gradual, evidence of the necessity of keeping strong armed forces in being. But as the administration of President Dwight D. Eisenhower relied primarily on nuclear weapons, the army was reduced by 1959 to 862,000 men. The Berlin crisis in 1962–63 brought a call-up of reserves that increased army strength to sixteen divisions again, and sixteen were maintained after the reserves were demobilized, with a strength of 975,000. Expansion began again with the decision to deploy ground forces in strength to Vietnam in mid-1965. By 1968 the army stood again at about the Korean peak. The gradual withdrawal from Vietnam, starting in 1968, brought army strength down to 800,500 by July 1973, with further cuts in prospect. The expansion in the Vietnam War was almost entirely achieved by a combination of draft and enlistment. Concomitant with the changes in its responsibilities and size, the army underwent a number of reorganizations.

Meanwhile, army forces overseas were distributed among army components of unified commands, the most important in Europe and the Pacific. The deployment pattern as it developed following the Korean War provided five divisions in Europe, two in Korea, and one in Hawaii—the balance of the divisions being in strategic reserve in the United States.

The army of the 1950's and 1960's employed increasingly sophisticated equipment and means of transportation and communication, necessitating new tactical organizations and an increasingly complex logistical support system.

The completion of the withdrawal from Vietnam in March 1973, after seven years of fighting, and the end of the draft on July 1, 1973, combined to mark the end of an era for the army. Since 1974 the army has been a volunteer force, as it had traditionally been in peacetime before World War II.

Peacetime Work. The army has throughout its history performed important peacetime tasks: exploration of the West; surveying of rail lines; improvement of rivers and harbors; building of the Panama Canal; occupation work in the South during Reconstruction and in other countries; building of many important public facilities; and contributions to modern medicine. The army has been called on to maintain order in civil disturbances, enforce federal laws, and help in the relief of natural disasters.

Army Aviation. Army aviation had its beginnings in World War II, when light observation aircraft (Piper Cubs) were made organic to field artillery units. When a separate air force was created in 1947, this type of aircraft remained under army control. Meanwhile, the army was experimenting with helicopters, which proved invaluable during the Korean and Vietnam wars for medical evacuation and other purposes. During the 1950's the army began development of many types of both fixed- and rotary-wing aircraft for observation, tactical movement of troops and supplies, aerial reconnaissance, command, liaison, and evacuation of casualties.

Army General Staff. Congress first created a general staff for the army, a group of heads of administrative bureaus, in 1813. The modern general staff dates from 1903, when Congress established the General Staff Corps and a chief of staff. The National Defense Act of 1916, reflecting congressional suspicions of a general staff, limited its numbers and functions; a new, more powerful one had to be created in 1918.

Major reorganizations took place under the National Defense Act of 1920, in 1942 and 1946, and under the Army Organization Act in 1950, 1955–56, and 1962–63.

Insignia of Rank. Insignia of rank date from the Revolution, when Washington ordered that field-grade officers wear colored cockades in their caps, general officers colored ribands across their coats, and noncommissioned officers stripes or epaulettes of colored cloth on arm or shoulder. In 1780 generals began to wear silver stars on their shoulders. The colonel's eagles date from 1832, and the various insignia for majors, captains, and lieutenants from 1836. In 1851 the silver leaf was prescribed for lieutenant-colonels, and the gold leaf for majors. In 1917 second lieutenants were authorized to wear the single gold bar. Meanwhile, the various chevrons of the noncommissioned officers were evolving into their present form.

Army Logistics. Logistics consists of providing the matériel and services a military force needs in peace or war: procurement, supply, transportation, maintenance, construction, evacuation and hospitalization, and other types of service.

During the American Revolution the Continental army had poor logistical support. The situation was not vastly improved in the War of 1812. Development of a system equal to the needs of 19th-century warfare came after 1812.

The Civil War saw the emergence of echeloned depots, classification of supplies, and methods of calculating requirements in terms of standard allowances for given bodies of men. A far-flung procurement organization emerged that performed well in drawing forth the material resources of the country. Railroads increased mobility and made possible the support of larger armies.

Logistics in the two world wars was vastly more complex. The United States had to support large forces overseas, and ocean shipping became the very center of army logistics. The total value of army procurement in World War II amounted to nearly $111 billion. There was a progressive increase in the quantity and variety of supplies and services needed to support a mechanized army.

The logistical systems developed during World War II have since undergone modification to keep pace with technological change. During the Vietnam War the vast majority of troops and many critical supplies were moved to the theater by air. Throughout the army's logistical establishment in the 1960's, automatic data processing became the central feature of logistical systems. (*See also* Logistics.)

Army Posts. Posts established by the army played their most important role in American history in the extension of the frontier westward. These posts were usually established at the western fringe of settlement or beyond at strategic places in Indian country. They were often the most important points along routes of travel and were trading centers as well as refuges for settlers. Many towns that grew up around these forts still retain their names. The sites of newer army posts have been selected for such reasons as suitability as training centers or proximity to transportation and industrial facilities and the availability of a supply of labor.

Army School System. Apart from the U.S. Military Academy, the first formal army school was for artillery instruction, at Fort Monroe, Va., in 1824. The School of Application for Infantry and Cavalry, later the Command and General Staff College, was established at Fort Leavenworth, Kans., in 1881. Between 1901 and 1914 a definite school system took shape, with the Army War College at the apex, including the Military Academy, the Command and General Staff College, and perhaps a dozen service schools for branch and specialist training.

During the 1920's a system of special service schools was developed to provide training of both regular and reserve officers and to train enlisted specialists. In 1924 the Army Industrial College was established, for training of regular officers in industrial mobilization and wartime procurement. After World War II the Army War College and the Industrial College formed the nuclei for the National War College and the Industrial College of the Armed Forces, which served all three services. The army, however, reestablished its own War College in 1950. By 1970 it was offering training in a vast multiplicity of specialties.

Army War College. The Army War College was established by Elihu Root in 1901 as the nucleus of a general staff. Its function has continuously been that of providing training of selected officers for higher command and general staff duties. In 1907 the college moved to Washington Barracks, D.C. (now Fort Lesley J. McNair). In 1917 it was closed and reopened in 1920. Classes were suspended again in 1940 and only resumed in 1950 at Fort Leavenworth, Kans., the Fort McNair location having meanwhile been taken over by the National War College. In July 1951 the college was moved to Carlisle Barracks, Pa.

Army Hospitals. Hospitals of a primitive sort were provided for soldiers during the Revolution, the War of 1812, and the Mexican War. The Civil War saw a considerable advance with the adoption of the system of evacuation to field hospitals set up in tents where the sick and wounded could get immediate attention and pavilion hospitals set up in permanent locations from which the seriously wounded could be evacuated. After the Civil War, at various army posts, army surgeons established small hospitals. The Spanish-American War saw the introduction of permanent general hospitals. The main improvement in the Korean and Vietnam wars was the development of mobile surgical hospitals operating close behind the lines and the use of helicopters for evacuation of the wounded.

ARMY ENLISTMENT. *See* **Enlistment.**

ARMY OF OCCUPATION (1918–23). The American Third Army, commanded by Maj. Gen. Joseph T. Dickman, crossed into Germany in December 1918, taking station in the north sector of the Coblenz bridgehead. Units engaged in duties of occupation and training, including participation in civil administration, until July 2, 1919, when the Third Army was succeeded by the "American Forces in Germany." Maj. Gen. Edward F. McGlachlin, Jr., assumed command until July 8, 1919, when Maj. Gen. Henry T. Allen, reported. At noon on Jan. 27, 1923, U.S. troops having left the Coblenz area, Allen relinquished command of the American area.

ARMY ON THE FRONTIER. The activities of the U.S. Army stationed near the frontier settlements from the beginning of national existence until about 1890, the end of the settlers' frontier. The principal functions were (1) guarding the frontier settlements from hostile Indians; (2) aiding the settlement of the West by developing and protecting the communication between the older settlements and the frontier, by exploring the West, constructing roads, and defending the overland trails, water routes, and later telegraph and railroad lines; and (3) policing the frontier until the civil governments could maintain order.

ARMY POSTS. *See* **Army, United States.**

ARMY SUPPLY. *See* **Army, United States.**

ARMY WAR COLLEGE. *See* **Army, United States.**

ARNOLD'S MARCH TO QUEBEC. In the summer of 1775 Col. Benedict Arnold laid before Commander in Chief George Washington a plan for attacking Canada. The old classic route by way of Lake George, Lake Champlain, and the Richelieu River was assigned to Gen. Richard Montgomery. Another passage by way of the Kennebec and Chaudière rivers, was assigned to Arnold. On Sept. 19, Arnold's command went by sea to and up the Kennebec and up the Dead River, full of ice, and through snowstorms, with insufficient food and clothing. At Sertigan, Arnold refreshed his exhausted detachment, so that it was able to go down the Chaudière and reach the St. Lawrence on Nov. 9. In the meantime, Montgomery had reached Montreal, but Arnold went on across the St. Lawrence and was actually in front of Quebec before Montgomery arrived. Guy Carleton, the British commander, got into Quebec before Montgomery could join Arnold on Dec. 2. Montgomery and Arnold assaulted Quebec on the night of Dec. 31. The effort failed; Montgomery was killed and Arnold wounded.

ARNOLD'S RAID IN VIRGINIA. In December of 1780 Commander in Chief Sir Henry Clinton of the British armies in North America determined to send an expedition into Virginia to conduct desultory raids and to block the mouth of the Chesapeake. The command was given to the traitor Benedict Arnold. On Dec. 30 Arnold seized boats on the James River and pushed up to Westover, Richmond, Westham, and Portsmouth, marauding and pillaging. In March he was joined and outranked by Maj. Gen. William Phillips. They led another devastating expedition through City Point and Petersburg. Arnold returned to Osborn's on the James, destroyed a small American fleet, and raided Manchester and Warwick. Throughout these movements the British were harassed by the inferior forces of the Marquis de Lafayette and Anthony Wayne.

ARNOLD'S TREASON. Brig. Gen. Benedict Arnold of the Continental army had fought gallantly for the American cause from Ticonderoga (1775) to Saratoga (1777). But by the spring of 1779 several motives led him to treason: (1) repeated slights by Congress, (2) resentment at the authorities of Pennsylvania who had court-martialed him, (3) need for money, and (4) opposition to the French alliance of 1778. Throughout the rest of 1779 and 1780 he transmitted military intelligence about the American army to the British. On July 12, 1780, he "accepted the command at West Point as a post in which I can render the most essential services" (to the British). He became a brigadier general in the British army, went to England after the defeat of the British, and died there June 14, 1801.

AROOSTOOK WAR (1838–39). An undeclared and bloodless war occasioned by the failure of the United States and Great Britain to determine the boundary between New Brunswick and what is now Maine. In 1820 Maine became a state. Almost immediately, ignoring the British contention that all land north of Mars Hill, in Aroostook County, was British, the Maine legislature, jointly with Massachusetts, made grants to settlers along both branches of the Aroostook River. Attempts at compromise failed, and by 1839, 10,000 Maine troops were either encamped along the Aroostook River or were on their way there. Gen. Winfield Scott was dispatched to negotiate a truce with the lieutenant governor of New Brunswick. This he did, and Great Britain agreed to a boundary commission, whose findings were incorporated in the Webster-Ashburton Treaty in 1842.

ARPENT. An old French unit of land measure, both linear and superficial, now standardized in Louisiana at 192 feet, or a square of that dimension (about five-sixths of an acre).

ARREST. The Fourth Amendment to the U.S. Constitution —applicable to state and city, as well as federal, law enforcement officers through the due process clause of the Fourteenth Amendment—guarantees "the right of the people to be secure in their persons . . . against unreasonable . . . seizures," and provides further that this right "shall not be violated . . . but upon probable cause." It is now established that an illegal arrest is an illegal "seizure" within the meaning of the amendment. Thus, although they commonly occur, arrests based on mere suspicion or common rumor or otherwise lacking "probable cause" are unconstitutional.

The Fourth Amendment provides that "no Warrants shall issue, but upon probable cause." Although the rule is otherwise with respect to searches, arrests for felonies may be made without warrants. (Most states permit warrantless arrests for misdemeanors only if committed in the officer's presence.) But the Fourth Amendment also prohibits "unreasonable searches and seizures" generally, and "probable cause" is also required in such circumstances. Probable cause exists where the information is sufficient to warrant a reasonable man to believe that a crime has, or is being, committed.

ARREST, ARBITRARY, DURING THE CIVIL WAR. Freedom from arbitrary arrest, guaranteed in the writ of habeas corpus, has become synonymous in Anglo-Saxon tradition with civil liberty. The right to restrict this freedom nevertheless is recognized as a constitutional exercise of power in time of "rebellion or invasion." Until 1861 this federal right had never been exercised, but the Civil War brought widespread restrictions of civil liberty. To cope with antiwar activities, President Lincoln issued several proclamations by which the privilege of the writ of habeas corpus was suspended.

The president's control of arbitrary arrest was frequently questioned, especially by Chief Justice Roger B. Taney, who held that the legislative branch rather than the executive had this constitutional authority. Lincoln ably defended himself against dictatorship charges in various open letters.

The Confederacy likewise made summary arrests to suppress disloyalty. Success was small, not only because political prisoners became popular martyrs, but because Confederate policy often met the additional resistance of states'-rights opposition.

ARROWSMITH'S MAP. *A Map Exhibiting All the New Discoveries in the Interior Part of North America* was published in London, Jan. 1, 1795, by Aaron Arrowsmith, "Hydrographer to His Majesty." A large-scale map on a globular projection, it was printed on six sheets, measuring when joined 48.5 by 57 inches. From notes furnished by the Hudson's Bay Company, additions and corrections were made on the basic map. More than seventeen editions were published between 1795 and 1850.

ARSENALS. An establishment for the manufacture, repair, receipt, storage, and issuance of ordnance. Historically, American arms manufacture favored governmental control rather than private production to insure quality and uniformity. The Springfield, Mass., and Harpers Ferry, W.Va., armories were established in 1794 and 1796, respectively. With the organization of the army's Ordnance Department on May 14, 1812, arsenals came under its direction. The expanded production needed in wartime was provided by the private sector. Since the Korean War, arsenals contribute to only a small portion of the army's total ordnance requirements.

ART. *See* **Painting.**

d'ARTAGUETTE'S DEFEAT (1736). The governor of Louisiana, Jean Baptiste Le Moyne, Sieur de Bienville, decided in 1736 to exterminate the Chickasaw because of their long and successful opposition to the French. He ordered Maj. Pierre d'Artaguette to lead a force from the north; Bienville, meanwhile, led a larger force from the south. In the battle d'Artaguette was wounded, and he and a score of his countrymen were captured. Bienville was defeated at the Battle of Ackia. The Chickasaw burned d'Artaguette and other captives at the stake.

ARTHUR D. LITTLE, INC. One of the first independent commercial research laboratories in the United States was founded by Arthur Dehon Little and Roger B. Griffin in Boston, Mass., in 1886 as a response to the slow pace of American industry in developing its own research facilities to utilize the rapid advances being made in science and technology. Initially most active in paper manufacture, the company branched out into coal derivatives, lubrication, forest products, and textiles. It was incorporated as Arthur D. Little, Inc., in 1909 and moved to its present headquarters in Cambridge, Mass., in 1917.

ARTICLES FOR GOVERNMENT OF THE NAVY. *See* **Uniform Code of Military Justice.**

ARTICLES OF CONFEDERATION. The Continental Congress decided even before independence that it was necessary to set up a confederacy based upon a written instrument. Congress was so engrossed in war problems, however, that debates dragged through more than a year. The principal disputes raged over whether taxes should be apportioned according to the gross number of inhabitants counting slaves or excluding them; whether large and small states should have equality in voting; whether Congress should regulate Indian affairs; and whether Congress should be permitted to fix the western boundaries of those states which claimed to the Mississippi. On Nov. 15, 1777, Congress finally approved a draft and sent it to the states to be ratified. The Articles did not become law until Mar. 1, 1781.

Although the Articles have been harshly criticized and critics at the time saw their inadequacy, they were generally regarded in 1781 as offering a sound national constitution. They provided for a "perpetual union" between the states. Each remained sovereign and independent and retained every right not expressly ceded to the general government. A single agency of government was established—the Congress; the states were to appoint from two to seven delegates annually to it, and each state was to have one vote. The costs of government and defense were to be defrayed from a common treasury, to which states were to contribute. The states were to supply quotas of troops. To Congress was entrusted the management of foreign affairs, war, and the postal service; it was empowered to borrow money, emit bills of credit, and determine the value of coin; it was to appoint naval officers and superior military officers, and control Indian affairs. But none of these powers was to be exercised save by vote of a majority of all states, and the more important could not be exercised save by the vote of nine.

It soon became evident that Congress was doomed to fail in its attempts to enforce the Articles. Demands for amendment and invigoration of the Articles were made even before they became effective. A committee which reported May 3, 1781, pointed to the chief defect of the Articles—they gave Congress no power to enforce its measures—and suggested a new article authorizing the employment of armed forces to compel recalcitrant states "to fulfill their Federal engagements." The close of 1786 found the Articles of Confederation in widespread discredit and many leaders eager to find a wholly new basis for union. Yet the Articles, soon to give way to the Constitution, had preserved the idea of union until national wisdom could adopt a more efficient system.

ARTICLES OF WAR. *See* **Uniform Code of Military Justice.**

ARTICLE X. *See* **League of Nations.**

ARTILLERY. Artillery in the U.S. Army dates from the revolutionary war, when units from Massachusetts and Rhode Island joined in the siege of Boston. The first artillery regiment of the Continental army was raised in January 1776; by 1777 four were operating. In the wars against the western Indians (1790–94) an artillery battalion was raised but was used mainly as infantry. Artillerymen manned the country's first coast defenses in 1794, leading to a traditional classification of U.S. Army artillery into field, siege and garrison, and coast artillery.

Between 1808 and 1901, artillery units served variously as light or horse artillery, infantry, or in coast defense, and grew from a few units to 98 batteries. In 1901 a major reorganization occurred. Seven regiments were broken into separate numbered batteries and companies of coast artillery within the Corps of Artillery. Coast and field artillery became full separate branches in 1907. Further reorganization took place during the world wars and in 1957, 1968, and 1969.

"AS GOES MAINE, SO GOES THE NATION." A saying based upon the supposed accuracy of Maine's September election as a political barometer for the country, originated by the Whigs after the presidential election of 1840.

ASHBURTON TREATY. *See* **Webster-Ashburton Treaty.**

ASHBY'S GAP (Va.). A pass in the Blue Ridge Mountains of Virginia leading from the Shenandoah Valley into eastern Virginia. In June 1863, J. E. B. Stuart held this gap to prevent Gen. Joseph Hooker from interfering with Robert E. Lee's march to Gettysburg.

ASH HOLLOW, BATTLE OF. *See* **Harney Expedition.**

ASHLAND (Ky.). An industrial city in the northeastern part of Kentucky, with a population of 27,064 in 1980. It was part of a major industrial complex, made up of cities in Ohio, West Virginia, and Kentucky, and considered as one metropolitan area. In 1980, the area population was reported as 311,350; its largest city center was at Huntington, W. Va.

Ashland was founded in 1815 by settlers from Virginia. It has been an important Ohio River port for over a century. Quantities of coal, oil, natural gas, and limestone are available in the vicinity, and the city has iron and steel mills, oil refineries, and plants for making bricks and other products.

ASHLEY EXPEDITIONS. Three expeditions sent out by William Henry Ashley aimed at launching the Rocky Mountain Fur Company in competition with the Hudson's Bay Company and the older established American companies.

Organized in St. Louis in 1822, the first expedition, commanded by Ashley's lieutenant, was attacked by the Blackfoot and driven out. Ashley headed another expedition, only to be attacked by the Arikara and forced to retreat. The third expedition, in the charge of Jedediah Smith, pushed on to the Yellowstone and penetrated to the Green River valley, the Utah trapping grounds. The party returned with a rich cache of furs, and Ashley set forth on a return winter trip. He crossed the continental divide by Bridger's Gap and reached the Green River near the crossing of the Oregon Trail. Ashley replaced the fixed trading post with the annual rendezvous for collecting furs.

ASIA, TRADE WITH. Trade with Asia burgeoned after the Revolution, which released American merchants from the restrictions of the British East India Company. Ships from Atlantic seaboard cities brought back tea, silks, and cottons from China and India and spices and coffee from the East Indies. The wars of the French Revolution delivered a great part of Europe's extracontinental trade into American hands. British and American commerce in opium from Turkey, India, and China balanced payments, east and west, for at least the first half of the 19th century, bringing China into the world trading and financial community and into the world political arena.

In the 19th century, America developed a mechanized textile industry that could undersell both Indian and Chinese cottons anywhere; the various East India companies lost their charters; Western merchants took the tea plant to India, Ceylon, and elsewhere; and Commodore Matthew C. Perry "opened" Japan in 1854. Thereafter, commerce with Asia became relatively less important. China was a significant market for the American coarse cottons industry, and Japan displaced China as America's major Asian trading partner. Japan's extraordinary economic development in the 20th century rendered American trade with Japan more important than that with the rest of Asia combined.

ASIENTO. A license granted in 1713 to the English South Sea Company by the Spanish government, as a result of the Treaty of Utrecht, whereby the company was given the exclusive right to sell a total of 144,000 African slaves in the Spanish colonies during thirty years or at the rate of 4,800 a year. For this privilege the company paid the Spanish crown $200,000.

ASSASSINATIONS, POLITICAL. By 1981 there had been eighty-four recorded assassinations or attempted assassinations of officeholders in the United States, excluding politically prominent nonofficeholders.

On Jan. 30, 1835, an unsuccessful attempt was made to kill Andrew Jackson. The assassination of Abraham Lincoln on Apr. 14, 1865, was the first of great political consequence in the United States. On July 2, 1880, Charles J. Guiteau, who had importuned James A. Garfield for a consular position, shot the president, who died on Sept. 19. On Sept. 6, 1901, William McKinley was mortally wounded by Leon F. Czolgosz, a young anarchist.

Former President Theodore Roosevelt was wounded in the chest on Oct. 14, 1912, as he made a campaign speech in Milwaukee, Wis. Franklin D. Roosevelt was the target of an assassination attempt on Feb. 15, 1933, in Florida by Joseph Zangara. On Nov. 1, 1950, two Puerto Ricans attempted to shoot their way into Blair House, the temporary residence of Harry Truman. On Nov. 22, 1963, President John F. Kennedy was shot and killed in Dallas, Tex. A commission concluded that Lee Harvey Oswald was the lone assassin. Kennedy's brother, Robert F. Kennedy, was killed on June 5, 1968, by Sirhan Sirhan immediately following a victory statement after the California presidential primary.

Political assassinations during the 1960's were associated with the domestic troubles of the civil rights movement and the war in Vietnam. The deadly series began with the 1963 murders of President Kennedy and civil rights leader Medgar W. Evers, followed by those of George Lincoln Rockwell, Martin Luther King, Jr., and Robert Kennedy, and ended with the 1972 unsuccessful attempt to kill presidential candidate George Wallace of Alabama. Afterward the political violence in the United States somewhat abated. There were two unsuccessful attempts on President Gerald Ford in September 1975. In April 1981, President Ronald Reagan was shot by John W. Hinckley, Jr. A bullet hit the president's chest, but he fully recovered within several months.

ASSAY OFFICES. Assaying is done at all federal mints, but special plants were established at New York in 1853; Boise, Idaho, 1869; Helena, Mont., 1874; Deadwood, S.Dak., and Seattle, Wash., 1896; and Salt Lake City, Utah, 1908, for the receipt, testing, melting, and refining of gold and silver bullion and foreign coins and for recasting into bars, ingots, or discs. The early mints at New Orleans, La., Charlotte, N.C., and Denver, Colo., later became assay offices. Other than the federal mints, there are now only two assay offices—New York and San Francisco. The New York office also receives gold and silver bars as settlement for international balances.

ASSEMBLY, FIRST AMERICAN. The Jamestown, Va., colony—under the charters of 1606, 1609, and 1612 of the Virginia Company of London—was governed by members of the company who assembled for quarter courts four times each year. In November 1618, the court ratified the Great Charter of Privileges, Orders, and Laws, giving the colony a generous measure of self-government. Sir George Yeardley, the new governor, convened an assembly as one step in the company's plan to give colonists the same "liberties, franchises, and immunities" as those enjoyed by residents of Britain. The first legislature in any American colony gathered in July 1619, attended by the governor, the four members of the council, and twenty-two burgesses.

ASSEMBLY, RIGHT OF. Right of assembly is protected by the federal and state constitutions. The First Amendment of the U.S. Constitution (1791) provides that Congress shall make no law abridging "the right of the people peaceably to assemble." Almost all constitutional clauses on the subject of assembly speak of "peaceful" or "orderly" assembly. Thus, the right of assembly is not unlimited. To sustain a charge of unlawful assembly it must be proved that the defendants "assembled together" and intended to commit an unlawful act—such as intimidation, threats, boycott, or assault—or a lawful act in a violent, boisterous, or tumultuous manner. At the same time, it is clearly established in the law that a meeting cannot be prohibited merely because unpopular changes may be advocated.

ASSEMBLY LINE. A system of manufacturing in which the work moves on a conveyor while each worker performs a specialized operation as the product goes by. The work operations may also be performed automatically. The assembly-line technique is largely an American development. In 1785 Oliver Evans built a gristmill near Wilmington, Del., in which a system of conveyors and chutes powered by waterwheels provided a continuous flow through the plant. This process became general in American flour milling. Subsequently, conveyor systems were used in meat-packing plants and foundry operations. The machine manufacture of standardized and interchangeable parts was actually of European origin but came to fruition in the United States through the work of men like Eli Whitney and Samuel Colt. By the 1850's it was known in Europe as the "American system of manufacture." Scientific management was initiated in the 1890's in the time-and-motion studies of Frederick W. Taylor.

These various elements of the assembly line converged in the American automobile industry, specifically in the Ford Motor Company, between 1908 and 1913. The company was faced with the problem of increasing the output of Model T cars while keeping the unit cost as low as possible. By Jan. 1, 1914, the production process was complete. It made possible complete chassis assembly in 1.5 hours instead of the 2.5 hours needed for stationary assembly, and engine assembly in 6 hours instead of 12. This technological breakthrough was followed by manufacturers of other commodities for which large output at low unit cost was wanted.

ASSESSMENT OF CANDIDATES. *See* **Political Assessments.**

ASSINIBOINE (or Assiniboin**).** A tribe of the northern Plains, the Assiniboine dwelled in the 18th century in Saskatchewan and Montana. Numbering about 10,000 in 1780, they played an important part in trade between whites and Indians, channeling firearms to other tribes. The Assiniboine made their way into Manitoba, gradually moving westward to maintain contact with the Hudson's Bay Company posts. They adopted the horse, the tipi, and related Plains traditions, waging war against their former Dakota relatives.

ASSINIBOINE, FORT. A port of the American Fur Company, west of Fort Union (near the present Montana–North Dakota border), which was the head of steamboat navigation on the Missouri River in 1834–35 and a depot for inland trade with the Assiniboine, Piegan, and Blackfoot.

ASSISTANCE CLAUSE. Election laws providing for the choice of an "honest and capable man" from each major party to "assist any voter in the preparation of his ballot when from any cause he is unable to do so" soon facilitated the delivery of bribed votes. The 20th century saw increasing state legislation to abolish the assistants and check fraud in connection with bona fide assistance to disabled voters.

ASSISTANT. The Massachusetts Bay Company Charter (1629) provided for eighteen assistants to be elected yearly by the freemen (stockholders). Seven, with the governor (or deputy governor), constituted a quorum (Court of Assistants) to manage the company's ordinary affairs. When the company became a commonwealth in Massachusetts, an assistant became a magistrate. Until deputies were admitted (1634), the Court of Assistants was the colony's sole legislature. As the colony's constitution matured, the assistants held four functions—legislative, executive, judicial, and "consultative." The Connecticut Charter (1662) provided twelve assistants.

ASSOCIATED LOYALISTS OF NEW ENGLAND (or Loyal Associated Refugees). Associations formed by Col. Edward Winslow, Jr., in Rhode Island during its British occupation (December 1776–October 1779), to chastise the Americans for losses and indignities. They made several naval raids in Long Island Sound.

ASSOCIATED PRESS (AP). The first successful attempt at cooperative news gathering on the eastern seaboard, the AP was formed in May 1848 at a meeting at the New York *Sun* office by the efforts of David Hale, co-owner of the New York *Journal of Commerce.* Other participating newspapers were the *Herald, Tribune, Express,* and *Courier and Enquirer.* Although the papers were strong competitors, they agreed to divide the expense of telegraphic transmission of news from Washington, D.C., and from Europe on its arrival by ship at Boston.

By the Civil War the AP reached out over the country through member newspapers that both collected and disseminated news that was objectively written and concisely edited. Monopolistic practices led to the shift in management from New York to Chicago. After the Illinois Supreme Court outlawed the AP's exclusion of competitors from membership, the headquarters returned to New York in 1900, where the company was incorporated as a nonprofit cooperative. By 1980 the AP served 1,365 U.S. daily newspapers and 3,600 U.S. television and radio stations and more than 10,000 newspapers and broadcast stations worldwide.

ASSOCIATIONS. Eighteenth-century merchant societies and political clubs organized by agreement and pledge of support for some particular purpose. After the passage of the Stamp Act, local organizations were linked through committees of correspondence into intercolonial associations, such as the "Sons of Liberty." In 1774, the First Continental Congress adopted the famous "association," the members pledging themselves and their constituents not to import, export, or consume British goods until their grievances were redressed. After the outbreak of hostilities, associations, both loyalist and patriot, were spontaneously formed, pledging the signers to serve their cause with their lives. During the war, the colonies found the association idea an effective device for recruiting troops.

ASSOCIATORS. A military organization formed by Benjamin Franklin in 1747, to defend Philadelphia. Revolting against the pacific policy of the Quakers, they formed military companies and erected two batteries on the Delaware River. The Associators disbanded after the peace of Aix-la-Chapelle in 1748.

ASSUMPTION AND FUNDING OF REVOLUTIONARY WAR DEBTS. At the time of the organization of the American national government under the U.S. Constitution Alexander Hamilton as secretary of the treasury proposed that the national government should assume the payment of the debts incurred by the individual states in carrying on the revolutionary war. This assumption of the state debts would increase the national debt by $18,271,786. From this proposal arose the "assumption" issue. Some of the states had paid part of their revolutionary war debt while others had paid little; also, some states were in better financial condition, since they had suffered little from the direct effects of the war. The southern states, whose population was smaller than that of the northern states, were especially hostile to this assumption, which would place increased taxation for its payment upon the entire country, themselves included.

The issue of assumption was at first defeated in Congress, but with the assistance of Thomas Jefferson, Hamilton procured an agreement by which southern votes in Congress were secured for the assumption of state debts in return for northern votes to locate the national capital on the banks of the Potomac River at the present city of Washington, D.C.

ASTOR FUR COMPANY. *See* **American Fur Company; Astoria; Pacific Fur Company.**

ASTORIA. A fur trading post established by John Jacob Astor at the mouth of the Columbia River in Oregon under Duncan McDougal in April 1811. The War of 1812 sounded the doom of the Astor enterprise. On Oct. 23, 1813, McDougal and his associates, whose sympathies were with the British, sold all the Astor interests on the Columbia to the North West Company. The post, renamed Fort George, was restored to the United States in 1818 in accordance with the Treaty of Ghent.

ASTOR PLACE RIOT (New York City, May 10, 1849). An outgrowth of a long-standing jealousy between the American actor Edwin Forrest and the English tragedian William

Charles Macready, and essentially an expression of anti-British feeling mingled with class hatred. When police failed to disperse a pro-Forrest mob outside the Astor Place Opera House, where Macready was playing *Macbeth,* the militia was called out; twenty-two people were killed and thirty-six wounded.

ASTRONAUTICS. Derived from "aeronautics" (the science or art of flight in aircraft) the word "astronautics" gained currency in the late 1950's. During the 1950's, combined with advances in high-performance military aviation; an arms race between the United States and the Soviet Union; the electronic computer revolution; and the development of telemetry, telecommunications, and various control systems, rocketry set the stage for man's escape from the gravitational envelope of the earth. In 1959 the new National Aeronautics and Space Administration (NASA) selected seven military test pilots to train to be orbital circumnavigators, or astronauts, as part of the U.S. manned ballistic satellite program, Project Mercury.

On May 25, 1961, President John F. Kennedy asked Congress to authorize and appropriate moneys to NASA for a manned lunar landing and return within the decade. At that date, the United States had had only fifteen minutes of experience in space with the suborbital Mercury-Redstone flight of Comdr. Alan B. Shepard, Jr. Project Apollo became a much larger and more complex program, designed to land on the moon rather than merely circumnavigate it.

The Mercury project achieved its goals in February 1962 with the three-orbit mission of Col. John H. Glenn. Project Gemini was created for two-man operations; so successful were its twelve missions (1965–66) that the United States finally gained a lead over the Soviet Union in the space race.

The Apollo program (1967), with spacecraft to accommodate three-man crews for two weeks and with Saturn launch vehicles that promised to inject over 100,000-pound payloads into translunar trajectories, were ready to launch a new era. In 1968, the *Saturn V* launch vehicle and the command and service modules were ready. Because the lunar landing module was not, the second manned flight of the Saturn-Apollo systems was assigned to make the first lunar circumnavigation. In December 1968, *Apollo 8*—carrying Frank Borman, James A. Lovell, Jr., and William A. Anders—first broke the hold of earth's gravisphere. They circled the moon at less than 100 nautical miles altitude on Christmas Eve. Two more test missions were equally impressive. On July 16, 1969, *Apollo 11* was launched. Four days later Neil A. Armstrong, followed by Edwin E. Aldrin, Jr., set foot upon the moon.

Six subsequent missions to the moon have been complemented by the achievements of three Skylab long-duration missions in earth orbit. Using modified Apollo spacecraft, a demonstration of international cooperation and rescue capabilities, the Apollo-Soyuz Test Project, took place in July 1975. The Soviet and American spacecrafts met and docked in space and for two days the five astronauts conducted tests. There followed unmanned spacecraft explorations of Mars, Venus, Jupiter, and Saturn. In 1976 the space shuttle project began. The space shuttle *Columbia*, with two astronauts at the controls, successfully orbited earth for the first time in April 1981, returned to earth, and became the first reusable spacecraft by making another flight in November and a third in March 1982.

ASTRONOMY. Until 1830 astronomy in the United States was largely limited to surveying and navigation. The years 1830–50 saw the founding of the first major American observatories—particularly the U.S. Naval Observatory in Washington, D.C. (1842), and Harvard Observatory in Cambridge, Mass. (1839). The principal achievements in this era were the use of the electric telegraph in determining geographical longitudes and William C. Bond's invention of the chronograph for the precise timing of observations. The pioneer experiments in celestial photography at Harvard Observatory were of great future significance.

American science was greatly stimulated through the importation of German methods, especially by Ferdinand Hassler, founder of the U.S. Coast Survey (1807); Benjamin Apthorp Gould, who founded the *Astronomical Journal* (1849); and Franz Brünnow, first director of the observatory at Ann Arbor, Mich. (1854). Alvan Clark of Massachusetts and his sons became the world's leading telescope makers. Simon Newcomb, director of the Nautical Almanac Office in Washington, D.C., prepared excellent tables of planetary motions with George W. Hill. Edward C. Pickering of Harvard Observatory greatly advanced celestial photography. Edward E. Barnard began photographing the Milky Way with short-focus, large-aperture lenses in 1889 at Lick Observatory in California.

Until 1900, most American astronomers were occupied with visual observations or with calculation of orbits of solar-system objects. Interest shifted increasingly toward astrophysics and stellar astronomy. Photographic observation methods quickly superseded visual ones, making study of stellar spectra a leading activity. At Lick Observatory, W. W. Campbell devised improved spectrographs for the 36-inch refractor. Frank Schlesinger perfected powerful new photographic techniques for measuring star distances between 1903 and 1905. Harvard Observatory's programs of spectral classification culminated in the nine-volume *Henry Draper Catalogue* of stars (1918–24).

Studies of the sun became prominent. Mount Wilson Solar Observatory in California was established in 1904; there George Ellery Hale detected magnetic fields in sunspots (1908) and Harlow Shapley studied the distances of globular star clusters. The 100-inch Mount Wilson reflector began operating in 1919; Edwin P. Hubble in 1923 detected Cepheid variables in the great Andromeda nebula and later formulated (1929) the relationship between the distances and red shifts of galaxies.

A profound reorientation and explosive growth of American astronomy was triggered by wartime technological advances. Powerful new equipment included the 200-inch Hale reflector on Palomar Mountain in California (January 1949). Also newly installed on Palomar was a 48-inch Schmidt telescope. Other improvements included photoelectric devices for more accurate photometry of faint stars. Very sensitive infrared photocells led to the detection of many extremely cool stars. During the 1950's and 1960's, image-intensifier tubes were developed at Westinghouse Laboratories useful as telescope accessories. Electronic computers revolutionized theoretical astronomy. Especially notable were the calculations of stellar models and their evolutionary changes and the refined studies of the moon's motion.

Radio astronomy was largely an outgrowth of wartime developments in radio engineering. In 1951, H. I. Ewen and E. M. Purcell observed microwave line radiation emitted by hydrogen in interstellar gas clouds, and many observatories and government laboratories built large radio telescopes to study it. The field of radio astronomy was broadened by discovery of violent bursts of radio noise from the planet Jupiter (1955). Strong radio sources outside our galaxy were first detected in 1949. Quasars remained a major unsolved mystery in the late 1970's, and from 1968 on, much attention was given to pulsars. Many species of molecules have been discovered in interstellar gas clouds. Large radar telescopes have been used very successfully for radar studies of the moon and planets.

Astronomical observations from above the earth's atmosphere began just after World War II. Instrumented artificial satellites launched by the National Aeronautics and Space Administration (NASA) from the mid-1960's observed the sun at ultraviolet, X-ray, and gamma-ray wavelengths. Orbiting astronomical observatory (OAO) satellites made extensive ultraviolet observations of stars, and the Uhuru satellite surveyed the heavens for X-ray sources. The moon was mapped in minute detail by Orbiter spacecraft, and its surface was inspected by Surveyor and Apollo landings, while the planet Mars was viewed at close hand by Mariner craft. American space probes *Pioneer* and *Voyager 1* and *2* flew past Jupiter and sent back photos, *Pioneer-Saturn* surveyed the surface of both Jupiter and Saturn, and *Mariner* photographed Venus and Mercury. The planet Venus was intensively explored by the Soviet Union, which sent six Venera probes there (five of them landed).

ATCHISON (Kans.). Located on the Missouri River; established by Missourians in 1854 as a center for efforts to make the territory a slave state. Three railroads subsequently were made to terminate at Atchison, including the Atchison, Topeka and Santa Fe. This made the city one of four river centers struggling to dominate the railroad traffic to the West. The city remains an important wholesale center.

ATCHISON, TOPEKA AND SANTA FE RAILROAD. *See* **Railroads, Sketches of Principal Lines.**

ATHAPASCAN INDIANS. One of the major groupings of Indian languages. Tribes speaking Athapascan languages occupied a large part of central Alaska, western Canada, and the southwestern United States (the Apache, for example).

ATHERTON COMPANY. Maj. Humphrey Atherton, Connecticut Gov. John Winthrop, the younger, and a group of speculators formed a company that, by purchase from the Indians (1659) and foreclosure of a questionable Indian mortgage (1662), claimed title to nearly all the Narragansett country. Jurisdiction was disputed between Connecticut and Rhode Island, and the company, by supporting Connecticut and selling land to settlers, precipitated armed incidents and rendered vain all attempts at decision until the English Board of Trade (1727) gave Rhode Island jurisdiction and left the company's heirs no tenable claims.

ATKINSON, FORT. An early post along the Santa Fe Trail in Kansas. It was built of sod in Ford County on the Arkansas River in 1850. For this reason it was called Fort Sod and later Fort Sodom. Abandoned in 1853, it was later temporarily reoccupied but was permanently abandoned in October 1854. Other forts of this name were located in Florida, Iowa, Nebraska, and Wisconsin.

ATLANTA (Ga.). Capital and largest city of Georgia; population 425,022 in 1980, center of metropolitan area including 2,029,617 people. Largest city and metropolitan area in the Southeast. Atlanta is a key transportation center and a leading manufacturing, commercial, and banking city.

Atlanta was founded in 1837, as "Terminus"—the western end of a railroad line extending to the sea at Savannah. The town grew as the railroad was extended. The town's name was changed twice and it developed as a warehousing and railroad service center. By the time of the Civil War, Atlanta was the nerve center of railroad and telegraph service for the southeastern states. It was, therefore, a major objective in the Civil War fighting (*see* Atlanta Campaign).

Rebuilding the city after Gen. Sherman burned it continued well into peacetime. Atlanta was named capital of Georgia in 1868. The city became home of two major educational organizations. Atlanta University began operations in 1867, and became the largest institution for college studies by Negroes in the South. Later, Georgia Tech was organized as the chief engineering school of the state.

ATLANTA CAMPAIGN (1864). The Union advance southward to Atlanta began May 5, 1864, simultaneously with Gen. U. S. Grant's advance to Richmond. Gen. William T. Sherman's Union army numbered 110,000 men; Gen. Joseph Johnston's Confederate troops, half that number. By July 6 Sherman had moved so near Atlanta that Johnston transferred his army south of the Chattahoochee River, into prepared positions along Peachtree Creek. On July 17 Johnston was relieved by a subordinate, John B. Hood. On July 20 Hood violently attacked, but was repulsed with heavy losses. During August, Sherman edged closer to Hood's supply line. By the 31st he was across it. Hood evacuated Atlanta, Sept. 1, and moved his army south.

On Sept. 1 Sherman telegraphed President Abraham Lincoln: "Atlanta is ours and fairly won." With the Confederates out of the city, all the people remaining in Atlanta were deported. After a brief rest, Hood started northward. Sherman followed, but soon returned to Atlanta. On Nov. 16, the famous March to the Sea was begun. Before setting out, Sherman ordered the complete destruction of the town.

ATLANTIC, BATTLE OF THE (1939–45). The struggle between Allied shipping and German submarines and Luftwaffe. Before the United States entered World War II, U.S. naval patrols gradually assumed the protection of anti-Axis merchantmen plying the broad neutrality zone. By 1941, the U.S. Navy was convoying ships to a line 400 miles west of Ireland. Before the American declaration of war, the Axis—at the cost of 59 German and 9 Italian submarines and 5 surface raiders—had sunk 2,162 ships.

A month after Pearl Harbor an offensive by a few U-boats in American waters had incredible success, since ships were still operating on a peacetime basis, unescorted and fully lighted. Belatedly, the United States organized the Tenth Fleet to bring all antisubmarine activities under a single command. An interlocking convoy system gradually developed from Gulf and Caribbean ports to Halifax in Nova Scotia or to Sydney on Cape Breton Island, where ships joined transatlantic convoys. German Adm. Karl Dönitz soon withdrew his U-boats to mid-ocean.

U-boats had great success against north Russian convoys, and the Allies soon abandoned this run as too dangerous in summer. But burgeoning U.S. naval strength, as well as scientific advances, operations analysis, and improved radar, began to thwart U-boats. Shaken, Dönitz largely abandoned attacks on convoys. Despite German improvements in structure and weapons, U-boats could never regain the initiative.

ATLANTIC AND PACIFIC RAILROAD. *See* **Railroads, Sketches of Principal Lines.**

ATLANTIC CABLE. *See* **Cables, Atlantic and Pacific.**

ATLANTIC CHARTER. The Atlantic Charter was signed Aug. 14, 1941, by President Franklin D. Roosevelt and Prime Minister Winston Churchill at a meeting in Argentia Bay off Newfoundland. The United States, still technically a neutral in World War II, already had taken a number of steps that brought it close to war. The charter expressed idealistic objectives for a postwar world: renunciation of territorial or other aggrandizement; opposition to territorial changes not approved by the people concerned; the right of people to choose their own form of government; equal access to trade and raw materials of the world; promotion of economic advancement, improved labor standards, and social security; freedom from fear and want; freedom of the seas; and disarmament of aggressor nations pending the establishment of a permanent system of peace. On Jan. 1, 1942, twenty-six countries (including the United States and Great Britain) signed the United Nations Declaration, which included among its provisions formal endorsement of the charter.

ATLANTIC COAST LINE RAILROAD. *See* **Railroads, Sketches of Principal Lines: Seaboard Coast Line.**

ATLANTIC COMMUNITY. A supposed feeling of community arising from a common culture, embracing at most the whole Western Hemisphere and much of Europe, but as more commonly interpreted only North America and Western Europe. The area envisaged is sometimes viewed as having specific common interests sufficiently important to justify a common political or economic policy—perhaps even political union. To some extent the North Atlantic Treaty Organization reflects this sentiment.

ATLANTIC FISHERIES DISPUTE. *See* **Fisheries Dispute, Arbitration of.**

ATOMIC BOMB. A military weapon deriving its energy from the fission or splitting of the nuclei of certain isotopes of the heavy elements uranium or plutonium. Feasibility studies had begun in 1942 under Vannevar Bush and James B. Conant of the Office of Scientific Research and Development. Enrico Fermi achieved the world's first sustained nuclear chain reaction in Chicago on Dec. 2.

The Manhattan District of the U.S. Army Corps of Engineers was responsible for design and construction of plants at Oak Ridge, Tenn., and Hanford, Wash., for the production of uranium-235 and plutonium, as well as for the design, fabrication, and testing of the weapon at a special laboratory at Los Alamos, N. Mex., of which J. Robert Oppenheimer was the director. A nuclear device using plutonium was tested by the United States at Alamogordo, N. Mex., on July 16, 1945; and a bomb of this type was dropped on Nagasaki, Japan, on Aug. 9, 1945. A bomb using uranium-235 was dropped on Hiroshima, Japan, on Aug. 6, 1945.

The atomic bombs dropped on Hiroshima and Nagasaki each released energy equivalent to about 20,000 tons of high explosive. More than 105,000 people died and 94,000 were wounded in these two attacks. Other nations soon produced atomic bombs—the Soviet Union in 1949; the United Kingdom in 1952; France in 1960; China in 1964; and India in 1974. During the 1970's the United States developed a small hydrogen bomb that releases high-speed neutrons in a radius of 200–300 yards. Called the neutron bomb, this new tactical weapon kills people but spares buildings. Its production was approved by the Carter administration in 1977.

ATOMIC ENERGY COMMISSION (AEC). The atomic bomb attacks on Japan in August 1945 thrust upon Congress the task of devising legislation for the control and development of atomic energy. President Harry Truman signed the Atomic Energy Act into law on Aug. 1, 1946. The new law created the AEC, five commissioners to be appointed by the president. All production facilities and nuclear reactors were to be government-owned; all technical information and research results were placed under AEC control; and all such information was excluded from the patent system.

The cold war required the AEC initially to devote most of its resources to weapon development and production. This effort accelerated after the first Soviet nuclear detonation in August 1949, with high-priority research on the hydrogen bomb. In addition, the commission constructed several experimental power reactors. The Atomic Energy Act of 1954 permitted private industry to own reactors and production facilities (but not fissionable material), and removed restrictions on dissemination of technical information to other nations, and removed the patent exclusion.

Although weapon development, testing, and production accelerated, the AEC cast its public image in terms of Dwight D. Eisenhower's "Atoms-for-Peace" plan, encouraging partnership with industry in building small-scale nuclear power plants and in establishing the International Atomic Energy Agency under the United Nations. Improvements in weapons became more difficult after the moratorium on atmospheric nuclear testing in 1958, and the demonstration power plants failed to achieve economically competitive civilian nuclear power.

In 1961 President John F. Kennedy appointed as chairman Glenn T. Seaborg, who launched a reappraisal of civilian nuclear power that helped to restore public confidence in its prospects and to concentrate resources in the most promising reactor systems. The AEC supported the Kennedy administration in negotiating the limited test ban treaty of 1963, advocated the development of nuclear explosives for peaceful purposes, expanded research and development, and closed most of its facilities for the production of special nuclear materials.

A decade of stability ended in 1971 with the appointment of James R. Schlesinger as chairman. Taking office during an intensive environmentalists' attack on the growing nuclear power industry, Schlesinger launched a broad reorganization of the AEC, expanding its regulatory staff, streamlining the licensing and regulatory procedure, carrying into the hardware stage the decision of the Seaborg commission to develop the fast-breeder power reactor, and opening new avenues for utilizing nuclear materials as an economic resource. In January 1975 the commission was replaced by two new agencies: Energy Research and Development Administration and Nuclear Regulatory Commission.

ATOMIC POWER REACTORS. The possibility of using the energy in the atomic nucleus as a power source was widely recognized soon after the discovery of nuclear fission late in 1938. On Dec. 2, 1942, Enrico Fermi and others achieved the first self-sustained chain reaction at the University of Chicago. This made possible the construction of three large plutonium-producing reactors; each generated about 250,000 kilowatts of energy, but they were not utilized for electric power production. Despite the initial popular belief that the use of nuclear power was imminent, the U.S. Atomic Energy Commission (AEC), facing extreme shortages of uranium ore, supported only three small reactor projects before 1950.

Growing industrial interest in nuclear power, a revision in atomic energy legislation in 1954, and increasing ore supplies made a more ambitious program possible. The AEC adopted a plan to test the feasibility of five different reactor systems. The results committed the United States almost exclusively to water-cooled reactors for the next two decades. By the end of 1957 the AEC had seven experimental reactors in operation, and American industry had started nine independent or cooperative projects expected to produce 800,000 kilowatts of electricity by the mid-1960's.

The AEC countered the pessimism resulting from greater progress by the United Kingdom, France, and the Soviet Union by predicting the imminence of economically competitive nuclear power and concentrating resources on water-cooled reactors for the immediate future and sodium-cooled breeder reactors for later decades in the century. This confidence was fulfilled by early 1964, when an American power company announced its decision to construct a nuclear power plant. Despite the temporary dampening effect of challenges from environmentalists and licensing delays, the trend toward nuclear power accelerated again in the early 1970's. By 1979 the total nuclear gross generating capacity of the United States provided 54 million electrical kilowatts generated in seventy-five operating plants. The Three Mile Island accident in March 1979, in which some radiation was released, provided a rallying point for antinuclear protests and led to numerous investigations and to an immediate closing of seven similar reactors.

ATTAINDER. A summary legal procedure whereby all the ordinary civil rights of the defendant are waived, the state proceeding against him by "bill," or legislative act. An attainted person suffered the loss of offices, property, and usually life, his children losing the inheritance of the estate and their noble rank, if any. The U.S. Constitution specifically prohibits the enactment of bills of attainder.

ATTICA. The most violent prison riot in American history occurred at the Attica State Correctional Facility, forty miles east of Buffalo, N.Y. On Sept. 9, 1971, approximately 1,000 of the 2,254 inmates (85 percent of whom were black) seized control of a portion of the compound. More than thirty guards and civilian employees were taken as hostages. The convicts issued demands for higher wages; religious and political freedom; dietary, medical, and recreational improvements; and total amnesty and freedom from reprisals upon surrendering of the hostages. On Sept. 13, 1971, after four days of negotiations, 1,500 heavily armed state troopers, sheriff's deputies, and prison guards began an assault. Twenty-nine inmates and ten hostages died from the assault. Three convicts and one guard had died prior to the attack.

ATTORNEY GENERAL. *See* **Justice, Department of.**

AUBRY'S RIDE (1848). Francis Xavier Aubry, after a successful trading venture in Santa Fe in 1848, determined to bring out a second caravan in the same year and allowed himself eight days to ride back to Missouri. He wagered a considerable sum on his ability to do so. His horse gave out on the Arkansas River. He pushed on fifteen or twenty miles to Mann's Fort, secured a remount, was pursued by Indians, but reached Independence within less than the time specified.

AUBURN PRISON SYSTEM. The details of the separate or silent system were originally worked out in the prison being erected by New York at Auburn in the years following 1819. An act of that year and another of 1821 called for individual cells to displace the discredited congregate system. Rows of cells, 3.5 by 7 by 7 feet in size were erected in tiers, back to back, forming a cell block inclosed by the outer walls of the building. The cells provided separate sleeping quarters, from which the convicts marched in lockstep to the shops of contractors in the prison yard. Strict rules of silence were enforced. The system was designed to isolate the convicts from each other and to encourage them to penitence without sacrificing the value of their labor.

AUDUBON SOCIETY, NATIONAL. A citizens' organization that has been a major force in shaping America's wildlife protection and conservation movement. The society's roots go back to the late 19th century, when there were virtually no effective game laws. In an early attempt to protect wildlife, an Audubon society, named for the artist and naturalist John James Audubon (1785–1851), was established in 1885. The organization was short-lived, but it led to the formation of a number of state Audubon societies. During the next several years it became clear that there was need for a coordinated national effort for federal regulation. In 1905 twenty-five state Audubon societies joined to form the National Audubon Society. The organization was concerned primarily with campaigning for bird protection laws and with direct protection of wildlife. But from its earliest days the society has also had broader wildlife and conservation interests. By providing educational materials and training teachers, the society in the 1930's began teaching a doctrine that was not to become of general concern for almost another forty years: ecology. In 1980, through its 412,000 members and 448 local chapters, it was working for wiser local and national policies to meet a wide range of environmental problems.

AUGHWICK. An Indian village on the Juniata River near the site of Fort Shirley, Pa., which in the 1750's served as a trading post and a home for Indian refugees from the Fort Duquesne vicinity.

AUGUSTA (Ga.). City located at the head of navigation on the Savannah River, founded in 1735 by Gen. James Edward Oglethorpe. Until 1773 it remained the northwestern outpost of Georgia, dominating Indian trade and relations. Largely Loyalist, it fell twice into British hands. For a short period it was the state capital. Upland cotton and steam transportation made the city, temporarily, the greatest inland cotton market in the world. A government arsenal and a large powder mill made it a major source of supply for Confederate armies. In the 20th century Augusta remained an important cotton trading center and developed into a major textile manufacturing city. Since World War II the population has steadily decreased, the 1980 census indicating 47,532 persons.

AUGUSTA (Maine). Capital city of Maine, with a population of 21,819 according to the 1980 census. The city is located forty-five miles from the open sea, on both banks of the Kennebec River; however, tides affect the river level as far upstream as Augusta, and it has been a seaport since its founding. It was designated capital in 1832.

The site on which Augusta is built was used in 1628 as a trading post by the Pilgrims from Plymouth. During the 18th century, a fort was built against Indian and French invasions from Canada. The first permanent settlers arrived in the 1750's. Small settlements on both banks of the Kennebec merged to form Augusta in 1797. During the 19th century, Augusta grew as a shipping center. In the years before refrigerators and ice-making machinery, ice was cut each winter and shipped to other cities. In addition to government activities, Augusta has factories which produce cotton cloth, paper, and leather products. It is also a center for Maine's poultry business.

***AUGUSTA*.** A British vessel that, in 1777, led the attack against Commodore John Hazelwood's fleet defending Fort Mercer on the Delaware River. The Americans resisted, forcing a British retreat. Defense construction may have caused channel changes, and the *Augusta* grounded. The Revolutionists attacked, and on Oct. 23, the *Augusta* exploded, losing over sixty men.

AUGUSTA, CONGRESS OF (Nov. 5–10, 1763). In response to orders from the British government to the governors of Virginia, North Carolina, South Carolina, and Georgia that they collect representatives of the southern Indians, inform them that the French and Indian war had ended, and bring about a general settlement on trade and boundary difficulties. The governors and John Stuart, superintendent of Indian affairs in the Southern District, met 700 Indians at Augusta, Ga., signed a treaty of friendship, and secured therein important land cessions in Georgia from the Creek.

AUGUSTA, FORT. Constructed by Pennsylvania in 1756, near the site of present Sunbury, to defend the frontier and to forestall the French who supposedly intended to fortify the forks of the Susquehanna River, it was abandoned after 1780.

AUGUSTA, TREATY OF (1773). Made by Gov. James Wright of Georgia, and John Stuart, superintendent of Indian affairs in the Southern District, with chiefs of the Creek and Cherokee nations, at the suggestion of the Indians, who were hopelessly in debt to white traders. By this agreement Georgia was ceded two tracts of land comprising more than 2.1 million acres, and from the sale of these lands the traders were to be paid.

AUGUSTA COUNTY (Va.). Named in honor of Princess Augusta, wife of the Prince of Wales; created on Nov. 1, 1738, from that portion of Orange County lying beyond the Blue Ridge. It included parts of the present states of Kentucky, Ohio, Indiana, Illinois, and Pennsylvania, and nearly all of West Virginia. Here the Virginians came into conflict with Pennsylvania's claims, for both colonies had settlers in those parts of Pennsylvania west of the Alleghenies. (*See* Pennsylvania-Virginia Boundary Dispute.)

AURARIA. First settlement in Colorado, established in October 1858, and one of the towns started at the juncture of Cherry Creek and the South Platte, following gold discoveries. In April 1860 it was consolidated with Denver, its rival, on the opposite bank of Cherry Creek.

AURORA. Philadelphia newspaper founded in 1790 by Benjamin Franklin Bache as the *General Advertiser,* becoming the Jeffersonian Republican mouthpiece. It was notorious for its violent personal abuse and its attacks on the administrations of George Washington and John Adams. Shortly after his arrest and parole in 1798 Bache died. The *Aurora* was continued by William Duane, but lost much of its effectiveness after 1800, when the capital was moved from Philadelphia to Washington.

AUSTIN (Tex.). Capital city of Texas, with a population of 345,496 in 1980; it was the center of a metropolitan area including 536,450 people. The first settlement on the site was named Waterloo, but the name was changed to honor the "Father of Texas," Stephen F. Austin, in 1839 when the site was selected as the capital of the Republic of Texas. The University of Texas is located in Austin. Austin has several local industries which are important in the state's economy, and it serves as a processing center for farm products. However, the state government, the university, and services for nearby U.S. Air Force bases employ most Austin workers.

AUSTIN COLONY. On Jan. 17, 1821, the Spanish authorities in Mexico granted to Moses Austin permission to settle 300 families in Texas. The Mexican provisional government later confirmed this concession to Stephen F. Austin, who obtained contracts to settle 900 additional families, most of whom he had introduced by 1833. Austin's colonies formed the nucleus of the Anglo-American occupation of Texas.

AUSTRALIAN BALLOT. *See* **Ballot.**

AUTOMATION. The word "automation" was coined in 1946 by D. S. Harder, vice-president of manufacturing for the Ford Motor Company. In 1948–49 the company built what was called the first automated factory, manufacturing automobile engines. The key elements of automation are automatic production machines; machines to transfer materials between, and feed materials into, production machines; and a control system that regulates the whole operation, including itself (feedback).

AUTOMOBILE. A revival of interest in highway transportation in the late 19th century provided a fertile climate for exploitation of the great advances made in automotive technology during 1860–90. More compact and efficient power units had been developed, and the idea of substituting a motor for the horse occurred independently in several nations. American accomplishment was most notable in steam-powered and electric-powered cars. German and French inventors were well ahead of their American counterparts by the 1890's in development of the gasoline-powered automobile. Credit for the first successful American gasoline automobile is generally given to Charles E. and J. Frank Duryea of Springfield, Mass., bicycle mechanics who built their first car in 1893. The Duryeas initiated the manufacture of motor vehicles for a commercial market in the United States in 1896, when they made the first sale of an American gasoline-powered car and produced twelve more of the same design. Allowing for changes of name and early failures, thirty American automobile manufacturers produced an estimated 2,500 motor vehicles in 1899. The most important of these was the Pope Manufacturing Company of Hartford, Conn.

The market for motorcars expanded rapidly as numerous races, tours, and tests demonstrated that the automobile was superior to the horse. Contrary to popular myth, there was great enthusiasm for the motorcar in the United States from its introduction. Some 458,500 motor vehicles were registered in the United States by 1910, making America the world's foremost automobile culture. There were some 515 separate automobile manufacturers by 1908, the year in which Henry Ford introduced the Model T and William C. Durant founded General Motors.

The Association of Licensed Automobile Manufacturers (ALAM), a trade association of thirty leading producers of gasoline-powered cars, was formed in 1903 to enforce an 1895 patent on the gasoline automobile originally applied for in 1879 by George B. Selden. The National Automobile Chamber of Commerce (which became the Automobile Manufacturers Association in 1932 and the Motor Vehicle Manufacturers Association in 1972) instituted a cross-licensing agreement among its members in 1914.

The ALAM companies tended to emphasize higher-priced models that brought high unit profits, while Henry Ford and many other independents were more committed to the volume production of low-priced cars. The $600, four-cylinder Ford Model N (1906–07) deserves credit as the first low-priced car with sufficient horsepower to be reliable. The rugged Ford Model T (1908–27) was even better adapted to the wretched rural roads of the day, and its immediate popularity skyrocketed Ford's share of the market for new cars to about 50 percent by the outbreak of World War I. Mass production techniques perfected at the Ford Highland Park, Mich., plant in 1913–14—especially the moving-belt assembly line—progressively reduced the price of the Model T to a low of $290 for the touring car by 1927, making mass personal automobility a reality. To compete with the Model T's progressively lower prices, the makers of moderately priced cars innovated modern consumer installment credit.

By the mid-1920's automobile manufacturing ranked first in value of product and third in value of exports among American industries. The automobile industry was the lifeblood of the petroleum industry; a chief customer of the steel industry; and the biggest consumer of many other industrial products, including plate glass, rubber, and lacquers. In 1929, the 26.7 million motor vehicles registered in the United States—one for every 4.5 persons—traveled an estimated 198 billion miles, and that year alone government spent over $2.2 billion on roads and collected $849 million in motor vehicle taxes.

Improvements during the 1920's included the self-starter, the closed-car design, ethyl gasoline, octane rating of fuels, better crankshaft balancing, four-wheel brakes, low-pressure "balloon" tires, syncromesh transmission, and safety plate glass. The trend was toward annually restyled, larger, more powerful, and faster six-cylinder cars. The number of active automobile manufacturers dropped from 108 to 44 between 1920 and 1929; and Ford, General Motors, and Chrysler came to be responsible for about 80 percent of the industry's total output.

The major innovations not yet incorporated by the late 1920's were the all-steel body, the automatic transmission, and drop-frame construction. Streamlined styling was pioneered in the 1930's. The automatic transmission was introduced in the 1939 Oldsmobile and by the 1970's became standard equipment along with power brakes, power steering, radios, and air conditioning. Development of the high-compression, overhead-cam, V-8 engine in the 1950's culminated in the "muscle cars" of the late 1960's. By the early 1970's Big Three production had shifted toward emphasis on smaller, sportier, more economical models.

The post–World War II American automobile industry could be considered a technologically stagnant industry, despite its progressive refinement of product and automation of assembly lines. The most promising improvements during the 1970's in the internal-combustion engine were being pioneered abroad. Detroit's share of the world market for cars slipped from about three-fourths in the mid-1950's to little more than a third by the mid-1970's.

Federal legislation affecting the industry proliferated from the New Deal era on. The National Labor Relations Act of 1935 encouraged the unionization of automobile workers; and with the capitulation of General Motors and Chrysler in 1937 and Ford in 1941, the United Automobile Workers became an institutionalized power. Automotive design came to be regulated by the federal government with passage of the Motor Vehicle Air Pollution Act of 1965 and the National Traffic and Motor Vehicle Safety Act of 1966. Prices for new cars, as well as the wages of automobile workers, were made subject to governmental approval with the establishment in 1971 of wage and price controls. These considerations notwithstanding, the automobile industry continued to flourish, with a steady increase of factory sales of passenger cars until 1973 (a record year with sales over 9.6 million).

The phenomenal post–World War II proliferation of the automobile was abruptly halted in 1973–74 by a fuel shortage, associated with a worldwide energy crisis. An embargo by the Arab oil-producing nations resulted by Jan. 1, 1974, in a ban on Sunday gasoline sales, a national 55-mph speed limit, five- to ten-gallon maximum limitations on gasoline purchases, and significantly higher prices at the pump. Despite short-range easing of the fuel shortage with the lifting of the Arab embargo, dwindling oil reserves promised, at the very least, increasingly higher gasoline prices (reaching $1.40 per gallon in 1981).

The sale of small cars increased to 39 percent of the American market for the first quarter of 1973. By December, for the first time in history, sales of compacts and subcompacts surpassed sales of standard-sized cars. Large cars piled up on storage lots and in dealers' showrooms, and massive layoffs of automobile workers accompanied the shifting of assembly lines to the production of smaller models. Independently of the fuel shortage, 1973 marked the beginning of diversion of the Highway Trust Fund into nonhighway transportation. Both General Motors and Ford inaugurated mass-transit divisions and were moving toward designing modular transportation systems for metropolitan areas.

AUTO RACING. The first road race occured at Chicago in 1895. The last important open road race was run in 1916 at Santa Monica, Calif., for the Vanderbilt Cup. The most famous closed-track event is the Indianapolis 500-mile race, run since 1911. Dirt-track racing has always been popular throughout the country, the cars ranging from specially designed midgets to modified stock cars. Drag racing became popular after World War II, with an annual competition on the Bonneville Salt Flats (Utah). Organized automobile racing and time trials were supervised by the American Automobile Association until taken over by the U.S. Automobile Club in 1955.

AUTOSSEE, BATTLE OF (Nov. 29, 1813). During the Creek War, Gen. John Floyd, commanding 940 Georgia militia and several hundred friendly Creek Indians, crossed the Chattahoochee River into Mississippi Territory and attacked at Autossee, a Creek village near Tuckabatchee. They drove the Creek from their villages, burned their houses, and killed 200.

AVERY SALT MINE (Avery Island, near New Iberia, La.). Although a brine spring was discovered in 1791, it was not until May 1862 that the existence of a rock salt mass was revealed. The Confederacy worked the mine until the Union forces seized it and destroyed the equipment in April 1863. The mine has been worked continuously since 1883.

AVERYSBORO, BATTLE OF (Mar.16, 1865). W. J. Hardee's corps of Gen. J. E. Johnston's Confederate army, retreating through North Carolina, entrenched at the village of Averysboro and gave a portion of Gen. W. T. Sherman's Union army a determined resistance for several hours; but inferior numbers compelled retreat during the night.

AVERY'S TRACE. In 1787 the North Carolina legislature provided for a lottery the proceeds of which were used to cut a way across the Cumberland Mountains in the Tennessee country. Peter Avery blazed and cut a trace through the sites of the present towns of Harriman, Monterey, and Cookeville. The Cherokee claimed the region traversed by the trace and demanded toll. Guards of militia were often necessary.

AVIATION. *See* **Air Transportation.**

AVIATION AGENCY, FEDERAL (FAA). A 1958 statute created the Federal Aviation Agency (Federal Aviation Administration since 1966), in part through the transfer of the Civil Aeronautics Administration and the safety-regulatory activities of the Civil Aeronautics Board. These older organizations were based on legislation of 1938. The newer agency promotes civil aeronautics, with particular attention to safety and efficiency in the use of navigable airspace. It promulgates safety regulations and air traffic rules; examines, inspects, and maintains surveillance over equipment and the regulated activities of airmen; plans, constructs, and operates aids to navigation and communication; administers grants-in-aid for airport developments; and engages in research on traffic and safety measures and devices. For some purposes its jurisdiction extends to military aviation.

AWAKENING, GREAT. *See* **Great Awakening.**

AWAKENING, SECOND. The great religious revival that swept over the United States in the late 18th and early 19th centuries. In the East it centered in the colleges. President Timothy Dwight of Yale University in chapel sermons and classroom discussions prepared the way for a renewed religious interest. A revival began in 1802 that resulted in the conversion of a third of the student body. The Awakening spread and soon young college graduates were entering every form of Christian work. In the West the Awakening was attended with great emotional excitement, under such evangelists as James McGready, Barton W. Stone, and William McKendree. At first largely Presbyterian, the revival soon became interdenominational and spread rapidly.

AYLLÓN, EXPEDITIONS OF DE. In 1521 Lucas Vásquez de Ayllón sent from the West Indies an expedition to the present Carolina coast, returning with a number of captured natives. In 1526 de Ayllón sailed with 600 prospective settlers, African slaves, and horses. His settlement, San Miguel de Gualdape, is recorded, but its site has yet to be determined. The Spaniards suffered malarial fevers, dissensions, and Indian assaults. The settlement was abandoned after one year and the survivors returned to the West Indies.

AYUBALE, BATTLE OF (Dec. 14, 1703). A frontier engagement between a force of 50 whites and 1,000 Indians under former Gov. James Moore of South Carolina and the defenders of the Spanish mission at Ayubale, near Tallahassee. He took Ayubale, devastated a wide area, badly crippled the Spanish in Florida, and carried away 1,300 Apalache Indians (or 600, according to the Spanish estimate), settling as Carolina dependents, on the east side of the lower course of the Savannah River, those not sold as slaves.

AYUNTAMIENTO (or *Cabildo*). A Spanish and Spanish-American municipal council, with administrative, legislative, and judicial functions. Citizens sometimes joined it in open meeting. Many cities in the United States were governed by *ayuntamientos.*

AZILIA, MARGRAVATE OF. The fantastic scheme of Sir Robert Montgomery to establish "a New Colony to the South of Carolina." Despite activities in Britain, he and others failed to settle the area between the Savannah and the Altamaha rivers, the Golden Islands region, within the three years conditioning his grant of 1717 from the Carolina proprietors.

BACHELOR HOUSES. To protect the colony from being burdened with the indigent and to maintain moral standards, Connecticut in 1636 forbade heads of families from entertaining single young men without permission. Nor could an unmarried young man keep house alone without consent under penalty of a fine. The Connecticut Code of 1650 and the New Haven laws of 1656 extended this to single persons of either sex. Similar laws are found in early Massachusetts codes.

BACKLASH. Entering the lexicon of American politics in the mid-1950's "backlash" initially referred to the hostile reaction of conservative southerners in the Democratic party to the liberal stance of the national Democratic party on domestic issues, particularly race relations. Passage of the Civil Rights Act of 1957 increased the alienation. In the 1960's the term achieved prominence, no longer limited to the South. The national Democratic party adopted programs to upgrade the social, economic, and political status of Afro-Americans: the Economic Opportunity Act of 1964, the Civil Rights Act of 1964, the Voting Rights Act of 1965, and the Open Housing Act of 1968. The hostile response among blocs of rank-and-file voters considered Democrats since at least the New Deal era was referred to as backlash.

During the 1960's the term was increasingly used to identify voters who supported Alabama Gov. George C. Wallace for the presidency. In his bid in 1968 under the American Independent party, Wallace's following was similarly said to be from the backlash of white citizens. The term was also used to characterize resistance to reform among white citizens who felt that Afro-Americans were demanding too much, too fast, with too much conflict and violence.

"BACK TO AFRICA" MOVEMENT. A major resurgence of the black-American colonization-of-Africa idea, the movement was founded by black leader Marcus Garvey in Jamaica (1914) as the United Negro Improvement Association. Moving the organization to New York in 1917, Garvey widely publicized the colonization idea through his weekly the *Negro World*. Despite much publicity and a large subscribed fund from the black community, nothing was ever accomplished.

BACKWOODS AND BACKCOUNTRY. The term "backwoodsman" became common when pioneers began advancing the frontier into and beyond the mountains of Pennsylvania, Virginia, and the Carolinas, regions which came to be known as the backcountry. During the Revolution backwoodsmen under George Rogers Clark took Kaskaskia and Vincennes from the British. An undisciplined but efficient army of backwoodsmen annihilated Maj. Patrick Ferguson's force at the Battle of King's Mountain. Later, under their idol, Andrew Jackson, they fought the Creek War and won the Battle of New Orleans. When Jackson was inaugurated in 1829 the backwoodsmen flocked to Washington, and the word "backwoodsman" acquired an opprobrium which it never lost.

BACON'S REBELLION (1676). A revolt in Virginia in 1676 led by Nathaniel Bacon, Jr., a young planter, against the aged royal governor, Sir William Berkeley. The revolt has usually been interpreted as an attempt at political reform directed against the allegedly oppressive rule of the governor. Recent scholarship has emphasized the controversy over Indian policy.

When Indian depredations occurred on the northern and western frontiers in the fall of 1675 and spring of 1676, Bacon ignored Berkeley's refusal of permission to retaliate, and led volunteers against the friendly Occaneechee and Pamunkey Indians. Bacon then drove Berkeley and his forces to the eastern shore of Virginia. Bacon died within a few months, and Berkeley returned to the mainland and reestablished his authority. Commissioners sent by Charles II severely censured Berkeley's strict policy toward the defeated rebels and attempted to remove him from the governorship. Berkeley returned to England in May 1677 to justify himself but died before seeing the king.

BACTERIOLOGY AND VIROLOGY. Cotton Mather—in his unpublished "Angel of Bethesda"—is the only American writer known to have given credence during the 18th century to the hypothesis that epidemic diseases are caused by, and spread through the agency of, microscopic organisms. Early in the 19th century John Crawford, a Baltimore physician, drew the ridicule of most of his colleagues for advocating a similar "germ" theory of disease.

During the 1830's and 1840's new potentialities for biomedical research arose with the appearance of greatly improved microscopes. A handful of American medical investigators tried to establish a connection between the organisms they observed and epidemic diseases. Their failure, together with the undeniable success of sanitary work based upon assumptions that disease arose in dirt and miasmas, brought further experiment almost to a halt during the 1860's and much of the 1870's. Only in the early 1880's was substantial interest in bacteriology rekindled in the United States, after a spate of advances in Europe—Joseph Lister's introduction of antiseptic surgery, Robert Koch's discovery of the tubercle bacillus and identification of the comma bacillus of cholera, and Louis Pasteur's successful inoculation against rabies and other animal diseases.

The number of American scientists pursuing bacteriological research mushroomed as the United States hastened to take advantage of, and catch up to, European scientific work. Many went to Europe to learn about the demanding new laboratory methods and bacteriological techniques. Others absorbed the new techniques from the rapidly proliferating literature. By the mid-1880's bacteriological instruction was being given at several universities. A few years later public health laboratories were established; early bacteriological activities included the testing of water supplies, the diagnosis of diphtheria, and the preparation of vaccines and sera.

Some of the most important bacteriological contributions by Americans before World War I were made in federal government laboratories. Daniel Salmon investigated the causal organism of swine cholera and in the 1890's organized a meat inspection service that used microscopes to detect trichinosis in pork for export. In 1893 Theobald Smith and F. L. Kilborne unraveled tick transmission of Texas cattle fever, one of the earliest demonstrations of the role of the insect vector. Smith subsequently carried out important studies in the bacteriology of human diseases, particularly tuberculosis. Significant bacteriological contributions were also made by the soil bacteriologist Charles Thom and the plant pathologist Erwin F. Smith. The zoologist Charles Wardell Stiles identified a new variety of American hookworm and played a leading role in eradicating and controlling it.

In the army George Sternberg was a productive pioneer in the early 1880's, through his isolation of the pneumococcus. Even more important was his success in 1893 in organizing the Army Medical School, amply justified within a few years by the notable findings in Cuba of the Yellow Fever Commission under Walter Reed, with its electrifying demonstration of transmission by the mosquito.

By the 20th century, bacteriologists began to organize societies and create journals and to spread out across the country to staff new university departments. Others joined developing research facilities. In the U.S. Marine Hospital Service, a one-man bacteriological research effort by J. J. Kinyoun expanded after 1900 with the formation of the Hygienic Laboratory, under Milton Rosenau. The laboratory became responsible for the standardization and control of vaccines and other biologicals, and after World War II its microbiological and other research developed enormously with its growth into the National Institutes of Health.

For much of the early 20th century, the nation's principal biomedical research center was the Rockefeller Institute for Medical Research, founded in 1906. Many of the difficult tasks of bacteriology still remained and were vigorously pursued, including probing the subbacterial world of the viruses. Steadily improved laboratory techniques and equipment greatly advanced all these studies—and none more than virology. Here the most dramatic impetus came with the introduction of the electron microscope, developed mainly in Europe during the 1930's but put into commercial production by the Radio Corporation of America just before World War II. With this instrument the American study of such long-frustrating virus diseases as poliomyelitis and influenza greatly accelerated after the war, a study climaxed by the development of the successful Salk and Sabin vaccines.

BAD AXE, BATTLE OF (Aug. 3, 1832). The Sauk and Fox Indians, dissatisfied with lands to which the federal government had moved them, recrossed the Mississippi River in April 1832 and, under Black Hawk's leadership, attacked white settlers. They were defeated by an American force of 1,300 men at the mouth of the Bad Axe River.

BAD LANDS. A severely eroded area in South Dakota, created by water erosion. A vast number of fossils have been exposed by the erosion. The federal government established the region as the Badlands National Monument in 1939. The term "badlands" is now used to describe any area with a similarly eroded topography.

BAGHDAD PACT. Originated on Feb. 24, 1955, as an agreement between Iraq and Turkey to "cooperate for their security and defense." Britain, Pakistan, and Iran also joined. The

United States never officially joined, not wishing to further sharpen Soviet and Egyptian opposition to it or to increase Israeli apprehensions. Nevertheless, the United States provided considerable assistance, especially financial.

By building Iraqi power and splitting the Arab world, the pact aroused the hostility of Egypt and Arab nationalists. Moreover, it was so unpopular in Iraq that it helped bring about the overthrow of the pro-Western monarchy of King Faisal II in 1958; the new government withdrew from the pact in March 1959. Following Iraq's withdrawal, the other members, with American support, re-formed as CENTO (Central Treaty Organization), headquartered in Ankara, Turkey.

BAGOT-RUSH AGREEMENT. *See* **Great Lakes Disarmament Agreement.**

BAHAMA ISLANDS. Former British colony, a chain of 760 islands fifty miles off the southeast coast of Florida (independent since July 1973.) Although granted to the Carolina proprietors in 1670, the Bahamas had only a meager development before 1718. Pirates found their innumerable harbors most convenient. After 1718, with separation from the Carolinas, colonists increased and pirates diminished. The islanders supported the American opponents of British policy and later aided them with military supplies. During the Civil War, the islands served as a base for blockade runners. During Prohibition the islands served as a port for rum-runners. During World War II the U.S. government leased areas for military bases, and in 1950 signed an agreement with Great Britain permitting the United States to establish a proving ground and missile-tracking station.

***BAILEY* V. *DREXEL FURNITURE COMPANY*, 259 U.S. 20 (1922).** A case in which the U.S. Supreme Court invalidated a 1919 act of Congress that had levied a 10 percent tax on the products of business concerns employing children under sixteen. The Court held that the measure was an attempt to bring under congressional control matters whose regulation belongs solely to the states.

BAKER, BOBBY, CASE. Robert G. ("Bobby") Baker, secretary to the U.S. Senate majority at the time of his resignation under fire in 1963, was one of the most powerful congressional staff members of his time. Baker rose from Senate page to top Senate assistant with the help of Majority Leader Lyndon B. Johnson and Sen. Robert S. Kerr of Oklahoma. Baker was indicted in January 1966. His conviction and prison sentence of from one to three years were based partly on evidence that he had pocketed about $100,000 in campaign payments and tried to conceal the transactions in his income tax declarations. After four years of appeals and litigation over admittedly illegal government eavesdropping, Baker entered Lewisburg Penitentiary in January 1971.

BAKER'S CABIN MASSACRE (Apr. 30, 1774). The murder of six or seven unarmed Mingo Indians by a party of whites at Baker's Cabin, on the Virginia side of the Ohio River, near present-day Steubenville, Ohio. As a result Chief Logan went on the warpath, charging that his sister and other near relatives had been killed.

***BAKER* V. *CARR*, 369 U.S. 186 (1962).** Decided by a six-to-two decision by the Supreme Court; established the rule that the federal courts could review claims of discrimination against voters arising out of legislative malapportionment. Nonjusticiability of malapportionment had been commented on in an extended opinion by Justice Felix Frankfurter in *Colegrove* v. *Green* (1946). The complaint in *Baker* was that although the Tennessee constitution had required since 1870 that a census be taken every ten years and that the legislature be apportioned according to the number of qualified voters in each county, all attempts to reapportion from 1901 to 1961 had failed. The impact of *Baker* was to open the doors to judicial consideration of issues related to apportionment. Although the Supreme Court did not rule on constitutional standards for apportionment until two years later, the *Baker* decision stimulated immediate judicial, legislative, or referendum actions on the issue of legislative apportionment in at least forty-three states.

BAKESHOP CASE. *See* ***Lochner* v. *New York*.**

BALANCE OF TRADE. An excess of merchandise exports over imports is usually called a favorable balance of trade, and the reverse, an unfavorable balance. The American colonies had an unfavorable balance because the colonists were constantly buying on credit or depending on England for capital for new undertakings.

After the Revolution the nation still wanted English manufactures but found it difficult to pay because England's markets were closed to many American products and trade with the British West Indies was illegal. The new trade to China, treaties with Prussia and Sweden, and Jay's Treaty improved matters, but the development of cotton growing and the outbreak of the Napoleonic wars helped much more. Both France and England bought heavily of U.S. products. After 1806 England took successful steps to stop American commercial growth, and from English intervention the War of 1812 developed. Following the war foreign manufactured goods flooded U.S. markets and hurt infant industries. Protection sentiment produced progressively higher tariffs. Foreign trade picked up after 1830. Europeans, particularly the English, invested about $150 million, much of it in American internal improvements. But European investment ended abruptly with the panic of 1837 and defalcation by several states. Between 1838 and 1849 the balance was slightly favorable. During the 1850's imports and exports expanded rapidly until the Civil War. Foreign trade declined during the war.

American foreign trade grew from $405 million in 1865 to $1.2 billion in 1873. In 1874 the trade balance again became favorable. During World War I the United States supplied the Allies with enormous quantities of food and war matériel. Between July 1, 1914, and Dec. 31, 1919, the U.S. trade balance was favorable by $18.6 billion. In 1916 the United

States ceased being a debtor nation and became a creditor.

The 1920's were prosperous. Since high tariffs made imports difficult, the only way to continue to sell abroad was to make heavy loans. The United States lent $12 billion during the decade, while foreigners invested $7 billion in the United States. Notable borrowers were Latin-American nations and Germany, which was thereby helped to pay reparations to the Allies, which in turn were able to pay on their war debts to the United States. With the crash of 1929, many Latin-American nations defaulted. U.S. loans to Germany declined, and after the Hoover moratorium in 1931 Germany ceased reparation and the Allies stopped paying debts.

U.S. foreign trade improved starting in 1934. Numerous reciprocal trade treaties lowered U.S. tariff walls and encouraged freer trade. World War II stimulated exports enormously, mostly in lend-lease shipments of war matériel to the Allies. The United States did not expect payment, but those who simultaneously provided imports did, so that in effect the nation had an unfavorable balance of trade between 1942 and 1945. During the next five years the United States exported vast quantities of goods to help rebuild a war-ravaged world. Despite the Korean War (1951–53) the favorable balance hovered around $5 billion until the mid-1960's. The balance of payments turned against the United States in 1958, and gold began to flow out of the nation on a regular basis. In 1966 even the favorable merchandise balance began to shrink, until in 1971 it turned unfavorable by $2 billion. It became favorable in 1973 and 1975, but then reached a record of minus $28.5 billion in 1978. Rising prices of American goods, increasingly efficient competition from abroad (notably Japan and Germany), the costly Vietnam War, and the tendency toward protection vis-à-vis the United States by the European Common Market explain the shift in some measure.

BALCONES ESCARPMENT. A geologic fault extending across Texas from Del Rio to Red River west of Denison. Visible on the surface eastward from Del Rio and northeastward from San Antonio to Austin, the fault continues below the surface to the east of Waco and Fort Worth. The region east of the fault is humid and contains nearly all of the most populous cities; the soil to the west is hard and dry.

BALFOUR AND VIVIANI-JOFFRE MISSIONS. In April 1917, after the United States entered World War I, a mission headed by Arthur James Balfour, British foreign secretary, and another by René Viviani, French minister of justice, and Marshal Joseph Joffre, former commander of the French armies, visited the United States. They discussed purchase of war materials, military equipment, merchant tonnage, cooperation of the navies, and creation of an American army. Balfour discussed terms of peace with E. M. House and President Woodrow Wilson.

BALIZE. A pilot village and fortification established in 1722 on the principal mouth of the Mississippi, about a half mile from the Gulf of Mexico. Built by the French as first line of defense for Louisiana, it afforded slight protection because the mud would not hold strong works and other passes were negotiable by light craft. The Spanish maintained it, but the United States abandoned it for defenses thirty miles upstream.

BALLADS. When George Lyman Kittredge wrote, in 1904, that "a ballad is a song that tells a story or a story told in song," only one collection of American folk songs had been published (*Allen's Slave Songs of the United States,* 1867). Since that time hundreds of titles have been added to the literature of American balladry. American ballads, composed by hard-handed miners, mountaineers, cowboys, sailors, and lumberjacks, are peopled with working-class characters. Undoubtedly the most popular are the occupational ballads ("Casey Jones," "The Erie Canal"), bad-man ballads (Jesse James), murder ballads (Pearl Bryant), and the vulgar or bawdy ballads popular in colleges.

Afro-American ballads stand in a class by themselves, for while the main body of Afro-American songs is not strictly narrative in form, it includes America's most original and interesting narrative songs in English—"John Henry," "Frankie," "Po' Laz'us."

BALLINGER-PINCHOT CONTROVERSY (1909–11). A bitter contention over the conservation of natural resources. Early in William H. Taft's administration an order of former President Theodore Roosevelt withdrawing from sale certain public lands containing waterpower sites in Montana and Wyoming was canceled. Gifford Pinchot, chief of the Forest Service, publicly charged Secretary of the Interior Richard A. Ballinger with favoritism toward corporations seeking waterpower sites. Pinchot defended L. R. Glavis, Land Office investigator, dismissed for accusing Ballinger of being a tool of private interests by favoring certain claims to valuable Alaskan mineral lands. Pinchot also was dismissed. A joint congressional investigating committee exonerated Ballinger, but failing to regain public confidence, he resigned in March 1911.

BALLOONS. In early June 1784—just a year after the success of the Montgolfier brothers in France—Peter Carnes raised a 35-foot, hot-air balloon at Bladensburg, Md. Later that month Carnes's tethered balloon carried Edward Warren aloft at Baltimore. The first American to make a free ascent, however, was John Jeffries, in the hydrogen balloon of Jean-Pierre Blanchard, a Frenchman, at London in late 1784. Blanchard made the first free ascent in the United States at Philadelphia in January 1793.

Not until 1830 did an American make a balloon ascent in the United States: Charles Ferson Durant, at Castle Garden (Battery Park) at the tip of Manhattan Island. The first aerial photographs in the U.S. were taken from a balloon in 1860, and the first telegraph message sent from the air in 1861. The Union used balloons in the Civil War. Captive balloons were used extensively for reconnaissance and fire control in World War I. In World War II Japan launched 9,000 unmanned bomb-carrying balloons to ride the jet stream toward the United States; about 10 percent reached America.

The U.S. Weather Bureau uses hundreds of small balloons

daily to study atmospheric conditions. In May 1961 the U.S. Navy's Strato Lab V polyethylene balloon, with a capacity of 10 million cubic feet, carried two men to a record altitude of 113,740 feet. Balloons are used in a wide variety of such scientific research as celestial measurements by infrared telescope and cosmic ray studies.

There were several unsuccessful attempts to cross the Atlantic in the 1970's, and finally in August 1978 three Americans, Max Anderson, Ben Abruzzo, and Larry Newman, completed the transatlantic crossing, lifting off from Maine and landing near Paris after 137 hours, 18 minutes aloft. In May 1980 Max Anderson and his son Kris were the first to fly nonstop across North America.

BALLOT. A method of voting by way of a form that lists the voter's options. In colonial times, voice voting and even letting corn or beans designate votes were used. With the formation of the Union, the paper ballot emerged as the dominant voting method, and many states allowed the voter to make up his own ballot at home. Almost immediately the political parties, motivated by a desire to influence the vote, started to print ballots. These ballots listed only the candidates of a single party and were peddled to the voters on or before election day. The parties were able to influence the vote by pressuring voters to take their ballot, virtually ensuring a straight-ticket vote, and forcing them to vote in public.

The system of party ballots led to widespread intimidation and corruption. Between 1888 and 1896, civic groups and "good government" people convinced over 90 percent of the states to adopt a new ballot patterned after one in Australia. The Australian ballot was official (being prepared and distributed by the government), consolidated (placing the candidates of both major parties on the same ballot), and secret (eliminating the "public vote"). Still in use in all states, it eliminated much of the partisan intimidation and vote fraud that had existed; it also facilitated split-ticket voting.

BALL'S BLUFF, BATTLE OF (Oct. 21, 1861). In this militarily inconsequential clash in Virginia, Union Col. E. D. Baker, senator from Oregon and a friend of President Abraham Lincoln, was killed; the Union troops, through mismanagement, were defeated. Discontented Radicals and a critical public blamed Gen. G. B. McClellan. Congress inaugurated the Committee on the Conduct of the War to investigate Ball's Bluff and other Union failures. McClellan arrested Gen. C. P. Stone for the defeat and for Baker's death. No formal charges were ever made. After six months' imprisonment Stone was released.

BALTIMORE (Md.). Seaport at the upper end of the Chesapeake Bay on the Patapsco River, and Maryland's largest city, Baltimore was founded in 1729 and named in honor of the second proprietor of Maryland, Charles Calvert, Baron Baltimore. Baltimore was not dissociated from the Roman Catholic tradition of Maryland and in 1808 became the seat of the first Roman Catholic archdiocese in the United States.

Needing an outlet for tobacco, the founders of Baltimore sought and obtained a port charter in 1729. With the discovery of markets for flour in Ireland and Scotland, many tobacco fields were converted to wheat. Shipbuilding grew with the development of the Baltimore clipper. At the outbreak of the Revolution, Baltimore was a busy seafaring and commercial town of 6,700 inhabitants. In 1790 the population had grown to 13,501, and in 1797 Baltimore became a city.

During the Revolution and the War of 1812 privateers built and manned in Baltimore played a conspicuous part. The tide was turned in the latter war when the port was successfully defended against the British.

Looking to the west for increasing wheat supplies for its flour trade and threatened by the opening of the Erie Canal in 1825, Baltimore began construction in 1827 of the Baltimore and Ohio Railroad, the first steam-operated railway in the United States. The tide of Baltimore's growth was stemmed during the second half of the 19th century by political strife and the Civil War, climaxed in 1904 by a fire that destroyed about 150 acres in the downtown area. After World War I the port revived. The restoration of active trading with the Caribbean changed the thrust of Baltimore's economy from commerce to heavy industry, as new iron mines and oil wells were opened in the Caribbean area. Shipbuilding continued, but the city's industry was dominated by primary metal manufacturing; the Bethlehem Steel Company, the largest tidewater steel mill in the United States, had an annual ingot capacity of 8.2 million tons. In the late 1970's the port was handling more than 46 million short tons of cargo annually. Baltimore's rank among the nation's cities had fallen to tenth, as its population decreased to 792,000 in 1980.

In 1867 Johns Hopkins founded Johns Hopkins Hospital and the Johns Hopkins University. In 1868 George Peabody founded the Peabody Institute, including a conservatory of music still highly ranked. After World War II, Baltimore pioneered in attacking urban blight and slum conditions.

BALTIMORE, BATTLE OF (Sept. 12, 1814). After the burning of Washington, D.C., a British land force of 8,000, commanded by Gen. Robert Ross, attempted to capture Baltimore. Ross, killed in battle, was successfully opposed by a force of Maryland and Pennsylvania militia and volunteers.

***BALTIMORE* AFFAIR** (1891–92). An attack by a Chilean mob in Valparaíso on Oct. 16, 1891, upon 117 sailors on shore leave from the U.S.S. *Baltimore* left two Americans dead and several wounded. This hostility emerged from the mistaken feeling that during Chile's civil war the United States had sympathized with the Chilean government. On Jan. 21, 1892, the United States threatened to end relations. Chile apologized on Jan. 26 and paid $75,000 to the injured and to relatives of the dead sailors.

BALTIMORE AND OHIO RAILROAD. *See* **Railroads, Sketches of Principal Lines: Chesapeake and Ohio.**

BALTIMORE BELL TEAMS. Named for the small bells suspended in metal arches over the hames to speed the horses and sound warning on narrow, crooked roads. These teams hauled country produce to Baltimore and returned with goods for homes and local merchants from points as far southwest as Knoxville, Tenn., and operated until 1850 or later, when they were superseded by canals and railroads.

BALTIMORE CLIPPER. The fast topsail schooner developed around Chesapeake Bay in the revolutionary period and later similar square-rigged vessels. In post-revolutionary days their speed enabled them to be used in privateering and the slave trade. *Ann McKim* (1833) was the ultimate expression of the type and is regarded by some as the link between the Baltimore clipper and the clipper ship.

BALTIMORE COUNCILS, PROVINCIAL AND PLENARY. Ecclesiastical legislation in the Roman Catholic church of the United States began with a synod of the priests under Bishop John Carroll of Baltimore in 1791. The regulations adopted served to administer church affairs until 1829, when the first Provincial Council of Baltimore was held. There were seven of these councils between 1829 and 1849. By 1852 the church had been divided into provinces; provincial councils were held under their archbishops, and three plenary councils were held in 1852, 1866, and 1884. The legislation of these three national assemblies concerned explanations of Catholic faith, administration of the sacraments, holy days, clerical discipline, ecclesiastical property tenure, and Catholic education and welfare agencies.

BALTIMORE FIRE (Feb. 7–8, 1904). The third greatest conflagration in American history. It destroyed most of the central business district over an area of 150 acres. Damages were estimated at about $150 million.

***BALTIMORE* INCIDENT.** While convoying merchant vessels to Havana during naval hostilities with France, Capt. Isaac Phillips in the U.S. sloop *Baltimore* encountered a British squadron on Nov. 16, 1798. Facing superior force, and with strict injunctions to avoid conflict with British vessels, Phillips, under protest, submitted to the mustering of his crew and removal of all seamen without papers showing American citizenship. Phillips was summarily dismissed from the navy, and stringent orders were issued requiring American national vessels to resist forcibly any similar insult.

BALTIMORE RIOT (Apr. 19, 1981). An attack on Pennsylvania and Massachusetts militia en route to Washington by Baltimoreans who considered them invaders. The railroad was not continuous through Baltimore, horses drawing the cars from one terminal to the other. After a few troops had gone through, the connecting tracks were blocked, which forced later contingents to march. The crowd pursued them with stones, bricks, and a few pistol shots. The militia fired back. Finally the police succeeded in holding the people back until the troops entrained. Four militiamen and twelve civilians were killed and an unknown number wounded.

BANK, FEDERAL RESERVE. *See* **Federal Reserve System.**

BANK DEPOSITS. Bank deposits fall into two categories. A saver may deposit money for safekeeping and to earn interest—a primary deposit. Or a bank may enter the amount of a loan on a borrower's checking account—a secondary, or created, deposit. Early banks had two basic ways of lending their credit, by issuing bank notes (the bank's demand promissory notes) or by creating deposits. It was long assumed that in the pre–Civil War period banks did most of their lending in the form of bank notes, but statements of both the first Bank of the United States and the second generally showed more deposits than bank notes. In rural areas bank notes were used more than deposits. The Farmer's Bank of Maryland was the first to pay interest on deposits (1804). After the National Banking System was set up in 1863, the use of checks drawn on demand deposits rapidly outdistanced bank notes. Between 1866 and 1913 the deposits of national banks grew from $565 million to over $6 billion, but their bank notes totaled only $727 million.

Between mid-1914 and mid-1920 (the Federal Reserve System opened on Nov. 16, 1914) demand deposits rose from $10.1 billion to $19.6 billion. Wartime needs of the government and sharply reduced reserve requirements against deposits in the Federal Reserve Act were responsible for these "invisible greenbacks" of World War I. Demand deposits rose from $18 billion in mid-1922 to $22.5 billion in mid-1929, but fell to a low of $14.4 billion in mid-1933—moves that reflected, and also helped cause, the boom and then the depression of those years. The Banking Act of 1933 forbade banks to pay interest on demand deposits, and the Banking Act of 1935 gave the Federal Reserve authority to double reserve requirements. During World War II demand deposits rose from $33.6 billion in mid-1940 to $88.8 billion in mid-1946, again playing the role of invisible greenbacks. They increased unduly again during the Korean War and grew from $132.3 billion to $169.6 billion from December 1964 to December 1970, the height of the war in Vietnam. One would expect a rise in population and real income to increase deposits, but wars and excessive government spending in peacetime can also cause a disproportionate increase.

BANK FAILURES. American financial history to 1934 was characterized by an appalling number of bank failures, because the majority of banks were local enterprises. It took only a serious crop failure or a business recession to precipitate dozens or even hundreds of bank failures. State-chartered banks had a particularly poor record.

The first bank to fail was the Farmers' Exchange Bank of Glocester, R.I., in 1809. The statistics of bank failures between 1789 and 1863 are inadequate, but the losses were unquestionably large. Not until after 1853 did banks' deposit liabilities exceed their note liabilities.

The establishment of the National Banking System in 1863 introduced needed regulations for national banks. These were more numerous than state banks to 1894, and were larger on the average. But even their record left much to be desired. There were 515 national bank suspensions during 1864–1913, while state banks suffered 2,491 failures. The nation had 1,532 banks in 1863 and 26,664 in 1913. The worst year was the panic year of 1893, with almost 500 failures. The establishment of the Federal Reserve System in 1913 did little to improve the record. By 1933 there were 14,771 banks, half as many as in 1920.

The bank holocaust of the early 1930's—9,106 bank failures in four years, 1,947 of them national banks—culminating in a nationwide bank moratorium in March 1933, produced needed reforms. Congress forbade Federal Reserve member banks to pay interest on demand deposits and founded the Federal Deposit Insurance Corporation (FDIC). The FDIC raised its initial capital by selling two kinds of stock. Class A stock (paying dividends) came from assessing every insured bank 0.5 percent of its total deposits—half paid in full, half subject to call. All member banks of the Federal Reserve System had to be insured and had to buy Class B stock (paying no dividends) with 0.5 percent of their surplus —half payable immediately, half subject to call. In addition, any bank desiring to be insured had to pay 0.083 percent of its average deposits annually. The FDIC first insured each depositor in a bank up to $2,500, and by 1974, to $40,000. At the end of 1971 the FDIC was insuring 98.6 percent of all commercial banks and fully protecting 99 percent of all depositors. But it was protecting only about 64 percent of all deposits, savings deposits at a high percentage but business deposits at only about 55 percent.

During the first nine years of the FDIC there were 487 closings because of financial difficulties, mostly of insured banks, and 387 of these received disbursements from the FDIC. During the years 1943 to 1974, the average number of closings dropped to 5 per year, but during 1975–80 the average was 10 closings annually. From 1934 to 1980 the corporation made disbursements in 568 cases representing $6.2 billion in deposits. Through this protection people today are spared that traumatic experience of past generations, a "run on the bank" and the loss of a large part of their savings.

BANK FOR INTERNATIONAL SETTLEMENTS (BIS). BIS evolved from the Hague Agreement of Jan. 20, 1930, predicated on the report in March 1929 of the committee of reparation experts headed by Owen D. Young. Located in Basel, it began business May 17, 1930, with an authorized capital of 500 million Swiss gold francs (about $100 million then), one-quarter paid in by 1961. The central banks of Belgium, Britain, France, Germany, and Italy and two banking groups, one Japanese and one American, guaranteed the original subscription. The Japanese group sold out in 1951.

Its chief activity is executing any banking operations the central banks request. It may also "act as trustee or agent in regard to international financial settlements." Since 1964 it has worked for the Group of Ten (representatives of the major banking nations) and more recently helped with the European Monetary Agreement. The BIS may not issue notes, accept bills of exchange, make advances to governments, or acquire a predominant interest in any business enterprise. Between 1971 and 1979 the BIS more than tripled its balance from 24 billion to 70 billion gold francs. The bank complements operations of the International Monetary Fund and the World Bank.

BANKHEAD COTTON ACT (Apr. 21, 1934). It was designed to supplement the Agricultural Adjustment Act of 1933. While not actually placing limits upon the growing of cotton by individual farmers, the act set a national quota and levied a tax of 50 percent of the central market price (but not less than 5 cents per pound) upon cotton ginned in excess of the individual quota. After the Supreme Court invalidated the Agricultural Adjustment Act, Congress repealed the Bankhead Act (Feb. 10, 1936).

BANK HOLIDAY. *See* **Banking Crisis of 1933.**

BANKING. There were no commercial banks in colonial times, although there were loan offices or land banks, which made loans on real estate security with limited issues of legal tender notes. Robert Morris founded the first commercial bank in the United States, the Bank of North America, chartered Dec. 31, 1781. It greatly assisted the financing of the closing stages of the Revolution. By 1811 there were eighty-eight state-chartered banks.

Alexander Hamilton's financial program included a central bank to serve the Treasury, provide a depository for public money, and be a regulator of the currency. Accordingly the first Bank of the United States—de facto the fifth—was founded Feb. 25, 1791, with a twenty-year charter. Its huge $10 million capital and favored relationship with the government aroused much anxiety, especially among Jeffersonians. The bank's sound but unpopular policy of promptly returning bank notes for redemption in specie and refusing those of non-specie-paying banks, together with a political feud, was largely responsible for its not being rechartered in 1811. Between 1811 and 1816 state banks increased to 246, and note circulation quadrupled. Nearly all but New England banks suspended specie payments in 1814 because of the War of 1812 and unregulated credit expansion.

Congress established the second Bank of the United States on Apr. 10, 1816, also with a twenty-year charter. The bank's $35 million capitalization and favored relationship with the Treasury likewise aroused anxiety. Instead of repairing the overexpanded credit situation, the bank aggravated it by generous lending policies, precipitating the panic of 1819. Thereafter, under Nicholas Biddle, it was well run. It required other banks to redeem their notes in specie, but most had come to accept that policy. The bank's downfall grew out of President Andrew Jackson's prejudice against banks and monopolies; the memory of the bank's role in the 1819 panic; and most of all, Biddle's decision to let rechartering be a main issue in the 1832 presidential election. Jackson vetoed the recharter. After Sept. 26, 1833, the government placed all its deposits with the "pet banks" (politically selected state banks) until it set up the Independent Treasury System in the 1840's. Between 1830 and 1837 the number of banks, note circulation, and loans all about tripled. Without the second bank to regulate them, the banks overextended themselves in lending to land speculators. The panic of 1837 resulted—bringing a suspension of specie payments, many failures, and a depression that lasted until 1844.

For thirty years the country was without an adequate regulator of bank currency. In some states the laws were very strict or banking was forbidden; in others the rules were lax. Banks made many long-term loans, especially on real estate, and resorted to subterfuges to avoid redeeming notes in specie. In parts of the Midwest and South there was some "wild-cat" banking—lending notes at town branches but redeeming in specie only at a main office hidden away in a remote spot. Bankers had to consult weekly publications, Bank Note Reporters, for the current discount on bank notes and turn to the latest Bank Note Detectors to distinguish counterfeits and notes of failed banks. In this bleak era of banking, however, there were successful banking systems in Massachusetts, New York, Indiana, Ohio, Iowa, and Louisiana.

Secretary of the Treasury Salmon P. Chase began agitating for an improved banking system in 1861. The National Banking Act created the National Banking System on Feb. 25, 1863, and was completely revised June 3, 1864. The system's head officer was the comptroller of currency. It was based on recent reforms, especially the Free Banking System's principle of bond-backed notes. But the reserve requirements for bank notes were high, and the law forbade real estate loans and branch banking, had stiff organization requirements, and imposed burdensome taxes. In 1865 Congress levied a prohibitive 10 percent tax on state bank notes, effective July 1, 1866, which drove most of these banks into the new system. There were 1,644 national banks by Oct. 1, 1866, and they were required to use "National" in their name. Checks had been increasing in popularity since before the Civil War, and by 1853 the total of bank deposits exceeded that of bank notes. By the 1890's about 85 percent of all business transactions were settled by check payments. Since state banks were less restricted, their number passed that of national banks in 1894. Most large banks were national, however. Improvements in state banking laws began about 1887.

The National Banking System constituted a substantial improvement over the pre–Civil War hodgepodge of banking systems, but it had three major faults: the perverse elasticity of the bond-secured bank notes, of which the supply did not vary in accordance with the needs of business; the decentralization of bank deposit reserves; and no central bank to take measures to forestall crises or to lend to deserving banks in times of distress.

Four times—1873, 1884, 1893, and 1907—panics highlighted the faults of the National Banking System. Improvised use of clearinghouse certificates in interbank settlements somewhat relieved money shortages in the first three cases; "voluntary" bank assessments collected and lent by a committee headed by J. P. Morgan gave relief in 1907. In 1908 Congress passed the Aldrich-Vreeland Act to investigate foreign central banking systems and suggest reforms and to permit emergency bank note issues. The Owen-Glass Act of 1913 superimposed a central system on the existing national system. It required all national banks to "join," which meant to buy stock equal to 3 percent of their capital and surplus, thus providing the funds to set up the Federal Reserve System (1914). State banks might also join, but by the end of 1916 only thirty-four had done so. A majority of the nation's banks have always remained outside the Federal Reserve System, although the larger banks have usually been members. Thus ended the need for the Independent Treasury System, which wound up its affairs in 1921.

Between the opening of the Federal Reserve System and 1979 the commercial banking system grew and changed, as might be expected in a nation whose population more than doubled and whose real national income septupled. The number of banks declined from 27,864 in mid-1914 to 14,712 in 1979; the number of national banks, from 7,518 to 4,564. (Bank failures between 1920 and 1933 were the principal cause.) Demand deposits meanwhile grew from $10 billion to $435 billion; and time deposits, from $8.6 billion to $674 billion. Loans grew from $15.2 billion to $814 billion; investments, on the other hand, rose from $5.5 billion to $288 billion—30 percent in Treasury securities. Wholesale prices quadrupled in that same period.

By 1921 there were 31,076 banks, the all-time peak; many were small family-owned state banks. Every year local crop failures, other disasters, or simply bad management wiped out several hundred of them. By 1929 the number of banks had declined to 25,568.

The 1930's witnessed many reforms growing out of the more than 9,000 bank failures between 1930 and 1933 and capped by the nationwide bank moratorium of Mar. 6–9, 1933. Congress passed two major banking laws, one on June 16, 1933, and the other on Aug. 23, 1935. These laws gave the Federal Reserve System firmer control, especially over member banks. They set up the Federal Deposit Insurance Corporation to insure bank deposits, and soon all but a few hundred small banks belonged.

During World War II the banks converted their excess reserves into government obligations and increased their own holdings from $16 billion in 1940 to $84 billion in 1945. Demand deposits more than doubled. Price levels nearly doubled during the 1940's.

By the Federal Reserve–Treasury "accord" of March 1951, the Federal Reserve System regained its freedom to curb credit expansion, and thereafter interest rates crept upward. That development improved bank profits and led banks to reduce somewhat their holdings of federal government obligations. Term loans (five to ten years) to industry and real estate loans increased. Banks also encountered stiff competition from rapidly growing rivals, such as savings and loan associations and personal finance companies.

Interest rates rose spectacularly during the 1960's, prime commercial paper reaching 9 percent in 1970, then dropped sharply in 1971, only to rise once more, hitting 20 percent in mid-1980. Whereas consumer prices had gone up 23 percent during the 1950's, they rose 31 percent during the 1960's, and climbed over 70 percent during the 1970's. Money supply figures played a major role in determining Federal Reserve credit policy from 1960 on.

BANKING, BRANCH AND GROUP. The first Bank of the United States had eight branches; the second, twenty-nine. Thereafter, what meager developments there were before the 20th century took place under state authority, very little occurring between 1860 and 1890. The National Banking Act of 1863 forbade national bank branches.

The Federal Reserve Act of 1913 permitted foreign branches to a limited degree; in 1918 state banks having branches and wanting to join the Federal Reserve System were authorized to keep them; and the McFadden-Pepper Act of 1927 allowed national banks a limited number of branches in the parent bank's city, provided the state permitted branch banking. The Banking Act of 1933 permitted national banks to establish branches.

In 1936 eighteen states permitted statewide branch banking, and seventeen within limited areas (3,581 branches in existence). In 1969 there were still eighteen states permitting branch banking; states permitting it within limits had increased to twenty. At the end of 1979 the 15,201 banks had 39,727 branches and "additional offices."

Where branch banking is prohibited or discouraged, resort has been made to chain or group banking: chains are owned by one or more individuals; groups, by holding companies. Such uncontrolled concentration of financial resources caused public concern, and Congress held hearings, finally passing the Bank Holding Company Act of 1956, which made the Federal Reserve's board of governors the supervisory agency in this field. In December 1970 there were 121 registered bank holding companies, holding $78 billion in deposits, or 16.2 percent of all commercial bank deposits. But holding companies controlling only one bank were exempt from the 1956 law; between 1955 and April 1970 their number grew from 117 to 1,116 and their deposits from $11.6 billion to $138.8 billion, or 32.6 percent of commercial deposits. Many carried on nonbanking activities. Alarmed by this rapid growth, Congress, by a Dec. 31, 1970, law ended the exemption of one-bank holding companies; all are now under Federal Reserve control. In 1979, there were 2,478 bank holding companies, with $745 billion in deposits, which represented 67 percent of commercial deposits.

BANKING, STATE. State investment in banks was common before the panic of 1837, with the idea that bank profits would lead to abolition of taxes. This had its roots in the early 18th century, when most colonies had loan offices or land banks. Interest payments from loans paid the expenses of the provincial governments.

In the 19th century sometimes the state was sole owner of a bank (South Carolina); more commonly it was part owner (Indiana). In some cases the ventures were profitable; in others, disastrous. In Louisiana, where bonds issued to aid banks amounted to $19 million, there was collapse and reform under the Specie Reserve System of 1842. Among the successful state-owned banks, the State Bank of Missouri was the most important. It operated through the panics of 1837 and 1857; and in 1862, when it entered the national system as a private bank, the state sold its stock for a premium.

State banking was one of three alternatives left the states following public distrust of banks after the panic of 1819, the political struggle with Andrew Jackson over renewing the charter of the second Bank of the United States, and the panic of 1837. Some states forbade banking altogether: seven of thirty-one states were doing so in 1852. The majority elected to regulate banking more closely. Still others made banking a state monopoly or set up a state-owned bank.

With the passage of the July 1865 amendment to the National Banking Act, imposing a 10 percent tax on state bank notes after July 1, 1866, to force all state banks to join the National Banking System, state-owned banks disappeared. State-chartered banks got around the law by encouraging borrowers to use check currency.

BANKING ACTS OF 1933 AND 1935. The Banking Act of 1933 contained (1) provisions to increase the power of the Federal Reserve Board to control credit, especially to brokers and customers secured by stocks and bonds; (2) provisions dealing with commercial banks, the most important providing for insurance of bank deposits under the Federal Deposit Insurance Corporation; and (3) provisions to separate commercial and investment banking functions.

Under the Banking Act of 1935, Title I amended the deposit insurance provisions of the Banking Act of 1933. Title II provided reorganization of the Federal Reserve Board and renamed it the Board of Governors of the Federal Reserve System. Powers over discount and open market operations of the Reserve banks were increased and centralized in the Board of Governors, and the discount base was very materially broadened. Title III contained technical amendments to the banking laws governing commercial banks.

BANKING CRISIS OF 1933. The large number of bank failures during 1931–32, combined with hoarding, markedly weakened the banking structure. Attempts of the Reconstruction Finance Corporation to avoid disaster were largely nullified by publication of names of borrowing banks. Bank moratoria were declared in five states by the end of February, and in seventeen additional states during the first three days of March. On Mar. 4, banks in the remaining states closed their doors.

Congress, called in special session by President Franklin D. Roosevelt, passed the Emergency Banking Act of 1933 on Mar. 9, providing machinery for reopening only sound banks. The bank moratorium, proclaimed by the president on Mar. 6, was extended a few days to permit the provisions of the act to be put into effect. Sound banks were reopened on Mar. 13, 14, and 15. By Mar. 15, banks controlling about 90 percent of the banking resources of the country were again in operation.

BANK NOTES. *See* **Money.**

***BANK OF AUGUSTA* V. *EARLE*,** 13 Peters 519 (1839). Involved the right of a Georgia bank to recover on a bill of exchange purchased in Alabama. The Supreme Court, speaking through Chief Justice Roger B. Taney, held that though a state might exclude the creature of another state, yet in the silence of any positive rule it would be presumed that "foreign" corporations were by comity permitted to make contracts. Taney's opinion became the leading authority on the law of foreign corporations.

***BANK OF COMMERCE* V. *NEW YORK CITY*, 2 Black 620 (1863).** The Supreme Court held that the state could not tax capital invested in federal securities—thereby strengthening the financial position of the government in the midst of the Civil War.

BANK OF NORTH AMERICA. America's first government-incorporated bank, chartered by the Continental Congress in 1781, commenced operations in Philadelphia on Jan. 7, 1782. Organized by Robert Morris, the bank supplied vital financial aid to the government during the closing months of the American Revolution.

BANK OF THE STATE OF SOUTH CAROLINA. *See* **South Carolina, State Bank of.**

BANK OF THE UNITED STATES. First Bank of the United States (1791–1811). As the result of a proposal by Secretary of the Treasury Alexander Hamilton, an act incorporating subscribers to the Bank of the United States was approved by President George Washington and became law on Feb. 25, 1791. The bank, located in Philadelphia, had capital of $10 million, 25,000 shares of $400 par value. One-fifth was subscribed by the government, the rest by private investors. Private subscriptions were limited to 1,000 shares, and no more than thirty votes. Foreign shareholders were not permitted to vote by proxy. The board of twenty-five directors, elected by the shareholders, elected a president to receive compensation, the directors serving without pay. Only American citizens might be directors. The bank was empowered to carry on commercial banking, was not permitted to deal in commodities or real estate, and was limited to a 6 percent interest charge on loans. The bank could issue circulating notes totaling up to $10 million.

The Bank of the United States opened on Dec. 12, 1791. It furnished the country, through its main office and eight branches, with sound banking service for twenty years. It served as fiscal agent for the government and exerted a salutary controlling influence on the note issues of the state banks by refusing to accept state bank notes not redeemable in specie. Nevertheless, its charter was not renewed in 1811, due to doubt as to its constitutionality. The bank eventually paid shareholders $434 on each share.

Second Bank of the United States (1811–36). After a brief and unsatisfactory period of state banking, the second Bank of the United States was incorporated on Apr. 10, 1816. Capital and note issue limits were increased to $35 million. The president of the United States was authorized to appoint five of the directors. The second bank was badly managed under its first president, William Jones. In 1819 Langdon Cheves succeeded Jones and got the bank back to a sound position. In 1823 Nicholas Biddle assumed the presidency, and the bank extended sound banking service through its main office and twenty-five branches. A dispute between Biddle and President Andrew Jackson made efforts to obtain a renewal of its charter futile, and the institution ceased to function as a national bank in 1836.

***BANK OF THE UNITED STATES* V. *HALSTEAD*, 10 Wheaton 51 (1825).** Concerned the applicability of state legislation regulating the procedural processes to federal courts within the respective states. The Supreme Court upheld the power of federal courts to alter forms of proceedings to meet changing conditions on general (implied) grounds relating to the judicial power and from specific legislative grants.

***BANK OF THE UNITED STATES* V. *PLANTER'S BANK OF GEORGIA*, 9 Wheaton 904 (1824).** Chief Justice John Marshall here enunciated the rule that a suit against a corporation chartered and partly owned by a state was not a suit against the state itself. The rule was later applied to banks wholly owned by a state (*see Briscoe* v. *Bank of the Commonwealth of Kentucky*).

BANKRUPTCY LAWS. The subject of bankruptcy laws was not considered by the federal convention of 1787 until late in its proceedings. Charles Pinckney's first draft of the bankruptcy clause of the Constitution was adopted with only one dissenting vote.

Congress did not immediately exercise the power to establish uniform bankruptcy laws. The first federal legislation was enacted in 1800 as a result of unsettled economic conditions from widespread speculation in new companies dealing in land and in government scrip, and closely resembled English statutes. It applied only to traders, merchants, and brokers and provided only for creditor-initiated proceedings. It was essentially a liquidation provision—the assets of the bankrupt being sold to satisfy creditors. A bankrupt was permitted to retain a certain percentage of his assets and could be discharged from any unsatisfied indebtedness by the consent of two-thirds of his creditors. The act was limited to five years. The return to prosperity, coupled with public dissatisfaction with the act, resulted in its repeal in 1803.

The second national bankruptcy act (1841) was also the product of hard times—the great panic of 1837 and the resulting depression. It permitted creditor- and debtor-initiated proceedings and eliminated creditor control of discharge. The act was repealed after eighteen months, as economic conditions improved. The Civil War resulted in the third statute (1867), following the patterns of its predecessors but extending both voluntary and involuntary bankruptcy to moneyed and commercial corporations. The act was repealed in 1878 partly because of abuses by the courts administering it.

During the intervals between federal bankruptcy acts, state laws governed the debtor-creditor relationship. Such laws were limited because of the constitutional grant of power to Congress, were not uniform, and often discriminated against out-of-state creditors. The panic of 1893 rekindled interest in national bankruptcy legislation, and in 1898 Congress enacted a bankruptcy bill drafted primarily for various commercial interests. The act has continued to the present day, and has been amended more than ninety times.

BANKS, EXPORT-IMPORT. Export-import banks of Washington have had as their goal the promotion of U.S. trade that might otherwise be lost because it seemed too risky to appeal to private business. The 1945 Export-Import Bank Act provides that the bank is not to compete with private capital—and at times its activities have, in effect, taken the form of subsidizing some U.S. exports, allegedly to help overcome barriers foreign governments have erected against U.S. imports.

The first Export-Import Bank of Washington was created by executive order and chartered Feb. 12, 1934, to facilitate trade with the Soviet Union; the second, in March 1934, to finance the purchase and minting of silver for Cuba. In June 1936 they merged, and on July 31, 1945, became an independent federal agency. The Reconstruction Finance Corporation provided most of its early funds. Trade with the USSR did not materialize, and the bank has chiefly aided Latin America, although China, European countries, and Canada have felt its benefits. It has extended credit for the export of agricultural products to firms seeking to export heavy machinery and railroad equipment and to firms unable to withdraw funds from countries with exchange restrictions.

The federal Treasury now owns all the Export-Import Bank's capital stock, $1 billion. The bank may borrow up to $6 billion from the Treasury on a revolving basis, although debt-ceiling restraints often limit its borrowings. It must get its authorizations annually from Congress. Other sources of funds are private capital markets and its own earnings. Losses have been minor. Theoretically it can support—through loans, guarantees, and insurance—trade to $16.125 billion. In practice, in fiscal 1977 it supported $8.5 billion of exports. From its inception through fiscal 1977 it supported $110 billion in export sales.

BANKS, INVESTMENT. *See* **Investment Banks.**

BANKS, LAND. *See* **Agriculture.**

BANKS, NATIONAL. *See* **Banking.**

BANKS, POSTAL SAVINGS. *See* **Postal Service, United States.**

BANKS, PRIVATE. Historically, private banks are the original form of banking, strictly defined as individuals or partnerships engaged in deposit, exchange, loan, discount, or sale of securities. Like any private business their obligations were originally protected by the personal liability of the individual or partnership. With the growth of social control of business the number of private banks declined. Some states prohibit their operations, and there has been a tendency to subject them to the same control as corporations and curtail the field of their operations. Private banks continued to exist because of a real need for their services, the lack of regulation, and a tradition of personal integrity. Perhaps the most famous house of private bankers has been that of J. P. Morgan.

BANKS, SAVINGS. The first savings bank in the United States was the Provident Institution for Savings in Boston, chartered Dec. 13, 1816. The Philadelphia Savings Fund Society was chartered on Dec. 2, but did not begin business until Feb. 25, 1819. Between 1816 and 1820 ten mutual savings banks were chartered in the Northeast. By 1914 there were 634, with nearly 8 million depositors and $4 billion in savings. By the end of 1979 there were 463 in eighteen states, still chiefly in the Northeast, with $158 billion in deposits.

After the Civil War stock savings banks were organized. Their number reached 1,529 by mid-1915 and declined to 341 in 1935, with $700 million in deposits. The Postal Savings System, founded in 1910 largely to serve immigrants, accepted savings at the post office but deposited them in savings banks; it experienced a temporarily rapid growth during the early 1930's when so many banks were failing. Its peak was 1947, with 4.2 million depositors and more than $3 billion in deposits. By mid-1965 it had only 1 million depositors, totaling $344 million. It was then outdated, since the Federal Deposit Insurance Corporation gave depositors adequate protection and other institutions paid higher interest rates. Congress terminated the system in March 1966.

Both state-chartered and national savings banks offer customers savings account service and are the most important form of savings institution. Time deposits totaled $674 billion in 1979. Savings and loan associations have given both savings and commercial banks severe competition: since 1929 their "deposits"—actually shares in the association—have grown from $6.2 billion to $470 billion, in 1979.

BANKS, WILDCAT. *See* **Banking.**

BANNOCK. A Great Basin tribe speaking a language of the Shoshonean branch of the Uto-Aztecan linguistic family, the Bannock ranged from southeastern Idaho west into the Snake River region in Idaho and east into Wyoming. Divided into small bands, the tribe moved widely, gathering wild seeds and insects and sometimes massing for communal rabbit and antelope hunts. When first contacted, some had assimilated Plains traits by virtue of the presence of horses, but did not adopt the Plains war pattern. Their small population was reduced early by smallpox and reservation confinement.

BANNOCK WAR (1878). One of the last major uprisings among American Indians in the Pacific Northwest. Threat of starvation impelled the Bannock to leave the Fort Hall Reservation in Idaho to find sustenance through gathering and hunting. They found the hogs of settlers rooting up the camass bulbs upon which they relied heavily for food, and under the leadership of Buffalo Horn, they began to attack settlers. Pursued by troops under Gen. O. O. Howard, the Indians suffered heavy losses, scattered in small groups, and gradually drifted back to the reservation.

BAPTIST CHURCHES. The Baptist movement originated in two strands of 17th-century English Puritanism: the Separate Puritan Congregation of John Smith and Thomas Helwys established in Holland in 1608, and the Particular Baptists, who separated from Henry Jacob's Southwark congregation in England in 1638. The latter was strongly related to Calvinist doctrine and to Non-Separating Congregationalist understanding of the church.

In the United States, Roger Williams helped establish the first Baptist congregation in Providence, R.I. (1639). The center of the Baptist movement was in the Middle Colonies, where the Philadelphia Baptist Association (1707) united churches from Virginia to Massachusetts. The Great Awakening led to the Ketochten Association in Virginia (1765) and the Warren Association in Rhode Island (1767).

In 1814, the Baptists established a General Convention to support the missionary work of Adoniram Judson in Burma. Others were established to handle publications and home missions. These were charitable organizations to which congregations voluntarily subscribed.

The Baptist churches split in 1845, largely over slavery. The Southern Baptist Convention adopted a more denominational pattern and empowered the central body to act semiautonomously. This centralizing tendency has continued until the late 1970's, when the actual polity of the church could be described as semipresbyterian. The Baptists in the North moved more slowly toward a centralized denominational organization and relied on the voluntary society model until 1907, when the Northern Baptist Convention was formed, becoming the American Baptist Convention in 1950 and the American Baptist Churches in the U.S.A. in 1973.

The Afro-American Baptists increased after the Civil War because of racial discrimination. In 1880, the National Baptist Convention of America was formed. This influential group split in 1907, the larger faction becoming the National Baptist Convention, U.S.A., Inc.

Tensions caused by modern trends in theology have plagued all Baptist groups. The Northern Baptists have split twice (1932, 1947), and the Southern Baptists have sacrificed several seminary professors to maintain unity. In the opinion of many Baptist theologians, these quarrels have seriously weakened the Baptist churches' capacity to bear witness to their distinctive beliefs: religious liberty, independence of the local congregation, and the doctrine of soul liberty. Most Baptists hold a theology derived from the Evangelical Calvinism of the 18th century. Although Baptists have adopted confessions of faith, these have been regarded as noncompulsory summaries of principles.

There are twenty-six Baptist denominations in the United States as well as many independent congregations. Approximately 95 percent of all Baptists belong to eight organizations: Southern Baptist Convention, 13 million members; National Baptist Convention, U.S.A., Inc., 6.3 million members; National Baptist Convention of America, 2.6 million members; American Baptist Churches in U.S.A., 1.2 million members; National Primitive Baptist Convention, 250,000 members; Conservative Baptist Association of America, 220,000 members; General Association of Regular Baptist Churches, 240,000 members, and Free-Will Baptists, 230,000 members.

BAR ASSOCIATION, AMERICAN. *See* **American Bar Association.**

BARATARIA. A bay, village, and bayou on the Gulf Coast of Louisiana inseparably connected in history and legend with the smuggling operations of Jean and Pierre Laffite, who maintained headquarters there from 1810 to 1815. Though regarded as pirates by the United States, the Laffites claimed to operate as privateers under letters issued by the Republic of Cartagena (now part of Colombia), which had declared its independence from Spain in 1810.

BARBARY WARS. Tripolitan War (1801–05). After the Revolution the United States, following the example of European nations, made annual payments to the Barbary states (Morocco, Algiers, Tripoli, and Tunis) for unmolested passage along North Africa's Barbary Coast. Constant difficulties ensued, and in 1801 Tripoli declared war and seized several American vessels. The war, entirely naval except for the Derna expedition, was feebly prosecuted until 1803, when Commodore Edward Preble was sent out with the *Constitution, Philadelphia,* and several brigs and schooners. After a naval demonstration before Tangiers, Preble set up a strict blockade of Tripoli. On Oct. 31, 1803, the *Philadelphia* ran on a reef and was captured. On Feb. 16, 1804, Lt. Stephen Decatur and his men recaptured and burned it. During August and September, Preble harassed the Tripolitan shipping and fortifications. On Sept. 4, the *Intrepid*, with a cargo of gunpowder and shells, was maneuvered into the harbor at night. Apparently the explosion occurred prematurely, for all participants were killed and little damage was done to Tripolitan shipping. New commanders were sent periodically, and by spring the Bey of Tripoli was ready to conclude peace, partly due to the success of the Derna expedition, which was threatening to march on Tripoli. The treaty (June 4, 1805) abolished all annual payments, but provided $60,000 ransom for the men of the *Philadelphia.*

War with Algiers (1815). Although payments were continued to the other Barbary states, the absence of American naval vessels preceding the War of 1812 encouraged Algiers to seize American merchantmen. Immediately after the determination of the war, Decatur, now a commodore, was ordered to the Mediterranean. By June 1815, forty days after his departure from New York, Decatur had captured the Algerian flagship *Mashuda* and secured a treaty—no future payments, restoration of American property, emancipation of Christian slaves escaping to American men-of-war, civilized treatment of prisoners of war, and $10,000 for a merchantman recently seized. As Tunis and Tripoli were forced to equally hard terms and an American squadron remained in the Mediterranean, the safety of American commerce was assured.

BARBECUE. Outdoor entertainment distinguished by the serving of meat cooked, often as whole carcasses, on racks over open pits of coals. Apparently originating in Virginia about 1700 in connection with local fairs, the barbecue was especially popular on the southwestern frontier.

BARBED WIRE. Following various patents on barbed wire (twisted wire with coiled barbs), in 1873 Joseph F. Glidden, a prairie farmer of Illinois, gave it commercial practicability and the next year sold the first piece. Factories developed.

Before the plains were fenced into pastures, cowmen cooperated to build drift fences across long distances. By 1890 most private range land had been fenced. With fencing came wire-cutting "wars" in Texas and elsewhere, but barbed wire revolutionized the whole range industry, cutting off trail driving and free grazing, making improvement of breeds and watering of the range by wells and tanks inevitable.

BARBED WIRE PATENT CASE, 143 U.S. 275 (1892). Settled a long dispute as to patent rights for barbed wire between Joseph Glidden and Jacob Haish. The latter claimed exclusive rights could not be set up because there were various types of barbed wire in use when the Glidden patent was granted. The court decided that Glidden had "taken the final step in the invention which has turned a failure into a [commercial] success."

BARGEMEN. A term used interchangeably with keelboatmen, bargers, and keelers, and applied to men engaged in operating river boats that traveled upstream as distinct from flatboats. French and American bargemen on the Missouri and upper Mississippi rivers were also hunters and trappers. Most full-time bargemen worked on the lower Mississippi and the Ohio River and its tributaries. After 1820 they gradually disappeared as the steamboat, turnpike, and railroad took over transportation.

BARNBURNERS. A progressive faction of the Democratic party in New York State in the 1840's; first called Radicals. The name "Barnburner" was given them as early as 1843, based on the story of the Dutch farmer willing to burn his barn to get rid of the rats. Barnburners opposed further expenditures for canals; wanted a limitation on the state debt and a direct state tax; advocated (and subsequently controlled) a constitutional convention; favored the Wilmot Proviso; and opposed the extension of slavery. They seceded from the state convention of 1847 and the 1848 Democratic National Convention, nominated Martin Van Buren for president, and united with the Free Soilers, defeating Lewis Cass, the Democratic candidate. They gradually returned to the Democratic party, but when the Republican party was formed, most of the younger Barnburners joined.

BARN RAISING. A combination of cooperative labor and social festivity common in frontier days, still surviving in some sections. Before the barn raising, carpenters cut the lumber. On the day of the event, neighboring farmers and their families would assemble. The men erected, with simple tools, the framework of the barn. Prizes were sometimes offered for the greatest feat of strength. Dinner prepared by the women was followed by games, athletic events, and a dance.

BARNSTORMING. In 1815 a theatrical troupe including Noah M. Ludlow was led by Samuel Drake from Albany into the West. They often slept in barns and played in theaters little better than barns, bringing contemporary farce and melodrama as well as Shakespeare and Sheridan to Cincinnati, St. Louis, Nashville, New Orleans, and many smaller frontier centers in the days before railroads. By analogy, itinerant fliers and stunt pilots about 1912–22 were also called barnstormers.

BARNUM'S MUSEUM. In December 1841, P. T. Barnum bought Scudder's American Museum at Broadway and Ann Street, New York. It was enlarged as Barnum's American Museum, exhibiting not only thousands of curios and relics but also living curiosities. There was also a lecture room seating 3,000, in which plays were given. Fire destroyed building and contents, July 13, 1865.

BARRIER FORTS, ATTACK ON (1856). The first use of armed force against China by the United States. On Nov. 15, during intermittent warfare between the Chinese and British, Commander A. H. Foote, in the sloop *Portsmouth* below Canton, was fired upon by the four Barrier Forts. Foote attacked the forts on Nov. 20 with a force of 287 sailors and marines, spiking the guns and blowing up the walls, securing greater safety for Americans trading in China.

***BARRON* V. *BALTIMORE*,** 7 Peters 243 (1833). John Barron, owner of a wharf in Baltimore, Md., contended that the city, by grading and paving streets, had diverted streams from their natural courses toward his facility, causing increased sedimentation that rendered his water too shallow for business. The city had deprived him of property without due process of law, violating the Fifth Amendment. The question was whether or not the specific amendment, and more generally the Bill of Rights, applied to state and local authority. Chief Justice John Marshall dismissed the case in a unanimous opinion of the Supreme Court, concluding that the Bill of Rights restrained the federal government alone and was not binding on the states. Subsequent Supreme Court rulings have modified this decision.

BARTER. The exchange of goods without using money, such as obtaining furs from Indians for beads, liquor, and firearms. As people on the frontier usually lacked money they bartered horses, farms, tobacco, wool, and rice. Barter is also involved in transactions carried on in terms of money but which utilize goods for part of the payment. Many real-estate deals are of this nature.

BARTLETT'S EXPLORATIONS. As U.S. commissioner on the Mexican boundary question, John Russell Bartlett made explorations in 1850–53 into Texas, New Mexico, California, and adjacent Mexican states. Scientists accompanied the party, and the results were published with interesting illustrations in 1854.

BASCOM, FORT. Established on the Canadian River in New Mexico in 1868 by Gen. George W. Getty under Gen. Philip H. Sheridan's orders, to protect the frontier against the Cheyenne, Kiowa, Comanche, and Arapaho.

BASEBALL. The early history of the national pastime is a farrago of mythology, unsubstantiated facts, and rampant sentimentality. All experts agree, however, that a game in which a bat, ball, and bases were used was being played throughout the United States during the early 19th century.

One myth is that the game was "invented" in 1839 by Abner Doubleday in Cooperstown, N.Y., where the National Baseball Hall of Fame and Museum was built in 1939. But baseball scholars have demonstrated that Doubleday had nothing to do with the game's beginnings or development. In any event, in 1845, a group of New York City sportsmen organized the Knickerbocker Baseball Club and drew up a set of rules. For the next few years baseball was played almost exclusively in and around New York City by the Knickerbockers and other teams composed of gentlemen sportsmen.

During the decade preceding the Civil War several clubs were organized in the larger cities of the Northeast, composed of players from all walks of life. By 1860 more than 50 clubs belonged to the National Association of Baseball Players; several played regular schedules and charged admission. The Civil War broke up the clubs but long before Appomattox baseball had become the most popular game among the troops. A short time after the war more than 200 clubs were members of the National Association. It would be at least another twenty-five years before the game was standardized.

Baseball soon became a business enterprise. The first all-professional team was the Cincinnati Red Stockings. Other professional teams were formed, but their success was jeopardized by bribery, gambling, and lack of organization. The clubowners quickly recognized the advantages of monopoly over unregulated competition and of organization over chaos. In 1876, teams from eight cities established the National League of Professional Baseball Clubs, introduced regularly scheduled games, and formulated and codified most of the current rules.

During the next half-century professional baseball became a complex, ingeniously organized industry dominated by the major-league clubowners. As early as 1882, the American Association was organized under rules set down by the National League. Minor leagues were established. The structure was completed with the formulation of the American League in 1901 and the establishment of the World Series in 1903.

Aside from practice games in spring training, the two major leagues have confined their rivalry to the World Series and All-Star games. In 1905 both leagues agreed to rules that regularized and institutionalized the World Series. Despite wars, depressions, and acts of nature, the World Series has been played every autumn since 1905 with the championship going to the winner of four games, except in the years 1919–21 when the title went to the team that won five games. The All-Star Game is played in midseason between teams of the outstanding representatives of both leagues.

Jackie Robinson broke the color line in organized baseball, playing for the Montreal Royals in the International League in 1946 and the Brooklyn Dodgers in the National League in following years. Television, while making new fans, did not necessarily create new customers, and it all but wrecked the minor leagues (in 1980 there were only eighteen minor leagues, as compared to fifty-nine in the late 1940's).

Despite changes in popular tastes and customs, professional baseball has remained not only a business but also a monopoly. After the formation of a new league was announced in 1959, organized baseball absorbed some of its potential competitors and expanded each league from eight to ten teams. The owners established new teams and shifted franchises to areas where it was hoped there were more paying customers, a larger television audience, and local officials willing to build new baseball parks. By 1980 the National League consisted of twelve teams and the American League of fourteen. At the same time, the owners had to contend with a players' union, which in April 1972 conducted a thirteen-day strike that forced the postponement of the regular opening of the season. The players, moreover, continued to agitate for an alteration in the "reserve clause," which bound a player to his club until he retired or was traded. In 1973 the players and the owners came to an agreement to have an outside arbitrator to hear grievances, and in 1975 the arbitrators ruled in the case of Andy Messersmith and Dave McNally that they were "free agents," baseball veterans who can refuse to sign a contract and then enter the free-agent draft. This system resulted in huge salary increases; in late 1981, several free agents signed contracts worth more than half a million dollars a year. The free-agent compensation led to the first midseason strike of major-league baseball players in June and July 1981. During the fourty-nine-day strike 712 games were canceled and major-league cities lost millions of dollars in business revenues.

BASKETBALL. The only major sport of wholly American origin, basketball was invented in 1891 by James Naismith, a physical education instructor at the Springfield, Mass., Young Men's Christian Association (YMCA) Training School. Having been forced indoors by cool weather, students balked at the dull exercises and gymnastics. Naismith devised a game that forbade running with the ball and tackling, discouraged high-velocity throwing, and allowed each participant to share in ball handling and scoring.

Naismith's first game was a success; within months, basketball was being played at other YMCA's, which began to form leagues in 1893. Women quickly took up the game. Smith and Vassar pioneered in college women's basketball, and Geneva College (Pa.), Mount Union College (Ohio), and the University of Iowa introduced the sport to male students in 1892. Intercollegiate leagues began forming in 1901. Professional, amateur, and industrial teams took form as well as intramural and competitive programs in public and private schools.

The game has become second only to soccer in worldwide popularity, and was introduced into the Olympic Games in 1936; since then the United States has monopolized gold medals in men's basketball except in 1972 when the Soviet Union's team won a disputed victory and in 1980 when the United States boycotted the Olympic games in Moscow.

In 1901 the Amateur Athletic Union (AAU) joined with the Springfield YMCA to form a basketball rules committee to control amateur and industrial teams. In 1908 college rules were drawn up by the National Collegiate Athletic Association (NCAA). The AAU, the YMCA, and the NCAA formed a Joint Basketball Rules Committee in 1915. The

National Basketball Committee of the United States and Canada now meets annually to effect rules changes for collegiate, high school, AAU, and YMCA basketball.

While basketball has been esteemed for its purely recreational values, the game has proved immensely popular as a competitive sport. The YMCA and the AAU sponsored leagues and tournaments from the earliest days of the game. Various promoters held national high school tournaments until the National Federation of State High School Athletic Associations banned them in 1934. College basketball reached big-time status in the 1930's, when air travel began to facilitate intersectional games. The National Association of Intercollegiate Athletics established a tournament in 1937 for small colleges. New York City sportswriters inaugurated the National Invitational Tournament in 1938. In the following year the NCAA held its first tournament; the winner is usually recognized as the national champion. The NCAA since 1957 has sponsored a college-division tournament in addition to the university division.

Professional teams appeared before 1900; a professional National Basketball League was formed in 1898 but lasted only until 1903. Players frequently played for several teams at once, the exclusive contract not becoming common until the 1920's. Early teams enjoyed great success on barnstorming tours, a tradition still carried on by the Harlem Globetrotters, organized in 1927. The National Basketball League (1938) and the Basketball Association of America (1946) merged in 1949 to form the National Basketball Association. This and the American Basketball Association (1967) now dominate professional basketball, regularly replenishing their ranks by organized drafting of outstanding college players.

BASTOGNE. A town in the Belgian Ardennes, scene of an epic defense by American troops during the Battle of the Bulge in World War II. Controlling a vital road network, Bastogne was an obvious goal when German armies on Dec. 16, 1944, launched a surprise counteroffensive. The Allied commander, Gen. Dwight D. Eisenhower, rushed armored and airborne divisions to Bastogne. The Fifth Panzer Army encircled Bastogne Dec. 20, but because the main German objective was to cross the Meuse River to the west, all-out attack was delayed. When the Germans on Dec. 22 demanded surrender, the American commander, Brig. Gen. Anthony C. McAuliffe, responded, "Nuts!" The U.S. Third Army began to drive to Bastogne's relief, and clearing weather enabled American planes to drop supplies. Although the Germans attacked strongly on Christmas Day, the defenses held; on Dec. 26 American tanks broke the siege. For a week the Germans tried to take the town. The defenses held, and on Jan. 3, 1945, the Third Army began eliminating the "bulge" the Germans had created in American lines.

BATAAN-CORREGIDOR CAMPAIGN. A few hours after the attack on Pearl Harbor, Dec. 7, 1941, Japanese air units from Taiwan attacked Clark Field to destroy American air power in the Philippines. Major landings by Lt. Gen. Masaharu Homma's army on Manila on Dec. 22 and 24 caught forces under Gen. Douglas MacArthur in a trap on the Bataan peninsula. His retreat was skillful. On Jan. 9, MacArthur's largely Filipino reservist army, backed up by American and Filipino Scout regulars, retreated to a secondary line and then held. By February Homma's attack had been defeated, but MacArthur's men were gravely short of supplies. A tight Japanese blockade had isolated the Philippines. In early March MacArthur broke through the blockade by PT boat to escape to Australia. On Apr. 9, 1942, Bataan surrendered; later many hundreds perished on the march to prison camps in central Luzon.

Corregidor, a fortress island in Manila Bay, held out for three weeks more under Gen. Jonathan M. Wainwright. Japanese artillery and aircraft bombarded the island, forcing thousands to take shelter in tunnels. On May 5–6 Japanese troops gained a foothold, inducing Wainwright to surrender.

BATEAU. A keelless, flat-bottomed, sharp-ended craft, built of plank and propelled by oars, setting poles, or square sails and steered by oar or rudder. Large bateaux employed eighteen or twenty rowers and carried forty tons or more. Missouri bateaux were often called Mackinaw boats. Bateaux were superseded on the Ohio and Mississippi rivers before 1800 by keelboats.

BATHTUBS AND BATHING. The first mention of bathtubs in the United States dates to the early 1820's. The most advanced installation took place in Philadelphia between 1832 and 1837 when the Stephen Girard estate built a row of model houses. The water rate for a bathtub in 1836 was $36.00 per year. In that year, despite an effort to ban them on sanitary grounds, Philadelphia had 1,530. In 1845 Boston made their use unlawful except on the advice of a physician. By 1860 most first-class New York hotels had bathtubs. The "rain bath" was introduced in the mid-19th century.

BATON ROUGE (La.). Capital city of Louisiana since 1849, located on the Mississippi River. Founded by the French about 1720 as a military and trading post, it became English in 1763, Spanish in 1783, French again in 1800, and was claimed by Spain at the time of the Louisiana Purchase (1803). After the West Florida Revolution in 1810 it was annexed to the United States. In 1822 the city became the site of the U.S. military post and arsenal for the southwestern district until 1877, except during a part of the Civil War.

During the 20th century Baton Rouge became an industrial center. Standard Oil Company built a huge refinery in 1909, attracted by its river port and the nearby oilfields. The city was an important synthetic rubber center during World War II. The population was 219,486 in 1980.

BATON ROUGE, BATTLE OF (Aug. 5, 1862). To regain control of the lower Mississippi, the Confederates planned to recapture Baton Rouge, La. Confederate Gen. John C. Breckinridge's forces were to be supported by the ironclad ram *Arkansas.* He attacked the town from the east and forced the Union troops to the levee, where their gunboats protected them. Unsupported by the *Arkansas,* which had broken down, Breckinridge withdrew.

BATON ROUGE, SEIZURE OF (September 1810). Baton Rouge, on the Mississippi River, was in a portion of Spanish West Florida to which the United States mistakenly asserted title as a part of the Louisiana Purchase. In September 1810, American settlers in West Florida seized Baton Rouge, organized a convention, declared their independence of Spain, and invited the United States to annex their territory. President James Madison promptly gave orders for the occupation of West Florida as territory belonging to the United States.

BATTELLE MEMORIAL INSTITUTE. Set up in Columbus, Ohio, by the will of steel industry heir Gordon Battelle to encourage creative research and invention, primarily in metallurgy. The institute began operations in 1929 with an endowment of about $3.5 million. Research was carried out exclusively by the staff on behalf of private industry. Battelle provided the model for the modern nonprofit contract research institute. Its endowment permitted institute-sponsored projects, but most research was for specific firms and governments. When helping to develop xerography gave the institute a share in its profits, its resources increased greatly. After World War II, branches were set up in Geneva, Frankfurt, and Richland, Wash. Work in all sciences was developed, and by 1979 Battelle did more than $300 million's worth of research and development annually.

BATTERY. The twenty-one-acre area at the southern tip of Manhattan Island at the confluence of the Hudson and East rivers. Originally fortified by the Dutch; in 1693 the British governor ordered the installation of a supplementary battery of cannon on the rocky island some 300 yards offshore. Construction of the large fort that dominates the park was begun in 1808; after the War of 1812 it was named Fort Clinton. The island was connected to the mainland by a drawbridge; by 1822 landfill had completely connected the two areas. The following year the fort was converted into an auditorium—Castle Garden. The surrounding park had become one of New York's most popular recreation areas. From 1855 to 1890 the building served as the immigration station for New York, and later housed the New York Aquarium. The fort was renamed Castle Clinton National Monument in 1946 and restored to its 19th-century appearance.

BATTLE FLEET CRUISE AROUND THE WORLD. Undertaken by order of President Theodore Roosevelt as a demonstration of national strength. Sixteen American battleships sailed from Hampton Roads, Va., bound for San Francisco, on Dec. 16, 1907, by way of Rio de Janeiro and the Strait of Magellan. On May 6, 1908, the fleet reached San Francisco, and sailed on July 7 for Hawaii, New Zealand, Australia, the Philippines, China, and Japan, returning by way of the Suez Canal and the Mediterranean. It reached Hampton Roads on Feb. 22, 1909.

"BATTLE HYMN OF THE REPUBLIC." One of the most popular and inspiring of American patriotic hymns, written by Julia Ward Howe. While in Washington, D.C., in 1861, Mrs. Howe heard soldiers singing "John Brown's Body," the music of which was written by William Steffe about 1852. Remarking that these were poor words for such a glorious tune, she wrote the entire hymn that night. Printed in the *Atlantic Monthly* for February 1862, it at once became popular and spread over the entire country.

BATTLE MONUMENTS COMMISSION, AMERICAN. *See* **Federal Agencies.**

BATTLESHIPS. *See* **Warships.**

BATTLESHIPS, DUMMY. On Feb. 24, 1863, a scow with turret of tar-smeared barrel staves, wooden guns, clay furnace, pork barrel funnel, and ludicrous mottoes on its false paddle box was floated down the Mississippi River by federal seamen, causing Confederates below Vicksburg to destroy the newly captured ironclad *Indianola.* A similar dummy on Feb. 20, 1865, drew fire from Confederate batteries along Cape Fear River.

BATTS-FALLAM EXPEDITION. First recorded crossing of the Appalachian Mountains. The expedition was sent from Fort Henry (site of Petersburg, Va.) in 1671. Led by Capt. Thomas Batts and journalized by Robert Fallam, the party of five, including an Appomattoc Indian chief, crossed the Blue Ridge and Allegheny range and pushed down the valley of the New River to the line of West Virginia.

BAYARD-CHAMBERLAIN TREATY. Drafted at Washington, D.C., Feb. 15, 1888, to clarify the respective powers and rights of Great Britain and the United States in the waters of Newfoundland and adjacent provinces. The new treaty defined U.S. rights in Canadian waters, recognized Canadian jurisdiction in narrow bays, remedied several U.S. grievances, and promised further concessions should the United States remove tariff duties on Canadian fish. The Senate rejected the treaty on Aug. 21, 1888, but in 1910, when the protracted fisheries dispute was arbitrated at The Hague, the substance of several of its provisions appeared in the award against U.S. claims.

BAYARD V. SINGLETON**,** North Carolina Superior Court (1787).The first reported decision under a written constitution overruling a law as unconstitutional. The defendant moved for dismissal according to an act of the legislature which required the courts to dismiss, upon affidavit, suits against persons holding forfeited Tory estates. The court overruled the motion and declared that the constitution of the state gives every man a right to a decision concerning property by jury trial.

BAYNTON, WHARTON AND MORGAN. A firm of Philadelphia merchants that virtually monopolized the rich western trade after the French and Indian War. Before the legal opening of Indian trade, the firm sent the first cargo of goods westward (1765), infuriating Pennsylvanian frontiersmen known as Black Boys, who attacked the pack train and destroyed the shipment. Soon, however, the firm had 600 pack horses and wagons on the road between Philadelphia and Pittsburgh and some 300 boatmen on the Ohio River.

Its unscrupulous business methods and other factors caused the company to enter into voluntary receivership and withdraw completely in 1772. To recoup its losses, with the firm of Simon, Trent, Levy and Franks, it organized the Indiana Company to secure land grants for losses incurred through Indian attacks. Sir William Johnson's ingenious handling of the Indians resulted in the Six Nations ceding to this company 2.5 million acres, now a part of West Virginia. Immediate objections arose, and Wharton and Trent were sent to London to negotiate for the Indiana Company. Here the claims of other groups brought about the formation in 1769 of the Grand Ohio Company, or Walpole Company, in which the Indiana land grant was merged. The outbreak of the Revolution caused this project to collapse.

BAY OF PIGS INVASION (Apr. 17, 1961)**.** The attempt by Cuban exiles—organized, financed, and led by the U.S. Central Intelligence Agency (CIA)—to overthrow the revolutionary regime of Premier Fidel Castro in Havana. The landing of 1,453 men on the swampy southwestern coast of Cuba was a total disaster as the Castro forces captured 1,179 and killed the rest. For the United States and President John F. Kennedy the Bay of Pigs was a bitter political defeat and a monumental failure in a large-scale intelligence enterprise. It inspired the Soviet Union to install missiles with nuclear warheads in Cuba the following year, leading to the most dangerous postwar crisis between Washington and Moscow. In December 1962, Castro released the 1,179 Bay of Pigs prisoners in exchange for $53 million worth of medical supplies and other goods.

BAYONNE DECREE. *See* **Napoleon's Decrees.**

BAYOU. In the South, especially in the Mississippi River delta region of Louisiana and Mississippi, numerous bays, creeks, sloughs, and small elongated lakes are called bayous. The word is more specifically used to distinguish the sluggish or stagnant offshoots of rivers that meander through the marshes or alluvial lowlands.

BAYOU TECHE EXPEDITION. A Union raid in April and May 1863, from Brashear City (Berwick Bay) to Alexandria, La., on Red River, to disperse the Confederate state government at Opelousas and thus prevent Confederate reinforcements from being sent to Vicksburg, then besieged by Gen. Ulysses S. Grant.

BAY PATH. A trail from the Connecticut River to Massachusetts Bay at or near Boston. The same trail from the bay to the Connecticut River would be the Connecticut Path. Some writers reserve the name Bay Path for such a trail in Massachusetts and that of Connecticut Path for one in Connecticut. There seems no question that from 1648 there was a route known as the New Path westward through Weston and Brimfield to Springfield. After 1683 another path ran southwestward from the vicinity of Boston to Woodstock, Conn., and thence westward to Hartford. Some claim that the second route was the Old Path used by the Thomas Hooker party in 1636 and by the other early colonists.

BAY PSALM BOOK**.** A hymnal used in Massachusetts Bay Colony, and the earliest book known to have been printed in the United States. Begun in 1639 and finished in 1640, it was printed in Cambridge, Mass., as *The Whole Booke of Psalmes* by Stephen Daye, the first printer of the English colonies. Eleven copies are known to exist.

BEALL'S RAID ON LAKE ERIE (Sept. 19, 1864). John Beall, a Confederate acting master in the navy, seized the steamer *Philo Parsons* on Lake Erie in an attempt to capture the Union revenue cutter *Michigan* and free Confederate prisoners on Johnson's Island, at the entrance to Sandusky Bay, Ohio. The plot failed when Beall's men revolted. He was captured three months later, tried, and executed.

BEAR FLAG REVOLT (1846)**.** Unlike American residents of Monterey and Los Angeles, those of northern central California formed a community by themselves. Restive under Mexican rule and overanxious to assert their "racial superiority," they feared the California authorities would completely control them. They believed the government planned to seize and expel all foreigners in the province.

When the news came (later proved false) that 250 Californians were advancing on Sacramento, the Americans immediately repaired to John C. Frémont's quarters at the Marysville Buttes. Next they seized a large band of government horses being driven to San José by way of Sutter's Fort and captured Sonoma, the chief stronghold of the Californians north of the Bay Region.

Then followed the erection of the Republic of California under William B. Ide. William Todd designed a flag from unbleached cloth five feet long and three feet wide. Facing a red star was a grizzly bear, which gave both the flag and the republic their familiar name. Before the new government could get under way, Commodore John D. Sloat reached Monterey, claiming California for the United States. On July 9, 1846, the American flag replaced the bear flag.

BEAR HUNTERS AND BEAR STORIES. When Lewis and Clark in 1806 returned from their historic expedition into the Far West, they published accounts of the grizzly bear and its ferocity. The grizzly is especially ferocious when cornered, and often imagines itself cornered when it is not. Stories of hand-to-hand fights with grizzlies and of fights between bulls and grizzlies became an enduring part of American lore. The discovery of the grizzly increased the fame of the more widespread black bear, known indeed to have killed a few men. Bear hunters became folk heroes as distinct as keelboatmen or Indian fighters. Although by 1925 the grizzly came dangerously close to extinction, it lives on in national parks.

BEAR PAW MOUNTAINS BATTLE (Oct. 1–5, 1877)**.** At the end of their long campaign the Nez Perce under Chief Joseph were surrounded by Gen. Nelson A. Miles's command in the Bear Paw Mountains of northern Montana. After a brave resistance, Joseph surrendered, ending the Nez Perce War.

BEAR RIVER. Site in California of gold deposits found in July 1848, six months after the strike at John Sutter's mill.

BEAR RIVER, BATTLE OF (Jan. 29, 1863). Utah Indians, among the more peaceful of American Indians, had occasionally preyed upon Mormon settlers and emigrants on the overland mail route. To subdue and control the Indians Col. Patrick E. Connor led his troops to Bear River. With scarcely 200 effectives, he fought four hours against 300 well-armed Indians, smashing their villages, capturing their animals and stores, and killing over 200 of them. His own loss was 15 killed and 48 wounded.

BEAUBIEN LAND CLAIM. An effort to homestead a portion of the Fort Dearborn military reservation at Chicago. Jean Baptiste Beaubien had long lived on the tract as a trader, and in 1835 entered some seventy-five acres of it at the land office. A prolonged legal contest ended in rejection by the U.S. Supreme Court in 1839.

BEAUFORT (S.C.). Second permanent settlement in South Carolina, founded by the British in 1711 on Port Royal Island. First visited in 1521 by the Spanish, early attempts at settlement were made by the French (1562), English (1670), and Scots (1684). The city remains a port of entry. Preservation of colonial buildings and other historic landmarks have made Beaufort a tourist center. The population in 1980 was 8,634.

BEAUHARNOIS, FORT. French post and Jesuit mission, erected in 1727 on Lake Pepin in Minnesota to keep the Sioux from attacking France's new line of communication between Lake Superior and the West and to prevent the Sioux from allying with the Fox Indians. Abandoned about 1728.

BEAVER DAM CREEK, BATTLE OF. *See* **Mechanicsville, Battle of.**

BEAVER DAMS, BATTLE OF (June 24, 1813). Col. C. G. Boerstler with a detachment of about 600 men left Fort George, near Niagara, N.Y., under orders to march to the De Cou house above Beaver Dams to disperse James Fitzgibbon's British irregulars and Indians. Fitzgibbon was warned and ambushed the Americans a little east of Beaver Dams. After two hours of fighting, the Americans surrendered.

BEAVER HATS. Men's beaver hats were imported until about the middle of the 17th century. Once begun, hat manufacture in America grew rapidly. By 1731 hatmakers of London were complaining. In 1732 Parliament forbade American makers to export hats, even among the American colonies. New England calmly ignored or evaded the law. Silk hat manufacture began in earnest about 1835 and the beaver hat diminished in popularity.

BEAVER MONEY. Lack of currency in the Pacific Northwest led to private gold coinage called beaver money because a beaver was pictured on each coin (1849). Illegal but useful, they quickly disappeared from circulation because they contained 8 percent more gold than U.S. coins.

BEAVER TRADE. *See* **Fur Trade.**

BECKNELL'S EXPEDITIONS. William Becknell, the "father of the Santa Fe Trail," left Franklin, Mo., for Santa Fe, N.Mex., June 10, 1821, on a trading expedition. He is believed to be the first American merchant to reach the New Mexican capital after the establishment of Mexican independence. After a profitable trade he returned to Missouri in January 1822. Later in the year he departed from the regular trail along the Arkansas River by crossing the Cimarron River, thus tracing out the Santa Fe Trail, and using wagons on the plains for the first time.

BEDFORD, FORT. Fort Raystown, Pa., built about 1750, was enlarged and strengthened during the French and Indian War. Renamed Fort Bedford (1759), it was the main depot for supplies and troops between Carlisle and Fort Pitt. The fort withstood a six weeks' siege during Pontiac's conspiracy, but in 1769 was bloodlessly yielded to James Smith's Black Boys. It was abandoned before the Revolution.

BEDFORD-STUYVESANT. A section of Brooklyn in New York City; core area of the largest contiguous Afro-American ghetto in the United States. Most of the 722,816 blacks residing in Brooklyn in 1980 lived in Bedford-Stuyvesant and adjoining areas, traditionally bounded by Washington Avenue, Myrtle Avenue, Broadway, and Atlantic Avenue.

During the late 19th century, Bedford and Stuyvesant were neighboring but distinct sections, overwhelmingly white and middle class. After World War I, blacks began moving in, in considerable numbers. By 1950 more than half the section's population was black and 61 percent of Brooklyn's blacks were concentrated there.

The political success of black Americans in Bedford-Stuyvesant began with the election of Bertram Baker to the state assembly in 1948. Shirley Chisholm's election to the U.S. House of Representatives in 1968 was a major advance.

BEDINI RIOTS. Public demonstrations against the papal nuncio, Monsignor Gaetano Bedini, in Cincinnati, Ohio. On Dec. 31, 1853, a mob marched to the cathedral rectory, but was dispersed after one citizen and one policeman had been injured fatally. On Jan. 14, 1854, an effigy of Monsignor Bedini was burned and threats were made against the Catholic clergy and churches.

BEECHER ISLAND, BATTLE OF (1868). Col. George A. Forsyth, leading fifty scouts in search of pillaging Indians, encamped on the Arikaree River south of Wray, Colo. Attacked by about 1,000 Cheyennes and Sioux, the scouts moved onto Beecher Island. The Indians made several unsuccessful charges, then settled to a siege. Despite wounds and five deaths, the scouts held on. Emissaries eluded the Indians at night, and on the ninth day troops arrived.

BEECHER'S BIBLES. Applied to Sharps rifles during the Kansas struggle between free-state and proslavery elements. In 1856, at New Haven, Conn., Henry Ward Beecher addressed a meeting at which a subscription was taken to equip a company of free-state emigrants to Kansas. He said that for slaveholders in Kansas a Sharps rifle was a greater moral argument than a Bible; the emigrants were, therefore, equipped with rifles.

BEEF TRUST CASES. In 1902 three large meat packers—Swift, Armour, and Morris—formed the National Packing Company to secure control of packing houses in Kansas City, East St. Louis, and Omaha. The government charged monopolistic practices. In 1905 the Supreme Court upheld the government charges for the most part, but failed to order dissolution of the company. The government sought an injunction, but the packers pleaded immunity because they had previously testified against themselves. In 1920, after Federal Trade Commission investigation, the packers agreed to dispose of varied stockyard interests, retail meat markets, and the wholesaling of lines not directly related to meat packing.

BEEKEEPING. The honeybee, *Apis mellifera,* is not native to North America. The common black bees of Europe were imported to Virginia in 1621, followed by Italian, Egyptian, Cyprian, Tunisian, Carniolan, and Caucasian strains.

Rev. Lorenzo L. Langstroth, of Andover, Mass., is the father of American beekeeping. His utilization of the ⅜-inch space between combs made possible development of the modern movable-frame hive (1852), which, with minor modifications, is still being used. The publication of books by Langstroth and by Moses Quinby in 1853 marked the real beginning of beekeeping in the United States. Their contributions led ultimately to a new industry: the wax foundation, the bee smoker, the honey extractor, and techniques of queen production revolutionized beekeeping. The American Bee Association (1860) was the first national organization of beekeepers. In 1980 there were two: the American Beekeeping Federation and the Honey Industry Council of America.

BEEKMAN PATENT. A tract sixteen miles square in Dutchess County, N.Y., embracing the present towns of Beekman, Union Vale, a portion of La Grange, and nearly all of Pawling and Dover, granted to Col. Henry Beekman on Apr. 22, 1697, by the British governor.

BEER. *See* **Brewing.**

BEES. A social gathering combining work, pleasure, and often competition. In the New England and middle colonies and on the frontiers, communal activities formed an important exception to the individualistic habits of American farm families. Machinery and specialized labor ended these practices except for the threshing ring, which continues where farms are not large and farming is diversified. Corn husking, barn raising, log rolling, cradling, threshing among men, sewing, quilting, apple paring among women, roused the competitive spirit, made sport of work, and gave recognition to champion workers. Courting opportunities were afforded the young people. Educational counterparts were spelling bees and ciphering matches. Maple sugaring-offs in the North, cane sorghum boilings in the South, and roundups in cattle country were adaptations of the same principle.

BEET SUGAR. Four small beet sugar factories were constructed in the United States between 1838 and 1856, but all failed. The first successful one was established by E. H. Dyer at Alvarado, Calif., in 1870 and operated through 1967. During the 1870's Maine and Delaware offered a bonus for beet sugar manufacture, and factories were built at Portland and Wilmington. Portland inaugurated the practice of contracting with farmers for a specific acreage of beets raised from seed furnished by the company. This plan has persisted to the present. Production has tended to concentrate in irrigated areas in the West.

By 1910 more beet than cane sugar was produced in the continental United States; in 1920 the output exceeded 1 million tons; and in 1978 it was about 3 million short tons, about 30 percent of the sugar consumed in the United States.

Beginning in the 1930's, machines for planting, cultivating, and harvesting beets were developed. Adoption was hastened by shortages of hand labor during the war and by postwar prosperity. The United States has protected its sugar industry by tariffs and other means since 1803. Since 1934 the secretary of agriculture has determined requirements and assigned quotas to U.S. and foreign production areas.

BELGIAN RELIEF. The means by which some 7.3 million Belgian civilians, inside the German army lines during World War I, received necessary food through the Allied blockade. Created in October 1914 by a group of Americans with government approval, the Commission for Relief in Belgium (CRB) became the neutral channel through which more than 5.1 million tons of provisions and supplies passed into Belgium. From 1915 some 1.8 million French civilians in occupied northern France were included. Relief requirements were met by gifts amounting to $52 million in cash and kind collected in the United States, the British Empire, and elsewhere; by British and French government subsidies totaling $314 million; and by U.S. government loans of $380 million made to Belgium and France in 1917–19.

BELKNAP, FORT. Built in 1850 on the Salt Fork of the Brazos River in central Texas to afford frontier protection and to guard the Lower Indian Reserve set aside by Texas. Tribes on the reserve were the Caddo, Anadarkho, Waco, Tahwaccaro, and Tonkawa. Named for Gen. William Goldsmith Belknap.

BELKNAP SCANDAL. One of the scandals of President Ulysses S. Grant's second administration. Cora Le Roy Belknap, first wife of Secretary of War William W. Belknap, secured a lucrative post tradership at Fort Sill for John S.

Evans, reportedly receiving $6,000 per year for this service. After her death it was alleged that the money was paid to Secretary Belknap. On Mar. 2, 1876, the House of Representatives voted unanimously to impeach the secretary and Belknap resigned. He was acquitted on grounds that the Senate had no jurisdiction over a resigned officer.

BELLEAU WOOD, BATTLE OF (June 6–21, 1918). One of the first sizable offensive battles of World War I, fought by the American 2nd Division led by Maj. Gen. Omar Bundy against the German 7th Army approaching the Marne at Château-Thierry. Against bitter resistance the Americans recaptured Bouresches, Vaux, and La Roche Wood. Nearly 8,000 Americans were killed, wounded, or missing. Approximately 1,600 German prisoners were taken.

BELLEFONTAINE. The first permanent English-speaking settlement in the Old Northwest. "La belle fontaine" was a spring located south of the present town of Waterloo, Ill. The first settlers, mainly veterans who had served with George Rogers Clark, established themselves in 1779. At an election in 1782 fifteen Americans voted. In 1800 it was the third largest settlement in the Illinois Territory. As Illinois became more populous, Bellefontaine gradually lost its identity.

BELLEFONTAINE, FORT. Built in 1805 on the south side of the Missouri River, four miles from its junction with the Mississippi. It was constructed on low land near Coldwater Creek and named for a spring there. After the flood of 1810 the fort was moved to the top of a nearby hill where it served as military headquarters for the Middle West until the erection of Jefferson Barracks in 1826.

BELLE ISLE. An island in the James River at Richmond, Va., used as a prison by the Confederacy. It held approximately 10,000 men under harsh conditions by the end of 1863. Because the prisoners constituted a drain on the food supply and were the objectives of several cavalry raids, the captives were sent to a new prison at Andersonville, Ga.

BELLEVUE WAR. William W. Brown, owner of a hotel at Bellevue, Jackson County, Iowa, was believed to lead a gang of outlaws. Sheriff William A. Warren attempted to arrest Brown and several other men on Apr. 1, 1840. Four of the posse and three of the alleged bandits (including Brown) were killed, and thirteen of Brown's band captured. Citizens voted for hanging or whipping; the men were flogged and sent down the Mississippi River.

BELL TELEPHONE LABORATORIES. The world's largest and probably best-known institution for organized industrial research. Bell Labs has provided much of the stimulus for an ongoing revolution in telecommunications based on solid-state electronics and information theory. Its prime responsibility is the engineering of the Bell telephone communications network as an integrated system, leading to a wide range of new technologies beneficial to many industries and the federal government in the military area.

Bell Labs was formally organized as a nonprofit corporation in 1925, although the Bell telephone system had supported scientific and engineering research since the 1880's. A succession of fundamental contributions emanated from Bell Labs prior to World War II: Karl G. Jansky's pioneering observations of extraterrestrial radio waves; the work of Harold S. Black on feedback amplifier theory and of George C. Southworth on waveguides; and Clinton J. Davisson's electron diffraction experiments. Fundamental work on noise in electronic circuits by H. Nyquist and J. B. Johnson led to the creation of the information theory by Claude E. Shannon in the 1940's. Bell Labs played a key role in the development of radar during World War II.

The successful development of the transistor (1948) initiated a new era of solid-state electronics, with wide-ranging applications to computers, satellite communications, and consumer goods. Other notable inventions and developments are the coaxial cable, the introduction of Boolean algebra for switching, and the invention of the AND and OR gates in the late 1930's, the latter making possible the digital computer. Further research has been related to development of solar batteries, optical masters, acoustics, magnetic materials, polymer science, and suboceanic and satellite communications. Headquarters are at Murray Hill, N.J.

BELMONT, BATTLE OF (Nov. 7, 1861). Ulysses S. Grant's first Civil War battle and first defeat. Gen. John C. Frémont ordered the attack on Belmont, Mo., to prevent Gen. Leonidas Polk at Columbus, Ky., from aiding the Confederates in Missouri. Steaming from Cairo, Ill., on the Ohio River, Grant landed five miles above Belmont and drove Gen. G. J. Pillow's men to the river and set fire to their camp. Polk, crossing with reinforcements and aided by the Columbus batteries, drove Grant to his transports and retreat.

"BELOVED MAN"/"BELOVED WOMAN." The equivalent terms in American Indian languages of the Southeast reflect an honorable status ascribed to persons because of achievement or birth. Suggested is status ranking, existent in aboriginal times among the Creek, Muskogee, Choctaw, Chickasaw, and Natchez.

BELTRÁN-ESPEJO EXPEDITION (1582–83). An expedition into New Mexico from Santa Barbara (southern Chihuahua) led by Bernardino Beltrán to rescue Franciscan missionaries Augustin Rodríguez and Francisco López. Upon reaching Pueblo country and learning that the missionaries had been killed, Beltrán and his soldiers, including Diego Perez de Luxán and Antonio de Espejo, stayed to explore. Their favorable reports of the country and people strengthened the resolve of secular and religious authorities to colonize New Mexico and evangelize its inhabitants.

BEMIS HEIGHTS, BATTLES OF. *See* **Freeman's Farm, Battles of.**

BENEFIT OF CLERGY. Originally a plea exempting clergy from criminal process; ultimately a commutation of the death sentence in certain felonies for all prisoners who could read, which last requirement was dropped by the 18th century. Statutes abolishing this privilege appear after the Revolution, but until the Civil War it was still used in southern states, sparing a master's valuable property in his slave.

BENNING, FORT. Camp Benning (Fort Benning after 1922) was established near Columbus, Ga., during World War I. By consolidation of the Small Arms Firing School (Camp Perry, Ohio), the Infantry School (Fort Sill, Okla.), and the Machine Gun School (Augusta, Ga.), a model infantry school was established (1920).

BENNINGTON, BATTLE OF (Aug. 16, 1777). British Gen. John Burgoyne planned a raid on the American stores at Bennington, Vt., to encourage Loyalists, frighten New England, replenish his provisions, and mount a regiment of heavily equipped German dragoons. Led by German Col. Frederick Baum, about 800 men—dragoons, Tories, Canadians, Indians, and a handful of English—neared Bennington, where American Gen. John Stark had assembled about 2,600 troops. Despite reinforcements sent by Burgoyne, the Americans won the battle.

BENTON, FORT. After 1830 the American Fur Company established several trading posts near the navigation-head of the Missouri River. One of these, Fort Lewis (1844), was moved in 1846 to the site of the present town of Fort Benton, Mont., where it was renamed in 1850 for Thomas Hart Benton. During the Montana gold rush (1862) Fort Benton became a main port of entry to the mines. A town sprang up around it and the fur company sold out to a mercantile firm in 1865.

BENTONVILLE, BATTLE OF (Mar. 19–21, 1865). Gen. J. E. Johnston and a small Confederate force in North Carolina, hoping to prevent a junction of the Union generals W. T. Sherman and U. S. Grant, attacked the left wing of Sherman's army. Though outnumbered, Johnston succeeded in fighting a drawn battle, but lost at least 2,000 men. By the night of Mar. 21 most of Sherman's army was concentrated at the spot, and Johnston retired.

BENT'S FORT. First known as Fort William, completed by William Bent, his three brothers, and Ceran St. Vrain about 1832, on the north bank of the Arkansas River, some seven miles east of present La Junta, Colo. Bent's Fort participated in both the mountain fur trade and the overland commerce to Santa Fe, becoming the outstanding trading post of the Southwest. The fort was a depot for military expeditions before and during the Mexican War. According to unverified tradition, the government wanted the fort, but offered an inadequate price. Bent thereupon partially destroyed it and deserted it in 1849. Moving forty miles downriver, he erected Bent's New Fort (1853), leased it to the government in 1859, and retired. Renamed Fort Wise and then Fort Lyon, it was moved twenty miles up the river to its present location.

***BEREA COLLEGE* V. *KENTUCKY*, 211 U.S. 45 (1908).** Involved the right of Berea College to teach black and white students at the same time in the same classroom. Kentucky law declared it illegal and the state supreme court upheld the statute. The U.S. Supreme Court dodged the major issue of interracial education and decided the case on narrow grounds involving the right of the state to change or amend the charter of a corporation. It held that the law did not prohibit the teaching of blacks and whites at the same place at different times or at different places at the same time, but provided the states with the means to outlaw interracial education. Such an amendment of the charter of Berea College was held to violate no provision of the Constitution. The decision reinforced and expanded the *Plessy* v. *Ferguson* ("separate, but equal") doctrine (1896).

BERGEN PRIZES. Capt. Pierre Landais of the *Alliance*, an American vessel of John Paul Jones's squadron in European waters, captured three British merchantmen in 1779. When bad weather forced Landais into Bergen, Norway, England requested and obtained restoration of the vessels from the Danish-Norwegian government. Jones demanded indemnification at Copenhagen. After years of negotiation, it was proved that an Anglo-Danish treaty of 1600 obligated Denmark to England. Hence it could not be forced to indemnify the United States. Congress reimbursed Landais in 1806 and the heirs of Jones in 1848.

BERING SEA DISPUTE. *See* **Pelagic Sealing Dispute.**

BERING SEA FISHERIES. *See* **Sealing.**

BERKELEY (Calif.). Home of the University of California; city population of 103,328 in 1980. Was founded as a seminary town and named after the English philosopher, Bishop George Berkeley. It was incorporated in 1878. Some of the most advanced scientific research in the world is conducted at the University of California.

BERLIN, TREATY OF. Separate peace treaty between the United States and Germany, signed Aug. 25, 1921, and proclaimed Nov. 14, entered into after the Senate rejected the Treaty of Versailles. Its provisions merely refer to those of the Treaty of Versailles that are either accepted or rejected by the United States. Provisions thus taken over were those with respect to colonies, disarmament, reparations, and responsibility for the war. The most important features rejected were the League of Nations, the International Labor Organization, and the boundaries provisions.

BERLIN AIRLIFT. History's largest exclusively aerial supply operation. For eleven months (1948–49) American and British planes sustained more than 2 million West Berliners and occupation troops after the Soviet Union blocked surface routes into Berlin. The American commander, Gen. Lucius D. Clay, obtained U.S. government approval for an airlift requiring a minimum of 140,000 tons per month. The Soviets harassed some flights, but stopped short of war. Hurt by reciprocal denial of imports from West Germany, they raised the blockade May 12, 1949, although the airlift continued into September. (*See* Berlin Blockade.)

BERLIN BLOCKADE. The Soviet blockade of Berlin, beginning June 23, 1948, and the responding American-British airlift were the most dramatic of the early cold-war confrontations. Initially seeking West Germany's recovery to promote the economic reconstruction and growth of Western Europe, the United States in early 1948 imposed stringent German currency reforms and moved toward a West German constitution and government. This precipitated the Soviet blockade of the western half of Berlin, to prevent the revival of West German power. Despite the stakes, both powers were unwilling to risk war. After 321 days of successful American and British sustenance of West Berlin's population, the Soviets terminated the blockade.

BERLIN DECREE. *See* **Napoleon's Decrees.**

BERLIN WALL. In 1961 Premier Nikita Khrushchev of the Soviet Union renewed his three-year-old threat to transform West Berlin into a "free city" before that year ended: if the West would not agree, the Soviets would sign a peace treaty with East Germany, abrogate the right of its World War II allies to be in Berlin, and make their further stay dependent upon East German consent. The Soviets hoped this would resolve the problem of a satellite whose population was escaping to West Berlin in ever larger numbers. The United States felt that Western presence and access to the western half of Berlin were nonnegotiable. When on Aug. 13, 1961, the Communists built a wall dividing Berlin, they put an end to the refugee issue. But American inaction left a profound impression of a lack of resolve at a time when many Europeans believed that the distribution of power was turning in favor of the Soviet Union.

***BERMUDA* ADMIRALTY CASE.** During the Civil War, British flag vessels made frequent sailings with war supplies for the Confederacy. Some ships, instead of running the blockade, delivered their cargoes to British islands near the Atlantic coast for delivery to the South. In 1862 the *Bermuda* sailed from Liverpool to St. George's in the Bermudas, and on Apr. 23 allegedly headed for Nassau. Its cargo included artillery, ammunition, small arms, and Confederate uniform insignia and postage stamps. On Apr. 27, some 400 miles from Charleston, S.C., it was captured by the Union.

The federal district court held that evidence proved the ship intended to deliver its cargo either at Nassau or to a Confederate port—by itself or by transshipment. The Supreme Court (Dec. 1865) upheld the lower court: the vessel and cargo, even if neutral, were condemned for the reason that ultimate destination was to ports under blockade (the doctrine of continuous voyage), which justified seizure and condemnation. Further, it was affirmed that such destination equally justified seizure of contraband en route to ports not under blockade.

BERMUDA CONFERENCE (1957). After the deep Anglo-American rift caused by the Suez War in 1956, President Dwight D. Eisenhower and Harold Macmillan, the new British prime minister, met in Bermuda to bring the two allies closer together again. European unity and the continued testing of nuclear weapons were stressed, and the two leaders announced an agreement whereby the United States would supply Britain with intermediate-range missiles.

BERMUDA ISLANDS. A cluster of more than 300 islands 570 miles east of Cape Hatteras, N.C. America has had close contact from the first colonists shipwrecked on their way to Virginia in 1609 to the present. From 1612 to 1615 the islands were included under the Virginia Company charter, but thereafter became a separate company colony and then a crown colony (1684). The settlers concentrated on tobacco, and there was considerable trade with the mainland. The inhabitants opposed British colonial policy and sent delegates to the Continental Congress to secure relief from the trade embargo against loyal colonies. They achieved their end by furnishing gunpowder and other supplies to the rebels. During Prohibition (1919–33) rum smuggling to the United States was highly profitable. In 1941 sites for U.S. naval and air bases were leased. Bermuda is now a popular tourist area, with a permanent population of 54,893 (1980).

BERNARD, FORT. A small trading post between Horse Creek and Fort Laramie in Wyoming on the Oregon Trail. A trappers' trail from Bent's Fort in Colorado joined the Oregon Trail at this post. Taos and Santa Fe traders freighted flour here to trade to emigrants bound for the coast.

BETHABARA. The first town planted (1753) by German Moravians from Pennsylvania in Wachovia, N.C. Its early settlers were noted for advanced agricultural practices, especially their "medicine garden," which produced over fifty kinds of herbs. Bethabara grew slowly and is now only a small village, known locally as Oldtown.

BETHEL COMMUNITY (1844–77). A communist experiment established in Shelby County, Mo., by William Keil and followers (chiefly German) from Ohio and Pittsburgh, Pa. Keil preached moral living, subscribing to no religious faith, and dominated an unincorporated, self-sustaining, orderly, prosperous community that expanded to four towns. Property and labor were shared, though private earnings were allowed. A sister colony was fostered in Aurora, Oreg., in 1855. Both dissolved, dividing their property upon Keil's death in 1877.

BETHESDA HOUSE OF MERCY. An orphanage and school, founded by Rev. George Whitefield, near Savannah, Ga., in 1739. Whitefield died in 1770, and the project faltered before 1800. Savannah's venerable Union Society, sponsor of present Bethesda, revived the orphanage in 1855.

BEVERAGES, NONALCOHOLIC. *See* **Soft Drink Industry.**

BIBLE. That the appearance of the two most widely used early English translations of the Bible was contemporaneous with English colonization of America is of great historical importance. The Genevan Bible, the work of Protestant scholars who had fled to Geneva to escape Catholic Queen Mary's persecutions, was the Puritan's Bible. Even after the appearance of the King James, or Authorized, Version (1611), the Genevan Bible held its own. During the entire colonial period the Bible was first among moral and cultural influences.

No single factor had a larger part in determining what moral direction the nation would take after the Revolution than the widespread distribution of the Bible throughout the West by such agencies as the American Bible Society (1816), the American Tract Society (1825), and the American Sunday School Union (1824). The Bible had an important role in advancing every reform movement in American history—antislavery, temperance, and peace movements. It also gave birth to numerous erratic movements.

Bible reading still exercises a wide influence, as indicated by the fact that the United Bible Societies, a world fellowship of fifty-six societies, distributed over 440 million Bibles, including almost 14 million Testaments in 1980, and the increase of Bible-related publications has not slackened (about 6,000 titles in 1981).

BIBLE COMMONWEALTH. Applied by modern historians to the Puritan colonies of Massachusetts and New Haven, Conn., where the right to vote was limited to church members and an effort was made to bring all activities into harmony with the Bible. This is best illustrated by *An Abstract of the Lawes of New England* . . . (London, 1641), a code prepared by John Cotton which became the basis for the government of the New Haven colony. Insofar as possible, all provisions were supported by marginal scriptural citations.

BIBLES, PRINTING OF. The first book printed in the United States of which any copy survives was the *Bay Psalm Book,* which contained portions of the Bible. The first complete Bible was John Eliot's translation into the Algonkin language printed at Cambridge in 1663. Partly because the printing of the King James Version was an Oxford monopoly, three editions of Martin Luther's Bible in German appeared in America before any were printed in English. Robert Aitken published the first American Bible in English in Philadelphia (1781–82). Isaiah Thomas printed the first Greek New Testament, Worcester (1800). The first printing of the Douay Version (Roman Catholic) was in Philadelphia in 1790.

BICAMERAL LEGISLATURES. Having as their antecedents the British Parliament and colonial legislatures, bicameral legislatures have been used by the national and almost all state governments since the adoption of the Constitution. The pattern prevailed in all states until Nebraska established a unicameral legislature in 1934.

The bicameral legislature was developed to resolve political conflict through compromise. A heterogeneous group of voters selects the members of both chambers. On the national level, the Senate gives equal representation to each state, and the House of Representatives has members apportioned on the basis of each state's population.

In a bicameral legislature, proponents claim, unwise and precipitous legislation is prevented: bills are reviewed more carefully, and checks and balances are promoted, although these assertions remain essentially unproven.

BICYCLING. Bicycles had their first vogue in America in the late 1860's. A decade later Albert A. Pope began importing them from England and later manufacturing them. Chiefly through his efforts, including propaganda for better roads, bicycling became, during the 1880's and 1890's, one of the most popular American sports. For a while it was pushed into the background by motorcycles, automobiles, and the development of golf, tennis, and other outdoor sports. A short revival of interest occurred in the 1930's, but the biggest resurgence occurred in the 1960's and 1970's. Numerous bicycle clubs were started and many cities and parks set aside bicycle paths. Bicycles were used for recreation and transportation to avoid automobile traffic congestion. It is estimated that in the 1970's approximately 75 million people in the United States participated in cycling sports.

BIDDLE MISSION. Charles A. Biddle, sent by President Andrew Jackson to Nicaragua, Guatemala, and Panama to determine expediency of Isthmus of Panama canal negotiations, secured from New Granada (Colombia) a concession (June 22, 1836) for himself and associates to construct a trans-isthmian road or railway, and for steam navigation of the Chagres River. Jackson, infuriated at Biddle's use of the mission to secure a private concession, disclaimed official connection with the affair. Biddle's death (Dec. 21, 1836) saved him a presidential reprimand.

BIDLACK TREATY (Dec. 12, 1846). Benjamin A. Bidlack, American chargé d'affaires in Bogotá, signed a treaty with New Granada (Colombia) removing tariff discrimination against American commerce and guaranteeing neutrality of the Isthmus of Panama and New Granada's rights of sovereignty over the isthmus. On thirteen occasions American troops were landed to protect the transit route. When Panama seceded (Nov. 3, 1903), it was held by the American government that the covenant ran with this land (*see* Hay-Bunau-Varilla Treaty).

"BIG APPLE." A term that gained currency in the 1960's and 1970's to designate New York City. It originated in the 1940's with jazz musicians.

BIG BLACK RIVER, BATTLE AT (May 16–17, 1863). After his defeat at Champion's Hill in Mississippi, Confederate Gen. John C. Pemberton retreated to the Big Black River, hoping to hold the river's bridge long enough for the army to cross before Gen. Ulysses S. Grant could attack. On May 17 Grant's advance troops appeared, and Pemberton was driven in retreat into Vicksburg.

BIG BONE LICK. A salt spring in Boone County, Ky., 1.5 miles east of the Ohio River. The earliest known white man to visit was Capt. Charles Lemoyne, Baron de Longueuil (1729). In 1773 James Douglas, a Virginia surveyor, described the fossils found on the surface: mastodon, Arctic elephant, and other animals of the glacial epochs. In 1803 and 1806 Dr. William Goforth entrusted fossils to the English traveler Thomas Ashe, who sold them to the Royal College of Surgeons in London and to private Irish and Scotch collectors. Thomas Jefferson made a collection, and natural history museums collected the remaining skeletons. Large prehistoric animals were attracted to the lick by the seepage of brine from an underlying basal coal measure. Pioneers found that 500 gallons of this water made one bushel of salt.

BIG BOTTOM MASSACRE (Jan. 2, 1791). Shawnee Indians surprised a new settlement on the Muskingum River in Ohio; stormed the blockhouse; and killed eleven men, one woman, and two children. Three settlers were captured; four escaped. The Ohio Company of Associates immediately provided greater protection for settlers.

BIG BROTHER MOVEMENT. In 1903, a small group of men in Cincinnati, Ohio, agreed to take an interest individually in fatherless boys in that city. The movement was formalized in New York City a year later. At present there are 400 member agencies of a national organization, Big Brothers/Big Sisters of America, formed in 1977 by merger of Big Sisters (dating from 1908) and Big Brothers of America. The headquarters is in Philadelphia, Pa.

BIG HOLE, BATTLE OF (Aug. 9, 1877). During the Nez Perce War, Col. John Gibbon, with volunteers and mounted infantrymen, attacked Chief Joseph's camp on the Big Hole River in Montana. The Nez Perce drove the soldiers back and disabled or killed sixty-nine. Eighty Indians died, over two-thirds women and children.

BIG HORN MOUNTAINS. A range of the Rocky Mountains mainly in north central Wyoming, extending into southern Montana. Discovered in 1743 by Pierre Gaultier de Varennes, Sieur de La Vérendrye; soon frequented by American fur traders. In 1811 crossed by Wilson Price Hunt and the overland Astoria expedition. Site of the Fetterman massacre (1866) and the Battle of the Little Bighorn (1876).

BIG KNIVES (Long Knives). Used by western Indians to designate English colonists; after 1750 restricted to colonists of Virginia. George Rogers Clark spoke of himself and his men as Big Knives in speeches to the Indians in 1778 after the capture of Illinois. From the latter part of the Revolution through the War of 1812, the term designated Americans. The origin is thought to be the steel knives and swords of colonists, contrasted with stone knives of the early Indians.

***BIGLOW PAPERS*.** Originally, nine satirical poems by James Russell Lowell in Yankee dialect directed against the Mexican War which had as their object the acquisition of slave territory. From 1846 to 1848 they spread from newspaper to newspaper. In 1848 Lowell gathered them into a collection, elaborating on them until the original intent was all but lost. To the spokesman Hosea Biglow was added the pundit editor Rev. Homer Wilbur.

Beginning in 1862, Lowell ran in the *Atlantic Monthly* a second series, this time satirizing the South, but the lyrics could not voice the national tragedy. As a result the final collection (1867), with its chaos of embellishment, its beautiful nature poetry, and its long essay on Yankee dialect, is hardly primarily satiric.

BIG MOCCASIN GAP. In extreme southwestern Virginia; admitted Daniel Boone and other pioneers through the Clinch Mountains into Kentucky. Not far from it were the blockhouses, built by Capt. John Anderson in 1777, where parties formed for the journey over the Wilderness Road. The line set by the Treaty of Lochaber (1768) and surveyed by John Donelson in 1770 crossed the road near this gap.

"BIG STICK" POLICY. President Theodore Roosevelt was fond of quoting an African proverb that if you speak softly and carry a big stick, you will go far. The "Big Stick" came to mean the power of the United States, and especially of the U.S. Navy, which Theodore Roosevelt did not hesitate to show off. He used his "Big Stick" to take over and manage the affairs of several Latin American countries and to prevent similar actions by European countries.

BILLETING. Quartering of military troops, a European practice rarely resorted to in America. Increased troop arrivals during the French and Indian War made billeting an issue, beginning in New York and Philadelphia, in 1756. To shelter soldiers, the Mutiny Act of 1765 required colonial governments, when barracks were not available, to billet troops in inns, barns, and uninhabited houses and to furnish certain provisions. Billeting aroused resistance in Charleston (1764), New York (1766), and Boston (1768), and led directly to the Boston Massacre. The Quartering Act of 1774, designed to permit billeting within Boston, had little to do with the final issue, which was already joined. Billeting was objected to in the Declaration of Independence and was prohibited in the Bill of Rights, in the Third Amendment.

BILL OF RIGHTS. The term "bill of rights" does not appear in the U.S. Constitution. It is, however, commonly used to designate the first ten amendments; often includes later amendments affecting rights or liberties, such as the Nineteenth Amendment, granting the right of suffrage to women.

At the constitutional convention in 1787 George Mason proposed that the Constitution be "prefaced with a bill of rights." Elbridge Gerry moved the appointment of a committee, but the motion lost. Accordingly, the Constitution as submitted for ratification contained no bill of rights. It did, however, include some important guarantees of personal rights and liberties: the privilege of the writ of habeas corpus was not to be suspended except in cases of rebellion or invasion; no bill of attainder or ex post facto law was to be passed;

all crimes were to be tried by jury; and no religious test could be required as a qualification to any office.

When the Constitution came before the ratifying conventions, its opponents joined with advocates of a bill of rights. They were answered by Federalists, in particular James Wilson and Alexander Hamilton, who argued that such personal guarantees were unnecessary and dangerous because their inclusion might imply that the federal government had powers that in fact had not been conferred on it. James Madison tended to think along the same line, but in time he was won over to the side that favored a bill of rights. The consequence of the debate over political philosophy and constitutional theory and interpretation was that states sent along with their ratifications more than a hundred amendments they wanted adopted by the new government.

After nearly three months of deliberation (June–August 1789), through a select committee of ten and later with the House itself as a committee of the whole, the House of Representatives proposed seventeen amendments for ratification. The House then forwarded them to the Senate.

The record of the Senate proceedings is extremely meager. It is doubtful that the Senate devoted more than two normal session days to the subject. On Sept. 21 the Senate asked for a conference with the House to straighten out differences. The House reduced its original seventeen amendments to twelve, and these the Senate approved on Sept. 25.

On Nov. 20, 1789, New Jersey became the first state to ratify the amendments; Virginia, on Dec. 15, 1791, was the eleventh, completing the ratification process. On the latter date the Bill of Rights became effective. Two amendments failed of ratification, those on the apportionment of representatives and the compensation of members of Congress.

In some four hundred words, the original Bill of Rights provides—in its more important articles—for freedom of religion, speech, press, and assembly and the right of petition (First Amendment); a guarantee against unreasonable searches and seizures (Fourth Amendment); prohibitions of double jeopardy, of coerced testimony against oneself in any criminal case, of depriving any person of his life, liberty, or property without due process of law, and of the taking of private property for public use without just compensation (Fifth Amendment); the right to a speedy and public trial, the right to be confronted by accusing witnesses, and the right to assistance of counsel (Sixth Amendment); the right to trial by jury (Seventh Amendment); a prohibition against excessive bail or fines and against cruel and unusual punishments (Eighth Amendment). The Ninth Amendment is a statement of the general principle that the provision of certain rights in the Constitution shall not imply the denial of other rights "retained by the people"; and so, too, the Tenth Amendment states that the powers not delegated to the federal government or prohibited to the states are reserved to the states or to the people.

The Supreme Court in 1833 declared that the first ten amendments were adopted to guard against abuses by the federal government and not against encroachments by the states. The first constitutional breakthrough came in *Meyer* v. *Nebraska* (1923), in which the Court declared unconstitutional a state statute that prohibited any school from teaching any subject in a language other than English. The Court's opinion broadly defined the "liberty" protected by the due process clause of the Fourteenth Amendment. And, two years later, in *Gitlow* v. *New York,* the Court said that it would "assume" that freedom of speech and press "are among the fundamental personal rights and 'liberties' protected by the due process clause of the Fourteenth Amendment from impairment by the states."

In subsequent cases decided in the 1930's the Court "assimilated" into the Fourteenth Amendment the First Amendment freedoms of religion and assembly. The Court has not, however, "incorporated" into the Fourteenth Amendment all the guarantees of the first eight amendments. The Court has proceeded slowly and on a case-by-case basis. It was not until 1963 that the Court, overruling a case it had decided in 1942, held that the Sixth Amendment right to counsel was applicable to the states under the due process clause of the Fourteenth Amendment.

BILLS OF CREDIT. Noninterest-bearing government obligations that circulate as money; commonly applied to issues by the colonies and by the Continental Congress and states during the revolutionary war. Bills of credit in the colonies began with an issue of £7,000, shortly increased to £40,000, in Massachusetts in 1690. This was followed by similar action by other colonies. In most cases the bills were issued to excess and depreciated sharply. Parliament prohibited such paper currency in New England in 1751 and in other colonies in 1764. As soon as the colonies broke away from England, they again began to emit bills of credit. The Continental Congress authorized $241,552,780 of bills from 1775 to 1779 inclusive, while various states put out $209,524,776 of bills during the same period. The bills became known as treasury notes or United States notes.

BILLS OF EXCHANGE. Paper orders, usually issued by a company engaged in international trade, to pay out a specified sum of money at some future time and place. They were used in the colonial period for buying and selling of goods in England and other foreign markets. They are still used, but are seldom actually "exchanged" between countries. International trade is frequently carried on by placing bills of exchange with banks in the native country of the businessman who issues the bill. The term is sometimes applied to a bank check used in business within the United States.

BILLS OF RIGHTS, STATE. The bill of rights adopted by Virginia in 1776 was the model for the national Bill of Rights, the first ten amendments of the U.S. Constitution. The Virginia declaration, largely the work of George Mason, was in large part a restatement of English principles drawn from such sources as Magna Carta, the Petition of Right, and the English Bill of Rights. It still stands in practically the original form in the constitution of Virginia.

While other state constitutions have copied the Virginia provisions somewhat, they have added other provisions according to local or contemporary needs. The second great bill of rights, the Declaration of Rights of the Commonwealth of Massachusetts (1780), also remains in force today. The bills of rights in other states show the results of contemporary events and are often more lengthy. Thus, slavery is prohibited in Maryland, Nevada, and almost all southern states, a direct result of the Civil War and Reconstruction.

BILOXI (Miss.). City in Mississippi on the Gulf of Mexico, the first settlement in, and capital of, the Louisiana Territory. Settled by Pierre Lemoyne, Sieur d'Iberville, in 1699, with 200 French colonists, as Fort Maurepas on the Biloxi Bay (near present Ocean Springs). Relocated to the present site in 1719. New Orleans became the capital in 1722. Biloxi was incorporated as a village in 1872 and as a city in 1896. Seafood is its chief industry. Its 1980 population was 43,927.

BIMETALLISM. In 1792 the U.S. Congress followed the world's leading countries in establishing a bimetallic monetary standard under which both silver and gold served as a basis of coinage. This policy was based on the theory offered by Alexander Hamilton, in his *Mint Report*, that under bimetallism there is a more plentiful supply of money. Another reason for bimetallism was the fact that the principle of subsidiary silver coinage (the use of silver alloys for coins of smaller denomination than the currency unit) was unknown, and bimetallism was a necessity if small units of silver were to be coined.

The bimetallic system was a failure. Revision of the legal ratio between the values of gold and silver in 1834 and 1837 created an adequate gold coinage but drove out the limited silver coinage in circulation, since the free-market value of silver was higher than its monetary value. From 1834 on, silver coins as standard money ceased to play a part in the life of the nation. The establishment by Congress of subsidiary silver coinage in 1853 confirmed this situation legally. But the 1853 statute accidentally left the silver dollar as a standard coin, although the market value of silver continued to make its coinage impossible. In a revision of the statutes in 1873 the unknown piece was dropped (*see* Crime of 1873).

In 1873 the world market ratio of silver to gold fell below 16 to 1 for the first time in history. This decline coincided with the opening of rich silver mines in the West, with the post–Civil War deflation, and with a deep depression that sorely afflicted the country (*see* Panic of 1873). The consequence was a political movement, promoted by the silver interests and embraced by agrarian and proinflation elements for the restoration of bimetallism. Eventually there developed in the Senate and less definitely in the House a nonpartisan "silver bloc," led by members from the sparsely populated western states in which mine owners gained great political influence. In the 1870's, 1890's, and 1930's, the efforts of this pressure group, reinforced by the popular clamor for inflation, almost achieved bimetallism and succeeded in extracting from Congress legislation giving a cash subsidy of some sort to the producers of silver (*see* Bland-Allison Act of 1878 and Sherman Silver Purchase Act of 1890).

The depression of the 1930's restored interest in bimetallism, the gold standard, and the money supply. On Apr. 5, 1933, President Franklin D. Roosevelt suspended the gold standard. The Thomas Amendment to the Agricultural Adjustment Act (May 12, 1933) authorized the president to restore bimetallism.

During the 1960's the United States abandoned all but a small vestige of a metallic standard. The acts of Mar. 3, 1965, and Mar. 18, 1968, eliminated the gold reserve against Federal Reserve deposits and Federal Reserve notes. An act of July 23, 1965, put an end to minting standard silver coins; and an act of Aug. 15, 1971, temporarily suspended the international right to convert dollars into gold.

BINGHAM PURCHASE. In 1786, when Massachusetts, which then included Maine, disposed of large tracts of unsettled timberlands in Maine by lottery, William Bingham, a wealthy Philadelphia banker, drew several townships and purchased others, with a total area of 1 million acres. Gen. Henry Knox had signed a contract to buy another tract of 1 million acres, but his duties as secretary of war prevented his developing it, and Bingham took that over also.

BIOCHEMISTRY. The origins of biochemistry in America derive from studies in Europe by Liebig, Pettenkofer, Voit, Hoppe-Seyler, and Kühne. American origins are obscure due to parallel developments in agricultural and medical chemistry in the 19th century, with no clear merging until the 1930's. American students of Liebig, Pettenkofer, and Voit were mostly concerned with agricultural problems involving plant growth and animal feeding; those of Hoppe-Seyler and Kühne, with problems of human physiology.

Proteins received a great deal of attention—agricultural chemists being concerned mainly with the protein content of feeds and their utilization by farm animals; and physiological chemists searching for underlying composition. In the late 19th century Thomas B. Osborne at the Connecticut Agricultural Experiment Station carried out work on isolation and purification of plant proteins and sought to unravel their amino acid composition. W. O. Atwater, F. G. Benedict, and H. P. Armsby did extensive studies on energy requirements of animals and energy values of various foods.

In the early decades of the 20th century agricultural chemists were largely responsible for the unfolding of nutritional knowledge of vitamins and minerals. In 1912 Sir Frederick Gowland Hopkins and Casimir Funk called attention to the dietary need of trace organic nutrients, and Funk introduced the term "vitamine." The work on vitamins A, B, D, and B-complex by such men as Osborne, Lafayette B. Mendel (Connecticut Agricultural Experimental Station), Elmer V. McCollum (Wisconsin station and Johns Hopkins University), Harry Steenbock (University of Wisconsin), Robert R. Williams, Joseph Gold-Berger (U.S. Public Health Service), Conrad A. Elvehjem (Wisconsin), and Roger Williams (Oregon State College) inaugurated a whole new understanding of nutrition and led, through practical application to food selection and fortification, to the virtual elimination of scurvy, rickets, beriberi, and pellagra.

Composition and properties of body fluids received much attention from physiological chemists associated with medical schools and research centers such as the Rockefeller Institute for Medical Research (D. D. Van Slyke), Harvard University (Lawrence J. Henderson and Otto Folin), University of Chicago (A. Baird Hastings), and Johns Hopkins University (W. H. Howell).

American biochemists pioneered in the study of intermediary metabolism with the use of isotopic tracers. At Columbia University in the 1930's Rudolf Schoenheimer and David Rittenberg utilized heavy hydrogen and nitrogen-15 to show the active breakdown of fats and proteins in animal tissues. Radioisotopes—particularly carbon-14, discovered by Reuben Kamin—were used extensively after World War II. Melvin Calvin at the University of California developed techniques necessary for the study of photosynthesis, used for the study of fermentation and metabolism. Vincent du Vigneaud carried out particularly significant work between 1935 and 1960 in the reactions of sulfur-containing compounds and of active methyl groups.

In 1926 James B. Sumner crystallized jack-bean urease, thus demonstrating the protein nature of enzymes. John H. Northrup crystallized pepsin a few years later, and by the mid-1970s more than a hundred enzymes had been prepared in crystalline form, many of them in America. In the 1960's William Stein and Stanford Moore of Rockefeller University and C. B. Anfinsen of the National Institutes of Health established the amino acid sequence and structure of ribonuclease. The nature of genetic mechanisms came under extensive study after O. T. Avery at the Rockefeller Institute recognized the role of nucleic acids in hereditary processes in 1944. James Watson joined Francis Crick of Cambridge University in 1951 to establish the double helix structure of DNA. American molecular biologists—notably Max Delbrück, A. D. Hershey, S. E. Luria, R. W. Holley, H. G. Khorana, and M. W. Nirenberg—played an important role in clarifying the function of nucleic acids in protein synthesis between 1950 and 1970. In the 1970's genetic research led many scientists to predict a new biological-industrial revolution. Recombinant DNA methods or gene-splicing techniques were developed at numerous research centers in the United States and in Europe, and the National Institutes of Health, which originally issued rather stringent rules about DNA research, relaxed its guidelines in 1980. Human interferon, an antiviral protein substance and potentially an important drug for treatment of viral infections and even cancer, was first produced in a laboratory by gene-splicing in January 1980.

BIOLOGY. *See* **Bacteriology and Virology; Botany; Ecology; Fish and Marine Life; Genetics; Herpetology; Mammals; Molecular Biology; Ornithology; Physiology**

BIRCH, JOHN, SOCIETY. *See* **John Birch Society.**

BIRCHARD LETTER. A public letter, June 29, 1863, to M. Birchard and eighteen other Ohio Democrats in which President Abraham Lincoln defended the administration's treatment of antiwar agitators. Lincoln offered to rescind the sentence of banishment (May 5, 1863) to the Confederacy of C. L. Vallandigham, an Ohio politician who had violated General Order No. 38, forbidding any expression of sympathy for the Confederacy, if a majority of those to whom the letter was addressed would subscribe to certain pledges in connection with the prosecution of the Civil War.

BIRCH BARK. The bark of the paper birch was used by Indians of the Great Lakes country and adjacent Canada for covering canoes, wigwams, food containers, and cooking vessels. A kettle of this bark will boil food safely if it does not touch the flames. Small sheets of birch bark were used for picture writing with a stylus by the Chippewa (Ojibwa) and a few other Indians.

BIRDS. *See* **Ornithology.**

BIRD SANCTUARIES. Natural areas set aside for birds, where they can nest, feed, or roost free from harm or disturbance by human beings. They are protected from hunters; from indirect effects of human action, such as disturbance that may frighten a nesting bird from its eggs; or from loss of vital habitat, as when a marsh is acquired as a sanctuary to prevent the area from being filled in, drained, or otherwise changed. Normally a place is picked because it has natural advantages, but there may also be man-made improvement, such as special planting or water impoundment.

When sanctuaries were first established around the turn of the 20th century, it was thought that a sanctuary should guard the protected birds against natural enemies. Most wildlife biologists now believe that predators are a vital part of the natural scheme of things and that, within reasonable limits, all wildlife within a sanctuary should be protected.

The first bird sanctuaries came into being when the American Ornithologists' Union and the National Audubon Society began providing funds to hire wardens to enforce wildlife laws. In 1903 President Theodore Roosevelt began setting aside some government-owned lands as federal bird reservations. A major development was the imposition in 1934 of a fee (duck stamp) for hunting waterfowl. Duck stamp monies are earmarked for acquisition of wildlife refuge lands. Today the National Wildlife Refuge System, under the U.S. Interior Department's Bureau of Sports, Fisheries, and Wildlife, maintains about 400 units, covering some 45 million acres.

The Audubon Society, which, with a string of more than sixty sanctuaries from Maine to California, maintains the nation's largest private refuge system, has for the most part left game-bird sanctuaries to the government and concentrated on nongame species.

BIRD'S INVASION OF KENTUCKY (1780). One phase of extensive operations by the British whereby the entire West, from Canada to Florida, was to be swept clear of Spaniards and colonists (*see* British Plan of Campaign in the West). From Detroit, Col. Henry Bird led an Indian army, with a few white men, against the settlers of Kentucky. Martin's Station and Ruddle's Station were easily overwhelmed, but lack of provisions compelled a retreat. Over 300 prisoners were taken back to Detroit.

BIRD'S POINT. Early fortification in Missouri, neighbor to both Charleston, Mo., and Cairo, Ill., opposite the mouth of the Ohio where it joins the Mississippi. Of strategic importance in guarding both rivers; first fortified by the Spanish in 1795. Col. U. S. Grant was in command of this district for a time, and a few skirmishes took place during the Civil War.

BIRMINGHAM (Ala.). Largest city in Alabama, with a population of 284,413 in 1980; center of a major metropolitan area including 847,360 people. Birmingham, often called the "Pittsburgh of the South," is a chief iron and steel producer, and one of the country's leading manufacturing centers. The city's industrial power is based on the high-quality iron ore, coal, and limestone within its immediate vicinity. The production of cast-iron pipe has been a specialty. The city itself dates from the beginning years of America's steel industry (1871). It grew rapidly, since good railroad connections linked it to markets in other parts of the country.

Birmingham is a major medical center for the state of Alabama and is the home of the Southern Research Institute, devoted to cancer research and high-temperature studies.

BIRTH CONTROL MOVEMENT. While most colonial and early national Americans were governed by the biblical injunction to increase and multiply, individual instances of birth control occurred, largely through sexual abstention and abortion. Family limitation was established practice in certain religious communities. Birth control became a concern of other Americans beginning in the 1830's and 1840's in the context of feminist and health reform agitation. Birth control publicists faced widespread disapproval and harassment. Nevertheless, there was some experimentation with contraceptive devices, plus a steady growth in demand for birth control information.

Beginning in 1873 the adoption of federal and state Comstock laws caused birth control pamphlets to be classed as obscene and barred from the mails and made it difficult even for physicians to write on scientific aspects of contraception. Not until 1912 did a president of the American Medical Association, the pediatrician Abraham Jacobi, endorse birth control in public.

Significant relaxation of legislation against birth control did not come until a decade or so later, when Margaret Sanger challenged the measures in the courts—first through publication of contraceptive information and then, in 1916, by opening a birth control clinic in Brooklyn, N.Y. With the rapid establishment of other clinics the National Birth Control League was formed in 1917, forerunner of the Planned Parenthood Federation of America. During the next several decades this body was the focal point of many legal battles and of the opposition to birth control of various civic and religious bodies, especially the Roman Catholic church. After World War II, however, there was a steady acceleration in public acceptance of family limitation—due partly to economic realities and partly to trends toward greater sexual freedom and women's rights. This acceptance has led to expanded educational and clinical programs by the Planned Parenthood Federation and other private organizations; greater support for medical research in related fields, such as reproductive biology; extensive programs to produce cheap and effective contraceptive devices and drugs; and, beginning in the 1960's, federal involvement in a variety of birth control activities.

BISHOP HILL COLONY. A theocratic communist colony, founded in Henry County, Ill., in 1846 by Erik Jansson, who brought there some 1,500 emigrants from Sweden, where they had been persecuted because of their conversion to perfectionism. The colony was incorporated in 1853 and was dissolved in 1860. In 1879 many members lost their farms to liquidate its debts and the costs of years of litigation.

BISMARCK (N. Dak.). Capital city of North Dakota, with a population of 44,485 in 1980; located near an important crossing place on the Missouri River, a ford used for many years before the American town was founded. Mandan Indian villages were located in the vicinity before white explorers reached the area. The city is an important transportation center, where railroads and airlines have terminals. Live cattle, meat, and lignite are its main products.

Bismarck was named in 1873 when the town and Dakota Territory were very much in need of railroad service. Settlers named the town in honor of the German chancellor, hoping to attract German money and enable the Northern Pacific track to be built through their town.

BISMARCK SEA, BATTLE OF (Mar. 2–4, 1943). To reinforce the Japanese garrison at Lae, New Guinea, eight Japanese transports carrying 7,000 troops, escorted by eight destroyers, left Rabaul, New Britain, on Feb. 28, 1943. Hidden initially by bad weather, the convoy was spotted by Allied patrol planes in the Bismarck Sea. Heavy bombers struck the ships on Mar. 2, but the biggest attack came on the 3rd as the convoy entered Huon Gulf. Brushing aside feeble Japanese air cover, more than 300 American and Australian bombers and fighters unleashed a devastating attack. These attacks and a quick strike by American motor torpedo boats sank all eight transports as well as four destroyers, at a cost of only four Allied planes.

BISON. *See* **Buffalo.**

BIT. An archaic term for one-eighth of a dollar, used chiefly in the South and Southwest, when depreciation of colonial paper money, problems of exchange, coinage, and lack of specie caused the circulation of the Spanish real, a silver coin of that value.

BIZERTE. City on the north coast of Tunisia, important during World War II. In November 1942, German and Italian forces occupied the area. On Apr. 22, 1943, when Gen. Sir Harold Alexander's Anglo-American troops attacked Gen. Jürgen von Arnim's Italo-German forces in the northeastern corner of Tunisia, Bizerte was the objective of the American forces. Gen. Omar N. Bradley's U.S. Second Corps entered Bizerte on May 7, the same day British units seized

Tunis. This Axis defeat (200,000 prisoners were taken) opened the way for future Allied operations across the Mediterranean into Europe.

BLACK BALL LINE. The first and most celebrated of the lines of transatlantic sailing packets from New York. Its nickname came from the black disk carried on the fore-topsail and the house flag. Regular monthly sailings started at Liverpool on Jan. 4, 1818, and at New York the next day. In 1822 service was increased to semimonthly with eight ships. The line continued for sixty years.

BLACK BELT. A crescent-shaped area extending along the Alabama River in Alabama and up the Tombigbee River in northeastern Mississippi. About three-fourths of its 5,000 square miles lies in Alabama; it derives its name from the black soil prevalent in contrast to the red clays to the north and south and is a prairie that lies much lower than the surrounding country because of the decomposition of the soft limestone rock under the soil. This decomposition has made it one of the best agricultural regions of the entire South. The Black Belt became a plantation region producing great cotton crops by slave labor from 1830 to 1860. All the rivers of Alabama, except the Tennessee, water the region.

With the coming of the Civil War, the Black Belt turned to raising foodstuffs and furnished a great part of the food supplies for the Confederate armies. After the war it again became the leading cotton-producing region of the South until 1880. Unable to meet the competition of Texas cotton, it turned more and more to diversified farming and the raising of food crops, although it remained the principal cotton region east of the Mississippi River.

BLACK BOYS. Pennsylvania frontiersmen who, under the leadership of James Smith, defended the frontier against the Indians. In 1765, fearful of traders who might supply guns to the Indians, the Black Boys burned a packhorse train belonging to Baynton, Wharton and Morgan, a company engaged in the Indian trade. The frontiersmen disguised themselves by blackening their faces.

BLACKBURN'S FORD, BATTLE AT (July 18, 1861). On his advance to Bull Run, Union Brig. Gen. Irvin McDowell ordered Gen. Daniel Tyler's division to reconnoiter toward Manassas Junction. Tyler found Confederate Gen. James Longstreet's brigade in position behind Bull Run at Blackburn's Ford, attacked, and was decisively repulsed.

BLACK CAPITALISM. Black economic development, with the objective of encouraging economic independence among Afro-Americans, through the ownership and operation of business enterprises and increased employment opportunities, especially at the managerial level.

Early federal programs were focused on the development of black enterprises catering chiefly to black populations. A new goal of making blacks integral participants in the overall enterprise system gradually emerged during the late 1960's. Primary barriers have been prejudice, lack of capital and entrepreneurs, and a paucity of business experience among Afro-Americans. Despite evident progress by 1977, blacks, constituting about 11.5 percent of the total population, owned 2.3 percent of all firms and took in 1.3 percent of total annual American business receipts; employed blacks constituted 10 percent of the total employed and an infinitesimal proportion of business managers.

The black economic development that began in the early 19th century (small grocery stores, food catering, gardening, and barbering) prospered until Reconstruction created a hostile climate, and 20th-century immigration spawned competition. The National Business League, founded by Booker T. Washington in 1900, helped Afro-Americans, and still helps, along with at least 140 other organizations that concentrate on assisting black businesses.

Since receiving increasing attention after the 1965 War on Poverty program encouraged black leaders and white businessmen, with federal assistance, to provide more economic opportunities for blacks, the fostering of black capitalism has become increasingly controversial.

BLACK CAVALRY IN THE WEST (1866–91). Established by an act of Congress in 1866, the Ninth and Tenth Cavalry regiments spent over twenty-five years on the frontier. These black troopers fought Indians, bandits, horse thieves, and Mexican revolutionaries. Both regiments served in the West with distinction and gallantry. Their service covered Kansas, Texas, Indian Territory, Nebraska, New Mexico, Arizona, Colorado, and the Dakotas. A dozen Medals of Honor decorated black cavalrymen, plus many commendations for valor. These troopers were respectfully called "buffalo soldiers" by the Indians, supposedly because they saw a similarity between the hair of the black troopers and that of their sacred animal of the plains.

BLACK CODES. Legislation enacted in the former Confederate states in 1865 and 1866 to limit the freedom of recently freed blacks. It is sometimes considered to include legislation that restricted the action and movements of slaves (slave codes). Persons using the term "black codes" to include all such laws see them as originating in the 17th century, continuing until the Civil War, and being reenacted in slightly modified form immediately after the war.

The laws passed in 1865–66 by the several states differed, but all were intended to replace the social controls of slavery swept away by the Emancipation Proclamation and the Thirteenth Amendment, and to assure the South that free blacks would remain subordinate to whites. Typical of the legislation were provisions for declaring blacks to be vagrants if they were unemployed and without permanent residence. They were subject to being arrested, fined, and bound out for a term of labor if unable to pay the fine. Penalties existed for refusing to complete a term of labor. Persons encouraging blacks to refuse to abide by these restrictive laws were themselves subject to penalties. Northern reaction helped to produce the Fourteenth and Fifteenth amendments, which temporarily removed such legislation from the books. Following Reconstruction, many of the provisions of the black codes were reenacted in the Jim Crow laws that continued in effect until the Civil Rights Act of 1964.

BLACKFOOT. One of the most numerous and powerful of the tribes of the northwestern Plains, the Siksika ("black feet") were so named because their moccasins were black. The Blackfoot nation at its peak, between 1700 and about 1870, may have had as many as 15,000 members. Spread from the North Saskatchewan River to the southern tributaries of the Missouri in Montana, the Blackfoot nation formed a military federation significant in the balance of power in the northwestern Plains in the 18th century. The Blackfoot complex is one of classic Plains culture: bison hunting; the war and coup-counting patterns; movements of individual bands; and the great seasonal convocations for intensive hunting. They had the best-developed system of military associations (divisions of warriors) based on age-grading.

BLACK FRIDAY (Sept. 24, 1869). The climactic day of an effort by Jay Gould, James Fisk, Jr., Abel Rathbone Corbin, Daniel Butterfield, and one or two associates to corner the ready gold supply of the United States. The nation being on a paper-money basis, gold was a speculative commodity on the New York exchange. On June 15, 1869, they entertained President Ulysses S. Grant on Fisk's steamboat, attempted to learn the Treasury's gold policy, and argued that it was important to keep gold high in order to facilitate sales of American grain in Europe. Grant was noncommittal. A gold corner did not seem difficult if government nonintervention could be assured. On Sept. 2 Gould began buying gold on a large scale; on the 15th Fisk began buying heavily and soon forced the price from $135 per ounce to $140. The movement excited much suspicion and fear; on the 23rd, with gold at $144, the New York panic grew serious.

The climax of Black Friday found Fisk driving gold higher and higher, business profoundly disturbed, and the New York gold room a pandemonium as scores were ruined. As the price rose to $160 Secretary of the Treasury Boutwell telegraphed an order to sell $4 million of the gold reserve. Gould had already begun selling, and gold sank rapidly to $135. The episode caused heavy indirect losses to business and an ugly smirch on the Grant administration. Gould and Fisk made an $11 million profit.

BLACK HAWK WAR (1832). A conflict between the United States and Sauk (Sac) and Fox Indians, mainly in Illinois and Wisconsin. The leader of the Sauk and Fox, an aging chief named Black Hawk, was the rival of another Sauk chief, Keokuk, who had ceded land to the whites under a treaty of 1804 and with his faction moved across the Mississippi to Iowa in 1823. Black Hawk, who had fought on the side of the British in the War of 1812, declined to evacuate his village at Rock Island, Ill. In 1831, when white settlers preempted Black Hawk's village, he threatened resistance. An army was assembled, and Black Hawk withdrew across the Mississippi.

Early in 1832, Black Hawk, with 400 warriors and their families, crossed back into Illinois and moved toward Rock Island. Gen. Henry Atkinson ordered Black Hawk to return to Iowa; emissaries from Black Hawk were shot in cold blood. Black Hawk retired up the Rock River, attacking and burning frontier settlements, with the soldiers in pursuit. Black Hawk made offers of peace, which were ignored. On July 28 he was overtaken and crushingly defeated.

The remnant of Black Hawk's forces was pursued across southern Wisconsin and massacred as it attempted to cross the Mississippi into Iowa. Black Hawk was later captured by the Winnebago, who turned him in for the reward. After imprisonment, he was taken to Washington, D.C., where, incongruously, he was honored. He was then allowed to return to the remnant of his tribe in Iowa.

BLACK HILLS. A group of mountains in western South Dakota and northeastern Wyoming, mainly in the Black Hills National Forest. The Black Hills were within the Great Sioux Reservation (Laramie Treaty of 1868). Gold was found in the hills by miners accompanying Gen. George A. Custer's expedition of 1874. The federal government sought to protect the rights of the Indians until these rights could be eliminated by treaty. When early efforts failed, the government raised the embargo and gold hunters rushed in. This led to the Black Hills War, the high point of which was the destruction of Custer's army on the Little Bighorn in June 1876. After this the government forced a treaty of relinquishment and civil government was established.

The miners first assembled at Custer, S.Dak., where 15,000 passed the winter of 1875–76. Gold having been found in Deadwood Gulch, there was a stampede from Custer to the new diggings early in 1876. The Homestake gold mine was established at Lead and for over a hundred years has yielded fabulous sums. Its engineers believe its stores of ore cannot be depleted for many years to come. Mica, spodumene, amblygonite, feldspar, arsenic, gold, silver, and galena are produced in commercial values. More than 100 valuable minerals are present. The region is also the site of Wind Cave National Park, Mount Rushmore National Memorial, and Jewel Cave (S.Dak.) and Devils Tower national monuments.

BLACK HILLS WAR (1876). The Black Hills of western South Dakota and adjacent northeastern Wyoming traditionally had been hunting grounds and sacred territory for the Sioux (Dakota). Under the Laramie Treaty of 1868, the Black Hills were part of the Great Sioux Reservation, but persistent rumors of mineral wealth attracted goldseekers. In 1874, the government sent troops into the Black Hills under Gen. George Armstrong Custer, ostensibly to establish sites for army posts. When Custer found gold, the gold rush was on.

When the Sioux threatened war, the government offered to purchase the land, but the Indians refused to sell. In November 1875 all Indians off the reservation hunting buffalo were ordered to report to their agents, but few complied. In March 1876 Gen. George Crook headed north from the Platte River to round up the absentee bands. In June they mounted a three-pronged invasion of the Indian country.

After their victory at the Little Bighorn, where Custer and his troops lost their lives, the Indians dispersed, celebrating and hunting, and were unable to cope with renewed offensives by the military. By spring 1877 most of the warriors had straggled in to the agencies to be disarmed. Under a treaty in 1877 the Sioux were obliged to cede the Black Hills for only a fraction of their value, and the area was opened to the gold-miners.

BLACK HORSE CAVALRY. A bipartisan group of corruptionists in the New York legislature who during the last quarter of the 19th century preyed particularly on corporations. They usually blackmailed by introducing bills that would be damaging to the business of corporations, but that would be killed if sufficient money were forthcoming.

BLACK INFANTRY IN THE WEST (1866–91). In the summer of 1866, Congress for the first time authorized six regiments of black troops to be included in the regular army. Two of the regiments were designated cavalry and four, infantry. The infantry regiments were assigned to the South and the West. In 1869 congressional reorganization of the army consolidated them into two regiments. In 1870 the black regiments moved out on the Texas frontier and began a tour of duty along the Rio Grande that was to last a decade.

The two regiments separated in 1880, one moving to Indian Territory, and later Arizona and New Mexico, and the other to Dakota Territory, where some units were assigned to guard Sitting Bull and his people at Fort Randall. In the summer of 1888 the latter was moved to Montana Territory.

BLACK JACK, BATTLE OF (June 2, 1856). The first engagement of the Kansas Border War. In retaliation for John Brown's massacre at Pottawatomie Creek, a Missouri band under Capt. Pate seized two of Brown's sons. Brown attacked Pate at Black Jack, near Baldwin, Kans. After minor casualties on each side Pate surrendered with twenty-one men. Both bands were dispersed by Col. Edwin V. Sumner of the regular army.

BLACK LAWS. Ohio enacted laws in 1804 and 1807 compelling registration of all Afro-Americans in the state, forbidding any free black to remain without giving $500 bond against his becoming a public charge, and denying validity to an Afro-American's testimony in trials where whites were involved. In the legislative session of 1848–49, with the Free Soil party leading the attack, the laws were repealed.

BLACK LEGION. A secret terrorist society active in Michigan in 1936 that murdered a number of blacks and whites whom it felt had violated its peculiar moral standards. The legion first attracted public notice by its murder, May 12, 1936, of Charles A. Poole of Detroit. The resultant criminal prosecutions and public condemnation soon drove the order into obscurity and to dissolution.

BLACKLEGS. A term, now used in a general sense, which once referred to professional gamblers with large capital, associated in perfectly organized gangs which robbed, murdered, and plundered with impunity in the old Southwest.

BLACKLISTING. A practice of employers to exclude from the job market individuals who are, or are believed to be, union men, labor agitators, or active in strike activities. Originating in the labor troubles of the 1830's, blacklisting was one of the most widely used antiunion weapons. Lists of suspects were usually available from an employer. The blacklist was a fact of life for American labor until the advent of the New Deal. The passage of the National Labor Relations Act, or Wagner Act, in 1935 brought a measure of effective control.

A new dimension emerged following World War II with the development of the cold war. Investigations into Communist activities in America resulted in the expulsion of Communists from trade unions and of Communist-dominated unions from national labor organizations. The most glaring example resulted from congressional investigations of government employees and persons employed in the arts, particularly in the motion picture industry. With the rise of McCarthyism in the early 1950's, the House Un-American Activities Committee, under Chairman John S. Wood, made an exhaustive investigation into Communist influence in the entertainment world. Saved by the Fifth Amendment from going to jail for contempt of Congress, unfriendly witnesses were consequently included in a show-business blacklist for the next decade.

BLACK MUSLIMS. The Black Muslim (Nation of Islam) movement was founded in Detroit in 1930 by Wali Farad. According to Black Muslim doctrine, Farad was an incarnation of God who came to America to rescue Afro-Americans from the white race. In 1934, Farad was succeeded by Elijah Muhammad; under his leadership, the Black Muslims established mosques in most major cities and achieved a membership of more than 100,000 by the early 1960's. One of the movement's most prominent leaders was Malcolm X, until his break with the sect in 1963. The Black Muslims denounce Christianity as a means of white oppression and preach black racial superiority, but have avoided confrontations with white authorities and have obeyed America's laws while minimizing contact with whites.

BLACK NATIONALISM. The belief that the African origins and the American experiences of blacks have created in the United States a nation within a nation and that the interest of Afro-Americans can best be served by recognition of this ethnic unity. Black-nationalist views include positive acceptance of blackness, some degree of separation from the white majority, and creation of a national homeland. In the 19th century it found expression in black churches and fraternal organizations, in emigration schemes sponsored by blacks, and in opposition to efforts to return blacks to Africa. In the 20th century cultural nationalism, pan-Africanism, community control, and a variety of separatist movements have characterized black nationalism.

BLACK PANTHERS. The Black Panther party, organized in Oakland, Calif., in 1966 by Afro-American militants Huey P. Newton and Bobby G. Seale, represents a synthesis of black nationalism and Marxism: the Panthers believe in black liberation and sponsor programs to develop cohesiveness in the black community, but they also favor coalitions with radical elements from other races.

In 1967, the Panthers organized Oakland's ghetto for self-defense against the police. On May 2 thirty armed Panthers demonstrated on the steps of the California capitol to protest passage of a bill that infringed on their right to bear arms. They immediately became a symbol of black militancy; party branches were established throughout the United States.

The Black Panthers achieved their greatest impact in 1968 when Eldridge Cleaver published *Soul On Ice,* a best-selling defense of black liberation. They merged briefly with the Student Nonviolent Coordinating Committee (SNCC). The Panthers' notoriety and militancy triggered police harassment. Newton and Seale were arrested on numerous occasions and subjected to lengthy trials and imprisonment before their release. In the early 1970's, in a dramatic change of tactics, they turned to electoral politics; Seale unsuccessfully ran for mayor of Oakland in 1973.

BLACK PATCH WAR. Attempts of Kentucky and Tennessee tobacco growers to overcome monopolistic control of markets and prices. In the Black Patch or fire-cured tobacco area of southwestern Kentucky and adjoining Tennessee, aggressive methods of association members and retaliation by nonmembers resulted in much violence. During 1907 and 1908 night riding by the "silent brigade" was prevalent. Speculation in warehouse receipts, increased production in unrestricted areas, adverse court decisions, and general friction, hostility, and suspicion doomed the movement.

BLACK POWER. Control by black people of political, social, economic, and cultural institutions that affect their daily lives. In 1966 Stokely Carmichael and Willie Ricks of the Student Nonviolent Coordinating Committee (SNCC) proclaimed it upon completion of the march through Mississippi begun by James Meredith. Initially, it meant that blacks should have political control of those areas in the South in which they constitute a majority. This was extended to the advocacy of black control of urban ghettos and all institutions that affect the lives and destinies of Afro-Americans. Black-power strategies cover the spectrum from black capitalism and electoral politics to armed struggle; goals range from pluralism (equal group status within American society) to separatism (an autonomous black city, county, state, or nation), to socialist revolution (replacing white American capitalism with black socialism).

BLACK ROCK, BOMBARDMENT OF (Oct. 13, 1812). In reprisal for the capture of two British sloops by the Americans, Black Rock (at the northern end of the village of Buffalo, N.Y.) was subjected to a heavy bombardment. The short range of the guns on the American shore prevented an effective answer. News came of the American defeat at Queenston Heights and a week's armistice was arranged to permit the burial of the dead.

BLACKSMITHING. In colonial times the blacksmith was an important factor of the community. The first colony at Jamestown, Va., in 1607, brought over a blacksmith. By 1810 Pennsylvania reported 2,562 blacksmith shops, doing $1,572,627 worth of work. In 1850 the United States had 100,000 blacksmiths and whitesmiths, in addition to gunsmiths and machinists.

The blacksmith not only made shoes for horses and oxen and applied them, but also made latches, hinges, andirons, farm tools, nails, hammers, axes, chisels, and carving tools; he welded and fitted wagon tires and hub rings and made and fitted all metal parts of wagons, carriages, and sleighs. He frequently furnished ice skates, toy wagons, and doll carriages, and was the single source of decorative ironwork for fine houses. Most skilled were those who shaped iron to the precise and intricate needs of ships. In the latter part of the 20th century blacksmiths had all but disappeared from the American scene.

BLACKSTOCK'S HILL, BATTLE OF. *See* **Enoree, Battle of.**

BLACK SWAMP. Once applied to much of northwestern Ohio but more accurately to an area lying chiefly in the drainage basin of the Maumee River. Most was once under Lake Erie. Drainage difficulties, malarial diseases, and its general inaccessibility long retarded settlement. After 1850, when drainage and transportation problems began to be solved, the region underwent a rapid development and today constitutes one of the richest farming sections of the state.

***BLACK WARRIOR* AFFAIR.** The *Black Warrior,* an American steamer, touched at Havana, Cuba, Feb. 28, 1854, on its eighteenth voyage to New York. In technical conformity with law, but contrary to informal agreements, a cargo manifest was demanded by Spanish authorities. Failing this, the ship was seized, but was restored to its owners on payment of a $6,000 fine. The issue hung fire until August 1855, when Spain paid an indemnity of $53,000.

BLACKWATER, BATTLE OF (Dec. 18, 1861). While campaigning against Confederate Gen. Sterling Price in Missouri, part of Gen. John Pope's command surrounded an enemy force at the Blackwater River at the mouth of Clear Creek (vicinity of Warrensburg), and compelled its surrender. This was part of Pope's campaign to strip Price of supplies and munitions.

BLADENSBURG, BATTLE OF (Aug. 24, 1814). Maj. Gen. Robert Ross, with 4,500 British troops, landed on the Patuxent River in Maryland, Aug. 19–20, compelling Commodore Joshua Barney to destroy his gunboat flotilla in that river. The British then turned toward Washington. About 6,000 militia, a few regulars, and Barney's seamen constituted the defensive force under Maj. Gen. William Winder. Ross reached Bladensburg Aug. 24. Across the river, on rising ground, Winder hastily and unskillfully posted his army. The British drove back the American light troops after crossing the bridge. Barney's naval contingent, firing eighteen-pounders, checked Ross for a time. Winder ordered a general retirement, the British being too exhausted to pursue vigorously. Halting briefly at Capitol Hill, the Americans marched on to Georgetown. Ross entered Washington and burned the Capitol, presidential mansion, and public buildings. A congressional investigation whitewashed all concerned, but Secretary of War John Armstrong was compelled to resign.

BLADENSBURG DUELING FIELD. Five miles from Washington, D.C., in the jurisdiction of Maryland, where statutes against dueling were more lax, thirty to fifty duels were fought by statesmen, military and naval officers, and civilians from 1802 until 1851. Most famous were the mortal wounding of Commodore Stephen Decatur by Commodore James Barron (1820) and the killing of Sen. A. T. Mason of Virginia by his brother-in-law, J. M. McCarthy (1819).

BLAND-ALLISON ACT. The depression following the panic of 1873 caused cheap-money advocates (led by Representative R. P. Bland of Missouri) to join with silver-producing interests in urging return to bimetallism. Free coinage, as the symbol of justice for the poor, was seized upon by greenbackers and others determined to prevent resumption of specie payments and to make government obligations payable in silver. When Bland's bill for free coinage, passed by the House (Nov. 5, 1877), jeopardized Secretary of the Treasury John Sherman's plans for resuming specie payments, Sherman substituted limited purchases for free coinage, through a Senate amendment sponsored by Sen. W. B. Allison of Iowa. The producers accepted the arrangement as likely to restore silver to $1.29. The law, passed Feb. 28, 1878, over President Rutherford B. Hayes's veto, required government purchase, at market prices, of $2–4 million worth of silver bullion monthly, and coinage into legal tender 16-to-1 dollars, exchangeable for $10 silver certificates receivable for public dues and reissuable.

BLAST FURNACES, EARLY. The first unsuccessful attempt to build blast furnaces in the colonies was made in Virginia by the London Company. The Puritans in Massachusetts established the first successful ironworks as early as 1644. Not until the 18th century did the smelting of iron in America become important. By the American Revolution there were more blast furnaces in the colonies than in England and Wales, and American furnaces produced more pig iron and castings than English furnaces.

BLEASE MOVEMENT. In the early 1900's, Coleman L. Blease, South Carolina politician, attempted to appeal to the political consciousness of the underprivileged white class by studiously imitating former Gov. Benjamin Tillman's vehement attacks on Afro-Americans, aristocrats, and clerical politicians. He was elected governor in 1910, and his administration was bizarre. He pardoned extravagantly and answered opposition with abusive language. He was reelected in 1912, but his influence declined.

BLEEDING KANSAS. *See* **Border War.**

BLENNERHASSETT ISLAND. In the Ohio River below the mouth of the Little Kanawha River and two miles south of Parkersburg, W.Va. First known as Backus Island for Elijah Backus, who purchased it in 1792. It is the site of Blennerhassett House, where Aaron Burr and Harman Blennerhassett, who purchased the north end of the island in 1798, are alleged to have plotted treason against the United States.

BLESSING OF THE BAY. Second seaworthy vessel built in the colonies, preceded only by the *Virginia* (1607). A thirty-ton bark, mostly of locust, it was built at a cost of £145 for Gov. John Winthrop at Mistick (now Medford), Mass., by Robert Molton and other shipwrights sent to New England in 1629 by the Company of the Massachusetts Bay.

BLIND. *See* **Handicapped, Education of the.**

BLIZZARDS. In popular terminology, any snowstorm of long duration or accompanied by appreciable wind is called a blizzard in both England and America. Records show that historic blizzards have occurred somewhere in the United States almost every year since chronicles began. In the northern plains eighteen notably disastrous blizzards occurred between 1871 and 1905; on the other hand, during the period 1905–23, only three blizzards were notable. The Dakotas and Minnesota were hit by five in the 1960's. Toward the south and east notable blizzards occur less often. The Great Lakes region has had relatively few blizzards (nine since 1894, the worst in 1970 in Chicago). New England suffers in about one year out of five; and the Deep South has had only seven notable blizzards since 1800. The Midwest was ravaged by severe blizzards in 1978 and 1979 (both left more than 100 dead), and the worst blizzard in New England history took place in 1978.

BLOCKADE. The closing by sea of the coasts and ports of an enemy to cut off entirely his maritime communications. As a nation with a small navy and a large merchant marine, the United States originally sought to limit the scope and uses of blockades. The Continental Congress in 1784 specified that only blockades maintained by actual patrolling squadrons in proximity to the enemy's coast and ports were legitimate. The American view of blockade was embodied in the Declaration of Paris, adopted by the great powers in 1856, stipulating that a blockade must be "maintained by a force sufficient really to prevent access to the coast of the enemy." (Ironically, the United States did not sign the Declaration because it objected to a provision outlawing privateers.)

At the onset of the Civil War, President Abraham Lincoln proclaimed a blockade of the entire coast of the Confederacy. This blockade, a major factor in the Union victory, was scrupulously observed by the British, who viewed it as a valuable precedent. The United States, finding itself the dominant naval power, resorted to other devices. One was the doctrine of continuous voyage, which held that ships destined for a neutral country could be seized if it could be proven that their cargo was destined ultimately for a blockaded port.

By the time of World War I the development of submarines, mines, and long-range artillery had made the traditional "close" blockade militarily impossible. Britain resorted to a "distant" blockade, utilizing mine fields and patrols of cruisers on the high-seas approaches to Germany. The United States protested, but it was the German "submarine blockade" of the British Isles that most outraged American opinion and eventually brought the United States into the war on the side of the Allies. In World War II the United States and Britain employed a long-range air and naval blockade against Germany, while the Germans again engaged in unrestricted submarine warfare against the Allies.

During the Cuban missile crisis of 1962 the United States imposed a "quarantine" of Cuba to halt the delivery of offensive weapons and force the removal of Soviet missiles installed there.

BLOCKADE RUNNERS, CONFEDERATE. On Apr. 16, 1861, President Abraham Lincoln proclaimed a naval blockade of the Confederacy's 3,500 miles of coastline. Trade with other countries by running the blockade proved highly lucrative to the Confederacy: 1.25 million bales of cotton were run out, and 600,000 small arms and other munitions, endless supplies of provisions, clothing, hospital stores, manufactures, and luxuries were run in, valued at $200 million. Had it not been for the blockade runners, the Confederate armies would have been on the verge of starvation; and except for the increasing stringency of the blockade, the runners would probably have enabled the South to win its independence by keeping a federal squadron of 600 vessels occupied.

"BLOCKS OF FIVE." During the Benjamin Harrison-Grover Cleveland election of 1888, W. W. Dudley, Republican campaign treasurer, issued a circular on Oct. 24, to Indiana followers, suggesting that they "divide the floaters into blocks of five," each in the charge of a trusted leader with the necessary bribes who would deliver the vote.

BLOCS. Organized voting groups in American legislative bodies, and more loosely, associations of pressure groups attempting to lobby in American legislatures. The purpose is to create a group of legislators who will vote together consistently on certain specified issues. The farm bloc, formed in the Senate in 1921, is perhaps the best example. Together with a parallel group of House members, it secured the passage of a number of bills in the 1920's. A liberal bloc in the House in the 1930's lent support to New Deal legislation. A protectionist bloc, a wet bloc, a dry bloc, and a veterans' bloc were all active in Congress around 1940. After World War II a labor bloc and a civil rights bloc rose to prominence.

"BLOOD IS THICKER THAN WATER." Commodore Josiah Tattnall, in command of the American squadron in the East Indies waters, made this adage a part of American history when explaining why he had given aid to the British squadron in an attack on Taku forts at the mouth of the Pai River, June 25, 1859, infringing strict American neutrality.

BLOODY ANGLE (May 12, 1864). The climax in the first phase of Gen. U. S. Grant's wilderness campaign in Virginia. Grant moved in force against the salient, or "bloody angle," in Gen. Robert E. Lee's line. Because of surprise, lack of artillery, and the force of the onslaught the salient was overrun. Lee led the counterattack; the Union advance was halted and forced back. All day and far into the night the battle raged. Neither side could advance. Early next morning Lee retired to prepared positions and the fighting ceased.

BLOODY ISLAND. Sand bar in the Mississippi River, opposite St. Louis, Mo., which became densely wooded and a rendezvous for duelists. Appearing first above water in 1798, its continuous growth menaced St. Louis harbor. Beginning in July 1837 Capt. Robert E. Lee, of the Army Corps of Engineers, devised and established a system of dikes and dams that washed out the western channel and ultimately joined the island to the Illinois shore.

BLOODY MARSH, BATTLE OF (July 7, 1742). The principal and decisive engagement in the War of Jenkins' Ear. A Spanish force collected in Havana and St. Augustine and invaded Georgia preparatory to attacking Frederica, the strongest English settlement in Georgia. James Oglethorpe immediately attacked. He routed the Spaniards, and in the retreat he posted in ambush on the edge of a marsh three platoons and a company of Highlanders. When about 400 Spaniards unsuspectingly marched into the glade, Oglethorpe's forces killed about 200 and forced the remainder to retreat to the south end of the island. A few days later the remaining force returned to Florida.

BLOODY MONDAY. Election riots, Aug. 6, 1855, in Louisville, Ky., which grew out of the bitter rivalry between the Democratic and Know-Nothing parties. Rumors started that foreigners and Catholics had interfered with the voting. A street fight occurred, twenty-two persons were killed, scores injured, and much property destroyed by fire.

BLOODY POND, BATTLE OF (Sept. 8, 1755). The British expedition to capture Crown Point, N.Y., under Sir William Johnson, had reached Lake George when word was received of the approach of 1,400 French, Canadians, and Indians. Johnson sent out 1,000 men; the troops fell into an ambush and the survivors retreated to camp, where an attack was beaten off. Several hundred Canadians and Indians returned to plunder the scene of the fight. They were resting by a pool when they were attacked by a scouting party. After a short but bloody fight, the Canadians and Indians fled. The bodies of the dead were thrown into the pool, henceforth called Bloody Pond.

BLOODY RUN, BATTLE OF (July 31, 1763). Pontiac's siege of Fort Detroit began May 9, 1763. During the night of July 30–31, Capt. James Dalzel and 280 relief troops marched eastward along the Grand Marias River to surprise Pontiac. Instead the column was itself furiously assailed at Parent's Creek (ever since called Bloody Run) and driven back to the fort. Dalzel was slain and sixty men killed or wounded.

BLOODY SHIRT. "Waving the bloody shirt" describes attempts in political campaigns (especially 1872 and 1876) by Radical Republicans to defeat Democrats by impassioned oratory designed to keep alive the hatreds and prejudices of the Civil War.

BLOOMER DRESS. A loose-fitting costume of knee-length dress and Turkish pantaloons buttoned at the ankle, introduced in Seneca Falls, N.Y., by Elizabeth Smith Miller in February 1851 and popularized by Amelia Bloomer, editor of the feminist journal *Lily.* For its physical comfort and as a symbol of the suffrage movement, the dress survived six years of ridicule until the revival of the hoopskirt.

BLOUNT CONSPIRACY. Named for William Blount, U.S. senator from Tennessee, 1796–97. The conspiracy was connected with the Yazoo land frauds of 1796, to raise the value of western lands by driving the Spaniards out of Louisiana and Florida by a land force of western frontiersmen and Indians with the aid of a British fleet. The conspiracy was exposed when an incriminating letter fell into the hands of the administration and was transmitted by President John Adams to the Senate (July 3, 1797). Blount was promptly expelled.

BLUE AND GRAY. Familiar names for the armies of the North and South during the Civil War, derived from the fact that the Union army wore blue uniforms while the Confederates wore gray.

BLUE-BACKED SPELLER. One of the most famous textbooks in U. S. educational history, by Noah Webster. A small book in blue covers, it included preferred American spellings of many words. The *American Spelling Book* (the proper title) appeared first in 1783, went through many editions, and was still in use a century later.

BLUEBACKS. Confederate paper currency, first issued under an act approved one month after the establishment of the Confederate government. From an initial issue of $1 million, the treasury notes grew to $800 million by Apr. 1, 1864, when deflationary measures were taken that reduced the outstanding currency to $480,036,095 on Oct. 1, 1864.

BLUE-COLLAR WORKERS. Members of the nonagricultural labor force who perform manual labor, whether skilled, semiskilled, or unskilled, and, typically, work for hourly wages. The percentage of manual workers in the total work force has changed only slightly since 1900 (from about one-third to nearly one-half), although the proportion of female blue-collar workers has significantly declined.

BLUE EAGLE EMBLEM. A blue American thunderbird, with outspread wings, proclaimed on July 20, 1933, as the symbol of industrial recovery by Hugh S. Johnson, head of the National Recovery Administration. All who accepted the president's Reemployment Agreement or a special Code of Fair Competition were permitted to display a poster with the blue eagle and the announcement "Member N.R.A. We Do Our Part." On Sept. 5, 1935, following the invalidation of the compulsory code system, the emblem was abolished and its future use as a symbol was prohibited.

BLUEGRASS COUNTRY. Some 8,000 square miles of east central Kentucky, encircled by the Ohio River on the north and the Knobs on the east, south, and west. The terrain, with some exceptions, has a gracefully undulating surface over a limestone foundation, and is specially adapted to the growth of bluegrass. The first settlers of Kentucky came to this region in one of the greatest migrations of American history, over the Wilderness Road, by way of Cumberland Gap. Here the pioneers Daniel Boone and Simon Kenton became national heroes.

BLUE LAWS. Originally, colonial laws regulating conduct, particularly on the Sabbath. Rev. Samuel A. Peters wrote an account of the so-called blue laws of Connecticut in *A General History of Connecticut, by a Gentleman of the Province,* published on blue paper in London in 1781. Rigid Sabbath, sex, and sumptuary regulations prevailed generally in Puritan New England. To some degree blue laws could be found in every one of the American colonies. Compulsory church attendance and laws forbidding sports, travel, and work on the Sabbath were found in the South as well.

BLUE LICKS, BATTLE OF (Aug. 19, 1782). An engagement between 182 Kentucky pioneers and 240 Indians and Canadians, in the British service, raiding into Kentucky from the Ohio country and the vicinity of Detroit. It occurred near the lower Blue Lick Springs on the middle fork of Licking River. A precipitate attack was launched by Kentuckians, from several pioneer stations, against the foe lying in ambush. After a fierce conflict of a few minutes, the right wing of the Kentuckians gave way and the entire body retreated.

BLUE LIGHTS. In December 1813, American frigates under Cmdr. Stephen Decatur prepared to run out of the harbor of New London, Conn., where they had been blockaded by the British. Decatur saw blue lights near the mouth of the river in sight of the British blockaders. Convinced that these were signals to betray his plans he abandoned the project. Suspicion was directed against members of Congress who pressed for peace, and the odious epithet "Blue-light Federalists" long was applied to extreme Federalists.

BLUE LODGES. Secret proslavery societies in western Missouri during 1854 to thwart northern antislavery designs to make Kansas a free territory under the Kansas-Nebraska Act. They promoted the migration of proslavery settlers to Kansas and crossed the border to participate in the election of proslavery members to the territorial government.

BLUE RIDGE TUNNEL. Constructed in 1850–58 by the Blue Ridge Railroad, the state of Virginia, and the Virginia Central Railroad, at a cost of $488,000, through Blue Ridge Mountain under Rockfish Gap, between Afton and Waynesboro, Va. It was for some time the longest tunnel in America. In 1870 the Chesapeake and Ohio Railroad acquired it.

BLUE SKY LAWS. Legislative enactments designed to prevent fraudulent flotation or sale of corporate stocks and bonds. Kansas enacted the first blue sky law in May 1911. There are three types: (1) fraud statutes, to follow and punish the security swindler; (2) dealers-license statutes, to prevent fraud by restricting security traffic; and (3) specific approval statutes, regulating and controlling only the securities sought to be sold within the state. Blue sky laws have been supplemented by the Securities Act of 1933 and the Securities Exchange Act of 1934, which regulate and control interstate dealings in securities and the operation of the organized security exchanges, respectively.

BLUESTEM PASTURES. Prior to 1929, called Flint Hills; a region in east central Kansas extending into Oklahoma between the Verdigris and Arkansas rivers (Osage pastures). During the late 1880's the pastures were fenced, and eventually the region became the most important pasture country in the central prairie-plains area.

BLUFFTON MOVEMENT. In South Carolina, an attempt in 1844 to invoke "separate state action" against the tariff of 1842, after John C. Calhoun's failure to secure the presidential nomination and the northern Democrats' abandonment of the South on the tariff. Though many Blufftonites undoubtedly contemplated disunion, the object of their leader, Robert Barnwell Rhett, seems to have been a "reform" of the Union giving further safeguards to southern interests. The movement collapsed within a short time, largely through its repudiation by Calhoun.

BLUNDER, FORT. *See* **Rouse's Point Boundary Controversy.**

BOARD OF TRADE AND PLANTATIONS. The main British colonial office from its creation, May 15, 1696, until the American Revolution. It was a paid board of five members, the chief officers of state being also ex officio members. It had charge of regular commercial relations with other nations, enforcement of trade and navigation acts, general supervision of colonial administration, and examination of colonial laws. It heard and investigated complaints of merchants, recommended imperial legislation in its field, and kept in touch with the regular consular service.

The board members changed with the usual party shifts. Under a dominant character like the Duke of Newcastle it had little power—most of the business being transferred directly to Newcastle's office. In 1748 George Dunk, Earl of Halifax, was appointed president of the board. He began at once to make his position important. Plans were developed for strengthening the royal governors. Judges were made dependent upon the crown for their salaries and terms of office, and the struggle began between agents of the crown and leaders of the colonial legislatures. Wills Hill, Earl of Hillsborough, who became a full secretary of state for the colonies, was directly responsible for many of the unfortunate policies between 1764 and 1772 that ultimately led to the Revolution.

BOARDS OF TRADE. *See* **Chambers of Commerce.**

BODY OF LIBERTIES. *See* **Massachusetts Body of Liberties.**

BOG IRON MINING. Bog ore, a brown hematite deposited in pond and bog bottoms, was found by the colonists in the coastal lowlands from Massachusetts to Delaware. It was the first important source of native iron, although superior but less accessible and tractable rock ores were also known to exist in America. These hematites were smelted with charcoal in small furnaces that cast, directly from the ore, kettles and other hollowware, as well as pig for refining into bars for nails and implements. Bog ores had been largely displaced by rock ores by the time of the Revolution.

BOISE (Idaho). Capital of Idaho, with a population of 102,451 in 1980. It is the center of a metropolitan area with a population of 173,036. Located on the Boise River, it provided an excellent base camp for gold prospectors in 1862, the year the city was founded. The capitol building is used as a center for government and also as a showcase for Idaho's minerals, forest products, and agricultural products. The city acts as principal market and manufacturing center for southwestern Idaho. Boise's refineries handle the sugar beets grown in Idaho, northern Nevada, and eastern Oregon.

BOISE, FORT. A fur trading post of the Hudson's Bay Company in Idaho. First built in 1834 on the Boise River about seven miles above its mouth, it was relocated in 1838 near the confluence of the Boise and Snake rivers. It was famous as a stopping point on the Oregon Trail. Partially destroyed by flood in 1853, it was abandoned after the Indian war of 1855.

BOLLMAN CASE (1807). In *ex parte* Bollman and Swartwout the Supreme Court upheld its power to issue a writ of habeas corpus to review a commitment by an inferior federal court, and ordered the release of two petitioners held on charges of treason as participants in the Burr conspiracy. Justus Erich Bollman and Samuel Swartwout, by separate routes, had carried a letter in cipher from Aaron Burr to Gen. James Wilkinson. Wilkinson arrested them and sent them to Washington. In holding that the evidence had been insufficient to support a charge of treason, Chief Justice John Marshall said that "there must be an actual assembling of men for the treasonable purpose, to constitute a levying of war." But, he added, if that be proved, then a conspirator, however remote from the scene of action, would be guilty.

BOLL WEEVIL. A beetle which eats the buds and young bolls of cotton; may have existed in Mexico and Central America for centuries. About 1892–93 it crossed into Texas; by 1923 it had reached the Atlantic coast. In 1930, 90 percent of cotton was infested. Since then the fight against it has decreased its ravages.

BOLTERS. Party members who do not support the regular nominee of their party or its platform. The "bolt" may occur at the convention or after the convention or primary.

BONANZA KINGS. John W. Mackay, James G. Fair, James C. Flood, and William S. O'Brien organized the Consolidated Virginia Silver Mine near Virginia City, Nev., from smaller claims on the Comstock lode, in 1871, later adding the nearby California mine. Production began to fall off in 1879, but in twenty-two years the two mines yielded $150 million in silver and gold and paid over $78 million in dividends. "Bonanza" was applied to the large ore body that lay in a vertical rift of the hanging wall of the Comstock lode.

BONANZA WHEAT FARMING. An important factor in the settlement and development of the Red River Valley spring wheat region. The Cass-Cheney farm, first and best known of the bonanzas, was established in 1875. By 1890 over 300 farms in the valley exceeded 1,000 acres; a half dozen or more exceeded 15,000 acres. Some were individually owned; others were corporations. Few were established after 1890, and most were broken up within the next quarter century.

BONDS, GOVERNMENT. *See* **Debt, Public.**

BONDS AND BOND MARKETS. A bond is a certificate which states that money has been loaned and that the issuer guarantees the money will be paid back at a certain time; meanwhile, a fixed rate of interest stated in the bond will be paid to the lender. Bonds are issued by individuals, companies, and government agencies. "Coupon" bonds are printed with coupons attached; a coupon is presented to a bank when an interest payment is due. "Savings" bonds are sold by the U.S. Treasury. The money is used for public purposes. Liberty Bonds were issued during World War I, and War Savings Bonds during and after World War II. "Municipal" bonds are issued by states, cities, towns, and government agencies. Holders ordinarily do not have to pay U.S. income tax on the interest they earn, so municipal bonds can be sold with lower interest payments than most corporation bonds. "Mortgage" bonds are issued by individuals or companies that need loans to buy property or special equipment. Bonds are also classified according to the length of their term and the degree to which they are secured by the assets of the borrower. They may be traded on any stock exchange.

***BONHOMME RICHARD–SERAPIS* ENCOUNTER** (Sept. 23, 1779). John Paul Jones's flagship, the *Bonhomme Richard,* was proceeding up the east coast of England in quest of English cargoes. Although worn-out and unseaworthy, it carried forty-two guns. Jones sighted two enemy ships, the *Serapis* and the *Countess of Scarborough,* and maneuvered close to the *Serapis*; both opened broadside fire. Two of his larger guns on the lower deck burst, killing and wounding several men and leaving only lighter guns and musketry. The slaughter on both sides was terrible, and the American ship was leaking badly. After an hour, Jones answered the British challenge to surrender: "I have not yet begun to fight." Two hours later the British surrendered.

BONITO IN CHACO CANYON. A large prehistoric pueblo ruin in N.Mex., northeast of Gallup, belonging to prehistoric Pueblo III, the Grand period in Pueblo culture. Bonito was occupied during 919–1130. It was originally four stories high with about 500 rooms, the architecture resembling modern Indian villages near Santa Fe. The ruin was partially excavated in 1896–99 by the Hyde Expedition and in 1921–23 by the National Geographic Society.

BONNEVILLE DAM. *See* **Hydroelectric Power.**

BONNEVILLE EXPEDITION (1832–34). Capt. B. L. E. Bonneville led a party of trappers and traders from Fort Osage, Missouri, May 1, 1832, along the Platte–South Pass route to Green River. Here Fort Bonneville was built. Bonneville moved to the headwaters of the Salmon River and then continued to cover the Rocky Mountains and the Columbia drainage basin. A branch expedition left Green River, July 1833, crossed Salt Lake Desert, descended Humboldt River, crossed the Sierras north of Yosemite Valley, and wintered at Monterey. It returned through the Sierras via Walker's Pass, across the Great Basin, and up Bear River, joining Bonneville June 1, 1834.

"BONNIE BLUE FLAG." A popular Confederate ballad. Authorities disagree as to the author, where it was first sung, and the meaning of "bonnie blue flag." It was, however, sung often by Harry McCarthy; it was sung in New Orleans and in Richmond theaters in 1861.

BONUS ARMY (1932). A spontaneous gathering of about 15,000 unemployed World War I veterans who in May, marched to Washington, D.C., seeking economic relief from Congress, eventually petitioning for immediate payment of the adjusted compensation, or "bonus," certificates approved by Congress in 1924 but not payable until 1945. The leader, Walter W. Waters, maintained almost military discipline. Although the police tried to provide quarters, most of the men built wretched hovels. In mid-June, Congress defeated the bonus bill, but the "Bonus Expeditionary Force" stayed on. Late in July, they were ordered to evacuate. An attempt to remove the remaining 2,000 resulted in the death of two policemen and two veterans. On July 28, U.S. troops drove them away using tanks, infantry, and cavalry.

BONUS BILL, CALHOUN'S. On Dec. 16, 1816, John C. Calhoun recommended that the House of Representatives inquire into creating a fund for internal improvements from profits from the second national bank. Calhoun, as chairman of the committee introduced a bill on December 23 to set apart as a permanent fund for internal improvements the $1.5 million bonus exacted from the bank as a price of the charter and the profits from the $7 million of the bank stock owned by the United States. Although the bill was passed, President James Madison vetoed it, Mar. 3, 1817, as unconstitutional.

BONUSES, MILITARY. Gratuities or benefits, usually paid in a lump sum, to veterans of military service, as distinguished from pensions, a continuing compensation paid to disabled veterans or their dependents. The practice began in 1776 when the Continental Congress voted to reward the Continental army with grants of land. In 1778 the Congress voted to give, at the end of the war, an additional five years' pay to commissioned officers and about $80 to others.

During the first half of the 19th century, bonuses took the exclusive form of land grants. Very little of the land was actually taken up by veterans, since the warrants could be sold or exchanged for interest-bearing or treasury scrip. A large market for the warrants developed and most of the bonus lands fell into the hands of speculators. Civil War veterans of the Union army received bonuses adjusted to the length of service, a maximum of $100 for three years' service.

Although servicemen received a bonus of $60 at the end of World War I, the American Legion, in 1919, took the position that ex-servicemen were entitled to "adjusted compensation"—the difference between money received in the service and the larger amount they could have earned at home. A bill to grant such a bonus was passed over President Calvin Coolidge's veto in 1924. Veterans were to receive $1.00 for each day of domestic service and $1.25 for each day served overseas, payment being in paid-up twenty-year endowment insurance policies, deferred until 1945. With the coming of the depression and massive unemployment, the Legion demanded immediate cash payment. In 1931 Congress passed over President Herbert Hoover's veto a compromise bill under which veterans could borrow 50 percent of the cash value at 4.5 percent interest. Subsequent demands were highlighted by the Bonus Army incident of 1932 (*see* Bonus Army). In January 1936 Congress passed over President Franklin D. Roosevelt's veto a bill for immediate payment.

Before the end of World War II, Congress passed the Servicemen's Readjustment Act of 1944, popularly called the GI Bill of Rights. The act provided unemployment compensation, education and job training, and guaranteed housing and business loans. The three programs ended in 1949, 1956, and 1962, respectively.

In July 1952 Congress passed the Veteran's Readjustment Act, which extended benefits to veterans of the Korean conflict honorably discharged on or before Jan. 31, 1955. Thus, veterans discharged after Feb. 1, 1955, were not eligible. Eleven years later Congress passed the Veteran's Readjustment Benefits Act of 1966, extending benefits to veterans of the conflict in Vietnam and retroactively to those who had served for more than 180 days after Jan. 31, 1955. In December 1974 Congress passed, over President Gerald Ford's veto, the Vietnam Era Veteran's Readjustment Act, extending the period of educational benefits from thirty-six to forty-five months and increasing the monthly payments to veterans enrolled in college by 23 percent.

BOODLE. Money used for graft or bribery, first applied by sensational newspapers (1884–86) to New York Aldermen charged with accepting bribes. Thereafter, the term came into common use to signify bribery in general and particularly in municipal governments.

BOOK AUCTIONS. The first book auction in America for which a definite record exists is the sale held by Ambrose Vincent in Boston, May 28, 1713. The auction spread rapidly to New York, Philadelphia, Virginia, and Charleston, S.C., in the second quarter of the century. Among the earliest and most active auctioneers was Robert Bell of Philadelphia, who held numerous sales from 1768 to 1784. In 1784 the Pennsylvania assembly passed an act requiring auctioneers to be appointed and licensed. By the late 19th century, activity centered in New York.

Noted sales include the later library of Thomas Jefferson (1829); the library of George Washington (1876); and the library of George Brinley of Hartford (1878–93), which was the largest collection of books relating to America ever formed. The Thomas Winthrop Streeter collection of North American history, particularly on the West, grossed more than $3 million (1966–69). The Robert Hoe library, rich in many fields, was the most valuable library ever sold by auction (1911–13) in America.

BOOK COLLECTING. *See* **Collecting: Books and Manuscripts.**

BOOK PUBLISHING. The history of book publishing in the United States began in 1638 with the arrival in Boston of a press that the Rev. Josse Glover, who died on the voyage over, had meant to set up. Glover's widow settled in Cambridge, where the press was set up and operated by two sons of Stephen Day. Eighteen-year-old Matthew Day, consequently, became the nation's first printer. In the hands of the Days and later of the family of Samuel Green, the Cambridge press printed more than 200 books before its demise in 1692. The *Whole Booke of Psalmes* (the *Bay Psalm Book*) was the first book printed in America (1640).

Book publishing was slow to rise. It was a cottage industry in the 17th and 18th centuries; for some time materials had to be imported, and a native literature was late in developing. The print shop also turned out magazines and newspapers.

In the 18th century, there were tentative starts in virtually every field of publishing. The center of the book trade was shifting from Boston toward Philadelphia and soon would shift to New York. The press also moved constantly westward. The long struggle for copyright was beginning, and specialized publishing was bringing new diversity. Children's books and textbooks were helping to broaden literacy.

Modern publishing began in the early 19th century, and Mathew Carey of Philadelphia is widely regarded as the first modern publisher. The house he founded still exists as Lea and Febiger. Books were sold before the Civil War through trade fairs, trade sales, and book auctions; in bookshops; and by subscription. Paperback publishing began in 1842. A technological revolution started about 1825 with the invention of the flatbed press and the revolving cylinder press. Thousands of volumes could be turned out in a short space of time. Cheap fiction, including the dime novel, came out of this revolution, which soon embraced hardcover books as well.

Most of the great houses known today were founded in the half-century before the Civil War. In New York, there were John Wiley and Sons, Harper, Appleton, A. S. Barnes, Putnam, Dodd, Mead, Baker and Scribner, D. Van Nostrand, and E. P. Dutton; in Philadelphia, besides Mathew Carey's successors, were J. B. Lippincott Company and the Blakiston Company; in Boston, Ticknor and Fields, Houghton Mifflin, and Little, Brown.

Between the Civil War and World War I publishing influenced the national culture more than any other medium until television. The leaders were Henry Holt, George E. Brett (who established the American branch of Macmillan), Thomas Y. Crowell, P. F. Collier, I. K. Funk, David McKay, Frank N. Doubleday, S. S. McClure, George Doran, Albert and Charles Boni, Alfred A. Knopf, and Ben W. Huebsch. The period also saw the rise of the university press, with Cornell University's appearing first (1869).

The mass market continued to expand with the help of public libraries and education. An overwhelming quantity of fiction was published between 1890 and 1910. The 1920's saw a literary renaissance and another generation of publishers: Bennett Cerf and Donald Klopfer (Random House), Leon Shimkin aand M. Lincoln Schuster (Simon and Schuster), and Alfred Harcourt and Donald Brace (Harcourt, Brace). During World War II millions of books were supplied to soldiers, leading to the growing importance of the paperback industry and to the phenomenon of the 1970's in which it was possible for an author to earn a million dollars from a book before publication, from paperback, motion picture, and other subsidiary rights.

BOOKS, CHILDREN'S. Reading matter for colonial children consisted largely of works to instruct or improve, like *Spiritual Milk for Boston Babes* (1646) by John Cotton and the *New England Primer* (published before 1690 by Benjamin Harris). Most were English imports or American printers' reissues, some with slight Americanization. Among the most significant were John Newbery's *The History of Little Goody Two Shoes* (1775 and 1787) and *Mother Goose's Melodies* (1786).

In the 1830's, Washington Irving and Christopher Pearse Cranch introduced American stories of the fantastic, and Samuel Griswold Goodrich and Jacob Abbott began their endless series of didactic geographical and travel stories. For decades the American Sunday School Union and other tract societies poured out little books advocating religion and condemning vice. By the 1850's Nathaniel Hawthorne was introducing Greek mythology in his *Wonder-Book for Boys and Girls* (1852) and *Tanglewood Tales* (1853). The 1860's and 1870's saw Mary Mapes Dodge creating *Hans Brinker* (1865); Louisa May Alcott, *Little Women* (1868) and its sequels; Thomas Bailey Aldrich, *The Story of a Bad Boy* (1870); and Mark Twain, *Tom Sawyer* (1876) and other stories. John Bennett's *Master Skylark* (1897) brought credit to the end of the century. From the 1880's on came dime novels and the formula-style Horatio Alger, Jr., series. While the boys had farm stories and western and sea adventures, the girls were offered pious heroines (such as Elsie Dinsmore) but also Susan Coolidge's "Katy" books (1872–86), Lucretia Hale's *The Peterkin Papers* (1880) and its sequel (1886), and Margaret Sidney's *Five Little Peppers* (1881) and its sequels. Joel Chandler Harris contributed his dialect stories from *Uncle Remus: His Songs and Sayings* (1880). The only lasting poetry for children was Sarah Josepha Hale's "Mary Had a Little Lamb" in her *Poems for Our Children* (1830) and Clement C. Moore's "A Visit from St. Nicholas" (1823).

The 20th century saw more English imports, translations from foreign-language books, and increased American production. L. Frank Baum achieved success with his Oz books, and other series writers also flourished. By 1922, critics began to recognize quality in children's literature through the annual John Newbery medal and, by 1938, the Randolph Caldecott medal for picture-book illustration—each established by Frederic G. Melcher and administered by the American Library Association. The first National Book Award for children's books was awarded in 1969.

BOOMER MOVEMENT (1879–85). Attempts to occupy an area in Indian Territory. The Five Civilized Tribes of Indians owned all of the present state of Oklahoma except the Panhandle. In 1866 for having participated in the Civil War on the side of the South, they were compelled to cede to the United States as a home for other Indians the western half of their domain. An unassigned fertile region of some 2 million acres near the center came to be known as the "unassigned lands" or Old Oklahoma.

Early in 1879 E. C. Boudinot published a newspaper article stating that this was public land, and so open to homestead entry. Colonies of homeseekers called "boomers" under the leadership of C. C. Carpenter (1879), David L. Payne (1880), and W. L. Couch (1884), attempted to settle the region but were ejected by soldiers. In 1889 the unassigned lands were opened to settlement by act of Congress.

BOOMTOWNS. Settlements that sprang up or rapidly increased in size as the result of some mineral or industrial development.

BOONDOGGLING. On Apr. 3, 1935, Robert C. Marshall testified that he taught various crafts, including "boondoggling," to workers on relief, and described "boondoggles" as gadgets or useful articles made out of scrap material. The term "boondoggling" was thereafter rather loosely used by critics of the New Deal to ridicule so-called useless make-work and unproductive projects for relief workers.

BOONE-CALLAWAY KIDNAPPING. Boonesborough on the Kentucky River had been left in peace by the Indians until July 14, 1776, when three girls were captured floating in a canoe: Jemima, daughter of Daniel Boone, and two daughters of Col. Richard Callaway. A rescue party was organized by Boone. Meanwhile the girls were hurried north toward the Shawnee towns across the Ohio River. The girls attempted to mark their trail until threatened by the Indians. The third morning the rescuers came up and the girls were escorted home in triumph.

BOONESBOROUGH. Former village on the south side of the Kentucky River, in the present county of Madison, founded Apr. 2, 1775, by Daniel Boone. Boone and his companions blazed a trail across Cumberland Gap and through the wilderness to the mouth of Otter Creek on the Kentucky River. There they erected a stout stockaded fort. On Apr. 15 and July 4, 1777, Boonesborough was subjected to Indian attacks. The fiercest siege and assault occurred Sept. 7–20, 1778, by a large body of Shawnee, but failed to bring about its downfall, and the Indians withdrew.

BOONE'S STATION. The stockaded home of Daniel Boone from 1780 to 1786, settled by Daniel's brother, Israel, in 1776, on Boone's Creek in Fayette County, Ky., near the present village of Athens.

BOONTON IRON WORKS. Important iron-making center, founded about 1770 by Samuel Ogden along the Rockaway River, near Boonton, Morris County, N.J. With the building of the Morris Canal in 1830 the New Jersey Iron Company was organized. Under Fuller and Lord (1852–76) the enterprise became an integrated industry with ore and timber reserves, canal boats, furnaces, mills, and auxiliary plants. The plant closed in 1911.

BOONVILLE, BATTLE OF (June 17, 1861). In the first engagement of the Civil War in Missouri, troops of the Missouri state guard (prosouthern) under Col. John S. Marmaduke were defeated by Gen. Nathaniel Lyon at Boonville, a strategic point on the Missouri River.

BOOT AND SHOE MANUFACTURING. Bootmakers and shoemakers arrived early in each of the colonies. Despite the widespread existence of these craftsmen, a nascent industry had begun to develop in eastern Massachusetts by the end of the colonial era. To supply the demands of a growing population after the revolutionary war, merchant capitalists slowly reorganized the trade. They purchased leather from American and foreign markets, cut the materials, hired craftsmen to make the shoes, and sold the finished products.

Factories and mechanization came after 1850, as entrepreneurs recognized the usefulness of consolidating various processes at one location, where better supervision could occur. Machines were perfected that imitated specific hand processes. Three developments proved most significant: the adaptation of the Howe sewing machine to stitching uppers; a device for sewing the upper to the sole; and the perfection of the welt-stitching machine for joining the upper and sole.

In 1895 employees formed the International Boot and Shoe Workers Union. In 1899 the principal producers of shoemaking machinery formed the United Shoe Machinery Company, which still controlled this industry in the mid-1970's. In 1905 shoe manufacturers formed the National Boot and Shoe Manufacturers Association, which changed names several times and in 1972 became American Footwear Manufacturers Association.

In 1977, 811 American shoe manufacturing establishments produced $3.7 billion worth, or 391 million pairs, of shoes, and provided work for 146,000 people.

***BOOTH* V. *UNITED STATES*,** 291 U.S. 339 (1934). In 1919 Congress passed an act permitting certain federal judges to retire with full pay, at the age of seventy. On June 16, 1933, new legislation reduced their pay 15 percent. Retired Judge Wilbur F. Booth thereupon sued the government. The Supreme Court unanimously ruled in his favor.

BOOTLEGGING. Derived from the early Indian traders' custom of carrying a bottle of liquor in the boot, especially applied to illicit deliveries of alcoholic beverages. The manufacture of illicit hard liquor is termed "moonshining," and the product, variously known, is often called mountain dew.

Bootlegging has little reason for being unless heavy taxation or legal efforts to prevent the sale of liquor create a demand. Between the effective date of the Eighteenth Amendment, prohibiting manufacture of or traffic in liquor (Jan. 16, 1920), and its repeal (Dec. 3, 1933) the consumption of bootleg liquor was 100 million gallons a year.

A limited number of bootleggers has always operated, but since the quality of their merchandise and public support are both uncertain, their sales volume remains relatively small. The federal Bureau of Alcohol, Tobacco, and Firearms reported seizing 15,000 stills in 1958. Only 1,300 were seized in 1974, but the bureau estimates that it confiscates one-third to one-half of all operating stills.

BORAX (sodium tetraborate). Important for cleaning the surfaces of metal pieces to be joined by being melted together. The key figure in the discovery of borax in North America was John A. Veatch, who found it in California in 1856. The California Borax Company was organized to exploit this source. In 1857 Veatch found borax in the waters of mud volcanoes in the Colorado Desert of southern California. Borax was soon found in surface encrustations in Nevada and southern California. In 1880 production began in Death Valley, Calif., where for a decade the famous twenty-mule-team wagons carried it to the railroad junction at Mojave, 160 miles away.

These surface deposits of borax were largely sodium calcium tetraborate (ulexite), and their conversion to true borax was mastered only in the mid-1880's. American producers drove the price down to a level that caused most of them to fail. The principal survivor, Francis M. ("Borax") Smith, promoted borax in a pamphlet advertising 200 "recipes" for borax. By 1896 Smith controlled nearly all American sources of borax, but was forced to merge with the English company Redwood and Sons to form a company now known as U.S. Borax. The exploitation of shallow deposits terminated after the beginning of mining operations in 1927 in the Mojave Desert, now marked by the company town, Boron. In the 1970's, production there and at Searles Lake, Calif., exceeded 1 million tons per year.

BORDER FORTS, EVACUATION OF (1796). With the Mississippi River and the line through the middle of the Great Lakes–St. Lawrence system as the western and northern boundaries of the new nation (*see* Definitive Treaty of Peace, 1783), Great Britain agreed to evacuate all places held by its armies within the United States "with all convenient speed." These included Carleton Island (Fort Haldimand), Oswego (Fort Ontario), Niagara, Detroit, and Michilimackinac, guarding the fur trade route between Montreal and the far Northwest. For a decade Great Britain pursued a policy of opportunism, meanwhile retaining the posts and exercising de facto control over the Northwest. In 1793, however, it entered the continental wars, while in America President George Washington was prosecuting the conquest of the Northwestern Indian Confederacy (*see* Wayne Campaign). Faced with a war in Europe, the British did not want another in America. By the Jay Treaty (ratified in 1795) the evacuation of the western posts by June 1, 1796, was promised. With the transfer American rule over the country adjacent to the Great Lakes was first established, but west of Lake Michigan and on Lake Superior British authority continued dominant until after the War of 1812.

BORDER RUFFIANS. Citizens of western Missouri who endeavored to establish slavery in Kansas Territory. The term originated in 1855 with Gen. B. F. Stringfellow's assault upon A. H. Reeder, governor of the territory, and was first used by the *New York Tribune.* Antislavery presses and orators soon expanded the term to include all proslavery southerners in Kansas.

BORDER SLAVE STATE CONVENTION (Feb. 4–27, 1861). Also called the Peace Convention or Peace Conference; met in Washington, D.C., to attempt to satisfy the states of the far South on the slavery issue. Twenty-two states were represented, with the border states most active. The Crittenden Compromise plan, which formed the basis of discussion, was so modified by further compromise that the convention satisfied no one. The recommendations, submitted to Congress on Feb. 27, constituted the last attempt at conciliation on the slavery question in the territories.

BORDER STATES. Slave states bordering on the North, consisting of Delaware, Maryland, Virginia, Kentucky, and Missouri. Largely southern in sentiment, many of their economic ties were with the North. None seceded except Virginia, from which West Virginia separated. Kentucky maintained for a few months in 1861 the unique policy of neutrality, and all except Delaware sent considerable numbers of soldiers to the Confederacy. Kentucky and Delaware were the only border states to cling to slavery until the Thirteenth Amendment abolished it.

BORDER WAR (1854–59). The opening of the Kansas Territory to slavery in 1854 promoted emigration from the Northeast of antislavery groups and the arrival of squatters and speculators. Recurring personal altercations led proslavery and free-state groups to organize regulating associations and guerrilla bands. The first eighteen months of settlement witnessed sporadic killings and robberies, including the Wakarusa War, December 1855, which brought over 1,000 border ruffians into the territory. "Bleeding Kansas" soon became a grim reality. The sack of Lawrence, May 21, 1856, by a posse of border ruffians and John Brown's massacre of five proslavery men at Pottawatomie three days later started a four months' reign of terror. Major conflict terminated in 1859, but sporadic disorders continued until the Civil War inaugurated a new chapter in Kansas-Missouri relations.

BORGNE, BATTLE OF LAKE (Dec. 14, 1814). The naval engagement preceding the Battle of New Orleans. The British captured five American gunboats guarding the Malheureux Island passage. This cleared the eastern approach to the city and avoided the fortifications along the river. The defeated Americans inflicted heavy losses upon their captors, delaying the attack on New Orleans, which made it possible for the lately arrived Gen. Andrew Jackson to organize the defense of the city.

BOROUGH. Numerous colonial towns were patterned after the English borough, a trading community or town with some degree of corporate organization and certain rights of self-government. Colonial boroughs received charters from the governors and were governed by a mayor and recorder, appointed by the governor, and aldermen elected by the freemen. They also handled both civil and criminal business. After the Revolution borough charters were granted by the state legislatures.

BOSQUE REDONDO. A reservation of forty square miles on the Pecos River in east-central New Mexico, near Fort Sumner, to which 8,000 Navaho and 400 Mescalero Apache were removed in 1863. The government planned to transform the Navaho into peaceful, sedentary farmers. Although the plan was unsuccessful, it did end the raiding. The Navaho were allowed to return to their homeland in 1868.

BOSSES AND BOSSISM, POLITICAL. Anyone who controls voters in an authoritative, organized, and arbitrary manner in an American political entity, especially a city, county, or state, is traditionally known as a political boss. Bossism is a phenomenon of the latter half of the 19th century and the first half of the 20th century and has been linked with the immigration, urbanization, and machine politics of that era. Although a boss is a practitioner of machine politics, not all machine political leaders are bosses. To be a boss in the classic sense means to dominate a polity—a city, county, or state. Machine politics concentrates on patronage, service, and favors in exchange for electoral loyalty. It minimizes issues, ideology, and impersonal rationality while maximizing personal contact and organized access to government.

Famous city bosses included William Marcy Tweed, Richard Croker, Charles Francis Murphy, Ed Flynn (all of New York), James McManes (Philadelphia), Frank Hague (Jersey City), James Michael Curley (Boston), Edward H. Crump (Memphis), Abraham Ruef (San Francisco), Thomas J. Pendergast (Kansas City, Mo.), and George B. Cox (Cincinnati). State bosses included Matthew Stanley Quay and his successor Boies Penrose (Pennsylvania), Thomas Collier Platt (New York), Thomas Taggart (Indiana), Huey P. Long (Louisiana), and Harry Flood Byrd (Virginia). City bosses could sometimes parlay their power into domination of state politics. Bosses have not come exclusively from either of the two major political parties, but more big-city and southern state bosses have been identified with the Democratic party. Richard J. Daley, mayor of Chicago until his death in 1976, was the last outstanding big-city boss, having dominated Chicago's Democratic machine for two decades, but by the 1970's he had become something of an anachronism.

BOSTON (Mass.). Capital of Massachusetts, located on Massachusetts Bay. Capt. John Smith explored and mapped the vicinity of Boston in 1614. In 1621 a party from Plymouth visited the site. Settlers located there and across the Charles River. Following the Great Migration of 1630, John Winthrop's group settled at Charlestown but soon moved over to the Shawmut peninsula. On September 7 it was ordained by the Court of Assistants, sitting at Charlestown, that the new town be named Boston. In 1632 Boston was made the capital of Massachusetts Bay Colony. In 1639 the first post office was opened; in 1652, a mint; in 1674, a printing press; and in 1686 the first bank in the colonies. Boston was becoming the largest and most important town in America. It was one of the earliest and chief centers of rebellion against the government of England, and the first armed conflicts of the revolutionary war took place in its environs.

Boston was merely a town administered by selectmen until 1822, when it received a city charter. During the 19th century it became the cultural center of the continent. It was the nation's leading port until well into the 19th century, when it lost its supremacy to New York.

By 1980 the metropolitan area included seventy-eight cities and towns; the population of the city proper was 562,994 and the metropolitan area, 13,887,800. Since World War II, Boston's industry has spread throughout the metropolitan area, while commerce has remained centered in the city; machinery, electrical goods, and shoes are high in the area's list of manufactures, and Boston is the world's leading wholesale wool market. Still a major fishing port, Boston is New England's main port, handling over 20 million metric tons of cargo annually. Boston is the home of twenty colleges and universities, including Boston and Northeastern universities. It is also a medical center, including the notable Massachusetts General Hospital. Boston's cultural tradition continues.

BOSTON, SIEGE OF (Mar. 4–17, 1776). On July 3, 1775, George Washington, chosen commander in chief by the Continental Congress, found the British holding Bunker Hill and Boston Neck. During the winter no serious operations were undertaken. In January 1776, the guns captured at Ticonderoga (May 10, 1775) reached Cambridge. On March 4, Washington seized Dorchester Heights, from which his guns commanded the city and harbor. The British forces were now in an untenable position, and on the 17th they embarked for Halifax. The Americans immediately occupied Boston.

BOSTON & MAINE. *See* **Railroads, Sketches of Principal Lines.**

***BOSTON-BERCEAU* ACTION** (Oct. 12, 1800). Off Guadeloupe, the U.S. frigate *Boston* (thirty-six guns) captured the French corvette *Berceau* (twenty-four guns) after a twelve-hour chase and a stubborn engagement. Though almost dismantled, the *Berceau* was towed into Boston as a prize.

BOSTON COMMITTEE OF CORRESPONDENCE. A revolutionary body of propaganda and administration that promoted American unity and made possible the first Continental Congress. The parent body was appointed by a Boston town meeting, Nov. 2, 1772, and consisted of twenty-one men. Within a few months eighty committees had been organized in Massachusetts. The committee also played a role in the early conduct of hostilities and facilitated the transition of Massachusetts to independent statehood.

BOSTON COMMON. A forty-five-acre tract in Boston, bought by the city in 1634 as a pasture and parade ground. Where the British troops were entrenched in 1775, people now walk under the trees while their children ride in the swan boats on the Frog Pond. Orators still speak at the Boston Common. In the Central Burying Ground lie many Bostonians and British soldiers killed at the Battle of Bunker Hill, and monuments to famous citizens border the paths.

BOSTON MANUFACTURING COMPANY. Organized in 1813 by Boston merchants previously engaged in the India trade, including Francis Cabot Lowell. It built at Waltham, Mass., the first complete textile factory in America, combining power spinning and weaving.

BOSTON MASSACRE (Mar. 5, 1770). British regulars arriving (Oct. 1, 1768) to maintain order in Boston produced soldier-civilian tensions that came to a head on Mar. 5, 1770. Seven grenadiers led by Capt. Thomas Preston marched to the relief of an eighth, on duty at the customhouse and beset by a taunting crowd of civilians. Preston, unable to disperse the crowd, loudly ordered his men, "Don't fire," while the mob was shouting "Fire and be damned!" The soldiers fired, killing five men.

In October 1770 Preston was tried for murder and acquitted by a Boston jury; some surviving documents suggest that the jury was "packed." The soldiers won acquittals a month later, the jurors coming from towns outside Boston. Four civilians accused of firing from the customhouse windows were tried in December 1770; the evidence against them was so thin that the jurors peremptorily acquitted all.

"BOSTON MEN". A term derived from the hailing place of the first Yankee ships trading along the northwest coast of America, used to distinguish Americans from Englishmen and Canadians. The expression was incorporated and used in the Chinook jargon.

"BOSTONNAIS" (or "Bastonais"). Once applied by French-Canadians to Americans. It dates back to the invasion of Canada under Gen. Richard Montgomery in 1775, and possibly to that of Sir William Phips in 1690. Meaning "people of Boston," it was given to all English colonists on the Atlantic seaboard and finally to all Americans.

***BOSTON NEWS-LETTER*.** The first newspaper published without interruption during the colonial period, beginning the week Apr. 17–24, 1704. The original publisher was John Campbell; the first printer, Bartholomew Green. In 1723 Green became the owner and changed its name to *The Weekly News-Letter.* When Green died in 1732 his son-in-law, John Draper, took over. Draper died in 1762, leaving the paper to his son, Richard, who changed the title to *The Boston Weekly News-Letter and New England Chronicle.* Richard Draper published his pro-British sentiments in the paper until his death in 1774. His widow continued publication until Feb. 22, 1776, when British troops and Loyalists, including Mrs. Draper, evacuated Boston.

BOSTON POLICE STRIKE (1919). About three-quarters of the Boston police force went on strike, Sept. 9, when the police commissioner refused to recognize their right to affiliate with the American Federation of Labor. Mayor Andrew J. Peters and a citizens' committee made compromise proposals relating to pay and working conditions, but the police commissioner rejected them. The strike left Boston almost unprotected, and riots, disorders, and robberies occurred. Peters called out the Boston militia, restored order, and broke the strike. With the city already under control, Governor Calvin Coolidge ordered the police commissioner again to take charge of the police and called out the entire Massachusetts militia. This action gave Coolidge a reputation as a courageous defender of law and order.

BOSTON PORT ACT. The first of the Coercion Acts, passed by Parliament on Mar. 31, 1774. To punish Boston for the Boston Tea Party, the act ordered the port of Boston closed on June 1, 1774, until the townspeople paid for the tea destroyed and proved they were peaceable subjects. The cry was raised in America that the Port Act was merely a prelude to a "massacre of American liberty"; the colonies rallied to Boston's aid; and the Continental Congress was called.

BOSTON RESOLUTIONS OF 1767. When New England's declining prosperity made economy essential and the Townshend Acts threatened fresh British oppression, Samuel Adams secured the passage in the Boston town meeting of resolutions pledging the citizens to abstain from the use of many British manufactures. Outside of New England, however, the movement had little success, and it was soon merged with the nonimportation agreement.

BOSTON RESOLUTIONS OF 1810. A forecast of New England separatism in the approaching War of 1812. In these resolutions, passed February 9, the Massachusetts legislature condemned the severity of President James Madison toward Francis James Jackson, the notorious British minister, exculpated Jackson, and endeavored to compel renewed diplomatic intercourse with Great Britain.

BOSTON TEA PARTY (Dec. 16, 1773). During the night, 342 chests of tea belonging to the East India Company were thrown into Boston harbor by American patriots, Sons of Liberty, disguised as Indians. This audacious destruction of British property was caused by the Boston Whigs' fear that if the tea were landed, its cheap price would prove an "invincible temptation" to the people, give the East India Company a monopoly of the American tea trade, and establish the right of Parliament to raise a colonial revenue by means of port duties. The Boston Tea Party marked the beginning of violence in the dispute between mother country and colonies, and it put the most radical patriots in command throughout America. The efforts of the British government to single out Massachusetts for punishment served only to unite the colonies and hasten them into war with England.

BOSTON TEN TOWNSHIPS. A tract of 230,400 acres north of the Susquehanna River in New York, claimed by both New York and Massachusetts until, by the Treaty of Hartford in 1786, New York was granted sovereignty and Massachusetts right of preemption of the soil. Subsequently, in 1787, right of purchase from the Indians was granted by Massachusetts to Samuel Brown and ten associates.

BOTANICAL GARDENS. Specialized parks that display the diversity among plants and provide regionally significant demonstrations of the most beautiful and cultivable flowering plants and ferns from the world catalog of more than 300,000 extant species. Among the earliest botanical gardens in the United States were John Bartram's Garden, established near Philadelphia in 1728 and now a public park; André Michaux's Garden, established at Charleston, S.C., in 1787, now part of that city; and the Elgin Botanical Garden, established in New York in 1801 where Rockefeller Center now stands. The oldest existing American garden is the Missouri Botanical Garden, founded in St. Louis in 1859.

Botanical gardens range from one acre to thousands of acres. Among the largest are the New York Botanical Garden and the Missouri Botanical Garden, both strongly oriented to research and professional training, and both maintaining large herbaria, libraries, and laboratories.

BOTANY. The study of American plants has attracted many naturalists, beginning with early explorers. Botanical specimens taken to Europe in the 16th and 17th centuries from the Florida-Georgia, Roanoke, and Virginia areas were included in John Gerard's *Herball* (1597) and John Parkinson's *Theatrum* (1640). The first book on North American plants was by a Paris physician, Jacques-Philippe Cornut, *Canadensium Plantarum* (1635). He relied on specimens growing in Parisian gardens. The earliest notable resident naturalist was John Banister, who came to America in 1678. The oldest Virginia specimens preserved today, taken by John Banister, were published separately by Robert Morison, John Ray, and Leonard Plukenet and, with Virginia specimens and descriptions sent by John Clayton to Johann Gronovius, Carl Linnaeus' associate in Leiden, were enumerated in *Flora virginica* (1739–43), the earliest book devoted to Atlantic coastal plain flora. The descriptions and drawings of Carolina plants in Mark Catesby's *Natural History* and important collections made by Pehr Kalm, especially from Pennsylvania and New Jersey, with a few specimens from Cadwalader Colden along the Hudson River and John Bartram along Delaware Bay, were the essence of Linnaeus' knowledge of the plants of the eastern United States, as incorporated in his pivotal *Species plantarum* (1753).

Bartram established the first botanic garden in 1728. With his son, William, he discovered plants endemic to the southeastern states, including *Franklinia;* William Bartram's *Travels* (1791) is an important source book for the naturalist today. Benjamin Smith Barton illustrated his *Elements of Botany* (1803), the first botany text published in the United States, largely with William Bartram's drawings. Barton planned a more comprehensive continental flora than André Michaux's (1801, 1803) and employed the German Frederick Pursh and, later, the Englishman Thomas Nuttall to botanize for him. Barton intended to include novelties of the Meriwether Lewis and William Clark expedition; but Pursh, apprehending inexorable delays, published his own *Flora Americae septentrionalis* (1814), the year before Barton's death. Nuttall botanized from Georgia to the mouth of the Columbia River and from San Diego to Michilimackinac. His *Genera* (1818), although in the already outmoded Linnaean classification, is a fundamental reference. François André Michaux had accompanied his father, André, on his American explorations, and in 1801 returned to America to continue the work. He explored west to the Mississippi and published *Histoire des arbres forestiers de l'Amérique septentrionale* (1810–13). Stephen H. Long's expedition to the Rocky Mountains was the first government-sponsored expedition to document floras and faunas. In his report on the expedition, John Torrey adopted the natural system of classification of Bernard de Jussieu. Edwin James, who also took part in the expedition, botanized (July 1820) on the summit of Pikes Peak. Botanical exploration increased rapidly, bearing fruit in Torrey and Asa Gray's *Flora of North America* (1838–43). Harvard's Gray, an advocate of Darwinism in America, became the leading botanist of the 19th century. The plants of the California coast were first collected in 1791 by Thaddaeus Haenke of Spain. In 1792–93 Martín Sessé and José Mariano Mociño led another Spanish botanical expedition to New Spain and southern California. British botanists Archibald Menzies, David Douglas, and Thomas Drummond collected many horticultural species in the West during the late 18th and early 19th centuries.

Many early American collectors in the West were attached to government exploring expeditions and, later, to government surveys. Regional floras for the West were often published by the federal government. Edward Lee Greene and Edward Palmer were notable plant collectors who often traveled alone in the West during the late 19th century.

The modern study of American plants depends heavily on collections in herbaria. The herbaria made in America during the 18th century commonly went to Europe, and in the 19th century those that stayed in the country often were inadequately preserved. Thus, many of the important herbarium collections in America are less than a century old.

Dimension was added to the study of botany when the first American microscope with an efficient achromatic lens appeared. Charles Edward Bessey opened the first student laboratory in 1871. Graduate work abroad (principally in Germany), immigrant botanists, Darwinian concepts, and the question of mechanism versus vitalism stimulated laboratory science and departmentalized botany. Edward Charles Jeffrey, for example, became the first professor of vegetable histology (later plant morphology) at Harvard in 1902; and his *Anatomy of Woody Plants* (1917) and C. J. Chamberlain's *Gymnosperms, Structure and Evolution* (1934) evidenced increasing interest in evolution and phylogeny. Plant physiology had been introduced by Joseph Priestley when he came to America as an exile in 1794, but little progress was made before the 20th century. D. T. MacDougal wrote the first American text on plant physiology (1901). The physicist L. J. Briggs and the plant ecologist H. L. Shantz worked out the wilting coefficients of plants. Between 1930 and 1940 knowledge of photosynthesis and hormone actions progressed. Tissue culture, initiated by W. J. Robbins in 1930, inspired research in factors necessary for growth and differentiation. With the advent of the electron microscope, morphogenesis and ultrastructure were favored by plant physiologists. Molecular biology, which originally concentrated on bacteria, now studies development in higher plants.

Plant pathology was first taught at Illinois in 1873. The ability of bacteria to induce plant disease was demonstrated in 1879–85. Understanding of viruses progressed when studies showed that no symptoms were produced in some hosts (1918) or under certain environmental conditions (1922), and virus strains were demonstrated in 1925. Wendell M. Stanley, Nobel laureate in 1946, purified a virus strain in 1935. Algal studies, at first taxonomic, were diversified as Gilbert Smith probed the origins of gametes and as physiological investigations led to algae as potential food in space travel.

The first American experiment in genetics, reported by Cotton Mather in 1716, concerned Indian corn. A development important to genetics was the opening of the West and the subsequent inauguration of land-grant colleges (1862), which stressed agricultural botany. Following the rediscovery of Mendelian inheritance in 1900, genetics attracted renewed botanical and zoological experimentation. Tomatoes and tobacco stimulated a new field of study, cytogenetics.

Paleobotany—originally purely descriptive because of an expanding coal industry and the discovery of fossil beds in the West—came to embrace the study of paleoclimates, fossil pollens, and migration of floras.

BOUCHARD EXPEDITION. An effort on the part of the Buenos Aires revolutionary authorities to bring into the anti-Spanish liberal cause the inhabitants of California. Hippolyte de Bouchard came to California and, Nov. 20, 1818, captured Monterey. Other landings showed that the Californians were not anxious for liberation from Spain. Accordingly, Bouchard sailed for Chile, and California remained in the Spanish empire until Apr. 11, 1822, when a special junta declared it dependent upon Agustín de Iturbide's Mexican empire.

BOUGAINVILLE. The amphibious landing on Bougainville, largest of the Solomon Islands, was made by the U.S. First Marine Amphibious Corps, at Cape Torokina on the western coast, on Nov. 1, 1943. The objective was to gain locations for airfields within easy striking distance of Rabaul, on New Britain Island. This was, at the time, the best-planned and executed amphibious operation of World War II. Even though the Japanese moved many troops into the Allied perimeter, by Nov. 30 the objective was achieved and the perimeter was well defended.

BOULDER DAM. *See* **Hydroelectric Power.**

BOUNDARIES OF THE UNITED STATES. The boundaries of the United States have changed many times during the nation's history. When the United States and Great Britain made their peace treaty in 1783, one of the main provisions was the recognition by Great Britain that the former colonies controlled certain land areas of North America. Thirteen British colonies had revolted against royal rule, but the land recognized as the United States covered the territory of twenty-four of the present states. The northern boundary was drawn through the Great Lakes and the St. Lawrence River, and across the northern edges of New York, Vermont, and New Hampshire.

The southern boundary was the boundary between Georgia and Florida, but secret clauses of the treaty set the boundary in two places. If Great Britain had to turn Florida back to Spain, the proper boundary of Florida lay at the line of 31° north latitude. The United States agreed to a more northerly border if the British continued to hold Florida.

Spain got Florida back from Great Britain in 1783, and found that the line of 31° had been set as the new border. This dispute led to Pinckney's Treaty in 1795: the border of Florida was agreed to be where the peace treaty with Great Britain had drawn it.

The Louisiana Purchase. In 1803, Thomas Jefferson's administration arranged for the largest single land addition to the United States through the Louisiana Purchase from France. The $15 million purchase price added large parts of thirteen new states. However, there was a good deal of question about where the Louisiana Purchase began and ended.

The northern border was to touch on the border of British-owned Canada. However, French claims based in Louisiana and in Canada overlapped. Also, the correct northwestern boundary as of 1783 was still unsettled.

The War of 1812 pitted the United States against Great Britain, with the control of the Great Lakes and Canada at stake. The Convention of 1818 took up the question of the old northwestern boundary of the United States and Canada (as of 1783) as well as the boundary between U.S.-owned Louisiana and the western sections of Canada. A line was drawn directly south from the northwest point of Lake of the Woods to the line of 49° north latitude. From that point out to the Rockies, the forty-ninth parallel was accepted as the boundary between the United States and Canada.

Florida Boundary and Transcontinental Treaty (1819). The Louisiana Purchase reopened boundary questions with Spain. French explorers and colonists had claimed parts of Florida. After the Louisiana Purchase the United States began to act as though these sections of West Florida were included in the Louisiana Purchase.

In 1810, the United States announced that it regarded the Perdido River as the boundary of Florida, and claimed the land between the Perdido and the Mississippi. Another step was taken to control West Florida in 1812, when the Territory of Mississippi was created with a strip of Gulf Coast from the Pearl to the Perdido River. Spain had neither the troops nor the power to cause any serious difficulty for American occupation. Today that section is divided between the states of Alabama and Mississippi.

Partly as a result of these acquisitions, and partly because Gen. Andrew Jackson had invaded Spanish Florida in pursuit of hostile Indians and their European allies, a treaty was drawn up to turn Florida as a whole over to the United States. This Florida cession, however, was only part of the Adams-Onís Treaty, sometimes called the Transcontinental Treaty. The treaty took up the question of the western and southern boundaries of Louisiana, where the former French possession touched on Texas and the Spanish claims in the Rocky Mountains. The treaty lent further support to U.S. claims to the extreme Northwest and the Pacific Coast.

The Maine Border Settlement (1842). The border between Maine and the Canadian province of New Brunswick had been a matter of dispute since the Peace of Paris. The peace treaty had referred to the course of the St. Croix River as part of the boundary. It took until 1798 for a mixed U.S.-British commission to agree on which branch of the St. Croix was to be used as the boundary. In the meantime, the king of the Netherlands attempted to solve the problem, and the so-called Aroostook War had nearly led to a third war between the United States and Britain. This dispute was settled in 1842 by the signing of the Webster-Ashburton Treaty.

Texas and the Mexican Cession. When the United States annexed the Republic of Texas, the question of boundaries between Texas and Mexico was inherited from the Lone Star

Republic. The Mexican War, in fact, began in the disputed territory which lay between the Rio Grande (which Texas and the United States claimed as the border) and the Nueces River (claimed by Mexico). This was the only border dispute in U.S. history which led to a major war.

After the Mexican War an enormous new portion of North America came under U.S. rule. The cession of land by Mexico included all of California, Utah and Nevada, plus most of Arizona and New Mexico. In 1854, the Gadsden Purchase treaty with Mexico added the southern strips of Arizona and New Mexico.

Oregon. The northwestern portion of the United States was generally called the Oregon Territory. It included modern Oregon, Washington, Idaho, and parts of Montana. Under the Louisiana Purchase, the United States claimed this land and much that lay farther north in what is now British Columbia. In 1819, the U.S. claims were reinforced by the acquisition of Spain's claim to the region.

A dispute arose with Great Britain over the territory. The Convention of 1818 said that the territory would be "jointly" occupied, not actually annexed by either country. American settlers moving into Oregon in the 1840's caused a great deal of tension with Great Britain.

In 1846, the extreme claims of Americans were withdrawn and a treaty was worked out with Great Britain. This treaty extended the boundary line of the 1818 convention (49° north latitude) to the Pacific, except for the large area of Vancouver Island, which remained in British hands.

Alaska. The purchase of Alaska from Russia in 1867 brought with it one other major question about U.S. boundaries. There was no question about the north-south boundary along the 141° west longitude line. The panhandle of Alaska, however, ran southward along the Pacific coast. This panhandle was defined in a treaty between Russia and Great Britain in 1825 as being a strip along the coast which was thirty miles in depth. The coastline of Alaska is extremely irregular, so the question arose, whether the thirty-mile strip was to extend inland from the inlets, or from "headland to headland" at the mouths of the bays and inlets.

The question became an important one in the 1890's, when gold was discovered in the Klondike region. Canadian interests tried to get the boundary drawn from headland to headland so that Canadians might have one open port of their own. The United States contended that the boundary should follow the actual shoreline. This dispute was settled by a joint committee of six lawyers, three from each side. The settlement, reached in 1903, found in favor of the United States. In spite of this experience, which was painful for Canadians, a new international joint commission was created in 1909. This commission handles questions that may arise between the United States and Canada regarding use of the waterways between the two countries. In the waters of the Great Lakes, Lake Champlain, and the St. Lawrence, the cooperation of the two nations has dated from 1818, when the Rush-Bagot Agreement led to the discontinuance of naval forces on the lakes. This agreement and its later application to the land boundary have led to a peaceful boundary between the United States and Canada.

BOUNDARY DISPUTES BETWEEN STATES. At the time of the adoption of the U.S. Constitution (1788), apparently only Pennsylvania and Maryland of the original thirteen states had no boundary question. Since the adoption, more than half the states have been involved in boundary disagreements. Probably the first to be settled was that between North Carolina and South Carolina. This was ended by a survey in 1815 that extended the 1772 line to the corner of Georgia. The Massachusetts–Rhode Island dispute originated in the Plymouth Colony grant of 1630 and the Rhode Island charter of 1663. In spite of a Supreme Court case in 1846 that Rhode Island lost, the dispute was not settled until the two states agreed on a boundary line by a compact assented to by Congress in 1858. The line was remarked in 1899 by mutual consent. The boundary dispute between Connecticut and New York, which began before 1650, was settled by the two states in 1880, Congress approving their action in 1881. The Massachusetts–New Hampshire boundary controversy, which originated in the Massachusetts charter of 1629, was settled in 1895.

The disputes settled by congressional action alone have related chiefly to boundaries originally established between territories by act of Congress. Notable among these are changes in the boundaries of Michigan with Indiana and Ohio. A protracted Illinois-Wisconsin dispute was settled with the admission of Wisconsin into the Union in 1848.

A relatively large number of boundary disputes between states have been settled by decisions of the Supreme Court where specific treaties have been involved. In the dispute between Missouri and Kentucky, the court upheld the treaty signed by France, Spain, and England in 1763 which set the Mississippi River as the boundary.

In boundary questions between states not involving specific treaties, the Supreme Court applies the principles of general international law. Water boundaries in rivers and bays have given rise to many more disputes than land boundaries. In this regard the Court has held that the doctrine of the thalweg (that is, that the main channel of navigation is the middle of a river rather than a line equidistant between the two banks) is applicable between states unless the boundary has been fixed in some other way. This principle was used by the Court in its determination of the boundary between New Jersey and Delaware on the Delaware River in 1934. Along the unstable Missouri River, boundary cases have been decided by application of the rules of international law concerning change by avulsion or accretion. International law regarding cession of territory on a river boundary was followed in determining the Ohio River boundary.

Boundaries in waters other than rivers have been disputed, and in many instances an economic factor has been involved: oyster beds in *Louisiana* v. *Mississippi,* 202 U.S. 1 (1906); fishing rights in *Michigan* v. *Wisconsin,* 272 U.S. 398 (1926), and *Wisconsin* v. *Michigan,* 297 U.S. 547 (1936); and oil wells in *Oklahoma* v. *Texas,* 269 U.S. 314 (1926).

Questions of state boundaries continue to arise, as in the

case of the Rio Grande, which was set as the boundary between the United States and Mexico by the Treaty of Guadalupe Hidalgo in 1848. In 1853, by the Gadsden Purchase, the United States acquired the territory from the Rio Grande west to the Colorado River. The boundary between Upper and Lower California was set by the Treaty of Guadalupe Hidalgo. The Rio Grande changed course in the vicinity of El Paso, and the resultant dispute was settled in 1963 (formalized in 1967) by the Chamizal Treaty.

BOUNTIES, COMMERCIAL. In the colonial period Great Britain paid bounties on the export from the American colonies of hemp, flax, tar, potash, indigo, and other commodities to stimulate their production and diminish Britain's dependence on foreign nations. The loss of these bounties after the Revolution brought disaster. The colonial governments also offered bounties on linen, woolens, iron, glass, brick, and salt, and after 1775 redoubled efforts to build up domestic manufacturers by combining cash bounties, financial subsidies, and tariff protection.

Following the Revolution, states continued bounties for wheat, flax, corn, hemp, glass, sailcloth, and silk. The federal government required the navy to buy only rope made from American hemp and sent scientists abroad to find better strains of sugarcane and other plants. On the eve of the Civil War the South, which felt that tariff protection and subsidies had chiefly benefited other sections, forbade them. The United States and states have both given bounties to the beet sugar industry, coupled with high tariff protection and huge subsidies in the Far West for irrigation projects.

In the 20th century bounties continued to be used by the states to rid them of wolves and other carnivorous animals, but tariffs and quotas have been relied upon by the United States to stimulate and protect industry.

BOUNTIES, FISHING. *See* **Fishing Bounties.**

BOUNTIES, LAND. *See* **Land Bounties.**

BOUNTIES, MILITARY. When war forces were raised by volunteering instead of by conscription or militia obligations, bounties stimulated recruiting. The practice was adopted during the Revolution by both Congress and the states. To fill militia quotas, states offered their own bounties, so that states and Congress bid against one another and sums mounted until Congress was offering $200 and New Jersey $1,000. Bounty jumping and reenlisting were prevalent.

Bounties shrank to $6 in 1791 for Indian campaigns, but climbed after the Whiskey Rebellion to $16 and 160 acres. During the War of 1812 offers increased to $124 and 320 acres. They were abolished in 1833 but were resumed in 1847 for the Mexican War. Civil War bounties repeated revolutionary history, with the exception of land grants. Bounties disappeared after Appomattox, and recruiting bounties were expressly forbidden by the Selective Service Act of 1917.

Civil War Bounties. The system of granting land as a bounty was not followed in the Civil War except for the favored position of servicemen under the Homestead Act. From 1861 states and localities stimulated recruiting by grants of money. Since July 1861, Congress had allowed a $100 bounty for three-year men. The passage of the Militia Draft Act in July 1862 provided $25 for nine-month and $50 for twelve-month volunteers.

Officials everywhere pressed for larger bounties, and on Mar. 3, 1863, Congress passed the Enrollment Act, which legalized the earlier practice of giving $100 to conscripts and substitutes. Also, since those able to do so could avoid the draft on payment of $300, for several months an equivalent sum was given to all three-year, and $400 to all five-year, volunteers.

A worse system prevailed for state bounties. It was considered a disgrace for any congressional district to have to submit to a draft, so funds were raised to the utmost limit to fill the quotas by offering bounties before the federal draft began.

In four years' time the federal government paid over $300 million in bounties, and in 1864–65 alone the states and localities paid about the same amount. The total mercenary fees for the war amounted to $750 million dollars.

BOUNTY JUMPER. A product of the system of military bounties in the Civil War. Aided and abetted by bounty brokers, men would enlist, collect bounties, desert, and then reenlist elsewhere, repeating the process until finally caught.

BOUQUET'S EXPEDITION (1763–65). At the outbreak of Pontiac's War, Col. Henry Bouquet was sent with 500 regulars to relieve Fort Pitt. Leaving Carlisle, Pa., and defeating the Indians at the Battle of Bushy Run, he relieved the fort. He collected 1,500 men and in October 1765 marched unopposed to a point near the Muskingum River. There he was met by chiefs bringing in eighteen white prisoners and suing for peace. Bouquet demanded the return of all the captives; and, taking the principal chiefs as hostages, he moved south to the Muskingum. He made peace with the Indians, directed them to go to Sir William Johnson to make treaties, and took hostages for the performance of this obligation and for the delivery of about 100 prisoners still in the hands of the Shawnee. He returned to Fort Pitt, where the Indians subsequently delivered the remaining captives. Bouquet's expedition ended the reign of terror on the border.

BOURBON COUNTY. Established by Georgia in 1785, on the Mississippi, north of the thirty-first parallel and extending to the mouth of the Yazoo River, above Natchez. Being largely a land speculation, it was to be governed by fourteen men; and when a land office should be opened, the price per acre should not be more than 25 cents. As Spain had not yet evacuated this territory and as the United States disputed Georgia's claim, the act was repealed three years later.

BOURBONS (Redeemers). White southern politicians who gained control of their state governments at the end of the Reconstruction era in the 1870's. They called themselves Redeemers because they believed they had redeemed their states from Republican and black control. Their detractors called them Bourbons, who, like the ruling monarchs of France, were so wedded to the ideas and practices of the past that they forgot nothing and learned nothing. Neither term accurately describes them. Most were conservative Democrats who openly aligned themselves with the Republican, industrial North to exploit the natural resources of the South. They sacrificed long-held tenets of agrarianism and states' rights, to advocate southern industrial development.

BOURGEOIS. Used in the fur trade, especially in the Northwest, to refer to the leader of a unit. The bourgeois was governor of the pack train, master of the canoe brigade, and despot of the trading post. His word was law and his orders were implicitly obeyed. He was responsible for the well-being of the men and the success of the trade venture.

BOURGMONT'S EXPLORATIONS. Étienne Veniard de Bourgmont, first French scientific explorer of the Missouri River, commanded Fort Detroit in 1706. By 1712 he was exploring the lower Missouri Valley, and by 1717 reached the Platte River. In 1723 Bourgmont led an expedition up the Mississippi from New Orleans and with the help of friendly Missouri Indians built Fort Orleans on the north bank of the Missouri River in Carroll County, Mo. In 1724 he conducted an overland trip to the village of the Kansas Indians near present Doniphan, Kans., effecting peace with them and, further to the southwest, with the Padouca.

BOUWERIES. When the Dutch West India Company took over Manhattan Island in 1626, it divided a large tract of land in what is now New York City's lower east side into six bouweries or farms, erected buildings on them, and leased them to tenants.

BOWDITCH'S AMERICAN PRACTICAL NAVIGATOR. In 1799 Nathaniel Bowditch published in the United States an expanded, corrected, revised edition of J. H. Moore's standard work, *The Practical Navigator.* By the third edition (1802), the work was so changed that it bore Bowditch's name and the new title *The New American Practical Navigator.* It quickly became the standard work used by American seamen.

BOWERY. A district in lower Manhattan in New York City which has developed around a street first known in the 17th century as Bouwerie Lane or Bouwerie Road, because it led from New Amsterdam out to the bouwerie or farm of Gov. Peter Stuyvesant. By 1800 the slums growing up around it determined its future character. It eventually attained worldwide notoriety because of its swindling, political chicanery, prostitution, crime, and gang warfare.

BOWIE KNIFE. Devised by Rezin P. Bowie or his brother James, who died at the Alamo, it has been the subject of heroic folk tales. It achieved fame in the Sandbar duel in 1827. It was for four decades a part of the regular equipment of frontiersmen, backwoodsmen, mountain men, Texas Rangers, and pirates. Its steel was of superb temper, the blade well guarded, handle and blade so balanced that it could be thrown.

BOWLES'S FILIBUSTERING EXPEDITIONS. William Augustus Bowles, after an adventurous life among the Creek Indians in the early 1780's, incited them against Spain in three Florida filibustering expeditions, 1788, 1791, and 1799. As agent for the trading house of Miller, Bonnamy and Company, Bowles sought the trade of the Creek, held by another English firm, Panton, Leslie and Company, who had secured their concessions from Spain and from Alexander McGillivray, the half-breed Creek chief. He eventually fell prey to Spanish duplicity and was held prisoner by the Spanish. He escaped and put out for Florida for his last filibustering expedition. In 1800 he seized the Spanish fort at St. Marks and held it for a few months. He escaped and was captured in 1803 and died two years later in Havana.

BOWLING GREEN. Park in New York City, originally a small open space in front of the fort at the foot of Broadway, sometimes called the Parade. It was leased for a bowling green in 1733.

BOWYER, FORT, ATTACK ON (Sept. 15, 1814). From this fort, commanding the entrance to Mobile Bay, Maj. William Lawrence, with 130 troops, inflicted a mortifying defeat upon a British combined land and sea force of six vessels and 1,300 men, killing 162 and wounding 70 British while suffering only 8 American casualties.

BOXER REBELLION (1900). An antiforeign uprising in China by a secret society known as Boxers; beginning in June, 231 foreigners and many Chinese Christians were murdered. On June 17 the Boxers began a siege of legations in Peking. The United States joined Great Britain, Russia, Germany, France, and Japan in a military expedition for relief of the legations, sending 5,000 troops and raising the siege on August 14. The United States did not join the punitive expedition under the German commander in chief and opposed the demand for a punitive indemnity. The Boxer protocol finally fixed the indemnity at $333 million, punished guilty Chinese officials, and permitted the major nations to maintain legation guards at Peking and between the capital and the sea. The U.S. share of the indemnity, originally set at $24.5 million but reduced to $12 million, was paid by 1924.

BOXING. *See* **Prizefighting.**

BOYCOTTING. Collective refusal to purchase commodities or services from a manufacturer or merchant whose employment or trade practices are regarded as unfair, occasionally used against aggressor nations. Its chief use is by organized workers to secure better conditions of employment. Means include the distribution of cards, handbills, and lists of grievances and picketing.

In the United States the courts have made a distinction between primary and secondary boycotts. The former involves refusal of patronage by employees directly concerned;

the latter involves attempts to persuade or coerce third parties to boycott an employer.

The boycott was held unlawful as early as 1886. In 1908 the Supreme Court decided that the secondary boycott constitutes a conspiracy in restraint of trade under the provisions of the Sherman Antitrust Act (1890). The Court held that treble damages might be recovered for losses sustained by the manufacturer through the interstate boycott. In 1911, the same tribunal decided that all means employed to make effective an unlawful boycott are illegal, even though in themselves such means are innocent.

An attempt to escape from restrictions of the Sherman Act was made through section 20 of the Clayton Antitrust Act (1914), which prohibits the use of the injunction to restrain employees from picketing, boycotting, and advising others to withhold patronage when such activities are peaceful and lawful. In 1921, however, the Supreme Court ruled that all methods employed to make effective interstate boycotts involving third parties are unlawful.

Boycotts have also been used by unorganized groups appealed to through the press, mail, radio or television, or, in local instances, person to person.

BOYDTON PLANK ROAD, ENGAGEMENT AT (Oct. 27–28, 1864). While moving Union troops on the Boydton Plank Road where it crossed Hatcher's Run, near Petersburg, Va., a gap opened between Gen. Winfield S. Hancock's Second Corps and Gen. G. K. Warren's Fifth Corps. Confederates pushed into this opening and attacked Hancock's right and rear, provoking a bloody battle.

BOYS' CLUBS OF AMERICA. An organization that sponsors about 600 clubs for boys in American cities; began operations in New England in the 1860's. It supports programs of physical and social activities for boys aged 8 to 18.

BOY SCOUTS OF AMERICA. Incorporated Feb. 8, 1910, and granted a federal charter by Congress June 15, 1916; based on principles established in England by scouting's founder, Lord Baden-Powell, in 1907. The purpose is to build desirable qualities of character, to teach the responsibilities of citizenship, and to develop physical and mental fitness.

There are three programs: Cub Scouting, for boys who have completed the second grade or are 8–10 years of age; Scouting, for boys who have completed the fifth grade or are 11–17 years of age; and Exploring, for young men and women who have completed the eighth grade or are 15–20 years of age. The scouting program depends on more than 1.5 million scoutmasters, den leaders, and Explorer advisers, who volunteer their time and talents. In 1980, the organization had 4.4 million members.

BOZEMAN TRAIL. Traced by John M. Bozeman, 1863–65, as the shortest and easiest route for emigrants to the gold fields of Virginia City, Mont. The trail continued the route from the South Platte at Julesburg (Fort Sedgwick), Colo., past Fort Laramie, where it crossed the Oregon Trail, to the Powder River crossing at Fort Connor, Wyo. Thence it passed east of the Big Horn Mountains to the Yellowstone River and westward to Virginia City. Notwithstanding the Treaty of Laramie in 1851 the Sioux resented the invasion, and when forts were established for emigrant protection, they went on the warpath. By 1868 all posts along the trail had been abandoned. Following suppression of the Sioux in 1877 the Bozeman Trail became an important cattle trail.

BRADDOCK'S EXPEDITION. On Apr. 14, 1755, Gen. Edward Braddock, commander of British forces in America, was dispatched for a campaign in the French and Indian War. The regulars and colonial forces rendezvoused at Fort Cumberland, to start for Fort Duquesne by the route later called Braddock's Road.

The army, 2,200 strong, started west June 7, but advanced slowly. Then, on the advice of Lt. Col. George Washington, his aide-de-camp, Braddock pushed on rapidly with some 1,200 men and a minimum of artillery, leaving a command under Col. William Dunbar to bring up the heavier goods.

From Fort Duquesne, Capt. Daniel Beaujeu led some 250 French and 600 Indians to oppose Braddock. He had not laid his ambush when the British opened fire, putting most of the French to flight and killing Beaujeu. His subordinate rallied the Indians and after three hours Braddock ordered a retreat. The general was mortally wounded; many of the officers were killed; the retreat became a rout. Dunbar, now in command, retreated rapidly to Fort Cumberland.

BRADDOCK'S ROAD. From the Potomac River at Wills Creek (Cumberland, Md.) to the Monongahela at Turtle Creek. From Wills Creek to the upper Youghiogheny River was opened by the Ohio Company, probably in 1752. In 1754 Lt. Col. George Washington improved the road to Great Meadows and extended it to six miles northeast of the present Uniontown, Pa. In 1755, Gen. Edward Braddock's expedition extended it almost to Fort Duquesne. After Braddock's defeat the road facilitated Indian raids; still later it became a highway for western emigration and part was incorporated in the National Road.

BRADSTREET'S FORT FRONTENAC EXPEDITION. After the disaster at Ticonderoga in July 1758, Lt. Col. John Bradstreet led a successful raid that went far to restore British morale during the French and Indian War.

Taking command in early August of 2,600 men secretly mobilized in the Mohawk Valley, Bradstreet reached Oswego on August 24 and, crossing Lake Ontario, captured Fort Frontenac at Cataraqui (present Kingston) on the 27th. The post and French ships were burned. This broke the French hold of the water routes by which the western posts were supplied, contributing to the evacuation of Fort Duquesne and the surrender of Fort Niagara.

BRADSTREET'S LAKE ERIE EXPEDITION (1764). Col. John Bradstreet led an expedition to the Great Lakes area to place Indian relations on a peace footing. On the shores of Lake Erie, Bradstreet revealed ignorance of Indian affairs by concluding improper treaties with unimportant delegations of Delaware and Shawnee, and did not recover possession of all prisoners. He proceeded to Detroit, where he was only partially successful. While returning, he failed to move on mutinous Scioto villages. Delaying on the Sandusky shore, Bradstreet's forces, near to mutiny, encountered severe hardships. His reputation as a popular hero did not survive.

BRADY PHOTOGRAPHS. Over 7,000 photographs taken by Mathew B. Brady and his associates during the Civil War for over $100,000. They included portraits of officers and soldiers and battle scenes. The project bankrupted Brady, and the War Department acquired the plates and some negatives at public auction in 1874 for $2,840. Some photos are in private hands. The largest collections are in the National Archives and the Library of Congress.

BRAIN TRUST. Prior to his nomination for the presidency in 1932, Franklin D. Roosevelt brought together Raymond Moley, Rexford G. Tugwell, and Adolph A. Berle, Jr., all professors at Columbia University. They helped Roosevelt during his campaign, and after his inauguration became prominent in his councils. They and all economists, lawyers, and scholars who subsequently joined the administration were indiscriminately dubbed the brain trust. The expression became a symbol for all New Deal experimentation.

BRANDS, PRIVATE AND NATIONAL. From the beginning of American commerce, much merchandise has been identified by marks of origin, ownership, or sponsorship. The trademarks of merchants or other distributors have been called private brands to distinguish them from the trademarks of national manufacturers.

Rivalry originated in the late 19th century, and became clearly evident in the 20th. Gradually, nationally advertised brands entered commodity fields where the dealer had been dominant. The manufacturer's brands, procurable through other channels, weakened his hold on his customers. For this reason and others, the large department stores, mail-order houses, and chains promoted the sale of private brands they controlled and established new ones. Often the only important difference was that one was sponsored by a manufacturer and bore a craftsman's mark, the other by a distributor and bore a merchant's mark.

BRANDY STATION, BATTLE OF (June 9, 1863). The greatest cavalry conflict of the Civil War, with Gen. Alfred Pleasonton's federal cavalry and infantry and John Buford's Union cavalry clashing with J. E. B. Stuart's Confederates at Fleetwood Hill and Brandy Station. The Confederates retained the field, but Pleasonton learned that Robert E. Lee's army was moving northward toward Maryland.

BRANDYWINE CREEK, BATTLE OF (Sept. 11, 1777). Fought in Chester County, Pa. British and Hessian troops composed a force of 18,000. The American army under Gen. George Washington numbered 11,000. Following a feint attack by the Hessians on the Americans at Chad's Ford, the British crossed the east side of the creek at Jeffrie's Ford, continued southward, and suddenly attacked Gen. John Sullivan's troops near Birmingham Meetinghouse. The Americans fought gallantly, but were compelled to retire. Washington withdrew his army toward Philadelphia.

BRANNAN PLAN. Farm price-support plan using direct payments to the farmer, under certain conditions, as a substitute for price supports; proposed by Charles Brannan, Secretary of Agriculture, in 1949. The plan has been urged in Congress a number of times, but has never been approved.

BRATTLEBORO. *See* **Drummer, Fort.**

BRAZIL, CONFEDERATE EXPATRIATES TO. Perhaps nearly half of the 8,000–10,000 Confederates who emigrated after the Civil War went to Brazil. Coming from every southern and some northern states, they represented every social class and profession. Most settled in colonies in the wilderness of the provinces of Paraná, São Paulo, Rio de Janeiro, Espírito Santo, and Pará. Most tried agriculture and stock raising. They were comparatively successful at Villa Americana, in the hinterland of São Paulo, which at its peak had several hundred families. The experiments broke up after a few months or at most a few years, the colonists going to São Paulo or returning to the United States.

BRAZITO, BATTLE AT (Dec. 25, 1846). En route to Chihuahua, N.Mex., Gen. Alexander W. Doniphan, with 500 Missouri volunteers, reached the east bank of the Rio Grande. He received Juan Ponce de León's messenger, under a black flag, demanding surrender. In a thirty-minute fight, the Americans' superior fire and tactics triumphed.

BREDA, PEACE OF (July 21, 1667). Signed by England and France after the naval war between England and Holland in which France joined the latter; provided for restoration of Acadia to France and confirmed English possession of New Netherland. King Charles II's order (1668) for Acadia's return was delayed by claims of Thomas Temple to part of the region. Restoration took place in 1670, France returning to England at the same time part of the island of St. Christopher.

BREED'S HILL. *See* **Bunker Hill.**

BRETHREN (Dunkers or Dunkards). Descendants of a pietist sect founded by Alexander Mack that began to migrate to America in 1719. The Brethren grew during the Great Awakening and have tended to assume an evangelical posture. Early congregations attached great importance to the Lord's Supper. In the past they emphasized plain dress. The largest denomination is the Church of the Brethren (175,000 members). Other denominations are the Fellowship of Grace Brethren Churches, 39,000; the Brethren Church (Ashland, Ohio), 15,000; and the Old German Baptist Brethren, 4,900.

BRETTON WOODS CONFERENCE (United Nations Monetary and Financial Conference). Held in New Hampshire, July 1–22, 1944, by forty-four nations, to plan postwar international economic cooperation. Agreement was reached for an International Monetary Fund of $8.8 billion (American quota $2.75 billion), to promote exchange stability and expansion of international trade, and for an International Bank for Reconstruction and Development (the World Bank) with authorized capital of $10 billion (American subscription $3.175 billion). Four nations attending did not sign—Haiti, Liberia, New Zealand, and the Soviet Union.

BREWING. Beer came from England to America with the earliest settlers; brewing was carried on by farmers and tavern keepers. Commercial breweries selling to local areas that could be reached by horse and wagon were soon started. Early American beer was of the English type. Near the middle of the 19th century German immigrants brought their type of beer. The milder and more aromatic German lager soon captured most of the beer market.

From 1875 on, technological and scientific changes made the small-scale operator unable to compete with the large brewery. The railroad made it possible for breweries to seek nationwide distribution—which required beer able to withstand temperature changes, bumping, and the lapse of time. From the 1880's on, pasteurization checked bacterial growth; chemical additives were eliminated; bottling became mechanized; and carbonation was controlled and artificial.

The brewing industry after Prohibition operated in a different environment. As Prohibition had accustomed people to drinking hard liquor, it took a dozen years to build the market for beer back to its size before World War I. There were only 95 breweries in 1977 as compared to 1,400 in 1914.

BRIAND-KELLOGG PACT. *See* **Kellogg-Briand Pact.**

BRIAR CREEK, BATTLE OF (Mar. 3, 1779). Col. Mark Prevost, British commander, trapped and routed a force of about 1,200 southern militia and regular Continentals under Col. John Ashe at Briar Creek, in Severn County, Ga. The American loss was 150 killed and wounded, 189 captured. The British lost but 16 killed and wounded.

BRICKER AMENDMENT (1952–57). A series of proposals to amend the U.S. Constitution, primarily to ensure that treaties and executive agreements inconsistent with the Constitution could not become effective in domestic law. These were sponsored as Senate joint resolutions, in the 82d through the 85th Congresses, by Sen. John W. Bricker of Ohio, but failed to obtain sufficient support for enactment.

BRIDGEPORT (Conn.). Second largest city in Connecticut, with a population of 142,546 in 1980; it was the center of a metropolitan area including 807,143 people. It is located on Long Island Sound, at the mouth of the Pequonock River. A drawbridge over the river gave the town its name, and the road became a major link between New York and Boston. Bridgeport manufactures a wide variety of products from wire to plumbing supplies, and including brass products, engines for ships, and drug supplies. During the 19th century, whaling vessels outfitted and based themselves in Bridgeport. In the early 20th century experimentation on, and production of, some automobiles and trucks was conducted there.

BRIDGER, FORT. Frontier trading post and later a fort of the U.S. Army, located on Black's Fork, Uinta County, Wyo. Built by James Bridger, trapper and scout, with Louis Vasquez, in 1843. Best known as a way station and supply point for emigrants bound for Oregon, Utah, and California and the beginning of caravan travel to the Pacific coast. Taken over by Mormon colonists about 1855, it was burned on the approach of U.S. troops in the Mormon War of 1857, rebuilt as a military post in 1858, and abandoned in 1890. For years it was famous as a mail, express, and telegraph station.

BRIDGES.

Timber and Masonry Bridges. The construction of permanent bridges was a costly enterprise the American colonies seldom undertook. The earliest were split logs or hewn timbers laid between timber cribs or rubble stone abutments. These were superseded by pile-and-beam structures of long stringers spanning between abutments and intermediate transverse rows of piles, each bound together by a horizontal cap piece and diagonal braces. Notable for size were the Great Bridge over the Charles River at Cambridge, Mass. (1662), and the York River bridge at York, Maine (1761). A variation was the span built by Enoch Hale over the Connecticut River at Bellows Falls, Vt., in 1785, in which the chief supporting elements were massive timbers arranged in the form of crude polygonal arches.

Timber bridge construction was inaugurated by Timothy Palmer, who built the first timber truss span over the Merrimack River at Newburyport, Mass. (1792), and the Permanent Bridge over the Schuylkill River at Philadelphia (1798–1806). Over the same stream was the Colossus of Lewis Wernwag (1809–13), which included wrought-iron bracing elements in place of timber trusses. Theodore Burr patented a combination arch and truss in 1817; Ithiel Town in 1820, the lattice truss. Simpler forms came with the patents of Stephen Long (1830), William Howe (1841), and Caleb and Thomas Pratt (1844).

Masonry bridges were extremely rare, because of the high cost of quarrying and dressing stone as well as laying up the blocks, until the advent of the railroad. The first two were built by the Baltimore and Ohio Railroad: the Carrollton Viaduct at Baltimore (1829) and the Philips Viaduct at Relay, Md. (1835), both still standing. The masonry arch was rapidly superseded by concrete around 1890.

Iron and Steel Truss Bridges. The first iron truss bridge was built by Earl Trumbull in 1840 over the Erie Canal at Frankfort, N.Y. The Howe truss was adopted for the first iron railroad bridge, at Manayunk, Pa., in 1845 by Richard Osborne, also the first bridge to contain both cast and wrought iron. The next decade was the heroic age of the iron truss: the Pratt invention was quickly adapted to iron construction, followed by patents of Squire Whipple (1847), Wendel Bollman (1852), and Albert Fink (1854). The Whipple truss was more widely used for big railroad bridges up to 1890 than the redundant Bollman and Fink trusses.

The rapid progress emboldened engineers to create massive iron and steel bridges required by broad waterways and heavy rail loads. The Ohio River proved to be the challenge: the first was built at Steubenville, Ohio, by the Pittsburgh and Steubenville Railroad (1863–65)—320 feet. The substitution of steel for iron in truss bridges came with the Chicago and Alton's Missouri River bridge at Glasgow, Mo. (1878–79).

The first use of the cantilever truss for rail loads was in the Kentucky River bridge of the Cincinnati Southern Railway (1876–77), by Charles Shaler Smith. It was followed by ever-lengthening spans at Niagara Falls (1883), Poughkeepsie, N.Y. (1886–88), and Memphis, Tenn. (1888–92), by which date steel had largely come to replace iron.

Iron and Steel Arch Bridges. The iron arch bridge was slow to develop—the first built by Richard Delafield at Brownsville, Pa., 1836–39. The Eads Bridge over the Mississippi River at Saint Louis, Mo. (1868–74), the triumph of James B. Eads, was the first in the United States built of steel and had the longest arch spans at the time. The hinged arch was introduced by Joseph M. Wilson of Philadelphia in 1869 and was adopted for the 509-foot spans of William R. Hutton's Washington Bridge in New York (1887–89).

Suspension Bridges. Chronologically, the suspension bridge antedates iron truss and arch forms, but these were derived from long-established timber and masonry prototypes. The suspension bridge with a rigid level deck carried by iron chains was invented by James Finley, who built the first one at Uniontown, Pa., in 1801. The wire-cable form was the achievement of Charles Ellet and John A. Roebling. Ellet's greatest bridge, at Wheeling, W. Va. (1846–49), failed in a storm and had to be rebuilt by Roebling, who had already established his reputation with suspension aqueducts. Roebling's triumphs came in stunning succession: Niagara Falls (1851–55), Cincinnati (1856–67), and Brooklyn, N.Y. (1869–83)—the last embracing the longest single span in the world at the time, 1,595 ft.

Steel and Concrete Bridges. The simple steel truss reached its greatest length, 746 feet, in the Chester Bridge in Chester, W.Va. (1977); and the longest of the continuous truss is the bridge over the Columbia River in Astoria, Ore., with a span of 1,232 feet (1966). Cantilever trusses made it possible to stretch the New Orleans Public Belt Highway Bridge to 1,575 feet in 1958, and the Commodore Barry Bridge in Chester, Pa., to 1,644 feet in 1970. One of the largest steel arch bridges is the Hell Gate Bridge at New York City (1914–16), designed by Gustav Lindenthal for a four-track rail line, and the longest steel arch, stretching 1,700 feet, is the New River Gorge Bridge at Fayetteville, W.Va. (1977).

New York's East River spans, following the Brooklyn Bridge, brought the steel tower to suspension bridges, forming precedents for the George Washington at New York (1927–31), its 3,500-foot double-deck main span once the longest and still the heaviest; Golden Gate at San Francisco (1933–37), for twenty-seven years the longest clear span at 4,200 feet; Verrazano-Narrows at New York (1959–64), its 4,260-foot main span now the longest in the world. Othmar Ammann was chief engineer of the New York bridges, and Joseph B. Strauss, of the San Francisco.

The first reinforced concrete bridge was built in Golden Gate Park, San Francisco, in 1889 by Ernest Ransome. The Tunkhannock Creek Viaduct of the D. L. and W. Railroad (1911–15) is still the largest concrete bridge in overall dimensions. The 460-foot arch ribs in the Westinghouse Bridge at Pittsburgh, Pa. (1930–31), were for more than thirty years the longest, but the length has been exceeded by two highway bridges in the state of Washington.

The introduction of rigid frames and box girders in the early 20th century led to a great increase in length and improvement in appearance of the conventional girder bridge that originally appeared in iron in 1841.

BRIDGEWATER, BATTLE OF. *See* **Lundy's Lane, Battle at.**

BRISCOE* V. *BANK OF THE COMMONWEALTH OF KENTUCKY, 11 Peters 257 (1837). The Bank of Kentucky was owned by the state, its officers and directors appointed by the state legislature. The question was whether notes issued constituted a subterfuge by which the state in effect was emitting bills of credit in the sense forbidden by the Constitution. The Supreme Court found the notes to be backed by the resources of the bank and not the credit of the state and the bank to be a separate entity capable of suing and being sued; therefore, such notes were not bills of credit in the prohibited sense. This case repudiated the decision in *Craig* v. *Missouri.*

BRISTOE CAMPAIGN (Oct. 9–22, 1863). Gen. Robert E. Lee crossed the Rapidan River in Virginia, October 9, turning the right flank of Union commander George G. Meade, and advanced toward Washington. Using parallel roads Meade marched rapidly to cover the capital. He reached Centreville first, his rear guard, under Gen. G. K. Warren, severely repulsing Gen. A. P. Hill's corps at Bristoe Station, October 14. Lee retreated to the Rappahannock River.

BRISTOL TRADE. During the early 16th century Bristol found its location in southwestern England a great advantage in capturing trade with America; by the 17th century it had become the foremost English port. In the later 17th century Bristol became the port of departure for many colonists bound for America. In the 18th century it still shared heavily in western enterprises, especially through slave trade and fisheries. On the eve of the American Revolution it was the second city in Britain, and its merchants greatly influenced British colonial policy.

BRITISH CAMPAIGN OF 1777. As 1776 ended, the British ministry came to think of the problem in America as one of reconquest, and in consultation with Gen. Sir John Burgoyne, provided for an expedition from Montreal southward along the Champlain-Hudson route. A large army moving up the Hudson from New York would meet Burgoyne at Albany, and a subsidiary force might proceed eastward down the Connecticut River. An auxiliary force would go up the St. Lawrence River to Oswego and, with Indian aid, strike into the Mohawk Valley.

The British force in the colonies would be reinforced from England. American Tories, Canadians, and Indians would be recruited, and foreign regular troops would be hired (*see* German Mercenaries). An unusual complement of guns was to be taken, as numerous forts would need to be besieged and reduced by gunfire.

The plan failed because of the shortcomings of the commanding general; the physical barriers of river, forest, and terrain, which impeded transport and troop movements; the difficulty of securing adequate supplies of food and munitions; the uncertain allegiance of Canada and American Tories; and overrating Indian cooperation. The American opposition capitalized on these handicaps.

BRITISH DEBTS. Debts owed by American colonial merchants and planters to British merchants before the Revolution continued a subject of dispute until 1802. The merchants of the North and the planters of the South bought most of their manufactured articles from English merchants. The merchants of the North depended on their trade and the South upon their crops to pay England. The result, from 1763 to 1775, was an indebtedness of £3 million—most owed by southern planters. Stoppage of payment was frequently resorted to in the fight against colonial legislation of Parliament. Wiping out the indebtedness by war was a contributing cause of the Revolution.

During the Revolution all states enacted laws affecting these debts. North of Maryland most debts were owed to Loyalists, while in the southern states most belonged to the British merchants. Some laws confiscated Loyalist estates, including debts; some laws sequestered or confiscated the debts due to British merchants; still others banished or restricted the activities of the agents of the British merchants. In Maryland £144,536 of debts due to British merchants were paid into the state treasury; in Virginia about £287,000; and in North Carolina over £50,000.

These debts were an important problem in the negotiation of the Definitive Treaty of Peace in 1782–83. John Adams was responsible for the provision (article IV) that the debts due before the war were to be paid in sterling. Article V required that Congress should recommend to the several states the restoration of the confiscated estates of the Loyalists. Article IV met with determined opposition in the southern states and article V in all of the states. Practically all of the states either delayed or refused compliance.

With adoption of the Constitution, opposed by many debtors, the federal courts facilitated collection of many debts, and the new administration negotiated more effectively with England relative to the infractions of the treaty of peace. After Governeur Morris's mission to London an English minister, George Hammond, was sent to the United States. Negotiations between Hammond and Thomas Jefferson failed to settle the debt question. The strained relations of 1792–93 led to the mission of John Jay and the famous Jay's Treaty. By article VI the United States accepted liability for debts that could not at that date be recovered due to legal impediments by the states. A five-man commission, to adjudicate the claims, sat at Philadelphia from May 29, 1797, to July 31, 1799. Claims of £5,638,629 8s. 1d. were received. The commissioners were unable to agree on jurisdiction of the commission, nature of legal impediments, the question of solvency of debtors, and wartime interest. The entire matter fell again into the regular diplomatic channels. A final settlement was negotiated by Rufus King and the ministry of Henry Addington on Jan. 8, 1802. The United States was to pay, in lieu of its liability under article VI of Jay's Treaty, the lump sum of £600,000. An English commission sat until 1811 adjusting the claims. It found only about 20–25 percent of the claims good, but even so was able to pay, with the £600,000, only about 45 percent of the approved claims.

BRITISH PLAN OF CAMPAIGN IN THE WEST. British authorities, during the spring of 1780, were prepared to recapture the Illinois country and to attack St. Louis, New Orleans, and other Spanish posts on the Mississippi River. Four simultaneous movements were begun. Col. Henry Bird with a force from Detroit was directed to "amuse" George Rogers Clark at the Falls of the Ohio. Gen. John Campbell, from Pensacola, after taking New Orleans was to proceed up the Mississippi to Natchez, where he was to be joined by a force which was to have captured St. Louis. Capt. Charles de Langlade was to advance down the Illinois River while another party was ordered to watch Vincennes. No part of the plan proved successful.

BROAD SEAL WAR. Following the closely contested election of 1838, two groups sought admission to Congress from New Jersey. Both held commissions bearing the great (broad) seal of the state; only the Whig commissions were legally executed and signed by the governor. Charging their opponents with fraud and facing loss of control of the House, the Democratic majority refused to seat all but one Whig. When it was proved that county clerks had suppressed some returns that would have given the Democrats a majority, the House, on Feb. 28, 1840, voted to seat the five Democrats.

BROADSIDES. A name given to sheets of paper printed on one side only. In 17th-century America broadsides were used for poetical effusions, news items, and political propaganda; in the Revolution, for political purposes, often reprinted in the printer's newspaper. Later they were used in political, antislavery, and temperance campaigns; also for song sheets, memorials, obituaries, accounts of trials, executions, official proclamations, and posters.

BROADWAY. A street in New York City running the length of Manhattan. Most of the lower course is said to follow old Indian trails. In New Amsterdam its first quarter mile was called the Heerewegh or Heere Straat, anglicized to Broadway about 1668. The first paving was done in 1707. The first sidewalks were laid in 1790. In 1852 a franchise was granted for a cable-car line on Broadway, then the city's chief residential street. The line, which was fought in the courts for over thirty years, was finally built in 1885, but by that time the street had become the main business thoroughfare. The first subway line was begun in 1900. In the late 19th century theaters congregated along it, first below and then above Longacre (now Times) Square, until its name became a symbol for the American theater. Brilliant lighting in the early 20th century brought it the nickname of the Great White Way.

BRODHEAD'S ALLEGHENY CAMPAIGN. Col. Daniel Broadhead set out from Fort Pitt, Aug. 11, 1779, with 600 regulars, volunteers, and a few Delaware warriors against the Seneca on the upper Allegheny. A party of Indians coming downstream was defeated, but warned the villages, and the inhabitants fled. After destroying their houses and corn, Brodhead returned to Pittsburgh. Provisional treaties were made with the Wyandot and a branch of the Shawnee that for a short time saved the frontier from invasion.

BRONCO. A Spanish word, early used in America to characterize hostile Indians. In time the Spaniards applied the adjective to wild horses, a usage peculiar to America. Loosely, a bronco is a range horse, a cow horse—more specifically and accurately, a range horse that pitches or bucks.

***BRONSON* V. *RODES*,** 7 Wallace 229 (1868). An action on a New York executor's bond of 1851 to repay a loan "in gold or silver coins." In 1865 the obligor tendered payment in U.S. notes, which Congress had declared "lawful money and a legal tender in payment of debts." The tender was refused and the obligor sued to cancel a mortgage securing the bond. Decrees in his favor by two state courts were reversed by the U.S. Supreme Court.

BROOK FARM INSTITUTE OF AGRICULTURE AND EDUCATION. A cooperative community that grew out of the realistic social criticism of the day, touched by German transcendentalism. George Ripley was the center of the group, which moved to a farm of 200 acres in West Roxbury, Mass., in 1841. The members built a community in which manual and intellectual labor might be united and men and women live in a simple but cultivated society.

An adaptation of the Fourier phalanx was adopted in 1845, with the primary departments of agricultural, domestic, and mechanic arts, and a large phalanstery was built. Fire destroyed it in 1846 while the members celebrated its completion. Money was depleted, and the experiment had to end.

BROOKINGS INSTITUTION. A pioneer in the organized, independent study of problems of government relating to organization and administration, development and evaluation of policies, and the training of public-service personnel. The antecedent Institute for Governmental Research was established in 1916. Robert S. Brookings, a public-spirited St. Louis businessman, arranged financial support and established the Institute for Economic Research and the Graduate School of Government and Economics. In 1928 he combined these to form the Brookings Institution.

Brookings Institution studies are generally viewed as being factually and analytically authoritative contributions to the public's consideration of policy issues. Some have had an immediate and direct impact upon federal actions, such as the organization of the Marshall Plan.

BROOKLYN. A borough of New York City at the southwestern extremity of Long Island. The earliest recorded land grants within present-day Brooklyn date from the mid-1630's. After ferry service was established between New Amsterdam and Long Island about 1640, a town called Breuckelen, after a village in Holland, was established about a mile from the ferry slip and organized in 1646. Breuckelen (also known as Brookland, Brooklyn, and other variants) was one of six small towns constituting Kings County in 1680. Population growth was spurred by more reliable steam ferries to and from New York City in 1814 and by Irish and German immigration. In 1816 Brooklyn village, population 4,000, was chartered. Brooklyn achieved city status in 1834 and became the dominant community in Kings County, annexing outlying areas until in 1896 it had become coterminous with Kings County. Brooklyn city then ranked fourth in the country in both population and manufactures and served as a major port facility. Despite its size and independence, Brooklyn never attained full freedom from neighboring New York City. Whereas the opening of the Brooklyn Bridge in 1883 encouraged continued growth in Brooklyn, it also connected it more securely to Manhattan, thus facilitating Brooklyn's merger with New York City in 1898.

By 1925 Brooklyn had become, and still remains, the most populous borough in New York City, totaling 2,230,936 in 1980. One-fourth of this population was black and concentrated in Bedford-Stuyvesant and its environs, the largest predominantly black ghetto in the United States.

BROOKLYN BRIDGE. First bridge built across the East River between New York City and Brooklyn, and at the time the world's longest suspension bridge. The corporation to build the structure was organized in 1867, the city of Brooklyn subscribing for $3 million of the stock and New York for $1.5 million. John A. Roebling was chosen chief engineer, but he died in 1869, and his son Washington completed the task. The bridge was thirteen years in building, and cost $15.5 million. It was opened on May 24, 1883.

BROOKLYN HEIGHTS, BATTLE OF. *See* **Long Island, Battle of.**

BROOKS-BAXTER WAR. A dispute between Elisha Baxter and his opponent, Rev. Joseph Brooks, in the 1872 election for Arkansas's governor. Brooks contested his loss, but the legislature supported Baxter. Baxter was inaugurated on Jan. 6, 1873. In the spring of 1874 Brooks secured a favorable state supreme court decision, but President Ulysses S. Grant ruled that the decision rested with the state legislature, which supported Baxter's claims, May 11, 1874.

BROOKS-SUMNER AFFAIR. Sen. Charles Sumner, in his speech "The Crime Against Kansas," on May 19, 1856, ridiculed Sen. Andrew P. Butler of South Carolina for his devotion to "the harlot, Slavery." Two days later Butler's nephew, Preston S. Brooks, a member of Congress from South Carolina, sought out the Massachusetts senator at his desk and struck him over the head repeatedly with a cane. Sumner received injuries that incapacitated him for some years. This demonstration, and the investigation ordered by the House, heightened the tension of the sectional controversy. Brooks, saved from expulsion by the two-thirds rule, was praised in the South and reelected.

BROTHERHOOD OF LOCOMOTIVE ENGINEERS. *See* **Railroad Brotherhoods.**

BROWN, FORT (Brownsville, Texas). Established in 1846 by Gen. Zachary Taylor; named for Maj. Jacob Brown, killed later that year in its defense against Mexicans. It was held briefly in 1859 by the Mexican brigand Juan Cortina and was taken from the Confederates by Union troops. From 1865 to 1944 its 288 acres were occupied by a U.S. garrison. It was declared surplus in 1946.

BROWNISTS. Groups in England (ca. 1580–1660) that separated from the established church; derived from Robert Browne, author of *Reformation Without Tarrying for Anie* (1583), who advocated an essentially Congregational polity, a church made up only of the visible elect who were to choose and install their own officers. Later Separatists, including the Pilgrims at Plymouth, probably owed much to Browne, as did the settlers of Massachusetts Bay.

BROWNSTOWN AND DETROIT TREATIES (1807–08). At Detroit, Nov. 17, 1807, Gov. William Hull negotiated cession of the Indian title to the southeast quarter of Michigan plus the portion of Ohio north of the Maumee. Between this tract and the settled portion of the United States lay an extensive area still in Indian possession. Accordingly, at Brownstown, Nov. 25, 1808, Hull negotiated a treaty whereby title to a roadway from Maumee Rapids to Lower Sandusky (modern Fremont) and thence southward to the Greenville Treaty line was secured, to make possible travel by land to Detroit without trespassing upon the Indian domain.

BROWNSVILLE AFFAIR. Around midnight on Aug. 13, 1906, in Brownsville, Tex., an armed group of men fired indiscriminately into homes and stores adjacent to Fort Brown, garrisoned by black soldiers. One townsman was killed and a policeman wounded. Witnesses alleged that those shooting were soldiers. A handful of cartridges used by the U.S. Army was found outside the fort; yet none of the men's rifles had been fired, and none of the fort's cartridges were missing. Military inquiries and civilian grand jury investigations failed to establish who did the shooting. On October 4 President Theodore Roosevelt stated that all would be discharged "without honor" unless they produced the guilty men. All maintained their innocence, and all 167 enlisted men who had been garrisoned at Brownsville were cashiered from the army. Their discharges stood until Sept. 22, 1972, when Secretary of the Army Robert F. Froehlke directed that the discharges be changed to "honorable."

BROWN UNIVERSITY. Founded in 1764 in Warren, R.I., as Rhode Island College. Established by Baptist clergy, the college set forth a liberal outlook in its charter, emphasizing nonsectarian principles. The first president, James Manning, was elected and the first students admitted in 1765; the first commencement was held in 1769. The school moved to Providence in 1770. During the Revolution, it was used as a barracks and hospital.

In 1804, the college was renamed Brown University in honor of Nicholas Brown, a generous benefactor. Francis Wayland, elected Brown's fourth president in 1827, introduced electives and emphasized applied science and engineering. The first master of arts degree was awarded in 1888, followed in 1889 by the first doctor of philosophy. Under Elisha Benjamin Andrews, elected president in 1889, nine new departments were created. In 1891, Pembroke College, a coordinate undergraduate school for women, was established. William Herbert Perry Faunce, president from 1899 to 1929, enlarged its curriculum, inaugurated study for honors, and formally established the graduate school. With the merger of Brown University and Pembroke College in 1971, all courses became coeducational.

***BROWN* V. *BOARD OF EDUCATION OF TOPEKA*.** Two cases reaching the U.S. Supreme Court in 1954 and 1955 concerned with separation by race in public education. In the first case the Court held that segregation at all levels was illegal. In the second it held that the pace of desegregation in schools was the responsibility of school authorities and should be carried out "with all deliberate speed." After the 1955 decision, the case was returned to federal district courts for implementation. The *Brown* decision reflected no major shift of positions by the Court. The furor caused by the decision is more of a reflection on the opposition to the finding than on the novelty of the legal position.

Oliver Brown sued the Topeka, Kans., Board of Education when his daughter was denied admission to the school near her home because of her race. En route to the Supreme Court the case was combined with cases from three other states and one from the District of Columbia. In 1954 the Court held that to separate Afro-American school children by race induces a sense of inferiority that retards educational and mental development, that "separate education facilities are inherently unequal," and that the plaintiffs were "deprived of the equal protection of the laws guaranteed by the Fourteenth Amendment." The decision limited its disapproval of "separate but equal" to education, but it was construed to mean that racial segregation was not permissible in other public facilities; later Court action supported this view.

BROWN* V. *MARYLAND, 12 Wheaton 419 (1827). A case relating to the right of a state to control the sale of imported merchandise. It afforded Justice John Marshall an opportunity to supplement his earlier opinion on the meaning of the commerce clause of the Constitution. Affirmed by the court of appeals, the case came to the Supreme Court on a writ of error. Marshall reversed the affirmation on the ground that the Constitution prohibits a state from levying imposts or duties on imports or exports except those "absolutely necessary for executing its inspection laws." The principles have been upheld by nearly all courts.

BRUSSELS MONETARY CONFERENCE (Nov. 22–Dec. 17, 1892). Authorized by the Sherman Silver Purchase Act, failed because Great Britain rejected American proposals for increasing silver coinage; the Americans rejected the British plan for small European silver purchases. This helped cause the repeal of the Sherman silver act.

BRYAN-CHAMORRO TREATY (Aug. 5, 1914). A treaty between the United States and Nicaragua. It granted to the United States in perpetuity the exclusive right to build an interoceanic canal in Nicaragua, subject to a subsequent agreement regarding details of construction and operation, and also a ninety-nine-year lease of Great and Little Corn islands and a right to establish a naval base in the Gulf of Fonseca. Nicaragua received $3 million.

Costa Rica and El Salvador protested the treaty and appealed to the Central American Court, which decided that Nicaragua had violated its neighbors' rights and should restore the legal status existing before the treaty. Nicaragua refused to accept the decision and the treaty remained in force. The proposed naval base was never established and the Corn Islands remained under Nicaraguan jurisdiction except for a small area used by the United States for a lighthouse.

BRYAN'S STATION. Established in 1779 in Kentucky (near Lexington) by four Bryan brothers from North Carolina. The occupants of this parallelogram of some forty cabins withstood several Indian attacks, the most important in August 1782, when they were besieged by about 300 Indians and Canadians under Capt. William Caldwell and Simon Girty.

BUCCANEERS (Freebooters). Adventurers who infested the West Indies in the 16th, 17th, and 18th centuries. Among themselves they were known as Brethren of the Coast. It seems probable that Normans settled on an island, perhaps Tortuga, living off wild animals and preying upon the neighboring Spanish colonies. The Spaniards soon began to attack these groups and destroy their cattle and swine. Driven finally to open warfare with Spain, they began a career of piracy, plunder, and murder. About 1670 a partial stop was put to this piracy and some went to the Pacific to continue their profession. By the Treaty of Ryswick in 1697 buccaneering was practically suppressed.

BUCKBOARDS. Originally designed for personal transportation in mountain regions, these distinctively American four-wheeled vehicles, with one seat resting upon elastic boards fastened directly to the axles, were widely used in newly settled sections.

BUCKLAND RACES (Oct. 19, 1863). Confederate Gen. J. E. B. Stuart, with Gen. Wade Hampton's cavalry division, covering Robert E. Lee's retirement from Bristoe to the Rappahannock near Buckland Mills, Va., turned on H. J. Kilpatrick's pursuing Union cavalry, while Fitzhugh Lee's division charged the Union flank. Kilpatrick was routed, fleeing five miles to Haymarket and Gainesville. The Confederates derisively called the affair "Buckland Races."

BUCKSHOT WAR. As a result of the state election of 1838, members of the Democratic party and the Whig and Anti-Masonic opposition both claimed control of the Pennsylvania House of Representatives. Two speakers were elected. A mob assembled in Harrisburg, threatened violence, and forced Thaddeus Stevens, leader of the opposition, and Charles B. Penrose and Thomas H. Burrowes to escape from the senate chamber through a window. Gov. Joseph Ritner called for U.S. troops, which President Andrew Jackson refused, whereupon the governor called out the Philadelphia militia, requisitioning thirteen rounds of buckshot cartridges, whence the name "Buckshot War." The opposition was defeated when three Whigs voted with the Democrats.

***BUCK STOVE AND RANGE* CASE.** In 1906 the metal polishers in the Buck Stove and Range Company, St. Louis, struck for a nine-hour day. The American Federation of Labor put the company on their "unfair list," whereupon the company obtained a sweeping injunction forbidding this boycott. For refusal to obey, Samuel Gompers, John Mitchell, and Frank Morrison were sentenced to prison for contempt, but did not serve. The case was outlawed in 1914 by the Supreme Court under the statute of limitations.

BUCKTAILS (1818–26). A faction of the New York Democratic Republican party opposed to the canal policy of Gov. DeWitt Clinton. The name was originally applied to Tammany Society members and was taken from the Tammany insignia, a deer's tail worn in the hat.

BUDGET, DIRECTOR OF THE. *See* **Office of Management and Budget.**

BUDGET, FEDERAL. The federal budget is drawn up each year by the U. S. Office of Management and Budget, under the president's direction. It makes plans to provide financing to carry out programs the president recommends. Each year, the president presents a "budget message" to Congress, indicating what he recommends for government activity and the kinds of tax income he hopes to receive. The president cannot actually impose a budget on the country, however. Congress has the right to approve budgeted items and to appropriate tax money.

In 1921, the Budget and Accounting Act was passed, by which the Bureau of the Budget was created to help the president draw up the annual federal budget.

If the federal budget is unbalanced because there is too little income, this can be remedied by deficit financing—the government can borrow money, promising to repay it in the future by selling government bonds. Each budget after the sale of the bonds must include interest to be paid to the banks, companies, or individuals who bought the bonds.

BUENAVENTURA RIVER. A mythical river, erroneously depicted on early Spanish and American maps. The maps showed a river flowing from the Rocky Mountains into Great Salt Lake and emptying into the Pacific Ocean. As late as 1844 John C. Frémont was searching for this river.

BUENA VISTA, BATTLE OF (Feb. 22–23, 1847). During the Mexican War, Gen. Zachary Taylor had advanced his army of 4,700 men from Monterrey to a mountain pass south of Saltillo. Near the hacienda of Buena Vista he encountered a Mexican force under Gen. Antonio López de Santa Anna three times the size of his own. Though the Americans lost ground the first day, they won a brilliant victory on the second, and the Mexicans withdrew.

BUFFALO. The American bison at the time of the discovery of the New World ranged over about one-third of the continent from Canada to Mexico, and from Oregon to western New York, Pennsylvania, Virginia, and the Carolinas. The chief habitat was the plains between the Missouri River and the Rocky Mountains. Easily hunted and of large size—the males reaching 2,000 pounds—the buffalo were a favorite food for Indians and frontier settlers. As civilization advanced westward, the animals were exterminated and by 1850 few if any remained east of the Mississippi. The dry plains, however, still contained vast numbers. Gen. Philip H. Sheridan, in 1866, estimated 100 million buffalo between Camp Supply in Indian Territory and Fort Dodge, Kans.

Plains Indians based their civilization and religion to a large extent on the buffalo. Every part of the buffalo was useful to the Indians, for food, shelter, weapons, and clothing. Natural increase kept pace with the slaughter until the advent of the Union Pacific and Kansas Pacific railroads led to disappearance of the animals in the central plains. In the 1870's hunters began systematic and wholesale destruction, shipping robes and meat to the East. By 1899 the buffalo was almost extinct.

William T. Hornaday, of the National Museum, first called the nation's attention to the virtual disappearance of the buffalo in 1886. His census in 1889 showed only 1,091 American bison existing throughout the world. In 1905 the American Bison Society was organized. Public consciousness was aroused and there are now managed herds on government reservations.

BUFFALO (N.Y.). Second largest city in New York State, at the eastern tip of Lake Erie, twenty miles southeast of Niagara Falls. When in 1799 Dutch land speculators bought most of the Phelps-Gorham purchase, they commissioned Joseph Ellicott to survey and offer for sale lots in a village on Buffalo Creek, to be called New Amsterdam. The Dutch name never was generally used, and when the village became the county seat in 1807 it officially took the new name. The town was completely burned in 1813, but was rapidly rebuilt. It became the terminus of the Erie Canal in 1825 and was a city by 1832.

Buffalo developed during the 20th century into a major industrial city and port. It has been a port on the St. Lawrence Seaway since 1957. It is connected to Canada by bridges. Its many industries, including steel, electric products, and grain storage, have access to the enormous amount of hydroelectric power supplied by Niagara Falls and have helped Buffalo grow to a city of over 357,810 by 1980.

BUFFALO CHIPS. The dried excrement of the American bison, widely used for fuel by American Indians and the first white men on the Great Plains.

BUFFALO TRAILS. The first thoroughfares of North America were the traces made by buffalo and deer in seasonal migration and in quest of feeding grounds and salt licks. Many of these routes were followed by the Indians to hunting grounds and as warriors' paths; they were invaluable to explorers and adopted by pioneers. Buffalo traces were characteristically north and south; but their major east-west trails anticipated the courses of trunk railways.

BUFFER STATE. *See* **Indian Barrier State.**

BUFFINGTON ISLAND SKIRMISH (July 19, 1863, Meigs County, Ohio). Contributed to the capture of the Confederate raider, Gen. John Morgan, seeking to escape across the Ohio River at a ford opposite Buffington Island. Delayed overnight, he was almost surrounded by Union cavalry next day and the battle ended in a rout. Morgan and 1,200 men escaped, but the raid finally ended in his capture on July 26.

BUFORD EXPEDITION. As part of the effort to make Kansas a slave state, Col. Jefferson Buford of Eufaula, Ala., in April 1856 organized and equipped for settlement, mostly at his own expense, 400 men mainly from Alabama, Georgia, and South Carolina. In Kansas, Buford's men participated in many of the conflicts between the free and slave state factions.

BUILDING AND LOAN ASSOCIATIONS. For a century after the founding of the first building and loan association in Frankford, Pa., in 1831, these were local private cooperative credit agencies lending on home mortgages, generally with monthly amortization payments. Sporadic failures during the depression of the 1890's became epidemic in the depression of the 1930's. The federal government provided subsidies to the building and loan associations that carried corresponding regulation. The Reconstruction Finance Corporation (1932) made loans to building associations; the Federal Home Loan Bank System provided a central credit facility for member institutions. The Home Owners Loan Act of 1933 promoted chartering associations under the Federal

Home Loan Bank Board, creating an organization somewhat like the Federal Reserve System. In 1934 the Federal Savings and Loan Insurance Corporation, guaranteeing mortgages, was a benefit of the National Housing Act.

Federal Housing Administration and Veterans Administration loans by building associations have increased, though in 1971 conventional loans still constituted almost 86 percent of the funds extended. The assets of savings and loan associations stood at the end of 1978 at $523.6 billion.

BUILDINGS. *See* **Architecture.**

BULGE, BATTLE OF THE. A German counteroffensive in World War II, so named from a forty-mile-wide and sixty-mile-deep bulge created in American lines. It was the greatest pitched battle ever fought by U.S. troops, involving 600,000 Americans.

As German armies retreated from France in late summer 1944, Adolf Hitler believed that he might regain the initiative by a counteroffensive in the semimountainous Ardennes region of Belgium and Luxembourg. Field Marshal Gerd von Rundstedt secretly massed more than 200,000 men and 1,200 tanks in the wooded Eifel region opposite the Ardennes. On Dec. 16, three German armies struck along a sixty-mile front against seven American divisions; surprise was total, but only at one point did the Germans achieve the swift breakthroughs essential to success of their plan: a tank-infantry task force penetrated north of St. Vith and continued westward virtually unchecked.

On the second day the supreme Allied commander, Gen. Dwight D. Eisenhower, and the Twelfth Army Group commander, Lt. Gen. Omar N. Bradley, rushed reinforcements. In spite of the American defense German gains by Dec. 19 had split the Twelfth Army Group. Eisenhower put the northern armies under Field Marshal Bernard L. Montgomery, which later led to recrimination when American commanders held that Montgomery claimed undue credit for the German defeat.

The Germans surrounded Bastogne on Dec. 20. The American Third Army on the 22nd began to drive to Bastogne's relief, and German panzer divisions striving for the Meuse River were slowed by gasoline shortages. On Dec. 23 the weather cleared, enabling Allied planes to attack German columns and drop supplies at Bastogne. Severe fighting continued, even after the Fourth Armored Division lifted the siege on Dec. 26. The First and Third armies, nevertheless, began to counterattack Jan. 3, 1945, driving to a juncture north of Bastogne at Houffalize on Jan. 16 and precipitating slow German withdrawal. The last of the "bulge" was eliminated on Jan. 28.

BULLBOATS. When Hudson's Bay Company traders first visited the Mandan Indians in 1790 they found that the tribe possessed tublike boats with frameworks of willow poles, covered with raw buffalo hides. From 1810 to 1830, American fur traders on the tributaries of the Missouri built boats eighteen to thirty feet long, using the methods employed by the Indians in making their circular boats.

BULLDOZE. In 1875, during the Reconstruction period, a federal marshal was investigating an attempt to assassinate a registrar of voters in East Feliciana Parish, La. The natives refused him all information, and he was approached by a half-witted German who shouted, "Bull dooza mit der hooza!" The expletive had no meaning whatsoever, but to the frightened marshal it sounded like a threat from the Ku Klux Klan and he fled; the term "bulldoze" came into general use throughout the South with the generic meaning to intimidate in a bullying manner.

BULL GARRISON HOUSE. On Tower Hill, South Kingstown, R.I. On Dec. 15, 1675, during King Philip's War, it was attacked and burned by Narragansett Indians, fifteen defenders losing their lives.

BULLION. *See* **Bimetallism.**

BULL MOOSE PARTY. Nickname of the Progressive party of 1912–16, which nominated Theodore Roosevelt for the presidency in 1912. The Progressives left the Republican party following the renomination of President William H. Taft. The name was a tribute to Roosevelt, who often used "bull moose" to describe the strength and vigor of a person.

The party was in large part reabsorbed into the Republican party in 1916, after the nomination of Charles Evans Hughes, who was acceptable to the leading Progressives.

BULL RUN, FIRST BATTLE OF (July 21, 1861). The first major engagement of the Civil War, known in the Confederacy as the Battle of Manassas. The principal Union army, under Gen. Irvin McDowell, was mobilized about Washington. Union Gen. Robert Patterson, with a smaller army, was sent to "retain" Confederate Gen. Joseph E. Johnston in the Shenandoah Valley. Gen. Pierre G. T. Beauregard, with his southern army, occupied the line of Bull Run Creek, which lies across the main highways from Washington southward. His advance force under Gen. M. L. Bonham was based at Fairfax Courthouse to watch McDowell's army.

Public opinion compelled President Abraham Lincoln to order McDowell forward. The Union advance guard drove in Bonham's pickets on July 17. In accordance with previous orders, Bonham withdrew to Centreville, waited until dark, and then retired behind Bull Run. Eluding Patterson, Johnston and part of his army reached Bull Run on Saturday, July 20, stationing his troops on the slope behind Beauregard's line. At dawn McDowell attacked. Fierce fighting raged from Bull Run to the Henry house plateau to which the Confederates were driven. Here Gen. T. J. Jackson won the nickname "Stonewall." The arrival of another portion of Johnston's army turned the tide in favor of the Confederates. The federal troops were driven across Bull Run in disorder, pursued along the Warrenton Turnpike. The Union withdrawal turned into a rout as the troops streamed back in the direction of Washington.

From some 13,000 men actually engaged, the Union lost about 500 killed, 1,000 wounded, and 1,200 missing; the Confederates, with about 11,000 engaged, lost about 400 killed, 1,600 wounded, and 13 missing. The Confederates also captured twenty-five guns and much other material.

BULL RUN, SECOND BATTLE OF (also known as the Battle of Manassas). Gen. Robert E. Lee, Aug. 24, 1862, at Jeffersonton, Va., sent the 23,000 troops of Gen. T. J. ("Stonewall") Jackson to break the communications of Maj. Gen. John Pope's Army of Virginia, unassailably placed on the upper stretches of the Rappahannock. On the 27th Jackson plundered Pope's base at Manassas Junction and proceeded to Groveton Heights. On the 28th, he attacked Gen. Rufus King's division. On Aug. 29 Pope attacked Jackson, who with difficulty beat off repeated assaults. Lee, meantime, had brought up the remainder of his army, 32,000 men, and had formed them on Jackson's right. Lee swept Pope from his positions. Heavy rain on Aug. 31 delayed pursuit and made possible the retreat by Pope within the Washington defenses. Pope was not again trusted with field command. Pope's losses, Aug. 16 to Sept. 2, were 1,747 killed, 8,452 wounded, and 4,263 missing or captured; those of Lee were 1,553 killed, 7,812 wounded, and 109 missing.

BULLWHACKER. *See* **Mule Skinner.**

BUMMERS. A nickname applied to foragers of Gen. W. T. Sherman's army during its march to the sea in 1864 and north through the Carolinas.

BUNCOMBE. *See* **Bunkum.**

BUNDLING. A mode of courtship in colonial days where the parties instead of sitting up together went to bed together, with their clothes on. This custom, inherited from Europe, apparently originated as a matter of convenience and necessity where space and heat were lacking. Its prevalence seems to have ended in the late 18th century with the general improvement of living conditions.

BUNKER HILL (June 17, 1775). To force the British from Boston, on the night of June 16 the American militia besieging the town sent 1,200 men to seize Bunker Hill, on the peninsula of Charlestown. Instead, the detachment built a small redoubt on Breed's Hill, nearer Boston but easily flanked. They were discovered at daybreak, and British warships opened an ineffective fire. Col. William Prescott, commanding in the redoubt, was joined by perhaps 2,000 men. Meanwhile, under Maj. Gen. Sir William Howe, 2,000 British infantry, with a few filed guns, landed below the redoubt. Howe's first two attacks were bloodily repulsed by the provincials. What would have happened had the Americans had enough powder cannot be known; but Prescott's men were out of ammunition and were forced to quit the redoubt. After an engagement lasting less than two hours, the British were masters of the peninsula, but with heavy casualties. At first regarded by the Americans as a defeat, Bunker Hill came to be regarded as a moral victory, leading to a dangerous overconfidence in unpreparedness.

BUNKER HILL MONUMENT. Commemorating the Bunker Hill battle during the Revolution, its cornerstone was laid by the Marquis de Lafayette in 1825 and it was dedicated in 1843, Daniel Webster being chief orator at both events.

BUNKUM (Buncombe). A term that, by 1828, had come into general use in Washington to mean speechmaking designed for show or public applause and, later, insincere public talk or action. It is reputed to have originated with a speech that Felix Walker made in Congress to please his Buncombe County, N.C., congressional district.

BURCHARD INCIDENT. Rev. Samuel D. Burchard, representing several hundred clergymen supporting the Republican presidential candidate James G. Blaine, addressed the candidate at New York's Fifth Avenue Hotel on Oct. 30, 1884. In his speech Burchard described the Democrats as the party of "rum, Romanism, and rebellion." Blaine's failure to offset the diatribe cost him Irish support and the election.

BUREAUCRACY. In its most general sense "bureaucracy" may refer to all administrative organizations, public or private. Most narrowly, it refers to the administration of government through bureaus, or specialized administrative units. As commonly used, bureaucracy refers primarily to government bodies and tends to carry negative connotations, with regard to excessive size, impersonality, and unresponsiveness.

BURGESSES, HOUSE OF. *See* **Colonial Assemblies.**

BURGHERS. Citizens of an incorporated city who, under the Dutch (1657), enjoyed great or small burgher rights, and under the English were entitled by birth or admission by the magistrates to the designation of freemen. In New York and Albany only freemen, who had paid the required fees, could do business or ply a trade.

BURGOYNE'S INVASION (1777). In the late spring Gen. John Burgoyne prepared to invade New York from Canada by the Lake Champlain–Hudson River route. Lt. Col. Barry St. Leger was given command of a small expedition, which was to ascend the St. Lawrence River, cross Lake Ontario, and advance on Albany by the Mohawk Valley. Their principal objective was junction with Sir William Howe. In July, Burgoyne's army of 3,700 British regulars, 3,000 German troops, 250 Canadians and Tories, and 400 Indians proceeded up Lake Champlain, captured Ticonderoga from Gen. Arthur St. Clair, and proceeded up Lake George to force the Americans under Gen. Philip Schuyler to retreat from Fort Edward.

Meanwhile Howe, evidently believing the rebellion nearly crushed, left Sir Henry Clinton at New York to make a sortie up the Hudson and went to Philadelphia.

Burgoyne's raiding force to secure patriot stores at Bennington, Vt., was overwhelmed. St. Leger, besieging Fort Stanwix, managed, at Oriskany, to repulse a body of militia under Gen. Nicholas Herkimer, but at news of the approach of a patriot force under Benedict Arnold, abandoned his campaign.

Gen. Horatio Gates, in command of the American army near the mouth of the Mohawk, reinforced by Gen. Daniel Morgan's Virginia riflemen, moved northward and entrenched at Bemis Heights, about eight miles south of Saratoga, now Schuylerville. Burgoyne, whose Indian scouts had fled, was close upon the American army before he realized its presence. The first Battle of Freeman's Farm was fought Sept. 19. Burgoyne waited Clinton's expected advance up the Hudson, but Clinton got no farther than the Highlands of the Hudson. By Oct. 7 Burgoyne's effective troops numbered about 5,000, while the Americans in front of him were nearly 8,000. An attack led by Gen. Arnold threatened their whole position (*see* Freeman's Farm, Second Battle of). Burgoyne fell back toward Saratoga. The Americans were able to surround him, and on Oct. 17 he surrendered to Gates.

BURKE ACT (1906). Amended the Dawes General Allotment Act of 1887. Under the Dawes Act the Indian became a citizen immediately upon receipt of a "trust patent," but did not receive title to his land for twenty-five years. The Burke Act provided that the Indian would become a citizen only at the end of the twenty-five-year trust period, when he became the unrestricted owner of his land. The secretary of the interior was given the right to abbreviate the probationary period in individual cases in which Indians had shown themselves competent to manage their own affairs. Accordingly, competency commissions were established to pass on the qualifications of Indian applicants.

BURLINGAME TREATY (July 28, 1868). Articles added to the Treaty of Tientsin (1858) between the United States and China. They acknowledged Chinese territorial jurisdiction in China, left trade privileges in China to the discretion of the Chinese government, and established free immigration between the countries. It placed China on the most-favored-nation plane with regard to treatment of consuls and immunity and privileges in travel, residence, and education of Chinese subjects in the United States. It guaranteed nonintervention by the United States in Chinese domestic administration. It was signed in Washington by William H. Seward, secretary of state; Anson Burlingame, acting as envoy extraordinary and minister plenipotentiary of the emperor of China; a Chinese envoy; and a Manchu envoy.

BURLINGTON (Vt.). Largest city in Vermont, with a population of 37,712 in 1980. Burlington is located in northwestern Vermont, facing Lake Champlain. An important lake port, it provides water transportation for Vermont products, ranging from wood to stone, and has contact through Lake Champlain with the St. Lawrence Seaway in the north and with New York harbor to the south.

Burlington was established in 1773 on land received by charter from New Hampshire. The city was an important objective of British troops during the War of 1812, but it was successfully defended and became a key American base.

It is connected by ferry to Port Kent, N.Y., by the oldest steamboat company still operating in the United States. The State University and several smaller colleges are in Burlington, and it is also Vermont's principal transportation and banking center.

BURLINGTON COMPANY. A group of eight investors of Burlington, N.J., which absorbed various mortgages of George Croghan between 1768 and 1770 issued to Gov. William Franklin and assigned by him to the company, including one for 3,000 on 40,000 acres of Croghan's Otsego, N.Y., purchase. Franklin, besides personal loans to Croghan, had purchased a 50 percent stock interest in the company for 1,500 (1772). The remaining original shareholders sold their stock and rights, including Franklin's mortgages, to Andrew Craig and William Cooper, who, without notifying Franklin, instituted sheriff's sale proceedings under a judgment of 1773 and, by questionable methods, purchased the Otsego tract for 2,700 (January 1786). Efforts of Franklin and Croghan's heirs to contest title proved fruitless.

BURLINGTON ROUTE. *See* **Railroads, Sketches of Principal Lines: Burlington Northern.**

BURLINGTON STRIKE. On Feb. 27, 1888, locomotive enginemen of the Burlington Railway, members of the Brotherhood of Locomotive Engineers, struck for higher wages and abandonment of the system of classification. Trains were wrecked, men shot, and property destroyed. The brotherhood finally gave in, and by Feb. 1, 1889, operations were normal.

BURMA ROAD AND LEDO ROAD. Construction of a 400-mile military highway from Ledo, India, to join an existing 717-mile road to Burma from Kunming, China, was one of the largest engineering projects of World War II.

In 1937 the Chinese had started a crash project to get a passable military road between Kunming and Lashio, Burma, a railhead on a railway to Rangoon. By 1940 the Burma Road was a backcountry highway which could carry ten tons. Japan's conquest of Burma in 1942 blockaded China's land route to Rangoon.

When Lashio fell, a Chinese division fled to India. In June 1942 Gen. Joseph W. Stilwell, American theater commander in China, Burma, and India, proposed using this army to retake north Burma and build a 400-mile military highway to link up with the Burma Road at Wanting. Chinese and British allies showed no enthusiasm for a second Burma campaign. Stilwell's strategy persisted. The Ledo Road project started in October 1942, but it made little progress during 1943. Stilwell's Chinese began gaining victories in early 1944, and the road moved toward China. The capture of Myitkyina, Burma, on Aug. 3, 1944, forecast the joining of the Ledo Road to the Burma Road and Kunming. Opened Jan. 27, 1945, the combined highways were officially named the Stilwell Road. The Ledo portion was engineered by 17,000 Americans, under Gen. Lewis A. Pick; fatalities totaled 1,133 men, 625 in combat. "Pick's Pike" cost $150 million.

BURNING SPRING. Located in present Kanawha County, W. Va., near Malden. It is not known when this "boiling pot," which could be ignited and extinguished at will, was first seen by white persons, but in 1755 Mary Ingles, a captive, assisted Indians in making salt there. The 250-acre tract on which the spring was located was patented by generals George Washington and Andrew Lewis. Washington's nephew later sold it to the owners of a salt plant.

BURNS FUGITIVE SLAVE CASE (1854). One of three famous fugitive slave cases arising in Boston, Mass., after the enactment of the Fugitive Slave Law of 1850. The Vigilance Committee (1850–61) planned to rescue Anthony Burns, an escaped slave, from the courthouse. They battered in a door of the building at night, May 26, and killed the U.S. marshal. Despite the committee's efforts, U.S. Commissioner Edward G. Loring remanded Burns to his owner in Alexandria, Va. Several rich citizens paid $1,300 for his freedom in 1855 and Burns returned to Massachusetts. Following the Burns case, enforcement of the Fugitive Slave Law declined.

BURNT CORN, BATTLE OF (July 27, 1813). An encounter between Creek Indians and Alabama frontiersmen on Burnt Corn Creek. On their return from Pensacola, where aid had been received from the British, a party of Creek Indians was attacked by frontiersmen under Col. James Caller. The Indians won, killing two and wounding fifteen.

BURR CONSPIRACY. The climax of the dramatic struggle for power between President Thomas Jefferson and Aaron Burr, vice-president during Jefferson's first term. Following his duel with Alexander Hamilton in 1804, Burr schemed to regain something of his onetime popularity and power. To accomplish this he chose land conquest or seizure in Spanish territory west of the Mississippi.

Failing to attach England to his cause, he enlisted those who might be of help, yet never disclosed his exact intentions. Harman Blennerhassett, a trusting, visionary Irishman, who lived on an island in the Ohio River, was one. Burr sought successively to draw France and Spain into his web of intrigue, but to no avail.

Before leaving Philadelphia in the summer of 1806, Burr wrote to his coconspirator Gen. James Wilkinson, who commanded the American army on the Mississippi, that the expedition would start for New Orleans before the end of the year. But Wilkinson declined to be involved further. Instead, when Burr's advance flotilla reached the lower Mississippi, Wilkinson ordered its members arrested. Burr, too, was seized and then paroled. He attempted to escape to Spanish territory, but was again captured and taken east for trial. Burr was acquitted of treason and high misdemeanor.

BURR-HAMILTON DUEL. The most famous duel in American history resulted in the mortal wounding of Alexander Hamilton by Aaron Burr, July 11, 1804. Burr issued his challenge ostensibly because Hamilton refused to disavow a "despicable opinion" of Burr, which he was reported to have expressed during Burr's unsuccessful New York governorship campaign in 1804. Actually, Burr vengefully blamed Hamilton for his defeat for the presidency in 1801.

Hamilton, morally opposed to dueling, doubted that his technical demurrer to Burr's charge would be accepted. The duel took place beneath the Palisades at Weehawken, N.J. As Hamilton fell, he discharged his pistol wildly and, his second believed, involuntarily. After suffering excruciating pain from the ball lodged in his spine, Hamilton died the next day. Amid shocked mourning for Hamilton, Burr fled from the murder findings of coroners' juries. The charges were quashed, but Burr's remaining years were doomed to discredit.

BURR TRIAL. Aaron Burr was indicted for treason in 1807 and brought to trial in the U.S. Circuit Court at Richmond, Va., before Chief Justice John Marshall sitting as a circuit judge. In guiding the jury as to the law of treason the chief justice gave an interpretation so restricting the meaning of the words "levying war" that in the case at hand only the assemblage at Blennerhassett Island could come within it. Burr, however much he may have counseled, advised, or planned that assemblage, was not present. Under the Marshall interpretation his absentee connection was not sufficient to render him guilty of treason. The chief justice was sharply criticized for inconsistency and bias, in that in an earlier case involving two of Burr's messengers (*see* Bollman Case) he had stated the law in a way which seemingly should have linked Burr with the treasonable assemblage.

BUSHWHACKERS. Originally used in the early 18th century to describe a backwoodsman; applied during the Civil War by federal soldiers to Confederate guerrilla fighters, with a distinct implication of private plunder. Used in Missouri for border ruffians, it was more commonly applied in the mountains of Virginia and Kentucky.

BUSHY RUN, BATTLE OF (Aug. 5–6, 1763). Col. Henry Bouquet's expedition to relieve Fort Pitt was attacked by Indians near Bushy Run, twenty-five miles east of Pittsburgh, Pa. After a day of indecisive fighting, the men rested. In the morning Bouquet, feigning retreat, drew the Indians forward to receive a flanking fire. The Indians, completely routed, fled, but the British had lost over 100 men.

BUSINESS, BIG. The concentration of industrial and financial power that began in the post–Civil War period. The United States was undergoing a rapid change from an agrarian, rural, handicraft economy to an industrial, urban, factory economy.

The first of the big businesses were the railroads, which proliferated in numbers and distances covered during the 1870's and 1880's. Entrepreneurs engaged in disastrous competition quickly saw the profitability of cooperation and consolidation. The extension of transcontinental railroads and the consolidation of competing lines resulted in the creation of a national transportation network and a national market.

As society became aware of real or imaginary abuses resulting from an economy that was becoming dominated by a single firm or several large firms in almost every area of activity, protesters first turned to producers' and consumers' cooperatives, but these attempts at self-help were unsuccessful. Soon protesters sought government action. Their efforts resulted in the passage of the Interstate Commerce Act (1887), intended to regulate railroad activities, and the Sherman Antitrust Act (1890), to regulate industrial size and competition. These acts, and subsequent legislation, proved ineffective. During the Progressive and New Deal eras, further regulatory legislation was passed.

Much of the difficulty of enacting effective regulatory legislation has been the result of the persuasiveness of business lobbies and the problem of eliminating the evils of size while retaining the benefits. Since the mid-20th century the problem of size and concentration of economic power has manifested itself in the creation of conglomerate enterprises.

BUSINESS, PUBLIC CONTROL OF. The American colonies inherited from England a penchant for competition in the production of goods and services. During the 17th century mercantilist government reliance on monopolies was waning, soon to be replaced by free individual initiative as the guarantee of an abundancy of products at reasonable prices. Certain types of proprietors—innkeepers, ferrymen, millers—since their enterprises were affected with a public interest, were forbidden to refuse their services to applicants. The holders of a monopoly, such as a bridge or toll road, were also regulated in their charges. With the development of public utilities, in which competition was wasteful, the grant of franchises presupposed the supervision of rates.

Railroads early came under state supervision. After the lines became interstate and competition led to discriminatory abuses, the Interstate Commerce Act of 1887 forbade unreasonable rates, favoritism to certain shippers, and unfairness to local communities served by a single line. The Interstate Commerce Commission for twenty years was frustrated in administering the act until aided by the Hepburn Act of 1906, the Mann-Elkins Act of 1910, and the Shipping Act of 1916.

The experiments with public restraints on transportation were matched by state and then federal statutes attempting to preserve competition in commerce. "Trust" became the generic term for a business combination, though mergers were resorted to also. The Sherman Antitrust Act of 1890 was short and simple, but subject to elusive interpretation. It made illegal "every contract, combination in the form of trust or otherwise, or conspiracy in restraint of trade . . . among the . . . States, or with foreign nations." The courts stood in the way of enforcement. The powerful movement toward business consolidation rendered invalid the desire for competition that had long prevailed among small businesses. Nevertheless, the Clayton Act of 1914 amended the Sherman law by punishing particular monopolistic practices. The Federal Trade Commission was set up in the same year, and by its cease-and-desist orders relieved the clogged court dockets.

During World War I it was evident that free-market forces alone could not be relied upon to direct materials, capital, and labor into defense uses. The War Industries Board, Food Administration, Fuel Administration, and Emergency Fleet Corporation were the chief agencies of government control at this time; as the railroads under private management proved unable to meet traffic needs, the government leased the lines and reduced waste in their operation.

Economic demobilization was prompt after World War I, on popular demand, and the nation entered the prosperous 1920's. Presidents in that decade were content to give business its head. After the stock market collapsed in 1929 and a catastrophic business year followed, President Herbert Hoover championed agricultural controls; federal appropriations for relief of the unemployed; and the Reconstruction Finance Corporation, to make loans to railroads, banks, and other major business enterprises.

President Franklin D. Roosevelt's inauguration occurred in a dreary scene of banks closing, industrial production shrunk to less than half, staple farm crops at giveaway prices, and a third of the nation's workers jobless. Swiftly the federal government came to the rescue. All but a few banks were reopened, ample credit was dispensed to financial enterprises, public relief payments were expanded, and homes were protected against foreclosure. The Agricultural Adjustment Act constituted a breadline for farmers, and the National Industrial Recovery Act gave manufactures and commerce the coveted liberty of collusion in return for minimum wages, maximum hours, and the right of workers to organize and bargain collectively. The antitrust acts were suspended.

With entrance of the United States into World War II, government controls were redoubled: government-set materials priorities; consumer rationing; price, wage, and profit limits. The next episodes of wage and price fixing—in 1971–73—were intended to reduce the inflation resulting from the long Vietnam War; they met with little or no success, though unemployment was somewhat lessened.

Significant developments in the policing of business after World War II involved federal action. Fair employment practices were mandated on behalf of minority groups. Consumer protection markedly increased by means of the Food and Drug Administration, a reanimated Federal Trade Commission, and the Environmental Protection Agency (1970). The Federal Power Commission was concerned with energy sources such as nuclear reactors, natural gas, offshore drilling for oil, and higher-voltage transmission lines for electricity. The Department of Transportation was established in 1967 to embrace numerous existing agencies. Distress of the railroads promoted a public corporation, Amtrak. The Department of Health, Education, and Welfare was formed in 1953; its 300 programs to improve living conditions modified and supplemented private enterprise. Efforts of the states toward business regulation have been encouraged by federal initiative and are subject to federal guidelines but remain relatively spasmodic and weakly staffed.

BUSINESS CYCLES. A fluctuation in economic activity, a business cycle consists of expansions occurring at about the same time in many economic activities, followed by similarly general recessions, contractions, and revivals which merge into the expansion phase of the next cycle. This sequence is recurrent but not periodic; in duration, business cycles may last from one year to ten or twelve years.

The chronology of business cycles in common use for the United States was developed by the National Bureau of Economic Research, Inc. On an annual basis, it extends from 1834 to 1970 and covers thirty-two expansions and thirty-two contractions. The monthly and quarterly chronology begins in 1854 and covers twenty-seven cycles. Most of the eleven business cycle contractions (recessions) in the United States from 1920 to 1970 have lasted about a year or less. Only two were substantially longer: the eighteen-month contraction during 1920–21 and the forty-three-month contraction during 1929–33. These intervals represent the consensus among a number of different measures of economic activity.

BUSINESS FORECASTING. The function of a group of specialists with its own professional organization, the National Association of Business Economists. Business forecasting takes place on three levels: at the national level; at the industry or market level; and at the individual firm level. Large corporations have their own economics departments for such forecasting.

Nearly all business forecasting in America is strongly quantitative. Numerical forecasts of the main national accounts, national economic indicators, industry time series, and firm accounting statements are regularly prepared. At a minimum, businesses need annual forecasts. It is popular to combine forecasts for one, two, or three years ahead and to include quarterly forecasts. Some firms need monthly or weekly forecasts, whereas others must peer into the future for two or three decades (life insurance corporations, forest product manufacturers, mining companies, public utilities).

The growth of multinational corporations has made it imperative to forecast the outlook for the whole world economy. Overseas activity levels, world trade, U.S. trade, and U.S. balance of payments are the main items that command the attention of present-day business forecasters.

By and large, there are two approaches to business forecasting. In the judgmental approach, economists with perceptive vision of the contemporary environment and prevailing trends fit the statistical magnitudes of the economy into future patterns that appear to be plausible. The other approach is through formal model building. Mathematical models with statistically estimated coefficients are fitted together into logical, dynamic systems.

BUSINESS MACHINES. The large-scale application of business machines began with the typewriter and the cash register; these were American inventions, in the sense that the first commercially successful examples were introduced in the United States. A typewriting machine was patented in England in 1714 by Henry Mill and was followed by many others. The first one patented in the United States was the typographer of W. A. Burt of Detroit (1829). The machine which gave the name "typewriter" to the whole class of such machines was developed between 1866 and 1873 by C. L. Sholes, Carlos Glidden, and Samuel Soulé of Milwaukee, Wis. Its success stemmed in part from the association of James Densmore, an astute businessman, and a manufacturing agreement (1873) with the prosperous firearms manufacturing company, E. Remington and Sons.

The cash register appeared at about the same time (1879), conceived by a Dayton, Ohio, businessman, James Ritty. Ritty's attempt to sell it failed until he was joined by Joseph Patterson, the legendary prototype of the supersalesman. Thus was launched the National Cash Register Company. The success of the typewriter and cash register owed more to promotion than to demand, and to the "invention" of the female typist. By the 1890's, schools flourished for teaching ladies to type.

A parade of successful inventions was led by the irrepressible Thomas A. Edison's mimeograph (1875), which began the history of the reproducing machine; his stock ticker (1868), the parent of the teletyping machine; and his phonograph (1877), soon adapted as a dictating machine.

A new principle for a multiplying machine, based on a gear wheel with retractable teeth was introduced in 1886 by Willgodt Odhner, a Swede living in St. Petersburg, Russia. The German version, Brunsviga, became the prototype of increasingly more complicated and versatile mathematical machines. Meanwhile, an American from Cincinnati, F. S. Baldwin, had apparently anticipated Odhner by a year with a machine based on the same principle. But Baldwin, a professional inventor, had sold only ten machines by 1886 when he retired to further experimentation. A calculating machine industry had developed by the time he associated himself in 1911 with Jay R. Monroe to form the Monroe Calculating Machine Company. This industry had grown up around the simple adding machine and particularly the comptometer introduced by Dorr E. Felt in 1885 and the W. S. Burroughs calculator of 1892. The United States came to rival Germany as the center of the calculating-machine industry.

Burroughs recognized the desirability of a printed record, and his machine was consequently adapted to this purpose; in 1894, the loose-leaf ledger was adapted to mechanical accounting. By 1910 the accountant had available a bookkeeping machine that performed all four arithmetic operations in a loose-leaf ledger without removing the sheets from the binder or the binder from the machine. The following year saw J. T. Underwood offering a typewriter modified into a billing machine with an adding register.

The first important calculating machine for science was the punched-card tabulating machine introduced by Herman Hollerith of Washington, D.C., for use in compiling the 1890 census. Hollerith's machine simultaneously sorted and counted cards on which data had been placed in a coded pattern of holes. Hollerith left the government to form his own factory, which in 1911 joined with others to form the C-T-R Company, now known as International Business Machines. A rival system by James Powers was marketed commercially (from 1927) by the Remington Rand Company, successor to the pioneer typewriter manufacturer. Both systems were shown by L. J. Comrie, in the late 1920's, to be adaptable to the needs of scientific calculation and were then merged into the evolving computer.

Of other business machines, the most remarkable development has taken place in the reproducing machine. Edison's mimeograph was joined about 1906 by a machine using a photographic process, and photostatic copies became predominant until about 1950. Since then, the most common process has been xerography, an electrostatic system invented in 1937 by Chester F. Carlson.

BUSING. The transporting of children by bus to school to achieve desegregation or racial balance. The Supreme Court ordered school desegregation in 1954, and the court's unanimous 1971 decision in *Swann* v. *Charlotte-Mecklenburg Board of Education* reaffirmed that busing was a legitimate tool. A 1971 Gallup poll found a 77 percent national opposition to busing, with blacks split almost evenly. In March 1972 President Richard M. Nixon proposed a package of antibusing measures. In June, Congress passed the Higher Education Act with compromise antibusing provisions, chiefly the Broomfield amendment (Rep. William S. Broomfield of Michigan), that delayed implementation of court busing orders until appeals had been exhausted. In May 1973 the Supreme Court upheld an appeals court ruling that barred Richmond, Va., from merging its predominantly black city schools with predominantly white suburban schools by busing across school district lines. In a landmark decision in July 1974 the Court ruled that the federal district and appeals courts in a Detroit case (*Bradley v. Milliken*) had unconstitutionally approved the merger of suburban and city schools for purposes of desegregation. Busing remained a legitimate instrument for furthering integration, but not across school district lines. It continued to be a controversial issue in the late 1970s, when even some supporters of desegration charged that court-ordered busing was counterproductive.

BUSY BEES OF DESERET. The Mormon settlers (1848) in the territory that became Utah. Deseret is the "land of honeybee" of the Book of Mormon.

BUTE, FORT (Manchac Post). Named for British prime minister, John Stuart, third Earl of Bute; established in 1763 at junction of Iberville River (or Bayou Manchac) with Mississippi River. Remained important British military and trading post in West Florida until captured by Spanish forces under Bernardo de Galvez of Louisiana on Sept. 7, 1779.

BUTLER'S ORDER NO. 28. Gen. Benjamin F. Butler became military commander of New Orleans, May 1, 1862, following its fall to Union troops. The marked hostility of the inhabitants was exhibited in insults by the women. On May 15, Butler issued an order that any female insulting or showing contempt for any officer or soldier of the United States should "be treated as a woman of the town plying her avocation." The order was a cause of Butler's removal from command of New Orleans, Dec. 16, 1862.

BUTLER'S RANGERS. A regiment of Loyalists recruited in 1777 by Col. John Butler to serve with the Indians against the colonists. From their headquarters at Fort Niagara, the Rangers embarked on forays that spread terror throughout New York and Pennsylvania. They perpetrated the Wyoming Valley invasion in July 1778 and took part in Sir John Johnson's raid on the Mohawk settlements in 1780. The regiment was disbanded in June 1784.

BUTTE DES MORTS COUNCIL. Lewis Cass, governor of Michigan Territory, and Thomas L. McKenney, Indian commissioner, held a council with the Chippewa, Menomini, and Winnebago at Little Butte des Morts, north of Lake Winnebago. A treaty was signed there Aug. 11, 1827, adjusting boundaries and the relations of these tribes with the Indians migrating to Wisconsin from New York.

BUTTERFIELD CLAIMS. In 1854 two ships, loaded with war materials, cleared at New York for St. Thomas in the Danish West Indies. Suspicion arose that they were destined for Venezuelan rebels. Because of lack of evidence they were cleared in a libel suit. When they arrived at St. Thomas, trouble arose again. The owners presented a large claim for damages because the vessels were detained by the Danish government. Negotiations finally ended in a Danish-American arbitration treaty (1888) disallowing the claim on the ground that the Danish government had observed strictly the neutrality laws involved. The name is derived from the firm that handled the negotiations.

BUTTERFIELD OVERLAND DISPATCH. Because of much travel to Colorado after the discovery of gold, D. A. Butterfield, backed by New York capital, organized a joint-stock express and passenger carrying service between the Missouri River and Denver. In July 1865, the route via the Smoky Hill River in central Kansas was surveyed, and soon thereafter coaches were in operation. Ben Holladay, acting for a competing organization, bought the Butterfield Overland Dispatch in March 1866.

BUTTERFIELD OVERLAND MAIL. *See* **Southern Overland Mail.**

BYRD'S POLAR FLIGHTS.

North Pole. On Apr. 5, 1926, Commander Richard E. Byrd sailed on the U.S.S. *Chantier* for Kings Bay, Spitsbergen, in Norway, which he intended using as the base for a flight to the North Pole. The vessel arrived in the bay on Apr. 29 with the big trimotor Fokker airplane, *Josephine Ford.* After being held up by defects in the plane's skis for some days, Byrd and his pilot, Floyd Bennett, took off for the North Pole shortly after midnight on May 9. At 9:02 A.M., Greenwich civil time, the pole was reached. After circling around it, they returned to Spitsbergen.

South Pole. Early in the Antarctic spring of 1929 Byrd made a flight from his base at Little America to the foot of the Queen Maud Mountains and laid down a gasoline base. On Nov. 29, 1929, at 3:29 P.M., the polar flight party took off in the Ford airplane, *Floyd Bennett,* for the pole. At 9:15 they started up the Liv Glacier Pass for the Polar Plateau. At 1:14, Greenwich civil time, the pole was reached. After a short flight to the east the plane was landed at the fuel base. At six o'clock the return journey to Little America began. Shortly after ten the party landed at the camp.

CABANNE'S TRADING POST. Established ten miles above Omaha on the west side of the Missouri River between 1822 and 1826 for the American Fur Company by John Pierre Cabanne. Between 1833 and 1840 the post was moved to Bellevue, Nebr., and placed under the management of Peter A. Sarpy.

CABEZA DE VACA, TRAVELS OF. Álvar Núñez Cabeza de Vaca went to America with the expedition of Pánfilo de Narváez, which landed near present Tampa, Fla., in April 1528. After a brief, disastrous exploration, the colonists built five horsehide boats and sailed for Cuba. A hurricane sank all but the one commanded by Cabeza de Vaca, and it soon was wrecked on the Texas coast. From 1528 to 1536 Cabeza de Vaca and his companions endured untold hardships, including imprisonment by Indians, in a 6,000-mile journey through the American Southwest and northern Mexico. After arriving safely in New Spain, Cabeza de Vaca returned to Old Spain to ask Charles V for the governorship of "La Florida." Instead he was given the governorship of Paraguay. His account of his travels was printed in 1555 at Valladolid, Spain, under the title *Relación y Comentarios.*

CABILDO. The Spanish governmental organization for the province of Louisiana. It was established by Alexander O'Reilly, an Irish officer in the Spanish army, in 1769, superseding the French superior council, and was abolished when France regained possession of the province in 1800. The cabildo met in the Government House (Casa Capitular or Principal), known today as the Cabildo.

CABINET. This body, which has existed since the presidency of George Washington, rests on the authority of custom rather than the Constitution or statute. It is generally composed of the heads of the major federal administrative departments: State; Treasury; Defense; Justice; Interior; Agriculture; Commerce; Labor; Health and Human Services; Housing and Urban Development; Transportation; Energy; Education. In terms of money spent, number of persons employed, and scope of legal authority, these are the most significant units of the administration. The heads of these departments are presidential appointees, subject to confirmation by the Senate.

Although all presidents have periodically held formal cabinet meetings, the role of the cabinet in presidential decision-making has generally been limited, depending on the particular president. The cabinet collectively may lack significance, but individual members may have great influence. Frequently and increasingly, cabinet members are overshadowed by the expanding White House staff.

CABIN RIGHTS ("tomahawk rights," "corn rights," "sugar-camp rights," or, later, "settlement rights"). Construction of a cabin, clearing of a small tract, or the making of other improvements on unoccupied and unclaimed land on the frontier was commonly held to be sufficient for granting title. At a later time when revenue needs led to the sale of public land, such improvements might entitle the squatter to a preferential or preemption right to buy the land from the government, state or federal, at the lowest established price.

CABLE CARS. Developed in the late 19th century as a form of street transportation. They operate by means of an underground cable in constant motion from one end of the route to the other. A system of clutches is used to hook the car on to the cable and to unhook it when the operator wishes to stop the car. Cable cars are still in operation in San Francisco, where they are maintained as a National Historic Landmark.

CABLES, ATLANTIC AND PACIFIC. Telegraphy had barely been successfully established on land in the mid-1840's when thoughts turned to bridging the Atlantic Ocean. American contributions to the first Atlantic cables centered around Cyrus Field, who with a few friends, financed a line up to and across Newfoundland, but the money and expertise for the ocean route were to be found in England. Money was raised primarily from the merchants of London, Liverpool, and Manchester; the British and American governments supplied guaranteed subsidies for a working cable as well as ships for the laying operations. The British steamship *Agamemnon* and the American steamship *Niagara,* each with half the cable, made an unsuccessful attempt to lay a transatlantic cable in 1857. In 1858 they met at mid ocean to try again. On August 5, a single-wire connection was made between Valencia, Ireland, and Trinity Bay, Newfoundland. Unfortunately, high-voltage pulses aggravated flaws in the cable; its condition deteriorated; and it failed entirely by October 20.

In 1865 the entire length of a transatlantic cable was loaded on board the *Great Eastern.* It broke two-thirds of the way across. But on Aug. 27, 1866, a renewed attempt was successful; the 1865 cable was then picked up and completed.

An additional cable was laid across the Atlantic in 1869, and in 1884 John W. Mackay and James Gordon Bennett laid the first two American-sponsored cables. Many others followed and improvements were made.

Strong interest in a Pacific cable was expressed in the United States and Canada from 1870 on, but commercial and political demands were not great enough, and not until 1902 was the first (British) Pacific cable laid; it ran from Vancouver to Australia and New Zealand. In 1903 the first link of an American Pacific cable (promoted by Mackay) was completed between San Francisco and Hawaii; it was later extended to Guam and the Philippines. After 1900 British interests lost some ground to other national interests, notably those of the American Telephone and Telegraph Company.

CABOT VOYAGES. In 1496 a petition was placed before Henry VII of England in the name of John Cabot, an Italian navigator, and his three sons, Sebastian, Lewis, and Sanctius, for the privilege of making explorations in the New World. Letters patent dated Mar. 5, 1496, were granted to the Cabots, and in the spring of 1497 they sailed west from Bristol. Coasting southward they discovered, it is believed, Cape Breton Island and Nova Scotia. The next year John Cabot made further explorations along the eastern coast of North America. His discoveries were supposedly recorded on a map and globe made by the explorer. Both are now lost.

CABRILLO EXPEDITION. In the hope of finding a direct route from Spain to the East Indies through Spanish waters, Juan Rodríguez Cabrillo and Bartolomé Ferrelo sailed on June 27, 1542, from Navidad, Mexico, and on September 28 reached a port they named San Miguel. They were in fact at San Diego Bay and thus were the discoverers of California. They got as far north as Drake's Bay but were forced back to the Santa Barbara Islands, where Rodríguez died. Ferrelo is believed to have reached the Rogue River in Oregon.

CABUSTO, BATTLE OF (November 1540). Cabusto, a Chickasaw town situated on the Black Warrior River near old Erie, Ala., was the scene of one of Hernando de Soto's conflicts with the Indians. With Cabusto as a base, de Soto broke through the palisaded defenses of the Indians north of the river and advanced up the Tombigbee Valley.

CACIQUE. A term adapted by the Spanish from the northern South American–Caribbean Carib language, in which it referred to a village, to a tribal chieftain or headman, or to both. The Spanish then came to apply it to chiefs elsewhere in their American domains. Among the Keresan-speaking Pueblos of the Rio Grande area the cacique, often a secret figure, represents peace and spiritual leadership, embodying in his presence and person the sense of tribal well-being.

CAHABA OLD TOWNS. A cluster of villages along the Cahaba River, some six miles northeast of Marion, Perry County, Ala. From Fort Claiborne in Monroe, Col. Gilbert Russell in the spring of 1814 was sent northward to Cahaba Old Towns in a futile effort to provide defense against the Creek Indians.

CAHOKIA (Ill.). The first permanent French settlement in Illinois, founded March 1699 by priests of the Seminary of Quebec who established the Mission of the Holy Family. Their chapel was located near the left bank of the Mississippi River, a short distance south of modern East St. Louis. Cahokia took its name from the adjacent Indian village.

The mission quickly attracted French settlers, principally from Canada, occasionally from Louisiana. Their number, however, was never large. A census in 1723 enumerated only twelve white residents. By 1800 its population had increased to 719. Throughout the 18th century Cahokia exemplified a typical French village. There was a common pasture land and a large common field divided into strips for cultivation. The church was the center of village life and the priest the most influential resident.

Although Cahokia became the seat of St. Clair County, its growth was not commensurate with that of the territory. In 1927 the village was incorporated, and in 1978 had a population of 18,904.

CAHOKIA MOUNDS. The prehistoric settlement of Cahokia in the alluvial plain of the Mississippi River valley, about four miles northeast of present-day East Saint Louis, is the largest archaeological site north of central Mexico. A focus of development of the Mississippian culture in the Midwest between A.D. 700 and about 1450, Cahokia probably attained the status of a true city with a population estimated at 30,000 by A.D. 1000–1100. The site was carefully planned with many of the mounds constructed with horizontal compass orientations in mind. At least 100 large platform and burial mounds and many smaller ones are within the six-square-mile tract or within its immediate area. Monks Mound, the largest platform mound at Cahokia and the third largest temple mound in the New World, is 300 by 200 meters at its base and 30 meters high. Several buildings of wattle and daub were apparently on the summit of this huge terraced earth construction, which covers fifteen acres. The inhabitants of this prehistoric city lived both within and outside a wooden palisade surrounding Monks Mound and other platform and burial mounds situated around the sides of a large central plaza. Rings of posts 240 to 480 feet in diameter that once stood outside the main palisade have been interpreted as calendrical wood henges. High-quality artifacts include polished, painted, and engraved ceramics tempered with crushed shell. Clearly the center of a chiefdom or early state-level society, Cahokia had immense influence throughout the Midwest. The cultural climax at Cahokia waned by A.D. 1300.

CAHUENGA, TREATY OF (Jan. 13, 1847). Ended California's part in the Mexican War. After preliminary negotiations, at the old Cahuenga ranch house, Capt. John C. Frémont and Andres Pico, leader of Mexican forces in California, signed a document, the liberal terms of which were in complete accord with President James Polk's conciliatory policy.

CAIRO (Ill.). City in southern Illinois, at the juncture of the Ohio and Mississippi rivers, founded in 1837 by the Cairo City and Canal Company. The sale of lots, which commenced in 1853, and the completion of the Illinois Central Railroad attracted settlers, and by 1860 the population exceeded 2,000. During the Civil War, Cairo was of great strategic importance, and for several months both Gen. U. S. Grant and Andrew H. Foote had headquarters there.

CAIRO CONFERENCES (1943). On their way to the Teheran Conference, President Franklin D. Roosevelt and Prime Minister Winston Churchill met with Generalissimo Chiang Kai-shek in Cairo, Egypt (November 22–26), to discuss the war against Japan and other Far Eastern matters. The three issued a declaration of intent: to take from Japan all the Pacific islands occupied by it since 1914; to restore to China all territory "stolen" by Japan, such as Manchuria, Formosa, and the Pescadores Islands; and to give Korea its independence "in due course."

Returning from Teheran, Roosevelt and Churchill met with President İsmet İnönü of Turkey at the second Cairo Conference (December 4–6). No significant agreements were reached, and İnönü declined to enter the war.

CAJON PASS. Between the San Gabriel and San Bernardino mountains; the best route from the Mojave Desert to southern California. It was probably first known to white men when in March 1776 it was traversed by Father Francisco Garcés. The first American to discover the pass was Jedediah Smith (November 1826). Shortly afterward it became a part of the route between California and Santa Fe.

CALAMITY HOWLER. A phrase contemptuously used by political opponents of the discontented Populists and agrarians during the late 1880's and 1890's. The term signifies a noisy pessimist, particularly one who disagrees with the measures and policies of the ruling party and who foretells the economic ruin of a geographical section or the nation.

***CALDER* V. *BULL*,** 3 Dallas 386 (1798). The *locus classicus* wherein the Supreme Court defined an ex post facto law: one which makes criminal an act that was not punishable when committed; or retrospectively increases the punishment; or alters the rules of evidence in order to convict the offender.

CALHOUN'S *DISQUISITION ON GOVERNMENT*. John C. Calhoun's reasoned views on government from the point of view of the permanent minority (the South). Begun in 1843, finished in 1848, it elaborates the doctrine of his *South Carolina Exposition and Protest.* Its keynote is the idea of a concurrent majority. Simple majority government always results in despotism over the minority unless some way is devised to secure the assent of all classes, sections, and interests. The argument is close-knit and convincing if one accepts the belief of Calhoun that the states retain absolute sovereignty over the Constitution and can do with it as they wish.

CALHOUN'S *EXPOSITION*. After passage of the Tariff of Abominations, and at the request of the South Carolina legislature, John C. Calhoun prepared his *South Carolina Exposition and Protest* declaring the tariff of 1828 "unconstitutional, unequal and oppressive; and calculated to corrupt public virtue and destroy the liberty of the country." Calhoun proposed nullification as the constitutional remedy: South Carolina should interpose the state's veto, to be binding upon its citizens and the general government unless three-fourths of the states should amend the Constitution. Amended and published, although not adopted, by the legislature, Calhoun's *Exposition* was applied four years later in the nullification of the tariff acts of 1828 and 1832.

CALICO RAILROAD. The derisive name applied to the proposed Lyons, Iowa, Central Railroad from Lyons to Council Bluffs. The company was organized in 1853. Iowa residents purchased stock, and counties voted bonds to help build the road. The funds, however, were inadequate and some were misappropriated. Work was stopped and some 2,000 were left without pay and work. The counties were compelled to redeem their bonds. The railroad company store at Lyons distributed goods, including a supply of calico, in partial payment to the workers.

CALIFORNIA. Extreme isolation made California nearly the last part of the Western Hemisphere to become a European colony. The name California was first applied to Baja (lower) California. Alta California was discovered in 1542 by Juan Rodríguez Cabrillo. In 1602–03 Sebastían Vizcaíno made the first usable maps of the coastline, and named and charted the Bay of Monterey. When a "sacred expedition" founded San Diego in 1769 and Monterey in 1770, Father Junípero Serra began what would ultimately be twenty-one Franciscan missions along El Camino Real from San Diego to Sonoma.

New Spain tried to make Spanish colonists out of the native Indians through the mission system, but this attempt failed, and when the missions were finally "secularized" under Mexican rule, the mission lands and cattle passed into the hands of a few hundred ranchers. California remained weak and unprosperous under Mexico. At the end of the Mexican period in 1846, the population other than full-blooded native Indians was only about 7,000.

When Mexico ceded California to the United States on Feb. 2, 1848, signers of the treaty were unaware that gold had been discovered at John A. Sutter's sawmill on the American River. Before the end of 1849 the gold rush had increased California's population above 60,000, the number required for statehood. State government was in *de facto* operation for nearly a year before Congress finally admitted California as part of the Compromise of 1850. The gold rush also brought tragic disappointment. At the peak in the early 1850's a miner might average $20 a day, but his expenses averaged $18. Thus, the state was full of disillusioned men who had no money to go home. The gold rush set a tone of greed, crime, violence, and disorder. Mistreatment of Indians, Mexicans, and Chinese introduced a long tradition of racial oppression in Anglo-American California.

Mining remained the dominant industry until the 1870's, for the discovery of the great silver deposits of the Comstock lode in 1859 made up for the gradual decline in gold. Manufacturing and farming developed slowly. A great drought in the early 1860's nearly wiped out the cattle industry; but wheat began to flourish, and wine production increased rapidly in Northern California. The citrus industry developed phenomenally in Southern California.

The Central Pacific, the western part of the first transcontinental railroad, was completed in 1869. The Southern Pacific, as it was later called, dominated the economy and the government and politics of California. The railroad failed to bring prosperity to California, and the 1870's were a time of depression and unemployment. The so-called Workingmen's party of California, organized in 1877, demanded radical change in general and Chinese exclusion in particular. Its followers were unemployed and unorganized. In 1878 the party elected most of the San Francisco delegates to the state constitutional convention that produced California's second constitution, ratified in 1879.

The new constitution attempted important political and economic reforms, but conservative forces were able to discredit and nullify these provisions. The Southern Pacific and various urban public-utility corporations were allied with corrupt politicians. In 1906 a graft prosecution in San Francisco began the process of overthrowing this system. Simultaneously a "good government" movement gained control in Los Angeles, and in 1907 these movements joined other California progressives to form the Lincoln-Roosevelt Republican League. In 1910 this organization won control of the statewide Republican party, and succeeded in nominating and electing Hiram W. Johnson as governor.

In a remarkable series of reforms in 1911, the progressives established effective regulation of the railroad and other public utilities, a workmen's compensation plan, and the state's first budget system, and enacted the initiative, the referendum, the recall, and the direct primary. This was carried to an extreme in 1913 with the adoption of the cross-filing system (in effect until 1959), which permitted a candidate to file for the nomination of more than one party. Such measures greatly weakened the power and responsibility of political parties in California.

Movies, Oil, and Water. Southern California remained thinly populated through the 1890's, but early in the 20th century the region's warm winters and moderate summers began to attract a great surge of population growth. The climate and varied landscape led the infant motion picture industry to "discover" California in 1907, and the movies in turn advertised Southern California. Within a few years the great majority of all motion pictures were being made in Hollywood, where the first studio was established in 1911.

Another industry that played a vital part in California's growth was oil. The first discoveries were made in Ventura County in the 1860's. By 1979 California had accounted for more than 11 percent of the nation's total oil output. The oil refining industry demanded enormous quantities of water; growing cities needed even more; and California's burgeoning agriculture depended on irrigation because of the long dry summers. San Francisco tapped Hetch Hetchy, a beautiful valley in Yosemite National Park, but the damming and flooding of Hetch Hetchy were delayed for many years by the Sierra Club. Long aqueducts brought water to Los Angeles —first from the Owens Valley in 1913, and then from the Colorado River, where Hoover Dam was finished in 1936. Irrigation water from the great Central Valley Project, begun in the 1930's and built by the Federal Bureau of Reclamation, could be sold only for units of land no larger than 160 acres. This limitation led the state government to undertake a vast project of its own to provide water for larger farms and for other uses. In 1960 the voters approved the largest bond issue in the history of an American state, for the Feather River Project to bring water from the northern Sierra to the arid western San Joaquin Valley and to Southern California.

California was particularly vulnerable to the depression of the 1930's. Its agriculture had specialized in luxury foods, such as oranges. Hundreds of thousands of elderly people had retired to Southern California, and had now lost their savings in bank failures. By 1934 nearly one-fifth of the people of California were on relief; more than one-fourth of the employable could find no jobs. Various governors' attempts at a New Deal for California were badly frustrated. The huge wartime expenditures of the federal government in California —largely for the building of ships and aircraft—not only brought the state out of the depression but launched it into a period of unprecedented growth.

In the 1960's, California passed New York to become the most populous state. California's annual production and income in 1965 were surpassed only by the United States, the Soviet Union, West Germany, Britain, and France. But in the later 1960's deep cutbacks in federal spending in the aircraft, aerospace, and electronics industries brought sudden unemployment to thousands of scientists, engineers, and technicians, and from 1969 to 1971 California shared in a nationwide economic recession, complicated by inflation. The unemployment in California in 1979 was 6.2 percent, almost the same rate as 6.3 nationwide unemployment.

In the field of race relations, the Japanese-Americans rebounded from their wartime oppression to achieve social advancement, but Afro-Americans, Mexican-Americans (Chicanos), and Indians remained in relative poverty. The liberal efforts of Governor Brown and the Democratic legislature to break down the residential segregation practices of the real estate industry produced a severe white backlash. Afro-American resentment contributed to the terrible riot in the black ghetto of Watts in Los Angeles in August 1965. The Mexican-Americans became by far the largest ethnic minority in California. In 1980, the people of Spanish origin (most of them Mexican-Americans) numbered 4.5 million out of the state's population of 24 million, or about 19 percent. Most of them were concentrated in the eastern part of Los Angeles and other urban barrios. Others engaged in migrant agricultural labor and lived in rural slums. Hope for improvement arose after César Chavez (himself from a family of migrant workers) established the first successful agricultural union, the National Farm Workers Association, in 1962 (now United Farm Workers of America). Farm workers gained the right to collective bargaining in 1975 when the Agricultural Labor Relations Act was adopted.

A period of mass disruptions on college and university campuses began with the "free speech movement" at Berkeley in 1964 and increased with American involvement in the war in Vietnam. Public resentment against student rebels and increased taxes produced a strong conservative reaction. Ronald Reagan swept into office as governor in 1966 as the leader of this revival of conservatism—on a pledge to "cut, squeeze, and trim" the costs of government, including the costs of public higher education. Reagan adopted the slogan "the Creative Society," stressing his belief that private enterprise with the greatest possible freedom from government control was the most important creative force in America. Richard M. Nixon became the first native son of California to be elected president of the United States.

Reagan was succeeded in 1975 by the Democrat Edmund G. Brown, Jr., son of the former governor. The shift in executive leadership from conservative to liberal coincided with a shift to a new set of general values: Californians were coming to feel that growth should be measured in qualitative rather than quantitative terms. Dissatisfied with the increased government spending, California's taxpayers attracted nationwide attention in 1978 by voting for the so-called Proposition 13, a constitutional amendment that reduced the local property tax by 57 percent.

CALIFORNIA ALIEN LAND LAW. To check the increasing competition of Japanese immigrant farmers, the California legislature passed the Alien Land Law of 1913, amended and extended in 1920, 1923, and 1927. These laws permitted aliens eligible for American citizenship to acquire, enjoy, and transfer real property in the state to the same extent as citizens. On the other hand, individual aliens who were not eligible for citizenship and corporations in which a majority of members were such aliens, or in which a majority of the capital stock was owned by them, were permitted to hold real property only as stipulated in existing treaties. The law was repealed in 1955 as violating the Fourteenth Amendment.

CALIFORNIA BANK NOTES. In the 1820's Californians depended on Boston ships for all goods of foreign manufacture and generally paid for them with hides, commonly known as California bank notes, and averaging $1.50 to $2.00 in value.

CALIFORNIA BATTALION. On July 5, 1846, at Sonoma, Capt. John C. Frémont absorbed most of the Americans who had begun the Bear Flag Revolt. The 234 men were at Monterey on July 23, enlisted by Commodore Robert F. Stockton as the Navy Battalion of Mounted Riflemen. The California Battalion served through the rest of the American campaign against the Spanish Californians. It was mustered out of service, unpaid, Apr. 1–19, 1847. The question of merging it with the regular U.S. forces under Gen. Stephen W. Kearny was an important part of the Kearny-Frémont controversy, which led to Frémont's later arrest and court-martial.

CALIFORNIA TRAIL. Various through trails to California, the earliest ones being up the peninsula (1769) and northwest from Sonora (1774). From Santa Fe the Old Spanish Trail followed the Chama River, crossed Colorado into Utah, and later extended southwest to Los Angeles. Early traders and trappers also went west through Zuni, then southwest by Salt River and west by the Gila, or (later) from Zuni west to the Mohave country. Still other trails followed the Rio Grande south, then struck west to the headwaters of the Gila. In the 1840's gold-seekers converged in the Salt Lake Valley via the Platte River, Pueblo–Fort Bridger, and Frémont trails, then continued west into northern California.

CALIFORNIA, UNIVERSITY OF. A state university, it was chartered in 1868, and instruction began in 1869 in Oakland; in 1873 it moved to the present site of the Berkeley campus. Other campuses are at Davis (1905), Irvine (1965); Los Angeles (1919); Riverside (1907); San Diego (1912); San Francisco (1873); Santa Barabara (established 1891, became part of university 1944); and Santa Cruz (1965). The university's system of campuses spread throughout the state became a model for other state university systems.

CALIFORNIA V. CENTRAL PACIFIC RAILROAD COMPANY (1888). The Supreme Court held that, under the commerce and other clauses, Congress has power to construct interstate means of transportation directly or by charter through corporations, and that California could not tax the franchise thus granted.

CALOMEL (mercurous chloride). Used throughout the 19th century as a medication, especially for malarial fevers. Although known in colonial days, calomel was first widely used after its administration as a purgative by Benjamin Rush in the Philadelphia yellow fever epidemic of 1793. John Esten Cooke extended the theory to practically all diseases, through his lectures and writings at Transylvania University (1827–37). A milder dosage known as Cooke's pills was popular for many years. While W. A. Hammond was surgeon general (1862–64), calomel and tarter emetic were banned, but later restored. Calomel is still being used as a cathartic, diuretic, and antiseptic.

CALUMET. *See* **Pipe, Indian.**

CALUMET AND HECLA MINES. Copper mines in the Keweenaw Peninsula of Lake Superior in northwest Michigan, discovered by Edwin J. Hulbert in 1859. Hulbert uncovered the conglomerate lode in 1864. The Calumet and Hecla mines opened under Hulbert's management, but in 1866 Alexander Agassiz was sent from Boston to superintend the initial development. In spite of difficulties the two mines paid dividends in 1869 and 1870, and in 1871 were consolidated into the Calumet and Hecla Mining Company. Other mining companies were opened in the vicinity, but by 1923 most had consolidated with the Calumet and Hecla Company.

CALVINISM. In its broadest sense, the entire body of conceptions arising from the teachings of John Calvin. Its fundamental principle is the conception of God as absolutely sovereign. The statement of Calvinism most influential in America was the Westminster Confession (1647), accepted by New England Congregationalists and embodied in their Cambridge Platform (1648). American Presbyterians were sternly Calvinistic. The Synod of Philadelphia, oldest general Presbyterian body in America, passed the Adopting Act in 1729 requiring all ministers and licentiates to subscribe to the

Westminster Confession. Other Calvinistic bodies in America are the Dutch and German reformed churches.

CALVO DOCTRINE. Enunciated in 1885 by Carlos Calvo, Argentinian diplomat and jurist; held that foreigners should be denied the right to appeal to their own governments for enforcement of contracts. Latin American governments often will include a Calvo clause in a contract with a foreigner. (*See also* Drago Doctrine.)

CAMBODIA, BOMBING OF. As part of the American involvement in the Vietnam War, bombing operations in Cambodia began on Mar. 18, 1969. The operations were initially conducted by B-52's to reduce a threat to U.S. ground forces being withdrawn as part of President Richard M. Nixon's program to end U.S. ground involvement. The North Vietnamese had established stockpiles of arms and munitions in Cambodian sanctuaries, from which they launched attacks across the border into South Vietnam. The air strikes, in conjunction with other factors—such as the reduction of the overall vulnerability of American forces as they relinquished the major combat roles to South Vietnamese forces—cut the number of American ground casualties in half. After the withdrawal of U.S. ground troops from Cambodia on June 30, 1970, tactical air and B-52 strikes continued at the request of the Cambodian government until Aug. 15, 1973, when they were terminated as a result of congressional action.

CAMBRIDGE (Mass.). Originally intended as the seat of government of the Massachusetts Bay Colony, the town was abandoned by Gov. John Winthrop and others in favor of Boston, leaving Deputy Gov. Thomas Dudley and Simon Bradstreet to found New Towne, as Cambridge was first called in 1630. For a time Rev. Thomas Hooker's company settled there (1632–36). Their places were taken by the company of Rev. Thomas Shepard, the first permanent minister of the town. The name was changed to Cambridge in 1638, two years after the founding of Harvard College. In 1639 Stephen Day set up the first printing press in North America at Cambridge. Since then the city has been a major cultural and literary center. The Massachusetts Institute of Technology, the Smithsonian Astrophysical Observatory, and Harvard University have made scientific and industrial research a major activity of the city. The 1980 population was 95,322.

CAMBRIDGE AGREEMENT (Aug. 26, 1629). A decision made and signed by Puritan members of the Massachusetts Bay Company that if the charter and company could be legally transferred to New England, they would migrate there with their families. By accepting the agreement, the company shifted its emphasis from commerce to religion.

CAMBRIDGE PLATFORM (August 1648). A resolution drawn up by a synod of ministers from Massachusetts and Connecticut by request of the Massachusetts General Court, who desired a formal statement of polity and a confession of faith because of the current Presbyterian ascendancy in England and the activities of local Presbyterians. The platform, written by Richard Mather, endorsed the Westminster Confession and for ecclesiastical organization upheld the existing congregational practice.

CAMDEN (N.J.). An industrial city with a population of 84,910, in 1980. Located on the Delaware River, directly across from Philadelphia, Camden was first settled in 1681 and was originally known as Cooper's Ferry because a man named Cooper provided ferry service at that point. Patriots renamed the city in 1773 for the Earl of Camden, an English nobleman who opposed the British government's repressive activities in America. Camden has several important industries. One of the largest soup kitchens in the country produces soups which are canned in one of the city's factories; other important products include radio and electronic equipment, chemicals, and leather goods.

CAMDEN, BATTLE OF (Aug. 16, 1780). Revolutionary War battle fought by Gen. Horatio Gates and his army of 3,500 regulars and militia against Lord Cornwallis and his 2,000 veterans. Exhausted from marching from Hillsboro, N.C., the militia fled at the first attack, near Camden, S.C. The regulars were almost annihilated. Gates returned to Hillsboro and vainly attempted to rally his men and recruit more militia. He was replaced by Nathanael Greene.

CAMDEN-YORKE OPINION. A written professional opinion given in 1769 by Lord Camden, lord chancellor of Great Britain, and Charles Yorke. It related to the rights of private persons who had taken conveyances of lands from native tribes of India, and supported such titles, grants from the king not being necessary. The opinion was seized on by certain western land companies in America as applicable to purchases they might make from aborigines as proprietors of the soil. When the matter came to judicial test after the Revolution, the contrary view prevailed: titles to lands acquired from the American Indian tribes were void when the state had not given consent; the real title was held to be in the state as sovereign.

CAMELS IN THE WEST. The Mexican War added to the United States 529,189 square miles. To establish fast express routes, Congress in 1855 appropriated $30,000 to purchase camels in Egypt and Asia. Seventy-six camels were brought to Texas (1856). Twenty-eight were taken to California (1857) for mail and express routes through the desert, but after a few trips their use was discontinued.

CAMINO DEL DIABLO (Devil's Highway). An old, difficult trail connecting a series of desert water holes northwestward from the Rio de Sonoita to the Gila River near its confluence with the Colorado. Apparently first traced by white men when the Jesuit missionary Eusebio Kino traversed it in February 1699. It was used by travelers to California.

CAMPAIGN RESOURCES. Both human and material resources are necessary to acquire, retain, and nurture political power. These resources can be purchased or volunteered and must be organized, patterned, and channeled in varying combinations. Human resources include personal energies, intelligence, and skills. Staff and volunteer energies must be structured into the manpower demands of modern campaigning. Professional and technical skills are necessary in the organizational, publicity, and financial management.

Material resources include money, goods, and services. Expenditures fall roughly into four general categories: (1) overhead, including maintenance of campaign headquarters and staff; (2) field activity, including meetings, rallies, and travel; (3) publicity; and (4) election-day activities, including expenditures for poll watchers, cars, and drivers. Goods and services paid for by a corporation or by a labor or other special-interest organization are prohibited under federal law and in some states. When "in-kind" contributions of goods and services are permitted, the law may require that they be disclosed and a value put upon them in the same manner as money contributions.

CAMPAIGN SONGS. Partisan ditties used in American political canvasses and especially in presidential contests. In the 19th century the words of these songs were commonly set to established melodies widely popular at the time. Perhaps the best known of them was "Tippecanoe and Tyler Too," in which words by Alexander C. Ross were adapted to the folk tune "Little Pigs." This song spread rapidly over the country, furnishing a party slogan to the Whigs of 1840. In 1872 an attempt was made to revive the air for "Greeley Is the Real True Blue." The words, sometimes with music, were distributed in paper-covered songbooks or songsters. Among these were the *Log Cabin Song Book* (1840) and *Hutchinson's Republican Songster for the Campaign of 1860.*

In the 20th century, with changes in campaigning, particularly the use of radio and then television, the campaign song declined in popularity. In his 1932 presidential campaign Franklin D. Roosevelt adopted the nonpolitical melody "Happy Days Are Here Again." By the 1960's campaign songs no longer presented issues, but instead presented an emotional feeling attached to a campaign, using adaptations of popular tunes.

CAMPAIGNS, POLITICAL. Organized efforts to win elections in order to gain public office or to gain power, influence, or prestige. Campaigns are drives for votes made by political parties and candidates and their auxiliary organizations, culminating in elections won by a majority or plurality, as determined by constitutional or legal provisions. Campaigns are held for nomination or election: nomination campaigns include primary and runoff primary elections, conventions, and caucuses; the final phase is the campaign for general or special election. If victory seems impossible, the campaign may attempt to affect the outcome (for example, splinter a potential majority in the electoral college); it may attempt to educate the electorate over a long period of time, as minor and single-issue parties do; it may attempt to crystallize an issue or series of issues, as factional contests do in primaries; or it may attempt to project an individual for future consideration for public office or for purposes of ego satisfaction.

In addition, campaigns are waged for or against initiatives, referenda, ballot measures, bond issues, and constitutional amendments in states and localities. Petition campaigns are undertaken to obtain enough voter signatures for the candidate or party to qualify on the ballot; petition drives may also be conducted when recall elections are permitted.

Campaigns are designed to reach a growing electorate, swelled both by natural increases and by the extension of the right of suffrage. In 1980 there were more than 160 million persons eligible to register and vote, and about 52 percent of them voted in the presidential election.

One vital campaign function is to convey information, knowledge, and opinions to potential voters, ideally to stimulate rational voting decisions. In actuality, campaigns are appeals to reason mixed with emotion. Competing philosophies require publicity, and in the American experience, supporters of differing views and candidates have been quick to take to the printed word, and not only at election times. The system of newspaper support of, or support by, one political faction or the other developed early. The printed word led to pictures, buttons, banners, and novelty items. Modern developments include rallies, radio and television presentations, public opinion polling, jet and helicopter travel, and use of computers for registration and voting analyses and for fund, mail, and telephone drives.

CAMPAIGNS, PRESIDENTIAL. Presidential campaigns have taken place in the United States every fourth year, beginning in 1788. They include both candidate nomination and the subsequent campaign for election. Since the 1830's, nomination has centered on national party conventions to choose individuals to run for president and vice-president and to adopt the party's platform. Delegate selection was for a long time wholly extralegal and determined by local party traditions. Early in the 20th century some states set up presidential primaries to choose delegates and record voter preferences. In the late 1960's further reform began to broaden the ability of party members to participate in delegate selection and reduce the influence of party organizations.

An incumbent president who desires renomination usually obtains it without a convention contest. If he does not want it or has already served two terms, the convention makes the final choice, sometimes only after a lengthy and bitter struggle. Since the late 1950's, rapid modes of transportation and ease of communication have often enabled one candidate to build up a strong lead prior to the convention and win on the first ballot. Thus, the preconvention campaign has become the decisive part of the nominating process. Once chosen, the presidential candidate selects a new national party chairman and sets up his campaign organization. In the 19th century the nominee himself did little stumping, but the 20th century saw increased candidate involvement. From the 1920's on, radio figured prominently in getting the candidates' messages disseminated; since 1952, television has been the key medium. Public relations experts and opinion pollsters have also come to occupy crucial roles.

Campaigns of 1788 and 1792. These first two campaigns had no formal nominations, only one presidential candidate, and little opposition to the second choice. The Constitution ratified, the Continental Congress delayed three months before fixing the first Wednesday in January 1789 for choosing electors, the first Wednesday in February for their voting, and the first Wednesday in March for starting the new government. Thirteen states could cast ninety-one votes; but two states had not ratified, and New York failed to elect or appoint electors; four electors failed to vote. George Washington received sixty-nine votes, one of the two votes of every elector. John Adams received thirty-four of the second votes, and ten others thirty-five.

In 1792 fifteen states could cast 132 electoral votes. Alexander Hamilton's financial measures and the consolidation of national power (*see* Federalist Party) roused an opposition (Jeffersonian Antifederalists), which centered its efforts on the defeat of Adams by the Antifederalist George Clinton, since to defeat Washington was seen to be futile. Washington's vote was again unanimous, and Adams defeated Clinton seventy-seven to fifty.

Campaign of 1796. For the first time, the national election was contested by political parties. The Federalists agreed upon John Adams and Thomas Pinckney. The Democratic-Republicans (*see* Republicans, Jeffersonian) chose Thomas Jefferson and Aaron Burr. Electors were chosen in sixteen states. Adams secured seventy-one electoral votes, Jefferson sixty-eight, Pinckney fifty-nine, Burr thirty, and the remaining forty-eight were divided among nine others.

Campaigns of 1800 and 1804. The election of 1800 marks a turning point in American political history. Burr had already established the nucleus of a political machine that was later to develop into Tammany Hall. He swept New York City with an outstanding legislative ticket, gained control of the state assembly, and secured the electoral votes of New York for the Democratic-Republicans (*see* Republicans, Jeffersonian). He had already secured a pledge from the Democratic-Republican members of Congress to support him equally with Jefferson. Hence the tie vote (seventy-three each) that gave him a dubious chance for the presidency. The Federalist candidates were John Adams, sixty-five votes, and Charles Cotesworth Pinckney, sixty-four votes.

Publicly disclaiming any intent to secure the presidency, Burr was, nevertheless, put forward by the Federalists in order to defeat Jefferson and bring about another election (*see* Jefferson-Burr Election Dispute). A slight majority in the House of Representatives enabled them to rally six states to Burr and divide the vote of two others, thus neutralizing the vote of the eight states that supported Jefferson. After thirty-five fruitless ballotings a sufficient number of Federalists cast blank ballots to give Jefferson ten states and the presidency.

This narrow escape from frustrating the popular will led to the Twelfth Amendment to the Constitution, separating the balloting for president and vice-president, in time for the 1804 election. Jefferson covertly helped eliminate Burr in New York, and the party caucus brought George Clinton forward as candidate for the vice-presidency. The Federalists selected Pinckney as their presidential candidate and Rufus King for the vice-presidency. Jefferson was triumphantly reelected in 1804 with Clinton as vice-president.

Campaigns of 1808 and 1812. Candidates for the Democratic-Republican nomination in 1808 were James Madison, the choice of Thomas Jefferson; James Monroe; and George Clinton. At the party caucus Madison received eighty-three votes; his rivals, three each.

The Federalist opposition was led by Charles Pinckney and Rufus King, but the chief obstacle to the Madison slate came from his own party. The malcontents finally voted the party ticket, and in the electoral college Madison obtained 122 out of 176 votes. Clinton ran far behind on the presidential ticket, but became vice-president by a wide margin.

In 1812 Madison secured his renomination by a tacit yielding to the demands of Henry Clay and the war hawks. Clinton having died in office, the vice-presidential nomination went to Elbridge Gerry of Massachusetts. Opposition to the party slate was led by DeWitt Clinton of New York, who finally accepted nomination from the prowar Republicans, with the endorsement of the Federalists. Jared Ingersoll of Pennsylvania was nominated as his running mate. The electoral college gave Madison 128 votes, Clinton 89.

Campaigns of 1816 and 1820. There was no campaign by parties in 1816 worth the name, none at all in 1820. President Madison's choice was James Monroe, secretary of state and war. Some Democratic-Republicans favored Gov. Daniel D. Tompkins of New York. Younger Republicans, interested in nationalist measures following the War of 1812, preferred William H. Crawford, secretary of the treasury and citizen of Georgia. They gave him fifty-four votes in the congressional caucus to sixty-five for Monroe. In the electoral college Monroe overwhelmed Rufus King, signer of the Constitution and statesman of note, but a Federalist whose party now was thoroughly discredited by the Hartford Convention. Monroe was given 183 votes to 34 for King.

Campaign of 1824. The next campaign marked the beginning of the transition from federalism to democracy with resulting voter realignment under new party emblems. In general, the politicians supported William H. Crawford; John Quincy Adams represented business; John C. Calhoun, the South and the rising slavocracy; Henry Clay, the expanding West; and Andrew Jackson, the people everywhere. The first three were cabinet members, Clay was speaker of the House, and Jackson was the country's most popular military figure.

Calhoun withdrew and became candidate for vice-president on both the Adams and Jackson tickets. No candidate received a majority electoral vote. Jackson secured the greatest number, 99; Adams, 84; Crawford, 41; and Clay, 37. Selection was made by the House of Representatives and Adams was chosen.

Campaigns of 1828 and 1832. In 1828 President John Quincy Adams stood for reelection on the National Republican ticket and Andrew Jackson of Tennessee made his second campaign for the presidency, his supporters now being called Democrats. Designated the people's candidate by the action of friends in the legislature of his own state, Jackson won. The campaign was waged throughout the administration of Adams. There was a great increase in the popular vote cast, 647,286 being cast for Jackson and 508,064 for Adams. The electoral vote stood 178 for Jackson to 83 for Adams. Calhoun was again elected vice-president.

Jackson stood for reelection in 1832, although he had spoken in favor of a single term. After December 1831, when Henry Clay returned to the Senate, he, rather than Adams, received the support of most of those who were opposed to Jackson. Clay was formally presented by a national convention in December 1831. A national convention of young men prepared a platform in May 1832. In that month a national convention of Jackson supporters nominated Martin Van Buren of New York for the vice-presidency. In this election the recently gathered Anti-Masonic party supported William Wirt of Maryland. Aside from the personal contest between Jackson and Clay, the main issue was Jackson's attack on the Bank of the United States and particularly his veto of the bill for the recharter of the bank, a bill that had the backing of the supporters of Clay in both houses of Congress. Twenty-four states participated in this election, and all except South Carolina provided a popular vote. The popular vote was Jackson, for the distribution of the vote in twenty-three states gave Jackson 687,502, Clay 530,189, and Wirt 101,051. In the electoral college the vote stood Jackson 219, Clay 49, Wirt 7, with 11 votes representing the vote of South Carolina cast for John Floyd of Virginia.

Campaign of 1836. Made up chiefly of Anti-Masons, National Republicans, and anti-Jackson Democrats, the Whig party, formed in 1834, naturally lacked unity. Because of this, the Whig leaders put forward several sectional candidates in the 1836 presidential campaign: Judge Hugh L. White by Tennessee and Alabama, Judge John McLean by Ohio (withdrew the following August), Sen. Daniel Webster by Massachusetts, and Gen. William H. Harrison, formally nominated by both Anti-Masonic and Whig state conventions in Pennsylvania.

At the Democratic National Convention in Baltimore, May 21–22, 1835, Martin Van Buren, President Jackson's choice, was unanimously nominated. No platform was adopted, but a committee drew up an address presenting Van Buren as one who would, if elected, continue "that wise course of national policy pursued by Gen. Jackson." This may be regarded as the first platform ever issued by the Democratic party.

Van Buren won the presidency with 170 electoral votes and a popular vote of 765,483 to 739,795 for his opponents. White received 26 electoral votes, Webster 14, and Harrison 73, while South Carolina bestowed its 11 votes on W. P. Mangum. No candidate for the vice-presidency received a majority of the electoral vote, so on Feb. 8, 1837, the Senate chose the Democratic candidate, Richard M. Johnson, over his leading rival, Francis Granger.

Campaign of 1840. Distinctive as the first national victory of the Whig party, the campaign of 1840 was unique for its popular and emotional appeal. The Whig convention, assembled at Harrisburg, Pa., Dec. 2, 1839, nominated Gen. William Henry Harrison of Indiana for president and John Tyler of Virginia for vice-president. The only bond uniting the various groups under the Whig banner was a determination to defeat the Democrats. The Democratic convention held at Baltimore, May 5, 1840, was united on Martin Van Buren. A platform on strict construction lines was adopted.

Harrison was adroitly celebrated as the "Hard Cider and Log Cabin" candidate, a phrase which the Democrats had used in contempt. Oratory, invective against Van Buren the aristocrat, songs and slogans ("Tippecanoe and Tyler Too") swamped the country. Harrison polled an electoral vote of 234, a popular vote of 1,274,624; Van Buren received 60 electoral votes and 1,127,781 popular votes. A minor feature was the appearance of an abolition (the Liberty) party, whose candidate, James G. Birney, received 7,069 votes.

Campaign of 1844. No outstanding Democratic candidate could muster the necessary two-thirds vote in the 1844 convention, so James K. Polk of Tennessee, the first "dark horse," was nominated, with George M. Dallas of Pennsylvania as running mate, on a platform demanding "the re-annexation of Texas and the re-occupation of Oregon" and in favor of tariff reform. The Whigs nominated Henry Clay of Kentucky and Theodore Frelinghuysen of New Jersey, on a platform favoring protective tariff and a national bank but quibbling on the Texas annexation issue, which alienated some of the Whigs. The Liberty party unanimously selected James G. Birney as its candidate. Polk was elected, with 170 electoral votes to 105 for Clay. The popular vote was Polk, 1,338,464; Clay, 1,300,097; Birney, 62,300.

Campaign of 1848. The Whig nominee, Zachary Taylor, who sidestepped the burning issue of slavery extension, won on his military reputation with Millard Fillmore as his vice-president. His Democratic opponent, Gen. Lewis Cass of Michigan, straddled the slavery extension question by advocating state sovereignty. The new Free Soil party, specifically opposed to extension and headed by Martin Van Buren, split the Democratic vote in New York and thus contributed to Taylor's triumph. (Gerrit Smith, the National Liberty party candidate and staunch abolitionist, advised those who would not vote for an abolitionist to vote for Van Buren, rather than Cass.) Taylor carried half the states, eight in the South and seven in the North. The popular vote was Taylor, 1,360,967; Cass, 1,222,342; Van Buren, 291,263; Smith, 2,733. The electoral vote was Taylor, 163; Cass, 127.

Campaign of 1852. The Whig party in 1852 was apathetic and demoralized by the slavery issue. Democratic victory seemed almost certain. After many ballots, the leading Democrats were eliminated and a dark horse, Franklin Pierce of New Hampshire, was nominated with William R. King of Alabama. The Whigs nominated the military hero Gen. Winfield Scott; the Free-Soilers nominated the antislavery leader John P. Hale of New Hampshire. Both major parties endorsed the Compromise of 1850, so there were no issues and little contest. Pierce carried all states save Massachusetts, Vermont, Kentucky, and Tennessee. The popular vote was Pierce, 1,601,117; Scott, 1,385,453; Hale, 155,825. The electoral vote was Pierce, 254; Scott, 42.

Campaign of 1856. The Republican party in its first presidential campaign nominated John C. Frémont of California. Its platform opposed slavery expansion and condemned slavery and Mormonism. The American, or Know-Nothing, party nominated Millard Fillmore, who had succeeded to the presidency following the death of Zachary Taylor. The Democrats nominated James Buchanan, with John C. Breckinridge as his running mate. Their conservative platform stressed states' rights, opposed sectionalism, and favored giving popular sovereignty to the territories. The electoral vote was Buchanan, 174; Frémont, 114; Fillmore, 8. The popular vote was Buchanan, 1,832,955; Frémont, 1,339,932; Fillmore, 871,731.

Campaign of 1860. The Democratic National Convention met amid great excitement and bitterness over the slavery issue, at Charleston, S.C., Apr. 23, 1860. The delegates from the eight states of the far South (Southern Democrats) demanded the platform provide that Congress should guarantee slave property in the territories. This was refused, and the convention adjourned to Baltimore on June 18. The convention nominated Stephen A. Douglas of Illinois for president, and later the national committee nominated Herschel V. Johnson of Georgia for vice-president. The platform pledged the party to stand by the Dred Scott decision or any future decision that dealt with the rights of property. Southern Democrat delegates met separately at Baltimore on June 28, and nominated John C. Breckinridge of Kentucky for president and Joseph Lane of Oregon for vice-president. The platform reaffirmed the extreme southern view of slavery. Meanwhile, the Whig and American (Know-Nothing) parties had met at Baltimore on May 9 and adopted the name of the Constitutional Union party, also the platform of "the Constitution of the country, the Union of the States and the enforcement of the laws." They nominated John Bell of Tennessee for president and Edward Everett of Massachusetts for vice-president and attempted to ignore the slavery and other sectional issues, with a plea for the preservation of the Union.

The Republican National Convention had met in Chicago on May 16, united on the platform issues of nonextension of slavery and of a homestead law and by advocacy of a protective tariff. The convention nominated Abraham Lincoln of Illinois with Hannibal Hamlin for vice-president.

The split in the Democratic party made possible the election of Lincoln, with 180 electoral votes against 72 for Breckinridge and 39 for Bell. Douglas received but 12. The popular vote totaled 1,865,593 for Lincoln, 1,382,713 for Douglas, 848,356 for Breckinridge, and 592,906 for Bell.

Campaign of 1864. A national convention was called by "the executive committee created by the national convention held in Chicago on the sixteenth day of May 1860." The use of the name Republican was carefully avoided. The convention met in Baltimore on June 7, 1864, and named itself the National Union Convention, to appeal to Union sentiment and do away as far as possible with partisan influence. The platform was a statement of "unconditional Union" principles and pledged the convention to put down rebellion by force of arms. Abraham Lincoln was nominated for a second term by the vote of every delegate except those from Missouri, who had been instructed to vote for Gen. Ulysses S. Grant. The nomination then was made unanimous. Andrew Johnson was nominated for vice-president.

The Democratic party met on Aug. 29, at Chicago. Its platform declared the war a failure and advocated the restoration of the Union by peaceable means. The convention nominated Gen. George B. McClellan for president and George H. Pendleton for vice-president. McClellan accepted but virtually repudiated the platform, for he was thoroughly loyal to the cause of the Union.

The victories of the Union army rallied the people to the support of Lincoln and Johnson and the Union cause. For the first time in U.S. history certain states, those of the South, deliberately declined to choose electors for the choice of president. Lincoln carried every state that took part in the election but New Jersey, Delaware, and Kentucky, with 212 electoral votes. McClellan received 21. Lincoln was given a popular majority of only 403,151 in a total of 4,010,725.

Campaigns of 1868 and 1872. Horatio Seymour of New York and Frank Blair of Missouri, the Democratic nominees, ran on a platform calling for a restoration of the rights of the southern states and payment of the war bonds in greenbacks. The Republicans nominated the war hero, Ulysses S. Grant, and Schuyler Colfax of Indiana. Their platform acclaimed the success of Reconstruction and denounced as repudiation the payment of the bonds in greenbacks.

Personal attacks on the candidates and Republican "waving the bloody shirt" marked the campaign. An effort to replace the Democratic nominees in October failed but foreshadowed defeat. Grant received 214 electoral votes to Seymour's 80, and nearly 53 percent of the popular vote, receiving 3,013,421 votes to 2,706,829 for Seymour.

Dissatisfaction with Reconstruction policy and a desire for reform led to a Liberal Republican party, which nominated Horace Greeley, with B. Gratz Brown of Missouri, to oppose Grant's reelection in 1872. (Grant's running mate was Henry Wilson of Massachusetts.) Its platform demanded civil-service reform, universal amnesty, and specie payment. The tariff issue was straddled to please Greeley, a protectionist. The Democrats accepted the Liberal Republican platform and nominees. The Greeley campaign lacked enthusiasm, and he was mercilessly lampooned. Grant received 286 electoral votes to Greeley's 66 and over 55 percent of the popular vote, receiving 3,596,745 votes to 2,843,446 for Greeley.

Campaign of 1876. Resulted in a disputed presidential election. At the Republican national convention James G. Blaine of Maine led the field for six ballots, but his involvement in a scandal caused a stampede to Rutherford B. Hayes of Ohio, who was nominated on the seventh ballot. William A. Wheeler of New York was named his running mate. The platform endorsed the Resumption Act and eulogized the Republican party for its work during the Civil War and Reconstruction.

The Democrats chose Gov. Samuel J. Tilden of New York, with Thomas A. Hendricks of Indiana as his running mate. The platform denounced the scandals of the Grant administration and declared reform to be the main issue.

The electoral college gave Tilden 184 unquestioned votes, Hayes 165. The 4 votes of Florida, the 8 votes of Louisiana, the 7 votes of South Carolina, and 1 vote of Oregon were claimed by both parties. After a protracted, bitter dispute, Congress created an electoral commission of five senators, five representatives, and five judges of the Supreme Court to help decide the result. (*See* Electoral Commission.)

In case the two houses of Congress voting separately refused to accept any return, the dispute was to be referred to the commission, whose decision was to be final unless it was rejected by both houses. The two houses, voting separately on strict party lines, did disagree. Decision, therefore, rested with the commission, which by a vote of eight to seven refused to go against the election results as certified by the state authorities and declared in favor of the Republican contenders. In each case the Senate accepted this decision, the House rejected it. All the disputed votes were counted for Hayes and Wheeler and they were declared elected.

Campaign of 1880. Republicans overcame a split between groups headed by James G. Blaine and Roscoe Conkling by naming James A. Garfield, a member of neither faction, over former President Ulysses S. Grant, supported by the Conkling wing for a third term. The Conkling faction was appeased by the nomination of Chester A. Arthur for the vice-presidency. The Democrats nominated Winfield Scott Hancock, a nonpolitical Civil War general; but their party had no positive program, was discredited by its factious opposition to the Hayes administration, and was defeated by a close vote. The popular vote was Garfield, 4,453,295; Hancock, 4,414,082. The electoral vote was Garfield, 214; Hancock, 155.

Campaign of 1884. Fought primarily between James G. Blaine, Republican, and Grover Cleveland, Democrat, the campaign was one of the most vituperative in American history. Blaine was believed to be allied with the spoils element in Republican politics; he had an unhappy record for baiting the South; he favored certain big business interests; and his railroad transactions had raised a suspicion that he had used his position as speaker of the House for personal profit. To divert attention from these attacks certain Republicans published evidence that Cleveland was the father of an illegitimate son. There were virtually no serious issues between the two parties. The two parties approached election day running neck and neck. Democratic victory was finally decided by the vote of New York State. Cleveland and his running mate, Thomas A. Hendricks, obtained a popular vote of 4,879,507 against Blaine's 4,850,293, and an electoral vote of 219 against Blaine's 182. Antimonopoly party candidate Benjamin F. Butler's popular vote was just over 175,000, and that of John P. St. John, Prohibition candidate, was just over 150,000.

Campaign of 1888. The tariff was the chief issue of this campaign, which resulted in the election of a candidate by a majority of the electoral college but not of the popular vote. The Republicans had scant hope of victory, for Cleveland had proved an admirable president, when his annual message of 1887, devoted entirely to arguments for tariff reform, gave them new heart. Benjamin Harrison, who represented extreme high-tariff demands, was nominated by the Republicans at Chicago on June 25. Levi P. Morton was named for vice-president. Harrison waged an aggressive campaign. His speechmaking abilities made a deep impression on the country. Cleveland, renominated by the Democrats at St. Louis early in June, felt that his presidential office made it improper for him to do active campaigning; his running mate, former Sen. Allen G. Thurman of Ohio, was too old and infirm to be anything but a liability to the party; and campaign funds were slender. Worst of all for the Democrats, their national chairman, Sen. Calvin S. Brice of Ohio, held high-tariff convictions, was allied with big business, and refused to put his heart into the battle. Cleveland received 5,537,857 popular votes, Harrison 5,447,129; but Cleveland had only 168 electors against Harrison's 233. Clinton B. Fisk of New Jersey, Prohibition candidate, polled 249,506 votes; Alson J. Streeter of Illinois, Union Labor nominee, 146,935.

Campaign of 1892. Grover Cleveland was reelected over Benjamin Harrison in 1892 by a surprising majority. Cleveland had been named on the first ballot at the Democratic convention in Chicago; Adlai E. Stevenson was selected for the vice-presidency. Harrison, who had estranged the professional politicians of his party; quarreled with its most popular figure, James G. Blaine; and impressed the country as cold and unlikable, was reluctantly accepted by the Republicans at Minneapolis on June 10. It was impossible to repudiate his administration. However, the McKinley Tariff of 1890 had excited widespread discontent, the Sherman Silver Purchase Act of the same year had angered the conservative East, and heavy federal expenditures had caused general uneasiness. Cleveland's firm stand on behalf of the gold standard and low tariffs and his known strength of character drew large numbers of independent voters. Cleveland, with a popular vote of 5,555,426, had 277 electors; Harrison, with a popular vote of 5,182,690, had 145; while the Populist candidate, James B. Weaver, won 22 electoral votes.

Campaign of 1896. This campaign and election ushered in a period of Republican domination which lasted until 1911. William McKinley of Ohio was named by the Republicans at

St. Louis, with Garret A. Hobart as vice-presidential candidate. The traditional platform was adopted except for a declaration for the gold standard until bimetallism could be secured by international agreement. A bloc of western delegates bolted and organized the Silver Republican party.

There was no dominant candidate for the Democratic nomination. The important contest was over the platform, favoring free silver at the sixteen-to-one ratio, criticizing injunctions in labor disputes, and denouncing the overthrow of the federal income tax. In its support William Jennings Bryan delivered his "Cross of Gold" oration. That speech gave impetus to Bryan's candidacy for the presidential nomination. The Populists, Silver Republicans, and National Silver party members joined the Democrats in his support. The administration Democrats placed a National Democratic ticket in the field to hold conservative Democratic votes away from him, nominating John M. Palmer of Illinois.

The campaign was highly spectacular. The Democrats exploited Bryan's oratory by sending him on speaking tours back and forth across the country. In sharp contrast, the Republican management kept McKinley at his home in Canton, Ohio, where carefully selected delegations made formal calls and listened to "front porch" speeches. More important were the flood of advertising, the funds for building local organizations, and the large group of speakers on the hustings. The popular vote was unusually large, each candidate receiving larger totals than any previous candidate of his party, McKinley's vote being 7,102,246 and Bryan's 6,492,559. The electoral vote was 271 and 176, respectively.

Campaign of 1900. The presidential candidates and most issues of 1896 were carried over to the 1900 campaign. With the trend of prices upward, the pressure for inflation had declined, and expansion of American control over new territories had created the issue of imperialism.

At the Republican convention in Philadelphia, President McKinley accepted Theodore Roosevelt as the vice-presidential candidate. The party's position on the new territories was American retention with a large measure of self-government.

When the Democrats met at Kansas City, they once again selected William Jennings Bryan. The 1896 platform was reindorsed, an antitrust plank added, and imperialism designated the "paramount issue." The popular vote was McKinley, 7,218,491; Bryan, 6,356,734. McKinley obtained 292 electoral votes to 155 for Bryan. This election made Roosevelt's elevation to the presidency automatic upon McKinley's death in September 1901.

Campaign of 1904. Theodore Roosevelt, who succeeded to the presidency on the death of William McKinley in 1901, ardently hoped to be nominated and elected "in his own right." The death of Marcus A. Hanna of Ohio, whom big business interests preferred, made possible the president's nomination by acclamation when the Republican convention met in Chicago, June 21. Charles W. Fairbanks of Indiana was chosen for the vice-presidency.

The Democrats, meeting at St. Louis, July 6, pointedly turned their backs upon "Bryanism" by omitting from their platform all reference to the money question (*see* Free Silver) and by nominating Alton B. Parker, a conservative New York judge who pledged to maintain the gold standard, and for vice-president, Henry Gassaway Davis, a wealthy West Virginia octogenarian. Business leaders, more afraid of the Democratic party than of Roosevelt, contributed heavily to the Republican campaign chest. Roosevelt won by a landslide that gave him 336 electoral votes to Parker's 140 and a popular plurality of 2,544,238.

Campaign of 1908. Theodore Roosevelt, although at the height of his popularity, refused to run for a second elective term in 1908, but swung his support to William Howard Taft. James S. Sherman of New York was selected for the vice-presidency.

The Democratic convention was dominated by William Jennings Bryan. Party differences were not significant. Bryan received about 44 percent of the popular vote, 6,412,294 to Taft's 7,675,320. Taft's electoral vote was 321; Bryan's 162.

Campaign of 1912. This campaign marked the culmination of the progressive movement in national politics and resulted in the return of the Democrats after sixteen years of Republican presidents.

The struggle for the Republican nomination became a battle between the progressive and conservative wings. In the beginning it was the progressive Sen. Robert M. LaFollette of Wisconsin against the incumbent, William Howard Taft. But former President Theodore Roosevelt entered the race to rally behind him Republicans who believed Taft had been too friendly with the conservative Old Guard. The conservative-controlled national committee placed Taft delegates on the temporary roll in all contests, and the small majority resulting gave Taft the nomination. Roosevelt was later nominated by the newly organized Progressive (Bull Moose) party, consisting largely of Republican bolters.

The contest for the Democratic nomination was also hard fought with both leading candidates accepted as progressives. Beauchamp ("Champ") Clark of Wisconsin had an actual majority in the convention for a time, but when William Jennings Bryan transferred his support to Woodrow Wilson, a shift began that resulted in the latter's nomination. The choice for vice-president was Thomas R. Marshall. All three party platforms were unusually favorable to progressive policies. Wilson, backed by a united party, won easily. Wilson's popular vote was 6,296,547, Roosevelt's was 4,118,571, and Taft's was 3,486,720. The electoral vote was, respectively, 435, 88, and 8. Eugene V. Debs, Socialist, secured approximately 900,000 votes.

Campaign of 1916. This campaign reunited the Republican party when, after the nomination of Charles Evans Hughes, Theodore Roosevelt, already nominated by the declining Progressive party, announced support of the ticket.

There was no opposition to the renomination of President Wilson and Vice-President Thomas R. Marshall. The Democrats defended the policies of the administration. The Republicans attacked them, promised a stronger foreign policy, and were supported by the more extreme partisans of both alliances in the European war.

Wilson won with an electoral vote of 277, against 254 for Hughes. The popular vote was Wilson, 9,127,695; Hughes, 8,533,507.

Campaign of 1920. The debate on the League of Nations determined the alignment of political forces in 1920. The Republicans met in Chicago, could not agree upon any of the leading preconvention candidates, and nominated Warren G. Harding, senator from Ohio. Calvin Coolidge, governor of Massachusetts, was nominated for the vice-presidency.

The Democrats met in San Francisco. None of the discussed candidates commanded a great following. James M. Cox, governor of Ohio, was nominated with Franklin D. Roosevelt as vice-presidential nominee. The Socialist party nominated Eugene Debs for the fifth time. A Farmer-Labor ticket appeared also.

None of the platforms was unexpected or significant on domestic issues. The Republicans attacked the president and opposed entrance into the League of Nations. The Democratic national committee supported Wilson's appeal for a "solemn referendum" on the covenant of the League. The total vote cast was 26,733,905. The Nineteenth Amendment had been proclaimed in August, and women were entitled to vote. Harding won over 60 percent of the vote cast. Cox received only 127 electoral votes to Harding's 404. The strength of all the third parties totaled only about 5.5 percent.

Campaign of 1924. As in 1920, the candidates in 1924 were new in a presidential canvass. The Republican convention in Cleveland nominated Calvin Coolidge, who had succeeded to the presidency in August 1923 when President Harding died. The vice-presidential nomination was accepted by Charles G. Dawes of Illinois. The platform was marked by extreme conservatism.

The Democrats met in New York for two and a half weeks. There was serious division on American adherence to the League of Nations, on proposed denunciation of the Ku Klux Klan, and on choice of the nominee. Each leading candidate, Alfred E. Smith and William G. McAdoo, was sufficiently powerful to prevent the nomination of the other, and finally the nomination went to John W. Davis of West Virginia. Gov. Charles W. Bryan of Nebraska was nominated for vice-president. The platform called for a popular referendum on the League of Nations.

The Conference for Progressive Political Action brought about widespread support of Sen. Robert M. La Follette in his independent candidacy, endorsed by the Socialist party and the officers of the American Federation of Labor.

The total vote cast exceeded that of 1920 by 2.36 million, Coolidge securing 15,718,211 votes, and Davis 8,385,283. La Follette (5 million) carried Wisconsin (13 electoral votes). Coolidge received 382 electoral votes, Davis, 136.

Campaign of 1928. On Aug. 2, 1927, President Coolidge announced that he did not choose to run in 1928. A popular movement forced the nomination of Secretary of Commerce Herbert Hoover at the Republican National Convention, which met at Kansas City, Mo., in June. The platform contained strong support of a protective tariff and sound business administration. It advocated rigorous enforcement of the Eighteenth Amendment. Charles Curtis of Kansas was nominated for vice-president.

The Democrats met at Houston and on June 28 nominated New York Gov. Alfred E. Smith, the first Catholic to be nominated for the presidency. They then nominated Arkansas Sen. Joseph T. Robinson for vice-president. The platform did not differ strikingly from that of the Republicans. The contest became one between rival personalities. Smith took a stand in favor of a change in the Prohibition amendment, and advocated that the question of Prohibition and its enforcement be left to the individual states.

Hoover won a landslide, with a total of 444 electoral votes over Smith's 87. The popular plurality of Hoover over Smith was 6,375,824 in a total vote of 36,879,414.

Campaigns of 1932 and 1936. At the Republican Convention at Chicago on June 14–16, 1932, President Hoover and Vice-President Curtis were renominated. The platform praised the Hoover record, including his program for combating the depression. A "wet-dry" plank on Prohibition favored a referendum on a repeal amendment.

The Democratic Convention was also held at Chicago, June 27–July 2. Gov. Franklin Delano Roosevelt of New York was nominated; John Nance Garner of Texas was selected as the vice-presidential candidate. The platform pledged economy, a sound currency, old-age and unemployment insurance under state laws, the "restoration of agriculture," and repeal of the Eighteenth Amendment together with immediate legalization of beer.

After a campaign featuring Roosevelt's promise of "a new deal," the popular vote was as follows: Democratic, 22,809,638; Republican, 15,758,901; Socialist, 881,951; Socialist-Labor, 33,276; Communist, 102,785; Prohibition, 81,869; Liberty, 53,425; and Farmer-Labor, 7,309. The electoral vote was 472 for the Democrats and 59 for the Republicans.

In 1936 the Republican Convention was held at Cleveland beginning on June 9. Gov. Alfred M. Landon of Kansas and Frank Knox, a Chicago publisher, were nominated for the presidency and vice-presidency, respectively. The platform strongly denounced the New Deal administration.

The Democratic Convention at Philadelphia on June 25 proved to be a ratification meeting for the New Deal. President Roosevelt and Vice-President Garner were renominated.

The Democrats again won an overwhelming victory. The popular vote was Democratic, 27,752,869; Republican, 16,674,665; Union, 882,479; Socialist, 187,720; Communist, 80,159; Prohibition, 37,847; and Socialist-Labor, 12,777. The Democrats received 523 electoral votes, Republicans 8.

Campaign of 1940. The Republican nomination was won by Wendell L. Willkie at Philadelphia, June 28. As president of a large utilities corporation Willkie had fought the New Deal, but in foreign affairs he was an internationalist, and with Europe at war, this commended him to the liberals. The nomination of a liberal by the Republicans, together with the international crisis, made the nomination of Franklin D. Roosevelt by the Democrats (Chicago, July 16) a practical certainty, even though his running for a third term was unprecedented. Both candidates promised aid to the Allies; both promised to keep the United States out of foreign wars. Roosevelt and Henry A. Wallace, secretary of agriculture, received 27,307,819 popular and 449 electoral votes against 22,321,018 popular and 82 electoral votes for Willkie and Charles L. McNary of Oregon.

Campaign of 1944. Thomas E. Dewey, governor of New York, was nominated by the Republican convention in Chicago on June 26 with little opposition, with John W. Bricker of Ohio as his running mate. President Roosevelt, running for a fourth term, encountered even less opposition at the Democratic convention in Chicago. The real struggle revolved around the vice-presidential candidate. Sen. Harry S. Truman of Missouri was finally nominated. Roosevelt received 25,606,585 popular and 432 electoral votes to Dewey's 22,014,745 popular and 99 electoral votes.

Campaign of 1948. The Republicans, having gained control of Congress in 1946, expected to turn the apparently unpopular Truman administration out of power, and for the first time in the party's history renominated a defeated candidate, Thomas E. Dewey, in Philadelphia on June 21. The Democrats, on the other hand, suffered from severe internal conflicts. Truman's nomination at Philadelphia on July 15 caused no enthusiasm. Radicals left the party and nominated Henry A. Wallace and Sen. Glen Taylor of Idaho as the candidates of the Progressive party. Southerners, offended by the civil rights planks of the platform, seceded and formed the States' Rights Democratic party, with Gov. J. Strom Thurmond of South Carolina and Gov. Fielding L. Wright of Mississippi as their candidates. The election was close—Truman and Alben W. Barkley of Kentucky polled 24,105,812 popular and 304 electoral votes against 21,970,065 popular and 189 electoral votes for Dewey and Gov. Earl Warren of California. Thurmond polled 1,169,063 popular votes and 38 electoral votes. Wallace won 1,157,172 popular votes.

Campaign of 1952. After a long and bitter struggle, the internationalist wing of the Republican party succeeded on July 11 in bringing about the nomination of Gen. Dwight D. Eisenhower against the opposition of Sen. Robert A. Taft and his supporters. The Democrats turned to Gov. Adlai E. Stevenson of Illinois. Stevenson suffered from revelations of corruption in the Truman administration, from widespread dissatisfaction with the war in Korea, and from the vague feeling that it was "time for a change." Eisenhower's personal appeal, moreover, was immense. He and Sen. Richard M. Nixon of California polled 33,936,234 votes to 27,314,987 for Stevenson and Sen. John J. Sparkman of Alabama. The Republicans carried the electoral college, 442 to 89.

Campaign of 1956. Adlai E. Stevenson was renominated on the first ballot by the Democrats at Chicago, with Sen. Estes Kefauver of Tennessee as his running mate. Eisenhower and Nixon were renominated by the Republicans at San Francisco. The campaign, however, was far from being a rehash of 1952. Stevenson, having been advised that his serious discussions of issues in 1952 had been over the voters' heads, pitched his campaign at a lower level. The results disappointed his more ardent supporters without winning him any votes. The Suez crisis, occurring on the eve of the election, further strengthened the administration's position by creating a national emergency. In the election the president polled 35,590,472 popular and 457 electoral votes to Stevenson's 26,022,752 popular and 73 electoral votes.

Campaign of 1960. The Democrats nominated Sen. John F. Kennedy of Massachusetts at Los Angeles in July, with Sen. Lyndon B. Johnson of Texas as his running mate. The Republicans, meeting at Chicago, nominated Vice-President Richard M. Nixon and Henry Cabot Lodge of Massachusetts. In a series of televised debates, the candidates submitted to questioning by panels of reporters. By sharing a national audience with his lesser-known opponent, Nixon may have injured his own cause. The final vote was not known until weeks after the election. Kennedy received 34,227,096, Nixon 34,108,546, and minor candidates 502,773. Despite the fact that Kennedy won by only 118,550 votes and had only 49.7 percent of the total vote as compared with 49.6 percent for Mr. Nixon, the President-elect won 303 electoral votes to Nixon's 219. At forty-three, Kennedy was the youngest man ever elected to the presidency (although not the youngest to occupy the office). He was also the first Roman Catholic ever to become president.

Campaign of 1964. Assuming office following the assassination of President John F. Kennedy in November 1963, Vice-President Lyndon B. Johnson acted quickly to restore public calm and to achieve many of Kennedy's legislative goals. Lyndon Johnson was subsequently nominated by acclamation by the Democrats, meeting in Atlantic City, N.J. The vice-presidential nominee was Minnesotan Hubert H. Humphrey, assistant majority leader of the Senate.

Conflict centered in the Republican party. New York's Gov. Nelson Rockefeller represented the moderate and liberal factions. A new, conservative group was led by Arizona's Sen. Barry M. Goldwater. Goldwater accumulated large numbers of delegates in the South and West, and sealed his first-ballot victory with a narrow win in the California primary. Rep. William E. Miller of New York was selected as his running mate.

Goldwater challenged the previous party consensus on a limited welfare state and the emerging Democratic policy of accommodation with the Communist world. The Democrats defended their record as bringing peace and prosperity, while pledging new social legislation to achieve a "Great Society." The armed conflict in Vietnam also drew some attention. In response to an alleged attack on American warships in the Gulf of Tonkin, the president ordered retaliatory bombing of North Vietnam, at the same time pledging "no wider war."

In the balloting, Lyndon Johnson was overwhelmingly elected, gaining 43,129,484 popular votes (61.1 percent), for

486 electoral votes. Goldwater won 27,178,188 votes (38.5 percent) and 52 electoral votes.

Campaign of 1968. The presidential election took place in an atmosphere of increasing American civil disorder, evidenced in protests over the Vietnam War, riots in black urban neighborhoods, and assassinations of political leaders. On Mar. 31, President Lyndon B. Johnson startled the nation by renouncing his candidacy for reelection. His withdrawal stimulated an intense contest for the Democratic nomination between Sen. Eugene McCarthy, Sen. Robert F. Kennedy, and Vice-President Hubert H. Humphrey. Kennedy appeared to have the greatest popular support, his campaign culminating in a narrow victory over McCarthy in the California primary. On the night of this victory, Kennedy was assassinated. At an emotional and contentious convention in Chicago, Humphrey was easily nominated on the first ballot. Maine's Sen. Edmund S. Muskie was selected as the vice-presidential candidate.

Former Vice-President Richard M. Nixon was the leading candidate for the Republican nomination. Gaining a clear majority of delegates on the first ballot at the party's convention in Miami Beach, he named Gov. Spiro T. Agnew of Maryland as his running mate. A new party, the American Independent party, was organized by Gov. George C. Wallace of Alabama and was able to win a ballot position in every state. Curtis LeMay, former air force general, was selected vice-presidential candidate.

The campaign centered on the record of the Johnson administration. Nixon denounced the conduct of the war and promised an "honorable peace" and withdrawal of American troops. He also pledged a vigorous effort to reduce urban crime and restrict school desegregation. Wallace denounced both parties, calling for strong action against North Vietnam, criminals, and civil rights protesters. Humphrey largely defended the Democratic record, while also proposing an end to American bombing of North Vietnam.

The balloting brought Nixon a narrow victory. With 31,785,480 votes, he won 301 electoral votes. Humphrey won 31,275,166 votes and 191 electoral votes. Wallace gained the largest popular vote for a third-party candidate since 1924—9,906,473 votes, or 13.5 percent of the popular total.

Campaign of 1972. The Nixon administration provided the campaign setting in 1972 by a series of American policy reversals, including the withdrawal of most American ground forces from Vietnam, the imposition of wage and price controls, and presidential missions to Communist China and the Soviet Union. President Richard M. Nixon's control of the Republican party was undisputed, resulting in a placid party convention in Miami, where he and Vice-President Spiro T. Agnew were renominated.

In the Democratic party, major reform resulted in increased representation at the convention of women, racial minorities, and persons under thirty. The contest became a two-man race between Sen. George S. McGovern and former Vice-President Hubert H. Humphrey. A series of upset primary victories and effective organization in local party caucuses culminated in a direct victory for McGovern in the California primary and a first-ballot nomination in Miami. The vice-presidential postion was awarded to Missouri's Sen. Thomas Eagleton. After it was revealed that Eagleton had been hospitalized three times for mental depression, he was persuaded to resign, and the Democratic National Committee named Sargent Shriver as his running mate.

The Democrats attempted to focus the campaign on the continuation of the war in Vietnam, electronic eavesdropping by the Republicans on the Democratic national headquarters at Washington's Watergate complex, and governmental favors for Republican party contributors. The full extent of those improprieties was not revealed, however, until the following year. Aside from defending the Nixon record, the Republicans attacked the Democratic candidate as advocating radical positions on such issues as amnesty for war resisters, marijuana usage, and abortion. Much attention centered on 25 million newly eligible voters, including the eighteen-year-olds enfranchised by constitutional amendment.

The final result was an overwhelming personal victory for Nixon, who won the highest total and proportion of the popular vote in electoral history. Nixon won 47,169,905 popular votes (60.7 percent) and 521 electoral votes from forty-nine states. McGovern won 29,170,383 popular votes (37.5 percent), but only 17 electoral votes.

Campaign of 1976. The 1976 campaign took place two years after the traumatic Watergate scandal, which forced President Nixon to resign. Gerald Ford, who had succeeded Spiro Agnew after his resignation in 1973, became the country's first unelected president in 1974. He was seriously challenged for presidential nomination by the conservative former governor of California, Ronald Reagan, and after winning a narrow victory at the Republican convention he chose Sen. Robert J. Dole, a Kansas conservative, to be his running mate. While in office Ford had gained sympathy for his decency and honesty, but he alienated many by pardoning Nixon and was also hampered by an economic slump.

The Democratic campaign was marked by the spectacular rise of Jimmy Carter to national prominence. Carter began preparations for the presidential campaign in January 1975, shortly after he left the office of governor of Georgia, but a year later he was still little known outside Georgia. Yet within a few months he proved his ability to get votes and after he won the first primary in New Hampshire he was easily nominated at first ballot. His vice-presidential choice was Sen. Walter F. Mondale of Minnesota.

Carter's campaign speeches had a strong moral tone but lacked specifics. He repeatedly stressed that he was not connected with the Washington bureaucracy and promised to install a decent, compassionate, and responsible government. But Carter's initial advantage over Ford diminished as the election approached. In three televised debates neither candidate gave an inspiring performance, and many voters remained undecided until the last moment.

Carter won a close victory in the polls, with 40,825,839 (50.4 percent) popular votes and 297 electoral votes; Ford received 39,147,770 (48.3 percent) popular votes and 240 electoral votes. The western half of the nation except Texas voted solidly for Ford, while Carter carried all southern states. Most black voters preferred Carter.

Campaign of 1980. The 1980 presidential campaign was overshadowed by American hostages in Iran, held since November 1979. President Carter was increasingly criticized for ineptitude, lack of leadership, and inability to solve the economic problems; some charged that during his presidency the United States became militarily inferior to the Soviet Union. Sen. Edward Kennedy challenged Carter for nomination but the convention renominated Carter and Mondale.

Following a rough primary campaign, former governor of California Ronald Reagan easily secured a nomination at the Republican convention. He asked former president Ford to join his ticket but finally selected George H. Bush, former U.N. ambassador, his leading rival for nomination.

Public disenchantment with both candidates led former Republican congressman from Illinois, John Anderson, to proclaim an independent candidacy. In October the League of Women Voters organized two television debates: first Reagan and Anderson and then Reagan and Carter (who refused to participate in the originally proposed debate of all three candidates). In an oppressively formal confrontation with Carter, Reagan asked the American public, "Are you better off than you were four years ago," and promised to cut taxes and "to take the government off the backs of the people," while Carter stressed the international aspects of the presidency and said that Reagan had "an extremely dangerous and belligerent attitude" toward nuclear arms control.

The election brought a landslide victory for Reagan, who received 43,898,770 (51 percent) popular votes and 489 electoral votes, while Carter got only 35,480,948 (41 percent) popular votes and 49 electoral votes. Anderson was chosen by 5,719,222 voters. Only seven states voted for Carter.

CAMPBELLITES. *See* **Disciples of Christ.**

CAMP BUTLER. A training camp for Illinois volunteers, established in 1861 and used until 1866, located six miles east of Springfield. Here nearly a third of the Illinois regiments were mustered into the federal service and later discharged. After 1862 Camp Butler was also used as a prison camp, housing as many as 3,600 Confederates.

CAMP CHASE. Located just west of Columbus, Ohio; served as training camp and military prison during the Civil War. Confederate prisoners were received in large numbers. In 1864 a Confederate plan to release the prisoners at Johnson's Island in Lake Erie, seize Sandusky, and release the prisoners at Camp Chase miscarried.

CAMP DOUGLAS. Established in September 1861 for the concentration and training of Illinois volunteers. It covered sixty acres near the then southern limit of Chicago. After 1862 Camp Douglas served also as a prison camp, 30,000 Confederates being confined there at one time or another. It was dismantled in November 1865.

CAMP FIRE GIRLS. An organization for girls through high school age, organized in 1910 by Dr. Luther Halsey Gulick. Dr. Gulick, a physician, was interested in providing an organization through which girls could make suitable friends, improve their own health, and perform community service. The organization's watchword, "Wohelo," summarizes its objectives of work, health, and love.

CAMP GRANT MASSACRE (Apr. 30, 1871). The Arivaipa band of Apache, hoping to settle down and lead peaceful lives, was encamped near Camp Grant, Ariz. In an early morning attack the sleeping Apache were slaughtered by a party of citizens of Tucson, assisted by Papago Indians. Most of the Arivaipa men were away hunting; of 108 Indians slain only 8 were men. Twenty-nine children were taken to be sold as slaves in Mexico. The perpetrators of the massacre were arrested, but acquitted at once by a Tucson jury.

CAMP JACKSON AFFAIR. Capt. Nathaniel Lyon, an antisecessionist in command of the U.S. arsenal in St. Louis, Mo., received information in 1861 that Missouri authorities, including the secessionist governor Claiborne F. Jackson, were planning to capture the arsenal to arm prosouthern troops. Lyon armed a number of politico-military organizations and removed the remaining guns to Illinois. Brig. Gen. D. M. Frost, a secessionist, set up Camp Jackson in the western part of St. Louis. On May 8, the camp received arms from Jefferson Davis. Lyon, with about 8,000 men, seized without resistance the militiamen at Camp Jackson. While being marched to the prison, a large crowd sympathetic to the prisoners had gathered. The crowd was fired upon by Lyon's troops and about twenty-eight were killed and a number wounded. Many of the militiamen were opponents of secession, and all were subsequently released on parole, subject to exchange as prisoners of war.

CAMP MEETINGS. Outdoor religious meetings were a feature of the evangelical revival in the 18th century. Baptists held meetings similar to the later camp meetings during the American Revolution. A meeting conducted by Presbyterian and Methodist ministers at Gasper River, in Logan County, Ky., in July 1800, is generally accepted as the first camp meeting. The encampments usually lasted four days or longer, with several services each day, and four or five ministers speaking. The evening services were usually tense with excitement and emotion. During the late 19th century, popular educational movements, such as Chautauqua (New York), and summer resort communities, such as Ocean Grove, N.J., developed from camp-meeting beginnings.

CAMPOBELLO FIASCO (April 1866). An attempt by the John O'Mahony Fenians to seize the island of Campobello, New Brunswick, for Ireland. The British sent a vessel to Eastport, Maine, and increased their garrisons. Three U.S. vessels and a number of troops intercepted shipments of Fenian arms and prevented violations of American neutrality laws. The Fenians returned home to plan anew.

CAMPS AND CANTONMENTS OF WORLD WAR I. To build the camps and cantonments for housing and training of U.S. National Guard and National Army divisions during World War I, the Construction Division of the army (later the Cantonment Division) was created in May 1917.

The secretary of war ordered sixteen cantonments with wooden barracks for the new National Army and sixteen National Guard camps where troops would be quartered in tents with wood floors, with wooden buildings for kitchens and mess halls. Construction was crowded practically within a ninety-day period. Each National Army cantonment could accommodate 28,000 men. The National Guard camps were built on a more limited scale.

By Sept. 1, 1917, the thirty-two construction projects were housing troops, and a month later all tent camps were substantially complete. On Nov. 15 the same was true of the cantonments. Physical work of building was done by civilian labor (reaching a peak of 200,000 men). In addition, three embarkation camps and two quartermaster camps were constructed. Total capacity for the National Army cantonments was 654,786; for the National Guard camps, 438,042.

CAMP WILDCAT. A natural fortification in the Rockcastle Hills of Laurel County, Ky., where Union troops, under Col. T. T. Garrard, decisively repulsed Gen. Felix Zollicoffer on Oct. 21, 1861.

CANADA, CONFEDERATE ACTIVITIES IN. Directed against northern prison camps and reported as early as November 1863, but unorganized until the arrival in Canada of Confederate commissioners Jacob Thompson, J. P. Holcombe, and C. C. Clay in May 1864. An effort was made to seize federal ships on Lake Erie in John Beall's raid in September, and an attack was made on St. Albans, Vt., in October. Plans to release Confederate prisoners in northern prison camps failed.

Plots to burn northern cities followed. In New York eleven hotels and Barnum's Museum were fired on Nov. 25, but the blazes were quickly extinguished. A train-wrecking effort near Buffalo, N.Y., to release Confederate generals failed and one plotter was executed.

Confederates in Canada supplied cash for buying gold, shipping it to England, and selling it in order to depress federal currency values. Two million dollars were shipped with no permanent result. About $300,000 was spent by Confederates in Canada.

CANADA AND THE AMERICAN REVOLUTION. Attempts at Alliance. For strategic reasons, it seemed essential to win Canada to the cause of the American Revolution. On Oct. 24, 1774, the Continental Congress dispatched a letter appealing to the Canadians, dwelling upon the supposed grievances of Canadians against the British government and inviting them to send delegates to the next Congress; if they refused to be friends, they would be treated as foes. Massachusetts made similar overtures, and early in 1775 sent John Brown to advance the cause. In the absence of any actual rising in the province, Congress later in the year decided to seize Canada by force. In 1776 it supplemented its military effort by sending to Montreal Benjamin Franklin, Samuel Chase, and Charles Carroll, equipped with a printing press to spread revolutionary propaganda. The mission made little impression upon Canadian opinion and retired from Canada after the siege of Quebec had been raised by troops from England.

American Invasion of Canada. In attempting the conquest of Canada, the Continental Congress wished to effect a diversion favorable to the colonial operations around Boston and to deprive Britain of a base for attack. The capture of Ticonderoga and Crown Point secured the route northward. Hopes of success were increased by the knowledge that there were few regular troops in Canada and the expectation of a rising of the French-Canadians. Congress authorized Gen. Philip Schuyler (June 27, 1775) to undertake the invasion. Active direction fell to Brig. Gen. Richard Montgomery.

A hasty enterprise against Montreal resulted only in the capture of Ethan Allen by the British (Sept. 25). The real gateway of Canada, St. Johns on the Richelieu River, fell after a siege lasting from Sept. 17 to Nov. 2. Montreal was occupied Nov. 13, 1775.

The one assault on Quebec by Benedict Arnold and Montgomery (Dec. 31) failed completely, Montgomery being killed; in spite of reinforcements, toward spring the siege ended abruptly with the opening of navigation, when the first of 10,000 regulars arrived from England (May 5, 1776). After defeats at Cedars and Three Rivers, the Americans evacuated Montreal (June 15) and St. Johns (June 18). British pursuit was delayed while they built a fleet, which destroyed Arnold's (*see* Valcour Island, Battle of), but it was too late in the season for further operations, and invasion of the colonies was postponed until 1777 (*see* Burgoyne's Invasion).

CANADA AND THE WAR OF 1812. Since the destruction of British power in Canada was a primary object of those responsible for bringing on the War of 1812, it was inevitable that the United States should attempt the conquest of the colony. In 1812 an attempted invasion on the Detroit frontier resulted in disaster and an enterprise on the Niagara met the same fate. The next year brought more success: Oliver Hazard Perry's victory in the Battle of Lake Erie permitted a successful invasion of western Upper Canada and the Detroit frontier region remained in American hands until the end of the war. Farther east, the Americans successfully raided York, but initial successes on the Niagara were followed by a check at Stoney Creek, and no permanent foothold was gained; the campaign against Montreal was a total failure. In 1814 the United States again attempted to invade Canada on the Niagara, but no conquest of territory resulted.

CANADIAN-AMERICAN RECIPROCITY. Faced with the ending of British imperial preference in the 19th century, Canada turned for trade to North America. Under threats of annexation to the United States originating in 1849 with Montreal merchants, the British government supported reciprocal trade with the Americans. In 1854, the Elgin-Marcy

Reciprocity Treaty, to remain in force for ten years from 1855 and abrogable on one year's notice, gave Americans access to Atlantic fisheries north of the thirty-sixth parallel and listed most Canadian raw materials and agricultural produce as goods reciprocally admitted duty-free. The United States abrogated the treaty in 1866, ostensibly because of the Civil War but principally because it was not economically advantageous. For British North America, confederation as the Dominion of Canada (1867) offered a new economic possibility.

From Confederation to 1911, reciprocity was an aim of all Canadian governments. The government of Sir Wilfrid Laurier fell in 1911 in an election fought in large part over a draft treaty supported by several prominent American politicians as a prelude to annexation. After 1911, reciprocity ceased to be a significant trade strategy.

CANADIAN-AMERICAN RELATIONS. The Canadian-American relationship is unusual. The two nations share one of the longest common borders in the world. This frontier is technically undefended. Canada and the United States are each other's best customers, with more goods moving across the Great Lakes than over any other localized water system in the world.

To understand the relationship, one must be aware of three problems: (1) Until the 20th century, Americans assumed that one day Canada would become part of the United States. (2) Canadians found themselves caught between the United States, which they feared would absorb them, and Great Britain, whose colony they were. (3) The Canadian population has been roughly one-third French-speaking for a century and a half, and this bilingual and bicultural condition has complicated the North American relationship.

The relationship has been marked by periods of sharp hostility tempered by an awareness of a shared continental environment and by the slow emergence of a Canadian foreign policy independent of either Great Britain or the United States. The original hostility arose from the four intercolonial wars in which the North American colonies of Britain and France were involved from 1689 until 1763. In the French and Indian War, Britain triumphed and Canada passed to the British by the Peace of Paris (1763). Thereafter, Canadians were caught up on the fringes of the American Revolution. The Treaty of Paris, in 1783, created the new United States and left what thereafter was called the British North American Provinces in British hands.

Loyalists in Canada resented the loss of their American property and, later, the renunciation by some American states of their debts for Loyalist property confiscated during the American Revolution. The British regained certain western forts on American soil, contrary to the treaty of 1783, to assure control over the Indians. Although Jay's Treaty of 1796 secured these forts for the United States, western Americans continued to covet Canada. This plus a controversy over British impressment of U.S. seamen and the problem of neutral rights on the seas led to war against Britain in 1812. Unsuccessful invasions of Canada nurtured anti-Americanism there, while the burning of York (now Toronto), the capital of Upper Canada, became an event for the Canadian imagination not unlike the stand at the Alamo. The Treaty of Ghent, signed in 1815, restored the status quo ante but ended British trade with American Indians. The Rush-Bagot Agreement of 1817 limited armed naval vessels on the Great Lakes and became the basis for the myth—since the agreement did not apply to land fortifications—that the Canadian-American border henceforth was undefended.

A second period of strain along the border began in 1837 and extended until 1871. Rebellions in Canada were put down by the British government, but not before American filibustering groups provoked a number of border incidents; further, the leaders of the rebellion sought refuge in the United States. A dispute over the Maine boundary led to a war scare. Although the border was settled by the Webster-Ashburton Treaty of 1842, the Oregon frontier remained in dispute until 1846. In the 1850's, Canada flourished, helped in part by trade with the United States encouraged by the Elgin-Marcy Reciprocity Treaty of 1854. During the Civil War, Canadians were felt to be antinorthern, and they bore the brunt of Union resentment over Queen Victoria's Proclamation of Neutrality. The *Trent* affair of 1861 brought genuine danger of war between the North and Britain and led to the reinforcement of the Canadian garrisons. Canadians anticipated a southern victory and an invasion by the northern army in search of compensatory land; therefore, detailed defensive plans were developed. Ultimately Canada enacted its own neutrality legislation. The American threat helped, in 1864, to bring the provinces together into a confederation, by the British North American Act in 1867.

Tensions were much eased by the Treaty of Washington in 1871. The frontier between the two countries became progressively "unguarded." Although this agreement strengthened the principle of arbitration and although Canada was represented for the first time in a diplomatic matter, the treaty was unpopular in Canada, giving rise to the charge that Britain was willing to "sell Canada on the block of Anglo-American harmony." Significantly, Canadians began to press for independent diplomatic representation.

Problems between Canada and the United States after 1871 were more economic and cultural than strictly diplomatic. Disputes over the Atlantic fisheries and fur seals in the Bering Sea were resolved by arbitration. As the United States refused to renew reciprocity of trade, Canada turned to tariff protection. The Alaska boundary question, unimportant until the discovery of gold in the Klondike, exacerbated old fears. Perhaps the last gasp of fear of direct annexation was heard in 1911, when the Canadian electorate indirectly but decisively turned back President William Howard Taft's attempt to gain a new reciprocity treaty. American neutrality in 1914, at the outbreak of World War I, was resented in English-speaking Canada, and relations remained at a low ebb until the United States entered the war in 1917.

A period of improved relations followed. With the coming of World War I, the economies of the two nations began to interlock more closely. In 1927 Canada achieved full diplomatic independence by exchanging its own minister with Washington. Canadians were disturbed that the United States failed to join the League of Nations, but welcomed U.S.

initiatives toward peacekeeping in the 1920's and 1930's. With the outbreak of World War II and the fall of France in 1940, Canadians were willing to accept the protection implied by President Franklin D. Roosevelt in his Ogdensburg Declaration of Aug. 18, and Roosevelt and Prime Minister William Lyon Mackenzie King established the Permanent Joint Board on Defense, which continues to exist.

Military cooperation continued during and after America's entry into World War II. The Alaska Highway was jointly constructed; Canadian forces helped against the Japanese in the Aleutian Islands; and both Canada and the United States became charter members of NATO in 1949. A collaborative series of three early-warning radar systems was constructed across Canada during the cold war, and in 1957 the North American Air Defense Command (NORAD) was created. Although Canada entered into trade relations with Cuba and Communist China when the United States opposed such relations, diplomatic relations remained harmonious. Nor did relations deteriorate when Canadians protested American nuclear testing in the far Pacific Northwest or when Canada gave refuge to 40,000 young Americans who sought, during the Vietnam War, to avoid military service.

This was offset by increased economic and cultural tension. In the 1930's the two countries erected preferential tariff barriers against each other, and despite an easing of competition in 1935, Canadians have continued to be apprehensive of the growing American influence in Canadian industry and labor. Disputes over the role of American subsidiary firms in Canada; over American business practices, oil import programs, and farm policy; and over the influence of American periodicals and television in Canada led to a resurgence of "Canada First" nationalism under Prime Minister John Diefenbaker in the late 1950's and early 1960's. Still, Queen Elizabeth II and President Dwight D. Eisenhower in 1959 together opened the St. Lawrence Seaway, long opposed by the United States, and the flow of Canadian immigrants to the United States continued. The growth of a French-Canadian separatist movement; diverging policies over the Caribbean and, until 1972, the People's Republic of China; American ownership of key Canadian industries; and disagreements over east coast maritime border and fish catch quotas promised a future not without dispute. Under the prime ministership of Pierre Trudeau (1968–79, 1980–) Canada has placed more emphasis on relations with Third World countries than with Western Europe and the United States, but Canada authorized construction of the Alaska Highway Gas Pipeline in July 1980 and supported the U.S.-led boycott of the Olympic Games in Moscow the same year.

CANADIAN-AMERICAN WATERWAYS. A large number of bodies of water on the North American continent extend across national boundaries. Since 1535, when Jacques Cartier first navigated the St. Lawrence River to what is now Montreal, attention has been focused particularly on the transportation potential of the St. Lawrence system and its links to the Great Lakes. Natural obstacles in the path of a fully navigable passageway from the lakes to the sea via the St. Lawrence have gradually been eliminated—at first by competition and subsequently by cooperation between the two countries. The Welland Canal, connecting Lake Ontario and Lake Erie, for example, was originally built by Upper Canadian interests in response to the American opening of the Erie Canal. American initiative during the Civil War constructed canals at Sault Ste. Marie, opening Lake Superior.

Not until the 1890's was serious consideration given to joint construction of a St. Lawrence waterway, and then various proposals were opposed by one nation or the other. Finally, in 1954, the U.S. Congress agreed to a Canadian initiative of 1951 for construction of a seaway capable of handling the largest oceangoing vessels. The St. Lawrence Seaway was officially opened in 1959 and handles largely bulk cargo, especially iron ore and wheat.

Since the 1960's transportation and navigation have played a decreasing role in Canadian-American waterway considerations. Most new factors—pollution, water supply, flood control, and hydroelectric power—were covered in the Boundary Waters Treaty of 1909. Many of the issues surfaced in the negotiations leading to the Columbia River Treaty of 1961 and its subsequent modification in 1964. While the United States and Canada have been able to agree in principle to clean up the Great Lakes, disagreement over responsibility and financial commitment has hampered action.

CANADIAN AND U.S. BOUNDARY DISPUTES. *See* **Northeast Boundary; Northwest Boundary Controversy.**

CANADIAN ANNEXATION MOVEMENT. In 1849 Canadian urban and commercial interests, primarily in Montreal, sponsored a movement to annex Canada to the United States to offset the serious decline in trade, prices, and property values in Canada. An annexation manifesto, issued on Oct. 10, 1849, received over 1,000 signatures, including some of the most prominent political and financial leaders of Montreal. Widespread opposition, counter manifestoes, and return of prosperity ended the movement within six months.

CANADIAN RIVER. Part of the Arkansas River system in the southwest United States. The name possibly was given to the river by early French hunters and traders who came from Canada. The upper part was called Rio Colorado by the Spanish. By the Treaty of Doak's Stand in 1820, Canadian River was made the northern boundary of the Choctaw nation. Early emigrants to California followed the south bank of the Canadian on to Santa Fe.

CANAL BOATS. *See* **Canals.**

CANAL LANDS. *See* **Canals.**

CANAL RING. A group of corrupt contractors and politicians who conspired shortly after the Civil War to defraud New York by overcharging for repairs and improvement of the state's canal system. It defied an investigation in 1868 and for years was powerful enough to prevent interference and to defeat unfriendly candidates for office.

CANALS. Since 1607, American river systems have provided an essential element in internal transportation. However, full-scale navigation ceased at the fall line (*see* Fall Line). The earliest canals—such as the Patowmack Company's works at Great Falls, Md. (constructed 1786–1808), and the Western Inland Lock Navigation Company's canal at Little Falls, N.Y. (1795)—bypassed the fall line. The Middlesex Canal (1793–1804), connecting Boston with the Merrimac River, and the Santee and Cooper Canal (1790's), connecting these two rivers above Charleston, S.C., fully launched America into canal construction.

Lack of skilled engineers, compounded by crude surveying equipment, hampered canal construction. Samuel Thompson erred over 30 feet in elevation in his Middlesex Canal survey. William Watson brought knowledge of English canals and more accurate surveying abilities to the project. The Erie Canal (1817–25) became the great school for American canal engineers and civil engineering in general. Benjamin Wright, its first chief engineer, derived his principal experience primarily from surveying the Erie route and working for the Western Inland Lock Navigation Company. Erie school engineers spread throughout the United States, working in all aspects of civil engineering. Nathan Roberts worked on the Pennsylvania Main Line Canal (1826–34) and the Chesapeake and Ohio (C & O) Canal (1828–50). Josiah White, a merchant, promoted the Lehigh Canal (1827–29) and held several patents for canal lock construction.

When a canal would open up a large new territory and its chances for financial success were limited, the state tended to provide the necessary capital. When a canal focused on a single natural resource or was linked to an established trade route, it usually was privately financed. Except for the Erie Canal, most state systems were financial disasters. Private companies usually escaped the problems of poor construction based on contract favoritism, fiscal mismanagement, and pressures to locate in certain areas for political rather than sound engineering or business reasons.

Financing took many forms. State systems received direct cash outlays or federal land subsidies. Both states and private companies issued stock. Other sources were company script, lotteries, tolls, or outright grants from towns to entice the canal into their area.

The principal engineering elements of a canal are the source of water supply, the canal bed, and locks to raise boats from one level to another. Other engineering elements are stop gates (to control water in long, open levels in case of a breach or during repairs), waste weirs, overflows, culverts, and aqueducts.

The most individual units on canals were the canalboats. Basically there were two types—packet (passenger) boats and freight boats. Packet boats lasted only until railroads developed. Freight boats were either company boats or private boats. Towing power was furnished from towpaths along the shore by horses, mules, and later electric motors or steam engines. In large canals today vessels travel under their own power except when passing through locks. Sometimes tugboats are used.

Canals continue to play a key role in America. Both the Erie Barge Canal and the Chesapeake and Delaware Ship Canal are vital transportation links. Canal landmarks are becoming the basis for parks, museums, and other recreational development and, in several cases, are being restored to their 19th-century operating order. (*See also* St. Lawrence Seaway; individual canals.)

CANAL ZONE. *See* **Panama Canal.**

CANARY ISLANDS. Spanish islands off the northwest coast of Africa, which served as a way station for Spain's New World voyages, besides supplying wine for Spanish America and skilled workers for West Indian sugar plantations. The New England colonies early began a profitable intercourse with the Canaries and Portugal's Madeiras and Azores, involving mainly the exchange of lumber and fish for wine. Although illegal according to English interpretation of the Navigation Act of 1663, trade with the Canaries continued until the early 19th century.

CANDLES. Candles lighted most American homes, public buildings, and streets until gas (1820's) and kerosene lamps (1850's) replaced them. Housewives made many kinds—bear grease, deer suet, bayberry, beeswax, tallow dip, and spermaceti. Every autumn the housekeepers filled their leather or tin candle boxes to last through the winter. First, women prepared wicks from rough hemp, milkweed, or cotton, then dipped or molded several hundred candles by hand. The homemaker was the only manufacturer until the 1700's, when an itinerant candlemaker could be hired. Later, professional chandlers prospered in the cities. Although factories were numerous after 1750, home-dipping continued as late as 1880.

CANE RIDGE REVIVAL. The culmination of a great spiritual awakening in Kentucky (*see* Great Revival). This occurred in August 1801, at a camp meeting of about 20,000 near the Cane Ridge Meeting House in Bourbon County. The revivalists underwent fervid physical and vocal exercises that indicated an extraordinary religious experience. The Disciples of Christ developed from the intellectual quickening of the movement.

CANNING INDUSTRY. Nicolas Appert, a Parisian confectioner, is generally considered the father of the canning process (1809). Appert's method consisted of the following steps: (1) enclosing in bottles the food to be preserved; (2) corking the bottles carefully; (3) submerging the bottles in boiling water for varying lengths of time, depending on the food; and (4) removing the bottles and cooling them.

Pioneers of American canning were Thomas Kensett, Sr., and his father-in-law, Ezra Daggett, working in New York beginning in 1819, and William Underwood, of Boston, who started in 1821. All three used the Appert method with bottles; the tin can did not come into widespread use until 1839. In 1895, William Lyman Underwood, grandson of the first Underwood, and Samuel Cate Prescott confirmed that bacteria caused food spoilage, as shown earlier by Louis Pasteur, and that heating to temperatures above the boiling point was needed for sterilization of the product.

Of the many developments since, that of the hydrostatic sterilizer stands out. In addition to providing consistent sterilization, this unit results in tremendous savings in steam and water costs and can adjust readily to different sizes of cans and bottles. Another development is that of huge aseptic tanks for storing partially processed tomatoes so that the finish processing can be done all year in accordance with market demands rather than only in season.

The trend toward big business is manifesting itself in the canning industry in two ways. The companies are getting larger as small ones are bought out, combine, or go out of business. Also, more and more growers are forming bargaining associations to negotiate with the canners on crop prices.

CANNONISM. A term common during Joseph G. Cannon's service as speaker of the House of Representatives (1903–11) when the great powers of that office were used in the interest of the ultraconservative elements and to defeat progressive legislation.

CANOE. The Algonkin-speaking Indians of the Northeast made birchbark canoes long before the whites reached North America, and the pioneers quickly adopted them. Until railroads became common, the canoe was the chief vehicle for reaching much of the northern part of the continent.

CANTIGNY, AMERICAN ATTACK AT (May 28, 1918). The American First Division, under Gen. Robert L. Bullard, on Apr. 25, 1918, joined the French First Army facing Cantigny, held by the German XVIII Army. To test the Americans' offensive ability in their first active sector, the French command ordered the new division to capture Cantigny. The Twenty-eighth Infantry attacked at 6:45 A.M. on May 28. The assailants, assisted by French tanks, took all objectives, with 250 prisoners, in forty-five minutes. The Americans repulsed several violent German counterattacks, losing 1,067 killed or wounded, but maintaining their position.

CANTON (Ohio). A city in northeastern Ohio with a population of 94,730 in 1980 and a metropolitan area including 404,421 people. Canton produces a large range of mechanical products from vacuum cleaners to office safes. Specialized steel products are turned out, including roller bearings for machinery, and a major steel mill of the electric-furnace type is operated there.

CANTON FUR TRADE. Developed from the search for some staple, other than specie, which American merchants could exchange for the teas and silks of China. The cargo of the first American vessel, the *Empress of China,* to Canton, Feb. 22, 1784, included furs, but only such rare furs as otter, seal, beaver, and fox were acceptable. Boston merchants decided to seek sea otter skins on the Northwest Coast. The *Columbia* (Sept. 30, 1787–Aug. 9, 1790) returned from Canton with a cargo of teas exchanged for sea otter skins. By 1796 American vessels were engaged in contraband fur trade with the Californians and by 1804 were borrowing Aleutian sea otter hunters, on shares, from the Russian governor at Novarkhangelsk. In 1783, in the southern Pacific, the mass slaughter of the fur seal had begun. When, after the War of 1812, the fur trade with Canton was renewed, the growing scarcity of the sea otter, increased competition, and a consequent decline in profits reduced the American vessels from thirteen in 1821 to two in 1830. Trading in furs with Canton became merely one aspect of a more general Pacific trade and by 1837 the old Northwest fur trade no longer existed.

CANTONMENTS. *See* **Camps and Cantonments of World War I.**

CANVASS. Describes two political processes. First, it means to ascertain by direct personal approach how citizens intend to vote in a coming election. Second, in a somewhat looser sense, to canvass means to make a campaign for the support of a given candidate, either by the candidate or his supporters, or for a party ticket.

CAPE ANN. Eastern peninsula of Massachusetts, known in 1605 to Samuel de Champlain as Le Cap aux Isles. Capt. John Smith in 1614 called it Cape Tragabigzanda, and it was renamed Cape Ann for the wife of James I. In 1623 the Dorchester Company of merchants in England established a fishing station at the cape, to which came disaffected settlers from Plymouth and Nantucket. Among these Roger Conant was a leader. In 1624 he quieted friction over fishing rights asserted for Plymouth by Myles Standish. For ships of that time the fishing grounds were too distant and, since the soil was poor, the enterprise failed in 1626. For twenty years the settlement languished, until Rev. Richard Blynman arrived in 1642. The city of Gloucester, on Cape Ann, began to grow as a deep-sea fishing port and has never lost its eminence.

A moorland section of the cape called Dogtown was abandoned after the 18th century, and its odd settlers became figures of rather sordid romance. Other sections, Annisquam and Pigeon Cove, were given over to artists.

CAPE BRETON EXPEDITION. *See* **Louisburg Expedition.**

CAPE CANAVERAL (Fla.). A low sandy promontory on the east coast of Florida. Until 1950, when a German V-2 rocket was fired from the cape, it was a stretch of barren sands. Since that date, complete facilities for the assembling and launching of ballistic and space vehicles have been installed there and a large community has grown up. Following the death of President John F. Kennedy in 1963 it was renamed Cape Kennedy, but it reverted to its original name in 1973.

CAPE COD. Peninsula in southeastern Massachusetts, possibly the Promontory of Vinland of the Norse voyagers (985–1025). Giovanni da Verrazano in 1524 approached it from the south, and Esteban Gomes the next year called it Cape St. James. Bartholomew Gosnold in 1602 gave it its present name. Samuel de Champlain charted its sand-silted harbors in 1606, and Henry Hudson landed there in 1609. Capt. John Smith noted it on his map of 1614, and the Pilgrims entered the "Cape Harbor" on Nov. 11, 1620.

Whaling and cod fishing arose in the 18th century. Oysters and clams still bring wealth to Wellfleet. Salt by evaporation of sea water became an industry before 1800. Cranberry growing started about 1816 at North Dennis. At Falmouth and elsewhere shipbuilding flourished before and after the Revolution. Sandwich was famous from 1825 to 1888 for its glassworks. Whaling started migration of Portuguese from Lisbon, the Azores, and the Cape Verde Islands. The cape has a long chronicle of shipwrecks. During the summer months the fishing ports are exceptionally busy, and the villages and towns become heavily populated resorts. In 1961 Cape Cod was designated a national seashore.

CAPE FEAR, ACTION AT. *See* **Fisher, Fort, Capture of.**

CAPE FEAR RIVER SETTLEMENTS. Discovered by Giovanni da Verrazano sailing for France in 1524, the Cape Fear region of North Carolina was the site of a short-lived Spanish colony in 1526. The first English settlement was made in 1662 by New England men under William Hilton. For unknown reasons the colony was abandoned, but Hilton returned the next year with a colony from Barbados to establish the county of Clarendon, which flourished until 1667. In 1713 Landgrave Thomas Smith of Carolina received a grant for Smith Island at the mouth of the Cape Fear River, and soon settlers from South Carolina and Albemarle, N.C., began to move into the region. In 1725 the town of Brunswick was laid out about fourteen miles from the sea. Wilmington was founded in 1733 and became the colony's chief port. From 1732 until 1775, thousands of Scottish Highlanders settled on the upper Cape Fear River. Naval stores, lumber, and rice became the most important products of the region.

CAPE GIRARDEAU. As early as 1765, a bend in the Mississippi sixty miles south of the French village of Ste. Geneviève in Missouri was referred to as Cape Girardot or Girardeau. The settlement dates from 1793 when the Spanish granted Louis Lorimier, a French-Canadian, the right of establishing a trading post. Lorimier was made commandant of the district and prospered from land sales and the Indian trade.

CAPE HORN. Southernmost point of the Americas. Traditionally the most dreaded of ocean headlands because of its almost ceaseless storms and the fact that it lies within the southern ice line, Cape Horn was first sighted by the Dutch navigators Jakob Le Maire and William Schouten in 1616. Schouten named the point Cape Hoorn after the town of Hoorn in Holland. The difficulty of making the westbound passage played a part in retarding the growth of California until the discovery of gold in 1848. This stimulus put American square-rigged ships in the forefront of the world. After the building of the Panama Canal, the importance of the route around Cape Horn rapidly declined.

CAPITAL, NATIONAL, LOCATION OF. Immediately after the Continental Congress adjourned (1783) from Philadelphia to New York, because of Pennsylvania's failure to protect it from the insults of mutinous soldiery, agitation was begun in Congress for establishing a permanent seat of government. Nearly every eastern and Middle Atlantic state offered a location. The struggle carried over into the Congress under the Constitution. In 1790 Alexander Hamilton, secretary of the Treasury, supposedly used the desire of the southern states to obtain the capital, and traded, through Secretary of State Thomas Jefferson, Pennsylvania support for the Potomac River location, in return for Virginia support for his plan of the assumption of the states' revolutionary war debts.

CAPITALISM. An economic system in which the ownership and control of land, natural resources, and capital; the production and marketing of goods; the employment of labor; and the organization and operation of the system as a whole are entrusted to private enterprise working under competitive conditions. The right to own property, the freedom to make contracts, and the freedom of entrepreneurs to make their own decisions, set prices, and make a profit are basic assumptions of the system. The accumulation, control, and use of capital (primarily by private enterprise) is the way that goal is most quickly reached.

The first two English colonies in America lacked capital and the profit motive. Little incentive existed in either Virginia or Plymouth for the individual to work hard to build up a surplus, since the settlers were expected to put all their produce into a common fund from which all would be supported and out of which the companies financing the expeditions would receive repayment and profit. When the settlers were permitted greater freedom of enterprise and allowed to accumulate private property, the colonies prospered. The Industrial Revolution was a spontaneous development, arriving when technology was sufficiently advanced and the rate of saving was about double the rate of capital depreciation.

In a truly capitalistic economy neither giant private monopolies nor government regulatory bodies should interfere with the operation of the free market system. But abuses by trusts in the late 19th century and after provided good reason for increasing government regulation. Later on, wars and major depressions provided others. After the mid-1960's, chronic inflation prompted still more regulation, including a growing amount of price fixing by government. Thus, by the late 1970's the federal government was regulating virtually every business in some way.

CAPITAL PUNISHMENT. The imposition of the death penalty as an optional or mandatory punishment for the commission of certain types of crimes, thereby known as capital crimes. No definitive agreement has existed among the capital punishment jurisdictions of the United States as to what constitutes a capital offense. Furthermore, most jurisdictions granted judges or juries the authority to decide whether the death penalty would be imposed. Capital crime can be divided into four categories: (1) crimes against the government, such as treason, espionage, and capital perjury; (2) crimes against property when life is threatened, such as arson, burglary, and train wrecking; (3) crimes against the person, including murder, rape, and felony murders associated with kidnapping, assault, and robbery; and (4) miscellaneous offenses created by panic legislation.

Capital punishment was adopted from the English system. The colonies retreated from it during and after the American Revolution. During the Civil War some states reinstated the death penalty. The opponents of capital punishment renewed their attack at the turn of the century. A clear trend away from capital punishment became evident by the late 1960's. Executions dropped from a high of 152 in 1947 to 7 in 1965, and only 4 after 1967. In 1971, thirty-nine of the fifty-four U.S. jurisdictions provided for the death penalty.

In 1972 the Supreme Court ruled in *Furman* v. *Georgia* (408 U.S. 238) that the optional death penalty was unconstitutional because it violated the Eighth (cruel and unusual punishment) and Fourteenth amendments. One immediate effect was commutation of the death sentence to life imprisonment for all six hundred prisoners awaiting execution, followed by a series of appellate court rulings that state laws imposing the optional death penalty were unconstitutional.

The decision stimulated an intense national discussion. National surveys indicated that public opinion favored the use of the death penalty in certain types of cases. Legislation reinstating the death sentence for specific crimes was introduced in Congress and some state legislatures. The states began to pass new capital punishment laws featuring optional and mandatory death penalties for specific crimes. New York's optional death sentence was one of the first to be tested in the courts. The Supreme Court, in refusing to review the appellate court ruling that declared that new law unconstitutional, reaffirmed its decision in *Furman.* By 1981 the death penalty had been restored in thirty-three states.

CAPITATION TAXES. The federal government is forbidden by the Constitution from levying a capitation (per capita) or other direct tax "unless in Proportion to the Census of Enumeration." Section 9, however, in accord with colonial practices of placing taxes on the importation of convicts and slaves, permits a tax on persons entering the United States, "not exceeding ten dollars for each person." The poll-tax restriction did not apply to states. Following colonial precedents, the state employed this tax, generally placed on all males above twenty-one, sometimes above sixteen. In southern states the poll tax was often made a prerequisite for voting, thus disqualifying the Afro-American or controlling his vote. Ratification of the Twenty-fourth Amendment in 1964 outlawed the poll tax in federal elections. In 1966 the Supreme Court ruled that the state poll tax was unconstitutional under the Fourteenth Amendment.

CAPITOL AT WASHINGTON. In a competition in 1791 of architectural plans for the capitol building, Stephen Hallet's, although not satisfactory, was judged the best. William Thornton submitted a more artistic design, and Hallet was employed to make working drawings of it and to superintend the construction. Accused of substituting his own plan, Hallet was dismissed in 1794 and James Hoban succeeded him. The cornerstone was laid with Masonic ceremonies by President George Washington, Sept. 18, 1793; but the center portion had not been erected when the British burned the public buildings in 1814. Rebuilding commenced under Benjamin H. Latrobe, and the center portion of Acquia freestone with a low dome, designed by Charles Bulfinch, was finished in 1827. The present north and south wings of Massachusetts marble were begun in 1851, from designs of Thomas Ustick Walter, and finished in 1857–59. The present dome of cast iron, an adaptation of Michelangelo's St. Peter's basilica (Rome) and Sir Christopher Wren's St. Paul's (London), was begun in 1856 and finished in 1865. It is surmounted by Crawford's heroic bronze of Freedom, 19.5 feet high. In 1959–60 the east front was extended over 30 feet.

CAPPER-VOLSTEAD ACT (Cooperative Marketing Act; Feb. 18, 1922). As a consequence of the depression of agricultural prices after World War I, farm organizations established a farm bloc in Congress. Sen. Arthur Capper was a member of this bloc. The act authorized agricultural producers to form voluntary cooperative associations for producing, handling, and marketing farm products—exempting such associations from antitrust laws. The secretary of agriculture was given power to prevent such associations from achieving and maintaining monopolies.

CAPRON TRAIL. An east-west trail in Florida, probably first run about 1850, the date of the establishment of Fort Capron (St. Lucie County). It passed from Fort Capron through Fort Vinton, Fort Drum, Fort Kissimmee, Fort Clinch, Fort Meade, to Fort Brooke (Tampa). The name commemorated the valor of Capt. Erastus A. Capron, killed at the Battle of Churubusco in Mexico.

CAPUCHINS. A branch of the Franciscan Friars Minor, founded by Matteo da Bascio of Urbino, Italy, in 1525. An arm of the 16th-century Counter-Reformation, the Capuchins dedicated themselves to missionary work in the 17th century. They were the first missionaries in Maine (1630) and established a central mission at Port Royal, Nova Scotia (1633). Placed in charge of missionary work in Louisiana in 1722, they expanded to the east bank of the Mississippi four years later. This latter area was ceded to the Jesuits in 1750. The French monks were replaced in 1766 by Spanish Capuchins until 1807. Modern history of the order begins in 1857 when two brothers, Gregory Haas and John Fry, established a friary at Mount Calvary, Wis. In the mid-1970's there were over 1,200 Capuchins in the United States.

CARACAS MIXED COMMISSIONS. Established after the 1902 Venezuelan debt crisis (*see* Venezuela, Blockade of). After negotiations at Washington, D.C., protocols were signed in 1903 between Venezuela and ten creditor powers, including the United States, providing for settlement of claims by commissions consisting of one member appointed by each party and a neutral umpire. Commissions sat at Caracas and awarded sums ranging from over 10 million bolivars (francs) to Belgium to 174,000 bolivars to Norway-Sweden.

CARAVAN TRAFFIC ON THE GREAT PLAINS. Existed from about 1825 to 1875, reaching its peak after the Civil War. Both immigrant and trade caravans were employed, particularly during the Oregon movement (1842), the Mormon migration (1847), and the California gold rush (1848).

The first important caravan traffic was via the Santa Fe Trail. William Becknell drove the first wagon from western Missouri to Santa Fe in 1822. Caravans of twenty-five wagons or more largely transported trade goods. The distance traveled from Franklin, Mo., to Santa Fe was 870 miles.

Caravan movements over the Oregon Trail were equally significant, although perhaps not so important commercially. Elm Grove, twelve miles southwest of Independence, Mo., was a favorite starting point, and later West Port. The caravan of 1842 traveled as far as Fort Hall, Idaho. From here the people traveled on foot, on horseback, or by raft down the Snake and Columbia rivers. The following year some immigrants reached the banks of the Columbia River.

Heavy freight caravans plied the routes between San Antonio and Chihuahua, between Santa Fe and Chihuahua, and from points in Nebraska, Kansas, and Colorado to the Far West by 1860. A well-known road from Council Bluffs to the Great Salt Lake via Fort Bridger was traveled by thousands of Mormon pilgrims from 1847 to 1860. In 1869 the first transcontinental railway was completed, but caravan trade and travel remained for a decade.

CARDIFF GIANT. In 1868 George Hall had a human figure weighing 2,966 pounds carved from Iowa gypsum in Chicago. He transported the "giant" to Cardiff, N.Y., and secretly buried it on the Newell farm. In 1869 it was discovered by men digging a well. It was exhibited as a petrified prehistoric giant, creating much excitement and deceiving many people until the hoax was exposed by Othniel C. Marsh of Yale.

CAREY DESERT LAND ACT (1894). Because the Desert Land Act of 1877 had failed to encourage the irrigation of desert lands of the western states, Congress in the Carey Desert Land Act encouraged the states to take the leadership in reclamation by granting them up to a million acres to be available to cooperating developers. Unfortunately, the units of land individuals could acquire were too small to attract capital for building diversionary dams and ditches. Larger projects, being interstate in character, were beyond individual state promotion. Congress next turned to the Department of the Interior, under the Newlands Reclamation Act of 1902, to use proceeds from public-land sales and mineral leases for irrigation projects.

CARIBBEAN POLICY. Up to the 1830's, Americans focused on Cuba, hoping that it would remain in Spain's weak hands and not fall to England or France. During the 1840's, U.S. policy toward Cuba became more assertive; attempts to purchase the island began and prominent southerners assisted efforts by some Cubans to annex their country to the United States. Central America became an object of American interest in a projected interoceanic canal; treaties were signed with Colombia, Nicaragua, and Honduras to assure U.S. rights to build the canal. This ran counter to British designs, but with the signing in 1850 of the Clayton-Bulwer Treaty, the two countries agreed to share jurisdiction over the canal. The United States next turned its attention to the Dominican Republic. In 1854 and 1866, negotiations were begun to permit use of that country's largest bay as a U.S. naval station, and in 1869 they were broadened to include annexation of the entire country. The move was unsuccessful, as was an effort to purchase the Danish West Indies in 1866.

By the 1890's the canal question again became primary. With Britain beset by challenges to its European position, the United States pursued a more aggressive policy to secure control of approaches to the canal, which culminated in 1898 in the Spanish-American War. The war left the Caribbean under U.S. hegemony, with Puerto Rico as an American colony and Cuba under temporary occupation (the latter would assume quasi-protectorate status in 1902 under the Platt Amendment). The question of jurisdiction over the canal was settled by the Hay-Pauncefote Treaty in 1900, wherein Britain renounced its claims. Construction was still delayed by Colombia's reluctance to grant the necessary strip of land across the Isthmus of Panama, but in 1903 a U.S.-instigated rebellion severed Panama from Colombia. The land was turned over to the United States, and construction began.

To remove any pretext for European intervention, the United States assumed the role of gendarme, a policy expressed officially in 1905 in the Roosevelt Corollary to the Monroe Doctrine. Interventions under President Woodrow Wilson included takeovers of the governments in Haiti and the Dominican Republic.

After World War I, U.S. policy became less overbearing. In Central America there was a shift toward intraregional arbitration and joint action. In Cuba the Crowder Commission, a special board managing Cuba's public finances, completed its functions in 1924; and in the same year intervention in the Dominican Republic ended. The trend continued during the administration of Herbert Hoover with the abrogation of the Roosevelt Corollary, and culminated in President Franklin D. Roosevelt's Good Neighbor Policy, officially abandoning military intervention in Latin America. The Platt Amendment was abrogated in 1933, as was a treaty with Panama also authorizing U.S. intervention. In 1934 the last troops were withdrawn from Haiti.

By the early 1950's, policy once again assumed a more aggressive character, influenced by the cold war and the fear of Communist infiltration. Such considerations led to the overthrow of President Jacobo Arbenz Guzmán's leftist regime in Guatemala, with U.S. support, in 1954. The aggressiveness became more pronounced in the 1960's after Cuba's gravitation toward the Soviet bloc. Accordingly, aid was given in 1961 to the abortive Bay of Pigs invasion of Cuba by anti-Castro exiles; in January 1962, on U.S. initiative, Cuba was excluded from the Organization of American States; and later in the year the island was blockaded during the missile crisis. The next assertion of U.S. power occurred in 1965 in the Dominican Republic, where 42,000 U.S. Marines were landed during a period of intense revolutionary unrest. An inter-American force soon replaced the marines and withdrew after elections the next year. In the late 1960's and the 1970's the United States paid scant attention to the Caribbean region. A friendlier approach characterized President Jimmy Carter's administration: the United States had limited government contacts with Cuba for the first time in twenty years, and in 1978 a treaty was concluded with Panama according to which Panama would assume full control over the canal by 2000. But after a leftist, Sandinist junta took power in Nicaragua in 1979 and civil war intensified in El Salvador in the early 1980's, U.S. policy became antagonistic again.

CARILLION, FORT. *See* **Ticonderoga, Fort.**

CARLISLE. Borough of southern Pennsylvania, founded 1751; center of Scotch-Irish settlement in the Cumberland Valley. The crossroads of important Indian trails and site of Fort Louther, it was a trading center for pioneers and site of a treaty between the Ohio Indians and Benjamin Franklin (1753). It was a station on the Underground Railroad.

CARLISLE COMMISSION. *See* **Peace Commission of 1778.**

CARLISLE INDIAN INDUSTRIAL SCHOOL. First off-reservation school for American Indians; established in 1879 in Pennsylvania by Capt. R. H. Pratt, under whose twenty-five-year direction it grew to 1,000 students. Instruction covered farming, horticulture, dressmaking, cooking, laundering, housekeeping, and twenty trades. Pupils, including the great athlete Jim Thorpe, were urged to spend a year working on farms or in homes or industries of the neighborhood. The school was closed in 1918.

CARLOTTA, CONFEDERATE COLONY OF. In 1865 many ex-Confederates left for Mexico. Emperor Maximilian encouraged this by appointing Commodore M. F. Maury imperial commissioner of immigration. Military and civil colonies were established along the railway between Veracruz and Mexico City. The best-known colony was Carlotta, 500,000 acres in the Cordova Valley, named for the empress. Among reasons for its failure were a hostile American press, lack of funds, improper colonization methods, forcible land seizure, political conditions in Mexico, local hostility, and opposition of the U.S. government.

CARLSBAD CAVERNS. The largest underground chambers ever discovered, in southeastern New Mexico, were found by Jim White, a Texas cowboy, in 1901. The caverns became a national monument in 1923 and a national park (46,753 acres) in 1930.

CARMELITES. Catholic order believed to have been founded by St. Berthold about 1195 in Palestine. Their rule has stressed extreme asceticism, absolute poverty, abstinence from meat, and solitude. In 1452 the Order of Carmelite Sisters was formed. The friars were temporarily assigned the care of eastern Louisiana in 1622. Only one brother is known to have gone to the area, which was transferred to the Capuchins in 1726. The first sisters entered the United States in 1790 and established a nunnery in Port Tobacco, Md.

CARNEGIE CORPORATION OF NEW YORK. A private grant-making foundation created by Andrew Carnegie in 1911 to promote understanding between the United States and the British Empire. Of its $135 million endowment, $10 million was to be used in the British dominions. Carnegie, personally, and the corporation in its early years provided more than $56 million for 2,509 library buildings. The library building program ended in 1917. In the 1970's grants were made primarily for the improvement of education at all levels. The corporation is also interested in governmental affairs, education opportunities for minorities, and education in developing countries.

CARNEGIE FOUNDATION FOR THE ADVANCEMENT OF TEACHING. A private operating foundation established in 1905 by Andrew Carnegie with an initial $10 million endowment (increased in 1908 to $15 million). It was incorporated in 1906 by an act of Congress. As of June 30, 1973, teacher pension payments of $82,877,862 had been given to 6,214 individuals. Once the foundation's primary purpose, the pension program was phased out in 1974.

Several notable studies have been undertaken by the foundation in medical, legal, engineering, and dental education; college athletics; and teacher-training. A program of tests for entrance to graduate and professional schools (1937–48) was merged with other testing organizations to create the Educational Testing Service. The Council on Policy Studies in Higher Education, the foundation's principal organ, was formed in 1974 to report on various educational problems.

CARNEGIE HERO FUND COMMISSION. Created in 1904 for making annual awards from a trust income of $5 million, given by Andrew Carnegie, to recognize acts of heroism in the United States and Canada. The commission awards medals and cash awards, pensions for dependents of those killed while performing a heroic act, pensions for those disabled while performing a heroic act, or, in the case of young heroes, funds for higher education.

CARNEGIE INSTITUTION OF WASHINGTON. In 1901 Andrew Carnegie offered the federal government $10 million in bonds of the U.S. Steel Corporation as an endowment to finance the advancement of knowledge. His gift was declined, and he gave it in 1902 to establish the private Carnegie Institution, renamed the Carnegie Institution of Washington when, in 1904, it received a congressional charter. The institution was to encourage original research by exceptional men by spending a small part on grants to individuals and the bulk on large, well-organized projects. Carnegie added $2 million to the endowment in 1907 and another $10 million in 1911. The institution created ten major departments in the physical and biological sciences, history, economics, and sociology. The ten departments evolved into six in different parts of the country: the Mount Wilson Observatory; the Geophysical Laboratory; the Department of Terrestrial Magnetism; the Division of Plant Biology; the Department of Embryology; and the Department of Genetics.

CARNIFEX FERRY, BATTLES AT (1861). An Ohio regiment posted at this river-crossing (Gauley River) in West Virginia was routed on Aug. 26 by a Confederate brigade under Gen. John B. Floyd, who entrenched and remained there until attacked on Sept. 10 by Gen. William S. Rosecrans's small army. After a sharp action, Floyd, slightly wounded, retreated with his command during the night.

CAROLANA. A colony projected by Daniel Coxe, British physician and land speculator, who by 1698 had acquired title to the region west of the Carolina settlements, including the lower Mississippi Valley. The expedition sent to plant the colony landed at Charleston, S.C., but one ship sailed up the Mississippi for 100 miles, turning back when informed on Sept. 15, 1699, that the French occupied the region. Coxe reasserted his claim, but his colony never materialized.

CAROLINA, FUNDAMENTAL CONSTITUTIONS OF. The most pretentious of the attempts to establish a feudal aristocracy in English America; drawn up in 1669 by John Locke under the direction of his patron, the Earl of Shaftesbury. It provided for a provincial nobility of proprietors, landgraves, and caciques having permanent ownership of two-fifths of the land; a grand council made up of proprietors and their councillors which should have the executive and judicial authority; an established Anglican Church and religious toleration; and serfdom and slavery. The system never went into effect and was rejected by the assembly about 1700.

CAROLINA PROPRIETORS. The first Carolina patent was granted by Charles I to Sir Robert Heath in 1629. The province extended from ocean to ocean between the thirty-first and thirty-sixth parallels. This patent was declared forfeited by Charles II on the ground of nonuse, and in 1663 he issued a charter to eight joint proprietors. In 1665 the boundaries were extended to include the territory from 29° to 36° 30′ north latitude. "Declarations and Proposals," the first organic law, issued by the proprietors in 1663, promised land to settlers who emigrated within five years, representation of freeholders in a provincial assembly, and liberty of conscience.

The enterprise resulting in loss, proprietary neglect became chronic. Proprietary orders destructive of provincial interests brought about a revolutionary movement in South Carolina (1719), which the crown thereupon took over as a royal colony, leaving North Carolina to the proprietors until purchase of the proprietorship of both provinces for the crown (1729).

CAROLINA ROAD. *See* **Virginia Path.**

CAROLINAS, SHERMAN'S MARCH THROUGH THE. In February 1865, Union Gen. William T. Sherman's army left Savannah on its way northward "to make South Carolina feel the severities of war" and to unite with Gen. Ulysses S. Grant in Virginia. By Feb. 17 the army was at Columbia, S.C., which was burned. On Mar. 10 the army was at Fayetteville, N.C. As Sherman advanced, opposition became stronger. At Bentonville on Mar. 19 the advance was delayed several days, but by Mar. 25 Sherman was at Goldsboro. On Apr. 13 he had reached Raleigh. The march of nearly 500 miles in about eight weeks was impeded as much by the multitude of slaves and their families who mingled with the marching troops as by the opposition.

CAROLINE, FORT. Built at the mouth of the St. Johns River in Florida in 1564 by a company of French Huguenots led by René de Laudonnière. Seen by the Spanish as a French threat to their dominions, Pedro Menéndez de Avilés was dispatched in 1565 both to settle Florida and expel the French. After establishing St. Augustine, Menéndez marched to Fort Caroline (Sept. 17–19, 1565), which he captured (Sept. 20), killing 132 French defenders in the first hour of the attack and massacring those taken prisoner. Renaming the fort San Mateo, Manéndez established a garrison there.

***CAROLINE* AFFAIR.** In November 1837, William Lyon Mackenzie launched a rebellion in Upper Canada. Defeated by government forces, Mackenzie and his followers fled to Navy Island in the Niagara River. Sympathizers on the American side of the river supplied them with food, arms, and recruits, using the steamer *Caroline.* On the night of Dec. 29, Canadian troops seized the *Caroline,* killing Amos Durfee, an American. The steamer was towed into midstream, set afire, and turned adrift. President Martin Van Buren protested to the British but was ignored. Steps were taken to forestall invasion from Canada and to prevent Americans from violating the frontier. The case dragged on for years and became complicated by the arrest, in New York, of Alexander McLeod, a Canadian sheriff, for the murder of Durfee. As an adjunct of the Webster-Ashburton Treaty the affair was settled in 1842 by an expression of regret by England.

CAROLINE ISLANDS. In the American drive across the Central Pacific in World War II, Truk atoll, near the center of the Caroline Islands, was originally targeted for an amphibious assault. After an air strike on Apr. 17–18, 1944, Truk was "neutralized" by a second fast-carrier raid on Apr. 29 and by land-based heavy bomber attacks.

To protect the right flank of Gen. Douglas MacArthur's return to the Philippines, key positions in the Palaus in the western Carolines were selected for amphibious landings. Pelelieu Island, strongly fortified and defended by 13,000 Japanese, was assaulted on Sept. 15. Organized resistance ended on Nov. 27 at the cost of almost 10,500 American casualties. Meanwhile, the infantry captured the neighboring island of Angaur and occupied undefended Ulithi atoll, 360 miles to the northeast, which became a major U.S. naval base.

***CARONDELET*.** A Mississippi River steamboat with a sloping iron casemate and thirteen guns, built at St. Louis by James B. Eads. It fought at Fort Henry and Fort Donelson. In April 1862, under Commander Henry Walke, it forced the evacuation of Island Number Ten by running past the batteries at night to safeguard Union troops crossing below.

CARONDELET CANAL. Named for the Spanish governor who sponsored it in 1794 as a navigation and drainage project. The canal extended a mile and a half from New Orleans to Bayou St. John, thus opening water communication between the city and Lake Pontchartrain and eliminating the necessity of the long Mississippi River voyage.

CARONDELET INTRIGUE. Baron Francisco Luis Hector de Carondelet was one of the governors of Spanish Louisiana who intrigued with western communities of the United States to detach them from the Union. His purpose was to deny the United States unchallenged access to the Mississippi River, an endangerment to Spanish Louisiana and New Spain. The movement ended with ratification (1795) of Pinckney's Treaty.

CARPENTERS' HALL (Philadelphia). Built by the Carpenters' Guild in 1770 as a meeting place. The first Continental Congress convened here on Sept. 5, 1774.

CARPETBAGGERS. Northerners who went to the South at the end of the Civil War and became active in politics as Republicans. The term was used to stigmatize them as so transitory and propertyless that their entire goods could be carried in carpetbags. Some individuals may have fitted this stereotype, but no single term can accurately describe the diverse group of northerners who participated in southern politics as Republicans during Reconstruction. Few carpetbaggers were wealthy or prominent when they came to the South, but few were penniless. Primarily they moved to improve their personal lives and status. Many had gained wartime experience in the South as soldiers in the Union army or as agents of the Treasury Department and the Freedmen's Bureau, or had been sent as missionaries to minister to the educational and religious needs of former slaves.

Most carpetbaggers arrived before the Reconstruction Act of 1867 offered them political opportunities by enfranchising black southerners and disqualifying many former Confederate officeholders. In 1867–68, they took an active part in shaping the new state constitutions. Hundreds of northerners served as Republican officials. At least forty-five sat in the U.S. House of Representatives and seventeen in the Senate; ten were governors. Their attitudes toward black southern Republicans varied from close, dedicated alliance to open, hostile opposition. They disappeared almost completely after the federal government in 1877 abandoned Reconstruction.

CARPET MANUFACTURE. Carpets first appeared in American homes about 1700, a product of households, itinerant handicraftsmen, or small shops supplied with carpets made in workers' homes. Aided by favorable tariff rates, the transition to the factory system began in 1791 when William P. Sprague set up a plant in Philadelphia. Linking the Jacquard apparatus (for weaving intricate patterns) to the hand looms in 1828 gave a further impetus, and by 1835 the industry was dominated by sizable mills. Inventions by Erastus B. Bigelow and Halcyon Skinner between 1840 and 1875 made power weaving possible, and production was organized along modern lines in large plants.

A marked shift in the industry's growth occurred after 1900. As carpets became increasingly widespread, they began to lose their prestige value. By 1950 output had been reduced to its 1870 level. From the low point reached at midcentury, the industry's growth trend once again shifted, and by the 1970's, output had quadrupled. Two developments enabled the industry to reduce prices: substitution of synthetic fibers and cotton for the more expensive carpet wool, and the shift from woven carpets and rugs to tufted floor coverings that are less durable but much less costly to manufacture.

CARRIAGE MAKING. Horse-drawn vehicles were made in the colonies from the earliest days of settlement. Prior to the Revolution, pleasure vehicles were rare. Extensive road building and a rapid increase of horse-drawn vehicles began with the birth of the Republic. Famous builders of wagons and stagecoaches established themselves at strategic points (*see* Concord Coach).

Except for carriages for the well-to-do, private conveyances developed along popular lines. The first example was the one-horse shay, or chaise, a light vehicle with two high wheels adapted to the rough roads. For fifty years these were so popular that proprietors of carriage shops were usually known as chaise-makers. By the mid-18th century the chaise was superseded by the four-wheel buggy. It was simpler, lighter, stronger, and cheaper.

Carriage making reached the height of its development in 1904 but then declined rapidly. The number of horse-drawn vehicles made in America in 1939 was less than 50,000, compared with 1.7 million thirty years earlier. By the 1950's the industry produced only racing sulkies and a few made-to-order buggies.

CARRIAGE TAX, CONSTITUTIONALITY OF. In the case of *Hylton* v. *United States* (1796), the question of whether a tax on carriages imposed by Congress (June 5, 1794) was a direct tax, and therefore subject to the rule of apportionment, was decided in the negative. Three justices, sitting without their colleagues, decided unanimously that the tax was an excise or duty and not a direct tax. The case was the first in which the constitutionality of an act of Congress was directly reviewed by the Court.

CARRION CROW BAYOU, BATTLE OF (Oct. 14–15, 1863). Confederates attempted to turn back a federal raid up the Bayou Teche from Berwick Bay to Opelousas and Washington, La. Other skirmishes occurred there later in the year (Nov. 3, 11, and 18), during the return of the federal raiders to New Iberia.

CARRIZAL, SKIRMISH OF (June 21, 1916). Two troops of the Tenth Cavalry, on a reconnaissance mission, attempted to force passage through the town of Carrizal in Chihuahua, Mexico. Four hundred Carranzistas, representatives of the

Mexican government, resisted. The Americans were defeated and withdrew, leaving forty-five men killed, wounded, or taken prisoner. This resulted in an exchange of sharp notes between the governments and the massing of troops. Further conflict was avoided by the appointment of a joint commission and the eventual withdrawal of American troops from Mexico. (*See* Mexico, Punitive Expedition into.)

CARSON CITY (Nev.). Capital of Nevada, with a population of 32,022 in 1980. Founded in 1858, it became the territorial capital in 1861, and the state capital in 1865 because it was close to the center of the Nevada silver-mining district. It is now a market center for stock-raising ranches. In the neighborhood, fossilized remains of prehistoric animals have been found.

CARTAGENA EXPEDITION. Organized in 1741 in England to capture the great Spanish stronghold of the Caribbean, it was composed of thirty ships of the line, ninety other vessels, 15,000 sailors, and 12,000 land troops. At Jamaica the expedition was reinforced by 3,600 troops from the colonies. The attacks on Cartagena, from Mar. 9 to Apr. 11, failed, and about two-thirds of the land force was lost from illness and in battle. (*See* King George's War.)

CARTER'S VALLEY SETTLEMENT. John Carter, later leader in the Watauga settlement, located a trading house on the west side of the Holston River in Tennessee country below Long Island of Holston and a few miles south of the Virginia line in 1770; that section of the Holston Valley has ever since borne the name Carter's Valley. Carter sold supplies to emigrants and to the Cherokee out on hunts. In 1772 the trading post was robbed by the Indians and abandoned by Carter, who removed to the Watauga. After another unsuccessful settlement in 1776, efforts were renewed by hardier pioneers in 1777, and they thereafter held the fertile region.

***CARTER* V. *CARTER COAL COMPANY*,** 298 U.S. 238 (1936). In this case the Guffey Coal Act, regulating wages, hours, conditions of work, and prices in the coal industry, was declared unconstitutional because the production of coal is not within the interstate commerce power and the act made an unconstitutional delegation of legislative power. The price-fixing provisions were not passed upon.

CARTHAGE, BATTLE OF (July 5, 1861). Defeated at Boonville, Missouri secessionists retreated into southwest Missouri, hoping for reinforcements from Arkansas. Near Carthage, Union forces attacked; defeated by the secessionists, they retreated to Springfield. Encouraged by victory and reinforcements, the secessionists prepared to advance on Springfield.

CARTOGRAPHY. Commercial Mapping. Commercial U.S. mapmaking began immediately after the Revolution with proposals by William Tatham, Thomas Hutchins, Simeon De Witt, and other topographers and geographers to compile maps of states and regions. The three most widely published and used types of maps are the geographical national and world atlases, county atlases, and individual maps. Geographical atlases and maps were first published in the United States in the early 1790's. Prior to the introduction of lithography about 1830, maps were printed from copper engravings. Lithography expedited publication of maps in variant forms and made them less expensive. The principal centers of publication during the 19th century were Philadelphia, Boston, New York, and Chicago.

By midcentury, map publication was accelerated by introduction of the rotary steam press, zinc plates, the transfer process, glazed paper, chromolithography, and application of photography to printing. August Hoen of Baltimore and Julius Bien of New York set the standards of cartographic excellence. The Hoen Company was still producing maps in the late 1970's. Beginning with the second half of the 19th century uniquely American commercial map publications were the county atlas and the city and town map. During this period the fire-insurance and underwriters map was developed and perfected in great detail; until the 1960's it was kept up to date by the Sanborn Map Company.

Commercial map publication during the 20th century expanded to include recreational, travel, road, automobile, airline, sports, and astronautical exploration maps. During and after World War II there was a rapid acceleration in commercial map production, mainly a response to the requirements of a nation at war in all parts of the world. Government agencies contracted out to commercial map publishing firms large orders for many kinds of maps and atlases. Aerial and satellite photography has become a fundamental source of information in map compilation.

Federal Mapmaking. In a resolution of the Continental Congress on July 25, 1777, Gen. George Washington was empowered to appoint Robert Erskine geographer and surveyor to Washington's headquarters staff. Under Erskine and his successors, Simeon De Witt and Thomas Hutchins, more than 130 manuscript maps were prepared. A considerable mapping program by the federal government has evolved that covers the world and, since 1964, the moon.

In 1785, Congress established the General Land Office, responsible for survey of the public domain. The activity of this office has continued to this day. Increase in maritime commerce brought about, in 1807, the creation of an office for survey of the coasts, which became the U.S. Coast and Geodetic Survey. The rapid movement of population to the West and large acquisition of lands by the Louisiana Purchase increased the need for exploration, survey, and mapping, much of which was accomplished by topographical engineers of the War Department.

Between 1819 and the Civil War, mapping activities increased greatly. A topographical bureau established in the War Department in 1819 was responsible for nationwide mapping. A cartographic office set up in the U.S. Navy Depot of Charts and Instruments in 1842 was instrumental in the mapping of the Arctic and Antarctic regions and the Pacific Ocean and in supplying the navy with charts. In the 1850's the Office of Explorations and Surveys was created for explorations, surveys, and maps of the West, especially for projected railroad routes to the Pacific coast.

During the Civil War the best European techniques were blended with those of U.S. cartographic establishments, especially in the armies. By the end of the war, U.S. mapmaking was equal to any in Europe. A few of the mapping agencies created between the Civil War and World War I to serve major continuous national needs include the Bureau of the Census (1875), the Geological Survey (1879), the Hydrographic Office of the navy (1866), the Corps of Engineers, and the Weather Bureau (1870).

World War I created a need for maps by the military in Europe. Mapmaking and reproduction units were established in France. Some maps were made from aerial photographs, the beginning of modern quantitative mapping. New techniques of compilation and drafting and improved methods of rapid reproduction were developed.

During the Great Depression many specialized agencies were created. Thematic and special-purpose maps came into their own. Significant among the specialized agencies were the Bureau of Agricultural Economics, the Tennessee Valley Authority, the Climatic and Physiographic Division, the National Resources Committee and Planning Board, and the Federal Housing Administration.

Mapping agencies proliferated during World War II, producing topographic maps, aeronautical and nautical charts, and thematic maps. The wide use of aerial photography during the depression was expanded to universal application, especially for large-scale topographic maps. The Aeronautical Chart and Information Service, the Hydrographic Office, and the Army Map Service were the primary agencies.

After World War II large-scale mapping spread into the Arctic and Antarctic regions. The development of color-sensitive photographic instruments, highly sophisticated cameras in space vehicles, automated cartography combining electronics with computer technology, sensing by satellites, and a host of other kinds of instrumentation made possible almost instantaneous mapping of any part of the earth.

CARTOONS, POLITICAL. Early cartoons were woodcuts or engravings. Benjamin Franklin printed his "Join or Die" snake cartoon in the *Pennsylvania Gazette,* May 9, 1754. Paul Revere and other artists depicted the Stamp Act and the Boston Massacre in separately issued engravings. The ratification of the Constitution was celebrated by Benjamin Russell with the rising columns of the "Federal Edifice" cartoon in the *Massachusetts Centinel* (1788); but woodcut cartoons were used sparingly in newspapers. From the Jackson period through the Civil War many poster cartoons, wood engravings, and lithographs contained portraits of political figures, with lettering issuing from their mouths. Civil War cartoons appeared in periodicals such as *Harper's Weekly* and *Vanity Fair.* The modern cartoon, a pen drawing with effective caricatures, was the creation of Thomas Nast of *Harper's Weekly* following the Civil War. The first newspaper editorial cartoons were those of Walt McDougall used by the *New York World* in 1884.

CARVER CLAIM. Grew out of the assertion that at St. Paul on May 1, 1767, the Sioux nation granted to Jonathan Carver, traveler and author, a tract embracing approximately the northwestern one-fourth of modern Wisconsin. The federal government rejected the claim early in the 19th century.

CARVER'S *TRAVELS*. The first person to visit and describe the region of the upper Great Lakes and the upper Mississippi was Capt. Jonathan Carver of Massachusetts. His tour (1766–68) was described in his *Travels,* first published in London in 1778. Many editions in several languages were issued. During the 20th century the reliability of the narrative has been debated by scholars.

CARY'S REBELLION. An uprising in colonial North Carolina occasioned by the disfranchisement of the numerous Quakers. In 1707 Thomas Cary, deputy governor, was deposed at the solicitation of the Quakers, but for two years refused to abandon his office. In 1710 the proprietors sent Edward Hyde as governor, and Cary revolted, although he had promised to support Hyde. With Virginia aid, Cary was defeated, captured, and sent to England on a treason charge, but was never tried.

CASABLANCA CONFERENCE (Jan. 14–24, 1943). A meeting between President Franklin D. Roosevelt and Prime Minister Winston Churchill to resolve military problems, primarily the strategy that was to follow victory in North Africa, and to unite the factions representing Free French forces. The American proposal to assault the European continent was overruled in favor of the British plan for an invasion of Sicily and Italy.

CASCADES OF THE COLUMBIA. Falls and rapids in the Columbia River at the present site of the Bonneville Dam. They were a cause of great difficulty to early explorers and fur traders and were dreaded by settlers, who often preferred crossing mountain passes to descending the cascades.

CASCO TREATY OF 1678. Ended war between the Indians of the Abnaki and Pennacook confederacies and the English settlers of Massachusetts Bay and sought to reestablish friendly relations that had characterized the northern settlements before King Philip's War in 1675. The treaty stipulated that all captives were to be surrendered without ransom and that the English should give the Indians one peck of corn annually for each family settled on Indian lands.

CASCO TREATY OF 1703. An unsuccessful attempt by Gov. Joseph Dudley of Massachusetts Bay to prevent further Indian hostilities along the northern frontier. War was already going on in Europe between England and France, and the Indians of the Abnaki and Pennacook confederacies in New England were under the influence of French Jesuits. Dudley arranged a meeting with the Indians in Casco, Maine, June 20, 1703. The Indians made professions of peace, disavowing any conspiracy with the French, presented the governor with a belt of wampum, and ended the ceremony with an exchange of volleys. Within two months the eastern Indians were again on the warpath.

"CASH AND CARRY" PROGRAM. In 1939 the United States revised its neutrality laws to permit "cash and carry" purchase of arms and other military equipment by any power engaged in warfare, repealing former provisions that prohibited the sale of equipment to war makers. The cash-and-carry arrangement required that no American money be loaned to belligerents and that no Americans or American ships be used to transport arms to warring countries. The law was designed to help the British and French, whose ships could easily sail to American ports during the opening months of World War II.

CASIMIR, FORT. *See* **New Castle.**

CASKET GIRLS. Women imported into Louisiana by the Compagnie des Indes as wives for settlers. Their name derives from the small chests (*cassettes*) in which they carried their clothes. Normally women were supplied to the colonists by raking the streets of Paris for undesirables or by emptying houses of correction. The casket girls, however, were recruited from church charitable institutions and were practically guaranteed to be virtuous. It later became a matter of pride in Louisiana to show descent from them. The first consignment reached Biloxi in 1719 and New Orleans in 1727–28.

CASTINE (Maine). A town on the east side of Penobscot Bay, Maine. Strategically located in respect to the Penobscot Indians and their trade and within the area in dispute between English and French, it was a center of international rivalry. The trading post established in 1630 by the Plymouth colonists passed to the French in 1635 by the Treaty of St.-Germain. English again by conquest in 1654, it was returned to the French in 1670 by the Treaty of Breda, trade being dominated by the Baron de St. Castine until 1701. From the beginning of the Indian wars in 1688 until 1759, the Indians, instigated by the French, prevented English settlement. Soon after 1763 the first English settlers took possession. It was incorporated in 1796.

CASTLE THUNDER. A tobacco warehouse in Richmond, Va., used (1861–65) by the Confederates to confine political prisoners and occasional spies and criminals charged with treason. Its officers were accused of brutality toward their charges. After the fall of Richmond the prison was used by the federal authorities to house Confederates charged with crimes under international law.

CASTORLAND COMPANY. Organized in Paris in 1792 as the Compagnie de New York to colonize French aristocrats and others following the French Revolution. Land in Lewis County, N.Y. was bought. Settlers arrived in 1796; within four years the colony had failed.

CATALINA, SANTA. Island located about twenty-five miles southeast of Los Angeles harbor, discovered Oct. 7, 1542, by Juan Rodríguez Cabrillo. In 1602 Sebastián Vizcaíno named it for St. Catherine of Alexandria. The chief bay, Avalon, during the Spanish and Mexican period was one of the most frequented ports of refuge for smugglers, hunters of sea otters and seals, and hide and tallow traders. The island became a resort area after purchase in 1919 by William Wrigley.

CATHOLICISM. During the colonial period most Roman Catholics in America lived in Maryland, founded by the Catholic Calvert family as a sanctuary for Christians. The Maryland Catholics were deprived of their religious freedom and many civil rights temporarily by the Puritans in the 1650's and permanently by the Anglicans after the Revolution of 1688. Nevertheless, a few became wealthy landowners. In the 18th century some Catholics settled in Pennsylvania. Hardly any were to be found in the other colonies, where their religion was proscribed. A majority of colonial Catholics supported the American Revolution, yet only gradually did the Catholics acquire full civil rights.

The spiritual care of colonial Catholics was provided mainly by Jesuits; the clergy and laity came under the jurisdiction of the vicar-apostolic of the London district until the Revolution. In 1784, Rome appointed as superior of the U.S. mission a native of Maryland, John Carroll. Five years later he was elected first bishop of Baltimore. There were then about 35,000 Roman Catholics, chiefly in the Middle Atlantic states and in the French villages of the western country. Carroll became an archbishop in 1808.

During and after the French Revolution many priests came from that country, and bishops of French birth were numerous in the early 19th century. Financial aid was furnished by the Society for the Propagation of the Faith (founded at Lyons in 1822); the Leopoldine Foundation (Vienna, 1828); and the Ludwig-Missionsverein (Munich, 1838).

Catholic educational and charitable institutions date from 1727, when the first French Ursulines arrived in New Orleans. In 1791, Georgetown Academy was opened for students of every religion, and the first seminary, St. Mary's, was founded by French Sulpicians in Baltimore. Elizabeth Bayley Seton, after founding the Sisters of Charity of St. Joseph, established a school for girls at Emmitsburg, Md., in 1809; members began the first Catholic orphanage and hospital in the East (Philadelphia) in 1814 and 1828, respectively. By 1840 there were at least 200 Catholic schools. The first Catholic weekly newspaper was the *United States Catholic Miscellany,* founded at Charleston, S.C., in 1822.

To ensure uniformity of discipline and cooperation in solving common problems, the bishops assembled seven times from 1829 to 1849 in the Provincial Councils of Baltimore. Three plenary councils were held at Baltimore in 1852, 1866, and 1884. From 1890 to World War I the archbishops met annually in different cities.

Between 1830 and 1860 the Roman Catholic population of the United States increased from 318,000 to 3,103,000; nearly 2 million were immigrants. This sudden influx gave rise to the

American nativist movement, which vilified "Romish" beliefs and practices and impugned the loyalty and patriotism of Catholics. Anti-Catholic sentiment exploded in the burning of the Ursuline convent at Charlestown, Mass. (1834), and riots in Philadelphia (1844). Organized nativism attacked the church through the American Protestant Association (1842) and the Know-Nothing party in the 1850's. After the Civil War, anti-Catholic bias was active only locally, except when stirred up nationally by the American Protective Association in the 1890's and the Ku Klux Klan in the 1920's.

On slavery and emancipation, Catholics divided along sectional lines, but the bishops maintained unity within the church by refraining from official statements. During the Civil War, Catholics fought on both sides. On the battlefields and in the military hospitals Catholic sisters rendered generous service as nurses.

In 1863 the country had about 100,000 Catholic Afro-Americans, slave and free; the majority lived in Louisiana. In spite of exhortations of the Plenary Council of 1866, the church made little progress among the blacks. After World War II, Catholic bishops ended racial segregation in churches and schools. In the 1960's black clerical, religious, and lay leaders formed organizations such as the National Office for Black Catholics to satisfy the needs of Afro-Americans. The number of black Catholics in 1980 was estimated at 1 million (about 3.3 percent of the black population).

The Catholic church in the United States remained under the direct supervision of the Congregatio de Propaganda Fide until 1908. It was not noticeably affected by the presence of an American minister at the papal court from 1848 to 1868. In 1869–70 the American church was represented at the First Vatican Council by forty-eight bishops and one abbot. The first American cardinal was John McCloskey, archbishop of New York (1875). Since 1893 the pope has had an apostolic delegate residing in Washington, D.C. Between 1962 and 1965, 246 American bishops and abbots, as well as several theologians and other scholars, attended sessions of the Second Vatican Council and contributed to the writing of its Declaration on Religious Freedom.

The greatest impetus to Catholic educational efforts in the United States was given by the Third Plenary Council of Baltimore (1884). Parents were commanded to procure a religious education for their children by sending them, if possible, to Catholic schools; priests were ordered to erect an elementary school in each parish, a goal never attained and abandoned in the 1960's. The Catholic University of America in Washington, D.C., was opened in 1889, and the National Catholic Educational Association was established in 1904. Since World War II certain forms of state aid to children attending Catholic schools have been upheld by the Supreme Court, but the attempts of some states to supplement the salaries of teachers of secular subjects or to purchase services for the teaching of secular subjects in nonpublic schools have been declared unconstitutional. Mainly because of the rising costs the number of Catholic schools and universities declined greatly by the 1970's.

It was through its school system that the church preserved the faith of the children of immigrants and eased their entrance into American society. Between 1881 and 1890 about 1.25 million Catholics immigrated to the United States, and only slightly fewer came in the next decade, bringing the total Catholic population to 12,041,000 at the turn of the century. The only large, lasting schism in American Catholicism began in 1907 with the organization of the Polish National Catholic Church. To foster the growth of the church in isolated districts, the Catholic Church Extension Society was founded in 1905 and the National Catholic Rural Life Conference in 1923.

The First American Catholic Missionary Congress (1908) aroused interest in missionary work. Three years later the first native American religious community intended exclusively for the foreign missions, the Maryknoll Fathers, was established at Maryknoll, N.Y. The Catholic Students' Mission Crusade was inaugurated in 1918. Foreign missionaries reached a peak of 9,655 in 1968 and by 1981 fell to 6,324.

Most American Catholics have belonged to the working class, and their leaders have long been concerned with the social order. In 1937 the Association of Catholic Trade Unionists was founded, and in the same decade the first labor schools opened. Catholics sought to forestall juvenile delinquency by founding the Catholic Youth Organization in Chicago in 1930.

In 1917 the National Catholic War Council was formed to coordinate the activities of the dioceses and societies with the national emergency; after the armistice it was transformed into the permanent National Catholic Welfare Conference. In 1966 it was reorganized into the National Conference of Catholic Bishops and its operational secretariat and service agency, the U.S. Catholic Conference.

American Roman Catholicism's only canonized saints are Mother Frances Xavier Cabrini (died 1917), a naturalized citizen who founded the Missionary Sisters of the Sacred Heart for the care of immigrants, and Elizabeth Bayley Seton (died 1821). Also remarkable for heroic virtue were Blessed Philippine Duchesne (died 1852) and Blessed John Nepomucene Neumann (died 1860).

Laymen have taken an increasingly active role in the church. Such men as Orestes A. Brownson and James McMaster wielded much influence as editors of Catholic magazines and newspapers in the 19th century; and local societies began to federate as early as 1855 in the German Catholic Central Verein. In the 20th century, lay organizations have been brought together successively in the American Federation of Catholic Societies and the National Council of Catholic Laity. After World War II the laity and clergy fostered the Cana Movement and the Christian Family Movement for the application of Catholic principles to the married state and parenthood, and the retreat movement for a deepening of the spiritual life amid secular occupations. The characteristic political defensiveness of Catholics, reinforced by the defeat of the Democratic party's Catholic candidate for the presidency in 1928, Alfred E. Smith, amid widespread anti-Catholic bigotry, was overcome to a large extent by the election of another Catholic, John F. Kennedy, in 1960.

The Second Vatican Council (1962–65) wrought striking changes in the American church. In some respects church discipline (mixed marriages, fasting, abstinence from meat) was relaxed. The liturgy, revised and translated into English, was introduced everywhere but was not universally welcomed; some radical groups began to hold unauthorized services. Friendly relations, common prayer, joint social action, and theological discussions with other Christian denominations and with Jews were promoted. The permanent diaconate, to which men over thirty-five, married or single, may be ordained, was established. The pentecostal or charismatic movement spread, as did the cursillo movement. While continuing to support their charitable institutions locally and the Catholic Relief Services (founded 1943) for overseas aid, Catholics joined in the struggle against poverty by launching the Campaign for Human Development in 1969.

In some areas, unrest and decline overshadowed the renewal intended by the Vatican Council. Although the program of studies for candidates for the priesthood was reformed, vocations decreased, so that of the 596 seminaries and novitiates with 48,992 students existing in 1965, only 328 with 12,468 students remained in 1980. Similarly, most religious orders rewrote their constitutions but lost many members and failed to enlist many new ones; the sisters dropped off most sharply from 181,421 in 1966 to 122,653 in 1980. Priests organized the National Federation of Priests' Councils in 1968. Meanwhile, their number fell from 59,892 in 1967 to 56,712 in 1974, but again increased to 58,398 in 1980. More effort was made to utilize the mass media, but the number and circulation of Catholic newspapers and magazines declined, and many Catholic publishing houses went out of business. Finances were strained by diminished church attendance, the expense of maintaining old parishes in inner cities while building new ones in the suburbs, and the need to provide spiritual care for the large numbers of Spanish-speaking in some places. Uncertainty about many Catholic doctrines increased. Although Pope John Paul II's U.S. visit in October 1979 won him the sympathy of Catholics and non-Catholics, his charisma only briefly overshadowed the continuing conflicts between American Catholics and the Vatican concerning birth control, abortion, homosexuality, ordination of women, social and political activism, and liturgical changes. Despite these conflicts, American Catholics ranks reached a new high of 50,449,842 in 1980.

CATLIN'S INDIAN PAINTINGS. From 1829 to 1838 artist George Catlin roamed the trans-Mississippi wilderness, sketching and painting some 600 Indian portraits, scenes of native life, and landscapes. He exhibited his collection in Europe after 1838 and added the 603 items of the so-called Catlin Cartoon Collection. The original collection, held as security for a loan, was presented to the Smithsonian Institution in 1879.

CATSKILL MOUNTAINS. Mountains of the Appalachian system in New York, named for the many wildcats roaming there in the early days of New Netherland. Since the mid-19th century, the mountains have been a major resort area.

CATTLE. Cattle were brought to America before 1600 by the Spanish settlers of Florida. In 1611 cattle raising started in Virginia, and the Pilgrims began with the Devonshire breed in 1624. Black and white Dutch cattle were brought to New Amsterdam in 1625 and Flemish cattle to Virginia in 1621. Large yellow cattle were imported from Denmark into New Hampshire in 1633. Cattle grazed upon common or public lands, giving rise to brands and roundups early in American history. Since controlled breeding was impossible, the types of cattle became intermingled and no distinction was made between dairy and beef animals. Some dairying was done even though milk yields were small and butter and cheese were generally of poor quality.

Interest in improved livestock came after the Revolution when Bakewell (improved Longhorn) cattle were imported, followed by Shorthorns (Durhams) and Devons. Herefords were first imported in 1817. Aberdeen Angus came from Scotland after the Civil War. By the 1880's some Shorthorns were being developed as dairy stock, and other dairy breeds had been established—the Holstein-Friesian, based upon stock from Holland, and the Brown Swiss. Earlier, Ayrshires, Jerseys, and Guernseys had become known as dairy cattle.

Meanwhile, a new cattle industry was rising in the Great Plains. During the Civil War long-horned cattle, descendants of Spanish stock, grew up unchecked on the Texas plains. John G. McCoy arranged to ship them from the railhead at Abilene, Kans., and in 1867 the long drives from Texas began. By 1880 more than 4 million cattle had been driven north. Many of the cattle were held for breeding on the northern plains, giving rise to the range cattle industry. Overgrazing, disastrous weather, and settlement by homesteaders brought the range cattle industry to an end after 1887.

The ranch cattle industry—based upon owned and leased land, winter pasture and feed, and controlled breeding—led to more effective beef production. The Hereford and Angus continued to dominate the beef breeds, but after World War II the Charolais, Santa Gertrudis, Brangus, and Beefmaster gained prominence.

While dairy breeds have not changed, productivity per cow has increased greatly; technology has improved; and the areas of supply have been extended. By 1978, 11 million dairy cows produced 122 million pounds of milk, and there were 116 million beef cattle and calves in the United States. About 40 million cattle and calves were slaughtered for food in 1978.

CATTLE ASSOCIATIONS. Organizations of cattlemen on the western ranges. The Colorado Cattle Growers' Association was formed in 1867. The Wyoming Stock Growers' Association, organized in 1873, had a membership of 400 in 1886 from nineteen states, with cattle, real estate, plants, and horses valued at $100 million. In 1884 the National Cattle and Horse Growers' Association was organized at St. Louis. The Southwestern Cattle Growers' Association of Kansas and the Montana Stock Growers' Association began in 1884. In the Wyoming Stock Growers' Association, brand inspectors supervised the sale and transportation of a million cattle in 1885. Roundup districts were laid out, rules for strays or mavericks adopted, and thousands of brands recorded.

CATTLE BRANDS. Peculiarly associated with ranching, as taken over from Mexico, the brand is a mark of ownership. They are burned on range horses also. Attempted substitutions for firebranding have proved impracticable. Brands are made up of letters, figures, and geometric designs, symbols, or representations of objects. Combinations are endless. Because brands reduce the value of hides and also induce screw worms, they are now generally small. Every legitimate brand is recorded by either state or county, thus preventing duplication within a given territory.

CATTLE DRIVES. The Spaniards, establishers of the ranching industry in the New World, drove herds northward from Mexico as far back as 1540. Notwithstanding antecedent examples, Texans established trail driving as a regular occupation. Before they revolted from Mexico in 1836, they had a "Beef Trail" to New Orleans. In the 1840's they extended their markets northward into Missouri. During the 1850's emigration and freighting from the Missouri River westward demanded many oxen, and Texas longhorn steers by the thousands were broken for work oxen. Herds of longhorns were driven to Chicago, and one herd at least to New York.

California also developed ranching, and during the 1830's and 1840's a limited number of cattle were trailed from there to Oregon. But the discovery of gold in California arrested for a while all development of the cattle industry and created a high demand for outside beef. During the 1850's the big drives were from Texas.

During the Civil War, Texas drove cattle throughout the states for the Confederate forces. After the war Texas had probably 5 million cattle—and no market. In 1866 there were many drives northward without a definite destination and without much financial success, and to the old but limited New Orleans market, following well-established trails to the wharves of Shreveport and Jefferson (Tex.). In 1867 Joseph G. McCoy opened a regular market at Abilene, Kans. The great cattle trails, moving successively westward, were established and trail driving boomed. In 1867 the Goodnight-Loving Trail opened up New Mexico and Colorado to Texas cattle. Tens of thousands were soon driven into Arizona.

In the 1870's Texas longhorns were driven by cowboys into Oklahoma, Kansas, Nebraska, the Dakotas, Wyoming, Montana, Nevada, and Idaho. The Long Trail extended into Canada. In the 1890's herds were still driven from the Panhandle of Texas to Montana, but by 1895 trail driving was virtually ended by barbed wire, railroads, and nesters.

CATTLE RUSTLERS. Cattle thieves have been a problem wherever cattle have been run on the range. Rustlers drove off cattle in herds when Texas was a republic; they now carry them off in trucks in many states. Their methods have varied from open and forceful taking of cattle in pitched battles to sneaking away with motherless calves. Cattle are branded to distinguish their ownership, but rustlers sometimes change the old brand into their own brand.

CATTLE TICK FEVER. The worst plague of the western range during the trail-driving days (1865–95). It caused widespread outbreaks of what was variously known as Spanish, Texas, and tick fever and pleuro-pneumonia, although for years the cause was unknown. Many states established quarantines against the Texas longhorns. The tick has now been virtually eradicated.

CAUCUS. A term applied to a meeting of party members in any community or legislative body for the purpose of discussing and promoting the affairs of their particular political party. There are various applications of the term.

First, "caucus" means a meeting of the respective party members in a local community to nominate candidates for office or elect delegates to party conventions. Such a caucus was used as early as 1725, particularly in Boston, where several clubs endorsed candidates and came to be known as caucus clubs. The gentry organized "parlor caucuses" for the same purpose; this method of nomination soon became the regular practice. It was entirely unregulated by law until 1866, but abuses became so flagrant that, despite some legal regulation after that date, control by bosses came under more and more criticism. By the early 1900's the caucus had given way to nominating conventions and later to the direct primary. A few states still permit the use of caucuses for nomination to local offices or selection of delegates to conventions.

"Caucus" also refers to a meeting of the respective party members in either house of Congress. The Federalists held party caucuses as early as 1796; the Republicans followed suit. In general, this caucus has three functions: to nominate candidates for speaker, president pro tem, and other House or Senate offices; to elect party officers and committees, such as the floor leader, whip, Committee on Committees, Steering Committee, Policy Committee; and to decide on policy or legislation.

A special application of the party caucus in Congress was the congressional caucus (1796–1824), the earliest method of nominating presidential candidates, but many thought it contrary to the spirit of the Constitution, if not actually unconstitutional. After 1824 the congressional caucus never met again, being succeeded in the next decade by the national convention system.

CAVALRY, HORSE. A branch of the U.S. Army, used up through the Indian wars in the West. In 1775 and 1776 the Continental army fought with a few mounted militia commands as its only cavalry. In December 1776 the Congress authorized 3,000 light horse and the army organized four regiments of cavalry. At the end of the war, all cavalry commands were discharged. During the next fifty years when regular cavalry units did exist, they were organized for short periods of time and comprised only a minute part of the army.

Indian trouble revived the need for federal horse soldiers. The six Mounted Volunteer Ranger companies showed the value of using mounted government troops in the West but also proved that a more efficient, less expensive force was needed. On Mar. 2, 1833, Congress replaced the Mounted Rangers with the Regiment of U.S. Dragoons, a ten-company force mounted for speed but trained to fight both mounted and dismounted. In May 1836 the Second Regiment of Dragoons was formed to fight in the Seminole War.

In 1846 Congress added a third dragoon unit, the Regiment of Mounted Riflemen for the Mexican War, and in 1855 the First and Second Cavalry. In 1861 the Civil War regiments were reorganized as First through Sixth Cavalry, with the Seventh through Tenth added in 1866. The Ninth and Tenth Cavalry were manned by black enlisted men and non-commissioned officers commanded by white officers (*see* Black Cavalry in the West). During the western Indian wars, the cavalry performed adequately under adverse conditions. Often there were too few troops for so vast a region and such determined foes; a cost-conscious Congress rarely provided adequate support.

When the Indian wars ended in the early 1890's, the horse cavalry declined in importance. Some troops served as infantry during the Spanish-American War, and the cavalry was revived briefly during Gen. John Pershing's punitive expedition into Mexico. But during World War I only four regiments were sent to France, after which the mechanization of armies made the horse cavalry obsolete.

CAVALRY, MECHANIZED. *See* **Armored Vehicles.**

CAVE-IN-ROCK. A cave in Hardin County, Ill., on the Ohio River, about thirty miles below the mouth of the Wabash. In pioneer times it was used as an inn patronized by flatboatmen. It often served as a rendezvous for outlaws who robbed flatboats going down the river.

CAYUSE WAR (1847–50). In 1836 a Presbyterian mission was established among the Cayuse Indians by the medical missionary Marcus Whitman at Waiilatpu, in southeastern Washington. By 1842 the Indians had become hostile and apprehensive at the increasing numbers of white immigrants. During the winter of 1846–47 many Cayuse died in a measles epidemic. Blaming the missionaries, the Cayuse destroyed the mission, killing Whitman, his wife, and twelve others. A military expedition pursued the Indians to the mountains. The struggle dragged on until the spring of 1850, when to make peace five Cayuse men gave themselves up. They were tried and hanged.

CEDAR CREEK, BATTLE OF (Oct. 19, 1864). Following the Battle of Fisher's Hill, Va., the Union and Confederate armies marched up and down the Shenandoah Valley, the former destroying property and crops. Union Gen. Philip H. Sheridan halted his army across Cedar Creek, east of Fisher's Hill. Shortly afterward he went to Washington. The Confederates unexpectedly attacked and, after defeating the Union troops, halted unnecessarily. Returning from Washington, Sheridan rode (*see* Sheridan's Ride) from Winchester, twenty miles away, and led his men back into battle. The Confederates were defeated, suffering heavy losses.

CEDAR MOUNTAIN, BATTLE OF (Aug. 9, 1862). The first encounter in the Second Bull Run campaign. Union Gen. John Pope's advance under Nathaniel Banks at Cedar Run, near Culpeper, Va., was opposed by Gen. T. J. Jackson's Confederate troops. Although outnumbered, Banks advanced, but his troops were repulsed. Following a brief pursuit Jackson withdrew to join Gen. Robert E. Lee's army.

CEDAR RAPIDS (Iowa). Second largest city in Iowa, with a population of 110,243 in 1980, and center of a metropolitan area of 169,720. It was settled in 1838, when cabins were built at the rapids of the Cedar River. The rapids made it necessary to ford the stream or to carry canoes around them, so the location was a natural one for a trading center. In time, the rapids were harnessed to provide power for mills.

For a time, the settlement was known as Rapid City, but the present name was used in 1849 when it was incorporated. During the years following the Civil War, Cedar Rapids was a major railroad junction. This helped promote its dry-cereal manufacturing industry in the late 19th and early 20th centuries. Cedar Rapids also has factories that assemble and produce trucks and tractors, radios, and electrical equipment. Coe College, established in 1881, is located in the city.

CÉLORON'S LEAD PLATES. Markers used by the French in the French-English rivalry over the Ohio Valley. By 1749 the English were pressing across the Alleghenies into the rich valley beyond the mountains. The governor of New France sent an army, led by Pierre Joseph Céloron, to enforce its authority on the Ohio. Céloron descended the river as far as the Great Miami, where he turned northward toward Detroit. En route he urged the Indians to cease all intercourse with the English and warned the English to leave the country. At strategic points along the Ohio, lead plates were planted, bearing an inscription reciting the French monarch's title to the country. Both the English and the Indians ignored the admonitions of Céloron; the ownership of the Ohio Valley remained to be determined by the French and Indian War.

CEMENT. Cement was first made of lime burned from oyster shells. In 1662 limestone was found at Providence, R.I., and manufacture of "stone" lime began. Not until 1791 did John Smeaton, English engineer, establish the fact that argillaceous (silica and alumina) impurity gave lime improved cementing value. Burning such limestones made hydraulic lime, a cement that hardens under water. After the beginning of the Erie Canal (1817), American engineers learned to make and use a true hydraulic cement (one that had to be pulverized after burning to slake, or react with water). Canvass White, subsequently chief engineer of the Erie Canal, obtained a patent and is credited with being the father of the American cement industry. During the canal and later railway building era, demand rapidly increased and suitable cement rocks were discovered in many localities.

After the Civil War, Portland cements, because of their more dependable qualities, began to be imported. The name Portland cement was given by an English bricklayer, Joseph Aspdin, in 1824, to a cement made by burning and pulverizing briquets of an artificial mixture of limestone (chalk) and clay, because the hardened cement resembled a building stone from the Isle of Portland. Manufacture was started at Coplay,

Pa., about 1870, by David O. Saylor, who selected from his natural cement rock of about the same composition as the Portland cement artificial mixture. By 1900 the Portland cement industry spread rapidly, and by 1977 there were 163 plants across the country. Production increased from 17,578 tons in 1910 to 76,340 tons in 1977.

CEMETERIES, NATIONAL. Before the Civil War, military dead were usually interred in cemetery plots at the man's post. The Mexican War set the precedent of burying American dead on foreign soil. The Civil War demonstrated the need for better military burial procedures. By War Department General Order 75 (1861), formal provisions for recording burials were established; and General Order 33 (1862) directed commanders to lay off plots near every battlefield for burying the dead. Also in 1862, Congress authorized the acquisition of land for national cemeteries; two types were developed: those near battlefields and those near major troop concentration areas, such as Arlington, Va. (1864).

After the Spanish-American War, Congress authorized the return of remains for burial in the United States at government expense if the next of kin desired it. Of Americans killed in World War I, approximately 40 percent were buried abroad. Only 12.5 percent of the number returned were interred in national cemeteries. Beginning in 1930, twenty-four cemeteries were transferred from the War Department to the Veterans Administration, and after 1933, thirteen more were given over to the Department of the Interior. After World War II, approximately three-fifths of the 281,000 Americans killed were returned to the United States, 37,000 of them to be interred in national cemeteries. By 1951, all permanent overseas cemeteries had been placed under the control of the American Battle Monuments Commission.

CENSORSHIP. The Press. Censorship of the printed word has been the focus of legal, political, and social conflict throughout American history. In colonial and early national periods, censorship was usually politically motivated. Despite the First Amendment, Federalists and Republicans prosecuted newspaper editors for seditious libel. By contrast, in 1836, Congress rejected, partly on grounds of freedom of the press, President Andrew Jackson's efforts to bar "incendiary" abolitionist publications from the mails. The major 20th-century outbreak of political censorship came under the war-inspired espionage and sedition laws of 1917–18. In *Schenck* v. *United States* (1919), the Supreme Court enunciated the "clear and present danger" test subsequently used to restrict sharply the government's powers of political censorship.

Since the mid-19th century, press censorship has more typically arisen from moral considerations. In the turbulent post–Civil War era, "obscene" books and magazines aroused great alarm; and in 1873 the New York Society for the Suppression of Vice and the New England Watch and Ward Society were founded. Spurred by Anthony Comstock of the New York antivice group, Congress outlawed the mailing of "obscene," "lewd," or "lascivious" publications. In succeeding years, many states enacted legislation against their sale.

From the outset, however, the censors had their critics, and with the new literary realism and a change in moral values in the 1920's, obscenity laws came under increasing challenge. A succession of novels attacked by Comstock's successor, John S. Sumner, were cleared in the New York courts, while in Boston the Watch and Ward Society met defeat in its efforts to suppress H. L. Mencken's *American Mercury* magazine (1926).

The issue of federal censorship emerged sharply in 1929–30, during debate over the Smoot-Hawley tariff, which provided that works should be judged as a whole rather than on isolated passages, that recognized classics should be treated in a special category, and that court proceedings should replace purely administrative censorship. Federal district judge John M. Woolsey, in a landmark decision of 1933, permitted the importation of James Joyce's hitherto banned *Ulysses.*

Postal censorship was supported by Roman Catholic groups such as the National Organization for Decent Literature, which had largely supplanted the Protestant-dominated vice societies; but many of the post office rulings were reversed in the courts, most notably in the *Esquire* magazine case of 1943.

The U.S. Supreme Court first addressed itself to the obscenity issue in *Roth* v. *United States* (1957), which set forth a more permissive legal definition of obscenity. Under this new standard, the Supreme Court cleared D. H. Lawrence's *Lady Chatterley's Lover* in 1960.

Although the broad trend from the 1920's was toward a decline in censorship, periodic upswings occurred, particularly in times of rapidly changing social and sexual mores. In 1966 the Supreme Court upheld the conviction and prison sentence of Ralph Ginzburg, publisher of *Eros* magazine, noting particularly his advertisements, appealing "to the prurient interests." In the Postal Act of 1967, Congress provided for criminal proceedings against mailers of "erotically arousing" or "sexually provocative" advertisements who continue to mail to any citizens who have formally indicated to the postal authorities their desire not to receive such unsolicited material. In 1973 the Supreme Court continued its tougher line on the obscenity issue, holding that lawmakers and the courts have the right to assume a causal connection between pornography and antisocial behavior.

Motion Pictures. As the popularity of motion pictures spread, so did efforts to regulate them, and numerous cities and states established licensing boards to ban or cut any film deemed obscene, immoral, or otherwise objectionable. In 1915 the Supreme Court upheld such prior-restraint censorship. In 1952 the Court reversed its 1915 position and declared motion pictures "a significant medium for the communication of ideas" and thus fully shielded by the First Amendment. In June 1973, a more conservative Supreme Court majority reopened the censorship door a bit, ruling that a movie (or book or periodical) that offended local community standards might legitimately be banned only in that area.

In 1968 the Bureau of Customs seized a Swedish film, *I Am Curious (Yellow),* an action reversed in federal court. By contrast, when New York City police in 1972 closed a theater exhibiting an explicit sex film, *Deep Throat,* the suppression was upheld in a criminal court trial. Of private censoring organizations, the most influential is the National Catholic Office for Motion Pictures (formerly the Legion of Decency), founded in 1934 by the American Catholic bishops.

Over the years the movie industry responded to censorship threats with various self-regulatory schemes. The National Board of Review, organized in 1909, soon lost credibility. In 1922, reacting to the establishment of a movie licensing board in New York State and the rise of censorship pressures elsewhere, the Motion Picture Producers and Distributors of America appointed former Postmaster General Will H. Hays as its president, with a mandate to oversee the moral tone of the movies. After considerable delay the "Hays Office" in 1930 promulgated a highly detailed, but initially ineffective, production code. Four years later, under continued censorship and boycott threats, the Production Code Administration was established. As the industry became less monolithic and public attitudes more permissive, the code lost effectiveness. In 1968, to forestall mandatory film classification, the industry began assigning each movie a rating. By the late 1970's, although the broad drift was clearly toward greater tolerance, censorship was still a far from negligible factor.

Radio and Television. In 1927 Congress established the Federal Radio Commission (FRC); in the Communications Act of 1934, the FRC was transformed into the Federal Communications Commission (FCC), with licensing and regulatory power over both radio and television broadcasting. The new agency was subjected to this explicit proviso: "Nothing in this Act shall be understood or construed to give the Federal Communications Commission the power of censorship." Aside from insisting that broadcasters present both sides of controversial issues, the FCC during its first thirty-five years generally construed its regulatory power quite narrowly. Under the chairmanship of Dean Burch, who took office in 1969, it moved in a more activist direction.

The Federal Trade Commission also exercises a regulatory function in radio and television advertising, and all states but Texas and Colorado have prohibited broadcasts of court proceedings. Commercial broadcasting has been shaped by a complex set of pressures rooted in considerations of the marketplace and in the industry's own assessment of the public taste, codified in the Television Code of the National Association of Broadcasters (founded 1922).

CENSORSHIP, MILITARY. It was not until the Civil War that systematic military censorship began. Vigorously enforced censorship included army control of telegraph lines; post office confiscation of disloyal newspapers; imprisonment of newspaper editors; and confiscation and sale of their presses. During the Spanish-American War slight attempts at controlling the press by exclusion from cable terminals in Florida were easily foiled by the use of dispatch boats carrying uncensored messages from Cuba.

In World War I the strongest military and civil censorship to date in America was to be seen in the Espionage Act of June 1915, certain executive orders issued by President Woodrow Wilson, and voluntary suppression of military information by the press. Field military censorship included some examination of outgoing mail sent by troops in France and control of correspondents' dispatches sent from the front. A censorship board in the United States controlled telephone, telegraph, and overseas cables.

By late evening of Dec. 7, 1941, the day Pearl Harbor was attacked, censorship of outgoing cables was executed by the navy in New York City, and within days, a combination of voluntary and official censorship of military information was operating. On Dec. 18 the Office of Censorship was established. Radio, land lines, and overseas cables became subject to censorship, and censorship codes for press and radio were created and enforced. Overseas censorship imposed on mail and press communications was the strongest in American history.

Mail was not screened in the Korean War, although press dispatches from the combat zone were censored. During the war in Vietnam there was no mail or press censorship, and information was protected from press disclosure only by security regulations preventing its release to the press.

CENSUS, U.S. BUREAU OF THE. Administers Section 2 of Article I of the U.S. Constitution, which provides for a decennial census to apportion the House of Representatives. With the progressive delegation over the years of many other data-gathering functions, the bureau has become the nation's leading producer of basic statistical sources.

The first census of 1790 could have been limited to statewide aggregates of population, but census takers were required to list heads of families; number of persons in each household; and, for an estimate of military or industrial manpower, the number of free white males at least sixteen years old. By 1850, Congress required details about every inhabitant except untaxed Indians.

Congress provided as a part of the census of 1810 for publication of data about domestic manufactures. Secretary of State John Quincy Adams developed a questionnaire for manufacturing establishments in the census of 1820. In 1840 social statistics (occupations, dependent persons, literacy, and schools) and data about economic institutions were included. The superintendent of the 1870 census, Gen. Francis Amasa Walker, directed the production of the *Statistical Atlas* (1874), which includes statistical charts, graphic illustrations of census data, and maps of rainfall, temperature, geology, and economic activities.

The tenth census was a comprehensive centennial survey planned originally for 1875 by Walker. It became, instead, the 1880 census, which included, for the first time, untaxed Indians. Statistics included detailed data about dependent and delinquent classes, the growth of cities, morbidity and mortality, police departments, benevolent and educational organizations, and religious bodies. Highly qualified special agents prepared reports on vital statistics, agriculture, major industries, use of power and machinery in industry, wages and prices, the factory system, and strikes and lockouts. The twenty-two volumes of special studies that resulted were supplements to the statistical *Compendium of the Tenth Census*

(June 1, 1880). The 1890 census was of comparable magnitude.

The Census Office abandoned the comprehensive inventory method in 1900, providing instead for the collection of non-population data during the intercensal decennial period. Since the late 1930's the Bureau of the Census has developed sampling techniques to estimate and publish current demographic and economic data. In 1941 the bureau was made responsible for statistics on foreign trade.

During the 19th century Congress delegated responsibility for the census reports successively to the president, State Department, and Department of the Interior. An act of Mar. 6, 1902, provided for a permanent census office within the Interior Department. This office was transferred the following year to the newly established Department of Commerce and Labor, where it later became known as the Bureau of the Census. (In 1913 the bureau was included in the separate Department of Commerce.)

CENT. The U.S. cent came from the adoption of the dollar and its division decimally. A privately issued coin dated 1783 (the "Washington cent") had the word "cent" on it. Vermont and Connecticut in 1785 coined cents, but Massachusetts, in 1786, was the first state to have the word on its coin. The Fugio, or Franklin, cent in 1787 was the first issued under the authority of the United States. Cents were minted regularly by the federal government starting in 1793.

CENTENNIAL EXPOSITION (Philadelphia, 1876). Celebrated the one-hundredth anniversary of the Declaration of Independence. It was ten years in the planning and building, covered over 450 acres in Fairmount Park, and cost over $11 million. Thirty-seven foreign nations constructed pavilions. The 167 buildings housed more than 30,000 exhibitors from fifty nations. The gates opened on May 10, and during the 159 days that followed there were 8,004,274 cash admissions. There were seven principal divisions: mining and metallurgy, manufactures, science and education, fine arts, machinery, agriculture, and horticulture. The Woman's Building was an innovation in expositions.

CENTINEL OF THE NORTH-WESTERN TERRITORY. Published in Cincinnati by William Maxwell; the first newspaper in the Northwest Territory. It appeared Nov. 9, 1793, and weekly thereafter until June 1796, when it was merged with *Freeman's Journal.*

CENTRAL AMERICAN COURT OF JUSTICE. A tribunal established in 1907 by the five Central American republics (Costa Rica, El Salvador, Guatemala, Honduras, and Nicaragua) in accordance with a treaty signed at the Central American Peace Conference held in Washington in 1907. It consisted of five judges, one selected by each signatory state. It was given jurisdiction over controversies that could not be settled by a diplomatic understanding and in cases of an international character brought by a citizen of one of the five republics against another. The court was installed at Cartago, Costa Rica, on May 25, 1908. When the period of ten years for which the court was established expired in 1918, nothing was done to renew it, and the court was dissolved.

CENTRAL INTELLIGENCE AGENCY. The surprise Japanese attack on Pearl Harbor in December 1941 revealed grave shortcomings in U.S. intelligence operations. Steps were taken to improve this situation, especially through the establishment of the Office of Strategic Services (OSS). President Harry S. Truman, on Jan. 22, 1946, established the Central Intelligence Group (CIG) to coordinate, correlate, evaluate, and disseminate intelligence information relating to the national security. In 1947 the National Security Act was passed by Congress, establishing the Central Intelligence Agency (CIA) under the direction of the National Security Council. Its functions, similar to those of the CIG, include the clandestine collection of foreign intelligence information.

The act also established the position of director of central intelligence. The director is the president's principal adviser on foreign intelligence and heads the U.S. Intelligence Board (composed of the heads of the principal intelligence agencies) and the CIA. The CIA does not make policy; it provides evaluated factual data for senior policymakers.

Since the 1950's, highly advanced scientific and technical methods for collection of intelligence have enabled the United States to negotiate and monitor adherence to agreements such as the Nuclear Test Ban Treaty and the Strategic Arms Limitation Treaty.

The activities of the CIA are monitored by the Armed Services and Appropriations committees of the Senate and the House of Representatives. In the 1970's, charges that the CIA abused its power in covert political actions overseas and at home increased public debate on its role and led to adjustments in both houses in committees appointed to oversee it.

CENTRALIZATION. In national affairs, centralization usually refers to the growing concentration of authority in the federal government. Centralization has been stimulated mainly through congressional legislation regulating and protecting interstate commerce, particularly through investigative and regulatory agencies centering in Washington. Centralization has been accelerated through federal appropriations of money for a great variety of state enterprises or needs. Through its power to appropriate money and to prescribe conditions with which a state must comply if it wishes to share in the federal funds, the national government is able to do indirectly what it cannot do directly.

Centralization is viewed with alarm by some, who fear that it will result in the reduction of the states to mere administrative areas of the national government. By others, it is viewed as inevitable once national unity has been attained.

In state affairs, centralization refers to the expanding activities of state governments, whereby they have assumed supervision, direct control, or actual performance of activities previously carried on inadequately, if at all, by counties, cities, or other local governments: support of schools, highway construction and maintenance, charities, correctional institutions, and public health.

CENTRAL OF GEORGIA RAILROAD. *See* **Railroads, Sketches of Principal Lines.**

CENTRAL OVERLAND CALIFORNIA AND PIKES PEAK EXPRESS. Chartered by the Kansas legislature in February 1860. It absorbed stage lines running from St. Joseph, Mo., to Denver and Salt Lake City. Its president, William H. Russell, launched the famous Pony Express. In May 1860 it obtained a contract for mail service from Utah to California. Maintenance of frequent stage service and heavy losses from the Pony Express brought embarrassment. On Mar. 21, 1862, Ben Holladay purchased the holdings at public sale for $100,000.

CENTRAL PACIFIC–UNION PACIFIC RACE. A construction contest between the two companies bidding for government subsidies, land grants, and public favor. The Pacific Railway Act (1862) authorized the Central Pacific to build eastward from the California line and the Union Pacific to build westward to the western Nevada boundary. This legislation was unpopular with the railroad companies, and they planned to build beyond the designated boundaries. Their attitude led to amendments to the act (1865–66) that authorized the roads to continue construction until they met. This precipitated a historic race in 1867–69, because the company building the most track would receive the larger subsidy.

When the two roads were about 100 miles apart, Congress passed a law compelling the companies to join their tracks at Promontory Point, Utah, some 50 miles from the end of each completed line. The final, and most spectacular, lap of the race was made toward this point in the winter and spring of 1869, the tracks being joined on May 10. Neither company won the race because there was no definite goal on Promontory Point and both tracks reached the immediate vicinity at about the same time.

CENTRAL ROUTE. The overland route used extensively after 1848, by immigrants bound for California. From Independence or other points on the Missouri River they followed the Platte, went through South Pass in Wyoming, north of Great Salt Lake, along the Humboldt River to the sinks, and by different passes through the Sierras. Beginning with 1851, mail service was maintained over this route.

***CENTURY OF DISHONOR*.** A book by Helen Maria Hunt Jackson, published in 1881, which publicized the cause of the American Indian. An indictment of the U.S. government for its repeated failure to keep treaties made with, and promises made to, native American Indians, it was influential in promoting reforms in Indian affairs.

CENTURY OF PROGRESS INTERNATIONAL EXPOSITION (Chicago, 1933–34). One of the greatest financial successes in the history of world fairs. It was planned during a period of prosperity and successfully held in the midst of a great depression to celebrate the one-hundredth anniversary of the founding of Chicago and to demonstrate a century's progress. The original plans were scaled down several times to meet shrinking budgets. Official foreign participation was extremely limited. The modernistic architecture of the exposition has exerted much influence and the color effects have made themselves clearly evident in commercial design.

CERAMICS. *See* **Pottery.**

CEREALS. Man's most important food source. In the United States, cereals ranking in importance according to acreage harvested are maize (corn), wheat, oats, sorghum, barley, rice, rye, and sugarcane.

Indians raised maize extensively long before the arrival of Columbus. European settlers quickly adopted it because the plants grew almost anywhere, required little attention, and yielded good returns. The "corn belt" developed in the 19th century from Ohio to Nebraska after a mechanical revolution harnessed the horsepower necessary for extensive cultivation.

Columbus introduced wheat, barley, and sugarcane in 1493. New York and Pennsylvania produced wheat extensively in the 17th century. After repeal of the English Corn Laws (1847), U.S. wheat exports increased. Improved plows, reapers, and threshers were available. Washington, California, and North Dakota became important wheat-producing states by 1890. As with maize, improved varieties that were drought- and disease-resistant and gave higher yields led to increased production on less land during the 20th century.

Since barley, oats, and rye withstand cold weather better than other cereals, they were grown in Montana, the Dakotas, and Minnesota. Besides being used as food, barley and rye were used to make alcoholic drinks. Oats were also valuable because of oat flour's antioxidant quality.

African slaves brought sorghum to America, but it remained unimportant until droughts and insect plagues ruined Great Plains farming in the 1880's. Farmers turned to sorghum because it was drought-resistant and immune to grasshopper attack. Texas has become the biggest producer.

Rice culture began when South Carolina settlers imported rice from Madagascar in 1695. By 1808, Georgia farmers were raising African rice on dry land. In 1980 Arkansas, Texas, Louisiana, and California grew the most rice.

Sugarcane came to Louisiana from San Domingo in 1742, but commercial production did not develop until 1795. The states producing most of America's sugarcane in 1980 were Louisiana, Florida, and Hawaii.

CEREALS, MANUFACTURE OF. Ferdinand Schumacher, a German immigrant, began the cereals revolution in 1854 with a hand oats grinder in a small store in Akron, Ohio. His German Mills American Oatmeal Company, the nation's first commercial oatmeal manufacturer, marketed the product as a substitute for breakfast pork. In 1877, Schumacher adopted the Quaker symbol, the first registered trademark for a breakfast cereal. Henry Parsons Crowell in 1882 and John Robert Stuart three years later followed suit. Crowell, operating at Ravenna, Ohio, consolidated all operations under one roof. Stuart's Chicago Imperial Mill and his mill in Cedar Rapids, Iowa, also offered formidable competition. In 1888 the three combined the nation's seven largest mills into the American Cereal Company. By 1900, Quaker Oats had a national market and produced yearly sales of $10 million.

Shredded wheat, probably the first ready-to-eat precooked cereal, appeared in Denver in 1893. Henry Perky, the developer, built the Shredded Wheat Company, which the National Biscuit Company purchased in 1928. William Danforth of the Robinson Commission Company began manufacturing dairy and chicken feed and Purina whole wheat cereal. Sales boomed, and cereal became a major part of the business. The Ralston-Purina Company early in the 20th century decided to concentrate on the feed business and became the nation's largest feed producer.

The primary thrust toward the new breakfast-food concept came in Michigan from John H. Kellogg, William K. Kellogg, and Charles W. Post. A medically trained Seventh-Day Adventist, Dr. John H. Kellogg experimented with cereals because of the dietary strictures of his faith. Granola was his first cereal product. In 1891, Kellogg applied for a patent for a flaked-food process, and two years later he formed the Kellogg's Sanitas Food Company. In 1895 he launched cornflakes, the success of which produced forty rival manufacturers in the Battle Creek area.

The most serious competition came from Charles W. Post, who began with Postum, a cereal coffee substitute, and created Grape-nuts and Post Toasties. Post's death in 1914 facilitated the merger of his company with the Jello firm and began the process of mergers that culminated in the powerful General Foods Corporation.

In 1906, William Kellogg established the Kellogg Toasted Corn Flake Company without his brother, Dr. Kellogg, moving rapidly away from his brother and the health food concept, opting for heavy advertising and commercial taste appeal. His signature became the company trademark. In 1925 William Kellogg introduced Rice Krispies. More durable packages with waxite liners insured freshness and better shipping. By 1930, Kellogg's produced 40 percent of U.S. ready-to-eat cereals and distributed products worldwide.

Early in the 20th century the Quaker Oats Company (formed in 1901 to replace the American Cereal Company) jumped into the world market. Its sales increased 150 percent in the century's first decade. Alexander Anderson's steam-pressure method of shooting rice from guns created puffed rice and wheat. The World War II boom boosted annual sales to $90 million, and by 1964 the firm sold over 200 products and grossed over $500 million.

National advertising facilitated the emergence in the 1920's of the fourth largest American cereal manufacturer, General Mills. In 1921, James Ford Bell, president of Wasburn, Crosby Company, a Minneapolis milling firm, began experimenting with rolled wheat flakes. Wheaties became the "Breakfast of Champions." In 1928 four milling companies in Minneapolis, California, Utah, Texas, Oklahoma, and Detroit consolidated as the General Mills Company. The new firm expanded packaged food sales by heavy advertising. Further product innovation and diversification brought total General Mills sales to over $500 million annually (18 percent in packaged foods) by the early 1950's.

In the 1970's the ready-to-eat cereal industry came full circle. Beginning with supposed health foods (Kellogg's original granola), the industry moved in less than a century back to health foods and even to the reintroduction of granola.

CERRO GORDO, BATTLE OF (Apr. 18, 1847). Advancing into the interior of Mexico after taking Veracruz, Gen. Winfield Scott found a Mexican army under Gen. Santa Anna entrenched on the National Road, eighteen miles below Jalapa. The Americans stormed two fortified hills and gained the rear of the position; the Mexicans fled. Santa Anna escaped, leaving 3,000 prisoners, guns, baggage, and $11,000 in specie. The American loss was 431.

CHAD'S FORD. *See* **Brandywine Creek, Battle of.**

CHAIN GANGS. A form of convict labor occasionally used by southern sheriffs in antebellum days, much as they had been used in debtor prisons in the North. The wide and systematic employment of chain gangs took place after the Civil War, when lessees took control over most convicts in the southern states. In place of the old ball-and-chain, the lessees substituted shackles fastened to both ankles and joined by a long chain to scores of other convicts, thus compelled to work, eat, and sleep together.

In the late 1880's, protests against the convict leases led to their gradual abandonment in favor of penal plantations, which usually dispensed with the chains. But soon an increasing demand for good roads prompted the county sheriffs to revive the chaingang system. By the late 1890's the major portion of the convicts of many southern states were coupled together in road gangs. The introduction of road-making machinery antiquated the chain gang.

CHAIN STORES. A group of retail stores in the same general kind of business under the same ownership or management. The U.S. Bureau of the Census in 1929 defined chains as firms with 4 or more stores. Beginning with the 1948 *Census of Business,* the Bureau abandoned the term "chain stores" and substituted "multiunit establishment firms." Seven categories of multiunit establishment firms range from 2 or 3 stores to 101 or more stores. Industry use of the term "chain stores" generally refers to 11 or more stores and includes the centralization of purchasing and warehousing. Multiunit department-store firms often do not include such centralized operations and so are not considered chains.

The date commonly cited as the beginning of modern chain-store history in the United States is 1859, with the Great Atlantic & Pacific Tea Company. Sears, Roebuck and Company, the world's largest retailer, began as a mail-order business in 1886 but did not start to build its chain of stores until the 1920's. Only fifty-eight chains existed in the entire United States in 1900. This number more than quadrupled by 1910 and tripled again by 1920. Diffusion of the chain-store phenomenon accelerated during the first three decades of the 20th century. By 1929 chain stores accounted for 22 percent of total U.S. retail sales.

The success of the chains was the result mainly of their

ability to charge lower prices than independents. Chain stores were able to reduce their costs by volume buying, purchasing directly from manufacturers, using specialized personnel, manufacturing goods, and contracting with manufacturers for the production of items with their own brand names. Their size made it possible for them to press manufacturers for lower prices.

One response of independent retailers and wholesalers was to use political power to neutralize the price economies of the chains. Many states passed anti–chain-store taxes during the 1930's that tended to raise chain prices. These discriminatory taxes were adverse to consumer interest in lower prices and were generally prohibited by judicial decisions before World War II. The focus then shifted to so-called fair-trade laws, which permit the establishment of legal minimum retail prices. Fair-trade laws are state laws that were made possible by the passage of the 1937 Miller-Tydings Enabling Amendment to the Sherman Antitrust Act. Enforcement has been difficult because consumers oppose them.

Even with the extensive growth of chains, single-store independents accounted for 66 percent of total U.S. retail sales in 1978. Chains are more important in certain areas, accounting for 80 percent of total variety-store sales and 58 percent of total grocery-store sales in 1978.

CHAIRMAKING. Among the numerous woodworking industries in the colonies, furniture making soon supplied articles for export to the South and to the Caribbean. The most common product was chairs. Their manufacture, already specialized before the Revolution, was recognized as a distinct branch of furniture making in the census of 1810. Rockers, said to be an American invention, were popular in Spanish America. Vessels leaving Baltimore for points around Cape Horn in a single day in 1827 carried 12,000 chairs.

Philadelphia chair shops had steam-driven machinery before 1825. About 1850 a Fitchburg, Mass., factory producing principally for export had a capacity of sixty-five dozen chairs a day and employed special machines to shape interchangeable parts that were boxed separately for shipment and assembled at their destination. Until after 1890, Massachusetts made more chairs than any other state.

Chair design has accommodated itself to period fashions, but popular types like the Windsor chair have remained in general use since introduced at Philadelphia about 1700, where they were known at first as Philadelphia chairs. (*See also* Furniture.)

CHALMETTE NATIONAL HISTORICAL PARK. Located about five miles below New Orleans, on the east bank of the Mississippi River; site of the Battle of New Orleans (1815). It was originally a sugar plantation owned by Ignace de Lino de Chalmette, a well-born French Creole.

CHAMBERSBURG, BURNING OF (July 30, 1864). Union Gen. David Hunter, defeated by the Confederate commander, Gen. Jubal A. Early, in the course of his retreat up the Shenandoah Valley, wantonly burned crops, homes, and villages. In retaliation, Early dispatched a cavalry force under Gen. John McCausland to Chambersburg, Pa., in adjacent Union territory, to demand a ransom of $100,000 in gold or $500,000 in greenbacks, failing the delivery of which, he was ordered to burn the town. No ransom of the amount demanded could be paid. The town was burned.

CHAMBERS OF COMMERCE. Voluntary associations of business and professional people approaching the problems of the community from the business angle. The Chamber of Commerce of New York is the oldest in America, its original charter having come from King George III in 1768.

In most older cities the chambers of commerce were developed from two types of previous organizations. The first of these was the Board of Trade, established originally for the purpose of regulating or supervising trading activities. Growth usually has been effected by merger with other types of organization, the basis of combination being a common concern with civic affairs. The second type was originally a group of taxpaying businessmen united for defense or to foster some civic interest.

Their activities include industrial and commercial development and dealing with problems connected with agriculture, transportation, publicity, charity solicitation, regulation and promotion of trade, and commercial arbitration.

CHAMBLY, FORT. A British fort built in 1775 and located at the foot of the Richelieu River rapids in Canada on the site of Fort St. Louis. The fort was captured by the Americans on Oct. 20, 1775, and held until spring 1776, when it was evacuated and burned as the Americans retreated southward to Ticonderoga (*see* Canada and the American Revolution).

CHAMPAGNE-MARNE OPERATION (July 15–18, 1918). This German offensive in France had several objectives. One was to correct their faulty supply in the Marne salient; another was to draw reserves to assure success in the offensive planned against the British in Flanders. The attack of the German army east of Reims was halted by the French army. West of Reims and east of Château-Thierry some fourteen divisions crossed the Marne, but unaided by the attack east of Reims and without artillery support, they soon withdrew, preparatory to a general withdrawal from the Marne salient. Approximately 85,000 Americans were engaged in the operation. (*See also* Aisne-Marne Operation.)

CHAMPAIGN COUNTY RESCUE CASES. An attempt to enforce the Fugitive Slave Act, involving a conflict of state and federal authorities. In April 1857 Udney Hyde harbored, on his farm near Mechanicsburg, Champaign County, Ohio, a fugitive slave from Kentucky. The slaveowner sent three U.S. deputy marshals and five Kentuckians for the slave on May 21. Friends summoned by Hyde from Mechanicsburg scared the posse away, but it returned six days later and carried off four citizens. The posse was overtaken by officers and a crowd and bound over to the Common Pleas Court of Clark County. Judge Humphrey H. Leavitt of the U.S. District Court at Cincinnati assumed jurisdiction and released the defendants as having rightfully performed their duties.

The payment of $950 by Hyde's neighbors for the slave's manumission terminated federal suits against leading obstructors.

CHAMP D'ASILE. In 1817 a group of Napoleonic exiles under Frédéric Lallemand made a fortified camp in Texas on the Trinity River, calling it Champ d'Asile. It was charged that they hoped to take Mexico and rescue Napoleon from St. Helena. The Spanish, who claimed the territory, forced the colonists to withdraw to Galveston Island. There they remained for weeks, the victims of hunger, sickness, and tropical storms. At last, aided by the pirate Jean Laffite, they made their way to the French settlements in Louisiana.

CHAMPION'S HILL, BATTLE OF (May 16, 1863). One of the battles in the Vicksburg campaign. Gen. U. S. Grant's army met the Confederate army of Gen. John C. Pemberton at Champion's Hill, defeating them and driving them from the field toward Vicksburg.

CHAMPLAIN, LAKE. *See* **Lake Champlain.**

CHAMPLAIN'S INDIAN ALLIANCE. In 1608 Samuel de Champlain made an alliance with the Indians of the St. Lawrence and with the Huron from the interior; in 1609 he assisted them in a campaign against the Iroquois. Two chiefs were killed by Champlain's arquebus. The Iroquois, astonished at the firearms, broke and fled. Champlain in 1610 and 1615 again attacked the Iroquois with his Indian allies. The strategic position of the Iroquois and their ability to obtain firearms from the Dutch at Albany made the Iroquois the natural enemies of New France. Champlain could not have foreseen that the Dutch would settle on the Hudson River and that without the alliance he could not have maintained his position at Quebec.

CHAMPLAIN'S VOYAGES. Samuel de Champlain's first Canadian voyage (1603) was as observer for the expedition of Aymar de Chaste, authorized by Henry IV of France. Champlain prepared a cartographic survey of the St. Lawrence region, resulting in a valuable account, *Des Sauvages.* In 1604 under Pierre du Guast, Sieur de Monts, he explored Nova Scotia. A year later he explored the New England coast, mapping 1,000 miles of coastline. With a commission as lieutenant governor, he set out in 1608 with a group of settlers who founded Quebec. Other voyages made him the acknowledged master of all that related to New France. His final voyage was in 1633.

CHAMPOEG CONVENTION. On May 2, 1843, Oregon settlers met at Champoeg to create a civil government to continue until either Great Britain or the United States established control over the Oregon country. This provisional government was the only one in the Pacific Northwest until the Oregon territorial government was established by the United States on Mar. 3, 1849.

CHANCELLORSVILLE, BATTLE OF (May 1–4, 1863). A major Civil War engagement fought between 130,000 Union men commanded by Gen. Joseph Hooker and 60,000 Confederates under Gen. Robert E. Lee. Lee's troops were entrenched behind Fredericksburg, Va., below the Rappahannock. Hooker crossed the river and advanced to attack from behind Chancellorsville. Lee and Gen. T. J. ("Stonewall") Jackson split their men, with Jackson taking his men around Hooker's right flank. Hooker, dazed by Jackson's attack, withdrew to the riverbank. Lee continued to advance and forced Hooker north of the river. Both sides suffered great casualties: Hooker lost 17,287 men (1,606 killed, 9,762 wounded, 5,919 missing); Lee 12,764 (1,665 killed, 9,081 wounded, 2,018 captured). It was the South's costliest victory, with Stonewall Jackson shot in the confusion of battle on May 2 by his own troops.

CHANTIER. In the fur trade of the Far West, signified the place near the larger posts where lumber was made up, boats and canoes built, and other craftsmanship necessary for the post performed. The word comes from the French *chantier* ("shipyard").

CHANTILLY, BATTLE OF (Sept. 1, 1862). Occurred during Union Gen. John Pope's withdrawal to Fairfax Courthouse in Virginia after his defeat at the second Battle of Bull Run. Confederate Gen. T. J. ("Stonewall") Jackson, seeking to command the road on which Pope was retreating, encountered federal troops protecting the line of retreat. Losses were heavy; Union generals Isaac I. Stevens and Philip Kearny were killed. Jackson could not interrupt Pope's retreat, and the federals reached Fairfax Courthouse.

CHAPARRAL. As used by Mexicans, who gave the word to the Southwest, any thick or thorny brush, but never timber. In California, chaparral is specifically the manzanita oak; in parts of Texas, it is called the black chaparral. Chaparral peculiar to arid and semiarid regions of the Southwest includes granjeno, mesquite, allthorn, and huisache; the bushes are often interspersed with cacti, agaves, and yuccas.

CHAPBOOKS. Cheap popular pamphlets, generally printed on a single sheet and folded to form twenty-four pages or less, often crudely illustrated with woodcuts, sold by chapmen. Published in the tens of thousands in America until about 1850, chapbooks were the beginning of popular literature in the United States, with emphasis on the wonderful, the sad, and the humorous. For over 100 years they often were the only literature available in the average home except the Bible, the almanac, and the newspaper.

CHAPLIN HILLS, BATTLE OF. *See* **Perryville, Battle of.**

CHAPULTEPEC, BATTLE OF (Sept. 13, 1847). The western approaches to Mexico City are commanded by Chapultepec, a rocky eminence, 200 feet high, crowned with stone buildings. During the Mexican War, after vigorous bombardment, Gen. Winfield Scott launched a division against the southern slopes. The garrison resisted desperately, but the Americans mounted the walls on scaling ladders and captured the castle. Two divisions attacked the Belén and San

Cosme gates, and the city surrendered. The American loss was 138 killed, 673 wounded. Mexican casualties are unknown, but 760 were captured.

CHARITY ORGANIZATION MOVEMENT. In founding the London Charity Organization Society in 1869, English poor-law reformers introduced the charity organization movement. It spread to the United States, and by 1904 there were 104 societies in America, the first in Germantown, Pa., dating from 1873. The movement had as its goals better handling of poverty cases by private agencies and the tightening of public policies toward indigents.

Philosophically, the charity organization movement favored the self-help concept; apart from those requiring institutional care, unfortunates in society were encouraged to elevate themselves through moral exertion and individual enterprise. These Victorian concepts were to guide poor relief through volunteer "friendly visitors" from the local Charity Organization Societies or Associated Charities, who would screen needy applicants and forward reports for action to private agencies.

In time the movement overshadowed the agencies it was to assist, taking on direct burdens of aid. The Charity Organization Society of the City of New York (1882) was a case in point. By the late 19th century it had established the Penny Provident Fund, to foster savings; the Provident Loan Society, to provide low-interest loans; workrooms to educate unskilled women in marketable occupations; and a woodyard, where beggars could labor for their daily bread.

The movement's paid visitors pioneered in the case method by treating families and individuals as separate problems. Social scientists used societal records for research. Journals, nationwide cooperation through the National Association of Societies for Organizing Charities (1888), and greater emphasis on professional preparation marked steps toward more rational and systematic treatment of poverty problems.

In the 20th century, growing specialization occurred in many areas of social welfare, including public health, housing, and recreation. Local, state, and national responsibility for resolving problems caused by poverty climaxed in creation of the cabinet-level departments of Health, Education, and Welfare (1953) and Housing and Urban Development (1965). The Family Welfare Association (1911) reflected a change in private relief work. Finally, formation of the American Association of Social Workers (1922) signified a new status for the profession.

CHARITY SCHOOLS. During the colonial period, free education generally meant instruction for poor and underprivileged children. Numerous schools were organized and supported by benevolent persons and societies, a practice that served to fasten on the idea of free education an odium that was difficult to remove. Schools were sometimes supported in part by rate bills: charges levied upon parents according to the number of their children in school. Declaration of poverty exempted parents from the payment of rate bills. In some instances the children were also provided with food, clothes, and lodging.

CHARIVARI. *See* **Shivaree.**

CHARLES RIVER BRIDGE CASE, 11 Peters 420 (1837). In 1785 the Massachusetts legislature incorporated the Proprietors of the Charles River Bridge to erect a toll bridge between Boston and Charlestown. In 1828 the legislature incorporated the Warren Bridge Company to build another bridge a few rods from the first. The new bridge was to become free to the public within six years. But the second charter's constitutionality was queried because it impaired the obligation of the first. (*See* Contract Clause.)

The case was carried to the Supreme Court in 1831, but because of absences and disagreement it was impossible to reach a decision until 1837. The Court upheld the constitutionality of the second charter with only two dissenting votes. In an opinion that marked the leaning against monopolistic power, Roger B. Taney, the new chief justice, developed the rule that corporate charters are to be construed strictly in favor of the public.

CHARLESTON (S.C.). Established in 1680 when the English, who had settled ten years earlier at Albemarle Point on the Ashley River, moved down to the present site on the peninsula between the confluence of the Ashley and Cooper rivers. By 1704, Charleston was a walled city. In 1706 Fort Johnson was built on James Island at the mouth of the harbor. Charleston was the capital of South Carolina until 1790.

Indian trade was the city's first source of wealth. Charleston merchants flourished from the 1730's to 1808, exporting rice and indigo to Europe and lumber to the West Indies and importing manufactured goods from England, household necessities from New England, and slaves from Africa. The city's merchants and planters sat in the Commons House of Assembly, and until 1730, Charleston was governed by commissions established by the assembly; subsequently the commissions were elected by the people of the city.

During the Revolution, Charleston was three times successfully defended against the British. Charleston was held by the British from May 12, 1780, until Dec. 14, 1782.

The city was incorporated on Aug. 13, 1783, and a city government with an intendant and thirteen wardens was established. The reassembling low-country elite had to consent to the demands of the growing backcountry planting interests to remove the capital from Charleston to Columbia.

During the French Revolutionary and Napoleonic wars, Charleston like other American ports had a new burst of commercial prosperity, giving rise to the many fine private houses and beautiful gardens. Charleston gardens benefited from the nurseries of André Michaux established on Charleston Neck in 1786. The Magnolia Gardens were created by the Rev. John Grimke Drayton in the 1840's and the Cypress Gardens by the Kittredge family in the 20th century.

President Thomas Jefferson's embargo of 1808, British Orders in Council, French decrees, and the War of 1812 disrupted trade. The merchants tied to European firms departed, their places gradually taken by representatives of northern firms, who redirected Carolina trade to Europe through northern ports. As steam replaced sail, this tendency increased, and the local merchant community declined. The city came to be dominated by rice and cotton planters. At the time of nullification (1832) the city was divided, but on Dec. 20, 1860, the convention that met in St. Andrew's Hall voted unanimously for secession from the Union.

The first shot in the Civil War was fired from Fort Johnson upon Fort Sumter, at the mouth of Charleston harbor, on Apr. 12, 1861. Fort Sumter, which was surrendered to the Confederates on Apr. 14, kept the Union navy out of Charleston harbor during the ensuing siege of Charleston. The victories at Secessionville on James Island on June 16, 1862, and at Battery Wagner on Morris Island on July 18, 1863, kept the Union troops at bay, but the city fell on Feb. 17, 1865. The great fire of Dec. 11, 1861, however, had done more damage than the enemy's bombardment.

Charleston made a beginning in postwar recovery with the development of the fertilizer industry in 1867. It was considerably damaged by an earthquake on Aug. 31, 1886. Since then, importation of ores has led to the development of a profitable oil-refining industry. Charleston's economy has been supported since 1901 by the presence of a U.S. Navy installation on the Cooper River. It is also the site of a military college, The Citadel, established in 1842. In 1978 Charleston ranked forty-fourth among harbors in the continental United States, having handled only slightly more than 6 million tons of cargo during the previous year. The city's population was 69,510 in 1980.

CHARLESTON (W.Va.). Capital of West Virginia; took its name from Charles Clendenin, whose son George acquired lands at the junction of the Elk and Kanawha rivers in 1787. Here was located Fort Lee, a refuge for wilderness settlers for a generation following the French and Indian War. Here Gen. Andrew Lewis halted his army in his march from Lewisburg to Point Pleasant in Dunmore's War. Its location made it a commercial center for both river valleys. In the early 19th century, salt deposits were discovered at Buffalo Lick. The salt was sold to boatmen and wagon train drivers headed westward.

Charleston was pivotal in the early part of the Civil War and changed hands between Confederate and Union forces a half-dozen times. When West Virginia became a state in 1863, there was much competition for the honor of being the state capital. Charleston served as capital in 1870–75. In 1885 it was designated the permanent capital.

Charleston had a population of 69,968 in 1980; it was the center of a metropolitan area including 269,595 people. Located close to deposits of soft coal and types of clay useful in making pottery and glass products, Charleston is a major producer of chlorine and dye products, synthetic fibers, and glass materials.

CHARLESTON AND HAMBURG RAILROAD. *See* **South Carolina Railroad.**

CHARLESTON HARBOR, DEFENSE OF (1776). On June 1, 1776, a British squadron, led by Sir Henry Clinton and Peter Parker, anchored off Sullivan's Island, at the entrance to Charleston Harbor, S.C. The city was held by 6,000 militia; a much smaller force was stationed on the island. On June 28 the British failed to batter down the island fort. After the loss of one ship, the British sailed for New York, ending the planned British invasion of the South.

CHARLESTON RIOT (Mar. 28, 1864). A fight occurred in Charleston, Ill., between soldiers on leave and Copperheads, resulting in nine killed and twelve wounded. Fifteen Copperheads were held for military trial but on President Abraham Lincoln's order were released to the civil authorities. Two were indicted, tried, and acquitted.

CHARLESTOWN. Former city of Massachusetts, now part of Boston, founded July 4, 1629. John Winthrop's company stopped here in 1630, before deciding to settle across the Charles River at Boston. The Battle of Bunker Hill was fought at Charlestown (June 1775), at which time the town was set afire by the British.

CHARLEVOIX'S JOURNEY. The journey of the French Jesuit Pierre François Xavier de Charlevoix to America and Canada (1720–22) was an attempt to discover a route to the Western Sea. The regent of France disguised it as a tour of inspection of posts and missions. Charlevoix went around the Great Lakes, entered Illinois, and voyaged down the Mississippi to New Orleans and Biloxi, interviewing Indians and traders along the way. He wrote of his experiences in *Histoire et description générale de la Nouvelle France* (1744).

CHARLOTINA. The name proposed for a colony suggested in a pamphlet in Edinburgh in 1763 entitled *The Expediency of Securing our American Colonies by Settling the Country Adjoining the River Mississippi, and the Country upon the Ohio, Considered.* It would have included the region lying between the Maumee, Wabash, and Ohio rivers, the upper Mississippi, and the Great Lakes.

CHARLOTTE (N.C.). Largest city in North Carolina, with a population of 314,447 in 1980; it is the center of a metropolitan area including 637,218 people. Charlotte is one of the most important U.S. textile manufacturing centers. It is located near the eastern edge of the cotton-producing areas of the South, and its convenient power supplies made it an ideal place for transforming raw cotton into fabric. Excellent land transportation routes enable the city to distribute its textile products to other parts of the country and to serve the Piedmont region of both Carolinas as a distribution center.

Charlotte was established in the 1760's and chartered as a town in 1768. It was named in honor of Queen Charlotte, wife of King George III. The local colonial court was held in Charlotte, and it was the market town for the farms opened up in the Piedmont during the 1760's and 1770's. The city was occupied by the British under Lord Cornwallis during the Revolutionary War. During the 19th century, Charlotte was the home of a U.S. mint, serving the goldfields in western North Carolina and northern Georgia.

CHARLOTTE, FORT. The name given to the French Fort Condé at Mobile when the English took over the town at the close of the French and Indian War in 1763. Fort Charlotte was captured by the Spaniards in March 1780 and held by them until U.S. troops took possession in April 1813. After the purchase of Florida by the United States in 1819, Fort Charlotte was gradually demolished. (*See* Mobile Seized.)

CHARLOTTE, TREATY OF CAMP (October 1774). Ended Lord Dunmore's War with the Shawnee. The site was on Pickaway Plains, Pickaway County, Ohio. Chief Cornstalk, defeated by Col. Andrew Lewis at Point Pleasant, agreed to give up all prisoners, not hunt south of the Ohio River, and obey trade regulations of the British.

CHARTER, ATLANTIC. *See* **Atlantic Charter.**

CHARTER COLONIES. Promoted through private enterprise under charters from the crown, charter colonies were founded by trading companies, squatters later incorporated, and lords proprietors. Colonies founded by trading companies either disappeared or changed their status early; thus, the Bermuda Company was the only trading company in control of a colony through most of the 17th century. Connecticut and Rhode Island, founded as squatter colonies by dissenters from Puritan Massachusetts, received charters of incorporation early in the Restoration period. The predominating type throughout the 17th century was the proprietary colony. Of this sort was James I's grant of all the Caribbean islands to the Earl of Carlisle, Maryland, and Maine, in the early part of the century, and after 1660 the Carolinas, New York, the Jerseys, the Bahamas, and Pennsylvania.

When the Restoration government turned its attention to the building of a colonial policy, it found charters an obstacle. Several colonies were royalized, and with the view to ultimate consolidation of all colonial possessions into a few large units, the Dominion of New England was established. Its failure brought temporary reaction in favor of charter colonies, but throughout the 18th century the process of royalization went on until by 1776 only two proprieties, Maryland and Pennsylvania, and two corporation colonies, Connecticut and Rhode Island, remained. Except in the corporation colonies the people seem to have preferred royal rule.

CHARTERED COMPANIES. British joint-stock companies that were formed for purposes of trade in the New World. Since production of certain desired articles required the transportation of laborers, colonization became a by-product of the trading company. The first English company to undertake successful colonization was the Virginia Company, chartered in 1606. The original project was enlarged and developed by later charters in 1609 and 1612 to the London branch of the Virginia Company and in 1620 to the Council for New England, the successor to the Plymouth branch. Down to the Puritan Revolution (1643–60) this method of sponsoring colonization predominated. The Newfoundland Company of 1610, the Bermuda Company of 1615, the Massachusetts Bay Company of 1629, and the Providence Island Company of 1630 represent the most important attempts at trade and colonization. After the Puritan Revolution, the lord proprietor superseded the trading company as preferred sponsor of colonization, both king and colonists becoming increasingly distrustful of corporations.

CHARTER OAK. *See* **Connecticut Charter of 1662.**

CHARTER OF LIBERTIES. Drafted in 1683 by New York's first assembly, approved by James, Duke of York. It described the framework of government and the functions of governor, council, and a legislative assembly representative of the qualified freeholders, and guaranteed the freedom of the assembly (which was to meet at least once in three years), trial by jury, due process of law in all proceedings, protection of the property of women, freedom from feudal exactions, exemption from quartering of soldiers, and especially religious toleration for all Christians.

CHARTER OF PRIVILEGES. Granted by William Penn to Pennsylvania, Oct. 28, 1701; guaranteed freedom of worship to all who professed faith in "One almighty God." All who believed in Jesus Christ were eligible for office. A unicameral legislature was established and the council ceased to be a representative body.

CHARTERS, MUNICIPAL. Written instruments authorized or granted by the state by which cities or similar entities are given their corporate existence, powers, structure of government, and legislative and administrative procedures. In the colonial period, municipal charters were confined to the royal and proprietary colonies and were granted by the governor. They dealt primarily with property rights, control of certain public institutions, and local courts.

With the Revolution, the granting of municipal charters became a function of state legislatures, first by a special act and later by general enabling acts, usually availed of by petition and popular election, sometimes by local selection of one of several optional laws. Beginning with Missouri in 1875, a majority of the states now provide, usually constitutionally, for home-rule charters. These charters are prepared by local commissions in already existing municipal corporations, adopted by the electorate, and amended by means of council or voter initiative and approval by the voters. Except as limited in home-rule states, the power of the legislature is paramount over a municipal charter.

CHARTRES, FORT DE. Seat of civil and military government in the Illinois country for more than half a century, near Kaskaskia in Randolph County, Ill., named in honor of the son of the regent of France. Built of wood, and exposed to the flood waters of the Mississippi River, the fort, begun in 1719, quickly fell into disrepair. In 1727 it was rebuilt, but by 1732 it was so dilapidated that Louis St. Ange, the commandant, built a new fort with the same name at some distance from the river. By 1747 this too had fallen into such bad condition that the garrison was withdrawn to Kaskaskia.

In 1751 the French decided to build a new fort at Kaskaskia, but the engineer chose a location near the old fort. Foundations were laid in 1753; three years later the structure was substantially finished. Costing 200,000 livres, the new fort was an irregular quadrangle capable of housing 400 men.

Fort de Chartres, transferred to the British on Oct. 10, 1765, was the last French post in North America to be surrendered under the Treaty of Paris. Renamed Fort Cavendish, it was the seat of British rule in the Illinois country until 1772, when it was abandoned.

CHARTRES, FORT DE, TREATY (1766). An agreement made by George Croghan, deputy superintendent of Indian affairs, with the western Indians in 1766, in which the Indians acknowledged the authority of the king of England and agreed to return prisoners and stolen horses and to permit the establishment of trading posts. The conference was held at Fort de Chartres, beginning on Aug. 25. Peace lasted for the duration of British rule in the Illinois country.

CHASE IMPEACHMENT. Part of a concerted Jeffersonian Republican effort to curb the power of the federal bench. Associate Justice Samuel Chase, an arbitrary personage with an abusive tongue and unswerving confidence in the Federalist party, was charged in articles of impeachment with unbecoming conduct and disregard of law. Chase was impeached by the House on May 12, 1804. The outcome of the Senate trial hinged on whether his conduct constituted "high crimes or misdemeanors." His acquittal (Mar. 1, 1805) was probably a distinct gain for judicial independence.

CHATEAUGAY, BATTLE OF (Oct. 25, 1813). Maj. Gen. Wade Hampton advanced along the Chateaugay River into Canada to Montreal with over 4,000 troops. On Oct. 22 he halted about fifteen miles from the St. Lawrence. Three days later, he attempted to dislodge 800 hostile troops. The British suffered only twenty-five casualties, the Americans double that number. Hampton abandoned his drive to Montreal.

CHÂTEAU-THIERRY BRIDGE, AMERICANS AT (May 31–June 1, 1918). German troops entered Château-Thierry on May 31, having broken the French front on the Aisne. French Gen. Ferdinand Foch sent the American Third Division, under the command of Joseph T. Dickman, to the region, where, aided by French Colonials, the Americans prevented the enemy from crossing the Marne on May 31 and June 1. German attacks ceased.

CHATTANOOGA (Tenn.). City in southeastern Tennessee, with a population of 169,565 in 1980, and the center of a metropolitan area of 426,540. It is located on the Tennessee River at a strategic crossing used for centuries as an Indian trading place. About 1815, John Ross established a landing in what is now downtown Chattanooga, known as Ross' Landing. In 1838 it was platted and renamed Chattanooga, the original name for Lookout Mountain, meaning "rock rising to a point." In 1839 it was incorporated as a town; in 1851 the state legislature granted a new charter and designated it a city. The town benefited from the construction of railroads in the 1840's. It was fought over in some of the most critical battles of the Civil War and was the base from which Union Gen. W. T. Sherman marched through Georgia.

Because of Chattanooga's location, the Tennessee Valley Authority provides the city with a tremendous supply of electricity. The TVA river-deepening projects ensure that barges can reach the city's docks year round. The city has become a major U.S. electrical-machinery-producing centers and has a wide range of other products, including chemicals, textiles, iron and steel, coal, and wood products.

CHATTANOOGA CAMPAIGN (October–November 1863). Before the Battle of Chickamauga, Union troops under Gen. U.S. Grant had begun to move eastward. Confederate Gen. Braxton Bragg had failed to follow through after Chickamauga. All he could do was "besiege" W. S. Rosecrans's Union army in Chattanooga, Tenn. Grant, placed in command of all Union forces in the West, replaced Rosecrans with G. H. Thomas and instructed him to hold Chattanooga "at all hazards." Reinforcements arrived. Vigorous action turned the tables on Bragg, who then awaited Grant's next move.

On Nov. 24, 1863, Union Gen. Joseph Hooker captured Lookout Mountain on the left of Bragg's line. The next day Grant attacked all along the line. The Confederate center on Missionary Ridge gave way; the left had retreated; only the right held firm and covered the retreat into northern Georgia. A rear-guard stand at Ringgold Gap halted Grant's pursuit. The Union troops returned to Chattanooga; the Confederate Army went into winter quarters at Dalton, Ga.

CHAUTAUQUA MOVEMENT. In an assembly held on Lake Chautauqua, N.Y., Aug. 4–18, 1874, John H. Vincent, a Methodist clergyman of New York, and Lewis Miller of Akron, Ohio, planned a course in Sunday-school organization, management, and teaching, and study of the Bible, which rapidly grew into a permanent summer colony. In 1878 the Literary and Scientific Circle (home-study courses) was launched. In 1879 a school for teachers in secular subjects and a school of languages, the College of Liberal Arts, were opened. Hundreds of local assemblies appeared in the United States and Canada. At least two of these, the Catholic Summer School at Lake Champlain and the Jewish Chautauqua Society at Atlantic City, N.J., have been permanent.

CHECK CURRENCY. Bank deposits against which the owner may write a check. The check itself is a type of draft, an order to the bank to pay. Checks may be written only against demand deposits, not against time deposits. Although extensively used for making payments in New York and other large cities as far back as the beginning of the 19th century, checks did not settle an amount of business equal to that settled by bank notes and coin until about 1853.

The Civil War was a turning point in the use of checks. Federal laws imposed high taxes, which ended the use of state bank notes and also led national banks to prefer deposit lending and educate their customers in the use of checks. By the end of the century 85–90 percent of all business was settled by checks, and this was still true in the late 20th century.

CHECKOFF. An arrangement by which union dues are to be deducted at the payroll source. Such an agreement is designed to simplify the collection of revenues. Because those agreements involve a third party—the union member—apprehension has been common that they are unfair to the payer. Section 320 of the Labor Management Relations Act of 1947 requires that if a checkoff agreement is negotiated, an authorization for the payroll deduction must be made in writing by each employee.

The checkoff agreement was first secured by Ohio miners in 1889. That clause was later formalized in the area agreements of bituminous miners after their sweeping strike victory in 1897. Unions supported their position by pointing out that for years operators had been deducting money from employee pay to cover such costs as rent, medical and hospital service, and purchases in company stores. The mineworkers attempted to extend their checkoff agreement by insisting, in 1904, that it be extended to all men employed by the employer, not to union members alone. In more recent times, unions have based their claims to fee payments at the payroll source from nonmembers on the grounds that they are obligated, under federal law, to represent both members and nonmembers in the bargaining unit equally. (*See also* Closed Shop; Labor; Taft-Hartley Act.)

CHECKS AND BALANCES. The separation of powers of government that was the underlying principle upon which the U. S. government was created by the Convention of 1787. This theory consists in setting off legislative and executive departments from each other and the courts against both. Each department is supposed to operate as far as possible within a separate sphere of administration. In order to prevent executive aggression, the system of checks and balances was introduced and provison was made for a federal judiciary. Furthermore, it was provided that the Senate and House of Representatives should act as checks upon each other in the national Congress.

CHEMICAL INDUSTRY. In 1608 the London Company sent eight Poles and Germans "skilled in making tar, pitch, glass, and potashes" to Jamestown, and in the same year some of these products were exported from the colony to London. By 1614 there was a saltworks near Jamestown, and an attempt was being made to produce saltpeter. These projects foundered, with the other enterprises of Jamestown; but there was a saltworks in Plymouth colony in the 1620's, and a glassworks in 1639. The Dutch had a distillery at New Amsterdam in 1638, and Salem had one ten years later. John Winthrop, Jr., organized a company to produce saltpeter in 1650, and the Connecticut colony granted him a monopoly on the production of a variety of minerals and chemicals. The Pennsylvania colony established a lime kiln (1681), a tannery (1683), and a paper mill (1690). Pottery manufacture was established at Burlington, Vt., in 1680. Calico printing was undertaken in Boston in 1712, and soap manufacture in 1716. Sugar refining began in New York in 1730.

The English Navigation Acts of 1661 were intended to reserve certain raw materials for England and to discourage colonial manufacture of goods exported by the mother country. Despite such constraints the success of this system was far from complete. At the time of the Revolution, the Continental Congress urged the quick establishment of the whole range of chemical industries, and many of the new states encouraged them with bounties. Such vital materials as salt and saltpeter were forthcoming in sufficient quantities. After the war Philadelphia became the center of a small, but variegated, chemical industry. Samuel Wetherill began the manufacture of white lead in 1789. In 1793, John Harrison constructed a manufactory for sulfuric acid. In 1801, Adam Seybert began to make mercurials.

In 1797 salt production began at the Onondaga reservation (near Syracuse, N.Y.) and Kanawha, W. Va. The Du Pont powder works was established near Wilmington, Del., in 1802. A substantial vitriol factory was established at Strafford, Vt., in 1807, and in 1811 the first alum works opened at Cape Sable, Md.

In 1815, U.S. chemical manufacturers initiated an often repeated appeal for tariff protection, alternately favored and rejected by the government into the 20th century. In 1816, Baltimore introduced the manufacture of coal gas for street illumination. In time, nearly every town had its gasworks.

In 1840–42 the virtues of phosphorus in fertilizers were publicized in Europe; manufacturers began treating bones, the main source of phosphorus, with sulfuric acid to produce superphosphate. Then mineral sources of phosphorus were found, first in Europe and next in large deposits in South Carolina and Florida. The first sulfuric acid works in the South was built in Charleston in 1868, to make superphosphate. In the 1860's the petroleum industry began its dramatic expansion, and with it grew a demand for sulfuric acid, which was used in removing impurities from the oil.

The sulfuric acid industry used sulfur as a raw material. Sulfur was widespread, but not in sufficient quantity. The problem was solved to some degree by the development of sulfur production as a by-product industry of metallurgy, where sulfide ores were often exploited. "Native" sulfur deposits were found in the 1860's on the Louisiana coast; but attempts to mine the deposits were repeatedly frustrated by quicksand until, in the 1890's, Hermann Frasch developed a method for pumping the sulfur out in a liquid state.

Plastics were another peculiarly American specialty. As early as 1819 Seth Boyden of Newark, N.J., invented patent leather, a leather coated with linseed oil. A more famous process of creating plastic was Charles Goodyear's successful vulcanization (treatment with sulfur) of rubber (1839). In 1854, J. Cutting of Boston patented nitrocellulose film for photography. Forming the material under heat and pressure (with the initial objective of making artificial billiard balls), John W. Hyatt of Albany introduced Celluloid about 1870. Made into dentures, collars, handles for toilet articles, and photographic film, Celluloid became a household word and ushered in the age of plastics.

The next plastic material to achieve wide use was introduced in 1909 by a Belgian immigrant, Leo H. Baekeland. Bakelite, made from phenol and formaldehyde, appeared just in time to fill the requirement of the new radio industry for insulating material.

The complex Solvay soda process was introduced in the

United States in 1884 in the Onondaga salt region. A decade later, yet another process, based on the inventions of Hamilton Y. Castner and consisting of the electrolysis of salt brine to yield sodium, chlorine, and their derivatives (such as soda), was installed by the Mathieson Alkali Company at Saltville, Va. By 1909 the United States was self-sufficient in soda.

The development of a practical dynamo in the 1870's led to the development of a commercially useful electric furnace by E. H. Cowles and A. H. Cowles (1885); the introduction of the most important process for making aluminum, by C. M. Hall (1886); the manufacture of bromine on a large scale at Midland, Mich., by H. H. Dow (1889); the introduction of carborundum (silicon carbide) by one of Thomas Edison's assistants, Edward G. Acheson (1891); and the commercial production of calcium carbide at Spray, N.C., by T. L. Willson (1893).

By 1900 the U.S. chemical industry's only significant chemical exports were sulfur and wood-distillation products. Fertilizer manufacture, the largest sector of the U.S. chemical industry, was almost entirely based on the production of superphosphate, for which the cotton and tobacco farmers were the chief market, and it relied on foreign sources for potash and nitrate fertilizers. An intense search for domestic mineral sources was rewarded in the 1920's; successfully exploited from 1931, underground deposits near Carlsbad, N.Mex., have since satisfied U.S. potash requirements.

The only significant U.S. firm in the new manufacture of synthetic organic chemicals was the then small Monsanto Chemical Company of St. Louis. Finally, highly sophisticated processes were being developed in Europe for nitrogen fixation—that is, for the conversion of atmospheric nitrogen into a chemically active form. For some time after the outbreak of war in 1914, dyes and drugs were imported from Germany by submarine. But spurred by the war, the U.S. government for the first time gave massive support to a chemical enterprise—namely, the attempt to create an industry for the fixation of nitrogen. By about 1925 the United States had an important industry for nitrogen fixation, and by 1928, thanks in part to the confiscation of the German dye patents, it was largely self-sufficient in dyes.

Thereafter, the U.S. industry came to resemble that of Europe, with large firms producing diverse, but interrelated, products, with an emphasis on complex chemical synthesis instead of the simple processing of raw materials. Amalgamation began in the fertilizer industry. In 1899 twelve manufacturers joined to form the General Chemical Company, which became the Allied Chemical and Dye Company in 1920. Meanwhile, the Du Pont Company began to interest itself about 1908 in products other than explosives, beginning with those using nitrocellulose (Celluloid, paint).

Wartime shortages, followed by preparations for another war in the 1930's, resulted in some spectacular chemical developments, especially the development of artificial rubber and synthetic gasoline from coal. New plastic materials were introduced, the most notable being the plastic fibers that ultimately supplanted cotton as the most popular textile material: viscose rayon and nylon. The element silicon began to yield its secrets in 1940, with the first of many hitherto unknown compounds called silicones. Thomas Midgley of the General Motors Corporation, who had developed ethyl gasoline, announced in 1930 the development of the refrigerant Freon, a compound of carbon, hydrogen, and fluorine. In the 1940's, in connection with the Manhattan Project, the U.S. chemical industry made fluorine in large quanties, and from this came the outstandingly corrosion-resistant fluorocarbons (such as Teflon). Following World War II, the fastest-expanding fields of the chemical industry have been plastics, pharmaceuticals, and petrochemicals.

CHEMICAL WARFARE. Chemical warfare denotes an emphasis on weapons of area destruction such as gases, defoliants, and herbicides. The Hague Convention of 1899 and the Geneva Protocol of 1925 placed restrictions on the use of chemical weapons, and the latter forbade the employment of poisonous or other gases. Although the Protocol was not ratified by the U.S. Senate until Dec. 16, 1974, the United States generally abided by its provisions and, except for mass incendiary bombing in World War II, has carefully refrained from initiating chemical warfare. After World War II, U.S. reliance on active deterrents did spur the development of a large chemical-biological arsenal. The extensive employment of chemical weapons in Southeast Asia marked a major change in American chemical warfare policy. Both herbicides and "incapacitating" gases were used extensively throughout the 1960's, although the complete scope of their employment has remained secret.

CHEMISTRY. The American Revolution coincided with the chemical revolution. In 1756, William Smith began teaching natural philosophy, including some chemistry, at the College and Academy of Philadelphia (now the University of Pennsylvania). A similar course was initiated by James Madison at the College of William and Mary in 1774 and by Charles Morton at Harvard in 1787. At the College and Academy of Philadelphia medical school, founded 1765, John Morgan offered a course in chemistry and materia medica. Two years later, the physician James Smith began teaching the same subject at Kings College (Columbia). By 1800 Dartmouth and Princeton also had instruction in chemistry.

In the half-century after independence, the Philadelphia area was the chemical center of the new nation. In addition to the manufacture of drugs, paints, bleach, sulfuric acid, and other acids, within fifty miles of the city mills and factories were turning out iron, glass, bleached paper, and gunpowder. Philadelphia was also preeminent in chemical education. At the University of Pennsylvania a succession of professors of great ability taught chemistry: Benjamin Rush, Caspar Wistar, James Woodhouse, and Robert Hare. In the 1830's Philadelphia lost its preeminence, at first chiefly to New England and by midcentury Washington and New York. Benjamin Silliman of Yale had much to do with this. Beginning his career in 1803, Silliman went on for half a century writing texts, editing the *American Journal of Science,* and popularizing chemistry through public lectures and demonstrations. He was also a leader in promoting college programs specifically directed toward training chemists, and he convinced Yale to establish the Sheffield Scientific School in 1847. Benjamin Silliman, Jr., and Benjamin Pitkin Norton were the first chemists at Sheffield. Its first doctorate was awarded in 1863 to the celebrated Josiah Willard Gibbs.

Similar developments were occurring at Harvard, where the Lawrence Scientific School was established in 1847. Eben Horsford was its first chemistry professor. His successor, Oliver W. Gibbs, took a strong interest in scientific societies. He was one of the founders of the National Academy of Sciences (1863).

The American Chemical Society, founded in 1877, became a national organization in the 1890's. The *Journal of the American Chemical Society* took its place among the most important of its type in the world. In the late 19th century a few American chemists achieved international renown, notably J. W. Gibbs at Yale, who applied thermodynamics to chemical equilibria, and Theodore W. Richards of Harvard, who won the Nobel Prize in 1914 for his meticulous determination of atomic mass. The first decades of the 20th century were of extraordinary importance to both practical and theoretical chemistry. The structure of the atom was being worked out. Exciting new research was opening up in radiochemistry, photochemistry, crystallography, pharmacy, spectroscopy, solution theory, acid-base theory, stereochemistry, polymer chemistry, and nutrition. Robert A. Millikan measured the charge on the electron; and Gilbert N. Lewis and Irving Langmuir helped to explain covalent and ionic bonding.

These achievements and the pressures of World War I were powerful stimuli. In the sudden absence of vital drugs and dyes from Germany and with huge orders for explosives and other chemicals for war pouring in, the entire chemical know-how of the country had to be mobilized. Strenuous efforts achieved spectacular results in purity, chemical variety, and quantity of production.

In nuclear chemistry Ernest O. Lawrence and Robert Jemison Van de Graaff pioneered in developing accelerators for probing into the structure of atoms and for making artificial isotopes. This work evolved to the making of elements not naturally found on the earth. The first were neptunium and plutonium, synthesized by Glenn T. Seaborg and his associates in 1944 at the University of California, Berkeley. Radioactive isotopes and deuterium, discovered by Harold Urey in 1932, proved invaluable in establishing reaction mechanisms and metabolic pathways. Willard F. Libby showed in 1946 how one could date ancient materials by the carbon-14 method. Scientists worked feverishly in secret during World War II to convert nuclear fission into an awesome weapon.

Significant contributions to organic chemistry were made between 1920 and 1950 by Linus Pauling and Moses Gomberg. Polymer chemists produced synthetic rubbers, numerous plastics, filaments like nylon, and epoxy cements. Other researchers determined the highly complex structure of various plant and animal components and secretions.

Inorganic chemistry came alive in the 1930's with the intensive investigation of coordination and chelation compounds by Kenneth Pitzer, Joel Hildebrand, John C. Bailar, and many others. Silicone was developed by the General Electric Company in the 1940's. In 1933, Pauling predicted that the so-called inert gases could react with fluorine and other halogens. In 1962 this was accomplished by Neil Bartlett in Canada. Geochemistry and cosmic chemistry have attracted many able researchers since the 1950's. The same is true for environmental chemistry, a field in which extremely sensitive methods of analysis have been devised. American analytical chemists have contributed substantially to spectroscopy, chromatography, ion exchange, and nuclear magnetic resonance procedures. But in both scientific and human importance the greatest advances from the 1930's into the 1970's have been in biochemistry (*see* Biochemistry).

CHEQUAMEGON BAY. On the southern coast of Lake Superior; site of the first dwelling occupied by white men in what is now Wisconsin. French traders built a hut on the west shore, probably in 1658. In 1693, Madeline, the largest of the islands in the bay (Apostle Islands), was occupied by a fort built by Pierre Le Sueur; it was abandoned before 1700. In 1718 a French fort, La Pointe, was built on the island, where Louis Denis de la Ronde had fur-trading and copper interests. A French garrison was there until 1759. The first English trader here was Alexander Henry, whose partner, Jean Baptiste Cadotte, founded a permanent trading post.

CHERBOURG. The capture of this French city, held by the Germans since June 1940, by American forces three weeks after the Normandy landings of June 6, 1944, gave the Allies their first great port in northwestern Europe. Cherbourg was needed to sustain the growing forces of the invasion. The Germans fought stubbornly, demolished the port, and blocked the harbor channels, but surrendered on June 26.

CHEROKEE. *See* **Five Civilized Tribes.**

***CHEROKEE NATION* V. *GEORGIA*,** 5 Peters 1 (1831). By a series of treaties the Cherokee ceded certain lands to the federal government, were guaranteed the remainder of their territory, and were recognized as a nation with their own laws. After the discovery of gold on Cherokee land in 1829 and encroachment by settlers, the Cherokee appealed to the Supreme Court (Dec. 12, 1830), to prevent Georgia from enforcing its laws within the Cherokee Nation. The majority opinion held that since the Cherokee were not U.S. citizens nor, as contended by them, a foreign nation, the Court lacked jurisdiction.

CHEROKEE RIVER. *See* **Tennessee River.**

CHEROKEE STRIP. Improperly applied to an area of about 12,000 square miles in Oklahoma. Guaranteed to the Cherokee by treaties of 1828 and 1833 as an outlet, it was not to be occupied for homes. The treaty of 1866 compelled the Cherokee Nation to sell portions to friendly Indians. The strip was leased by the Cherokee Nation in 1883 to the Cherokee Strip Livestock Association. In 1891 the United States purchased the Cherokee Strip for $8,595,736.12. Opened by a land run on Sept. 16, 1893, it became part of the territory of Oklahoma.

CHEROKEE TRAIL (Trappers' Trail). Laid out and marked in 1848 by Lt. Abraham Buford. It extended from the vicinity of Fort Gibson up the Arkansas River to the mouth of the Cimarron and up the latter stream to a point in northwestern Oklahoma. From here it ran west to the Sante Fe Trail, joining it at Middle Cimarron Spring.

CHEROKEE WARS (1776–81). The Cherokee had generally sided with the English against the French, but encroachment of the British upon their lands provoked the Cherokee in 1760 into a two-year war with Carolina colonists. Agreements were subsequently approved by some Cherokee chiefs to cede lands to the Carolinas, Georgia, and Virginia.

During the Revolution, the Cherokee sided with the British and were soon engaged in a general war on the frontiers of the Carolinas, Virginia, and Georgia. Punitive expeditions of militiamen converged upon the Cherokee. Nearly all the Cherokee towns were plundered and burned. Several hundred Cherokee fled to British protection in Florida. Cherokee elders sued for peace in June and July 1777, at the price of further cessions of Cherokee lands.

The dissident and more warlike faction, the Chickamauga, separated from the rest of the tribe, pushing down the Tennessee River and establishing new settlements on Chickamauga Creek. In 1779 the Overhill Cherokee joined the Chickamauga and some Creek in cooperating with the British in attacking some colonial settlements. Again a Virginia–North Carolina expedition devastated the Cherokee towns. In spring 1781 a treaty with the Cherokee confirmed the land cessions of 1777. The treaty was thereafter strictly observed by all the Cherokee except the Chickamauga.

CHERRY VALLEY MASSACRE (Nov. 11, 1778). An attack by Col. John Butler's Rangers, a Loyalist regiment, and Indians under the Mohawk leader Joseph Brant, on the colonial outpost at Cherry Valley in the upper Susquehanna Valley. Thirty colonials were killed, all the buildings burned, and cattle taken.

CHESAPEAKE AND DELAWARE CANAL. As early as 1764 a survey was made for a canal route between Chesapeake and Delaware bays. The canal, thirteen and five-eighths miles long, with three locks, was built 1825–29. A cut ninety feet deep through earth and stone was the heaviest engineering project yet undertaken in America. In 1919 the government purchased it and made it into a sea-level ship canal.

CHESAPEAKE AND OHIO CANAL (the "Old Ditch"). A joint project of the United States, Maryland, and Virginia; the legal successor of the Potomac Company in the attempt to connect the Chesapeake Bay with the Ohio River. The plan was to construct a series of locks and canals around the rapids and falls of the Potomac from Georgetown to Cumberland. From there the Ohio was to be reached at the Youghiogheny. Ground was broken in 1828, and the canal was completed to Cumberland by 1850. The corporation was not successful in reaching the Ohio because of the inherent difficulty of the task and because of competition from the Baltimore and Ohio Railroad, which reached Wheeling about 1852.

CHESAPEAKE AND OHIO RAILROAD. *See* **Railroads, Sketches of Principal Lines.**

CHESAPEAKE CAPES, BATTLE OF. *See* **Virginia Capes, Battle of.**

CHESAPEAKE-LEOPARD **INCIDENT** (June 22, 1807). Off Hampton Roads, Va., the American frigate *Chesapeake* was stopped by the British *Leopard* and ordered to surrender four deserters. Upon refusal by Capt. James Barron, the *Leopard* opened fire. The American vessel was unprepared for battle and replied with only one gun. After the *Chesapeake* had been irreparably injured and its crew had three men killed and twenty wounded, Barron surrendered. The British recovered only one deserter, but three American seamen were also removed. The British captain forced the *Chesapeake* to creep back into port. Barron was court-martialed and suspended for five years. Negotiations were prolonged by Great Britain until 1811 when it disavowed the act and returned two of the Americans, the third having died.

CHESAPEAKE-SHANNON **FIGHT** (June 1, 1813). The U.S. frigate *Chesapeake,* commanded by Capt. James Lawrence with an untrained crew, sailed out of Boston. At 5:45 P.M. it met the British frigate *Shannon,* commanded by Capt. Philip Vere Broke with a highly trained crew of 330 men. By 5:55, all the American officers were dead or wounded and the crew was in a panic. Lawrence, dying, gave his last order, "Don't give up the ship." Leading his crew, Broke boarded, and by 6:05 had taken the *Chesapeake.*

CHEYENNE. The Cheyenne Indians ranged, in the 17th century, through western South Dakota, eastern Montana, and northern Wyoming; a branch of the tribe pushed well into Colorado. They appeared on the Minnesota River before 1700. The Cheyenne pushed into the Missouri River valley by 1800. In the setting of the high Plains, they abandoned farming and pottery making and, becoming superior horsemen, took over the classic Plains encampment organization.

Between 1832 and 1851, some Cheyenne settled on the upper Arkansas River at Bent's Fort; others remained near the headwaters of the Platte and Yellowstone. The southern groups fought the Kiowa but later allied with them, while the northern segment was involved with the Dakota, fighting Gen. George Armstrong Custer.

CHEYENNE (Wyo.). Capital of Wyoming since 1869; established in 1867 by the Union Pacific Railroad. It became the chief outfitting point for gold seekers flocking into the Sweetwater region and the Black Hills, and, as home of the Wyoming Stock Growers' Association, the administrative and social metropolis of the cattlemen's range of the northern Plains. The collapse of the cattle boom of the 1880's ended its great days. The population in 1980 was 47,283.

CHICAGO (Ill.). Second largest city in the United States, located on Lake Michigan, in northeastern Illinois, at the mouth of the Chicago River. The French explorers Louis Jolliet and Jacques Marquette were the first known white visitors, in September 1673. The first permanent settlement was not founded until about 1790. With the Treaty of Greenville in 1795, a six-square-mile tract at the mouth of the Chicago River was ceded to the United States, and in 1803 Fort Dearborn was erected. Its evacuation during the War of 1812 precipitated a massacre by the Potawatomi. By 1825 there were only about forty inhabitants. A final treaty in 1833 by which the Indians ceded land claims gave impetus to a massive wave of immigration. The population grew to 4,170 by 1837, when Chicago was formally incorporated as a city.

In 1848 the Illinois and Michigan Canal linked Chicago with the Mississippi River system and the eastern seaboard, and the spreading web of railroads established Chicago as the country's main freight transfer point. Soon there were blast furnaces and factories manufacturing agricultural machinery and railroad sleeping cars. Livestock, hauled to the mile-square Union Stock Yards, was slaughtered and packed at the Armour and Swift companies' plants.

On the evening of Oct. 8, 1871, disaster struck with the great Chicago Fire, the cause of which remains undetermined (*see* Chicago Fire). Reconstruction began immediately, following the former grid pattern of streets and conforming with modern fire regulations.

Expanding industries offered a breeding ground for strikes and labor unrest after the Panic of 1873 and the ensuing depression. Meanwhile, architectural innovations transformed the city, while ghetto shanties housed a great wave of foreign immigration. With Prohibition came bootlegging, gang warfare, lawlessness, and municipal corruption. The administration of Mayor Edward J. Kelley (1933–47) saw the establishment of a powerful political machine that initiated serious reform. Mayor Richard J. Daley, elected to an unprecedented sixth four-year term in 1975, was also head of the Cook County Democratic Party, the nation's largest urban political machine. Daley and Chicago hosted the tumultuous 1968 Democratic National Convention (*see* Chicago Seven). Daley died in 1976, and in 1979 his former associate, Jane Byrne, became the city's first woman mayor after receiving 82 percent of the vote.

Chicago is the Midwest's leading economic and cultural center, with a population of 3,005,072 (metropolitan area 7,102,328) in 1980. Although the Union Stock Yards ended meat-packing activities by the early 1970's, Chicago remains a major center of food-processing and surpasses Pittsburgh as the leading producer of iron and steel. The manufacture of electrical equipment, machinery, metal products, and chemicals, and publishing and printing also are important.

CHICAGO AND NORTHWESTERN RAILWAY. *See* **Railroads, Sketches of Principal Lines.**

CHICAGO BOARD OF TRADE. *See* **"Pit."**

CHICAGO, BURLINGTON AND QUINCY RAILROAD. *See* **Railroads, Sketches of Principal Lines: Burlington Northern.**

CHICAGO DRAINAGE CANAL. In 1886 an investigation by a city council commission resulted in construction (1893–1900) of a drainage canal from Chicago to Lockport, whereby the flow of the Chicago River was reversed and the city sewage, diluted with water from Lake Michigan, was sent down the Illinois. Diversion of the lake water provoked opposition of adjoining states and Canada, finally inducing the federal government to compel the city to provide other means of sewage disposal.

CHICAGO FIRE. In 1871 a scorching wind blew up from the plains of the Southwest week after week and made the structures of pine-built Chicago dry as tinder. Fire began on Sunday evening, Oct. 8, 1871. Where it started is clear; how it started no one knows. The traditional story is that Mrs. O'Leary went out to the barn to milk her cow; her lamp was upset and cow, stable, and Chicago were engulfed in one common ruin. But Mrs. O'Leary testified under oath that she was safe abed and knew nothing about the fire until she was called by a friend. Five square miles, including the central business district of the city, were burned, over 17,500 buildings destroyed, and 100,000 people rendered homeless. Direct property loss was about $200 million. The loss of human lives is estimated at 200–300.

CHICAGO, MILWAUKEE AND SAINT PAUL RAILWAY COMPANY V. MINNESOTA, 134 U.S. 418 (1890). An act of the Minnesota legislature (1887) established the Minnesota Railroad and Warehouse Commission and defined its duties in relation to common carriers. The state supreme court held that rates published by the commission should be final. The U.S. Supreme Court declared the act unconstitutional because it deprived a railroad of property without due process of law and deprived it of equal protection of the law.

CHICAGO, MILWAUKEE, SAINT PAUL AND PACIFIC RAILROAD. *See* **Railroads, Sketches of Principal Lines.**

CHICAGO PORTAGE. The Des Plaines River runs close to the head of the Chicago River; over the land between, a traveler could transport his boat from the Great Lakes–St. Lawrence to the Mississippi River system. During spring floods boats might sometimes pass between Lake Michigan and the Illinois River without any land carriage, while in dry seasons a portage of 100 miles, to LaSalle, was often necessary. In 1848 completion of the Illinois and Michigan Canal ended the importance of the Chicago Portage.

CHICAGO ROAD. Early highway from Detroit to Chicago. For generations it was an important Indian trail, the explorer Robert Cavelier, Sieur de La Salle, in 1680 being probably the first white man to travel it. In 1824 Congress appropriated money for the survey of roads of national importance and the president allocated one-third of the entire sum to surveying a military highway connecting Detroit with Fort Dearborn at Chicago. From about 1830 on, thousands moved to the Northwest over the Chicago Road.

CHICAGO, ROCK ISLAND AND PACIFIC RAILROAD. *See* **Railroads, Sketches of Principal Lines.**

CHICAGO SANITARY DISTRICT CASE, *Wisconsin* v. *Illinois,* 289 U.S. 395, 710 (1933). The increasing diversion of Great Lakes waters by the city of Chicago to carry off sewage through the long-established drainage canal was claimed to be lowering lake levels, thus impairing transportation facilities of bordering states. In 1930 the Supreme Court had fixed maximum diversion at a point below that necessary to continued use of the drainage canal system alone, thus requiring the construction of sewage disposal works, but the city and state delayed. The 1933 opinion settled finally the authority of the United States to intervene to enforce action by a state.

CHICAGO SEVEN (also Chicago Eight or Chicago Ten). Following rioting at the Chicago Democratic convention of 1968, Abbie Hoffman, Rennie Davis, John Froines, Tom Hayden, Lee Weiner, David Dellinger, Jerry Rubin, and Bobby Seale were indicted for crossing state lines to riot or to conspire to use interstate commerce to induce rioting. The trial exploded into a marathon (1969–70). Judge Julius J. Hoffman's obvious bias provoked defiant behavior from the defendants. A mistrial was finally declared in the case of Bobby Seale. William M. Kunstler, chief defense lawyer, became a hero to some for utilizing the court as a political forum. The jury ultimately acquitted all defendants on the conspiracy charge and found only five guilty of crossing state lines to riot. These convictions were reversed on appeal, and the government decided to drop the charges.

CHICAGO TREATIES. In August 1821, 3,000 Indians conferred at Chicago with the U.S. government, which desired to procure from the Potawatomi and allied tribes the southwestern part of Michigan. They proved amenable.

In 1833 the government wished to acquire several million acres lying between Lake Michigan and Rock River in northeastern Illinois and southeastern Wisconsin and to remove Indians living there to new homes west of the Mississippi. Several thousand Indians attended the council. Eventually, the Indians moved from the region.

CHICAGO, UNIVERSITY OF. Founded in 1890 by John D. Rockefeller as a Baptist university, it opened its doors on Oct. 1, 1892. Growth was rapid under the first president, William Rainey Harper (1890–1906), and the university gained a reputation as a center of research. Harper established junior and senior college divisions, of two years each, which prevailed until 1931, when the Chicago plan was instituted. Under the Chicago plan, yearlong integrated courses covering broad fields of knowledge were developed; students met the requirements for the bachelor's degree by passing, either through comprehensive examinations or placement tests, fourteen required courses. The plan was extended in 1941 to provide a four-year liberal arts curriculum, and modified in 1954.

CHICKAMAUGA, BATTLE OF (Sept. 19–20, 1863). A Civil War battle in the valley of Chickamauga Creek between the Army of the Cumberland, under Union Gen. W. S. Rosecrans, and an inferior Confederate force under Gen. Braxton Bragg. Bragg's poorly coordinated attacks on the first day were matched by Rosecrans's blunders on the second. Gen. George H. Thomas, commanding the Union left, with the aid of troops under Gordon Granger, held the army together and after nightfall withdrew into Chattanooga.

CHICKASAW. *See* **Five Civilized Tribes.**

CHICKASAW BLUFFS. The high bank of the Mississippi River at the mouth of the Wolf River, site of several forts dating from as early as 1682. Much intrigue with the Chickasaw centered around this post, especially during the Spanish occupation of Louisiana. Near Fort Pickering, John Overton settled the town of Memphis in 1820.

CHICKASAW BLUFFS, BATTLE OF (Dec. 29, 1862). Union Gen. W. T. Sherman's attack from the Chickasaw Bayou, off the Yazoo River in Mississippi, was part of a threefold federal plan to reduce and capture Vicksburg. The repulse of Sherman's troops at Chickasaw Bluffs demonstrated the futility of any attack from the Yazoo.

CHICKASAW COUNCIL HOUSE, TREATY OF (Sept. 20, 1816). Negotiated by Andrew Jackson and other commissioners, it promised an annuity to the Chickasaw Nation, money and land to chiefs and warriors, and exclusion of peddlers from their country. In exchange, the Chickasaw ceded land on both sides of the Tennessee River.

CHICKASAW-CREEK WAR. On Feb. 13, 1793, the Chickasaw declared war against the Creek, to avenge the murder of two hunters. Piomingo, a Chickasaw chief attributing the murders to Creek resentment at the Chickasaw refusal to join an alliance against the Anglo-Americans, sought U.S. aid. The government promised support in return for peace and friendship, but refused armed intervention. On Oct. 28, Spanish officials of Louisiana and West Florida engineered a treaty of the Chickasaw, Creek, and other southern tribes with one another and with Spain.

CHICKASAW-FRENCH WAR (1736–40). Supplied with guns and ammunition by English traders, the Chickasaw Indians by 1734 had virtually halted French travel on the Mississippi. The governor of the Louisiana colony, Jean Baptiste Le Moyne, Sieur de Bienville, in 1736 planned a two-pronged attack against them. A French-Choctaw army moved north from Mobile, while another army under Maj. Pierre d'Artaguette, descended the Mississippi from Illinois. D'Artaguette's troops were wiped out by the Chickasaw and Bienville's force was decisively routed at the Battle of Ackia.

During Bienville's second campaign in 1739–40 troops were assembled from both Illinois and Louisiana at Chickasaw Bluffs. No attack was attempted, however, since the French were stricken with fever. The Chickasaw, mistaking a small party of French for the advance party of a much larger force, nevertheless agreed to peace.

CHICKASAW OLD FIELDS. On the north bank of the Tennessee River, four miles below the mouth of the Flint River, in present Madison County, Ala., where the Chickasaw fixed their easternmost villages when they migrated east to the Mississippi. The Chickasaw defended their claim to the adjacent land by driving out the Shawnee in 1714 and by overwhelming the Cherokee in 1769. The Old Fields were claimed by the Chickasaw until 1805, when they were included in a land cession to the United States.

CHICKASAW TREATY (1783). Negotiated by Virginia's commissioners with the Chickasaw, at Nashborough (Nashville), removing the claim of the tribe to territory between the Cumberland River and the ridge dividing the waters of that river from those of the Tennessee. Although failing to obtain a cession of western Kentucky, the commissioners, treating on North Carolina soil, cleared for North Carolina the Indian title to one of the most fertile stretches in the West and cemented friendship between settlers and the Chickasaw.

CHICORA. A portion of northern Spanish Florida, in the present-day Carolinas, thought to have been inhabited in the 16th century by Indians of great wealth but of strange form, some having tails, others having feet so large they could be used as umbrellas, and some having an eye in the middle of their chests.

CHIEF JOSEPH'S CAMPAIGN. *See* **Nez Perce War.**

CHIHUAHUA TRAIL. In the late 16th century Spanish colonization had advanced from Mexico City northward to Santa Fe. Until Mexican independence (1821) all contact between New Mexico and the outer world was restricted to this 1,500-mile trail. Superseded by railroads, the highway was revived as a great automobile highway of Mexico.

CHILD LABOR. Once thought to have been virtually eliminated except in agriculture; again became a social issue in the 1970's. Juvenile employment probably existed in the spinning schools established early in the colonies. Textile mills founded after the Revolution are known to have employed children for excessively long hours. Two-fifths of the factory workers in New England in 1832 were reported to be children. Agitation for compulsory school-attendance legislation had appeared in the previous decade. In the 1840's Connecticut, Massachusetts, and Pennsylvania passed laws limiting the hours of employment of minors in textile factories.

The child labor problem had grown to the point of national significance by 1870. The Knights of Labor projected a campaign for child labor legislation in the 1870's and 1880's that resulted in many state laws. Insistence on improved standards of legislation and their adequate enforcement led to the formation of the National Child Labor Committee in 1904 to promote the welfare of America's working children. By 1920, census reports began to reflect a decline in child labor.

The Fair Labor Standards Act (1938) set the minimum working age at fourteen for employment outside of school hours in nonmanufacturing, at sixteen for employment during school hours in interstate commerce, and at eighteen for occupations called hazardous by the secretary of labor. The Public Contracts Act (1936) set the minimum age at sixteen years for boys and at eighteen for girls employed in firms that supply goods under federal contract. The Sugar Act (1937) set the minimum age at fourteen for employment in cultivating and harvesting sugar beets and cane.

Since the passage of the 1938 act and of a 1948 amendment prohibiting children from farm work during school hours almost no modification has been made in the federal law. In May 1974 the first major amendments covering children who work in agriculture prohibited work by any child under twelve on a farm covered by minimum-wage regulations. Twelve- and thirteen-year-olds would be permitted to work on such farms only with written permission of their parents. In 1977 new legislation permitted children between ten and twelve to work on farms during summer "under certain conditions."

CHILDREN'S COURTS. *See* **Juvenile Courts.**

CHILLICOTHE. One of four tribal divisions of the Shawnee. Also the chief town of the tribe and some half dozen other places bore this designation. Three were located in Ohio. The first is the Chillicothe of Dunmore's War. Better known was the "Old Chillicothe" on the Little Miami, north of present Xenia. Another was on the Great Miami at Piqua.

CHILLICOTHE JUNTO. A group of Chillicothe (Ohio) Jeffersonian Republican politicians who brought about the admission of Ohio as a state (1803).

CHIMNEY ROCK. A landmark visible at forty miles from any direction in Morrill County in western Nebraska. The peak is 4,242 feet high.

CHINA, U.S. ARMED FORCES IN. The Chinese Revolution of 1911 brought a reinforcement of foreign garrisons in China. A battalion-sized U.S. Marine legation guard was at Peking and the Fifteenth U.S. Infantry Regiment was at Tientsin. Elements of the Asiatic Fleet frequented the treaty ports, and a river patrol was established on the Yangtze. In the 1920's there were periodic additions to U.S. garrisons in China. Sino-Japanese hostilities beginning in 1931 caused further deployments of U.S. troops to China. In December 1937 the U.S. gunboat *Panay* was sunk in the Yangtze by Japanese air attack. In 1938 the Sixth Marines departed, as did the Fifteenth U.S. Infantry from Tientsin. The Fourth Marines left Shanghai in late November 1941.

The China-Burma-India (CBI) Theater was created in January 1942 with Chiang Kai-shek as commander in chief and Lt. Gen. Joseph W. Stilwell as his chief of staff. Maj. Gen. Claire L. Chennault, who had organized the American Volunteer Corps ("Flying Tigers"), was given command of the U.S. China Air Task Force, which later became the Fourteenth Air Force. In May 1944, B-29's were deployed to Chinese airfields from which they could reach Manchuria, Korea, and Japan itself. The Japanese reacted with a sixteen-division offensive that overran most of the airfields, causing the B-29's to be withdrawn to India. Chiang asked for Stilwell's recall. The CBI was split into two theaters—China and India-Burma—and Lt. Gen. Albert C. Wedemeyer was sent to replace Stilwell in China.

With the end of the war, the 55,000-man Third Marine Amphibious Corps was sent to North China. In January 1946, Gen. George C. Marshall arrived to arbitrate between the Nationalists and Communists, but he failed. The U.S. Marine occupation force in China was reduced until by the spring of 1949 just two battalions were left. By the end of June, the last marine and naval forces had left Tsing-tao.

CHINA, U.S. RELATIONS WITH. In 1789 fifteen American vessels were carrying on trade with China, seen by Americans as a great, ancient, and exotic culture devoted to the arts and sciences. Once the seafaring Yankees of the Canton trade established actual contact with the Chinese, American attitudes changed drastically. Merchants and missionaries now began to see China as a backward nation.

The first American emissary to China was Caleb Cushing, who in 1844 arrived with four naval vessels to formalize the first Sino-American treaty, which granted the United States commercial privileges equal to those granted to Britain. In 1899 Secretary of State John Hay dispatched a circular memorandum in which he asked England, Russia, Germany, France, Italy, and Japan to observe trade equality for everyone. The "Open Door notes" were quickly overtaken by events when, in June 1900, the Boxers laid siege to Peking. By August 1900 an international relief expedition, including 2,500 American troops, was on its way to break the siege.

The U.S. attitude of moral superiority gave way to an age of alliance during the tenure of the Nationalist government of Sun Yat-sen and Chiang Kai-shek on the mainland of China. Up until World War II, most Americans perceived the two Nationalist leaders in a very favorable light. Only during the civil war of 1945–49, when Chiang Kai-shek's mandate began to slip, did American disillusionment begin to set in. A mission headed by Gen. George C. Marshall to mediate between Mao and Chiang failed.

When the Communists took over the mainland in 1949 and drove Chiang to Formosa, most Americans perceived this event as a victory of evil over good. This was reflected in the determination of the American government during the next twenty-three years not to recognize the Communist regime, to oppose its entry into the United Nations, and to maintain a military alliance with the Chiang Kai-shek regime on Formosa. In late 1950, Chinese Communist soldiers intervened in the war in Korea and encountered U.S. troops. This encounter lasted for almost two years and ended in a stalemate.

President Richard Nixon reversed U.S. policy with his historic trip to Peking in 1972. American attitudes toward mainland China began to mellow once again. Exchanges between athletes, scholars, journalists, and commercial interests began to develop. (In October 1971 the People's Republic of China had been seated in the United Nations and the Taiwan regime ousted.) In 1973 the United States opened a liaison office in Peking, and on Jan. 1, 1979, full diplomatic relations were established; diplomatic relations and a defense treaty with Taiwan were terminated, but more than fifty other agreements with Taiwan continued in effect. In the early 1980's the U.S.-Chinese relations were businesslike, without serious frictions. In the meantime the American defense treaty with Taiwan remained intact, although the alliance was no longer widely proclaimed to the American public.

***CHINA CLIPPER*.** The first hydroplane in the San Francisco–Manila transpacific service. This airliner took off from Alameda, near San Francisco, for the first transpacific mail flight on Nov. 22, 1935.

***CHINA* INCIDENT.** A World War I analogue of the *Trent* affair. In February 1916 a British cruiser removed thirty-eight enemy aliens, including fifteen reservists, from the American ship *China* in the Yellow Sea. The prisoners were released on American demand, but the British assertion that enemy reservists were legally liable to seizure from neutral vessels remained untested.

CHINA TRADE. In the years following the Revolution, American merchants, cut off from the West Indian trade, discovered new opportunities in the China trade. The early cargoes carried to China comprised chiefly silver dollars and North American ginseng. In 1787, John Kendrick in the *Columbia* and Robert Gray in the *Lady Washington* sailed from Boston for the northwest coast of America. Then Gray, with a load of sea otter peltries, continued to Canton. For the next two decades Americans exchanged clothing, hardware, and various knickknacks in the Northwest for sea otter and other furs. As sea otters gradually disappeared, traders shifted to seals. Sandalwood, obtained in Hawaii and other Pacific islands, also became an important trade item. American sea captains brought back tea, china, enameled ware, nankeens, and silks.

After the Opium War (1840–42) between Great Britain and China, China was forced to open four additional ports to British trade. Similar rights for Americans were obtained in 1844 by the Treaty of Wanghia.

CHINCH BUG. An agricultural pest that ranges over most of North America. Discovered in North Carolina in 1785, chinch bugs were first described in 1831 by Thomas Say.

CHINESE EXCLUSION ACTS. *See* **Chinese Immigration and Labor.**

CHINESE IMMIGRATION AND LABOR. The immigration of Chinese to the United States, almost exclusively from Kwantung Province, began just before the California gold rush of 1849. The Chinese formed an important segment of the labor force of California, the American West, and western Canada. Peak Chinese population in the 19th-century United States was about 125,000.

The presence of the Chinese immigrants aroused great antagonism among white workers. The anti-Chinese movement solidified the San Francisco–centered trade union movement in California, where the union label was devised to differentiate goods made by white, as opposed to Chinese, workers. On Nov. 17, 1880, a commission headed by James B. Angell signed a treaty with China permitting restrictions upon the immigration of laborers but not teachers, students, merchants, and travelers. As anti-Chinese sentiment filled the West, the Chinese were systematically persecuted.

The Exclusion Act of 1882, the first of many purely ethnic bars written into American immigration law, suspended Chinese immigration for ten years, was extended in 1892, and made "permanent" in 1902. Following the Boxer Rebellion in 1900 and the establishment of the republic in 1911, friction over the exclusion policy disappeared. China, as a wartime ally, was given a token quota of 105 in 1943; and, in the general revision of immigration law in 1965, all ethnic bars were removed.

CHINOOK JARGON. The Chinook, an aboriginal American Indian tribe, occupied the Columbia River basin from the river mouth as far east as The Dalles. A strategic location on the Columbia enhanced their role as traders. The jargon incorporated elements of English, Spanish, French, and Russian. Considering the great linguistic diversity of the Northwest Coast, a trade language or jargon might be anticipated. From northeastern California to southeastern Alaska the Chinook jargon was used by traders, government agents, and missionaries in the mid-19th century.

CHINOOK WINDS. Peculiar to the Pacific Northwest; took their name from the Chinook Indians. Blowing east and southeast from the Pacific during winter and early spring, they penetrate far into the interior, even to the eastern slope of the Rockies, melting and evaporating ice and snow and bringing sudden relief from the most severe winter weather.

CHIPEWYAN. A tribe of Canadian Indians, the Chipewyan were drawn into the 18th-century fur trade and association with the Hudson's Bay Company. They pushed from an original habitat around Great Slave Lake and Lake Athabasca toward Hudson Bay and the domain of the Cree.

CHIPPEWA (or Ojibwa). Like many other native peoples of the Eastern Woodlands of North America, the Chippewa lacked any sense of tribal or national solidarity. Scattered today on what were formerly reservations in Minnesota, Wisconsin, and Ontario, with remnants in Oklahoma and the Dakotas, the Chippewa constitute the second largest tribe in North America, with a population of about 80,000.

The Chippewa were first encountered in the middle Great Lakes regions in the 16th century by the French fur trade. As a result, the Chippewa became middlemen on the French trade routes. Originally hunters, divided into small bands with informal headmen, dependent on birch bark for the making of houses, containers, and canoes, the Chippewa adopted metal tools and firearms at an early date. Although not farmers, the tribe made a special adaptation to the Minnesota-Wisconsin lakes in developing the wild rice resource.

CHIPPEWA, BATTLE OF (July 5, 1814). On the north bank of Chippewa River in the Niagara region, Gen. Sir Phineas Riall commanded a British force of about 2,000. Gen. Jacob Brown with 4,000 Americans was encamped nearby. Both sides attacked simultaneously. The Americans were repulsed. Winfield Scott's brigade and artillery engaged the British on the plain south of the Chippewa, compelling the British to retire in confusion.

CHISHOLM TRAIL. A cattle trail from San Antonio, Tex., across Oklahoma to Abilene, Kans., apparently named for Jesse Chisholm, who followed a part of this route in freighting supplies and may have guided a detachment of soldiers over it soon after the Civil War. After the war Texas ranchmen used it to drive large herds north to market. The Chisholm Trail decreased in importance after 1871, when Abilene lost its preeminence as a shipping point for cattle. The extension of the Atchison, Topeka and Santa Fe Railway to Caldwell, Kans., in 1880, again made the trail an important cattle route until the building of trunk lines into Texas.

CHISHOLM* V. *GEORGIA, 2 Dallas 419 (1793). Heirs of Alexander Chisholm of South Carolina sued Georgia to enforce payment of claims against that state. Georgia refused to defend the suit; the Supreme Court, upholding the right of citizens of one state to sue another, ordered judgment by default against Georgia. No writ of execution was attempted because of threats by the Georgia legislature.

CHISWELL'S MINES. Known from the first discovery of what is now Wythe County, Va., when the mines were operated by Col. John Chiswell. Fort Chiswell was built in 1758. In 1776 the state took over the iron mines. During the revolt of the Loyalists in 1779 and 1780, a plot to seize the mines was thwarted. The mines continued to produce throughout the Revolution.

CHIVINGTON'S MASSACRE. *See* **Sand Creek Massacre.**

CHOCTAW. *See* **Five Civilized Tribes.**

CHOCTAW LAND FRAUDS. After ceding their lands to the United States in 1830, most Choctaw removed west of the

Mississippi, those remaining behind being promised lands in Mississippi. Unscrupulous speculators acquired this Indian land scrip, on which they claimed title to $6 million worth of government land. The fraud was exposed and eventually resulted in an order postponing the land sales.

CHOCTAW TRADING HOUSE, TREATY OF. *See* **Indian Removal.**

CHOCTAW TRAIL. Any of several Indian paths through Choctaw country—central and southern Mississippi and western Alabama. Most important was a trail from the Natchez country (Mississippi River) to the Mobile area. Some met the Creek trails to Carolina called the Great Trading Path; another became part of the Natchez Trace.

CHOISEUL RAID (Oct. 27–Nov. 4, 1943). By October 1943, U.S. military forces had secured the central Solomon Islands and were preparing to seize the island of Bougainville. The island of Choiseul was the object of a diversionary attack. On the night of Oct. 27–28, a 725-man force landed on Choiseul without opposition, established a hidden operating base, and for the next six days conducted coastal forays to the north and south. This limited operation had little effect on Japanese dispositions.

CHOLERA. In June 1832 Asiatic cholera, an enteric disorder associated with crowding and poor sanitary conditions, reached North America. In New York City it killed more than 3,000 persons. It reached New Orleans in October; within three weeks 4,340 had died. Only Boston and Charleston among America's major cities escaped this first onslaught. The disorder coursed along American waterways and land routes until it reached the western frontier. After 1833 the disease virtually disappeared for fifteen years.

In December 1848 cholera again appeared in American port cities and struck down more than 5,000 in New York City. It spread rapidly, bringing death to even the remotest areas. The major attack of 1848–49 was followed by sporadic outbreaks for the next six years.

The last major epidemic of cholera threatened American ports late in 1865. Prompt work by the newly organized Metropolitan Board of Health kept the death toll to about 600 in New York City, but other American towns and cities were not so fortunate. The medical profession, however, had learned that a mild supportive treatment was far better than the rigorous treatment of earlier days. A higher standard of living and an emphasis on sanitation helped to reduce both incidence and mortality. Cholera continued to flare up sporadically until 1868, disappeared, and then returned briefly in 1873. In the succeeding years, occasional cases of cholera were found aboard incoming vessels.

CHOUTEAU AND COMPANY. Successor to Pratte, Chouteau and Company, the Western Department of the American Fur Company, which was sold out by John Jacob Astor to Bartholomew Berthold, Bernard Pratte, Pierre Chouteau, Jr., and Jean Pierre Cabanne in 1834. The company became P. Chouteau, Jr., and Company in 1838 and carried on business until about 1866.

CHOUTEAU'S TRADING POSTS. Trading largely among the Great Osage and Little Osage Indians, Pierre and Auguste Chouteau in 1794 erected Fort Carondelet in what is now Bates County, Mo. The Spanish government gave them the exclusive right to trade with these Indians for six years. Then Pierre Chouteau persuaded the Osage to move to the Arkansas River, where a fur-trading rendezvous was established. In 1809, Pierre and his son, A. P. Chouteau, became stockholders in the St. Louis Missouri Fur Company.

In 1822 Col. A. P. Chouteau occupied the La Saline trading post (now Salina, Okla.). He later established a trading house just below the falls of the Verdigris. In 1836 he built a stockade fort, near present Purcell, Okla., and traded with the Comanche, Kiowa, Wichita, and allied tribes.

François G. Chouteau established a post on an island three miles below the mouth of the Kansas. This was washed into the river in 1826 and another built ten miles up the Kansas.

CHRISTIANA FUGITIVE AFFAIR. In 1851 Edward Gorsuch, a Maryland farmer, accompanied by neighbors, attempted to recover four runaway slaves in Christiana, Pa., at the home of William Parker, an Afro-American. When Parker refused to turn them over, the group threatened to burn down his house. Parker's neighbors gathered, and a fight broke out during which Gorsuch was killed. Thirty-eight of Parker's neighbors were tried for treason, but were acquitted.

CHRISTIAN AND MISSIONARY ALLIANCE. Founded by A. B. Simpson in the 1880's to work among the masses in New York City. Theologically the denomination is mildly perfectionist and fundamentalist, and it emphasizes evangelism. It is known for its ministry among neglected groups in the United States and abroad.

CHRISTIAN CHURCHES. *See* **Disciples of Christ.**

CHRISTIAN COMMISSION. The largely church-supported United States Christian Commission was formed in New York in 1861 to provide comforts and supplies to the armies and navies not furnished by the federal government.

CHRISTIAN SCIENCE. *See* **Church of Christ, Scientist.**

CHRISTINA, FORT. Established by Peter Minuit and Swedish settlers on Mar. 29, 1638. It was the capital of New Sweden until 1643 and again in 1654. The following year, it was surrendered to the Dutch, who surrendered it to the English in 1664. The town around the fort was the first permanent white settlement in the Delaware River valley. Thomas Penn, the proprietor, renamed it Wilmington.

CHRYSLER'S FIELD, BATTLE OF (Nov. 11, 1813). The American army, bent on capturing Montreal, halted a mile east of Chrysler's farm on the north bank overlooking the St. Lawrence River. British gunboats began firing upon the

American rear. Gen. James Wilkinson directed Gen. John P. Boyd to drive the enemy back, but the troops were poorly organized and ineptly led. The Americans, after heavy casualties, retreated to their boats. The British had suffered heavily and made no efforts to pursue.

CHURCH AND STATE, SEPARATION OF. *See* **Religion.**

CHURCHES, ESTABLISHED. *See* **Religion.**

CHURCH MEMBERSHIP SUFFRAGE. When the Puritans in the trading company of Massachusetts Bay retreated to America with their charter, they established a theocracy without disturbing the trading company structure. They could maintain this theocracy only so long as they could control the freemen or stockholders, which necessitated limiting freemanship to those who approved of the theocracy. When pressure from dissatisfied nonfreemen became too great, they decided to accept a limited number on condition of orthodox church membership. The colony of New Haven also adopted the principle of church membership suffrage. By the fusion of Connecticut and New Haven in the charter of 1662 the narrow suffrage ended in the latter colony, as it did in Massachusetts when the charter was annulled in 1684.

CHURCH OF CHRIST, SCIENTIST. A religious movement founded by Mary Baker Eddy. Although the Christian Science Association was chartered in 1876, Mrs. Eddy consolidated the movement in 1879 by uniting all Christian Scientists in the Mother Church, the First Church of Christ, Scientist, located in Boston. There are some 3,200 branches worldwide. At the heart of Christian Science is its claim to be able to cure disease. The Christian Scientists have a large number of practitioners who heal through mental suggestion and personal influence. The church publishes the *Christian Science Monitor.*

CHURCH OF ENGLAND IN THE COLONIES. The first successful English settlement in America was made by members of the established church at Jamestown in 1607. All the southern colonies, except Maryland, were founded under the leadership of members of the Church of England. Maryland was founded by a Roman Catholic proprietor, but the Protestant settlers by 1702 had established the Church of England. In New York the church was established in the four leading counties. In the other northern colonies it depended largely upon the English Society for the Propagation of the Gospel in Foreign Parts (1701). During the 18th century the Church of England advanced in the colonies where it was not established and lost ground in those where it was. The American Revolution confronted it with the problem of forming a national organization and obtaining a native episcopate.

CHURCH SCHISMS OVER SLAVERY ISSUE. At the opening of the Civil War three of the great American churches, Presbyterian, Baptist, and Methodist, had already divided into northern and southern branches over the slavery issue. The secession of the southern states also brought division to the Episcopalians. The Roman Catholics experienced no divisions and very little controversy as a result of either slavery or the Civil War. Other churches, like the Congregational, avoided splits because they were confined almost entirely to the North, while such bodies as the Quakers excluded slave owners. The Disciples, a religious body confined mostly to the border, experienced no real division.

CHURUBUSCO, BATTLE OF (Aug. 20, 1847). Victorious at Contreras, Gen. Winfield Scott encountered Santa Anna's principal army at Churubusco, near Mexico City. Mexican engineers had prepared scientifically constructed works of great strength covering the bridge over the Churubusco River and fortified a massive convent nearby. These Scott assaulted simultaneously. The defenders resisted stubbornly, but were routed and retreated to the capital.

CIBOLA. An Indian name for the villages of the Zuni in what is now western New Mexico, rumored in the early 16th century to be fabulously wealthy. The Spaniards in Mexico in 1539 dispatched the expedition of the friar Marcos de Niza. His report inspired a stronger expedition the next year under Francisco Vásquez de Coronado.

CIMARRON, PROPOSED TERRITORY OF (Public Land Strip, or No Man's Land). Settled by squatters and cattlemen, the territory had no law. A movement was started to organize the country into Cimarron Territory in 1887. The proposal was referred to the committee on territories in Congress, and there it remained. The area now constitutes the panhandle of Oklahoma.

CINCINNATI (Ohio). A city in southwestern Ohio, part of the Miami Purchase of 1788, first settled opposite the mouth of the Licking River. The original name of Losantiville was changed to Cincinnati by Gov. Arthur St. Clair, who made it the capital of the Northwest Territory, 1790–1800. Fort Washington served as a base of military operations against the Indians. Cincinnati was incorporated as a town in 1802 and as a city in 1819.

Well located on the Ohio River to command western and southern markets, it ranked third in manufacturing among American cities by 1860. Cincinnati's leadership passed away as meat packing moved westward and trunkline railroads reduced the importance of the Ohio River. During the 20th century, the city retained some importance as one of the nation's largest inland coal ports. The city's population in 1980 was 385,457, ranking it as Ohio's third largest city.

CINCINNATI, SOCIETY OF THE. Organized in May 1783, the society was established by officers of the American Continental army, then about to disband. The name was an allusion to Cincinnatus, the Roman general who retired quietly to his farmstead after leading his army to victory. With a permanent fund for widows and the indigent, the founders also provided for the perpetuation of the society by making membership hereditary. There were thirteen state societies and an association in France for the French officers. Because of opposition, the failure of heirs, and the extinguishing of the French society by the revolution of 1792, the society entered upon a quiescent period. About 1900 a revival of interest enlarged the membership and procured a headquarters and public museum, Anderson House, in Washington, D.C. In the 1970's membership was about 2,800.

CINCINNATI RIOTS. In 1883 the criminal courts of Cincinnati, Ohio, had sentenced to death only four of the fifty men accused of murder in that year, leading the citizens to believe that the courts had become corrupt. On Mar. 28, 1884, a mob lynched two youths convicted of manslaughter instead of murder. The next night mobs broke into gun stores and armed themselves, attacked the jail again, and set fire to the courthouse. Troops with artillery were rushed in and hard fighting ensued. Not until the sixth day were street barricades removed. At least 45 persons had been killed and 138 injured.

CIO. *See* **American Federation of Labor–Congress of Industrial Organizations.**

CIPHER DISPATCHES. Code telegrams on the possible use of money to insure the votes of Florida and South Carolina for Samuel J. Tilden, the Democratic candidate, in the presidential campaign of 1876. Their publication in 1878 helped nullify the effect of the reputedly questionable proceedings of the Republicans in winning electoral votes.

CIRCUIT COURTS. *See* **Judiciary.**

CIRCUIT RIDERS. Ministerial circuit riding was devised by John Wesley for carrying on his religious movement in England. A circuit consisted of numerous preaching places scattered over a relatively large district served by one or more lay preachers. The original American circuit riders introduced Methodism into the colonies. By the end of the American Revolution there were about 100 U.S. circuit riders. With the formation of the Methodist Episcopal church in 1784, Francis Asbury was chosen bishop, several of the circuit riders were ordained, and the system was widely extended. Other religious bodies partially adopted it, particularly the Cumberland Presbyterians.

CIRCUITS, JUDICIAL. When the federal judicial system, under the Constitution, was established, the United States was divided into three circuits (Eastern, Middle, and Southern) to each of which were assigned two justices of the Supreme Court. These justices were required to hold the courts twice a year, sitting with district judges. During the first three years of its existence, the Supreme Court had practically no business to transact and the chief justice and his associates found employment in riding the circuits. Some relief was granted in 1793 in a change by which only one justice was required to sit with a district judge; and thereafter the justices rode the circuits in turn. In 1869, circuit judges were appointed, most of whom traveled over several states.

In the states, from the outset, circuit courts existed, and in the early days the judge, accompanied by many lawyers, rode large circuits.

CIRCUS. A performance of a variety of acts, traditionally including performing horses and riders, trained wild animals, acrobats, clowns, and aerialists. John William Ricketts founded the first circus in America, at Philadelphia in 1793. Early circuses performed in semipermanent structures, moved infrequently, and were predominantly shows of horsemanship. Starting in 1796 with the appearance of the first elephant in America, the traveling menagerie developed independently. About 1825, circuses and menageries began to merge. Tents and portable seats were in use by 1828. By 1835 seventeen horse-drawn overland circuses existed. Triumphal entry into town by the entire caravan led by a band typifies the beginnings of the American circus street parade.

Wild animal acts are an integral part of today's circus. Isaac A. Van Amburgh is credited with pioneering this type of act between 1820 and 1835 when he first entered a cage containing a lion, a tiger, a leopard, and a panther. The Nixon and Kemp Circus of 1857 introduced the steam calliope.

Phineas T. Barnum and William C. Coup organized Barnum's Circus in 1871. A year later they initiated the century of giant rail-transported circuses. In 1881 James A. Bailey joined with Barnum, and in 1888 the show first used the title Barnum & Bailey Circus. The five Ringling brothers of Baraboo, Wis., founded their circus in 1884. In 1907 the Ringlings purchased Barnum & Bailey and in 1919 merged the two circuses into Ringling Bros. and Barnum & Bailey Combined Shows. In 1956, economics forced it to give up tents in favor of appearing in permanent buildings. In 1969 a separate, second unit of the Ringling circus was formed.

CITIZENS' ALLIANCES. Organizations formed first in Kansas, Iowa, and Nebraska, by townsmen who supported the Farmers' Alliances. When the supreme council of the Southern Alliance met at Ocala, Fla., in December 1890, it assisted in the organization of these groups into the National Citizens' Alliance as a kind of auxiliary. Members were prominent in conventions that led to the formation of the People's party, into which their order was speedily absorbed.

CITIZENSHIP. Membership in a political community attended by certain privileges and responsibilities. In the United States, most persons have a dual citizenship of a special sort, federal and state. Since it is by the terms of the Fourteenth Amendment of the Constitution that a U.S. citizen is automatically made a citizen of the state in which he is a legal resident, U.S. citizenship is primary and state citizenship derivative.

U.S. citizenship can be acquired either by birth or by naturalization. Two basic rules govern citizenship by birth: place of birth and parentage. The only qualification is that persons must be born under U.S. jurisdiction as well as in U.S. territory. This qualification affects children of U.S. diplomats, those born on foreign public ships in U.S. territorial waters, those born of enemies during hostilities on American soil, children of American parents resident in foreign countries, and children of American Indians living in tribal relations. This last group was removed from the list in 1924, when Congress conferred citizenship upon all noncitizen American Indians born within the territorial limits of the United States.

The process of acquiring citizenship by naturalization may involve either collective or individual naturalization. The former is a conferring of citizenship on a group as a whole either by statute or by treaty. Individual naturalization involves a detailed process in which the alien himself seeks citizenship.

Loss of citizenship is possible by the acquisition of citizenship in another country or by a variety of actions such as service in the armed forces of another country. Citizenship secured illegally or fraudulently may be revoked.

CITIZENSHIP, DUAL. Can arise in several ways. A child born in the United States to foreign parents acquires U.S. citizenship at birth; at the same time, he may acquire the citizenship of his parents, under the law of their country. The converse can arise when a child is born to American parents in a foreign country. Dual citizenship can also arise when a woman marries a citizen of another country and upon her marriage becomes a citizen of that country under its laws, or when a person becomes a naturalized citizen in a foreign country, but retains his citizenship under the laws of his country of origin.

CITRUS INDUSTRY. Citrus are tropical and semitropical fruit trees that produce such commonly known fruits as the orange, lemon, lime, citron, grapefruit, tangerine, and pummelo. Citrus was introduced to the Americas by the Spanish *conquistadores* and early colonists. The citrus industry grew slowly in Florida and was of minor importance before the Civil War. During the Reconstruction period enterprising northern capitalists saw possibilities for profit in the citrus industry. Henry S. Sanford opened central Florida to the orange culture in the early 1870's. With citrus stock imported from various parts of the world, Sanford helped transform the orange industry into a money-making business. Following World War II, Florida passed California in production of citrus fruit. Today citrus is Florida's most valuable crop; Florida groves constitute over 70 percent of the U.S. citrus acreage. California leads in lemon production and ranks second in oranges and grapefruit. Arizona, Texas, and Louisiana also have significant citrus acreages.

CITY COUNCILS. The principal policymaking bodies for the nation's municipal governments are structured in four different ways. The most common form, the mayor-council, places both legislative and administrative power in the city council itself. The council-manager form allocates legislative power to the council and administrative power to a chief administrator, or manager. Infrequently found is the commission form, in which each council member serves as the head of an administrative department; and the fourth is New England's town meeting form.

Early American cities were governed by unicameral city councils, which often were also entrusted with judicial powers. After 1800, following the initiative of Baltimore and Philadelphia, many cities adopted the bicameral pattern of Congress and state legislatures; but this proved too cumbersome, and in the late 1970's fewer than five bicameral city councils remained in the United States.

CITY GOVERNMENT. *See* **Local Government; Municipal Government.**

CITY MANAGER PLAN. A simplified form of municipal government that originated in 1908 in Staunton, Va., but did not attract much attention until its adoption in Dayton, Ohio, in 1913. Then it spread rapidly, particularly in states that have the home-rule charter system, to more than 1,500 cities.

The essential features are a small council elected by the voters of the city on a nonpartisan ballot and the appointment by this council of a chief administrative officer known as the city manager, who assumes full responsibility for municipal administration. In some cases a member of the council serves as titular mayor.

CITY PLANNING. Colonial Towns. One of the best early colonial city plans was the one prepared for New Haven, Conn., in 1638: nine large square plots in rows of three, with the central square serving as the town common or green. This became a distinctive feature of colonial New England.

In contrast, the architectural square was characteristic of the courthouse towns of Virginia, consisting of a smaller green square closely surrounded by private residences, shops, a stately courthouse, and usually one or two churches.

Of the important seaport cities, Boston contained an unplanned maze of narrow winding streets, while Charleston, Philadelphia, Annapolis, Williamsburg, and Savannah contained axes, radials, diagonals, and squares patterned after monumental European renaissance plans.

Post-Revolution and 19th-Century Plans. The growth of commerce following the American Revolution brought a new grandeur to city planning: sweeping radials and diagonals, squares, ovals, and circles, designed to provide nobler settings for imposing public buildings; notably, Pierre L'Enfant's plan for Washington, D.C. These plans were ultimately overshadowed by the simplicity of the gridiron pattern.

The demand for textiles created the first planned company mill towns in New England, while wooden boomtowns of gridiron pattern were being hastily developed in the eastern coal fields and midwestern Plains states. The railroad promoted new railroad towns, while the Industrial Revolution was creating factory towns along the railroads in the East, designed as complete communities for industrial workers, close to the factories. In contrast to these notorious industrial slums, a few model company towns were designed.

The Civil War hastened industrial growth and urbanization. Cities rapidly being covered by the unimaginative gridiron pattern were neglecting environmental needs of residents in an effort to accommodate exploding urban populations.

Improvements in urban mass transit were causing rapid fringe expansion along the main transportation routes, creating prototypes of today's suburban communities. Tall buildings appeared in the latter half of the 19th century to relieve the monotonous horizontal pattern of urban development, while parks and landscaped residential avenues introduced much-needed open space.

City Beautiful Movement and Modern City Planning. In 1893 the World's Columbian Exposition in Chicago launched the City Beautiful movement. Cities appointed special civic art commissions to carry out vast self-improvement projects that yielded civic and cultural centers, tree-lined avenues, and waterfront improvements. Pierre L'Enfant's partially effectuated plan for Washington was reactivated. The almost universal disregard of environmental considerations in city plans aroused the disdain of literary writers and social reformers in the late 19th century whose advocacy of social surveys ultimately led to their inclusion in the planning process.

A number of imaginatively planned housing developments emerged following World War I, financed by large corporations and insurance companies. They were designed on standard city blocks to demonstrate the advantages in appearance and open space over the traditional tight row-tenement development. In 1927 America's first garden city, Radburn, N.J., introduced the concept of the superblock—a large residential planning unit free from vehicular encroachment, providing uninterrupted pedestrian access from every building to a large recreation area within the center and pedestrian underpasses at major arteries.

The legal framework for modern city planning practice began with the zoning ordinance, based on the police power to control land use and thereby protect the interests of the individual and the community. The growing number of abuses in zoning and the lack of direction in its application resulted in a master plan as the official document showing the pattern of development for the community.

Federal Involvement. Under President Franklin D. Roosevelt's New Deal, the federal government initiated strong leadership in housing programs. The National Housing Act of 1934 created the Federal Housing Administration (FHA). The National Housing Act of 1937 created the U.S. Housing Authority.

After World War II the National Housing Act of 1949 authorized federal assistance for slum clearance and urban redevelopment, a program broadened through the Housing Act of 1954, to become known as urban renewal. The Urban Planning Assistance Program gave direct assistance to municipalities under 50,000 in population. The Workable Program for Community Improvement required annual recertification of comprehensive master plans in order for cities to continue to be eligible. Other features were the Community Renewal Program and the General Neighborhood Renewal Plan. The achievement of racial, social, and economic mix was a strong requirement to receive federal funds.

The establishment in 1965 of the cabinet-level Department of Housing and Urban Development (HUD) was the culminating action of the federal government. The Demonstration Cities and Metropolitan Development Act of 1966 provided for grants to 147 selected "model cities" for urban improvement. This program never really had an opportunity to prove its worth because of changes in priorities during the administration of President Richard M. Nixon.

Landmark and historic preservation were aided by the 1966 National Historic Preservation Act, which focused on preservation policies in the Department of the Interior.

Housing programs for low- and middle-income families and the elderly on fixed incomes have had limited success, mainly because of the lack of continuity in programs initiated by Congress. The Housing and Urban Development Act of 1968 provided the most ambitious and versatile program. The production of 26 million new and rehabilitated housing units had lagged so badly by 1972 that President Nixon called a moratorium on all federally subsidized housing in January 1973. Subsequently the federal housing program took the form of housing allowances and government-leased housing.

The Housing and Community Development Act of 1974 effected an important change. Existing "categorical" grants were consolidated into a new single program of community-development "block" grants giving localities greater control over how the money was to be spent. President Jimmy Carter submitted about 15 bills on urban problems, but the only measure authorized by Congress was financial aid to industrial cities of the Northeast and the Midwest. President Ronald Reagan embarked on replacing grant programs with federal tax relief to entice small businesses to the cities in "enterprise zones."

New York's Urban Development Corporation. The New York State Urban Development Corporation (created 1968) is (as of 1980) the only public benefit corporation of its kind. Its purpose is to renew neighborhoods in older cities and create orderly growth of new urban areas. Its projects include low- and moderate-income housing, industrial plants, commercial development, community facilities, and new towns.

Private Developments. Private developments of planned residential communities, notably for retired persons on fixed incomes, proliferated during the 1960's, mostly in the Southeast and Southwest. For many younger families and those unable to pay the rising cost of more permanent housing, the mobile home community was one of the answers.

The New Communities Act of 1968, which authorized for the first time the development of new towns through a federal program of guaranteed obligations to private developers, resulted in two new communities. The Urban Growth and New Community Development Act of 1970 led to the funding of thirteen more projects, but all of them failed by 1978.

By the mid-1970's the most remarkable accomplishments of federally assisted urban renewal were Boston's Government Center; Lincoln Center for the Performing Arts, a cultural center for New York City; Hartford's Constitution Plaza; San Francisco's Gateway Center (Embarcadero); Los Angeles's Bunker Hill, with its related World Trade and Financial Center; Battery Park City, a truly vertical city next to New York's World Trade Center complex; and San Francisco's Japanese Trade and Cultural Center.

American city planners are certified by their own professional organization, the American Institute of Planners (AIP), founded in 1917.

CIVIL AERONAUTICS ACT (1938). The Civilian Aviation Act of 1926 established a commercial aviation bureau in the Department of Commerce to map airways, improve landing facilities, and establish beacons; it provided regulations for civilian fliers and the operation of civilian air routes. The Lea-McCarren Civil Aeronautics Act created the Civil Aeronautics Administration (CAA). Its five members, appointed by the president, had jurisdiction over aviation and combined some authority formerly exercised by the Bureau of Commercial Aviation, the Post Office Department, and the Interstate Commerce Commission. A safety board of five members, known as the Civil Aeronautics Board (CAB), was established with the CAA's governance. In 1978 Congress passed the Airline Deregulation Act, which provided for the dissolution of CAB by 1985. (*See* Federal Agencies.)

CIVIL AERONAUTICS BOARD. *See* **Civil Aeronautics Act; Federal Agencies.**

CIVIL DEFENSE. Those activities designed to minimize the effects upon the civilian population of an enemy attack on the United States; to deal with the immediate postattack emergency conditions; and to effectuate repairs or restoration of vital utilities and facilities damaged by such an attack. Modern civil defense dates from World War II, although precedents existed in World War I liberty gardens and scrap drives. President Franklin D. Roosevelt created the Office of Civil Defense (OCD) on May 20, 1941, but the air-raid warning systems, wardens, shelters, rescue workers, and fire-fighting activities were obfuscated by victory gardens, physical-fitness programs, and the rapid diminution of possible air threat. President Harry S. Truman abolished the OCD in 1945. Since then, the military services have been chary of involvement, and the American public has been unprepared to accept the viability of civil defense in an era of nuclear overkill. Civil defense administration shifted after 1961 to the Department of Defense.

CIVIL DISOBEDIENCE. An overt action that goes beyond the traditional legal challenges to laws or institutions. Direct action attempts to force negotiations on the law or institution considered unjust. For example, persons denied service in a public facility may simply sit down and refuse to leave (a sit-in). Civil disobedience may also involve deliberate violation of the "unjust" law or resistance to other laws.

CIVIL ENGINEERING. A branch of engineering that deals with construction of buildings, roads and other transportation systems, and public facilities such as water supply systems. The civil engineer deals with surveying, designing, and constructing reservoirs, sewage disposal systems, railroads, docks, bridges, and buildings for residential, commercial, or industrial purposes. Civil engineers cooperate with architects and with chemical, electrical, and mechanical engineers.

CIVILIAN CONSERVATION CORPS (CCC). Created in March 1933, the CCC was the first New Deal agency specifically charged with providing relief for unemployed young people. The federal government placed nearly 3 million single men on conservation tasks between 1933 and 1942. Reforestation was the most important, but enrollees were also engaged in erosion control, fire prevention, drought relief, land reclamation, and pest eradication. The CCC, probably the most widely accepted of the New Deal agencies, was abolished in 1942 because burgeoning reemployment caused by World War II rendered its continued existence unnecessary.

CIVILIZED TRIBES, FIVE. *See* **Five Civilized Tribes.**

CIVIL RELIGION. A term popularized by sociologist Robert Bellah and used to describe the relationship between religion and national identity in the United States. The basic theory is that there exists an informal civil religion that relates God and the American people. This civil religion provides the nation with a sense of unity and mission similar to that supplied by more traditional faiths in other lands. According to the theology of this faith, God chose the American people for a special mission in the world. He called the nation into being through His providence in the great acts of colonization and the American Revolution and tested its devotion in the Civil War. Ultimately, God will insure that American values are achieved throughout the world.

CIVIL RIGHTS, COMMISSION ON. *See* **Federal Agencies.**

CIVIL RIGHTS AND LIBERTIES. The various spheres of individual and group freedoms that are deemed to be so fundamental as not to tolerate governmental infringement. Constitutional provisions, statutes, and court decisions have been the principal means of acknowledging the civil rights and liberties of individuals.

The U.S. Constitution guarantees habeas corpus; no bill of attainder or ex post facto law; jury trial; privileges and immunities; and no religious test for public office. The Bill of Rights guarantees certain substantive rights (notably freedom of speech, the press, assembly, and religious worship) and certain procedural rights in both civil and criminal actions (notably a speedy and public trial by an impartial jury). In 1833 the Supreme Court ruled that these amendments did not apply to state and local governments. This position prevailed throughout the 19th and early 20th centuries, despite efforts of attorneys arguing that the intent of the framers of the Fourteenth Amendment's due process clause (1868) was to extend the protection of the Bill of Rights to the actions of states and localities. From 1925 through 1969, Supreme Court rulings had the effect of incorporating most of the major provisions of the Bill of Rights into the due process clause of the Fourteenth Amendment, thereby making them applicable to states and localities.

The Thirteenth, Fourteenth, and Fifteenth amendments and the five general civil rights acts spanning the years 1866–75 established the bases for a vast expansion of federal authority. Although the Thirteenth abolished slavery and involuntary servitude and the Fifteenth prohibited the abridgment of the right to vote because of race, color, or previous condition of servitude, the Fourteenth proved to be of greatest import to the development of individual rights.

CIVIL RIGHTS MOVEMENT. The civil rights movement is generally dated from the Supreme Court's decision of 1954 in *Brown* v. *Board of Education of Topeka* to the passage in 1965 of the Voting Rights Act. It was a nonviolent, direct-action campaign by black organizations and individuals and their white allies to achieve full integration of blacks.

Although an extension of past struggles, the civil rights movement was the direct outgrowth of liberalized racial views and victories by increased black agitation for equal rights since World War II. Prior to the 1960's, litigation in the courts, primarily by lawyers of the National Association for the Advancement of Colored People (NAACP), was the governing strategy of the civil rights movement. The Supreme Court had begun in the New Deal era to strike down Jim Crow practices in voting, interstate travel, housing, and education. This trend culminated in the *Brown* decision.

The expectations of Afro-Americans, particularly those of an expanding black middle class, were significantly heightened by the Warren court's decision. The first dramatic sign of a changed attitude appeared in December 1955, when Rosa Parks, a black, boarded a bus in Montgomery, Ala., and took a seat in the section for whites. Because she refused to surrender her place to a white, Mrs. Parks was arrested and jailed. Black community leaders organized the Montgomery Improvement Association, which under Martin Luther King, Jr., conducted a year-long boycott of the bus system that resulted in its desegregation. This not only publicized the deep-seated nature of American racism but significantly raised black consciousness in the United States, established King as the leader of the civil rights movement, and popularized among Afro-Americans the philosophy of nonviolence and civil disobedience.

One hundred congressmen issued a southern manifesto in March 1956, censuring the Supreme Court and praising state efforts to resist forced integration by lawful means. White citizens' councils sprang up in numerous southern communities, ostensibly to protect the constitutional rights of whites, but actually to prevent the free access of blacks to public schools. A revived Ku Klux Klan found considerable support among hard-core segregationists. President Eisenhower was compelled in 1957 by white mob violence to use federal marshals and troops to ensure the right of black children to attend the previously all-white Central High School in Little Rock, Ark.

The first phase of the civil rights movement, with its heavy emphasis on court action, ended in 1960 when four black students from North Carolina Agricultural and Technical University in Greensboro sat down at a segregated lunch counter and ordered coffee. When refused service, they continued to sit in silent protest until the store closed. Soon a wave of student-led sit-ins, wade-ins, and sleep-ins directed against segregated public facilities had engulfed the nation. Under the mounting black offensive, public places were desegregated with relative ease.

To ensure cooperation between various student groups, the Student Nonviolent Coordinating Committee (SNCC) was formed in Raleigh, N.C., in April 1960. In May 1961, members of the Congress of Racial Equality (CORE) began a series of "freedom rides" through the Deep South to test a Supreme Court decision banning segregation in interstate bus terminals. Their efforts produced a new order from the Interstate Commerce Commission desegregating all facilities used in interstate transportation.

By the end of 1961, SNCC and CORE, along with the Southern Christian Leadership Conference, were clearly in the vanguard of the movement. The staid NAACP and National Urban League had been eclipsed by the younger advocates of direct action. In 1962 and 1963 a coalition of SNCC, CORE, SCLC, and the NAACP, called the Council of Federated Organizations (COFO), was organized to register black votes in the South. In 1963 King led large demonstrations to desegregate Birmingham, Ala. The brutal force used by the police and the slaying of Medgar Evers, NAACP field secretary in Mississippi, a month later moved President John F. Kennedy in June 1963 to ask Congress to enact a comprehensive civil rights law.

By sending federal troops to the University of Mississippi in September 1962 to ensure the admission of black student James Meredith and by its general support of civil rights, the Kennedy administration had established itself in the eyes of most Afro-Americans as a friend and protector of their rights. Congress, however, did not enact any new measures until after the civil rights movement peaked on Aug. 28, 1963, when some 200,000 persons participated in a march on Washington to demonstrate their support for the civil rights bill. The bill was made law in July 1964. However, inadequacies in the law concerning voting rights and the murder of three civil rights workers in the summer of 1964 led to additional demonstrations. To dramatize the urgency of further legislation and to focus attention on Alabama, where only 2 percent of voting-age blacks were registered, King planned a march in Alabama from Selma to Montgomery, the state capital, in March 1965. The vicious beatings and murder of some of the marchers, followed by an impassioned plea of President Johnson for racial accord, prompted Congress to pass the Voting Rights Act of August 1965.

Passage of the 1965 Voting Rights Act marked the end of a decade of large-scale demonstrations to desegregate American society. Then, many Afro-Americans rejected the assimilationist and middle-class aims of the civil rights movement as illusory and turned toward the nationalist goals of "black power" and self-determination. Since the late 1960's, the nationalist philosophy, encompassing various shades of conservative, moderate, and radical politics, has dominated the thrust of the black liberation struggle.

CIVIL SERVICE. The appointed civilian employees of a governmental unit, as distinct from elected officials and military personnel. Under President George Washington and his successors through John Quincy Adams, the federal civil service was stable and characterized by relative competence and efficiency. However, under Jacksonian egalitarian democracy the federal, state, and local services were largely governed by a spoils system that gave little or no consideration to competence.

The unprecedented corruption and scandals of the post–Civil War era generated civil service reform. An act of 1871 authorized the president to utilize examinations in the appointing process, and President Ulysses S. Grant appointed the first U.S. Civil Service Commission in that year. But Congress refused appropriations; full statutory support for reform waited until 1883 and the Pendleton Act, still the federal government's central civil service law. This act reestablished the Civil Service Commission, created a modern merit system for many offices, and authorized the president to expand this system.

The 1930's saw a near doubling of the federal civil service and a renaissance of patronage politics, especially in the administration of work relief. With public and congressional support during his second term, President Franklin D. Roosevelt was empowered to, and did, expand the competitive system to most positions in the new agencies.

After World War II, federal personnel management, which had formerly consisted mainly of administering examinations and policing the patronage, further expanded its functions. These developments and a full-scale labor relations system transformed 19th-century merit system notions into public personnel management as advanced as any in the world. In a federal civil service of 3 million, there are fewer than 15,000 patronage posts of any consequence.

Beginning in the late 19th century, civil service reform came to many state and local governments. In 1883 New York State adopted the first state civil service act. By 1940 one-third of the states had comprehensive merit systems; in the 1970's two-thirds had them.

CIVIL WAR (1861–65). Sectional tension grew ominously in the 1850's and a major southern crisis followed the election of President Abraham Lincoln in November 1860. By early February 1861, the seven states of the Lower South (South Carolina, Mississippi, Florida, Alabama, Georgia, Louisiana, and Texas) had withdrawn from the Union and had begun the establishment of the southern Confederacy (*see* Confederate States of America). The sending of an expedition by Lincoln to relieve the federal garrison at Fort Sumter in Charleston harbor precipitated a southern attack upon that fort, which was surrendered on Apr. 13. This was the opening of the war. Each side claimed that the other began it.

Lincoln's Sumter policy involved the sending of the provisioning expedition and, after the fort had been fired upon, the call for 75,000 militia to be furnished by the states. This policy, while it produced a united North, served equally to unite the South; it was not until after Lincoln's call for militia that the four important states of the Upper South (Virginia, Arkansas, Tennessee, and North Carolina) withdrew from the Union and joined the Confederacy.

The Union had twenty-three states with 22 million people, as against eleven states and 9 million people (including 3.5 million slaves) within the Confederacy. In wealth and population, as well as in industrial, commercial, and financial strength, the Union was definitely superior to the Confederacy. The South had the advantage of bold leadership, gallant tradition, martial spirit, unopposed seizure of many federal forts and arsenals, interior military lines, and unusual ability among its generals. Its military problem was that of defense, which required far fewer men than offensive campaigns and widely extended hostile occupation.

Legally the war began with Lincoln's proclamation of Apr. 15, 1861, which summoned the militia to suppress "combinations" in the seven states of the Lower South, and the proclamations of Apr. 19 and Apr. 27, 1861, which launched a blockade of southern ports. Before Congress met in July 1861, the president had taken those measures that gave to Union war policy its controlling character. Besides proclaiming an insurrection, declaring a blockade, and summoning the militia, he had suspended habeas corpus, expanded the regular army, directed emergency expenditures, and in general had assumed executive functions beyond existing law. A tardy ratification of his acts was passed by Congress on Aug. 6, 1861, and in 1863 these strongly contested executive measures were given sanction by the Supreme Court.

Militarily, both sides were unprepared. The first Battle of Bull Run (July 21) was the only large-scale engagement in 1861. Although a Union defeat, it was, like most of the battles, an indecisive struggle. Except during the generalship of Union officers George B. McClellan, George G. Meade, and Ulysses S. Grant, the southerners had the undoubted advantage of military leadership on the main eastern front; Robert E. Lee's notable but indecisive victories of second Bull Run, Fredericksburg, and Chancellorsville were won against John Pope, A. E. Burnside, and Joseph Hooker. At Antietam, however, McClellan stopped Lee's northern invasion of September 1862, while the ambitious Confederate offensive of 1863 was checked at Gettysburg. In the West most of the operations were favorable to the Union side. This was especially true of the "river war" (resulting in the capture of Columbus, forts Henry and Donelson, Nashville, Corinth, and Memphis); the Union half-victory of Shiloh; and the important Union victories of 1863 at Vicksburg and Chattanooga. Later campaigns involved Confederate Gen. J. E. Johnston's unsuccessful operations against William Tecumseh Sherman in upper Georgia, Sherman's capture of Atlanta and his famous raid through Georgia and the Carolinas, Union Gen. Philip H. Sheridan's devastating operations in the Valley of Virginia, the Grant-Meade operations against Lee in Virginia, the J. B. Hood–G. H. Thomas campaign in Tennessee, and final operations in the Petersburg and Appomattox areas, which culminated in the fall of Richmond and the close of the war. In the naval aspects, Union superiority was impressively shown in the blockade of southern ports, the capture and occupation of coastal positions, the cooperation of western flotillas with the armies, the seizure of New

Orleans in April 1862, the complete control of the Mississippi River after the fall of Vicksburg and Port Hudson in July 1863, and the defeat and sinking of the Confederacy's proudest ship, the *Alabama*, by the *Kearsarge* (June 19, 1864). On the other hand, Confederate cruisers and privateers did considerable damage to Union commerce, the Union Navy failed in the operations against Richmond, and several ports remained in southern hands until late in the war.

War aims changed as the conflict progressed; the declaration of Congress on July 22, 1861, that the war was waged merely for the restoration of the Union was belied by the Radical Republicans, who by 1864 had determined in the event of victory to treat the South as a subordinate section upon which drastic modifications would be imposed. The relation of the war to the slavery question appeared in various emancipating measures passed by Congress, in Lincoln's Emancipation Proclamation as well as his abortive compensated emancipation scheme, in state measures of abolition, and finally in the antislavery amendment to the Constitution. Gen. Marcus J. Wright, a Confederate officer attached to the War Department after the war, estimated Confederate manpower at 600,000 to 700,000. Confederate dead have been estimated at 258,000; Union dead, at 360,000. The stupendous economic and material loss has never been more than roughly estimated.

Aside from the obvious consequences of slaughter and destruction, the results of the war involved suppression of the "heresy" of secession, legal fixation of an "indestructible" Union, national abolition of slavery, overthrow of the southern planter class, rise of middle-class power in the South, decline of the merchant marine, ascendancy of the Republican party, inauguration of a high-tariff policy, far-reaching capitalistic growth associated with centralization of government functions, and adoption of the Fourteenth Amendment. (*See also* Army, Confederate; Army, Union; Confederate States of America; Navy, Confederate; and articles on specific battles by title.)

Civil War Diplomacy. The basic diplomatic policy of the United States during the Civil War was twofold: to prevent foreign intervention in behalf of the southern Confederacy and to gain the acquiescence of England and France in the vast extension of maritime belligerent rights, which was considered necessary to crush the South. Since France and England were great maritime powers and none too friendly toward the United States at the time, they seemed to offer the only serious danger of foreign intervention.

In the very beginning, Secretary of State William H. Seward deliberately gave the British government the impression that he was willing, if not anxious, to fight Great Britain should that country show undue sympathy for the Confederacy. The launching of the Confederate cruisers and the building of the Confederate rams in England and France gave the Union even stronger grounds for complaint, as did the sale of munitions and the colossal blockade-running business carried on with the Confederacy. French intervention in Mexico was an added score against France. The piling up of grievances by the United States against France and England helped create the very definite belief that intervention meant a declaration of war by the United States. As for war, neither France nor England cared to pay such a price to see the United States permanently divided. These grievances of the United States were used to counteract the grievances of England and France in the blockade of their West Indian ports and the seizure of their merchant vessels, under the doctrine of ultimate destination, hundreds of miles from the Confederate coast when apparently destined to neutral ports.

The objective of Confederate diplomacy was to obtain foreign assistance in gaining independence. The Confederate government based its plans, first, upon European dependence upon southern cotton and, second, upon the well-known desire of England to see a powerful commercial rival weakened and of Napoleon III to see the champion of the Monroe Doctrine rendered impotent to frustrate his attempted annexation of Mexico. The Confederacy failed to obtain foreign intervention because the things to be gained by war on the part of England and France would not offset war losses.

Propaganda and Undercover Activities. The abolition crusade and the proslavery reaction laid the psychological bases for the Civil War. Upon the outbreak of the conflict, press and pulpit further stirred the emotions of the people. In the South, propagandists devoted their efforts to asserting the right to secede and to proving that the aggressive North was invading southern territory. In the North, the preservation of the Union, patriotism, and the crusade against slavery were the major themes. On both sides, atrocity stories abounded. Both sides attempted to influence European opinion, and Lincoln sent journalists and ecclesiastics to England and the Continent to create favorable sentiment.

Despite these efforts, many on both sides remained unconvinced. The prosouthern Knights of the Golden Circle in the North were paralleled by numerous secret pronorthern "peace" societies in the South. These organizations encouraged desertion; aided fugitive slaves, refugees, and escaping prisoners; and occasionally attempted direct sabotage.

Munitions. The standard equipment of the Union army was muzzle-loading Springfield or Enfield rifles and cannon. Many early regiments, however, went to the front with nondescript arms of their own procuring. Other hundreds of thousands of rifles were furnished by contractors who took all the antiquated, castoff weapons of European armies. Some proved more dangerous to the man behind the breech. Before 1861 various American companies had been making breech-loading repeating rifles that would fire fifteen times as rapidly as the best of muzzle-loaders, with equal accuracy and force, and with greater ease of manipulation. But the backwardness of the War Department and its staff prevented the use of such improved weapons until the closing months of the war.

The munitions of the Confederacy were inferior to those of the North. Battlefield captures, raiding expeditions, imports from Europe, and an increasing production from southern munitions plants kept the troops armed. Largely cut off by the blockade from European supplies and with little industrial development, plants had to be built and manned, and materials obtained and prepared. Yet, in 1864, lead-smelting works, bronze foundries, a cannon foundry, and rifle, carbine, and pistol factories were operating. The big problem of supply was the lack of adequate transportation.

Freedom of the Seas. The blockade of the Confederacy set up by the federal government was far from satisfying the stringent requirements of international law and of previous U.S. diplomatic practice. Further, the Supreme Court applied the doctrine of continuous voyage to confiscate neutral property, contraband or no contraband, in transit between Great Britain and the British West Indies, when that property was ultimately destined, by a subsequent maritime leg of an essentially continuous voyage, to a blockaded Confederate port. (*See also Trent* Affair.)

Union Cotton Trade. At the beginning of the war the U.S. government decided to permit a restricted trade in cotton in cotton-growing areas held by Union forces, partly because of the foreign demand for cotton and partly to enable destitute southerners to buy necessities. The commerce was restricted to treasury agents; private individuals and members of the military and naval forces were not allowed to participate in the traffic, and there was to be no commercial intercourse with the Confederates. These rules could not be enforced. The trade, legal and illegal, attained immense size. In the spring and summer of 1864 enough cotton went North to supply the factories, while each week $500,000 worth of goods was going South through Memphis. The results of the trade were harmful to the Union cause. According to many officers, it prolonged the war at least a year.

War Supply Contracts. In the first year of the war, the federal government and a score of states were bidding against each other for war supplies, with disgraceful consequences. Several of the great personal fortunes had their origins in Civil War contracts. Furthermore, goods of inferior quality often found readier sales than first-class products. After a year of this profiteering the War Department began serious efforts at reform, but the contract business remained slightly malodorous until the end of the war. The situation seems to have been not much better in the Confederacy.

Surrender of the Confederate Armies. The most important surrender after Lee's Appomattox (Apr. 9, 1865) was that of Confederate Gen. Joseph E. Johnston to William T. Sherman at the Bennett house near Durham Station, N.C., Apr. 26. Parole was granted to 37,047 prisoners on the same terms Ulysses S. Grant had given Robert E. Lee. The capitulation of the rest of the Confederate forces followed as a matter of course. On May 4, Gen. Richard Taylor surrendered to Gen. Edward R. S. Canby at Citronelle, Ala., thus ending Confederate forces east of the Mississippi. Six days later Jefferson Davis was captured by James H. Wilson's cavalry near Irwinville, Ga., and was imprisoned at Fortress Monroe. The final act was the surrender of Kirby-Smith and the trans-Mississippi troops to Canby at New Orleans on May 26. The total number surrendered and paroled from Apr. 9 to May 26 was 174,223.

Economic Consequences in the North. Destructive as it was of material as well as of human values, the Civil War proved to be a great stimulus to the economic life of the North. Government contracts, paper-money inflation, and a new protective tariff system brought a rapid expansion of capital and a new prosperity to northern industry, with large-scale industry increasingly common. Woolen manufacturing, munitions and war supplies, the petroleum industry, telegraphs and railways, the banking system, and agriculture experienced new gains. With wages lagging far behind a price rise, labor turned new energies toward organizing national craft unions. The burden of taxation was borne with little complaint. Thus was secured one-fifth of the wartime needs of the government. The rest was borrowed directly or indirectly; the war ended with a federal debt of over $2.6 billion. Yet the national wealth had been greatly increased and a new era of American capitalism was ahead.

Economic Consequences in the South. The Civil War brought economic suffering, devastation, and ruin to the South. As a result of the blockade, the interruption of intercourse with the North, and the strain of supporting the armed forces, the people were subjected to extreme privation. Large land areas were laid waste by military operations. Accumulated capital resources were dissipated. Railroads were either destroyed or deteriorated to the point of worthlessness. Livestock was reduced by almost two-thirds. Slave property valued at about $2 billion was wiped out. About a fourth of the productive white male population was killed or incapacitated. Land values were undermined; agricultural production was greatly retarded; trade was disrupted; banks and mercantile houses were forced into bankruptcy; the credit system was disorganized; and commercial ties with foreign nations were broken. (*See also* Reconstruction.)

The war also brought sweeping changes in the economy of the South. The destruction of slavery together with the devastation wrought by the conflict forced the plantation system to give way to sharecropper, tenancy, and small farm systems. With the breakup of the plantations there occurred a great increase in the number and economic importance of the small towns and their inhabitants.

The war caused a diminution in the part the South played in the determination of national economic policies. During the postwar period, tariff, monetary, railroad, banking, and other such matters were generally decided without any consideration for the South. The result was economic exploitation of the South by other sections of the nation.

CIVIL WAR GENERAL ORDER NO. 100. A code comprising 157 articles "for the government of [Union] armies in the field" according to the "laws and usages of war." It later formed the basis for the conventions of the Hague conferences of 1899 and 1907.

CIVIL WORKS ADMINISTRATION. *See* **New Deal.**

CLAIBORNE SETTLEMENT. Acting upon a trading license, William Claiborne established in 1631 a plantation on Kent Island in upper Chesapeake Bay, an outpost of Virginia represented in its general assembly. In 1638 Gov. Leonard Calvert seized Kent Island; during the civil war in England Claiborne temporarily regained control.

CLAIM ASSOCIATIONS. Frontier institutions designed to provide a quasi-legal land system in areas where no land law existed. Settlers who preceded the government surveyor into a new area and established their homes therein or who located on public land not yet offered at public auction made improvements with no certainty of continued ownership. Claim associations, or claim clubs, appeared early in the 19th century and were found in practically every part of the public land area that received settlers before 1870. Their heyday was in the 1840's and 1850's in Iowa, Kansas, and Nebraska. The squatters would come together and adopt a more or less stereotyped constitution or bylaws guaranteeing mutual protection to each claimant of 160 or 320 acres who met the simple requirements for improvements. Claim jumpers were dealt with in summary fashion by these associations.

The Preemption Law of 1841 legalized squatting upon surveyed lands and gave the settler the right of preempting his claim before the public sale, thereby protecting him against competitive bidding, but only if he could raise the funds to pay for the land.

CLAIM JUMPER. One who drove a squatter from his claim or, in his absence, seized it.

CLAIMS, FEDERAL COURT OF. Created by Congress in 1855. The court investigates contractual claims against the United States by private parties or referred to it by an executive department or by Congress. In some cases the decisions of the court are final, subject to appeal to the Supreme Court; in others, the court merely reports its findings to Congress or to the department concerned.

CLARK, FORT. A frontier post built in 1813 where Peoria, Ill., now stands. A wooden stockade mounting cannon, named in honor of George Rogers Clark, it was an effective restraint upon hostile Indians during the War of 1812. Unoccupied, it was destroyed by Indians in 1819.

CLARK, FORT, IN MISSOURI. *See* **Osage, Fort.**

CLARK'S NORTHWEST CAMPAIGN. During the early years of the Revolution, the British exercised undisputed control over the country northwest of the Ohio River. Their most important center of influence was Detroit, the headquarters of the posts and the key to the control of the fur trade and the Indian tribes. George Rogers Clark, leader of harassed Kentucky settlers, perceived that Kentucky could best be defended by the conquest of Detroit. He directed his first blow against the French towns in Illinois. Kaskaskia was occupied in July 1778, and the remaining Illinois towns were easily persuaded to join the rebel standard. British Lt. Gov. Henry Hamilton of Detroit marched upon Vincennes, which was retaken, Dec. 17; but instead of pushing on against Kaskaskia, Hamilton settled down for the winter. Clark led his army of 170 men across Illinois to tempt his fate at Vincennes. After thirty-six hours of battle, Hamilton yielded his fort and garrison to the rebel leader, Feb. 24, 1779. Although Detroit was never attained, Clark retained his grip upon the southern end of the Northwest until the close of the war.

CLAYTON ANTITRUST ACT (1914). Major reform legislation in the New Freedom program of President Woodrow Wilson, outlawing certain monopolistic or restrictive trade practices not specifically covered by the Sherman Antitrust Act (1890). It prohibited discrimination in prices among purchasers; exclusive dealing and contracts tying a purchaser to a single supplier; acquisition of competing companies; interlocking directorates in industrial corporations capitalized at $1 million or more and in banks with assets of more than $5 million; and interlocking shareholdings through the purchase of stock in competing firms. The act stipulated that neither trade unions nor farm organizations lawfully seeking to attain legitimate objectives should be construed as illegal combinations in restraint of trade. Supreme Court rulings in the decade after 1914 demonstrated that the act had not conferred upon trade unions broad immunity from antitrust prosecution. The most important amendments of the Clayton Antitrust Act were the Robinson-Patman Act of 1936, dealing with price discrimination, and the Celler-Kefauver Act of 1950, which outlawed corporate mergers that tended to stifle competition or to promote monopoly.

After 1945 the government made a concerted effort to challenge giant mergers and to check anticompetitive practices; but the effectiveness of the Clayton Antitrust Act was undercut by congressional exemption of various industries, the tendency of the executive branch to equate large firms with technological efficiency and economies of production, and the failure to evolve an antitrust doctrine aimed at curbing conglomerates.

CLAYTON-BULWER TREATY (1850). A compromise arrangement resulting from conflicting British and U.S. interests in Central America. In the late 1840's Great Britain was occupying the Bay Islands and the eastern coast of Central America. After the Mexican War broke out, the British quickly saw that the assured U.S. victory would stimulate U.S. interest in a ship canal across the isthmus. Therefore, on Jan. 1, 1848, British authorities seized the mouth of the San Juan River, the logical eastern terminus of any future canal.

Strained relations at once developed, but each government assured the other that it had no selfish designs on the transit route. Sir Henry Bulwer was sent to Washington, where, with Secretary of State John M. Clayton, he negotiated the treaty, which provided that England and the United States should jointly control and protect the canal that would soon be built. The interpretation of the treaty led to further bitter disputes, over continuing British occupations, but Great Britain, valuing its U.S. cotton trade more than its claims in Central America, withdrew in 1858–60. When, after several decades, the canal was still unbuilt, popular demand grew for abrogation of the agreement, to make possible construction of a U.S.-controlled canal. Finally, in 1901, the Hay-Pauncefote Treaty superseded the Clayton-Bulwer arrangement.

CLAYTON COMPROMISE (1848). The plan drawn up by a bipartisan Senate committee headed by John M. Clayton for organizing Oregon and the Southwest. It excluded slavery from Oregon, prohibited the territorial legislatures of New Mexico and California from acting on slavery, and provided for appeal of all slavery cases from the territorial courts to the Supreme Court. It passed the Senate but was tabled in the House of Representatives.

CLEARINGHOUSE, NEW YORK. In 1853 thirty-eight New York City banks organized the first U.S. bank clearinghouse. The previous system of Friday settlements had created enormous confusion and danger of loss as runners with bags of currency dashed about the financial district. Even more serious was the possibility that some bank might accumulate large adverse balances during the week and threaten the stability of the whole group. The change to daily settlements was so effective that the more reckless banks were obliged to close.

The inflexible currency of this period and the impotence of the Independent Treasury forced the new clearinghouse to take a position of leadership. After the crisis of 1857 it required its members to hold reserves against their deposits. Ten times between 1860 and 1914, in order to tide the banks over a crisis, the New York Clearinghouse issued loan certificates for use in the settlement of daily balances. It has steadily increased its daily clearings and activities, including clearings of stock certificates, coupons, and foreign trade bills as well as checks of member banks.

CLEARINGHOUSES. The principle of clearing has been in use for centuries by many kinds of organizations, to achieve economy and simplicity of operation. It consists basically of matching offsetting items so that only the net result needs to be dealt with. The most common use of clearing in the United States has been in connection with bank checks. By the end of the Civil War there were clearinghouses in New York, Boston, Philadelphia, and Chicago. In 1900 there were 87 U.S. clearinghouses; the number reached a peak of 198 in 1920.

Many clearinghouses assumed certain responsibilities for the banking community until the Federal Reserve period: they conducted examinations of their members, published reports of their condition, and aided those in difficulty by issuing loan certificates. Many stock and commodity exchanges instituted clearings for the transactions of their own members. Greatly increased use of charge accounts and credit cards reduced the number of transactions by increasing the average size of check payments. Gradual adoption of accounting machinery and computers was another factor in altering the nature of clearing.

CLEARWATER RIVER, BATTLE ON (July 11–13, 1877). During Chief Joseph's campaign, the Nez Percé established camp on the Clearwater River, west of Kamiah, Idaho. Gen. Oliver O. Howard attacked with infantry, cavalry, and artillery. The Indians were eventually driven in retreat past Kamiah to the Lolo Trail leading into Montana.

CLEVELAND (Ohio). Port of entry and largest city in Ohio. In 1796 the Connecticut Land Company sent Moses Cleaveland to lay out a "capital" city and survey the Western Reserve lands it had purchased from Connecticut. Cleaveland chose the mouth of the Cuyahoga River, on Lake Erie, as the site. The Ohio legislature designated Cleveland the seat of Cuyahoga County in 1810 and incorporated it as a village in 1814. Cleveland gained access to the Atlantic Ocean with completion of the Erie Canal in 1825 and to the Ohio River with completion of the Ohio Canal in 1832. It was incorporated as a city in 1836, and in 1854 merged with Ohio City.

The Ohio Canal offered an outlet for agricultural products and provided the transportation necessary for industrial development, particularly iron and steel manufacturing. Allied industries, especially toolmaking, multiplied in the post–Civil War decades. Oil refining became significant after 1870.

The original New England settlers became a minority as European immigrants and black and white migrants from the South responded to labor needs created by Cleveland's industrial growth. The population in 1980 was 573,822 (metropolitan area 1,898,720).

CLEVELAND DEMOCRATS. Democrats who during President Grover Cleveland's second administration continued to support him after silverites, high-tariff men, and other dissident elements had broken from his leadership. In the Democratic National Convention of 1896, the Cleveland Democrats, led by William C. Whitney and William E. Russell, were decisively defeated; their refusal to accept the result brought about the formation of the National Democratic Party (Gold Democrats).

CLIFF DWELLERS. *See* **Anasazi.**

CLINTON RIOT (Sept. 4, 1875). One of the worst disturbances during Reconstruction in Mississippi. Four whites and an undetermined number of blacks were killed. President U. S. Grant refused to send the army, thus allowing the whites to discard radical Reconstruction.

CLIPPER SHIPS. Long, narrow wooden sailing vessels, with lofty canvas; from about 1843 to 1868, the greatest sailing ship in speed and beauty. Trade in tea from China profited from quicker delivery of that perishable product. The discovery of gold in California induced many from 1849 to 1859 to make the voyage around Cape Horn in fast clipper ships. The discovery of gold in Australia in 1851 also gave a great impetus to the building of clipper ships.

The first real clipper was the *Ann McKim,* built in Baltimore in 1832. Beginning about 1850 the California clippers increased rapidly in size, ranging from 1,500 to 2,000 tons register. It was more than a quarter of a century before the steamship was able to break the record of the fastest clippers.

CLOCK AND WATCH INDUSTRY. The first clockmaker of record in America was Thomas Nash of New Haven in 1638. Throughout the 17th century, eight-day striking clocks with brass movements were produced in Connecticut. The wooden clock was not made in America until the 18th century. By 1745 Benjamin Cheney of East Hartford was producing wooden clocks; there is evidence that these clocks were being made as early as 1715 near New Haven. Benjamin Willard, founder of the Willard Clock dynasty of Massachusetts, was apprenticed to Cheney.

The main line of descent of the American clock and watch industry derives from Thomas Harland, who emigrated from England in 1773 and opened a shop in Norwich, Conn. Harland trained many clockmakers, the most famous of whom was Daniel Burnap, who established his own business in East Windsor about 1780. Harland and Burnap were the forerunners of the modern, industrial era of clockmaking. Eli Terry, the first to systematize clock production, was apprenticed to Daniel Burnap in 1786. Terry commenced business at Plymouth, Conn., in 1794. After 1800 he began to produce wooden clocks in quantity and in 1808 contracted with the Porter brothers of Waterbury for the production of 4,000 wooden clock movements at $4 each. About 1814, Terry designed and manufactured the thirty-hour wooden shelf clock.

Seth Thomas and Chauncey Jerome, both of whom worked for Terry, elaborated factory production and carried the industry into its distinctly modern phase. Jerome engaged in itinerant clockmaking and repairing, moving to Bristol in 1821. In 1825 he designed the bronze looking-glass clock, and developed the commercial possibilities of the thirty-hour rolled-brass movement in 1838. By 1855 almost all common clocks in America were brass.

The earliest production of watches in some volume is accorded to Thomas Harland. Between 1809 and 1817 Luther Goddard of Shrewsbury, Mass., produced about 500 movements. Goddard learned the art of clockmaking from his cousin Simon Willard, son of Benjamin Willard; thus, this line of mechanical influence can be traced from Benjamin Cheney. Between 1836 and 1841 James and Henry Pitkin of East Hartford, Conn., made perhaps 800 movements, using the most elaborate tools known in America up to that time. Shortly before 1850, Aaron Dennison and Edward Howard made plans to manufacture watches on a volume basis, using a system of interchangeable parts. This venture resulted in the formation of Dennison, Howard, and Davis, predecessor of the Waltham Watch Company. Howard had been apprenticed to Aaron Willard, Jr.

Watchmaking helped establish and carry forward a new standard of accuracy in American metalworking. Other men who contributed prominently to this development in the 19th century were Ambrose Webster, Charles Mosley, Edward Marsh, and Charles Vander Woerd.

Electricity was also adapted to several small battery-operated clocks of little influence, put out by various short-duration makers. An example was the electric clock invented by Henry E. Warren of Ashland, Mass., in 1909. Warren's patents of 1918 for an entirely different clock led to the most pervasive development in 20th-century timekeeping, the electric "clock." This is not a true clock because it contains no timekeeping element and is not capable of regulation or of functioning independent of an electric system. It keeps close time as long as the current is on, without need for any of the attentions, such as winding, regulating, and cleaning, that purely mechanical clocks require. In the 1970's digital watches and clocks (battery- or line-powered) became popular. The most accurate electric clocks now contain a tiny vibrating quartz crystal.

CLOSED SHOP. A union security clause in labor-management contracts that stipulates that all persons who are to be employed must be members of a specified union as a precondition for such employment. The closed shop was a dominant feature of early unionism in the United States, a natural outgrowth of the guild features of craft organization of work. Closed-shop arrangements were pervasive early in the 20th century and a source of controversy.

CLOTHING INDUSTRY. In the 18th century, U.S. clothing manufacture was largely a household industry. In the colonies, fine imported textiles were costly. By the 1790's, French fashion prints were copied by women who wanted to dress in the current mode. Shops produced up-to-date, custom-made clothing for the rich, but in the average family women and children made plain, durable clothes of wool or linsey-woolsey. The preliminary stages of spinning and weaving were eliminated from home work after the 1830's, when textile manufacture became an established industry.

The ready-to-wear industry made a tentative beginning in the late 18th century, with the establishment of slop shops, which sold rough clothing to sailors. Custom tailors also began to make up some clothing in slack times. The first clothing factory was in New York City in 1831. Early stores, such as Brooks Brothers, sold both custom- and ready-made clothing at midcentury. But the output of ready-made clothing was inconsequential compared to the amount homemade.

The Civil War demand for uniforms, which coincided with the widespread adoption of the sewing machine, led to standardized sizes. Women's clothing began to be ready-made; and many women found employment in the women's wear industry. The sewing machine's low cost, portability, and simplicity promoted a decentralized industry based on unskilled labor, piecework, and low capital investment. In the men's wear trade, there were some large, integrated firms ("inside shops") that controlled all stages of manufacture on their own premises. But since adding more machines introduced few technical economies of scale, a manufacturer's greatest cost was labor. Consequently, most production was carried on by small, marginal firms ("outside shops").

With thousands of small contractors competing in selling finished clothes, workers had to work long hours for low pay to retain their jobs. In addition, the clothing worker's earnings were highly seasonal. Workers were jammed into tenement rooms with no adequate heat, ventilation, light, or sanitary conditions. In 1896 and 1897, New York State's new factory legislation banned families' living and working in the same quarters, but workers were still crowded together in empty tenement rooms and lofts.

The many immigrant workers employed in the needle trades, made labor organization chaotic and sporadic in the 19th century. The traditional craft bias of American unions was inadequate to deal with the differences of skill, national background, and sex that divided clothing workers. Organizing them required a concept of industrial unionism, first employed effectively in the men's wear industry. In 1910 workers struck at the Hart, Shaffner, and Marx factory in Chicago. Despite lack of support from the craft-based United Garment Workers of America (UGW), they won an agreement in 1911 to arbitration of future disputes, which resulted in a wage increase, a 54-hour week, and a preferential union shop. At the 1914 UGW convention, dissident sentiment led to the formation of the Amalgamated Clothing Workers of America (ACW). Ignoring jurisdictional disputes with the UGW, the ACW concentrated on organizing the men's wear branches of the industry.

The International Ladies Garment Workers Union (ILGWU), founded in 1900, emerged as the primary organizing force in the women's wear industry. In 1909, New York City shirt-waist makers struck in a protest remarkable for its high number of women strikers, more than 80 percent. Five months later fifty to sixty thousand cloak and suit makers, mostly men, walked out in the Great Revolt. The so-called Protocol of Peace, which ended the strike, was the first collective settlement by owners in the industry.

From World War I through the 1930's, the unions acted as an important force in stabilizing the industry. In the late 1920's both the ACW and ILGWU suffered a period of internal disunion when they expelled Communist elements, but both met the depression with renewed organizing drives and supported the National Recovery Administration codes. In 1937 they finally achieved industrywide collective bargaining. Statistics on the growth of the ready-made clothing industry throughout the 20th century attest to its increased importance in the economy. In the late 1970's the United States produced more apparel than any other country in the world, but a substantial portion of ready-made clothing sold to American consumers came from the Far East.

CLOTURE. A procedure used by the U.S. Senate since 1917 to curtail prolonged debate or filibuster in order to reach a final vote. Cloture must be proposed by sixteen senators; if approved, each senator thereafter is limited to one hour of speaking time.

CLOVIS CULTURE (or Llano culture). The earliest and most famous of the Late Lithic big-game hunting cultures, located in the North American High Plains and the Southwest; it existed in late Pleistocene environments with now extinct animal species 11,250 years ago. The settlements are identified archaeologically by the presence of bones of mammoths, bison, horse, and tapir, and Clovis fluted projectile points. These points were attached to the ends of lances or darts and atlatls (throwing sticks). Other artifacts include prismatic blades and stonecutting and scraping tools.

Clovis fluted points are also found scattered across the rest of the continent. The relationship between the Clovis culture and contemporary cultures to the east and west is an unsolved puzzle, as is the origin of the culture.

COAHUILA AND TEXAS, STATE OF. On May 7, 1824, the Mexican Congress united the former Spanish provinces of Coahuila and Texas, declaring that Texas might become a state when it acquired the necessary population and resources. The union was ended by the Texas revolution.

COAL. Coal is a major U.S. energy source. The U.S. Geological Survey ranks coal by chemical and physical characteristics. Anthracite, which contains the greatest percentage of carbon, ranks highest; lignite, with the smallest percentage, ranks lowest. Between them is a class called bituminous coals, subdivided into intermediate categories of fixed carbon and heating values. Bituminous coal is the most abundant rank in the United States and the one most commonly used.

Coal is widespread throughout the United States. The U.S. Geological Survey estimates that the potential recoverable reserves of coal are some 400 billion tons. With technological innovations and increased efficiencies in mining methods, these reserves could be greatly extended. Total U.S. production for 1978 was a bituminous and lignite coal output of 665 million tons and an anthracite output of about 5 million tons.

Coal is mined by two principal methods, underground and surface operations. Coal seams within 200 feet of the earth's surface are generally more adaptable to surface mining methods. Mechanization of underground mining operations received its greatest impetus with the introduction of Joy loading machines in the early 1920's; earlier attempts to introduce machinery proved unsuccessful except for an undercutting machine, introduced in 1877. The introduction of rubber-tired haulage units in 1936 gave further impetus to underground mechanization, and during the late 1940's, total mechanization of underground operations was begun. For surface mining operations, large earth-moving machines with big bucket capacities (200 cubic yards) have been introduced. U.S. coal production rose rapidly during the 19th century from an annual production in 1800 of 120,000 tons to 265 million tons by 1900. In the late 1960's, the industry was hampered by stiffening federal and state regulations designed to meet environmental considerations. The energy crisis in the 1970's led to renewed emphasis on coal.

COAL MINING AND ORGANIZED LABOR. Always dirty and exceedingly dangerous, coal mining has been historically an industry plagued by instabilities of production, consumption, and price. A gamut of dispersed production units has made private, as well as governmental, supervision, inspection, and regulation extremely difficult.

Unionization of mine labor began in the 1840's. It was variously a response to fraternal impulses among workers, dangerous working conditions, unsatisfactory wages, truck payments (payment in goods), abuses by company towns and privatized police, introduction of scab labor, blacklisting and yellow dog contracts, and unemployment. Unionization was complicated by the presence of thousands of immigrant workers in the pits; ethnic, cultural, racial, and linguistic barriers; the isolation of miners from one another; their relative immobility; and dual unionism and organizational mistakes.

Since January 1890, miners have been chiefly represented by the United Mine Workers of America (UMWA), an industrial union founded by bituminous miners from Pennsylvania, Ohio, Indiana, and Michigan but quickly encompassed anthracite miners also. Earlier, abortive unionization attempts were nearly all led by immigrants; nearly all, contrary to myth, were moderate and conciliatory, favoring arbitration over strikes. The UMWA, in this tradition, rose to power under two of the most famous and conservative unionists of their generations, John Mitchell and John L. Lewis. In 1980, the UMWA had 245,000 members.

COAST AND GEODETIC SURVEY. Upon the recommendation of President Thomas Jefferson, Congress on Feb. 10, 1807, enacted a law authorizing a survey of U.S. coasts. Swiss-born mathematician and geodesist Ferdinand Rudolph Hassler was chosen to administer the plan that he himself had submitted. He went to Europe in 1811 to procure the necessary scientific books and instruments. Numerous delays and misunderstandings brought a modification of the law on Apr. 14, 1818, authorizing the employment of military and naval officers only, thereby excluding Hassler and leading to a practical suspension of activities.

On July 10, 1832, Congress reactivated the Survey Act of 1807. Hassler was reappointed superintendent, to carry on concurrently his work as superintendent of the U.S. standards of weights and measures, a responsibility that then became a function of the Survey of the Coast.

Various operations of a geodetic survey were encompassed on land, including basic triangulations over 9,000 square miles and 1,600 miles of shoreline, and the hydrography of the adjacent waters. Field data were accumulated for maps.

The field operations were extended by Congress on Mar. 3, 1871, to a geodetic connection between the Atlantic, Gulf, and Pacific coasts. The 2,500-mile arc of triangulation along the thirty-ninth parallel of latitude was completed in 1895, an important achievement in the history of geodesy. The Eastern Oblique Arc from the Bay of Fundy to New Orleans, started by Hassler in 1816, was completed in 1889. In 1878, the bureau was renamed the Coast and Geodetic Survey.

The survey participated in several eclipse expeditions and boundary demarcations with Mexico and with Canada. Gravity observations have also been conducted in various parts of the world. Hydrographic observations furnish navigational information and nautical charts. Aeronautical charts are produced; topographic operations are carried on along the coastline; inshore and offshore hydrography and wire-drag surveys are made; ocean current studies, tidal observations and predictions, and certain features of oceanography are given attention. The geodetic survey itself investigates the size and shape of the earth. Geomagnetic studies determine the direction and intensity of the earth's magnetic field, and astronomical observations determine time, latitude, longitude, and azimuth in the mapping of stations used by the survey.

On July 13, 1965, the Coast and Geodetic Survey and the Weather Bureau became branches of the Environmental Science Services Administration (ESSA), which was absorbed by the National Oceanic and Atmospheric Administration of the Department of Commerce on July 9, 1970.

COAST GUARD, UNITED STATES. One of the armed forces of the United States and the principal federal agency for marine safety and maritime law enforcement. It operates under the Department of Transportation except when serving as a part of the navy.

The Coast Guard's parent service, the U.S. Revenue Marine (later the Revenue Cutter Service), was established by Congress on Aug. 4, 1790. The act authorized Alexander Hamilton, secretary of the treasury, to construct and operate ten small cutters to ensure the collection of customs duties on imports imposed by the Revenue Act of 1789. The cutter service soon became well known for expertise and daring in aiding ships and seamen in distress. At the time of the Quasi-War with France, there being no other U.S. naval force, Congress on July 1, 1797, authorized the president to cause the cutters "to defend the seacoast and to repel any hostility to their vessels and commerce." The service soon began to distinguish itself as a fighting force. After the establishment of the navy (1798), Congress decreed that the cutters "cooperate with the Navy . . . whenever the President shall so direct." Since then, cutters have sailed with the navy against all armed enemies of the United States.

The necessity for federal action in other areas of law enforcement and marine safety led early Congresses to establish several other essentially unifunctional agencies. The first was the Lighthouse Service, launched by an act of Aug. 7, 1789. In 1838, Congress created the Steamboat Inspection Service (later known as the Bureau of Marine Inspection and Navigation). Meanwhile, such hazardous areas as Cape Cod and North Carolina's Outer Banks became veritable graveyards for sailing ships and seamen of all nations. Legislation soon formally established the Life-Saving Service, a chain of lifeboats stationed along the coasts.

Successive efforts led eventually to the amalgamation of all these agencies as the U.S. Coast Guard (Jan. 28, 1915). On Apr. 1, 1967, in a sweeping reorganization, the Coast Guard was relocated from the Treasury Department to the new Department of Transportation.

The modern Coast Guard performs a multitude of duties: search and rescue; maintaining ocean stations to furnish meteorological data; military readiness; enforcing laws of the high seas and customs, immigration, and conservation laws; merchant marine and boating safety; aids to navigation, such as lighthouses and buoys; ice-breaking; port security; oceanography; and research.

COASTING TRADE. Until after 1850, shipping along the coasts was the principal means of transportation and communication between sections of the new country. In the colonial period it served to distribute European imports; manufactured goods of the Northeast were exchanged for the cotton and tobacco of the South, while agricultural products of the Mississippi Valley came to the Atlantic coast by way of New Orleans. Following the completion of railroad trunk lines after 1850, such bulk cargoes as coal, lumber, ice, iron, steel, and oil were still shipped by sea.

Colonial coasting trade was reserved to British and American vessels by the Navigation Acts of 1651 and 1660; and with the formation of the Union, the policy was continued, a prohibitive tax being placed on foreign-built and owned ships in 1789, followed by their total exclusion from coastwise competition under the Navigation Act of 1817.

COASTWISE STEAMSHIP LINES. American steamers made coastwise voyages as early as 1809, but the first regular lines operated in the sheltered waters of Long Island Sound and between Boston and Maine about 1825. Local services were established in the Gulf of Mexico in 1835; the United States Mail Steamship Company opened a regular line from New York to Charleston, S.C., Havana, New Orleans, and the Isthmus of Panama in 1848. In 1849 the Pacific Mail Steamship Company pioneered the route from Panama to San Francisco and Oregon. Competition from railroads, motor buses, and trucks, mounting operating costs, and labor difficulties resulted in the withdrawal of most service by 1937.

COBB, FORT. Established by Maj. W. H. Emory, Oct. 1, 1859, on the Washita River in Indian Territory. The Confederates occupied it for a time. Reoccupied by troops under Col. W. B. Hazen in November 1868 to protect the nearby Indian agency, it was once more abandoned in favor of Fort Sill.

COCHISE INCIDENT. *See* **Apache Pass Expedition.**

CODE NAPOLÉON. The unification and simplification of French laws under Napoleon Bonaparte's direction, promulgated in 1804 as the French civil code. It served as model for the civil laws of Orleans Territory, promulgated in 1808 and commonly called the Old Louisiana Code, which, revised and amended, remains the basic law of Louisiana.

CODE NOIR (Black Code). Commonly applied to the Edict Concerning the Negro Slaves in Louisiana, issued by Louis XV in 1724. The Code Noir fixed the legal status of slaves and imposed certain specific obligations and prohibitions on them and their masters and on freed or free blacks. Article I decreed expulsion of Jews from the colony. Article III prohibited any religious creed other than Roman Catholicism, and article IV decreed confiscation of slaves placed under any person not a Catholic. The essential provisions of the code remained in force in Louisiana until 1803, and many of them were embodied in later American Black Codes.

CODE, UNITED STATES. A consolidation of the general and permanent laws of Congress, private laws of limited applicability and temporary emergency measures being excluded. Its volumes are arranged by fifty subject titles. In authorizing the *United States Code* in 1924, the purpose of Congress was to supplement the *Statutes at Large,* which are arranged chronologically and contain numerous enactments later repealed, amended, or allowed to expire. The *Code* is the handiest source for statutory law in force at a given time.

CODES OF FAIR COMPETITION. The agreements negotiated under the authority of the National Industrial Recovery Act of June 16, 1933. The rules of fair trade practice promulgated by the Federal Trade Commission in 1923–33 were taken more seriously than previous codes of business ethics, but the sanctions supporting them were inadequate for full effectiveness. Violation of any provision of the National Industrial Recovery Act codes was made a misdemeanor. This, and the penalty of being deprived of the blue-eagle symbol, encouraged general compliance.

COD FISHERIES. North American cod fisheries lie off the coasts of New England, Newfoundland, and Labrador. The first fishermen came from Spain and France, attracted by the fisheries off Newfoundland. In the 16th century, Englishmen made frequent fishing voyages to the Grand Banks. Within a few years of Capt. John Smith's successful fishing venture in 1614 off New England, fishing colonies were established in Massachusetts and Maine.

The final defeat of France in the great colonial struggle with England left France with restricted fishing privileges. The New England cod fisheries expected to benefit, but new discontent appeared when Parliament passed the Sugar Act of 1764. Its enforcement threatened to ruin the profitable trade with the French West Indies that was based on the exchange of the poorer grade of cod for sugar and molasses.

Codfishing suffered severely from the revolutionary war, but the United States secured extensive fishing privileges from England in the Definitive Treaty of Peace (1783).

The Peace of Ghent (1814) did not provide for continuance of fishing privileges in British colonial waters. The Convention of 1818 attempted to settle the fisheries question, but it continued to be a sore spot until the Hague Tribunal of Arbitration in 1910.

After the War of 1812 the cod and mackerel fisheries expanded. The European market declined, but the domestic market more than offset this loss. After the Civil War the cod lost the distinction of being the principal food fish of the American seas. From about 1885 the cod fisheries began to decline in relation to other American fisheries.

COERCION ACTS (Restraining Acts or Intolerable Acts). Four measures passed by the English Parliament in 1774, partly in retaliation for such incidents as the Boston Tea Party. The Boston Port Act closed the harbor until the town had indemnified the East India Company for the destruction of its tea. The Massachusetts Government Act reduced Massachusetts to a crown colony. The Act for the Impartial Administration of Justice provided that judges, soldiers, and revenue officers indicted for murder in Massachusetts should be taken to England for trial. The Quartering Act removed all obstacles to the billeting of troops in Massachusetts.

COETUS-CONFERENTIE **CONTROVERSY.** A conflict in the 18th century between the progressive and conservative parties in the Dutch Reformed churches, now the Reformed Church in America. Beginning in 1628 the churches had been under authority of the church in Holland. A century later positive movement for freedom began. An assembly known as a *coetus*, assuming some power, was formed in 1737. Its opponents gradually grouped themselves in a so-called *conferentie*. In 1771 a plan of union brought from Holland reconciled the parties and established virtually complete independence of the church in America.

COEUR D'ALENE MISSION. A Roman Catholic Indian mission established (1842) near Cataldo, Idaho. In 1877 the mission was removed to the vicinity of Desmet, in present Benewah County.

COEUR D'ALENE RIOTS. Resulted from a strike of union miners in the lead and silver mines of northern Idaho in 1892. The mine owners protected nonunion labor with armed guards and obtained injunctions against the unions. On July 11, armed union miners expelled nonunion men from the district, a mill was dynamited, and a pitched battle was fought. State and federal troops took charge and martial law was proclaimed. In 1893 the local miners' unions affiliated with the Western Federation of Miners. In strikes in 1894 and 1899, federal troops suppressed violence.

COFFEEHOUSES. Soon after coffee was introduced into England from the Near East in 1650, establishments that served coffee became popular gathering places. Similar establishments soon arose in all the major ports and towns of the colonies, and such prominent coffeehouses as the London Coffee House (Philadelphia) and the Merchants' Coffee House (New York) assumed active roles in 18th-century colonial business and political life.

COFFEE'S TRADING POSTS. Maintained by Holland Coffee and others under the name of Coffee, Calville and Company. In 1834 they located a post on the north bank of Red River. Shortly thereafter they established another post on the same river above the mouth of Walnut Bayou in Oklahoma. During the late 1830's, Coffee exercised a strong influence over the Indians and ransomed numbers of white captives brought from Texas.

***COHENS* V. *VIRGINIA*,** 6 Wheaton 264 (1821). The case in which the Supreme Court upheld its jurisdiction to review the judgment of a state court where, in a criminal case, it was alleged that the conviction violated some right under the Constitution or federal laws.

COINAGE. The colonies had an inadequate volume of coins. Unlike the Spaniards, the English denied their American colonies the right to possess local mints. Colonists in backward or poor areas were forced to use wampum, beaver skins, and other commodity money. Elsewhere the lack of an adequate amount of English specie was compensated by French, Dutch, Portuguese, and above all Spanish coins.

The present U.S. coinage system was established by the Coinage Act of Apr. 2, 1792. The dollar was fixed at about the same weight of silver as the Spanish peso. Robert Morris, Thomas Jefferson, and Alexander Hamilton decided on a decimal system of coinage, the world's first. For accounting purposes they divided the dollar into 100 "cents" (a new term) and also into half-dollars; quarter-dollars; "dismes" or dimes; and half-dismes. The actual coins were to be of silver, except for the copper cents and half-cents. In addition there were to be gold coins as multiples: "eagles," or ten-dollar pieces; half-eagles; and quarter-eagles. But the gold-silver ratio that was chosen, 1–15, meant that a satisfactory bimetallic system was very difficult to maintain; at this rate gold was heavily undervalued. The United States produced only a trickle of precious metal. For three decades after 1806 no silver dollars were coined; the many half-dollars that were struck tended to be hoarded or exported. To encourage gold coinage, the government in 1834 changed the mint ratio to 1–16; thus, it was silver's turn to be undervalued.

By 1850 California gold was driving up the price of silver so rapidly that there was a severe decline in the already insufficient amount of silver coinage. Congress in 1851 authorized the first billon (mixed silver and copper) coin, a three-cent piece. The coin was an immediate success. In 1853 Congress ruled that all the other silver coins (except the dollar) also be turned into subsidiary coins.

In 1856 the United States made its first experiment with coinage made from nickel: the "flying eagle" one-cent piece, called a nickel until a five-cent piece of the same metal appeared ten years later. Gold production in California and Australia was making it easy to supply the country with coins of large denomination, including "double eagles" ($20).

Coinage after the Civil War has little proper history of its own. As the use of notes increased, the volume of coinage shrank. The Bland-Allison Act of 1878, the Sherman Act of 1890, and the Silver Purchase Act of 1934 attempted to force more silver into circulation by requiring the government to buy set amounts of silver each year and to strike at least some silver dollars, which had been inadvertently outlawed in the coinage law of 1873 but came to be struck again in enormous volumes. Apart from regions in the West, silver dollars never became popular except when the market price of silver jumped. The lack of American concern over the silver content of coins was highlighted when, in 1964–65, part-silver half-dollars, quarters, and dimes were withdrawn and replaced by nickel-clad copper coins. A $1 coin with the image of Susan B. Anthony was introduced in 1979, but it proved so unpopular that it was abandoned in 1981.

***COIN'S FINANCIAL SCHOOL*.** Written by W. H. ("Coin") Harvey to gain support for bimetallism, at 16–1, from people suffering from the hard times prevailing in 1894.

COLBERT'S GANG. A band of whites, half-breeds, and Chickasaw led by James Colbert that assisted the British at Mobile and Pensacola against the Spaniards (allies of the colonies) in the Revolution. Later, by harrying the Spaniards from Chickasaw Bluffs, it saved the east bank of the Mississippi River for Britain, and ultimately the United States.

COLD HARBOR, BATTLE OF (June 3, 1864). Following failures to smash and outflank Gen. Robert E. Lee at Spotsylvania, Gen. U. S. Grant on May 20 directed the Army of the Potomac southeast on a turning movement. Lee retired behind the North Anna River. Grant continued sideslipping toward Richmond until the Confederates stood on a six-mile front without reserves. Grant's assault against well-entrenched lines cost 5,600 Union casualties and failed completely. Grant dug in, held Lee in position until June 12, then resumed sideslipping, and, crossing the James River, threatened Richmond through Petersburg.

COLD SPRING HARBOR BIOLOGICAL LABORATORY. Founded in 1890 at Cold Spring Harbor, N.Y., as a summer school in the biological sciences. As the Cold Spring Harbor Laboratory for Quantitative Biology (since 1963), it became one of the world's foremost centers for biological research. The Carnegie Institute of Washington established the Station for Experimental Evolution in 1904, and Mrs. E. H. Harriman donated funds for the Eugenics Record Office in 1910. In 1921, the latter two merged to become the Department of Genetics of the Carnegie Institute. In succeeding years, year-round housing was built so that the laboratory's facilities could be used by members of the staff and visiting scholars for ongoing research projects. Private gifts, government research funds, and foundation grants proved inadequate as research costs soared, and in 1963 the laboratory was placed under the aegis of a consortium of universities.

COLD WAR. The struggle for world supremacy between the United States and the Soviet Union following World War II. It was waged by diplomatic means, propaganda, and threats of force, rather than by outright military force—except in limited, local wars fought largely by proxies of the great powers—because the strains imposed by World War II and the threat of nuclear devastation deterred recourse to a "hot war." The cold war was a product of the polarization of power after World War II, when the United States and the Soviet Union overshadowed all other powers. The 1960's saw the emergence of substantial concentrations of political, economic, and sometimes military power independent of the two superpowers, in China, Western Europe, and Japan. This development made diplomatic alignments far more complex.

The U.S. government, as well as official and otherwise sympathetic historians, have seen the hostility between the American and Soviet blocs and the American containment policy as the necessary results of a Soviet intention to impose Communist power wherever non-Communist weakness permitted. The United States, according to this view, thus was moved to respond to an expansionist Soviet empire by building positions of military and economic strength all around the borders of the Communist world.

The threat of massive nuclear retaliation may well have been indispensable to keeping the contest merely cold as the superpowers confronted each other through the Korean War and a series of Berlin, Middle Eastern, and Eastern European crises in the 1950's. In the 1960's, however, not only did the end of the polarization of world power help force both superpowers into new diplomatic postures, but each of the superpowers found habitual cold war policies leading it into frustration—the Soviet Union in the Cuban missile crisis of 1962 and the United States in Vietnam. As a result, more flexible policies and a Soviet-American détente could more readily recommend themselves. Détente culminated in the Helsinki agreements on European security and cooperation in 1975. In the late 1970's, U.S.-Soviet relations again deteriorated, mainly because of Soviet internal repression and the invasion of Afghanistan in 1979. When President Ronald Reagan assumed office in 1981, some commentators described the international atmosphere as "cold peace."

COLLECTIVE BARGAINING. A two-party, rule-making process important in relationships between employers, or their associations, and workers represented by their unions. It is institutionalized in the United States, where it is widely practiced and highly sophisticated, as an alternative to rule-making by employers alone or by government through legislation, compulsory arbitration, or edict. Although this two-party process is private rather than governmental, government does exert an influence.

Collective bargaining in the United States arose out of the need by workers for a voice in, and some control of, the determination of wages, hours, and conditions of employment. The free pursuit of economic self-interest became a legal basis for unionism and collective bargaining. The early landmark decision in *Commonwealth of Massachusetts* v. *Hunt* (1842) practically freed unions from the crime of conspiracy, yet antiunion judges easily found illegality in objectives and actions of unions. Later, injunctions were used to block organizing or other efforts of unions. Unions also suffered from inclusion under the Sherman Antitrust Act (1890) and did not escape with enactment of the Clayton Act (1914). Yet the principle of free pursuit of self-interest was more and more affirmed by liberal judges. In 1932 the Norris–La Guardia Act (Anti-injunction Act) denied federal courts the power to issue injunctions in labor disputes. The National Industrial Recovery Act (1933) and the National Labor Relations Act (1935) gave direct government support to the practice of collective bargaining. Support of unions was modified and the role of government broadened by the Taft-Hartley Act (1947) and the Landrum-Griffin Act (1959).

Some bargaining structures are local; others, national. Some are highly centralized; others, decentralized. Some are multiunit, comprising several companies or unions. At the beginning of a negotiating situation, neither party knows what terms the other is willing to settle for. What takes place in the process is contrived and used to find out the settlement position of the other party without prematurely revealing one's own position. Exorbitant demands, numerous meetings, deadlines, marathon sessions prior to the deadline, eleventh-hour and "corridor" settlements rather than settlements at the bargaining table, are typical. Settlements are commonly reached without resorting to overt power, although the ever-present possibility of a strike is an important factor. Central to the process is that the respective constituencies accept the bargain finally struck.

***COLLECTOR* V. *DAY*,** 11 Wallace 113 (1871). Probate Judge Day of Barnstable County, Mass., having paid the Civil War income tax on his salary under protest, brought suit to recover it and obtained judgment. The tax collector then sued out a writ of error. The U.S. Supreme Court in 1871 decided that it was not competent for Congress to levy a tax upon the salary of a judicial officer.

COLLEGES AND UNIVERSITIES. American colleges and universities began in 1636 with Harvard College (now University). Other colonial colleges were the College of William and Mary, chartered in 1693; the Collegiate School (Yale University), founded in 1701; the College of New Jersey (Princeton University), chartered in 1746; King's College (Columbia University), founded in 1754; the College, Academy, and Charitable School of Philadelphia (University of Pennsylvania), chartered in 1755; the College of Rhode Island (Brown University), chartered in 1764; Queen's College (Rutgers—the State University), chartered in 1766; and Dartmouth College, chartered in 1769. At first, the colleges had a Protestant character, but with the advent of the Enlightenment the curriculum was modified by the addition of medicine, law, the sciences, and modern languages.

American usage of the term *university* dates from 1779, with the rechartering of the College of Philadelphia as the University of the State of Pennsylvania. State-controlled colleges and universities appeared in Georgia, North Carolina, and Tennessee by 1800. The Dartmouth College decision (1819) by the U.S. Supreme Court, a ruling that supported freedom from state interference, proved to be the Magna Charta of private and denominational colleges.

After the Civil War, the number of colleges and universities continued to increase. New institutions opened for women, Afro-Americans, American Indians, and members of various faiths. The opening of the Johns Hopkins University (1876) brought German standards of research and scholarship to American higher education. Other changes included the institution of the undergraduate elective system at Harvard and of agricultural and engineering colleges.

During the 20th century, enrollment in colleges and universities climbed sharply upward, but in the late 1970's the rate of increase slowed down. The number of women students and faculty members has increased perceptibly, as has the number of members of racial and ethnic minority groups.

By the late 1970's, 43 percent of the 2,900 colleges and universities were under governmental (mostly state) control and had 75 percent of the total enrollment. The private sector comprises institutions under denominational direction and those under the governance of self-perpetuating secular boards of trustees. A number of denominational colleges, though, have secularized the composition of their boards of trustees so as to qualify for much needed public funds.

Colleges and universities in the 1970's faced increasing financial difficulties. Other serious issues, especially for the junior faculty, were academic freedom and tenure. The question of equal opportunity remains perplexing and controversial. Although barriers to higher education have fallen for racial and ethnic minorities and for women, complaints of discrimination continue, notably by the handicapped.

Black colleges. A number of private and public institutions have drawn all or the majority of their students from among Afro-Americans. The private ones began with Lincoln University in Pennsylvania in 1854 and Wilberforce University in Ohio in 1856. Still extant in 1980 were Hampton Institute (1868), Fisk University (1866), Talladega College (1867), Howard University (1867), Atlanta University (1865), Johnson C. Smith University (1867), St. Augustine's College (1867), and Tuskegee Institute (1881). Public colleges for blacks were established mostly in the 20th century. Discriminatory practices caused these to be far less well supported financially than state institutions for whites. Black colleges increased in enrollment even as blacks entered institutions from which they had previously been excluded.

Denominational colleges. Of the approximately 900 colleges established in America by 1861, only 182 survived; of these some 160 were founded by fifteen religious denominations, about 140 under the control of the Presbyterians, Methodists, Baptists, Congregationalists, Roman Catholics, and Episcopalians. After the Civil War the church colleges' prominent position in American higher education was weakened by the impact of Darwinian ideas, industrial growth, development of modern science and technology, spread of humanistic and antireligious thought, declining financial status, and competition with prestigious secular institutions.

COLLOT'S JOURNEY. French Gen. Victor Collot came to Philadelphia after the British, in 1794, took possession of Guadeloupe, West Indies, where he had been governor. When litigation prevented his departure for France, he left McKeesport, Pa., June 6, 1796, visited the Ohio River settlements and the Illinois country, and then turned back down the Mississippi to New Orleans. His journal shows an appreciation of the potentialities of the American West.

COLOMBIA, CANAL CONTROVERSY WITH. The Hay-Herrán Treaty, signed between the United States and Colombia (January 1903), authorized the building of a canal across Panama (then a province of Colombia) under American auspices; but the Colombian senate failed to ratify the agreement. The province of Panama, resentful over this failure, revolted in November 1903 and, with U.S. aid, established its independence. The United States at once made a canal treaty with the infant republic (*see* Hay–Bunau-Varilla Treaty). Colombia repeatedly demanded amends. Finally, in 1921, the United States paid Colombia $25 million.

COLONIAL AGENT. A representative sent to England by the colonies in America during the 17th and 18th centuries who formed an indispensable link between the mother country and colony. In the 17th century agents went to England only on special missions. In the 18th century, when the business of colonial administration had greatly increased, the agent remained at his post year after year. Benjamin Franklin was in England from 1757 to 1762 as agent of the Pennsylvania assembly. The agent was not necessarily a colonist; frequently an Englishman especially interested in the American colonies was appointed. He served as a clearinghouse of information at a time when ignorance of colonial conditions was widespread; attended hearings on various matters held by the Board of Trade and the Privy Council; prepared petitions embodying specific claims or requests; worked on the perennial Indian problems; and wrestled with boundary disputes.

COLONIAL ASSEMBLIES. Began with the Virginia House of Burgesses called by Gov. George Yeardley in 1619. The first Virginia assembly, unicameral in organization, was composed of the governor, his council, and two burgesses elected for each of the towns, plantations, and hundreds. In the late 17th century the elected element separated from the parent assembly, resulting in a bicameral legislative body.

Plymouth colony set up a popular assembly of all qualified freemen. With the growth of out-settlements this evolved into a representative bicameral body. In Massachusetts Bay, Gov. John Winthrop and his supporters tried to concentrate legislative authority in the Court of Assistants. This failed, and a representative bicameral system eventually evolved.

In Rhode Island, Providence, Portsmouth, Newport, and Warwick were empowered to initiate legislation that was thereupon referred to the assembly; the assembly would also refer measures to the towns. The system was ineffective, and the charter of 1663 gave the assembly a dominating role.

Connecticut had the General Court, which was both a representative body and, upon sitting as a court of election, a primary assembly. The latter feature disappeared in the 18th century in favor of local election of colonial officials.

The Maryland proprietor, Cecil Calvert, Lord Baltimore, called an assembly of freemen. He attempted to establish the principle that the proprietor alone might initiate legislation, and sent over drafts of measures. The assembly rejected them, claiming sole powers of initiation, and passed a number of bills framed by its own members. Baltimore finally admitted the competence of the assembly to initiate laws but insisted they be submitted to him for approval.

Lawmaking processes in Carolina were confused by the divergent aims of the eight proprietors and the settlers. The settlers were determined to uphold the binding nature of the Concessions and Agreement of 1665, which provided for a popularly elected assembly of freeholders. The proprietors attempted to enforce the feudal Fundamental Constitutions with its extraordinarily complicated lawmaking machinery, designed to guarantee proprietarial control of legislation.

New York under the Duke of York for many years had no popularly elected body. With the retirement of Gov. Edmund Andros to England in 1680, the settlers refused to pay imposts. The Duke of York granted an assembly, sending Thomas Dongan as governor; but the laws passed by the deputies were never ratified; under James II, assemblies were forbidden but reappeared under William III.

Pennsylvania was provided with a popularly elected assembly. After the withdrawal of the charter of Massachusetts Bay in 1684, consolidation took place under the Dominion of New England; the assemblies were suppressed and lawmaking powers were centered in the appointed Dominion council. New York, East New Jersey, and West New Jersey, the last two with popularly elected assemblies, were also embodied in the Dominion before it collapsed in 1689.

During the 18th century the assemblies frequently came into collision with the governors, as a rule leaving the assemblies in a strongly entrenched position, in spite of the continued control of legislation by the Privy Council. With the approach of the Revolution, breaches took place between the assemblies and their governors in all but the two corporate colonies (Connecticut and Rhode Island).

COLONIAL CHARTERS. Royal charters represented the king's authorization of colonization under private enterprise and his definition of the relationship of the colony to England. Charters to trading companies vested powers of government in the company in England, which determined officers, laws, and ordinances necessary for the colony. In proprietary charters, authority was granted to the lord proprietor. According to the corporation charters of Connecticut and Rhode Island, government was to be administered by governor, council, and house of representatives, with the house chosen directly, the governor indirectly, by the people.

In the late 17th century the king tried to substitute the royal province for corporation and proprietary governments. By 1776 there remained only two proprietary provinces, Maryland and Pennsylvania, and two corporation colonies, Connecticut and Rhode Island. Massachusetts operated under a charter but was governed in the 18th century as a royal province.

COLONIAL COMMERCE. Several forms existed. There was the two-way commerce, between a colony and England, between two colonies, or between a colony and a West Indian port. Triangular trade was common, as between a colony, the African coast, and the West Indies, typified by Rhode Island's trade in rum, slaves, and molasses.

Commerce was carried on, as a rule, in American-built ships. When ships themselves were articles of commerce, they were generally built in New England, loaded in a southern port, and sent to their destination. The two greatest commercial centers before the American Revolution were Boston and Philadelphia. Colonial commerce involved not only barter, specie transactions in Spanish or Portuguese coins, and bills of exchange, but credit extensions on a great scale.

The development of restrictions on the colonies, outside of early restrictions by the crown on the sale of tobacco, is associated with the trade and navigation acts. Certain colonial products, such as American woolens or beaver hats, could not enter into commerce; certain other products could be carried directly only to the mother country or to another colony. Ships engaged in colonial commerce were confined, with certain exceptions in favor of prizes captured, to vessels of English, later British, or colonial construction and manned chiefly by those owing allegiance to the crown; they were required to have a British or colonial registry, to be commanded by British or colonial officers, to sail under British colors, and to import European commodities only through a British port, with the exception of a few specified articles.

COLONIAL COUNCILS. Existed in all the colonies. In general they represented the same control as the governor. In the royal provinces they were appointed directly by the crown. In the proprietary colonies they were appointed by the proprietor; in Massachusetts, Rhode Island, and Connecticut the councils were elective. Councils varied in size, although practice tended to a council of twelve in the royal provinces. Colonial councils acted as the upper house of the legislature, and when so acting, the governor was not to be present. The council, together with the governor, formed a supreme court of appeals in civil cases. The council was an executive and administrative body for the governor, and many of his acts could be carried out only with the approval of the council.

COLONIAL CURRENCY. *See* **Money.**

COLONIAL DAMES OF AMERICA. A society of women descended from ancestors who came to reside in America prior to 1750 and founded a town that has survived and developed, held important positions, or helped achieve American independence. The society, organized in 1890, collects relics and mementos for preservation and fosters interest in American history. Membership in 1980 was about 2,000.

COLONIAL GOVERNORS. The chief civil officers in the American colonies before the Revolution. Some were appointed by the king, as was the governor of the royal colony of Virginia; others were nominated by a proprietor, such as William Penn, and were approved by the crown; and those of the chartered colonies were elected by deputies of the freemen of the community.

The tasks of the executive of the chartered colonies were relatively simple. Chosen by his own people and linked by only nebulous bonds to the mother country, he suffered no conflict of loyalties. The position of the governor of the royal or proprietary colonies, however, was often unpleasant. Saddled with definite instructions, he faced a provincially minded and stubborn assembly that controlled the purse strings. After the Restoration, England attempted to establish uniform government in the colonies, but the assemblies became the real executives and soon learned the art of self-government.

COLONIAL GOVERNORS' INSTRUCTIONS. Instructions were issued in the king's name by the Privy Council to every royal governor of a province. They touched upon nearly every subject involved in colonial government, from the council and assembly and the governor's relations thereto, legislation, finance, justice, military and naval matters, to religion and morals. Because of opposition by the colonists or ignorance of colonial conditions on the part of the ministry, instructions were often unenforced and unenforceable.

COLONIAL JUDICIARY. Every colony created a judiciary by act of the assembly and followed the general pattern of English procedure. Each colony had a system of local courts to try petty offenses. Most colonies had a county court presided over by one of the superior judges who traveled on circuit. There was a superior court presided over by a chief justice. Each colony had an attorney general. In the royal provinces the chief justice and the judges of the superior court were at first appointed directly by the crown. Governors were authorized to fill vacancies when they occurred.

The death of George II in 1760 terminated all judicial commissions. The Board of Trade insisted that all renewals should be "at the pleasure of the Crown." This deprived Englishmen in America of rights guaranteed to Englishmen in England, and is one of the specific acts of tyranny charged against George III in the Declaration of Independence.

COLONIAL PLANS OF UNION. The separate founding of the colonies, coupled with difficulties of travel, prevented effective union until the Revolution. However, many proposals for union grew out of the common problems faced by the colonies. The chief plans, which varied widely in origin and the number of colonies to be included, were as follows:

1. The United Colonies of New England, 1643–84. Massachusetts Bay, Plymouth, Connecticut, and New Haven, united for frontier defense.

2. Dominion of New England, 1688. The British crown made Sir Edmund Andros governor-general of all the New England colonies, New York, and East and West Jersey.

3. Intercolonial Congress, 1689–91. New York, Massachusetts, Plymouth, and Connecticut entered a temporary military league for frontier defense.

4. William Penn's "Briefe and Plaine Scheam" for Union, 1697, a proposal for a loose confederation.

5. Union under the Earl of Bellomont, 1698–1701, governor of New York, Massachusetts, and New Hampshire, and commander of the military forces of Connecticut, Rhode Island, and the Jerseys.

6. Hamilton's Plan, 1699, for frontier defense and production of naval supplies for the Royal Navy proposed by the deputy-governor of Pennsylvania. An intercolonial assembly was to levy a poll tax to finance the work, to be done by British regulars.

7. "A Virginian's Plan of Union," 1701, advocated uniting the colonies under a congress and governor-general.

8. Robert Livingston's Plan, 1701, proposed that the colonies be grouped into three units coordinated by the Council of Trade for frontier defense.

9. Earl of Stair's Plan, 1721, was to include all the continental colonies and the British West Indies.

10. The Lords of Trade Plan, 1721, was essentially a brief outline of the Stair plan.

11. Daniel Coxe's Plan, 1722, proposed a union of all the continental colonies under one governor, represented by a lieutenant in each colony.

12. The Kennedy-Franklin Plan, 1751, was published by Archibald Kennedy, receiver-general of New York, in a pamphlet on Indian trade and frontier defense. Benjamin

Franklin added some details that closely resembled his later Albany Plan.

13. The Albany Plan, 1754. Largely the work of Franklin, it called for an intercolonial council with membership apportioned according to wealth and population. The president-general was to be appointed by the crown. Control of Indian affairs and frontier defense was to be administered by this royal officer and his council.

COLONIAL POLICY, BRITISH. This policy promoted domestic industry, foreign trade, the fisheries and shipping, and the planting of crown lands in the New World with the establishment of settlements or exploitation of resources through such companies as the Hudson's Bay Company. It also included utilization of the vast labor resources of Africa in the establishment and maintenance of plantations for the production of "colonial staples."

The earliest English colonial policies are embodied in the 16th-century patents to Sir Humphrey Gilbert and Sir Walter Raleigh; in 1606, patents were granted to the London and Plymouth companies of Virginia in connection with which a settlement policy was laid down embodying the idea of direct crown control; but in 1609 this was modified in favor of the Virginia Company substituting indirect control. Direct control made its reappearance in 1624, when Virginia took its place as the first "royal colony" under a system of government that permitted the survival of the colonial assembly. In 1629 appeared the corporate colony of Massachusetts Bay with a charter that permitted the transfer of the government of the company to the New World; 1632 saw the proprietaryship of Maryland. Thus, three types of colonial government appeared: royal, proprietary, and charter.

With the outbreak of the English Civil War, the Long Parliament assumed control from the crown, making the Earl of Warwick governor-in-chief and lord high admiral of all the English colonies in America. Various regulations strictly controlled colonial commerce in favor of English shipping and manufactures. The Restoration added measures beginning with the Navigation Act of 1660 and culminating in the comprehensive Act of 1696. The growth in importance of the colonies led to various experiments in their supervision.

Colonial policy in the 18th century was characterized by efforts to reduce the colonies to a uniform type—the royal colony—and by increased restrictions upon colonial enterprise. An important modification of policy came with the growing menace of French competition. Side by side with mercantilism, modern imperialism made its appearance. In order to secure direct revenue from the colonies, Parliament passed the Stamp Act of 1765 and the Townshend Acts of 1767, helping to bring on a crisis that led to the Revolution.

COLONIAL POLICY OF THE UNITED STATES. *See* **Insular Possessions.**

COLONIAL SETTLEMENTS. Various colonies were planted along the Atlantic coast for different reasons. Sir Humphrey Gilbert landed with his company for a few months on Newfoundland's shores in 1584. Sir Walter Raleigh in 1585 settled a few colonists on Roanoke Island (Carolina coast), but failed to keep the venture alive. The close of war with Spain in 1604 freed England to turn to America. Joint-stock companies, combining capital and credit, entered into colonization. In 1607 the Plymouth Company tried a settlement on the Kennebec River (Maine), the London Company on the James River (Virginia). A rigorous winter and the death of the chief promoter soon sent the Kennebec settlers away. The London Company persisted. During its existence about 5,500 emigrants left England for Virginia; in 1625 about a thousand were living in the colony. The long voyage, disease, starvation, and Indians took a deadly toll. Virginia became the first permanent English colony.

In 1624 the Dutch West India Company founded New Amsterdam and Fort Orange (Albany). In 1638 the New Sweden Company began Fort Christina on the Delaware, but New Sweden ceased to be when captured by the Dutch in 1655.

The economic motive was not the only factor in colonial enterprise. Abundant land meant little without people. Settlers came in 1620 when the Pilgrims planted the colony of Plymouth. The primary motive was to establish in Massachusetts a city of God. Villagers from Massachusetts Bay, in 1635, founded the colony of Connecticut. In 1638 Puritans began the colony of New Haven, which was merged with Connecticut in 1662. Intolerable conditions in Massachusetts peopled Rhode Island. Massachusetts added Maine by purchase and secured Plymouth colony by merger, and before 1700 the Bay province had over 50,000 people. New Hampshire harbored a few people under the proprietorship of Capt. John Mason. Maryland owed its genesis to Lord Baltimore, who desired a refuge for Catholics.

The circle of English colonies was completed in 1664 by the conquest of New Netherland, renamed New York and granted to the Duke of York. He subgranted New Jersey to Sir George Carteret and Lord John Berkeley. Carolina, granted to eight men by charter in 1663, divided into North Carolina, peopled from Virginia, and South Carolina, settled by discontented planters from Barbados and persecuted Protestants from France and England. The Quakers established their own colonies on the Delaware. In 1674 Berkeley sold West Jersey, which the Quakers settled along the Delaware River at Burlington. East Jersey, purchased from the Carteret estate in 1680, went to a large board in which the Quakers were prominent. In 1681 William Penn received a charter for Pennsylvania, where he tried a "Holy Experiment" in Quaker principles. The province became a haven of refuge for the persecuted, welcoming English, Welsh, and Irish Quakers, and Germans. Delaware, granted to Penn by the Duke of York and governed at first as part of Pennsylvania, in 1704 became a province with Penn as proprietor. Georgia came into existence in 1732 in response to humanitarian motives, harboring debtors from English jails.

COLONIAL SHIPS. The ships that brought the first settlers to the New World were very small. Sir Humphrey Gilbert's vessel weighed 10 tons. Christopher Newport's three ships, in which the first Virginians came to America, were 100, 40, and

20 tons, respectively. The *Mayflower* was 180 tons, its keel length 64 feet, beam width 26 feet, and depth from beam to keel 11 feet, while the full length was 90 feet. The *Dove* and the *Ark,* which carried Lord Baltimore's company to Maryland, were 50 and 400 tons, respectively. Vessels were soon being made in the colonies. By 1676, 730 ships had been built in Massachusetts alone, and hundreds more in other New England colonies.

COLONIAL SOCIETY. Colonial society was a product of Old World institutions and the New World environment. English settlers brought traditional concepts of the social order, in which deference was due the upper levels of society. But in America an abundance of land and a shortage of manpower created the opportunity for upward mobility and a large, open middle class of propertied farmers, artisans, merchants, and professionals. Newly freed indentured servants and casual laborers, the bottom rank of colonial society, were not permanently locked in that position.

The instability resulting from such mobility, coupled with the attempt to tighten imperial authority after the Restoration, caused a series of rebellions. By the end of the 17th century, violent challenges to established authority subsided as the indigenous elite won acceptance of their social and political leadership. By the 1720's the social structure had begun to rigidify. The Revolution helped to arrest this process and to open new avenues of opportunity and mobility.

The bulk of those migrating in the 17th century came from the English middle and lower classes. Unlike the religiously motivated Puritans, most came to better their economic conditions or to escape political persecution.

The effect of non-English migration on colonial society was primarily cultural, not political. Most non-English settlers found colonial political practices more enlightened than those they had known and had little desire to alter them. On the other hand, the non-English brought with them a diversity of religions; this and the presence of thousands of dissenters encouraged the practice of religious toleration.

COLONIAL WARS. Colonial wars were not mere New World phases of Old World conflicts. America's natural resources and the supposed advantages of controlling American markets led Europeans to seek vast holdings here, and economic rivalries among the colonials themselves were intensified by racial and religious antagonisms. Louis XIV gave little practical support to offensives in America; thus, in King William's War (1689–97), Louis de Buade, Comte de Frontenac, resorted to Indian allies in ruthless border raids. Similar raids were utilized, chiefly by the French, in Queen Anne's War (1702–13), King George's War (1744–48), and the French and Indian War (1754–63); and by the English against the Spanish in the War of Jenkin's Ear (1739–1742).

COLONIES, MANUFACTURING IN THE. *See* **Industries, Colonial.**

COLONIZATION MOVEMENT. Aimed at sending all or part of the black population in the United States to colonize Africa or Central America. As early as 1776, Thomas Jefferson proposed a plan to colonize U.S. blacks in Africa. After the Revolution, groups of blacks sought support from state governments to emigrate. In 1815 Paul Cuffe, a black merchant, transported thirty-eight persons to Sierra Leone at his own expense. Various colonization resolutions were passed by state legislatures in the early years of the Republic. In 1817 the American Colonization Society was established. It sent free blacks to Sierra Leone until 1821, when land that eventually became Liberia was purchased for the settlement.

There was some increased interest in the 1850's among blacks after passage of the Fugitive Slave Act of 1850. In 1854 the National Emigration Convention of Colored People was organized to consider colonization in Central America. It waned with the advent of Radical Reconstruction, but schemes continued to develop until the end of the century.

The major resurgence of the colonization idea in the 20th century was in the United Negro Improvement Association of Marcus Garvey in the 1920's. Garvey's "Back-to-Africa" movement was even less successful than its predecessors.

COLORADO. First visited by white men led by the Spanish *conquistador* Francisco Vásquez de Coronado, in 1541. Juan de Ulibarri took formal possession for Spain in 1706, but Frenchmen pushed southwestward and disputed Spanish claims. The Treaty of Paris (1763) made Spain undisputed owner of the Colorado region.

The western part of Colorado was retroceded to France in 1800, and through the Louisiana Purchase in 1803, the United States acquired it. The major part of what is now Colorado belonged to Spain and then to Mexico, until the Mexican War and the Treaty of Guadalupe Hidalgo (1848) gave the whole area to the United States. Subsequent boundary adjustments expanded Colorado to its present limits.

The most thorough exploration of the region was effected by fur trappers and traders. Trading posts were the first fixed habitations of white men in Colorado. The first towns in Colorado were founded in the 1850's by Spanish settlers from New Mexico, who developed irrigated agriculture and grazing. Need for protection from Indians caused the establishment in 1852 of Fort Massachusetts. In 1858 the Pikes Peak gold rush resulted in widespread settlement. Jefferson Territory became Colorado Territory in 1861. Colorado troops sustained the Union in the Civil War.

Refractory ores, Indian wars, and the Civil War retarded Colorado's growth in the 1860's. The end of the wars, the coming of the railroads in 1870, and the development of agriculture improved conditions. Increased population helped bring statehood on Aug. 1, 1876. The range cattle industry, the extension of railroads, the discovery of great silver lodes at Leadville and Aspen, and the smelting industry furthered prosperity. Demonetization of silver and the panic of 1893 brought economic distress. Abrupt reduction in silver output was offset by the rise of the great gold camp of Cripple Creek. Coal and petroleum production has also been important to Colorado. By 1960, farm products were valued at about thirty-five times the output of precious metals. Then manufacturing became the leading industry.

Colorado, with fifty-five named peaks higher than 14,000 feet, has a mean elevation of 6,800 feet. The scenic beauty and climate of the state have made the tourist business a leading industry. Colorado's population was 2,888,834 in 1980.

COLORADO COAL STRIKES (1903–04; 1913–14). Caused by refusal of the mine operators in Trinidad, Colo., to recognize the right of unionization and demands by workers for better pay and working conditions, as well as for the right to board, trade, and seek medical attention wherever they pleased. In both cases, troops were called in. In 1904 the strikers returned to work without having won any material advantages, but in 1914 they won more satisfactory working conditions, the state enacted legislation to prevent similar occurrences, and the Colorado Fuel and Iron Company adopted a more constructive labor policy.

COLORADO NARROW-GAUGE RAILROADS. Beginning in the late 1860's Colorado became the center of the construction of narrow-gauge (three feet) railroads. In 1873 over half the narrow-gauge mileage in the United States was in Colorado. Close study had shown that a gauge of three feet was practicable in mountainous regions. About a half-dozen narrow-gauge railroads are still in operation in Colorado.

COLORADO RIVER EXPLORATIONS. In 1539 the Spanish explorer Francisco de Ulloa reached the mouth of the Colorado, in the Gulf of California, without knowing of the river's existence. The actual discovery was made in 1540 by Hernando de Alarcón. He did not make a junction with the expedition under Francisco Vásquez de Coronado, two of whose officers, Melchior Díaz and García López de Cárdenas, reached the Colorado. Cárdenas went on to discover the Grand Canyon. In the next two centuries, exploration of the river was in the hands of Franciscan missionaries.

In the early 19th century, exploration was mostly by trappers and fur traders. In 1826 a British naval officer, Lt. R. W. H. Hardy, explored the lower Colorado and wrote the first dependable description of the country near the mouth.

With the establishment of a military post at the mouth of the Gila River, one of the major tributaries, the U.S. government became interested in scientific exploration of the Colorado. The topographical engineers of the War Department sent several expeditions. John Wesley Powell's blueprinting of the stream was completed by the Geological Survey. George A. Johnson first ascended the river to the head of navigation, above the Black Canyon, in his steamer, the *General Jessup,* in 1857. Only in the 1920's did the river begin to be exploited for irrigation and hydroelectric power.

COLORADO RIVER PROJECTS. The Colorado River Compact (1922) set down a plan for apportioning the waters of the Colorado between the Lower Basin (Arizona, California, and Nevada) and the Upper Basin (Colorado, New Mexico, Utah, and Wyoming). Failing ratification by Arizona, the plan was approved by Congress as a six-state agreement in the Boulder Canyon Project Act (1928). In 1930 a program to coordinate Lower Basin power and water use was initiated by the secretary of the interior. Initial operating contracts included the use of Hoover (Boulder) Dam power in California, reservation of waters for Arizona, and construction of the All-American Canal from hydroelectric-power revenues. Beginning with Hoover Dam (1936), nine major and many smaller dams have been built, as well as related water-diversion works. The Colorado River Storage Act (1956) authorized construction of major reservoirs in both basins.

There have been long-standing differences between the Basin states concerning release of water from the Upper Basin. The Colorado River Basin Project Act (1968) provided a ten-year moratorium on studies of any plan to import water into the Colorado River basin. Major additional facilities authorized by this act are the Central Arizona Project; the Southern Nevada Water Project; and the Dixie Project, which will supply southern Utah. Even so, a water deficiency of 1.5 million acre-feet is predicted for the Lower Basin.

COLORADO SPRINGS (Colo.). Second largest city in Colorado, with a population of 215,150 (1980); center of a metropolitan area of 317,458. The U.S. Air Force Academy and several other colleges are there. One of the leading tourist cities in Colorado, situated in the eastern Rocky Mountains, Colorado Springs was established as a town in 1891, when silver and gold were discovered at Cripple Creek.

COLT SIX-SHOOTER. The invention of Samuel Colt. With the rifle, it revolutionized methods of warfare and was an important link between the muzzle-loading musket and the magazine rifles and machine guns of today.

Its manufacture began at Paterson, N.J., in 1836. Colt's patent covered the revolution and locking of the cylinder firmly in place, so that the chambers of the cylinder came in line with the barrel by simply pulling the hammer back to full cock. It did not at first receive endorsement of government officials, and the company failed in 1842.

A few Colt arms used by army officers and Texas Rangers proved the worth of the "revolving pistol," and a supply was ordered by the government in January 1847. The first two or three thousand were made at the plant of Eli Whitney, son of the inventor, in New Haven, Conn. These .44-caliber revolvers soon became the standard of the U.S. Army and the Texas Rangers. Colt resumed the manufacture of revolvers at Hartford, Conn., in 1848. Large quantities of these arms were used during the Civil War by both sides. Colt revolvers, up to the early 1870's, were made to shoot loose powder and lead bullets, the powder being ignited by a percussion cap. From that period, envelope cartridges, enclosing powder and bullet, were used until the advent of metallic ammunition.

COLUMBIA. One symbol of the United States is a goddess-like figure called Columbia. She appeared very often in 19th-century drawings and cartoons as a representation of the United States. The figure has been used on coins and stamps.

COLUMBIA (S.C.). The capital and largest city of South Carolina, with a population of 99,296 (1980), and the center of a metropolitan area of 408,176. Its industries include the manufacture of textiles, clothing, building materials, electronic equipment, and plastic products. It is the home of the University of South Carolina, several smaller colleges, and an agricultural research station maintained by the U.S. Department of Agriculture and Clemson University.

Columbia was made state capital in 1786. Shortly after the city was captured by Union troops in February 1865, a major fire destroyed homes and offices, but not the public buildings.

COLUMBIA, BURNING OF. Gen. William Tecumseh Sherman's Union army reached Columbia, S.C., Feb. 17, 1865, on its famous march through the Carolinas. Columbia was the capital of the state held responsible for the war (South Carolina was the first to secede), which probably accounts for its burning. Sherman's assertion that the fire spread from bales of cotton ignited by evacuating Confederates is not acceptable, for the cotton appears to have been drenched by fire engines long before the fires gained headway. Who started the fire has never been definitively established.

COLUMBIA FUR COMPANY. Founded by Joseph Renville about 1822 and operated in the countries of the Sioux and Omaha, as far west as the Missouri River and as far east as the Great Lakes. By 1827 it had become a serious competitor and soon a part of the Astor American Fur Company, thereafter transacting business under the name of the Upper Missouri Outfit in the territory above the mouth of the Big Sioux River in South Dakota.

COLUMBIAN EXPOSITION. *See* **World's Columbian Exposition.**

COLUMBIA RIVER EXPLORATION AND SETTLEMENT. The estuary of the Columbia River in the northwest United States was first seen, described, and mapped in 1775 by Capt. Bruno Hezeta. In 1792, Capt. Robert Gray of Boston sailed 10 miles up the river proper, naming it Columbia's River after his ship, and W. R. Broughton of Capt. George Vancouver's party surveyed and charted to Cottonwood Point, 119 statute miles from the Pacific Ocean.

The Lewis and Clark expedition, in 1805, explored from the Yakima to Cottonwood Point, 214 miles. In 1807, David Thompson explored for 111 miles, from its mouth to its source in Columbia Lake; and in 1811, Finan McDonald navigated from Kettle Falls to Death Rapids, 255 miles, and Thompson navigated the entire river.

Prior to the great wagon train of 1843, settlements had been started along the river. The posts of the fur traders included those of the North West and Astoria companies. The wagon train rapidly opened the country.

COLUMBIA RIVER TREATY. A waterpower and water-storage agreement between the United States and Canada to run for sixty years, signed in Washington, D.C., Jan. 17, 1961. The construction of the Libby Dam on the Kootenay branch of the Columbia River (northern Montana) was completed within five years after joint ratification. Canada built dams at Arrow Lake, Duncan Lake, Lower Bonnington, and Mica Creek in British Columbia. These supply hydroelectric power to Washington, Oregon, Idaho, Montana, British Columbia, and Alberta.

COLUMBIA UNIVERSITY. A private, nonsectarian institution and one of the oldest major American universities; formally established by royal charter in 1754. Founded as the College of the Province of New-York, the school was known as King's College. The first president, Samuel Johnson, constituted the entire faculty. Instruction began in the Trinity Church schoolhouse in New York City; enrollment was limited to men. By 1760 the college had its first permanent home, in lower Manhattan.

Myles Cooper, who succeeded Johnson in 1763, developed the college along English lines. A medical school was added in 1767. Forced to close at the outbreak of the Revolution, the school was rechartered in 1784 as Columbia College under the Regents of the University of the State of New York. The medical school was merged in 1813 with the College of Physicians and Surgeons, which was reestablished within the college in 1860.

Under Charles King (1849–64) the college moved to midtown. King established the School of Law (1858) and the School of Mines (1864), now the School of Engineering. The first graduate faculty, political science, was established in 1880, and the School of Architecture was added in 1881.

The university moved to its present site on Morningside Heights in 1897. The faculties of philosophy (1890) and pure science (1892) had already been established, and Teachers College was added the following year. Nicholas Murray Butler (1902–45) established the schools of Pharmaceutical Sciences (1904), Journalism (1912), Business (1916), Dental and Oral Surgery (1916), Public Health and Administrative Medicine (1921), Library Service (1926), and Social Work (1940). The School of International Affairs (1946), General Studies (1947), and the School of the Arts (1965) were subsequently consolidated.

Founded in 1889 and incorporated into the university in 1900, Barnard College offers women a four-year liberal arts curriculum. In 1973, under Martha E. Peterson, all undergraduate courses at Columbia were opened to Barnard students, and vice versa.

COLUMBUS (Ohio). Capital of Ohio, with a population of 564,871 in 1980; center of a metropolitan area of 1,093,293. It is a major industrial center as well. Aircraft, auto parts, machinery, and coal-mining and oil-well equipment, are leading products, and it includes one of the largest factories in the world for the production of oilcloth. Ohio State University and the Battelle Memorial Institute are there.

The state capital since 1812, Columbus grew rapidly with improved transportation. The Ohio and Erie Canal extended a spur to Columbus in 1831; the Cumberland Road (or National Road) reached it in 1833.

COMANCHE. The most famous Indian tribe of the Plains; dominated southwestern Texas and southwestern Oklahoma from their acquisition of the horse in the early 18th century until their reservation confinement in 1875. Against their depredations the Texas Rangers were organized. By 1719, independent bands occupied a section of southwestern Kansas on the northern bank of the Arkansas River. Pushing south, they expelled the Jicarilla and Lipan Apache. The Comanche thereafter regarded the Apache as enemies. They also carried on attacks against Spanish settlers and against Americans. They were gradually subdued and located with the Kiowa on two Texas reservations in 1854, ceding these in 1867 in favor of an Oklahoma parcel. Only after uprisings in 1874–75 did they adapt to reservation life.

COMBINE. A farm machine that makes harvesting and threshing a single process. It was developed by 1828, but not perfected until the 1870's. Between 1870 and 1873 the U.S. Patent Office recorded the invention of six harvester-threshers; and by 1880 the combine was commercially established.

COMIC STRIPS AND FUNNY PAPERS. *See* **Newspapers.**

COMMANDER IN CHIEF OF BRITISH FORCES. A position of high importance in North America in the last half of the 18th century, held by Horatio Sharpe (1754), Edward Braddock (1755), William Shirley (1755–56), John Campbell, Earl of Loudoun (1756–57), James Abercrombie (1758), Jeffrey Amherst (1758–63), Thomas Gage (1763–75); Sir William Howe (1775–78), Sir Henry Clinton (1778–82), and Sir Guy Carleton (1782–83). All were supervised directly by the British ministry.

COMMERCE. *See* **Trade, Domestic; Trade, Foreign.**

COMMERCE, COURT OF. Created by act of Congress, June 18, 1910, as a tribunal for complex trade litigation. Five judges were appointed by the president for five-year terms, with new members assigned by the chief justice of the Supreme Court from among the circuit judges. Its jurisdiction covered all civil suits arising under the Interstate Commerce Act, the Elkins Act, and the orders of the Interstate Commerce Commission. When one member, Judge Robert W. Archbald, was impeached, convicted of corruption, and removed from the bench, Congress dissolved the court, Oct. 22, 1913.

COMMERCE, DEPARTMENT OF. Created by an act of Congress on Mar. 4, 1913. The secretary of commerce is appointed by the president and is a member of the cabinet. The original mission of the Department of Commerce was "to foster, promote, and develop the foreign and domestic commerce" of the United States. Now the department participates in the creation of national policy, promoting progressive business policies and growth; assisting states, communities, and individuals toward economic progress; strengthening the international economic position of the United States; improving use of the physical environment; assuring effective use and growth of scientific and technical resources; and acquiring, analyzing, and disseminating information concerning the nation and the economy.

COMMERCE CLAUSE. Article I, Section 8, Paragraph 3, of the U.S. Constitution gives Congress the power "to regulate Commerce with foreign Nations, and among the several States, and with the Indian Tribes." The judicial history of the clause begins with *Gibbons* v. *Ogden* (1824); Chief Justice John Marshall ruled that commerce encompassed "every species of commercial intercourse" and that if Congress had legislated in that area, federal power was plenary. The Court under Chief Justice Roger B. Taney resolved the issue of the extent of state power in the absence of federal legislation: when Congress was silent, the states might act, unless the specific subject required "uniform national control."

The Sherman Antitrust Act (1890) found constitutional justification in the clause, as it seemed to afford broad federal authority to prohibit combinations in restraint of trade and general market monopolization. The Court, however, relying on a distinction between production and distribution, held the statute inapplicable to a monopoly that had acquired nearly complete control over the manufacture of refined sugar (*United States* v. *E. C. Knight Company,* 1895). Over the next forty years, the Court applied the same restrictive principle to the control of mining, fishing, farming, oil production, and the generation of hydroelectric power. Similarly, the Court, in *Knight,* evolved the "direct effect" doctrine: only if a local activity directly affected interstate commerce was federal control valid.

Regulation-minded Progressive leaders of the early 20th century sought rulings that would expand the sweep of the clause. In the Minnesota Rate Cases (1913), Justice Charles Evans Hughes made clear that "direct" regulation of foreign or interstate commerce by the states was out of the question. In the Shreveport Rate Case (1914) he took the next step, stating that "when interstate and intrastate activities are so related that the government of the one involves the control of the other, it is Congress and not the states that is entitled to prescribe the final and dominant rule."

The Progressives also sought to use the clause to evolve a national police power, through legislation prohibiting lottery tickets, impure food and drugs, adulterated meat, transportation of women across state lines for immoral purposes, and child labor. The Court generally sustained such use. The exception was the case of child labor, in which the Court returned to limiting federal power.

On this broad judicial view of the clause, New Dealers based the National Industrial Recovery Act (1933) and other broad measures, such as the Bituminous Coal Act (1935). Judicial response to these acts was not only hostile but entailed a sharp return to older formulas. Charging that the Court had returned the country to a "horse-and-buggy" definition of interstate commerce, Franklin D. Roosevelt tried to induce the Court to embrace broad commerce precedents. The success he achieved was notable. Starting with *National Labor Relations Board* v. *Jones and Laughlin Steel Corporation* (1937), the Court not only rejected the whole battery of narrow commerce formulas but also validated the clause as the principal constitutional base for later New Deal programs, authorizing broad federal control of labor relations, wages and hours, agriculture, business, and navigable streams. In the Civil Rights Act of 1964, Congress banned racial discrimination in all public accommodations. The constitutional foundations for it were the commerce and equal protection clauses of the Fourteenth Amendment.

COMMERCE COMMISSION. *See* **Interstate Commerce Commission.**

COMMERCIAL CABLE COMPANY. Founded in 1883 by John W. Mackay and James Gordon Bennett; principal competitor of Western Union in the field of communications. In 1884 it laid two transatlantic cables to compete with those leased by Western Union from the American Telegraph and Cable Company. Its land lines were operated in conjunction with the Postal Telegraph.

COMMERCIAL COMMITTEE. One of the principal standing committees of the Continental Congress during the Revolution. Originating as the "secret committee," appointed (Sept. 19, 1775) to make purchase of powder, its functions were gradually enlarged until it became the chief agency of Congress in the extensive business of exchanging American products for arms and ammunition abroad. It was reconstituted July 5, 1777, with the name Committee of Commerce, and again Dec. 14, 1778. Its chief figure was Robert Morris.

COMMISSION GOVERNMENT. A system of municipal government characterized by an absence of separation of powers with regard to executive and legislative functions; a commission serves both as executive and as legislature. The system was developed in Galveston, Tex., in 1900, and became popular in the next two decades; about 500 cities had commission government by 1917. As the cities using this structure grew and urban problems became more complex, the demands placed upon the commissioners became more numerous and intricate. Those interested in reform placed increasing emphasis on professionalism in government, and the commission members in most large communities did not have sufficient background to manage efficiently the complex functions under their control. In the early 1980's, only 107 municipalities had commission government.

COMMISSION MERCHANTS AND FACTORS. Legally "a factor is an agent employed to purchase or sell goods on commission in his own name, or in the name of his principal." The factorage system was introduced soon after the dissolution of the Virginia Company (1624) and probably was of most importance from 1815 to 1860, when staple crops were produced in the South for markets in the Northeast and Europe. Commission merchants advanced money to planters and manufacturers, in return for which products were consigned to them for sale. The development of the commodity exchanges, the tremendous increase of industrial capital, and improved methods of transportation and communication ended the dominant position of the commission merchant.

COMMISSION ON CIVIL RIGHTS. *See* **Federal Agencies.**

COMMITTEE FOR INDUSTRIAL ORGANIZATION. *See* **American Federation of Labor–Congress of Industrial Organizations.**

COMMITTEE GOVERNMENT IN THE REVOLUTION. *See* **Revolutionary Committees.**

COMMITTEE OF THE STATES. The Articles of Confederation empowered Congress to appoint a committee consisting of one delegate from each state to sit in the recess of Congress and to exercise such powers as Congress, "by the consent of nine states, shall from time to time think expedient to vest them with," with the proviso that it not be authorized to do any act requiring the voice of nine states. Only once, in June 1784, was the committee called into existence.

COMMITTEE OF THE WHOLE. A parliamentary device employed by the House of Representatives principally to expedite consideration and amendment of bills. In effect, the House temporarily discards its legislative role and constitutes itself a deliberative committee, operating under more flexible rules. A quorum consists of 100 members, and legislation is open to freer debate and section-by-section amendment. All actions of the Committee of the Whole must be approved or turned down by the House itself.

COMMITTEE OF THIRTEEN (1850). A select committee of the U.S. Senate, agreed to on Apr. 18, 1850, to which were to be sent the compromise resolutions of senators Henry Clay of Kentucky and John Bell of Tennessee on the slavery issue. On May 8 the committee reported, offering two bills: an omnibus bill providing for the admission of California as a free state, the territorial organization of Utah and New Mexico, a settlement of the disputed Texas boundary, and a bill to end the slave trade in the District of Columbia. A lengthy amendment to the fugitive slave law was also submitted.

COMMITTEE OF THIRTEEN (1860). A select committee of the U.S. Senate, constituted Dec. 18, 1860, to consider the compromise proposals of Sen. John J. Crittenden on the slavery issue. The committee rejected the test compromise proposal concerning slavery in the territories and made no recommendation.

COMMITTEE OF THIRTY-THREE. A select committee of the U.S. House of Representatives, constituted Dec. 6, 1860. Composed of one member from each state, the committee was established to consider Sen. John J. Crittenden's compromise measures on the slavery issue. No decision was reached, and no report made.

COMMITTEE ON PUBLIC INFORMATION. Set up by order of President Woodrow Wilson, Apr. 14, 1917, consisting of the secretaries of state, war, and the navy, with the journalist George Creel as civilian chairman, the committee was responsible for uniting American support behind the World War I effort.

COMMITTEE ON THE CONDUCT OF THE WAR. A joint committee of Congress to inquire into the management of Union military and civilian policies in the Civil War. It was organized on Dec. 20, 1861, and continued until ninety days after the close of the Thirty-eighth Congress (June 1865). Its eight published volumes deal chiefly with military campaigns and the competency of commanding officers.

COMMITTEES OF CORRESPONDENCE. Organized by the colonies as part of the machinery that spread propaganda and coordinated the patriot party. Samuel Adams persuaded Boston to establish the first standing committee of correspondence (Nov. 2, 1772) to send a statement of rights and grievances to other towns in the colony. These committees exercised at times judicial, legislative, and executive functions and gave rise to the later committee system.

COMMITTEES OF SAFETY. Carried on and extended the work of the revolutionary Committee of Correspondence. The Second Continental Congress on July 18, 1775, recommended the establishment of such committees in the colonies to carry on the important functions of government. Many of these committees supplied the armies with men and equipment and apprehended Tories. With the adoption of state constitutions, the committees were largely replaced by constitutional agencies.

COMMODITIES AS MONEY. Used chiefly in the colonial period where there was a scarcity of coin or other suitable currency. By 1700 the use of commodity currencies was giving way to coin payments in the towns and cities, although it remained common for some years in the rural districts.

COMMODITIES EXCHANGE ACT (1936). Designed to prevent and remove obstructions and burdens on interstate commerce caused by market manipulation and excessive speculation on exchanges dealing in agricultural commodities.

COMMODITY EXCHANGES. The enormous expansion of markets after 1850 required organizations that could handle exchanges of commodities on a large scale. The Chicago Board of Trade was organized in 1848. The New York Produce Exchange was formed in 1850. The Merchants Exchange of St. Louis had the characteristics of a modern exchange about 1854. The New York Cotton Exchange was organized in 1870, and the New York Coffee Exchange in 1882.

COMMODITY PRICES. *See* **Prices.**

COMMODORES. *See* **Admirals and Commodores.**

COMMON LANDS. Lands held in common by the proprietors, in which each owner had fractional rights and carried on farming in accordance with open field practices; or, more generally, undivided and unallotted land on the outskirts of the New England settlements, used for pasturage and woodland.

COMMON LAW. The principles declared and developed in the decisions of the courts when adjudicating upon the private law in countries of Anglo-Saxon origins. It is usually not incorporated in the constitution or written statutes of a country. The early settlers of the United States claimed, and were in fact supposed, to have brought with them to America their inherent common-law rights of person and property. The common-law rights of the individual, as generally accepted, have been stated at various times in American history. The Declaration of Independence says that all men "are endowed by their Creator with certain unalienable rights, that among these are life, liberty, and the pursuit of happiness." Also the Bill of Rights and the bills of rights in the various state constitutions are in whole or in large part made up of statements of common-law rights.

COMMON SENSE. A tract by Thomas Paine, published in Philadelphia, January 1776. He maintained that, being of age, the colonies were qualified for independence and that their future interest demanded it. In its first three months 120,000 copies circulated.

COMMONWEALTH* V. *HUNT (1842). Decided by the supreme court of Massachusetts; held the defendant, the Boston Journeymen Bootmakers Society, a trade union, to be a lawful organization. Previously, associations of workers had been judged unlawful conspiracies.

COMMUNES. Communal-living experiments in the United States antedate the Revolution, experiencing their greatest vitality in the early 19th century, when hundreds of planned communities, some religious and others secular, were established. Of those only the Shakers and Hutterites remain.

In the late 1960's a new wave of youthful communitarians fanned out through California and New Mexico to establish rural communes, expanded across the country, and attracted a sizable minority of single and married adults, many with children. In the late 1970's there were estimated to be over 3,000 communes in forty or more states.

Communitarians of the 1970's differed as radically as their 19th-century ancestors, but certain beliefs were widely held. There was an emphasis on the return to the land as a spiritually enriching way of life, and a rejection of technological advance, materialistic values, competitive endeavor, and establishment goals. Communitarians in general laud peace, nonviolence, natural diet, simple crafts, sexual freedom, and communal raising of children.

COMMUNICATION INDUSTRIES. *See* **Book Publishing; Magazines; Newspapers; Printing; Radio; Telegraph; Telephone; Television.**

COMMUNICATION SATELLITES. The launching of Sputnik 1 by the Soviet Union on Oct. 4, 1957, and coincidental work in employing the moon as a passive reflector for communications stimulated thinking toward artificial satellites. On Dec. 18, 1958, an Atlas B rocket launched the SCORE communications satellite. On Aug. 12, 1960, the National Aeronautics and Space Administration (NASA) launched Echo 1, a giant balloon reflector that relayed voice and some television signals. The U.S. Army's Courier 1B satellite, launched Oct. 4, 1960, was the first active repeater. However, Telstar 1—built by the Bell System and launched by NASA on July 10, 1962—provided the crucial test for superiority of the active satellite and the capability of COMSATS in providing multichannel, wideband transmission. Syncom 2 (July 26, 1963) achieved a geostationary orbit synchronous with the earth's rotation.

In 1962 the United States established the Communications Satellite Corporation to represent the United States in a worldwide satellite system. In 1964 nineteen nations, under UN auspices, formed the International Telecommunications Satellite Consortium (Intelsat), whose governing body developed the first practical global system.

The first commercial synchronous satellite, Intelsat 1 (Early Bird), was launched for transatlantic service Apr. 6, 1965. In the 1970's, satellites revolutionized international communications, and by 1980 five series of Intelsat satellites served almost 100 nations. A keen competition developed in the American domestic satellites field. In 1981 the North American domestic series included Westar, Satcom, Anik (Canadian), Comstar, and Communications Technology Satellite (joint U.S.-Canadian). Two main types of systems emerged: one serving a large number of customers and the other tailored to specialized needs, such as the SBS-1 satellite for high-speed business communications (1980). Sixty-four international, domestic, and military communications satellites orbited the earth in 1980.

COMMUNICATIONS COMMISSION, FEDERAL. *See* **Federal Communications Commission.**

COMMUNIST PARTY UNITED STATES OF AMERICA. Began in Chicago in 1919, when a schism split the Socialist party (SP), and radical, doctrinaire Bolsheviks rejected the progressive gradualism of the SP. The left wing that emerged from the SP was split into the Communist party (CP) and the Communist Labor party (CLP). When the U.S. Department of Labor and attorney general launched antisubversive programs in 1919–20, the two factions went underground, continuing their rivalry. In 1920 the United Communist party (UCP) was created; it was, in the main, the old CLP with a handful of CP members. The CP maintained a separate organization, and the split persisted.

Unity was imposed on the fighting factions by the Communist International (Comintern) in 1921, when it told the Americans to unite or be reorganized from without. The CP and the UCP then created the Communist Party of America. The Comintern urged the American Communist movement to operate in the open and to participate in electoral and other parliamentary activities. Accordingly, in December 1921, the Workers Party of America was created. The Communist Party of America formally dissolved in 1923. In 1925 the name was changed to Workers (Communist) Party of America, and in 1929 it became the Communist Party, United States of America (CPUSA).

The change in 1929 was more than a change in name. After the death of Lenin in 1924, Joseph Stalin emerged as Soviet chief of state, following a series of actions against rivals of left and right in the Russian party. In the American party a leftist tendency appeared under James P. Cannon, and a rightist faction, under Jay Lovestone, which argued that conditions in the United States justified modification of Communist policy. Both factions were expelled from the CPUSA in 1928–29, and the Stalinist element came to prevail under the leadership of William Z. Foster.

With the Stalinization of the American party in 1929, a strategy of alienation was undertaken to combat traditional labor unions by creating rival organizations; the party also struggled against all other leftist groups. The strategy assumed that all other parties had to be opposed and liquidated to prepare the CPUSA for its historically prescribed duty upon the collapse of capitalism.

The rigid alienation continued until 1935. Because of the growing Nazi menace, the international party line was changed. The Seventh World Congress of the Comintern in Moscow in 1935 laid down a new policy of making common cause with liberal elements, even capitalists. It was to be proper for U.S. Communists to support their own government. The Popular Front ushered in a "strategy of enticement." Foster was replaced by Earl Browder. Recriminations against the New Deal ended, and Washington, Lincoln, Jefferson, and, of course, Stalin were called fighters for the people.

The period of the Popular Front (1935–39) was the time of the party's greatest vogue. Leaders manipulated hundreds of front organizations. Instead of fighting the trade-union movement, the Communists joined it and established strong centers of influence. In 1939 the Soviet Union negotiated a nonaggression pact with Nazi Germany. The shock in the United States was seismic. Thousands in the party and front organizations immediately left the party.

On June 21, 1941, German armies invaded the Soviet Union. From 1941 to 1945 the CPUSA was in the forefront of patriotic striving because the military aims of the United States and the Soviet Union coincided. In 1943 the Soviet Union, in a gesture of amity, abolished the Comintern; and in 1944 Earl Browder abolished the CPUSA and created the Communist Political Association.

Browder believed that the postwar period would be one of class collaboration and that the goals of Communism would be achieved without class warfare. But with the end of World War II the international Communist line changed again and the cold war began. As a consequence, Browder was deposed by his American colleagues; the Communist Political Association was abolished; and the CPUSA was reestablished under William Z. Foster.

By 1957 the party was brought to the point of collapse by three developments. First, Foster's ultra-leftism fastened on the party a view that the years ahead would be years of war, fascism, and U.S. imperialism and that the party should be prepared to resume a hard line. Second, the CPUSA was put under strong pressure by government authorities. The most effective action against the Communist party was the Smith Act of 1940, which made it a crime to advocate or teach the necessity of the violent overthrow of government or to conspire to do so. The eleven top leaders of the CPUSA were convicted in October 1949 of advocating violent overthrow of the government, and the Supreme Court upheld the convictions in *Dennis* v. *United States* in 1951. Other prosecutions followed. The most immediate effect of these actions on the party as a whole was a decision to go underground. Only a skeletal public organization was maintained.

The denunciation of Stalin by Nikita Khrushchev at the Twentieth Congress of the Soviet Communist party in 1956 traumatized many American party members. Stalin was condemned by Khrushchev for having promoted a "cult of personality," which was alien to Marxist-Leninist principles, and for having established a personal tyranny. Contrary to the dogma of the past, it was also said that war with the capitalist states was not inevitable and that peaceful coexistence could obtain. The shock of these pronouncements shattered the American party.

Between 1930 and 1955, party membership went from about 7,500 to 22,600, with peaks of 55,000 in 1938 and 65,000 in 1945. In 1978 the party claimed a membership of 18,000.

COMMUNITIES. Among the earliest communistic experiments were the short-lived one founded by Pieter Plockhoy, a Dutch Mennonite, on Delaware Bay in 1661; the Labadist Community of Protestant Mystics, founded in northern Maryland in 1680; the Mennonite Community at Germantown, Pa., founded in 1683; and the Women in the Wilderness in Pennsylvania, in 1694. Conrad Beissel adopted the Dunker religion and founded, in 1732, the Ephrata Community.

The first Shaker community was the Jerusalem Community, founded in 1786 by Jemima Wilkinson at Gates County, N.Y. The main branch followed Ann Lee; their first permanent community was set up in 1787 at Mt. Lebanon, N.Y.

The Harmony Community and the Zoar Community were founded by groups of Separatists from Württemberg, Germany, led by George Rapp and Joseph Blaumiler, respectively. The Harmony Society was originally, in 1805, in Butler County, Pa.; in 1814 the Harmonists moved to Indiana, and in 1825 to Economy, Pa. Zoar was founded in Ohio in 1817 and continued until 1898.

Other religious communities were Perfectionists at Oneida, N.Y., Brooklyn, N.Y., and Wallingford, Conn.; the Hopedale Community, Massachusetts (1842–57); the Amana Community in New York, and later in Iowa (1842–1932); the Bishop Hill Colony in Illinois (1848–62); the Mormon Community at Orderville, Utah (1874–84), and the Hutterian Brethren.

Nonreligious communities experimented in economic or social philosophy. An example of the former was Robert Owen's unsuccessful experiment at New Harmony, Ind., which he purchased from the Rappists in 1825. In 1841, Boston intellectuals established the literary West Rexburg Community. In 1842 they transformed their society into a Fourierist phalanx, the Brook Farm Association. Other Fourierist communities were the Wisconsin Phalanx (1844–50) and the North American Phalanx, New Jersey (1843–56).

Other settlements founded on social or economic communism were at Teutonia, Pa. (1843), Icania, Iowa (1848–98), Equity, Ohio (1830–32), Eutopia, Ohio (1847–51), and Modern Times, Long Island, N.Y. (1851–60).

COMMUNITY ACTION PROGRAM. Probably the most controversial feature of President Lyndon B. Johnson's War on Poverty, title IIA, section 202(a) of the Economic Opportunity Act of 1964, provided funds and a rationale for about 1,000 community action organizations formed within the next three years.

The concept of the program grew out of comprehensive antidelinquency projects planned and implemented during the administration of John F. Kennedy. The Mobilization for Youth Project, the first of these, contained most of the essential features of what later became community action.

The Economic Opportunity Act was signed into law on Aug. 20, 1964, and the initiative passed from the federal government to the localities. Besides bringing poverty to public attention, community action programs soon generated strong criticism of the "social service establishment" for regulating the poor while maintaining them at or near subsistence levels. Criticism soon led to demonstrations, class-action lawsuits against state and federal agencies, and demands that the poor be granted representation on agencies dealing with problems of poverty. Several community action programs moved in 1965–66 toward granting majority control to poor people or their representatives. City administrations (most of them Democratic) countered with pressure to curb the programs at the federal level. Administrative and congressional reaction took a variety of forms: the budgets of the Office of Economic Opportunity (OEO) were repeatedly attacked after 1964, and Congress revised legislation, earmarking funds for less controversial and more controllable programs, such as Project Headstart. In 1967 the Green amendment to the Economic Opportunity Act made it difficult for community action programs to be controlled by poor people.

With the choices to be made at the community level reduced after 1967, community action programs rapidly declined, and the reform energies that had previously gone into community action shifted to a variety of advocacy and social action movements independent of federal sponsorship. President Richard M. Nixon tried to further curtail community action programs, but a compromise bill signed on Jan. 4, 1975, extended OEO programs through 1977 and replaced the agency with the Community Services Administration. The Economic Opportunity Act, extended in 1972, 1974, and 1978, fell victim to budget cuts during the first year of President Ronald Reagan's administration and expired in 1981; the Community Services Administration was abolished the same year.

COMMUTATION BILL (1783). The Continental Congress voted to commute the half-pay promised officers of the army on disbandment into a lump sum equal to five years' full pay, to be discharged by certificates bearing 6 percent interest.

COMPACT THEORY. The idea that the basis of government is in the agreement of the people. Its appearance in America coincides with the first settlements, and it is implicit in the Mayflower Compact. Church covenants and trading company charters gave support to the compact philosophy. The idea of compact is therefore equally valid as the basis of ecclesiastical and civil government. As a political philosophy, it was taken for granted by Thomas Jefferson in compiling the Declaration of Independence.

COMPAGNIE DE L'OCCIDENT. Also known as the Western Company, the Mississippi Company, or Mississippi Bubble. A French trading company organized by John Law in 1717 for exploiting the resources of Louisiana. In 1719 it became the Compagnie des Indes (Company of the Indies), which retained control of Louisiana until 1731.

COMPANY OF ONE HUNDRED ASSOCIATES. A privileged commercial company established by Cardinal Richelieu in 1627 for the colonization of New France (Canada), also known as the Company of New France. Since it was more interested in trade than in colonization, the colony failed to prosper; the charter was revoked in 1663.

COMPROMISE MOVEMENT OF 1860. An attempt to check the movement toward secession and to avert war, by meeting the grievances of the South in regard to slavery. When Congress rejected the Crittenden Compromise, the movement continued in the Border Slave State Convention of February 1861. No agreement was reached on the chief demand of the South—the recognition of property rights in slavery in the territories.

COMPROMISE OF 1790. In return for Alexander Hamilton's agreement to provide the congressional votes needed to locate the national capital on the Potomac River, Thomas Jefferson and James Madison promised enough votes to assure enactment of Hamilton's plan for assumption of the revolutionary war debts of the states by the federal government.

COMPROMISE OF 1850. Five statutes enacted in September 1850, following a bitter controversy between the representatives of the North and South on issues of states' rights and extension of slavery. Henry Clay's select committee of thirteen recommended an "omnibus bill" providing for the admission of California under its free-state constitution, territorial governments for Utah and New Mexico silent on slavery, settlement of the boundary dispute between Texas and the United States, abolition of the slave trade in the District of Columbia, and an amendment to the fugitive slave law.

Compromise failed; its ground was covered in five statutes formerly included as sections of the proposed omnibus bill. The act establishing a territorial government for Utah (Sept. 9) contained the important popular sovereignty clause providing that any state or states formed out of this territory should be admitted with or without slavery as their constitutions should prescribe. An identical clause was appended to the New Mexico territorial act (Sept. 9), which also resolved the conflict between Texas and the federal government over the Santa Fe region by a cession, with compensation to Texas, to the newly created territory. On the same date, the act admitting California under its constitution prohibiting slavery in the new state was approved. The Fugitive Slave Act of Sept. 18, 1850, heavily amended the original statute of Feb. 12, 1793. The Act Abolishing the Slave Trade in the District of Columbia was approved on Sept. 20. These statutes were presented to the country as a series of compromise measures. It was not until 1852, after a storm of partisan protest, that the country at large made clear its acquiescence.

COMPROMISE OF 1890. The Republican majority in the U.S. Senate broke a legislative logjam at the expense of black suffrage. Three major bills jockeyed for position: a bill to expand the government purchase and coinage of silver; a bill to increase tariff protection for industrial goods and agricultural staples; and a federal elections bill. The elections bill sought to redeem the promise of the Fifteenth Amendment and to revive the obligation of the federal government to supervise elections on behalf of the rights of the freedman. The Compromise of 1890 saw the federal elections bill sacrificed to sectional accommodation and to passage of the Sherman Silver Purchase Act and the McKinley Tariff Act.

COMPROMISES OF THE U.S. CONSTITUTION. To a great extent the whole work of the Convention of 1787 was a compromise among the views of thirteen independent and autonomous nations. It was a question of whether to strengthen this league or create an entirely new national government. The so-called Virginia Plan aimed to create a national government that would largely disregard the autonomy of the separate states. The New Jersey Plan provided for a revision of the Articles of Confederation and an increase in the powers of the extant national government. But that government was to operate only on the states as such.

The compromise was agreed upon that the national legislative body (Congress) should consist of two houses: in one (the Senate) the states should have equal representation, in the other (the House of Representatives) the representation should be based on population. This at once brought up the question of the slave population. Northern states claimed that slaves were property and should not be counted. Southern states claimed that they were individuals and should be included. These arguments were compromised by the provision that representatives should be apportioned by adding to the numbers of free persons, "including those bound to service for a term of years and excluding Indians not taxed, three-fifths of all other persons."

The third compromise concerned the slave trade. The northern states wanted it prohibited but also wanted Congress empowered to pass navigation acts and regulate commerce. South Carolina and Georgia wished a continuation of the slave trade but feared national control of navigation acts and commerce. Congress was granted the power to pass navigation acts and regulate commerce but was prohibited from taxing exports. The northern states consented to a continuance of the slave trade for twenty years.

COMPROMISE TARIFF OF 1833. *See* **Tariff.**

COMPTROLLER GENERAL OF THE UNITED STATES. Head of the General Accounting Office, created by the Budget and Accounting Act of June 10, 1921. He is appointed by the president for a fifteen-year term and is subject to removal only by a joint resolution of Congress for specified causes or by impeachment. The comptroller general directs an independent agency formed to assist Congress in providing legislative control over the receipt, disbursement, and application of public funds through a postaudit function.

COMPTROLLER OF THE CURRENCY. Created by Congress on Feb. 25, 1863. The comptroller is appointed by the president for a term of five years, to provide administrative regulation and supervision over the country's national banks, numbering 4,437 in 1980.

COMPUTERS. The first person to envision what is now described as a card-programmed general-purpose automatic calculator was Charles Babbage (1835). Although never completed, his analytic engine was surprisingly similar to the modern computer. It contained a memory ("store") in which numbers were stored; an arithmetic unit ("mill") that performed all four arithmetic operations; punched card data and program input; and a punched card or printed output.

Development of digital computers was made possible by the developing technology of the first half of the 20th century: electronic means of storing information and controlling flow of information, electronic amplification, and the ability to accept input from users and provide readable output.

The first large-scale digital computer was the Automatic Sequence Control Calculator (Mark I) at Harvard University. In 1937, Howard Aiken gave a detailed description of a calculating device based on conventional punched-card machines. In 1939, Harvard signed a contract with International Business Machines (IBM) Corporation to build this massive device; it was completed in 1944 and presented to Harvard; it went into immediate operation on war-related calculations. After the war, Aiken built the Mark II (a relay machine) and the Marks III and IV, which were electronic.

George Stibitz at Bell Telephone Laboratories constructed the first relay-calculating device, the Complex Calculator, in 1939. The first electronic computer, ENIAC, was a result of the collaboration of John Mauchly and J. Presper Eckert of the Moore School of Engineering at the University of Pennsylvania. Mauchly's memo outlining a high-speed electronic device led to funding of the project at Aberdeen Proving Ground. By fall 1945, ENIAC was working on ballistics tables, atomic energy problems, and assorted mathematical problems. The collaboration of John von Neumann with the ENIAC project resulted in the first logical design of an electronic computer in which the program could be stored and modified electronically. EDVAC took another quantum jump beyond ENIAC—an internally stored program, general-purpose computer.

The first generation of electronic computers was plagued by many difficulties; the foremost problem was with the memory unit. ENIAC had a memory of only twenty words using the vacuum tube. This limitation was overcome with Eckert's development of an acoustic delay-line memory. This enabled the designers to think in terms of building a memory of, say, 512 or 1,024 words with only a few tubes, in contrast to the large tube requirement for ENIAC's small memory capacity. The first internally stored program computer, the EDSAC, was designed and built at Cambridge University by Maurice Wilkes. BINAC, a computer built by the Eckert-Mauchly Corporation (formed 1946) for Northrop Aircraft Corporation, had its first successful run in Philadelphia in 1949.

Two other forms of memory commonly used by first-generation computers were electrostatic tubes and magnetic drums. The electrostatic-tube memory was developed in England by F. C. Williams of Manchester University.

Most of the computers conceived and developed in the decade after World War II were one-of-a-kind machines. Some were dead ends in terms of immediate impact, while others had clearly spawned offspring. One of the most prolific was built at the Institute for Advanced Study. Its progeny included MANIAC, ILLIAC, JOHNNIAC, ORDVAC, AVIDAC, SILLIAC, and WEIZAC.

Another major computer of this period was Whirlwind, built at the Massachusetts Institute of Technology. The project began in 1944 when Gordon Brown was asked to build an aircraft simulator for the navy in his MIT Servomechanism Laboratory. In 1946, under Jay Forrester, the project evolved into a design for what eventually became the digital computer Whirlwind I, which went into operation in about 1951. While on the Whirlwind project, Forrester developed the first effective magnetic-core memory.

With the delivery of UNIVAC I in 1951 to the Bureau of the Census by Eckert-Mauchly, individual computers lost their uniqueness. They also began to be recognized as having a variety of practical applications. IBM's entry into the electronic digital computer field came with the development, beginning in 1951, of the Defense Calculator. Other milestones include the developmental work at the National Bureau of Standards (SEAC and SWAC) and such computers as Raytheon Corporation's RAYDAC, the Bendix G-15, Librascope's LGP-30, the IBM 650, and the Burroughs 220.

The years 1955–65 saw many new accomplishments. One of the most significant was the development of computer languages. The first was FORTRAN, developed at IBM. In 1959 the first automated computerized process control system was installed (at a Texaco refinery); the banking industry adopted MICR (Magnetic Ink Character Recognition); and transistors began to replace vacuum tubes, due to developments in the semiconductor industry. Semiconductors are a class of solids whose electrical conductivity is between that of an insulator and a conductor; metal-oxide semiconductors led to greater component densities than could be achieved with the older bipolar devices. The advent of the transistor in 1948 enabled the size of electronic devices to be reduced by a factor of 100,000 by the 1970's. Major external stimuli for the astonishing achievements in miniaturization were provided by the aerospace programs, in missile guidance systems, and by the telephone industry. The miniaturized circuits can contain 1,500 elements on chips an eighth of an inch square. By the mid-1970's the impact of microelectronics on consumer products was already substantial, as in the pocket-sized electronic calculator and electronic timepieces. The miniaturization of electronic components in the late 1970's and early 1980's (a computer memory chip that could store 288,000 bits of information was produced in 1981) led to the introduction of portable desk-top computers and to a rapidly increasing use of computers in schools, libraries, businesses, banks, retailing, publishing, and art. Personal computers and video games became very popular, and a growing number of workers began to do office work at home on small computers or terminals with typewriter keyboards.

COMSTOCK LODE. One of the richest deposits of precious ores ever discovered, in Virginia City, Nev. From its discovery in 1859 to its decline in 1879, more than $500 million in silver and gold were taken from it.

CONCEPCIÓN, BATTLE OF (Oct. 28, 1835). A vanguard action by 92 Texans, led by Gen. Stephen F. Austin, preliminary to a tighter siege of San Antonio, against 400 Mexicans from the garrison who sought to isolate the detachment near Mission Concepción. The Mexicans made a surprise attack, but Texan rifle fire smothered it.

CONCESSIONS AND AGREEMENT (1664–65). Issued by John Lord Berkeley and Sir George Carteret to encourage immigration to New Jersey. The document provided for a liberal government, freedom of conscience, and land on reasonable terms with exemption from quitrents for five years. Similar constitutions were published for Carolina, Pennsylvania, and West Jersey.

CONCILIATION, LABOR. The settlement of industrial disputes either by conference between employers and employees or by joint boards representing them, without the assistance of outside agencies. When an outside agent intervenes, the procedure is known technically as mediation.

CONCILIATION COURTS, DOMESTIC. Conciliation is an informal process whereby a third party seeks to secure an agreement between the parties to a controversy. Just prior to the Civil War, provisions for the use of the conciliation process were established in the constitutions of six states, but no use of this power was made until after 1910.

CONCORD (N.H.). Capital of New Hampshire, with a population of 30,400 in 1980. Located on the Merrimack River close to the center of New Hampshire, Concord is a business center for warehousing agricultural products of the Merrimack valley (chiefly apples and similar fruits) and for granite quarrying and shipping.

Concord was named in 1765, although a settlement had been made on the site as early as 1725. After it became state capital (1808), Concord developed into one of the leading suppliers of coaches and wagons for stagecoach routes in the United States. Concord firms produced wagons and ambulances during the Civil War and continued to manufacture coaches and wagons into the 20th century.

CONCORD COACH. The most famous type of American stagecoach, manufactured by Abbot, Downing and Company of Concord, N.H., from about 1813.

CONCORD GROUP. A group of notables living in Concord, Mass., in the 19th century, including Henry David Thoreau, Ralph Waldo Emerson, Nathaniel Hawthorne, A. Bronson Alcott, and William Ellery Channing.

CONCURRENT RESOLUTIONS. *See* **Resolutions, Legislative.**

CONDÉ, FORT. The second Fort Louis de la Mobile, erected in 1711 by the French under Jean Baptiste Le Moyne, Sieur de Bienville, on the site of the present Mobile, Ala. It remained an important French fort until transferred to the British in 1763, who renamed it Fort Charlotte.

CONESTOGA MASSACRE. *See* **Paxton Boys.**

CONESTOGA WAGON. First came into general use on the overland routes across the Alleghenies just after the American Revolution. The Conestoga wagon was huge, heavily built, with broad wheels suited to dirt roads and a bed higher at either end of the wagon than in the middle, to prevent its contents spilling as it went up and down hills. Its canvas-covered top presaged the prairie schooner. It was drawn by four to six horses, with the driver usually riding wheelhorses.

CONFEDERACY, SOUTHERN. *See* **Confederate States of America.**

CONFEDERATE AGENTS. The skill, energy, and resourcefulness of Confederate agents abroad brought results on the battlefield in the Civil War. States and even railroads were represented in Mexico, Europe, and Canada. Purchasing agents of the war, navy, treasury, commissary, and quartermaster departments were aided by commercial agents to expedite forwarding of supplies through the blockade.

CONFEDERATE ARMY. *See* **Army, Confederate.**

CONFEDERATE FLAG. Three times during the Civil War, the Confederate Congress designated an official flag. The Stars and Bars was the first. This is the flag most commonly thought of as the Confederate flag. The second was a white field twice as long as it was wide, with the battle flag as a union two-thirds the width of the flag. The third was similar to the second except for proportions and the addition of a vertical red bar at the outer edge. There were still other designs for the Confederate navy.

CONFEDERATE NAVY. *See* **Navy, Confederate.**

CONFEDERATE PRISON CAMPS. About 200,000 prisoners were taken by the Confederates in the Civil War. An exchange of prisoners, arranged in 1862, was ended in 1863, and captives were held in scattered prison camps until near the end of the war. The majority consisted of tobacco warehouses or open stockades. Poor quarters, insufficient rations and clothing, and lack of medicines produced much disease and a high death rate. Some relief was obtained when southerners permitted the Union to send food, clothing, and drugs through the lines.

CONFEDERATE STATES OF AMERICA. A confederacy of eleven southern states founded primarily to preserve slavery and protest against centralizing tendencies of the federal government that advanced the economic interests of the North to the disadvantage of the agrarian South.

Constitution. The provisional Confederate Constitution, adopted on Feb. 8, 1861, at Montgomery, Ala., carried out these purposes. Omitting the general welfare clause of the U.S. Constitution, which tended toward centralization, the provisional constitution safeguarded the sovereignty of its member states, although it was silent on secession. It forbade the Confederate congress to pass any law impairing property rights in slaves or restricting the interstate slave trade and guaranteed the right to take slaves into the territories; but it prohibited the African slave trade and permitted non-slaveholding states to join the new Confederacy. The conservative mood of the framers preserved intact most of the provisions of the U.S. Constitution.

Cabinet. After the adoption of the provisional constitution, the convention elected Jefferson Davis president and Alexander H. Stephens vice-president. Robert Toombs of Georgia became secretary of state; Christopher Memminger of South Carolina, secretary of the treasury; Leroy Pope Walker of Alabama, secretary of war; Stephen Mallory of Florida, secretary of navy; John H. Reagan of Texas, postmaster general; and Judah P. Benjamin, attorney general.

Judicial System. One serious weakness of the Confederate government was the refusal of its congress to establish a supreme court as provided by the constitution. State supreme courts filled the void somewhat by upholding acts of the government, and the district courts were active in trying federal cases and sustaining the central government.

Congress. President Abraham Lincoln's policy of coercion led to the secession of four states of the upper South: Virginia, Arkansas, Tennessee, and North Carolina. As soon as Virginia officially ratified the secession ordinance by a vote of the people on May 23, 1861, the Confederate congress voted to remove the capital to Richmond, despite its vulnerable position. The provisional congress had governed as a unicameral body, but when the permanent government was established on Feb. 22, 1862, it was succeeded by a congress of two chambers. Throughout the war the Confederate congress proved ineffective. It became bitterly divided into anti-Davis and pro-Davis factions. After the fall elections of 1863, President Davis lost his majority in congress.

Decision Leading to War. A pressing task was to secure recognition both by the U.S. government and European nations. Secretary of State William Seward refused to see the southern commissioners, but spoke with Supreme Court Justice John A. Campbell of Alabama, who acted as an intermediary. Seward gave him the impression that Fort Sumter, at Charleston, S.C., would be evacuated. Instead, Lincoln sent ships with provisions to relieve the garrison at Charleston. The decision that Davis and his cabinet made to fire on the approaching expedition started the war he had hoped to avoid. Lincoln responded by issuing the order for a blockade of the southern coasts and the raising of 75,000 troops.

Manpower. The disproportion in manpower and economic resources between the North and the South in 1860 was so great that the Confederacy had little chance to win the war. Reasonable estimate is that the superiority of the Union over the Confederate army was about two to one.

Diplomacy. The first objective of the Confederate commissioners to England and France was to secure recognition of the Confederacy as an independent government. They met with no success except that England and France recognized the belligerency of the Confederacy. Throughout the war, Russia, influenced by antislavery sentiment and wishing to keep the United States united and strong as a counterbalance against the British Empire, was hostile to the Confederacy.

Blockade-Runners. Although Europe refused to recognize the Confederacy or to break the blockade, it rendered it great material aid. This was accomplished largely through the blockade-runners—the swift, small steamers that slipped into southern harbors on dark nights. The crews and financial backing for these ships were largely British. At first they operated principally from Nassau but later also from Bermuda; their main port of entry was Wilmington, N.C., protected by Fort Fisher. The Union navy was, until the last year of the war, ineffective in stopping the blockade-runners.

The Confederacy could not have fought without blockade-runners. At least 1.5 million bales of cotton were exported from the Confederacy by the blockade-runners through the Mexican port of Matamoros. Blockade-runners brought into the Confederacy 330,000 stands of arms, principally Enfield rifles, for the Confederate troops and at least 270,000 for the states and private persons.

Ordnance. Although the Confederacy relied largely on Europe for small arms, it made remarkable progress in manufacturing gunpowder and cannons. This success was the doing of Gen. Josiah Gorgas, a northerner who joined the Confederacy and was appointed chief of ordnance, and Col. George Washington Rains, who was placed in charge of the manufacture of powder. Rains built a modern factory at Augusta, Ga., that produced a superior type of gunpowder at one-third the cost of powder brought through the blockade. Gorgas established arsenals and foundries that manufactured guns, pistols, sabers, and cannons.

Clothing and Food. The Confederacy was poorly prepared for carrying on a war; in 1860 the eleven states produced only 10 percent of the manufactured goods of the country. Because of dwindling supplies of leather, many Confederate soldiers marched and fought without shoes. People in the cities suffered from lack of food, in part because of inflation; there seems to have been adequate food in the country. The great trouble was distribution, largely because of the destruction of the railroads. Thus, the Confederate congress enacted the Impressment Act of Mar. 26, 1863, which provided a procedure for the impressment of goods and agricultural produce. Impressment caused discontent and contributed to the growth of the peace movement in the South.

Finance. The government relied on issuing bonds and paper money, with only a relatively few foreign loans. During the four years of war, the Confederacy operated on only $27 million in cash. The bullion in U.S. customhouses and mints within the Confederacy, amounting to $718,294, was seized; sequestration of enemy property and appropriation of the gold and silver of the New Orleans banks just before the capture of the city brought $11,661,082.

So recklessly did congress authorize the issuance of treasury notes that by the end of 1863 five times more currency was circulating than needed. Thus, congress, on Feb. 17, 1864, passed a law requiring all currency above $5 to be exchanged for bonds. New issues of paper currency were to be exchanged at the rate of two new dollars for three old. Nevertheless, nothing could stop the high inflation. The total Confederate debt is conservatively estimated at $2.3 billion.

Taxation. This financial disaster might have been avoided, but not until after two years of war did congress pass a drastic tax law. The belief existed that future generations should share the expense of winning independence through long-term bonds. The Confederacy raised only about 1 percent of its income in taxes.

Desertion. Inflation and the low pay that the soldiers received contributed greatly to the loss of morale in the army and among civilians. Also, the high incidence of illness in the army and the extreme inadequacy of the medical service weakened the desire to fight. Letters from home describing lack of food, marauders, and other hardships caused soldiers to desert. The legislatures of the states provided some relief for poor families by requiring each county to levy a local property tax for this purpose, but it proved inadequate.

Peace Movements. Under such conditions, serious peace movements arose in the Confederacy. After the defeat at Gettysburg and the fall of Vicksburg in 1863, many southerners thought the cause was lost. By this time they realized that Europe would not intervene. The peace advocates were often organized into secret societies, notably the Heroes of America, that elected local officers, protected deserters, and tried to sabotage the Confederate cause by bushwhacking activities and by burning railroads. Much more important than the peace movements in weakening the will to fight was the revival of states' rights feeling.

Alarmed by the strength of the peace movement, President Davis appointed Vice-President Stephens, Sen. R. M. T. Hunter of Virginia, and former Supreme Court Justice Campbell as commissioners to carry on negotiations. They met on Feb. 3, 1865, with Lincoln and Secretary of State Seward on the *River Queen* at Hampton Roads, Va. Lincoln insisted on the restoration of the Union and the abolition of slavery as indispensable terms of peace. The Confederacy refused.

Causes of Collapse. The end of the Confederate States came with the surrender of Lee at Appomattox on Apr. 9, 1865; the surrender of Gen. J. E. Johnston at Durham, N.C., on Apr. 26; the flight of the cabinet; the arrest of Davis at Irvinville, Ga., on May 10; and the surrender of Gen. Edmund Kirby-Smith in the trans-Mississippi West on May 26. The collapse of the Confederacy was caused by the conjunction of adverse circumstances mentioned above and the questionable leadership of President Davis as compared with the superior leadership of President Lincoln.

CONFEDERATION. The period from 1781 to 1788 and the government under the Articles of Confederation, the nation's first constitution. On Mar. 1, 1781, the Articles became the framework of central government in the new country. A unicameral legislature with one vote per state, no power of taxation, no power to regulate commerce, and no authority to coerce a state—all of these indicated that Americans intended to prevent a recurrence of their problems under the British.

The Confederation Congress adopted the administrative structure developed under the Second Continental Congress, with a secretary for foreign affairs, a secretary of war, and a superintendent of finance. One issue had delayed adoption of the articles—control of the domain west of the Appalachian Mountains. The Confederation had committed itself to creating new states there that would eventually be equal with the original thirteen. Thomas Jefferson's proposals became the basis of the Ordinances of 1784 and 1785. The former divided the West into territories with much self-government and provided for each territory's entrance into the union on a basis of equality with the original thirteen once it reached the population of the smallest state. The Ordinance of 1785 provided for the orderly disposition of lands to settlers.

However, Congress's real hope for revenue from land sales depended on speculators rather than settlers, and the more restrictive Northwest Ordinance (1787) replaced Jefferson's 1784 one. At first, Congress would appoint territorial officials; when 5,000 males inhabited the territory, they would elect an assembly that would nominate candidates for the governor's council; when 60,000 free adults lived in the territory, it could apply for equal statehood.

The Confederation's inability to regulate either foreign or domestic commerce left the new nation at the mercy of the major trading nations. America competed against the mercantilistic systems of England, France, and Spain without imposing any restrictions in retaliation. Each attempt by Congress to secure authority to do so met with rejection; any one state could withhold authority. Individual states competed economically with one another, and Congress could do nothing about it.

The Confederation also could not resolve diplomatic difficulties with other nations, because of its inability to offer advantages or to make threats. Spain presented problems to the United States as westward expansion brought the two close to one another on the Gulf coast.

Lacking a reliable source of revenue, the Confederation found itself in dire straits. It could not tax but could only requisition funds from the states, which rarely met their quotas. Moreover, the Continental Congress had borrowed during the Revolution from private individuals, states, and foreign governments, and the Confederation now had to assume and rationalize these debts.

State governments, with strong tax powers, did not face the same dilemma, and private individuals had a significant quantity of specie available to them. However, Continental currency soon drove sound money into hiding. Marginal farmers and artisans were hardest hit by continuing deflation, and they led the demand for mortgage moratoria and issuance of legal-tender paper currency.

Although seven states succumbed to this pressure for inflationary policies, inflationist tactics alarmed conservatives in every state. Fears of more frontal assaults on property rights, such as Daniel Shays's rebellion in Massachusetts, led conservatives to demand a reformation of the central government, leading directly to the Philadelphia Convention of 1787 and to the eventual adoption of the U.S. Constitution.

CONFEDERATION, ARTICLES OF. *See* **Articles of Confederation.**

CONFEDERATION, FORT. A Spanish post, built in Alabama in 1794 on the site of the French Fort Tombecbe, itself built in 1736 on the Tombigbee River. It was named to commemorate the newly formed union of Indian tribes consummated by the Treaty of Nogales. The fort was dismantled in 1797, in accordance with Pinckney's Treaty of 1795. U.S. troops rebuilt and occupied it soon after the Spanish left.

CONFERENCES. *See under specific name of conference, as in* **Bretton Woods Conference.**

CONFIRMATION BY THE SENATE. The constitutional requirement that appointments by the president be made "by and with the Advice and Consent of the Senate." Although Congress may waive this requirement in the case of "inferior Officers, as they think proper" and has done so for the great majority of such positions, by 1980 there were over 300 office titles whose holders required confirmation by the Senate.

CONFISCATION ACTS (1861–64). During the Civil War the Confederate and Union governments punished opposing populations by confiscations of private property. The federal law of Aug. 6, 1861, authorized Union seizure and condemnation of property put to hostile use and declared forfeited all claims to the labor of slaves who bore arms or worked in military or naval service with permission of Confederate masters. The act of July 17, 1862, designated local, state, and Confederate officials as citizens whose property was subject to seizure. The Confederate Congress had retaliated on Aug. 30, 1861, by providing for the sequestration of property and credits of Union adherents. The federal Captured and Abandoned Property acts of Mar. 12, 1863, and July 2, 1864, were confiscatory, but the proceeds from seizure were recoverable within two years after the cessation of war.

CONFISCATION OF PROPERTY. Property has been confiscated in the United States during wartime ever since the revolutionary war. As a means of financing hostilities against England, the Continental Congress declared in 1776 that the property of Loyalists was subject to seizure. During the Civil War both the North and the South confiscated property (*see* Confiscation Acts). World War I and World War II witnessed a revival of property seizure when Congress enacted the Trading with the Enemy Act on Oct. 6, 1917. This created the Office of the Alien Property Custodian, which took over and operated in trust about $700 million of enemy-owned or enemy-controlled property. After the war Congress decided to return most property; in 1935 the office was abolished.

During World War II, Congress amended the original act and reestablished the office. Millions of dollars of enemy property were again frozen. After the war Congress enacted the War Claims acts of 1948 and 1962, under which enemy property held in trust by the United States was vested and used to satisfy war claims of U.S. citizens. During the postwar period the United States continued freezing, rather than vesting, alien property in the absence of special agreement.

CONFISCATION OF U.S. PROPERTY ABROAD. *See* **Nationalization of U.S. Property Abroad.**

CONGLOMERATES. Business organizations built on acquisitions of firms usually not in a business directly related to that of any of the other corporate divisions of the parent company. Conglomerates existed before World War II but became increasingly popular in the late 1950's and 1960's.

In 1969, antitrust indictments challenged some of them. Also, securities manipulations became widely publicized. As the economy began to slow down in the early 1970's, the managers of some conglomerates were proved to have been far less efficient than supposed. By 1980, business mergers and acquisitions had decreased.

CONGREGATIONAL CHURCHES. One can trace their ancestry to the Non-Separating Puritans who originally settled the New England colonies. Their Cambridge Platform (1648) accepted the Calvinist Westminster Confession of Faith and affirmed the policy of admitting to the sacraments only those who could relate a conversion experience. After considerable controversy, the Halfway Covenant, which included those who could not relate a conversion experience, was adopted in 1662.

The Great Awakening (1733–46) was a period of crisis for Congregationalism. The more extreme evangelicals withdrew to establish their own churches, and many Boston liberals accelerated their movement toward Unitarianism.

Despite general Congregationalist support of the revolutionary war, Congregational churches were gradually disestablished in its aftermath. The early 19th century saw the splitting off of the Unitarian churches, primarily in Boston.

During the second half of the 19th century, Congregationalism continued in a more liberal direction. A national council was formed in 1871, and in 1913 a liberal confession of faith was adopted at Kansas City.

In 1931, the Congregationalists merged with the Christian Churches to become the Congregational Christian Churches. This denomination in turn merged with the Evangelical and Reformed Church to form the United Church of Christ in 1957 (1,745,533 members in 1980). Some Congregational Christian Churches and the Conservative Congregational Christian Conference remained separate.

The Unitarian Universalist Association should be considered a member of the Congregational family. The Unitarians, who withdrew from orthodox Congregationalism in the early 19th century, have been moving progressively away from distinctively Christian affirmations, and now stress an intellectual humanism rooted in the values of all religions.

John Murray gathered the first Universalist church in Gloucester, Mass., in 1779, but the greatest influence on American Universalism was Hosea Ballou, who, a generation later, moved Universalism in a more Unitarian direction. In 1961, the Unitarians and the Universalists formally merged in the Unitarian Universalist Association, which in 1980 had 139,052 members.

CONGREGATION DE PROPAGANDA FIDE. The Sacred Congregation de Propaganda Fide, founded in 1622, was the completion of the formative stage of the Catholic reform instituted by the Council of Trent (1545–64). Its officials were, after the pope, the highest court of appeal for the church in the United States to 1908, when the United States ceased to be a missionary territory.

CONGRESS, CONTINENTAL. *See* **Continental Congress.**

CONGRESS, UNITED STATES. The U.S. Congress was conceived by the makers of the Constitution to achieve maximum individual liberty in conjunction with social order. The 1787 Constitutional Convention created a Congress of two houses—a Senate in which each state would have equal representation and a House of Representatives in which states would be represented according to population. The Constitution created a legislative branch coequal in stature and authority with the executive and judicial branches.

Functions and Powers. (1) Through the passage of bills that become law, Congress determines national policies to be carried out by the executive branch. (2) Congress raises and appropriates the money to carry out these policies. (3) Congress oversees the executive branch to determine whether such national policies are being carried out. (4) Congressmen enhance public understanding of national issues. (5) Congressmen seek to bring justice out of conflicts between citizens and their government. (6) Congress seeks solutions to the issues that divide the nation.

The basic powers are to tax, spend, and borrow; to regulate foreign and interstate commerce; to maintain a defense establishment; to declare war; to admit new states; and to propose constitutional amendments. Congress also has an almost unlimited power of investigation. Congress may not tax exports, grant titles of nobility, or pass ex post facto laws. The Bill of Rights prohibits Congress from abridging freedom of speech, the press, the free exercise of religion, the right of peaceful assembly, the right of petition, and other freedoms.

Since it has the constitutional power to ratify treaties and confirm cabinet and ambassadorial nominees, the Senate regards itself as the president's chief foreign policy adviser. Not all presidents have agreed to such a role for the Senate. Congress has other nonlegislative powers in connection with the presidency. If no candidate receives a majority of the electoral votes, the House of Representatives determines the president and the Senate determines the vice-president. If the vice-presidency becomes vacant, the House and Senate must both confirm the president's nominee to fill the vacancy. In the case of presidential disability, Congress has grave, complicated duties. Congress alone has the power to impeach and remove from office the president and all federal civil officers.

Membership. Congress has grown with the nation. The First Congress (1789–91) consisted of 26 senators and 65 representatives; the Ninety-seventh (1981–83) had 100 senators and 435 representatives. The Constitution provides that representation in the House be kept up to date through a federal census every ten years. The Supreme Court in *Wesberry* v. *Sanders* (1964) laid down the one-man, one-vote doctrine, ruling that congressional districts must be substantially equal in population.

Representatives have two-year terms; senators, six. Minimum age for House members is twenty-five; for senators, thirty. All must be citizens and, at the time of election, must reside in the state from which elected.

Rules and Procedures. Under the Constitution, the Congress must meet every January; the president may call special sessions of either body. The Constitution provides that the vice-president shall preside over the Senate without a vote except in case of a tie. The House chooses its own presiding officer, the speaker of the House, from its membership. Any member may introduce a bill or resolution on any subject except that all bills for raising revenue must originate in the House but may be amended freely by the Senate.

The House and Senate must make a journal of their proceedings except for secret matters. Recent procedural reforms have made voting, both on the floor and in committee, a matter of public record. Of great historical importance is the *Congressional Record,* a record of debate with much additional material.

Committee System. Not envisioned by the makers of the Constitution, the committee system, evolved through trial and error, is still evolving. The committees have specific, written jurisdictions. Working usually through hundreds of subcommittees, committees choose which bills to consider, amend, rewrite, kill, or recommend for passage, with or without public hearings.

The House committee system is more powerful than that of the Senate. The House performs most technical work through committees; committee recommendations have an excellent chance of being adopted by the entire House, usually without major amendments. The smaller Senate, with historic pride in its freedom of debate, more often makes major changes in committee recommendations.

House and Senate. A notable difference in House and Senate operating methods is debate. For decades senators regarded themselves as answerable to no one save their states. This created the tradition of unlimited debate. As it rapidly grew in numbers, the House found it necessary to put rigid limits on debate.

Despite frequent references to the Senate as the upper house, the Constitution clearly created two equal, coordinate bodies, neither superior to the other. No bill can be sent to the president until it passes both houses in identical form; neither house can adjourn for more than three days without permission of the other; and senators and representatives receive identical salaries. The U.S. Congress is the most powerful legislative body in the world.

CONGRESS, 1ST TO 97TH. The second clause of Article I, Section 4, of the Constitution, now superseded by Section 2 of the Twentieth Amendment, provided that Congress should assemble at least once yearly, on the first Monday of December, unless a different day should be appointed by law. The beginning and end of the terms of senators and representatives, and therefore the calendar limits of each Congress, were determined by the Confederation Congress in designating Mar. 4, 1789, as the day the new government under the federal Constitution was to begin. The Twentieth Amendment, which declared that the terms of senators and representatives should end at noon on Jan. 3, and thereby shortened the term of the 73rd Congress by two months, was adopted in 1933.

The following table gives the years within which each term of Congress began and ended, the speakers of the House of Representatives, and the presidential administrations.

Congress	Speaker	Administration
1st (1789–91)	F. A. Muhlenberg	Washington
2nd (1791–93)	Jonathan Trumbull	Washington
3rd (1793–95)	F. A. Muhlenberg	Washington
4th (1795–97)	Jonathan Dayton	Washington
5th (1797–99)	Jonathan Dayton	Adams
6th (1799–1801)	Theodore Sedgwick	Adams
7th (1801–03)	Nathaniel Macon	Jefferson
8th (1803–05)	Nathaniel Macon	Jefferson
9th (1805–07)	Nathaniel Macon	Jefferson
10th (1807–09)	Joseph B. Varnum	Jefferson
11th (1809–11)	Joseph B. Varnum	Madison
12th (1811–13)	Henry Clay	Madison
13th (1813–15)	Henry Clay (1813–14) Langdon Cheves (1814–15)	Madison
14th (1815–17)	Henry Clay	Madison
15th (1817–19)	Henry Clay	Monroe
16th (1819–21)	Henry Clay (1819–20) John W. Taylor (1820–21)	Monroe
17th (1821–23)	Philip P. Barbour	Monroe
18th (1823–25)	Henry Clay	Monroe
19th (1825–27)	John W. Taylor	Adams
20th (1827–29)	Andrew Stevenson	Adams
21st (1829–31)	Andrew Stevenson	Jackson
22nd (1831–33)	Andrew Stevenson	Jackson
23rd (1833–35)	Andrew Stevenson (1833–34) John Bell (1834–35)	Jackson
24th (1835–37)	James K. Polk	Jackson
25th (1837–39)	James K. Polk	Van Buren
26th (1839–41)	R. M. T. Hunter	Van Buren
27th (1841–43)	John White	Harrison (1841) Tyler (1841–43)
28th (1843–45)	John W. Jones	Tyler
29th (1845–47)	John W. Davis	Polk
30th (1847–49)	Robert C. Winthrop	Polk
31st (1849–51)	Howell Cobb	Taylor (1849–50) Fillmore (1850–51)
32nd (1851–53)	Lynn Boyd	Fillmore
33rd (1853–55)	Lynn Boyd	Pierce
34th (1855–57)	Nathaniel P. Banks	Pierce
35th (1857–59)	James L. Orr	Buchanan
36th (1859–61)	William Pennington	Buchanan
37th (1861–63)	Galusha A. Grow	Lincoln
38th (1863–65)	Schuyler Colfax	Lincoln
39th (1865–67)	Schuyler Colfax	Lincoln (1865) Johnson (1865–67)
40th (1867–69)	Schuyler Colfax	Johnson
41st (1869–71)	James G. Blaine	Grant

Congress	Speaker	Administration
42nd (1871–73)	James G. Blaine	Grant
43rd (1873–75)	James G. Blaine	Grant
44th (1875–77)	Michael C. Kerr (1875–76) Samuel J. Randall (1876–77)	Grant
45th (1877–79)	Samuel J. Randall	Hayes
46th (1879–81)	Samuel J. Randall	Hayes
47th (1881–83)	Joseph W. Keifer	Garfield (1881) Arthur (1881–83)
48th (1883–85)	John G. Carlisle	Arthur
49th (1885–87)	John G. Carlisle	Cleveland
50th (1887–89)	John G. Carlisle	Cleveland
51st (1889–91)	Thomas B. Reed	Harrison
52nd (1891–93)	Charles F. Crisp	Harrison
53rd (1893–95)	Charles F. Crisp	Cleveland
54th (1895–97)	Thomas B. Reed	Cleveland
55th (1897–99)	Thomas B. Reed	McKinley
56th (1899–1901)	David B. Henderson	McKinley
57th (1901–03)	David B. Henderson	McKinley (1901) Roosevelt (1901–03)
58th (1903–05)	Joseph G. Cannon	Roosevelt
59th (1905–07)	Joseph G. Cannon	Roosevelt
60th (1907–09)	Joseph G. Cannon	Roosevelt
61st (1909–11)	Joseph G. Cannon	Taft
62nd (1911–13)	Champ Clark	Taft
63rd (1913–15)	Champ Clark	Wilson
64th (1915–17)	Champ Clark	Wilson
65th (1917–19)	Champ Clark	Wilson
66th (1919–21)	Frederick H. Gillett	Wilson
67th (1921–23)	Frederick H. Gillett	Harding
68th (1923–25)	Frederick H. Gillett	Harding (1923) Coolidge (1923–25)
69th (1925–27)	Nicholas Longworth	Coolidge
70th (1927–29)	Nicholas Longworth	Coolidge
71st (1929–31)	Nicholas Longworth	Hoover
72nd (1931–33)	John N. Garner	Hoover
73rd (1933–35)	Henry T. Rainey	Roosevelt
74th (1935–37)	Joseph W. Byrnes (1935–36) William B. Bankhead (1936–37)	Roosevelt
75th (1937–39)	William B. Bankhead	Roosevelt
76th (1939–41)	William B. Bankhead (1939–40) Sam Rayburn (1940–41)	Roosevelt
77th (1941–43)	Sam Rayburn	Roosevelt
78th (1943–45)	Sam Rayburn	Roosevelt
79th (1945–47)	Sam Rayburn	Roosevelt (1945) Truman (1945–47)
80th (1947–49)	Joseph W. Martin, Jr.	Truman
81st (1949–51)	Sam Rayburn	Truman
82nd (1951–53)	Sam Rayburn	Truman
83rd (1953–55)	Joseph W. Martin, Jr.	Eisenhower
84th (1955–57)	Sam Rayburn	Eisenhower
85th (1957–59)	Sam Rayburn	Eisenhower
86th (1959–61)	Sam Rayburn	Eisenhower
87th (1961–63)	Sam Rayburn (1961) John W. McCormack (1962–63)	Kennedy
88th (1963–65)	John W. McCormack	Kennedy (1963) Johnson (1963–65)
89th (1965–67)	John W. McCormack	Johnson
90th (1967–69)	John W. McCormack	Johnson
91st (1969–71)	John W. McCormack	Nixon
92nd (1971–73)	Carl Albert	Nixon
93rd (1973–75)	Carl Albert	Nixon (1973–74) Ford (1974–75)
94th (1975–77)	Carl Albert	Ford
95th (1977–79)	Thomas P. O'Neill, Jr.	Carter
96th (1979–81)	Thomas P. O'Neill, Jr.	Carter
97th (1981–83)	Thomas P. O'Neill, Jr.	Reagan

CONGRESSIONAL APPORTIONMENT. *See* **Apportionment.**

CONGRESSIONAL FILIBUSTER. *See* **Filibuster, Congressional.**

CONGRESSIONAL RECORD. A daily, unofficial publication of the proceedings of Congress. The Senate and House journals contain the official records. Published by Congress since 1873, it was preceded by the *Annals of Congress* (1789–1824), *Register of Debates* (1824–37), and *Congressional Globe* (1834–73), all privately published.

CONGRESSIONAL REGULATORY POWERS. Powers granted Congress by the Constitution to enact controls in certain areas and to make laws or regulations needed to implement such powers. Most regulatory legislation is passed by Congress in pursuance of the delegated power to tax, spend for the general welfare, and regulate interstate commerce. In recent years, Congress has passed on to administrative agencies the power to issue specific regulations controlling most social and economic activities. Congress spells out broad operating boundaries subject to alteration for practical or political reasons.

The power of Congress to control law in domestic matters is virtually plenary. Control over foreign policy is shared with the president. Officially, Congress is given the power to declare war and to appropriate all monies expended in war efforts; but since the Constitution assigns the president the power to command the armed forces, the deployment of such forces can virtually commit the Congress to support undeclared war efforts, such as those in Korea and Vietnam. Historically, Congress has granted the president authority to act according to his judgment during periods of domestic and international conflict.

CONGRESS OF INDUSTRIAL ORGANIZATIONS. *See* **American Federation of Labor–Congress of Industrial Organizations.**

CONGRESS OF RACIAL EQUALITY (CORE). Founded in 1942, CORE was originally an interracial group employing Gandhian tactics of nonviolent direct action in the struggle for racial equality. Although it invented the "sit-in," it remained a minor organization until the southern black college student sit-ins of 1960. CORE became nationally famous with its "freedom ride" of 1961, in which interracial teams dramatically challenged southern segregation while traveling in Alabama and Mississippi. By the mid-1960's, with the rise of nationalist tendencies in the black community and the disillusionment resulting from defeats suffered by the movement, CORE reversed its goal from integration to racial separatism, but declined sharply in membership and influence.

CONNECTICUT. The Connecticut River valley and the shoreline of Long Island Sound were thickly settled by Indians when Adriaen Block, a Dutchman, sailed up the river in 1614. In the 1630's, settlers from Massachusetts Bay arrived at what is now Windsor. Purchasing land from Indians, they displaced a Dutch trading post at Hartford and also settled Wethersfield. To these three "river towns" were added a military settlement at Saybrook (1635) and a Puritan colony at New Haven (1638). By 1740 the colony had been organized into incorporated towns. Connecticut Colony was first organized under the Fundamental Orders (1639), the first organic document of government in U.S. history. The orders were superseded by the royal charter of 1662, which was supplanted by a constitution in 1818.

Demands for a constitution lacked wide support until the rise of Jeffersonian Republicanism. In 1818 a genuine constitution was adopted. With numerous amendments the constitution continued in force until 1965. The 1965 document, necessitated by application to Connecticut of the U.S. Supreme Court's apportionment ruling in *Baker* v. *Carr* (*Butterworth* v. *Dempsey,* 1964), provided for the least possible alteration of government structure. State senatorial and house districts were made to conform to the one-man, one-vote principle by dividing and grouping towns.

Agricultural changes due to hostile topography, soil depletion, and a growing livestock production led to vast migrations from the state during the half-century following the Revolution, and population became fairly stable until the development of the industrial sector. The difficulty of earning a living from farming, together with the presence of an unusually well-educated population aided by mercantile capital, turned many Connecticuters to invention and manufacturing. Metals (especially brass), rubber products, small arms, machine tools, electrical equipment, and aircraft and other military production have dominated.

Urbanization continued steadily to about 1920. The dominant movement since the depression, however, has been suburban. Connecticut vies year after year with one or two other states for the highest per capita wealth in the country. The population in 1980 was 3,107,576.

CONNECTICUT, FUNDAMENTAL ORDERS OF. As founded in 1635, Connecticut consisted of the three river towns—Windsor, Hartford, and Wethersfield—with Springfield temporarily included. The river towns were established within territory to which the planters had neither patent nor title. They established a court, which, from Apr. 26, 1636, until Apr. 5, 1638, exercised jurisdiction over such matters as necessary. During the spring of 1638, there was a general assembly of the planters to establish a more satisfactory form of government. Out of this meeting came the Fundamental Orders, "voted" on Jan. 14, 1639. They were put into their final form by Roger Ludlow.

The document recognized no higher authority than the freemen of the three towns and provided for the calling of general assemblies; the election of a governor and magistrates; and the qualification of voters. It specified how deputies to the court were to be elected; how elections were to be called; how courts were to be organized and empowered; and how taxes were to be apportioned among the towns.

Superseded by the Connecticut Charter of Apr. 23, 1662, the Orders had their essential features incorporated into the charter, which was replaced by a new state constitution in 1818; the constitution retained these fundamentals.

CONNECTICUT, OLD PATENT OF. The first grant to Connecticut, known only from conflicting claims made under its authority and from what purports to be a copy of a deed made by Sir Robert Rich, Earl of Warwick, on Mar. 19, 1632, of a strip of land including part of the present state of Connecticut. Warwick had no right to make the grant; nor did the grantees make any move to take possession until, in 1635, actual settlement was under way at the river towns of Windsor, Hartford, and Wethersfield. At that time the grantees announced their claim and began erecting a fort at the mouth of the Connecticut River. In 1644 the fort and, presumably, the rights under the patent were sold to the planters of the river towns, who had from the beginning regarded themselves as the colony of Connecticut. The nebulous Warwick Patent undoubtedly played a large part in securing for Connecticut the limits set forth in the Charter of 1662.

CONNECTICUT CHARTER OF 1662. Following the accession of Charles II, the people of Connecticut petitioned the king to grant them a charter for the colony, as they considered that the Old, or Warwick, Patent gave them only an uncertain tenure. Carrying a draft of a charter based upon the Warwick Patent and letters to several persons of note, Gov. John Winthrop sailed for England in 1661. His efforts were rewarded by the granting of a charter dated Apr. 23, 1662.

In 1685 James II endeavored to annul many existing charters. The colony petitioned him to continue as before; but Sir Edmond Andros was sent over late in 1686 to receive their charter. On Nov. 1, 1687, Andros formally annexed the colony to his Dominion of New England. According to tradition, Andros called for the charter. After it had been brought in, and while Gov. Robert Treat was orating against its surrender, the lights were suddenly extinguished. When they were relighted, the charter was gone, having been taken by Joseph Wadsworth and secreted in a hollow tree, known later as the Charter Oak. Wadsworth preserved the charter and retained it for some years, for the General Assembly formally recognized his act. Andros administered the government for about two years. Then, with the overthrow of King James, Connecticut resumed its charter government. The charter continued as the basic law of Connecticut until 1818.

CONNECTICUT COMPROMISE. In the Constitutional Convention of 1787, the larger states supported the Virginia Plan, which would create a bicameral legislature in which "the rights of suffrage . . . ought to be proportioned to the Quotas of contributions, or to the number of free inhabitants." The small states demanded equality in a unicameral house. Roger Sherman of Connecticut proposed a compromise: two houses, the one with equal and the other proportional representation. Amendments linking direct taxes and representation in the House and representation on the basis of the total white population and three-fifths of the slave population were added. Sherman's proposal was adopted.

CONNECTICUT CONSTITUTIONAL CONVENTION. Two hundred and one delegates met at Hartford, Conn., on Aug. 26–Sept. 16, 1818, to frame a constitution to replace the Connecticut Charter of 1662. The final draft represented a moderately liberal advance. All Christian sects were put on an equal basis; small-town control of the lower house of the legislature was continued; the governor was given slightly more power; and an independent judiciary was established. The constitution was ratified by the electorate on Oct. 5.

CONNECTICUT WESTERN LANDS. The Connecticut Charter of 1662 granted the territory that the state now occupies plus a seventy-mile-wide strip from the Delaware River to the Pacific Ocean. Conflicts over the western boundary were resolved in 1786 when Connecticut ceded to the United States all its western territories except the Western Reserve (an area extending 120 miles from Pennsylvania's western boundary along Lake Erie), most of which it sold in 1795 to the Connecticut Land Company for $1.2 million, thereby establishing its educational fund. It retained a half-million-acre tract in the western part of the Reserve, the Firelands, set aside to compensate Connecticut families for losses in the Revolution.

CONNECTICUT WITS. *See* **Hartford Wits.**

CONNOLLY'S PLOT (1775). John Connolly, a Loyalist officer who had lived at Fort Pitt, proposed to John Murray, Lord Dunmore, that he should capture Fort Pitt and join Lord Dunmore in putting down the rebellion in Virginia. George Washington had been warned, however, and Connolly was captured Nov. 20, at Hagerstown, Md.

CONNOR, FORT. Headquarters for operations against the Cheyenne and Sioux, established by Gen. P. E. Connor, Aug. 19, 1865, at the Bozeman Trail crossing on Powder River, Wyo. It was abandoned and rebuilt on a different site as Fort Reno. It was again abandoned after the Red Cloud War.

CONQUISTADORES (conquerors). Leaders of the Spanish conquest of the Americas. Juan Ponce de León, in search of the fabled fountain of youth, had landed on the shores of Florida (1513) before Hernando Cortes took Mexico in 1519. Immediately thereafter, other *conquistadores* began exploring and subduing lands northward. Notable among them were Pánfilo de Narváez, Álvar Núñez Cabeza de Vaca, Hernando de Soto, Francisco Vásquez de Coronado, Antonio de Espejo, Juan de Oñate, and Alonso de León.

CONSCIENCE WHIGS. Dissident New England members of the Whig party, so-called because of their vigorous opposition to slavery. The faction favored the adoption in 1846 of the Wilmot Proviso, limiting or forbidding the spread of slavery in new territories, and when the 1848 Whig National Convention refused to endorse it, they bolted and joined the Free Soil party. The terms "Woolly Heads" and "Amalgamationists" were also applied to the group.

CONSCIENTIOUS OBJECTORS. Originally persons of various religious and social sects who opposed war as contrary to their faiths and creeds. Since the Civil War the U.S. government has broadened the definition to include persons objecting to participation in, and support of, all wars on moral and intellectual grounds.

The American Revolution produced the first major conflicts between religious objectors (particularly Quakers, Mennonites, and Dunkards) and governmental demands for militia service. Some colonies levied fines; and in some instances such believers were labeled Tory sympathizers.

During the Civil War the Confederacy provided military exemptions to religious objectors who furnished substitutes or paid a tax of $500; the South generally treated conscientious objectors as pro-Union sympathizers. The Union provided exemptions if an individual obtained a substitute or paid $300. In February 1864, Congress provided noncombatant alternative service for religious objectors.

World War I introduced the concept in the United States that military service was "personal, universal, and absolute" for those liable to the draft, with provision allowing conscientious objectors alternative noncombatant military or civilian duties. Many refused noncombatant status and were court-martialed and sentenced to prison. President Wilson granted amnesty to most objectors by 1919.

During World War II and the Korean War, provisions again were made for noncombatant status. During the Vietnam War, traditional conscientious objectors took religious stands opposed to active participation, but thousands of others objected to the war on moral grounds and refused military service by going to Canada and Europe; others publicly burned draft cards as a symbol of protest. (*See also* Amnesty.)

CONSCRIPTION. U.S. laws before and after independence required able-bodied males to enroll in the militia. The Continental Congress in 1778 recommended the states draft men from their militias for one year's service in the Continental army; but this failed to fill the Continental ranks.

Although both sides resorted to conscription during the Civil War, the system worked effectively for neither. The Confederate congress on Apr. 16, 1862, passed an act requiring military service from all males aged eighteen to thirty-five not legally exempt. The U.S. Congress followed on July 17, 1862, with an act authorizing a draft within a state when it could not meet its quota with volunteers. This failed, and on Mar. 3, 1863, Congress passed the first genuine national conscription law, setting up under the Union army elaborate machinery for drafting men between twenty and forty-five.

In 1917, Woodrow Wilson decided to rely on conscription, rather than enlistment, for World War I. The Selective Service Act of May 18, 1917, was carefully drawn to remedy the defects in the Civil War system. In 1917–18, 24 million men were registered and nearly 3 million inducted into the military services, with little resistance.

The Selective Service and Training Act of Sept. 14, 1940, instituted national conscription in peacetime, requiring registration of all men between twenty-one and forty-five, with selection for one year's service by a national lottery. The term of service was extended by a year in August 1941 and, after Pearl Harbor, to the duration of the war plus six months and requiring registration of all men eighteen to sixty-four.

The World War II draft expired in March 1947, but conscription was revived in 1948. The Universal Military Training and Service Act of 1951 theoretically placed a military obligation on all men between the ages of eighteen and a half and twenty-six for a total of eight years of combined active and reserve military duty. The act was extended and variously amended at four-year intervals and provided options of various types of reserve service for the basic two years of active duty required. Various deferments for educational and other reasons were provided for, as well as exemptions subject to abuse. Opposition to operations of the Selective Service System was a central feature of the movement against the Vietnam War. The draft law was renewed for only two years in 1971. Meanwhile, President Richard M. Nixon in 1969 restored the system of selection by lottery. In June 1973 he ended the draft entirely and reverted to all-volunteer forces. On June 27, 1980, President Jimmy Carter signed the unpopular bill providing for peacetime draft registration. His successor, President Ronald Reagan, continued the draft.

CONSERVATION. The wise use of resources, including not only land but the people living on it, water, wildlife, and minerals. Historically, one group of conservationists has promoted natural resource development or use, and another group has promoted preservation or nonuse.

During the colonial period several significant attempts were made in America to regulate the use of resources: cutting and sale of timber were regulated in Plymouth, and Newport, R.I., allowed deer hunting only six months of the year.

Little was done with respect to conservation by the U.S. government until in 1849 the U.S. Department of the Interior was established. Carl Schurz, its secretary from 1877 to 1881, recommended scientific care of forests and establishment of federal forest reservations. The Forest Reserve Act was signed in 1891, permitting President Benjamin Harrison to set aside 13 million acres as reservations. Yellowstone National Park was established in 1872, and Yosemite in 1891. Several societies and clubs emphasizing conservation were created, including the Sierra Club in 1892 and the National Audubon Society in 1905.

Conservation as a social movement was initiated by President Theodore Roosevelt, an active outdoorsman. The chief influence on him was Gifford Pinchot, a professional forester named head of the Division of Forestry in 1898. Some lasting achievements of the Roosevelt-Pinchot era were the Reclamation Act of 1902, fostering western development; the Antiquities Act of 1906, setting aside federal land as natural monuments; and the North American Conservation Conference of 1909, where delegates from the United States, Canada, and Mexico met to analyze resources.

The American Game Protective and Propagation Association was founded in 1911, the Save-the-Redwoods League in 1918, and the Izaak Walton League in 1922. Although legislation was limited, the National Park Service Act was passed in 1916; the Migratory Bird Treaty Act with Canada, restricting hunting of migratory species, became law in 1918; and the Mineral Leasing Act, regulating mining on federal lands, and the Federal Water Power Act, giving the Federal Power Commission authority to issue licenses for hydropower development on public lands, were both passed in 1920.

The period 1933–39 has been called the "golden age of conservation." The primary conservation emphasis during the administration of Franklin D. Roosevelt was on land planning. The Soil Erosion Service, Civilian Conservation Corps, Tennessee Valley Authority, Soil Conservation Service, and Resettlement Administration were established.

The Conservation Foundation and Resources for the Future, founded in 1948 and 1952, respectively, were particularly active in promoting conservation research and education. In the spirit of Theodore Roosevelt, President John F. Kennedy called a White House conference on conservation in May 1962 to draw up plans to facilitate the elimination of resource problems. The following year saw the Clean Air Act, which appropriated federal funds for a cooperative attack on air pollution; and the establishment of the Bureau of Outdoor Recreation within the Department of the Interior to coordinate federal efforts in that area. President Lyndon B. Johnson continued the Kennedy emphasis on conservation.

In the 1970's the primary focus became environmental quality. The National Environmental Policy Act of 1969 established the Council of Environmental Quality to oversee efforts in dealing with pollution and to make environmental policy recommendations to the president. The Environmental Protection Agency (EPA) has proposed several national quality standards pursuant to the mandates of such legislation as the Clean Air Act of 1967 and the Water Quality Improvement Act of 1970. Conservationists won an important battle against developers in 1980 when President Jimmy Carter signed a bill designating over 104 million acres in Alaska as national conservation areas, but the succeeding administration, especially Secretary of the Interior James Watt, was accused of undermining basic conservation laws.

CONSERVATISM. American conservatism, it is generally agreed, has not been as strong a force as American liberalism. Although a colonial America that included slaveholders and Puritans was in part a conservative society, the American Revolution and the Declaration of Independence were plainly at odds with the standing order. Even so, the Constitution and organization of a strong national government blunted the edge of this revolutionary radicalism.

Conservatism itself was hard pressed after Thomas Jefferson defeated the Federalists in 1800. John Marshall, chief justice of the Supreme Court, and the famous senatorial triumvirate of Henry Clay, John C. Calhoun, and Daniel Webster later furnished dramatic leadership for the conservative minority's hostility to Jacksonian democracy.

After the Civil War certain values identified with Jefferson and Jackson, such as democracy and individualism, were taken over by the Republican party and adapted to the needs of the rising business community. Both the Republican party and big business were conservative in their resistance to social reforms and to government regulation of the economy.

In the early 20th century, modern mass society provoked a reconsideration of conservatism. In national politics, however, Herbert Hoover's defeat in 1932 ended an era of generally conservative Republican control. Thereafter, conservatives were forced to react defensively to the policies of Franklin D. Roosevelt and the New Deal.

Even the revival of the Republican party under President Dwight D. Eisenhower after World War II made no fundamental change in the New Deal pattern of social and economic planning. Conservative politics accordingly came to be identified with the military ethos or with the radical right.

By the 1960's the most interesting phenomenon in American conservatism was the ideological rapprochement between right-wing libertarians and young New Left radicals, who were really more anarchistic than socialistic. What united the components of this strange amalgam was its opposition to the modern big-business, big-government establishment forged by the cold war. The new libertarians also rejected the formal conservatism of the Richard M. Nixon administration.

A shift to conservatism occurred in 1980 when the Senate came under Republican control and Ronald Reagan overwhelmingly defeated President Jimmy Carter, whose liberal policies (with some populist elements) were undermined by inefficiency. Hailed as the first true conservative president in many years, Reagan began to dismantle many social and economic programs originating in the New Deal.

***CONSOLATO DEL MARE* PRINCIPLE.** One of the principles in a code of sea law in the early Middle Ages. It avows that a belligerent state has the right to take enemy property, even noncontraband, from a neutral ship. The United States has traditionally opposed the principle by the opposite dictum of free ships, free goods.

CONSPIRACIES ACTS OF 1861 AND 1862. Attempts to suppress antiwar activities in the North during the Civil War. One statute (July 31, 1861) provided for a fine and imprisonment for those who conspired by threats, intimidation, or force to obstruct or overthrow the government. The act of July 17, 1862, identified antiwar activity as treason and softened the death penalty for treason to the alternative of death or imprisonment and fine.

***CONSTELLATION-INSURGENTE* ENCOUNTER** (Feb. 9, 1799). Near Nevis Island in the West Indies, during naval hostilities with France, American Commodore Thomas Truxtun in the frigate *Constellation* defeated the French frigate *Insurgente* in a sharp engagement. In this and in the subsequent *Constellation-Vengeance* action, Truxtun not only gave vigorous backing to the U.S. policy of commerce protection, but set high standards for its new navy.

***CONSTELLATION-VENGEANCE* ENCOUNTER** (Feb. 1–2, 1800). The U.S.S. *Constellation,* heading for Guadeloupe, sighted the French frigate *Vengeance.* Commodore Thomas Truxtun of the *Constellation* ordered his men to aim at the hull. The French fired into the American ship's rigging to prevent being chased; they suffered about four times the losses of the Americans. When the *Constellation*'s mainmast fell, the French escaped.

***CONSTITUTION*.** An American 44-gun frigate launched Oct. 21, 1797. In the naval war with France it served as Commodore Silas Talbot's flagship, and in the Tripolitan War, as the flagship of Commodore Edward Preble. The *Constitution* was victorious in several single-ship engagements in the War of 1812. During the fight with the *Guerrière* a seaman gave it the nickname "Old Ironsides." Ordered broken up in 1830 by the Department of the Navy, the frigate was retained in deference to public opinion aroused by Oliver Wendell Holmes's poem "Old Ironsides." It was rebuilt in 1833, served as a training ship at Portsmouth, Va., from 1860 to 1865, was partially rebuilt in 1877 and again in 1925, and, except for one cruise, has been docked at the Boston navy yard since 1897.

CONSTITUTION, BRITISH. The statement of principles and practices involved in government by the king and Parliament. It is not set forth in a single document like the Constitution of the United States but consists partly of basic statutes, of which Magna Charta (1215) is one of the earliest examples, and partly of customs and common-law principles formerly thought of as embodying "natural" rights.

CONSTITUTIONAL APPORTIONMENT. *See* **Apportionment.**

CONSTITUTIONAL CONVENTION. The U.S. Constitution was the work of a convention that sat at Philadelphia from late May 1787 until mid-September, the culmination of a lengthy campaign for constitutional reform staged by nationalistic political leaders, above all James Madison and Alexander Hamilton, both of whom had long been convinced that the Articles of Confederation were hopelessly deficient.

Twelve states sent delegates to the convention. Rhode Island, then in the grip of a paper-money faction fearful of federal monetary reform, boycotted the meeting. The participating states appointed seventy-four delegates, of whom fifty-five put in an appearance. Of these, some fifteen or twenty were responsible for virtually all of the convention's work.

Dominating from the beginning was a group of delegates intent on creating a genuinely national government possessed of powers adequate to promote the security, financial stability, commercial prosperity, and general well-being of all of the states: George Washington, James Madison, James Wilson, Gouverneur Morris, Rufus King, Charles Cotesworth Pinckney, John Rutledge, Benjamin Franklin, Edmund Randolph, and Alexander Hamilton.

The nationalists commanded on most occasions the support of a moderate group that accepted the necessity for strong central government but was willing to compromise substantially with the convention's states' rights bloc when that proved necessary: Elbridge Gerry, Oliver Ellsworth, Roger Sherman, and Abraham Baldwin.

A small, but significant, bloc of states' rights delegates was firmly opposed to the creation of a sovereign national government. Its leaders included William Paterson, author of the New Jersey Plan; John Dickinson; Gunning Bedford; John Lansing; and Robert Yates. These men recognized the necessity for constitutional reform but believed strongly that a confederation type of government ought to be retained.

Voting in the convention was by states, each state having one vote. The nationalist faction demonstrated its power at the very outset of the proceedings. Following organization for business, Randolph presented what has since become known as the Virginia Plan—a proposal for a thoroughly nationalistic frame of government—which the convention accepted without debate as the basis for its further deliberations. The plan called for a genuinely national government rather than one based upon state sovereignty (*see* Virginia Plan).

This meant junking the Articles of Confederation outright and erecting a powerful national government, federal only in that it would still leave to the states a separate if unspecified area of sovereignty. To make this clear, the nationalists put forward a resolution submitted by Randolph and Morris declaring that "no Union of States merely federal" would be sufficient; instead, "a national government ought to be established, consisting of a supreme legislative, executive, and judiciary." The Randolph-Morris resolution carried almost unanimously, Connecticut alone voting opposition.

The most serious conflict between the nationalist and states' rights factions came over the composition of the legislature. The nationalists began the debate with the demand that both houses of Congress be apportioned according to representation and that the lower house, at least, be elected directly by the people of the several states. The states' rights faction early made it clear that it would accept nothing less than state equality in at least one house. In mid-June, to emphasize its point, it introduced the New Jersey Plan, which called for a one-chamber legislature based upon state equality —that is, a continuation of the Confederation Congress (*see* New Jersey Plan). The plan met prompt defeat, but the impasse remained. The ultimate solution was found in the so-called Great Compromise. This provided that the lower house of Congress be apportioned according to population, that each state have one vote in the upper house, but that all bills for raising revenue originate in the lower house. A further resolution, offered by Elbridge Gerry, provided that senators were to vote as individuals and not as state delegations. After two weeks of further debate, the nationalists yielded and accepted the compromise.

The debate on the executive proved to be protracted and difficult, but it too was a victory for a strong national government. The delegates accepted an idea originally advanced by Wilson: choice of the president by electors chosen by the several states (*see* Electoral College).

Equally nationalistic was the convention's resort to the judiciary to guarantee federal sovereignty and national supremacy against incursion by the states. The convention early rejected coercion of derelict states as inconsistent with the prospective government's sovereign character. Surprisingly, the states' rights–oriented New Jersey Plan supplied the final solution: it carried a clause declaring the Constitution, treaties, and laws of the national government the "supreme law of the respective states" and binding the state courts to enforce them as such. Incorporation of the supremacy clause in the new Constitution was a victory in disguise for the nationalist cause. On the surface the clause made the state courts the final judge of the limits of both federal and state sovereignty. But the convention had also provided for the establishment of a national judiciary and had vested in the federal courts jurisdiction over all cases arising under the Constitution, treaties, and laws of the United States. This meant that the Supreme Court would possess the ultimate power to settle questions involving state and federal sovereignty.

Meanwhile, in a concession to the states' rights party, the convention had dropped the delegation to Congress of power to legislate in all cases in which the states were severally "incompetent" and had resorted instead to a specific enumeration of the powers of Congress. The convention in its final draft incorporated an important clause giving Congress the power to enact "necessary and proper" legislation in fulfillment of its delegated powers, and it accepted a vaguely drafted "general welfare clause" that, with the "necessary and proper" provisions, was to serve in the 20th century as the basis for a tremendous expansion of federal power. In mid-September 1787 the convention put its various resolutions and decisions into a finished draft and submitted the Constitution to the states for approval. (*See* Constitution of the United States.)

CONSTITUTIONAL UNION PARTY. Late in 1859 old-line Whigs and members of the American (Know-Nothing) party, alarmed at excesses of partyism and sectionalism and fearing secession, began to form a new party. Meeting in 1860 in Baltimore, they chose John Bell and Edward Everett as candidates for president and vice-president. Polling only 590,000 votes and carrying only Kentucky, Virginia, and Tennessee, the party succeeded, nevertheless, in temporarily allaying disunion sentiment.

CONSTITUTION*-*CYANE AND -***LEVANT*** ENGAGEMENT (Feb. 20, 1815). The *Constitution,* commanded by Capt. Charles Stewart, captured the British frigate *Cyane* and sloop of war *Levant* 200 miles northeast of the Madeiras.

CONSTITUTION FORT. Erected in 1775 on what is now Constitution Island in the Hudson River opposite West Point, N.Y. Some forty guns and mortars were mounted, and a log boom stretched across the channel. Early in 1776 defensive efforts were transferred south, and Constitution Fort was abandoned. After Sir Henry Clinton's withdrawal, George Washington issued orders for a new defense system, based on West Point, which included part of the old works of Constitution Fort restored as redoubts.

CONSTITUTION-GUERRIÈRE **ENGAGEMENT** (Aug. 19, 1812). The capture of the British frigate *Guerrière* (Capt. James R. Dacres) by the *Constitution* (Capt. Isaac Hull) was the first important naval victory of the War of 1812 and did much to win enthusiasm for the war from New Englanders. It took place 750 miles east of Boston while Hull was watching for British merchantmen on their usual course between Halifax and Bermuda.

The British lost twenty-three killed and fifty-six wounded, including Dacres; the American loss was only seven killed and seven wounded. The *Constitution* was nearly 50 percent superior in all features, but it was Hull's superior seamanship that made them count. To the British, the superiority of the new American type of frigate was the most important factor.

CONSTITUTION-JAVA **ENGAGEMENT** (Dec. 19, 1812). While cruising off South America, Commodore William Bainbridge on the U.S.S. *Constitution* sighted the British *Java.* After a battle of two hours, the British surrendered. Its losses were nearly five times those of the American ship and included its commander, Capt. Henry Lambert.

CONSTITUTION OF THE UNITED STATES. The Constitution, which has served since 1789 as the basic frame of government of the republic of the United States, was the work of a constitutional convention that sat at Philadelphia from late May 1787 until mid-September of that year (*see* Constitutional Convention).

Ratification. In mid-September 1787 the convention put its various resolutions and decisions into a finished draft and submitted the Constitution to the states for approval. The convention had provided for ratification of the Constitution by state conventions, stipulating that ratification by any nine states would put the Constitution into effect. The Federalists, as the proponents of ratification soon became known, in the next ten months carried every state but Rhode Island and North Carolina. Their impressive victory resulted from their positive and imaginative remedy for the country's grave constitutional ills. Their opponents, the Antifederalists, could offer no constructive proposal of their own.

Dates of ratification by states:

December 1787	Delaware (unanimous)
December 1787	Pennsylvania (vote 46–23)
December 1787	New Jersey (unanimous)
January 1788	Georgia (unanimous)
January 1788	Connecticut (128–40)
February 1788	Massachusetts (187–168, with a request for a Bill of Rights)
April 1788	Maryland (63–11)
May 1788	South Carolina (149–73)
June 1788	New Hampshire (57–47, with request for twelve amendments)
*June 1788	Virginia (89–79, with request for a Bill of Rights)
*June 1788	New York (30–27)
*November 1788	North Carolina (194–77; after Bill of Rights had been proposed)
*May 1790	Rhode Island (34–32)

*Ratified Constitution after the ninth state adoption

Amendments to the Constitution. Constitutional growth since 1789 has made the present-day "living Constitution" a very different thing from the charter drafted at Philadelphia in the late 18th century. The doctrine of broad construction has led since 1880 to a vast increase in federal powers, as the national government has adapted itself to modern urbanization and industrialization. Yet the fundamental ordering of power in government that the framers decreed, their pervasive provisions for limited government, and their profound concern for individual liberty still lie at the very heart of the American constitutional system.

Twenty-six amendments have been adopted since 1789. The first ten were drafted to meet the protests in numerous state ratifying conventions against the absence of a bill of rights in the Constitution. On the initiative of James Madison, the First Congress submitted twelve amendments to the states; ten of these were ratified (1791) and constitute the Bill of Rights, which limits the powers of the federal government but not the powers of the states (*see Barron* v. *Baltimore*). The subsequent sixteen amendments are listed below with the copy of the Constitution.

CONSTITUTION OF THE UNITED STATES

Preamble

WE THE PEOPLE of the United States, in Order to form a more perfect Union, establish Justice, insure domestic Tranquility, provide for the common defence, promote the general Welfare, and secure the Blessings of Liberty to ourselves and our Posterity, do ordain and establish this Constitution for the United States of America.

Article I

Section 1. All legislative Powers herein granted shall be vested in a Congress of the United States, which shall consist of a Senate and House of Representatives.

Section 2. The House of Representatives shall be composed of Members chosen every second Year by the People of the several States, and the Electors in each State shall have the Qualifications requisite for Electors of the most numerous Branch of the State Legislature.

No Person shall be a Representative who shall not have attained to the age of twenty five Years, and been seven Years a Citizen of the United States, and who shall not, when elected, be an Inhabitant of that State in which he shall be chosen.

Representatives and direct Taxes shall be apportioned among the several States which may be included within this Union, according to their respective Numbers, which shall be determined by adding to the whole Number of free Persons, including those bound to Service for a Term of Years, and excluding Indians not taxed, three fifths of all other Persons. The actual Enumeration shall be made within three Years after the first Meeting of the Congress of the United States, and within every subsequent Term of ten Years, in such Manner as they shall by Law direct. The Number of Representatives shall not exceed one for every thirty Thousand, but each State shall have at Least one Representative; and until such enumeration shall be made, the State of New Hampshire shall be entitled to chuse three, Massachusetts eight, Rhode-Island and Providence Plantations one, Connecticut five, New-York six, New Jersey four, Pennsylvania eight, Delaware one, Maryland six, Virginia ten, North Carolina five, South Carolina five, and Georgia three.

When vacancies happen in the Representation from any State, the Executive Authority thereof shall issue Writs of Election to fill such Vacancies.

The House of Representatives shall chuse their Speaker and other Officers; and shall have the sole Power of Impeachment.

Section 3. The Senate of the United States shall be composed of two Senators from each State, chosen by the Legislature thereof, for six Years; and each Senator shall have one Vote.

Immediately after they shall be assembled in Consequence of the first Election, they shall be divided as equally as may be into three Classes. The Seats of the Senators of the first Class shall be vacated at the Expiration of the second Year, of the second Class at the Expiration of the fourth Year, and of the third Class at the Expiration of the sixth Year, so that one third may be chosen every second Year; and if Vacancies happen by Resignation, or otherwise, during the Recess of the Legislature of any State, the Executive thereof may make temporary Appointments until the next Meeting of the Legislature, which shall then fill such Vacancies.

No Person shall be a Senator who shall not have attained to the Age of thirty Years, and been nine Years a Citizen of the United States, and who shall not, when elected, be an Inhabitant of that State for which he shall be chosen.

The Vice-President of the United States shall be President of the Senate, but shall have no Vote, unless they be equally divided.

The Senate shall chuse their other Officers, and also a President pro tempore, in the Absence of the Vice-President, or when he shall exercise the Office of President of the United States.

The Senate shall have the sole Power to try all Impeachments. When sitting for that Purpose, they shall be on Oath or Affirmation. When the President of the United States is tried, the Chief Justice shall preside: And no Person shall be convicted without the Concurrence of two thirds of the Members present.

Judgment in Cases of Impeachment shall not extend further than to removal from Office, and disqualification to hold and enjoy any Office of honor, Trust or Profit under the United States: but the Party convicted shall nevertheless be liable and subject to Indictment, Trial, Judgment and Punishment, according to Law.

Section 4. The Times, Places and Manner of holding Elections for Senators and Representatives, shall be prescribed in each State by the Legislature thereof; but the Congress may at any time by Law make or alter such Regulations, except as to the Places of chusing Senators.

The Congress shall assemble at least once in every Year, and such Meeting shall be on the first Monday in December, unless they shall by Law appoint a different Day.

Section 5. Each House shall be the Judge of the Elections, Returns and Qualifications of its own Members, and a Majority of each shall constitute a Quorum to do Business; but a smaller Number may adjourn from day to day and may be authorized to compel the Attendance of absent Members, in such Manner, and under such Penalties as each House may provide.

Each House may determine the Rules of its Proceedings, punish its Members for disorderly Behaviour, and, with the Concurrence of two thirds, expel a Member.

Each House shall keep a Journal of its Proceedings, and from time to time publish the same, excepting such Parts as may in their Judgment require Secrecy; and the Yeas and Nays of the Members of either House on any question shall, at the Desire of one fifth of those Present, be entered on the Journal.

Neither House, during the Session of Congress, shall, without the Consent of the other, adjourn for more than three days, nor to any other Place than that in which the two Houses shall be sitting.

Section 6. The Senators and Representatives shall receive a Compensation for their Services, to be ascertained by Law, and paid out of the Treasury of the United States. They shall in all Cases, except Treason, Felony and Breach of the Peace, be privileged from Arrest during their Attendance at the Session of their respective Houses, and in going to and returning from the same; and for any Speech or Debate in either House, they shall not be questioned in any other Place.

No Senator or Representative shall, during the Time for which he was elected, be appointed to any civil Office under the Authority of the United States, which shall have been created, or the Emoluments whereof shall have been encreased during such time; and no Person holding any Office under the United States, shall be a Member of either House during his Continuance in Office.

Section 7. All Bills for raising Revenue shall originate in the House of Representatives; but the Senate may propose or concur with Amendments as on other Bills.

Every Bill which shall have passed the House of Representatives and the Senate, shall, before it become a Law, be presented to the President of the United States; If he approve he shall sign it, but if not he shall return it, with his Objections to that House in which it shall have originated, who shall enter the Objections at large on their Journal, and proceed to reconsider it. If after such Reconsideration two thirds of that House shall agree to pass the Bill, it shall be sent, together with the Objections, to the other House, by which it shall likewise be reconsidered, and if approved by two thirds of that House, it shall become a Law. But in all such Cases the Votes of both Houses shall be determined by yeas and Nays, and the Names of the Persons voting for and against the Bill shall be entered on the Journal of each House respectively. If any Bill shall not be returned by the President within ten Days (Sundays excepted) after it shall have been presented to him, the Same shall be a Law, in like Manner as if he had signed it, unless the Congress by their Adjournment prevent its Return, in which Case it shall not be a Law.

Every Order, Resolution, or Vote to which the Concurrence of the Senate and House of Representatives may be necessary (except on a question of Adjournment) shall be presented to the President of the United States; and before the Same shall take Effect, shall be approved by him, or being disapproved by him, shall be repassed by two thirds of the Senate and House of Representatives, according to the Rules and Limitations prescribed in the Case of a Bill.

Section 8. The Congress shall have Power To lay and collect Taxes, Duties, Imposts and Excises, to pay the Debts and provide for the common Defence and general Welfare of the United States; but all Duties, Imposts and Excises shall be uniform throughout the United States;

To borrow Money on the credit of the United States;

To regulate Commerce with foreign Nations, and among the several States, and with the Indian Tribes;

To establish an uniform Rule of Naturalization, and uniform Laws on the subject of Bankruptcies throughout the United States;

To coin Money, regulate the Value thereof, and of foreign Coin, and fix the Standard of Weights and Measures;

To provide for the Punishment of counterfeiting the Securities and current Coin of the United States;

To establish Post Offices and post Roads;

To promote the Progress of Science and useful Arts, by securing for limited Times to Authors and Inventors the exclusive Right to their respective Writings and Discoveries;

To constitute Tribunals inferior to the supreme Court;

To define and punish Piracies and Felonies committed on the high Seas, and Offences against the Law of Nations;

To declare War, grant Letters of Marque and Reprisal, and make Rules concerning Captures on Land and Water;

To raise and support Armies, but no Appropriation of Money to that Use shall be for a longer Term than two Years;

To provide and maintain a Navy;

To make Rules for the Government and Regulation of the land and naval Forces;

To provide for calling for the Militia to execute the Laws of the Union, suppress Insurrections and repel Invasions;

To provide for organizing, arming, and disciplining, the Militia, and for governing such Part of them as may be employed in the Service of the United States, reserving to the States respectively, the Appointment of the Officers, and the Authority of training the Militia according to the discipline prescribed by Congress;

To exercise exclusive Legislation in all Cases whatsoever, over such District (not exceeding ten Miles square) as may, by Cession of particular States, and the Acceptance of Congress, become the Seat of the Government of the United States, and to exercise like Authority over all Places purchased by the Consent of the Legislature of the State in which the Same shall be, for the Erection of Forts, Magazines, Arsenals, dock-Yards, and other needful Buildings;—And

To make all Laws which shall be necessary and proper for carrying into Execution the foregoing Powers, and all other Powers vested by this Constitution in the Government of the United States, or in any Department or Officer thereof.

Section 9. The Migration or Importation of such Persons as any of the States now existing shall think proper to admit, shall not be prohibited by the Congress prior to the Year one thousand eight hundred and eight, but a Tax or duty may be imposed on such Importation, not exceeding ten dollars for each Person.

The Privilege of the Writ of Habeas Corpus shall not be suspended, unless when in Cases of Rebellion or Invasion the public Safety may require it.

No Bill of Attainder or ex post facto Law shall be passed.

No Capitation, or other direct, Tax shall be laid, unless in Proportion to the Census or Enumeration herein before directed to be taken.

No Tax or Duty shall be laid on Articles exported from any State.

No Preference shall be given by any Regulation of Commerce or Revenue to the Ports of one State over those of another; nor shall Vessels bound to, or from, one State, be obliged to enter, clear or pay Duties in another.

No Money shall be drawn from the Treasury, but in Consequence of Appropriations made by Law; and a regular Statement and Account of the Receipts and Expenditures of all public Money shall be published from time to time.

No Title of Nobility shall be granted by the United States: And no Person holding any Office of Profit or Trust under them, shall, without the Consent of the Congress, accept of any present, Emolument, Office, or Title, of any kind whatever, from any King, Prince, or foreign State.

Section 10. No State shall enter into any Treaty, Alliance, or Confederation; grant Letters of Marque and Reprisal; coin Money; emit Bills of Credit; make any Thing but gold and silver Coin a Tender in Payment of Debts; pass any Bill of Attainder, ex post facto Law, or Law impairing the Obligation of Contracts, or grant any Title of Nobility.

No State shall, without the Consent of the Congress, lay any Imposts or Duties on Imports or Exports, except what may be absolutely necessary for executing its inspection Laws: and the net Produce of all Duties and Imposts, laid by any State on Imports or Exports, shall be for the Use of the Treasury of the United States; and all such Laws shall be subject to the Revision and Controul of the Congress.

No State shall, without the Consent of Congress, lay any Duty of Tonnage, keep Troops, or Ships of War in time of Peace, enter into any Agreement or Compact with another state, or with a foreign Power, or engage in War, unless actually invaded, or in such imminent Danger as will not admit of delay.

Article II

Section 1. The executive Power shall be vested in a President of the United States of America. He shall hold his Office during the Term of four Years, and, together with the Vice-President, chosen for the same Term, be elected, as follows.

Each State shall appoint, in such Manner as the Legislature thereof may direct, a Number of Electors, equal to the whole Number of Senators and Representatives to which the State may be entitled in the Congress: but no Senator or Representative, or Person holding an Office of Trust or Profit under the United States, shall be appointed an Elector.

The Electors shall meet in their respective States, and vote by Ballot for two Persons, of whom one at least shall not be an Inhabitant of the same State with themselves. And they shall make a List of all the Persons voted for, and of the Number of Votes for each; which List they shall sign and certify, and transmit sealed to the Seat of the Government of the United States, directed to the President of the Senate. The President of the Senate shall, in the Presence of the Senate and House of Representatives, open all the Certificates, and the Votes shall then be counted. The Person having the greatest Number of Votes shall be the President, if such Number be a Majority of the whole Number of Electors appointed; and if there be more than one who have such Majority, and have an equal Number of Votes, then the House of Representatives shall immediately chuse by Ballot one of them for President; and if no Person have a Majority, then from the five highest on the List the said House shall in like Manner chuse the President. But in chusing the President, the Votes shall be taken by States, the Representation from each State having one Vote; A quorum for this Purpose shall consist of a Member or Members from two thirds of the States, and a Majority of all the States shall be necessary to a Choice. In every Case, after the Choice of the President, the Person having the greatest Number of Votes of the Electors shall be the Vice-President. But if there should remain two or more who have equal Votes, the Senate shall chuse from them by Ballot the Vice-President.

The Congress may determine the Time of chusing the Electors, and the Day on which they shall give their Votes; which Day shall be the same throughout the United States.

No Person except a natural born Citizen, or a Citizen of the United States, at the time of the Adoption of this Constitution, shall be eligible to the Office of President; neither shall any Person be eligible to that Office who shall not have attained to the Age of thirty five Years, and been fourteen Years a Resident within the United States.

In Case of the Removal of the President from Office, or of his Death, Resignation, or Inability to discharge the Powers and Duties of the said Office, the Same shall devolve on the Vice-President, and the Congress may by Law provide for the Case of Removal, Death, Resignation or Inability, both of the President and Vice-President, declaring what Officer shall then act as President, and such Officer shall act accordingly, until the Disability be removed, or a President shall be elected.

The President shall, at stated Times, receive for his Services, a Compensation, which shall neither be encreased nor diminished during the Period for which he shall have been elected, and he shall not receive within that Period any other Emolument from the United States, or any of them.

Before he enter on the Execution of his Office, he shall take the following Oath or Affirmation:—"I do solemnly swear (or affirm) that I will faithfully execute the Office of President of the United States, and will to the best of my Ability, preserve, protect and defend the Constitution of the United States."

Section 2. The President shall be Commander in Chief of the Army and Navy of the United States, and of the Militia of the several States, when called into the actual Service of the United States; he may require the Opinion, in writing, of the principal Officer in each of the executive Departments, upon any Subject relating to the Duties of their respective Offices, and he shall have Power to grant Reprieves and Pardons for Offences against the United States, except in Casses of Impeachment.

He shall have Power, by and with the Advice and Consent of the Senate, to make Treaties, provided two thirds of the Senators present concur; and he shall nominate, and by and with the Advice and Consent of the Senate, shall appoint Ambassadors, other public Ministers and Consuls, Judges of the supreme Court, and all other Officers of the United States, whose Appointments are not herein otherwise provided for, and which shall be established by Law: but the Congress may by Law vest the Appointment of such inferior Officers, as they think proper, in the President alone, in the Courts of Law, or in the Heads of Departments.

The President shall have Power to fill up all Vacancies that may happen during the Recess of the Senate, by granting Commissions which shall expire at the End of their next Session.

Section 3. He shall from time to time give to the Congress Information of the State of the Union, and recommend to their Consideration such Measures as he shall judge necessary and expedient; he may, on extraordinary Occasions, convene both Houses, or either of them, and in Case of Disagreement between them, with Respect to the Time of Adjournment, he may adjourn them to such Time as he shall think proper; he shall receive Ambassadors and other public Ministers; he shall take Care that the Laws be faithfully executed, and shall Commission all the Officers of the United States.

Section 4. The President, Vice-President and all civil Officers of the United States, shall be removed from Office on Impeachment for, and Conviction of, Treason, Bribery, or other high Crimes and Misdemeanors.

Article III

Section 1. The judicial Power of the United States, shall be vested in one supreme Court, and in such inferior Courts as the Congress may from time to time ordain and establish. The Judges, both of the supreme and inferior Courts, shall hold their Offices during good Behaviour, and shall, at stated Times, receive for their Services, a Compensation, which shall not be diminished during their Continuance in Office.

Section 2. The judicial Power shall extend to all Cases, in Law and Equity, arising under this Constitution, the Laws of the United States, and Treaties made, or which shall be made, under their Authority;—to all Cases affecting Ambassadors, other public Ministers and Consuls;—to all Cases of admiralty and maritime Jurisdiction;—to Controversies to which the United States shall be a party;—to Controversies between two or more States;—between a State and Citizens of another State;—between Citizens of different States;—between Citizens of the same State claiming Lands under Grants of different States, and between a State, or the Citizens thereof, and foreign States, Citizens or Subjects.

In all Cases affecting Ambassadors, other public Ministers and Consuls, and those in which a State shall be Party, the supreme Court shall have original Jurisdiction. In all the other Cases before mentioned, the supreme Court shall have appellate Jurisdiction, both as to Law and Fact, with such Exceptions, and under such Regulations as the Congress shall make.

The Trial of all Crimes, except in Cases of Impeachment, shall be by Jury; and such Trial shall be held in the State where the said Crimes shall have been committed; but when not committed within any State, the Trial shall be at such Place or Places as the Congress may by Law have directed.

Section 3. Treason against the United States, shall consist only in levying War against them, or in adhering to their Enemies, giving them Aid and Comfort. No Person shall be convicted of Treason unless on the Testimony of two Witnesses to the same overt Act, or on Confession in open Court.

The Congress shall have Power to declare the Punishment of Treason, but no Attainder of Treason shall work Corruption of Blood, or Forfeiture except during the Life of the Person attainted.

Article IV

Section 1. Full Faith and Credit shall be given in each State to the public Acts, Records, and judicial Proceedings of every other State. And the Congress may by general Laws prescribe the Manner in which such Acts, Records and Proceedings shall be proved, and the Effect thereof.

Section 2. The Citizens of each State shall be entitled to all Privileges and Immunities of Citizens in the several States.

A Person charged in any State with Treason, Felony, or

other Crime, who shall flee from Justice, and be found in another State, shall on Demand of the executive Authority of the State from which he fled, be delivered up, to be removed to the State having Jurisdiction of the Crime.

No Person held to Service or Labour in one State, under the Laws thereof, escaping into another, shall, in Consequence of any Law or Regulation therein, be discharged from such Service or Labour, but shall be delivered up on Claim of the Party to whom such Service or Labour may be due.

Section 3. New States may be admitted by the Congress into this Union; but no new States shall be formed or erected within the Jurisdiction of any other State; nor any State be formed by the Junction of two or more States, or Parts of States, without the Consent of the Legislatures of the States concerned as well as of the Congress.

The Congress shall have Power to dispose of and make all needful Rules and Regulations respecting the Territory or other Property belonging to the United States; and nothing in this Constitution shall be so construed as to Prejudice any Claims of the United States, or of any particular State.

Section 4. The United States shall guarantee to every State in this Union a Republican Form of Government, and shall protect each of them against Invasion; and on Application of the Legislature, or of the Executive (when the Legislature cannot be convened) against domestic Violence.

ARTICLE V

The Congress, whenever two thirds of both Houses shall deem it necessary, shall propose Amendments to this Constitution, or, on the Application of the Legislatures of two thirds of the several States, shall call a Convention for proposing Amendments, which, in either Case, shall be valid to all Intents and Purposes, as Part of this Constitution, when ratified by the Legislatures of three fourths of the several States, or by Conventions in three fourths thereof, as the one or the other Mode of Ratification may be proposed by the Congress; Provided that no Amendment which may be made prior to the Year One thousand eight hundred and eight shall in any Manner affect the first and fourth Clauses in the Ninth Section of the first Article; and that no State, without its Consent, shall be deprived of its equal Suffrage in the Senate.

ARTICLE VI

All Debts contracted and Engagements entered into, before the Adoption of this Constitution, shall be as valid against the United States under this Constitution, as under the Confederation.

This Constitution, and the Laws of the United States which shall be made in Pursuance thereof; and all Treaties made, or which shall be made, under the Authority of the United States, shall be the supreme Law of the Land; and the Judges in every State shall be bound thereby, any Thing in the Constitution or Laws of any State to the Contrary notwithstanding.

The Senators and Representatives before mentioned, and the Members of the several State Legislatures, and all executive and judicial Officers, both of the United States and of the several States, shall be bound by Oath or Affirmation, to support this Constitution; but no religious Test shall ever be required as a Qualification to any Office or public Trust under the United States.

ARTICLE VII

The Ratification of the Conventions of nine States, shall be sufficient for the Establishment of this Constitution between the States so ratifying the Same.

AMENDMENTS TO THE CONSTITUTION

Resolved by the Senate and House of Representatives of the United States of America, in Congress assembled, two thirds of both Houses concurring, that the following Articles be proposed to the Legislatures of the several States, as Amendments to the Constitution of the United States, all, or any of which Articles, when ratified by three fourths of the said Legislatures, to be valid to all intents and purposes, as part of the said Constitution, viz.

ARTICLE I

Congress shall make no law respecting an establishment of religion, or prohibiting the free exercise thereof; or abridging the freedom of speech, or of the press; or the right of the people peaceably to assemble, and to petition the Government for a redress of grievances.

ARTICLE II

A well regulated Militia, being necessary to the security of a free State, the right of the people to keep and bear Arms, shall not be infringed.

ARTICLE III

No Soldier shall, in time of peace be quartered in any house, without the consent of the Owner, nor in time of war, but in a manner to be prescribed by law.

ARTICLE IV

The right of the people to be secure in their persons, houses, papers, and effects, against unreasonable searches and seizures, shall not be violated, and no Warrants shall issue, but upon probable cause, supported by Oath or affirmation, and particularly describing the place to be searched, and the persons or things to be seized.

ARTICLE V

No person shall be held to answer for a capital, or otherwise infamous crime, unless on a presentment or indictment of a Grand Jury, except in cases arising in the land or naval forces, or in the Militia, when in actual service in time of War or public danger; nor shall any person be subject for the same offence to be twice put in jeopardy of life or limb; nor shall be compelled in any criminal case to be a witness against himself, nor be deprived of life, liberty, or property, without due process of law; nor shall private property be taken for public use, without just compensation.

ARTICLE VI

In all criminal prosecutions, the accused shall enjoy the right to a speedy and public trial, by an impartial jury of the State and district wherein the crime shall have been committed, which district shall have been previously ascertained by law, and to be informed of the nature and cause of the accusation; to be confronted with the witnesses against him; to have compulsory process for obtaining witnesses in his favor, and to have the Assistance of Counsel for his defence.

ARTICLE VII

In Suits at common law, where the value in controversy shall exceed twenty dollars, the right of trial by jury shall be preserved, and no fact tried by a jury, shall be otherwise re-examined in any Court of the United States, than according to the rules of the common law.

ARTICLE VIII

Excessive bail shall not be required, nor excessive fines imposed, nor cruel and unusual punishments inflicted.

ARTICLE IX

The enumeration in the Constitution, of certain rights, shall not be construed to deny or disparage others retained by the people.

ARTICLE X

The powers not delegated to the United States by the Constitution, nor prohibited by it to the States, are reserved to the States respectively, or to the people.

ARTICLE XI

The Judicial power of the United States shall not be construed to extend to any suit in law or equity, commenced or prosecuted against one of the United States by Citizens of another State, or by Citizens or Subjects of any Foreign State.

ARTICLE XII

The Electors shall meet in their respective states and vote by ballot for President and Vice-President, one of whom, at least, shall not be an inhabitant of the same state with themselves; they shall name in their ballots the person voted for as President, and in distinct ballots the person voted for as Vice-President, and they shall make distinct lists of all persons voted for as President, and of all persons voted for as Vice-President, and of the number of votes for each, which lists they shall sign and certify, and transmit sealed to the seat of the government of the United States, directed to the President of the Senate;—The President of the Senate shall, in the presence of the Senate and House of Representatives, open all the certificates and the votes shall then be counted;—The person having the greatest number of votes for President, shall be the President, if such number be a majority of the whole number of Electors appointed; and if no person have such majority, then from the persons having the highest numbers not exceeding three on the list of those voted for as President, the House of Representatives shall choose immediately, by ballot, the President. But in choosing the President, the votes shall be taken by states, the representation from each state having one vote; a quorum for this purpose shall consist of a member or members from two-thirds of the states, and a majority of all the states shall be necessary to a choice. And if the House of Representatives shall not choose a President whenever the right of choice shall devolve upon them, before the fourth day of March next following, then the Vice-President shall act as President, as in the case of the death or other constitutional disability of the President.—The person having the greatest number of votes as Vice-President, shall be the Vice-President, if such number be a majority of the whole number of Electors appointed, and if no person have a majority, then from the two highest numbers on the list, the Senate shall choose the Vice-President; a quorum for the purpose shall consist of two-thirds of the whole number of Senators, and a majority of the whole number shall be necessary to a choice. But no person constitutionally ineligible to the office of President shall be eligible to that of Vice-President of the United States.

ARTICLE XIII

Section 1. Neither slavery nor involuntary servitude, except as a punishment for crime whereof the party shall have been duly convicted, shall exist within the United States, or any place subject to their jurisdiction.

Section 2. Congress shall have power to enforce this article by appropriate legislation.

ARTICLE XIV

Section 1. All persons born or naturalized in the United States, and subject to the jurisdiction thereof, are citizens of the United States and of the State wherein they reside. No State shall make or enforce any law which shall abridge the privileges or immunities of citizens of the United States; nor shall any State deprive any person of life, liberty, or property, without due process of law; nor deny to any person within its jurisdiction the equal protection of the laws.

Section 2. Representatives shall be apportioned among the several States according to their respective numbers, counting the whole number of persons in each State, excluding Indians not taxed. But when the right to vote at any election for the choice of electors for President and Vice-President of the

United States, Representatives in Congress, the Executive and Judicial officers of a State, or the members of the Legislature thereof, is denied to any of the male inhabitants of such State, being twenty-one years of age, and citizens of the United States, or in any way abridged, except for participation in rebellion, or other crime, the basis of representation therein shall be reduced in the proportion which the number of such male citizens shall bear to the whole number of male citizens twenty-one years of age in such State.

Section 3. No person shall be a Senator or Representative in Congress, or elector of President and Vice-President, or hold any office, civil or military, under the United States, or under any State, who, having previously taken an oath, as a member of Congress, or as an officer of the United States, or as a member of any State legislature, or as an executive or judicial officer of any State, to support the Constitution of the United States, shall have engaged in insurrection or rebellion against the same, or given aid or comfort to the enemies thereof. But Congress may by a vote of two-thirds of each House, remove such disability.

Section 4. The validity of the public debt of the United States, authorized by law, including debts incurred for payment of pensions and bounties for services in suppressing insurrection or rebellion, shall not be questioned. But neither the United States nor any State shall assume or pay any debt or obligation incurred in aid of insurrection or rebellion against the United States, or any claim for the loss or emancipation of any slave; but all such debts, obligations and claims shall be held illegal and void.

Section 5. The Congress shall have power to enforce, by appropriate legislation, the provisions of this article.

Article XV

Section 1. The right of citizens of the United States to vote shall not be denied or abridged by the United States or by any State on account of race, color, or previous condition of servitude.

Section 2. The Congress shall have power to enforce this article by appropriate legislation.

Article XVI

The Congress shall have power to lay and collect taxes on incomes, from whatever source derived, without apportionment among the several States, and without regard to any census or enumeration.

Article XVII

Section 1. The Senate of the United States shall be composed of two Senators from each State, elected by the people thereof, for six years; and each Senator shall have one vote. The electors in each State shall have the qualifications requisite for electors of the most numerous branch of the State legislatures.

Section 2. When vacancies happen in the representation of any State in the Senate, the executive authority of such State shall issue writs of election to fill such vacancies: Provided, That the legislature of any State may empower the executive thereof to make temporary appointments until the people fill the vacancies by election as the legislature may direct.

Section 3. This amendment shall not be so construed as to affect the election or term of any Senator chosen before it becomes valid as part of the Constitution.

Article XVIII

Section 1. After one year from the ratification of this article the manufacture, sale, or transportation of intoxicating liquors within, the importation thereof into, or the exportation thereof from the United States and all territory subject to the jurisdiction thereof for beverage purposes is hereby prohibited.

Section 2. The Congress and the several States shall have concurrent power to enforce this article by appropriate legislation.

Section 3. This article shall be inoperative unless it shall have been ratified as an amendment to the Constitution by the legislatures of the several States, as provided in the Constitution, within seven years from the date of the submission hereof to the States by the Congress.

Article XIX

Section 1. The right of citizens of the United States to vote shall not be denied or abridged by the United States or by any State on account of sex.

Section 2. Congress shall have power to enforce this article by appropriate legislation.

Article XX

Section 1. The terms of the President and Vice-President shall end at noon on the 20th day of January, and the terms of Senators and Representatives at noon on the 3d day of January, of the years in which such terms would have ended if this article had not been ratified; and the terms of their successors shall then begin.

Section 2. The Congress shall assemble at least once in every year, and such meeting shall begin at noon on the 3d day of January, unless they shall by law appoint a different day.

Section 3. If, at the time fixed for the beginning of the term of the President, the President elect shall have died, the Vice-President elect shall become President. If a President shall not have been chosen before the time fixed for the beginning of his term, or if the President elect shall have failed to qualify, then the Vice-President elect shall act as President until a President shall have qualified; and the Congress may by law provide for the case wherein neither a President elect nor a Vice-President elect shall have qualified, declaring who shall then act as President, or the manner in which one who is to act shall be selected, and such person shall act accordingly until a President or Vice-President shall have qualified.

Section 4. The Congress may by law provide for the case of the death of any of the persons from whom the House of Representatives may choose a President whenever the right of choice shall have devolved upon them, and for the case of the death of any of the persons from whom the Senate may choose a Vice-President whenever the right of choice shall have devolved upon them.

Section 5. Sections 1 and 2 shall take effect on the 15th day of October following the ratification of this article.

Section 6. This article shall be inoperative unless it shall have been ratified as an amendment to the Constitution by the legislatures of three-fourths of the several States within seven years from the date of its submission.

Article XXI

Section 1. The Eighteenth Article of amendment to the Constitution of the United States is hereby repealed.

Section 2. The transportation or importation into any State, Territory, or possession of the United States for delivery or use therein of intoxicating liquors, in violation of the laws thereof, is hereby prohibited.

Section 3. This article shall be inoperative unless it shall have been ratified as an amendment to the Constitution by conventions in the several States, as provided in the Constitution, within seven years from the date of the submission hereof to the States by the Congress.

Article XXII

Section 1. No person shall be elected to the office of the President more than twice, and no person who has held the office of President, or acted as President, for more than two years of a term to which some other person was elected President shall be elected to the office of the President more than once. But this Article shall not apply to any person holding the office of President when this Article was proposed by the Congress, and shall not prevent any person who may be holding the office of President, or acting as President, during the term within which this Article becomes operative from holding the office of President or acting as President during the remainder of such term.

Section 2. This article shall be inoperative unless it shall have been ratified as an amendment to the Constitution by the legislatures of three-fourths of the several States within seven years from the date of its submission to the States by the Congress.

Article XXIII

Section 1. The District constituting the seat of government of the United States shall appoint in such manner as the Congress may direct:

A number of electors of President and Vice-President equal to the whole number of Senators and Representatives in Congress to which the District would be entitled if it were a State, but in no event more than the least populous State; they shall be in addition to those appointed by the States, but they shall be considered, for the purposes of the election of President and Vice-President, to be electors appointed by a State; and they shall meet in the District and perform such duties as provided by the twelfth article of amendment.

Section 2. The Congress shall have power to enforce this article by appropriate legislation.

Article XXIV

Section 1. The right of citizens of the United States to vote in any primary or other election for President or Vice-President, for electors for President or Vice-President, or for Senator or Representative in Congress, shall not be denied or abridged by the United States or any State by reason of failure to pay any poll tax or other tax.

Section 2. The Congress shall have power to enforce this article by appropriate legislation.

Article XXV

Section 1. In case of the removal of the President from office or of his death or resignation, the Vice-President shall become President.

Section 2. Whenever there is a vacancy in the office of the Vice-President, the President shall nominate a Vice-President who shall take office upon confirmation by a majority vote of both Houses of Congress.

Section 3. Whenever the President transmits to the President pro tempore of the Senate and the Speaker of the House of Representatives his written declaration that he is unable to discharge the powers and duties of his office, and until he transmits to them a written declaration to the contrary, such powers and duties shall be discharged by the Vice-President as Acting President.

Section 4. Whenever the Vice-President and a majority of either the principal officers of the executive departments or of such other body as Congress may by law provide, transmit to the President pro tempore of the Senate and the Speaker of the House of Representatives their written declaration that the President is unable to discharge the powers and duties of his office, the Vice-President shall immediately assume the powers and duties of the office as Acting President.

Thereafter, when the President transmits to the President pro tempore of the Senate and the Speaker of the House of Representatives his written declaration that no inability exists, he shall resume the powers and duties of his office unless the Vice-President and a majority of either the principal officers of the executive department or of such other body as Congress may by law provide, transmit within four days to the President pro tempore of the Senate and the Speaker of the House of Representatives their written declaration that the President is unable to discharge the powers and duties of his office. Thereupon Congress shall decide the issue, assembling within forty-eight hours for that purpose if not in session. If the Congress, within twenty-one days after receipt of the latter written declaration, or, if Congress is not in session, within twenty-one days after Congress is required to assemble, determines by two-thirds vote of both Houses that the President is unable to discharge the powers and duties of his office, the Vice-President shall continue to discharge the same as Acting President; otherwise, the President shall resume the powers and duties of his office.

ARTICLE XXVI

Section 1. The right of citizens of the United States, who are 18 years of age or older, to vote shall not be denied or abridged by the United States or any State on account of age.

Section 2. The Congress shall have the power to enforce this article by appropriate legislation.

CONSTITUTIONS, STATE. *See* **State Constitutions.**

CONSULAR CONVENTION. In 1782, Benjamin Franklin signed a convention with the French foreign minister that departed materially from Franklin's instructions from Congress. It contained the threat of extraterritoriality. John Jay advised against ratification. Negotiations resulted in the more favorable treaty of 1788, which regulated the functions of consuls exchanged between France and the United States under the Franco-American Alliance of 1778. It was abrogated in 1798 and replaced by the Convention of 1800.

CONSULAR SERVICE. *See* **Foreign Service.**

CONSUMER PROTECTION. In early American agrarian communities the buyer was effectively shielded by his knowledge of products and by strong community sanctions against fraudulent practices. With the rise of specialization and of division of labor, the modern corporation became a distant market force and the growing power of product advertising allowed sellers to make exaggerated claims. Growing consumer skepticism ensued, followed by the enactment of legislation designed to afford the consumer protection. Among early protective laws was that banning the use of the mails for perpetration of fraud, passed in 1872. State and local governments also early provided "sealers" to inspect the accuracy of weights and measures and inspectors to check on sanitation standards. By 1906 the Pure Food and Drug Act was passed. In 1914 the Federal Trade Commission was created to monitor false and misleading advertising.

Self-policing attempts by Better Business Bureaus eliminated some superlatives but left consumers bewildered by rival product claims. The demand for more legislative protection brought in 1928 the appearance of Consumers Research, a private nonprofit organization designed to substitute the publication of laboratory test results for partisan advertising claims. Consumers Research was soon overshadowed by Consumers Union (1936), which had a subscription roster of 2.8 million for its magazine *Consumer Reports* by 1981.

These consumer testing efforts greatly accelerated the growth of consumer legislation and provided increased support for federal, state, and local governmental agencies. In 1961 President John F. Kennedy formed the Consumer Advisory Council, and during the administration of Lyndon B. Johnson the position of special assistant on consumer affairs and the President's Committee on Consumer Interests were established. National, state, and local consumer organizations were formed in the 1960's and 1970's under the Consumer Federation of America, to assist in handling buyers' complaints, to lobby for legislation, and to introduce consumer education into the schools.

CONSUMER PURCHASING POWER. The exchange value, or monetary value, of the good or service produced by an individual in relation to the goods and services produced by all other productive members of society. The productive members of society in the United States are all those over age fourteen who produce goods or stand ready to provide services designed primarily for sale in the marketplace.

The average consumer is often unable to determine the degree to which inflation affects his purchasing power or whether inflation exists. If the purchasing power of a consumer, as evidenced by increasing income, increases at the same rate as inflation, the consumer is able to maintain the same relative standard of living. If income increases faster than prices, living standards rise. The federal government, through its Consumer Price Index (CPI), prepared monthly by the Bureau of Labor Statistics of the Department of Labor, attempts to measure changes in purchasing power by collecting data on some 400 selected items making up the expenditure pattern of a "typical" urban working family. The CPI is the best measure for the consumer to judge his purchasing-power position compared with that of a base period.

CONTEMPT OF CONGRESS. Although the power to punish for contempt of Congress is essentially judicial in character, the Supreme Court has held repeatedly that either the House of Representatives or the Senate may hold private persons in contempt. At one time Congress executed its power to punish for contempt directly by resolutions calling for summary punishment. More recently, under an 1857 statute, Congress passes a resolution on the contempt charge, which is then turned over to the U.S. attorney for the District of Columbia for possible grand jury action and prosecution. Any resulting punishment is judicially imposed.

CONTI, FORT. Two redoubts built on the east side of the Niagara River at Lake Ontario in 1679 by order of Robert Cavelier, Sieur de La Salle, to protect the base of supplies for his expedition, but destroyed by fire within the year.

CONTINENTAL. A term used in Revolutionary times to distinguish British colonies on the mainland of North America (from Georgia to Massachusetts) from British colonies off the continent (such as Bermuda). During the Revolutionary War, the word was applied to certain members of the American army—the Continentals. These units were established by Congress, as distinguished from militia units, which remained under colony or state control. The word was also used to describe the paper money (bills of credit) issued by the United States during the war, called Continental currency.

CONTINENTAL ASSOCIATION. An attempt by the American colonies to force Great Britain to recognize their political rights by means of economic coercion. Formed in 1774 by the Continental Congress, it provided for nonexportation and nonimportation and was controlled by the people, working through committees, rather than by merchants. The British discovered new sources of trade to replace the lost American market. The association had not been in effect six months before it was clear that the dispute was not to be decided by a bloodless economic war.

CONTINENTAL CONGRESS. The body of delegates of the American colonies first assembled in September 1774 and again in May 1775 as an advisory council of the colonies. It eventually became the central government of the union until it was superseded on Mar. 4, 1789, by the new government under the Constitution.

The First Continental Congress, which sat at Philadelphia from Sept. 5 to Oct. 26, 1774, consisted of fifty-six delegates from twelve colonies (Georgia did not elect or send delegates) convened to seek measures for the recovery of colonial rights and liberties held to have been violated by a succession of acts of the British government. The principal measures were the adoption of the Declaration of Rights (Oct. 14), of an association (Oct. 20) binding the colonies in a nonimportation, nonconsumption, and nonexportation agreement, and of a resolution that, unless the grievances were redressed, another congress should be assembled on May 10, 1775.

The grievances were not redressed, and the Second Continental Congress met in Philadelphia the following May. Meanwhile, something close to war had broken out between Massachusetts and the British military forces (*see* Lexington and Concord), whereupon Congress resolved to give aid to Massachusetts, took over the provincial army at Boston, and appointed George Washington commander in chief. The idea of independence laid its grip upon the public mind, and so, on July 2, 1776, Congress adopted a resolution "that these United Colonies are, and of right ought to be, free and independent States"; two days later it adopted the Declaration of Independence.

Congress at once set about to frame an instrument of union. It was not until after nearly a year and a half of effort and numerous controversies that Congress agreed upon that framework of government known as the Articles of Confederation (Nov. 15, 1777). Ratification of the Articles by the several states was still necessary, and it was only on Mar. 1, 1781, that the last of the thirteen ratifications, that of Maryland, was obtained. (*See* Articles of Confederation.)

With the war and its impelling power for unity at an end, the states lost their concern for the Congress of their union and even drifted toward dissolving it; Congress, for its part, advanced not from strength to strength but from weakness to weakness. Only the determination of a small group to save the union led, through the Annapolis Convention, to the Convention of 1787 and finally to the newly framed Constitution.

CONTINUOUS VOYAGE DOCTRINE. *See* **Enemy Destination.**

CONTRABAND, SLAVES AS. A doctrine set up by Gen. Benjamin F. Butler, in May 1861, as applicable to the problem of fugitive slaves of secessionists seeking refuge in Union military camps. He used the term "contraband" in explaining that he treated "the able-bodied negroes, fit to work in the trenches, as property, liable to be used in aid of rebellion, and so contraband of war." Contraband as doctrine disappeared after the passage of the Confiscation Act on Aug. 6, 1861, but "contraband" as a slang term for "slave" was widely used.

***CONTRABANDISTAS*.** Yankee skippers who began to trade with the Spaniards of the California coast towns after the War of 1812. Such trade was prohibited by the Spanish government, and until 1818 many American cargoes were confiscated and the crews thrown into prison. After that date, the Spanish demand for Yankee notions and an outlet for their own cattle hides caused a relaxation of the regulations.

CONTRABAND OF WAR. A term in international law deriving from a belligerent's claim of its right to prevent an enemy from receiving goods of value in waging war and to declare such goods shipped by neutrals as liable to seizure and condemnation, usually on the high seas.

In the wars of the 1790's, Britain and France, acting to cut off imports from each other by blockade or decree, arbitrarily seized hundreds of U.S. ships, charging contraband violations. The U.S. Navy consequently fought the Quasi-War with France (1798–1800) to defend the right to transport noncontraband cargoes.

During the Civil War, U.S. cruisers on the high seas captured British ships with cargo ostensibly for British ports in the Bahamas but, in fact, for transshipment to the Confederacy by a "continuous voyage."

During World War I, Britain imposed broad categories of contraband on neutral shipping destined for the enemy, virtually ending U.S. trade with Germany. Germany's unrestricted submarine warfare against Allied shipping hastened U.S. entry into the war on the side of the Allies. In November 1941, in a move to remove all restrictions on aid to the Allies, Congress partially repealed the Neutrality Act of 1939, allowing U.S. merchant ships to carry any cargo, including contraband, through war zones to and from Great Britain. After World War II, the 1949 Geneva convention called for free passage of medical and religious objects, as well as foodstuffs, clothing, and tonics for children and maternity cases.

CONTRACT CLAUSE. Article I, Section 10, of the U.S. Constitution provides that no state shall pass any law "impairing the Obligation of Contracts." Broad interpretation of this clause by the Supreme Court under Chief Justice John Marshall made it the basic constitutional instrument for the protection of private property in the 19th century—a primary link between law and economic growth and a basic source of national authority over the states. The clause was thought to embrace only contracts between individuals, but even interpreting it in this limited sense, the Court was able to impose controls on state bankruptcy, insolvency, and stay laws.

By extending the clause beyond the intent of the framers to embrace public contracts—an interpretation begun on the circuit level in the 1790's—the Court gained jurisdiction over state land grants and tax exemptions, municipal bonds, and agreements between the state and its political subunits. Especially crucial in shaping national economic development was the Dartmouth College decision.

Beginning in the 1890's, the more flexible due process clause of the Fourteenth Amendment progressively replaced the contract clause as the constitutional bulwark of property. More important, the complexities of urban, technological society have necessitated legislative modification of absolute property rights.

CONTRACT LABOR, FOREIGN. During the Civil War a shortage of skilled industrial labor and a sharp decline in immigration led the Union government to adopt a contract labor law (Act to Encourage Immigration, July 4, 1864) allowing foreign workers to enter into agreements providing their services to employers in return for prepaid transportation to the United States. Comparatively few firms imported contract labor under the system, mainly because it lacked adequate guarantees against contract breaking; in all, not more than a few hundred workers were thus brought to the United States. The contract labor law was repealed in 1868.

During the economic recession of the mid-1880's craft unionists demanded curbs on foreign contract labor. On Feb. 26, 1885, Congress passed the Foran Act, an anti-contract-labor law, prohibiting the prepaid passage of an immigrant in return for a promise of his services. The statute specifically exempted actors, artists, lecturers, singers, and domestic servants, as well as skilled labor required for new industries. The act was supplemented in 1891, 1903, 1907, and 1910. The act of 1903 extended the exemptions to any recognized learned profession, including teachers.

CONTRERAS, BATTLE OF (Aug. 19–20, 1847). An engagement in Gen. Winfield Scott's advance on Mexico City. Scott was forced to take the difficult road across the lava bed south of Lake Chalco. This route was commanded by the heights of Contreras, held by Gen. Gabriel Valencia. After severe fighting, the Americans drove Valencia from Contreras and captured Churubusco.

CONVENTION, DIPLOMATIC. An agreement between countries to follow a particular course of action. It is not quite so solemn an agreement as a treaty, but it is considered binding. Conventions regularly deal with treatment of prisoners of war and sick or injured people, postal rates, or airplane routes. Often, conventions clarify agreements previously reached in a treaty but not spelled out in detail.

CONVENTION ARMY. British Gen. John Burgoyne's army after it had been surrendered in 1777 by a "convention" (Convention of Saratoga) rather than by the customary "capitulation." It was marched from Saratoga, N.Y., to Cambridge, Mass., there to return to England. But the transports did not arrive and the troops remained in various locations until the war ended. The Definitive Treaty of Peace of 1783 released all prisoners of war. By this time, the army had been reduced by paroles, exchanges, deaths, and desertions to about half its original 5,000. Some of the men remained in the United States, but most returned to their native lands.

CONVENTION OF 1787. *See* **Constitution of the United States.**

CONVENTION OF 1800. Signed by the United States and France at Mortefontaine on Sept. 30; tacitly detached the United States from its alliance with France at the price of American claims for damages resulting from French actions against U.S. commerce since the beginnings of the French revolutionary wars. It secured U.S. release from the treaties of 1778 and 1788. The final French terms posed problems: if the alliance were to be terminated, so would American claims; indemnities would be considered only if the treaties were still in force. The commissioners agreed to defer both indemnities and treaties, in effect abandoning both. The convention thus ended the Quasi-War with mutual restoration of captured naval vessels and liberalization of the treatment of American ships in French ports.

CONVENTION OF 1818 WITH ENGLAND. A treaty signed at London, Oct. 20. Ratifications were exchanged at Washington, D.C., on Jan. 30, 1819. It gave U.S. citizens the right to fish on portions of the coasts of Newfoundland, the Magdalen Islands, and Labrador; established the Northwest boundary from the Lake of the Woods west to the Rocky Mountains along the forty-ninth parallel, north latitude; stipulated that territory west of the Rockies claimed by either should be open to both for ten years, without affecting any territorial rights; renewed the terms of the commercial convention of July 1815 for ten years; and referred U.S. claims to indemnification for slaves seized by British forces in the Revolution to arbitration by a friendly sovereign.

CONVENTIONS, PARTY NOMINATING. Held at both state and national levels to nominate party candidates and conduct other party business. Such conventions were common in all states during the 19th century; since then, most states have resorted to primary elections. National conventions to nominate candidates for president were first held at Baltimore in preparation for the election of 1832.

Each national convention is composed of delegations from each of the states, the District of Columbia, and the territories. Much of the preparatory work and other business of the conventions is carried on by committees of delegates that meet before the convention. Committees hear rival claims to delegate status and recommend who shall be seated, recommend rules for the convention and for the conduct of the party's business between conventions, and prepare the party platform for adoption by the convention.

CONVICT LABOR SYSTEMS. In the early 1800's, manufacturers began to contract for prison labor. Under the contract system, the manufacturer supplied raw materials, supervised the inmates, marketed the finished products, and paid the state for the services of the inmates; the state housed the prisoners. Under the piece-price system, prison authorities supervised the work and received money from the manufacturer for the finished products. The lease system permitted convicts to work outside the walls of penal institutions, most often as railroad construction laborers and in mines, sawmills, and brickyards.

After the Civil War many southern states looked to this practice as a way of resolving their postwar monetary problems, but publicity concerning abuses caused most of them to abandon the practice by 1904; by 1936 every state had abolished it. Replacing it was the public account system, under which the state functioned as a manufacturer, producing and marketing prison-made goods, as well as maintaining control over the workers. Opposition from private producers caused this system to be short-lived. Several southern states then began to lease convicts to counties for road work.

After World War II the state-use system became the preferred method. Convicts worked for the state, their services or products used or purchased only by agencies of the state or its political subdivisions. Convicts have never been paid more than a few cents per day.

CONVOYS. Early in the conquest of America, Spain employed close escorts and support forces to safeguard its homeward-bound treasure galleons. English overseas expansion required resolute enforcement of the convoy acts, dating from 1650, regulating the organization of convoys and provided for arming merchantmen. During the Quasi-War (1798–1800), U.S. frigates escorted British convoys in the Caribbean. With the establishment of the Pax Britannica, the vital role of convoys rapidly diminished. The British Admiralty in 1872 abolished the Compulsory Convoy Act of 1798, relying thereafter on naval patrol of threatened sea routes. That policy proved disastrous during World War I against commerce-raiding German U-boats. Not until May 1917, when shipping losses threatened Britain with imminent starvation and U.S. escort vessels became available, did the Admiralty reinstitute convoys. Allied convoy systems during World War II achieved virtually worldwide dimensions, owing to the phenomenal range of the German commerce-raiding effort. With the advent of nuclear weaponry, the wide dispersion of convoyed shipping and the employment of aerial transports, as during the Berlin airlift (1948–49), became characteristic elements of convoy operations.

CONWAY CABAL. The New England coterie in the Continental Congress and its efforts (1777–78) to regain control of the army and the Revolution, both of which had passed from its hands when Congress took over the war and elected George Washington commander in chief. Maj. Gen. Thomas Conway's indiscreet letter to Gen. Horatio Gates revealed the military side of the cabal, which aimed at the removal of Washington as the main obstacle to Massachusetts's regaining control of the army. Conway's letter and the subsequent public revelations rallied support for Washington, overwhelming conspirators both in Congress and in the army.

COOCH'S BRIDGE, BATTLE OF (Sept. 3, 1777). British and Hessian troops, after debarking at Elk Ferry, Md., were proceeding toward Philadelphia. They were attacked by Gen. William Maxwell's expert marksmen and cavalry, which, from the woods, Cooch's Bridge, and the Welsh Baptist Church, delivered close, well-directed firing from 9 A.M. until noon, when the enemy was forced to retire. It is claimed this was the first battle under the Stars and Stripes.

COOKE, JAY, AND COMPANY. A private investment bank, established in Philadelphia in 1861. When the Treasury's sale of U.S. loans brought inadequate funds early in the Civil War, Cooke was appointed special agent to sell U.S. Treasury bonds known as "five-twenties." By 1865, Jay Cooke and Company was regarded as the leading U.S. banking house, but peace brought difficulties. Failing to get sufficient government business, Cooke turned to railroad finance. First he sold minor issues, and in 1869 he tried to finance the

Northern Pacific. In 1873 the company failed because of heavy advances to the railroads.

COOK'S SEARCH FOR THE NORTHWEST PASSAGE (1776–80). Capt. James Cook of the British navy sailed from England on July 12, 1776, with the ships *Resolution* and *Discovery* to determine the existence of a northwest passage through America. Cook sailed along the coast north into the Arctic Ocean until his way was blocked by ice. Sailing along the Alaska coast, he passed through the inlet named for him, and found his way through the Aleutian Islands. He touched the continent of Asia and finally sailed through Bering Strait and far into the Arctic Ocean. He proved that there was no navigable northwest passage. The expedition wintered during 1779 in the Hawaiian Islands, where Cook met death (Feb. 14) at the hands of the natives.

COOLEY* V. *BOARD OF WARDENS OF PORT OF PHILADELPHIA, 12 Howard 299 (1852). Chief Justice John Marshall had intimated (1824) that the Constitution gave Congress an exclusive power over interstate and foreign commerce. Chief Justice Roger B. Taney later held that state regulations of commerce were valid if not in conflict with any law of Congress. In the Cooley case, Justice Benjamin R. Curtis formulated a solution. Where the subject seems to demand a uniform rule, local regulations will be struck down. But where the subject admits of diversity, the states remain free to act during the silence of Congress. This solution has remained the accepted doctrine.

COOPERATIVES, CONSUMERS'. Stores set up by associations of consumers to distribute consumption goods. Over the years new services have been added, and some have broadened the concept to cover all cooperative buying, whether for production or for consumption purposes.

One of the earliest Americans to form a cooperative was Benjamin Franklin, who in 1752 organized the Philadelphia Contributorship for the Insurance of Houses from Loss by Fire. By 1961 the number of U.S. consumer cooperatives was less than 38,000, varying in kind from 50 community consumer health plans to 22,000 credit unions. Consumer stores and consumer goods centers numbered over 1,000, with 50 of them reaching annual sales of $1 million or more.

COOPERATIVES, FARMERS'. Farmer associations for marketing products, purchasing farm supplies, and providing such services as insurance, credit, electricity, and irrigation. In general, they function as democratic self-help organizations on a cost-of-service basis. U.S. farmers' cooperatives go back to the early 19th century. They began to develop rapidly after the Civil War with promotion by the Granger movement. Their intensive development started about 1900, and they have expanded steadily. Since 1946, cooperatives have played an important role in modernizing U.S. agriculture. Many are now large, integrated organizations serving tens of thousands of farmers. Many large cooperatives are federations of local cooperatives; others are centralized associations that the farmers join directly. There were 6,736 farmers' cooperatives in 1977.

COOPERATIVES, TOBACCO. Associations for the marketing of tobacco were formed after the Civil War by the Grangers, but the first major effort by an organized group came with the attempt of the American Society of Equity to control tobacco prices early in the 20th century. The effort by "night riders" to force growers to market through pools led to violence and failed in its objective. The drastic fall in tobacco prices in 1921 led to the promotion by Aaron Sapiro, a California lawyer, of strong, centralized tobacco-marketing associations in several of the major producing areas. In 1925, internal weaknesses and the difficulties inherent in the concept of monopoly control led to their collapse.

A number of tobacco cooperatives perform marketing functions for their members; many maintain auction warehouses or perform selling or related services. But the principal function is to facilitate the administration of the government mandatory price-support program for tobacco.

COOPER UNION FOR THE ADVANCEMENT OF SCIENCE AND ART. An institution for the free instruction of men and women in applied science, art, and social and political science, opened in New York City in 1859. Peter Cooper furnished the inspiration and, at a cost of some $630,000, the large site and building on Astor Place; Abram S. Hewitt was chiefly responsible for the plan of instruction and the early administration. In addition to the Art School and the School of Engineering, a department of humanities provides a program of socio-humanistic studies. Cooper Union maintains the Museum for the Arts of Decoration and a library.

COPPAGE* V. *KANSAS, 236 U.S. 1 (1915). By 1915 thirteen states had laws prohibiting an employer from requiring as a condition of employment the signing of individual contracts not to affiliate with unions. In *Coppage* the Supreme Court held that such statutes violated the Fourteenth Amendment and that the ruling in *Adair* v. *United States* (1908)—that employers could discharge workers because of their affiliation with unions—illegally implied the right to insist upon nonunion pledges as a condition of employment.

COPPERHEADS. Originally a term used to designate the Democratic followers of Andrew Beaumont in Luzerne County, Pa., about 1840, who were opposed to the Democratic faction led by Hendrick B. Wright. It was revived during the Civil War to describe the Democrats opposed to the war policy of President Lincoln. Strongest in Ohio, Indiana, and Illinois, the Copperheads (Butternuts or Peace Democrats) were encouraged by Democratic successes in the elections of 1862.

The Copperheads advocated a union restored by negotiation rather than war. They denounced military arrests, conscription, emancipation, and other war measures, but their lack of sympathy for the Confederates was shown in July 1863, when they joined unionists in defending Indiana and

Ohio during Col. John H. Morgan's raid. Persecuted by the military and the Union League, they organized in 1862 the Knights of the Golden Circle, borrowing the name and ritual of a southern rights organization of the 1850's. The organization was known as the Order of American Knights in 1863 and the Sons of Liberty in 1864, when the Copperheads' chief spokesman C. L. Vallandigham of Ohio became supreme commander. The successful termination of the war discredited the Copperheads, and the Democratic party was handicapped for some years because of its Copperhead affiliates.

COPPER INDUSTRY. American Indians used virgin copper prior to the coming of Europeans, but the U.S. copper industry is dated from the discovery of a vein of copper ore at Simsbury, Conn., in 1705. In 1709 copper production began, followed by the development of other deposits. English colonial law forbade smelting in the colonies, so most ore was shipped to England.

It was not until exploitation of the rich ore deposits of the Upper Peninsula of Michigan in the early 1850's that U.S. copper production exceeded a few hundred tons per year. Production increased from 728 tons in 1850 to more than 30,000 tons in 1880. In the early 1850's the U.S. copper industry was dominated by the Calumet and Hecla Mining Company in Michigan.

The first discovery of copper in Montana was at Butte in 1866, in the Parrot silver mine. Later, the Anaconda Copper Mining Company gained control of most of the mining properties in the Butte area, and exploitation of the southwestern oxidized silver copper deposits also began. In Arizona the operations of the Bisbee and Copper Queen mines were merged in 1885, forming the basis for copper mining in Arizona, which in the 1970's accounted for about one-half of the domestic production of primary copper.

In the 1860's the emerging electrical industry created a new demand for metals for conductors. Copper proved to be best. Advances in technology had considerable impact on the U.S. industry. Introduction of the Bessemer steel converter for smelting copper in the late 1880's made it possible to treat much lower-grade ores. The beginning of open-pit mining in 1907 permitted profitable exploitation of the huge bodies of low-grade disseminated copper sulfide ores in the Southwest.

World War I provided tremendous impetus to the domestic copper industry. The United States became the copper clearinghouse for the whole world. World War II brought the copper industry to all-time high production records. Following World War II, hydrometallurgy grew as a commercial method of extracting copper in the United States. Dissolution and precipitation—collectively referred to as "leaching"—are now used extensively for treating copper-bearing mine waste and for processing oxide ores. In the 1970's refining output soared to about 1.5 million tons annually. Even so, U.S. needs outstripped domestic production, and by 1979, imports accounted for 13 percent of the domestic supply.

COPPOC CASE. During the winter of 1857–58, John Brown quartered some of his followers on a farm near Springdale, Cedar County, Iowa. Edwin and Barclay Coppoc joined Brown in July 1859 and participated in his attack on Harpers Ferry. Edwin Coppoc was captured and executed. Barclay Coppoc escaped but was later compelled to leave Springdale to evade extradition by Virginia authorities.

COPYRIGHT. Provides protection to authors of literary, dramatic, musical, and other artistic and intellectual works (Title 17, U.S. Code). It vests in the owner certain exclusive rights, which include printing, reprinting, copying, selling, performing, or recording the work. Copyrighted works must be registered with the Copyright Office of the U.S. Library of Congress, which is headed by a registrar of copyrights. The term of copyright protection is twenty-eight years from the date of publication or of registration. Renewal for a second term of twenty-eight years may be granted on application. A copyright may be transferred or assigned by an instrument in writing signed by the copyright owner.

Article I, Section 8, of the U.S. Constitution gives Congress the power to "promote the Progress of Science and useful Arts, by securing for limited Times to Authors and Inventors the exclusive Right to their respective Writings and Discoveries." Congress passed the first federal copyright legislation on May 31, 1790. It provided for the protection of books, maps, and charts for fourteen years and for the privilege of renewal for fourteen years. Between 1831 and 1909, revisions were made to add music, dramatic compositions, photographs, works of art, periodicals, and performances of music, and to extend the initial and renewal terms. Efforts to revise substantially the copyright law so that it reflects the impact of new technologies, such as microfilm, xerography, cable television, and electronic information storage and reproduction, were brought to fruition in 1976. The new law extended the copyright protection to the lifetime of the author plus fifty years; imposed copyright liability on public broadcasters, cable television, and jukebox operators; and codified the "fair use" doctrine for photocopying.

CORAL SEA, BATTLE OF THE (May 7–8, 1942). As part of its World War II plan to isolate Australia, Japan sought to capture Port Moresby, in southeastern New Guinea. In early May 1942, Rear Adm. Sadamichi Kajioka's invasion force, including the light carrier *Shoho,* and Vice Adm. Takeo Takagi's covering force, built around the two large carriers *Shokaku* and *Zuikaku,* moved into the Coral Sea, east of New Guinea. U.S. intelligence had broken the Japanese code providing warning of the assault; a task force under Rear Adm. Frank J. Fletcher, including the carriers *Lexington* and *Yorktown,* was in position to intercept.

The Battle of the Coral Sea was history's first carrier battle and the first large naval battle in which surface ships did not exchange fire. It was tactically a draw: the Americans lost more ships, and the Japanese, more planes. But it was an American strategic victory. As a result of the day's action, the Japanese called off the Port Moresby invasion.

CORINTH, BATTLE AT (Oct. 3–4, 1862). After the Battle of Shiloh, the Union troops occupied Corinth, Miss. On Oct.

3, Confederate Gen. Earl Van Dorn attacked with 20,000 men. The advance lines of Union Gen. W. S. Rosecrans, who had about equal numbers, were broken, and next morning the Confederates assaulted his main position. Suffering heavy losses, the Confederates retreated to Holly Springs, Miss.

CORN. Indian corn, or maize, America's most valuable crop, was developed by American Indians in prehistoric times. By the time Europeans arrived in the New World, corn was widely grown in both North and South America. Many types, including sweet corn and popcorn, had been developed. From the Indians, the English settlers learned to grow corn in hills and to fertilize each hill with fish. Jamestown and Plymouth owed their survival to the grain. The grain could be eaten green. It could be dried or parched and ground into meal, to be made into cornbread or johnnycake. Corn was excellent feed for hogs, cattle, and poultry. Any surplus could be distilled into whiskey, either for home consumption or for sale.

Prior to the Civil War, corn, rather than cotton, was the most valuable crop in the South. The varieties grown were flint and gourdseed, plus a mixture of the two called dents. As the yellow dents were making the American corn belt one of the most productive agricultural areas in the world, researchers published studies showing how corn could be bred for certain characteristics, including high yield. In 1926 the Pioneer Hi-Bred Corn Company offered hybrid seed corn for sale on a continuing commercial basis, and thereafter more and more hybrid corn seed companies emerged. Corn yields increased at a spectacular rate.

Just prior to World War I, the United States produced two-thirds of the world supply of corn. In 1979 it was producing one-half of the world total. Of the 60 million acres of corn harvested annually in the United States, 86 percent is used for grain and the remainder for forage and silage.

CORN BELT. The uniquely fertile region of the "prairie triangle" in the upper Mississippi Valley, stretching from Ohio to Nebraska, in which farmers since the mid-19th century have specialized in the corn crop. In 1920 about 50 percent of U.S. corn was grown in the six central states of the corn belt—Nebraska, Iowa, Missouri, Illinois, Indiana, and Ohio; by 1979 this proportion was 65 percent.

CORN BORER, EUROPEAN. Introduced into the United States from southern Europe in broom corn about 1910, the European corn borer had spread over nearly all major U.S. corn-growing areas by 1949 and had caused an estimated loss of 313,819,000 bushels of grain corn in that year. The insect attacks nearly all herbaceous plants large enough for its larvae to enter. Although the insect still causes considerable damage, the introduction of inbred corn lines and hybrids resistant to the borers, the development of controls involving the use of insecticides, and the introduction of parasites have materially reduced the loss caused by the pest.

CORNELL UNIVERSITY. A coeducational, land-grant institution of higher learning founded by Ezra Cornell in 1865 at Ithaca, N.Y. In 1868 it was opened for instruction under Andrew D. White, its first president. Henry W. Sage, chairman of the board, made a spectacular success of the investment in Wisconsin pinelands that Ezra Cornell had acquired with the land scrip, leading to a vast endowment. The College of Agriculture, Veterinary College, College of Home Economics, and School of Industrial and Labor Relations are state schools. The School of Nutrition is partly state-funded. The colleges of Engineering, Arts and Sciences, Medicine, and Architecture, and the schools of Hotel, Business, and Public Administration; Nursing; and Law and the graduate school have always been entirely private. Cornell first admitted women in 1872. Among its innovations is the elective system, in operation from the very first.

CORNET. The lowest-ranking commissioned officer in a cavalry troop, who carried the cornet, or standard. Designated second lieutenants in 1799, they were redesignated cornets from 1800 to 1802 and from 1808 to 1815.

CORN-HOG ECONOMY. The classic "corn-hog" system involves raising hogs for sale to markets, and corn-raising to feed the hogs. This system was prevalent in the corn-belt states of the Midwest, but today the economy of most corn-belt states involves cattle feeding as well as hog-raising, and the raising of other crops, such as soybeans, as well as corn.

CORNING LETTER. A public letter, dated June 12, 1863, from President Abraham Lincoln to Congressman Erastus Corning and other New York Democrats, in reply to their letter in which they denounced the arrest of C. L. Vallandigham, a Copperhead spokesman, as unconstitutional. In his reply Lincoln explained his use of arbitrary arrest by inquiring rhetorically: "Must I shoot a simpleminded soldier boy who deserts, while I must not touch a hair of a wily agitator who induces him to desert?"

CORONADO'S EXPEDITION (1540–42). In 1540 the Spanish nobleman Francisco Vásquez de Coronado started north from Mexico to locate the incredibly wealthy Seven Cities of Cibola reported by Marcos de Niza. The expedition crossed Arizona into the Zuni country of New Mexico, but found no treasures. Other branches of the expedition explored farther northeast; García López de Cárdenas discovered the Grand Canyon. Coronado, proceeding east, set up headquarters for a while at Tiguex, a large Tiwa pueblo on the Rio Grande in New Mexico. Lured on by tales of the wealthy country of Quivira, Coronado in 1541 pushed east into the Plains. The expedition found the grass huts of the Quivirans, who were Wichita, in what is now Kansas. They had no treasures. Coronado wintered again on the Rio Grande and then returned to Mexico in 1542. His journey acquainted the Spaniards with the Pueblo and opened the Southwest to future exploration and settlement.

CORPORATIONS. The trading companies chartered in the 16th and 17th centuries by the English monarchs were the first corporations in American history. The London, Plymouth, Massachusetts Bay, and Hudson's Bay companies played a large part in the establishment and support of European colonies in North America. The royal charter of such companies made legitimate a wide range of essentially governmental functions. By the 18th century, corporations had become primarily trading companies. Furthermore, their monopoly in trade was held by judges to exclude competition only from other chartered companies; unincorporated companies could lawfully compete with them.

From 1780 to 1801, U.S. state legislatures chartered 317 business corporations. Almost all were created for such public purposes as supplying water, transport, insurance, or banking services. During the 19th century, as mining and manufacturing grew relative to agriculture in the U.S. economy, corporations came to be used more and more for general business purposes. As early as 1811, New York had enacted a general incorporating statute, but it was of limited application. The New Jersey incorporating act of 1875 embodied many provisions long sought by business and gained in individual instances by particular companies only through special enactment. In the 1870's, however, the privileges granted by corporate charters remained insufficient to facilitate as much centralization of control of manufacturing as some businessmen desired. As the U.S. transportation network grew and markets became interstate in character, multistate business entities arose in the form of trusts. In several industries, trustees exercised control by holding the stock of a number of corporations operating throughout the country.

In 1890, Congress enacted the Sherman Antitrust Act, declaring combinations in restraint of trade to be illegal. But between 1887 and 1893 the New Jersey legislature enacted a series of statutes greatly liberalizing its 1875 law and making resort to the trust device unnecessary. Whereas earlier general incorporation had typically delimited the geographical region, New Jersey in 1887 amended its law to allow foreign corporations to own real estate in New Jersey and in 1892 removed all restrictions on its own corporations doing business outside the state.

Although the U.S. Constitution makes no reference to corporations, it gives Congress the power to regulate commerce between the several states and with foreign nations. Congress used this power in chartering national banks and transcontinental railroads in the 19th century. Since 1890, the federal government has played the major role in constraining the power of state-chartered corporations to centralize control of economic activity throughout the nation and the world. In addition to specifically regulating such industries as transportation, radio broadcasting, and atomic energy, the federal government regulates corporations engaged in interstate and foreign commerce through antitrust laws.

CORPUS CHRISTI (Tex.). A city on the Gulf Coast of Texas, with a population of 231,999 in 1980; the center of a metropolitan area of 326,228. Corpus Christi houses many oil refineries and chemical factories, and is the home for a part of the Texas fishing fleets. On a well-protected harbor in Corpus Christi Bay, which was named by Spanish explorers in 1519, a town was laid out in 1839 by Pennsylvania immigrant Henry Kinney. Many stories are told of pirates having used the port in earlier days. Gen. Zachary Taylor used it as a base for his operations against Mexico during the Mexican War. During the 19th century the town became an important center for cotton and wool trading. Deep-water channels have been dredged so the port can handle oceangoing vessels. It is connected with other coastal ports by the Gulf Intercoastal Waterway.

CORREGIDOR. An island lying near the mouth of Manila Bay in the Philippines. It became an important fort, since it could prevent ships from entering or leaving Manila Bay. On May 6, 1942, U.S. forces on Corregidor were overrun and forced to surrender to the Japanese after weeks of bombing and siege. On Feb. 27, 1945, the island fortress was retaken by American troops. A paratroop unit landed on a high point of the island while amphibious troops stormed ashore. The Japanese defenders fought almost to the last man.

CORRICK'S FORD, SKIRMISH AT (July 14, 1861). Threatened by the force under Union Gen. George B. McClellan, Confederate troops retreated eastward after an unsuccessful stand at Rich Mountain, and were overtaken at Corrick's Ford, Va., ending the first Confederate invasion of northwest Virginia.

CORRUPT BARGAIN. The charge made by the Jacksonians in 1825 that Henry Clay had supported John Quincy Adams in the House presidential election in return for the office of secretary of state.

CORRUPTION, POLITICAL. The first principal meaning is patently illegal behavior in the sphere of politics; bribery is a prime example. The second relates to governmental practices that, while legal, may be improper or unethical. To some people, patronage is such a practice. A third meaning involves conflicts of interest on the part of public officials. The fourth meaning relates to political behavior that is not responsive to the public interest. The Watergate scandal provides a vivid example.

Corruption has been a constant feature of U.S. politics since the birth of the Republic. The 19th century witnessed corruption on a grand scale, generally in connection with the spoils system. Among the most prominent instances were the Indian land frauds, the scandals of Ulysses S. Grant's administration, and the murky bargaining after the 1876 presidential election, resulting in the "election" of Rutherford B. Hayes. Between 1863 and 1883, every speaker of the House of Representatives who was in office for at least one full term was charged with corruption. The Senate, too, was rife with corruption and scandal. Bribery and "influence peddling" among state legislators were widespread.

The Teapot Dome affair was probably the most significant episode to occur during the first half of the 20th century. In the 1960's, Bobby Baker, secretary of the Senate majority, engaged in "influence peddling." The Watergate scandal of the Richard M. Nixon era involved corruption on a vaster scale. It included illegal political contributions, the "laundering" of campaign funds, the "sale" of ambassadorships, and the use of government agencies by the administration for personal and political gain.

Instances of corruption at state and local governmental levels have also been numerous and varied. They have included illicit or improper dealings in contracts, franchises, prostitution, drugs, and countless other goods and services.

Controls over political corruption take three forms: conflict and competition between the different branches of government, political parties, interest groups, and the mass media; laws defining certain acts as illegal and prescribing appropriate punishments; and regulations limiting the excesses of the spoils system, governing financial matters, and controlling lobbying. The Pendleton Act of 1883, establishing the civil service, was the first of these. Statutes adopted in 1907, 1910, and 1925 have served to regulate campaign funding, and the Regulation of Lobbying Act of 1946 sets limits on the activities of paid lobbyists. These and other laws have been amended, and still others have been enacted, in an effort to close loopholes in the system of controls.

CORRUPT PRACTICES ACTS. Adopted by the federal government, beginning with the Pendleton Act of 1883, and by all the states and territories, beginning with New York in 1890, in order to inject an element of equal opportunity and fairness into election campaigns and elections. Such laws are also supposed to enable persons without private wealth to run for elective office without becoming dependent on organizations or persons who will seek political favors. These laws regulate political contributions and expenditures and look for improper activity in the actual conduct of elections, such as illegal registration, bribery, and falsification of election returns. Specifically, there are limitations on the sources of funds; the amount of money involved; and the purposes for which the money can be spent. Publicity is required in the form of reports about contributions and expenditures.

The Hatch Act of 1939, with later amendments, restricts the political activities of employees of the federal government as well as administrative employees of state governments working in connection with a federally funded activity.

The corrupt practices acts of the states in general follow the lines of federal legislation.

CORWIN-DOBLADO TREATY (Apr. 6, 1862). Negotiated to enable Mexico to prevent foreign intervention to force payment of debts, and to improve trade between the United States and Mexico. The United States was to lend Mexico $11 million, and Mexico was to pay 6 percent interest semiannually. The loan was to be secured by unsold nationalized mortmain property of the Catholic church in Mexico and Mexican government lands, and administered by a mixed commission chosen by the two governments. The treaty was ratified by Mexico, but not by the United States.

COSMETICS. Ceremonial body paints were used by male members of American Indian tribes long before the European discovery of the New World. While the paints and dyes developed by the Indians had little appeal for the colonists, cosmetics then in use in Europe were valued, and some apparently arrived in North America along with the first settlers. As the colonial population grew, so did the import of hair powder, perfume, rouge, wigs, and bosom bottles. After 1700, domestic producers began supplying cosmetics.

For approximately two decades following the American Revolution only a sparing application of powder and rouge was considered fashionable. Except for light applications of scent and hair oil, the use of cosmetics by men remained socially unacceptable. The domestic production of cosmetics continued to expand after 1800, but growth was relatively slow throughout the greater part of the 19th century. Demand was largely confined to wealthy, fashion-conscious women living in the major urban communities.

Output of the cosmetics industry moved up sharply during the 20th century. Among the major contributors to this trend were further urbanization, higher income levels, a general relaxation of the Victorian standards of social behavior, a proliferation of beauty parlors, the introduction of a great variety of medium- and low-priced beauty aids, and the growing custom of emulating movie actresses and society leaders. In addition, there were extensive advertising and sales promotion campaigns.

COST OF GOVERNMENT. National, state, and local expenditures from taxes and other, limited, general purpose revenues. Until the 1930's, census reports generally equated such expenditures with cash outgo. Since then, the census provides data on several series of expenditures. Here the "direct general expenditures" series is used after 1930, which includes, for the particular government level, expenditures from its own taxes as well as grants or shared taxes supplied by another government and excludes expenditures of such facilities as government-owned utilities, liquor stores, and insurance trust funds.

Growing populations, the demand for a higher standard of public services, and wars and depressions have produced ever-increasing governmental expenditures. The federal government spent $5 million in 1792; in 1978, more than $400 billion. Collectively national, state, and local governments spent $10.59 billion in 1927; in 1978, over $745 billion. The largest single federal program cost has been for national defense and international relations. Education and highways accounted for more than half of state and local budgets before the depression; education, welfare, and highways have accounted for more than half subsequently.

In 1979 the national government provided $53.5 billion in grants to the states and $19.6 billion to local governments. The states provided their local governments with $61.1 billion in grants and shared revenues in 1977. The already substantial transfer of funds from the national government to state and local governments was augmented, beginning in late 1972, by congressional passage of the first national general revenue-sharing act, providing for the return by the federal government of more than $5 billion annually to state and local governments for general expenditures for the five-year term of the act. The revenue-sharing act was extended in 1976 and again in 1980.

COST OF LIVING. Measured as the percentage of change in the index of retail prices of necessities or as the average family-consumption expenditures. It has been a chief concern of nonfarm families during epochs of inflation, when prices commonly advance faster and in greater percentages than wages. Farm families favor higher prices because they depend on the sales value of their produce.

Wage earners must have suffered declines in real income during the colonial era, when commodity prices were highly unstable. Inflation during the Revolution also undoubtedly hurt them in the eastern centers. In the early 1790's, prices began another sharp rise, leading to the earliest U.S. strikes on record, among Philadelphia craftsmen.

Continuous urban retail price quotations for the years 1789–1850 are practically nonexistent. Ethel D. Hoover's cost-of-living index for 1800–50, overstates U.S. living costs before midcentury. Another index, compiled by the Federal Reserve Bank of New York and relying on different criteria, gives much lower figures beginning in 1820 and an upward trend until 1850. A third measure, an implicit consumption price index since 1789, lies halfway between the Hoover and Federal Reserve indexes in 1820 if all are converted to the same base (1913). According to this index, real consumption expenditures per capital tended to rise at an average of 1.3 percent per annum, going from $46 in 1789 to $106 in 1850.

Over the interval 1850–1913 the general cost-of-living pattern resembled that of the consumption price index of 1789–1850 in basic outline. The Hoover, Federal Reserve, and consumer-price indexes come into much closer agreement. Civil War inflation saw wages lagging far behind living costs—a disparity particularly severe in Confederate currency and relatively mild on the West Coast, where gold remained in circulation. Nevertheless, real consumption per capita reached some $301 by 1913, which represents an average annual increase of 1.67 percent since 1850.

From 1913 to the 1980's, the statistical materials are far superior to those before 1913, thanks to the U.S. Bureau of Labor Statistics (BLS). Its monthly Consumer Price Index (CPI), known until 1945 as the Index of the Cost of Living, has improved its coverage and, by the 1970's, provided quotations in twenty-three selected areas on about 304 commodities and services.

The BLS Index underwent its first large increase during World War I, rising to 203 percent in 1920. The cost of living so far outran increases in wage rates that the annual number of work stoppages grew tremendously. After 1920 the index remained at about 175 percent for a decade, then dipped to 131 in 1933, and recovered slowly to 142 by 1940 (1913 base).

America underwent a new experience in World War II by placing a fairly firm lid on living costs. The BLS Index inched upward to 182 by 1945. Since wage controls were comparatively flexible and employment was extremely brisk, the vast majority of civilians enjoyed a notable increase in real income. The actual cost of living increased somewhat more than the BLS Index indicated, because of such factors as ceiling-price violations and the black markets that emerged in scarce commodities.

Unfortunately, no plans were made for the demobilization period. Buying pressure, originating with huge federal deficits, burst forth and, instead of intensifying controls, the government lifted them. The CPI spurted upward in 1946 until it reached 243 percent by 1950. The effort to contain prices during wartime turned out to be a postponement of inflation. Pensioners and others on fixed incomes began to suffer notable reductions in real income. Those who had purchased savings bonds during the war took heavy losses in the purchasing power of their savings.

Following world prices in general, the CPI drifted upward after 1950, with slight declines during some recessions. By 1960 it attained 299 percent, and 525 at the end of 1974 (1913 base). America began to face a new problem: inflation during periods of depression and unemployment. Swollen federal deficits aggravated the problem during the Korean and Vietnam wars: the administrations of Harry Truman and Richard Nixon fought retreating battles by jawboning business and labor leaders or by imposing selective controls on a temporary basis. The 20th century became marked by more or less chronic inflation; and the future for stability in the cost of living was not bright, partly because of more cost elements. Taxes, energy, and environmental protection are examples, along with steep expenses for all building and equipment.

Fortunately, American productivity advanced rapidly enough between 1913 and 1975 to permit wage rates to keep up with the cost of living and, in the long run, to surpass it. Real consumption per capita dropped to some extent during World War I and again during the depression, but by and large, it has continued to grow. From $301 in 1913, it expanded to $971 in 1973, equivalent to an increase of 2 percent per annum.

COSTUME. *See* **Dress.**

CÔTE DES ALLEMANDS. A forty-mile area along the right bank of the Mississippi River about thirty miles north of New Orleans. It was named for the many German settlers in the area. By land grants in 1721, Jean Baptiste Le Moyne, Sieur de Bienville, induced Alsatian colonists, who planned to return to Germany from John Law's Arkansas River concession following the collapse of Law's financial schemes, to settle in this district.

COTENTIN PENINSULA. That part of Normandy bounded by Cherbourg on the north, Avranches on the south, the Vire River on the east, and the English Channel on the west. Its hedgerows are natural defensive positions for soldiers. The area also has peat bogs impassable to vehicles. Military forces are thus constrained to well-defined corridors of advance. Half of the American forces invading Normandy on June 6, 1944, the VII Corps of the First U.S. Army, entered into the Cotentin. By the end of the month, troops that had landed elsewhere reached the Cotentin western shore, sealed off Cherbourg, and captured this port. From

July 3 to 18, they launched the "battle of the hedgerows" and moved south about seven miles at a cost of 40,000 casualties. They then initiated the "Cobra" battle, broke the German defenses, and on July 31 seized Avranches.

COTTON. Although grown in the South since the founding of Jamestown in 1607, cotton did not become a cash crop during the colonial period. Most was consumed locally in domestic manufacture. By the late 18th century, revolutionary inventions in the English textile industry began the process that would transform the U.S. South into the "cotton kingdom." When trade with England reopened after the Revolution (1783), planters in the coastal areas of South Carolina and Georgia found a lucrative market for their cotton.

When in 1793 Eli Whitney invented his cotton gin, which quickly and cheaply separated the seeds from the staple, Georgia and South Carolina planters expanded production. Exports increased from 500,000 pounds in 1793 to 18 million pounds by 1800 and more than 90 million pounds a decade later. The cotton belt rapidly expanded westward into Alabama, Mississippi, Louisiana, Arkansas, Tennessee, and Texas. In 1860, the United States produced more than 2 billion pounds (4.5 million bales) of cotton. About 75 percent was exported, mainly to England. Southerners proclaimed that "cotton was king."

The Civil War proved that cotton was not king. The Union blockade separated the South from its markets and sources of supply. The war left most cotton farmers destitute, their fields and equipment in neglect or ruin, and their black labor force free. Gradually the South returned to cotton but under a much altered system. Land was rented out in small parcels, usually under the sharecropping system. In 1880, 36 percent of cotton farmers were tenants; in 1935 it had risen to over 60 percent. Meanwhile, cotton production increased. Within a decade after the Civil War, the prewar high was equaled, reaching 10 million bales by 1900 and 16 million by World War I. Acreage increased from fewer than 8 million acres in 1869 to 25 million in 1900 and more than 35 million in 1914.

By this time there were signs of serious trouble in the southern cotton belt. Declining prices and production inefficiencies brought poverty to millions of cotton growers, a condition worsened by the boll weevil infestation that entered Texas in 1892 and gradually spread to Georgia and South Carolina by 1922. The United States lost its domination of the raw cotton markets as other countries increased production. Rich, irrigated lands in California, Arizona, and New Mexico were shifted to cotton production; and these areas—free from the uncertainties of weather, the boll weevil, and weed infestation—offered disastrous competition to the older cotton areas. With the Great Depression, cotton prices dropped still lower and conditions reached crisis proportions.

Cotton acreage, almost 45 million acres in 1925, dropped to the lowest point in 1975, less than 9 million acres, but then increased again to 12.8 million in 1979. Production also declined, but at a slower rate: from 16 million bales in the mid-1920's to 8.3 million in 1975. In 1979 the production increased to 14.6 million bales. Work on better lands became mechanized with the introduction of tractors, plows, weeders, and automatic pickers. Output per man-hour increased nine times between 1940 and 1973. The eastern cotton states became minor producers as the cotton belt shifted west. In 1979, Texas was the largest producer, followed by California, Mississippi, Arizona, Louisiana, and Arkansas. Although the United States remained the world's leading cotton producer, its onetime near monopoly was gone. By the early 1960's, its share of world production had dropped to less than 30 percent, and by 1980, to 17 percent.

COTTON CONTROL ACT. *See* **Bankhead Cotton Act.**

COTTON GIN. The implement or machine used to pull the cotton fibers from the seed. There are many varieties of cotton, but two basic types—black-seed cotton, from which the fibers pull away easily, and green-seed cotton, from which it is difficult to free the fibers. The roller gin was used in the colonies by the mid-18th century. The cotton fibers were fed between two hand-turned rollers, which pulled the cotton from the seed. The roller gin could not be used on green-seed cotton because it crushed the seeds and stained the fiber.

Eli Whitney was granted a patent on Mar. 14, 1794, for a machine that used spiked teeth set into a wooden cylinder to pull the cotton fibers through the slots in a metal breastplate; the slots were too small to allow the seeds to pass through. A second cylinder with brushes freed the fibers from the teeth. In 1796, Hogden Holmes patented a cotton gin in which the teeth were cut into circular saws mounted on the cylinder. In a court suit, it was judged that the Holmes patent did not disallow the control of the principle of the earlier Whitney patent. Whitney and his partner, Phineas Miller, determined to keep the gin under their immediate control, sold ginning services, not machines. Because of a fire in their New Haven shop, shipment of gins was delayed, and southern blacksmiths began making them as needed. After years of court suits, several southern states finally paid Whitney almost $100,000 for the patent rights. Patented improvements of the earlier roller gin began in the 1830's, and improvements in the saw gin continued throughout the 19th century.

COTTON KINGDOM. Between 1830 and 1860, the region reaching from South Carolina to Texas. Characteristic of the Cotton Kingdom were the plantation system and slavery. The plantation system developed because cotton was most cheaply produced on a large scale. Slavery supplied a cheap and abundant supply of unskilled labor. (*See* "King Cotton.")

COTTON MONEY. Certificates issued by banks on baled cotton, generally used by planters in the Old South. When secession demoralized the cotton exchanges, growers called on the Confederacy to issue cotton money. Mississippi, the only state to comply, issued $5 million in treasury notes to be advanced on 1861 cotton stored and pledged for delivery by owners. Before the money was repudiated in 1869 as part of the Confederate debt, over half of it had been redeemed.

COTTON STATES AND INTERNATIONAL EXPOSITION. *See* **International Exposition of 1895.**

COTTON WHIGS. *See* **Conscience Whigs.**

COUNCIL, CITY. *See* **City Councils.**

COUNCIL BLUFFS (Iowa). On the Missouri River in southwestern Iowa; began as a Potawatomi village clustered about an army blockhouse built in 1837. A year later it was given to a Jesuit missionary. Mormons began to arrive in June 1846, and named the town Kanesville; wagon trains were organized there for the long journey to Great Salt Lake and to the goldfields of California. In 1853 the state legislature changed the name to Council Bluffs. It became a major railroad terminus. The population in 1980 was 56,449.

COUNCIL FOR FOREIGN PLANTATIONS. One successor to Oliver Cromwell's Colonial Board (the other being the Council for Trade). Appointed in 1660 to secure a more uniform system of colonial government and to enforce the new Navigation Act, its members included statesmen, merchants, and colonial administrators. The council functioned chiefly as a bureau of investigation and reported to the Privy Council. In 1665 it expired, its work being assumed by a Privy Council committee, but five years later it was revived. In 1672, merged with the Council for Trade, it became the Council for Trade and Plantations. It was abolished again in 1674, and in 1675 its duties were entrusted to the Committee for Trade and Plantations, also known as the Lords of Trades and Plantations, of the Privy Council.

COUNCIL FOR NEW ENGLAND. The name under which the survivors of the Plymouth branch of the Virginia Company, chartered in 1606, were incorporated by a charter in 1620. The council received the land extending from Long Island to the Bay of Fundy, the authority to colonize and govern, and monopolistic trade and fishing rights. It resembled the royal council of the Virginia Company, for in the charter no mention was made of general courts or freemen, and it was a closed corporation of forty members. From the outset its members, who were nobles and landed gentry rather than merchants, were more interested in developing the land than in trade. This they planned to do by granting most of the region to its members as fiefs and manors. The rest of the land was to be given to others, singly or in groups, with rights of local self-government, but subject to the superior authority of the council's governor general.

Sir Ferdinando Gorges was president of the council. His son Robert was appointed the first governor-general and went to New England in 1623. He succeeded no better than most members of the council and soon departed for England. The enterprise as a whole failed, but New England was colonized through the unexpected success of two small grants to nonmembers. The first of these patents was that of the Pilgrims, who settled on Cape Cod in 1620, and the other was the Massachusetts Bay patent of 1628, confirmed the following year by royal charter.

COUNCIL GROVE (Kans.). City in east central Kansas named for a grove at the Neosho River crossing, where early western travelers gathered to form wagon trains. In 1847, Seth Hays established at Council Grove the first settlement on the trail west of Westport (now part of Kansas City), Mo. It was the jumping-off point for the wagon trek to Santa Fe. Located in the rich dairy and grain area of northeastern Kansas, Council Grove is the county seat of Morris County. The population in 1980 was 2,381.

COUNCIL OF APPOINTMENT, NEW YORK. A body created by the first state constitution (1777) to check the appointive power of the governor. It consisted of the governor and one senator from each of the four great districts, elected annually by the assembly. The claim of the council members to have concurrent right of nomination with the governor was upheld by the constitutional convention of 1801. The council became the nucleus of a powerful political machine that by 1821 could dispense patronage of 14,950 offices with an aggregate salary of over a million dollars. It was abolished by New York's second constitution in 1821.

COUNCIL OF CENSORS. A council created in Pennsylvania by its 1776 constitution, to be composed of two men from each city and county, elected for seven years, and authorized to inquire into the efficiency of the executive and legislative departments and to amend the constitution. Meeting only once, it failed in its purpose.

COUNCIL OF ECONOMIC ADVISERS. See **Federal Agencies.**

COUNCIL OF NATIONAL DEFENSE. A council of six cabinet members and an unpaid civilian advisory committee, created by Congress on Aug. 29, 1916, to investigate transportation and industrial mobilization problems and manage the utilization of U.S. resources in wartime. Organization was not completed until March 1917, and lack of appropriations after 1920 limited its experience to the war period itself. As the parent body of the War Industries Board, it was useful in the early stages of industrial mobilization.

COUNCIL OF REVISION, NEW YORK. Part of the system of checks and balances incorporated in the first state constitution (1777). The veto power was vested in this council, composed of the chancellor, the judges of the state supreme court, or any two of them, plus the governor. It was abolished by the constitution of 1821.

COUNTERFEITING. To counterfeit means to imitate with intent to defraud. Most counterfeit paper money can be classified into: (1) imitations of legitimate notes; (2) alterations of legitimate notes, including notes raised to a higher denomination; and (3) fakes represented as obligations of institutions that do not exist. Counterfeit notes prior to the Civil War also had to be distinguished not only from ordinary legal tender but also from legitimate paper money circulating at a discount, because it represented obligations of broken or failed banks and was therefore only fractionally valuable.

The circulation of both counterfeit notes and valid, but discounted, notes of commercial banks gave rise to pamphlets known as Bank Note Reporters and Counterfeit Detectors, published by money brokers in centers of financial activity. These pamphlets gave up-to-date information on the validity and value of notes currently in use. After the effective end of state banknote issues in 1867, the Bank Note Reporters became unnecessary because all bank-note and government-issued currency thenceforth circulated at par.

The Confederate States of America legalized existing counterfeit issues during the Civil War. In an effort to spare the possibly innocent individual detected with a counterfeit note, the Confederate government legalized the acceptance of bogus notes late in the war. It had little choice. Hardly anyone could tell the difference between the real and the imitation. Frequently the counterfeit notes were of better quality.

COUNTRY STORE (general store). The dominant form of mercantile establishment in the early years of U.S. settlement. Because the isolation of the community compelled farmers to obtain most things locally, country storekeepers carried a varied assortment of goods: coffee, tea, sugar, salt, clothing, medicine, books, and hardware. In accepting farm products for store goods, the merchant acted as a marketing agent. Many country merchants also served as local postmasters. The social importance of the store made it the chief contact with the outside world and a social center for the community.

COUNTY. *See* **County Government.**

COUNTY FAIRS. A peculiarly American agricultural institution that arose in the early 19th century. They differed markedly from the fairs for buying and selling held during the colonial period. Their major impetus came from Elkanah Watson and his Berkshire Agricultural Society. Watson exhibited Merino sheep in the village square in Pittsfield, Mass., in 1807 and persuaded neighbors to join him in a livestock show in 1810. The Berkshire Society was organized in 1811 and began sponsoring an annual fair. By 1820, agricultural societies had been organized in many counties. The states made grants to the societies, mainly for prizes for products exhibited at fairs. The emphasis was upon growing greater and better-looking crops and fatter animals. During the late 1820's and 1830's the movement declined but was revived in the 1840's; well into the 20th century the number of fairs and attendance showed a steady increase. After World War II the number of fairs declined again as the farm population shrank.

COUNTY GOVERNMENT. The institutions of government in the more than 3,000 counties in the United States owe their origins to the colonies, which borrowed extensively from English practice. In most states these have persisted without substantial change. County governments exist in all states except Rhode Island, Connecticut (which abolished counties in 1959), and Alaska, whose boroughs differ from counties in some respects; in Louisiana counties are called parishes.

Although there is wide variation in structure, the typical county still operates through an elective governing body, whose functions are largely administrative, and a set of elective "row" officers—such as sheriff, attorney, treasurer, registrar of deeds, and coroner. The commonest type is a board of three or five elective commissioners, but in a few states a much larger board (100 or more) is used, made up of town supervisors and, frequently, city councilmen.

A small number of counties have centralized administrative responsibility in an elective or appointive executive. In some states variation in government from county to county is now permitted. In a few instances, city and county governments have been consolidated. Many county governments furnish services usually provided by municipalities—such as libraries, parks, and airports—in addition to functioning as administrative agencies. State laws largely determine county government structure, functions, and authority. Property tax is the principal local source of county revenues, but a large and increasing part of county budgets comes from state and federal aids, from shared state taxes, and, since 1972, from federal revenue-sharing funds.

COUNTY-SEAT WARS. In the "boomtown" craze after the Civil War, several western states were disturbed by controversies over the location of county seats. In Kansas there were twenty-eight such contests. Nebraska and the two Dakotas experienced county-seat troubles to a lesser extent.

COUREURS DE BOIS (or bushrangers). Men who left the early French settlements in Canada and took to the wilderness, actuated by adventure and the fur trade. During the late 17th century the exodus seriously weakened the colony of New France. In spite of government edicts and the hostility of the Jesuits, the bushrangers flourished. While they were accused of debauching the Indians, they did render valuable service as explorers and pioneers in the fur trade.

COURTESY OF THE SENATE. A time-honored custom observed by the U.S. Senate when considering presidential nominations to federal offices. If a nominee is objected to by one or both of his home-state senators, the Senate will generally refuse to confirm the appointment if the objecting senator belongs to the same party as the president.

COURTHOUSE ROCK. A notable landmark on the Oregon Trail, located about five miles south of present Bridgeport, Nebr. In 1846 the trail ran seven miles from this natural formation. This rock-and-clay, castlelike landmark, estimated to be 250 feet high and to cover an acre, is said to have been named by the fur traders because of its likeness to the courthouse in St. Louis.

COURT LEET. In English law, a court exercising the jurisdiction of the sheriff's tourn over petty criminal matters. In colonial Maryland leet jurisdiction was exercised by the proprietors of manors of 2,000 or more acres under authority issued by the proprietary in 1636. Both freeholders and leaseholders sat in the court and a presenting jury was employed.

COURT OF INTERNATIONAL JUSTICE, PERMANENT. *See* **International Court of Justice.**

COURTS-MARTIAL. Military courts established to try individuals subject to military jurisdiction. The Continental Congress passed an act on Sept. 29, 1789, continuing the British courts-martial system, already in use in the colonies. American courts-martial now derive their authority from the constitutional authority of Congress "to make Rules for the Government and Regulation of the land and naval forces."

COURTS OF THE PLAINS. Under Mexican law the enforcement of range bandos and the settlement of disputes between rancheros and vaqueros were vested in the *jueces del Campos* (judges of the Plains). These officers attended stock roundups on the great ranches and settled conflicting claims of ownership. They were also peace officers. The courts of the Plains functioned until the breaking up of the great land-grant estates in the late 1870's.

The term was also applied to the impromptu popular tribunals set up for the enforcement of justice along the emigrant trails across the Great Plains. They met the necessity for punishing crime and enforcing law and order in the absence of other courts and law enforcement officers. The members of these courts of the Plains were usually chosen from the most able, conservative, and respected men of the community.

***COUTUME DE PARIS*.** The law administered in the courts of French colonial Canada and Louisiana, originally the customary feudal law of the provostship and viscounty of Paris. Under British rule, after 1763, the military commandants, assisted by popularly elected justices, acted as judges in administering the *coutumes.* Although the English criminal code was introduced by the Quebec Act of 1774, French civil law was retained until 1792. This legal system, modified by the Virginia Declaration of Rights, was continued on the American occupation of the Illinois country in 1778; and the laws of the Northwest Territory also guaranteed to the French inhabitants existing *coutumes* in family relations and in descent and conveyance of property. In Louisiana, the *coutumes* remained in force until the arrival of Alexander O'Reilly, Irish soldier in the Spanish army, who imposed Spanish law in 1769.

COUTURE'S OPERATIONS. Jean Couture, a carpenter, was left in command of Arkansas Post in 1686. After La Salle's failure to establish a colony at the mouth of the Mississippi and the temporary suspension of French activities in that quarter, Couture deserted the French service. By 1696 he had found his way to Carolina, and in 1700 guided an English expedition from Charleston through the Cherokee country and down the Tennessee, Ohio, and Mississippi rivers to the mouth of the Arkansas.

COVENANT, CHURCH. The formal and public act of mutual engagement that, according to the theory of the New England clergy, should be entered into by the founders of a particular church and without which no church could come into being. All New England churches were founded upon such an agreement, and later recruits subscribed to the covenant; at times of revival the covenant was often unanimously "renewed." Insistence upon this theory was one of the peculiar characteristics of Congregational or Independent theologians.

COVERED WAGON. The means of transcontinental transportation used for two centuries in America. Born in Pennsylvania as the Conestoga wagon, constructed under various names but always of strength and capacity, it served nomadic America as no other vehicle could have done. The covered wagon was basically a wagon box with a framework of hoop-shaped slats over which a canvas tent was stretched. Each was drawn by several teams of horses, mules, or oxen. Many were boat-shaped with oarlocks so that they might be floated over streams, the animals swimming across.

COVODE INVESTIGATION (1860). A partisan committee, headed by Republican Rep. John Covode of Pennsylvania, to investigate President James Buchanan's use of money and patronage to influence congressmen. The committee uncovered a few sinecures and some irregularities in printing contracts. The major purpose—to obtain campaign material for the 1860 election—was realized in a voluminous report denouncing the Democratic administration.

COWBOYS. The cowboy began his career when the first cattle were unloaded on the Caribbean coast of Mexico during the conquest by Hernando Cortes in 1519. The cattle ate their way northward and sometimes were brought into the future United States by soldiers and missionaries. Along the way, methods for tending cattle without fences were evolved, and when settlers began moving into Texas in the 1820's, they adopted Mexican methods for herding and handling cattle.

The heyday of the cowboy began in 1867. The founding of the first real cow town, Abilene, Kans., enabled Texas cattle, several million strong after years of neglect because of the Civil War, to be trailed to a railhead without encountering farmers. Over the next quarter-century over 10 million cattle were trailed from Texas into Kansas, Nebraska, New Mexico, Colorado, Wyoming, and Montana.

One reason the cowboy so captured the popular imagination was his unique working gear, most of it borrowed from the Mexican vaquero. Furthermore, the cowboy represented courage and devotion to duty. In fact, so dangerous was the life that seven years was the average limit of the cowboy's riding life. The discovery of the cowboy by the "penny dreadfuls" (popular novels of violent adventure that originally sold for a penny) gave the nation a hero who represented an ideal of physical prowess and courage that accorded well with the mores of the day.

The 20th-century cowboy still fascinates, although he tends his cattle from a truck, eats hot food from the ranch-house galley, and sleeps in a bed. On some spreads he even tends cattle by helicopter.

COWBOYS AND SKINNERS. Bands of guerrillas and irregular cavalry who operated chiefly in the "Neutral

Ground" of Westchester County, N.Y., during the American Revolution.

"Cowboys" was a name given to the Westchester Light Horse Battalion, a Loyalist provincial corps of the British army, commanded by Col. James de Lancey. The Westchester Light Horse was organized in 1777 and was an irregular unit of the British army until the end of the war, taking part in some of the principal battles.

The "Skinners," ironically named after Gen. Cortland Skinner's Brigade of New Jersey Volunteers, had no regular organization. They were separate bands of mounted banditti who plundered, burned, and ravished the "Neutral Ground" from 1778 to 1783, and sold their plunder to both sides. They were sometimes employed as scouts and spies, although both sides hanged or shot them whenever they were caught.

COWBOY SONGS. On cattle drives, one danger was that any unusual noise after the cattle were asleep might send them into a wild and destructive stampede. To drown those disturbing noises, the cowboys came to croon or yodel to the cattle. From these cattle calls grew some of the trail songs descriptive of cowboy life. They also sang around the campfire and in the cow-town saloons to amuse themselves. They sang the old ballads along with the sentimental songs of Tin Pan Alley, and they made up new songs and adapted old ones that told about themselves in their own lingo.

Jack Thorpe of New Mexico published locally a small pamphlet collection of cowboy songs without music in 1907. John A. Lomax's *Cowboy Songs and Other Frontier Ballads* (1911) was the first printing of cowboy music. Radio and motion pictures gave cowboy songs a tremendous vogue.

COW COUNTRY. Vast region in the West occupied by the range cattle industry. Its central portion was the Great Plains area. The cow country came into existence after the Civil War and grew rapidly until shortly after 1880, when it covered the greatest area and reached the height of its importance. At its height it included most of the region from Mexico to Canada and from the central part of the second tier of states west of the Mississippi nearly to the Pacific coast. After about 1885 the cow country rapidly declined, as a result of the westward advance of settlers. By the 20th century a definite cow country ceased to exist.

COW CUSTOM. The unwritten or common law of the range when the range cattle industry flourished on the western plains in the second half of the 19th century. Cow custom dealt with such matters as prior rights to grazing areas, boundaries of ranges, roundups, movements of cattle on trails, branding of unmarked animals, rights to water, erection of drift fences, and cooperative measures in preventing prairie fires, protecting a neighbor's cattle, or caring for stray animals. Much was later translated into statutory law by such states as Wyoming and Texas.

COWPENS, BATTLE OF (Jan. 17, 1781). One of the most brilliant American victories in the Revolution. Gen. Daniel Morgan, with Andrew Pickens's militia, drew up 940 men in three lines on the slope of a hill near Cowpens, S.C. As Col. Banastre Tarleton's 1,150 British approached, the first two lines of Morgan's army fired and fell back. The British thought they had won, advanced in disorder, and were met by a deadly fire and bayonet attack. Cavalry struck them on the right and militia on the left. Surrounded, they surrendered. British losses were 600 prisoners and over 200 killed and wounded; American, 72 killed and wounded.

COWPUNCHER (puncher, cowpoke). "Cowboy," as word and fact peculiar to U.S. ranching, originated in Texas about 1836. "Cowpuncher" came into use around fifty years later, when cowboys used prods to force cattle through chutes into stock cars and, accompanying cattle on trains, carried prods to punch up any animal that got down in a car.

COW TOWNS. As the Chisholm Trail was established for cattle drives in 1867 and the great drives accompanied the expansion of the cattle-range industry, the cow towns of history arose in all their gaudy glory. The first was Abilene, Kans. Others grew up in other parts of Kansas and in Missouri, Nebraska, Wyoming, Montana, the Dakotas, Texas, Arizona, Colorado, and New Mexico. There were two kinds of cow towns: those that marked the ends of the trails; and those that acted as distributing points for vast range areas and, after railroads were built, as shipping points. Cattle owners made these towns headquarters for buying and selling.

COX, INSURRECTION OF (1798). On July 17, Zachariah Cox, a land speculator, embarked down the Ohio River from Smithland, Ky., with an armed force of eighty. Gen. James Wilkinson charged Cox with plotting insurrection, presumably against Spain, and sent a warning to Gov. Winthrop Sargent of Mississippi. Cox arrived in Natchez with only thirteen men on Aug. 11, and Sargent arrested him. He escaped to New Orleans, only to be rearrested in Nashville, where he was finally released. Cox insisted he had merely intended to explore Spanish territories west of the Mississippi, and the circumstances substantiate his contention. In 1803, Congress declared his arrest illegal but denied his claim for damages.

COXEY'S ARMY. Jacob Sechler Coxey, of Massillon, Ohio, was a self-made businessman and a reformer with a special interest in fiat money. During the depression following the panic of 1893 he worked out a plan to save the country. He wanted two bills enacted that would provide for large issues of legal-tender currency to be spent for good roads and other public improvements, thus furnishing work to the unemployed. His device to arouse public and congressional interest in these bills was the march of a "living petition" of the unemployed to Washington, D.C. They marched out of Massillon on Easter Sunday 1894, with about a hundred men, followed by half as many reporters. Instead of the 100,000 he had predicted, Coxey had about 500 men when he arrived in Washington in time for a great demonstration on May Day. When he tried to speak from the Capitol steps, he was arrested, fined, and sent to jail for carrying banners and walking on the grass in the Capitol grounds.

Meanwhile, "industrial armies" larger than Coxey's had been formed by the unemployed on the Pacific coast and elsewhere, planning to join Coxey in Washington. Many armies disintegrated before reaching Washington, and only about 1,200 straggled in. The District of Columbia finally paid their way home.

CRAB ORCHARD. An early important station in Kentucky on the Wilderness Road. It was near Logan's Fort in what is now Lincoln County. Here travelers formed parties for protection against the Indians as they journeyed toward Cumberland Gap and settlements east of the mountains.

"CRACKER LINE." A term used by soldiers in the Civil War for a food-supply line. It was especially used by the short-rationed Union soldiers in Chattanooga in the fall of 1863, when, with the railroad cut off by the Confederates, a steamboat line was opened on the Tennessee River to bring foodstuffs up from Bridgeport.

"CRACKERS." Usually used disparagingly to describe poor whites of the pine barrens area of the South, also referred to as piney woods people, sand hillers, and clay-eaters. The term is said to have originated in colonial Georgia from the practice of teamsters cracking their huge whips as they drove their teams long distances to markets with farm produce.

***CRAIG* V. *STATE OF MISSOURI*,** 4 Peters 410 (1830). The Missouri legislature, in 1821, established a loan office for issuing paper money to be lent to debt-burdened Missouri farmers. Suit was brought in the circuit court to force payment of a note Hiram Craig had given for a loan of loan-office certificates. This court and the Missouri Supreme Court decided that Craig must pay. The U.S. Supreme Court reversed the decision, holding loan-office certificates unconstitutional because they were bills of credit emitted by a state.

CRANEY ISLAND. At the mouth of the Elizabeth River in Virginia, fortified during the War of 1812 to command Norfolk harbor. A powerful British fleet attacked, June 22, 1813, landing a force on Nansemond Point and sending barges against the island. Virginia militia defeated those at Nansemond while the fort's batteries drove off the barge force. The enemy lost 200 killed and wounded. This American victory saved Norfolk, Portsmouth, and Gosport.

CRATER. A gigantic hole in the Confederate fortifications east of Petersburg, Va., produced on July 30, 1864, by the detonation of a huge powder mine laid by the Union army.

CRATER LAKE NATIONAL PARK. Located in southwestern Oregon; surrounds Crater Lake, which fills the core of a long-dead volcano, Mount Mazama. The lake is the deepest in the United States (2,000 feet) and is six miles wide. Crater Lake includes several islands created by later volcanic action: Wizard Island is a cone itself, rising to almost 2,000 feet. The park was established in 1902.

CRAWFORD, FORT. Built in 1816 under supervision of Gen. T. A. Smith at Prairie du Chien, Wis., the fort commanded the junction of the Wisconsin and Mississippi rivers. It was an important military outpost in the period of fur trading and lead mining. Here several important Indian treaties were signed. The fort lost its significance following the defeat of Black Hawk in 1832.

CRAZY SNAKE REBELLION (1900–1901). Crazy Snake, with certain Creek Indians objecting to the government's plan to allot their tribal lands, set up a government of their own at Hickory Ground, in Indian Territory, in October 1900. Warned to disperse by the U.S. marshal, they did so; but, reassembling in January 1901, they threatened law-abiding Indians and punished violators of their own so-called laws. The marshal, an armed posse, and a troop of U.S. cavalry arrested ninety-four Indians. The leaders were tried and, pledged to make no further trouble, were released on their own recognizance.

CREDIT. In any society it is likely that some individuals or firms will desire to spend more income than they receive and others might be willing to advance part of their current income if they are adequately compensated. Those advances are called "credit." In the United States the demand for credit probably dates back to the day of first settlement, and since the economy had little transport or manufacturing, the investment demand for credit was largely mercantile and agricultural. What credit existed was usually extended by individuals or by merchants as a part of their commercial activities.

Early banks were largely devoted to supplying credit needs of the mercantile community. While they mobilized the savings of stockholders and a few depositors, they also issued bank notes in exchange for commercial paper. After 1865 the creation of demand deposits (checking accounts) largely replaced note issue.

In the 19th century, local banks were the dominant institution in the short-term credit market in the North and West; in the South a combination of merchants and cotton factors provided much the same service. Because of legal restrictions there were few mechanisms to effect the interregional movement of credit. This was partly overcome by commercial paper houses. These institutions began in the East in the 1840's and moved into the Midwest in the early 1870's and to the Pacific coast by the turn of the century. They were simple arbitragers, buying commercial paper from banks in high-interest regions and reselling it to banks in lower-interest areas. Their function has been largely taken over by national firms capable of obtaining credit in one market and using it in another.

The emergence in the 1820's, 1830's, and 1840's of capital-intensive transportation and manufacturing firms and a new finance-intensive technology in agriculture increased demand for long-term credit. At first these demands were partly met by commercial banks and the new industrial banks. But the panic of 1837 and the depression of 1839–42 convinced some bankers that long-term loans were unsafe; their views received reinforcement from new banking legislation that made it difficult for commercial banks to make long-term loans.

Other institutions emerged as major suppliers of long-term credit. Although the first savings bank did not open its doors until 1816, the idea spread rapidly. From the late 1830's until the end of the century the savings bank remained the most important supplier of long-term credit. Nevertheless, the savings banks mobilized only the savings of the poor and were never important outside the Northeast. There were large markets in the East, Midwest, and South still unserved. Life insurance companies came to meet a substantial part of their demands. Life insurance companies passed savings banks in importance in the early 20th century and remain the most important supplier of long-term institutional credit.

The rapid development of the corporate form of industry in the 19th century and the increase in government obligations produced a situation in which a substantial demand for credit and an ability to issue debt instruments coincided. The development of the formal capital markets was called for to facilitate the transfer of this kind of credit, and the New York Stock Exchange was formally organized in 1817. Soon local markets emerged in Boston and Philadelphia, and by the 1830's there were local markets as far inland as St. Louis. These exchanges moved into transportation securities in the early 19th century and into public utilities shortly thereafter. By 1900 they were handling manufacturing securities, and by World War I the market served to mobilize credit for almost all branches of American activity (agriculture was an exception). Although the system suffered a temporary setback after the crash of 1929, it rebounded during World War II and remains a major route for the extension of long-term credit.

CREDIT ISLAND, BATTLE OF (Sept. 5–6, 1814). During the summer of 1814 the Americans attempted to regain control of the upper Mississippi from the British. Maj. Zachary Taylor, with 334 men in eight boats, was attacked at Credit Island (now part of Davenport, Iowa) by a few British and many Indians and was compelled to return to St. Louis.

CRÉDIT MOBILIER OF AMERICA. A company used by a group of leaders of the Union Pacific Railroad to enable them to pocket exorbitant profits in the construction of the line. Involved were T. C. Durant, Oakes Ames, and Oliver Ames. According to a Senate investigation, the managers stripped the Union Pacific of what Congress had intended should be a permanent endowment and lined their own pockets with $23 million. When Congress convened on Nov. 21, 1867, it was evident that the Union Pacific–Crédit Mobilier combination might come under fire. Oakes Ames therefore took 343 shares of Crédit Mobilier stock and distributed at least 160 shares among senators and representatives. Late in the presidential campaign of 1872 the *New York Sun* made charges that resulted in both House and Senate investigations which ruined the reputation of Oakes Ames; of James Brooks (New York), who also was formally censured by the House; of New Hampshire Sen. James W. Patterson, who was recommended for expulsion, although no action was taken since his term was about to expire; and of Speaker Schuyler Colfax. Other men, including James A. Garfield, then a representative from Ohio, were badly damaged in public esteem.

CREDIT OF THE NATION. A term implying both the ability and the willingness of a nation to meet its obligations and faith on the part of its creditors that repayment of the debt will be made at a future date. A nation that defaults on its external debt has its credit standing impaired in the capital markets of the world. A nation that repudiates its debts directly or through their repayment in worthless "printing-press money" virtually loses its national credit.

CREEK INDIANS. *See* **Five Civilized Tribes.**

CREEK WAR (1813–14). The only serious revolt of the Creek Indians of Alabama and Georgia against the Americans, emanating principally from the forced acculturation of the Indians. The Creeks had split into two factions because of disagreements over how best to cope with the intrusions. A strong opposition to the proposed "civilization" developed among the Upper Creek of central Alabama. The Upper Creek, known as the Red Sticks, were hostile, while the Lower Creek, or White Sticks, remained loyal to the United States. Prophets arose among the Red Sticks, inciting them to war. Gen. Andrew Jackson began a campaign against the Red Sticks in late 1813. On Mar. 27, 1814, Jackson almost wiped out the Red Stick forces at the Horseshoe Bend of the Tallapoosa River in eastern Alabama, killing an estimated 900 warriors and making prisoners of 500 women and children. Ironically, the White Sticks, despite having aided Jackson in the war, were compelled to sign the Treaty of Fort Jackson (Aug. 9, 1814), ceding more than 20 million acres.

CREOLES. "Creole" was originally employed to distinguish Europeans born in the American colonies from their fellow nationals born in the mother countries; but in later times it has been restricted to individuals of French, Spanish, or Portuguese ancestry born in the Americas. In parts of the South, Afro-Americans of French or Spanish ancestry and retaining some European culture are also known as Creoles.

***CREOLE* SLAVE CASE.** On Nov. 7, 1841, the 135 slaves of the *Creole,* sailing from Hampton Roads, Va., to New Orleans, overpowered the crew, killed one white man, and took the vessel into the English port of Nassau, in the Bahamas, where the authorities freed all but those charged with murder. Secretary of State Daniel Webster demanded surrender of all the slaves, but the British, who had abolished slavery, refused. In 1853, an Anglo-American commission agreed on an indemnity of $110,330 to the United States.

CRESAP'S WAR (1774). Desultory warfare, under Capt. Michael Cresap, with the Ohio River Indians. Among other incidents, on Apr. 30, 1774, the family of Logan, a noted chieftain, was lured across the Ohio from its camp on Yellow Creek River, made intoxicated, and brutally murdered, prompting the ravages of Logan and his followers. Later it was shown that Daniel Greathouse, and not Cresap, was the leader in the massacre.

CRÈVECOEUR, FORT. The first fort built in the West by the French. In January 1680, Robert Cavelier, Sieur de La Salle, entered the string of small lakes above modern Peoria, Ill. As protection from the Iroquois, he built a temporary fort within a few weeks. On his way east, La Salle sent an order to Henry de Tonti to inspect Starved Rock as the site for a permanent fort. During Tonti's absence, Fort Crèvecoeur was destroyed by the Frenchmen in charge. The fort was on the bank of the Illinois River opposite present-day Peoria.

CRIME. Criminal proscriptions in colonial New England derived from the English common law and the ascetic Christianity of the Puritans. Intoxication, sexual irregularities, irreverence, and other departures from biblical strictures were the commonest crimes; heresy and witchcraft were the ultimate offenses. Punishment was swift and relied heavily on corporal pain and public humiliation. Adding to the problem, courts in England transported to the southern colonies convicts who had been offered the alternative of indentured servitude on plantations. Maritime traffic encouraged piracy, transformed into privateering during the Revolution.

Post-Revolution national development proceeded far more rapidly than institutions of social control. Violent gangs in New York, Boston, Baltimore, and Philadelphia carried on their predations; river pirates terrorized inland waterways; large numbers of runaway youths and vagrants supported themselves by theft.

The expansion of the western frontier in the 19th century provided the setting for the exploits of notorious outlaws and resolute law officers. Prostitution, gambling, and predacious crime flourished. Interpersonal conflict boiled over into assault with a deadly weapon, manslaughter, or murder; armed robbery thrived. Countermeasures were severe: lynch law, perfunctory trials, and harsh punishments were dispensed by peace officers as remorseless as the criminals.

Massive immigration during the century set the stage for gangster-controlled organized crime. Patterns of criminal behavior indigenous to southern Italy and Sicily were adapted to meet the demand for goods and services proscribed by U.S. laws. This criminal activity took the form, principally, of illicit trade in alcoholic beverages during Prohibition; networks of prostitution rings; gambling syndicates; and international coordination of the production and distribution of narcotics. As late as the 1950's, intergang rivalries were still frequently erupting into vendetta slayings, and mob-related killings continued. There have been increasing indications since the 1960's of the displacement of white racketeers by blacks in the control of gambling and narcotics operations in the urban ghetto. In 1951, the U.S. Senate Committee to Investigate Organized Crime produced extensive evidence of the infiltration of more than seventy separate kinds of legitimate business by organized crime. The relatively infrequent crime of kidnapping wealthy persons for purposes of ransom achieved its highest incidence in the 1930's.

The common varieties of property and assaultive crimes have had their highest incidence in settings of low socioeconomic status, characterized by family instability, unemployment, low educational attainment, and migrant population. Official crime statistics published annually since 1930 in the *Uniform Crime Reports* indicate a striking increase generally in rates of serious crime. Historical studies of police records of major urban centers, however, contest the popular view that the actual current crime rate is higher than it was in the 19th century. Federal Bureau of Investigation statistics show a decline in criminal homicide rates.

Changes in technology and social organization have created new patterns. Car theft, for example, has replaced horse theft. The civil rights movement of the 1960's, although on the whole peaceable, touched off some bloody, costly riots. The vulnerability of air transportation has posed fresh challenges to law enforcement. White-collar crime—violations committed in the course of performing business and professional duties—has become more common as the social class structure has broadened at the middle and upper levels. The widespread use of computers has produced a new variety of crime. Computer crime usually involves theft of information or embezzlement.

CRIME, ORGANIZED. Entrepreneurial activities that provide customers with illegal goods or services, including prostitution, gambling, bootlegging, and the sale of narcotics. During the colonial period, seacoast cities offered groggeries, prostitutes, and gambling for sailors, dockworkers, and travelers, plus elite houses of prostitution and gambling for a more select clientele.

After the Revolution the burgeoning commercial cities of the Midwest also provided prostitution and gambling. Transportation lines became centers for entertainment, and the colorful Mississippi riverboat gambler entered into American folklore. In the Far West, mining towns attracted itinerant gamblers and prostitutes.

After the Civil War, entertainment, or red-light, districts developed in the larger cities. Con men, pickpockets, and burglars hung out in saloons and gambling halls. In the red-light districts were concentrated the Chinese opium dens and drugstores that sold morphine or cocaine. Changes in gambling brought increasing syndication. Horse racing became an important urban leisure activity. By the 1880's, bookmakers were paying the tracks $100 daily for the privilege of managing betting between the fans. Gamblers also developed offtrack bookmaking syndicates.

Policy gambling also became a syndicate activity after the Civil War. As early as the 18th century, policy (in which a bettor chose a number or numbers that would appear in a drawing) had been run as a sideline to legal lotteries. With the beginning in the 1830's of the progressive banning of lotteries by the states, policy shops independent of lotteries sprang up. Policy and bookmaking syndicates were closely tied to politics. Syndicate leaders supported politicians with money, while many local political organizations and gambling syndicates had overlapping memberships. The Irish were instrumental in putting together the system of organized crime, they dominated gambling outside the southern cities by 1900.

From 1890 to 1905, organized crime may have reached its high point in the United States. In the decade preceding World War I, a movement to enforce gambling laws closed racetracks in all but five states and thus virtually eliminated ontrack bookmaking. It also forced gambling houses, policy operations, and offtrack bookmaking to operate in a more clandestine manner. A movement against prostitution, particularly after 1907, eliminated the open red-light districts in city after city. The generally more clandestine operations decreased the extent and profitability of prostitution. Passage of the Harrison Act (1914), which controlled interstate shipments of opiates and cocaine, rapidly reduced the illegal sale of such narcotics.

The moral crusades that brought decline to gambling, prostitution, and narcotics in the early part of the 20th century were climaxed by passage of the Eighteenth (Prohibition) Amendment to the U.S. Constitution (1919). With sale of alcoholic beverages illegal, a market for illicit enterprise opened up. Those who rose to prominence as bootleggers were primarily distributors. They often opened their own distilleries and breweries and operated their own import services. Because of the rapid rise of bootlegging gangs and their efforts to expand, disputes often occurred. The 1920's ushered in a level of violence that persisted well beyond the decade. When Prohibition ended in 1933, many continued careers in gambling, labor racketeering, and other illicit activities. New ethnic groups came into prominence in organized crime. Although Jews and Italians had made important inroads into the operation of red-light districts before World War I, bootlegging greatly accelerated their rise. The creation of black ghettos in northern cities during World War I allowed the formation of black-controlled policy operations (as well as the closely related numbers rackets).

Other forms of gambling, too, expanded in the 1920's and 1930's. Horse racing made a comeback. Betting on baseball and football rapidly expanded in the 1920's and began to rival betting on horse races. Slot machines, in existence since at least the 1890's, also flourished in the 1920's.

Two expanding areas of criminal opportunity became important after World War II. One was the sale of heroin. By the 1950's there was a fairly stable system by which poppies were harvested in Turkey and the Near East, processed into heroin near Marseilles, and then shipped to the United States. The second area was the loansharking racket, made possible when many states tightened their laws with regard to maximum interest rates and strengthened enforcement.

Between 1930 and 1960 some Italians emerged in crucial positions in organized crime. Partly this was the result of the fact that the old-time Irish and Jewish crime leaders were not always replaced by young men from their own ethnic groups. During the 1930's and 1940's, Italian criminals in the New York–New Jersey region coalesced into some five or six major "families." In Providence, Buffalo, Detroit, Chicago, New Orleans, and Kansas City coalitions that were primarily Italian achieved important positions within organized crime by the 1940's and 1950's.

As a result of U.S. Senate hearings under Estes Kefauver (Special Committee to Investigate Organized Crime in Interstate Commerce) in 1950–51; the meeting of large numbers of Italian criminals at Apalachin, N.Y., in November 1957; and testimony by Joseph Valachi before the McClellan committee in 1963, political leaders, law enforcement officials, and the media discovered the strong Italian influence in organized crime, leading to the myth that a Mafia or Cosa Nostra controlled crime throughout the nation. In the 1960's, therefore, law enforcement agencies focused upon Italian criminals.

A number of other factors in the 1960's threatened Italian importance in organized crime and created a transition period. The rapid expansion of heroin use, especially in black ghettos, meant that new groups began importing and distributing drugs, especially Latin-Americans. The use of marijuana and psychedelic drugs spread rapidly. Large numbers of entrepreneurs became importers, manufacturers, distributors, and pushers of drugs. Their operations were largely independent of traditional, organized criminal groups. Changes in black and Puerto Rican ghetto culture led to the growth of independently operated indigenous drug distribution and numbers gambling operations.

By the late 1960's there were movements to modify or repeal some of the laws making certain goods or services illegal and thus creating the markets for organized crime. As a result of a series of U.S. Supreme Court decisions, the possibility of successful prosecution of pornography sellers became so difficult that "adult book" stores multiplied. As a result of legislative changes in a few states, but especially as a result of Supreme Court decisions, abortion ceased to be illegal under most circumstances, if performed under medical supervision. Similarly, a concerted effort began to persuade legislators to modify or eliminate the laws against marijuana and to convince the courts that such laws be found unconstitutional. Finally, a number of states established lotteries, and New York established a government-run offtrack betting (OTB) system. Proponents argue that state-run gambling helps the states to raise much-needed revenue and will also reduce the profits of illegal gambling.

CRIME AGAINST KANSAS. *See* **Brooks-Summer Affair.**

CRIME COMMISSIONS. Although entering the American sociopolitical scene only at the beginning of the 20th century, crime commissions had their genesis in the civic action groups formed during the previous three decades to counter inefficiency and corruption in law enforcement. Notable among these forerunners were the Society for the Suppression of Vice (New York City, 1873), the New England Watch and Ward Society (Boston, 1878), and the Society for the Prevention of Crime (New York City, 1878). Between 1900 and 1950, major urban and state commissions were established to research problems of the administration of justice and to propose amelioration. After World War II the formation of commissions mushroomed. Crime commissions have sought to initiate research and educate the public and the profession concerning crime and law enforcement. One of the most productive commissions has been the National Council on Crime and Delinquency, founded as the National Probation and Parole Association in 1907. More recently, federal crime commissions have been established for special purposes: the National Commission on Law Observance and Enforcement (1925–31), the U.S. Senate (Kefauver) Committee to Investigate Organized Crime (1950–51), and the President's Commission on Law Enforcement and Administration of Justice (1965).

CRIME CONTROL ACTS (1934). To counteract a rapid increase in racketeering, kidnaping, and other forms of crime, six new crime laws were enacted (May 18) by Congress. These laws empowered the federal government to punish persons assaulting, resisting, killing, or interfering with federal agents performing their duties and authorized the death penalty for kidnapers taking their victims across state lines. The federal criminal code was further strengthened by the Crime Prevention Compact Act (June 16), which permitted the states to enter into compacts for the prevention of crime and the enforcement of criminal laws.

CRIME OF 1873. Applied to the coinage law of Feb. 12, 1873. The law constituted a virtual codification of the then extant laws relating to the mints and coinage. The omission of the standard silver dollar became, for more than two decades after 1876, the Crime of 1873. The movement for the free coinage of silver began about 1876, when decreased use of silver as a monetary metal and increased production caused the price of silver to decline. The leaders defended the bimetallic standard and charged that the demonetization of silver was the result of a conspiracy entered into by British and American financial interests to secure the adoption of the gold standard in the United States. The "silverites" clung to the plot theory in spite of the fact that the 1873 act was simply a legal recognition that the silver dollar had not been in circulation for decades; that the act was considered in five sessions of Congress, read repeatedly, debated exhaustively, and discussed frequently by Treasury officials. For two decades millions of people thought that a crime had been committed and voted their convictions at every opportunity.

CRIPPLE CREEK MINING BOOM. The district immediately southwest of Pikes Peak in Colorado was a cattle ranch until Robert Womack discovered a promising gold vein in January 1891. On July 4, W. S. Stratton staked the Independence claim that was to bring him wealth and preeminence as a mine operator. A mining district was organized. The owners of the cattle ranch plotted the city of Cripple Creek. Fires and serious labor strikes interrupted production during the 1890's. The district's gold output reached $50 million in 1900 and thereafter declined. More than $500 million worth of gold has been taken from mines in Cripple Creek.

CRIPPLE CREEK STRIKES. In August 1893 the mine workers of Cripple Creek, Colo., by striking, prevented the lengthening of the working day. A period of rapid unionization of the miners and organization of the mine operators was followed by a serious strike in January 1894. A period of peace was ended by the bitter strike of 1903–04 when well-organized, well-financed, and politically powerful unions were defeated by the mine owners. Loss of life, destruction of property, abuse of the state militia power, and the practical elimination of unions in the mining district resulted.

***CRISIS*.** A series of patriotic political pamphlets written by Thomas Paine during the Revolution. The first appeared in the *Pennsylvania Journal* on Dec. 19, 1776, and began with the famous sentence "These are the times which try men's souls." There were twelve major pamphlets and four supernumerary ones. *The Crisis* was also the title of a states' rights pamphlet written by Robert J. Turnbull in 1827.

CRITTENDEN COMPROMISE (1860). The most important proposal made in the attempt to resolve the conflict between North and South peacefully. The plan, presented to the U.S. Senate on Dec. 18 by Sen. J. J. Crittenden of Kentucky, proposed six articles as amendments to the Constitution and four resolutions. The heart of the compromise was in the first article, which provided that north of 36°30′, the line of the Missouri Compromise, in all territory then held or thereafter acquired, slavery would be prohibited and that south of the line slavery would be protected as property.

The plan was the chief subject of consideration by the Senate Committee of Thirteen, the House Committee of Thirty-three, and the Peace Convention in Washington. It was defeated on Dec. 22 in the crucial Committee of Thirteen, chiefly because the Republicans, in consultation with Abraham Lincoln, then president-elect, refused to yield on prohibition of slavery in the territories.

CRITTENDEN RESOLUTION (July 22, 1861). The House of Representative announced, in a resolution put forward by J. J. Crittenden of Kentucky, that the North's objectives in the Civil War were to preserve the Constitution and the Union and not to interfere with slavery or to subjugate the South. A similar resolution introduced in the Senate by Andrew Johnson was passed July 25.

CROGHAN'S EXPEDITIONS TO ILLINOIS (1765). French cession of the Illinois country was included in the Treaty of Paris of 1763. For two years, however, the victorious British were frustrated in attempts to occupy the country because of hostile Indians. Peaceful negotiation fell to George Croghan, a renowned Indian agent. On May 15, he left Fort Pitt and proceeded down the Ohio with two boatloads of gifts and a contingent of deputies from friendly Ohio tribes. On June 8, a short distance below the mouth of the Wabash, the party was attacked by Kickapoo and Mascouten warriors. Croghan was tomahawked, taken prisoner, and forced to march to Ouiatenon, near present-day Lafayette, Ind. A dawning awareness of Croghan's importance and a fear of reprisals led to his release on July 1; the Wabash tribes agreed to peace and future British occupation. A short time later, deputies of the Illinois tribes arrived in Ouiatenon, conferred with Croghan, and accepted British authority.

Croghan's second expedition to Illinois, consisting of seventeen bateaux, set out from Fort Pitt on June 18, 1766. His ostensible purpose was to meet with the tribes and distribute gifts, but he also wanted to assess prospects for a colony there. He arrived at Fort de Chartres on Aug. 20, and in conferences on Aug. 25–26 the Indians formally confirmed their acceptance of British authority.

CROMPTON LOOM. The first successful power loom for making fancy cotton fabrics; invented and patented in 1837 by William Crompton, an English weaver who had settled in Massachusetts. Crompton adapted this loom to the manufacture of fancy cassimeres at Lowell and thus introduced a new era in wool manufacture.

CROP LOAN ACT (Feb. 23, 1934). Authorized the Farm Credit Administration to extend loans to farmers for crop production and harvesting. A fund of $40 million was set up for this purpose. Approximately $38 million was loaned.

CROSS KEYS, BATTLE OF (June 8, 1862). An engagement near Harrisonburg, Va., during Confederate Gen. T. J. "Stonewall" Jackson's retreat up the Shenandoah Valley. Confederate Gen. Richard Ewell, with 6,000 infantry and 500 cavalry, repulsed an attack by Gen. John Frémont's Union force of 10,000 infantry and 2,000 cavalry.

"CROSS OF GOLD" SPEECH. "You shall not press down upon the brow of labor this crown of thorns, you shall not crucify mankind upon a cross of gold." So William Jennings Bryan, a delegate from Nebraska, concluded his attack upon the single gold standard before the Democratic National Convention at Chicago on July 8, 1896. The free-silver delegates, recognizing in Bryan the leader they had sought, made him the convention nominee.

CROSWELL LIBEL SUIT. Harry Croswell in 1802 published in the *Wasp* an attack on President Thomas Jefferson for which he was convicted of criminal libel. According to traditional legal procedure, no evidence except the fact of publication was admitted. In an appeal to the state supreme court Alexander Hamilton argued for the right to submit the truth of the case in evidence. His plea was instrumental in liberalizing the libel law of the state by an act of Apr. 6, 1805, and achieved an outstanding victory for freedom of the press.

CROWBAR LAW OF OHIO (Feb. 8, 1819). Taxed branches of the Bank of the United States and authorized the state officers, if necessary, to collect the tax by opening every chest of the bank. Despite an injunction, state officers took $100,000 from the branch at Chillicothe. The Supreme Court forced the return of the money, holding that a state could not tax a federal instrumentality.

CROWN LANDS. When America was colonized by the English, all lands available for settlement were considered land pertaining to the crown. Therefore, England was able to alienate these lands through royal patent, under whatever conditions seemed desirable. This land was, therefore, crown land. When land became either proprietorial land or land belonging to the corporate colonies, it was subject only to those incidental charges laid down in the patents, such as mining precious metals or protecting white-pine masting timber.

CROWN POINT. A promontory on the west shore of Lake Champlain in northern New York, a bone of contention between New France and the English colonies. In 1690 a scouting party from Albany erected the temporary Little Stone Fort near Crown Point. Gov. Charles de Beauharnois of New France in 1730 sent a small force to the point to intercept traders from Albany, and in the next year Louis XV ordered a fort built. It was named Fort St. Frederic.

Only 110 miles from Albany, Fort St. Frederic served as a base for French raiding parties against New York and New England. Not until July 31, 1759, did Lord Jeffrey Amherst force the French to blow up the fort and retreat. Amherst then built a huge new fortress, called Crown Point or Amherst by the British, but in 1773 it was almost completely destroyed by fire. Col. Seth Warner and the Green Mountain Boys easily took Crown Point from its small garrison on May 12, 1775. During the Revolution it served mainly as an advance post of Fort Ticonderoga. In 1910 it became a state park.

CROWN POINT TO NO. 4. After the capture of Crown Point by Gen. Jeffrey Amherst in 1759, in the French and Indian War, he ordered a road cut through the wilderness of what is now Vermont to old Post No. 4 at Charlestown on the Connecticut River. The road facilitated movement of troops and supplies from the east in Amherst's campaign against Montreal and also served as an important military pathway during the Revolution.

CROW WING, BATTLE OF. *See* **Sioux-Chippewa War.**

CROZAT GRANT. France, in 1712, granted Antoine Crozat a charter of government and monopoly over Louisiana. He was responsible for all expense of government. His governor secured few results, so Crozat gave up his grant in 1717.

CRUISERS. *See* **Warships.**

CRYSTAL PALACE EXPOSITION. *See* **Exhibition of the Industry of all Nations.**

C.S.A. COTTON. In 1861–63 the Confederates issued bonds that were paid for in baled cotton. Owing to the marking on the bales, this was commonly known as C.S.A. (Confederate States of America) cotton.

CUBA. American commercial interest in Cuba predates the American Revolution, which was in fact precipitated partly by British restriction of colonial trade with Cuba. Although economic interest became a crucial determinant, early U.S. policy emphasized strategic considerations. The United States was willing to allow a weak Spain to maintain its colonial occupation, with the expectation that Cuba would gravitate into American control once Spain lost its colony. The United States vetoed foreign proposals to liberate the island during the Spanish-American independence wars (1810–24) and discouraged Cuban independence.

U.S. interest in acquiring Cuba heightened during the 1840's and 1850's. In 1853, President Franklin Pierce offered to purchase the island but was sharply refused. In response, the American minister to Madrid, Pierre Soulé, in collaboration with England and France, issued the Ostend Manifesto (1854), which claimed the right of the United States either to purchase Cuba or take it without Spanish consent. The document was officially repudiated, but it revealed the depth of American sentiment. Southern expansionists desired to add Cuba as a slave state. Although American slaveowners found some support among Cuban planters, their efforts were blocked by northern antislavery opposition. The Civil War effectively ended efforts to purchase Cuba.

In 1868, Cuban insurgents launched the first of their wars for independence. The Ten Years' War cost heavily in lives and property. Unable to overcome Spain alone, the rebels sought U.S. aid. Arms and matériel were sent despite an official policy of neutrality. An agreement between Spain and Cuba ended the war in 1878, but the provisions for home rule and amnesty were not implemented. New taxes and restrictions were imposed, and in 1894 Spain canceled Cuba's trade agreement with the United States.

In February 1895, Cubans reopened their war for independence; as before, the United States maintained official neutrality, but Cuban exiles led by José Martí used it as a base for operations. A government-in-exile was established; funds were raised; men recruited and trained; and an invasion prepared. Initial landings and campaigns in Cuba were successful, but the Spanish recovered and the war dragged on.

Several factors combined to force a declaration of war against Spain by the United States in April 1898: pro-Cuban sentiment, the expansionist spirit of late 19th-century America, and public anger over the sinking of the battleship *Maine* on Feb. 15, 1898, in Havana harbor. Following a brief campaign, American forces occupied Cuba. The occupation, lasting from 1898 to 1902, was limited by the Teller Amendment, which forbade the United States to exercise sovereignty over the island longer than necessary to assure pacification. Nevertheless, demands for complete independence increased. Washington instructed the military authorities to call a constitutional assembly in 1900.

By February 1901 the Cuban assembly had written a constitution, but it had failed to define Cuba's relationship with the United States. The result was the Platt Amendment, which limited Cuba's treaty-making power and freedom to contract debts; permitted the United States to establish naval bases in Cuba; and allowed American intervention to preserve independence or internal order.

From 1902, when the American occupation ended, until 1934, when the Platt Amendment was abrogated, the United States did intervene. The first intervention occurred in 1906, following a revolt against Cuban president Tomás Estrada Palma. Following another revolt in 1917 over a fraudulent election, American troops again restored order. In January 1921, when the Cuban economy collapsed as a result of falling sugar prices, President Woodrow Wilson sent Gen. Enoch Crowder to Havana as an adviser. During this era, foreign capital (mostly American) poured into Cuba as private investment and public loans. In 1933 economic stress and disenchantment with the corrupt presidency of Gerardo Machado y Morales resulted in the final American intervention under the Platt Amendment. In May 1933, President Franklin D. Roosevelt sent Sumner Welles as ambassador. Welles offered to cancel the Platt Amendment; in return he sought guarantees for U.S. economic interests. Machado was deposed before he could achieve any results. Roosevelt refused to recognize the reform-minded liberal government that was established, forcing the installation of conservatives. By 1934 civilian government was restored, backed by Cuban army strongman Fulgencio Batista Zaldívar. Washington then abrogated the Platt Amendment; further, Cuba was assigned a quota of U.S. sugar and preferential treatment for other products; the Cubans conceded preferential treatment to a long list of U.S. industrial products.

During the Batista era (1934–59), relations were close. American capital was welcome, and no official objections were raised over the U.S. presence at the Guantánamo Bay naval base.

The United States responded moderately to the revolutionary government of Fidel Castro when it came to power in January 1959, despite the expropriation of American properties. However, in July 1960, responding to congressional pressure and Castro's allegations of U.S. economic aggression, President Dwight Eisenhower canceled the sugar quota and embargoed exports to Cuba. Relations strained as Cuba nationalized American properties, sought closer ties to the Soviet bloc, and promoted revolutionary activities in Latin America. In January 1961 the United States severed relations with Cuba.

Beginning in the summer of 1960, Cuban groups opposed to the Castro regime were funded and trained by the U.S. Central Intelligence Agency (CIA). In April 1961, President John F. Kennedy authorized a CIA-organized invasion by opposition groups that hoped to depose Castro. The landing, at the Bay of Pigs, resulted in total defeat.

In January 1962 the United States obtained Cuba's expulsion from the Organization of American States (OAS) on the ground that Cuba was supporting subversion in the hemisphere. Cuba turned to the Soviet Union. The Soviets provided economic and military support, including nuclear missiles. President Kennedy declared a quarantine on the shipment of offensive weapons to Cuba on Oct. 24, 1962, and an American invasion force was prepared. Less than a week later the Soviet Union agreed to withdraw all nuclear missiles.

Throughout the 1960's, relations remained hostile. The United States continued economic sanctions and exerted diplomatic pressure on trading partners of Cuba outside the Soviet bloc. However, by the early 1970's several Latin-American governments renewed relations with Cuba, while the administration of President Richard Nixon appeared to be reappraising its Cuban policy.

Some improvement in relations was expected after a five-year agreement to curb aircraft and ship hijackings between the two countries was signed in 1973. However, the United States continued its diplomatic and trade boycott, and the Cubans refused to negotiate while the boycott existed. In 1974 the United States refused to support an OAS vote to end sanctions against Cuba. This contributed to the defeat of the motion. But in 1975 relations began to improve. On Mar. 1, Secretary of State Henry Kissinger said that the United States was "prepared to move in a new direction" in its Cuban policy, and Castro called for improved relations with the United States. In 1977, partial diplomatic relations were renewed with the establishment of the U.S. "interest section" in Havana. But the U.S.-Cuban détente was hampered because of the continuing U.S. economic blockade, unsettled claims by Americans, and Cuba's presence in Africa. In 1980, Castro let some 120,000 Cubans, including about 1,800 criminals, emigrate to the United States, which further strained relations. The conservative policy of the Ronald Reagan administration in the early 1980's saw a growing tension between the two countries.

CUBAN MISSILE CRISIS (1962). By August it was common knowledge that the Soviet Union was engaged in a large-scale military buildup in Cuba. As Soviet arms and men piled up in Cuba, the public clamor for President John F. Kennedy to "do something" increased. On Sept. 26, Congress adopted a resolution that Kennedy interpreted as a demand for action if the Cubans threatened violence to the rest of the hemisphere. On Oct. 21 he went on television to announce that he was putting a strict quarantine on all offensive military equipment being shipped to Cuba; had ordered stepped-up surveillance of Cuba, and had directed the armed forces "to prepare for any eventualities." On Oct. 24 the deadline for the imposition of the quarantine passed without incident. Soviet ships approaching Cuba changed course. Soviet Premier Nikita Khrushchev, in a letter to British pacifist Bertrand Russell, castigated the United States but also suggested a summit meeting to avert war. On Oct. 28, Khrushchev formally capitulated.

CULLOM COMMITTEE. Sen. Shelby M. Cullom of Illinois was made chairman of the Committee on Interstate Commerce in 1883. Cullom launched an investigation of the railroads, out of the findings of which developed the Interstate Commerce Act of 1887.

CULPEPER'S REBELLION (1677–79). The Albemarle colony in the northern part of Carolina raised tobacco. The 17th-century navigation acts denied it a free market outside England, and heavy duties kept northern merchants from coming to buy. Feelings of repression found an object in the acting governor, Thomas Miller, also customs collector. The insurrection came to a head in 1677 with John Culpeper and George Durant as leaders. They imprisoned Miller and most of his council, took over all public records, established courts of justice, and convened an assembly. For two years they administered affairs. Culpeper went to England, promising submission to proper authority. Miller in the meantime escaped, went to England, and charged Culpeper with treason and embezzlement. Culpeper found support in the Earl of Shaftesbury, a proprietor of Carolina, who maintained that no regular government had existed in Carolina at the time of the rebellion, since Miller's appointment had been improperly made, and that the colonists' actions were not treasonable. Culpeper was acquitted.

CUMBERLAND, ARMY OF THE. Originally the Army of the Ohio, commanded by Gen. D. C. Buell, but renamed when Gen. W. S. Rosecrans took command on Oct. 30, 1862. Rosecrans was succeeded by Gen. George H. Thomas on Oct. 16, 1863. The Army of the Cumberland played an important part in many battles and in Sherman's Atlanta campaign.

CUMBERLAND, FORT. At the junction of the Potomac River and Wills Creek, within the present limits of Cumberland, Md., the Ohio Company of Virginia built a storehouse in 1750. In 1754 a small fort was constructed by colonial troops and called Fort Mount Pleasant. A larger fort was erected in 1755 for Edward Braddock's expedition against Fort Duquesne and was renamed Fort Cumberland in honor of the Duke of Cumberland. Abandoned in 1765, it was not occupied again except during the Whiskey Rebellion.

CUMBERLAND COMPACT. *See* **Cumberland Settlements.**

CUMBERLAND GAP. A pass in the Appalachian Highlands about forty-five miles northeast of Knoxville, Tenn. For centuries, the defile allowed the Warrior's Path of Kentucky to connect with the trails used by Indians and buffalo. Dr. Thomas Walker named the gap in 1750; by 1800, thousands of hunters and settlers had used the pass to enter Kentucky. Through it passed Daniel Boone's party and the Long Hunters in the late 1760's and in 1775. A mail route through the gap to Danville was established in 1792. In 1797 the first tollgate in Kentucky was located on this road. During the Civil War, Confederates occupied the gap very early but retired in June 1862 to strengthen their hold on Chattanooga. On Aug. 30 they occupied it again. Union forces retook it in September 1863. Railroads reached the pass in 1889 and 1890, and today a major highway uses the gateway.

CUMBERLAND PRESBYTERIAN CHURCH. Formed in 1810 by a separation of the Cumberland presbytery of eastern Tennessee and Kentucky from the Presbyterian church, caused by the Synod of Kentucky (1806) dissolving the Cumberland presbytery for ordaining uneducated ministers during the Great Revival. The church grew rapidly and, in 1813, formed the Cumberland Synod of three presbyteries; in 1829 a general assembly was formed. In 1906 they united with the Southern Presbyterian Church (the Presbyterian Church in the United States). In 1980 the Cumberland Presbyterian Church had 94,574 members.

CUMBERLAND RIVER. Flows through southern Kentucky and northern Tennessee; named by Dr. Thomas Walker in 1750. Near it and not far from Barbourville, Ky., Walker's exploring party built the first known cabin in Kentucky and there spent the winter of 1750–51.

CUMBERLAND ROAD (United States Road, National Road, National Turnpike). First national road in the United States. Congress in March 1806 provided for the marketing and construction of the road from Cumberland, Md., as the eastern terminus, to the Ohio River. Construction began in 1811, and by 1818 the U.S. mail was running over it to Wheeling, now in West Virginia. In general, the route followed Braddock's Road. Maryland, Pennsylvania, and Ohio each gave permission for the building of the road within their boundaries. In March 1825, Congress appropriated funds for extending the road from Wheeling to Zanesville, Ohio. Over this route the highway followed Zane's Trace, which at Zanesville turned southwestward to Lancaster, Chillicothe, and the Ohio River. Parts were later turned over to Maryland, Pennsylvania, Ohio, and Virginia (1831–34), some tollgates being erected by the states. The highway was completed in Indiana and Illinois only after the federal government had relinquished control. The road to Vandalia, Ill., its western terminus, was 591 miles in length, built at a cost of almost $7 million to the federal government. The Cumberland Road is now U.S. Route 40.

CUMBERLAND ROAD, TENNESSEE. Ran from eastern Tennessee to the Cumberland settlements (not to be confused with the national Cumberland Road); was opened in 1795. It began at Southwest Point, ran through Cherokee territory to Fort Blount on the Cumberland, and down the north side of the river to Nashville. It became a post route in 1797.

CUMBERLAND SETTLEMENTS. The immense domain acquired from the Cherokee by the Transylvania Company in March 1775 by the Treaty of Sycamore Shoals covered lands on the Cumberland River and below. Richard Henderson, leader of the Transylvania Company, had several forts constructed, around which settlements formed. After the survey of the state line demonstrated that the region was in North Carolina and not Virginia, Henderson went to French Lick (Nashville, Tenn.) in April 1780 and organized a government under articles drafted by him known as the Cumberland Compact. This instrument embodied agreements between the Transylvania Company and the settlers respecting lands to be acquired from the company. The legislature of North Carolina, in 1783, declared the Transylvania purchase void but provided for Henderson and his associates a consolation grant of 200,000 acres of land on Clinch and Powell rivers.

***CUMMINGS* V. *MISSOURI*,** 4 Wallace 277 (1866). The U.S. Supreme Court invalidated a provision in the Missouri constitution of 1865 requiring public and corporation officers, attorneys, teachers, and clergymen to take an expurgatory oath before practicing their professions, since it violated the federal constitutional prohibition of bills of attainder.

CURFEW BELL. A bell that was tolled at a fixed hour of night. The curfew signal still survives in some towns to apprise citizens of the time. Legal measures prohibiting nocturnal activities of various kinds are often referred to as curfew laws. In the South, slaves were warned from the streets after nine o'clock unless they had a pass from their owners.

CURRENCY. *See* **Coinage; Money.**

CURRENCY, CONTINENTAL. Bills of credit issued by the Continental Congress and the states to assist in financing the Revolution. The first issue, $2 million, was voted on June 22, 1775, shortly after the Battle of Bunker Hill. Between then and Nov. 29, 1779, the Continental Congress authorized total issues of $241,552,780. The states issued bills in the amount of $209,524,776. This was a tremendous amount of currency, considering the population, and it shortly began to depreciate. By January 1781, it was valued at 100–1 and by May had practically lost its value. The phrase "not worth a Continental" comes from this period. Finally, under the funding act of 1790, the old continental issues were accepted in subscription of U.S. stock (bonds) at the rate of 100–1.

CURRENCY, RED DOG AND BLUE PUP. Nicknames applied to state bank notes in the era following the end of the Second Bank of the United States when the circulating medium was largely the badly secured and fluctuating paper of the "wildcat" banks. The name probably comes from engraved designs in some of the notes.

CURRIER & IVES. Nathaniel Currier, a lithographer, began issuing original colored prints in New York City in 1835. James M. Ives joined the firm in 1850, and in 1857 became a partner. The firm's prints—sentimental, journalistic, sporting, humorous, and historical—became tremendously popular. Currier retired in 1880, and his son Edward succeeded him. When Ives died in 1895, his interests were inherited by his son Chauncey. In 1902, Chauncey Ives bought out Currier. In 1907, Ives sold the firm to Daniel Logan, who went out of business a few years later.

CUSHING'S TREATY (or Treaty of Wanghia; July 3, 1844). Opened political relations between the United States and China and, through establishment of the most-favored-nation doctrine in matters of commerce, secured for the United States the trading privileges won by England as a result of the Opium War. It introduced the principle of extraterritoriality in the relations between China and the West.

CUSTOMS SERVICE, UNITED STATES. Colonial Period. As early as 1621, the Navigation Acts of the British Empire specified the colony of Virginia as a port of entry for goods and the collection of customs. In 1671, Virginia's royal customs officer, first in the colonies, was appointed. Colonial customs administration was as concerned with the detection of fraud and smuggling as with assessment of duties. Many collectors suffered rough treatment and even death. By 1767 the British saw the need for a Board of Customs Commissioners in Boston, but the customs machinery could not prevent the growth of smuggling.

The New Republic. Under the Articles of Confederation (1781), it soon became apparent that the national treasury could not rely on the states for funds. Consequently, the Constitution gave Congress the power "to lay and collect Taxes, Duties, Imposts, and Excises [and] to regulate Commerce with foreign Nations." The first Tariff Act was passed on July 4, 1789. Customs districts, ports of entry, and customs officers were established.

Tariff Administration. The first Tariff Act was protective. A 5 percent duty was retained on all goods not otherwise enumerated. Higher ad valorem rates were fixed on certain luxury items. Specific duties intended to stimulate domestic production were imposed on selected articles.

Protectionism caused a continuing battle between the North, which wanted high rates on manufactured goods and low rates on raw materials, and the South, which wanted the opposite. This was a contributing cause of the Civil War. Even after the war, the debate continued in national politics.

The Tariff Acts of 1922 and 1930 created some semblance of stability. The 1930 act set tariff rates and granted authority to the Treasury Department to issue customs regulations for its administration. Its many amendments include the Antismuggling Act of 1935, trade agreements, the Customs Administration Act of 1938, and customs simplification acts. Later, rates of duty were drastically reduced, especially by the Kennedy Round of tariff negotiations (1964–67).

Revenue. During the first year of operation (1789–90), the Customs Service collected duties of over $2 million. Until 1860 (except during the low-tariff decade 1831–40), duties comprised 80–90 percent of the government's revenues, and thereafter until 1910, from 45–55 percent. Following passage of personal income tax legislation in 1913, customs revenues became only a fraction of total federal receipts, thus largely divorcing tariff considerations from those of revenue. Customs revenues totaled about $7.5 billion in 1980.

Administration. For sixty years, salaries and other expenses of the U.S. Customs Service were deducted from duties and the balance transferred to the treasury. Congress amended the law in 1849 so that all receipts would be paid into the treasury. In 1875 the Division of Customs was created. In 1913, 49 customs districts replaced 126 districts and 38 independent ports. Customs collectors were placed on a regular salary.

The Bureau of Customs, created in 1927, provided for a commissioner appointed by the secretary of the treasury. The bureau also assumed the investigative functions of the Special Agency Service to combat fraud and smuggling.

The customs border patrol was transferred to the Customs Agency Service in 1936, and four patrol districts were created. In March 1960, customs enforcement officers were transferred to the offices of supervising customs agents and the headquarters office was renamed the Division of Investigations and Enforcement (later the Office of Investigations).

The expansion of the economy and growth of international trade and commerce prompted decentralization of the Customs Service in 1965. A field organization consisting of nine regional offices and more than forty districts was established to supervise nearly 300 ports of entry. Presidentially appointed collectors and comptrollers of customs were eliminated, and all field positions filled by Civil Service selection.

Mission and Responsibilities. Many laws passed after the first tariff act added to customs officers' duties. In 1790 they were directed to pay military pensions. An act of July 16, 1798, created the Marine Hospital Service and required collectors to gather hospital dues of 20 cents a month for the relief of sick and disabled seamen. Early collectors also reported statistics on imports and exports and supervised the revenue cutter service. Other acts concerned the safety of passengers and the collection of statistics on immigrants.

Succeeding congresses charged the Customs Service with more and more functions. In 1917 it was chosen to enforce the Espionage Act and the Trading with the Enemy Act, acts that required increased examination of outgoing and incoming passengers and ships. Customs officers also acted as local agents of the Bureau of War Risk Insurance.

In April 1917, customs officers seized sixty-five German and fourteen Austrian ships lying in American ports for violations of neutrality laws. The Port of New York, soon the key staging area in the country's war effort, became the headquarters of the Customs Intelligence Bureau (CIB). The CIB issued certificates of citizenship to American seamen, mustered crews of incoming vessels and issued identification cards, guarded vessels to prevent persons from landing or boarding without permits, and maintained surveillance of all craft to prevent acts of sabotage. This unit was disbanded in 1919. During World War II, customs handled similar responsibilities, including censorship. During Prohibition (1920–33) the U.S. Customs Border Patrol chased rumrunners on the Great Lakes and the Atlantic and Gulf coasts and along both borders.

Although the customs work force nearly doubled from 1965 to 1975, its work load more than quadrupled. A major responsibility in the 1970's has been the war to halt the flow of narcotics and dangerous drugs into the country. During the skyjacking crisis, customs recruited and trained over 1,000 air security officers. New laws protecting the environment and the quality of life added to customs responsibilities, including motor vehicle safety and emissions control, pesticide control, and marine mammal protection.

CYCLES, BUSINESS. *See* **Business Cycles.**

CYCLONES. *See* **Tornadoes.**

DADE MASSACRE (Dec. 28, 1835)**.** On Dec. 23, 1835, at the outbreak of the Second Seminole War, Maj. Francis L. Dade, with a force of 112, left Fort Brooke on Tampa Bay to reinforce the garrison at Fort King, about 130 miles to the northeast. The Indians learned of the troop movements and decided on open country for their attack. The morning of Dec. 28 was chilly, and the soldiers were unprepared, having buttoned their overcoats over their ammunition boxes. The Indians hid in patches of saw palmetto, and at eight o'clock they launched their attack. There were only four survivors.

DAHLGREN'S AND KILPATRICK'S RAID (Mar. 1, 1864). Planning to release the Union prisoners in Richmond, Va., Gen. Judson Kilpatrick, with 4,000 cavalry, arrived north of Richmond. Some skirmishing took place while he awaited the arrival of Col. Ulric Dahlgren with 500 men. Dahlgren arrived several miles from Richmond and encountered heavy musketry; he decided to delay his attack. Kilpatrick, not realizing Dahlgren was nearby, abandoned his attempt to enter Richmond. The next day, Dahlgren advanced on the city, but was killed and many of his men captured.

DAIRY INDUSTRY. Cattle were imported into the colonies in the early 17th century. There were no specific dairy breeds; animals were identified by size and color, and they soon lost weight and shape through poor management and interbreeding. Only in New England, where animals grazed under the care of a town cowherd, was there much control over breeding. Almost every farm and most town households kept one or two cows. In winter the milk was used for butter and cheese. Some dairy produce was exported before 1700. By the mid-18th century, some areas were noted for prime butter or cheese. Exports stimulated better management even before the Revolution. Between 1790 and 1805, cheese exports exceeded 1 million pounds annually.

Commercial growth was rapid from the late 1820's. In 1840, dairy manufactures, valued at $33.8 million, were reported from all thirty states. New York, Pennsylvania, and Massachusetts were the largest producers, Vermont and New Hampshire the most specialized. Outside the Northeast, only Ohio and Virginia were large producers. By 1860, butter output increased notably in Vermont, New York, Pennsylvania, Ohio, and Illinois. Cheese output, concentrated in Vermont, New York, and Ohio, lagged after 1850. New York remained the heart of "America's dairyland" until displaced by Wisconsin in the opening decades of the 20th century.

The perishable nature of milk limited the city milk trade, the most profitable branch of dairying. Fresh milk was only available locally in season. Most big-city milk supplies were watered, adulterated, expensive, and more lethal than city water. Between 1856 and 1861, Massachusetts outlawed adulteration and slop feeding and instituted nominal inspection. New York and five other states followed suit, but until local milk trains—put into operation around Boston and New York City in the early 1840's—had supplanted barges, wagons, and slop-milk systems, little progress was made. Gail Borden began to make patented condensed milk in 1859. Dr. Harvey D. Thatcher's sanitary dairy bottle (1884) and Dr. Henry L. Coit's medically "certified milk" (1894) eased contamination; but the real solution, pasteurization, was demonstrated by New York philanthropist Nathan Strauss in 1893. By the 1920's, milk from tuberculin-tested herds was also on the market. Finally, between 1924 and 1927 the U.S. Public Health Service developed a model uniform sanitary regulation for voluntary adoption by state and municipal authorities.

A radical change in the dairy industry began with the shift from farm to factory cheesemaking. The factory system of cheesemaking, inaugurated by Jesse Williams of Oneida County, N.Y., in 1851, spread during the Civil War decade; annual output soared to 172 million pounds by 1880, the most notable increase coming in Wisconsin, already third after New York and Ohio. By 1876, exports of cheddar-type American cheese regularly absorbed half the nation's output. Wisconsin became the banner cheese state by 1905.

The first butter factory, or "creamery," was established by Alanson Slaughter of Orange County, N.Y., in 1861, but farm production of butter increased until about 1900. Creamery output (notably in Iowa, Illinois, Wisconsin, and Pennsylvania) did not accelerate before the 1880's, when over 3,000 refrigerator cars were already in service. In 1878, Dr. Carl G. DeLaval of Sweden patented a continuous centrifugal cream separator, which proved much more efficient than gravity methods; after 1885 he also marketed small hand separators for use on farms.

All dairymen benefited from a butterfat test perfected by Wisconsin chemist Stephen M. Babcock in 1890. The test measured the fat content of milk and furnished a more objective and equitable basis for payments to farmers by processing plants and city dealers. Babcock also did the basic research on milk enzymes that culminated after 1903 in the more efficient "cold curing" of cheese. State dairy and food commissions were appointed to police the industry, and the promotional energies of dairymen's associations were diverted into lobbying actions to secure tariff protection (1894) and curbs and taxes on oleomargarine. By 1950, when the discriminatory Oleomargarine Act of 1902 was repealed, margarine output was rapidly overtaking that of butter.

Advances in dairy husbandry began in the 1880's with the practice of feeding the animals ensilage (such fodder as unripened corn, clover, and alfalfa). The storage of feed in silos lengthened the milking season up to 10 weeks, allowing manufacturing plants to stay open throughout the year. Adaptation of German scientific feeding principles resulted in a balanced dairy ration. These farms adopted milking machines in the 1920's and installed cooling equipment later. Milk output doubled between 1900 and 1960 and peaked at 124 billion pounds in 1979. The greatest relative increases occurred in new dairy states such as Florida, Arizona, and California. Between 1950 and 1970, the number of farms reporting milk cows fell by 80 percent and thousands of small dairymen went out of business. Nevertheless, milk products were second only to sales of cattle and calves in cash value to U.S. farmers.

DAKOTA (Indians). The Dakota are represented in western Minnesota, North Dakota, South Dakota, and eastern Montana and Wyoming by seven main tribes and a number of lesser tribal or band groupings. These are groups sometimes categorized as Sioux, primarily a linguistic reference. The Siouan-speaking peoples—including the Hidatsa, Assiniboine, and linguistically more remote Mandan—appear to have come out of the Woodlands into the Plains in late prehistoric or early historic times.

The Dakota gave primary allegiance to the band, the broadly spread local group, rather than to the tribe as such. Convocations of several bands for bison hunting or war gave rise to a tribal sense. Taken together, the Dakota peoples formed one of the larger Plains Indian groups, numbering about 25,000 in 1780. By this time the equestrian mode of life was fully integrated in the Plains; by then horticulture had been abandoned in favor of the classic Plains hunting pattern. With the horse, the Dakota moved as bands across their vast territory, exploiting the bison in the grasslands and engaging in warfare. Given their basic Plains orientation, the various Dakota took on all the material, social, and ceremonial trappings associated with the area: the tipi, the use of buckskin, beadwork, skin painting, extremely strong social ties, and the ritual and religious features of vision quest, Sun Dance, and medicine bundles or fetish objects.

The gold rush of the 1870's into the Black Hills, with its encroachment on Indian lands, created solidarity among the Dakota peoples. Their alliance, fanned by the spread of the Ghost Dance, brought the Dakota, notably the Teton, together with the Cheyenne and culminated in the 1876 battle at the Little Bighorn. A second Ghost Dance movement resulted in the Battle of Wounded Knee in December 1890. Dakota are currently to be found on former Indian land reserves in North and South Dakota.

DAKOTA EXPEDITIONS OF SIBLEY AND SULLY (1863–65). In 1863, Union Gen. H. H. Sibley was ordered to march from Camp Pope against the Dakota and drive them west toward the Missouri River, where Gen. Alfred Sully was to intercept the Indians before they could cross the river. Sibley set out on June 16 and established his field base at Camp Atcheson, in what is now Griggs County, N.Dak. He defeated the Indians at Big Mound, Dead Buffalo Lake, and Stony Lake. He established his camp at the mouth of Apple Creek, near the site of present Bismarck, N.Dak., and waited for news of Sully's command. On Aug. 1 he began his return march to Fort Abercrombie, which he reached Aug. 23.

Meanwhile, Sully had established his headquarters at Sioux City, Iowa. He was seriously delayed by lack of equipment and the low stage of the Missouri River. The steamboat accompanying him carried his supplies to Fort Pierre, S.Dak. On Aug. 13 he left for a quick march northward. On Aug. 30 he learned that Sibley's army had already left the area and Indians had recrossed the Missouri. On Sept. 3 he won a battle at the present site of Whitestone Hill, N.Dak., and returned to Fort Pierre.

The second campaign was conducted by Sully in the summer of 1864. His army proceeded up the Missouri River from Sioux City to the site of the new army post at Fort Rice, N.Dak. Leaving part of his force to construct the fort, he marched northwest to the Indian camp located in the Killdeer Mountains. A battle was fought July 28, and the Indians were defeated and scattered.

The third expedition into Dakota Territory was made by Sully in 1865. His force moved up the Missouri River to Fort Rice and marched north of Devils Lake. On Aug. 2 he set out for the Mouse (Souris) River and from there marched southwest to Fort Berthold. His force returned to Fort Rice on Sept. 8.

DAKOTA GOLD RUSH. *See* **Black Hills.**

DAKOTA LAND COMPANY. Organized by Minnesota territorial officials in 1857 to secure eligible town sites, establish the capital of the Dakota region at Sioux Falls, and control territorial official appointments and public contracts. In 1858 it entered Dakota and secured several town sites on the Big Sioux River and prospected others on the James and Missouri rivers. The promoters set up a provisional government at Sioux Falls, elected a legislature, and chose a delegate to Congress, but they failed to secure recognition by the federal government. The election of President Abraham Lincoln cut off their control of patronage; the outbreak of Indian hostilities in Minnesota in 1862 ended the project.

DAKOTA TERRITORY. Created by act of Congress, Mar. 2, 1861. It corresponded to the present states of North Dakota, South Dakota, and much of Wyoming and Montana. Montana Territory, with the present state limits, was cut off from Dakota Territory in 1864. When Wyoming Territory was created, in 1868, Dakota Territory was reduced to the region comprising the two Dakotas of today.

The first legislative assembly of the territory convened at Yankton on Mar. 17, 1862. Yankton was the capital until 1883, when it was moved to Bismarck. In 1889 the territory was divided into North Dakota and South Dakota.

DALE'S LAWS OF VIRGINIA. A criminal code issued by Sir Thomas Dale for colonial Virginia (1611–16). When Dale arrived in Jamestown, he found the colonists rebellious and disinclined to work. He placed them under martial law and issued a code notable for its pitiless severity.

DALLAS (Tex.). Second most populous city in Texas, with a population of 904,078 in 1980; the center of a metropolitan area that included 2,974,878 people. "Big D" is the business center of Texas and much of the Southwest. It is located at the forks of the Trinity River, a natural site for a trading post. French traders who bootlegged goods into Spanish Texas in the 18th century traded there with the Indians. John Neely Bryan, the first American on the scene, set up a trading post in 1840 named in honor of George Mifflin Dallas.

The town grew moderately until the 1860's. Although a Confederate force used it as a base during the Civil War, the city was never involved in combat. After the war, many farmers began to raise cotton. Railroads reached it in 1872. Cotton and wheat were brought there to be shipped. Cattle were turned into meat and leather and sent on for sale. New businesses and good connections with the rest of the Southeast led the Federal Reserve System to designate Dallas in 1914 as the home of one of its district banks.

Dallas underwent a major flood in 1908, which led to the creation of a "master plan" for rebuilding the city by George E. Kessler. Railroads serving the city were rerouted around the center of town and new street plans were provided. Meanwhile, Dallas had grown into a textile center. Oil began to influence Dallas's growth when East Texas oil fields were discovered and developed during the 1930's. The period following World War II saw the development of aircraft factories, electrical manufacturing establishments, and construction of chemical works and oil refineries. Dallas had a moment of unwanted world-wide attention in 1963. President John F. Kennedy was murdered there on Nov. 22.

DALLAS-CLARENDON CONVENTION (1856). An Anglo-American agreement, signed Oct. 17, by George Mifflin Dallas, U.S. minister to Great Britain, and George William Frederick Villiers, Earl of Clarendon, British foreign secretary, intended to clear up conflicting interpretations of the Clayton-Bulwer Treaty of 1850. Great Britain agreed to withdraw from Nicaragua and Honduras, while the United States conceded an enlarged British Honduras.

***DALLAS REPORTS*.** The first four volumes of reported decisions of the U.S. Supreme Court, 1790–1800. The reporter of these decisions was Alexander J. Dallas, an eminent Philadelphia lawyer and secretary of the treasury under President James Madison.

DALLES, THE. About 70 miles east of Portland, Oreg., The Dalles of the Columbia River—referring both to a stretch of the river and the adjacent shore—was one of the most dangerous points in the early fur trade of the Pacific Northwest, because of both navigation difficulties and Indian hostilities. The City of The Dalles was incorporated in 1857. The reservoir formed by the Dalles Dam (1957), three miles above the city, covered the rapids and gorge of The Dalles. The city is a busy inland port, ships moving through the locks of the dam after passing through the Bonneville Dam 50 miles downstream. The population of the city in 1980 was 10,820.

DAME SCHOOL. A type of school transplanted to American colonies from England, usually conducted by a woman in her home. Young children were taught the alphabet, the hornbook, elements of reading, and moral and religious subjects. In New England such schools prepared boys for admission to the town schools.

"DAMN THE TORPEDOES." A reply by Union Adm. David Glasgow Farragut to a warning of the dangerous proximity of submerged torpedoes (now called mines) at the critical juncture of the Battle of Mobile Bay (Aug. 5, 1864). As the Union fleet approached the harbor entrance, which was known to be nearly closed by mines, the monitor *Tecumseh* struck a mine and sank. Threatened with early defeat by a heavy cross fire from Confederate forts and fleet, Farragut in the flagship *Hartford* took the lead and steamed safely through the mine fields.

DAMS. *See* **Hydroelectric Power.**

DANBURY, BURNING OF. In 1776, Danbury, Conn., was a depot of patriot army stores. In 1777, British Col. William Tryon planned to destroy these supplies. On Apr. 25 he landed and marched on Danbury. The villagers, warned of the invaders, fled, and the Continental troops retired, taking part of the stores. Tryon destroyed miscellaneous supplies. Apprised by a Loyalist that the patriot militia was gathering at Bethel, Tryon on Apr. 27 set fire to nineteen dwellings, twenty-two stores and barns, and a meetinghouse, valued at $80,000. His retreat was hampered by generals Gold S. Silliman, David Wooster, and Benedict Arnold. Wooster was killed, and Tryon struggled back to his ships.

DANBURY HATTERS' CASE (*Loewe v. Lawlor,* 208 U.S. 274 [1908]). In 1901–02 a union, the United Hatters of North America, attempted to force the unionization of the employees of Dietrich Loewe and partners, a hatmaking concern in Danbury, Conn. The Loewe company resisted, and a strike and nationwide boycott were instituted by the union. Loewe brought action against the local union as violators of the Sherman Antitrust Act. A district court agreed and fixed $74,000 as damages due the company. The circuit court of appeals overruled this verdict, but in 1908 the U.S. Supreme Court reversed the circuit court ruling and sent the case back for trial. In 1912 the court of appeals decided upon $80,000 as Loewe's damage, which, under the law, was to be trebled, the total sum with costs being more than $250,000. The union not being incorporated, the defendants were individually liable for their shares of the penalty. In 1917 the district court ordered the sale of the homes of 140 workmen in Danbury, Bethel, and neighboring towns to satisfy the judgment.

DANCE. American Indian dance. There is a great range of dance styles and forms in the various native American areas. Underlying these native dance forms everywhere are various kinds of drums, ranging from the Eskimo tambourine to the cylinder drum of the Plains Indians and Pueblo; the many rattles; the panpipes of California; flutes; and ubiquitous singing.

The simplest was the round dance of the Great Basin, dancers shuffling in a circle. There, dancing was a social event marking the coming together of socioeconomic bands at prescribed times of the year. Among the Pueblo, dancing was intimately bound up with religious life. Social dances there were, but the masked impersonations of the rain beings marked the ceremonial highlight of a complex ritual calendar. California too had its impersonation of spiritual beings. Masked dancing reached a peak on the Northwest Coast. There, as in the renowned Plains Sun Dance, an element of frenzy might be introduced.

Theatrical dance. Theatrical dancing in the colonial period was at a primitive level, and the first classical ballet performers were European—in particular, French—artists who toured extensively. The earliest notable American dancers were products of the French school—John Durang, Augusta Maywood, and Mary Ann Lee. Throughout the 19th century, the art of serious theatrical dancing languished. The roots of popular show dancing drew mainly from English models and were influenced strongly by dance forms brought from Africa. Black performers had a difficult time being seen in the white theater, although William Henry Lane (Juba) achieved popularity.

The popular theater of the 1880's and 1890's attracted Loie Fuller, Isadora Duncan, Ruth St. Denis, and Maude Allan, but there were very few ballet schools and no ballet companies to appear in. The combination spurred the development of indigenous expressionist dance, subsequently known as modern dance. The most influential figures in the succeeding generation were Martha Graham and Doris Humphrey. Among others who were active dancers and choreographers in the 1930's and 1940's were Helen Tamiris (*Negro Spirituals*) and Lester Horton.

Classic ballet revisited America through the efforts of touring foreign troupes. The most famous of these were the Anna Pavlova Company, which mounted a production of *Swan Lake* in New York in the early 1920's, and the Ballet Russe of Sergei Diaghilev. Pavlova produced a group of aspiring dancers; and members of the Diaghilev company, notably Adolph Bolm and Mikhail Mordkin, took up residence in the United States, established dance schools, and eventually created companies for their students. The first domestic company staffed entirely by Americans was the Littlefield Ballet (later the Philadelphia Ballet), 1935–42, established by Catherine Littlefield. The company staged the first complete *Sleeping Beauty* seen in the United States. In Chicago, Ruth Page sustained ballet activities during the 1930's in the Page-Stone Company, succeeded by the Chicago Opera Ballet, and Ruth Page's International Ballet.

George Balanchine was among the choreographers stranded in France after the demise of the Diaghilev Ballet Russe. Lincoln Kirstein, a writer and fledgling artist, formed the idea of transplanting the ballet to the United States by establishing a school and company modeled on the traditional Russian pattern. Balanchine agreed to be in charge of the school, and in 1933 it was established in New York. The American Ballet gave its first public performance two years later in the Wadsworth Athenaeum in Hartford, Conn., and subsequently became the resident company of the Metropolitan Opera House. After an unsatisfactory artistic association, the company disbanded in 1938. Uniting briefly for a South American tour in 1941, it suspended operation again during World War II.

At the war's end, the company was re-formed under the name Ballet Society. The director of the New York City Center, Morton Baum, asked the company to become a constituent of the City Center in 1948, at which point the company changed its name to the New York City Ballet and began regular fall and spring seasons. It moved to its present home at State Theater in Lincoln Center in 1964. Its chief choreographer from its inception was Balanchine, although a substantial contribution was made by Jerome Robbins after 1949.

New York's other company, Ballet Theatre, opened its first season in 1940. In 1957 the company, changed its name to American Ballet Theatre. It has maintained an eclectic approach that was begun when the company was first organized with the idea that it would be a museum of the dance —that is, a repository for the finest classic and contemporary works.

The end of World War II brought an enormous expansion of public interest in ballet and modern dance and in cooperative productions between the two. Modern-dance choreographers Martha Graham, Merce Cunningham, Alvin Ailey, Glen Tetley, and Twyla Tharp have created pieces with ballet companies, such as American Ballet Theatre, New York City Ballet, and the City Center Joffrey Ballet.

Dancing in the popular theater drew heavily from the Afro-American dancers. Minstrel shows became enormously popular in the 19th century and the mixed bill of dancers along with other specialty acts succeeded as genuinely broad public entertainment until the advent of the movies. The earliest modern dancers performed as parts of these vaudeville shows, as did ballet dancers. At the same time, dancing on the legitimate stage generally declined to a decorative function almost extraneous to the musical play into which it was inserted.

The advent of talking pictures in 1927 started a demand for dancers who could exploit the new form's possibilities. Dancer and choreographer Fred Astaire elaborately tapped out the delights of the carefree, while Busby Berkeley filled movie screens with glamorous and sumptuous formations of dancers. Broadway continued to send choreographers to Hollywood in the persons of Balanchine, Agnes De Mille, and Robbins to duplicate their stage triumphs.

Popular dance. Social dancing, until the advent of ragtime at the turn of the century, was modeled on traditional European examples. Before World War I, ragtime banished the waltz, the schottische, and other dances. The ballroom was invaded by dances that propelled dancers into rambunctious contact, which was continued through the 1920's with the Charleston. The restraint of an earlier time was only partially restored by the fox-trot after World War I.

Latin rhythms of the tango, rhumba, and samba entered the field, as did the merengue. The jazz-derived lindy became popular in the middle 1930's, and all of these dances comprised the repertory of the average social dancer until individualistic rock-and-roll dancing swept them aside in the late 1950's and early 1960's. As the wave of anarchic individualism subsided in the 1970's, a modified return was made to paired social dancing. In the late 1970's, dancing to the "New Wave" music in discotheques, many with lavish video systems, became popular.

DANCING RABBIT CREEK, TREATY OF (Sept. 27, 1830). Provided for the final extinction of Choctaw claims to land in Mississippi and the removal of the nation west of the

Mississippi. Greenwood Leflore, a chief of the Choctaw, persuaded his nation to accede to the white demands and was well rewarded. The cession totaled 7,796,000 acres; many speculative frauds followed.

DANISH SPOLIATION OF AMERICAN COMMERCE (1807–11). Attempting to escape Danish privateers, many British merchantmen secured false papers and hoisted the American flag. In Danish attempts to capture vessels under false flag, many neutral American vessels were also captured, libeled, and condemned. The total U.S. number captured was 187. The United States presented claims to Denmark, but the Danish government made delays. It was finally through the personal intervention of King Frederick VI that a compromise was effected, by which Denmark paid $650,000. The treaty was ratified in June 1830.

DANISH WEST INDIES. *See* **Virgin Islands.**

DANITES (Sons of Dan). A Mormon secret order, established about 1838, whose members were reputed to be pledged to follow the dictates of the Prophet regardless of law or accepted morality.

D'ARGES COLONY. *See* **Arges.**

DARIEN, BANK OF. Chartered in 1818 at Darien, Ga., largely to promote that town as an export point for products of the state. It was capitalized at $1 million, half reserved for the state government. With power to issue notes, within a few years the bank had outstanding almost $2 million, which soon depreciated and led temporarily to the suspension of specie payments. Attacked by various rival interests, it became the center of political storms throughout its life. Its charter was repealed in 1841, and it came to an end the next year.

DARK AND BLOODY GROUND. The name given Kentucky at the time of settlement in the mid-18th century. There was a tug of war for its possession between northern and southern tribes, particularly Cherokee and Shawnee. When the Transylvania Land Company signed the Treaty of Sycamore Shoals in 1775, Chief Dragging Canoe of the Cherokee said they had secured "a dark and bloody ground." The whites realized this was so as a result of years of fighting the Indians. In later periods Kentucky has been called "a dark and bloody ground" because of its feuds and civil outbreaks.

DARK DAY (May 19, 1780). In New England, the sun rose clear and bright, but at about nine o'clock in the morning darkness gradually developed. That evening the moon appeared blood red, and the earth was wrapped in impenetrable darkness. Religious people thought these phenomena to be a direct fulfillment of Bible prophecy. Scientists conjecture they were caused by smoke from fires on the frontier.

DARK HORSE. A compromise candidate selected as party nominee when a deadlock arises among leading candidates. The candidate is usually substantially colorless with respect to current issues, unidentified with party factions, and unobjectionable in his public and private life.

D'ARTAGUETTE'S DEFEAT. *See* **Artaguette.**

DARTMOOR PRISON (Devonshire, England). Used for American naval prisoners during the War of 1812. By April 1815, there were 5,542 Americans confined, 252 of whom died. On Apr. 6, 1815, the captives, indignant because of their continued confinement more than three months beyond the conclusion of peace, staged a noisy demonstration. The commandant called for troops, who fired on the Americans, killing seven and wounding sixty. A joint English-American commission exonerated the commandant but blamed the soldiers for firing after the prisoners had retreated. The British provided for the families of the slain and pensioned the disabled. The prisoners were released at the end of April 1815.

DARTMOUTH COLLEGE. In 1755, Congregational clergyman Eleazar Wheelock founded Moor's Indian Charity School in Lebanon (now Columbia), Conn. Wheelock wanted to establish a college to train missionaries. He found governmental authorization and a location in Hanover, New Hampshire. Gov. John Wentworth secured for Wheelock in 1769 a sizable grant of land and a royal charter for the college, named for the Earl of Dartmouth. Wheelock assembled the first class of twenty of Dartmouth College in 1770 in a small hut. Enrollment rose rapidly, in part because it stayed open during the Revolution. Four students were graduated in 1771, by 1780 the college had graduated almost a hundred.

Wheelock died in 1779 and was succeeded by his son John until 1815. The Dartmouth Medical School was founded in 1797 by Nathan Smith. John Wheelock's presidency witnessed a bitter contest between the trustees and the State of New Hampshire for control of the college (*see* Dartmouth College Case). The struggle left the college in a demoralized and impoverished state, and it fell to Nathan Lord, president from 1828 to 1863, to restore its health and spirit. Lord and his successors embarked on a broad program of expansion that before the end of the century gave Dartmouth a greatly increased endowment, additional buildings, and a strong faculty. A separate scientific school was started, and an agricultural and mechanical school. The Thayer School of Engineering was founded in 1871 by Sylvanus Thayer. In 1900 the Amos Tuck School of Business Administration was added.

In the 20th century Dartmouth experienced its greatest growth. A computer center, a center for the arts, facilities for graduate work in a number of fields, and a library of 1.2 million volumes have been added. Under President John G. Kemeny, who took office in 1970, the college expanded its medical school and adopted a plan to increase undergraduate enrollment to 4,000 students.

DARTMOUTH COLLEGE CASE. In 1819 the U.S. Supreme Court, in *Trustees of Dartmouth College v. Woodward,* 4 Wheaton 518, declared private-corporation charters to be contracts and hence, by the contract clause of the Constitution, immune from impairment by state legislative action.

The president of Dartmouth, John Wheelock, was deposed (Aug. 26, 1815) by the self-perpetuating board of trustees established under the charter of 1769. New Hampshire presently altered the charter and brought the institution under state control, changing its name to Dartmouth University. The college sued William H. Woodward, an adherent of the university faction and former secretary-treasurer of the college, for recovery of the charter, seal, and other documents. After a state court decision favorable to the university faction, Daniel Webster argued the case before the Supreme Court. Chief Justice John Marshall's opinion held that the New Hampshire law was invalid, as it impaired contractual (charter) obligations. This decision freed existing corporations from control by the states that created them. Control was largely restored by state legislation and judicial decisions.

DAUGHTERS OF 1812. A U.S. national society, founded in 1892 to promote patriotism and increase knowledge of U.S. history by preserving records, teaching, site marking, and commemorations. Membership is based on ancestor's civil, military, or naval service in the period 1784–1815.

DAUGHTERS OF THE AMERICAN REVOLUTION (DAR). A national patriotic society organized in 1890 by Caroline Scott Harrison, wife of President Benjamin Harrison, and chartered by Congress in 1895. Membership requires descent from an ancestor who served in a military or civilian capacity during the American Revolution and "acceptability" to the local chapter. Membership in 1980 was 209,000.

DAUGHTERS OF THE CONFEDERACY, UNITED. *See* **United Daughters of the Confederacy.**

DAUPHIN ISLAND. In the Gulf of Mexico near the entrance to Mobile Bay; discovered by Pierre Lemoyne, Sieur d'Iberville, in 1699. First named Massacre Island by the French because they found large quantities of human bones.

DAVENPORT (Iowa). Third largest city in Iowa, with a population of 103,264 in 1980. It is part of a major metropolitan area that includes the cities of Moline and Rock Island, Ill.; the metropolitan area had 383,958 people in 1980. The city was established in 1836 by Antoine de Claire and Col. George Davenport. With several partners, they outlined the town on ground they had visited and worked on in the army.

Davenport is an important commercial center. The first bridge across the Mississippi River, which also had the first railroad service in Iowa, was located there. A large flood-control dam, and locks to permit ships to pass it, was constructed at Davenport. Since World War II, Davenport has become an important aluminum manufacturing center, adding to the city's cement works and food-processing plants.

DAVIDS. *See* **Submarines and Torpedoes, Civil War.**

DAVIS, FORT. Named for Jefferson Davis; established in 1854 in western Texas to protect settlers and mail along the Overland Trail. During the Civil War, Union and Confederate troops successively occupied the post. When the railroad passed twenty miles southward, need for protection from Indians ceased, and the fort was abandoned, July 1891.

DAVIS, IMPRISONMENT AND TRIAL OF. After Jefferson Davis's last official meeting with his cabinet as president of the Confederacy, probably at Charlotte, N.C., Apr. 26, 1865, he proceeded with some of his staff to Washington, Ga., where he took definite steps to escape to Europe. On May 2, 1865, President Andrew Johnson offered $100,000 for the arrest of Davis, charged with planning the assassination of Abraham Lincoln. On May 10, Davis was captured near Irwinville, Ga., by Col. Benjamin D. Pritchard. He was imprisoned in Fortress Monroe, Va., in May 1865, charged with treason and complicity in Lincoln's assassination. Since it was legally requisite that he be tried in Virginia, he could not be prosecuted until the federal courts resumed their functions in that state. In May 1867 the U.S. circuit judges were ready, but the prosecution was not prepared. Given that a Virginia jury might refuse to convict, Davis was released on bail after two years of confinement.

A new indictment was drawn and preparations made to try Davis in May 1868. The Johnson impeachment trial interfered, and it was not until November 1868 that proceedings actually commenced. Davis's counsel pleaded that the Fourteenth Amendment had already punished Davis by abridging his voting rights and denying him the right to hold federal office, and a trial would put him in double jeopardy. The case was referred to the Supreme Court. In the meantime, on Christmas Day, 1868, Johnson issued a general amnesty proclamation, and on Feb. 26, 1869, a *nolle prosequi* was entered in the case.

DAVIS-JOHNSTON CONTROVERSY. Factional differences between the Confederacy's president, Jefferson Davis, and his friends, and Gen. J. E. Johnston and his partisans concerned (1) the relative ranking of general officers after the First Battle of Bull Run; (2) Johnston's relief from command of the Army of Northern Virginia after the Battle of Fair Oaks in spring 1862 and the transfer of command to Gen. Robert E. Lee; (3) the assignment of Johnston to command the forces in Tennessee, where he served in the winter of 1862–63; (4) the unsuccessful defense of Vicksburg with Gen. J. C. Pemberton in summer 1863; and (5) Johnston's relief by Gen. J. B. Hood during the Atlanta campaign in 1864, and his restoration nearly a year later after Hood had wrecked his army and the Confederacy was near collapse.

DAWES COMMISSION. Commonly called the Commission to the Five Civilized Tribes; appointed by President Grover Cleveland in 1893 to negotiate with the Cherokee, Creek, Choctaw, Chickasaw, and Seminole to induce these Indians to abolish their tribal governments and come under state and federal laws. Having secured the necessary agreements, the commission made up tribal rolls, classified the tribal lands, and allotted to each citizen his rightful share of the common property. It also had large governmental functions. The commission was abolished on July 1, 1905.

DAWES GENERAL ALLOTMENT ACT (1887). Provided for the breakup of the Indian tribal relationship and the abandonment of the domestic nation theory. Reservations were to be surveyed and allotments of 40 to 160 acres assigned to heads of families, orphans, and children; surplus lands were to be opened to white settlement. Although the allotments were inalienable for twenty-five years, they quickly fell into the hands of whites, who thus acquired the best lands within the reservations. In 1934, the allotment policy was halted by the Indian Reorganization Act, and efforts were made to restore tribal organization and to recover lost land.

DAWES PLAN. Adopted in August 1924; resulted from the German default on World War I reparations, December 1922–January 1923. A group headed by Charles G. Dawes, former director of the Bureau of the Budget, was chosen in November 1923 to devise annual payments that Germany could meet, but no total payment was set. They worked out a plan of payments to start with 1 billion gold marks in 1924–25, to be increased to 2.5 billion in 1928–29. The sources of payments were an external loan, revenue from bonds and preferred stock of a company organized to take over the German government railroads, debentures issued against German industry, a transport tax, and the budget. The plan operated successfully until replaced by the Young Plan in May 1930.

DAYLIGHT SAVING TIME. A movement originated in England by William Willett in 1907 to utilize summer daylight by advancing the clock in spring and turning it back in fall. A law was passed by Congress, effective Mar. 30, 1918, requiring the time of day to be advanced by one hour on the last Sunday of March of each year and turned back one hour the last Sunday in October. There was much opposition, and a bill was passed repealing the law, over the veto of President Wilson, on Aug. 20, 1919. Daylight saving time became a matter of state and municipal option. On Feb. 6, 1942, daylight saving time, then called "war time," was instituted nationwide on a year-round basis until September 1945, when local option was restored. In 1966 the Uniform Time Act called for all states to adopt daylight saving time from the last Sunday in April through the last Sunday in October; it permitted states to exempt themselves by state legislation. In January 1974, nationwide daylight saving time was again instituted to reduce expenditure of fuel for lighting and heating, but public opposition and minimal conservation of energy brought about repeal within the year. Except for two states and parts of three others standard time was restored from the last Sunday in October until the last Sunday in February 1975, when daylight saving time was once again introduced.

DAYTON (Ohio). City located in southwestern Ohio, with a population of 203,588 in 1980; center of a metropolitan area of 830,070. Dayton helps make Ohio a major producer of industrial goods. It is best known as the home of the Wright brothers, who developed the design of their airplane in their bicycle repair shop. The Wrights opened a flying school in Dayton and produced many planes in local factories. Wright-Patterson Air Base is the center for air force research and development, and the home of a museum of aviation.

Dayton is a center for the manufacture of precision tools and machinery, including cash registers, electrical ignition systems for automobiles, and heavy-duty weighing scales.

D DAY. A U.S. military term designating the target date for an operation. It was first used by the American Expeditionary Forces in 1918 but became widely known in relation to the Normandy invasion of June 6, 1944. "D" is merely a reiteration of the first letter of day.

DEARBORN, FORT. By the Treaty of Greenville in 1795, the cession of a tract six miles square at the mouth of the Chicago River, was exacted from the Indians, to serve as the site for a future fort, and in 1803 its establishment was decreed. It was named after Gen. Henry Dearborn, then secretary of war. With the outbreak of the War of 1812 several hundred Indians assembled at Chicago. On July 29, Gen. William Hull at Detroit ordered the commandant to evacuate Fort Dearborn. His command was destroyed by the Indians a short distance from the fort. Four years later, Chicago was reoccupied and erection of the second Fort Dearborn was begun. It was garrisoned until 1823, when the shifting of Indian trade and population induced the government to withdraw the garrison. Increasing trouble with the Winnebago and other tribes compelled its restoration in 1828. Three years later, the garrison was again removed, but the outbreak of the Black Hawk War brought back the troops in 1832. The development of modern Chicago began in 1833. The Indians vanished, and in 1836 Fort Dearborn was finally evacuated. Its military reservation became Chicago's Grant Park.

DEARBORN WAGON. A light, four-wheeled vehicle, usually with a top, perhaps with side curtains, and pulled by one horse. It was said to have been designed by Gen. Henry Dearborn. It was in almost universal use in the United States about 1819–50.

DEATH VALLEY. A desert valley about 140 miles long, in California near the Nevada line, the driest and hottest area in North America, known for its production of borax. It is the bottom of a volcanic fault or trough, the lowest point in the United States (282 feet below sea level). It was named by the Manly-Hunt party of emigrants, many of whom perished there in 1849. At Emigrant Spring a rich silver deposit was found, the first of many lost mines in the valley; the best-known is Death Valley Scotty. In 1933, Death Valley was proclaimed a national monument.

DEBATABLE LAND. The part of southeastern North America that came to be Georgia. There the Spanish, English, and French clashed. Pedro Menéndez de Avilés sailed up the Georgia coast in 1566 and secured the region for Spain. The English planted a settlement at Charleston, S.C., in 1670 and began an encroachment southward, which led to the settlement of Georgia in 1733. An intensive diplomatic battle began that broke into the War of Jenkins' Ear in 1739. Not until the end of the French and Indian War in 1763, when England secured Florida, was the contest finally ended.

***DE BOW'S REVIEW*.** A monthly journal important in helping to mold public opinion in the antebellum South. The editor was James Dunwoody Brownson De Bow. The *Commercial Review of the South and West,* published in New Orleans beginning in January 1846, went through several official changes of title, but was soon known almost everywhere simply as *De Bow's Review.* The *Review* strongly advocated raising health and educational levels in the South, but its major avowed purpose was to encourage the independent economic expansion of the region. The *Review* defended slavery and joined in the fight to reopen the slave trade from Africa. After 1858 it became an champion of secession and supported the Confederacy until the disruption of supplies and the breakdown of communications brought its efforts to a halt after August 1862. After the war it devoted itself to the economic recovery of the South. The magazine continued to be published until June 1880.

DEBS, IN RE **(158 U.S. 564).** Influenced by his attorney general, Richard Olney, and convinced that the Pullman strike of June–July 1894 was interfering with interstate commerce and the delivery of mails, President Grover Cleveland ordered troops into Chicago and moved against the strikers in the courts. Olney secured from the U.S. court in Chicago an injunction based on the Sherman Antitrust Act and on the law prohibiting obstruction of the mails. It forbade Eugene V. Debs, president of the American Railway Union, and other officers "from in any way or manner interfering with, hindering, obstructing or stopping" the business of the railroads entering Chicago. Arrested for alleged violation of the injunction on July 10, Debs and other leaders were found guilty, Dec. 14, of contempt and sentenced to three to six months. Carried to the Supreme Court on a writ of habeas corpus, the sentence was upheld, May 27, 1895.

DEBT, IMPRISONMENT FOR. The practice of imprisoning debtors until they gave satisfaction was brought to the colonies from England. A common modification provided that a debtor might be sold into service for a period to discharge his debt.

Popular reaction against imprisonment for debt appeared about 1775: humanitarian societies modeled after the Thatched House Society of London began to operate, supplying food to poor prisoners and raising funds to settle small claims. The efforts of the humanitarians were reinforced by those of utilitarian legal reformers, who wished to substitute direct means of attaching a debtor's property and to provide a system of distribution that would protect the interests of all creditors. From meliorative programs, the reformers passed to agitation for a complete abolition of imprisonment for debt; between 1820 and 1868, laws or constitutional provisions narrowly restricting the conditions for imprisonment were adopted by most of the states.

DEBT, PUBLIC. With the establishment of the national government, debts created by the Continental Congress and the states became of pressing importance. The foreign debt, $11,710,000, was assumed by the federal government, but there was less unity of opinion about the domestic debt.

Alexander Hamilton, first secretary of the treasury, held that the federal government should also assume the domestic debt. He estimated that this debt (exclusive of state debts) amounted to $27,383,000, plus accrued interest of $13,030,000. The question was debated at length in Congress; it was finally provided that all holders of outstanding certificates were to receive their face value with interest, except for outstanding Continental bills of credit, which were to be redeemed at 100 for 1 in specie. Hamilton was also successful with his plan for the assumption of state debts, some $18,271,786 of these obligations being actually assumed by the federal government.

From 1791 until 1806 the public debt fluctuated between $75 million and $87 million, declining to a low of just over $45 million in 1812. The War of 1812 brought an increase to $127,334,933 in 1816. Thereafter, the debt was reduced steadily to only $37,513,000 in 1835. From 1835 on, it varied considerably, but remained below $100 million until 1862.

The Civil War brought a heavy increase, to a peak of $2,322,331,208 in 1866. After 1866 the debt decreased, although the interest-bearing debt did not fall below $1 billion until 1888, reaching a low of $585,029,230 in 1892. A moderate expansion of the federal debt to slightly over $1 billion in 1899 took place, after which it fell again slightly, remaining somewhat under $1 billion from 1901 to 1916.

Beginning in 1917, World War I, with its issues of Liberty Bonds, brought the public debt to $25,234,496,274 in 1919. A reduction to $15,770,000,000 was effected by 1930. As the recession in business became severe, government revenues fell off and expenditures increased. The debt increased steadily to $22,158,000,000 by June 1933. Through the 1930's, revenues continued to be inadequate to meet expenses.

The huge increase of both federal debt and gross national product (GNP) during World War II clarified the relationship between the two, and economists came to think of all debts in terms of their relations to GNP. On this basis the federal debt exceeded GNP by more than 20 percent in 1945. All administrations from 1950 on operated on the basis of a bookkeeping deficit, but one not large enough to prevent the relative decrease in magnitude of the federal debt. By 1980 the debt was about 36 percent of the GNP, a ratio lower than in the depression years of the 1930's but higher than the 25 percent level of the prosperous years of the early 1920's.

The federal trend from 1946 to 1980 was toward lower public indebtedness. The same was not true of state and local debts. Combined, they stood at 7.5 percent of GNP in 1945 and at about double that by 1970, while interest rates were rising even faster. In the 1970's, state and local debts decreased and by 1978 represented 13 percent of GNP. In the climate of opinion of the 1970's, it appeared unlikely that any type of public indebtedness would be substantially reduced.

DEBT AND INVESTMENT, FOREIGN. The net of all the claims on people or governments of foreign nations held in the United States, less the reverse claims held by foreigners, is the foreign debt owed to or by this country. Actually the obligations are of many different types, some representing borrowing and some representing investments in the equity of foreign companies.

Prior to World War I, "foreign debt" meant the amount the United States owed abroad. Before independence, Americans had been deeply indebted to English merchants. The Revolution forced the Continental Congress to borrow money from France and Holland. In the 1790's, Alexander Hamilton hoped that sound government finance would attract European capital, but wars in Europe prevented this from happening to any marked degree. With peace in Europe, English capital gradually flowed into state bonds. After the mid-19th century, American railroads and other utilities were able to borrow privately in European markets and to market common stock. By 1914, there was $7.2 billion of foreign capital in the United States, and Americans owned about $3.5 billion in foreign obligations.

World War I reversed these relations. By 1920, European governments owed the U.S. government $12 billion. European investors had drawn their U.S. balances down to $3 billion, while American private interests had sent an additional $4 billion abroad. The debts of the European governments to the United States seemed too large to repay over ten or twenty years without disrupting world trade. Consequently, arrangements were made in the 1920's for gradual payment and low interest rates.

The Great Depression temporarily checked U.S. foreign investment and, together with World War II, ended the hope of substantial collection of the old war debts. Financial assistance by the United States in the war took the form of lend-lease, a euphemism for outright gifts, so that no large burden of current indebtedness remained at the close of the war.

To make capital available for postwar reconstruction, the United Nations sponsored the International Monetary Fund and the International Bank for Reconstruction and Development, with the United States as the largest subscriber to both. The American government did not entirely withdraw from direct intergovernmental loans, but the few billion lent was small in comparison to the economic and military aid supplied freely under the Marshall Plan and successive laws. In 1950 the total foreign investment was only $19 billion, of which $11 billion represented direct ownership. As Europe began to prosper in the late 1950's, the situation changed rapidly. By 1965, American private investment abroad was $81 billion, of which nearly $50 billion was direct ownership.

These large exports of capital made it impossible for the United States to avoid large deficits in the balance of international payments. Consequently, the federal government tried by means of taxes to slow down the capital outflow. The 1969–71 recession operated strongly in the same direction. Meanwhile, nearly $100 million in dollar exchange accumulated abroad, chiefly in the hands of bankers and oil-exporting nations. Therefore, while the United States remained by far the leading creditor nation, with foreign claims of one type or another reaching $168 billion in 1980, these claims were balanced by expatriated currency.

DEBTS, COLONIAL AND CONTINENTAL. Because custom, imperial restrictions, and local circumstances led the American colonies to raise extraordinary public funds by lotteries and emission of paper currency rather than by borrowing, colonial debts, in the present sense, were not heavy. Massachusetts first issued paper currency in 1690 to meet the expenses of King William's War; the subsequent struggles with the French and Indians forced other colonies to follow suit and resort to borrowing funds for public purposes. In 1775 these debts, plus others incurred by British attempts at imperial reorganization, totaled over £2.5 million. The states incurred heavy debts during the Revolution. The federal government actually funded and assumed state debts (1790) in a total of $18,271,786, to which more than $3 million was subsequently added.

The Second Continental Congress and the Congress of the Confederation also incurred heavy debts. Despite constitutional weaknesses, the Continental Congress authorized (Oct. 3, 1776) a domestic loan of $5 million. When interest was raised from 4 percent to 6 percent and Congress began using foreign loans to pay interest on domestic debts, domestic loans rose to $11,585,506 (specie value); certificates of indebtedness for war supplies added $16,708,000, and the total domestic debt (1790) was $40,423,085. Moreover, the congresses had gained credit abroad. Foreign loans negotiated between 1777 and 1783 totaled $7,830,517. After the war the Confederation sank further into debt abroad, and as Congress was unable to pay all interest and installments on foreign loans, the foreign debt rose to $11,763,110 by Jan. 1, 1790.

DEBTS, STATE. One of the problems to be solved during the formation of the national government, from 1787 to 1789, was the disagreement over the assumption by the proposed federal government of the debts incurred by the states during the Revolution. The assumption of debts having been carried out, nearly all the states found themselves debt-free or with small debts. (*See* Debt, Public).

Between 1820 and 1840 the states, especially those west of the Appalachians and east of the Mississippi River, entered into extensive borrowing for canals, turnpikes, railroads, and manufacturing enterprises. The panic of 1837 caused revenues from the projects to decline, and with a reduction in the tax collections of the states, many issues went into default. Large amounts of these bonds had been sold to foreign investors. From 1840 to 1860 the states were engaged in repaying funds borrowed earlier. During this period it was common practice to write rigid debt limits into state constitutions. To avoid these limits, some states created state corporations to construct public works and repay borrowing through user charges. With the outbreak of the Civil War, borrowing by the states increased to support the war. A condition for ending the war was repudiation of the debts incurred by the states of the Confederacy.

From the post–Civil War period to the 1930's, most of the borrowing was to finance public buildings and, toward the end of the period, to finance the construction of highways. The 1930's saw states borrowing to finance general relief expenditures. Overall, though, the period was one of repayment of state debts.

State indebtedness was $3.59 billion in 1940, dropped to $2.4 billion in 1946, but rose to nearly $5.3 billion in 1950. The reduction during 1940–46 was a direct result of World War II, when no capital improvements that did not further the war effort were undertaken. The rise in the late 1940's was the result of borrowing for maintenance of facilities neglected during the war, granting state bonuses to those who served in the military forces, and expanding highway systems. Between 1950 and 1957 the indebtedness of the states rose to $8.5 billion. This increase went for public offices, welfare institutions, the educational system, and highways.

During the 1960's the debt of the states more than doubled, to $39.5 billion in 1969. An increase to $54.5 billion occurred in 1972, and by 1978 the outstanding debt of the states reached $103 billion. Expanded programs of public works and construction of penal institutions, hospitals, educational facilities, and recreational facilities led to the increase. General price levels were rising, which caused larger amounts to be borrowed. Statutory and constitutional changes in the 1960's also gave legislatures greater flexibility in creating state debt. Debt limits were increased in some states, while others adopted sliding limitations based on average revenue receipts. Even with these changes, the state component in local government debt—including counties, municipalities, school districts, and special districts—remains the smallest.

DECATUR'S CRUISE TO ALGIERS. On May 20, 1815, during the U.S. war on Algiers (*see* Barbary Wars), Capt. Stephen Decatur sailed with three frigates, three brigs, two schooners, and a sloop, the *Guerrière*, his flagship. Off Cape Gata, Spain, on June 17, he captured the Algerian frigate *Mashuda.* Arriving at Algiers on June 28, Decatur immediately negotiated a treaty with the dey of Algiers.

DECIUS LETTERS. An anonymous attack on Patrick Henry for his opposition to the Constitution. Written by James Montgomery or John Nicholas, the letters appeared in the *Independent Chronicle* of Richmond, Va., between December 1788 and March 1789.

DECLARATION OF INDEPENDENCE. There were two declarations of independence—the first a decision by the Continental Congress made on July 2, 1776, and the second a paper written by Thomas Jefferson that Congress entitled "The unanimous Declaration of the thirteen united States of America" and released to the world on July 4. Both sprang from a resolution introduced in Congress on June 7 by Richard Henry Lee, who, speaking for Virginia, asked his colleagues to resolve that "these United Colonies are, and of right ought to be, free and independent States . . . and that all political connection between them and the State of Great Britain is, and ought to be, totally dissolved." On June 10 it was agreed that Lee's resolution be postponed for three weeks and that a committee be appointed to prepare a declaration to the effect of the resolution. The committee consisted of Thomas Jefferson, John Adams, Benjamin Franklin, Roger Sherman, and Robert R. Livingston. Jefferson, elected with the most votes, by custom automatically became chairman of the committee and thus the assignment of preparing a declaration of independence fell to him.

From the time Jefferson completed his draft until he laid it before Congress, some thirty-one changes were made in the Declaration by Jefferson or his committee. Franklin, abed with gout, made five more minor changes. Jefferson then drew up a fair copy of the Declaration and placed it on the desk of the secretary of the Continental Congress on June 28.

Congress assembled on July 1 prepared to vote on Lee's resolution. But first John Dickinson of Pennsylvania argued reconciliation. John Adams's reply rehearsed all the arguments for independence made in Congress during the past six months. Neither speech changed delegates' minds. An unofficial vote taken while Congress sat as a committee of the whole showed nine colonies for independence and four either against, split, or forced to abstain for lack of instructions from the home government. A formal vote was postponed until the next day in the hope that recalcitrant delegates could be brought around. The delay worked. On July 2, by a unanimous vote (New York abstaining), Congress resolved for independence.

Immediately after the vote, Congress turned to editing Jefferson's paper, upon which it worked for more than two days. In spite of some forty additions and extensive cuts that reduced the paper by one-quarter, Congress left the document pretty much intact. Congress completed its revision of the Declaration in the early evening of July 4.

Signing of the Declaration. Few facts are known about the signing of the Declaration of Independence. The Declaration was printed July 4 bearing only the names of John Hancock, as president, and Charles Thomson, as secretary of Congress. On July 19, after learning New York had approved the Declaration, Congress voted that the document "be fairly engrossed . . . on parchment with the title and style of 'The unanimous Declaration of the thirteen united States of America.' " On Aug. 2, the *Journal* of the Continental Congress notes, "The Declaration of Independence being engrossed and compared at the table was signed by the members." The names of the signers were kept secret until Jan. 19, 1777, when they were released to the world.

DECLARATION OF INDEPENDENCE

In Congress, July 4, 1776

The unanimous Declaration of the thirteen united States of America

WHEN in the Course of human Events, it becomes necessary for one people to dissolve the political bands which have connected them with another, and to assume among the powers of the earth, the separate and equal station to which the Laws of Nature and of Nature's God entitle them, a decent respect to the opinions of mankind requires that they should declare the causes which impel them to the separation.—We hold these truths to be self-evident, that all men are created equal, that they are endowed by their Creator with certain unalienable Rights, that among these are Life, Liberty and the pursuit of Happiness.—That to secure these rights, Governments are instituted among Men, deriving their just powers from the consent of the governed,—That whenever any Form of Government becomes destructive of these ends, it is the Right of the People to alter or to abolish it, and to institute new Government, laying its foundation on such principles and organizing its powers in such form, as to them shall seem most likely to effect their Safety and Happiness. Prudence, indeed, will dictate that Governments long established should not be changed for light and transient causes; and accordingly all experience hath shewn, that mankind are more disposed to suffer, while evils are sufferable, than to right themselves by abolishing the forms to which they are accustomed. But when a long train of abuses and usurpations, pursuing invariably the same Object, evinces a design to reduce them under absolute Despotism, it is their right, it is their duty, to throw off such Government, and to provide new Guards for their future security.—Such has been the patient sufferance of these Colonies; and such is now the necessity which constrains them to alter their former Systems of Government. The history of the present King of Great Britain is a history of repeated injuries and usurpations, all having in direct object the establishment of an absolute Tyranny over these States. To prove this, let Facts be submitted to a candid world.—He has refused his Assent to Laws, the most wholesome and necessary for the public good.—He has forbidden his Governors to pass Laws of immediate and pressing importance, unless suspended in their operation till his Assent should be obtained; and when so suspended, he has utterly neglected to attend to them.—He has refused to pass other laws for the accommodation of large districts of people, unless those people would relinquish the right of Representation in the Legislature, a right inestimable to them and formidable to tyrants only.—He has called together legislative bodies at places unusual, uncomfortable, and distant from the depository of their public Records, for the sole purpose of fatiguing them into compliance with his measures.—He has dissolved Representative Houses repeatedly, for opposing with manly firmness his invasions on the rights of the people.—He has refused for a long time, after such dissolutions, to cause others to be elected; whereby the Legislative powers, incapable of Annihilation, have returned to the People at large for their exercise; the State remaining in the mean time exposed to all the dangers of invasion from without, and convulsions within.—He has endeavoured to prevent the population of these States; for that purpose obstructing the Laws for Naturalization of Foreigners; refusing to pass others to encourage their migrations hither, and raising the conditions of new Appropriations of Lands.—He has obstructed the Administration of Justice, by refusing his Assent to Laws for establishing Judiciary powers.—He has made Judges dependent on his Will alone, for the tenure of their offices, and the amount and payment of their salaries.—He has erected a multitude of new offices, and sent hither swarms of Officers to harass our people and eat out their substance.—He has kept among us, in times of peace, Standing Armies without the Consent of our legislatures.—He has affected to render the Military independent of and superior to the Civil power.—He has combined with others to subject us to a jurisdiction foreign to our constitution, and unacknowledged by our laws; giving his Assent to their Acts of pretended Legislation:—For quartering large bodies of armed troops among us:—For protecting them, by a mock Trial, from punishment for any Murders which they should commit on the Inhabitants of these States: —For cutting off our Trade with all parts of the world:—For imposing Taxes on us without our Consent:—For depriving us in many cases, of the benefits of Trial by Jury:—For transporting us beyond Seas to be tried for pretended offences:—For abolishing the free System of English Laws in a neighbouring Province, establishing therein an Arbitrary government, and enlarging its Boundaries, so as to render it at once an example and fit instrument for introducing the same absolute rule into these Colonies:—For taking away our Charters, abolishing our most valuable Laws, and altering fundamentally the Forms of our Governments:—For suspending our own Legislatures and declaring themselves invested with power to legislate for us in all cases whatsoever.—He has abdicated Government here, by declaring us out of his Protection and waging War against us.—He has plundered our seas, ravaged our Coasts, burnt our towns, and destroyed the lives of our people.—He is at this time, transporting large Armies of foreign Mercenaries to compleat the works of death, desolation and tyranny, already begun with circumstances of cruelty & perfidy scarcely paralleled in the most barbarous ages, and totally unworthy the Head of a civilized nation.—He has constrained our fellow Citizens taken Captive on the high Seas to bear Arms against their Country, to become the executioners of their friends and Brethren, or to fall themselves by their Hands.—He has excited domestic insurrections amongst us, and has endeavoured to bring on the inhabitants of our frontiers, the merciless Indian Savages, whose known rule of warfare, is an undistinguished destruction, of all ages, sexes and conditions. In every stage of these Oppressions We have Petitioned for Redress in the most humble terms: Our repeated Petitions have been answered only by repeated injury. A Prince, whose character is thus marked by every act which may define a Tyrant, is unfit to be the ruler of a free people. Nor have we been wanting in Attentions to our British brethren. We have warned them from time to time of Attempts by their legislature to extend an unwarrantable jurisdiction over us. We have reminded them of the circumstances of our emigration and settlement here. We have appealed to their native justice and magnanimity, and we have conjured them by the ties of our common kindred to disavow these usurpations, which, would inevitably interrupt our connections and correspondence. They too have been deaf to the voice of justice and of consanguinity. We must, therefore, acquiesce in the necessity, which denounces our Separation, and hold them, as we hold the rest of mankind, Enemies in War, in Peace Friends.

WE, THEREFORE, the Representatives of the UNITED STATES OF AMERICA, in General Congress, Assembled, appealing to the Supreme Judge of the world for the rectitude of our intentions, do, in the Name, and by Authority of the good People of these Colonies, solemnly publish and declare, That these United Colonies are, and of Right ought to be FREE AND INDEPENDENT STATES; that they are absolved from all Allegiance to the British Crown, and that all political connection between them and the State of Great Britain, is and ought to be totally dissolved; and that as Free and Independent States, they have full Power to levy War, conclude Peace, contract Alliances, establish Commerce, and to do all other Acts and Things which Independent States may of right do.—And for the support of this Declaration, with a firm reliance on the protection of divine Providence, we mutually pledge to each other our Lives, our Fortunes and our sacred Honor. [signatures]

DECLARATION OF RIGHTS (1774). In response to an appeal from Massachusetts, representatives of all the colonies except Georgia met in September 1774 in Philadelphia to deliberate upon redress of their grievances against England. In this First Continental Congress a committee of two from each colony reported on violation of the rights of the colonies. On Oct. 14 a resolution embodying the views of the Congress was passed, becoming known as the Declaration of Rights. In the introduction it was asserted that the British Parliament had assumed the authority of compelling the colonists to submit to a policy that deprived them of their rights as Englishmen (*see* Constitution, British). Eleven specific resolutions defined these rights and declared they had been violated. It was stated that by the "principles of the English Constitution" the colonists were entitled to "life, liberty, and property" and that removal to the colonies did not result in the loss of the rights of Englishmen. It was insisted that the rights of the colonists were violated by the Stamp Act of 1765, the Townshend Revenue Act of 1767, and the Coercive Acts and Quebec Act of 1774. It was hoped that this declaration would impress British statesmen sufficiently to bring about the desired relief.

DECLARATORY ACT (1766). Intended by the British to be an important constitutional compromise with the American colonies and to clarify the colonies' relationship to Parliament and the crown, for the Stamp Act of 1765 had aroused a great constitutional controversy. The Declaratory Act (1) recited the claims of the colonies to a legal exclusive right of taxation; (2) asserted that the colonies were subordinate to the crown and Parliament; (3) declared the king and Parliament had full power and authority to make laws and statutes of sufficient force and validity to bind the colonies of America; (4) declared all votes, resolutions, and proceedings of the colonies calling in question the authority of Parliament as null and void. A declaratory act clarifying the British constitution was favored by William Pitt the Elder and other friends of America, but the act went far beyond their wishes; it thus became an active cause of grievance and a standing threat to colonial self-government, instead of a constitutional compromise.

DECLARATORY JUDGMENT LAWS. Permit courts, when petitioned, to render judgments clearing any doubts as to a person's legal status, a title to property, or the meaning of a contract, before the parties have suffered loss or injury. Such laws are relative latecomers: 19th- and early 20th-century courts demonstrated a reluctance to render such opinions. Passage of a federal declaratory judgment law was impeded by the Supreme Court's holding that declaratory proceedings in federal courts must involve an actual "case" or "controversy." To avoid the constitutional objection, the first enduring state declaratory judgment statutes limited the remedy to "cases of actual controversy" (California and Kansas in 1921). When these statutes survived court tests, similar legislation was enacted in other states, and by the 1970's nearly all states had adopted declaratory judgment laws. Since 1934 a federal declaratory judgments act permits federal courts to declare legal relations.

DECORATION DAY. *See* **Memorial Day.**

DECORATIONS, MILITARY.

Medal of Honor. The highest U.S. decoration for valor. In separate army, navy, and air force versions, it is awarded by the president in the name of Congress to a member of the armed forces who distinguishes himself conspicuously by gallantry and intrepidity at the risk of his life, above and beyond the call of duty, while engaged in armed conflict in either declared or undeclared war. In December 1861, Congress approved a Navy Medal of Honor for enlisted personnel. An Army Medal of Honor for enlisted men was authorized in July 1862; in March 1863 it was extended to army officers and made retroactive to the start of the Civil War. Provisions to award the Navy Medal of Honor to navy and Marine Corps officers came in 1915, and the air force received authority in 1949. In 1963, members of the Coast Guard, who from the first were eligible while serving with the navy, were accorded eligibility. On rare occasions the Medal of Honor has been awarded in peacetime, (to Charles A. Lindbergh in 1927 and Commander Richard E. Byrd in 1926). About 3,200 medals have been awarded. Those receiving it are granted special privileges, such as a pension of $100 a month.

Distinguished Service, Navy, and Air Force Crosses. Ranking next below the Medal of Honor, the Distinguished Service Cross was established for the army on June 2, 1918; the Navy Cross on Feb. 4, 1919; and the Air Force Cross on July 6, 1960 (its members until then had been eligible for the Distinguished Service Cross). The award is made to an armed forces member who distinguishes himself by extraordinary heroism not justifying the award of a Medal of Honor while engaged in an action against an enemy; while engaged in military operations involving conflict with an opposing foreign force; or while serving with friendly foreign forces engaged in an armed conflict against an opposing armed force in which the United States is not a belligerent party.

Distinguished Service Medal. The Distinguished Service Medal is awarded to those who, while serving in any capacity, distinguish themselves by exceptionally meritorious service in a duty of great responsibility. The Distinguished Service Medal is the highest award for merit and ranks third in order of precedence of all American decorations. The army version was authorized by Congress on July 6, 1918, and made retroactive to Apr. 6, 1917. Members of the air force received this version until July 6, 1960, when their own distinctive award was authorized. The navy version was authorized on Feb. 4, 1919, retroactive to Apr. 6, 1917. This version is also awarded to Marine Corps personnel. The Coast Guard medal was authorized in 1951 for peacetime service, when that service is not under navy control.

Silver Star. The Silver Star was authorized for all services on July 9, 1918, as a three-sixteenths of an inch silver star to be worn on the appropriate campaign service ribbon. The award was made for gallantry in action as cited in published orders issued by the headquarters of a general officer. Since it was made retroactive, many individuals from the Spanish-American War received the citation star. The Silver Star is the third highest award for combat heroism and ranks fourth in overall precedence. The medal, changed in 1932 to its present form, is a gilded bronze five-pointed star with the original silver star superimposed in a wreath at the center.

Legion of Merit. Ranking just below the Silver Star, the Legion of Merit was created by Act of Congress on July 20, 1942, retroactive to Sept. 8, 1939, the date that President Franklin D. Roosevelt proclaimed a state of emergency before World War II. It is awarded to members of the armed forces both of the United States and of friendly foreign nations who "have distinguished themselves by exceptionally meritorious conduct in the performance of outstanding services." The Legion of Merit is the only U.S. decoration with specific degrees of rank. The size, design, and method of wear differ with each of the four degrees. It replaced the Purple Heart as the award for meritorious service.

Distinguished Flying Cross. First authorized by Congress on July 2, 1926, and amended by executive order on Jan. 8, 1938, the Distinguished Flying Cross was made retroactive to Nov. 11, 1918, for heroism or extraordinary achievement while participating in aerial flight. A special provision allowed the award to be made to individuals who were recommended for, but did not receive, the Medal of Honor, Distinguished Service Cross, Navy Cross, or Distinguished Service Medal. Amelia Earhart is the only civilian recipient. The criteria for the award are the same for all services.

Soldier's Medal. The Soldier's Medal is a noncombat award given to any person who, while serving in any capacity with the army, distinguishes himself by heroism not involving actual conflict with an enemy after July 2, 1926. It is a highly respected sign of personal bravery usually indicating risk of life. On July 6, 1960, Congress authorized the equivalent Airman's Medal.

Navy and Marine Corps Medal. Authorized by Congress on Aug. 7, 1942, the Navy and Marine Corps Medal parallels the Soldier's Medal and is awarded to anyone who, while serving in any capacity with the navy or the Marine Corps, distinguishes himself by heroism not involving actual conflict with an enemy after Dec. 6, 1941. The award may also be made to any person to whom the secretary of the navy, before Aug. 7, 1942, awarded a letter of commendation for heroism.

Bronze Star Medal. First authorized in 1944, the regulations covering the Bronze Star have undergone numerous revisions. As of Nov. 28, 1967, the Bronze Star may be awarded by the secretary of a military department, or by the secretary of transportation with regard to the Coast Guard when it is not operating as a service in the navy, to any person who, while serving in any capacity in or with the army, navy, air force, Marine Corps, or Coast Guard after Dec. 6, 1941, distinguishes himself by heroic or meritorious achievement or service not involving aerial flight during military operations. It can also be awarded to all personnel authorized the Combat Infantry Badge or Combat Medical Badge between Dec. 7, 1941, and Sept. 2, 1945.

Air Medal. Established on May 11, 1942, the Air Medal is given to any person who, while serving with the armed forces subsequent to Sept. 8, 1939, distinguishes himself by meritorious achievement while participating in aerial flight.

Purple Heart, Order of the. Established by George Washington on Aug. 7, 1782, as a reward for meritorious service and extraordinary fidelity; originally called the Badge of Military Merit. It is America's oldest military decoration. After the Revolution it fell into disuse until it was reestablished in 1932. The new regulation interpreted a "singularly meritorious act" to include wounds received in action and was made retroactive to Apr. 5, 1917, authorizing the medal to all individuals who received Meritorious Service Citation Certificates and wound chevrons in World War I. Since 1942, when the Legion of Merit was established, the Purple Heart has been awarded to members of the armed forces and, in some cases, civilians, for injuries received in action.

DEERFIELD MASSACRE. Early on Feb. 29, 1704, 50 French soldiers and 200 Indian allies from Canada, under Maj. Hertel de Rouville, entered the snowdrifted stockade at Deerfield, Mass., and overcame the 300 sleeping inhabitants; about 50 were killed, 137 escaped, and 111 were taken captive. During the journey to Canada 17 captives died from exposure or at the hands of their captors. After negotiations lasting several years, 60 captives were allowed to return home; some, however, preferred to remain in Canada.

DEFENSE, DEPARTMENT OF. Created in 1947 by the National Security Act. The department is headed by the secretary of defense, the third ranking member of the president's cabinet. It was set up following World War II in order to "unify" the armed forces. It replaced the War and Navy departments. The experience of World War II indicated that a unified command of the armed forces would be wise. One movement was to unite the armed forces under a single direction; the other was to create a separate and equal military force to direct air power. The Department of Defense was the result of an effort to accomplish both objectives. It was a single civilian-headed organization to direct all the military activities, but was made up of three subordinate departments —Army, Navy, and Air Force.

The secretary of defense heads a large organization with two tasks: it represents the president in directing and managing the armed forces, and it represents the armed forces before Congress by requesting support and direction in organizing defense policies. The Joint Chiefs of Staff is an organization of the heads of the U.S. Army, Navy, Marine Corps, and Air Force. These officers serve directly under the secretary of defense as the principal military advisers to the president, the secretary of defense, and the National Security Council. Under the Department of Defense, the three "service" departments are headed by civilian officials, the secretaries of the army, the navy, and the air force.

DEFENSE, NATIONAL. The pursuit of all national interests by military means. In 1789 the U.S. Constitution gave the federal government powers to provide for the common defense, balanced by state control of the militia and the right of the citizenry to bear arms. The Congress was empowered to levy taxes, declare war, raise armies, and provide for a navy. The president was named commander in chief and in 1795 received authority to call out the militia. The Militia Act of 1792 established the principle of universal obligation to military service for all free white male citizens between eighteen and forty-five.

DEFIANCE, FORT. The strongest post built by Gen. Anthony Wayne during his 1794 campaign against the Indians of the region, at the junction of the Auglaize and Maumee rivers within the present Defiance, Ohio. From it, Wayne moved down the Maumee Valley to the victory of Fallen Timbers, near present Toledo, Ohio.

DEFICIT, FEDERAL. Since the federal government's annual receipts and expenditures never balance exactly, a surplus or deficit must result. All wars and most major depressions have caused a deficit. There were eighty-nine annual deficits during 1791–1980. Minor ones, financed by bank loans or bond issues, have been paid off by higher taxes or greater tax receipts in better times. Major ones have been financed by inflation, borrowing, or taxation.

The American Revolution was financed largely by domestic loans and issues of paper money, most later repudiated or redeemed at very low rates. The War of 1812 caused a four-year deficit of $68 million, financed by internal loans and circulating treasury notes. The Mexican War produced a three-year deficit of $53 million taken care of by government borrowing. The Civil War was accompanied by a four-year deficit of $2.619 billion, financed largely by borrowing on long-term bonds and interest-bearing notes. The Spanish-American War caused a two-year deficit of $127 million, financed by a "popular loan" and increased internal taxes. World War I produced a three-year deficit of $24.9 billion. The government met immediate needs by selling the banks short-term treasury notes. These were soon retired with the proceeds of the next Liberty Loan. There were five such loans. Banks cooperated by lending to people who wanted to buy the bonds and accepting the bonds as security. The government then drew checks on the deposits thus created. A deposit currency inflation resulted, accentuated by the lower reserve requirements set by the Federal Reserve Act of 1913. Consumer prices almost doubled between 1916 and 1920.

Not until after 1929 did a depression constitute a major emergency. From 1913 through 1941 the government had an annual deficit averaging almost $3 billion a year, 54 percent over receipts. The thinking was that deficit spending was necessary to bring about economic recovery. The deficits were financed by the sale of government obligations to the public and to banks. At the end of 1941, member banks and Federal Reserve banks held $22 billion worth of government obligations, roughly 44 percent of the federal debt.

World War II produced a deficit of $183 billion during 1942–46 and precipitated a price inflation fed not only by its own enormous cost but by the government spending of the 1930's. Consumer prices almost doubled from 1939 to 1952.

The Korean War, the cold war, and foreign aid to nations devastated by World War II were largely responsible for the next deficit, $16.6 billion, in 1952–54. The inflationary effects were mild. Another large federal deficit began in 1961 and may be attributed to the costs of the war in Vietnam, extensive social welfare reforms, the cold war, and space exploration. The sum of all deficits in 1961–73, less the 1969 surplus, totaled almost $150 billion at the end of fiscal 1973 (June 30). This deficit, moreover, had over half its growth in the last three years of the period. To a degree, incurring annual deficits has become a way of life for the federal government.

After a relatively small deficit of $4.7 billion in 1974, the federal deficits soared in an unprecedented way: from 1975 to 1980 they amounted to about $286 billion, with the record high of $66.4 billion in fiscal 1976. Factors contributing to this were the fourfold increase of oil prices, mushrooming bureaucracy and grants to state and local governments, cost of social programs, and growing defense budgets. Federal deficits are the most basic cause of price inflation. Between 1950 and 1980, consumer prices increased about 300 percent; the average annual inflation rose from 6.7 percent during 1970–75 to 7.8 percent in 1975–79, and in two consecutive years, 1979 and 1980, there was a double-digit (11.3 and 12.4, respectively) inflation.

DEFINITIVE TREATY OF PEACE (1783). This treaty between Great Britain and the United States, signed at Paris on Sept. 3, marked the consummation of the revolutionary war. Coincidentally were signed peace treaties between Great Britain and France, the ally of the United States, and Spain, the ally of France. A preliminary peace between Great Britain and the Netherlands had been signed on Sept. 2, 1783.

The principal terms of the Anglo-American definitive treaty were independence of the United States; evacuation "with all convenient speed" of British troops; guarantee against obstacles to the collection, in sterling money, of private prewar debts to British creditors; boundary on the north corresponding to the present one as far west as the Lake of the Woods in present-day Minnesota, on the west the Mississippi, and on the south Florida; and "liberty" to fish in Atlantic inshore fisheries of remaining British North America.

DEGOLYER CASE (1874). A congressional committee investigated excessive expenditures for municipal paving in Washington, D.C., under the territorial governor, Alexander R. ("Boss") Shepherd. The DeGolyer Company, which laid the pavement, had paid a large retaining fee to Congressman James A. Garfield to present its merits before the Board of Public Works. Garfield stated that, as a House member, he had no connection with the government of the District of Columbia. The investigation also revealed that Boss Shepherd had been awarding municipal contracts to friends. The investigation led to the abolition of territorial government in Washington and the institution of commission rule.

DE HAVEN'S EXPEDITION (1850–51). Undertaken by the federal government and financed by Henry Grinnell, to rescue Sir John Franklin, an English explorer lost in the Arctic in 1845. The expedition, under the command of Lt. Edwin Jesse De Haven of the U.S. Navy, left New York City, May 22, 1850. De Haven began his search in Baffin Bay, sailing westward into Barrow Strait, where he found evidence of Franklin's encampments. De Haven did not find Franklin, but he discovered and named Grinnell Land. The expedition returned to New York, Sept. 30, 1851.

DEISM. Belief in the existence of a supreme being, but rejecting revelation and the supernatural doctrines of Christianity; introduced into America in the latter 18th century. Its influence was particularly felt during and immediately following the Revolution.

DELAWARE. The second smallest state in area; lies in the middle of the Atlantic coastal plain halfway between Washington, D.C., and New York City. In 1980 its population was 595,225.

Delaware was settled in 1631 by the Dutch, superseded briefly by the Swedes in 1638. The Dutch recovered control in 1655, only to be overthrown by the English, who gave the state its present name. When William Penn became proprietor of Pennsylvania, the "three lower counties on Delaware" were given him by the Duke of York. In 1776 these counties became the "Delaware State." On Dec. 7, 1789, Delaware, by being first to ratify the Constitution of the United States, gained the honor of becoming the first state, with Dover as its capital.

After the Revolution, industrialization began in the northern part of the state with powder mills along the Brandywine. The southern area remained agricultural, specializing in grains and fruits. Because of slave interests, some of its citizens supported the Confederacy, but the state itself remained loyal to the Union cause. The Democratic party was in control until 1889, when a Republican senator was elected. From the turn of the century the state has been largely Republican.

By the end of World War I, New Castle County had become largely industrial and the home of the Du Pont Company. The southern part remained agricultural until about 1950, when local industries began to compete with farming. New Castle County at the close of World War II was industrial, commercial, and largely suburban in character.

DELAWARE (Indians). The history of the Delaware tribe, located in New Jersey, western Long Island, and Staten and Manhattan islands, mirrors the fate of many Atlantic seaboard Indians: a gradual movement westward until their final settlement in Oklahoma. This tribe, first contacted by the Dutch in 1609, is alleged to have sold Manhattan Island in 1626. Gradually the Delaware gave up their coastal villages. In the course of their long odyssey westward, they were involved with the French and Spanish, fought the British, became converted to Moravian Christianity, and so generally lost their earlier cultural associations.

Considering that change had come to the Delaware as early as the 17th century, it is difficult to give a precise description of the native culture. They were Algonkin-speakers of the Atlantic Coast, often identified with the Abnaki. A dependence on hunting and basic maize agriculture can be supposed. Bark houses and containers, village autonomy with village chiefs, and political alliances with others of the same language grouping might be expected.

DELAWARE, WASHINGTON CROSSING THE (1776). The turning point of the Revolution, Gen. George Washington's crossing of the Delaware River and subsequent defeat of the British in New Jersey checked the British advance toward Philadelphia and restored American morale. On Christmas Day, 1776, some 2,400 men set out from the Pennsylvania side of the Delaware River north of Trenton, N.J., to surprise the British forces, chiefly Hessians. Although the supporting columns failed or refused to make the crossing because of the treacherous weather and the floating ice, Washington's command made its way across. It marched to Trenton, surprised the Hessian garrison, killed some, including the commander, Col. Johann Rall, and took 946 prisoners. It then recrossed the Delaware, with half its number disabled by the cold. Emanuel Leutze's famous painting *Washington Crossing the Delaware,* although more fanciful than accurate in detail, has become a symbol of Washington's great exploit.

DELAWARE AND HUDSON. *See* **Railroads, Sketches of Principal Lines.**

DELAWARE AND HUDSON CANAL. Projected by the Wurts brothers to carry anthracite from their Pennsylvania coalfield to New York City, the Delaware and Hudson Canal was built, 1825–28, from the Delaware River at Honesdale, Pa., to the Hudson River at Kingston, N.Y. The canal was enormously profitable for a number of years, but by 1900, with the rise of the railroads, it had ceased operation.

DELAWARE AND RARITAN CANAL. The idea of connecting New York and Philadelphia directly by water was discussed before 1800, but it was not until 1830 that the

Delaware and Raritan Canal Company was organized. The Camden and Amboy Railroad, a parallel competitor chartered on the same day, soon made a deal by which the two became essentially one. The canal, extending from the Raritan River estuary to tidewater on the Delaware, was opened in 1834 and was of enormous importance to commerce. In 1871 it passed completely under the domination of the Pennsylvania Railroad. By 1930 its traffic had almost ceased.

DELAWARE BAY. Between the east coast of Delaware and the southwest coast of New Jersey; Henry Hudson discovered it on Aug. 28, 1609. The South Bay and River, as the Dutch called them, were visited by a number of Dutch navigators, among them Capt. Cornelis Jacobsen Mey, in 1614, for whom Cape May is named. These were followed in 1631 by an expedition under David P. De Vries which founded Zwaanendael near present Lewes, Del. During 1632–33 he visited "Godyn's Bay" and reported that the English called it "My Lord Delaware's Bay." Thomas West, Lord De La Warr, the first governor of Virginia, probably never saw the bay and river named for him by Capt. Samuel Argall, who arrived at the bay in the *Discovery* on Aug. 27, 1610.

DELAWARE CIRCLE. The northern boundary of the state of Delaware. It was first mentioned in the royal grant from Charles II to his brother, James, Duke of York, in March 1682. In order to define the boundaries of Chester and New Castle counties, both of the province of Pennsylvania, Isaac Taylor and Thomas Pierson in 1701 surveyed a line with a twelve-mile radius from New Castle. In 1765 Charles Mason and Jeremiah Dixon surveyed their lines tangent to the circle.

DELAWARE COUNTIES ACT OF UNION (1682). Passed Dec. 7, in answer to a petition from the counties of New Castle, St. Jones, and Whorekill, or Deale (now New Castle, Kent, and Sussex, which constitute the state of Delaware). The petitioners asked that the three counties might "be favoured with an act of union" with Pennsylvania so that they might have the same rights as those in that province.

DELAWARE, LACKAWANNA AND WESTERN. *See* **Railroads, Sketches of Principal Lines: Erie Lackawanna.**

DELAWARE PROPHET (Neolin?). Started a nativistic movement among the Delaware Indians near Lake Erie in 1762. Claiming to be preaching by divine command, he called for a cessation of wars among Indians in favor of a holy war against the whites and a return to the ways of their ancestors. The message had a strong appeal to the other tribes of the region, and it influenced the Ottawa chief Pontiac in his uprising and attack on Detroit in 1763.

DELEGATION OF POWERS. The courts have often said that Congress as a recipient of delegated power from the people through the Constitution may not further delegate its legislative powers to other agencies of government. At the same time, they have admitted that Congress can adopt only a general policy, which must be implemented by others in unanticipated circumstances and contexts. The U.S. Supreme Court stated in 1940 that "delegation by Congress has long been recognized as necessary in order that the exertion of legislative power does not become a futility."

Three types of delegation can be identified. The first leaves to a person or agency the task of filling in the details and elaborating the general policy. This is exemplified in the Interstate Commerce Commission being directed to insure that railroad rates are "reasonable." A second type is contingency delegation. Legislation is passed that will go into effect or be suspended when the executive branch determines that a specified situation exists. Tariff laws, for example, usually give the president power to change duties if other countries make changes. The third type occurs in foreign affairs, where courts have approved broader delegations of power to the president.

Limits exist on the ability of Congress to delegate legislative power to administrative agencies. Congress must define the subject to be regulated and provide a standard to guide its agent's actions. Delegation must be to public officials, not to private groups or individuals. Penal sanctions for violation of administrative orders can be provided only by Congress.

***DELIMA* V. *BIDWELL*,** 182 U.S. (1901). First of the Insular Cases, following the Spanish-American War. The protectionists' claim that Puerto Rico was a foreign country, and so subject to the Dingley Tariff, was rejected by the Supreme Court; Congress was permitted on other grounds to regulate the tariff relations of dependent states.

DEMARCATION LINE. In 1493, Pope Alexander VI issued a bull to King Ferdinand II and Queen Isabella I, monarchs of Spain, granting them all lands in South America west of a line 100 leagues west of the Azores and Cape Verde Islands. On June 7, 1494, by the Treaty of Tordesillas the demarcation line between Spain and Portugal was placed 370 leagues west of the Cape Verde Islands. This line, north by south, struck South America near the mouth of the Amazon River.

DEMOBILIZATION. Dismissal of troops to civilian life and the winding down of a war industry at the end of hostilities or a national emergency. Because American wars have been fought predominantly with volunteers, militia, or drafted civilians, the sudden return of these individuals to civilian life often has had the proportions of an avalanche.

In the Revolutionary War and the War of 1812, demobilization was a continuous process because of short-term enlistments and because poor transportation and communications made it impractical or impossible to shift troops from one engagement to another.

In the Mexican War, Gen. Winfield Scott experienced a demobilization of 40 percent of his troops when their one-year enlistments expired. From then on, volunteers were enlisted for the duration of the conflict. At the end of the war 41,000 men were dispersed over the Southwest and Mexico; they were finally transported to New Orleans by boat.

The problems of releasing 1,034,064 men after the Civil War dwarfed previous demobilization efforts and were compounded by the lack of a detailed plan. Demobilization took as long as eighteen months for volunteers; it took longer for regular troops because of the French threat in Mexico and the need for occupation troops during Reconstruction.

After the sudden victory of the United States in the Spanish-American War (1898), mustering-out procedures were changed midway through demobilization, causing much confusion. Some regiments were held until 1902 because of the insurrection in the Philippines.

World War I ended with an abruptness that again caught military planners without a demobilization plan. Over 3 million men were eligible for discharge. Release by military unit was the method considered most equitable and least disruptive of the economy.

World War II demobilization planning began in the last two years of the war and required the efforts of a special planning division. The task was herculean: 8 million soldiers had to be demobilized, 5 million of whom were deployed worldwide and had to be returned home; in addition, a four-year logistical buildup had to be liquidated. Troop release was by individuals, not units; and a point system governed the sequence. By June 1946 the army was reduced in strength by half. This sudden release of personnel greatly inhibited the proper disposition of war matériel, because not enough troops were left to handle the assignment efficiently. The limited wars of the post–World War II period used reserve call-ups and drafted troops who were rotated on an individual twelve-month basis; thus, demobilization was continuous.

DEMOCRACY. A system of government in which the authority to govern is exercised by public officials responsible to a broad electorate that periodically chooses from among competing candidates for office in free elections. Democracy may be said to exist where most adults have the right to stand for office and to vote; freedom of association in competing political parties is recognized and protected; and public opinion is informed through an unfettered press, freedom of speech, and general education.

Democracy developed gradually in the course of American history. As the colonial period progressed, there were democratic developments, notably the rise of locally elected popular branches of the legislatures to positions of self-confidence and power. The American Revolution advanced the cause of democracy by eliminating the monarchy and a hereditary titled aristocracy from the American scene and by broadening the base of social, economic, and political power. The party line of the American Revolution was that all men are endowed by their Creator with equal natural, inalienable rights and that government rests upon the consent of the governed. The right to vote and hold office without regard to property qualifications was greatly expanded during the Jacksonian period. The right to vote was extended to free blacks by state action in only six states in 1860. The Fifteenth Amendment to the Constitution in 1870 forbade the denial of the right to vote because of race or color and gave Congress the power to enforce this concept by appropriate legislation. The struggle to translate this commitment into reality, culminated in the Voting Rights Act of 1965. By 1920, fifteen states had extended the suffrage to women, and the right of women to vote was nationalized by the Nineteenth Amendment in 1920. Finally, the voting age was reduced in 1971 to eighteen by the Twenty-sixth Amendment.

DEMOCRACY, JACKSONIAN. *See* **Jacksonian Democracy.**

DEMOCRACY, JEFFERSONIAN. *See* **Jeffersonian Democracy.**

DEMOCRACY, WORLD SAFE FOR. Slogan from President Woodrow Wilson's message to Congress, Apr. 2, 1917, asking for a declaration of war: "The world must be made safe for democracy. Its peace must be planted upon the tested foundations of political liberty."

DEMOCRATIC CLUBS. *See* **Jacobin Clubs.**

DEMOCRATIC PARTY. Conventionally, the Democratic party is dated to the formative decade immediately following the ratification of the Constitution in 1789. Indeed, the Antifederalists of that seminal period were, as often as not, individuals who had opposed ratification. The policies proposed as alternatives to those of the completely dominant Federalist party were based principally on constitutional interpretations. Despite policy debates, the American party system emerged not so much because of them as because of the deep divisions engendered by the dominant Federalists' frequent rejection of the legitimacy of organized partisan opposition. Nevertheless, the U.S. party system that emerged during the first two decades of the 19th century was characterized by a general acceptance of the legitimacy of a party in opposition to a regime in power and by the fuller development of a national arena for political conflict and development. The Democratic party, or its predecessor the Democratic-Republican party, played a critical role in the establishment of legitimate two-party competition.

Although the Democratic-Republicans were originally identified as the party of strict or narrow construction of the Constitution, the party position in each state was often determined by political expediency. Although it remained in ascendancy into the third decade of the 19th century, it disintegrated into competing factions, and in 1824 a viable opposition party, successor to the Federalist party, emerged, first designated National Republican and later Whig.

The Democratic party in the Jacksonian era was substantially consistent in its opposition to a national bank, to the tariff, and, on the whole, to federal internal improvements. Subsequently, the failure of the Whig party and the Democratic party to resolve the slavery issue resulted in the former's disintegration and replacement by the Republican party (1856) and the latter's massive defeat in national politics (1860). While the post–Civil War era brought a long period of presidential losses to the Democratic party, it also saw sectional party divisions that gave the Democrats almost unchallenged control of the South until the mid-20th century. The Southern Democratic constituency brought with it a generally conservative ideology, and William Jennings Bryan gave the Democratic party a rural and anticorporate policy orientation. By 1896 the party had lost the bulk of its urban voters, and only through the circumstance of the William H. Taft–Theodore Roosevelt split of 1912 did the party achieve victory in that year. After Woodrow Wilson's presidency, the Democratic party appeared once again to sink into the role of a minority party. The impact of the Great Depression provided the basis for Franklin D. Roosevelt's landslide victory of 1932. His coalition-building skills brought urban labor into the ranks of the Democratic party and laid the foundation for successive victories until 1952.

After eight years of a Republican administration, the Democratic party was reinvigorated by the election of John F. Kennedy and by "New Frontier" policies. His sweeping social and civil rights reforms were continued under President Lyndon B. Johnson, but during his presidency the Democratic party became deeply divided over the war in Vietnam. In the 1970's the Democrats briefly exploited the discrediting of the Republican party by the Watergate scandals, but worsening economic conditions and the Iranian crisis during President Jimmy Carter's term in office led to an overwhelming Democratic defeat in 1980, with the Senate coming under Republican control for the first time since 1954.

DEMOCRATIC-REPUBLICAN PARTY. An offshoot of the Anti-Federalist party, and ancestor of the modern Democratic party. It organized around Thomas Jefferson's Republican party's opposition to the policies of Alexander Hamilton in the 1790's. Jefferson's Republican party was based on a number of "Republican Clubs" and "Democratic Clubs" already formed in different states. The party expressed opposition to strong central government, the economic policies of Hamilton, and to the support of England during the wars of the French Revolution. It advocated an agrarian democracy, strict construction of the Constitution, and reforms eliminating aristocratic control of government. (*See* Democratic Party).

DEMOGRAPHY. The quantitative and statistical analysis of populations that focuses upon birth, marriage, death, and geographical mobility. Two basic methods of analysis have been employed by historical demographers: aggregative analysis, which involves the collection of vital data for a whole population by month and year, accumulated for substantial periods of time, thus providing graphic evidence for long-term trends in births, marriages, and deaths for specific communities; and family reconstitution, which involves the detailed recovery of vital events for each individual and family in specific communities, thus providing a remarkably complete collection of data on many of the most intimate aspects of human experience.

The first serious U.S. contributions in the field of demography were made by historians of early America whose work began to appear during the mid-1960's. Focusing upon specific communities, colonies, or groups, many historians began to make use of European historical demographic methods and to demonstrate for the first time what actually happened to people living in 17th- and 18th-century American communities. These studies represent only a tiny fraction of the total population. In the 1970's, historians began to probe the demographic history of the United States during the 19th century. The analysis of census listings in particular was providing new information and insights into the demographic experience.

***DEMOLOGOS*.** Officially christened *Fulton the First;* Robert Fulton's steam warship, designed during the War of 1812 for the defense of New York's harbor. After a detailed study of Fulton's design by a panel of naval experts, Congress authorized its construction; it was launched on Oct. 29, 1814. The ship cruised New York Harbor in 1815, but it never saw battle. It lay at the navy yard until 1829, when it blew up.

DEMONETIZATION. *See* **Silver Legislation.**

DENONVILLE, FORT. A palisaded wooden fortress, erected by order of the governor of Canada, Jacques René de Brisay, Marquis de Denonville, on the east side of the Niagara River at Lake Ontario in 1687, to protect the French trade. Depleted by starvation during the winter, it was relieved in spring 1688 and abandoned in September.

DENONVILLE'S INVASION (1687). Determined to subdue the Iroquois, the governor of Canada, Jacques René de Brisay, Marquis de Denonville, summoned Henry de Tonti and Daniel Greysolon, Sieur Duluth, to organize the French forces, including Indian allies, and proceed to Irondequoit Bay on Lake Ontario. The main army under Denonville embarked at Montreal for Irondequoit Bay, where the western forces soon joined them.

Denonville advanced against the Seneca, July 12. On the second day, while approaching a village reported deserted, the army was ambushed and 100 soldiers and 10 Indian allies were lost. The following day Denonville ordered an advance against the village, but the Seneca had burned it during their retreat. The French destroyed three other villages and surrounding fields before returning to Irondequoit Bay.

DENTISTRY. In early America dentistry was largely a matter of occasional toothdrawing, chiefly by physicians. The earliest known specialist was James Reading in New York about 1733. Little is known beyond the advertising notices in colonial newspapers. Most dentists were itinerants. The best also cleaned and filled teeth and prepared artificial dentures. Apprenticeship was the sole method of learning. The first American dental book was *A Treatise on the Human Teeth* (1801), by R. C. Skinner. Between 1801 and 1839 a few more dental books were published, and lectures on dentistry were sporadically offered at the University of Maryland. In Bainbridge, Ohio, Dr. John Harris opened a short-lived private medical school where he also taught dentistry. The first organized effort to combat quacks and incompetents was by the Society of Surgeon Dentists of the City and State of New York, organized in 1834.

Literature, education, and organization became realities in dentistry beginning in 1839, when the *American Journal of*

Dental Science, the first journal of its kind in the world, edited by Chapin A. Harris and others, and Harris's textbook *The Dental Art: A Practical Treatise on Dental Surgery* appeared. Harris and Horace H. Hayden, dean of Baltimore dentists, organized the Baltimore College of Dental Surgery (now the Dental School of the University of Maryland), chartered in 1840. The Ohio College of Dental Surgery followed in 1845 and other colleges in the 1850's. In 1840, Harris, Hayden, Solyman, Brown, and others founded the American Society of Dental Surgeons. The society acquired the reputation of a clique and dissolved in 1856. Meanwhile, in 1855 dissidents founded the American Dental Convention (ADC), open to virtually all who applied. Four years later the American Dental Association (ADA) was organized representing local societies and dental schools. The two organizations coexisted until 1883, when the ADC dissolved. The ADA (named the National Dental Association from 1897 to 1922) has remained the spokesman of the organized dental profession.

After the Civil War, one of the primary problems was the improvement of educational standards. During the 1860's several local dentistry societies began requiring a diploma from a dental college. In 1875 the ADA also added this requirement. State licensing laws made the need for standards even more critical if the diploma was the key to a license. The National Association of Dental Examiners (1883) and the National Association of Dental Faculties (1884) carried much of the burden. The Dental Faculties Association of American Universities was formed in 1909. The critical nature of the problem may be illustrated by the precipitous drop in the entering class at Northwestern University Dental School from 166 to 66 when the admission requirement was raised from two years of high school to high school graduation. A major step came in 1916 when the Dental Educational Council, a joint body including the ADA, established specifications for class A, B, and C schools. The Dental Educational Council and the American Association of Dental Schools (1923) pushed through curricular and other changes that raised dentistry to a university-educated profession.

The pioneering *American Journal of Dental Science* was followed by a succession of proprietary journals published by dental manufacturing companies. In 1913 the ADA inaugurated its own quarterly *Bulletin,* later the monthly *Journal of the American Dental Association.* The ADA also started the *Journal of Dental Research* in 1919.

Meanwhile, advances in scientific dental knowledge and techniques were also paving the way to improved dental health. Through most of the 19th century, improvements were chiefly mechanical. New drills and other instruments were devised. The foot-operated cord-driven dental engine, introduced in 1871, proved to be of fundamental importance. Artificial teeth and dentures were improved when porcelain teeth began to replace those made of ivory. The discovery of anesthesia in 1846, making extraction relatively painless, and the invention of vulcanite by Charles Goodyear in the 1850's made cheap dentures widely available. The dental engine made possible adequate preparation of the teeth to receive fixed crowns and bridges. In 1907 William H. Taggart developed a casting process that made gold inlay fillings possible.

In the latter 19th century, a more scientific attitude toward dentistry began to appear. Prominent in this development was the work of Greene Vardiman Black. Among his more important achievements were the establishment of proper techniques of cavity preparation to prevent further decay (1891) and the development of a method of making stable amalgams (1895). His final contribution was a pioneer article with Frederick S. McKay on mottled enamel.

Improvements in the early 20th century were more careful antiseptic techniques and judicious extractions, as well as increasing use of X rays to determine conditions within the bone. Concern with bacterial infection as a cause of tooth decay led to increasing attention to oral disease, oral hygiene, and preventive dentistry. Far more promising as a mass preventive measure was the introduction of fluoridation of water supplies in the 1940's.

In 1928 the ADA inaugurated a continuing and fruitful arrangement with the National Bureau of Standards that led to important advances in dental materials and instrumentation. A dental research program at the National Institutes of Health (1932) led to the creation of the National Institute of Dental Health in 1948.

One effect of the oral hygiene movement and the growth of public health dentistry, combined with the scientific improvements in dentistry itself, was a growing public demand for dental services, but the cost of dental care also came to the fore. Various insurance and panel practice schemes were suggested without a solution being found. Provision of dental services remained a challenging problem in the 1970's.

DENVER (Colo.). Capital of Colorado, located in the northeastern part of the state; founded in 1858 by a gold-seeking party who named it for J. W. Denver, governor of the Kansas Territory. Located near the foot of the Rocky Mountains, Denver became the supply depot for the mines. Development was slowed by the Civil War, Indian uprisings, and refractory ores, but with its designation as state capital (1867), the coming of the railroad (1870), and improved smelting methods, the city began to grow rapidly. Great silver camps grew, railroads multiplied, and agriculture flourished nearby. Although demonetization of silver and the panic of 1893 retarded Denver's growth, the Cripple Creek gold strike (1891) brought renewed expansion.

In the first decade after 1900, Denver won home rule from Colorado, began to beautify itself, and doubled its population to 213,381. A slump in mining after World War I closed Denver's smelters, but other businesses grew. Over 20,000 acres of mountain parks were acquired for recreation. World War II brought large war industries to Denver. The impressive Stapleton Airport was expanded, and in 1965 one of the world's foremost air-training centers was added. Denver became an important distribution, trade, tourist, and cultural center. The city's population was 491,396 in 1980; Denver-Boulder metropolitan area included 1,615,442 people.

DENVER AND RIO GRANDE WESTERN. *See* **Railroads, Sketches of Principal Lines.**

DEPARTMENT STORES. In the early 1880's, large downtown retail establishments, divided into departments and selling clothing, soft goods, furniture, and home appliances, were the first to be called department stores. Individual departments were sometimes leased to outside operators.

The Census Bureau defines department stores as "establishments normally employing 25 people or more, having sales of apparel and soft goods combined amounting to 20 percent or more of total sales, and engaged in selling each of the following: furniture, home furnishings, appliances, radios and TV sets; apparel; and household linens and dry goods."

The share in total retail sales for department stores was 2 percent in 1899, 8 percent in 1929, and 10 percent in 1980. In 1977, about 8,800 establishments were classified by the bureau as department stores, with $77 billion in sales and 1,644,000 employees. Of these stores only some 600 were independent units; the remainder were owned by chains varying in size and scope—more than one-half of them having more than 100 units. A trend toward moving to suburban or even rural locations began in the 1950's and accelerated in the 1960's and 1970's, so that independent operation in urban centers became less typical of department stores.

DEPLETION ALLOWANCE. An amount of money that may be deducted from the taxable income of a person because of the use of some asset that cannot be replaced. Depletion allowances are granted to mine or oil-well owners, for example, because their products cannot be replaced once they have been extracted from the ground. In practice, depletion allowances permit owners to deduct from their taxable income a percentage of the income from the mines or wells.

DEPORTATION. Governmental expulsion of an unwanted alien. Deportation laws often have encountered criticism because of the alleged harshness of their impact on deportees. This was true, for example, of the Alien Act of 1798 (expired 1800) and also of U.S. policy in the 1920's. The first U.S. deportation law of modern times (1888) provided for the deportation of contract laborers (typically Chinese) within one year after illegal entry. The 1891 Immigration Act extended the penalty to all illegal immigrants. Subsequent amendments expanded the categories of deportees and increased the period after entry, until the 1952 deportation law eliminated all time restrictions on most deportations.

An average of 336 deportations per year between 1892 and 1900 rose to 995 by 1907. New amendments raised 1908–20 deportations to 2,676 per year. Since 1920, deportations have ranged between 90,000 and 130,000 in each decade. The 1920's saw peak deportation of subversives, public charges, and those with mental or physical defects. The 1930's saw peaks for deportation of those involved in prostitution, criminals, and illiterates. Deportation of narcotics violators reached a high in the 1960's. Lack of proper documents, inspection avoidance, falsified statements, and violation of nonimmigrant status have been major reasons for deportation since the introduction of national-origin quotas in 1924.

In the 1970's the emphasis in deportation was on expulsion of illegally present Mexican laborers; in the year ending Sept. 30, 1977, almost 18,000 Mexicans who entered without inspection were deported. In 1980 the United States wanted to deport 1,800 Cuban "undesirables" who had come in "freedom flotillas" in the spring of that year, but secret talks with Cuba on the issue collapsed Jan. 16, 1981. Other deportation problems occurred in 1981 when between 1,000 and 1,500 Haitian refugees came to the United States illegally by boat each month. They were held in overcrowded detention centers.

DEPOSIT, FORT. Established in Alabama, on the Tennessee River, Oct. 23, 1813, by Gen. Andrew Jackson as a base for his operations during the Creek War (*see* Horseshoe Bend, Battle of).

DEPOSIT, RIGHT OF. By article IV of Pinckney's Treaty (1795), Spain recognized the U.S. claim to free navigation of the Mississippi River. Article XXII gave U.S. citizens the privilege of depositing and reexporting their property duty-free at New Orleans for three years; at the end of that period Spain should either continue this permission or assign an equivalent establishment at another place on the banks of the Mississippi. Opened in April 1798, the New Orleans deposit was extensively used until the intendant of Louisiana closed it, Oct. 16, 1802. Under threat of war Spain reopened the deposit at New Orleans, Apr. 19, 1803. It remained open until the United States took possession of New Orleans in December 1803, by virtue of the Louisiana Purchase.

DEPOSIT ACT OF 1836. Provided for distribution of the U.S. Treasury surplus, except for $5 million, to the states on the basis of representation in Congress. The act rid the government of the surplus (from tariff proceeds and public-land sales) that many wanted to share in; made inadvisable a reduction in the price of the government land the West wanted so much; benefited the old states much more than the new; diverted attention from Henry Clay's distribution bill, which President Andrew Jackson was pledged to veto; and won the president's reluctant approval. Deposits were halted when the panic of 1837 turned the surplus into a deficit.

DEPRESSION, GREAT. *See* **Great Depression.**

DEPRESSION OF 1920. Prosperity prevailed in the early part of 1920, as an aftermath of World War I. As prices rose, rumors of a buyers' strike spread. After reaching a peak in May, commodity prices declined rapidly and gave rise to unprecedented cancellation of orders. Money was extremely tight, although the stringency did not become acute until autumn. A flight of gold from the country caused a marked advance in money rates, and the end of the year saw a 30 percent decline in industrial stocks. Depression continued throughout 1921, characterized by inactive industries, business failures, and a decline in foreign trade.

DEPRESSIONS. *See under* individual Panics; Depressions; Business Cycles.

DERNA EXPEDITION (1805). In the last year of the Tripolitan War, William Eaton, formerly U.S. consul at Tunis, in an effort to dethrone the Bey of Tripoli and replace him with his brother Hamet, organized at Alexandria an expedition of 600 men. After leading them across 500 miles of desert, he captured Derna by assault. Before his force marched on Tripoli, news arrived of the signing of a peace treaty.

DESERET, STATE OF. Taken from the Book of Mormon, the name "Deseret," meaning "land of the honeybee," was given to the provisional state formed by the Mormons in 1849. It included the immense area of land, acquired in the Mexican War, east of the Sierra Nevada and west of the Rocky Mountains. At a convention on Mar. 4, a constitution was drafted, and Salt Lake City made the capital. Brigham Young was chosen governor. Almon W. Babbitt was elected delegate to petition Congress to admit Deseret to statehood. Congress, after voting unfavorably on the bill, created the Territory of Utah in 1850. The Mormons accepted this as a temporary measure. Remnants of the Deseret government were preserved for a number of years after 1850 and statehood was sought until 1883.

DESERT, GREAT AMERICAN. *See* **Great American Desert.**

DESERT CULTURE (Western Archaic culture). Part of the continentwide Archaic stage in prehistoric America. Both the lifeway and the artifacts were adjustments to arid land, sparse vegetation, and seasonal exploitation of wild plants and animals. The area encompasses the Great Basin, the Intermontane region, parts of the Colorado plateau, coastal California, Arizona southward into the central plateau of Mexico, and sections of the Plains south into Texas. Among the features are small social units, seed harvesting, fur cloth, woven sandals, basketry, flat milling stones, and a wide variety of small projectile points, choppers, scrapers, and bone tools. Most radiocarbon dates indicate that the formative development of the Desert culture began between 11,000 and 9,000 years ago. Sequences in development have been unearthed in a number of caves. The Desert culture persisted into the historic period in many areas.

DESERTION. Desertion from military service has been a continual phenomenon in the United States. The armed forces require enlisted men and women to serve tours of duty of specific duration; unlike commissioned officers, enlisted personnel are not legally permitted to resign before the end of that period. Thus, desertion—being absent without authorization for over a month—constitutes the enlisted person's repudiation of his legal obligation.

In peacetime, there has been a direct correlation between desertion rates and the business cycle. During a depression and labor surplus, fewer soldiers have abandoned the army; in an expanding economy, many more have forsaken the high job security but low monetary rewards of the army. The highest peacetime desertion rates in American history were reached during the periods of economic growth in the 1820's, early 1850's, early 1870's, 1880's, early 1900's, and 1920's (7–15 percent each year). A peak of 32.6 percent was recorded in 1871 in protest against a pay cut.

During wartime, desertion rates have varied widely but have generally been lower than in peacetime service—perhaps reflecting the increased numbers of troops, national spirit, and more severe penalties prescribed for combat desertion. The termination of hostilities has generally been accompanied by a dramatic flight from military duty.

In the Revolution, desertion depleted both the state militias and the Continental army after such reverses as the British seizure of New York City; at spring planting or fall harvesting time, when farmer-soldiers returned to their fields; and as veterans deserted in order to reenlist, seeking the increased bounties of cash or land that the states offered for new enlistees. Widespread desertion, even in the midst of battle, plagued the military during the War of 1812. In the Mexican War, 6,825 men, or nearly 7 percent of the army, deserted.

The Civil War produced the highest American wartime desertion rates because of its bloody battles, new enlistment bounties, and the relative ease with which deserters could escape capture in the interior regions. The Union armies recorded 278,644 cases of desertion, representing 11 percent of the troops. Confederate deserters numbered 104,428, or 10 percent of the armies of the South.

The Spanish-American War resulted in 5,285 desertions, or less than 2 percent in 1898. The rate climbed to 4 percent during the Philippine Insurrection of 1900–02. In World War I, because Selective Service regulations classified anyone failing to report for induction at the prescribed time as a deserter, the records of 1917–18 showed 363,022 deserters (more appropriately, draft evaders). Traditional deserters amounted to 21,282, or less than 1 percent. In World War II, desertion rates reached 6.3 percent in 1944, but dropped to 4.5 percent by 1945. The use of short-term service and the rotation system during the Korean War kept desertion rates down to 1.4 percent in 1951 and to 2.2 percent in 1953.

The unpopular war in Vietnam generated the highest percentage of wartime desertion since the Civil War. From 13,177 cases, or 1.6 percent in 1965, the annual desertion statistics mounted to 2.9 percent in 1968, 4.2 percent in 1969, 5.2 percent in 1970, and 7.4 percent (79,027) in 1971. Like the draft resisters, many deserters sought sanctuary in Canada, Mexico, or Sweden. In 1974 the Defense Department reported that there had been 503,926 incidents of desertion between July 1, 1966, and Dec. 31, 1973.

DESERT LAND ACT (1877). The second step taken by Congress to adjust the homestead unit of 160 acres to the requirements of farming in the semiarid West, the first being the Timber Culture Act of 1873. After 1877 it was possible for settlers to acquire 1,120 acres of public lands, 160 acres each under the Homestead, Pre-emption, and Timber Culture acts, and 640 acres under the Desert Land Act, which was designed to permit settlers to acquire a large enough tract of land to justify diversion dams and ditches for irrigation. Payment of 25 cents an acre was required upon making the entry and $1 an acre after three years. The act was taken advantage of by dummy entrymen operating for large capitalistic interests and by speculators hoping the government-irrigated land would become enormously valuable. Despite scandals and fraud, the act remained in operation with minor amendment into the 20th century.

DES MOINES (Iowa). Capital and largest city of Iowa, with a population of 191,003 in 1980. It was the center of a metropolitan area of 236,101 people. The city was incorporated in 1851 and became the capital in 1857. Des Moines is located at the confluence of the Raccoon and Des Moines rivers. This strategic location made it possible for soldiers to protect and control a wide section of Iowa territory, and forts were located at Des Moines as early as 1843. The fort and city became a stopping place for wagon trains bound across Iowa during the 1840's and 1850's. After the Civil War, Des Moines became an important stop on the direct rail route to Omaha, where the transcontinental rail lines began.

Several large insurance companies have headquarters in Des Moines; home and farm magazines are published there. It is also the shopping and warehousing depot for much of central Iowa. Much food processing is done in the city, using the farm products of central Iowa. Tools, machinery, and clothing are also produced.

DE SOTO EXPEDITION (1539–43). Hernando de Soto, a Spanish conquistador who had been involved in Francisco Pizarro's conquest of the Inca of Peru, secured a royal grant for the conquest of Florida. Sailing from Havana with about 600 men, he landed on Tampa Bay in 1539; a four-year journey in search of riches that he never found then took him halfway across the continent. As he traveled, de Soto pillaged and massacred thousands of Indians, while many of his followers were killed or died of disease and exposure.

In May 1541, de Soto discovered and crossed the Mississippi River. The Spaniards spent the winter of 1541–42 in northeastern Arkansas, and in spring 1542 they moved down the Arkansas River to the Mississippi once more. De Soto fell ill and died near Natchez on May 21, 1542. After fighting off Indian attacks in east Texas, the Spaniards built barges to float down the Mississippi, finally reaching the Gulf of Mexico. On Sept. 10, 1543, 320 survivors landed at the mouth of the Pánuco River in Mexico.

DESTROYER DEAL. On Sept. 3, 1940, President Franklin D. Roosevelt announced a "destroyer deal" with Great Britain, agreeing to turn over fifty old U.S. destroyers to the Royal Navy to help British convoys defend themselves against German submarine attacks. In exchange, the British gave the United States the right to build naval and air bases at several British-owned locations: Placentia Bay, Newfoundland; Bermuda; the Bahamas; Jamaica; St. Lucia; Trinidad; Antigua; and Georgetown, British Guiana.

Roosevelt was attacked by political opponents and American "isolationists," who argued that the deal constituted a treaty and should have been submitted to the Senate for approval. Roosevelt contended that it was a military agreement within his power as commander in chief.

DESTROYERS. *See* **Warships.**

DETROIT (Mich.). City located on the Detroit River, in southeast Michigan; began as a French community, when Antoine de la Mothe Cadillac, in 1701, founded a strategic garrison and fur-trading post. In 1760, the French garrison surrendered to a British military force. The Detroit community prospered as a fur-trading depot and a major cosmopolitan gateway for the Great Lakes. In 1783, Detroit was included within the new United States. The British, however, continued to administer Detroit until, by Jay's Treaty, their troops withdrew in 1796.

By 1805, Detroit was designated the capital of the new Michigan Territory. In 1805 also, the town was destroyed by fire and rebuilt. After the War of 1812, Detroit enjoyed an almost uninterrupted growth. In the post–Civil War era, it grew to be a modern city with highly diversified industries. In the first decade of the 20th century, Detroit became the automotive capital of the nation. The industry began in 1899 when R. E. Olds established a small factory in Detroit. Henry Ford brought even greater fame to Detroit with the introduction of the assembly line, the $5-a-day minimum wage, and his famous Model T. During World War I, the city's civilian and military production astounded the nation.

By the late 1920's, Detroit had become the boom city of the nation, since its high wages and unusual employment opportunities made the community a mecca for workers. The Great Depression brought widespread unemployment and devastating deflation. Recovery began with the awarding of defense contracts in 1940.

Postwar Detroit gradually evolved into a true metropolitan area. By 1980 the metropolitan area ranked fifth in the nation, with a population of 4,344,139; the city proper had 1,203,339 people. The economy of the area remains dependent largely on the automotive industry; because of the severe slump in car production in the late 1970's, unemployment in Detroit was almost double the national rate. The strains of growth and tensions in the inner city led to the race riots of 1943 and contributed to the destructive civil disorders of 1967. Detroit's cultural attractions include the municipal Detroit Institute of Arts and two large universities, Wayne State University and the University of Detroit.

DETROIT, FORT. From the 18th century through the early 19th century, several forts bearing different names existed at Detroit. The earliest, built by the French in 1701, was Fort Pontchartrain du Détroit. In November 1760 the fort surrendered to the British, who shortened its name to Detroit.

In May 1763 Ottawa chief Pontiac took to open warfare after his plan to seize Detroit by stratagem failed. Pontiac's siege of Detroit was broken after fifteen months (1764). Throughout the Revolution, Detroit was the chief center of British power in the West, and the goal of the American armies. All their efforts to reach Detroit were defeated, and the British greatly enlarged the fort. On July 11, 1796, in pursuance of Jay's Treaty, the British at length yielded Detroit to the Americans. In 1812, American Gen. William Hull invaded Canada from Detroit, but instead of conquering the country, he retreated and surrendered his army and all Michigan Territory to the British. For over a year the Americans made extensive efforts to recover Detroit; Commodore Oliver

Hazard Perry's victory on Lake Erie on Sept. 10, 1813, determined the issue. Conveyed across Lake Erie by Perry's fleet, Gen. William Henry Harrison quickly occupied Detroit and to the fortifications he gave the new name Fort Shelby. Fort Detroit continued for another decade as military headquarters of the Department of the Lakes, after which the city ceased to require its protection, and its site was devoted to peaceful pursuits.

DETROIT, SURRENDER OF (Aug. 16, 1812). On the eve of the War of 1812, Gen. William Hull was ordered to Detroit in Michigan Territory. The War Department ordered Hull to capture Malden in Canada. Hull crossed into Canada on July 11 and remained there until Aug. 7. He did not attack Malden, as he did not believe he could carry the place without heavy artillery. This could not be removed from Detroit until the rotten gun carriages had been replaced. After the fall to the British of the American post at Mackinac in July, many Indians flocked to the British, and a party of them cut Hull's communications, forcing him to return to the American side. Gen. Isaac Brock, lieutenant-governor of Upper Canada, arrived and demanded the surrender of Detroit. Hull yielded, Aug. 16, without resistance.

Hull was subsequently court-martialed and found guilty of cowardice and neglect of duty, and sentenced to be executed. President James Madison remanded the execution because of Hull's service during the Revolution.

DETROIT, WOODWARD PLAN OF. Augustus B. Woodward was appointed by President Thomas Jefferson one of three judges to administer, with Gov. William Hull, the newly created Michigan Territory. Finding the century-old French town of Detroit completely burned (*see* Detroit Fire), he planned a modern city similar to the Washington, D.C., plan made by his friend Pierre L'Enfant—notably streets radiating from local centers. Much of Woodward's plan is still fundamental in Detroit.

DETROIT FIRE (June 11, 1805). In early Detroit, a stockaded town of narrow streets and crowded buildings, the barn of John Harvey, a baker, caught fire. The blaze spread with astonishing speed, so that the entire town was wrapped in one common conflagration. By midafternoon every building but one had vanished. The disaster was appalling, but it gave opportunity to build a new Detroit (*see* Detroit, Woodward Plan of).

DEVALUATION. A downward adjustment of the price of a currency in terms of other currencies, in a system in which each currency has a gold par value; it may be achieved through a devaluation of one currency, an upward revaluation of other currencies, or a combination of the two. The U.S. dollar had been devalued four times by the end of 1973.

The gold content of the U.S. dollar, established at 24.75 grains (Apr. 2, 1792), was reduced to 23.2 grains (June 28, 1834) and then raised to 23.22 grains (Jan. 18, 1837). The gold content was reduced to 13.71 grains on Jan. 31, 1934. Under President Richard M. Nixon the gold content was reduced to 12.63 grains (Mar. 31, 1972) and then another 10 percent to 11.368 grains (Feb. 12, 1973). Since convertibility of the dollar into gold was suspended Aug. 15, 1971, the devaluations in terms of gold were pro forma only. The new gold prices were merely devices for measuring the downward adjustment of the U.S. dollar relative to other currencies set by the Smithsonian Accord (Dec. 17–18, 1971) to help correct a deficit in the U.S. international payments balance.

DEVIL'S HOLE, AMBUSCADE OF (Sept. 14, 1763). About a mile below the whirlpool on the east side of the Niagara River, John Stedman, the keeper of the portage, and twenty-four men were passing over the portage road in several wagons, when they were ambushed by a band of Seneca. With the exception of Stedman and one or two others, all were killed. The Seneca also successfully ambushed the relief companies. Five officers and sixty privates were killed; eight or nine were wounded. The Seneca had also successfully closed a source of supply for Detroit by killing or seizing the cattle at Niagara, thus making transportation over the portage impossible for that season.

DEWITT'S COLONY. Green DeWitt obtained from the Mexican governor of Texas, on Apr. 15, 1825, a contract to settle 400 families in Texas. DeWitt issued under this contract 181 land titles. In this colony, at Gonzales, the first shot in the Texas revolution was fired, Oct. 2, 1835.

DEW LINE. On Sept. 27, 1954, the United States and Canada agreed to establish a third radar line, "Distant Early Warning" (DEW) Line, across Arctic Canada from Alaska to Greenland. This supplemented the Pinetree Chain of radar stations extending across the continent north of the U.S.–Canadian border and the "Mid-Canada Line." DEW Line began operation on July 1, 1957.

DIAMOND ISLAND FIGHT (Sept. 23, 1777). Colonial troops fought British defenders of Diamond Island in Lake George, N.Y., as part of a movement designed to cut British Gen. Burgoyne's communications on the lake, but it was unsuccessful.

DICTIONARIES. Early American lexicographers imitated English models, especially Samuel Johnson's *Dictionary of the English Language* (1755). Although exhibiting Johnsonian skill in definition, the first American dictionaries—*A Compendious Dictionary of the English Language* (1806) and the two-volume *An American Dictionary of the English Language* (1828, rev. 1847) by Noah Webster—were strongly nationalistic and often idiosyncratic in spellings and punctuations. Webster's dictionaries were continued by his publishers, George and Charles Merriam. Their major work is the *International* series, beginning with the *International* of 1890, with first and second editions of the *New International* in 1909 and 1934 and the *Third New International* (450,000 entries) in 1961. The abridged series (1898–   ) has set the pattern for household dictionaries.

Competition with Webster's dictionaries has been sporadic. The six-volume *Century Dictionary* (1889–91), edited by William Dwight Whitney—the nearest analogue to the *Oxford English Dictionary*—was last published in 1909. The Funk and Wagnall's *Standard Dictionary of the English Language* (1893–95) was followed by the *New Standard* in 1913.

For many years Funk and Wagnall's was also the chief competitor with Merriam in dictionaries for home, school, and office use; its *New Standard College Dictionary,* the latest version, appeared in 1963. Other outstanding competitors have been published including the *American Heritage Dictionary* (1969).

Two research dictionaries—the *Dictionary of American English* (Craigie and Hulbert, 1936–44 and 1960) and the *Dictionary of Americanisms* (M. M. Mathews, 1951 and 1956)—follow the *Oxford* in presenting the history of the American vocabulary through dated citations. The best dictionary of American slang is that published by Wentworth and Flexner (1961; third edition, 1976). Frederick Cassidy's *Dictionary of American Regional English* (1975–) provided a new standard for dialect lexicography.

DICTIONARY OF AMERICAN BIOGRAPHY. A cooperative reference work sponsored by the American Council of Learned Societies; originally published between 1928 and 1936 in twenty volumes containing 13,633 biographical sketches of Americans written by 2,243 contributors. No person who died after Jan. 1, 1935, was included. Since 1936 a series of supplementary volumes has been published.

DIGHTON ROCK. A petroglyph on the Taunton River in Massachusetts, first observed in 1680. Its intricate and not easily decipherable inscriptions have been attributed to Phoenicians, Norsemen, and some thirty other unprovable sources. It is now certain that most of its designs were relatively meaningless scribblings by Indians in colonial times. There are fairly conclusive indications, based upon photographs, that the first inscription may have been made by the lost Portuguese explorer Miguel Corte-Real in 1511.

DILLON ROUND. Tariff reductions reached at an international meeting held in Geneva, Switzerland. The agreement, concluded on Jan. 16, 1962, involved the United States and the European Economic Community, and it bound all signers to reduce their tariffs on a reciprocal basis. It was one "round" in the series of meetings dealing with tariffs and is so called because of the role played in it by U.S. Secretary of the Treasury C. Douglas Dillon.

DIME. Coin of U.S. currency having the value of ten cents, or one-tenth of a dollar. First spelled "disme," it was so marked on the trial pieces minted under the act of Apr. 2, 1792. The first put into circulation were issued in 1796.

DIME NOVELS. Mrs. Ann S. Stephens wrote the first novel of record published in paper covers to sell for ten cents, *Malaeska: The Indian Wife of the White Hunter.* It was published in 1860 by Erastus F. Beadle, Irwin P. Beadle, and Robert Adams, who had begun business in New York with the idea of publishing "dollar books for a dime." Their series quickly fell into the style that the dime novel was to maintain throughout its existence—continuous suspense, violent action, and bloodshed, but a high standard of morals. Irwin Beadle left the firm in 1862, and in 1866 he formed a partnership with George P. Munro, a former Beadle and Adams employee, to launch a series called New Dime Novels. Beadle and Adams about the same time tried a series of longer stories (50,000 words or more) at twenty cents a copy, but they were not a great success. By 1880 dime novels were being denounced as a menace to youth. Nevertheless, their circulation increased; one story is known to have sold nearly 500,000 copies. Some series began to be sold for five cents, catering to the boys' trade. By 1910 the newsprint or pulp paper magazines were replacing the paperback novels, although the character of the fiction remained much the same.

DINGLEY TARIFF. *See* **Tariff.**

DINWIDDIE COURTHOUSE. *See* **Five Forks, Battle of.**

DIPLOMACY, SECRET. Some confusion exists in differentiating diplomacy and foreign policy. Diplomacy is, properly speaking, the tactics of international relations, whereas foreign policy is the strategy. Diplomats of all nations practice secret diplomacy; negotiators of democratic nations usually have refrained from secret foreign policy.

As for the larger meaning of secret diplomacy (that is, secretive foreign policy), the foreign policy of the United States became increasingly secretive through executive agreements from the 1950's to the 1970's. The constitutions of democratic states often provide for ratification of treaties by popularly elected legislative bodies, which usually means immediate publication of the texts as well as public hearings and debates. After World War II the U.S. government concluded an ever-increasing number of executive agreements as compared to treaties. There were also over 400 secret agreements, the nature of which the State Department declined to reveal. Moreover, thousands of other executive agreements were evidently concluded by other government agencies, particularly by the Defense Department. After discovery of secret executive agreements signed in the 1960's with Ethiopia, Laos, Thailand, South Korea, and Spain, legislation passed Congress that provided that all international agreements must go to Congress for its information.

DIPLOMATIC MISSIONS. The use of diplomatic missions has varied throughout American history. The Constitution provided for appointment and confirmation of diplomatic representatives, and presidents for the most part conformed to those requirements. From time to time, there would be special missions to negotiate treaties. The work of these special negotiators was as open and obvious as the diplomacy of the regular representatives and amounted only to the bringing-in of special negotiating talents. By and large, 18th- and 19th-century presidents conducted diplomacy through regularly appointed envoys, usually the local American ministers and (beginning in 1893, when the rank was authorized) ambassadors. In the 20th century, the complexities of international affairs having increased and the domestic political repercussions of foreign relations having become much more important, presidents became more inclined to negotiate not merely through regularly accredited representatives but also through special envoys. Despite the provisions of the Logan Act of 1799 (still in force in the 1970's), which forbids unauthorized negotiations by private individuals, such pourparlers also have occurred.

DIPLOMATIC SERVICE. *See* **Foreign Service.**

DIRECT PRIMARY. *See* **Primary, Direct.**

DIRECTORIES, CITY. The first American city directory was *Macpherson's Directory for the City and Suburbs of Philadelphia* (1785), a work that assigned numbers to houses and lots and made possible a uniform system of residential identification. The second appeared in New York in 1786; Boston followed in 1789. Most of these books contained advertising, historical information, directions and advice to visitors, data on mails and import duties, and statistics. Their greatest early value was in assisting merchants to reach prospective customers. Today no city is without its directory.

DIRIGIBLES. Motor-driven lighter-than-air craft that can be flown against the wind and steered; first constructed in America by Caesar Spiegler. His first dirigible made its maiden flight July 3, 1878. Thomas Scott Baldwin built the first dirigible for the U.S. government; it was 96 feet long and had a 20-horsepower engine. Called the *SC-1,* it made its first flight at Fort Meyer, Va., in August 1908.

When the United States entered World War I, the U.S. Navy ordered sixteen dirigibles of the nonrigid type, developed from a British model used for antisubmarine patrols. The English nickname, "blimp," was brought back by U.S. Navy personnel. By the end of the war, the navy had twenty B-type blimps (77,000–84,000 cubic feet; single engine) and ten C-type blimps (182,000 cubic feet; twin engine).

In 1917 an army-navy joint board delegated the development of the much larger and more complex rigid airship to the navy, and in July 1919 Congress authorized the procurement of two rigid airships. The Lakehurst Naval Air Station was placed in commission in 1921, and for the next forty-one years it was the center of U.S. lighter-than-air aeronautics.

Meanwhile, the army also operated dirigibles, concentrating on the semirigid type and blimps. In 1921 the army purchased the Italian semirigid T-34 airship named *Roma,* 412 feet long, having a gas volume of 1.2 million cubic feet, and powered by six 400-horsepower Anasaldo engines. During a trial flight on Feb. 21, 1922, the *Roma* flew into a high-voltage electrical transmission line, went up in flames, and crashed. In 1925 the army procured the semirigid *RS-1,* fabricated by the Goodyear-Zeppelin Corporation and erected by the army at Scott Field, Ill. Shortly after its last flight on Oct. 16, 1928, during which it was seriously damaged, the *RS-1* was dismantled.

The navy progressed in the development of rigid airships. To begin with, it purchased the British airship *R-38,* which became the *ZR-2.* On Aug. 24, 1921, the *ZR-2* crashed near Hull, England. The navy's own first rigid dirigible, the *ZR-1,* was 677 feet long, had a gas volume of 2.235 million cubic feet, and was powered by six 300-horsepower Packard engines. It made its first flight on Sept. 4, 1923, and was the first rigid airship in the world to be inflated with nonflammable helium gas; the first airship to use helium rather than hydrogen was the navy blimp *C-7,* Dec. 1, 1921. On Oct. 10, 1923, the *ZR-1* was formally christened *Shenandoah.* On Sept. 3, 1925, it broke up in a violent thunderstorm and crashed near Ava, Ohio.

At the end of World War I the navy was to have received two German zeppelins as spoils of war, but their crews destroyed them before they could be delivered. Germany was obliged to build a new zeppelin, the navy's *ZR-3,* best known as the *Los Angeles.* The *Los Angeles* was 658 feet long, had a gas volume of 2.762 million cubic feet, and was powered by five 530-horsepower Maybach engines. It made its delivery flight to the United States, Oct. 12–15, 1924, and served as a training and experimental airship for the navy. It was decommissioned on June 30, 1932, but was retained at Lakehurst until scrapped in 1940.

In 1928 the Goodyear-Zeppelin Corporation built two rigid airships for the navy, the *ZRS-4* and *ZRS-5,* 785 feet long, with a gas volume of 6.850 million cubic feet and eight 560-horsepower Maybach engines. At that time they were the largest airships in the world, exceeded only by the German airship *Hindenburg* of 1936. They could carry five fighter planes in their hulls; the planes were equipped with skyhooks, and the airships could launch and retrieve planes in flight by means of a trapeze lowered from their undersides.

The *ZRS-4,* christened *Akron,* made its first flight on Sept. 25, 1931. On the night of Apr. 4, 1933, the *Akron* was lost in a violent electrical storm over the Atlantic. The *ZRS-5,* christened *Macon,* made its first flight on Apr. 21, 1933. It made fifty-four flights totaling 1,798 hours and participated in several war games with the U.S. fleet. On Feb. 12, 1935, it suffered a structural failure and crashed in the Pacific.

The loss of the *Macon* ended the navy's development of the rigid airship. But the blimp remained. During World War II the navy's blimp forces were expanded to more than 160 airships for antisubmarine patrols. The basic training airship was the L-type blimp (146 feet long, 123,000 cubic feet gas volume, two 145-horsepower Warner engines). The backbone of the antisubmarine patrol forces was the K-type blimp (251 feet, 425,000 cubic feet gas volume, two 425-horsepower Pratt & Whitney engines).

After the war the navy increased the airships' size, lift, endurance, and versatility. In 1954 the ZPG-1-type blimp appeared (324 feet, 875,000 cubic feet, two 800-horsepower engines), unusual in the new configuration of its tail surfaces; the ZPG-1 and all navy airships thereafter had their tail surfaces disposed in an X configuration, which contributed to increased maneuverability. In 1957 a ZPG-2 made a nonstop circumnavigation of the North Atlantic, being in the air for 264 hours. Like all other navy blimps, it was an antisubmarine aircraft. Five were modified into ZPG-2W's to carry a large air-search radar for airborne early-warning duty. In 1956 four ZPG-3W's were procured to carry an even larger radar. With a gas volume of 1.5 million cubic feet, the ZPG-3W was the largest nonrigid airship ever built. By 1960 high-speed, deep-cruising nuclear submarines rendered the blimp's antisubmarine capabilities less effective. In June 1961 the navy's blimp squadrons were decommissioned, and on Aug. 31, 1962, all flight operations by airships were terminated.

Since the 1920's the Goodyear Tire & Rubber Company has maintained a small fleet of advertising blimps. The Goodyear fleet was at maximum strength in the 1930's, when it operated six airships, all of which had been turned over to the navy as training ships by 1942. Goodyear had only one blimp remaining when a study revealed the blimp was a unique advertising vehicle, and "blimp" had become synonymous with "Goodyear." Since 1969 three Goodyear blimps have been cruising the skies of the United States; a fourth operates in Western Europe. Goodyear's was the only organized airship operation in the world in the 1970's.

DISARMAMENT. Reduction of the number and type of weapons with which wars can be fought, in order that world peace may be secured. Complete disarmament would require elimination of all major offensive and defensive weapons, and reduction of the armed forces of a nation to police functions, patrol of land borders, and coast guard operations. No major nation has continued complete disarmament for very long.

Partial disarmament has been attempted in various ways. One of these is effectual disarmament in a particular area. In 1817, for example, the United States and Great Britain agreed that only very small naval vessels should be stationed on the Great Lakes, and since 1871, the border between the United States and Canada has been free of military posts or forces.

Limitation of the size of armed forces by international agreement is another method of partial disarmament. By such voluntary agreements, the naval forces of the United States, Great Britain, France, Italy, and Japan were limited in size at several times during the period between World Wars I and II. Conventions, by which nations have agreed to ban the use of particular kinds of weapons in war, have been successfully employed. Poison gas, for example, although used in World War I, was outlawed by international convention and played no important part in World War II.

Disarmament or arms limitation is an extremely important issue in today's international relations. Since World War II, the United Nations has been especially active in trying to work out a satisfactory limit on nuclear weapons. The United States, Great Britain, and the Soviet Union agreed in 1963 to limit the testing of nuclear weapons. In 1967, a treaty went into effect by which the nuclear powers agreed not to use nuclear weapons in outer space, nor to construct military bases on the moon. Another effort to limit arms led to the beginning of Strategic Arms Limitations Talks (SALT) between the United States and the Soviet Union in 1969. The first SALT treaty was concluded in 1972, but U.S.–Soviet relations deteriorated in the late 1970's, and although the second SALT treaty was signed in June 1979, it was from the beginning harshly criticized in Congress and was shelved in January 1980 after the Soviet invasion of Afghanistan. When President Ronald Reagan assumed office, arms-limitation efforts were overshadowed by an increased military buildup. (*See also* Arms Race with the Soviet Union; Geneva Conferences; Strategic Arms Limitation Talks.)

DISASTERS. The following is a selected list of major disasters that have occurred in American history.

Aviation. Sept. 17, 1908. The first airplane crash involving a fatality, at Fort Myer, Va. A plane flown by Orville Wright and Thomas E. Selfridge hit a bracing wire. Wright was badly injured, and Selfridge was killed.

July 2, 1912. The dirigible *Akron* blew up over Atlantic City, N.J.; the builder and 4 crew members were killed.

Apr. 4, 1933. The second dirigible *Akron* was forced down in a violent storm near Barnegat, N.J. It fell into the sea and broke up, killing 73.

May 6, 1937. The 830-foot dirigible *Hindenburg* exploded at Lakehurst Naval Air Station in New Jersey while tying up to its mooring mast. It crashed in flames, killing 13 passengers and 22 of the crew.

Aug. 31, 1940. A Pennsylvania Central Airlines plane crashed near Lorettsville, Va., killing 25.

Jan. 16, 1942. A transport plane on tour for Victory Loans crashed in Las Vegas, Nev. Fifteen army ferry pilots, actress Carole Lombard, and 6 others were killed.

Sept. 11, 1942. A flaming plane nose-dived into the Curtiss-Wright airplane factory in Buffalo, N.Y. Twelve were killed and 35 injured.

Jan. 31, 1943. The charred wreckage of a navy seaplane was found near Boonville, Calif. En route from Pearl Harbor to California, the plane had been missing for 20 days. The 19 people aboard were killed.

June 3, 1943. The wreckage of an army transport plane, missing since May 31, was discovered in Austin, Nev. Col. P. R. Love, an associate of Charles Lindbergh, was among the 15 dead.

July 28, 1945. A B-26 army bomber crashed into the Empire State Building in New York City between the 78th and 79th floors, setting fire to the upper part of the building. The pilot and 12 others were killed; 26 were injured.

Dec. 6, 1945. Five navy torpedo bombers were mysteriously lost off the Florida east coast in the Bermuda Triangle. A navy rescue plane sent out the same day to search for the bombers also disappeared.

Oct. 24, 1947. A United Airlines DC-6 caught fire and crashed into a hillside in Bryce Canyon, Utah, killing 46 passengers and 6 crew members.

June 7, 1949. A C-46 carrying 75 Puerto Ricans to the United States crashed in the coastal waters of Puerto Rico; 54 were killed.

June 23, 1950. A Northwest Airlines DC-4, en route to Minneapolis, crashed in Lake Michigan during stormy weather. The crash killed all 58 aboard.

June 18, 1953. A U.S. Air Force C-124 Globemaster crashed near Tokyo, Japan, killing all 129 aboard.

Oct. 6, 1955. An unexplained course change by the pilot of

a United Airlines DC-4 on a New York–San Francisco flight is believed to have caused the plane to crash into the 12,005-foot-high Medicine Bow Peak in Wyoming. All 66 aboard were killed.

June 30, 1956. A TWA Lockheed Super Constellation and a United Airlines DC-7, both on Visual Flight Rules, collided on parallel courses over the Grand Canyon, killing all on board both planes (128).

Feb. 3, 1959. An American Airlines Lockheed Electra airliner crashed into the East River near La Guardia Airport in New York City during an instrument landing in heavy fog. Sixty-five of the 73 people aboard died.

Feb. 25, 1960. A Brazilian DC-3 airliner and a U.S. Navy plane collided over Rio de Janeiro Bay. Sixty-one of 64 aboard were killed, including a section of the U.S. Navy band.

Dec. 16, 1960. A midair collision in a snowstorm between a United Airlines DC-8 and a TWA Super Constellation occurred over Staten Island, N.Y. The 127 passengers and crew and 8 people on the ground were killed.

Feb. 15, 1961. Eighteen members of the U.S. figure skating team were killed when a Sabena Airlines Boeing 707 crashed near the Brussels airport; 55 others were also killed.

Mar. 1, 1962. An American Airlines Boeing 707 crashed in Jamaica Bay, N.Y., shortly after takeoff. All 95 aboard were killed.

June 3, 1962. An Air France Boeing 707 crashed and burned shortly after takeoff at Orly Airport, Paris. Of the 130 killed, 121 were cultural leaders from Atlanta.

Jan. 27, 1967. Astronauts Virgil I. Grissom, Edward H. White, and Roger B. Chaffee were killed in a flash fire in the Apollo spacecraft during tests on the launch pad.

July 19, 1967. An off-course Cessna 310 hit a Piedmont Airlines Boeing 727 over Asheville, N.C., killing the 79 aboard the jet, including secretary of the navy-designate, John T. McNaughton. The 3 people aboard the Cessna were also killed.

Sept. 9, 1969. A Piper Cherokee, flown by a student pilot, hit a DC-9 over Shelbyville, Ind. The student pilot plus the 82 aboard the DC-9 were killed.

Oct. 2, 1970. A Martin 440 lost power over Silver Plume, Colo., and crashed trying to land on a highway. Of the 40 aboard 31 were killed, including 14 members of the Wichita State University football team.

Nov. 14, 1970. A chartered DC-9 jet, carrying the Marshall University football team, exploded over Huntsville, W. Va., during a foggy rainstorm, killing all 75 aboard.

Sept. 4, 1971. A Boeing 727, carrying 111 persons, crashed into a mountainside while approaching the airport at Juneau, Alaska, and fell into a deep gorge; all aboard died.

Sept. 24, 1972. A surplus F-86 Sabrejet, being flown by an inexperienced pilot, failed in its takeoff from Sacramento, Calif., and smashed into an ice-cream parlor, killing 12 children and 10 adults; the pilot survived.

Dec. 29, 1972. An Eastern Airlines L-1011 TriStar jumbo jet crashed in the Florida Everglades during its landing approach. Of the 176 aboard, 101 died.

July 31, 1973. A Delta Airlines DC-9, attempting to land in fog at Boston's Logan International Airport, crashed into an embankment and burst into flames. Eighty-eight of the 89 aboard were killed.

Dec. 1, 1974. During a heavy rainstorm a TWA Boeing 727 crashed into a mountain near Upperville, Va., while approaching Dulles International Airport in Washington, D.C. All 92 aboard were killed.

June 24, 1975. An Eastern Airlines Boeing 727 jetliner crashed in flames at the edge of Kennedy International Airport in New York City while attempting to land during an electrical storm. Of the 116 passengers and crew of 8 aboard, 112 people died.

Mar. 27, 1977. In aviation's worst disaster, a KLM Boeing 747 carrying tourists from Netherlands and a chartered PANAM Boeing 747 collided in a heavy fog on a runway in Tenerife, Canary Islands. Both jets burst into flames and all persons aboard the KLM were killed; the death toll was 579. Only 65 people survived.

Apr. 4, 1977. A Southern Airways DC-9 crashed in a hailstorm while attempting to land on a highway at New Hope, Ga. The death toll was 58 passengers, 4 crew members, and 8 persons on the ground.

Sept. 25, 1978. A Pacific Southwest Boeing 727 and a Cessna 172, with a student pilot and an instructor, collided over San Diego, Calif. All persons in both planes were killed; with 13 more people on the ground the total was 150.

May 25, 1979. An American Airlines DC-10 lost an engine and crashed after takeoff at O'Hare International Airport, Chicago; 272 people aboard the plane and 3 men on the ground were killed. It was the highest death toll in U.S. aviation history.

Oct. 31, 1979. A Western Airlines DC-10 crashed on landing at the Mexico City airport, killing 71 people on board and 3 on the ground. There were 19 survivors.

Sept. 13, 1980. A Florida Commuter Airlines DC-3 crashed into the Atlantic off Freeport, Bahamas. All 34 people on board were killed.

May 26, 1981. A U.S. Marine combat jet crashed on the flight deck of the aircraft carrier *Nimitz,* killing 14 and injuring 43; also, 19 aircraft were damaged. The autopsy revealed that the pilot had a high dosage of the drug brompheniramin.

Jan. 13, 1982. An Air Florida Boeing 737, bound for Florida, crashed in a snowstorm shortly after takeoff on the crowded 14th Street bridge in Washington, D.C., and plunged into the ice-covered river. Of the 76 people aboard 71 died; in addition, 7 people on the bridge were killed.

Earthquakes and Volcanic Eruptions. Nov. 18, 1755. A serious earthquake centered north of Boston, Mass., caused serious damage. Miraculously no deaths were reported.

Dec. 16, 1811; Jan. 23, 1812; Feb. 7, 1812. A series of large earthquakes centering around New Madrid, Mo., and covering about 40,000 square miles. The largest earthquake in U.S. history, fatalities, although unknown, were slight due to the sparse settlement of the region. In 1815, Congress passed the first national disaster relief act as a result of the quake.

Aug. 31, 1886. A major earthquake shook Charleston,

S.C., causing more than $5 million in damage and killing 110.

Apr. 18, 1906. San Francisco earthquake *(see separate article).*

Mar. 27, 1964. One of the most powerful earthquakes to strike anywhere in the world hit southern Alaska, killing at least 115 people and causing over $500 million damage. A tidal wave that resulted covered Crescent City, Calif., and killed 12 persons.

Feb. 9, 1971. The Los Angeles area of California was struck by an earthquake of moderate intensity that killed 65 people, 47 of whom were patients at the San Fernando Veterans Administration Hospital. The most costly earthquake in U.S. history, damage was estimated at $1 billion.

May 18, 1980. After 123 years of dormancy Mt. St. Helens in the Cascade Mountains in southwestern Washington exploded and hurled ash and steam about 60,000 feet high. Smaller explosions occurred in late May, June, July, August, and October. Damages were estimated at $2.7 billion; 34 people were killed.

Fires, Explosions, and Collapses.

1676. Fire destroyed one-third of the city of Boston, Mass.

Sept. 21, 1776. Fire destroyed nearly one quarter of New York City five days after the British occupation.

March 21, 1788. Fire destroyed 856 buildings in New Orleans, La.

Dec. 16, 1835. Fire destroyed 650 buildings in New York City's financial district. Its $22 million in damage bankrupted most of New York's insurance companies.

Oct. 8–9, 1871. Chicago fire *(see separate article).*

Oct. 8–14, 1871. Violent forest fires swept through Michigan and Wisconsin and created superheated air and gases that killed over 2,000 people.

June 30, 1900. A steamship and pier at Hoboken, N.J., caught fire, killing 326 persons and causing over $4 million in property damage.

Dec. 30, 1903. Locked emergency exits, a fire escape with no ladder, and carelessness by stagehands contributed to the deaths of 639 people at the Iroquois Theater in Chicago following the outbreak of a fire on stage.

Mar. 25, 1911. Triangle Shirtwaist Company fire (*see* Triangle Fire).

May 2, 1929. Poisonous fumes from burning X-ray film in the Clinic Hospital in Cleveland, Ohio, killed 125 people.

Apr. 21, 1930. Fire broke out at a construction site in the Ohio State Penitentiary at Columbus and spread to the tarpaper roof. Most of the prisoners were kept in their cells until escape was impossible; 317 died and 231 were injured.

Mar. 18, 1937. Carelessness in using an unauthorized gas tap caused a violent explosion that killed 413 children and 14 teachers at a schoolhouse in New London, Tex.

Nov. 28, 1942. Lack of exit doors, doors that opened inward, and flammable material contributed to the death of 493 people at the Cocoanut Grove nightclub in Boston.

July 6, 1944. A Ringling Brothers, Barnum and Bailey circus tent, weatherproofed with a highly flammable substance, caught fire and collapsed in Hartford, Conn. Blocked exits prevented escape for many of the 7,000 attending the show; 163 were killed and 261 injured.

Sept. 30, 1944. Liquid-gas tanks exploded in Cleveland, Ohio, setting off a fire over a 50-block area. Property damage was estimated at $10 million, about 100 lost their lives, and more than 200 were injured.

Oct. 20, 1944. A liquid-gas tank exploded in Cleveland; hundreds were left homeless and 121 died.

Dec. 7, 1946. Fire broke out in the "fireproof" Winecoff Hotel in Atlanta, killing 119 people and injuring 168.

Dec. 1, 1958. Eighty-seven children and 3 nuns were killed in a raging fire at Our Lady of the Angels parochial school in Chicago.

Dec. 19, 1960. At Brooklyn Navy Yard in New York City a fire broke out aboard the aircraft carrier *Constellation,* causing $75 million damage and killing 50 workmen.

Apr. 6, 1968. The business district of Richmond, Ind., was shaken by an explosion in a sporting goods store; it destroyed 8 buildings, killed at least 43, and injured close to 100.

Sept. 25–30, 1970. Five days of forest fires destroyed over 200,000 acres in southern California. Damage was more than $175 million, 1,500 buildings were destroyed, and 14 died.

Feb. 10, 1973. Forty workmen were killed in Staten Island, N.Y., when a 287-foot circular storage tank for liquefied gas exploded; damage totaled $31 million.

June 30, 1974. The lights failed at a two-level discotheque in Port Chester, N.Y., after a fire broke out next door. Many patrons were trampled to death attempting blindly to find exits through flames and heavy smoke; 24 died.

Oct. 25, 1976. A fire at the Puerto Rican Social Club in Bronx, N.Y., claimed 25 lives; 3 men were convicted for arson.

May 28, 1977. A fire broke out in a private dining room at a Southgate, Ky., nightclub killing 164; over 100 people were injured.

June 26, 1977. A sixteen-year-old inmate in the Columbia, Tenn., jail set fire to the padding material in his cell with a cigarette; the fire spread, and 38 inmates and 8 visitors died.

Dec. 22, 1977. An explosion at a 250-foot-high grain elevator at Westwego, La., caused 35 deaths; most victims were caught in the adjoining office building.

Apr. 27, 1978. The scaffolding on a power plant cooling tower under construction at St. Marys, W.Va., collapsed; all 51 workers on the scaffolding were killed.

Jan. 20, 1979. A fire in a Hoboken, N.J., tenement house killed 21 people; it was apparently set by an arsonist.

Apr. 2, 1979. A fire caused by a short circuit in an electrical cable broke out in Straughan Wayside Inn retirement home at Farmington, Mo.; 25 people died.

Nov. 21, 1980. A fire in the 26-story MGM Grand resort luxury hotel and casino in Las Vegas killed 84 people and injured 500.

Dec. 4, 1980. An electrical flash fire in the Stouffer's Inn conference center at Harrison, N.Y., killed 26 people and injured 40; most of the victims were corporate executives. An ex-busboy was later charged with arson.

Jan. 9, 1981. A fire in a two-story nursing home for the

elderly and mentally retarded at Keansburg, N.J., killed 30 people, most trapped in their bedrooms.

July 17, 1981. Two concrete and steel "sky bridges" over the lobby of the Hyatt Regency Hotel in Kansas City, Mo., gave way and fell on the dancers below, killing 113 and injuring 186.

Marine. Jan. 13, 1840. Near Eaton's Neck, N.Y., the steamboat *Lexington* caught fire, killing 140 persons.

June 17, 1850. A fire aboard the steamer *Griffith* on Lake Erie took the lives of all 300 aboard.

Dec. 24, 1853. En route to California, the steamer *San Francisco* foundered off the Mexican coast; of its 700 passengers, 240 drowned.

Nov. 13, 1854. En route to New York City from Bremen, Germany, an immigrant ship, the *New Era,* was wrecked off the New Jersey coast, killing more than 300 people.

Sept. 7–8, 1860. The steamer *Lady Elgin* collided with the schooner *Augusta* on Lake Michigan; almost 400 drowned.

Apr. 27, 1865. The coal-burning Mississippi steamer *Sultana,* licensed to carry 376 persons, including crew, departed from New Orleans on Apr. 21 with 75 passengers and a ship's company of 85. Arriving at Vicksburg, Miss., on Apr. 23, boiler repairs were effected while 25 passengers and 2,400 paroled Union soldiers boarded the steamer. Leaving Vicksburg on Apr. 25, the *Sultana* arrived at Memphis, Apr. 26. At 2:00 A.M. on Apr. 27, less than an hour after sailing from Memphis, the ship's boilers burst. Those who survived the explosion and fire jumped into the Mississippi. Many drowned attempting to reach the distant banks of the river or to float downstream to Memphis. Fewer than 1,000 survived.

Oct. 3, 1866. En route to New Orleans from New York City, the steamer *Evening Star* foundered; 250 were lost.

June 15, 1904. The wood paddle steamer *General Slocum,* under Capt. William Van Shaick, caught fire in New York's East River with 740 children and 640 adults aboard. The captain continued to steer the ship into the wind at normal speed. The ship was finally beached and the decks collapsed. Lifeboats were tied down with wire, the crew was inexperienced, the water pumps failed to work, and the life jackets had not been inspected for more than 10 years. Many of the 1,021 who were killed were drowned or caught in the paddle wheels in an attempt to escape. Van Shaick was sentenced to ten years in prison but served only two.

July 24, 1915. An excursion steamer, the *Eastland,* overturned while in port in Chicago, killing over 800 people.

Sept. 8, 1934. A fire broke out on the cruise ship *Morro Castle* on its return from Havana to New York. On the evening before, the captain had died and the ship was under the command of the chief officer, William Warms. Warms neglected to send an SOS and continued to sail the ship into a 20-knot wind, turning the ship into an inferno. The crew lowered lifeboats for themselves and rowed to safety. The chief engineer left in the first lifeboat with 30 other crew members and only 1 passenger. Of the 562 aboard, 134 perished.

Apr. 10, 1963. About 220 miles off Cape Code, Mass., the U.S.S. *Thresher,* a nuclear submarine, mysteriously sank with 129 aboard. Designed to cruise at 1,000 feet, the *Thresher* sank to the bottom of the ocean, a depth of 8,400 feet.

July 29, 1967. The U.S. aircraft carrier *Forrestal* broke into flames following an explosion on the flight deck, off the coast of North Vietnam; 134 died and 100 others were injured. Sixty planes and helicopters were destroyed or damaged.

Jan. 14, 1969. The U.S. nuclear aircraft carrier *Enterprise* was swept with fire at Pearl Harbor, Hawaii, following explosions on the flight and hangar decks; 27 were killed and 82 were injured.

June 2, 1969. The *Frank E. Evans,* a U.S. Navy destroyer, while on SEATO maneuvers, misinterpreted an order and was cut in two by the Australian carrier *Melbourne.* The forward section of the ship sank with 74 men; 200 others were rescued.

Mar. 2, 1971. On a run from Port Arthur, Tex., to Boston, the 661-foot tanker *Texaco Oklahoma,* ran into heavy seas off Cape Hatteras, N.C., and broke in two; 28 of 44 crew members were missing and presumed dead.

Nov. 10, 1975. A U.S. ore carrier, *Edmund Fitzgerald,* sank in a storm on Lake Superior; 29 crewmen died.

Oct. 20, 1976. The 664-foot Norwegian tanker *Frosta* and the 120-foot ferry *George Prince* collided on the Mississippi at Luling, La.; 71 bodies were recovered, and 18 ferry passengers survived.

Jan. 17, 1977. A U.S. launch and a Spanish freighter collided in Barcelona harbor; 46 U.S. sailors and marines died.

Jan. 28, 1980. A U.S. Coast Guard cutter, *Blackthorn,* collided with the oil tanker *Texas Capricorn* in Tampa Bay, Fla.; 23 crewmen of *Blackthorn* were killed.

May 9, 1980. In a sudden storm the phosphate carrier *Summit Venture* rammed into the Sunshine Skyway Bridge over Tampa Bay, Fla. A section of roadway fell into the bay with several passenger cars and a Greyhound bus; 35 died.

Mining. May 1, 1900. Two hundred miners were killed in an underground explosion at a Scofield, Utah, mine.

May 19, 1902. A mine at Coal Creek, Tenn., exploded, killing 184 workers.

Dec. 6, 1907. An explosion at a Monongah, W. Va., mine killed 361 miners.

Dec. 19, 1907. A coal mine explosion at Jacob's Creek, Pa., resulted in the death of 239 miners.

Nov. 13, 1909. Fire broke out in a mine at Cherry, Ill., killing 259.

Oct. 22, 1913. A mine explosion at Dawson, N.Mex., killed 263 men.

May 19, 1928. A coal mine explosion at Mather, Pa., killed 195 miners; some of the 78 survivors were rescued after 5 days.

Mar. 6, 1968. Fire broke out in a shaft of the Belle Isle, La., salt mine, killing all 21 miners at the bottom of the 1,200-foot shaft.

Nov. 20, 1968. Explosions and fires killed 78 miners trapped in the No. 9 mine in Mannington, W.Va.; the mine was sealed when rescue proved impossible.

May 2, 1972. A fire in the Sunshine Silver Mine in Kellogg, Idaho, spread flames and carbon monoxide fumes throughout the mine's corridors, blocking hoist exits; 91 perished at lower levels (below 4,600 feet). Two miners were found alive after 7 days.

Railroads and Bridges. July 17, 1856. A train crash near Philadelphia, Pa., killed 66 children on a school outing.

Dec. 29, 1876. The bridge spanning a gorge in Ashtabula, Ohio, collapsed as a passenger train was passing over it; the train fell into the gorge, killing 84.

Aug. 10, 1887. A train passing over a burning bridge at Chatsworth, Ill., fell when the bridge collapsed, killing 100 of the 800 aboard.

Nov. 22, 1950. A Babylon-bound Long Island Railroad commuter train hit a Hempstead-bound train at Rockville Center, N.Y.; 153 were injured and 79 were killed.

Feb. 6, 1951. A Pennsylvania Railroad commuter train fell through a temporary trestle at Woodbridge, N.J., that had opened only 3 hours before, killing 85 and injuring 330.

Sept. 15, 1958. A New York City–bound Jersey Central commuter train fell through an open lift bridge into Newark Bay, killing 48 persons. Warning signals and derailing devices had failed to stop the train. The motorman died either just before or during the crash.

Dec. 15, 1967. The Silver Bridge over the Ohio River connecting Kanauga, Ohio, and Point Pleasant, W.Va., collapsed during the evening rush hour, plunging 75 cars and trucks into the river; 40 deaths resulted.

Oct. 30, 1972. An Illinois Central commuter train rammed into a new Illinois Central train during morning rush hour as the new train was backing up, having overshot the station; 45 were killed and about 320 injured.

Feb. 4, 1977. During rush hour a Chicago Transit Authority elevated train hit the rear of a standing train. Two cars plunged into a busy intersection; 11 passengers and pedestrians were killed, and 189 people were injured.

Storms and Floods. Aug. 10, 1856. Île Dernier (Last Island) off the coast of Louisiana was turned from a resort into a desolate sandy beach by a hurricane that killed more than 250 of the island's 300 inhabitants.

Mar. 11–13, 1888. A blizzard struck New York City, isolating most of the city with winds of 84 miles per hour and snowdrifts up to 18 feet. Property damage was in the millions, and more than 200 people died.

May 31, 1889. The Conemaugh River in Johnstown, Pa., flooded after heavy rains and burst its dam, sending a 40-foot wave down on the village of South Fork, which had been alerted. Telegraph lines being down, Johnstown was not warned and was buried under 30 feet of water. Over 2,500 were killed, some 300 by a fire started by spilled petroleum.

May 27, 1896. St. Louis and East St. Louis were struck by a tornado that left 5,000 homeless, killed 306, injured over 100, and caused damage estimated at $13 million.

Sept. 8–9, 1900. Galveston storm *(see separate article)*.

May 31, 1903. Over $4 million in property damage was caused by the overflowing of the Kansas, Missouri, and Des Moines rivers; 200 drowned and 8,000 were left homeless.

Sept. 12–14, 1919. Winds of 84 miles per hour during a hurricane in Florida, Texas, and Louisiana caught 488 persons at sea; all drowned. An additional 284 people were killed on land, and $22 million property damage resulted.

Mar. 18, 1925. Thirty-five towns were destroyed by a series of tornadoes in Missouri, Illinois, Indiana, Kentucky, Tennessee, and Alabama; property damage was estimated at $18 million, 15,000 were left homeless, 792 died, and 13,000 were injured.

Sept. 18, 1926. Florida was hit by a hurricane that caused $165 million damage, made 40,000 homeless, and killed 373; an additional 6,000 were injured.

Sept. 29, 1927. Ninety died as a tornado struck St. Louis; 6,000 were injured, and $40 million worth of property damage resulted.

Sept. 16–17, 1928. Florida was struck by a hurricane that killed more than 1,800 people, mainly in the Lake Okeechobee area; heavy winds (160 miles per hour) caused the lake to overflow into heavily populated areas.

Aug. 31–Sept. 8, 1935. Florida was struck by a hurricane that killed 376 and caused property damage estimated at $6 million, including the railroad from Key West to Florida City.

Sept. 21, 1938. A hurricane struck Long Island, N.Y., and New England, killing 680 people and causing $400 million damage; nearly 2,000 were injured.

July 11–19, 1951. Heavy rains caused floods in Kansas and Missouri that resulted in $1 billion damage and killed 41. Hundreds of thousands were left homeless.

Mar. 21–22, 1952. Mississippi, Missouri, Alabama, Arkansas, Kentucky, and Tennessee were hit by tornadoes that killed 239 people and injured over 1,000.

June 8, 1953. Michigan and Ohio were hit by tornadoes that caused $15 million damage, killed 139, and injured nearly 1,000.

Aug. 31–Sept. 1, 1954. Hurricane Carol caused $500 million damage from Maine to North Carolina; 68 were killed.

Oct. 12–18, 1954. Hurricane Hazel hit North Carolina and moved up the East Coast, hitting New York and Canada; 99 were killed in the United States and 85 in Canada; over $100 million damage was caused.

Aug. 17–19, 1955. Hurricane Diane struck six northeastern states, causing heavy floods in southern New England; 191 died, nearly 7,000 were injured, and $457 million in property was damaged.

June 26–28, 1957. Hurricane Audrey and a tidal wave hit Texas and Louisiana, wiping out the town of Cameron, La., killing over 500, and causing $150 million property damage.

Jan. 20–26, 1959. Floods and tornadoes in Ohio and Pennsylvania and the Southwest rendered 25,000 homeless and killed over 100 people.

Sept. 6–12, 1960. Hurricane Donna hit Florida and the Atlantic coast, killing 30, injuring 600, and destroying more property than any earlier hurricane.

Jan. 26–27, 1967. Heavy snowfalls struck Wisconsin, Illinois, Indiana, Michigan, and Ohio, killing 80.

Apr. 21, 1967. Tornadoes hit northern Illinois, killing 56, injuring 1,500, and causing damage over $20 million.

May 16, 1968. Eleven states were hit by tornadoes, the

heaviest damage in Indiana, Iowa, Illinois, and Arkansas; 70 were killed, 1,000 injured, and thousands made homeless.

Jan. 18–26, 1969. Heavy rains over a 9-day period turned most of southern California to a sea of mud. One hundred died, $60 million in property damage occurred, and 9,000 homes were destroyed.

Feb. 9–10, 1969. New England, New York, New Jersey, and Pennsylvania were hit by a 2-day snowstorm that left over 15 inches of snow; 166 died, and loss of business was estimated at $25 million.

Feb. 23–26, 1969. Heavy rains struck southern California for the second time in a month, causing mudslides and killing 18; an additional 12,500 were rendered homeless.

Feb. 24–27, 1969. New York and New England were struck again by heavy snows (up to 3 feet), causing 54 more deaths.

Aug. 17–20, 1969. Hurricane Camille hit the South, mainly Louisiana, Mississippi, Alabama, and Virginia, causing $1 billion damage; 400 were dead or missing.

Aug. 4, 1970. Hurricane Celia hit Florida and Corpus Christi, Tex., with winds of over 160 miles per hour, killing 27. Damage in Corpus Christi was estimated at $300 million.

Feb. 21, 1971. Tornadoes hit Mississippi and Louisiana, causing $7.5 million damage, killing 115, and injuring 500.

Feb. 26, 1972. A coal-refuse dam in Buffalo Creek, W.Va., collapsed, spreading water and sludge into the valley below; 118 died and 4,000 were rendered homeless.

June 9–10, 1972. Heavy rains in the Black Hills of South Dakota caused floods that raged down Rapid Creek. Rapid City was covered with water, knocking out railroads, bridges, roads, and communications. There were $100 million damage and 235 deaths.

June 15–25, 1972. Hurricane Agnes hit Florida and then the rest of the Atlantic coast up to New York with heavy rains. The death toll for Cuba and the United States was 134; $60 billion in damage was done to homes and businesses.

Apr. 3, 1974. Nearly 100 tornadoes struck 11 southern and midwestern states and Canada during an 8-hour period, killing more than 325 and causing $1 billion property damage.

July 31, 1976. A flash flood along route 34 in Big Thompson Canyon, Colo., killed 138 vacationers; damages were estimated at $50 million.

Apr. 3–6, 1977. Tornadoes and floods in the South and Appalachia killed about 40 people and caused $275 million damages.

July 19–20, 1977. Nine inches of rain resulted in a flash flood in Johnstown, Pa.; 68 people died, and the damage was estimated at $200 million.

Sept. 12–13, 1977. After 12 inches of rain in 24 hours, a flash flood devastated metropolitan Kansas City, Mo. There were 26 dead, and about $140 million damage.

Nov. 6, 1977. After four days of heavy rain, the Kelly Barnes dam in Toccoa, Ga., burst and flooded the campus of Toccoa Falls Bible College, killing 39 people, including 20 children.

Aug. 4–8, 1978. After a week of heavy rains in southern and central Texas, flash floods caused 26 deaths and resulted in $50 million damage.

Apr. 9–11, 1979. Tornadoes in Texas and Oklahoma killed 60, injured 800, and caused $300 million damage. It was the most deadly tornado to strike Texas in 25 years.

Feb. 13–22, 1980. Thirteen inches of rain caused floods in southern California and Arizona; 26 people were killed, and damages were estimated over $300 million.

DISCIPLES OF CHRIST. The Disciples, or Christian, movement was a product of the Second Great Awakening in the frontier camp meetings (1795–1810). Alexander Campbell and Barton Stone were its leading theorists. Campbell, following the "restorationist" teachings of his father, Thomas, had joined the Baptists in 1813. As he developed his own views in the *Christian Baptist* (1823–30), he moved away from traditional Baptist affirmations. He and his followers became an independent denomination in 1827. He published the *Millennial Harbinger* (1830–66) to spread his views. Stone, the evangelist who conducted the Cane Ridge Revival (1801), near Paris, Ky., had also moved in a restorationist direction, and his followers joined Campbell in 1832.

Despite minor differences between Campbell and Stone, the basic idea was a restoration of the primitive church as it was described in the New Testament. For the early Disciples of Christ, this meant a rigorous congregationalism, faith in the sense of intellectual assent, repudiation of creeds and speculative theology, rejection of sectarianism, believer's baptism by immersion only, and weekly communion.

In 1849 the Disciples formed the American Christian Missionary Society. Other voluntary societies for such purposes as benevolence and ministerial relief quickly followed. These innovations caused a deep split in the movement. The conservatives, who were to become the Churches of Christ, rejected them and also resisted such changes as the introduction of church music. The largest branch of the movement, its membership can be estimated as about 3 million. The progressives, who were to become the Christian Church (Disciples of Christ), accepted the innovations and went on to develop a more classical denominational form. They have been supporters of the ecumenical movement and have joined the Federal, National, and World Councils of Churches. Membership in 1980 was about 1.2 million.

DISCOVERY. Name of two British war vessels during the discovery of the Northwest Coast of America. The first was a small vessel of 300 tons used as the companion ship to the *Resolution* in Capt. James Cook's third voyage (1776–80), on which he explored the Northwest Coast to the Arctic Ocean. The second ship was a sloop of war of about 400 tons' burden, the chief ship of Capt. George Vancouver's explorations of North America (1792–94).

DISFRANCHISEMENT OF THE SOUTHERN BLACK. *See* **Suffrage, Afro-American.**

DISMAL SWAMP. A swamp in North Carolina and Virginia, covering about 750 square miles. In the center is the circular Lake Drummond, 3.5 miles in diameter. The swamp was named by William Byrd in 1728, and 4,000 acres were owned by George Washington. In the 1970's a controversial drainage and agricultural development program aroused conservationists.

DISSENTERS. Those who disagreed with the doctrines of the established Church of England and, later, to other religious establishments. There consequently grew up separate "dissenting" bodies. The most important were Congregationalists, Baptists, Quakers, Presbyterians, and Wesleyans, or Methodists. "Nonconformist" was applied at first to those who refused to agree to the practices of an established church. In the 19th century the term came to be applied to all who in any way disagreed with the established church. Since that time "nonconformist" and "dissenter" have come to be used without distinction.

DISTILLING. Almost as quickly as colonists arrived in the New World, they began producing alcoholic beverages. The settlers at Roanoke Island brewed a crude ale from maize, and New Englanders made wine from wild grapes. Commercial distilleries were operating in New Amsterdam as early as 1640 and shortly thereafter in Boston (1654) and in Charleston, S.C. (1682).

Rum and brandy were the two most popular distilled beverages throughout the colonial period. Rum distilled from West Indian sugar was an important colonial industry, significant in the commerce of the British Empire. Among frontier farmers whiskey was always available and often preferred. Isolated western farmers distilled whiskey from corn, rye, and barley. Besides being a popular beverage, frontier whiskey served as a medicine, a commodity for exchange, and a cash crop.

By 1791, Kentuckians already had enough interest in whiskey to warrant a convention opposing the excise or whiskey tax of the federal government (*see* Whiskey Rebellion). The federal government eventually proved to be at least as good a customer as it was a taxing agent: the army, until 1832, and the navy, until 1862, provided enlisted personnel with a liquor ration. Whiskey distillers also benefited indirectly from the Embargo Act of 1807 and the War of 1812. Rum distilleries were blockaded from their sources of cane sugar and molasses, so rum drinkers were forced to develop a taste for whiskey, especially Kentucky (or Bourbon) whiskey.

After the repeal of Prohibition in 1933, the distilling industry did not resume its older pattern of many small, often family-owned distilleries. Few distillers possessed the capital or marketing capabilities to resume operations. In the late 1970's, although about a hundred separate establishments annually produced over $2 billion worth of distilled beverages and had about 16,000 employees, most liquor was produced by half a dozen major corporations.

DISTRIBUTION ACT. *See* **Deposit Act of 1836.**

DISTRIBUTION OF GOODS AND SERVICES. Involves creating a demand for goods, creating the goods to correspond with the demand, determining who should get what goods and how much each should receive, and moving the goods to the point of consumption.

In the United States an advancing technology interacting with changing social customs and activated by competition between 12 million businesses has resulted in a flow of products that influences the way of life and creates needs for additional products. These 12 million businesses include retailers, wholesalers, service industries, farms, forests, mines, and fisheries as well as over 400,000 manufacturers and processors. With the aid of consumer feedback and market research they are primarily responsible for creating a demand for an expanding flow of new products and discarding those that become obsolete. Only one in five products succeeds. To reduce risks, manufacturers engage in research and test marketing by placing products on trial. To inform consumers and motivate them to buy, business firms in 1979 expended $14.5 billion in newspaper advertising, $10 billion in television advertising, $3 billion in magazine advertising, and $19.5 billion in other forms of advertising.

Agents, wholesalers, and retailers are responsible for moving products from the manufacturer to the consumer. Agents represent manufacturers and primary producers as sellers or represent wholesalers and retailers as buyers. They help to buy, sell, price, finance, transport, or store; they do not take title to the product. Merchant-wholesalers perform some or all the above functions and do take title to the goods. Manufacturers also sell to retailers and wholesalers through 31,000 sales branches. This distributive activity linking the origin of the goods to the retailer or consumer, generally described as "wholesaling," has increased at a faster rate than retailing. Between 1948 and 1977 wholesale sales increased by 1,150 percent and retail sales by only 454 percent.

The forces of supply and demand are the dominant influence on the activity of the distribution, and interplay of these forces in the marketplace is the strategic factor in allocating the products and services. But from the turn of the century on, legislation was needed to assure fair competition and to protect the consumer. In the early 1950's, business firms began to emphasize coordinating their products with consumer demand. This approach became known as the marketing concept. Another influence on distribution is an awakening interest among consumers in protecting their interests. Stimulated by Ralph Nader and others, large numbers of consumers are showing increasing initiative in bringing influence to bear on business firms to reduce consumer abuse and increase distribution efficiency.

DISTRICT, CONGRESSIONAL. The electoral unit by which members of the U.S. House of Representatives are selected. Although in early American history some states frequently elected congressmen-at-large, the single-member district has generally prevailed since the 1840's. The total number of House seats to which each state is entitled is set by the federal government after each census (reapportionment), but each state legislature has to set up the boundary lines for such districts (redistricting).

Congress at one time suggested districting guidelines, which were generally disregarded. In 1964 the Supreme Court ruled in *Wesberry* v. *Sanders* that districts must be substantially equal in population. Previously, great population inequalities developed in many states, either as a result of a failure to redistrict (a "silent gerrymander") or as a result of deliberate efforts to maximize the political position of a particular political party by manipulating the shape of the district without regard to population (a gerrymander).

DISTRICT OF COLUMBIA. Established in order that the nation's capital city could be built on territory outside the control and influence of any one state. The decision to locate the District of Columbia on the Potomac River was reached as part of the first major political deal between the Federalists (Alexander Hamilton's friends) and the Republicans (Thomas Jefferson's followers). In return for an agreement to locate the capital in the South, Jefferson agreed to support Hamilton's proposal for the U.S. government to assume the state debts from the Revolutionary War. This compromise was reached in 1790, and President George Washington was authorized to select the site along the Potomac.

The original one-hundred square mile site was carved out of both Virginia and Maryland. In 1846, Virginia requested the government to restore the land that once belonged to Virginia. As a result, the District of Columbia was reduced to sixty square miles, all of it at one time within Maryland, north of the Potomac River.

The District of Columbia, since it does not belong to a state, has a very unusual legal status. Its residents do not elect representatives to a state legislature, nor do they have senators or representatives in Congress. There are elected officials, however, and residents elect a nonvoting delegate to the House of Representatives. The Twenty-third Amendment to the Constitution (Mar. 29, 1961) finally gave residents of the District of Columbia—by that time, entirely occupied by the city of Washington—the right to choose electors for president, with at least as many electoral votes as the "least populous state." The District casts three electoral votes. (*See also* Washington, D.C.)

DISTURNELL'S MAP *(Mapa de los Estados Unidos de Méjico, Segun lo organizado y definido por las varias actas del Congreso de dicha República: y construido por las mejores autoridades. Lo publican J. Disturnell, 102 Broadway. Nueva York. 1846)*. This map, used in the Treaty of Guadalupe Hidalgo, is a reprint of a map published in 1828 by White, Gallaher and White, which had plagiarized H. S. Tanner's *Map of the United States of Mexico,* 1825. John Disturnell published twenty-three editions between 1846 and 1858.

DIVINE PROVIDENCES. In New England, events that came to pass through the agency of natural causes and yet appeared to be specifically ordained by the will of God. New England theologians believed that the age of miracles had passed, but that God still achieved His desired ends, not by reversing or suspending the laws of nature, but rather by guiding the laws according to their proper natures. In the late 17th century, the doctrine was particularly stressed as a defense against the materialism, atheism, and mechanism of Thomas Hobbes's philosophy; it was also emphasized by Increase and Cotton Mather as a device to arouse the sluggish emotions of what they believed to be a backsliding generation.

DIVISION ACT OF 1800. Divided the Northwest Territory by a line running from the Ohio River opposite the mouth of the Kentucky River north to Fort Recovery, Ohio, and thence due north to the Canadian boundary. Indiana Territory was created west of the line, while the eastern division retained the original name. Vincennes and Chillicothe, Ohio, were made the respective capitals. William Henry Harrison, territorial delegate from the Northwest Territory, was responsible for the war. (*See also* Harrison Land Act.)

DIVORCE. Consonant with the Puritan moral precept that it is one's duty to love one's spouse, the New England colonies created the institution of judicial divorce for those who could not. They went further in declaring that marriage was not a sacrament, as the Catholic church had claimed, and developed divorce in secular courts. There had been a few legislative divorces in New England in the 1600's, but by the early 1700's the laws putting the process into the hands of the judiciary were complete. This meant that the adversary system was applied and one party had to be guilty, and that the court had to have grounds for deciding when to grant divorce. Those most commonly found were adultery, neglect, and physical cruelty. Some states, especially those that stemmed from the Church of England rather than Reformist sects, did not readily accept judicial divorce. South Carolina permitted no divorce until 1949; New York recognized adultery as the sole ground until the 1960's.

In the early 20th century, divorce was taken up by the women's suffrage movement. Some of the earliest achievements of the suffrage movement were more rights for women in divorce. In the 1960's, many social currents came together to create another definition of marriage and new bases for divorce. Marriage was seen as a partnership that requires both spouses actively to work at it. The implication is that if one or both parties fails to do so, the marriage is dead; what remains is to get the rights of all parties straightened out financially and legally. The California divorce law of 1969 was the first to be based on these new principles. The U.S. divorce rate has risen steadily. Although in the 1970's it was among the highest for record-keeping societies, it was conservative from a broader comparative point of view.

DIXIE. A name for the southern states of the United States. Many theories are offered to explain the origin of the term. The earliest printed use is in an 1850 play entitled *The United States Mail and Dixie in Difficulty,* Dixie being the play's principal black character. Daniel D. Emmett, the author of the song "Dixie" and a noted minstrel, contended that show people referred to the South as "Dixie's land." He wrote "Dixie" as a walkaround for Bryant's Minstrel Troupe of New York in April 1859. The tune's popularity attracted numerous versions of its lyrics. It was used as a Confederate anthem and marching song.

DIXON-YATES CONTRACT. A contract approved on Oct. 5, 1954, by the Atomic Energy Commission under which the Middle South Utilities, Inc., and the Southern Company (Dixon-Yates group) were to build a generating plant at West Memphis to feed power into the TVA system to supply Memphis. The contract was an issue during the 1954 congressional elections because of charges of conflict of interest. President Eisenhower canceled the contract on July 11, 1955, after Memphis voted to build its own steam-generating plant.

DODGE CITY (Kans.). City in southern Kansas on the Arkansas River; site of several temporary army camps until Fort Dodge was built in 1864. Upon completion of the Santa Fe Railroad to this site in 1872, a town sprang up as an outfitting center for buffalo hunters. When cattle succeeded buffalo, Dodge City became a rendezvous for cowboys and the shipping station of millions of head of cattle per year until 1886, when the government closed the free range. In the 20th century it became an industrial city and center of trade in wheat, agricultural equipment, livestock, and sorghum. The 1980 population was 18,001.

DODGE CITY TRAIL. A cattle trail from west Texas to the railway terminal in Kansas. Herds were gathered along the trail at several Texas points. Crossing the Red River near Vernon, the herds continued through Fort Supply in western Oklahoma to Dodge City.

DODGE-LEAVENWORTH EXPEDITION (1834). U.S. Dragoons and delegations of Osage, Cherokee, Delaware, and Seneca Indians, under the leadership of Col. Henry Dodge. Its chief purpose was to impress the Indians of the Plains who had been committing depredations on newly arrived Indians from the east and upon white settlers. Starting from Fort Gibson on the Arkansas River on June 21, the expedition continued southwest to the Pawnee Pict village on the north fork of the Red River. Delegations of Plains Indians returned to Fort Gibson with the expedition, and conferences between them and the immigrant tribes led to peace. Treaties were concluded in 1835 and 1837, but subsequent years brought bitter warfare.

DOHRMAN'S GRANT. A section of land (23,040 acres) in the southeastern part of Tuscarawas County, Ohio, granted by the Congress of the Confederation on Oct. 1, 1787, to Arnold Henry Dohrman, in appreciation for the aid and shelter which he, as merchant and agent of the United States at Lisbon, Portugal, rendered American cruisers and vessels of war during the American Revolution. Congress also granted Dohrman a salary, retroactive, for his services.

DOLLAR. The term "dollar" comes from the English corruption of the word "thaler," a widely circulated silver coin from the Joachimsthal in Germany. The English and their colonists applied the term indiscriminately to thalers, to French silver "dollars" (écus), and to the Spanish "pieces (pesos) of eight," or eight reals. In keeping accounts, colonists and colonial governments reckoned usually in pounds, shillings, and pence; but the most common coins were probably the real (nominally a sixpence, but usually rated at seven or eight pence) and the eight-real piece, or "dollar."

The standard unit of U.S. currency is the dollar, established under Secretary of the Treasury Alexander Hamilton. A decimal system of money was devised, in which the dollar was divisible into one hundred "cents" or ten "dimes." This decimal system was novel for the late 18th century and provided a much more easily managed system of money than the British system. (*See also* Coinage; Money.)

DOLLAR, SILVER. *See* **Coinage.**

DOLLAR-A-YEAR MAN. When the United States entered World War I in 1917, a large number of prominent merchants, manufacturers, bankers, professional men, and others entered the service of the government as executives in departments in which they were expert, receiving as token salary a dollar per year, plus expenses.

DOLLAR DIPLOMACY. The policy of promoting a nation's economic interests abroad and strengthening its power to effect its policy objectives by using its economic resources. In the United States it received its most explicit expression by President William Howard Taft. In a message to Congress on Dec. 3, 1912, Taft stated that American diplomacy "is an effort frankly directed to an increase of American trade." The term was particularly applied to U.S. policies in the Caribbean and Central America. This policy was as old as the nation, but its statement at this time set off a bitter debate. William Jennings Bryan and President Woodrow Wilson were among the severe critics of Taft's and Theodore Roosevelt's policy; yet they practiced dollar diplomacy in the negotiation of the Bryan-Chamorro Treaty with Nicaragua (1914) and in the occupation of Haiti and the Dominican Republic. Pejorative use of the term declined in later years, but post–World War II foreign economic and military aid programs constituted a revival and extension of dollar diplomacy on a broad scale.

DOLLAR SIGN. Popular belief ascribes the dollar sign ($) to a mark on government mailbags standing for U.S., or Uncle Sam, or to the pillars of Hercules on the Spanish dollar. It also might be a conversion of the old Spanish symbol for the Spanish dollar. Most probably it is a conventionalized combination of the letters *p* and *s* for "pesos." Such a mark was used by a government clerk as early as 1788.

***DOLPHIN* ADMIRALTY CASE** (1863). The contraband-laden *Dolphin,* obviously destined for the Confederacy, was captured on Mar. 25, 1863, between neutral ports of call. At Key West, Fla., Judge William Marvin, elaborating on the continuous voyage doctrine, held that all segments of such a voyage are illegal if the voyage "would be illegal if not so divided."

DOMAIN, EMINENT. *See* **Eminent Domain.**

DOMAIN, PUBLIC. *See* **Public Domain.**

DOMESTIC RELATIONS, COURTS OF. In the first decade of the 20th century it became clear that a vast number of family problems need intelligent, scientific adjustments by legal process. Thus, the courts of family relations were evolved by degrees and finally established as a permanent part of the U.S. judicial system. These courts deal with family maladjustments, desertion, immorality, child and family neglect, illegitimacy, social disease, divorce, impairment of the morals of minors, and similar problems.

DOMESTIC TRADE. *See* **Trade, Domestic.**

DOMINICAN REPUBLIC. Almost as soon as the Dominican Republic won its independence from Haiti in 1844, it was threatened by conflicting interests of Haiti, the United States, France, and Great Britain. In 1846 the United States began to investigate the Bay of Samaná as a potential naval base. When Emperor Faustin I of Haiti invaded the Dominican Republic in 1849 and 1850, Britain and France intervened to compel him to sign a truce (Oct. 16, 1851) for one year. When Faustin refused to negotiate a truce or a treaty for ten years, the three powers prepared to forestall any new attempt by Faustin. When President Pedro Santana of the Dominican Republic, on Mar. 18, 1861, proclaimed its annexation by Spain, the United States was prevented by the Civil War from opposing a clear violation of the Monroe Doctrine. But in the Dominican Republic bitter opposition to the restoration of Spanish rule forced the Spanish troops to withdraw on July 20, 1865. Secretary of State William H. Seward and President Andrew Johnson sought during 1868–69 to annex both Haiti and the Dominican Republic but failed. In 1869, President Ulysses S. Grant renewed efforts to annex the Dominican Republic. Because of charges of corruption and opposition by the press (inspired in part by the Haitian minister), Grant did not pursue his efforts.

A partial customs receivership begun by the United States in 1904 was extended in 1905 to the entire Dominican Republic. A treaty (Feb. 8, 1907) provided for a U.S. customs receivership to secure a funding loan floated by U.S. bankers.

The assassination on Nov. 19, 1911, of President Rámon Cáceres led to insurrections and near anarchy. In 1912, Secretary of State Philander C. Knox, an exponent of "dollar diplomacy," threatened to withhold customs revenues from the Dominican president unless he accepted a government selected by the United States. The following year Secretary of State William Jennings Bryan obtained the post of general receiver of the Dominican customs revenues. Resistance by the Dominican government to another such appointment without its consent gave President Woodrow Wilson the opportunity to proclaim martial law on Nov. 29, 1916, with the government headed by an officer of the U.S. Navy.

After World War I, criticism of the American occupation by Latin-American nations and some Americans led to a consultative committee of prominent Dominican citizens, which resigned Jan. 9, 1920, primarily because of increasing censorship by the military governor. Criticism by Republicans hastened the initial steps for ending U.S. rule. Secretary of State Charles Evans Hughes engineered the withdrawal. When the Dominican government refused to accept his proposal, Hughes appointed Sumner Welles to effect a new agreement. Under this agreement (Sept. 19, 1922), elections were to be held for a provisional president, after which the executive departments would be turned over to a Dominican cabinet. The provisional government was to hold elections for a constitutional government. After prolonged negotiations, Hughes agreed to revisions of the 1907 treaty. The last of the marines left on Sept. 18, 1924.

Less than six years later, new turmoil paved the way for the dictatorship of Rafael Trujillo. Despite his despotic rule, he was supported by the U.S. government, largely because he favored American business interests. A new "permanent agreement" was made in 1934, permitting substantial reductions in Dominican debt payments in exchange for more powers for the American general receiver of customs. The United States relinquished its financial controls in the Dominican Republic completely in 1940.

Instability after the assassination in 1961 of Trujillo culminated in a civil war that began on Apr. 24, 1965, providing the United States with an opportunity to intervene (Apr. 28). Although giving decisive support to the forces opposing the revolution, U.S. policy was stated as neutral, with the hope of restoring Dominican "democracy." U.S. intervention was severely criticized by the United Nations Security Council and the Organization of American States (OAS). An OAS peace commission arranged an accommodation on Aug. 30 that provided for a provisional president, but new fighting began in December. The American troops were finally withdrawn under OAS supervision in September 1966. Thereafter, the United States gave the Dominican Republic substantial economic assistance. Despite renewed strife in the early 1970's, the United States did not intervene.

DOMINICAN REPUBLIC, PROPOSED ANNEXATION OF. In 1868, Buenaventura Báez, dictator of Santo Domingo, asked the United States to assume a protectorate of his nation preliminary to annexation. Secretary of State William H. Seward first discouraged, but later approved, the plan; but the administration of Andrew Johnson took no action. President Ulysses S. Grant's private secretary, Orville E. Babcock, was sent to the island in 1869 and signed an informal agreement committing the United States to annexation and an agreement for a naval station at Samaná Bay, to be used if the treaty should fail. In the U.S. Senate, annexation met strong opposition. Grant induced Congress to send a commission to the island to investigate, but the Senate in June 1871 killed the treaty and the project.

DOMINICANS, or Order of Preachers (O.P.). Part of a worldwide Roman Catholic religious community of friars founded in 1216 by St. Dominic. The Dominicans arrived in America with the Spanish explorers. The first community was established at St. Rose in Springfield, Ky., in 1806 by

Edward Dominic Fenwick, along with the first Catholic school for boys west of the Alleghenies (1806) and the first Catholic church in Ohio, at Somerset, in 1818. Fenwick became the first bishop of Cincinnati. In the Far West, community life was established by José Sadoc Alemany, appointed bishop of Monterey (1851) and later the first archbishop of San Francisco (1853). The Dominicans also established themselves in Washington, D.C. (1852), and New York (1867).

In 1980 there were four Dominican provinces in the United States, with 1,110 priests, brothers, and novices. In addition to many priories, the Dominicans staff Providence College in Rhode Island, some high schools, and their own seminaries. In 1909, they organized the Holy Name Society, which is administered in the United States by the National Association of the Holy Name Society. The Dominicans' intellectual mission includes teaching in universities; publishing scholarly periodicals; producing other publications, especially the writings of St. Thomas Aquinas; and foreign missionary work.

DOMINION OF NEW ENGLAND. *See* **New England, Dominion of.**

DOMINION THEORY. A theory holding that since the colonies were not part of the British realm, but individual realms subject to the king, Parliament had no authority over them. The theory was best expressed by John Adams in his *Novanglus* letters of Dec. 1774 – Apr. 1775, written in response to the Tory viewpoint of "Massachusettensis" (Daniel Leonard).

DONATION LANDS. Given by states or the federal government to reward citizens for services or to encourage settlement in remote or dangerous regions. Probably first used for the lands in northwestern Pennsylvania granted in 1785 as bounty for soldiers of the Revolution. In 1842, 1850, and 1854, Congress passed donation acts for the territories of East Florida, Oregon, Washington, and New Mexico.

DONELSON, FORT, CAPTURE OF (Feb. 15, 1862). In January 1862, the Confederate line of defense in the West extended from Cumberland Gap westward across Kentucky to Columbus on the lower Ohio. After the capture of Fort Henry, early in February 1862, Fort Donelson, twenty miles westward on the Cumberland River, was the only obstacle to a Union advance all along the line. Gen. Ulysses S. Grant proposed to destroy the fort, but difficulties imposed by terrain, rain, and cold weather delayed him. On Feb. 13, Grant's troops assaulted Fort Donelson unsuccessfully. The Confederates counterattacked without success. On Feb. 15 the fort and over 14,000 men were surrendered.

DONELSON'S LINE. Between Virginia and Cherokee territory; run in 1771 by Col. John Donelson of Virginia to establish the boundary agreed upon in the Treaty of Lochaber, from a point on the Holston River six miles above Long Island to the mouth of Kanawha River. In some devious way, the line was fixed and reported to run with the Kentucky River. Thus, the Virginians found encouragement to settle above the Kentucky River on land that, according to the treaty, belonged to the Cherokee.

DONGAN CHARTERS. Gov. Richard Nicolls in 1665 chartered New Harlem and Manhattan as a city with a mayor, aldermen, and minor officers. New York City in 1683 petitioned Gov. Thomas Dongan for a new charter, which set up a government consisting of a mayor, six aldermen, six common councillors, recorder, clerk, sheriff, treasurer, coroner, constables, overseers, assessors, and courts (1686). Dongan also granted charters to towns on Long Island.

DONIPHAN'S EXPEDITION (1846–47). After the capture of Santa Fe in 1846, Col. Alexander W. Doniphan, commander of the First Regiment of Missouri Mounted Volunteers, part of Gen. Stephen W. Kearny's command, was ordered to lead an expeditionary force southward to Chihuahua. On Christmas Day he defeated 600 Mexicans at Brazito. The town of El Paso was occupied two days later. On Feb. 8, 1847, now reinforced, Doniphan set out with 924 men for Chihuahua. Twenty miles north of Chihuahua City, on Feb. 28, the Americans met over 3,000 Mexicans. Doniphan was victorious, in the Battle of the Sacramento, and the city was occupied the next day.

DONNER PARTY. Eighty-seven California-bound emigrants, whose nucleus was the Donner and Read families from Sangamon County, Ill., were blocked by snows south of the Great Salt Lake. Camping at Truckee Lake in November 1846, the party suffered indescribable hardships, the survivors escaping starvation only by eating the flesh of those who died. Rescue parties from California broke through and led out, with heavy loss of life, those who were able to travel. Forty-seven of the original group survived.

"DON'T FIRE TILL YOU SEE THE WHITE OF THEIR EYES." The origin of this alleged command to the patriots at Bunker Hill, June 17, 1775, may have been Col. William Prescott's order to reserve fire and aim low because powder was scarce. It is said to have been passed on by Israel Putnam in these words: "Men, you are all marksmen—don't one of you fire until you see the white of their eyes."

"DON'T GIVE UP THE SHIP." Spoken by James Lawrence, commander of the American frigate *Chesapeake,* after he fell fatally wounded in the engagement with the British frigate *Shannon,* thirty miles off Boston harbor, on June 1, 1813. The *Chesapeake* was captured, and Lawrence died four days later.

DORCHESTER. Residential district in south Boston, settled in June 1630 by the vanguard of the Great Migration, which came on the *Mary and John.* A town-meeting form of government was set up, reportedly the first of its kind in the colonies, in 1633. In 1868, Dorchester was incorporated into Boston.

DORCHESTER COMPANY. Certain English merchants, having ships sailing from Weymouth to fish off the banks of

Newfoundland, in 1622 decided that a settlement on the coast of New England would be to their advantage. The merchants obtained a license to search for a site for their colony, and a month later Sir Walter Erle became a patentee.

The promoters met on May 26, 1624, at Dorchester, England, under the auspices of Sir Walter Erle and Rev. John White. A joint-stock company was formed, and £3,000 were subscribed. A ship, the *Fellowship,* was purchased, fitted out, and dispatched. In September 1625, it reached its home port. Two ships were sent out the following year; and three, one laden with kine, in 1627.

By that time about fifty men had been left at Cape Ann, and some men from Plymouth Colony who disliked the separatist rule there joined them; that undertaking did not flourish, chiefly because "fishermen would not work on land neither husbandmen make good fishermen." Great losses had almost ruined the company, so it was decided to establish a new company. An appeal was made to London merchants holding similar views on religion, and a new joint-stock company, the New England Company, was formed.

DORR'S REBELLION (1841–42). As late as 1841, Rhode Island was still using as its constitution the charter granted by King Charles II in 1663. The limitation of the suffrage to the owners of freehold estates and their oldest sons disfranchised more than half the adult male population. For some years the masses, under Thomas W. Dorr, had been clamoring for wider participation in the government. Finally, the malcontents called a convention in October 1841 and drew up a People's Constitution. A convention chosen by the qualified electors met in November 1841 and framed the Landholders' Constitution. Both constitutions provided for an enlargement of the suffrage, but the voting franchise was to be somewhat more liberal under the People's Constitution. The latter was submitted for ratification in December 1841, and all adult male citizens were asked to vote. The constitution was ratified by a majority. The Landholders' Constitution was submitted in March 1842 to those who were qualified to vote under its provisions. It was rejected by a small margin, and the government continued to function under the charter. A new government was organized under the People's Constitution with Dorr as governor. The governor of the old party, Samuel W. King, appealed to President John Tyler to lend military assistance. Tyler recognized the legality of the old, or charter, government and promised aid if violence were committed by the insurgents. King sent the state militia to attack the Dorrites, fortified in the northwestern part of the state. Many of Dorr's followers fled, and Dorr surrendered. A sentence of life imprisonment was imposed upon Dorr, but was rescinded. The conservatives yielded to the demands of the people, and a third constitution was adopted; it provided for manhood suffrage with slight restrictions.

DOUBLOON. A Spanish gold piece, so called because its value was double that of a pistole. Its value varied from $8.25 in 1730–72 to about $7.84 in 1786–1848. It was freely used in the West Indies and South American trade, and southerners in the colonial period often had their cash assets in Spanish gold.

DOUGHBOY. "Doughboy" was universally used in the U.S. Army to mean an American infantryman, until World War II when it was replaced with "GI." It was already in use on the Texas border in 1854. The explanation was that the infantrymen wore white belts and had to clean them with "dough" made of pipe clay.

DOUGHFACES. Northerners who, before the Civil War, supported southern policies relative to territorial expansion and slavery. The word was coined in 1819 by John Randolph of Virginia as a term of contempt.

DOVE. *See* **Ark and Dove.**

DOVER (Del.). Capital of Delaware, with a population of 23,512 in 1980. It is basically a government town with little industry other than food processing. Its farming area specializes in poultry and fruit growing, and the city provides marketing and processing centers for these products.

William Penn ordered that a town be created at the site of Dover in 1683. It was not actually surveyed and laid out until 1717. A number of the buildings date from the 18th century, when it was the home of several influential Delaware families. The original state capital of New Castle was abandoned in 1777 for fear the British army or fleet would capture it. Dover was less accessible from the sea and easier to defend.

DOVES. Those who opposed American participation in the war in Vietnam, based on the symbolic "dove of peace." It gained currency during the presidency of Lyndon B. Johnson. Supporters of the war were called hawks.

DRAFT. Selection of some of the male population for compulsory military service. The concepts of universal military training and compulsory military service in time of emergency were established in the United States under the legal systems of all the colonial powers. They were rigorously applied in some colonies. In Massachusetts the Minutemen were a body selected from the mass of the universal, or "common," militia. The compulsory militia laws were used sporadically during the Revolution both for local defense and for the Continental army. Service in the latter could be avoided by hiring a substitute or by payment of a fee. Compulsory universal-militia service was written into the constitutions of the states and remains in force in most state codes. The U.S. Constitution provides for the training of state militias under standards to be prescribed by Congress. The Militia Act of May 8, 1792, provided a broad organizational structure for the militia but no means of enforcing training. The act's inadequacies and the disappearance of any continuing military threat in the more populous eastern states led to disintegration of the old universal-militia concept.

From the end of the Revolution until 1863, American military manpower procurement for the regular services was based entirely on volunteers. The only viable units of the militia were also composed of volunteers. The armies of both the Union and the Confederacy were organized on the same basis (that is, a mass of state volunteer militia units organized around a nucleus of regulars from the prewar U.S. Army).

When neither voluntary enlistment nor the erratic pattern of state compulsory service produced the manpower needed, both the North and the South resorted to a federal draft. The implementing legislation in the North was the Enrollment Act of 1863. Hiring substitutes or paying fees in lieu of service continued to be authorized. Bitter opposition to the draft continued throughout the war.

From the end of the Civil War until 1903, military manpower procurement reverted to the prewar voluntary system. During this same period American military policy was reexamined by a group of theoreticians whose work manifested itself in a series of legislative acts between 1903 and 1916. The state volunteer militia—by now known as the National Guard—was brought under greater federal control. A federal military reserve was created under the War and Navy departments. The foundation was laid for an army that, once mobilized, could be supported only by a federal draft. Organization of an effective army general staff helped make possible a review of the mistakes of the Civil War draft and the development of plans for a more efficient and equitable system.

These plans were ordered into effect by the Selective Service Act of 1917. The hiring of substitutes and the payment of bounties were outlawed. Enrollment and selection were to be done by local civilian boards organized under federally appointed state directors and operating under uniform federal regulations. Civilians established the categories of deferment and acted on appeals. Manpower requirements were developed by the army general staff and apportioned as state quotas. The order of induction was determined by lottery. The World War I draft was found by the Supreme Court to be constitutional. In general, the new Selective Service program was accepted by the public as fair and reasonable. Opposition to any continuing program of compulsory service in peacetime continued to be overwhelming.

The fall of France and the worsening of U.S. relations with Japan led to the enactment of the nation's first peacetime draft with the passage of the Selective Training and Service Act of 1940. The impact of the World War II draft was pervasive. Over 10 million men were inducted, representing the most extensive mobilization of the nation's manpower in its history. Draftees were assigned to all the armed services. With the exception of one year (March 1947 to March 1948), the draft was in continuous operation from 1940 to Jan. 27, 1973. The administrative machinery established during World War II had been modified but never dismantled. From 1940 until 1967 the Selective Service System was geared to the requirements of total war and total mobilization. Military manpower requirements of the Korean and Vietnam conflicts were much smaller. Requirements between those wars were even more limited. Successive administrations dealt with this problem by liberalizing deferments.

By offering deferment to those who enlisted in the National Guard or one of the federal reserve forces, a direct link was established for the first time between the draft and the civilian reserves. The remaining draft eligibles consisted largely of young men who had not chosen to marry and to father a child in their teens, who were not successfully enrolled in college, and who upon graduation from college had not taken jobs in teaching or some other exempted occupations. As the manpower requirements of the Vietnam War and the personal risks of service increased, the consequences of the deferment policies could no longer be accepted.

The response by the administrations of presidents Lyndon B. Johnson and Richard M. Nixon was a return to the lottery as a substitute for obviously discriminatory deferments. Early in 1973 the Nixon administration ended the draft, returning to a reliance on volunteers, but with maintenance of the Selective Service System in a standby, or "zero draft," status. The manpower requirements of the active and reserve forces were met by large increases in pay and related incentives. In April 1975 the Selective Service System was discontinued by President Gerald Ford. President Jimmy Carter was originally against draft registration, but after the Soviet invasion of Afghanistan in December 1979, he proposed a registration plan, which was approved by Congress in June 1980. A registration of all males nineteen and twenty years old took place between July 21 and Aug. 2. It was revived by president Ronald Reagan.

DRAFT RIOTS (1863). Although there had been minor disturbances connected with personal enrollments, or conscription, under the Civil War act of Mar. 3, 1863, actual violence awaited the draft itself. Minor riots occurred in Rutland, Vt.; Wooster, Ohio; Boston, Mass.; and Portsmouth, N.H.; but none equaled those in New York City. Objection to the draft rested chiefly on the provision for money payments in lieu of service. Shortly after the drawing of lots commenced on July 13 at the Ninth Congressional District draft headquarters, a mob, mostly of foreign-born laborers, stormed the building; overpowered attendants, police, firemen, and militia; attacked residences, other draft district headquarters, saloons, hotels, restaurants, and even railway tracks. Four days of rioting resulted in a thousand casualties and $1.5 million in property loss. On July 15, militia regiments sent toward Gettysburg began to return, and order was restored. Picked troops from the Army of the Potomac were brought in, and on Aug. 19 drawings proceeded peaceably.

DRAGO DOCTRINE. After Great Britain, Germany, and Italy undertook by force of arms to compel Venezuela to pay certain claims, Luis María Drago, Argentina's minister of foreign affairs, sent a protest to the United States on Dec 19, 1902. Drago held that the payment of its debts was binding, but the debtor government had the right to choose the manner and the time of payment. He denounced armed intervention as a means of collecting debts. An amended version of this doctrine was adopted by the Second Hague Conference in 1907.

DRAKE AT CALIFORNIA. Sir Francis Drake, in 1577, left England with five ships to open Oriental and Pacific trade and deliver a blow at Spanish commercial and colonial monopoly. After harassing the Spaniards in the Atlantic Ocean, Drake passed through the Strait of Magellan, and in his one remaining ship, the *Golden Hind,* plundered the Pacific coast of South America. Prevented by unfavorable winds from sailing west to the Molucca Islands, Drake, in June 1579, entered Drake's Bay, Calif., to repair his ship. Claiming the land for

England and naming it New Albion, Drake remained there thirty-six days, exploring and establishing friendly relations with the Indians. Before departing for the Moluccas, he nailed up a brass plate as evidence of England's claim. In 1936 the plate, dated June 17, 1579, was discovered on the western shore of San Francisco Bay, where it had been discarded not long before, its value unrecognized, after having been brought from the vicinity of Drake's Bay.

DRAKE'S OIL WELL. E. L. Drake of New Haven, Conn., was sent by the Pennsylvania Rock Oil Company in 1858 to Titusville, Pa., where he experimented in drilling for petroleum, the first venture of the sort in America. He had many difficulties, his partners lost faith, and his own resources were strained to the limit when, on Aug. 28, 1859, he found oil at a depth of 69.5 feet. It rose to within 10 feet of the surface, and for some time forty barrels were pumped daily, selling at $20 a barrel. The oil strike precipitated a rush to the oilfield.

DRAMA. *See* **Theater.**

DRAPER'S MEADOWS. The first settlement west of the great Allegheny divide, on the present site of Blacksburg, Va.; founded in 1748 in the New River section by John Draper, Thomas Ingles, and other Scottish and Irish immigrants from Pennsylvania. On July 8, 1755, the settlement was destroyed by Shawnee Indians.

DREADNOUGHT. A type of battleship that derived its name from the British warship *Dreadnought* (1906). This ship made obsolete every battleship afloat. It had a displacement of 17,900 tons, a speed of 21.6 knots, and a cruising radius of 5,800 sea miles. It was protected by 11-inch armor and was the first battleship to be driven by turbines. Its main battery consisted of ten 12-inch guns, making it the first all-big-gun ship in the world. From its launching until World War I, every battleship built with a main armament entirely of big guns all of one caliber was considered to be in the *Dreadnought* class.

The *Dreadnought* inaugurated a race in building battleships of this type between Great Britain, the United States, and other naval powers. In the United States, two ships of this type were designed and authorized in 1905 but were not launched until 1908. Fifteen others were built by the United States before World War I. On Aug. 29, 1916, Congress authorized ten dreadnoughts. During the war this program was discontinued in favor of building destroyers for overseas duty but was resumed after the armistice. It was finally halted by the Washington Naval Conference of 1922.

DRED SCOTT CASE (*Dred Scott* v. *John F. A. Sanford,* 19 Howard 393). Decided by the Supreme Court on Mar. 6, 1857. The basic judgment was that Scott, because he was a slave, was neither a citizen of Missouri nor a citizen of the United States and had no constitutional right to sue in the federal courts. Dred Scott began his litigation in 1846 in the state courts of Missouri, in a bona fide freedom suit based on Missouri law and his earlier residence in free territory. The lower court declared him free, but the Missouri Supreme Court reversed the decision. A new suit was instituted, in the federal courts, also seeking a broader Supreme Court decision that might settle the disputes over slavery in the territories. When the decision finally was rendered, each judge wrote a separate opinion. Chief Justice Roger B. Taney's was considered the opinion of the Court. Six other judges presented concurring opinions; two dissented.

The only judgment rendered by an undeniable majority was that a slave could not be a citizen. Other principles laid down whose legality was disputed were that (1) blacks could not be citizens; (2) black slaves were a species of property protected by the Constitution and, hence, Congress had no authority to abolish slavery in the territories and the Missouri Compromise was unconstitutional; and (3) a black slave, even though freed by residence in a free state or territory, was remanded to slavery when he returned to a slave state. The decision stirred inflammatory reactions that helped precipitate the Civil War. After the war, the Thirteenth and Fourteenth amendments superseded the Dred Scott decision.

DRESS. Early American colonists dressed in an approximation of the prevailing English mode. In Jamestown, Va. (1607), women's bodices and men's doublets were long waisted, boned, and stiffly padded, with high, starched, fan-shaped whisk collars or ruffs. Men wore padded trunk hose and tights, sometimes with boots to mid-thigh, and leather jerkins. Women dressed in full skirts over a hoop. Both sexes wore wide-brimmed hats with high crowns and shoes with heels. The Pilgrims at Plymouth, Mass. (1620), and the Dutch of Manhattan, N.Y. (1623), wore simple versions of this style, with unpadded doublets and full breeches. The women preferred hoods and the short-waisted Dutch bodice. Pilgrim attire was plain and somber, with woolen stockings and heavy shoes. Dutch clothing was made of satin and velvet, with jewelry accessories.

By 1630, male garb consisted of a skirted doublet with slashed sleeves over a full-sleeved linen shirt with wide, lace-edged collar. Gathered breeches, heeled boots with turned-down cuffs, swords, broad-brimmed hats with plumes, mustaches, and pointed chin beards underlined the dashing effect. Women wore high-waisted bodices with low necklines and three-quarter-length sleeves. They covered their full skirts with silk aprons; added jewelry, fans, and muffs; and adorned their faces with beauty patches. The Puritans of the Massachusetts Bay Colony (1630) wore a modified version, minus ribbon and lace trimmings.

About 1670 the three-piece suit (coat, waistcoat, and breeches) came into existence. Throughout the 18th century a fitted knee-length coat with flared skirt and matching breeches was worn over a vest, often embroidered in colored silks. Powdered wig, cravat, silk stockings, and heeled shoes with buckles completed the costume. Men wore three-cornered hats and greatcoats with capes. A scarlet woolen cape was popular with both sexes. Women's dresses had low necks, tight elbow-length sleeves edged with deep ruffles, and full skirts worn over hoops. Sheer white fichus crossed over the bodice. A deep bonnet was worn out of doors. Coiffures grew increasingly high and by 1770 had assumed the shape of a sugarloaf. The most characteristic accessory was the folding fan. Wealthy men and women imported silk brocades and velvets for their clothing. The less wealthy wore homespun and buckskin breeches or coarse woolens and linens of English manufacture.

After the American Revolution the new country copied everything French. Extravagant dress was abandoned for simplicity and natural lines. Men wore high-waisted, double-breasted, cutaway coats with wide lapels and high collars over tight midcalf breeches. The top hat of beaver appeared, worn over unpowdered hair. Women wore high-waisted neoclassic gowns of lightweight embroidered muslins and short coiffures with ringlets, plumes, or turbans; carried beaded purses; and walked in flat-heeled slippers.

By 1820, men had adopted full-length trousers, wool cutaways or skirted frock coats, patterned velvet vests, and stiff black cravats. By 1830, women's clothing was made of warmer silks and woolens, the waistline had descended to its natural place, and vast leg-of-mutton sleeves appeared, and enormous hats and cashmere shawls. Cone-shaped, gored skirts reached to the ankle, revealing shoes with small heels. Toward 1840 a deep oval bonnet concealed the face, the sleeve diminished, and the skirt began to expand. Its flounces and multiple petticoats were replaced in the 1850's by the crinoline, a cage of metal hoops joined by vertical cotton tapes. Dresses were of plaid silks or striped velvets with ribbon trim and lace collars and undersleeves. Tiny folding parasols, drop earrings, and brooches were popular.

By the mid–19th century, Americans could purchase a variety of woven textiles and, ultimately, ready-made clothing. Elias Howe patented the sewing machine (1846), and during the Civil War machine-sewn uniforms were issued. By the late 1860's, mass-produced clothing for men was widely accepted. Women purchased ready-made capes and underwear but made their own dresses from paper patterns devised by Ebenezer Butterick (1863) or had them made. The fashionable purchased their wardrobes in Paris, and their rural sisters, from the Montgomery Ward catalog.

The most significant indigenous innovation of the 1850's was the blue denim work pants made by Levi Strauss. Originally worn during the California gold rush, levis were adopted by lumberjacks, railroad workers, and cowboys. Men began to wear neckties, caps, straw hats, and black silk top hats. The 1860's saw the matching three-piece suit and the sack jacket. The bowler hat was introduced in the 1870's; the belted Norfolk jacket and knickerbockers, shortly after.

In 1860, women's skirts reached their maximum circumference, and in 1865 the fullness began to move to the rear, evolving into the bustle and train. Dresses were combinations of heavy fabrics trimmed with jet, fringes, and tassels. Dainty boots, small hats, large parasols, and cameo brooches were worn. Tightly laced corsets culminated in the hour-glass figure of the 1890's, personified by the Gibson girl, her hair in a high pompadour, dressed in the new tailored suit and flat straw sailor hat. In the first decade of the 20th century the silhouette was an S-curve, with bosom thrust forward and hips back. High, boned collars and lace trimmed the popular shirtwaist. Just before World War I, women wore narrow hobble skirts, ostrich boas, and enormous plumed hats. During the war many of them served in uniform. Their roles necessitated drastic reforms, and corsets and floor-length skirts were abandoned. In the 1920's, hems rose gradually to the knee, legs were encased in flesh-colored silk stockings, arms were bare, and hair was worn short under cloche hats. Dresses were tubular and low waisted. With the depression of the 1930's the hem dropped to midcalf, and to floor length for evening. The bias-cut, clinging dress with defined waistline replaced the flapper silhouette. In the late 1930's, U.S. designers like Claire McCardell began to make clothes specifically for the life-style of American women. Slacks were popular at resorts, and Hollywood was an important influence. Adrian, who dressed many of the stars, popularized the square, padded shoulders, which remained in style until 1947. It was accompanied by upswept hair, tiny veiled hats perched over one eye, and high-heeled platform shoes with ankle straps. The classic sportswear look appeared on American campuses in the 1930's. Women wore sweaters and skirts; men wore pullover sweaters or tweed jackets with flannel trousers. Bobby socks, saddle shoes, and double-breasted camel's hair coats were worn by both sexes.

Nylon stockings were introduced in 1940. The first completely man-made fiber, nylon started a trend to synthetics that all but eclipsed natural fibers by the 1970's because of their low cost and ease of care. During the war, skirts remained short and narrow because of government restrictions on textiles. When Christian Dior created the New Look (1947), hemlines dropped on both sides of the Atlantic. Full skirts appeared over stiff nylon petticoats, and cinched waists and rounded shoulders replaced angularity. Ten years later, the chemise, a beltless style evocative of the 1920's, was in vogue. By 1961 it had become the sleeveless, knee-length, body-skimming dress popularized by the fashionable wife of President John F. Kennedy. Her pearls, pillbox hat, low-heeled pumps, and short white gloves were copied by millions of women. The extremely short minidress was introduced in the mid-1960's, accompanied by white plastic boots, enormous sunglasses, and a long mane of hair. Hats were no longer fashionable.

By 1970, pants were worn by women of all ages for every occasion. As the Women's Liberation movement grew, the demarcation between the sexes diminished in dress. Both wore long hair, platform sandals, shoulder bags, jewelry, and decorated blue jeans. The counterculture initiated the craze for handcrafts, and all adorned their costumes with leather and string accessories. The prosperity of the 1960's and early 1970's created a demand for novelty, and fads like ethnic and nostalgic clothes followed each other in rapid succession. Consumer goods had become so plentiful that the old rules of appropriateness, like Sunday best, Easter outfit, party dress, and other special-occasion clothing, formerly part of the buying ritual, ceased to exist. Informality became the keynote. In the mid-1970's many of the young claimed to be totally disinterested in clothes, but their dress reflected a deliberate, studied rejection of the past. The late 1970's saw a partial return to a more tailored look, and a suit gradually became a standard dress for professional women. Another expression of this trend was the popularity of "prep school" apparel around 1980. Meanwhile, designer jeans, pushed in aggressive television campaigns, turned into status symbols.

DREWRY'S BLUFF, BATTLE AT (May 12–16, 1864). As part of the overland movement against Richmond, Gen. Ulysses S. Grant put Gen. B. F. Butler in charge of the Union forces operating from the Yorktown peninsula in Virginia. Landing at Bermuda Hundred, Butler sought to attack Confederate forces in rear of Richmond. At Drewry's Bluff he was defeated by Gen. P. G. T. Beauregard.

DRIED FRUITS AND VEGETABLES. In colonial times great quantities of apples were dried in the sun and by artificial means. Prior to 1795, drying and the use of salt and sugar were the principal methods of preserving foods. In 1854, it was estimated, Maine could furnish the nation's supply of dried apples. The perfection of fruit evaporators in 1870–75 increased exports of dried-fruit products. Of nearly a half-billion pounds of dried apples exported in 1909, 83 percent came from California. Later, new drying processes and machinery enlarged outputs. New methods of preserving foods in their fresh state reduced the necessity for dried foods, and they have become delicacies.

DROGHER TRADE. A type of shipping carried on from about 1825 to 1834, between American firms, mostly in Boston, and Spaniards in California, by means of which New England manufactures were exchanged for cattle hides. "Drogher" is a West Indian word applied to slow and clumsy coast vessels.

DROUGHTS. Droughts in the United States fall into two general classes. One is of a transitory nature, usually affecting a comparatively small area or lasting for a single season, to be followed quickly by enough rainfall for current needs. In the other, more important class rainfall is abnormally low for several years. Transitory droughts may be expected every year in some areas, but annual droughts over a long period of time are infrequent.

Rainfall records show that an extended drought in the midwestern area culminated in the 1840's, after which more abundant precipitation reached a maximum phase in the 1870's and 1880's. Again, in 1886–95 an extensive drought prevailed, followed by years of abundant rainfall. Another dry phase began about 1930 and continued, with few fairly good years, up through 1941. There were three extremely dry years—1930, 1934, and 1936—the first being most pronounced in the central-eastern portion of the country and the other two affecting most extensively the interior valleys and Great Plains. The dry period was terminated by torrential rains through the Great Plains and the Southwest in late September and October of 1941.

In 1950 a drought began in the Southwest; after it ended with heavy rains in summer 1957, a long drought started in the Atlantic coast states, and by the mid-1960's water tables, rivers, and reservoirs reached dangerously low levels. A series of hurricanes raked the Appalachins during 1967–72, bringing rivers and water tables back to the level of the predrought years.

An extremely widely spread drought plagued the country in 1976–77. California and the Pacific Northwest were hit hardest, but crop damages in the Atlantic states were also considerable. After two wet years, a hot dry wave in 1980 resulted in a moderate drought and water shortages in northeastern states.

DRUG ADDICTION. The regular use of a drug from which the addict cannot abstain without physical or psychological discomfort.

In the early 19th century, opium could be purchased in the United States as an alcoholic extract or in various proprietary medicines. The smoking of opium was commonly associated with Chinese laborers. Crude opium itself was easily obtainable, since state restrictions were not widely enacted until the end of the 19th century. Scientific and technological advances in the 19th century dramatically altered the forms and manner in which opium could be administered. In the first decade morphine was isolated from crude opium. In 1832, U.S. pharmaceutical manufacturers began commercial extraction of morphine from opium, and by 1900 most imported opium was destined to meet this demand. The introduction of the hypodermic syringe gave physicians a simple method of introducing drugs into the body. By the 1890's opium importation reached about a half-million pounds annually. In 1898 diacetylmorphine, under the trade name Heroin, was marketed as a cough suppressant, but soon its addictive nature became apparent. Within a few decades heroin replaced morphine as the preferred drug for addicts.

Prior to cocaine's isolation from the coca leaf and commercial production in the late 19th century, coca was mostly used as an alcoholic extract. After the 1880's, cocaine became popular in many forms. Besides the stimulating and euphoric qualities it imparted to tonics, soda pop, and elixirs, cocaine had other valuable characteristics. It was employed as a surface anesthetic for the eye, used as a remedy for hay fever and sinusitis, and injected near nerves to block pain stimuli. By about 1900 fear of cocaine as an incitement to crime and debauchery was followed by strict state controls. Illicit cocaine became fairly rare in the United States until the 1960's, when it again appeared in quantity on the illegal market.

Legislatively, the narcotics have often been confused. The Pure Food and Drug Act (1906) sought to insure that proprietary medicines would be labeled as to narcotic content. At about the same time, the United States was drawn into a world campaign to monitor international traffic in narcotics and to limit their use to strictly medical needs. American leadership progressed from the Shanghai Opium Commission (1909) to the International Opium Conference at the Hague (1911–12), which prepared the Hague Opium Convention (1912), the first international treaty for the control of narcotics traffic. The Harrison Narcotic Act of 1914 sought to record most narcotics transactions, including those by health professionals. The severest restrictions on addiction maintenance continued to be the American attitude toward narcotics until the 1960's, when an upsurge of heroin use helped justify maintenance programs using methadone, a synthetic narcotic, as a legal substitute for heroin. Federal and state penalties against narcotics sales and smuggling, which had reached severely punitive levels by 1960, were moderated; in 1970 many of the laws regarding narcotics were harmonized and made more flexible by passage of the Comprehensive Drug Abuse Prevention and Control Act.

In the late 1970's and early 1980's, medical researchers began to stress the health problems caused by marijuana, which had been considered by many a "safe drug." By 1981 marijuana use among young people ceased to rise, but heroin trade increased. Federal contributions to enforcement and treatment programs aimed at narcotic and other drug abuse grew enormously after 1967, following recommendations of the President's Commission on Law Enforcement and Administration of Justice.

DRY DOCKS. Employed for construction and repair of ships, dry docks have constituted the foundations of naval architecture. They are erected on an inclined plane, to facilitate launchings, or erected below water level by means of cofferdams and fitted with watertight gates. The first federal dry dock in the United States was a 253-foot graving dock completed at Boston in 1833. Equipped with copper-sheathed turning gates and a caisson (floating gate), substantial pump wells, pumping machines, discharge culverts, capstans, and keel blocking. The New York Navy Yard's 307-foot dock (1851) boasted the world's first all-metal cofferdam.

After floating dry docks were introduced, the U.S. Navy constructed, such "balance" docks at Portsmouth, N.H. (1800), and Pensacola, Fla., and a floating sectional dry dock at Mare Island, Calif. (1853). The advent of steel construction and the increase in warship dimensions necessitated larger all-masonry docks. Following the Spanish-American War, 740-foot graving docks were constructed at Portsmouth, Boston, Philadelphia, and Mare Island. Subsequently, the navy established dry docks at Puget Sound and Pearl Harbor. During World War I, 1,005-foot dry docks equipped with massive traveling cranes were built at Norfolk, Philadelphia, and San Francisco. In World War II, graving docks with reinforced concrete walls over 20 feet thick were constructed at Norfolk and Philadelphia. The rapid strategic movement of naval forces dictated that the floating dry dock join the U.S. Fleet's mobile service force. During 1942–45, twenty-seven 457-foot LSD's (landing ship dock) were launched, many joining the Pacific fleet as combined dry docks and landing craft carriers.

DRY FARMING. The conducting of agricultural operations without irrigation in a climate with a deficiency of moisture. It involves the raising of crops that are drought resistant or drought evasive (maturing in late spring or fall) and makes the best use of a limited water supply by maintaining good surface conditions. In California, during the 1850's, Americans began to raise crops, such as winter wheat, whose principal growing season coincided with the winter rainfall season. By 1863 dry farming was practiced in Utah. In some interior valleys of the Pacific Northwest, dry farming was reported before 1880. In the Great Plains, adaptation to dry farming methods was associated with the small-farmer invasion of the late 1880's. State agricultural experiment stations of the Great Plains inaugurated experimental activities under government auspices, and the federal Department of Agriculture created the Office of Dry Land Agriculture in 1905. The drought cycles of the 1930's intensified experimental work and the invention of machinery for special soil cultural processes.

DUAL CITIZENSHIP. *See* **Citizenship, Dual.**

DUBUQUE (Iowa). City in northeastern Iowa named for Julien Dubuque, a French-Canadian lead miner. Permanent settlement began in 1833. Lead mining gradually waned, but log rafts were floated down the Mississippi to entrench the lumber industry. The oldest city in Iowa, Dubuque is an important river port and industrial center. Its population in 1980 was 93,745.

DUBUQUE MINING DISTRICT. *See* **Galena-Dubuque Mining District.**

DUCKING STOOL. A rude armchair used from the 17th century to the early 19th century for punishment of certain offenses, including witchcraft, scolding, and prostitution. It was used to humiliate offenders publicly. The chair was usually fastened to a long wooden beam fixed as a seesaw on the edge of a pond or stream. The offender was strapped into the chair and briefly immersed.

DUDLEY'S MASSACRE. *See* **Meigs, Fort.**

DUELING. A private fight between two persons, prearranged and fought with deadly weapons, usually in the presence of two witnesses called seconds who regulate the mode of fighting and enforce the rules agreed upon, having for its object to decide a personal quarrel. The first such affair in the English colonies occurred at Plymouth in 1621. It lost favor in the North after the Revolution but spread in the antebellum South.

Agitation against dueling began in the 18th century. Most states eventually decreed a challenge a breach of the peace, the wounding of an opponent an attempt at murder, and the killing of a combatant a homicide, seconds being held equally guilty. The army and navy condemned the practice late in the 18th century; in the late 19th century, public opinion and ridicule brought an end to the custom.

DUE PROCESS OF LAW. Perhaps the most important provision of the Constitution of the United States, appearing in both the Fifth and Fourteenth amendments. The provision is that neither the federal nor any state government may "deprive any person of life, liberty, or property, without due process of law." The Supreme Court in effect divided the constitutional provision into two different guarantees. One was the guarantee of substantive rights to life, liberty, and property, of which a person may not be deprived, no matter how fair the procedure might be when considered by itself; the other was a guarantee of fair procedures by the judicial or administrative bodies.

The original Bill of Rights, including the Fifth Amendment, was held to be a limit only on the federal government. The Fourteenth Amendment, with its due process clause, was expressly intended as a limit on the states. For the first thirty years after ratification of the latter in 1868, the Supreme Court was reluctant to use its powers to enforce the amendment, believing that the original federal equilibrium ought to be maintained. In 1873, Justice Noah H. Swayne stated that liberty in the Fourteenth Amendment "is freedom from all restraints but such as are justly imposed by law." Leading state courts followed this line by stressing the substantive, rather than the procedural, aspects of the state due process clauses. The result was the doctrine of freedom of contract, which read a laissez-faire ideology of private enterprise into the due process clauses of the Fifth and Fourteenth amendments as interpreted by the Supreme Court from 1897 to 1937. In 1925 the Court held that "liberty" in the Fourteenth Amendment puts the same restraints on the state that the First Amendment does on the federal government.

Under the impact of New Deal legislation and its underlying liberal philosophy, the Supreme Court in 1937 said that it would no longer substitute its own social and economic beliefs for the judgment of the legislatures. This meant the end of substantive due process with respect to economic and social legislation affecting property rights and relations.

But substantive due process did not end; it only shifted its locus from property to life and liberty. A parallel development has taken place with respect to procedural due process. While substantive due process with respect to property and freedom of contract was flourishing, the Supreme Court was reluctant to apply the due process clause to correct injustices in state criminal trials; but beginning in the early 1930's the Court began to apply the clause to set aside state criminal convictions and, moving on a case-by-case basis, the Court applied to state criminal procedures most of the procedural requirements spelled out in the Bill of Rights as requirements for federal cases.

DUGOUT. A temporary home of the Plains country, built in the side of a ravine or hill. Three sides were made of earth. The front, made of logs or sod, had a door and a window. The roof, sloping back onto the hill, was a framework of poles, covered with brush, slough hay, and sod. (*See also* Sod House.)

DUG SPRINGS, BATTLE AT (Aug. 2, 1861). Gen. Nathaniel Lyon, operating near Wilson Creek, Mo., defeated a Confederate force of the Missouri State Guard under Gen. James S. Rains.

DUKE OF YORK'S LAWS (1665). A code of laws drawn up by Gov. Matthias Nicolls to bring a more uniform system of government to the towns of Long Island, N.Y. The laws were drawn largely from the existing codes of Massachusetts and New Haven. A civil and criminal code was set up; elaborate provisions made for local governments; a general provincial organization of the courts and militia provided; Indian affairs, ecclesiastical establishments, social and domestic relations regulated; standards of weights and measures provided; and legal forms and methods of keeping records fixed. The code was gradually extended to include the whole province.

DULL KNIFE CAMPAIGN (1878–79). Northern Cheyenne held on a reservation at Darlington, in Indian Territory, escaped Sept. 9, 1878, and started for their home in Montana, led by Dull Knife and Little Wolf. They crossed the Kansas border, killing cowmen and hunters. The band contained 89 warriors and 246 women and children. Although troops were sent to head them off, the Cheyenne eluded or defeated them.

In October the Cheyenne crossed the South Platte River, and the camps separated. Dull Knife's people were captured on Oct. 23 and taken to Fort Robinson, Nebr. The commandant received orders on Jan. 5, 1879, to transport the Indians back to Oklahoma, but they refused to go. When, five days later, the chiefs Wild Hog and Crow were arrested, the rest of the band broke out. It was not until Jan. 22 that the last of the Indians were killed or captured. Dull Knife escaped to the Sioux. Little Wolf's band was induced to surrender on Mar. 25 but was permitted to remain in Montana.

DULUTH (Minn.). Third largest city in Minnesota, with a population of 92,811 in 1980. It is the center of a metropolitan area that includes Superior, Wis., and numbers 265,430. Duluth is located at the western end of Lake Superior, where the St. Louis River empties into the lake, the farthest point inland that ships can reach through the St. Lawrence Seaway and the Great Lakes. Although this access is only good for part of the year (the Great Lakes are blocked by ice in winter), it has increased the shipping business in Duluth.

The city is named after a French explorer who visited the area in 1679, Daniel Greysolon, Sieur Duluth. His interest, fur-trading, remained important in the area until the late 1840's. Duluth was incorporated in 1857. The city's great boom came with railroads. Jay Cooke selected Duluth as the terminal for his railroad from St. Paul to the shores of Lake Superior. (1870).

The discovery of iron ore in the Mesabi Range turned Duluth into a major port on the Great Lakes. Iron ore from the Mesabi was brought to Duluth for shipment from the 1890's on. Grain elevators were built during the early 20th century to store wheat for later shipment over the Great Lakes. The opening of the St. Lawrence Seaway led to additional elevators, and Duluth became an important wheat port.

DULUTH'S EXPLORATIONS. Louis de Buade, Count Frontenac, governor of New France, was eager to find, if possible, a route to the western sea. In 1678 he gave secret instructions to Daniel Greysolon, Sieur Duluth (Dulhut), to explore westward from Lake Superior. Duluth made friends with the Chippewa near Sault Ste. Marie and in 1679 moved across to the western end of the lake, where he had a rendezvous with the Sioux near the site of present Duluth. He accompanied the Sioux through the Savanna portage to Lake Mille Lac near the source of the Mississippi.

Returning to Lake Superior, he met the Assiniboine Indians on the Kaministikwia portage and explored part of the northern shore. In 1680 he determined to open a new route to the Mississippi, via the Brulé–St. Croix portage. He pushed westward from the Sioux country and crossed Minnesota to the land of the Teton Sioux on Big Stone Lake. Thereafter his efforts were utilized in the Iroquois wars and in safeguarding the French in the West. In 1683 he built a post on the St. Croix portage, the first interior fort in Wisconsin. In 1688, Duluth again visited the Sioux region, approaching via the Green Bay–Fox-Wisconsin route to the Mississippi.

DUMBARTON OAKS CONFERENCE (Aug. 21–Oct. 7, 1944). Held at an estate in Georgetown, Washington, D.C., to prepare a charter for a "general international organization," as stipulated in the Declaration of Four Nations at Moscow in November 1943. The meetings were conducted in two phases: until Sept. 28 with representatives of the United States, Great Britain, and the Soviet Union; from Sept. 29 to Oct. 7 the Republic of China replaced the Soviet Union. Preliminary negotiations had established a Security Council and a General Assembly. Discussion encompassed areas of jurisdiction, economic and social as well as security matters; membership in the bodies; voting procedure; veto privileges; and provision for economic and military sanctions. Among the unresolved issues were the Soviet demand for sixteen seats in the General Assembly, great-power veto in the Security Council, and arrangements for a full United Nations conference to agree on the final charter. Proposals were published by the four governments on Oct. 9, 1944.

DUMMER, FORT. The first permanent English settlement in what is now Vermont, erected in 1724, on the present site of Brattleboro, by the colony of Massachusetts, to protect its northern frontier. The blockhouse was also used as a trading post. Numerous scouting parties operated out of the fort. On Oct. 11, 1724, it was subjected to Indian attack.

DUMMER'S WAR (1724–25). French governors of Canada, in an effort to obstruct English border settlements, provoked a boundary dispute between the Abnaki Indians and Maine and Vermont settlers. On Aug. 23, 1724, and May 19, 1725, the whites defeated superior Indian forces and killed the Jesuit missionary Sebastian Rasle. This war was named for William Dummer, acting governor of Massachusetts, who then held jurisdiction over Maine and Vermont.

DUMPLIN CREEK, TREATY OF (June 10, 1785). Entered into on Dumplin Creek of the French Broad River by John Sevier, governor of the state of Franklin (eastern Tennessee) and chiefs of the Overhill Cherokee. It had for its purpose procuring the consent of the Indians to settlement of the region between French Broad River and the ridge dividing the Little Tennessee and Little rivers.

DUNBAR'S EXPEDITION (1804–05). President Thomas Jefferson asked William Dunbar, a Mississippi scientist, to explore the Red River of the South. Dr. George Hunter, a Philadelphia chemist, was appointed to aid him. They headed an expedition of seventeen that left Natchez, Miss., in October 1804. They entered the Red from the Mississippi but higher up turned into its confluent, the Ouachita (Washita). After penetrating into Arkansas as far as Hot Springs, they returned to Natchez in January 1805.

DUNBAR'S LINE. Sometimes applied to the thirty-first parallel between the Mississippi and Chattahoochee rivers, recognized by the Pinckney Treaty of 1795 as the international boundary between the United States and Spanish West Florida. It was surveyed by Andrew Ellicott for the United States and William Dunbar for Spain in 1798.

DUNKARDS. *See* **Brethren.**

DUNMORE'S WAR (1774). Early in 1774, Col. John Connolly, agent of John Murray, Earl of Dunmore, royal governor of Virginia, took possession of Fort Pitt, renamed it Fort Dunmore, and attempted retaliation for Indian outrages. The Shawnee were eager for war. The governor called out the militia of southwest Virginia, which, under Gen. Andrew Lewis, prepared for an expedition to the Shawnee towns beyond the Ohio.

Early in August some Virginia militia under Maj. Angus McDonald raided the Wapatomica towns on the Muskingum River. Dunmore advanced to Fort Dunmore, where he opened a land office; in September he called on the neighboring militia to join in an expedition against the hostiles. Before he could join Lewis, the Shawnee warriors led by Cornstalk attacked Lewis's division at the mouth of the Great Kanawha. At Point Pleasant the whites won a decisive victory. The Indians fled back to their Ohio towns, and the chiefs sought Dunmore's camp and offered peace. Dunmore marched to the Pickaway Plains, where he established Camp Charlotte and made a treaty, which was sealed by the delivery of hostages. The militias returned to Virginia.

DUQUESNE, FORT. In 1753 the Marquis Duquesne de Menneville, governor of New France, moved to occupy the Ohio Valley. Robert Dinwiddie, British lieutenant-governor, sent George Washington to warn the French. The French refused to desist. In February 1754, 800 Frenchmen left Montreal, and on Apr. 17 took possession of the fort being built by the Ohio Company at the forks of the Ohio. The French destroyed this and constructed Fort Duquesne.

Troops left Fort Duquesne to defeat Washington at Great Meadows in 1754 and to rout Gen. Edward Braddock's expedition in 1755. The French then held undisputed possession of the Ohio Valley for three years, administering their military occupation from Fort Duquesne and stimulating Indian raids. Finally, on Nov. 24, 1758, when Gen. John Forbes's expedition neared the forks of the Ohio, the French destroyed Fort Duquesne and retreated.

DUST BOWL. The area within the Great Plains devastated by the climatic storms that spread dust across the nation during the drought of the 1930's. The dust clouds were the product of a dry spell lasting several years; the vegetative cover became so depleted that the fields were directly exposed to wind action. The bowl was centered in the region of New Mexico, Texas, Oklahoma, Kansas, and Colorado.

DUTCH BANKERS' LOANS. The financial independence of the United States was assured when John Adams, minister to the Hague, secured in June 1782 the flotation of a $2 million loan through certain Amsterdam banking houses. Although the full loan was not immediately subscribed to, necessitating a more attractive issue in 1784, it was the most important financial resource possessed by Robert Morris as superintendent of finance from 1781 to 1783.

DUTCH FORK OF SOUTH CAROLINA. A district about forty miles long between the Broad and Saluda rivers. Settled compactly by South Germans in the years 1740–60, it kept the German language for a century.

DUTCH GAP CANAL. After Confederate Gen. P. G. T. Beauregard foiled Gen. B. F. Butler's attempt to move on Richmond, Butler fell back to Bermuda Hundred, Va., with his army of 35,000. Some miles above this place, the James River makes an almost complete loop, approaching to within 174 yards of itself to form a neck called Dutch Gap. Butler decided to cut a channel through this neck, hoping to move up the river by boat, saving miles of travel and avoiding powerful Confederate batteries. The canal was begun on Aug. 10, 1864, and completed on Jan. 1, 1865. It was a failure and was never used by the army, but after the war it was enlarged and used by river steamboats.

DUTCH-INDIAN WAR (1643–45). Brought desolation and distress to the struggling colony of New Netherland; caused by the brutal Indian policy of William Kieft, director-general of the colony. In February 1643, Kieft attacked Indians at Pavonia and murdered about eighty in their sleep. The tribes rose in fury. Kieft asked the colonists to elect a board to advise with him, and "the Eight" were chosen. With the director they armed the colonists and company servants and hired as soldiers a number of English settlers. Long Island, Westchester, and Manhattan were laid waste. With the exception of distant Fort Orange and Rensselaerswyck, safety was to be found only in the immediate vicinity of Fort Amsterdam on Manhattan Island. The fort itself offered poor refuge. The colonists faced starvation. Hostile Indians, 1,500 strong, threatened attack. Fortunately, the Indians had no common or sustained plan of attack, and raiding parties from the fort met with some success. Over a year dragged by before a general peace was signed on Aug. 29, 1645.

DUTCH MERCHANTS AT ALBANY. In 1614, agents of the United New Netherland Company erected Fort Nassau on Castle Island and traded in furs for several years. The Dutch West India Company built Fort Orange in 1624 and expected to reap a fortune out of peltries. Their first cargo of furs sold for 28,000 guilders, and the trade continued to be lucrative. In addition, a number of private merchants and "petty traders" located in Fort Orange and its vicinity. The Dutch merchants continued their profitable operations long after the English conquest in 1664. (*See* Albany).

DUTCH WEST INDIA COMPANY. Organized by a group of Dutch merchants and chartered by the States General in 1621. The company's enormous powers included the exclusive right to trade on the west coast of Africa, in the West Indies, on the east and west coasts of America, and in Australia. The company was empowered to make alliances with the natives, build forts, and plant colonies. In 1624 the company planted a settlement at Fort Orange and, in 1625, on Manhattan Island, the colony of New Netherland. Strict obedience was imposed on all colonists. The director and council acted under instruction from the company. Continued despotic control and the company's interest in trade rather than in colonization were detrimental to the colony.

DUTIES, AD VALOREM AND SPECIFIC. Ad valorem duties are assessed as a stated percentage of the value of imported goods; in contrast, specific duties are expressed as a certain sum of money per unit of imported goods, defined by physical characteristics, such as weight or quantity. Ad valorem duties are more equitable in effect, as the tax rate rises proportionately with value; in contrast, specific duties have a regressive effect. Ad valorem duties provide constant protection during an inflationary period. Specific duties are comparatively easy to administer, requiring no valuation of the commodities, and are more predictable in their generation of customs revenues, a characteristic particularly important during the years prior to the Civil War, when customs revenues provided 85 percent of federal revenues. The U.S. tariff structure in the 1970's used ad valorem and specific duties in roughly equal proportion.

DUZINE. Form of government (1728) by which one descendant from each of the twelve original Huguenot patentees of New Paltz, N.Y. (1677), chosen annually at town meeting, exercised legislative, judicial, and executive powers. Although powers were curtailed when New Paltz was incorporated (1785), elections continued until about 1820.

EADS BRIDGE. A steel and iron structure spanning the Mississippi River at St. Louis, Mo., designed and built, 1868–74, by James B. Eads. The first bridge across the Mississippi, it was for years the only one that far south.

EADS GUNBOATS. In 1861 the federal government awarded James B. Eads a contract to build ironclad gunboats to be used to blockade southern ports and attack Confederate forts along the western rivers. Eads built seven gunboats, the first federal fleet of ironclads. Their sloping casemates, plated with 2.5-inch iron and pierced for thirteen guns of various sizes, were mounted on flat-bottom scows and propelled by paddle wheels in the stern. They performed indispensable service against the Confederacy.

EADS JETTIES. A system of jetties designed to maintain the depth of the Mississippi River at its mouth. Sediment carried down by the Mississippi prevented oceangoing vessels from entering the river and constituted a serious threat to the commerce of New Orleans. Congress entered into a contract in 1875 with James B. Eads for deepening the channel of the middle pass to 30 feet. This was accomplished by constructing jetties or bulwarks on both sides of the channel. The work was successfully completed by 1879 at a cost of $5 million.

EAGLE, AMERICAN (the bald eagle, *Haliaeetus leucocephalus*). The eagle, from ancient times a military emblem and symbol of strength, probably first appeared as an American symbol on a Massachusetts copper cent coined in 1776. In 1782 the eagle, the distinctively American bald, or white-headed, eagle was placed on the Great Seal of the United States. It has appeared on the reverse of some U.S. coins since the beginning of coinage. The bald eagle is an endangered species and is protected in every state under the National Emblem Act (1940).

EARTHQUAKES. The historical record of U.S. earthquakes goes back to 1638 in New England and to about 1800 in California. One of the earliest major earthquakes to affect the colonies occurred in the Three Rivers area north of Quebec, along the lower St. Lawrence River, on Feb. 5, 1663.

The western United States exhibits the greatest seismic activity in the country—especially Alaska, California, Nevada, Utah, and Montana—although the upper part of the Mississippi embayment, southwest Kentucky, southern Illinois, and southeastern Missouri are also seismically active. The great San Francisco earthquake of Apr. 18, 1906, was associated with a rupture of the San Andreas fault (*see* San Francisco Earthquake). In New Madrid, Mo., large earthquakes occurred in 1811–12. An earthquake near Charleston, S.C., on Aug. 31, 1886, did considerable damage and killed about sixty people.

Two measures of the size of an earthquake are used. First, earthquake intensity is measured by damage to the works of man and to the ground surface and by human reaction. Intensity assessments depend on the Modified Mercalli Scale of intensity ranges of from I to XII (total damage). Second, earthquake magnitude is measured from the maximum wave amplitude recorded on a seismograph. (*See also* Disasters.)

EASTERN ARCHAIC CULTURE. An adjustment of a multifocused hunting and gathering lifeway to the forests and river valleys of prehistoric eastern North America. In contrast to the earlier game-focused subsistence patterns of the Lithic, the Archaic was characterized by the hunting of a variety of animals, extensive utilization of wild plants, fishing, and shellfish gathering. The transition is particularly well documented in midsouthern states south of the major glacial ice lobes (Kentucky, Georgia, Tennessee, Alabama, southern Illinois, and southern Missouri) between about 7000 and 5000 B.C. By 3000 B.C., technologically versatile tool kits had developed. The adjustment to forested conditions is evident in axes, adzes, wedges, gouges, and other large woodworking tools. Large notched and stemmed projectile points became common, and bone, horn, ivory, and shell artifacts became abundant. Ground slate projectile points and knives, plummets, pipes, stone bowls, weights for throwing sticks, and stone beads are also found in some areas. Copper was pounded into knives, projectile points, spuds, and a variety of additional utilitarian tools in the Old Copper culture of Wisconsin and neighboring states. Ornaments and ceremonial objects also became common.

Earthworks, burial mounds, formalized burials, pottery, sedentism, and cultigens first appear in eastern North America among Archaic cultures. The importance of plant foods is reflected in specialized grinding equipment, such as mortars and pestles. Pottery has been dated as early as 2500 B.C. at Stallings Island, Ga., and a squash seed has been tentatively identified from a Poverty Point, La., site dating to 1000 B.C. Semisedentary and even sedentary existence became possible along the major rivers, giving rise to the Riverine Archaic culture. Poverty Point, with its huge octagonal earth ridges, is one of the most impressive archaeological sites in North America. The Archaic was eventually replaced throughout the warmer and moister areas of the East by the Formulative culture, a lifeway sustained primarily by domesticated plant foods, about A.D. 500.

EASTERN ORTHODOXY. The first American Eastern Orthodox churches were the 19th-century Russian missions in Alaska. Main growth of the Orthodox churches in the United States resulted from the heavy immigration from eastern Europe at the end of the 19th and beginning of the 20th centuries. The American history of these churches has been a story of division and controversy, as Old World issues have been perpetuated. Since the mid-20th century, there have been signs that this period of controversy is drawing to a close: The patriarch of Moscow healed some of the schisms among the American Russian Orthodox in 1970 and declared the American church to be autocephalous; the various Greek churches also seemed to be moving toward a greater degree of unity, largely the result of the work of a series of excellent archbishops of North America, Michael, Iakovos, and Athenagoras, who have centralized the church's operations. Many of the Eastern Orthodox churches in the United States have been active in the ecumenical movement and have joined both the National Council of Churches and the World Council of Churches. In the late 1970's there were twenty-one Orthodox churches, with a combined membership of more than 4 million. The two largest churches were the Greek Orthodox Archdiocese of North and South America (1.95 million members) and the Orthodox Church in America (1 million members).

EASTERN SOLOMONS, BATTLE OF THE (Aug. 24, 1942). To reinforce the embattled island of Guadalcanal, in the Solomon Islands, the Japanese dispatched a convoy carrying 1,500 troops from Truk, in the Carolines, in August 1942. But long-range American aerial reconnaissance brought word of the approaching enemy armada. Rear Adm. Frank J. Fletcher's task force moved into position east of the southern Solomons to intercept the Japanese advance. Fletcher's efforts to attack on Aug. 23 were unsuccessful; that night, misled by erroneous intelligence reports that the Japanese had retired, he detached one of his carrier groups to refuel, cutting his strength by nearly a third. This left him at a slight disadvantage in the battle that took place on Aug. 24.

Night brought an end to the battle, and both sides retired. At a cost to Fletcher of only seventeen planes and damage to the carrier *Enterprise,* he had sunk a Japanese carrier, crippled the seaplane tender *Chitose,* and taken a heavy toll of Japanese planes and pilots. The 1,500 Japanese reinforcements did not get through to Guadalcanal; U.S. Marine dive-bombers from that island sank their transport the next day.

EAST FLORIDA. *See* Florida.

EAST INDIA COMPANY, ENGLISH (1600–1874). One of the longest-lived and richest trading companies. Not until the era of the American Revolution did the company figure in American affairs, and then briefly. At that time, to strengthen its foothold at Canton, the company purchased larger amounts of tea. After Britain's imposition of the tea tax in 1767, American boycotts greatly reduced their consumption of tea. With its warehouses overflowing, the company surrendered part of its political power for the right to export tea directly to America. This right, acquired in 1773 under Frederick, Lord North's Regulating Act, had unhappy results. Because it allowed the East India Company to ship tea to America duty free while it required Americans to pay a tax on the tea, the act contributed to the colonial feeling of repression by England and precipitated many anti-British activities leading up to the Revolution. After the Revolution, the company had little or no contact with America.

EAST INDIES TRADE. East Indian commerce included "all countries lying beyond the Cape of Good Hope or the Straits of Magellan." Characteristic were voyages from Salem, Mass., beginning in 1784, with provisions to the Cape of Good Hope and Mauritius; from there, perhaps, with bills, sometimes freight, to Bombay, for cotton to be sold in Canton for teas; perhaps from Mauritius to Madras, or Calcutta, thence home, with cottons; or to Batavia (present-day Netherlands), with iron, wine, and ginseng, thence to Canton, perhaps with freight. A Salem vessel opened a trade in pepper from Sumatra in 1793, and another, in 1799, the coffee trade with Mocha, a Yemen seaport. The end of the East India Company's monopoly in 1813 and the end of the Napoleonic wars in 1814 increased competition until it was sometimes cheaper to buy Indian goods in London. The prohibitive tariff of 1816 on cheap cotton cloths turned East India merchants to saltpeter, indigo, sugar, spices, drugs, cotton, hides, and gunnies. By 1840, American merchants were importing Calcutta goods from Manchester, England, and shipping cloth from Lowell, Mass., to India.

EAST JERSEY. A separate province formed in 1676 by the Quintipartite Deed between the Quakers Edward Billing and John Fenwick, on one side, and Sir George Carteret, on the other. This deed divided New Jersey from "the most southwardly point of the east side of Little Egg Harbor" to the Delaware River at the forty-first parallel. The territory east of this line, East Jersey, went to Carteret. In 1682 his heirs sold their portion to William Penn and eleven associates, each of whom sold one-half of his share to a new associate, making a board of twenty-four proprietors. Save for two short periods, this board governed the province until the close of the proprietary period. The population included Puritans, Scottish Presbyterians, and some Quakers. To promote trade, Perth Amboy was founded and became the capital in 1686. On Apr. 15, 1702, the proprietors surrendered their government to the crown but retained all rights to the soil.

EASTLAND. An excursion steamer that overturned in the Chicago River, July 24, 1915, at the moment of departure for a day's outing on Lake Michigan. Of some 2,000 passengers, more than 800 lost their lives.

EASTON, TREATY OF (Oct. 26, 1758). Signed at the fourth (Oct. 8–26, 1758) of a series of conferences held by Pennsylvania in 1756–58 to divert the Delaware Indians of the upper Delaware and Susquehanna river valleys from aiding the French. Besides the Delaware, representatives of the Iroquois were present. Peace was made possible when the Pennsylvanians, led by Gov. William Denny, persuaded the Iroquois to abrogate the treaty made at the Albany Congress of 1754, by which they had ceded most of the lands of the western Susquehanna Valley to the English. The Iroquois also promised the Delaware the right to live and hunt in security in these western Susquehanna lands, to which most Delaware subsequently migrated.

EAST TEXAS MISSIONS. Spanish border institutions designed to check French aggression and Christianize the Indians. Two were founded on the Neches River in 1690 but abandoned in 1693. Renewed French encroachments led to the founding of six missions in 1716, five near Nacogdoches, Tex., and one in present Louisiana. In 1756 a mission was established on the lower Trinity River. Unsuccessful, three of them were moved to San Antonio, Tex., in 1730, and shortly after the transfer of Louisiana to Spain (1762), the others were suppressed.

EAST TEXAS OILFIELD. Located in east Texas about 140 miles from the Gulf coast, where oil would not be expected from a scientific standpoint. The discovery was made Sept. 8, 1930, by C. M. ("Dad") Joiner. By Aug. 16, 1931, there were 1,815 wells with a production of 295,000 barrels. By late 1935 there were 19,507 wells producing 820 million barrels, valued at $648 million. The field in 1935 covered about 137,000 acres. By 1975, 13,207 wells produced 72 million barrels annually. Producing acreage was 63,000. The field continues to operate under the Texas Railroad Commission.

EATON AFFAIR. In 1816, Margaret ("Peggy") O'Neale, daughter of a Washington, D.C., innkeeper, at age sixteen married John B. Timberlake, a purser in the U.S. Navy. In 1828, her husband died. For a decade, she and her husband had been on friendly terms with Sen. John H. Eaton of

Tennessee, who had often stayed at the O'Neale establishment. On Jan. 1, 1829, with the approval of President-elect Andrew Jackson, Eaton married her. Their relations continued to be a subject for scandalmongers.

For over two years, Washington society was disturbed by an undercover social war revolving about Mrs. Eaton. After Eaton was appointed secretary of war, the social status of his wife became a political issue. Other cabinet members attempted to ostracize her. Martin Van Buren was the only cabinet member to support the Eatons.

The Eaton affair contributed to the break between Jackson and John C. Calhoun in 1830, followed the next spring by a cabinet reorganization, which brought the Eaton affair into the open: Van Buren and Eaton resigned, and three pro-Calhoun cabinet members were forced to do the same.

ECHO. A slave ship captured with 300 native Africans on board and brought to Charleston, S.C., in 1858. The Africans were returned to Africa, to the newly formed republic of Liberia; the *Echo* was condemned as a slaver and sold. The captain and crew were tried under the federal act condemning the African slave trade as piracy. Although a conclusive case was established, the jury brought in an acquittal.

ECOLOGY. The science of ecology came to the United States during the 1890's as a result of European studies in limnology, oceanography, plant ecology, and animal ecology. The main activity of naturalists during the 18th and 19th centuries was describing native species and their geographical distributions, but in doing so, they often made protoecological observations, noting how distributions of species were correlated with topography, soil, climate, and associated species. The practical aspects of man's relation to nature stimulated considerable interest during the 19th century in agricultural insect pests, and economic entomology was strengthened by the discovery that certain species are important vectors of diseases. A large and useful entomological literature was published. Alpheus S. Packard illustrated the ecological significance of Darwin's theory of evolution in his monograph on the cave fauna of North America (1888).

Limnology was the first ecological science to be formally organized, largely the achievement of the Swiss scientist François Alphonse Forel. During most of his career he investigated the physical attributes of lake waters as influences on organisms in lakes. In America, the study of limnology arose in the 1890's in Illinois, Wisconsin, Michigan, Indiana, and Ohio, accompanied in each case by the establishment of a biological research station. The most notable scientists in this field were Stephen A. Forbes, Edward A. Birge, C. Dwight Marsh, Chancey Juday, Jacob E. Reighard, Carl H. Eigenmann, and David S. Kellicot.

Marine research stations have an earlier origin in America and have provided an important impetus for ecology. Three of them have been established at the earliest site, Woods Hole, Mass.: the Bureau of Commercial Fisheries Laboratory (1885), the Marine Biology Laboratory (1888), and the Woods Hole Oceanographic Institute (1930).

Plant ecology began in America primarily in response to the work of Europeans. Professors of botany Charles E. Bessey and John M. Coulter, at the University of Nebraska and the University of Chicago, respectively, decided to train graduate students in this new branch. Bessey's most outstanding student was Frederic E. Clements; Coulter's was Henry C. Cowles. Clements's first study was a phytogeographical survey of Nebraska, with Roscoe Pound (1897); most of his subsequent publications were devoted to climatic influence upon plant succession. Cowles began with a study of dune plant communities on Lake Michigan (1899–1901).

Animal ecology in the United States has a broader origin than either limnology or plant ecology. Its early history was partly built upon those studies as well as upon pure and applied zoology. One of the first prominent animal ecologists in America was Victor E. Shelford; trained at the University of Chicago, he brought into animal ecology both the physiological and descriptive emphases of Cowles. The diversity of early studies in animal ecology is indicated by the diversity of chapters in the 1913 bibliographical guide to the subject by Charles C. Adams.

ECONOCHACA, BATTLE OF. *See* **Creek War.**

ECONOMIC ADVISERS, COUNCIL OF. The council consists of three professional economists appointed by the president with the approval of the Senate. It is part of the Executive Office of the President and is responsible for providing the president with expert opinion on economic matters and help in preparing his annual economic report.

ECONOMIC ROYALISTS. President Franklin D. Roosevelt, in his speech of acceptance of the Democratic nomination for a second term, delivered at Philadelphia, June 27, 1936, spoke of "economic royalists," persons prominent in finance and industry who were in general opposed to his tendency to centralize the government and to put it into competition with private enterprise.

ECORSE RIVER COUNCIL (Apr. 27, 1763). An Indian council convened by Chief Pontiac at the mouth of the Ecorse, a few miles west of Detroit. A project was formed for a union of the tribes to drive the English from the country. (*See* Pontiac's War.)

EDENTON (N.C.). A town on Albemarle Sound laid out in 1712. It was known as "the town on Queen Anne's Creek" until 1722, when it was enlarged and incorporated as Edenton (named for Charles Eden, former governor). The town, capital of the colony from 1722 until about 1743, became a center of shipbuilding and trade. On Oct. 25, 1774, fifty-one women gathered and signed an agreement not to drink tea or wear clothes made in England until the tax on tea was repealed. Their action at this "Edenton Tea Party" is the earliest recorded instance of political activity by American women. In 1980 the town had 5,357 people.

EDGE HILL, BATTLE OF (Dec. 5–7, 1777). A series of small skirmishes in which Gen. William Howe tested the strength of Gen. George Washington's fortified camp near Whitemarsh, three miles above the present Philadelphia city limits. The British took Edge Hill, but Howe decided that Washington could not be displaced, and on Dec. 8 withdrew to Philadelphia.

EDUCATION. The earliest educational efforts took place at home. Orphans and children whose parents could not afford to pay for schooling were enabled, through apprenticeship laws, to obtain vocational training and instruction in reading and religion. A law passed by the General Court of Massachusetts in 1642 required town authorities to make certain that children were educated and imposed fines for neglect. Success was not achieved, and the court passed in 1647 the Old Deluder Satan Act, which required that each township of fifty families engage a teacher to instruct children in reading and writing and that each township of a hundred families establish a "grammar schoole." Similar laws were enacted in all the New England colonies except Rhode Island, where education was considered a private matter. Although there were private schools, the most important educational work was accomplished in the town schools. The schools were publicly supported and publicly controlled, but they were sectarian, since for much of the colonial period there was cooperation between church and government. In the 18th century the "moving school" arose, a teacher being located for a few months at a time in each of the villages surrounding a town. Probably the most widely circulated elementary textbook in the colonial era was *The New England Primer* (Boston, 1690).

Secondary education in New England began with the Boston Latin School in 1635. These schools featured teaching of the Latin and Greek language and literature. During the mid-18th century, the academy, which offered nonclassical and practical subjects, became increasingly attended. Higher education was inaugurated in 1636, when the Massachusetts General Court decided to allot £400 "towards a schoole or colledge," later named Harvard College. Harvard was chartered in 1650. Yale opened in 1701, Brown in 1764, and Dartmouth in 1769.

Education in the middle colonies varied from area to area. The Dutch in New Netherland set up public elementary schools. Under the English in the 18th century, the poor were taught in schools of the Society for the Propagation of the Gospel in Foreign Parts, an Anglican association founded in 1701. Grammar schools were founded in New York, including one that prepared students for King's College (now Columbia University), chartered in 1754 under Anglican auspices.

In New York, Pennsylvania, New Jersey, Rhode Island, Maryland, and Delaware, various religious sects established elementary schools of their own. In secondary education Pennsylvania led the middle colonies with the founding in 1689 of the Friends' Public School of Philadelphia (now the William Penn Charter School); the establishment of secondary schools to train ministers; and the founding of the Academy in Philadelphia, proposed by Benjamin Franklin in 1743 and opened in 1751. By an act of the Maryland General Assembly, King William's Secondary School, a free public school, was founded at Annapolis in 1696. In addition to King's College, higher education in the middle colonies comprised the College of New Jersey (Princeton University), founded in 1746; the College of Philadelphia (University of Pennsylvania), the new name for Franklin's Academy by the rechartering of 1755; and Queen's College (Rutgers University), chartered in 1766.

The southern colonial school policy may be characterized as laissez-faire and pauper education. The geographical, social, and economic conditions in the South resulted in a system of colonial laws for apprentice training of poor and orphaned children; charity schools for the poor; private schools and tutorial training for the children of wealthy parents; and so-called Old Field Schools, elementary schools established on abandoned wasteland. A particularly significant type of elementary school was the school with an endowment from a will or bequest. The Syms-Eaton School in Virginia originated with the will of Benjamin Syms in 1634 and was enlarged with funds from Thomas Eaton's will of 1659; probably the first endowed lower-educational institution in the colonies. There were instances of educational provisions for black children, mainly because plantation owners were interested in teaching them Christianity. The only college in the South during the colonial period was the College of William and Mary in Williamsburg, Va., which, although chartered in 1693, was only a grammar school in reality and did not confer degrees until 1700.

The Revolution led to a greater awareness that new educational forms and policies were necessary. Proposals were made for a national school system based on democratic principles, and a national university was urged. Most early state constitutions included some provisions for education. Some states—such as Georgia in 1785, North Carolina in 1789, Vermont in 1791, and Tennessee in 1794—granted charters for state universities.

The U.S. Constitution makes no reference to education, and therefore, under the provisions of the Tenth Amendment to the Constitution, educational control is reserved to the several states. However, by virtue of the principle of "general welfare" in the Preamble and the doctrine of implied powers, the federal government has spent billions of dollars on educational projects. In the Land Ordinance of 1785, Congress reserved a lot, known as Section Sixteen, in every township in the Western Territory "for the maintenance of public schools." By means of the land-grant policy the federal government furnished the basic aid necessary for the promotion of a public school system, especially in the Middle West and the Far West.

Until the early 19th century, New England was the only region that could lay claim to anything resembling a public school system. A Massachusetts law of 1789 legally established the district school system and in 1827 the district school system was made compulsory. New York State was active in setting up a statewide school system during this period. In 1784 it organized, and in 1787 reorganized, the University of the State of New York, a centralized school system. In 1812 the state set up a system of administration, with Gideon Hawley as the first state superintendent of schools. Considerable effort was expended all over the young nation to create educational systems. Voluntary groups came into being, such as the Free (later the Public) School Society of New York City, which offered free educational opportunities from 1805 until its merger with the city's board of education in 1852. Funds for education were raised by lotteries, license fees, direct state appropriations, fines, sales of public lands, rate bills (tuition fees) in accordance with the number of children of the family attending school, and local taxes.

Important new textbooks were written by Noah Webster, Jedediah Morse, and Samuel G. Goodrich (Peter Parley). Later, textbooks embodied the pedagogical principles of Johann Heinrich Pestalozzi; among the writers were Warren Colburn, William C. Woodbridge, and Lowell Mason. Moral training was promoted, often in a religious context—so much so that Catholics, Jews, and various Protestant minorities found themselves forced to open their own schools to escape sectarian instruction in the public schools.

In secondary education the Latin grammar school gave ground to the English grammar school, to the academy, and finally to the high school. The academy was characterized by a curriculum of many subjects, including astronomy, geology, and other theoretical and practical sciences; foreign languages; philosophy, art, and music; rhetoric and oratory; and English language and literature. The high school was first introduced into Boston in 1821 as the English classical school, renamed the English high school in 1824.

The American college, recovering from the Revolution, inaugurated a broader curriculum in response to social demands. The natural and physical sciences, modern foreign languages, law, and the social sciences made their appearance as well as studies for the profession of medicine. Gradually the religious influence was replaced by the secular. Professional schools were opened for the training of engineers, physicians, clergymen, and lawyers. The Dartmouth College decision handed down by the U.S. Supreme Court in 1819 prevented state control of a chartered private college. The ultimate impact of this was that private and denominational schools were founded in large numbers and state legislatures established their own colleges and universities.

One of the major arguments in higher education was allowing students to choose some of their courses. The elective system was favored in principle in the Amherst College faculty report of 1826, but it was repudiated by the Yale College faculty report of 1828.

Teacher training received an impetus before 1830 through the publication of several treatises on pedagogy, such as Joseph Neef's "Sketch of a Plan and Method of Education" (1808) and Samuel Read Hall's "Lectures on School-Keeping" (1829); the opening of private teachers' seminaries by Hall in 1823 and by James Gordon Carter in 1826; and the publication of teachers' journals.

Through the efforts of James Carter and Horace Mann, Massachusetts set up a state board of education in 1837. In 1852, Massachusetts pioneered in enacting legislation to make school attendance compulsory. The kindergarten was first established in America in 1856 by Mrs. Carl Schurz, as a German-speaking school in Watertown, Wis. A private English-language kindergarten was opened in 1860 by Elizabeth Palmer Peabody in Boston, and the first public school kindergarten was set up in 1873 by Susan Blow in St. Louis, Mo., under the philosopher William Torrey Harris.

The Pestalozzian ideas were revived by Supt. Edward A. Sheldon of the Oswego, N.Y., schools in 1859. The theory and the practice of Johann Friedrich Herbart were introduced, especially in connection with the teaching of social studies and character. Also contributing to character training were the widely used readers of William Holmes McGuffey. New ideas stressing a curriculum and a methodology based on child growth, development, and interest were first put into operation by Francis Wayland Parker in Quincy, Mass. The elementary school founded by John Dewey at the University of Chicago (1896–1904) experimented with these ideas and served as a model for progressive school education. The testing movement began in the 1890's. The entire curriculum of the elementary school came under scrutiny in the *Report of the Committee of Fifteen on Elementary Education,* prepared in 1895 for the National Education Association (NEA).

The high school grew in prestige throughout the 19th century, taking the place of the academy as the favored form of secondary education. It received legal recognition in 1874, insofar as support by public taxes was concerned, by the Kalamazoo Case decision in the Michigan Supreme Court. Thereafter, it became the typically American school of the people—free, public, universal, comprehensive in curriculum, and both academic and vocational.

Higher education in the 19th century showed several new tendencies: emergence of new subjects, such as agriculture, sociology, anthropology, and education; secularization of colleges and universities, in part under the influence of Darwinian ideas; a steady increase in private and public institutions of higher learning; and greater emphasis given to creative scholarship. The subject of science received considerable emphasis during the century. The passing of the first Morrill Act by Congress in 1862 made land grants to the states for the establishment of colleges in which "agriculture and the mechanic arts" would be taught. This law and the Morrill Act of 1890 brought an expansion of state universities in the Middle West and Far West.

Women's higher education was provided in parts of the country before the Civil War on a private, denominational basis. The earliest graduates were given the degree of Domina Scientiarum. High academic standards were characteristic of Elmira Female College (1855) and Vassar Female College (1865), both in New York State. Coeducation began with Oberlin Collegiate Institute (1833) and Antioch College (1853), both in Ohio, and at the state universities of Utah (1850), Iowa (1855), and Washington (1861). Other important developments in the century were the granting of the earned Ph.D. degree in 1861 by Yale, the introduction of the elective system at Harvard by President Charles Eliot in 1869, and the founding of the Johns Hopkins University in 1876 as the first graduate school in the United States.

Teacher education was characterized by the raising of standards of training in the normal schools and the admission of educational psychology, history of education, and other courses in education into the university curriculum.

Professional education flourished with the opening of the Massachusetts Institute of Technology (1861), the establishment of the American Medical Association (1847) and the Association of American Medical Colleges (1890), and the founding of the Association of American Law Schools (1900).

Religious education was given in parochial schools by Episcopalians, Presbyterians, Lutherans, Catholics, and Jews. The Roman Catholic Bishops' Third Plenary Council in Baltimore (1884) decreed that all Catholic parents must send their children to the parochial schools to be erected in every parish.

For Afro-Americans opportunities for education were limited, although some colleges were opened for them before the Civil War. After the Civil War, from the establishment of the Freedmen's Bureau in 1865, schooling of all kinds—most of it racially segregated—was made available to blacks. The legal precedent for segregated schools, "separate but equal" education, was set by the decision of the U.S. Supreme Court in 1896 in the case of *Plessy* v. *Ferguson.*

The elementary school grew at a rapid pace after 1900. The nursery school was introduced about 1920, and preschool education was later supported by the federal government, especially during the depression years and World War II. Curriculum changes in the 1950's involved an emphasis on science and the inclusion of foreign languages. Tests of intelligence and achievement and diagnosis and prognosis came to be frequently used. The doctrines and practices of John Dewey, Edward Lee Thorndike, and William H. Kilpatrick exerted a deep influence. The parent-teacher association became an outstanding feature. The impact of the federal government on elementary education was, of necessity, indirect—for example, through the National School Lunch Act of 1946 and other temporary, supportive measures; the White House Conferences on Children and Youth in 1940, 1950, 1960, and 1970–71; and the White House Conferences on Education in 1955 and 1965. The Supreme Court handed down a number of influential decisions, declaring invalid a Nebraska law against teaching foreign languages in private elementary schools (1923); upholding the constitutionality of religious and other private schools (1925); allowing states to furnish bus transportation for parochial schools (1947); permitting released time for religious instruction, but only outside the public school (1948, 1952); requiring public schools to discontinue the segregation of black pupils (1954, 1955); ordering immediate desegregation of public schools (1969); supporting the constitutionality of pupil busing to bring about desegregation (1962); upholding the ban on public school prayers (1962) and Bible reading in public schools (1963); and upholding the supplying of free secular textbooks to parochial school students (1968) and the prohibiting of public financial aid to parochial school teachers (1971).

The junior high school first appeared in Berkeley, Calif., about 1910. In the 1960's, the middle school appeared, a four- or three-year school following grade five or six.

The secondary school curriculum was the subject of many investigations. The report by NEA in 1918 set down the Seven Cardinal Principles of Secondary Education, which have exerted an influence on the curriculum of the American high school: health, vocation, command of fundamental processes, worthy home membership, worthy use of leisure, citizenship, and ethical character. Vocational education was promoted by the Smith-Hughes Act passed by Congress in 1917, the Vocational Education Act of 1963, and the federal campaign for career education beginning in 1970.

In 1900 the Association of American Universities was formed to promote high standards among the institutions of higher education. The public junior college had its start in 1902 at Joliet, Ill. After World War II it began to multiply under the name of community college.

Among the other significant developments in 20th-century higher education was that of federal government activity. The government aided higher education through the GI Bill of Rights for veterans of World War II (1943, 1944), the Korean War (1952), and the Vietnam War (1966); the Fulbright (1946), the Smith-Mundt (1948), and the Fulbright-Hays (1961) acts for the exchange of students, faculty, and research workers with foreign countries; the National Defense Education Act of 1958; the Higher Education Act of 1965; and the Education Professions Development Act of 1967.

In the field of teacher education, the normal schools of the 19th and the early 20th century became teachers colleges that granted degrees, and after World War II many of them were transformed into state colleges with liberal arts programs added to professional teacher training. During 1958–60, professors of academic subjects and professors of education made a national effort to arrive at a common policy on the education and certification of teachers.

The standards of medical education were raised sharply with the publication in 1910 of a report by Abraham Flexner for the Carnegie Foundation for the Advancement of Teaching. The other professions also concerned themselves with the modification of curriculum and the upgrading of standards.

The education of Afro-Americans, which had been encouraged by the philanthropy of George Peabody (1867) and John F. Slater (1882), was further benefited by funds set up in the names of John D. Rockefeller in 1903, Anna T. Jeanes in 1905, Phelps-Stokes in 1909, and Julius Rosenwald in 1911. Although opportunities increased for Afro-Americans at all levels of public and private education, the South and part of the North continued to practice racial segregation in education. The most fundamental civil rights events in education were the U.S. Supreme Court decisions of 1954 and 1955, which declared segregation in public schools contrary to the doctrine of equality as guaranteed by the Constitution and ordered desegregation to be carried out "with all deliberate speed." Racial integration of the public schools and various actions to equalize the educational opportunities of Afro-Americans were accelerated by the Civil Rights Act of 1964, which provided for the withholding of federal funds from public school districts in which racial segregation was practiced. State and federal court decisions, including those by the U.S. Supreme Court in 1970 and 1971, required speedier desegregation and confirmed the constitutionality of cross-town conveyance of children by buses to achieve integration in public schools. During the 1970's the campaign in behalf of racial equality in education was fully under way on both the *de jure* and *de facto* fronts, in the South and in the North.

EDUCATION, BOARDS OF. Boards of education go back to the founding in 1784 of the University of the State of New York, under centralized control. Another important milestone was the organization in 1837 of the Board of Education in Massachusetts, with Horace Mann as secretary. Since then, state, county, and local government units have appointed, or citizens have elected, committees or boards of citizens representative of the population to conduct public educational institutions and affairs.

State boards of education define the educational policies for administrative and teaching staffs from nursery school to graduate school. Frequently, the state board appoints a state superintendent of public instruction. In many states there are several specialized boards of education. There is a trend toward reduction of the number of boards and increasing centralization of educational control within a single board.

On the local government level, there are some 15,000 school districts in the United States. These are directed by boards or committees of education responsible for such functions as purchase and sale of real property; construction of school buildings; procurement of materials and facilities; appointment of personnel; development of policies and programs in accordance with state law; and, in numerous instances, power to raise taxes for the school budget.

EDUCATION, LAND GRANTS FOR. *See* **Land Grants for Education.**

EDUCATION, UNITED STATES OFFICE OF. Established by Congress on Mar. 2, 1867. Designated as an independent, subcabinet Department of Education under the direction of Henry Barnard as commissioner, this unit functioned "for the purpose of collecting of such statistics and facts as shall show the condition and progress of education in the several States and Territories, and of diffusing such information respecting the organization and management of school systems, and methods of teaching, as shall aid the people of the United States in the establishment and maintenance of efficient school systems, and otherwise promote the cause of education throughout the country." Another provision required the commissioner to present an annual report to Congress and his recommendations for future actions.

Renamed Office of Education in 1869, the division was placed in the Department of the Interior. From 1870 to 1929 it was known as the Bureau of Education. During 1939–53 it was located in the Federal Security Agency, and in 1953, it became a constituent division within the Department of Health, Education, and Welfare.

In addition to the annual reports, the Bureau of Education began to publish, in 1896, bulletins and studies of educational developments in the United States and abroad.

Office of Education activities included administration of federal participation in vocational education, grants and loans for improvement of state and local educational programs, and aid for education of the handicapped. The office grew from 250 persons in 1950 to 2,642 in 1970. The total budget grew from $700 million in 1963 to $4.7 billion in 1972. The significance of the research functions declined with the establishment, in 1972, of the independent National Institute of Education. The Office of Education ceased to exist as a separate entity in 1980 when it was absorbed by the new Department of Education (created in 1979).

EDWARD, FORT. Colonial base built in 1755 by Gen. Phineas Lyman to back up Col. William Johnson in the French and Indian War. It was located at the Great Carrying Place, on the east side of the Hudson River, fourteen miles south of Lake George, and stood at the junction of two Indian trails to Lake Champlain. It was originally called Fort Lyman, but after the Battle of Lake George, Johnson changed its name to Fort Edward in honor of a grandson of King George II. Allowed to fall into disrepair, the fort was abandoned in July 1777 by the Americans in the face of Gen. John Burgoyne's advance. There is now a village, Fort Edward, N.Y., on the site, whose main industry is pulp and paper mills.

EDWARDS, FORT. Frontier post built (1816–17) at the present site of Warsaw, Ill. It supplanted a cantonment built in 1815, which in turn had replaced Fort Johnson, erected by Maj. Zachary Taylor in September 1814 and destroyed the following month. After 1818, a government factory for Indian trade was located there. Except for short periods, Fort Edwards was garrisoned by small detachments of U.S. regulars until its abandonment in July 1824.

EDWARDSEAN THEOLOGY. The evangelical philosophy of Jonathan Edwards, preacher of the Great Awakening in the 1730's. To his contemporaries a conventional though brilliant Calvinist, Edwards appeared to later generations a radical theologian who had endeavored to bring contemporary thought (primarily British) and Christian orthodoxy to terms in his posthumous writings on metaphysics and ethics. His empirical study of varieties of religious experience led to *The Nature of the Religious Affections,* for which the Great Awakening supplied ample case material. He had helped initiate the revival by his solution to the Calvinistic dilemma of divine sovereignty and human initiative. His sermons at that time (1735), directed against the passivism that is the nemesis of Calvinism, found full-fledged expression in his most famous dissertation, *Freedom of the Will.*

EFFECTIVE OCCUPATION. When rivals seriously challenged Spain's monopolistic claims in the New World, Spain sought to justify its title by right of prior discovery. In answer the argument was advanced that the exclusion of others was warranted only where the Spaniards, in Queen Elizabeth's words, had "actually settled and continued to inhabit." The English were joined by the French and Dutch in giving practical application to this principle of effective occupation. When Spain by the Treaty of Madrid in 1670 formally recognized England's rights to the areas it had occupied, the general acceptance of the principle was complete. An important doctrine in modern international law, the tests of effective occupation have been the subject of frequent definition.

EGG HARBOR ENGAGEMENT (Oct. 15, 1778). Gen. Casimir Pulaski, a Polish volunteer in the Continental army, had been sent eastward with his legion from Princeton, N.J., to protect American vessels operating against British shipping at Egg Harbor, N.J. Before daylight, guided by information from a deserter, a British detachment attacked and surprised the American encampment, inflicting heavy loss.

"EGYPT." A colloquial term applied to the southernmost quarter of Illinois. The term probably resulted from the delta-like character of the Cairo region and several Egyptian place-names. There is written record of the use of "Egypt" as early as 1855, but evidence indicates that it was common long before that.

EIGHTEENTH AMENDMENT, also known as the Prohibition Amendment (1919–33). It prohibited the manufacture, sale, transportation, import, or export of intoxicating liquors for beverage purposes and authorized Congress and the several states to enforce this by appropriate legislation.

The Anti-Saloon League launched its campaign for national prohibition in 1913. A joint resolution of Congress failed to get the necessary two-thirds vote in the House in 1914. Three years later both houses voted to submit the proposed amendment to the states. Nebraska, the thirty-sixth state to ratify, acted on Jan. 13, 1919, making the amendment effective. In the meantime, Prohibition had been voted as a war measure for the duration of World War I. On Oct. 27, 1919, the Volstead Act was passed to enforce the amendment.

By 1932 public support of the amendment was definitely waning. The Republican platform demanded return to state option; the Democratic platform favored repeal. A better than two-thirds vote in Congress started a repealing amendment (*see* Twenty-first Amendment) to the states in February 1933, providing for the first time in American history that ratification should be by special convention rather than legislative action. On Dec. 5, 1933, the Eighteenth Amendment was repealed.

EIGHT-HOUR DAY, MOVEMENT FOR. *See* **Wages and Hours of Labor, Regulation of.**

EISENHOWER DOCTRINE. In an address to Congress, Jan. 5, 1957, President Dwight D. Eisenhower declared that U.S. military and economic power would be used to protect the Middle East against Communist aggression. The doctrine was designed to reassure Western allies that the United States regarded the Middle East as vital to its security. At the president's insistence the doctrine took the form of a congressional resolution, which was signed into law on Mar. 9.

ELBE RIVER. The Elbe and a tributary, the Mulde, served as a dividing line between Soviet and Allied forces of the West when World War II in Europe ended. American troops of the Second Armored Division were first to reach the river, on Apr. 11, 1945. Yet, the Allied high command had already decided to forgo a drive on Berlin and to use the Elbe and Mulde as readily discernible terrain features to avoid clashes between converging Western and Soviet troops. Patrols from other American units along the Mulde subsequently pushed to the upper Elbe in hope of being first to contact the Soviets. On Apr. 25 a patrol met the Soviets at Torgau.

EL CANEY, BATTLE OF. *See* **San Juan Hill and El Caney, Battles of.**

EL DORADO OIL FIELD. Oil was first struck at the El Dorado Oil Field, Kans., in 1915. The Trapshooters Well, drilled in 1917, gushed out 24,000 barrels in a single day, overflowed all tank space, and filled hastily built ponds. The field's peak production of 30 million barrels annually was in 1918. A total of 2,005 wells have been drilled at the field, but many have since been abandoned. In 1972, there were 819 wells producing nearly 1.5 million barrels of oil annually.

ELECTION LAWS. Until the late 1950's, laws governing elections in the United States were within the province of the states, although the Constitution specifically provided for the election of president and vice-president. The right to vote had been guaranteed by the Constitution to all persons over twenty-one who were duly qualified. The U.S. Supreme Court had from time to time declared state election laws unconstitutional because they discriminated against blacks. Congress passed a series of civil rights acts beginning in 1957, culminating in the Voting Rights Act of 1965. This act authorized direct federal action in registering voters in states in which 50 percent or more of eligible citizens had not been registered, and charged federal officials to see that votes were properly recorded. Decisions by the Supreme Court in 1966 and passage of the Twenty-fourth Amendment eliminated the collection of poll taxes, thus enfranchising many black citizens in the South. In 1970 the Court upheld the Voting Rights Act of that year, which extended the right to vote in federal elections to persons eighteen years of age. The Twenty-sixth Amendment gave the suffrage to eighteen-year-olds in state elections.

In spite of the increased extension of federal authority over elections, the states still establish the general basis for voting. Election of local and state officials, representatives to state legislatures, members of Congress, and presidential electors takes place at the state level. Fraudulent voting, improper electioneering, misuse of campaign funds, and bribery and intimidation of voters are subject to state legislation if committed in state elections. State law also establishes machinery for the conduct of elections. Contested elections are usually settled by court order under state legislation. Control over party primaries and state conventions is exercised by the states. The welter of state electoral law makes it extremely difficult to present a precise account of electoral procedures.

ELECTION OF THE PRESIDENT. Derives directly from the structure of the U.S. Constitution and from the two-party system it helped create. After prolonged discussion, the drafters of the Constitution provided that the president would be chosen by electors, especially selected as the legislature of each state should prescribe. Each state was to be entitled to "a number of electors equal to the whole number of Senators and Representatives to which the State may be entitled in the Congress." (In 1962 the Twenty-third Amendment added three electoral votes for the District of Columbia.) Each elector was to cast two votes; the candidate who received the largest number was to become president and the runner-up was to become vice-president, provided the largest number of votes constituted a majority. Should no candidate receive a majority, selection was to fall to the House of Representatives, where each state would be entitled to one vote.

The early development of a two-party system in the United States produced notable changes in the projections of the framers of the Constitution. Consequently, the Twelfth Amendment was passed in 1804, requiring electors to vote once for president and once for vice-president. The development of the party system has virtually guaranteed one presidential candidate a majority of the electoral vote; since its maturation after 1824 the House of Representatives has never had to elect a president.

During the first decades of the Republic the state legislatures selected the electors. By 1828 the present practice of selecting electors by popular, partisan vote was nearly universal. The presidential candidates still campaign, technically, for the election of their electors, because all states now provide that the electors shall be chosen by the people at the general election.

All the electoral votes of each state go to the candidate receiving the most votes in the state. This allows the designation of a president who has received fewer popular votes than his opponent, and the electoral college has twice elected such presidents: Rutherford B. Hayes in 1876 and Benjamin Harrison in 1888.

Nominations for president and vice-president are made at national party conventions whose delegates have been selected through party primaries, state party conventions, or state party central committees. The national committees of each party raise campaign funds, develop organizations to influence the voter, and assist in research and public relations.

ELECTIONS. An election is an act of individuals duly qualified to vote who indicate individually and select collectively their choices from among candidates for office or remove an officeholder from office. The three types of elections are primary, general, and recall. A primary precedes a general, or final, election; its purpose is nominating candidates for office. The purpose of a general election is to make a final selection from among candidates, who may have been chosen in a primary or nominated by some other system. A recall is an election providing for removal of an elected official.

The U.S. Constitution requires a congressional election every two years to elect all 435 members of the House of Representatives for two-year terms and one-third of the Senate for six-year terms. Every four years a president must be elected. Each state constitution contains provisions for what officers are to be elected, the requirement of the secret ballot, times of elections, and qualifications of voters.

Only duly qualified voters may vote in an election. The Fifteenth and Nineteenth amendments to the Constitution prohibit exclusion because of "race, color, or previous condition of servitude" and sex. The equal protection clause of the Fourteenth Amendment is further protection against exclusion. Except for federal elections, the states have jurisdiction over the qualifications required of each citizen to vote.

In early American history, such voting requirements as social status and ownership of land existed. In 1962, the last vestige, the poll tax, was outlawed by the Twenty-fourth Amendment, for national elections. The states do not have uniform voting requirements, but the types of qualifications are similar: (1) U.S. citizenship; (2) minimum period of residency in the state; (3) age (eighteen years); (4) requirement to register before given deadlines. To prevent fraud, registration of voters is mandatory. In some areas periodic registration is necessary. Permanent registration requires that the voter appear only once if he remains in a voting district.

On election day, the polls are held in each precinct or neighborhood from morning until evening. Usually, two judges of election representing the two major parties, one inspector, and several clerks are required in each precinct. The clerks check the voter's name against the registration list. The voter is given a blank ballot, goes to a booth, votes, and deposits the ballot in the ballot box; or he casts his vote through a voting machine.

Absentee voting is allowed both for civilians and for military personnel. The absent qualified voter must apply for an absentee ballot within a prescribed period preceding the election; a ballot, with a return envelope, is sent to the voter by an election official; and, after a notary public or other official signs the ballot envelope, the voted ballot is returned to the official with an affidavit that the voter has complied with the election laws.

After the polls close, the clerks and judges count the votes, put the poll book and tally sheets in the ballot box, seal it, and return it to the city or county clerk, board of election, or canvassing board. The secretary of state is responsible for collection of all state and national returns in his state and issues certificates of election to the winners.

Most state and county elections are held in the fall of even-numbered years at the same time as presidential and congressional elections. Most township, school district, and municipal elections are held in the spring of odd-numbered years. But there is no universal rule about the time for holding state and local elections. Federal general elections are held the first Tuesday after the first Monday in November of even-numbered years.

The cost of elections is borne by both the government and the private sector. The government role lies in paying for the administration of elections and keeping election records. Money spent by the private sector amounts to hundreds of millions of dollars each year. The most serious threat to honesty and fairness in elections is in the area of financing campaigns. Despite passage by Congress of the 1971 campaign financing law, which limits amounts that can be spent on certain methods of campaigning, as in the mass media, there is still no ceiling on the total amount that can be spent.

ELECTIONS, CONTESTED. Often called a "recount," a contested election is an election in which the results are challenged. Usually elections are contested on one or more of the following grounds: (1) irregularities in canvass of the votes; (2) irregularities in conduct of the election; (3) violations of the provisions of the election laws; and (4) ineligibility of the person declared elected. The contest proceedings are brought to court in the manner provided for trial of civil actions insofar as possible. Once an election contest is instituted, either the contestant or the contestee may have the ballots of designated precincts inspected for the trial. A recounting of the votes may be held as evidence for the trial. The contest is judged by the authority empowered to admit winners of elections to the office for which they are running.

ELECTIONS, DISPUTED. *See* **Campaigns, Presidential: Campaign of 1824, Campaign of 1876; Jefferson-Burr Election Dispute.**

ELECTIONS, PRIMARY. *See* **Primary, Direct; Primary, Run-off; Primary, White.**

ELECTORAL COLLEGE. The concept of the electoral college emerged at the Constitutional Convention as a compromise between diverse plans for selecting the chief executive. The plan adopted provided for selection of the president and vice-president by electors from each state. Each state was to be entitled to the same number of electors as it had senators and representatives in Congress. Originally the electors were selected by state legislatures. With the development of a party system by the late 1820's, voters were asked to choose from among slates of electors put forth by the parties and generally pledged to particular candidates. Although at first some electors were selected by districts, a statewide system of electors has generally prevailed since the 1830's.

Under the present system, voters designate their presidential choice by voting for a slate of electors pledged to a party's candidates for president and vice-president. The party ticket receiving the most popular votes in a state receives all the electoral votes of that state. The winning slate of electors of each state convenes in its state capital in December, and the electors cast their votes. In early January the electoral votes are counted before a joint session of Congress. The Constitution requires that the votes be cast separately for president and vice-president and that each receive an absolute majority. If a majority does not exist, election is by the House of Representatives, where the members choose from the three candidates having the greatest number of votes. Each state has one vote. If a contingency election is required for vice-president, it is carried out by the Senate, each member having one vote.

In most instances the electoral college simply ratifies the results of the popular vote. It has failed, however, in three instances to select a president (1800, 1824, 1876). In the first two instances, the decision was made in the House. In 1876, Congress established an electoral commission to rule on disputed sets of electoral returns from several states. In two cases the candidate selected in the electoral college had fewer popular votes than his opponent (1876, 1888), producing a "minority president."

ELECTORAL COMMISSION. In the 1876 election for president, four states reported conflicting sets of voting returns. The election was so close that one vote from the four states would have made Samuel J. Tilden, the Democrat, president of the United States over the Republican, Rutherford B. Hayes. Reconstruction was nearly over, but military units were guarding polling places and occupying state buildings in three southern states—Florida, Louisiana, and South Carolina. There was one disputed vote in Oregon, but the three southern states had sent in completely different returns. The Reconstruction governments reported Republican victories in all three; the Democrats claimed that voting records had been tampered with and that Democrats had been barred from voting. The election, they said, was rightfully theirs.

Congress itself was tightly balanced between the two parties. It was finally agreed that a commission made up of five senators, five representatives, and five judges of the U.S. Supreme Court would examine the returns. The parties would be evenly represented, with two Democratic and two Republican judges selecting the fifth (supposedly impartial) judge. As it turned out, the fifth judge was a Republican. The Electoral Commission recognized the returns as certified by the state officials (that is, as Republican) and declared Hayes the winner by a strictly party vote of 8–7.

ELECTORAL COUNT ACT (Feb. 3, 1887). Designed to prevent a disputed national election, made each state the absolute judge over electoral appointment and returns, specifying congressional acceptance of electoral returns certified by a state in accordance with its own electoral law. Congress can intervene only if the state itself is unable to decide or has decided irregularly. In such cases, a concurrent vote of Congress is decisive, but should the two houses disagree, the votes of those electors whose appointment is certified by the governor are counted.

ELECTORATE. *See* **Franchise.**

ELECTRIC POWER AND LIGHT INDUSTRY. The electric power and light industry began its rapid development during the last quarter of the 19th century. The arc-lighting industry became the first sector of the electric light and power industry to achieve a substantial commercial success. Charles F. Brush of Cleveland, Ohio, became the pioneer innovator in arc lighting in America. His first commercial installation was in Philadelphia in 1878, and the Brush system was soon adopted in other cities. Numerous competitors soon entered the field: the Thomson-Houston Electric Company, organized by Elihu Thomson and E. J. Houston of Philadelphia, and the Sperry Electric Light, Motor and Car Brake Company of Elmer A. Sperry, both founded in 1883. Thomson was responsible for several improvements in arc lighting, including an automatic current regulator and a lightning arrester. Sperry devised a current regulator and invented an automatic regulator of electrode spacing in the arc light. The Thomson-Houston Company became dominant in the industry by 1890. By 1895 the industry was facing strong competition from both incandescent gas and electric lights.

Thomas A. Edison and his associates at Menlo Park, N.J., were largely responsible for the successful incandescent lighting system. Edison turned his attention to the problem of indoor electric lighting in 1878. The Edison Light Company attracted substantial financial support from J. P. Morgan and other investment bankers. After a careful study of the existing gaslight industry, Edison decided that a high-resistance lamp was necessary to permit the economical subdivision of electric energy generated by a central station. A systematic search resulted in the development of the carbon filament high-vacuum lamp by late 1879. The Menlo Park team also developed a series of new dynamos of unprecedented efficiency and power capacity. The first commercial central station, on Pearl Street in New York City, began operation in 1882. Three separate manufacturing companies were organized to produce lamps, dynamos, and transmission cables, but these were later combined in 1889 to form the Edison General Electric Company. The subsequent merger of this company with the Thomson-Houston Company in 1892 resulted in the General Electric Company.

George Westinghouse became the pioneering innovator in the introduction of an incandescent lighting system using alternating current, which proved to have decisive advantages over the Edison direct-current system. A key element of the new system was the transformer. Although the principle of the transformer had been known since Faraday's experiments of 1831, its development reached a level suitable for use in the lighting industry only around 1885. Westinghouse organized the Westinghouse Electric Company in 1886 to begin the manufacture of transformers, alternators, and other alternating-current apparatus. The first commercial installation was located in Buffalo, N.Y., late in 1886. Shortly thereafter, the Thomson-Houston Company also entered the field and was the only serious competitor of Westinghouse in America until the formation of the General Electric Company. The advent of the Westinghouse alternating-current system precipitated the "battle of the systems," during which spokesmen of the Edison Company argued that alternating current was much more dangerous than direct current. But the economic advantages of alternating current were such that the battle was soon over.

During the late 1880's, urban streetcars were electrified through the use of large direct-current motors. Similar techniques were soon used in electric elevators in skyscrapers and for telpherage systems in heavy industry. The first successful large-scale electric streetcar system was introduced by Frank J. Sprague, who organized the Sprague Electric Railway and Motor Company in 1884. Sprague had developed an efficient 15-horsepower direct-current motor by 1885 and obtained a contract to build a forty-car system in Richmond, Va., in 1887. The Richmond installation became the prototype for the industry. The Westinghouse Company began to manufacture railway motors in 1890, and General Electric's entry was effective in 1892 following the merger with Thomson-Houston, which had acquired the Van Depoele patents. These two companies soon dominated the field. Sprague became the pioneer in the electrification of elevated railways. His company was purchased by General Electric in 1902.

The next major innovation was the introduction of alternating-current machines during the 1890's. The Westinghouse Company acquired the strategic alternating-current motor patents of the Serbian immigrant Nikola Tesla. The company led in the development of practical alternating-current motors for use in interurban railroads and in industry. Westinghouse demonstrated a two-phase transmission system that provided power for incandescent lighting and for a variety of alternating-current motors and rotary converters at the World's Columbian Exposition in Chicago, in 1893. In October of the same year, they received the contract to construct the generating equipment for the Niagara Falls Power project. The great success of this project in generating enormous amounts of power and transmitting it efficiently up to 20 miles clearly established the superiority of alternating current for hydroelectric power.

Charles P. Steinmetz, who joined the General Electric Company as an electrical engineer in 1893, presented a classic paper on the use of complex algebra in alternating-current analysis at the International Electrical Congress in Chicago the same year. He also formulated a law of magnetic hysteresis that became a basis for the rational design of transformers and alternators.

Sidney B. Paine of General Electric was responsible for the first major use of alternating-current motors in industry. He persuaded a new textile factory in Columbia, S.C., to abandon the traditional system of giant steam engines and to adopt polyphase induction motors to drive machines. The new system spread throughout the industry. Direct-current motors continued to be widely used in applications requiring variable speed, such as in steel mills and for machine tools.

One of the most significant events in the history of the electric light and power industry was the introduction of high-speed turboelectric generators in central power stations during the first decade of the 20th century. However, the higher speeds of the turbogenerators (up to 2,000 revolutions per minute) necessitated the use of stronger materials, such as nickel-steel alloys, to withstand the increased mechanical stresses. New rotor designs were also necessary to reduce air resistance and improve ventilation. Both Westinghouse and General Electric decided to manufacture their own turbines. The first large commercial installation was a 5,000-kilowatt unit built by General Electric under the direction of W. L. R. Emmet for the Commonwealth Edison Company of Chicago in 1903. This was replaced by a 12,000-kilowatt turbogenerator in 1909. One interesting consequence of the revolution was the entry of the Allis-Chalmers Company of Milwaukee as a "third force" in 1904. The primary economic significance of the turboelectric generator was that it made possible economies of scale that made it more economical for most consumers to purchase electric power from central generating stations than to install their own isolated generating plants.

The first two decades of the 20th century were marked by a competition between the steam locomotive and the electric locomotive, using either direct current or alternating current. The battle was won by the older steam technology, with the alternating-current locomotive finishing a poor third. Most electrified interurban transportation was installed in areas having high population density or requiring tunnels, where the smoke from steam locomotives was a problem. The mileage of "electrified track" reached 250 in 1905 and about 3,000 in 1914. After a fairly rapid growth during 1904–08, alternating-current rail systems were not further expanded until the electrification of the New York–Washington, D.C., line of the Pennsylvania Railroad during the 1930's.

Another major trend during the 20th century has been toward higher transmission voltages in order to increase the distances over which electrical energy can be transmitted economically. The technical knowledge required for improved insulators and reduction of corona loss was accumulated particularly by Charles Scott, Harris J. Ryan, and Frank W. Peek. Transmission distances in excess of 300 miles became feasible with the adoption of 345 kilovolts as a standard transmission line voltage in the 1950's. Transmission voltages of up to 1,000 kilovolts have recently come into use on an experimental basis. Coincident with these developments has been a rising concern for the conservation of nonrenewable resources, such as coal. This concern, which reached a crest just prior to World War I, led to the formulation of a policy for the rational development of the nation's hydroelectric power resources. This policy was articulated by conservationists and supported by leading engineers. Their program was implemented by numerous privately and publicly owned hydroelectric power projects, especially in the South and West, including the well-known impoundments built by the Tennessee Valley Authority (TVA) beginning during the 1930's.

The growth of hydroelectric generating stations and the realization by Samuel Insull and others in the electric utility industry that even further economies could be achieved through the creation of power "pools," or "superpower systems," led to a consolidation movement beginning around 1910. Insull organized the Middle West Utilities Company as a combination of several smaller plants in 1912. After World War I, Insull established a utilities empire financed by the sale of holding-company stock to the public. The 1929 stock market crash ruined Insull financially and led to his trial for mail fraud and embezzlement, although he was finally acquitted. This episode discredited the electric light and power industry and helped provide the rationale for the TVA experiment. Despite this setback, the trend toward larger interconnected power systems resumed and has been further stimulated by the advent of computer control since World War II.

The impact of industrial research laboratories on the power and light industry was especially evident just prior to World War I. A leading role was played by the General Electric Research Laboratory (1900), responsible for the development of gas-filled tungsten-filament lamps, which quickly supplanted the carbon-filament vacuum lamps and enabled the production of lamps in a range of sizes with unprecedented efficiency. Lamp production increased enormously following these innovations, and more than 14 million residential homes had been wired for electricity by 1925. Other domestic uses of electricity developed during the 1920's, including electric stoves, refrigerators, irons, and washing machines. The establishment of the Rural Electrification Administration in the 1930's accelerated the spread of power lines into areas of low population density.

A federal program to develop nuclear reactors for power production was launched in 1954 and resulted in an installation located in Shippingport, Pa., which began generating electric power in 1957. Several other installations have since gone into operation, but fossil fuel power plants continue to supply the bulk of the nation's electricity, for there is a continuing controversy over the safety of nuclear technology and possible adverse environmental effects from nuclear wastes.

ELECTRIFICATION, HOUSEHOLD. Electricity became commercially available in America in the 1880's, as incandescent lighting began to brighten homes. The telephone followed, and together they set the stage for the development of electrified housework. However, certain barriers delayed the implementation of the developing technology until about 1920. Utility companies were reluctant to encourage home appliances, because the companies were making substantial investments simply to meet the demand for industrial power and domestic lighting. Moreover, many utilities had complementary interests in supplying gas for home cooking and heating. Gradually it became clear that the morning and evening power needs of households complemented perfectly the peak loads supplied to industry. The new demand broadened the distribution of the load over the day, without requiring any substantial increase in capital investment. The second major obstacle was the timidity and conservative attitudes of American consumers. In addition, the initial costs of electrical appliances were prohibitively high, both in equipment investments and in the cost of the electricity they consumed; and they were extremely inefficient. Finally, the early appliances were unreliable and short-lived. It was not until the refinement of electrical technology in the early 20th century that would allow for the rapid electrification of household appliances after World War I.

Two major innovations: the invention of a low-cost, nondegradable electrical resistance, and the perfection of a high-speed, fractional-horsepower electric motor subsume all electrical appliances under the functions of heating and powering.

Electric heat had interested scientists long before it became commercially practical. Its status began to change during the 1890's, when it became conspicuous at expositions and international trade fairs. Probably the most spectacular display was that of an all-electric kitchen at the World's Columbian Exposition in Chicago in 1893.

Platinum resistance was the earliest used in electrical heating appliances. Its high melting point and resistance to chemical degradation from oxidation made platinum ideal for long-term performances. About 1892, nickel-steel alloys began to be used. These could endure temperatures greater than 1,000°F., although chemical oxidation remained a serious problem unless the alloys were carefully embedded in enamel. But in 1904, the Simplex Electric Heating Company announced the superiority of its enamel coating by which the heating resistance was embedded and sealed in an insulating coat of enamel burned onto the article to be heated.

Two years later, A. L. Marsh patented the Nichrome wire resistor, and this discovery became the foundation of all subsequent electrical heating apparatuses. This nickel-chromium alloy had a high electrical resistance, very high melting point, and little susceptibility to oxidation; also, it was economical to produce. The first electric range using the Marsh resistance was built by George Hughes and demonstrated at the National Electric Light Association exhibit in St. Louis in 1910. By 1914, at least seven major firms were manufacturing cooking and heating appliances under the Marsh patent. In 1918, Hughes Electric Heating merged with General Electric and Hotpoint, to establish the Hotpoint Division of General Electric. Throughout the 1920's, the Hotpoint Division continued to innovate in electric range development.

The second major technological advance was the creation of a practical, high-speed, fractional-horsepower electric motor. Westinghouse built the earliest fractional-horsepower alternating-current motors in the 1890's, based on the engineering designs of Nikola Tesla; but most of these units were dedicated to industrial purposes. In 1913, General Electric widened the field with a motor designed to power washing machines. Subsequent improvements made the motor more durable, reduced its size, and increased its torque. Improved tolerances, improved manufacturing tools, and self-lubricated motors were the most important developments.

Between 1910 and 1914, washing actions vied with one another for the approval of customers of electric washing machines. They included the dolly agitator, the cylinder rotator, the oscillator cleaner, and the suction cleaner.

In the early 1920's the Maytag Company redesigned its milk-stool agitator into one that had a greater hydrodynamic efficiency in churning the water. This propeller concept was soon widely imitated. James B. Kirby as early as 1913 experimented with a centrifugal dryer innovation that quickly displaced the wringer. Kirby sold the first washer and spin dryer in 1926, under the Laun-Dry-Ette trademark. Other major improvements in home laundering included the evolution of the tub from a basic wooden construction to colored enamels and acrylic finishes in the 1970's. In 1925, A. W. Altorfer made an important improvement by suggesting a high, center agitator post. The automatic washer was invented by Rex Bassett and John W. Chamberlain (1932). The first Bendix automatic washer appeared five years later.

The earliest domestic refrigerator was patented in 1908 by Marcel Audiffron and Henry Stengrum. This U.S. patent was too heavy and too expensive to manufacture for domestic use. General Electric bought the patent in 1911, but its development was delayed six years by technical problems. Fred D. Wolf made an independent start on a smaller, practical domestic refrigerator, and in 1914 sold his first model. This unit used anhydrous ammonia as a coolant and had a 244-pound refrigerating capacity. Wolf's patents changed hands several times, until they were bought in 1920 by Frigidaire, a subsidiary of General Motors.

Another pioneering group in domestic refrigerator technology was led by E. J. Copeland and A. H. Goss. They formed the Electro-Automatic Refrigerator Company in 1914 and built their first model that same year. Two years later, the company reorganized to sell its first sulfur-dioxide refrigerated machine under the name of Kelvinator. For many years Kelvinator specialized in converting iceboxes into electrically refrigerated units by building compressors, condensers, and evaporators into the iceboxes. In 1936, Thomas Midgley, Jr., discovered a new synthetic refrigerant with an almost ideal set of physical properties: Freon was odorless, nontoxic, and a very good refrigerant. It soon replaced sulfur dioxide as a coolant.

David D. Kenney patented a vacuum cleaner to clean railroad cars in 1902. All subsequent vacuum cleaners were manufactured under his patent. But it was the great marketing success of W. H. Hoover, beginning in 1907, that made vacuum cleaning widely accepted.

The structure of the home appliance industry has altered radically since the 1910's when many small manufacturers specialized in a specific type of appliance. During the early 1930's, electric appliance sales were badly depressed. Sales did not climb back to their 1929 level until 1935. This forced many small manufacturers out of business. Perhaps even more important in altering the structure of the industry were mass marketing techniques after World War II. Consolidations and mergers concentrated production in the hands of major full-appliance line manufacturers, such as General Electric, Westinghouse, Philco, RCA, and Frigidaire. Independent distributors became less important. Building contractors replaced salesmen as the most important distributors. In the late 1950's, a swing away from exclusive brand name retail distribution developed with the proliferation of discount houses, variety stores, and supermarket sales. With a saturation of the market in the 1960's with electric mixers, toasters, coffeemakers, can openers, knives, and other appliances, and the threat of an energy shortage and the rise of the price of electricity in the 1970's, many large manufacturers began to abandon the appliance industry.

ELECTROCHEMICAL INDUSTRY. Although the electrochemical industry began with the production of electric batteries in the early 19th century, a multifaceted electrochemical industry appeared only after the development of efficient mechanical generators of electricity (dynamos) in the late 1870's, when the first important contributions were made in the United States, thanks to the use of hydraulic turbines to drive dynamos and to the activity of Thomas A. Edison and his assistants.

One consequence of the availability of cheaper mechanically generated electricity was the electric furnace, which utilized the passage of a current through resistant materials to cause intense heat. Such furnaces, first developed by Sir William Siemens in England about 1880, attained higher temperatures than before. In 1885, E. H. and A. H. Cowles developed an important resistance furnace, which led to two important discoveries by E. G. Acheson: the artificial abrasive material carborundum (1891) and artificial graphite, theretofore a rare mineral form of carbon. In 1892, T. L. Willson, an Englishman working at a hydroelectric power site at Spray, N.C., patented "carbide" (actually calcium carbide). It reacts strongly with water to produce the gas acetylene, the most familiar use being as a heating and illuminating gas in camp stoves and lanterns.

The German chemist Friedrich Wöhler, who first identified calcium carbide, also made the first identification of aluminum (1845). The lateness of this discovery indicates the difficulties encountered in extracting aluminum from ores. In 1854 the French chemist H. Sainte-Clair Deville succeeded in reducing the ore to aluminum, through the action of sodium (itself an electrochemical product). Deville was aware that aluminum could also be produced by passing an electric current through the molten ore; but this was not economically feasible until development of the dynamo. Most early workers in the development of the electric furnace had aimed vaguely at the discovery of an economical way of making aluminum, their other discoveries usually being by-products of this effort. Such was the case with H. Y. Castner, who became one of the most productive electrochemical inventors. In 1886, a few years after leaving the Columbia University School of Mines, Castner discovered a more efficient process for making sodium. In 1894 he invented an electrolytic process for making caustic soda (sodium hydroxide).

The aluminum problem was solved by the combined effects of electrolysis and the electric furnace. In 1884, Richard Grätzel, in Germany, produced aluminum by the electrolysis of melted aluminum chloride or fluoride. His process was not commercially successful, nor was another introduced by the Cowleses in 1885, in which aluminum plus another metal (that is, an alloy) were made in the electric furnace. Finally, P. L. T. Héroult, the leading French authority on electric-furnace processes, made aluminum by the electrolysis of aluminum oxide liquefied in an electric arc; and C. M. Hall, a student at Oberlin College, made aluminum by the electrolysis of aluminum oxide dissolved in the mineral fluorite (aluminum fluoride). The Aluminum Company of America was founded on the basis of Hall's process.

The tremendous hydroelectric power source developed at Niagara Falls in the 1890's gave the United States and Canada peculiar importance in electrochemistry. To this was added in the 1930's immense hydroelectric power in Tennessee, at Muscle Shoals (on the Tennessee River in Alabama) and elsewhere, in an interconnected network of the Tennessee Valley Authority (TVA). TVA both widened the geographical range of the electrochemical industry and made possible cheap electrochemical production methods for materials, such as phosphorus. All major metals except iron and steel are now made or refined electrically. The polished metallic surfaces on appliances are electroplated. Perhaps the most noteworthy subsequent industries are those for producing metallic magnesium from the magnesium salts in seawater, developed between 1915 and 1929 by the Dow Chemical Company, and for producing fluorine, developed during World War II. Electrochemical methods were also introduced during World War II for the isotope separation of uranium, for which additional hydroelectric sites were constructed on the Columbia River at Hanford, Wash.

ELECTRONICS. The branch of technology dealing with devices and methods that depend on the controlled motion of electrons for their functioning. The rise of electronics may be traced to the discovery of the electron and the beginnings of radiotelegraphy. The electron was discovered at Cambridge University by J. J. Thomson in 1897; by 1903, R. A. Millikan had begun high-vacuum electronic researches at the University of Chicago that were to lead him to the measurement of electronic charge. Development of the first cathode-ray oscillograph by Germany's K. F. Braun in 1897 found an echo in America nine years later, when Lee De Forest invented the thermionic vacuum-tube amplifier—the triode—in which electrons from a heated electrode serve to amplify electric signals. Guglielmo Marconi first demonstrated "wireless" telegraphy in Great Britain in the mid-1890's.

The early successes of radiotelegraphy (for instance, Marconi's bridging the Atlantic in 1901) were based on devices that depend on electronics processes in solids, notably at junctions of conductors and semiconductors. An early successful type of detector, the "cat's whisker" crystal rectifier, achieved new importance as a detector of ultra-high-frequency waves in radar sets. De Forest's triode remained a curiosity for several years, in part because he did not appreciate the importance of maintaining the highest possible vacuum. That was demonstrated by the American Telephone and Telegraph Company, which needed an efficient telephone "repeater" (amplifier) for the transcontinental telephone line that would link New York with San Francisco.

The growing number of applications for the triode was accompanied by increasing sophistication of radio receivers. Four inventions stand out in that connection: the feedback (regenerative) circuit, the superheterodyne circuit, superregeneration, and frequency modulation (FM). All four were invented by E. H. Armstrong, a professor of engineering at Columbia University.

During the second decade of the 20th century Great Britain, Germany, and the United States were the leaders in radiocommunications. Commercial developments followed a surprisingly uniform pattern everywhere: major manufacturers of electrical equipment shied away from large-scale participation in radiocommunications, preferring instead to form new companies in whose favor they would slough off their patent and other interests. This led to the formation of the Radio Corporation of America (RCA) in 1919; it took over the Marconi Wireless Telegraph Company of America with the support of the General Electric Company and the encouragement of the U.S. Navy.

Up to then, radiocommunications meant point-to-point communications. No one had systematically broadcast to a large audience. In 1919 a Westinghouse engineer, Frank Conrad, also a radio amateur, received a favorable response when he substituted records of music for the spoken word during tests. He began mentioning the local music store from which he got the records—the first "commercially sponsored" broadcast. A Pittsburgh department store contracted for broadcast announcements advertising sets with which to receive the broadcasts. Westinghouse established the first commercial broadcast station, KDKA in Pittsburgh, in 1920. During the period between the two world wars, American broadcasting developed into a giant industry involving enormous investments in transmitters, receivers, a branch of the entertainment industry, and advertising and other commercial developments.

Point-to-point communications also developed into a major industry, notably through the application of radio to telephony, local services such as police communications, and aviation and marine communications. Most shipping lines began to equip their vessels with radio after the liner *Titanic* summoned help by radio before sinking (1912). The military importance of communicating with units or ships also received prompt recognition.

The only other major electronics industry during this interwar period involved the recording and reproduction of sound and motion pictures. "Talking" movies were introduced in 1927. The change from mechanical to electronic phonograph recording and reproduction in the 1920's led to a new level of quality unsurpassed until development of the long-playing record, magnetic tape, and stereophonic recording.

World War II gave a tremendous push to the American electronics industry. The strategic demands of communications in a global war led to a great increase in industrial capacity. The proximity fuze and atomic weapons depended heavily on electronics for their development. Antiaircraft fire control and the exigencies of artillery tables led, respectively, to the development of servomechanisms and mechanical computers. The most spectacular development was radar ("radio detection and ranging").

Radar developed in at least seven countries almost independently, but most successfully in Great Britain, which was particularly vulnerable to airborne attack. American development of radar goes back to U.S. Navy observations in the 1920's and U.S. Army developments in the 1930's, and limited numbers of radar sets were available on land and in warships at the outbreak of World War II; but the operational use of these sets was not well thought out and lagged several years behind the British systems. However, British experience and American industrial know-how combined to produce excellent equipment after the two nations agreed to share resources, and superiority in radar contributed significantly to the Allied victory.

After World War II the American electronics industry faced substantial cutbacks; it seemed by no means certain that the manufacturing and manpower resources developed during the war could continue to find employment. Only a few realized that the industry was poised for an immense leap forward, of a magnitude unequaled since the Industrial Revolution. This leap forward has been labeled the Second Industrial Revolution. As in the initial developments in electronics half a century earlier, an important feature was dependence on related advances in modern physics; but in the second round, scientific developments were consciously exploited with a view to advancing electronics technology.

An outstanding example of the conscious exploitation of scientific developments was the invention of a new kind of amplifier requiring neither vacuum nor heated electrodes—the transistor—at the Bell Laboratories, whose primary interest is the improvement of telecommunications. The transistor was the most important electronic invention since De Forest's triode and contributed substantially to the extension of the communications arts to television, telemetry, and space flight; the ubiquity of electronics in the economy; and the development of computers.

Television, like radar, developed most quickly in Great Britain, even though the two most important features of modern television, an all-electronic receiver and an electronic camera tube, had been developed in the United States. But again America rapidly caught up. Armstrong's FM invention also came into its own, and sound recording and reproduction were considerably enhanced by the long-playing record and audiotapes. Refinements such as stereophonic recording and color television helped launch electronics as a multibillion-dollar industry.

Wartime radar and other telecommunications advances found ready applications in civilian fields such as aviation, marine communications, and local services ranging from railways to taxicabs. Research and development on military applications continued and were intensified by the cold war and the Vietnam War.

Even more spectacular advances were made in the fields of telemetry and remote control. American electronics technology made it possible for the first American satellite (*Explorer 1,* January 1958) to perform complex measurements of considerable scientific interest, including confirmation of the existence of the Van Allen belts of radiation surrounding the earth. Under a vigorous program initiated by President John F. Kennedy, a series of landings on the moon by American astronauts began in 1969.

The space program served to step up technology much as war had—but largely for peaceful purposes. An outstanding example was the stationary communications satellite, an orbiting vehicle crammed full of electronics gear powered by solar cells and placed into orbit at a height (23,000 miles above the earth) that synchronizes its speed with the earth's rotation, so that the satellite appears stationary. They regularly receive, amplify, and relay signals between two or more earth stations and can carry thousands of telephone conversations and several television programs simultaneously.

In the late 20th century, electronics technology entered into countless new fields. Progress in medicine, industrial control, food technology, and a host of consumer fields ranging from materials processing to the printing of books was made possible by the introduction of electronic methods.

The most pervasive development of all was the electronic computer. Whereas earlier machines had made it possible to substitute mechanical power for human or animal muscle, the electronic computer made it possible to enhance and multiply the capabilities of the human brain.

The electronic computer is derived from mechanical computers such as those designed at the Massachusetts Institute of Technology during the second quarter of the 20th century.

The first digital electronic computer was developed around 1940 by Howard Aiken at Harvard University with the help of the International Business Machines Corporation (IBM). (A parallel project at the University of Pennsylvania, led by J. W. Mauchly and J. P. Eckert, Jr., had a similar result for the Sperry-Rand group through its UNIVAC division.)

The single most important physical element in the development of the modern computer was the substitution of transistors for the less reliable vacuum tubes. Almost equally important was the substitution of tiny magnetic elements called "cores" for mechanical relays to perform switching operations. These two hardware advances were accompanied by software developments such as the binary system and the "stored program." In the late 1970's, the introduction of home computers and electronic video games was rapidly transforming the American household and assured the growth of the electronics industry.

ELECTRONIC SURVEILLANCE. Since 1934, telephone wiretapping in the United States has been outlawed by federal statute but widely engaged in by federal and state law enforcement authorities as well as by private persons. Bugging of rooms and offices was not forbidden, but it was made subject to other constitutional restrictions when the bug involved some physical penetration into the place under surveillance. In two decisions in 1967, the Supreme Court laid out a set of restrictions and conditions for the constitutionality of any legislation permitting wiretapping or bugging. Congress enacted legislation in 1968 that authorized federal and state officials to wiretap and bug for a wide variety of suspected offenses if they first obtained a court order. The federal government has installed hundreds of wiretaps, mostly in gambling cases and a few in drug cases. On the state level as well, most of the surveillance has been for the purpose of detecting illegal gambling.

The federal government has also sought the right to use electronic surveillance for national security purposes without any judicial supervision. The Supreme Court unanimously denied them this power in 1972 insofar as purely domestic groups were concerned. The issue still remains open with respect to surveillance without judicial controls insofar as national security involving foreign intelligence is concerned. Electronic surveillance played a significant part in the Watergate affair (*see* Watergate).

ELEMENTARY AND SECONDARY SCHOOL EDUCATION ACT (1965). Passed by Congress and signed by President Lyndon B. Johnson. It was the first act of Congress which provided general financial assistance to elementary and secondary schools; its major aim was to provide funds to help states educate poor children. Its provisions established a number of categories under which aid was available to states.

ELEPHANT BUTTE DAM. *See* **Hydroelectric Power.**

ELEVATED RAILWAYS. During the second half of the 19th century, the congestion of city streets necessitated forms of rapid transit. New York was the first locus of experiment. The first elevated railway line, from Battery Place to Thirtieth Street, was built in 1866–67. Ultimately lines were built the length of Manhattan Island on Third, Sixth, and Ninth avenues and extended into the Bronx and Brooklyn, employing steam locomotives; in 1903 the lines were electrified. Chicago relied (and still relies) heavily on the elevated railway for its rapid transit. Its first line was opened in 1893. Boston's elevated railway connected the North and South railroad stations over Atlantic Avenue (1901). In Philadelphia the Market Street subway was brought onto an elevated structure west of the Schuylkill River.

On unballasted tracks the passage of railway cars was noisy; the structure was unsightly; and the steel supports were an obstruction to surface traffic. Consequently, when subway construction became less costly, new rapid transit construction tended to be placed underground. Construction of New York's Independent Subway System in the 1930's permitted removal of most elevated lines.

Modern elevated construction can be made attractive in appearance; tracks can be carried on ballasted concrete slabs to reduce noise; and spaces under elevated structures can be used as parking areas. Several new rapid transit systems—monorail and sky bus, for example—are intended for elevated alignments. What can be done to alleviate the opposition the old-style elevated structures generated is apparent in the design of the elevated sections of the San Francisco Bay Area Rapid Transit (BART) System.

ELEVATORS. The development of the modern elevator began with the use of the steam engine to provide power to drive the machines in mills. Most mills were multistoried, so it was necessary to have a hoisting machine between floors. This machine, like all others in the mill, was powered by the central steam engine. Starting and stopping were effected by a rope that passed through the car and that, when pulled by the operator, controlled the rotation of the hoisting machine. Later, the desirability of having a separate steam engine for the elevator became apparent.

Almost all hoists or elevators functioned by winding a rope on a drum to raise the platform, and since the possibility of rope breakage created a hazard, they were not used to carry passengers until the invention of the safety elevator by Elisha Otis, a mechanic in a mattress factory in Yonkers, N.Y. During the New York Crystal Palace exhibition in 1854, he gave dramatic demonstrations of a safety device that would grip the elevator guide rails if the hoist ropes parted. With passenger safety demonstrated, Otis built the first passenger elevator in 1857 in a china and glass store in New York City.

Use of the drum machine for elevators was restricted to low-rise buildings because the length and weight of the drum imposed a severe restriction on the building structure and on the height the elevator could travel. By 1870 a rope-geared hydraulic system was developed whereby the elevator was raised and lowered by a piston acting through a system of sheaves (complex pulleys) over which the hoist ropes passed in a manner similar to that of a reversed block and tackle. This eliminated the winding drum. By 1880 both these systems were in general use. The development of the electric motor had only a minor effect on the operation of elevators at first, when it was used to replace the steam engine that powered the pumps used on hydraulic systems. Then Otis designed a drum machine that used an electric motor to drive the drum (1889).

The beginning of the modern high-speed elevator occurred about 1900, when the traction machine was developed. The traction machine depends on friction between the driving sheave or pulley and the hoist ropes and does not require the ropes to be wound on a drum. With the traction machine, elevators can serve buildings of any height and are limited in speed only by the height of the building. In 1904 the Otis Company installed the first gearless traction machine in Chicago, which was to make high elevator speeds practical. In this machine the drive sheave is mounted directly on the motor shaft and there are no gears. The result is a quiet and smooth-running elevator, even at speeds of 2,000 feet per minute. Further control developments were made during the 1920's and 1930's by Otis, Westinghouse, and other companies. These systems provided automatic landing of the elevators at floor level and automatic floor selection by the pressing of buttons for the desired stop. Completely automatic elevators that did not require the presence of an operator were developed in the 1920's but did not come into general use until 1950. By 1960, the installation of any elevator requiring an operator was a rarity.

ELEVATORS, GRAIN. Oliver Evans first applied machinery to the task of lifting grain to the top floors of the mechanized, integrated flour mills he designed on the Brandywine River at the end of the 18th century. His "elevator" was simply a series of iron buckets attached to an endless, moving belt that extended from the storage room to the waterway or road alongside the mill. In 1842 a Buffalo grain merchant, Joseph Dart, built an elevating apparatus for unloading grain directly from vessels into his waterfront warehouse, using a steam engine to provide the power. Within a few years every new grain warehouse featured similar machinery; the devices grew more powerful and efficient, the storage bins larger and taller. The fusing of the elevating and warehousing functions had become common by the mid-1850's; midwesterners referred to the entire structure as a "grain elevator." This technology spread slowly from the Great Lakes ports. In the 1870's the major transfer points on the Mississippi River route and on the eastern seaboard began adopting it. By the 1880's, railroads spreading feeder lines into emerging grain belts west of the Mississippi River encouraged the construction of elevators at each station. Grain elevators now consist of enormous clusters of concrete silos or steel tanks, receive grain carried by trucks from farms, and handle the grain by pneumatic machinery.

ELEVENTH AMENDMENT. After the decision of the Supreme Court in *Chisholm* v. *Georgia* (1793), a surge of states' rights sentiment developed. This resulted in the submission of the Eleventh Amendment on Mar. 5, 1794, proclaimed by the president, Jan. 8, 1798. Whereas the Court had held that a state could be sued by a citizen of another state in case of an alleged breach of contract, the amendment declared that "the judicial power of the United States shall not be construed to extend to any suit in law or equity, commenced or prosecuted against one of the United States by citizens of another state, or by citizens or subjects of any foreign state."

ELGIN-MARCY TREATY (June 5, 1854). Also known as the Reciprocity Treaty of 1854, this treaty established Canadian-American reciprocity. It was negotiated by James Bruce, Lord Elgin, governor-general of Canada, and U.S. Secretary of War William L. Marcy. The treaty secured Canadian loyalty and allayed the tension over American use of the fisheries, relieving British diplomacy during the Crimean War. The United States abrogated the treaty in 1866.

ELIZABETH (N.J.). City in northeastern New Jersey, with a population of 106,201, according to the 1980 census. Located just south of Newark, Elizabeth has an extensive port facility, Port Elizabeth. Many foreign-made products pass through the port. The city is an important manufacturing center as well, with special products such as sewing machines and paper products. The city was the first home (in 1746) of the College of New Jersey (now Princeton University). (*See* Elizabethtown Associates.)

ELIZABETHTOWN ASSOCIATES. The first group to be granted permission by the English government to settle in New Jersey. On Sept. 30, 1664, Gov. Richard Nicolls consented to a petition of six residents of Jamaica, L.I., to purchase and settle 400,000 acres of land west of the Arthur Kill, in New Jersey. By deed of Oct. 28, confirmed by patent from Nicolls on Dec. 1, the associates purchased a broad tract from the Indians. The associates, limiting their number to eighty, admitted Gov. Philip Carteret when he purchased rights of a prior associate, and together they founded Elizabethtown (now Elizabeth). The original settlers were Puritans from New England and Long Island; later, immigrants from Scotland arrived. The town was capital of the province until 1676 and of East Jersey until 1686. On Feb. 8, 1740, George II granted a charter for the Free Borough and Town of Elizabeth. (*See* Elizabeth.)

ELK HILLS OIL SCANDAL. In May 1921, the administration of the naval oil reserves was transferred from the Department of the Navy to the Interior. Investigation by a Senate committee brought out the fact that Secretary of the Interior Albert B. Fall, who executed the lease of the Elk Hills, Calif., oil reserve to the Pan-American Petroleum Company in 1922, had "borrowed" $100,000 from E. L. Doheny, president of the company. A resolution by Congress, January 1924, directed President Calvin Coolidge to institute criminal prosecutions and a civil suit to cancel the lease. Litigation resulted in cancellation, and the company was ordered to pay for all petroleum taken out. Doheny was acquitted of bribery, and both Fall and Doheny of criminal conspiracy; but Fall was eventually convicted (1931) of bribery and sentenced to one year. (*See also* Teapot Dome Oil Scandal.)

ELKHORN, BATTLE OF. *See* **Pea Ridge, Battle of.**

ELKINS ACT (1903). Required railroads to hold to their published rates and forbade rate cutting and rebates. The act was favored by the railroads to prevent loss of revenue. It supplemented the Interstate Commerce Act of 1887 by providing more specific methods of procedure and penalties for its nonobservance. (*See also* Hepburn Act of 1906.)

ELK RIVER, BATTLE OF (May 1–2, 1862). The Louisiana cavalry, operating under Gen. P. G. T. Beauregard in the vicinity of Elk River, Ala., defeated Gen. Ormsby Mitchell's Union forces, capturing many stores and inflicting severe casualties.

ELLENTON RIOT (Sept. 16–19, 1876). The bloodiest Reconstruction incident in South Carolina; resulted from the pursuit of a black criminal by white riflemen who surrounded terrified blacks near Ellenton. Federal troops checked the disorders. Two whites and between 15 and 100 blacks died.

ELLICOTT'S MISSION. Andrew Ellicott, U.S. surveyor general, arrived at Natchez, Miss., on Feb. 23, 1797, to join a Spanish commission in running the line (thirty-first parallel) established as the boundary between the United States and the Spanish possessions by the Treaty of San Lorenzo. Ellicott got them to evacuate Natchez and completed the line to the Chattahoochee River by September 1800.

ELLIS, FORT. A defense against the Sioux built in 1867 on the East Gallatin River, near present Bozeman, Mont. From this fort Gen. John Gibbon marched in 1876 following the Battle of the Little Bighorn to bury the dead. The fort ceased to function in 1886.

ELLIS ISLAND. In 1890 the U.S. government assumed complete responsibility for screening immigrant arrivals at the Port of New York. New York's reception facilities on Manhattan Island (the Battery) were viewed as unsatisfactory by Congress, which selected Ellis Island as more suitable. Owned by the federal government since 1808, this island one mile southwest of Manhattan received its first immigrants in 1892. More than 16 million immigrants passed through Ellis Island, almost three-fourths of all immigrants to the United States having landed there. Both World War I and restrictive immigration legislation in the 1920's reduced the importance of Ellis Island. By World War II, the island handled only new arrivals being detained and aliens being deported. In 1954 its facilities were closed. In 1965 the Statue of Liberty National Monument assumed control of Ellis Island.

ELLSWORTH'S ZOUAVES. The U.S. Zouave Cadets of Chicago, Ill., were organized in 1859 as a volunteer militia company and fraternal club by Elmer E. Ellsworth. Drill and uniform were derived from the Algerian Zouaves in the French army. The 4,000-mile exhibition tour of the Zouave Cadets attracted wide attention. In 1861, Ellsworth organized the First New York Fire Zouaves, a regiment of firemen that served in the Union army.

ELMIRA, BATTLE OF (Aug. 29, 1779). At Newtown, near present Elmira, N.Y., the Iroquois Indians and Loyalists made their only stand against the armies of Gen. John Sullivan and Gen. James Clinton. Fatalities on both sides were not large. The Indians and Loyalists fled, the former being frightened by the cannon.

ELMIRA PRISON. A Union prison camp in New York State, established in July 1864 by the federal government. The enclosure consisted of thirty acres in which 12,123 captives were housed in barracks and tents. Although the camp was well equipped and efficiently managed, exceptional hardships marked the prison's history. A stagnant pond used as a sink became a cesspool; scurvy resulted from lack of vegetables; smallpox spread; a cold winter and inadequate fuel added to the suffering; and melting snows produced a flood. As a result, 24 percent of the prisoners died before the closing of the prison in 1865.

EL PASO (Tex.). A city and port of entry in west Texas on the Rio Grande. Largest of the U.S.-Mexican border cities, located opposite its twin city, Juárez. The site was first recognized in 1598 by Juan de Oñate, who named it El Paso del Norte. A Franciscan mission was established there in 1659. The site became U.S. territory in 1848, and Fort Bliss was established to protect the inhabitants and travelers from the Apache. In 1849 its settlers were furnishing supplies to the California immigrants. By 1857, transcontinental mail coaches were using the old routes through American El Paso. The transcontinental railroads in 1881 followed the long-marked trails to El Paso. Thereafter, growth was rapid.

El Paso grew into a major commercial and manufacturing center in the 20th century, in an area famous for cattle raising, cotton growing, and mineral production. It is one of the largest antiaircraft and guided missile centers in the country. Serving as a gateway to Mexico, it attracts many tourists. The population of El Paso increased from little more than 10,000 in 1890 to 425,259 in 1980.

EMANCIPATION, COMPENSATED. A device for eliminating slavery by having the government buy the slaves. The constitutional convention of Virginia in 1829–30 proposed an amendment to the Constitution giving Congress the power to purchase and colonize slaves. With the decline of the colonization movement, interest in compensated emancipation declined also.

The Republican party revived interest. Their 1860 platform recognized it as desirable. President Abraham Lincoln believed it to be the best solution to the slavery problem. In a special message to Congress, Mar. 6, 1862, he asked the adoption of a joint resolution pledging financial aid to any state adopting gradual emancipation. The resolution was passed, but none of the border states would accept the offer.

The only successful attempt at compensated emancipation was in the District of Columbia.

The last effort was made in Lincoln's message of Dec. 1, 1862. He proposed a constitutional amendment permitting an issue of government bonds to any state adopting gradual emancipation. With the Emancipation Proclamation all interest in the scheme disappeared.

EMANCIPATION MOVEMENT. Organized antislavery forces, both conservative and radical, were active between 1816 and 1840. The conservative American Colonization Society (1817) was instrumental in sending some freedmen to the colony of Liberia in Africa. In 1830, the more aggressive American Anti-Slavery Society urged immediate or gradual emancipation begun at once. Slaveowners objected to claims of the Anti-Slavery Society that slaveowning was sinful, and the general public was also not supportive. Although these groups failed to induce planters to free their slaves, their campaign kept the issue before the public. Leadership passed to increasingly militant abolitionists after the 1830's.

EMANCIPATION ORDERS, FRÉMONT AND HUNTER. A cardinal policy of President Lincoln in the early months of the Civil War was to save the border slave states for the Union by reassuring them that the war was not against slavery. On Aug. 30, 1861, Gen. John C. Frémont, commanding the Department of the West, on his own initiative issued a military proclamation declaring free the slaves of all persons in Missouri supporting the Confederacy. Lincoln wrote Frémont asking that he conform to the Confiscation Act of Aug. 6, 1861, which declared forfeit the claim of owners to slaves used "in aid of the insurrection." Frémont refused unless openly commanded by the president. On Sept. 11, the president so commanded. On May 9, 1862, Gen. David Hunter, commanding the Department of the South, issued an order declaring free all slaves in South Carolina, Georgia, and Florida. Lincoln voided the order on May 19.

EMANCIPATION PROCLAMATION (Jan. 1, 1863). Abraham Lincoln's grant of freedom to slaves in states then in rebellion. In conformity with the preliminary proclamation of Sept. 22, 1862, it declared that all persons held as slaves within the insurgent states—with the exception of Tennessee, southern Louisiana, and parts of Virginia, then within Union lines—"are and henceforth shall be, free." Admonishing the freedmen to abstain from violence, it invited them to join the armed forces of the United States and pledged the government to uphold their new status. Unlike the preliminary proclamation, it contained no references to colonization of the freed slaves. The mere fact of its promulgation ensured the death of slavery in the event of a northern victory. The Emancipation Proclamation may thus be regarded as a milestone on the road to final freedom as expressed in the Thirteenth Amendment, declared in force on Dec. 18, 1865.

EMANCIPATOR. A monthly abolitionist newspaper published in 1820 at Jonesboro, Tenn., by Elihu Embree. One of the first antislavery newspapers, it preceded *The Genius of Universal Emancipation* by seven months. From 1833 to 1850 an antislavery newspaper was edited by R. G. Williams in New York and Boston under the successive titles *Emancipator and Republican, Emancipator and Journal of Public Morals, Emancipator and Free America,* and *Emancipator and Free Soil Press.* Like William Lloyd Garrison's *The Liberator,* it espoused extreme abolitionism.

"EMBALMED BEEF." Meat canned by Chicago packers and issued to Union armies was often called "embalmed beef" by the soldiers. Soldiers in the Spanish-American War insisted that the canned meat issued to them in Florida, Cuba, and the Philippines was "embalmed beef" of Civil War issue. During World War I canned Argentine beef was issued to the Allied armies. The British soldiers called it "bully beef," but the American soldiers, accustomed to red meats, called it contemptuously "embalmed beef" or "monkey meat."

EMBARGO. An official order that prohibits the shipment of goods to or from a particular place. Some embargoes are general; others may apply to one or two commodities. An arms embargo is frequently imposed when one country is trying to remain neutral in a war between two or more others.

EMBARGO ACT (1807). A measure taken by Thomas Jefferson to deal with abuses to U.S. shipping by England and France in the early stages of the Napoleonic wars. The United States had grown wealthy as the chief of neutral carriers at a time when British shipping was dedicated to war purposes, but the Orders in Council of Jan. 7 and Nov. 11, 1807, and the Berlin and Milan decrees of Nov. 21, 1806, and Dec. 17, 1807, respectively, threatened direst penalties to any neutral venturing into a port of the enemy of either belligerent. There was the added goad of the humiliating *Chesapeake* incident of June 22, 1807, in which the British boarded an American ship and impressed four sailors, claiming that they were British. The embargo aimed to secure a submission that could not be achieved by armed forces.

The embargo was effective to a degree. Exports experienced a 75 percent decline against a 50 percent decline in imports. But throughout 1808 it became increasingly apparent that America lacked the unity and energy to press the embargo to its ultimate conclusion. Opposition to the embargo grew steadily. It became a point of honor with Jefferson for the embargo to survive his second term of office. But the act was repealed three days before his term expired in March 1809.

EMBASSIES. Missions of the highest diplomatic rank accredited to foreign states. Each ambassador represents the U.S. president to the head of the state to which he is accredited and, by custom, has the right of audience with the sovereign. In practice, a U.S. ambassador reports to the U.S. State Department and, for the most part, deals with the ministry of foreign affairs of the nation to which he is accredited.

U.S. ambassadors are appointed by the president, under the Constitution (Article II, Section 2), "by and with the

Advice and Consent of the Senate." The early Republic was represented abroad by ministers; the first U.S. ambassador was appointed in 1893. By 1981 the United States had exchanged ambassadors with 144 countries.

U.S. embassies vary greatly in size. In late 1968 the nine largest embassies each had as many as 1,000 U.S. citizens attached—about a fifth from the State Department proper, the remainder from thirty-four other agencies. Although expected to coordinate the activities of representatives of a broad spectrum of U.S. government agencies, U.S. ambassadors had no direct control over them until 1961.

U.S. embassies, regardless of size, usually have four main subdivisions: political, economic, cultural, and consular affairs. To coordinate the work of the many non–Foreign Service personnel representing the other U.S. agencies, resort is made to the "country team" concept, by which the senior representatives of these agencies constitute, along with the senior Foreign Service Officers attached to the embassy, a "cabinet" for the U.S. chief of mission. U.S. missions abroad, as of June 30, 1979, employed a total of 19,121 U.S. nationals.

EMBLEMS, PARTY. Symbols of political parties used in the United States since the black cockade of the Federalists. Party emblems are placed at the top of party column ballots in a number of states. A crowing rooster or a star usually serves for the Democrats, an elephant or an eagle for the Republicans, hands clasped against the background of a hemisphere for the Socialists, and the crossed hammer and sickle for the Communists. Emblems have enabled the illiterate elector to vote a straight ticket without difficulty.

EMERGENCY FLEET CORPORATION. Because of the need during World War I to build ships rapidly, the U.S. Shipping Board incorporated, on Apr. 16, 1917, the Emergency Fleet Corporation, to build, own, and operate a merchant fleet for the U.S. government. The Fleet Corporation began by requisitioning the 431 steel ships being built in America for foreign operators. Second, the corporation built, through private agency companies, three great steel shipyards (the largest being the Hog Island yard in Pennsylvania), and invested in many other yards, increasing total ways capable of building oceangoing ships from 256 to 934. The peak construction program in October 1918 comprised 3,116 ships (two-thirds of steel) of 17 million tons. But by Oct. 31, 1918, only 378 steel ships (2.3 million tons) had been put in service. World War I ended as the army general staff faced the prospect of inadequate supply ships by July 1919. After the armistice, when 218 yards (385,000 workers) were building under contract for the Fleet Corporation, contracts totaling 25 percent of the original program were cancelled, despite protests by shipbuilders and workers. But the balance of construction was continued on the assumption that the market value of the ships would be greater than the savings of further cancellations. Not until 1922 was the last vessel delivered to the Fleet Corporation.

EMERGENCY RAILROAD TRANSPORTATION ACT (June 16, 1933). Applied to carriers and subsidiaries subject to the Interstate Commerce Act. It was designed to avoid unnecessary duplication of services and facilities, to promote financial reorganization of the carriers, and to provide for the study of improving rail transportation. The act repealed the "recapture" clause of the Transportation Act of 1920, placed railroad holding companies under the supervision of the Interstate Commerce Commission, provided for a simpler rule of rate making, and created the office of federal coordinator of transportation.

EMERGENCY RELIEF ADMINISTRATION. *See* **New Deal.**

EMIGRANT AID MOVEMENT. A plan to promote free-state migration to Kansas Territory, conceived by Eli Thayer in March 1854. The movement was largely confined to the Northeast. In the Northwest, where the vote on territoriality was the deciding factor in making Kansas free, there was little organized effort. Settlers went at their own expense, but aid companies secured reduction in transportation costs, founded a few towns, and forwarded supplies and mechanical equipment. In 1855, renewed activity of promoters and Kansas radicals and the inception of supplementary aid committees resulted in larger patronage, but tangible results were negligible. By 1857 the movement was rapidly drawing to a close. (*See also* New England Emigrant Aid Company.)

EMIGRANT COMPANIES. *See* **Overland Companies.**

EMIGRATION. The repatriation of immigrants to their native lands from the United States, whether after long residence or a brief sojourn, has appeared to many Americans a betrayal of their hospitality. Expatriates have seemed even more ungrateful. Demographers suggest that during the era of the great migration extending from the 1830's to the 1920's, allowance for the volume of emigrants returning to their native lands would reduce the net gains in population attributed to immigration by 20–50 percent of the accepted totals. Progressively, the proportion of emigrants increased. Between 1908 and 1923 the predominance of southern and eastern European male immigrants whose overpowering aim was to save money to return home and buy land; acute spasms of political and cultural self-consciousness; and the hostility of native Americans contributed to an exceptionally high incidence of repatriation, which reached 89 percent among Balkan immigrants. During four years of the Great Depression, emigrants exceeded immigrants. In periods of extreme crisis and disillusionment—beginning with the 80,000 to 100,000 Loyalists who left the country during the American revolutionary era—expatriates have augmented repatriates, thus adding to the emigrant exodus. Despite the discontent in the United States of the 1960's, no more than 24,000 Americans living abroad failed to retain their citizenship.

EMINENT DOMAIN. The inherent right of a sovereign power to take private property for public use without the owner's consent. The Fifth Amendment of the U.S. Constitution implicitly acknowledges this right of the national government by providing that private property shall not "be taken for public use, without just compensation." By Supreme Court interpretation of the due process clause of the Fourteenth Amendment, the same right and limitation have been attributed to state governments.

EMORY'S MILITARY RECONNAISSANCE (1846). Part of the military movement against Mexico, led by Lt. W. H. Emory of the U.S. Topographical Engineers. The party was attached to Gen. Stephen Watts Kearny's army of the West. Emory's reconnaissance included a portion of the Rio Grande and the Gila River to the Colorado River, and thence to the California coast. This was the first American official survey of this region.

EMPLOYERS' LIABILITY LAWS. During the 18th century and early 19th century, common law recognized the duties of the "master" both to provide the "servant" a reasonably safe place to work and to establish safety rules. An injured employee could maintain an action in negligence against an employer when the latter had breached one of the above duties, but many industrial accidents were not traceable to negligence but to the inherent risk of the work. As the common law developed, the employer was absolved of liability (1) by the "assumption of risk" doctrine, applied when the injured worker knew of dangerous conditions and defects resulting from the employer's negligence; (2) by the "fellow-servant" doctrine, applied when injury was caused by the negligence of a co-worker; and (3) by the "contributory negligence" doctrine, applied when the injured worker's own carelessness contributed to the accident.

Georgia became the first state to chip away at the employer's three common-law defenses, abolishing the fellow-servant rule in 1855. Gradually most states enacted employers' liability laws that abrogated or mitigated the fellow-servant and assumption-of-risk defenses. Some also eased the harsh effect of contributory negligence, establishing a "comparative negligence" doctrine that did not bar the employee's recovery against the employer but only diminished it by the percentage of negligence attributable to the employee. The Federal Employers' Liability Act of 1908 virtually eliminated the common-law defenses when interstate carriers were employers; the Jones Act of 1915 dictated similar protection for seamen.

The most notable inadequacy of the employers' liability acts is that the employee is required to show the employer's negligence and its proximate cause of the injury. Many workers are unable to afford the process of lengthy, expensive litigation, especially when there is the possibility of minimal or no recovery of damages.

Beginning in Maryland in 1902, workmen's compensation laws have been enacted for the purpose of taking the unreasonable financial strain off the injured employee. Relatively quick and widespread acceptance of such laws indicated that they were an efficacious way to meet a felt need. Workmen's compensation laws have over the years effectively preempted employer liability statutes. Standard provisions of these compensation laws ensure that an injured or sick employee (or the beneficiary of a deceased employee) will receive cash or medical benefits without proof of fault. Compensation is awarded by administrative, not judicial, bodies and according to definite payment schedules, so that money is received a short time after injury or death. By 1973 all fifty states had comprehensive workmen's compensation statutes.

Coverage has continued to expand in scope: by 1960 about 80 percent of the U.S. work force was protected by state compensation laws and most of the remaining 20 percent was covered by other programs.

EMPLOYMENT ACT OF 1946 (Feb. 20, 1946). Reaffirming a continuing federal policy to promote maximum employment, production, and purchasing power, the Employment Act required the president to submit an annual economic report. It also created a three-member Council of Economic Advisers to assist the president and a Joint Economic Committee of the Congress.

EMPLOYMENT SERVICE, UNITED STATES (USES). In 1914 the Immigration Service developed the beginnings of a nationwide information system about employment opportunities. At the time of U.S. entry into World War I the federal government established an employment unit in the Department of Labor, the USES, to mobilize the nation's manpower for the war effort, but at the end of the war the USES ceased to exist.

The Wagner-Peyser Act of 1933 reestablished the USES to set minimum standards, develop uniform administrative and statistical procedures, publish employment information, and promote a system of "clearing labor" between states. During the Great Depression the USES had a large responsibility in developing essential information about local job opportunities, in seeking to match workers to jobs, and in placing the unemployed on the many government work projects developed during the 1930's. With the passage of the Social Security Act in 1935, a state employment service was required, since unemployment insurance benefits could in most cases be paid only through a public employment office. By the time of U.S. entry into World War II, a state employment service operating in collaboration with the USES had been established in all states.

During World War II the nation relied heavily upon the public employment services for the allocation of manpower. Since World War II enormous changes have forced reconsideration of the role and services of governmental agencies in combating unemployment. The expanded role of the USES now requires the federal service to make labor surveys, certify training needs, provide testing and counseling, expand job placement for persons trained, and provide information and guidance on occupational needs.

EMPRESARIO SYSTEM. Empresario was the title given those who obtained contracts to settle colonists in Mexican Texas. Contracts, granted by the governor, authorized the empresario to introduce a specified number of families into an area within six years. For his services, he was entitled to receive 23,025 acres of land for each hundred families that he introduced, up to 800 families. He could exact moderate fees from the colonists for his service. The empresario was obligated to introduce only families of Catholic religion and good moral character and to establish schools and churches. He controlled the land within the generous limits of his grant, and no titles could issue therein without his consent; but he owned only those lands that he acquired by purchase or as a "premium" for introducing colonists. Misunderstanding of the legal status of an empresario with relation to his grant was at the bottom of considerable U.S. speculation in Texas lands.

EMPRESS AUGUSTA BAY, BATTLE OF (Nov. 2, 1943). Fought at night some fifty miles west of Bougainville, the largest of the Solomon Islands, which the Allies were endeavoring to secure as part of their Pacific counteroffensive in World War II. A Japanese force (under Rear Adm. S. Omori) of two heavy cruisers, two light cruisers, and six destroyers had as its objective the destruction of American amphibious forces on Bougainville. The American force (under Rear Adm. A. S. Merrill) included four light cruisers and eight destroyers. For the first time in the war, American destroyers of a battle group were used offensively. The destroyers were to make a torpedo attack on the Japanese warships; the cruisers were to hold their gunfire until the torpedoes struck the enemy. The Japanese withdrew after an hour and ten minutes, with the loss of one light cruiser and one destroyer sunk, two heavy cruisers and two destroyers damaged. American casualties were one cruiser and two destroyers damaged.

EMUCKFAU VILLAGE AND ENOTACHOPCO CREEK, BATTLE AT. *See* **Creek War.**

ENABLING ACTS. Congress early provided for the admission of new states. The people of a territory desiring statehood had to petition Congress for an enabling act, which authorizes holding a constitutional convention, provides for the election of delegates, and may seek to impose certain conditions on the convention and on the new state itself. For example, Utah was required to prohibit polygamous marriage forever. In 1911 the Supreme Court held that such restrictions were not binding when they related to matters concerning which the states have jurisdiction under the Constitution. An exception is when the conditions imposed relate to the use of lands granted to a state by Congress (*see* Public Domain) for a specific purpose.

ENCOMIENDA SYSTEM. A Spanish institution, originally the granting of an estate by the king for service against the Moors, introduced into the New World with the conquests. The king granted deserving individuals an estate and the right to receive and collect for themselves the tributes of the Indians who lived on it, who were given them in trust, for their life and the life of one heir.

ENCOMIUM. An American brig sailing from Charleston, S.C., to New Orleans, with forty-five slaves owned by North Carolina planters, was wrecked on Feb. 4, 1834, in the British Bahamas. The slaves were seized and liberated at Nassau. The case was presented to the British government with the earlier, similar case of the *Comet.* Liberal indemnification for the slaves was secured in 1839.

ENCYCLOPEDIAS. The *Encyclopaedia Britannica,* established in Edinburgh in 1768, was successful enough to be pirated in the United States in 1798 by Thomas Dobson of Philadelphia. Despite its name, the *Britannica* has been managed by Americans since the beginning of the 20th century, passing into American ownership in 1920. The fifteenth edition (popularly known as *Britannica 3* because of its tripartite organization) represents the most complete revision since the eleventh.

The *Encyclopedia Americana,* edited by Francis Lieber, a German immigrant, appeared in Philadelphia in 1829–33, based on the seventh edition of Friedrich Brockhaus's *Konversations-Lexikon,* a standard German work. The *Americana* lapsed in 1858; a new work under the same title was first published in 1902–04 and continues.

The first encyclopedia based mainly on American contributions was the sixteen-volume *New American Cyclopaedia,* edited by George Ripley in 1858–63. Another innovation was the *American Annual Encyclopedia,* a book of about 800 pages, issued annually 1861–74 and continued as *Appleton's Annual Cyclopaedia* until 1902. The success of these and other 19th-century reference works and lowered printing costs led to the development of many other encyclopedias.

One of the major 20th-century developments has been the great success of encyclopedias for children, which began during the mid-19th century. Among them have been *The Book of Knowledge* (based on *The Children's Cyclopaedia,* first issued in London in 1910) and *The World Book,* which began in 1917–18.

Among the most important American encyclopedias have been the great scholarly specialized reference tools: to name a few, the *International Encyclopedia of the Social Sciences,* the *Encyclopedia of Religion and Ethics,* the *Encyclopedia of World Art,* and the *Encyclopedia of Science and Technology.*

END POVERTY IN CALIFORNIA. *See* **EPIC.**

ENEMY ALIENS IN THE WORLD WARS. The Alien Enemies Act of 1798, reaffirmed by the Supreme Court in 1948, authorizes the president to expel from the country any alien whom he regards as dangerous to the public peace or safety or whom he believes to be plotting against the country. The Internal Security Act of 1950 and the Immigration and Nationality Act (McCarran-Walter Act) of 1952 give the attorney general authority to hold an alien in custody without bail. The Espionage Act of June 15, 1917, allowed for imprisonment of up to twenty years and a fine of $10,000 for disloyal statements or attempts to interfere with recruitment and enlistment. Furthermore, the president ordered enemy aliens to stay away from military camps and munition factories, and they were not allowed to enter or leave the United States without special permission. Although the total number of enemy aliens interned was comparatively small—2,300 of the

6,300 arrested—procedural protection was minimal, and suspects were often arrested and held without trial. Alien property came under the jurisdiction of the Office of the Alien Property Custodian, established by the Trading with the Enemy Act of 1917. Enemy aliens lost jobs because of suspicion, and vigilante groups and amateur spy catchers harassed them. Popular idiocy reached its zenith with the renaming of sauerkraut "liberty cabbage"; of dachsunds "liberty pups"; and of German measles "liberty measles."

By contrast the treatment of enemy aliens during World War II, with the lamentable exception of the Japanese (*see* Japanese-Americans in World War II), was more enlightened at both the public and official levels. Unfortunately, the deep-seated West Coast prejudice toward Orientals, combined with the hysteria of the early war years, produced enough pressure to cause exclusionary action by President Franklin Roosevelt. In 1942, Executive Order No. 9066 gave the secretary of war the power to restrict designated military areas. About 110,000 Japanese-Americans, some 70,000 of whom were U.S. citizens, were then transferred from California, Oregon, Washington, and Arizona to relocation camps in the interior. Vigilante action against aliens was virtually unknown during World War II, and the excesses of anti-German feeling did not reappear, although enemy aliens from Germany, Italy, and Japan were required to be fingerprinted (as all aliens were) and to carry identification cards. By the middle of the war 4,132 dangerous enemy aliens had been interned.

ENEMY DESTINATION. A doctrine of the international law of neutrality legalizing seizures on the high seas (or, in recent wars, after diversion into control ports) of contraband cargoes carried in neutral ships between neutral ports, when there is evidence of enemy destination. To prevent neutrals from taking over the trade between the French colonies and France during the 18th century and from taking over the Spanish colonial trade later, British courts held neutral ships to be part of the enemy merchant marine when neutral trade exceeded limits customary in time of peace (Rule of the War of 1756). To circumvent the British rule, Americans carried goods from the French West Indies to American ports and reshipped them to France, ostensibly independent voyages from neutral ports. The British then developed the doctrine that such shipments constituted continuous voyages between the enemy ports of origin and ultimate destinations. This rule was applied to contraband by 1761 and to blockade by 1804.

Although Americans denied the validity of the rule throughout the Napoleonic period, they embraced it during the Civil War. Seizures occurred in the first lap, when ships went from England to a neutral West Indian port, with intent to proceed to Confederate ports shown by evidence of absolute contraband, open bills of lading, or incriminating correspondence. Although intent to run the blockade was mentioned by courts, it was not a necessary element in view of proof of contraband. In the *Peterhoff* incident the continuous "voyage" was overland, an antecedent of frequent continuous transportation situations in the two world wars. The London Naval Conference of 1909 recommended application of the doctrine of continuous voyage to absolute, but not to conditional, contraband or to blockade; nevertheless the British applied it to all these situations in the world wars, and U.S. protests during the period of American neutrality were abandoned after entry into the wars.

ENFORCEMENT ACTS. *See* **Force Acts.**

ENGAGÉ. *See* **Voyageurs.**

ENGINEERING EDUCATION. The earliest and, for a time, most prominent engineering school in America was the U.S. Military Academy at West Point, N.Y. (1802), particularly after 1817, when Sylvanus Thayer remodeled the institution along the lines of France's École Polytechnique. In the 1830's and 1840's, many Americans went abroad for scientific and technical training or to analyze and report on European methods of technical instruction. By that process, many institutions begun in a mood of democratic reform during the Jacksonian era to educate the working classes were transformed into specialized schools for advanced study. Thus, Amos Eaton's Rensselaer school, founded in 1824 to teach science to the children of farmers and artisans, was by the late 1840's metamorphosed into a polytechnic institute for the training of professional engineers. Professional technical instruction was begun at Harvard (1847), Yale (1847), the University of Pennsylvania (1847), Dartmouth (1851), and the University of Michigan (1852).

To 19th-century Americans, it seemed more democratic to locate technical instruction at an advanced level; a less intellectually ambitious vocational kind of training smacked of class distinctions. And yet, the European emphasis on rigorous preparation in mathematics and science ran counter to a persistent pattern in the United States of practically oriented, on-the-job training for engineers, and the new American schools were faced with determining the relative importance of practical and theoretical content in their programs. Technical educators tended to emphasize engineering theory. Employers, however, wanted engineers who could directly and profitably solve the problems of field and factory.

William Barton Rogers's first ideas for the Massachusetts Institute of Technology, founded in 1859, called for a school of such intellectual strength that it "would soon overtop the universities of the land" but which at the same time would teach practical knowledge of direct utility. Most of the agricultural and mechanical colleges founded after passage of the Morrill Act in 1862 tried the same combination.

Coleman Sellers, one of the founders of the American Society of Mechanical Engineers (1880), was a spokesman for the view that engineers should be trained broadly in order to participate effectively in social and political life, but engineering schools were dominated by the attitude that technological progress demanded specialized education and separate facilities. Robert H. Thurston, dean of engineering at Cornell University, insisted that engineering departments flourished best the further removed they were from nontechnical departments. Thurston's version of an ideal system of engineering education encompassed a complete range of institutions—from grammar schools where children would be taught only technical terminology to advanced research institutes that would also serve to guide government policy in technological matters. Thurston's concept of an elementary education was never realized, but engineering educators found his arguments for thoroughly professional training attractive. The formation of the American Society for Engineering Education (1893) gave technical educators a mechanism to explore both their needs and the perplexing curricular questions of a separate, but intellectually equal, university program.

Another compelling factor in shaping engineering education along specialized lines was an increasing industrial demand for skilled technicians. Stevens Institute of Technology (1870) in New Jersey, for example, was established specifically to provide advanced training in mechanical engineering. Case Institute (1880) in Ohio, Georgia Institute of Technology (1888), and the California Institute of Technology (1891) were also begun in response to the needs of new and technically sophisticated manufacturing activities. Two world wars further revealed the importance of trained engineers, and such schools as the California Institute of Technology and the Massachusetts Institute of Technology came to fulfill Thurston's hopes for technical institutions of intellectual prestige and political power.

Stimulated by federal funds, engineering schools found their enrollments increasing dramatically in the postwar period. The tensions of the cold war and the shock of *Sputnik 1* provided a windfall in the form of funds from the public purse—first, in the formation of the National Science Foundation (1950), which pumped money into basic research, and then by the passage of the National Defense Education Act (1958), which explicitly tied the country's security to scientific and technical training.

ENGINEERING SOCIETIES. The first engineering societies were local. The Boston Society of Civil Engineers (1848), the Engineers Club of St. Louis (1868), and the Western Society of Engineers of Chicago (1869) were among the first but were gradually overshadowed by national ones. The American Society of Civil Engineers, founded in 1852, did not become active nationally until revitalized in 1867. It set high professional standards and claimed to represent all nonmilitary engineers, a claim made moot in 1871 by the founding of the American Institute of Mining and Metallurgical Engineers. The increased employment of engineers in industry led to the formation of the American Society of Mechanical Engineers in 1880 and the American Institute of Electrical Engineers in 1884.

The headlong progress of technology created new technical specialties almost yearly, and new societies were founded to meet their needs, such as the Society of Automotive Engineers (1905), the American Institute of Chemical Engineers (1908), and the Institute of Radio Engineers (1912), which merged with the American Institute of Electrical Engineers in 1963 to form the Institute of Electrical and Electronic Engineers.

One of the first groups to express a spirit of professional unity was the American Association of Engineers, founded in 1915, which lobbied vigorously for state licensing laws for engineers and on other issues. Internal dissensions weakened this organization, but much of its program was continued by the National Society of Professional Engineers (1934).

The profession's social responsibility was a theme of many agencies sponsored by societies. The first, the Engineering Council (1917), assisted the government in mobilizing engineering talent during World War I. It was replaced in 1920 by the more representative Federated American Engineering Societies; Herbert Hoover was first president of the federation. The reports of these committees were critical of business practices and antagonized powerful conservative elements within the founder societies. In 1924 the American Institute of Mining Engineers withdrew from the federation, which was reorganized as the American Engineering Council and became a spokesman for right-wing views until dissolved in 1939. A new unity organization, the Engineers Joint Council (1945), helped to secure the creation of the National Academy of Engineering in 1964, under the charter of the National Academy of Science, to advise the nation on public policy.

ENGINEERS, CORPS OF. The world's largest engineering force, the U.S. Army Corps of Engineers is the only organization of its kind that fulfills both military and civil missions. Within the army it acts as a combat arm and a technical service; within the federal government, as a national construction agency. It built the breastworks at Bunker Hill, the Cumberland Road, the Panama Canal, Fort Peck Dam, and the Manhattan Project.

On June 16, 1775, the Continental Congress authorized a chief engineer for the Grand Army and three years later provided for three companies of sappers and miners. The corps helped assure the success of George Washington's Fabian strategy and the decisive siege at Yorktown. Disbanded in 1783, engineer units reappeared in 1794 as elements of the short-lived Corps of Artillerists and Engineers.

The present organization dates from 1802, when President Thomas Jefferson signed a bill providing for a corps of engineers to be stationed at West Point, N.Y., and to "constitute a military academy." The first engineering school in the United States, West Point was also the leading one until the Civil War. Composed almost exclusively of top academy graduates, the Corps of Engineers with its temporary offshoot, the Corps of Topographical Engineers, formed the only sizable group of trained engineers in the country.

In the 19th century, the corps built roads, canals, piers, and lighthouses, and took part in surveys and explorations. From 1824 onward, Congress assigned the corps increasing responsibility for river and harbor projects for building thousands of miles of inland waterways and hundreds of deep-water harbors, with far-reaching benefits in flood control, power production, water conservation, pollution abatement, and recreation. Since the 1950's the corps has also been active in space, missile, and postal construction.

ENGLISH COMPROMISE OF 1858. During the fight in Congress over admission of Kansas as a slave or free state,

Rep. William Hayden English of Indiana offered an amendment, passed on May 4, providing for an election on Aug. 2 in which Kansans would vote on the acceptance of a large government land grant to Kansas. If accepted, Kansas would become a state under the proslavery Lecompton Constitution. If rejected, statehood would be postponed until Kansas had a larger population. The voters rejected the proposition.

ENGLISH SETTLEMENT (Ill.). A colony for English artisans and laborers established by Morris Birkbeck and George Flower in Edwards County, Ill. The first immigrants arrived in 1818. Thereafter, for nearly thirty-five years, new groups from England arrived periodically, enabling the settlement to retain its homogeneity. Two towns were established: Wanborough, which soon died, and Albion, a town that in 1980 had a population of 12,285.

ENLISTMENT. While in colonial times service in the militia was compulsory in most colonies, forces raised for long expeditions outside the colony or for extended service were usually composed of volunteers. Voluntary enlistment was also the method by which Continental forces were raised. It was initially for one year, but in 1777 was increased to three years or the duration of the war; the one-year term was restored in 1778 because of the failure to secure enough long-term volunteers, despite bounties, land grants, and other incentives.

In 1783, the country began a peacetime dependence on volunteer enlistments in the armed forces that endured down to the passage of the first peacetime conscription act in 1940. Enlistment in volunteer units under state auspices was the primary method of raising forces in all American wars down to World War I.

In the world wars the draft supplanted army enlistment, but the navy and the marines relied on volunteers until 1943. Between 1945 and 1973 only the army relied on the draft as well as on enlistment to fill its ranks. On June 30, 1973, the postwar draft came to an end, and all the services again recruited by enlistment. The terms of enlistment have varied but have generally been for from three to five years.

ENLISTMENT IN THE UNION ARMY. In the Civil War, Union enlistment was largely in the hands of state officials. Bounties, often immense, were offered from the start. Enlistments during the war were for various periods: three, six, nine, and twelve months, or two, three, and five years. The president's delay in calling Congress in 1861 did much to cool the fervor for enlistment at a time when there was a large labor surplus and a holiday attitude toward joining the army and crushing the secessionists. Nevertheless, the seasonal agricultural labor surplus in the fall of 1861 made it possible to assemble a volunteer army of 640,000 by December.

On Dec. 3, 1861, Gen. George B. McClellan decreed a complete reorganization of the recruiting service, which, however, was dismantled by Secretary of War Edwin M. Stanton in a burst of overconfidence on Apr. 3, 1862. The wasting of the army by death, desertion, and sickness in early 1862 convinced Stanton to revive the service on June 6. Enlistment had almost ceased, so Secretary of State William H. Seward schemed to get the governors to appeal to the president for a call for troops to clinch a final victory, presumed to be imminent. On July 17, 1862, a law was passed calling for a draft of 300,000 militia for nine months of service. When that failed, the Enrollment Act of Mar. 3, 1863, was passed to draft 300,000 men for three years. From then on, adequate enlistment was had only by means of bounties stimulated by fear of the draft. The total number of enlistments for the war was 2,865,028.

ENOREE, BATTLE OF (Nov. 20, 1780). Thomas Sumter drew Sir Banastre Tarleton into battle at Blackstock's Plantation between the Tyger and Enoree rivers in South Carolina. Sumter was wounded, but Tarleton lost more than ninety killed and as many wounded. American losses were three killed and five wounded.

ENSIGN. The lowest commissioned rank in the U.S. Navy and Coast Guard. In the colonial militia, in the Revolution infantry, and in the regular army until 1815 (except for 1799–1800) it was a rank lower than first, second, or third lieutenant; in the navy, it superseded midshipman in 1862.

ENTAIL OF ESTATE. Under feudal law the grantee of an estate could not sell or give away any of it, and on his death it was inherited by his eldest son; common law, however, favored free disposition of such tenures. Entailing of estates was relatively common in colonial America, especially in the agricultural South and Middle States. Stout opposition developed because of the belief that it was dangerous to perpetuate a political bloc of landed aristocrats in America. In several colonies, recourse was had to common recovery; in others, legislative acts allowed free disposition. By the Revolution, colonial opinion was opposed to entail. Many of the original states followed the lead taken by Virginia in 1776 in abolishing entail.

ENTANGLING ALLIANCES. A phrase turned by Thomas Jefferson, not George Washington. Washington advised against "permanent alliances," while Jefferson, in his inaugural address (Mar. 4, 1801), declared his devotion to "peace, commerce, and honest friendship with all nations, entangling alliances with none." It is a pet phrase of isolationists warning against foreign commitments.

***ENTERPRISE-BOXER* ENGAGEMENT** (Sept. 5, 1813). Off Monhegan Island, Maine, the U.S. brig *Enterprise,* commanded by Lt. William Burrows, defeated the British brig *Boxer,* commanded by Capt. Samuel Blyth, in a hard-fought forty-minute action.

***ENTRADA*.** A term denoting the entrance of *conquistadores* into lands being explored or settled. The most significant *entradas* were highly spectacular as well as forcible. Juan de Oñate's *entrada* into New Mexico for colonization purposes was marked by a carriage of household goods and gods as well as military equipment.

ENUMERATED COMMODITIES. Colonial products permitted to be exported only to limited destinations, generally to Great Britain or its colonies. The first article enumerated was tobacco in 1621, by order in council. Later enumerations were by specific acts of Parliament and included sugar, tobacco, and other common commodities. The object of much of this legislation was to prevent important colonial products from reaching European markets except by way of England. There was one exception to the regulation: direct trade from the colonies was permitted to points in Europe south of Cape Finisterre, Spain, for rice, 1730; sugar, 1739; and all additional colonial products enumerated, 1766–67. After 1765 rice could be exported to any place south of Finisterre and was not limited to Europe, giving American rice an open market in the Spanish colonies. (*See also* Navigation Acts.)

ENUMERATED POWERS. Powers specifically given to the federal government by the U.S. Constitution to avoid encroachment on the powers of the states or the people thereof. Those given to Congress are contained in large part in Articles I (especially Section 8), IV, and V. Article II creates the office of president of the United States and vests him with the executive power. Enumerated powers are, by the Ninth and Tenth amendments in the Bill of Rights, "not to be construed to deny or disparage others retained by the people," and "the powers not delegated to the United States by the Constitution, nor prohibited by it to the States, are reserved to the States respectively, or to the people."

ENVOY EXTRAORDINARY. *See* **Ambassadors.**

EPHRATA. A communal organization founded near Lancaster, Pa., in 1735 as a religious retreat by German Seventh Day Baptists led by Conrad Beissel. The institution comprised, besides householders, two monastic orders, Sisters and Brethren. The community operated numerous mills; a tannery; a bakehouse; a bookbindery; and, most famous, a printing press, set up in 1745, which produced the first printed music in America. The Sisters did fine pen and needlework. Ephrata won renown for its vocal music, its academy, and its Sunday school. The monastic features of the community had died out by 1800, and the congregation ceased to exist shortly after Ephrata became a borough of Pennsylvania in 1891.

EPIC. An acronym for End Poverty in California, a scheme devised by Upton Sinclair, Democratic candidate in 1934 for the governorship. The twelve principles of EPIC and its twelve political planks appealed to an electorate concerned about the depression. Sinclair was defeated by a small margin.

EPIDEMICS. "Epidemic" is a relative term depending upon the availability and reliability of vital statistics. Prior to the 20th century, statistics on mortality and morbidity were scarce and unreliable, so many outbreaks of disease passed unnoticed. To be considered epidemic, a disease had to reach large enough proportions to attract general attention.

In the colonial period, the chief epidemic diseases were smallpox; yellow fever; and diphtheria, which first swept the colonies in 1735. These disorders on occasion decimated towns and cities. In addition, periodic outbreaks of measles, scarlet fever, influenza, and other diseases aroused concern.

In the 19th century, smallpox was brought under control in some measure by vaccination, and the incidence of diphtheria declined. A series of yellow fever epidemics, beginning in Philadelphia in 1793, struck at every major American port city for the next twelve years. The attacks on southern ports peaked in the 1850's. In New Orleans, La., three epidemics during that decade killed 14,000 residents. Yellow fever then spread far up the inland waterways. Yellow fever epidemics tapered off after the Civil War, the last outbreak occurring in New Orleans in 1905.

The second major epidemic disease of the 19th century was Asiatic cholera, which struck twice with a major impact, in 1832–35 and 1849–55. As a filth disease, it fell before the advancing sanitary movement of the mid-19th century. In the 20th century the only comparable outbreak of disease was the great influenza epidemic of 1918–19, with a death toll of 450,000. (*See also* Cholera; Influenza; Poliomyelitis.)

EPISCOPAL CHURCH. The Protestant Episcopal church is the representative of the Anglican communion in the United States. The Revolution left the church divided and weakened. The New England wing of the church, which had been moving in a High Church direction, and the more moderate wing, located primarily in the southern and Middle Atlantic states, met in general convention in Philadelphia in 1785 and ironed out their differences. The result was the adoption of a modified Book of Common Prayer and a church government that united the historic values of episcopacy with considerable local and lay control.

Clashes between the new Anglo-Catholic theology of the Oxford movement (Tractarianism) and more traditional understandings of the episcopal position were common in the 19th century. The general convention became a testing ground of the opposing factions, and although the issue seldom appeared in formal resolutions, it lay behind other actions. The last serious eruption of the controversy occurred in 1873, when a small party withdrew from the church to establish the Reformed Episcopal church.

In the 20th century the Protestant Episcopal church has maintained a moderately liberal theological position that comprehends all positions. Heavily influenced by the so-called Social Gospel, it has stressed its social services and urban ministries. In the 1970's the church began to ordain women and revised the American Prayer Book, causing deep dissension. The 1980 membership was 2.8 million.

E PLURIBUS UNUM **("from the many, one").** Motto on the seal of the United States, selected by Benjamin Franklin, John Adams, and Thomas Jefferson (1776).

EQUAL EMPLOYMENT OPPORTUNITY COMMISSION. A federal agency created to administer Title VII of the Civil Rights Act of 1964, which prohibits discrimination in employment based on race, color, religion, sex, or national origin. Its mandate covers all employment conditions, including hiring, job classification, job assignment, pay, promotion, layoff, and firing. The commission descends from the Fair Employment Practices Committee (FEPC), created in 1941 by executive order to monitor fair employment practices in federal civil service and in industries essential to the war effort or holding government contracts and terminated in 1946. Legislative support for such an agency did not exist until 1964.

EQUALITY, DOCTRINE OF. The modern doctrine of equality is rooted in the Hobbesian-Lockean assertion of the equal right of every man to his own self-preservation in the state of nature. In *Leviathan* (1651), English philosopher Thomas Hobbes reasons that the right of self-preservation is the fundamental natural right, and the equality of that right makes men equal in the most fundamental respect. Thus, they must have equal rights in determining the means.

In his *Second Treatise of Government* (1690), English philosopher John Locke asserts that the equality of humans rests in their being members of a single species; thus, no man is by nature governor over another and all men are free. This same order—equality first and freedom second—appears in the Declaration of Independence. That "all men are created equal" is regarded as a self-evident truth; and the rights of life, liberty, and the pursuit of happiness are seen to be derivative from it. The declaration implies that men lived as individuals in the state of nature. In the predominantly Lockean understanding of the declaration, however, civil society is constituted by a movement away from the condition in which the equality of all men is actual. In Abraham Lincoln's reinterpretation of the declaration during the slavery controversy, civil society is constituted by a movement toward that condition and equality is ultimately secured to all by the law of the land.

EQUALIZATION FEE. *See* **McNary-Haugen Bill.**

EQUAL PROTECTION OF THE LAW. The Fourteenth Amendment of the U.S. Constitution provides that no state shall deny any person the equal protection of the law. Since the clause does not forbid reasonable classification if individuals within each category are accorded equal treatment, in the *Civil Rights Cases* (1883) the Supreme Court accepted racial classification, even though the provision's clear purpose was to protect newly emancipated Afro-Americans. It confined the clause's applicability to state-enacted discriminations.

In *Plessy* v. *Ferguson* (1896) the Court sanctioned state-imposed segregation, provided that the separate accommodations were substantially equal. Everyone ignored the duty to keep the accommodations equal, until in 1938 the Court began moving toward a literal reading of the equal protection clause; it narrowed the definition of state action, declaring a state party to discrimination if it does not try to eliminate it.

From the *Gaines* case (1938) to *Brown* v. *Board of Education* (1954) the Court applied the clause with increasing rigor, concluding in *Brown* that separate facilities equal in every tangible respect deny equal protection because of the emotional damage to those set apart solely because of race. In 1957, Congress passed the first federal civil rights act in eighty-two years, followed by others in 1960, 1964, 1965, and 1968.

The clause was also invoked in *Baker* v. *Carr* (1962) and *Reynolds* v. *Sims* (1964), in which the Court laid down the one-man, one-vote principle, holding that the equal protection clause requires all members of state legislatures to be elected from districts roughly equal in population. The clause was invoked to forbid laws against interracial marriage; denial of welfare benefits to resident aliens; laws hampering minor parties; requirement of extraordinary majorities to approve bond issues; and discrimination against women in employment.

EQUAL RIGHTS AMENDMENT (ERA). Providing "equality of rights under the law shall not be denied or abridged by the United States or by any state on account of sex," the bill was first introduced to Congress in 1923, but remained bottled up in the House Judiciary Committee for forty-seven years. It was finally passed by Congress on Mar. 22, 1972, and sent to the states for ratification. By 1975, thirty-five states (of the thirty-eight needed) had ratified the proposed amendment, but only one legislature did so after 1975. After heated debate, Congress in 1978 extended the deadline for ratification from Mar. 22, 1979, to June 30, 1982. Although ERA supporters made an intensive lobbying effort to get the final three necessary state endorsements, Idaho federal judge Marion Callister ruled on Dec. 23, 1981, that Congress had acted illegally in extending the ratification deadline, and that five states that had nullified their previous endorsements be removed from the ratification list. ERA supporters appealed to the Supreme Court, but by June 30, 1982, ratification was still three states short, and the measure was defeated.

EQUAL RIGHTS PARTY. A minor political party, 1884–88, which had as its objective the enfranchisement of women. It also advocated repression of the liquor traffic; uniform legislation with respect to marriage, divorce, and property; civil service reform; and an end to war. Its candidate for president was Belva A. Lockwood. The party failed to receive support even from the suffrage organizations and polled at most 2,000 votes.

ERA. *See* **Equal Rights Amendment.**

ERA OF GOOD FEELING (1817–24). A phrase originated by the *Columbian Centinel* (Boston, Mass., July 12, 1817) and widely used to describe President James Monroe's two administrations. The demise of the Federalist party gave the appearance of political union in strong nationalism, illustrated by the tariff act of 1816, the second National Bank, and western development. Monroe weathered the panic of 1819, and received all but one electoral vote in 1820.

ERIE (Pa.). Pennsylvania city facing on Lake Erie, with a population of 119,123 according to the 1980 census; it was the center of a metropolitan area of 263,654. The only lake port in the state, it is an important business and manufacturing center, with paper mills and machinery-making and electrical-equipment factories. The port is well protected by Presque Isle peninsula, which had been the French headquarters on Lake Erie in the 1750's. The U.S. lake squadron that fought the Battle of Lake Erie had been built there. Erie became a vital industrial center after the completion of the Erie and Pittsburgh Canal in 1844. The canal, and railroads that followed it, made Erie the chief port for gathering iron ore from Michigan and Minnesota to be shipped to Pittsburgh.

ERIE, FORT. A British fort erected on the left bank of the Niagara River at Lake Erie by Capt. John Montresor in 1764. It was destroyed in 1779 and rebuilt a short distance south in 1791. The new fort was damaged by storm in 1803, and another was started on higher ground in 1805. In the War of 1812 it changed hands several times until the fortifications were destroyed by the Americans on Nov. 5, 1814.

ERIE, LAKE. The fourth largest of the Great Lakes. It was named after the Erie (or Cat Nation), an Indian tribe living south of the lake who were exterminated by the Iroquois about 1655. The first white man on its waters was Louis Jolliet, who, in 1669, followed its northern shore on a return trip from the upper lakes. Two missionaries, François Dollier de Casson and René de Bréhant de Galinée, took formal possession for Louis XIV. In 1679, Robert Cavelier, Sieur de La Salle, launched the first ship on Lake Erie, the *Griffon,* which disappeared on a return voyage from the upper lakes. Rivalries between French and English over the western fur trade gave the lake a strategic importance. Holding Detroit and Niagara, the French were secure until the end of the French and Indian War.

From 1763 until 1796, British-Indian control was maintained despite the Definitive Treaty of Peace of 1783, which placed the international boundary in the middle of the lake. With the surrender of the border posts by Jay's Treaty (1794), American settlements spread along the southern shore. In the War of 1812 a British fleet took control of the lake until the Battle of Lake Erie. In the peace negotiations the British were compelled to yield the lakes (*see* Ghent, Treaty of). In 1818 the Rush-Bagot Agreement neutralized all the Great Lakes.

The completion of the Erie Canal, the construction of Ohio's canal system, and the spread of settlement increased lake traffic rapidly. As part of the St. Lawrence Seaway, it has contributed to the economic development of Buffalo, N.Y.; Erie, Pa.; the Ohio lake ports; and Detroit, Mich.

ERIE, LAKE, BATTLE OF (Sept. 10, 1813). The major naval engagement on the Great Lakes in the War of 1812 insured American control of Lake Erie and thus the freedom to invade Canada. It also forestalled any cession of territory in the Northwest to Great Britain in the treaty of peace (*see* Ghent, Treaty of).

Commodore Oliver Hazard Perry's fleet of one captured brig and the two brigs and six schooners he had built at Erie, Pa., blockaded Malden, the British base, obliging the British force of three brigs and three schooners to come out for supplies. The fleets met soon after noon, with Perry having the advantage of the windward position. Perry ordered the *Caledonia* and the *Niagara* to support the *Lawrence* in concentrating on the head of the British line. Because of previous orders, Jesse D. Elliott of the *Niagara* felt he must keep behind the *Caledonia* rather than use his superior sailing power to pass ahead (*see* Perry-Elliott Controversy). As a result of the light air and the slow sailing of the *Caledonia,* the *Lawrence,* unsupported, sustained the fire of the larger British ships for over two hours until 80 percent of its crew was killed or wounded and the ship badly damaged. At 2:30 P.M., Perry was rowed through dangerous fire to the *Niagara,* which he ordered into close action. Securing a position ahead of the two strongest British ships, the *Detroit* and the *Queen Charlotte,* Perry poured in raking broadsides. Robert H. Barclay, the British commander, soon surrendered. From the *Lawrence,* Perry sent his famous message to Gen. William Henry Harrison, the commander of the American army in the Northwest, "We have met the enemy, and they are ours."

ERIE CANAL. The New York legislature in 1808 authorized a survey and in 1810 set up a commission that selected Lake Erie for the western terminus of an artificial waterway to the Great Lakes through the Mohawk Gateway. DeWitt Clinton, later governor (1817–22, 1824–28), was responsible for its execution. He prodded the legislature in 1817 to authorize construction.

The 4-foot-deep ditch was 363 miles long, with eighty-three locks lifting boats a total of over 600 feet; it cost over $7 million. In 1825, Clinton led a procession of canal boats from Buffalo to New York City.

The success of the Erie Canal led to a "canal mania." The legislature constructed branches in Oswego, Chenango, Genesee Valley, Black River, Cayuga, and Seneca. By the 1870's canal tonnage had fallen substantially because of competition from the railroads. The abolition of tolls in 1882 did not check the Erie's decline. The Erie Canal became part of the New York State Barge Canal system, built between 1909 and 1918.

ERIE LACKAWANNA. *See* **Railroads, Sketches of Principal Lines.**

ERIE RAILROAD. *See* **Railroads, Sketches of Principal Lines: Erie Lackawanna.**

***ERIE RAILROAD COMPANY* V. *TOMPKINS*,** 304 U.S. 64 (1938). The Judiciary Act of 1789 provides that in diversity-of-citizenship cases federal courts must apply "the laws of the several states, except where the Constitution, treaties, or statutes of the United States shall otherwise require." In 1842, in *Swift* v. *Tyson,* the Supreme Court held that the act had encompassed only state statutory law; henceforth federal courts would be free to ignore state common law and to apply their own. In *Erie* v. *Tompkins,* the Court overruled *Swift* as an unconstitutional assumption of power by federal courts. The doctrine that has evolved from the *Erie* ruling generally requires that federal courts in diversity-of-citizenship cases apply state statutory and common law within the framework of the Federal Rules of Civil Procedure.

ERIE TRIANGLE. About 200,000 acres bounded by Lake Erie, N.Y., and the forty-second parallel was part of the territory ceded to the United States by New York and Massachusetts in 1781 and 1785, respectively. Pennsylvania bought it in 1788.

ERSKINE'S AGREEMENT (Apr. 18–19, 1809). David M. Erskine of Great Britain and Secretary of State Robert Smith agreed on a withdrawal of the British Orders in Council of January and November 1807 against U.S. trade and restoration of U.S. commercial intercourse. Erskine was recalled and relations between England and America grew worse, because he failed to get a U.S. agreement not to trade with colonies of Britain's enemies.

ESCALANTE-DOMÍNGUEZ EXPEDITION (1776–77). To open intercourse between Santa Fe, N.Mex., and the new port of Monterey, Calif., and to explore for new Indian peoples to evangelize, a party headed by Fray Silvestre Vélez de Escalante and Fray Francisco Atanacio Domínguez started from Santa Fe, July 29, 1776. It followed the Chama River, crossed the San Juan (or Navajoo), and reached the Great Salt Lake Valley. Unable to secure native guides, it abandoned the effort to reach Monterey. Turning south through Cedar Valley, it went eastward through the "Arizona strip" and crossed the Colorado at the Ford of the Fathers (later, Lee's Ferry). After reaching Oraibi, it followed known trails to Zuni, Acoma, Laguna, and Isleta, and arrived in Santa Fe on Jan. 3, 1777. In five months it had covered about 2,000 miles and extended Spanish claims northward nearly to the forty-second parallel.

ESCALATOR CLAUSE. Article 21 of the London Naval Treaty of Apr. 22, 1930, permitted the United States, Great Britain, and Japan to increase their tonnage in cruisers, destroyers, and submarines, in the same proportions as agreed upon in the treaty if the new construction of other powers "materially affected" their own security. This principle was maintained in the London Naval Treaty of Mar. 25, 1936, between the United States, Great Britain, and France.

ESCH-CUMMINS ACT. *See* **Transportation Act of 1920.**

ESKIMO. The Eskimo (or Inuit), one of the most widely distributed peoples of the world, inhabit the area from southeastern Alaska around the Arctic coasts to eastern Greenland. Yet a mode of life based on hunting has tended to limit population growth. At no point do the Eskimo appear to have exceeded 60,000, excluding 16,000 Aleut, a linguistically related people.

The Eskimo are the one people in the world whose physical type, language, and basic culture are common to the entire population. The uniqueness of the Eskimo is manifested in the presence of the language phylum, Eskaleut, appearing nowhere else in the world; and a social organization based on the hunting of sea and land mammals.

They have made use of every hunting resource available to them. Whaling, for example, was practiced in north Alaska, in fragile skin-covered boats. Where no other game was available, the ubiquitous seal served as the economic mainstay. Some Eskimo pushed inland to make capital of the caribou. In line with the demands of the environment the Eskimo were highly inventive. The central Eskimo invented the iglu for quasi-permanent residence and for temporary shelter on the hunt. The harpoon with detachable shaft, the saucerlike stone lamp, tailored clothing, special footgear, boats, sleds and sledges, dog traction, and the use of driftwood are elements of the Eskimo culture. Yet the stress on the material tended to limit the growth of their society. There are no chiefs, and the community lacks corporate reality because of the stress on lines of kinship.

ESOPUS. *See* **Kingston.**

ESOPUS WAR (1659–64). The Esopus, a division of the Munsee Indians, were part of the Delaware Confederacy. The war was started by settlers at the mouth of the Esopus River (present-day Kingston, N.Y.) who fired into a group of intoxicated Esopus Indians, who retaliated by attacking the Dutch village. The Dutch declared war and routed the tribes. A truce was declared, but Peter Stuyvesant had sent some Indian captives to Curaçao as slaves and this remained a source of grievance. Three years later the Indians suddenly attacked the settlements at the Esopus, killing twenty-one persons and taking forty-five prisoners, most of whom were recovered. In May 1664, a treaty of peace was signed.

ESPIONAGE, INDUSTRIAL. The systematic use of spies by American companies to report on their employees began after the Civil War. Employers originally recruited spies from the work force but eventually hired trained men. Spies reported on various matters, such as inefficiency, theft, worker unrest, and union activity. In 1937 the U.S. Senate Committee on Education and Labor stated that American companies employed labor spies in virtually every plant and union. The maturation of labor-management relations after World War II brought a virtual end to antiunion espionage. Industrial espionage is now largely confined to spying by companies upon each other. The practice is systematic among competitive industries affected by changes in fashion or taste.

ESPIONAGE ACT (War and National Defense Act; June 15, 1917). Authorized severe punishments for any person transmitting information, or attempting to do so, regarding the national defense, or for interfering with the national forces in any way. Material urging insurrection, treason, or forcible resistance to U.S. laws was declared to be nonmailable. On May 16, 1918, amendments, generally referred to as the Sedition Act, were added to provide heavy punishment for anyone who should, during war, "utter, print, write, or publish any disloyal, profane, scurrilous, or abusive language" about the flag, the armed forces, the Constitution, or the form of government. Under the act more than 1,500 persons were arrested, one of whom was Socialist leader Eugene Debs, who was later pardoned by President Warren G. Harding (1921). By World War II the 1917 act had been modified by an act of Mar. 28, 1940, and under its provisions 160 wartime cases of espionage were tried. In the postwar period, Ethel and Julius Rosenberg were found guilty of spying for the Soviet Union and executed in 1953. Present-day espionage laws show numerous amendments and clarifications found in Title 18, U.S. Code (1970).

***ESSEX*, ACTIONS OF THE** (1812–14). During the War of 1812 the *Essex*, under Capt. David Porter, inflicted a loss of $6 million on British whaling in the South Pacific. The *Essex*, the first U.S. warship to round Cape Horn, captured British whalers around the Galápagos Islands in March–September 1813. Outside of Valparaíso, in neutral waters, on Mar. 28, 1814, it was attacked by the British frigate *Phoebe* and the sloop *Cherub*. Hampered by the loss of his maintopmast in a squall, Porter resisted stubbornly for two hours but was compelled to surrender.

***ESSEX* CASE** (1804). A prize case decided by the British High Court of Admiralty in August 1804 that further refined the doctrine of continuous voyage. The court ruled that "the mere touching at any port without importing the cargo into the common stocks of the country" constituted a continuous voyage and the goods therefore were forfeit. The decision increased the seizures of U.S. vessels and aggravated the tension between Great Britain and the United States.

ESSEX JUNTO. A group of "men of education and property," representatives of Essex County, Mass., who came together at Ipswich in April 1778 to consider a new state constitution. Their adverse opinion, expressed in the "Essex Result," of the proposals of John Hancock caused him to so name the group. They long were the dominant group in the Federalist party and favored adoption of the federal Constitution and Alexander Hamilton's financial program, and opposed the Embargo Act of 1807, bringing about its repeal. Because of bitter opposition to Jefferson and to the War of 1812, the junto came to be called the "British faction." Its continued opposition to the war led to the calling of the Hartford Convention.

ESSEX WILDCAT BANK. At Guildhall, Essex County, Vt., chartered Nov. 7, 1832, it was one of the numerous wildcat banks that issued irredeemable currency before the National Banking Act of 1863. The bank had issued a large amount of currency on no capital whatever, except $2,000 in stockholders' notes.

ESTABLISHED CHURCHES. Churches supported by tax funds or by direct grants of aid. The Congregational Church was established in several New England colonies and the Church of England in part of New York and some southern colonies. Churches were disestablished during and after the Revolution.

ETERNAL CENTER. The first large crude oil strike in present West Virginia. It was in the Burning Springs Field (Wirt County) and was made in December 1860.

ETHNOLOGY, BUREAU OF AMERICAN. Established Mar. 3, 1879, as the Bureau of Ethnology, when Congress transferred to the Smithsonian Institution ethnological investigations of the American Indians. Maj. John Wesley Powell headed the bureau. With limited resources, the foremost center for the scientific study of the American Indians produced many publications on linguistics, ethnology, archaeology, physical anthropology, and Indian history. In 1964 the bureau was merged into the Department of Anthropology of the U.S. National Museum.

EUTAW SPRINGS, BATTLE OF (Sept. 8, 1781). The last important engagement of the Revolution in South Carolina. It was forced on the British Col. Alexander Stewart by Gen. Nathanael Greene to prevent aid to Lord Cornwallis, should he return to the state. Both commanders attacked successfully with their right wings, but the British forced Greene from the field. Stewart, however, was unable to retain his position and retreated next day. The battle had no effect on the Yorktown campaign, but British losses made them retire to Charleston for the remainder of the war.

EVANGELICAL ALLIANCE. An early attempt at cooperation among Protestants. The alliance was formed in London in 1846 at a convention of fifty evangelical bodies of Europe and America. Its father in America was Samuel S. Schmucker of Gettysburg Theological Seminary, who had published a *Plan for Protestant Union* in 1838. A branch of the alliance was formed in America in 1867. The greatest international conference of the alliance was held in New York in 1873. By 1900 the alliance's influence was waning; in 1908 the Federal Council of the Churches of Christ in America replaced it.

***EVANGELINE*.** Henry Wadsworth Longfellow poem, published in 1847. The tale of betrothed lovers accidentally separated when the Acadians were exiled by the British in 1755 reflects the popular idea of the ruthlessness of the British in tearing the Acadians from their homeland, though the facts differ from the legend presented.

EVANGELISM, EVANGELICALISM, AND REVIVALISM. Technically, "evangelism" refers to any process by which a Christian church recruits new members. "Evangelical" originally referred to the followers of Martin Luther, and it appears regularly in the official names of Lutheran congregations. In the late 18th and early 19th centuries those English Christians who either were Methodists or similar to the

Methodists came to be called Evangelicals. In the late 1930's and 1940's, many American religious conservatives came to prefer "Evangelical" as a self-designation, believing that "fundamentalist" had come to have negative connotations. "Revivalism," strictly speaking, refers to evangelism that demands that the convert pass through the experience of the New Birth (a personal awareness of salvation) and adopt a moralistic style of life.

The history of American religion could be written as the history of American evangelicalism. Religious diversity was characteristic of the new land, and each church had to recruit its own membership. The Great Awakening of the 1730's and 1740's suggested one method of coping with the problem—a spontaneous outbreak of renewed religious feeling and the need for each man to experience the New Birth. Such theologians as Jonathan Edwards and Gilbert Tennent studied the revivals closely and developed a theology of revivalism.

After the Revolution a large revival broke out in Kentucky and expanded through the South; it formed the basis of the characteristically southern form of piety. In the North, Charles G. Finney developed a new form of revivalism that stressed the use of proven techniques. It ripened into the big-city campaigns of such men as Dwight Moody, Billy Sunday, and Billy Graham.

Of other methods of evangelism the most important is the Sunday school, the primary recruiting agency of Protestantism. In addition, the churches developed many youth and special-interest associations in the latter part of the 19th century. Roman Catholicism was an enthusiastic participant in this kind of evangelism, using a wide variety of mutual-aid and devotional organizations to tie the immigrant to his faith. In the 20th century, radio and then television, expanded the methods by which converts were recruited. Use of the media by fundamentalist groups became highly controversial by the late 1970's.

EVANS'S *GENERAL MAP OF THE MIDDLE BRITISH COLONIES IN AMERICA*. A map prepared by Lewis Evans, engraved by James Turner, and published in 1755 by Franklin and Hull of Philadelphia and Dodsley of London. It was accompanied by an important topographical discussion entitled *Geographical, Historical, Political, Philosophical and Mechanical Essays.* The esteem in which the map was held is evidenced by seventeen reissues and plagiarisms of the map before 1814.

EVANSVILLE (Ind.). A city in southwestern Indiana, with a population of 130,496, according to the 1980 census. It was the center of a metropolitan area with 309,408 people. It is located on the north bank of the Ohio River and possesses one of the best U.S. natural inland harbors. Its industries include a large aluminum factory and the distribution of agricultural equipment. It is also a collection depot for farm products and soft coal mined in the vicinity.

The first settlers reached Evansville in 1812, when Hugh McGary began a ferry service there across the Ohio. After Gen. Robert Evans arrived, the town came to be known as Evansville and became county seat. When steamboats began to work the Ohio in the 1820's, Evansville became a prosperous river port until the mid-1850's, when railroads by-passed the river traffic.

EVERGLADES NATIONAL PARK. Located in southern and southwestern Florida. The Everglades is a swampy region famous as the home of alligators and a wide variety of wildlife, especially many species of birds. The park was established in 1947 to insure that much of the Everglades would remain in its natural state. A considerable area outside the park has been drained and turned into sugar cane fields or cattle grazing lands.

EXCESS PROFITS TAX. A predominantly wartime tax to capture profits in excess of normal peacetime profits. The first effective national excess profits tax was enacted in 1917, with rates graduated from 20 to 60 percent on the profits of all businesses in excess of prewar earnings but not less than 7 percent or more than 9 percent of invested capital. In 1918 the tax was limited to corporations and the rates increased; in 1921 it was repealed. In 1933 and 1935, two mild excess profits taxes supplemented a capital stock tax.

Four excess profits statutes were passed in 1940–43. The 1940 rates were 25–50 percent, and the 1941 ones, 35–60 percent. In 1942 a flat rate of 90 percent was adopted, with a postwar refund of 10 percent; in 1943 the rate was increased to 95 percent. The tax was repealed on Jan. 1, 1946. The Korean War, however, induced Congress to reimpose an excess profits tax (July 1, 1950–Dec. 31, 1953) of 30 percent, with a 70 percent ceiling for the combined corporation and excess profits taxes.

EXCHANGE, BILLS OF. A written unconditional order signed by the drawer to another person, called the drawee, to pay a certain sum to a third party, called the payee, on demand or at a fixed date. Initially it was an instrument of indebtedness, a promise to pay that was incurred in one currency and was to be settled in another currency. As such, it was a way of coping with the early mercantilist prohibition on the exportation of gold and silver and of avoiding the risk of transporting bullion over long distances. Concomitantly, the parliamentary interdiction on the use of gold and silver in the colonies restricted the export of English coins and prohibited the colonials from minting their own coinage. The use of the bill of exchange declined in the late 19th century with the increased self-financing of industry, the growing tendency to eliminate the wholesale merchant with increasing industrialization, the rapid growth of railroads, and the increased use of telegraphic transfers of funds.

EXCHANGE OF PRISONERS. The exchange of prisoners of war was an established practice by the time of the American Revolution. The exchange of captured British soldiers for Massachusetts militiamen shortly after the battles at Lexington and Concord set a precedent for other states. In July 1776 the Continental Congress authorized military commanders to negotiate exchanges, and in 1780 it appointed a commissary general of prisoners, assuming responsibility for exchanges. A cartel trading American prisoners confined in England for British prisoners interned in France was signed in March

1780. A general exchange of prisoners occurred in 1783.

Battlefield exchanges occurred during the War of 1812; a general British-American cartel for exchanging prisoners was signed in May 1813. None was negotiated during the war with Mexico, but many Mexican prisoners were released on condition that they remain out of combat and most U.S. prisoners were released at the end of hostilities.

During the Civil War the Dix-Hill Cartel was concluded in July 1862, providing for parole of captured personnel. The cartel became ineffective as the tide of battle changed, and commanders resorted to the traditional battlefield exchange of prisoners. Most Confederate prisoners were released at the end of the war. Except for the exchange of a few Spanish soldiers for American sailors, no exchange of prisoners occurred during the Spanish-American War.

During World War I prisoners were exchanged after the armistice. Throughout World War II the United States negotiated through neutral nations with the Axis powers for the exchange of prisoners. A general exchange did not occur until after the Axis defeat.

In the Korean War exchange of prisoners was delayed until the issue of voluntary repatriation was resolved and an armistice signed. A general exchange occurred in August 1952; twenty-one Americans chose not to be repatriated.

During the Vietnam War each side released prisoners from time to time, but most American prisoners held by the North Vietnamese were released between the signing of the Paris Agreement of Jan. 27, 1973, and the withdrawal of U.S. military personnel from South Vietnam in March.

EXCHANGES. Since the commercial revolution of the 16th century, exchanges have provided a permanent, institutionalized auction market for buyers and sellers of paper commodities (company shares, bank stock, and governmental obligations). Dating from the 16th and 17th centuries in Amsterdam and London, they facilitated the marketing of governmental securities and the obligations of quasi-governmental joint-stock companies such as the Royal African Company and the Virginia Company.

The New York Stock Exchange, first active in the late 18th century and formally organized in 1817, grew initially in response to the need for a regular market for the new United States. The Chicago Board of Trade, organized in 1848, dealt in grains and provisions, while the New York Produce Exchange, founded in 1850, traded in flour, hay, and naval stores. The New York Cotton Exchange, organized in 1870, dealt only in cotton; exchanges for sugar, coffee, rubber, silk, hides, and mine products were created between the late 19th century and the 1920's. Regional stock exchanges emerged in the 19th century in Boston, Philadelphia, Buffalo, Chicago, San Francisco, and Los Angeles.

Until World War I, American commodity and stock exchanges remained basically private clubs that promulgated and enforced their own trading rules, and disciplined violators. Self-regulation was a frail mechanism for preventing members from manipulating markets for personal profit: insiders could rig markets by means of short selling, wash sales, and pools that depressed or raised prices. Since 1916, when Congress adopted the Cotton Futures Act and the Grain Standards Act, American exchanges gradually became subject to governmental regulations, notably the Securities Act (1933) and the Securities Exchange Act (1934).

Prior to the 1930's, U.S. commercial banks participated heavily and without regulation in marketing of corporate securities and lent funds for the purchase of securities on credit (margin). Stock prices therefore had a direct, frequently devastating impact on normal deposit banking and commercial credit, the greatest debacle being the panic of 1929. The Glass-Steagall Act of 1933 severed commercial banks from investment operations, and in 1934 Congress assigned regulation of margin transactions to the Federal Reserve Board. During the early 20th century, stock exchanges provided a ready source of capital for new corporate ventures; today most securities actively traded represent old obligations rather than venture capital.

EXCHANGE STUDENTS. Colonial Americans studied—particularly medicine—in Britain, Ireland, the Netherlands, Italy, Germany, and Sweden. In the early Republic, study abroad was opposed by George Washington, Thomas Jefferson, and Noah Webster, but nonetheless young Americans enrolled in European universities for medical and graduate studies. These exchange students and their 19th-century successors brought back not only German doctorates but German ideas for raising the standards of higher education and of academic freedom. During the 20th century, attendance by Americans in European universities increased greatly under the stimulation of the Rhodes scholarships and the Fulbright exchange program enacted by Congress (1946).

Foreign study in American institutions began at Yale (1784). By 1904, 2,673 men and women from 74 countries were enrolled in American higher institutions. Under the Fulbright and the Fulbright-Hays (1961) acts, the number of foreign students in the United States increased sharply. By 1980, 286,000 foreign students were enrolled in U.S. institutions of higher learning.

EXCISE TAXES. Internal taxes on items or services that are produced and sold in the United States. One of the earliest excise taxes was the tax on whiskey, which led to the Whiskey Rebellion, the first great test of the federal government's power to enforce obedience to its laws.

EXECUTIVE, CHIEF. *See* **Governor; President.**

EXECUTIVE AGENT. An agent appointed by the president of the United States for the purpose of conducting negotiations or investigations dealing with foreign countries. Senate confirmation is not required. The first use of an executive agent was by President George Washington, who asked Gouverneur Morris to go to London to investigate certain questions affecting the U.S.-British relations.

EXECUTIVE AGREEMENTS. International agreements concluded by the president, as distinguished from treaties, which can be ratified by the president only with consent of the Senate. They are as effective as formal treaties in conferring rights and obligations. The Constitution mentions them obliquely as "agreements" or "compacts." Although administrative agreements, many have determined significant policies, such as the Rush-Bagot Agreement (1817); the exchange of notes enunciating the Open Door Policy in China (1899, 1900); the armistices after the Revolution, the Spanish-American War, and the two world wars; and the Moscow, Teheran, Yalta, and Potsdam agreements during World War II (1943, 1945).

They can be classified according to whether they are (1) based on prior legislation; (2) implemented by subsequent legislation; (3) based on prior treaties; (4) based on prior treaties and implemented by legislation; (5) made under the president's constitutional powers; or (6) based in part on presidential powers and in part on legislation or treaty. Some form of congressional approval occurs in all but the fifth.

EXECUTIVE AND CONGRESS. The makers of the Constitution created a strong executive and a strong Congress, endowed each branch with independent power, and provided a minimum of structuring of the relations between them. Some key functions, such as appointments, lawmaking, and treaties, are shared, an arrangement that facilitates the encroachment of the branches upon each other. Few functions not deliberately designed to be shared are the exclusive province of one branch. Thus, although Congress declares war, the president also initiates it. The history of relations between these two branches has been one of struggle, with the predominant share of successes, and therefore of enlarging power, accruing to the executive.

Several patterns of executive-congressional relations are discernible. In one, the executive achieves clear ascendance, if not dominance. The most sweeping assertion of presidential power occurred when President Abraham Lincoln, under what he termed the "war power," expanded the armed forces, drew unappropriated funds from the Treasury, closed the Post Office to "treasonable correspondence," and suspended the writ of habeas corpus.

In an opposite pattern, Congress is ascendant. For all of President Woodrow Wilson's commitment to the League of Nations, it was the Senate that decided that the United States was not to join.

In another pattern, Congress and the executive are drawn together in consensus and cooperation, as in Franklin Roosevelt's New Deal program and Lyndon Johnson's Great Society program. Typically, such efforts involve highly effective presidential leadership that rallies public sentiment and evokes congressional support through manipulation of executive largess and deft bargaining.

Finally, legislative-executive relations may repose in deadlock. In his 1960 campaign, John F. Kennedy advocated an ambitious program to move the country forward again, but only a minor part bore fruit during his lifetime.

EXECUTIVE OFFICE OF THE PRESIDENT. Established by the Reorganization Act of 1939, principally as a staff aid, to assist the president in effectively controlling and coordinating the rest of the executive branch. Within this agency, the White House Office helps the president maintain communication with Congress, the executive agencies, and the public; it handles his correspondence, appointments, engagements, and paperwork. The Bureau of the Budget, established in the Treasury Department in 1921 and transferred to the Executive Office in 1939, was reorganized and redesignated the Office of Management and Budget in 1970. This office aids the president in collating, controlling, and presenting to Congress the agencies' budgetary requests; in coordinating legislative proposals that originate in the executive branch; and in improving governmental management and statistical activities. The Council of Economic Advisers, created by the Employment Act of 1946, informs the president of economic trends and suggests policies related to them. It also helps prepare the annual economic report to Congress. The National Security Council was instituted by the National Security Act of 1947. It advises the president on the integration of diplomatic measures, military programs, and domestic policies. Under its direction, the Central Intelligence Agency, established by the same act, coordinates the civil and military intelligence activities of other agencies. The Office of Emergency Preparedness (established in 1968) is the successor to the Office of Emergency Planning (established in 1962), which itself was the successor to the Office of Civil and Defense Mobilization (established in 1958); this office brings together numerous planning and control functions on the civil side of war and disaster mobilization.

The Executive Office of the President has been considerably expanded to include the following: National Aeronautics and Space Council (1958), Office of Science and Technology (1962), Office of the Special Representative for Trade Negotiations (1963), Office of Consumer Affairs (1964), Office of Economic Opportunity (1964), Office of Intergovernmental Relations (1969), Council on Environmental Quality (1969), Domestic Council (1970), Office of Telecommunications Policy (1970), Council on International Economic Policy (1971), and Special Action Office for Drug Abuse Prevention (1971).

EXECUTIVE ORDERS. Executive orders deal with a wide variety of internal administrative matters of the executive branch, such as departmental reorganization and the promulgation of civil service rules and regulations, and are based on his constitutional powers or derive from statutory authority.

The courts have regularly ruled that executive orders have the same force of law as if they were included in an act of Congress, but only if they have a basis in constitutional or statutory law. Thus, President Harry Truman's seizure of steel mills during the Korean War, implemented through executive orders, was held unconstitutional. Congress too may object to executive orders.

Until 1907, executive orders were unnumbered. Since then, they have been numbered chronologically. Orders are published in the *Federal Register* and incorporated annually in the *Code of Federal Regulations.*

EXECUTIVE PRIVILEGE. From the very beginning of the constitutional system, legislative investigatory authority and executive assertions of immunity from investigation have been a major area of conflict between the executive and legislative branches. The strongest argument for executive immunity was essentially a Federalist position stated most clearly by Vice-President John Adams and Congressman Fisher Ames in the 1790's. They not only supported the position that executive officials are not required to disclose matters involving their confidential relations with the president but also asserted that the president was not answerable to any judicial process except impeachment. These positions were vigorously opposed by Antifederalist Sen. William Maclay, who deemed these and other Federalist assertions of strong executive power evidences of monarchical tendencies. In the 20th century, Edward S. Corwin argued that the president's power to provide executive immunity was a power likely to collide head-on with the inherent power of Congress to investigate all matters within its legislative capability. But nowhere did Corwin find that immunity extended to impeachment proceedings against the president himself. To accept so broad an interpretation of executive privilege would be to alter fundamentally the political system itself.

During the Watergate controversy of 1974, the U.S. Supreme Court upheld the order of District Judge John Sirica requiring President Richard Nixon to surrender sixty-four taped White House conversations. The interests of fairness in the administration of justice were held to outweigh President Nixon's claim of absolute presidential authority to determine the application of claimed executive privilege.

EXETER COMPACT. A group of settlers at the town of Exeter, N.H., signed a compact (based on the Mayflower Compact) on July 14, 1639. They were refugees from Massachusetts Bay, where their religious views had caused them difficulty. The compact was an attempt to provide a frame of government for the town. Exeter and several other towns founded in the same way were eventually annexed to Massachusetts and remained under its control from 1643 to 1680, when New Hampshire was established as a royal colony.

EXHIBITION OF THE INDUSTRY OF ALL NATIONS. Better known as the Crystal Palace Exhibition, it was held in New York City in 1853. It was the first international exposition held in the United States. Inspired by and imitating London's Crystal Palace exhibition of 1851, a group of New York civic and business leaders, led by Horace Greeley, raised the necessary funds; the city leased them Reservoir Square (now Bryant Park). The glass-and-iron structure, built in the form of a Greek cross, contained almost 250,000 square feet. Almost half of the 4,854 exhibitors came from twenty-three foreign nations. The opening, set for May 1, was delayed until July 14; many exhibits were not ready until September. This "Iliad of the Nineteenth Century" cost $640,000 and incurred a deficit of $300,000. It closed on Dec. 1; efforts to revive it came to naught. The Crystal Palace was itself destroyed by fire on Oct. 5, 1858.

EXPANSIONISM. The causes of U.S. expansion have varied between regions and between periods. A fear of the power of Napoleonic France motivated the Louisiana Purchase (1803) and the expansion of the country from the Appalachians to the Missouri Valley. A belief in geographic determinism was the primary motive for the prolonged effort to annex Florida (1810–19). Missionary zeal, in its secular manifestation as Manifest Destiny, was important in the territorial acquisitions of the 1840's, while strategic necessity was the dominant consideration in the annexation of Puerto Rico (1898) and the Panama Canal Zone (1903). In the form of land hunger, economic ambition fueled the unsuccessful effort to conquer Canada in the War of 1812 and, translated as a desire for foreign markets, led to the decision to retain the Philippine Islands after the Spanish-American War.

Advocates of expansion enjoyed majority support only at intervals, usually as a result of external and fortuitous circumstances. The difficulties of the European powers periodically served to give reality to the ambitions of expansionists. This was particularly true during the first wave of expansion (1803–19), when the United States acquired the Louisiana Territory and the Floridas.

The most dramatic increase in the nation's size came in the 1840's, when the western boundary of the United States reached the Pacific Ocean. Except for the acquisition of southern Arizona with the Gadsden Purchase (1853) and the purchase of Alaska (1867), the continental boundaries of the United States were completed with the Treaty of Guadalupe Hidalgo in 1848. The quarter-century following the Civil War was a time of industrial growth and internal consolidation, and although the expansionist urge did not disappear, it found neither opportunity nor public sympathy.

The expansionism of the 1890's was imperial in tone, colonial in method, and insular in direction. In part the product of the needs of industrial capitalism, it was more economic in motive than earlier waves of expansionism. It culminated in the establishment of a protectorate over Cuba and the annexation of Puerto Rico and islands in the Pacific. Although cold war competition after World War II inspired the establishment of U.S. bases and military and economic aid programs throughout the globe, the United States has seemingly rejected the association of mission with territorial conquest.

EXPATRIATION. The right of a citizen or subject to transfer his allegiance from one political state to another. Under English rule of the colonies this right could be exercised only with the consent of the government, but in the United States the Congress in 1868 by statute recognized that all persons possessed this right. Later legislation set conditions under which expatriation would occur in the case of both native-born and naturalized citizens.

The Supreme Court in the 1950's and 1960's declared unconstitutional a number of such provisions, so that expatriation is now basically a voluntary matter and cannot be imposed on a citizen against his wishes, even as punishment. About all that remains is that naturalization can be canceled for fraud.

EXPENDITURES, FEDERAL. The Constitution of the United States provides, in Article I, Section 9, for "Appropriations made by Law," but no limitation on the amount of federal expenditures. Although Congress is limited by the Constitution to taxing "to pay the Debts and provide for the common Defence and general Welfare of the United States," in practice, money derived by taxation or borrowing may be spent for any purpose enacted by Congress.

When the federal government began its operation, its functions were few and its expenditures small. As new functions were added and old functions were expanded, federal expenditures were vastly increased. Thus, in 1791, expenditures amounted to only $3,097,000, but in 1974 expenditures totaled $268,342,952,000. Whereas the per capita expenditure in 1791 was only 76 cents, in 1974 it was in excess of $1,000.

Wars have been the chief factor in causing federal expenditures to rise. The Civil War cost the federal government nearly $13 billion; World War I, $112 billion; and World War II, $664 billion. After each war in which the United States participated (excluding Vietnam) federal expenditures fell markedly but failed to drop even close to the prewar level. During the Vietnam War federal expenditures increased enormously, nearly tripling from approximately $87.8 billion in 1962 to $246.5 billion in 1973. By far the largest percentage of the federal budget after World War II was allocated to national defense. However, even though the dollar output on national defense has soared ($50 billion in 1965, $80 billion in 1970, and $135.9 billion in 1980), the percentage of total national expenditures allocated to defense has actually decreased (41.9 percent in 1965, 40.8 percent in 1970, and 23.4 percent in 1980). In 1973, for the first time since before the Korean War, the largest allocation of federal expenditures went to an area other than national defense—human resources. The 1980 budget dollar was allocated as follows: 48.1 cents for payments to individuals; 23.4 cents for national defense; 16.2 cents for grants to states and localities; 9.3 cents for interest; and 3 cents for other federal operations.

EXPORT DEBENTURE PLAN. During the 1920's several bills for an export debenture plan were introduced into Congress. The principle of this plan was government payment of a bounty on exports of certain farm products in the form of negotiable instruments (debentures) that could be used in paying customs duties. Thus, farm products would not be sold domestically for less than the export price plus the bounty; farmers could then sell their whole crop at prices higher than otherwise would obtain. None of these bills became law.

EXPORT-IMPORT BANKS. *See* **Banks, Export-Import.**

EXPORTS. *See* **Trade, Foreign.**

EXPORT TAXES. Some delegates at the Constitutional Convention thought that the ease with which the government could raise money by taxing exports would tempt it to tax large-scale exports of a few states, with consequent inequality. In the end, the power to tax exports was prohibited in the Constitution (Article I, Section 9). Article I, Section 10, also withheld this power from the individual states.

EXPOSITIONS. *See under name of exposition, as in* **Louisiana Purchase Exposition** *or* **New York World's Fair.**

EXPUNGING RESOLUTION. When a legislative body wishes to express its disapproval of an action previously taken by itself or by its predecessors in office, a resolution is passed requiring the clerk to expunge the action from the record.

EXTRADITION. The surrender by one sovereign government to another of a fugitive from justice. Requests are made only under definite treaty arrangements, which usually establish reciprocity in such matters.

A second meaning of extradition in the United States refers to Article IV, Section 2, of the Constitution, which states, "A Person charged in any State with Treason, Felony or other Crime, who shall flee from Justice, and be found in another State, shall, on Demand of the executive Authority of the State from which he fled, be delivered up, to be removed to the State having jurisdiction of the crime." This apparently mandatory provision has been held by the Supreme Court to be discretionary. The governor of the state of refuge may hold a hearing to examine the facts. The usual grounds for denial are that the act complained of is not a crime in the state of refuge, or that the accused will not receive a fair trial if returned, or that the person sought to be extradited has become an upright citizen.

EXTRA SESSIONS. The president is empowered by Article II, Section 3, of the Constitution, "on extraordinary Occasions" to "convene both Houses, [of Congress] or either of them." "Extra," or "special," sessions of Congress have been called often. The Senate alone has often been convened to confirm appointments made by a newly inaugurated president. The need for extra sessions was diminished by the Twentieth Amendment, which provides that the inauguration and the convening of the regular sessions of Congress will take place in the same month.

Unlike many state governors, the president cannot limit the agenda, once a special session is called. Congress has no obligation to even consider the matters for which the president convened the session. Except for the provision involving the disability of the president (the Twenty-fifth Amendment), the national and state constitutions are silent on the question of whether or not legislative bodies may convene extra sessions on their own initiative.

EXTRATERRITORIALITY, RIGHT OF. Immunity to the laws of a country granted to nationals of another country. In Oriental countries extraterritorial courts were set up to administer Western law. Treaties with the Turkish suzerainties of Morocco, Tripoli, Tunis, and Algiers gave the United States modified privileges of extraterritoriality when the Treaty of 1830 between the United States and Turkey conferred upon American citizens exemption from Islamic law. This exemption was given up in 1923. Americans enjoyed consular jurisdiction in Egypt by virtue of this treaty.

The United States had extraterritorial privileges in China (1844; *see* Cushing's Treaty), Japan (1858), Muscat (1833), Siam (1833), and Persia (1856). Americans and British formed the Foreign Settlement at Shanghai (1863), a municipal administration exempt from Chinese jurisdiction. In 1906 the U.S. Court for China was established. As states that had been obliged to grant extraterritoriality grew in strength, the United States cooperated with them in their efforts to rid themselves of the inferior position implied by the grant.

EZRA CHURCH, BATTLE OF (July 28, 1964). To halt Gen. William Tecumseh Sherman's continued southward march, Gen. John B. Hood, defending Atlanta, ordered S. D. Lee's Confederate corps to attack the surrounding Union army near Ezra Church. Neither side could gain any advantage. At nightfall Lee withdrew into the Atlanta defense line. Sherman continued his march.

FACTORS AND FACTORAGE. *See* **Commission Merchants and Factors.**

FACTORY MANAGEMENT. *See* **Industrial Management.**

FACTORY SYSTEM. Workers are brought together in a factory for the purpose of making a product or products. Raw materials, tools, and supervision are provided and wages are paid to the workers for their labor. U.S. factory production began in the 18th century and dominated manufacturing in the 19th century, when power-driven machinery and organized systems of production were introduced.

FACTORY SYSTEM, INDIAN. The chain of government-owned and operated stores that existed from 1795 to 1822. Twenty-eight posts were established, but only seven or eight were extant at any given time. The first stores were established at Coleraine, Ga., and Tellico, Tenn. The most important ones were located at Green Bay and Prairie du Chien, Wis.; Detroit and Mackinac, Mich.; Chicago, Ill.; Fort Wayne, Ind.; Chickasaw Bluffs, Miss.; and Natchitoches, La. The purposes of the system were to strengthen military policy, to promote peace, to protect the Indians against exploitation by private traders, and to offset the influence of the British and the Spanish.

Factors sold the goods to the Indians in exchange for furs, skins, bear oil, beeswax, and other products. These furs and products were shipped to the superintendent, who sold them at auction or in foreign markets. Many difficulties arose. Freight rates were excessively high; delays were constant; the superintendent was limited to the domestic market in making his purchases and, as a result, frequently secured goods of inferior quality; skins and furs were often improperly treated, resulting in considerable losses; and the factors were forced to disobey instructions and sell on credit, thus creating many losses resulting from uncollected accounts. The factory system was never accepted as a permanent policy.

FAIR DEAL. The phrase adopted by President Harry S. Truman to characterize his program of domestic legislation in his State of the Union message of Jan. 5, 1949. The program included a full-employment law, a request that the wartime Fair Employment Practices Committee be put on a permanent basis, and legislation on housing, health insurance, aid to education, atomic energy, and the development of the St. Lawrence Seaway. In general, Congress did not respond, but the Employment Act of 1946 was passed in accordance with his wishes and under it the Council of Economic Advisers was set up.

After his surprising 1948 victory, the president gathered together many of the proposals he had made in previous years in his annual message to Congress in January 1949. He asked for laws on housing, full employment, higher minimum wages, better price supports for farmers, more organizations like the Tennessee Valley Authority, the extension of social security, and fair employment practices. An anti-poll-tax law and a fair employment practices bill failed, but the Housing Act of 1949 facilitated slum clearance, the minimum wage level was lifted from 40 to 75 cents an hour, and the Social Security Act of 1950 extended benefits to 10 million more people.

FAIR EMPLOYMENT PRACTICES COMMITTEE (FEPC). During 1941, U.S. industry was organized to produce war goods and to supply aid for the British. Many industries and unions denied equal job opportunities to members of minority groups, so, on June 25, 1941, President Franklin D. Roosevelt ordered the creation of the FEPC, within the Office of Production Management, to ensure equal access to jobs for qualified people, regardless of race or national origin.

The FEPC operated throughout World War II, but was never fully accepted by employers or union leaders and was discontinued in 1946. In 1948, President Harry S. Truman urged that the FEPC be made permanent and created a similar board within the Civil Service Commission. Although FEPC was not revived as a separate unit, its basic purposes became accepted elements of national labor practice.

FAIRFAX COURTHOUSE. *See* **Chantilly, Battle of.**

FAIRFAX PROPRIETARY. Rested on a patent issued by James II to Thomas, Lord Culpeper, in 1688, counter to the wishes of the inhabitants of Virginia. The patentee was given rights to the soil in the region between the Rappahannock and Potomac rivers and the right to make grants of land and collect quitrents. For purposes of government, however, the Northern Neck, or Fairfax proprietary, remained an integral part of Virginia. The proprietary later passed to Thomas, sixth Lord Fairfax of Cameron.

Westward expansion precipitated an acute controversy about the grant. In 1745 a committee of the Privy Council confirmed proprietary rights over more than 5 million acres, including much of the best land in Virginia, to Fairfax. The American Revolution reopened the question of his rights. A year after his death in 1781, the Virginia assembly sequestered the quitrents of the Northern Neck, and in 1785 abolished them and other seignorial rights of the proprietors.

Since the Definitive Treaty of Peace of 1783 had prohibited

further confiscation of Loyalist property, the Fairfax heirs contended that the Virginia act of 1785 could not affect their title to lands held in fee. In 1793 a syndicate undertook to acquire the interest held in fee under the Fairfax title. In 1796 the state agreed to relinquish claim to all lands specifically appropriated by Fairfax to his own use in return for all lands that were "waste and unappropriated" at his death.

FAIR LABOR STANDARDS ACT (1938). Popularly known as the Wages and Hours Bill, it ended several years of endeavor by proponents of federal regulation of hours and wages. The National Industrial Recovery Act of 1933 established the National Recovery Administration (NRA) to regulate the operation of industries under industrial codes, which included the regulation of prices, trade practices, wages, hours, collective bargaining, and labor conditions, but in 1935, the Supreme Court invalidated it. Congress responded by enacting the Bituminous Coal Conservation Act of 1935, which regulated wage and hour standards in the industry, but in 1936, the Court invalidated the act without ruling on the power of Congress to regulate wages.

President Franklin D. Roosevelt in 1937 urged a federal wage-and-hour law, culminating in the Fair Labor Standards Act, an omnibus bill that regulated hours of labor, wages, and child labor and created the Wage and Hour Division in the Department of Labor. The act applies in industries affecting or producing goods for interstate commerce. A minimum wage was established; child labor under the age of sixteen was prohibited, with certain exceptions; specific hazardous occupations were forbidden to youths under eighteen; time-and-a-half pay was required for overtime employment; and criminal penalties for violation of the act were provided, including exclusion from interstate commerce of such goods as were not produced in accordance with its standards. The Supreme Court upheld the validity of the act in 1941, but the act has remained the source of substantial litigation.

FAIR OAKS, BATTLE OF (May 31–June 1, 1862), also known as the **Battle of Seven Pines.** On May 27, Union Gen. George B. McClellan's army was concentrated near Fair Oaks Station, ten miles east of Richmond. Confederate Gen. J. E. Johnston attacked in driving rain, on May 31. Confusion, misunderstanding of orders, and lack of effective staff work prevented proper advantage being taken of initial Confederate successes. About sunset Johnston was wounded; Gen. G. W. Smith succeeded him. The Confederate attack was renewed early the next day in the hope of cutting McClellan's line of communications, but with little chance of success. At the close of the day the Confederates retired to await McClellan's next move (*see* Peninsular Campaign).

FAIRS. *See* **County Fairs; State Fairs.**

FAIR-TRADE LAWS. Laws for resale price maintenance or the control by a supplier of the selling prices of his branded goods at subsequent stages of distribution by means of contractual agreement. California was the first state to enact a fair-trade law (1931). Thereafter, all except Missouri, Texas, and Vermont and the District of Columbia passed similar legislation.

In 1936 the U.S. Supreme Court ruled that state fair-trade laws were legitimate means of protecting a manufacturer's goodwill as symbolized by his trademark. In 1937 the Miller-Tydings Amendment to the Sherman Antitrust Act of 1890 exempted interstate fair-trade agreements from the antitrust laws but made no reference to nonsigners' clauses, whereby the manufacturer by making a contract with one retailer (or wholesaler) in a fair-trade state could legally bind all other retailers (or wholesalers) in that state to maintain his stipulated resale prices. However, in May 1951 the Supreme Court invalidated all fair-trade price structures in interstate commerce that were based on the use of nonsigners' clauses. The Fair Trade Enabling Act (or McGuire Act), passed in July 1952, restored to manufacturers the power to require retailers and wholesalers to adhere to fixed minimum price schedules whether they had signed fair-trade contracts or not.

But fair trade became caught up in a crossfire of court action at the state level. By August 1956, eight state supreme courts had handed down adverse decisions on fair trade, rendering it virtually inoperative in some areas, and many others had ruled that nonsigners' clauses violated state constitutions. A quiet campaign to put through a new federal resale price maintenance law failed in Congress in 1964. By mid-1975 only twenty-five states still had fair-trade laws of any kind on the books, and the federal government seemed on the verge of wiping out the two federal laws (the Miller-Tydings Amendment and the McGuire Act) that still made surviving state fair-trade laws viable in interstate commerce. Subcommittees in both houses of Congress had approved bills repealing fair trade, backed by President Gerald R. Ford.

FAJARDO CASE (1824). In October, during the U.S. campaign against pirates in the West Indies, the alcalde of Fajardo, Puerto Rico, insulted and imprisoned Lt. C. T. Platt of the West Indian Squadron. The squadron commander, David Porter, sent seamen and marines ashore and secured an abject apology. The Navy Department, hostile to Porter, court-martialed and suspended him for six months. Porter resigned from the navy in August 1826.

FALKLAND ISLANDS. In 1831 the Argentine Republic, claiming the islands as heir of Spain, seized three U.S. sealing and whaling vessels. Unduly strong protests were made by the U.S. representative in Buenos Aires, and Comdr. Silas Duncan of the U.S.S. *Lexington* made an unauthorized attack on an Argentinian colony in the Falklands and transported the inhabitants to the mainland. When Great Britain took possession of the Falkland Islands on the basis of 18th-century claims, Argentina claimed that the inhabitants could have fought the British off if they had not been removed. The United States persisted in refusing to consider Argentinian claims for the losses occasioned by the raid. In 1982, in the midst of seemingly stalemated talks with Britian on its sovereignty in the Falklands, Argentina seized the islands. A large British force rewon the islands after several weeks of fighting. The fiasco caused the collapse of Argentina's military junta.

FALLEN TIMBERS, BATTLE OF (Aug. 20, 1794). When Gen. Anthony Wayne set out from Fort Greenville in what is now Ohio, on July 28, 1794, the British and Little Turtle, the Indian leader, warned of Wayne's advance, hastily gathered 1,300 Indians in northwest Ohio at the rapids of the Maumee in a region called Fallen Timbers. Fewer than 800 Indians engaged in the two-hour battle. Wayne won decisively, paving the way for the frontier enforcement of Jay's Treaty and the British evacuation of the border forts.

FALLING WATERS SKIRMISH (July 13–14, 1863). Confederate Gen. Robert E. Lee, retreating from Gettysburg, Pa., entrenched north of the swollen Potomac River, around Williamsport, Md. His army crossed at Falling Waters. The Confederate rear guard, Gen. Henry Heth's division of Gen. A. P. Hill's corps, was attacked by Gen. John Buford's and Gen. Hugh J. Kilpatrick's cavalry divisions. Confederate Gen. James J. Pettigrew was mortally wounded, but Heth's division retired safely into Virginia.

FALL LINE. A line roughly parallel to the Atlantic coast dividing the coastal plain from the Appalachian foothills (or Piedmont), created by the difference in geologic structure of the two areas. Streams flowing from the mountains over the higher, erosion-resistant rock of the Piedmont descend suddenly onto the more easily eroded coastal plain and create waterfalls or rapids at these points—thus its name.

The fall line produced sectionalism, especially in the South during the colonial period. The tidewater area, conducive to a large-plantation economy based on tobacco, rice, and indigo, was the home of wealthy, conservative slaveowners, who controlled the local governments. By contrast, the backcountry nurtured a small-farm economy. Cut off from direct access to European influence, people in the western counties were rougher in manner and more turbulent in politics. Western antagonism toward the tidewater over such issues as taxation and representation in the legislature occasionally led to mob violence.

FALMOUTH, BURNING OF (Oct. 18, 1775). Part of the British plan to cripple seaport towns—Falmouth being a part of Portland, Me.—and to punish rebels for giving aid to Continental troops in besieged Boston. On Oct. 16, Capt. Henry Mowat sailed into Falmouth harbor in Casco Bay and shelled the town. Unable to come to terms with the inhabitants, he fired the town after the townspeople had withdrawn.

FAMILY. A small kinship-structured group with the key function of nurturant socialization of the newborn. In America the family system has varied according to region, economic conditions, and time. Despite regional and ethnic variations, and social experiments, certain characteristics may be applied to the American family structure: a nuclear family unit (parents and children); a high degree of equality between the sexes and of freedom given to young people in courtship; and the concept of marriage to one's love choice.

FAMILY COMPACT (1761). Alliance between the Bourbon families of France and Spain, directed primarily against England. The contracting parties promised common action by land and sea and stipulated that no peace should be made by either save by common consent.

FANEUIL HALL. Public market and meeting hall erected in 1742 as a gift to Boston by merchant Peter Faneuil. The site of public protests against unpopular British measures before the Revolution, it became known as the Cradle of Liberty. Designed by the painter John Smibert, the building was destroyed by fire in 1761, only its exterior walls remaining. It was enlarged and rebuilt before the Revolution, and restructured by Charles Bulfinch in 1805, with a third floor added. It was designated a national historic landmark in 1967.

FAR EASTERN POLICY. U.S. Far Eastern policy worked for commercial opportunity and, to this end, legal and diplomatic protection for its businessmen in Asia via exterritoriality arrangements. Moreover, U.S. missionary activity among the Chinese led to diplomatic efforts to protect and maintain religious properties. Fundamental to the achievement of these purposes were the preservation of the territorial and administrative integrity of China and the maintenance of its independence. As a result, American policy displayed a spectrum of tactics and strategies ranging from the national to the multinational, beginning with the treaties of Wanghia (1844) and Tientsin (1858). U.S. policy with Japan, opened to the West by Commodore Matthew Perry in 1854, and the treaty negotiated by Townsend Harris in 1858, also concerned extraterritoriality and commercial privileges. In addition, American racist attitudes and legislation affected U.S. relations with both countries similarly, as in the Burlingame Treaty of 1868, the Gentlemen's Agreement of 1907, and the Immigration Act of 1924.

The watershed of Far Eastern policy came in 1899–1900 with Secretary of State John Hay's declarations of the Open Door, pledging (and asking other nations to pledge) equality of trade opportunity and the territorial and administrative integrity of China. This policy outlook became entwined in tension between the United States and Japan and between the United States and China, as exhibited in President Theodore Roosevelt's concern for Japan's emergence in eastern Asia, resulting in the Taft-Katsura Agreement (1905), the Root-Taahira Agreement (1908), and the dollar-diplomacy episodes in Manchuria and China from 1908 to 1913.

From 1913 through the 1920's, U.S. policy trumpeted humanitarian Open Door concern for China. Yet at China's expense it also gave way to Japan's ambitions in Manchuria at the Versailles conference and then attempted through the Washington Conference treaties of 1922 to encourage an international coalition to implement the Open Door concept.

Japan's invasion of Manchuria in 1931 caused the United States to invoke the Kellogg-Briand pact and resulted in the Stimson doctrine of nonrecognition (1932). Thereafter, U.S. policy tended to favor China and exhibited apprehension about Japan's aspirations, especially toward the French and Dutch possessions in Southeast Asia.

At the Cairo Conference in 1943, at Yalta in 1945, and at Potsdam in 1945, U.S. policy was modified by the emergence of the Soviet Union as a power in the struggle for China between Nationalist and Communist forces. Containment of Soviet influence came to be a doctrine in U.S. foreign affairs. The resulting tension saw the buildup of North Korea by the Soviets, while the United States supported Syngman Rhee's South Korean regime. The Korean War brought China into direct conflict with the United States.

President Dwight D. Eisenhower and Secretary of State John Foster Dulles mixed national caution, moralistic rhetoric, and diplomatic maneuvers designed to isolate the People's Republic of China, which they refused to recognize, and drew up a mutual security pact with Chiang. Trade restrictions by the United States, the influencing of UN votes against admission of Mao's regime, and recurring crises over the offshore islands of Quemoy and Ma-tsu were major manifestations of tension between Peking and Washington.

Far Eastern policy faced a crisis in the 1960's when the U.S. struggle in Vietnam rocked the very stability of the nation at home and abroad. American reluctance to approve fully of the 1954 Geneva settlement, the development of the ineffective Southeast Asia Treaty Organization, and the complex maneuvers designed to keep Laos out of Communist hands led only to a tragic military commitment begun by President Kennedy and carried through by Johnson and Nixon. With U.S. withdrawal from Vietnam in 1972 came an end to the notion that through such policies as the Open Door and humanitarian idealism, the United States might attain a position of leadership in the Far East. (*See also* articles under China, Japan, Korea, and individual entries such as Southeast Asia Treaty Organization.)

FARGO (N. Dak.). Largest city in North Dakota, had a population of 61,308 according to the 1980 census. Fargo is located at a one-time ferry crossing where travelers crossed the Red River of the North from Minnesota into North Dakota. Founded in 1872 and named in honor of William G. Fargo, of the Wells-Fargo Express Company, it became the most important shipping point for the rich wheat farmland near the river in the later 1870's and 1880's, and it is still a very important wheat-shipping city. Fargo is an oil pipeline terminal, servicing the oil produced in North Dakota fields, and a center of the livestock trade.

FARIBAULT CLAIM. Jean Baptiste Faribault, fur trader, and his Sioux wife, Pélagie, were granted title to Pike's Island, near Fort Snelling, Minn., in an unratified treaty with the Sioux negotiated by Col. Henry Leavenworth in 1820. In 1838, Faribault offered to compound for $12,000, but the government never recognized the claim.

FARIBAULT PLAN. In 1891, Archbishop John Ireland arranged with the boards of education in Faribault and Stillwater, Minn., for a parochial school in each of these two towns to be regarded during class hours as a state school, while retaining its own teachers and preserving its character as a distinctly Catholic school during the remainder of each day.

FARM BOARD, FEDERAL. *See* **Agriculture.**

FARM BUREAU. *See* **Agriculture.**

FARM CREDIT AGENCIES. *See* **Agriculture.**

FARMER-LABOR PARTY OF MINNESOTA. The most successful third party in U.S. history. It was forged from a coalition of agrarian and labor organizations between 1918 and 1944. It fell heir to a sizable voting base among the farmers of western Minnesota from the Nonpartisan League. The league-labor forces worked together and entered their candidates on the 1918 ballot under the label Farmer-Labor. Although it lost the election, the new coalition displaced the Democratic party as a major political force in the state. The stronghold of the Nonpartisan League in the state had been the largely Scandinavian farmers of northwestern and west-central Minnesota and the state's Socialist movement. To this base were added the German-American population, alienated by U.S. entry into the war; labor in Minneapolis, St. Paul, Duluth, and the iron ranges of northeastern Minnesota; and the radical Progressives.

In July 1919, the Minnesota State Federation of Labor established the Working People's Nonpartisan Political League as a parallel political organization to the farmer-oriented Nonpartisan League. Selected by both organizations as their candidate for governor in the Republican primary was Henrik Shipstead. The third-party label was preserved by filing additional candidates for other offices under the "Farmer-Labor" designation. Shipstead lost to the regular Republican candidate, but two league-endorsed candidates were elected to the House of Representatives. In 1922 the two leagues together endorsed a full slate of candidates. A Farmer-Labor ballot appeared in the primary elections. In the general election Shipstead won a seat in the Senate. Also elected to Congress was Knud Wefald. In 1923 the two leagues formed the Farmer-Labor Federation and captured the state's second U.S. Senate seat by getting Magnus Johnson elected in a special election. In 1924 the party failed to win the governorship and lost Johnson's Senate seat, but it won three of the state's ten congressional seats and retained a firm grip on Shipstead's Senate seat and the House seat in the Red River valley.

In 1930, Floyd B. Olson, the Farmer-Labor party's foremost leader, was easily elected governor. Re-elected in 1932 and 1934, he served until his death in 1936. Despite hostile legislatures Olson secured large appropriations for the relief of unemployment, a two-year moratorium on farm mortgage foreclosures, old-age pensions, measures to extend conservation, and the state's first income tax (1933). The party's 1934 platform proposed public ownership of all industry, banking, insurance, and public utilities and the formation of a "cooperative commonwealth." Elmer A. Benson was elected governor in 1936. More radical and doctrinaire than Olson, Benson was far less skillful in leading a coalition of dissenting political groups. The Republican candidate for governor in 1938, Harold E. Stassen, who leveled charges of corruption and communism at Benson, overwhelmed him in the election. The Farmer-Labor party never recovered its vitality, retaining only one Senate seat until 1941 and one congressional seat until 1944, when it merged with the Democratic party. Nationally, the party's presidential candidates were Robert M. La Follette in 1924 and Franklin D. Roosevelt in 1932, 1936, and 1940.

FARMER-LABOR PARTY OF 1920. A transitory effort to create a national third party. In November 1919, delegates of state and local labor groups from forty states met in Chicago and organized the National Labor party. The first platform, promulgated as "Labor's Fourteen Points," was based on the fundamental ideal that workers and farmers should exercise controlling power. It called for the nationalization of all public utilities, basic industries, and banks. In 1920, when the party met in Chicago, its name was changed to Farmer-Labor party to attract farmer support. The convention intended to nominate Robert M. La Follette, but he rejected the public ownership plank as too sweeping. It turned to Parley P. Christiansen of Utah as candidate for president and Max S. Hayes as his running mate. In the election, the party failed to secure the support of the American Federation of Labor, the Committee of Forty-eight, the Nonpartisan League, and the Socialist Eugene V. Debs; and drew fewer than 300,000 votes. At a convention in Chicago in 1923, representatives of the Workers' Party of America (Communist) gained control, and the farmer-labor leaders withdrew from the movement.

FARMERS' ALLIANCE. The name commonly given to either or both of two powerful agricultural organizations. The National Farmers' Alliance, also known as the Northern, or Northwestern, Alliance, founded in 1880 to combat the unfair discrimination of the railroads against the rural classes (*see* Granger Movement). In the late 1880's, hard-pressed farmers of the "middle border" joined it hoping they could curb the railroads and the trusts and bring about a lowering of interest rates. When established parties failed to bring results, the alliance went into politics, and by 1890 third-party tickets for state and local offices were general throughout the Northwest.

The National Farmers' Alliance and Industrial Union originated about 1874 in Lampasas County, Tex., when farmers united in a secret, ritualistic alliance against cattle kings and land sharks. Dormant in the late 1870's it revived in Parker County, Tex., as the Farmers' State Alliance in 1879. It absorbed the Louisiana Farmers' Union, the Arkansas Agricultural Wheel, and local farmers' clubs all over the South. Business exchanges were founded, but most failed. Avoiding third-party action, the alliance set out to capture the Democratic party of the South, and by 1890 it was succeeding. Meantime, a subordinate Colored Farmers' Alliance and Cooperative Union had been founded to look after the welfare of blacks.

Efforts to unite the two alliances failed because of divergent economic interests and the formation, mainly under the auspices of the Northwestern Alliance, of the People's, or Populist, party in 1892.

FARMER'S ALMANAC. Published continuously since its founding by Robert Bailey Thomas at Sterling, Mass., in 1793. Its homely presentation of scientific subjects and its general moral and literary character were imitated by others. The later issues appeared in several editions aimed to appeal to sectional interests. (*See also* Almanacs.)

FARMERS' COOPERATIVES. *See* **Cooperatives, Farmers'.**

FARMERS INSTITUTES. The first genuine example was held at Yale in 1860. By 1870 many state farm organizations made some provision for lectures to farmers. The classic form of the farmers institute was put into operation generally during the 1880's. By 1885 the plan was systematized and state appropriations granted for carrying it out; by 1889 the movement was in full swing.

Sponsored by a county agricultural society, a county grange, or a farmers club; directed by state lecturers; and participated in by leading local farmers, the programs were commonly arranged for a two-day meeting in winter. Farm problems were discussed in the light of the best scientific and practical knowledge. Discussion of household economy was added for farm women. Political partisanship was shunned, but questions of public policy affecting agriculture received attention. National attendance was as high as 4 million. After 1914 agricultural extension on a national scale absorbed institutes' functions.

FARMER'S LETTERS, DICKINSON'S. The most effective presentation of the colonial objections to the Townshend Acts of 1767. Written by John Dickinson, a lawyer and gentleman farmer of Pennsylvania, the twelve letters appeared in the newspapers in 1767–68. Reprinted as a collection and circulated throughout the colonies, their influence was great. They emphasized the right of Parliament to regulate trade but not to legislate for the colonies in cases in which revenue was the primary objective. They shifted the emphasis of colonial disapproval from the form of parliamentary law to its purpose, which soon drove the colonists to the position that Parliament had no right to legislate for the colonies at all.

FARMERS' ORGANIZATIONS. The earliest agricultural societies in the United States were scientific groups. Two organized in 1785: the South Carolina Society for Promoting and Improving Agriculture, and the Philadelphia Society for Promoting Agriculture. These, and similar organizations in other states, were made up largely of large landowners who were interested in finding the best kinds of plants or animals to raise on their land. In 1852, the U.S. Agricultural Society was formed to encourage Congress to organize the Department of Agriculture. In 1867, the first large farm organization appeared, when Oliver Kelley organized the Patrons of Husbandry, a semi-secret organization, open only to farmers, who met in local groups known as Granges. The group was soon referred to as "Grangers," and was prominent in the 1870's and 1880's. Farmers suffering from low profits and bad weather organized into Farmers' Alliances, which demanded that the government take over the ownership and operation of railroads. Cooperative farmers' stores were to be found in many farm communities, run by farmers for their own good. In 1902, the National Farmers Union was established as an agency mainly of small-farm owners and low-income farmers. It specifically aimed at united action between farmers and trade unions.

While there were several efforts to organize a national political party representative of farmers and laboring people, no such national party developed. Local Farmer-Labor parties did appear in several states, and the Farmer-Labor party came to dominate Minnesota in the 1920's and 1930's. As the Democratic-Farmer-Labor party it consistently elected Democratic legislators in the 1940's and 1950's.

Instead of a political organization as such, a new group of farm organizations developed as farm bureaus, which advised farmers of their rights to services from their county farm agents. The bureaus were combined in 1920 into the American Farm Bureau Federation. Its objectives were to keep the farmers informed and to represent farmers' interests in government circles. It was one of the leading influences on agricultural legislation during the New Deal.

Other farm organizations are frequently put together for special purposes. The most obvious example would be the Rural Electric Cooperatives Association, which is made up of the people throughout rural America who use electric power through electric cooperatives. There are many other "cooperatives" in American farm areas.

FARMING. *See* **Agriculture.**

FARM MACHINERY. *See* **Agricultural Machinery.**

FARM MORTGAGE FORECLOSURE ACT (1934). During the massive farm foreclosures of the Great Depression, Congress authorized the Land Bank commissioner to extend loans to farmers to enable them to recover farm properties owned by them prior to foreclosure.

FARM MORTGAGE REFINANCING ACT (1934). Established the Federal Farm Mortgage Corporation (FFMC) under the Farm Credit Administration and authorized it to issue up to $2 billion in guaranteed bonds. The purpose was to further the refinancing of farm debts by exchanging FFMC bonds for consolidated farm loan bonds and investing them directly in mortgage loans.

FARM RELIEF. *See* **Agriculture.**

FARM TENANCY. *See* **Agriculture.**

FAR WEST (Mo.). A town in Missouri founded on Aug. 8, 1836, by Mormons who had been expelled from Clay County. In 1837 the town became the seat of Caldwell County. By 1838 it had become the center of a community of some 10,000 Mormons. On Oct. 31, 1838, during the anti-Mormon movement in Missouri, Far West was surrendered to Gen. Robert Lucas. The governor of Missouri, Lillburn W. Boggs, expelled the Mormons from the state.

***FAR WEST*.** A light-draft stern wheeler owned by the Coulson Packet Company. It was the supply boat of the Yellowstone expedition under Gen. Alfred H. Terry, including Gen. George A. Custer's cavalry. After the Battle of the Little Bighorn it carried Maj. Marcus A. Reno's wounded to Fort Abraham Lincoln, N.Dak.

FAST DAYS. Days of humiliation and of thanksgiving, in colonial New England, officially dedicated to seeking the forgiveness of God or expressing gratitude to Him. Both fast days and thanksgiving days were celebrated with a sermon; on a thanksgiving day the service was followed by feasting, but a fast day did not necessarily mean entire abstinence from food, though abstinence from secular pursuits was called for.

FATHER OF HIS COUNTRY. Used as a descriptive designation of George Washington in Pennsylvania as early as 1778. The first known publication of it was by Francis Bailey, an Ephrata-trained printer, on the cover of his *Nord Americanische Kalender* for 1779.

FATHER OF WATERS (Mississippi River). An inexact translation of the Algonkin words *misi* ("great") and *sipi* ("water"). First heard from Indians by Frenchmen on the upper reaches of the river.

FAVORITE SON. A presidential candidate proposed by his own state political committee and offered to the convention as the choice of his home state. This enables a delegation to remain out of the contest between better-known candidates until it can make its most effective choice.

FAYETTE, FORT. Dedicated 1792, on the Allegheny River, a quarter of a mile above Fort Pitt, in what is now downtown Pittsburgh, Pa., it served first as headquarters for generals Anthony Wayne and James Wilkinson and later as a supply depot. Wayne gathered his army there for his campaign against the Ohio Indians (*see* Fallen Timbers, Battle of). In the War of 1812 it served as a recruiting station. It was abandoned about 1816.

FEATHERBEDDING. A slang term applied to the union practice of insisting that workers be employed and paid even though management claims that they are not performing any useful tasks. The charge has been made, for example, that some railroad work rules involve featherbedding, but unions insist that the extra men, such as firemen on diesel locomotives, have an important emergency function to perform.

FEDERAL AGENCIES. Under authority implied in the U.S. Constitution, numerous agencies to execute or administer national legislation have been created by statute or executive order. The existing federal agency system has been considerably influenced by three major study groups: the President's Committee on Administrative Management (1936–37); the Commission on Organization of the Executive Branch of the Government (1947–49), known as the Hoover Commission; and the President's Advisory Council on Executive Organization (1969–71), known as the Ash Committee. The Executive Reorganization Act of 1949, which is an outgrowth of the Hoover group's report, authorized the president for a four-year period (consistently extended thereafter, typically for two-year periods) to prepare plans to create, abolish, transfer, or modify any part of the executive branch. Congress may overrule a change.

The agency closest to the president himself is the Executive Office of the President; set up by the Reorganization Act of 1939. The Bureau of the Budget, established in the Treasury Department in 1921 and transferred to the Executive Office in 1939, was reorganized and redesignated the Office of Management and Budget in 1970. The Council of Economic Advisers was created by the Employment Act of 1946. The National Security Council was instituted by the National Security Act of 1947. The Office of Emergency Preparedness (established in 1968) is the successor to the Office of Emergency Planning (established in 1962), which itself was the successor to the Office of Civil and Defense Mobilization (established in 1958).

As part of a continuing effort to provide the president with more staff help, the Executive Office of the President has been considerably expanded to include the following: National Aeronautics and Space Council (1958), Office of Science and Technology (1962), Office of the Special Representative for Trade Negotiations (1963), Office of Consumer Affairs (1964), Office of Economic Opportunity (1964), Office of Intergovernmental Relations (1969), Council on Environmental Quality (1969), Domestic Council (1970), Office of Telecommunications Policy (1970), Council on International Economic Policy (1971), and Special Action Office for Drug Abuse Prevention (1971).

There are eleven agencies whose heads, by tradition, constitute the president's cabinet. These are the executive departments in order of their official rank: State; Treasury; Defense (combining departments of the army, the navy, and the air force); Justice; Interior; Agriculture; Commerce; Labor; Health, Education, and Welfare; Housing and Urban Development; and Transportation. From 1829 until 1971 the postmaster general was a member of the cabinet. In 1971 the U.S. Postal Service was created as an "independent establishment of the executive branch" to replace the department.

There are a number of important federal agencies similar in structure to executive departments, although they are too small or relatively not so important as to warrant cabinet status. The National Aeronautics and Space Administration, the Veterans Administration, the Federal Reserve System, the Smithsonian Institution, and the National Science Foundation are typical. The General Services Administration was established by the Federal Property and Administrative Services Act of 1949.

The Small Business Administration, established by Congress in 1953, carried over and expanded in peacetime the essential functions of two wartime predecessors: the Smaller War Plants Corporation (1942–47) of World War II and the Small Defense Plants Administration (1951–53) of the Korean conflict. A 1958 statute created the Federal Aviation Agency (Federal Aviation Administration since 1966), in part through the transfer of the Civil Aeronautics Administration and the safety-regulatory activities of the Civil Aeronautics Board. These older organizations were based on legislation of 1938. The U.S. Information Agency was created by Reorganization Plan 8 of 1953, which consolidated several propaganda and informational activities directed to foreign countries, among them the Office of War Information, which was under the aegis of the State Department. The Federal Mediation and Conciliation Service was set up by the Labor-Management Relations (Taft-Hartley) Act of 1947 to replace the U.S. Conciliation Service situated in the Department of Labor (1913).

Several agencies, instead of having a single head, have plural leadership—often as a device to assure representation of diverse interests. The Railroad Retirement Board, created by Congress in 1935, follows this pattern. Congress established the Renegotiation Board in 1951, absorbing functions of the War Contracts Price Adjustment Board. The Subversive Activities Control Board, set up by statute in 1950, met its demise in 1974. It had been charged with determining, upon application, whether various organizations were "Communist action," "Communist-front," or "Communist-infiltrated" organizations within the meaning of the Subversive Activities Control Act of 1950. The American Battle Monuments Commission, created by law in 1923, administers American military cemeteries abroad; regulates the design of monuments erected in them; and plans, constructs, and maintains other memorials that commemorate the service of American armed forces in foreign countries. The Commission on Civil Rights was established by statute in 1957.

A special category of plural agency is the independent regulatory commission, which is characterized by unusual discretion in making rules for specified segments of the national economy, by some quasijudicial power in applying the rules, by mandatory bipartisan membership (usually), and by special insulation of its members against arbitrary presidential interference. The exceptional powers of regulation and adjudication possessed by agencies of this type appear necessary for flexible control over technically complex activities, and the very scope of these powers occasions the requirement of insulation. The first such agency and the prototype of the others was the Interstate Commerce Commission; the latest agency of this type is the Atomic Energy Commission. Two other important independent regulatory commissions are the Federal Communications Commission and the National Labor Relations Board. The Civil Aeronautics Board, also an independent regulatory commission, was established by Congress in 1938 as the Civil Aeronautics Authority and renamed under the presidential Reorganization Plan of 1940. The Federal Power Commission was created by statute in 1930, replacing an earlier commission of the same name (1920). Congress instituted the Federal Trade Commission in 1914 and substantially expanded its duties in later laws.

Under a 1934 act to amend the Railway Labor Act of 1926, the National Mediation Board was set up to replace the U.S. Board of Mediation (1926). The Securities and Exchange Commission was created by statute in 1934, absorbing certain functions that the Securities Act of 1933 had assigned to the Federal Trade Commission; subsequent legislation has enlarged these.

The Tax Court of the United States does not readily fit any classification of executive agency. The court was originally established by the Revenue Act of 1924 as the U.S. Board of Tax Appeals and was renamed by the Revenue Act of 1942.

Another type of federal agency comprises those that furnish credit for certain types of private or public financial ventures, such as the Farm Credit Administration. The Export-Import Bank of the United States (the Export-Import Bank of Washington until 1968) is a banking corporation, first authorized by executive order in 1934. The Federal Deposit Insurance Corporation was organized under the Federal Reserve Act of 1933. The Federal Home Loan Bank Board was first established by law in 1932 and has undergone several changes of name, status, and function through later legislation (1955) and through Reorganization Plan 3 of 1947. The board directs the Federal Home Loan Banks System and the Federal Savings and Loan Insurance Corporation.

The Tennessee Valley Authority is an example of another type of executive agency—a government corporation—for at times Congress has felt that it would enable agencies involved in business activities to be more effective if they were provided the legal attributes of business corporations. Other agencies that have been established as corporations include the Federal Savings and Loan Insurance Corporation (1934), the Federal Crop Insurance Corporation (1938), the St. Lawrence Seaway Development Corporation (1954), the Export-Import Bank, the Panama Canal Company (1950), the Inter-American Foundation (1969), and the Overseas Private Investment Corporation (1969).

A few federal agencies belong to the judicial or legislative, rather than the executive, establishment. The Administrative Office of the U.S. Courts, created by statute in 1939; the Government Printing Office, established as a congressional agency by joint resolution in 1860; the Library of Congress, created by law in 1800 to serve Congress; and the General Accounting Office, established by the Budget and Accounting Act of 1921 and headed by the comptroller general of the United States.

FEDERAL AID. The granting of financial assistance to the states by the federal government. Prior to the Great Depression, grants to the states of land and money for canals, railroads, education, and roads supplemented private enterprise and state resources for developments judged to be economically and socially desirable. During and after the Great Depression, the initial incentive was to relieve the distress of the population, and the assistance took on unprecedented variety and magnitude. Only national rescue could relieve the hunger and homelessness of one-fifth of the population and the collapse of agriculture, industry, and credit. Federal aid thereafter grew in complexity and scale.

Federal assistance takes the forms of cash payments, tax credits, payments in kind, and loans below the market rate of interest. The object may be to persuade recipients to take certain actions (for example, make capital investments) or to refrain from others (overproduction in agriculture, emission of industrial pollutants). Other aims are income redistribution, economic growth, price stability, increase of employment, foreign trade balance, slum clearance and decent low-cost housing, health care, education, and efficient means of travel and transport.

FEDERAL-AID HIGHWAY PROGRAM. About 43,000 miles of interstate and defense highways have been built, largely at federal expense, the states having contributed only 10 percent of total cost of construction. In addition, more than 900,000 miles of primary and secondary roads are maintained on a 50–50 basis by the federal and state governments acting jointly. The Federal Highway Administration is charged with administration of the Federal-Aid Highway Construction Program.

Following the passage of the Federal-Aid Highway acts of 1916 and 1921, the Bureau of Public Roads became the chief agency for promoting a national network of highways. The bureau was moved to the Federal Works Agency; to the Department of Commerce; and finally, in 1967, to the Department of Transportation. In 1970 it was reorganized and its duties assigned to the Federal Highway Administration.

FEDERAL AID ROAD ACT. *See* **Rural Post Roads Act.**

FEDERAL AVIATION ADMINISTRATION (FAA). A 1958 statute created the Federal Aviation Agency (Federal Aviation Administration since 1966), in part through the transfer of the Civil Aeronautics Administration and the safety-regulatory activities of the Civil Aeronautics Board. The FAA promotes civil aeronautics, with particular attention to safety and efficiency in the use of navigable airspace. It promulgates safety regulations and air traffic rules; examines, inspects, and maintains surveillance over equipment and the regulated activities of airmen; plans, constructs, and operates aids to navigation and communication; administers grants-in-aid for airport development; and engages in research on traffic and safety measures and devices. For some purposes its jurisdiction extends to military aviation.

FEDERAL AVIATION AGENCY. *See* **Aviation; Federal Agencies.**

FEDERAL BUREAU OF INVESTIGATION (FBI). Established July 26, 1908, by Attorney General Charles J. Bonaparte, the investigative arm of the U.S. Department of Justice was known originally as the Bureau of Investigation until the adoption of its present name on July 1, 1935. Reorganized in 1924 following the appointment of J. Edgar Hoover as director, the FBI is a fact-gathering and fact-reporting agency with headquarters in Washington, D.C., and field offices throughout the United States.

FBI jurisdiction covers a wide range of federal investigative matters in the criminal, civil, and security fields, including espionage, sabotage, and subversive activities. In general, the FBI is responsible for enforcing most federal criminal statutes. It reports to the attorney general, chief legal officer of the United States; to his assistants; and to the U.S. attorneys in federal districts for decisions about prosecutive action. Its National Crime Information Center (NCIC), established in 1967, maintains a computerized communications network linking law enforcement agencies in every state, the District of Columbia, and the Royal Canadian Mounted Police headquarters in Ottawa, Canada.

FEDERAL COMMUNICATIONS COMMISSION (FCC). Created by the Communications Act of 1934, superseding the Federal Radio Commission of 1927, the FCC is an independent agency that regulates interstate and foreign communications by radio, television, telegraph, wire, and cable. It is responsible for the development and operation—but not censorship—of broadcast services and for efficient telephone and telegraph service at reasonable rates. It also coordinates the Emergency Broadcast System of the national defense effort.

The commission consists of seven members appointed, with the Senate's approval, for seven-year terms by the president and a chairman who serves at the president's pleasure. The principal operating sections are the Cable Television Bureau, the Common Carrier Bureau, the Broadcast Bureau, the Safety and Special Radio Services Bureau, and the Field Engineering Bureau. The commission's jurisdiction covers the fifty states, Guam, Puerto Rico, and the Virgin Islands; its decisions may be appealed to the courts.

FEDERAL CONVENTION. *See* **Constitution of the United States.**

FEDERAL DEPOSIT INSURANCE CORPORATION (FDIC). Set up by Congress in 1933 to provide bank depositors insurance against loss of their deposits. All member banks of the Federal Reserve System must be insured. Other banks can choose to be insured; 97.8 percent of all commercial banks were covered by 1978. The insurance costs the banks a small percentage of their average deposits annually. Originally, deposits of up to $2,500 were insured, but this limit has been raised; in 1979 it stood at $40,000. The FDIC also examines bank operations. (*See also* Federal Savings and Loan Insurance Corporation.)

FEDERAL ELECTION CAMPAIGN ACT (1972). This act repealed the Corrupt Practices Act of 1925 and limited the amount candidates or their families could contribute to their own campaign. The act also limited to 10 cents per voter the amount that could be spent by congressional and the presidential candidates for media advertising, and strengthened the requirements for reporting of campaign receipts and expenditures, including names and addresses of all persons who made contributions in excess of $100.

FEDERAL EMERGENCY RELIEF ACT (1933). This act created the Federal Emergency Relief Administration (FERA) and authorized an appropriation of $500 million, allotting half this amount as direct relief to the states and the balance for distribution on the basis of $1 of federal aid for every $3 of state and local funds spent for relief. The act left the establishment of work relief projects to state and local bodies and authorized the RFC to supply the funds for distribution to the states through a relief administrator.

FEDERAL FARM BANKRUPTCY ACT. *See* **Frazier-Lemke Farm Bankruptcy Act.**

FEDERAL GOVERNMENT. The national political system created at the Constitutional Convention of 1787: the institutions of government (Congress, the presidency, and the Supreme Court); the basic roles and powers assigned to each of the three branches; the federal system, which divides power between national and state governments; the principle of separation of powers; and the checks-and-balances system, designed to protect the jurisdiction of each branch from the other two.

FEDERAL HIGHWAY ACT. *See* **Federal-Aid Highway Program.**

FEDERAL HOME LOAN BANK. The Federal Home Loan Bank Board was established by the Federal Home Loan Bank Act of 1932, a measure recommended to Congress by President Hoover in 1931. The act established a five-member board and created a series of discount banks for home mortgages. The Home Owners Loan Act of 1933 promoted the chartering of associations under the board, creating a system somewhat like the Federal Reserve System. It authorized the establishment of eight to twelve banks in different parts of the country with a total capital of $125 million. Eligible for membership in the system were building and loan associations, savings banks, and insurance companies. The board has undergone several changes of name, status, and function through Reorganization Plan 3 of 1947 and later legislation (1955). The board directs the Federal Home Loan Banks System and the Federal Savings and Loan Insurance Corporation.

FEDERAL HOUSING ADMINISTRATION. *See* **Housing and Urban Development, Department of.**

FEDERALIST. A collection of essays, also known as the *Federalist Papers,* written by James Madison, Alexander Hamilton, and John Jay following the Constitutional Convention of 1787, to influence ratification in New York of the Constitution of the United States. All the papers appeared over the signature Publius in reply to anonymous papers in the press condemning the new government.

FEDERALIST PARTY. The first Federalists were a cluster of nationalists within the Continental Congress (including Robert Morris, James Madison, George Washington, and John Jay) who were instrumental in calling the Constitutional Convention in 1787. Believing in a strong central government, virtually all members of the First Congress counted themselves Federalists; so did the president and all the members of the cabinet.

Initially Federalism was compatible with a wide range of opinion. But the First Congress quickly developed pro- and anti-administration alignments, most noticeably on financial policy, on foreign policy, on the location of the capital city, and on the breadth of executive discretionary power. In all areas except Virginia the established elites were Federalist.

The party also attracted strong and continuing support from frontier farmers in New York, who were pleased with the maintenance of stable relations with Indians, and farmers in western Virginia, who were skeptical of the tidewater planters. Nevertheless, in the 1790's supporters became alienated by a fiscal policy keyed to the interests of northern merchants and commercial farmers and a foreign policy they regarded as unduly dependent on maintaining good relations with England. By 1795 it was clear that an opposition party had mobilized around the agrarian philosophy of Thomas Jefferson (*see* Republicans, Jeffersonian). In the election of 1796, Federalist John Adams barely won the presidency against the Democratic-Republican candidate; in 1800, the Federalist party lost the presidency to Jefferson. After 1800 they did not again win a national election, but continued to offer opposition to their opponents for local and national office.

In 1804 a small cluster of impatient Federalists toyed with schemes of disunion. Thereafter Federalists expressed antiembargo and antiwar sentiments by mobilizing public dissent in corresponding committees and state conventions (*see* Hartford Convention). Although many drifted into the Republican party during the War of 1812, Federalists continued to control the state governments of Maryland, Delaware, Connecticut, and Massachusetts and to represent large popular minorities in other states; but the party disintegrated during the 1820's.

FEDERAL MEDIATION AND CONCILIATION SERVICE. The Federal Mediation and Conciliation Service was set up by the Labor-Management Relations (Taft-Hartley) Act of 1947 to replace the U.S. Conciliation Service situated in the Department of Labor (1913). The service seeks to minimize or prevent interruptions of commerce caused by labor-management disputes. On its own initiative or at the request of either party it lends assistance in conciliating or mediating differences over new contract terms or over grievances arising under existing contracts. The service has no law enforcement authority; refusal by either party to accept a recommendation of the agency violates no duty under the act. In its mediatory operations, it also tries to foster better day-to-day relations between labor and management.

FEDERAL POWER COMMISSION. The Federal Power Commission was created by statute in 1930, replacing an earlier commission of the same name (1920). The 1930 statute was amended by the Public Utility Act of 1935 and the Natural Gas Act of 1938. In the field of hydroelectric power and natural gas, the agency has purposes like those of other regulatory commissions. It works with other agencies in planning multipurpose river-basin development; licenses construction of power projects on navigable waters or government lands; and regulates the rates, the securities, the accounting practices, and the mergers of companies transmitting or wholesaling electrical energy. The commission exercises similar controls over interstate commerce in natural gas.

***FEDERAL REGISTER*.** The official journal of the U.S. government, authorized by Congress in 1935; in it are published all presidential proclamations, executive orders, and regulations having general application or legal effect, and such other documents as the president or Congress may direct.

FEDERAL RESERVE SYSTEM. The central bank of the United States, founded by the Owen-Glass Act of Dec. 23, 1913; comprised of twelve regional banks coordinated by a central board in Washington, D.C. A central bank is a bank for banks: it holds their deposits (their legal reserves) for safekeeping; it makes them loans; and it creates its own credit in the form of created deposits (additional legal reserves) or bank notes (Federal Reserve notes). It also has the responsibility of promoting economic stability by control of credit.

All national banks had to subscribe immediately 3 percent of their capital and surplus for stock in the Federal Reserve System; state banks might also become "members." The Federal Reserve System was thus superimposed on the National Banking System. In addition to providing a central bank, the new law supplied an elastic note issue of Federal Reserve notes based on commercial paper, whose supply rose and fell with the needs of business; it required member banks to keep half their legal reserves (after mid-1917, all of them) in their district Federal Reserve banks; and it improved the check-clearing system. The seven-man board took office Aug. 10, 1914, and the banks opened for business Nov. 16. At first the Federal Reserve's chief responsibilities were to create enough credit to carry on the nation's part of World War I and to process Liberty Bond sales.

The Federal Reserve did too little too late to stop the speculative boom that culminated in the 1929 crash. In the years 1930–33, more than 9,000 banks failed. The bank holocaust brought on congressional investigations and demands for reforms. By the act of Feb. 27, 1932, Congress temporarily permitted the Federal Reserve to use federal government obligations, as well as gold and commercial paper, to back Federal Reserve notes and deposits; the law soon became permanent.The Banking Act of June 16, 1933; parts of the Securities Act of May 27, 1933, and of the Securities Exchange Act of June 19, 1934; and the Banking Act of Aug. 23, 1935, increased the powers of the Federal Reserve System. The board was reorganized, without the secretary of the Treasury; it was given more control over member banks and over open-market operations; and it got important new credit-regulating powers.

In World War II, the Federal Reserve assisted with bond drives and saw to it that the federal government and member banks had ample funds for the war effort. Its regulation limiting consumer credit, price controls, and the depression before the war were mainly responsible for there being somewhat less inflation with somewhat more provocation than during World War I. Securities support purchases (1941–45), executed for the system by the New York Federal Reserve Bank, raised the system's holdings of Treasury obligations from about $2 billion to $24 billion. The Federal Reserve was not fully relieved of the duty to support federal government security prices until it concluded its "accord" with the Treasury, reported on Mar. 4, 1951.

A law of July 28, 1959, reduced member banks to two

classifications: 295 reserve city banks in fifty-one cities and about 6,000 "country" banks, starting not later than July 28, 1962. According to this law, member banks might count their vault cash as legal reserves; thereafter, the requirement for legal reserves against demand deposits was 10–22 percent for member city banks and 7–14 percent for member country banks. In 1979, members of the Federal Reserve System included 5,425 banks of 14,738 in the United States; they held about 75 percent of all U.S. bank deposits. (*See also* Banking.)

FEDERAL SAVINGS AND LOAN ASSOCIATIONS. *See* **Banking; Savings and Loan Associations.**

FEDERAL SAVINGS AND LOAN INSURANCE CORPORATION. A benefit of the National Housing Act, the Federal Savings and Loan Insurance Corporation was created by a law of June 27, 1934, to guarantee mortgages and insure savings accounts. Established as a corporation, capital stock was financed by the Home Owners Loan Corporation. It is directed by the Home Loan Bank Board. State member associations are not obliged to belong to it, although most do.

FEDERAL SECURITIES ACT (1933). Compelled full disclosure to investors of information relating to new securities issues offered publicly or through the mails or in interstate commerce. It required that with certain exceptions (federal, state, or municipal bonds; railroad securities; and securities of religious, charitable, and educational bodies) all new issues were to be registered with the Federal Trade Commission.

FEDERAL SPENDING POWER. *See* **Expenditures, Federal.**

FEDERAL-STATE RELATIONS. The Constitution defined federal powers but did not make clear the extent of state powers. To remedy this, the Tenth Amendment was added in 1791 as a part of the Bill of Rights, specifically reserving to the respective state or to the people "the powers not delegated to the United States by the Constitution, nor prohibited by it to the States." The amendment failed to draw a clear line, but it helped to establish the principle of dualism: matters of local concern should be handled by the states, while affairs of general importance should be taken care of by the federal government.

From the establishment of the first Bank of the United States in 1791 onward, the broad constructionists have gradually extended federal authority into the field reserved to the states. Prior to the Civil War, through the Kentucky and Virginia Resolutions of 1798 and 1799, the South Carolina nullification ordinance of 1832, and the secession in 1860–61 of eleven states, states' rights adherents sought to stop the centralizing tendencies of the federal government. Since the defeat of the Confederacy in 1865 there has been little effective resistance to the trend toward centralization.

The federal constitution itself limits the states in many ways; for example, in Article I, Section 10, and in Article IV, Sections 1 and 2 (*see* Constitution of the United States). Given the restrictions on the financial autonomy of the states, federal-state relations in the sphere of finance have become more and more important. With the passage of the first Social Security legislation in 1935, federal grants-in-aid to the states for the first time became substantial; they expanded significantly beyond the field of social welfare with the passage of the Federal-Aid Highway Act in 1956. By the mid-1970's the relative financial responsibilities of the federal government and the states and municipalities had become a strident issue, as state governors sent up the cry that urban development and public transportation, for example, were matters of national concern and that a proportion of revenues from federally levied taxes in fact belonged to the states. In January 1982, President Ronald Reagan presented his "new federalism" plan, according to which some forty federal programs would be transferred to individual states; the plan encountered opposition from many quarters.

FEDERAL TRADE COMMISSION (FTC). Created by Act of Congress (1914) to investigate any evidence of unfair business competition between companies engaged in interstate commerce. The commission consists of five members, no more than three of whom may belong to a single political party. An independent federal agency whose decisions have the force of law, it can require a company to stop unfair practices and can impose criminal penalties on firms when fraudulent intent or harm to health can be proved. The commission also controls radio and television advertising.

FEMINIST MOVEMENT. *See* **Woman's Rights Movement.**

FENCE VIEWERS. Local officers in New England, who verify property boundaries and administer laws relating to these boundaries. Except in Connecticut, where their duties are usually performed by selectmen, two or more are chosen at the annual town meeting for the ensuing year. They have the power to settle the location of the line fence and apportion the proper share of its cost on the owners.

FENCE WAR. The struggle that ensued when ranchmen began using barbed wire in the cattle country. In the early 1880's fence cutting became so serious in Texas that the full state ranger force was required to supplement the local authorities. (*See also* Barbed Wire.)

FENCING AND FENCING LAWS. Virginia in 1632 required crops to be fenced and in 1646 defined a legal, or "sufficient," fence. In Maryland the laws were similar, and in North Carolina, more rigid. Fencing law advanced with the movement of the frontier. Settlers insisted upon using unsold public land, and as settlement increased, the demand for fencing of pasture, rather than crops, arose and spread westward. The problem was general in the older states and became increasingly serious with the growing scarcity of timber. In 1867, Illinois passed a permissive law allowing local governmental units to require stock to be fenced in. Five years later, a law for preventing stock from running at large was made general unless suspended by local option. In 1870, Iowa passed a local-option law.

In sections of the East, stones from the fields were laid into fences. The zigzag, or Virginia rail, fence spread with the frontier; as timber became more scarce, post-and-pole, picket, and board fences became common and wire fencing came into use. Between 1850 and 1870, waves of enthusiasm for hedge fences swept from New England to Texas. In the treeless plains, cattlemen took possession of large areas, and were driving cattle to the railroad (*see* Cattle Drives); settlers could not protect their crops until the advent of barbed wire, when the frontier again began to move. Advancing settlers fenced their farms and the free open range began to disappear. Cattlemen fenced their own land, and until curbed by federal legislation in 1885, they frequently enclosed government land. In areas of mixed husbandry, the woven wire fence came into use near the close of the century.

FENIAN MOVEMENT. Originated in 1858 among Irish-Americans under John O'Mahony, to raise money, supply equipment, and provide leaders to aid the Irish Republican, or Revolutionary, Brotherhood in an uprising against Great Britain. Membership rose to 250,000. In October 1865 the Fenians established an "Irish Republic" in New York and ordered bond issues. A group called "the men of action" broke from the parent organization and conducted raids into Canada. Opposed by the federal government and the Roman Catholic church, members deserted to join the Land League and Home Rule movements. Their last congress was held on Jan. 28, 1876. O'Mahony's death, Feb. 6, 1877, virtually ended the brotherhood. (*See also* Campobello Fiasco.)

FERGUSON IMPEACHMENT. James E. Ferguson, previously unknown in Texas politics, was elected governor in 1914 and reelected in 1916. Soon after his second inauguration, the state house of representatives preferred twenty-one impeachment charges against him, including misappropriation of state funds, falsifications of records, unwarranted interference with the control of the University of Texas, and refusal to divulge the source of a personal loan of $156,500. He was found guilty on ten charges, removed from office, and disqualified from holding public office.

FERRIES. Used to cross all large streams in colonial days, they were only gradually replaced by bridges or tunnels. The island position of Manhattan necessitated ferry connections with Staten Island, Long Island, and the west bank of the Hudson. Ferries were also important in Boston Harbor; Hampton Roads, Va.; and across the Delaware between Philadelphia and Camden, N.J. In the West, ferries persisted between San Francisco and the East Bay well after construction of the Bay Bridge and, in the early 1980's, in Puget Sound. Car ferries had an important role across lakes Michigan, Erie, and Ontario; the Straits of Mackinac; the lower Mississippi; the Detroit River; and Suisun Bay. In 1982 some Lake Michigan ferries were still operating. A resurgence of ferryboats, resulting from the energy crisis and environmental considerations, occurred in the late 1970's.

FERRIS WHEEL. A noted feature of the World's Columbian Exposition at Chicago in 1893 was a huge upright steel wheel with passenger cars swung around its rim—the first of many such wheels. It was built by George W. G. Ferris, a Pittsburgh engineer.

FERROUS METALS. Iron leads all metals produced from domestic ores in the United States, in both quantity and value. Of the other metals of commerce in the ferrous group—manganese, chromium, nickel, cobalt, columbium, molybdenum, vanadium, and tungsten—only nickel, molybdenum, and vanadium are produced in any commercial quantity from U.S. ores. The importance of these metals lies largely in the use of iron for making steel and in the combining of several metals to form special alloys.

Iron. The first use of iron ore in the United States was apparently by the Indians: natural iron oxides were used for war paint and other coloring purposes. American colonial ironmaking ventures began in the early 1600's, at sites near iron ore deposits. Mining began in Virginia, but the first successful integrated ironmaking operation was in Massachusetts. Mining of a vast iron ore district in the Lake Superior region began in 1846, and by 1892 the Mesabi Range was the leading domestic source. As the better ores became depleted following World War II, the industry turned to low-grade ores of the taconite type. Subsequently the federal government provided aid for the exploration of domestic iron ore and for rapid amortization of taconite plants, through the Defense Production Act of 1950. Taconite ores continue to compete with high-grade foreign ores and have gradually replaced the lower-grade domestic direct-shipping ores. More than 90 percent of domestic iron ore was being mined in the 1970's from large open pits, underground mines having been closed because of high costs. In the late 1970's domestic mines produced over two-thirds of U.S. iron ore needs, the remainder being supplied largely by Canada, Venezuela, and Brazil. Total consumption of iron ore and agglomerates amounted to 125 million tons in 1979, averaging 62.5 percent iron content. Reserves of iron ore were estimated at approximately 2 billion tons of recoverable metal. (*See also* Iron and Steel Industry.)

Manganese. Mining of manganese in the United States dates from 1837, when ore was produced for use in coloring earthenware. It was mined in quantity for use in steelmaking in several states during the period from the Civil War to the early 1900's, and production of iron-manganese alloys was started in the 1870's. Although manganese deposits are found throughout the United States, they are either small or of very low grade; as early as 1905 domestic production was insignificant in comparison with imports. Industrial consumption of manganese ore in the United States was 1.4 million short tons in 1979, essentially all converted to alloy form for the iron and steel industry.

Chromium. Chromite, the principal chromium mineral, was first found in the United States in Maryland in 1827 and used for pigment purposes. This source proved small and was soon depleted, but a second mine was opened in 1829 in Lancaster County, Pa., and operated on a small scale for about fifty years. Other eastern discoveries were not large, and by 1896 production shifted to California, Montana, and Oregon, before being replaced by imports from the Near East near the end of the century. The Defense Production Act of 1950 stimulated domestic production; it was terminated in 1958, when stockpile objectives were reached. No ore has been mined since 1961. Domestic resources were estimated in the 1970's at somewhat less than 2 million tons of equivalent metal contained in over 20 million tons of chromite material, all located in the West and Alaska.

Nickel. Small amounts of nickel ore were obtained from mining operations near Lancaster Gap, Pa., and Fredericktown, Mo., in 1853–93, but until 1954, when a mine was opened at Riddle, Oreg., domestic primary nickel was produced mainly as a by-product of copper refining. In the 1970's domestic reserves were estimated at about 400 million equivalent pounds of metal in deposits near the Riddle, Oreg.; low-grade nickel resources existed in Minnesota and Wisconsin.

Cobalt. Cobalt is a relatively rare element in the earth's crust. Limited amounts have been produced in the United States as a by-product of iron, nickel, copper, and zinc-refining operations; small quantities of cobalt ore were mined beginning in the 1900's. Ore from the Blackbird district of Idaho was refined in a plant at Garfield, Utah (1953–59). Beginning in the 1940's by-product cobalt was produced from concentrate obtained at the Cornwall, Pa., iron-mining operation of Bethlehem Steel Corporation. Production ceased in 1971, leaving domestic needs dependent on imports and stockpiled materials.

Columbium. In 1801, Charles Hachett, an English chemist, discovered a new element while analyzing a heavy black mineral previously found in New England; he named the element columbium after the poetic alias of its country of origin, "Columbia." Only small amounts have been located in the eastern United States since then, and the first sizable domestic commercial production was recorded in 1918, when columbite, containing its sister metal tantalum, was mined in the Black Hills of South Dakota. Columbium and tantalum are generally interchangeable for steel alloy use (tantalum is of particular importance for electronic uses). Limited domestic mining continued through the 1920's and 1930's, mostly in the western states. In the early 1940's columbium demand began to increase, and foreign sources were turned to almost exclusively. Under the stimulus of a government purchase plan (1952–59), concentrates of columbium and tantalum were produced and stockpiled. In the 1960's and 1970's, production of columbium was essentially from imported concentrates, slags, and ferrocolumbium; no domestic ore has been produced since 1971. National stockpile inventories have been maintained.

Molybdenum. Production of molybdenum is centered in the United States, where more than 50 percent of identified world resources are located. The principal U.S. source is a vast deposit at Climax, Colo., which was developed, along with the Questa deposit in New Mexico, to meet World War I demands. The Climax deposit, the largest known, is mined by underground caving methods. U.S. molybdenum reserves were estimated in the late 1970's at 4 million tons.

Vanadium. At the beginning of the 20th century both vanadium and uranium-vanadium ores were discovered in Colorado. In 1906 two reduction plants were erected near Newmire, Colo., to process the ores, recovered vanadium being used principally as a steel additive. Further explorations uncovered ores in several other states, principally in the Four Corners area of the Southwest. World War I stimulated production, and in 1918 about half the world's vanadium production came from the area. By 1929, U.S. production had decreased to less than 20 percent of the world's reported output. World War II resulted in a rapid recovery of the vanadium industry; after the war, vanadium output further increased as a by-product of uranium-vanadium ores processed to recover uranium, and from the late 1940's to 1960 the United States was the world's principal source, with some being exported. Electric-furnace smelting of western phosphate ores to elemental phosphorus has resulted in some vanadium recovery from the ferrophosphorus produced as a by-product, and mining of vanadium ore is done in Arkansas. Domestic consumption of vanadium was 6,719 short tons in 1979, domestic production, 5,758 short tons.

Tungsten. The existence of tungsten-ore deposits in the United States was known as early as 1872, but an appreciable demand did not occur until the 1900's, when Frederick W. Taylor and Maunsel White developed tungsten steel with the unique property of holding a cutting edge at dull red heat. Tungsten has been produced in the area between the Rocky Mountains and the Pacific coast. In the 1970's almost all domestic tungsten production was associated with other metals, mainly molybdenum, recovered in western mining operations. An estimated 10 percent of the world's tungsten resources is located in the United States.

FERTILIZERS. Early colonists farmed poor soils that were rapidly depleted in fertility. Through necessity, farmlands were fertilized with animal manure, waste fish, seaweed, tannery wastes, and slaughterhouse by-products. The use of gypsum was introduced from France by Benjamin Franklin; it had considerable popularity, along with lime, among the German farmers of Pennsylvania. Edmund Ruffin began experimenting with lime, in the form of marl, on his rundown plantation in Virginia. Favorable results led to his *Essay on Calcareous Manures* (1832). When European chemists revealed that phosphorus, potassium (potash), and nitrogen were chemicals of critical importance in plant growth, America turned to chemical fertilizers. Superphosphate began to be produced in Baltimore in 1849. In 1850, Thomas and P. S. Chappell obtained a patent for mixed fertilizer consisting of bones, sulfuric acid, ammoniacal liquors, and residues of chemical processing industries. U.S. phosphate deposits were developed as the century progressed. St. Julien Ravenel recognized the importance of rock phosphate deposits along the Ashley and Cooper rivers in South Carolina; his ammoniated and acidified phosphates, developed from 1867 onward, were an important factor in the revival of agriculture in the South. There was rapid growth of the fertilizer industry around Charleston until 1881, when Florida deposits of rock phosphate began to be developed. After 1893, Tennessee also became a major producer.

Organic wastes (fish, slaughterhouse wastes) were the principal sources of fertilizer nitrogen until the mid-19th century. Guano began to be imported from islands off the coast of Peru in significant quantities after 1848. However, ruthless exploitation curtailed the supply. Saltpeter (sodium nitrate) was mined on a high desert plateau in northern Chile, although production and marketing were controlled by British firms. Ammonium sulfate, made available by the extraction of ammonia from coal gas, took on increasing importance during the 19th century as the coking and illuminating gas industries expanded. The cyanamide process for fixation of atmospheric nitrogen utilized the electric furnace to produce calcium cyanamide from limestone, coke, and air; initiated in Germany, it had substantial development in the United States during and after World War I. The product was a potential source of ammonia but could also be used directly as a fertilizer. After World War II, farm equipment was developed for the direct use of anhydrous (water-free and liquid) ammonia as a fertilizer. Potassium became available as a mineral salt for fertilizer compounding in the late 19th century, with the development of the Stassfurt salt deposits in Germany; the German chemical industry subsequently developed a world monopoly in potash. When supplies were cut off during World War I, American agriculture was severely handicapped. During the 1920's the United States became self-sufficient by development of potash resources found in the brines of Searles Lake, Calif.; in the salt flats near Wendover, Utah; and in the desert near Carlsbad, N.Mex.

In the 1970's the fertilizer industry faced serious problems with respect to future sources of raw materials (phosphate rock, potash salts, and hydrogen from petroleum and natural gas for synthesis of ammonia). Fertilizers were also coming under criticism from environmentalists, since water runoff from heavily fertilized lands caused serious eutrophication of nearby lakes and streams. Use of chemical fertilizers in the United States was 51.1 million tons in 1979, double the figure of 1960. Exports in 1979 were valued at $1.4 billion, while imports were valued at $976 million.

FETTERMAN MASSACRE (Dec. 21, 1866). The chief victory of the Sioux and Cheyenne during Red Cloud's war against Fort Phil Kearny, Wyo. Capt. William Fetterman was sent with eighty men from the fort to relieve a wood transport train that had been attacked by Indians. Although instructed not to cross a line of hills called Lodge Trail Ridge, Fetterman was lured by Crazy Horse and a decoy party of mounted warriors until his command was trapped on the other side of the ridge. Every man in the command was killed. (*See also* Sioux Wars.)

FEUDALISM. One of the motives prompting colonization of the New World was the desire on the part of noblemen to establish feudal domains in America, as in the proprietary colonies. For example, the Maryland grant bestowed on Lord Baltimore and his heirs extensive seignorial rights and made the entire area a barony. The feudal idea also appeared in the Carolinas, New Jersey, Delaware, and the Dutch settlements along the Hudson River.

Many feudal legal principles and practices have influenced American law. Feudalism's greatest contribution to English and American political institutions came from the contractual element that existed between lord and vassal. This concept was translated to the relations existing between the crown and its subjects; the idea that the crown must live within the law was brought to the New World and exists today in the political philosophy that government should be subject to a higher law, whether it be natural law or the Constitution.

FEUDS, APPALACHIAN MOUNTAIN. In the mountainous regions of Kentucky, Tennessee, North Carolina, Virginia, and West Virginia in 1860, the topography of the country and the sparsity of population made law enforcement difficult, and the people were distrustful of the courts as institutions of justice. Bitter disputes arose between mountaineers over even trifling matters; straying livestock, the "wronging" of a woman, or the killing of a dog could set friend against friend. The greatest single cause for dispute was the division of sentiment over the Civil War, when armed bands of regulators attempted to intimidate people on both sides of the national issue. Most outstanding of the mountain feuds were those of Hatfield-McCoy (1880–87), Martin-Tolliver (1874–87), French-Eversole (1885–94), and Hargis-Callahan-Cockrell (1899–1903).

FFV. The initials of "First Families of Virginia," a term first used satirically in the North in the 19th century to denominate aristocratic families of Virginia who were proud of their descent from the early settlers of the colony; only a few of these families—such as Wyatt, Throckmorton, Peyton, and Fairfax—can claim a direct lineage from the peerage.

FIAT MONEY. *See* **Money.**

FIDDLERS AND FIDDLE TUNES. Fiddlers have flourished mainly in the South. Religious revivals of the 18th century and the association of the fiddle with licentiousness brought fiddling into a disrepute expressed by the phrase "thick as fiddlers in hell"; but the fiddle held its own, as attested by the widespread tradition of "The Arkansas Traveler" toward the middle of the 19th century. Lecturing on "The Fiddle and the Bow," Robert L. (Bob) Taylor fiddled himself into the governorship of Tennessee in 1887. Texas cowboys at night fiddled popular tunes to appreciative longhorns.

FIELD MUSEUM OF NATURAL HISTORY. Chartered Sept. 16, 1893, as the Columbian Museum of Chicago to contain most of the exhibits from the World's Columbian

Exposition of that year. Funded largely by Marshall Field, it opened in the Palace of Fine Arts, Jackson Park, on June 2, 1894, with departments of geology, botany, zoology, and anthropology, and moved to its present building in Grant Park in 1921. The museum is also noted for its expeditions, publications, and public education program.

***FIELD* V. *CLARK*,** 143 U.S. 649 (1892). The Supreme Court ruled that the McKinley Tariff Act of 1890—which empowered the president to take certain articles off the free list if he found that the countries exporting such products to the United States unreasonably discriminated against American agricultural products—was a delegation of discretion as to the facts, not the law, and thus was not unconstitutional.

FIFTEENTH AMENDMENT (proclaimed Mar. 30, 1870). In an attempt to guarantee the franchise to the newly emancipated slaves, the Fifteenth Amendment forbids federal and state governments to deny or abridge the right to vote "on account of race, color, or previous condition of servitude" and empowers the Congress "to enforce this article by appropriate legislation." It evoked endless countermeasures in the southern states, some purporting to be legal and others frankly defying the law, relying upon violence, intimidation, and fraud (*see* Grandfather Clause; Literacy Test; Poll Tax; Primary, White). Blacks were kept from the polls until the Civil Rights acts of 1957, 1960, and 1964, and especially the Voting Rights Act of 1965, drastically diminished the force of discriminatory tactics.

FIFTHS MINING TAX. The provision that one-fifth of all metals mined belonged to the crown is found in Spanish and Mexican law as well as English colonial charters. William Penn reserved an additional fifth in his subgrants. The Continental Congress in 1785 reserved a third for the government. The United States did not adopt this principle and definitely rejected it in the Mineral Patent Law of 1866.

"FIFTY-FOUR FORTY OR FIGHT." The Oregon country between the Rocky Mountains and the Pacific Ocean, from California to Alaska, or between 42° and 54° 40′ north latitude, was long claimed, and jointly occupied, by both England and the United States. In July 1843 an Oregon convention at Cincinnati, Ohio, adopted a resolution demanding 54° 40′ as the American boundary. In a speech in the Senate in 1844, Sen. William Allen of Ohio used the phrase "Fifty-four forty or fight," and the slogan became the battle cry of the expansionist Democrats. Emigrants for Oregon in the spring of 1846 painted the legend "Fifty-four forty" on their wagon covers. (*See also* Oregon Treaty of 1846.)

"FIGHT IT OUT ON THIS LINE IF IT TAKES ALL SUMMER." A line in a message of May 11, 1864, from Gen. Ulysses S. Grant to Gen. Henry Wager Halleck, written at Spotsylvania Courthouse, Va., after the Battles of the Wilderness; it expressed Grant's determination to continue his plan of advance on Richmond despite heavy losses and only partial successes.

FIGUREHEADS. Ships have used figureheads since ancient Egyptian times. The figurehead was used on American ships as early as the Revolution. John Paul Jones is credited with designing a goddess of Liberty for the *America*, the first ship-of-the-line of the United States. William Rush of Philadelphia, a famous figurehead carver, designed heads for the frigates *Constellation* and *United States*. The *Constitution* carried five different figureheads during its long career, the most notable being that of Andrew Jackson. In 1909, by the Navy Department's order, figureheads were removed from the navy's fighting ships.

FILIBUSTER, CONGRESSIONAL. The practice in the U.S. Senate of prolonging debate and using other delaying tactics to prevent action by forcing the body to end its consideration of a proposal. Although supported as a means to promote full and open debate on issues, it has been used more frequently simply to frustrate attempts to pass legislation. In 1917 the Senate adopted cloture provisions for limiting debate; since then more than fifty major filibusters have been recorded on such measures as civil rights bills, the communications satellite bill, and reform of the military draft system. The longest filibuster ranged over seventy-five days in 1964; the individual record belongs to Sen. J. Strom Thurmond, who in 1957 held the floor for over twenty-four hours.

FILIBUSTERING. The word "filibuster" is an English corruption of the Dutch *Vrijbuiter* ("freebooter"); in the mid-19th century it came to be applied to American adventurers engaged in armed expeditions against countries with which the United States was at peace. The Burr conspiracy and Essex Junto are examples. Expansionist sentiment in the Far West and in the Lower South caused the filibustering activities of 1850–60. In 1849, 1850, and 1851, Narciso López, a former Spanish general, supported by several prominent southern leaders, led three unsuccessful expeditions against Cuba (*see* López Filibustering Expeditions). In California, in 1851–52 two stranded Frenchmen, the Marquis de Pindray and Count Gaston Raoul de Raousset-Boulbon, mustered several hundred discontented compatriots for two independent expeditions into the Mexican state of Sonora. In 1853, William Walker, a lawyer and editor, sailed from San Francisco with a small force and landed in Lower California, which he then proclaimed an independent republic; shortly thereafter he "annexed" neighboring Sonora. In 1855, Walker turned his attention to Nicaragua (*see* Walker Filibustering Expeditions). Filibustering was halted by the Civil War and never again became the problem that it was in the 1850's.

FILLMORE, FORT. Established 1851 in New Mexico, about thirty-six miles north of El Paso, Tex. On July 26, 1861, the Union troops at this fort evacuated it and subsequently surrendered. Reoccupied by Union forces on Aug. 11, 1862, the fort does not appear to have been used after the Civil War.

FILMS. *See* **Motion Pictures.**

FILSON'S MAP. "This map of Kentucke," drawn by John Filson, was engraved by Henry D. Pursell and printed by T. Rook in Philadelphia in 1784. It was based on surveys made by Daniel Boone and others, and supplemented Filson's *The Discovery, Settlement and Present State of Kentucke,* (Wilmington, Del., 1784). Although crude, the map was popular; at least 1,500 copies were printed and there were at least six different issues.

FINCASTLE, FORT. *See* **Henry, Fort.**

FINCASTLE COUNTY. The name given by the Virginia Assembly in 1772 to the part of the colony west of the Kanawha River and south of the Ohio; it included all of the present state of Kentucky. In 1776, Fincastle County was divided into three new counties, Kentucky being the name for one.

FINNEY, FORT, TREATY OF (Jan. 31, 1786). An agreement with the Indians of the lower Ohio Valley and the Lake country concerning lands in the Old Northwest ceded to the United States by England in 1783 by the Definitive Treaty of Peace. Negotiations were undertaken for the purpose of inducing the Shawnee, Miami, Ouiatenon, Piankashaw, Potawatomi, and Kickapoo to consent to the assignment of areas for their hunting grounds and to waive their claims to lands previously wrung from the Iroquois by the Treaty of Fort Stanwix (November 1768) and from the Delaware and Wyandot at Fort McIntosh (January 1785). Only the Shawnee met the U.S. commissioners at Fort Finney, near the junction of the Great Miami and Ohio rivers. Obliged by threats of force to sign what was called a treaty of cession and to consent to moving to a district between the Wabash and Great Miami, the Shawnee later repudiated the treaty; the United States did not attempt to enforce it.

FINNEY REVIVALS. Evangelist Charles G. Finney began preaching at revivals in central New York about 1825; from 1827 to 1835, meetings held in most large cities resulted in thousands of conversions. The revivals aroused much opposition because of Finney's "new measures," especially his introduction of the "anxious bench," where awakened sinners sat in public view. His converts furnished leadership for the many reform movements preceding the Civil War.

FIRE-EATERS. Southern proslavery extremists who, as early as the 1840's, advocated secession and the formation of a separate confederacy; among those who preached such doctrines were R. B. Rhett, Edmund Ruffin, and W. L. Yancey. Few acquired responsible positions after the Confederacy materialized.

FIRE FIGHTING. In colonial times city householders and businesses were required by law to keep a specified number of leather buckets on hand for fire emergencies. Some of the larger cities owned hooked ladders; smaller towns had no protection. In 1730, New York City imported from Holland two hand-pumping machines. Companies were all volunteer, the members running to the engine house and drawing the machine by hand to the conflagration; water had to be pumped from wells, ponds, or streams. The first telegraph fire-signal system was put into operation in Boston, in 1852. The steam fire engine was introduced in 1829–30; Cincinnati, Ohio, installed the first salaried steam fire department in 1853. New York City's volunteer firemen were not abolished until 1865. In the later 19th century, fireproof or fire-resistant buildings began to be built, the chemical fire extinguisher was developed, and the sprinkling system came into use.

In the 20th century, fire departments were motorized. By 1910, high-pressure hydrant systems were being introduced. Beginning in the late 1950's, new and improved equipment was introduced throughout the United States: the super pumper, capable of pumping 8,000 gallons of water per minute at very high pressure (necessary for fighting fires in very tall structures); the snorkel truck, equipped with a cherry picker boom to replace the traditional extension ladder; foam, for fighting oil fires.

FIRELANDS. A tract of 500,000 acres, largely within the two westernmost counties (Huron and Erie) of the Western Reserve, granted by the state of Connecticut to citizens of nine "suffering towns" for losses totaling $538,495.26 resulting from British raids during the Revolution. The proprietors were incorporated by law of Connecticut (1796) and Ohio (1803). Lands were partitioned in 1808, and settlement began.

FIRES, GREAT. *See* **Disasters.**

"FIRESIDE CHATS." On Mar. 12, 1933, President Franklin D. Roosevelt initiated the practice of addressing the American public by nationwide radio broadcast. The so-called "fireside chat" became customary during his administration, and has been used by other elected officials, most notably President Jimmy Carter.

"FIRE WHEN YOU ARE READY, GRIDLEY." An order given by Commodore George Dewey to Capt. Charles V. Gridley on board the flagship *Olympia* at the opening of the Battle of Manila Bay in the Philippines (May 1, 1898).

"FIRST IN WAR, FIRST IN PEACE, AND FIRST IN THE HEARTS OF HIS COUNTRYMEN." Words written by Gen. Henry ("Light-Horse Harry") Lee as a part of the resolutions offered by John Marshall in Congress on the death of George Washington. They were repeated in Lee's memorial oration in Philadelphia, Dec. 26, 1799.

FIRST LADY OF THE LAND. The wife of the president of the United States or the woman designated to be hostess at the White House. The unofficial title of "First Lady" originated during the first half of the 19th century. The phrase "First Lady of the Land," surrounded by quotation marks, was applied to Lucy Webb Hayes by Mary Clemmer Ames in 1877; it does not seem to have had a wide journalistic use until after the production (1911–12) of Charles Frederic Nirdlinger's play about Dolley Madison, entitled *The First Lady of the Land.*

FISH AND MARINE BIOLOGY. The history of the study of American fishes can be roughly divided into two periods: the first, primarily one of exploration and description, and the second (from about 1870) one of biology and management. Thomas Harriot's *Briefe and True Report of the New Found Land of Virginia* (1588) contained two paragraphs on fish and one on fishing. More important were the drawings that John White made of fish and other wildlife on his voyages to Roanoke (1584–90). Capt. John Smith listed fishes found in both Virginia and New England in the account of his travels (1624); Thomas Morton discussed thirteen kinds of saltwater fish of importance as food in his *New English Canaan* (1637); and John Josselyn listed in his *New England Rarities* (1672) over eighty kinds of fish found in the coastal region of Massachusetts. In his *New Voyage to Carolina* (1709) John Lawson listed thirty-seven salt- and twenty-one freshwater fishes. John Brickell incorporated much of Lawson's information in *The Natural History of North Carolina* (1737). Mark Catesby, in *Natural History of Carolina, Florida and the Bahama Islands* (1731–43), illustrated forty-six fishes (four copied from White's drawings). Carl Linnaeus requested that Alexander Garden, a Scotsman living in Charleston, S.C., send him fish specimens; Linnaeus included the description of forty new species in his *Systema naturae* (12th ed., 3 vols., 1766–68). Johann David Schoepf, a surgeon with the Hessian troops during the American Revolution, wrote a paper on the fishes of New York that was published at Berlin in 1787; it was the first ichthyological paper written in America and the first concerned solely with American species.

Jeremy Belknap provided a list of the various species of fish to be found in his state and a discussion of the conservation of the river species in his *History of New Hampshire* (vol. III, 1792). The Meriwether Lewis and William Clark expedition (1803–06) brought back twelve new species of fish from the West. Samuel Latham Mitchill, assisted by Samuel Akerly and S. G. Mott, published a lengthy illustrated paper on the fishes of New York (1814). The first book on American fishes was written by Constantine Rafinesque; while professor of botany and natural history at Transylvania University (Lexington, Ky.), he published *Ichthyologia Ohioensis, or Natural History of the Fishes Inhabiting the River Ohio and Its Tributary Streams* (1820). Useful works on the fishes of particular areas were later published by Jerome V. C. Smith (Massachusetts, 1833), James E. De Kay (New York, 1842), John Edwards Holbrook (South Carolina, 1855–60), and Louis Agassiz (Lake Superior, 1850).

Institutional support improved considerably with establishment of the Smithsonian Institution (1846), the Museum of Comparative Zoology at Harvard University (1859), and the American Museum of Natural History (1869). Spencer Fullerton Baird directed the natural history research that went on in the Smithsonian Institution and in the West. Agassiz was responsible for the founding of the Museum of Comparative Zoology and trained many outstanding naturalists, including the ichthyologists Charles Frederic Girard, David Starr Jordan, and his own son, Alexander Agassiz. Jordan was the foremost ichthyologist in America from the 1870's until the 1920's; his *Synopsis of the Fishes of North America* (1883) and *Fishes of North and Middle America* (1896–1900) are indicative of the broad scope of his studies. Also prominent during that period were Theodore N. Gill, Charles Henry Gilbert, and Barton Warren Evermann. The study of fossil fish flourished under the leadership of Edward D. Cope, Charles R. Eastman, and Louis Hussakoff.

In 1870 there was an important shift of emphasis from exploration to management. First, the American Fish Culturists' Association was founded in that year in New York City; this organization, which changed its name in 1886 to the American Fisheries Society, has played a leading role in the development of fishery biology. Second, in 1870 Baird began his successful efforts to establish the U.S. Fish Commission; he was appointed its first commissioner in 1871. His assistant, George Brown Goode, edited and partly wrote the commission's detailed survey on *The Fisheries and Fishery Industries of the United States* (8 vols., 1884–87). The commission's work was concentrated upon oceanic and Great Lakes fisheries, other freshwater fish being left to the state fish and wildlife services for study. During the 1870's and 1880's there was an unwise reliance upon untested large-scale fish-stocking programs; as a result of widespread failures, management studies were eventually placed on a broad ecological base.

Management studies depend in part upon exploratory and descriptive studies, of which Stephen A. Forbes and Robert E. Richardson published an outstanding example, *The Fishes of Illinois* (1908). Others of note were written by David H. Storer (Massachusetts, 1867), Tarleton H. Bean (Pennsylvania, 1893; New York, 1901–05), Hugh M. Smith (North Carolina, 1907), Theodore D. A. Cockerell (Rocky Mountain region, 1908), and John O. Snyder (surveys of fishes of various rivers in the Far West, 1900–20). Goode published a manual on the food and game fishes of America in 1888, as did Jordan and Evermann in 1902. Goode and Bean also published a treatise on oceanic ichthyology in 1896. John T. Nichols founded *Copeia* in 1914; it became the official journal of the new American Society of Ichthyologists and Herpetologists in 1916.

Down to the end of World War II the management of American fisheries steadily worsened in spite of a slow increase in understanding. After the war, however, state and federal funds were more generously invested in management and management research, and fishery training programs were greatly expanded in universities across the country. The investigation and regulation of the Pacific tuna fishery before it reached the danger point are illustrative of the management capabilities that the fishery biologists have achieved.

Marine Life. Congressional interest in the development of marine biology can be traced back to the establishment of such agencies as the Coast and Geodetic Survey (1807). From its beginning the U.S. Navy encouraged voyages of exploration and publication of results. In 1838, Congress placed Charles Wilkes in command of the U.S. Exploring Expedition, which included a philologist, conchologist, botanist, horticulturist, mineralogist, two naturalists, and two draftsmen. Matthew Fontaine Maury, a U.S. naval officer and noted navigator, helped stimulate interest in deep-sea marine organisms through his *Physical Geography of the Sea* (1855). Beginning in 1850, the U.S. Coast and Geodetic Survey assisted in extended biological surveys of the East and Gulf coasts. In 1877 the survey invited Alexander Agassiz of the Museum of Comparative Zoology at Harvard to take charge of an expedition to examine the physical and biological conditions of the Gulf Stream and the waters around Cuba, Key West, Yucatán, and the Tortuga Islands, using their steamer *Blake*. The *Blake* carried on marine studies into the early 20th century.

In 1882 the *Albatross*, the first ship to be built especially for marine research by any government, was built for the Bureau of Fisheries; it amassed one of the greatest collections of marine organisms made by a single ship. The *Albatross* was sold in 1921; the *Fish Hawk*, a specially designed ichthyological research vessel, was disposed of in 1926. The navy then transferred the ocean tug *Patuxent*, renamed *Albatross II*, to the bureau; it went out of service in 1934. The *Harvard*, built (1926) as a New England steam trawler, was sold in 1939 to the Bureau of Fisheries for $1 and renamed *Albatross III;* it served as a fisheries research ship from 1948 until 1959. The *Albatross IV* was built in 1963 for National Marine Fisheries Service research in the northwest Atlantic; in the mid-1970's, *Albatross IV* operated out of the Marine Biological Laboratory at Woods Hole. The Bureau of Sport Fisheries and Wildlife, established in 1956 and renamed the U.S. Fish and Wildlife Service (Department of the Interior) in 1974, supported in the late 1970's thirteen fish-and-wildlife laboratories and ninety-one national fish hatcheries.

During the second and third decades of the 19th century the foundation of scientific societies, such as the Philadelphia Academy of Natural Sciences (1812), and of scientific periodicals exercised an important influence on the study of marine life. In 1846, James Dwight Dana published his epoch-making *Report on the Zoophytes*, followed by Joseph Leidy's work on some of the parasites of marine fauna. After Louis Agassiz's death in 1873 the distinctive school that he founded flourished under the leadership of his son, Alexander, and E. L. Mark at Harvard University and W. K. Brooks at the Johns Hopkins University. From these two centers the study of marine invertebrates spread across the country.

FISH COMMISSION, UNITED STATES. By joint resolution (Feb. 9, 1871) Congress directed the appointment of a commissioner of fish and fisheries to investigate and propose remedies for the declining productivity of American fisheries. The first commissioner (1871–87) was zoologist Spencer Fullerton Baird. The commission sponsored investigations in marine biology, operating a scientific laboratory at Woods Hole, Mass., and the research ship *Albatross*. In 1872, working with state agencies, it began to propagate and distribute game and commercial fish species. In 1877 it also began to collect data for American fisheries and to aid commercial fishermen in locating new fishing grounds and improving fishing techniques. In 1903 the Fish Commission became the Bureau of Fisheries of the new Department of Commerce and Labor.

FISHDAM FORD, BATTLE OF (Nov. 9, 1780). Gen. Thomas Sumter with nearly 600 men was in camp at Fishdam Ford on Broad River, in northwestern South Carolina, on the night of Nov. 8–9, 1780. The encampment was attacked by British Maj. James Wemyss, about 1 A.M.; Sumter's men repelled the attack, wounding and capturing Wemyss.

FISHER, FORT, CAPTURE OF (1864–65). Fort Fisher, N.C., kept the Cape Fear River open for use by blockade runners during the Civil War. In winter 1864, Gen. Robert E. Lee, wrote from Petersburg that the post must be held because without it he could not provision his army. On Dec. 24, 1864, a Union fleet of sixty vessels under Adm. David Porter, carrying infantry under Gen. B. F. Butler, bombarded the fort for several hours and landed the infantry; realizing the position could not be taken, the soldiers and fleet withdrew. On Jan. 13, 1865, the fleet returned and bombarded the fortification for two days and nights; on Jan. 15 a force of 2,000 sailors and marines landed and attacked the ocean front of the fortress, but were repulsed. Shortly afterward, the infantry penetrated a rear salient, and the fort was taken.

FISHERIES DISPUTE, ARBITRATION OF. The Definitive Treaty of Peace of 1783 between Great Britain and the United States recognized the liberty of U.S. citizens to fish within the territorial waters of British North America. The War of 1812 put an end to this treaty. The Convention of 1818 respecting fisheries, boundary, and the restoration of slaves again recognized the "liberty forever," but only in stipulated territorial waters—on the western and northern coasts of Newfoundland, the shores of the Magdalen Islands, and the coast of Labrador; it allowed landing privileges for refreshment of fishermen in the renounced areas. Serious disputes over the exercise of these liberties and landing privileges occurred from 1836 to 1854, when the fisheries question was again adjusted as a part of the Canadian-American Reciprocity Treaty. The Treaty of Washington (1871) restored to U.S. citizens the privileges renounced by the Convention of 1818 and temporarily recaptured by the reciprocity treaty.

The fishery article of the Treaty of Washington came to an end in 1885; from then until 1909 the precise liberties of American fishermen in British territorial waters according to the Convention of 1818 were the matter of constant bitter dispute, particularly concerning the territorial jurisdiction of Great Britain in nontreaty waters, over bays less than six miles across from headland to headland. The dispute was referred by an agreement of both governments (Jan. 27, 1909) to the Permanent Court of Arbitration at The Hague, which laid down (Sept. 7, 1910) definitive decisions and regulations.

FISHERIES DISPUTES. Independence from Great Britain led to a number of disputes over the right to fish in waters off the British-held territories of Nova Scotia, Labrador, and Canada; these fishing "banks" were used regularly by American fishing fleets from Gloucester, Boston, Newport, New Haven, and New York (*see* Fisheries Dispute, Arbitration of). Disputes have also taken place with other powers. Since World War II, a number of Russian fleets have operated in the same areas as U.S. fishing boats; there has been disagreement over the proper way to control the catch of certain species to insure that the fish will not be exhausted as a resource; and there have been arguments over the use of "territorial waters" close to each other's land areas. In the 1960's serious arguments occurred with Peru, which claimed the right to control fishing within 200 miles of its coastline. The Peruvian coast guard and navy have captured U.S. ships catching tuna in waters claimed by Peru. This has led to fines charged to the owners and the U.S. government having to compensate boat owners for the fines. In 1969, the United States, Peru, Chile, and Ecuador agreed to conduct a conference to settle the fishing rights question, but that conference has not reached any firm agreements. Further disputes about fisheries took place after the United States, Canada, and Mexico extended their fishing zones to 200 miles in 1977 (Mexico in 1976). Canada seized several U.S. fishing boats in the late 1970's and the U.S.-Canadian fishing treaty from 1979 has remained stalled; Mexico, after several years of unsuccessful negotiations, renounced fishing accords with the United States in December 1980.

FISHER'S HILL, BATTLE AT (Sept. 22, 1864). After his defeat by Union Gen. Philip H. Sheridan at Winchester, Va., Gen. Jubal A. Early retired southward to Strasburg and formed a line of battle about Fisher's Hill, west of the town, to await Sheridan's attack. Several days later the Confederates were flanked and driven from the field. Early continued his retreat southward.

FISHERS ISLAND (N.Y.). Between the south coast of Connecticut and the east end of Long Island, N.Y., it was first noted by Adrian Block in 1614. It was included in the Connecticut patent granted by Charles II in 1662 but was also within the patent of the Duke of York; the question of state ownership was not legally settled until 1879.

FISHING AND FISHERIES. Fishing boats were active off North America while the earliest explorations were going on, and Europeans were busily drying fish ashore before bringing it back to Europe for sale. The fishing grounds off New England, Nova Scotia, Labrador, and the Gulf of St. Lawrence provided an enormous resource for the early colonists. An extensive colonial fishing industry developed off Cape Hatteras and in the Chesapeake Bay region.

In 1978 the United States stood fourth among the world's fishing nations, behind Japan, the Soviet Union, and China. The U.S. fishing industry employed directly or indirectly about half a million people. In 1978 over 6 billion pounds of fish were caught and processed. Since 1956, a government program to help fishing-boat owners improve their vessels and increase their efficiency has been in operation; this program was extended in 1970 for a ten-year period.

In addition to cod, mackerel, flounder, and blackfish, northeast coast fishermen do an extensive business in lobsters, clams, and oysters. The largest fleets are based in Portland, Maine; Gloucester and Boston, Mass.; New York; Philadelphia; Baltimore; and Savannah, Ga.

The Gulf Coast provides a base for a very valuable shrimp fishery; shellfish of many types are taken from the waters close to shore; and there is extensive fishing for snapper and pompano. The chief fishing ports on the gulf are New Orleans, Biloxi, Mobile, and Jacksonville.

The Pacific Coast and Alaska provided extensive grounds for two of the most valuable fish caught—salmon in the north, and tuna off central and southern California. The tuna fishery business is carried on seasonally, fleets following the tuna schools as they migrate between California and Peru; Americans account for one-fifth of the world's tuna catch. Salmon are taken extensively in the inlets and rivers of Alaska, Washington, Oregon, and northern California. King crab are caught extensively off Alaska and shipped throughout the country. The major fishing ports on the Pacific Coast include Juneau and Ketchikan, Alaska; Seattle, Wash.; Portland, Oreg.; and San Francisco and San Diego, Calif. In Hawaii, fishing is carried on from ports in every island.

A movement has developed toward turning fishing vessels into floating factories, aboard which fish are not only caught and stored but also processed. Canning accounts for nearly all the preservation of fish for long periods of time. However, all but fish which are to be eaten immediately are now ordinarily frozen to prevent spoilage. The industry has developed two important new markets, other than the direct selling of fish for human food. One of these is agriculture: fish and fish parts that are not suitable for human use are ground and dried until they can be spread on fields as fertilizer. Another development has been the study of fish as a source of concentrated protein for human food, or for livestock and chicken feed. The fish are ground, packed solid, and often turned into grains or pellets for use as food.

One of the most dangerous problems of the fishing industry is posed by chemical pollution of the waters from which fish are taken. Another cause for concern is the danger that certain types of seafood may be eliminated by unwise catching policies. This has been an issue between the United States and other countries on several occasions (*see* Pelagic Sealing Disputes; Whaling). A special conservation problem is presented by the salmon, which are easily caught en route to their home waters for spawning.

Most states have special agencies concerned with fish conservation. These ordinarily require licenses for fishermen, whether commercial or sport fishermen, and post "open" and "closed" seasons to protect their fish from extinction. Fish hatcheries are maintained in many states to insure a plentiful supply of fish in lakes and streams.

Several U.S. government agencies concern themselves with fishing. The State Department, for example, argues the case for the right of American fishermen to use the high seas for fishing and for the protection of endangered species through international agreements. Within the Department of Commerce, the National Oceanic and Atmospheric Administration includes many agencies directly concerned with the business of fishing, primarily the National Marine Fisheries Service and the National Ocean Survey. The U.S. Fish and Wildlife Service, an agency of the Department of the Interior, is concerned with conservation of sports fish and with the preservation of natural wetlands and spawning grounds. The Food and Drug Administration is responsible for checking on whether individual lots of canned fish are usable and on whether fish from particular fishing grounds ought to be banned from sale because of possible pollution.

FISHING BOUNTIES. From 1789 until 1807 the federal government levied duties on imported salt and paid allowances, in lieu of drawback, on fish and meat cured with foreign salt and then exported; this allowance, or bounty, primarily affected the cod fisheries. It was revived in 1813. Beginning in 1828 the salt duty was lowered, while the bounty remained unchanged; becoming in effect a true bounty, it continued until 1866.

FISHING CREEK, ACTION AT (Aug. 18, 1780). Col. Banastre Tarleton, under command of British Gen. Charles Cornwallis, pursued Gen. Thomas Sumter to his encampment at Fishing Creek, S.C., near the Catawba River. Completely surprised, the Americans were routed. This defeat laid South Carolina open to royalist troops.

FISHING CREEK CONFEDERACY. The name given to local disturbances during the Civil War in the Fishing Creek Valley (mainly in Columbia County, Pa.) in 1864. These grew out of draft resistance and may have had some connection with the Knights of the Golden Circle. It was reported that a fort had been built by recalcitrant drafted men and Confederate sympathizers in the mountains of the northern end of the county, and Union forces were dispatched to deal with the emergency; the "fort" was never found. Ardent Republicans in the county cooperated with Union troops, who were guilty of some abuse of civilians. A number of citizens were arrested, but only a few were convicted by court-martial.

FISK OVERLAND EXPEDITIONS (1862–66). Congress in 1862 authorized an armed escort for a proposed emigrant train going from St. Paul, Minn., westward through the Indian country. Capt. James Liberty Fisk led this expedition by way of forts Abercrombie, Union, and Benton to the mines in Deer Lodge, Mont., and Bannock, Idaho. In 1863 he led a second expedition to Virginia City, Mont. In 1864 he followed in the rear of Gen. Alfred Sully's punitive expedition against the Indians as far as Fort Rice on the Missouri River and then struck directly west toward the Yellowstone and Bighorn rivers. After being attacked in the hilly country south of the North Dakota Bad Lands by the Sioux, he was rescued by a detachment of Sully's army and brought back to Fort Rice. In 1866, Fisk led an expedition of miners and homeseekers to Helena, Mont.; the Great Northern Railroad was later built along his route.

FISK UNIVERSITY. Founded in Nashville, Tenn., in 1865, as a school for black students. In the 1960's it began to operate an integrated campus.

FITCH'S STEAMBOAT EXPERIMENTS. John Fitch claimed to have considered the use of the steam engine for ships before he heard of similar plans by other inventors. In 1785 he made a model and sought funds from Congress and the Virginia assembly. He eventually received from New Jersey (1786) and from Virginia, Delaware, Pennsylvania, and New York (1787) the exclusive rights to steam navigation in their waters for fourteen years. In April 1786 he organized a joint stock company in Philadelphia. An engine was built by Henry Voight, a watchmaker, and installed on a small boat to drive twelve paddles, six on a side. The vessel was successfully tried out, Aug. 22, 1787, on the Delaware River with members of the Constitutional Convention looking on. A more powerful boat went upstream to Burlington, N.J., in July 1788, but the boiler broke down. A third boat made regular runs to Trenton, N.J., in the summer of 1790, but it failed to earn expenses. A U.S. patent was granted to the company in 1791. A fourth boat was wrecked by a storm. Fitch and Voight quarreled, and their associates did not continue the enterprise.

FIVE-AND-TEN-CENT STORES. Also known as variety stores, they originally limited their stock to modestly priced items; they now carry moderately and popularly priced stationery, apparel and accessories, housewares, toys, toilet articles, and hardwares.

The first five-cent store was opened in 1879 in Utica, N.Y., by Frank W. Woolworth; the store failed, but Woolworth opened a successful five-and-ten-cent store in Lancaster, Pa., the same year. By 1899 there were 54 such Woolworth stores, and by 1919, 1,081 stores, many acquired through mergers with other developing variety chains, among them S. H. Knox and Company, F. M. Kirby and Company, and E. P. Charlton and Company. During this growth period other famous chains were established: J. J. McCrory opened in Scottsdale, Pa., in 1882; S. S. Kresge, a former partner of McCrory, opened in 1897; and S. H. Kress and Company opened in Tennessee in 1896. Other well-known chains of the early 1900's included W. T. Grant and Company, H. L. Green, J. J. Newberry and Company, Neisner Brothers, G. C. Murphy and Company, and McClellan Stores Company. By 1929 there were 12,110 variety stores; by 1948, 20,210.

Most five-and-ten-cent chain stores have become multifaceted corporations responding to changes in the business climate, consumer demand, and shopping habits and to innovative competitors. In 1977 there were 17,400 variety stores in the United States, with sales estimated at $7.095 billion; variety chains accounted for $5.8 billion of the total.

FIVE CIVILIZED TRIBES. The term "civilized" came to be applied to the Choctaw, Chickasaw, Creek, and Cherokee, when they were removed, along with the Seminole, a Creek or Hitchiti offshoot, to the Indian Territory of Oklahoma, because of their readiness to adapt to Europeanized institutions. The Cherokee spoke a language related to that of the Iroquois and occupied regions in what is now Tennessee and North Carolina at the southern end of the Appalachian chain; the four other tribes are linguistically assigned to the Muskhogean (Muskogean) grouping, which had a tradition of western origin and may have fanned into the southeastern states in late prehistoric times.

In 1539–42, Hernando de Soto found the Creek, Choctaw, Chickasaw, and Cherokee in locations that remained fairly fixed until the exodus of the 19th century (the Seminole were a composite tribe that developed in the late 18th century). Estimates of population vary over the three centuries before removal, but it seems clear that none of the tribes was very large. The largest was the Cherokee, with a population of perhaps 22,000 in 1650; by 1715 it had been reduced by half as a result of smallpox. Even the earliest accounts suggest tribal federations in the area. One of these, the Creek Confederacy, was a political and military organization made up of several tribes who clustered for mutual aid and defense around the dominant Muskhogee tribe. The emphasis of such federations on political organization is the hallmark of the area. All five tribes were intensively agricultural, planting maize and related plants in the neighborhood of palisaded villages. All built a religious system around fertility and world renewal, adjusting to a ceremonial calendar and stressing the ceremonial ball game. The stress in the area was on matrilineal and matrifocal institutions; important were tribal councils to regulate tribal interrelations, war, and peace.

The Choctaw, who had nearly destroyed the de Soto expedition, came to ally with the British; the other tribes sometimes tied to the British and at other times asserting independence, played varying parts. By the early 19th century many Indians had abandoned their former modes of life and taken on European patterns of political organization, systems of land tenure, and agriculture. The plantation system, not excluding African slaves, was adopted by many. Between 1809 and 1821, Sequoya, a Cherokee, invented a system of syllabic writing for the native language, suggesting the influence of European culture.

Beginning in the administration of President Andrew Jackson, attempts were made to dispossess the southeastern Indians and to move them to Indian Territory west of the Mississippi; their removal was effected in 1835–42 and involved the forced migration of massed Cherokee in 1838, the so-called Trail of Tears. It was not accomplished without rebellion, notably the second Seminole War (1835–42). Most southeastern Indians were removed to Indian Territory, although a remnant fled to the Florida Everglades, where their descendants are still to be found. Several hundred Cherokee hid out in the mountains and in 1842 were granted permission to remain on lands in western North Carolina; their descendants still reside there. In Indian Territory the five tribes, including most of the Seminole, established autonomous states, employing the constitutional model of the United States; it was the presence of these states that gave rise to the use of the term "civilized" to designate the tribes. The five tribes retained their autonomy until Oklahoma acquired statehood in 1907.

FIVE FORKS, BATTLE OF (Apr. 1, 1865). Fought about twenty-five miles south of Richmond, Va. Union Gen. P. H. Sheridan, driven back on Mar. 31, concentrated at Dinwiddie Courthouse nearby, so disposing his superior forces as to require extended deployment by Confederate troops; on Apr. 1 he successfully attacked Gen. George E. Pickett, capturing much artillery and many prisoners. Evacuation of Richmond followed the next day.

FIVE NATIONS. The five original tribes of the Iroquois Indian Confederacy: Mohawk, Oneida, Onondaga, Cayuga, and Seneca, all based in central and western New York State. In 1722 the group accepted a sixth "nation," the Tuscarora tribe from North Carolina.

FIVE-POWER NAVAL TREATY (Feb. 6, 1922). One of the treaties negotiated at the Washington Naval Conference on limitation of armaments. It placed limitations upon capital ships, aircraft carriers, and Far Eastern naval bases; declared a ten-year holiday on capital ship construction; and restricted aggregate battleship tonnage to 525,000 for the United States and Great Britain, 315,000 for Japan, and 175,000 for France and Italy.

FIVE-TWENTIES. A large issue of U.S. bonds sold during the Civil War; redeemable after five years and payable after twenty, they bore 6 percent interest. Proposals to redeem them with greenbacks resulted in much controversy.

FIVE VILLAGES. Large, fortified villages of earth-covered lodges of the Mandan and Hidatsa, on the west side of the Missouri River between the Heart and Little Missouri rivers, in North Dakota. In 1738 the Hidatsa were living in three of the villages and the Mandan in two. White traders and other travelers customarily made the villages their rendezvous. The Hudson's Bay Company and other companies had traders there as early as 1772, and they were doing a thriving business when the Lewis and Clark expedition reached the villages in 1804. The smallpox epidemic of 1837 reduced the Indian population of the upper Missouri so drastically that the survivors consolidated to build new villages farther up the river. By 1858 the remnants of the five villages had found refuge from the Sioux in a single village named Like-a-fish-hook, adjacent to the trading post of Fort Berthold, N.Dak.

FLACO'S RIDE (Sept. 24–30, 1846). On Aug. 13, 1846, Los Angeles, Calif., surrendered to Commodore Robert F. Stockton—the first step in his attempt to conquer California for the United States. Stockton left the pueblo in charge of Lt. Archibald H. Gillespie and a force of fifty men early in September; the southern Californians took up arms and besieged Los Angeles. John Brown, called Juan Flaco ("Lean John"), eluded the besiegers and in less than five days' riding time carried a request for aid 500 miles to San Francisco.

FLAG, PRESIDENTIAL. First designed in 1882. The present flag (approved July 1960) consists of a blue field with a slight modification of the Great Seal of the United States, surrounded by a circle of fifty stars, in the center.

FLAG DAY (June 14). Presidents Woodrow Wilson and Calvin Coolidge suggested that June 14 be observed as Flag Day, marking the anniversary of the adoption by Congress in 1777 of the Stars and Stripes as emblem of the nation; the National Flag Day Act (Aug. 3, 1949) gave it official status.

FLAG OF THE CONFEDERATE STATES. *See* **Confederate Flag.**

FLAG OF THE UNITED STATES. On June 14, 1777, the Continental Congress resolved "that the flag of the thirteen United States be thirteen stripes, alternate red and white; that the union be thirteen stars, white in a blue field, representing a new constellation." Vermont and Kentucky, after being admitted to the Union, requested to be included in the symbolism of the flag; Congress provided that after May 1, 1795, the flag have fifteen stripes, with fifteen white stars in a blue field in the union. On Apr. 4, 1818, President James Monroe signed a bill providing that from July 4, 1818, "the flag of the United States be thirteen horizontal stripes of alternate red and white; that the union have twenty white stars in a blue field; that one star be added on the admission of every new state in the Union." The exact proportions were established by executive order of President Woodrow Wilson in 1916. On June 22, 1942, the rules and customs relating to the civilian use of the flag were codified by Congress.

FLAGS.

State and City. Each state of the Union has a distinctive flag. In most of the flags of the original thirteen states some memorial of colonial or revolutionary history is incorporated; Maryland's flag bears Lord Baltimore's coat of arms; Massachusetts' is a representation of the famous "Pine Tree" flag flown by George Washington's first navy.

Most large cities have city flags. New York City has an official emblem combining the colors of the United Netherlands with the municipal seal under which English authority replaced the Dutch. The flag of the District of Columbia is symbolic of the coat of arms of the Washington family.

Military. The Navy Department assigns personal flags to admirals and pennants to various commands. The naval reserve has a merchant marine flag and a yacht pennant; the naval militia, a commission pennant and a distinguishing flag. The U.S. Marine Corps has distinct colors, regimental flags, and flags for general officers on ships or at posts. The Department of the Army provides personal flags for the chief of staff and generals on the general staff; also distinctive flags for army transports and for the Quartermaster Corps, Engineer Corps, Signal Corps, and Ordnance Department. The banners (U.S. flag) of the infantry are called "colors"; of the cavalry, "guidons"; and of the navy, "ensigns." The Coast Guard uses the U.S. ensign in the same manner as the navy but flies the Coast Guard ensign at fore as a distinguishing flag. This service has a flag for commandant and pennants for broad command, senior officer, and commissioned personnel. Government offices, such as the Commerce Department and the Public Health Service, also have distinct flags. Foreign services (diplomatic and consular) use the consular flag.

FLAPPERS. Young women in the 1920's who broke with traditional conventionality. They were called flappers for wearing loose garments and not buckling the clasps on either their coats or boots. Cartoonist John Held immortalized them; the actress Clara Bow epitomized them.

FLATBOATMEN. Men who worked on flatboats—roughly made rafts, invented in 1750, that carried goods downstream, especially on the Mississippi, and then were broken up for timber. They were usually farmers or laborers out to see the country or to dispose of the products of their farms. Flatboatmen bore a reputation for thievery, debauchery, and quarrelsomeness (their battles with keelboatmen are well known). Wages were usually about $50 for the voyage. In the late 18th century, flatboatmen returned north by sea or by the Natchez Trace; after regular steam service began on the Mississippi (1817) they returned by steamboat. (*See also* Store Boats.)

FLEET, UNITED STATES. *See* **Navy, United States.**

FLEETWOOD, BATTLE AT. *See* **Brandy Station, Battle of.**

***FLETCHER* V. *PECK*,** 6 Cranch 87 (1810). The legislature of Georgia had been persuaded to authorize (1795) the issuance of grants of certain land along the Yazoo River belonging to the state. A later legislature (1796) annulled these grants on the ground of fraud. Meanwhile, a part of the land had passed through several innocent holders to one Peck, who conveyed to Fletcher with a covenant that the title had not been impaired by the subsequent act of the Georgia legislature. Fletcher sued Peck for a breach of this covenant. The question before the Court was whether or not the original grant by Georgia was a binding contract. Chief Justice John Marshall held that the term "contract" applies to a grant from a state as well as to executed contracts between individuals and that there was no breach of covenant by Peck —the first time a state law was invalidated as contrary to the Constitution. (*See also* Dartmouth College Case; *Sturges* v. *Crowninshield.*)

FLINT (Mich.). Located about fifty miles northwest of Detroit, with a 1980 population of 159,611 in the center of a metropolitan area of 521,589, Flint is almost completely devoted to automobile manufacturing. It was the scene in 1936 of the first sit-down strike (in the Buick factory). Most local wage-earners work for General Motors and belong to the United Auto Workers Union; the average wages are among the highest in the country. Educational institutions in Flint include a branch of the University of Michigan, the Michigan School for the Deaf, and General Motors Technical Institute.

FLOATING BATTERIES. Heavily armed vessels with protective armor but with comparatively weak motive power, used in the United States as early as 1776 (on the Delaware River in the defense of Philadelphia). The first steam warship in the world, the *Demologos,* built by Robert Fulton in 1814–15, should be considered a floating battery.

FLOGGING. Whipping, a common form of punishment during the colonial period; originally a whip constructed of knotted rawhide was used, but it was replaced by the cat-o'-nine-tails, which consisted of several bound leather strips. Offenders who were flogged received no additional punishment until prisons came into being in the 19th century; thereafter, malefactors frequently were first whipped and then incarcerated for a short term. Flogging was a common method of punishing recalcitrant prisoners until the early 20th century. It has now been outlawed in all the states except Delaware, where it may be administered for twenty-five different crimes.

FLOOD CONTROL ACT (1936). Extended the Flood Control Act of 1928, which had authorized $325 million for levee work in the Mississippi Valley, to cover all river basins in the nation. For the first time it asserted federal responsibility for controlling floods. Major responsibility was assigned to the Army Corps of Engineers.

FLOODS. Not all floods are destructive—the controlled annual floods of the Mississippi and Nile rivers, for example, are the main factor in the fertility and economy of those agricultural areas—but when floods are uncontrolled, the economic and human losses exceed those of most other disasters.

The most notable flood of the 19th century was the Johnstown flood of May 31–June 1, 1889, which caused over 2,200 deaths, when a dam failed above Johnstown, Pa. (*see* Johnstown Flood). The greatest human disaster resulting from flooding in the United States was caused by the Galveston hurricane of Sept. 8–9, 1900, when an estimated 6,000 people died (*see* Galveston Storm). The most widespread flood in American history was the great Lower Mississippi Valley flood of March–June 1927, in which 313 lives were lost and $300 million damage was inflicted. The region has been visited by great floods about once in every decade since the earliest settlements. One of the longest floods occurred during the three-month period from March to May 1965 in the upper Mississippi, when deep snow melted over a wide area. Record floods have also occurred in the region of the Potomac River and adjacent basins (1889, 1936, 1937, 1942, and 1972). (*See also* Disasters: Storms and Floods.)

In the United States the average annual loss of life from flooding during 1925–70 was only 83; property losses in the 1951–70 period rose to $450 million annually, with 75,000 people driven from their homes on an average each year. (In 1972 alone, 200,000 were evacuated during several floods.

FLOOR LEADER. The senator or representative in Congress who acts as leader of his party on the floor of the chamber of which he is a member. Originally there was such a recognized floor leader only in the House of Representatives and only for the majority party, his function being to assist the speaker of the House in arranging and pushing through the legislative program; he was informally designated by the speaker. Since the reduction of the speaker's power in 1910–11, floor leaders have been more formally chosen for each party by the respective party caucuses in each house; thus, both chambers now have a majority leader and a minority leader, whose chief function is to direct the parliamentary strategy of their parties.

FLORIDA. Southernmost state of the United States, bounded on the north by Alabama and Georgia, on the east by the Atlantic, and on the west by the Gulf of Mexico and Alabama. The coast of Florida was discovered by Juan Ponce de León in 1513, and the area was explored by Lucas Vázquez de Ayllón, Pánfilo de Narváez, and Hernando de Soto.

Jean Ribault reached the upper east coast of Florida in 1562 with 150 colonists and claimed this territory for France (he landed first near St. Augustine, but made his settlement on an island near present-day Beaufort, S.C.). Two years later René Goulaine de Laudonnière, who had accompanied Ribault, came to Florida with another company of Huguenots. They settled near the mouth of the St. Johns River, where they built Fort Caroline. In 1565, Ribault returned with 300 additional colonists but was attacked by the Spanish admiral Pedro Menéndez de Avilés; subsequently a storm wrecked Ribault's fleet. Starvation soon drove the stranded Frenchmen toward the Spanish settlement of St. Augustine, where most of them were massacred. Dominique de Gourgues avenged the French in 1568 by killing the Spanish garrison at San Mateo (Fort Caroline).

Menéndez established St. Augustine, San Mateo, and a number of garrisons along the east and west coasts of the peninsula, and up the Atlantic coast as far as Santa Elena. In the 17th century, Spanish settlement consisted of a Franciscan mission system (*see* Florida, Spanish Missions in). In 1698 a fort was erected at Pensacola to block French expansion in the Mississippi region. English pressure from the north led to the destruction of the Spanish missions, frontier warfare in the debatable land between Florida and Georgia, and the eventual cession of Spanish Florida to England by the Treaty of Paris (1763) in exchange for Cuba.

The Proclamation of 1763 established colonial government and divided the region at the Apalachicola River into East Florida and West Florida. After 1775 thousands of Loyalists poured into East Florida; it was the objective of several attacks by the Americans (1776–78) and assisted the southern campaign of the British in 1778. West Florida was part of the Anglo-Spanish Mississippi rivalry. The region became involved in the Revolution through the efforts of Americans to get supplies at New Orleans (*see* Gibson-Linn Episode; Willing Expedition) and Spain's declaration of war against England (1779). By the Definitive Treaty of Peace (1783), both East Florida and West Florida were returned to Spain.

West Florida was claimed by the United States as part of the Louisiana Purchase in 1803 and was occupied in 1813; Spain ceded the rest of Florida to the United States under the terms of the Adams-Onís Treaty (1819). Gen. Andrew Jackson, first American governor, restored semicivil government to Florida, with judges, attorneys, and collectors functioning as civilian employees. The appointive legislative council, authorized by Congress for the Florida territory in 1822, became elective in 1826. In 1824, Tallahassee, an abandoned Indian town located midway between East Florida and West Florida, was selected as the territorial capital. Numerous cotton plantations developed between the Suwannee and the Apalachicola rivers; oranges, lumber, sugarcane, tobacco, corn, and rice were also produced. Economic development came to an abrupt halt in 1837: the second Seminole War (1835–42) and the panic of 1837 closed every bank and wiped out most white settlements south of St. Augustine (*see* Seminole Wars).

In 1845, Florida was permitted admission as a slave state. The first elections for state officials were held in May 1845. The Internal Improvement Act of 1855 encouraged generous land subsidies to private companies engaged in construction of railroads. Cattle ranches multiplied on the open range, and population doubled in the first fifteen years of statehood. On Jan. 10, 1861, Florida seceded from the Union. The only major battle fought in Florida was Olustee (Feb. 20, 1864), in which the Confederates successfully defended the interior of the state. In May 1865 a mixed garrison of Union soldiers and emancipated slaves introduced Reconstruction. Because the revised state constitution did not provide ballots or other civil rights for blacks, it was not acceptable to Congress, and Florida was placed under military rule in March 1867. A new constitution (1868) revised the criminal code and made public education the responsibility of the state. Florida Reconstruction was brought to an end with the election of conservative Democrat George F. Drew as governor in 1876.

The Drew administration (1877–81) ushered in an era of "Bourbon democracy," so called because it was dedicated to commercialization and industrialization of the state, even avowing a willingness to cooperate with Yankee investors. Encouraged by land subsidies from the Bourbons, the railroad tycoons came to Florida, and railroads brought a rapid influx of settlers and tourists. Promotional literature was partially responsible for the expansion of citrus groves from Jacksonville south to Biscayne Bay in the 1880's. The Great Freeze of 1895 destroyed most of the trees, but it resulted in improved techniques of citrus production that brought exports up to 5 million boxes by 1905. Pebble deposits of phosphate rock were found in the Peace River near Bartow in 1885, and hard rock deposits were uncovered at Dunnellon in 1889; by 1900, Florida was exporting 5.5 million tons of phosphate.

In the 1890's, Florida agrarians reacted to Bourbonism by joining the Populist movement. The Populist party held its national convention in Ocala, Fla., in 1890 (*see* Ocala Platform) and provided issues for progressive reform in the 20th century. Gov. Napoleon Bonaparte Broward (1905–09) pioneered reform in education, conservation, and taxation, including unification of all state-supported universities under the Board of Regents (1905) and drainage operation in the Everglades (initiated 1906). Other significant 20th-century developments have been the land boom (1921–25); selection of Cape Canaveral as the site for the U.S. space program; and the opening of Disney World near Orlando in 1971, boosting the economy of central Florida, and attracting more than a million visitors in its first year. Population growth in the 20th century has been spectacular: from 500,000 in the early 1900's to 9.7 million in 1980.

FLORIDA (or *Oreto*). A ship cleared from Liverpool, England, on Mar. 22, 1862; upon arrival at Nassau, it was delivered to Confederate Comdr. John N. Maffitt, having until then been registered as an English ship. With a crew crippled by yellow fever and with incomplete batteries, Maffitt ran the blockade into Mobile, Ala.; four months later, the *Florida* escaped through the blockade and embarked on several long raiding cruises, sweeping from the latitude of New York to the Brazilian coast. In October 1864, at Bahia, Brazil, a Union sloop, the *Wachusett,* in violation of international law, forced the *Florida's* surrender and towed it to Hampton Roads, Va., where it was sunk. (*See also* Alabama Claims.)

FLORIDA, JACKSON'S SEIZURE OF. *See* **Arbuthnot and Ambrister, Case of.**

FLORIDA, PURCHASE OF. The so-called sale of Florida to the United States by Spain for $5 million, effected by the transcontinental boundary and claims settlement of the Adams-Onís Treaty (1819). Since the Floridas were then prominent in public interest and the United States assumed liability for claims of its citizens against Spain up to $5 million, many viewed the bargain as a purchase. Its negotiators, however, had no idea that that figure represented the value of the Floridas (*see* Adams-Onís Treaty).

FLORIDA, SPANISH MISSIONS IN. There were three phases in the attempts to set up missions in Spanish Florida: the abortive attempts prior to 1565; Jesuit missions, 1566–71; and Franciscan missions, 1573–1763. The first phase is characterized by the martyrdom of the Dominican Luis Cancer de Babastro on his first entrance into Florida (1549) and by the unsuccessful expedition of Tristán de Luna (1559–61). Florida then lay fallow, except for the luckless Huguenot settlement, until 1565, when Pedro Menéndez de Avilés settled St. Augustine and the Jesuits were called upon to undertake organized mission work. The first expedition (1566) resulted in the martyrdom of Father Pedro Martínez, probably somewhere north of the St. Johns River. A second expedition (1568) produced extremely few converts, but one of the lay brothers compiled the first catechism and grammar in the Yamasee language—both now lost. In 1570 an attempt was made to missionize the region called Ajacan (Virginia), but through treachery eight fathers and brothers were massacred in 1571. In 1573 the first Franciscans arrived. They were able to extend their work among the Indians north, south, and west from St. Augustine. The region called Gualé in Georgia, the Apalache region toward the west, and the immediate regions around St. Augustine formed the principal foci for the Franciscans (*see also* Georgia, Spanish Missions in), who made and kept thousands of Indian converts. The decline of the missions came with the founding of Charleston, S.C. (1670), and the aggression of the English (*see* Apalache Massacre). By 1763, when Florida was ceded to England, the missions had disappeared.

FLORIDA, STRAITS OF (also called the New Bahama Channel and the Gulf of Florida). The straits connect the Gulf of Mexico with the Atlantic Ocean and separate Florida from Cuba. Their total length exceeds 300 miles; the width varies from 60 to 100 miles; and the main channel has been sounded to a depth of 6,000 feet.

FLORIDA BOUNDARY. The 16th-century La Florida included all Spanish North America east of the Mississippi River. In 1670 the Treaty of Madrid recognized British occupation as far south as Charleston, S.C., and in 1743 British conquest reached the St. Marys River. In 1719 Spain accepted the Perdido River (the present western limit of Florida, where it adjoins Alabama) as the Florida-Louisiana boundary. England took the region in 1763 and set up two provinces, East Florida and West Florida, the latter extending from the Apalachicola to the Iberville (almost to New Orleans); in 1764 the northwestern limit was placed at the shifting mouth of the Yazoo River, then about 32° 26′ north latitude, on the Mississippi. Spain regained the Floridas in 1783, and the southern boundary of the United States was drawn along the thirty-first parallel, north latitude, from the Mississippi to the Apalachicola, down the Apalachicola to the Flint, eastward to the head of the St. Marys River, and along that river to the Atlantic Ocean. The United States claimed West Florida as part of the Louisiana Purchase (1803). The portion west of the Pearl River was included in the state of Louisiana in 1812; the part east to the Perdido was added to the territory of Mississippi in 1813, although both were still legally Spanish. The Adams-Onís Treaty of 1819 evaded defining the previous ownership of West Florida and left East Florida's limits unchanged. The latter was made a territory in 1821, and a state in 1845.

FLORIDA EAST COAST RAILROAD. *See* **Railroads, Sketches of Principal Lines.**

FLORIDA LAND BOOM OF THE 1920's. Prior to 1925 there was a great increase in activity in the buying and selling of Florida real estate. The rapid growth of cities is illustrated by Miami's growth from 5,471 inhabitants in 1910 to 69,754 in 1925. Real estate assessments between February 1920 and February 1925 went from $253,785,338 to $475,908,261. Bank deposits more than doubled between Jan. 1, 1924, and Jan. 1, 1925. Causes of the boom included the opening of far southern Florida to railway transportation prior to 1900; drainage of the Everglades, begun in 1906; a constantly increasing tourist trade; and ratification of a state constitutional amendment in November 1924 prohibiting state collection of income and inheritance taxes. By mid-1925 the rise in real estate values was completely out of hand. By September it was evident that the beginning of the end had come; many who had made heavy down payments on property could no longer unload it on others.

FLORIDA RANGERS (or East Florida Rangers). A Tory corps formed at St. Augustine by Col. Thomas Browne under a commission of June 1, 1776. In November 1777 they numbered 130 and guarded the frontier, with some Indians, at Fort Tonyn on St. Marys River. In March 1778 they captured Fort Barrington, Ga.; on July 2 they burned Fort Tonyn to prevent its capture by American troops. The corps was at Fort Picolata, East Florida, in June 1783, and probably settled in the Bahamas.

FLORIDA WAR. *See* **Seminole Wars.**

FLOUR MILLING.

Technology. Colonists in the 17th century introduced European grains along the eastern seaboard, built windmills and water mills, and developed New York as a milling and marketing center for flour. Oliver Evans's mill in which grain and meal moved mechanically (completed 1785) constituted the beginning of automation in industry. From 1815 to 1860, a limited market justified little expansion in merchant milling. Important technological developments in farming, transportation, and grain storage, however, established the potential for rapid growth during and after the Civil War. Inventions of agricultural machinery allowed farmers to handle grain in greater amounts. The Erie Canal, opened in 1825, cut freight costs between the Genesee Valley and New York by 90 percent per ton. Joseph Dart installed automatic machinery in his mills at Buffalo and applied steam power to operate grain storage elevators in 1843.

Before 1860, U.S. millers ground soft winter wheat between millstones set close together. "Low" milling extracted as much meal as was possible from one grinding but pulverized the wheat berry—and wheat germ enzymes and bran moisture impaired the flour's durability. By 1870, millers were experimenting with a technique of "high" grinding and gradual reduction, which involved several grindings with the stones set progressively closer; bolting between grindings helped separate the bran from the flour. This produced a finer flour and more flour per bushel of wheat. Minneapolis flour shipments rose from 1 million to 5 million barrels between 1876 and 1884.

Hard spring wheat, grown increasingly in the Dakotas and Minnesota after 1865, required certain improvements in the gradual-reduction system, because of its higher gluten content and more easily shattered bran. In 1873, Edmund La Croix and George T. Smith patented middlings purifiers that separated the dust, bran, middlings, and flour more completely by blowing air through screens so meshed as to sort the different particles. Chilled iron corrugated rollers began to replace millstones for grinding at about the same time the middlings purifier was introduced. Roller breaking twisted the grain rather than crushing or shearing it; it allowed more precise spacing between the grinding surfaces and more even stock-feeding than burrstones. Germ scalpers—machines that sifted off wheat germ after flattening it out—came into use after R. L. Downton's invention in 1875. Carl Haggenmacher, a Hungarian, patented a plansifter in 1888 that improved the separation of the chop between grindings. O. M. Morse invented a "cyclone" dust collector in 1886 that reduced the hazard of explosions in mills. Electric power came into use in the mills as early as 1887, in Laramie, Wyo., but steam- and waterpower predominated until about 1920.

Testing flour for strength and quality became standard procedure after A. W. Howard set up the first testing laboratory in Minneapolis in 1886. By the early 20th century the major milling companies operated scientific laboratories not only to test the baking qualities of flour but to find industrial uses for wheat derivatives.

During World War II the National Research Council recommended that flour for military use be vitamin-enriched; thereafter, millers commonly added thiamine, riboflavin, niacin, and iron to household flour. The impact of enriched flour reduced some vitamin-deficiency diseases and eliminated others. After World War II, engineers devised a mechanical system for refining flour, beyond ordinary milling, using airflow dynamics. Turbogrinders, introduced in 1959, generate high-velocity air vortices in which flour particles become smaller as they rub against each other. Air classifiers then separate the micron-sized particles into protein and starch fractions. With air grinding and classification, millers can process flours of two or three times the normal protein content. Since the mid-1960's, airflow systems have also been used in conveying and storing flour. Pneumatic conveyors have largely replaced bucket elevators, eliminating certain dust and insect problems, while making one-floor mill layouts possible. The pneumatic lines connect to storage bins and from there to Air-Slide railroad cars to facilitate bulk flour transportation.

Industry. After 1700, mills supplied with an abundance of wheat from the Middle Atlantic region met domestic needs as well as the demands of markets in Europe and in the West Indies. By 1750, Philadelphia was a leading flour center; merchants purchased the products of nearby mills, hoping either to ship the barreled staple worldwide or to speculate on the domestic grain market. By 1780 a combination of new technology, waterpower, grain supply, and entrepreneurial skill had produced milling centers of unusual capacity, such as the Brandywine Mills on the Brandywine Creek near Wilmington, Del. This group of twelve "merchant mills" (so called because they ground specifically for export; "custom mills" supplied local needs) ground annually more than 50,000 barrels of flour of all grades—superfine, common, middling, ship stuff, and cornmeal.

Large-scale milling began with the growth of Baltimore and Richmond as milling centers in the first half of the 19th century. By 1860, Rochester, N.Y. (with the fine white wheat of the Genesee Valley), and St. Louis and Milwaukee (with the surrounding region's soft red winter wheat) were the leading flour-manufacturing centers. After 1870 the mills in Minneapolis burgeoned, aided by the concentration of wheat growing in Minnesota and the Dakotas, a ready source of waterpower in St. Anthony Falls, and the invention of the middlings purifier. C. A. Pillsbury and Company was organized in Minneapolis in 1874. In 1880, Minneapolis produced more than 2 million barrels of flour. A movement toward concentration created the "flour trust" in the 1890's. Thomas A. McIntyre organized the trust, the United States Flour Milling Company, in 1898. Trusts, as management manipulations, more often brought excesses in unfair competition, price fixing, overcapitalization, and speculation than in improved products. The Sherman and Clayton antitrust laws helped curb the monopoly trend.

A decline in demand for flour in foreign markets and the growth of southwestern and Pacific Coast wheat regions geographically decentralized the milling industry. Kansas, Oklahoma, and Texas produced enormous quantities of hard winter wheat, while California and Washington grew much white wheat. Kansas City, Dallas, Seattle, and San Francisco developed as milling centers and grain markets. Buffalo, on the Great Lakes, took the lead from Minneapolis as the largest milling center after 1920. The Chicago Board of Trade became a major institution in the grain exchange.

Changes in the locations of wheat-growing areas and transportation, the introduction of the Alsop process of artificial bleaching in 1904, and the beginning of large-scale commercial baking have influenced milling since 1900. The growth of competition in flour marketing and changes in flour consumption stimulated the formation of such regional and national combinations as Pillsbury Flour Mills (1923), General Mills (1928), and Gold Dust Corporation (1929).

FLYING CLOUD. A clipper ship built at East Boston by Donald McKay in 1850. It was an extreme type of its class and long held top place for beauty and speed; it made the run from New York to San Francisco in the record time of 89 days, and to Hong Kong in 127 sailing days.

FLYING THE HUMP. U.S. officials in 1941 saw a vital need to keep China in the war; yet Japan's early conquests had cut off all means of supplying China other than by air. When Burma fell, the only air route left open was from eastern Assam across the High Himalayas to K'unming in Yunnan province. The air distance from the principal U.S. base at Dinjan was only 500 miles, but the route led over the 10,000-foot Patkai Range and the 14,000-foot Kumon Range; the main "hump," which gave its name to the massif and the air route, is the 15,000-foot-high Satsung Range between the Salween and Mekong rivers. Turbulence, severe icing, enemy aircraft, and a monsoon season lasting from mid-May to October posed grave hazards. Yet for nearly three years, the U.S. Army Army Air Forces Air Transport Command transported supplies and passengers to China; from 1942 the airlift delivered a total of 650,000 tons, with a monthly maximum of 71,042 tons reached in July 1945. The Hump was the proving ground of massive strategic airlift.

FLYING TIGERS (American Volunteer Group)**.** The most ambitious and famous undertaking to promote China's air effort against Japan entailed furnishing China with U.S. military pilots, U.S.-made fighter planes, and aircraft support personnel. This expedition, the American Volunteer Group (AVG), known as the Flying Tigers, was conceived in large measure by Claire L. Chennault, an American military aviator, who in 1937 retired to accept employment as an adviser to the Chinese. After undergoing strenuous training, the AVG forces were divided—one segment to defend Rangoon, the other to defend the skies over K'unming, the terminus of the Burma Road. They first engaged the Japanese on Dec. 20, 1941. The Chinese technically owned and controlled the group, but on July 4, 1942, with Chinese concurrence, the AVG was brought under American auspices and redesignated the China Air Task Force. During seven months of fighting over Burma, China, Thailand, and French Indochina, the AVG destroyed approximately 300 Japanese aircraft and recorded a like number of probable kills.

FOLK ART. The term most often used to describe aesthetically pleasing artistic efforts of those who have received little or no formal training in the principles of academic art; other terms include "naive," "primitive," "provincial," "popular," and "nonacademic." Folk art flourished especially between the Revolution and the Civil War, mainly in New England, New York, and Pennsylvania, where a growing middle class could afford the services of itinerant artisans. It was created by, and for, ordinary people. For many it was a means of support which was combined with other occupations, such as schoolteaching, preaching, shopkeeping, and even legal or medical practice.

Some motifs found in American folk art indicate a response to specific national events: following George Washington's death his image appeared on trade signs, ships' figureheads, weather vanes, toys, food molds, and bedcovers. Other patriotic emblems included the Indian; the closely related figures of Liberty and Columbia; carved portraits of such political giants as Thomas Jefferson, Andrew Jackson, and Abraham Lincoln; and the bald eagle.

First-rate folk art is individual in style and unself-conscious. In painting the emphasis is on color, decorative surface patterns, and flat, unmodeled, two-dimensional shapes; in sculpture, bold and simple forms are used to produce unique creations. Lack of sophistication or technical skill is outweighed by simplicity of line and form, often combined with deliberate attention to details, a straightforward utility of purpose, and an engaging originality of design or decoration. Even today there are untutored individuals who produce works of considerable aesthetic accomplishment.

FOLKLORE. Europeans who colonized the Atlantic seaboard related wonders of natural history. The new settlers also repeated accounts of magical feats performed by Indian sorcerers. Afro-American folk expression covers a spectrum of interrelated forms: animal and "Old Marster" tales; spirituals, blues, work songs, and hollers; toasts; hoodoo practices; dance steps; and formulaic sermons. These undercover spoken, sung, and recited traditions are indebted less to African sources than to American conditions. From the Tennessee backwoods of Davy Crockett, the hunter; across the Mississippi of Mike Fink, the keelboatman; to the Rockies of Jim Bridger, the mountain man, the westering frontiers created a breed of ring-tailed roarers who could put a rifle ball through the moon, tote a steamboat on their backs, and whip their weight in wildcats. These boasters echoed the midcentury spirit of Manifest Destiny: Davy Crockett said he had the world by the tail with a downhill pull.

The waves of Irish, Germans, Scandinavians, Eastern Europeans, and Italians who poured into the promised land in the 19th and 20th centuries produced an ethnic lore comprising Old World survivals, such as the belief in the maleficent power of the evil eye, and New World forms, such as the humorous dialect stories mimicking the accents and intonations of the newcomer and the sad-funny tales of immigrants' cultural mistakes. Certain industries generated their own lores—notably lumbering, mining, cattle raising, railroading, and oil drilling. Whether in ballads of death—at the steam engine's throttle, in a cave-in deep underground, in a log jam, or in a cattle stampede—or in anecdotes of oil field, cow camp, and lumber shanty, one common figure emerged: that of a skilled and dedicated workman, faithful to his employer, to his fellows, and to the free-enterprise system. In the 1920's and 1930's a pantheon of pseudo heroes, led by Paul Bunyan, the giant lumberjack, and Pecos Bill, the giant cowboy, caught the public fancy. Mechanized, mass-culture America is also echoed in folklore. A cycle of urban legends revolves around the automobile: the Vanishing Hitchhiker, the Stolen Grandmother, the Killer in the Back Seat.

FOLK MEDICINE. The American colonists found the Indians using an effective system of natural medicine, and they were quick to add to their own medical practice various plant, animal, and mineral substances. The basis of the settlers' own knowledge was the medical and folk-medical regimen that had come to northwestern Europe from classical times and during the ascendancy of Arabic medicine. Perhaps the most influential folk-medical chapbook in America was the *Long Lost Friend* of John George Hohman, published in its German version at Reading, Pa., in 1820; along with the so-called *Egyptian Secrets* ascribed to Albertus Magnus, it spawned many recipe books. These persist and even flourish in the 20th century.

FOLKSONGS. *See* **Ballads; Music.**

FOLSOM CULTURE COMPLEX. A Paleo-Indian culture, named from the initial discovery at a kill site near Folsom, N.Mex. (1926); several other kill sites and camping places were subsequently found in an area extending from Saskatchewan, Canada, south to northern Mexico. Evidences of Folsom man include distinctive fluted lance points, scrapers, knives, gravers, and other tools; remains are almost always found with bison, especially *Bison taylori,* an animal typical of the Late Wisconsin period. The Folsom hunters roamed the high plains from 9,000 to 8,000 B.C.

FONDA'S EXPEDITION. Led by John H. Fonda in the spring of 1823 from the vicinity of Fort Towson in southeastern Oklahoma, to Santa Fe, N.Mex. His route probably ran west on the Red River to Mustang Creek; thence north to the Canadian River, west on the Canadian to San Miguel,

N.Mex.; and from there to Santa Fe. Fonda then pushed on to Taos, where he wintered, and returned to St. Louis, Mo., via Santa Fe the following October.

FONTAINEBLEAU, TREATY OF (Nov. 3, 1762). In providing for the cession of the Isle of Orleans and all Louisiana west of the Mississippi River to Spain, Louis XV and his minister, Étienne François de Choiseul, desired to compensate their ally for its impending loss of Florida to Great Britain, to strengthen the Family Compact of 1761, and to win Spain's consent to an immediate settlement of the French and Indian War (*see* Paris, Treaty of).

FOOD. Maize ("Indian corn") was the staple of the Indian diet from the eastern shores down to the arid plains of the Southwest. It was eaten raw, cooked, and even popped, sometimes coated with maple syrup, but mostly dried to be cooked whole as hominy or crushed into meal for grain. Eastern tribes cultivated corn, beans, peas, red peppers, onions, pumpkins, and squash (and sweet potatoes and melons in the warmer South). Maple sap, nut oils, fish oils, bear grease, and fats were used to flavor foods. The woods held walnuts, hickories, butternuts, and chestnuts, as well as wild-growing grapes, blueberries, blackberries, cranberries, and raspberries. For game the Indians hunted elk, moose, deer, bear, grouse, partridge, wild ducks and geese, smaller edible animals, wild turkeys, and passenger pigeons.

Around the Great Lakes, a ricelike grain grew wild in the marshy shallows; this "wild rice" has become a modern delicacy. Rivers and lakes yielded trout, bass, pike, pickerel, catfish, perch, and eel, while along the ocean quahogs (on which the Pilgrims survived until their first crop came in), clams, oysters, and crabs abounded.

Indians of the Great Plains (the "Buffalo Hunters") relied on a meat diet of bison, antelope, and wild dog. A good season's kill was preserved by slicing the meat into thin strips and drying it, making jerky, a process also used by the Northwest Coast Indians to preserve their huge yearly salmon catches. Nevada, Utah, and southern California's "Digger Indians" ate whatever they came across: grasshoppers; field mice; grubs; roots; wild grass seed; and acorn.

Columbus introduced barley, grapes, sugarcane, and horses to the New World. Cattle were taken to North America in stages: by the Spanish in 1525; by the French in 1608; by the Dutch in 1614; by the English in Virginia in 1611. Sheep were taken to Virginia in 1609. Game was abundant; but until salt and other spices became available, colonists had trouble preserving meat. New Englanders liked to "corn" (cure in brine) their beef, eating it boiled with root vegetables. By the mid-17th century, cattle were numerous enough to permit a limited slaughter. A typical day's fare for a Dutch colonial family in New Amsterdam would start off with a draft of beer or ale for each family member, followed by a breakfast of *suppawn* (corn meal porridge boiled in milk), rye bread, butter, grated cheeses, and headcheese (a sausage of cooked hogsfeet and hogshead mixed with vinegar and spices). *Hutspot* (hodgepodge), a stewlike porridge of meat and root vegetables, was a midday meal favorite, as were pork and cabbage, and roast duck with dumplings. Supper was likely to be *suppawn* again, or perhaps a hearty soup served with coleslaw, and for dessert, *oliekoeken,* an ancestor of the doughnut. The Dutch also observed a teatime to see them through the long hungry afternoons.

New Englanders fished during the winter months, bringing home cod, haddock, halibut, and mackerel. New England traders brought cargoes of sugar, molasses, and tea. In the South in preplantation days, corn was the primary food and remained important as hoecake, hush puppies, corn pone, and bourbon whiskey. But a big plantation dinner might start with syllabub, a concoction of cream and wine; continue with turtle soup, ham, boiled mutton, scalloped oysters, roast turkey, rice, hot biscuits, and vegetables; and end with plum pudding, apple pie, blancmange, cheese, fruit, sherry, and Madeira and claret wines.

In the early 1800's the rise of cities meant that fewer Americans were growing their own food; many poor in the cities could not afford wheat grain and were lucky to eat meat once a week. In contrast, the frontiersmen were eating salt meat three times a day and drowning the salt taste in large quantities of corn liquor. The worst aspect of America's diet was its limited use of milk, fresh fruits, and leafy vegetables —protective foods that only the affluent could afford. Everyone seemed to be able to afford spirits, and dyspepsia was widespread. Diluted with water, hard liquor was drunk even by children.

The 19th-century industrial tycoons cultivated a taste for fine foods, and a restaurant culture arose in America, cradled in New York City. By the late 19th century it had reached Chicago and joined forces with another new phenomenon, the steak; America became beef-conscious. European visitors to America in the first half of the 19th century marveled at the variety of foods and, especially, at the amount of meat in the diet. From the mid-19th century the variety and freshness of America's foods greatly increased. Pineapples, coconuts, and bananas began to be imported from the West Indies, Cuba, and Central America. Fresh vegetables were shipped by rail from southern ports to northern cities. After the Civil War, canning helped to vary the American diet even further. In 1865 a government report stated that people had learned to eat tomatoes and that they could learn to like oranges also.

In the late 19th century the world was alerted to a new, microscopic enemy, bacteria; but it took the impetus of Upton Sinclair's scathing indictment of the filthy Chicago meatpacking plants in his book *The Jungle* (1906) to turn American apathy to outraged concern. Congress legislated a permanent appropriation for meat inspection and passed the Pure Food and Drug Act of 1906. In 1929, the depression left the country with more food than people could buy, and the Federal Surplus Commodity Corporation was established to buy up excess commodities and distribute them to the millions of needy. During World War II and the postwar years, farm output expanded rapidly. From 1950 to the early 1970's, technological improvements afforded over a 50 percent increase in farm output, using 5 percent fewer acres and 60 percent less labor. Food for Peace programs, school lunches, food stamps for the poor, and many other programs resulted from a food surplus.

Even with marketing developments that have standardized America's tastes, it is still a land of regional palates and ethnic traditions. In the cities, where over 94 percent of the population lives, high-income families spend proportionately less of their income for food than low-income families, but they tend to buy more and pay more for food and to use more meat, poultry, and fish per week. Farm families consume more milk, milk products, grains, sugars, and fats; they also eat fewer vegetables and fruits, but proportionately more of their produce is either fresh or canned or frozen at home.

FOOD AND DRUG ADMINISTRATION (FDA). The Food, Drug, and Insecticide Administration was created by Congress (1927) to enforce the Pure Food and Drug Act of 1906, the Insecticide Act of 1910, and several minor statutes. In 1930, Congress shortened the name to Food and Drug Administration. In 1940 the FDA was transferred from the Department of Agriculture to the Federal Security Agency. In 1953, Congress converted the loosely knit Federal Security Agency units into the Department of Health, Education, and Welfare; the FDA became a part of that department, the FDA commissioner being responsible directly to its secretary. In 1968 the secretary of the Department of Health, Education, and Welfare fused the FDA with two other agencies to form the Consumer Protection and Environmental Health Service (CPEHS), but the next year that step was reversed.

The FDA has responsibility for the safety of foods and their appropriate labeling; the safety, efficacy, and labeling of prescription and nonprescription drugs and the accuracy of prescription-drug advertising; the certification of antibiotics and insulin; the safety of veterinary drugs and animal feed; and the safety of cosmetics, health devices, and man-made sources of radiation. In 1972, Congress transferred to the FDA from the National Institutes of Health control over serums, vaccines, and other biological products.

FOOD PRESERVATION. The early English settlers at Jamestown and Plymouth subsisted on dry corn and beans that the Indians had stored for winter use; later, western explorers and traders found the Plains Indians cutting buffalo meat into thin strips and drying it in the sun on wooden frames. In the early 1800's a Frenchman, Nicolas Appert, developed canning. Commercial canning began in the United States with pickles and ketchup in Boston in 1819 and seafood in Baltimore in 1820. The cooking in boiling water took five or six hours, but this was sharply reduced in 1860 when Isaac Solomon added calcium chloride to the water, raising its boiling point. The introduction of the pressure cooker, or retort, in 1874 was an even more important step, permitting much more rapid processing, with no loss through bursting cans. Home canning of all types of food, mainly in glass jars, was encouraged after about 1900 as a means of utilizing home garden products and providing better diets. Many people still can and preserve at home, just as some farmers slaughter animals and salt or smoke the meat; but the widespread use of freezers has made home canning less important.

In 1803, Thomas Moore, a Maryland dairy farmer who lived about twenty miles from Washington, D.C., began transporting butter to the capital in an icebox of his own design. Moore patented his refrigerator and published a pamphlet describing it; by the 1840's, American families were beginning to use iceboxes for food storage and preservation. One of the first recorded refrigerated rail shipments was in 1851. In 1868, William Davis patented a refrigerator car with metal tanks along the sides that were filled with ice from the top. Beginning in the 1830's, various systems of mechanical refrigeration were patented. In the home, the mechanical refrigerator began to replace the icebox in about 1920.

In 1912, Clarence Birdseye was in Labrador and noticed that freshly caught fish pulled through the ice quickly froze solid; when thawed, the physical character of the tissue and its taste remained the same. Birdseye succeeded in inventing a machine for quick-freezing food products by conduction—that is, by pressing the food directly between very cold metal plates; in 1923 he established a frozen seafood company. Frozen concentrated orange juice, based on a process developed in the U.S. Department of Agriculture, became widely used after World War II. As frozen foods became more prevalent, deep-freeze compartments were included in many home refrigerators. Central frozen-food lockers became popular in many small towns to preserve meat. By the late 1970's one household in three had its own deep-freeze unit.

World War II supplied a strong impetus to the development of improved methods of drying food. Spray drying improved the quality of dried eggs and powdered milk; other methods produced potatoes, soup mixes, fruit juices, and other items that could be conveniently shipped and stored before being reconstituted for consumption. Freeze drying developed after World War II. In this process, the product is frozen and the moisture is then removed as a vapor by sublimation; the resulting food, after reconstitution, retains much of its original flavor, color, and texture. By the 1970's, freeze drying was widely used for coffee, soup mixes, and other convenience foods. Some meat was freeze dried, and other developments kept meats edible for prolonged periods of time; antibiotics introduced into chilling tanks, for example, prolonged the freshness of poultry.

FOOD STAMP PROGRAM. A program for better nutrition among low-income families: food coupons are used to increase purchasing power. Families taking part in the program purchase food coupons according to a scale of purchase requirements based on the size of the family and its income. "Bonus" coupons are provided free by the U.S. Department of Agriculture, to give the family the buying power for an economy-level diet. Participants shop for food in any authorized food store; they may buy all foods for human consumption, including seeds and plants for use in gardening. Retailers are first trained, and then authorized to accept coupons, which they redeem through banks or authorized food dealers; in turn, local banks send the coupons to Federal Reserve banks. After the program proved effective, the Food Stamp Act was signed into law on Aug. 31, 1964. In the early 1970's the program was sharply expanded as increased resources were made available. A 1977 revision eliminated the purchase requirement and thus made food stamps available to extremely poor people; this, along with rising unemployment and inflation, contributed to a substantial increase in participation and cost. In 1981 some 23 million Americans received food stamps. Long criticized for alleged fraud, waste, and abuse, the program became one of the victims of budget cutting during the first year of Ronald Reagan's administration: most benefits were cut and about 1 million people were eliminated from the program.

FOOTBALL. In November 1869, Princeton and Rutgers universities met in the first recorded intercollegiate game of what has been called football but was in reality a type of association football or soccer. In the next few years rugby supplanted soccer in popularity, and within a short time English rugby was transformed into American football; in 1880 the newly established Intercollegiate Football Association accepted a set of regulations that recognized and codified the changes that had taken place on the field, and what was virtually a new game had been established. It enjoyed enormous popularity; by World War I the game was the nation's leading intercollegiate sport. After World War II many colleges were compelled by rising costs to drop football as an intercollegiate sport. Among those retaining football, there was a trend toward the establishment of intercollegiate associations or conferences made up of teams of roughly the same caliber; this device helped to produce a system under which institutions that placed a high premium on football victories played only among themselves.

Professional football originated in the industrial towns of Ohio and the mining regions of western Pennsylvania in the years preceding World War I. Most of the teams were made up of former college stars who held other jobs or undergraduates who played professionally on Sundays under assumed names. In 1920 the American Professional Football Association was formed, and a year later its name was changed to the National Football League; it consisted for the most part of teams from the smaller cities in the Middle West. By the 1930's, however, many of the nation's largest cities had obtained league franchises. In 1946 the All-America Conference was established as a rival league; but after four years of intensive competition for players and spectators, it collapsed, and three of its teams joined the National Football League. The American Football League, formed in 1959, also sought to challenge the National Football League, but competition for players and the resulting increase in salaries again forced the two to merge. In 1966, the new league agreed to join the National Football League in 1970 in a merger that Congress exempted from antitrust suits; the restructured National Football League now consists of twenty-eight teams divided into two conferences, with the winner of each conference meeting for the championship in the Super Bowl.

FORAKER ACT (effective May 1, 1900). This act set up the government of Puerto Rico, annexed from Spain in 1898, at the conclusion of the Spanish-American War. The executive department of the government of Puerto Rico, an unorganized territory, was to be composed of a council of eleven members: six heads of administrative departments and five other persons, appointed by the U.S. president. Legislative authority was vested in this council and in an elective house of delegates. Provision was also made for a district court. U.S. laws not locally inapplicable, except as otherwise provided, were to be in force. Native inhabitants were considered "citizens of Puerto Rico" and entitled to the protection of the United States. A special tariff of 15 percent of the Dingley rates was levied upon all goods shipped between the United States and Puerto Rico.

FORBES EXPEDITION (1758). A major campaign of the French and Indian War, directed against Fort Duquesne, focus of French territorial and trading control of the upper Ohio River valley, at the site of present-day Pittsburgh, Pa. Gen. John Forbes commanded a force of more than 6,500 men composed of Pennsylvanians, Virginians, regulars of the Highland and North American regiments, and Marylanders. From April to September, Forbes was invalided by illness, but Col. Henry Bouquet of the Royal Americans proved a brilliant associate, directing the arduous training of the volunteers and influencing the decision to cut a wagon-wide swath through Pennsylvania, the Forbes Road. From Carlisle and Winchester, the main body and the Virginia troops advanced respectively to Fort Bedford and Fort Cumberland in July. Bouquet occupied the advance post of Loyalhanna (Ligonier). In mid-September the Virginians moved to Fort Bedford and shortly, with Forbes's artillery, joined the main body for an anticipated final push. On being told of the desperate situation of the French at Fort Duquesne—their Indian allies deserting and their communication with Canada cut—Forbes ordered a forward press. On Nov. 25, English-speaking people took permanent possession of Fort Duquesne.

FORBES PURCHASE. A 150,000-acre tract along the Apalachicola River in Florida, ceded by the Seminole and Creek to John Forbes and Company in 1804 and 1811. In 1817, prior to the cession of Florida to the United States, the tract was sold to Colin Mitchel. The American commissioners declared the title invalid, but with the exception of the military reservation of St. Marks, it was confirmed to Mitchel in 1835 by the U.S. Supreme Court.

FORBES ROAD. Built in 1758 across western Pennsylvania for the use of the Forbes Expedition, beginning just west of Bedford—in continuation of the established route from eastern Pennsylvania by way of Lancaster, Carlisle, and Chambersburg—and passing through Ligonier to Pittsburgh. For thirty years it was the chief highway to the Ohio Valley (*see* Wagoners of the Alleghenies).

FORCE ACTS. Name applied to various federal statutes passed to enforce certain national laws and constitutional amendments, particularly in the South. The act of Mar. 2, 1833, authorizing President Andrew Jackson to use the army and navy, if necessary, to collect customs duties, was a reply to South Carolina's vigorous defiance of the tariffs of 1828 and 1832 in its ordinance of nullification, Nov. 24, 1832.

Four acts enforced recognition of the freedmen's civil and political rights as guaranteed by the Fourteenth and Fifteenth amendments: the Act of May 31, 1870, reenacted the Civil Rights Act of Apr. 9, 1866; the federal election law of Feb. 28, 1871; the act to enforce the Fourteenth Amendment, Apr. 20, 1871, extended the earlier acts; the Supplementary Civil Rights Act of Mar. 1, 1875. In 1894 Congress repealed most of the provisions of the force acts, after an unsuccessful attempt in 1890 to pass a new force bill.

FORCE'S TRACTS (in full, *Tracts and Other Papers, Relating Principally to the Origin, Settlement, and Progress of the Colonies in North America*). Reprints of scarce and important historical writings dealing with the American colonies, published in four volumes (1836–46) by Peter Force.

FORD'S PEACE SHIP. Henry Ford financed an unofficial mission in World War I to the Scandinavian countries in the hope that neutral governments might be induced to offer an armistice to the belligerents; *Oscar II* sailed from Hoboken, N.J., on Dec. 4, 1915. The movement, largely initiated by the Hungarian feminist and pacifist Rosika Schwimmer, led to the establishment of the Neutral Conference for Continuous Mediation, an unofficial committee with headquarters at Stockholm.

FOREIGN AFFAIRS, COMMITTEE FOR. *See* **Revolutionary Committees.**

FOREIGN AID. A prominent instrument of U.S. foreign policy since the beginning of World War II, although some aid had been made available before then in the form of loans, credits, and gifts. The Lend-Lease Act of March 1941 authorized the president to "lend, lease, or otherwise dispose of" arms, equipment, and supplies to any country whose defense he deemed vital to U.S. security. About $50 billion worth of resources was transferred to America's allies (1941–45), most without expectation of repayment.

Three organizations were created during the war to assist postwar reconstruction: the United Nations Relief and Rehabilitation Agency (UNRRA), to provide relief to devastated areas; the International Bank for Reconstruction and Development (IBRD), to encourage private investment and to provide long-term capital for projects that did not interest private investors; and the International Monetary Fund (IMF), to help resolve international payments difficulties. The United States put up most of the capital for these multilateral agencies. However, revival of the international economic system required immediate, large-scale aid far beyond the resources of these organizations. Washington officials did not hesitate to employ U.S. economic power to gain political objectives. Thus, aid to Great Britain in the form of a $3.75 billion loan in 1946 was made conditional upon Britain's willingness to dismantle the imperial preference system. A proposed loan of between $1 billion and $6 billion to the Soviet Union was never made because the Soviets refused to accept the political conditions attached to it. In early 1947, $400 million in military and economic aid was given to Greece and Turkey for the purpose of resisting the expanding Soviet influence there (*see* Truman Doctrine). In June 1947, Secretary of State George C. Marshall announced the willingness of the United States to support the reconstruction and rehabilitation of Europe to make that continent less vulnerable to Communist subversion and increase the volume of international trade (*see* Marshall Plan); Congress approved extending some $17 billion in aid over a four-year period.

Early in 1949, President Truman broadened the geographical scope of foreign aid by proposing Point Four, a program of technical assistance to underdeveloped countries. Late in 1949, the United States began making military assistance available to the members of the North Atlantic Treaty Organization to create a Western European army capable of resisting a Soviet attack. In 1950, aid to the French in Indochina and to the Nationalist Chinese on Formosa was stepped up (only limited aid had been given to Chiang Kai-shek during 1947–49). During the 1950's, the preponderance of U.S. expenditures for foreign aid was devoted to military assistance to nations along the periphery of the Soviet Union and Communist China. The administration of Dwight D. Eisenhower placed primary emphasis on attracting private capital for investment, and not until 1957 did the government commit itself, through creation of the Development Loan Fund, to the use of soft loans as a technique for stimulating economic development.

The Kennedy administration's aid policy had two main thrusts: the Peace Corps, an elaboration of Truman's Point Four program that involved sending young American volunteers to underdeveloped parts of the world to furnish technical aid; and the Alliance for Progress, a plan to spend $20 billion over a ten-year period for economic development in Latin America. By the 1970's, both domestic critics and overseas recipients of aid worried that economic assistance programs might lead, as they had in Vietnam, to military involvement, and defenders of the program found it difficult to explain what tangible contribution the $125 billion in U.S. aid since World War II had made to American security.

FOREIGN INVESTMENTS IN THE UNITED STATES. The British invested more money in American enterprises and advanced more credit to them than the money men of any other nation, from the colonial period until the United States became a creditor nation during World War I. The first investment began in the early 17th century when two English joint stock companies, the Virginia Company and the Massachusetts Bay Company, seeded America's development with money raised in London. By 1899, British investments in the United States were ten times greater than those of the Netherlands, which ranked second. The Germans, Swiss, Belgians, and French were also active investors, although French investments declined considerably at the beginning of the 20th century.

American Revolution to the Civil War. When the Revolution began, American colonists owed British creditors an estimated $28 million, an amount approximating some two years of colonial imports; French, Dutch, and Spanish loans of approximately $7.8 million had helped the colonies win their independence, but British merchants were anxious to reenter the American market. By the early 19th century, competition between British capitalists was so keen that they extended credit to U.S. merchants for periods of from twelve to eighteen months. These credits financed American trade in all parts of the world and also provided the financial base for opening up much of America's west. After the War of 1812, mercantile credit grew substantially; it was estimated at $100 million in 1837, almost all of it British.

The British had a large interest in the second Bank of the United States (1816), and the bond issue of $11.25 million for the purchase of Louisiana (1803) found Britishers taking up $9.25 million of the bonds. Estimates made in 1837 placed foreign long-term holdings in America at $200 million. These funds went largely into state and municipal securities, which were used for internal improvements or for social overhead, at a time when the federal government would finance neither. New York State bonds of over $7 million, almost all held in England, financed the Erie Canal (1817–25). Concurrently, Anglo-American banking houses, through the London money market, underwrote the Deep South cotton lands. By 1838, 50 percent of all state securities, some $85 million, were in British hands.

Investment opportunities were halted after the financial crisis of 1837–43, which found nine states defaulting on their interest payments; Mississippi, Florida, and Arkansas repudiated their debts entirely. But by 1848, political disturbances on the European continent once again made American governmental securities popular. American railways also attracted investors. Sound estimates put America's foreign indebtedness in 1857 at no less than $400 million, about two-thirds in securities and the remainder in mercantile credit. Direct private investments by foreigners in American enterprise were not included in these figures: although much smaller in amount, they were likely to be concentrated in a key industry or sector and often had an accelerating influence on growth. The Civil War caused some foreign capital to be brought home, but 1863–64 saw renewed foreign investment in the United States.

Civil War to World War I. In the post–Civil War era the United States developed new connections with Frankfurt and Amsterdam through the recently arrived German-American merchant bankers and investment houses. Other continental European investment firms were coming heavily into the American market, but British capital for governmental, as well as railway, securities dominated the U.S. demand for foreign funds. In this period European capital financed about 40 percent of U.S. railway construction. Sixty-seven British mining companies registered between 1870 and 1873 in Colorado, Utah, and Nevada. British management also became significant in such ventures as mortgage companies and ranches. Several Dundee and Edinburgh trusts organized for investment in the United States in 1873 and played a dominant role in financing the newer railways in the South and Southwest. Scotland invested more per capita in the development of the United States than any other nation in the post–Civil War period; many ranching and mortgage companies and financial and investment trusts that were based in London raised their capital in Scotland. The mortgage companies developed large reserve funds in American securities, and by 1914 were as much investment trusts as mortgage companies.

Although interrupted by the panic of 1873, foreign investment in the United States increased during the 1880's to about $2 billion, of which $1.53 billion was in railroad securities. In 1899 it was estimated that the British were still by far the largest investors at $2.5 billion; the Dutch next at $241 million; then the Germans at $105 million; the Swiss at $75 million; and the French at $50 million. By 1914, according to a reliable estimate, Britain still held 63 percent of foreign-owned American securities. Overall, government figures for foreign long-term investment in the United States show an increase from $200 million in 1843 to $400 million in 1860 and $600 million by 1866; by 1869 the figure had grown to $1.5 billion, and it reached $6.7 billion in 1914.

Post–World War I. By the end of World War I, the United States was well advanced as a creditor nation. The holdings of American long-term portfolio investments by Europeans had declined from $5.4 billion in 1914 to $1.6 billion; direct long-term investment dropped from $1.3 billion to $900 million. Britain sold back about two-thirds of its U.S. investments in order to finance the war, while France sold back a larger proportion. By 1920, Britain owed America $4.2 billion, France owed $3 billion, and other European countries owed large amounts also. The prosperity of the 1920's tempted new capital; total foreign long-term investment in the United States peaked in 1930 at $5.7 billion, dropped to $2.3 billion in 1931, but by 1940 reached $8.1 billion.

By 1950 total foreign investment in the United States was $19.4 billion—$7.7 billion long-term; and $11.7 billion short-term private and U.S. government obligations. In 1978 the book value at year's end for direct foreign investment in the United States was $52.3 billion; figures from the Treasury Department and the Department of Commerce show foreign portfolio investment at $49.8 billion.

The new force in the world economy after World War II was the multinational corporation. The huge size and consumer buying power of the United States have led many such companies to make direct investments in America; the majority are British and Anglo-Dutch in origin, but during the 1960's German and Japanese companies grew rapidly. In 1973 the Japanese broke ground for their first steel mill in the United States, and in 1978, Japanese direct foreign investment was $2.7 billion. Britain still had the highest level of permanent direct investment, $7.6 billion in 1978, but insurance had yielded first place to manufacturing. In 1974, European-American, a New York State bank owned by a consortium of six European shareholder banks with assets in that year of $112 billion, took over selected assets of Franklin National, the twentieth largest bank in the United States (*see* Bank Failures). The OPEC states, with huge surpluses of petrodollars, invested in the 1970's in real estate, banks, manufacturing, and oil companies, but their combined direct investment of $576 million in 1980 represented less than 1 percent of the total foreign investment in the United States.

FOREIGN POLICY. Based on what is conceived to be the national interest of the American people, U.S. foreign policy is affected by economic interests, political forces, and social influences.

Beginnings: 1776–1825. Early policy was concerned with establishing the viability of independence, avoiding entanglement in European wars, and reducing dangers from the bordering European colonies by opportune expansion at their expense. Aid from France (1776) and a subsequent alliance (1778) assured independence from Britain. Jay's Treaty (1794) removed British troops from the Northwest, and Pinckney's Treaty (1795) certified the southern boundary with Spain. President George Washington, in his farewell address (1796), urged abstention from permanent alliances and an independent course for America in foreign affairs; the address became a foundation stone of American isolationism.

President Thomas Jefferson attempted to win respect for American trading rights, which were being violated on the high seas by the British and French belligerents. These problems subsequently brought on the War of 1812 with Britain; the Treaty of Ghent (1814) ended the war without remedying any of the problems that had caused it. But the nation's international involvements also worked to its advantage, forcing Napoleon to sell Louisiana (1803) to the United States for $15 million.

Experience dictated the principles enunciated in the Monroe Doctrine of 1823: "the American continents are henceforth not to be considered as subject for further colonization"; the United States should not intervene in the internal concerns of Europe; and European powers should not "extend their system to any other portion of this hemisphere." This doctrine and Washington's farewell address framed the basic foreign policies of the United States for over a century.

Nationalist Expansion: 1825–1889. With a weak Canada and Mexico on its borders, the United States began a period of expansion. The doctrine of Manifest Destiny encouraged James K. Polk in demanding all of Oregon from Britain; he gladly settled for the area south of the forty-ninth parallel, because he had the war with Mexico to contend with. Ostensibly growing out of a border clash, the war was sought by Polk after his purchase plans failed. The Treaty of Guadalupe Hidalgo (1848) added the Southwest to the United States. The Gadsden Purchase (1854) in Arizona completed the southern boundary. Seward's opportune purchase of Alaska from Russia (1867) removed another potential enemy from the continent; at the same time, his success in ousting France from Mexico and Spain from Peru gave credence in Europe to the Monroe Doctrine.

Emergence as a World Power: 1889–1945. As Europe divided into rival alliances, Anglo-American differences were settled in a series of arbitral awards that fed a growing confidence in legality and morality as bases of foreign policy. At the same time, expansionists argued for the "large policy" that culminated in the Spanish-American War (1898), which gave Puerto Rico, Guam, and the Philippines to the United States. Hawaii was added by joint congressional resolution (1898), and the Platt Amendment (1901) gave the United States its first protectorate in Cuba.

In China the United States followed in the wake of the British, picking up through the "most-favored nation" treaties the same rights Britain won by war. When these rights were jeopardized in 1899, Secretary of State John Hay addressed notes to the powers advocating respect for the Open Door policy. Theodore Roosevelt played a large role in making American power a reality in the Far East. Equally active in the Caribbean, he obtained the right to build the Panama Canal by approving an arranged revolution. In 1905, he issued the Roosevelt Corollary to the Monroe Doctrine, claiming the right of the United States to intervene in Latin America when the Monroe Doctrine might be threatened.

The outbreak of World War I brought Woodrow Wilson's proclamation of neutrality; yet his dogmatic stand on neutral rights and his concern for structuring a new international order brought the country into the war. During the interwar period, the United States concentrated on attempting to collect its war debts and to build peace through multilateral arms reduction. But the Washington Naval Conference treaties (1922), dealing largely with the Far East, and the Kellogg-Briand Pact (1928), outlawing war as an instrument of national policy, contained no enforcement provisions; they fell apart when Japan challenged the agreements in Manchuria in 1931. The United States issued a weak protest in the Stimson Nonrecognition Doctrine (1932). As peace disintegrated in Europe, Congress passed a series of neutrality laws (1935–37). In Latin America, Franklin D. Roosevelt's administration renounced the right of intervention (1933); abrogated the Platt Amendment; called the troops home from the former protectorates; and, in the Declaration of Lima (1938), initiated a collective security structure. The Good Neighbor policy was well received in Latin America, and the Reciprocal Trade Agreements Act (1934) aroused hopes for restoring international trade. After the outbreak of World War II, Roosevelt revised the neutrality laws, leased destroyers to Britain, and created lend-lease aid to the Allies.

Post–World War II Policy: 1945–62. Postwar U.S. foreign policy developed in three stages. In the first period (1945–47) it sought to maintain wartime cooperation and to build the United Nations; it proposed international control in nuclear affairs and signed peace treaties with Eastern Europe that were highly favorable to Soviet desires.

The early cold war (1947–53) marked the initiation of the containment policy in the Truman Doctrine (1947), which extended aid to people resisting subjugation. Truman responded to the Soviet blockade of Berlin with a giant airlift to the city, went forward with unification plans, and, most important, signed the North Atlantic Pact (1949), which bound the United States to the defense of Western Europe. The Communist takeover in China and the outbreak of the Korean War (June 1950) globalized the containment policy.

The third period (1953–62) was characterized by a weapons race and a hardened bipolarity of power. Dwight D. Eisenhower recognized the sovereignty of West Germany and made its forces a major part of the North Atlantic Treaty Organization (NATO); the Soviet Union responded with the Warsaw Pact while it preached coexistence. The Soviets launched *Sputnik I* (1957), denoting a missile delivery advantage; Eisenhower installed American missiles in European sites to offset the advantage. Nikita Khrushchev demanded the four-power evacuation of Berlin within six months, threatening to turn the access routes over to East Germany; this threat was removed at talks at Camp David, Md., during Khrushchev's visit to the United States (1959).

John F. Kennedy was also committed to the containment of Communism, gaining respect with his successful neutralization of Laos (1962). His bold use of power in the Cuban missile crisis (1962) may have induced the Soviets to sign the Nuclear Test Ban Treaty (1963), the first breakthrough in the control of nuclear weaponry. Kennedy believed the future lay with the underdeveloped world, as witnessed by his Alliance for Progress (1961) and the Peace Corps (1961), but his dispatch of troops to Vietnam indicated unmistakably that the security of the Third World was a primary concern in American policy.

Vietnam and After. President Lyndon B. Johnson continued the Kennedy policies, in his own style. He intervened in Santo Domingo, made a military pact with West Germany (1964), and accepted France's troop withdrawal from NATO. He approved the Kennedy Round of agreements with the Common Market for tariff reduction (1967) and initialed the Nonproliferation Treaty with the Soviets. Early in his administration Johnson escalated American involvement to save South Vietnam while that country straightened out its political turmoil; the Gulf of Tonkin Resolution (1964) authorized the president to use all measures necessary in Vietnam. By the summer of 1965 he had begun regular bombing of North Vietnam and had committed American ground forces. The Tet offensive and public discontent with the war eventuated in the president's ordering a bombing halt and beginning talks with Hanoi's representatives in Paris.

Richard M. Nixon continued Kennedy's and Johnson's practice of concentrating foreign policy decisions within the White House staff, and appointed Henry Kissinger as his chief adviser. They began the so-called Vietnamization policy and a graduated reduction of American ground troops in Vietnam. Meanwhile, Nixon acceded to the admission of Communist China to the United Nations. In May 1972, with Leonid Brezhnev, he signed agreements on scientific exchanges and cooperation in space and a strategic arms limitation treaty (SALT). A bombing cutoff on Aug. 15, 1973, brought the American war in Southeast Asia to an end. The Arab-Israeli October war erupted soon after; and Henry Kissinger, by then secretary of state, focused on the search for a settlement.

Gerald Ford retained the Nixon cabinet and assured the nation that he would pursue the Nixon foreign policies of negotiation for peace, pursuit of détente, maintenance of the alliances, and sharing with other nations the responsibility for peace. The détente with the Soviet Union reached its climax in the Helsinki agreement on security and cooperation in Europe in 1975; shortly thereafter U.S.-Soviet relations deteriorated when President Jimmy Carter made human rights one of the main themes of his foreign policy. Although the SALT II treaty was signed in June 1979, it was never ratified. Carter's greatest international achievement was the September 1978 Camp David agreement, which led to the formal peace treaty between Israel and Egypt in March 1979. Another high point, although more controversial, occurred in January 1979 when the United States broke formal ties with Taiwan and established full diplomatic relations with China. The Panama Canal treaties, signed in 1977 and ratified one year later, were also a victory for Carter. These successes, however, became overshadowed by the storming of the U.S. embassy in Teheran on Nov. 4, 1979, after the deposed Iranian shah arrived in the United States. Despite diplomatic efforts and a rescue attempt that failed completely, more than fifty American hostages remained in Iran for over fifteen months. When President Ronald Reagan assumed office in 1981, he turned his attention to domestic affairs; his foreign policy was characterized by harsh criticism of Soviet aggressiveness and by increases in defense spending.

FOREIGN SERVICE. The forerunners of the diplomatic and consular services were secret agents named by the Continental Congress in 1775–76 to seek European support in the conflict with Great Britain. The generally high quality of the early diplomatic and consular personnel soon faded, especially after the administration of President Andrew Jackson, when the spoils system took hold. A major effort at improvement came with the passage of an act (1856) that increased salaries for diplomatic positions and fixed salaries in lieu of retaining fees for principal consular positions, enacted administrative controls, and made a first small move toward a merit system by providing for "consular pupils."

Congress reorganized the consular service in 1906 but failed to take appointments out of politics; President Theodore Roosevelt immediately corrected the omission by extending the merit system to consular officers. The Rogers Act of 1924 provided for (1) amalgamation of the diplomatic and consular services into a unified Foreign Service of the United States with meritoriously selected and competitively promoted officers; (2) appointments to classes, not to positions, thus allowing for greater flexibility in transferring officers; (3) increased salaries and representation allowances; and (4) a retirement system to avoid keeping officers of advanced age in service at the cost of efficiency. The Rogers Act was ultimately replaced by the Foreign Service Act of 1946. The new unified service had 633 officers. World War II demands for foreign duty were largely met from outside the Foreign Service; the service itself covered a wartime personnel insufficiency by recruiting a temporary Foreign Service Auxiliary.

The post–World War II period was one of uncertainty and change for the Foreign Service. The Foreign Service was subjected to substantial criticism; a number of special committee reports urged reform, the most important being the

Wriston Report (1954); the Herter Report (1962); the American Foreign Service Association Report (1968); and the State Department Task Forces Report (1970). The recommendations were for amalgamation of foreign and domestic personnel, which has been almost completely implemented; unification of overseas services at the officer level within the Department of State and among the foreign-affairs agencies; and establishment of functional specialization at the middle grades, which has been accomplished at least in form. A measurable impact of these developments was a rapid rise in the number of Foreign Service officers from under 1,300 in early 1954 to over 3,400 by the end of 1957, accomplished primarily through lateral entry by civil service and Foreign Service staff personnel (a process called Wristonization).

FOREIGN TRADE. *See* **Trade, Foreign.**

FORESTRY. The practice of "scientific management of forests for the continuous production of goods and services" evolved slowly. During the colonial period, one of the most famous attempts to prevent indiscriminate cutting was William Penn's briefly enforced ordinance for Pennsylvania. In 1864, George P. Marsh, an American diplomat and traveler, warned that continued deforestation invited desolation and decay. A tree-planting movement led to the first federal timber culture act (1873). Three years later Congress, at the insistence of a committee of the American Association for the Advancement of Science, appropriated $2,000 for a study of American forest conditions and European forestry methods. During the 1880's several states established forest boards or commissions, and the American Forestry Association launched an effort for the study and protection of forests. In 1891, Congress authorized the president to establish forest reserves from the public domain.

The practice of forestry in the United States began in 1892 under the direction of Gifford Pinchot at Biltmore, the Vanderbilt estate in western North Carolina. Pinchot became the federal government's chief forester in 1898 and assumed administration of the national forest system under the newly created Forest Service in 1905. He showed the nation the practicality and profitability of managing forests for continuous timber crops. The early 20th century witnessed the extension of national forests to the eastern states under the Weeks Law of 1911; the organization of programs in forestry research; and the beginning of a forestry profession. Important milestones in the use of forests for recreational purposes were reached with the establishment of the National Park Service in 1916 and the designation in 1924 of the nation's first "wilderness" area in New Mexico. In the late 1970's the national wilderness system covered about 13 million acres.

The economic depression of the 1930's prompted federal public works programs that advanced the practice of forestry. The Civilian Conservation Corps enrolled some 2 million youths, approximately half of whom were engaged in forest protection and reforestation projects. Improved forestry practices were also promoted by the Soil Conservation Service, the Tennessee Valley Authority, and the short-lived National Recovery Administration. The dust storms of the 1930's prompted the federal government to establish the Prairie States Forestry Project, in which some 30,000 farmers helped to plant 217 million trees in 18,000 miles of shelterbelts to reduce the harmful effects of such storms.

After World War II the Forest Service and American Forestry Association called for a national program providing increased forest protection, improved timber-cutting practices, and wider application of the principle of multiple use in forest management (the adjustment of one forest use to another so that a net public benefit results). The Multiple Use–Sustained Yield Act of 1960 stressed that timber harvest and growth should be balanced over a period of time so that forest yield will be continued into perpetuity.

FOREST SERVICE, UNITED STATES. The Forest Service traces its beginning to an 1876 act of Congress authorizing Franklin B. Hough, a forestry agent in what is now the U.S. Department of Agriculture, to investigate the supply and uses of forest products in the United States; to seek out means successfully used abroad to manage and renew forests; and to investigate the influence of forests on climate. A Division of Forestry was set up in 1881; Gifford Pinchot became first chief of the renamed Forest Service in 1905, when the agency took over the forest reserves from the Department of the Interior's General Land Office., The first experiment station was established near Flagstaff, Ariz., in 1908, for the study of range conditions. The Forest Products Laboratory was established in cooperation with the University of Wisconsin at Madison in 1910. Most national forest land in the East was acquired under the Weeks Act (1911), which also set up a program for cooperation with the states in fire protection. The Clarke-McNary Act of 1924 expanded the Weeks Act by allowing for the purchase of lands needed for the production of timber; it also provided for cooperation with the states in producing and distributing forest-tree seedlings and gave impetus to the establishment of state forestry agencies. The Forest Service's 14-million-acre wilderness and primitive area system began in 1924, with the setting aside of the 1-million-acre Gila Wilderness in New Mexico; the first primitive area was set aside in 1930.

In 1928 the McSweeney-McNary Act authorized a program of forest research and the first comprehensive nationwide survey of forest resources. Tree planting in national forests was expanded under the Knutson-Vandenberg Act of 1930. Later legislation expanded the agency's activities into cooperative river-basin projects for flood control. In 1953 it acquired 7 million acres of submarginal farmland, mostly in the western Great Plains, much of it now rehabilitated in the national grasslands. A landmark forestry law, the Multiple Use–Sustained Yield Act (1960), confirmed long-standing policy. Under the Land and Water Fund Conservation Act of 1965 the agency acquired land specifically for public outdoor recreation in national forests. Under the Endangered Species Preservation Act of 1966, the Forest Service expanded its protection of rare wildlife, and under the Environmental Quality Act of 1969, it has minimized undesirable impacts of forest uses. By 1979 the Forest Service was overseeing about 188 million acres of public lands in 154 national forests and 19 national grasslands—including 15.7 million acres of reserved wilderness and primitive areas—in forty-one states and Puerto Rico, and carrying on a broad program of research. The national forests are administered from ten regional headquarters; national headquarters are in Washington, D.C. Some 350 research projects are coordinated by eight experiment station headquarters. There is an Institute of Tropical Forestry in Rio Piedras, P.R.; an Institute of Northern Forestry in Juneau; and an Institute of Pacific Islands Forestry in Honolulu.

FORGES, COLONIAL. In the 17th century a few ironworks were established near the bog ores of the coastal region of New England but not until the early 18th century did the iron industry became important in colonial economic life. Two types of early forges existed: at bloomery forges (bloomeries) bars of wrought iron were obtained by heating iron ore to a semimolten mass and hammering it under heavy hammers driven by water power; at refinery forges, pig iron from blast furnaces was heated and hammered, reheated and rehammered, under ponderous water-driven hammers until a refined form of wrought iron was produced. The bar iron was shaped into finished products by hundreds of blacksmith shops scattered over the colonies. By 1775 there were more forges in the colonies than in England and Wales, and the output of bar iron was larger in America than in England.

"FORGOTTEN MAN." The title of a public lecture (1883) delivered by William Graham Sumner of Yale University. By this term he identified the "honest, industrious, economical" man who "pays" for the political and social extravagance of others. The term was revived—but used to refer to the underprivileged—by Franklin D. Roosevelt in an address at Warm Springs, Ga. (May 18, 1932).

FORMAN'S COLONY. A settlement in present-day Mississippi planned (1789) by Gen. David Forman of New Jersey and Diego de Gardoquí, Spanish minister to the United States, on behalf of Ezekiel Forman. Actual settlement (1790) of sixty slaves was made with the aid of Maj. Samuel S. Forman on 500 acres of land on the St. Catherine River, four miles from Natchez.

FORMAN'S MASSACRE (1777). At the time of the Indian attack on Fort Henry (W. Va.), Capt. William Forman came to the rescue of the fort. Not finding Indians, he went on a scouting expedition and was surprised in McMechen Narrows, midway between present Moundsville and Wheeling; he and twenty companions were killed.

FORSYTH'S FIGHT. *See* **Beecher Island, Battle of.**

FORT. *See under identifying name of fort, as in* **Recovery, Fort,** *except where the designation has become attached to a continuing city.*

FORT BENTON (Mont.). After 1830 the American Fur Company established several trading posts near the head of navigation of the Missouri River. One of these, Fort Lewis, (1844), was moved in 1846 to the site of the present town of Fort Benton; it retained its original name until 1850, when it was renamed for Thomas Hart Benton. During the Montana gold rush Fort Benton became a main port of entry to the mines; a town sprang up around it, and the fur company sold out to a mercantile firm in 1865.

FORT HILL LETTER. John C. Calhoun's definitive statement of his nullification doctrine, written at his home, Fort Hill (S.C.), Aug. 28, 1832, addressed to Gov. James Hamilton. It proposed, as solutions of the tariff and similar dilemmas, constitutional amendment, compromise, or abandonment by the federal government, and, as a last resort, secession.

FORTIFICATIONS. In the colonial period, fortifications ranged from small, improvised earthworks and palisaded stockades to masonry works of substantial size. Frontier forts were established in large numbers until the late 19th century; built to resist Indians equipped with nothing heavier than small arms, these were generally of timber or adobe construction, depending on location.

From the 1790's the construction of fortifications against naval attack was a major item in the nation's defense expenditures and also the principal representative of its military architecture. Among the best known of these, all completed before the Civil War, were Fort Monroe, Va.; Fort Sumter, S.C.; Fort Pulaski, Ga.; Fort Morgan, Ala.; and Fort Jackson, La. The appearance of rifled artillery in the Civil War ended the construction of these massive vertical-walled masonry forts. The wartime defenses for both North and South were simple low-profile earthwork forts revetted by timber or sandbags; hundreds of these were built, in a few cases to ring large cities, such as Atlanta, Ga., and Washington, D. C.

Following the Civil War, construction was limited for a time to new earthwork defenses of a more durable style. In the 1890's powerful 10- and 12-inch breech-loading rifles were mounted on disappearing carriages that lowered the guns after each firing to protected positions behind many feet of earth and concrete. Along with 12-inch mortars, such armament was installed between 1893 and 1918 along both continental coasts, in the Philippines and Hawaiian Islands, and at both entrances to the Panama Canal.

A final fortification effort (1937–45) was characterized by concrete and steel emplacements that provided overhead cover for guns of up to 16-inch caliber; included in the program were defenses in Alaska and in the Caribbean area, as well as for the Atlantic bases acquired from Great Britain. By 1950, all such fortifications were abandoned, to be replaced by newer defense systems utilizing aircraft and guided missiles.

FORT LAUDERDALE (Fla.). Established (1838) as a military post commanded by Maj. William Lauderdale during the Seminole War. The city, famous for its miles of canals and riverfront that have carved it up into a number of islands, developed during the 20th century, as railroads and the Intercoastal Waterway provided easy access. It is one of the fastest-growing cities in Florida, with a population of 153,256 in 1980. Prominent as a resort town, its chief local industries are boat building and services, and shipping and warehousing of locally produced foods, including citrus and dairy products. Port Everglades, two miles south, is an important seaport.

FORTUNES, GREAT. In colonial America great landed estates were created alongside and within the proprietary grants. Other sources of colonial fortunes were overseas trade; the fur trade; the slave trade; and moneylending. As early as 1680, thirty merchants in Massachusetts were estimated to have fortunes ranging between $50,000 and $100,000. John Robinson of Virginia, who died in 1766, was probably the first millionaire.

The period after the American Revolution marked the emergence of the millionaire class. Stephen Girard (1750–1831) amassed $7 million in Philadelphia from astute speculative ventures. The largest fortune in the period prior to 1860 was that of John Jacob Astor (1763–1848), a German immigrant involved in the fur trade, especially through the American Fur Company, and in real estate; he left an estate of at least $20 million. In the field of transportation Cornelius Vanderbilt (1794–1877) stands out for his investments, first in sailing ships and steamboats and then in railroads; his estate of $100 million was the basis for the long-term domination by his descendants, in cooperation with the Whitney and Webb families, of the New York Central Railroad and its affiliates. Another railroad magnate was Jay Gould (1836–92), who gained a fortune of some $50 million. In California four great fortunes arose out of the construction (1863–69) and management of the Central Pacific Railroad by Leland Stanford, Collis P. Huntington, Charles Crocker, and Mark Hopkins. Edward H. Harriman (1848–1909) dominated the Union Pacific, Southern Pacific, and Central Pacific; a rival was James J. Hill (1838–1916), who won control of the Great Northern and the Northern Pacific.

In post–Civil War banking, centered in New York City, the giant figure was John Pierpont Morgan (1837–1913); he was the American agent for a London banking house headed by his father and then became a partner in Drexel, Morgan and Company in 1871, which he reorganized in 1895 as J. P. Morgan and Company. Morgan left a net estate of more than $68 million. Among other financial personalities, Russell Sage (1816–1906) was known as a railroad promoter and moneylender who acquired a fortune of some $70 million. August Belmont (1816–90) started as an agent for the Rothschilds but created his own firm and a large family fortune in banking and railroads. A banking family that came to have tremendous wealth and industrial power was that of the Pittsburgh banker Thomas Mellon (1813–1908), an Irish immigrant, and his sons, Andrew W., Richard B., and James R. Mellon; Andrew W. Mellon (1855–1937) built up a fortune reputed to be $1 billion. Among the notable steel magnates were Andrew Carnegie (1835–1919), a Scottish immigrant who disposed of some $350 million in gifts to benefit education and libraries; John W. Gates, a leader of the U.S. wire industry; Charles M. Schwab, organizer of Bethlehem Steel; and Henry C. Frick. The meat-packing industry was another source for millionaires: Philip D. Armour (1832–1901) built up an estate of $50 million, and Gustavus F. Swift (1839–1903) accumulated $25 million. Cyrus H. McCormick (1809–84), inventor of the reaper, became its leading manufacturer and founded a Chicago dynasty of great wealth, while George M. Pullman (1831–97) built his dynasty upon the manufacture of sleeping and dining cars.

Oil refining and oil production were the basis of the greatest American fortune prior to 1913, that of John Davison Rockefeller (1839–1937). His formation of the Standard Oil trust and his investments led to a fortune estimated in 1913 to be about $900 million; his donations to religious and other causes exceeded $500 million. Another massively wealthy family is that of Eleuthère Irénée Du Pont (1771–1834), a French émigré who established a gunpowder plant near Wilmington, Del., in 1802. George Hearst (1820–91) gained millions through his holdings in Utah silver, Montana copper, and the Homestake Gold Mine in South Dakota; his fortune was greatly increased by both his widow and his son, William Randolph Hearst (1863–1951), in newspapers, South American copper, and other investments. William A. Clark (1839–1925) was Montana's wealthiest copper magnate. And copper mining in the United States, Chile, and the Belgian Congo was the basis for the fortune of Meyer Guggenheim (1828–1905). Fortunes were made in sugar refining by Henry O. Havemeyer (1847–1907) of New York City and Claus Spreckels (1828–1908) of San Francisco; in lumber by Frederick Weyerhaeuser (1834–1914) of St. Paul; in electric street railroads by Peter A. B. Widener (1834–1915) of Philadelphia; and in the retail tobacco trade by Washington Duke (1820–1905) and his sons James B. and Benjamin N. Duke of Durham, N.C.

The development of the automobile after 1900 enabled pioneers in automobile manufacture and management—Henry Ford, Walter P. Chrysler, William C. Durant, and Pierre S. Du Pont—to build up vast fortunes. Among the most publicized fortunes acquired in the 20th century are those created in oil production and refining by J. Paul Getty and Haroldson L. Hunt, in aircraft by Howard R. Hughes, in public construction and shipbuilding by Henry J. Kaiser, in tanker shipbuilding by Daniel K. Ludwig, and in electronics by James J. Ling.

FORT WAYNE (Ind.). Named for Gen. Anthony Wayne, who established a frontier fort at the site (1794) during his campaign to put down a major Indian revolt; the location had been the center of the Miami Indians, and a French fort had been built there early in the 18th century. It was an important outpost for the American army in the War of 1812; besieged by British-led Indians and Canadians, it was the first American fort in the old Northwest Territory to hold out.

The St. Joseph and St. Mary rivers combine at Fort Wayne to form the Maumee River. The water transportation network made Fort Wayne important as a gateway to northern Indiana; it was a principal point on the canal system linking Lake Erie with the Wabash River in western Indiana. It later became an important rail center. In 1980 it was the second largest city in Indiana, with a population of 172,196 (metropolitan area 382,961). Local industrial plants produce trucks, radios and television equipment, and other machinery.

FORT WORTH (Tex.). The federal government sought to protect the border settlements of Texas after annexation in 1845 by erecting a chain of forts. Fort Worth, thirty-five miles west of the village of Dallas, was one of these; it was built by Company F, the Second Dragoons, under Maj. Ripley A. Arnold in 1849. Settlements soon sprang up to the west and the post was abandoned (1853). The location became a thriving town, supplying the needs of the border settlements, an important cattle shipping point after 1874. A number of giant meat-packing plants opened in 1902, and the city gradually became the meat-packing center of the Southwest. Since the discovery of oil in 1920 Fort Worth has been one of the most active oil-producing areas in the United States. In April 1949 aviation manufacturing began in the city. In 1980 the population of Fort Worth was 385,141.

FORT WORTH FRONTIER CENTENNIAL EXPOSITION (July 1–Dec. 1, 1936). One of the series of celebrations marking the centennial of Texan independence; in size and importance it was second only to that held in Dallas. It was revived on a smaller scale the following year.

"FORTY ACRES AND A MULE." An expression common among blacks in the South after the Civil War, describing the homestead that each family expected from the confiscation of plantations. This expectation probably arose from the division among freedmen of lands on the southeast coast by Gen. William T. Sherman's order of January 1865.

FORTY-EIGHTERS. The Revolution of 1848 in Germany led to the migration to the United States of many Germans of significant attainment. German influence increased greatly in Cincinnati, Milwaukee, St. Louis, and Chicago; it helped the National Union party decisively in the congressional election of 1862 and the national election of 1864.

FORTY FORT (Pa.). A frontier fort, erected 1772 in what is now Forty Fort Borough in Wyoming Valley, and named for the first forty settlers sent (1769) by the Susquehanna Company of Connecticut to take up the Wyoming lands. Enlarged in 1777.

FORTY-MILE DESERT. Between the sink of Humboldt River and the Carson or Truckee River routes, this was the worst stretch of the entire journey for the goldseekers who traveled through Nevada to California (*see* Death Valley; Donner Party). Neither water nor grass was to be found, and the loss of life was high.

FORTY-NINERS. Gold-seekers who trekked to California when the news reached them that on Jan. 24, 1848, James Wilson Marshall had discovered gold in the tailrace of a sawmill that he and John A. Sutter were erecting on the South Fork of the American River, about fifty miles northeast of the present city of Sacramento.

FOUNDATIONS, ENDOWED. In America a foundation is a nongovernmental, nonprofit organization, having funds and a program managed by its own trustees or directors, established to maintain or to aid social, educational, charitable, religious, or other activities serving the common welfare. The first notable funds approaching the modern concept of a foundation were the two established in 1791 under the will of Benjamin Franklin in the cities of Boston and Philadelphia, to assist "young married artificers" of good character, each of whom might be lent $300 at 5 percent. Portions of these funds were to accumulate for 200 years and are still accumulating. The first substantial foundation to meet the present definition was the Peabody Education Fund (1867), set up by George Peabody with a principal sum of over $2 million to aid the stricken South; its final balance was transferred in 1914 to the John F. Slater Fund.

Early in the 20th century endowments were set up, often in perpetuity but frequently with wide latitude in their use. "To promote the well-being of mankind throughout the world," the purpose clause of the Rockefeller Foundation, was not unusual in its breadth. The funds of foundations were largely the venture capital of philanthropy, best spent in enterprises requiring risk and foresight, ones not likely to be supported by government or by private individuals. Andrew Carnegie was a chief proponent of these ideas. In 1902 he set up the Carnegie Institution of Washington, "to encourage, in the broadest and most liberal manner, investigation, research, and discovery, and the application of knowledge to the improvement of mankind." In the same year, the General Education Board was set up, a Rockefeller benefaction of which Carnegie was an active trustee. Others followed rapidly: the Milbank Memorial Fund and the Carnegie Foundation for the Advancement of Teaching (1905); the Russell Sage Foundation (1907); the New York Foundation (1909); the Carnegie Endowment for International Peace (1910); the Carnegie Corporation of New York, largest and most general of the Carnegie benefactions (1911); the Rockefeller Foundation, giant of the early foundations (1913); and the Cleveland Foundation, first of the community trusts (1914).

Foundations have undergone four major congressional investigations and a number of special hearings. The Federal Commission on Industrial Relations (1915) looked into the charge that foundations were dominated by big business and were exerting a strong reactionary influence; the Select (Cox) Committee of the House in 1952, the Special (Reece) Committee in 1953–54, and an investigation begun by Congressman Wright Patman in 1962 took the position that foundations may be tending to weaken the capitalistic system and favor socialistic change. Increasing use of foundations and colleges as tax shelters for business operations in the late 1940's led to the Revenue Act of 1950, under which foundation income derived from business operations not related to their exempt purposes is fully taxed. The Tax Reform Act of 1969 imposed an annual 4 percent excise tax on net investment income; strict prohibitions on self-dealing; a requirement to spend currently full investment income or the equivalent of 5.5 percent of fair market value of assets; limitations on stock holdings in any one corporation; a requirement to provide more detailed reporting; and a requirement that grants to individuals meet approved standards. The bill has resulted in dissolution of some foundations and a slowing in the creation of new ones. In 1979 some 3,140 foundations disbursed a total of $2 billion.

FOUNDING FATHERS. The political leaders of the United States during the years of the American Revolution and the writing of the Constitution.

FOUR CHAPLAINS. On Feb. 3, 1943, the troopship *Dorchester* was torpedoed and sunk. Aboard were four Army chaplains (George L. Fox, Alexander D. Goode, Clark V. Poling, and John P. Washington), who went down with the ship, having given up their life preservers to soldiers. Their joint sacrifice was dramatized as a sign of interfaith cooperation for the good of men and is commemorated in a U.S. postage stamp.

FOUR FREEDOMS. President Franklin D. Roosevelt, in a major speech before Congress (Jan. 6, 1941) urged "a world founded upon four essential human freedoms: (1) freedom of speech and expression everywhere in the world; (2) freedom of every person to worship God in his own way everywhere in the world; (3) freedom from want . . . everywhere in the world; (4) freedom from fear—which . . . means a worldwide reduction of armaments to such a point . . . that no nation will be in a position to commit an act of physical aggression against any neighbor—anywhere in the world."

FOUR-H (4-H) CLUBS. A rural youth movement originating in 1902 in Ohio and Illinois. Albert B. Graham taught boys and girls in Springfield Township, Ohio, how to test the soil on their farms for acid content with litmus paper; O. J. Kern of Winnebago County, Ill., interested students in seed corn development. The corn clubs or experiment clubs, as they became known, were encouraged by production contests offering prizes. In 1910, Iowa used three-leaf and four-leaf clover pins to recognize achievement among club members. The next year the clover emblem appeared on labels marking 4-H brand tomatoes, salmon, corn, potatoes, and apples that members had grown, picked, caught, preserved, and marketed. The name "4-H" came into general use after World War I; the H's stand for head, heart, hands, and health.

The Smith-Lever Act (1914) provides federal support; private support is provided by the National 4-H Service Committee (founded 1921) and the National 4-H Club Foundation (founded 1948). The U.S. Department of Agriculture and the Cooperative Extension Service of the state land-grant universities share administrative responsibilities for 4-H. About 4 million young Americans belonged to the movement in 1980.

FOUR HUNDRED. In 1892, Mrs. William Astor, finding that her list of guests exceeded her ballroom's capacity, asked Ward McAllister, social arbiter in the Gilded Age, to reduce it to 400. The Four Hundred became a cliché denoting social exclusiveness anywhere.

FOURIERISM. Charles Fourier (1772–1837), a French Socialist, conceived of an ideal community consisting of 1,600 persons living on a self-supporting estate of several thousand acres; out of the common gain, subsistence would be provided and surpluses equitably distributed among the three groups: labor, capital, and talent. In 1834, Albert Brisbane, a young humanitarian, returned to the United States from France, where he had studied under Fourier; he publicized Fourierism by lecturing, writing books, and contributing to newspapers. Some forty small experiments sprang up as a result of the excitement. Brook Farm was one of the more impressive experiments; its failure in 1846 marked the end of the association movement in the United States.

FOUR-MILE STRIP. According to a treaty of peace signed Aug. 6, 1764, at Fort Niagara, by Sir William Johnson, British superintendent of Indian affairs, and the Seneca, the latter ceded to the crown, reserving the hunting right, a strip of land four miles wide on each side of the Niagara River from Lake Ontario to Lake Erie.

FOUR-MINUTE MEN. Members of a volunteer national organization who gave four-minute speeches before motion-picture and other audiences in 1917–18 to promote the sale of World War I Liberty Loan bonds.

FOUR-POWER TREATY (Dec. 13, 1921). One of seven treaties that emerged from the Conference on Limitation of Armaments held in Washington from November 1921 to February 1922; it acted as the necessary preliminary to the other treaties and resolutions of the conference. The signatories (the United States, Great Britain, France, and Japan) bound themselves to respect each other's "rights in relation to their insular possessions and insular dominions in the region of the Pacific Ocean." The treaty was to run for ten years, and thereafter until denounced by one of the signatories. A declaration of the same date applied the treaty to the mandated islands of the Pacific, but without preventing the United States from negotiating about the mandates. By a supplementary treaty (Feb. 6, 1922) the signatories declared that "insular possessions and insular dominions," when applied to Japan, included only Korafuto (southern portion of Sakhalin), Formosa, the Pescadores, and the islands under the mandate of Japan.

FOURTEEN POINTS. Following publication by the Soviet government in late 1917 of secret treaties among the Allies, President Woodrow Wilson addressed Congress on Jan. 8, 1918, and stated in fourteen points America's terms of peace: (1) "open covenants of peace openly arrived at"; (2) freedom of the seas; (3) removal of economic barriers and equality of trade conditions; (4) reduction of armaments to the lowest point consistent with domestic safety; (5) impartial adjustment of colonial claims; (6) evacuation of Russian territory and Russian self-determination; (7) evacuation and restoration of Belgium; (8) evacuation of France and restoration of Alsace-Lorraine to France; (9) readjustment of Italian frontiers; (10) autonomous development for the peoples of

Austria-Hungary; (11) readjustments in the Balkans; (12) autonomous development for the non-Turkish nationalities of the Ottoman Empire and the opening of the Dardanelles; (13) restoration of an independent Poland with access to the sea; (14) establishment of a general association of nations. The fourteen points were accepted by the Allies on Nov. 4, 1918 —with the reservation that they had "complete freedom" on the subject of freedom of the seas and that "compensation will be made by Germany for all damage done to the civilian population of the Allies and their property"—and became the legal basis for the ensuing treaty of peace.

FOURTEENTH AMENDMENT (1868). The second of three Civil War amendments to the Constitution, designed primarily to restrain the states from abridging the civil rights and liberties of individual citizens, especially those of emancipated slaves.

Section 1 is composed of four primary clauses: the citizenship clause; the privileges and immunities clause; the due process clause; and the equal protection clause. Federal and state citizenship was granted to "all persons born or naturalized in the United States"; this clause has been the basis for Supreme Court decisions on congressional power to expatriate citizens (*Afroyim* v. *Rusk* [1967] and *Rogers* v. *Bellei* [1971]).

In 1873 the Supreme Court (*see* Slaughterhouse Cases) interpreted the privileges and immunities clause in such a restrictive manner that its potential significance has never been realized; it held that civil rights were primarily derivatives of state citizenship and that only rights of U.S. citizenship were protected by the privileges and immunities clause from state abridgment.

The due process clause states: "nor shall any State deprive any person of life, liberty, or property without due process of law." Most significant in terms of free speech and criminal procedure, this is a reiteration of the same guarantee in the Fifth Amendment, raising the question whether the Fourteenth Amendment was intended to "incorporate" the Bill of Rights. Incorporation would have made the Bill of Rights applicable to the states, thereby overruling *Barron* v. *Baltimore* (1833).

The equal protection clause is the basis for many racial discrimination decisions. *Brown* v. *Board of Education* (1954) declared segregated public schools to be "inherently unequal" and therefore in violation of the equal protection clause; it overruled *Plessy* v. *Ferguson* (1896), which had held that "separate but equal" facilities did not violate equal-protection requirements. In *Reynolds* v. *Sims* (1964) the Supreme Court held that apportionment of representation in both houses of bicameral state legislatures must be based upon the criterion of "one man, one vote" in order to satisfy the equal protection clause; geographic representation was thereby prohibited. Decisions since 1964 have extended the *Reynolds* rule.

Sections 2, 3, and 4 of the amendment pertain to issues arising directly from the Civil War, such as the basis for determining state populations for purposes of apportionment and the status of war debts. Section 5 is an enabling clause, permitting Congress to enforce the provisions of the amendment by appropriate legislation.

FOURTEENTH COLONY. A designation sometimes improperly used for Transylvania (western Virginia), Franklin (in what is now eastern Tennessee), or Vermont. Transylvania, founded May 1775, was intended to be a colony, but it received no official recognition; Virginia made the region a county late in 1776. Franklin had no better claim (*see* Franklin, State of). Vermont has perhaps the best claim; the inhabitants of the New Hampshire grants called a convention on Apr. 11, 1775, to consider organizing a royal colony. Subsequent meetings, however, resulted in a state organization that failed to be recognized until 1790.

FOURTH OF JULY. *See* **Independence Day.**

FOWLER EXPEDITION (or Glenn-Fowler expedition). Jacob Fowler and Hugh Glenn desired to open a road and trade with Santa Fe. They departed from Covington, Ky., in June 1821 and traveled by way of Missouri and Kansas to the Arkansas River and on into Colorado, where they met a number of Indian tribes. In the vicinity of Pueblo, they were met by a Mexican party that conducted Glenn and four companions to Santa Fe, while Fowler and his companions built a house on the site used by Zebulon M. Pike fifteen years before. Learning of Mexican independence in early winter, they went over the Sangre de Cristo pass to Taos. The return trip was made in May 1822.

FOWLTOWN, BATTLE OF (Nov. 21, 1817). The attack by U.S. troops on the Indian village of Fowltown, fourteen miles east of Fort Scott, Ga., started the first Seminole War. The Indians, having refused to give up lands ceded by the Treaty of Fort Jackson in 1814, were ordered removed; Maj. David E. Twiggs and 250 men attempted to surround the town, but were fired upon by the fleeing Indians. The village was later destroyed.

FOX. The Fox Indians originally possessed a Woodland culture and were traditionally allied with the Sauk (with whom they shared an Algonkin language) and with the Kickapoo; all three are believed to have moved into Wisconsin from Michigan in the early 17th century. The relatively small Fox tribe found itself in conflict with both the French and the Chippewa. Displacing the Illinois, the Fox moved southward and were caught in Iowa with the Sauk in the Black Hawk War in 1832. Moving to Kansas, they separated from the Sauk and returned to a reservation in Iowa on land they purchased themselves.

FOX-FRENCH WARS. The first direct contact between the Fox Indians and the French came in 1665. The Fox subsequently exacted a toll for portage between the Fox and Wisconsin rivers in central Wisconsin. Some of the Fox who went to Montreal in 1671 were ill-treated; seeking revenge, they opposed French attempts to push westward to trade with the Chippewa (Ojibwa) and the Siouans, and they began to plunder the French trading canoes. Meanwhile, the French were furnishing firearms to the Chippewa, enemies of the Fox. In 1712 the Fox mounted an unsuccessful attack on Detroit; the surviving Fox fled to Wisconsin, where they began to stir up war among other Indians against the French and their Indian allies. A French punitive expedition in 1716 laid siege to a palisaded Fox village and succeeded in extracting hostages and a promise to end the war. After keeping the peace for ten years, the Fox attacked the Illinois allies of the French; in 1728 a force of nearly 500 French and 1,200 Indians moved against the Fox and destroyed two of their villages. In 1730 the Fox were defeated in eastern Illinois; they took refuge among the Sauk (or Sac), and from that time the two tribes were merged. Guerrilla warfare continued between the French and the Sauk and Fox until 1738.

FOX-WISCONSIN WATERWAY. One of the best-known portage routes from the upper Great Lakes to the Mississippi River and the main artery of transportation through what is now Wisconsin. Between a bend of the Wisconsin River (just below the narrows called the Dells) and the upper Fox River, now connected by a canal, there was a portage about a mile and a half in length, over level ground. This waterway was known to the Indians from prehistoric times. The first recorded travelers were the French explorers Louis Jolliet and Jacques Marquette (1673). Thereafter it was much used by the French. During the British regime posts and towns were built at each end of the waterway, at Green Bay and Prairie du Chien. The Americans in 1816 safeguarded the portage route by building Fort Howard at its eastern end and Fort Crawford at the western. In 1828, after a serious uprising of the Winnebago, Fort Winnebago was built at the portage and garrisoned until the 1840's. The Fox-Wisconsin became the chief artery between the lead-mining region in southwest Wisconsin and the older settled community around Green Bay. Improvement of the route was one of the first plans of American entrepreneurs. A canal was dug across the portage, and the falls and rapids of the lower Fox were overcome by locks. Financed by a land grant from Congress (1846), by 1850 the portage canal was finished and a steamboat went through. In 1853 the Fox-Wisconsin Improvement Company was organized, but its work did not make the route navigable.

FRACTIONAL CURRENCY. *See* **Money.**

FRAME OF GOVERNMENT, 1682. *See* **Penn's Frame of Government.**

FRANCE, AMERICAN JOINT COMMISSION TO. An American mission to France to seek arms and aid for the Revolution. In 1776, Congress appointed Silas Deane, already in Paris; Arthur Lee, its agent in London; and Benjamin Franklin, then in Philadelphia and a member of the Congress. They had instructions, based on the Plan of 1776, to negotiate treaties with whatever powers they could, especially France and Spain. Spain was unwilling to set a bad example of revolt for its own American colonies and turned Arthur Lee back when he entered Spain in 1777. The commission was not formally received by the French king until Mar. 20, 1778, after the signature of the alliance of Feb. 6, 1778. After the signing of the treaties of 1778 the joint commission continued to function until, later that year, Franklin was made the U.S. minister plenipotentiary in France.

FRANCE, CONVENTION WITH. *See* **Convention of 1800.**

FRANCHISE. A franchise is a special privilege of any sort granted to an individual or a group of individuals (for example, the right to establish a corporation and to exercise corporate powers). More specifically, in the constitutional or statutory sense, the term denotes the right of suffrage. Persons upon whom this privilege is conferred are voters or electors; collectively, they make up the electorate, which may be defined as that part of the people of a state who are legally qualified to declare their will in direct primaries and general elections, on initiative and referendum measures, and in recall elections. Qualifications for voting laid down by federal and state constitutions and laws have dealt with such matters as age, sex, race, nationality, literacy, property holding, payment of taxes, and periods of residence. The history of the suffrage in the United States has had three distinct lines of development: the movement toward universal suffrage beginning in 1789; efforts to establish suffrage for black Americans, from the Civil War to the present; and the movement to remove the suffrage from state to national control, beginning in the second half of the 20th century. The proportion of the total population that possessed the franchise increased from only 6 percent in 1789 to about 70 percent in the late 1970's, as the franchise was extended legally from propertied white males to black American males, to women, and to eighteen-year-olds. (*See also* Suffrage, Afro-American; Voting Rights Act; Woman's Suffrage.)

FRANCISCANS. Members of the Order of Friars Minor (O.F.M.), founded by St. Francis of Assisi in 1209. They were preeminent in the discovery, exploration, and settlement of Spanish North America. In the sections of North America belonging to France, where they were known as the Recollects, they were less active. In the English colony of Maryland they joined the Jesuits in 1672 and were active there until 1720, when the last of their group died. It is probable that from Maryland they penetrated into Pennsylvania. Following the American Revolution various provinces in Europe sent Franciscans to the United States; the Franciscans labored chiefly in the "new" West and Northwest. The present era of Franciscan activity in the United States, chiefly in parishes and schools, began in the 1850's. In 1973 there were 3,326 Franciscans (priests, scholastics, and lay brothers) working in 352 foundations (friaries, schools, and Indian missions). There are also 92 foundations abroad (Bolivia, Brazil, Central America, Japan, Peru, and the Philippines) directed by U.S. Franciscans.

FRANCO-AMERICAN ALLIANCE OF 1778. On Feb. 6, 1778, the French foreign minister, Charles Gravier, Comte de Vergennes, signed two treaties with the independent United

States, one a treaty of amity and commerce based on the freedom of the seas, the other a treaty of alliance in case recognition of the United States should bring war with Great Britain, as it did. The alliance provided that neither party would make peace without the consent of the other and that there should be no peace until the independence of the United States, absolute and unlimited, was secured by treaty or by truce. Thereafter, France would guarantee the independence of the United States and the United States would guarantee the possession by France of its West Indian islands. The alliance brought the conflict to a victorious end, thanks to the joint efforts culminating at Yorktown and to continued French loans (35 million livres, or $6,352,000, paid back 1792–95) and subsidies (10.5 million livres, or $1,996,500).

FRANCO-AMERICAN MISUNDERSTANDING. When the French learned of Jay's Treaty of 1794, they were so angered that they declined to receive the American minister, refused any longer to observe the treaty of 1778, and issued the decree of 1796, which declared that the French would treat American ships the same way the British did; later decrees ordered that American ships carrying British goods would be seized and American citizens on British warships would be treated as pirates. Damages suffered by Americans amounted to over $12 million between 1796 and 1800 (*see* French Spoliation Claims). In 1798, President John Adams sent a special mission to France, consisting of C. C. Pinckney, John Marshall, and Elbridge Gerry, to renew relations and negotiate with France a treaty similar to Jay's Treaty. The endeavor failed because the American representatives refused to pay bribes to three agents of Charles Maurice de Talleyrand-Périgord (*see* XYZ affair); this so aroused the United States that war was contemplated. Appropriations were made by Congress; the navy was enlarged; and American warships were allowed to engage in naval warfare with French armed vessels (*see* Naval War With France). The French government became more conciliatory toward the United States in order to prevent an Anglo-American alliance; Adams reciprocated by appointing a mission that was able to negotiate the Convention of 1800.

FRANCO-AMERICAN RELATIONS. Mutual interest led to the Franco-American alliance of 1778; indeed, French aid during the American Revolution was essential to American success, but suspicion of French motives led the Americans to open separate negotiations and conclude peace with England in September 1783. The radicalization of the French Revolution and outbreak of war between France and England in February 1793 left American opinion deeply divided. President George Washington's proclamation of neutrality in April 1793 was taken by the French as an ungrateful act; relations deteriorated rapidly. Jay's Treaty with England (1794) was seen by the French as the height of perfidy. They campaigned against the Federalists in the election of 1796 and refused to receive the American minister sent to Paris that year. Attempts by the Directory to extort money from American commissioners in Paris led to the so-called XYZ affair in 1798. France seized ships carrying British goods, causing the United States over $12 million in damages between 1796 and 1800; Congress reacted in 1798, unilaterally abrogating the French alliance and authorizing the capture of armed French vessels. An undeclared naval war (*see* Naval War With France) taxed the resources of both nations until it was terminated by the Convention of 1800.

Franco-American relations were frequently tenuous during Napoleon Bonaparte's rule (1799–1814); although the sale of Louisiana to the United States (1803) removed one potential source of friction, Bonaparte's arbitrary treatment of U.S. shipping led American statesmen to consider declaring war against France as well as England in 1812. A Franco-American commercial treaty was signed in 1822, but there was little mutual enthusiasm during the period of the Bourbon Restoration (1815–30). American recognition of the independence of the former Spanish provinces in South America (1822) was resented by the French, as was the Monroe Doctrine of 1823. President Andrew Jackson's vigorous campaign for the collection of damages to American shipping during the Napoleonic period ended in 1836 with a French payment of 25 million francs, but mistrust remained mutual.

The revolution of February 1848 that established the Second Republic was well received in the United States, but America's unsympathetic attitude toward the Crimean War (1854–56) and general contempt for Napoleon III was matched by Napoleon's proposed mediation in the American Civil War, his sympathy for the southern cause, and his intervention in Mexico. Conflict between the two nations was avoided by the withdrawal of French troops from Mexico in 1867. Nevertheless, the United States was the first nation to recognize France's Third Republic. Sentimental Franco-American amity was manifested in the gift of the Statue of Liberty in 1886, and occasional Franco-American colonial disputes (Panama Canal, Liberia, Tunisia, Madagascar, Indochina) failed to become as serious as they had in the past.

Decisive improvement in Franco-American relations took place under the initiative of Théophile Delcassé, French foreign minister from 1898 to 1905. French neutrality and successful mediation in the Spanish-American War were appreciated by America. Rapprochement was cemented by a mutually beneficial trade convention in 1899 and by U.S. support of France during the first Moroccan crisis of 1905 and at the Algeciras Conference (1906).

The U.S. Senate's refusal to ratify the Treaty of Versailles after World War I or to enter the League of Nations was resented by the French, as was America's unwillingness to link the reduction of German reparations payments with French war debts owed to the United States; reciprocally, the suspension of payments in 1932, following the spread of the Great Depression to France, caused a furor in America. Despite American assistance in freeing France from German troops in World War II, the legacy of mistrust remained; matters were complicated by early American recognition of the Vichy government and by Anglo-American insults to Gen. Charles de Gaulle, leader of Free France.

With the resignation of De Gaulle as interim president of France in January 1946, Franco-American relations were on the whole good for the remainder of the Fourth Republic

(1945–58). Marshall Plan aid was essential in the reconstruction of France, which joined the North Atlantic Treaty Organization (NATO) in 1949. Nonetheless, by the late 1950's, most Frenchmen desired a more independent foreign policy. De Gaulle became president of the Fifth Republic in 1958; dissatisfied with America's refusal to give France equality in the Atlantic alliance, he undertook a diplomatic and economic offensive against Anglo-American interests, blocking England's entry into the Common Market in 1963 and withdrawing French forces from NATO in 1966. Franco-American relations were less strained after De Gaulle's retirement in 1969 and the end of French objections to English entry into the Common Market. In the post-Vietnam era, official Franco-American relations seemed to improve somewhat under the presidency of Georges Pompidou (1969–74) and even more so under that of Valéry Giscard d'Estaing (1974–81), but with the election of Socialist François Mitterrand in 1981, popular rapprochement appeared unlikely.

FRANCO-AMERICAN WAR PRIZE CASES. Claims by U.S. citizens for indemnity from the French government because of illegal captures, detentions, seizures, condemnations, and confiscations prior to Sept. 30, 1800. In negotiating the Convention of 1800, Napoleon insisted that claims for spoliations (about $20 million) be relinquished, as a condition for abandonment of the old treaties of 1778. The American claimants then turned to the U.S. government for indemnification. On Jan. 20, 1885, Congress passed an act whereby the United States assumed liability to its own nationals for damage done by the illegal acts of the French state. Between 1885 and 1925 the claimants and their descendants finally received a total of $5 million. (*See also* French Spoliation Claims.)

FRANKFORT (Ky.). Capital of Kentucky, with a population of 25,973 in 1980. The town got its name from a resident, Stephen Frank, who was killed by Indians while trying to cross a ford in the Kentucky River; "Frank's Ford" became the modern Frankfort. The city was laid out and developed by Gen. James Wilkinson, who got the Virginia legislature to approve the site in 1786. Wilkinson had hoped to create a major river port and business center; although these plans failed, the first Kentucky legislature designated the town as state capital (1793). Frankfort is now an important marketing and shipping town, with several liquor distilleries.

FRANKING. The privilege of sending a letter or package through the mails without charge, introduced in the United States in 1776. Abuses accompanied its growth, and in 1873 franking was discontinued. In 1874 the free-in-county mailing privilege for newspapers was renewed; free mailing has since been extended to congressional franked mail, official penalty mail for certain departments of the government in penalty envelopes, and personal free mail under signature for authorized persons.

FRANKLIN, BATTLE OF (Nov. 30, 1864). Confederate Gen. John B. Hood, in his march from Atlanta to Tennessee, failed to cut off Gen. John M. Schofield at Spring Hill, Tenn. The following day, Hood pursued Schofield northward to Franklin, Tenn.; he rashly attacked, and suffered several bloody repulses. After dark Schofield retired to Nashville.

FRANKLIN, STATE OF. North Carolina in 1784 ceded its western lands to the United States. Residents of the eastern part of the ceded region, known as Wataugans, assembled at Jonesboro, Tenn., in August and December 1784 and organized the state of Franklin. North Carolina immediately repealed the cession act and attempted to woo back the westerners. John Sevier and other western leaders, unable to check the Franklin movement, seized power and adopted a constitution validating North Carolina land titles. With Sevier as governor, the state maintained a precarious existence for four years, characterized by Indian troubles, intrigues with the Spanish (*see* Spanish Conspiracy), and ineffectual efforts to obtain recognition from Congress and North Carolina. The opposition of a faction led by John Tipton contributed materially to North Carolina's success in reestablishing jurisdiction by 1789.

FRANKLIN INSTITUTE. Most prominent of American mechanics institutes, established in Philadelphia (1824) primarily through the efforts of Samuel Merrick and William H. Keating. The organization expressed the broad conviction that America's future depended on a combination of technology and democracy. The institute began a series of evening lectures in March 1824 on the principles and applications of science, and in the same year established a school of mechanical and architectural drawing. Exhibitions were begun in October 1824 to stimulate interest in industrial development and technical advance. The *Journal of the Franklin Institute* began publication in 1826 as the *Franklin Journal and American Mechanics' Magazine* and soon became an important medium for the transmission of advances in technology. Experimental investigations were the institute's most dramatic activity. In 1932 the institute redirected its educational program by opening a museum of technology. Experimental investigations did not again figure prominently in its efforts until World War II, when defense research led to the establishment of a peacetime industrial research laboratory.

FRANKLIN STOVE. Invented 1742 by Benjamin Franklin, in cooperation with Robert Grace, it consisted of a low stove, equipped with loosely fitting iron plates through which air might circulate and be warmed before passage into the room. This "New Pennsylvania Fireplace" avoided drafts, gave more even temperatures throughout the room, and checked loss of heat through the chimney. Designed to be used in an already existing hearth, it did not resemble what are now called Franklin stoves.

FRANQUELIN'S MAPS. Jean Baptiste Louis Franquelin came to New France about 1672; in 1678 he began making maps of the New World and in 1687 became hydrographer for the king. Franquelin interviewed the French explorers and recorded their explorations. Twenty of his maps, most of them signed, have been identified, extending in time from 1678 to 1708.

FRAUNCES TAVERN. A reconstructed 18th-century house at Broad and Pearl streets in New York City, it was originally built by Stephen De Lancey in 1719 and opened as a tavern by Samuel Fraunces, a West Indian black, in 1762. In the Long Room, on Dec. 4, 1783, Gen. George Washington said farewell to his officers. The tavern was purchased by the Sons of the Revolution in 1904; designated a landmark in 1965, it contains a museum of revolutionary war memorabilia and a library.

FRAYSER'S FARM, BATTLE OF (June 30, 1862). One of the Seven Days' Battles, in which Union Gen. George B. McClellan retreated from Richmond, Va., to the James River. After McClellan had held off the Confederates at Savage's Station, he got his force across White Oak Swamp. Near Frayser's Farm and the settlement of Glendale, Confederate generals James Longstreet and A. P. Hill struck east, but they were checked after slight successes; the Confederates then failed to carry out Gen. Robert E. Lee's converging plan and encircle McClellan, who withdrew to Malvern Hill. (*See also* Peninsular Campaign.)

FRAZIER-LEMKE FARM BANKRUPTCY ACT (June 28, 1934). Enacted by Congress to relieve farmers burdened by mortgages on which foreclosure was threatened; it authorized courts to grant such farmers a five-year moratorium under certain conditions. The Supreme Court (May 27, 1935) unanimously held this act to be a violation of the due process clause of the Fifth Amendment. Congress then passed the Frazier-Lemke Farm Mortgage Moratorium Act (Aug. 29, 1935), modifying the terms of the moratorium and limiting it to a three-year period; this law was unanimously sustained by the Supreme Court (Mar. 29, 1937).

FREDERICA (Ga.). A fortified town on St. Simons Island, laid out (1736) by James E. Oglethorpe as a defense against inland attack by the Spaniards in Florida. It consisted of a fort and barracks, made of tabby, and many houses, some of brick, all surrounded by earthen fortifications. It was abandoned as a fortified post in 1748, and by the time of the Revolution it had fallen into ruins.

FREDERICK (Md.). The town was laid out in 1745, having been settled several years before by a group of Germans led by John Thomas Schley; in 1755, Gen. Edward Braddock had his headquarters there for a brief period. During the Revolution the residents were active in the patriot cause. During the Civil War, with the battles of South Mountain, Antietam, Gettysburg, and Monocacy being fought nearby, the town was often in the path of marching troops. The 1980 population of the city was 27,557.

FREDERICKSBURG, BATTLE OF (Dec. 13, 1862). Gen. Robert E. Lee outmarched Union Gen. Ambrose E. Burnside to Fredericksburg and placed his army of about 78,000 on the high ground from one to two miles south of the Rappahannock River, roughly paralleling the river for more than six miles. Burnside slowly concentrated his 122,000 troops on the northern bank, drove the Confederate sharpshooters out of Fredericksburg, and crossed to the southern bank, where he drew his lines for battle on Dec. 13. The main battle was fought at the base of Marye's Heights, where a sunken road provided a natural breastwork for the Confederates; the Union infantry was rolled back by the devastating fire from this road. Nightfall ended the battle, with 10,208 Unionists and 5,209 Confederates killed or wounded. Burnside withdrew north of the Rappahannock during the night of Dec. 15.

FREDERICKTOWN, ACTION AT (Oct. 21, 1861). Union forces under Col. J. B. Plummer and Col. William P. Carlin defeated Brig. Gen. M. Jeff Thompson's forces of the Missouri State Guard at Fredericktown, Mo., breaking up the Confederate advance into southeast Missouri.

FREDONIAN REVOLT. In 1826, Haden Edwards, an impresario in eastern Texas, became involved in a quarrel with some of the old settlers in his colony; when Mexican officials annulled Edwards's contract, he and his followers resisted and proclaimed the Republic of Fredonia. The revolt was suppressed in 1827 without bloodshed.

FREE BANKING SYSTEM. In the United States, free banking came to mean the abolition of the special privileges banks enjoyed by virtue of special charters; it also meant a note issue protected by a deposit of public securities. The basic law and model for other states was the New York act of Apr. 18, 1838, that ended the practice of granting special legislative charters. The issuance of notes was delegated to a comptroller at Albany who was authorized to issue registered bills to any bank upon the deposit of an equal amount in bonds of the United States, New York, or other approved states. This system, strengthened by later amendments, evolved into one of the strongest in the nation. Its principles of freedom of incorporation, individual stockholder liability, and a note issue protected by public securities were adopted by sixteen states and Canada and were incorporated into the National Banking System of 1863. (*See also* Banking.)

FREE BLACKS. The 1790 census counted approximately 60,000 free blacks in the United States, and by 1860, approximately 500,000. Some were descendants of those who had never been slaves; the remainder had been freed under a variety of circumstances. All the northern states abolished slavery shortly after the Revolution. In the slave states of the South the transition from slave to free was difficult. Some slaves purchased their freedom; others ran away to the North. Those who remained in the South had been freed by their masters (a practice discouraged and sometimes specifically prohibited by slave states in the 19th century). Visible racial differences kept most free blacks in a servile position. The Civil War ended the peculiar legal status of the free black. (*See* Afro-Americans; Suffrage, Afro-American.)

FREEDMAN'S SAVINGS BANK. A bank for Afro-Americans, incorporated under the Freedman's Bank Act of Mar. 3, 1865. Headquarters were established in the District of Columbia, with branches in various states. The bank was mismanaged and closed its doors on June 29, 1874.

FREEDMEN'S BUREAU. On Mar. 3, 1865, Congress established the Bureau of Refugees, Freedmen, and Abandoned Lands. The bureau provided emergency food and shelter to people dislocated by the Civil War and was expected to define how former slaves would provide for their own subsistence; it established schools, conducted military courts to hear complaints of both former slaves and former masters, and supervised the arrangements for work made by the freedmen. The bureau was assigned to the War Department and Maj. Gen. O. O. Howard of Maine was named commissioner. Assistant commissioners were appointed in the seceded states to direct the work of other officials, known generally as Freedmen's Bureau agents, who were sent into the field. The most important contribution of the Freedmen's Bureau was in education. Private freedmen's aid societies supplied teachers and their salaries; the bureau supplied buildings and transportation. By 1871 eleven colleges and universities and sixty-one normal schools had been founded. In its seven years of existence, the bureau spent over $6 million for its schools and educational work, and appropriated more than $15 million for food and other aid distributed throughout the southern and border states. Bureau agents also registered black voters under the Congress's radical Reconstruction plan.

FREEDOM OF SPEECH. A basic right protected from abridgment by Congress, by virtue of the First Amendment. This provision in the Constitution has neither clear analogue nor predecessor in English and colonial common law. It was the great debate after passage of the Alien and Sedition Acts of 1798 that "first crystallized a national awareness of the central meaning of the First Amendment" (*New York Times Company* v. *Sullivan* [1964]). A growing libertarian interpretation was sporadically invoked during debates over rights of abolitionists in the 1850's and of anarchists in the last quarter of the 19th century, but it took real shape only with World War I and the prosecutions arising from opposition to it. Justice Oliver Wendell Holmes then formulated the clear-and-present-danger rule as a proposed boundary line, first in the majority decision in *Schenck* v. *United States* (1919) and later in dissent; it reemerged as the dominant rule for more than two decades, from the 1930's until the decision in *Dennis* v. *United States* (1951), which exposed inadequacies in the approach. More significant, the Court in *Gitlow* v. *New York* (1925) extended the protection of the First Amendment to state action. Since the *Dennis* case the Court has avoided a single overarching rule. It has retained clear-and-present danger as a test for crowd situations but has developed a multiplicity of tests in various types of situations that underscore "the principle that debate on public issues should be uninhibited, robust, and wide-open" (*New York Times Company* v. *Sullivan*).

FREEDOM OF THE PRESS. A constitutional restraint on government that, in the language of the Supreme Court, "was fashioned to assure unfettered interchange of ideas for the bringing about of political and social changes desired by the people" (*Roth* v. *United States,* 1957). The federal sedition acts of 1798–1801 authorized the defense of truth; however, antigovernment editors were, upon conviction, fined and committed to prison. In the 19th century, antislavery publications were suppressed under state criminal laws in the South, and Copperhead newspapers were harassed in the North during episodes of martial law. During World War I the federal Espionage Act of 1917 and similar state laws were used in a two-year frenzy of prosecution during which freedom of the press temporarily disappeared.

Although the First Amendment has never been held to be absolute, state prepublication censorship (*Near* v. *Minnesota* [1931]) and guilt by association (*De Jonge* v. *Oregon* [1937]) were denounced by the Supreme Court; the *Near* case decision began forty years of steady expansion of First Amendment freedoms under court protection. A major First Amendment opinion (*Bridges* v. *California* [1941]) stopped state and federal judges from punishing their journalistic critics in criminal contempt trials without a jury. During President Franklin D. Roosevelt's second term the Court frequently used the First Amendment against the states, and increased the scope and number of cases taken for review. During the 1950's and 1960's the desegregation issue provoked cases that also expanded freedom of the press; in 1964 the Court denied damages to Alabama officials suing the *New York Times* for libel and, stating a new rule, singled out and required public officials suing thereafter to prove either that the newspaper or broadcasting station knew its words were false or that it showed reckless disregard of whether they were false or not. This rule was extended the same year to criminal libel and in 1967 to persons in public life. (*See also* Censorship.)

FREEDOM OF THE SEAS. A principle of international law prohibiting acquisition or exclusive control by states of high seas, as distinct from territorial seas and inland waters. It extends to nearly landlocked seas (for example, the Baltic Sea and the Black Sea) if connected by international waterways with oceans, as well as to the connecting waterways, which include, by convention, interoceanic canals. (*See also* Territorial Waters.)

FREEDOM RIDERS. Blacks and whites, many associated with the Congress of Racial Equality (CORE), who traveled in buses from Atlanta to Alabama in the spring of 1961 and to Mississippi in November 1961 in protest against segregation at bus terminals in the South.

FREEDOMS, FOUR. *See* **Four Freedoms.**

FREEHOLDER. The owner of a land or estate, either for life or with inheritance rights. Seven colonies restricted the suffrage to freeholders, the others permitting persons owning enough of other forms of property to vote; statutes defined the minimum freehold for town or rural residents.

FREE LAND. A term used to refer to the American frontier, the outer edge of settlement; squatters could settle here and eventually expect either to acquire title by purchase or to sell their claims to later comers. Free grants were given in the colonial period, and in Oregon and Florida before 1862. After 1862 all public land that was surveyed and opened to settlement was free, with some exceptions, under the Homestead Act. This law, last applied in Alaska, was repealed in 1974.

FREEMAN'S EXPEDITION. Organized by President Thomas Jefferson's orders (1805) to explore the Red River of Louisiana and Texas. With a party of twenty-five and three boats, Thomas Freeman left Fort Adams, Miss., at the mouth of Red River in April 1806. At a point 635 miles from the mouth of the Red River the group was turned back by a Spanish military party, having added little to knowledge of the new Louisiana Purchase.

FREEMAN'S FARM, FIRST BATTLE OF (Sept. 19, 1777; also known as the first Battle of Bemis Heights, or Stillwater). British Gen. John Burgoyne led his army south against Gen. Horatio Gates, who was headquartered about four miles away at Bemis Heights, just below Saratoga, N.Y. (*see* Burgoyne's Invasion); at Freeman's Farm, over a mile from Gates's headquarters, the English encountered American troops; in the late afternoon reinforcements from the left enabled the Americans to hold firm. With darkness, the field of battle was left in the hands of the British, who had lost 600 killed, wounded, or taken. American casualties were little over half that number. Burgoyne had been thwarted in opening a way to Albany.

FREEMAN'S FARM, SECOND BATTLE OF (Oct. 7, 1777; also known as the second Battle of Bemis Heights, or Stillwater). British Gen. John Burgoyne sent out 1,500 troops to reconnoiter Gen. Horatio Gates's position at Bemis Heights. By 2:30 P.M. they were hotly engaged; suffering more than 400 casualties in less than an hour, they began to fall back. Benedict Arnold pursued the British to their entrenched camp. Burgoyne had inflicted slight losses; his only recourse was retreat. (*See* Burgoyne's Invasion.)

FREEMAN'S JOURNAL. A newspaper started by Francis Bailey in Philadelphia, Apr. 25, 1781, and edited by the anti-British Philip Freneau. It claimed to be "open to all parties but influenced by none"; it was filled with invective and abuse. Aligning itself with the Constitutionalists, it invited opposition and changed the entire outlook on journalism. It ceased publication May 16, 1792.

FREEMASONS. British Masons established modern Freemasonry in America in the 1730's. Henry Price founded a grand lodge in Boston, Mass., in 1733; by 1734, some 6,000 Freemasons were estimated to live in the Atlantic seaboard colonies. The first Scottish Rite lodge was installed at Albany, N.Y., in 1768. The first Ancient's lodge was established in 1781, in New York City. Early in 1775, the Rev. Prince Hall and several other Afro-Americans were initiated into Military Lodge No. 58 at Boston; on July 3, Hall organized the first lodge of "Colored Masons" in North America, known first as African Lodge and later as Prince Hall Grand Lodge. William Morgan's death in 1826, allegedly because of his threat to expose the secrets of Freemasonry (*see* Morgan Trails), raised a political storm against Masonry and caused it to decline; but by the 1840's, Masonry was spreading rapidly throughout the nation, and in the 1970's there were approximately 4 million Masons in the United States.

Best known of the appendant orders of Freemasons, the Shrine (Ancient Arabic Order of Nobles of the Mystic Shrine) was established in the United States in 1870. In 1922 the Shrine established a program of hospitals for the care of crippled children, and within the next thirty years seventeen such hospitals had been founded, supported by annual assessments of members, contributions, fund-raising projects, and estate benefits. In 1980, this order had 40,000 members.

FREEMEN. In the colonial period "freemen" meant freeholders, possessors of land in fee simple (*see* Freeholders). In some communities admission by the magistrates to the freedom was necessary in addition to ownership of land. In Massachusetts and other New England colonies religious qualifications or guaranty of good conduct were required. Only in the chartered cities of New York and Albany did the term "freeman" have economic significance: the charters of these cities forbade any merchant to do business or any craftsman to ply his trade without admission to the freedom by the magistrates and payment of the required fees.

FREEPORT DOCTRINE. Stephen Douglas's doctrine, advanced at the Lincoln-Douglas debates of 1858 in Freeport, Ill., that in spite of the Dred Scott decision slavery could be excluded from territories of the United States by local legislation. By thus answering Abraham Lincoln's questions on slavery, Douglas secured reelection to the Senate, but lost southern support for the presidency in 1860.

FREE SHIPS, FREE GOODS. A phrase referring to the claim of neutrals that cargoes in neutral ships, except contraband, are not subject to seizure by belligerents. The United States has been a consistent champion of the formula. This interpretation was not accepted by England at the time of the War of 1812, and both England and Germany opposed it in 1914. (*See also* Enemy Destination.)

FREE SILVER. Meaning specifically the unlimited coinage of silver by the U.S. government for anyone bringing the metal into the U.S. Mint, this functioned as an important political slogan in the late 19th century when social unrest (largely the result of unstable economic factors causing depressions of considerable magnitude in the mid-1870's and the early 1890's), political ambitions, and vested economic interests combined sporadically to cause a powerful push for legislation to increase the money supply. (*See* Bland-Allison Act; Sherman Silver Purchase Act.) Although government subsidy of silver production recurred occasionally in the 20th century, the end of free silver as an effective implement of American politics was indicated in 1900 by the passage of the Gold Standard Act; it declared the gold dollar to be the U.S. standard of value (as indeed it had been ever since 1834).

FREE SOCIETY OF TRADERS. A commercial company to which William Penn sold 20,000 acres of land in Pennsylvania and granted a charter (Mar. 24, 1681) with large powers and privileges, including manorial rights. All goods were to be consigned to an agent in London; two or more general factories were to be set up in Pennsylvania. Little came of the expectations.

"FREE SOIL, FREE SPEECH, FREE MEN AND FRÉMONT." The Free Soil platform of 1848 declared, "We inscribe upon our banner: Free Soil, Free Speech, Free Labor and Free Men." In the campaign of 1856 the Republicans adopted the slogan with varying changes and added the name of their presidential candidate, John C. Frémont.

FREE SOIL PARTY. A political party, organized at Buffalo, N.Y. (Aug. 9, 1848), that opposed the extension of slavery into the western territories; it nominated a ticket of Martin Van Buren and Charles Francis Adams with the platform of "no more slave states and no more slave territory" and of free homesteads to actual settlers. Van Buren polled 291,263 votes, largely in New York State and in the Northwest. The election of a dozen members of Congress, who later held the balance of power in the House, and a considerable number of state legislators indicated a fair success for the movement. Four years later its disorganized remnants became absorbed in the new Republican party.

FREE-STATE PARTY. *See* **Kansas Free-State Party.**

FREETHINKING. Religious thought based on reason as opposed to established religions. Ethan Allen's *Reason the Only Oracle of Man* (1784) attacked miraculous revelation and biblical infallibility and advocated a natural religion premised on man's moral freedom. Deistic principles and societies spread rapidly; Thomas Paine's *Age of Reason* appeared (1794–96). But a reaction had set in by 1800. The Great Revival reduced freethinkers to a respectable minority of Unitarians and Universalists.

The next important phase of American freethinking centered in the transcendentalism of William Ellery Channing, Ralph Waldo Emerson, and Theodore Parker, who in the 1830's and 1840's proclaimed the divinity of man and his kinship to nature and God. This pantheism, limited largely to Unitarian circles, suffered a more striking eclipse than deism, although its humanitarianism triumphed.

Evolutionary views spread rapidly in the United States after the Civil War, causing a "war" between science and religion; Henry Ward Beecher's theological latitude and tolerance infused a more liberal spirit into American Christianity; and "higher criticism" began to apply scientific inquiry to the authority of the Bible. American pragmatism asserted itself through the psychology of religion, sociology, and anthropology, and mild freethinking developed within, rather than outside, established religion. In the 1930's and 1940's, freethinking leveled off; it continued on the wane in the 1970's.

FREE TRADE. If trade is free, certain goods and services can be obtained at lower cost abroad than if domestic substitutes are produced in their place; this concept has each country producing for export those goods in which production is relatively efficient, thereby financing the import of goods that would be inefficiently produced at home. Free trade is therefore thought to facilitate the optimal use of economic resources.

FREIGHTERS. *See* **Merchant Marine.**

FREIGHTERS OF THE OVERLAND TRAILS. *See* **Overland Freighting.**

FREMONT (Calif.). A city at the southeastern end of San Francisco Bay, established as a municipality in 1956 after several residential towns were consolidated. Its population grew rapidly, from 43,790 in 1960 to 131,945 in 1980. While still largely a residential center, it is also home to a major automobile assembly plant.

FRÉMONT'S EXPLORATIONS. John Charles Frémont led five expeditions into the Far West. From June to October 1842, he investigated the Oregon Trail, crossing the plains and mountains to southern Wyoming and ascending Frémont's Peak. In 1843–44 he explored the region north of the Great Salt Lake, the Snake and Columbia river valleys, the Klamath Lake country, and eastern Nevada, going through Kit Carson Pass to Sutter's Fort and returning east by way of the San Joaquin Valley and the Old Spanish Trail. In July 1845 he went through the Sacramento Valley to Oregon and returned by way of the valley to California, where the last official expedition was terminated when he became involved in the conquest of California in June 1846 (*see* Bear Flag Revolt). His fourth and fifth expeditions (1848–49; 1853–54) explored a route for a railroad across the Rocky Mountains in the vicinity of 37° and 38° north latitude; they were privately financed, and contributed no practical information.

FRENCH ALLIANCE. *See* **Franco-American Alliance of 1778.**

FRENCH AND INDIAN WAR (1754–63). The final struggle between the French and the English for control of North America. The French and British colonists attempted to project their control into the Ohio region between 1748 and 1753 by peaceful penetration. The area was dominated by the Iroquois League, which favored the British; the French found allies among the Delaware, Shawnee, Wyandot, and smaller tribes. (*see* French Claims in Ohio.)

The war originated in the plan of the governor of Canada, Roland Michel Barrin, Marquis de La Galissonière, to construct some nine forts on the Great Lakes, the Ohio and its tributaries, and the Mississippi to New Orleans. He put some 1,500 troops into the Ohio venture and only a few score in each of the other forts. His move south of Lake Erie encroached on territory claimed by Virginia, whose governor sent George Washington on a mission (November 1753) to Fort Le Boeuf to warn the French that they were trespassing; overwhelming French forces pushed Washington back and into a capitulation at Great Meadows, compelling him to return to Virginia. Prime Minister Thomas Pellam-Holles, Duke of Newcastle, was stirred into action by the news, but he clearly did not comprehend the realities of war in the forests of America, particularly that the French had the great advantage of river and lake passages to the battlefields and that the British would have to make roads; in 1755 he dispatched, under Gen. Edward Braddock, only 800 regulars, who were to be guided from Fort Cumberland by some 600 Virginians under Washington to the scene of the 1753 humiliation. Braddock's expedition cut a way toward Fort Duquesne, only to be surprised just below the fort and badly defeated by an inferior force of French and Indians. Meanwhile, Sir William Johnson, with 3,000 militia and 300 Iroquois, marched north from Albany to Lake George. As a springboard, Johnson established Fort Edward on the Hudson; at Lake George, in hard fighting, including the Battle of Bloody Pond, he won a victory that was not pursued.

In 1756, Newcastle's government abstained from any operations in America except for building a few frontier forts. The colonists' concentration of 7,000 at Albany fumed in exasperation; sickness slew some 3,000, which was blamed on the dilatory commander in chief, John Campbell, Earl of Loudoun. Meanwhile, the French commander, Marquis Louis Joseph de Montcalm, reached Quebec and swept the British from their foothold at Oswego. The Oswego disaster persuaded Lord Loudoun to avoid the forests and to utilize the navy to strike directly up the St. Lawrence to Quebec, first attacking the fortress of Louisburg. Frustrated by the slowness of the navy, however, he jumped without escort to Halifax; by the time his battle fleet arrived there in July 1757, the French had a superior one protecting Louisburg, and Loudoun abandoned the attack. The colonists demanded his relief, for during his absence Montcalm had seized the forward post of Fort William Henry at Lake George, hard won by Johnson in 1755.

By 1759, William Pitt the Elder had come to power in Britain and was determined to drive the French from the American continent. The capture of Quebec by Gen. James Wolfe was to be the main effort: his Louisburg force, assisted by the navy, was to be joined at Quebec by another, led by Gen. Jeffrey Amherst, coming via Lake Champlain, while Gen. John Prideaux and Johnson were to take Niagara and thence endeavor to reach the rear of Montreal. The juncture of Wolfe and Amherst was frustrated by the excellent delaying strategy of Gen. François de Bourlamaque and his 3,600 troops, pitted against Amherst's 12,000; harassment by hovering Abnaki and a drenching by October storms at last stopped Amherst for the winter. Concurrently, the siege of Niagara was successful. The fort was surrendered on July 25, a victory that cut French water communication to Louisiana and opened the back door to Montreal. By necessitating the detachment of troops for the protection of Montreal, it had the additional effect of weakening Montcalm at Quebec.

Wolfe's victory on the Plains of Abraham (Sept. 13, 1759) did not guarantee a British hold on Quebec, and his death in the battle was a serious loss. Some 10,000 French still held Montreal under the governor, Pierre François de Rigaud, Marquis de Vaudreuil-Cavagnal, who had succeeded to the French command, and the outcome for 1760 depended upon whose navy would first reach the St. Lawrence. In the winter of 1759–60 the 7,000 troops of Gen. James Murray, icebound in Quebec, became victims of Wolfe's previous destruction of neighboring farms: lack of fresh provisions caused scurvy, and by April 1760, Murray had barely 3,000 active men when Gen. François Gaston de Lévis marched with 9,000 from Montreal to try to recapture Quebec. On May 9, it was a British frigate that hove first into view of besieged and besiegers. The French then retreated upon Montreal, but the convergence of troops under Amherst, Col. William Haviland, and Murray caused Vaudreuil to surrender on Sept. 8 without useless bloodshed.

Canada was won by the British, but anxious times remained. In 1761, Amherst received orders at his new headquarters in New York City to dispatch his veterans to West Indian operations, 2,000 to Dominica and 7,000 to Martinique, even as British replacement of French authority in the interior was unsettling the Indians, notably the Shawnee and Oneida. Upon Spain's declaration of war against Britain in 1762, Amherst had to part with 4,000 more troops to participate in the British seizure of rich Havana; in late June a small French squadron of 1,500 troops from Brest audaciously pounced upon the fishery town of St. John's, Newfoundland, and destroyed 500 vessels. Because of the stripping of his army, Amherst had to collect the garrisons of Nova Scotia for the recapture, led by his younger brother William, in September.

Britain, France, and Spain signed the Treaty of Paris on Feb. 10, 1763. The British had only 8,000 weary troops in America when Pontiac convoked the Ecorse River Council on Apr. 27 and took to open warfare (*see* Pontiac's War).

FRENCH ARMY, MARCH OF ROCHAMBEAU'S. During the Revolution, a French force of 6,000 under Jean de Vimeur, Comte de Rochambeau, was landed at Newport, R.I., July 10, 1780, to aid the American colonists under George Washington's command. Blockaded in Narragansett Bay by a British fleet, the army lay idle in Rhode Island for a year (*see* Newport, French Army at). On May 22, 1781, Washington and Rochambeau agreed to attack New York; Rochambeau's troops left Rhode Island in June, and an advance legion participated in a skirmish near the Harlem River on July 2. On July 6, Rochambeau joined Washington at Dobbs Ferry on the Hudson River. Lord Charles Cornwallis's move to Virginia had changed Washington's plan, and on Aug. 19, Washington began his march toward Yorktown with 2,000 of his own soldiers and 4,000 French. On Sept. 5–6 they reached the head of Chesapeake Bay, where most of the men sailed for Yorktown; others proceeded via Baltimore or went all the way by land. (*See* Yorktown Campaign.)

FRENCH-CANADIAN IMMIGRATION. *See* **Immigration.**

FRENCH CLAIMS IN OHIO. On Apr. 9, 1682, Robert Cavelier, Sieur de La Salle, took possession of all the land drained by the Mississippi River and its tributaries in the name of the king of France. The French placed the Alleghenies as the western boundary of the British colonies; the British contested this claim, and the crown continued to make grants of land extending westward to the Pacific Ocean. In 1749 the expedition of Pierre Joseph de Céloron de Blainville explored the region along the Ohio River and buried leaden plates claiming the territory in the name of France; a grant to the Ohio Company by the English crown was regarded by the French as an encroachment. The French built forts at Presque Isle on Lake Erie, down the Ohio, and down the Mississippi to its mouth, placing them in actual possession of the lands south of the Great Lakes and east of the Mississippi to the Alleghenies, and precipitating the French and Indian War.

FRENCH CREEK, ACTION AT (Nov. 1–2, 1813). Gen. James Wilkinson, operating along the St. Lawrence River with Montreal as his objective, ordered a brigade to French Creek in Clayton, N.Y., where it was attacked, Nov. 1, by a British flotilla; an American battery at Bartlett's Point on the western shore repulsed the British attack, which was renewed Nov. 2. The British were defeated and suffered heavy losses.

FRENCH DECREES. Laws whose purpose was to blockade England. The decree of 1793 ordered the capture of all provisions going to Great Britain; those of 1794 and 1796 declared that France would treat neutral vessels in the same manner that England did; that of 1797 was similar to the decree of 1793; the decree of 1798 ordered that neutral vessels carrying British goods should be treated as if they were British; and for one month in 1799 a decree classified neutral citizens on a British ship as pirates. James Monroe's mission to Paris obtained exemption from the first two decrees for American vessels during 1795; the decrees after 1795 applied to the United States until the conclusion of the Franco-American Convention of 1800. In the second period of decrees (1806–12) the Berlin Decree (1806), the Milan Decree (1807), and the Bayonne Decree (1808) proclaimed a blockade around the British Isles and ordered the capture of all neutral vessels entering British ports, paying British duties, or submitting to British search (*see* Napoleon's Decrees). These decrees struck particularly at American commerce and led the United States to retaliate unsuccessfully with the Embargo Act (1807), the Nonintercourse Act (1809), and the Macon Bill No. 2 (1810).

FRENCH EXPLORATION IN THE WEST. Samuel de Champlain discovered Lake Champlain in 1609 and visited lakes Huron and Ontario in 1615. His subordinate, Jean Nicolet, discovered Lake Michigan while on his way to the Winnebago of present-day Wisconsin in 1634. Systematic exploration of the Mississippi basin began with Robert Cavelier, Sieur de La Salle, in 1669. Louis Jolliet and Jacques Marquette voyaged in 1673 from Green Bay up the Fox River and down the Wisconsin (*see* Fox-Wisconsin Waterway) to the Mississippi, descended the Mississippi to the Arkansas, and went back to Lake Michigan by way of the Illinois. Exploration of the Mississippi to the Gulf was completed by La Salle in 1682. In the north, Daniel Greysolon, Sieur Duluth, pushed southwest from Lake Superior and there met Father Louis Hennepin, who ascended the Mississippi from the Illinois in 1680. La Salle landed at Matagorda Bay in January 1685 and built Fort St. Louis, the first Texas settlement. After La Salle's death, Henri Joutel, a lieutenant, led six of the colonists to Canada, exploring much of present Texas and Arkansas en route (*see* La Salle, Spanish Searches for). Henri de Tonti ascended the Red River from the Mississippi as far as Texas in 1690.

The westward march across the Great Plains commenced in 1713 when Louis Juchereau de St. Denis traveled from Natchitoches on the Red River to San Juan on the Rio Grande in an unsuccessful effort to trade with Mexico. Four years later an expedition under Bernard de la Harpe advanced from Natchitoches up the Red River, continued almost to the Wichita Mountains, turned northeast to the Arkansas, and followed it back to the Mississippi; another, led by Claude Charles du Tisne, traveled from Kaskaskia up the Missouri and cross country from the Osage village to the Wichita village on the Arkansas. Étienne Venyard, Sieur de Bourgmont, built Fort Orleans on the Missouri in 1723, whence he led an expedition to the Comanche in the Smoky Hill Valley of present Kansas in 1724. The first known Frenchmen to complete the crossing of the Great Plains to the Rockies were Pierre and Paul Mallet, who journeyed from the confluence of the Missouri and Platte rivers to Santa Fe in 1738, and, crossing back to the Arkansas the following year, returned to the Mississippi. First to arrive at the Rockies in the north were two sons of Pierre Gaultier de Varennes, Sieur de La Vérendrye: all three left the Manitoba lakes in 1739 and blazed a trail to the Mandan village on the Missouri in present North Dakota; three years later the two sons passed the Big Horn Range to the Rockies. Other traders and trappers threaded their way up every important stream of the Mississippi basin.

FRENCH FRONTIER FORTS. After New France was reorganized by Louis XIV, a host of brilliant adventurers overran the Great Lakes and the Mississippi Valley; milestones in this expansion were the founding of Fort Frontenac, later also called Cataraqui (Kingston, Ont.) in 1673, Fort Miami (St. Joseph, Mich.) in 1679, Fort St. Louis and Fort Crèvecoeur (in Illinois) in 1680–82, Fort Biloxi (Miss.) in 1699, Mobile in 1702, and New Orleans in 1717. New France now extended from the Gulf of St. Lawrence to the Gulf of Mexico, and to safeguard it, strategic intermediate points were occupied: Fort Pontchartrain (Detroit) in 1701; Fort Michilimackinac (Mich., a reoccupation) about 1715; Fort de Chartres (Ill.) in 1717; and Fort Niagara (N.Y.) about 1721.

The danger point then became the upper Ohio Valley; in quick succession forts Presque Isle (Erie), Le Boeuf (Waterford), Machault (near Venango), Venango, and Duquesne (Pittsburgh) were established in Pennsylvania. The French and Indian War began in this area and ended in the complete downfall of New France, whose frontier forts passed into English hands or into oblivion.

FRENCH GRANTS. Land given to French settlers in America by the U.S. government, including two tracts of 24,000 acres and 1,200 acres granted in 1795 and 1798, respectively. These tracts, in present Scioto County, Ohio, on the Ohio River opposite the mouth of Little Sandy Creek, were granted to settlers who had been induced to migrate to the United States in 1791 by agents of the speculative Scioto Company: the settlers had found that their land titles were worthless and that their settlement at Gallipolis, Ohio, was on land belonging to the Ohio Company of Associates. Altogether, 101 persons were compensated by the two congressional grants, but very few actually settled on their lands.

FRENCH IN THE PENOBSCOT REGION. In colonial times the region of the Penobscot River (in present-day Maine) was strategically important as a buffer between the northern limits of Sagadahoc, claimed by the English, and the southern limits of Acadia, claimed by the French. Baron Vincent de Castine established a trading post in the town that now bears his name, and the French cultivated friendship with the Indians through Jesuit priests. After the Treaty of Utrecht (1713) and Dummer's Indian War (1723–25) this French influence was strongly contested by the English; lands along the west bank of the Penobscot River included in the Muscongus Patent were taken up. In 1759, with the French and Indian War in progress, the governor of Massachusetts proposed to erect a fort at what is now Fort Point, and the English took active possession of the Penobscot River, which they came permanently to possess by the terms of the Treaty of Paris (1763).

FRENCH MILLS (N.Y.). Shortly after the outbreak of the War of 1812, the town of French Mills, on the St. Lawrence River, was temporarily held by the British. On Nov. 13, 1813, James Wilkinson reached it with his demoralized army (*see* Montreal, Wilkinson's Expedition Against). The weather turned bitter and the troops had little shelter; rations were short, clothing inadequate, and pay in arrears. Many died; many deserted. During February 1814 the site was evacuated, troops moving to Plattsburgh and Sacket's Harbor, N.Y.

FRENCH PRIVATEERS. French ships acting against neutral vessels in accordance with French decrees. The American secretary of state reported in 1797 documentary evidence of the capture by French privateers of 32 American merchant ships (the newspapers claimed that 308 others had been taken). The crews of the ships were treated with inhumanity, and early in 1798 the climax was reached with French captures in American harbors. During the ensuing state of war, lasting until Feb. 1, 1801, about eighty-four French privateers were captured (*see* Naval War With France).

FRENCH REFUGEES. French Protestants (Huguenots) tried unsuccessfully to settle in Florida and Brazil in the 16th century. Subsequently many went to South Carolina, Virginia, and other British colonies. French-speaking Walloons went early to New Netherland, and French-Swiss groups, to Pennsylvania and North Carolina. The Huguenots enriched the commercial, social, and professional life of Boston, New York, and Charleston. The French Revolution brought a succession of political refugees: aristocratic émigrés, former plantation owners from Santo Domingo, exiled revolutionaries, and, after Waterloo, many Bonapartists.

FRENCH SPOLIATION CLAIMS. Claims made by American citizens for losses sustained through France's enforcement of its English blockade. These claims cover two general time periods, those arising between 1793 and 1798 (*see* Franco-American Misunderstanding) and those arising chiefly between 1800 and the end of the Napoleonic Wars. The first were settled in part through ratification of the Convention of 1800 (*see* Franco-American War Prize Cases). A further disposition of early claims was made in the Louisiana Purchase Treaty of 1803.

The second, more controversial group of claims grew chiefly out of French seizures and confiscations of American ships and cargoes under a series of decrees issued by Napoleon between 1806 and 1810 (*see* Napoleon's Decrees). The total claims amounted to over $12 million, exclusive of interest. During the administrations of presidents James Madison, James Monroe, and John Quincy Adams, unsuccessful attempts were made to secure a settlement. When Andrew Jackson became president (1829), he sent William C. Rives to Paris as minister with instructions to press the subject vigorously. Following the July Revolution (1830), a commission was appointed that eventually decided that 25 million francs should be paid in settlement of the claims. A treaty was concluded on July 4, 1831, and was proclaimed about a year later. The money was to be paid in six annual installments beginning one year from the date of ratification. When that time arrived, the American government discovered that no appropriation for the payment had been provided by the French parliament. The controversy that followed came to a climax early in 1836, when diplomatic relations were suspended. The British offered to mediate. The French paid the four installments that were past due and paid the remainder when due; thereafter, 1,567 claimants were awarded the money received pro rata. The special commission had awarded $9,352,193, while the six installments with interest paid by France yielded $5,558,108.

FRENZIED FINANCE. A term for furious speculation. In a series of articles in *Everybody's Magazine* (1904–05) Thomas W. Lawson described in detail the methods by which Standard Oil interests reorganized the Anaconda and other mining interests as the Amalgamated Copper Company. These articles created a sensation and were republished under the title *Frenzied Finance* (1905).

FRESNO (Calif.). Located in the San Joaquin Valley, at the center of one of the richest agricultural regions in the nation; although the area is a natural desert, its soil is rich and is irrigated by a system of deep wells and long-distance canals. Its most profitable crop is cotton; its best-known product is wine. Other industries include raisin-packing, shipping and processing equipment for farm products, manufacture of airplane parts, and airplane servicing. In 1980 the population was 218,202 in the center of a metropolitan area of 515,013.

FRIENDLY ASSOCIATION. The governor and council of Pennsylvania declared war against the Delaware Indians and their confederates on Apr. 14, 1756; the Indians had suffered under the unjust land policies of the non-Quaker proprietors and, with French support, had revolted openly. On Nov. 2 the Quakers formally established an extralegal organization, the Friendly Association for Regaining and Preserving Peace With the Indians by Pacific Measures, which functioned as mediator in a series of conferences. The proprietary interests charged the association with political motives, although it expended £7,000 or more to help satisfy the Indians' claims. The association probably ended in 1764.

FRIENDS, SOCIETY OF. *See* **Quakers.**

FRIENDS OF DOMESTIC INDUSTRY. The name assumed by a convention of 500 delegates from New England and the northern states, including Ohio and Virginia, who met at New York (1831) to promote public opinion in favor of retaining a protective tariff.

FRIES'S REBELLION (1799). The armed resistance of certain farmers in Bucks and Northampton counties in Pennsylvania to a federal tax on land and houses. The houses were evaluated by the number and size of their windows, which the farmers understood to imply a window tax. Women in protest poured scalding water on the assessors when they were measuring the windows, from which came the term "Hot Water Rebellion." The insurgents, led by John Fries, a traveling auctioneer, forcibly prevented the assessors from functioning in Bucks County; federal troops were sent, and the rebellion was put down.

FRIGATES. *See* **Warships.**

FRINK AND WALKER STAGE LINES. A firm that operated most of the stages in Illinois and many in several adjoining states from about 1836 to 1855.

FRITCHIE, BARBARA, AND THE FLAG. A Civil War legend given life by the poet John Greenleaf Whittier: Mrs. Fritchie, aged ninety-six, lived in Frederick, Md., when the Confederates passed through in September 1862; seeing a Union flag in her window, Gen. Thomas J. "Stonewall" Jackson ordered his men to fire at it. The old lady rushed to the window, seized the flag, and waved it defiantly; Jackson thereupon decreed death to any soldier who molested her. The story was untrue. Mrs. Fritchie waved a small Union flag from her porch when federal troops marched through six days later, but she and Jackson never saw each other.

FRONTENAC, FORT. Erected at Cataraqui (present Kingston, Ontario) by Louis de Buade, Comte de Frontenac, in 1673; in 1675 the seigniory was granted to Robert Cavelier, Sieur de La Salle, who built Fort Frontenac on the earlier foundation. In 1683 the post was confiscated by Antoine Lefèbvre La Barre; it was abandoned in 1684. In 1687 the Marquis de Denonville garrisoned the post. The fortifications were later blown up under orders of Denonville, and in 1695 they were destroyed further by the Indians. In 1696, Frontenac repaired the fortress and regarrisoned it, and it was used then as a base for trade. On Aug. 27, 1758, it was captured and destroyed by Col. John Bradstreet. In 1789, wooden living quarters were constructed within the old fort and enclosed within a stockade; the old French tower in the northeast angle was used as a magazine. In 1819 the fort was demolished.

FRONTENAC DESTROYS ONONDAGA (1696). To punish the Iroquois for raids on the French settlements and for interfering with trade, Louis de Buade, Comte de Frontenac, left Montreal July 4, with an expedition composed of French regulars, Canadians, and their Indian allies; they reached Fort Frontenac within twelve days. Leaving a small force to garrison this post, they crossed Lake Ontario and arrived at the mouth of the Oswego River on July 28, passed up the river to the vicinity of the Onondaga village, and erected fortifications. The Onondaga fired their village and retired. Frontenac's army advanced and found the village in flames. A detachment then proceeded against a nearby Oneida village and found thirty-five men who wished to welcome them as friends; these they took prisoner. Destroying the village and fields, the army now retraced its steps, harried by the enraged Onondaga.

FRONTIER. As most commonly conceived, the frontier was the line separating the settled regions from those as yet unoccupied; or it was the region on either side of that line (sometimes defined as having from two to six inhabitants to the square mile) whose inhabitants had as their chief concern the breaking of land.

FRONTIER DEFENSE. The theory and practice of frontier defense evolved slowly. In completed form the frontier included five aspects or phases: (1) the commercial frontier, represented by the fur trader, trapper, and hunter; (2) the military frontier, represented by an irregular line of army posts (*see* Army on the Frontier; Army Posts); (3) the cession frontier, which marked the limit of land that had been officially acquired from the Indians; (4) the public-land frontier, the limit of lands that had been surveyed and opened for sale and settlement; and (5) the frontier of settlement, determined by the density of population, which in turn rested upon the fertility and accessibility of the land. Defense involved attention at various times to each of these frontiers and involved a number of activities. The army surveyed rivers, lakes, and harbors; cut roads; built bridges; protected transportation; ejected squatters and established legal claimants; and restrained and regulated hunters and trappers. It assisted officers of the law, protected whites against Indians and Indians against whites, and fought occasional battles.

FRONTIER MERCHANT. The frontier merchant replaced the itinerant peddler on the fringes of settlement as soon as population became dense enough to support a store, and remained a feature of community life until the increase in population in his section made economic specialization possible; he ran a general store, carrying dry goods, groceries, hardware, medicines—anything frontier settlers might buy. Lack of ready cash made it necessary for him to barter his store goods for the crops and products of the settlers. Through the barter system the storekeeper enabled communities without banking facilities to carry on trade with the outside world. The frontier store was a social center where the scattered population could gather to trade and exchange the topics of the day; in many cases villages developed with the store as a nucleus.

FRONTIER PREACHING. The four principal frontier religious bodies—Baptists, Disciples, Methodists, and Presbyterians—all dwelt on the uncertainty of life, the imminence of death, and the endless fiery punishment that awaited unrepentant sinners. There was much outdoor preaching at the camp meetings, often characterized by strong emotionalism.

FRONTIER THESIS, TURNER'S. The frontier acquired the meaning of process when, in 1893, Frederick Jackson Turner produced a paper on "The Significance of the Frontier in American History." He inquired why the United States was as it was, noting that the children of the immigrants had begun by the 18th century to be not Europeans, but Americans. He looked for causes for the transformation, and with the notion that the open frontier with its cheap land might have been a causal factor, he had a new perspective on America. Turner suggested that in the process of occupying the continent, forces were created or released that built the mental structure of Americans, shaped their ideas of government, and contributed to the development of their institutions.

FRONTIERSMEN. *See* **Pioneers.**

FRONT ROYAL, BATTLE AT (May 23, 1862). Gen. Thomas J. "Stonewall" Jackson, moving his Confederate troops down the Luray Valley in Virginia to cut off Gen. Nathaniel P. Banks's retreat from Strasburg to Winchester, defeated the Union forces at Front Royal, twelve miles east of Strasburg (*see* Jackson's Valley Campaign).

FROST-BITTEN CONVENTION (Dec. 14, 1836). In May 1835 a state constitution for Michigan was adopted, with the southern boundary laid down in the Ordinance of 1787. Admission to the Union was refused by Congress without a boundary redrawn to give the mouth of the Maumee River to Ohio. Michigan refused, and a two-year deadlock ensued. An irregular assembly at Ann Arbor (known as the Frost-Bitten Convention) finally gave in; Michigan entered the Union, Jan. 26, 1837.

FRUIT GROWING. Columbus, on his second journey to the New World, planted the seeds of lemons, limes, and sweet oranges to augment the strange new diet of the colonists in Hispaniola. By 1566, other Spaniards were planting olives, dates, figs, oranges, lemons, and limes on the coast of what is now Georgia; by 1769 they had planted orchards of fruit trees all the way from Texas to California. Capt. John Smith reported in 1629 that residents of Jamestown were growing apples, pears, peaches, apricots, and many other fruits.

The orange, introduced into Florida when St. Augustine was settled (1565), did not become firmly established as a commercial crop until Florida became a state in 1821; it was the largest fruit industry in the United States in 1973, with a tonnage of over 9 million and leading its nearest competitor, grape growing, by a volume of over two to one. Department of Agriculture shipments of seedless orange-tree cuttings from Brazil began California's navel orange industry in 1871. U.S. lemon production centered in California and Arizona in the 1970's.

The earliest settlers in the New World brought with them both seed and propagating wood of apples. Large orchards quickly developed; apples from New England were being exported to the West Indies at least by 1741, and Albemarle pippins were sent from Virginia to England as early as 1759. The movement of settlers westward seems to have been preceded by the distribution of apple seedlings by Indians, trappers, and itinerants.

Grape growing was not established as an industry in California until about 1830. In 1863, when an American louse called Phylloxera, which attacks the roots of vines, was accidentally imported into Europe, massive vine-growing areas were destroyed; nearly 2.5 million acres of land were estimated to have been ruined in France alone. The ravages were checked eventually by the importation of louse-resistant stocks from California onto which the older vines were grafted; in time the American vines completely replaced the pre-Phylloxera European vines.

The total small-fruits industry of the United States, including blackberries, dewberries, raspberries, cranberries, blueberries, strawberries, and gooseberries, returns about $100 million a year to the growers. Few small fruits were grown commercially until after 1825, when wild plants were domesticated. The avocado, date, and mango are the most important tropical fruits grown commercially in the continental United States. When Hawaii was added as a state, pineapples, bananas, and papaya gained in prominence.

Commercial fruit growing was seldom profitable until after the Civil War, because of the lack of reliable rapid transportation to population centers. Much of the fruit grown commercially is consumed fresh and is sold on the open market; the remainder is processed for sale frozen or canned, or is made into such products as jams and preserves.

FRUITLANDS. A cooperative community established by Bronson Alcott as an experiment in "consocial" living and transcendental idealism at Harvard, Mass. With his wife and daughters (the "little women") and nine other idealists, he moved to Fruitlands (1843) to live with physical asceticism and spiritual beauty. The men sowed eleven acres, but failed as farmers. Winter drove them from Fruitlands after seven months' residence.

FUEL ADMINISTRATION. A World War I agency instituted Aug. 23, 1917, under authority of the Lever Act, to control the production, distribution, and price of coal and oil. Its five main activities were (1) to stimulate an adequate increase in the production of fuel; (2) to encourage voluntary economy in the private consumption of fuel; (3) to restrict consumption by industries not essential to winning the war; (4) to regulate the distribution of coal through a zoning system; and (5) to fix maximum prices within each zone. Its methods were effective.

FUELS. The first fuel used in the colonial and early national periods was firewood; the rich forest resources were used to heat homes, to power early steam locomotives and steamboats, and to make charcoal for use in the iron forges of the early 19th century. During the 19th century, the great U.S. coal supplies were tapped and used as basic fuels for steam locomotives and other industrial uses. Anthracite coal was the preferred fuel for home heating during the last decades of the 19th century.

During the 20th century, petroleum and natural gas came to be used in power plants, in automobile and aircraft engines, and in heating homes and office buildings. The demand for fuel oils grew so markedly that the United States changed from an exporter to an importer of crude oil during the middle years of the 20th century. Following World War II, nuclear fuels became available, generating heat by the process of nuclear fission. Uranium-based nuclear fuels were introduced in naval vessels and electric power generating plants. In 1970, the U.S. consumption of fuels included petroleum (43 percent); natural gas (32.8 percent); soft coal (19.8 percent); and hard coal (0.3 percent).

FUGIOS (also known as **Franklin Cents**). The earliest coins issued by the United States, all dated 1787 and made in conformity with a resolution of Congress dated July 6, 1787.

FUGITIVE SLAVE ACTS. A series of local, state, and federal acts intended to discourage runaways among slaves, to punish those who harbored such persons, and to make possible the recovery by slaveowners of their slave property. In 1672 legislation in Virginia authorized killing a runaway who resisted arrest and public payment of his value; a similar law existed in Maryland. Persons harboring fugitives were required to make payments to owners. An act of 1741 rewarded persons who captured a runaway and increased the fine on harborers. The Northwest Ordinance of 1787 rendered the status of fugitive slaves in free territory a problem. It recognized the right of owners to reclaim slaves, and the Constitution provided similar support.

Congress passed two Fugitive Slave acts. The act of 1793 authorized the claimant or his agent to arrest runaways in any state or territory and to prove before a magistrate that the fugitive owed service; any person knowingly harboring a fugitive or obstructing his arrest was liable to a $500 fine for each offense. The Fugitive Slave Act of 1850 (part of the Compromise of 1850) was intended to supplant the ineffective 1793 law. U.S. commissioners were added to the usual courts to issue warrants for the arrest of fugitives and certificates for their removal from the state. The claimant's affidavit was all that was necessary to establish ownership. Once arrested, an alleged fugitive was taken before a commissioner, who determined the matter summarily. Anyone harboring, concealing, or rescuing a fugitive was liable to a fine of $1,000, six months' imprisonment, and civil damages of $1,000 for each runaway with whom he was involved.

FULBRIGHT ACT AND GRANTS. The Fulbright Act of 1946 (Public Law 584) was sponsored by Sen. J. William Fulbright of Arkansas to initiate and finance international educational exchange programs with funds in foreign currencies accruing to the United States from the sale of property abroad considered surplus after World War II. Subsequent acts of Congress, including the Fulbright-Hays Act (Mutual Education and Cultural Exchange Act) of 1961, broadened the programs and authorized the use of such currencies from other sources and the appropriation of dollars if needed. Programs were developed by executive agreements with interested, eligible nations. By 1973 they numbered more than 126 countries and territories in every region of the world. The act originated the largest program in history of international exchange grants made to individuals.

"FULL DINNER PAIL." A Republican campaign slogan in the 1900 presidential election campaign, used to emphasize the prosperity of William McKinley's first term and to appeal to the labor vote.

FULTON. A wooden side-wheel steamer built in 1837 in New York for harbor defense. It was the second steam warship in the U.S. navy. Given new engines in 1852, it took part in the Paraguay expedition. It was burned during the Civil War.

FULTON'S FOLLY. In 1807, Robert Fulton, with the financial backing of Robert R. Livingston, built the *Clermont,* a steamboat that became known as Fulton's Folly. It made the 150-mile run from New York City to Albany in thirty-two hours. A regular passenger service was inaugurated, and a new era in water transportation began. In 1809, Fulton obtained a federal patent. (*See also* Steamboat Monopolies.)

FUNDAMENTAL CONSTITUTIONS. English colonists carried to the New World the conception of a supreme and fundamental constitution to which all laws must conform, but which was not embodied in one comprehensive written document. The rights and privileges of that constitution were extended to them through royal charters. Promoters in turn often issued patents to individuals or groups of people; these patents, besides giving land, usually accorded the right of local autonomy, but required subordination to the superior provincial government. The grantees usually issued additional concessions, which assumed the position of fundamental law. Early in the Restoration period the proprietors of the Carolinas and Jerseys granted concessions and agreements followed by fundamental constitutions (*see* Carolina, Fundamental Constitutions of); these, with William Penn's Frame of Government, were an attempt to compromise with the new conflicting concept of sovereignty in the people that had developed in the northern colonies. The precursor of this concept was the Mayflower Compact, which served as an emergency constitution for the Pilgrims until they could replace the legal patent given to them by the Virginia Company. The Fundamental Orders of Connecticut and of New Haven, and the Providence Agreements are similar except that they were made to be permanent; these two corporation colonies were much more independent of the mother country than colonies of any other type and furnished the pattern on which the state constitutions of the new United States were modeled.

FUNDAMENTAL ORDERS OF CONNECTICUT. *See* **Connecticut, Fundamental Orders of.**

FUNDING OF REVOLUTIONARY DEBT. *See* **Assumption and Funding of Revolutionary Debt.**

FUNSTON'S CAPTURE OF AGUINALDO (Mar. 14–25, 1901). When organized Filipino resistance to U.S. rule collapsed, Emilio Aguinaldo, the insurgent president, fled to Palanan, an inaccessible village in northeastern Luzon (*see* Philippine Insurrection). One of his officers, bearing dispatches to southern Filipino leaders, surrendered himself. Gen. Frederick Funston decoded the cipher dispatches and prepared forged replies that were transmitted to Aguinaldo in Palanan, stating that a Tagalog insurgent band was joining him and bringing five American prisoners. Funston, four white officers impersonating prisoners, and eighty Macabebe scouts proceeded by sea to the east coast of Luzon, landing secretly in Casiguran Bay. Deceiving local inhabitants, they marched to Palanan, where they dispersed Aguinaldo's bodyguard, seized him, and returned to the coast. Aguinaldo took the oath of allegiance, and other leaders of the rebellion followed his example.

FURNITURE. Stylistically, American furniture has always been closely related to Old World models—particularly those of the middle class and of English origin—but with pronounced regional characteristics.

17th Century. Simple board furniture was nailed together by house carpenters. More sophisticated furniture was made by joiners, who also fashioned interior architectural trim. With mortise-and-tenon joints, joiners made heavy, low, rectangular chests, tables, chairs, bedsteads, and cupboards of oak, using pine and maple for interior parts. Case pieces were often carved in low-relief foliate or geometrical patterns. Turners, employing lathes, made chairs of maple and ash and did piecework for joiners, producing table legs, bedposts, balusters for stair rails, and split spindles and bosses to be applied as ornament on chests, cupboards, and boxes. Much early furniture was painted in strong earth colors, principally black, red, and ocher, and less often in blue, green, and white.

Restoration and William and Mary Styles (1690–1730). The 1690's brought lighter new forms and classical proportions. Innovations included thin drawer linings, dovetail construction, moldings around drawers, and teardrop or chased-brass mounts instead of iron escutcheons and wooden knobs. Most furniture was made of native walnut or maple, although surfaces of the finest case pieces were occasionally ornamented with burled veneers of walnut or ash or with japanning in imitation of oriental lacquer. New forms included cane-back, banister-back, slat-back, leather-back, and easy (upholstered) chairs; tall clocks; high chests of drawers (highboys) on trumpet-shaped legs and matching dressing tables (lowboys); slant-top desks; and gateleg and butterfly tables.

Baroque and Rococo Furniture in Queen Anne and Chippendale Styles (1730–90). In the Queen Anne style case furniture in particular was highly architectural, with molded cornices, scroll pediments, dentils, and flutes and reeds as well as proportions based on Palladian principles. In chairs the cyma curve dominated regional designs, which featured backs with solid, vase-shaped splats and bow-shaped crests. Sometimes the knees of cabriole legs were carved with scallop shells and volutes, but usually there was little ornament. In about 1760 cabriole legs with pad, trifid, or pointed slipper feet, the hallmark of the Queen Anne style, were supplanted by cabriole legs with claw-and-ball feet or by straight, square supports (Marlborough legs).

Increasingly comfortable furniture was made, and more easy chairs and sofas produced; tea and card tables, desks and bookcases, and firescreens were popular new forms. After the introduction of the Chippendale style (about 1760) mahogany superseded walnut for high-style furniture, although walnut, maple, and cherry continued to be used, especially outside urban centers. Chippendale chair-back splats were pierced; case pieces continued in the Palladian manner, with the addition of carved ornament in French, Chinese, or Gothic taste. The high chest on cabriole legs was "modernized" in Philadelphia with rococo leaf carving. Bombé double chests and desk-and-bookcases were a specialty in Boston, where blocked-front desks and chests of drawers with a vertical concave panel flanked by two convex panels originated. In Newport, R.I., Quaker cabinetmakers of the Goddard and Townsend families brought block-front furniture design to its highest development by capping each vertical panel with a large carved shell.

Manufacture of the American Windsor chair was begun in Philadelphia before 1750. An outgrowth of an English type, American Windsors were lighter and stronger, with lathe-turned legs and stretchers; bows for the back were shaped by steaming. Universally popular, Windsors were forerunners of inexpensive 19th-century painted and stencilled fancy chairs.

Federal Furniture in the Neoclassical Style (1790–1825). London furniture designs by George Hepplewhite, Thomas Shearer, and Thomas Sheraton in the new neoclassical taste, giving an overall effect of delicacy with inlaid or veneered ovals, rectangles, squares, and circles, were widely accepted in America by the early 1790's. The urn was a common element in the new vocabulary of ornament, which included the anthemion, the bellflower, the patera, swags of drapery, fretwork, beading, fluting and reeding, the rinceau band, griffins, steer skulls, busts and figures of ancients, and the new United States seal, the American eagle. Columns and pilasters were more attenuated than formerly.

Mahogany was often applied as veneer. New forms were ladies' desks, sewing tables, pembroke tables, sideboards, gentlemen's secretary desks, and lolling, shield, oval, and square-back chairs with thin square, tapered, or round reeded legs.

Today called "Empire" after furniture designed for the first empire of Napoleon in France, the style based on ancient Greek and Roman forms was brought to America by émigré cabinetmakers—notably Charles-Honoré Lannuier, who arrived in New York in 1803—and through English pattern books of George Smith. Mahogany tables (often with gilt ornamentation and marble tops), chests, and sofas in this style produced between 1810 and 1835 became increasingly heavy and robust.

Trends in American furniture making during its first century and a half include (1) labor-saving practices (machine-made banisters and leather, instead of caned, chair backs), (2) rich effects at low cost (painted surfaces to simulate a rich wood or marble or gilded in imitation of bronze mounts), (3) predominantly English styles, although Dutch influences in New York and German influences in Pennsylvania were strong, (4) simplification of ornament and outline (lean and taut, as in New England, and thin, streamlined forms devoid of ornament, as in the furniture made by the Shakers), and (5) conservative attitudes about relinquishing favored forms, coupled with a desire to be fashionable, leading to new ornament on old forms (the Philadelphia highboy).

Victorian Styles (1835–1901). About 1835, revival styles were introduced. Loosely called Victorian, after the Queen of England (1837–1901), elements of several styles were often combined. In the 1850's, John Henry Belter of New York pioneered in the use of laminated wood for curved forms that were elaborately carved, and at the same time, the importation began of Michael Thonet's Viennese bentwood chairs of unadorned surface and clean outline. The New York Crystal Palace Exhibition of 1853, the Philadelphia Centennial Exposition of 1876, and successive international fairs brought America foreign fashions that were quickly interpreted in the home market.

Charles Locke Eastlake's *Hints on Household Taste* (London, 1868; Boston, 1872) had a profound influence in simplifying American furniture design of the 1870's and 1880's and was responsible for the widespread production of "Eastlake" furniture of simple rectilinear design with incised carving. A purification of style was also effected by oak furniture designed by the architects Henry Hobson Richardson (in the Queen Anne revival style), Frank Lloyd Wright (rectangular, often barred, vertical, and expressionistic), and Charles and Henry Greene; and by the Mission furniture of Gustav Stickley and Elbert Hubbard (four-square and broader in profile than Wright's).

After 1825 metal was increasingly used in furniture—in cast-iron, wire, and patent furniture, in wire springs for upholstery, in bedsprings, and in innerspring mattresses. Wire ice-cream parlor chairs were widely produced.

Twentieth Century. Parallel to the development of the modern or international school of architecture was 20th-century furniture by architects and professional designers who conceived new forms to take advantage of industrial processes. In the early 1930's members of the Bauhaus School in Weimar came to the United States. They exploited technology and new materials—stainless steel and chromed metal, glass and plastic, and leather. Their furniture, organic and functional in design, has been lauded for its precision of form, intense simplicity, and hygienic elegance. In contrast, the Art Deco style, which flourished in America after the Exposition Internationale des Artes Décoratifs et Industriels of 1925, is one of ornament with exotic motifs from many sources—Egyptian, Aztec, and Southwest Indian art; the Russian ballet; and the electric flash. Its outlines are jagged and fragmented; its materials are plastic, chrome, china, veneered woods, and patterned fabrics. Strains of these two styles coexisted and intertwined during the 1920's and 1930's.

In 1940, Charles Eames and Eero Saarinen won a competition in organic design with their one-piece, molded plywood chair. In 1946, Eames, with his wife, Ray, developed the spider-legged side chair of contoured plywood elements with resilient rubber mounts. Two years later the Eameses, in conjunction with a group at the University of California at Los Angeles, produced the first fiberglass plastic chair, which was followed by plastic stacking chairs in 1950. George Nelson introduced the storage-wall room divider with interchangeable elements in 1945.

Concurrent with the use of modern materials, solid wood is widely used for much furniture in Tudor, colonial, and other revival styles, sold to an increasingly mobile people who seek to create a sense of tradition and roots. Some companies produce exact and authentic reproductions of early American furniture. Modern housing with many built-in conveniences has reduced the need for most domestic forms except tables and chairs.

FURNITURE INDUSTRY. As city populations grew large enough to support specialized occupations, the skills of furniture making were subdivided into a dozen crafts, including chairmaking, clockmaking, looking-glass making, carving, turning, gilding, painting, and japanning; the cabinetmaker—succeeding the joiner—emerged as the primary furniture craftsman. The furniture of the best American craftsmen—such as the Townsend and Goddard families, who popularized the block-front style; Samuel McIntire, the Salem, Mass., carver; Duncan Phyfe of New York City; and Benjamin Randolph of Philadelphia—was equal in finish and design to the finest European pieces.

Even in the era of hand production there were trends toward the standardization of parts and the subdivision of labor. The 17th-century chair industry began the specialized manufacture of chair parts, such as arms and legs. In cabinetmaking shops the same patterns might be used over many years to make elements of a piece of furniture.

The export of furniture, begun in the early 1700's with coastwise shipments from New England ports, expanded by the 1790's to South America and Africa. Active in this trade was a consortium of Salem, Mass., cabinetmakers and allied craftsmen headed by Deacon Elijah Sanderson. To supply the rapidly expanding southern markets, some New York and Philadelphia cabinetmakers and chairmakers migrated to Charleston, S.C., Savannah, Ga., and New Orleans, La. Others established branch shops in the South. By 1820 the export and local sales of Duncan Phyfe required the services of 100 workmen, each specializing in his own craft and all working under one roof.

By the 1830's, woodworking machinery was available to cabinetmakers. By the 1850's the largest furniture firms were true factories, using steam-powered mortising, tenoning, and carving machines; steam-powered lathes; and steam-powered jig, scroll, band, and circular saws. New and refined techniques of bending wood and pressing wood scraps into molds for ornaments were also in use. Smaller shops mechanized relatively slowly, and late into the 19th century, many shops continued to use simple mortising and jig or scroll saws powered by foot treadles; but by 1870 the mechanization of that part of the industry producing for the commercial, as opposed to the custom, market was virtually complete.

From its early seaboard centers, the furniture industry moved westward as the interior markets of America developed. New York and New England continued to produce large quantities of furniture in the 19th century; but by 1850, Cincinnati was a furniture center, and after the Civil War, first Chicago and then Grand Rapids, with its proximity to western timber stands, became manufacturing centers. In general, the western factories utilized cheap water transportation as a basis for the mass production and mass marketing of less expensive grades of furniture, sometimes called "cottage furniture." In the 20th century a new center of furniture production, based on supplies of hardwood and cheap labor, appeared in the southern states, especially North Carolina.

The system of wholesaling furniture through drummers, auctions, or warerooms maintained by individual manufacturers was replaced in the 1890's by the institutionalization of the furniture exposition. Semiannual expositions, open only to dealers, at which any manufacturer could show his current line, were first held in New York City and then in Chicago and Grand Rapids. After World War I the major exposition center was High Point, N.C. Throughout the 20th century the expansion of the furniture industry kept pace with the population growth; after the post–World War II jump in home construction, the furniture industry ranked as the second largest U.S. consumer durable goods industry, exceeded only by the automobile industry in gross sales.

FUR TRADE. The traffic in furs and skins began with the first contacts between European explorers and the Indians along the shores of North America, and has continued without interruption. Furs were almost the only New World commodity that afforded immediate returns.

New England Fur Trade. Trade with the Indians in the New England area continued throughout the colonial period, but declined in importance after King Philip's War. The economic basis of the earliest settlements, especially Plymouth, consisted largely in the fur trade, but the geographical situation prevented any considerable expansion: there were no great waterways leading to the interior of the continent, and the presence of New Netherland on the west and New France on the north held trade in check. At first the Dutch in the Connecticut Valley (*see* House of Hope) had a monopoly, but in the 1630's, Massachusetts traders succeeded in breaking it up. William Pynchon founded a post on the site of Springfield, Mass., and he and his son John dominated the fur trade of this region for many years; meanwhile, Massachusetts traders were pushing up the Concord and Merrimac rivers and northeastward along the Maine coast. The United Colonies of New England (1643) had as one object the protection of the trading interests of its members. From 1694 until the Revolution, Massachusetts Bay tried to limit the trade to government truck houses, which showed no commercial profit but probably aided in keeping peace with the Indians.

Middle Atlantic States. The trade in furs and coarser skins constituted an important element in the economic life of this area during the 17th and 18th centuries. At first, proprietary and governmental authorities tended to reserve the trade for themselves, but it proved impossible to maintain an effective monopoly, and trade fell gradually under the control of the merchant class.

The trade of the New York area, which dominated the Hudson-Mohawk route to the Great Lakes and the Northwest, was established by the Dutch, monopoly rights being granted in turn to the New Netherland Company and the Dutch West India Company (chartered 1621); important posts were established at Fort Orange (later Albany), and the House of Hope, on the Connecticut River. The Dutch at Fort Orange laid the foundations of trade with the Iroquois, who acted as middlemen for tribes farther west. The English took New Netherland in 1664 and continued the trade along much the same lines, but they soon came into conflict with the French; the fur trade became a vital factor in the Anglo-French rivalry that did not end until 1763. The English in 1722 established the post of Oswego (N.Y.) to intercept the French trade with the interior; they enjoyed an advantage in the form of cheap goods of superior quality, but the Albany merchants caused embarrassment by trading with the French at Montreal in spite of regulations. After 1763 a considerable part of the New York trade was diverted to Canada.

The Dutch and Swedes pioneered the fur trade of the middle region but were soon supplanted by the English. By 1750 the trade had reached the Wabash and Maumee rivers, where the English clashed with the French (*see* French Claims in Ohio). Pennsylvania enjoyed the advantage of position in exploiting the Ohio region; Philadelphia and Lancaster became important centers of the trade, and prior to the Revolution large companies grew up, among them Baynton, Wharton and Morgan, and David Franks and Company.

Great Lakes Region. This region was one of the rich fur-bearing areas of North America, and the peltry trade flourished on a large scale for some 200 years. Beaver skins were the most important, but the country also yielded raccoon, otter, mink, muskrat, fox, and many other animals.

New France had its genesis largely in the fur trade. Quebec was founded by Samuel de Champlain in 1608; with this settlement as a base, the trade extended to the interior with amazing rapidity. The French authorities devoted much attention to matters of regulation and control, and at times the fur trade largely overshadowed all other interests. The privilege of exporting furs to France was vested in a succession of companies, including the Company of the Hundred Associates, founded in 1628, the Company of the West Indies, the Company of Canada, and the Company of the West. At first the Indians were encouraged to bring their furs down to great annual fairs held at Three Rivers or Montreal, but gradually French traders established various posts; among the most important were Niagara, Detroit, Michilimackinac, Sault Ste. Marie, La Baye, St. Joseph's, and Vincennes. As a rule the trade of particular posts was farmed out to individuals with monopoly privileges.

Bitter rivalry grew up between the French and English traders from New York and Pennsylvania, and the struggle for the fur trade became one of the causes of the intercolonial wars. Following the capitulation of Montreal in 1760, there was an influx of British merchants and a rapid expansion of the trade. The British abandoned the system of government monopoly, but a new trend toward economic monopoly appeared, centered in the hands of a few companies, among which the North West Company became the most powerful. The "merchants of Montreal" extended their operations to the upper Missouri and into the region northwest of Lake Superior. The British refused to surrender the Northwest posts to the United States until 1796 (*see* Border Forts, Evacuation of).

After 1796, American interests made a strong bid for commercial control, although British influence among the Indians remained strong until after the War of 1812. In 1795 the United States inaugurated a system of government factories (*see* Factory System, Indian) to undermine British influence; the system was not a success and was discontinued in 1822. From the close of the War of 1812 until his retirement in 1834, John Jacob Astor virtually controlled the trade of the Great Lakes region (*see* American Fur Company). In 1834, Ramsay Crooks took over the Northern Department, which continued under the name of the American Fur Company until it failed in 1842. The Great Lakes fur trade continued sporadically thereafter.

Rocky Mountains. During the early 19th century this was the most attractive U.S. fur-trading area. The trade was developed almost entirely by Americans; Frenchmen had pushed up the Missouri River, and Spaniards had made a few attempts to trade for furs in the Southwest, but after the purchase of Louisiana, Americans entered vigorously into the trade of the newly acquired region. In 1807, Manuel Lisa of St. Louis led an expedition up the Missouri and Yellowstone rivers and established a trading post at the mouth of the Bighorn River. The St. Louis Missouri Fur Company (founded 1809) and the Missouri Fur Company (founded 1814) extended their operations as far west as southwestern Montana. In 1824 the traders of the Rocky Mountain Fur Company abandoned the Missouri River and the practice of establishing trading posts, struck out boldly into the mountains, and inaugurated the famous rendezvous (*see* Trappers' Rendezvous) at such places as Jackson Hole and Pierre's Hole. From 1832 to 1834 this company competed bitterly with Astor's American Fur Company, which had entered the upper Missouri trade a few years earlier. The American Fur Company won out, and thereafter dominated the trade of the area. It also introduced steamboats on the upper Missouri.

Several smaller groups and numerous individual "free trappers" operated in the Rocky Mountain area. Some, like Ceran St. Vrain and Charles and William Bent, erected forts or trading houses that became landmarks. Others, including Capt. Benjamin L. E. Bonneville, Nathaniel J. Wyeth, Jacob Fowler, Sylvester and James O. Pattie, and Ewing Young, headed parties of traders who made extensive expeditions into the mountains.

Southeast and Lower Mississippi. English traders from Carolina were already on the Cumberland and Tennessee rivers when La Salle claimed the Mississippi Valley for France in 1682; by 1700 the English were passing down these rivers to the Ohio and Mississippi. Permanent French settlement in the lower Mississippi Valley after 1699 brought on a struggle; by 1717 the French had won over all important tribes except the Cherokee and deprived the Carolina traders of half their Indian traffic, but the French policies and their war with the Natchez enabled British traders to recover their former position by 1730.

After Louisiana reverted to royal control in 1732, French traders operating from Mobile offered English goods to the Indians, but wars between England and France (1744–63) severely handicapped the French. After expulsion of France from the Mississippi Valley in 1763, British traders controlled the southeastern fur trade until the close of the American Revolution. The Louisiana Purchase (1803) brought the fur trade centering in New Orleans under U.S. control, the War of 1812 loosened the hold of the British traders at Mobile and Pensacola, and the acquisition of the Floridas in 1821 brought the entire southeastern fur trade into American hands. The fur trade gradually decreased in importance with the expansion of agriculture, although it continued well into the 20th century.

Upper Mississippi and Missouri Rivers. As early as 1694, Frenchmen from Illinois began dealing with the Osage Indians. French settlements were built up in Kaskaskia and Cahokia (Illinois) about 1700, and in 1723, Fort Orleans was established on the Missouri, in present Carroll County, Mo. In 1763, when Great Britain acquired the territory east of the Mississippi, the French were carrying on trade by land and by water up the Mississippi, along the Wisconsin, Fox, Chicago, and Illinois rivers to the Great Lakes, and up the Ohio to the territory inhabited by the Wabash Indians. Pierre Laclède Ligueste moved up the Mississippi from New Orleans, reaching the present site of St. Louis late in 1763, and established a trading post there; English competition restricted traders operating from St. Louis principally to the Mississippi below the Des Moines and the Missouri with its tributaries. After the British lost this territory to the American colonies the St. Louis traders moved again into the upper Mississippi and Missouri to fight it out with the North West and the Hudson's Bay companies.

In 1794 the Spanish Commercial Exploration Company was promoted by Missouri Lt. Gov. Zenon Trudeau to exploit the fur trade of the upper Missouri, combining the capital and energies of prominent merchants of St. Louis, and subsidized by the Spanish government. After the return of Meriwether Lewis and William Clark, the St. Louis Missouri Fur Company was organized; other companies and individuals followed and forts were erected along the Missouri and its tributaries. P. Chouteau, Jr., and Company became the largest and most successful fur-trading company until it went out of business in 1866.

FUR TRADE OF THE PACIFIC COAST. *See* **Canton Fur Trade; China Trade.**

FURUSETH SEAMEN'S ACT. *See* **Seamen's Act of 1915.**

FUTURE FARMERS OF AMERICA. A youth organization, founded in 1928, to encourage young people to enter farming, to develop knowledge and skills useful in agriculture, and to encourage good citizenship. It has annual conventions in Kansas City, Mo.

GABRIEL'S INSURRECTION (1800). A conspiracy of Gabriel and other slaves near Richmond, Va., to seek freedom; the conspirators were arrested before they could strike.

GADSDEN, FORT. Built by Gen. Andrew Jackson on the east bank of the Apalachicola River, fifteen miles above its mouth, during his invasion of Florida in spring 1818 (*see* Arbuthnot and Ambrister, Case of) and maintained by the United States through the rest of the Spanish occupancy.

GADSDEN PURCHASE. Following the Treaty of Guadalupe Hidalgo (1848), the United States was charged with not enforcing Article XI, which promised Mexico protection from inroads by American Indians; a boundary-line dispute also arose involving territory for a southern railroad route to the Pacific Ocean. In 1849, P. A. Hargous purchased the Garay grant, made by Mexico in 1842 to open a transit concession across the Isthmus of Tehuantepec; this was nullified in 1851 by Mexico, but in 1853, A. G. Sloo was given a similar grant. Both Hargous and Sloo demanded U.S. protection for their concessions. In July 1853, James Gadsden, minister to Mexico, negotiated a treaty whereby territory in northern Mexico was sold to the United States and Article XI of the Treaty of Guadalupe Hidalgo was abrogated; the United States was to pay Mexico $15 million; to assume all claims of its citizens against Mexico, including the Hargous claim; and to cooperate in suppressing filibustering expeditions. The Senate ratified the treaty on Apr. 25, 1854, but reduced the territory to be acquired to that considered essential for the railroad route; all mention of private claims and filibustering expeditions was deleted; the payment to Mexico was lowered to $10 million; and an article was inserted promising U.S. protection to the Sloo grantees. The United States secured 45,535 square miles of territory, which became known as the Gadsden Purchase and comprises the southern part of Arizona and New Mexico.

GAG RULE, ANTISLAVERY (May 26, 1836). Adopted by the House of Representatives to hold back the flood of antislavery petitions following the growth of antislavery sentiment, by preventing discussion of antislavery proposals. Rescinded Dec. 3, 1844, after northern support had fallen away. It strengthened the antislavery movement by adding the issue of deprivation of the right of petition.

GAINES, FORT. Erected in 1822 on the eastern end of Dauphin Island in Mobile Bay, to guard the bay's entrance. In 1861 it was seized and held by the Confederacy, until recaptured by Union troops in 1864. In 1898 the fort was recommissioned, but was later abandoned.

GAINES CASE. One of America's longest lawsuits, instituted in 1834 by Myra Clark Whitney (later Mrs. Gaines) to recover property in New Orleans from the estate of her father, Daniel Clark. The issues were her legitimacy and the validity of Clark's will made in 1813 and assertedly destroyed by his executor. Both points were eventually decided in Mrs. Gaines's favor, and in 1877 the nonexistent will was admitted to probate and she recovered property worth $250,000. In 1890, five years after her death, the so-called Blanc Tract suit was decided against New Orleans; four years later the city paid the Gaines heirs $1,925,667.

GAINES' MILL, BATTLE OF (June 27, 1862). After the opening of the Seven Days' Battles at Oak Grove and Mechanicsville, Va. (June 25–26), the Union right wing north of the Chickahominy River, under Gen. Fitz-John Porter, was withdrawn to high ground east of Gaines' Mill and south of Cold Harbor, because of knowledge that Gen. Robert E. Lee had sent Gen. T. J. ("Stonewall") Jackson's corps on a northward flanking detour. Lee attacked with the major portion of his army shortly after noon on June 27; when Jackson arrived in midafternoon, Lee had double Porter's numbers, but the latter was in a strong position. Just before dusk the Confederates pierced the Union line and captured twenty-two guns. That night Porter's force was withdrawn to the south side of the Chickahominy.

GAINES' TRACE. Indian trail made into a highway for the transportation of government merchandise (1810) by the factor at St. Stephens, Ala., George S. Gaines, to avoid Spanish revenue authorities at Mobile. It began at Colbert's Ferry on the Tennessee River near the Muscle Shoals and crossed the divide to Cotton Gin Port on the Tombigbee.

GALÁPAGOS ISLANDS. An archipelago 600 miles off the coast of Ecuador, whose strategic importance was realized during the administration of President Franklin Pierce (1853–57); rumors of French and British interest (1862–66, 1892, 1899–1902) kept American diplomats alert. The

Venezuela and Panama crises (1902–03) aroused Ecuadorian fear that the United States would seize the islands, and later negotiations to build a U.S. coaling station failed. During World War II the United States established weather and signal stations there.

GALENA-DUBUQUE MINING DISTRICT (southwestern Wisconsin, northwestern Illinois, and Dubuque County, Iowa). Nicolas Perrot first mined lead there in 1690. The Fox granted Julien Dubuque permission to work the mines in 1788; when he died (1810), the Fox prevented his creditors from continuing operations. It was not until 1833 that miners returned to Dubuque. In 1810, Henry Shreve took a barge of lead to New Orleans from the Galena River mines, where the Indians that year melted 400,000 pounds; George Davenport floated the first flatboat cargo downstream in 1816. The first government leases to mine lead at the Galena settlements were granted in 1822; during the first quarter-century, about 472 million pounds of lead, valued at $14.2 million, was shipped downstream.

GALLATIN'S REPORT ON MANUFACTURES. On Apr. 10, 1810, Albert Gallatin, secretary of the treasury, sent to the House of Representatives a report (requested in 1809) on encouraging manufactures. He suggested moderate increases in protective duties, the rates to hold for a certain period so that the manufacturers could count on them; he also suggested that to supply capital, the United States should issue its obligations and lend them to the manufacturers.

GALLATIN'S REPORT ON ROADS, CANALS, HARBORS, AND RIVERS. Acting on a Senate resolution of 1807, Secretary of the Treasury Albert Gallatin prepared an analysis and program for transportation improvement (1808). He urged the building of a series of canals along the Atlantic seaboard from Massachusetts to the Carolinas; the establishment of communication between the Atlantic and midwestern rivers and with the St. Lawrence and the Great Lakes; and interior canals and roads. He thought that all the improvements could be made for $20 million, and the debt be paid in ten years; this proposed indebtedness, the first of its sort in U.S. history, was bitterly denounced by many. The War of 1812 stopped all thought of the projects; after the war, four roads were built. Most of the works advocated by Gallatin were later completed either by the federal government (the intracoastal waterway) or by the states (the Erie Canal).

GALLEY BOATS. On the Ohio River, small shiplike craft designed to use both sails and oars—the same craft known after 1800 as barges. The French and Spanish maintained galleys on the Mississippi for military purposes. The federal government built two galleys, the *President Adams* and the *Senator Ross,* which were launched at Pittsburgh in 1798 and 1799, respectively.

GALLIPOLIS (Ohio). Founded in 1790 by French immigrants. About 600 prospective settlers, called the French Five Hundred, holding fraudulent land titles from the Scioto Land Company, sailed from Le Havre to Alexandria, Va. On learning the facts, the company disbanded; some were transported to a site on the right bank of the Ohio River about three miles below the mouth of the Great Kanawha River, where cabins had been erected for them by Marietta settlers. (*See* French Grants.)

GALLOWAY'S PLAN OF UNION. On Sept. 28, 1774, Joseph Galloway of Pennsylvania submitted a plan to the Continental Congress attempting to settle the conflict between England and the colonies by establishing an American legislature with a president-general appointed by the king and a grand council chosen by the colonial assemblies; the legislature was to be considered a branch of the British Parliament, and the assent of both bodies would be necessary to make laws governing the colonies valid. Congress rejected it by the vote of one colony.

GALPHIN CLAIM. For goods, in the amount of £9,791, supplied to the Creek and Cherokee prior to 1773. The principal was paid in 1849 by the Treasury Department; in 1850 the interest, amounting to $191,352, was paid under unusual circumstances.

GALVANIZED YANKEES. Confederate soldiers captured and imprisoned during the Civil War who were given their freedom in exchange for taking an oath of allegiance to the United States and enlisting in the Union army; about 6,000 were enrolled into six regiments of U.S. volunteers in 1864–65; a few hundred others were placed in state volunteer units. The six regiments were ordered to the western frontier so that they would not be required to fight against former comrades-in-arms. Samuel Bowles used the sobriquet "Galvanized Yankees" in a dispatch from Nebraska to the *Springfield* (Mass.) *Republican,* May 24, 1865. The term was also applied occasionally to captured Union soldiers who turned Confederate.

GALVESTON (Tex.). An important seaport on the Gulf Coast, with a population of 61,902 in 1980. Together with Texas City, it was the center of a metropolitan region including 195,940 people. Galveston is located on a sandy island that stretches along the coast, protecting Galveston Bay from the direct actions of the Gulf of Mexico; the city itself, therefore, has often been affected by hurricanes and other storms sweeping in from the Gulf.

Galveston island and bay were, in the early 19th century, a center for piratical activities. After Texas became independent, the area was used as a base for the Texas navy, and it remained an important base under U.S. government. The city and port were fought over during the Civil War. During the early 20th century Galveston became a leader in new types of city government: the "Galveston Plan" introduced the idea of having individual commissioners elected by the people to operate the major branches of city services. Galveston and Texas City manufacture petrochemicals and machinery for the oil industry and operate a major portion of the Texas-based Gulf fishing fleets.

GALVESTON, LOSS AND RECAPTURE OF (1862–63). A Union naval squadron forced the Confederates to evacuate the island of Galveston, Tex., in October 1862 and enabled Union troops to occupy the island just before Christmas. On New Year's Eve Confederate Gen. John B. Magruder attacked Union vessels in Galveston harbor with two steamers brought from Houston, while about 1,000 Confederates with cannon crossed Galveston Bay and attacked by land. The Union troops surrendered the island on Jan. 1, 1863.

GALVESTON PIRATES. Lawless men, former Baratarian pirates and other adventurers, headquartered on Galveston Island, in the Gulf of Mexico, during the early 19th century. They swore allegiance to the revolutionary government of Mexico and pretended to be privateers engaged in capturing Spanish merchant vessels, but in reality they were slave traders and pirates. Their first leader was Luis Aury, who was later joined by a Captain Perry. These men abandoned the island in November 1816, but their place was taken by Jean Laffite, whose establishment soon numbered nearly 1,000. A U.S. naval vessel put an end to their activities in 1821.

GALVESTON STORM (Sept. 8, 1900). The U.S. Weather Bureau began on Sept. 4, 1900, to post daily telegraphic bulletins on the progress of a tropical cyclone, but the storm broke over Galveston, Tex., on the morning of Sept. 8 before the populace realized its approach; by 4 P.M. the entire city was under from one to five feet of water. All connections with the mainland were severed by 5:15 P.M., when the wind reached 96 miles an hour. The climax came at 8 P.M., when the wind, at an estimated 130 miles an hour, shifted from east to southeast, whereupon a tidal wave four to six feet high swept the city, piling up a great wall of crushed buildings almost half a mile inland from the gulf; most of the estimated loss of 7,000 lives occurred at that time. The storm abated after midnight.

GAMBLING. The first extensive public gambling in the United States was by means of the lottery; by 1750, lotteries had become an integral part of public financing and were operated for the benefit of municipalities, churches, public utility companies, and schools. There was a wave of legislation abolishing lotteries in the 1830's; from 1895 to 1963 they were illegal everywhere in the country. In 1964, New Hampshire introduced a state lottery to help pay for its schools; its example was followed by New York in 1967 and later by other states. An outgrowth of the lottery, policy (originally called lottery insurance) and the numbers game (essentially the same) have been the most widespread forms of gambling in America since the late 19th century, with an annual gross income in the 1970's estimated at $500 million.

Horse racing, football, and other sports attract a large volume of betting. In many states, betting on horse races (and in Florida, dog races) is now legal if done at the tracks, and in some by off-track betting (Nevada legalized all forms of gambling in 1931); but betting in general is still carried on illegally in the United States.

Faro, roulette, poker, and craps entered America through New Orleans, and there the first houses devoted exclusively to gambling were opened at about the time of the Louisiana Purchase (1803). From there the professional sharper moved northward along the Atlantic coast, up the Mississippi and Ohio rivers, and into the West and Southwest. The most spectacular of these gamblers operated on the Mississippi River steamboats; river gambling reached its peak in the 1850's when 2,000 professional gamblers regularly worked the boats between New Orleans and St. Louis.

By the late 1820's, gambling houses were palatial; the finest was probably the Club House at Saratoga Springs, N.Y., established in 1867 by John Morrissey and owned 1894–1906 by Richard Canfield. The play at Canfield's houses was the highest in the world, roulette limits being twice as high as at Monte Carlo. Since World War II, Las Vegas, Nev., and Atlantic City, N.J., have become the centers for high-stake gambling in the United States.

GANGSTERS. *See* **Crime, Organized.**

GAR. *See* **Grand Army of the Republic.**

GARCÉS-ANZA ROUTE. The route from Sonora to southern California, based on discoveries in 1771 of the Spanish priest Francisco Garcés and in 1773 of the Indian Tarabal. Garcés and Juan Bautista de Anza proved its practicability (Jan. 8, 1774–May 26, 1775) and thereby made possible the Anza expedition.

GARCÍA, MESSAGE TO. A legend popularized by Elbert Hubbard's article in the *Philistine* of March 1899, according to which President William McKinley, shortly after the outbreak of the Spanish-American War, wanted to send a message to Gen. Calixto García Íñiguez, a Cuban revolutionary, whose whereabouts were unknown; someone said, "There is a fellow by the name of Rowan who can find García if anybody can." In fact, Lt. A. S. Rowan set out for Jamaica early in April 1898, on a mission of inquiry about the size and location of Spanish and Cuban forces. When war broke out, Rowan crossed to Portillo, Cuba; he met García on May 1 at Bayamo and left Cuba on May 5, and made his way to Washington, D.C., with valuable messages *from* García.

GARDENING.

Vegetable Gardens. In the 1540's members of Hernando de Soto's exploring party adapted Indian forms of gardening to achieve self-sufficiency. Early subsistence gardens, located near population centers, developed into market gardens. Greenhouse production of fruits and vegetables began sometime between 1709 and 1737 near Boston; at Mount Vernon in the 1780's, George Washington had an orangery that was heated by vents under the floor. Greenhouse crops of the 19th century consisted largely of lettuce, cucumbers, and tomatoes.

In the 1930's many urban residents moved to small garden plots in the country to grow their own food. During World War I, World War II, and the Korean War, the government encouraged backyard gardens; in 1943, 40 percent of the vegetables raised for fresh consumption were grown in such "victory gardens." Inflation trends of the 1970's indicated yet another turn toward home gardening. Interest in organic gardening (that is, without use of insecticides or other chemicals) increased in the 1970's.

Flower Gardens. Such flower gardens as there were in colonial America tended to remain traditional. The Spanish walled patio garden of the American Southwest and Florida, the formal English gardens of New England, and the national variations of Dutch, German, and French gardens in the 17th century all observed the rectilinear ground plan of the formal garden. Famous gardens in early America include the Longwood gardens near Wilmington, Del., begun by George Pierce in 1701; John Bartram's garden, begun near Philadelphia in 1730; and the governing trustee's garden in Georgia, established in 1733, the world's first economic test garden.

Records of European shipments of roses to America predate 1700. Early colonial references often mention the flower; George Washington is credited with the development of a new variety of rose, the "Mary Washington," based on the native *Rosa setigera* at his Mount Vernon estate. Rock gardening, the incorporation of natural designs of rock, plants, sand, and water, was introduced to the New World by Ralph Hancock, an Englishman, during the 1920's; it became popular because of its ease in construction and care.

GARDINER AWARD. Granted by the commission established under the Treaty of Guadalupe Hidalgo (1848) to settle outstanding claims of Americans against Mexico. George A. Gardiner asked $500,000 for loss of mining property in San Luis Potosí during the Mexican War; the commission awarded $428,747.50 to Gardiner and W. W. Corcoran (an assignee in good faith), and $153,330 to John O. Mears, an accomplice. In 1852 a Senate committee found conclusive evidence of fraud; Gardiner was convicted of forgery and perjury and committed suicide. By 1859 the United States had recovered $250,000. (*See also* American-Mexican Mixed Claims Commissions.)

GARDINERS ISLAND (N.Y.). In Gardiners Bay at the eastern end of Long Island; purchased by Lion Gardiner, who came to America in 1635. The Indian deed (May 3, 1639) states the consideration was "ten coates of trading cloath." Later Gardiner received from Sir William Alexander, Earl of Stirling, a proprietary grant to the island; title has never gone out of the Gardiner family. On Sept. 11, 1686, Gov. Thomas Dongan of New York confirmed the former grants and erected the island into the "Lordship and Manor of Gardiner's Island." In 1699, John Gardiner entertained Capt. William Kidd, the pirate, who hid much treasure on the island.

GARFIELD-BLAINE-CONKLING CONTROVERSY. Sen. Roscoe Conkling of New York quarreled with President Rutherford B. Hayes, who denied the senator's claim, under the custom of senatorial courtesy, to control all federal appointments in his state. When James A. Garfield, Hayes's spokesman, was nominated as a presidential candidate (1880), Conkling refused to support the ticket until assured that Garfield would consult him about appointments; when the president ignored senatorial courtesy and recognized the anti-Conkling wing by nominating William Henry Robertson for collector of the Port of New York, he suspected Secretary of State James G. Blaine's influence and denounced Garfield for a breach of faith. He succeeded for a time in blocking the appointment, but then resigned and vainly sought vindication by reelection. It was to avenge this "injustice to Conkling" that Charles J. Guiteau assassinated Garfield.

GARLAND CASE, 4 Wallace 333–39 (1867). In December 1860, Augustus Hill Garland took the oath required to practice law in the federal courts. In 1865, after the Civil War, Congress passed a law requiring attorneys to swear they had not borne arms voluntarily against the United States or accepted office under a government hostile to it; Garland had served in the Confederate congress, but not in the army. Having a pardon from President Andrew Johnson, Garland petitioned the Supreme Court to practice without taking the new oath. The Court held that the oath was substantially a bill of attainder and an ex post facto law and, so, unconstitutional; the president's pardon was held to be complete.

GARRISON MOB. In Boston, Oct. 14, 1835, a mob burst into the office of the *Liberator,* seeking George Thompson, British abolition emissary. Discovering William Lloyd Garrison, the editor of the antislavery *Liberator,* the mob hustled him along the streets to the city hall, nearly killing him.

GARY (Ind.). An important steel-producing city with a population of 151,953, in 1980; Gary is the third largest city in Indiana. It was founded in 1906, when the United States Steel Corporation decided to construct its largest steel mill in an entirely new city, and was named for Elbert Gary, the executive who promoted the plan. An artificial harbor was built facing Lake Michigan; one branch of the Calumet River was diverted; sand dunes on the site were flattened and the sand used to fill in the swampy land. The city was considered the most modern industrial town in the world; its steel mill was the largest in the world for over thirty years. The "Gary Plan" for schools was considered an important innovation: it involved alternating periods of play with study and making the school a community center. Gary was also a pioneer community in religious cooperation: in the 1920's a number of different religious groups used the same facilities for church-related school and social activities.

GAS, NATURAL, INDUSTRY. *See* **Natural Gas Industry.**

GAS IN WARFARE. *See* **Chemical Warfare.**

GASOLINE TAXES. The first gasoline taxes came into existence independently in three states in 1919: Oregon, Colorado, and New Mexico. Those who wanted to use highways paid for them, and the amount was nominal at first. Collected from wholesalers at very small cost to governments, the tax soon grew. By 1930, when all states had gasoline taxes, revenues amounted to $500 million annually and

854,000 miles of surfaced highways had been built for the 2.7 million motor vehicles registered in the United States. Beginning in 1932 the federal government levied an excise on gasoline, but not until 1956 was the connection of the tax to highways made explicit, when the Highway Trust Fund was created. In the mid-1970's, using the tax to control the price of gasoline appeared to be an attractive method of cutting consumption for conservation purposes; pressure mounted to use gas tax monies for nonhighway purposes, particularly for mass transit.

***GASPÉE,* BURNING OF THE** (June 9, 1772). In March 1772, H.M.S. *Gaspée* arrived in Narragansett Bay, R.I., to attack the problem of widespread smuggling, and proceeded to stop even small market boats. On June 9 the *Gaspée* ran ashore on Namquit (now Gaspée) Point in Warwick, R.I. An angry group met in Providence and plotted to burn the ship. John Brown, a leading Providence merchant, supplied eight boats; the men armed themselves and with muffled oars proceeded down the river, boarded the *Gaspée* without resistance; bound and put the crew on shore, and set the *Gaspée* on fire. A proclamation was issued to apprehend the participants in the raid, and although they were widely known in Providence, no substantial evidence was obtained and no one was brought to trial.

GASTONIA RIOTS (1929). Soon after Fred E. Beal, of the National Textile Workers Union, arrived in Gastonia, N.C., to organize textile mill workers, a strike was called to secure union recognition. On June 7, the Gastonia chief of police, O. F. Aderholt, was killed while attempting to disband a strikers' meeting, and in the fighting that followed seven strikers were reported killed. Beal and six other men were convicted of murdering Aderholt; they were released on bail, and all fled to Russia.

GATLING GUN. The most famous of multiple-barrel rapid-fire arms, patented Nov. 4, 1862, by Richard Jordan Gatling. Adopted in 1866, its first conspicuous use was in the siege of Santiago, Cuba (1898), by which time it was being superseded by the machine gun. The barrels, six to ten in number, were placed in a circular frame that was made to revolve by means of a crank, each barrel in turn being automatically loaded and fired; a rate of 400 shots a minute was attained.

GAUGERS, TOWN. Officials in colonial New England, chosen annually by the general court to gauge or measure all vessels used for any sale commodity.

GAUGES, RAILROAD, STANDARDIZATION OF. *See* **Railroads.**

"GAUNTLET, RUNNING THE." When a captive warrior was brought to an Iroquois village, the women and children, armed with sticks, formed two lines between which the prisoner was required to run; if he survived the ordeal, he was often permitted to live. The *Jesuit Relations* cite the custom in 1647 as common to the Iroquois and the Abnaki but do not use the term "running the gauntlet"; the term originated in Europe as "gantlope" (1646), a form of punishment in which one ran between rows of men armed with belts or sticks, and later (1661) appeared as "gauntlet."

GELPCKE* V. *DUBUQUE, 1 Wallace 175 (1864). The supreme court of Iowa, after declaring constitutional the statute authorizing the city of Dubuque to issue bonds for funds with which to buy railroad stock, reversed itself. The city attempted to escape payment on grounds that the bonds were unauthorized. The U.S. Supreme Court held that the state law, as interpreted by the state supreme court at the time the bonds were issued, governed the obligation of the contract, an obligation protected by the U.S. Constitution from subsequent impairment by a legislative act or judicial decision.

GENERAL ACCOUNTING OFFICE. *See* **Federal Agencies.**

GENERAL AGREEMENT ON TARIFFS AND TRADE. *See* **Reciprocal Trade Agreements.**

***GENERAL ARMSTRONG*.** Within the space of a few hours on Sept. 26, 1814, during the War of 1812, the U.S. privateer *General Armstrong* and a British squadron arrived in Faial, the Azores. British longboats approached the *General Armstrong;* they were warned to stand away and were then fired on. The American consul requested support of the port authorities, but the *General Armstrong* was destroyed by the British. The United States believed Portugal negligent in its duty as a neutral and pressed a claim for damages, which was submitted to Napoleon III for arbitration. The award was in favor of Portugal, for the Americans had opened fire before requesting assistance.

GENERAL COURT, COLONIAL. The Massachusetts Bay colony charter gave full powers of governing, correcting, punishing, and ruling to a body known as the general court, consisting of the governor, eighteen assistants, and the freemen of the company. The assistants voted themselves the power of British magistrates. The charter provided for four meetings of the general court each year, at which additional freemen were admitted, rules for governing the province adopted, taxes levied, fines assessed, and undesirable immigrants ordered returned to England. The large meeting came eventually to exercise mainly legislative powers, but under the first charter some judicial business was transacted.

The other New England colonies followed the Massachusetts practice. Plymouth called the members of its smaller body "assistants"; Connecticut and New Haven used the term "magistrates"; all used the term "general court" for a meeting of the governor, the assistants, or magistrates, and the freemen or their representatives.

GENERAL ELECTRIC RESEARCH LABORATORY. One of the earliest American industrial laboratories for basic research, established in 1900 in Schenectady, N.Y., under the auspices of the General Electric Company. Its first director, Willis R. Whitney, a chemist, gathered about him an able group including W. D. Coolidge, who succeeded Whitney as director in 1932, and Irving Langmuir, who was to win the Nobel Prize for chemistry in 1932. The early successful researches gave General Electric a powerful position in the lamp industry in the early 20th century and encouraged the establishment of similar laboratories elsewhere in American industry. By 1975 the research laboratory had a staff of 1,800, including 600 professionals, and was only one of many laboratories within General Electric.

GENERAL ORDER NO. 38 (Apr. 13, 1863). Issued by Union Gen. Ambrose E. Burnside, commander of the Department of the Ohio, it forbade expressing sympathy for the Confederacy. Clement L. Vallandigham, the Ohio Copperhead leader, denounced it in a speech at Mount Vernon, Ohio, on May 1; he was arrested May 5, tried by military commission, and banished beyond the Union lines (*see* Vallandigham Incident).

GENERAL ORDER NO. 100. *See* **Civil War General Order No. 100.**

GENERAL SERVICES ADMINISTRATION. *See* **Federal Agencies.**

GENERAL STAFF, ARMY. *See* **Army, United States.**

GENERAL TIME CONVENTION. *See* **American Railway Association.**

GENERAL WELFARE CLAUSE. Article I, Section 8, of the U.S. Constitution grants to Congress the "Power To lay and collect Taxes, Duties, Imposts and Excises, to pay the Debts and provide for the common Defence and general Welfare of the United States." There was a long-standing dispute about whether the welfare clause had a content independent of the other enumerated powers, Alexander Hamilton holding that it did and James Madison holding that it did not. Congress, preferring the Hamiltonian version, has used tax money for subsidies and "internal improvements." It was not until the depression of the 1930's that the Supreme Court ruled on the meaning of the clause in a case of any significance. In *United States* v. *Butler* (1936), Justice Owen J. Roberts regarded Madison's view as rendering the clause "mere tautology," and concluded that the general welfare power was limited only by the rest of the taxing and spending clause, not by the rest of Section 8, which lists the substantive powers of Congress. The general welfare clause is thus not susceptible to precise definition: it is, in effect, as broad as Congress wishes to make it. The choice of how to spend tax money "belongs to Congress, unless the choice is clearly wrong, a display of arbitrary power, not an exercise of judgment" (*Helvering* v. *Davis,* 301 U.S. 619 [1937]).

GENESEE ROAD. Built in 1797 to cross New York from Fort Schuyler to Geneva by authority of the New York legislature; it was financed by lotteries, supplemented by labor subscribed by the inhabitants along the route. It was open for 100 miles, was 64 feet wide, and bridged through the low country with logs and gravel; it was made a turnpike in 1800 and became a part of the Mohawk route from Albany to the West after the War of 1812.

GENETICS. Named in 1906 by William Bateson, it then included the fields of heredity, variation, and evolution; it has since come to encompass the cytological and biochemical aspects of heredity. The major developments in 20th-century genetics, largely developed in the United States, include the chromosome theory of heredity, the theory of the gene, the chemical basis of heredity, the double-helix model of the gene, the genetic control of protein synthesis, the genetic code, and the regulation of gene action.

The theory relating chromosome behavior during sex cell formation to Mendel's laws of heredity was developed by Walter Sutton and E. B. Wilson at Columbia University beginning in 1902. In 1910–20 the Drosophila Group at Columbia—T. H. Morgan and his students A. H. Sturtevant, H. J. Muller, and C. B. Bridges—collected experimental evidence using fruit flies (*Drosophila melanogaster*) and published (1915) *The Mechanism of Mendelian Heredity,* which rapidly won acceptance for the chromosome theory. Muller demonstrated that genes are stable, mutating infrequently; that they control all aspects of metabolism and morphology; and that life itself has its origins in the gene's ability to reproduce its errors or mutations. In 1926 at the University of Texas he was able to measure induced mutations with X rays. In 1940, G. W. Beadle and E. L. Tatum at Stanford University induced in the mold *Neurospora crassa* mutations that lacked biochemical products ordinarily synthesized by the mold. The genetic material itself was shown by O. Avery, C. MacLeod, and M. McCarty, at the Rockefeller Institute in 1944, to be deoxyribonucleic acid (DNA) in bacterial cells. In 1952, Alfred D. Hershey and Martha Chase, at the Cold Spring Harbor Biological Station, showed that the life cycle of the bacteriophage virus could be carried out by DNA in the absence of the viral protein. In 1953 the mechanism by which genes replicate their variations was analyzed by J. D. Watson, an American, and F. H. C. Crick at the Cavendish Laboratory at Cambridge University with their double-helix model of DNA. Their associated genetic dogma proposed that the coded sequences in DNA were transcribed into a related molecular substance, ribonucleic acid (RNA), which was translated, or decoded, into proteins. Proof of the dogma was completed in the early 1960's, especially through the experiments initiated at the National Institutes of Health by M. Nirenberg.

Concurrent with the growth of genetics as a pure and applied science was the unsuccessful development of the American eugenics movement (*see* Genetics, Applied). Human genetics has developed, largely since the mid-1950's, as a basic science independent of the earlier eugenics movement; it includes chromosome analysis of birth defects, and prenatal diagnosis of fetal defects in chromosome number, as well as of a small number of metabolic disorders.

GENETICS, APPLIED. A commonsense movement emerged in the late 19th century to protect America from obvious familial perpetuation of social liabilities, specifically criminality and pauperism. The most famous document of this movement was Richard L. Dugdale's account of the Jukes family (1874), almost all of whom were dangerous or dependent. Following the rediscovery of Mendelian theory at the turn of the century, a vigorous eugenics movement (largely inspired from England) sprang up to try to improve national heredity. The American Breeders Association (1903) provided the organizational expression of the eugenics movement. Charles B. Davenport, a distinguished experimental biologist, led the movement from the well-financed Eugenics Record Office at Cold Spring Harbor, N.Y., of which he was director (1910–34). Feeblemindedness became the object of reform of the eugenicists, many of whom began to define heredity in terms of middle-class values and racial strains; becoming identified with nativist and anti-immigration campaigns in the 1910's and 1920's, they were discredited. Nevertheless a number of state legislatures passed laws permitting the sterilization of certain defective persons.

Hermann J. Muller's discovery (1926) that genes could be altered by external application of radiation was soon utilized by agriculturists. In the post–World War II era the possibilities for applying knowledge of genetics took on a new dimension with discovery of the chemical processes involved in heredity, but it was only privately that scientists discussed a new genetic engineering in which chemical changes in traits would be possible. In 1963 the debate broke into the open. Progress continued, and by the mid-1970's a number of biochemists had turned away from particular lines of inquiry for fear that the public might in some way make improper use of their research into controlling inheritance.

GENÊT MISSION. Citizen Edmond Charles Édouard Genêt, designated by the Girondists as minister from France to the United States (Nov. 19, 1792), landed at Charleston, S.C., on Apr. 8, 1793. He became a factor in the conflict between Alexander Hamilton and Thomas Jefferson, the latter his friend. Even Jefferson was alienated, however, by Genêt's violation of U.S. neutrality by outfitting privateers to be used against Spain and his handling of the *Little Sarah,* an interned privateer, which in defiance of a formal pledge of neutrality had been permitted to go to sea; Genêt had proceeded on the philosophy that he was the minister of a people to a people, not of a government to a government. The administration demanded his recall but permitted him unofficial residence.

GENEVA ACCORDS OF 1954. A series of agreements reached at a conference held at Geneva, Switzerland (May 8–July 21, 1954) intended to settle the first Indochina War (1946–54), between France and the Vietnamese Communist forces led by Ho Chi Minh. The conference had been called by the Soviet Union, Great Britain, the United States, and France, and included the People's Republic of China, the Democratic Republic of Vietnam (Vietminh), and the Associated States of Vietnam, Laos, and Cambodia, which were still within the French Union. Great Britain and the Soviet Union served as cochairmen. The result was four separate documents: cease-fire agreements between the French and Vietminh for Vietnam, Laos, and Cambodia, and a "final declaration" to which all participants except the State of Vietnam (South Vietnam) and the United States expressed either tacit or verbal assent.

The cease-fire agreement for Vietnam temporarily divided that country into two zones, with a provisional demarcation line, bordered on either side by a demilitarized area, at approximately the seventeenth parallel; within 300 days French Union forces were to withdraw to the south of this line, and the Vietminh to the north of it. In each zone civil administration, pending general elections, was to be "in the hands of the party whose forces [were] regrouped there." Until movements of troops were completed, civilians in either zone were to be free to move permanently to the other zone. No new foreign military personnel or weapons were to be introduced into either zone; no new military bases could be constructed, and neither zone could participate in military alliances with foreign governments. The International Control Commission, made up of representatives from India, Canada, and Poland, was to supervise implementation of the cease-fire.

The cease-fire agreements for Laos and Cambodia provided for the withdrawal of French Union and Vietminh forces from both of these countries, although the French were to be allowed to maintain a small force in Laos for the purpose of training the Laotian national army. The Khmer Issarak, Cambodian allies of the Vietminh, were to be demobilized. The Pathet Lao, Laotian allies of the Vietminh, were to regroup in the provinces of Phong Saly and Sam Neua, in northern and northwestern Laos. The International Control Commission was to supervise implementation of the cease-fire in both countries. The governments of Laos and Cambodia pledged themselves not to join any military alliances inconsistent with the cease-fire agreements or the United Nations Charter and not to accept foreign military aid except for the purpose of defense.

GENEVA CONFERENCES. In the 20th century the United States participated in several diplomatic conferences held at Geneva, Switzerland. The first major one was a naval disarmament conference (*see* Geneva Three-Power Naval Conference), called by President Calvin Coolidge in 1927. In 1932–34 there was a general disarmament conference called by the League of Nations and attended by fifty-eight other nations; it concentrated on land armaments. The United States proposed the abolition of all offensive armaments and, when this was rejected, countered with a proposal for a 30 percent reduction; Germany, Italy, and the Soviet Union welcomed the plan, but France, concerned about Germany's increasing power, rejected it. Germany withdrew from the league in October 1933.

In 1947 an international tariff conference prepared a draft charter for a proposed international trade organization and produced a General Agreement on Trade and Tariffs, signed by twenty-three nations, which resulted in tariff reductions on many items. In 1954 an international conference tried to reach a settlement on the problems of Korea and Indochina (*see* Geneva Accords of 1954).

In July 1955 a summit conference was held in which the principal participants were the United States, Great Britain, France, and the Soviet Union. It was notable for President Dwight Eisenhower's proposal of an "open skies" inspection plan that would have allowed Americans and Russians to conduct aerial reconnaissance over each other's territory. The Soviet Union countered with a proposal for the mutual withdrawal of foreign forces stationed in Europe. No substantive agreements came out of the conference, but it offered some hope that the tensions of the cold war might be easing. In May 1961 a fourteen-nation conference convened at Geneva in an attempt to resolve the conflict in Laos between the government and the forces of the pro-Communist Pathet Lao; the negotiations were influenced by the decision of President John F. Kennedy and Premier Khrushchev to declare their support for a neutral and independent Laos. After prolonged discussions the conferees agreed (July 1962) to the establishment of a neutral coalition government in Laos.

The United States has also participated in a series of conferences on the international control of nuclear weapons, held intermittently since 1958, which helped to prepare the way for the Nuclear Test Ban Treaty (1963), the Nuclear Nonproliferation Treaty (1968), and the Treaty on the Limitation of Strategic Armaments (1972).

GENEVA CONVENTIONS. A series of international agreements drafted in Geneva, Switzerland, for the amelioration of the treatment of the sick and wounded, in particular, but also of all prisoners, in land and sea warfare. The first Geneva Convention (1864), ratified by the United States, most other American countries, and twelve European nations, covered only field armies. An 1868 convention, while not ratified, expanded the earlier agreement to include naval warfare. Another conference was held in 1906, at which the conventions were revised; these were then adopted by the Hague Peace Conference of 1907. In 1929 the conventions, signed by forty-seven nations, were widened to improve the lot of prisoners of war. The convention of 1949 was ratified by sixty-one countries, including the United States. It covered the amelioration of conditions of the wounded and sick in the armed forces, including those in the field and those shipwrecked at sea; the treatment of prisoners of war; and, in response to Nazi atrocities in World War II, the treatment and legal status of noncombatants in wartime.

GENEVA THREE-POWER NAVAL CONFERENCE (1927). President Calvin Coolidge invited Great Britain, Japan, France, and Italy to a conference at Geneva, Switzerland, to impose a limit on the tonnage of cruisers, destroyers, and submarines. Great Britain and Japan accepted the invitation; France and Italy declined. The negotiations failed, partly because of the U.S. insistence on parity in tonnage with Great Britain. The U.S. policy of freedom of the seas also clashed with the possible status of Great Britain as a belligerent in a war to fulfill obligations under the covenant of the League of Nations. The collapse of the conference strengthened the agitation of the advocates of a big U.S. navy.

GENIUS OF UNIVERSAL EMANCIPATION. An abolition periodical, established by Benjamin Lundy at Mount Pleasant, Ohio, in January 1821. Later that year it was moved to Jonesboro, Tenn., where it was published until 1824; thereafter it was issued from Baltimore (1824–30), Washington, D.C. (1830–34), Philadelphia (1834–36), and Hennepin, Ill. (1838–39). Publication, frequently irregular, ceased after Lundy's death.

GENIZARO. Non-Pueblo Indians who lived somewhat in the Spanish style in 18th-century New Mexico. Many had been captives among the Plains Indians and then ransomed or taken by the Spaniards; they were servants, became Christianized, and learned the Spanish language. Some were settled in a special section of Santa Fe, and others separately in villages located where they would bear the brunt of initial attacks by Apache, Ute, and Comanche. As auxiliary soldiers, they became known as genizaros, a term that derives from a Spanish translation of the Turkish word *yenicheri* (in English, "janissary"), referring to Turkish infantry recruited from compulsory converts and conscripts taken from among Christian subjects.

"GENTLEMEN'S AGREEMENT." In diplomatic relations between countries, an informal arrangement by which two countries agree to a particular action without making a regular written treaty, based on the idea that one gentleman's word is enough to satisfy another. The most famous such agreement was that reached between the United States and Japan in 1907. President Theodore Roosevelt agreed to see to it that Japanese residents already in the United States would receive good treatment in exchange for a promise that the Japanese government would prevent Japanese laborers from coming to the United States.

GEOGRAPHER'S LINE. Surveyed by Thomas Hutchins, geographer of the United States, according to a plan in the Ordinance of 1785. It was to begin at the point at which the Pennsylvania boundary intersected the Ohio River and was to run due west forty-two miles. The line is located at 40° 38′ 2″ north latitude, but the inaccuracies of the survey (begun 1785–86) caused it to deviate a mile to the north at its western end. Every six miles, at right angles to the line, the meridians marking the boundaries of the Seven Ranges were drawn, while parallel to it, at six-mile intervals, east-west lines were drawn to complete the township boundaries.

GEOLOGICAL SURVEY, UNITED STATES. Established as a bureau of the Department of the Interior by act of Congress (1879) primarily to help in the discovery and exploitation of mineral and mineral-fuel deposits, initially for the western mining industry. Over a fifty-year period, some sixty geologists made extraordinary contributions to economic geology. In 1905 the bureau's Waldemar Lindgren and several colleagues founded a journal, *Economic Geology,* to carry American knowledge and theory all over the world. By 1921, bureau petrologists had communicated the optical properties of hundreds of minerals, and in 1924, bureau chemists published an important volume on changes and reactions in rock masses, *Data of Geochemistry.*

In 1882 a program was launched to make a national map, but this goal remains on the distant horizon, as the demand for maps of larger scale and greater accuracy has diverted funds from the general project. In 1907–08 a water resources branch was founded to administer surface and groundwater studies; a land classification board was established; and maps of the national forests were published. During the first two decades of the 20th century research was intensified in coal, oil, and gas; the bureau sought to determine the geological conditions favorable to phosphate and potash deposits; and beginning in 1913, Congress appropriated money to encourage the discovery of potash. Under the Mineral Leasing Act of 1920 the Geological Survey administered the prospecting and leasing of the promising public lands in all these energy and nonenergy resources. During World War I the bureau lent most of its topographic staff to the army and turned to the search for strategic mineral reserves; during World War II it was particularly successful in finding bauxite, used in making aluminum. In 1956 the Geological Survey concluded the search for uranium on the Colorado plateau. Abroad, the military geology branch provided the geological facts necessary to select sites for U.S. forces of occupation and to design and construct offensive and defensive installations.

The Geological Survey of the mid-1970's periodically reviewed the nation's mineral wealth; it had been in the Antarctic since 1954; it had collaborated with the Woods Hole Oceanographic Institution since 1962 to investigate the continental shelf and slope of the Atlantic coast; and it was mapping the moon. In 1973 the executive branch of the U.S. government moved other federal groups dealing with seismology and solid earth physics into the Geological Survey's National Center for Earthquake Research, established in 1965 at Menlo Park, Calif.

GEOLOGICAL SURVEYS, STATE. From 1824 until about 1860, state geological surveys contributed significantly to the development of economic and intellectual life, and were closely related to the transportation revolution. Construction engineers were often hired as state geologists, and vice versa.

The movement for state geological surveys began in North Carolina: Denison Olmsted, science professor, was appointed to prosecute a survey in 1824; Elisha Mitchell inherited the job in 1826 and finished the survey in 1828. South Carolina had Lardner Vanuxem examine the state's minerals and strata in 1825–1826. Tennessee (1831–50), Maryland (1833–42), Virginia (1835–42), and the other southern states established more comprehensive surveys. The Massachusetts survey (1830–33) was connected with an attempt to map the state accurately; Edward Hitchcock, its geologist, persuaded the legislature to include botany and zoology, making the survey one of natural history as well as geology. New York and Pennsylvania organized and financed important surveys beginning in 1836. Nearly every state had a geological survey done or in progress by the beginning of the Civil War.

State surveys led to the creation of the American Association for the Advancement of Science (1848), which grew from a meeting of the state geologists in 1840 to share field results. They contributed also to the development of geological theory; they were a significant source of employment for American scientists before the rise of universities, a focus for high-level research of both practical and theoretical benefit, and a training school analogous to a modern graduate school.

After the Civil War state geological surveys came to be eclipsed by other organizations. By the end of the 19th century, state surveys were directed toward two goals that occasionally conflicted: to assist entrepreneurs in exploiting mineral resources and to promote conservation.

GEOPHYSICAL EXPLORATION. For 19th-century America, geophysics was rather an instrumental component of geographic surveys than a conceptual framework for geologic interpretation; after Darwin this pattern was incorporated into an evolutionary paradigm that supplied the theoretical context for over a century. Concern with applying physical theories and techniques gradually created an informal alliance between three scientific groups. Planetary astronomy addressed such problems as the formation, age, and structure of the earth; "dynamical" geology attempted to explain earth processes in terms of mechanics and physical laws; and mining engineering provided technical training in metallurgy, mathematics, and physics. Many of the instruments of geophysics and many of the explorations that used them stemmed from high-level prospecting, especially for oil.

In the exploration of the American West, Grove Karl Gilbert framed quantitative geologic observations into rational systems of natural laws organized on the principle of dynamic equilibrium. Clarence E. Dutton conceived the idea of isostasy, or the gravitational equilibrium of the earth's crust. Samuel F. Emmons, Clarence King, and George F. Becker applied geochemical and geophysical analysis to the problems of orogeny and igneous ore formation. Becker explicitly attempted mathematical and mechanical models to describe ore genesis and the distribution of stress in the earth's crust; he was also instrumental in the establishment of the Carnegie Institution's Geophysical Laboratory. Geophysics advanced in the context of a symbiosis of field exploration and laboratory investigation. Explanations developed for glacial epochs best epitomized the status of the science: attempts to relate glacial movements to astrophysical cycles provided a common ground for geology, geophysics, astronomy, and meteorology, but the results were rarely integrated successfully. In developing the planetesimal hypothesis in 1904, Thomas C. Chamberlin preserved a naturalistic understanding of earth geology, while F. R. Moulton supplied the mathematical physics. Geophysics remained more an analytic tool than a synthetic science.

After World War II, with new instruments and techniques developed for mining and military purposes, with additional subjects (especially oceanography), and with a theoretical topic to organize its research (continental drift), geophysics developed both an identity and a distinctive exploring tradition, well exemplified by the International Geophysical Year (IGY), planned for 1957 and 1958 but extended to 1959. Although aborted in 1963, Project Mohole, to drill into the interior of the earth, was superseded by other oceanic drill projects, especially the Joint Oceanographic Institutes Deep Earth Sampling Program (JOIDES), begun in 1964. The International Upper Mantle Project (1968–72) formed a bridge between IGY and research under the multinational Geodynamics Project (1974–79), which proposed to discover the force behind crustal movements.

GEORGE, FORT. On the Canadian side of the Niagara River at its entrance into Lake Ontario; captured by the Americans May 27, 1813, as part of the plan to capture York (now Toronto). At the same time, the Americans secured control of Lake Ontario and occupied British Fort Erie, remaining in possession of the entire western shore until the failure of the expedition against Montreal and the evacuation of Fort George in December.

***GEORGE WASHINGTON*.** Arriving at Algiers in 1800 with the annual tribute paid to the dey of Algiers to buy immunity from pirates, this American ship was ordered to carry gifts to the sultan of Turkey. As his ship and crew were at the mercy of the dey, Capt. William Bainbridge obeyed. President Thomas Jefferson approved Bainbridge's conduct but issued orders for defensive and offensive measures against the dey's forces to prevent future humiliations.

GEORGIA. Youngest of the original colonies, Georgia was founded to erect a buffer against the Spaniards in Florida and the French in Louisiana; to produce silks and other special raw materials; to rehabilitate the unfortunate debtors of London; and to offer a refuge for persecuted Protestants. The charter (1732) provided for a board of trustees to govern the colony for twenty-one years, after which control reverted to the crown. The colony comprised that territory between the Savannah and Altamaha rivers and lines drawn due west from their headwaters to the Pacific. The first colonists (1733) settled Savannah. Opposition by Spain led to the War of Jenkins' Ear (1739–44). Not until the crown assumed control did the colony begin to flourish. Georgia was slow to join the Revolution because of gratitude to England for large grants of money and fear of attack by the king's forces in Florida and by Creek and Cherokee on the west and north, but did join in time to be represented in the Second Continental Congress. In 1778 the British seized Savannah; within the next few months the state was almost completely subjugated. The next year royal government was restored. Defeat elsewhere forced the British to evacuate Savannah in 1782.

Georgia was the first southern state to ratify the federal Constitution (by unanimous vote, Jan. 2, 1788); however, until 1838 there were quarrels with the federal government involving the territorial rights of the Creek and Cherokee and Georgia's boundaries. In the Georgia Compact, the state accepted the Chattahoochee River as its western boundary land the federal government promised to remove the Indians (*see Cherokee Nation* v. *Georgia*). Following removal of the Indians (1838), Georgia for a time was the greatest cotton-producing region in the world.

Georgia seceded from the Union on Jan. 19, 1861, but was almost free from invasion until 1864, when Gen. William Tecumseh Sherman made his devastating march through Georgia and left bitter feelings. Reconstructed with the other Confederate states, Georgia was first readmitted to the Union in 1868; expulsion of Afro-American members of the Georgia legislature led to a second Reconstruction phase, after which the state was readmitted to the Union, July 15, 1870.

After the removal of federal troops (1871) a group of conservative Democrats regained control; Joseph E. Brown, John B. Gordon, and Alfred H. Colquitt—the Bourbon triumvirate—dominated state politics until 1890. In the 1890's the threat of splitting the white vote to permit blacks and their Republican allies to hold the balance of power provided an effective argument against the Populists and made white supremacy analogous to Democratic control. Leaders of both parties supported a registration law of 1908, which practically eliminated the black voter and prostrated the Republicans. The Populists declined rapidly after 1900, but Thomas E. Watson was able to dictate the course of state politics for almost two decades afterward.

The two main features of the political system after 1917 were legislative apportionment, giving political control to conservative rural voters, and the county unit rule to which it was tied, both voided by U.S. courts in 1962. Following the elimination of the white primary (1945), there was a rapid increase in the number of black voters, most of whom became Democrats; black officeholders steadily increased after 1950. Georgia voted Republican for the first time in its history in the presidential election of 1964.

Economic recovery was slow following Reconstruction. Until World War II, Georgia's industries were largely engaged in primary processing, particularly in lumber and textiles. Cotton began to lose its hegemony under the New Deal, and after the middle of the 20th century, livestock, grain, poultry, and forest products became dominant in the state's agriculture, as mechanization increased and landholdings grew in size. Many new industries appeared after 1945.

***GEORGIA*.** A Confederate cruiser purchased in Scotland (March 1863) by Matthew F. Maury, Confederate agent. It cruised successfully for seven months, capturing or destroying nine vessels worth $406,000. After eluding all Union cruisers, it was sold at Liverpool on June 1, 1864.

GEORGIA, PURITAN MIGRATION TO. Descendants of Puritans who had arrived in Massachusetts in 1630 and who two generations later (1695) had left for South Carolina secured a grant of 32,350 acres in the Midway District of coastal Georgia and settled (1752) at Dorchester, the name they had given to their previous settlements. In 1758 they founded Sunbury and developed it into an important port. About 350 whites came, bringing with them 1,500 slaves.

GEORGIA, SOUTHERN BOUNDARY OF. According to Georgia's colonial charter, the Altamaha River was its southern boundary, but in 1763 the boundary was extended southward to the St. Marys River and to a straight line joining the source of the river with the confluence of the Flint and Chattahoochee rivers. The same boundary was agreed to by Spain (then owning Florida) in Pinckney's Treaty of 1795. Five years later acting U.S. commissioner, Andrew Ellicott, with the Spanish commissioner, fixed the two points to be joined by the straight line (*see* Southern Boundary, Survey of) and erected a mound near where he considered the source of the St. Marys to be. By 1830 Georgia had rejected Ellicott's mound as the true head of the St. Marys, claiming a point a dozen miles to the south; at issue were 2,500 square miles. Finally, a line was surveyed in 1859, using Ellicott's points; it was accepted in 1861 by Florida and in 1866 by Georgia.

GEORGIA, SPANISH MISSIONS IN. Established first along the inland passage; the Jesuits started the work (1569) but were soon succeeded by Franciscans. Seven missions were founded, and in 1612 the Atlantic coast became the province of Santa Helena. Friars also visited central Georgia, and Spaniards were in regular communication with Christian Indians within present South Carolina. In 1632 a mission was established at Apalache, and in 1681 one was established on the Chattahoochee at Sábacola. Attacks by Indians, slave traders, and Caribbean pirates compelled the removal of the missions south below the St. Marys River in 1686. In 1702, Gov. James Moore of South Carolina led a drive against them, seized three friars, and captured many Indians. The following year he marched against the Apalache missions; two friars were killed, Christian Indians were tortured, and hundreds were carried off to be sold to West Indian planters, effectively ending the Georgia missions.

GEORGIA, WAYNE'S OPERATIONS IN (1782). After the surrender of Gen. Charles Cornwallis at Yorktown (October 1781), Gen. Anthony Wayne was sent south to drive the British into Savannah and capture them. Crossing the Savannah River on Jan. 12 and making his headquarters at Ebenezer, Wayne carried out various expeditions against outlying British forces; a band of Creek seeking to enter the city was cut to pieces, and a force of British regulars was routed on the Ogeechee Road. Peace having been voted by Parliament, the British surrendered Savannah to Wayne on July 12.

GEORGIA COMPACT (Apr. 24, 1802). This provided for the cession of Georgia's western lands on several conditions, chiefly that the United States would pay Georgia $1.25 million out of the first net proceeds of the land sales; validate Georgian, British, and Spanish land grants; assume the Yazoo claims; and extinguish the Indian title to land in Georgia (*see Cherokee Nation* v. *Georgia*).

GEORGIA LAND LOTTERY SYSTEM. Georgia abandoned the headright method of disposing of its public land and adopted the lottery system in a series of acts (1803–31) that set aside additional tracts for distribution. In general, all Georgian men twenty-one years of age, widows, and orphans were eligible; service in the Revolution and in other stated wars entitled the veteran to an additional draw or to some other advantage. The land was divided into lots, generally of 202.5 acres, and the lucky drawer was required to pay a fee of from $15 to $20.

GEORGIA-MISSISSIPPI COMPANY. One of four companies to which land was granted in 1795 in the second Yazoo sales; its tract lay between the Mississippi and Tombigbee rivers and embraced about 12 million acres, for which it was charged $155,000. In January 1796 it sold its holdings to Massachusetts speculators, who organized the New England Mississippi Company. This company became the chief contender with Congress for a settlement of the dispute of ownership (*see* Yazoo Fraud).

GEORGIANA. Name chosen (in honor of the king of England) by the Company of Military Adventurers for a colony it proposed to establish on the Mississippi, below the Ohio, after the close of the French and Indian War (1763). Under Gen. Phineas Lyman of Connecticut, the colony was to be settled mainly by former soldiers; Lyman repeatedly petitioned the British government, but his only reward was a land grant near Natchez in 1770. In 1774 he led a few hundred families, chiefly from Connecticut and Massachusetts, to the Natchez region, but because of the British policy of leaving the lands along the Mississippi as Indian territory (*see* Proclamation of 1763), his settlers secured only squatters' rights to their lands.

GEORGIA PLATFORM. Resolutions written by Charles J. Jenkins and adopted December 1850 by a convention held in Milledgeville, Ga., regarding the Compromise of 1850. They accepted what had been done, but warned that further encroachments on the rights of the South would lead to the disruption of the Union.

GEORGIA RAILROAD. *See* **Railroads, Sketches: Western and Atlantic Railroad.**

***GEORGIA* V. *STANTON*,** 6 Wallace 50 (1867). A Supreme Court case initiated by Gov. Charles J. Jenkins for the state of Georgia to restrain Edwin Stanton, secretary of war; Ulysses Grant, general of the army; and John Pope, commander of the military district, from enforcing the Reconstruction Acts of Congress of 1867, alleging that the acts would overthrow the existing constitutional government of the state. The Court ruled that the defendants represented the executive authority of the government and to grant the petition would place the Court in the position of passing judgment on political questions.

GERMAINE GIRL CAPTIVES. Four children captured by the Cheyenne. Two were recaptured in Texas on Nov. 8, 1874. Gen. Nelson A. Miles demanded surrender of the other two sisters and the return of the tribe to their reservation, or annihilation. The order was obeyed.

GERMAN-AMERICAN BUND. Founded (1932) as Friends of the New Germany, to indoctrinate people of German descent living abroad. Under Fritz Kuhn, a naturalized American, the Bund gained notoriety (1936–39) through its use of uniformed storm troopers, special training camps, and blatant racist propaganda. Membership estimates vary from 6,000 to 25,000. The movement collapsed when Kuhn was convicted (1939) of embezzling Bund funds.

GERMAN-AMERICAN DEBT AGREEMENT. By the Treaty of Berlin (Aug. 25, 1921) Germany accepted responsibility for the costs of the U.S. army of occupation and for adjudicated claims of American citizens for damages against Germany ($120 million, plus interest at 5 percent). In the German-American Debt Funding Agreement of 1930 the occupation costs were fixed at $247,865,645, payment of which, and also of the percentage of awards to U.S. citizens that still remained unpaid by the War Settlements Act of 1928, was effected by delivery to the U.S. government of two sets of long-term bonds, noninterest bearing. On the first series Germany suspended payment in 1932 after paying in annual installments a total of $65,998,512.13; on the second series Germany suspended payment in 1935.

GERMAN COAST. *See* **Côte des Allemands.**

GERMAN FLATS. Meadowlands in New York south of the Mohawk River, opposite the present village of Herkimer, granted for settlement to the Palatines as a protection against French attack (probably in 1723–24). In 1757 the settlement was attacked by the French and Indians and 200 persons killed or captured. In September 1778, German Flats was laid waste for ten miles along the river.

GERMAN IMMIGRATION. *See* **Immigration.**

GERMAN MERCENARIES (known as Hessians). The troops hired by Great Britain from several German princes to fight against the rebelling American colonies. In the course of the revolutionary war a total of 29,875 such German officers and men were sent to America; they constituted about one-third of all the land forces fighting for the king in North America. These auxiliaries fought under three successive commanders: Leopold Philip von Heister, Baron Wilhelm von Knyphausen, and Friedrich Wilhelm von Lossberg—all Hessians. Usually they operated as brigades, regiments, or corps in conjunction with British troops and under British commanders.

GERMANNA (Va.). The oldest white settlement in Orange County, named by Alexander Spotswood because of the Germans located there in 1714 and later to work his mines.

GERMANTOWN (Pa.). Founded (Oct. 24, 1683) by German Quakers and Mennonites led by Francis Daniel Pastorius, agent for the Frankfort Land Company, which purchased from William Penn 25,000 acres six miles from Philadelphia. Germantown (also German Town or Germanopolis) never became large, because it was a base for the distribution of the Germans into the interior.

GERMANTOWN, BATTLE OF (Oct. 4, 1777). Gen. William Howe disposed his main force around Germantown, Pa., while Gen. Charles Cornwallis's division occupied Philadelphia. With a poorly trained force, Gen. George Washington planned to converge at dawn on Germantown, drive the British army back on the Schuylkill River, and force its surrender. The night march of Oct. 3–4 was beset with delays, and at dawn a dense fog prevailed. The right wing struck an advance post of the British and drove it back to the mansion of the Chew family; a detachment was left to besiege them and the rest pressed on. The left wing was slow to reach the scene, but victory seemed assured when Gen. Adam Stephen, of the left wing, coming up behind Gen. Anthony Wayne of the right in the fog, mistook the latter for the enemy and fired. Wayne's men, beset on both sides, fell back in confusion. The Americans continued to press the attack and then fell back. Cornwallis, hearing the firing, rushed two battalions to the field. The Americans retreated in good order, bringing off all their cannon as well as some captured British guns. Washington's daring and strategy deeply impressed Europe and helped gain the aid of France.

GERMANY, AIR BATTLE OF. On the eve of World War II the German Air Force (GAF) was the most powerful in the world, but it was designed primarily for the direct support of ground armies. Air superiority was made the formal objective for both the British Royal Air Force (RAF) and U.S. Army Air Forces (USAAF) at the Casablanca Conference (January 1943) and accounts for the USAAF early emphasis on bombing the German aircraft and ball-bearing industries. During 1943, USAAF bombers operating over Germany beyond the reach of escort fighters suffered severe losses; in 1944, long-range escort fighters began to accompany them all the way to their targets. The GAF could not make effective use of its growing number of aircraft, because of the loss of experienced GAF pilots, and sharp reductions in the availability of aviation gasoline beginning in May 1944. In late 1944, USAAF bombers began to concentrate on synthetic-oil producing plants and on the transportation network; the GAF, hopelessly outnumbered and undergoing unceasing attack by day and night, had lost the battle.

GERMANY, AMERICAN OCCUPATION OF. Begun when troops of the U.S. First Army crossed the German border (Sept. 11, 1944), the American occupation of Germany came into full force with Germany's surrender (May 8, 1945). On June 5, Germany was partitioned into four occupation zones—American, British, French, and Russian; Berlin, in the Soviet zone, was also divided. Gen. Dwight D. Eisenhower became U.S. military governor in Germany. Responsibility for governmental activities in the American-occupied areas was passed to the military government detachments and agencies, which carried on the work of the troops and reestablished the civil administration. On Sept. 21, 1949, the authority of the U.S. military governor was transferred to John J. McCloy, first U.S. high commissioner for Germany, marking the end of military government; U.S. forces continued to occupy Germany until May 5, 1955, when High Commissioner James B. Conant relinquished occupation powers.

GERONIMO'S CAMPAIGNS. *See* **Apache Wars.**

GERRYMANDER. A term first used during Elbridge Gerry's second term as governor of Massachusetts, when a bill (Feb. 11, 1812) redistricted the state to give the Jeffersonian Republicans an advantage in the election of state senators; it derived from a caricature representing a strangely shaped Republican district as a salamander, which quickly became "gerrymander." The purpose of partisan gerrymandering is to strengthen one party by concentrating the opposing party's voters into only a few districts. The purpose of racial gerrymandering is to limit the number of districts in which the unfavored group is dominant. The U.S. Supreme Court since 1964 has mandated that districts must be essentially equal in population; it has outlawed racial gerrymandering, but has yet to limit partisan gerrymandering.

GETTYSBURG, BATTLE OF (July 1–3, 1863). Confederate Gen. James J. Pettigrew's North Carolina brigade, attempting to raid Gettysburg (June 30), reported to Gen. Robert E. Lee that it had encountered Union cavalry. Lee sent Gen. A. P. Hill's Third Corps toward the town. On July 1, near Willoughby Run, Hill was repulsed; but the Confederate Second Corps of Gen. Richard S. Ewell, marching southward, drove the Union forces to Cemetery Hill, south of the town. Lee ordered up Gen. James Longstreet's corps, then the rear guard, and advanced Hill to Seminary Ridge. On July 2 Union Gen. George G. Meade had his Second, Third, and Fifth Corps on Cemetery Ridge, his Twelfth Corps on Culp's Hill, and his Eleventh Corps in support of the battered First Corps on Cemetery Hill. The Sixth Corps was in general reserve. When Longstreet attacked in the late afternoon, his only material gain was the capture of a good artillery position. Ewell easily captured Culp's Hill; one of his divisions almost reached Cemetery Hill but had to fall back for lack of support. Lee felt his one hope of victory was to break the Union center by a direct assault on Cemetery Ridge; he chose Gen. George E. Pickett's fresh division of the First Corps, Gen. Henry Heth's division of the Third Corps, and two brigades of Gen. William D. Pender's division of the Third. About 125 guns were placed to cover the advance. It was two o'clock on July 3 before Longstreet reluctantly ordered Pickett's charge against the front of the Second Corps, which failed. The only counterstroke, a cavalry attack on the Confederate right, was easily beaten off by Gen. J. E. B. Stuart's men. Back on Seminary Ridge with the survivors, Lee learned that Ewell had been able to accomplish nothing; retreat was the only course left. Left dead or wounded were 20,000 Confederate casualties. Meade had lost 23,000 men; his admirable defense had largely achieved the Union victory. The turning point in the Civil War, it marked the defeat of Lee's attempt to invade Pennsylvania and reach Washington.

GETTYSBURG ADDRESS (Nov. 19, 1863). Delivered by President Abraham Lincoln at the dedication of the national cemetery at Gettysburg, Pa. The address was not, as reported, written while Lincoln was traveling by train, but was completed in Washington, although Lincoln made minor changes at Gettysburg.

GHENT, TREATY OF (signed 1814). Negotiations leading to this treaty, which effected the end of the War of 1812, were begun on June 26, 1812, when the American government made preliminary overtures; on Sept. 21, the Russian chancellor proffered a mediation, accepted at Washington, D.C. (Mar. 11, 1813), but rejected at London. The British foreign secretary, Robert Stewart, Viscount Castlereagh, on Nov. 4, 1813, offered a direct negotiation, which was accepted on Jan. 15, 1814. Negotiations took place at Ghent, Belgium. On Nov. 13 details were worked out which were mutually acceptable: American rights in the Newfoundland fisheries were acknowledged; both parties agreed to employ their best efforts to abolish the slave trade; and boundary commissions were provided for subsequent negotiations. A treaty was signed on Dec. 24, 1814. It reached the United States on Feb. 11, 1815, and was formally ratified on Feb. 17.

GHOST DANCE. A nativistic or messianic movement that originated among the Paiute Indians of Nevada. In 1869 a prophet named Wodziwob claimed that the world would end, thus eliminating white men, after which all dead Indians would return to rebuild the world; he instructed his followers to dance a circle dance and sing certain divinely revealed songs. The movement spread to the Indians of southern Oregon and northern California, but gradually subsided when the promised events did not occur. In 1889 there was a resurgence of the Ghost Dance when the Paiute messiah Wovoka, or Jack Wilson, claimed to have seen God, who directed him to announce to the Indians that by dancing and singing certain songs, they would cause the disappearance of the whites, restore their hunting grounds, and reunite with departed friends. The revitalized Ghost Dance gained its principal strength among tribes to the east and among some Plains tribes, including the Sioux, Cheyenne, Arapaho, and Comanche; it became a militant movement among former warriors confined to reservations. (*See also* Wounded Knee, Battle of.)

GI. American servicemen in World War II were referred to as "GI's," stemming from the expression "government issue" used for uniforms and other equipment supplied by the Army.

GIARD TRACT. One of three Spanish land claims in present Iowa. It is named for Basil Giard, who traded with the Indians on the west bank of the Mississippi River and did some farming as early as 1779; in 1800 he petitioned the Spanish government of Upper Louisiana for a grant of land and was given 5,760 acres. The conveyance was approved by Congress in 1816. The village of McGregor is on the site of the tract.

***GIBBONS* V. *OGDEN*,** 9 Wheaton 1 (1824). Robert R. Livingston and Robert Fulton had secured from the New York legislature a grant of monopoly rights for a period of years for the operation of steamboats on the waters of the state; the demands of the monopoly threatened strife over interstate commerce. *Gibbons* v. *Ogden* arose when Aaron Ogden, who held a license from the monopoly for operation between points in New York and New Jersey, sought an injunction in a New York court to eliminate competition from Thomas

Gibbons, who had a license from the federal government under an act of Congress regulating the coasting trade.

Chief Justice John Marshall wrote an opinion (characterized as having done more to knit the nation together than anything except war) interpreting the word "commerce" broadly, to include not only buying, selling, and barter but also other forms of intercourse, including navigation: commerce among the states could not stop at state lines; as against federal regulations of interstate commerce in the waters of a state, conflicting state regulations must fall; and the New York grant of monopoly rights was therefore unconstitutional insofar as it was in conflict with the act of Congress regulating the coasting trade.

GI BILL OF RIGHTS. The Servicemen's Readjustment Act (1944), the so-called GI Bill of Rights, provided government aid for veterans' hospitals and vocational rehabilitation; for the purchase by veterans of houses, farms, and businesses; and for four years of college education for veterans—$500 a year for tuition and books and a monthly allowance of $50 (later progressively raised). The act was extended to veterans of the Korean War. The Readjustment Benefits Act of 1966 gave similar rights to all veterans of service in the U.S. armed forces, whether during wartime or peacetime. (*See also* Bonuses, Military.)

GIBSON, FORT. Established in 1824 on the left bank of the Neosho River, near its confluence with the Arkansas in eastern Indian Territory. It was abandoned in 1857; reoccupied, 1863; abandoned, 1871; regarrisoned, 1872; and finally relinquished as a military reservation, 1891.

"GIBSON GIRL." Illustrator Charles Dana Gibson (1867–1944) portrayed active, wasp-waisted women at various occupations at the end of the nineteenth century. These illustrations caught the popular fancy, and the term "Gibson Girl" soon came to delineate a type of American woman.

GIBSON-LINN EPISODE. In the American Revolution, supplies of gunpowder and arms, formerly purchased in England and the West Indies, were cut off. Col. George Gibson, serving on the Virginia line, conceived the plan of attempting to procure a supply of powder from New Orleans. Gibson, Lt. William Linn, and fifteen others, disguised as traders, arrived at New Orleans in August 1776. Oliver Pollock, an American trader, protected them from British spies; arranged an audience with the Spanish governor; and persuaded the governor to sell Gibson 10,000 pounds of powder. Linn set out with 9,000 pounds of the powder up the Mississippi River for Fort Pitt, Pa., and arrived early in May 1777; Gibson arrived at Philadelphia in October 1777 with the remaining powder.

GIDDINGS RESOLUTIONS (1842). A series of resolutions proposed by Ohio Whig congressman Joshua R. Giddings on Mar. 21–22 as a result of the *Creole* case and directed against slavery and the coastal trade in slaves. The resolutions angered Southern representatives. When a censuring resolution was adopted by a substantial House majority, he resigned from Congress on Mar. 23. A majority of more than 3,000 voters returned him to his seat in a special election in April.

GIDEON CASE. In *Powell* v. *Alabama* (1932), the U.S. Supreme Court held that a state prosecution of indigent defendants for a capital crime without effective appointment of defense counsel violated the due process clause of the Fourteenth Amendment to the U.S. Constitution; but in *Betts* v. *Brady* (1942) the Court declined to require the states to provide counsel in most noncapital cases. In 1962, Clarence Earl Gideon was prosecuted for burglary in a Florida state court; his request that counsel be appointed to defend him was denied. Gideon was convicted, but he insisted at his trial that "the U.S. Supreme Court says I am entitled to counsel." A year later, in *Gideon* v. *Wainwright* (372 U.S. 335), the Supreme Court agreed with him; overruling *Betts,* it held that at least in all felony cases "any person . . . too poor to hire a lawyer cannot be assured a fair trial unless counsel is provided for him." Many states quickly implemented the decision by establishing public defender systems.

GIDEON SOCIETY. In 1899, Samuel Eugene Hill, John H. Nicholson, and Will J. Knights founded the Gideons, an organization for Christian commercial travelers. A few years later the work of distributing Bibles was undertaken; by 1975 more than 10 million copies had been placed in hotels, hospitals, and similar institutions, in the United States and abroad.

GILA TRAIL. An early trade and emigrant route following the Gila River and its branches between Yuma, Ariz., and several points along the upper Rio Grande from Santa Fe to El Paso. It was followed by early Spanish travelers and by fur trappers. The Mormon Battalion marked a wagon road by way of Guadalupe Pass from the Rio Grande to Tucson, the Pima villages, and the lower Gila. The southern Gila routes were used by many migrating to California; the Southern Pacific Railway still follows them in part through Arizona.

GILBERT ISLANDS. The capture of key positions in the Japanese-occupied Gilbert Islands (November 1943) was the first step in the American drive across the Central Pacific toward Japan. In charge of the operation was Adm. Chester W. Nimitz, commander in chief of the U.S. Pacific Fleet and Pacific Ocean Areas. After a two-hour preliminary bombardment, army troops captured Butaritari Island in Makin Atoll on the morning of Nov. 23. Betio Island in Tarawa Atoll was heavily fortified and bitterly defended; between the morning of Nov. 20 and the afternoon of Nov. 23 the Second Marine Division suffered more than 3,300 casualties in one of the bloodiest battles of the Pacific War.

GILBERT'S PATENT. In 1578, Sir Humphrey Gilbert was granted letters patent by Queen Elizabeth I to discover lands and plant colonies in America within a six-year period. Lands he discovered were to be held as a royal fief; one-fifth of all gold and silver was to be reserved to the crown; Gilbert was authorized to set up a government, grant lands, and make trade concessions; all laws and religious policies were to conform to English practice. In 1583, Gilbert's fleet reached Newfoundland. The colony failed and Gilbert was lost at sea. On Mar. 25, 1584, Gilbert's patent was renewed in the name of his half brother, Sir Walter Raleigh.

GILDED AGE. The period of currency inflation, widespread speculation, overexpansion of industry, loose business and political morals, and flashy manners that extended from the end of the Civil War in 1865 to the Panic of 1873. The title "Gilded Age" came from the novel published by Mark Twain and Charles Dudley Warner (1873).

GINSENG, AMERICAN (*Panax quinquefolium*). A plant growing in the Hudson Valley and elsewhere that resembled a root native to Korea and northern China, to which the Chinese imputed extraordinary properties. On Feb. 22, 1784, Robert Morris dispatched the *Empress of China* from New York with American ginseng for China; the voyage netted $30,000. The China trade in ginseng boomed, restricted only by the limited quantities available, and continued into the 20th century. Wisconsin is the principal producer.

GIRL SCOUTS OF THE UNITED STATES OF AMERICA. Founded on Mar. 12, 1912, by Juliette Gordon Low, of Savannah, Ga., who patterned the movement after the Girl Guides of England; chartered by special act of Congress on Mar. 16, 1950; member of the World Association of Girl Guides and Girl Scouts. Girls, in partnership with adult volunteers, share in activities and projects that encourage their active participation as individuals and citizens in their homes and communities. Emphasis is placed on the development of awareness, values, relating to others, and contributing to the betterment of society.

The U.S. Girl Scout organization is divided into six geographical regions, each with a branch office; national headquarters is in New York. Local Girl Scout councils (353 as of 1980) provide programs for four age levels—Brownie Girl Scouts, ages six through eight; Junior Girl Scouts, nine through eleven; Cadette Girl Scouts, twelve through fourteen; and Senior Girl Scouts, fourteen through seventeen. The national organization maintains four Girl Scout National Centers—Potomac, Md.; Savannah, Ga.; Briarcliff Manor, N.Y.; and Ten Sleep, Wyo.—for the use of Girl Scout traveling groups and for program and training activities.

GIST, TRAVELS AND JOURNALS OF. In 1750 the Ohio Company sent Christopher Gist, a surveyor and frontiersman, to explore the Ohio Valley. He left Wills Creek, the site of Cumberland, Md., crossed the Allegheny, and explored north of the Ohio as far as the Miami River. In March 1751 he crossed the Ohio at the Scioto and traveled in Kentucky, reaching his home on the Yadkin in May. From November 1751 to May 1752 he explored between the Monongahela and the Little Kanawha, east of the Ohio. His journals discuss the suitability of the western lands for colonization and throw light on Indians, fur traders, and the conflict between France and England for the Ohio Valley. Gist also kept a journal of an expedition in the West in 1753, when he went with George Washington to Fort Le Boeuf in Pennsylvania.

"GIVE ME LIBERTY OR GIVE ME DEATH!" In the Virginia Provincial Convention, Patrick Henry offered resolutions (Mar. 23, 1775) to organize the militia and put the colony on a footing of defense. When met with opposition, he is quoted as saying, "Is life so dear or peace so sweet as to be purchased at the price of chains and slavery? Forbid it, Almighty God! I know not what course others may take, but as for me, give me liberty or give me death!"

GLACIER NATIONAL PARK. Established in 1910 in the Rocky Mountains of northern Montana. Across the Canadian border is the much larger Wharton National Park; together, the two are known as the Wharton-Glacier International Peace Park. Glacier National Park straddles the continental divide. The park's 1 million acres include extensive areas for the preservation of wildlife.

GLASGOW, ACTION AT (Oct. 15, 1864). During Confederate Gen. Sterling Price's expedition into Missouri, Confederate forces captured the Union garrison at Glasgow. Army supplies were the objective.

GLASSBORO SUMMIT CONFERENCE (June 23–25, 1967). An impromptu "summit" held at Glassboro State College, N.J., between President Lyndon B. Johnson and Soviet Premier Aleksei N. Kosygin. It was held at the end of Kosygin's visit to the United Nations in New York to present Soviet views on the Middle East to the General Assembly. The summit had nebulous results.

GLASSMAKING. Glass is principally sand and silicon dioxide, with other compounds added as coloring agents. The raw materials are mixed as crushed solids, melted, and made into objects by manipulation of the molten glass. In the American colonies glass was first made into windows and containers at Jamestown, Va. (1608–09). In the 18th century there were three fairly successful glass houses, all run by German immigrants: Henry William Stiegel worked at Manheim, Pa., 1763–74; Caspar Wistar and his son Richard worked at Alloway, N.J., 1739–80; John Frederick Amelung operated the New Bremen Glass Manufactory near Frederick, Md., 1784–95. All these glasshouses made free-blown and expanded-blown molded glass. In the early 19th century two important developments occurred. The first was an improvement in the use of multipart metal molds that could be incised with designs, permitting the rapid blowing of objects of identical size and decoration. The technique—generically known as "blown three-mold" because most of the molds were in three parts—provided an alternative to the laborious wheel-cutting technique. The second advance was the perfecting of means for pressing glass in metallic molds. Developed either in the factories of Pittsburgh, Pa.; Boston, Mass.; or Sandwich, Mass., between 1823 and 1825, it revolutionized the glass-manufacturing process. With improvements in technology, lower prices made glass accessible to everyone.

Until the early 19th century, window glass was made by blowing a large sphere, attaching a solid punty on the opposite side from the blowpipe, cutting the sphere into two hemispheres, and then rotating each hemisphere to create flat, circular sheets. The cylinder method consisted of blowing a large cylinder of glass, allowing it to cool, scoring it down the middle, removing the ends, and reheating it so that could be opened to form a flat, rectangular sheet. This technique gained ascendancy in the 19th century and produced larger panes, which gradually led to a change in architectural styles. In the 20th century, glass technology developed a method by which plate glass is made either by pulling sheets up from a pool of glass or by casting it on molten tin.

In Europe and in America, glassmaking, which had been primarily a manual, family enterprise, had by the 1850's become a well-organized industry. European processes, furnaces, and machines were emulated and perfected by a number of American glass manufacturers, and new methods were introduced—notably by Michael Owens, whose Owens bottle machine (between 1899 and 1903) revolutionized the beverage industry. As the 20th century opened, scientific research, chemical analysis, and the development of new formulas enabled glass to fill new functions. Heat-resistant glasses, developed toward the end of the 19th century, were perfected and became basic household utensils. Electricity required a tremendous number of glass envelopes for light bulbs; in 1926, Corning Glass Works developed the ribbon machine, capable of producing up to 2,000 light bulbs a minute. The rise of the automobile led to mass-produced safety glasses that would cause minimum injury on breakage.

From an artistic standpoint, American glass manufacturing exerted a vast influence abroad, particularly through the contribution of Louis C. Tiffany. In the first half of the 20th century, the most influential factory was the Steuben Glass Company.

GLASS-STEAGALL ACT (Feb. 27, 1932). An emergency banking measure designed to permit groups of five member banks in difficulties and individual member banks with a capital not in excess of $5 million to borrow at the Federal Reserve banks on collateral not normally eligible for rediscount, at a rate 1 percent above the rate on normally eligible paper. Section 3 authorized the Federal Reserve Board, until Mar. 3, 1933 (later extended), to permit Federal Reserve banks to use U.S. government obligations, in addition to gold and eligible paper, as security for Federal Reserve notes. The Banking Act of 1933 is also sometimes known as the Glass-Steagall Act.

GLEBES. Lands set aside for the clergy by American colonists, in pursuance of English tradition, motivated in some measure by the belief that the presence of a minister would be an inducement to people to migrate to the new community.

GLENDALE, BATTLE OF. *See* **Frayser's Farm, Battle of.**

GLIDERS, MILITARY. A weapon system unique to World War II, first used by the Germans in 1940. The British and Americans implemented glider operations designed to land, in a small area, large numbers of fully armed troops ready for immediate combat, eliminating the time required to assemble paratroopers; gliders also made possible the delivery of vehicles and heavy weapons that could not be dropped by parachute. The largest Allied glider mission, part of Operation Market-Garden in September 1944, employed 2,596 gliders to secure a bridgehead across the Rhine at Arnhem.

***GLOBE, WASHINGTON*.** Successor to the *United States Telegraph* as "official organ" of Andrew Jackson's administration; first issued Dec. 7, 1830. Its editor was Francis Preston Blair. In 1845 it was replaced by the *Washington Union.*

GLORIETA, BATTLE OF (Mar. 28, 1862). On Mar. 27, a Confederate force, following the Santa Fe Trail, encountered a Union force in Apache Cañon and was defeated. The Union troops fell back to Pidgin's ranch, just east of Glorieta Pass. The next day, both sides having been reinforced, they fought the battle that proved the turning point for the Confederate cause in the Far West. The Union force finally fell back to Kosloski's ranch; the Confederates held the field, but a Union detachment had gained the Confederate rear and destroyed the baggage and supply train in Cañoncito. The Confederate survivors retreated to Santa Fe and down the Rio Grande.

GNADENHUTTEN (Ohio). A Delaware village on the Tuscarawas River (site of the present town), founded in 1772 by Christianized Indians and Moravian missionaries migrating from Pennsylvania. During the Revolution the pacifism of the Moravian Indians made them suspect to both sides, and in 1781, hostile Indians forced their removal to the Sandusky Valley. Parties of them returned for food during the ensuing winter, and in February 1782, warriors who had accompanied them attacked settlers in Washington County, Pa. Militiamen surrounded Gnadenhutten on Mar. 7, intending to destroy the town and take the unresisting Indians to Fort Pitt, Pa.; but when one of the Indian women was seen in the dress of a captured settler, the enraged frontiersmen voted to kill the entire band. The Indians made no resistance, and about a hundred men, women, and children were executed.

GNP. *See* **Gross National Product.**

***GODEY'S LADY'S BOOK*.** First published in Philadelphia (1830) by Louis Godey as the *Lady's Book.* In 1837, Godey bought the *Ladies Magazine* of Boston and made its editor, Sarah Josepha Hale, his literary editor; during the forty years of their association *Godey's* became one of the most influential periodicals in America in matters of fashions, etiquette, and home economics, with a monthly circulation of 150,000. In 1877 the magazine was moved to New York, where it expired in 1892.

GOEBEL AFFAIR. William Goebel was a northern Kentucky politician who became known as a friend of the common people. In 1899 he won the Democratic nomination for the governorship; after a hotly contested campaign, his Republican opponent, William S. Taylor, was declared the winner.

The election returns were contested, and mountaineers from the eastern counties went to Frankfort, the capital, in large numbers. On Jan. 30, 1900, Goebel was shot by an unidentified rifleman. The legislature declared him elected, and on Jan. 31, he was sworn in as governor. He died Feb. 3.

GOLD ACT (June 17, 1864). The depreciation of greenbacks was measured by the premium on gold, and speculators were blamed for the fluctuations in the premiums; this act therefore made it unlawful to buy or sell gold for future delivery or to buy or sell foreign exchange to be delivered after ten days. The result was such an increase in the fluctuation of the price of gold that the act was repealed on July 2, 1864.

GOLD BUGS. The free silverites' name for those in favor of the gold standard in the campaigns that culminated in 1896.

GOLD CERTIFICATES. *See* **Money.**

GOLD CLAUSE CASES. A joint resolution of Congress (June 5, 1933) abrogated the gold clause (which had provided for the payment of principal and interest in gold in existing governmental and private contracts) and made almost all kinds of money legal tender in the satisfaction of such obligations. As a result, four suits were brought, two against the government and two against railroad companies: one plaintiff was the holder of a Liberty bond; one, the holder of gold certificates; and two, the holders of railroad obligations.

The Supreme Court rendered a decision on Feb. 18, 1935. In the two cases involving private contracts (railroad bonds), the decision was against the plaintiffs: private contracts were held powerless to interfere with the constitutional right of the Congress "to coin money and regulate the value thereof." In the case of the Liberty bond, the Court declared the action of the government unconstitutional, but refused to grant the plaintiff damages, for he had neither shown nor attempted to show loss of buying power. With regard to gold certificates the Court decided against the plaintiff, pointing out that had he received gold dollars, he would have immediately had to turn them over to the government for other forms of currency under the law (*see* Gold Standard).

GOLD DEMOCRATS. Repudiating the radical free-silver platform of their presidential candidate, William Jennings Bryan, a group of Democrats organized the National Democratic party at Indianapolis, Ind., on Sept. 2–3, 1896, and nominated Sen. J. M. Palmer of Illinois on a conservative, gold platform. Many Gold Democrats either voted for Republican William McKinley or avoided voting, and Palmer polled only 134,635 votes.

GOLDEN GATE BRIDGE. Erected across the entrance of the harbor at San Francisco, Calif., at a cost of $35 million, by the Golden Gate Bridge and Highway District, created by the California legislature (1923, 1928). The central span is 4,200 feet long; the total length, including approaching viaducts, is 1.75 miles. Construction work began on Jan. 5, 1933, and the bridge was opened to traffic on May 28, 1937.

GOLDEN GATE INTERNATIONAL EXPOSITION (February–October 1939). Built on Treasure Island, a man-made island (430 acres) in the center of San Francisco Bay, it was dedicated to the glorification of western and Pacific achievements and to transportation and communications. There were 10,496,203 paid admissions. At the close of the fair there was $500,000 in cash in the treasury; claims against the corporation totaled $4.6 million.

GOLDEN HILL, BATTLE OF (Jan. 19, 1770). The Liberty Boys of New York City had for three years been at odds with the British soldiery. Three soldiers who were posting insulting placards were seized by several Liberty Boys. Others rushed to the rescue, and a street fight took place at Golden Hill (in the vicinity of William Street above Wall Street). Sixty soldiers charged with cutlass and bayonet; several citizens were wounded, and it is said that one died of his injuries. There was another sharp clash on the following day.

***GOLDEN HIND*.** Originally named the *Pelican,* the first English vessel to circumnavigate the globe sailed from Plymouth, England, on Dec. 13, 1577. It was renamed by its captain, Sir Francis Drake, in Magellan Strait. Sailing up the South American coast, it reached the San Francisco area, June 15, 1579; sailed round the Cape of Good Hope; and reached Plymouth on Sept. 26, 1580.

GOLD EXCHANGE. Organized in New York City in the autumn of 1862. Any respectable citizen could become a member by paying $100 a year to defray expenses, and 450 men became members. At first, gold was actually delivered. In 1863 the Treasury Department facilitated dealings by issuing gold certificates of deposit; when business increased, the Gold Exchange Bank was organized, and sales and purchases were cleared each day, payment of balances only being made. The gold exchange served a useful purpose until the United States resumed gold redemption at the beginning of 1879.

GOLD HOARDS, FEDERAL. In 1933, gold coin was recalled from circulation, and the Gold Reserve Act of 1934 required Federal Reserve banks to turn their gold holdings over to the Treasury Department in exchange for credits or a new noncirculating gold certificate. The safeguarding of the entire gold reserve thus fell to the federal government. The Fort Knox military reservation in Kentucky became the site for a gold depository in 1936.

GOLD IN CALIFORNIA. James W. Marshall discovered gold on Jan. 24, 1848, at the site of a sawmill he was building in partnership with Capt. John A. Sutter at Coloma, on the south fork of the American River about forty miles from Sacramento. Four days later, with several ounces of the metal, he rode to Sutter's Fort, at present Sacramento. Sutter and Marshall agreed to keep the discovery secret until the completion of pending business operations and pledged the others who knew of the find to silence. Nevertheless, the news was soon out, and the gold rush began.

GOLD MINES AND MINING. Gold mining in the United States began in the foothills of the Appalachian Mountains in North Carolina following the chance discovery of a nugget in 1799. Limited but continuous activity there and in Georgia after the opening of gold deposits in 1828–29 resulted in the production of an estimated $24.5 million in gold in the years before 1848. The first decade of California mining, 1848–58, saw some $550 million in gold extracted.

The early California mines were placer deposits of free, or pure, gold mixed with sand and gravel. The gold was recovered by agitating water and debris in a mining pan; the gold, being heavier, settled to the bottom of the pan. Refinements such as the rocker, sluice, tom, dredge, and hydraulic nozzle all washed the gold-bearing debris with water. The only chemical process used was mercury-gold amalgamation: separated from other debris, the amalgam can be heated, driving the mercury off as a vapor, leaving a residue of free gold. When placer deposits began to be exhausted, interest turned to lode mining, the mining of free gold in veins embedded in quartz or rock; this called for relatively complicated and expensive methods of crushing the ore, and early tools were soon replaced by steam-powered stamp mills. The Empire and the North Star mines at Grass Valley were California's most successful lode mines.

In 1859 the Comstock lode was discovered in Nevada. The year before, small placer deposits had been found near Cherry Creek in what was to become Colorado, touching off the Pikes Peak rush in the spring of 1859. In the next decade camps were opened in Idaho and Montana, and the Black Hills region of South Dakota experienced the same pattern after 1875. The Alaska fields were first mined in the 1880's, with later and richer discoveries in 1898 near Cape Nome and in 1902–03 in the Fairbanks region. Goldfield and Tonopah provided Nevada with a second rush in 1903–05.

As mines were extended farther and deeper, more extensive methods were required to extract the ore. The Comstock operations in Nevada in 1865–75 were especially noted for application of new techniques, such as the compressed-air drill and the diamond-studded rotary drill (borrowed from France) and the new explosives nitroglycerine and dynamite (from Sweden). One of the first successful chemical processes for separation of refractory ores was the cyanide process (1887), which involved the placing of finely crushed gold ores in a solution of potassium cyanide. This process and others such as chlorination and oil-flotation were available when the Cripple Creek fields of Colorado were opened in 1891, and the nation's richest mining district developed from the telluride ores of Cripple Creek. The new chemical processes also made possible the reworking of older mines to recover gold from low-grade ores, and the development of new areas in which low-grade ores existed, such as the San Juan region of Colorado.

Mine production reached its highest levels in the decade 1905–15, when an annual average of 4,513,480 fine ounces of gold was produced. In 1970 three states (South Dakota, Nevada, and Utah) mined 84 percent of the 1,743,000 fine ounces of gold produced in the United States.

GOLD PURCHASE PLAN. Formulated by President Franklin D. Roosevelt's financial adviser, George F. Warren, and sometimes referred to as the Warren Plan, it was put into operation Oct. 25, 1933, and continued until late January 1934. The Reconstruction Finance Corporation was authorized to buy gold newly mined in the United States and, if necessary, on the world markets, at prices to be determined after consultation with the president and the secretary of the treasury. The initial price of $31.36 per ounce was raised, at first daily, to $34.45 by Jan. 16, 1934. It remained there until the formal devaluation of Jan. 31 fixed a price of $35.

GOLD REPEAL JOINT RESOLUTION (June 5, 1933). A joint resolution of Congress which canceled the gold clauses in public and private debts that required the debtor to repay the creditor in gold dollars of the same weight and fineness as those borrowed.

GOLD RESERVE ACT (Jan. 30, 1934). At the request of President Franklin D. Roosevelt, Congress nationalized all gold by ordering the Federal Reserve banks to turn over their supply to the U.S. Treasury; in return such banks were to receive gold certificates to be used as reserves against deposits and Federal Reserve notes. The act also authorized the president to devalue the gold dollar so that it would have not more than 60 percent of its existing weight; on Jan. 31, 1934, the value of the gold dollar was fixed at 59.06 cents.

GOLD STANDARD. A monetary system in which the unit of value consists of the value of a fixed quantity of gold in a free gold market. U.S. experience with the gold standard began in the 1870's. In accordance with the Resumption Act of 1875, paper dollars became officially redeemable in gold on Jan. 2, 1879, but many banks had begun redemption by Dec. 17, 1878. Under the gold standard as it then operated, the unit of value was the gold dollar, which contained 23.22 grains of pure gold; an ounce of gold could be coined into $20.67, the "mint price" of gold. The Gold Standard Act of 1900 made legally definitive a system that had existed *de facto* since 1879, declaring that the gold dollar "shall be the standard unit of value, and all forms of money issued or coined by the United States shall be maintained at a parity of value with this standard." That meant that the value of every dollar of paper money; of silver, nickel, and copper coins; and of every dollar payable by bank check was equal to the value of 23.22 grains of pure gold coined into money. Anything therefore that affected the value of gold in the world's markets affected the value of the gold dollar.

While gold as a monetary standard during 1879–1933 was far from stable in value, it was more stable than silver, and its historical record was much better than that of paper money. After World War I not many nations could afford a gold coin standard; instead, they used the gold bullion standard (the smallest "coin" was a gold ingot worth, say $8,000) or the even more economical gold exchange standard. In the latter case the country would not redeem in its own gold coin or bullion but only in drafts on the central bank of some country on the gold coin or gold bullion standard with which its treasury "banked." As operated in the 1920's, this parasitic gold standard, preferentially dependent on the central banks of Great Britain, France, and the

United States, allowed credit expansion on the same reserves by two countries. In 1931 the gold standards of Austria, Germany, and Great Britain successively collapsed, the last dragging down several nations on the gold exchange standard with it.

In the United States the gold coin standard continued in full operation until March 1933 (except during the World War I embargo on gold exports, Sept. 10, 1917–June 9, 1919). Bank failures in late 1932 severely shook public confidence in the economy, and in February 1933 a frightened public began to hoard gold. On Mar. 6, 1933, President Roosevelt declared a nationwide bank moratorium for four days and forbade banks to pay out gold or to export it. On Apr. 5 the president ordered all gold coins and gold certificates in hoards over $100 turned in for other money; the government took in $300 million of gold coin and $470 million of gold certificates by May 10. On Apr. 20, Roosevelt imposed a permanent embargo on gold exports. By the Thomas Amendment to the Agricultural Adjustment Act of May 12, 1933, Congress gave Roosevelt power to reduce the gold content of the dollar as much as 50 percent. A joint resolution of Congress on June 5 abrogated the gold clauses to be found in many public and private obligations requiring the debtor to repay the creditor in gold dollars of the same weight and fineness as those borrowed. During autumn 1933 the Treasury bid up the price of gold under the Gold Purchase Plan and finally set it at $35 an ounce under the Gold Reserve Act of Jan. 30, 1934. This made the new gold dollar 13.71 grains of pure gold, although the act forbade the actual coinage of gold. The United States was now back on a gold standard (the free gold market was in London), but of a completely new kind: a "qualified gold-bullion standard" with only external, and not internal, convertibility. The $35-an-ounce price greatly overvalued gold, stimulating gold mining all over the world and causing gold to pour into the United States. U.S. holdings grew from $6.8 billion in January 1934 to $24.7 billion in September 1949.

After World War II a new international institution complemented the U.S. gold standard. The International Monetary Fund (IMF) went into effect in 1947. Each member nation was assigned a quota of gold and of its own currency to pay to the IMF and might, over a period of years, borrow up to double its quota from the IMF. Admittedly, under the IMF a nation might devalue its currency more easily than before. But a greater hazard lay in the fact that many nations kept part of their central bank reserves in dollars, which, being redeemable in gold, were regarded as being as good as gold. Possessing more dollars than they wanted and preferring gold, some nations—France in particular—demanded gold for dollars. American gold reserves fell from $23 billion in December 1947 to $15.5 billion in 1963. To reassure foreign creditors, Congress, on Feb. 18, 1965, removed the 25 percent gold certificate requirement against deposits in Federal Reserve banks, and on Mar. 18, 1968, it removed a similar requirement against Federal Reserve notes. Repeatedly the Treasury took steps to discourage foreign creditors from exercising their right to demand gold for dollars. By late 1967, American gold reserves were less than $12 billion. Meanwhile, sales of gold in London to hold down the price of gold on the free market there were becoming unbearably large. In March 1968 the Treasury abandoned them, and so did other nations, letting the free market price soar above the mint price of $35 an ounce. On Aug. 15, 1971, President Richard M. Nixon announced that the U.S. Treasury would no longer redeem dollars in gold for any foreign treasury or central bank.

GOLD STAR MOTHERS. An organization founded in 1928 by the mothers of men or women who had died in military service during wartime. It took its name from the service flags that were displayed by families and organizations to which soldiers or sailors belonged during the world wars: blue stars were used to denote men or women in the services; gold stars were for those who had died during wartime.

GOLD TELEGRAM OF PARKER. Sent to the Democratic National Convention at St. Louis, July 9, 1904, by Alton B. Parker, the presidential nominee, informing the convention that since the platform was silent on money, he desired to affirm his adherence to the gold standard so that the convention could nominate another candidate if it wanted to. Neither platform nor nominee was changed.

GOLF. The word "golf" is derived from the Dutch *kolf,* akin to the Germanic *Kolbe,* meaning "club." The game is historically Scottish. In the United States the number of players far surpasses that of any other game. It has been estimated that more than 12 million Americans play a minimum of ten rounds a year and that there are at least 8,000 golf courses. The first golf club to be founded in the United States was the South Carolina Golf Club, established in 1786 in Charleston. Its records stopped in 1812; it was reincorporated in 1969 at Sea Pines Plantation on Hilton Head. The oldest continuing golf club is the St. Andrews Golf Club, founded in 1888 in Yonkers, N.Y., relocated in nearby Mount Hope in 1897. Golf is governed by the U.S. Golf Association (USGA), established in 1894.

American golf first received international recognition for its quality in 1913 during the USGA's Open championship—open, that is, to both amateurs and professionals. (The first U.S. Open was held in 1894).

Americans began to dominate the game during the next decade, particularly in the persons of Robert T. ("Bobby") Jones, Jr., an amateur from Atlanta, Ga., and Walter Hagen, a professional from Detroit, Mich. During 1923–30, Jones won thirteen of the thirty-two men's championship tournaments sponsored by the USGA and the Royal and Ancient Golf Club (Scotland)—the Open and amateur tournaments held by each annually. Hagen won eleven national championships in 1914–29, five of them in tournaments of the U.S. Professional Golfers Association (founded 1916).

Jones founded (1934) the Masters Tournament, played annually at Augusta, Ga. An open competition, it soon came to be recognized as a major world tournament because of the prestige of its field. Among the many famous winners were Gene Sarazen, Sam Snead, Ben Hogan, Arnold Palmer, Gary Player, and Jack Nicklaus. By 1973, between them, Nicklaus and Player had won twenty-seven of the internationally recognized championships.

The USGA initiated its first Women's Amateur Championship in 1895 at the Meadowbrook Golf Club at Hempstead, L.I. In 1928, Glenna Collett (later Glenna Vare) won the first of her record six championships. In 1975 she was still recognized as America's greatest female amateur. In 1946 the USGA inaugurated an open championship for women; the first winner was Patty Berg, who went on to innumerable other titles. Mildred ("Babe") Didrikson Zaharias won two Open tournaments and one amateur but virtually dominated professional golf right up to her death at the age of forty-one.

GOLIAD, MASSACRE AT (Mar. 27, 1836). Col. James W. Fannin, Jr., of the Texan army, surrendered to the Mexicans his force of about 400 Anglo-Americans, near Goliad, Tex., as prisoners of war to be returned to the United States. Pursuant to a Mexican decree that foreigners taken on Mexican soil be treated as pirates, they were shot down one week after their surrender.

GONZALES, BATTLE OF (Oct. 2, 1835). First battle of the Texas Revolution, caused by the demand of the Mexican military commander at San Antonio that the people of Gonzales surrender a cannon. The demand was refused, whereupon a force of 100 men was sent to seize the gun; a band of Texas volunteers routed the force a few miles from Gonzales.

GOOD NEIGHBOR POLICY. In his first inaugural address (1933), President Franklin D. Roosevelt stated: "In the field of world policy I would dedicate this nation to the policy of the good neighbor—the neighbor who resolutely respects himself and, because he does so, respects the rights of others." U.S commitment to this policy and the spelling out of its practical meaning were tested and established through experience. The first action required was the cessation by the United States of a well-established practice of sending armed forces to Latin-American countries to maintain political stability or to protect the lives of U.S. citizens; the protocol on nonintervention at the 1936 Buenos Aires Conference of American States declared intervention "inadmissible . . . for whatever reason, in the internal or external affairs of any other of the Parties." By "intervention" Roosevelt meant the landing of U.S. armed forces, and neither he nor his successors violated the pledge made at Buenos Aires until the intervention in the Dominican Republic in 1965. A further renunciation was made, that of refusing to interpose or offer "advice" about domestic political developments in Latin-American and Caribbean countries.

The Good Neighbor policy aided the United States in securing the strong support of nearly all Latin-American countries during World War II. Following the war, successors of the Roosevelt administration followed different principles, so that the term of the Good Neighbor policy may best be regarded as spanning the years 1933–46.

GOODNIGHT-LOVING TRAIL. A cattle trail named for Charles Goodnight and Oliver Loving, who drove the first herd over this route in 1866. Starting near Fort Belknap, Tex., it ran southwest and west to the Horsehead crossing of the Pecos and then up the Pecos to Fort Sumner, N.Mex., where the cattle were sold to the U.S. government. An extension of the trail continued north to Denver and Cheyenne.

GORE. A small piece of land, generally triangular, lying between larger areas; in Maine and Vermont, and formerly in Massachusetts, a minor unorganized territorial division, usually irregular in shape and lying between two towns. The term has also been used for small areas that have been the subject of boundary disputes, and for long narrow strips of land cut off by bends in large rivers.

GORE-McLEMORE RESOLUTIONS (1916). In reaction to a German declaration that all armed enemy merchant vessels would be sunk without warning after Mar. 1, Representative Jeff McLemore of Texas introduced a resolution in Congress on Feb. 17 requesting the president to warn Americans not to travel on armed vessels. Senator Thomas P. Gore of Oklahoma introduced a resolution on Feb. 25 to deny passports to Americans seeking passage on armed belligerent vessels and demanded protection of American trade in noncontraband from the Allied restrictions. Under pressure from President Woodrow Wilson, who construed the resolutions as a test of his leadership, the Gore resolution was tabled.

GORGES' PROVINCE OF MAINE. Ferdinando Gorges, a member of the Council of New England, received as his portion of the territory the land lying between the Piscataqua River, and its tributary, the Newichawannock (the Salmon Falls), and the Kennebec River, and extending 120 miles inland. He received a charter in 1639. Gorges attempted to establish a detailed feudal regime. His difficulties were increased by the fact that grants of land had already been made by the council within the limits of his grant, leaving him in control of only Kittery, Agamenticus (York), and part of Wells.

The complete form of government authorized was never established. Gorges governed through his appointed councillors, who held the first general court of the province on June 25, 1640. The proprietor incorporated Agamenticus as a market and borough town in 1641 and as the city of Gorgeana in 1642. Gorges' own manor, Point Christian, and one at Ogunquit granted to Thomas Gorges, were the only manors set up. After the death of the proprietor in 1647, the province was neglected; in 1649 the inhabitants of the three towns formed a government under Edward Godfrey. In 1652, Massachusetts Bay Colony forcibly extended its jurisdiction over them. In March 1678 the Bay colony purchased Maine from the heirs, for £1,250. Maine became an integral part of the province of Massachusetts Bay under the charter of 1691, and Gorges' province became the county of York.

GORTONITES. Rhode Island disciples of Samuel Gorton, who in 1643 was imprisoned by the general court of Massachusetts Bay for blasphemy and then banished. His teaching, a species of Antinomian mysticism, attacked learning in the ministry; declared that every man was his own priest, that outward ordinances should be abolished, and that the believer became united with Christ and so partook of the perfection of God; and denied the existence of heaven and hell.

GOTHIC LINE. In June 1944, when the Germans gave up Rome to the Allies, Adolf Hitler ordered his troops in Italy to fight a delaying action north about 150 miles to a fortified zone in the Apennines, there to make a protracted defensive stand. This position, protecting the Po River valley, was the Gothic Line, a belt of fortifications 10–12 miles deep in naturally strong defensive terrain, about 200 miles long, roughly from Carrara to Pesaro. By August, 2,400 machine-gun posts, 500 gun and mortar positions, 120,000 meters of barbed wire, several Panther tank-gun turrets embedded in steel and concrete bases, and many miles of antitank ditches had been incorporated into the line. In April 1945 the Allies finally broke the Gothic Line. American troops entered the valley and took Bologna on Apr. 21. The German commander agreed to an unconditional surrender on Apr. 29.

"GOVERNMENT BY INJUNCTION." A phrase that gained currency during the Pullman Strike of 1894, it is attributed to Judge Murray F. Tuley of Chicago and was popularized by Gov. John P. Altgeld of Illinois, who wrote the words into the state Democratic platform of 1896 and again into the national party platform.

GOVERNMENT CORPORATIONS. Public enterprises characterized by a preponderance of public control; use of corporate organization (board of directors and general manager) for "business-type" purposes (where there is regular income from goods or services); and much independence from the traditional governmental supervision. Examples are the Tennessee Valley Authority, the Federal Deposit Insurance Corporation, the Export-Import Bank, and the U.S. Postal Service. The Government Corporation Control Act of 1945 reduced most federal corporations almost to the fiscal and personnel status of ordinary departments. State and local governments form corporate entities for many purposes, such as transportation, waterworks, and utilities.

GOVERNMENT NEWSPAPERS. Newspapers published in or near the national capital that benefited from being, in effect, the government printer before the Government Printing Office was established (1860). The earliest such newspaper was the *Gazette of the United States,* published in Philadelphia beginning in 1789. Government printing favors came and went with the changing administrations.

"GOVERNMENT OF THE PEOPLE, BY THE PEOPLE, FOR THE PEOPLE." The definition of democracy that President Abraham Lincoln incorporated in the concluding sentence of his Gettysburg Address, Nov. 19, 1863.

GOVERNMENT OWNERSHIP (sometimes called public ownership). The theory that land and natural resources belong to the whole people or to the ruler as representative of the people dates back to the beginnings of government. The doctrine of eminent domain, enshrined in state and federal constitutions, represents the idea that government may, with proper compensation, take privately owned land, buildings, or enterprises for public purposes. The economist Henry George and his followers advocated what was in effect public ownership of all land. Some Populists were strong advocates of expanded government ownership, and the Socialist movement encouraged it. Government ownership has taken various forms. Some enterprises may be administered as so-called regular government departments. Others may be public corporations (*see* Government Corporations).

GOVERNMENT PRINTING OFFICE. *See* **Government Publications.**

GOVERNMENT PUBLICATIONS. The documentation and interpretation of American history rely heavily on publications of the U.S. government. "Government authors" are agencies and departments, not individuals. Printing and distribution of government publications were at first undertaken by commercial publishers on a contract basis. The Government Printing Office (GPO), established within the legislative branch in 1860, has gradually come to monopolize this business; it issues the major publications of Congress; the departments, agencies, and independent establishments; and the Supreme Court. Dependence on commercial publishers continues on a small scale, as in the publication of rulings of U.S. district courts and courts of appeals. Under federal legislation, designated libraries in every state receive specified GPO publications free of charge.

GOVERNMENT REGULATION OF BUSINESS. *See* **Business, Public Control of.**

GOVERNMENT SPENDING. During the colonial era, government expenditures amounted to less than $1 per person annually in some colonies. Annual per capita federal expenditures in 1800 were $2 and remained at about that figure until 1860. In the 1860's defense, war debt interest, and veterans' benefits used most of the federal monies. State and local government expenditures were for internal improvements and education. From the Civil War to World War I, state and local spending doubled; federal spending was less than $30 per capita on the eve of World War I.

Federal expenditures per capita in 1971 were $2,700. Government spending (including trust funds, and state and local spending) has been an important economic factor since the 1930's and in the 1970's accounted for one-third of the U.S. gross national product (GNP). Most of the long-range growth in the government sector has come from social-welfare spending during the New Deal; the Fair Deal; and, more especially, in the administrations of Lyndon Johnson and Richard Nixon. A temporary inverse correlation exists between spending for the two world wars and spending for social welfare at the federal level.

GOVERNOR. Chief executive of the state governments. Colonial governors, and particularly royal governors, incurred such disfavor that when the first state constitutions were written, the powers granted the state governors were drastically curtailed. In 1917 a movement for state administrative reorganization began in Illinois and in the next decade gave the governor real administrative control over the departments and agencies of the government. The modern governor has great power and responsibility.

GOVERNORS, CONFERENCES OF. Formal organization of the National Governors' Conference began in 1908 as a result of an invitation by President Theodore Roosevelt to consider conservation needs. Two national meetings were held in 1910; since that time, except for 1917, they have been held annually. A bipartisan executive committee plans the agenda; meetings are held throughout the United States. Chairmanship of the conference alternates between Republican and Democratic governors. There are six standing committees: Executive Management and Fiscal Affairs; Human Resources; Crime Reduction and Public Safety; Natural Resources and Environmental Management; Rural and Urban Development; and Transportation, Commerce, and Technology. There are also five regional conferences: midwestern, southern, western, New England, and mid-Atlantic. In addition to the fifty states, the Virgin Islands, Guam, Puerto Rico, and Samoa attend the national conference.

GOVERNORS ISLAND (N.Y.). A small island near the southern tip of Manhattan. Called Nooten, or Nutten, Island by the Dutch, it was bought from the Indians by Wouter Van Twiller. In 1698 it became part of the military area of New York City and a rustic retreat for the colonial governors. The island was made a part of New York City in 1730; the first small fortification was placed on it in 1776. In 1800, New York State ceded it to the U.S. government, and during the next decade two forts, Castle William and Fort Columbus (renamed Fort Jay) were erected. In 1821 it became federal military headquarters for the New York area, and during the Civil War served as a military prison camp. In 1966 it became U.S. Coast Guard headquarters for the eastern area.

"GO WEST, YOUNG MAN, GO WEST." First used by John Babsone Lane Soule in the *Terre Haute* (Ind.) *Express* in 1851. It appealed to Horace Greeley, who wrote in an editorial in the *New York Tribune,* July 13, 1865, "Go West, young man, and grow up with the country." When the phrase gained popularity, Greeley printed Soule's article.

GRADUATION ACT (Aug. 3, 1854). Authorized a reduction in the price of government land that had been subject to sale for ten years or more; the previous price of $1.25 per acre was reduced to $1 for land that had been on sale for ten years and, through various graduations, to 12.5 cents per acre for land that had been on sale for thirty years.

GRAFTON* V. *UNITED STATES (1907). In this case the Supreme Court held that since both civil and military tribunals in the Philippines derived their authority from the U.S. government, an American soldier in the Philippines, after trial by court-martial, could not be brought before the civil courts for the same offense.

GRAIN, TRADE IN. *See* **"Pit."**

GRAIN FUTURES ACT (Sept. 21, 1922). Government control over commodity exchanges had been nullified by invalidation of an act of Aug. 24, 1921; omitting tax provisions, Congress reenacted similar regulations, which were upheld. The Grain Futures Administration assisted the secretary of agriculture in enforcement of the provision that all trading in grain futures must be at grain exchanges designated as contract markets submitting daily reports.

GRAND ARMY OF THE REPUBLIC (GAR). Founded by Benjamin F. Stephenson as an association for Union veterans of the Civil War. On Apr. 6, 1866, the first post was established at Decatur, Ill.; the first national encampment was held at Indianapolis on Nov. 20. The GAR quickly attained a preeminent place among veterans organizations, but its membership grew slowly. The peak was reached in 1890, with 409,489 members. At the last encampment (1949) only six members attended; the last member died in 1956.

Early in its history partisan purposes were forbidden, but for many years the organization was a powerful political force. Its unremitting efforts for benefits for veterans and their dependents led both major political parties to bid for its support. The GAR had auxiliary societies—the Woman's Relief Corps (organized on a national basis in 1883), the Ladies of the Grand Army of the Republic (1886), and the Sons of Union Veterans of the Civil War (1881)—which carry on the work begun by the GAR in the establishment and improvement of veterans facilities.

GRAND BANKS. A submerged (about 240 feet) tableland between Newfoundland, Canada, and deep water, reaching to the latitude of Boston and east for 500 miles. The meeting of Arctic current and Gulf Stream produces almost constant fog. By 1578, Spanish, Portuguese, French, Breton, and English ships were fishing there for cod, whales, and walruses; in the 1960's, 2 billion tons of cod were taken annually.

GRAND CANYON (Ariz.). A gorge of the Colorado River, 4–18 miles wide and in places more than a mile deep, winding some 280 miles from Marble Canyon, near the Utah line, to Grand Wash Cliffs, in northern Mohave County. The first description of the canyon by white men is to be found in Pedro de Castañeda's narrative of the Coronado expedition. The canyon was little known until Lt. Joseph C. Ives and Dr. J. S. Newberry visited the lower end in April 1858 and brought back the first geological description of the region. The Grand Canyon National Park, 673,575 acres, was created by Congress on Feb. 26, 1919. In 1932 an additional 198,280 acres containing Toroweap Point of the canyon was set aside as the Grand Canyon National Monument.

GRAND COULEE DAM. *See* **Hydroelectric Power.**

GRANDFATHER CLAUSE. A device in southern state constitutions to circumvent the suffrage requirements of the Fifteenth Amendment: exemption from property-owning, tax-paying, or educational requirements in state suffrage laws was granted to those who had had the right to vote on Jan. 1, 1867 (thus excluding blacks), and to their lineal descendants. In 1915 the Supreme Court declared the grandfather clause unconstitutional (*see Guinn and Beal* v. *United States*).

GRAND GULF, BATTLE AT (Apr. 29, 1863). To secure a landing for Gen. Ulysses S. Grant's army below Vicksburg, Miss., was the main objective of Adm. David D. Porter's daylight bombardment of Grand Gulf, Miss. The ironclads proved too fragile to cope with shore batteries, and Grant had to land his men farther down.

GRAND OHIO COMPANY. Formed in 1769 by Samuel Wharton and Thomas Walpole to purchase 2.4 million acres of the land ceded to the British by the Six Nations at the Treaty of Fort Stanwix in 1768. The company was reorganized and its scheme expanded to include the establishment of a new colony on the Ohio River to be known as Pittsylvania (later changed to Vandalia). After the Revolution the company was reorganized in America as the Vandalia Company.

GRAND PORTAGE (Minn.). Name given by voyageurs to the nine miles between Lake Superior and navigable waters on the Pigeon River. About 1780 the name came to be applied to the British North West Company post at the lake end of the portage; at the height of its prosperity (about 1795) it had a stockade, sixteen buildings, and schooner connection with Sault Ste. Marie. About 1797 a fort was built at Grand Portage by a rival, the X Y Company, which coalesced with the larger group in 1804. In that year the transfer of activities from Grand Portage to Fort William, Ontario, was completed as a result of Jay's Treaty of 1794.

GRAND PRAIRIE. A geographical division of north Texas extending about 200 miles south from the Red River, two to three counties in width. Its period of settlement and county organization was 1846–58. It was the first important cattle-grazing region of Texas and an early prairie farming area.

GRAND RAPIDS (Mich.). Settled first as a Baptist Indian mission (1826) on the site of an old Indian village and a fur-trading post of the American Fur Company. Many settlers were Dutch immigrants, some of whom began the manufacture of furniture before the Civil War. The city developed into the principal center of American furniture manufacture; it has remained the styling center for many furniture companies. Other industries include auto parts manufacture and other metal-working plants. It was Michigan's second-largest city in 1980, with a population of 181,843.

GRAND RIVER MASSACRE. *See* **Messiah War.**

GRAND TRUNK WESTERN. *See* **Railroads, Sketches of Principal Lines.**

GRANGER CASES. Between 1869 and 1874 the legislatures of Illinois, Iowa, Wisconsin, and Minnesota passed statutes, known generally as the Granger laws, for the regulation of railroads and warehouses within their respective borders. Efforts at enforcement led to a large number of lawsuits, a series of which, the so-called Granger Cases, were decided by the U.S. Supreme Court in March 1877. At issue was the right of a state to regulate, on the ground that the business concerned was public in nature, a corporation that was privately owned and managed. Attorneys for the railroads argued that any such assumption of power on the part of the state amounted to a deprivation of property without due process of law. The Court held that regulation, even to the setting of maximum rates, was within the constitutional right of the states. The case most frequently cited in this connection is *Munn* v. *Illinois.* In 1886 the Court modified the Granger decisions, restricting state regulation to strictly intrastate business.

GRANGER MOVEMENT. In 1867, Oliver Hudson Kelley founded a farmers' lodge, the Patrons of Husbandry, to educate farmers in the newer methods of agriculture; each local unit was called a Grange. When the panic of 1873 broke, there were Granges in every state but four, but the center of Granger activity remained in the grain-growing region of the upper Mississippi Valley. By then the Grange had become far more political than educational and, assisted by a host of unaffiliated farmers clubs, was in the thick of the fight for state regulation of railroads and elevators.

The grievances that drove the farmers to revolt grew out of their almost complete dependence on outside markets for the disposal of their produce and on corporation-owned elevators and railroads for its handling. Elevators, often owned by the railroads, charged high prices for their services, weighed and graded grain without supervision, and used their influence with the railroads to ensure that cars were not available to farmers who sought to evade elevator service.

At Granger lodge meetings and picnics the farmers exhorted one another to nominate and elect to office only those who shared their views and to form independent, reform, or antimonopoly parties through which to carry on the fight. So many farmers made Independence Day 1873 an occasion for airing these views that the celebration was long remembered as the Farmers' Fourth of July. Victories at the polls led to the passage of a series of so-called Granger laws for the regulation of railroads and warehouses (*see* Granger Cases).

Hardly less important than the political activities of the Granges were their business ventures. Numerous cooperative elevators, creameries, and general stores were founded, although most of these establishments failed. Other experiments included buying through purchasing agents or through dealers who quoted special prices to Grangers, patronizing mail-order houses, and manufacturing farm machinery. The last-mentioned undertaking resulted in serious financial reverses and had much to do with the sudden decline that, beginning about 1876, brought the movement to an end.

GRAN QUIVIRA. Quivira was the name used by Francisco Vásquez de Coronado for the Indian villages he sought in the plains of Kansas in 1541, and was probably the native name used by the Wichita and the Pawnee. Gran Quivira was later used to designate the ruins of a Piro village in New Mexico and its Spanish mission, built in 1629, abandoned in 1670, and now a national monument.

GRANT'S HILL, BATTLE OF (Sept. 14, 1758). While Ligonier, the advance post of Gen. John Forbes's expedition, was harried by small parties of Indians, Col. Henry Bouquet ordered a counterdemonstration against the Indian encampments near Fort Duquesne. Maj. James Grant marched with 842 men, taking position on the hill in Pittsburgh that now bears his name. Advancing at daybreak, the detachment was overwhelmed as French and Indians attacked from front and flanks. The British defeat was bloody and inglorious.

GRANTS-IN-AID. Federal grants-in-aid are grants of money to state and local governments. The first large grants (1862) were the gifts of public lands to benefit new state land-grant universities. The constitutionality of grants was not seriously questioned until the cases of *Massachusetts* v. *Mellon* and *Frothingham* v. *Mellon* (1923): the Supreme Court found that grants were not a violation of the Constitution and that states were not coerced by a grant they could refuse. Broad use of grants began in the 1930's, with New Deal legislation. After World War II the number of grants multiplied until it reached an estimated maximum of 1,500, some of which were highly specific; since then, there has been some consolidation of grants in the public health field. Grants-in-aid are sometimes made for fixed amounts and called closed-end grants; there are also special-project grants, awarded only to successful applicants. In addition, the federal government makes open-end grants, promising to match all approved state expenditures, especially in the field of public assistance, in which expenditures vary considerably. Few grants are unconditional. In the mid-1970's federal grants to states and localities approximated $50 billion a year, and state grants to local units amounted to $45 billion a year. (*See also* Revenue Sharing.)

GRANVILLE GRANT. When, in 1728, the Carolina proprietors sold their rights to the crown, one of the eight proprietors, Lord John Carteret, later Earl Granville, refused to sell. Yielding governmental rights, he received a grant from the king of one-eighth of the original proprietorship, located between the Virginia line and 35°34′ north latitude and extending westward to the Mississippi River; it included approximately one-half the territory of the royal colony of North Carolina and most of its population and wealth. The estate was confiscated by the patriot government of North Carolina during the Revolution. The efforts of the Granvilles to recover this property after the war ended in an adverse decision by the U.S. Supreme Court (1817).

GRASSHOPPERS. These insects fall roughly into two groups: migratory (locusts) and nonmigratory. Every species has done damage in one place or another in America, the locusts in sparsely settled regions and local grasshopper species in the more settled regions. Especially serious attacks occurred in New England in 1743, 1749, 1754, and 1756. The California missions suffered heavily in the 1820's, as did farm areas of Missouri and Minnesota. Grasshoppers appeared in the Great Basin and on the Great Plains in 1855 and at intervals thereafter, with great plagues in 1874–76. The hopperdozer, a device for catching and killing insects, made its first recorded appearance in 1878, but may have been used as early as 1858. It consisted of a shallow pan on skids with a large screen behind the pan, which farmers pulled across fields; grasshoppers jumped up, hit the screen, and fell into the pan, which was filled with kerosene or poison. Control by poison bran was first used in 1885 and remained the chief effective control until the discovery of the hydrocarbon insecticides, such as chlordane, in the mid-1940's. In the 20th century the worst grasshopper attack was the plague of 1936, which destroyed crops and forage throughout the Midwest, the South, and especially the Great Plains. The menace of grasshoppers declined during World War II, and thereafter the use of new insecticides has kept grasshoppers in check.

GRASS ROOTS CONFERENCE (June 1935). A meeting at Springfield, Ill., of about 5,000 representatives of the Republican party in the midwestern states, held to consider ways to revitalize the party and rebuild its shattered organization, in preparation for the presidential campaign of 1936. It adopted an extended declaration of principles—the preservation of the Constitution, the maintenance of the separation of powers, the mutual independence of the federal and state governments, and the "political and economic system as established by our forefathers."

GRATTAN INCIDENT (Aug. 19, 1854). Lt. John L. Grattan, with twenty-nine men and an interpreter, marched from Fort Laramie, Wyo., to the Sioux villages eight miles east, to apprehend a Miniconjou who had attacked a Mormon emigrant near the post. When peaceful measures failed, the lieutenant determined to use force; in the ensuing engagement the Indians annihilated his detachment. (*See also* Sioux Wars.)

GREAT AMERICAN DESERT. The myth of a great desert between the Rocky Mountains and the Missouri and Mississippi rivers, uninhabitable by all but the Indians, originated in the reports of early travelers, such as Zebulon M. Pike. This notion formed the basis of the government's policy of removing Indian tribes from east of the Mississippi to the country between that line and the Rocky Mountains. As the Indian removal policy was being inaugurated, the destruction of the myth of the Great American Desert was begun by the Sante Fe traders. During the 1840's the existence of a desert was disproved.

GREAT AWAKENING. The period of religious fervor that began with the arrival in Philadelphia of English evangelist George Whitefield, in 1739. It spread as Whitefield traveled through the colonies preaching a revivalistic message and ended roughly in 1744 as ministerial and popular enthusiasm gave way to reinvigorated institutionalized religion. It was foreshadowed by Solomon Stoddard in western Massachusetts in the late 17th century, Theodorus Frelinghuysen and Gilbert Tennent in the Delaware River valley in the 1720's, and Jonathan Edwards in Northampton, Mass., in 1734. The process of the Great Awakening can be discerned as a response to a call for conversion and reformation. It was at first welcomed by most regular religious figures, for the complacency of the laity was generally discerned. But as it provoked ever more enthusiastic outbursts, particularly in New England and the middle colonies, the ministers split: some adopted extreme enthusiasm and by their preaching further intensified the Great Awakening and spread it geographically, but others hardened against enthusiasm. In the quarreling among ministers and between ministers and their congregations, ministerial authority was weakened and, as some have argued, the entire authority structure of Anglo-America shaken.

GREAT BASIN. A 189,000-square-mile region that lies between the Wasatch Mountains on the east and the Sierra Nevada on the west, including most of Nevada and the western third of Utah. It was explored and mapped by John Charles Frémont (1843–46).

GREAT BRIDGE, BATTLE AT (Dec. 9, 1775). The governor of Virginia, John Murray, Earl of Dunmore, placed his colony under martial law in November 1775 and began recruiting a Loyalist army. He fortified the passage of Elizabeth River at Great Bridge, near Norfolk; on Dec. 9 he attacked the Virginia militia and was badly defeated.

GREAT DEPRESSION. The period from late 1929 until 1940 is often called the Great Depression. This depression actually began in Europe, where business conditions were very poor through the late 1920's. It made its onset in the United States with the greatest stock market panic of U.S. history, beginning on Oct. 24, 1929. The prices of shares in American industries (stocks) were inflated far beyond true value. Many people (even bank officers) had invested their savings and company funds in the stock market. Many industries, meanwhile, had overproduced and overpriced goods that could not easily be sold abroad or to American farmers, whose incomes were low. When investors realized this, the panic of selling began. The stock market crash of 1929 "broke" many individuals and businesses whose money had been used for speculation. Businesses were forced to close, throwing many people out of work. Neither businesses nor individuals could then buy many things that had already been manufactured. Production of goods and services dropped almost 30 percent by 1932. Unemployment rose from 1.5 million in 1929 to 12.1 million people in 1932. As a result of the prolonged depression and panic, people drew their savings out of banks and spent them. Bank loans could not be repaid on mortgages and business warehouses, factories, and inventories. A major banking crisis had developed by the time Franklin D. Roosevelt was sworn in as president (*see* New Deal).

GREAT EASTERN. The world's largest ship up to its time, built in England, 1854–58. In 1864 the Atlantic Telegraph Company engaged the *Great Eastern* as a cable layer; it laid the first Atlantic cable in 1866. It was broken up in 1888.

"GREAT JEHOVAH." "In the name of the great Jehovah, and the Continental Congress" were the words Ethan Allen said he used in calling on Capt. William Delaplace to surrender Fort Ticonderoga, N.Y. (May 10, 1775). The phrase was made widely known when it appeared in Washington Irving's *Life of Washington* (1855–59).

GREAT LAKES. The largest group of lakes in the world, consisting of Lake Superior, Lake Huron, Lake Erie, Lake Michigan, and Lake Ontario. The U.S.-Canada border runs through all the lakes except Lake Michigan, which is entirely in the United States. Apart from climatic considerations, the Great Lakes have influenced American history chiefly as highways of trade and travel. When the French first effected a lodgment on the lower St. Lawrence River, they were searching for a water route to the Indies. The hostile Iroquois long barred the French from direct access to the lower lakes, but the Ottawa River route to Georgian Bay and the upper lakes was traversed by Samuel de Champlain as early as 1615. Lake Michigan was visited by Jean Nicolet in 1634 and Sault Ste. Marie by Isaac Jogues and Charles Raymbault in 1641. Thirty years later (1672) the Jesuits published a map of Lake Superior that was not materially improved upon until the 19th century. Father Louis Hennepin in 1683 first delineated with approximate accuracy all five of the Great Lakes.

Aided by the Iroquois the English gained access to Lake Ontario. To bar them from the region farther west, Antoine de La Mothe Cadillac founded Detroit, commanding lakes Erie and Huron, in 1701, which became the center of French control of all the upper country. By the surrender of Canada in 1760 (*see* French and Indian War) the British became masters of the Great Lakes, but by the Definitive Treaty of Peace of 1783 they agreed to share control with the United States. During the War of 1812 the American government established naval dominance of all the lakes. The Rush-Bagot Agreement of 1817 established limitations on naval forces on the lakes (*see* Great Lakes Disarmament Agreement).

Commerce and industry in the region burgeoned after the opening of the Erie Canal in 1825. Products are transported across the lakes, through the St. Lawrence Seaway and the New York State Barge Canal to Canada and the Atlantic Ocean. Commercial fishing has declined as an industry since 1945, one reason being the pollution that has resulted from using the lakes for the discharge of sewage.

GREAT LAKES, NAVAL POWER ON THE. The French had no naval establishment on the Great Lakes. In 1761 a British shipyard was established at Navy Island above Niagara Falls; in 1771 a second shipyard was established at Detroit, which became thereafter the principal naval center on the upper lakes. Following the advent of American authority on the lakes (1796) both governments supported armed vessels as necessary to maintain their authority.

The War of 1812 demonstrated the necessity of naval supremacy on the Great Lakes. Lacking it, the Americans could not hold Detroit and other parts of Michigan; when it was regained by the Battle of Lake Erie (Sept. 10, 1813), the British abandoned Detroit and fled eastward, hotly pursued (*see* Thames, Battle of the). On Lake Ontario, meanwhile, the struggle for naval supremacy was largely indecisive.

With the return of peace, both nations faced the necessity of building new fleets on the lakes; this prospect was happily averted through an agreement initiated by President James Monroe in 1815 and effected two years later (*see* Great Lakes Disarmament Agreement) that is still in force.

GREAT LAKES DISARMAMENT AGREEMENT (1817). Effected by an exchange of notes between British Minister Charles Bagot (Apr. 28) and Acting Secretary of State Richard Rush (Apr. 29), in which the United States and Great Britain agreed to limit their naval forces on the Great Lakes. Each was to have only one vessel of not more than 100 tons with one 18-pound cannon on Lake Ontario, two similarly limited ships on the upper lakes (meant to include Lake Erie), and one such on Lake Champlain. The Senate unanimously gave its approval and consent on Apr. 16, 1818. The agreement has since served as a model of effective disarmament.

GREAT LAKES EXPOSITION–CLEVELAND CENTENNIAL (1936–37). The 150 acres of the exposition, which dramatized the romance of iron, steel, and the manufacturing of the entire Great Lakes region, extended for a mile along the shore of Lake Erie. Built in eighty working days, it was purely local in character and participation.

GREAT LAKES NAVAL CAMPAIGN OF 1812. At the start of hostilities, eight American schooners attempting to escape from Sackets Harbor on Lake Ontario were pursued by British armed vessels; two were captured and the others driven to Ogdensburg, on the St. Lawrence River. In May 1812 the British schooner *Lord Nelson* was captured and taken to Sackets Harbor, but the British squadron controlled the lake. On July 29 the British bombarded Sackets Harbor but were forced to withdraw.

The British had undisputed control of the upper lakes when American Commodore Isaac Chauncey ordered Lt. Jesse D. Elliott to select a base and purchase vessels for a fleet on the upper lakes. Black Rock, on the site of Buffalo, was selected as the navy yard. On Oct. 8, Elliott was informed that two British ships had cast anchor across the Niagara off Fort Erie; early the following morning, with a picked force, he boarded and captured the ships. On Nov. 8 ten vessels left Sackets Harbor to intercept the British fleet returning southward from Fort George; the flagship *Royal George* was pursued into Kingston harbor, at the eastern end of Lake Ontario, but there, with the aid of the shore batteries, it drove off the American fleet. On Oct. 11 the British schooner *Simcoe* was destroyed, and before the campaign closed three merchant ships were captured by the Americans.

GREAT LAKES–ST. LAWRENCE WATERWAY PROJECT. *See* **St. Lawrence Seaway.**

GREAT LAKES STEAMSHIPS. *See* **Lakers.**

GREAT LAW OF PENNSYLVANIA (Dec. 7, 1682). Enacted by an assembly of freeholders called at Upland (Chester) by William Penn, it was an amplification of a body of laws submitted by Penn to England (*see* Penn's Frame of Government). It established liberty of conscience, extended the suffrage, limited the death penalty to relatively few offenses, attempted to legislate a perfectly moral state, and remained the basis of law for colonial Pennsylvania.

GREAT MASSACRE (April 1622). The Indian assault that almost annihilated the English settlement in Virginia. It was planned by Opechancanough, Powhatan's brother and successor. Men, women, and children were slain, some by their Indian guests of the night before. Jamestown was saved by the warning of Chanco, a young Indian convert whose white godfather, Richard Pace, carried warning through the night to the colonial capital.

GREAT MEADOWS (Pa.). Ten miles east of present-day Uniontown, on the Cumberland Road; site of Maj. George Washington's first battle and the first engagement of the French and Indian War. In April 1754, Washington left Alexandria with part of the Virginia regiment. A council of war at Wills Creek, Md., determined on an advance across the mountains to open the road for the forces to follow; the expedition left Wills Creek by the trail later called Braddock's Road, marching into Pennsylvania, and on May 24 some 150 men encamped at the open place known as the Great Meadows. There, on May 27, Washington learned that a small French force was hidden a few miles to the north. Leaving a guard behind, he made a night march and in a surprise attack killed ten of the French and took twenty-one prisoners. Washington sent the prisoners to Williamsburg and, returning to Great Meadows, erected Fort Necessity.

In June the rest of the Virginia regiment and an independent company from South Carolina augmented the force to about 360. Fort Necessity was enlarged and strengthened, and on July 3 it was attacked by about 500 French and 400 Indians. Both sides nearly exhausted their ammunition without sustaining great damage. At length, his provisions almost gone, Washington capitulated; the English marched on foot to Virginia, carrying their wounded.

GREAT MIGRATION. During the reign of Charles I (1625–49) discontent in England was such that 60,000 persons emigrated. About one-third went to New England, founding the colonies of Massachusetts Bay, Connecticut, and Rhode Island; others settled in Old Providence, in the Caribbean, and elsewhere. The basic cause for the Great Migration was Puritan discontent, as evidenced by its end when the English scene became more hopeful after the Long Parliament assembled, but depression in agriculture and the cloth trade led many others to emigrate for economic betterment.

GREAT NINE PARTNERS' PATENT. A large New York land grant secured by speculators during the regime of Gov. Benjamin Fletcher (1692–98). North of the Rumbout and Beekman patents, it included most of the northern half of Dutchess County.

GREAT NORTHERN RAILROAD. *See* **Railroads, Sketches of Principal Lines: Burlington Northern.**

GREAT PLAINS. Historically the Great Plains may be roughly defined as the region lying between the ninety-eighth meridian and the Rocky Mountains. With some exceptions, the area has a level surface sloping gradually upward to the foothills of the mountains. It is almost treeless and is subhumid or semiarid, with little rainfall. Before white occupation the Great Plains were the grazing area of huge herds of buffalo and the home of such Indian tribes as the Sioux, Cheyenne, Arapaho, Pawnee, Comanche, and Apache.

Americans in general knew very little of the region when the northern portion was transferred to the United States by the Louisiana Purchase. Discouraging reports concerning the habitability of the Great Plains were given by the explorers Meriwether Lewis and William Clark, Zebulon M. Pike, and Stephen H. Long (*see* Great American Desert). By 1840 the area was included in what was designated as the permanent Indian country. During the 1840's the region was crossed by emigrants to Oregon, by military and exploring expeditions, by the Mormons on their way to Utah, and by thousands of gold seekers rushing to California. During the 1850's commissioners and Indian agents made treaties with the Indians by which the tribesmen ceded territory, agreed to move, or gave permission for laying out roads and establishing military posts. Emigrants continued to pour west over the trails. Stagecoaches carrying mail and passengers to California began running early in the decade. In the early 1860's a vast wagon-freighting business was developed, and the pony express greatly expedited mail service. By the close of the Civil War the area was aflame with Indian wars (*see* Sioux Wars). During this same period the Union Pacific Railroad was built westward, to be followed soon by other railroads.

Beginning late in the 1860's and during the ensuing two decades the region was the scene of the great range cattle industry; the decline of this activity was due chiefly to the relentless pressure of the settlers, who narrowed the open range until it finally disappeared before the end of the century (*see* Barbed Wire). During the 1930's, dust storms devastated many sections of the Great Plains. Between 1930 and 1970 the rural population of the area decreased by more than 30 percent, while urban population increased by 166 percent.

GREAT REVIVAL (1801). The peak of a western religious revival movement that began under the vehement preaching of James McGready, a Presbyterian minister, in Logan County, Ky. Methodists, Presbyterians, and Baptists often united in conducting the larger meetings, generally held in encampments. Strange bodily manifestations intensified the religious revival, which quickly spread through the West. The climax was reached in a sacramental camp meeting at Cane Ridge, Ky., in August 1801; attendance has been estimated between 10,000 and 25,000. Emphasis upon emotional appeal brought extravagances, but the revival contributed much of value toward developing the western region. Church membership increased tremendously. The Methodist and Baptist denominations were strengthened, but the Presbyterians suffered from schisms; out of the dissent developed the Cumberland Presbyterian church, which, with the Methodist church, continued to use the camp meeting revival.

GREAT RIVER ROAD. Part of the U.S. network of interstate highways. It is intended to be one of the major north-south highway arteries, running along the course of the Mississippi River.

GREAT SALT LAKE (Utah). Located in northwestern Utah; about fifty-one miles wide and eighty-three miles long, averaging 25 to 30 feet in depth. From wet periods to dry, the salt content ranges from 20 to 27 percent by weight. Louis Armand de Lom d'Arce, Baron de Lahontan, claimed to have discovered the River "Long" and to have heard (January 1689) Indians describe "a salt lake 300 leagues in circumference." It was discovered in 1824 by James Bridger, a fur trapper, who mistook it for an arm of the Pacific Ocean. John C. Frémont made a preliminary instrument survey of the lake in 1843 and described it in his reports; Howard Stansbury made a more thorough survey in 1849–50. The most exhaustive studies were made in the 1880's by Grove K. Gilbert for his monograph *Lake Bonneville.*

GREAT SERPENT MOUND (Ohio). Outstanding prehistoric example of effigy earthworks peculiar to the upper Mississippi Basin; now a state park. It represents a crawling serpent 1,330 feet long, from 2 to 3 feet high, resting on a promontory overlooking the valley of a creek. It is not associated with burials.

GREAT SMOKY MOUNTAINS. A group of the Appalachian Mountains along the North Carolina–Tennessee boundary, about fifty miles in length, and containing sixteen peaks over 6,000 feet high. Originally inhabited by Cherokee Indians and known as Iron Mountains until about 1789. Extensively explored by Samuel B. Buckley, Thomas L. Clingman, and Arnold Henry Guyot in the 1850's. The mountains are so called because of the blue haze characteristic of the region. In 1934 the Great Smoky Mountains National Park, twenty miles wide and fifty-four miles long (516,626 acres), was established.

GREAT SOCIETY. The theme of President Lyndon B. Johnson's presidential campaign of 1964, announced May 22 at Ann Arbor, Mich. By the phrase, the president meant a society in which poverty would be abolished, education would be available for all, peace would prevail, and every man would be free to develop his potential.

"GREAT SPIRIT." In general, an idea of a single divine being is alien to native American thinking. Even though concepts of spirit and soul are common in pre-Columbian religions, they are generally built around cosmologies based on zoomorphic figures. Some Californian tribes and some groups in the Plateau and in sections of the Northwest Coast had an idea of an Earth-Maker, an anthropomorphic figure who made the world but who was indifferent to it. To some the creator was an animal, often in the West a coyote or raven. The idea of the "Great Spirit" is usually associated with the Algonkin-speaking peoples of the Great Lakes and Eastern Woodlands areas and in some measure with the peoples of the eastern Plains, but it appears that this idea may have been a Christian one integrated by missionized Indians into their native religious pattern.

GREAT SWAMP FIGHT (Dec. 19, 1675). During King Philip's War, the combined forces of Massachusetts Bay, Plymouth, and Connecticut, over 1,000 soldiers with about 150 Indian allies, marched on Dec. 18–19, 1675, from Smith's Garrison House (now Wickford, R.I.) to the island in the Great Swamp (site of South Kingstown, R.I.), which had been fortified by the Narraganset. After three hours of desperate fighting, the fort was forced at the rear and the Indians routed. This battle did not end the war, but it broke forever the power of the Narraganset.

GREAT TRADING AND WAR PATH. An Indian path that ran down the Shenandoah Valley to the valleys of the New and Holston rivers to the Overhill Cherokee towns in the Tennessee country, and thence to the Coosa River, where it connected with the warpath of the Creek Indians. One of its prongs ran from the Holston through Cumberland Gap; another, through Boone's Gap of the Alleghenies to the middle towns of the Cherokee. It was over this path that the northern Indians went to war with the Cherokee. A great stream of white migration flowed along it from Pennsylvania, Maryland, and Virginia to the Southwest from 1770 onward.

GREAT TRAIL. An Indian thoroughfare leading from the Forks of the Ohio to the site of Detroit. It followed the north bank of the Ohio River to the mouth of Big Beaver Creek, traversed the watershed to the "Crossing-place on the Muskingum," where Bolivar (Fort Lawrence) now is, and then bore northwest, passing near the sites of the present towns of Wooster, Fremont, and Toledo. During the late 18th century it was the most important trail north of the Ohio.

GREAT VALLEY. The large area in California between the Sierra Nevada and the Coast Ranges, drained by the San Joaquin and Sacramento rivers. First explored and trapped by Jedediah Smith in 1822. The valleys, known as the Central Valley, are the agricultural heartland of California.

GREELY ARCTIC EXPEDITION. Lt. Adolphus W. Greely, U.S. Army, led an expedition to Grinnell Land for three years of exploration and scientific observation in 1881. A supply ship, sent in 1882, was prevented by ice from reaching either prearranged rendezvous and returned to the United States; a second ship, sent in 1883, was sunk by ice. The Greely party had meanwhile explored some 6,000 square miles of newly discovered land and reached a point then farthest north, but its food supply was limited. Secretary of the Navy William Eaton Chandler purchased, on his own responsibility, two Scotch whalers, the *Bear* and the *Thetis,* and dispatched them northward in the spring of 1884; with them was the *Alert,* a vessel specially designed for polar exploration, contributed by Queen Victoria. Seven survivors, including Greely, were discovered on June 22 in a tent on Cape Sabine, 250 miles south of their base on Ellesmere Island; all but one completely recovered.

GREENBACK MOVEMENT. A reaction against the tendency to reestablish specie payments in place of the greenback standard of exchange that had prevailed since 1862 (see Greenbacks). It made its strongest appeal to debtor farmers. Its most essential demand was that greenbacks be given complete legal-tender status and be issued freely. It also united opposition to national banks and their currency with resentment against the handsome profits that holders of Civil War bonds were to take out of the funds raised by taxes. Although its ideas had strong support in both major parties in rural areas and received partial endorsement in the national Democratic convention in 1868, the greenback movement thereafter became chiefly one for minor parties. The campaign of 1872 found the only organized support of greenback policies in the new National Labor Reform party. Independent state Granger parties sprang up following the panic of 1873; two of them, in Indiana and Illinois, furnished the leadership to create a new national party committed to greenback policies (*see* Greenback Party). The achievement of the resumption of specie payments undermined the appeal of its program; the growing disparity of values between silver and gold made free coinage of silver a far more feasible political goal than greenback inflation. The movement was a significant predecessor of many agrarian and labor political movements and trained leaders of the Populist crusade.

GREENBACK PARTY. In 1867–68, there was a movement in Ohio to require the government to pay off its Civil War bonds with greenbacks instead of gold (*see* Greenback Movement; Ohio Idea). In 1872, greenbacks were approved as currency by a small, new party, the Labor Reform party. By 1876, the Labor Reform party and several midwestern Granger groups had merged to form the Greenback party, which nominated Peter Cooper of New York for president. He won only about 80,000 votes, nearly all in the Midwest. The most evident results of the campaign of 1876 were the election to the Illinois legislature of a number of Greenback party members and their combination with Democrats to elect Justice David Davis of the U.S. Supreme Court to the Senate, a move that may have kept Samuel J. Tilden from becoming president. Historians credit the party with over 1 million votes in the 1878 election. Strikes and labor trouble caused a number of workers to join the farmers who were the main strength of the party. The party picked up the argument that silver should be coined freely, and it began to demand that government should limit the hours of labor; that Chinese laborers should be excluded from the United States; and that public lands be granted only to people who actually settled on them. These ideas were popular enough to elect fourteen or fifteen Greenback congressmen and a much larger number of friendly Democratic or Republican congressmen.

By 1880, many Americans had become convinced that the country would do well on a gold standard. The Greenbackers' nominee for president was James B. Weaver, who got 300,000 votes. The party's congressional strength dropped to ten members. The last Greenback presidential campaign was in 1884, when the party nominated Gen. Benjamin F. Butler. Butler tried to win the Democratic nomination that same year, but in the election he finished a dismal third behind Cleveland and Blaine. Many Greenbackers then drifted into the new Populist party.

GREENBACKS. Popular name for the U.S. notes issued during the Civil War as legal tender for all debts except tariff duties and interest on the public debt. They served as the standard of value in ordinary commercial transactions after their issue in 1862. Depreciated during the Civil War, they were brought to par by the Resumption Act (1875) by 1879.

GREEN BAY (Wis.). Formerly known as La Baye and La Baye des Puans; site of the earliest white settlement west of Lake Michigan. Discovered by the French explorer Jean Nicolet in 1634, the region was not visited by other Frenchmen for more than twenty years. The first French fort was built on the site in 1684 and was called Fort St. François Xavier; it was evacuated in 1695. A French post was rebuilt there in 1717 during the first Fox war and called Fort La Baye. It was abandoned and reestablished several times, until in 1760 the last French soldiers withdrew. British troops arrived the next year, renamed it Fort Edward Augustus, and maintained it until Pontiac's conspiracy.

Meanwhile a considerable settlement had grown up; although French in language and customs, the inhabitants took the oath of allegiance in 1761 to the British sovereign. Green Bay became a fur-trade emporium, commanding the eastern end of the Fox-Wisconsin portage route to the Mississippi. In the War of 1812, Green Bay traders sided with Great Britain. They were impoverished by their war contributions and regarded with dislike the coming of the Americans and the building of Fort Howard in 1816. A village was laid out in 1829, and the city of Green Bay was incorporated in 1854. It developed into an agricultural and lumbering center, and continues to produce large quantities of dairy, lumber, and paper products. Its port handles millions of tons of shipping each year. The 1980 population was 87,889.

GREENBRIER COMPANY. A land company organized (1745) by John Robinson, speaker of the Virginia House of Burgesses, and Thomas Nelson, later governor of Virginia; it received a grant for 100,000 acres in the Greenbrier Valley in West Virginia. Rival of the more famous Ohio Company.

GREEN MOUNTAIN BOYS. In 1749, Gov. Benning Wentworth of New Hampshire began to grant lands in the region west of the Connecticut River that is today Vermont, even though New York put in a strong claim to the area. In 1770 the New York Supreme Court held that all Hampshire patents were invalid and that persons who had settled under New Hampshire had to rebuy their lands. The people of the New Hampshire grants west of the Green Mountains resolved to keep their lands by force if necessary, formed military companies, and elected Ethan Allen colonel commandant of the Green Mountain Boys. Settlers under New York jurisdiction were terrorized. Rude fortresses were built on Otter Creek and Onion, or Winooski, River. New York sheriffs were driven off. With the coming of the revolutionary war, the Green Mountain Boys espoused the patriot cause. Led by Ira Allen, Thomas Chittenden, and Jonas Fay, they declared an independent republic of Vermont in 1777. In 1790, New York relinquished its claim, and in 1791 the Green Mountain state was admitted into the Union.

GREEN RIVER. Tributary of the Colorado, flowing south and west from the Wind River Mountains in west central Wyoming. Spanish parties noted its course and named it Rio Verde. In the nineteenth century the upper Green River became a favorite place of meeting for the powerful tribes: Snake, Nez Perce, Flathead, Blackfoot, and Crow, who assembled for annual exchange of pelts for trade goods supplied by the Rocky Mountain Fur Company and the American Fur Company. Henry's Fork, Fort Bonneville, Ham's Fork, and Horse Creek were the sites of six of the rendezvous of the mountain men held between 1824 and 1840.

GREEN RIVER KNIFE. Counterpart of the Bowie knife, made famous by the mountain men, after whose favorite rendezvous ground it was named. The trade name "Green River" was incised on the blade near the hilt. "Up to Green River" became a synonym for "up to the hilt."

GREENSBORO (N.C.). Eastern point of a "triad" of cities (with High Point and Winston-Salem) which together are the center of the state's largest metropolitan area. During the Revolution, Gen. Nathanael Green commanded the American troops in a major battle at Guilford Courthouse. After the Revolution the courthouse was abandoned and a new one built a few miles away on the site of the modern city, which was named in honor of the general. Greensboro became an educational center during the 19th century, when several colleges located in its vicinity. It has become a leading insurance center of the South, with the home offices of several major insurance firms. In addition, the city houses large textile companies and chemical and machinery firms. In 1980 it had a population of 155,642.

***GREEN* V. *FRAZIER*,** 253 U.S. 233 (1920). At issue was whether North Dakota might utilize tax funds to create publicly owned grain elevators and banks. The Supreme Court ruled that where the "united action of the people, legislature and court" agree upon the 'public purpose' nature of a proposed expenditure, the Court is "not at liberty to interfere, unless it is clear beyond reasonable controversy that rights secured by the Federal Constitution have been violated."

GREENVILLE, FORT (Ohio). Built late in 1793; one of a line of fortifications erected between Cincinnati and Lake Erie during Gen. Anthony Wayne's campaign against the Indians, it served also as a storage place for supplies and as a rendezvous for the army. At the fort, on Aug. 3, 1795, the Northwest tribes signed the Treaty of Greenville. Soon thereafter the fort was abandoned.

GREENVILLE, TREATY OF (Aug. 3, 1795). Sequel to Gen. Anthony Wayne's defeat of the Indians at Fallen Timbers, Ohio (August 1794). Negotiated by Wayne and the chiefs of the Delaware, Shawnee, Wyandot, Miami Confederacy, and other tribes, the treaty established a definite boundary between Indian lands and those open to settlement. Running up the Cuyahoga, the line followed the portage to the Tuscarawas, thence to Fort Lawrence, to Loramie Creek, to Fort Recovery, and to the Ohio River opposite the mouth of the Kentucky. The land westward and northward of this line was conceded to the Indians, except Detroit and the other French settlements and several trading-post sites with highways between them. Also, the United States reserved 150,000 acres on the Ohio opposite Louisville, Ky. The result of the treaty was an era of greatly increased immigration into the Northwest Territory.

GREER COUNTY DISPUTE. Greer County, 1,511,576 acres in the Oklahoma triangle between the north and south forks of Red River, was claimed by both Texas and the U.S. government under the Adams-Onís Treaty (*see* Marcy's Exploring Expedition). In order to determine its status the U.S. attorney general instituted suit against Texas in the early 1890's; on Mar. 16, 1896, the case was decided in favor of the United States.

GRENVILLE ACT, or **Sugar Act** (1764). Passed by Parliament during George Grenville's ministry, it imposed duties on sugar, coffee, wine, and other items imported into the American colonies from foreign countries and lowered the duty on molasses. It called for a stricter enforcement of the customs laws and provided that the taxes collected be paid into the British exchequer, to be used for "defending, protecting, and securing" the British colonies in America.

GRIERSON'S RAID (Apr. 17–May 2, 1863). In conjunction with Gen. Ulysses S. Grant's attack on Vicksburg, Miss., Union Col. B. H. Grierson led 1,700 cavalrymen from La Grange, Tenn., through Mississippi to Baton Rouge, La., in order to disrupt communications and transportation and to draw Confederate forces away from Vicksburg. Grierson covered over 600 miles in sixteen days, destroying bridges as well as railway and telegraph lines.

GRIFFIN, FORT (Tex.). Established in 1867 on the Clear Fork of the Brazos River, in what is now Sheckelford County, to protect the border settlements against the incursions of hostile Comanche and Kiowa. In the late 1870's it became a thriving commercial center for buffalo-hide buyers and cattlemen. It was abandoned in 1881.

GRIFFON. First sailing vessel on the upper Great Lakes, built in 1679 by Robert Cavelier, Sieur de La Salle, to transport men and supplies between Niagara and his projected Illinois colony. In August of that year the *Griffon* carried La Salle to Green Bay, from which the ship was sent back to Niagara laden with furs; vessel and crew disappeared on the voyage, and their fate remains a mystery. Frequent reports of the discovery of its remains have been published, but all have lacked substantial foundation.

GRINGO. A nickname, perverted from the Spanish word *griego* ("Greek"), applied in several Spanish-American countries to foreigners who "talk Greek," or unintelligibly.

GRISTMILLS. The gristmill met an important local need for more than two centuries, grinding the farmers' grain and levying toll, usually in kind, for the service.

***GROSJEAN* V. *AMERICAN PRESS COMPANY*,** 297 U.S. 233 (1936). To cripple political enemies, Gov. Huey Long persuaded the Louisiana legislature to put a license tax on the selling of advertising in newspapers. When the law was challenged in *Grosjean* v. *American Press Company,* the Supreme Court held that (1) freedom of the press in the sense of freedom from prior restraint is a liberty protected from state legislative action by the due process clause of the Fourteenth Amendment; (2) a corporation is a person within the purview of that amendment; and (3) the license tax was designed to regulate rather than to raise revenue and thus violated the right of the press to freedom from prior restraint.

GROSS NATIONAL PRODUCT (GNP). A figure showing the value of all U.S. goods and services produced in a given year. It includes (at market prices) the purchases by consumers and government organizations, the private investments in U.S. business and farm activities, and the value of all exports.

GROS VENTRE. Name applied by the French to Indians of the Atsina and Hidatsa tribes, later distinguished as Gros Ventres of the Missouri and Gros Ventres of the Prairie.

GROVETON, BATTLE OF (Aug. 28–29, 1862). Gen. Thomas J. ("Stonewall") Jackson assembled his three divisions behind an unfinished railroad north and west of Groveton, Va., on Aug. 28, after destroying Union stores at Manassas Junction. Late that afternoon he attacked a Union division on the Warrenton pike, and on Aug. 28 he resisted the assaults of three corps and a division, enabling Gen. Robert E. Lee to assemble his victorious force for the second Battle of Bull Run on Aug. 30.

GUADALCANAL (August 1942–February 1943). To check the Japanese advance, the Allies planned to seize bases in the southern Solomon Islands. When the Japanese began building an airfield on Guadalcanal in July 1942, Allied preparations were hurried to send an invasion force supported by a three-carrier task force. On Aug. 7, the marines landed on Guadalcanal and nearby Tulagi, scattering small Japanese forces on both islands. Japanese reaction was swift. In a night attack against Allied naval forces early on Aug. 9 (Battle of Savo Island), seven Japanese cruisers and a destroyer sank three U.S. cruisers, an Australian cruiser, and a U.S. destroyer, forcing withdrawal of Allied naval units from the area. Left unsupported, the marines dug in to defend the airfield, Henderson Field.

Marine planes flew in, while the Japanese landed 1,000 ground troops. A second Japanese reinforcement effort was defeated in the naval battle of the Eastern Solomons (Aug. 23–25), but the Japanese continued to bring in small elements in nightly destroyer runs ("Tokyo Express"). In mid-September the Japanese made a major effort to crush the marine positions (Battle of Bloody Ridge), only to be repulsed.

For the next month, heavy air and sea battles took place. By mid-October, there were more than 23,000 Allied troops ashore, but the Japanese had almost as many. Further Japanese efforts to reinforce their troops were frustrated in a series of naval actions. U.S. marines were soon replaced by more than 50,000 army troops. The Japanese, now short on supplies and weakened by disease, fell back before heavy American attacks. During the first week of February 1943, the Japanese survivors were evacuated in night operations.

GUADALUPE HIDALGO, TREATY OF (Feb. 2, 1848). Signed at Guadalupe Hidalgo near Mexico City, it specified the terms of peace at the close of the Mexican War. It was negotiated by Nicholas P. Trist, the chief clerk of the Department of State. It provided for the establishment of the U.S.-Mexican boundary at the middle of the Rio Grande from the Gulf of Mexico to a point where that river met the southern boundary of New Mexico; west on this southern boundary of New Mexico to the western line of New Mexico; north along that western line until it intersected the first branch of the Gila River; down that branch and the middle of the Gila to the Colorado River; and direct to the Pacific at a point one marine league south of the southernmost point of the port of San Diego. The treaty also provided for the cession to the United States by Mexico of the territory of New Mexico and Upper California for a payment of $15 million. It was ratified, with amendments, by the Senate, Mar. 10, 1848.

Because the surveyors could not agree on the identity of the first branch of the Gila, the line between the Rio Grande and the Gila was never marked; its international importance was ended by the negotiation of the Gadsden Purchase of 1853.

GUAM. Southernmost of the Mariana Islands and westernmost territory of the United States, captured by American forces (June 1898) during the Spanish-American War and ceded to the United States by the Treaty of Paris (Dec. 10, 1898). Ferdinand Magellan is credited with discovery of the island in 1521. Following its cession in 1898, Guam was administered by naval officers. In 1950 its administration was transferred to the Department of the Interior under the Organic Act. Until 1970, under this act, the chief executive of Guam was a governor appointed by the president, but a 1968 amendment provided for popular election thereafter. There is a unicameral legislature of twenty-one members; a court with the jurisdiction of a federal district court and local jurisdiction has been established, its decisions subject to appeal to the U.S. Court of Appeals. The people of Guam have been citizens of the United States since 1950.

During World War II, Guam was occupied by Japanese forces (December 1941–July 21, 1944). It has since played a key role in U.S. Pacific defenses. Its 1980 population of 105,-816 was largely employed in military-related pursuits, but tourism provides an increasing source of economic activity.

GUANO. A manure first imported into the United States in 1824 by John S. Skinner, agriculturalist and editor of *American Farmer.* The press urged the trial of this form of manure, often presenting fabulous stories of its productive power, but its use was insignificant until the 1840's and was never widespread. Its high price, owing in part to Peruvian monopoly of the principal source, led to decline in its use after 1854.

GUANTÁNAMO BAY. U.S. naval base near the eastern end of the south coast of Cuba, 40 miles east of Santiago. It comprises 36,000 acres, including the port at Caimanera. Under the terms of the Platt Amendment of 1901, the United States obtained the right to intervene in Cuba and to buy or lease territory for naval stations; the specific site was acquired on lease by a treaty signed July 2, 1903. A new treaty (1934) eliminated the right of intervention but reasserted prior stipulations in regard to Guantánamo Bay, which were to remain in effect until both parties agreed to modify or abrogate them. Fidel Castro denied the validity of the treaties, but the United States retained the base. Facilities include a fleet anchorage and operating base, U.S. Marine Corps base, naval air station, and underground hospital and oil-storage facilities.

GUERRILLAS. A term originally applied to quasi-military and irregular groups of Spanish partisans who fought against Napoleon (1808). The spectrum of guerrilla activity runs from conventional military operations by organized groups to uncoordinated, spontaneous, individual acts of sabotage, subversion, or terrorism carried out against an enemy. Guerrillas normally operate outside of constituted authority.

GUFFEY COAL ACTS. Sponsored by the United Mine Workers Union and guided through Congress by Sen. Joseph Guffey (Pa.) in August 1935, the Bituminous Coal Conservation Act formed an integral part of the Franklin D. Roosevelt administration's effort to create federal regulatory power under the National Industrial Recovery Act. It sought to establish price controls and production quotas; afford protection to labor; retire marginal coal lands; and, generally, treat the bituminous coal industry as a public utility. Before portions of the act were operative, the U.S. Supreme Court declared it unconstitutional (see *Carter* v. *Carter Çoal Company*). Recast and amended, it was redesignated the Guffey Coal Act of 1937 and easily passed by the Congress. Administration of the act, embodying the most complex and comprehensive administrative power ever granted a regulatory agency in peacetime, was vested in the National Bituminous Coal Commission. Although Congress subsequently extended the act through 1943, it was largely unsuccessful.

GUILFORD COURTHOUSE, BATTLE OF (Mar. 15, 1781). Retreating northward through North Carolina, Gen. Nathanael Greene crossed the Dan River into Virginia, closely followed by Gen. Charles Cornwallis. Collecting recruits, Greene recrossed the Dan with 4,404 men and marched rapidly to Guilford Courthouse, N.C., where he offered battle. Cornwallis, with 2,213 veterans, attacked; the battle that ensued was one of the most severe of the revolutionary war. The British held the field, but the battle was a strategic victory for the Americans. Cornwallis soon withdrew to Wilmington, N.C., abandoning all the Carolinas save two or three coast towns (*see* Southern Campaigns).

***GUINN AND BEAL* V. *UNITED STATES*,** 238 U.S. 347 (1915). The state of Oklahoma attempted to include in its constitution, on a permanent basis, the grandfather-clause principle earlier applied on a statutory and temporary basis in other southern states. The Supreme Court decided that the provision represented a clear violation of the purpose and intent of the Fifteenth Amendment.

GUION'S EXPEDITION (1797). In accordance with Pinckney's Treaty of 1795 the United States was authorized to occupy Spanish posts along the east side of the Mississippi down to the new southern boundary. A detachment, commanded by Capt. Isaac Guion, was sent from Fort Washington (Cincinnati) early in June and occupied Chickasaw Bluffs and Walnut Hills, Miss., arriving at Natchez in December.

GULF, MOBILE AND OHIO. *See* **Railroads, Sketches of Principal Lines: Illinois Central Gulf.**

GULF STREAM. In the North Atlantic, the western boundary current and its eastward-flowing extension. More properly, the Gulf Stream system consists of three sections along the western and northern edges of the clockwise gyre that fills the center of the ocean; the Florida current flows from the Gulf of Mexico northeastward along the coast to Cape Hatteras, N.C.; from Hatteras to the Grand Banks of Newfoundland is the Gulf Stream proper, a strong current but not as well defined as the Florida current in either breadth or depth; east of the Grand Banks is an even less well-defined, weaker current alleged to carry warmth to western Europe.

The Gulf Stream has been the most intensively studied of all ocean currents. By 1519, Spanish seafarers had learned to avoid the Gulf Stream on outward passages to the Caribbean and to follow it on homeward passages. Scientific study of the Gulf Stream began when Benjamin Franklin learned that American merchant captains shortened their passages by avoiding the Gulf Stream as they sailed westward; in 1775, he made the first of a series of surface temperature measurements across the Atlantic, identifying the Gulf Stream by its core of warm water carried from lower latitudes. In 1844 the U.S. Coast Survey began the first major study of the Gulf Stream; chief among the results was the discovery of cold veins within the warm current. The Coast Survey's work climaxed in the current and temperature measurements made in the Florida Straits by Lt. John E. Pillsbury beginning in 1885. Pillsbury's results strongly supported the notion that the Gulf Stream is driven primarily by the prevailing winds rather than by density differences. At the beginning of the 20th century the students of Vilhelm Bjerknes in Norway and Sweden showed the Gulf Stream to be a boundary current between the warmer, lighter waters of the Sargasso Sea and the colder, heavier waters along the continental shelf and slope. In 1948, Henry Stommel showed theoretically that western boundary currents result from the variation of the deflecting force of the earth's rotation. Since then, the apparent conflict between wind-stress and density differences as the primary driving force of the Gulf Stream has been resolved by sophisticated theories that require both.

GULLAH (also known as **Geechee**). A dialect spoken by descendants of slaves in coastal Georgia and South Carolina, or a member of the group speaking this dialect.

GUNBOATS. In the simplest sense, tiny men-of-war extremely overgunned in proportion to size. They significantly entered U.S. history in the 1776 Battle of Valcour Island on Lake Champlain. In America's first Barbary War, there proved to be a need for gunboats. Typically carrying twenty to twenty-three men and two 24- or 32-pounders (cannon) in a hull 70 feet long, 18 feet broad, and nearly 5 feet deep, the boats were effective only along a coast, since for them to be stable on the open sea, their crews had to stow the cannon along the keel, making the vessels defenseless. Gunboats were useful in the suppression of West Indian piracy and in the Seminole Wars. In the Civil War, improvised gunboats were found on embattled rivers everywhere. The innovative ironclads, especially the unseaworthy monitors, were basically of use against forts rather than against other ships.

In the decades before the Spanish-American War, European neocolonialism introduced "gunboat diplomacy," calling for larger, hybrid craft that could safely cross oceans; assume a year-round anchorage on a foreign strand; possess sufficiently shallow draft to go up a river; and carry heavy armament. The 1892 U.S.S. *Castine,* for example, was 204 feet overall, weighed 1,177 tons, and had eight 4-inch rifles. The 1936 *Erie* had a very successful rough-weather design and was adopted by the Coast Guard for the Campbell class, outstanding in the Battle of the Atlantic. The *Erie* at 2,000 tons was between a destroyer and a light cruiser in size, and was armed with four 6-inch rifles. The inshore fighting of World War II called for small gunboats (patrol gunboat, or PG) and still smaller motor gunboats (patrol gunboat motor, or PGM), with the emphasis on a multiplicity of automatic weapons and on rocket launchers for shore bombardment. The gunboat concept of relatively enormous firepower in a small vessel had a new impetus from rocket weaponry. The

U.S. Navy had no interest in modernizing gunboats until the Vietnam War spawned a variety of tiny types used in swarms either to police the shoreline or to penetrate the riverways. The heaviest types revived the name of "monitor." In the 1970's the Navy was testing designs seeking great speeds.

GUNDELOW. A type of small vessel known only in New England in the 1870's, used mostly for lightering cotton and coal from ships in Portsmouth, R.I., and Newburyport, Mass., to the mills on the rivers. It was lateen rigged, with a single very short mast and long yard with high peak. Gundelows disappeared at the turn of the century. The name (a corruption of "gondola") was also applied to a small gunboat with one high mast and square sail used by the colonial army against the British on Lake Champlain.

GUNNISON MASSACRE (Oct. 26, 1853). Capt. John W. Gunnison and seven companions, engaged in surveying for a Pacific railroad, were slain at their camp, near Deseret, Utah. It was charged that the murder had been instigated by Mormons; actually, the attack was made by Indians to avenge the death of a Ute warrior slain by emigrants.

GUSTAV LINE. A belt of German field fortifications in southern Italy during World War II. Running from Minturno on the west coast, through Cassino, across the Apennines, and behind the Sangro River to the Adriatic, it blocked the approaches to Rome through Avezzano in the east and through the Liri Valley in the west. On May 11, 1944, Gen. Alphonse Juin's French Expeditionary Corps broke the Gustav Line, enabling Polish troops to take Monte Cassino, British and Canadian forces to move up the Liri Valley, and American units to advance up the coast to Anzio.

GUTIÉRREZ-MAGEE EXPEDITION. Bernardo Gutiérrez de Lara, a Mexican, joined forces at Natchitoches, La., in September 1812 with A. W. Magee, former lieutenant in the U.S. Army, for the purpose of invading Texas and wresting it from Spanish control. Magee soon died, but he was followed by Samuel Kemper and later by a Capt. Perry. The filibusters captured San Antonio in March 1813. The Spanish governor of Texas and twelve of his staff were made prisoners of war and later killed. In August the army, a force of 3,000, was ambushed by the Spanish and destroyed.

GWINNETT-McINTOSH DUEL (May 16, 1777). The challenge of Button Gwinnett to Gen. Lachlan McIntosh grew out of a military rivalry and was precipitated when McIntosh called him "a scoundrel and lying rascal." They fought on the outskirts of Savannah, Ga.; each was wounded in the leg; Gwinnett died of gangrene three days later.

GWYNN'S ISLAND (Va.). After the burning of Norfolk (January 1776), John Murray, Earl of Dunmore, the royal governor, sailed in his fleet from Hampton Roads, and in May 1776 made a camp on Gwynn's Island in Chesapeake Bay. There he threw up entrenchments and built a stockade. Gen. Andrew Lewis, by order of the Committee of Safety, brought up batteries and shelled the fleet and the camp, which Dunmore abandoned on July 10.

HABEAS CORPUS, WRIT OF. A legal process through which someone who alleges that he is being detained illegally may secure a quick judicial inquiry into the lawfulness of his detention. Detention takes many forms: incarceration in a penitentiary pursuant to court judgment; detention in a police station following arrest; commitment to a mental institution; service in the armed forces; detention through quarantine regulations; and restraint through private authority, as in the custody of children. The writ is addressed to the person responsible for the detention and requires him to produce the petitioner quickly. There is no statute of limitations. The writ may be petitioned for by a relative or friend if the concerned individual is unable to apply on his own.

The writ is traceable to Section 39 of Magna Charta (1215); its availability as a remedy against the crown dates from the late 15th century. In the American colonies the writ was available as part of the common law. After independence was declared, it was guaranteed in most of the revolutionary state constitutions, and the U.S. Constitution in Article 1, Section 9, Clause 2, forbade its suspension "unless when in Cases of Rebellion or Invasion the public Safety may require it." Habeas corpus statutes do not attempt to describe which detentions are illegal; all they provide for is a procedure by which a court may look into the matter. If the court concludes that the detention is illegal, the petitioner is freed by the judge at once. A state prisoner is not eligible to apply to a federal judge for habeas corpus until he has first exhausted whatever remedies are available to him under state law, including litigation of his federal claim. Similarly, a member of the armed forces is not entitled to bring a habeas corpus proceeding in a federal district court until he has exhausted the remedies provided by the military court system.

President Abraham Lincoln suspended the writ at the beginning of the Civil War (*see* Arrest, Arbitrary, During the Civil War). The limited suspensions of the writ in 1871 and 1905 were announced by the president pursuant to statute; a suspension in 1941, in Hawaii, without statutory authorization, was held by the Supreme Court to be without legal authority (*Duncan* v. *Kahanamoku,* 327 U.S. 304 [1946]).

HAGUE COURT OF ARBITRATION. *See* **Permanent Court of Arbitration.**

HAGUE PEACE CONFERENCES (1899, 1907). Delegates from twenty-six nations, including only the United States and Mexico from the Americas, assembled May 18–July 29, 1899, at The Hague in the Netherlands. Czar Nicholas II of Russia, who called the meeting, hoped to advance peace through the discussions, especially on arms limitations. This first conference reached modest agreement on rules of land and maritime warfare but failed to make headway on limiting arms. All participating nations agreed to the Convention for the Pacific Settlement of International Disputes, and they created the Permanent Court of Arbitration.

The second conference met June 15–Oct. 18, 1907. Forty-four governments sent delegates, including nineteen from the Americas. Armament discussions again failed; but conventions appeared on laws of war, naval warfare, and neutrality, plus one renouncing the right to use force to collect debts. The Convention for the Pacific Settlement of International Disputes was revised; delegates could not agree on how to create a court of arbitral justice, but adopted a resolution supporting "the principle of obligatory arbitration." The precedents of 1899 and 1907 in the form of conventions, declarations, and stated desires, contributed substantially to later and more fully developed international institutions, including the League of Nations, the United Nations, and international courts of justice.

***HAGUE V. COMMITTEE ON INDUSTRIAL ORGANIZATION*, 207 U.S. 496 (1939).** Mayor Frank Hague of Jersey City, N.J., attempted to suppress the disruptive activities of the Committee on Industrial Organization. His ordinances empowering the director of public safety to deny permits for public meetings when he felt public order might be endangered and forbidding distribution of printed matter were declared by the Supreme Court to be a violation of the Fourteenth Amendment, an important decision involving a review of the history and meaning of civil liberty.

HAIDA. A tribe of the northern sector of the Northwest Coast; despite some differences in social organization and language, it possessed a generally uniform culture with the Tlingit and Tsimshian. About 10,000 Tlingit and 6,000 Tsimshian were living on the coastal mainland of the Alaska panhandle and the northwestern coasts of adjacent British Columbia in 1760, while 8,000 Na-Déné-speaking Haida were located on Queen Charlotte and Prince of Wales islands. Intensive missionization and trade, especially through the Hudson's Bay Company, affected the culture of all three tribes. The native societies were characterized by the system of ceremonial and social exchanges of property, the potlatches, by which an individual validated his place in an elaborate social hierarchy; large communal houses of cedar planks; totem poles (a reflection of the emphasis on social position); and intervillage feasting, reciprocities, and war. Characteristic of the area were exquisite carving and painting. The pressures exerted by the Alaskan gold rush, the presence of salmon canneries, and the introduction of a moneyed economy have brought about far-reaching social changes since 1900.

"HAIL COLUMBIA." First national hymn of the United States, the direct outgrowth of President George Washington's neutrality policy in the war between France and England. In 1798, Joseph Hopkinson, a young lawyer who had a reputation as a poet and patron of the arts, composed a song to the music of "The President's March," which had been written in the early 1790's by Philip Roth. Hopkinson, a strong Federalist and admirer of Washington, avoided reference to either France or England, and gave voice to a national feeling of independence and a determination to protect America's honor and rights.

HAINES' BLUFF (Miss.). Overlooking the Yazoo River about fourteen miles northwest of Vicksburg, it was fortified by the Confederates to protect Vicksburg's right flank and the Chickasaw Bayou region (*see* Chickasaw Bluffs, Battle of). Union Gen. William Tecumseh Sherman made a demonstration against Haines' Bluff, Apr. 30, 1863, to divert Confederate attention while Gen. Ulysses S. Grant ran his transports past the Vicksburg batteries. Grant's movement caused the Confederates to evacuate Haines' Bluff on May 18.

"HAIR BUYER." Epithet fixed on the British lieutenant governor of Detroit, Henry Hamilton, by Kentucky military leader George Rogers Clark. In late 1776, Hamilton promoted Indian raids on settlements of the Ohio frontier, including Boonesborough, Harrodsburg, and Logan's Fort. Clark charged that Hamilton encouraged the Indians to commit inhuman acts, but the charge was unsupported by trustworthy evidence.

HAIR STYLES. The few ladies and gentlewomen in the colonies at the close of the 17th century succumbed briefly to the fashion of elaborate, often outlandish constructions of hair, some of which towered several feet into the air. In the early 1700's hair was worn close to the head and often adorned with gray or white powder. Some sixty years later, architectural innovation again took hold, and hair was arranged around elaborate structures of wire or basketry and adorned with flowers, feathers, fruit, and even small sculptures. About 1800, women's hair became shorter, and soon after, side curls appeared. These evolved, in the early 1840's, into the typical Victorian style of flat pads that covered the ears. In the 1880's the fringe appeared and gradually developed, by being turned back, into the elaborate coiffures associated with the Gay Nineties.

In 1908 the permanent wave, a technique of rapidly softening the hair with alkaline solutions and then styling it before the alkali could damage the hair, was imported into the United States, where it effectively revolutionized women's hair styling. Originally only hair that conformed to the recommended length of three feet was permanent-waved, but about 1915, the dancer Irene Castle popularized bobbed hair, and with that style permanent-waving became a fixture in American culture; innovations, such as the cold wave (introduced in the early 1930's), improved on the process. Hair coloring, originally intended to conceal women's graying hair, became popular as a styling device after World War II. In the 1960's and 1970's, many women adopted hair styles that were freer and less formalized.

By the end of the 17th century gentlemen in America wore the lavish, full-bottomed wigs so popular at the court of Louis XIV of France. These soon gave way to the more practical "travel" and "campaign" wigs, and by the time of the American Revolution many men had abandoned wigs entirely and were tying their hair into pigtails—a single queue at the nape—and using powder to simulate wigs. Men's hair became shorter at the end of the 18th century, and wigs were all but abandoned. (Members of the military and legal professions continued to wear queues into the early 19th century.) During the 19th and 20th centuries there have been few changes in men's hair styles except for length.

Beards and mustaches have had a checkered history. One Joseph Palmer, who died in 1840, has inscribed on his tombstone "Persecuted for growing the beard." A scant twenty years later, beards were regarded as symbols of sincerity and solidity. They vanished just before World War I and then reappeared, first among hippies and later among more conventional men, in the 1950's. Wigs for men appeared in profusion in the 1960's, along with false facial hair, as much for frivolity as for cosmetic purposes.

HAITI, INTERVENTION IN. To protect American life and property in Haiti following a revolution in January 1915, President Woodrow Wilson sent a commission to negotiate a treaty that would give the United States a naval base on the island. The new government, under Gen. Vilburn Guillaume Sam, refused to negotiate. During the summer of 1915, Sam executed 167 political prisoners, and, on July 28, the people of Port-au-Prince rose against the government and killed Sam. That same day, U.S. Marines occupied the island and established almost complete control. The National Assembly elected a president, Sudre Dartiguenave, favorable to the United States. On Sept. 16, Dartiguenave signed a treaty that the Haitian Senate ratified on Nov. 11; under its terms, Americans nominated by the U.S. president but serving as officials of the puppet Haitian government assumed control of the country's finances, police force, public works, and sanitation.

The *caco* (guerrilla) revolt against forced labor in 1918–20 led to an investigation by the U.S. Senate in 1921. The committee's report criticized forced labor but recommended that the marine garrison be maintained. Under Gen. John H. Russell, American high commissioner (1922–30), a few roads were built and yaws was practically eliminated. Civil liberties were infringed by the military and governmental censorship. Only a small part of a $16 million loan obtained from the National City Bank of New York in 1922 was used for public works or productive enterprises. Under the transitory provisions of the constitution of 1918, an appointed council of state exercised the legislative power and elected the president. This "double dictatorship," hatred of the American occupation, and economic distress led to an uprising in 1929. In 1930 President Herbert Hoover appointed a commission to study the problem of terminating the intervention. A popularly elected government took office in 1930; most American officials were gradually withdrawn; and in 1934 the military occupation ended. American financial control continued in accordance with the terms of the 1922 loan.

HAKLUYT'S *VOYAGES*. Short title of a collection of original records of English voyages before 1600; the full title is *The Principall Navigations, Voiages, and Discoveries of the English Nation* (1589). The editor was Richard Hakluyt, clergyman, geographer, and promoter and historiographer of the English expansion. Materials he collected after 1600 were in part included in the work of Samuel Purchas, *Purchas his Pilgrimes* (1625). For virtually every voyage of importance, Hakluyt procured a full narrative by a participant and added many official documents and private letters. He thus preserved the records of the voyages of Jacques Cartier, Sir John Hawkins, Sir Francis Drake, Sir Martin Frobisher, John Davys, Thomas Cavendish, Sir Walter Raleigh (to Guiana), and (in Purchas) Henry Hudson and William Baffin. He also preserved the records of the colonial projects of French Florida, Adrian Gilbert's Newfoundland, and Raleigh's Virginia.

HALDIMAND NEGOTIATIONS. When the Republic of Vermont, established during the revolutionary war at New York's territorial expense, failed to gain admission to the United States, Lord George Germain authorized the British commanders in America to offer Vermont self-government under the crown. In 1780, the Vermont leaders sounded out Gen. Frederick Haldimand, who commanded at Quebec, by proposing an exchange of prisioners. A cartel for exchange of prisoners was arranged, and under cover of this arrangement Haldimand negotiated for Vermont to reunite with Great Britain for the remainder of the American Revolution. The Vermont negotiators were a small group dominated by Ira and Ethan Allen and Gov. Thomas Chittenden, whose guiding principles were to perpetuate Vermont and safeguard its landed interests regardless of who won the war. Haldimand offered Vermont a liberal constitution, preferment for the leaders, confirmation of land titles, and territorial expansion; the Vermonters temporized and only promised to make their land neutral. In 1782, considering that they had again been shabbily treated by Congress and that Vermont might even be suppressed after the war, they sent emissaries to Quebec with proposals for a reunion as soon as Great Britain could protect and subsidize them. But Haldimand delayed and avoided any commitment.

HALE, EXECUTION OF (Sept. 22, 1776). When George Washington desired information as to the British strength and positions, Nathan Hale volunteered to act as a spy. Posing as a schoolmaster, he entered the British lines on Long Island and procured the information. He was returning to his own lines when he was arrested and executed. His last words are said to have been, "I only regret that I have but one life to lose for my country," a paraphrase of a line from Joseph Addison's *Cato*.

HALE OBSERVATORIES. In 1969 the names of the Mount Wilson and Palomar observatories were together changed to the Hale Observatories, in honor of George Ellery Hale (1868–1938). In 1904, Hale, eager to study the sun with the most advanced equipment and under the best atmospheric conditions, led an expedition to Mount Wilson in Southern California; his results were so promising that the Carnegie Institution of Washington provided funds for the Mount Wilson Solar Observatory. The word "Solar" was later dropped from the name, and a substantial amount of research was devoted to stellar, nebular, and galactic composition, evolution, and distribution.

The equatorially mounted reflecting telescopes on Mount

Wilson were designed specifically for long-exposure celestial photography. The 60-inch telescope was completed in 1908, and the 100-inch Hooker telescope, then the largest in the world, in 1918. In 1928 the Rockefeller Foundation agreed to fund, and the California Institute of Technology together with the Mount Wilson Observatory agreed to supervise, the construction and operation of a 200-inch reflector. At its dedication in 1948, the 200-inch instrument was formally named the Hale telescope. A companion telescope was the 48-inch Schmidt camera, designed to yield particularly wide-angle celestial photographs. Since the steady sprawl of Los Angeles has caused the seeing from the observatory to deteriorate, the new telescopes were placed on Mount Palomar, about 45 miles north-northeast of San Diego. Despite their physical separation, the two observatories have always been operated as one research installation.

HALF-BREEDS. A term originally applied to the children of white men and Indian women, but soon extended to include all degrees of racial intermixture. Some half-breeds were the off-spring of Indian fathers and white women who had been captured by the Indians. In the Great Lakes area many French voyageurs and fur trappers married Indian women from such tribes as the Huron, Cree, and Chippewa, and their offspring became known as *métis* (mixed bloods).

HALF-BREED TRACT. The 121,000 acres of land in a triangle between the Mississippi and Des Moines rivers in southeastern Iowa, set aside for the use of half-breeds by a treaty of 1824 with the Sac and Fox Indians. In 1831, Congress gave the half-breeds the right to convey their land. In 1841, after much turmoil between squatters and buyers of the rights, the New York Land Company acquired ownership of 41 of the 101 rights—48,000 acres—through a court decree. When agents of the company tried to sell the land that squatters were improving and to eject the squatters who did not buy, trouble developed. The state adopted occupancy legislation that would assure settlers the value of their improvements in the event of ejection. Only after long and expensive litigation were titles to property in the tract made safe.

***HALF MOON*.** The ship the Dutch East India Company provided for the voyage of exploration made by Henry Hudson in 1609, in the course of which the Hudson River was discovered. A vessel of 80 tons, it was a flat-bottomed two-master of the *vlieboot* type. Later employed in the East India trade, the *Half Moon* was wrecked in 1615 on the shore of the island of Mauritius.

HALFWAY COVENANT (June 1657). If, as they reached adulthood, children of the founders of Massachusetts and Connecticut gave no acceptable proof of spiritual regeneration, should they be granted full church membership? An intercolonial ministerial conference at Boston attempted to answer through the Halfway Covenant, whereby membership was granted to the children whose parents had experienced regeneration but, pending regeneration of their own, participation in the Lord's Supper and voting in the church were withheld. A Massachusetts synod proclaimed it for all Massachusetts churches (1662), but controversy continued for more than a century.

HALIFAX, FORT (Maine). Built in 1754 on a point of land at the confluence of the Sebasticook and the Kennebec rivers, it was one of the last of the line of forts erected by the British to enforce their claim to the Kennebec region.

HALIFAX FISHERIES AWARD. The Marcy-Elgin Reciprocity Treaty of 1854 provided for extension of the inshore fishing "liberties" of the Convention of 1818 to all (instead of stipulated) Atlantic coastal waters of British North America, with reciprocal privileges for British subjects in American coastal waters as far south as 36° north latitude. The treaty expired in 1866. The Treaty of Washington of 1871 secured for American citizens the right to use Canadian fisheries for ten years (extended to expire in 1885), without the reciprocal provision for Canada; a special mixed commission sitting at Halifax awarded $5.5 million in gold to Great Britain as compensation for its abandonment of the reciprocal privilege in American territorial waters.

HALL, FORT (Idaho). A fur-trading post on the left bank of the Snake River near its junction with the Portneuf, built in the summer of 1834 and named in honor of Henry Hall of Boston. In 1837 the fort was sold to the Hudson's Bay Company, which abandoned it in 1855. Fort Hall was a center for trade with Indians and a stopping and trading point for Oregon Trail immigrants (1841–55).

HAMBURG RIOT (July 8, 1876). The most important act of violence in the struggle between the Radical Republicans and the Democrats for the control of South Carolina. Several hundred armed white men gathered in Hamburg to force the disarming of a black militia company accused of obstructing the streets; one white man and seven blacks were killed. Daniel H. Chamberlain, the Republican governor, called the affair a massacre engineered for political purposes. His remarks alienated his white supporters and assured the victory in the state Democratic convention the following August of those who favored no compromise with the Radicals.

HAMILTON, FORT (Ohio). Built in September 1791 on the Miami River, it was the first and one of the most important of a line of posts between Fort Washington (Cincinnati) and Fort Defiance (Maumee Valley).

HAMILTON'S FISCAL POLICIES. When Alexander Hamilton was appointed the first secretary of the treasury (Sept. 11, 1789), he was confronted with disrupted commercial and revenue systems, inadequate currency, a host of unsettled claims, and a very considerable foreign and domestic debt. As a strong proponent of economic nationalism, he considered essential the revival of confidence in public credit at home and abroad, a sound currency, an integrated system of manufactures, the revival of foreign trade, and the establishment of a national bank and a mint. Fortunately for his plans, the congressional act establishing the treasury gave the secretary considerable authority. On Jan. 14, 1790, he presented to Congress the first of his plans for fiscal reforms. The national debt, he believed, should be discharged according to the terms of the original contract. Arrears of interest, as well as the original debt, should be paid eventually. The state debts contracted during the Revolution should be assumed along with the national debt. He proposed a reorganized and orderly system of collecting duties on imports and tonnage, implemented by a duty on imported wines, spirits, coffee, and teas and an excise on domestically distilled spirits. These revenues would provide for the interest on the debt and for the current expenses of government. The payments of principal due on the foreign debt could be provided for by floating new loans abroad; interest would be paid out of the excise. He pointed out as a fundamental maxim that "the creation of debt should always be accompanied with the means of extinguishing it." Provision for the payment of the debt itself would be carried out through the establishment of a sinking fund, under the administration of a board of commissioners who would make judicious purchases of the debt when the purchase price was below par, resulting in the double benefit of retiring the debt and raising the price of stock. Virtually all Hamilton's proposals were enacted.

Unlike the domestic debt, about which there was room for compromise between debtor and creditor, the foreign debt—principal and interest—had to be paid promptly according to the schedule of the original contracts. Acting under two congressional acts (Aug. 4 and Aug. 12, 1790) that authorized the borrowing of $14 million to support public credit, Hamilton and his European agent, William Short, proceeded to negotiate a series of European loans.

A crucial aspect of Hamilton's plans for economic development was the creation of a national bank, which would act as a means of increasing capital, discouraging speculation, and supplying through its bank notes a ready medium of exchange (*see* Bank of the United States). During Hamilton's tenure the bank was a useful agent of the treasury, helping to regulate the currency, facilitate the collection of taxes, prevent the proliferation of state banks, and provide a ready source of loans for the federal government. The mint was established in 1792, but to Hamilton's disappointment, it was placed under the State Department rather than Treasury.

Hamilton's plans for the future of American manufacturing were an integral part of his economic program, but were ignored by Congress, largely because his plan for providing tariff protection and bounties for infant industries was regarded as inimical to the interests of agriculture and as providing special favor to a small economic class (*see* Hamilton's Report on Manufactures).

HAMILTON'S REPORT ON MANUFACTURES (Dec. 5, 1791). As the first secretary of the treasury, Alexander Hamilton insisted that development of the nation required mercantilist policies rather than pursuit of laissez-faire. He set aside the vexing question of the comparative productivity of agriculture and manufactures in favor of the practical benefits of a balanced national economy. He also argued that international commerce was subject to interruptions and that the United States needed to be able to supply itself with the materials of war. Hamilton demonstrated that manufactures were not hostile to agriculture but instead would furnish domestic demand for farm products. To this "home market" argument he added arguments for the propriety of public promotion and the protection of infant industries. In his scheme, agriculture, industry, and commerce would enliven each other. He proposed protective duties on competing imports, but his main emphasis was on bounties and premiums to both domestic manufactures and agriculture, because such bounties and premiums would not make goods scarce or raise prices. The proposals of the report were only partially adopted until the War of 1812 demonstrated their wisdom.

HAMLET CASE (1850). The first recorded case under the Fugitive Slave Law of 1850, it exemplified the charge of abolitionists that the law would facilitate the kidnapping of free blacks. James Hamlet, a free black of New York City, was arrested and taken to a Baltimore jail, in strict accordance with the law. He was redeemed shortly thereafter through the contributions of New York abolitionists.

***HAMMER* V. *DAGENHART*,** 247 U.S. 251 (1918). The U.S. Supreme Court held unconstitutional the Keating-Owen law prohibiting the shipment in interstate commerce of products of mines and factories that employed child labor. A subsequent congressional effort to prohibit child labor through use of its taxing power was also held unconstitutional in *Bailey* v. *Drexel Furniture Company* (259 U.S. 20) in 1922. (*See also* Child Labor.)

HAMPDEN EXPEDITION (1814). Part of the general plan of the British during the War of 1812 to take possession of northeastern Maine in order to gain a direct route from Halifax to Quebec. The British occupied Castine at the mouth of the Penobscot River on Sept. 1, 1814, and proceeded up the river. The militia at Hampden offered but slight resistance, and Capt. Charles Morris of the U.S. corvette *Adams* was forced to fire his vessel and flee. The towns of Bangor (Sept. 3) and Frankfort (Sept. 6) surrendered without resistance.

HAMPTON (Va.). A city facing Chesapeake Bay opposite Norfolk, with a population of 122,617 in 1980. Established in 1610, it claims the title of the oldest continuously occupied English settlement in the New World. Hampton's growth as a city has been relatively recent; it was not incorporated until 1887, although it had been a military objective during the revolutionary war, the War of 1812, and the Civil War, when it was occupied by Union forces. A major U.S. Air Force base is located in Hampton, and a research center of the National Aeronautics and Space Administration. Local industries include processing shellfish and producing a variety of light metal products.

HAMPTON ROADS CONFERENCE (Feb. 3, 1865). In response to an unofficial attempt by Francis P. Blair, Sr., to bring about peace when the collapse of the Confederacy was evident, Jefferson Davis wrote that he was willing to enter into a conference "with a view to secure peace to the two countries." On seeing this letter Abraham Lincoln wrote Blair of his readiness to bring peace "to the people of our one common country." The conference was held on the *River Queen* in Hampton Roads, Va. Lincoln offered peace on the basis of reunion, emancipation, and the disbanding of Confederate troops; the Confederate representatives (Alexander H. Stephens, R. M. T. Hunter, and J. A. Campbell) were not empowered to accept any terms except independence, and so the conference adjourned.

HANDICAPPED, EDUCATION OF THE. The education of the physically handicapped is distinct from that of the mentally, emotionally, socially, and economically handicapped, although there may be an interrelationship or combination of these types in some cases. The education of children with physical handicaps comes under the field of special, or exceptional, education.

The earliest American effort to deal with the problem of educating the physically handicapped began in 1817, when Thomas H. Gallaudet opened a private school for the deaf in Hartford, Conn. He utilized the French manual, or sign, method of communication; his example resulted in the opening of schools in Massachusetts, New York, Pennsylvania, Ohio, and Kentucky. Eventually, the oral method gained ground, but many schools have combined both procedures. Higher education for the deaf was inaugurated in 1864 by Edward M. Gallaudet, son of Thomas, with the establishment of the National Deaf-Mute (now Gallaudet) College in Washington, D.C. A public day school for the deaf using the oral method opened in Boston in 1869. Considerable impetus to the education of the deaf was given by Samuel Gridley Howe and Alexander Graham Bell; the latter helped found the Volta Bureau (1880) and became the first president of the American Association to Promote the Teaching of Speech to the Deaf (1890). A New York State law (1936) required the annual testing of pupils' hearing. In 1979 about 86,000 deaf and hard-of-hearing pupils received special assistance.

The education of the blind was first promoted in the United States by Howe, who organized private schools in Boston (1832), New York, and Philadelphia. After the opening of special public classes in Chicago (1900) and a special school in New York (1909), the trend was to avoid the isolation of the blind in institutions. The American Printing House for the Blind, founded in 1855 in Louisville, Ky., received annual federal grants from 1879. Library facilities for the blind were made available by the Boston Public Library (1868), the New York State Education Department (1896), and the Library of Congress (1897). Congressional laws (1931, 1952) provided library services to blind adults, adolescents, and children. In 1979 about 33,000 blind pupils received special assistance.

The first public school system to provide special schools for the crippled was that of Chicago (1899); New York followed in 1906. In 1937, 301 public school systems had special schools and classes for crippled pupils. Since the mid-1960's children homebound with serious physical defects have been aided by radio, television, and telephone; those in regular schools have benefited from more thoughtfully designed buildings, furniture, and buses. Moreover, wheelchairs have been made available to enable crippled children to become more mobile. In 1979 about 178,000 crippled pupils received special instruction or aid in public schools.

The largest category of the physically handicapped in the schools is that of the speech-defective. In 1979 about 1,216,000 speech-impaired children were undergoing special education. These include the deaf-mute, the stutterers, and those with cleft palate and spastic speech. In the 1970's there was an increase in the number of speech correction programs administered by trained personnel in schools, hospitals, and university clinics.

Health-impaired children have been the subject of nationwide publicity and collection campaigns. The needs of children afflicted with tuberculosis, poliomyelitis, cystic fibrosis, muscular dystrophy, and cerebral palsy have received such special attention at least since the 1930's.

The education of the physically handicapped has been aided by the federal government through the Fogarty-McGovern Act (1958) and the Handicapped Children's Educational Assistance Act (1968), both administered by the Bureau of Education for the Handicapped of the U.S. Office of Education. Education of the handicapped was named as a national priority for the 1970's. In 1980 the needs of handicapped children became the responsibility of the Office of Special Education and Rehabilitative Services within the new Department of Education.

HANDSOME LAKE CULT. An Iroquois nativistic movement founded by a Seneca prophet named Handsome Lake in 1799. It spread rapidly to the other tribes of the Six Nations. The doctrine combined native Iroquois beliefs with those of the Quakers, among whom Handsome Lake had been reared, and it stressed both ethical prescriptions and ritual purification. Handsome Lake told his people to purge their lives of all that was worldly and profane, to live in peace with the whites, and to revive their ancient ceremonies. The religion, which provides for congregational worship in the longhouse, still survives in an altered form.

HANGING. A method of execution brought over from England by the early settlers of America. With the adoption of the Constitution, which prohibited "cruel and unusual punishment," hanging became the sole legal means of effecting capital punishment until the innovation of electrocution and the use of lethal gas. Nevertheless, hanging, as it was conducted, was cruel. It was the occasion of festivities, during which a body was often left suspended for an entire day. The condemned man was frequently flung from a ladder, or placed on a cart that was wheeled from under him, and suffered the agonies of slow strangulation. The 19th century brought about the adoption of more humane and scientific principles. The scaffold was established and the hangman's knot developed; the combined effect of both creates a snapping of the spinal column that results, presumably, in a swift and painless end. All hangings became private and by 1981 only four states had this form of capital punishment.

HANGING ROCK, ACTION AT (Aug. 6, 1780). Gen. Thomas Sumter, with a force practically stripped of ammunition, attacked British regulars, Provincials, and Tories at Hanging Rock, S.C., and defeated it. The Tories fled the field. Had not Sumter's men stopped to plunder the British camp of liquor, their victory could have been made decisive.

HANNASTOWN (Pa.). When the Pennsylvania colonial government organized its westernmost lands into Westmoreland County in 1773, the county seat was established at Robert Hanna's tavern on the old Forbes Road, thirty-five miles east of Pittsburgh. The settlement was an important rendezvous for expeditions against the Indians, who, on July 13, 1782, attacked and burned it. In 1787 the county seat was moved three miles south to Greensburg.

HANNASTOWN RESOLUTION (1775). Upon receipt of the news of the clash at Lexington, Mass., in April, the frontier inhabitants of Westmoreland County, Pa., met at Hannastown on May 16 and declared it the duty of Americans to resist English oppression.

HANNIBAL AND ST. JOSEPH RAILROAD. *See* **Railroads, Sketches of Principal Lines.**

HANOVER CAVALRY ENGAGEMENT (June 30, 1863). On June 25, Confederate Gen. J. E. B. Stuart left Robert E. Lee's advancing army and raided around the Army of the Potomac. Wanting to rejoin Lee, he was forced to detour and moved northward toward Carlisle, Pa. At Hanover, Pa., he was opposed by Gen. Judson Kilpatrick; unable to break through, he turned eastward and arrived on July 1 in Carlisle.

"HAPPY HUNTING GROUND." The "Happy Hunting Ground," where men lived on after death, appears as a concept among the Algonkin-speaking people of the Eastern Woodlands and some adjacent tribes. It is suggestive of Christian values, perhaps stemming from the Jesuits in the area in the 17th century; neither the notion of a "Great Spirit" nor that of a "Happy Hunting Ground" seems integral or organically related to the beliefs of native Americans before their contact with Europeans.

HARD-CIDER CAMPAIGN. *See* **Campaigns, Presidential: Campaign of 1840.**

HARD LABOR, TREATY OF (Oct. 14, 1768). To prevent war between white settlers and Indians, Sir William Petty, Lord Shelburne, sent instructions from London to the superintendents of Indian affairs in southwest Virginia to call the Indian tribes who claimed the western lands into conferences to agree on dividing lines. Supt. John Stuart convened the Cherokee at Hard Labor, S.C., where a treaty was signed fixing the line to run from Tryon Mountain of the Blue Ridge Mountains straight to Chiswell's Mine on the New River and from there in a straight line to the confluence of the Kanawha and Ohio rivers. Virginians were not satisfied; the line as fixed left white settlers in Indian country. Agitation led to a shift of the line farther west by the later Treaty of Lochaber.

HARD MONEY. A term for specie, that is, gold and silver coin. During much of the 18th century, many Americans suffered from the inflation of paper money. The Constitution says that "no State shall . . . make any Thing but gold and silver Coin a Tender in Payment of Debts" (Article I, Section 10), which put the United States on a hard money basis. Since then debtor classes and some business groups have repeatedly tried, often with success, to modify the intent of these words, until on Aug. 15, 1971, the United States took the final step in establishing an irredeemable paper money standard. (*See also* Gold Standard; Money.)

HARDWARE TRADE. The commercial manufacture in the colonies of some iron products, such as wire and nails, began about the middle of the 17th century and increased fairly steadily thereafter. Domestic production did not outpace imports until about 1860. By 1900, U.S. hardware exports exceeded imports. The general store was the main retail hardware outlet, especially in rural America, until the middle of the 19th century. The storekeepers obtained their supplies from urban commission merchants, who usually acted as the agents of the producers, which eliminated the risk of loss to the commission house if prices declined or the products remained unsold. Specialized hardware stores gradually gained in importance during the 19th century. These new retailers and the larger general stores required a greater assortment of goods and more services than the commission merchants could furnish. Hardware wholesalers developed to fill this need and have remained the major source of supply for hardware dealers. The number of hardware stores in the United States peaked at about 35,000 establishments between 1948 and 1958 and then declined to about 26,500 in 1977. Although sales per establishment have increased, a growing share of total hardware sales has been going through new types of outlets, starting with mail-order firms and downtown department stores in the late 19th century and more recently including discount stores, mail-order company retail store units, and now "home centers" (large combination lumber and hardware dealerships).

HARE. A small caribou-hunting grouping of Na-Déné–speaking Indians, living at the edge of the tundra, west and northwest of Great Bear Lake. Their life before contact with Europeans depended on the small socioeconomic band, related tribal segments tied to a hunting and trapping territory; beyond the component bands, which came together locally from time to time, they lacked any sense of tribal organization. Since the 18th century the Hare and their neighbors have been drawn into trade and, today, are being drawn into the changing industrialized patterns of the Canadian north. The group numbered 500–700 in 1800.

HARGIS-CALLAHAN-COCKRELL FEUD. In the 1899 local election in Breathitt County, Ky., James Hargis and Edward Callahan were elected county judge and sheriff, respectively, on the Democratic ticket. When the election was contested, Tom Cockrell, the town marshall of Jackson, and his brother Jim arrested Hargis. In July 1902, Tom Cockrell was accused of killing Hargis's brother Ben in a pistol fight. The feud continued with the killing of many friends and relatives of the Hargis-Callahan faction and the Cockrell family (more than 100 by 1912).

HARLEM. The Dutch who settled during the 1600's in the upper part of New Amsterdam (Manhattan Island) called it Nieuw Haarlem, or New Harlem, after the town in Holland. The early settlers built ground houses and planted large farms. After the British takeover of New Amsterdam in 1664, Harlem became a British community but did not become a part of New York City until 1873. During the 19th century the community attracted many Europeans. The wealthy immigrants lived in luxurious brownstone houses, and many East European Jews moved to lower Harlem from the lower East Side of Manhattan. By the close of the century, real estate speculators had overbuilt Harlem and began to have difficulties in renting some of the new apartments.

The mass settlement of blacks in Harlem started in 1900, after New York's disastrous race riot; one of the spiritual leaders of the movement was Rev. Adam Clayton Powell, Sr. Frightened whites began to move out, and by 1910 they were in full flight. In less than ten years Harlem was a predominantly black community; it later became the culture capital of the black world (*see* Harlem Renaissance).

Politics was a form of community activity in Harlem from its beginning as a black settlement. After 1900 public recognition was accorded this fact: requests made by Harlem politicians for offices and appointments in the 1890's were now reconsidered, and spokesmen at all levels of municipal politics demanded greater recognition of the community. After World War I, Harlem first used its political strength to gain control of the institutions that affect power in the community. During the depression of the 1930's new men and movements appeared, notably Adam Clayton Powell, Jr., a clergyman who became city councilman from Harlem and then the first black congressman from the community. The most noted of the new movements was Father Divine's Peace Kingdoms, which had its greatest development in Harlem.

During and after World War II the Harlem community expanded to accommodate new arrivals from the South. By the 1960's the world's most famous ethnic community was in decline, but in the 1970's it contained over half of New York's million-plus black people.

HARLEM, BATTLE OF (Sept. 16, 1776). After the Battle of Long Island, George Washington withdrew to Manhattan Island and established a line from the mouth of the Harlem River across the island to Harlem (now Morningside) Heights. Morale was low, and groups of soldiers were leaving camp almost daily and going home. On the morning of Sept. 16, about 1,000 British appeared on the Harlem Plains, and skirmishing began; with reinforcements sent down from the heights, the British were repulsed and driven back. This small victory greatly heartened the American troops, and Washington held his position for another month.

HARLEM RENAISSANCE. A black cultural movement during the 1920's that centered in the Harlem ghetto of New York City. Under the influence of W.E.B. DuBois and poet and novelist James Weldon Johnson, the movement was characterized by racial pride and interest in African culture. The burst of black creativity in the literary and visual arts attracted white financial patronage, which disappeared with the Great Depression. Nevertheless, the movement had a broad impact upon American literature, music, and theater.

HARMAR, FORT (Ohio). Built (1785–86) at the junction of the Muskingum and Ohio rivers by Maj. John Doughty and named for Col. Josiah Harmar, who occupied it for a time. Its troops furnished protection to the surveyors of the seven ranges and later to the early settlers at nearby Marietta. After the Treaty of Greenville (1795) the troops were withdrawn.

HARMAR, FORT, TREATIES OF (Jan. 9, 1789). Negotiated by Arthur St. Clair, governor of the Northwest Territory. A treaty with the Six Nations (excepting the Mohawk, not represented) renewed and confirmed the Treaty of Fort Stanwix of 1784. It fixed the western limits of the possessions of the Six Nations; a separate article provided severe punishment for Indians or whites guilty of stealing horses; and goods to the value of $3,000 were given the Indians. The other treaty, with the Wyandot, Delaware, Ottawa, Chippewa, Potawatomi, and Sauk nations, renewed and confirmed the treaty of Fort McIntosh of 1785; these nations were to serve as buffer nations against unfriendly Indians, and for $6,000, the Indians relinquished all claim to lands beyond the limits set forth in the treaty.

HARMAR'S EXPEDITION. In October 1790, Gen. Josiah Harmar marched from Fort Washington (Cincinnati) against the Indian towns at present-day Fort Wayne; two hotly contested battles were fought (Oct. 18, 22). In both battles important detachments of Harmar's troops were defeated, whereupon Harmar retreated to Fort Washington.

HARMONY SOCIETY. Established in Butler County, Pa., in 1804, by German Separatists under the leadership of George Rapp and his adopted son, Frederick Reichert. The Harmonists emigrated from Württemberg, Germany, to escape persecution. Economic necessity and the egalitarianism inherent in their pietistic beliefs led them to organize communistically in 1805. In 1815 the society moved to Posey County, Ind., but it returned in 1825 to a permanent home at Economy, Pa., twenty miles below Pittsburgh on the Ohio River. The Harmonists engaged in agriculture and industry with remarkable success, but late in the century their wealth was dissipated by unwise investments and poor management. They had adopted celibacy in 1807 and, despite occasional new members, their numbers diminished. Most of the property was sold by 1903 and the society came to an end.

HARNESS. For several generations the ox yoke took the place of the harness in the American colonies. The heavy draft harness appeared about 1800 with the advent of post roads, cast-iron plows, and other light agricultural machinery; at the same time, harness and saddle hardware began to be manufactured with allied trades in Connecticut. During the stagecoach period, which lasted from early in the century until the Civil War, harness factories were established at Hartford, Conn.; Newark, N.J.; Wheeling, W. Va.; Louisville, Ky.; Cincinnati, Ohio; and other market centers. With the popularization of the buggy about 1850 a demand arose for a light harness that would be graceful and decorative as well as durable. Harness-making machinery was perfected, culminating in the sewing machine, and accelerated the concentration of manufacturing in quantity-production factories. Harness-making declined with the rise of the motor car.

HARNEY EXPEDITION (1855). Aroused by depredations of Sioux Indians on the frontiers (*see* Grattan Incident) and along the California Trail, the federal government in March ordered Gen. W. S. Harney to punish the offending tribes and occupy their country. Harney left Fort Leavenworth, Kans., on Aug. 5, with 1,200 troops. Proceeding west of Fort Kearney, Nebr., on Sept. 3, he nearly annihilated Little Thunder's band of Brulé Sioux at Ash Hollow. Marching from Ash Hollow by way of Fort Laramie and the White and Cheyenne rivers, Harney reached the Missouri, Oct. 19, at Fort Pierre in Dakota country. In the spring of 1856, Harney built Fort Randall, 150 miles farther down the Missouri.

HARO CHANNEL DISPUTE. The Oregon Treaty of 1846 set the marine boundary between Washington and British Columbia as the middle of the channel that separates Vancouver Island from the continent; but two channels, the Haro Strait and the Rosario Strait, exist, and between them lies the San Juan archipelago, capable of being fortified. An arbitral decision (Oct. 21, 1872), designating the Haro Strait as the channel referred to in the treaty, awarded the archipelago to the United States.

HARPERS FERRY (W. Va.). Located where the Shenandoah River joins the Potomac, it was a key transportation center for western Virginia, Pennsylvania, and Maryland during most of the 19th century. Founded in 1747 by George Harper, the town was designated by President Washington as the site of a federal arsenal in 1796. The arsenal was the objective of John Brown's raid in 1859 and was a principal objective of both Confederate and Union forces during the Civil War. Harpers Ferry commanded access to the rich farmlands and food-raising areas of western Virginia. Union forces took the town early in the Civil War, but Confederate Gen. Thomas J. ("Stonewall") Jackson won a major victory there on Sept. 15, 1862. Retaken by Union troops, it was again retaken by Confederates in 1863.

HARPERS FERRY, CAPTURE OF (Sept. 15, 1862). On Sept. 9, at Frederick, Md., Gen. Robert E. Lee directed Gen. Thomas J. ("Stonewall") Jackson to make a wide march to the southwest, capture the garrison at Harpers Ferry, Va. (now West Virginia), and then hurry northward to rejoin the main army. The main army was to advance westward through South Mountain and meet Jackson as he came north from Harpers Ferry. The combined forces would then move into Pennsylvania. By Sept. 14, Jackson was beginning his siege of Harpers Ferry, but the Union forces at Harpers Ferry put up unexpected resistance and did not surrender until the following day. Lee had advanced to Sharpsburg, expecting Jackson; Jackson was twenty-four hours behind schedule, a delay that was nearly disastrous.

HARPERS FERRY, RAID ON (Oct. 16–18, 1859). A one-man war on the institution of slavery, which created such public discussion and political turmoil that, for the first time, national thought was aroused on the issue. John Brown, a farmer and wool factor, planned to invade the South in a series of raids along the line of the Allegheny Mountains, liberating the slaves and organizing the country under a plan of government of his own devising. At a convention at Chatham, Canada, on May 8, 1858, a provisional constitution was adopted, a paper government set up, and a provisional army established with Brown himself as commander in chief. Harpers Ferry, Va. (now West Virginia), was selected for attack because it offered an easy gateway to the South and the slaveholding sections and because it was the site of the U.S. armory and arsenal. Brown arrived there on July 3, 1859, and established headquarters at the nearby Kennedy farm in Maryland. He moved to the assault on Sunday night, Oct. 16, with seventeen whites and five blacks. The venture failed, for not one slave willingly joined the army of liberation. Besieged by Virginia and Maryland troops, the survivors were driven into a fire engine house on the government reservation. Tuesday morning, Oct. 18, a force of U.S. Marines battered down the doors and captured the insurgents. Brown and six of his men were hanged at Charles Town, the county seat.

HARPER'S WEEKLY. A pictoral magazine founded (1857) by Fletcher Harper of the publishing firm of Harper and Brothers. It exerted great political influence during the Civil War and was famous for the cartoons of Thomas Nast, who became its staff artist in 1862. In 1916, *Harper's Weekly* was consolidated with the *Independent.*

HARRISBURG (Pa.). Located on the Susquehanna River on the site of Harris' Ferry. Selected as state capital (1812) because it was closer to the "western" settlements than the earlier capitals (Philadelphia and Lancaster) but was not too far for eastern lawmakers to travel to it. Besides housing government buildings, the city is an industrial and shipping center. Iron and coal are mined in the vicinity, and several steel mills and factories produce metal products and machinery; food packing and processing plants serving the surrounding farm region. Population in 1980 was 53,264.

HARRISBURG CONVENTION (July 30–Aug. 3, 1827). After the Tariff of 1824 proved unsatisfactory to the woolen interests and the Woolens Bill of 1827 had been defeated, meetings were held in the northern states and 100 delegates from thirteen states met at Harrisburg, Pa., to agree on a new bill. A memorandum to Congress set forth the special needs of the woolens manufacturers and the value of protection, but the demands of the memorandum were ignored.

HARRIS' FERRY (Pa.). John Harris settled on the Susquehanna River shortly before 1719, and later operated a public ferry there; the settlement was known as Harris' Ferry. In 1785 his son, John Harris, Jr., had a city laid out around his home called Louisbourg in honor of King Louis XVI; by 1791 it was known by its present name, Harrisburg.

HARRISON, FORT (Ind.). Named for Gen. William Henry Harrison. Built in 1811 on the east bank of the Wabash River, where Terre Haute now stands, as a protection against depredations by the Indians Tecumseh and the Prophet.

HARRISON LAND ACT (May 10, 1800). Named after William Henry Harrison, first delegate from the Northwest Territory and chairman of the Committee on Public Lands responsible for its framing; it amended and democratized the terms of the act of 1796, reflecting the demands of the frontier (*see* Land Act of 1796), by facilitating individual purchases of land on easier terms (*see also* Division Act of 1800). The act provided for the sale of land west of the Muskingum River in units as small as 320 acres. East of the river tracts of 640 acres would still be offered. The credit system was made more flexible; a four-year term was offered, during which time payments might be completed and penalties for forfeiture abated. The minimum price of $2 an acre and the auction system were retained. Four land districts were established, each with a land office—Cincinnati, Chillicothe, Marietta, and Steubenville (all in present-day Ohio). Annual auction sales were to be held at each but private sales might take place in the intervening periods. The office of register was instituted to administer the land sales and records in each district.

HARRISON'S LANDING LETTER, McCLELLAN'S. In July 1862, Union Gen. George B. McClellan prepared a letter in which he set out his personal views concerning the existing state of the rebellion. He handed it to President Abraham Lincoln at Harrison's Landing, Va., on the James River, where Lincoln had come following the Seven Days' Battles. McClellan did not intend the letter to be published, but the contents soon became publicly known. The views of McClellan were in opposition to those of the radical element of the Republican party, whose renewed opposition ultimately led to McClellan's downfall a few months later.

HARRODSBURG (Ky.). The earliest white settlement in Kentucky was begun at Harrod's Town (or Harrodsburg) in June 1774 by James Harrod. It became the principal base of operation for the Virginia pioneers.

HARTFORD (Conn.). Capital and largest city in Connecticut, with a population of 136,392 in 1980. It is located on the Connecticut River, about forty miles from the mouth of the river (as far inland as ships of the early days could travel). A Dutch trading post known as Fort Good Hope was established at the site in 1633; a whole town of Massachusetts settlers, directed by the Rev. Thomas Hooker, moved there in 1635. The English settlers far outnumbered the Dutch and took over the Dutch post in 1654. In 1662 a royal charter issued to Connecticut caused the original "river towns" of Connecticut to absorb the New Haven colony; there was a great deal of rivalry between the towns of New Haven and Hartford, and they were both listed as state capital from 1662 to 1875, when Hartford's position was finally established. Hartford is the home of over forty insurance companies and many precision manufacturing industries. A 19th-century industrial specialty, the Colt .45 revolver, provided the city with its start in precision tool making; firearms are still produced in the city.

HARTFORD. A wooden-screw steam sloop-of-war, 2,790 tons, 226 feet by 43 feet, named for Hartford, Conn., and launched at Boston, Nov. 22, 1858. During the Civil War it became famous as the flagship of Adm. David Glasgow Farragut in the passage of forts Jackson and St. Philip, in the bombardment and passage of the batteries at Vicksburg, Miss., and at Port Hudson, La., and in the Battle of Mobile Bay. In 1939 it was taken to Norfolk, Va.; it sank in 1956.

HARTFORD, TREATY OF (1650). Signed by Peter Stuyvesant, governor of New Netherland, and the commissioners of the United Colonies of New England after quarrels over the ownership of the Connecticut Valley, the detention of fugitives, trade by the Dutch with the Connecticut Indians, the expulsion of English traders along the Delaware River, and Stuyvesant's seizure of a Dutch ship in New Haven harbor. Stuyvesant visited Hartford, where four arbitrators presented an award that left the Delaware question open; accepted Stuyvesant's explanation of the ship seizure; and established a boundary line between the English and Dutch drawn, on Long Island, across the island from Oyster Bay, and, on the mainland, from Greenwich twenty miles northward into the country. The Estates-General ratified this agreement in 1656; England never ratified it.

HARTFORD CONVENTION (Dec. 15, 1814–Jan. 5, 1815). At the invitation of the Massachusetts legislature twenty-six New England Federalist delegates, elected by the legislatures, were sent from Massachusetts, Connecticut, and Rhode Island. Vermont and New Hampshire failed to cooperate, although some counties sent delegates. The convention was held in secret sessions at Hartford, Conn., to consider the advisability of calling a general convention to revise the Constitution. The resolutions adopted for the consideration of New England legislatures recommended interstate cooperation in repelling British attacks; the use of federal revenues in state defense; the protection of citizens against unconstitutional military acts; and constitutional amendments that would limit southern political power, commercial embargoes and trade restrictions, declarations of war, admission of new states into the Union, and officeholding by naturalized citizens. Because of its secrecy and because of the immediate end of the war, the convention was laid open to ridicule and charges of treasonable intent.

HARTFORD WITS. In the late 18th century a small group of young writers, chiefly Yale graduates, banded together as an informal literary club at Hartford, Conn. They achieved wide recognition through their timely satiric verse and were dubbed the Hartford (or Connecticut) Wits. The principal members were John Trumbull, Joel Barlow, David Humphreys, Timothy Dwight, Theodore Dwight, Richard Alsop, and Lemuel Hopkins. Their chief writings in collaboration were *The Anarchiad, The Political Greenhouse for the Year 1798,* and *The Echo,* which satirized educational curricula and Jeffersonian democracy.

HARVARD UNIVERSITY. Oldest college in the United States. Founded in 1636 at Cambridge, Mass., with a grant of £400 from the Massachusetts General Court; its first classes were held in 1638. Named for John Harvard, a graduate of Emmanuel College in Cambridge, England, who left the institution half his property and his entire library. According to the charter of 1650, college affairs are administered by the Corporation (consisting of the president and five fellows, given perpetual succession) and by the Board of Overseers. In 1780 Harvard became a university; in 1782 a medical school was established; and in 1817 a law school was added. Under John T. Kirkland (president, 1810–1828), the college acquired professors with European training.

The greatest advances were made under Charles William Eliot (president, 1869–1909), who turned Harvard from a provincial college into a great national university; he laid the foundations of the graduate school in 1872, revived the law school by appointing Christopher Columbus Langdell dean, and reformed the medical school. Believing that students should not be forced to study subjects in which they had absolutely no interest, Eliot introduced the elective system.

Tempering Eliot's emphasis on the elective system, Abbott Lawrence Lowell (president, 1909–1933) asked undergraduates to concentrate in one discipline and introduced the tutorial system. He also introduced the house plan, financed by Edward S. Harkness; in this plan the three upper classes were lodged with their tutors in residential units.

HASTINGS' CUTOFF. Named for Lansford W. Hastings, who first advocated its use in 1846. A route to California that crossed the Great Salt Desert and the Sierra Nevada instead of proceeding north to Fort Hall, Idaho, and then branching southward. It was shorter, but the desert produced terrible suffering among emigrants driving slow-moving ox teams.

HATCH ACT (Aug. 2, 1939). Sen. Carl Hatch of New Mexico and many others had become concerned about the political manipulation during the 1930's of the rapidly expanding federal service. Since 1883 the Pendleton Civil Service Reform Act had, with some success, controlled partisan political activity by career civil servants. The Hatch Act applied the same restrictions to all federal employees except those in policy posts; a 1940 amendment brought under the act all state and local employees paid in full or in part by federal funds. The new statute required nonpayment and removal of violators, a penalty that, by a 1950 amendment, could be reduced to ninety days' suspension without pay.

The Hatch Act was upheld in 1947 by a divided Supreme Court, which accepted the view that public employment was a privilege subject to reasonable conditions, one of which could be the limitation of overt partisan activity. A 1972 U.S. district court ruling held, by a two-to-one vote, that the Hatch Act was vague, overly broad, and counter to the First Amendment. By a six-to-three decision on June 25, 1973, the Supreme Court again upheld the constitutionality of the Hatch Act. A companion decision upheld so-called Little Hatch Acts of state and local governments.

HATCHER'S RUN, BATTLE OF. *See* **Boydton Plank Road, Engagement at.**

HATCHET, CARRIE NATION'S. Carrie Nation (1846–1911) led demonstrations against saloons, praying and preaching at the doors of the illegal bars in Barber County, Kans., where she lived. She decided that more drastic measures were necessary, and in 1900 wrecked several saloons with stones and iron bars, in an attempt to get herself arrested; in arresting her, the town officials would have acknowledged the existence of the illegal saloons. In Wichita, on Jan. 21, 1901, she first used a hatchet. Saloon smashing was copied by women throughout the United States.

HATFIELD-McCOY FEUD. Anderson (Anse) Hatfield, clan leader, and many of his kinsmen lived in or near Williamson, W. Va.; the McCoys lived just across the border in Kentucky. Their animosity dated back to the Civil War, but the feud proper began in 1880, after a Hatfield had been accused of stealing a hog belonging to Randolph McCoy. In 1882 three sons of Randolph were seized by a squad of Hatfields led by a constable and a justice of the peace, on pretense of arrest for the killing of Ellison Hatfield; instead, the sons were brutally murdered. The feud continued savagely until 1888, when Kentucky officers made several raids into West Virginia, killing at least two Hatfield clansmen and capturing nine more. Two of the men were executed, and the others sent to prison. By 1890, except for occasional killings, the feud was ended.

HAT MANUFACTURE, COLONIAL RESTRICTIONS ON. Colonial manufacturers, especially in New England and New York, exported hats to neighboring colonies, the West Indies, and southern Europe. In 1732 the influential Company of Felt-Makers in London persuaded Parliament to forbid colonial exportation of hats, to require a seven years' apprenticeship, to exclude blacks, and to limit each manufacturer to two apprentices. The industry's rapid growth after 1783 suggests that the law had had an inhibiting effect.

HATTERAS INLET, CAPTURE OF (Aug. 28–29, 1861). At Hatteras Inlet, the key to Pamlico Sound, the Confederates had erected two weak forts. These were attacked by six Union steam warships and one sailing sloop under Flag Officer S. H. Stringham. By using chiefly his large-shell guns and steaming at varying ranges, Stringham made it impossible for the defenders to reply effectively with their old short-range smooth-bores, and soon demolished the forts, forcing the garrison to surrender.

HAUN'S MILL MASSACRE (Oct. 30, 1838). An armed mob in Caldwell County, Mo., seeking to drive a colony of Mormons from the state, suddenly appeared at the settlement, killed seventeen colonists, robbed their homes, and ordered the survivors to leave the country on pain of death.

HAVANNA, ACT OF (July 30, 1940). Designed to prevent the transfer to Germany of European colonies in the Western Hemisphere, the act was unanimously approved by the Pan-American Union. It provided that the American republics, collectively or individually, might in the interest of common defense take over and administer any European possession in the New World endangered by aggression.

HAVANA CONFERENCE (Jan. 16–Feb. 20, 1928). The sixth international conference of American states. It improved the organization of the Pan American Union and produced definite progress toward international conciliation and intellectual cooperation, but the principle of nonintervention was not agreed to by the participants.

HAVASUPAI. One of three Yuman-speaking small tribes located in the middle course of the Colorado River in western Arizona. The three—Havasupai, Walapai, and Yavapai—appear not to have numbered more than 1,000 at any time. Although a Basin-type people and former gatherers, they took over river-bottom farming of maize and its associated food plants. They have been an isolated and marginal cultural segment in the American Southwest and maintained their tribal autonomy and cultural norms until the 20th century.

HAWAII. A group of Pacific islands some 2,000 to 3,600 miles west-southwest of California, which became the fiftieth of the United States in 1959. The islands were discovered in 1778 by the English navigator Capt. James Cook, who called them the Sandwich Islands. The first American known to have reached Hawaii was John Ledyard of Connecticut, who sailed with Cook. Merchants from New England were established at Honolulu, the major deepwater port of Hawaii, by 1820, when they were joined by missionaries and whalers from the same region. From 1820 to 1860, Hawaii's commercial life centered on whaling; 80 percent of the ships were American, and shops, warehouses, and shipyards ashore were largely American-owned. American missionaries became trusted advisers of the chiefs and influenced the development of law and government. The monarchy, created by Kamehameha I (1784–1810), was modified in the 1840's by a written constitution and laws based on those of American states; monarchs ruled until 1893, with many Americans among their ministers and officials.

In 1826 a treaty between Hawaii and the United States was signed by the commander of the U.S.S. *Peacock;* it was respected by Hawaii but never ratified by the United States. Formal diplomatic relations began in 1843, with the appointment of a U.S. commissioner. A commercial treaty was completed in 1849. Increased contact between the islands and the coast led to an American sentiment for annexation of Hawaii. In 1854 a treaty providing for admission of the island kingdom as a state was actually signed, but failed of approval because of the death of King Kamehameha III.

From an estimated 300,000 at the time of Cook, the population declined to fewer than 60,000 by 1870, mainly because of introduced diseases and out-migration. Whaling was replaced by sugar-growing as the mainstay of the economy after 1860; rapid growth of the industry brought ever-closer ties with the United States. Sugar's growth demanded an enlarged labor supply, and supplementary labor was sought from China, Japan, Portugal, northern Europe, and the Pacific islands. By 1900 the population was again on the rise, but the Hawaiians were outnumbered by aliens, chiefly from Asia. Unrest under King Kalakaua and his sister, Queen Liliuokalani, was further stimulated by the effects of the 1890 McKinley Tariff on the market for Hawaii's sugar. The queen's attempt to lessen American influence in her government led to a revolt and overthrow of the monarchy in 1893, with U.S. Minister John L. Stevens deeply involved in the revolution. The leaders of the new provisional government immediately petitioned Washington for annexation, but a treaty signed for that purpose was withdrawn from the U.S. Senate by President Grover Cleveland.

From 1894 to 1898 the Republic of Hawaii, led by President Sanford B. Dole, awaited a friendly Washington administration; a joint resolution of Congress finally brought annexation. The bulk of the Hawaiian population opposed the ending of their independence, but only one minor attempt at armed opposition (1895) took place.

Under the 1900 Organic Act the immigration laws of the United States were extended to the Territory of Hawaii, cutting off the importation of contract workers first from China and then from Japan; after 1906 the Philippines became the major source of workers. Sugar continued to be the dominant industry, paralleled after 1900 by the growth of pineapple production. As early as 1873, Maj. Gen. John Schofield had investigated the military value of Pearl Harbor, on the island of Oahu, and exclusive U.S. use of that potential base had been secured as a condition of renewal of a trade treaty in 1887. In 1908 work on opening Pearl Harbor for a naval station was begun. During World War I a major army installation was built at Schofield Barracks, also on Oahu. After the Japanese attack on Pearl Harbor and other military bases on Dec. 7, 1941, Hawaii was a major command center for the Pacific war; federal expenditures became the major source of income. Wartime population reached more than 800,000.

At the time of annexation, statehood for Hawaii received scant consideration, chiefly for ethnic reasons. A campaign for statehood in the 1930's was frustrated by concern over

Japanese expansion in the Pacific. Even after World War II, political maneuvers delayed passage of a statehood law until 1959. By the 1970's Hawaii's population was being changed by migration from the mainland and from the Philippines and Samoa. Japanese and Chinese percentages dropped to 28 and 5 percent, respectively. In 1980 the population was 965,000 and Hawaii ranked fortieth among the states. Tourism had become the single most important industry.

HAWES-CUTTING ACT. *See* **Tydings-McDuffie Act.**

HAWKS. Name applied to those who enthusiastically supported American participation in the Vietnam War. It gained currency during the presidency of Lyndon B. Johnson.

HAWK'S PEAK EPISODE (Mar. 6–9, 1846). When John C. Frémont was ordered by the Mexicans to leave California, he occupied Gavilan (Hawk's) Peak, some twenty-five miles from Monterey, Calif., built a log fort, and raised the American flag. After three days he set out for Oregon. The affair may be regarded as a direct cause of the Bear Flag Revolt.

HAWLEY-SMOOT TARIFF. *See* **Smoot-Hawley Tariff.**

HAW RIVER, BATTLE OF (Feb. 25, 1781). While in pursuit of Sir Banastre Tarleton and his British troops, Col. Henry Lee crossed the Haw River in North Carolina, pretended his forces were reinforcements hurrying to Tarleton, and nearly annihilated a local Loyalist force. This deterred many local Tories from espousing the Loyalist cause.

HAY–BUNAU-VARILLA TREATY (Nov. 18, 1903). Signed by Secretary John M. Hay and Philippe Bunau-Varilla, envoy at Washington of the Panama republic. The United States guaranteed the independence of the republic of Panama, while that republic granted the United States in perpetuity "the use, occupation, and control of a strip of land ten miles wide for the construction of a canal"; in return for sovereign rights over this zone and the adjacent waters, the United States agreed to pay $10 million when ratifications were exchanged and, beginning nine years later, an annuity of $250,000. (*See also* Hay-Herrán Treaty.)

HAY BURNING. When settlement moved beyond the timber belt, the homesteaders burned buffalo chips for fuel; when these were gone, they turned to hay. It was twisted into convenient hanks called "cats" and burned like sticks of wood. Mechanical devices were invented to twist these cats, as were special types of hay-burning stoves.

HAYBURN'S CASE (1792). The first case involving the constitutionality of an act of Congress to reach the federal courts, it arose out of a pension law authorizing circuit judges to pass on claims subject to review by the secretary of war and Congress. The decision of the Pennsylvania circuit, declining to hear the petition of William Hayburn on the ground that the law was inconsistent with the Constitution, led the attorney general to appeal to the Supreme Court for a mandamus. The justices refused to act on the motion, but took under advisement one in behalf of Hayburn; before a decision was announced, other relief for pensioners was provided. The decision in the Pennsylvania circuit is sometimes styled the "first Hayburn case" to distinguish it from the motion before the Supreme Court.

HAYES AWARD (Nov. 12, 1878). A decision ending an Argentine-Paraguayan dispute over territory between the Verde and Pilcomayo rivers. In 1876 the two governments had agreed to submit the question of title to the president of the United States; in 1878, Rutherford B. Hayes rendered an award upholding Paraguay's claims.

HAYES-TILDEN CONTROVERSY. *See* **Campaigns, Presidential: Campaign of 1876.**

HAYFIELD FIGHT (Aug. 1, 1867). A battle between the Miniconjou Sioux and soldiers of Fort C. F. Smith, Mont. It took place 2.5 miles from the fort with no decisive victory for either side. (*See* Sioux Wars.)

HAY-HERRÁN TREATY (Jan. 22, 1903). Signed by Secretary of State John M. Hay and Dr. Tomás Herrán, the Colombian minister. It allowed the New Panama Canal Company, which held an option on the canal route, to sell its properties to the United States. The treaty further provided that Colombia would lease to the United States a strip of land across the Isthmus of Panama for the construction of a canal, in return for $10 million cash and, after nine years, an annuity of $250,000. It was ratified by the U.S. Senate, but not by the Colombian congress. (*See also* Hay–Bunau-Varilla Treaty; Panama Canal.)

HAYMARKET RIOT (May 4, 1886). An incident of the militant movement in 1886 in Chicago for an eight-hour working day. In protest against the shooting of several workmen, August Spies, editor of the semianarchist *Arbeiter-Zeitung,* issued circulars demanding revenge and announcing a mass meeting at the Haymarket. In anticipation of violence, large police reserves were concentrated nearby. Despite Mayor Carter H. Harrison's advice, 180 police advanced on the meeting and ordered the crowd to disperse. At this point, a bomb fell among the police, resulting in seven deaths and seventy injured. Eight alleged anarchists were convicted on a conspiracy charge and four were hanged. The eight-hour movement collapsed beneath the stigma of radicalism. Gov. John P. Altgeld pardoned the three surviving prisoners in 1893, declaring that the trial had been a farce.

HAY-PAUNCEFOTE TREATIES. The first Hay-Pauncefote Treaty, signed Feb. 5, 1900, by Secretary of State John Hay and Sir Julian Pauncefote, the British ambassador, modified the Clayton-Bulwer Treaty of 1850, which provided for a joint protectorate by England and the United States of any transisthmian canal. It permitted the construction and maintenance of a canal under the sole auspices of the United States. The U.S. Senate amended the treaty to have it supersede the Clayton-Bulwer Treaty and to give the United States the right to fortify the canal; Great Britain declined to accept the Senate amendments. The second Hay-Pauncefote Treaty, signed Nov. 18, 1901, declared that it should supersede the Clayton-Bulwer Treaty and provided that a canal might be constructed under the auspices of the United States, which would have all the rights incident to such construction as well as the right to manage the canal. It stipulated that the canal should be free and open to the vessels of all nations "on terms of entire equality" and that the charges of traffic should be "just and equitable" (*see* Panama Tolls Question). The United States was virtually accorded sole power to assure the neutrality of transisthmian transit.

HAYS, FORT (Kans.). Built in 1867, one of a system of military posts established to combat hostile Plains Indians. Gen. Philip H. Sheridan for a time made his headquarters at Fort Hays, as did Gen. George A. Custer. When the Kansas Pacific Railroad reached this point, Hays City was settled; it became the most turbulent town on the Plains while it was the railhead. Here James Butler ("Wild Bill") Hickok began his career as a frontier marshal in 1869.

HAYWOOD-MOYER-PETTIBONE CASE. Former Gov. Frank Steunenberg of Idaho was killed in 1905 by a bomb planted at his home by Harry Orchard. The assassin turned state's evidence and implicated the principal officers of the old Western Federation of Miners, generally viewed as a radical union: Charles H. Moyer, president; William D. Haywood, secretary-treasurer; and George A. Pettibone. Through questionable extradition proceedings, these men were taken from Colorado to Idaho. A jury of farmers and ranchmen acquitted Haywood; later, Pettibone was tried and acquitted, and Moyer was released without trial.

HAZELWOOD REPUBLIC. Organized July 29, 1856, by Rev. Stephen R. Riggs at his Hazelwood Mission near Yellow Medicine, Upper Sioux Agency, in western Minnesota. The constitution, signed by seventeen Indians and eight half-breeds, professed belief in God and His Word, education, agriculture, adoption of the dress and habits of white men, and obedience to U.S. laws. A president, secretary, and three judges were elected biennially. The republic numbered eighty-two full bloods by 1858. Weakened by hostilities of "blanket" Indians, it disbanded about 1860.

"HEADQUARTERS IN THE SADDLE." When Gen. John Pope was brought from the western front in 1862 to take command of the Union Army of Virginia, he issued a proclamation to the soldiers and was credited with saying that his headquarters would be in the saddle. The expression was used by Gen. W. J. Worth as early as the Seminole War in 1841; Pope said later that it was a standing joke at West Point before he graduated in 1842 and denied that he would have used anything so stale.

HEADRIGHT. The system in most of the English colonies, especially in the 17th century, of granting a certain number of acres, usually fifty, for each settler. The grant was made either to the settler himself or to the person who paid for his transportation. This principle was also found in the early land laws of Texas (*see* Empresario System).

HEALTH, EDUCATION, AND WELFARE, DEPARTMENT OF (HEW). Established on Apr. 11, 1953, under the president's Reorganization Plan No. 1, supplanting the Federal Security Agency. The new cabinet-status department had four operating agencies: the Office of Education; the Social Security Administration; the Social and Rehabilitation Service; and the Public Health Service. This last consisted of the National Institutes of Health; the Food and Drug Administration; the Alcohol, Drug Abuse and Mental Health Administration; the Center for Disease Control; the Health Resources Administration; and the Health Services Administration. In 1979, as a result of lobbying of the National Education Association, a new Department of Education was formed; HEW became the Department of Health and Human Services.

HEALTH, PUBLIC. *See* **Public Health.**

HEATH PATENT (Oct. 30, 1629). A proprietary grant by Charles I to Sir Robert Heath of the region south of Virginia between 31° and 36° north latitude, to be known as Carolana, later styled Carolina. Heath's colonists landed in Virginia in 1633 but could not obtain passage to Carolana. Busy in London, Heath in 1638 transferred his patent to Henry Frederick Howard, Lord Maltravers, who appointed officers and directed them to encourage Virginians to settle in Carolana. The region was explored and land purchased from Indians but not settled. In 1663 the Privy Council declared the Heath patent forfeited because of failure to plant a settlement.

HEATING AND AIR CONDITIONING. House warming depended on the primitive fireplace, often without a chimney, through the 17th century. In 1744, Benjamin Franklin issued a pamphlet describing his "Pennsylvania fireplace." Stoves used in America at that time were not "scientific," but Franklin's stove was (*see* Franklin Stove). The stove was not particularly popular, but it ushered in a fever of invention of what came to be called Franklin stoves, Rittenhouse stoves, or Rumford stoves. The stove gradually became independent of the fireplace, which it replaced as the household hearth. Stove plates—that is, the sides and backs of stoves—became the largest single product of the American iron industry.

Central heating had been known in ancient times to the Romans and the Chinese, both of whom made hollow heating ducts in the floors and walls of houses. The American architect B. H. Latrobe made such an installation in the U.S. Capitol building (1806). More common was the central heating introduced (1808) by Daniel Pettibone in the Pennsylvania Hospital in Philadelphia: a stove in which the smokepipe was enclosed within a larger pipe through which hot air circulated. Heating by passing hot water through pipes was subsequently used to heat buildings as they became too large to be heated efficiently by stoves. Many factories were heated by the "waste" heat from the steam engines with which they were powered, and piped steam became an alternative to hot water. Both systems were installed in the skyscrapers that began to appear in Chicago in the 1880's.

A demand for artificial ventilation arose out of the conception that unpleasant odors and night air both caused disease; the chimneylike ventilator that had long been common on ships was applied to a few hospitals, and ordinary fireplaces were sometimes activated in summer, merely to draw in "fresh air." In the 1860's Americans could buy small blowers that would operate for a few hours through the force of a weight or spring. Twenty years later the electric motor was developed; the electric fan was one of the first applications of this motor. In 1902, Willis H. Carrier of Buffalo introduced a cooling coil on which water condensed, dehumidifying the air. In 1906 the term "air conditioning" was introduced to describe the control of temperature, humidity, circulation, and purity of air in closed spaces. In the 1840's Dr. John Gorrie had developed an ice machine to make ice for the cooling of hospital rooms, but cooling was an incidental effect of the first air-conditioning systems; Carrier wrote in 1910 of the cooling effect of the new installation in the U.S. Capitol, but actually what the installation did was to reduce the humidity. Home air conditioners awaited the development of the small and reliably automatic refrigeration machine, which became available in the 1930's.

"HE KEPT US OUT OF WAR." The phrase epitomizing President Woodrow Wilson's success, up to that time, in avoiding the European war was first used in the Democratic platform of 1916 and echoed by William Jennings Bryan at the St. Louis convention. It became a campaign slogan and aided in Wilson's reelection.

HELDERBERG WAR. *See* **Antirent War.**

HELENA (Mont.). The capital of Montana, with a population of 23,938, in the census of 1980. Settlement began in 1864 when four prospectors struck gold in what they called "Last Chance Gulch." In the fall of 1864, a town was organized and named Helena. After the first rush was over, gold locked in quartz rocks was found and regular mining equipment was needed to handle that kind of ore. The town had its own newspaper, a land-office, and a bank within two years of its founding. In 1875, it became the capital of Montana Territory. It was named capital of the state as a result of a series of statewide elections in 1892 and 1894.

Helena developed rapidly after mining firms found silver and lead in the vicinity. After the Northern Pacific and the Great Northern railroads crossed in the town, Helena became an important shipping center. The main local industry is the mining and smelting of lead. In addition, the city is a supply center for sheep and cattle ranching and farming.

HELENA, BATTLE OF (July 4, 1863). A Confederate force attempted to take Helena, Ark., which was strongly fortified and held by Union troops. The Confederate right wing stormed the Union works, but the left was defeated, and the right was finally driven back, the whole attack failing.

HELENA MINING CAMP. Established in 1864 with the discovery of gold in Last Chance Gulch, Prickly Pear Valley, just east of the Continental Divide; the most productive mining camp in Montana. Gold seekers hurried to the new diggings, which soon adopted the name Helena; the district became known as Rattlesnake.

HELICOPTERS, MILITARY. With the development of the single-rotor type by Igor Sikorsky in the United States in 1939–41, the helicopter became a practical aircraft capable of carrying a useful load and having almost limitless commercial and military applications because of its unique ability to land and take off vertically, to hover in the air, and to maneuver readily in all directions at slow flight speeds. During the latter part of World War II, helicopters flew numerous lifesaving missions; about 500 helicopters had been produced by the close of the war. In 1947 the navy introduced helicopters on aircraft carriers to rescue downed pilots and crews. The Korean War saw increasing use of the helicopter in rescue and supply missions and in battlefield evacuation; it also saw its first application as a tactical weapon in 1951, when helicopters were employed by the U.S. Marine Corps as assault transports to move troops into battlefield positions over inaccessible terrain. Helicopters also became an essential component of antisubmarine warfare by carrying dunking sonar, magnetic airborne detection equipment, and homing torpedoes. During the Vietnam War, helicopters equipped with machine guns, rockets, and small guided missiles were developed specifically for armed escort of transports and ground interdiction; another development was the employment of large helicopters as flying cranes in construction work and to resupply ships at sea. The number of helicopters purchased annually by the military averaged about 1,500 per year after 1967, exceeding the number of fixed-wing aircraft produced for the military during the same period. In the mid-1970's about 12,000 helicopters were in service.

"HELL ON WHEELS." A term applied, because of their turbulent character, to the temporary rails-end towns, or construction camps, of the Union Pacific Railroad, built 1865–69.

HELPER'S *IMPENDING CRISIS OF THE SOUTH*. Published in 1857, an economic appeal to nonslaveholders of the South written by Hinton Rowan Helper, a North Carolinian of the small-farmer class. Using the census reports of 1790 and 1850, he contrasted northern and southern states to show that the South, with slave labor, was unable to keep pace with the "free" North in population, agriculture, industry, and commerce; by selecting and misinterpreting his figures, he convinced many northerners, uninfluenced by the moral appeal, that slavery was an economic fallacy. By the end of 1857, 13,000 copies had been sold; by 1860, 142,000. A *Compendium,* published in 1859, was widely circulated as Republican campaign literature. In the South copies were publicly burned, and individuals were jailed for buying or possessing it. "Helperites" were deprived of positions and privileges. A Virginian, Samuel M. Wolfe, refuted Helper in a book entitled *Helper's Impending Crisis Dissected* (1860).

HEMP. England early sought hemp from the colonies to rig its sailing ships. It never became an important export crop, but hemp patches were attached to many colonial homesteads, hemp and tow cloth were familiar household manufactures, and local cordage supplied colonial shipyards. After the Revolution, hemp became a staple crop in Kentucky. Output peaked about 1860, when 74,000 tons were raised in the United States, of which Kentucky produced 40,000 tons and Missouri 20,000 tons. Thereafter, the advent of the steamship, the substitution of steel for hemp cordage, and the introduction of artificial fibers lessened demand; U.S. production of hemp for fiber ceased shortly after World War II.

HEMPSTEAD (N.Y.). One of the oldest towns on Long Island, settled in 1643 by Englishmen from Wethersfield and Stamford, Conn. The land was granted by Gov. William Kieft and by the Massapeague, Merrick, and Rockaway Indians. A fort, a meetinghouse, and the first dwellings were built within a palisade. Popularly thought to have been named for Hemel Hempstead in England, but other authorities claim it was named by the Dutch for a town in Holland (until about 1700 the name was spelled Heemstede). In 1683, Hempstead was made part of Queens County, and in 1899, part of Nassau County. In the early 1900's the rural town began its expansion as an urban community with the arrival of the Long Island Railroad. The 1980 population was 40,404.

HENDERSON LAND COMPANY. After the voiding of the Transylvania Company's title to lands in the Kentucky country by the Virginia legislature, Richard Henderson went to French Lick, North Carolina, and opened a land office for the promotion and sale of lands in the Tennessee country. Nashborough, later Nashville, was the center of the company's operations until 1783, when the North Carolina legislature declared the title of the company void.

HENING'S STATUTES. A collection in thirteen volumes of all the public laws of Virginia from the first session of the legislature (1619) to the session ending Dec. 28, 1792, compiled and edited by William Waller Hening, pursuant to an act of the Virginia assembly (1808). The first four volumes were published in 1809; by an act of 1819 an enlarged edition (thirteen volumes) was made possible, and by an act of 1823 the set was completed. In 1835–36 three supplements appeared, bringing the collection down to February 1808.

HENNEPIN NARRATIVES. Louis Hennepin, a Franciscan friar, accompanied Robert Cavelier, Sieur de La Salle, on his first voyage to Illinois (1675) and was sent from there in 1680 with two companions to explore the upper Mississippi River. They were taken captive by the Sioux. Hennepin saw and named a number of sites, including the Falls of St. Anthony, where modern Minneapolis stands. The captives were rescued by Daniel Greysolon, Sieur Duluth. Hennepin returned to France, where he wrote *Description de la Louisiane* (Paris, 1683), a largely truthful narrative. He later published *Nouvelle découverte d' un très grand pays situe dans l'Amerique* (Utrecht, 1697); translated and published in England as the *New Discovery of a Very Large Country Situated in America,* (1698), in which he claimed for himself the prior discovery of the lower Mississippi, plagiarizing his descriptions of the lower river from those of Zénobe Membré, who accompanied La Salle on his voyage of 1682.

Hennepin wrote a third book of travels, *Le nouveau voyage* (Utrecht, 1698), which is a patchwork of citations from his other books and those of his contemporaries. His writings were bestsellers in their day. He gave European readers an account of the flora and fauna (animal and human) of North America that was standard for a generation or more.

HENRY, FORT (Tenn.), **CAPTURE OF** (Feb. 6, 1862). Union troops under Gen. Ulysses S. Grant, supported by gunboats under Commodore Andrew Foote, moved by water against Fort Henry on the Tennessee River, initiating the successful Mississippi campaign. Outgunned and outnumbered, Confederate Gen. Lloyd Tilghman safely evacuated most of his small garrison before surrendering. Grant moved immediately on Fort Donelson, twenty miles to the west.

HENRY, FORT (W. Va.). Built as Fort Fincastle in June 1774, on the Ohio River, on the site of what is now Wheeling, W. Va. In 1776 the name was changed to Fort Henry in honor of Patrick Henry, governor of Virginia. On Sept. 10, 1782, the fort was attacked by Indians and British in what historians claim was "the last battle of the American Revolution."

HENRY LETTERS. In 1809, John Henry, a British agent, investigated the extent of secessionist sentiment in New England for Sir James H. Craig, governor-general of Canada. Angered because the British did not pay him for his reports, Henry sold copies of the letters for $50,000 to President James Madison, who published the correspondence in 1812 in an effort to discredit New England Federalist opposition.

HENRYS FORK (Idaho). A branch of Snake River named for Andrew Henry, a partner of the St. Louis Missouri Fur Company, who built a fort there in 1809 in the heart of the Blackfoot fur country.

HEPBURN ACT OF 1906. Regulatory legislation designed to clarify certain powers previously granted to the Interstate Commerce Commission and to increase its authority. It authorized the commission to determine and prescribe just and reasonable maximum rates upon complaint and investigation; establish through routes and prescribe maximum joint rates and proper rate divisions between participating carriers; and determine, prescribe, and enforce uniform systems of accounts. The commission's orders on carriers subject to its jurisdiction were made binding without court action. The law strengthened the Elkins Act of 1903 dealing with personal discrimination; forbade railroads from transporting any commodity, other than timber and its manufactured products, in which they were financially interested, except for their own use; restricted the granting of free passes to certain groups; and increased the number of commissioners from five to seven.

HERD LAW VERSUS FREE GRASS. At issue in the newly settled West in the late 19th century was whether livestock or growing crops must be fenced. The livestock owner who planted little or no crops favored free grass, or the fencing of fields and allowing animals to run at large. The homesteader who owned few animals believed in herd law—the enclosure of pasture lands, with cultivated fields left unfenced. State laws usually provided that each township or county unit should decide the question for itself by local election. The controversy resulted at times in violence, destruction of property, and even loss of life. As communities became more thickly settled and prosperous, adequate fences were constructed and the controversy died out.

HERMITAGE. The estate of Andrew Jackson, near Nashville, Tenn., bought in 1795. He moved to it in 1804, selling all but 6,000 acres of the original 28,000. The log cabin was replaced by a brick house in 1819; this burned in 1834, and the present building was erected on the old site. It was bought by Tennessee in 1856 to be preserved as a shrine.

***HERMOSA* CASE.** On Oct. 19, 1840, the American schooner *Hermosa* was wrecked on the key of Abaco. Wreckers took off the crew, cargo, and thirty-eight slaves, and put in at Nassau, where the slaves were liberated because slavery was not recognized on British territory. The United States took the position that there could be no alteration of the status of master and slave in cases where the vessel was unwillingly taken within British waters. The case was settled by an award of $16,000 to the slaveowners.

HERPETOLOGY. Early contributions to the study of American reptiles were contained in Mark Catesby's *The Natural History of Carolina, Florida, and the Bahama Islands* (1731–43) and William Bartram's *Travels Through North and South Carolina, Georgia, East and West Florida* (1791). Some American reptiles were described by Carolus Linnaeus in his *Systema Naturae* (1758). In the late 1700's and early 1800's, foreign naturalists such as Constantine S. Rafinesque, Charles A. Lesueur, and Prince Maximilian zu Wied traveled in America and described the reptiles they saw; others worked on American reptiles that had been sent to them. Studies were also made by John Eaton LeConte of the U.S. Army; Thomas Say, who traveled with the Stephen H. Long expedition to the Rocky Mountains (1820); and Richard Harlan, a practicing physician, who published *Genera of North American Reptiles and a Synopsis of the Species* (1826–27) and *American Herpetology* (1827).

John Edwards Holbrook, a Charleston, S.C., physician, produced the first major contribution to U.S. knowledge of American reptiles, *North American Herpetology* (1836, 1842); its success and influence related to its completeness for the time and to the superb color lithographs. His work brought a measure of recognition to the rise of science in America. In the following decades a number of expeditions sponsored by the U.S. government were organized to explore the American West; it was to the credit of Spencer Fullerton Baird that large collections of reptiles were brought back to museums, in particular the U.S. National Museum, and were studied by a number of scientists, including Baird, Charles F. Girard, Henry C. Yarrow, and Charles Pickering. By 1880 most of the expeditions to the West had been completed and the results published. Concomitant with the work on western reptiles, serveral state herpetofaunal surveys were published, including those by David Humphreys Storer for Massachusetts (1839) and James E. DeKay for New York (1842–44).

Samuel Garman of the Museum of Comparative Zoology at Harvard brought together much information published in scattered reports of various U.S. exploring expeditions; his *North American Reptilia, Part I, Ophidia* (1883) remained of considerable value until outdated by *The Crocodilians, Lizards, and Snakes of North America* (1900) by Edward Drinker Cope. Leonhard Hess Stejneger of the U.S. National Museum introduced the careful designation of type specimens and type localities into the description of new species, produced *The Poisonous Snakes of North America* (1895), and later coauthored with Thomas Barbour five editions of *A Check List of North American Amphibians and Reptiles* (1917). Alexander G. Ruthven of the Museum of Zoology, University of Michigan, introduced the use of biometric methods in his monograph on garter snakes (1908).

Since the 1920's, American universities have become the primary centers for herpetological studies. Some of the more important contributors have been Frank N. Blanchard, who pioneered in field studies of reptiles and developed marking techniques, and Henry Fitch, who subsequently produced some of the most complete field studies of reptiles to date. Clifford H. Pope published *The Turtles of North America* (1939). Archie Carr greatly expanded the knowledge of North American turtles with shorter papers and his *Handbook of Turtles* (1952); he later made pioneering contributions on sea turtles and their conservation. Hobart M. Smith provided an excellent summary with his *Handbook of Lizards* (1946). Alfred S. Romer's *Osteology of the Reptiles* (1956) was still the standard reference for that field of research twenty years later. Albert Hazen Wright coauthored with his wife Anna the scholarly *Handbook of Snakes of the United States and Canada* (1957), which drew together all the information prior to that date. Laurence M. Klauber made many contributions on western reptiles and introduced refined statistical techniques. Albert M. Reese published widely on the development and anatomy of the American alligator, including *The Alligator and Its Allies* (1915).

During the 20th century several scientists produced semipopular works that served to generate wide interest in reptiles. Raymond Lee Ditmars's *Reptile Book* (1907) was one of the most stimulating to young naturalists. Karl P. Schmidt produced the *Field Book of Snakes* (1941) in coauthorship with D. Dwight Davis. Roger Conant wrote the first of the newest type of field guides, *A Field Guide to Reptiles and*

Amphibians (1958), that contained range maps, color illustrations, and synoptic information about the organisms. Herpetofaunal surveys have been written for most of the states.

Three major societies sponsor scholarly periodicals within the field of herpetology: *Copeia* (founded 1913) is published by the American Society of Ichthyologists and Herpetologists, *Herpetologica* (1936) is published by the Herpetologists' League, and the *Journal of Herpetology* (1968) is published by the Society for the Study of Amphibians and Reptiles.

HERRIN MASSACRE (June 22, 1922). Outgrowth of an attempt to operate a strip mine in Williamson County, Ill., with nonunion labor during a coal strike. Forty-seven men working at the mine surrendered, under a promise of safe conduct, to an armed force of several hundred striking union miners. The captives were marched to a spot near Herrin and then ordered to run for their lives under fire; twenty-one were killed. A special grand jury returned 214 indictments for murder and related crimes, but at the trial, local sentiment prevented convictions.

HESSIANS. *See* **German Mercenaries.**

***HESTER* CASE.** In December 1698 the *Hester,* about to sail from Perth Amboy, N.J., was seized by authorities for nonpayment of duties to New York. The proprietors appealed to England, claiming port privileges under statutes of 1673 and 1696 and the action of the customs commissioners in erecting the port. In 1700, damages were awarded the vessel's owners and the right of New Jersey to ports of its own confirmed.

HEXING. A form of witchcraft practiced by the Pennsylvania Dutch.

HICKORY GROUND. A Creek town (Oticiapolfa) on the east bank of the Coosa. Just below the Hickory Ground, on the site of the French Fort Toulouse, a detachment of Andrew Jackson's soldiers erected Fort Jackson. Here, on Aug. 9, 1814, Jackson made a treaty with the remnants of the Creek, which ceded their lands in southern Georgia and central Alabama to the United States. (*See* Creek Wars.)

HICKSITES. A split in the Society of Friends brought about by the preaching of Elias Hicks, a Long Island Quaker, led to the formation of the Hicksite sect in 1827 in Philadelphia; other separations took place the following year in New York, Baltimore, and elsewhere. The Hicksites established Swarthmore College and several schools. Seven of the Hicksite synods met in 1902 to form the Friends General Conference, designed to foster cooperation among the yearly meetings. (*See also* Quakers.)

HIDE AND TALLOW TRADE. In Spanish California, missions and ranchmen depended chiefly on the sale of hides and tallow for a livelihood. In 1822, William A. Gale, ex-fur trader, interested Bryant, Sturgis and Company of Boston in the products; Boston ships soon took over the trade, with a direct commerce between California and the eastern seaboard of the United States. In the Plains region few cattle were killed for hides alone. Buffalo hide had long been an important article of commerce; with the coming of the railroad, buffalo were slaughtered in huge numbers.

HIGH COMMISSION, COURT OF. A term applied to a series of English commissions created by royal letters patent, 1535–1641. Originally instruments of the Privy Council to protect the crown against heresy and treason, the commissioners matured into a full-fledged court of law, "the Star Chamber for ecclesiastical cases." In 1625 any three commissioners were authorized to conduct trials, whereby proceedings could be held simultaneously in several places. The court became William Laud's most effective means to root out Puritan nonconformity. Proceedings, or threat of proceedings, in High Commission caused many Puritan ministers to flee to Holland and the New World.

HIGHER CRITICISM. The historical and textual study of the Bible, introduced into America in the late 19th century from Germany and England. President William R. Harper of the University of Chicago and professors Charles A. Briggs of Union Theological Seminary and C. E. Bacon of Yale Divinity School were among the leaders of this new approach. They and their colleagues were bitterly denounced by those who continued to hold the old view of an infallible Bible, but by the end of the century their findings were beginning to receive wide acceptance among ministers and leading laymen.

HIGHER EDUCATION. *See* **Colleges and Universities; Education.**

HIGHER EDUCATION FACILITIES ACT (Aug. 14, 1963). Authorized a five-year program of federal grants and loans for the construction or improvement of public and private higher educational facilities.

HIGHER-LAW DOCTRINE. During the debate on the Compromise of 1850, Sen. William H. Seward declared in a speech (Mar. 11) that the proposed fugitive slave act might be constitutional, but there was a "higher law than the Constitution." The higher-law doctrine was an appeal to conscience as superior in authority to the laws of Congress.

HIGHLANDS OF THE HUDSON. A rugged hill mass extending along the Hudson River from eight miles above West Point to eight miles below, chosen by the Provincial Congress of New York as a defense area against the British. In the fall and winter of 1775, fortifications were constructed on Martelaer's Rock (now Constitution Island), directly across from West Point. Early in 1776 the defense effort was shifted to forts Clinton and Montgomery, on the rocky knobs flanking both sides of the mouth of Popolopen Creek (Pooploop's Kill), four miles below West Point.

Sir Henry Clinton stormed the forts on Oct. 6, 1777, taking them after heavy losses. With the capture of Fort Constitution on Oct. 7 and the breach of river obstructions, the Hudson Highland defenses were in British hands. Following the withdrawal of the British ten days later, after Burgoyne's surrender at Saratoga, Gen. George Washington demanded an impregnable defense for the "key to America." Col. Thaddeus Kosciusko was placed in charge of the construction of the works at West Point in 1778. A massive chain was stretched across the river between West Point and Constitution Island, protected downstream by a log boom. Water batteries and redoubts on both sides of the river ensured a three-mile fire-swept zone along the line of the river—principally downstream. Redoubts and forts on the hills farther inland assured proper protection against a land attack.

HIGH LICENSE. A method of regulating the liquor traffic through the exaction of high fees for licenses to sell liquor, originating in Nebraska in 1881 with radical temperance men. Until then a license fee of $200 a year had been considered high; under the Nebraska law, fees ranged from $500 to $1,000, in order to reduce the number and improve the character of the places licensed. The system was soon adopted in many states, and is still widely used.

HIGH-MINDED MEN. Forty (later fifty-one) anti-Clintonian Federalists who urged the election of Vice-President Daniel D. Tompkins, the Republican candidate for governor of New York in 1820. In a publication dated Apr. 14, 1820, the group deplored Gov. DeWitt Clinton's "personal party," declared the Federalist party dissolved, and allied themselves with the Tammany faction. As they had often referred to themselves as "high-minded men" in the anti-Clintonian *New York American,* they were henceforth ridiculed by the opposition as "high-minded Federalists."

HIGH SCHOOLS. *See* **Education.**

HIGHWAY ACT (June 29, 1956). Authorized $32 billion over the following thirteen years for the construction of a 41,000-mile interstate highway system and for the completion of the federal-aid system of highways. The federal government was to provide 90 percent of the construction costs for the interstates and 50 percent for the federal-aid system. The act also provided for new taxes on gasoline and other highway-user items for a Highway Trust Fund to finance construction costs.

HIGHWAYS. *See* **Roads.**

HIJACKING. *See* **Crime, Organized.**

HIJACKING, AERIAL. Piracy of aircraft, principally commercial airliners; also called "skyjacking." The first air hijacking on record occurred Feb. 21, 1931, in Peru, when revolutionists seized an aircraft and ordered it flown out of the country, tossing out propaganda leaflets on their way. After 1931 no more attempts were made until 1947; between 1947 and 1980 there were 625 hijack attempts worldwide. The most popular destination for hijackers during this period was Cuba; the Middle East ranked second.

Between 1967 and 1972, political disaffection in the United States, militant left-wing and urban guerrilla action in some Latin-American countries, intensified political oppression in some Eastern European countries, the Palestinian guerrilla movements in the Middle East, the plight of the so-called homesick Cuban, and criminals with "get-rich-quick" extortion schemes caused aerial piracy to reach epidemic proportions. In 1969 there were ninety hijack attempts, of which seventy-one were successful; in 1970, eighty-nine attempts, of which fifty-five were successful; in 1971, sixty-three attempts, of which twenty-four were successful; and in 1972, seventy attempts, of which twenty-five were successful. The decline of successful hijackings in 1971 was the direct result of tough security measures put into effect by the U.S. Federal Aviation Administration, the airlines, and government law-enforcement agencies worldwide. These measures included specially trained sky marshals riding shotgun on flights, and searches of passengers and carry-on luggage before boarding. By 1973 search of passengers and carry-on luggage using metal detection and X-ray devices was mandatory at all U.S. airports.

Aviation industry representatives and world governments, led by the United Nations, sought acceptance of several international treaties to deal with the apprehension, extradition, and punishment of air pirates. These treaties included Tokyo (1963), The Hague (1970), and Montreal (1971) conventions and special legislation proposed by the International Civil Aviation Organization, an arm of the U.N. However, by late 1975, not all nations had ratified these agreements; nor was it certain that some nations ever would. On Feb. 15, 1973, the United States and Cuba signed a "memorandum of understanding" that calls for the punishment or return of skyjackers to the country in which the act is committed unless political asylum is clearly indicated. Canada and Cuba soon followed suit with a similar treaty, and other countries began informal talks with Cuba on the subject. In August 1980, Cuban refugees who had come to the United States in the previous spring hijacked six planes to Cuba; most of the hijackers were prosecuted by Cuban authorities.

HILLABEE TOWNS. Five Creek Indian towns located on a western tributary of the Tallapoosa in eastern Alabama. The Hillabee were one of the twelve major divisions of the Creek and numbered about 800. They took part in the Creek War; their towns were captured in November 1813 by a combined force of Cherokee and Tennessee militia; the towns were devastated, and 316 inhabitants killed or captured.

HINDMAN, FORT. *See* **Arkansas Post, Battle of.**

HIPPIES AND YIPPIES. The term "hippy" originated with jazz musicians' "hip" in the 1940's, meaning someone who was sharp and aware of things. In the 1960's, the term was adopted by young people who were attempting to lead a life outside of American middle-class conventionality. Among certain characteristics were the rejection of materialist values, the adoption of bright and bizarre clothing, and a life characterized by rootlessness.

Yippies were an outgrowth of the hippy philosophy. The term stands for Youth International Party. The Yippy philosophy was to satirize all conventional institutions, particularly the political. The Yippies were most prominent during the 1968 Democratic Convention in Chicago.

HISE TREATY (June 21, 1849). Unauthorized treaty made with Nicaragua by Elijah Hise, an American diplomat sent to Central America by President James K. Polk. In return for exclusive right to the Nicaraguan route for a possible interoceanic canal, the United States guaranteed the territorial integrity of Nicaragua, including its claim to the town of San Juan, then a British protectorate. Although not adopted, the treaty was important as the first of a series of incidents that excited the U.S. public against England (*see* Squier Treaty).

HISS CASE. In August 1948, Whittaker Chambers, a self-professed member of a Communist spy ring, testified before the House Un-American Activities Committee that he knew Alger Hiss, an adviser to the State Department on economic and political affairs, to have been a member of the same spy ring in the 1930's and that Hiss had passed secret documents to him in 1938. Hiss denied the charges under oath. He was indicted in December 1948 on two counts of perjury (the statute of limitations for espionage charges had run out). The first trial ended in July 1949 in a hung jury; on Jan. 21, 1950, at a second trial, Hiss was found guilty and sentenced to five years in prison. After serving three years, he was released.

HISTORICAL SOCIETIES. The first historical organizations to appear after the American Revolution were state and local societies, beginning with the Massachusetts Historical Society (1791) and followed by New York City, 1804; American Antiquarian Society, Worcester, Mass., 1812; Rhode Island, 1822; Maine, 1823; New Hampshire, 1823; Pennsylvania, 1824; Connecticut, 1825; Indiana, 1830; Ohio, 1831; Virginia, 1831; Louisiana, 1836; Vermont, 1838; Georgia, 1839; Maryland, 1844; Tennessee, 1849; Wisconsin, 1849; and Minnesota, 1849. Frequently, the founders were actively engaged in promoting the growth of their area, and they viewed history as a means of furthering local interests. The collection policies of the early groups were generally broad, and many societies became repositories for some surprising items, such as the New-York Historical Society's collection of Egyptian mummies and artifacts and the Kansas Historical Society's collection of stuffed birds. The early publications of transactions and collections contain not only historical documents but also archaeological, anthropological, and geological data.

There were two attempts at national organization prior to the Civil War. The American Antiquarian Society (Worcester, Mass., 1812) took the nation's past as its field, but its membership was largely local. The short-lived American Historical Society (1838–40) consisted mainly of congressmen. In 1884 the American Historical Association (AHA) was founded. In 1904 the Conference of State and Local Historical Societies was created as part of a program of the AHA; in 1940 it became the independent American Association for State and Local History.

Historians were not entirely satisfied with the single yearly meeting of the AHA. In 1895 a group of southerners founded the Southern History Association in Washington, D.C.; the organization died in 1907 from lack of funds, but left eleven volumes of publications and a solid precedent for the formation in 1934 of the healthier Southern Historical Association. In 1904, West Coast historians organized the Pacific Coast Branch of the AHA. In 1907, historical societies of the Midwest formed the Mississippi Valley Historical Association, which quickly became national in scope; in 1964 it changed its name to the Organization of American Historians.

Topical organizations represent the trend toward specialization among historians, with the exception of such societies as the Railway and Locomotive Historical Society and the Steamship Historical Society of America, which were largely the product of nostalgia. Ethnic historical agencies, such as the American-Swedish Historical Museum (1926) and the Swiss-American Historical Society (1928), were formed at a time when immigration was being restricted; the Association for the Study of Negro Life and History was founded in 1915 during a period of aggressive activity by Afro-Americans to win their civil rights. Family historical societies, trusts, and libraries were primarily a development of the 20th century.

Collection and preservation of manuscripts, documents, books, pamphlets, newspapers, and artifacts, as well as publication of articles, essays, documents, and memoirs, remain the most important work of historical societies. Publication in the 19th century took place in volumes of collections and transactions. Beginning with the *Maryland Magazine of History* in 1906, societies issued periodicals; these have developed into slick, illustrated magazines since the 1950's.

HISTORIOGRAPHY, AMERICAN. Sagas of Norse voyages to America were written down by Adam of Bremen in his description of the *Northerly Lands* (ca. 1070). Great English compendiums of accounts of voyages to the New World were also made: Richard Eden, *The Decades of the Newe Worlde* (1555); Richard Hakluyt, *The Principal Navigations, Voyages and Discoveries of the English Nation* (1589); and Samuel Purchas, *Hakluytus Posthumus, or Purchas, His Pilgrims* (1625). Many firsthand accounts of the early colonial settlements survive, including Capt. John Smith's *The General History of Virginia, New England and Summer Isles* (1624). Puritan historians conceived of history as a way of spreading religious truth and chronicling God's will on earth. William Bradford, governor of Plymouth Colony, wrote the story of Plymouth Plantation between 1630 and 1651, seen in the framework of a struggle between God and the Devil. Gov. John Winthrop did the same in his journal for the Massachusetts Bay Colony.

In the 18th century, colonial historical writing took on a more naturalistic cast and secular aims, presenting the colonies as outposts of the British Empire and explaining events in natural terms. Two such histories are Thomas Prince's *Chronological History of New England* (1736) and William

Smith's *The History of the Province of New York* (1757). The movement leading to the Revolution generated a spate of partisan histories, almost all taking substantial portions of their information from Edmund Burke's *Annual Register.* An outspoken, and perhaps the most original, history was written in 1805 by Mercy Otis Warren, *History of the Rise, Progress, and Termination of the American Revolution.*

With independence and the establishment of the Constitution, there developed a historical consciousness that generated the founding of historical societies and the publication of documents. The most famous of the editors of historical documents was Jared Sparks, a Unitarian minister and editor of the *North American Review* who published in twelve volumes the *Diplomatic Correspondence of the American Revolution* (1829–30). Government agencies too began publishing select portions of their records, but it was not until the National Archives Act of 1934 established the National Archives and a historical publications commission, and the Works Progress Administration launched its Historical Records Survey, that there was any systematic means of location and publication of historical materials on a national scale.

Biography served as a popular form of history in the early Republic. It turned historical figures into legendary heroes and national symbols, and stimulated the collection of private papers of state and national leaders. Sparks published twelve volumes of the *Writings of George Washington* (1834–37) and edited the works of Benjamin Franklin in ten volumes (1836–40). It was Sparks who first attempted to compile a national history through the collected biographies of local heroes, in the twenty-five volume *Library of American Biography.* The capstone of the new school of academically trained historians' work as applied to biography was the twenty-volume *Dictionary of American Biography* (1928–36), sponsored by the American Council of Learned Societies and edited by Allen Johnson and Dumas Malone. In the 1960's American historians turned to prosopography, the use of biographical data to determine common sociological and behavioral patterns of such groups as abolitionists and progressive congressmen, and to the techniques of psychology to develop new insights into the behavior of historical figures and social movements.

By the 1830's patriotic clamor for a national literature, history, and character had begun to find a response in the work of a group of literary historians. George Bancroft, in his ten-volume *History of the United States from the Discovery of the American Continent* (1834–74), expanded the theme of the Chosen People from the exclusive concept of the Puritans of New England to include the whole country, and translated the democratic faith into the language of German romanticism. Francis Parkman took as his thesis the superiority of the Anglo-Saxon race as a civilizing force in the struggle for the "great American forest" and wrote an epic history of France and England in North America, blending the influences of the romantic movement with the main current of American historiography. Bancroft initiated the genre of multivolume national histories, written by individual historians. The best of these in the 19th century is Henry Adams' *History of the United States During the Administrations of Jefferson and Madison* (nine volumes, 1889–91).

The critical historians arose in the 1850's partly in reaction to the bravura of the literary historians; they were influenced by a developing respect for science and factual data and were for the most part local or church historians. The group found its organ in the *Historical Magazine;* the monument to their work was the eight-volume *Narrative and Critical History of the Americas* (1884–89), edited by Justin Winsor. This new group of professionals, who were trained for the most part in German universities and who taught in the new American universities, signalized their appearance by establishing (1884) the American Historical Association.

A younger generation of historians pursued several new directions. Herbert Levi Osgood, Charles M. Andrews, and Lawrence Henry Gipson were the leaders of the imperial school of colonial historiography, maintaining that American colonial history can be understood only in the context of the whole of the British Empire. Frederick Jackson Turner, on the other hand, helped to internalize the study of national history with his frontier and sectional interpretations. All the work of the first generation of American-trained historians is summed up in *The American Nation: A History* (twenty-six volumes, 1904–08), edited by Albert Bushnell Hart.

Economic interpretation and the so-called new history were products of the Progressive era and were particularly the work of Charles A. Beard in *An Economic Interpretation of the Constitution* (1913) and, with his wife, Mary, *The Rise of American Civilization* (1927); and James Harvey Robinson, a historian of Europe, in *The New History* (1912). The economic interpretation spurred historians in the 1920's and 1930's to find economic bases and motivations in all areas of American history, emphasizing periods of struggle between social classes. The new history also produced the field of intellectual history, first cultivated by Vernon Lewis Parrington, in *Main Currents in American Thought* (1928–30); by Merle E. Curti, in *The Growth of American Thought* (1943); and by Perry Miller, in *The New England Mind* (1939).

After World War II and during the cold war, American historians began to look for continuities in their past. Daniel Boorstin, in his three-volume social history *The Americans* (1958–73), not only explored new fields but documented the thesis that the consistent genius of America lay in the ability of its people, free of ideological blinders, to approach and solve problems pragmatically. Clinton Rossiter, in *Seedtime of the Republic* (1953), and Edmund Morgan, in *Stamp Act Crisis* (with Helen M. Morgan, 1953) and other works, found the American Revolution a conservative effort to preserve liberties already won. Arthur Schlesinger, Jr., in his *Age of Roosevelt* (three volumes, 1957–60), found the roots of the New Deal in the Progressive era and the 1920's, as did Arthur Link, biographer of Woodrow Wilson, and Eric Goldman, in *Rendezvous with Destiny* (1952).

HISTORY, AMERICAN, SOURCES OF.

Material. Archives, manuscripts, newspapers, and printed government documents are four basic types of literary sources. Archives constitute the official records and working papers of an organization. Manuscripts are the private, nonofficial records of individuals, even if those individuals are in public posts; they would include unpublished letters, diaries, memoirs, and autobiographies. Because of the availability of newspapers from virtually every period and place in American history, historians have found them an important, if often unreliable, source. Printed government documents reflect a great deal more than the workings of the government: the reports of many agencies deal with the multiple economic and social facets of American life; congressional committee hearings reveal varying viewpoints on any phase of the national existence affected by federal law.

Much of the quantitative data used by historians is generated from government documents, especially those emanating from the census bureau. Political historians can get at the wellsprings of American politics through careful analysis of voting statistics. Artifacts also constitute an important research source. Houses, furniture, tools, handicrafts, and machine-made products tell much about the American experience. Similarly, maps, prints, photographs, and paintings can furnish contemporary visual conceptions of the past.

Locations. Archival sources are usually located close to the organization that generated them. Thus, government records are found in capital cities, and county or city records in courthouses or city halls. Churches most often maintain archives at the headquarters of a regional jurisdiction.

Federal records are administered by the National Archives and Records Service (NARS). Included in NARS are the National Archives in Washington, D.C.; twelve regional federal archives and records centers; and six presidential libraries. Since 1940 the National Archives has microfilmed its documents of highest historical value. These films are available for sale, and each regional records center has copies.

The Library of Congress Manuscript Division contains 30 million items related to American history, such as presidential papers (all on microfilms available for sale or on interlibrary loan) and inactive records of such organizations as the National Association for the Advancement of Colored People, the National Urban League, and the American Historical Association. Other components of the library rich in Americana are the law library, government documents division, prints and photographs division, map division, music division, newspaper collection, and delta (pornography) collection. University libraries, archives, and special collections are also good sources of American history. Great private libraries, such as the Huntington in San Marino, Calif., and the Newberry in Chicago, have important sources dealing with literature and the frontier experience. The American Antiquarian Society in Worcester, Mass., specializes in early newspapers and other printed sources.

Historical societies constitute a highly important resource. Along the East Coast, most of the state historical societies have printed their colonial archives. Since 1964 many societies, along with universities, have cooperated with the National Historical Publications and Records Commission in microfilming collections of national importance. A detailed finding aid accompanies each publication.

Guides. The *Guide to Archives and Manuscripts in the United States* (Philip M. Hamer, ed.) was published in 1961; arranged geographically, it printed responses from repositories throughout the nation. In 1962 the initial volume of the *National Union Catalog of Manuscript Collections (NUCMC)* appeared, with succeeding volumes following annually. Prepared by the Library of Congress, *NUCMC* has entries for individual collections and an extensive index, combining names, repositories, and subjects. As yet, *NUCMC* has not made the Hamer *Guide* obsolete, and both must be employed in a thorough search for sources. Many repositories have published excellent guides to their collections, but recent acquisitions are not reported to the research community unless the guide is updated.

HITCHCOCK RESERVATIONS (1919). At the time of the first vote by the Senate on the Peace Treaty of Versailles and the League of Nations, Sen. Gilbert M. Hitchcock of Nebraska, Democratic leader, endeavored to reconcile the opposition by the following reservations: the right of Congress to authorize or forbid the use of American forces for league sanctions; interpretation of the Monroe Doctrine by the United States; equality of voting power with the British Empire, inclusive of the Dominions; the right of withdrawal; and exemption of domestic questions from the league's jurisdiction. Republicans prevented consideration of these reservations and adopted instead the reservations proposed by Sen. Henry Cabot Lodge (*see* Lodge Reservations).

***HITCHMAN COAL COMPANY* V. *MITCHELL*,** 245 U.S. 229 (1917). The United Mine Workers attempted to organize the West Virginia coalfields and thereby protect their bargaining power in neighboring, unionized fields. After a strike in 1906, the Hitchman Company required all returning employees to forgo union affiliation. The union sent in organizers, and the company secured an injunction, which was upheld by the Supreme Court on the ground that the economic interest of the union in fortifying its bargaining position did not constitute "just cause or excuse" for interfering with existing amicable employment relations.

***HIT OR MISS*.** First boat to be carried over the Allegheny crest on the Allegheny Portage Railway (October 1834). Bearing a westbound emigrant, the flatboat was placed on a railroad car at Hollidaysburg, Pa.; at Johnstown it was returned to canal waters. The experiment encouraged the building of "portable" boat bodies on which freight could be sent over the canal system between Philadelphia and Pittsburgh without transshipment.

HOBKIRK'S HILL, BATTLE OF (Apr. 25, 1781). After the Battle of Guilford Courthouse, Gen. Nathanael Greene invaded South Carolina and marched toward the British post at Camden, where Lord Francis Rawdon-Hastings was in command. At Hobkirk's Hill, north of Camden, he was attacked by Rawdon. Two of his regiments fell into confusion through loss of a commander and a misunderstanding of orders, and the battle was lost. However, the fall of Fort Watson in his rear made Rawdon's position untenable; on May 10 he retreated southward, abandoning Camden.

HOBSON'S CHOICE. An English proverbial phrase meaning no choice at all. It was the name given by Gen. Anthony Wayne (May 1793) to the encampment site selected for his army about 400 yards below the frontier village of Cincinnati on the north bank of the Ohio River. Here the troops remained for about six months undergoing training.

HOCKEY. Three Canadian cities, Montreal, Kingston, and Halifax, all claim to have been hockey's birthplace during the second half of the 19th century. The name "hockey" is believed to come either from *hoquet,* the French word for an implement closely resembling the modern hockey stick that shepherds used to control their flocks, or from *hogee,* the Mohawk word meaning "to hurt" (in the late 1700's British soldiers stationed in Canada played a rudimentary form of hockey with the Mohawk on frozen lakes and ponds). Canada established itself as the leader in ice hockey by being the first to institutionalize the game: a meeting at McGill University in Montreal (1879) produced the first standardized rules, based largely on those of lacrosse and rugby. In 1885 the Canadian Amateur Hockey Association was formed. It was not until 1893 that ice hockey was introduced in the United States, the year in which the Stanley Cup was put up for competition in Canada by the governor-general, Frederick Arthur Stanley. Since 1926 only professional teams have competed for this trophy.

The National Hockey League (NHL) was formed in Canada in 1917 following the dissolution of the National Hockey Association, which had been the strongest league since 1909. Beginning in 1924, U.S. teams were admitted to the NHL. In 1981 the league had twenty-two teams, fourteen of them U.S. teams; most of the players have been Canadian. The World Hockey Association (WHA) was founded in 1972 as a second professional league also made up of teams from Canada and the United States; in 1975 it had fourteen teams, five Canadian and nine U.S. In 1979, the WHA merged with the NHL.

Yale and Johns Hopkins universities both claim to have introduced hockey as a game to the United States in 1893. By 1980 hundreds of amateur high school, college, and community hockey teams existed. The governing body of amateur hockey in the United States is the Amateur Hockey Association of the United States (AHAUS); it holds membership in the International Ice Hockey Federation, and it sponsors the U.S. Olympic team in the winter games.

HOG ISLAND SHIPYARD. Built on the Delaware River during World War I by the Emergency Fleet Corporation, to produce merchant ships and transports faster than German submarines could sink them. Its maximum capacity was for fifty ships on the ways and twenty-eight at piers; it completed one 7,500-ton steel, oil-burning vessel every seventy-two hours. Ships actually built totaled 110, the last finished in January 1921. The yard was sold in 1930.

HOG REEVE. A town officer in colonial New England, with the duty of impounding swine that strayed from the common lands and with appraising damage done by them.

HOGS. In 1539, Hernando de Soto introduced hogs into the continental United States. Importation of hogs into the thirteen colonies accompanied the establishment of Jamestown in 1607; this was soon followed by their introduction in the Massachusetts Bay area and in the Delaware River region of Pennsylvania and New Jersey. By the late 17th century, hogs were well established in the Middle Atlantic and New England colonies, as was the practice of finishing them for market by feeding them Indian corn. American breeds were developed from these early sources, but more significant development took place after extensive importations from western Europe during the first half of the 19th century. The eight leading breeds in the 1970's included the Chester White, Duroc, Hampshire, Poland China, and Spotted, all developed in the United States in the 19th century; the Berkshire and Yorkshire, developed mainly in England; and the American Landrace, developed from the Danish Landrace, first imported in 1934, with later additions of Norwegian and Swedish Landrace lines. Since the 1930's, as a result of changes in consumer preference and a decline in the use of lard, a meat-type hog, providing an increased yield of preferred lean cuts and a reduced yield of fat, has been developed.

During the early 1800's herds were driven to cities on the eastern seaboard. Later, with population shifts and the development of transportation systems, packing centers were established at Cincinnati and Chicago; after World War II, as other Midwest stockyards became increasingly important, that of Chicago declined. By the mid-1970's the production of hogs was one of the major U.S. agricultural enterprises. In 1979 the total gross income from the sale of hogs, pork, and pork products amounted to $8,853,000,000.

HOHOKAM. A prehistoric culture that developed along the Salt and Gila rivers in the low, hot desert of southern Arizona and New Mexico by 100 B.C., and climaxed A.D. 1200–1400. Evidences of more than a thousand years of Hohokam culture are revealed at the Snaketown site in the lower Gila Valley, southeast of Phoenix, Ariz. Sedentary village life and irrigation systems were well established by A.D. 500. During the climactic period, multistoried great houses with mud walls up to 2 meters thick were built, and the canal system reached its greatest extent (about 150 miles). A widespread drought, beginning as early as A.D. 1200, resulted in population shifts and a decline in agricultural productivity; many areas were eventually abandoned.

Many features of the Hohokam culture had Middle American prototypes, including luxury objects of turquoise, shell, and copper; the cotton-cloth complex; and ceremonial earthworks. Plant cultivation supported the economy, supplemented by hunting and gathering; large numbers of chipped stone and bone tools, grinding stones, stone bowls, axes, and painted ceramic vessels litter the settlements. The dominant decorative themes are lizards, frogs, bears, and other animals.

HOLDEN PEACE MOVEMENT (1863–64). Although he never completely revealed his plans, it is probable that William W. Holden, editor of the (Raleigh) *North Carolina Standard,* intended to detach North Carolina from the Confederacy and make a separate peace with the United States. Through editorials, public meetings, and petitions demanding peace negotiations, he weakened the southern cause and alarmed its leaders. In January 1864, Gov. Zebulon B. Vance, convinced that Holden planned to force the calling of a state convention for the negotiation of peace directly with the North, severed political relations with him. Holden immediately announced his candidacy for the governorship, but Vance crushingly defeated him in August 1864. Vance's victory killed the peace movement in North Carolina.

HOLDING COMPANY. A company characterized by its ownership of securities (generally common stock) of other companies for the purpose of influencing the management of those subsidiary companies, rather than for investment or other purposes. "Pure" holding companies confine their operations to the ownership and management of other firms, and are not themselves operating companies; until the passage of limiting legislation (the Public Utility Holding Company Act of 1935 and the Bank Holding Company Act of 1956), they were free of all regulations imposed on operating companies. The holding company emerged as a common form of business organization around 1900, some decades after its first use in railroads (1853) and communications (1832).

HOLES OF THE MOUNTAINS. Mountain valleys where fur trappers were accustomed to camp, trap beaver, and meet at annual rendezvous. Among the most famous were Jackson Hole along the east base of the Teton Range in Wyoming, Pierre's Hole on the western slope of the same range, and Ogden's Hole at the site of the present city of Ogden, Utah.

HOLLADAY OVERLAND STAGE COMPANY. In 1862, Ben Holladay bought the interests of the firm of Russell, Majors and Waddell. By 1866 he operated over 2,760 miles of western road, used 6,000 horses and mules, 260 coaches, and many wagons, and employed hundreds of men. The federal government paid him $650,000 annually to carry the mail over these lines. In 1866 he sold his properties to Wells, Fargo and Company.

HOLLAND LAND COMPANY. In 1789 four Dutch banking houses—Stadnitski and Son, Van Staphorst, Van Eeghen, and Ten Cate and Vollenhoven—interested in speculating in U.S. funds, sent Théophile Cazenove to the United States as their agent. In 1792, lands were purchased in the Genesee Valley and in Pennsylvania. In 1796 the Hollandsche Land Compagnie (or Holland Land Company) was organized. The stock was divided into shares representing ownership of 1.3 million acres in the Genesee Valley, 900,000 acres east of the Allegheny River, and 499,660 acres west of the Allegheny. The company was never very successful, and its assets were liquidated in the 1830's and 1840's.

HOLLAND PATENT. In accordance with a mandamus of King George III and council (July 20, 1764), 20,000 acres of land were surveyed in Albany County, N.Y., for Henry Fox, Lord Holland; a patent was granted on Mar. 17, 1769. He sold the tract to Seth Johnson, Andrew Craigie, and Horace Johnson. A few settlers were on the property in 1797.

HOLLAND SUBMARINE TORPEDO BOAT. Designed by John P. Holland and purchased by the Navy Department on Apr. 11, 1900. A cigar-shaped craft, 53 feet long, propelled by a gasoline motor on the surface and by an electric motor under water; it could dive, rise, and be held at a desired level by the action of horizontal rudders placed at its stern. Its armament consisted of one bow torpedo tube, one bow pneumatic dynamite gun, and three short Whitehead torpedoes.

HOLLY SPRINGS (Miss.). Gen. Ulysses S. Grant's 1862 overland campaign south from Tennessee depended on accumulated supplies at Holly Springs, Miss. Surprise attacks by the Confederate generals N. B. Forrest and Earl Van Dorn incapacitated the railway and destroyed Grant's depot (Dec. 20). Grant withdrew northward and thereafter approached Vicksburg, Miss., from the river.

HOLLYWOOD (Calif.). A section of Los Angeles, first settled in 1853. Incorporated as the City of Hollywood in 1903; became a district of Los Angeles in 1910. In 1911, the Nester Film Studio was the first motion picture studio in Hollywood; by year's end, fifteen more had located there. By the 1920's, Hollywood was the center of the nation's motion picture industry. Since that time it has been synonymous with that industry.

HOLMES COUNTY REBELLION (June 1863). A Civil War draft resistance incident in Ohio. After seizing four men from an enrolling officer, an armed group ignored an order to disperse. A skirmish with troops in which two objectors were wounded ended the resistance. Thirteen men were surrendered for trial and the troops withdrew.

HOLMES* V. *WALTON (1780). One precedent for the doctrine of judicial review. The N.J. Supreme Court declared unconstitutional a statute that provided in certain classes of cases that a jury might consist of six men; the legislature subsequently repealed the voided portion of the act. Thus, the right of the courts to pass upon the constitutionality of legislation was not denied, but the legislature claimed the final power to define the functions of each department of government.

HOLSTON TREATY (July 2, 1791). Gov. William Blount of the Southwest Territory (now Tennessee) met the representatives of the Cherokee at White's Fort (Knoxville), some four miles below the junction of the French Broad and Holston rivers. Their treaty made the Cherokee-American boundary the watershed between the Little and the Little Tennessee rivers and guaranteed to the Cherokee the possession of the lands still retained by them.

HOLSTON VALLEY SETTLEMENTS. The Holston River, discovered in 1743 south of the New River, was explored by Stephen Holston (1748). Progress of settlement down the Holston Valley was slow because the Cherokee opposed encroachments south of New River. The treaty of 1768 at Fort Stanwix caused an inrush and permanent settlements on the Holston and its tributaries below Virginia's southern boundary line. Donelson's line (1771) fixed the boundary between the Cherokee and Virginia at Holston River; the Holston settlement, a large part of which was in North Carolina until 1777, was governed by Virginia. West of Donelson's line a distinct settlement known as Pendleton District was formed on the Holston River.

HOLT'S *JOURNAL*. John Holt staunchly supported the revolting colonists during the Revolution; forced from New York City by the British, he established his *Journal* upstate at Kingston. He later moved to Poughkeepsie, where he remained with several interruptions until returning to New York City in 1783.

HOLY CROSS, PRIESTS OF. Members of the religious congregation (in Latin, *Congregatio a Sancta Cruce*) formed by Basil Anthony Moreau near Le Mans, France, in 1837 to assist in local parishes, hospitals, and educational institutions and to work in foreign missions. In 1841, Edward Sorin, C.S.C., introduced the congregation into the United States and the following year founded the University of Notre Dame near South Bend, Ind. The Priests of Holy Cross teach and assist at King's College in Wilkes-Barre, Pa.; Stonehill College in North Easton, Mass.; and the University of Portland in Portland, Oreg. They serve as parish priests in several dioceses and as missionaries in Asia, Africa, and South America.

HOLY EXPERIMENT. William Penn's term for the ideal government he established in Pennsylvania in 1681. It laid "the foundation of a free colony for all mankind" and guaranteed civil liberty, religious freedom, and economic opportunity. The people shared fully in government, with a constitution and code of laws chosen by them. No restrictions were placed on immigration; oaths were abolished; and peace was established. This government succeeded for seventy years.

"HOLY LORD" HINGES. The commonest of housedoor hinges used in colonial America, shaped like the letters H and HL, were imported from England after 1700. They were made of plain wrought iron and were left unpainted. A symbolic meaning—"Holy" and "Holy Lord"—may have led to their use as a protection against witchcraft.

HOME LOAN BANK, FEDERAL. *See* **Federal Agencies.**

HOMEOPATHY. A pharmacotherapeutic technique that relies on the ability of medicinal substances to act curatively when administered to the sick in accordance with the "law of similars." Introduced in 1796 by Samuel Hahnemann, who lived and worked in Leipzig and Paris, it was brought to the United States in the 1820's; throughout the century the American school was the world leader of homeopathy.

Its role in American medicine is still a source of controversy. It secured a strong position in the cities of the Northeast and Middle Atlantic regions, drawing its clients from among the rich and the socially and politically prominent; its other major focus was among the German immigrants in the Midwest. In the 1840's and 1850's, homeopathic physicians were expelled from medical societies and subjected to professional ostracism by orthodox (allopathic) physicians. The founding of the American Medical Association in 1847 was in part a reaction to the 1844 creation of the American Institute of Homeopathy. Nevertheless, the small, or "infinitesimal," doses of homeopathic physicians provoked a decline in the prevalent "heroic" prescribing, and some of the new medicines introduced by homeopathy were eventually adopted by allopaths and manufactured by leading drug companies.

The admission of homeopathic physicians to the American Medical Association in 1903 was one cause of the decline of homeopathy after World War I to the present level of about 1,000 physicians in the United States. Another factor in this decline was the 1910 Flexner Report on American medical education, which held that a separate system of homeopathic schools was no longer needed.

HOME OWNERS' LOAN CORPORATION (HOLC). Created in 1933 for a three-year period by the Federal Home Loan Bank Board as directed by act of Congress, it assisted homeowners unable to meet mortgage payments during the Great Depression. In its three years of lending operations it made a million loans for a total of over $3 billion. The HOLC could lend 80 percent of the appraised value or $14,000—whichever was smaller—on homes having a value not exceeding $20,000. It issued its own bonds for delinquent mortgages and liens, refinancing the indebtedness on liberal terms to the homeowner, who thereupon made his payments direct to the HOLC. In addition, it financed the capital stock of the Federal Savings and Loan Insurance Corporation and invested in federal savings and loan associations and other lending institutions.

HOME RULE. The policy that permits cities and counties to draft their own charters, to establish their own governmental structures, and to control matters that are local in nature. The policy may be established by state legislation alone, by the state constitution supplemented by enabling legislation, or by self-executing constitutional provisions. The primary impact of home rule has been to permit variations in governmental structure.

HOME RULE IN THE SOUTH, RESTORATION OF. Virginia, by a quick appeal to Congress, escaped the rigors of Reconstruction. In Tennessee a conservative constitution was ratified (March 1870) and a Democratic administration elected (November) to take office in October 1871. Georgia, although admitted to the Union, was reorganized under military direction when black members of the legislature were denied seats, and was forced to ratify the Fifteenth Amendment before being readmitted (July 15, 1870); in the following election the Democrats gained control of the legislature (Nov. 1, 1871) and impeached Gov. Rufus B. Bullock. In North Carolina a "reform legislature" impeached Gov. William W. Holden (1871), but it was not until Zebulon B. Vance's election (1876) that the Democrats got full control. Texas was under carpetbag rule until Jan. 17, 1874, when the Radical governor, failing to get the support of President U. S. Grant, surrendered his office to a Democrat. In Arkansas a Democratic-Conservative governor took office in 1874.

In the remaining states to be "redeemed" the strife was more prolonged and the national significance greater. In 1875 the Mississippi Democrats, while ostensibly drawing no color line, organized on the "Mississippi Plan" of armed "companies"; on election day (Nov. 2) the Democrats, through threats and multiple voting, won a victory in the legislature. The lieutenant-governor was impeached, the governor resigned, and Radical rule came to an end on Mar. 29, 1876.

The South Carolina Democrats nominated a "straight-out" ticket and organized the semimilitary "Red Shirts." The election (Nov. 7, 1876) was characterized by many irregularities, and each side claimed the victory. The dangerous situation resulting from the establishment of a dual government continued until President Rutherford B. Hayes withdrew the federal soldiers and the Republicans gave way on Apr. 11, 1877. A like situation in Florida came to an end when the Florida Supreme Court ruled against going behind the election returns and Gov. George F. Drew was inaugurated on Jan. 2, 1877. A similar election and contest in Louisiana were not settled until Hayes sent a commission to negotiate an agreement. On Apr. 24, 1877, home rule was established under Gov. Francis T. Nicholls.

HOMESTEAD ACT (May 20, 1862). An important step in developing U.S. land policy, this law provided that an American citizen, or a person who had announced his intention of becoming a citizen, could get title to a farm of 160 acres of public land for use as a "homestead." The purpose of the act was to make it easy for farmers to move into the open public lands of the West. The homesteader was required to build a house on the 160 acres and to begin farming on it; after five years of work on the land, it would become his personal property. A small registration fee (from $26 to $34) was required to file the necessary papers. Between 1862 and 1900, about 80 million acres were "homesteaded."

HOMESTEAD MOVEMENT. Free land was ingrained in the thoughts and desires of westward-moving settlers from early colonial days, but until the West became politically powerful the demand passed unheeded. Congress began very early to receive petitions asking that land in certain regions be given without price to settlers. In 1797 such a petition came from the Ohio River area, and two years later one came from Mississippi Territory. In 1812, Rep. Jeremiah Morrow of Ohio presented a request from the True American Society, whose members considered "every man entitled by nature to a portion of the soil of the country." In 1825, Thomas Hart Benton moved that an inquiry be made into the expediency of donating lands to settlers; the House committee on public lands reported in favor of such a policy in 1828. In his message of Dec. 4, 1832, President Andrew Jackson expressed the opinion that "the public lands should cease as soon as practicable to be a source of revenue." The National Trades Union Convention in 1834 and 1836 adopted resolutions favoring giving land to settlers. Perhaps the most active leader in the movement was George Henry Evans, who became the editor of *The Working Men's Advocate,* established in 1844. Horace Greeley also espoused the cause and brought it the powerful aid of his *New York Tribune.* The increasing public agitation was reflected in Congress by resolutions, petitions, and, in 1846, the introduction of homestead bills by Felix G. McConnell of Alabama and Andrew Johnson of Tennessee. Special laws donating land to settlers in Florida and Oregon under certain conditions were passed in 1842 and 1850, respectively.

The homestead movement first became a definite political issue in 1848, when the Free Soil party declared in favor of free land to actual settlers, but no major party came to the support of a homestead policy until 1860. Most southerners opposed homestead legislation, believing it would result in the peopling of the territories by antislavery settlers. Many easterners disapproved of the movement because of their fear of its effect on the economic situation in eastern states. Besides these sectional antagonisms, there was the opposition of the Know-Nothing party and other antialien groups to any proposal to give free land to foreign immigrants. In 1860 a homestead bill, introduced by Galusha A. Grow of Pennsylvania and amended in the process of debate and conference, passed both houses. Although this law as finally passed retained a price of 25 cents an acre, it was vetoed by President James Buchanan; the effort to override the veto failed by a small margin. The new Republican party in 1860 declared that "we demand the passage by Congress of the complete and satisfactory Homestead measure." The victory of the Republicans and the secession of the South left the triumphant party free to carry out its program. On May 20, 1862, President Abraham Lincoln signed the Homestead Act.

HOMESTEAD STRIKE OF 1892. The Amalgamated Association of Iron, Steel and Tin Workers was a powerful labor organization, which had established working relations with the Carnegie Steel Company at Homestead, Pa. Henry Clay Frick, chairman of the company, was determined to break the power of the union and demanded that its members accept a decrease in wages. When the union refused, Frick brought in nonunion labor. The ensuing violence and disorder led to the militia being called in, and organized labor's first struggle with large-scale capital ended in failure.

"HOME, SWEET HOME." Song written by John Howard Payne while living in Paris, set to music from a Sicilian air by Henry Bishop. It was first sung by Maria Tree in Payne's operetta *Clari,* at Covent Garden Theatre, London (May 8, 1823), and at the Park Theatre, New York (Nov. 12).

HONDURAS PROPOSED LOAN TREATY (signed Jan. 10, 1911). This treaty would have made possible a loan to Honduras by American bankers, to refund defaulted British bonds and to provide money for public works. It contemplated American control of Honduras' customs through a collector general nominated by the fiscal agents of the loan with the approval of the president of the United States; it was rejected by the Honduran congress and the U.S. Senate.

HONEY ISLAND (Pearl River, Miss.). A refuge for conscripts and deserters from the Confederate army. In April 1864, so many were in this region that Confederate Col. Robert Lowry was ordered "to move upon Honey Island and clear it out."

HONEY WAR (1839). Popular name for hostile activities in northeast Missouri when the Iowa-Missouri boundary dispute was at its height. Aroused over resistance in collecting taxes and disagreement as to ownership of bee trees, the two governors ordered their militia to enforce the respective state laws. Compromise prevented armed conflict.

HONKY-TONK GIRLS (or Hurdy-Gurdies). Entertainers engaged by saloon keepers and proprietors of social resorts in frontier mining towns to dance with all comers. They were mostly sturdy country girls, many of them German, and were usually engaged in sets of four with a chaperone who accompanied them at all times.

HONOLULU (Hawaii). Capital and largest city of Hawaii, with a 1980 population of 365,048. It lies on the southern shore of the island of Oahu beside a sheltered harbor, almost surrounded by coral reefs ("Honolulu" means "safe harbor"). British sea captains suggested to King Kamehameha I that the harbor would be a good site for his capital, which it became in 1820. During the 19th century, Honolulu became the "Crossroads of the Pacific"; it was an important port of call for trading ships, a harbor to which whalers came to refresh their crews and get supplies, and the shipping center for Hawaiian products. Sugar cane needs processing before sugar can be shipped, so Honolulu's first factories were sugar mills.

The city was an essential naval and air base during World War II. Following the war, some naval facilities were converted to civilian uses and to accommodate the booming tourist trade. Honolulu's Waikiki Beach is famous. Diamond Head, an extinct volcano at the eastern edge of the city, was named by sailors who thought that some of the volcanic sands were diamonds. Two of the city's cultural institutions play an important role in the entire Pacific area: the University of Hawaii, and the Bishop Museum of Polynesian Ethnology and Natural History.

HONOLULU CONFERENCE (Feb. 6–8, 1966). President Lyndon B. Johnson and Premier Nguyen Cao Ky of South Vietnam met for an exchange of views on military affairs, with the undeclared goal of consulting on arrangements for increasing the U.S. commitment in South Vietnam and to express American confidence in the Ky regime.

"HONORED MEN." *See* **"Beloved Man"/"Beloved Woman."**

HOOD'S TENNESSEE CAMPAIGN (October–December 1864). Early in October, Confederate Gen. J. B. Hood's army was in the vicinity of Dalton, Ga. Sherman followed from Atlanta. Hood marched off westward to Tuscumbia on the Tennessee River and awaited Sherman's pursuit. Instead, Sherman detached reinforcements under Gen. J. M. Schofield to Col. George H. Thomas at Nashville and returned to Atlanta. On Nov. 19, Hood decided to ignore Sherman and push into Tennessee to scatter the Union forces gathering at Nashville. On Nov. 29 he nearly cut off Schofield's retreating army at Spring Hill. The next day he assaulted Schofield's army at Franklin and was repulsed with heavy losses. Schofield hurriedly retreated into Nashville. Hood followed, but did not attack, awaiting Thomas's move. On Dec. 15, Thomas attacked and crushed the left of Hood's line; he renewed his attack the next day and was successful (*see* Nashville, Battle of). Thomas's cavalry pursued vigorously, but was unable to disperse Hood's army, which crossed the Tennessee River and turned westward to Corinth, Miss.

HOOKWORM. An intestinal parasite prevalent in the sandy soils of warm climates, spread by soil pollution. It inhibits growth and development in children and is generally debilitating in adults, weakening their resistance to other diseases. Known as "miner's anemia" in Italy, the disease was diagnosed in 1838. It was first noted in Puerto Rico in 1899, while Charles Stiles, helminthologist for the U.S. Natural History Museum, described in 1900 the differences between European hookworm and the new variety, which he named American killer. Stiles then studied the disease in the southern United States and convinced John D. Rockefeller, Sr., to fund the Rockefeller Sanitary Commission for the Eradication of Hookworm Disease in 1909. The commission's goals were to eradicate the disease itself, to strengthen public health administration, and to educate the public in health and hygiene. When the commission was dissolved in 1914, many of its activities were taken up by individual public health agencies.

HOOSAC MILLS CASE (*United States* v. *Butler*, 297 U.S. 1 [1936]). The Agricultural Adjustment Act (1933) empowered the secretary of agriculture to enter into contracts with farmers to restrict production in return for cash benefits and to lay processing taxes, the proceeds of which were to be devoted to the benefit payments. In the Hoosac Mills case the Supreme Court declared the processing taxes invalid because the payment of cash benefits to farmers to get them to cooperate was coercive and was an attempt on the part of Congress to regulate agricultural production—a matter solely within the jurisdiction of the states.

HOOSAC TUNNEL. Opened in 1876, extending 4.73 miles through the Hoosac Mountains of Massachusetts. Started in 1855 by the Troy and Greenfield Railroad; the state was forced to take it over when the railroad failed in 1863. In 1887 it was turned over to the Fitchburg Railroad (part of the Boston and Maine). The first use of compressed air drills in the United States (1866) was in its construction.

HOOSIER. A term applied to the inhabitants of Indiana since pioneer days. The oldest theory of its origin is that it is a corruption of "Who's here" *(hyer* or *yere),* as pronounced by the early inhabitants in answer to a knock on the door. Other explanations are that it originated from the word "husher," meaning a bully who could quickly hush or quiet an antagonist, or from the English dialect "hoozer," meaning anything large or awkward.

HOOVER COMMISSIONS. Two nonpartisan commissions on organization of the executive branch of government, set up by unanimous votes of the two chambers of the U.S. Congress and chaired by former President Herbert Hoover. The first (1947–49) dealt with the growth of government during World War II; the second, with growth during the Korean War. Both sought to reduce expenditures and to end duplication and overlapping of services or activities. Of the personnel for each, four were named by the president, four by the vice-president, and four by the speaker of the House. Task forces reported to the commissions, which, after studies by their staffs and members, reported their findings to Congress. More than 70 percent of the recommendations were put into effect, including passage of the Military Unification Act of 1949; creation of the General Services Agency; and formation of the Department of Health, Education, and Welfare.

HOOVER DAM. A concrete arch dam built by the Bureau of Reclamation at Boulder City, Nev., on the Colorado River. It was completed in 1936 and has a height of 726 feet, length of 1,244 feet, and volume of 4.4 million cubic yards. The power generating capacity is 1,345,000 kilowatts. The dam is notable for its height and for the size of the lake, Lake Mead, which at more than 31 million acre-feet is the largest man-made lake in the United States. The dam was known as Boulder Dam for a number of years following its completion.

HOPEDALE COMMUNITY (Milford, Mass.). Created in 1842 under the guidance of the Rev. Adin Ballou as "an experiment in the science of a divine order of society." It was a joint-stock company that shifted between the extremes of communism and individualism; it ended in 1856, surrendering its property to its two heaviest stockholders. Ballou believed it too Christian in principle for its time.

HOPEWELL. The first great cultural climax in prehistoric North America, 300 B.C.–A.D. 250. Less a culture than an exchange system or cult, the Hopewell complex probably developed in Illinois but soon spread to southern Ohio, where impressive earthworks were constructed. The regional cultures shared design motifs and ornamental or ceremonial objects, such as clay figurines, platform pipes, carved stone tablets, copper head and chest ornaments, earspools, panpipes, and flat celts, but also maintained distinctive local styles. Raw materials included mica, copper, shell, pipestone, meteoric iron, shark and alligator teeth, bear teeth, obsidian, and tortoiseshell. The Hopewell burial-mound-and-log-tomb complex was often built in two stages; many of the bodies were first cremated. Corn apparently never became a staple in the economic systems of the Hopewell; the harvesting of a wide variety of wild plants and animals probably sustained the Illinois populations.

HOPEWELL, TREATY OF (Nov. 28, 1785). Made at Hopewell, S.C., between the Cherokee and commissioners of the United States; the following January the same commissioners made almost identical treaties with the Choctaw and Chickasaw. The treaties fixed boundaries between the different tribes and between Indians and whites, and gave the United States sovereignty over the three tribes and control of their trade. The Treaty of Hopewell is significant as the first general Indian treaty made by the United States.

HOPEWELL IRON WORKS. Two apparently independent enterprises by this name were located in southeastern Pennsylvania: the Hopewell Forge belonging to the Cornwall mines opened by Peter Grubb in 1742 in Lancaster (now Lebanon) County; and the Hopewell Furnace and Forge begun by William Bird in 1744 in Berks County, which failed in 1784. The Lancaster forge continued for many years under the ownership of Robert Coleman.

HOPI. Classic representatives of Pueblo culture, occupying three mesas (tablelands) at the edge of the Painted Desert in northeastern Arizona. They numbered about 6,500 in the early 1980's. Each of the seven towns forms a basic social unit; there is thus no tribe as such. The Hopi speak a Shoshonean language remotely related to the Tanoan languages spoken by the people of the Rio Grande pueblos to the east. It is suggested that they are deeply rooted in time in their present location.

The Hopi are divided into maternal units, or clans: the individual takes his group affiliation from his mother, and ownership of house, farmland, and the important ceremonial paraphernalia pass from mother to daughter. Political authority passes to men through the female line of descent. Ceremonial activity—involving initiation and the impersonation of spirits or gods with masked dancing—aims at agricultural fertility, world renewal, and societal stability. Although the Hopi fought defensive wars, especially against the intrusive Navaho (on whose culture they left a strong imprint), the primary orientations of their society are directed toward peace. Like the other Pueblo, they have adopted the pattern of intensive agriculture, despite the desert conditions under which they live. Water is carefully controlled; crops are planted at the base of a mesa to catch even the morning dew;

and rainmaking rituals form a vital part of Hopi religious observances. The so-called Snake Dance, carried on by priests of the Snake society in alternate years, embodies a symbolism that identifies the snake, lightning, and rain. The Hopi have successfully maintained their native culture against pressures from outsiders, including the expedition of Francisco Vásquez de Coronado in 1540; Franciscan missionization, begun in 1629; and the effects of the Pueblo Revolt of 1680, which forced the movement of some Hopi.

HORIZONTAL TARIFF BILL (May 1, 1872). A federal tariff law that cut protective duties 10 percent. it was repealed in 1875 to meet an alleged need for more revenue.

HORNBOOK. The primer or first reading book used in the colonial schools, transplanted to America by the English colonists; it was simply a sheet of paper mounted on a board and covered with transparent horn. The board ended in a handle that was perforated for attachment to the child's belt. Hornbooks contained the alphabet in capital and small letters; combinations of vowels with consonants to form syllables; the Lord's Prayer; and Roman numerals.

***HORNET-PEACOCK* ENGAGEMENT** (Feb. 24, 1813). Off British Guiana, the U.S. sloop *Hornet* captured the British brig *Peacock* after a spirited action of fifteen minutes. Soon afterward the *Peacock* sank.

***HORNET-PENGUIN* ENGAGEMENT** (Mar. 23, 1815). The U.S. sloop of war *Hornet* engaged the British brig *Penguin* off the island of Tristan da Cunha in the south Atlantic. The *Penguin* was so badly damaged it had to be destroyed; the *Hornet* did not receive a single shot through its hull.

HORSE. The horse in America dates at least from the single-hoofed *Equus caballus* that emerged in late Pleistocene times, about 1 million years ago. Paleontologists suspect that the horse became extinct in America not more than, and possibly less than, 10,000 years ago; none of the historic Indians living in the New World has any tradition of such an animal. It was reintroduced into the Western Hemisphere at the end of the 15th century by Christopher Columbus, who landed twenty-five horses on the island Hispaniola. The Spanish crown encouraged the sending of breeding stock to the Caribbean islands; the Spanish horses acclimated rapidly and within twenty years formed the chief supply for the Spanish mainland expeditions. By the mid–16th century outstanding horse breeders in Cuba, Jamaica, Chiapas, and Oaxaca sold their products on two continents. While Jamestown was being settled (1607) by the English, Juan de Oñate was establishing Spanish ranches in New Mexico. The Jesuit missionary Eusebio Francisco Kino and his companions pushed a second wedge into Arizona, where they established many stock ranches by 1700. Gaspar de Portolá from Baja (Lower) California and Juan Bautista de Anza from Arizona took horses into Alta (Upper) California, where they increased prodigiously. Exportation from California to Hawaii began in 1803 and reached extensive proportions by 1830. Horses became so numerous in California that thousands were driven off cliffs or into the sea to drown. Indian revolts and English depredations at the close of the 1600's tended to spread the horse north from Florida into the English colonies. On the outskirts of Virginia they multiplied in a feral state—like the mustangs of the Southwest—until they were a menace to the crops and were hunted for sport. These horses were generally small, with bad points, but new blood was frequently obtained from the Spanish stock west of the Mississippi; until the 19th century the Spanish horse presented the nearest, and in many respects the best, breed available.

Before settled agricultural systems developed, oxen were preferred for draft purposes, but horses and ponies were essential for inland travel and military excursions. In the British colonies as a whole, horses were valued for riding, hunting, and racing at market fairs. Horses and mules drew canalboat and railcar. The western pony served the hunter, trapper, and miner, and later the cow horse provided the mounts for the long drives and herding activities of the cowboy. The original cow horse belonged essentially to the mustang breed. The cow pony had to have bottom (stamina and spirit), surefootedness, and "cow sense"—a quality lacking in many finely bred horses. The elite were the cutting horses: agile, intelligent, and trained to cut, or part, animals from a herd. Extractive industries, manufactures, and city distributive systems were all dependent on horsepower, as were military operations.

New England carried on the first extensive American horse breeding. The horse Justin Morgan foaled in Massachusetts in 1793, founding a line notable not only for speed but also for light draft and providing the nearest attainment to a distinct American breed; Rhode Island developed the noted Narragansett pacer, a fast, easy-gaited saddle horse. In direct contrast to these was the Conestoga of the Pennsylvania-German farmers; the product of selection and careful handling, these animals were distinguished for size, strength, and endurance. The general usage of the standard draft breeds, pure or grade, was a part of the agricultural revolution taking place just after the Civil War. The Percheron was widely imported in the 1850's to become the most popular type. The other leading breeds, Belgian, Clydesdale, and Shire, were bred for the market from the 1870's. The corn belt from Ohio to Iowa was the center of the draft horse supply.

The revolution worked by the internal-combustion engine resulted in a displacement of horses for power and transportation. From about 26 million farm horses and mules in the United States in 1920, the number declined to about 3 million horses and mules on farms in in the 1970's.

HORSEHEAD CROSSING. Two river crossings were so designated, one in Texas and the other in Arizona. In Texas the Goodnight-Loving cattle trail passed the Pecos River at Horsehead Crossing near the present town of Ficklin. In Arizona, travel bound for Concho and Fort Apache passed the Puerco River at Horsehead Crossing just below its junction with the Little Colorado.

HORSE MARINES. A term ordinarily referring to cavalrymen doing the work of marines, or vice versa; it may designate almost any military or naval incongruity. It became associated with an episode in 1836, following the Battle of San Jacinto: Maj. Isaac Burton's Texas Rangers were making a reconnaissance along the coast to establish the extent and speed of the Mexican withdrawal; near Copano, Tex., Burton sighted and by ruse captured three Mexican supply ships. Burton's detachment became known as the Horse Marines.

HORSE RACING. The original Virginia colonists began racing at the first opportunity, over forest pathways or roads. Course racing began on Long Island, N.Y., in 1665; races were also run in the other colonies during the 17th century. Racing spread as the nation grew, until in the early 1980's pari-mutuel racing (as distinguished from amateur sport) was legal in about twenty-five states. Although some thoroughbreds are raised in every state, in 1971 more than half the crop of 24,000 thoroughbred foals came from just five states—California, Kentucky, Florida, Maryland, and Virginia. The preeminence of Kentucky as a breeding state was formerly attributed to the limestone in the soil and water of the Bluegrass region, but with modern nutritional techniques it is possible to raise horses almost anywhere.

In the early colonial matches the owner of each horse put up a stake, and the stakes made up the winner's purse. Auction pools (in which the contestants were auctioned off and the purchaser of the winner collected the pool less a commission to the pool seller) were developed prior to the Civil War, and bookmakers had appeared on the scene by the last half of the 19th century. Purses continued to be modest, and the manipulation (real or imagined) of horses' form for betting purposes led to such public indignation that racing was outlawed in a number of states. The adoption of the pari-mutuel system of wagering in 1908 gave racing a new aspect: from being a semiprivate sport, it became a vast public entertainment business in which not only racing associations and horsemen but also state governments derived income directly proportional to volume of wagering. Over the years the states increased their shares of pari-mutuel handle to the point at which the average tax has become a burdensome 7.4 percent. Total revenue to the racing states from racing in 1980 amounted to about $713 million.

Night racing has been the mainstay of harness racing, especially in metropolitan areas. Thoroughbred races are also run under lights, but not at the major tracks. In the 1970's racing on Sundays, which had previously been illegal, became permissible in several states, and the development of synthetic surfaces and the construction of enclosed, heated grandstands have made year-round racing possible. Some states have established lotteries based on races. New York State, Connecticut, and Nevada have authorized off-track betting.

HORSESHOE BEND, BATTLE OF (Mar. 27, 1814)**.** After a six-months' campaign during the War of 1812, Maj. Gen. Andrew Jackson attacked 800 Creek Indians strongly entrenched at the Horseshoe Bend of the Tallapoosa River, now in Alabama; the battle lasted about seven hours. Their breastworks overrun, the Indian warriors refused to surrender and all but about 50 were killed. The battle broke forever the military power of the southern Indians.

HORSE STEALING. In the West and Southwest the value that range people put on horses is summed up in the saying, "A man on foot is no man at all." "As lowdown as a horse thief" expressed the nadir of the social scale. A majority of "cottonwood blossoms"—men hanging, usually without benefit of jury, from limbs of cottonwood trees—were horse thieves. During the lawless decades following the Civil War, gangs of horse thieves operated out of Texas into the Old South and the West. They had hideouts for stolen horses, which would be sold or traded off only after having been driven hundreds of miles from home.

HORTALEZ AND COMPANY. To enable France and Spain to secretly assist the American colonists in their fight for independence from Great Britain, the dummy firm of Roderique Hortalez and Company was organized (August 1776); within a year it had sent the Americans eight shiploads of military stores worth over 6 million livres. Notwithstanding the formal alliance of 1778 between France and the colonists, the company continued in business until 1783. Its total disbursements exceeded 21 million livres.

HOSPITALS. In the British-American colonies, workhouse or almshouse infirmaries sometimes developed into public general hospitals (Philadelphia General Hospital opened as the infirmary of an almshouse in 1732); but the Pennsylvania Hospital in Philadelphia (1751) was the first permanent British-American institution created solely for the care of the sick. In French colonial areas along the Gulf of Mexico, hospitals were established by the government or the Mississippi Company even earlier (Mobile, 1713; New Orleans, ca. 1722). After the Revolution, general hospitals appeared in urban centers (New York Hospital, 1791; Massachusetts General in Boston, 1811); they were privately supported charitable institutions designed to provide short-term care for those who could not be nursed at home. Patients with incurable or terminal illnesses were sent to the public almshouse.

In the 17th century, communities often set up temporary pesthouses to isolate and care for the sick during epidemics; after the middle of the 18th century when smallpox inoculation became accepted, private inoculation hospitals sprang up. To care for the insane, custodial institutions developed, such as Eastern State Hospital at Williamsburg, Va. (1773). To fill military needs, the federal government created temporary hospitals; the oldest permanent federally supported hospital system was the Marine Hospital Service (1798). Throughout the 19th century, America had a mixture of city, state, and federally supported institutions and private philanthropic hospitals, the latter often established by ethnic, religious, or benevolent societies or Masonic groups. Hospitals devoted to the treatment of a single disease, organ, or age group evolved (for example, New York Eye Infirmary, 1820). Until midcentury the private patient scarcely existed. Those with private means expected to be cared for in their homes. The first U.S. hospital survey (1873) showed that there were only 149 hospitals, one-third of which were for mental patients; fifty years later there were 6,762 hospitals, a growth caused chiefly by changes in the hospital's function.

Before the germ theory was accepted, infectious diseases were attributed to vitiated air and lack of sunlight, and hospital wards were usually constructed on a pavilion plan with high ceilings and tall windows for good ventilation and light. The Nightingale ward, a long narrow room with twenty beds against each wall between tall windows, was in vogue until World War I. By the 1920's rising land values, advancing medical technology, and additional hospital functions caused the pavilion plan to be abandoned in favor of the vertical monoblock. As the public image of the hospital changed, from that of hospice for the sick poor to that of a diagnostic and treatment center for all classes, the number of private or semiprivate rooms steadily increased. St. Vincent's Hospital in New York (1849) was among the first to provide private rooms; since the mid-20th century, private and semiprivate rooms have predominated. Scientific laboratories and special therapy areas began to appear in 1889. X rays, discovered in 1895, furthered the trend toward making the hospital the workshop of medicine. In 1918 the American College of Surgeons sponsored a program of hospital standardization that set forth minimum requirements for properly equipped hospitals. Through annual surveys, the college ratings exposed substandard institutions. In 1918, only 12.9 percent of U.S. hospitals were approved; by 1936, 72.2 percent met the standards.

After World War II the hospital began to assume a new role as community health center, as a substitute for the rapidly vanishing general practitioner. Although the number of U.S. hospitals has increased only slightly (by 1979 there were 6,988 hospitals), they have so expanded as to almost double the number of beds available to about 1.37 million.

"HOT OIL" CASE *(Panama Refining Company* v. *Ryan,* 293 U.S. 388 [1935]). The National Industrial Recovery Act of 1933 authorized the president to prohibit the transportation in interstate and foreign commerce of oil produced or withdrawn from storage in excess of the amount permitted to be produced by the state from which the oil was shipped. The Supreme Court invalidated this provision, holding that Congress had delegated essential legislative power to the president.

HOT WATER, BATTLE OF (June 26, 1781). A skirmish about six miles from Williamsburg, Va., between Americans of the Pennsylvania Line and a force of British troops. It is also called the Battle of Jamestown and the Battle of Green Spring. Hot Water is the old name of the plantation adjoining Green Spring plantation.

HOT WATER REBELLION. *See* **Fries's Rebellion.**

HOUMA. An Indian tribe originally located in Mississippi; early in the 18th century it was living near the site of New Orleans, but later moved to Bayou Lafourche in southern Louisiana. By the 20th century the Houma had become a group of mixed ancestry: Indian (comprising the remnant of several Muskhogean groups), Afro-American, and white. They are French-speaking, are of variable physical type, and in the 1970's numbered about 2,500, living in scattered settlements of their own along the bayous. They have persistently fought against being identified with Afro-Americans.

HOUSATONIC. A large sloop of war, one of the Union fleet blockading Charleston in 1863–64. On Feb. 17, 1864, a Confederate hand-operated submarine torpedoed the *Housatonic* and sank with it; most of the *Housatonic*'s crew was saved.

HOUSE COMMITTEE ON UN-AMERICAN ACTIVITIES (HUAC). In 1938 a resolution of the House of Representatives authorized appointment of a special committee to investigate "un-American propaganda activities in the United States." HUAC was established in the same year under the chairmanship of Democratic Rep. Martin Dies, Jr., of Texas. It won five renewals by overwhelming votes, and in 1945 it was made a standing committee of the House of Representatives. It was renamed the Internal Security Committee in 1969 and was abolished in 1975.

Chief sponsor of the move to set up the committee was Democratic Rep. Samuel Dickstein of New York, who expected it to concentrate on ferreting out foreign agents. However, the committee, although giving due attention to Communists and Fascists, directed much of its fire at New Deal liberals, intellectuals, artists, labor leaders, and immigrants. After World War II a parade of turncoat radicals and publicity-seekers came before it to testify against alleged subversives in government, labor unions, the press, religious organizations, and Hollywood. Committee hearings were characterized by the badgering of unfriendly witnesses and by scant regard for due process. HUAC declined in prominence with the rise in the early 1950's of the flamboyant Sen. Joseph R. McCarthy of Wisconsin (*see* McCarthy-Army Hearings).

"HOUSE DIVIDED." Accepting the Republican nomination to the U.S. Senate at Springfield, Ill. (June 16, 1858), Abraham Lincoln paraphrased a sentence from the Bible (Mark 3:25): "A house divided against itself cannot stand." He continued, "I believe this government cannot endure permanently half slave and half free. I do not expect the Union to be dissolved—I do not expect the house to fall—but I do expect it will cease to be divided."

HOUSE-GREY MEMORANDUM (Feb. 22, 1916). Signed by Col. Edward M. House, President Woodrow Wilson's adviser, and Sir Edward Grey, British foreign secretary, the memorandum stated that Wilson would summon a conference for ending World War I when England and France considered the time right. Should Germany refuse to meet at the conference, the United States would probably enter the war against Germany. Nothing came of the plan.

HOUSE OF HOPE (or Fort Good Hope, Conn.). Built by Jacob van Curler at Dutch Point on the south bank of the Little or Park River at its junction with the Connecticut

River, within the present city of Hartford. As the first European settlement in Connecticut (June 1633), its purpose was to tap the trade of the Connecticut Valley, especially in furs. In 1635–36, English colonists from Massachusetts Bay Colony settled north and west of the fort, so narrowly circumscribing the fort that it had little value strategically or commercially. When war broke out between England and the Dutch in 1653, Capt. John Underhill seized the fort; by the following year it was completely under English control.

HOUSE OF REPRESENTATIVES. *See* **Congress, United States.**

HOUSING. On each successive frontier settlers built themselves primitive shelters, which were gradually replaced by better structures as family resources expanded. The free-standing house, individually owned, is still the dominant and favored building type wherever land prices and convenience permit. But the colonial towns of the eastern seaboard apparently exercised a high degree of community responsibility for the period, in terms of elementary municipal services and regulations with respect to roads, fire safety, and minimal sanitation. In the higher-density centers, wooden structures were outlawed in favor of the brick row house. Piped water systems were beginning to reach homes in several communities before the Revolution.

In the early stages, industrialization and the immigrant flood led to factory enclaves with company-built housing, but the major result was big cities with slums that neither individual nor commercial enterprise has been able to remedy. Meanwhile, the great public health revolution created a new concept of "minimum standards," and municipalities slowly began to develop the vast present-day network of sanitary services and housing regulations. The automobile, following the railroad and trolley car, opened up vast areas of cheap suburban land for middle- and upper-class home ownership, inaugurating a period of chaotic metropolitan expansion. The old slums still accommodated low-income immigrants, and there were ever-widening rings of blight, decay, and overcrowding in once-adequate residential districts.

A series of national emergencies sparked direct public action. In 1917 the federal government built housing projects for war workers. In the postwar shortage, several state and local governments took tentative steps. With the depression of 1929 came disaster in the housing market, and many kinds of federal measures, including subsidies for low-rent public housing. World War II and its aftermath again brought emergency shortages, with a big federal program for war workers and special aids for veterans. But the decay in central districts continued. Federal grants for redevelopment were inaugurated in 1949, with added incentives since 1954. Federal mortgage insurance and other credit aids stimulated millions of suburban tract houses, sporadic rental construction, some cooperatives, and some housing initiative for the elderly. Several states provided additional aids, and most residential development became subject to public guidance through local planning and zoning as well as building regulations, but little effective planning or housing responsibility was shown at the metropolitan level. In 1965 the cabinet-level Department of Housing and Urban Development (HUD) was established by Congress to alleviate some of these problems.

HOUSING ACTS. The National Housing Act of 1934 established the Federal Housing Authority (FHA), and was designed to stimulate residential construction, promote improvement in housing standards, and create a sound system of home financing. The National Housing Act of 1937 (Wagner-Steagall Act) created the U.S. Housing Authority (USHA) and was designed to provide public housing for low-income groups. The Housing Act of 1954 authorized the construction of 35,000 houses over a one-year period to house families displaced by urban renewal and slum clearance programs, increase the amount of the maximum mortgage on both sale and rental housing, lower down payments, and lengthen amortization periods. Provision was also included to curb future abuses of the FHA home-loan program. The Housing Act of 1955 authorized the construction of an additional 45,000 public housing units for the next two years. The Housing Act of 1957 raised maximum amounts in a number of FHA programs and cut cash requirements. The Housing Act of 1958 further liberalized minimum down payments and increased the funds available for home mortgages; another housing bill passed in 1959 provided $650 million for slum clearance and urban renewal, and a stopgap housing bill passed in 1960 extended the FHA loan improvement program. The Housing Act of 1961 was the most comprehensive since the 1958 act. It attempted to reduce urban blight, to improve lower income housing, and to stimulate the economy through an increase in housing construction. The Housing and Urban Development Act of 1968 provided $5.3 billion for a three-year program designed to provide more than 1.7 million units of new and rehabilitated housing for low-income families and included subsidies to help the poor buy houses and rent apartments. The Housing and Community Development Act of 1974 shifted the responsibility for low-income housing to local communities.

HOUSING AND URBAN DEVELOPMENT, DEPARTMENT OF (HUD). Created by act of Congress in 1965, HUD centralizes at cabinet level the federal activities started under the provisions of the National Housing Act of 1934, which created the still-extant Federal Housing Administration (FHA) and other agencies to deal with the housing emergency caused by the Great Depression. It insured first-mortgage loans up to 80 percent of the value of homes (but not in excess of $14,000) and of low-cost rental housing provided by limited-dividend corporations. Reamortizations were extended up to twenty years. By 1937 all states had removed obstacles to lending under the national statute. By 1954 the mortgage insurance premiums paid by lenders had enabled the FHA to return to the Treasury the sums advanced by it, and the agency has since been self-sustaining.

Under the Housing and Urban Development Act of 1968, interest subsidies were introduced for low- and middle-income homeowners and for financing cooperative and rental housing for low-income families. Those subsidies opened the way to replacing substandard housing on a scale not previously possible. HUD began to carry out its mandate for urban development beyond the mere provision of shelter. It concerned itself particularly with ensuring nondiscrimination in construction projects in which it was involved; applicants for mortgage insurance were required to make positive efforts to attract buyers or tenants of all races, and the department favored cities with records of nondiscrimination. Grants for neighborhood facilities, parks, and water and sewerage were made. Professional housing managers were trained to cope with the problems of physical maintenance and tenant relationships. Rehabilitation of old housing was financed. Assistance in construction of hospitals and homes for the elderly was emphasized. The Model Cities program encouraged local governments, with citizen participation, to make and execute plans for improved living standards. A nationwide registry of minority-group contractors and subcontractors and a manual on minority business opportunities connected with housing were distributed and publicized.

By 1973 the housing program had suffered from centralized control, as well as benefited from it. The Housing and Community Development Act of 1974 shifted initiative to localities.

HOUSTON (Tex.). Founded in 1836 by two brothers, Augustus and John Allen, on the site of an earlier town, and named for Gen. Sam Houston, who defeated the Mexicans at San Jacinto, it was the new republic's first capital (1837–39). The town was established on low land near the Buffalo Bayou, a slow-moving stream that lacked a clear mouth on the Gulf of Mexico; however, it was near good farmland and near the sea. Docks were developed along the Buffalo Bayou, and attempts were made to improve the channel into the Gulf. Houston became one of the earliest railroad centers in Texas; the lines extended inland to gathering points for cotton and other agricultural products, including beef. By 1900, Congress had approved a project to deepen the waterway.

The city's great growth came in the 20th century. The discovery of oil to the north turned Houston from a lumber and cotton town into an oil city. After the oil was piped to Houston, it was either shipped out as crude oil or refined in Houston itself; the pipelines terminated near the Houston Ship Channel, and tank farms, oil refineries, and chemical plants were erected along the waterway. The concentration of chemical and petroleum engineering activities produced an unusual number of scientifically trained individuals in the area, which in turn began to attract other businesses. The large sums made in these new businesses made the city a financial center.

Houston became the nation's space headquarters during the 1960's when the Manned Spacecraft Center was established at the suburb Clear Lake. Among Houston's educational institutions, Rice Institute (founded 1912) had a national reputation as a center for engineering studies; as Rice University, it expanded its offerings during the 1950's and 1960's. Houston's medical center won worldwide attention during the 1960's as a result of the heart-transplant work done by Dr. Michael De Bakey. Population in 1980 was 1,594,086, making it the fifth largest U.S. city.

HOUSTON SHIP CHANNEL. Opened in 1919, but deepened to a minimum of 36 feet and greatly improved since that time, it furnishes Houston with a fifty-seven-mile outlet to the Gulf of Mexico for seagoing vessels and has made the city a close rival of New York City in volume of exports.

HOWARD, FORT (Wis.). Built in 1816 on the site of the former French Fort La Baye and of the British Fort Edward Augustus, it was the first American post at Green Bay and was of value in Americanizing the French settlement. The garrison was withdrawn in 1841; troops were again brought there at the close of the Mexican War.

HOWARD UNIVERSITY. Established in 1867 in Washington, D.C., as a school for black students, in the 20th century it began a policy of admitting students regardless of race. The university consists of sixteen schools and colleges, including professional schools of engineering, architecture, medicine, dentistry, pharmacy, law, and social work. It was named for Oliver Otis Howard, a Civil War officer who headed the Freedmen's Bureau in 1865–72. The university is operated by an independent board of trustees, but receives part of its funds from the U.S. government.

HUBBARDTON, BATTLE OF (July 7, 1777). British Gen. Simon Fraser defeated an American force under Seth Warner at Hubbardton, Vt., as it retreated from Ticonderoga, N.Y. One American detachment was completely surprised and the men ran off; the leader of another was killed, and his men dispersed.

HUDSON-FULTON CELEBRATION (1909). Commemorating the 300th anniversary of Henry Hudson's exploration of the Hudson River (1609) and the 100th anniversary of the first successful application of steam to marine navigation on that river by Robert Fulton (1807), replicas of the *Half Moon* and the *Clermont* traveled up the Hudson River valley for local ceremonies; the principal part of the celebration occurred in New York City from Sept. 25 to Oct. 11.

HUDSON RIVER. Giovanni da Verrazano was probably the first white man to see the Hudson River (1524), which he ascended for about half a league. French traders traversed it during the 16th century, trading with the Mohawk Indians, and founded a small fort near the site of Albany in 1540. Henry Hudson, exploring for the Dutch West India Company, ascended the river in 1609 as far as Albany and sent some of his men to explore it some twenty-five miles farther, past the mouth of the Mohawk; it thereupon became an artery for Dutch colonization, with Albany founded as a fur-trading station in 1614. A party of persecuted Walloons emigrated to what is now Ulster County in 1660, founding Kingston and other villages, while Germans from the Palatinate settled in the valley in 1710. The British took over the Dutch possessions in 1664.

For more than two centuries the Hudson was the chief avenue of travel and transportation from what is now upper New York State to New York City and the coast. Completion of the Erie Canal (1825) and the Champlain Canal added more business. Robert Fulton's *Clermont* was tested on the Hudson in 1807, and thereafter steamboats began to displace sloops. Large and elegant passenger steamboats plied the river in the mid–19th century. The completion (1851) of the Hudson River Railroad along its eastern bank brought about a steady diminution of the river's freight traffic.

The river is so wide and deep, its banks for the most part so rugged, that below Albany, nearly 150 miles from its mouth, it was not bridged until 1889, when a cantilever railroad structure was completed at Poughkeepsie; the next bridging was at Bear Mountain in 1925; and the first bridge to cross at New York City was the George Washington suspension bridge, in 1931. (The Pennsylvania Railroad completed a tunnel connection under the river in 1910; the Holland Tunnel, connecting Manhattan and New Jersey, was completed in 1927.)

HUDSON RIVER CHAIN. On May 1, 1778, a chain was stretched across the Hudson River between West Point and Constitution Island as a barrier to British shipping. It was constructed in approximately six weeks from iron mined in Orange County. The individual links were slightly over 2 feet long and 2.5 inches thick and weighed 140 pounds. The chain, weighing 180 tons, was attached to huge blocks on either shore, supported by protecting batteries; it was buoyed at frequent intervals in midstream.

HUDSON RIVER LAND PATENTS. The Dutch practice of making large grants was followed by the English, with the result that by 1738 there was little unpatented land left on the Hudson River below Albany. At Albany the great manor of Kiliaen Van Rensselaer, called Rensselaerswyck, lay on both sides of the river. To the south was the manor of Robert Livingston in Columbia County, Col. Henry Beekman's great tract in Dutchess County, Frederick Philipse's Highland patent in Putnam, and the manors of Scarsdale, Pelham, Morrisania, Fordham, and Philipsborough in Westchester. Large tracts such as the Great Nine Partners patent in Dutchess County and the Kakiate and Chesecocks patents in Orange County were secured and held for financial speculation.

HUDSON'S BAY COMPANY. One of the oldest commercial corporations in existence, chartered on May 2, 1670, as the Governor and Company of Adventurers of England Trading into Hudson's Bay. During the heyday of the fur trade, the company had posts in most parts of what is now Canada. It also had a few forts on U.S. soil, mostly along the boundary line west from Grand Portage, where a bitter struggle was carried on with the North West Company. In Minnesota and North Dakota missionaries were sent to the Indians and half-breeds under the aegis of the company. Missionaries also played an important part in the company's relations to the history of the Oregon country, where company men appeared after the union of the two companies in 1821 to carry on the fur trade begun years earlier by the North West Company. By welcoming Americans, Dr. John McLoughlin, the company's chief factor, helped Oregon to become American.

HUE AND CRY. In old English law when a felony was committed, the hue and cry was raised, and all who heard it were obligated to join in the chase. Later, "hue and cry" came to mean the chase itself, and then a proclamation authorizing the capture of a criminal. In the American colonies, individuals suspected of felonies, escaped prisoners, and runaway servants and slaves could by law be pursued by hue and cry from town to town. The hue and cry would justify arrests of idlers, vagrants, or other suspicious characters. In following persons on a hue and cry, officers were authorized to impress men, horses, and boats.

HUERTGEN FOREST. A stretch of primarily coniferous woodland twenty miles long and ten miles wide lying close to the Belgian border of Germany, southeast of Aachen; scene of some of the most intense fighting of World War II. Designed to control flooding of the Roer River, the Urft and Schwammenauel dams (the Roer Dams) form big reservoirs in southern reaches of the forest. In early September 1944, the U.S. First Army made its main effort north of the forest but deemed it necessary to clear the forest to achieve flank protection. The convoluted terrain, dense trees, pillboxes of the Siegfried Line, and dearth of roads afforded the defender sharp advantage. In attacks in September and October the Americans gained less than two miles at a cost of 4,500 casualties; an attack in November resulted in 6,000 casualties. In succession five other divisions attacked in the forest; everywhere the fighting was costly. The stalwart German defense was attributable in part to German plans for a major counteroffensive to be launched farther south in December (the Battle of the Bulge), which would have been jeopardized had the Americans crossed the Roer River; and in part to the presence of the Roer Dams, which might be used to flood the Roer and isolate any American force that crossed. Not until mid-December was most of the forest taken, and following the German counteroffensive, the Americans still had to capture the Roer Dams (February 1945).

HUGUENOTS. "Huguenot," of unknown origin, was first applied to French Protestants during the religious struggles of the 16th century. About 300,000 French Huguenots fled to Prussia, Switzerland, Holland, England, and America. Attempted settlements in Florida and South Carolina (1562 and 1564) failed. In 1623, Huguenots settled New Amsterdam. Fort Orange (Albany), Kingston, and New Paltz in New York were Huguenot settlements. Some 200 or 300 Huguenot families came to Boston after the Dragonades.

After 1685 increasing numbers of Huguenots came to America, settling in Rhode Island; in Hartford and Milford, Conn.; and in New Rochelle, N.Y. In Delaware, Maryland, and Pennsylvania they were called Dutchmen and confused with German settlers. Three shiploads coming to Manakintowne, Va., in 1700 made up the largest single settlements of

Huguenots in America; King William Parish was set aside for them, but they soon mingled with the English of the colony.

In South Carolina, Huguenots began coming in 1670, played a large part in the settlement of Charleston in 1680, and by 1687 had established four settlements largely or wholly French: Jamestown on the Santee River, the "Orange Quarter" on the Cooper River, St. John's Berkeley, and Charleston. They preserved their identity in South Carolina more completely than in other colonies; the only Huguenot church in America is in Charleston. Their religion was Calvinistic in theology, ritual in form, presbyterian in government, and tolerant in principle.

HULL, COURT-MARTIAL OF. Gen. William Hull's surrender of Detroit in 1812 was followed by his court-martial at Albany two years later. Martin Van Buren and Philip S. Parker conducted the case for the government; Hull acted in his own defense. He was charged with treason, cowardice, and unofficerlike conduct. Hull was denied access to official records; denied, in effect, the right of representation by counsel; and tried before a packed court under Gen. Henry Dearborn's presidency. Hull should not have invaded Canada before perfecting his defenses at Detroit, and should have exercised greater care in preventing the severing of his communications. But the government was also to blame; the secretary of war neglected to inform him that war had begun, and Dearborn had signed an armistice in which Hull was not included and of which he was not informed, thus allowing the British to throw their entire force against Detroit. Hull was acquitted of treason. He was found guilty of the other charges and sentenced to death, although the court recommended mercy. President James Madison pardoned him.

HULL HOUSE. A settlement house established (1889) in Chicago, Ill., by Jane Addams. It showed how neighborhood services could be combined with formal and informal educational and cultural activities.

HULL'S ESCAPE FROM BROKE'S SQUADRON. On July 17, 1812, the *Constitution,* commanded by Capt. Isaac Hull, off Barnegat, N.J., fell in with a British squadron of six vessels commanded by Capt. P. B. V. Broke. A chase lasting over sixty hours ensued, during which Hull escaped from what more than once appeared to be certain capture.

HULL'S TRAIL. Cut by Gen. William Hull through forest and swamp on his march to Detroit in 1812. Starting at Urbana, Ohio, it passed through forts McArthur and Findlay, north through Portage and Bowling Green, and crossed the Maumee River near Turkeyfoot Rock; then down the river through the site of Maumee anu along Detroit Avenue in the city of Toledo; then to Monroe (Frenchtown), Mich., on the Raisin River and on to Brownstown on the Huron; and then followed the old river road northward through Monguagon, Wyandotte, Ecorse, and Springwells to Detroit.

HULL TREATY (Nov. 17, 1807). Following a council with the Ottawa, Chippewa, Wyandot, and Potawatomi at Detroit, much of the land in southeastern Michigan Territory was ceded by the Indians. The new Indian boundary was a line about seventy-five miles west of the Detroit River and extending north to the line of White Rock in Lake Huron.

HÜLSEMANN INCIDENT. During the unsuccessful Hungarian Revolution of 1849, President Zachary Taylor sent Ambrose Dudley Mann to Hungary to report its prospects of success, with a view toward recognition. This unneutral action inflamed the Austrian chargé d'affaires, Chevalier J. G. Hülsemann, to a series of intemperate protests in September 1850. The protests were answered by Secretary of State Daniel Webster and William L. Marcy who defended America's right to take an interest in the revolution.

HUMANE SOCIETIES. *See* **Animal Protective Societies.**

HUMAN RIGHTS. As early as 1639 the "Act for the liberties of the people" was approved by the Maryland General Assembly; it provided that all freemen should "have and enjoy all such rights liberties immunities privileges and free customs . . . as any natural born subject of England hath or ought to have or enjoy." Its foundation was the idea that certain rights and liberties are inseparable from the citizen as a free man and are beyond the power of any government to give or to take away. In 1789, when the U.S. Constitution was ratified, Congress undertook to fulfill the wish of the American people to add a bill of rights; this was accomplished by the first ten amendments (ratified in 1791). While the amendments enumerated specific guarantees, the Ninth Amendment was designed to foreclose the argument that rights that were not named were necessarily excluded. The Supreme Court has, in fact, recognized rights and liberties that have not been expressly enumerated, as well as "peripheral rights" that help secure the guaranteed rights. Thus, human rights continue to be in a process of evolution and differentiation. Some receive recognition only because they are provided for in a written constitution, while others, whether written or unwritten, have come to receive a high priority because they are considered indispensable for life in a free and just society; it is the latter that have come to be known as human rights and have received international recognition or sanction, as in the Nuremberg trials of the Nazi war criminals and in the declarations of human rights adopted by the United Nations and the Council of Europe.

HUMPHREY'S EXECUTOR* V. *UNITED STATES, 295 U.S. 602 (1935). In the Federal Trade Commission Act, Congress provided that any commissioner might be removed by the president for inefficiency, neglect of duty, or malfeasance in office. In October 1933, President Franklin D. Roosevelt removed Commissioner William E. Humphrey, not on any of the stipulated grounds, but because of differences of opinion as to policy. After Humphrey's death, his executor sued for recovery of the deceased's salary. The Supreme Court held that Congress intended to create the FTC as an independent body of experts, and therefore meant to limit the president's removal power to the causes enumerated in the act. The FTC duties are predominantly quasi-legislative and quasi-judicial; Congress has authority, the Court declared, to require such a body to act independently of executive control, and may forbid removal except for cause.

HUNDRED. The hundred in England was of varying size but supposed to have been originally an area occupied by 100 families, with administrative officials and a court. Very early in Virginia the hundred was adopted as a territorial division for judicial, military, and political purposes and included, in theory at least, 100 families, but was far more extensive than in England and soon became strictly territorial, without regard to the number of persons. The hundreds gradually lost their influence, but their names persisted. In Maryland in the early period, the hundred was the unit of representation for the legislature (two burgesses from every hundred) and the unit for judicial, fiscal, and military purposes. Even after counties were established, the importance of hundreds long continued. In Delaware, under English control, the hundred was adopted and was in operation by 1690. After counties were established the hundreds continued as the important subdivisions of counties, persisting to the present.

"HUNDRED DAYS." The special session (Mar. 9–June 16, 1933) of the 73rd Congress during which it enacted much of the legislation of the first New Deal. President Franklin D. Roosevelt had called the special session to deal with the banking crisis, but decided to hold Congress in session to deal with unemployment and farm relief.

HUNGARIAN IMMIGRATION. *See* **Immigration.**

HUNKERS. Name applied to the conservative faction of New York's Democratic party in the 1840's. Hunkers favored spending state surpluses on canals, making internal improvements, liberal chartering of state banks, and James K. Polk for president; they deprecated antislavery agitation. Distribution of state patronage promoted discord with the progressive element of the party known as Barnburners. By 1853 the terms "Hards" and "Softs" were being used to replace the labels "Hunkers" and "Barnburners."

HUNTERS AND CHASERS OF THE EASTERN FRONTIER. A secret society formed in the United States by extremists and Canadian refugees who favored Canada's independence from Great Britain. The first Hunters "lodge" was established in Vermont in May 1838. The Hunters later absorbed four similar secret societies. At their height (1839) they probably had 40,000 members. In September 1838 they established headquarters at Cleveland and proclaimed the Republican Government of Upper Canada; they launched unsuccessful attacks against Prescott and Windsor, Canada, in November and December. Sporadic attacks continued until 1841, but the lodges began to disintegrate as the "patriots" began to distrust their leaders and learned of the severe treatment prisoners were given by Canadian authorities. (*See also* Caroline Affair.)

HUNTING GROUNDS. This term may be applied to a vast area like the Great Plains, which was the range of the buffalo and was shared by many different Indian tribes; or it may refer to a limited and fairly well-defined region recognized as the exclusive preserve of a certain tribe. The geographic location and extent of the Indians' hunting grounds depended on the animal life within a region and its seasonal migration; the accessibility of such areas and the trails leading to them; and tribal custom, together with the hostile or friendly relations between neighboring tribes. Sometimes different tribes shared the same hunting grounds. In other cases, a tribal council might allocate certain limited areas to small hunting parties belonging to the tribe in question.

HUNTSVILLE (Ala.). First town in the state; originally called Twickenham and renamed Huntsville in 1811 after John Hunt, a pioneer Tennessean. When Madison County was organized out of the Mississippi Territory (1808), Huntsville became the county seat. Inhabited by land-hungry immigrants from Tennessee, Georgia, and Virginia, it soon became a thriving center of civilization. Burned by Union troops in 1862, the city regained its position as a commercial center after the war. The Marshall Space Flight Center was developed in Huntsville during the 1950's, and the city grew from a post–World War II population of just over 16,000 to 142,-513 in 1980.

HURON, LAKE. Second largest of the Great Lakes, bounded on the north and east by Ontario, Canada, and on the south and west by Michigan. The part known as Georgian Bay was discovered by Father Joseph Le Caron in 1615. Samuel de Champlain reached the lake the same year and named it the Mer Douce; its present name is from the Huron Indians, who inhabited the area. It became the route for explorers, missionaries, and fur traders to the Mississippi and western Plains. It is part of the St. Lawrence Seaway.

HURRICANES. Intense revolving storms that occur in tropical or subtropical waters and frequently extend into continental regions. The winds of 75 to more than 200 miles per hour inflict tremendous damage. The most damage from hurricanes has been caused by the accompanying storm tides that inundate coastal areas or by the general floods that result from excessive rainfall (12–18 inches). For instance, Hurricane Agnes of June 19–24, 1972, the greatest natural disaster in American history, resulted in the loss of about 130 lives and economic losses of over $2 billion in the Atlantic states from Florida to New York. The Galveston hurricane of Sept. 7–8, 1900, was the most deadly human disaster in American history, with 6,000 drowned by the storm tide; from 500 to 2,000 people drowned in similar storm tides of 1804, 1881, 1893, and 1928 in Georgia, Florida, South Carolina, and along the Gulf coast. On June 27, 1957, about 550 people drowned in Cameron Parish, La., as a result of Hurricane Audrey. Another tragedy occurred in the James River Basin on Aug. 20, 1969, when dying Hurricane Camille, after inflicting $1 billion in flood damage and 137 deaths on the Gulf coast (Aug. 17), moved up the Appalachians dumping 27–31 inches of rain and drowning 155 people in the flash floods. Floods did most of the damage in Pennsylvania and the New York, Maryland, and Virginia basins during Hurricane Agnes (June 19–24, 1972); in many of the New England hurricanes, such as those in 1954 and 1955; and during Hurricane Diane (Aug. 17–19, 1955), which swept into Pennsylvania, New York, Connecticut, and Ontario, leaving 200 dead and $900 million in damage.

Other memorable hurricanes include the Miami hurricane of Sept. 18, 1926, when 400 died; the Lake Okeechobee hurricane just two years later, when 2,000 drowned; the Labor Day hurricane of Aug. 31 to Sept. 3, 1935, when 400 died on the Florida Keys; the New England hurricane of Sept. 21, 1938, that devastated the coastal resorts and villages from Long Island to Cape Cod (with 600 dead); that on Sept. 14–15, 1944, in the same region (400 dead); the Homestead, Fla., hurricane of Sept. 15–16, 1945 (with 170-mile per hour winds); hurricanes Carol and Edna of Aug. 31 and Sept. 11, 1954 (81 dead and $500 million damage in New England); and Hurricane Betsy of Sept. 8–10, 1965 ($1.4 billion damage in Florida and Louisiana).

HURTADO* V. *CALIFORNIA **(1884).** At issue was whether a conviction for murder without grand jury indictment was a violation of the due process clause of the Fourteenth Amendment. California had provided a criminal procedure based merely on information or formal accusation by the prosecution. The Supreme Court held that such conviction was not outlawed: due process of law meant that either old or new procedure could be followed.

HUSKING BEES. *See* **Bees.**

HUTCHINSONIAN CONTROVERSY. *See* **Antinomian Controversy.**

HUTCHINSON LETTERS. Letters from Thomas Hutchinson, governor of Massachusetts, soliciting troops and urging abridgment of American liberties were transmitted from London to the colonies by Benjamin Franklin. At Boston early in 1773 they caused a stir that encouraged the Massachusetts legislature to petition Hutchinson's removal. Franklin was denounced before the Privy Council and punished by the loss of his post as deputy postmaster-general of the colonies.

HYDER ALI. A converted merchantman of sixteen guns belonging to Pennsylvania. On Apr. 8, 1782, in Delaware Bay, it captured the British brig *General Monk,* which had eighteen to twenty guns.

HYDROELECTRIC POWER. The era of hydroelectric power in America began during the 1880's with the installation of direct-current generators at a number of sites. A power installation was established at Niagara Falls in 1880, using a small water-driven dynamo to provide power for two arc lamps in a nearby park. Another early plant was installed in Appleton, Wis., in 1882, using a 12.5-kilowatt Edison dynamo; but development remained limited until the introduction of alternating-current generating and transmission systems. The first installation in America to utilize alternating current was located on the Willamette River in Oregon in 1889 and produced more than 500 kilowatts at 4,000 volts. The first three-phase hydroelectric plant in America was located on Mill Creek in California in 1892, using two generators of 250 kilowatts each. The most spectacular hydroelectric power project of the 19th century was completed at Niagara Falls during the 1890's; it became the most influential example of the method of high-voltage power distribution that has become dominant in the 20th century. During 1902–07 the nation's hydroelectric power capacity grew from 438,472 horsepower to 1,349,087 horsepower.

A conference on natural resources held at the White House in 1908 stressed the necessity of exploiting more fully the nation's hydroelectric power capacity of more than 30 million horsepower in order to conserve nonrenewable fossil fuels. The movement culminated in the passage of the Water Power Act of 1920, which created the Federal Power Commission to regulate the further development of hydroelectric power. One of the major limitations of most hydroelectric plants—the wide annual fluctuation of stream flow—was overcome during 1910–30 by the creation of power pools, which integrated large numbers of hydroelectric and steam-generating stations into a single distribution network. Associated with the creation of power pools was a growing tendency to consolidate small power companies by merger, which resulted not only in economies of scale but in standardization of methods and equipment. In 1928 the output of hydroelectric power plants reached 43 percent of the total electric power generated in the United States.

An extensive and controversial system of hydroelectric plants was built on the Tennessee River and its tributaries following the passage of the Tennessee Valley Authority (TVA) act of 1933. This development was undertaken as a large-scale experiment in regional planning and resource management; its most controversial aspect was the prospect that the TVA would generate and sell electric power in competition with privately owned companies. The outbreak of World War II brought a demand for large quantities of electric power and led to an enormous increase in the capacity of the TVA system. Twelve dams were simultaneously under construction in 1942, and the hydroelectric power generated by TVA increased from about 2 billion kilowatt hours in 1939 to 12 billion kilowatt hours in 1945 and to 27 billion kilowatt hours in 1978, almost 10 percent of total national production of hydroelectric power.

The most important innovation in hydroelectric power technology since World War II has been the introduction of pumped storage. During periods of low demand, water may be pumped from one reservoir to another at a higher elevation. The pumped water may then be released to generate electricity during a period of high demand, giving a considerable increase in overall system economy.

The *Register of Dams in the United States* (1963) included 3,400 projects. The dams described below were chosen on the basis of exceptional size, capacity, or historical significance. (*See also* Hoover Dam.)

Bonneville (1938). This project on the Columbia River (Wash.) was authorized as a public works project during the Great Depression. It was constructed and is still operated by the U.S. Army Corps of Engineers. The dam is 122 feet in height and contains 1.168 million cubic yards of concrete. The original generating capacity was 86,400 kilowatts, since increased to 518,400 kilowatts.

Cherokee (1942). Part of the TVA system, located on the Holston River (Tenn.). The dam has a height of 175 feet, length of 6,760 feet, and volume of 4 million cubic yards. The generating capacity is 120,000 kilowatts.

Chickamauga (1940). A TVA installation on the Tennessee River. The dam has a height of 129 feet, length of 5,800 feet, and volume of 3.3 million cubic yards. The power capacity is 108,000 kilowatts.

Chief Joseph (1955). Constructed by the Army Corps of Engineers on the Columbia River (Wash.). It has a height of 245 feet, length of 4,383 feet, and volume of 1.8 million cubic yards. The generating capacity was 1,879,000 kilowatts in 1980, to be increased to 2,069,000 kilowatts.

Cowans Ford (1971). Part of the Duke Power Company System, on the Catawba River (N.C.). The dam has a height of 130 feet, length of 7,387 feet, and volume of 1.27 million cubic yards. The generating capacity is 372,000 kilowatts.

Dalles (1957). Built by the Army Corps of Engineers, upstream from the Bonneville Dam, on the Columbia River. The dam has a height of 300 feet, length of 8,875 feet, and volume of 3.06 million cubic yards. The power capacity in 1980 was 1,807,000 kilowatts.

Denison (1944). Constructed by the Army Corps of Engineers on the Red River on the Texas-Oklahoma border. An earth dam with a height of 165 feet, length of 17,200 feet, and volume of 18.8 million cubic yards. The power capacity is 175,000 kilowatts.

Douglas (1943). A TVA dam on the French Broad River (Tenn.). It has a height of 202 feet, length of 1,705 feet, and volume of 0.68 million cubic yards. The power capacity is 113,500 kilowatts.

Fontana (1945). Highest of the TVA dams, on the Little Tennessee River (N.C.). It has a height of 480 feet, length of 2,365 feet, and volume of 3.57 million cubic yards. The generating capacity is 225,000 kilowatts.

Fort Loudoun (1943). A TVA dam on the Tennessee River (Tenn.). It has a height of 122 feet, length of 4,190 feet, and volume of 4.18 million cubic yards. The generating capacity is 131,190 kilowatts.

Fort Peck (1940). An earth dam built by the Army Corps of Engineers on the Missouri River (Mont.). It has a height of 250 feet, length of 21,026 feet, and volume of 125 million cubic yards. The power capacity is 165,000 kilowatts.

Fort Randall (1956). An earth dam built by the Army Corps of Engineers on the Missouri River (S.D.). It has a height of 165 feet, length of 10,700 feet, and volume of 50.2 million cubic yards. The power capacity is 320,000 kilowatts.

Garrison (1960). A large earth dam built by the Army Corps of Engineers on the Missouri River (N.D.). It has a height of 210 feet, length of 11,300 feet, and volume of 66.5 million cubic yards. The power capacity is 400,000 kilowatts. Its lake of 24.4 million acre-feet is one of the largest U.S. man-made lakes.

Glen Canyon (1964). A concrete arch dam built by the Bureau of Reclamation on the Colorado River (Ariz.). The height is 710 feet, the length 1,550 feet, and the volume 4.86 million cubic yards. Notable for both the height of the dam and the size of the lake, which is 27 million acre-feet.

Grand Coulee (1942). A concrete gravity dam constructed by the Bureau of Reclamation on the Columbia River (Wash.). It has a height of 550 feet, length of 4,173 feet, and volume of 10.6 million cubic yards. The power capacity was 7,460,000 kilowatts in 1980, to be increased to an ultimate capacity of 10,830,000. kilowatts. It is one of the largest concrete dams and one of the largest power producers in the United States.

Guntersville (1939). A TVA dam on the Tennessee River (Ala.). It has a height of 94 feet, length of 3,979 feet, and volume of 1.18 million cubic yards. The power capacity is 97,200 kilowatts.

Hoover. *See* Hoover Dam.

Hungry Horse (1953). An arch dam built by the Bureau of Reclamation on the Flathead River (Mont.). It has a height of 564 feet, length of 2,115 feet, and volume of 3.086 million cubic yards. The generating capacity is 285,000 kilowatts.

Ice Harbor (1961). An earth gravity dam built by the Army Corps of Engineers on the Snake River (Wash.). It has a height of 208 feet, length of 2,700 feet, and volume of 2.14 million cubic yards. The power capacity is 270,000 kilowatts.

Kentucky (1944). A TVA dam on the Tennessee River (Ky.). It has a height of 206 feet, length of 8,422 feet, and volume of 6.9 million cubic yards. The power capacity is 170,000 kilowatts.

Lookout Point (1955). Built by the Army Corps of Engineers on the Willamette River (Oreg.). It has a height of 258 feet, length of 3,381 feet, and volume of 8.59 million cubic yards. The generating capacity is 120,000 kilowatts.

McNary (1953). Constructed by the Army Corps of Engineers on the Columbia River (Oreg.). It has a height of 220 feet, length of 7,365 feet, and volume of 3.95 million cubic yards. The power capacity is 980,000 kilowatts.

Merwin (1931). Owned by the Pacific Power and Light Company, on the Lewis River (Wash.). It has a height of 313 feet, length of 1,250 feet, and volume of 0.307 million cubic yards. The power capacity is 135,000 kilowatts. The first arch gravity dam in the Northwest.

Nickajack. Construction on this TVA dam began in 1967 on the Tennessee River (Tenn.). It has a height of 81 feet, length of 3,767 feet, and a power capacity of 100,350 kilowatts (1979). It replaced the Hales Bar Dam a few miles upstream, in use since 1913.

Norris (1936). A TVA dam on the Clinch River (Tenn.). It has a height of 265 feet, length of 1,860 feet, volume of 1.18 million cubic yards, and a power capacity of 100,800 kilowatts.

Palisades (1957). Built by the Bureau of Reclamation on the Snake River (Idaho). It has a height of 270 feet, length of 2,100 feet, and volume of 13.5 million cubic yards. The power capacity is 114,000 kilowatts.

Pickwick Landing (1938). A TVA dam on the Tennessee River (Tenn.). It has a height of 113 feet, length of 7,715 feet, and volume of 3.76 million cubic yards. The generating capacity is 216,000 kilowatts.

Trinity (1962). Built by the Bureau of Reclamation on the Trinity River (Calif.). It has a height of 537 feet, length of 2,600 feet, and volume of 29.2 million cubic yards. The power capacity is 100,000 kilowatts.

Watts Bar (1942). A TVA dam on the Tennessee River. It has a height of 112 feet, length of 2,960 feet, and volume of 1.69 million cubic yards. The power capacity is 150,000 kilowatts.

Wheeler (1936). A TVA dam on the Tennessee River (Ala.). It has a height of 72 feet, length of 6,342 feet, and volume of 0.808 million cubic yards. The power capacity is 356,400 kilowatts.

Wilson (1925). A TVA dam on the Tennessee River (Ala.). It has a height of 137 feet, length of 4,535 feet, and volume of 1.28 million cubic yards. The power capacity is 629,840 kilowatts. First installation of the TVA system and a focal point of controversy over the issue of public versus private development of hydroelectric power.

HYDROGEN BOMB. A type of military weapon that derives its energy from the fusion of the nuclei of one or more light elements, particularly the deuterium and tritium isotopes of hydrogen. Although the United States had developed and used the atomic (fission) bomb by 1945, only modest theoretical research on thermonuclear fusion was done until the Soviet Union first detonated an atomic bomb in September 1949. During the next six months a debate took place at the highest levels in the administration of Harry S. Truman over whether to develop the hydrogen bomb; on Jan. 31, 1950, Truman announced his decision to accelerate work on the hydrogen bomb, thereby ending the debate. In February 1951, Stanislaw M. Ulam and Edward Teller devised a new design principle that was incorporated in the first test device detonated at Eniwetok Atoll in the Pacific Ocean on Oct. 31, 1952.

HYDROGRAPHIC SURVEYS. Conducted by the U.S. Naval Oceanographic Office in coastal waters or shoal regions, to chart ocean depths and currents in order to facilitate the safe navigation of ships. (*See also* Oceanographic Survey.)

HYGIENE. By 1832 most of the larger American cities had created boards of health that enacted various kinds of regulations, and twenty states had adopted licensure regulations for practitioners. In their care of patients, though, American practitioners did not, as a profession, honor the traditions of attention to hygienic practices. A few individual physicians, beginning with Benjamin Rush, evinced a special interest in hygiene. New British works on health were acknowledged, and some European treatises were translated. Elisha Bartlett, John Bell, and Robley Dunglison prepared original monographs on personal hygiene. Like other physician-authors of the period, Bell discussed skin care, dress, exercise, diet, longevity, and certain aspects of public hygiene. Some citizens of Boston founded the American Physiological Society in 1837 in order to learn "that part of Human Physiology which teaches the influence of air, cleanliness, exercise, sleep, food, drink, medicine, etc., on human health and longevity," reflecting a growing concern among Americans.

By 1876 there was still no comprehensive American treatise on hygiene. The situation changed abruptly with the growth of bacteriology and the emergence of a preventive medicine begun by Louis Pasteur and continued by many others during the last quarter of the century, which provided justification for new kinds of specific hygienic practices, both personal and public, that have become widespread in the 20th century. At the same time, American physicians and other health professionals began to give significant attention to occupational hygiene and the prevention of diseases associated with particular occupations. In medical schools, hygiene was taught as public health or preventive medicine; personal hygiene was viewed primarily as a matter of infectious disease control. With the surge of scientific knowledge about ways to prevent disease and maintain health, hygiene is assuming its original and rightful position as an integral component of medical and liberal education. (*See also* Mental Hygiene Movement; Public Health.)

HYMNS. American hymns are derived in part from New England's earlier psalmody; the *Bay Psalm Book* (1640) superseded older (English) metrical versions of the Psalms. Probably the only book of hymns before the Revolution was one issued at Newport in 1766 by the Baptists. A Methodist selection of English origin appeared in 1790, was revised in 1802, and had an American supplement added in 1808. During the last decade of the 18th century and the first third of the 19th century the Protestant Episcopal, Universalist, Lutheran, Unitarian, Congregational, and Presbyterian churches issued collections; almost no hymns by Americans appeared in these books.

Samuel Davies (1723–61) was the first American to write hymns that have survived. American missionary hymnody had its beginnings in Asahel Nettleton's *Village Hymns* (1824). The writing of popular hymn tunes in the late 18th and early 19th centuries by William Billings, Daniel Read, Timothy Swan, and Oliver Holden stimulated hymn writing. Pioneer conditions and the early Sunday schools, prayer meetings, and camp meetings aided in the development of the enormously popular gospel songs. Mid–19th-century denominational hymnody suffered from sectarian controversies and deteriorated because of the inroads of gospel songs. Early in the 20th century there was a notable revival of hymn writing in the United States. Until 1880 less than 14 percent of the hymns included in the chief denominational hymn books were by native writers; in sixty years the number rose to about 35 percent. Frank Mason North, Frederick Lucian Hosmer, Harry Emerson Fosdick, and others have made distinct contributions. The 20th century ecumenical movement has also inspired a number of American hymns. The Hymn Society of America, founded in 1922, has continued to encourage the composition of new works.

IBERO-AMERICAN IMMIGRATION. *See* **Immigration.**

IBERVILLE RIVER. Originally named for Pierre Lemoyne, Sieur d'Iberville, who traversed it in 1699, it is now called Bayou Manchac; it leaves the Mississippi fifteen miles below Baton Rouge, La., and empties into the Amite River about twenty-five miles to the east. Since it forms part of the northern boundary of the so-called Isle of Orleans, it became a link in the boundary between British and Spanish possessions after the Treaty of Paris (1763). The British made it navigable by dredging, permitting their ships to enter the Mississippi and thus rendering their commerce independent of the Spanish authorities at New Orleans. Spain regarded the Iberville as part of the international boundary between Louisiana and Spanish West Florida after the Louisiana Purchase in 1803. The Iberville formed part of the southern boundary of the short-lived West Florida Republic, established in 1810 after a successful revolt against Spain. (*See also* Bute, Fort.)

ICARIA. The perfect commonwealth described by the French Communist Étienne Cabet in *Voyage en Icarie* (1840); all property was to be held in common, and all the products of labor were to be divided according to need. The book led to attempts to put the theory into practice in the United States: in Fannin County, Tex., in 1848; at Nauvoo, Ill., in 1849, under Cabet's personal leadership; at Cheltenham, Mo.; and in Iowa, near Corning. In 1881 former members of the Cheltenham group founded a community at Cloverdale, Calif. (Icaria-Speranza); it was dissolved in 1887.

ICELAND, U.S. FORCES IN. Fearing that Germany might take over Iceland, the British swiftly occupied the island on May 10, 1940. The Icelanders hoped instead to entrust their protection to a nonbelligerent of the Western Hemisphere and asked the United States to place the island under the protection of the Monroe Doctrine. The U.S. government agreed to relieve the British in Iceland. The first American troops arrived on July 7, 1941. After the United States entered World War II, U.S. forces increased prodigiously. By mid-1943 a peak strength was reached of approximately 40,000 soldiers and seventy-five fighter-interceptor planes. As the battle tide turned against Germany, the Icelandic garrison was gradually reduced. The remaining force left in April 1947. American forces returned in February 1951, as the North Atlantic Treaty Organization, of which Iceland had become a member, sought to bolster its defenses. Troops were stabilized during the early 1970's at approximately 1,000, serving as personnel for antisubmarine defenses, a fighter squadron, and a radar base.

ICHTHYOLOGY. *See* **Fish and Marine Life.**

IDAHO. Last of the fifty states to be seen by white men—when Meriwether Lewis and William Clark reached the continental divide in 1805. After 1808, British and Canadian trappers and traders explored most of the region; when mountain men from St. Louis began to compete with these trappers after 1824, it became a disputed borderland. Under British control from the War of 1812 until the signing of the Oregon Treaty of 1846, Idaho became part of the Oregon Territory in 1848. After formation of the Washington Territory (1853), Congress carved the new Idaho Territory out of Washington, Dakota, and Nebraska in response to the sudden concentration of population following the discovery of gold in the Clearwater and Salmon rivers region in 1860; established in 1863, it straddled the continental divide and encompassed an area substantially larger than Texas—eastern Washington Territory, western Dakota Territory (including all of what is now Montana), and almost all of Wyoming. Vast uninhabited tracts were returned to the Dakota Territory in 1864 when Montana Territory was formed. With the loss of Montana, Idaho became geographically anomalous—two distinct sections separated by the massive central Salmon River mountain barrier, with the capital, Boise, in the south. On July 3, 1890, it became a state.

Improved rail transportation (1878–84) encouraged both a gradual transition from placer to quartz mining in Idaho and the development of important lead-silver discoveries on the Wood River (1880) and in the Coeur d'Alene Mountains (1884). Coeur d'Alene production of more than $2 billion made Idaho the nation's leading silver state in less than eighty years. Ordinary farming in the north and irrigated farming in the south also expanded rapidly. Successful reclamation projects under the aegis of the Carey Act of 1894 and the U.S. Reclamation Service were undertaken in the Twin Falls country and at Boise and Minidoka; giant dams and reservoirs being built at Arrowrock, American Falls, Anderson Ranch, and Palisades; major tracts of desert were transformed for the production of potatoes, sugar beets, alfalfa, seed corn, fruits, and other specialized crops. Idaho's forests cover 40 percent of the state's area; until about 1960, timber and minerals followed agriculture in the state's economy, but tourism has gained importance, as has manufacturing. Idaho is one of the most rural states in the nation—46 percent of the total 1980 population of 943,935.

"I HAD RATHER BE RIGHT THAN BE PRESIDENT." Expression used by Sen. Henry Clay of Kentucky early in 1839 in a conversation with Sen. William C. Preston of South Carolina. Clay, alarmed by the growth of abolitionism in the North, had decided to attack the movement publicly; he consulted Preston, who suggested that a public speech against abolitionism might be injurious to Clay's political fortunes. This advice, according to Preston, elicited the famous reply.

ILLINOIS. The first Europeans to see Illinois are believed to have been Father Jacques Marquette and Louis Jolliet, in 1673. Marquette established a mission at the Great Village of the Illinois (near present-day Utica) in 1675; and Robert Cavelier, Sieur de La Salle, constructed Fort Crèvecoeur (near present-day Peoria) in 1680 and Fort St. Louis at Starved Rock (near present-day La Salle) in 1682. French activity shifted to the south in 1699, with establishment of the Holy Family mission at Cahokia. In the American Bottom (the land along the Illinois side of the Mississippi, between the mouths of the Illinois and Kaskaskia rivers), the town of Kaskaskia was founded in 1703; Fort de Chartres was built nearby in 1720. Eventually some 2,000 French and blacks populated the area, exporting grain to New Orleans and furs to Quebec.

When the Treaty of Paris was signed (1763), control over Illinois passed to Great Britain; the first British soldiers arrived at Fort de Chartres in October 1765. The Quebec Act of 1774 annexed Illinois to the Province of Quebec. On July 4, 1778, George Rogers Clark captured Kaskaskia and Cahokia in the name of the state of Virginia and later seized Vincennes, Ind., assuring American control of the Illinois Country. Illinois was a county of Virginia until Mar. 1, 1784; three years later it became a part of the Northwest Territory. After the War of 1812, settlers flooded into Illinois, mainly from the Carolinas, Virginia, Tennessee, and the Southeast. Illinois became the twenty-first state on Dec. 3, 1818; the northern boundary was set at 42°30′, giving it shoreline on Lake Michigan and the city of Chicago. In 1820 the capital was moved from Kaskaskia to Vandalia and, in 1837, to Springfield. The defeat of the Sauk and Fox Indians in the Black Hawk War of 1832 was followed by treaties in which the Indians relinquished their last Illinois lands.

In 1837 the assembly passed an internal improvements act, pledging the state's credit to a grandiose scheme of railroad and canal construction and river improvements; the system collapsed, and Illinois was saddled with a tremendous debt.

Illinois has been a leader in agriculture since before the Civil War; by 1870 the state ranked first in wheat and corn production and in value of livestock, and second in hog production. In 1971 it set a new per-acre high for winter wheat. The number and size of farms follow the national pattern: in 1870 there were 202,803 farms with an average size of 127.6 acres, while a hundred years later there were 124,900 farming units that averaged 235 acres in size. Manufacturing continued to expand: by 1870 the value of manufactured products almost equaled the value of agricultural products; in 1880 manufactured products had five times the value of agricultural products; the ratio was 8–1 in 1977.

ILLINOIS, BRITISH ATTEMPTS TO REACH. By the Treaty of Paris (1763), title to the Illinois Country passed from France to Great Britain. However, Pontiac, chief of the Ottawa, attacked the British frontier garrisons at Fort Pitt, and the approach to Illinois from the east was abandoned. A detachment from Mobile, Ala., began fitting out at New Orleans in January 1764. On Feb. 27 the ascent of the Mississippi River was begun; three weeks later an Indian attack halted the expedition. By the summer of 1764 Pontiac's conspiracy had collapsed, and diplomacy seemed to be worth trying. From Mobile, Lt. John Ross and Hugh Campbell were sent to meet with the Indians; they reached their destination in February 1765, but found the Indians defiant and accomplished nothing. Lt. Alexander Fraser reached Fort Chartres in late April 1765 but found the Indians hostile; by the time George Croghan, deputy superintendent of Indian affairs, reached Fort Ouiatenon in July, he was able to hold a great council at which Pontiac promised to abandon resistance to the advance of the British troops. On Aug. 24, 100 men of the Black Watch began the descent of the Ohio from Fort Pitt. On Oct. 9 they reached their destination, Fort Chartres. The French garrison was formally relieved on the following day.

ILLINOIS, GREAT VILLAGE OF THE. On the north side of the Illinois River about midway between the present cities of La Salle and Ottawa, Père Jacques Marquette in 1673 found a Kaskaskia village made up of 74 cabins; four years later another Jesuit missionary found eight Illinois tribes located there in 351 cabins. In 1680 the Great Village extended along the river for more than three miles and contained perhaps 7,000 inhabitants; in September of that year it was destroyed and its inhabitants dispersed by the Iroquois.

ILLINOIS AND MICHIGAN CANAL. Built by the state of Illinois (1836–48), connecting Lake Michigan and the Mississippi River by a channel from Chicago to LaSalle on the Illinois River. It was profitable from its opening; tolls exceeded expenses of operation until 1879. In the 20th century traffic dwindled almost to nothing, but sections of the canal continued in use until 1930. Of all North American artificial waterways only the Erie Canal outranked it in importance to the development of its region.

ILLINOIS AND WABASH COMPANY. Formed in 1779 by merging the Illinois Land Company and the Wabash Land Company. The original companies had been organized by the same man, William Murray of Philadelphia; both companies held claims to land in the Illinois Country, and both sought to establish towns and develop trade. George Ross of Philadelphia was elected president of the combined companies; William Murray and John Campbell were designated agents to carry out the actual operations. The company's activity apparently terminated in 1784 after Virginia ceded its western lands to the federal government.

ILLINOIS BAND. Organized (1829) by seven students in the Yale Divinity School. Bearing commissions from the American Home Missionary Society, the members of the band went to Illinois in 1829, engaged in home missionary activities, and helped found Illinois College at Jacksonville.

ILLINOIS CAMPAIGN OF GEORGE ROGERS CLARK. *See* **Clark's Northwest Campaign.**

ILLINOIS CENTRAL RAILROAD. *See* **Railroads, Sketches of Principal Lines: Illinois Central Gulf.**

ILLINOIS COUNTRY. The term commonly applied in the 17th and 18th centuries to the region that became the state of the same name. As originally used by French explorers, it designated the country occupied by the Illinois Indians; when white settlements took root along the Illinois and Mississippi rivers, it referred to the area of which these were nuclei.

ILLINOIS COUNTY. Created by Virginia in 1778 for the government of the Northwest Territory, it survived as a unit of Virginia civil jurisdiction only until 1784.

ILLINOIS FUR BRIGADE. One of several trading expeditions sent out annually, beginning about 1816, by the American Fur Company from its headquarters at Mackinac. The brigade, usually numbering ten or twelve bateaux loaded with trade goods, made its way down Lake Michigan and through the Chicago portage and Des Plaines River to the Illinois River, where it divided into small parties that spent the winter bartering with Indians for furs. In the spring the brigade reassembled and returned to Mackinac. The Illinois brigade made annual expeditions until 1827; in 1828 the American Fur Company sold its Illinois interests to Gurdon S. Hubbard, the brigade's commander.

ILLUMINATI OF NEW ENGLAND. Certain political meetings between 1790 and 1800 of New England clergymen, influenced by the French Revolution, gave rise, about 1798, to rumors that the Illuminati, a European cult inimical to government and religion founded by Adam Weishaupt, had penetrated American society and aimed at the overthrow of American civil and religious institutions. Statesmen viewed the matter with grave concern. The Freemasons were suspected of being involved. The Theistical Society of New York, organized in 1802, was also suspect and was nicknamed the Columbian Illuminati. The alarm soon died out.

***I'M ALONE* CASE.** On Mar. 22, 1929, the *I'm Alone,* a vessel of Canadian registry (but American ownership) engaged in smuggling liquor into the United States, was sunk by gunfire from a U.S. Coast Guard cutter while more than 200 miles offshore. A treaty of 1924 had given the United States rights of search and seizure over British vessels suspected of rum-running, but had specified that these rights did not extend farther than a distance of one hour's steaming from the coast. The sinking caused considerable outcry in Canada, the more so as a member of the crew had lost his life. The question was arbitrated by a commission composed of the chief justice of Canada and a justice of the U.S. Supreme Court; the final report (Jan. 5, 1935) recommended an apology by the United States to Canada, the payment of indemnities to the master and crew and to the dead man's widow, and the additional payment to Canada of $25,000 as a "material amend." These recommendations were fully carried out.

IMBODEN-JONES RAID (Apr. 20–May 14, 1863). Entering West Virginia through mountain gaps near Harrisonburg, Va., Confederate Gen. William E. Jones marched to the Baltimore and Ohio Railroad at the Cheat River, near the northwestern boundary of Maryland. Simultaneously Gen. John D. Imboden moved on Beverly and Weston. Jones traversed 700 miles of territory, destroying railroad bridges, barreled petroleum, and other property and collecting supplies and livestock, which he moved to Virginia, in preparation for the Gettysburg campaign. Imboden accomplished similar results in a smaller territory.

IMMEDIATISM. A term employed by the British antislavery movement in its drive for the immediate abolition of West Indian slavery. Adopted by American abolitionists in 1831, it was redefined to signify merely an immediate beginning of measures looking to the ultimate extinction of slavery.

IMMIGRANT LABOR. *See* **Labor.**

IMMIGRATION. Immigrants are persons who have voluntarily and permanently carried themselves and their goods from their native environment to the United States for the purpose of settling and establishing a new life: they are aliens, other than returning resident aliens, who are admitted into the United States for permanent residence. The flow of migrants to the central regions of the North American continent constitutes the greatest movement of peoples in Western history. In the years 1820–1979 the total of immigrants was 49,125,413; they came at an average annual rate of 3.7 newcomers per 1,000 of population. Germany alone sent 14.2 percent of the total; Italy, 10.8 percent; Great Britain, 10 percent; Ireland, 9.7 percent; Austria-Hungary, 8.8 percent; Canada, 8.4 percent; Russia and the Soviet Union, 6.9 percent; Mexico, 4.4 percent; and Sweden, 2.6 percent. France, Greece, Norway, Poland, China, and the West Indies each sent from 1 percent to 1.99 percent of the total.

Included in the total population of 76 million in the continental United States in 1900 were 10.5 million born in Europe and 26 million more with at least one foreign-born parent. In 1940 the foreign-born and persons with at least one foreign-born parent amounted to 26 percent of the total; in 1930, near 31 percent; in 1950, 22.3 percent; in 1960, 18 percent; in 1970, 15.5 percent; and in 1979, 16.4 percent. The relative decline in the foreign stock reflects in a graphic way the changes in policy expressed in the restriction laws of 1921, 1924, 1952, and 1965 (*see* Immigration Restriction).

Colonial Immigration (1607–1776). The Dutch colony of New Netherland for fifty years separated the English colonies of New England and those of the South. Throughout the English settlements American blood was already decidedly mixed by 1776: there were large settlements of Scotch-Irish on the frontier; Huguenot French in the larger cities; small Jewish groups from Spain and Portugal in Rhode Island; Welsh in Pennsylvania; Germans in Pennsylvania and scattered throughout the South; Swedes in Delaware; and Danes, Scotch, Irish, and Finns in Philadelphia. Proprietors and speculators especially encouraged the flow of immigration as an adjunct to direct colonization, and thousands came as indentured servants and redemptioners. The resulting diversity of religions made religious toleration a necessity, and the final separation of church and state, apart from its being a matter of democratic theory, became inescapable under colonial circumstances.

The Scotch-Irish and the Germans are numerically the most prominent of colonial immigrant groups. There were more than 350,000 Scotch-Irish and Irish in the colonies in 1776, settled predominantly in Pennsylvania and the Appalachian frontier. At the same time, there were about 225,000 people of German blood in the United States, of which 33 percent resided in Pennsylvania; the great majority came from the Rhine country, especially from the Palatinate and Württemberg, victims of political and religious persecution and of economic disorders.

The Old Immigration (1776–1890). From 1790 to 1820 the influx of immigration was relatively slow. After the War of 1812 and the Napoleonic Wars, the rapid modern growth of population in Europe suddenly made itself felt, stimulated by the rapid development of steamship and railroad transport and encouraged with vigor by the governments of the new states of the Midwest, whose primary need in those years was to build up a population. European peasants, artisans, and intellectuals became expatriates out of dissatisfaction with conditions in Europe and a belief that they would be favorable in the United States. Whole sections of the rural and lower middle classes in one locality after another fell victim to a class movement—popularly known as America fever—that spread from parish to parish, transmitted most effectively by hundreds of thousands of "America letters" written by enthusiastic immigrants to relatives and friends.

The Irish Wave. Irish immigration increased rapidly after 1820, rising from 54,338 during 1821–30, to 207,381 during 1831–40, to 1,694,838 during 1841–60. In general the Irish came as individuals and sent for their families and friends; they were of the artisan, small-farmer class, many the victims of land clearances and consolidations. They settled largely in coastal cities or in growing towns along the road, canal, and railroad construction projects on which they worked, and they accounted for the rapid growth of cities and provided the cheap labor necessary for incipient industries. Despite the Civil War, during which agents of the U.S. northern states in Ireland sought labor and, no doubt, potential volunteers, the decade 1861–70 saw 435,778 Irish enter the United States.

Until 1890 the influx remained at about 500,000 Irish per decade, after which it declined as the Irish laborers in America came into competition with continental immigrants and as conditions in Ireland improved. The rise of a new nationalism in Ireland in the early 20th century brought the number of immigrants down to 146,181 in 1911–20. In 1921–30 admissions stood at 221,000; in 1931–40, at 13,167; in 1951–60, at 57,332; in 1961–70, at 37,461; and in 1971–79, 10,600.

The German Wave. From 1860 to 1890, Germany ranked highest in American immigration statistics; and in 1840–60 and 1890–1900 it held second place. From 1820 to 1979 the total of immigrants from Germany to the United States was 6,983,000. From eastern and northern Germany came peasants who were conservative in politics and religious belief. From southwestern Germany and the Rhineland came political exiles and agnostics, university-trained men and intellectuals. They were called *Dreissiger* (or Grays) and Forty-eighters (or Greens), the former having emigrated after the political disturbances of 1830 and the latter within a few years after the revolutions of 1848. A strong contingent of "Old Lutherans" left Saxony and laid the foundations of the powerful Missouri Synod, in the decade of the 1840's. After the Civil War, political and religious considerations were overshadowed by the economic motive. Agricultural America had a special appeal for rural Germans whose homeland was in the process of industrial development.

German immigrants distributed themselves throughout the United States, but certain sections and cities were more favored than others: the northern Mississippi Valley; Milwaukee; St. Paul; St. Louis; Chicago; Cincinnati; Cleveland; and Davenport, Iowa.

Swiss immigration amounted to 278,187 between 1820 and 1924; the greatest influx was in 1881–83, with more than 10,000 arrivals. A number of group settlements were carried out by the Swiss, notably a colony in Switzerland County, Ind., shortly after 1800, and the farming community of New Glarus, in Green County, Wis., in 1845.

The Scandinavians. From 1820 to 1979, immigration from Sweden totaled 1,273,000; that of Norway amounted to 856,000. For Norway the peak decade was 1901–10, with 190,505 arrivals, while Sweden at the same time sent 249,534. For the 1850's the figures are Norway, 22,935 and Sweden, 21,697; for the 1860's, Norway, 15,484 and Sweden, 17,116. Figures for Denmark and Finland run parallel with those for the two larger countries. Overall, Denmark accounts for 0.7 percent of all immigration since 1820 and Finland for 0.1 percent.

The New Immigration (after 1890). The new immigration had as its principal source the crowded and relatively backward agricultural communities of eastern and southern Europe. Once upon American shores, these immigrants became factory wage-earners or laboring hands in the mining camps; they often remained segregated from the mainstream of American life and institutions. Agitation for restriction on immigration was directed in large part against the alleged characteristics of this group.

Strikingly new patterns of immigration may be observed between 1931 and 1979. In 1931–40 the total of immigration from all countries fell from 4.1 million to slightly over a half million, with the countries of origin ranked as follows: Germany-Austria (117,000), Canada (109,000), Italy (68,000), Mexico (22,000), England (22,000), Poland (17,000), Czechoslovakia (14,000), Ireland (13,000), and France (13,000). In 1971–79 these countries were ranked by place of last permanent residence as follows: Germany-Austria (77,000), sixteenth; Canada (156,200), sixth; Italy (123,900), tenth; Mexico (583,700), first; Great Britain (121,500), eleventh; Poland (32,500), twenty-fifth; Czechoslovakia (5,000), forty-third; Ireland (10,600), thirty-eighth; and France (22,700), thirty-second. In addition to those cited above, by 1971–79 the following moved high in the ranking: Philippines (312,700), second; Cuba (249,700), third; West Indies (237,400), fourth; Korea (235,400), fifth; India (141,400), seventh; the Dominican Republic (130,800), eighth; Vietnam (129,300), ninth; and Hong Kong (109,500), twelfth.

The Italians. In 1930, New York City had more people of Italian stock than Rome; during 1907, the peak year of Italian immigration, more Italians were admitted than the 1960 population of Venice. From 1820 to 1930, over 4,628,000 Italian immigrants arrived. Before 1860, only 14,000 Italians, mainly from the northern provinces, migrated to the United States, including a few goldseekers who early founded the Italian colony in California. Since 1890 more than one-half of the Italian population has resided in New Jersey, New York, and Pennsylvania; about 15 percent in New England; and slightly less than 15 percent in Illinois, Indiana, and Ohio.

The Mexicans. The average annual influx of Mexicans was well under 100 until 1900. The record since then displays a rapid rise in rate and in absolute numbers: 1901–10, 49,642; 1911–20, 219,004; 1921–30, 459,287; 1931–40, 22,319; 1941–50, 61,000; 1951–60, 299,000; 1961–70, 453,000; 1971–80, 583,700. The total recorded for the entire period 1820–1980 is 2,177,100.

The Canadians and French Canadians. Statistics on the immigration of French Canadians are incomplete and unreliable, but according to U.S. Census reports, French Canadians residing in the United States in 1890, 1910, and 1930 numbered 302,496; 385,083; and 370,852, respectively. French Canadians are estimated to have made up about 33 percent of the total of 3,991,417 persons who emigrated to the United States from Canada and Newfoundland after the passage of the act of 1921; most settled in highly industrialized regions of New England and found employment in factories, particularly in the textile industry. They and their children have adhered tenaciously to the Roman Catholicism and the language and customs of their native provinces.

The Iberians. Immigrants from Portugal began to arrive in the United States in relatively large numbers in the 1870's, and became known to coastal New Englanders as resourceful fishermen and skilled artisans. The peak influx of Spanish laborers and skilled workmen was reached in 1911–20, when 68,000 were counted, but Spanish immigration was appreciably smaller than the Portuguese. Portuguese numbering 93,300 constituted 2.4 percent of the total number of immigrants in 1971–79.

The Peoples of Eastern Europe. To the year 1900, immigration from the Balkan states and eastern Europe, exclusive of Russia, was ascribed in official U.S. reports either to Poland, European Turkey, or Austria-Hungary, the latter designation embracing a number of distinct nationalities and ethnic groups.

While 4 million Austro-Hungarians were admitted since 1820, the peak years of migration were the decade 1901–10, when a total of 2,145,261 of them were recorded. The national affiliation or province of origin of these peoples cannot be specified. However, a report that identifies the land of origin of a total of 205,961 émigrés of a twelve-month period in 1902–03 suggests that the relatively smaller groups of proto-Czechoslovakians were sending a somewhat disproportionally large number of immigrants to the United States when compared with the later Yugoslavian lands.

Refugees and Displaced Persons. The Displaced Persons Act of 1948 was the first of eight special acts (1948–60) that provided for the admission of refugees from Communist-dominated countries, victims of natural calamities, and orphan children. A total of 185,256 refugees were admitted from East Europe between 1954 and 1979, as follows: Bulgaria, 3,607; Czechoslovakia, 11,868; Romania, 17,967; Poland, 20,993; Soviet Union, 28,334; Yugoslavia, 50,029; and Hungary, 52,458.

The Polish. Over a half million persons have been counted as immigrants from Poland between 1820 and 1979, but these figures are known to be low: they omit the two full decades from 1899 to 1919, and the numerous boundary changes in the 19th century that led to discrepancies in the counts of persons who belonged ethnically and culturally to the Polish nation. Recent admission figures are 1951–60, 128,000; 1961–70, 73,300; 1971–79, 38,700. The area of residence of the foreign-born Polish people is predominantly the Middle Atlantic, the East North Central, and the Northeast regions.

The Czechoslovakians. Census data show the modern Czechoslovak component in the foreign-born white population at the level of 319,972 (2.8 percent) in 1940 and 278,268 (2.7 percent) in 1950. Immigration since the 1950's has been moderate: 21,400 Czechoslovakians entered in 1961–70 and 9,100 in 1971–79. The Czechoslovak peoples in the United States are concentrated most heavily in the Middle Atlantic and East North Central regions.

The Yugoslavians. The 1950 census counted 143,956 Yugoslavians (1.4 percent) among the foreign-born white population. By far the greater part of the immigration of nearly 145,000 persons in 1951–79 has been in the categories of displaced persons and refugees. The Yugoslavs have settled in the industrial centers of the East North Central, Middle Atlantic, and Pacific regions.

The Hungarians. The total of Austrians and Hungarians emigrating from Austria-Hungary to America between 1861 and 1951, counting by nationality composition, was 4,181,927. Since 1905 the total arriving from Hungary alone is listed at 484,758; in 1911–20, the decade of peak immigration, 422,693 were counted. Hungarians settled in the urban industrial centers of the East and Midwest.

The Russians. In 1940 and 1950 the Russian component in the foreign-born white population of the United States was 1,040,884 (9.1 percent) and 894,844 (8.8 percent), respectively. Immigration from the Soviet Union, tallied according to country of birth, was 15,700 in 1961–70 and 32,500 in 1971–79. The Bureau of the Census reports the largest concentration of Russian-born immigrants, Jewish and non-Jewish, as having settled in the Middle Atlantic region.

Asia. In 1820–1951, 954,230 immigrants were recorded from Asiatic countries: China, 399,217; India, 11,743; Japan (since 1861), 279,407; Asian Turkey (since 1869), 205,584; other, 58,279. The immigration acts of 1921, 1924, and later had the direct effect of suppressing the opportunity for migration to the United States from Asiatic lands. In the years 1954–79 refugees admitted from Asia by provision of the special refugee acts of 1948–60, by country of birth, show a total of 196,216, over half of these coming from Vietnam. Immigrants from Asia are located principally in the Middle Atlantic, the Pacific coast, the East North Central, and the New England regions.

Trends of the 1960's and 1970's. The work regulations specified in the Immigration Act of 1965 tended to curtail the flow of laborers from northern Europe and South America; and the high priority given relatives in the new law increased the influx from southern Europe, Mexico, Canada, and Asia. For the year ending Sept. 30, 1979, the countries of origin ranked as follows: Mexico, 52,500; Philippines, 40,800; West Indies, 33,500; Korea, 28,700; Canada, 20,200; Vietnam, 19,100; India, 18,600; the Dominican Republic, 17,500; Hong Kong, 16,800; Great Britain, 15,500; Cuba, 14,000; China, 12,300; and Colombia, 10,500. Also notable was an overall decline in immigration from Europe. In 1931–40, Europe as a whole sent 348,000 persons as compared with 160,000 for all the Western Hemisphere, but in 1971–79, Europe sent 728,200 persons and the countries of the American continents from Canada to Chile sent 1,778,300. The figures for the continent of Asia rose from under 3 percent of the total in 1931–40 to 1,352,100, or 34.1 percent in 1971–79.

IMMIGRATION RESTRICTION. Restrictionism originated in several quarters that tended to coalesce about the time of World War I in a drive to limit "new" immigrants, particularly the "less American" Asians, Slavs, Italians, and Jews. The earliest opponents of unlimited immigration were labor spokesmen, for economic and possibly racial reasons. After the Supreme Court ruled in 1876 that the federal government had responsibility for immigration regulation, western leaders urged Congress to bar Chinese, claiming that they undercut American wages. The Chinese Exclusion Act prohibiting the immigration of Chinese for ten years was passed in 1882 and was made permanent in 1902. An 1885 law prohibited the importing of workers under contract. The influx of Japanese labor that began in the 1890's led the United States to exchange a series of notes with Japan, in 1907–08, whereby the latter agreed to stop emigration of some of its unskilled workmen. Down to the 1920's the American Federation of Labor continually supported restriction to protect American workers. Anti-Catholicism, directed at specific nationalities, aroused massive restrictionist support under the leadership of the American Protective Association in the 1890's and the Ku Klux Klan in the 1920's. A third group advocating immigration restriction was made up of American intellectuals, mainly from New England, who advocated so-called Anglo-Saxon superiority as the basis of American achievements. An early practical attempt to preserve Anglo-Saxon America was a bill proposing a literacy test for admission; vetoed by presidents Grover Cleveland, William H. Taft, and Woodrow Wilson, it became law in 1917, but the test was abandoned in the next decade.

The first quota law, the Immigration Act of 1921, limited immigration substantially and, more important, selected arrivals by national-origin quotas, which favored northwestern Europeans. It reduced arrivals in one year from 805,228 to 309,556 in 1922. A more basic law was the Johnson-Reed Act of 1924, which further reduced total immigration from Europe and Asia and maintained the national-origins idea, although it did not restrict arrivals from the Western Hemisphere and repealed the Chinese and Japanese exclusion laws. It provided for an annual quota of 164,667 until July 1, 1927, when the quota was to be fixed at 150,000 and the admission of persons of any national group eligible for naturalization was to be limited to the percentage of that base figure that that national group had constituted in the total population in 1920. The Immigration and Nationality (McCarran-Walter) Act of 1952 simplified the national-origins formula of 1924 by basing the annual quotas of national groups on a flat one-sixth of 1 percent of the population by the 1920 census. New quotas, effective Jan. 1, 1953, were established in a series of presidential proclamations for each country or quota area, and these were put in force at a level of 160,000 per annum.

The Act of 1965 (Public Law 89-236), effective Dec. 1 of that year and amended in 1976, set aside the system of quota by national origin. With respect to the Eastern Hemisphere, it set up instead an overall limit of 170,000 immigrants per year and an annual limit of 20,000 for natives of any single foreign state. (Immediate relatives and "special immigrants" were to be admitted without regard to numerical limitations.) The issuance of entry visas was made subject to a new preference system; high priority to persons who desired reunification with their families and relatives; second priority to persons who brought special abilities, whether artistic, scientific, or professional; next, skilled workers; then, unskilled labor; and finally, displaced persons or refugees from political, racial, or religious discrimination. Effective July 1, 1968, a ceiling figure of 120,000 with respect to the total of Western Hemisphere natives was set; a limit of 20,000 immigrants per country was established in 1976 (immediate relatives and special immigrants were exempted from the ceiling). In regard to all applicants in the categories of skilled and unskilled laborers, the new law required that the U.S. Department of Labor certify that their entry would not adversely affect the wages and working conditions of U.S. workers in similar employment. Advocates of population limitation, critics of Vietnam War refugee resettlement, and complainants of the economic recession of the 1970's have revived demands for further immigration restriction. In 1982, the Senate passed the Simpson bill, a sweeping revision of the nation's immigration laws, including a new system of fines and prison terms for employers who knowingly hire illegal aliens.

IMMUNITY BATH. A phrase that seems to have been first used in March 1906, when Judge J. O. Humphrey of the U.S. District Court for Northern Illinois was considering the question of ordering the discharge of sixteen defendants of the beef trust, then under indictment for violation of the Sherman Antitrust Act. In his argument opposing such action, U.S. Attorney General W. H. Moody declared ironically that the defendants' discharge would amount to giving them an "immunity bath." The phrase has since been applied to the practice, under federal and state laws, of granting immunity from prosecution to implicated persons who disclose evidence of crime that would otherwise go unpunished.

IMMUNITY OF PRIVATE PROPERTY. The law of maritime warfare recognizes the right of a belligerent to capture and confiscate property belonging to nationals of the enemy state, when found on the high seas. This liability of private property to capture encouraged the widespread practice of privateering from colonial times through the War of 1812. Privateering was abolished by the states signing the Declaration of Paris of 1856; the United States refused to become a party to the declaration unless it also established the immunity of private property from capture on the high seas. Again, at the Hague peace conferences of 1899 and 1907, the United States proposed a rule abolishing the capture of private property in maritime warfare.

IMPEACHMENT. The U.S. Constitution provides that "the President, Vice-President, and all civil Officers of the United States, shall be removed from Office on Impeachment for, and Conviction of, Treason, Bribery, or other high Crimes and Misdemeanors" (Article II, Section 4). There are no specific instructions concerning the manner in which impeachment proceedings shall originate other than the section granting the House of Representatives "the sole Power of Impeachment" (Article I, Section 2, Paragraph 5). In contrast, Section 3, Paragraph 6, of the same article provides that "the Senate . . . shall have the sole Power to try all Impeachments." It then states that "when sitting for that Purpose, they [the Senators] shall be on Oath or Affirmation. When the President of the United States is tried, the Chief Justice shall preside: and no Person shall be convicted without the Concurrence of two thirds of the Members present." Article I, Section 2, Paragraph 7, also holds that "Judgment in Cases of Impeachment shall not extend further than to removal from Office, and disqualification to hold and enjoy any Office of Honor, Trust or Profit under the United States: but the Party convicted shall nevertheless be liable and subject to Indictment, Trial, Judgment and Punishment, according to Law."

Impeachments have been voted by the House of Representatives and tried by the Senate of the United States on a number of occasions, primarily involving judges. The two-thirds vote of the Senate necessary for conviction has been obtained in only three cases.

Within the states the impeachment power has not been used extensively. The impeachment of judges from partisan motives was carried out in several instances in Pennsylvania and Ohio at the beginning of the 19th century. In 1913, Gov. William Sulzer of New York was impeached and removed from office, the charges resting on broad grounds of unfitness and involving offenses committed by Sulzer prior to his election. Subsequently, governors in Texas and Oklahoma were removed from office after impeachment and conviction. The most significant developments relating to the impeachment power occurred at the federal level. Indeed, the most direct 20th-century invocation of the power as a curb on a president was made in the early 1970's, against President Richard M. Nixon. Impeachment proceedings against Nixon were begun in October 1973. In July 1974 the House Judiciary Committee recommended three articles of impeachment to the House of Representatives, but Nixon resigned before a full House vote could be taken on the matter. The impeachment power was not fully invoked, but the purposes of the impeachment process were perhaps partially fulfilled. (*See also* Chase Impeachment; Impeachment Trial of Andrew Johnson; Nixon, Resignation of; Presidential Exemption From Subpoena.)

IMPEACHMENT TRIAL OF ANDREW JOHNSON. The greatest state trial in the United States followed the impeachment of President Andrew Johnson in 1868, the first and only American president to suffer this ordeal. Johnson was elected vice-president in 1864 as President Abraham Lincoln's running mate. On Lincoln's death he became president and promptly took his stand for Lincoln's plan of Reconstruction. The Radical Republicans began at once maneuvering to thwart him. Above all else, they wanted the continuance of Edwin M. Stanton as the secretary of war, which was the object of the Tenure of Office Act passed on Mar. 2, 1867, over Johnson's veto. On Feb. 21, 1868, Johnson removed Stanton from office, and three days later the House of Representatives, by a vote of 126 to 47, impeached the president for removing Stanton in defiance of the Tenure of Office Act. On Mar. 13, 1868, the Senate trial began. The evidence for the prosecution consisted largely in establishing that Johnson had in fact removed Stanton. The defense was that under the Constitution the president had the right to do so and that the Tenure of Office Act, in seeking to deprive him of that right, was unconstitutional. Johnson himself did not attend the trial. On May 16, 1868, the roll was called first on the eleventh article of the thirteen to be voted on. Thirty-five senators voted guilty and nineteen not guilty; two-thirds not having pronounced guilty, the chief justice declared that the president was "acquitted on this article." The court then adjourned to permit the representatives and senators to attend the Republican National Convention. On May 28 the Senate reconvened to vote on the second and third articles; again thirty-five senators voted for conviction and nineteen for acquittal. The remaining articles were never voted on.

IMPENDING CRISIS. *See* **Helper's *Impending Crisis of the South*.**

IMPERIAL IDEA, PREREVOLUTIONARY. Implicit in the imperial idea was mercantilism, a complex of political, military, and economic considerations that aimed at a self-sufficient empire in which colonies and mother country would be knit together, the former providing raw materials to sustain the economy and enhance the military potential of the latter. This relationship was defined in various Navigation Acts passed between 1651 and 1696 and in a number of laws after 1699 dealing with the colonial wool, hat, and iron industries. Together with prohibitions on the issue of colonial paper currency, the whole produced a colonial economy that was integrated with, but subordinate to, that of Britain. The political corollary was that the colonies possessed only such self-government as was extended by "royal grace and favor."

Practice did not always conform to theory. In the political sphere the powers of imperial government became in fact decentralized, or federalized, as Britain, before 1763, permitted the colonial assemblies a wide measure of autonomy and failed to support royal governors in their conflicts with local legislatures. By 1774 the view was being publicized that the colonial assemblies and Parliament were coequal sovereignties under the crown, and in the First Continental Congress, James Galloway proposed an American parliament coequal with Britain's in colonial affairs. The rejection by the Continental Congress of the Galloway plan in 1774 demonstrated that even colonial Americans had ceased thinking of empire and were moving toward independence.

IMPERIALISM. Most precisely, this means the forcible extension of governmental control over foreign areas not destined for incorporation as integral parts of the nation; the term is often used more broadly to signify any important degree of national influence, public or private, over other societies, while to some it refers principally to foreign economic exploitation with or without other actions. In the case of the United States, the purchase of Alaska in 1867 ended the period when all new territory was assumed to be on the path to eventual statehood, and thereafter U.S. expansionism took forms more properly labeled "imperialistic." Early and abortive post–Civil War moves to annex or control the Dominican Republic, the Danish West Indies (Virgin Islands), Samoa, and Hawaii were followed by the beginnings of a modern navy and a quickening quest for new overseas markets beyond traditional trade ties to western Europe. The Cuban revolt against Spanish rule simultaneously mobilized these growing interests and embroiled the United States in war with Spain (1898), after which the victorious United States assumed responsibility for most of the remaining Spanish empire. Puerto Rico, Guam, and the Philippine Islands became outright colonies, while Cuba was made a self-governing protectorate after two years of U.S. occupation. Hawaii, which later gained old-style territorial status in 1900, was also annexed during the war. These developments occasioned a national debate over imperialism; the annexation of the Philippines set off the hottest battle. The decision to annex was defended on the grounds that the Filipinos needed enlightened U.S. rule and that the islands' possession would aid greatly in American penetration of a supposedly vast and growing China market. The actual result was a Filipino rebellion against the United States, crushed only after three years of warfare, a circumstance that helped to end the vogue of colonial annexations of the traditional type. The United States continued to spread its influence through the use of various types of protectorates. The establishment of a protectorate in Cuba (1901) was followed by similar actions in Panama (1903), the Dominican Republic (1905, 1916), Nicaragua (1912), and Haiti (1915), and by the purchase of the Virgin Islands (1917). The Open Door notes (1899, 1900) marked a U.S. attempt to impose its own commercial and diplomatic guidelines upon the great-power rivalry in China.

After World War I a period of retrenchment seemed to mark the end of U.S. imperialism. Caribbean military occupations were liquidated, and the Good Neighbor policy of the 1930's involved a general abandonment of formal protectorates. In 1934, Congress provided for eventual Philippine independence via a transitional period ending in 1946. However, the unique position of power and wealth which the United States assumed after World War II enabled it to reach unprecedented levels of global influence, while the cold-war rivalry with the Soviet Union became the justification for a proliferation of alliances, military commitments, and client states. Those who define imperialism broadly argue that the postwar complex of U.S. overseas military bases, foreign aid, multinational corporations, intervention, and limited wars can best be described by that term.

IMPLIED POWERS. At the end of Section 8 of Article I of the U.S. Constitution, which enumerates the powers of Congress, the following clause appears: "The Congress shall have Power . . . to make all Laws which shall be necessary and proper for carrying into execution the foregoing Powers, and all other Powers vested by this Constitution in the Government of the United States, or in any Department or Officer thereof." This clause is the source of the doctrine of implied powers.

During President George Washington's administration the Federalists favored broad construction of the Constitution so as to maximize the powers of the new central government, while Antifederalists sought to minimize those powers. Both groups seized upon the idea of implied powers. Alexander Hamilton argued that the necessary-and-proper clause means that Congress is not strictly limited to the enumerated "foregoing powers" but also has any powers that can be reasonably implied therefrom; Thomas Jefferson argued, on the contrary, that a law must be both necessary and proper to the existence of one of the enumerated powers. The Hamiltonian theory has always won out ultimately, because it makes better sense in an evolving world. Together with the misnamed "doctrine of national supremacy" (national acts are supreme over state acts if both are otherwise constitutional), the doctrine of implied powers has enabled the Supreme Court to uphold the vast expansion of federal law and federal power necessary to meet the changing problems with which the nation has been confronted.

IMPORTS. *See* **Trade, Foreign.**

IMPOSTS. Article I of the U.S. Constitution empowers Congress to levy "Taxes, Duties, Imposts and Excises" (Section 8) and forbids the states to "lay any Imposts or Duties on Imports or Exports" (Section 10). Inasmuch as Congress lacks the power to impose taxes on exports (Section 9), it is apparent that the little-used word "imposts" is synonymous with import duties (*see* Tariff).

IMPRESSMENT, CONFEDERATE. From the early part of the Civil War, the Confederate War Department—first without, and after March 1863 with, congressional approval—seized from producers supplies for the army and slaves for work on fortifications. Criticism of the administration of the law and the law itself increased with the growing suffering. By the winter of 1864–65 the system was abandoned.

IMPRESSMENT OF SEAMEN. The drafting of men into a navy, it was a chief cause of bad relations between Great Britain and the United States between 1790 and 1815. Under cover of the belligerent right of search British boarding parties removed from the decks of foreign neutrals any seamen "deemed" British. It is estimated that between 1790 and 1815, about 20,000 British seamen signed up on American ships, but in no circumstances was naturalization as a U.S. citizen a protection to the seaman. The British left determining of nationality to the press gangs and boarding officers. The British returned native-born American seamen to the United States, without indemnity, if their citizenship could be established, but took little responsibility to determine citizenship; each separate case had to be handled by the American government. As early as 1796 the United States issued certificates of citizenship to its mariners in an effort to protect them, but these were easily lost or were sold to British subjects. The British consequently refused to honor the certificates. In 1792, President Thomas Jefferson tried to proceed on the rule "that the vessel being American shall be evidence that the seamen on board of her are such." Great Britain refused any concessions whatever to the principle. Three times the United States tried to negotiate a treaty in which each party would deny itself the right to impress persons from the other's ships. In 1812, Congress alleged impressment to be the principal cause of the declaration of war against Great Britain.

INAUGURATION OF THE PRESIDENT. According to the Constitution only one thing is required for the inauguration of a president: Article II, Section 1, provides that "before he enter on the Execution of his Office, he shall take the following Oath or Affirmation:—'I do solemnly swear (or affirm) that I will faithfully execute the Office of the President of the United States, and will to the best of my Ability, preserve, protect and defend the Constitution of the United States.' " The ceremony has been expanded into a day-long festival that begins with the taking of the oath of office on a platform at the east front of the Capitol in Washington, D.C. The oath is usually administered by the chief justice of the Supreme Court. The president then delivers his inaugural address. The afternoon is devoted to a parade from the Capitol, down Pennsylvania Avenue to the White House, led by the president and the First Lady. In the evening the celebration concludes with several inaugural balls. The official date for the inauguration was first set as Mar. 4 by the Twelfth Amendment of the Constitution, passed in 1804; in 1933 the Twentieth Amendment set it at Jan. 20. When the vice-president takes the oath of office at the death of a president, all ceremonial formalities are dispensed with; the oath is administered as soon as possible by a justice or civil authority wherever the person assuming office happens to be.

INCOME TAX CASES (*Pollock* v. *Farmer's Loan and Trust Company,* 157 U.S. 429; *Rehearing,* 158 U.S. 601 [1895]). The 1894 tax of 2 percent on incomes over $4,000 was designed by southern and western congressmen to rectify the federal government's regressive revenue system (the tariff and excise taxes) and commence the taxation of large incomes. Conservative opponents saw the tax as the first step in a majoritarian attack on the upper classes. On Apr. 8, 1895, the Court delivered a partial decision, holding by six to two (one justice was ill) that the tax on income from real property was a direct tax and had to be apportioned. On other important issues the Court was announced as divided, four to four. A rehearing was held, and on May 20 the entire tax was found unconstitutional, five to four. Not until 1913, after adoption of the Sixteenth Amendment, could a federal income tax be levied.

INCOME TAXES. *See* **Taxation.**

INDEMNITIES. As used in diplomacy and international law, a term for payments exacted to recoup military costs of a victor state or to compensate for damages suffered by a state or its nationals from injuries by another state or its nationals. It usually connotes blanket settlement of claims, public or private, by a political agreement. Political considerations affect forms of settlement. For example, U.S. spoliation claims against the French for seizure of American merchant ships in the 1790's were settled partly by indemnity paid by France, partly by compositions entailing U.S. assumption of liability for many of its nationals' claims in return for release from the 1778 alliance with France, and partly as part-payment for the Louisiana Purchase (1803). The effort to collect German reparations after World War I and World War II showed the impracticability of full compensation for losses in major wars. The 20th century has brought many repudiations of national debts by revolutionary regimes and large-scale nationalizations of alien property, which under existing international law created liability for prompt and adequate compensation; yet payment of indemnities has been problematic and unequal. Use of force to collect such debts has been largely abandoned.

INDENTURED SERVANTS. In colonial America these were for the most part adult white persons who were bound to labor for a period of years. There were three well-known classes: the free-willers, or redemptioners; those who were kidnapped or forced to leave their home country because of poverty or for political or religious reasons; and convicts. Most of the colonies regulated the treatment of indentured servants. Runaway servants could be compelled to return to their masters and serve out their terms, additional periods being added for the time they had been absent. Indentured service of the colonial genre ceased after the American Revolution. (*See also* Contract Labor, Foreign.)

INDEPENDENCE (Mo.). In the 1820's when overland freighting from Missouri to upper Mexico began, goods were shipped from St. Louis to the town farthest west on the Missouri River. To meet the demand for a more western depot near the bend of the river, Independence was founded in 1827, ten miles from the state border. At the head of the Santa Fe and Oregon-California trails, it became known as the jumping-off place of the American frontier. Independence supplied between 6,000 and 8,000 emigrants in 1849 and claimed 1,600 inhabitants and thirty stores. However, it did not long remain the farthest west point on the Missouri. In the mid-20th century Independence emerged from obscurity, becoming known as the home of President Harry S. Truman and subsequently as the site of the Truman library and research center. The population of the city in 1980 was 111,806.

INDEPENDENCE DAY. The adoption of the Declaration of Independence on July 4, 1776, has caused that day to be taken as the birth date of the United States of America. The first anniversary does not appear to have been commemorated throughout the thirteen states, but there were elaborate celebrations in the principal cities. The practice of commemorating the Fourth soon spread widely after the adoption of the Constitution, but it was not formally established as a national holiday by act of Congress until 1941.

INDEPENDENCE HALL. A red-brick structure, not far from the center of Philadelphia, where the Declaration of Independence, Articles of Confederation, and Constitution were signed. Built (1732–57) to serve as provincial Pennsylvania's state house, it became the meeting place of the Continental Congress during the American Revolution. It adjoins Congress Hall, where the House and Senate met during the 1790's, and Old City Hall, where the Supreme Court deliberated, on Independence Square. It was made a part of Independence National Historical Park in 1948.

INDEPENDENCE ROCK. A granite boulder on the north bank of the Sweetwater River in Wyoming, it is a landmark on the Oregon Trail.

INDEPENDENT OFFICES APPROPRIATIONS ACT. (Mar. 28, 1934). This act, passed by Congress on Mar. 26, restored the cuts made by the Economy Act of 1933, increased the salaries of government employees, and the allowances of World War I veterans. President Franklin D. Roosevelt vetoed the bill on Mar. 27, but Congress overrode his veto the following day. It is important for being the first defeat Roosevelt sustained at the hands of Congress.

INDEPENDENTS (Political). Registered voters not affiliated with any political party. Since the 1960's, the independents have become a major political factor.

INDEPENDENTS (Religious). *See* **Separatists.**

INDEPENDENT TREASURY SYSTEM. The alternative, supported by Democrats, to a central bank, desired by the hard-money advocates. By late 1837 the nation had twice experienced living under a central bank, had seen it liquidated, had suffered the abuses of pet banks, and then had endured a panic and depression. The Democrats blamed it all on banks and wanted the Treasury to operate independently of them and all public dues to be paid in hard money. In June 1840, Congress passed a bill setting up the Independent Treasury System that, after June 30, 1843, was to accept only specie, but the first act of the Whig administration of President William Henry Harrison in March 1841 was to repeal the bill. One of the major planks in Democratic candidate James K. Polk's platform in 1844 was to recreate the Independent Treasury System. Congress set one up in August 1846 to receive and pay only in specie at subtreasuries located in major cities. Because the system operated badly, the government made increasing use of banks, which promptly loaned money left in their hands. In 1914 the Federal Reserve System, a central bank, went into operation, and in 1921 the Independent Treasury System ended.

INDIANA. A state whose name means "land of the Indians," it was visited by white men as early as the 1670's. Robert Cavelier, Sieur de La Salle, was the first to explore the region. During the French occupation small settlements were established—Fort Miami (about 1704); Fort Ouiatenon (about 1719); and Fort Vincennes (about 1732). With the end of the French and Indian War, the region was ceded to the English in 1763. During the Revolution, George Rogers Clark captured Vincennes and a small part of the Old Northwest.

By the Treaty of Paris of 1783, the region between the Appalachians and the Mississippi River became a part of the United States. Clarksville, the earliest authorized American settlement in the Old Northwest, was founded in 1784 on the Ohio River, opposite Louisville, by Clark and fellow soldiers. In 1788 the Northwest Territory was organized under the terms of the Ordinance of 1787, with Indiana included therein. Intermittent warfare between Americans and Indians continued. Indiana became a separate territory in 1800, with its capital at Vincennes. The Americans and Indians renewed their conflict at Tippecanoe in 1811 and during the War of 1812, resulting in bitter defeat for the Indians.

On Dec. 11, 1816, Indiana became the nineteenth state of the United States, with approximately 80,000 inhabitants. Until about 1800 its population had been mainly French and Indian. From 1800 until 1830 most settlers came from Virginia, Kentucky, the Carolinas, Maryland, and Tennessee. In the next three decades many settlers came from Ohio and the

Middle Atlantic states; immigrants from other countries, predominantly Germans with the Irish a distant second, arrived in increasing numbers. In 1860 a majority of the 1,350,000 residents still lived in southern Indiana.

Agriculture was the chief occupation of the pioneers; corn and hogs were the main products. By 1860 the Indians had, for the most part, been removed, and nearly all the land had been surveyed and sold. Rural areas accounted for 91 percent of the population in 1860 and almost 66 percent in 1900. Not until 1920, when there were close to 3 million residents, was the population slightly more urban than rural. While up to the early 1900's manufacturing was based chiefly on agriculture and lumbering, it has since come to depend principally on metals (mainly steel). Railroad mileage, only 228 miles in 1850, soared to a peak of 7,426 miles in 1920. The rapid development of east-west railroad traffic and the advance of manufacturing augmented economic and political ties between Indiana and eastern states at the expense of former connections with southern states. Since 1920 Indiana has become a more urban and industrial commonwealth. In 1980 a little over two-thirds of its nearly 5.5 million residents lived in urban areas; a large majority of them also lived in the northern half of the state.

INDIANA COMPANY. A group of Indian traders lost goods at the hands of the Indians on the outbreak of Pontiac's War in 1763; as compensation, the chiefs of the Six Nations, at the Treaty of Fort Stanwix in 1768, presented the traders with a tract of land between the southern boundary of Pennsylvania and the Little Kanawha River. Two of the merchants went to England to get a royal confirmation of the title, but the claim was swallowed up in the project for the Grand Ohio Company. On the outbreak of the Revolution, the Indiana Company was reorganized and proceeded to sell land, but its operations were blocked by Virginia, which claimed that this land lay within its borders. The company appealed to the Continental Congress, and the Committee on Western Lands approved the Indiana claim, but Virginia denied the jurisdiction of the Congress over western lands. New Jersey took up the claim and appealed to Congress, but to no avail. After the Constitution became effective in 1789 the Indiana Company brought suit against Virginia in the U.S. Supreme Court (*Grayson* v. *Virginia*), but the case was delayed pending the adoption of the Eleventh Amendment to the Constitution, after which it was dismissed on the ground that the Court had no jurisdiction.

INDIAN AFFAIRS, BUREAU OF (BIA). The principal federal agency responsible for Indian programs; referred to at times as the Office of Indian Affairs, the Indian Department, and the Indian Service, it has been known as the Bureau of Indian Affairs since the 1950's. Established by order of the secretary of war in 1824, the bureau received congressional blessing ten years later. It remained within the War Department until 1849 when it was transferred to the newly created Home Department, later the Department of the Interior. The head of the bureau has always been called the commissioner of Indian Affairs. The forerunner of the bureau was the Office of the Superintendent of Indian Trade (1806–22). While regulation of trade with the Indians has continued to be a function of the bureau, other responsibilities have surpassed it in importance: land and resource management and development, education, vocational training and placement, law and order, and social welfare. Until 1954, when the Indian Health Service was established within the Department of Health, Education, and Welfare, the bureau also provided health care for reservation Indians. Because of strong criticism of the bureau, Congress in 1869 set up a Board of Indian Commissioners to exercise joint control with the secretary of the interior over Indian appropriations. The board was highly influential in Indian affairs until the early 1900's. President Franklin D. Roosevelt abolished it by executive order in 1933.

Since the 1950's the BIA has had three principal levels of administrative responsibility: (1) a national headquarters with a small policy staff in Washington, D.C.; (2) area offices composed of both technical and supervisory personnel at strategic locations throughout the country; and (3) local offices, usually known as agencies (*see* Indian Agencies). A major feature of Indian policy in the 1970's was the transfer of authority and responsibility for various programs from the BIA to the individual tribes.

INDIAN AGENCIES. Local administrative units of the Bureau of Indian Affairs that most directly affect reservation Indians. An agency may have jurisdiction over a single reservation, a part of a reservation, or several reservations. Since early 20th century the principal federal official at each agency, formerly called the agent, has been called the superintendent, and sometimes agencies have been referred to as superintendencies. Since it was in 1796 that Congress authorized the establishment of government-owned trading houses, each of which was headed by an "Indian agent," it is likely that the term "agency" came into use at that time, continuing after the abolition of government trading houses in 1822. Since 1834 the number of agencies has varied from year to year as dictated by administrative and political considerations; the total number since World War II has never exceeded 100 and has generally been between 70 and 80. Agency employees, many of whom are Indian, are a part of the federal civil service system. On large reservations with abundant resources agency personnel may include specialists in most or all of the following fields: education, law enforcement, social welfare, road construction, irrigation engineering, forestry, soil conservation, real estate appraisal, range management, industrial development, adult vocational training, employment assistance, housing, and tribal government.

INDIANAPOLIS (Ind.). Capital and largest city of Indiana, with a population of 700,807 in 1980. It is the marketing center for very rich farmland; its industrial plants include several that process meat and other foods. A large number of manufacturing industries are located in the city, with emphasis on making equipment for various types of transportation. There are also several precision machine companies, and chemical works. In addition, the city houses a concentration of insurance companies and a leading textbook publishing company. Among its cultural institutions are Butler University and the Indiana University Medical Center.

The legislature of Indiana decided in 1820 that the state should have a new capital city, preferably located near the center of the expected population; the site selected lies at an important crossing of the White River. The city was planned, beginning in 1821. The name, compounded of the state's name and the Greek word *polis,* meaning "city," was chosen by the legislature. A great increase in the city's size and business importance came in 1830, when the National Road (Cumberland Road) reached Indianapolis and put it in the path of westward traffic from Pennsylvania, Maryland, and Ohio. Rail service arrived in 1847, beginning a long development of the city as a railroad center. It was the first city to have a railroad "belt system" that put freight service on a circuit of the city, rather than have it run directly into the center of town before being distributed; it was also a pioneer in the development of electric-powered trolleys and electric train service to other cities.

Before the Civil War, a number of German immigrants settled in and near Indianapolis, providing some skills and background in mechanical work; by 1861, the city was an important factory town. It became one of the centers for the developing automobile industry; auto designers began "road testing" their designs on a closed track there, and the track developed into a race track for automobiles. The "Indianapolis 500" began its series of 500-mile auto races in 1911, and has been run annually since then.

INDIANA STATE CANALS. The Wabash and Erie Canal, to connect Lake Erie and the Ohio River through Indiana, was that state's first internal improvement project, planned in conjunction with Ohio in 1829 and begun in 1832. In 1836 a great internal improvement bill, carrying total appropriations of $13 million, provided for the building of a canal along the Whitewater River northward from the Ohio; another, the Central Canal, from the Wabash west of Fort Wayne via Indianapolis and the White River to Evansville; a railroad; and some turnpikes. However, by 1840 the state was nearly bankrupt. The short completed portions of the Central Canal were sold to private interests for $2,425. Before the Wabash and Erie reached the Ohio River in 1853, railroads were destroying its reason for being. The Whitewater Canal, taken over by a private corporation in 1846, was dead before 1870. Financial failures though they were, the canals played a large part in the development of the Middle West.

INDIAN BARRIER STATE. The idea of a neutral barrier state closed to white settlement but open for Indian trade was first proposed in the negotiations of 1755 designed to settle the claims of France and Britain to the Ohio Valley; it was again put forward in the treaty plans of 1761–62, whereby Canada was to be ceded to Britain (*see* Paris, Treaty of). With the end of the Revolution the proposal came to the fore again in the negotiations between Great Britain, on the one hand, and the United States, France, and Spain, on the other (*see* Definitive Treaty of Peace). Britain, after the 1783 treaty, proposed that a barrier region be erected around the Great Lakes, in which both nations should have freedom of trade but no right of settlement. The American secretary of state declined to consider the British offer. Meanwhile the United States asserted its authority over the Indian confederacy, and the idea of an Indian barrier state was dropped.

INDIAN BIBLE, ELIOT'S. A 1200-page translation into Algonkin by John Eliot, minister at Roxbury, Mass. Composed 1650–58, it was printed on the hand press in the Harvard Yard, in Cambridge, and completed in 1663. Eliot had not only to learn the language but also to invent an orthography. His version was used among the converted Indians on Martha's Vineyard for over a century.

INDIAN BRIGADE. Three Union regiments composed largely of Cherokee, Creek, and Seminole, formed in 1862: two regiments were enlisted in Kansas from Indians loyal to the Union; these, together with some white troops, invaded the Indian Territory, where they were joined by a sufficient number of Indians formerly allied with the Confederacy to make up a third regiment. The brigade fought many minor engagements in northeastern Indian Territory.

INDIAN CLAIMS COMMISSION. Established by act of Congress in 1946 to hear and settle, once and for all, claims by Indian tribes for compensation for lands taken from them. The hearings did not begin until 1951, but within a specified time limit (five years), 852 claims were filed by Indian tribes for judgments against the United States. The claims pertained primarily to alleged undervaluation of the tribal lands by the United States at the times of treaties and purchases. Many of them involved grievances of a social and cultural nature, among them the socioeconomic effects on Indian cultures of governmental policies. As the slowness of the process of adjudicating the claims became apparent, it was found to be necessary to extend the tenure of the commission five times. The commission expired in 1978 and all remaining cases were transferred to the Court of Claims. By 1980 almost $400 million had been awarded to claimant tribes, although the amounts of the awards represented far less than the amounts claimed in most cases.

INDIAN COMMISSIONS. President Andrew Johnson in 1865 appointed a peace commission, including military and civilian members, to negotiate treaties with the Indians of the Great Plains and the Southwest. This commission enjoyed a limited success in its negotiations with southwestern tribes but failed completely to secure peace in the upper Great Plains. In February 1867, Congress authorized the establishment of a new commission to investigate the Fetterman Massacre of the previous December; early in July 1867 this commission reported that most of the Indians were ready for peace and recommended that aggressive warfare against them cease at once. Responding to this information, Congress enacted a bill providing for still another peace commission. After an initial meeting in St. Louis in August 1867, the commissioners went to North Platte, Nebr., where they met with the Ogalala and Brulé Sioux and the Northern Cheyenne; unsuccessful in obtaining a treaty of peace here, they moved southward and in October negotiated a treaty with the Kiowa, Arapaho, Southern Cheyenne, Plains Apache, and Comanche at Medicine Lodge Creek in southwestern Kansas. Shortly thereafter they went to Fort Laramie, Wyo., where they were able to persuade Sioux chief Red Cloud to cease hostilities pending a renewal of negotiations in the spring. In April 1868 the commissioners concluded the Treaty of Fort Laramie, which ended Red Cloud's war, but by the fall of 1868 tribes with whom the peace commissioners had dealt were again fighting. In April 1869, Congress authorized the president to appoint a permanent Board of Indian Commissioners, with a membership not to exceed ten, that would exercise joint control with the secretary of the interior over a fund to promote peace and civilization among the Indians; the board was abolished by executive order in 1933. One of the last of the Indian commissions established for a specific, temporary purpose was the Commission to the Five Civilized Tribes (*see* Dawes Commission); it was established by Congress in 1893 and completed its work in 1905.

INDIAN COUNTRY. A term used to designate territory to which the Indian title had not been extinguished; more specifically, it applies to the area set aside for the Indians in pursuance of the Indian removal policy formulated in 1825. By 1840 a definite Indian Country had been created, extending from Texas to Canada. The eastern boundary ran west from Green Bay to the Mississippi, down that river to northeastern Iowa, southwestward a short distance into Iowa, south to the Missouri line, west on that line to the Missouri River, down that river to the western boundary of Missouri, and thence along that boundary and the western boundary of Arkansas to the Texas line. The western limits were the western boundary of the United States as defined by the Adams-Onís Treaty (1819) and the eastern line of the old Oregon Country.

Within a few years the pressure of settlers led to treaties with various tribes by which the boundary of Indian Country was pushed almost entirely beyond the limits of Wisconsin and Iowa. In 1851 the eastern Sioux agreed to give up claim to almost all lands in Iowa and Minnesota; in 1854 the tribes that had been located along the eastern border of Indian Country were induced to make treaties ceding lands and agreeing to move. After the passage of the Kansas-Nebraska Act in 1854, Indian Country was reduced to the region west of Arkansas and between Kansas and Texas, known as the Indian Territory. When Oklahoma became a state in 1907, the last remnant of the Indian Country disappeared. (*See also* Indian Policy, National; Indian Territory.)

INDIAN CULTURE, AMERICAN. Ethnologists and archaeologists agree that American Indians are descended from peoples of northeastern Asia who made a series of migrations from across the Bering Strait and into North America. It has been suggested that human migrations began as early as 25,000 years ago. Having a common arctic or subarctic orientation, different migratory groups fanned out from an original point of entry in Alaska, became isolated, and began to assume both cultural and linguistic identities. Physically, the American Indian peoples relate to a general East Asian Mongoloid strain. But given isolation and genetic drift over a long period of time, physical types display great diversity. The skin color of American Indians has been popularly designated "red," stemming from John Cabot's 1497 voyage and his description of the extinct Beothuk of Newfoundland, a group that smeared the body with a mixture of bear grease and red ocher. Although it is possible that American Indians brought with them a common East Asian language that became differentiated over a period of time, not one of the native American languages has been proven to be related to a Eurasian speech family. If one defines a distinct language as one not intelligible outside a particular group, over 600 separate languages—not dialects—were spoken in North America in 1492; until the introduction of variously conceived phonetic alphabets, these languages were unwritten.

Two primary patterns are discernible beneath the diversity in cultural development. In the northern reaches of North America and in southern South America the initial arctic and subarctic hunting adaptation persisted. The natives of both areas used the transportable skin tent and similar modes of dressing skins, tailoring clothes, and working stone; their food and its preparation and weapon assemblage were similar; and their social, political, and religious structures appear also to have had much in common. In the temperate, subtropical, and tropical regions the migrants became settled, their cultures based on various forms of wild-seed gathering; from this gathering adaptation, centered in Middle America, the basic agricultural inventions of the American Indians proceeded. The most intensive cultural developments of pre-Columbian America occurred in Mexico, Peru, the American Southwest, and the lower Mississippi. Farther to the north and south, clusters of population were smaller; agricultural practices, more attenuated; and integration of tribal units, in social, political, and religious terms, less well defined.

There is no evidence of any protracted or significant contact between pre-Columbian America and the Old World before 1492, although there was superficial contact with Norsemen in northeastern North America and probably some exchange between South American Indians and Polynesians. The uniquely American array of domesticated plants and animals, as well as tools and equipment associated with them, are evidence of a native American cultural development independent of Europe and Asia. The wheel and wheeled vehicles were never known to the American Indian. Although there are some cultural parallels, in cotton farming and weaving, in the use of bronze (but not iron), and in the development of calendrical systems and mathematics, these developments were differently integrated into the general cultural patterns of the Old World and the New World.

A conservative estimate suggests a population of 8.5 million American Indians in both North and South America at the time of the discovery of the New World. The areas of intensive agriculture show the greatest density, and there is a sharp decline in population as one moves northward and southward. A minimum estimate sets the native Indian population of North America north of Mexico at 1.1 million in 1492, while Mexico itself, with its greater control of food production, is assigned 3.5 million. In the Sacramento–San Joaquin drainage, despite the primary dependence on acorns, there seems to have been an exceptionally large population, estimated at 200,000. Native populations declined after contact with Europeans. Diseases and epidemics of Old World origin wiped out many groups. In the 1920's, however, the Indian populations of North America began to increase.

Native American cultural diversity broadly reflects the adaptations of farmers, gatherers, and hunters to their natural surroundings; historical generalization must be brought into play in differentiating groups on the basis of culture area, for example, the American Indians of the Plains area did not develop a vital culture until after 1750, when they so successfully adapted to the use of the imported horse.

Eskimo Culture Area. So distinct are the Eskimo (or Inuit) culturally from other native Americans that they are often accorded an identity all their own. Theories about their origins differ; they may have been the last arrivals in North America from Asia, spreading out from the western American arctic about A.D. 1000, moving as far to the east as Angmagssalik in Greenland. The recency of the Eskimo movement is indicated by the presence of a mutually intelligible language from Norton Sound to Greenland. Their subsistence is gained basically through hunting. Their maritime adaptation was based on the exploitation of all available sea mammals: whaling in northern Alaska, beluga hunting in Hudson Bay and the central arctic, and sealing everywhere. Land animals were trapped widely, but greatest dependence was on the slaughter of the caribou.

Social and political patterns. The Eskimo lacked any tribal or political sense. Stress was laid on familial relationships, membership in a group being determined by ties of kinship. Chieftainship was lacking except for the emergence from time to time of a hunt organizer. Social relationships beyond the extended family group lay in cooperative hunting relationships.

Art and technology. Eskimo inventions include the harpoon with detachable head, the saucerlike lamp fueled by seal oil, tailored skin and fur clothing, and several types of boat, including the kayak. Sod and stone houses were in general use, although some central groups lived in the domed ice lodge. Some groups developed depictions of spirit forms, masks in the west suggesting Northwest Coast conventions, while in the east monsters and spirits were freely drawn.

Religion, myth, and folklore. The basic element in Eskimo religion was a world view according to which the inhabitants of the animal world were seen as morally superior to men, allowing themselves, if the proper rituals were carried out, to be taken for food. A second element was shamanism, marked by the presence of curers or doctors.

North American Subarctic Culture Area. The subarctic area is perhaps the least readily defined, because the peoples resident in the interior both of Alaska and of northwest Canada and those in the northern reaches of Quebec were influenced by the more vital cultures nearest them. The subarctic peoples were characterized by an inland adaptation to tundra and boreal forest. The chief adjustment of the area in the west was to the caribou, those in the east coming to depend on moose and deer. In the west, caribou were taken by most groups by the herding of the game into corrals where they were lanced. Both areas exploited game resources to the full; an amazing series of traps was developed, although fur trapping did not come into its own until after the 17th century.

Social and political patterns. The principal designations of tribal groups in the subarctic depend on language, linguistic subgrouping, or dialect. Tribes had no political sense; the socioeconomic band was the primary functioning unit. Bands were made up generally on the basis of kinship. They moved about in the course of a year for hunting, trapping, and fishing and might at intervals meet with other bands of the same area and language for a communal caribou drive, ceremonials, and arrangement of marriages. Hunt leaders emerged as men of prestige, possessing only informal political roles.

Art and technology. The hunting-trapping complex gave rise to some distinctive inventions: babiche, caribou rawhide, was used for lines, netting, and the round and tailed snowshoe; the cache for preserving food was common; pemmican—pounded fat, berries, and meat—was also a characteristic. Clothing was tailored from tanned skins of caribou, moose, and deer. The portable skin tent presaged the Plains tipi.

Religion, myth, and folklore. Religion was similar to that of the Eskimo, with recognition of animal spirits, shamanism, and group ceremonies involving hunting. A special development of the area was the girls' rite, a year of seclusion for girls following the onset of the menses; the bringing of such young women back into the band was the major ceremonial event.

Northwest Coast Culture Area. Stretching from southeastern Alaska down the mountainous coast of British Columbia to Puget Sound, this culture area was exclusively maritime. Although basically oriented to hunting, cultural development was accented by the presence of the salmon. Despite the absence of agriculture, the native peoples experimented with planting clover as food. The aboriginal population seems never to have been large; the area was populated over a period of time by thrusts of various peoples who were gradually assimilated into native cultural patterns but retained their linguistic identity.

Social and political patterns. Small villages were the rule, groups federated by commonality of language and especially by kinship relationships. A defined tribal sense evolved, which allowed for cultural and linguistic distinctiveness. The unit was the village, a row of cedar-plank extended-family houses inhabited by as many as thirty or forty people. Because of the profusion of the produce of the sea and other hunted and gathered materials, the native cultures possessed a remarkable surplus and capitalism arose to which the prestige of persons and groups was related. Prestige and status were achieved through dissemination of property, and thus potlatch gift-giving originated: one village feasted another, or there was exchange feasting between groups within a village. Social life was intimately bound up with the feasting system. The Kwakiutl of Vancouver Island turned the system of feasting into a mechanism of vengeance; their potlatches served to advance status in that increasingly rich feasts required reciprocation from economic and social rivals. Among the Haida, Tlingit, and Tsimshian, in the north, inheritance and group affiliation were through the mother; one inherited a house from a mother's brother. Tlingit and Haida were divided into two exogamous groups, Raven and Wolf, membership in which was maternally focused. The two halves, or moieties, regularly feasted each other, built each other's houses, and buried each other's dead. Property rights were generally passed on to the children of one's sister; a man's children would fall into the opposite grouping, whereas his sister's children would not. In the center of the area such groups as the Kwakiutl emphasized both the maternal and paternal sides; paternal organizations appeared in the south. Chiefs were those of high title. Political power, however, resided in the group rather than in the individual.

Art and technology. Salmon and other fish were netted, seined, and lured. They were eaten fresh, stored as pemmican, stored with berries, smoked, or soaked in oil in cedar boxes. Sealing, whaling, and deep-sea fishing for halibut were known. Horn and antler wedges were used to split cedar logs into planks, the trees having been felled by burning and wedging. Elaborate dugout canoes with sewed gunwale planks were common. The house was the hallmark of the area; cedar planks, painted or carved, were set upright to form a squared structure with a gabled roof; the inhabitants sat and slept on a plank platform, with a central firepit. The roof was of planking, bent so that sections of the roof could be pushed on and off as needed. The totem pole, a familial device, was erected at the center of the house front, the mouth of one of the human or animal figures on the pole serving as the entrance. The relationship between family and kindred and the animal world was continually reaffirmed; on the totem pole, animal and quasi-human figures flowed into one another. All surfaces—including house walls, box sides, and canoes—were decorated. There was also a realistic convention, manifested in carved portrait masks of both human and animal figures.

Religion, myth, and folklore. The principal ceremonial was the First Salmon Rite, a kind of first-fruits ritual. Animals represented on the totem pole were those with which an ancestor had had a mystic experience, and these experiences were ritually repeated, giving rise to a notion of a guardian spirit. Also present in the area was a modified form of the vision guest.

Western Culture Areas: Plateau, Basin, and California. Although the Plateau, Basin, and California cultures differed, they had a common basic dependence on wild-seed gathering and were all topographically isolated. The Plateau culture area borders on the western subarctic in the north and is shut off from the Northwest Coast by the coastal mountain chain. Toward the south the area shades off gradually into the Great Basin, a desert complex stretching from the Sierra Nevada to the eastern Rockies and reaching to the San Juan plateau of New Mexico and the Grand Canyon region. The culture area of native California, equally isolated, had generally the same boundaries as the state. Its focus lay in the Sacramento–San Joaquin drainage, with some variations appearing in the south and in the Basin-style configuration around the Gulf of California and in Baja California. In southeastern California, among such groups as the Mohave and Yuma, influence by the strong agricultural development of the American Southwest was manifested in river-bottom farming of maize and in pottery making. Nowhere else does agriculture appear in these western regions.

Social and political patterns. The Plateau peoples, divided into fairly distinct tribal-linguistic units, paralleled native California peoples in the development of the village. Among both, a sense of village and tribal autonomy was general. While chieftainship depended on force of personality and speaking skills, the office of the chief per se assumed some importance in village affairs. Villages were generally small, and several villages in both areas might make up a tribe. California developed some patterns of social organization, as, for example, moiety structures among the Miwok and Yokut and rudimentary exogamous clan units among other groups.

Economically the Plateau peoples depended on the gathering of various wild root crops; on hunting; and on salmon, taken in large quantities as they moved from the coast up the freshwater streams to spawn. In the Basin, under often rigorous desert conditions, hunting of deer and rabbits was interspersed with gathering of juniper berries and pine nuts; a wide variety of insects was obtained for food. Eastern Basin and Plateau tribes east of the continental divide were influenced by the Plains people after 1700, taking on the horse and the Plains manner of warfare. California was characterized by the gathering of acorns, supplemented with hunting and fishing, and this dependency on the acorn gave the area its distinctive separatism; a single tribelet inhabiting a single village might renounce all contact with other groups, and warfare might result from trespass.

Art and technology. Of the three areas, the Basin had the simplest technology; inventions and adaptations were made by the Californians especially. The acorns gathered in California were subjected to leaching in baskets, hot water being employed to remove the bitter tannin. California also achieved proficiency in the making of stone points for both the dart and the arrow. Houses varied greatly, from the brush shelter of the Basin (wickiup) to the plank houses of the Yurok and Hupa, pale reflections of the Northwest Coast. Between lay a great range of tent-like shelters, brush houses, and semisubterranean dwellings of sections of the Plateau. Footgear and clothing were minimal. The entire Western area made use of the rabbitskin blanket for warmth. Basketry and, to a lesser degree, matting were the high points of artistic achievement in the Basin area; geometric designs were created by using multicolored materials. The widest range of baskets appears in California, with remarkable shapes and decorative motifs.

Religion, myth, and folklore. Religion was simplest among the Basin peoples. Although they engaged in social and ceremonial dancing, shamanism, and the girls' rite, these practices were less elaborate among them than in California and the Plateau. The Plateau peoples had a version of the First Salmon Rite, and of the vision guest. In California, world renewal was associated with the dead and was thus a mourning ritual; in some groups the dead were impersonated by men, initiated members of secret associations. California also had the myth of the Lecherous Father, a figure who feigns illness and death and returns to achieve his incestuous aims. Throughout the western area was the motif of the Trickster who transforms, changes, and creates.

Plains Culture Area. Before the advent of the horse the area known as the Plains encompassed a number of largely undifferentiated cultures. Much of the western area appears to have been moderately nomadic. The portable skin tent was dragged by dogs on the travois, tent poles pulled behind the animal, on which goods could be piled. Bison were hunted and often stampeded over cliffs. Horses appear to have been obtained from the Spanish expeditions. Escaped horses thrived on the Plains—the Indians, capturing them, achieved a horse domestication of their own, although using a few Spanish elements such as the lance. Although bone bits were known, saddles were rare and stirrups almost never used. Plains culture and its associated war patterns had come into their own by 1780, by which time the equestrian development had been fully integrated. The horse permitted the Plains Indian to obtain in far greater numbers the bison that roamed the grasslands of the area between the Rocky Mountains and the Mississippi River. The traditional tipi of the Plains could become larger, and communication between wandering bands could be more readily achieved.

Another Plains development lay among the sedentary or agricultural peoples: patterns of maize farming, diffused from the lower Mississippi and moving up the valley through both eastern and western tributaries, including the Missouri, characterized the riverine peoples of the eastern Plains. A twofold ecological system thus arose; sedentary Plains groups, such as the Omaha and Osage, although strongly influenced by the horse and by bison hunting, stood in rather sharp contrast to the exclusively equestrian tribes, such as the Crow, Blackfoot, Kiowa, and Comanche. The area at large was always in a state of flux. Problems of communication between groups of different languages were surmounted by the development of sign language, a convention common to the whole area but not elsewhere. Plains Indian culture reached its peak in the period 1700–1870.

Social and political patterns. Tribal entities in the Plains were definable by territory, language, and common cultural convention. The hunting and war patterns created the basic band unit, the group at times augmented by association with other bands at the time of intensive bison hunting. Within this basic pattern, forms of social structure varied considerably: strong maternal clan institutions appeared in the northwest, while the eastern tribes, such as the Omaha, developed equally strong paternal stress. Political structure was generally vague. There were no paramount chiefs but rather leaders for various activities: hunt chiefs, war leaders, heads of warrior groups or of the important sodalities or clubs, priests, and curers. In hunting, both nomadic and sedentary, the Plains Indian acted as though at war. The hunt was rigorously policed, groups of warriors acting to keep other hunters in line, destroying the property of any who acted prematurely. Plains Indian warfare was highly conventionalized. Status was achieved on the basis of a system of formal counting of acts of bravery, or coups. A coup might be striking an enemy with the hand, touching his horse or his tipi, or running off his horses; it was witnessed and recognized in solemn conclave of warriors and leaders. War was neither for territorial expansion nor necessarily, except for horses, for booty. There was seldom a practical need to kill an enemy, nor did custom require killing.

Art and technology. Every part of the bison was used: the skins for robes, the sinew for thread, the paunch for cooking. Holes in the ground were lined with the bison paunch, soup and blood being heated by dropping in hot stones to bring the liquid to a boil. The flesh was jerked, pounded with berries, dried, and boiled. Decoration appeared on fringed buckskin garments, painted or embroidered with porcupine quills, and in painted parfleches, or rawhide containers.

Religion, myth, and folklore. Religious life was a mixture of acts of war and benign ceremonies for tribal good. In the Sun Dance, for example, a common ritual throughout the area, accompanied by the display of related fetish objects, there was a vague sense of tribal benefit to be obtained from the sun; yet at the same time the dance was a vow of vengeance. The major religious preoccupation of the Plains was the quest of a vision by which an individual sought to achieve power. A neophyte, in young manhood, solemnly approached the spirit world, fasting, humbling himself, and frequently engaging in self-torture. He then went off in search of a spirit that would become his special guardian. On his return the neophyte was catechized by the older men to be certain that the vision was in keeping with proper tradition. An amulet given by the spirit, wrapped in buckskin, was the individual's medicine bundle, which might come to take on tribal importance. The men entrusted with the care of such fetish bundles became priests, bringing out these tribal symbols on certain occasions, unwrapping them ceremonially, singing the appropriate songs, and following defined ritual patterns. The aim of such rituals was to ensure tribal well-being.

Eastern Culture Areas: Eastern Woodlands (Northeast) and Southeast. The area from the Great Lakes to the Gulf of Mexico and from the Atlantic coast to the Mississippi River showed a unified cultural focus. The center of the eastern development lay generally in the Gulf states. Strong Mexican influences contributed both intensive farming and, in prehistoric times, the development of elaborate earthworks and mounds. (Moundbuilding, of which there are remains in Illinois and Wisconsin, moved northward to the Ohio River system.) The Southeast was apparently the source of a series of population movements that took place before European contact; the five—and later six—tribes of the Iroquois were a reflection of those movements from the South to upper New York and adjacent Canada. Many northeastern Algonkin-speaking tribes extended the influence of the Southeast culture area by adopting patterns of farming, dress, warfare, and political organization of the Iroquois. Similarly the Siouan-speaking peoples may have moved from the Southeast into the northern Plains. With the advent of Europeans this trend was reinforced by the displacement of native coastal populations.

Social and political patterns. The hallmark of the Southeast culture area was its political organization. A tribal sense was fostered, amounting almost to nationalism. Groups such as the Creek, Cherokee, Choctaw, and Iroquois developed strongly defined political systems involving well-defined official positions and political federations. From such federations and their protocol derive the peace pipe, wampum, the sachem, and the tomahawk. The Southeastern peoples tended generally to build palisaded villages, a pattern that carried over into the Northeast, and to raise their crops around the village walls. Villages belonged to the greater tribe and sent representatives to a tribal council, a practice best exemplified in the League of the Iroquois. Political organization was generally linked with strong matrilineal institutions: office was obtained by inheritance through females; women could warn and ultimately depose a chief; women as a group achieved a virtual gynocracy.

Among the Creek and their neighbors, men were warriors, hunters, and farmers; women owned the land and the house; and a man married into the wife's community. War patterns involved conquest, subjugation of other groups, and enslavement. Yet the Gulf groups, especially the Creek, were divided into two major social groupings, the red and the white, the former aligned to war, the latter to peace. Towns were directed toward one activity or the other, it being the duty of white town chiefs to speak for peace. All men went to war, regardless of white or red background, and much attention was given to deliberations about war. The two moieties played against each other in a ball game (called by such names as shinny or lacrosse) having ceremonial importance as a form of world renewal. A town had its fields, its palisades, cabins (matrilocal L-shaped houses of wattle and daub), and its game yard, a virtual stadium. In addition, some tribes of the Gulf region had a ceremonial structure, a temple-like circular building, often on a mound. This, the House of Heat, was the center of warrior activity. Tribal bundles, or palladia, were kept there to be brought out at appropriate times by priests. A spiral fire was kept burning in the temple all year, extinguished and rekindled at the time of the Busk, the annual world-renewal ceremony.

The Eastern Woodland peoples were less well defined in tribal estate and social structure than the Southeastern, but many developed federations out of fear of the Iroquois. In the Northeast groups stressed the patrilineal family. Tribalism existed as a force in the Woodlands, related to hunting territory. There was no formalized structure of chieftainship, although there was a vague status based on wealth. The poor begged of the rich in certain ceremonies. Of these, among the western Algonkins, the Midewiwin, the great medicine society, was of paramount importance.

Art and technology. In the Southeast tobacco was strongly developed. Corn was ground in mortars as meal but also treated with wood ash to make hominy. Succotash, mixed corn and beans, was a Southeastern invention. Persimmons were raised for making a flour and bread. Poisons were used in fishing and in war. The blowgun was used by the Iroquois in the hunting of small game. The upper Ohio Valley, sections of the St. Lawrence River, the southern Great Lakes, and New England showed a modified agriculture—maize cultivation of the simplest kind, corn, beans, and squashes planted together in a hill, often with fish as fertilizer. The corn crib appeared in this area. In the west the Ojibwa experimented with the wild rice. The nonagricultural groups made extensive use of birchbark for canoes, housing, and containers. High levels of art and material achievement were reached, as in the carved posts of the Iroquois.

Religion, myth, and folklore. Southeastern religion was based on agriculture, stressing fertility and rituals designed to enhance the growing of food. Animal spirits and the fetish object or bundle were not unknown, and there is a suggestion of a parallel to the Plains vision quest. Clans within the tribe, both among the Iroquois and the Gulf peoples, claimed animal ancestors. There were shamanistic curers, but priests or ritualists were more important. The ceremonies involved purification, fasting, ritual emetics, and solemnity. The groups to the west had an elaborate mythology, including the Hiawatha legend, Manebush, and the "Great Spirit."

Southwestern Culture Area. The American Southwest shows considerable cultural diversity and linguistic variation. Two major foci existed in the prehistoric past: the Pueblo development in the San Juan plateau of northern Arizona and New Mexico, and the Hohokam culture of the Gila and Salt valleys in southern Arizona. The so-called Basket-Maker cultures, the two major civilizations, and several ancillary ones —similar to the Basin cultures at the beginning of the Christian era—arose to a peak of development between A.D. 1000 and A.D. 1300. The culture area reached well into Mexico, into the lower Colorado River valley, and into the southern Basin. The Athapascan-speaking Navaho and Apache, who reached the area in late prehistoric times, were closely drawn into the Southwestern cultural orbit. What is most remarkable about the area is the development of intensive agriculture in the face of desert conditions.

The Spanish term *pueblo* relates to the permanent villages of adobe and stone, with houses of one or more stories, of the San Juan plateau. The multistoried houses were characteristic a millennium ago, reflected in the Mesa Verde monument and Chaco Canyon. In many cases the entire pueblo consisted of a single building of three or four stories with 200 to 500 rooms. The towns—variable in population, rarely having more than 3,000 people and sometimes as few as 250—were arranged according to local tradition. The Hopi towns, as well as Acoma, were built on mesa tops, the houses aligned according to the contours of the mesa itself. In the Rio Grande valley several blocks of houses might be put together in rows, as at Jemez; sometimes there was a central plaza. The important structure was the kiva, the ceremonial chamber, semisubterranean, round or rectangular, depending on the local tradition, with a roof entrance.

Social and political patterns. The Pueblo possessed a tightly knit society. Each pueblo regarded itself as the hub of the universe. The tendency was toward village endogamy, and patterns of kinship relationship were well defined. In the west, as at Hopi and Zuni, a matrilineal clan system was paramount: men inherited clan membership from the mother and were reared in the maternal household, leaving it at marriage; preferentially a man married the daughter of a mother's brother and resided in the household of his wife and her mother and sisters; women owned the house and the land that the men worked. In the central Pueblo area, among the Keresan Pueblo, matriarchy was less strong, there being a bilateral mode of descent. In the east, among the Tanoans, the paternal dual system arose, with moiety organization, the society being divided into exogamous halves. The Spanish, especially after the Pueblo Revolt of 1680, introduced elected secular officials among the Pueblo with some success. A governor, for example, was affirmed to deal with the outside, acting in general as chief. Most pueblos had an official peacemaker, an obscure and mystic figure often designated by the Spanish term "cacique," who was required to do no work but to concentrate on communal good, acting as the bearer of peace. There were warrior societies, the leader often being balanced against the cacique.

The Navaho and Apache, drawn into the Pueblo cultural orbit, gradually became maize farmers, although not on the intensive Pueblo scale. Maternal institutions, an apparent reflection of Hopi contact, were adopted by both, an imprint more strongly felt by the Navaho. Yet these groups never took on a settled economy in the same degree as their neighbors. Both were quick to adapt to sheep and cattle and retained a pattern of modified agriculture and sheep and cattle raising. The eastern groups of Apache were drawn into the Plains bison-hunting and war complex.

Art and technology. Pueblo economic activity centered on intensive agriculture. Planting was done under extremely adverse conditions; the Hopi, for example, planted maize at the base of a mesa to catch moisture from the morning dew. The complex of corn, beans, and squashes was basic. Tobacco was raised and also a variety of cotton. Maize was of many varieties and colors. The Pueblo wove textiles, making kilts, sashes, and the long navy-blue woman's dress. Men did the weaving in the western pueblos; women made the pottery, an ancient agricultural tradition reaching its highest artistic achievement among these peoples. Footgear was generally a buckskin moccasin. Navaho women developed the weaving of rugs and blankets into a notable art. Symbolic art characterizes the American Southwest, where design elements may suggest clouds, rain, and lightning. Both groups used the dry or sand painting, creating symbolic figures of spiritual beings and natural phenomena.

Religion, myth, and folklore. Religion provided the major cohesive element in Pueblo society. Primary emphasis lay on communal and group activity; curing, for example, was done by groups. Each pueblo had a set of cultlike associations. Among these groups were the wearers of the kachina masks —fetishes kept in the kiva, fed, given aspersions of holy water and tobacco, and worn when the occasion required imitation of the generally ancestral, rainmaking personalities. Religion was directed principally toward a reaffirmation of a tie with the traditional supernatural beings. Given origins lying far to the north, the presence among the Apache of the girls' rite as a major ceremonial occasions little surprise. This underlay other aspects of Apache religion. The Navaho, more influenced by the Pueblo, stressed curing as a major ceremonial preoccupation. The curing paraphernalia are Pueblo, but the orientations are distinctly Navaho: sand or dry painting and the ritual use of tobacco, corn pollen, water, and masks are among directly borrowed elements; the elaborate system of Navaho chants, designed to effect the well-being of the entire society as well as to cure the patient, some lasting over extended four-day periods, has no parallel among the Pueblo.

Twentieth-Century Indian Culture. The census of 1980 enumerated 1,418,000 Indians and Alaska natives in the United States, as compared with a total of 523,591 in 1960, the most rapidly increasing group in the United States. Moreover, most Indians were young; in 1980 more than half were under the age of twenty. According to some estimates, more than 50 percent of U.S. Indians now live in urban areas (*see* Relocation Program, Voluntary).

The greatest numbers of urban Indians lived in Chicago, Los Angeles, the San Francisco Bay area, and Minneapolis–St. Paul in 1970; Los Angeles had the largest Indian population of any city in the United States, an estimated 50,000 in the metropolitan area. Urban Indians do not usually live in enclaves but are widely scattered in the cities among people of varied ethnic and national origins. Indians who had not migrated lived on approximately 200 reservations, the largest populations being in Arizona, Oklahoma, New Mexico, California, North Dakota, South Dakota, Montana, Minnesota, and North Carolina. More than 30 percent of American Indians were Navaho, Cherokee, Sioux, or Chippewa. The Navaho, located mainly in Arizona and New Mexico, constituted by far the largest tribe, having a population of 140,000.

The best-preserved Indian cultures were in the Southwest, including those of the Hopi, Zuni, and Navaho, although no Indian culture had been completely unaltered by contact with whites. Nevertheless, the rate of acculturation for many tribes had been slow. Numerous aspects of Indian cultures persisted, and more than fifty Indian languages were still alive.

The Indians of the 1970's were increasingly insistent on their right to retain their identity as Indians. The Pan-Indian movement was growing, and a number of intertribal organizations were involved in political action of various kinds (*see* American Indian Movement; National Congress of American Indians; National Indian Youth Council). As a group they were still the most deprived in the nation, ranking at the very bottom in indices of health, education, income, and employment. In 1970 the average annual income per Indian family was only $1,500, while the unemployment rate was ten times the national average. It was estimated that 70 percent of all Indian housing was substandard. The average age of death was only forty-four, about 33 percent lower than the national average. The educational level of all Indians remained below that of the nation as a whole, with an estimated fifth-grade median; Indian dropout rates from schools were 100 percent higher than the national average.

Indians by no means speak with one voice. Still, there are many issues on which most Indians are agreed, such as opposition to the termination of the reservation system. Most wish to retain their Indian cultures and their identity as Indians. They want the right to control their own affairs and their own funds without paternalistic governmental interference. They wish to determine their own destinies rather than have decisions made for them by non-Indians. At the same time, they insist that the nation must honor its treaty obligations and that it should continue to assist them financially and in other ways.

INDIAN FACTORY OF VIRGINIA. During the French and Indian War, in 1757, a board of trustees was set up in Virginia to facilitate trade with, and the recruitment of warriors from, Cherokee country. Supplies were ordered from England; pending their arrival, the trustees requested patience of the Cherokee. When, in 1759, the first cargo was approaching Indian Country, it had to be recalled, owing to the outbreak of hostilities that enlarged into the Cherokee War of 1760–62. The trustees were instructed to sell their stocks and to balance accounts with the provincial treasurer. In 1765 the assembly recreated the trustees, appropriated £ 2,500, and decreed trade without profit. Factor David Ross journeyed to the Cherokee and discussed with them problems of trade; upon his return he reported to the trustees that a traffic such as that projected would be attended by "inconveniences." The trustees dropped the scheme and made preparations to dispose of their goods. The Privy Council in England, meanwhile, had nullified the act reestablishing the trustees. (*See also* Factory System, Indian.)

INDIAN KEY MASSACRE. An Indian attempt, during the second Seminole War, to destroy a settlement on Indian Key, halfway between the present cities of Miami and Key West, Fla. The Indians were discovered before they attacked, on Aug. 7, 1840, and all but six whites escaped in the darkness.

INDIAN MEDICINE. The Eskimo, along with other native American hunters—all western and interior subarctic peoples—developed the concept of the shaman, often popularly termed a "medicine man." Since it was believed among the Eskimo that improper behavior toward the animal spirits caused the soul or essence of the person to wander away and illness to result, the shaman was called on to restore the soul by ritual and magic. Other peoples with the shamanistic institution held that illness was caused by a "pain" that intruded into the body; among them, the practitioner removed the object, usually by sleight of hand or by sucking. The hunting cultures recognized other aspects of illness in a more practical way: toothache, broken bones, sleeplessness, and constipation were attacked by a complex series of potions, infusions, and poultices.

Curing and medicines were more complex among agricultural peoples. The Pueblo stressed curing as part of a total religious ritual, developing curing groups, clubs, or societies that had secret rituals. (*See also* Midewiwin.) The Navaho of the Southwest built a religious system based on curing and evolved an elaborate series of curing chants and rituals. Gulf tribes, such as the Creek, gave special training to curers. Sweat bathing was used for cures in that area, as in much of North America. Buckskin-wrapped sacred objects, acquired in individual spirit-vision quests among the Plains tribes and passed on as sacred tribal symbols, were termed "medicine bundles" and were thought to have curing properties, but their primary function was ceremonial.

Native South Americans contributed more to medical knowledge than did native North Americans. From the tropical forests comes curare, originally a poison but used medicinally today; rubber products, including tubing and the enema syringe; and quinine, coca, and ipecac.

INDIAN MISSIONS. During the colonial period efforts to Christianize the Indians were made by Spanish Franciscans in Florida and Upper California; French Jesuits in the South and New York; Spanish missionaries in New Mexico, Arizona, and Texas; Roger Williams, John Eliot, and David Brainerd in New England and the Middle Atlantic region; and the Moravians among various tribes. Definite missionary work was begun by boards and societies as follows: in 1787 the Society for Propagating the Gospel among the Indian and Others in North America; in 1796 the New York Missionary Society; in 1797 the Northern Missionary Society; in 1802 the Western Missionary Society (the three latter organizations forming in 1817 the United Foreign Missionary Society, later absorbed by the American Board of Commissioners for Foreign Missions, supported by the Congregational, Dutch Reformed, and Presbyterian churches); in 1803 the General Assembly of the Presbyterian Church; in 1817 the General Missionary Convention of the Baptist denomination; in 1821 the Methodist Episcopal Church; in 1842 the American Indian Mission Association; and in 1845 boards of the Southern Baptist Convention and the Methodist Episcopal Church, South.

INDIAN POLICY, COLONIAL. **British Policy Prior to 1755.** From the earliest colonial times Indian title to the soil was construed by the British to be one of occupancy, with the ultimate fee in the crown and colony. Before 1755 Indian affairs were largely controlled by the individual colonies. Policies were initiated by the colonial governors; assemblies appropriated money to pay the expenses involved and passed laws to regulate Indian trade. Treaties, involving extinguishment of Indian title and other matters, were negotiated by colonial officials or representatives of the crown and signed by both parties. Colonial control resulted in the native Americans' being robbed of their lands and cheated in trade; many tribes, therefore, allied themselves with the French during the French and Indian War.

British Policy After 1755. To win Indian support, the British inaugurated a system of imperial management in 1755 and 1756 by creating two separate Indian departments and appointing a superintendent for each. By 1761 the right to buy Indian lands had been denied the American colonies and was directed by the home government. The Proclamation of 1763 guaranteed to the Indians "for the present" the lands between the Appalachians and the Mississippi; no trader was permitted within the reservation without a license obtained from the colony in which he resided. This administrative system subordinated the Indian superintendents to the military authorities, and so in 1764 they presented a plan designed to give them more independence. The proposal provided that they be permitted to regulate such Indian affairs as treaties, trade, land purchases, and matters pertaining to peace or war without political or military interference; that all Indian traders were to be placed under the control of the superintendent; that civil cases were to be tried by the Indian agents and appeals taken to the superintendent; and that all provincial laws relating to Indian affairs were to be repealed. Although Parliament never sanctioned the plan, the superintendents proceeded to administer Indian affairs according to it.

In 1767 a compromise between imperial and colonial control was effected: it was agreed that the regulation of Indian trade should be transferred to the colonies and a definite Indian boundary surveyed; if ever permitted, westward colonization was to be under imperial control. Boundary agreements were accordingly negotiated, and the surveys were made. The real problem then was to prevent encroachments upon the frontier lands. Despite the efforts of the superintendents to prevent Indian land cessions to individuals and to companies, these continued until the Revolution.

The Indians were paid very little for land cessions, and permanent annuities were never granted during the colonial period. The British, nevertheless, succeeded in retaining the friendship of the major tribes throughout the Revolution.

INDIAN POLICY, NATIONAL. American Indian policy was modeled on that of the British. Two basic elements have been especially important: legal recognition of the fact that Indians have ownership interests in the lands they traditionally used and occupied; and the notion that Indians require government assistance and protection because they are not sophisticated in the ways of European society. Those who drafted the Articles of Confederation insisted upon placing full authority over Indian affairs in the hands of the federal government. The Constitution is much less specific in this regard, although, in Article I, Section 8, it does endow Congress with the power to "regulate Commerce with foreign Nations, and among the several States, and with the Indian Tribes." Powers deriving from other portions of the Constitution have also been used to develop legislation for the implementation of federal Indian policy. Among these are the powers to make expenditures for the general welfare, to control the property of the United States, and to make treaties. Important too are the powers of Congress to admit new states and prescribe the terms of their admission, to make war, to establish post roads, to create tribunals inferior to the Supreme Court, and to promulgate a "uniform Rule of Naturalization."

Indians in the American Revolution. In March 1775 the Massachusetts Provincial Congress accepted the offer of the Indians of Stockbridge to serve the patriots as minutemen. Thereafter overtures were made to others—the Iroquois, Penobscot, and St. Francis. In turn, the British superintendent of Indian affairs in the north tried to induce the Indians to ally themselves with the English, culminating in a council at Oswego in July 1775. The American invasion of Canada cut off supplies and made possible a treaty of neutrality between Continental commissioners and some of the Iroquois at Albany in September and another at Fort Pitt in October, securing the neutrality of the Ohio and Lake tribes.

The first Indian involvement in the war occurred in 1776 on the Virginia–North Carolina frontier when the Cherokee, counting on English help in removing the white intruders from the Watauga and Nolichuckey valleys, plunged the frontier into conflict; the result was an overwhelming defeat of the Cherokee, the purging of the area of Tories, and the cession of the lands in question in the Treaty of Long Island of Holston on July 2, 1777.

In the North the failure of the Canadian invasion started the conversion of northern tribes to the British. First the Mingo, in 1776, sought to nip the Kentucky settlement in the bud. In 1777 a Mohawk, Joseph Brant, led the Iroquois (except the Oneida and Tuscarora) in cooperating in the Burgoyne–St. Leger campaign, and terrorized the frontier until they were silenced by the Clinton-Sullivan-Brodhead campaign in 1779. In 1777 the Shawnee went over to the British after the murder, by Virginia militia, of Chief Cornstalk. In 1778 British supplies brought over the Wyandot, Ottawa, Miami, and other Lake tribes. The Delaware went over to the British in 1781 after years of vain waiting for the American reoccupation of Fort Laurens, south of Lake Erie, and a campaign against Detroit. The war ended in the Old Northwest with the Indians confident that they had successfully defended their hunting grounds as the result of the victory of Blue Licks, Ky., and the defeat of the expedition of Col. William Crawford, both in 1782.

In the South, the Cherokee had resumed their attacks on the Americans in the fall of 1780, only to be crushed again in the Battle of Boyd's Creek. The Creek in general refrained from warfare until 1781 when they made a futile attempt to relieve the British forces at Savannah.

Early Federal Policy. Before the War of 1812, U.S. Indian policy had two principal objectives: to keep Indians pacified and to gain control of Indian trade. Both the British and the French tried to incite the Indians against the Americans and to persuade the Indians to trade furs and other items to them rather than to the Americans. When Congress established the War Department in 1789, it made the new department responsible for administering Indian affairs. Between 1798 and 1822 the department operated trading houses where Indians were guaranteed fair prices for the goods they had to sell and those they wished to buy (*see* Factory System, Indian). The first federal official within the department to have primary responsibilities in Indian administration was the superintendent of Indian trade, whose office was established in 1806. Indian trade fell increasingly into the hands of private citizens after 1820, and the Office of the Superintendent of Indian Trade was eliminated two years later.

Land Cessions and Treaties. When the United States came into existence, it was held that the ultimate title to the soil resided in the federal government, although the Indians had a right to the use and occupancy of the lands they claimed that could be extinguished only by their consent. Negotiations for Indian land cessions were to be conducted only by agents of the federal government except in certain cases in which the original states were permitted to act. A proclamation of Sept. 22, 1783, prohibited any person from "purchasing or receiving any gift or cession of such lands or claim without the express authority and direction of the United States in Congress assembled."

For nearly a century after the founding of the United States, Indian land cessions were accomplished by means of treaties couched in the formal language of an international covenant. These treaties were negotiated with Indian chieftains and leaders by appointees of the executive branch of the federal government, signed by both parties, and ratified by the U.S. Senate. In 1871 the fiction of regarding the Indian tribes as independent nations was abandoned, and thereafter simple agreements were made with them. This change of practice seems to have been dictated mainly by the determination of the House of Representatives to have a voice in the making of commitments entailing appropriations of money, for the agreements required the approval of both houses of Congress.

The first treaty made by the United States with any Indian tribe was that made with the Delaware in 1778; the first Indian land cession to the new nation was that made by the Six Nations, or Iroquois, by the second Treaty of Fort Stanwix (1784) by which land in northwestern Pennsylvania and in the extreme western part of New York was ceded. The following are brief summaries of selections from the long list of Indian land cessions made between 1784 and 1871:

Treaty of Hopewell, 1785, with the Cherokee, ceding land in North Carolina west of the Blue Ridge and in Tennessee and Kentucky south of the Cumberland River.

Treaty of New York City, 1790, with the Creek, ceding a large tract in eastern Georgia (*see* McGillivray Incident).

Treaty of the Holston River, 1791, with the Cherokee, ceding land in western North Carolina and northeastern Tennessee.

Treaty of Greenville, 1795, with the Wyandot, Delaware, Shawnee, Ottawa, Chippewa, Potawatomi, Miami, Eel River, Wea, Kickapoo, Piankashaw, and Kaskaskia, ceding large areas in southern and eastern Ohio comprising nearly two-thirds of the present state, some land in southeastern Indiana, and small tracts around Michilimackinac in Michigan.

Treaty of Tellico, 1798, with the Cherokee, ceding three tracts of land, most of it in eastern Tennessee.

Treaty of Buffalo Creek, 1802, with the Seneca, ceding lands in western New York involved in the purchase of the Holland Land Company (an unusual treaty in that the land was ceded directly to the company).

Treaty of Vincennes, 1803, with the Kaskaskia, ceding a large area in central and southeastern Illinois comprising about half the present state—other tribes ceding their claims to this area in the Treaties of Edwardsville, 1818 and 1819.

Treaty of Fort Clark, 1808, with the Osage, ceding land between the Arkansas and Missouri rivers, comprising nearly one-half of Arkansas and two-thirds of Missouri.

Treaty of Fort Jackson, 1814, with the Creek, ceding large areas of southern Georgia and central and southern Alabama.

Treaty of St. Louis, 1816, with the Ottawa, Chippewa, and Potawatomi, ceding land between the Illinois and Mississippi in Illinois and in southwestern Wisconsin.

Treaty of Old Town, 1818, with the Chickasaw, ceding land between the Tennessee and Mississippi rivers in Tennessee and Kentucky.

Treaty of Saginaw, 1819, with the Chippewa, ceding a large area surrounding Saginaw Bay and numerous other scattered tracts in the present state of Michigan.

Treaty of Doak's Stand, 1820, with the Choctaw, ceding land in west-central Mississippi.

Treaty of Chicago, 1821, with the Ottawa, Chippewa, and Potawatomi, ceding land in southern Michigan and northern Indiana.

Treaties of St. Louis, 1823, with the Osage and Kansa, ceding extensive areas of land in the present states of Missouri, Kansas, and Oklahoma.

Treaty of Prairie du Chien, 1830, with the Sauk and Fox, Sioux, and other tribes, ceding land in western Iowa, southwestern Minnesota, and northwestern Missouri.

Treaty of Fort Armstrong, 1832, with the Sauk and Fox, ceding a 50-mile strip of land along the west bank of the Mississippi in Iowa (known as the Black Hawk Purchase).

Treaty of Sauk and Fox Agency, 1842, with the Sauk and Fox, ceding all of south-central Iowa.

Treaty of Traverse des Sioux, 1851, with the Sisseton and Wahpeton bands of the Sioux, ceding claims to lands in southern Minnesota, comprising more than one-third of the present state, and in northern Iowa.

Treaty of Fort Laramie, 1851, with the Sioux, Cheyenne, Arapaho, and other tribes, ceding land in North Dakota, Montana, and Wyoming (the provisions being altered by the Senate and never ratified by the Indians).

Treaty of Table Rock, 1853, with the Rogue River Indians, ceding land in southern Oregon.

Groups of treaties were negotiated in the light of particular national developments. In 1854, in order to make way for the organization of Kansas and Nebraska territories, there were a number of treaties in which land was ceded by Indian tribes that, for the most part, had been located along the eastern border of the Indian Country. After the discovery of gold in California the center of interest shifted to the region of the Great Plains; in 1861, for instance, the Arapaho and Cheyenne ceded their claims to enormous tracts of land in the present states of Nebraska, Kansas, Colorado, and Wyoming. Before the end of the 1860's the old Indian Country on the Great Plains was reduced to the area known as the Indian Territory. During the same period the extinguishment of Indian titles was proceeding rapidly from the Rocky Mountain region to the Pacific coast. By 1871 there was complete federal control of the land from coast to coast.

Many of these treaties came at the close of wars: for example, the Treaty of Greenville in 1795, at the conclusion of Gen. Anthony Wayne's campaign in the Old Northwest; the

Treaty of Fort Jackson (1814) following Gen. Andrew Jackson's military activities in the Old Southwest; the Treaty of Fort Armstrong (1832) at the end of the Black Hawk War; and the numerous treaties concluding the Indian wars on the Plains after the Civil War (*see* Indian Commissions). Many other treaties were negotiated because of the pressure of westward movement or because the government had plans it wished to carry out: for example, the Treaty of Fort Wayne (1809) made by William Henry Harrison; the scores of treaties with both eastern tribes and the Indians of the Plains when the federal government's Indian removal policy was being carried into effect following the passage of the Indian Removal Act of 1830; the treaties that marked the abandonment of this policy in the early 1850's; and the Treaty of Fort Atkinson (1853) in which various Plains tribes agreed to permit roads and military posts within their territories.

Compensation to the Indians for the land ceded by them consisted of livestock, various kinds of merchandise (often including guns and ammunition), and annuities. A government report of 1883 indicates that up to 1880 the federal government had expended more than $187 million for the extinguishment of Indian land titles.

Removal Policy. The predominant theme in U.S. government Indian policy between the War of 1812 and the middle of the 19th century was that of transferring to lands in the West all those Indians east of the Mississippi River who wished to continue their tribal status, the so-called removal program. The seeds of a removal program were sown in the series of negotiations with southeastern tribes that began with the first Treaty of Hopewell in 1785. In 1802 when Georgia was asked to cede the lands from which the states of Alabama and Mississippi were later created, its officials insisted that, in return, the federal government promise to "peaceably obtain, on reasonable terms," the Indian title to all lands inside the state. In 1804 Congress enacted legislation authorizing the president to work out an exchange of eastern lands for those in the West. By 1809 substantial opposition to removal had developed among the eastern tribes, motivated in part by the experiences of Cherokee, Delaware, and Shawnee who had voluntarily gone westward in the years between 1785 and 1800.

Successful conclusion of the War of 1812 was followed by renewed interest in Indian removal, which became a basic item in a majority of the Indian treaties negotiated thereafter. In 1817 John C. Calhoun, secretary of the War Department in President James Monroe's cabinet, joined forces with war hero Gen. Andrew Jackson and Lewis Cass, governor of Michigan Territory, in urging formal adoption of a removal policy. The first major removal treaty was that signed by the Delaware in 1818; others soon followed. Monroe gave his full support to a removal policy in January 1825 as the only means of solving "the Indian problem." Immediately thereafter, Calhoun issued a report calling for the resettlement of nearly 100,000 eastern Indians. Jackson entered the White House in January 1829 and quickly let it be known that he would espouse a national policy of Indian removal. The following year Congress passed the national Indian Removal Act, which authorized the president to set up districts within the so-called Indian Territory for the reception of tribes agreeing to land exchanges. The act also provided for payment of indemnities to the Indians, for assistance in accomplishing their resettlement, for protection in their new locations, and for a continuance of the "superintendency and care" previously accorded them. The sum of $500,000 was authorized to carry out the act. Treaty negotiators set to work both east and west of the Mississippi to secure the permission of the indigenous tribes in Indian Territory who were being asked to accept strangers onto their lands and to obtain the approval of those tribes to be removed. The Shawnee gave up their lands in Ohio in 1831 in exchange for 100,000 acres in the Indian Territory. In the same year, the Ottawa ceded Ohio lands for a promise of 30,000 acres on the Kansas River. The Wyandot sold their Ohio acreage in 1832, thus effectively ending Indian settlement in that state. Illinois and Indiana were similarly cleared of Indians in the early 1830's. The remaining Kickapoo of Illinois, under the prophet Kanakuk, held out until 1832, when they agreed peacefully to relocate to lands in Kansas. Among the other tribes moved at that time were the Chippewa, who were pushed into Wisconsin and Minnesota; the Sauk and Fox, Winnebago and Potawatomi, who were resettled in what is now Iowa; and the Ottawa, Kaskaskia, Peoria, Miami, and some New York Indians, all of whom were assigned tracts in the Indian Territory along the western border of Missouri. The greatest resistance to removal came from the Indians of the Southeast; even the small Seminole tribe chose to fight rather than consent to removal. The most tragic story, however, is that of the Cherokee (*see* Trail of Tears). By 1850 the period of Indian removal was essentially over. The 1850's and 1860's saw the holdings of the relocated Indians further reduced as new states were created out of the lands that had once been regarded as permanently set aside for Indian occupancy.

By no means all the Indians east of the Mississippi River moved westward. Small pockets remained in many eastern states. Among the Indians escaping removal was a small band of several hundred fugitive Cherokee who fled to the mountains on the border between North Carolina and Tennessee; in 1842 they received federal permission to remain on lands set apart for their use in western North Carolina. These lands make up the Qualla Reservation, one of the largest Indian areas under federal supervision in the eastern United States.

By 1850 the federal government had concluded 245 separate Indian treaties, by means of which it had acquired more than 450 million acres of Indian land at a total estimated cost of $90 million. As the Civil War neared, new features of Indian policy were developed. Important among them was land allotment. The treaty of 1854 with the Omaha contained the first comprehensive provision for the division of Indian land into individual holdings and provided a model both for other treaties and for the general allotment act that followed thirty-three years later.

Indians in the Civil War. Indian Territory lay between Arkansas and Texas, and there, under authority of the Removal Act of 1830, lived the great tribes of the South (*see*

Five Civilized Tribes), the more influential of whom were slaveholders. The five tribes, distrusting both the federal government and the individual southern states, would have preferred remaining neutral, but Union troops were early withdrawn from the frontier posts and the Indians were exposed to southern influence without hindrance. In May 1861, Confederate agents appeared to negotiate treaties of amity and alliance. They began with the Cherokee, who held out for neutrality until August. The other tribes yielded more readily; but some groups persisted in adherence to the Union. Creek loyalists were among the most stubborn. They prepared to withstand coercion by resort to arms, but soon fled northward to Kansas. Meanwhile a group of Indians led by Confederate Gen. Albert Pike had participated in the Battle of Pea Ridge. Afterward Pike labored to have the Indian regiments restricted to the home-guard duty, for which they were originally intended, but he only partially succeeded. Repeated Confederate defeats in Missouri and Arkansas had a calamitous effect on the Indian alliance, as did the Emancipation Proclamation and the Amnesty Proclamation. In 1863 the Cherokee, through their national council, nullified their alliance, other tribes later doing likewise. Before long organized Indian participation in the war had ceased altogether.

Assimilation Policy. The major thrust of federal policy following the Civil War was toward subduing the still-hostile western tribes and placing their members on reservations. Congress, in an 1871 appropriations bill, decreed that the federal government would not enter into any further treaties with Indian tribes. In the 1870's many missionary groups began to advocate policies aimed at Indian assimilation. Foremost among these was land allotment designed to break up the communal holdings of each tribe and distribute the land among its members. Many serious-minded persons were convinced that an allotment program would make yeoman farmers of the Indians, thereby placing them on the road to assimilation. In 1887 the Dawes General Allotment Act was passed, providing for the breakup of the reservations. Another element of the forced assimilation policy prevailing after the 1880's was the off-reservation boarding school. It was widely believed that if Indian youngsters could be educated in the ways of the white men, the Indian "problem" would be solved.

Education Policy. Following the revolutionary war the first Indian treaty to include an educational provision was that of 1794 with the Oneida, Tuscarora, and Stockbridge. An 1803 treaty with the Kaskaskia authorized the hiring of a Catholic priest to teach literature. Provisions covering other aspects of education were included in many of the treaties negotiated thereafter. Congress in 1802 authorized the first federal appropriation for "civilizing" the Indians—an amount not to exceed $15,000 per year. Seventeen years later it enacted the law that remains the legal basis for most of the education program of the Bureau of Indian Affairs. The act provided that the president of the United States might employ "capable persons of good moral character" to instruct Indians, and provided for an annual appropriation of $10,000 for introducing among the Indians "the habits and arts of civilization." By midcentury there were more than 100 schools financed in part from the "civilization fund," all operated by religious organizations. The Five Civilized Tribes began administering their own schools following their removal to Oklahoma between 1831 and 1848 and did so until the early 20th century.

Religious influence in Indian education waned after 1870, when the federal government undertook to operate, as well as finance, Indian schools. The first federal boarding school for Indians was established in 1879 at Carlisle, Pa. In the 1890's the Bureau of Indian Affairs began contracting with local public school districts for educating Indian youngsters, and Congress outlawed as contrary to federal policy the payment of subsidies to sectarian schools.

An important study of Indian education was undertaken by the Institute for Government Research in 1926: the Meriam Report recommended the establishment of more schools that the Indians could attend on a daily basis and a corresponding reduction in the use of off-reservation boarding schools. The Johnson-O'Malley Act of 1934 provided that monies appropriated by Congress for Indian education could be turned over to states, territories, and their political subdivisions as well as to certain other public and private agencies. By the 1970's the public school had become the principal vehicle for Indian education, accounting for the enrollment of nearly two-thirds of all school-age Indian youngsters.

Since 1968 the government has encouraged a new direction in the administration of education programs for Indians in federally operated schools: the placement of responsibility and authority in the hands of local Indian communities with continuing financial subsidies provided by the federal government. Indian school boards have been established for these federal schools, including the off-reservation boarding schools, and in a few instances tribes or local communities have assumed full responsibility for school administration. The Bureau of Indian Affairs receives annual appropriations for the administration of college scholarships, and since 1956 it has operated an extensive program of adult vocational training. The respective allocations for these programs in 1974–75 were about $32 million and $19 million.

Citizenship Policy. Some early Indian treaties, such as that of 1830 with the Choctaw, provided for grants of citizenship to individual Indians. The Kickapoo Treaty of 1862 made citizenship dependent upon acceptance of an allotment of land in severalty. Other treaties of the Civil War period required submission of evidence of fitness for citizenship and empowered an administrative body or official to determine whether the Indian applicant conformed to the standards called for in the treaties.

Following ratification of the Fourteenth Amendment in 1868 several Indian naturalization acts were passed by Congress, most of them similar to an 1870 law relating to the Winnebago of Minnesota which provided that an Indian might apply to the federal district court for citizenship but must prove to the satisfaction of the court that he was sufficiently intelligent and prudent to manage his own affairs, that he had adopted the habits of civilized life, and that he had supported himself and his family for the preceding five years.

The Dawes General Allotment Act (1887) gave citizenship to Indians born within the United States who had received allotments as well as to those who had voluntarily moved away from their tribes and adopted "the habits of civilized life." The following year Congress extended citizenship to Indian women marrying persons who were already U.S. citizens. Approximately two-thirds of the Indians of the United States had become citizens by 1924; in that year Congress passed a general Indian citizenship act, as a result of which all native-born Indians came to enjoy full citizenship status.

Twentieth-Century Policy. The 1920's were years of confusion as new policy proposals were made and considered. The Meriam Report of 1928 recommended the abandonment of the allotment program, the continuance of federal trusteeship over lands already allotted, and the construction of schools near the homes of Indian youngsters. These recommendations and others from the report were incorporated by Commissioner John Collier into the Indian Reorganization Act of 1934. The act also provided for the establishment of democratic local government on the reservations, and established the policy of Indian preference with respect to employment in the Bureau of Indian Affairs. The Indian Claims Act of 1946 made it possible for tribes to bring suit against the U.S. government before a special tribunal known as the Indian Claims Commission, whereas previously Indians had been able to sue the government in the Court of Claims only through special acts of Congress.

The dominant policy theme during much of the 1950's was that of withdrawing special federal services from Indians and elevating them to a status of equality with other citizens. The institution of this policy, known to the Indians as "termination," produced protest from nearly all the reservations, and Indian defense organizations united in their effort to have it overturned; it ceased to be a major policy thrust after about 1958. Beginning in the 1960's and continuing throughout the early 1970's, the principal trend was toward placement of administrative responsibility for reservation services in the hands of Indians, while the federal government continued to finance these services. Special legislation to permit the Bureau of Indian Affairs to contract with Indian tribes and make grants to them was passed by Congress in January 1975.

INDIAN QUEEN. A tavern on the east side of Fourth Street above Chestnut, one of the noted hostelries of 18th-century Philadelphia, which served as headquarters for many congressmen when Philadelphia was the capital of the United States. It was destroyed in 1851.

INDIAN RESERVATIONS. The word "reservation" has been loosely employed to designate any land area set aside for Indian use and occupancy; it has no particular legal meaning, although it appears often in federal statutes. Although some states have created small reservations, the vast majority of such areas are under the supervision of the U.S. Bureau of Indian Affairs, which administers more than 400 discrete Indian land units. The types of reservations under federal supervision are those created by treaty or acts of Congress before 1871; those created by acts of Congress after 1871; and those brought into being through executive orders setting public lands apart for Indian use. Depending on the manner in which they were established, reservations may be inhabited by a single tribe, or several tribes. The Indian Reorganization Act of 1934 provided legal authority for the residents of a single reservation, regardless of how many tribes they might represent, to establish a unified local government.

Although the lands of some reservations, especially those in the Southwest, are still held in common ownership, it is more usual for reservations to be a combination of tribally and individually owned lands. In the latter instance, the federal government, through the Bureau of Indian Affairs, is the trustee for both tribal and individual owners and enforces restrictions against mortgage and sale. In some areas of the United States, notably the Great Plains and the Pacific Northwest, much land inside the original boundaries of reservations was acquired by non-Indians prior to passage of the Indian Reorganization Act. A confusing combination of state, tribal, and federal jurisdiction prevails within the boundaries of such reservations.

INDIAN SPRINGS, TREATIES OF (1821, 1825). By the treaty of 1821 the Creek ceded to the United States a large tract of land east of the Flint and Chattahoochee rivers, in exchange for $200,000 and the assumption of $250,000 worth of claims. In the treaty of 1825 they agreed to migrate west of the Mississippi and ceded all their lands in Georgia, together with a large tract lying west of that state; they were to receive an equal number of acres west of the Mississippi and the sum of $400,000. This second treaty caused such widespread disagreement among the Creek that the United States rendered it null and void in the Treaty of Washington, 1826, in which the Creek ceded all their land east of the Chattahoochee and a considerable area west of that river.

INDIAN STREAM REPUBLIC. Since the international boundary around the sources of the Connecticut River, in the extreme northerly part of New Hampshire, was uncertain, the settlers based their land titles on a purchase from the native Indians in 1796 and established their own government, admitting little control by New Hampshire. A constitution was adopted in 1832, and legislatures met in 1833, 1834, and 1835. The claim of independence, or, failing that, of belonging to the United States, but not to New Hampshire, was rejected by both state and federal governments. This caused many to wish to join Canada; bad feeling and violence resulted. In April 1836 the people voted to join New Hampshire and were incorporated as the town of Pittsburg in 1840. The Webster-Ashburton Treaty of 1842 settled the boundary.

INDIAN TERRITORY. This originally included all the present state of Oklahoma except the panhandle; it was never an organized territory, but was set aside as a home for the Five Civilized Tribes, who were removed to it in the period 1820–42. In 1866 they ceded the western part to the United States as a home for other tribes. The reduced land of the Five Civilized Tribes, then called Indian Territory, was occupied by more than 75,000 Indians. Lands were held in common, and each tribe had its own government.

INDIAN TRADE AND INTERCOURSE ACT (1834). Before 1834 the policy of the federal government in removing Indians from areas in which frontiersmen were settling to new areas was not supplemented by any guarantees that their new homes would be reserved to them against future inroads by whites. This act and subsequent treaties with various tribes set aside a permanent Indian Country. White settlers were rigidly excluded from it; trading was permitted only under federal license; and other safeguards were established to protect the Indians from white men's exploitation or interference. The guarantees remained in effect only so long as whites were not interested in the territory (*see* Indian Country).

INDIAN TRADE AND TRADERS. When explorers and settlers arrived in America they found vast potential wealth in furs and skins awaiting exploitation. The beaver was the most important fur-bearing animal, and often the term "beaver trade" was used as synonymous with "Indian trade" in general; in southern latitudes the trade was mainly in coarse skins and hides, such as those of the deer, bear, and buffalo. (*See also* Fur Trade.) As the Indian was drawn into the orbit of European commerce, his manner of living and hunting was altered, and he became increasingly dependent on European goods. The Indian trade was at first carried on by settlers or small merchants, but conditions soon demanded new methods and forms of organization. Trade was based largely on credit and required a considerable capital outlay; complex problems of marketing and transportation called for more efficient business methods. The small firms and partnerships formed at important trade centers often gave way to large companies that were monopolistic in nature. Commission houses were established at such centers as Montreal, New York, Philadelphia, Charleston, and St. Louis; sometimes these commission merchants established companies that directly managed the business in all its stages, from the wilderness hut to the European market.

A complete roster of the fur trade would include hundreds of persons, from whom the following were selected more or less at random. Pierre Esprit Radisson and Médart Chouart, Sieur de Groseilliers, penetrated the Great Lakes region in the late 1650's; later came Alexander Henry, John Long, Peter Pond, Robert Dickson, John Askin, John Jacob Astor, and Ramsay Crooks. The merchants of Montreal included Isaac Todd, James McGill, Simon McTavish, and Benjamin and Joseph Frobisher. George Croghan and William Trent operated in the Ohio Valley, while the name of the Chouteau family is associated with the trade based upon St. Louis, Mo., founded by René Auguste Chouteau and Pierre Laclède in 1764. A great many of these attained prominence in fields other than the fur trade.

INDIAN TRIBAL COURTS. Created in the late 19th century by an order of the Office of Indian Affairs and consisting usually of one, two, or three Indian judges, they are held on various reservations with populations over 200–300 to try minor cases in which the parties are Indians; they are sometimes called courts of Indian offenses. Judges are appointed by the superintendent of the reservation; with the assistance of the superintendent they make their own rules of procedure and evidence. Decisions must be approved by the superintendent before going into effect.

INDIES, COMPANY OF THE. *See* **Mississippi Bubble.**

INDIGO CULTURE. Introduced into South Carolina at the inception of that colony; shown by Eliza Lucas in 1744 to be practical with slave labor. Neighboring planters promptly adopted her idea as a supplement to the cultivation of rice. Stability was given to the industry by the granting (1748) by the British government of a bounty of sixpence a pound on indigo shipped to England. For some thirty years indigo, after rice, was the colony's most important crop; on the eve of the American Revolution more than a million pounds were exported annually. Production then declined rapidly.

INDUSTRIAL BROTHERHOOD (1868). At first, a purely fraternal order. At the 1874 convention of the Industrial Congress called by the trade unions, the brotherhood agreed to fuse its organization with the congress and contribute its name and ritual (other organizations at the convention were the Patrons of Husbandry and Sovereigns of Industry). An attempt was made to organize the brotherhood by states, but the depression of the 1870's caused loss of strength and eventual absorption in other labor organizations.

INDUSTRIAL EDUCATION. *See* **Education.**

INDUSTRIAL MANAGEMENT. In the early decades of the 20th century the term "industrial management" was used interchangeably with "scientific management," as exemplified in the work of Frederick W. Taylor (*see* Scientific Management). The establishment of schools of industrial management at the Massachusetts Institute of Technology and elsewhere is indicative of the wide acceptance of the term. Many participants in the study and practice of business administration gradually found that they could achieve satisfactory mastery of the body of available data only through specialization. They concentrated their attention on personnel management, financial management, or some other specialty. By the 1940's "industrial management" had come to mean primarily "factory management." By the 1970's the use of the term "industrial management" was becoming less common. Systems analysis was being applied to the field, and pertinent courses in schools of business administration were beginning to be taught under the rubric "production" or "production and operations management." At the same time, schools retaining industrial management courses were incorporating in their classes the latest research on finance, human behavior in organizations, and marketing as well as on planning, coordination, and control.

INDUSTRIAL RELATIONS. Also known as personnel management, human resources management, and employer-employee relations, its functional area includes the recruitment of the work force; the matching of the job and the man, including the analysis and classification of the job into the pay hierarchy; the evaluation of the performance on the job; the designing of a system of rewards for satisfactory performance and penalties for substandard performance; the training program for required manpower; the designing of safety programs to avoid occupation accidents; the designing of communications systems between subordinates and superiors; and the institutionalization of auxiliary benefits, including medical and dental care, old-age pensions, and casualty insurance. Finally, it must subordinate all these functions to a system of due process known as collective bargaining.

The personnel movement is traceable to Robert Owen, the British textile-mill owner and utopian Socialist who discovered that productivity could be increased if workers were treated with dignity. He influenced men like Ordway Tead, who promoted the organization of personnel departments in corporations during the second decade of the 20th century. In the 1920's management associations promoted the use of personnel departments as substitutes for unions.

Industrial psychologists have contributed techniques for the selection of workers to fit the various jobs; work sociologists have contributed detailed studies of the appropriate organization structures into which workers should be fitted to work most effectively; industrial engineers have contributed the technique of motion-and-time study to standardize and measure performance. All of the techniques have been challenged at one time or another and contribute to worker grievances. (*See also* Collective Bargaining.)

INDUSTRIAL RESEARCH. In the mid-17th century, John Winthrop, Jr., applied the scientific knowledge of his day to the establishment of iron and salt manufacturing in New England and conducted experiments on the preparation of indigo that have been called "the first industrial research within the present borders of the United States." Later in the colonial era the American Philosophical Society promoted scientific investigations in distilling, brewing, ore assaying, and "all new arts, trades, and manufactures, that may be proposed or thought of." Such studies continued in the early national period, particularly by Philadelphia chemists including James Woodhouse, who studied the production of starch and the reaction of metals to acids; Robert Hare, inventor of the oxyhydrogen blowpipe and various improvements in illumination; and John Harrison, pioneer American manufacturer of sulfuric acid. An outstanding industrial scientist of the antebellum era was Samuel L. Dana, who served as chemist for the Merrimack Manufacturing Company at Lowell, Mass. (1834–68), developing the "American system of bleaching" and improvements in dyeing and calico printing.

Not until the late 19th century did the value of industrial research become widely apparent to business leaders. A typical industrial scientist of the period was Charles Benjamin Dudley, who conducted studies for the Pennsylvania Railroad on the composition of rails and establishing standards and specifications for the mechanical equipment used by that firm. In 1898, Dudley helped found the American Society for Testing Materials; three years later Congress responded to growing business pressure by establishing the U.S. Bureau of Standards, which assisted manufacturers in devising uniform specifications for products and processes.

By the 20th century entrepreneurs were increasingly aware that the application of science could be used for profitable innovation and product development. Herman Frasch helped demonstrate this principle by devising a process that made it possible for the Standard Oil Company to utilize sulfurous petroleum deposits. Further illustrations were provided by the development in the 1890's by Edward G. Acheson of carborundum (silicon carbide), a valuable abrasive; and the invention by Leo Baekeland of an extremely useful synthetic plastic, the phenol-formaldehyde resin known as Bakelite. Acheson worked for the company that Thomas A. Edison had founded in the 1870's for the primary purpose of conducting industrial research. Even more exclusively concerned with research was the company founded by Arthur D. Little in 1886. These firms inspired large manufacturing firms to establish research laboratories, particularly in the electrical industry. In 1900, General Electric founded the first large American industrial research laboratory at Schenectady, N.Y.; in 1902 the Du Pont Company established an explosives laboratory at Gibbstown, N.J., followed later by an "experimental station" at Wilmington, Del.; the Eastman Kodak Company set up an energetic research program at Rochester, N.Y.; in 1907 the American Telephone and Telegraph Company established a laboratory that ultimately became the largest of its type in the country.

Industrial research in America gained maturity during the 1920's. The automobile industry became heavily committed to applied science as General Motors launched a varied research program under Charles F. Kettering. The growing scale and capital requirements of successful innovation led increasingly to cooperative ventures. The depression of the 1930's stimulated some companies to push such cost-cutting innovations as the continuous casting of aluminum and the development of diesel traction for locomotives. The federal government became increasingly concerned about the concentration of research capability in the hands of a relatively few large corporations. A Works Projects Administration survey issued late in the decade showed that about half the nation's industrial scientists were employed by only forty-five companies.

World War II provided an awesome example of the potential of scientific research and development when the federal government, in concert with such industrial giants as Du Pont, produced the atomic bomb through the Manhattan Project. The tendency toward bigness and concentration became pronounced in the postwar era as the scope of industrial research grew ever larger; it was buttressed by increasing federal involvement, manifested in massive federal financial investment in research and in the government's cooperation with business in applying science to peacetime and war-related goals. By 1981 American industry was spending nearly $34 billion on research and development—matched by about the same amount in government funds. The continuing connection between government and industrial research was highlighted by the cooperation of the Atomic Energy Commission and electrical companies in producing nuclear power and by the partnership of the National Aeronautics and Space Administration and the Bell Telephone Company in launching and operating communications satellites.

INDUSTRIAL REVOLUTION. The period during which mechanical devices were generally substituted for human skills and inanimate power or energy was substituted for animate power, with consequent changes in transportation and the use of raw materials; some scholars apply the term only to the initial development of steam-powered iron or steel machinery, and others to the whole process of industrial growth that is still continuing. In America it is popularly confined to the time when the economy was based on coal, steam, and iron, a period that began after the War of 1812 and reached its apogee around 1900, to be superseded by a stage, sometimes called the "second industrial revolution," when more oil, electricity, and automotive power were used.

INDUSTRIAL WORKERS OF THE WORLD (IWW). A radical labor organization founded in Chicago in June 1905 as an alternative to the more moderate and exclusive American Federation of Labor. From 1909 to 1918 it achieved success and notoriety as the most militant and dangerous institution on the American Left. The IWW appealed to all workers regardless of skill, nationality, race, or sex; it sought to organize them into vast industrial unions that would use direct economic action to seize control of industry and abolish capitalism. At its peak in 1917 the IWW had no more than 150,000 members (often called Wobblies), but more than 3 million workers had passed through its ranks and many more had come under its influence. During World War I, federal and state governments convicted over 200 IWW officials on sedition and espionage charges. The IWW survives today as a skeletal organization on the fringes of U.S. radicalism. It had forty-two local groups in 1980.

INDUSTRIES, COLONIAL. During the colonial period most people engaged in agriculture, which was greatly diversified in the North, while tobacco was of extreme importance in the South. Naval stores, including tar, pitch, rosin, and turpentine, the products of pine forests, as well as masts and spars, were exported from all sections of the seaboard, especially from the southern colonies; planks, boards, shingles, barrel staves, and even house frames were produced at sawmills and exported to the West Indies and elsewhere. Potash and pearl ash, incidental to the clearing of land, being made from wood ashes, were in demand, especially in England, for bleaching and soapmaking.

Boston, Salem, New Haven, Portsmouth, and Philadelphia became shipbuilding centers. Shipbuilding created or stimulated many other industries, such as the making of sails, rope, nails, spikes, anchors, and chain-plates, and caulking and painting. In New England fishing for cod, mackerel, bass, herring, halibut, hake, sturgeon, and other ocean fish at the banks developed into a leading industry, as did whaling. By the close of the 17th century, Plymouth, Salem, and Nantucket, Mass., and villages on the eastern end of Long Island were doing a profitable business in spermaceti, sperm oil, whalebone, and ambergris. After the opening of the 18th century whaling expanded to a remarkable extent, whalers often pursuing their prey to Arctic waters.

The production of textiles was largely a household industry; almost every home had its spinning wheel and hand loom to produce rough serges and linsey-woolseys. Before the Revolution a few shops were established in New England and in other places where several looms were brought together under one roof. Other home manufactures were furniture, tools and other implements, wagons, harnesses, and nails.

Ironmaking reached large proportions; the basic mining and smelting processes were generally conducted on plantations or large estates where fuel for the ironworks and food for the workers could be obtained. Among other industrial enterprises were tanneries and leatherworking establishments, fulling mills, gristmills, powder mills, saltworks, paper mills, printing shops, glassworks, brick kilns, firearms shops, copper shops, breweries, and distilleries. (*See also* Fishing and Fisheries; Fur Trade; Iron and Steel Industry; Textiles; Whaling.)

INDUSTRY. *See* **Manufacturing** *and specific industries.*

INDUSTRY, FORT (Ohio). At the mouth of the Maumee River, on the site of present-day Toledo; scene of a treaty (July 4, 1805) whereby the leading Indian tribes of the Ohio-Indiana-Michigan area ceded to the United States 2,726,812 acres, constituting that part of the Western Reserve lying west of the Cuyahoga River and a section immediately south of it extending to the Greenville Treaty line.

INFLATION. A rapid rise in the price of commodities and services. According to traditional analysis, such price rises are caused by an increase in the quantity of money that is not paralleled by a corresponding increase in the quantity of goods and services coming on the market. The 1950's produced a new analysis of inflation, the "wage-cost push" theory, according to which higher money wages in excess of increased labor productivity engender higher operating costs and thus force producers to raise their selling prices to consumers. Inflation resulting from the wage-cost push is of the creeping variety; that is, it consists of relatively small, but regular, increases in the price level extending over a long period, as opposed to the more violent type of inflation that has occurred chiefly as a result of war and its aftermath.

Prior to the Revolution, inflation occurred in many of the colonies where bills of credit were issued by the government and made legal tender. With the outbreak of the revolutionary war, bills of credit were put into circulation on a large scale by both the states and the Continental Congress. By January 1781, this currency was valued at 100 to 1 in relation to specie, and by May it had lost its value almost completely.

After the collapse of the Continental currency and the establishment of the Union, prices remained moderate until the War of 1812, when another inflation occurred, caused by the overissuance of bank notes. Prices peaked in 1814–15;

thereafter the price level receded sharply until 1821.

The next major inflation occurred during the Civil War: in order to help finance the war, Congress authorized three issues of greenbacks of $150 million each; the currency was thus inflated, and prices rose rapidly, reaching a peak in 1864–65. The price level dropped rapidly after 1865 until 1880. With the outbreak of World War I prices began to rise rapidly; the peak was reached in spring 1920, when the wholesale price index stood at 244 percent of the prewar level.

Because of the introduction of price, wage, and other direct controls in 1942, official price indexes during World War II rose only moderately (10 to 15 percent); with the removal of controls in mid-1946, the unleashing of monetary purchasing power built up during the war drove prices up again. They reached their highest level in fall 1948, rising to an inflationary peak approximately equaling that of World War I.

Beginning in the late 1950's the United States suffered from disturbingly high annual rates of inflation. After 1967 the Vietnam War and a series of extremely unbalanced federal budgets raised the annual rate of inflation above the "creeping" 2 percent level to an economically upsetting range above 5 percent. From 1971 to 1974 the administration of Richard Nixon entered into price control by administrative decrees and commissions. The Arab oil embargo of 1973–74 raised energy and petrochemical costs to heights that disrupted the entire price structure. The market forces set in motion by the energy squeeze produced both recession and an 11 percent inflation in 1974. In 1976 inflation dropped to 5.8 percent, but in 1977 a four-year increase of the inflation rate began: 6.5 in 1977, 7.7 in 1978, 11.3 in 1979, and 13.5 in 1980. President Ronald Reagan's extensive budget cuts and a prolonged economic recession resulted in a decrease in inflation to 10.4 percent in 1981.

INFLATION IN THE CONFEDERACY. An issue of $20 million of non-interest-bearing treasury notes was authorized on May 16, 1861, by the Confederate congress. The issuance of treasury notes was increased throughout the remainder of the year, there being $105 million in such notes outstanding at the end of 1861. Taxation was not resorted to on any great scale, and Confederate bonds found but a meager market; consequently, government expenses were met in large measure by the issuance of ever-increasing amounts of treasury notes. By the end of 1864 the amount of currency had risen to $1 billion, and the gold quotation was 40 for 1. The currency was in great confusion, complicated by state, city, and private issues of notes. Large quantities of notes were also issued by the banks, which had been freed from the compulsion to redeem notes in specie early in the war. Although the collapse of the currency came with the loss of the war, it would have occurred shortly in any event.

INFLUENZA. Commonly called the "flu," the first epidemic struck colonial America in 1647. Some form of respiratory disease reached major epidemic proportions in 1675, 1688, 1732–33, 1737, 1747–50, 1761, and 1789–91. The disease was widespread in Europe and America in 1830, 1837, and 1847; eased up for a long period; and then broke out on a worldwide scale 1889–93. In the summer of 1918, a deceptively mild wave swept through army camps in Europe and America and was immediately followed by the second and third waves of the greatest recorded pandemic of influenza in history. This pandemic is estimated to have killed 15 million individuals; approximately 28 percent of the U.S. population was attacked by the disease, and the death toll amounted to 450,000. Several outbreaks occurred in the 1920's, but the morbidity and mortality from influenza gradually declined in the succeeding years. The introduction of new therapeutics in the 1940's led to a steady drop in the overall influenza mortality rate until the outbreaks of Asiatic influenza in 1957, 1958, and 1960. The influenza death rate per 100,000 reached 4.4 in the latter year, the last time this figure exceeded 4. In three epidemic years since 1960 (1963, 1968, and 1969) the annual death rate for influenza was successively 3.8, 3.5, and 3.4 per 100,000. In 1933, the influenza virus now known as influenza virus A was identified, and subsequently other strains were recovered. Influenza vaccines had had only limited value by the mid-1970's.

INFORMATION AGENCY, U.S. (USIA). A government agency which has the task of presenting accurate information about the United States to foreigners. Its work ranges from setting up libraries in foreign cities, to operating the Voice of America radio system. Since 1948, the agency has been handling cultural exchange programs and the exchange of students and professors between the United States and foreign countries. In 1953 it was officially created as a separate government agency under the president. The USIA works in close cooperation with the State Department; the director of the agency also serves as an adviser to the president.

IN GOD WE TRUST. The motto that has appeared on most issues of U.S. coins since about 1864. Its use on the coins stems from the rise of religious sentiment during the Civil War; there is no law that requires it to be used.

INHERENT POWERS. As a general rule only those powers that are expressly conferred upon national agencies by the U.S. Constitution, or that may be reasonably inferred therefrom, can be exercised by the national government, but the Supreme Court has on a number of occasions asserted that the national government has other powers that arise out of its character as a sovereign state. These powers it has called "inherent." Specific examples include the power of the president to prohibit the sale of munitions to certain warring nations (*United States* v. *Curtiss-Wright Export Corporation,* 299 U.S. 304); the power to acquire territory by discovery and occupation (*Jones* v. *United States,* 137 U.S. 202); the power to expel undesirable aliens (*Fong Yue Ting* v. *United States,* 149 U.S. 698); and the power to make such international agreements as do not constitute treaties in the constitutional sense (*Altman and Company* v. *United States,* 224 U.S. 583).

INHERITANCE TAX LAWS. Two types of death duties are popularly called inheritance taxes; both in theory are taxes on the transfer of property at death rather than on the property itself. One, of which the prime example is the federal estate tax, is a tax based on the value of the entire net estate. The other, the inheritance tax of many states, is based on the value of the shares received by individual heirs, rates being progressive with respect to both the amount of the distributive share and the degree of relationship of the distributee to the deceased, the rate increasing as the relationship becomes more distant. The tax normally applies whether the transfer is by testate or intestate succession.

The federal government adopted an estate tax in 1916 that became a permanent part of the federal tax system. Prior to that, it had resorted to an inheritance tax on three occasions: 1797–1802, 1862–70, and 1898–1902; the acts of 1797 and 1898 being limited to personal property. The first really successful state act was the New York inheritance tax law of 1885. By 1902, twenty-six states had levied inheritance taxes of one kind or another; all states except Nevada ultimately adopted some form of death duty.

The federal estate tax was levied until 1976 on estates in excess of $60,000. The marital deduction on estates was raised in 1976 to $250,000, and a further liberalization in 1981 led to an increase of cumulative transfers exempt from estate and gift taxes from $175,625 in 1981 to $600,000 in 1987, when less than 1 percent of all estates would be taxed.

INITIATIVE. A process by which citizens, either directly or indirectly, propose legislation or constitutional amendments; it is operative only within the context of state or local government, there being no provision for the initiative at the federal level. Under the direct initiative, someone draws up a proposed bill or constitutional amendment and secures the signatures of a specified percentage of voters (usually about 10 percent) on a petition; the legislation thus initiated is placed on the ballot for a decision on its passage by the voters, a referendum. The indirect system provides that the legislation or amendment that is proposed must go to the legislature for decision; if it is not acted upon by that body within a specified time period, it is removed from the legislature and brought to a vote of the people. Under either system the legislation is usually declared to be passed if a majority of those who vote on the issue voted for the bill; however, some jurisdictions require that a majority of those who vote in the election vote for the bill. It is quite common to require an extraordinary majority, usually of two-thirds, for the approval of both constitutional amendments and bond issues.

INJUNCTIONS. Restraining court orders, which have played a major role in U.S. labor history. The use of the injunction began in the 1880's, but became prominent for the first time in the Pullman strike of 1894. Many labor injunctions were issued after 1890, 1920–30 showing the greatest number. Based upon the common-law doctrines of conspiracy and restraint of trade and coupled with a broad view by the courts of the "property" concept as applied to the employer's right to do business, the injunction embittered labor. Alleged abuses of the injunction included the lack of jury trial in contempt cases, the issuance of injunctions upon insufficient grounds, the blanket character of many injunctions, and the wide definition of "property" by the courts.

The Clayton Antitrust Act of 1914 was hailed by organized labor; it was believed that the act largely exempted unions from the antitrust laws, and that injunction procedure had been favorably modified. But later cases indicated that the injunction remained a rigorous antiunion weapon. The Norris–La Guardia Anti-injunction Act of 1932 imposed a number of restrictions upon the issuance of injunctions by federal courts, specified actions by unions that might not be enjoined, and limited the doctrine of restraint of trade as applied to labor disputes. A number of states subsequently enacted similar legislation. The Labor-Management Relations Act of 1947 (the Taft-Hartley Act), diminished the anti-injunction effectiveness of the Norris–La Guardia Act by making it possible for the federal courts to issue an injunction against a union if an actual or threatened strike endangered the nation's health or safety.

INLAND LOCK NAVIGATION. In 1792 the New York legislature granted charters to the Western Inland Lock Navigation Company to open water communication along the Mohawk River between the Hudson River and lakes Ontario and Seneca, and to the Northern Inland Lock Navigation Company to connect the Hudson with lakes George and Champlain (never accomplished). The Western company, by locks and short canals, opened a crude navigation between the Hudson and the lakes, but it never earned a profit and was eliminated by the completion of the Erie Canal (1825).

INLAND WATERWAYS COMMISSION. Appointed by President Theodore Roosevelt in 1907 to prepare "a comprehensive plan for the improvement and control" of U.S. river systems. In 1908 it submitted a bulky preliminary report urging that future plans for improvement of navigation take account of water purification, power development, flood control, and land reclamation. In 1909 the National Waterways Commission was created to carry on its work.

INNS. *See* **Taverns.**

INQUIRY. An organization set up by the federal government shortly after the United States entered World War I (1917) to conduct studies of the problems of peacemaking that would claim attention at the close of the war. When the American delegation sailed for France in December 1918, books, maps, memoranda, bibliographies, and statistical material accompanied it. A series of base maps of problem areas permitted daily preparation of maps in duplicate for all Allied commissions that required them. All delegations at Paris also made wide use of the so-called Black Book and Red Book, prepared by former members of the Inquiry; these were assemblages of proposed solutions—the Black Book of European problems mainly, the Red Book of colonial problems.

INQUISITION, SPANISH (or Holy Office). Informal, sporadic activity in the New World began as early as 1524; it was permanently established in Mexico City in 1571, its jurisdiction extending eventually from the Isthmus of Panama to the Spanish borderlands now within the United States. It was suppressed in 1813, restored for a while, and abolished in

1820. The tribunal took cognizance not only of heresy but also of blasphemy, perjury, forgery, bigamy, and piracy; and exercised an elaborate censorship of books. Non-Catholics and Indians were exempt. The penalties included fines, flogging, confiscation, and imprisonment; the death sentence was rare. The Inquisition was only slightly active in upper California and in Florida. In New Mexico, where Franciscans were officers of the Inquisition, some alcaldes and governors were charged with offenses. The Inquisition was never introduced into Spanish Louisiana.

INSANE, TREATMENT OF THE. *See* **Mental Hygiene Movement; Mental Illness, Treatment of.**

INSCRIPTION ROCK (or El Morro). A varicolored sandstone rising 200 feet out of a lava-strewn valley in Valencia County (N.Mex.), it derives its name from inscriptions carved by early Spanish and subsequent explorers; the name of Don Juan de Oñate, Apr. 16, 1606 (an error for 1605), is the earliest. It was created a national monument in 1906.

INSECTICIDES AND HERBICIDES. An insecticide is a chemical used to control or destroy unwanted insects. Insecticides are manufactured in five forms; wettable powders, emulsions, solutions, dusts, and aerosols; they are applied by means of hand equipment, ground machinery, and airplanes. The recommended use of arsenical compounds as insecticides dates from 1681, and they (primarily Paris green and London purple) became the main stomach poisons of chewing insects in the later 19th and early 20th centuries. Paris green, a coloring agent, was first used as an insecticide against the Colorado potato beetle in the 1880's. Farmers disinfected stored grain and controlled root lice with carbon bisulfide. California citrus growers in 1886 used hydrocyanic acid gas to fumigate trees. In 1880 lime-sulfur was employed against the San Jose scale, and in 1882 the grape phylloxera was controlled with napthalene. Kerosine and kerosine emulsions, with soap and milk, suffocated sucking insects: thrips, lice, and plant bugs. Pyrethrum, a contact insecticide nonpoisonous to humans, killed household insects. Lead arsenate, first used against the gypsy moth in New England forests in 1892, was used against the cotton boll weevil until the development of calcium arsenate in 1916. In 1906 the U.S. Department of Agriculture began using arsenical dips against the Texas fever-carrying cattle tick.

During World War II many new chlorinated hydrocarbon insecticides were produced, DDT being the most effective and widely used. The organic, contact insecticides (usually attacking the nervous system) proved more effective than the long-used inorganic internal arsenicals, which often scorched or proved toxic to plants. The chlorinated hydrocarbons also presented the problem of a transmittable residue, and the Environmental Protection Agency banned most uses of DDT in 1972. The organophosphorous insecticides generally circumvented the residue problem but were more toxic to man and animals during application. The U.S. Department of Agriculture also developed systemic insecticides to protect plants and animals; in 1958 ronnel became the first systemic insecticide ingested by cattle to kill the cattle grub.

In the 19th century several states enacted laws requiring farmers to control weeds. Along fencerows, roads, and wherever else it was desirable to kill all vegetation, farmers distributed herbicides, or weed killers, in the form of ashes and salt. During 1896–1910, scientists discovered that copper salts selectively killed broad-leaved weeds in cereal crops. Carbolic acid, caustic soda, arsenical compounds, and kerosine were other effective herbicides. The synthesizing of the growth regulant 2,4–D in 1941, and the proof of its efficacy as a selective herbicide in 1944, brought a new era in chemical weed control. Unlike the earlier contact herbicides, organic 2,4–D is a systemic growth regulant that is translocated throughout the plant, killing all parts. Its low cost, noncorrosive qualities, nontoxicity to man and animals, and selectivity make it ideal for agricultural uses. The number of systemic herbicides and temporary soil sterilants and their use have burgeoned: farmers spent $15 million treating 30 million acres in 1950 but $2,869 million treating 285 million acres in 1978. Research in the 1970's emphasized the use of biological (predators and parasites) and cultural (planting and cultivation) control methods.

INSECTS AND INSECT BLIGHTS. Many insect problems are raised by pests, such as moths or cockroaches, which attack human food or certain kinds of clothing and destroy them, or termites, which chew through the wooden supports of buildings. Insects are a threat to successful farming, and to tree or animal raising. The boll weevil is a major hazard for cotton raising; ticks attack cattle and other livestock; and beetles or grasshoppers are common insect threats to many crops. The greatest danger presented by insects is the possibility of spreading diseases such as malaria and yellow fever. Until late in the 19th century, Americans were more concerned about insect damage to crops or livestock than about the possibility that insects could spread disease among humans. During the mid–20th century, a number of new insecticides were developed (*see* Insecticides and Herbicides).

INSIGNIA OF RANK. *See* **Army, United States; Navy, United States.**

INSPECTION, COMMITTEES OF. The Townshend Acts of 1767 created a storm of protest against Great Britain in the American colonies. To force their repeal, the nonimportation agreement of 1765 was revived. In New York City on Mar. 13, 1768, a special committee was named to "inspect all European importations." The life of this committee was short, but similar committees in the other colonies, notably Boston, continued to function, inspecting the correspondence and accounts of merchants (*see* Revolutionary Committees).

INSPECTION, GOVERNMENTAL. The role of state and federal governments in the inspection of the means of production and of goods and services. Governmental activities adjunctive to the process of private industry—such as airport maintenance, public roads, postal service, and navigational aids—are also inspected, and inspection has been extended to the administration of laws covering immigration, migrant labor, voting procedures, the armed services, national parklands, forests, and timber management. Among some of the older federal inspection agencies are the Steamboat Inspection Service (1838), the Interstate Commerce Commission (1887), and the Food and Drug Administration (1927).

States have inspection laws governing the operation of factories, mines, hospitals, schools, public utilities, buildings, and restaurants. In all large urban centers, and in most suburban areas, control over water and sewer services is exercised by state or local authorities. Inspection of agricultural products began about 1890–93 in New York and Wisconsin; the federal government has also used extensive authority over the movement of meat products in interstate commerce, beginning in 1894. As state and federal governments have expanded their roles into the areas of health and welfare, there has been an increase in their inspection of the manner in which grants-in-aid are made and used. Also, recent moves to establish the office of ombudsman for investigating citizens' grievances against state and local officials have resulted in increased investigation of administrative activities.

INSTALLMENT BUYING, SELLING, AND FINANCING. The use of short- and intermediate-term credit to finance the purchase of goods and services for personal consumption, scheduled to be repaid in two or more installments; its origin lies in the open-book credit provided by retailers in colonial times. Consumer installment selling was first introduced in 1807 by the furniture firm of Cowperthwaite and Sons. The single largest component of consumer installment credit is automobile credit, which began in 1910. Wanamaker's of Philadelphia introduced the first revolving credit plan for soft goods in 1938; although the permitted payment period was four months, no charge was made for the use of the credit service. The modern revolving charge account emerged as a credit arrangement that enables a consumer to buy from time to time, charging purchases against an open line of credit, and to repay at least from one-tenth to one-sixth of the unpaid balance outstanding at the end of a billing cycle, with a monthly charge ranging from 1 to 1.5 percent of a specified unpaid balance. Bank charge-credit plans were inaugurated by the Franklin National Bank of New York in 1951.

At the state level the Uniform Consumer Credit Code was introduced in 1968 to replace existing segmented state laws affecting consumer credit. At the federal level the Consumer Credit Protection (or Truth-in-Lending) Act (1969) requires disclosure of finance charges as annual percentage rates; the Fair Credit Billing Act (1974) is intended to protect consumers against inaccurate and unfair credit billing and credit card practices; the Equal Credit Opportunity Act (1974) requires credit grantors to make credit equally available to all creditworthy customers, without regard to sex or marital status.

INSTITUTE FOR ADVANCED STUDY. Formally coming into existence in 1930, the Institute for Advanced Study started operations three years later at Princeton, N.J. It was conceived by Abraham Flexner, its first director (to 1939), who obtained financial support from Louis Bamberger and Mrs. Felix Fuld. The establishing letter of the founding donors abjured undergraduate teaching but contemplated granting Ph.D.'s. The institute was first housed at Princeton University; Flexner implicitly viewed it as a postgraduate arm of the university. Oswald Veblen became the leader of the institute's School of Mathematics, the most prestigious part of the organization; he moved strongly for the construction of a new building for the institute away from the Princeton campus, and selected the site of the present institute building. Both Flexner and Veblen supported the inclusion of the humanities within the institute. Persecution or lack of intellectual freedom in Europe sent many great scholars to the institute in the 1930's. In addition to being a center for mathematicians and physicists, notably Albert Einstein, it has been home to such distinguished scholars as art historian Erwin Panofsky and diplomatic historian George Kennan.

INSULAR CASES (1901–22). A succession of cases in which the Supreme Court determined the status of the outlying possessions and dependencies of the United States. The Court held that such territories and possessions were of two kinds, incorporated and unincorporated; it further held that Congress, in legislating for incorporated territories, is bound by all provisions of the Constitution, but in legislating for unincorporated territories, is bound only by certain "fundamental" provisions of the same (*Downes* v. *Bidwell,* 1901). That Hawaii and Alaska were incorporated territories was determined by the Court in *Hawaii* v. *Mankichi* (1903) and *Rasmussen* v. *United States* (1905). The Philippine Islands were held to be unincorporated in *Dorr* v. *United States* (1904). That Puerto Rico was also not incorporated was held in *Porto Rico* v. *Tapia* (1918) and again, with a full statement of the reasoning involved, in *Balzac* v. *People of Porto Rico* (1922).

INSULAR POSSESSIONS. In 1898 the United States annexed Hawaii and obtained Puerto Rico, the Philippines, and Guam as a result of the war with Spain. American Samoa was occupied in 1899, under a treaty with Great Britain and Germany and by agreement with the native chiefs. The Virgin Islands were purchased from Denmark in 1917, and responsibility for the Trust Territory of the Pacific Islands was assumed in 1947 as a result of World War II. Smaller islands, including Midway, acquired in 1867, and Wake, occupied in 1898, are important chiefly as stopping places on air routes or as sites for lighthouses or communication facilities. Canton and Enderbury islands in the central Pacific are jointly administered by the United States and Great Britain.

The status of U.S. insular possessions has changed over the years. The Philippines became independent in 1946; Puerto Rico became an autonomous commonwealth in 1952; and Hawaii became a state in 1959. The Ryukyu and Daito islands, captured from Japan in World War II, were returned by treaty in 1971. Guam is an organized, unincorporated territory whose inhabitants have U.S. citizenship; American Samoa is an unorganized, unincorporated territory whose inhabitants are U.S. nationals but not U.S. citizens; and the

Virgin Islands, like Guam, is an organized, unincorporated territory whose residents enjoy U.S. citizenship. The Trust Territory of the Pacific Islands continues to be administered under the agreement made in 1947 with the United Nations. *(See also articles on specific islands and island groups.)*

INSURANCE. The insurance business has its roots in the early years of the Republic, when the business was carried on primarily in seaport coffeehouses. Marine and fire insurance were the earliest forms of the property and liability branch of the insurance business; later additions include inland marine, aviation, workmen's compensation, automobile, multiple line, and suretyship insurance. The other major branch of insurance, life and health, did not assume importance until the 1840's. Health insurance began as accident insurance about 1850. The first auto insurance was issued in 1898.

Marine Insurance. In the 17th century agents of English underwriters brought their operation to the colonies, underwriting most of the marine risks before the Revolution. Credit for the first American marine insurance advertisement goes to John Copson of Philadelphia in 1721. During the Revolution, Philadelphia became the headquarters for marine underwriting; it was there that plans were made for the formation of the Insurance Company of North America, the first stock insurance company in the nation and the first American company capable of writing satisfactory marine contracts (1792). Marine premium receipts increased over 300 percent between 1843 and 1858, due to the tremendous volume of underwriting created by the clipper trade. The invention of the steamship made the clipper ship obsolete, ending underwriting prosperity. Civil War insurance rates handicapped merchantmen carrying the American flag. In 1866, when foreign commerce was again prosperous, only 25 percent of American cargo was carried by American ships. Marine underwriters were forced to find new risks; many added general fire underwriting. After the depression of 1893, Congress limited the coastal trade to U.S. ships; new ships were built, and American marine underwriters found their business increasing again. The greatest growth came with World War I. The Bureau of War Risk Insurance, created by Congress in 1914, made it possible to quote stable rates. Fire insurance companies entered marine underwriting; foreign companies established brokerage capacity. Between the end of World War I and the beginning of World War II, there was an overcapacity in marine underwriting. Congressional encouragement of risk-spreading through syndicates made underwriting insurance on merchant vessels possible between the Neutrality Act of Nov. 4, 1939, and April 1942, when the government requisitioned all American vessels. At the request of the Maritime Commission the American Hull Syndicate wrote war risk insurance on hulls, and the American Cargo War Risk Exchange made vital shipping possible by creating a market large enough to spread the results among many marine underwriters. The McCarran-Ferguson Act of 1945 reiterated sections of the Shipping Act of 1920 that exempted marine insurance from the antitrust laws, making American marine insurance competitive in world markets. In 1980 the premium volume of U.S. ocean marine insurance was over $1 billion.

Inland Marine Insurance. Initially designed to insure cargo on inland waterways, inland marine insurance expanded to include movement on land. Some of the first policies insured the possessions of traveling salesmen; in the 20th century, tourist baggage and postal shipments have been added. Bridges and tunnels used for transportation are also included in inland marine insurance. Premiums grew from $196 million in 1948 to $2,061 million in 1979.

Aviation Insurance. Aviation insurance covers the hull and liability hazards of both commercial airlines and private aircraft; it does not include accidental injury or death coverage. The two principal aviation underwriting pools in the United States are Associated Aviation Underwriters and U.S. Aviation Underwriters, Inc. In the late 1970's a thousand American companies participated in aviation insurance; U.S. aviation premium volume was $171 million in 1980, including both direct business and reinsurance.

Fire Insurance. The first U.S. fire insurance company was the Philadelphia Contributionship for Insurance of Houses From Loss by Fire (1752). Primarily a marine underwriter, the Insurance Company of North America became (1794) the first company to market insurance coverage on both buildings and their contents, and the first to underwrite fire risk beyond the city limits. Also, this was the first time fire insurance was underwritten by a stock company. In New England in 1835 Zachariah Allen and other mill owners formed the Manufacturer's Mutual Fire Insurance Company, the first of the factory mutuals. In 1866 the fire companies formed the National Board of Fire Underwriters, which disseminated information on the compensation of agents, fire prevention, and the discovery and prevention of arson. In 1909 Kansas enacted a law that gave the state insurance commissioner power over rates. In 1910 in New York the Merritt committee was appointed to investigate the affairs of insurance companies in that state; the laws that came out of its recommendations served as models for other states. In 1948 almost $1.3 billion in premiums were written; in 1979, $4.8 billion. Since the 1950's the trend toward multiple-line coverage and packaging of property and casualty lines in either indivisible or divisible premium contracts has grown.

Workmen's Compensation Insurance. Prior to the development of workmen's compensation an injured worker's legal right was based upon common law. Employers' liability statutes began to be written toward the end of the 18th century, and some modification of the common-law defenses had been adopted by most states by 1908. Between 1909 and 1919, forty investigatory commissions were established. The consensus was that employers' liability legislation should be replaced with workmen's compensation laws based on a new legal concept—liability without regard to fault. Industrial accidents and disease were seen as hazards of industry, and the cost of insurance was incorporated into the price of the product. The trend has been toward more comprehensive coverage for a larger group of workers. In 1934, only 33 percent of the total work force was covered; in the mid-1970's about 75 percent was included. Premiums in 1979 were $13.2 billion. (*See also* Employer's Liability Laws.)

Automobile Insurance. The first automobile insurance policy was issued by the Travelers Insurance Companies in 1898. In 1979, automobile insurance premiums reached $36.6 billion. More and more states are making the purchase of automobile insurance by car owners compulsory. General dissatisfaction with the system under which loss recoveries by automobile accident victims are often dependent on proving who caused the accident has led to no-fault "first party" laws by more than twenty states and consideration of similar action by most other states; these laws permit accident victims to recover medical and hospital expenses and lost income from their own insurance companies, and usually place some restrictions on the right to sue.

Life Insurance. The earliest life insurance policies in America were written as a sideline by marine underwriters on the lives of sea captains for the duration of a voyage. The Presbyterian Ministers' Fund (1759) and the Episcopal Corporation (1769) were organized as annuity funds for the clergy. The tontine, a life insurance lottery, first appeared in 1790 (*see* Tontine Plan). Subscribers to the Universal Tontine used their funds to form an insurance company in 1792; the tontine policy was not used again until 1867. The growth of stock life insurance companies characterized the business in the early 19th century. The Girard Life Insurance, Annuity and Trust Company of Philadelphia was the first company to write life insurance on a commercial basis and to allow its policyholders to participate in the profits. The expansion of the economy in 1830–37 engendered the founding of large stock insurance companies, but the recession after 1837 gave impetus to the mutuals. In 1855 Massachusetts became the first state to establish an insurance department; Elizur Wright, commissioner from 1858 to 1867, developed the first American table for establishing policy reserves and in 1861 promoted the first nonforfeiture law. By 1890 most states had established insurance departments. The first mortality table based on the experience of insured lives in America was published in 1868. Level-premium insurance was firmly established. The period following the Civil War was characterized by extreme competition between companies; companies falsified statements to make better showings. The rate of termination by lapse was high because of high-pressure sales methods, with consequent loss to the policyholder. Life insurance companies invested in every phase of the economic expansion of the United States and became competitors of the investment bankers. In July 1905 the New York assembly and senate directed a committee to investigate life insurance companies. The committee's report (1906) brought to light numerous practices detrimental to policyholders' interests. Recommendations by the committee brought about a fundamental change in the life insurance business. Most important was the recommendation in favor of mutual life insurance on the level-premium plan with statutory reserves; mutual companies were to be prohibited from writing nonparticipating policy contracts; stock companies were to be required to issue either participating or nonparticipating policies. The McCarran-Ferguson bill (1945) strengthened state regulation and helped to guarantee more qualified insurance management. Entry into mutual funds and variable annuities by the life insurance companies made them subject to the federal securities laws. Members of the Midwest stock exchange began selling life insurance in 1970, and other exchanges permitted their members to follow this lead. Nearly 1,950 legal reserve life insurance companies owned assets of $480 billion in 1980.

Group Insurance. The first group life insurance policy was issued by the Equitable Life Assurance Company in June 1911. In the 1970's, low-cost group life, health, and disability coverages were available through companies with twenty-five or more employees (and through many associations to their members as well); group insurance was almost a necessity for an employer wanting to attract and hold employees.

Industrial Life Insurance. The first industrial life insurance policy in America was issued in 1875 by the Prudential Insurance Company. Primarily for the industrial worker, premiums, usually weekly, are collected at home by an insurance agent; policies require no medical examination and are written with a face value of less than $1,000. The personal contact provided by the agent has led to a very low rate of lapse. Home service agents wrote 3 million policies in 1980, and $36 billion of industrial life insurance was in force.

Fraternal Life Insurance. This insurance first appeared in 1869 with the formation of the Ancient Order of United Workmen. Primarily social or religious organizations, the fraternals were at first actuarially unsound, but the National Fraternal Congress achieved legislation, through the state regulatory agencies, that assured a sound actuarial basis. In 1980 about 200 fraternal benefit societies in the United States and Canada had insurance in the amount of $58.3 billion.

Health Insurance. Rail and steamboat accidents in the 19th century precipitated the first demand for an insurance policy to protect against loss of income because of accident. Although the Franklin Health Assurance Company of Massachusetts is credited with being the first insurer to write accident insurance in America in 1850, the Travelers Insurance Company, founded 1863, was the first company to write health insurance that provides a schedule of stated benefits payable to the insured for each illness or injury. The Massachusetts Health Insurance Company of Boston, incorporated 1847, was the first American company to write individual health insurance. The Fidelity and Casualty Company of New York issued the first contract to protect against loss of income from accident and from certain diseases (1891). Workmen's compensation laws stimulated an interest in group health insurance contracts for illness and nonwork injuries not covered by the law, and in 1914 the Metropolitan Life Insurance Company issued the first group health contract, covering its home office employees. The depression of the 1930's was a stimulus to group health insurance, as was increasing awareness of the rising cost of medical care. Blue Cross in 1948 had its beginning when a group of schoolteachers entered an agreement with Baylor Hospital in Dallas, Tex., to provide them with hospital care on a prepayment basis. To compete with Blue Cross, traditional insurance companies have developed reimbursement policies for hospital and surgical care. During World War II group health insurance became an important part of fringe benefit packages. The postwar period was attended by sharply escalating costs for health care and continued improvement of health insurance. Perhaps most significant was the development of major medical insurance; in the mid-1970's, by using deductibles and coinsurance to control claim cost and claim frequency, such policies provided for benefits up to $250,000. During the 1950's the health insurance industry also began to provide long-term disability income coverage. The advent of Medicare in 1966 caused many companies to modify their coverages to avoid duplicating Medicare benefits. Dental insurance plans are a development of the 1970's, on the part of both Blue Cross and commercial insurance companies.

INSURRECTIONS, DOMESTIC. An insurrection may be defined as an organized uprising against the duly constituted authorities of a sovereign state, with the objective of accomplishing some public political purpose; as such it is to be distinguished from criminal activity, however formidable, which has no public purpose, and from a riot, which has no coherent organized character. A rebellion, to be properly classified as such, must profess statehood as its objective. By this standard, the establishment of the Confederacy of 1861–65 was a true rebellion, while the Whiskey Rebellion of 1794 was no more than an insurrection.

Most of the insurrections occurring in the American colonies or in the United States before 1861 fall into one of two categories: frontier or agrarian uprisings directed against a tidewater government controlled by a planter or mercantile establishment; or servile insurrections by blacks held in slavery. The first frontier-agrarian insurrection clearly distinguishable as such was Bacon's Rebellion (1675–76) in Virginia. The Regulator movement on the Carolina frontier in the late 1760's and early 1770's was in the same category, as were Shays's Rebellion of 1786–87, the Whiskey Rebellion, and Fries's Rebellion (1799). The ill-starred Dorr's Rebellion of 1842 in Rhode Island was essentially a democratic egalitarian movement to replace the outworn colonial character of 1662 with one providing for universal manhood suffrage. Shays's Rebellion, the Whiskey Rebellion, and Dorr's Rebellion were all doubtless inspired in part by the prevailing natural-rights philosophy, which, as the Declaration of Independence proclaimed, embraced a "right of revolution" against an oppressive government.

Of a different order were the slave revolts of the two and a half centuries before passage of the Thirteenth Amendment. How many such uprisings attained a sufficiently organized and coherent character to be classified properly as insurrections is a matter of some dispute. Cautious historians believe that there were only two or three true servile insurrections in the colonial period: those in New York City in 1712 and 1741, and the large uprising at Stono, S.C., in 1739. In the first three decades of the 19th century, at least three serious black servile insurrections took place, inspired in part, perhaps, by the success of the black revolutionary republic in Haiti: the Gabriel uprising in 1800 in Virginia, the abortive Denmark Vesey uprising in Charleston in 1822, and the insurrection led by Nat Turner in Virginia in 1831. All these had black freedom as their objective; all failed, as did John Brown's celebrated insurrection of 1859—a white-led uprising for the same purpose. (*See also articles on individual insurrections.*)

INTEGRATION. The Revolution led to the abolition of slavery north of the Mason-Dixon line and in the Northwest Territories. But the Constitution indirectly sanctioned slavery by counting each slave as three-fifths of a person for purposes of taxation and the apportionment of representatives—a compromise demanded by the South. Chattel slavery was basically incompatible with racial segregation; and although the civil and social status of blacks was rigidly subordinate, racial mingling and miscegenation in the South were widespread. The Jim Crow pattern first emerged in the antebellum North, where Afro-Americans were disfranchised in New Jersey, Pennsylvania, and Connecticut, and a property qualification for voting, for blacks only, was established in New York. Blacks were not allowed to testify in court against whites in Illinois, Ohio, Indiana, Iowa, and California.

Four years of civil war led to the destruction of slavery both physically and, through the Thirteenth Amendment of 1865, constitutionally. The Reconstruction period (1865–77) witnessed the passage of the Fourteenth Amendment (1868), which recognized Afro-Americans as citizens, guaranteed them equal protection under the laws, and secured their civic privileges and immunities from state violation; and the Fifteenth Amendment (1870), which barred disfranchisement on grounds of race, color, or previous condition of servitude. The period also produced a battery of enforcement acts and civil rights laws designed to guarantee civic equality to Afro-Americans, but subsequently the conservative Supreme Court so narrowly interpreted the Fourteenth Amendment (the 1883 Civil Rights Cases) and the Fifteenth Amendment (*United States* v. *Reese*, 1876) that Afro-Americans were for the most part denied the intended benefits of emancipation. When poor black and white southerners threatened to coalesce in the Populist revolt of the 1890's, the conservative southern state regimes successfully disfranchised almost all blacks and masses of poor whites also, and shortly thereafter these states adopted the full range of Jim Crow ordinances.

A 20th-century demographic revolution gave Afro-Americans a power base and, together with changing domestic attitudes and political alignments and the pressures of world opinion, conditioned the events that were to culminate in a second Reconstruction. For almost 300 years Afro-Americans had been 90 percent southern and overwhelmingly rural. But their 20th-century flight from southern rural poverty and discrimination produced a different demographic pattern: of the Afro-American population, 40 percent lived outside the South and 73 percent in cities by midcentury. The New Deal created a newly dominant liberal ideology that eventually reached to the Supreme Court. And after World War II an invigorated civil rights coalition, especially through the National Association for the Advancement of Colored People, won dramatic gains from the federal government.

Integration was most successfully achieved in public accommodations: federal court decisions banned segregation in transportation and recreation, and the Civil Rights Act of 1964 effectively integrated such privately owned facilities as hotels and restaurants. In 1965 the Voting Rights Act led to the massive enfranchisement of southern Afro-Americans. School desegregation was also effected, after *Brown* v. *Board of Education of Topeka* (1954) had produced a decade of token integration. The Elementary and Secondary Education Act of 1965 provided massive federal aid to education, and the Department of Health, Education and Welfare was authorized to withhold funds from school districts not complying with desegregation directives. By 1970 school integration in the South had outstripped that in the North and West.

Most resistant to integration were the areas of jobs, because unions and seniority blunted integration drives, and housing, because whites fled integrating city neighborhoods for the suburbs. Black discontent with the slow pace of integration in these vital areas fueled the urban rioting of the late 1960's. Despite the controversy over school busing and the rhetoric of black separatism, integration in sports and the communications media was dramatic, and public opinion surveys continued to indicate that most blacks preferred integration and that white prejudice was continuing to erode.

INTELLIGENCE, MILITARY AND STRATEGIC. Military intelligence is information on the capabilities of the armed forces of potentially hostile or allied countries, acquired by covert or open means, and implies the existence of counterintelligence, the employment of techniques or agents to deny similar defense information to likely enemies. In combat, military intelligence serves to provide a field commander with detailed assessments of the enemy's strength, the composition of hostile forces, and an opponent's probable plans. Since World War II, military intelligence in the United States has been subsumed under the concept of strategic, or national, intelligence, the term applied to information collected and analyzed by the United States concerning the defense, industrial, economic, scientific, transportation, and communications capabilities; the plans; the resources; the political life; and even the geographic, meteorological, and demographic characteristics of other nations, allied or hostile, for the purpose of formulating national policy.

In 1885 the U.S. War Department first formed a section to supervise military intelligence. Intelligence staffs have continued to exist within the U.S. Army and the U.S. Navy since then (and within the U.S. Air Force since 1947), although their areas of competence continue to change with the concentration of functions in higher echelons of the Department of Defense. The World War II Joint Chiefs of Staff Intelligence Committee evolved into the J-2 section of the Joint Chiefs after the war. The inefficiency of intelligence efforts of World War II, especially as revealed in the postwar investigation into the Pearl Harbor attack, raised demands for a centralized structure, which the Congress provided for in the National Security Act of 1947. The act established the National Security Council (NSC) and the Central Intelligence Agency (CIA). The U.S. Intelligence Board (established 1959) serves as the major forum initiated by the NSC to evolve consensus and to produce finished intelligence summations. The CIA plays a predominant role in coordinating the work of the board's members in producing information for the NSC's deliberations. The State Department's Bureau of Intelligence and Research contributes current political information on foreign governments. Establishment of the controversial Defense Intelligence Agency (DIA) in 1961 displaced the J-2 member of the board with a DIA member responsible for defense intelligence. The National Security Agency (NSA) deals in communications, cryptology, and the information gleaned from breaking or monitoring foreign coded message transmissions. Also represented on the Intelligence Board are the Atomic Energy Commission, the Federal Bureau of Investigation, and the Treasury Department. The Intelligence Resources Advisory Board (created 1971) is chiefly concerned with the efficient allocation of intelligence budgets. (*See also* Central Intelligence Agency; National Security Council; Office of Strategic Services.)

INTELLIGENCE TESTS. The first mental testing took place in England and Germany in the late 19th century. Beginning in 1888 an American, James McKeen Cattell, applied the theory of Sir Francis Galton that psychological traits could be used to investigate the differences between individuals. By the 1910's a number of Americans, concerned often with the great social problem of "feeblemindedness," had begun working with adaptations of the tests originated by the French physician Alfred Binet. Binet was interested in testing normal intelligence of children. The most successful of Binet's followers was Lewis M. Terman, who in 1916 produced the definitive Stanford-Binet intelligence test. Terman made two innovations that laid the basis for the later spectacular growth of intelligence testing in the United States: large-scale standardization and the intelligence quotient (IQ), which had been suggested by the German Louis William Stern to describe a constant degree of intelligence regardless of age. Shortly after the turn of the century, a number of workers, particularly Robert Yerkes, had devised point scales to correlate with age the number of test items accomplished successfully. Psychological statisticians, notably Truman L. Kelley and L. L. Thurstone, devised systems of multiple-factor analysis in the late 1930's so that the measurement of individual differences could be read. One particular development necessary for the mass application of intelligence testing was the written group test; the most successful was that devised by Arthur S. Otis (1918). During World War I, psychologists under the leadership of Yerkes utilized intelligence testing of all army recruits to demonstrate the usefulness of such tests. After the war, industrial and business firms utilized intelligence tests and in the schools intelligence testing became an integral part of the educational system. In 1960 J. P. Guilford of the University of Southern California suggested adding creativity as an intelligence factor. For decades critics have pointed out the class and ethnic biases of the tests and bewailed the harmful effects of typing pupils by IQ when the children might in fact with proper training improve their scores. Since the 1950's, attempts have been made to devise tests that do not depend on environmental factors.

INTERCHANGEABLE MANUFACTURE. A system by which components may be made so similar in size and shape that they can be assembled to close limits without fitting. Printers' type was probably the earliest application. In mid-18th-century France Gen. Jean B. V. de Gribeauval applied interchangeability to field guns and their carriages; Honoré Le Blanc, inspector general of arms, applied the concept to small arms. Thomas Jefferson attempted to introduce the system to the United States; Jefferson and Eli Whitney corresponded, and it is believed that an account of Le Blanc's work may have readied Whitney and inclined him toward his 1798 contract to make 10,000 muskets. The first U.S. contract specifying interchangeable work was issued to Simeon North in 1813. The true milling machine appeared at North's works between 1816 and 1820; it became the most important machine tool of the century. Interchangeability was fully realized at Springfield Armory between 1844 and 1848 and then introduced at Harpers Ferry and the contract armories. Thus, interchangeable work in metalworking was finally achieved. It had already been achieved in woodworking. In the 1790's Gideon Roberts was the first of a group of makers of wooden clocks in Connecticut to develop special machinery. Eli Terry led in the realization of the potentials of such machinery; he had his factory organized on a productive basis by 1818. The clockmakers did not work to close limits, and the degree of interchangeability that they achieved was incidental to production by machine. By the 1970's interchangeable work to extremely close limits was practiced on an international scale.

INTEREST LAWS AND INTEREST RATES. Laws regulating interest rates are directed primarily at lenders (which include institutional investors such as banks) and are of two types: (1) those governing the amount that can be charged borrowers, generally termed usury laws, and (2) those governing the interest that lenders can pay to induce the public to invest with them funds to be used as capital to lend other borrowers.

A usury law was first enacted in Massachusetts in 1661; by 1791 such laws had been enacted by all the thirteen original states, initial limitations ranging from 6 percent to 10 percent. The National Bank Act of 1864 and the Banking Act of 1933 tied national bank rates to state usury laws; the latter act gave national banks the option of charging up to the maximum rate fixed by the state or 1 percent above the Federal Reserve Bank rate. In 1969 Congress enacted the Consumer Credit Protection (or Truth-in-Lending) Act, which regulates most commercial lenders and has extensive disclosure requirements, including a showing of the total cost of borrowing as an annual percentage rate. Some states have enacted similar legislation that complements the federal act. The Credit Control Act of 1969 empowers the Federal Reserve Board to set maximum and minimum interest rates on credit transactions.

The payment of interest on deposits has been the primary method used by banks to attract private funds. Such interest was originally paid only on time deposits (savings accounts and certificates of deposit), but in the late 19th century, demand deposits (checking accounts) grew so substantially that banks began paying interest on them as well. Interest-rate competition for demand deposits was believed to be a factor contributing to the banking collapse of the 1930's. By the Banking Acts of 1933 and 1935 Congress (1) prohibited the payment of interest on demand deposits by all Federal Reserve member banks and by nonmember banks insured by the Federal Deposit Insurance Corporation (FDIC) and (2) limited the payment of interest on time deposits to maximum rates set by the Federal Reserve Board and the FDIC.

"INTERESTS" (or "vested interests"). An expression popularly used around the opening of the 20th century to designate the gigantic business corporations that then dominated the American scene. Among these interests were the so-called money trust, sugar trust, tobacco trust, oil trust, beef trust, and steel trust.

INTERIOR, DEPARTMENT OF THE. Established in 1849 as the sixth department of cabinet rank, with responsibility for the General Land Office, the Indian Office, the Pension Office, the Bureau of the Census, the Patent Office, and several minor supervisory agencies. Its role has gradually changed from general housekeeper to guardian of the nation's natural resources. Each of its six organization units is headed by an assistant secretary: Management; Program Development and Budget; Fish, Wildlife, and Parks; Land and Water Resources; Energy and Minerals; and Congressional and Legislative Affairs. Subsidiary organizations include the Bureau of Land Management, caretaker of 450 million acres of public domain; the National Park Service; the Geological Survey; the Bureau of Indian Affairs; the Fish and Wildlife Service, which maintains 377 wildlife refuges (32 million acres) and operates 90 hatcheries to keep federal waters stocked with fish; the Bureau of Outdoor Recreation, which administers the Land and Water Conservation Fund; the Bureau of Mines; the Mining Enforcement and Safety Administration; the Bureau of Reclamation, whose irrigation projects have transformed deserts and dry prairies into fertile farmlands; the Office of Saline Water; the Office of Water Research and Technology; and four regional electric power administrations: Bonneville Power Administration, in the Pacific Northwest; Southwestern Power Administration; Southeastern Power Administration; and Alaska Power Administration.

INTERIOR DECORATION. The finishing, furnishing, and decorating of rooms by a person having a special skill in laying out a general plan. The term "interior decoration" fell into disrepute in the second half of the 20th century, being replaced by the term "interior design." Practically, the work of the interior designer lies in the selection of the furnishings of a room, from wall coverings to ashtrays. The task is one the owner of a house often takes on for himself.

The earliest historical evidence of interior decorating is the 18th-century drawings of interiors that were occasionally made by craftsmen or architects to suggest how to arrange the furnishings of a given room. The architect Robert Adam, who worked in London between the 1750's and the 1790's, approached the decorator's role when he designed furniture and metalwork for many of his interiors.

In the 19th century, people had more choices of furnishing styles, and householders who built homes without architects began seeking advice. Moreover, decorating ideas were included in architectural handbooks. A prime American example is the *Architecture of Country Houses* (1840), by A. J. Downing, which has one section devoted to furnishing interiors. In the middle of the 19th century all-around interior detail work, furnishing, and the decorating of walls and floors were first undertaken as a package by a few furniture shops.

The interior decoration movement, per se, emerged at the end of the 19th century. Whether filled with reproductions of earlier styles or eclectic and innovative, interiors designed after the 1860's were complex combinations of ornament and utility. The more affluent but less confident sought professional aid in making selections, and so the first modern interior decorators began to help them choose and place objects. No documentation exists to suggest when the first decorator began, but during this period books offered advice to the middle classes, and architects of the grander houses designed the furnishings, which were then made by one of the decorating companies. In 1904, when a magazine called *The Interior Decorator* was first published, the several interior decorators listed were clearly advisers rather than craftsmen.

At the turn of the century, interior decoration reflected several distinctively separate approaches. The traditionalists concentrated on employing objects that represented established earlier styles; often a room was meant to look as if it was furnished with old family possessions. The other extreme was represented by the more innovative designers, who attempted to develop new styles inspired by concepts of reform. On the international level, art nouveau, at the turn of the century, was the first in the series of modern styles; it was succeeded by two kinds of adventuresome design: Bauhaus was largely functional, while art deco, although embellished with new motifs, was essentially traditional in construction. The basic objective of interior designers since the turn of the century has been to provide an interior environment that is congenial to the householder and his guests. From being solely the luxury of the affluent, interior decoration has become a profession supplying business and middle-class domestic needs as well.

INTERMARRIED CITIZEN. A person who, through marriage to an Indian, became a citizen of the tribe; most commonly applied to a white person who married a member of one of the Five Civilized Tribes. Intermarried citizens shared equally with citizens by blood in lands and other tribal property.

INTERMEDIATE CREDIT BANKS. The twelve Federal Intermediate Credit Banks, each serving a farm-credit district, were established by congressional legislation in 1923 to increase the supply of credit available to farmers. The capital of the banks was originally provided by the government, but it was retired in full in 1968, and the outstanding stock was transferred to the Production Credit Association. The banks could supply credit for agricultural purposes by discounting or purchasing notes or bills of exchange that had been acquired from farmers by banks, agricultural credit associations, livestock companies, or cooperative marketing associations. In 1933 Congress authorized the creation of local production credit associations to make operating loans to farmers directly with funds supplied by the Federal Intermediate Credit Banks. Funds for these credit activities are obtained by the banks through the issuance of consolidated collateral trust debentures, consisting primarily of short-term issues. They are not direct obligations of the U.S. Treasury, but rather involve federal sponsorship.

INTERNAL IMPROVEMENTS. The first internal improvements, such as turnpikes and some short canals, were begun by private groups. Even the Middlesex Canal connecting Boston with the Merrimac River, the first important canal to be built, was completed without public aid in 1803. The Erie Canal was completed in 1825, and its success in rapidly developing upstate New York amazed the country (*see* Erie Canal). Other states attempted to duplicate the feat by building their own canals; most states that undertook canal construction severely strained their credit, and some defaulted on their obligations. Poorly developed frontier states, not able to finance costly canal and road construction, looked to the national government for assistance. The first national enterprise was the Cumberland Road to connect Cumberland, Md., with Wheeling, W.Va., in 1806. Meantime, the insistent demand of other areas for aid to canal and road construction induced Albert Gallatin, secretary of the treasury, to prepare a report in 1808 on internal improvements, in which he outlined a comprehensive system of canals and roads for federal construction. No action was then taken, but the agitation continued and in 1816 Rep. John C. Calhoun of South Carolina and others drove through Congress the Bonus Bill (*see* Bonus Bill, Calhoun's). Presidents James Madison and James Monroe insisted that there was nothing in the Constitution to authorize Congress to use public funds for internal improvements and urged that recourse be had to an amendment to the Constitution. The demand of the West for federal aid to internal improvements found its champion in Henry Clay of Kentucky. Clay favored federal aid to roads and canals. His so-called American System included protective tariffs to encourage the development of industries and internal improvements to make possible the easy flow of domestic commerce. Clay's views on internal improvements had the sympathetic support of President John Quincy Adams, during whose administration subsidies were granted to many canals. At the same time, river and harbor appropriations began to appear with regularity. Few of the enterprises were of lasting significance.

In the mid-1830's the craze for internal improvements seemed to seize most of the country. Schemes were adopted without consideration of their feasibility and ultimate cost; states piled up debts to finance elaborate programs; absurd prices were paid for necessary lands; and other costs, even wages, were driven to high levels as a result of the competition of contractors for employees. The panic of 1837 wrought havoc with these programs; many of the states were forced to suspend work, to dismiss employees, and to default on their obligations (*see* Repudiation of State Debts). There was a revulsion against state ownership and construction of such facilities, and when business conditions revived in the late 1840's, private capital generally was forced to take the initiative, with little state assistance. Many of the state projects were sold to private groups.

By 1850, the railroad net was beginning to reveal its modern outline. Although constructed by private groups, many eastern railroads received aid from state and local governments. The relatively undeveloped West was not so fortunate: in that area the cry went up for federal grants of land to aid railroads. In 1850 a new era in federal aid to internal improvements began when Congress granted 3.75 million acres of land to aid in constructing a railroad from Illinois to Mobile, Ala. In the next twenty-one years more than 131 million acres of land were given as subsidies to railroads.

Since the 1920's the federal and state governments have been continuously engaged in programs of road construction. Federal expenditure on harbors, waterways, and airports has also remained at a high level. Federal grants, as distinct from loans, for the building of roads began to be made by 1944. In 1956 Congress enacted the Highway Revenue Act, which provided for matching grants to the states, on a nine-to-one basis, for the construction of a great toll-free interstate and defense highway system.

By the 1960's many were beginning to question the wisdom of huge state and federal expenditures for thruways and freeways. These expressways had displaced thousands of urban dwellers, adversely affected local property taxes, and caused the loss of valuable farmland. The declining passenger business of the railroads led them to contract and finally virtually to end their passenger service except for a few commuter lines. Rapid-transit facilities in the major cities were seriously affected by high wage levels and other costs. As profits disappeared, elevated and subway train lines and most urban bus routes were taken over by public authorities; but to keep them in operation and to prevent fares from becoming prohibitively high, further public aid became necessary. Governments used various methods of providing that essential aid: tax exemption; outright grants by city, state, and federal governments; use of profits from bridge and tunnel tolls to aid rapid-transit lines; and levies of higher parking and use fees to discourage commuters from driving their cars. Congested traffic in the cities, made worse by thruways that bring cars into central cities, has inspired a revival of interest in the building of rapid transit lines. (*See also* Bridges; Canals; Cumberland Road; Railroads; Roads; Transportation and Travel; Tunnels.)

INTERNAL REVENUE. *See* **Taxation.**

INTERNATIONAL CONTROL COMMISSION. Consisting of India, Canada, and Poland, it was established for Laos in 1954 and dissolved in 1958. Its revival was proposed by a conference that assembled in Geneva (May 12, 1961) to work out a cease-fire in Laos. The commission was reactivated in July 1962 to supervise a Laotian settlement if one could be reached. No settlement was made.

INTERNATIONAL COURT OF JUSTICE (sometimes called the Hague Court or World Court). Established under the United Nations charter in 1946, the court is the successor to the Permanent Court of International Justice, organized in 1922 to supplement the Permanent Court of Arbitration. It is composed of fifteen members, no two of the same nationality, nominated by nations and recognized private organizations and elected for a term of nine years, in staggered groups of five every three years, by the concurring separate votes of a majority of the Security Council and the General Assembly of the United Nations. The court adopts its own rules of procedure, which were completely revised in 1972. It has two types of jurisdiction: first, a true legal jurisdiction to decide cases; and second, an advisory jurisdiction with respect to internal matters of international organizations. In its true legal jurisdiction, only nations may be parties in cases before the court. As a general principle, the court may hear cases only with the consent of the states that are parties before it, but states may by declaration give a general consent to the court's jurisdiction in matters relating to a question of international law.

INTERNATIONAL EXPOSITION OF 1895. Plans for this exposition, held in Atlanta, Ga., were conceived late in 1893 by business and civic leaders who felt that the South had been inadequately represented in the World's Columbian Exposition of 1893. Many foreign nations and many American states participated. The promotion of Pan-Americanism was one of the principal objects of the exposition; buildings were also devoted to Afro-Americans and to women.

INTERNATIONAL GEOPHYSICAL YEAR (July 1, 1957–Dec. 31, 1958). Eighteen months of geophysical observations by about 30,000 scientists and technicians representing more than seventy countries; the extension of the program for an additional year (until Dec. 31, 1959) was officially called International Geophysical Cooperation (IGC), but that period is generally included in the term "International Geophysical Year" (IGY). The IGY and IGC attempted simultaneous observations in eleven fields of earth, near-earth, and solar physics: aurora and airglow, cosmic rays, geomagnetism, glaciology, gravity, ionospheric physics, latitude and longitude determination, meteorology, oceanography, seismology, and solar activity. More than 2,500 stations were occupied at a cost of about $500 million. Two of the most prominent achievements of the IGY, are the discovery of the Van Allen radiation belts, and the calculation of a new, pear-shaped model of the shape of the earth.

INTERNATIONAL HARVESTER COMPANY. As a solution to the bitter competition among manufacturers of farm machinery a consolidation of the leading companies was effected in 1902 at the instigation of Cyrus Hall McCormick, Jr. It included McCormick Harvesting Machine Company; Deering Harvester Company; Plano Manufacturing Company; Warder, Bushnell and Glessner Company; and Milwaukee Harvester Company. Action was brought against the company by the federal government, and in 1914 the Court held that under the Sherman Antitrust Act the company was an illegal combination in undue restraint of trade and ordered the property of the company divided among distinct independent corporations (*United States* v. *International Harvester Company,* 214 U.S. 987).

INTERNATIONAL JOINT COMMISSION. Created by the Boundary Waters Treaty of 1909; consists of three American and three Canadian members with jurisdiction over cases involving the use of boundary waters or of rivers crossing the U.S.-Canadian boundary. It may also settle any problem of any nature that the two governments agree to refer to it.

INTERNATIONAL LABOR ORGANIZATION (ILO). An intergovernmental agency established by the 1919 peace treaty, on recommendation of the Commission on International Labor Legislation chaired by Samuel Gompers. Since 1945–46, the ILO has been a specialized agency of the United Nations, governed under the terms of its own constitution and financed independently by annual assessments on its member states. The permanent secretariat of the ILO is the International Labor Office, headquartered in Geneva, Switzerland. In 1981 a total of 145 countries belonged to the ILO; continuous U.S. membership goes back to 1934. To its traditional tasks of setting international labor standards, the ILO has added a broad range of technical assistance programs to help less-developed countries improve their services in the labor field. In 1969 it was awarded the Nobel Peace Prize.

INTERNATIONAL LAW. The body of rules and principles of action binding states and international agencies in relationships with each other. An exclusive attitude within the European community prevented admission of non-European states to this international legal system before the 19th century, with the exception of the United States. The U.S. Constitution authorizes Congress to "define and punish Piracies and Felonies committed on the high Seas, and Offenses against the Law of Nations" (Article I, Section 8, Clause 10). U.S. courts routinely apply international law in litigations within the United States that present issues within its rules —for example, acquisition and delimitation of territory; conflicts of nationality; rights of aliens; limitations of national jurisdiction over persons, corporations, and ships; diplomatic and consular privileges and immunities; the effect to be given treaties; and enforcement of neutrality obligations. Rules stem from the customary practice of nations, evidenced by diplomatic documents and determined by courts, or from positive lawmaking treaties. Even when the latter lack enough ratifications to be universally obligatory, they may stimulate new customary law that has this effect. (*See also* Blockade; Freedom of the Seas; Geneva Conventions; Intervention; League of Nations; Monroe Doctrine; Neutrality; Recognition, Policy of; United Nations; War, Laws of.)

INTERNATIONAL MONETARY FUND (IMF). On July 1, 1944, delegates of forty-four nations met at Bretton Woods, N.H., and proposed the IMF to promote stability of currencies and international cooperation on a multilateral basis. The IMF came into existence on Dec. 27, 1945, and began operations on Mar. 1, 1947, with headquarters in Washington, D.C. Member nations' currencies were denominated in gold or the U.S. dollar, itself based on gold at $35 an ounce (the function of gold as a value unit was eliminated in 1976). Each nation subscribed an amount appropriate to its economic importance. From this fund any member may temporarily draw out monies to help meet international trade deficits. In 1969 the IMF established a new monetary facility, the Special Drawing Rights (SDR's), which became by the late 1970's one of the principal reserve assets of the international monetary system. In 1980 the IMF had 141 members, and had assets of 43.8 billion SDR's.

INTERSTATE COMMERCE. *See* **Trade, Domestic.**

INTERSTATE COMMERCE COMMISSION (ICC). The first of the independent regulatory commissions, the ICC was created by the Interstate Commerce Act of 1887. The Supreme Court had ruled (*Wabash, Saint Louis and Pacific Railroad Company* v. *Illinois,* 118 U.S. 557) that the states had no power to regulate interstate shipments. Congress responded with its first broad regulatory statute aimed at major private enterprise. The act provided for a five-person commission—later increased to seven and then to eleven—appointed by the president and confirmed by the Senate. In 1970 an annually rotating chairman was replaced by one presidentially appointed.

The principal task of the ICC has been the regulation of railroads and, since 1935, motor carriers. The initial law was aimed at rates, but increasing complaints brought about legislation that greatly broadened the commission's powers. The supervision of safety was added by the Railroad Safety Appliance Act of 1893 and remained with the ICC until transferred to the Department of Transportation in 1967. The Elkins Act of 1903 and the Mann-Elkins Act of 1910 were aimed at discriminatory practices among shippers. The Hepburn Act of 1906 strengthened the rate-making authority of the ICC and extended its jurisdiction to pipelines and express companies. The Esch-Cummins Railway Act of 1920 gave the ICC broad powers to prescribe rates for railroads and to encourage reorganization of the companies into more efficient economic units. Authority over telephone, telegraph, and cable service, granted in 1888, was transferred to the Federal Communications Commission in 1934. Through the Motor Carrier Act of 1935, ICC authority was extended to trucking. The Transportation Act of 1940 gave the commission power over certain interstate common water carriers. The Rail Passenger Act of 1970, which established Amtrak, authorized the ICC to assist Amtrak, establish standards of service, and report on its operations. A possible trend away from regulation began when four deregulation bills (airlines, 1978; trucking and railroad, 1980; and busing, 1981) decreased the power of the ICC.

INTERSTATE COMMERCE LAWS. The Constitution specifically grants the federal government power "to regulate Commerce . . . among the several States." But for a century there was little federal regulation of interstate commerce other than transportation and communications. It was not until the post–Civil War period, when the power of the modern corporation became clearly evident, that the national political environment began to change. The Interstate Commerce Act of 1887 was the first major federal statute. The Sherman Antitrust Act of 1890, aimed at curbing monopolies, was supported in 1914 by the Clayton Antitrust Act (which in addition exempted labor organizations from the antitrust laws) and by the creation of the Federal Trade Commission in 1914. The food and drug acts of 1906 and 1938 as amended have been aimed at preventing adulteration and mislabeling. Powers given to the Federal Trade Commission in 1938 forbid false advertising. The Truth-in-Packaging Act of 1966 and the Consumer Credit Protection (Truth-in-Lending) Act of 1969 have brought further protection to consumers. The publicity acts of 1903 and 1909 were forerunners of the Securities and Exchange Act of 1934, all aimed at the sale of fraudulent securities.

Controls over additional modes of transport came with the Shipping Act of 1916, which established the U.S. Shipping Board, whose authority was reestablished in 1936 under the Maritime Commission. Federal regulation of utilities came with the creation in 1920 of the Federal Power Commission. The Federal Radio Commission of 1927 was broadened into the Federal Communications Commission in 1934. Regulation of the labor relations of industries engaged in interstate commerce culminated in the formation of the National Labor Relations Board in 1935, whose powers and duties were revised by the Taft-Hartley Act of 1947 and amendments to it. The Civil Aeronautics Act of 1938, setting up the Civil Aeronautics Authority (later Civil Aeronautics Board), concluded formation of the series of agencies known as the independent regulatory commissions.

Interstate commerce laws are not limited to regulative and punitive measures. Subsidies are available, for example, to maritime shipping and to large segments of agriculture. Many federal agencies engage in research of interest to business and commercial organizations. The Tennessee Valley Authority (TVA) was created in 1933 to help in the development of an entire area.

The views of the Supreme Court on federal powers under the interstate commerce clause have gradually broadened. For some decades the implementation of certain statutes was modified or negated by the Court's opinions on what constituted interstate commerce. Not until the late 1930's did the Court include manufacturing plants and processes, for example, within the scope of regulation under the commerce clause. By 1946, in the case of the *American Power and Light Company* v. *Securities and Exchange Commission,* the Court concluded that "the Federal commerce power is as broad as the economic needs of the nation."

INTERSTATE COMPACTS. Article I, Section 10, of the U.S. Constitution states that "no state shall, without the Consent of Congress, . . . enter into any Agreement or Compact with another State, or with a foreign Power." Over the years this provision has been interpreted to mean that interstate agreements that in any way affect the balance of the federal system must receive the approval of Congress. Such agreements appeared early in U.S. history. In the colonial period nine agreements on boundaries existed, and four more were made under the Articles of Confederation. Compacts were limited chiefly to a few boundary agreements in the first century of the Republic; only 24 were ratified from 1783 to 1900. The increase in compacts began in the 1930's, when the Council of State Governments and other organizations began to encourage interstate cooperation as an alternative to federal administration of all interstate issues. During 1950–70, the number of new compacts increased dramatically, but in the 1970's the growth slowed down. By 1979 the number of compacts approved was 176.

Perhaps the most significant are the river development compacts, dealing with irrigation, pollution control, fishing, and navigation. Federal sponsorship of the Colorado River Compact (1928) did not succeed in precluding a long litigation between Arizona and California. The Delaware River Basin Compact (1936) included the federal government as well as New York, New Jersey, Pennsylvania, and Delaware. The New England Interstate Water Pollution Control Commission (1947) expanded its powers to include regulatory activities in the early 1970's. The Susquehanna River Basin Compact of 1969 (which deals with planning land use), like the Delaware, also includes federal participation. The Lake Tahoe Regional Planning Commission (1968) endeavored to prevent overdevelopment. New Jersey, New York, and Connecticut have a Tri-State Regional Planning Commission. The Southern Growth Policies Agreement was established in 1971 to help promote expansion by bringing new industries to the region.

A large number of compacts deal with social questions. The Interstate Compact on the Placement of Children had been ratified by forty-four states by 1979. The Interstate Agreement on Qualification of Educational Personnel had been ratified by thirty-one states by 1979.

One of the many important compacts is the Port of New York Authority (1921), which does a multibillion dollar business involving airports, bridges, and tunnels. The Interstate Compact to Conserve Oil and Gas, formed in the 1930's, has had tremendous power in limiting production of petroleum products in an effort to maintain prices. The Interstate Compact for the Supervision of Probationers and Parolees, also formed in the 1930's, has been effective in the administration of criminal law. A new kind of compact appeared in 1981 when the Northwest Interstate Compact on Low-Level Radioactive Waste Management was developed; another compact on radioactive waste disposal was drafted by the Southern states at the same time.

INTERSTATE TRADE BARRIERS. Commercial blockages between the colonies were widened and intensified by states during the Confederation, and a principal reason for calling the Constitutional Convention of 1787 was to eliminate this cause of friction. The Constitution gave authority over interstate commerce to Congress, except for "absolutely necessary . . . inspection" provisions, and for nearly a century and a half the United States had the most extensive free trade area in the world. The Great Depression, beginning in 1929, witnessed more limitations by the states to raise revenue for hard-pressed state treasuries and to protect intrastate business against the competition of neighbors. Devices included taxes on incoming goods and on out-of-state corporations; requirements for inspection of commodities and in some cases lengthy quarantine; demands that incoming trucks pay fees and have certain equipment; and the setting up of state "ports of entry." California went so far as to restrict "immigration" to those possessing a certain amount of cash. The threat that the United States would be "Balkanized" led to a conference of state governments in 1939, but in the following twenty-five years restraints increased. The Supreme Court struck down the most undisguised discriminations but was tolerant of exactions that furnished to the states revenues that would otherwise have had to be supplied by the federal government. A committee of the House of Representatives, after hearings in 1965, concluded that the system of state taxation worked badly and that standardization of state restrictions was preferable to rigid enforcement of constitutional prohibition. States, in the face of increasing dependence on federal aid and discipline, pled states' rights. By the early 1980's Congress had not acted on pending corrective legislation.

INTERURBAN ELECTRIC LINES. Electric interurban railways appeared in America shortly after the introduction of urban electric streetcars. The first interurban service started in Ohio in 1889–90, and other short lines soon followed. Many of the first interurban electric lines were built in order to improve local and branch line railroad passenger service. By 1900 more than 2,100 miles of such interurban lines were in service. In the early 20th century, a major investment boom occurred in the interurban industry. Between 1901 and 1908 more than 9,000 miles of interurban electric lines were constructed in the nation. When the peak mileage of 15,580 miles was reached in 1916, almost two-thirds was located in Illinois, Indiana, Michigan, Ohio, Pennsylvania, and New York. One could travel by interurban railway, using many different lines, from Elkhart Lake, near Sheboygan, Wis., to Oneonta, N.Y., a distance of 1,087 miles. First in mileage was Ohio, and the 2,798 miles in that state served every city of 10,000 or more.

The hope for profits rarely materialized for the numerous interurban lines. Even in the best years, the rate of return for the entire industry was just 3 percent, or only two-thirds that of the steam railroads. After World War I, expanding automobile traffic brought increased operating ratios, deficits, and extensive abandonment. During the 1920's more than 5,000 miles of line were abandoned, and 7,000 miles were given up during the 1930's. Interurban mileage dropped to only 200 miles by 1960.

INTERVENTION. In the 18th and 19th centuries, European concepts of international law permitted nations to intervene in other sovereign states to protect the lives and property of their own citizens. The United States subscribed to that idea, and throughout its early history American forces raided pirate villages, bombarded foreign towns in reprisal for offenses to U.S. traders and missionaries, and landed marines in other nations to protect Americans during upheavals.

Although the United States showed few compunctions about intervention to protect its own citizens, it was leery of politically motivated intervention. Initially it feared that reactionary powers might intervene in the United States. Thus, strategic and ideological forces brought Americans to consider themselves the leading antiinterventionists in the world. During the Revolution, when French help was desperately needed, Congress instructed its ministers to France to offer only commercial favors in exchange for French economic and naval help and to avoid any political ties. Necessity compelled Congress to accept a political alliance in the end. A few years later France declared war on Great Britain, triggering a debate about U.S. obligations under the French treaty. In 1793, President George Washington announced an impartial neutrality within the bounds of treaty agreements with France. And in 1796 he enunciated his foreign policy principles in his farewell address: "in extending our commercial relations, to have as little *political* connection as possible." President James Monroe and Secretary of State John Quincy Adams continued the principle of nonintervention, citing it in support for recognizing the new governments of Latin America. In 1823 they made it the basis of the Monroe Doctrine. Clearly Monroe and Adams did not regard America's intervention in the Western Hemisphere as the equivalent of American intervention in Europe. They found little difficulty in rationalizing U.S. intervention in Spanish Florida. West Florida had been occupied in 1810 under the pretext that the boundary of the Louisiana Purchase included it. In 1818 Monroe ordered Andrew Jackson to cross into East Florida and punish the Indians who had been raiding the United States across the border, arguing that Spain was unable to maintain order there.

America's interventions increased in number and magnitude. Some, like that in China to put down the Boxer Rebellion of 1900, could be justified on the old ground of protecting the lives and property of U.S. citizens. But others had obvious political intentions, and new justifications had to be found. In 1898, President William McKinley announced he was intervening in the Cuban revolution against Spain not only to protect Americans but also on general humanitarian grounds. President Theodore Roosevelt intervened to prevent Colombia's suppression of a revolution in Panama in 1903 and thus secured the Panama Canal route, justifying his action by citing treaty rights and the interests of collective civilization. Then Roosevelt began what became a long series of interventions in the Caribbean, asserting the U.S. right to interfere in any Western Hemisphere nation to prevent "chronic wrongdoing" or the collapse of public order. U.S. forces undertook "preventive intervention" in Cuba (1906), Nicaragua (1912), Haiti (1915), the Dominican Republic (1916), and Mexico (1914 and 1916).

America's participation in World War I and the Allied intervention in Siberia in 1918 disillusioned many Americans about interventionism. Under pressure from Latin-American nations, the United States agreed at the Montevideo Conference of 1933 that "no state has the right to intervene in the internal or external affairs of another." President Franklin D. Roosevelt's government inserted a reservation concerning the lack of definitions in the agreement and reserving America's rights under international law, but reiterated this pledge three years later at Buenos Aires.

After World War II the United States returned to a policy of "protective intervention" but extended the policy beyond the Western Hemisphere. Alarmed by the rise of the Soviet Union the United States adopted a policy designed to contain Communism. Added to the strategic, ideological, and cultural factors behind containment was a vast expansion of trade and investments abroad. U.S. interventions were seen by Americans as attempts to prevent Communist subversion of legitimate and friendly governments. Even so, the United States betrayed some uneasiness about its policies. It tried to hide its involvement in the overthrow of the Guatemalan government in 1954 and the invasion of Cuba at the Bay of Pigs in 1961. Interventions in Greece (1947–49), Korea (1950–53), Lebanon (1958), and Vietnam (1965–73) were justified by the invitation of what the United States considered to be legitimate governments resisting invasion or overthrow by an armed tyrannical minority. Intervention in the Dominican Republic in 1965 was justified on the ground that the United States was seeking only to protect its own citizens in the midst of a civil war, although it was later admitted that the real purpose was to prevent a Communist seizure of power. The blockade of Cuba during the missile crisis of 1962 was justified on the ground that the introduction of Soviet missiles would suddenly alter the balance of power. Popular disillusionment in America with the war in Vietnam led to a noticeable decline in interventionist sentiment.

INTESTATE ESTATES. In the colonial South, New York, and Rhode Island, the lands of a person dying without making a will descended to his eldest son, while chattels were distributed to the children equally. New England and Pennsylvania assimilated real and personal property and provided for division among the children, a double portion going to the eldest son; even in 18th-century New England, however, land in fee tail was generally held to descend to the eldest son. The revolutionary era ushered in a legislative offensive against primogeniture. The rule has since obtained in the United States that, on the death of an intestate seized of real property in fee simple, such property descends to his or her children equally, subject to the varying rights of the surviving husband or wife.

INTOLERABLE ACTS (in part also known as the Coercion Acts). Five acts of Parliament (March–June 1774): the Boston Port Act, the Massachusetts Bay Regulating Act, the Act for the Impartial Administration of Justice, the Quartering Act, and the Quebec Act. The first four acts were designed to punish Boston for the Tea Party and to reinforce royal authority at the expense of popular liberty by alterations in the Massachusetts charter; the Quebec Act, although lumped by Americans with the Coercion Acts, was not a punitive measure, but in the hands of colonial propagandists it was made to appear a menace to the religious as well as the civil liberties of the colonists. These acts, intended to restore peace and order in America and to isolate Massachusetts, threw the colonies into ferment and became the justification for calling the first Continental Congress in September 1774.

INTREPID. Formerly the Tripolitan ketch *Mastico;* captured by Stephen Decatur during the war with Tripoli and used by him on Feb. 16, 1804, in burning the *Philadelphia,* which had been captured by the Tripolitans. On the night of Sept. 4, 1804, the vessel, carrying powder, large shells, solid shot, and combustibles, was sailed into the harbor of Tripoli by Lt. Richard Somers, where it exploded before getting sufficiently near the enemy gunboats to destroy them.

INVESTIGATING COMMITTEES. The practices of Parliament and the colonial assemblies were considered ample precedent for using investigatory powers in the state and federal constitutional systems that emerged after the American Revolution; the power of legislative bodies to conduct investigations was considered inherent in the performance of legislative functions. The House of Representatives created a special committee in 1792 to inquire into the reasons for the defeat of Maj. Gen. Arthur St. Clair's expedition against the Indians of the Northwest in the previous year. For Congress the expansion of investigatory authority concerning potential legislation came slowly and in the face of substantial internal opposition. As late as 1827, for example, the House voted only 102 to 88 in favor of a statute to compel testimony—the argument for the statute being principally that only through compulsion of testimony could the facts essential to the development of new legislation be ascertained. In the Senate, investigations to aid legislation were also opposed strongly. The first major Senate inquiry of this type, approved in 1859, sprang from John Brown's raid on the federal arsenal at Harpers Ferry, Va.

During the first four decades of its existence Congress invoked common-law principles to punish recalcitrant witnesses for contempt. In 1827 Congress imposed a statutory penalty for refusal to appear, to answer germane questions, or to produce papers before an investigating committee. In *Kilbourn* v. *Thompson* (1880) the Supreme Court declared that the cases in which the power of contempt might be invoked were limited; in 1897 the Supreme Court, in *In re Chapman,* upheld congressional power to punish for contempt. The power to invoke common-law authority considerably undermined the *Kilbourn* doctrine. In 1927, in the case of *McGrain* v. *Daugherty,* the Court unanimously upheld an even broader construction of congressional power to investigate.

In the mid-20th century attention came to be concentrated upon the abuses of congressional or state legislative investigating committees, often—as in the hearings of the McCarthy committee (Senate Permanent Committee on Investigations) or the House Un-American Activities Committee—involving serious effects upon the public or private reputations or careers of some of the witnesses. Although *Watkins* v. *United States* (1957) was cited as limiting investigation that was merely for "the exposure of individual behavior," *Barenblatt* v. *United States* (1959) indicated that the Court was generally willing to permit broad investigatory activities.

Historically, the most serious limitation on the investigating power of congressional committees has been the invocation of the doctrine of separation of powers by presidents who chose to refuse to permit divulgence of information or papers. The confrontation, in 1973, between the Senate Select Committee for Investigating into Presidential Campaign Activities (the Ervin committee) and President Richard M. Nixon about the right of the committee to review tape recordings of conversations of the president raised the issue in its most direct form. Whether it would be resolved on the basis of a broad assertion of executive privilege or of Archibald Cox's contention that "even the highest executive officials are subject to the rule of law" was the salient issue in the controversy. Cox's view prevailed in *United States* v. *Nixon* (1974).

INVESTMENT BANKS. The modern investment bank has three parts: it investigates and judges the stocks and bonds that business concerns, seeking to raise capital, ask it to market for them; it buys these securities for a negotiated price, frequently borrowing most of the funds needed from a commercial bank; and in cooperation with other firms it markets the securities, either wholesale or retail at a profit. The presence of stock exchanges, on which buyers know they may resell securities, makes it easier for the investment banker to sell his wares in the first place.

Early in the 19th century well-known brokerage houses, such as Prime, Ward and King of New York or Alexander Brown and Sons of Baltimore, or commercial bankers, such as Nicholas Biddle, sold securities (chiefly governments') to wealthy clients or to investment houses overseas. During the Civil War, Jay Cooke developed a large organization of bond salesmen to sell government bonds to the public. After the war the House of Junius Morgan and of his son, J. P. Morgan, assumed leadership in investment sales. But Morgan carried his dislike for wasteful competition and his dictation too far when he helped to found such monopolies as the Northern Securities Company and the United States Steel Company about 1901. In consequence, Theodore Roosevelt's trustbusting activities and in 1912 the Pujo Money Trust investigation followed. The latter found that Morgan headed a huge security merchandising monopoly. During the 1920's giant commercial banks, such as New York's Chase National and National City developed large investment affiliates to market securities. Irresponsible management of these contributed to the 1929 panic. Revelations before Congress between 1931 and 1933 led to the prohibition of affiliates and to the passage of the Securities Act of May 27, 1933, and the Securities Exchange Act of June 6, 1934. These laws obliged the investment banker to "tell all" in his prospectus about the security he was offering, under severe penalty if he failed to do so. Investment banking declined sharply in the 1930's; indeed, government agencies, such as the Reconstruction Finance Corporation were the big suppliers of capital. Other regulations included the Chandler Act of June 1938, reducing the once dominant role of the investment banker in reorganizations; the Maloney Act of June 25, 1938, policing over-the-counter markets; and the Investment Company Act of 1940, regulating investment trusts, chiefly mutual funds.

In March 1937, William O. Douglas of the Securities and Exchange Commission (SEC) urged compulsory competitive bidding for new securities. On Apr. 8, 1941, the SEC announced Rule U-50, essentially effecting such a policy. Within a few years, purchase syndicates grew in size, and selling groups, which were supposed to benefit from U-50, almost ceased to exist. Meanwhile, on Oct. 30, 1947, the Justice Department brought suit against seventeen major firms and the Investment Bankers Association for being a monopoly. The case lasted six years, but the U.S. Circuit Court held that there was insufficient evidence of monopoly.

Between 1900 and 1980 economic and political pressures considerably altered investment banking: capital became less scarce, which made investment houses less influential; most firms were no longer partnerships but corporations; bonds fell in importance and stocks rose; railroads declined and utilities grew; investment banking was more competitive; and public disclosure was the rule. In the 1930's, direct or private placements became an important method of marketing: large insurance companies, for example, bypassed the investment bankers and bought directly. Investment firms performed a greater variety of services, such as advising investors, evaluating securities, serving as professional negotiators for clients contemplating merger, and arranging direct placements themselves.

INVESTMENT COMPANIES. Financial organizations (sometimes trusts but more usually corporations) that sell their shares to numerous public investors in order to place the proceeds in a diversified investment portfolio. The main advantages to the investor are diversification, liquidity, and continuous professional supervision, otherwise available only to investors of means. The first investment company, the Foreign and Colonial Government Trust, was founded in Great Britain in 1868. A few investment companies were organized in the United States during the late 19th century. They proliferated in the 1920's, reaching a market value of nearly $7 billion. All but a handful were closed-end. The 1929 market collapse revealed unsound investment policies by some managers that gave investment trusts a bad name—hence the change of name to "investment companies." The half-dozen open-end mutual funds founded in the 1920's survived the depression; thereafter the mutual fund became the dominant form, eventually comprising over 90 percent of investment company assets. By 1980, 564 mutual funds had 12 million stockholders and assets of $135 billion.

IOWA. In June 1673, Louis Jolliet and Jacques Marquette entered Iowa and encountered such tribes as the Mascoutens, the Peoria, and the Miami. Iowa belonged to France from 1673 to 1762, when Louisiana west of the Mississippi was ceded to Spain. The Spanish made three private land grants —to Julien Dubuque in 1796, to Louis H. Tesson in 1799, and to Basil Giard in 1800. At Napoleon's command Spain retroceded Louisiana in 1800, only to see the United States acquire it three years later through the Louisiana Purchase. Thereafter Iowa land was included in the District of Louisiana until 1805; in the Territory of Louisiana until 1812; and in the Territory of Missouri until 1821. It was unorganized territory until attached to Michigan Territory in 1834. In 1836, Iowa formed a part of Wisconsin Territory.

The Sauk, Fox, Potawatomi, Iowa, Winnebago, and Sioux peopled the region. The only pitched battle between Indians and whites on Iowa soil occurred at present-day Des Moines on Apr. 19, 1735. The Black Hawk War (1832) resulted in the first Indian cession of Iowa land. Between 1832 and 1851 the United States acquired title to the land of Iowa from the Indians for less than 10 cents an acre. After 1851 only two significant Indian episodes occurred: the return of the Fox Indians in 1856 to establish the Tama Reservation, and the Spirit Lake Massacre in 1857.

In 1833 permanent settlement began. The first public surveys were begun in 1837, and two land offices were established the following year. The Territory of Iowa, including present Iowa, Minnesota, and that part of North and South Dakota east of the Missouri River, was created on July 4, 1838, having been named after the Iowa River, which in turn derived its name from the Iowa Indians. A clamor for statehood culminated in the constitution of 1844. Iowa was admitted to the Union on Dec. 28, 1846, with the present area (56,290 square miles), under a second constitution. The Democrats dominated state politics until 1858; from then on until the New Deal era the Republicans were mostly in control.

Iowa is an agricultural state. Farmers drew up the constitution of 1846, formed the first agricultural societies in 1852, founded an agricultural college in 1858, and established the state dairy association in 1877. The value of Iowa livestock and livestock products exceeds that of any other state, although by 1980 industrial production slightly exceeded farm income. The population in 1980 was 2,913,387; 57.2 percent of Iowans lived in urban areas.

IOWA BAND. A group of eleven ministers from Andover Theological Seminary who came to Iowa in 1843 as missionaries of the American Home Missionary Society. Their hope was that each one should found a church and that together they might found a college. Each man founded one or more Congregational churches, and the group was instrumental in founding Iowa College, which opened at Davenport in November 1848. (*See also* Illinois Band.)

IPSWICH PROTEST. Acting legally, Gov. Edmund Andros, in March 1687, ordered certain New England tax levies. Led by their pastor, John Wise, the men of Ipswich, Mass., refused payment; their formal remonstrance was the Ipswich Protest. Arrest and punishment followed; but the incident indicates the nascent colonial antagonism toward any taxation program not self-devised.

IRAN, U.S. RELATIONS WITH. Until World War II, U.S. relations with Iran were closely linked with British policy. In 1907 an Anglo-Russian convention divided the country, then known as Persia, into two spheres. British attempts to establish a protectorate over the region were defeated in 1919. In 1921, Gen. Reza Pahlavi seized the government, and three years later was elected hereditary shah. During World War II, increased pro-Axis activity led to an Allied occupation in 1941 and the deposition of the shah in favor of his son, Mohammed Reza Pahlavi. At the Teheran Conference (1943), the United States, Great Britain, and the Soviet Union, agreed to maintain Iran's independence.

After World War II, U.S. policy was dominated by its interest in Iran's vast oil reserves. In 1950, Ali Razmara became premier on a program to restore honesty to the corrupt government but was assassinated after nine months in office in a coup by Mohammed Mossadegh. The United States, with oil in mind, at first sympathized with Mossadegh, but Secretary of State John Foster Dulles reversed that policy and aided in Mossadegh's overthrow and the restoration of the shah in 1953. The new premier, Fazollah Zahedi, established closer relations with the United States. At the same time, the United States began a vast program of economic and military aid. In 1955, Iran joined the Central Treaty Organization (or Baghdad Pact). Iran became America's strongest ally in the Middle East, and although a founding member of the Organization of Petroleum Exporting Nations (OPEC), it continued to support U.S. interests in the region.

With increasing discontent within Iran, U.S. aid became closely linked by the Iranian population to the shah's unpopular government; American support for the shah alienated that country's population. In January 1979, the shah was overthrown by Moslem fanatics led by Ayatollah Khomeni. On Nov. 4, 1979, Iranian militants seized the U.S. embassy in Teheran and held fifty-two American hostage for 444 days (*see* Iranian Captivity). With the Moslem revolutionaries in control of the government, relations between Iran and the United States continued to remain tense.

IRANIAN CAPTIVITY (Nov. 4, 1979–Jan. 20, 1981). On Nov. 4, 1979, several hundred Iranian militants seized the U.S. embassy in Teheran and took some ninety people hostage. About sixty were U.S. citizens. The militants announced that the Americans would be held until the deposed shah,

Mohammad Reza Pahlavi, undergoing medical treatment in a New York City hospital, was returned to Iran to stand trial for crimes allegedly committed during the years he ruled the country. President Jimmy Carter declared that he would not extradite the shah and retaliated by reviewing the visas of 45,000 Iranians in the United States; cutting off purchases of Iranian oil; and freezing all official Iranian assets in the country. On Nov. 19 and 20, the Iranians released thirteen women and blacks in the hope of gaining the support of U.S. minority groups. On Feb. 11, 1980, Iranian President Bani-Sadr announced Iranian conditions for the release of the hostages: that the United States acknowledge "past crimes"; recognize Iran's right to obtain extradition of the deposed shah and take control of his fortune; and promise not to interfere in Iran's internal affairs. Twelve days later a United Nations commission tried to secure the hostages' release, to no avail. On Apr. 7, Carter severed all diplomatic relations with Iran and imposed an embargo on all U.S. exports, except food and medicine, to that country. On Apr. 17, he announced further sanctions, including a ban on all imports from Iran. The president and his advisers also formulated a daring rescue to free the captives. On Apr. 24, American helicopters and transport planes flew to a secret base in the desert of eastern Iran. Because of mechanical failures three of the helicopters did not finish the trip, and the mission had to be called off. During the withdrawal, a helicopter crashed into a transport and eight American servicemen died. The feared retaliation against the hostages did not occur, but many of them were moved to locations outside Teheran.

The failed rescue mission was followed by a lull in diplomatic efforts. that lasted through the summer. On July 11, however, a hostage was released due to illness. On July 27, the shah died, but it was not until the presidential campaign of 1980 that efforts for the release of the hostages brightened. On Oct. 28, President Carter reiterated that he was prepared to free Iranian assets and resume some trade. On Nov. 2, Iran's parliament endorsed a special commission's conditions for freeing the hostages, but Carter's defeat by Ronald Reagan clouded the negotiations. Negotiations continued with Algerian diplomats acting as intermediaries. On Jan. 20, 1981, presidential inauguration day, the fifty-two hostages, after 444 days in captivity, were released.

IRISH IMMIGRATION. *See* **Immigration.**

IRISH TRACT. That portion of the Valley of Virginia and the bordering region on the northwest that was settled by the Scotch-Irish. It may now be identified as the counties of Augusta, Rockbridge, and Bath, together with the southwest fourth of Rockingham and portions of Highland, Alleghany, Botetourt, Roanoke, Craig, and Montgomery.

IRON ACT OF 1750. Passed by Parliament because of commercial difficulties with Sweden, where England obtained most of the bar iron, and in the hope that the colonies would supply such iron instead. It provided that colonial pig iron could enter Great Britain free of duties and that colonial bar iron could be imported into London duty-free (after 1757 into all English ports). Through the influence of English manufacturers, restrictive clauses were placed in the law. Slitting mills, steel furnaces, and plating mills could not be erected in the colonies, although those already in operation could continue. The law was not very successful. Increasing amounts of colonial iron were sent to England, but not in such quantities as were expected. The restrictive aspects of the law were not observed, and many ironworks were erected.

IRON AND STEEL INDUSTRY. The American iron industry was founded in the 17th century by British capitalists who sought to profit from America's abundance of iron and timber. The Virginia Company under Sir Edwin Sandys founded an ironworks at Falling Creek, but the plant was destroyed in the Indian massacre of 1622. John Winthrop, Jr., was more successful. He persuaded a group of English capitalists to finance the undertaking, imported skilled ironworkers, and in 1645 built a large plant at Braintree, Mass., but the site lacked sufficient waterpower. The plant failed, and Winthrop was replaced by Richard Leader, who established an entirely new plant on the Saugus near Lynn. The Lynn works was a technical success but a financial failure, mainly because of the high cost of skilled labor. But the transplantation of iron technology succeeded; skilled ironworkers founded smaller, more primitive, ironworks that gradually spread throughout the colonies. By the outbreak of the Revolution, the colonies were producing almost 15 percent of the world's iron. Ironworks had been built in every colony except Georgia, but Pennsylvania was emerging as the leader in iron production. The typical unit was an iron plantation, containing a mansion house for the owner and homes for the workers, located on an estate of several thousand acres on which timber was abundant. Blast furnaces consumed enormous quantities of charcoal, and after one region was deforested, the plantation could be reestablished farther west. The colonies also produced steel, an alloy of iron and carbon. It was produced as "blister" steel by the cementation process that involved prolonged heating of wrought iron with carbon. Used for sharp-edged tools, swords, and bayonets, steel was expensive and constituted only a small part of the industry.

From the Revolution to the Civil War, America lagged behind in the transformation of the iron industry taking place in Europe. By the late 18th century, the British had switched from coal to coke in iron smelting; but Americans continued to rely on charcoal through the 1850's. By that time America, an exporter of iron in the colonial period, was importing huge quantities of iron for industrial purposes. In 1817 the puddling furnace and rolling mill for making wrought iron was introduced in America. Eleven years later James Neilson of Scotland developed the hot-blast technique, employed by Americans to achieve the higher temperatures needed to utilize anthracite coal in place of charcoal in blast furnaces. Coke was successfully employed in America in 1837, but it was not widely used until the 1860's.

America's rapid rise to world leadership between the Civil War and World War I came with the substitution of steel for iron. The basic European innovations, the Bessemer and open-hearth processes, were refined and mechanized in such a way as to give American producers a significant advantage. In 1856 Sir Henry Bessemer in England invented his process for removing excess carbon from molten pig iron by blowing air through it. William Kelly, a Kentucky ironmaster, had been experimenting with the same idea, and his priority was recognized by the U.S. Patent Office in 1857. In 1864 a company in Wyandotte, Mich., attempted to make steel under Kelly's patent, and in 1865 a company in Troy, N.Y., began to make steel under Bessemer's patent. In 1866 the two groups pooled their patents and formed the Bessemer Steel Association. Alexander L. Holley, of the Troy group, altered Bessemer's process in many ways. He used two converters, each with a detachable bottom, and attempted to make a batch process into one approximating continuous operation. He also favored large, integrated plants that would gain the economies inherent in large-scale operation. The open-hearth (or Siemens-Martin) process was introduced to America in 1868. By 1890 it had begun to supplant the Bessemer process. Being slower, it was easier to control with precision. But another factor was Samuel T. Wellman's invention of devices that mechanized the loading of the furnace, thus cutting labor costs drastically.

From 1875 to 1920 American steel production increased from 380,000 tons to 60 million tons annually, and America became the uncontested world leader in the manufacture of iron and steel. This growth was made possible by solid technological foundations, the protective tariff, and the rapid growth of the American economy. Another factor was America's natural resources. Iron ore was reasonably abundant in the eastern United States. But the Lake Superior region contained vast deposits of exceedingly rich ore. In 1844 the Marquette Range in Michigan was discovered. Other discoveries followed, the greatest being the Mesabi range in Minnesota. From 1855 to 1900 the axis of the iron industry shifted from the East to the Midwest. Iron ore was brought to ports on Lake Michigan and Lake Erie, and great steel centers grew up in Pittsburgh, Pa.; Youngstown, Ohio; and Gary, Ind. Other rich ore deposits were found in the Birmingham region of Alabama and were developed after the Civil War.

Since the early 1950's the American industry, while continuing to grow, has lost ground relative to the rest of the world; in 1950 U.S. steel production was 46.4 percent of the world production, while in 1980 the ratio decreased to 14.1 percent. By the 1960's the richer, more easily worked, iron ores were nearly exhausted. A major crisis was averted by shifting to the less rich and harder taconite ores of the Lake Superior region. This move brought about a major technological innovation by the American industry: it involved constructing benefication plants to enrich the ore and convert it into pellets. The basic oxygen process of steelmaking, developed in Germany and Austria, rapidly gained ground over the open-hearth process for making steel during the 1960's. In 1980, 67.6 million tons out of the total U.S. production of 111.8 million tons, were produced by this process.

IRONCLAD OATH. An oath prescribed by act of Congress, as part of the Reconstruction legislation of 1867, by which every person elected or appointed to any federal office of honor or profit, civil or military, had to swear allegiance to the Constitution and declare that he had never voluntarily borne arms against the United States or aided, recognized, or supported jurisdiction hostile to the Constitution. This oath was the key to the disqualifications that the Radical Republicans imposed during Reconstruction.

IRONCLADS, CONFEDERATE, ON INLAND WATERS. The use of ironclads was principally confined to the Mississippi River and its affluents. At the Head of the Passes, on Oct. 12, 1861, the Confederate privateer ram *Manassas* became the world's first ironclad steamer in action. Although the Confederates continued to achieve individual successes, such as the *Arkansas*' single-handed passage of the combined fleets of Adm. David G. Farragut and Adm. Charles H. Davis above Vicksburg, Miss., July 15, 1862, the United States, through the efforts of its War and Navy departments, quickly gained ironclad superiority. The ironclad war on inland waters ended with the surrender of the Confederate ship *Missouri* in the Red River, June 3, 1865.

IRONCLAD WARSHIPS. Thickening a ship's sides with fitted armor against penetration by shot was common practice in the first half of the 19th century. The first U.S. ironclad was the *Stevens Battery,* begun in 1842 but never completed. In the Civil War inadequate shipbuilding facilities forced the Confederates to fit armor on existing hulls; the captured Union steam frigate *Merrimack* (renamed *Virginia*) was the first so converted. Although similar conversions were made by both sides on the Mississippi River (*see* Eads Gunboats), the Union generally relied on newly constructed iron or wooden vessels designed to carry metal armor. The *Monitor* was the first completed, and its success against the *Virginia* on Mar. 9, 1862, led to the construction of many others of the same type—characterized by a very low freeboard, vertically armored sides, and armored revolving gun turrets.

IRON CURTAIN. In an address at Westminster College at Fulton, Mo., on Mar. 5, 1946, Winston Churchill, retired prime minister of Great Britain, spoke of Eastern Europe as an area where an iron curtain had descended, behind which Soviet control was increasing. The expression came to connote controls over influences of any kind entering Communist countries from the outside or circulating within them.

IRON SHIP. The popular name for the *Michigan,* the first iron ship in the U.S. Navy. It was launched at Erie, Pa., in 1844 and was long the only naval vessel on the upper Great Lakes. It is preserved as a historical memorial in Erie.

IROQUOIS. The Iroquoian-speaking tribes were intrusive into the Northeast, having moved up from the South before contact with Europeans. Settling in the lake region and Mohawk Valley in north central New York, the Seneca, Cayuga, Oneida, Onondaga, and Mohawk formed a political union that for two centuries dominated the Algonkin peoples. Legend ascribes the formation of the famous League of the Iroquois (Five Nations) to the heroes Dekanawida and Hiawatha, and it was said that the confederation aimed at peace. Joined after 1712 by the linguistically related Tuscarora, whose conflicts with European settlers in North Carolina resulted in their alliance with the Oneida, the league became known as the Six Tribes. The confederacy was fully integrated by 1700, and political reciprocities between the original five were so well defined that the beginnings of the union can probably be dated early in the 16th century, although 1570 is an often quoted date. Each tribe had a council to regulate its own local affairs, and a great council, consisting of fifty peace chiefs, or sachems, met once yearly at Onondaga, N.Y. Judicial, legislative, and military questions were resolved first within the individual tribes and then passed on to the representative body, where unanimous consensus was required, there being no concept of majority voting. The number of sachems for each tribe was fixed by a developing tradition in the representative council. Ambassadors traveled to advise of decisions, questions, and times of meeting; they carried the tubular beads of accreditation, the wampum. Both councils, tribal and intertribal, were highly susceptible to public opinion. The unanimous decisions were reached only after discussion, all opinions being heard in an atmosphere of dignified oratory.

The various ranks of chieftainship, together with such rights and privileges as might accrue to sachem status, passed on matrilineally through the clans that made up the society of the five tribes. A sachem received political office by virtue of its matrilineal inheritance by the clan and his designation to it by the women of the clan. Through their power to appoint, the women of the clan had a vital political role; but in addition, the women of a chief's clan in the generation of his mother had the power to warn and depose him. Although they held no political office as such, women were free to speak, to initiate political issues, and by the pressures they were able to exert, to direct events.

The development of stockaded villages with communal dwellings for clan segments (the so-called long houses), elaboration of maize cultivation, and matrilineal descent suggest the southeastern peoples. The Iroquoian languages also have affinities with the speech of southern native Americans, relating to Cherokee, and are related ultimately to a Siouan or Hokan-Siouan phylum. Public festivals, elaborate myths, and the important role of dreams also suggest southern origins. Distinctive, however, are the Iroquois curing groups, the "false face" curers, related to secret lodges, a tradition suggestive of northeastern, or Algonkin, origins.

The league ceased to be effective after the American Revolution, and the tribes, in part at least, were forced to disperse. A flurry of messianism, reflecting a cultural revival, began in 1799 with the advent of the prophet Handsome Lake, founder of a syncretistic pagan-Christian movement among the Seneca. In 1979 about 8,800 Iroquois lived on six reservations in New York state; the headquarters of the league was at Onondaga Reservation south of Syracuse.

IROQUOIS BEAVER LAND DEED. At Albany, July 10, 1701, the Iroquois deeded in trust to England their conquered Huron lands in Canada and a portion of their own ancient holdings, in all a tract 800 miles long and 400 miles broad, north and northwest of lakes Erie and Ontario, and the southern shores. This action was designed to prevent French claims, to put the Iroquois under the protection of the British, and to secure to the English colonies the rich fur trade of the region; but neither this deed nor a more definitive one given later to lands south of the lakes was intended by the Indians to transfer title to the land itself.

IROQUOIS THEATER FIRE (Dec. 30, 1903). A fire during a matinee at the Iroquois Theater in the loop district of Chicago resulted in the deaths of over 600 people. Advertised to be the "finest and safest in America," the new Iroquois theater proved, upon investigation, to be a firetrap, built of the cheapest materials, many of them highly flammable, and lacking adequate exits. As a result of the tragedy a wave of safety legislation swept the country.

IROQUOIS TREATY. At Albany on July 13, 1684, Gov. Thomas Dongan of New York; Lord Howard of Effingham, governor of Virginia; delegates from both colonies; and Col. Stephen Cortland, one of the Council of New York, representing Massachusetts Bay, met in council with seventeen sachems of the Mohawk, Onondaga, Oneida, and Cayuga nations. Gov. Howard rebuked the Indians for breaking treaties and allowing their warriors to attack the settlers and Indians of Virginia. The Mohawk denied that they had broken faith, advocated peace for all nations, and asked that the Duke of York's arms be placed upon their castles. The other nations, with ceremony, agreed to live at peace with the English. On Aug. 2, the Onondaga and Cayuga declared themselves and their lands under the sovereignty of the Duke of York. On Aug. 5, the Seneca arrived and confirmed the action of the other nations.

"IRREPRESSIBLE CONFLICT." A term used by Sen. William H. Seward in his Rochester speech on Oct. 25, 1858, in which he forecast that the socioeconomic institutions of the North and of the South were headed for a collision.

IRRIGATION. Streams were used by the Indians of the Southwest in pre-Columbian times and by their Spanish conquerors. Farther to the north the first irrigators were the fur traders, especially the factors of the Hudson's Bay Company in the Columbia Valley in the 1830's. They were succeeded by the missionaries Marcus Whitman near Walla Walla, Wash. (1839), and Father Pierre Jean De Smet in the Bitterroot Valley of Montana (1842). Irrigation on a large scale within the United States was first practiced by the Mormons in Utah; by 1850 they had 16,333 acres under cultivation.

The first ditches were short and narrow, dug with pick, shovel, plow, and scraper, to irrigate the bottom lands bordering the streams. To irrigate the higher bench lands, greater financial resources were necessary. These were supplied initially by colonies and commercial companies. In California a group of Germans founded the Anaheim Colony near Los

Angeles in 1857, diverting water from the Santa Ana River to irrigate their vineyards. In 1870 the Southern California Colony Association, under the leadership of John W. North, located the Riverside Colony on the banks of the same river and dug a thirteen-mile canal costing $50,000. In the same year, the Union Colony of Nathan C. Meeker at Greeley in northern Colorado began the construction of two canals. Corporations such as the Colorado Mortgage and Investment Company constructed many of the larger canals during 1870–1900. Thereafter, conflicts between the water-users and the companies demonstrated that this institution was ill suited to the needs of irrigated agriculture.

More suitable was the mutual irrigation company—which originated in Utah—a form of agricultural cooperative in which the irrigation facilities are owned and operated by the water-users and in which stock certificates represent shares of water. Since it lacked the authority to tax, it could not accumulate the funds necessary to construct the diversion dams and storage reservoirs of the larger systems. In response to this need, Californians, in formulating the Wright Act of 1887, invented the irrigation district with power to levy taxes and issue bonds. Within thirty years each of the seventeen contiguous western states had authorized the creation of such districts. A further problem emerged in that while the irrigation district had the power to levy taxes only upon agricultural lands, city dwellers also benefited from irrigation development. To remove this inequity, Coloradoans in 1937 created the water conservancy district. In spite of the invention of the irrigation district, the construction of projects with expensive dams remained beyond the means of local communities; consequently, western irrigators turned to the federal government for assistance, which they received through the Carey Act of 1894, and the Reclamation Act of 1902.

Initially, the doctrine of riparian rights prevailed. Since it restricted these rights to riparian owners and forbade diminution of stream flow, it was soon modified or abrogated. The California courts modified it by allowing stream diminution, but the Rocky Mountain states abrogated it and adopted a water law embodying the doctrine of prior appropriation. This necessitated the invention of methods of acquisition, adjudication, and administration. Through laws enacted in 1879 and 1881 the Colorado legislature pioneered in the creation of these methods, and the framers of the constitution of Wyoming, with the assistance of the teritorial engineer, Elwood Mead, improved upon them. The Wyoming system, which has influenced the irrigation institutions of all the western states with the exception of those of Colorado, provides for state control of the appropriative right. A dispute between Colorado and Kansas over the use of the Arkansas River led the Supreme Court in *Kansas* v. *Colorado* (1907) to enunciate the principle of equitable apportionment. Subsequently Colorado initiated the use of interstate compacts to settle interstate disputes by signing on Nov. 24, 1922, the Colorado River Compact with its neighbors in the Colorado watershed. Since then, state governments have negotiated compacts governing the utilization of nearly every western interstate stream.

Since 1940 there has been a spectacular increase in the number of acres irrigated from wells. The first extensive irrigation from these sources occurred in southern California in 1868. By 1890 more than 2,000 flowing wells were irrigating 38,378 acres in California. Thereafter, with lowering water levels, pumped wells became more numerous, and by 1899, there were 152,506 acres being irrigated in California from groundwater. After 1900, Louisiana and Arkansas rice growers resorted to well irrigation in considerable numbers, as did the farmers of the Pecos Valley in New Mexico. With the development and manufacture of small deep-well turbine pumps and the availability of low-cost electricity in the 1930's, groundwater became an important source of irrigation.

The common-law rule of absolute ownership, which governed the utilization of groundwater, proved unsuited to the needs of western farmers. The decline of water levels in southern California led the supreme court of that state, in *Katz* v. *Walkinshaw* (1902), to formulate the rule of correlative rights, giving those using water from a common groundwater basin equitable rights to it. New Mexico by legislative enactment in 1927 applied the appropriation doctrine to the use of groundwater, and fifteen western states followed its example in some measure. In 1978 the irrigated land in the United States comprised 51 million acres.

ISLAND NUMBER TEN, OPERATIONS AT (Mar. 15–Apr. 7, 1862). Six ironclads and ten mortar boats commanded by Union Flag Officer Andrew H. Foote cooperated with Maj. Gen. John Pope's 25,000 men in capturing Island Number Ten, located in the upper part of a triple bend of the Mississippi, fifty-five miles below Cairo, Ill. It was the first achievement in the campaign to divide the Confederacy by gaining control of the Mississippi.

ISLEÑOS. An industrious group of Canary Islanders, who came to Spanish Louisiana in 1779, settling at Terre aux Boeufs near Lake Borgne, at Galveztown near the junction of the Iberville River (now the Bayou Manchac) and the Amite, and at Valenzuela on Bayou Lafourche.

ISLE OF ORLEANS. A tract of some 2,800 square miles, bounded by the Iberville River, lakes Maurepas and Pontchartrain, the Gulf of Mexico, and the Mississippi. It was exempted by France when all else east of the Mississippi was ceded to England by the Treaty of Paris, 1763, and later, in the hands of Spain (*see* Fontainebleau, Treaty of) became a barrier to American navigation of the Mississippi (*see* Deposit, Right of). It was sought by the United States from Spain during the Nootka Sound affair in 1790 and was a factor in the negotiations for the Louisiana Purchase.

ISLE OF PINES. A historically Cuban island in the northwest Caribbean Sea, it was excepted from Cuban territory by the Platt Amendment in 1903 for its strategic value as a potential naval base guarding the Yucatán entrance to the Gulf of Mexico. By 1904 the United States was more interested in European routes to Panama and, having secured Guantánamo, drafted the Hay-Quesada Treaty relinquishing claim to the Isle of Pines. Because of sentiment favoring Caribbean hegemony the treaty languished unratified until Mar. 13, 1925.

ISLES OF SHOALS. A group of small, rocky islands ten miles off Portsmouth, N.H., of which Duck, Appledore, Cedar, and Smuttynose belong to Maine and of which White, Lunging, and Star belong to New Hampshire. Visited by fishermen from the 16th century on, mentioned by Samuel de Champlain in 1605, and described by Capt. John Smith after his voyage of 1614, they were given to the Laconia Company in 1631. In 1635 they were divided between Sir Ferdinando Gorges and Capt. John Mason and thus added to their properties in Maine and New Hampshire. The islands were permanently settled in the 1630's and for a time were the center of much fishing and commerce, with a population of over 600. By the 19th century, the islands had become almost uninhabited, but Appledore and Star in particular have become summer resorts.

ISOLATIONISM. American noninterventionist and unilateralist attitudes and concomitant opposition to involvement in foreign alliances and wars. Although isolationism developed early in American history, the term itself gained prominence only in the 20th century. Isolationists did not want to cut the United States off from the rest of the world. They did not oppose foreign trade and did not necessarily oppose American expansion. They were not pacifists; they favored maintaining military forces to guard American interests and security in the Western Hemisphere. They distrusted Europe and England in particular.

The efforts by President John Adams (1797–1801) to avoid war with France were part of the isolationist tradition. In his first inaugural address, in 1801, President Thomas Jefferson advised against "entangling alliances." Even the War of 1812 against England was not waged in alliance with any European belligerents and the United States did not send troops to fight in Europe. The Monroe Doctrine of 1823 advised America "not to interfere in the internal concerns" of Europe. Continental territorial expansion from 1803 to 1867 was accomplished within the isolationist framework. Even the extensive U.S. acquisition of territories in the Caribbean and the Pacific in the 19th and early 20th centuries was accomplished through unilateral actions, not joint actions with European states.

U.S. efforts to stay out of World War I and rejection of membership in the League of Nations afterward were consistent with isolationism. In the 1920's and 1930's isolationists led by senators William E. Borah, Hiram W. Johnson, Gerald P. Nye, and Arthur H. Vandenberg vigorously opposed involvement in European controversies. The Senate Munitions Investigating Committee under Nye (1934–36) was part of that noninterventionist effort, as was the enactment of neutrality laws from 1935 to 1937. When World War II erupted, isolationists fought a last-ditch battle against involvement abroad. In 1940–41 many of them worked through the America First Committee, the leading noninterventionist pressure group before the attack on Pearl Harbor.

With American entry into World War II, isolationism lost the strong position it had had in American thought. It became an enfeebled legacy of America's past, although controversies that surrounded U.S. involvement in the Vietnam War gave renewed currency to some arguments advanced by isolationists a generation before.

ISRAELI-AMERICAN RELATIONS. Effective U.S. support for the establishment of Israel began after World War II. President Harry Truman placed pressure on England to withdraw from Palestine and the ensuing debates culminated on Nov. 29, 1947, in a resolution for the partition of Palestine between Arabs and Jews. Although Truman withdrew support for partition in March 1948, opting instead for a temporary trusteeship, he immediately extended *de facto* recognition to Israel following its proclamation of independence on May 14, 1948. The United States, out of concern for its relations with the more economically and strategically important Arab states, remained neutral in the first Arab-Israeli war, 1948–49. Following the armistice of July 1949, the United States attempted to act as mediator in the Middle East. It aided Israel economically through a $100 million loan from the U.S. Export-Import Bank in 1949, governmental grants-in-aid, and technical assistance under the Point Four program. On May 25, 1950, the United States, England, and France issued a tripartite declaration that guaranteed the borders of Israel and its neighbors and placed a limited arms embargo on the region, generally successful until the first Soviet-Egyptian arms deal of September 1955.

Extensive Soviet military aid to Egypt, complete closing of the Gulf of 'Aqaba (September 1955), increased terrorist raids, and Jordanian entry into the Syrian-Egyptian military pact in October 1956 led to Israel's "preventive" attack against Egypt on Oct. 29 in conjunction with an Anglo-French bombardment and occupation of the area flanking the Suez Canal, nationalized by Egypt in July 1956. The Suez crisis was the nadir in Israeli-American relations, for the United States and the Soviet Union forced England and France to withdraw and pressured Israel to return the Gaza Strip and the Sinai Peninsula to Egypt. Israel completed its evacuation during March 1957, after President Dwight D. Eisenhower guaranteed it access to the Gulf of 'Aqaba.

Relations then improved as the United States generally supported Israel in the United Nations and began to supply it with military as well as economic aid. After nearly a decade of relative peace, a cycle of terrorist raids and Israeli reprisals began in 1965. Egypt's President Gamal Abdel Nasser suddenly forced the withdrawal of the UN Emergency Force on May 18, 1967; closed the Gulf of 'Aqaba on May 22; and signed a military agreement with Jordan on May 30, catching Israel and the United States by surprise. Convinced that Western aid would not be forthcoming and fearing aggression, Israel attacked Egypt on June 5. The scope of Israel's victory against Egypt, Jordan, and Syria in the Six-Day War surprised the world. Determined not to relinquish advantageous military positions without the complete normalization of relations with the Arab states and unwilling to return the old city of Jerusalem in any case, Israel resisted pressure that it withdraw to the prewar boundaries. The United States chose not to force the issue even after it became the sole supplier of military aircraft to Israel after the cooling of Franco-Israeli relations between 1967 and 1969. Although Israeli and American views had points of divergence, the United States became Israel's major source of support.

The strong American-Israeli relationship was tested in October 1973 when a coordinated Syrian-Egyptian attack, supported by other Arab nations and made possible by sophisticated Soviet military equipment, inaugurated the fourth Arab-Israeli war, but the United States continued to be Israel's crucial prop. The impressive American resupply effort was of vital importance to Israel, and President Richard M. Nixon's request on Oct. 19 for $2.2 billion in emergency military aid for Israel was quickly approved by Congress. America's Defense Condition Three worldwide military alert undertaken on Oct. 25 may have served to prevent direct Soviet military involvement in the conflict. On the other hand, the jointly sponsored Soviet-American cease-fire resolutions passed by the UN Security Council on Oct. 22–23 prevented Israel from destroying the surrounded Egyptian Third Army and reaching a more decisive military victory.

The Arab oil embargo in 1974 ushered in a new period in which the U.S. attitude was marked by an increasing effort to pressure the Israelis to make greater concessions to the Arabs. The election of the conservative Menachem Begin to prime ministership in 1977, on the other hand, boded ill for any Israeli-Arab rapprochement. There was a breakthrough in 1978 when President Jimmy Carter scored his major foreign policy victory by engineering the Camp David agreement that led to Egyptian-Israeli peace treaty in March 1979; but Egypt's initiative was not followed by other Arab nations. In the late 1970's and early 1980's PLO terrorist attacks grew in number, and Israel responded by massive retaliations, invading Lebanon four times (in 1975, 1978, 1980, and 1982). These incursions and the Israeli policy of establishing new settlements in the occupied areas led to disagreements with the United States. In the summer of 1982 a U.S. envoy arranged for an internationally supervised removal of PLO guerrillas from Beirut (besieged by Israeli armed forces), but U.S.-Israeli relations were at a low point.

ISTHMIAN CANAL. *See* **Panama Canal and Canal Zone.**

ITALIAN IMMIGRATION. *See* **Immigration.**

ITAMA. A series of prehistoric big-game-hunting people of the North American High Plains between about 9200 and 5000 B.C. Two main phases of the Itama culture are identified by archaeologists. The earlier, Folsom phase (9200 B.C.–8000 B.C.) is characterized by sites containing the remains of large-horned extinct bison and distinctive fluted projectile points made of stone. The later, more widespread Plano phase (8000 B.C.–5000 B.C.) is typified by sites containing modern fauna, such as smaller-horned bison or antelope, and unfluted projectile points. Settlements of both phases are principally small campsites and kill sites. Folsom settlements have been excavated at Lindenmeier, Colo.; Folsom, N.Mex.; and Blackwater Draw, N.Mex. The Plano phase gradually differentiated into smaller regional traditions, a trend observable in other areas of North America by 5000 B.C.

ITEM VETO. A specific form of the veto that enables a chief executive to disapprove one item in a bill while approving the rest—usually limited to appropriation bills. It first appeared in America in the Confederacy. It was adopted by Georgia in 1865 and spread rapidly to other states and to some local governmental units, particularly municipalities. In the late 1970's the governors of forty-three states had the power to veto items in appropriation bills. The president does not have an item veto.

IUKA, BATTLE OF (Sept. 19, 1862). To deter Union Gen. William S. Rosecrans from joining Gen. Don Carlos Buell in opposing Confederate Gen. Braxton Bragg's advance toward Louisville, Ky., Confederate Gen. Stirling Price, with 14,000 men, moved from Baldwyn to Iuka, Miss. Gen. Ulysses S. Grant, at Memphis, Tenn., ordered Rosecrans, with 9,000 troops, to attack Price from the south while Gen. E. O. C. Ord, 8,000 strong, struck him from the northwest. Discovering Rosecrans' approach, Price assailed his column in dense woods with Gen. Henry Little's division of 3,200 men. Little was killed, but Union Col. Charles S. Hamilton's division was driven back. Darkness halted the operations, and Ord, failing to hear the battle, did not attack. That night Price retired from a dangerous salient to Baldwyn.

IWO JIMA (Feb. 16–Mar. 17, 1945). One of the Volcano Islands, 750 miles south of Tokyo, Iwo gave Japan two hours' warning of U.S. B-29 raids from the Mariana Islands and provided a fighter base for the harassment of U.S. bombers. To reverse this situation and afford a haven for crippled American aircraft, the Joint Chiefs of Staff directed that Iwo Jima be seized. Lt. Gen. Tadamichi Kuribayashi, with 21,000 troops, defended Iwo. The marine commander, Lt. Gen. H. M. Smith, was supported by Adm. R. K. Turner. The 82,000-man landing force (Third, Fourth, and Fifth marine divisions) was commanded by Lt. Gen. H. Schmidt. Following three days' bombardment, the marines landed on Feb. 19 under cover of the heaviest prelanding bombardment of the war. Because of the massive preparation, beach casualties were moderate, but capture of the remainder of the island required the most bitter battle of the Pacific, and heavy casualties were inflicted on both sides. Seizure of Mount Suribachi (Feb. 23) by the Twenty-eighth Marines gave attackers the dominant terrain, from which was carried on a ten-day struggle to overrun the fireswept airfields and capture the ridges, buttes, and deep caves in which Kuribayashi made his last desperate stand. Although Iwo Jima was officially declared secured on Mar. 17, resistance was not extinguished until nine days later. The battle cost the United States 4,590 dead and 24,096 wounded; more than 20,000 Japanese were killed and 1,083 captured.

JACKSON (Miss.). The capital and largest city of Mississippi, with a population of 202,895 in 1980; the center of a metropolitan area of 316,252. Located on a bluff next to the Pearl River, Jackson is a major railroad and trading city. Several oil companies have their Mississippi headquarters in Jackson. Natural gas and petroleum have been discovered in the area since 1920. Local industries deal in lumber and cottonseed, textile products, and small metal products.

The site for the capital city was selected in 1821, because of its central location to Mississippi's population at that time. The old Natchez Trace, a major road across the state, crossed the Pearl River at the site. Originally called Le Fleur's Bluff because a French trader named Louis Le Fleur had a trading post there since the 1790's, the new capital was named in honor of Andrew Jackson.

During the Civil War, there was hard fighting in and around Jackson. The state capital was moved in 1863 before the city fell to Union troops. The war destroyed much of the city and its transportation facilities, leaving a major rebuilding task after the end of the fighting. State government activities returned in 1865.

JACKSON, BATTLE OF (May 14, 1863). An action leading to Union success in the campaign against Vicksburg, Miss., in the Civil War. After the Battle of Raymond, about twenty miles southwest of Jackson, Miss., Gen. Ulysses S. Grant hurried to seize Jackson and protect his rear when he turned westward to drive Confederate Gen. John C. Pemberton into Vicksburg. The small force at Jackson, commanded by Gen. J. E. Johnston, being no match for Grant's army, withdrew.

JACKSON, FORT, TREATY OF. *See* **Creek War.**

JACKSON AND ST. PHILIP, FORTS. *See* **Mississippi River, Opening of the.**

JACKSON HOLE (Wyo.). A valley in western Wyoming, east of the Teton Range and south of Yellowstone Park, was a trappers' rendezvous. It was apparently named for David E. Jackson, who spent the winter of 1829 there.

JACKSONIAN DEMOCRACY. The association of the Democratic party with the rise and triumph of democracy during Andrew Jackson's presidency (1829–37). The term "Jacksonian Democracy" is of unknown origin. Contemporaries of President Jackson did not use it, although Jackson's supporters frequently did make claims that the president represented the will of the people. During the last quarter of the 19th century the term does appear in the writings of several historians, but it was used in a narrow sense to refer to the programs and policies embraced by the Democratic party under Jackson's leadership. The historian most responsible for broadening the concept to signify a general democratic upheaval was Frederick Jackson Turner.

JACKSON'S VALLEY CAMPAIGN (1862). In early 1862, when Union Gen. George B. McClellan removed his army to the Virginia Peninsula (*see* Peninsular Campaign) for a march on Richmond, all available Confederate troops were sent there except a small force in the Shenandoah Valley under Gen. Thomas J. ("Stonewall") Jackson. President Abraham Lincoln had directed that a large Union force under Gen. Irwin McDowell be detained at Fredericksburg and vicinity to protect Washington from attack and to watch Jackson. It was planned to send McDowell to McClellan at the proper time. It became Jackson's mission to harass the Union troops in the valley, thus directing Lincoln's attention from Richmond to the defense of Washington. It was hoped to keep McDowell from joining McClellan. In a masterly campaign of deception and unexpected maneuver, Jackson managed to have a superior force at the point of contact. He struck first at Kernstown on Mar. 23, 1862. Although repulsed, he created much alarm. Six weeks later, as McClellan approached Richmond, Jackson defeated Gen. Robert H. Milroy at McDowell and drove him down the valley. Two weeks later, at Front Royal and at Strasburg, Jackson struck again. Lincoln canceled McDowell's orders to join McClellan. Sharp fights at Cross Keys and at Port Republic followed. The Union forces were scattered; the Washington authorities were distracted. Jackson controlled the situation in the valley. His objective had been accomplished. In thirty-five days he had marched 250 miles, fought four battles, and won them all. On June 21 he began to transfer his command to Robert E. Lee's army at Richmond (*see* Seven Days' Battles).

JACKSONVILLE (Fla.). Jacksonville, which has the largest land area of any city in the United States, had a population of 540,898 in 1980; its metropolitan area included 736,343 people. Located on the St. John's River, it is an important commercial and industrial city. Major industries and exports are wood products, "naval stores" such as turpentine, paper, and wood pulp. It is also notable for food packing and processing, cigar making, and various chemical industries. Jacksonville is one of the leading U.S. ports for the import of coffee and it serves as a distributing center for a wide area of the South Atlantic states.

Jacksonville includes the sites of some of the earliest attempted settlements in America. Fort Caroline, a French post set up in 1564, was located at the mouth of the St. John's River at a site now maintained as a National Memorial. Spanish and English forts were also located; a British road was laid out across Cow Ford, a stretch on the St. John's River near the center of the modern city.

Jacksonville received its name in 1822 when the name "Cow Ford" was changed to honor Andrew Jackson. During the Seminole War, Jacksonville served as a supply base for American troops. The vicinity of Jacksonville has had orange groves since Spanish colonial days. Before the Civil War, Jacksonville developed as a market town for oranges, for tars and turpentine, and for cotton.

During the Civil War, Jacksonville was a supply base and an operating base for Confederate blockade runners and commerce raiders. The city was occupied several times by Union troops who landed from naval vessels; in 1863 the town was extensively damaged. Following the war, it was rebuilt and became Florida's first resort city.

Jacksonville's central city population began to drop in the

1950's and the city seemed unable to handle all the government problems and rebuilding costs that it faced. The merging of the city and Duval County in 1967 created a single metropolitan city government which has become an object of study by other cities and counties with similar problems.

JACOBIN CLUBS (or Democratic Societies). Organized in Philadelphia, and later in other cities, after the arrival of French minister Edmond Charles Genêt (Citizen Genêt) in 1793. Modeled after the Jacobin Clubs in Paris, they sought to propagate democratic views on American politics and to arouse support for the principles of the French Revolution. They opposed most of the measures of George Washington's administration.

JAMES, ARMY OF THE. In existence from April to December in 1864, consisted of the Tenth and Eighteenth Corps, commanded by Union Gen. B. F. Butler. It constituted the left wing of Gen. Ulysses S. Grant's army. Butler was instructed to occupy City Point, threaten Richmond, and await Grant's arrival in the James River region of Virginia. He was checked at Drewry's Bluff and bottled up at Bermuda Hundred. Most of his command was later transferred to the Army of the Potomac and served until the surrender at Appomattox.

JAMES EXPEDITION (1820). Attached to that of Maj. Stephen H. Long, which explored the trans-Missouri country. It was led by Edwin James, a botanist and geologist. With two others he climbed Pikes Peak (Colorado) in July. The report of the expedition was compiled by James, who agreed with Zebulon M. Pike's report that the Plains were unfit for habitation by white men.

JAMES RIVER AND KANAWHA COMPANY. Begun in 1785 as the James River Company, in 1832 the river improvement scheme was broadened to include a canal to connect Richmond, Va., with the Ohio by way of the James, Greenbrier, New, and Kanawha rivers. Virginia and the cities of Richmond and Lynchburg subscribed most of the funds, and the canal was finished to Buchanan in 1851, where construction was abandoned owing to financial difficulties. In 1880 it was sold to the Chesapeake and Ohio Railroad, which abandoned the canal and used its towpath for a railroad.

JAMES RIVER COMPANY. Fathered by George Washington and chartered by Virginia in 1785, proposed to improve the navigation of the James River with canals and locks around the rapids and falls at Richmond and westward through the Blue Ridge. It opened navigation about 220 miles inland to the Shenandoah Valley and became one of the most successful corporations of the day. In 1832 it was superseded by the more ambitious project of the James River and Kanawha Company.

JAMESTOWN. The Virginia Company of London, or London Company, sent three vessels in late 1606 under Capt. Christopher Newport to create a colony in Virginia, find gold, and discover a route to the Pacific Ocean. In May 1607 the settlers landed on a marshy island in the James River estuary and by mid-June had built a triangular fort and planted grain. Disease appeared quickly, probably malaria and dysentery, and many settlers died during the first summer. Friendly Indians, who supplied corn and wild meat, enabled the colonists to survive the first winter, although the number of colonists dropped from over 100 to about 40 by December, when Newport brought in 120 more settlers.

In 1608, Capt. John Smith took firm control of the settlement, but after Smith returned to England in the fall of 1609, the colony almost collapsed in the winter of 1609–10; 90 percent of the settlers died. As governor, Sir Thomas Dale brought about a revival of the colony in the summer of 1610 by introducing a more stringent legal code and by abandoning the colony's communal system of production. Although the colony exported shipmasts and lumber, it never turned a profit for the London Company. John Rolfe in 1612 experimented with tobacco, and tobacco cultivation soon dominated the colony.

The year 1619 saw the beginning of prosperity in Jamestown and the arrival of the first blacks in Virginia; in the same year, the town became the seat of the first legislative assembly in the New World. In March 1622, Virginia shuddered under an Indian attack, and Jamestown became a refuge for the survivors. By 1625, 124 persons resided in Jamestown, which had twenty-two houses, three stores, and a church. As the colony prospered and expanded, however, Jamestown lost its preeminence. In 1631 an effort was made to make it the colony's exclusive port; but not even the government could contradict the edicts of geography. In 1676 the town was burned during Bacon's Rebellion, and it never regained its limited vitality. In 1698 another fire ravaged Jamestown, and the government was moved to Williamsburg in 1699.

In 1930 the Colonial National Historical Park was established, including most of Jamestown Island. The upper end of the island, site of the first representative legislative government on the continent, was declared a national historic si[illegible] in 1940.

JAMESTOWN EXPOSITION (1907). Planned to celebrate the tercentenary of the establishment of the first permanent English settlement in America, on Jamestown Island in the James River, was held at Norfolk, Va., from Apr. 26 to Dec. 1, 1907. A popular subscription of $1 million was supplemented by $1.2 million from the federal government, which held an international naval demonstration at Hampton Roads. The 340 acres of the exposition itself were located across the water from Old Point Comfort. Many nations participated in the ceremonies, but the exhibits were chiefly by Virginia and the federal government. Admissions totaled 2,850,735.

JAPAN, AIR WAR AGAINST. American airmen attacked Japan for the first time in World War II on Apr. 18, 1942. They flew sixteen twin-engine B-25's off the carrier *Hornet* about 688 miles west of Japan and hit Tokyo and other nearby targets before heading for landings in China. This isolated raid was led by Lt. Col. James H. Doolittle. By late 1943, anxious to begin a sustained air campaign against

Japan, President Franklin D. Roosevelt arranged with British and Chinese authorities to build bases in India and western China. On June 14, 1944, B-29 crews struck Japan from China for the first time. Sixty-three planes bombed a steel plant on Kyūshū but caused only minor damage. Seven planes and fifty-five crewmen were lost on the raid. Because the island of Kyūshū was at the extreme end of the B-29's 1,500-mile maximum combat radius, the U.S. airmen flew only five other missions against Japan from China.

Sustained air war against Japan did not begin until U.S. forces had seized the Mariana Islands, beginning their assault on June 15, 1944. From Saipan, Tinian, and Guam, the B-29's could reach Japan's major industrial cities. The first bomber reached Saipan on Oct. 12, carrying Maj. Gen. Haywood S. Hansell, commander of the B-29 force. On Nov. 24 Hansell launched the first air raid against Tokyo since Dolittle's. Nearly ninety B-29's struck at the city from an altitude of more than 25,000 feet. These high-altitude bombing raids proved ineffective, and Gen. Curtis E. LeMay took over from Hansell in January 1945. Other important changes followed. Washington directed that the B-29's carry more incendiaries on future raids, to take advantage of the known flammability of Japanese buildings. On Feb. 4 a heavy incendiary strike against Kōbe destroyed 2.5 million square feet of the city.

On Feb. 16, 1945. a U.S. Navy fast carrier force sailed into Tokyo harbor and launched more than 1,200 aircraft against Honshū targets, destroying some 500 Japanese planes. Navy carrier pilots returned to Japan on eighteen more occasions, bombing and strafing enemy facilities. The B-29's, however, wreaked the greatest damage on Japan, LeMay having ordered his airmen to attack with incendiaries at altitudes of less than 8,000 feet and individually rather than in formation. These tactics were employed for the first time on the night of Mar. 9–10, when 285 bombers dropped 2,000 tons of incendiaries on Tokyo. High winds fanned the flames into a huge fire storm that gutted 16 square miles of the city, killing 83,783 and injuring 40,918; one million Japanese were made homeless. Similar fire raids were subsequently flown against Nagoya, Osaka, Kōbe, and fifty smaller Japanese cities.

JAPAN, U.S. RELATIONS WITH. The United States was the first Western nation to arrange for full and open trade relations with Japan. Prior to 1854, only a small amount of trade was permitted by the Japanese through Dutch merchants at a single Japanese port. A U.S. Navy squadron, commanded by Commodore Matthew C. Perry, visited Japan twice. In March 1854, relations between Japan and the United States were instituted by the treaty of Kanagawa. Later missions succeeded in opening Japanese ports to further Western trade, and also opened Japanese eyes to the advantages of Western manufacturing, military organization, and trading customs. Japanese missions visited the United States in 1860 and in 1872.

By the late 19th century, the Japanese had built an army and navy of considerable strength. Japanese businessmen became interested in China, Hawaii, Korea, and other Pacific areas; in several of these areas they competed with American businessmen. After Japan defeated the Chinese Empire in a war (1894–95), there was fear that the Japanese might take over large parts of China and exclude foreign trade from those areas. In 1897, Japan objected to the American annexation of Hawaii.

In 1904, a surprise Japanese naval attack on a Russian fleet began the Russo-Japanese War. President Theodore Roosevelt arranged the peace treaty which ended that war and he was thought by the Russians to have been too favorable to Japan. In 1905, a treaty was arranged by which Japan agreed to recognize U.S. rule over the Philippine Islands, while the United States recognized Japanese control of Korea.

The first real crisis between the United States and Japan came about in 1906 when the public school board in San Francisco prevented Japanese immigrants from sending their children to school. This attitude insulted the Japanese and President Roosevelt had to persuade the school board to change its anti-Japanese rule and in the "Gentlemen's Agreement" (1907) the Japanese government promised to keep Japanese emigrants from leaving for America.

Relations between the United States and Japan began to strain during World War I. In 1915, Japan presented a set of demands to the Chinese government. The United States intervened to assist China and to prevent Japan from taking control of parts of China. In the peace settlement after World War I (in which the United States and Japan were associated against the Central Powers), Japan tried to force a statement on racial equality into the peace treaties. This was not done and the failure caused a further strain in relations. This same racial question provoked severe Japanese objections in 1924 when a U.S. immigration law was passed, prohibiting any Japanese from entering as permanent residents.

Japan, an important naval power, was involved in serious disputes with the United States and with Great Britain over the naval disarmament treaties that were drawn up in Washington and in London during the 1920's. In 1931, the Japanese government fell into the hands of military leaders who led their country into an invasion of Chinese territory. This armed attack was met with American words. Secretary of State Henry L. Stimson announced that the United States would not recognize any land captured by such tactics as belonging to Japan. In 1934, the Japanese government announced that it would no longer observe the limits set on naval vessels by the Washington Naval Treaty. A number of tensions followed which led to World War II.

After Japan surrendered at the end of World War II (Aug. 15, 1945), the United States became the chief occupying power and the country was run by Allied forces commanded by Gen. Douglas MacArthur. During military occupation, MacArthur encouraged the Japanese to develop a new constitution that prohibited military forces, and helped rebuild their industries for peaceful purposes. This work was done so successfully that Japan became the strongest industrial country in eastern Asia. A final peace treaty was signed between the United States and Japan, on Sept. 8, 1951. An unusual consequence was a "bi-lateral security" treaty. U.S. bases were permitted on Japanese territory and U.S. equipment was provided for the Japanese defense forces. The treaty arrangements have been altered from time to time since 1951 (each time reducing in some respects the use of Japanese land by U.S. forces), but the working alliance and trade agreements between the two countries continued. Outlying islands that had belonged to Japan were restored to Japanese rule. These included Iwo Jima and Okinawa, returned in 1971.

Trade relations between the two countries have been marked by vigorous competition in the fields of electronic equipment, textiles, and automobiles. An important problem for the two governments to solve concerns how much of each other's products each will admit to home markets.

JAPANESE-AMERICAN AGREEMENT. *See* **Lansing-Ishii Agreement.**

JAPANESE-AMERICAN RELOCATION. The relocation of Americans of Japanese ancestry during World War II began with a presidential order of Feb. 19, 1942, which authorized military authorities to designate certain restricted military areas from which any or all persons might be excluded, and in March, Congress gave Roosevelt's order statutory approval. There followed in swift succession a military order designating the West Coast a restricted zone, the imposition of an 8:00 P.M. to 6:00 A.M. curfew on Japanese-Americans and on German and Italian nationals within the zone, an order prohibiting Japanese-Americans from leaving the coastal zone, and a subsequent contradictory order excluding them from the same region. This network of commands in effect forced Japanese-Americans to report to designated centers for shipment out of the zone to a number of "relocation centers." There were ten such centers in all, in California, Arizona, Idaho, Utah, Wyoming, and Arkansas. Members of the Japanese-American West Coast minority were confined for up to four years and then resettled outside the coastal zone. About 112,000 persons were involved, more than 70,000 of whom were American citizens, or Nisei.

JAPANESE CHERRY TREES. The cherry trees in Potomac Park, Washington, D.C., were presented by Tokyo as a token of goodwill to the people of the United States. The first shipment in 1909 had to be destroyed because of insect pests. Tokyo then, in a special nursery, grafted flowering cherry trees on wild cherry stock; these reached Washington in perfect condition. The first two were planted Mar. 27, 1912.

JAPANESE EXCLUSION ACTS. In the late 19th century opposition to Asian immigrants developed principally in the West, because of a widespread belief that the Asians' lower standard of living was detrimental to the interests of American labor and agriculture. After demands to restrict Asian immigration had produced the Chinese Exclusion Act of 1882, efforts were made to extend restrictions to the Japanese. In order to head off the demands, President Theodore Roosevelt in 1901 negotiated an agreement with Japan whereby the latter vowed to limit severely the issuance of passports to Japanese laborers, but it was ineffective. In 1907 negotiations were reopened and led to the conclusion of the so-called Gentlemen's Agreement with Japan. In 1924 Congress enacted a law imposing numerical restrictions on immigration from all countries outside the Western Hemisphere. One provision of this law, known as the Johnson Act, completely barred the immigration of aliens who were ineligible for citizenship, a provision designed to exclude Japanese, who were statutorily barred from naturalization at that time. A change in public sentiment after World War II resulted in the elimination of the immigration restrictions on Asians. The Chinese Exclusion Act was repealed in 1943. The more general provision excluding aliens ineligible for citizenship was repealed by the McCarran-Walter Act of 1952.

JAVA SEA, BATTLE OF (Feb. 27, 1942). A fleet comprising American, British, Dutch, and Australian units, under Rear Adm. Karel Doorman attempted to halt a Japanese invasion of Java. Trying to find Japanese transports, Doorman encountered a covering force under Rear Adm. T. Takagi. The Japanese alone had air support and the heavy cruisers U.S.S. *Houston* and H.M.S. *Exeter* were outgunned by two Japanese cruisers. In the first clash the *Exeter* was severely damaged and two Allied destroyers were sunk. Retiring in hope of shaking off Takagi and finding the transports, Doorman lost another destroyer to a mine and, after dark, again ran into Takagi's fleet and lost two light cruisers, including his own flagship. The surviving ships retired. Neither the *Houston* nor any of the five U.S. destroyers was damaged; but the next day, as the *Houston* and the light cruiser H.M.S. *Perth* tried to escape southward, they encountered the main Japanese armada. Four Japanese transports were sunk, but both the *Houston* and *Perth* were lost and the Japanese invasion proceeded.

JAY-GARDOQUI NEGOTIATIONS. The beginning of diplomatic relations between Spain and the United States in 1783 found serious issues existing between the two nations. Don Diego de Gardoqui came to the United States as Spanish minister in 1785 and endeavored to make a treaty with John Jay, American secretary of foreign affairs. The two diplomats agreed on the main terms of a treaty (never signed) in 1786, by which the United States would have "forborne" to exercise the navigation of the Mississippi for thirty years in return for favorable commercial privileges in Spanish European ports and by which the southern U.S. boundary presumably would have been settled by a compromise that would have given the United States nearly all it claimed. Opposition of the southern states, with their western (Mississippi) appanages, blocked any chance of ratification; indeed, this opposition was one of the principal reasons for the inclusion in the Constitution of a provision requiring a two-thirds majority of senators present for the ratification of any treaty.

JAYHAWKERS. Free-state bands that played a large part in the Kansas-Missouri border war between 1856 and 1859, particularly the band captained by Charles R. Jennison and Union guerrilla bands during the Civil War. The name was applied also to the Seventh Kansas Cavalry, commanded by Jennison. Because of real and alleged depredations committed by the Jayhawkers, the term became one of opprobrium. The origin of the word is uncertain, but it may have been coined by a party of goldseekers from Galesburg, Ill., in 1849, and used in California. Since the Civil War "Jayhawker" has become the popular nickname for a Kansan.

JAY'S TREATY (Nov. 19, 1794). Adjusted a group of serious Anglo-American diplomatic issues arising out of the Definitive Treaty of Peace of 1783, subsequent commercial difficulties, and issues over neutral rights. The principal issues arising out of the treaty were Great Britain's deliberate refusal to evacuate six controlling frontier forts in American territory along the northern river-and-lake boundary established by the treaty (*see* Border Forts, Evacuation of); obstacles in state courts to the collection of prewar debts by British creditors, despite the guarantees of the treaty (*see* British Debts); alleged confiscation by states of property of returning Loyalists in violation of treaty protection against any such acts after the peace; and unsettled boundary gaps. To these grievances were added Britain's refusal to admit American ships into the ports of its remaining colonies in North America and the West Indies; its refusal to make a treaty of commerce, or even to exchange diplomatic representatives, during the period of the Confederation, 1783–89; and its active intrigue with the western Indian tribes that had been its allies during the Revolution but were left within the boundaries of the United States. British Prime Minister William Pitt (the younger) sent George Hammond to the United States in 1791 to discuss issues. The discussions had produced nothing by the time war broke out between France and Great Britain on Feb. 1, 1793.

Arbitrary British naval orders in 1793 and the consequent capture of hundreds of American neutral ships, combined with a bellicose speech of Sir Guy Carleton, Baron Dorchester, the governor-general of Canada, to the western Indians, precipitated the war crisis of 1794. Hamilton and the Federalist leaders pressed Washington to stop short of commercial reprisals (Congress did vote an embargo for two months), and Chief Justice John Jay was sent to London as minister plenipotentiary and envoy extraordinary on a special peace mission. In the negotiations with William Wyndham Grenville, British secretary for foreign affairs, Jay acquiesced in British maritime measures for the duration of the war, in return for the creation of a mixed commission to adjudicate American spoliation claims ($10,345,200 paid by 1802) for damages made "under color" of British Orders in Council (not in themselves repudiated); Great Britain agreed to evacuate the frontier posts by June 1, 1796 (executed substantially on time); the United States guaranteed the payment of British private prewar debts, the amount to be worked out by another mixed commission (£600,000 *en bloc* settlement made in 1802); and two mixed boundary commissions were set up to establish the line in the northwest (this one never met) and in the northeast (agreed on identity of the St. Croix River). Washington got the treaty through the Senate and the House (where the Jeffersonian Republicans tried to block the necessary appropriations) only with great difficulty.

JAZZ. *See* **Music.**

JAZZ AGE. A term first used by young people after World War I to describe "modernity" and associated with the rising popularity of jazz. It gained wide currency after F. Scott Fitzgerald published *Tales of the Jazz Age* in 1922, and subsequently came to be used to describe the period from World War I to 1929.

JEFFERSON, FORT (Ill.). Begun during the spring of 1780, on the east bank of the Mississippi River, twelve miles below the mouth of the Ohio, by George Rogers Clark to aid in his control over the Illinois country and protect communication with New Orleans. The garrison survived an attack by Chickasaw and Choctaw warriors, but owing to desertions by soldiers and settlers, the fort was evacuated in June 1781.

JEFFERSON, FORT (Ohio). Built by Gen. Arthur St. Clair, six miles south of the present Greenville, during his campaign against the Indians in 1791. Chiefly a depot for supplies, it was a link in the chain of posts between Fort Washington (Cincinnati) and the rapids of the Maumee.

JEFFERSON BARRACKS. Built in 1826 on the Mississippi River ten miles south of St. Louis, Mo., Jefferson Barracks was established by Secretary of War James Barbour as an infantry school for the U.S. Army. In the Civil War it became a hospital center, and in 1898 it served as a basic training camp for Spanish-American War volunteers. During World Wars I and II the army used the barracks for inducting and mustering out troops, and later part of it became an Air Force Reserve facility. In 1950, St. Louis County acquired some of the land for a historical park.

JEFFERSON-BURR ELECTORAL DISPUTE (1800). Thomas Jefferson and Aaron Burr were the Democratic-Republican candidates for the presidency and vice-presidency, respectively, in the acrimonious campaign of 1800. Because of the growing effectiveness of the two-party system the Democratic-Republican candidates each received seventy-three votes in the electoral college, and the Federalist vote split sixty-five for John Adams, sixty-four for Charles Cotesworth Pinckney, and one for John Jay. Thus, the election went to the Democratic-Republicans. But since the votes for Jefferson and Burr were exactly equal, the election was thrown into the House. The Federalists, still in control from the elections of 1798—despite the opposition of Alexander Hamilton and other leaders and in cynical disregard of popular interest—schemed to put Burr into the presidency. Jefferson received the vote of eight states and Burr of six; the representatives of Maryland and Vermont were equally divided. Thus, there was no majority among the sixteen states then belonging to the Union. For weeks intrigue went on amid rumors of forcible resistance should the scheme succeed. On Feb. 17, on the thirty-sixth ballot, the Federalist members from Maryland and Vermont declined to vote, with the result that Jefferson had the votes of ten states and was declared elected.

JEFFERSON CITY (Mo.). The capital of Missouri had a population of 33,619, according to the 1980 census. The city is located on the south bank of the Missouri River. It was designated as the capital on Dec. 31, 1821, when the first Missouri legislature decided that the capital should be located centrally rather than at St. Louis. It was named in honor of Thomas Jefferson. During the Civil War, Jefferson City was occupied by Union troops in order to keep Confederate sympathizers in the vicinity from helping the armies of the South. The state government is the chief employer and chief activity in Jefferson City.

JEFFERSONIAN ARCHITECTURE. A type of building, both domestic and public, planned or suggested by Thomas Jefferson, under the influence of Andrea Palladio, 16th-century Italian classicist. The buildings are a direct adaptation of classic models to contemporary local needs, and their proportions are calculated mathematically.

JEFFERSONIAN DEMOCRACY. Thomas Jefferson's philosophy of a democracy based on a citizenry of small, educated, independent freeholders. He fought against both primogeniture and entail because of his fear that the small freeholder, even in ample America, might be squeezed out if families could keep large landholdings permanently in their own hands. Although a firm believer in the right of private property, he did not believe in its maldistribution or tying it up permanently, but in its wide distribution among the capable, energetic, and thrifty.

His theory of state education is particularly illuminating for his doctrine of democracy. He considered an educated citizenry essential; he believed that society would benefit by utilizing all the talent available by paying to educate those who could not afford to educate themselves. In his plan—the foundation for the modern French system, but not the American—all children were to receive an education in the lower grades, above which a steady sifting process was to go on, leading certain selected students through higher grades and college. His carefully worked out system for state education is a most important gloss on his generalization that all men are created equal.

To his essentials for democracy, he added freedom of religion, speech, and the press. Without them he believed democracy impossible. He did not believe it possible everywhere and under all circumstances. All his writings and acts indicate fear of democracy except in a nation of small country freeholders, with few city wage earners.

He believed in limiting governmental functions to the minimum; in a strict construction of the Constitution and in reserving to the states as much power as possible; in majority rule as a working compromise that could not be rightful unless it recognized the equal rights of minorities; in "the honest payment of our debts and sacred preservation of the public faith"; in economy on the part of government so that "labor may be lightly burthened"; in freedom of trade; and in as small a debt as possible.

JEFFERSONIAN REPUBLICAN PARTY. *See* **Republicans, Jeffersonian.**

JEFFERSON'S LIBRARY. *See* **Library of Congress.**

JEFFERSON'S PROPOSED STATES. Virginia ceded its western land claims to the United States, Mar. 1, 1784. The same day Thomas Jefferson submitted to Congress a committee report, drafted by himself, for the future disposition of the western lands. The report, variously amended, was enacted Apr. 23, and is known as the Ordinance of 1784. Although the ordinance never became operative, being superseded by the Ordinance of 1787, some of its provisions contributed to the development of the nascent American constitutional system. It provided for the division of the western country into convenient units, whose citizens might set up temporary governments, which on attaining 20,000 free inhabitants should be replaced by permanent state governments, republican in form and duly subordinate to the federal government. Slavery (after 1800), nullification, and secession were to be forever prohibited. The area embraced by it was from Florida to Canada and from Pennsylvania to the Mississippi. This was to be subdivided by parallels of latitude 2° apart, beginning at the thirty-first, and by meridians of longitude running through the Falls of the Ohio and the mouth of the Great Kanawha. Provision was thus made for sixteen future states. Since the states south of Virginia had not yet ceded their western claims, the report identified and named only the ten states included within the Virginia cession. Apart from that of Washington, which occupied the eastern part of modern Ohio, these states comprised two tiers, running from north to south. Beginning at the north, those in the eastern tier were named Cherronesus, Metropotamia, Saratoga, and Pelisipia; the states in the western tier were named Sylvania, Michigania, Assenisipia, Illinoia, and Polypotamia.

JEFFERSON TERRITORY. Established under a spontaneously formed provisional government that had a precarious existence in Colorado from 1859 to 1861. Legally, the new settlements that grew up in Pikes Peak country following the discovery of gold near the site of Denver in 1858, were within the jurisdiction of Kansas; actually, they were so far from the seat of government that it appeared unlikely that the authority of that territory could be made effective. The first step toward the organization of a new government was taken in November 1858, when the inhabitants of Denver elected a delegate to Congress and asked that a new territory be created. Torn with dissension over slavery, Congress did not act until January 1861. Meanwhile, through several successive conventions and elections Jefferson Territory was formed without authorization from Congress; a constitution was adopted; and officials were chosen. Two sessions of the territorial legislature were held; laws regarding personal and civil rights were passed; and counties and courts were created—but the attempt to collect taxes generally failed. This provisional government had two rivals: some settlers gave allegiance to Arapahoe County, Kans., and in the majority of mining camps the local miners' courts were the chief means of maintaining law and order. Jefferson Territory came to an end after Congress created the Territory of Colorado in 1861.

JEHOVAH'S WITNESSES. An Adventist and apocalyptic sect founded by Charles Taze Russell in 1872, they were known as Millennial Dawnists, Russellites, and International Bible Students until 1931, when the current name was adopted. Since 1879 the principal means of spreading the Witnesses' message has been the *Watchtower,* a publication that gives the Witnesses' views on life. In 1884 the movement was incorporated as the Watchtower Bible and Tract Society. Jehovah's Witnesses believe in an Arian Christology—the nontrinitarian belief that Christ was an archangel—and in the imminence of the millennium. In that golden age, they believe, 144,000 will share in the kingly rule of Christ; others may escape destruction, but only if they work with the Witnesses in the present. The movement is tightly organized and engages in widespread evangelistic activities. Jehovah's Witnesses have been at the center of a number of court cases because of their claim to exemption from military service and their proselytizing activities; beginning in the 1940's legal controversy arose from their refusal to join in the pledge of allegiance to the flag. Despite popular animosity their right to dissent has been consistently affirmed by the courts. In 1981 the membership of the movement in the United States was 565,309. U.S. headquarters are located in Brooklyn, N.Y.

JENCKS ACT (Aug. 30, 1957). As a result of the Supreme Court's decision in *Jencks* v. *U.S.* (1957), which had given the defendant in a federal trial the right to see all evidence in government files, Congress passed this act, which provided that only material in FBI files relating to the subject of a witness' testimony at a trial might be produced in court after his direct examination.

JENKINS' EAR, WAR OF (1739–43). A struggle between England and Spain, preliminary to and merging into the War of the Austrian Succession (King George's War), which lasted until 1748. It was named for Robert Jenkins, a British seaman who lost an ear in a brush with the Spaniards off the coast of Florida. Commercial rivalry on the seas and disputes over the ownership of Georgia caused for the conflict. War was declared in June 1739, with the Caribbean the center of naval operations and the Georgia-Florida borderlands the scene of military warfare. Adm. Edward Vernon captured Puerto Bello on the Isthmus of Panama in 1739, but in 1740 met with disastrous failure before Cartagena, the principal port of Colombia. James Edward Oglethorpe, after having clinched a friendship with the Creek at a great meeting on the Chattahoochee, invaded Florida early in 1740 and seized two forts on the St. Johns River. In the following summer he attacked St. Augustine, but failed to take it. In 1742 the Spaniards, with a force of 5,000 men, sought to end the Georgia colony, but were turned back at the Battle of Bloody Marsh, on St. Simon Island. The next year Oglethorpe again invaded Florida without success.

JENKINS FERRY, BATTLE AT (Apr. 30, 1864). A campaign was planned wherein columns under Union generals Nathaniel P. Banks and Frederick Steele would converge toward Shreveport, La. (*see* Red River Campaign). While so engaged, Steele learned that Banks had withdrawn after the Battle of Pleasant Hill and that Confederate Gen. Sterling Price had received reinforcements. Steele immediately withdrew toward Little Rock, Ark., harassed by Edmund Kirby-Smith and Price. At Jenkins Ferry about fifty miles south of Little Rock, on the Saline River, Steele, delayed by the swollen stream, repulsed a severe Confederate attack.

JERSEY CITY (N.J.). The second largest city in the state, it had a population of 223,532 according to the 1980 census; it was the center of a metropolitan area of 555,483. Jersey City is the New Jersey community which has the longest continuous history. Michael Pauw, a Dutch patroon, had attempted to settle fifty families in the area beginning in 1629. Jersey City got its present name in 1820 when its residents received a charter as the "City of Jersey." It is a major industrial and shipping center. Its chief industrial products include electrical machinery, chemicals, soaps, oil products, and clothing. Its transportation facilities include eleven miles of waterfront, most of it improved with docks and wharves; an extensive network of roads and highways; a major vehicular tunnel under the Hudson to New York City; and excellent railroad connections. Jersey City Medical Center is the principal teaching hospital in the state of New Jersey and one of the leading medical treatment and research centers in the eastern United States.

JERSEY PRISON SHIP. A dismantled sixty-four-gun British man-of-war, moored in Wallabout Bay, later the site of the Brooklyn Navy Yard, in New York City, and used for the confinement of American naval prisoners during the Revolution. Although only one of several prison ships in New York harbor, it became notorious for the ill-use of prisoners.

JESSIE SCOUTS. Bands of Union soldiers or guerrillas, usually disguised as Confederates, who operated during the later years of the Civil War in northern Virginia and the adjacent sections of West Virginia.

JESUIT MISSIONS. Jesuit Indian missions within the boundaries of the present United States existed in two distinct phases, separated by a period of worldwide suppression of the order by the Holy See between 1773 and 1814 (for the United States, 1805). In the first, or colonial, phase, Jesuits and Franciscans formed the cutting edge of empire along the Spanish borderlands. The few Jesuits tolerated in the central part of the English colonies managed to do only minor work among tribes in the Potomac-Chesapeake region, particularly the Patuxent, Anacostan, and Piscataway. After the restoration of the order, the Jesuits soon became the major Indian missionary force in the trans-Mississippi West.

The efforts of Spanish Jesuits to penetrate the seaboard tribes from Virginia to Georgia proved abortive and bloody (1566–71). More solid was the later advance into Baja California and Arizona; especially notable was the Tyrolese Eusebio Kino (1645–1711), known as the Apostle of Arizona, who founded twenty-four missions. When Spain suppressed the order in its own dominions in 1767, Jesuits controlled 70 percent of New Spain's one million mission Indians.

French Jesuits arrived at Acadia in 1611 and Quebec in 1625; they greatly expanded their activities between 1632 and 1690. Their mission networks among the Huron, Algonquin, and Iroquois confederations involved penetration of the Abnaki of Maine and the Mohawk of New York. By 1670, converts numbering 2,000 were to be counted among the Five Nations of the Iroquois. The mission-thrust ranged down the St. Lawrence River to the tribes around the Great Lakes. Claude Allouez (1622–89)—the Apostle of the West—and his fellow Jesuits instructed tens of thousands from such tribes as the Fox, Illinois, Neutral, Nipissing, Ottawa, Potawatomi, Sac, and eastern Sioux. After Jacques Marquette opened the Mississippi River to the Gulf of Mexico in 1673 missions reached the Alabama, Arkansas, Chickasaw, Choctaw, Natchez, and Yazoo of the south. Ignace Guignas reached the western Sioux around 1730, and Charles Mesaiger the Assiniboine and Cree around 1735. Among the twenty-two French Jesuit martyrs, Jean Pierre Aulneau was killed by the Sioux, Paul Du Poisson by the Arkansas, Antoine Senat by the Chickasaw, and Jean Souel by the Yazoo. The sparsely manned missions (only fifty-one Jesuits in 1750), torn by intertribal wars, suffered heavy blows when the English conquest of Canada (1760) curtailed their manpower and when Spain's acquisition of the Louisiana territories (1762) discouraged French missionary presence there; then France suppressed the order in 1763.

Reestablished by the pope in 1805, the Jesuits lacked manpower and resources. Bishop Louis Dubourg, responsible for Catholicism in Indian country, had petitioned Rome five times by 1822 for Jesuits. Secretary of War John C. Calhoun encouraged his search, and President James Monroe contributed money to the bishop's plan for Indian reductions. Consequently a dozen Jesuit recruits flatboated down the Ohio in 1823 to open an Indian school at St. Louis, Mo. (1824–30). In 1833 the American hierarchy assigned the removed tribes of the West to the Jesuits, who soon opened missions in Kansas among the Kickapoo (1836–39) and Miami (1839–41) and in Iowa among the Potawatomi (1838–41). More solidly they established in Kansas a Potawatomi mission (1837) and an Osage mission (1847), which endured until the reservation policy broke them up in 1867. From these bases, a handful of Jesuits also worked out among the Arapaho, Cherokee, Cheyenne, Delaware, Kansas, Ponca, Seneca, Shawnee, Sioux, and other accessible tribes. Many tribes petitioned for missions of their own but had to be denied. The most notable plea came from 2,000 miles away via the four Flathead–Nez Perce delegations from the Rocky Mountains to the Jesuit headquarters at St. Louis, from 1831 to 1839, all but the first led by French-speaking Catholic Iroquois. The Belgian Jesuit Pierre Jean De Smet responded to the Flathead plea by founding a mission network from the Rockies to the Pacific (1840–46). Crises, wars, and gold rushes caused the network to contract, while recruits and new opportunities led it to expand; nine units were reported in 1847, six in 1849, and eighteen in 1863. After the 1850's the network expanded to include missions for the Cayuse, Nez Perce, and Blackfoot. Soon the network was to absorb the Sioux missions and spread over Alaska. Activities to the south were far less intensive, though the Jesuits did help revive (1864) the great mission of San Xavier del Bac (1700) near Tucson for the Papago and Pima, and through the 1870's the Osage missionaries sporadically visited the Oklahoma Indian Territory. The Jesuit mission system has continued, but with a relatively low priority among the many Jesuit apostolates.

JESUIT *RELATIONS*. Each Jesuit missionary in colonial and frontier America was required to report every year to his superior the events of his mission, the prospects for exploration, and all he had learned of the regions in which he dwelt. These reports were then made up into annual volumes entitled *Relations* and forwarded to the chief of the order in France or Rome. The *Relations* were published, beginning in 1632. In 1673 the publication was suspended; the missionaries, however, continued to send in reports, which remained in manuscript for almost two centuries. In all, forty-one separate *Relations* were published. In 1896 an edition was begun that included not only the published *Relations* but also other documents secured from many sources in America and Europe. This edition, edited by Reuben G. Thwaites, known as the *Jesuit Relations and Allied Documents,* extended from 1610 to 1791. It was published in seventy-three volumes.

JESUITS (members of the Society of Jesus). A religious order of men founded by St. Ignatius Loyola (1491–1556) and formally approved by the Holy See on Sept. 27, 1540. The Jesuits were an influence in colonial America through their explorations and missions. They were associated with the Calverts in the founding of Maryland, 1634; they inaugurated the Catholic ministry in the Middle Atlantic states, the upper Great Lakes region, and the Mississippi Valley. Jesuit activities in post-colonial America date from the organization of the Maryland Mission of the order in 1805. From Maryland the order spread to the Middle West, opening in 1823 at Florissant, in Missouri, what proved to be a starting point of subsequent far-flung expansion. In 1841 it became established in the Pacific Northwest and in 1849 in California. Jesuit houses opened in Kentucky, 1832; Louisiana, 1837; and New York, 1846. Activities of the American Jesuits include foreign missions; parochial ministry; the pastoral care of Indian reservations; the direction of retreats built about the *Spiritual Exercises* of St. Ignatius Loyola; chaplaincies in the armed forces, prisons, and hospitals; and inner-city programs. But the major interest of the Jesuits is education. The first American Jesuit college, Georgetown University, in Washington, D.C., dates from 1789. St. Louis University, in Missouri, the oldest school of university grade west of the Mississippi, has been conducted by the Jesuits since 1829. Over seventy educational institutions, parochial schools apart, were under their management in the United States in the early 1980's. The American

Jesuits, organized into ten provinces or administrative units, numbered over 7,600 in 1980.

JESUP, FORT. A U.S. military post on the watershed between the Red and Sabine rivers, about twenty-five miles west of Natchitoches, La., established in 1822. It was abandoned after the annexation of Texas in 1845 and the Mexican War of 1846–48.

JET PROPULSION LABORATORY. A federally owned installation in Pasadena, Calif., primarily engaged in applied research and development related to the exploration of deep space. Although owned by the government, it was originally established in 1944 by the California Institute of Technology (Caltech), which continues to staff and operate the laboratory under contract with the National Aeronautics and Space Administration (NASA).

In June 1944, U.S. Army ordnance awarded Caltech a contract to develop complete long-range missiles. For this mission its Rocket Research Project was reorganized and renamed the Jet Propulsion Laboratory (JPL), on Nov. 1, 1944. During the same period, the laboratory participated in the V-2 Bumper-WAC program and pioneered in the development of FM-FM radio telemetry and various radio and inertial guidance systems. In 1957 the JPL provided an earth satellite vehicle as well as the necessary space-to-ground communications and instrumentation to army ordnance. On Dec. 3, 1958, all contract functions and the government-owned facilities of the JPL were transferred from the army to the newly created NASA in support of that agency's civilian space mission. The JPL redirected its research and development efforts from missile systems to lunar and planetary exploration. After 1958 it became responsible for a number of deep-space missions executed for the NASA Office of Space Science. Under the NASA Office of Tracking and Data Acquisition, the JPL developed and operates the Deep Space Network—a worldwide system that tracks, commands, controls, and receives data from lunar and planetary spacecraft. The laboratory also pursues basic and applied research in support of these programs, and in transportation, medicine, and energy for other government and private organizations.

JEWS. *See* **Judaism, American.**

JIM CROW LAWS. First enacted by some southern legislatures in 1865 to separate the races in public conveyances; came to embrace racial segregation in all areas of southern life. Origins of the term "Jim Crow" are obscure; it was used before the Civil War in reference to racial separation on the railroads in Massachusetts. (*See* Segregation.)

JIMSONWEED CULT. A cult that featured the drinking of the potent narcotic jimsonweed—or toloache (from the Aztec *toloatzin*), as it was called by the Spanish—and was dedicated to an all-powerful deity, Chungishnish. It developed relatively late in the 18th century among the Gabrielino Indians of what is now Los Angeles County, after they had been introduced to mission life; thus, Christian influence is probable in the cult's conception of an omnipresent, omnipotent deity. The cult spread to most of the tribes of southern California, reaching the Diegueño of San Diego County in the early 19th century. Jimsonweed includes plants of the genus *Datura.* The visions and dreams that occurred under its influence were believed to foretell the future. Shamans often took it in order to "see sickness," and it was given to initiates in the boys' puberty rite.

JINGOISM. In American usage, a term for the blatant demand for an aggressive foreign policy. The word is probably derived from the "by jingo" of a music-hall song popularized by Gilbert Hastings Macdermott in England during a crisis with Russia in 1877–78.

JOB CORPS. When President Lyndon B. Johnson signed the Economic Opportunity Act on Aug. 20, 1964, the Job Corps was created as a major arm of the antipoverty program. Under Sargent Shriver, director of the Office of Economic Opportunity, the Job Corps was dedicated to providing general and vocational education, technical training, and useful work experience at residential centers for young people from poverty backgrounds, aged sixteen through twenty-one, to prepare them for responsible citizenship and productive employment. By the peak year of 1967 over 42,000 young people (about 75 percent were men) were enrolled in more than 100 Job Corps centers. The total expenditure of federal funds for the agency from 1965 to 1973 was more than $1.8 billion. Most of the centers were administered by private industrial firms; others were administered by universities, the Department of Agriculture, the Department of the Interior, and state agencies. During the administration of President Richard M. Nixon many of the Job Corps centers were closed and budgets were curtailed; what remained of the agency was transferred to the Manpower Administration in the Department of Labor. Emphasis was shifted from residential centers to centers within commuting distance of the enrollees' homes. Also, general remedial education was largely replaced by technical training. Since 1973 the Job Corps has operated under the provisions of the Comprehensive Employment and Training Act of 1973. The enrollment in 1980 was 39,000.

JOCKEY HOLLOW. Site of the encampment of the Continental army under Gen. George Washington during the bitter winter of 1779–80. About four miles southwest of the general's headquarters at Morristown, N.J., ten brigades of some 12,000 men were meagerly hutted there.

"JOE BOWERS." A song about the folk hero of the forty-niners. Dated around 1850, the song is a document straight from American soil. To the words and tune of this ballad oxen pulled a nation westward.

JOHN, FORT. Name given to Fort Laramie when bought by the American Fur Company, after John B. Sarpy, a partner. Built on the Laramie River in Wyoming Territory in 1834. The fort was still referred to as Laramie.

JOHN BIRCH SOCIETY. An ultraconservative organization founded in 1958 by Robert H. W. Welch, Jr. Named after John Birch, a Fundamentalist Baptist missionary from Georgia. Welch never knew Birch, who, while serving as a U.S. intelligence officer, was killed by Chinese Communists ten days after V-J Day, 1945, making him the first hero of the cold war, according to the society. The declared aim of the society is to fight Communism on an intellectual basis. It advocates a return to minimum federal government and abandonment of the Federal Reserve System, the Commodity Credit Corporation, and the veterans' hospitals. The organization is composed of a semisecret network of "Americanists" and publishes a journal, *American Opinion.* Its main headquarters are in Belmont, Mass.

JOHNS HOPKINS UNIVERSITY. A private, nonsectarian institution of higher learning; established in 1876 in Baltimore, Md., as a unique experiment that combined the European, especially German, emphasis on advanced study and serious research, and the traditional American emphasis on the liberal arts and the classics. It also included the first graduate school in the United States. The university was founded by the Quaker merchant Johns Hopkins with his bequest of $7 million.

The twelve trustees installed Daniel Coit Gilman as the first president. Gilman traveled on the Continent and in England to recruit a research faculty. In October 1876 Johns Hopkins University opened in buildings in downtown Baltimore. Among Gilman's innovations from Europe was an emphasis on teaching laboratories, student research, and the seminar. While students and masters gathered in such groups as the philological, historical, scientific, and archaeological associations, the Mathematical Society, or Peirce's Metaphysical Club, the young university also quickly became a center for new journals, usually the first in their fields in the United States. The need for a central publication agency resulted in the founding of the Johns Hopkins University Press in 1878.

Although the establishment of a medical school and hospital was integral to Johns Hopkins' testamentary bequest, their creation occupied many years and the energies of Gilman and two pioneers of American medicine, John Shaw Billings and William H. Welch. Together with Ira Remsen in chemistry and Henry Newell Martin in physiology, Billings and Welch constituted the first medical faculty almost a decade before the opening of the medical school itself. They conceived the first premedical program, projected a rigorous four-year medical course, and drew upon British and German innovations in the design of the hospital buildings and laboratory facilities. The hospital finally opened its doors in May 1889. The first medical residency system in the United States was established on William Osler's initiative. The School of Nursing was established under Isabelle Hampton later that year. In 1893 the medical school with Welch as its dean admitted its first students; this was made possible by an emergency fund raised by Mary E. Garrett and her associates with the provision that women be admitted on equal terms with men. As at the graduate school, new journals appeared at the medical school. In 1898 the elective system was instituted for the first time.

Notable achievements were made in many fields, and new services and departments were created: the Henry Phipps Psychiatric Clinic (1910), the Institute of the History of Medicine (1926), and the School of Health Services (1971). The undergraduate, graduate, and extension school were moved to the present Homewood campus (1916). Under subsequent presidents, the university assumed responsibility for the Applied Physics Laboratory in Silver Spring, Md., and the School of Advanced International Studies (SAIS) in Washington, D.C. SAIS activities were extended to Bologna, Italy, the first American graduate school in Europe, during 1953–56. During the administration of Lincoln Gordon (1967–71), the university began the Center for Metropolitan Planning and the Greater Homewood Corporation and admitted women to the undergraduate school.

JOHNSON AND GRAHAM'S LESSEE* V. *McINTOSH, 8 Wheaton 544 (1823). Established the constitutional principle that grants of land made to private individuals by Indian tribes are invalid. Successors to the grantees of a large tract of land in Illinois and Indiana, made by chiefs of the Illinois and Piankashaw in 1773 and 1775, challenged the ownership of a portion of the tract by William McIntosh, whose title derived from the U.S. government in 1818.

JOHNSON-CLARENDON CONVENTION (Jan. 14, 1869). Covered American claims against the British from 1853 onward. British concessions were so slight that the convention was rejected in the Senate, Apr. 13, 1869, by a vote of fifty-four to one. Settlement of Civil War claims was thereby postponed until the Treaty of Washington, 1871, and the subsequent, arbitrated Geneva award (1872).

JOHNSON COUNTY WAR. *See* **Rustler War.**

JOHNSON DOCTRINE. An expansion of the Roosevelt Corollary to the Monroe Doctrine enunciated on May 2, 1965, by President Lyndon B. Johnson in justification of his dispatch of U.S. Marines to quell civil disorders in the Dominican Republic. It stated that "the American nations . . . will not permit the establishment of another Communist government in the Western Hemisphere."

JOHNSON HALL. Built in 1761–62; the last home of Sir William Johnson, colonial superintendent of northern Indian affairs. Half a mile from Johnstown, N.Y., the hall was the scene of many conferences between the British and Indians and the mecca for travelers in the Mohawk Valley. Restored almost to its original appearance by the State of New York.

JOHNSON'S ISLAND. In Sandusky Bay, Lake Erie; used as a prison for captured Confederate officers from 1862 to the end of the Civil War. In the closing months of the war more than 3,000 were on the island. The proximity of Johnson's Island to Canada, where Confederate agents were stationed, invited plots and attempts to escape, in which members of northern antiwar secret societies (*see* Canada, Confederate Activities in) were also involved.

JOHNSTOWN FLOOD (1889). Occurred in Pennsylvania resulting from the collapse of the Conemaugh Reservoir during exceptionally heavy rainfall. The dam, constructed in 1852 and immediately abandoned, had been rebuilt during 1879–81 to a height of 80 feet by Pittsburgh sportsmen to quadruple the size of the reservoir, situated 275 feet above the Johnstown low flats; but they skimped the work and omitted the original discharge pipes and spillway. On Friday morning, May 31, 1889, at 3:30 P.M. the earthen walls yielded, inundating the valley in a powerful downward thrust. Halted by the Pennsylvania railway viaduct, just above Johnstown proper, the flood receded, causing destructive vortices, inducing a huge conflagration in the Cambria Iron Works, and annihilating most of Johnstown and its suburbs. Over 2,500 persons perished. Property losses totaled over $10 million.

JOINT COMMISSIONS. The arbitration of international disputes by joint commissions is usually distinguished from the negotiation of formal treaties by more than one diplomatic agent. Most arbitrations are the work of joint commissions. Of the many arbitrations to which the United States has been a party, some important ones were conducted for settling pre-Revolution American debts to the British, British spoliation claims, and the Maine-Canada boundary, under the Jay Treaty of 1794; for settling French spoliation claims in 1803, 1831, and 1880; for determining various articles under the Treaty of Ghent; for claims of U.S. citizens against Mexico, in 1839, 1849, and 1868; for U.S. claims against Columbia in 1861 and Peru in 1863; and for Spanish claims in 1871. Most significant of all was the Alabama Claims dispute, leading to the Geneva award of 1872.

JOINT COMMITTEE ON RECONSTRUCTION. On Dec. 4, 1865, Thaddeus Stevens, representative from Pennsylvania, moved the appointment of a joint committee from House and Senate to report conditions on which the late "so-called Confederate states" might be received back into the Union. The committee was appointed Dec. 13, 1865, with six members from the Senate and nine from the House. Their chief work was the formulation of the Fourteenth Amendment and the Reconstruction Act of Mar. 2, 1867.

JOINT OCCUPATION. The agreement reached by the United States and Great Britain with regard to Oregon Country under the Convention of 1818. The parties were unable to determine the boundary west of the Rocky Mountains because of rival claims. It was agreed that either nation could trade and settle in the region for ten years. On Aug. 6, 1827, the agreement was renewed, to continue until one party gave a year's notice of termination. Following the "Fifty-four Forty or Fight" campaign in 1846, Congress instructed President James K. Polk to serve notice upon Great Britain that the agreement was to end. The settlement of the boundary question by treaty, June 15, 1846, ended the joint occupation.

JOINT RESOLUTIONS. *See* **Resolutions, Legislative.**

JOINT-STOCK LAND BANKS. Chartered under the Federal Farm Loan Act, July 17, 1916. These banks were financed with private capital and were permitted to make agricultural loans in the states in which they were chartered and one contiguous state. About eighty-seven charters were granted, but not all the banks opened. The joint-stock banks had their largest growth in the better agricultural areas—Iowa, Illinois, Minnesota, Missouri, Texas, and California. The act was amended in 1923, limiting loans to one borrower to $50,000. The amount of a loan was limited to a percentage of the value of the appraised land and buildings. These banks did a thriving business during the World War I land booms but declined in the late 1920's. Many failed. The Emergency Farm Mortgage Act of 1933 ordered them liquidated. To aid in this, the Farm Credit Act of 1933 provided the Land Bank Commission with $100 million for two years, and renewed the provision for two more years in 1935.

JOLLIET AND MARQUETTE DISCOVERY. Louis Jolliet was a native of New France who embarked on a career of exploration. On one of his voyages to Lake Superior in 1669 he met the Jesuit missionary Jacques Marquette. Three years later the authorities of New France commissioned Jolliet to explore the Mississippi. Jolliet requested that Marquette be appointed chaplain.

On May 17, 1673, the two explorers left the mission of St. Ignace on the north shore of Mackinac Strait in two canoes with five voyageurs. They went by way of Lake Michigan, Green Bay, and the Fox River (*see* Fox-Wisconsin Waterway). A month from the time of departure their canoes shot out from the Wisconsin into the Mississippi. The two explorers drifted down the river as far as the Arkansas. From the Arkansas they turned back upstream, fearing to encounter Spaniards. Acting on Indian advice, they ascended the Illinois and the Des Plaines, portaging at Chicago to Lake Michigan. Marquette remained at the mission at De Pere to regain his health. Jolliet went in 1674 to Canada to report his discovery. Just before he reached Montreal, his canoe overturned in the rapids, and he lost all his journals, notes, and maps. Thus, Marquette's journal has become the official account of the voyage.

JONATHAN (Brother Jonathan)**.** Nickname for a typical American. The story, unknown until 1846, attributing it to George Washington's affection for Jonathan Trumbull, the Connecticut politician who was once on his staff, is without foundation. In the Revolution the term was employed by Loyalists and British soldiers in mild derision of patriots. After 1783 the term was often applied by New Englanders to country bumpkins, and by 1812 had become established as a national sobriquet.

JONES ACT (Organic Act of the Philippine Islands)**.** Passed by Congress on Aug. 29, 1916, provided for the government of the Philippines and committed the United States to the future independence of the archipelago. All inhabitants who were Spanish subjects on Apr. 11, 1899, and their descendants were designated as citizens. The right to vote was given to all literate male citizens over twenty-one years old. The two houses of the Philippine congress were made wholly elective; the president of the United States was to appoint, subject to confirmation by the Senate, justices of the Philippine supreme court and a governor-general.

JONES-CONNALLY FARM RELIEF ACT (Apr. 7, 1934). This act extended the list of enumerated basic agricultural commodities to the Agricultural Adjustment Act of 1933. It provided for benefit payments to cattle ranchers and the growers of barley, flax, peanuts, grain sorghums, and rye.

JONES-COSTIGAN SUGAR ACT (May 9, 1934). An amendment to the Agricultural Adjustment Act of 1933. It provided for benefit payments, under the terms of that act, to growers of sugar cane and sugar beets. It also sought to stabilize the price of sugar by authorizing limitation on the national production of these crops and empowered the secretary of agriculture to put all sugar imports on a quota basis. The Supreme Court's decision in *U.S.* v. *Butler* (1936) invalidated the tax features of this act.

JONES COUNTY, SECESSION OF. No evidence in documents supports the secession of Jones County from the state of Mississippi during the Civil War. It apparently derives from the antisecession sentiment of the county, a piney-woods area where there were no plantations, few blacks, and a small population and from the formation there in 1862 of a company of 125 raiders who cooperated with the Union army.

JONESTOWN MASSACRE (Nov. 18, 1978). In the 1950's, James (Jim) Warren Jones established himself as a charismatic churchman who championed the rights of the underprivileged. He established a cult, known as the People's Temple, and moved its headquarters to San Francisco. For years the press and cult defectors accused Jones of physical, sexual, and financial abuse, and in the mid-1970's he took most of his congregation to Guyana, where they established a commune, Jonestown. Continuing complaints of abuses within the cult failed to bring action by either the U.S. or Guyanese governments. Late in November 1978, Rep. Leo Ryan of California visited the commune to investigate the charges. As Ryan's party was preparing to leave on Nov. 18 from the nearby Port Kaituma airstrip, they were attacked by Temple members; five people, including Ryan, were killed. Jones, who had become increasingly paranoid, told the members of the commune that they were threatened by outsiders and must now commit suicide. Children were forced to drink a poisoned punch, and then the adults consumed the lethal drink. Members who resisted were either shot or injected with cyanide. When Guyanese troops reached Jonestown the following day, they found almost the entire commune dead; a few had escaped into the jungle. The death toll was 913 people, including Jones and 200 children.

***JONES* V. *VAN ZANDT*,** 5 Howard 215 (1846). Followed *Prigg* v. *Pennsylvania* in sustaining the federal Fugitive Slave Law of 1793. The Supreme Court unanimously declared that the Constitution not only made slavery a political question to be settled by each state for itself but also required each to allow the restoration of the slave property of others.

JORNADA DEL MUERTO (journey of death). A ninety-mile strip of desert extending from Valverde, N. Mex., to El Paso. The road follows a dry plain where many tragedies occurred because of the absence of water.

JOUETT'S RIDE (June 3, 1781). Capt. John Jouett, Jr., was spending the night at Cuckoo Tavern, Louisa, Va., when he saw Col. Banastre Tarleton's British troops go by toward Charlottesville, where the Virginia legislature was in session. Jouett rode by hidden paths the forty-five miles to Charlottesville before dawn, to warn the legislature, thus saving four signers of the Declaration of Independence—Thomas Jefferson, Thomas Nelson, Jr., Richard Henry Lee, and Benjamin Harrison—plus Patrick Henry and Edmund Randolph.

JOURNALISM. *See* **Newspapers.**

***JOURNAL OF CONGRESS*.** The official record of the proceedings of Congress. The Continental Congress in 1774 appointed Charles Thomson as secretary; he kept a manuscript journal recording resolves, decisions, and attendance, published contemporaneously in thirteen volumes. Thomson also kept a secret journal, not published until 1821. These journals, together with auxiliary records and papers, were used in the thirty-four-volume Library of Congress edition of the *Journals of the Continental Congress,* published 1904–37, to reconstruct the activities of the Congress from 1774 to 1789. At the end of each session since 1789, verbatim reports have been published with indexes. After the burning of the Capitol in 1814, when all printed copies were destroyed, the journals of the first thirteen congresses were reprinted (1820–26). The journals are substantially incorporated in the *Annals of Congress* (1789–1824), *Register of Debates* (1824–37), *Congressional Globe* (1833–73), and in the *Congressional Record* since 1873. The Senate also keeps an executive journal, published from time to time.

JOURNEYMAN. In skilled trades, a worker who has completed an apprenticeship or on-the-job training and has enough formal schooling to qualify as a full-fledged workman. Journeyman as a title is used in such trades as plumbing and carpentry. The title dates back to the medieval guilds.

JUCHEREAU'S TANNERY. Established by Louis Juchereau de St. Denys on or near the site of modern Cairo, Ill., in 1702. It included a missionary priest, more than a hundred tradesmen, and many Mascouten hunters. Decline commenced in 1703, when an epidemic caused the death of St. Denys and many of his men. Lambert Mandeville attempted to carry on, but in 1704 it was abandoned.

JUDAISM, AMERICAN. With the expulsion of Jews from Spain in 1492 and Portugal in 1497, Spanish and Portuguese Jews (Sephardim) had settled in the Iberian colonies in the Western Hemisphere. A settlement flourished in Brazil after the Dutch captured the area in 1630. When the Portuguese returned in 1654, Jews were obliged to migrate. Twenty-three landed in Dutch New Amsterdam (New York), establishing the first Jewish community in North America. Other Jews came to North America, mostly from northern Europe. Although they frequently had to struggle to obtain political and religious liberties, by the mid-1700's they enjoyed greater freedom in the English colonies than anywhere else in the world. With the outbreak of the American Revolution, remaining civic disabilities were gradually overcome.

Although Jews of Germanic descent (Ashkenazim) constituted the majority of American Jews by the 1720's, the Sephardim dominated Jewish spiritual life. The synagogue was characterized by a dignified orthodoxy. As there were no rabbis in the United States before 1840, services were led by a *hazzan* (cantor). By the late 18th century the 2,000–3,000 Jews in America had for the most part prospered. Many were involved in mercantile activities, and several had amassed considerable wealth. Immigration from Germany after Napoleon's defeat changed the entire nature of American Jewry. In 1850 there were about 50,000 Jews in the United States; in 1880, over 250,000. Most immigrants had settled initially on the East Coast and become peddlers, clerks, and artisans, eventually moving westward. Rising status was facilitated by broad social acceptance of Jews before the Civil War and by the tremendous industrial and financial expansion of the postwar period.

The Ashkenazic migration brought not only its poor but its educated middle-class laymen and scholarly rabbis. Classical Reform emphasized the progressive nature of Jewish law and interpreted prophetic Judaism as a faith rather than a national identity. Extensive changes were made in the tone and content of services, prayers, and traditional rituals. Of the influential rabbis, Isaac Mayer Wise was the most important. Having come to the United States in 1846, Wise established himself in Cincinnati in 1854; he issued a modern Hebrew prayer book in 1857 and played the major role in organizing the liberal Union of American Hebrew Congregations in 1873, the Hebrew Union College in 1875, and the Central Conference of American Rabbis in 1889. Attempts by traditionalists to stem the tide and organize parallel institutions met with scant success. As a result of the proliferation of congregations and secular Jewish societies—particularly the powerful B'nai B'rith organization (1843)—the synagogue was no longer the center of Jewish life.

The mass migration set in motion by serious pogroms in the Russian empire in 1881 and debilitating anti-Jewish legislation in 1882 caught the American Jewish community unprepared. The new arrivals were characterized by religious orthodoxy, political radicalism, and Zionist leanings. Anti-Semitism was making its first noticeable appearance in the United States. Nonetheless, a number of relief organizations, immigration aid societies, and school programs were established by American Jews to aid the newcomers.

The great majority settled in congested slums. In New York—where 46 percent of American Jews still lived in 1939—the largest urban community of Jews in history was consolidated. In these slums Jews formed a proletariat, particularly in the garment industry. Such Jews took the lead in establishing powerful trade unions to ameliorate sweatshop conditions. A fusion of the Germanic and Eastern European Jewish community was accelerated by increasing anti-Semitism in the United States, the growing proclivity of American Jews toward Zionism following the Balfour Declaration in 1917, the rise of Adolf Hitler in the 1930's. Despite anti-Semitism Jews began to play a much greater role in American politics, serving on the local and national level. As the Democrats became the party of urban-oriented reform, Jews flocked to its support. On the eve of the destruction of European Jewry, a relatively well-organized, secure, and yet highly self-conscious American Jewish community of about 5 million had developed.

The newcomers expanded the cultural and religious horizons of American Jewry. In New York and other major cities a vital, secularist Yiddish literature, press, and theater flourished from the 1910's into the 1930's. Jews also began to play an important role in the mainstream of American culture, particularly in the area of motion picture entertainment.

Although the confrontation of Orthodoxy and modern, secular American culture most frequently led to rapid secularization, numerous Orthodox synagogues sprang up. In 1887 the Orthodox established a talmudical academy in New York, which merged with a *yeshiva* ("high school") in 1915 and became Yeshiva College in 1928. They quickly took over the moderate Union of Orthodox Jewish Congregations, founded in 1898, and established the Union of Orthodox Rabbis in 1902 and the Rabbinical Council of America in 1935.

The newcomers also gave vitality to Conservative Judaism, which permitted change within traditional continuity. The Jewish Theological Seminary Association, founded in 1887, was revitalized by Solomon Schechter. In 1913 Schechter founded the Conservative United Synagogue of America. The central organization for Conservative rabbis, the Rabbinical Assembly of America, was established in 1919.

Under the impact of the growth of Jewish life in Palestine, Hitler's impact in Europe, and the influence of Eastern European Jews in the United States, Reform Judaism took a conservative turn. The Central Conference of American Rabbis adopted a more traditional statement of principles in 1937 and published a more traditional prayer book in 1940. At the same time, Jewish education began to reflect a new synthesis of religion, modern Hebrew culture, and Zionism. The Reconstructionist movement—founded in 1935 by Mordecai Kaplan—stressed the role of Judaism as a "religious civilization" and advocated the centralization of Jewish community life to include all varieties of Jewishness.

The decimation of European Jewry during World War II stimulated Zionism among American Jews, who played a crucial role in obtaining support for the establishment of the state of Israel in 1948. In the approach and aftermath of World War II the community was augmented by over 200,000 highly educated German Jews and intensely religious Eastern European Jews, including many Hasidim.

Except for many of the aged and certain pockets of poorer Orthodox Jews, the great majority of American Jews achieved middle- and upper-middle-class status. This was facilitated by the decline in anti-Semitism, which, being associated with nazism, came to be considered un-American. During the 1950's American Jews broke down the quota system in most colleges and universities. Jews flocked into the professions, notably law, medicine, accounting, and teaching;

although 6 million Jews constituted about 2.7 percent of the U.S. population in 1980, some 10 percent of American college professors were Jews.

The postwar years also saw a tremendous expansion in synagogue construction. Although the Conservative movement made the greatest gains, all three major branches benefited. Judaism became accepted as one of the "three American religions."

By the end of the 1960's the longstanding Afro-American-Jewish alliance in the fight for civil rights was undermined as militant blacks frequently singled out Jews as their oppressors. Many Jews came to fear they might have to pay a disproportionate price for Afro-American progress in professional jobs and in colleges and universities, as a result of affirmative action programs. The New Left, in particular, attacked Israel and Zionism in terms that aroused fears of rising left-wing anti-Semitism. Moreover, young Jews as well as many Jewish leaders criticized the American Jewish community for its growing conservatism and materialism. There were, at the same time, signs that the Jewish community was on the threshold of a cultural, and perhaps spiritual, renaissance. Newer and older forms of worship and social organization were being experimented with. The Israeli experience, moreover, exercised a highly beneficial impact on the Jews' self-image, and there was strong support for aiding the beleaguered Soviet Jews. Although low fertility rates and intermarriages in the 1970's indicated that the U.S. Jewish population might decline in the next decades, there was little fear that it would necessarily result in a loss of Jewish vitality.

JUDGE'S BILL (Feb. 13, 1925). A continuing increase in the work-load of the U.S. Supreme Court led a committee of justices—Willis Van Devanter, James C. McReynolds, and George Sutherland—to draft a proposal to Congress for limiting cases. The bill provided that most appeals from federal district courts would go directly to the Courts of Appeals (created in 1891). Appeals as a right by way of a Writ of Appeal from the Courts of Appeals and state courts to the Supreme Court were severely limited and the Supreme Court achieved substantial control of the cases it would hear through a *writ of certiorari* granted or denied at the court's descretion.

JUDICIAL REVIEW. The power of courts to hold that legislative enactments or executive decisions violate a written constitution. Although the Constitution makes no direct statement on the subject, it has always been assumed that American courts, when confronted with conflicting rules of law, must prefer the law of superior obligation to a rule of inferior standing. For the Supreme Court this thesis was first spelled out by Chief Justice John Marshall, in 1803, in the celebrated case of *Marbury* v. *Madison* (1 Cranch 137). If the Constitution is the superior paramount law, then a statute contrary to it cannot be law. He added that since judges must take an oath to support the Constitution, they are obliged to invalidate any statute that conflicts with it. The American doctrine of judicial review was the natural result of practices and ideas that were well known when the Constitution was written. Furthermore, at that time, there was widespread distrust of legislative power and a deep conviction that security from the abuse of such power would be found in written constitutions, the separation of powers, and checks and balances. Most of the leading members of the Constitutional Convention of 1787 and many members of the early congresses indicated that they accepted the propriety of judicial review. In addition, many state appellate courts rendered decisions prior to 1803 holding state statutes invalid on constitutional grounds.

JUDICIARY. Tribunals in the colonies, similar to those of England, enforced acts of Parliament and the principles of the common law and equity. The judiciary in the colonies was inadequate in significant respects because of the subjection of judicial institutions, procedures, and rulings to the will and purposes of England. Several of these inadequacies are outlined in the Declaration of Independence as complaints against the king.

Colonial and Constitutional Origins. At the base of the colonial judiciary was the office of justice of the peace, for dealing with minor civil and criminal matters. Above that office was the county court. A right of appeal to the colonial assembly existed in some colonies. There was in some cases a right of appeal to the judicial committee of the Privy Council in England. After the colonies became independent states, their court systems remained fundamentally the same, except for the development of courts of appeals with full-time professional judges.

All proposed plans submitted to the Constitutional Convention of 1787 provided for a national judiciary distinct from the judicial systems of the states. The adoption of the Constitution introduced two major breaks with the past: state judiciaries were subordinated to the federal judiciary in that the Constitution and federal laws and treaties were made the supreme law of the land, and an independent judiciary was explicitly created under the doctrine of the separation of powers.

Section 1 of Article III of the Constitution provided that the judicial power of the United States should be vested in a Supreme Court and such inferior courts as Congress might establish. It provided also that all federal judges were to hold office during good behavior and that their salaries were not to be diminished during their service in office. By Article II, the president was authorized to nominate, and, by and with the advice and consent of the Senate, to appoint Supreme Court judges. Section 2 of Article III prescribed the content of federal judicial power. Within the limits of that power the original jurisdiction of the Supreme Court was defined. The first ten amendments (Bill of Rights), added in 1791, included additional prescriptions with respect to the courts.

The judiciary provisions of the Constitution were given effect in the Judiciary Act of 1789, enacted after eleven states had ratified the Constitution. The Supreme Court consisted of a chief justice and five associate justices. Below were three circuit courts which were conducted by two Supreme Court judges and a district judge. Below the circuit courts were thirteen district courts, for each of which a district judge was to be appointed by the president.

The Federal Judiciary. The federal judiciary has seen a steady expansion, stemming from increases in territory, population, litigation and legislation; and the development of an increasingly complex society. The district courts have undergone drastic jurisdictional changes, assuming in 1891 all the trial court responsibility originally allocated to both them and the circuit courts. The circuit court system was modified repeatedly from 1801 until the early 20th century, particularly as the jurisdiction of the district courts expanded. Permanent judges were provided for the new circuit courts of appeals. The membership of the Supreme Court was increased to an all-time high of ten in 1863 and established at nine in 1869. It was not until 1891, however, that Supreme Court justices were relieved of obligations to ride circuit and much of their appellate jurisdiction.

To enable the Supreme Court to keep up with the growing stream of important cases, further jurisdictional reductions were made from time to time, particularly by limiting the classes of cases that might be taken to the Supreme Court as a matter of right, in contrast with those that might be accepted or rejected by the Court after a preliminary scrutiny to determine their public importance. Provisions with respect to appellate jurisdiction are complex. The purpose of Congress in prescribing the appellate jurisdiction of the courts is to provide for the expeditious appeal to the highest court of cases of greatest public importance, while moving those of less importance at a slower pace and limiting the right of appeal with respect to them or cutting it off altogether.

Although the federal judiciary consists only of courts created pursuant to Article III, the exercise of certain powers requires Congress to create other tribunals to exercise judicial functions—for example, the powers to govern territories, to grant patents, and to appropriate money to pay claims against the United States. These tribunals are known as legislative courts. These include those established in the territories of the United States, the Court of Claims, the Court of Customs and Patent Appeals, and the Tax Court of the United States. Bearing some resemblance to legislative courts are numerous independent agencies, such as the Interstate Commerce Commission, the Federal Trade Commission, and the National Labor Relations Board, which exercise functions judicial in character.

The appointment of federal judges by the president with the consent of the Senate has been criticized, but there has been no serious movement for popular elections, such as the movement that took place in connection with state judges. The provision for lifelong tenure during good behavior has been regarded as a serious defect in the system. Many judges have proved unwilling to resign even after reaching senility. A constitutional amendment authorizing compulsory retirement of judges at a fixed age has been much discussed and has attracted widespread support but has never been implemented, except that chief judges of circuit and district courts are required to step down at the age of seventy.

A barrier to efficiency in the federal courts has been the technicality and diversity in rules of practice. In 1792 Congress empowered the Supreme Court to adopt uniform rules of practice for the federal courts in equity and admiralty cases, and in 1898 in bankruptcy cases. Concerning actions at law, however, it was provided in the Conformity Act of 1872 that the federal courts should conform to the practice in effect in the state courts. Federal practice, therefore, varied from state to state. Congress in 1934 authorized the Supreme Court to adopt and promulgate uniform rules of civil procedure for the federal courts—effective in 1938. These rules have undergone revision and similar rules of criminal and appellate procedure have been adopted. In 1973 new federal rules pertaining to evidence were adopted.

Congress in 1922 provided for a Judicial Conference of the senior circuit judges, to be presided over by the chief justice. Later representative district and special judges were added to it. The conference met annually, and it was charged with making policy related to all aspects of the federal courts.

The Administrative Office Act of 1939 fundamentally changed the federal judicial system. The Judicial Conference was given a central administrative arm, the Administrative Office of the United States Courts. Circuit councils were also created as regional administrative structures.

State, County, and Municipal Courts. The state judicial systems differ greatly among themselves and from the federal system in matters of appointment, tenure, jurisdiction, organization, and procedure. Selection of state judges may be made by state legislatures, by cooperation between governors and legislatures or senates, by popular election, or by a nonpartisan appointive-elective method. Tenure varies from lifetime appointment to specific terms of service to mandatory retirement at a certain age.

The expansion of court work and the increase in tribunals created a need for centralized control of the judiciaries of the states. In the 1920's and 1930's a number of states, some in advance of the federal government and some later, organized judicial councils. The replacement of justice-of-peace courts with municipal courts within cities, beginning in the 1920's, was a step toward increased efficiency and consistency. In the 1960's and 1970's court structure was being modified by the establishment of unified state court systems, with central administrative responsibility vested in the state's chief justice and supreme court. Over half of the states had adopted the unified state court model by 1973.

The geographical jurisdiction of general trial courts over criminal cases and civil disputes is usually organized on a county or multicounty basis, while municipal courts are organized on the basis of the city or borough. General trial courts have subject matter jurisdiction over felony criminal cases, all juvenile, domestic relations, and probate cases, and civil actions involving claims in excess of $5,000. Municipal courts generally have jurisdiction over the remainder of state cases, including criminal misdemeanors, local ordinances, and minor civil cases. One way of simplifying this web of jurisdictional responsibility is the consolidation of state trial courts into a single-level trial court organized in a county or multicounty area. In the 1960's and 1970's this approach was increasingly adopted. In addition, professional managers are increasingly employed by courts, and only six did not have professional state court administrative staff by 1973.

Complexities of procedure have embarrassed the states as well as the federal government. An attempt at broad simplification was made in the 1920's and 1930's, led by the American Law Institute. After World War II significant progress occurred in the form of model codes promulgated by the American Bar Association and with groups of lawyers. In 1973 all but three states operated under Modern Rules of Criminal and/or Civil Procedure.

The Status Quo and Reform. Although there is no complete separation of powers in any state or in the federal government, the several judiciaries have maintained their strength against legislative and executive departments. Nevertheless, there is great concern about the courts' ability to keep pace with the acute increase in litigation. Increasingly efforts at reform are directed toward diverting case flow away from the courts. Although the prestige and power of the courts are often strained because of both the volume of work and the explosiveness of the issues to be resolved (particularly at the U.S. Supreme Court and other appellate courts), their pivotal position within government seems assured.

JUDICIARY ACT OF 1789. Implemented the judiciary clause of the Constitution; first organized the federal judiciary. It provided for a Supreme Court of six members, three intermediate circuit courts comprising two Supreme Court justices and a district judge, and thirteen district courts, corresponding roughly to state boundaries, with a judge for each. Probably most important was Section 25 granting the Court, through writs of error, the right to hear and decide certain appeals from state courts. In the act is established the doctrine of judicial review of state legislation, first exercised in the case of *Fletcher* v. *Peck* (1810). The section, through its assignment of jurisdiction to the Supreme Court on writs of error in cases of conflict between state and federal authority, also became one of the strongest bulwarks of federal power against the attacks of the states' rights school.

JUDICIARY ACT OF 1801. Erroneously viewed principally in the light of the election of 1800, leading to the assertion that the outgoing Federalists planned to perpetuate nationalism through the judiciary. Judicial reform was needed, had for some time been considered, was recommended by John Adams in 1799, and had been carefully prepared. The act reduced the membership of the Supreme Court to five and relieved its justices of circuit court duty; set up six circuits, five presided over by three circuit judges each and the sixth by a circuit and a district judge; and established five new judicial districts. Democratic-Republicans repealed the act in 1802. This action, at least as partisan as that of 1801, restored the Judiciary Act of 1789 to full force.

***JUILLIARD* V. *GREENMAN*,** 110 U.S. 421 (1884). The Supreme Court upheld the implied power of Congress to make U.S. government notes legal tender (and therefore money) in peacetime as well as in wartime. In 1870 the Court had held the legal-tender acts of 1862 and 1863 unconstitutional, but in 1871 the Court reversed this decision and upheld the legal-tender acts as a war measure. *Juilliard* v. *Greenman* upheld the acts without reference to the war power.

"JUKES" FAMILY. In 1874 Richard L. Dugdale, investigating county jails for the Prison Association of New York, found in a jail six blood relations who were guilty of theft, burglary, rape, and murderous assault. He further learned that of twenty-nine males, immediate kin of these six, seventeen were criminals and fifteen had received a total of seventy-one years of sentences. Of the women, 52 percent were harlots. This led him to a study in heredity, a two-century record of a degenerate family, called the Jukes to protect its more worthy members. Dugdale's report was published in 1875. In 1915 a continuation of it by Arthur H. Eastabrook was published by the Carnegie Institution.

JUMPING-OFF PLACES. Towns along the border of U.S. frontier settlement where emigrants completed their outfitting for the journey west in the 1840's and 1850's. Independence, Mo., was the best known.

JUNEAU (Alaska)**.** Capital of Alaska, with a population of 19,529 in 1980. Juneau was founded in 1880 and named after a pioneer gold-prospector, Joe Juneau. It is on the Alaska Panhandle and can be reached by water from the Puget Sound region. Juneau is supplied by sea or air from Seattle and Ketchikan. There is no year-round land transportation to the city because of the high mountains inland from it.

The chief activities are governmental, but the city is also a lumbering center. Since it is close to Mendenhall Glacier, it attracts some tourists each year who sail up the "Inland Passage" from Seattle. The capital of Alaska was shifted from the old Russian town of Sitka (or New Archangel) in 1900.

JUNIOR COLLEGES. *See* **Education.**

JUNIUS, LETTERS OF. Published in the *London Public Advertiser* from Jan. 21, 1769, to Jan. 21, 1772. The writer was possibly Sir Philip Francis, a disaffected British government official. A well-informed Whig, Junius poured brilliantly slanderous invective upon Tory-minded English ministers for a "series of inconsistent measures" that allegedly ruined England and drove the colonies "into excesses little short of rebellion." The letters were frequently reprinted in colonial and other English newspapers.

***JÜRGEN LORENTZEN* PRIZE CASE.** In 1861 the U.S. warship *Morning Light,* commanded by Capt. H. T. Moore, captured the Danish bark *Jürgen Lorentzen* sailing from Rio de Janeiro to Havana, Cuba, in the course of the blockade of the Confederacy. Moore, suspecting the bark was bound for a Confederate port, took it to New York City. An investigation turned out favorably for the *Jürgen Lorentzen.* A joint Danish-American commission was established to ascertain the damages and Congress made provision for the settlement.

JURY TRIAL. The characteristic mode of determining issues of fact at common law was transplanted from England to the American colonies and became an integral part of their legal system in both civil and criminal common-law cases. The Constitution as proposed in 1787 contained the provision that "the Trial of all Crimes, except in cases of Impeachment, shall be by Jury." No mention was made of jury trial in civil cases. It was argued by some that failure to include the requirement of jury trial in civil cases was in effect to abolish it. The Constitution was adopted without any provision for jury trial in civil cases, but in the articles of amendment adopted soon afterward a provision was included to the effect that in common law suits involving more than $20 the right of trial by jury should be preserved. The Sixth Amendment elaborated on the subject of jury trial in criminal cases by providing that "the accused shall enjoy the right to a speedy and public trial, by an impartial jury of the State and district wherein the crime shall have been committed."

Some states, however, have not adhered rigidly to the old common-law requirement that the jury be composed of not more or less than twelve persons and the requirement that the verdict be unanimous. For the federal government, these changes are held to be forbidden by the Constitution.

Jury trial has not been required in cases involving petty offenses, and in all cases, including cases involving serious crimes, the right of trial by jury may be waived by the parties.

JUSTICE, DEPARTMENT OF. Established June 22, 1870, by act of Congress. However, the office of attorney general had been created by Congress in the Judiciary Act of 1789. It reached cabinet rank when the first attorney general, Edmund Randolph, attended his initial cabinet meeting on Mar. 31, 1792. For many years the attorney general served almost solely as the legal counsel to the president and had no department as such. The proliferation of federal offenses proscribed by statute and the growth of civil litigation between private parties and the government transformed the office of attorney general. By the Civil War he was conducting most federal cases, both civil and criminal. He had a growing staff and was devoting all his time to the task. Direction of U.S. attorneys and U.S. marshals had been transferred from the courts to his office. This trend was formalized by the act that created the Department of Justice under the attorney general.

As early as 1871 the federal prison system was placed under the department's jurisdiction. The growth of laws specifying federal criminal offenses necessitated a Criminal Division (1909). Increased federal interest in developing the public lands brought creation of the Lands Division (later the Land and Natural Resources Division) in 1910. In the extensive departmental reorganization of 1933, several offices were made into divisions, including the Antitrust Division, the Tax Division, and the Claims Division (later the Civil Division). The Internal Security Division was created in 1954 and the Civil Rights Division in 1957. As legislation for the protection of the public continued to increase, the Pollution Control Section in the Land and Natural Resources Division (1970), the Consumer Affairs Section in the Antitrust Division (1971), and the Economic Stabilization Section in the Civil Division (1971) were created.

Meanwhile, enforcement duties were added. The Bureau of Investigation (later the Federal Bureau of Investigation) was created in 1908. The Immigration and Naturalization Service was transferred from the Department of Labor to the Department of Justice in 1940. Antinarcotics enforcement was concentrated in the Department of Justice with the creation of the Bureau of Narcotics and Dangerous Drugs in 1968. In 1972 the president created within the Department of Justice the Office for Drug Abuse Law Enforcement, to coordinate all such federal and state efforts, and the Office of National Narcotics Intelligence.

In the 1960's the department was assigned functions beyond litigative and enforcement. The Office of Criminal Justice, charged with examining and proposing improvements in the entire criminal justice process, was created in 1964. Providing federal financial aid to help states and localities upgrade their criminal justice systems was the task given in 1965 to the Office of Law Enforcement Assistance (greatly enlarged under the Law Enforcement Assistance Administration in 1968). The Community Relations Service, created by the Civil Rights Act of 1964 and charged with assisting minority groups, was transferred from the Department of Commerce to the Department of Justice in 1966.

JUSTICE OF THE PEACE. An official authorized to keep the peace and try felonies and trespasses and in more recent times to deal with numerous other affairs of local government. The office flourished in the colonies. The justice exercised both a criminal and a civil jurisdiction. In most of the colonies the justices in court sessions exercised sweeping local executive and administrative powers, drew up the levy, collected the tax, appointed road commissioners and supervised highways, made disbursements, granted licenses to keep taverns and retail liquors, and appointed and controlled administrators, executors, and guardians. They generally took acknowledgments of deeds and depositions and performed marriage ceremonies. While the institution still exists in some states, the justice's criminal jurisdiction has been curtailed, and he is in the main a committing magistrate. An appointive officer in colonial times, he is now generally elected.

JUVENILE COURTS. The formal inception of a specialized juvenile court in the United States occurred on July 1, 1899, with the implementation of an Illinois legislative act establishing the juvenile court division of the circuit court for Cook County. Civic leaders sought to separate children and youth from the ugly conditions in prisons and improve their opportunities for constructive citizenship. Various American institutions had developed in the 19th century: privately operated houses of refuge, where juveniles toiled long hours in manufacturing tasks within an overall repressive environment, (1820's and 1830's); probation (1868); and separate hearings for juveniles accused of criminal violations (1879).

The Illinois legislation not only established separate courts for juveniles but also incorporated other reforms. Legal proceedings were kept simple and summary, and lawyers were eschewed as unnecessary. Social workers and behavioral scientists assisted the judge. Court wards to be confined were segregated from adult offenders and placed in training and industrial schools, private foster homes, or institutions. Probation officers facilitated a child's adjustment in his own home. By 1925, a juvenile court existed in every state except two.

Constitutional challenges to juvenile court practice and procedure were consistently overruled until the 1960's. Concerns that children were denied a right to bail, counsel, public trials, jury trials, and immunity against self-incrimination, and that they could be convicted on hearsay testimony or by only a preponderance of the evidence, were swept aside by state appellate court rulings. Legislative reform in California and New York in 1961 and 1962, respectively, began to place a more regularized procedure on the historically informal juvenile court practices. In 1967 the U.S. Supreme Court ruled that constitutional due process protected the juvenile and mandated formal fact-finding hearings, together with the juvenile's right to be represented by an attorney and to avoid self-incrimination. The Court ruled in 1970 that the criminal system's principle of proof beyond a reasonable doubt must be utilized in juvenile court trials, but also in 1971 that juveniles were not entitled to a jury trial under the Constitution. These Supreme Court rulings stimulated an ongoing legal challenge of juvenile court practice and procedure and the beginning of a conspicuous role for lawyers in juvenile courts. Although the customary maximum age limit for juvenile court jurisdiction is eighteen, public concerns stimulated efforts in the 1970's to lower the age, to make more serious offenses subject exclusively to criminal court sanction.

KADIAK ISLAND. *See* **Kodiak Island.**

KAKIATE PATENT. Located in what is now Rockland County, N.Y.; purchased from the Indians in 1696 by Daniel Honan and Michael Hawdon. Known as the Hackyackawck or Kakiate patent, it was confirmed by Gov. Benjamin Fletcher. Quarrels over the northern boundary with the owners of the Chesecocks patent delayed partition and settlement.

KALAMAZOO (Mich.). The county seat of Kalamazoo county, settlement was first made in 1829 by Titus Bronson, who built a cabin on the Kalamazoo River at its confluence with Portage Creek. Kalamazoo was incorporated in 1843 as a town; it became a city in 1884. Paper manufacturing was begun in 1867, and has remained the city's largest industry. In 1957 Kalamazoo was selected by the U.S. Information Agency as the typical American city and was subsequently portrayed as such in the agency's exhibits abroad. In 1980 the population was 79,722.

KALAMAZOO CASE (*Charles E. Stuart et al.* v. *School District No. 1 of the Village of Kalamazoo,* 30 Michigan 69). Decided by the Michigan Supreme Court in 1874. Charles E. Stuart and other citizens of Kalamazoo sought to restrain school authorities from collecting taxes for support of a public high school and a nonteaching superintendent. The court held that the levying of these taxes was consistent with the educational policy of Michigan since 1817 and was legal under the constitution of 1850. The decision confirmed the right of the state to establish, at public expense, a complete system of education and set an important precedent.

"KALLIKAK" FAMILY. Fictitious surname of two New Jersey kinship groups investigated by American psychologist Henry Herbert Goddard (1866–1957). The study originated in the detailed genealogical history of an inmate at Goddard's training school for retarded children. The "bad blood" branch of the family, resulting from the illegitimate union during the Revolution of a soldier and a feebleminded girl, yielded 480 known descendants, 143 of whom were retarded. This group comprised criminal, alcoholic, illegitimate, epileptic, blind, deaf, and insane offspring as well; only 46 were normal. The "good blood" branch, derived from a subsequent marriage to a normal woman, consisted almost entirely of normal individuals, many superior or prominent. Goddard concluded that feeblemindedness is inherited as a recessive unit character. The study later came to be regarded as having underplayed the influence of societally conditioned and environmentally determined factors in mental ability.

KANAWHA, BATTLE OF THE. *See* **Point Pleasant, Battle of.**

KANAWHA SALT WORKS. Although it was known to the Indians, colonists did not learn of the salt along the Kanawha River, near present Charleston, W. Va., until 1755. The land on which the salt springs were located was bought by Joseph Ruffner in 1794, and leased by him to Elisha Brooks, who built a furnace there in 1797. Later the Ruffner brothers took over the saltmaking, improving methods and drilling the first deep well in 1808. By 1817 there were twenty brine wells and thirty furnaces producing 600,000 to 700,000 bushels of salt per year. Bitter competition caused the organization of a "Salt Trust" in 1817. Saltmaking was the dominant industry in the Kanawha area for more than fifty years.

KANSAS. Popularly known as the "Sunflower State," admitted to the Union on Jan. 29, 1861. It is located in the geographic center of the United States, and it is the site of the geodetic datum of North America from which all the United States, Canadian, and Mexican maps are made. There are rich deposits of oil, gas, coal, lead, zinc, and salt.

When the first white men arrived in Kansas, the resident Indian tribes were the Kansa, Osage, Wichita, Pawnee, and Pueblo. Hunter tribes of Kiowa, Comanche, Arapaho, Cheyenne, and Apache roamed over western Kansas.

The recorded history of Kansas began when Francisco Vásquez de Coronado's expedition from Mexico reached central Kansas in 1541. From 1682 to 1739 several French explorers crossed the area. England, France, and Spain claimed the area at various times, but real interest in exploration did not come until the purchase of the Louisiana Territory from France by the United States in 1803. The area was well explored in the decades to follow by Lewis and Clark, Zebulon Pike, Stephen Long, and others.

Preterritorial Kansas was on the way to the West. The Santa Fe Trail was used regularly after 1821. Pioneers on their way to Oregon and California opened new overland routes. The need for frontier defense led to the establishment of Fort Leavenworth (1827), Fort Scott (1842), and Fort Riley (1853). Fort Larned and Fort Hays are good examples of modern restoration.

Since Kansas was regarded as an arid land, nearly one-fourth of the state's present area was set aside by the federal government as a permanent home for the Indians. Some twenty tribes were sent to this reserved area by the Indian removal acts of 1830 and 1850.

When Kansas was organized as a territory in 1854 under the Kansas-Nebraska Act, the primary incentive was rivalry between the North and the South, partly over a railroad to the Pacific and partly over the issue of the extension of slavery. Thus began the six-year period when the area was referred to as "Bleeding Kansas." The Indian's land vanished rapidly as federal legislation and Indian treaties opened territory to white settlement. During the territorial period four constitutions were drafted. The first three failed, largely because of the fight over slavery. The fourth, adopted in 1859 and usually referred to as the Wyandotte Constitution, made Kansas a free-soil state in 1861.

Kansas faced severe drought and famine in 1860, and the strain of the Civil War shortly after admission to statehood. With fewer than 30,000 men between the ages of eighteen and forty-five, the state furnished over 20,000 men for the Union army. After the war Indian tribes were removed to Indian Territory, but Kansans were harassed by Indian raids until the late 1870's.

On July 10, 1860, the first "iron horse" arrived on Kansas soil. Liberal state and federal aid between 1864 and 1890 led to the creation of more than 200 railroad companies and more than 8,700 miles of track. The Union Pacific in 1869 and the Santa Fe in 1872 reached western Kansas. Railway towns became the western terminals for the "long drive" of Texas cattle. Hard winter wheat was introduced into the agricultural economy, and abundant mineral resources were exploited. Kansas increased its industrialization during World War I and afterward. By the mid-1970's Kansas produced about one-fifth of the nation's wheat. Livestock production was of even greater value. Airplanes, farm machinery, and numerous industrial goods were among the state's major manufactures. Its industrial income is derived mainly from oil, natural gas, coal, salt, clay products, and stone.

Politically, the history of Kansas has been basically Republican. But economic problems frequently led voters to join political movements outside the mainstream. Kansas furnished leadership and supported issues in the Granger movement (1870's), the Farmer's Alliance (1880's), the Populist revolt (1890's), and the Progressive movement (1901–17). Kansas was a heartland for populism and progressivism. In 1980 Kansas had a population of 2,363,208.

KANSAS, PROHIBITION IN. Kansas was opened for settlement just eight years after the enactment in 1846 of the first Maine Prohibitory Law, prohibiting the manufacture and sale of alcoholic beverages, and the prohibition idea was brought to Kansas by New Englanders. As early as 1856 Rep. John Brown, Jr., son of the antislavery crusader, presented to the free-state legislature a petition for passage of a "Maine law." Sentiment grew until 1880, when the people adopted a prohibition amendment to the state constitution. For twenty-six years enforcement was resisted where saloons were operated under a system of city fines, collected in lieu of licenses. Carry Nation advertised this flagrant violation by leading women zealots in saloon-smashing raids, commencing in 1899. Enforcement became more effective in 1906 when Gov. Edward W. Hoch and Fred S. Jackson, state attorney general, hit on the plan of ousting local authorities who failed to keep their oath to support the state constitution. Their success stimulated neighboring states to adopt the Kansas plan. But when the federal government enacted Prohibition, resentment against the Eighteenth Amendment spread to Kansas. Following repeal of national Prohibition in 1933, Kansas juries, in many instances, failed to convict liquor dealers. Prohibition gained new strength in 1934 when a state repeal amendment was defeated. Beer was legalized in 1937. In 1948 the state prohibition amendment was repealed.

KANSAS BORDER WAR. *See* **Border War.**

KANSAS CITY (Mo). City in western Missouri at the confluence of the Missouri and Kansas rivers. About 1800 Louis Bartholet established a trading camp, but the first permanent settlement was a trading post at Randolph Bluffs, built by François Chouteau in 1821. Floods caused this post in 1826 to be moved upstream near the mouth of the Kansas, at the apex of the big bend of the Missouri.

On the Santa Fe Trail, a few miles west of Independence, its terminus, John McCoy laid out Westport in 1833, four miles south of the mouth of the Kansas River. A company headed by William Sublette, noted fur trader, platted the Town of Kansas on the river in 1838, but a clouded title prevented its development until 1846, and it was called derisively Westport Landing. By 1846 the settlement was competing for its share of the Santa Fe trade with Independence, Westport, and Leavenworth. In 1853 the name was changed to the City of Kansas and in 1889 to Kansas City. During the border difficulties preceding Kansas statehood, it was a focus of proslavery activity, and near Westport the Civil War battle of that name was fought. Kansas City became a railroad and packing center after the Civil War and absorbed Westport. Kansas City, Kans., a separate municipality, is separated from Kansas City, Mo., only by the state line.

Kansas City has developed into an important manufacturing city. It is a major railway terminus, shipping livestock, chemicals, and grain. Kansas City is the second largest city in Missouri and in 1980 had a population of 448,159.

KANSAS-COLORADO WATER RIGHTS. In 1875–85, Kansas and Colorado developed irrigation systems by appropriation and diversion of water from the Arkansas River and by pumping water from the underground water supply in the river valley. Kansas claimed that the excessive use of water in Colorado endangered Kansas crops. In 1901 Kansas filed suit against Colorado contending that the state and its citizens suffered material damage from such illegal diversion. The Supreme Court in *Colorado* v. *Kansas,* 320 U.S. 383 (1907), recognized that each state had rights to the water—but the Court could not force a settlement. Litigation continued until 1943, when the Court recommended settlement through the compact clause of the Constitution (Article I, Section 10). The dispute was resolved in 1949 with the federal approval of the Arkansas River Compact. The building of the John Martin reservoir, near Lamar, Colo., was the key. Under the compact Colorado uses 60 percent of the normal flow of the river and Kansas 40 percent.

KANSAS COMMITTEE, NATIONAL. During civil war in Kansas Territory over slavery, emigrant aid societies and Kansas relief committees sprang up throughout the free states. On July 9, 1856, representatives of these groups and of older organizations met at Buffalo, N.Y., and formed a National Kansas Committee with headquarters in Chicago. It raised and spent some $200,000, sending arms, supplies, and recruits to the Free-State (antislavery) party in Kansas.

KANSAS FREE-STATE PARTY. Originated at the Big Springs Convention, Sept. 5, 1855. Opponents of slavery in the territory, defeated in previous elections, saw the necessity of consolidating all antislavery opinion. A platform, largely the work of James H. Lane, urged Whigs and Democrats to unite in a party devoted to the exclusion of slavery and of free blacks. A subsequent convention, meeting at Topeka on Sept. 19, called an election of delegates to a constitutional convention and provided for the appointment of an executive committee which, with Lane as chairman, directed the party's quest for statehood. Factionalism became more pronounced. Lane headed the conservative group; Charles Robinson, Kansas agent of the New England Emigrant Aid Company, led the radical wing. The chief tests of strength came over popular sovereignty, which was defeated; and over the exclusion of free blacks, which was referred to the voters and approved along with the Topeka Constitution. The Wakarusa War in December hastened Lane's transition to radicalism and gave him undisputed leadership of the western element in the territory. The Free-State party failed to obtain immediate statehood. Ignoring the Lecompton movement, it captured control of the territorial legislature in 1857. Although the party endorsed Republican doctrine in 1856, it was not supplanted by a Republican organization until Horace Greeley visited the territory in 1859.

KANSAS-NEBRASKA ACT (1854). The historical context of the Kansas-Nebraska bill is complex, but frontier expansion was a major factor. With the Compromise of 1850, it had been hoped that further controversy over slavery would be avoided. But it soon arose again, largely because of schemes for building a transcontinental railroad. The bill was introduced by Sen. Stephen A. Douglas of Illinois, a Chicago resident who wanted his region to be the eastern terminus of the proposed railroad to the Pacific. Although Douglas is usually regarded as the bill's author, there is significant evidence that the political reason for the bill's introduction lay more in the infighting taking place in the Democratic party in Missouri in 1853–54. Douglas, chairman of the Senate Committee on Territories, reported the bill for territorial organization of Kansas and Nebraska out of his committee in January 1854, including a provision that, by indirection, repealed the Missouri Compromise. The bill asserted that the Compromise of 1850 had superseded the 1820 principle that 36°30′ north latitude was the northern demarcation line for slave states; the bill also stated that the question of slavery in the territories should be settled by the people living in them. The final bill explicitly repealed the Missouri Compromise, and the possibility of slavery in the new territories was made real. Kansas and Nebraska were promptly opened for settlement in 1854. Although Nebraska remained relatively quiet, settlers came to Kansas not only to develop the frontier but also to lend their weight in the determination of whether Kansas would be free or slave.

KANSAS PACIFIC RAILROAD. Railroad system from Kansas City to Cheyenne, Wyo. Chartered by the Kansas territorial legislature in 1855 as the Leavenworth, Pawnee and Western Railroad, it was included in the Pacific Railway Act of 1862 and allowed to connect with the Union Pacific at the hundredth meridian. The route was changed in 1864. In 1863 Gen. John C. Frémont and Samuel Hallett secured control and changed its name to Union Pacific Railway Company, Eastern Division. After many factional difficulties the road passed into the control of a group headed by John D. Perry, who built to Denver and connected with the Union Pacific at Cheyenne by the use of the Denver Pacific. It served the Texas cattle trade and brought many immigrants to Kansas. In 1880 it was consolidated with the Union Pacific to form the Union Pacific Railway Company.

KANSAS STRUGGLE. *See* **Border War; Kansas; Kansas Free-State Party; Kansas-Nebraska Act; Lecompton Constitution.**

KAPOSIA, BATTLE OF (Battle of Pine Coulie). Late in June 1842, about a hundred Chippewa, coming overland from Lake St. Croix, established an ambush on the east bank of the Mississippi opposite Little Crow's Sioux village of Kaposia on the site of South St. Paul, Minn. Premature firing killed two Sioux women, giving the alarm. In a running fight lasting several hours the Chippewa were repulsed after heavy casualties to the Sioux.

KASKASKIA. Metropolis of the Illinois Country in the 18th century; founded in 1703 when the Jesuit Gabriel Marest moved the Mission of the Immaculate Conception from the site of present St. Louis to the right bank of the Kaskaskia River seven miles above its then junction with the Mississippi. With him went the Kaskaskia tribe of the Illinois Indians.

For fifteen years Kaskaskia was primarily an Indian village in which a few French lived. Growth commenced in 1717, when it became a part of the district of Louisiana. By 1770, it was said to contain 500 whites and nearly that many blacks.

The French and Indian villages had been separated by

Pierre Duque Boisbriant in 1719. By the end of the century only a handful of Indians remained. Under Boisbriant, commandant from 1718 to 1724, the characteristic land system of the French village was established. Agriculture flourished, and grain was shipped as far as Detroit and New Orleans.

In the late 18th century many changes took place in Kaskaskia. In 1765, after the cession of Illinois Country to Great Britain, a British garrison was established there, and traders replaced in part the former inhabitants, who moved across the Mississippi. On July 4, 1778, British rule ended with George Rogers Clark's capture of the town. For a decade American rule was ineffective, and Kaskaskia was sunk in anarchy. Its population declined to 349 whites in 1787.

By 1800 Kaskaskia had recovered somewhat, and had become perhaps half American. The creation of Illinois Territory in 1809, and its designation as the territorial capital, resulted in further revival. In 1818, it became the first state capital. When the state offices were removed to Vandalia in 1820, rapid decline set in. A disastrous flood in 1844 almost destroyed it and led to the removal of the county seat. In 1881 the Mississippi broke through the tongue of land on which Kaskaskia stood and began to flow through the channel of the Kaskaskia River. Gradually it encroached upon the town site. By 1910 it had obliterated the ancient settlement.

KASSERINE PASS, BATTLE OF (Jan. 30–Feb. 25, 1943). In a series of engagements in Tunisia during World War II that reached a climax near the Algerian border at the Kasserine Pass, combined Italian and German forces in February 1943 drove American and French troops back about fifty miles from the Eastern to the Western Dorsale mountains. The Americans were inexperienced and overconfident, and the French lacked modern, mechanized weapons and equipment. There were too few men for the large area they defended, and the forces were thinly dispersed. On Feb. 14, American forces were marooned on Lessouda and Ksaira hills. Allied troops abandoned Gafsa, Fériana, and Thélepte after destroying equipment and supplies, including facilities at two airfields, and the Americans were forced out of Sbeïtla. German Gen. Erwin Rommel continued the offensive on Feb. 19. He sent two columns through the Kasserine Pass, one probing toward Tebéssa, the main effort toward Thala. After fierce fighting, all were stopped by heroic defensive work. On Feb. 22, Rommel sent his units back to Mareth to prepare for Montgomery's inevitable attack. Unaware of Rommel's withdrawal, the Allies retook the Kasserine Pass on Feb. 25 and found the Italians and Germans gone.

KASSON TREATIES. Named after John Adams Kasson, charged with their negotiation. Treaties of reciprocity authorized under the Dingley Act of 1897, they provided for reciprocal tariff concessions with other nations: Denmark, the Dominican Republic, Nicaragua, Ecuador, Argentina, France, and Great Britain. None of the treaties was ratified by the Senate.

KAYODEROSSERAS PATENT. Through sixty years colonial New York's relations with the Mohawk were affected adversely by the Kayoderosseras, or Queensborough, patent. This tract of about 300,000 acres formed a rough parallelogram along the Mohawk River. The patent was applied for in 1703, and granted later to thirteen persons. Title was disputed by tribal leaders alleging fraud. In 1768, Gov. Sir Henry Moore and Indian Superintendent Sir William Johnson effected a settlement under which the patentees released part of the land and the Mohawk received $5,000 in compensation for the balance.

KEARNEYITES. Followers of Denis Kearney, a California labor agitator, who, in 1877, organized the Workingmen's party of California as a protest against unemployment, dishonest banking, inequitable taxation, land monopoly, railroad domination, Chinese coolie labor competition, and other economic and political evils. Fifty-one were elected delegates to the California constitutional convention of 1879, but appear to have had little direct influence. The new constitution seemed to meet, at least partially, the demands of the Kearneyites; and Kearney advocated its ratification. By 1880 the party had practically disappeared.

KEARNY, FORT. To protect the frontier, Congress passed a law in 1836 providing for a military road from the Mississippi near its junction with the Des Moines River, to the Red River. Col. Stephen W. Kearny and Nathan Boone selected a site (present Nebraska City) for a fort on the Missouri River. Fort Kearny was established in 1846, but was abandoned two years later in favor of a new Fort Kearny on the Platte. This location on the Oregon Trail was selected to furnish protection for emigrants en route and to keep the Indians at peace. The fort remained in use until 1871.

KEARNY, FORT PHIL. Principal military post on the Bozeman Trail; built by Col. H. B. Carrington in the Bighorn foothills on Piney Fork, in northern Wyoming. Construction, starting in July 1866, was opposed by the Sioux, who harassed it constantly. The Fetterman disaster of Dec. 21 reduced the garrison to perilous weakness, but Portugee Phillips, a frontiersman, rode 236 miles to Fort Laramie and secured help. The Wagon Box Fight, Aug. 2, 1867, ended in sharp defeat for the Sioux, but at no time were there enough troops for anything but defense. The fort was burned by Indians after its abandonment under the Treaty of Fort Laramie in 1868.

KEARNY-FRÉMONT QUARREL (1847). The quarrel between Gen. Stephen Watts Kearny and Col. John C. Frémont started in January with the appointment of Frémont as governor of California, and the removal of Kearny from the command of all forces in California except a small force of dragoons, by Commodore Robert F. Stockton, following Navy Department orders. New instructions arrived in March, ordering Kearny to set up a government, but Frémont continued to act as governor in Los Angeles. Frémont's actions led to his trial by court-martial. The trial in Washington, D.C., lasted from Nov. 2, 1847, until Jan. 31, 1848. The verdict was guilty with a recommendation for clemency. President James I. Polk pardoned Frémont and restored his position in the army, but he refused to accept either the verdict or the restoration of rank and resigned from the army.

KEARNY'S MARCH TO CALIFORNIA (1846). Gen. Stephen Watts Kearny left Santa Fe on Sept. 25, to conquer and possess California. Near Socorro, N.Mex., on Oct. 6, the column met Kit Carson on the way to Washington, D.C., with dispatches from Commodore Robert F. Stockton and John C. Frémont, announcing the conquest of California. Kearny reduced his force, depending on troops routed by sea for future campaigns. He ordered Carson to accompany him as a guide, and sent the dispatches by Thomas Fitzpatrick. The party soon found itself faced with lack of provisions and water, and had to abandon the wagons. From some Mexicans they learned that the Mexicans in California had succeeded in expelling the Americans from Santa Barbara, Los Angeles, and other places. On Dec. 6 Kearny attacked the enemy at San Pasqual. Kearny and his staff, plus about forty dragoons, led the pursuit and became separated from the others. More than 150 Mexicans turned on them and did much damage with their lances. In fifteen minutes of hand-to-hand fighting, the Americans drove them off. With 100 dragoons Kearny, twice wounded, fought his way through some 900 miles of grueling campaign, to reach San Diego, Calif., on Dec. 12.

KEARNY'S MISSION TO CHINA (1842). Dispatched to the Far East to protect American trading interests in China, Commodore Lawrence Kearny arrived in Canton at the close of the Anglo-Chinese War (Opium War). After issuing a statement that the United States would not under any circumstances sanction trade in opium, Kearny sent a note to the Chinese high commissioner, expressing the hope that the trade and citizens of the United States would be "placed upon the same footing as the merchants of the nation most favored." The reply gave assurances this would be done, and was subsequently incorporated in Cushing's Treaty, the first U.S. treaty with China. This exchange of notes constituted the genesis of the later Open Door doctrine.

***KEARSARGE* AND *ALABAMA* ENCOUNTER** (June 19, 1864). The Confederate ship *Alabama,* commanded by Capt. Raphael Semmes, arrived at Cherbourg, France, on June 11, 1864, for repairs and to land prisoners of war. Three days later, the U.S.S. *Kearsarge,* commanded by Capt. John A. Winslow, entered port to secure the released captives. Winslow's intention was denied by the French authorities, and he withdrew beyond the neutrality limits. Meanwhile, Semmes sent him word that he intended to come out and offer combat as soon as he could take on coal. The engagement was fought five days later. The *Alabama,* choosing to circle, fired the opening gun. The *Kearsarge,* fresh from overhauling, enjoyed every advantage of condition over the sea-weary *Alabama.* The *Alabama* was badly hit on its seventh rotation and turned toward Cherbourg, thereby presenting its port broadside. Winslow ordered a raking fire, and the sinking *Alabama* surrendered.

KEELBOAT. A craft used on American rivers, chiefly in the West. The earliest keelboat seems to have been a skiff with a plank nailed the length of the bottom to make the boat easier to steer, but by about 1790 the keelboat had become a long narrow craft built on a keel and ribs, with a long cargo box amidships. It was steered by a special oar and propelled by oars or poles, pulled by a cordelle, or fitted with sails.

KEFAUVER INVESTIGATIONS (Senate Special Committee to Investigate Organized Crime in Interstate Commerce). Senate investigations into organized crime originated with a bill sponsored by Democratic Sen. Estes Kefauver of Tennessee. In 1950, the Senate established a five-member crime committee with Kefauver as chairman. Kefauver's intensive investigations into crime in the nation's major cities, and the adept use of television coverage, made the public aware of the extensive nature of organized crime, spurred prosecutions, and made Kefauver a national figure.

KEGS, BATTLE OF THE (Jan. 7, 1778). Derisive name given to indiscriminate British firing, at Philadelphia, Pa., on David Bushnell's crudely built mines, designed to float down the Delaware River to explode upon contact with the British warships. No ships were harmed, but one gun-powder-filled keg exploded, killing four British sailors. The alarmed British garrison fired furiously on every floating object. The panic did not subside until nightfall.

KEITH CONTROVERSY. Religious in origin, it had political repercussions in Pennsylvania. In 1691 George Keith, a Quaker leader formerly prominent in England, violently criticized the Pennsylvania Friends' Meetings on doctrinal grounds and failure to strictly observe established discipline. Thomas Lloyd, a Quaker minister and William Penn's deputy governor, led the opposition to Keith. In 1692 Keith and his followers formed the "Christian Quakers." Keith was forbidden to preach by the regular meeting and also ran afoul of civil authority because of a seditious pamphlet he wrote attacking a Quaker magistrate. Keith went to England in 1693 to plead the orthodoxy of his group. The London Yearly Meeting, however, disowned him in 1695.

KELLOGG-BRIAND PACT (Pact of Paris). An agreement signed in Paris by fifteen nations on Aug. 27, 1928. Eventually nearly all other governments adhered to the treaty. Negotiations had begun between the United States, represented by Secretary of State Frank B. Kellogg, and France, represented by the foreign minister Aristide Briand. Article I provides that the parties renounce war as an instrument of national policy in their relations with one another. Article II provides that the settlement of disputes between the parties shall never be sought except by pacific means. The treaty did not prevent wars of self-defense, was not inconsistent with the Covenant of the League of Nations, and did not interfere with the rendering of aid under the Locarno treaties and the so-called treaties of neutrality.

KELLY'S FORD (Nov. 7, 1863). The Union army under Gen. George G. Meade, moving forward in the Mine Run Campaign, successfully attacked the Confederate works on the Rappahannock River at Kelly's Ford, Va., and at the crossing of the Orange and Alexandria Railroad, a short distance above the ford.

KELLY'S INDUSTRIAL ARMY. One of a number of "industrial armies" born of the panic of 1893. It was organized in California by Charles T. Kelly. Consisting of 1,500 men, most unemployed, it left California aboard railroad boxcars in 1894 to join Coxey's "army," in Washington, D.C. Coxey's army of 500 men had marched from Ohio to bring attention to the unemployed and press for relief legislation. At Council Bluffs, Iowa, the railroad ejected "General" Kelly's army, and they started on foot for Washington. A remnant reached the capital.

KEMPER RAID (1804). Many in West Florida, led by the Kemper brothers—Reuben, Nathan, and Samuel—expected the United States to take possession of that region under the Louisiana Purchase treaty of 1803. When this did not happen, the Kempers headed a party of about 100 in an abortive attempt to seize control of the region for the United States.

KENDALL* V. *UNITED STATES, 12 Peters 534 (1838). Held that administrative officers must conform to the law when entrusted by Congress with purely ministerial duties having no executive or discretionary character. Postmaster General Amos Kendall had maintained that he was responsible only to the president in performing such duties with respect to certain postal claims, but the Court overruled his argument because its acceptance would clothe the president with dispensing powers not contemplated by the Constitution.

KENESAW MOUNTAIN, BATTLE OF (June 27, 1864). As Union Gen. William Tecumseh Sherman advanced from Chattanooga, Tenn., toward Atlanta, he usually was able by flanking movements to avoid serious fighting. As he neared Atlanta, Sherman came upon the Confederate army occupying the crest of Kenesaw Mountain. He decided on a frontal attack. After a furious cannonade, the Union troops moved forward, but were everywhere repulsed with heavy losses. Several days later Sherman resumed his flanking movements. The unnecessary assault on Kenesaw Mountain was one of Sherman's few serious errors in the campaign.

KENNEBEC RIVER SETTLEMENTS. The English idea of colonizing what was later called the Province of Maine dates from David Ingram's tales of jewels and furs. Queen Elizabeth sent Sir Walter Raleigh, John Davys, and Adrian Gilbert westward. The Virginia Company was formed. Bartholomew Gosnold (1602), Martin Pring (1603), and George Weymouth (1605) visited the Maine coast and reported rich resources there. In 1607 the Popham plantation was established at the mouth of the Kennebec. But in 1608 it was abandoned. Fishermen were undoubtedly the first permanent settlers on the Kennebec. In 1625 the first deed drawn up in Maine was given to John Brown of New Harbor by Abnaki sagamores. Abraham Shurt settled on Monhegan in 1626. The Pilgrims established a trading post at Cushenoc, far up the Kennebec. There were eighty-four families near the Kennebec's mouth in 1630. There was a stout fort at Pemaquid. The Lygonia and Plough patents to Kennebec lands are dated 1630 and 1631. A settlement sprang up on Sheepscot Bay. John Parker acquired the lower west bank of the Kennebec in 1648; he bought Georgetown Island from Robinhood, a Kennebec chief. Robert Gutch bought, and settled in 1661 on, the site of what is now Bath. These settlements flourished until the Indian wars, when most of them except Monhegan were destroyed and had to be rebuilt.

KENNEBEC TRADING POST. Trading was the first link that bound Maine to the Massachusetts Bay Colony. From 1622 on, the Pilgrims of Plymouth traded in the Kennebec River region. William Bradford obtained an exclusive patent to river land at Cushenoc, now Augusta, head of tide, and built the Kennebec Trading Post. Pilgrim control of the river lasted until 1661.

KENNEDY, JOHN F., ASSASSINATION (Nov. 22, 1963). At 12:30 P.M. (central standard time), President John F. Kennedy was assassinated while riding in a motorcade in Dallas, Tex. Also in the motorcade were Texas Gov. John B. Connally, Vice-President Lyndon B. Johnson, and Mrs. Kennedy. Three shots were fired from the sixth floor of the Texas Public School Book Depository. The president was shot twice, in the lower neck and, fatally, in the head. Gov. Connally, was also hit and seriously wounded. Kennedy was killed instantly. Within an hour Lee Harvey Oswald, a twenty-four-year-old Dallas resident, was arrested as a suspect in the murder of a Dallas policeman; before midnight Oswald was charged with Kennedy's murder. Within forty-eight hours of his capture he was fatally shot by Jack Ruby of Dallas. A presidential commission under Chief Justice Earl Warren concluded that Oswald was the sole assassin.

KENNEDY, ROBERT F., ASSASSINATION (June 5, 1968). At 12:16 A.M. (Pacific standard time) in the Ambassador Hotel in Los Angeles, Sen. Robert F. Kennedy was shot three times. He was fatally wounded by one bullet, and pronounced dead on June 6. The senator's assailant was a twenty-four-year-old emigrant from Jerusalem and an Arab nationalist, Sirhan B. Sirhan. He was caught with the murder weapon in his hand and was convicted and sentenced to death. The sentence was commuted to life imprisonment in 1972, and he remained in prison in California.

KENSINGTON STONE. Found by a Swedish immigrant, Olof Ohman, on his farm in Kensington, Minn., in 1898. The stone bears a long inscription in runic characters telling of the difficulties of eight Goths and twenty-two Norwegians on a journey of exploration "from Vinland to the west." These events supposedly took place in the year 1362, but 19th-century scholarly opinion dated the inscription to the 19th century. The subject of the stone's authenticity was reopened in 1907 by H. R. Holand, but his elaborate historical conjectures foundered on a lack of evidence. Since 1967 O. G. Landsverk and A. Mongé have sought to prove the inscription's authenticity by a demonstration of its cryptographic nature. The claim has found little favor with orthodox expert opinion. The Kensington Stone is now the central feature of the Rune Stone Museum in Alexandria, Minn.

KENT ISLAND COLONY. *See* **Claiborne Settlement.**

KENT STATE PROTEST (1970). In April, Kent State University (21,000 students) in Kent, Ohio (28,000 population), was markedly less radical than comparable institutions across the United States. Opinions differ sharply about what triggered trouble on Friday, May 1. Activists were outraged by President Nixon's invasion of Cambodia. That night students and many hangers-on gathered at bars on North Water Street, far from the campus, and created a minor disturbance. Police responded late and inexpertly. A real riot developed, in which damage estimated at either $10,000 or $100,000 was done. A curfew was imposed. On Saturday night students burned down the Reserve Officers' Training Corps (ROTC) building. Students refused to allow firemen to fight the blaze. More than 400 Ohio National Guardsmen came to restore order. On Sunday most observers judged the crisis to be over.

On Monday, May 4, about 2,000 students gathered casually, but Gen. Robert Canterbury, commanding the Guardsmen, believed that an order of his had outlawed such assembly. The riot act was read, but the students ignored it. Canterbury thereupon gave the order for his troops to clear the campus. Guardsmen wearing gas masks, carrying M-79 tear-gas launchers, and armed with M-1 high-powered rifles set forth. With bad luck they marched into a cul-de-sac at the football field. They fell into confusion while students threw rocks at them, lobbed back their own gas cannisters, and subjected them to strident and obscene verbal abuse. The Guardsmen had no option but to retreat. Students interpreted the retreat as victory, and pursued the soldiers. Canterbury claimed that rampaging students "threatened the lives of my men," but numerous photographs taken at the time fail to confirm this. At 12:24, with an escape route open before them, the Guardsmen wheeled, turned back to where they had been humiliated, and fired for thirteen seconds, discharging fifty-five M-1 bullets, five pistol shots, and one shotgun blast. The student nearest the Guardsmen was twenty yards distant. Thirteen students were struck by bullets. Four were killed. Of the thirteen students hit, the majority had been passing to their next class.

A state grand jury was convoked. It quickly exonerated the Guardsmen, then brought in thirty-one indictments covering forty-three different offenses allegedly committed by twenty-five young people. The jury then added a long, intemperate obiter dictum, castigating the university and its professors. A federal court of review ordered the obiter dictum deleted. Belatedly, the trials started, but after one man was found guilty of obstructing firemen, public opinion forced the state to drop all charges. In 1974 a federal judge in Cleveland dismissed a criminal trial of seven selected Guardsmen accused of firing on the students. A major consequence of the tragedy was the closing down, in sympathy, of some 700 colleges and universities.

KENTUCKY. Fifteenth state of the Union; formed from the trans-Appalachian territory of Virginia. Geographically the state encompasses three distinct topographical areas. The eastern-northeastern third is a mountainous region, originally heavily forested, veined with innumerable streams. The inner dome, or Bluegrass plateau, lies near the center of the state. To the southwest lies the southwestern Mississippian embayment and the Jackson Purchase area.

Kentucky is truly a border state. It was the first state organized on the Ohio River frontier and forms a political and economic link between the North and the South, with characteristics of both regions. The discovery and earliest exploration of the territory are obscure. The actual dawning of Kentucky history followed the French and Indian War. In the period of serious exploration (1768–74), John Finley, Daniel Boone, Simon Kenton, James Harrod, and the McAfee brothers became indelibly associated with pioneering and settlement. Harrodsburg and Boonesborough were two of the first settlements.

Kentucky's beginnings coincided with the American Revolution. The area was caught in constant Indian raiding from both above and below the Ohio, much of this stimulated by the British. George Rogers Clark organized his Northwest campaign at Harrodsburg and the Falls of the Ohio. Boone, Benjamin Logan, John Bowman, and others defended the home front against ever-threatening raids.

The availability of abundant virgin land attracted more than 70,000 settlers overland by 1790. Conflict and confusion over land claims was almost as dramatic as that of Indian fighting. Kentucky was to become a rural state primarily dependent on agriculture and livestock production. The decade 1782–92 saw the pioneers engaged in a political struggle to establish local county governments, to separate the region west of the mountains from the political control of Virginia, and to establish an independent commonwealth (*see* Kentucky Conventions). Kentucky entered the Union on June 1, 1792.

Kentucky citizens were predominantly Jeffersonian in outlook, as demonstrated in the adoption of the Kentucky Resolution in 1798 and later in support of the Louisiana Purchase. From the outset, politics in Kentucky has had a strong personal flavor and been a popular preoccupation.

The western phases of the War of 1812 were heavily supported by the Kentucky political contingent in both the statehouse and Congress and by the volunteer militia in the field. The war produced a generous new crop of military-hero politicians. It also had an enormous bearing on social and economic development. The runaway inflation after 1815 saw the state banking system overexpanded and then bankrupted in the depression of 1819.

Between 1820 and 1860, Kentucky generally prospered. Its agriculture reached a high degree of development, and farmers became affluent, especially in the Bluegrass. Yet these were decades of frustration and failure for universities and colleges. Slavery with all its attendant social and economic problems created social and political friction and division. Never did Kentucky reflect its border location more markedly than in the troubled history of slavery.

The Civil War placed a severe strain on Kentucky; technically the state was neutral, but actually it was sharply divided internally. Approximately 35,000 volunteers fought with the Confederacy, and more than twice that number with the

Union. An appreciable number of officers of general rank fought on both sides, and both Abraham Lincoln and Jefferson Davis were born in Kentucky.

In the post–Civil War era Kentucky made sectional political adjustments, exploited its rich timber and mineral resources, and reestablished trade and industry. This period was marred by constant political infighting in which both major parties sought to grasp control. Bloody violence, especially among the Appalachian highlands, marred state history. Great family and community blood feuds were fought over a period of years.

In 1900 governor-elect William Goebel was murdered. This almost led to civil war in Kentucky and cast a shadow across state politics and social relations. There followed the Black Patch War (1906–08), in which tobacco farmers in the western part of the state revolted against the discriminatory practices of the purchasing companies. These marketing conditions also effected the farmers of central Kentucky, who by 1920 organized a cooperative marketing system in which tobacco was sold on an open auction floor.

From 1908 on, Kentucky was engaged in a major crusade to improve its educational system, accompanied by increases in public financial support of schools. Hand-in-glove with the educational reforms was the drive after 1918 to organize a modern highway authority and to build roads. By 1975, Kentucky had an extensive system of intrastate roads and perhaps the most extensive system of toll roads in the nation.

Since 1920 Kentucky has shifted from its agrarian economic base to a more highly industrialized one. World War I gave great impetus to the development of coal mining. Both western and eastern coalfields have been highly productive since the 1920's. Since 1940 an active issue in the state has been the controversy over strip mining.

Out on the Ohio River frontier, Kentucky has become highly industrialized. Among the significant industries are nuclear-produced electricity, hydroelectricity, whiskey, tobacco, textiles, small tools, electric typewriters, glass, electronics, automobiles and trucks, paper, packing, and chemicals. Although agriculture is still of major importance, Kentucky has become both urban and industrialized. The state's population in 1980 was 3,661,433.

KENTUCKY, INVASION OF (1862). In July Confederate Gen. Braxton Bragg moved his army from northern Mississippi to the vicinity of Chattanooga, Tenn., preparatory to a movement through middle Tennessee into Kentucky. Bragg's army left Chattanooga late in August, arriving at Bowling Green, Ky., in mid-September. Gen. Don Carlos Buell, commanding the Union defense, hastily gathered troops to oppose Bragg. On Sept. 14 Bragg wasted five valuable days to attack Munfordville. Buell made good use of this time. When Bragg resumed his march, he went to Bardstown. Buell concentrated his forces at Louisville. While Buell prepared to march southward, Bragg waited for an army under Edmund Kirby-Smith coming from eastern Kentucky. Confused by Buell's energy, Bragg moved eastward toward Kirby-Smith. On Oct. 8 Bragg unexpectedly encountered Buell's army near Perryville. A bloody battle followed. Bragg achieved a tactical success, but after dark withdrew to join Kirby-Smith. Two days later it was decided to leave Kentucky rather than chance defeat in enemy territory.

KENTUCKY AND VIRGINIA RESOLUTIONS. *See* **Virginia and Kentucky Resolutions.**

KENTUCKY CONVENTIONS. In 1784 the Kentucky frontier, then part of Virginia, was subject to frequent Indian attacks. A convention was called to meet in Danville to petition Virginia for assistance. Between 1784 and 1790 nine conventions were held. A tenth convention met in April 1792 to frame the constitution. Specific gains were made in broadening Virginia's laws for frontier defense and in passing four enabling acts: they provided specific rules for registry of land, established definite terms of separation, and secured Kentucky representation in the Congress of the Confederation. Navigation and trade rights down the Mississippi River were partially guaranteed, the Spanish conspiracy was defeated, and a fairly democratic constitution was drafted.

KENTUCKY COUNTY. Created by the Virginia assembly on Dec. 31, 1776, on petition of the Harrodsburg settlers, presented by George Rogers Clark and John Gabriel Jones. The new county included all of Fincastle County south of the Ohio River and west of the Big Sandy River and Cumberland Mountains. It was divided into three counties in 1780.

KENTUCKY'S NEUTRALITY DOCTRINE. When the secession of the southern states began in 1860, Kentucky was the only state to attempt to apply the doctrine of neutrality. On May 16, 1861, the Kentucky house of representatives resolved that the state would "take no part in the civil war now being waged, except as mediators and friends to the belligerent parties; and that Kentucky should, during the contest, occupy the position of strict neutrality." Four days later Gov. Beriah Magoffin issued a strict neutrality proclamation, warning all armed forces against entering Kentucky. On May 20, the Kentucky senate ratified neutrality.

In 1861, feeling that the cotton South had precipitated the crisis without consulting the border states, and believing that by remaining neutral it could stay the forces of war, Kentucky attempted to apply its system of neutrality until early September, when warring forces swamped it from all sides.

***KENTUCKY* V. *DENNISON*, 24 Howard 66 (1861).** The state of Kentucky petitioned for mandamus in the U.S. Supreme Court to compel the governor of Ohio to "honor a requisition of the Governor of Kentucky for the surrender of a violator of a state law relative to slaves." The Court held the duty of the Ohio governor mandatory but denied the federal government power to coerce him to perform the act. Otherwise the federal government could destroy the states.

KERMIS (kermess). An annual fair brought by the Dutch settlers to New Netherland in the 17th century. The first regular kermis in New Amsterdam began in October 1659 and lasted six weeks.

KERNSTOWN, BATTLE AT (Mar. 23, 1862). Obeying instructions to detain Union forces in the Shenandoah Valley, Gen. Thomas J. ("Stonewall") Jackson engaged Gen. James Shields's division at Kernstown, Va. Union Gen. Nathan Kimball, commanding after Shields was wounded, repulsed Jackson, who retreated up the valley.

KEROSINE OIL. In Prince Edward Island, Canada, 1846, Abram Gessner distilled kerosine (from the Greek *keros,* wax, and *elaion,* oil) from local coal. He shortly came to the United States and took out patents that he sold to the North American Kerosene Gas Light Company of New York, which began commercial manufacture in 1854. By 1859 the country had between fifty and sixty companies making kerosine from coal, shale, and other carbons. The business was crowding such older illuminants as whale oil and camphine out of the markets.

Although Kier had begun distilling kerosine or "carbon oil" from petroleum in 1850, the effective pioneer was Col. A. C. Ferris of New York. Obtaining most of the output of the Tarentum, Pa., wells, he began shipping it to New York, where various manufacturers distilled it. In 1858 the crude-petroleum business of the United States amounted to 1,183 barrels. Then in 1859 E. L. Drake made his momentous oil strike in western Pennsylvania. Works for making kerosine from coal died or were converted into oil refineries. By 1860 more than 200 patents had been granted on kerosine lamps. Within a few years kerosine became the world's principal illuminant. About 1880 a kerosine stove was perfected by the Standard Oil Company.

During the 20th century, additional uses were found for kerosine—as an ingredient in jet engine fuel, for domestic heating, and as a cleaning solvent and insecticide. In 1980 approximately 50 million barrels (42 gallons each) of kerosine were produced in the United States.

KETCH. A small yawllike vessel with two masts—main and mizzen—used originally as a yacht but later used in navies as a bomb vessel because of the space forward of the mainmast.

KETTLE CREEK, BATTLE OF (Feb. 14, 1779). After Savannah had fallen to the British, British troops quickly overran Georgia until they were rebuffed on Kettle Creek. Patriots surprised and scattered about 700 Loyalists. Nine Americans and seventy British were killed. The British retired from Augusta, and loyalism in Georgia and South Carolina was severely checked.

KEY WEST (Fla.). Southernmost city of the continental United States (Florida). Grant of the island was made to Juan Pablo Salas on Aug. 26, 1815, by the Spanish governor of Florida. Salas sold his grant to John W. Simonton on Jan. 19, 1822, who soon disposed of three-fourths of his rights to four other persons. The first settlers, chiefly from South Carolina and St. Augustine, came in 1822. The city became a major ship salvaging center. Key West has always been a key military point for the United States. The city has also developed into a popular resort. The 1980 population was 24,292.

KIDDER MASSACRE. On June 29, 1867, Lt. L. S. Kidder, with eleven men, left Fort Sedgwick, Colo., with dispatches for Gen. George A. Custer. Custer had moved, and in following his trail Kidder, in July, encountered 500 Cheyenne under Roman Nose. Surrounded in a gully on Beaver Creek, Kidder and all his men were killed.

KIDNAPPING OF FREE BLACKS. The kidnapping of northern free blacks to be sold into slavery in the South was a common business, notwithstanding laws to the contrary in southern states. Kidnappers were not easily punished because blacks were disqualified as witnesses. In 1793 and 1850, Congress passed fugitive slave laws that empowered federal officers to seize runaway slaves in free-soil states and return them to their masters. These laws, and the lust of federal magistrates for fees, made it easy to seize free blacks and hasten them into slavery under pretext of law. Free-soil states passed statutes that afforded some protection to free blacks.

***KILBOURN* V. *THOMPSON*,** 103 U.S. 168 (1880). A Supreme Court case in which it was declared that Congress had no "general power of making inquiry into the private affairs of the citizens," and that since the inquiry being conducted was judicial rather than legislative, the House could not hold Hallett Kilbourn in contempt for refusing to answer questions. Kilbourn could sue the House's sergeant at arms, John G. Thompson, who arrested him, but not representatives advocating his arrest.

KILLDEER MOUNTAIN, BATTLE OF (July 28, 1864). On July 23, 1864, information reached Gen. Alfred Sully's northwestern Indian expedition of a heavy concentration of Indians on Knife River. Coraling his heavy wagons and emigrant train, with 2,200 mounted men and light wagons carrying provisions and supplies, Sully found some 5,000 Sioux forces posted on Killdeer Mountain (N.Dak.). Through skillful use of cavalry charges, while artillery shelled the ravines, the mountain was occupied by dark, together with the abandoned Indian camp. Sully's casualties were 15 killed and wounded; Indian losses were estimated at 100.

KING, MARTIN LUTHER, ASSASSINATION (Apr. 4, 1968). The Rev. Dr. Martin Luther King, Jr., a clergyman and leader of the nonviolent movement for civil rights in the United States, had gone to Memphis Tenn. to prepare the community for a march in support of the striking Sanitation Worker's Union. Preparing to leave the Lorraine Motel, King went out on the second-floor balcony and was hit by a bullet fired from a rooming house across from the motel. He died one hour later (7:05 P.M.) at St. Joseph's Hospital.

President Lyndon B. Johnson proclaimed Apr. 7 a national day of mourning. The U.S. flag was flown at half-staff at all federal facilities until King's interment. Many public schools, libraries, and businesses were closed as memorial services and marches were held. King's body was flown to Atlanta, Ga.

The assassination was followed by rioting, looting, and arson in black districts of more than a hundred cities. Thousands were injured and forty-six people were killed. In the nation's capital racial violence devastated several blocks and brought about the death of ten.

The search for the assassin ended on June 8 when James Earl Ray was arrested at Heathrow Airport, London. Ray pleaded guilty on Mar. 10, 1969, to the charge of murder and was sentenced to ninety-nine years in prison. A report by a House of Representatives committee in July 1979 stated that King's assassination was "probably" the result of a conspiracy of right-wing St. Louis businessmen. Ray remained in prison, despite several appeals for a new trial and his claim that he had been urged to plead guilty by his lawyers.

"KING COTTON." An expression much used before the Civil War drawn from the book, *Cotton Is King,* by David Christy in 1855. In the U.S. Senate, Mar. 4, 1858, James H. Hammond declared, "You dare not make war upon cotton! No power on earth dares make war upon it. Cotton is king." The phrase expressed the southern belief that cotton was so essential that those who controlled it might dictate economic and political policies.

KING GEORGE, FORT. A cypress plank blockhouse built on the lower Altamaha River in Georgia in 1721, by Col. John Barnwell of South Carolina. The fort initiated a system of American defenses endorsed by the English Board of Trade to offset French expansion. Until it was burned in 1725, it challenged Spanish claims to a region that James E. Oglethorpe later dominated from Frederica, Ga.

KING GEORGE'S WAR (1744–48). France and England developed irreconcilable conflicts over boundaries in Canada and northern New England and possession of the Ohio Valley. When England's commercial war with Spain merged into the War of the Austrian Succession (1740–48), England and France declared war (Mar. 15, 1744). The French at Louisburg (Cape Breton Island) surprised and captured Canso on May 13 but failed to take Annapolis (Port Royal). In retaliation New Englanders captured Louisburg (June 15, 1745) and planned, with English aid, to attack Quebec and Montreal simultaneously. English help did not arrive and the colonials disbanded the next year. Meanwhile, France had sent a great fleet to recapture Louisburg and devastate English colonial seaports, but storms, disease, and the death of the fleet's commander frustrated the attempt. A second fleet was defeated on the open sea by combined British squadrons. Gruesome raids along the New England–New York borders by both parties and their Indian allies characterized the remainder of the war. The warring parties signed the Peace of Aix-la-Chapelle in October 1748, granting mutual restoration of conquests (Louisburg for Madras, India), but leaving colonial questions unsolved.

KING PHILIP'S WAR (1675–76). When Massasoit died (1662), new Indian leaders rejected friendship with the English, and were suspected of conspiring against New Englanders. Chief conspirator was Massasoit's second son, Metacom, or Philip, sachem of the Wampanoag. Despite peace covenants between Philip and the colonists, war eventually broke out. Swift, devastating raids on Swansea and neighboring towns threw the colonists into panic, intensified when the militia found no Indians to fight—for the Indians never made a stand. The war was a series of Indian raids with retaliatory expeditions by the English. The English counterattack was ill planned and indecisive and antagonized other tribes. The soldiers were poorly equipped and ignorant of Indian warfare.

Before the end of 1675, disaster overtook New England on all sides. Mendon, Brookfield, Deerfield, Northfield, and other towns were devastated, abandoned, or both. Similar raids devastated New Hampshire and Maine settlements. The English in turn destroyed the Narragansett in the Great Swamp Fight.

In 1676 the war turned temporarily against the English. The Indians fell on Lancaster and threatened Plymouth, Providence, and towns near Boston. Meanwhile, the colonies reorganized their forces, destroyed Narragansett food supplies, and captured and executed Canonchet. The Mohawk threatened to attack the valley Indians from the west, thereby helping the English; and Capt. William Turner with 180 men surprised and massacred the Indians at Deerfield. By the end of May the tide had turned in the west. Capt. Benjamin Church, assisted by able scouts, captured Philip's wife and son on Aug. 1, surrounded his camp, and shot and killed Philip as he tried to escape on Aug. 12. On Apr. 12, 1678, articles of peace were signed at Casco, Maine, with mutual restoration of captives and property.

KING'S COLLEGE. *See* **Columbia University.**

KING'S MESSENGER. A royal official during colonial times for the arresting of prisoners of state. When the Regicides—Edward Whalley, William Goffe, and John Dixwell—fled to New England on the accession of Charles II, two king's messengers were sent to arrest them.

KING'S MOUNTAIN, BATTLE OF (Oct. 7, 1780). In 1780 Maj. Patrick Ferguson, in command of about 1,000 soldiers from the British army of Gen. Charles Cornwallis, made a foray into western North Carolina. The "mountain men" of the backcountry had been stirred up by the ill conduct of the British troops in the South; and from the western Carolinas and Virginia, as well as from the present states of Kentucky and Tennessee, about 2,000 frontiersmen gathered. Hearing of this possible resistance, Ferguson beat a hasty retreat, but the American forces caught up to him at King's Mountain, now in York County, S.C. Ferguson took his position atop the mountain on Oct. 6. The next day he was entirely surrounded by the Americans. On Oct. 7 the Americans attacked up the mountain from all sides. After about an hour's fighting, Ferguson was killed. Capt. Abraham De Peyster succeeded to the command and raised the white flag. The British force was composed principally of Loyalists, and the bitterness felt by the mountain men was exceedingly deep. There were charges of atrocities on both sides. Practically all the British were either killed, wounded, or captured, and they lost over 1,000 stand of arms to the Americans.

KING'S PROVINCE. That portion of the mainland of Rhode Island between the Pawcatuck River and Narragansett Bay, known as the Narragansett Country and claimed by Rhode Island, Connecticut, and Massachusetts. A royal commission, in 1665, named this territory the King's Province and placed it under the jurisdiction of Rhode Island. Connecticut still claimed authority over it, but the matter was settled when Sir Edmund Andros took possession of both colonies. In 1729 this territory became Kings County, Rhode Island, and in 1781, Washington County.

KINGSTON (N.Y.). Formerly known as Esopus; a city on the Hudson River. It was settled in 1652 by Thomas Chambers, followed by Dutch settlers. Soon it became the scene of the Esopus War, and was later a center for trade and the third largest town in the colony. When the British took New York City, the Provincial convention moved to Kingston and adopted the first New York constitution in April 1777. Gov. George Clinton took office in July, the legislature met in August, and the courts opened in September. After the British approached in October and burned the town, the government left and never returned. An active industrial city in the 20th century, the 1980 population of Kingston was 24,481.

KING'S WOODS. In parts of colonial New England surveyors of the king's woods marked with a broad arrow all pine trees two feet or more in diameter suitable for use as masts in the Royal Navy. Even after the land had passed into private hands, trees previously so marked were reserved to the crown, thus taking from the colonists much of their best timber. Tactless enforcement of the law by the surveyors contributed to the growth of sentiment for independence.

KING WILLIAM'S WAR (1689–97). The first of the French and Indian wars. When Louis de Buade, Comte de Frontenac, arrived in Canada in 1689 to begin his second term as governor, he found the colony terror-stricken by Iroquoian raids. To revive the courage of the French and regain allegiance of Indian allies, he sent out three war parties: the first destroyed Schenectady, the second attacked and burned Salmon Falls on the New Hampshire border, and the third forced the surrender of Fort Loyal.

Massachusetts raised a fleet of seven ships, under Sir William Phips, who captured and plundered Port Royal, Nova Scotia. In May 1690, at the invitation of Leisler, representatives of Massachusetts, Plymouth, Connecticut, and New York met in New York City. A united attack by land on Montreal was planned with the promised cooperation of the Iroquois; Massachusetts and the other New England colonies undertook to attack Quebec at the same time by sea. Both expeditions were failures. The leaders of the colonies made repeated appeals to the English government for help. In 1693, a fleet was dispatched under Sir Francis Wheeler. This fleet reached Boston with fever-stricken crews, and as no preparations had been made to cooperate with it, nothing was accomplished. Frontenac also made urgent appeals for help, with no better luck. The French squadron failed to capture Boston.

The results were favorable to the French. Their Indian allies were always available for raids on the English frontier. Pemaquid, which had been rebuilt, was again captured by the French, and the New England frontier suffered cruelly. New York suffered less, but the Iroquois, frightened by French attacks, were with difficulty held to their alliance. The Treaty of Ryswick (1697) ended the fighting, but did little to settle the questions under dispute.

KINKAIDERS. Before 1904 homesteaders generally avoided the western third of Nebraska because of its aridity and poor soil. Some Nebraskans thought that if the homestead unit were enlarged settlers might be attracted. In 1904 they persuaded Congress to adopt the Kinkaid Act, which increased the unit in western Nebraska to 640 acres. A rush of settlers, called Kinkaiders, met disappointment from the outset. Unproductive soil, drought, dust storms, warfare with cattlemen and sheepmen, and insufficient capital defeated them.

KINSEY REPORT. In 1948 Alfred C. Kinsey, professor of zoology at Indiana University, and his associates published the results of their interviews with more than 5,000 American males concerning sexual behavior (*Sexual Behavior in the Human Male.*) In 1953 a comparable book on almost 6,000 females (*Sexual Behavior in the Human Female*) was published. Hundreds of articles and books discussed the research and findings. Because Kinsey's in-depth interviews were so numerous, his statements carried far more weight than earlier similar studies.

KIOWA. American Indians of the Plains. Dependence on the bison, aggressive raids for horses, war patterns, the vision quest, and Plains technology, including the use of buckskin and the tipi, were all characteristic of the Kiowa as well as their Plains neighbors. Despite small numbers, an estimated 2,000 in 1780, the Kiowa, always fiercely resistant to the inroads of settlers, moved slowly through the Plains in their search for hunting territory and horses. Tradition has it that they originated at the headwaters of the Missouri or in the northern Basin. On a gradual movement southward through the 18th century, the Kiowa moved from the Black Hills to the Arkansas River. Conflicting at first with the Arapaho and Comanche, they formed an alliance with the Comanche. They raided far into Mexico and terrorized sections of present Oklahoma and Texas during the 1860's and 1870's. The Kiowa are not to be confused with the Kiowa-Apache, a tribe in western Texas.

KIOWA, FORT. Built for the American Fur Company about 1822, near Fort Lookout, on the right bank of the Missouri River about ten miles above present Chamberlain, S. Dak. It was abandoned after the decline of the fur trade.

KITCHEN CABINET. A title derisively applied by President Andrew Jackson's political enemies to an informal group of advisers credited with exercising more influence on the president than his regular cabinet, especially from 1829 until 1831, when the cabinet was reorganized. The most important members of the Kitchen Cabinet were Amos Kendall, Francis Preston Blair, Sr., William B. Lewis, A. J. Donelson, Martin Van Buren, and John H. Eaton.

KITTANNING CAMPAIGN (August–September 1756). During the French and Indian War the Delaware village of Kittanning, on the Allegheny River, was a base for Indian raids on the Pennsylvania frontier. In retaliation, Col. John Armstrong led some 300 men against the Delaware. In a surprise attack, the militia and volunteers burned the town, destroyed ammunition and supplies, released eleven white prisoners, and killed thirty or forty Indians. The victory prevented further raids from Kittanning.

KLAMATH-MODOC. The Klamath and Modoc Indians spoke dialects of the same language and preserved a tradition of relationship, but differed somewhat in habitat and ecological adaptation. The Klamath lived in the lakes and marshes of south-central Oregon, and the Modoc at the edges of the Basin in northeastern California. In 1780 there were about 1,200 Klamath and 4,500 Modoc.

Although wild-seed gathering and hunting characterized both, the Klamath exploited the marshlands in which they lived, depending on seeds and roots of lake plants, whereas the Modoc, in a less well-watered area, gathered a variety of dry seeds, following generally the patterns of the Great Basin. Each tribe lacked any sense of extended political organization. Following the Californian configuration, small hamlets with a few communally inhabited semisubterranean winter earth lodges were the rule. Family life was centered in the hamlet. Petty and community chiefs were present, but their functions were largely those of speaker and moral leader. In neither tribe were religious ceremonials, art—except perhaps basketry—and social organizations elaborated.

Contact with the United States came after 1830. The tribes were relegated to the Klamath Reservation in Oregon in 1864. When some of the group resisted, leaving the reservation under the leadership of Kintpuash (Captain Jack), attempts were made to subdue them. The Modoc War of 1872–73, following a series of atrocities on both sides, involved evicting the tribesmen from the northern California lava beds. The contemporary tribes have been involved in litigation surrounding termination of reservation status.

KLONDIKE RUSH. On Aug. 16, 1896, gold was discovered on Bonanza Creek of the Klondike (Ton-Dac) River, a tributary of the Yukon River in Canada's Yukon Territory. News of the discovery reached the United States in January 1897, and in the spring many departed by boat up the Yukon or up the Inside Passage. On July 14, 1897, the steamer *Excelsior* arrived at San Francisco with $750,000 in gold; on July 17, the *Portland* arrived at Seattle with $800,000. The peak occurred during 1897–99, when some 100,000 persons left for Alaska. Passage was facilitated by construction of the White Pass and Yukon Railroad from Skagway to White Horse. Miners worked claims for the coarse gold and then sold them—principally to the Guggenheim Exploration Company, which introduced scientific methods of gold recovery. By 1900, $27 million in gold per year was being taken, but the richer deposits were soon exhausted.

KNIGHTS OF LABOR. A secret league founded by Uriah Stevens and other garment workers in Philadelphia in December 1869. During the early 1880's it became an open organization. In 1886 it included between 600,000 and 700,000 persons. Organized into mixed local and district assemblies, its aim was to weld the whole labor movement into a single disciplined army. All gainfully employed persons except lawyers, bankers, professional gamblers or stockbrokers, saloon keepers, and (prior to 1881) physicians were eligible.

Several factors contributed to rapid decline after 1886: unsuccessful outcome of the strike policy, internal friction, and the depletion of union finances. Of more basic importance were the centralized control and the mixed character of local and district assemblies, which inevitably invited difficulties with the job-conscious trade unions affiliated in the Federation of Organized Trades and Labor Unions (called American Federation of Labor after 1886). By 1890 their federated organization overshadowed the Knights of Labor.

KNIGHTS OF THE GOLDEN CIRCLE. A secret order first recruited in the South about 1855 by George Bickley, a Cincinnati physician, to support slavery and conquest of Mexico. During the Civil War it was introduced into Indiana as Peace Democrats, or Copperheads, to oppose President Lincoln's war policy. Although connected with minor violence, the order did not promote any serious plots against the government. It was reorganized in 1863 as the Order of American Knights and in 1864 as the Sons of Liberty, involved in the Northwest conspiracy in 1864. Soon thereafter the organization went into decline.

KNIGHTS OF THE GOLDEN HORSESHOE. Gov. Alexander Spotswood of Virginia undertook a journey in 1716 into the western wilderness. On Aug. 20 he left Williamsburg. The governor and his associates wended their way up the valley of the Rappahannock River. It was a picturesque cavalcade of gentlemen, rangers, pioneers, and Indians, followed by packhorses and servants. In two weeks they gained the summit of the Blue Ridge Mountains. Here they gazed on the beauty before them and offered one toast after another. When he returned to Virginia, Spotswood had some miniature gold horseshoes made for each gentlemen who accompanied him. Hence the participants were designated Knights of the Golden Horseshoe.

KNIGHTS OF THE WHITE CAMELIA. A secret organization that arose in New Orleans in 1867 and spread rapidly over the South with the aim of maintaining supremacy of the white race, which was threatened by Radical Reconstruction. It was much like the Ku Klux Klan in its aims and in having councils along state, county, and community lines.

KNOW-NOTHING PARTY. *See* **American Party.**

"KNOW YE" PARTY. Because of revolutionary war debts and depreciated paper currency worth only 16 cents on the dollar, Rhode Island passed a forcing act in May 1786 compelling creditors to accept payment in paper money at face value. If they refused, the money could be deposited with the court, which issued a certificate discharging the debt. These certificates were published in the newspapers and began with the words "Know Ye." The party became known as the Paper Money, or "Know Ye," party. Business conditions became so bad that the state was sometimes referred to as Rogue's Island. The act was declared unconstitutional in September 1786 in *Trevett* v. *Weeden.*

KNOX, FORT (Ind.). From 1763 to 1777, Vincennes, in present-day Indiana, though under British sovereignty, had no civil government. In May 1777, the town was officially occupied and the small stockaded Fort Sackville was built. It was occupied for George Rogers Clark in 1778, but abandoned on the approach of a British force. Captured by Clark on Feb. 23, 1779, it was renamed Fort Patrick Henry. In 1788 Maj. J. F. Hamtramck built a new fort named Fort Knox, after Secretary of War Henry Knox. The post was again abandoned in 1794.

KNOX, FORT (Ky.). In 1918 an army camp called Camp Knox was established in Kentucky, thirty-one miles southwest of Louisville. Made permanent in 1932 as Fort Knox, the post became the main repository of U.S. gold in 1937. Billions of dollars worth of gold are kept in the two-story granite, steel, and concrete vault by the Treasury Department; the door of the vault weighs more than 20 tons. The fort is also known for training armored divisions and for Godman Army Air Field.

***KNOX* V. *LEE*.** *See* **Legal Tender Cases.**

KNOXVILLE (Tenn.). Major city in eastern Tennessee, with a population of 183,139 in 1980; the center of a metropolitan area including 475,109 people. Knoxville is field headquarters of the Tennessee Valley Authority, and home of the University of Tennessee. Its industries include manufacturing businesses and one of the world's largest marble plants. It is an important railroad center and a marketing city for livestock and tobacco. In 1982 it hosted the World's Fair.

The first settlers arrived in 1787. The town, named in honor of Gen. Henry Knox, was selected as the capital of the Territory South of the River Ohio, which was admitted to the Union as the State of Tennessee in 1796. Knoxville served as state capital twice. The city was a trading center from the start. During the Civil War, it was held by Union troops and besieged by Confederates in 1863; a great part of the city was destroyed.

KNOXVILLE, SIEGE OF (November–December 1863). During the Civil War Confederate Gen. James Longstreet's command was detached toward Knoxville to capture Gen. Ambrose E. Burnside and occupy Knoxville. Longstreet was delayed and Burnside retired into Knoxville. Longstreet arrived on Nov. 17 and laid siege to the town. On Nov. 29 he unsuccessfully assaulted Fort Sanders. Longstreet's detachment was unnecessary. Nothing had been accomplished beyond depriving Gen. Braxton Bragg, at a critical period, of needed men and a skillful leader.

KODIAK (Alaska). A small city on the island of the same name, with a population of 4,756 in 1980. It is a fishing port, widely known as the home of Kodiak king crabs. The oldest city in Alaska, it was founded in 1792 by Russians under Aleksandr Baranov. It was originally a fur-gathering station but fishing became its chief activity during the 19th century when fur sealing reduced the number of animals. A U.S. Naval Station was established there in 1939.

KODIAK ISLAND (Kadiak Island). Located in the Gulf of Alaska east of Alaska Peninsula. Here, in 1784, Grigori Shelikof established the first Russian settlement in North America. The island is the habitat of the Kodiak bear and the king crab. It is also the site of a U.S. naval base.

KOMANDORSKIYE ISLANDS, BATTLE OF THE (Mar. 26, 1943). During World War II, while bringing reinforcements to the Japanese-occupied island of Attu in the western Aleutians, Vice Adm. Moshiro Hosogaya's four cruisers and four destroyers ran into an American force barely half as strong under Rear Adm. Charles H. McMorris. For more than three hours the two groups fought a long-range gun and torpedo duel south of the Komandorskiye Islands. Unable to get through to the transports Hosogaya was escorting, McMorris inflicted as much damage as he received, and finally broke off the action when his sole heavy cruiser was crippled. A bold torpedo attack by American destroyers saved the cruiser from complete destruction and helped persuade Hosogaya to retire to the west.

KOREA, WAR WITH (1871). By ancient custom, violation of Korean seclusion was a capital offense. In August 1866, W. B. Preston, an American merchant of Chefoo, China, dispatched the armed schooner *General Sherman* to Ping-yang (now Heijo) to open trade. The schooner grounded on a sandbar in the Ping-yang River. The Koreans, acting by royal command, burned the ship and murdered the entire crew.

The U.S.S. *Shenandoah,* sent from Chefoo to investigate, was denied all communication with the capital. A punitive expedition was authorized to demand an audience with the king and to secure satisfaction. The *Monocacy,* the *Palos,* and four steam launches arrived at the mouth of the Han River (then called Salée, or Seoul, River) on May 26, 1871. Local officials were advised that the squadron was friendly and sought merely to survey the coast and confer with the king. When no favorable reply was received, the ships started upriver. On June 1, masked batteries on either side of the stream suddenly opened fire. Two Americans were wounded. The Americans returned the fire. The *Monocacy* then struck a rock and withdrew.

The guardian-general of Fu-Ping prefecture formally complained of the American penetration of Korean waters, but declared himself too humble a person to dare communicate the American message to his king. The Americans sent a second expedition on June 10 to reduce the Korean forts. In the battles, on June 11, 250 enemy dead were left on the field. The American loss was 3 killed and 9 wounded. The squadron withdrew to consult with Washington. No treaty was secured until 1882.

KOREAN WAR (1950–53). The Soviet land grab of Japanese Manchuria during the last week of World War II was halted in Korea by American occupation northward to the thirty-eighth parallel, which became the divider between zones of trusteeship scheduled to end within five years with an independent, united Korea. By late 1947, the United States invoked the jurisdiction of the United Nations to arrange Korea-wide free elections. The North Koreans, refusing to participate, established in February 1948 a Soviet-satellite government, the Democratic People's Republic (DPR) of Korea. In July UN-sponsored measures resulted in the Republic of Korea (ROK), with Syngman Rhee as president.

To the majority of the UN General Assembly, Rhee's government had the legal status for ruling all Korea; the Soviet bloc claimed the same for the DPR. Through revolts, sabotage, and the inexperience of his administration Rhee found his political power waning in the May 1950 elections. The North Koreans in early June masked plans for military action by asking the UN to supervise elections for an all-Korea government. Then, on June 25, the North Korean army, trained and armed by the Russians, suddenly attacked across the parallel with 100,000 troops.

By then U.S. military commitments had been reduced to 500 advisers training the 95,000 recruits of the new ROK army. The North Koreans advanced, ignoring a UN cease-fire order. President Harry S. Truman authorized Gen. Douglas MacArthur to commit U.S. occupation forces in Japan, which were joined by UN contingents from fifteen other countries.

At the outset, except for U.S. Air Force sorties from Japan and U.S. Navy carrier strikes, the ROK army fought alone. Seoul, the capital, fell on June 28. On July 7, 700 men, constituting the first UN aid in ground action, spearheaded the understrength U.S. Twenty-fourth Infantry Division being airlifted from Japan to Pusan. U.S. Cavalry, Infantry, Marines, and a Regimental Combat Team arrived between July 18 and Aug. 3, stiffening the battered ROK formations and checking the North Korean momentum. A perimeter was established enclosing a meager 500 square miles hinged on Pusan. The Korean conflict has been called the first jet air war, and in the initial weeks American jet pilots quickly destroyed the North Korean air force, a small but effective force of Russian-built aircraft.

MacArthur exploited UN sea and air supremacy to plan a bold "end run" around the victorious North Koreans by striking amphibiously at Inchon, the port of Seoul, and the invaders' logistic base. On Sept. 15, 1950, U.S. Marines took Inchon. On Sept. 17 American forces captured Seoul. The UN forces at Pusan commanded by U.S. Gen. W. H. Walker advanced northward toward Seoul, meeting a southward drive of the marines on Sept. 26. The North Koreans became disorganized and fragmented. MacArthur was authorized by the UN to pursue across the thirty-eighth parallel and to demilitarize the aggressors. Pyongyang, the DPR capital, fell on Oct. 19. Terrain features and overconfidence began to divide the UN troops into eastern and western segments. Between these, a gap of 80 miles opened as they neared the Yalu River, the border with Red China.

Since the Korean War was dominated by the possibility of a third world war, Red China observed the letter of neutrality but freed large numbers of "volunteers" that suddenly and skillfully struck between the UN columns. In November 1950 Chinese Communist MIG-15 jet fighters appeared at the Yalu River and overwhelming Chinese armies poured into Korea. The UN forces were compelled to retreat. Pyongyang was given up on Dec. 5 and Seoul on Jan. 4, 1951.

MacArthur was forbidden to strike across the Yalu, and nuclear armament, still a U.S. monopoly, was withheld. Under these conditions, the war could not be concluded on satisfactory military terms. The MIG-15s' efforts to establish air superiority were thwarted by the U.S. Air Force F-86 Sabre fighter screens, which destroyed 792 MIGs at a cost of 78 F-86s. UN air power also provided close air support to outnumbered ground forces. MacArthur's objective became the destruction of Communist forces in Korea. This was to be achieved by Operation Killer. In two months Operation Killer restored a defensible battle line slightly north of the parallel. MacArthur's conviction that the war could not be won without decisive measures against Red China led Truman to replace him with Gen. M. B. Ridgway on Apr. 11, 1951.

Peace negotiations commenced at Kaesong in July 1951, were resumed at Panmunjom in October 1951, and dragged out to an armistice signed on July 27, 1953.

Except for a slightly rectified frontier, the *status quo ante bellum* was restored and the basic problem of Korean unity left unsolved. Both sides claimed victory. If strategic and tactical victory remained out of the grasp of the military on either side, the war was a political success for the UN.

The United States put 1.6 million servicemen into the war zones. Losses were 54,246 killed, 4,675 captured, and 103,284 wounded. The war cost the United States about $20 billion.

KOSSUTH'S VISIT (1851). Lajos Kossuth, Hungarian revolutionary leader, landed in New York City in December 1851. His visit was in response to an invitation extended by a joint congressional resolution, signed by President Fillmore. Everywhere he went he received great ovations. Although the

American government did not render official aid, Kossuth aroused nationwide support for his revolutionary causes.

KOSZTA CASE. Martin Koszta, following the Hungarian Revolution of 1848, fled to Turkey and then to the United States. After taking out first citizenship papers, he returned to Smyrna in Asiatic Turkey, where he was kidnapped by Austrians. On July 2, 1853, an American warship intervened, but his captors surrendered him to the French consul general. Upon strong representations by Secretary of State William L. Marcy, Koszta was released.

KU KLUX ACT (Apr. 20, 1871). One of the Force Acts, it was passed as the result of Republican efforts to give the president extraordinary powers to maintain Republican governments in southern states. President Grant used his power to suspend the writ of habeas corpus only once, on Oct. 17, 1871, in nine South Carolina counties. Federal troops were to be used in destroying the Ku Klux Klan and other "conspiracies" against enforcement of the Fourteenth Amendment, and cases were to be tried in federal courts. The act was declared unconstitutional in *United States* v. *Harris* (1882).

KU KLUX KLAN. 19th Century. The Ku Klux Klan was relied upon by southern whites to recoup their prestige, destroyed by the Civil War and Radical Reconstruction. Organized in May 1866 in Pulaski, Tenn., by a group of young veterans, it had a potential for intimidating freedmen that was soon discovered. At Nashville, in 1867, the Ku Klux Klan was organized into the "Invisible Empire of the South" ruled by a Grand Wizard; the Realms (states) were ruled by Grand Dragons; the Provinces (counties) were headed by Grand Titans; the individual Dens were under the authority of a Grand Cyclops. The Dens had couriers known as Night Hawks. Secret, the organization wanted to protect the white people from what they felt was humiliation by freedmen and to open the way for the reassertion of the supremacy of the whites.

The Klansmen wore white robes, masked their faces, wore high, cardboard hats, and rode robed horses with muffled feet. One of their favorite practices was to ride out of woods, surprising blacks walking home in the darkness from meetings of the Union League, an organization that sought to direct their votes into the proper Republican channels. The Klan also intimidated carpetbaggers and scalawags and played unseen influential roles in many trials in the South. It was responsible for floggings, lynchings, and other acts of violence and lawlessness. It was formally disbanded in the spring of 1869, but it did not die.

In 1871 the Ku Klux Act was passed, empowering the president to use federal troops and to suspend the writ of habeas corpus, to abolish the "conspiracy" against the federal government in the South. The gradual resumption of political power by whites saw the activities of the Klan decline.

20th Century. The reborn Klan has also been a secret, fraternal, and vigilante organization for native-born, white, Protestant Americans. In 1915, prompted by southern negrophobia and D. W. Griffith's epic movie, "The Birth of a Nation," an Alabama fraternalist, "Col." William J. Simmons, recreated the Klan at Stone Mountain, Ga. After World War I, the Klan spread nationwide. At its mid-1920's peak, it had perhaps 3 million members. The Klan was sworn to protect small-town values from foreigners, immorality, and change. The enemy was the outsider-alien, symbolized by Roman Catholicism. Although the Klan did well in inland and western cities, its violence was primarily restricted to the South and Southwest. Poor leadership, internal conflict, violence, community disruptiveness, corruption, and immorality soon destroyed its power.

The depression-era Klan discovered Communism, the Jews, and the Congress of Industrial Organizations, but its ranks were thin, and its influence outside of the Southeast was gone. The Dallas dentist Hiram W. Evans, who wrested the Klan away from Simmons in 1922, sold it to a Terre Haute, Ind., veterinarian, James A. Colescott, in 1939. Back taxes, bad publicity over German-American Bund connections, and World War II temporarily retired the Klan.

When its postwar resuscitator, Atlanta obstetrician Samuel Green, died in 1949, the Klan fragmented chaotically until a Tuscaloosa rubber worker, Robert M. Shelton, Jr., brought some order and unity in the 1960's and early 1970's. Despite occasional violence and friends in office in Alabama and Georgia, the Klan offered little resistance to integration. In the late 1970's, the Klan experienced a rebirth under such vocal leaders as Bill Wilkinson and David Duke; the membership grew from about 2,000 in 1975 to an estimated 10,000 in 1980. An increasing number of violent incidents occurred, the worst among them being the killing of five members of the Communist Workers Party at an anti-Klan rally in Greensboro, N.C., in November 1979.

KWAKIUTL. Resident on the northern coasts of Vancouver Island and sections of the adjacent mainland of western Canada, the Kwakiutl are the best known of the native tribes of the Northwest Coast culture area. Their fame arises from the detailed ethnographic studies of them by the distinguished anthropologist Franz Boas and his students.

The Kwakiutl speak a language usually classified as Wakashan. Although the Kwakiutl lacked political solidarity, they were bound together by socioeconomic networks based principally on the potlatch, a system of exchanges of property that enhanced social status and rank. The twenty-five villages of the Kwakiutl—with a population of perhaps 4,500 on Vancouver Island prior to contact with Europeans about 1775—passed property, food, manufactured objects, and surplus materials of all kinds from hand to hand within a defined system of social rank, and concepts of property and status became very elaborate.

Like others on the Northwest Coast, the Kwakiutl, dependent on the salmon and maritime village organization, stressed spirit visions and experiences. As with wealth, the Kwakiutl appear to have systematized their religious institutions more than did other tribes; they emphasized secret religious societies whose winter activities and initiations stood side by side with the potlatches in importance.

LABADISTS. Followers of the French religious reformer Jean de Labadie belonged to the Calvinist school. A colony settled in Bohemia Manor, Md., in 1683 under Augustine Herrmann and another shortly thereafter in New York.

LA BALME'S EXPEDITION (1780). French Col. Augustin Mottin de La Balme proposed a raid against the British at Detroit; enrolling in Illinois a body of French inhabitants, he crossed the Wabash, where he was joined by a party from Vincennes, captured by George Rogers Clark the previous year. They advanced to the Miami village where Fort Wayne, Ind., now stands. This village and the traders' stores were pillaged; then, not feeling strong enough to attack Detroit, La Balme began a hasty retreat. The Miami under Little Turtle pursued. La Balme was killed and his men dispersed.

LA BAYE. *See* **Green Bay.**

LA BELLE FAMILLE, BATTLE OF (July 24, 1759). In response to the massive British campaign to end the French and Indian War in 1759, 1,200 French soldiers and a large force of Indians marched to relieve Fort Niagara, N.Y. They were intercepted at La Belle Famille (Youngstown, N.Y.) by the British and Indians and utterly routed; only 200 of the French escaped capture or death.

LABOR. Unsuccessful in attempts to utilize native American Indians as a labor force, the American colonies in the 17th century looked to western Europe. Impoverished or propertyless laborers were induced to migrate through the promise of a better life. Until 1920, labor was in short supply.

Common interests of artisans resulted in some degree of organization in the 17th century, but it was not until the end of the 18th century that labor unionism came into being.In the 1780's, short-lived groups were founded, but not until the 1790's did more permanent unions appear. In 1792, Philadelphia shoemakers formed a protective organization, and in 1794 the Typographical Society of New York was founded. In addition to higher wages, shorter hours, and better working conditions, these bodies also sponsored fraternal benefits for sickness and burials.

The extension of democratic ideals in the 1820's created a more favorable climate for trade union success. Renewed activity found expression in the first recorded strike of women workers, when in 1824 the Pawtucket, R.I., women weavers left work for higher wages. In the larger cities many workers formed fairly stable trade unions. The recognition by many workmen that they had many problems in common prompted fifteen Philadelphia unions in 1827 to form the first city central trade council, the Mechanics Union of Trade Associations. By 1836 thirteen other cities had followed.

Although democracy under President Andrew Jackson did not completely free unions from legal disabilities, it gave an impetus to more liberal interpretations of labor's rights. The decision written by Massachusetts' chief justice Lemuel Shaw in the 1842 case of *Commonwealth* v. *Hunt,* recognized the legality of unions and their right to strike for a closed shop.

Under the leadership of Thomas Skidmore and William Leggett in New York and John Ferral and William English in Philadelphia, labor sought to achieve certain objectives through political action. In 1828 workingmen's parties were formed. Among their goals were the reduction of the workday to ten hours, abolition of imprisonment for debt, abolition of prison contract labor, enactment of mechanics' lien laws, curbs on banks and other monopolies, universal education, and free public land to settlers. In a few years these parties disappeared.

Despite organized labor's support of Andrew Jackson, the first use of federal troops in a labor dispute was ordered under his administration, in 1834. When Irish workers on the Chesapeake and Ohio Canal in Maryland struck for a closed shop and violence ensued, Jackson directed the War Department to restore peaceful conditions. In that same year the New York General Trades Union called a convention of delegates from other city centrals to discuss nonpolitical trade union objectives. From this emerged the first national federation of labor organizations, the National Trades Union. The panic of 1837 saw the disappearance of the National Trades Union, city centrals, and almost all local trade unions.

Social panaceas, utopianism, and the ten-hour-day movement dominated labor thinking during the next decade and a half. Lack of success of the first two alienated the workers, and they turned increasingly to trade unionism. The ten-hour-day movement was, on paper, more successful. Ten-hour legislation was passed in seven states during the 1840's and 1850's, but in all cases loopholes allowed workers to toil longer if they contracted a longer workday. By 1860, although the ten-hour day was widely accepted for skilled craftsmen, it was still not the norm for unskilled workers.

Improved economic conditions spurred on by increased industrialization and gold finds in California caused a resurgence of labor union activities. Many locals were formed, and some ten national unions were organized in the 1850's. These unions were so solidly formed that even the panic of 1857 did not destroy all of them.

The Civil War occasioned a severe labor shortage, since industrial expansion was needed in the midst of military recruitment. Congress, in 1864, authorized importation of contract labor. Inflation caused real wages to decline by one-third by 1865. Although few strikes were called during the war, labor considered the Conscription Act of 1863 unfair.

Favorable wartime conditions acted as a spur to union organization. National organizations and city centrals expanded their hold. During and after the war the railway brotherhoods were founded. The shoemakers' organization, the Order of the Knights of St. Crispin (1867) had attained a membership of over 50,000 by 1870, but soon failed. The iron molders and the anthracite coal miners were the two most powerful unions during the period after the Civil War, but both weakened in the early 1870's.

Encouraged by reformers seeking an eight-hour day—a movement pioneered by Ira Steward of Boston—the National Labor Union was established in Baltimore in 1866. Under the leadership of William Sylvis of the Molders and Richard F. Trevellick of the Ship Carpenters and Caulkers International, the National Labor Union concentrated upon producers' cooperatives and national political action. The failure of the cooperatives and the minimizing of trade union methods and objectives caused many national unions to withdraw from the federation. In 1872 the organization converted itself into the National Labor Reform party, which nominated David Davis of Illinois for president. Davis' withdrawal, after failing to capture the Democratic nomination, resulted in the collapse of the party and the National Labor Union. This short-lived federation was not a complete failure, for through its efforts Congress passed a law in 1868 limiting the hours of federal employees (laborers and mechanics) to eight a day.

Following the panic of 1873, of the thirty national unions, fewer than ten were able to survive. One casualty of the depression was the miners' union. In its absence anarchy ruled. In Pennsylvania a secret organization of Irish miners called the Molly Maguires was accused of spreading violence. Twenty-four Molly Maguires were convicted of murder in 1875 and ten were hanged in 1876.

A series of wage reductions sparked a militant labor demonstration in 1877, when a general strike tied up railroads. Local workingmen's parties combined with the Greenbackers to form the National Greenback Labor party at Toledo, Ohio, in 1878. Although this party elected fifteen members to Congress, its success was short-lived. The resumption of specie payment on Jan. 1, 1879, and the cleavage between currency reformers and labor people in the party caused its decline. Marxian and Lassallean socialism had some influence after 1876, and the headquarters of the First International was moved from Basel to New York City. The Marxists organized a workingmen's party in 1876, and a year later its name was changed to Socialist Labor party. This party succeeded only among unions that had a high proportion of German immigrants, as did the cigarmakers' and furniture workers' unions. In San Francisco the Workingmen's Party of California, under Denis Kearney, gained some political success. Anti-Chinese riots in 1877 were stimulated by this party and it elected a mayor of San Francisco in 1879. Although the party had disintegrated by 1881, its anti-Chinese agitation led to the Chinese Exclusion Act of 1882.

Antagonism to labor organizations throughout the depression years led to secret societies and orders. The Noble Order of the Knights of Labor began as a secret society. Founded in 1869 by Philadelphia garment cutters led by Uriah S. Stephens, it gained strength after the violence of 1876–77. By 1886 the Knights had a membership of 700,000. Under the leadership of Terence V. Powderly, its secret nature was abolished in 1881; for a short time it was the most powerful single labor organization in the United States.

The eight-hour movement reached its climax in May 1886. The national unions set the first of that month as the deadline. Labor demonstrations and clashes with the police were commonplace. Aroused by the shooting of several workmen in Chicago, the anarchist newspaper *Die Arbeiter Zeitung* called for a mass protest at the Haymarket. A bomb caused the death of seven policemen and the injury of many. Branded as radical because of the Haymarket incident, the eight-hour movement suffered a serious setback.

In the wake of the disastrous depression years of 1873–79, Samuel Gompers and Adolph Strasser of the New York Cigarmakers Union began looking to the British and their Trades Union Congress as models. A catastrophic strike virtually destroyed the Cigarmakers Union in 1877, but Gompers and Strasser reorganized it along British lines. Centralized control of the locals, effective collection of strike funds, and concern only for the immediate economic objectives of the cigarworkers were the principal guides. The promoters of the new unionism felt that a national federation of trade unions was essential. Consequently Gompers and Strasser seized upon a call for a national convention issued by two secret societies in 1881. On Nov. 15, 1881, the Federation of Organized Trades and Labor Unions was formed in Pittsburgh. For a short time this federation and the Knights of Labor tried to cooperate, but when this failed, the trade unions called another convention, at Columbus, Ohio. There on Dec. 8, 1886, the American Federation of Labor (AFL) was organized, and the Federation of Organized Trades and Labor Unions was disbanded.

Through collective bargaining, the strike, boycott, and picketing, the AFL sought to improve the economic status of its members. It sought public support through a campaign to popularize the union label. The AFL stressed job security, favored curbing immigration, espoused laws favorable to labor, and demanded relief from technological unemployment. It rejected independent political action, seeking only to lobby on behalf of its members.

The AFL made slow progress in the beginning. The membership of its affiliated unions rose from somewhat less than 200,000 in 1886 to more than 1,750,000 in 1904. In the 1890's the electrical workers, teamsters, musicians, and building laborers were formed into national unions. The proportion of workers organized in unions still lagged behind the growth of the labor force. The AFL persisted in concentrating its attention on the skilled crafts. Only the United Mine Workers (UMW), founded in 1890 as a result of an amalgamation of the AFL miners with those affiliated with the Knights, was initially organized along industrial lines.

More typical was the experience of the Amalgamated Association of Iron, Steel, and Tin Workers. In 1890 this union, restricted to skilled workers, claimed 24,000 members. In 1892 the union had a contract with the Carnegie Company at Homestead, Pa. Henry Clay Frick, manager of the steel works, realizing that the union did not represent the majority of the Homestead workers, who were mainly Slavic unskilled laborers, refused to accord recognition to the union and ordered a reduction in wages. The strike that followed involved the entire labor force of the steel works, Pinkerton guards, and the state militia. A number of deaths occurred. The strike was broken under the protection of the militia. The Association lost support in other steel mills and the steel industry was destined to be free of union controls for many more years.

The Coeur d'Alene district of northern Idaho was rocked by violence at the same time. A strike of the Western Federation of Miners, a sometime AFL affiliate, was marked by pitched battles, the dynamiting of a mill, and the proclamation of martial law. Federal and state troops restored order, but in 1894 and 1899 the events of 1892 were repeated.

The Socialists were critical of the job-conscious approach to unionism of the AFL under Gompers and its focus on skilled labor. Largely as a result of their efforts, Gompers was defeated for the AFL presidency in 1894, but when his successor proved unequal to the task, Gompers was returned to office. Then the Socialists, led by Daniel De Leon, sought to win control of the almost defunct Knights of Labor. In 1895, when this effort failed, the Socialist Labor party established an independent federation, the Socialist Trade and Labor Alliance. This alienated many Socialists, who defected from the Socialist Labor party and in 1897 formed the Social Democracy. In 1900 this organization united with another faction of the party to create the Socialist Party of America, which became the largest Socialist group in the United States and continued to challenge Gompers' policies, but from within the ranks of the constituent unions of the AFL.

The failure of the railroad brotherhoods to create a federation of railroad unions caused Eugene V. Debs, a former secretary of the Brotherhood of Locomotive Firemen, to attempt a new type of organization. In 1893 the American Railway Union was founded as an industrial union open to all railroad workers, including the unskilled. The Union was able to attract a membership of 150,000 after it had conducted a successful strike against the Great Northern Railroad in April 1894. The union was forced almost immediately into a strike by the Pullman Company, and the strike quickly assumed nationwide proportions.

From 1898 to 1904, the AFL unions received wide recognition from employers and were able to increase membership substantially—with the assistance of the National Consumers' League, National Civic Federation, National Child Labor Committee, and American Association for Labor Legislation. The success was reflected in the action of President Theodore Roosevelt when John Mitchell, president of the UMW, called a strike in 1902: Roosevelt compelled the mine owners to accept arbitration by a commission appointed by the president, and the commission's award of a 10 percent wage increase for the anthracite miners was the first known example of the federal government's intervention in a labor dispute on the workers' behalf. The International Ladies' Garment Workers' Union (ILGWU) was organized in 1900.

Trade union success caused a noticeable stiffening of attitudes among some employers. The National Association of Manufacturers (NAM), organized in 1895, spearheaded a campaign against trade unionism by sponsoring an open-shop drive. The unions were dealt a heavy blow by the courts during this open-shop campaign, when boycotts were ruled to be violations of the Sherman Antitrust Act.

At the same time, the AFL trade union concepts of craft exclusiveness and autonomy were challenged from the left. In Chicago, in June 1905, delegates from the Western Federation of Miners and from Daniel De Leon's Socialist Trade and Labor Alliance and some individual Socialists, notably Debs, joined to found the Industrial Workers of the World (IWW), with the objective of uniting all workers into one centralized industrial organization. The IWW called for abolition of the wage system and stressed direct action, the general strike, boycott, and sabotage.

The early years of the 20th century saw a change in the public attitude toward the problems of the worker, and protective legislation for labor's benefit was enacted in most states as well as at the national level. State laws were passed limiting child labor, setting standards for hours and wages for women, providing controls over sanitary and safety conditions, and attempting to establish accident insurance.

Woodrow Wilson's election as president in 1912 and his subsequent use of Gompers as his unofficial and official labor adviser meant that organized labor for the first time had access to an administration that paid serious attention to its needs. Under friendly pressure from the Wilson administration, Congress passed several laws favorable to labor. In 1913 the Newlands Act created a four-member Board of Mediation and Conciliation for the settlement of railroad labor disputes. In 1915 the La Follette Seamen's Act regulated conditions for maritime workers. The Adamson Act established an eight-hour day and time-and-a-half pay for overtime on interstate railroads. The Keating-Owen Act sought to bar the products of child labor from interstate commerce, but the Supreme Court in 1918 ruled against this law. A subsequent act passed in 1919 sought to tax the products of child labor out of existence, but this too was declared unconstitutional in 1922. During the period 1913–21 labor's cause found particular support in the fact that the Department of Labor, created in 1913, was headed by a labor leader, William B. Wilson, a former official of the UMW.

Of greatest concern to organized labor was the use by the courts of the Sherman Antitrust Act to frustrate its organizational drives. Consequently, when the Wilson administration in 1914 sponsored a revision of the antitrust laws, the resulting Clayton Antitrust Act contained provisions that prompted Gompers to call it "the Magna Carta of labor." Under the act's provisions, labor was not a commodity; labor organizations were not illegal; and the injunction was not to be used except to prevent irreparable property damage. Strikes, boycotts, and peaceful picketing were recognized as legal rights of labor, and jury trials were mandated in contempt cases except where the offense was committed in the court's presence. Judicial interpretation soon substantially weakened most of the labor provisions of the Clayton Act.

During World War I the number of organized workers increased from 2.75 million in 1916 to 4.25 million in 1919. A million women were recruited into the labor force; thousands of blacks migrated North from the rural South; and the U.S. Department of Labor expanded the activities of its employment service. Since the AFL enthusiastically supported the war effort, Gompers was appointed to the Council of National Defense and the Advisory Committee on National Defense. The Mediation Commission and the War Labor Board were created in 1917 and 1918, respectively. The Railroad Wage Commission and adjustment boards were established to ensure movement of the railroads. In recognition of labor's role in winning the war, an international conference was sponsored by the victorious powers in Washington in 1919, out of which came the International Labor Organization.

Although the standard workday declined to the desired

eight-hour norm, failure of wages to keep significantly ahead of rising prices, coupled with growing hostility to organized labor because of the opposition of labor's left wing to the war, meant a resurgence of labor unrest after the armistice. In 1919 over 4 million wage earners were involved in strikes, as compared to 1.25 million the year before. The most significant strike was called under AFL auspices against the U.S. Steel Corporation to end the twelve-hour day, and gain union recognition, collective bargaining rights, and wage increases. The refusal to bargain by Judge Elbert H. Gary, chairman of the board of U.S. Steel; the use of black strikebreakers; and the division of the strike committee into twenty-four craft committees spelled the doom of the walkout.

The 1920's, a decade of massive economic growth, saw real wages and per capita income rise, except for textile workers and coal miners, saw membership of unions decline from 5 million in 1921 to 3.4 million in 1929. Unions lost another 500,000 members during the depression from 1929 to 1933. The continued failure of the craft-oriented leadership of the AFL to organize unskilled labor allowed this task to be taken over by a new militant revolutionary movement, the Communists. Manufacturers' associations and chambers of commerce conducted a successful open-shop drive. Company unions founded and controlled by management grew in number and influence; by 1926 some 400 such unions had a membership of 1.4 million, and by 1935, 2.5 million. Labor spies and agents provocateurs were used increasingly to destroy legitimate unions. Expansion of fringe benefits helped discourage workers from remaining in unions. Finally, effective publicity campaigns blamed organized labor for the high cost of living and for increased radical and Communist activities.

The actions of the Supreme Court in rejecting labor's contention that the Clayton Act protected it from injunction proceedings and the overturning of a Washington, D.C., minimum-wage law for women convinced the AFL leadership that it must reverse its traditional attitude to political action. Consequently, the AFL joined with railroad brotherhoods, disgruntled liberals, reformers, farm groups, and Socialists in endorsing Sen. Robert M. La Follette of Wisconsin for president of the United States on the Progressive party ticket in 1924. The unwillingness of La Follette's supporters to create a permanent third party ended this effort.

The economic collapse of the nation that began in 1929 found the labor movement completely unprepared. Unemployment surpassed 13 million by 1933, and millions were employed only part-time. Although employment had declined 35.4 percent by 1933, the total national payroll had declined 56 percent. Local relief organizations and private charitable institutions sought to ameliorate some of the more extreme effects of the depression, but soon their funds were exhausted. The Communist party organized hunger marches, but the largest demonstration, by veterans in Washington in 1932 demanding the payment of bonuses, was not run by Communists. Until 1932 President Herbert Hoover sought to extend aid by assisting needy businesses and expecting that this would affect workers. Finally the president authorized loans to the states for emergency relief.

AFL membership declined by nearly 1 million from 1929 to 1933. Green had the federation reconsider its opposition to compulsory welfare schemes. In 1932 the AFL began advocating a compulsory system of unemployment insurance as well as large-scale public works projects, while attempting to hold the line on wages. Wisconsin enacted the first unemployment insurance law. A Congress more friendly to organized labor passed the Norris–La Guardia Act in 1932, which curtailed the federal courts' power to issue injunctions against peaceful strikes and made antiunion employment contracts unenforceable in the courts.

The New Deal of President Franklin D. Roosevelt came into being. Seeking to minimize the effects of unemployment, Congress authorized the Federal Emergency Relief Administration. The Civilian Conservation Corps was authorized for providing work for jobless young people. Under the National Industrial Recovery Act (NIRA), the Public Works Administration was established. The Civil Works Administration was created to employ 4 million jobless on public works to cushion the economic distress of the winter of 1933–34. With the passage of the National Employment Service Act, the U.S. Employment Service was expanded and the state bodies were coordinated with the federal agency. In 1935 the federal government withdrew from direct relief when Congress created the Works Progress Administration (WPA)—after 1939 the Works Projects Administration—to establish a massive national public works program for the jobless. Until 1943 the WPA spent $11 billion and employed 8.5 million different people on some 1.4 million projects. It was not until the defense and war production demands of the 1940's caused industry to boom that unemployment declined appreciably.

The codes of industrial self-regulation drawn up under the National Recovery Administration, established under the NIRA, prescribed minimum wages and maximum hours and eliminated child labor. The Walsh-Healey Government Contracts Act of 1936 sought to establish fair labor standards among contractors accepting government work. In 1938 the Fair Labor Standards Act established minimum wages, maximum hours, and abolition of child labor for all businesses engaged in interstate commerce. A joint federal-state system of unemployment insurance financed by a tax on employers' payrolls, coupled with a system of old-age and survivors' insurance financed by a payroll tax on both employers and employees, was adopted as the Social Security Act of 1935.

Strengthening the power of organized labor was a further objective of the New Deal. The NIRA proclaimed the workers' "right to organize and bargain collectively through representatives of their own choosing" and prohibited the employers from any "interference, restraint, or coercion" on this process. The National Labor Board, chaired by Sen. Robert F. Wagner of New York, was created to settle differences and in 1934 was authorized to hold elections of employees to determine their bargaining representatives. Although some organizing successes were made among garment workers and coal miners, the NIRA stimulated the successful expansion of company unions and gave inordinate power to large corporate employers through the codemaking provisions of the act. When the automobile labor codes were interpreted in favor of the Big Three auto makers, labor's disillusionment with the NIRA was complete. Frustrated high expectations triggered massive strikes in Toledo, San Francisco, and Minneapolis during the spring and summer of 1934. Federal and state governmental intervention resolved these strikes, and beginnings were made in collective bargaining in these heretofore open-shop cities.

Although the NIRA was invalidated by the Supreme Court in 1935, Congress reenacted the labor provisions in the same year by passing the Wagner-Connery National Labor Relations Act. A new three-man National Labor Relations Board (NLRB) was created for supervising union elections, designating bargaining agents, and holding hearings to determine unfair employer practices.

Reacting to the stimulus, the labor movement reawakened from its decade-long lethargy to begin a massive organizational drive. Noncompany union membership increased from 3 million in 1933 to 20.5 million in 1978.

The three industrial unions within the AFL—the UMW, the ILGWU, and the Amalgamated Clothing Workers of America—reestablished themselves as effective bodies of organized workers as early as 1933. At the 1935 AFL convention the delegates split on the question of craft versus industrial unions for the mass production industries; and after the traditional craft-oriented position won out, the minority leaders established the Committee for Industrial Organization (CIO)—after 1938 the Congress of Industrial Organizations —with John L. Lewis of the UMW as chairman. As the CIO successfully carried out its efforts in the mass production industries, the AFL unions also continued to expand. The Teamsters Union grew from 95,000 to 350,000 in the 1930's and became the largest union in the AFL.

Financed from the coffers of the UMW, the CIO set up committees to establish unions for rubber, automobile, steel, electrical, and textile workers. Using a dramatic technique, the sit-down strike—a device whereby the workers remained in the plants rather than vacating them and giving the companies an opportunity to utilize strikebreakers—the CIO United Automobile Workers Union (UAW) won recognition from the General Motors Corporation and the Chrysler Corporation early in 1937. By September it had bargaining agreements with every automobile producer except the Ford Motor Company and boasted of a membership of over 300,000. Ford finally recognized the union in 1941.

The Steel Workers' Organizing Committee, led by Philip Murray, then vice-president of the UMW, was ready to tackle U.S. Steel in 1937. Rather than risk a strike, U.S. Steel capitulated to the union, and in March 1937 its subsidiaries agreed to grant union recognition, wage increases, and the forty-hour week. The rest of the steel companies, known collectively as Little Steel, offered stiff resistance. The strike that followed was marked by violence and deaths. An investigation revealed that the companies had violated the Wagner-Connery Act, maintained spies, and collected weapons for use against the strikers; the NLRB demanded that the companies bargain in good faith with the union. In 1941 Little Steel capitulated.

Organized labor recognized its debt to the Roosevelt administration. In 1936 John L. Lewis contributed heavily to Roosevelt's reelection campaign; the New York labor leaders organized the American Labor party; and the AFL cautiously and quietly worked for the president's reelection through labor's Nonpartisan League. The situation was different in 1940 when Roosevelt ran for a third term. Lewis, piqued that he did not become the president's labor adviser and critical of Roosevelt's international policies, backed Republican Wendell L. Willkie. When Roosevelt won, Lewis resigned as president of the CIO and was replaced by Philip Murray.

Production and employment boomed with the increase of U.S. defense spending and shipments of war materials to the Allies in 1940. Sidney Hillman of the Amalgamated Clothing Workers of America was made codirector of the Office of Production Management in 1941, and in the same year, the National Defense Mediation Board was established. This body soon proved ineffective. Strikes of coal miners in 1941 raised Roosevelt's ire and caused public opinion to turn against the unions for subordinating the nation's interests to their own.

When the United States entered the war, a no-strike pledge was given at a conference of labor leaders called by Roosevelt. The National War Labor Board (NWLB) was created in January 1942. To the demand of the unions for the spread of the closed shop in war industries, the NWLB devised a compromise of "maintenance of membership" by which unionized workers were obliged to remain in their unions in order to continue employment.

The necessity of holding the wage and price levels stable caused further difficulty for the NWLB, and in July 1942 the board devised the Little Steel formula, by which it tied wage increases to rises in the cost of living after January 1941. Roosevelt ordered the freezing of wages and prices in April 1943, causing discontent. Lewis dramatized this discontent by refusing to appear before the NWLB and calling a strike of soft-coal and anthracite miners in May 1943. The seizure of the mines by the federal government quickly halted the strike but not before Congress passed the Smith-Connally War Labor Disputes Act over the president's veto. In December 1943, the railroads were temporarily taken over by the army in the face of a strike threat.

The need to expand the labor force during wartime was met by women and black workers. The Fair Employment Practice Committee (FEPC) was established by executive order in June 1941, and in May 1943 the government required nondiscrimination clauses in all war contracts. Attempts to make the national FEPC permanent failed to pass the Senate after the war, but by 1946 five states had created such commissions.

The CIO's political activities during the war were more vigorous than those attempted by the AFL. The CIO organized the Political Action Committee to work for Roosevelt's reelection in 1944 and to support congressional candidates favorable to labor's cause, and Hillman was asked to give labor's approval before Harry S. Truman was nominated for the vice-presidency by the Democratic party in 1944. The

AFL, although supporting Roosevelt in 1944, refused to give him its open endorsement.

The end of the war saw the beginning of a cyclic increase in wages and prices that frightened the public into an antiunion attitude. Strikes to keep up with the rising cost of living were widespread in 1945 and 1946, the most dramatic being the two strikes of the miners in 1946. The inflationary spiral, the feeling that unions had grown too powerful with the help of favorable legislation, the existence of a few corrupt labor officials, and the control of some unions by Communists resulted in public hostility to unions that was translated into congressional action. In June 1947 the Taft-Hartley Act was passed over Truman's veto.

Several factors paved the way for the long-desired merger of the AFL and CIO: the purge of the Communists from the CIO in 1949 and 1950; the appearance of new presidents of the rival federations when George Meany and Walter Reuther succeeded Green and Murray; and the beginning of vigorous anticorruption activity by the AFL. The merger occurred in 1955, and the new federation, calling itself the AFL-CIO, elected Meany president and Reuther head of the industrial union department. The most urgent task facing the merged federation was the elimination of corrupt elements. An ethical practices committee investigated and recommended the expulsion of a number of national unions—notably the Teamsters Union in 1957. Even so, evidences of sharp practices uncovered in 1957 by a Senate committee headed by John L. McClellan resulted in legislation that further restricted organized labor. The Landrum-Griffin Labor Management Reporting and Disclosure Act of 1959 restricted secondary boycotts, called for precise controls over union elections, demanded strict reporting of a union's financial transactions, outlawed extortion picketing, authorized state jurisdiction over labor disputes not handled by the NLRB, and modified union security provisions for the construction and garment industries.

Public-sector employment grew spectacularly during the 1960's as a consequence of new federal, state, and municipal programs, and the labor movement's continuing success in organizing public employees shows that union organizing techniques can be effectively applied outside private-sector, profit-oriented enterprises.

President John F. Kennedy's Executive Order No. 10988, issued Jan. 17, 1962, gave federal employees the right to organize and bargain collectively. This established the legal foundation for labor organization among federal governmental employees and stimulated the rapid growth of public-sector bargaining. State and municipal employees were granted similar rights when state legislatures passed public employee labor relations acts. So successfully have public-sector unions responded to their members' felt needs that the American Federation of State, County, and Municipal Employees (AFSCME), founded in 1936 but greatly expanded under Jerry Wurf after 1964, had become the eleventh largest national union by 1971, with some 550,000 members; the American Federation of Government Employees (federal government jurisdiction) ranked as the seventeenth largest, with 300,000.

The unionization of teachers grew significantly in the 1960's and early 1970's, under the aegis of the American Federation of Teachers (AFT). After the militancy of the AFT affiliate in New York City succeeded in winning a collective bargaining agreement there in 1961, union organization spread into almost every major school system in the country. Labor militancy even affected the National Educational Association (NEA), and this venerable professional association increasingly took on trade union characteristics; but efforts to create a merger between the AFT and the NEA had not come to fruition by 1980. Even college and university faculties began to move toward unionization: only five colleges had collective bargaining agreements in 1966, whereas over 500 colleges were organized by 1978. In 1972 the American Association of University Professors (AAUP) joined the organizational scramble for college and university bargaining rights for faculty with the AFT and the NEA.

Convinced of the necessity for political action, three organizations of public employees—the AFSCME, the NEA, and the International Association of Fire Fighters—formed the Coalition of American Public Employees (CAPE) in 1973. In addition, the AFT prevailed upon the AFL-CIO to create a public employee department within the federation and urged AFSCME to leave CAPE as a means of stimulating an AFT-NEA merger.

During the 1960's increasing militancy led to leadership upheavals. James Carey, longtime leader of the electrical workers (IUE), was replaced by Paul Jennings in 1964; David McDonald was replaced by I. W. Abel as president of the steelworkers (USWA) in 1965; and Arnold R. Miller replaced W. A. "Tony" Boyle as president of the UMW in 1972, after the murder of Joseph A. Yablonski and his family during a bitter rank-and-file contest within that union in 1969. (In April 1974 Boyle was found guilty of murder and sentenced to life imprisonment.) These changes did not stop criticism of the AFL-CIO for alleged inaction in organizing the low-income, unskilled workers; and this, together with the criticism of the "hawkish" stance of the federation on cold war foreign policy, led the UAW to discontinue affiliation with the AFL-CIO in 1968. Reuther joined with Frank E. Fitzsimmons, acting president of the Teamsters—whose president, James R. Hoffa, had been sent to jail in 1967 for jury tampering—to form the Alliance for Labor Action (ALA). With Reuther's death in 1970, the ALA lost its spark and disappeared.

Successful efforts to organize unskilled workers were attempted. The 1974 amendment to the National Labor Relations Act extending NLRB jurisdiction to health-care institutions laid the basis for the recruitment of larger numbers of low-paid, unskilled, nonwhite service workers into drug and hospital workers unions. A particularly significant effort was made to organize agricultural field hands in California by the United Farm Workers (UFW), under the leadership of César Chávez and with the assistance of the AFL-CIO.

A strike by automobile workers in the Chevrolet automobile manufacturing plant at Lordstown, Ohio, in 1971 awakened interest in questions of work satisfaction. To help resolve problems that were identified, efforts were sought to increase work satisfaction and to decrease the depersonalization of the worker by decentralizing the assembly line; some suggested increased worker participation in corporate or job decisionmaking. These efforts ended when the economy took a tailspin in 1973 and unemployment became the problem of the 1970's.

The environmental movement of the late 1960's and 1970's gave rise to a major debate over environmental protection vis-à-vis jobs. The economic impact of an environmental protection program was often ignored or the burden of sacrifice fell on the workers. Even so, the labor movement generally supported public programs to prevent ecological damage and to insure a healthy environment. Through these efforts the Occupational Safety and Health Act of 1970 was passed. The labor movement also insisted that the debate over jobs vis-á-vis environment could only be resolved through a strategy of full employment.

Even though the Full Employment Act of 1946 established full employment as a national goal, it was an increasingly elusive objective in the 1970's and early 1980's. With unemployment rising to over 10 percent in late 1982 and economists modifying their definitions of "acceptable" unemployment levels upward, achieving full employment was the major challenge for American labor.

LABOR, DEPARTMENT OF. Established as an executive department by President William Howard Taft on Mar. 4, 1913. Demands for a department of labor had originated with a conference of labor representatives held in Louisville, Ky., in 1865 to deal with labor problems, and the National Labor Union took up the demands. Following the example of Massachusetts in 1869, thirteen other states established bureaus of labor by 1883. In 1884, the Bureau of Labor was established by statute in the Department of the Interior. The bureau was elevated to an independent, but noncabinet, status as the Department of Labor in 1888. Legislation in 1903 established the Department of Commerce and Labor with cabinet status, with the Bureau of Labor continuing to study labor conditions. Renamed the Bureau of Labor Statistics, the bureau was installed in the new Department of Labor in 1913.

The new department was to "foster, promote and develop the welfare of wage-earners, to improve their working conditions, and to advance their opportunities for profitable employment." Besides the Bureau of Labor Statistics, it included the Children's Bureau and the Bureau of Immigration and Naturalization, with the addition of the Conciliation Service in 1918 and the Women's Bureau in 1920. The Wagner-Peyser Act established the U.S. Employment Service in the department in 1933. Administration of working conditions for construction workers was assigned under the Davis-Bacon Act of 1931 and for other workers under the Public Contracts Act of 1936. Administration of national minimum-wage levels was assigned under the Fair Labor Standards Act of 1938. The Welfare and Pension Plans Disclosure Act and the Labor-Management Reporting and Disclosure Act were passed in 1958–59. The impact of technology on the growing labor force resulted in the department's development of national manpower policies under the Manpower Development and Training Act of 1962. And the development of national standards of work-place safety and health was added under the Occupational Safety and Health Act of 1970.

The Department of Labor remains the smallest of the executive departments, with a staff that increased from about 5,000 in 1930 to 7,100 in 1960 and to 12,700 in 1972. Growth in the responsibilities of the department is reflected in a budget of $4.5 billion in 1972, as against $11 million in 1930 and $1.2 billion in 1961. This growth has been accompanied by functional organization, with assistant secretaries bearing line responsibility for such individual organizations as the Manpower Administration, the Labor-Management Services Administration, the Employment Standards Administration, and the Occupational and Safety Administration. The Bureau of Labor Statistics remains a separate administrative entity.

LABOR CONTRACTS, FOREIGN. *See* **Contract Labor, Foreign.**

LABOR DAY. On May 8, 1882, Peter J. McGuire, carpenters' union founder, proposed to the New York City Central Labor Union the designation of an annual "labor day." He recommended the first Monday in September. A parade and a festival were sponsored by the New York group the following Sept. 5. Oregon was the first state officially to designate a labor day holiday (1887), and thirty-one states had followed when President Grover Cleveland signed the bill, June 28, 1894, designating the first Monday in September as Labor Day and a federal legal holiday.

LABOR DISPUTES JOINT RESOLUTION (June 19, 1934). Established the National Labor Relations Board to replace the National Labor Board, established in 1933.

LABOR IN THE COLONIES. The scarcity of labor is evident from the use of labor impressment and labor cooperation. In New England, legislation occasionally gave constables power to compel artificers and mechanics to work in the harvest fields of their neighbors to save crops. Under labor cooperation, neighbors cooperated in large tasks. Slave labor, introduced in Virginia in 1619, in time became popular in the tobacco and rice colonies. Indentured servitude and apprenticeship, existed to some extent in all the colonies.

Hours of work were usually from daylight until dark. Remuneration was fair, partly because of the abundance of free or cheap land, but legislation at times interfered with wages. In Massachusetts a law in 1633 set a maximum wage of 2 shillings a day for most skilled mechanics when they boarded themselves and 14 pence when their employers supplied board. During most of the colonial period wages varied from 25 cents a day to four times that amount, the lowest wages usually including board.

LABOR LEGISLATION AND ADMINISTRATION. Up to the depression of the 1930's, the legal protection of labor was considered the exclusive responsibility of the states. The federal government confined its protective efforts to its own employees, to persons working for government contractors, and to those engaged in interstate transportation. Even state protections were slow in coming, because of the popular faith in individual competitiveness.

With the development of technology, an increase in occupational injuries led the industrial states gradually to adopt safety laws enforced by factory inspections (Massachusetts was first in 1877). Compulsory "no-fault" workmen's compensation insurance was adopted first in Wisconsin, in 1911; in virtually all the states by 1920.

There were early attempts to protect the health of industrial workers by state laws reducing excessive hours of work. At first, such laws applied only to women but later also to men. The Supreme Court ruled uncertainly as to the constitutionality of these statutes—deciding by close votes and then reversing itself—until 1917 when, in *Bunting* v. *Oregon,* it affirmed the propriety of such laws for both men and women.

Pennsylvania established a minimum age (twelve) for child labor in 1848; many states by 1900 still had no such statutes; and in 1923 only a handful of states had protective legislation for women workers. In that year, the Supreme Court curbed even the power of the states to adopt minimum wage legislation for women and children. It held in *Adkins* v. *Children's Hospital* that such laws abridged freedom of contract in violation of the due process clauses of the Constitution.

The Supreme Court reversed itself as to the powers both of the states and of the federal government. In *West Coast Hotel* v. *Parrish* (1937), the Court overruled the *Adkins* decision and upheld the state of Washington's minimum-wage statute. At the same time, Congress, under the leadership of President Franklin D. Roosevelt, was writing into federal law most of the reforms that had been creeping through the legislatures of the progressive states; and the Supreme Court upheld the constitutionality of these new measures.

A system of compulsory public insurance for the unemployed and for retired workers was provided in the Social Security Act (1935). A schedule of minimum wages and compulsory overtime rules was made applicable to both men and women in the Fair Labor Standards Act (1938); extensive rules limiting the employment of children were also included.

In the 1950's and 1960's an elaborate system of labor laws had two new objectives: (1) to extend basic protections, such as occupational safety, minimum wages, and social security, to virtually every category of labor; and (2) to introduce new programs to strengthen the positions of groups of disadvantaged workers—the technologically displaced, women, and ethnic minorities. The latter may be illustrated by the Manpower Development and Training Act (1962), the Equal Pay Act (1963), and the "equal employment opportunity" sections of the Civil Rights Act (1964). The new statutes proved cumbersome in administration—first, because of their extensive coverage and, second, because of the lack of a comprehensive manpower policy. The goals of equal opportunity, special protections, and compensatory aid were contradictory. Many older protections for women workers had to be repealed or nullified in order to ensure equality of treatment; while "equal opportunities" for the ethnic minorities had to be supplemented by unequal compensatory services known as "affirmative action" programs.

LABOR PARTIES. The first labor parties, which appeared in American cities after 1828, supported causes important to workers but failed to develop into a national force and did not survive the depression that began in 1837. Since then, the city labor party has been a recurring phenomenon. The movement in New York between 1886 and 1888, for instance, attracted national interest by supporting the candidacy of Henry George for mayor. Similar labor parties in other cities occasionally grew to state-level organizations. In 1900 organized labor in San Francisco promoted a Union Labor party.

The first labor organization of national scope, the National Labor Union, formed a short-lived party between 1870 and 1872. As well as supporting demands of labor such as the eight-hour day, its platform reflected greenback agitation. The Greenback Labor party, founded nationally in 1878, received the support of the Knights of Labor, whose division into district and local assemblies was suited to political activity. T. V. Powderly, leader of the Knights, was elected mayor of Scranton, Pa., on a Greenback Labor ticket in 1878 and was active in the founding of the Populist party in 1889. By then, the American Federation of Labor (AFL) was replacing the Knights as the chief national labor organization.

Socialist trade unionists, chiefly of German origin, had founded the Socialist Labor party in 1877. After the foundation of the more moderate Socialist Party of America in 1901, its members within the AFL constantly argued for endorsement of the Socialist party, but never succeeded.

After World War I a labor party finally did emerge. The National Labor party, formed in 1919, renewed the earlier policy of alliance with farmers' groups by organizing the Farmer-Labor party the following year. The AFL remained aloof. Only in 1924 did it join a coalition of farmers, labor groups, and Socialists in support of Robert M. La Follette's presidential candidacy under the banner of the Conference for Progressive Political Action (CPPA). Disappointing hopes for a new national party, the CPPA disintegrated after the election. The Farmer-Labor party survived in Minnesota, and small minorities of trade unionists continued to support the Socialist Party of America, the Socialist Labor party, and the Communist party (under different names). The American Labor party (now the Liberal party) was a means by which mainly old-guard Socialists of the garment trades could support Franklin D. Roosevelt and still retain a separate identity from the Democratic party. In general, the state of the American Left since 1924 has made the traditional "nonpartisan" policy of the AFL seem all the sounder. Adopted in 1906, this policy has aimed at "rewarding friends and punishing enemies" irrespective of party. In practice it has usually involved close alliance with the Democratic party.

LABOR PENSION REPORTING ACT (Aug. 28, 1958). In order to prevent abuses of employee pension funds, Congress passed this act requiring that all employee pension and welfare plans covering more than twenty-five employees, whether operated by employees, unions, or both in combination, be reported and their full nature disclosed.

LABOR UNIONS. *See* **Labor.**

LABRADOR FISHERIES. First attracted the cod and whale fishermen of New England during the colonial period. The Definitive Treaty of Peace, 1783, granted to American fishermen liberal privileges along the Labrador coast. As the economy of New England changed, fewer American fishermen found it worthwhile to go to Labrador for cod. Fishing on the Labrador coast is now limited from June to October, conducted by people of the east coast of Newfoundland.

LACOLLE MILL, BATTLE OF (Mar. 30, 1814). Defending their position in Canada during the War of 1812, the British had stationed 200 troops at a stone mill on the Lacolle River, five miles north of the international boundary. Taking 4,000 men from Plattsburgh, N.Y., Gen. James Wilkinson marched against this outpost. The defenders stoutly repulsed his ill-directed attack. Threatening weather and 200 casualties caused Wilkinson to retreat.

LACONIA GRANT. As John Mason and Sir Ferdinando Gorges were dividing their Province of Maine, they saw a chance to secure part of the rich fur trade formerly held by France and obtained a new grant of land from the Council for New England on Nov. 17, 1629. The area, believed to contain many lakes, was named the Province of Laconia. Its indefinite limits ran from Lake Champlain westward halfway to Lake Ontario and north to the St. Lawrence. The proprietors were authorized to cross other lands and to take as a coastal station as many as 1,000 acres of ungranted land. Mason, Gorges, and six others formed the Laconia Company to develop the grant and sent settlers to the Piscataqua. Despite several attempts to find a trade route to Laconia, the grant was never located. A second patent of Nov. 13, 1631, included land on both banks of the Piscataqua and the Isles of Shoals. In 1634 the company was dissolved.

LADD'S PEACE PLAN. In his *Essay on a Congress of Nations,* published in Boston in 1840, William Ladd, a New England philanthropist and reformer, proposed a periodic congress of nations for formulating international law and for promoting the general welfare of nations and a related but independent court for settling disputes by judicial decision or by arbitration. The essential features of the plan were in part realized in the Hague conferences of 1899 and 1907 and the establishment of the League of Nations and Permanent Court of International Justice after World War I.

LADIES' REPOSITORY. A monthly devoted to "literature and religion," published by the Methodist Book Concern from 1841 through 1876 (thirty-six volumes) and continued for four more years as the *National Repository.* Started at Cincinnati under the editorship of Leonidas L. Hamline, a Methodist clergyman, it once had 30,000 subscribers.

LAE AND SALAMAUA. On Mar. 8, 1942, the Japanese seized the ports of Lae and Salamaua, on the northeast coast of New Guinea. From there they dominated eastern New Guinea and threatened Allied shipping in the Coral Sea. Gen. Douglas MacArthur's forces began an attack on Salamaua at the beginning of July 1943. Two months of fierce combat ensued, before a combined American-Australian attack resulted in the seizure of the Salamaua airstrip, still five miles from the town. Overcoming a Japanese counterattack, the Allied force finally captured Salamaua on Sept. 12.

On Sept. 4, after a heavy naval and air bombardment, Australian troops stormed ashore east of Lae. A day later, U.S. paratroops seized Nadzab, northeast of Lae, where they were joined by other Australian forces. Although Japanese survivors of the Salamaua garrison retreated to Lae, the Lae defenders found themselves in an ever-tightening vise. Faced with being crushed between two forces, the Japanese decided to withdraw inland. Allied troops converging on Lae met only delaying forces and seized the town on Sept. 16.

LA FAMINE, TREATY OF (Sept. 5, 1684). Gov. Le Febvre de La Barre of New France, in charge of an expedition against the Seneca, was met at La Famine, at the confluence of the Salmon and Connecticut rivers, by the Onondaga orator Otreouati (also known as Grangula or Haaskouan) and fourteen deputies from the Onondaga, Oneida, and Cayuga nations. Otreouati countered all of La Barre's accusations, demanded the withdrawal of the army, and reserved the right to make war upon the Illinois. Although enraged by this defiance, La Barre was forced by sickness throughout the army to make peace and withdraw his army to Montreal.

LAFAYETTE, FORT. Situated on a shoal at the Narrows entrance to New York harbor. Construction began in 1812, and the fort was adapted only for guns of small caliber. During the Civil War it was used as a prison for political offenders. Impaired by fire in 1868, it was replaced by fortifications mounting considerably larger armament.

LAFAYETTE ESCADRILLE. A squadron of volunteer American aviators who fought for France before U.S. entry into World War I. Formed on Apr. 17, 1916, with 7 pilots, as the Escadrille Américaine, it changed its name after German protest to Washington. A total of 267 men enlisted, of which 224 qualified and 180 saw combat. Since only 12–15 pilots made up a squadron, many flew with French units; but all were deemed members of the Lafayette Flying Corps. They wore French uniforms and most had noncommissioned officer rank. On Feb. 18, 1918, the squadron was incorporated into the U.S. Air Service as the 103rd Pursuit Squadron.

LAFAYETTE'S VISIT TO AMERICA. In February 1824, President James Monroe invited the Marquis de Lafayette—Marie Joseph du Motier—to visit the United States. Lafayette accepted, but would not permit a government vessel to be sent for him, as Congress wished. He sailed in an American ship and reached New York on Aug. 16, 1824. After a tumultuous reception in New York and a four-day stay he toured New England, visited Albany, N.Y., and returned to New York City twice. Then he traveled slowly southward through Philadelphia and Baltimore, making leisurely stays everywhere.

After a long stop at Washington, D.C., where all government officials joined in doing him honor, he visited Thomas Jefferson at Monticello and went southward through the coastal states and then westward to New Orleans. Coming northward into the Middle West, he suffered shipwreck when a steamboat sank with him on the Ohio below Louisville, Ky., but despite his age (sixty-seven) he came through the disaster without severe shock. His progress everywhere was met by ovation. He visited Braddock's Field, Lake Erie, Niagara, and other American war scenes, after which he returned to Boston for the celebration of the fiftieth anniversary of the Battle of Bunker Hill. He visited New York City for the fourth time, and finally returned to Washington, from which he sailed for home on Dec. 7, 1825. Congress made him a gift of $200,000 in cash and a township of land.

"LAFAYETTE, WE ARE HERE." Following U.S. entry into World War I, the American Expeditionary Forces, commanded by Gen. John J. Pershing, landed in France on June 28, 1917—and on July 4, 1917, Paris enthusiastically celebrated American Independence Day. A battalion of the U.S. Sixteenth Infantry was reviewed by President Raymond Poincaré and then marched to the Picpus Cemetery, where several speeches were made at the tomb of the Marquis de Lafayette. Pershing was present but spoke very briefly, having designated Col. Charles E. Stanton of his staff to speak for him. Stanton uttered the historic words on that occasion, "Lafayette, nous voilà" ("Lafayette, we are here"), that have been popularly, but erroneously, attributed to Pershing.

LA FOLLETTE PROGRESSIVE PARTY. As a part of the Progressive movement that had begun about 1908, Sen. Robert M. La Follette of Wisconsin took the lead in forming in 1922 the Conference for Progressive Political Action. It was a loose federation of various Progressive groups, such as the farmers' Nonpartisan League, the Farmer-Labor party, the Single Tax League, and several labor organizations, including the sixteen railroad brotherhoods. The purpose at first was not to organize another political party, but to secure the election of Progressives to Congress, regardless of party, and to promote the enactment of liberal legislation.

A national convention was held in Cleveland, Ohio, July 4–6, 1924, at which La Follette was nominated for president and Sen. Burton K. Wheeler of Montana, a Democrat, for vice president. The new party, officially named the Progressive party, although generally known as the La Follette party, was also endorsed by the Socialist party and by the American Federation of Labor. The platform was largely a reproduction of La Follette's personal views on public questions, with particular emphasis on the needs of agriculture and labor. The party polled nearly 5 million votes—about 17 percent of all votes cast—chiefly in the Middle and Far West; it displaced the Democratic party as the second party in eleven states and carried Wisconsin.

LA FOLLETTE'S SEAMEN'S ACT. *See* **Seamen's Act of 1915.**

LA GALETTE, FORT. After the founding of the mission of La Présentation, at the mouth of the Oswegatchie, near modern Ogdensburg, N.Y., in 1749, the French missionary François Picquet, founder of the mission, persuaded the governor of Canada to build a substantial fort to protect Montreal against invasion from the Oswegatchie. It was captured by British Gen. Jeffrey Amherst in 1760.

LAIRD RAMS. Two double-turreted, ironclad steamers, one equipped with a ram and each armed with four 9-inch rifled guns, ordered in 1862 by James D. Bulloch, Confederate naval agent, from John Laird and Sons, shipbuilders, of Birkenhead, England. They were designed for use in breaking the Union blockade during the Civil War. They were both launched in the summer of 1863. On Sept. 3, 1863, Lord John Russell, British foreign secretary, suspecting that the ironclads were destined for the Confederacy, and influenced by the Union victories of Gettysburg and Vicksburg, ordered the ships detained. In October 1863 they were formally seized by the British government, which, in May 1864, purchased them for the royal navy. (*See also* Alabama Claims.)

LAISSEZ-FAIRE. A term originated by the disciples of the 18th-century school of economists in France known as the Physiocrats and given added meaning and widespread influence in the last quarter of the century by the Scottish economist Adam Smith. Translated literally as "let (people) do (as they choose)," and freely as "let things alone," the term designates a doctrine that the economic well-being and progress of society are assured when individuals are free to apply their capital and their labor without hindrance by the state.

LAKE CHAMPLAIN. Strategically located on the New York–Vermont border and extending six miles into Canada, was discovered in 1609 by Samuel de Champlain. Lake George drains into Lake Champlain by cascades and a 30-foot falls at Ticonderoga.

Both English and French colonial forces, augmented by their Indian allies, found Lake Champlain a convenient route for expeditions into enemy territory. In the 1640's the French fortified the Richelieu River at the northern end of the lake. The establishment of Fort Carillon at the southern end of the lake in 1756 gave the French control of the pathway. The French built Fort St. Frédéric on the western shore in 1731, as the base for raids against New England and New York during the mid-18th century. With the outbreak of hostilities between France and England in 1754, it became one of the prime military objectives of the British. In 1755 a fort was laid out by the French at Ticonderoga as an outpost for the defense of Fort St. Frédéric. An expedition led by British Gen. James Abercromby against Ticonderoga met disastrous defeat on July 8, 1758, but in the next year Gen. Jeffrey Amherst compelled the French to blow up Fort Carillon at Ticonderoga and Fort St. Frédéric and to retreat to Isle aux Noix at the northern end of Lake Champlain. The fall of Montreal on Sept. 8, 1760, brought the fighting to an end.

During the Revolution both Americans and British were

determined to control Lake Champlain. Commanded by Col. Ethan Allen, the American Green Mountain Boys seized Ticonderoga and Crown Point (formerly Fort St. Frédéric) in May 1775 but were unable to hold St. Johns. During the summer the expedition against Canada under Gen. Richard Montgomery, using Crown Point as a base, moved on to capture St. Johns and Montreal. The commander of the British forces in Canada, Sir Guy Carleton, Baron Dorchester, in fall 1776 moved down Lake Champlain with a flotilla but was delayed off Valcour Island by Gen. Benedict Arnold and his seagoing farmer boys; cold weather set in before the British could take the forts. In 1777 British Gen. John Burgoyne's army appeared on the lake (*see* Burgoyne's Invasion), compelled Gen. Arthur Saint Clair to evacuate Ticonderoga, beat the retreating Americans at Hubbardton, and captured Skenesboro, N.Y. Col. John Brown of Pittsfield, Mass., unsuccessfully attempted to seize Ticonderoga and to capture the supplies on Diamond Island in Lake George. After Burgoyne's defeat at Saratoga in October 1777, the British continued to control the Champlain Valley.

During the War of 1812, England threatened the United States from the north by both land and water, and considerable bodies of U.S. regulars and militia, supported by a naval force, were stationed at Burlington, Vt., and Plattsburgh, N.Y., and other spots along the lake. In command of the American fleet was Lt. Thomas Macdonough. On June 3, 1813, the Americans lost two vessels to the English. The next month, British Col. John Murray, with over 1,400 troops and marines, destroyed several military buildings near Plattsburgh. A few days later, Aug. 2, three British ships appeared off Burlington, but were driven off by Macdonough's ships and the shore battery. Macdonough sought out the English fleet, but it declined battle. In the fall of 1814 came the general advance of the English, the decisive engagement taking place on Sept. 11, when Sir George Prevost led more than 14,000 troops against 4,700 American regulars and militia under Gen. Alexander Macomb, who had taken up their position on the south bank of the Saranac River near Plattsburgh. At the same time, the British fleet attacked Macdonough off nearby Cumberland Head. The American land force and naval force were both victorious. Lake Champlain is now a link in the Hudson–St. Lawrence waterway, and the surrounding region is a noted resort area.

LAKE GEORGE, BATTLE OF (Sept. 8, 1755). William Johnson, major general of the New York militia, moved north against the French Fort St. Frédéric in midsummer 1755. At the southern end of Lake George his encamped force was threatened by Gen. Ludwig August Dieskau commanding 1,700 French and Indians. On Sept. 8 Johnson sent 1,200 men south to locate the French. Division proved costly; the French drove the Americans back with severe losses. At the camp barricades the reunited provincials beat off repeated charges; the day ended with the French retreating. Both commanders were wounded; Dieskau was captured. Provincial forces lost 260 killed, 91 wounded; the French, about as many. Johnson could not proceed, and capture of their commander stopped the French offensive.

LAKE OF THE WOODS BOUNDARY PROBLEM. Projected by the Definitive Treaty of Peace of 1783, which provided that the northern boundary should extend westward from the northwestern point of Lake of the Woods, in northern Minnesota, to the Mississippi. Since such a line was geographically impossible, it was agreed in 1818 that the boundary should be drawn south from the northwest point of the lake to 49° north latitude, creating the Northwest Angle.

LAKERS. Great Lakes bulk carrier steamships; a long, narrow, and deep vessel with machinery in the stern, navigating bridge forward, and crew quarters both forward an aft. Dating from 1816, by 1927 their number had grown to 765. Bulk cargoes consisted primarily of iron ore, coal, limestone, and wheat. The largest laker was 633 feet long, with a 70 foot beam and a 29-foot Depth.

LAKES, GREAT. *See* **Erie, Lake; Great Lakes; Huron, Lake; Michigan, Lake; Ontario, Lake; Superior, Lake.**

LAKES-TO-GULF DEEP WATERWAY. In 1673 Louis Jolliet noted the possibilities for a canal to connect the Great Lakes with the Des Plaines, Illinois, and Mississippi rivers. Aided by a right-of-way and a land grant provided by Congress, Illinois in 1848 completed the Illinois and Michigan Canal. The first 30-mile section, to a point below Lockport, was rendered obsolete by the completion in 1900 and the extension (1910) of the Chicago Sanitary and Ship Canal. Sponsored by the Chicago Sanitary District and representing an investment of $36,820,878, this new canal had a width of over 160 feet and a depth of 24 feet. In 1921, Illinois started construction of five locks and four dams between Lockport and Utica. Taken over in 1930 by the federal government, which spent $7,407,707 finishing the structures, the project was completed in 1933 with a channel depth of 9 feet. A similar minimum depth was achieved in the Illinois Waterway below Utica and in the Mississippi River to Cairo, Ill. Locks and dams at Peoria, La Grange, and Alton, Ill., were completed during 1938–39. Near St. Louis, Mo., a lateral canal with locks was opened in 1953, and a dam was finished in 1964.

LAME-DUCK AMENDMENT. The Twentieth Amendment (1933) to the Constitution of the United States abolished lame-duck sessions of Congress, from December of even-numbered years until the following Mar. 4. These sessions included numerous members who had failed of reelection (the lame ducks) a month before the session opened. Yet the law permitted them to sit and function until their terms ended, while a newly elected Congress stood by inactive and unorganized, usually for thirteen months. In the last lame-duck session, opening in December 1932, there were 158 defeated members sitting in the Senate and House. The amendment, sponsored by Sen. George W. Norris of Nebraska, did away with the lame-duck session by moving back the day on which terms of senators and representatives begin from Mar. 4 to Jan. 3, and by requiring Congress to convene each year on Jan. 3. The amendment also set back the date of the president's inauguration to Jan. 20. Other provisions related to the choice of president under certain contingencies.

L'AMISTAD* SLAVE CASE.** *See* ***Amistad **Case.**

LAMP, INCANDESCENT. As early as 1820 scientists had begun to work on the development of an incandescent lamp, but it remained for Thomas A. Edison at Menlo Park, N.J., on Oct. 21, 1879, to make the first successful high-resistance carbon lamp. The carbon lamp was gradually improved through minor changes in construction, many of which were introduced by American inventors. In 1905 Willis R. Whitney, head of the Research Laboratory of the General Electric Company at Schenectady, N.Y., succeeded in changing the character of the carbon filament to give it metallic characteristics. In 1910 William D. Coolidge of the General Electric Research Laboratory succeeded in making ductile tungsten. The drawn wire tungsten filament lamp shortly superseded all other forms. All lamps up to this time operated filaments in a vacuum. In 1913 Irving Langmuir, one of Whitney's assistants, discovered that with the largest sizes of lamps, if the filaments were coiled and the bulbs filled with inert gases the efficiency could be increased. Although fluorescent lamps provide more light with greater efficiency, incandescent lamps continue to be used because of their simplicity and low cost.

LANCASTER, FORT. A trading post on the South Platte River, Colo., in use during the early 19th century. It was noted by John Charles Frémont in 1843 as a trading post of a Mr. Lupton, apparently synonymous with Fort Lupton. By 1857 it was abandoned.

LANCASTER, TREATY OF (June 22–July 4, 1744). Negotiated in Pennsylvania, settled disputes between the Six Nations and Maryland and Virginia over land claims. For considerations of goods and money, the Six Nations surrendered claims to a large region in western Maryland and Virginia. The Six Nations were won to the support of England in the ensuing struggle with France (*see* King George's War).

LANCASTER PIKE. The first turnpike built in the United States, begun in 1791, completed in 1794, and freed from tolls, by state purchase, in 1917. In 1770 commissioners were appointed to lay out a 60-foot road, but the plan failed. William Bingham then secured a charter for the Philadelphia and Lancaster Turnpike Company, offering for public sale 1,000 shares of stock, $300 par, to be one-tenth paid up at once. The offering was heavily oversubscribed, and the surplus was reduced by a lottery. In 1807 the charter was made perpetual. The Pike lost heavily when the main line of the Pennsylvania Railroad, begun in 1846, paralleled its course. Free roads close by the Lancaster Pike also cut away its trade. The perpetual charter was, accordingly, surrendered.

LAND, INDIAN CONCEPT OF OWNERSHIP OF. To the American Indian land was not susceptible of individualistic sale and transfer. Land was an integral part of nature, which sustained the beings that lived upon it. The only Indian concept that corresponded to the European concept of land ownership was that geographic sections of that unity of nature were capable of being used particularly by different tribes. Friction and warfare could thus come about between groups. But as for individuals, Indians believed that the "Great Spirit made the earth and all that it contains for the common good of mankind."

LAND, LEASING OF AMERICAN INDIAN. Although Indian reservation land cannot be sold without an explicit act of Congress, it is possible for tribes or individual Indian owners of land allotments to lease land under the Trade and Intercourse Act of 1834. Tribal councils may also lease tracts of land as well as mineral rights.

LAND ACT OF 1796. This act established the office of surveyor general and reenacted the rectangular system of survey embodied in the Land Ordinance of 1785. Half of the townships were to be offered in 5,120-acre blocks, and the smallest unit that could be bought was 640 acres. The lands were to be sold at public auction, at or above the minimum price of $2 per acre. Full payment was required within a year after purchase, and a 10 percent reduction was offered for advance payment. The act failed because of the high minimum price and the large unit of entry deterred purchasing.

LAND ACT OF 1800. *See* **Harrison Land Act.**

LAND ACT OF 1820. The credit system in the disposition of the public lands inaugurated by the Land Act of 1796 and extended by the Harrison Land Act of 1800 had become an evident failure by 1820. Many settlers found it impossible to make the deferred payments on their lands; arrearages piled up rapidly, and Congress was forced to pass law after law for the relief of the settlers. After considerable agitation Congress enacted the law of Apr. 24, 1820, abolishing the credit system. The minimum price at the public auctions and at private sale thereafter was reduced from $2 to $1.25 per acre, the entire amount to be paid at the time of purchase. The smallest purchasable unit of land was fixed at 80 acres.

LAND BANKS. *See* **Agriculture.**

LAND BOUNTIES. The American colonies and, after the Revolution, the states and the national government all granted land bounties instead of cash subsidies to reward military service in past wars, to encourage enlistment, and to aid various groups. Virginia gave generous bounties the most; a special Virginia military district was reserved north of the Ohio for these grants. During the Revolution Congress promised land bounties to British deserters and to enlisted officers and men. During the War of 1812 and the Mexican War land bounties were offered as inducements to enlist and as rewards for service (*see* Bounties, Military). Land bounties were also granted to those whose appeals to Congress received strong political support. (*See also* Land Scrip.)

LAND DISTRIBUTION BILL, CLAY'S. The proposal made by Sen. Henry Clay of Kentucky for the distribution of the net proceeds from the public land sales among the states. Clay's bill, introduced in 1832, provided that 10 percent of the net proceeds be distributed to the states in which a sale occurred and that the remaining 90 percent be distributed among all the states and territories in proportion to their population. The advocates of distribution made a concession to the West by adding to Clay's bill a provision for preemption. Before the bill was adopted in 1841, it was further provided that if tariff rates were raised above 20 percent, distribution would automatically be suspended. In 1842 the tariff was raised, and Clay's political measure was suspended. (*See also* Surplus Revenue, Distribution of.)

LAND GRANT ACT. *See* **Morrill Act.**

LAND GRANTS, COLONIAL. Claims to land rested upon discovery, exploration, and occupation, which vested the title in the sovereign of a particular nation. According to this European concept, it was the prerogative of the sovereign who had taken title to terminate the claims of native Americans; the title to all English America was in the king, and from him all later titles stemmed. Royal land grants took the form of charters, and the whole Atlantic seaboard, except Florida, was, between 1606 and 1732, parceled out to the London and Plymouth companies; the Council for New England; James, Duke of York; William Penn and associates; George Calvert, Lord Baltimore; Edward Hyde, Earl of Clarendon, and associates; and James Oglethorpe and associates. From some of these in turn came grants to individuals and groups, which were gradually incorporated into regular colonial governments with boundaries based upon the earlier charters. Many of the original grants ran westward to the sea and became the foundation for the western claims of the original states, which were finally surrendered to the national government between 1778 and 1781 (*see* Western Lands).

Local land titles came from the colonial government or the proprietor, depending on who held the direct title from the king. The practice of New England was for the general court in each colony to grant a tract, called a township, to a body of settlers, who in turn issued deeds to individuals.

In Maryland there were some manorial grants of 1,000 acres or more, although most of the grants were small and made to actual settlers. The practice in Pennsylvania was to grant land to actual settlers in small parcels but to retain title to vast acreage in the settled areas. Thus, the proprietor not only held title to the ungranted regions but was also the largest landowner in the developed eastern counties and collected rents as from any other private estate.

In Virginia there was at first a system of grants based on headrights—fifty acres for each person arriving in Virginia—and belonging to the individual who paid the transportation. This led to abuses and gradually degenerated into a simple fee system at the land office. Anyone who could pay the fees could acquire original title to as many acres as he could pay for. Under this system large plantations grew up that were far too big to be fully cultivated.

Grants were not infrequently used to promote settlements in the backcountry. These were usually conditioned upon the transportation and settlement of a minimum number of families within a limited time. The best known is the Ohio Company grant of 500,000 acres near the Forks of the Ohio in 1749.

In New York and South Carolina there were vast individual grants and extensive engrossment. In New York the practice had begun under the Dutch by the creation of the patroon estates, which were recognized as valid by the English. Henry Hyde, Viscount Cornbury, and other royal governors issued enormous grants to their favorites.

To be valid, a grant had to come from the colonial government in which the land was situated. Undefined boundaries led to conflicts over titles, such as the troubles in Vermont, where settlers claimed land under grants from both New York and New Hampshire, and in the Wyoming Valley, where settlers from Connecticut were expelled as trespassers by those with titles from Pennsylvania (*see* Yankee-Pennamite Wars).

Land grants as bounties for military service became especially important after 1750. The Virginia grants were made in what is now West Virginia. Individual soldiers or officers could either use their warrants or sell them; the purchaser in turn could use them singly or in groups (*see* Washington's Western Lands). The British made extensive military grants in the Floridas after their acquisition from Spain.

Indian titles were presumed to be extinguished by the local colonial government as the representative of the king before land was granted to individual settlers. This was not always the case, and after 1750 frontiersmen commonly purchased lands directly from the Indians and secured confirmation later. In other instances settlers secured grants before Indian titles were extinguished—this being one of the causes of Pontiac's War. The Proclamation of 1763 was issued to stop encroachments of this kind. On the other hand, the expansion into Kentucky and Tennessee in the late 1760's and in the 1770's was based upon the assumption that Indian titles alone were valid.

The vast interior of the continent tempted Americans and Englishmen to seek grants to the rich lands west of the mountains. On the eve of the Revolution patents were pending in England for proprietary grants to form four new colonies (Vandalia, Transylvania, Georgiana, and Mississippi) in the region west of the Alleghenies and south and east of the Ohio and Mississippi rivers. Large purchases from Indians north of the Ohio also awaited confirmation.

Spain and France made grants similar to those made by England. When new areas came under the control of England, or later of the United States, the earlier foreign colonial land grants were accepted as valid (*see* Land Grants, Spanish and Mexican).

LAND GRANTS, SPANISH AND MEXICAN. The title records of these early grants before American control were in poor shape, some of them being entirely lost. Most grants had been made on conditions, and in many instances these had not been fulfilled. When these areas came under American jurisdiction, there was a scramble for the most promising locations. All the grants had to be tested in the courts by American judges attempting to apply Spanish and Mexican law and American equity. Unfortunately, the swift rise in land values encouraged the fabrication of grants through forged documents and professional witnesses who, for a fee, would swear to anything the lawyers asked of them. Although it took a generation before the cost of the claims was patented, it is doubtful that any number of them with an equitable or other legal basis was rejected. Altogether 20,059 claims were confirmed for a total of 30,519,605 acres. The largest numbers of claims were in Louisiana, Missouri, and Mississippi, and the largest acreages, in New Mexico, California, and Louisiana. The larger claims in Florida, Louisiana, and California contributed to a concentrated pattern of land ownership that survived into the last third of the 20th century.

LAND GRANTS FOR EDUCATION. The practice of making land grants to aid in supporting public schools was generally followed by the American colonies. The Confederation, borrowing from the New England land system, provided in the Land Ordinance of 1785 that the sixteenth section (640 acres) of each township, or one thirty-sixth of the acreage of the public land states, should be granted to the states for public schools. New states after 1848 were given two sections, or 1,280 acres, in each township, and Utah, Arizona, New Mexico, and Oklahoma were given four sections in each township when they entered the Union. At the same time, they were also given a minimum of two townships, or 46,080 acres, to aid in founding state universities.

In 1862 the Land Grant College Act, called the Morrill Act, gave each state 30,000 acres of public land for each representative and senator it had in Congress, to aid in establishing colleges of agriculture and mechanical arts. States that had no public lands received scrip that could be exchanged for public lands open to entry elsewhere. As a result, agricultural colleges were established in every state, with two each in southern states because of their insistence on segregation. Special land grants have also been made to endow other schools.

Congress was unusually generous in sharing public lands with Alaska for education and other purposes upon the state's admission to the Union in 1959. In place of numerous grants for education, internal improvements, and public buildings, Congress granted a total of 103,350,000 acres to be allocated as the new state wished. It also promised 5 percent of its net return from all land sales in the state for schools.

LAND GRANTS FOR RAILWAYS. When, in 1850, the proposed railroad scheme for Illinois was made intersectional by a plan to extend it to the Gulf of Mexico, Congress gave Illinois, Mississippi, and Alabama a right-of-way through the public lands for a distance of six miles on both sides of the road, amounting to 3,840 acres for each mile of railroad. The government-reserved sections within the twelve-mile area were to be priced at double the ordinary minimum of $1.25 an acre, which enabled strict constructionists to maintain that building the road would assure the government as much return from half the land as it might receive for the whole without the line. The government was promised free transportation for troops and supplies and rate concessions for transporting mails. Success produced a scramble for railroad land grants in all existing public land states. Land grants between 1850 and 1871 totaled 176 million acres. Most important were the transcontinental railways. First of the transcontinentals to be chartered and given a land grant, plus loans (in 1862), were the Union Pacific, to build west from Omaha, and the Central Pacific, to build east from Sacramento. In 1864 the Southern Pacific, the Atlantic and Pacific (a portion of which later became part of the Atchison, Topeka and Santa Fe), and the Northern Pacific were generously endowed with land, the latter receiving 39 million acres.

All land grant railroads undertook advertising campaigns to attract immigrants. When settlers found it difficult to meet their payments, complaints against the policies of the land grant railroads began to be made. Forfeiture of their undeveloped and unsold land was demanded. Reformers condemned the land grants as inconsistent with the free homestead policy, and in 1871 they succeeded in halting further grants. Continued agitation over the large amount of land claimed by railroads led to the General Forfeiture Act of 1890, which required the return to the government of land along projected lines that had not been built. In 1940 it was proposed that the railroads be required to return the unsold portion of their grants, but Congress did not so provide. Retention of these unsold lands by the railroads has been a sore point with many westerners, and agitation for compelling the forfeiture of these lands continued in the 1970's.

LANDGRAVE. A German title proposed for the second order of provincial nobility provided for in the Fundamental Constitutions of Carolina by the lords proprietors. Their inability to enforce the Constitutions made the title of little meaning save as an occasion for gifts of land to favorites, and as a title for the governors.

LAND OFFICE, U.S. GENERAL. Organized in 1812 as a bureau in the Treasury Department, to manage the public lands of the United States. The increasing burdens of the secretary of the treasury brought about the creation of the office of commissioner of the General Land Office. The commissioner's responsibility for more than a billion acres of land and for the patenting of tracts to hundreds of thousands of buyers made him a powerful political figure and made the Land Office one of the most important of federal bureaus. As revenue from the public land became diminishingly important, the office seemed less related to the Treasury Department. In 1849 it was transferred to the newly created Department of the Interior. It made detailed reports on minerals, agricultural possibilities, and forests of the West. The General Land Office became increasingly settler-minded until free lands were provided by the Homestead Act of 1862. Timbered areas of the public lands were withdrawn from entry under the Forest Reserve Act of 1891 for conservation and public management, and in 1905, they were transferred to the

National Forest Service in the Department of Agriculture. By 1947 the land disposal responsibilities of the General Land Office, which had been chiefly concerned with transferring public lands into private ownership rather than with conserving them in public ownership, were largely over. In 1946 the activities of the office were transferred to the new Bureau of Land Management. By 1978 the bureau administered 417 million acres of public lands and the leasing and sale of mineral rights on an additional 169 million acres. The bureau's aims are to protect the public lands and to preserve them for economic use, recreation, wildlife, and scenic beauty.

LAND ORDINANCES. *See* **Ordinances of 1784, 1785, and 1787.**

LAND POLICY. Because the new government of the United States needed revenue, the Land Ordinance of 1785 was passed, decreeing that the public lands should be sold for what was then a high price, $1.00 an acre—raised to $2.00 an acre in 1796 and lowered to $1.25 after 1820. Not until 1811 did the revenue from land sales amount to as much as $1 million, but thereafter it increased, until in 1836 the public lands produced 48 percent of the revenue of the federal government. As late as 1855 the income from this source was 17 percent of the total federal income. Western settlers insisted it was unfair to require them to pay $1.25 an acre for raw land, a price that added heavily to the capital cost of making a farm. Supported by Horace Greeley and his powerful *New York Tribune* and by eastern workingmen, the demand for free land gradually won converts. In 1862 they won their objective with the adoption of the Homestead Act.

Congress, responsive to western interests, had previously aided the building of canals, roads, and railroads in the public land states by generous grants of land. It had also made grants of land for public schools, public buildings, state universities, agricultural colleges, and other public institutions, on the assumption that such grants enhanced the value of the remaining lands and encouraged their sale and settlement. All such institutions were expected to sell their lands to produce the greatest possible revenue at the same time that the United States was giving land to settlers. Through these lavish donations, free grants to settlers, and huge purchases by speculators, the public lands were rapidly alienated.

Little thought was given to the consequences of this speedy transfer of lands to private ownership until the threatened exhaustion of the forest resources of the Great Lakes states and the rising price of timber raised fundamental questions about the wisdom of past disposal policies. By the turn of the century, conservation of the remaining resources under federal ownership was being vigorously advocated by John Muir, Gifford Pinchot, and Theodore Roosevelt. National forests were set aside as permanent reservations under controlled management. Places of special scenic beauty were created national parks; Yellowstone was the first, in 1872. In 1934 the remaining rangelands in public ownership were organized into management districts under the Taylor Grazing Act, thereby virtually ending the era of free land.

LANDRUM-GRIFFIN ACT (Sept. 14, 1959). Also known as the Labor Management Reporting and Disclosure Act, the act was designed to suppress organized crime in labor organizations. Its provisions also included anticorruption, fair election, and trusteeship guarantees; criminal penalties for unfair actions against union members by their unions; and revision of the ban on secondary boycotts under the Taft-Hartley Act to prohibit unions from coercing an employer or employee to stop doing business with another firm or handling its goods.

LANDS, PUBLIC. *See* **Public Domain; Public Land Commissions; Public Land Sales; Public Land States.**

LANDSCAPE ARCHITECTURE. The shaping and planting of a garden or tract of land. American landscape architecture has been dominated by two styles: the classical, or formal; and the picturesque, or informal. The classical sprang from the Renaissance and is distinguished by straight paths, straight rows of trees, clipped shrubbery, flower bedding, fountains, formal bodies of water, and the use of architecture and sculpture. The picturesque, originating in 18th-century England, is characterized by winding paths, irregular planting, spreading lawns, and irregular bodies of water, and little, if any, architecture and sculpture.

The first American gardens, mostly for vegetables, had plain geometric designs. In the 18th century, gardens became elaborate, especially in the South. The picturesque caught on in the 1840's. Andrew Jackson Downing, who favored the picturesque, laid out private estates along the Hudson River and promoted the style in several popular books. His successors Frederick Law Olmsted and Calvert Vaux adopted the picturesque style in 1858 for Central Park in New York City, and from that time on, the style has been the dominant one for urban parks. In the 1960's and 1970's it was also found along parkways and in suburban developments.

Although the picturesque style has prevailed since the 1840's, it was swept aside by the classical—at least in the private section—during the American Renaissance (1880–1930). The World's Columbian Exposition of 1893 proved to be the most important single factor in making it popular.

LAND SCRIP. Along with land warrants it became a kind of land-office money acceptable for entry of public lands. Congress never drew any clear distinction between the two in the forty-nine statutes (mostly between 1820 and 1880) that authorized issues of scrip, some directly, others only after trial of claims before special commissions or the courts. Congress placed restrictions on the use of certain kinds of scrip. Scrip was used primarily to reward veterans, to give allotments to half-breed Indians, to make possible exchanges of private land for public land, to indemnify people who had lost valid claims through errors of the General Land Office, and to subsidize agricultural colleges.

The greatest volume of scrip or warrants was given to soldiers of the American Revolution, the War of 1812, and the Mexican War and, in 1855, to veterans of all wars who had not previously received a land bounty or who had received less than 160 acres. Warrants of the first two wars were to be located in military tracts set aside for that purpose; those of the Mexican War could be entered anywhere on surveyed public land open to purchase at $1.25 an acre. A total of 68,300,652 acres were thus conveyed to 426,879 veterans, their heirs, or their assignees.

In treaties with the Choctaw (1830) and Chickasaw (1832) of Mississippi and Alabama these Indians were given several million acres in individual allotments and land scrip, all of which became the object of speculation by whites, including a number of prominent political leaders. For the next thirty years treaties with Indian tribes were almost impossible to negotiate without the inclusion of similar provisions for allotments and scrip. Three issues of scrip to two bands of Chippewa and Sioux half-breeds in the 1850's and 1860's similarly fell into the hands of speculators, who used them to acquire valuable timberland in Minnesota and California that they would otherwise have been unable to acquire legally.

In the Morrill Act of 1862, Congress granted land to states containing public domain, but other states were given scrip that they had to sell to third parties to enter land in public domain states.

The next major scrip measure was the Soldiers' and Sailors' Additional Homestead Act of 1872, which allowed veterans of the Civil War to count their military service toward the five years required to gain title to a free homestead and authorized those who had homesteaded on less than 160 acres to make an additional entry to bring their total acreage to 160 acres.

Other measures were enacted to indemnify holders of public-land claims that were confirmed long after the land had been patented to settlers; the claimants were provided with scrip equivalent to the loss they had sustained. Indemnity scrip for some 1,265,000 acres was issued, most of which was subject to entry only on surveyed land open to purchase at $1.25 an acre. These rare forms of scrip could be used to acquire town and bridge sites, islands, tracts adjacent to such booming cities as Las Vegas, or water holes controlling the use of large acreages of rangelands, and they came into great demand. Their value reached $75 to $100 an acre in 1888.

Least defensible of all the scrip measures were the carelessly drawn Forest Management Act of 1897 and the Mount Rainier Act of 1899, which allowed owners within the national forests and Mount Rainier National Park to exchange their lands for public lands outside the forests and park.

As the public lands rapidly diminished and the demand for land to own intensified, values of scattered undeveloped land increased, and so did the value of the various forms of scrip, without which it was impossible to acquire these tracts, as public land sales had been halted in 1889. In the 20th century, speculators bid up quotations to $500, $1,000, and even $4,000 an acre. By 1966, administrative relaxation had wiped out some of the distinctions between types of scrip; Valentine, Porterfield, and Sioux Half-Breed were all accepted for land having an appraised value of $1,386 an acre, and Soldiers' and Sailors' Additional Homestead and Forest Management lieu scrip could be exchanged for land having a value from $275 to $385 an acre. At that time 3,655 acres of the most valuable scrip and 7,259 acres of that with more limitations on use were outstanding.

LAND SPECULATION. Land speculation began with the first settlements. The proprietors of Virginia granted themselves great tracts of land from which they hoped to draw substantial incomes. Similarly, the Penns and Calverts in Pennsylvania and Maryland and the early proprietors of New York, New Jersey, and the Carolinas speculated in lands in an imperial way. Later in the colonial period English and colonial speculators sought both title to and political control over great tracts in the Mississippi Valley. The land companies attracted some of the ablest colonial leaders into their ranks: George Washington, Richard Henry Lee, Benjamin Franklin, the Whartons, and George Croghan. The struggles of these rival companies for charters and grants played an important role in British colonial policy. Company rivalries were matched by the rival land claims of the colonies.

The largest purchase and most stupendous fraud was the sale in 1795 of 21.5 million acres in Yazoo River country by the legislature of Georgia to four companies for 1.5 cents an acre. The next legislature canceled the sale, but the purchasers, frequently innocent third parties, waged a long fight to secure justice, claiming that the obligation of the contract clause in the Constitution prevented the Georgia legislature from reversing the original sale. The Supreme Court, in *Fletcher v. Peck* (1810), agreed.

When the public domain of the United States was created by the donations of the states with western land claims, speculative interests converged upon Congress with requests to purchase tracts of land north of the Ohio. There were three great periods of land speculation: 1817–19, 1834–37, and 1853–57. Land companies again were organized. The New York and Boston Illinois Land Company acquired 900,000 acres in the Military Tract of Illinois; the American Land Company had estates in Indiana, Illinois, Michigan, Wisconsin, Mississippi, and Arkansas; and the Boston and Western Land Company owned 60,000 acres in Illinois and Wisconsin.

The land reform movement with its corollary limitation of land sales had as its objective the retention of the public lands for free homesteads for settlers. Beginning in 1841, sales were restricted to 160 or 320 acres by new land acts—such as the Pre-emption Act (1841), the Graduation Act (1854), the Homestead Act (1862), the Timber Culture Act (1873), and the Timber and Stone Act (1878). But the cash sale system was retained, although after 1862 very little new land was opened to unrestricted entry and large purchases could be made only in areas previously opened to sale. Although reformers had tolerated the granting of land to railroads in the 1850's and 1860's, they later turned against this practice and began a move to have forfeited the grants unearned by failure to build railroads. In 1888–91 Congress adopted the Land Forfeiture Act of 1890, which required return of unearned grants to the public domain, and enacted other measures to end the cash sale system, to limit the amount of land that an individual could acquire from the government to 320 acres, and to make it more difficult to abuse the settlement laws. However, through the use of dummy entrymen and the connivance of local land officers, land accumulation continued.

Speculation in urban property was not so well structured

as was speculation in rural lands, but it was widely indulged in and subject to the same excesses in periods of active industrial growth and to a similar drastic deflation in values following the economic crises of 1837, 1857, 1873, and 1930–33. During the boom years, prices for choice real estate in New York and other rapidly growing cities skyrocketed, only to decline during depressions. The best known speculator is John Jacob Astor. Between 1800 and 1840 Astor invested $2 million in land in Greenwich Village and elsewhere in Manhattan. By his death his rent roll alone was bringing in $200,000 annually. His estate, valued at from $18 million to $20 million, mostly invested in real estate that was rapidly appreciating, had made him the richest man in the country. In two successive generations the family fortune, still concentrated in Manhattan real estate, increased to $50 million and $100 million.

In every dynamically growing city, similar increases in land values have occurred. In Chicago, for example, lots on State Street between Monroe and Adams climbed from $25 per front foot in 1836 to $27,500 in 1931, a depression year. Each generation produced its new millionaires. Their spendthrift life-style aroused resentment, especially among the followers of Henry George. To tax the unearned increment in rising land values for the social good, George proposed a single tax on land so that the enhanced value of land that stemmed from society's growth would benefit the government directly. The United States did not accept Henry George's view, but it has increasingly sought to restrict property owners' rights by zoning regulations in both rural and urban areas. The law curbs the creation of subdivisions with numerous small sites for second homes.

LAND SURVEYING. *See* **Public Lands, Surveying of.**

LAND SYSTEM, NATIONAL. The American land system was established as an adaptation of European land systems. Two general land systems prevailed. In New England the holding was patterned after the farms of England and consisted of several separate pieces of land, altogether making a small unit. There was the home lot, usually in a village; a modest-size tract of arable land; a smaller piece of meadow; a wood lot; and a share in a common. In the South, the grants of land were generally, to a family, a few hundred acres, and not infrequently, to the influential, a few thousand acres. These tracts were surveyed privately, and the sites chosen by the grantee virtually at will. Through these liberal grants, the foundation was laid for the plantation system.

The basic system of the North was found suitable for settlers as they moved westward, but the complications characterizing the New England holding were done away with. Farms came to be of one piece, and the village idea was abandoned as fear of the Indians disappeared. For a long time the farms of the North were small because each family did most of its own work and, until about the middle of the 19th century, with comparatively little machinery.

The U.S. land system is adapted to individualistic, private ownership (*see* Land Titles), modified by the power of taxation and by zoning ordinances. Zoning embodies the right of the public to decide the use to which land shall be put.

LAND TENURE. Applies to both farm and urban property and the status of the occupant or farmer who holds it either temporarily or permanently. The two classes of people from the tenure standpoint are the owner, or landlord, and the tenant, or lessee. Outside New England, tenures were patterned most closely on models from the Old World. Lands were held in entail and passed by primogeniture, and they were subject to payment of quitrents. But even in those colonies in which large estates flourished, the abundance of land available for settlement and the increasing liberality in granting land to small owners weakened the old system. Many large estates disappeared in the American Revolution. In the Hudson River valley the only surviving Dutch manor—Rensselaerwyck—and some large English grants operated by tenants continued until the mid-19th century. In the antebellum South, tenancy was not common. In New England self-government, the nature of the land, and the nature of the inhabitants led to the establishment of small family farms and little tenancy.

After 1865 the freedmen had no alternative but to accept small (40-acre) allotments of land with a mule, plow, and means of subsistence from a landlord, not uncommonly their former owner, with whom they shared the crop. Since the landlord provided everything, he resorted to crop liens to protect his equity; state laws helped further to tie the sharecropper to the land in virtual peonage. The number of sharecroppers increased, until by 1930 they constituted 43 percent of the farmers of Mississippi, 38 percent of those of Georgia, and 31 percent of those of Arkansas. In the sixteen states of the South sharecroppers and cash tenants constituted 55 percent of the farm families, but in the principal cotton counties the number of tenant-operated farms ranged up to 94 percent.

In the upper Mississippi Valley, tenancy began to appear during the first generation of development. Contributing to the emergence of tenancy was the public land policy of permitting large speculative purchases, which made land more expensive to those who used it. Settlers had to begin their farm operations heavily in debt for the land itself just when they needed all their capital to erect their cabins, fence their cultivated land, purchase livestock and machinery, and carry themselves for a year or more until their farming began to pay. Tenancy data, first collected in 1880, showed that in the richest prairie counties of Indiana and Illinois, one-third to one-half of all farms were operated by tenants.

Technology and the crop control program combined with other government boons, particularly irrigation projects, to bring about a rapid increase in the average size of farms and to eliminate thousands of farm families from rural life. Tenancy declined from 42.4 percent in 1930 to 13 percent in 1978. The small-scale, part-time, or diversified farmer was being eliminated.

The United States has experimented with reserving the mineral rights from lands it was alienating. In 1862 and 1864 it retained ownership of all minerals other than coal and iron from lands thereafter granted to railroads. In Theodore Roosevelt's administration many millions of acres of public lands were withdrawn from all forms of entry, because they were suspected of containing valuable minerals. In 1910 and 1914 homesteading was allowed on these withdrawn lands, but subsurface rights were retained by the government.

Urban tenures did not escape this complexity, as witness the drilling for oil and gas in Oklahoma City and in Long Beach, Calif. Also, in larger cities owners of desirable business locations may lease the bare site at a "ground rent" for long periods, ranging from twenty to ninety-nine years. At the end of the leasing period, ground and buildings revert to the owner of the fee unless some provision is included in the contract for compensation for the improvements.

LAND TITLES. In the United States land titles are called "allodial" or "fee simple," which terms have come to be used synonymously. "Allodial" means free of rent or services demanded by some lord or other claimant, leaving the exclusive right to land, or real estate, in the hands of an owner, subject only to the demands of the state or a third party to which the right of eminent domain has been granted. "Fee simple," means free of any condition or limitation imposed respecting the exclusive right to real property, exclusive ownership limited only as noted in the definition of "allodial."

Titles are required to go back to grants made by the state, and, to be perfect, must show that at no time, no matter how remote, has any claim been left unsatisfied or unacknowledged. The title must start with a grant, or, in case of direct conveyance of title to an individual, with a patent. A patent is in every respect a deed, giving the recipient full fee-simple ownership. Where a grant, usually of a larger tract, is made to a company, such as a colonizing company or a railroad, the company comes into possession of the land in fee simple and can therefore sell, passing all rights on to the buyer. This type of title is found in all parts of the country that at any time belonged to the federal government as a part of the public domain. In the thirteen original states the land systems varied. The rulers of the 17th century granted land to colonies, to colonizing companies, and to individuals. The title came from the king to the colony, from the colony to a town or land company, and from the town or company to the individual.

In the case of settlement on land before it became U.S. territory, as with the Florida and Louisiana purchases and the Mexican cession, an agreement was made to the effect that bona fide settlers should be respected in their titles. In the Spanish territory of the Southwest grants were lavish and vague; the titles to these lands are now on a par with other titles of the country, they became such through court action (*see* Land Grants, Spanish and Mexican).

A feature of U.S. land titles is the requirement of a complete schedule of all transfers, called an abstract of title, showing all transfers from the beginning to date. The result has been in numerous cases that certain small tracts of land are not worth the cost of the abstracts. A way out of this difficulty is provided in the Torrens system, involving the registration of titles and a state guarantee of their validity.

***LANE* V. *OREGON*,** 4 Wallace 71 (1869). The U.S. Supreme Court ruled that the Legal Tender Act of 1862 could not interfere with state taxation. Under the Constitution the state government controls the problems pertaining to taxation. It was a victory for states' rights and strict construction.

LAND WARRANTS. Certificates issued to veterans of many of the colonial wars, and also of the early wars of the United States. A land warrant promised the veteran that he would receive a specified amount of public land from his colonial government, his state government, or the federal government. This was a sort of bonus for his services during the war. Land warrants were an ideal arrangement for a government because governments ordinarily had little cash and were anxious to encourage settlement on their frontiers where the public land was located. Connecticut and Virginia retained title to some lands in the Northwest Territory (in Ohio) as areas within which their Revolutionary War veterans might claim land. Land warrants were sometimes issued for other purposes; the state of Connecticut, for example, issued land warrants to people who had suffered from British raids during the revolutionary war.

LANGLEY AERONAUTICAL LABORATORY. In 1915, Congress established the National Advisory Committee for Aeronautics (NACA). This committee, containing unpaid members from various governmental and nongovernmental areas interested in aviation, was made responsible for aerodynamic research. The Langley Memorial Aeronautical Laboratory (renamed Langley Aeronautical Laboratory in 1948 and Langley Research Center in 1958) near Hampton, Va., opened on June 11, 1920.

The parent organization, NACA, published the research results in the form of technical reports, available to both military aviation branches and civilian aircraft companies. Also, laboratory personnel over the years designed and constructed many innovative research tools, the most important of which was a series of wind tunnels. These innovations significantly increased the safety of testing; radical design changes could be investigated without endangering the life of a test pilot. After World War II, Langley engineers played a major role in the U.S. space program and eventually became one of the many installations of the National Aeronautics and Space Administration.

LANSING (Mich.). Capital of Michigan, with a population of 130,414 in 1980; it was the center of a metropolitan area of 467,584. Lansing is an important commercial and industrial center. Several important motor factories are located there, and the city houses banking and insurance companies that service central Michigan.

Lansing was selected as the capital of the state in 1847. As capital, it attracted railroad service and grew rapidly after rail connections were completed in the 1870's.

LANSING-ISHII AGREEMENT (Nov. 2, 1917). Concluded by an exchange of notes between Robert Lansing, U.S. secretary of state, and Viscount Kikujiro Ishii, head of a Japanese special mission to the United States. Its purpose was to reconcile conflicting points in American and Japanese policy in the Far East as a measure of cooperation in World War I. (Japan also undertook to win from the United States what Ishii termed Japan's "paramount interest" in China. The secret protocol on China was not made public until 1935.) The men expressed the two governments' reaffirmation of the

Open Door policy and of the territorial integrity of China. Ambiguously, the notes included a statement of U.S. recognition that Japan had "special interests in China, particularly in the part to which her possessions are contiguous." Its ambiguity was recognized at the time of the Washington Conference of 1921–22, and on Mar. 30, 1923, a further exchange of notes declared that "in the light of the understanding arrived at by the Washington Conference," the correspondence between Lansing and Ishii was considered canceled.

LAOS, INTERVENTION IN (1954–74). In 1954 independent Laos was established with the partition of French Indochina. The government of Laos was to encompass all political factions, including the Communist Pathet Lao. By August 1956 the government of Laotian Prime Minister Souvanna Phouma had reached agreement with the Pathet Lao for a coalition government which America opposed. In an effort to change Laotian policy, the United States periodically suspended aid to the government and increasingly turned to covert intervention in Laotian political affairs. U.S. action was motivated by a commitment to the containment of Communism. Following Communist successes in the May 1958 elections, the United States began to aid various anti-Communist political groups. After 1958, the United States began to direct its support to right-wing elements within the Laotian army. When civil war began in September 1960, the United States channeled its aid to right-wing army leaders rather than to Souvanna Phouma. As a consequence he opened diplomatic relations with the Soviet Union and moved to bring the Pathet Lao into the government. American activity seemed to be undermining its policy goals, but President John F. Kennedy looked with some favor on the neutralization of Laos and relaxed pressure on Souvanna Phouma. In July 1962 the Pathet Lao, the rightists, and the neutralists agreed to a government of national union and a neutralist foreign policy. Unable to agree on military matters, the coalition broke up in April 1963. Souvanna then asked for, and received, U.S. help against the Pathet Lao.

Beginning in 1964, American policy in Laos was linked with events in Vietnam. U.S. intervention increased in degree and in kind through the training of Meo tribesmen for guerrilla activity, the introduction of Thai mercenaries, and the development of a clandestine army independent of the regular Laotian army. No U.S. ground combat troops were used in Laos, but for the next seven years the United States fought a secret war in Laos, supporting ground troops and bombing the Ho Chi Minh Trail and Communist positions in northern Laos. In February 1974 a new Laotian coalition government was formed. All foreign troops were ordered from Laos; as had been the case in 1956, the coalition included the Communists and favored a neutralist foreign policy. Following the final Communist victory in South Vietnam, the influence of Laotian neutralists and Communists increased. In the spring of 1975 they forced the withdrawal of the administrators of the American aid program and a further reduction in American influence in Laos.

LA POINTE, TREATY OF (Oct. 5, 1842). Provided for the cession by the Chippewa to the United States of the western half of the upper peninsula of Michigan and a large tract in northern Wisconsin, extending westward to Minnesota.

LAPWAI INDIAN COUNCIL. *See* **Nez Perce War.**

LAPWAI MISSION. Established in November 1836, by the Rev. and Mrs. Henry Harmon Spalding, co-workers of the physician-missionary Marcus Whitman, at a site eleven miles above Lewiston, Idaho, where the Lapwai Creek empties into the Clearwater River. In 1839 the mission secured a printing press from Hawaii and sent it to Lapwai, the first press in the Pacific Northwest. The mission was closed after the murder of Whitman and twelve of his companions by Indians in 1847. In 1871 the Presbyterian Church resumed the work.

LARAMIE, FORT. Established in June 1834, by fur traders William Sublette and Robert Campbell. The first structure, built of logs, was named Fort William. Located near the junction of the Laramie and North Platte rivers, it became the trade center for a large area. The American Fur Company purchased the fort in 1836. They replaced the log stockade with adobe walls in 1841 and christened the structure Fort John, but the name did not take; "Fort Laramie" supplanted it. Emigrants to Oregon used this fort, on the Oregon Trail, as a supply and refitting depot. The government purchased the post from the trading company in 1849 and converted it into a military fort. It became the great way station on the principal road to the Far West. The Grattan and the Harney incidents near the fort in 1854 and 1856 foreshadowed the Indian war that followed, and Fort Laramie became headquarters for the military campaigns. It was abandoned in 1890. In 1960 it became a national historic site.

LARAMIE, FORT, TREATY OF (1851). In 1849 Thomas Fitzpatrick, Indian agent to the tribes of the upper Platte and Arkansas, requested authorization and funds for a general treaty with his wards. In February 1851, Congress responded with a $100,000 appropriation. At a council for Sept. 1 at Fort Laramie in Wyoming, the Sioux, Cheyenne, Arapaho, and Shoshone gathered. After twenty days of negotiations a treaty was signed that provided for peace, for territorial boundaries for individual tribes, for a $50,000 annuity to the Indians, and for establishment of forts and roads in the Indian country. The treaty was never ratified by the Indians.

LARAMIE, FORT, TREATY OF (1868). In 1866 the Sioux had agreed to the opening of the Bozeman Trail to Montana. Before negotiations were completed, Col. Henry B. Carrington arrived with troops and began erection of forts on the new road. The Indians objected and war ensued (*see* Red Cloud's War). The government changed policy and in 1867 sent peace commissioners, but the Indians refused to negotiate while the forts remained. The commissioners came again in April 1868, acceded to Indian demands, and drafted a treaty. They agreed to withdraw the forts and to recognize the country north of the North Platte and east of the Big Horn Mountains in northern Wyoming as unceded Indian territory in which no whites might settle. All that part of present South Dakota west of the Missouri River was formed into a Sioux reservation.

LARNED, FORT. Established on the Pawnee fork of the Arkansas River, in Kansas, Oct. 22, 1859. It was named for Col. B. F. Larned, paymaster-general of the U.S. Army. Gen. W.S. Hancock used it as a base for his expedition against the Cheyenne in 1867, and troops operated from it in the Dull Knife campaign of 1878, the year it was abandoned.

LA SALLE, EXPLORATIONS OF. Robert Cavelier, Sieur de La Salle, came to Canada in 1666 and began near Montreal the development of a seigniory. Soon, he became absorbed in the possibilities inherent in the Indian trade. In 1674, Gov. Louis de Buade, Comte de Frontenac sent La Salle to France to enlighten Louis XIV concerning his expansionist designs. The king approved his plans, and La Salle returned with a patent of nobility for himself and the grant of Fort Frontenac as a seigniory. In 1677 La Salle again went to France to seek royal approval of a colony in the country south of the Great Lakes and a trade monopoly of the region to be developed and authority to build forts and govern it. The king approved all but the idea of colonizing, and in 1678 La Salle was back in New France making preparations for the actual invasion of the West, to be launched the following season. A small vessel, the *Griffon,* was built above Niagara, and in August 1679, La Salle set sail for Green Bay. From there the *Griffon* was sent back to Niagara while La Salle journeyed southward by canoe around Lake Michigan to the mouth of the St. Joseph River. There he tarried until December, building Fort Miami and awaiting the return of the *Griffon,* which had vanished. He ascended the St. Joseph to South Bend, Ind., where he crossed to the Kankakee and descended that stream and the Illinois to Lake Peoria, where he built Fort Crèvecoeur and a vessel in which to descend the Mississippi. He also dispatched Franciscan missionary Louis Hennepin and two companions to explore the upper Mississippi, while he set out in midwinter for Fort Frontenac to procure supplies.

In 1681, La Salle was at Fort Miami ready to renew his push for the sea. Descending the Illinois, he reached the Mississippi on Feb. 2, 1682, and on Apr. 9 was at the Gulf of Mexico, where he formally claimed the entire Mississippi Valley for his king and named it Louisiana. The realization of his plans seemed assured, when Frontenac was replaced by a bitter enemy of La Salle. Facing utter ruin, La Salle went to France to appeal to his monarch in person. His requests were approved, and in 1684 he sailed for the Gulf of Mexico, equipped with men and means to establish a post on the lower Mississippi to serve as the southern outlet of his colony. He was unable to find the river's mouth, and the colonists were landed on the coast of Texas, where most of them perished (*see* St. Louis of Texas; La Salle, Spanish Searches for). La Salle was murdered by mutineers in 1687.

LA SALLE, SPANISH SEARCHES FOR. The alarm felt by the Spaniards over La Salle's intrusion in the Gulf of Mexico was revealed by the intensity of their search for his colony. Between 1685 and 1688 five maritime expeditions combed the Gulf coast, but failed to find the French settlement in Texas. By land, one expedition searched westward from Florida; four expeditions, led by Alonso De Leon, went northeastward from Mexico; and a number of minor searches were instituted by provincial officials. On his fourth expedition De Leon, in 1689, found the remains of La Salle's colony, three months after it had been destroyed by Indians.

LAS ANIMAS LAND GRANT. On Dec. 9, 1843, the Mexican government granted to Cornelio Vigil and Ceran Saint Vrain a tract of 4 million acres lying southwesterly from the Arkansas River to the Sangre de Cristo Mountains with the valleys of the Huerfano and the Purgatoire (Animas) rivers as side lines. On June 21, 1860, Congress confirmed only 97,651 acres of this grant on the ground that a grant of more than eleven square leagues to one individual was illegal under Mexican law. Dissatisfied claimants appealed unsuccessfully to a special court of private land claims from 1891 until 1904 and finally to the U.S. Supreme Court.

LASSEN'S TRADING POST AND RANCH. Near the mouth of Deer Creek in northeastern California, at the head of Sacramento Valley, it was an important center both in early exploration and in the gold rush. It was named after Peter Lassen, an early pioneer. John Charles Frémont was using the ranch as headquarters for exploring the region when war was declared against Mexico in May 1846.

LAST ISLAND CATASTROPHE (Aug. 10, 1856). Last Island, in the Gulf of Mexico opposite the mouth of Bayou Lafourche, which had become a summer resort, was devastated by a tropical hurricane. More than 100 persons perished.

LAS VEGAS (Nev.). The population of Las Vegas, the largest city in Nevada, was 164,674 in 1980; its metropolitan area included 462,218 people, more than half the total population of the state. Las Vegas began its history in 1905 and remained a rather small desert town until the end of World War II. Las Vegas is home to a large number of gambling casinos, luxurious hotels, and restaurants. The nearby Lake Mead National Recreation Area provides fishing, boating, and swimming. Hoover Dam, which created the lake, provides ready electric power for Las Vegas business concerns.

LATIN AMERICA, U.S. RELATIONS WITH. With the Latin-American wars for independence in 1810, leaders of the newly formed governments sought U.S. support. President James Madison issued a neutrality proclamation on Sept. 1, 1815, that had the effect of conceding belligerency rights to the rebellious colonies. The first nation accorded diplomatic recognition by the United States was Colombia in June 1822, and similar action was soon taken with respect to Mexico, the Federation of Central America, Brazil, Chile, the United Provinces of La Plata, and Peru. U.S. opposition to any effort on the part of European powers to reestablish colonial rule was articulated in the Monroe Doctrine in 1823, and the concept was gradually extended to signify that the American government viewed the entire Western Hemisphere as an area of special concern.

Early efforts to initiate general discourse between the American republics came to naught. Simón Bolívar convened a conference at Panama in 1826, but U.S. delegates did not arrive and resolutions adopted by delegates of the four participating states were never ratified. Soon U.S. relationships with Latin America focused on issues deriving from national expansion across North America and establishment of American hegemony in the Caribbean. War with Mexico in 1846–48 ended with that country ceding its extensive northern territories to the United States, and gestures were made toward the annexation of Cuba and the Dominican Republic. A diplomatic conflict with Great Britain over control of a canal route across the Central American isthmus resulted in British withdrawal from a dominant role in the Caribbean and cleared the way for the United States to construct a canal at Panama. The preeminence of the United States in the Caribbean was firmly established by the Spanish-American War in 1898–99, which concluded with the annexation of Puerto Rico and the creation of a protectorate over Cuba.

North American investments and trade became important in Mexico and Cuba in the late 19th century, but commercial relationships with the rest of Latin America remained of minor importance. The first important step toward closer relations with the Latin-American republics was initiated by Secretary of State James G. Blaine. In 1889 Blaine presided over the First International Conference of American States convened in Washington, D.C., by invitation of the United States. The only lasting result of the conference was the creation in Washington of a Commercial Bureau of American Republics, which later became the Pan American Union.

Subsequent inter-American conferences at Mexico City in 1901–02, Rio de Janeiro in 1906, and Buenos Aires in 1910 accomplished little. A growing hostility toward the American government was manifest as early as the second conference, reflecting in part a strong resentment of its increasingly interventionist role in the Caribbean area. Although the Pan American Union was created by the Buenos Aires meeting, the location of its headquarters in Washington and the chairing of its governing board by the U.S. secretary of state suggested that Pan-Americanism was designed to further American commercial and political interests.

Once the American government decided to build the Panama Canal, security of the waterway made it imperative that states in the vicinity not be permitted to fall under the domination of a potentially hostile power. In accordance with Theodore Roosevelt's corollary to the Monroe Doctrine, the United States undertook to eliminate political disorder and financial mismanagement in states whose internal difficulties exposed them to European intervention. The American government sent military forces into Cuba frequently, into Haiti in 1915, into the Dominican Republic in 1916, and into Nicaragua in 1912 and in 1926–27. In 1914 and in 1916 the United States intervened militarily in Mexico. These actions created fear and distrust of American intentions.

World War I brought about improved political relationships as well as a marked increase in commercial activity. North American capital discovered new opportunities in Central and South American mines, railroads, and public utilities, and the pace of investment quickened during the 1920's. A number of governments borrowed heavily from American banks to undertake public improvements. But the sixth inter-American meeting, held at Havana in 1928, unleashed a wave of acrimonious attack on American policies, particularly its intervention in Nicaragua.

U.S. policy began to change during the administration of President Herbert Hoover, and he withdrew the remaining marines from Nicaragua in 1933. He also took steps to end the American military presence in Haiti, which had continued since the 1915 intervention. President Franklin D. Roosevelt specifically repudiated intervention, announcing instead the Good Neighbor policy. Secretary of State Cordell Hull, at the seventh inter-American conference in Montevideo in 1933, signed a convention that forbade intervention by any state in the external or internal affairs of another. Subsequently, the United States terminated its military protectorates over Cuba and Panama. Latin-American relations improved, and at a special conference at Buenos Aires in 1936 and the eighth inter-American conference at Lima in 1938 a far more cordial atmosphere prevailed.

When World War II broke out in Europe, the foreign ministers of the American republics held meetings to formulate hemispheric defense policy. A meeting at Rio de Janeiro in January 1942 recommended that the American governments break off diplomatic relations with the Axis powers. All did so promptly except Chile and Argentina. Eventually, both countries took the recommended step, but Argentina was ruled by a pro-Axis government and the rupture of relations constituted a meaningless gesture. In contrast, Brazil sent an expeditionary force to join in the Italian campaign, and Mexico sent an air squadron to the Pacific theater.

Plans for strengthening the inter-American system were formulated at a conference held at Mexico City in 1945. These resulted in the Inter-American Treaty of Reciprocal Assistance signed at Rio de Janeiro in 1947 and in the creation of the Organization of American States (OAS) at the ninth inter-American conference at Bogotá in 1948. With a left-leaning government in power in Guatemala, the tenth inter-American conference at Caracas in 1954 devoted much of its attention to the efforts of the American government to secure approval of a resolution supporting collective action against any Communist threat. Secretary of State John Foster Dulles was successful, but only after bitter exchanges with the Guatemalan representative, with whom many sympathized, and the conference adjourned under a cloud of renewed resentment against the United States. No subsequent inter-American conference was held. In 1967 an extraordinary conference of the OAS in Buenos Aires approved a reform protocol, which modified the charter to substitute an annual general assembly for the inter-American conference.

The leftist Guatemalan government was shortly overthrown by revolution, but with the emergence of a Communist regime in Cuba after Fidel Castro's overthrow of Fulgencio Batista in 1959 and the Soviet Union's subsequent support of Castro, the Communist threat became a reality.

Having broken relations with Cuba, the American government supported an abortive invasion by counterrevolutionary forces in April 1961, which further undercut Latin-American sympathy for the U.S. position. Only during and after the Soviet effort to install long-range nuclear missiles in Cuba in October 1962 was anything approaching a united front achieved. Before ordering the successful interdiction of weapons delivery on Oct. 23, President John F. Kennedy obtained from the OAS council a resolution demanding Soviet withdrawal from Cuba of all weapons with offensive capability. Subsequently, all Latin-American countries with the exception of Mexico broke relations with the Castro regime.

The United States intervened militarily in the Dominican Republic in April 1965 to prevent a Communist takeover, and OAS support for the action was sought and obtained only after initiation of the invasion. Adverse reaction throughout Latin America was eased by the subsequent arrival of Brazilian military forces, as well as token troops from Costa Rica, Nicaragua, and Honduras, and the placing of a Brazilian general in charge of the "peacekeeping" force. Withdrawal took place after a new election in 1966.

In 1970 a Socialist-Communist government was elected in Chile, and it moved rapidly to expropriate the properties of American companies. A new Cuba-type crisis was avoided by the Chilean government's continued adherence to constitutional form and by moderation on the part of the United States. The almost complete solidarity in the isolation of Cuba was soon broken by Chile's reestablishment of full relations with Castro's government, and in mid-1972 Peru followed Chile's example. By early 1973 even the American position appeared to be softening when an agreement between Cuba and the United States to curtail aircraft hijacking was arranged through intermediaries. Country after country reopened embassies in Havana.

In September 1973 the Chilean armed forces overthrew the Marxist government of President Salvador Allende, who allegedly committed suicide. Congressional inquiries in the United States subsequently brought to light U.S. Central Intelligence Agency involvement in financing anti-Communist groups in Chile both prior to and during Allende's rule. The revelation did little to improve the U.S. image in the region.

Both the Nixon administration and that of President Gerald Ford were criticized by many Latin-American leaders as neglectful of their countries' interests. During President Jimmy Carter's administration the U.S.–Latin-American relations improved, partially because of Carter's stress on human rights and the new Panama Canal treaties (ratified in 1978), which stipulated for a gradual takeover of the canal by Panama. Even relations with Cuba became more friendly, and a liaison office was established in 1977. But as the 1970's were ending, turmoil in Central America provoked new antagonism. Deeply upset about the socialist Sandinist rule in Nicaragua (installed after the overthrow of the Somoza government in 1979) and the civil war in El Salvador, the administration of President Ronald Reagan irritated several Latin-American countries with its rhetoric about the Communist takeover of Central America.

The American government's program to extend technical aid and economic assistance to the less-developed countries of the world after World War II aroused hopes in Latin America of rapid economic and social progress. Technical and military assistance was provided, but the administration of Dwight D. Eisenhower made clear to Latin-American governments that they would have to look to private American capital to finance their industrialization programs. The relatively modest aid program the United States did offer to Latin America seemed to favor pro-American dictatorships rather than countries seeking to couple economic and social development with structural reforms and popular democracy.

The Inter-American Development Bank was launched in 1959, with the United States contributing a significant part of the capital. This move was followed in March 1961 by President Kennedy's proposal for the Alliance for Progress, the charter of which was approved at Punta del Este, Uruguay, in August of that year. The alliance involved a massive effort to combine national development planning with basic social, educational, land-tenure, and taxation reforms. In spite of an auspicious beginning and some significant successes, the goals of the alliance proved far more difficult to achieve than its creators had anticipated. Government instability, resistance to social and economic reforms, financing below promised levels by the United States, and vacillation in American aid policy all served to impede progress and to create disillusionment. A meeting of presidents of the participating countries at Punta del Este in 1967 sought to revive waning enthusiasm; but President Lyndon B. Johnson spoke without the support of Congress, and his colleagues knew it. The Nixon administration showed no inclination to revive the moribund Alliance for Progress.

The Good Neighbor policy, the emergence of the United States as a world power after World War II, and the Alliance for Progress each contributed to a gradual, but increasingly significant, political, economic, and cultural orientation of Latin America toward the United States. Thousands of Latin-American students choose to pursue their education in the United States rather than Europe, and business and commercial ties have grown steadily closer. On the other hand, opposition to the American government's policies has also increased, stemming in part from a fear of American economic power and military interventionism and, rather paradoxically, from a sense of neglect and the relatively low priority accorded Latin America in American international concerns. A growing sense of national power and cultural autonomy has come to infuse the outlook of such countries as Brazil, Mexico, and Argentina. By the early 1980's new centers of power were emerging that could not fail to alter old relationships.

LATIN-AMERICAN REPUBLICS, RECOGNITION OF. Both the government of the United States and public opinion were openly sympathetic to the cause of Latin-American independence from Spain in the early years of the 19th century. In 1810, during President James Madison's administration, Joel Poinsett was sent to Buenos Aires and Chile to promote commercial relations with the colonies and to express the friendly feeling of the United States. Other agents and consuls were sent in the following years. Officially the United States was neutral in the war, but private citizens engaged in filibustering and many Latin-American privateers were fitted out in

American ports despite official opposition.

The uncertain character of the struggle postponed for some years any serious consideration of diplomatic recognition. In 1817, three commissioners were sent to Buenos Aires to investigate the propriety of entering into relations with the government there, but no action was taken. Later in the same year Rep. Henry Clay began to advocate recognition in Congress. In 1821 he procured the passage of a resolution in the House of Representatives expressing sympathy with Latin America and a readiness to support the president when he felt that the time for recognition had come. Meanwhile Monroe and John Quincy Adams, his secretary of state, had proceeded cautiously, though the president had spoken sympathetically of the Latin-American cause in his message to Congress in 1819. The treaty with Spain for the purchase of Florida, signed Feb. 22, 1819 (*see* Adams-Onís Treaty), was still pending, and the administration did not wish to offend Spain until the exchange of ratifications on Feb. 22, 1821. By that time the patriots in South America had won important victories, and in the same year Mexico proclaimed its independence. Spanish forces still held the greater part of Peru, but the revolution in Spain had made their situation difficult.

On Mar. 8, 1822, Monroe recommended that the Latin-American republics be recognized. A bill authorizing diplomatic missions to them was signed by the president on May 4, and on June 19 Manuel Torres was received by the president as chargé d'affaires from Colombia. In the following months the United States also entered into diplomatic relations with Argentina, Chile, Mexico, Brazil, and Central America.

LATIN SCHOOLS. The earliest educational institutions set up in the American colonies, they grew out of the influence of the Renaissance and were patterned on the Latin schools of England. They appeared in all the colonies except Georgia, but reached their greatest growth in New England. The first successful attempt to establish a Latin school was made in Boston in 1635; it was the principal school in that city for nearly a half century. Latin schools were planned, supported, and managed by the well-to-do. Tuition fees were generally charged, and the curriculum was confined almost entirely to a study of Latin, Greek, religion, and mathematics. The Latin schools had begun to decline in importance by the mid-18th century, when they began to give way to the academies.

LATITUDINARIANS. A school of thought in the Church of England in the 18th century that emphasized the fundamental principles of the Christian religion rather than any specific doctrinal position. In America the name has been given to those who have not been primarily concerned about the interpretation of a creed and have been liberal in their judgments of those who hold other than standard views.

LATROBE'S FOLLY. The Thomas Viaduct, the Baltimore and Ohio Railroad's stone arch bridge over the Patapsco River, near Relay, Md., designed by and constructed under the direction of Benjamin H. Latrobe, Jr., in 1832. His engineering contemporaries insisted that the bridge could not be built, that it would not stand up under its own weight, let alone the weight of the 6-ton locomotives then in service, with their trains. But the viaduct was a complete success to the extent that a century after its construction 300-ton engines were passing over it in safety.

LATTER-DAY SAINTS, CHURCH OF JESUS CHRIST OF (known as Mormons)**.** The Mormons are members of a religious movement that originated in western New York during the Second Great Awakening. The church was founded in 1830 by Joseph Smith, who claimed to have discovered and translated the Book of Mormon on the basis of visions from heaven. After his work was finished, Smith maintained that the golden plates on which the message had been written were taken away into heaven. The Book of Mormon purports to be the history of certain of the lost tribes of Israel that fled to America after the conquest of their homeland. After Christ's Resurrection, these tribes were visited by Him and lived as Christians until, after a series of disasters and wars, they either lost the faith or were destroyed.

After the publication of Smith's initial revelation, the Mormons moved in 1831 to Kirtland, Ohio, where Smith hoped to found an ideal community. Unfortunately, the movement rested its fortunes on a shaky, and possibly illegal, bank that collapsed during the panic of 1837. Some Mormons fled to Missouri, where they quickly became unpopular with the "gentile" (non-Mormon) population. They next attempted to establish their ideal community in Nauvoo, Ill., a new city said to have been planned by Smith. By 1843, it was the largest town in the state. It was during this time that Smith received the revelations that separated Mormonism from other frontier evangelical movements. The most important was Smith's vision of the Temple and his elaboration of its sacerdotal system, which bears some relationship to Masonic rites. Smith taught that there was more than one God, that Christ was a separate deity, that the goods and relationships of this life would continue in the next, and that polygamy conformed to the will of God. The rumor that the community was ready to implement this latter revelation, plus gentile resentment of the community's political power, provoked the attack that carried Smith prisoner to Carthage, Ill. He was murdered there on June 27, 1844.

The death of the prophet caused a crisis, but Brigham Young (1801–77), Smith's second in command and *de facto* leader of the group, led the survivors across the Great Plains to form the state of Deseret in the valley of the Great Salt Lake. Here the Mormons were able to build their Zion. Tightly organized by Young, they built an island of prosperity that virtually became an independent nation. After the Mexican War, the Mormons were forced to abjure polygamy and admit non-Mormons to the territory.

In the 1970's the Mormons were one of the fastest-growing religious groups in the United States, with every Mormon male being obligated to spend at least two years as a missionary. Their influence remains worldwide, and they have churches throughout Europe. There were four Mormon denominations in 1978: Church of Jesus Christ of Latter-Day Saints, the main body, with a U.S. membership of 2,592,000; Reorganized Church of Jesus Christ of Latter-Day Saints, 185,636 members; Church of Jesus Christ (Bickertonites), 2,551 members; and Church of Christ, 2,400 members.

LAUD COMMISSION (Commission for Foreign Plantations). Established as a subdivision of the Privy Council in April 1634 to supervise the American colonies. Despite its broad powers, the commission, named after its chairman, the Anglican primate William Laud, accomplished little. Most supervisory activities continued to be carried on by special Privy Council committees or other outside groups. In 1641 the Commission was abolished by the Long Parliament.

LAURENS, FORT. On the Tuscarawas River, in northeastern Ohio, erected in 1778 by Gen. Lachlan McIntosh, to serve as an advance base for an expedition against Detroit. Hostile Indians harassed it in the fall of 1778. The next spring a seige by Indians under a British officer was raised only by a relief expedition. Soon thereafter, when Col. Daniel Brodhead succeeded McIntosh in the West, Fort Laurens was abandoned.

LAUSANNE AGREEMENT (1932). At a conference of the European allies of World War I at Lausanne, Switzerland, in 1932, the creditors of Germany for reparations under the Treaty of Versailles effected the last write-off of the staggering total originally imposed on the defeated enemy. They conditionally canceled nine-tenths of the obligations still surviving under the Young Plan and lumped the total due into one easily supportable bonded indebtedness of $750 million bearing 5 percent interest, to be redeemed at the rate of 1 percent per annum, plus service on the international loans to Germany previously made under the Dawes Plan and Young Plan. The signatories made the Lausanne Agreement dependent on cancellation of their debts to the United States. The U.S. government never accepted the arrangement.

LA VÉRENDRYE EXPLORATIONS. In 1728 Pierre Gaultier de Varennes, Sieur de La Vérendrye, was stationed by the French government of Canada at a small outpost on Lake Nipigon, thirty-five miles north of Lake Superior. There he heard from the Indians of a river flowing west into a salt sea. He conceived the idea of an overland commerce between Lake Superior and the Pacific Ocean to bring the goods of the Far East to France by way of Montreal. Obtaining a trade monopoly in this vast territory, he established a line of posts westward from Lake Superior to Lake-of-the-Woods and Lake Winnipeg, and up the Red and Assiniboine rivers. On the latter stream he built Fort La Reine, now Portage la Prairie. In 1738, in search of the westward-flowing river, he led a party south from this point to Star Mound in Canada. In 1742 La Vérendrye sent his two sons from Fort La Reine across the Missouri River at Old Crossing. From the account in their journal, the party traveled west and southwest until they came within sight of the Big Horn Mountains, west of the Black Hills. Here, on the banks of the North Platte River (erroneously called by their guides the Missouri), they buried a lead plate inscribed with the date and the names of three of the party (*see* La Vérendrye Plate).

LA VÉRENDRYE PLATE. A sheet of lead, 7 inches by 8 inches, buried upon the hill at the junction of the Bad and Missouri rivers in Fort Pierre, S.Dak., Mar. 30, 1743, by the sons of Pierre Gaultier de Varennes, Sieur de La Vérendrye, to certify the French claim to the upper Missouri Valley. It was recovered on Feb. 17, 1913. It is now in possession of the South Dakota Historical Society, Pierre.

***LAWRENCE*.** A twenty-gun brig built by Capt. Oliver Hazard Perry at Erie, N.Y., in 1813, and his flagship at the Battle of Lake Erie. In July 1815 it was sunk as useless, but it was raised in 1875 and exhibited at the Centennial Exhibition until accidentally destroyed by fire.

LAWRENCE, SACK OF (May 21, 1856). The beginning of actual civil war in the Kansas conflict (*see* Border War). A proslavery grand jury had indicted several free-state leaders for treason and had started legal action against the New England Emigrant Aid Company's Free-State Hotel, believed to have been built as a fort, and the newspapers *Herald of Freedom* and *Free State* as nuisances. A U.S. marshal appeared before the village with a posse of 700–800 men to serve the warrants. Having made his arrests unopposed, he relinquished his posse to the proslavery sheriff, S. J. Jones. Led by Jones and former Sen. David R. Atchison of Missouri, the mob burned the hotel and wrecked the newspaper offices. News of the sack aroused the entire North, led to the formation of the National Kansas Committee, and provided the Republican party with the issue of "Bleeding Kansas."

LAWRENCE RADIATION LABORATORY. On the Berkeley campus of the University of California, named in honor of its first director, Ernest O. Lawrence. In the early 1930's several nuclear particle accelerators were devised, none more successful than Lawrence's cyclotron. His first few machines were small, just a few inches in diameter; the largest component was the electromagnet needed to turn the particles in their circular paths. When toward the end of 1931 Lawrence retrieved from an unused radio transmitter a 75-ton magnet whose 27-inch-diameter pole faces determined the size of the next cyclotron, he installed it in an old frame warehouse near the Berkeley physics building. This structure he christened the Radiation Laboratory, a name made official in 1936, when the university's regents designated it a separate unit of the physics department. Upon Lawrence's death in 1958, the name was changed to the Lawrence Radiation Laboratory and later to the Lawrence Berkeley Laboratory.

During the 1930's the laboratory's primary activity was the study of nuclear reactions. Lawrence's brother, John, initiated biological investigations in 1935; and other important work in nuclear chemistry, engineering, detection and recording, linear acceleration, and other fields was performed. This wide-ranging experimental activity at the Radiation Laboratory was a major factor in raising American science to a position of world eminence. Work on a 184-inch cyclotron was interrupted by World War II, during which much of the laboratory's efforts were devoted to problems involving construction of the first atomic bombs. The first two elements heavier than uranium, neptunium and plutonium, were produced there in the early 1940's. By the end of 1946, the 184-inch machine, called a synchrocyclotron, was completed. In the next generation of much larger particle accelerators was the proton synchrotron, completed in 1954, with which antiparticles, such as the antiproton, were discovered.

Prior to World War II, funding for such research came from university and private foundation sources. Since 1942, support has come from the federal government, mostly via the Atomic Energy Commission. As part of the University of California, faculty and graduate students conduct research in the laboratory.

LAWRENCE RAID. *See* **Quantrill's Raid.**

LAWRENCE SCIENTIFIC SCHOOL. Established at Harvard University in 1847 by a gift of $50,000 from industrialist Abbott Lawrence, who wished to support applied science in eastern Massachusetts. The school existed until 1906 but enjoyed only mixed success, since Harvard presidents Edward Everett and Charles W. Eliot did not favor applied subjects in their liberal arts university. Everett thought the school would be a means for bringing a German university to Cambridge and from the start tried to direct the school into advanced studies of pure science. His first move was to get Eben N. Horsford, one of Justus von Liebig's best American students, to teach pure and applied chemistry. His second move was to appoint Louis Agassiz, the Swiss naturalist, to teach zoology and geology rather than the mining engineering Lawrence would have preferred. The school was most popular as an engineering school under Henry L. Eustis.

The school had an uneven history. It had only modest enrollments in the 1850's and went into a decline in the 1860's from which it did not recover until the late 1880's. Since it was unable to compete with the Sheffield Scientific School at Yale and the Massachusetts Institute of Technology (MIT), then in Boston, Eliot tried repeatedly to transfer its programs to MIT. After several such attempts failed, Nathaniel S. Shaler, a Lawrence alumnus and Agassiz's successor on the faculty, became dean in 1891 and devoted himself to building up the school. Despite his success (the enrollment reached 584 in 1902, an all-time high) and a 1903 bequest of approximately $30 million from shoe manufacturer Gordon McKay, Eliot tried another merger with MIT in 1904. To protect the new endowment and to preserve a place for applied science at Harvard, Shaler agreed in 1906 to dissolve the Lawrence Scientific School and send its remaining undergraduate programs to Harvard College in return for a new Graduate School of Applied Science, which survives.

LAWRENCE STRIKE (1912). Textile workers in Lawrence, Mass., struck against a wage cut that employers alleged was necessitated by legislation curtailing working hours, from Jan. 11 to Mar. 14, 1912. Perhaps its most sensational feature was the success of the Industrial Workers of the World (IWW) in organizing the mill workers into a militant cooperative body. The IWW had until then been a minor factor in eastern labor disputes, and its appearance in New England created widespread perturbation. The strike involved lawless practices common in American industrial warfare but resulted in increased wage scales.

LAW SCHOOLS. Until after the Civil War, lawyers were trained by apprenticeship. Some Americans went to London to study at the Inns of Court, but their training, too, was chiefly by apprenticeship. The best known of the first U.S. law schools was the Litchfield School in Connecticut (1784–1833). By the 19th century there were a dozen schools, in all of which study was heavily based on Sir William Blackstone's *Commentaries on the Laws of England.* The first law professor was George Wythe, Thomas Jefferson's teacher, appointed at William and Mary in 1779. For prestige and the power to grant degrees, some law schools attached themselves loosely to colleges, as was the case at Harvard in 1817 and at Yale in 1824; by 1840, the nine university-affiliated law schools had a total enrollment of 345, about half of them at Harvard.

By 1860 there were twenty-one law schools. Although Columbia had great influence after Theordore W. Dwight came there in 1858, it was overshadowed by Harvard, especially after Christopher Columbus Langdell became dean in 1870. Langdell introduced the case and the Socratic methods of study, the pattern for many schools. In 1899 Harvard made law a three-year course of study; it took ten more years before law became a graduate course of study. Harvard pioneered with strict entrance requirements and rigorous examinations. These reforms greatly influenced law schools generally.

But criticism was widespread, too: the case method was repetitive; while the case book was useful to teach the common law, it was not as useful for teaching statutory law; only the exceptional student participated in the Socratic debate; the case method encouraged a large ratio of students per professor and, so, fed the profit motive; the schools neglected legal history, clinical experience, systematic study, and scholarship; there was more to the law than could be learned from a study of appellate court opinions.

Columbia in the 1920's introduced functionally organized courses in legal economics and trade regulation, but the experiment failed, in part because law teachers believed that law schools should be devoted to teaching for the profession rather than to research. In the 1930's Yale was dominated by a spirit of legal skepticism and by the idea that law should be used for social engineering. In 1937 Chicago offered the option of a four-year curriculum, with courses in economics, accounting, ethics, psychology, English constitutional history, and political theory, but this course of study was dropped in 1949; Minnesota had a similar option, which it discontinued in 1958. Yale in 1933 offered a program combined with the Harvard School of Business Administration, but this was dropped in 1938 because of lack of enrollment.

A tendency developed to replace the pure case books with books called "Cases and Other Materials"; and electives were added to allow seminars. In the 1960's and 1970's more teaching was offered in the public-law area—administrative law, labor law, tax law, poverty law, law and medicine, law and science and technology, civil rights, civil liberties, law and society, housing and planning law, consumer rights, and social legislation. Courses oriented toward problems rather than cases were introduced. Clinical legal education was started in the 1940's, and interest in such work was intensified in the 1960's and 1970's.

The American Bar Association (ABA), founded in 1878, almost from its beginning showed an interest in legal education. In 1900 the Association of American Law Schools (AALS) was established for the purpose of setting standards for its institutional members. These organizations represented only the elite of the law profession; real power rested in the state legislatures and courts. Accordingly, many night, part-time, and even proprietary schools were allowed to develop; their clientele were the disadvantaged groups, including the recent immigrants and their children. The ABA and the AALS were generally hostile to these schools, but the legislatures were not eager to destroy them. What the ABA and the AALS could not accomplish was accomplished by the Great Depression and the World War II selective-service draft. In 1935 there were 127 unapproved schools, but by 1947 there were only 47. In 1972 there were 28 unapproved law schools, 18 of them in California.

In the 1960's law school enrollment went up sharply; by 1978 it reached 220,000. In 1979, 25,180 men and 10,026 women received law degrees at 175 institutions. The fall of 1973 was the first time that there was not a single unfilled seat in the entering class of an approved law school. Law schools have almost completely pushed out study by apprenticeship. In the late 1970's, only three states still permitted qualification by apprenticeship study.

LAWS, CONCESSIONS AND AGREEMENTS. *See* **West Jersey Concessions.**

LEAD INDUSTRY. In 1750, sustained lead mining and smelting began in Dutchess County, N.Y., and at the Austinville mine in Virginia. The demand for lead bullets and shot in the revolutionary war prompted the working of small deposits in Massachusetts, Connecticut, Maryland, Pennsylvania, and North Carolina. French trappers discovered lead in the upper Mississippi Valley about 1690, and by 1763 the district near Galena, Ill., had become a regular producer of lead. The French-Canadian Julien Dubuque operated lead mines and furnaces in Iowa, Wisconsin, and Illinois from the 1770's until his death in 1810. The Fox and Sauk Indian tribes continued to mine and smelt the ore until the 1820's, when they were largely dispossessed.

In 1797 Moses Austin migrated to southeast Missouri, where lead had been mined sporadically at Mine La Motte and other mines by early French explorers since about 1724. Austin set up a large furnace and shot tower on the Mississippi River in 1798 and by 1819 was producing 3 million pounds of lead per year.

Peter Lorimier built a Scotch hearth in 1834 near Dubuque, Iowa; this new technology greatly lowered production costs through improved productivity. Development of the lead region from Galena into southern Wisconsin and Dubuque proceeded rapidly, so that by 1845 the district produced 54,495,000 pounds of lead.

From 1845 until the 1860's, domestic lead production continued to be primarily from shallow galena (lead sulfide) workings in three districts: Austinville, Wisconsin-Illinois-Iowa, and southeast Missouri. Throughout the Civil War all these areas were largely controlled by the Confederacy, so that the Union had to rely on the melting of lead gutters, pewter housewares, and lead pipe and on purchase from foreign sources. In 1863 lead associated with silver was discovered in Little Cottonwood Canyon in Utah. Completion of the transcontinental railroad in 1869 gave the needed impetus to the growth of the intermountain lead-silver industry, including several smelters in Montana, Idaho, Utah, Nevada, California, and Colorado. Rich silver-lead ore was discovered at Leadville, Colo., in 1876, and for a time this was the world's largest lead-producing area. The large high-grade ore body found at Bunker Hill, Idaho, in 1885 was the basis for the development of the Coeur d'Alene as an important lead-silver-zinc producing area.

In 1869 the first diamond drill to be used in the United States was brought into the southeast Missouri district from France, and deeper, horizontally bedded deposits of lead ore were located at depths of 120 feet and more, with thicknesses of up to 500 feet. This area of nearly pure lead ore became one of the largest in the world. In 1872 the railway from St. Louis to Joplin, Mo., in the vicinity of which new ore bodies had been discovered, was completed, and the zinc-lead mining activity began to accelerate. About 1895, natural-gas discoveries were made in the Kansas and Oklahoma part of the Joplin, or tristate, district, providing cheap fuel for zinc smelting and further stimulating mining activities. Since lead was a coproduct of zinc in the ore, lead production was also augmented and several smelters were constructed in the vicinity of St. Louis.

The lead blast furnace first came into use in the United States in the late 1860's. With new concentrating methods of tabling, jigging, and doing selective flotation, the fine grinding of the ore required to permit upgrading produced unsuitable feed material for the smelters. Adoption of a new technique —sintering (desulfurizing and agglomerating) the fine ore concentrate, then reducing it to lead bullion in a blast furnace —again gave the industry an economic boost. Requiring greater amounts of capital, the new technologies brought consolidation into a few large companies within the industry around the turn of the century.

Having provided the lead needs of the nation during the first half of the 20th century, the older mining districts gradually became depleted, so that a new find was most welcome. Such was the case with the discovery of a "New Lead Belt" (some 50 miles from the Old Lead Belt) called the Viburnum Trend in southeast Missouri during the late 1950's. As the mines came into full production, Missouri lead output more than tripled, approaching a half million tons, or 80 percent of the total U.S. production in the late 1970's.

Large-scale peacetime reuse of lead became significant in

the United States about 1907. Secondary recovery now accounts for half the domestic lead supply. In 1980 the United States used 1.2 million short tons of lead, which was supplied by 745,000 tons recycled from scrap and 560,000 tons from domestic mines, the remainder coming from imports.

LEADVILLE MINING DISTRICT (Colo.). Named for a lead carbonate ore that abounded in the region and contained large amounts of silver, it is located near the headwaters of the Arkansas River. The first settlement resulted from the discovery in 1860 of rich placer deposits in California Gulch, which yielded over $3 million in gold before they were exhausted in 1867. Ten years of sporadic prospecting culminated, in 1875, in the discovery of the true nature of the carbonate ore by W. H. Stevens and A. B. Wood. Then occurred a mining rush on a grand scale. The Little Pittsburg, Matchless, Robert E. Lee, and other famous mines were developed. On Jan. 26, 1878, the city of Leadville was organized with H. A. W. Tabor, who was to become the district's best-known bonanza king, as the first mayor. During the period 1858–1925 the district produced nearly $200 million in silver and over $50 million in gold. Molybdenum was also discovered in the district, and by 1960, 90 percent of the world's supply was being produced at Climax, near the city of Leadville.

LEAGUE OF ARMED NEUTRALITY. *See* **Armed Neutrality of 1780.**

LEAGUE OF NATIONS. An international body formed on the basis of the first twenty-six articles of the Treaty of Versailles, which ended World War I. In the United States during the war the League to Enforce Peace, numbering among its members such prominent figures as former President William Howard Taft, favored a postwar association of nations that would guarantee peace through economic and military sanctions. In 1916, President Woodrow Wilson spoke before this group and set forth his own developing ideas on the subject. The president included self-determination and freedom from wars of aggression as prerequisites of a stable peace. Most important, he wanted to see the United States take the lead in a "universal association of the nations."

At the Versailles peace conference in 1919, Wilson battled those who wanted to postpone discussion of a league until the spoils of war had been divided, but succeeded in getting the League of Nations tentatively adopted. The heart of the League of Nations Covenant was Article X, which stated that the signatory nations agreed "to respect and preserve as against external aggression the territorial integrity and existing political independence" of all members. Other key articles were Article VIII, calling for the reduction of national armaments; Article XI, making "any war or threat of war . . . a matter of concern" to the league; Article XII, proposing arbitration or submission to the executive council of disputes between members; Article XVI, providing for economic and, if necessary, military sanctions against members violating Article XI; Article XVIII, entrusting the league with supervision of the arms trade when necessary for the common good; and Article XXII, establishing a mandate system over formerly German colonies.

The league structure consisted of a nine-member executive council, an assembly of all the members, the Permanent Court of International Justice, and a secretariat. Various commissions were established to oversee particular areas of concern. When the final Treaty of Versailles was signed with Germany in June 1919, the Covenant made up the first section of the treaty. By integrating the league with the general peace settlement, Wilson believed that any mistakes could be rectified later through the league.

Wilson's attempt to persuade the Senate to approve the treaty and bring the United States into the league became one of the classic executive-legislative struggles in American history. Sen. Henry Cabot Lodge united the Republican senators and a few Democrats behind a series of reservations to the treaty, the most important of which disavowed U.S. obligations to uphold the peacekeeping articles of the league unless Congress should so provide. Wilson rejected these reservations, contending that they were contrary to the spirit of the league and that because they made substantive changes in the treaty, they would necessitate reopening the peace conference. He agreed to accept a few "interpretations" to the treaty that would not change its substance. This impasse reflected real or perceived ideological differences over the direction of American foreign policy as well as senatorial jealousy of its prerogatives and the partisanship of Republicans and Democrats. In March 1920, the Senate failed to give the Treaty of Versailles the necessary two-thirds approval.

The United States maintained informal relations with the league in the 1920's and 1930's and, at times, acted jointly with it. The league served as an example for those who founded the United Nations after World War II. It ceased to function politically early in 1940, and its physical assets were turned over to the United Nations in April 1946.

LEAGUE OF UNITED SOUTHERNERS. An organization of southern leaders created in 1858 by Edmund Ruffin, a Virginia planter, and William L. Yancey, an Alabama politician, to promote southern political unity. It met with such indifference that the founders, in 1859, abandoned it.

LEAGUE OF WOMEN VOTERS OF THE UNITED STATES. Founded in 1920 to help the newly enfranchised women make intelligent use of voting privileges, it has become an outstanding agency for nonpartisan political education and a sponsor for legislation and policies judged by the league to be desirable for public welfare. The league had about 122,000 members in 1980.

LEARNED SOCIETIES. The first learned society founded in the United States was the American Philosophical Society (1743), whose origins have been traced to a club set up by Benjamin Franklin in Philadelphia in 1727. It was followed by the establishment of the American Academy of Arts and Sciences in Boston in 1780, John Adams being its prime mover. A few national societies were founded prior to the Civil War by those who were interested in a particular branch of knowledge represented by the society. They include the American Antiquarian Society, founded in Worcester, Mass. (1812), and the American Statistical Association, in Boston (1839). Local and regional societies were also created during this period. For example, the oldest historical society in America, the Massachusetts Historical Society, was founded in Boston in 1791, and the Chemical Society of Philadelphia, in 1792.

The Civil War saw increasing specialization in American life, which in turn was reflected in the character and number of American learned societies. American universities created many new departments devoted to particular disciplines. Faculty members began to form societies for the exchange of information and other activities regarding these disciplines. Thousands of local and regional societies played significant roles at their respective levels, but much greater importance was assumed by the approximately fifty national specialized learned societies, such as the American Chemical Society (1876), the American Historical Association (1884), the American Economic Association (1885), the American Psychological Association (1892), the American Anthropological Association (1902), and the American Society of Parasitologists (1924). A major difference between these specialized societies and earlier ones is that they have been open to all interested persons and some now have memberships in the thousands. An exception to these trends was the founding in 1898 of the National Institute of Arts and Letters and in 1904 of its affiliate, the American Academy of Arts and Letters; membership in both societies was honorific. In 1976 these organizations were merged into the American Academy and Institute of Arts and Letters; the membership is limited to 250 accomplished artists, writers, and composers.

An awareness gradually developed of the need to span gaps between disciplines and to coordinate knowledge and societal efforts at the national level. The Medieval Academy of America (1925) and the Renaissance Society of America (1954) were set up to cut across different disciplines in their respective periods of study. Founded in 1848, the American Association for the Advancement of Science had developed into a coordinating entity by the 1870's. Other societies in various areas of the natural sciences include the Federation of American Societies for Experimental Biology (1912), the American Institute of Physics (1931), the American Institute of Biological Sciences (1948), and the American Geological Institute (1948). In the period around World War I three overall coordinating councils were formed: the National Research Council (1916), natural sciences; the American Council of Learned Societies (1919), humanities and social sciences; and the Social Science Research Council (1923), social sciences.

Three international councils were formed to coordinate the activities of learned societies from various countries. They are the International Research Council (1919), after 1931 known as the International Council of Scientific Unions; the International Academic Union (1919), which in 1954 became a subsidiary of the International Council for Philosophy and Humanistic Studies; and the International Social Science Council (1952).

LEASEHOLD. A system of land tenure characteristic of the southeastern portion of the colony and state of New York. The tenant was bound to a perpetual payment of rent in money, produce, labor, or all three. This system was abolished by the middle of the 19th century by the constitution of 1846 and the decisions of the courts (*see* Antirent War).

LEATHER INDUSTRY. The American Indians processed their raw hides by means of the chamois method, which utilized animal fats, livers, and brains; the white buckskin that resulted was admired by the colonists as well as the Indians. Massachusetts had tanneries before 1650. In the Middle Colonies the presence of the leather crafts was coincidental with settlement. An abundance of hides, plus quantities of bark for tanning, made the Middle Atlantic region the leading leather-producing area. In the South, the tannery was a common feature of all well-managed plantations.

By 1840, the census of manufacturers reported 8,229 U.S. tanneries. They were widely scattered small operations taking place in small towns and employing local labor. Steam came late to the leather factory, and when it did, steam power was unspectacularly harnessed to old techniques.

After the Civil War, many procedures were mechanized, interest in the chemical aspects of tanning increased, and steam power turned most of the machinery. The demand for shoes, harnesses for animals, belts for machines, and upholstery for carriages and automobiles created an immense market. Midwestern meatpackers, who entered the leather business in the 1890's, contracted tanners to process hides at fixed prices and hold the leather until market prices were suitably high. The consolidation of big business did not bypass the leather industry. In 1917 the meatpackers, shoe manufacturers, and two large corporations tanned approximately 40 percent of the cattle-hide leather made in America. The most important contributions to the technology of tanning after 1850 were the chrome processes of Jackson Schultz, Robert Foerderer, and Martin Dennis. The chrome process was an inorganic method using chromate salts instead of bark extract as the tanning agent. This process reduced tanning time.

The leather industry boomed during World War I, but thereafter, the demand for leather dropped drastically. Full prosperity did not return until production was stimulated by World War II. The prosperity was short-lived: excess capacity, competition from substitute materials, and a lack of reliable foreign sources for hides curtailed production.

The Eagle Ottawa Leather Company of Grand Haven, Mich., developed solvent tanning in the late 1950's. The result was a uniformly soft piece of leather, but the costs of the process to date have proved too high for its universal use. Synthetic leather was developed in the 1960's. In 1977 there were 3,075 leather tanning and finishing establishments in the United States, employing 243,000 people.

LEATHERWOOD GOD. Leatherwood Valley in Guernsey County, Ohio, was the scene of a camp meeting in 1828. During the meeting a stranger appeared, who gave his name as Joseph C. Dylks. He would shout "Salvation!" and then make a sound like the snort of a frightened horse. He claimed that he was a celestial being, could perform miracles, and was the true Messiah. He disappeared from the community as mysteriously as he had appeared.

LEAVENWORTH (Kans.). In 1827, Col. Henry Leavenworth built Fort Leavenworth, three miles from the present site of the city on the Missouri River, to protect settlers traveling along the Santa Fe Trail. Squatters from across the river at Weston, Mo., moved into the area in June 1854, and soon formed a town association. Leavenworth was incorporated in 1855. It became the headquarters of the freighting firm of Russell, Majors and Waddell and the terminus of a number of overland mails. The Kansas border troubles brought a reign of terror to the town. Siding with the Union during the Civil War, the town prospered. With the advent of the railroads during the 1860's, Leavenworth became an important commercial center. The 1980 population was 33,-656. (*See also* Leavenworth, Fort.)

LEAVENWORTH, FORT. In 1824 some citizens of Missouri petitioned Congress for a military post at the Arkansas River crossing of the Santa Fe Trail to protect traders journeying to New Mexico. Secretary of War James Barbout in 1827 decided to erect a fort near the western boundary of Missouri. It was named Cantonment Leavenworth. Because of an epidemic of malaria, it was almost evacuated in May 1829; but late in that summer it was reoccupied. During 1832 it was renamed Fort Leavenworth. The post became important as a starting point for a number of military expeditions to the Far West, as a meeting place for Indian councils, and as a supply depot for forts and camps on the frontier. It rose to national prominence during the Mexican War, when the Army of the West was organized there and began a long march to occupy the Far Southwest (*see* Kearny's March to California). Occupying a strategic position in the West during the Civil War, it was at various times headquarters of the Department of the West, the Department of Kansas, and the Department of Missouri. The Fort Leavenworth military reservation was the seat of an arsenal between 1859 and 1874, and it was the U.S. Disciplinary Barracks in 1874–95 and 1906–29. To the military post were added the U.S. Army Command and General Staff School in 1881 and a federal penitentiary in 1895.

LEAVENWORTH AND PIKES PEAK EXPRESS. Launched by W. H. Russell and J. S. Jones to serve the Pikes Peak region of Colorado after the discovery of gold near Cherry Creek in 1858 (*see* Pikes Peak Gold Rush). The first coach reached Denver, May 7, 1859. The first route, along the Republican River, was changed to the Platte River Trail in June 1859. The express ran weekly. The Central Overland California and Pikes Peak Express absorbed the Leavenworth and Pikes Peak Express in 1860.

LEAVENWORTH EXPEDITION (1823). At the Arikara villages on the upper Missouri a party of the Rocky Mountain Fur Company under Gen. William Henry Ashley, en route to the Yellowstone, was attacked on June 2, and thirteen men were killed. Col. Henry Leavenworth promptly started up the Missouri from Fort Atkinson, at Council Bluffs, Nebr., with six companies of the Sixth Infantry and some artillery. Joined on the way by Joshua Pilcher's party of the Missouri Fur Company, by Ashley's survivors, and 750 Sioux, Leavenworth reached Grand River, Aug. 9. The next day he attacked the Arikara fortified villages, forcing their submission.

LEBANON, U.S. LANDING IN (1958). Under the threat of civil war in May, President Camille Chamoun of Lebanon in early July appealed to the United States for military forces to maintain order. By directive of President Dwight D. Eisenhower, approximately 5,600 U.S. Marines landed on Lebanese beaches on July 15 and 16 and secured port facilities and the international airport at Beirut. U.S. Army troops from stations in Germany began landing by air on July 19, with the last of a force totaling 8,500 arriving by sea on Aug. 5. The overall commander was Maj. Gen. Paul D. Adams. Although the populace cheered the troops, Lebanese army officers were bitter at first, the landings apparently having forestalled a coup d'etat aimed at replacing Chamoun with the army commander, Gen. Fuad Shehab. Only an occasional minor encounter between dissidents and American troops occurred. On July 31 the Lebanese Chamber of Deputies elected Shehab president, but Chamoun refused for several weeks to resign, so that Shehab was not inaugurated until Sept. 23. At that point the Lebanese army acted firmly to restore and maintain order, and the last U.S. forces departed on Oct. 25.

LEBOEUF, FORT, WASHINGTON'S MISSION TO. In 1753 the French erected forts Presque Isle and LeBoeuf in northwest Pennsylvania. Gov. Robert Dinwiddie of Virginia selected George Washington to deliver a letter to the French demanding their withdrawal. With frontiersman Christopher Gist and five others, Washington traveled from Wills Creek over the trail later known as Braddock's Road to the forks of the Ohio and thence to LeBoeuf. The commandant at LeBoeuf received Dinwiddie's letter and answered that he would forward it to Duquesne. Washington and his companions noted the strength of fort and garrison and the large number of canoes there, indicating a contemplated expedition down the Ohio. After two narrow escapes from death on the return journey, Washington arrived at Williamsburg on Jan. 16, 1754.

LECOMPTON CONSTITUTION. From Sept. 7 to Nov. 8, 1857, during the dispute over the admission of Kansas to the Union as a free or slave state, a convention of proslavery Kansans met at Lecompton and framed a state constitution. The constitution provided for the usual forms and functions of a state government, but an article covering slavery declared slave property inviolable, denied the power of the legislature to prohibit immigrants from bringing in slaves or to emancipate them without compensation and the owner's consent, and empowered the legislature to protect slaves against inhuman treatment. The schedule provided for a vote on a "constitution with slavery" or a "constitution with no slavery," the latter actually meaning no interference with slavery.

Other provisions prevented amendment before 1865 and placed responsibility for canvassing returns upon the presiding officer. On Dec. 21 the slavery clause was approved, 6,226 to 569 (although it was later learned that 2,720 of the votes were fraudulent), antislavery men declining to vote. The antislavery legislature (there being two legislatures—one proslavery and one antislavery—in Kansas at the time) called an election for Jan. 4, 1858, at which time the Lecompton Constitution was rejected, 10,226 to 162.

President James Buchanan recommended on Feb. 2 that Kansas be admitted to the Union under the Lecompton Constitution. The constitution was approved by the U.S. Senate, but Republicans, Democratic allies of Sen. Stephen A. Douglas, and others united to defeat it in the House. A compromise bill was suggested by Rep. William H. English of Indiana. It provided for a referendum in which Kansans would vote on the acceptance of a government land grant to Kansas, rather than on the constitution. If the Kansans accepted the land grant (5 million acres of land), Kansas would become a state under the proslavery Lecompton Constitution. If rejected, statehood would be postponed until the territory had a larger population. On Aug. 2 the Kansans rejected the land grant.

LECTURE DAYS. Midweek gatherings in the colonial New England churches for sermons on doctrinal points. In 1633 the general court ordered the lectures confined to afternoons so that the people would not lose a full working day, and in 1639 it attempted to reduce their number. When the clergy protested, it rescinded the order, but shortly thereafter lectures were generally abandoned.

LEDERER'S EXPLORING EXPEDITIONS (1669–70). John Lederer made tours of western exploration for Sir William Berkeley, governor of Virginia and a proprietor of Carolina. Lederer, starting from the site of Richmond, claimed to have reached the summit of the Appalachian Mountains, but in fact he reached only the eastern foothills of the Blue Ridge. He reached as far south as upper South Carolina, visiting many Indian tribes, some of whose customs he recorded in a book published in London in 1672.

LEDO ROAD. *See* **Burma Road and Ledo Road.**

LEE, FORT (N.J.). Originally called Fort Constitution, was built on Gen. George Washington's orders on the summit of the palisades of New Jersey opposite Fort Washington, on Manhattan Island, during the summer of 1776. The two forts, with obstructions placed between them in the Hudson River, were intended to prevent the passage of enemy vessels, but they failed in this purpose. After the fall of Fort Washington (1776), Fort Lee was abandoned when Gen. Charles Cornwallis crossed the Hudson.

The present borough of Fort Lee (Bergen County) was incorporated in 1904. During 1907–19 it was the motion-picture capital of the world. Fort Lee is now one of the world's largest film-processing centers. The population in 1980 was 32,449.

LEECH LAKE, INDIAN COUNCIL AT (Feb. 16, 1806). Maj. Zebulon M. Pike held a council with local Chippewa bands at the North West Company's trading post on Leech Lake in north central Minnesota. The Indians agreed to make peace with the Sioux, to yield up their British flags and medals, and to send two warriors to St. Louis with Pike.

LEECH LAKE UPRISING (1898). The previously friendly Pillager band of Chippewa in northern Minnesota had, by 1898, been irritated beyond patience. Being haled long distances to court as liquor witnesses and then abandoned caused the Pillagers to resist apprehension as material witnesses. U.S. sheriffs called in troops to help make arrests. Regular soldiers from Fort Snelling crossed Leech Lake to corral the fugitives. A gun accidentally discharged by a raw recruit upset a tense situation. General shooting followed. Soldiers, pinned to the ground in a clearing, and under hostile fire from noon to dark on Oct. 5, suffered several casualties before being rescued two days later. Reinforcements rushed up; and the Pillagers withdrew. Troops were withdrawn, and agents induced many Indians to surrender; executive clemency reduced the prison sentences.

LEGAL TENDER. Anything that, by law, a debtor may require his creditor to receive in payment of a debt, in the absence of the appearance in the contract itself of an agreement for payment in some other manner. The tender is an admission of the debt and in some jurisdictions, if refused, discharges the debt. There were two periods of American history when the question of legal tender was an important political issue. The first was between 1776 and 1789; the second was just after the Civil War. In the first period the question was whether the states should be permitted to print currency and require its acceptance by creditors regardless of its severe depreciation in value. In the second period the question was whether Congress had power, under the Constitution, to cause the issuance of paper money (greenbacks) that would be legal tender in payment of private debts (*see* Legal Tender Cases).

LEGAL TENDER ACT (1862). To finance Civil War, Congress issued fiat money. By the act of Feb. 25, 1862, and successive acts, the government put into circulation about $450 million of paper money dubbed "greenbacks." No specific gold reserve was set aside, nor was any date announced for their redemption. To insure their negotiability, Congress declared these notes legal tender. Wall Street and the metropolitan press opposed this measure. On the Pacific coast the law was frequently evaded through the passage of acts allowing exceptions on the basis of specific contracts. In 1870 the Supreme Court declared the Legal Tender Act unconstitutional and void in respect to debts contracted prior to its passage, but after two vacancies were filled the Court reversed its decision (*see* Legal Tender Cases).

LEGAL TENDER CASES. Concerned the constitutionality of the measures enacted by the U.S. Congress during the Civil War for the issue of treasury notes to circulate as money without provision for redemption. The constitutional question hinged not on the power of the government to issue the notes but on its power to make them legal tender for the payment of debts, particularly those contracted before the legislation was enacted. The Supreme Court ruled on the question first on Feb. 7, 1870, in the case of *Hepburn* v. *Griswold* (8 Wallace 603). The majority of the Court held that Congress had no power to enact the legal-tender provisions. The opinion against the constitutionality of the legislation was written by Chief Justice Salmon P. Chase, who as the secretary of the treasury had shared responsibility for the original enactments. Nominations of two new members of the Supreme Court were sent to the Senate on the day on which the decision was announced. At the ensuing term, over the protest of the four members who had previously constituted the majority, the Court heard the reargument of the constitutional question in another case. On May 1, 1871, the Court reversed the *Hepburn* decision in *Knox* v. *Lee* and *Parker* v. *Davis* (12 Wallace 457). Some of the notes issued were withdrawn by the Treasury, but some were reissued under a later statute enacted without reference to wartime conditions. This statute was upheld on Mar. 3, 1884, in *Juilliard* v. *Greenman.*

LEGION OF MERIT. *See* **Decorations, Military.**

LEGISLATIVE REORGANIZATION ACTS. The Act of Aug. 2, 1946, cut the number of congressional standing committees from forty-eight to nineteen in the House of Representatives, from thirty-three to fifteen in the Senate, and required regular meetings and records. The act also provided for an annual budget to complement the presidential budget and established the Legislative Reference Service as a branch of the Library of Congress to provide Congress with information on legislation. The legislative budget was abandoned in 1949. Title III, the Federal Regulation of Lobbying Act, required lobbyists to register and report lobbying expenses. The elimination of standing committees led to proliferation of subcommittees of Congress. The Act of Oct. 26, 1970, provided for public recording of committee roll-call votes as well as liberalization of committee procedures.

LEGISLATURE. Law making bodies on the national, state, and local levels have shown infinite variety in detail, but great similarity in broad outline. The U.S. Congress has provided the norm. Under a constitutional system of separation of powers in which the chief executive is popularly elected, rather than being chosen by and from the legislature, the president and others of the administration are excluded from direct participation in Congress. The legislature is bicameral, with a Senate that gives equal representation to each state and a House of Representatives that has members apportioned on the basis of each state's population. The two major political parties, Democratic and Republican, elect the overwhelming majority of the members of both houses. Their parliamentary members choose their own leaders, and the party with a majority organizes each house. More than in most systems, in which the executive is part of the legislature, the party leaders have to share their power with the leaders of the standing committees of the two houses.

All state constitutions provide for separation of powers. Nearly all have bicameral legislatures. Georgia, Pennsylvania, and Vermont experimented with unicameralism in their early history. Nebraska has been operating with a single chamber since 1934. The most common bases of representation have been population and units of local government.

Local governments have departed furthest from the traditional pattern. In the 20th century a number of local governments, especially those of middle-sized cities, have experimented with unification of powers. The manager form of government provides for a chief executive chosen by, but not from, the legislature, much as superintendents are chosen by school boards. The great majority of local governments have abandoned bicameralism. They have also frequently departed from the pattern of electing legislators from single-member districts, in many cases choosing them citywide. Less likely to have two-party competition, many local governments have organized their elections on a nonpartisan basis.

LEHIGH VALLEY RAILROAD. *See* **Railroads, Sketches.**

LEISLER REBELLION (1689). The Glorious Revolution in England was followed by uprisings in America. On May 31, 1689, Fort James on Manhattan Island was seized, and soon after, Capt. Jacob Leisler usurped control of southern New York. The following spring, at his suggestion, representatives from Massachusetts, Connecticut, and New York met in New York City to concert measures for a united offensive against Canada. Leisler assumed charge of operations, but lack of cooperation from the other colonies and his tactlessness spoiled his efforts. In March 1691, Col. Henry Sloughter was commissioned governor of New York by William and Mary. Leisler was tried for treason and executed.

***LEISY* V. *HARDIN*.** *See* **Original Package Doctrine.**

LEND-LEASE. A subsidy for America's allies that provided the economic and military aid they needed during World War II. Its primary purpose was to provide the sinews of war for Great Britain, the Soviet Union, China, and various members of the British Commonwealth of Nations, although many smaller participants also received lend-lease goods. By the close of the war a total of $47.9 billion of lend-lease aid had been extended by the United States to thirty-eight different countries—most of it in the form of military supplies, although a substantial amount of agricultural goods, raw materials, and manufactured goods also was distributed. Even exchanges of certain scientific information, particularly between Britain and the United States, fell under the provisions of the Lend-Lease Act of 1941.

***LETTERS FROM A PENNSYLVANIA FARMER*.** *See* **Farmer's Letters, Dickinson's.**

"LET US HAVE PEACE." In his letter of May 29, 1868, accepting the Republican nomination for the presidency,

Gen. Ulysses S. Grant endeavored to speak a word to calm feelings excited by civil war, reconstruction, and impeachment. His phrase "Let us have peace" became the keynote of his successful campaign.

LEVER ACT (Aug. 10, 1917). Sponsored by Rep. A. F. Lever of South Carolina to mobilize food and fuel resources for World War I, it authorized price fixing of commodities and licensing of producers and distributors and prohibited "unfair" trade practices. The Price-Fixing Committee, the Food and Fuel Administrations, and the Grain Corporation were created by executive orders to administer the law.

LEVY. An English project in the early 19th century to recruit recent British arrivals in the United States and Canada for an enterprise against Napoleon's French possessions in the West Indies. Charles Williamson, a British officer captured during the Revolution, was delegated to organize the Levy in 1803. He proposed to cooperate with Francisco de Miranda in an attack against Spanish possessions in Florida, Mexico, and South America. The Levy may have been offered to Aaron Burr but no organization was effected. Miranda and Burr both failed; Williamson returned to England.

LEWES, BOMBARDMENT OF (1813). A British attempt to stop shipping in the Delaware River and on Delaware Bay during the War of 1812. On Mar. 14, a squadron of ten British vessels anchored off Lewes, on Delaware Bay, ravaged shipping and threatened to destroy the town if provisions were not supplied. By delaying their reply, the Americans gained time to march militia to complete the construction of batteries. On Apr. 6 the British squadron began firing at the town, but the British shots passed high over the town, with the result that after over two days, of bombardment, no one at Lewes was killed or wounded and only a few houses were damaged. Shortly afterward the British vessels withdrew.

LEWIS AND CLARK CENTENNIAL EXPOSITION (1905). Held at Portland, Oreg., from June 1 to Oct. 15, commemorated the historic expedition of Meriwether Lewis and William Clark in opening up the Oregon country to settlement. It occupied 402 acres on the site of Willamette Heights. The federal government and nineteen states participated. Twice the anticipated number of visitors attended and made it a conspicuous financial success.

LEWIS AND CLARK EXPEDITION (1804–06). President Thomas Jefferson was deeply interested in scientific discoveries, and the Louisiana Purchase in 1803 afforded him a pretext for sending an expedition to explore the western country. Meriwether Lewis, Jefferson's private secretary, was appointed to command the expedition, and he associated his friend, William Clark, in the leadership. The party was assembled near St. Louis late in 1803 in readiness to start up the Missouri River the following spring. In the spring of 1804 it ascended the river by flatboat and keelboat to the group of Mandan and Arikara towns in west central North Dakota.

On Apr. 7, 1805, the explorers, in six canoes and two keelboats, set their faces toward the unknown West. Besides the two leaders, the party included twenty-six soldiers; George Drouillard and Toussaint Charbonneau, interpreters; Clark's servant, York; and Charbonneau's Indian slave companion, Sacajawea, and her infant son. On Nov. 7, 1805, the explorers gazed upon the Pacific Ocean. They had ascended the Missouri and its Jefferson fork to the mountains, which they had crossed to the Snake; thence down the Snake and the Columbia to the sea. The winter was passed in a shelter (named Fort Clatsop) near present-day Astoria, Oreg., and in March 1806 the return journey was begun. After crossing the Rockies the explorers separated into three groups to make a more extensive examination of the country than a single party could accomplish. Thus, both the Missouri and the Yellowstone rivers were descended, near whose junction the groups reunited. From here the party passed rapidly downriver to St. Louis, on Sept. 23, 1806, where the expedition ended.

LEXINGTON (Ky.). Second largest city in Kentucky, with a population of 204,165 in 1980; it was the center of a metropolitan area including 316,098 people. Lexington was named before it was settled. In June 1775, a group of pioneers was on the site when they received news of the battle of Lexington and they promptly named the place in honor of the battle. The first permanent settlement was not made until 1779 and the city was chartered by Virginia in 1782.

Lexington is the center of Kentucky's bluegrass region, one of the most important horse-breeding and horse-raising sections in the world. From its founding, Lexington has had fine animals, many brought west from Maryland and Virginia by the wealthier pioneers in the 1780's and 1790's. The town had its first horse races in 1787 and a short time later it had achieved its status of a center for horse racing and breeding.

During the early 19th century, Lexington was the shipping and shopping place for an important agricultural region; the earliest "cash" crop was hemp, from which ropes were made for the rigging of ships and Ohio River barges. Tobacco was also raised. After the Civil War the tobacco business dominated Lexington, which became the leading auction center for "burley" tobacco, a light-leaf strain. Following World War II, Lexington saw the introduction of a major factory for electric typewriters and the building of other plants. It is the home of the University of Kentucky. The federal government maintains a treatment center in Lexington, for persons suffering from narcotics addiction.

LEXINGTON. A name given to four American ships: (1) A Continental brig that, under Capt. John Barry, captured the British sloop *Edward* in April 1776, off Chesapeake Bay. In 1777 it cruised about Ireland under Henry Johnson, but was captured in September of that year. (2) A store ship that, under Lt. Theodorus Bailey, captured San Blas, Mexico, in 1848, in the final naval operation of the Mexican War. (3) A Union sidewheeler, later armored, that fought at Belmont, Miss., Fort Henry, Tenn., and on the Red River, 1861–63. At Shiloh it saved Gen. Ulysses S. Grant's army from being driven back in utter defeat the first day of the battle. (4) A World War II aircraft carrier that participated in the Battle of the Coral Sea, May 7–8, 1942, the first major check to Japan's advance in the Pacific. The *Lexington* was so badly damaged that it had to be sunk by an American destroyer.

LEXINGTON, SIEGE OF (Sept. 12–20, 1861). After the Battle of Wilson's Creek, Confederate Gen. Sterling Price of the Missouri State Guard moved his 1,500 men northward toward Lexington, Mo. Lexington was defended by 2,640 men under Union Col. J. A. Mulligan, who entrenched on a hill around the Masonic College. Price surrounded them and constructed a breastwork of hemp bales that enabled him to move within close range of the defenders in comparative safety. On Sept. 20 Mulligan surrendered.

LEXINGTON AND CONCORD (1775). On the evening of Apr. 18, the British military governor of Massachusetts sent out from Boston a detachment of about 700 troops to destroy military stores collected by the colonists at Concord. Detecting the plan, the Whigs in Boston sent out Paul Revere and William Dawes with warnings. The detachment found at Lexington, at sunrise on Apr. 19, a part of the minuteman company already assembled on the green. At the command of British Maj. John Pitcairn, the regulars fired and cleared the ground. Eight Americans were killed and ten were wounded. The regulars marched for Concord.

At Concord the Americans, outnumbered, retired over the North Bridge and waited for reinforcements. The British occupied the town, held the North Bridge with about a hundred regulars, and searched for stores. Of these they found few; but the smoke of those they burned in the town alarmed the watching Americans; reinforced to the number of about 450, they marched down to the bridge, led by Maj. John Buttrick. The regulars hastily formed on the farther side to receive them and began to take up the planks of the bridge. The front ranks of the regulars fired, killing two Americans and wounding more. The response of the Americans and their continued advance were too much for the British, who broke and fled. The Americans did not follow up their success, and after a dangerous delay the British marched for Boston about noon. At Meriam's Corner their rear guard was fired upon by the men of Reading, and from there to Lexington a skirmish fire was poured upon the British from all available cover. By the time they reached that town the regulars were almost out of ammunition and completely demoralized. They were saved from slaughter or surrender only by the arrival of a column from Boston, under Sir Hugh Percy. Forty-nine Americans and seventy-three British were killed.

LEXINGTON AND OHIO RAILROAD. *See* **Railroads, Sketches of Principal Lines..**

LEXOW COMMITTEE (1894). Appointed by the New York State Senate to investigate the New York City Police Department, it revealed widespread organized graft, called the "system." The system had been evolving for half a century, and although it was not politically organized, it found special protection under the Tammany Hall leadership of Richard Croker, beginning about 1886. Opponents of the system "were abused, clubbed and imprisoned, and even convicted of crime on false testimony by policemen and their accomplices." Legitimate businesses were forced to pay graft. The comparative success of the committee, of which Clarence Lexow, a Republican, was chairman, was brought about chiefly by its fearless counsel, John W. Goff, a Democrat.

LEYTE GULF, BATTLE OF (Oct. 23–25, 1944). As the first step in recapturing the Philippines from the Japanese, a U.S. armada descended on Leyte Island in mid-October 1944. Vice Adm. Thomas C. Kinkaid's Seventh Fleet included some 700 combat, support, and transport vessels and 500 aircraft. Supporting it was the Third Fleet, under Adm. William F. Halsey, a force of nearly 100 warships and more than 1,000 planes. Japanese naval units (64 warships) moved to oppose the invasion. From the north, a decoy group of aircraft carriers under Vice Adm. Jisaburo Ozawa sought to lure Halsey away so that a powerful battleship force under Vice Adm. Takeo Kurita and a smaller cruiser force under Vice Adm. Kiyohide Shima could move through the central Philippines and fall upon the exposed American amphibious assault units in Leyte Gulf. A much smaller force under Vice Adm. Shoji Nishimura moved through the Sulu Sea toward Surigao Strait, the southern entrance to Leyte Gulf, which he planned to enter simultaneously with Kurita.

Early on Oct. 23, two American submarines attacked Kurita, sinking two heavy cruisers and badly damaging a third. Alerted by this contact, planes from Halsey's carriers began hitting Kurita the next day. In five separate strikes, they sank the 64,000-ton super-battleship *Musashi,* crippled a heavy cruiser, and damaged many other targets; land-based Japanese aircraft managed to sink one of Halsey's carriers and damage a cruiser. But Kurita, badly shaken, turned back just as he was approaching San Bernardino Strait. Late in the day, he reversed course and headed once more for Leyte Gulf, too late for his rendezvous with Nishimura and Shima. To the south, Kinkaid was ready to intercept Nishimura in Surigao Strait. The American battleships and cruisers formed a line across the northern end of the strait. First contact came about midnight of Oct. 24–25, and within a few hours Nishimura was destroyed. Shima's small force, which arrived shortly thereafter, escaped with only small damage. Pursuing American ships and planes sank another cruiser and destroyer.

Before dawn on Oct. 25, Kurita's force debouched from San Bernardino Strait and headed for Leyte Gulf. Halsey, who should have intercepted him, had rushed north to attack Ozawa. Shortly after sunrise, Kurita struck Kinkaid's northernmost unit. For more than two hours, the tiny American force fought off the powerful Japanese fleet. American destroyers made repeated attacks to cover the fleeing escort carriers, whose planes constantly harassed Kurita. Suddenly, Kurita broke off his attack, convinced that he was being attacked by heavy units of the American fleet and that he could no longer reach Leyte Gulf in time to do significant damage. He turned north and escaped. Far to the north, Halsey struck Ozawa's decoy force. By afternoon on Oct. 25, in the final action of the far-flung battle, he had sunk four Japanese carriers, a cruiser, and two destroyers. The great one-sided American victory destroyed the Japanese fleet as an effective fighting force.

LIBBY PRISON. A notorious Confederate prison. When the captives from the first Battle of Bull Run arrived in Richmond in the summer of 1861, Gen. John H. Winder, provost marshal of the city, commandeered a number of vacant tobacco warehouses, among them one belonging to the firm of Libby and Son. Commissioned officers were confined there until after the fall of Richmond in 1865. After the failure of the cartel for the exchange of prisoners, Libby became crowded, and a shortage of food supplies during December 1863 and January 1864 caused extensive suffering. In February 109 officers escaped through a tunnel, and 61 made their way to the Union lines. On Feb. 28 and Mar. 4, 1864, two cavalry raids were made on Richmond for the purpose of releasing the prisoners (*see* Dahlgren's Raid). As a result, the Confederates established a new prison for officers at Macon, Ga., in May 1864. Thereafter Libby Prison was used only as a temporary station for captives en route to Macon.

LIBEL. In Anglo-American law includes defamatory matter in some such permanent form as writing, printing, or painting, the less permanent or oral form being designated as slander. English political libel suits were paralleled in colonial America. The most celebrated prosecution was that of John Peter Zenger, New York printer, in 1735. In this case the prosecution contended that only the fact of publication could be determined by the jury, while the court was to determine whether the publication was libelous. Andrew Hamilton, counsel for the prisoner, persuaded the jury to judge both law and fact and secured Zenger's acquittal.

The Sedition Act of 1798 allowed the defense to give evidence of the truth of the matter contained in the publication charged as a libel, the jury having the right to determine the law and the fact. Although the law expired in 1801, the whole question was brought to a head by the trial in New York of Harry Croswell, publisher of the *Hudson* (N.Y.) *Wasp,* for a libel on President Thomas Jefferson. As a result of Alexander Hamilton's arguments, the same ruling as in the Zenger case prevailed, and a precedent was set for the American common law. In 1805 a statute was enacted by New York State embodying the result of this decision, permitting the defendant to give truth in justification, provided it was published "with good motives and for justifiable ends."

While technically at common law oral defamation was a tort rather than a crime, in the colonial courts a flood of criminal prosecutions, as well as civil suits, for defamatory utterance gave unusual color and vitality to the court minutes of that period. In modern times criminal slander is not recognized in law, and civil suits for oral defamation have greatly declined in number and frequency. There is still judicial disagreement concerning whether oral defamation through the means of radio and television is libel or slander.

LIBERALISM. Believing in the rationality of man and the dignity of the individual, committed to freedom, equal justice, and equal opportunity, liberals have always been reformers with little reverence for tradition and great faith in the power of human intelligence to establish a more just society. They have distrusted power and privilege, felt sympathy for the exploited and deprived, and relied upon rational and enlightened social and economic policies to rehabilitate even the lowest elements of society.

The Anglo-American liberalism of the 18th and 19th centuries, traceable to John Locke and Adam Smith, was a reaction against powerful monarchies. It espoused a strictly limited, decentralized government. The natural rights of the individual—most frequently identified as rights to life, liberty, property, and the pursuit of happiness—had to be protected from the state. This supposition underlay the American Revolution, the Bill of Rights, Jeffersonian Democracy, Jacksonian Democracy, and the antislavery movement. The liberalism of the antebellum American republic was a persuasion well suited to an individualistic agrarian society hardly touched by the forces of industrial capitalism. In the late 19th century liberalism began to find new definitions. As private power structures appeared to be the greatest threats to the natural rights of the individual, the state emerged as a protector. Laissez-faire no longer seemed a viable formula for a newly complex society with increasingly visible injustices; the ideal of a strong activist government promoting the welfare of its citizens was developed. The Populist movement, primarily the vehicle of depressed southern and midwestern farmers, advocated a wide range of reforms. The multifaceted Progressive movement of the early 20th century, more urban and middle class, struggled to curb corporate power through either trust-busting (the New Freedom) or trust regulation (the New Nationalism). The Progressives formulated the beginnings of a social welfare state that would work for the goals of human dignity and equal opportunity through active government programs in behalf of the underprivileged. The New Deal was based upon the intellectual heritage of Progressivism. By the late 20th century liberalism was in some measure in disrepute. Large, expensive neo–New Deal social welfare programs appeared to have achieved scant success in resolving the discontent of the underprivileged. The unhappy American venture in Vietnam, brought to its peak by a liberal president, had divided the liberal movement and left it without a solid foreign policy orientation. Liberal reformers faced the task of redefining their objectives.

LIBERAL REPUBLICAN PARTY. The result of revolt of the reform element in the Republican party during President Ulysses S. Grant's first administration (1869–73). It advocated a conciliatory policy toward the South (*see* Reconstruction) and civil service reform and condemned political corruption. Some members favored tariff revision. The movement was led by B. Gratz Brown, Carl Schurz, Charles Sumner, Charles Francis Adams, and Horace Greeley. Greeley was named for president and Brown for vice-president in 1872, and both were later endorsed by the Democrats.

***LIBERATOR*.** A weekly antislavery newspaper edited by William Lloyd Garrison, published in Boston, Jan. 1, 1831, to Dec. 29, 1865. Its circulation never exceeded 3,000. The paper was influential in turning the antislavery movement from the advocacy of gradual emancipation to a demand for immediate, uncompensated emancipation. It aided Garrison's work in organizing the New England Anti-Slavery Society in 1832 and the American Anti-Slavery Society in 1833.

LIBERIA. On the western coast of Africa, the continent's oldest republic covers 43,000 square miles, mostly dense tropical rain forest. The estimated population in 1980 was 1,860,000; 2.5 percent belong to the Americo-Liberian elite, descended from liberated slaves and black American freedmen repatriated to Africa in the 19th century by the American Colonization Society. Since the founding of Liberia in 1822, the United States has maintained a policy of relative detachment. The colony declared itself independent in 1847, but the United States, embroiled in controversy over slavery, withheld recognition until 1862.

Relatively prosperous during the mid-19th century, Liberia became territorially overextended and declined disastrously when faced with European commercial and colonial competition. British and French traders and diplomats reduced Liberian territory by one-third before the United States quietly applied pressure around 1900 to preserve Liberian independence. By 1912 Liberia was badly in default to European creditors and, in return for a U.S. loan agreed to accept American customs officers and a military mission. Heavy investment by the Firestone Tire and Rubber Company in Liberian rubber plantations after 1926 partially alleviated financial strains. The United States suspended diplomatic relations from 1930 to 1935 over alleged forced labor abuses and cooperated with Liberian and League of Nations authorities in investigating the charges. U.S. influence peaked during World War II when the Liberian capital, Monrovia, became a major supply depot. Exports of high-grade iron ore began to revolutionize the country in the 1960's. European and Asian influence and capital now compete heavily with American.

The Liberian constitution replicates the U.S. form. The True Whig party has ruled continuously since 1877, perpetuating the Americo-Liberian oligarchy. Legislative and judicial branches have atrophied and power has been concentrated in the executive, especially under President William V. S. Tubman (1944–71). Tubman's National Unification Plan, supposed to close the gap between the oligarchy and indigenous peoples, was only a marginal success. Following a military coup in April 1980, which installed a People's Redemption Council, the constitution was suspended and political parties were banned.

LIBERTY, CONCEPT OF. Liberty may be understood as a relationship between men living in society under government. The present concept of liberty has its roots in modern natural-right teaching. According to that teaching, developed primarily by Thomas Hobbes and John Locke, the right to liberty is a necessary inference from the right of self-preservation, or is conceived as implicit in the exercise of that primary or natural right. From this point of view, the activities of the state should be directed toward providing security for life and for liberty, with the people as a whole judging the legitimacy of the exercise of that authority. On the basis of the Constitution, the American regime places central emphasis on individual liberty enforced through law and the delicate processes of government, which include separation of powers and a system of checks and balances.

***LIBERTY*, SEIZURE OF THE** (June 10, 1768). An incident in the Boston agitation against the Sugar Acts. When British customs officials learned that a wharf official had been locked in the cabin of John Hancock's sloop *Liberty* so that Madiera wine could be landed without payment of duty, they ordered the seizure of Hancock's vessel. The *Liberty* was towed from her wharf and anchored close to the British Fleet. A crowd assaulted customs officials on the dock and demonstrated before their homes. The next day the customs officials fled to Castle William in Boston harbor.

"LIBERTY, SONG OF." Written in 1768 by John Dickinson to unite Americans against British oppression by expressing in popular verse his convictions of the necessity of colonial union. The song enjoyed immense popularity.

LIBERTY BELL. Ordered by the Philadelphia provincial council in 1751 for the golden jubilee of William Penn's Charter of Privileges, the bell was cracked in testing upon arrival and recast by John Pass and Charles Stow. It was installed in the Philadelphia state house and proclaimed American independence following the reading there on July 8, 1776, of the Declaration of Independence. During the years 1777–78, it was hidden from the British in Allentown, Pa. The bell was strained tolling the obsequies of Chief Justice John Marshall in 1835 and was fatally cracked during the celebration of George Washington's birthday in 1846. It was first called the Liberty Bell by the antislavery movement in 1839. The Liberty Bell weighs over 2,080 pounds, and is inscribed "Proclaim Liberty throughout all the land unto all the inhabitants thereof." It is now housed in Independence National Historical Park.

LIBERTY BONDS. *See* **Liberty Loans.**

LIBERTY BOYS. *See* **Sons of Liberty (American Revolution).**

LIBERTY CAP. A sharp-pointed apex tilted forward. Probably Phrygian in origin and apparently used in Rome as a token of manumission, a cap of this form was used by revolutionists in France after 1789. With the extension of French revolutionary sentiment in America in the next decade, radical Jeffersonian Republicans sometimes donned liberty caps.

LIBERTY-CAP CENT. A U.S. coin, about an inch in diameter, struck by the U.S. mint at Philadelphia, 1793–96. On the obverse is a bust of Liberty with a pole over the left shoulder surmounted by a liberty cap.

LIBERTY LEAGUE. Dissatisfaction with the policies of the New Deal led a number of conservative Democrats, including former Democratic presidential candidate Alfred E. Smith, to form the League in August 1934. The League drew most of its following from wealthy Democrats and those who felt that the New Deal was a departure from the Constitution. During the 1936 presidential campaign, the League actively supported the Republican candidate, Alfred M. Landon.

LIBERTY LOANS. Upon U.S. entry into World War I in April 1917, it at once became apparent that large sums in excess of tax receipts would be needed both to provide funds for European allies and to conduct the war activities of the nation. The Treasury resorted to borrowing through a series of bond issues. The first four issues were known as liberty loans; the fifth and last was called the victory loan. The issues were brought out between May 14, 1917, and Apr. 21, 1919, in the total amount of $21,478,356,250. The separate issues were as follows: first liberty loan, $2 billion; second liberty loan, $3,808,766,150; third liberty loan, $4,176,516,850; fourth liberty loan, $6,993,073,250; and victory loan, $4.5 billion. The liberty loans were long-term bonds bearing from 3.5 to 4.25 percent interest, and the victory loan consisted of two series of three- and four-year notes bearing interest at 3.75 and 4.75 percent. The issues were all oversubscribed. The disposal of this vast amount of obligations was accomplished by direct sales to the people. Liberty loan committees were organized in all sections of the country.

LIBERTY PARTY. The first antislavery political party, was formed by opponents of William Lloyd Garrison's abolitionists in 1839. James G. Birney, the party's candidate for president in 1840, won about 7,000 votes in the election. In 1844 he won more than 62,000, drawing enough votes from Henry Clay to give New York and the election to James K. Polk. In 1848 the party nominated John P. Hale, but he withdrew and the party merged with the Free Soil organization. The leaders of the Liberty party included Salmon P. Chase, Gerrit Smith, Myron Holley, and Charles Torrey.

LIBERTY POLES (or liberty trees). Symbols before which Sons of Liberty assembled and "pledged their fortunes and their sacred honors in the cause of liberty" just before the American Revolution. Numerology played a part in the erection of liberty poles, particularly the numbers ninety-two and forty-five. The former symbolized the issue of John Wilkes's newspaper that had criticized the king, and the latter symbolized the votes in the Massachusetts legislature in 1768 against rescission of the circular letter to the other twelve colonies calling for united action against British abuses of power. The original liberty tree was an elm at the intersection of Washington and Essex streets, Boston; it was a rallying place for Sons of Liberty. It was cut down by British soldiers in 1775.

LIBRARIES. After the founding of the Harvard College Library in 1638, libraries in the colonies developed sporadically until well into the 18th century. Capt. Robert Keayne willed a sum to the city of Boston in 1655 for various public purposes, including a town library, and the city erected a public building in which a room was set aside for a library. In 1689 a number of church-related libraries were established along the Atlantic seaboard by Thomas Bray, a clergyman. At the turn of the century libraries were established with the founding of William and Mary College and Yale College in 1693 and 1701, respectively. In 1731 the first subscription library was founded by Benjamin Franklin, the Library Company of Philadelphia. Other social libraries were soon founded in Durham and Lebanon, Conn., and in 1750 the Redwood Library, which is the oldest library in the United States, was erected in Newport, R.I.

As the country turned increasingly to manufacturing and mercantile pursuits the need for greater access to educational materials in population centers found expression in social libraries. There were two basic types: proprietary and subscription. The proprietary library was, in effect, a joint-stock company, whereas the subscription library was a corporation to which a member paid an annual fee for service. Proprietary libraries levied assessments on shareholders and in some cases permitted others to use the library for an annual fee. Between 1733 and 1850 more than 1,000 social libraries were established. Although these collections were small and members few, the fees were low enough to make the organizations attractive to many classes of society. There were, for example, social libraries for mechanics, clerks, juveniles, and factory workers. The major weaknesses, lack of continuity beyond the founding group and uncertain financial support, contributed to the decline of the social library and its replacement by the free, public, tax-supported library in the mid-19th century.

Free public libraries for juveniles had been founded in Salisbury, Conn., in 1803 and in Lexington, Mass., in 1827. But it was Peterborough, N.H., that first took advantage of state education funds to found a free public town library, opened in 1833 and supported by annual appropriations. In 1852 the Boston Public Library came into being. The report of its trustees issued in July of that year is still recognized as the most comprehensive statement of purpose, functions, and objectives for the modern American public library. Encouraged by a commitment to free, popular education and permissive state legislation, public libraries quickly began to spread. Several states followed the pattern set by New York in permitting school districts to levy a tax to establish and support public libraries. By the Civil War, the concept of the public library had been established, and the nation boasted more than 500 libraries.

Several developments significant in modern library history occurred in 1876. At a meeting held during the Centennial Exposition in Philadelphia, Oct. 4–6, a group of librarians voted to form the American Library Association. Among them was Melvil Dewey, who was to be a dominant force in the library world for the next thirty years. In the same year the U.S. Office of Education issued its first report on libraries, *Public Libraries in the United States of America: Their History, Condition and Management.* The first part contained the results of a survey of over 3,800 public libraries. The second part comprised Rules for a Printed Dictionary Catalogue by Charles Ammi Cutter, librarian of the Boston Athenaeum. These rules were quickly adopted by libraries for both printed and card catalogs. The first library periodical, *Library Journal,* was founded in 1876, and Dewey's famous decimal classification scheme appeared in the same year.

In 1900 the library school at Columbia College had produced its first graduates. Within a few years every major type of library was represented in the United States and most were well established, headed by the Library of Congress. Closely related to the Library of Congress by their support for research, but separate in development, are the many research libraries in the United States. University libraries dominate this category, although a few research libraries—such as the Newberry Library in Chicago, the Henry E. Huntington Library in San Marino, Cal., and the Library Company of Philadelphia—remain private and independent. The growing demands of scholarly research are reflected in the fact that in 1876 only two libraries—Harvard and Yale—held more than 100,000 volumes, whereas by 1891 the number had grown to five; by the early 1980's thirty-four university libraries contained over 2 million volumes. In 1981 there were 4,796 academic libraries in the United States.

From their beginnings in the late 19th century through the first half of the 20th century, school libraries had minimal educational influence, primarily because elementary and secondary education remained textbook-oriented until the 1940's. With the passage of the National Defense Education Act in 1958 massive financial assistance became available to school libraries, and in 1965 the Elementary and Secondary Education Act augmented that assistance. With those new sources of funds such libraries soon came to constitute the largest category of libraries and continue a growing, vital force in American education.

Almost 10,000 U.S. libraries are devoted to special subject matter or a specialized clientele. Among these are libraries of private companies—banking, insurance, research, manufacturing—and those associated with public institutions, including government agencies.

The public library has pioneered in the development of most of the significant concepts of American librarianship—for example, the open shelf, by the Cleveland Public Library, and subject divisional organization, by the Providence Public Library. In 1981 the United States had 14,831 public libraries (including branches).

LIBRARY OF CONGRESS. Established by the same act of Congress, approved Apr. 24, 1800, that made provision for the removal of the government of the United States to the new federal city, Washington, D.C. The original collections of the library, obtained from London, consisted of 152 works in 740 volumes and a few maps. In 1802 Congress provided that a librarian be appointed, and President Thomas Jefferson named John James Beckley, clerk of the House of Representatives, who held both posts until his death.

When British troops burned the Capitol in 1814, the library of some 3,000 volumes was lost. To replace it, Congress purchased Jefferson's personal library, consisting of an estimated 6,487 books, for $23,950. In 1851 a Christmas Eve fire destroyed some 35,000 volumes, including two-thirds of the Jefferson library. By the end of 1864, the collections had grown to some 82,000 volumes, but they were far from distinguished. Then Congress passed four laws that cast the library in the mold of greatness: an act of Mar. 3, 1865, requiring the deposit in the library of a copy of all books and other materials on which copyright was claimed, with loss of copyright for failure to deposit; an act of Apr. 5, 1866, transferring to the Library of Congress the Smithsonian Institution's unique collection (40,000 volumes plus future increments) of scientific materials and transactions of learned societies, gathered from all over the world; an act of Mar. 2, 1867, strengthening international exchange of official publications and making the library the beneficiary; and an appropriations act of Mar. 2, 1867, providing $100,000 for the purchase of the Peter Force collection of Americana—the first major purchase since the Jefferson library and the library's first distinguished research collection. The 19th century also saw the creation (1832) of the Law Library in the Library of Congress, the assignment (1870) to the library of responsibility for the administration of the copyright law, and the first substantial gift to the library by a private citizen—Dr. Joseph Meredith Toner's collection of medical literature and of materials for the study of American history and biography, in 1882.

In 1897 the library, which had grown to nearly a million volumes, moved from the Capitol to its own building. In an appropriations act of Feb. 19, 1897, Congress provided for the appointment of the librarian by the president, with the advice and consent of the Senate. The collections are housed in the main building; in the annex, which was occupied in 1939; and in James Madison Memorial Building, dedicated in 1981.

The functions of the library were extended by Congress until it became, in effect, the national library, serving the Congress, federal agencies, other libraries, and the public. It provides research and reference services to the Congress; for example, over 376,000 requests were directed in 1981 to the Congressional Research Service, one of the six departments of the library, by members of Congress. The library's collections are open for reference use, and the use of the collections is extended through interlibrary loans and the Photoduplication Service.

The library contains the national Copyright Office for the registration of claims to copyright, and its collections are enriched from the copyright deposits. It has exchange agreements with private research institutions throughout the world. It also purchases materials, obtains them through official transfer, and receives gifts to the nation in the form of personal papers, rare books, and other valuable materials.

During the 20th century, the Library of Congress emerged as a library "universal in scope, national in service," as Librarian Herbert Putnam termed it. By 1981 the collections totaled over 78.6 million items and constituted unparalleled resources for research.

LICENSE CASES, 5 Howard 504 (1847). Involved laws of three states fixing conditions of, and requiring licenses for, the sale of certain goods imported from other states. In upholding the laws the U.S. Supreme Court weakened the doctrine of exclusive federal control of interstate commerce as laid down in *Gibbons* v. *Ogden* in 1824. That earlier doctrine was reasserted, however, with modifications, when, in *Cooley* v. *Port Wardens* (1851), the Court held that with reference to subjects not demanding uniformity, states might impose regulations on interstate commerce until Congress exercised its rights to establish uniform regulations.

LICENSES TO TRADE. Licenses to trade granted in the colonies reflected the English common law, which recognized the power of the sovereign to regulate the "common callings," such as innkeeping, carrying goods and persons, or operating a bridge. By the 19th century the scope of licenses to trade, now granted by states and municipalities, extended to a much wider variety of occupations and began to include professions such as medicine and architecture. The growing concern of the states in the regulation of business after the Civil War led to reliance on licenses to trade for the control of such diverse industries as ice manufacture and the operation of grain elevators. As late as the early 1930's, the U.S. Supreme Court effectively limited control of business by holding the due process clause of the Constitution to be a bar to much of such state action, including the issuance of restrictive licenses to trade. As the New Deal progressed in the 1930's, the Supreme Court retreated, so that by the 1970's wide areas of the economy were affected by state licensing without serious constitutional doubts. The growth of huge, national corporations began to weaken the effectiveness of state licensing of trade as a means to control business, so that federal licensing of trade has become effective in banking, electric power, gas distribution, telecommunications, and interstate transport in the air and on highways. At the municipal level licenses to trade continue to reflect local concerns with sanitation, orderly trade, and protection of local tradespeople from outside competition.

LIFE EXPECTANCY. The life span is the greatest number of years that a human being can live. Although the life span has remained unchanged, the average length of life, or the expectation of life at birth, has increased greatly in the United States since the colonial period. A life table (or mortality table) shows the probability of surviving from any age to any subsequent age in terms of the age-specific death rates prevailing at a particular time and place.

Until the 1930's reasonably complete records of death had not been kept for the United States. As a result, only fragmentary data are available for historical analysis. During the colonial period records of births and deaths were kept by families and churches. Except for the limited evidence provided by family Bibles, diaries, gravestones, and similar sources, there are practically no vital statistics for the 17th century, nor is the situation much better for the 18th century. Accurate death records began to be kept in New York in 1804. Mortality statistics were published by Boston in 1813, Philadelphia in 1825, and Baltimore in 1836. For about thirty years around 1900, complete records of deaths are available for what is known as the "original" death registration area, comprising ten states (Connecticut, Indiana, Maine, Massachusetts, New Hampshire, New Jersey, New York, Michigan, Rhode Island, Vermont). After 1910 the number of states requiring registration of births and deaths increased rapidly. In 1933 the registration areas included all the states for the first time. Since then, accurate and reasonably complete recording of births and deaths has been secured for the whole United States.

The earliest American life table, for Massachusetts and New Hampshire, was published by Edward Wigglesworth, a clergyman, in 1793. It was based on information from sixty-two communities and dealt with 4,983 deaths, of which 1,942 (39.2 percent) occurred during the first five years. This table was used for many years in Massachusetts for legal and actuarial purposes. In 1857, E. B. Elliots, an actuary, published in the *Proceedings* of the American Association for the Advancement of Science the first "Massachusetts Life, Population and Annuity Table," which he had constructed for the New England Life Insurance Company in Boston. Further advances were made by John Shaw Billings, a physician, who founded the surgeon general's library and who had charge of vital statistics in the censuses of 1880 and 1890. Through his efforts mortality schedules of probability were first used by the census office as a supplement to mortality enumeration. In connection with the census of 1880, Billings also constructed a number of local life tables. In 1881, Levi W. Meech, an actuary, developed the American Experience Table from the records and experience of thirty insurance companies. The value of this table was limited, because life insurance experience cannot fully substitute for general population data. Moreover, the large population changes of this period caused by immigration made all mortality tables less than satisfactory. For these reasons, Samuel W. Abbott, a physician and secretary of the Massachusetts Board of Health, arranged for the publication in 1898 of the Second Massachusetts Life Table, based upon the experience of the period 1893–97. Abbott used the table as an index of the health status of the people of the state. A comprehensive and trustworthy national life table was first prepared in 1910 by Samuel Lyle Rogers, director of the census from 1915 to 1921, and James W. Glover, of the University of Michigan.

Although mortality data for the nation as a whole are limited before the early 20th century, it is clear that a huge increase in life expectancy at birth has been achieved since the colonial period. In the 17th century, life expectancy at birth is believed to have been between 25 and 30 years. It has been estimated that during the colonial period half of all children died before the age of 10. The average length of life in the 1770's was probably about 35 years. By the early 19th century, some observers felt that health conditions were improving, but the evidence on declining mortality is sketchy and uncertain. Between 1820 and 1850 rising death rates were reported from large cities, a consequence largely of immigration, poverty, and rapid urban growth. Estimates based on data for several states place the expectation of life around 1850 at about 40 years.

A gradual improvement began after the Civil War and accelerated after 1900 as a result of improved living conditions and, more specifically, of sanitary reform and the application of microbiological discoveries. Beginning about 1870, a continuing downward trend in mortality ensued because of a decline in the frequency of such communicable diseases as smallpox, diphtheria, typhoid and typhus fevers, tuberculosis, and malaria. As an example, the death rate for diphtheria among children up to 10 years of age in New York City was 785 per 100,000 in 1894, declining to less than 300 in 1900, and in 1920, when active immunization of schoolchildren began, it fell below 100. By 1940 the disease had been virtually eliminated.

Initially, the saving of lives was limited chiefly to children over 5. The mortality of infants and children under 5 years of age did not decrease materially until about 1900. At the turn of the century, largely because of improper feeding, poor sanitation, overcrowding, and poverty, the common killers among infants were diarrhea and pneumonia. As infant feeding improved, clean milk and water became available, and social conditions were ameliorated, infant mortality declined.

The increase in life expectancy since 1900 has been striking. That year life expectancy at birth was 49.2 years, with women living an average of two years longer than men; in 1979 it was 70.6 years for men and 78.3 for women.

In 1900 expectation of life at birth for nonwhites was 33 years, 14.6 years less than that of whites. By 1979 the life expectancy for nonwhites had risen to 69.9 years, but was still 4.5 years below that of whites. This difference resulted from a higher infant and maternal mortality among blacks, as well as higher death rates from certain infectious diseases.

LIFEGUARD, WASHINGTON'S. A corps of infantry and cavalry attached to Gen. George Washington and responsible also for the safety of baggage and papers. Organized in 1776, it was augmented at Valley Forge by 120 picked men as a model corps to be trained by Baron Friedrich von Steuben. Its official title was the Commander in Chief's Guard.

LIFE INSURANCE. *See* **Insurance.**

LIFESAVING SERVICE. In 1789 the Massachusetts Humane Society began erecting huts on portions of that state's coast for the shelter of persons escaped from shipwrecks. In 1807 the society established at Cohasset the first lifesaving station in America and soon afterward another at Lovell's Island, both in the area of Boston Bay. It continued to be the only organized lifesaving agency in the nation until 1837, when Congress authorized the president to employ ships to cruise along the shores and render aid to distressed navigators. Rep. William A. Newell of New Jersey, introduced a bill in 1848 for aiding shipwrecked persons. An appropriation of $10,000 was made, and eight lifesaving stations were set up between Sandy Hook and Little Egg Harbor, N.J. The crews were all volunteers from the vicinity, but they were under the direction of officers appointed by the Revenue Marine Service and the Life Saving Benevolent Society of New York, organized in 1849. This society awarded medals for bravery and otherwise aided the work. Another appropriation in 1849 financed the establishment of four more stations on the New Jersey and Long Island coasts, all with volunteer crews. Sumner I. Kimball, chief of the Revenue Cutter Service, induced Congress in 1870–71 to appropriate $200,000 and to authorize the organization of a government lifesaving service, under control of the Treasury Department. On Jan. 28, 1915, this service lost its identity, being merged with the Revenue Cutter Service to form the U.S. Coast Guard. It then had 203 stations on the coasts of the Atlantic and Gulf of Mexico, 62 on the Great Lakes, 19 on the Pacific coast, and one at the falls of the Ohio River at Louisville, Ky.

LIGHTHOUSE BOARD. Although the federal government took control of navigational aids in 1789, before 1820 the commissioner of revenue supervised them; from then until the creation of the Lighthouse Board, they were under the wing of the fifth auditor of the treasury. In 1851 a board recommended the creation of the Lighthouse Board to govern federal aids to navigation. Two naval officers, two army engineers, and two civilians made up the board; except for the years 1871–78, when Joseph Henry was chairman, the board was headed by commissioned officers. Technical officers on detail supervised construction and routine operations in the field. The board itself operated through committees supervising particular aspects of the work. With the decline of the American merchant marine after the Civil War, the board's relative importance declined, as did its innovating role. In 1910 the board was supplanted by the Bureau of Lighthouses.

LIGHTING. Domestic lighting in America prior to about 1815 included lamps fueled by oil derived from animal or vegetable sources, tallow or bayberry candles, and pinewood torches. The late 18th-century chemical revolution stimulated dramatic improvements in both lamp design and candle composition. These included a lamp with a tubular wick and shaped glass chimney invented in the early 1780's by Aimé Argand and introduced into the United States during the administration of George Washington. The Argand lamp was approximately ten times as efficient as previous oil lamps and was widely used in lighthouses, in public buildings, and in the homes of the affluent. European chemists also isolated stearine, which was used in "snuffless candles," so called because they had self-consuming wicks. The candles became available during the 1820's and were produced on a mass scale in candle factories.

After an efficient means of producing inflammable gas from coal was discovered by European scientists, a new era of lighting began during the first decade of the 19th century. Baltimore became the first American city to employ gas streetlights in 1816, but the gaslight industry did not enter its rapid-growth phase until after 1850. Capital investment increased from less than $7 million in 1850 to $150 million in 1880. The electric light industry emerged during the last two decades of the century. Improvements such as the Welsbach mantle kept gas lighting competitive until World War I. Rural residents continued to rely on candles or oil lamps throughout most of the 19th century because coal gas could not be economically distributed in areas of low population density. The discovery of petroleum in Pennsylvania in 1859 soon led to the development of the kerosine lamp.

Two competing systems of electric lighting developed rapidly after the invention of large self-excited electric generators capable of producing great quantities of inexpensive electrical energy. The American engineer Charles F. Brush developed an effective street-lighting system using arc lamps beginning in 1876. One of Brush's inventions was a device that prevented an entire series circuit of arc lamps from being disabled by the failure of a single lamp. Brush's first commercial central arc-light stations were installed in 1879.

Thomas A. Edison became the innovator of the incandescent-lighting industry. Beginning in 1878 he made an intensive study of the gaslight industry and determined that he could develop an electric system that would provide equivalent illumination without some of the defects and at a competitive cost. Crucial to his success was an efficient and long-lived high-resistance lamp that would allow for the same necessary subdivision of light that had been achieved in gas lighting but not in arc lighting. Edison and his assistants at his Menlo Park, N.J., laboratory solved this problem by means of a carbon filament lamp in 1879. The successful introduction of the incandescent lamp on a commercial scale at the Pearl Street (New York City) generating station in 1882 was a tribute to Edison's use of organized systems research.

The thirty-year period after 1880 was a time of intense market competition between the gaslight, arc light, and incandescent light industries and between the direct-current distribution system of Edison and the alternating-current system introduced by George Westinghouse. Incandescent lighting with alternating-current distribution ultimately emerged as the leader. The General Electric Company, which was organized in 1892 by a consolidation of the Edison Company and the Thomson-Houston Company, became the dominant lamp manufacturer, followed by Westinghouse.

An important event in the history of electric lighting was the formation of the General Electric Research Laboratory under Willis R. Whitney in 1900. A dramatic improvement in the incandescent lamp was achieved by William D. Coolidge of this laboratory in 1910 with the discovery of a process for making ductile tungsten wire. The more durable and efficient tungsten lamps quickly supplanted the carbon filament lamp. Irving Langmuir, also a General Electric scientist, completed development of a gas-filled tungsten lamp in 1912. This lamp, which was less susceptible to blackening of the bulb than the older high-vacuum lamp, was introduced commercially in 1913.

Development of a new type of electric light began at General Electric in 1935. This was the low-voltage fluorescent lamp, which came on the market in 1938. The fluorescent lamp had several advantages over the incandescent lamp, including higher efficiency and a larger surface area, which provided a more uniform source of illumination with less glare. It also required special fixtures and auxiliary elements. This lamp has come into wide usage, especially in office buildings and schools. High-intensity mercury-vapor lamps came into general use for street lighting after World War II.

LIGONIER, FORT. At the site of the Pennsylvania town so named, was built by Col. Henry Bouquet in 1758. After the Battle of Grant's Hill, French and Indians attacked Bouquet at Ligonier but were repulsed (*see* Loyalhanna, Battle of the). Thereafter the fort was an important link in the chain of communications between eastern Pennsylvania and Fort Pitt. During Pontiac's War, Ligonier was the only small fort west of the mountains in Pennsylvania that did not fall in the early attacks; its retention made possible the relief of Fort Pitt by Bouquet's forced march in 1763.

LIMA CONFERENCE. *See* **Latin America, U.S. Relations With.**

LIMITATIONS, STATUTES OF. *See* **Statutes of Limitations.**

LIMPING STANDARD. A term formerly used to describe the U.S. monetary standard in the late 19th and early 20th centuries. The standard was no longer bimetallic because the revision of the Coinage Laws Act of 1873 (later called the Crime of '73) had eliminated free coinage of the silver dollar. Yet it was more than a gold standard, because the Bland-Allison Act of 1878 and the Sherman Silver Purchase Act of 1890, laws passed in an unsuccessful effort to restore bimetallism, gave the silver dollars authorized by Congress status as "standard" money. These coins were full legal tender.

LINCOLN (Nebr.). Capital of Nebraska, with a population of 171,932 in 1980; the center of a metropolitan area in which 192,779 people lived. It has been the capital of Nebraska since 1867. A small settlement named Lancaster had been located on the site because there were salt wells in the vicinity. Lancaster was renamed Lincoln in honor of the recently assassinated president.

Lincoln's capitol, completed in 1932, is topped by a tall statue of a sower, thus identifying the building with the farming industry that is the state's leading activity. Lincoln is also the location of the University of Nebraska and includes memorials to William Jennings Bryan (its most famous resident) and to Gen. John J. Pershing, the World War I commander who had lived, studied, and taught at the University of Nebraska. The city is also important as a trading center and food processing center for its area of eastern Nebraska.

LINCOLN, ASSASSINATION OF (Apr. 14, 1865). At 10:15 P.M., while attending a performance of "Our American Cousin" at Ford's Theatre in Washington, D.C., President Abraham Lincoln was shot in the back of the head by John Wilkes Booth. Lincoln was carried to a lodging house opposite the theater. There, without regaining consciousness, he died at 7:22 on the following morning.

Despite the fact that Booth broke his leg in jumping from the presidential box to the stage, he made his way from the theater and, with David E. Herold, escaped from Washington in the direction of Virginia. They first went to the house of Dr. Samuel A. Mudd, who set Booth's leg, and then to the Potomac River, where they hid in a pine thicket. During their wait, a farmer, Thomas A. Jones, brought them food. It was not until Apr. 26 that Booth and Herold were surrounded in a tobacco shed on the farm belonging to Richard H. Garrett, near Port Royal, Va. There Herold surrendered, but Booth defied his captors and was shot.

Before the death of Booth the government had implicated nine persons in the assassination—George A. Atzerodt, Lewis Payne, Herold, Mary E. Surratt and her son John H. Surratt, Edward Spangler, Samuel Arnold Mudd, Michael O'Laughlin, and Booth. All except John H. Surratt were tried before a military commission, May 9–June 30, 1865. All were found guilty, although the verdict in the case of Mary Surratt was certainly a miscarriage of justice. Atzerodt, Payne, Herold, and Mary Surratt were hanged on July 7. Arnold, Mudd, and O'Laughlin were sentenced to life imprisonment while Spangler was given six years; the four were imprisoned in Fort Jefferson, Dry Tortugas, in the Florida Keys. Jones and Garrett were not indicted. John H. Surratt was brought to trial in 1867, but the jury failed to agree, and his case was later dismissed. By Mar. 4, 1869, President Andrew Johnson had pardoned all the imprisoned men, except for O'Laughlin, who had died in 1867.

LINCOLN COUNTY WAR. A struggle that began in 1876 between two rival groups of ranchers and businessmen in southeastern New Mexico. One faction was headed by Maj. L. G. Murphy and the other by John Chisum and Alexander A. McSween. A series of murders and depredations culminated in July 1878 in a three-day battle at the town of Lincoln, in which McSween and several others were killed. William H. Bonney, better known as Billy the Kid, was a prominent figure in this struggle.

LINCOLN-DOUGLAS DEBATES (1858). Took place between Republican Abraham Lincoln and the Democratic incumbent, Stephen A. Douglas, during the senatorial campaign in Illinois. Douglas' opening speeches in his reelection drive, with their effective frontal attack on Lincoln's "house divided" doctrine, alarmed Lincoln's managers and led him to issue a formal challenge to Douglas. Douglas agreed to one debate in each of seven congressional districts.

About 12,000 gathered at Ottawa, Aug. 21, for the first debate. Douglas' theme was the sectional bias, the strife-fomenting nature, of Republican doctrine. He read a series of resolutions he mistakenly believed had been adopted when the party was formed in Illinois in 1854 and pressed Lincoln to deny his endorsement of them. Douglas likewise assailed Lincoln's own position on the slavery issue.

Lincoln went to Freeport for the second debate on Aug. 27 determined to impale Douglas on the horns of a dilemma. There he asked the Freeport questions, related to the Supreme Court's ruling in the Dred Scott case. Either Douglas must accept the Supreme Court's decision, which would mean that slavery could go anywhere, or he must cease urging the sanctity of Supreme Court decisions. It was not a new issue for Douglas, who was more realist than dialectician. "Slavery cannot exist a day," he answered, "or an hour, anywhere, unless it is supported by local police regulations." This was an effective counter in the debate.

The third took place on Sept. 15 at Jonesboro, in the southernmost region of the state, where neither antagonist had many partisans. At Charleston, three days later, the crowd was fairly evenly divided. Lincoln, smarting under Douglas' charges that he favored equality for blacks, toned down his earlier statements. Thereupon Douglas said his opponent's views were "jet black" in the North, "a decent mulatto" in the center, and "almost white" in Egypt.

On Oct. 7 the fifth debate took place at Galesburg, an abolitionist stronghold. On Oct. 13 the two men grappled at Quincy, and the last debate was two days later at Alton. There Lincoln and Douglas epitomized again their points of view. Lincoln repeated the charge that Douglas looked to "no end of the institution of slavery." But Douglas said: "I care more for the great principle of self-government, the right of the people to rule, than I do for all the Negroes in Christendom. I would not endanger the perpetuity of this Union."

Lincoln lost the election, but the debates brought him to the attention of the nation.

LINCOLN HIGHWAY. The idea of a coast-to-coast highway originated with Carl G. Fisher in 1912. In September Fisher laid the proposition before the leaders of the automobile industry and, giving $1,000 himself, obtained pledges of more than $4 million for construction. To add a patriotic touch, he gave the name "Lincoln" to the proposed road in 1913, and the Lincoln Highway Association was formed to further the project. States and individuals made contributions and cement manufacturers donated material for "demonstration miles." By an act of 1921 the federal government increased its aid to states in road building, which greatly helped this project. From Jersey City the route chosen passed through Philadelphia, Gettysburg, and Pittsburgh, Pa., and Fort Wayne, Ind.; near Chicago; through Omaha, Nebr., Cheyenne, Wyo., Salt Lake City, Utah, and Sacramento, Calif. It ended in San Francisco. The original course was 3,389 miles, later cut by more than 50 miles. Work began in October 1914 but proceeded slowly. When the association closed its offices on Dec. 31, 1927, $90 million had been spent. In 1925 the road became U.S. Highway 30.

LINDBERGH KIDNAPPING CASE. On the night of Mar. 1, 1932, the eighteen-month-old son of Col. Charles A. Lindbergh was abducted from his parents' country home near Hopewell, N.J. The kidnapper climbed to the window of the second-story nursery by a ladder brought with him. He left a note demanding $50,000 ransom. John F. Condon, a retired New York teacher, acting as intermediary, succeeded in having two night interviews with the man in a cemetery. On the second occasion, Apr. 8, the money was paid the kidnapper upon his promise to deliver the child, but the child had been slain. Its body was found on May 12 near the Lindbergh home. The serial number of every note of the ransom money was made public. On Sept. 15, 1934, a carpenter named Bruno Hauptmann passed one of the bills at a New York filling station and was arrested. More than $14,000 of the ransom money was found concealed about his house. At his trial at Flemington, N.J., in January–February 1935 the ladder was identified as having been made with plank taken from his attic. He was convicted, and executed on Apr. 3, 1936.

LINDBERGH'S ATLANTIC FLIGHT (1927). The first nonstop flight between New York and Paris, and the first one-man crossing of the Atlantic by air, was made by Charles

A. Lindbergh, May 20–21, 1927. Backed by a group of St. Louis businessmen, Lindbergh supervised the construction of a Ryan monoplane, christened the *Spirit of St. Louis.* On the morning of May 20, 1927, Lindbergh took off from Roosevelt Field with a load of 425 gallons of gasoline. Encountering fog and sleet, the aviator was compelled to fly blind part of the way at an altitude of 1,500 feet. Sighting the coast of Ireland, he turned his course toward France. After flying over England, he crossed the English Channel and at ten o'clock in the evening saw the lights of Paris. After circling the Eiffel Tower, he made for the Le Bourget airfield, where he landed, after having flown 3,605 miles in thirty-three hours and thirty minutes. The reception in France was enthusiastic. He became a symbol of daring, courage, and international fraternity. In Brussels, Berlin, and London he was received with equal enthusiasm. He returned to the United States from Cherbourg on the U.S.S. *Memphis,* sent by command of President Calvin Coolidge.

LIND'S AMERICAN TOUR (1850–1852). After opening at Castle Garden in New York City, Sept. 11, 1850, Jenny Lind, the "Swedish Nightingale," toured the eastern United States. Under the astute management of P. T. Barnum, she gave ninety-five concerts, the last on June 9, 1851. Tickets were auctioned before the concerts and often sold at fantastic prices, one at $650. Thereafter she gave many concerts under her own management before returning to Europe in 1852.

LIND'S MISSION TO MEXICO (1913). After the overthrow of President Francisco Madero of Mexico in February 1913, the government of the United States refused to recognize the government set up by Victoriano Huerta. In August John Lind of Minnesota was commissioned by President Woodrow Wilson as his personal representative in Mexico City, to use his influence to set up a constitutional government worthy of recognition. Lind's efforts failed.

LINEN INDUSTRY. Flax was the principal textile fabric in colonial America, where it was raised and made into linen on the farm. Some colonies subsidized its manufacture into sailcloth. For two centuries dressed flax and yarn were common articles of barter; homespun was familiar merchandise in country trade; and linsey-woolsey, made of flax and wool, was a common clothing fabric. With the coming of the cotton gin and of Arkwright machinery, cotton displaced flax. Small linen mills were established subsequently, but few were permanent, and none grew into sizable enterprises. The most successful manufactured thread and canvas. The Civil War cotton shortage stimulated efforts to revive the industry, but the high cost of dressing domestic flax and duties on imported fiber prevented its extension. Some linen goods, mostly thread and towels, are still manufactured in America, but the industry is a minor one, and most of the linen products now used in the United States are imported.

LINGAYEN GULF. Situated on the northwest coast of Luzon Island in the Philippines, Lingayen Gulf suffered two invasions in World War II: the first, in 1941, by the Japanese; the second, three years later, by the returning Americans.

In December 1941, the shores of Lingayen Gulf were defended by Filipino and American troops commanded by Gen. Douglas MacArthur. The invasion force of Japanese Lt. Gen. Masaharu Homma began landing before dawn on Dec. 22 along the eastern shore of Lingayen Gulf. A few artillery rounds and ineffective attacks by a handful of American submarines and bombers were all the defenders could muster. Homma quickly secured his initial objectives and began to drive inland. A day later, MacArthur issued the order to withdraw to Bataan.

Three years later, the situation was reversed. The Japanese, commanded by Gen. Tomoyuki Yamashita, lacked air and naval support and were no match for the powerful ground, sea, and air forces that MacArthur had marshaled for his return to Luzon. Yamashita planned, therefore, to offer little resistance to the American invaders, and to fall back to inland delaying positions for a final stand. Other than Japanese suicide planes that punished the American convoys, there was no real opposition to the invasion. After a devastating preassault bombardment, the landing began at 9:30 A.M. on Jan. 9, 1945, on the south shore of Lingayen Gulf. By evening the Americans had secured a wide and deep beachhead, in preparation for the drive on Manila. The shores of Lingayen Gulf soon became a vast supply depot to support American operations inland.

LINSEY-WOOLSEY. A stout homespun cloth having a wool weft and commonly a flax warp, although hemp or cotton was sometimes used, extensively manufactured in the American colonies and on the frontier.

LIQUOR. *See* **Bootlegging; Rum Trade; Whiskey.**

LIQUOR LAWS. Early liquor laws were enacted primarily as efforts to encourage temperance and what was perceived as morality. Although liquor legislation for perceived moral reasons is still a common goal, mid-20th-century statutes reflect a desire to protect those whose rights are threatened by liquor sellers and abusers.

As early as 1619 the colony of Virginia outlawed gaming, drunkenness, and other excesses. A little later, it enacted a number of liquor acts, including legislation against drunkenness among the clergy, and in 1676 it penalized judges who drank to excess on court days. Beginning in 1633 and during the rest of the 17th century, Massachusetts passed progressively stricter laws against drunkenness. New York first restricted the liquor business in 1638, and the remaining colonies soon did the same. The colonies one after another forbade the sale of liquor to Indians, with Connecticut first in 1645. Paradoxically, at the same time the colonies started to reap considerable income from liquor taxes.

By 1800 drinking had become enough of a problem to excite a temperance movement. In 1829 Maine was the first state to pass a local-option law, which permitted small subdivisions, such as counties, to prohibit liquor sales within their boundaries. The period 1830–45 was an era of local option, but in 1846 Maine initiated a trend of statewide prohibition. In 1890 the Supreme Court held that the states' power to regulate commerce was preempted by that of the federal government under the Constitution and that they could not prohibit interstate liquor traffic without congressional sanction (*Leisy* v. *Hardin,* 135 U.S. 100). Congress then attempted to protect the "dry" states from liquor shipments with the Wilson Act (1890) and the more effective Webb-Kenyon Act (1913). The increasing momentum of the temperance movement stimulated twenty-eight states to go dry by 1918.

The violent Prohibition era lasted from Jan. 16, 1920, until the ratification of the Twenty-first Amendment on Dec. 5, 1933, which repealed the Eighteenth Amendment. The Twenty-first Amendment has been held to mandate the preeminence of states in liquor regulation, and a resultant diversity of legislation exists among the states. Although no state is completely dry any longer, several states permit local options. To control the liquor traffic better, some states have established a government monopoly on liquor sales.

All states outlaw sales of liquor to minors, the adult age varying from eighteen to twenty-one. All states forbid automobile operators from driving while intoxicated, with a multitude of definitions of "intoxicated." There are 2 million arrests each year in the United States based on state public-drunkenness statutes. Since passage of the Twenty-first Amendment the federal government has had no legal basis for involving itself in liquor control.

LISA, FORT. Near the present site of Omaha, Nebr., it was established by Manuel Lisa, probably in the spring of 1813, when he was forced to abandon Fort Manuel, in what is now Montana. The most important post on the Missouri River from 1813 to 1822, it controlled the trade of the Omaha, Pawnee, Oto, and neighboring Indians.

LISA AND COMPANY. Consisted of Manuel Lisa, Gregoire Sarpy, François M. Benoist, and Charles Sanguinet. After Auguste and Pierre Chouteau failed to renew their fur trade monopoly and moved their activities to the Arkansas River, Manuel Lisa and Company, in 1802, obtained the exclusive trade with the Osage on the waters of the Missouri and Osage rivers. This monopoly ended with the establishment of U.S. territorial government in Upper Louisiana in 1804. In 1807 another firm called Manuel Lisa and Company was organized by Lisa, William Morrison, and Pierre Menard, with a capital of $16,000.

LITCHFIELD LAW SCHOOL. Established in 1784 in Litchfield, Conn., by Tapping Reeve, who was its only teacher until 1798. In that year he was succeeded by James Gould, who developed an institution that in the early 19th century gave legal training to hundreds of young men from almost every state and numbered among its graduates some of the most prominent men in the public life of the next generation, including Henry Clay. Before it closed in 1833, the Litchfield school had sent out more than a thousand graduates.

LITERACY. Usually defined as the ability to read and write in any language. The United States has enjoyed a very high rate of literacy among its people as a result of a strong American tradition of interest in schooling and a great emphasis on the printed word as a means of communication. A person who cannot read and write at all is identified as being "illiterate." Some experts call individuals "functionally illiterate" if they do not have the skills learned by schoolwork through the fourth- or sixth-grade level. An estimate of the number of "functional illiterates" in the United States as of 1980 was about 20 million adults. Estimates of complete illiterates run to about 1,120,000 people.

LITERACY TEST. Has been used by the federal government as an adjunct to its immigration and naturalization laws and by many states as a device to determine qualifications for voting. The federal government's use of the literacy test has not been a matter of major controversy, and the passage of immigration reform legislation in 1965, which abolished the national-origins system, removed one of the primary objections raised when the literacy test act was passed in 1917.

As used by the states, the literacy test gained notoriety as a means for denying the franchise to blacks. Effective federal action to counter this discrimination did not occur until the 1960's. In 1964, the Civil Rights Act provided that literacy tests used as a qualification for voting in federal elections be administered wholly in writing and only to persons who had not completed six years of formal education. The 1965 Voting Rights Act suspended the use of literacy tests in all states or political subdivisions in which fewer than 50 percent of the voting-age residents were registered as of Nov. 1, 1964, or had voted in the 1964 presidential election. In a series of cases, the Supreme Court upheld the legislation and restricted the use of literacy tests for non-English-speaking citizens. Under the 1970 extension of the Voting Rights Act, the use of the literacy test was suspended in all states and their political subdivisions until Aug. 6, 1975. The suspension of the literacy test led to significant increases in black registration in the seven southern states covered by the 1965 law, and the registration problems faced by non-English-speaking citizens have been eased by subsequent judicial and legislative actions.

LITERARY SOCIETIES. Common in rural districts throughout the West during the last quarter of the 19th century and, in some remote communities, well into the 20th century. Their objectives were social, since they sought to create or stimulate interest in "things literary" and at the same time provide entertainment and an opportunity for social contacts. Meetings were generally held once or twice a month, usually at the schoolhouse, and consisted of readings; short plays, commonly called dialogues; debates on various subjects; and sometimes a vocal solo, duet, or quartet.

LITERATURE. The American mind has its beginnings in the literature of discovery, exploration, and settlement from Richard Hakluyt's *Principal Navigations, Voyages, Traffiques and Discoveries* (1589) onward. A library of narratives by Capt. John Smith, Gov. William Bradford, Gov. John Winthrop, Edward Johnson, Thomas Morton, George Alsop, Mary Rowlandson, and others describes and interprets the first ventures of the English people into the New World. The writing shares the intellectual excitement of the eras of John Milton and Francis Bacon; it develops theories of history, of salvation, and of the relation of church and state that had a profound influence on American thought. The highest expression of the New England mind came in the work of Jonathan Edwards: *A Faithful Narrative of the Surprising Work of God* (1737) and *Enquiry Into the Modern Prevailing Notions of Freedom of the Will* (1754). Virginia neatly counterpointed the metaphysics of Edwards with the secularity of William Byrd, whose *History of the Dividing Line* (1738, first printed 1841 in *The Westover Manuscripts*) remains a humorous minor masterpiece; whose secret journals, not published until 1941 and 1942, reveal an American Samuel Pepys; and whose career is a blend of the Renaissance and the Enlightenment. The erudite Cotton Mather, in *Magnalia Christi Americana* (1702), brought the New England mind face to face with the Enlightenment. More widely read than any of these, the first American to have worldwide influence was Benjamin Franklin, whose adroit *Autobiography* is a classic of Western literature and whose letters, satires, bagatelles, almanacs, and scientific writings are the work of a citizen of the world.

The intellectual brilliance of American thought between the end of the Seven Years' War (1763) and the creation of the federal government (1789) is among the wonders of the history of ideas. Franklin participated, but so did Samuel Adams, John Adams, Thomas Paine, Thomas Jefferson, and others. Of this group Paine, the propagandist, whose *Common Sense* (1776) and *The Crisis* (1776–83) awakened American enthusiasm, and Jefferson, the principal author of the Declaration of Independence and the author of an unrivaled collection of letters and papers, are best remembered today.

The Revolution created a drive toward cultural independence. The satires of Philip Freneau, Francis Hopkinson, and John Trumbull are mainly of interest to scholars, but Freneau, in lyric poetry and in an exercise in Gothic romanticism, *The House of Night* (1779), marks the transition from the Enlightenment to romanticism. Trumbull was one of the Connecticut Wits, a group conscientiously endeavoring to create a national literature. The romances of Charles Brockden Brown have more vitality; *Wieland* (1798), *Arthur Mervyn* (1799), and *Edgar Huntley* (1799).

Maturer years began with three writers associated with New York. William Cullen Bryant—whose "Thanatopsis" (1817) was the product of a wunderkind and whose philosophical poems, such as "The Prairies," have intellectual dignity—edited the *New York Evening Post* from 1829 to 1878, giving space in its columns to advocates of liberal and radical movements. More popular was Washington Irving, whose *History of New York by Diedrich Knickerbocker* (1809) gave that city a symbolic figure, whose *Sketch Book* (1819–20) created Rip Van Winkle and Ichobod Crane, and whose *Alhambra* (1832), an exercise in the sentimental exotic, scarcely prophesied his *Tour of the Prairies* (1835) and his substantial biographies. The third was James Fenimore Cooper, of worldwide fame, whose Leatherstocking series (*The Pioneers,* 1823; *The Last of the Mohicans,* 1826; *The Prairie,* 1827; *The Pathfinder,* 1840; *The Deerslayer,* 1841) has been called an American prose epic.

Of those who sought a cosmopolitan solution to the question of what literary culture should be, the Cambridge poets —James Russell Lowell, Oliver Wendell Holmes, and Henry Wadsworth Longfellow—are characteristic. The most influential was Longfellow, who appealed to religious, patriotic, and cultural desires, in translations (his version of Dante Alighieri, 1865–69, is notable), short lyrics, remarkable sonnets, and narrative poems of special interest to the American of the 19th century—*Evangeline* (1847), *The Song of Hiawatha* (1855), *The Courtship of Miles Standish* (1858), and *Tales of a Wayside Inn* (1863, 1872, 1873). Holmes sought to liberate Americans from the tyranny of theology, and Lowell, from cultural provincialism. Associated with this group is the Quaker abolitionist John Greenleaf Whittier, whose *Snow-Bound* (1866) is an unforgettable vignette of rural America.

Moderns find the Concord group—Ralph Waldo Emerson, Henry David Thoreau, Nathaniel Hawthorne, and, a little apart from them, Herman Melville—more exciting. Emerson was the mover and shaker in 19th-century American idealism, with *Nature* (1836), "The American Scholar" (1837), "The Divinity School Address" (1838), and the *Essays* (1841, 1844). Industrial society pays more attention to Thoreau, whose *Walden* (1854) is more widely read and whose vigorous essays on what Americans of the late 20th century call civil rights are applicable to present problems. The modern appeal of Hawthorne in such books as *The Scarlet Letter* (1850), *The House of the Seven Gables* (1851), and *The Marble Faun* (1860), as well as in his short stories, was heightened in the 20th century with a spurt of interest in neo-Calvinist theories of human nature. A later, drastic revolution in literary values has placed Melville among the literary giants for much the same reason; and *Mardi* (1849), *Moby-Dick* (1851), *Pierre* (1852), and *Billy Budd* (not available until 1924) are studied for their symbolism of good and evil.

Only one antebellum author from the South was of comparable stature: Edgar Allan Poe. Although the present tendency is to derogate his genius, his influence as critic, short-story writer (*Tales of the Grotesque and Arabesque,* 1840), and poet has been worldwide.

Harriet Beecher Stowe's *Uncle Tom's Cabin* (1852), partisan, sentimental, and melodramatic, went around the world. After a great deal of unsuccessful hack writing, Walt Whitman produced the first version of *Leaves of Grass* (1855), a work he continued to rewrite and expand until 1892. Famous as metrical experimentation, this gospel was part of the 19th-century religion of humanity. In *Calamus* (1860), *Drum Taps* (1865), *Democratic Vistas* (1871), and *Specimen Days and Collect* (1882), Whitman caught the epic quality of the Civil War, as Abraham Lincoln caught its mystic quality in the Gettysburg Address (1863), and denounced political corruption as Mark Twain and Charles Dudley Warner did in the uneven novel they wrote together, *The Gilded Age* (1873).

The Civil War divides the culture of agrarian America from that of industrial America. One result of that conflict was curiosity about the far-flung nation; and the increasing effectiveness of literary periodicals, notable in the creation of the *Atlantic Monthly* in 1857, gave rise to a varied literature of local color. The postwar years also saw the rise of a mature literature of biography, history, and expository prose. American biography really struck its stride with James Parton's *Life and Times of Benjamin Franklin* (1864) and has continued to produce masterly works ever since. American achievement in historical writing begins early and matures in such books as William Hickling Prescott's *History of the Conquest of Mexico* (1843) and Francis Parkman's distinguished series *France and England in North America* (1851–92)—these two, together with John Lothrop Motley, being classed as "romantic" historians. Stylistic craftsmanship is most evident in the work of Henry Adams, whose *History of the United States During the Administrations of Jefferson and Madison* (1889–91) challenges the literary supremacy of Parkman.

Henry George's *Progress and Poverty* (1877–79) and Edward Bellamy's *Looking Backward* (1888) were very influential; and a varied literature of science, philosophy, and theology developed as the country discovered Charles Darwin. Andrew Dickson White's powerful, if uneven, *History of the Warfare of Science With Theology in Christendom* (1896) is perhaps the single best monument of this debate. All this is the background for William James's classic *Principles of Psychology* (1890), the prelude to pragmatism; *The Will to Believe and Other Essays* appeared in 1897.

American fiction came of age in the late 19th century, however great the contributions of Hawthorne's generation. In *The Adventures of Huckleberry Finn* (1884), Mark Twain created a classic work; and if his collected writings are uneven, he moved steadily from the "oral" manner of *The Innocents Abroad* (1869) to the Voltairean irony of *The Mysterious Stranger* (1916) as hilarity gave way to pessimism. But the gathering forces of realism found their spokesman in William Dean Howells. His *Criticism and Fiction* (1891) summed up realistic, but not naturalistic, theory; in *A Modern Instance* (1881), *The Rise of Silas Lapham* (1884), and *A Hazard of New Fortunes* (1890), he showed that the business of literature was with the here and now, not with trumpet-and-drum romances and sentimental tales. Beneath the serene surface of his prose there is a sardonic feeling, an ironic vision. Realists and naturalists (none of them consistent) were grouped around him—Hamlin Garland, Stephen Crane, Frank Norris, and others; and out of the excitement emerged the slow, awkward genius of Theodore Dreiser, whose *Sister Carrie* (1900) marks the transition in fiction between the realism of the 19th century and that of the 20th.

By 1887 Charles W. Chestnutt had made his mark as a short-story writer with the publication of "The Goophered Grapevine." Born in Ohio, Chesnutt taught in the South and then returned to the North and studied law. His novels—*The House Behind the Cedars* (1900), *The Marrow of Tradition* (1901), and *The Colonel's Dream* (1905)—are considered to be overwritten, but the short stories present folk customs and beliefs effectively. During the same period Paul Laurence Dunbar became prominent as a poet, writing both in dialect and in formal English.

While realists, sentimentalists, naturalists, and idealists argued, Henry James, self-exiled, opened the modern manner in fiction by concentrating on the subjective world. His progress from *The American* (1877) through *The Portrait of a Lady* (1881) to *The Wings of the Dove* (1902), *The Golden Bowl* (1904), and *The Sense of the Past* (1917) is for admirers a march toward subtlety of insight and of craftsmanship. He was a theorist of literary art (for example, *Notes on Novelists,* 1914); and his example has profoundly influenced contemporaries and successors of the rank of Edith Wharton (*The House of Mirth,* 1905), Willa Cather (*A Lost Lady,* 1923), and Ellen Glasgow (*The Sheltered Life,* 1932).

In the early 20th century, poetry seemed to recapture the great audiences it had lost since Longfellow, when Vachel Lindsay, Edgar Lee Masters, Edwin Arlington Robinson, Carl Sandburg, and Robert Frost achieved vast publics. But foreign influences from France and Italy and the impact of World War I, summed up in T. S. Eliot's *The Waste Land* (1922) and in the energetic propaganda of Ezra Pound, diverted poetry into the more difficult styles of Conrad Aiken, Wallace Stevens, Hart Crane, and Marianne Moore.

Reacting against the canons of the 19th century, critical theory, whether it concerned literature or culture, took on new importance about 1910. Van Wyck Brooks, in *America's Coming of Age* (1915), campaigned for a "usable past," which he created in later volumes; H. L. Mencken demanded "sophistication" in various books of *Prejudices* (1919–27); and Walter Lippmann in *A Preface to Morals* (1929) and Joseph Wood Krutch in *The Modern Temper* (1929) declined to accept traditional canons of the dignity of man. In vain the neohumanists—Irving Babbitt, Paul Elmer More, Stuart P. Sherman, and others—asserted that long-run sagacity lay with tradition. The distinguished prose of Lewis Mumford, in such books as *Sticks and Stones* (1924) and *The Brown Decades* (1931), demonstrated that the modern spirit was not identical with iconoclasm.

The 1920's began with the smashing success of Sinclair Lewis' *Main Street* (1920) and closed with the troubled rhetoric of Thomas Wolfe's *Look Homeward, Angel* (1929), a singular specimen of the confessional literature associated with the European romantics. The brilliant decade included F. Scott Fitzgerald's *The Great Gatsby* (1925) and the works of Ernest Hemingway; James Boyd's *Drums* (1925), which was a historical novel; and a spate of "sophisticated" writers, including James Branch Cabell, Joseph Hergesheimer, and Carl Van Vechten. Possibly the soundest products of the self-conscious school were Thornton Wilder's philosophical contes, such as *The Bridge of San Luis Rey* (1927).

From the cultural mix in Harlem in New York City and the sponsorship of artistic talent there the Harlem Renaissance erupted in 1921. Carl Van Vechten was the best known of the patrons. The range of production was broad, from poetry on West Indian themes by Claude McKay to Countee Cullen's lyrics in the style of John Keats and E. A. Robinson to Langston Hughes's scenes of the city and the novels of James Weldon Johnson, Wallace Thurman, and Zora Neale Hurston.

The angry thirties, as they have been called, took revenge by nourishing proletarian fiction that included the *Studs Lonigan* trilogy (1932–35) of James T. Farrell, John Dos Passos' *U.S.A.* (1937), and John Steinbeck's *In Dubious Bat-*

tle (1936) and *The Grapes of Wrath* (1939). The neonaturalistic novel also emphasized environment as the shaper of lives, especially in the social protest of Nelson Algren and the exposés of the black's plight in the work of Richard Wright, Erskine Caldwell, and Lillian Smith. The emerging genius of the 1930's was William Faulkner, who used his native Mississippi for a background to his criticism of modern society. A somber view of human failure and of race relations, *The Sound and the Fury* (1929), was followed by *Light in August* (1932), *Absalom, Absalom!* (1936), and twelve other novels. Foreign reporting of unexampled penetration by John Gunther, Edgar Snow, Vincent Sheean, and others not only pictured the death of Europe but also prepared Americans for a second world war. The spate of novels concerning World War I—John Dos Passos' *Three Soldiers* (1921), E. E. Cummings' *The Enormous Room* (1922), and Hemingway's *The Sun Also Rises* (1926) and *A Farewell to Arms* (1929) are examples—were at once the result of shock and of a return to European literary techniques. The novels of World War II lacked the shock techniques, but were frequently disturbing indictments and even previsions of future problems, notably James Gould Cozzens' *Guard of Honor* (1948), Norman Mailer's massive *The Naked and the Dead* (1948), James Jones' *From Here to Eternity* (1951), and Joseph Heller's surreal *Catch-22* (1961).

The first three decades after World War II saw powerful pressures on the literary arts, the novelist and the poet have had to compete with an increasing public interest in theology and philosophy, history and sociology, and the phenomenon known as "the new journalism." David Riesman's study of human behavior, *The Lonely Crowd* (1950); Paul Tillich's argument for religious existentialism, *The Courage To Be* (1952); Erik H. Erikson's *Childhood and Society* (1950); the historical studies of C. Vann Woodward; the psychoanalytic critiques of Norman O. Brown; and revivals of Oriental mysticism have had wide currency. Even more popular are the essays of certain journalists who combine autobiography with polemic, historical facts with anecdote: such black writers as James Baldwin and Eldridge Cleaver; such novelists turned journalists as Mailer, Truman Capote, Wright Morris, and Gore Vidal; and such cultural observers as Tom Wolfe and John Cage.

Deriving from the works of Nathanael West and Henry Roth in the 1930's, the postwar Jewish novel has flourished in the fiction of J. D. Salinger, Saul Bellow, Bernard Malamud, Philip Roth, Leslie Epstein, Isaac Bashevis Singer, and Joseph Heller. The southern novel retains older traditions and more diverse talents, notably Eudora Welty, Carson McCullers, Flannery O'Connor, and William Styron. The fantasists express their subjectivism in satire, parody, and absurdist humor (Kurt Vonnegut, John Barth, Donald Barthelme, Jerzy Kosinski, John Hawkes, Thomas Pynchon, Thomas Berger) or in the prophetic visions of science fiction (Ray Bradbury, Robert A. Heinlein, Isaac Asimov). Virtuoso novelists and storytellers such as Vladimir Nabokov (*Lolita,* 1955), John Updike (*Rabbit, Run,* 1960; *Rabbit Redux,* 1971; *Rabbit is Rich,* 1981), John Cheever, and Joyce Carol Oates have kept the genre alive by sheer linguistic agility. The major war and postwar black writers have included Richard Wright (*Native Son,* 1940), Ralph Ellison (*Invisible Man,* 1952), James Baldwin, poet-dramatist LeRoi Jones (who in 1969 changed his name to Imamu Amiri Baraka), and Eldridge Cleaver.

The postwar poets have had a more difficult time. Chief among them was Robert Lowell. Lowell's early Catholic visions in clotted, elliptical verse forms gave way to intensely personal confessions (*Life Studies,* 1959) and public utterances on civil issues (*For the Union Dead,* 1964; *Notebook, 1967–1968,* 1969) that mark a major talent, a poet who has found his right métier. Had they lived past middle age, Theodore Roethke, a romantic lyricist and mystic; John Berryman, a learned, idiosyncratic original, the inventor of "dream songs"; and Randall Jarrell, the witty poet-critic-teacher, might have achieved Lowell's eminence. Had they not dissolved almost as quickly as they assembled, several groups of poets—namely, the Black Mountain poets (Charles Olson, Robert Creeley), the beat generation (Allen Ginsberg, Gregory Corso), the San Francisco group (Lawrence Ferlinghetti, Gary Snyder), the New York school (John Ashbery, Frank O'Hara, Kenneth Koch)—might have left a deeper impress upon American literary history.

The impress made by playwrights is probably even slighter, and Eugene O'Neill continues to be the leading dramatist of this century. Except for the meteoric careers of Arthur Miller and Tennessee Williams during the later 1940's and 1950's and the brief promise of Edward Albee in the 1960's, American writing for the theater declined.

Literary criticism seems also to have weakened. The death of Edmund Wilson in 1972 (*Axel's Castle,* 1931; *To the Finland Station,* 1940; *Memoirs of Hecate County,* 1946) removed from the scene America's one true man of letters, albeit Alfred Kazin (*On Native Grounds,* 1932; *The Inmost Leaf,* 1955), and Lionel Trilling (*The Liberal Imagination,* 1950; *Beyond Culture,* 1965) maintained an intellectual tradition. Writers such as Leslie Fiedler and Richard Poirier breathe life into literary polemics, and E. B. White has kept the essay form alive. But belles lettres no longer hold the position of eminence they held in the 19th century.

LITTLE AMERICA. Name given by Richard E. Byrd to the Antarctic base which he established in 1929. Byrd used the base area of Little America in several of his Antarctic expeditions and the area has continued to be known by that name.

LITTLE BELT AFFAIR. *See* **President.**

LITTLE BIGHORN, BATTLE OF (June 25, 1876)**.** The Sioux in Dakota Territory bitterly resented the opening of the Black Hills to settlers in violation of the Treaty of Fort Laramie of 1868. Owing also to official graft and negligence they were facing starvation in the fall of 1875. They began to leave their reservations, contrary to orders, to engage in their annual buffalo hunt. They were joined by tribesmen from other reservations until the movement took on the proportions of a serious revolt. An order originating with the Bureau of Indian Affairs was sent to all reservation officials early in December, directing them to notify the Indians to return by Jan. 31 under penalty of being attacked by the U.S. Army.

Early in 1876 Gen. Philip H. Sheridan ordered a concentration of troops on the upper Yellowstone River, to capture or disperse the numerous bands of Dakota who were hunting there. In June Gen. Alfred H. Terry, department commander, and Col. George A. Custer, with his regiment from Fort Abraham Lincoln, marched overland to the Yellowstone. At the mouth of Rosebud Creek, a tributary of the Yellowstone, Custer received his final orders from Terry—to locate and disperse the Indians. With twelve companies of the Seventh Cavalry, Custer set out and soon discovered the Sioux camped on the south bank of the Little Bighorn River. He sent Maj. Marcus Reno with three companies of cavalry and all the Arikara scouts across the upper ford of the river to attack the southern end of the Sioux camp. Capt. Frederick Benteen, with three companies, was sent to the left of Reno's line of march. Custer led five companies of the Seventh Cavalry down the river to the lower ford for an attack on the upper part of the camp. One company was detailed to bring up the pack train. This plan of battle, typical of Custer, was in the beginning completely successful. Suddenly faced by a vigorous double offensive, the Indians at first thought only of retreat. At this critical juncture Reno became utterly confused and ordered his men to fall back across the river. Thereupon the whole force of the Indian attack was concentrated upon Custer's command, compelling him to retreat from the river to a position at which his force was later annihilated.

An official inquiry into Reno's conduct in the battle was made in 1879, and he was cleared of all responsibility for the disaster. Since that time the judgment of military experts has tended to reverse this conclusion and to hold both Reno and Benteen gravely at fault.

LITTLE CHURCH AROUND THE CORNER. In 1870 the rector of a New York church refused a burial service to George Holland because he had been an actor, but remarked, "I believe there is a little church around the corner where they do such things." He referred to the Church of the Transfiguration on Twenty-ninth Street, built 1849–56, which thereupon became a favorite sanctuary for actors.

"LITTLE GIANT." The nickname given Stephen A. Douglas at a political rally in Jacksonville, Ill., 1834.

"LITTLE GROUP OF WILLFUL MEN." By a five-day filibuster ending Sunday, Mar. 4, 1917, the passage of a bill to arm merchant ships against German submarines was prevented by a group of eleven senators: Robert M. La Follette, Frank Norris, Albert Baird Cummins, Asle J. Gronna, Moses E. Clapp, John D. Works (Republicans); William J. Stone, James A. O'Gorman, William F. Kirby, Harry Lane, James K. Vardaman (Democrats). Citing the passage of the bill by the House of Representatives, 403–13, President Woodrow Wilson, in a public statement, stigmatized the senators as "a little group of willful men, representing no opinion but their own, [who] have rendered the great government of the United States helpless and contemptible."

LITTLE NIAGARA. *See* **Niagara, Carrying Place of.**

LITTLE NINE PARTNERS' PATENT. Granted Apr. 10, 1706, to Samuel Broughton and seven associates, it was in the northeastern part of Dutchess County, N.Y., and included the present towns of Milan and Pine Plains, the north half of North East, and small portions of Clinton and Stanford. The colonial assembly authorized its partition in 1734.

LITTLE RED SCHOOLHOUSE. From the 18th century well into the 20th, the small, one-room country school, usually located on a small piece of wasteland that the farmers could readily spare, was painted, if at all, with red or yellow ochre, the cheapest possible paint. Such schoolhouses were commonly found along country roads, and served several farm families in a central place. Pictures of such buildings became a sort of patriotic fetish with the American Protective Association, successor of the Know-Nothing party, at the close of the 19th century.

LITTLE ROCK (Ark.). Capital and largest city in Arkansas, with a population of 158,461 in 1980; the center of a metropolitan area of 393,781. It was the capital of Arkansas Territory from 1820. The business and processing center for central Arkansas' cotton raising and general farming activities, it has excellent transportation facilities, including highways, air connections, rail, and riverboat service. The city's industries include food processing, agricultural feed production, and manufacturing of electrical equipment such as light bulbs, or building materials made either of wood or brick. State government activities occupy a great part of the city's population.

Little Rock was named by a French explorer in the 18th century because of a rocky obstacle discovered in the Arkansas River. The city was captured by Union Army forces in 1863 and the Confederate state government moved temporarily to Washington, a town in southwestern Arkansas. Little Rock was the center of a bitter argument over the integration of its high school in 1957. The U.S. Supreme Court ordered the admission of black children to the school. When local and state officials refused to do so, President Dwight D. Eisenhower used army troops to enforce the court order.

***LITTLE SARAH*.** An English ship captured by French privateers in 1793 and interned at Philadelphia. The French minister, Edmond Charles Genêt, by equipping the vessel and permitting its departure under the name *Little Democrat* in defiance of Secretary of State Thomas Jefferson's protest of July 12, forfeited the confidence of President George Washington and even of Jefferson, whose pro-French sympathies were outraged. Demand for Genêt's recall became insistent, imposing a strain upon Franco-American relations.

LIVESTOCK INDUSTRY. Importations of livestock to America began in 1609 and the introduction of new breeds never fully ceased. The bulk of the livestock consisted of cattle, swine, sheep, and horses; but there were also some goats and mules. Extensive animal husbandry long characterized frontier farming. Animals grazed with little attention paid to them. They were rounded up periodically, marked to indicate ownership, and herded and trailed to market. Livestock trailed over long distances became tough and lean. As early as the 18th century some farmers near urban markets specialized in fattening livestock.

Intensive animal husbandry in areas of denser settlement involved fencing the animals, growing feed for them, giving them shelter, and maintaining more animals on less land. It demanded more capital for barns, fences, feed, and machinery. From 1900 on, the livestock industry became progressively more intensive and more productive.

Technological advances, particularly the discovery in 1874 of silage and the development of the gasoline tractor (1892), helped change the industry. The tractor also caused a decline in the numbers of horses and mules, which by 1960 were so few that the Bureau of the Census did not count them. Advances in veterinary medicine, including the discovery of insect disease vectors (for example, tick fever, 1889), helped reduce losses, as did the discovery of antibiotics. Predator ravages declined as the industry intensified.

Most of the processing of animal products was done on the farm before 1800. Slaughtering, processing, and marketing soon became a specialized industry. Coastal towns had developed meat-packing industries to supply the trade with the West Indies and Europe in the 18th century. Philadelphia led in the business before and after the Revolution. Processing shifted westward, and by the 1840's Cincinnati was a great processing center. Other centers arose, and Chicago had become "hog butcher of the world" by the 1870's.

Advances in refrigeration on both railroads and ships allowed packers to reach vast markets in America and abroad. The chief advantages of centering operations in Chicago and Omaha seemed to be that the industry could better exploit labor in those cities and that the railroads tended to direct the animals to central points. In the 1930's, changes in labor laws reduced the advantages of central location at the same time that the truck was gradually replacing the railroad. Slaughtering and processing drifted to the countryside. The Chicago Union Stock Yards, established in 1865, closed in 1971 for lack of business. The advent of chain stores accelerated the shift to small rural auction markets and to decentralized processing. Grocery chains and packers occasionally operated their own farms and feedlots, especially during the 1950's and 1960's, but did not gain control of that aspect of the industry. Between 1960 and 1980, the number of animals slaughtered rose by only 3 percent, from 135 million head to 139.6 million. (*See also* Cattle; Hogs.)

LLANO ESTACADO. *See* **Staked Plain.**

LOBBIES. Groups of individuals acting for themselves or others who seek to influence the decisions of government officials primarily by informal off-the-record communications and exchanges. Their tactics range from bribery, threats of electoral retaliation, and mass mailings to supplying research and information in support of their views. Intermediate forms of influence include campaign contributions and persuasion.

In the 19th and early 20th centuries the typical lobbyist focused on the legislative arena and used high-pressure methods, including bribery, to influence legislators. By the 1950's many lobbyists had enlarged their focus to include the executive branch and shifted to soft-sell tactics. Congress began investigating lobbies in 1913 with a study of the National Association of Manufacturers (NAM). Since that time there had been at least one major investigation in every decade. The investigations were followed first by piecemeal legislation and then, in Title III of the Legislative Reorganization Act of 1946, by general legislation to regulate lobbies. Loopholes in the legislation, however, permit many lobbies to avoid registration and full disclosure of their activities. An effort in 1980 to strengthen the 1946 law through disclosure of grass-root lobbying and major contributors was easily defeated. Nevertheless, lobbies have tried to seek a lower profile by moving away from high-pressure methods in recent decades.

With the rise of the executive branch as initiator of legislation and the growth of the administrative bureaucracy, the focus of lobbyists began to shift from legislative bodies to executives offices. As a corollary, the growing proportion of lobbying that occurs outside the legislative limelight reduces its overall visibility. Increasingly, chief executives and bureaucratic agencies lobby for legislative passage of bills they have initiated. They often appear to be the sole influence on legislation, even though it is not uncommon for regulatory agencies to be lobbying in the interests of the clientele they are supposed to be regulating.

In the 1970's most lobbyists were still acting for associations with an economic interest—business, farm, labor, and the professions. Over half of all registered lobbyists in Washington, D.C., are specialized business associations such as the American Petroleum Institute and Aerospace Industries Association. Although multiinterest associations such as the AFL–CIO, the Farm Bureau Federation, and the NAM continue to lobby on a variety of congressional issues, critics of lobbying have moved on to new targets—for example, the "military-industrial complex" and the impact of corporate campaign contributions on executive policymaking. In addition to primarily economic lobbies, the 20th century has seen major lobbying efforts by prohibition groups like the Anti-Saloon League, civil rights groups like the National Association for the Advancement of Colored People (NAACP), reform groups like Common Cause, and peace groups like the National Peace Action Committee.

LOCAL GOVERNMENT. The designation given to all units of government in the United States below the state level. In the original colonial settlements on the Atlantic coast, towns and counties played the most significant local governmental role. In New England the town was of central importance; counties formed the dominant pattern in the South. Increasing urbanization in the 19th century shifted the emphasis gradually to municipalities. By the mid-20th century, 70 percent of the population lived in incorporated urban places and received local government services through them.

The functions of local government have remained relatively constant throughout American history. They include law enforcement, fire protection, welfare, public health, public schools, construction and maintenance of roads, election administration, and assessment and collection of the property tax. The New England town that developed as a small unit devoted to direct democracy continues to be an important general purpose unit of government in rural New England, but increased population and governmental complexity have forced many towns to abandon direct democracy in favor of representative government. In other regions the county has followed much the same pattern as the New England town —maintaining its significance primarily in rural areas. But even in highly urbanized areas, the county frequently plays an important role in welfare, public health, tax assessment and collection, and election administration. Furthermore, as urban problems have outgrown the boundaries of municipal governments, more and more urban counties have begun to assume major general governmental responsibilities.

City governments in the United States initially followed the English model, with a mayor and a council. In the late 18th and early 19th centuries, fear of strong executives and a desire to copy the U.S. Constitution led to institutionally weak mayors and to bicameral councils. The bicameral council was gradually abandoned, and most major cities provided for some strengthening of the office of mayor in the late 19th and early 20th centuries. In the first half of the 20th century several hundred cities experimented with a commission structure in which legislative and executive function were combined in one body. This experiment proved to be unsatisfactory in all but a few communities, and only about 190 cities used this form of government in the late 1970's.

Council-manager government has been much more popular, particularly in socially and economically homogeneous medium-sized cities. This type of structure began in Staunton, Va., in 1908 and spread rapidly, until by the late 1970's almost 40 percent of all cities used it. Its major feature is a strong, centralized, professional executive branch under a city manager who is hired by the city council.

Widespread consolidations have reduced drastically the number of school districts in the United States. In the 1930's the U.S. Census Bureau reported over 128,000 such governmental units. By 1977 the number had been reduced to 15,-000. Some school systems are administered by counties, towns, or municipalities, but most have separate governmental structures designed to insulate them from the normal political arena and to provide them with a separate tax base.

Other special districts have proliferated, particularly in the mid-20th century. The majority of these local governments are established to provide a single service or to perform a single function, such as fire protection, water, sewerage, mosquito abatement, parks and recreation, and airports. Two major reasons exist for the rapid growth of special districts. First, many potential service areas do not coincide with the boundaries of existing local governments, and special districts can fit these service areas. Second, many local governments have exhausted the taxing and bonding authority granted to them by the state legislatures, and each special district can begin with a new grant of authority to tax and to borrow.

As the density of urban population increased and local governments began to overlap functionally and geographically, reformers suggested a rationalization of governmental structures. The most far-reaching suggestion would have merged counties and cities into a single unit of metropolitan government. This suggestion was followed with some modification in Nashville, Tenn.; Jacksonville, Fla.; and Indianapolis, Ind. Other reform efforts attempted to reallocate local governmental functions among counties and municipalities on an areawide rather than a local basis. The outstanding example of this approach is Miami-Dade County in Florida. One increasingly popular device is the intergovernmental agreement, through which existing governments can band together to provide services that single units are unable to afford.

LOCAL OPTION. *See* **Liquor Laws.**

LOCHABER, TREATY OF (Oct. 18, 1770). Negotiated by Col. John Donelson for Virginia with the Cherokee. Its purpose was to exclude from the Indian lands whites who had settled west of the line fixed by the Treaty of Hard Labor of 1768. By the new treaty the dividing line was moved westward, to begin six miles east of Long Island of the Holston, running thence to the mouth of the Kanawha River, adding a vast area to Virginia. In the running of the Donelson Line a wide departure from the treaty was made in fixing the northern terminus.

***LOCHNER* V. *NEW YORK*,** 198 U.S. 45 (1905). At about the same time that Utah attempted to regulate hours of labor for men in dangerous industries, New York sought to extend such regulation to workers in baking and confectionary establishments. Although the Supreme Court upheld the Utah statute in *Holden* v. *Hardy,* 169 U.S. 366 (1898), it declared the New York statute invalid seven years later in *Lochner* v. *New York.* The law provided for a maximum sixty-hour week, with an average ten-hour day. Lochner, proprietor of a Utica bakery, had been convicted for violation of the law. On appeal to the Supreme Court, attorneys for the defendant argued that while such protections might be justified in dangerous industries, they were unnecessary in industries that, by their nature, required extreme care in matters of cleanliness and sanitation. The Court accepted this reasoning, holding the act void as a violation of freedom of contract. It held that this right is a part of the liberty of the individual, protected by the Fourteenth Amendment, along with the right to purchase or sell labor. The statute did not come under the legitimate police power of the state as a proper regulation of the health, safety, or morals of the people. (*See also West Coast Hotel* v. *Parrish.*)

LOCHRY'S DEFEAT (1781). When George Rogers Clark's proposed expedition against Fort Detroit mobilized at Wheeling, Col. Archibald Lochry and about a hundred Pennsylvania volunteers had not arrived. On Aug. 8 Clark started down the Ohio with his Virginia and regular troops, leaving word for Lochry to follow. Separated thus from Clark, Lochry and his men were attacked on Aug. 24 about twenty miles below the site of Cincinnati by a band of Indians under Joseph Brant and Alexander McKee. A third of Lochry's men were killed, the rest captured; several of the captives, including Lochry, were later killed.

LOCKE'S POLITICAL PHILOSOPHY. John Locke (1632–1704), one of the leading English philosophers of the 17th century, carried political theory to an advanced state of democratic development. His most characteristic contribution was his doctrine of natural rights. He maintained that life, liberty, and property were the inalienable rights of every individual and that the happiness and security of the individual were the ends for which government came into being.

Locke believed in the social contract not only as a means of securing the grant of political authority but also as a means of securing political and social liberty. The contract not only originates and delegates the powers which a government is to possess but also indicates the extent of liberty which the individual should retain. Locke justified the right of revolution not on the ground of hostile acts of the people but on usurpations of authority on the part of those to whom such authority has been delegated. In other words, the possession of authority by governmental officials is strictly on a fiduciary basis. However, the popular right of revolution should not be exercised for trivial reasons but only with the consent of the majority of the people. A controlling public opinion has the right to pass upon the acts of government. At the time of the American Revolution, Locke was perhaps the most influential political authority and his theories were regarded with the greatest respect by the leaders of the American cause.

LOCKOUT. The temporary withholding of work by an employer or employer group, generally for one or more of the following purposes: to defeat an organizational campaign; to undermine an incumbent union; to defend a multiemployer unit against "whipsaw strikes"; to avoid extraordinary losses from a partial strike or an anticipated strike; or to secure a better bargain. There are many more strikes than lockouts, but the distinction between them is often essentially formal, because either may be a response to the prospect or actuality of the other. At common law, lockouts were largely unrestricted. The National Labor Relations Act (1935), as amended, produced unstable adjudications regarding the legality of lockouts. In the 1970's, only lockouts based on one of the first two foregoing purposes were clearly prohibited, but notice and waiting periods were required for some lockouts. Federal legislation restricts lockouts, as well as strikes, that imperil national health, safety, or essential transportation.

LOCKS AND WATERWAYS. In the late 18th century dams and locks began to be employed to make rough rivers, such as the Mohawk, navigable for arks and flatboats. Usually, short canals with locks were built around falls or rapids: for example, one around the rapids of the James at Richmond, built 1785–89; five along the Potomac, built 1785–1808; several on the Connecticut and Merrimack rivers, constructed between 1790 and 1800. The height of the locks was then very modest. The Bellows Falls Canal on the Connecticut required nine locks in less than a mile to overcome a fall of fifty feet—or less than six feet of lift to each lock. The Chemung Canal, completed in 1833, connecting Seneca Lake with the Susquehanna River, though only twenty-three miles long had forty-nine locks.

For the sake of economy, the lock walls of some early canals, such as the Middlesex between Boston and Lowell (built 1794–1803), were of wood, and in some instances they began to bulge and warp almost as soon as completed. Until cement rock was discovered in central New York in 1818, most stone lock walls had to be built with ordinary lime mortar, as cement imported from Europe was too costly. With the aid of cement, locks became higher, and in 1830 one with a lift of seventeen feet was built on the Delaware Division of the Pennsylvania Canal system.

Larger rivers were canalized—that is, improved with dams and locks—early in the 19th century. When the canal fervor swept Pennsylvania, beginning in 1826, not only was the Monongahela thus improved for a hundred miles, but also small streams, such as Bald Eagle Creek and Conestoga Creek from Lancaster to the Susquehanna. In Ohio nearly a hundred miles of the Muskingum were canalized between 1836 and 1840, and there for the first time in America the locks—36 feet wide and 180 feet long—were made large enough for steamboats. Before the end of the 19th century navigation dams and locks were placed on the upper Ohio and the Mississippi. With the growth of steamboat traffic, improvement of small rivers and creeks by locks became a favorite form of congressional patronage. (*See also* Canals.)

LOCOFOCO PARTY. A radical faction of the Democratic party in New York allied with Jacksonian Democracy. At a meeting in Tammany Hall, Oct. 29, 1835, it wrested control of the city caucus from the conservatives by producing candles and lighting them with locofoco matches and thus continuing the meeting when opponents had darkened the hall by turning off the gas. Newspapers derisively called this faction the Locofoco party. Its program embraced suppression of paper money, curtailment of banking privileges, and protection of labor unions. From 1837 to 1860 the term was applied to the national Democratic party by its opponents.

LOCOMOTIVES. Steam had been applied on railroads in England early in the 19th century. These developments were known in the United States, and efforts were made to generate interest in the construction of railroads. In 1825 Col. John Stevens of Hoboken, N.J., built an experimental locomotive and demonstrated it on a circular track. The Baltimore and Ohio Railroad, chartered in 1827 as the first common-carrier railroad in the United States, early faced the question of what form of power to use. Peter Cooper of New York City, a director of the railroad, built the "Tom Thumb" for demonstration purposes. Success was sufficient to lead the railroad to sponsor a competition to secure a commercially useful locomotive. The competition was won by Phineas Davis of York, Pa., in 1831. His "York" was the predecessor of a considerable group of vertical-boilered locomotives called "grasshoppers" that had walking-beam power transmission.

Meanwhile "Best Friend of Charleston," the first locomotive intended for commercial service, had been built by the West Point Foundry in New York for the South Carolina Canal and Railroad Company. Locomotives were imported from England during the early experimental period, but they proved ill adapted to the light and uneven track of early American railroads and to the sharp curvature and heavy grades that were often employed. American locomotive design began to depart from British practice in order to adapt to these conditions. The early locomotive builders, Matthias W. Baldwin and William Norris of Philadelphia, proved to be inventive contributors to locomotive development. The Baldwin works, first in Philadelphia and later in Eddystone, Pa., became the nation's largest locomotive builder.

Numerous small locomotive works operated in the early period, ranging from the William Mason Company at Taunton, Mass., to the Richmond Locomotive Works at Richmond, Va. Some ultimately disappeared; a number merged to form the American Locomotive Company, second of the country's great locomotive builders. Several railroads built locomotives in their own shops, but none so many as the Pennsylvania Railroad. The Pennsylvania also pioneered in the standardization of locomotives, beginning in the 1870's.

The steam locomotive demonstrated its speed capabilities early, having attained 60 miles an hour by 1848. Hauling capability developed more slowly. The typical locomotive for freight and passenger work in the 1870's had four driving wheels and a tractive effort of 8,000 to 12,000 pounds. Locomotives for heavy freight work were built with six or eight driving wheels. The Consolidation type, first built for the Lehigh Valley Railroad in 1866, became the most popular. Tractive efforts of leading specimens of this locomotive type increased from 24,000 pounds in the 1870's to 46,000 pounds by the end of the century. Between 1895 and 1910, a series of innovations—trailing wheels to enable a wide firebox to be carried behind the rear drivers and the boilers to be lengthened, the brick arch, piston valves, and outside valve motion—enabled more than a doubling of tractive power. Most important was the introduction of superheating, which allowed very hot, dry steam to be delivered to the cylinders, reducing condensation and increasing cylinder horsepower within existing dimensions. In 1904 the first Mallet type of articulated locomotive was placed in service on the Baltimore and Ohio Railroad. Of particular use on lines of heavy gradient, the articulated locomotive increased rapidly in size, and by 1920 some examples exerted 120,000 pounds of tractive effort when working single expansion. The mechanical stoker, essential for firing such locomotives, had been perfected by then.

The need for greater horsepower to permit sustained high-speed operation with heavy loads led to a series of experiments from which emerged the first "superpower" locomotive, completed by the Lima Locomotive Works in 1925. This locomotive combined the elements already noted with a feed-water heater and four-wheel trailing truck to permit a much enlarged firebox. It became the prototype for hundreds of locomotives. By this time the manufacture of locomotives was confined to Baldwin, American Locomotive, and Lima. Railroad shops, especially those of the Pennsylvania, Norfolk and Western, and Burlington railroads, also continued to build new power. The depression of the 1930's brought a near-paralysis of locomotive building during the years 1932–35. Revival of railroad purchasing was marked by the development of a new generation of locomotives—single-expansion articulateds especially made for service on the western transcontinental roads and several of the coal-hauling roads in the East. These locomotives combined the starting tractive effort of the Mallets with the speed capabilities of the later superpower locomotives. In these designs the steam locomotive reached its peak of development in the United States: it could haul 18,000 tons or more in coal or ore service or move a 7,000-ton manifest freight at 70 miles per hour. World War II interrupted steam locomotive development. So great had been the progress in diesel locomotives that many railroads bought no more steam power afterward. The last steam locomotives built by Baldwin for service in the United States were delivered in 1949, and Lima's last locomotive for an American railroad, in the same year.

Straight electric locomotives were never extensively employed on American railroads. Although the Baltimore and Ohio used them after 1895 in its Baltimore tunnels, the Pennsylvania electrified the approaches to Pennsylvania Station in New York City in 1908, and the suburban lines out of Grand Central Station were electrified in the period 1906–13, use of the electric locomotive was always confined to special circumstances. The Milwaukee employed it over 641 route miles across the Rocky, Bitter Root, and Cascade ranges, the Great Northern between Skykomish and Wenatchee, Wash., and the Norfolk and Western and the Virginian on heavy-grade lines. The outstanding electrification was that of the Pennsylvania between New York and Washington, which was later extended over the main line to Harrisburg. The first segment, between New York and Philadelphia, was opened in 1932. Exceptionally heavy traffic density was considered to justify the investment in power transmission and distribution. Of the several types of locomotive employed on this 11,000-volt a.c. electrification, the GG-1 was outstanding, developing 8,500 horsepower on short-period rating.

Except over the limited electrified mileage and on a few short lines, all service of American railroads was powered in the 1970's by diesel-electric locomotives. These use diesel engines to power generators that supply direct current to the traction motors. The first such locomotives were delivered for switching service in 1925. Baldwin and American Locomotive both went into their manufacture, but the Electric Motive Division of General Motors pioneered in the application of the diesel to both passenger and freight road service in the late 1930's. The diesel locomotive has the advantage of high efficiency and availability, compared with the steam locomotive. It can be operated in multiple units, any number of locomotives being controlled by a single engineman. Midtrain helper locomotives can now be controlled from the head end, making for a better distribution of power in long and heavy trains. Although the first diesel road freight unit was tested in 1940, third-generation diesels were coming into service in the 1970's. Single units have been produced that generate more horsepower than four units of the original 5,400-horsepower freight diesel; yet locomotives in the 2,500-horsepower range remain popular.

LODE MINING. Gold, silver, and other metals are generally found in streaks that may range from a few inches to many feet in width and that are frequently traceable for a mile or more in length. These streaks are called lodes, veins, or ledges. A lode has been legally defined as mineral-bearing rock in place; tracting such rock from the earth is lode mining. Distinguished from placer mining, geared to metals found in alluvial deposits near the surface, lode mining is conducted in hard rock and almost entirely underground. The ore is mined either by shafts or by tunnels. The discoverer of a new lode, according to the laws of the early mining districts, could stake out two claims along the lode; others, one claim. Local laws set the size of the claim, which was recognized by the first U.S. mineral patent law in 1866. On May 10, 1872, Congress fixed the size of lode claims at 600 feet wide and 1,500 feet long. Famous lodes are the Mother Lode in California and the Comstock Lode in Nevada.

LODGE COROLLARY. *See* **Magdalena Bay Resolution.**

LODGE RESERVATIONS. The reservations attached to the Treaty of Versailles and the covenant of the League of Nations by the Senate in November 1919, and again in March 1920, bore the name of Sen. Henry Cabot Lodge as chairman of the Committee on Foreign Relations.

The committee first reported to the Senate a series of reservations to the treaty in early September. Republican senators who supported the League of Nations rejected them and a number of amendments proposed by senators opposed to the treaty and the league. During the next two months the pro-league Republicans negotiated a set of milder reservations. They asserted the Senate's right to advise and consent to league agreements individually and to approve appointment of U.S. league representatives, reaffirmed congressional authority to appropriate funds for participating in league activities, and stated that the United States alone should determine what questions lay within its domestic jurisdiction or involved its national honor and vital interest. Sen. Porter James McCumber proposed the most vital reservation, declaring that Congress should decide what U.S. obligations were in each instance under Article X of the covenant. Under orders from President Woodrow Wilson the Democrats boycotted these negotiations and voted against the reservations. Combining with the league's opponents they defeated ratification in November.

In January 1920, a bipartisan committee headed by Lodge and Sen. Gilbert Monell Hitchcock negotiated a third group of reservations. Against the advice of his supporters, the president rejected even those compromises. A majority of Democrats then broke with the president to support the bipartisan compromises. When Wilson threatened to pocket veto any treaty with reservations attached, enough remained loyal to him to defeat ratification the second time.

***LOEWE* V. *LAWLOR*.** *See* **Danbury Hatters' Case.**

LOFTUS HEIGHTS. The eastern bank of the Mississippi, first called Roche à Davion for a French missionary (1699). It took its name from an incident during the expedition led by British Maj. Arthur Loftus in 1764, from Mobile, to take possession of the Illinois country in accordance with the Treaty of Paris of 1763. At Roche à Davion the Loftus party of 300 was fired on by the Tunica Indians. Several men were killed, and Loftus retreated down the Mississippi. Dominating the Spanish-American boundary on the Mississippi, it became the site of Fort Adams, built 1798–99.

LOGAN ACT (Jan. 30, 1799). The act was the result of a private visit to France by Dr. George Logan, a Philadelphia Quaker, who had gone there in an effort to preserve peace between France and the United States during the Quasi-War. The act made it a high misdemeanor subject to fine and imprisonment for any citizen to carry on correspondence with a foreign government in any controversy in which the United States is engaged. The act is still on the statute books.

LOGAN'S FORT (or St. Asaph Station). Located near Stanford, Ky.; founded by Benjamin Logan, who arrived in Kentucky in 1775. On May 20, 1777, the fort was assaulted by Indians. Logan, by sheer courage and surprising athletic prowess, became the mainstay in his fort's defense. Stories of these exploits have given this station an important place in Kentucky's history.

LOGAN'S SPEECH. Popularly regarded as the most famous example of American Indian oratory, was made by the Mingo warrior John Logan, or Tahgahjute. The speech was made to John Gibson, who had been sent from Camp Charlotte (in present Pickaway County, Ohio) by the governor of Virginia to persuade Logan, then at his cabin a few miles distant, to attend the peace negotiations at the close of Dunmore's War (1774). Logan refused to come and recited his grievances in a speech so moving that Gibson translated and recorded it from memory. Thomas Jefferson later inserted it in his *Notes on the State of Virginia.*

LOG CABIN. It has been asserted that log construction was introduced by the Swedes who settled on the lower Delaware in 1638. But a log blockhouse, the McIntyre Garrison at York, Maine, built about 1640–45, is cited by others as evidence that the New England colonists had learned log construction for themselves. Such construction increased rapidly in the 17th century, and the one-room or two-room log cabin became the typical American pioneer home, being supplemented by outbuildings also of log construction.

LOG CABIN AND HARD CIDER CAMPAIGN. *See* **Campaigns, Presidential: Campaign of 1840.**

LOG COLLEGE. At Neshaminy, Pa., about twenty miles from Philadelphia, William Tennent, an Irish Presbyterian minister, erected a log schoolhouse. During 1726–42, it served to emphasize the need for an institution for the instruction of Presbyterian ministerial candidates. The Presbyterian Synod recognized this need, and in 1746 the charter for the organization of a college at Princeton, N.J. (later Princeton University), was issued.

LOGROLLING. A practice among members of Congress of trading votes for each other's pet bills. The term is derived from the frontiersmen's practice of helping one another in cutting down trees and rolling up the logs for building.

LOGSTOWN. An Indian village eighteen miles below the forks of the Ohio near present Ambridge, Pa., probably founded by the Shawnee about 1728; it became a mixed village of Shawnee, Delaware, and Iroquois. From 1747 to 1753 it was the most important Indian village on the upper Ohio, being the center of trade and the scene of Indian councils.

LOGSTOWN, TREATY OF (June 13, 1752). Opening to settlement lands west of the Allegheny Mountains, it was negotiated with the Iroquois, Delaware, Shawnee, Wyandot, and Miami Indians resident in western Pennsylvania, Ohio, and Indiana. In 1751 negotiations with the same Indians had been conducted at Logstown by George Croghan of Pennsylvania, but the Pennsylvania assembly had refused funds for erecting forts to hold the region against the French. In 1752 commissioners from Virginia distributed a royal present to the Indians and, with the help of Croghan and of Christopher Gist representing the Ohio Company, secured permission for Virginians to make settlements south of the Ohio and to build two fortified trading houses on the river.

LOGWOOD TRADE. Logwood, also called blockwood and sometimes known as campeachy wood or, improperly, Brasiletto or Jamaica wood, comes from the leguminous tree *Haematoxylen campechianum,* found in Central America and the West Indies. Its chief use (prohibited in England from 1581 to 1662) was in dyeing, blacks and blues. English activity in the trade, begun by the buccaneers and soon supplemented by colonial traders, centered in Spanish territory, first at Cape Catoche, then at Campeche Bay, Mexico, and finally around Belize (now British Honduras) and along the Mosquito Coast of Nicaragua. Most of the American colonists' logwood came from Yucatan and Honduras. Logwood grown in an English colony was regulated by the Navigation Acts, but foreign logwood could be exported freely, and approximately one-fifth of the 3,480 tons exported in 1770 from the continental colonies went directly to Europe.

LOMBOK STRAIT, BATTLE OF (Feb. 19–20, 1942). Allied naval forces opposing the Japanese invasion of the Netherlands East Indies consisted of a group of American, British, and Dutch cruisers and destroyers commanded by Dutch Rear Adm. Karel Doorman. On the evening of Feb. 19, 1942, Doorman set out to attack Japanese transports on the island of Bali. With his warships scattered as a result of earlier actions and with no time to concentrate them, Doorman was forced to carry out a disjointed and confused operation. In two uncoordinated attacks, before and after midnight, a Japanese transport and destroyer were damaged, while Doorman lost a destroyer and sustained damage to another destroyer and a light cruiser. Other Japanese warships caught Doorman's second group of raiders as they were retiring, increasing the damage to the cruiser but suffering hits on one of their own destroyers. A raid on the Japanese anchorage by motor torpedo boats just before dawn on Feb. 20 revealed that the enemy ships had already departed. The Japanese beachhead on Bali was established.

LONDON, DECLARATION OF (Feb. 26, 1909). A code of laws relating to maritime warfare drafted by the London Naval Conference. Ten naval powers thereby achieved a compromise agreement in the hope of enabling the international prize court, proposed at the second Hague Conference in 1907, to function. Conspicuous in the declaration was the treatment of the issues of contraband and continuous voyage, entailing peculiar difficulties between belligerents and neutrals. Agreement was reached on definite lists of absolute and conditional contraband and on a third classification of goods that could not be declared contraband. Barring this third classification, a belligerent might add to the absolute and conditional lists. Noteworthy in the free list were raw cotton and metallic ores. Continuous voyage was restricted in application to absolute contraband, thus voiding in large part the precedents of the American Civil War. Thus, arms (absolute contraband) were seizable anywhere on the high seas, if destined for the enemy; foodstuffs (conditional contraband) and cotton and copper (on the free list) were seizable only for violation of blockade. Since a blockading force could not bar access to a neutral port, neutral commerce was to be free from interruption except in cases of absolute contraband. The declaration went unratified, but the United States, with the experience of the Napoleonic Wars in mind, tried to make it an important instrument of policy.

LONDON, TREATY OF (1604). Ended the formal warfare that had been waged since 1585 between England and Spain, endangering English colonization in the New World. The treaty temporarily eradicated this danger and, among other things, reopened "free commerce" between the two kingdoms "where commerce existed before the war." Spain intended this clause to exclude English merchants from its colonies overseas, but the English gave it the opposite interpretation, causing continued warfare "beyond the Line" (*see* "No Peace Beyond the Line") and the rise of the buccaneers.

LONDON COMPANY. *See* **Virginia Company of London.**

LONDON ECONOMIC CONFERENCE (June 12–July 27, 1933). Officially called the World Monetary and Economic Conference. President Herbert Hoover had pledged American participation in this conference called by the League of Nations at the request of the Lausanne Conference for the purpose of halting the world depression through international economic cooperation. Meanwhile, Franklin D. Roosevelt had assumed the presidency and the U.S. had abandoned the gold standard. Commodity agreements were negotiated by silver- and wheat-producing nations, but attempts to bring about currency stabilization and tariff reductions failed. Roosevelt would not support a currency-stablizing program supported by the gold-bloc nations, which refused to discuss tariff reductions until agreement could be reached on that matter. The U.S. delegates also refused to discuss the issue of war debts. While the conference was still in session, Roosevelt recalled the American delegation.

LONDON NAVAL TREATY OF 1930. Ramsay MacDonald, British prime minister, convened a naval conference at London in 1930, attended by representatives of the United States, Great Britain, Japan, France, and Italy. The object was to reach an agreement to limit the size and number of warships, left unlimited by the Washington Treaty of 1922. The U.S.–British disagreement over parity and large cruisers was settled by compromise. The success of the conference was endangered by the French demand for a tonnage beyond Italian needs and for a security pact with Great Britain, and by the Japanese claim for a 10:10:7 ratio in place of the 5:5:3 ratio agreed to in 1922. The British were unwilling to give a guarantee to the French without American support, and the United States rejected the idea. The final treaty was a three-power pact with provisions to include France and Italy if agreeable in the future. The 5:5:3 ratio was applied to large cruisers, but Japan won a 10:10:7 ratio in small cruisers and destroyers and equality in submarines, each nation being permitted to maintain a tonnage of 52,700 in the latter category.

LONDON NAVAL TREATY OF 1936. The Japanese government having, on Dec. 29, 1934, denounced the Washington Naval Treaty of 1922, a conference of the principal naval powers was held in London from Dec. 9, 1935, to Mar. 25, 1936. Great Britain and the United States refused to recognize the Japanese claim to parity or to accept a "common upper limit" for naval construction. Japan thereupon withdrew from the conference. By the treaty of Mar. 25, 1936, Great Britain, France, and the United States agreed not to exceed specified maximum limits for various types of warships and to exchange information concerning their building programs. But it was provided that the limits agreed upon might be set aside in the event of war or in the event they were exceeded by a power not a party to the treaty. Italy, indignant at the application of sanctions in the Ethiopian war, refused to sign the treaty. (*See* Naval Limitation Conferences.)

LONE JACK, ACTION AT (Aug. 16, 1862). Fought in southeastern Jackson County, Mo., between the Union state militia under Maj. Emory S. Foster and Confederates under Gen. Upton Hays, Col. John F. Coffee, and Col. Vard Cockrell. The Confederates attacked early in the morning and a six-hour fight ensued. The Union artillery was captured. About 800 men were in each force, and each side sustained losses of about 125 killed and wounded.

LONG, HUEY, ASSASSINATION (Sept. 8, 1935). Sen. Huey P. Long was shot at the state capitol at Baton Rouge, La., by Carl A. Weiss, the son-in-law of Judge B. H. Pavy, leader of an anti-Long faction. Weiss was shot dead on the capitol steps by Long's bodyguards; Long died two days later.

LONG BEACH (Calif.). Fifth largest city in California, with a population of 361,334 in 1980. It is part of the Los Angeles metropolitan area, the second largest metropolitan area in the United States. It is located on San Pedro Bay, to the south of Los Angeles. This location has provided Long Beach with a fine harbor. U.S. Navy ships are based at Long Beach and shipyards in the city are important builders of naval and civilian vessels. The city was granted rights to its tidal lands by the state government in 1911 with the condition that any money made from these lands would be used to improve business, fisheries, and shipping facilities. When oil was discovered under the harbor (and under most of the city), Long Beach began to produce a great income for its own use. The city has improved its harbor with oil royalties, and provides a fine system of parks and water sports facilities. Its major business activities include an important aircraft factory, shipyards, fishing, and work for the petroleum industry. Long Beach State College, a unit in the California system of higher education, is located in the city.

LONG DRIVE. Beginning in 1866, cowboys drove herds of cattle overland to rail points on the northern Plains. The time consumed in driving a herd these hundreds of miles was from six weeks to two months (*see* Cattle Drives).

LONG EXPEDITION. To actively protest against the Adams-Onís Treaty with Spain, by which the United States relinquished claims to Texas, a meeting of the citizens of Natchez, Miss., was held in 1819 and an expedition into Texas was planned. James Long of Virginia was chosen as leader. He left Natchez in June 1819 with about 75 men; the number had increased to more than 300 soon after his arrival at Nacogdoches. There he promptly declared Texas free and independent and set up a provisional government, a republic. Long was elected president and made immediate military arrangements for conquering and holding the entire province. Failing to receive expected aid from the pirate Jean Laffite, and facing an overwhelming Spanish force, his entire scheme collapsed. In 1821 he returned to Texas from New Orleans with reinforcements and captured La Bahia, south of San Antonio. After holding it for a few days, he learned of Mexican independence from Spain and accepted an invitation from the new government to visit Mexico City, where he was killed in 1822.

LONGHORNS, TEXAS. Although predominantly descended from cattle that Spaniards began bringing to Mexico in 1521, longhorn cattle achieved character and fame as a Texas product about 1845. A strain out of cattle imported from southern states combined with the climate and ranges of Texas to develop an animal heavier and more "rangy" than Mexican cattle but sharply different from cattle elsewhere in the United States. Long of leg, body, and tail, a Texas steer carried horns that spread from 3 to 5 feet from tip to tip and occasionally over 8 feet. For driving thousands of miles and for stocking vast ranges vacated by buffalo and Indians, the breed was ideal (*see* Cattle Drives).

LONGHOUSES OF THE IROQUOIS. *See* **Architecture.**

LONG HUNTERS. Residents of settled American frontier communities who, in the 1760's, spent months in hunting game together in the western wilds. Daniel Boone was one of the earliest and the most noted.

LONG ISLAND. A part of New York State, 118 miles long and 1,682 square miles in area, it lies parallel to the southern shore of Connecticut and is bounded on the north by Long Island Sound and on the south by the Atlantic Ocean. In 1620 it was included in the grant given by James I to the Virginia Company of Plymouth. In 1635 Long Island was assigned to William Alexander, Earl of Stirling.

In 1636, when Wouter Van Twiller was director general of New Netherland, Jacobus Van Curler (or Corlaer) was given the first Dutch patent for land on Long Island. During the Dutch period farms spread along the Long Island shore opposite Manhattan Island, and several settlements, both Dutch and English, sprang up in the interior.

While the western end was being settled as a part of New Netherland, Puritan towns were planted along the northern and southern forks of the island's eastern end. In 1640 English settlers from New Haven, Conn., laid out Southold, and others from Lynn in Massachusetts Bay settled Southampton. Conflicting Dutch and English claims were settled by a treaty signed at Hartford in 1650, which fixed a boundary by drawing a line southward across the island from Oyster Bay. The eastern towns in time fell under Connecticut jurisdiction, and eastern Long Island was politically a part of New England when the English conquered New Netherland in 1664. Charles II at that time granted all of Long Island to his brother, James, Duke of York. Reconquest brought the Dutch back to the western district in 1673, but the Treaty of Westminster (1674) finally established Long Island's status as part of the English colony of New York.

In 1683 the island was divided into three counties: Queens, Kings, and Suffolk. A fourth county, Nassau, was created in 1898–99 by three townships formerly in the eastern part of Queens County, while the rest of Queens County became a borough of New York City. Kings County was gradually absorbed by the city of Brooklyn, so that by the end of the 19th century city and county were coterminous. In 1898 Brooklyn (and Kings County) became a borough of New York City. During the American Revolution the Battle of Long Island took place at Brooklyn on Aug. 27, 1776.

During the 18th, 19th, and early 20th centuries Long Island was chiefly an agricultural region, with fishing, whaling, and shipbuilding as the important industries. In the 19th century Sag Harbor, on Gardiners Bay, was the main whaling port, its most prosperous period occurring during 1840–60. In Great South Bay and Peconic Bay the oyster industry became very important during the 19th and early 20th centuries. The shipbuilding industry flourished in a number of north shore communities, such as Port Jefferson. In the 20th century Nassau and Suffolk, witnessed extensive construction of single-family homes, especially after World War II, which helped increase their combined population from 604,103 in 1940 to 2,605,813 in 1980. Long Island's early concentration on agriculture, fishing, and shipbuilding gave way to industrial development in the western section—especially in Queens and Kings counties. Aircraft manufacture became an important industry in Nassau County. Numerous summer resort areas developed in the eastern end, especially at East Hampton, Southampton, and Montauk.

LONG ISLAND, BATTLE OF (Aug. 27, 1776). Between Aug. 22 and Aug. 25, 1776, British Gen. William Howe brought all but one of his brigades across from Staten Island in New York, landing them on Gravesend Bay beach, on the southwestern tip of Long Island. Gen. George Washington's outpost line was along Brooklyn Heights. Washington strengthened his force by placing nearly a third of the American army on Long Island under Gen. Israel Putnam. On the night of Aug. 26–27 Howe captured Col. Samuel Miles's rifle regiment and most of Gen. William Alexander's command. The British then struck Washington's main position. Had this attack been pushed, all American forces on Long Island could have been captured. Instead, Howe switched to siege tactics. Realizing his danger, Washington determined to withdraw his forces to Manhattan, while giving the impression he was reinforcing, on Aug. 29–30.

LONG ISLAND FLATS, BATTLE OF (July 20, 1776). In June 1776 the Overhill Cherokee, under British incitement, determined to make war on whites settled in upper east Tennessee and southwest Virginia. Their 700 warriors were divided into three parties: the right wing, under Chief Old Abraham, was to strike Fort Watauga; the center, under Chief Dragging Canoe, was to attack Eaton's Station near Long Island of Holston; a smaller detachment was to strike settlers in Carter's Valley. Near Long Island and Eaton's Station were level lands or flats, where a sharp battle was fought. The Indians were routed, with more than forty killed.

LONG ISLAND OF HOLSTON, TREATY OF (1777). The militia of southwest Virginia and North Carolina under Col. William Christian and Col. Joseph Williams made a successful punitive expedition in the fall of 1776 against the Cherokee, following raids by the Indians and the Battle of Long Island Flats in northeast Tennessee. A pledge was extorted from the Cherokee that they would come into a treaty the following year. In June and July 1777 the Cherokee met and negotiated with commissioners of the two states at Long Island, and ceded lands.

LONG KNIVES. *See* **Big Knives.**

LONG'S EXPLORATIONS. In summer 1819 Maj. Stephen H. Long, in the steamboat *Western Engineer,* left St. Louis in command of the scientific part of the Yellowstone Expedition. Because of the delay and expense of the expedition,

Congress refused further funds. As a compromise Long was authorized to make a scientific exploration to the Rocky Mountains. On June 6, 1820, Long and twenty men set out to explore the Platte, Arkansas, and Red rivers. Marching up the Platte to the mountains, he discovered Long's Peak, Colo. Edwin James of his staff made the first recorded ascent of Pikes Peak. Capt. J. R. Bell marched down the Arkansas with part of the force; but Long, misled by Spanish information, explored the Canadian River and found it was not the Red only when he came to its confluence with the Arkansas.

On Apr. 20, 1823, Long set out on another exploration, from Fort Snelling, Minn., and thence up the St. Peter's (Minnesota) River. His mission was to explore the country, establish the location of 49° north latitude, and take possession of all the territory below this boundary line (*see* Convention of 1818 With England). The colony at Pembina and North West Company posts in the Red River country were visited. The return trip was begun in August, the party going down the Red River to Lake Winnipeg and thence eastward to Lake Superior, through the Great Lakes to Niagara Falls, and on southward to Philadelphia, where they arrived Oct. 26, 1823.

LOOKOUT MOUNTAIN, BATTLE ON (Nov. 24, 1863). An action in which Union Gen. Joseph Hooker, commanding the right wing of Gen. Ulysses S. Grant's army of about 56,000 men, cleared Lookout Mountain, Tenn., of the Confederate troops who had held it since the Battle of Chickamauga two months earlier. It is popularly known as the "battle of the clouds." The withdrawal of Confederate Gen. James Longstreet's corps from Lookout Mountain had left the Confederate left wing dangerously weak. Hooker's troops, scrambling up the mountain, drove off the remaining Confederates, swept on across Chattanooga Creek, and the next day participated in the fighting on Missionary Ridge.

LOOM. Primitive English looms, brought to America by the first settlers, were soon displaced by improved Dutch looms, to which the fly shuttle (invented by John Kay in 1733), which speeded their operation, was added. Power looms were invented in England, but original American types, adapted from the Scottish loom, were perfected by the Boston Manufacturing Company. Between 1825 and 1850 Samuel Batchelder, William Mason, and William Crompton of Massachusetts improved these looms to weave wool as well as cotton and to make pattern as well as plain fabrics, and Erastus B. Bigelow of the same state invented power looms to weave ingrain carpets and eventually Brussels and Wilton carpets. Another era of rapid improvement occurred after the Civil War, when James H. Northrop and George Draper perfected improvements that automatically changed shuttles and stopped a loom when a single warp thread broke. Early in the 20th century refinements were embodied in the Crompton loom and its successors. New, more completely automated looms were developed to offset the rising costs in labor and also to handle man-made yarns. One important development that has taken place in the 20th century is the shuttleless loom, including the water-jet loom, which uses a jet of water to force the weft between the warp. (*See also* Textiles.)

LOOMIS GANG. Consisting chiefly of the six Loomis brothers, it terrorized Madison County, N.Y., during the 1850's and 1860's. Burglary, horse stealing, and even murder finally aroused the community. Vigilantes killed the oldest brother, burned the Loomis farmhouse, and frightened the remainder of the gang into quiescence.

LOOSE CONSTRUCTION. A liberal interpretation of what the U.S. government is allowed to do under the Constitution. A "loose construction" view of the Constitution permits a use of more power by Congress than a "strict construction" view, which permits only the use of powers specifically granted by the Constitution.

LÓPEZ FILIBUSTERING EXPEDITIONS (1850–51). Armed attempts by Cuban revolutionists led by Narciso López and American annexationists to free Cuba from Spain. The expeditions were recruited and at least partly financed in the United States, and both set out from New Orleans. The first, consisting of 750 men, reached Cuba on May 18, 1850, and captured the Spanish garrison at Cárdenas, but was dispersed. The second expedition, consisting of 450 men, landed on Aug. 11, 1851; but it was captured and its members either executed or imprisoned.

LORAMIE'S STORE. A trading post on the Miami-Maumee portage in western Ohio, founded by Pierre Louis Lorimier (Anglicized to Peter Loramie) about 1769. It remained an important center of British influence among the Ohio Indians until destroyed by George Rogers Clark in 1782. Gen. Anthony Wayne erected a fort on the site in 1794. "Loramie's" was used as a significant point of identification for the Indian boundary in the Treaty of Greenville in 1814.

LORDS AND GENTLEMEN. A designation applied by the people of Massachusetts to William Fiennes, Viscount Saye and Sele; Robert Greville, Baron Brooke; and others who, under the Old Patent of Connecticut, designed a settlement at Saybrook in 1635.

LORDS OF TRADE AND PLANTATION. Beginning in 1624, British colonial administration was directed by special committees advising the Privy Council. To create an informed personnel with vigor and continuity in colonial policy, Charles II organized on Mar. 12, 1675, the Lords of Trade and Plantation, twenty-one privy councillors, nine of whom held "the immediate Care and Intendency" of colonies, any five constituting a quorum. Holding 857 meetings (1675–96) in offices in Scotland Yard, they established a permanent salaried secretary, assistant secretary, and clerical staff to handle colonial correspondence; became a bureau of colonial information by sending inquiries to colonial governors and agents to colonies; recommended appointees as royal governors to crown colonies and prepared their commissions and instructions; developed the technique of judicial review of colonial cases appealed to the Privy Council; assaulted, in the interests of unity and efficiency, the charters of colonies; and instituted the policy of consolidating colonies (the Dominion of New England). Their last meeting was on Apr. 18, 1696.

LORDS PROPRIETORS. *See* **Proprietary Provinces.**

L'ORIENT. Now Lorient, an important French port and naval base on the Bay of Biscay, from which, early in 1777, the ship *Amphitrite* cleared with a cargo of cannon, ammunition, tents, and other matériel for the American revolutionary army and succeeded in landing it safely at Portsmouth, N.H. In November 1777 two American frigates brought prizes into L'Orient and sold them. The port was thereafter a place of departure for American munitions and of entry for American products sold to the French during the Revolution.

LORIMER CASE. On May 26, 1909, the Illinois legislature, after a deadlock of nearly five months, elected William Lorimer, a Republican, as U.S. senator. About a year later sensational charges of bribery and corruption were made in connection with this election. After an investigation the Senate by a close vote, on Mar. 1, 1911, declined to unseat him. After a committee of the Illinois Senate had produced new evidence of corruption, the Senate ordered a second investigation, and on July 13, 1912, ousted him from his seat.

LOS ADAES. A Spanish garrison in Louisiana established east of the Sabine River about 1718 to prevent French encroachment from Natchitoches, twenty miles eastward on the Red River. It remained a Spanish military and trading post on the route between Natchitoches and San Antonio until surrendered to the United States in the Louisiana-Texas boundary settlement of 1821 (*see* Adams-Onís Treaty).

LOS ANGELES (Calif.). Largest city in California, with a population of 2,966,763 in 1980. It ranked third among all American cities in population, behind New York and Chicago. The metropolitan area of 7,445,721 was the second largest in America. The population of Los Angeles has been growing rapidly: between 1950 and 1980 it increased by 50 percent (the population of New York and Chicago during the same period decreased by 11 and 18 percent, respectively).

The site of Los Angeles was explored by Spaniards during the late 1760's. In 1769 Gaspar de Portolá visited the area with an expedition. A mission was set up just outside the modern city limits by the Father Junipero Serra in 1771—Mission San Gabriel. In 1781 Felipe de Neve, Spanish governor of California, established "El Pueblo de Nuestra Señora la Reina de Los Angeles de Porciuncula" ("The Town of Our Lady, Queen of the Angels of Porciuncula"), quickly shortened to "Los Angeles."

Los Angeles grew slowly under Spanish rule. When Mexico declared its independence from Spain in 1822, Los Angeles passed under Mexican rule. American trading vessels visited Los Angeles in the early 19th century and the town became a center for cattle trade. When the Mexican War broke out, Los Angeles was seized by U.S. Marines.

Native Californians (*Angelenos* or *Californios*) seemed willing to permit the Americans to take over until the Marine commander upset good relations by some of his orders. As a result, the Marines were surrounded by Californian Mexicans and forced to agree to leave the area. The commander arranged for a man to ride north, to get help. Juan Flaco, who rode for nearly five days to the San Francisco Bay area, is sometimes called the "Paul Revere of California." American troops reentered Los Angeles on Jan. 13, 1847, after a battle at La Mesa. The city, together with all of California, was turned over to U.S. rule by the Treaty of Guadalupe Hidalgo.

Los Angeles grew during 1848–60, largely as a result of the gold rush in northern California. It was incorporated in 1850. The Los Angeles area proved an excellent supply center. Like "cow towns" in other parts of the country, Los Angeles developed a reputation for lawless behavior by visiting cowhands. In addition, Americans and Mexicans distrusted each other and many law suits over land ownership were pressed in the courts. While the city grew in population, its growth was slow compared to the burst of growth in northern California.

Through the late 19th and early 20th centuries, Los Angeles produced large amounts of food; citrus groves, vineyards, and farms were quite productive. The arrival of the railroads connected Los Angeles with the San Francisco Bay area and with the eastern United States. A railroad rate war was waged between the Southern Pacific and the Santa Fe railroads during the 1880's. This resulted in unusually low rail fares to Los Angeles from the Middle West and a wave of population swept into the area. Dozens of new towns were laid out within the present city limits and there was a "boom" in land sales. The combination of good climate, fruit raising, and easy connections with the Middle West brought the city population by 1900 to over 100,000.

The first valuable oil deposits in the Los Angeles area were found in the early 1890's; by 1900 there was more oil available in Los Angeles than could be sold there. The development of automobile transportation provided a great boom for the oil industry. During the 20th century Los Angeles expanded as a city in which the automobile was the key to travel and the chief connection between the different sections of town.

Partly because of the need to ship surplus oil, engineers were set to work to provide a good harbor for Los Angeles. The U.S. Army Corps of Engineers designed and laid out Los Angeles harbor in a strip of shoreline facing San Pedro Bay. This harbor project is one of the most ambitious in U.S. history. It turned a shallow bay into a deepwater seaport with excellent facilities for all kinds of freighters and tankers. The work on the harbor breakwater began in 1899 and developments have been added from time to time ever since.

Water supply was another factor in the city's growth. In 1907 work was begun on the Owens Valley aqueduct—a pipeline which brought water from the Sierras across desert country to Los Angeles. The Owens Valley water supply convinced several nearby towns that they should join Los Angeles, extending the city limits far from the old "downtown" sections.

During the 20th century Los Angeles became a leading seaport on the Pacific coast of the United States. Its ideal combination of a fine harbor facility, a petroleum supply, and the network of railroads was reinforced when the Panama Canal was opened in 1914. Air transportation also developed rapidly in Los Angeles. The weather conditions in the area are close to ideal for flying (the sun appears eight of nine days, year round), and aviation activities grew rapidly. World War II stimulated a growth in the aircraft industry with the result that Los Angeles produces more planes than any other American city. Other important activities in Los Angeles include the manufacture of radio and electronic equipment and clothing.

Los Angeles has had an unhappy series of riots in its history. During 1871 there was a widespread riot in which over twenty Chinese were killed by white Americans. A long series of labor disputes was climaxed in 1910 by a major explosion in the building operated by the Los Angeles *Times.* Twenty were killed in the blast, caused by a bomb planted by labor organizers. One of the largest and bloodiest race riots of the 20th century took place in the Watts section of Los Angeles in 1965: 35 persons were killed and property damage was about $200 million. Relations between Mexican-Americans and English-speaking Americans are also a serious problem.

Hollywood, center of the theatre and television industries, is inside the Los Angeles city limits. The city has had a Philharmonic Orchestra since 1919 and maintains a number of outdoor music programs for serious modern and classical music. The educational institutions in and near Los Angeles include the state-owned University of California at Los Angeles, California Institute of Technology at Pasadena, and the University of Southern California. Mount Wilson Observatory, north of the city, is one of the most important centers for the study of astronomy in the United States.

LOST BATTALION. A misnomer applied to part of the U.S. 77th Division, which, during the Meuse-Argonne offensive in World War I, was surrounded in Charlevaux Ravine by German troops. The force was composed of companies A, B, C, E, G, and H, 308th Infantry; Company K, 307th Infantry; and two platoons from companies C and D, 306th Machine Gun Battalion, all under command of Maj. Charles W. Whittlesey. Adjoining French and American attacks launched Oct. 2, 1918, failed, whereas Whittlesey penetrated to his objective, where he was promptly encircled. For five days, from the morning of Oct. 3 until the evening of Oct. 7, he maintained a heroic defense against great odds until American relief troops broke through. Strictly speaking, Whittlesey's force was not a battalion, nor was it at any time lost.

"LOST CAUSE." A symbolic term descriptive of the ideals, aspirations, and memories of the southern Confederacy. It was probably first used by E. A. Pollard, a Richmond newspaperman, in a book *The Lost Cause,* published in 1866.

LOST COLONY. *See* **Raleigh's Lost Colony.**

LOST GENERATION. A group of American writers, notably Hart Crane, E. E. Cummings, John Dos Passos, William Faulkner, F. Scott Fitzgerald, Ernest Hemingway, Thornton Wilder, and Thomas Wolfe, most of whom were born in the last decade of the 19th century. The early adult years of these writers were framed not so much by their American cultural heritage as by World War I and by self-imposed exile from the mainstream of American life, whether in Europe or in Greenwich Village in New York City—or, in Faulkner's case, in the small Mississippi town of his birth. Although the origin of the phrase is disputed, it probably derives from a remark made in the presence of Gertrude Stein by a hotel owner in Paris shortly after the end of World War I. In 1926 Hemingway used it as the epigraph to *The Sun Also Rises.*

LOST ORDER, LEE'S. As the Confederate army advanced into Maryland in September 1862, Gen. Robert E. Lee, at Frederick, planned to capture Harpers Ferry and concentrate his army for an advance into Pennsylvania. Accordingly, on Sept. 9, he issued Special Order No. 191, outlining routes and objectives. Copies were sent to division commanders concerned. Gen. David H. Hill's division, formerly under Gen. Thomas J. ("Stonewall") Jackson's orders, had been transferred. Jackson, receiving the order before learning of Hill's transfer, sent him a copy in his own hand—which Hill preserved. Another copy from Lee's headquarters, also sent to Hill, was lost and later found by a Union soldier. It was sent to Union Gen. George B. McClellan, who sought to act on the information but moved too slowly, thus allowing Lee to concentrate his scattered troops. The loss of the order nearly brought about Lee's complete defeat.

LOTTERIES. A lottery may be defined as a scheme for the distribution of prizes by lot or chance; legally, it is a chance to win a prize for a price. A distinction historically exists between public and private lotteries. Governments have authorized lotteries for financial and eleemosynary purposes; private lotteries seek a private profit.

The earliest lawful form of lottery involving the United States, designed to overcome a dearth of company finances, is found in King James's third charter of Virginia (1612). The American colonies speedily seized upon this method of raising money; by 1699, lotteries were numerous enough for a New England ecclesiastical assembly to denounce them. One of the earliest printed references to lotteries occurs in Andrew Bradford's *American Weekly Mercury* for Feb. 23, 1720. To the end of that century lotteries were increasingly employed by most states to fund schools, roads, bridges, canals, and other expenses.

Between 1820 and 1833 the traffic in lottery tickets rose to extraordinary proportions. Philadelphia's lottery offices increased from 3 to more than 200 between 1809 and 1833, and New York had fifty-two drawings in 1830, with the prizes aggregating $9.27 million. It is estimated that, nationally, 420 lotteries at that time offered annual prizes totaling about $53 million. No consistent attempt was made to suppress lotteries until Pennsylvania and Massachusetts passed repressive laws in 1833; New York followed the next year.

The earliest antilottery society appeared in Philadelphia in 1833. During the next two decades one state after another ended lotteries, until they survived only in Louisiana (*see* Louisiana Lottery). In 1890 Congress, acting under its postal powers, made it a misdemeanor to use the mails to advertise or distribute lottery tickets; two years later Louisiana abolished its own internal lottery, and since then it has prohibited lotteries. In 1894 and 1897 Congress also forbade importing or advertising lottery tickets, and in 1895 it further exercised its commerce powers by excluding and making illegal any "lottery traffic through national and interstate commerce." Four years later the 1895 statute was challenged, but in 1903 the Supreme Court held that the national legislature could enact such laws in order to guard the people from the "pestilence of lotteries." Despite these federal laws, states may hold or permit lotteries within their own borders so long as no federal-state conflict arises. The constitutions and laws of the fifty states have reflected the changing times, so that in 1980 fourteen states had some type of lottery. The lottery revenues increased from $776 million in 1975 to $2,107 million in 1980.

LOUDON, FORT (Pa.). Built by Col. John Armstrong of the Pennsylvania militia in 1756 as a protection against Indian forays into the Conococheague Valley. During the 1758 expedition of Gen. John Forbes it was used as a military storehouse and convalescents' camp. Lt. Charles Grant with a detachment of Highlanders occupied the post when, in November 1765, the Black Boys demanded the return of several guns that Grant had impounded following an assault upon a pack train of trading goods. Refused, they fired upon the fort, forcing its surrender and evacuation.

LOUDOUN, FORT (Tenn.). Built in 1756, to meet the French menace in the Old Southwest. Erected on the Little Tennessee River west of the Alleghenies by the English of South Carolina, it was named for John Campbell, Earl of Loudoun, commander of the British forces in America. It stood until 1760, when, under French incitement, it was besieged by the Cherokee, and surrendered on Aug. 7. The troops marched out only to be attacked by the Indians on Aug. 10, when four officers, twenty-three privates, and some women and children were massacred. The fort was burned.

LOUISBURG EXPEDITION (1745). After the loss of Acadia in 1713, France settled Louisburg on Cape Breton Island, constructing a fortress and naval station. When King George's War began in 1744, Gov. William Shirley of Massachusetts determined to attack Louisburg. Well advised about French conditions, Shirley prevailed upon the general court (Jan. 25, 1745) to raise 3,000 men and necessary supplies and enlisted support from neighboring colonies. Shirley hoped to capture Louisburg before the French fleet arrived in the spring. On Mar. 24 about 4,300 men, commanded by Sir William Pepperell, sailed from Boston. Landing at Canso, across the strait from Cape Breton Island, they were cheered by the arrival on Apr. 23 of Commodore Peter Warren with three English warships (eight others arrived later). On Apr. 30, while Warren blockaded Louisburg harbor, Pepperell landed his men at Gabarus Bay and laid siege to the town. Fortunate in capturing (May 3) the French battery of thirty heavy cannon, which they turned on the town, the colonials forced Louisburg to capitulate (June 15), and captured the vessels of the French fleet as they arrived. The colonists were embittered when, by the Treaty of Aix-la-Chapelle of 1748, England scarificed Louisburg for Madras.

LOUISIANA. Spanish explorers touched the Louisiana coast before 1520, and Hernando de Soto died in the interior in 1542 while searching for mines of precious metals. Spain then abandoned the region. In 1682 Robert Cavelier, Sieur de La Salle, coming from Canada, followed the Mississippi to its mouth and claimed the entire valley for Louis XIV of France, in whose honor it was named Louisiana. La Salle's expedition to plant a colony at the mouth of the Mississippi in 1684 missed its intended destination and landed on the Texas coast, and in 1687 he was assassinated. Pierre Lemoyne, Sieur d'Iberville, planted the first permanent French colony on the Gulf coast in 1699 (*see* Biloxi), while Jean Baptiste Le Moyne, Sieur de Bienville, further explored the region. In 1712 Louis XIV, faced with an empty treasury, granted to Antoine Crozat the exclusive privilege of exploiting the area. Crozat exhausted his resources in futile searches for sources of quick wealth, and in 1717 surrendered his charter.

John Law, a Scotsman recognized in France as a successful banker and financier, organized the Western Company, which assumed control of Louisiana on Jan. 1, 1718. The scope of its operations was soon enlarged and its name changed to Company of the Indies. In 1720 the company failed, and Law passed off the scene (*see* Mississippi Bubble).

Louisiana then passed under royal control. It developed slowly, handicapped by strife between France and England. France undertook to unite Louisiana with Canada by erecting fortified posts to exclude the English from the Mississippi Valley. The British quickly accepted the challenge, and King George's War (1744–48) and the French and Indian War (1754–63) culminated in the expulsion of the French from the mainland of North America. In 1762 Louisiana west of the Mississippi and the Isle of Orleans were ceded to Spain, and the remainder of Louisiana was surrendered to England in 1763 (*see* Fontainebleau, Treaty of; Paris, Treaty of).

Resentment of the French inhabitants at the transfer, Spain's tardiness in taking possession of the colony, general economic distress, and the unpopular measures of Antonio de Ulloa, the first Spanish governor, led to his expulsion in the so-called Revolution of 1768. But Alexander O'Reilly, an Irish soldier in Spanish service, crushed the rebellion and firmly established Spanish authority in 1769. Louisiana experienced a steady development under Spanish rule despite many difficulties. It played an important part in the American Revolution. Needed supplies were forwarded from New Orleans to the patriot forces in the West (*see* Pollock's Aid to the American Revolution), and when Spain entered the war as an ally of France in 1779, Bernardo de Galvez, operating from Louisiana, captured the British posts in West Florida. Spanish discontent with the Definitive Treaty of Peace of 1783 led to intrigues with the Indians and with some of the western leaders for protecting Louisiana by holding back the influx of American settlers or detaching the trans-Allegheny region from the United States (*see* Western Separatism). The Nootka Sound controversy between England and Spain in

1790 and the mission of Edmond Charles Genêt in 1793, involving threats of western attack upon Louisiana, alarmed Spanish authorities. Disputes between the United States and Spain over navigation of the Mississippi and the northern boundary of West Florida were adjusted by Pinckney's Treaty of 1795, but Spain still feared the outcome of American expansion in the Southwest. By the Treaty of San Ildefonso (Oct. 1, 1800) Spain retroceded Louisiana to France; but before France had taken possession of the colony, Napoleon sold Louisiana to the United States in 1803 (*see* Louisiana Purchase).

Louisiana was admitted to the Union in 1812. Agriculture and commerce expanded rapidly. Sugar culture, stimulated by a protective tariff and the introduction of hardier varieties of cane and improved processes of manufacture, became the favorite crop in lower Louisiana, extending to the Red River by 1845. Cotton culture expanded greatly, particularly after the settlement of the region north of the Red River about 1840. The steamboat made New Orleans the commercial emporium of the Mississippi Valley. Expansion necessitated better transportation and banking facilities, and the state adopted the unsound policy of financing internal improvements by chartering several "improvement banks" backed by state credit, which brought financial distress in the panic of 1837. This prompted the development of a sound state banking system and a saner program of internal improvements. Agriculture and commerce soon revived, followed by a new era of railroad and levee construction in the 1850's.

Cultural activities flourished in antebellum New Orleans. Over a score of European operas received their American premieres in New Orleans, and the city's newspapers—some of them bilingual—were among the nation's best.

Louisiana had been denied any exposure to democratic ideas or institutions from its establishment in 1699 to 1803. After its admission to the Union, the state was controlled for many years by powerful oligarchies of planters, lawyers, and businessmen. Louisiana shared with South Carolina on the eve of the Civil War the distinction of being the most aristocratic, conservative, and property-conscious state in the South.

The sixth state to secede, Louisiana early suffered from federal military and naval superiority. New Orleans was captured on May 1, 1862, and vital sections of the state remained in federal hands throughout the war. During the war President Abraham Lincoln used Louisiana as a laboratory for testing his reconstruction theories. Louisiana emerged from the war with virtually no capital, an impoverished population, its traditional racial mores in limbo, and many of its leaders dead, discredited, or exiled. Radical Reconstruction (1868–77) imposed upon the state a baleful legacy of corruption, violence, racial animosity, and political cynicism.

A reactionary group of "home-rule Democrats" was voted into power (somewhat questionably) in 1877. For the next twenty years these men retained control of the state government by means of racist slogans, vote stealing, and other forms of repression. Property and literacy qualifications for the franchise were written into the state constitution of 1898. By then Louisiana had become the most illiterate state in the nation. The state's poor and ignorant farmers, black and white alike, were eliminated by the thousands from the voting rolls, leaving the Democrats of 1898 and their successors in secure possession of the government.

Louisiana's industrial development began about 1900, with the exploitation of petroleum and natural gas resources, as well as salt, sulfur, and timber. Limited social progress followed economic prosperity. Public education began to receive more support, yellow fever was eliminated and malaria brought under control, better levees were constructed, the tax base was broadened, a network of gravel roads was constructed, and the state university was gradually upgraded.

A mild spirit of progressivism entered Louisiana politics about 1920 and became militant with the advent of Huey P. Long as governor in 1928. Long carried through in record time an elaborate program of public improvement and social amelioration. Paved roads and free bridges replaced gravel roads and toll ferries on main highways, a magnificent new state capitol was erected, more adequate financial support was accorded to educational and charitable institutions, free textbooks were supplied to all children, and the burden of taxation was more equitably distributed. But Long was ruthless in suppressing those who opposed him, and he was shot to death in 1935 by a relative of one of his political foes.

From the time of Long's death until the 1960's, Louisiana politics operated within a "bifactional" state Democratic party, one faction appealing for voter support on the Longite platform of expanded public services, the other stressing the more conservative tenets of the anti-Longite opposition. Several factors, however, have combined to relegate the labels "Longite" and "anti-Longite" to history: (1) the continuing shift of population from countryside to cities and suburbs, (2) the migration into Louisiana of people from other states and nations, (3) the dramatic rise in Louisiana's standard of living as a result of the boom years of World War II and after, and (4) the resurgence of the Republican party in Louisiana.

Louisiana in the 1970's continued to enjoy the fruits of industrialization, mechanization of agriculture, and technological progress. Between 1970 and 1980 the population increased by 15 percent (to 4,203,972 inhabitants), and the state's ranking in per capita income moved up from forty-fifth to thirty-fourth place among the fifty states.

LOUISIANA, UPPER. The Spanish designation for that part of Louisiana stretching from Hope Encampment on the Mississippi northward to Canada and westward to the Rocky Mountains. Beginning in 1770, St. Louis was the seat of government, presided over by a lieutenant governor, subordinate only to the governor of Louisiana at New Orleans. The United States called Upper Louisiana the District of Louisiana, distinguishing Lower Louisiana with the name of Territory of Orleans. Upper Louisiana was further divided after the Louisiana Purchase in 1803 into five districts.

LOUISIANA LOTTERY. Chartered by the Louisiana legislature in August 1868 for twenty-five years. In return for its monopoly of the lottery business in Louisiana, the company paid $40,000 annually to the state, but was exempt from other taxation. In March 1879 the legislature repealed the charter, but the U.S. District Court for Louisiana held that this was a violation of contract. In 1890 the company, through John A. Morris, one of its founders, offered the state $500,000 annually for an extension of twenty-five years. This offer was subsequently raised to $1 million and then to $1.25 million. An act calling for a constitutional amendment embodying the lottery company's franchise was passed. This was vetoed by Gov. Francis T. Nicholls. The house passed the bill over his veto, but the senate failed to do so. The latter body approved a resolution denying the governor's right to veto a bill proposing a constitutional amendment, whereupon the house sent the bill to the secretary of state to be promulgated. This the official refused to do. Morris took the matter into the courts, which decided against the secretary of state. On Sept. 19, 1890, the U.S. Post Office Department denied the lottery company the use of the mails. Morris thereupon withdrew his proposition. In the meantime a political organization unfavorable to the lottery had been formed and held a convention in Baton Rouge, Aug. 7, 1890. The agitation thus initiated resulted in the election of Murphy J. Foster to the governorship. After his election, Foster approved acts (June 28 and July 12, 1892) making the sale of lottery tickets unlawful in Louisiana. The lottery company continued in business in New Orleans until 1895 (*see* Lotteries), when it transferred its domicile to Honduras. From there it continued to sell tickets in the United States until April 1906, when the U.S. Department of Justice succeeded in breaking up the business.

LOUISIANA PURCHASE (1803). The French province of Louisiana embraced the Isle of Orleans on the east bank of the Mississippi and the vast area between that river, the Rocky Mountains, and the Spanish possessions in the Southwest. For a generation Louisiana had been a pawn in European diplomacy. France ceded it to Spain in 1762 (*see* Fontainebleau, Treaty of). The first French minister to the United States, Edmond Charles Genêt, planned to attack it from the United States in 1793, but France turned to diplomacy as a means of recovering it between 1795 and 1799. By the Treaty of San Ildefonso, Oct. 1, 1800, and the Convention of Aranjuez, Mar. 21, 1801, Napoleon Bonaparte acquired Louisiana for France in return for placing the son-in-law of the Spanish king on the newly erected throne of Etruria.

The Treaty of San Lorenzo, Spain, in 1795, granted American citizens the privilege of depositing goods at New Orleans for reshipment on oceangoing vessels. The United States was deeply aroused when Juan Ventura Morales, the acting intendant of Louisiana, revoked this right of deposit on Oct. 16, 1802, and failed to provide another site, as the treaty required. President Thomas Jefferson appointed James Monroe as special envoy to assist Robert R. Livingston, the minister at Paris, in securing American rights. Monroe's instructions authorized an offer of $10 million for the Isle of Orleans, on which New Orleans stood, and the Floridas. In the meantime Livingston urged the cession to the United States of the Isle of Orleans and all the trans-Mississippi country above the Arkansas River.

By the spring of 1803 Napoleon's plans for his American empire had all gone astray. Spain refused to round out his possessions by ceding the Floridas. War with Great Britain was imminent. In the United States there was growing hostility to France and talk of an Anglo-American alliance. Disturbed at such a prospect, Napoleon decided to reap a profit and placate the Americans by selling them all of Louisiana.

When Monroe arrived in Paris on Apr. 12, the first consul had already appointed François de Barbé-Marbois, minister of the public treasury, to conduct the negotiations. On Apr. 11, Talleyrand had amazed Livingston by asking what the United States would give for the entire colony. Barbé-Marbois conferred with Livingston on the evening of Apr. 13, thereby initiating the negotiations before the formal presentation of Monroe. Some jealousy arose between the American negotiators, but it did not handicap their work. Monroe was at first less inclined than Livingston to exceed their instructions and purchase all of Louisiana. By a treaty and two conventions, all dated Apr. 30, the United States paid $11.25 million for Louisiana, set aside $3.75 million to pay the claims of its own citizens against France, and placed France and Spain on an equal commercial basis with the United States in the colony for a period of twelve years. On Nov. 30, 1803, Spain formally delivered the colony to Pierre-Clément Laussat, the French colonial prefect, who on Dec. 20 transferred the territory to William C. C. Claiborne and Gen. James Wilkinson, the American commissioners.

LOUISIANA PURCHASE, BOUNDARIES OF. The United States purchased Louisiana "with the same extent that it now has in the hands of Spain, and that it had when France possessed it; and Such as it Should be after the Treaties subsequently entered into between Spain and other States." The treaty of cession, incorporating these words, quoted verbatim from the treaty by which Spain retroceded Louisiana to France in 1800. France, original settler of Louisiana, had not reoccupied it at the time of the U.S. purchase, but the extent of the region "in the hands of Spain" was ill defined. Before 1763 France claimed the entire Mississippi watershed eastward to the Alleghenies and westward to undetermined limits, as well as the Gulf coast eastward to the Perdido River. Between French Louisiana and French Canada no clear line had been drawn.

France ceded western Louisiana to Spain in 1762 (*see* Fontainebleau, Treaty of), but there is no evidence that the two countries made a boundary delineation. Great Britain, by the Treaty of Paris, in 1763 completed its possession of all North America east of the Mississippi except New Orleans, making that river the eastern boundary of Louisiana. The province of West Florida was joined with the province of Louisiana, in administration only, from 1783, when Spain recovered both Floridas (*see* Definitive Treaty of Peace), until 1803, when Spain governed West Florida separately and asserted its independence of Louisiana (*see* West Florida, Annexation of). Meanwhile Spain's acquisition of Louisiana in 1762 had postponed the need for a Texas-Louisiana delineation. The United States took French colonial exploration and the instructions to the intended French captain-general of Louisiana in 1802 as bases for its claim that the purchase extended to the Rio Grande.

Since colonial occupation gave no ground for boundary

claims farther north, it was logical to assume that the purchase included the natural watershed of the Mississippi. President Thomas Jefferson's claim that Oregon was included had no foundation and no international recognition. An assertion that the northern boundary was defined in the Treaty of Utrecht of 1713 was ignored. In the Convention of 1818 a practical agreement between the United States and England placed the boundary at 49° north latitude, from the Lake of the Woods to the Rocky Mountains.

LOUISIANA PURCHASE EXPOSITION (Apr. 30–Dec. 1, 1904). Its 1,240 acres in St. Louis, Mo., made it the largest of international expositions to date; its cost was more than $31.5 million and its attendance 19,694,855. Six years of preparation went to the celebration of the centennial of the purchase of the Louisiana territory. Architecturally the fair followed the grandiloquent French style, and the ensemble formed an astonishing pattern of elaborate and universal chaos. The foreign governments contributed to this by building, for the most part, replicas of great European buildings and palaces—thus enhancing the architectural confusion.

LOUISIANA REVOLUTION OF 1768. The French inhabitants of Louisiana keenly resented being transferred to Spain by the Treaty of Fontainebleau of Nov. 3, 1762, and Spain's tardiness in taking possession of the colony induced the inhabitants to hope that the actual transfer would never take place. Economic distress, loyalty to France, and the unpopularity of Antonio de Ulloa, the first Spanish governor of Louisiana, culminated in Ulloa's expulsion from the colony in the so-called revolution of October 1768.

LOUISIANA SPECIE RESERVE BANKING SYSTEM. The panic of 1837 destroyed the loose banking system of Louisiana. As a result, there was a banking reform movement that culminated in the act of 1842, setting up a board of currency with large powers of supervision over all banks. The banks were required to separate their loans into two types: those made from capital and those made from deposits. Capital loans could be made on long-term paper, but those from deposits were limited to ninety-day paper, nonrenewable. In addition to this deposit protection was a requirement for a one-third specie reserve. Banks were prohibited from dealing in speculative ventures, and daily exchanges of notes and weekly specie settlements were required. The strength of the Louisiana system was demonstrated during the panic of 1857, which had less effect in New Orleans than in any commercial city of the nation. The Louisiana system exerted a marked influence on the national banking system.

LOUISVILLE (Ky.). Largest city in Kentucky, with a population of 298,451 in 1980; the center of a metropolitan area including 901,970 people. Louisville is located on the south bank of the Ohio River at the Falls of the Ohio, a natural stopping place and shipping point for traffic on the river.

The town was surveyed and laid out in 1773 by Thomas Bullitt, an agent of the Virginia colony, but it was not settled at that time. Men who accompanied George Rogers Clark on his sweep of the Ohio valley and capture of Vincennes established themselves at Louisville in a fort in the winter of 1778–79. The next year, additional settlers arrived and the place was named "Louisville" in honor of King Louis XVI.

In 1830 a canal was opened around the falls of the Ohio, and Louisville's commerce picked up until it became one of the busiest river ports in America. The city became an exchange point for goods and money from New Orleans and from the Midwest and New England. During the Civil War, the city was an important supply base for Union armies.

Louisville's industries include a major farm equipment factory and one of the world's largest electric appliance factories. The liquor industry in Louisville produces close to a quarter of all liquor manufactured in the United States. One of the attractions of Louisville is the Kentucky Derby, a horse race run annually at Churchill Downs since 1875.

LOUISVILLE AND NASHVILLE RAILROAD. *See* **Railroads, Sketches of Principal Lines.**

LOUISVILLE AND PORTLAND CANAL. Around the Falls of the Ohio, at Louisville, constructed by a Kentucky corporation chartered in 1825. The canal was begun in 1825 and opened in 1830. The original construction cost $742,869.94. The federal government, which had subscribed heavily to the project, acquired possession of the canal in 1872, reducing tolls to a nominal sum and none after 1880. The canal was twice enlarged, 1861–66 and 1870–82, and in 1927 was rebuilt with federal aid to permit through navigation.

LOVEJOY RIOTS. Elijah P. Lovejoy, an abolitionist clergyman, established a weekly newspaper, *The Observer,* at St. Louis in 1833. Threatened by proslavery men for editorials against slavery in 1834, he moved his press to Alton, Ill., in 1836; there it was smashed on the Alton dock by local citizens. Sympathizers helped to purchase a new press, but when Lovejoy came out for immediate abolition and a state antislavery society (July 1837), a mob destroyed the press (August), smashed a third (Sept. 21), and, in an effort to destroy the fourth (Nov. 7), shot its defenders and killed Lovejoy, who immediately came to be considered a martyr.

LOVELY'S PURCHASE. W. L. Lovely, Cherokee Indian agent in Arkansas, in an informal peace conference between Osage and Cherokee at the confluence of the Verdigris and Arkansas rivers in eastern Oklahoma, on July 9, 1816, obtained consent of the Osage to cede a large tract of land lying east of that stream if the government would pay claims for depredations held against them by white people. At St. Louis, Sept. 25, 1818, representative members of the Osage ratified this cession in consideration of payment by the government of claims amounting to $4,000.

LOVEWELL'S FIGHT. Occurred at Pigwacket (Fryeburg), Maine, May 9 (o.s.), 1725. Capt. John Lovewell, with thirty-three volunteers, was out for scalp bounty, and a chaplain with the party had just scalped an Indian when the troop was ambushed by about eighty Pequawkets (a branch of the Abnaki). Twelve white men, including Lovewell, fell at the onset; one deserted; and twenty-one were left. Ensign Seth

Wyman, the only officer, placed his men for a finish fight. Toward nightfall, seeing the Indians preparing for a fresh attack, Wyman shot the medicine man. This ended the fight. Eighteen men eventually reached home. Rev. Thomas Symmes in his contemporary account changed the date from May 9 to May 8, supposedly to divert from the chaplain, who died, the odium of scalp hunting on Sunday.

LOWELL (Mass.). A small settlement at the juncture of the Merimack and Concord rivers arose in the 18th century. In 1801 a carding mill was built; and in 1804 the Middlesex canal was completed around the Pawtucket falls. Water provided by these falls resulted in the development of a large textile industry. In 1826 the town was incorporated and named for Francis Cabot Lowell, the developer of America's textile industry. In 1836 it was chartered as a city. In the early nineteenth century it was frequently visited as a model industrial town. Much of its labor force was supplied by young women known as Lowell Girls. Lowell remained the textile center of America until the Great Depression when the industry began to move to the South. It is the home of the Lowell Textile Institute (1897) and Lowell State Teachers College (1894). In 1980 the population was 92,418.

LOWER CALIFORNIA (also known as **Bàja California**). Discovered in 1533 by Fortún Jiménez, a navigator in the service of Hernando Cortes. It was separated from Spanish Upper (Alta) California in 1772. The cession of the peninsula by Mexico was vainly sought by Nicholas P. Trist in making the peace treaty of Guadalupe Hidalgo in 1848. It was also the objective of William Walker's futile filibustering expedition of 1853–54; and James Gadsden failed to obtain it as part of the Gadsden Purchase in 1854. A number of efforts to purchase it for the United States in 1857, 1859, and later years were equally fruitless. The U.S. Navy for several years made use of Magdalena Bay on the west coast of the peninsula as a maneuvers base, by courtesy of the Mexican government; and an alleged Japanese effort to lease the bay in 1910–11 was the occasion leading to the Lodge Resolution of 1912.

LOWER COUNTIES-ON-DELAWARE. Comprising the counties of New Castle, Kent, and Sussex, or the present state of Delaware, evolved from Swedish and Dutch settlements. They were conveyed by the Duke of York (later James II) in 1682 to William Penn and shortly afterward annexed to the Province of Pennsylvania by the Act of Union. Because of disagreement in the provincial assembly, the Lower Counties seceded from that body in 1704 and formed, at New Castle, their own assembly, by which they continued to be governed until the adoption of the constitution of Delaware in 1776.

LOWER LAKES. *See* **Upper and Lower Lakes.**

LOWER SOUTH. That part of the South lying within the cotton belt: South Carolina, Georgia, Florida, Alabama, Mississippi, Louisiana, and Texas. In the later antebellum period these states (Florida excepted) secured political leadership in the South, based on large-scale, slave-labor cotton culture and its concomitants.

LOYAL, FORT, CAPTURE OF (May 20, 1690). Toward the beginning of King William's War, under the command of the governor of New France, Louis de Buade, Comte de Frontenac, a mixed force of French and Indians besieged Fort Loyal on Casco Bay, Maine, and compelled its commander, Capt. Sylvanus Davis, to surrender. Many of the captured were tortured and murdered.

LOYALHANNA, BATTLE OF THE (Oct. 12, 1758). At Ligonier, Pa., 600 French and Indians made an unsuccessful attack on 1,500 men, in an entrenched encampment, commanded by Col. James Burd, to delay the expedition of Gen. John Forbes. The French retired, after a four-hour conflict and slight losses. Burd's losses were considerable.

LOYALISTS (Tories). Those loyal to Great Britain during the American Revolution comprised about one-third of the colonial population. While a few of the more conservative stood for the rigid execution of imperial law, the majority opposed the objectionable acts of the British Parliament, served on the early extralegal committees, and were not hostile to the calling of the first Continental Congress in 1774, working hard to elect delegates of their own convictions. Although anxious to maintain their rights, in some cases even by a show of force, they were strongly opposed to separation from the empire.

After the Battle of Lexington great numbers of Loyalists flocked to the royal colors or organized militia companies of their own under commissions from the crown. Although they probably contributed 60,000 soldiers, their military service was not commensurate with their numerical strength: their only outstanding exploits were an expedition against the coast towns of Connecticut; frontier raids; and a savage guerrilla warfare against patriots in the South. As the struggle progressed, all who refused to take an oath of allegiance to the new governments were denied the rights of citizenship and could not vote, hold office, or enjoy court protection. In many cases Loyalists were forbidden to pursue professions or to acquire or dispose of property. Free speech was denied them, and they were not allowed to communicate with the British. When these laws failed of their purpose, the more ardent Loyalists were jailed, put on parole, sent to detention camps, or tarred and feathered. Nearly all the new state governments enacted legislation banishing those who refused to swear allegiance. About 200,000 Loyalists died, were exiled, or became voluntary refugees.

LOYAL LAND COMPANY. The first grant to a company organized to deal in western lands was to the Loyal Land Company. A grant of 800,000 acres was made to it by the Council of State of Virginia, on July 12, 1748. Thomas Walker, in 1750, led a tour of the Tennessee and Kentucky country east of the Cumberland Mountains. By the autumn of 1754 lands had been sold to about 200 settlers. The French and Indian War ended activities, and the Proclamation of 1763 gave the company trouble. To render lands west of the proclamation line available, Walker took an active part in removing the claims of the Indian tribes to the region. He participated in negotiating the treaties of Fort Stanwix and Lochaber in 1768 and 1770.

LOYAL LEAGUES. Generically the Union League of America, they were formed to restore northern morale, shaken by reverses in 1862. The movement had its origin at Pekin, Ill., on June 25, 1862. A convention assembled at Cleveland, May 20–21, 1863, to create the national Grand Council with headquarters at Washington, D.C. Union leagues insisted upon unconditional loyalty, promoted the Union party, and contributed to the reelection of President Abraham Lincoln. Many leagues continued mainly as local social clubs.

LOYAL LEGION, MILITARY ORDER OF THE. *See* **Military Order of the Loyal Legion of the U.S.A.**

LOYAL PUBLICATION SOCIETIES. Formed during the Civil War to distribute "journals and documents of unquestionable loyalty." Strongly opposing Copperheads and Democrats, they were active in state politics and the national campaign of 1864. Under Francis Lieber, the New York society from 1862 to 1865 raised $30,000, with which it published 900,000 copies of ninety pamphlets. The New England society spent $4,000 to print more than 200 broadsides.

LOYALTY OATHS. In the earliest colonial charters all those immigrating were required to take oaths of loyalty to the crown and to the colonial regime. During the American Revolution, loyalty oaths were used by radicals to enforce boycotts against the Tories, and both rebel and royal loyalty oaths were freely employed to maintain the security of the conflicting forces. In the Constitution, a specified oath is required of the president in Article II, Section 1, Clause 8; and Article VI requires an oath of all federal and state officers to "support this Constitution."

During the Civil War, test oaths were enforced in both the North and the South. The center of Abraham Lincoln's program for reconstruction in 1863 was a pledge of future loyalty to the Union, unlike the test oath enacted by Congress in 1862, which required pledges of past loyalty. The Supreme Court in *Cummings* v. *Missouri* (1866) held unconstitutional a state oath requiring voters, teachers, candidates for public office, and others to swear that they had not participated in rebellion against the United States. On the same day, in *Ex parte Garland,* the Court held unconstitutional a congressional statute requiring a similar oath of attorneys.

Oaths did not play a primary role in either of the two world wars, but the Hatch Act of 1938 required as a condition of federal employment that the applicant swear that he did not belong to an organization advocating the violent overthrow of the government. In the agitation over Communists in the postwar period, loyalty testing became a prominent activity in the executive establishment. It was also a principal feature of the work of congressional committees, and punishments for contempt or perjury were meted out to many who refused to make exculpatory statements or who swore falsely. Many state legislatures and municipal bodies required loyalty oaths of teachers, public and private, and governmental employees, most of which were upheld by the Supreme Court.

LOYALTY REVIEW BOARD. In 1947, the Loyalty Review Board was created within the Civil Service Commission to review evidence and conclusions in cases concerning the loyalty of individual federal employees to the United States. The board was abolished in 1953.

LUBBOCK (Tex.)**.** Eighth largest city in Texas, with a population of 173,979 in 1980; the center for a metropolitan area of 211,861. The city is located on the high plains of west Texas in an area devoted to cattle raising when the town was founded in 1891. Cotton is raised on very extensive farms (once cattle ranches) in a highly mechanized manner. "Agribusinesses" specialize in widespread raising of crops for sale to others. The city is a center for the west Texas oil industry and home of the Texas Technological College.

LUDLOW RESOLUTION. A proposed constitutional amendment introduced by Rep. Louis Ludlow of Indiana in 1935. It would have limited the power of Congress by requiring a popular referendum to ratify a declaration of war except in case of actual attack on the United States or its outlying territories. Only strenuous efforts by President Franklin D. Roosevelt's administration prevented its coming to a final vote in the House of Representatives in January 1938.

LUDLOW'S CODE. The general court of Connecticut in 1646 requested Roger Ludlow, a member of the court, to compile a body of laws for the commonwealth. The result was Ludlow's Code of 1650, which remains the foundation of the laws of the state.

LUMBEE (or Croatan, Indians)**.** Numbering more than 40,000, they have a mixed ancestry of white, Indian, and black strains. They seem to constitute a hybridized remnant of once-powerful Atlantic coast tribes and claim to be descendants of Sir Walter Raleigh's lost colony intermarried with the Hatteras Indians. They speak no Indian language and have few distinctively Indian traits. The group is centered in Robeson County, N.C., although some 2,000 urban Lumbee live in Baltimore, Md.

LUMBER INDUSTRY. The farmer cut down all of the trees that shaded his fields, but the lumberman specialized in a single species of tree. The lumberman logged the white pine north from Maine into New Brunswick and west into Pennsylvania. By the 1890's the pursuit of this tree led to the area around Spokane, Wash. Others began to cut the Norway pine and other species, or moved south to stands of southern pine and cypress, or to the West Coast, with redwoods, Douglas fir, Port Orford cedar, and other giant trees. Southern forests also provided oak for the stout warships of the Old Ironsides era and pitch, tar, and turpentine from the pine barrens of the Carolinas.

The chain saw has almost completely displaced the ax and handsaw; even greater technological advances have been made in sawmills. Pit sawing, in which a log was inched over a pit or trestle and sawed into boards or planks, was replaced in colonial times by the muley saw, operated by waterpower. Early in the 19th century the buzz, or circular, saw partially replaced the muley saw. It was fast and reliable but turned much of the log into sawdust. The increasing value of hardwoods led to the introduction of the band saw, which reduced the amount of wood wasted in sawdust. A toy in the 18th century, the band saw became a practical tool with the development of special steels, hard rubber, and resistant glues. Today sawmills, planing mills, drying kilns, and other associated plants are largely automated. Important developments since the middle of the 19th century include the making of paper from wood pulp, the burgeoning of the plywood industry, and the use of wood fibers for insulating material or wallboard.

The lumber industry has been the principal target of the conservationists over the years. Cheap raw material, unfavorable land laws, a cutting cycle that might vary from 15 to 150 years, and unfair local taxes led to desolate, eroded hillsides, or to thickets of weed trees and brush. Many large companies now maintain tree farms, practice conservation measures, and plan for a century ahead, but some small loggers still pursue ruthless ways. However, many of America's timber reserves are in the national forests and are subject to the rules established by the U.S. Forest Service. The U.S. lumber production increased by 14 percent between 1960 and 1979, while the consumption increased by 30 percent.

"LUNATIC FRINGE." A phrase used by Theodore Roosevelt in his *Autobiography* to characterize the "foolish fanatics," such as extreme pacifists, "who form the lunatic fringe in all reform movements." The term has since been used to describe those who proclaim impractical schemes.

LUNDY'S LANE, BATTLE AT (July 25, 1814). The most sharply contended engagement in the War of 1812, occurred when Gen. Jacob Brown's army, invading Canada, encountered the British under Gen. Phineas Riall at Lundy's Lane near Bridgewater and Niagara Falls. Col. Winfield Scott's First Brigade failed to carry the position in a frontal attack and was reinforced by Gen. Eleazar Ripley and Col. Peter B. Porter's brigades. Maj. Thomas Jesup, with the Twenty-fifth Infantry, drove in the British left, capturing Riall. Gen. Gordon Drummond, arriving with reinforcements, took command. Col. James Miller's Twenty-first Infantry stormed the hill and took the British artillery, the Americans repulsing counterattacks until midnight. Brown and Scott, both severely wounded, withdrew. Ripley, left in command, brought off the army when ammunition failed, but lacking horses, abandoned the captured cannon. Both sides claimed victory, but Drummond held the field. Losses were heavy: British, 30 percent; American, slightly less.

***LUSITANIA*, SINKING OF THE** (May 7, 1915). The Cunard liner *Lusitania* was sunk without warning by the German submarine U-20 off Old Head of Kinsale, Ireland. Of the 1,959 passengers and crew, 1,198 perished, including 128 Americans. Since on May 1, the day of sailing, the German embassy in Washington, D.C., had published an advertisement in American papers warning Atlantic travelers that they sailed in Allied ships at their own risk, it was widely believed that the sinking was premeditated. The log of the U-20 shows, however, that the submarine had sunk other ships, met the *Lusitania* by chance, and sank it from fear of being rammed. The cargo of 4,200 cases of small-arms ammunition and 1,250 shrapnel cases may have exploded and contributed to the rapid (eighteen minutes) sinking of the ship. The catastrophe created intense indignation in the United States.

LUSK COMMITTEE. Authorized in 1919 by the New York legislature and headed by state senator Clayton R. Lusk. It published a monumental report of 4,450 pages on radical and seditious activities.

LUTHERAN CHURCHES. Historically, Lutheranism has placed heavy emphasis on its confessional statements. The Augsburg Confession, drawn up by Melanchthon in 1530, is the primary doctrinal symbol, but many Lutherans also adhere to the 1580 Book of Concord. Lutheran theology is centered around the doctrine of justification by faith and stresses the role of the Word of God and the sacraments of baptism and the Lord's Supper as the communication of grace.

The primary growth of colonial Lutheranism was the result of German immigration. Salzburg Lutherans began settling in Georgia in 1734, but even larger numbers immigrated to Pennsylvania. The outstanding leader of the young church was Henry Melchior Mühlenberg, who managed to unite the various pastors in the colony in the Ministerium of Philadelphia (1748). The church did not have a national organization until the General Synod was formed in 1820.

In the early 19th century conflict arose between those who supported the emerging "American Lutheranism" and those who wished to emphasize tradition. The leader of the "American" Lutherans was the theologian Samuel S. Schmucker. In his *Fraternal Appeal to the American Churches* (1838), he called for an organization similar to the present National Council of Churches, and he was both a founder and an active member of the Evangelical Alliance. His principal opponent was Charles Philip Krauth. The controversy reached its climax in 1853 when the Definite Synodical Program was presented to the General Synod. It called for a revision of the Augsburg Confession in the direction of commonly held American religious beliefs and provoked a decade of conflict that effectively removed the partisans of American-oriented Lutheranism from power.

In many ways, the pattern of immigration made the dispute academic. Most new German immigrants had been influenced by the confessional revival in Europe, and they moved the church in that direction. Immigration also tended to fragment Lutheranism; different synods, representing different European communities, struggled to provide an adequate ministry and to find marks of distinction.

One of the most successful of these immigrant churches was the Missouri Synod, founded by Saxon immigrants. Its theology was both pietist and confessional. The synod affirmed a congregational polity and a "low" transfer theory of the ministry; it affirmed pure doctrine and the need for a strict theological consensus. In the 20th century, this confessional stance has led to controversy over the higher criticism of the Bible.

In the early 1980's about 95 percent of all Lutherans were members of three synods: the Lutheran Church in America (2,925,188 members), the American Lutheran Church (2,-352,431 members), and the Lutheran Church–Missouri Synod (2,719,319 members). The first two, together with the Association of Evangelical Lutheran Churches (121,000 members), voted in September 1982 to merge and form a new Lutheran church. It will be the fourth largest church in the country. The seven remaining Lutheran denominations had a combined membership of 477,996 in 1980, the largest being the Wisconsin Evangelical Lutheran Synod (407,987 members).

***LUTHER* V. *BORDEN*,** 7 Howard 1 (1848). An attempt to make the Supreme Court decide between the charter government of Rhode Island and the new government arising from the rebellion led by Thomas W. Dorr in 1842. Chief Justice Roger B. Taney's opinion evaded that issue, recognized state law and state courts as completely competent, and declared existing state authority legally empowered to use martial methods to maintain itself against violence.

LYCEUM MOVEMENT. A phase of the early adult education and public school movements, utilizing, principally, lectures and debates. It was begun by an article in the *American Journal of Education* (October 1826) by Josiah Holbrook, containing a plan for "Associations of Adults for Mutual Education." The first society was organized by Holbrook in November 1826 at Millbury, Mass. By 1831 lyceums existed in all the New England states and in northern New York. In the same year the New York State Lyceum called a meeting in New York City to organize a national lyceum. Holbrook journeyed as far west as Missouri and found active interest in the western states, including Kentucky and Tennessee. National lyceums were held each year until 1839, although often poorly attended. The town lyceums, estimated by Holbrook at 3,000 in 1835, increased greatly until the early 20th century. In 1915 their number was estimated at 12,000. In 1924–25 it was found that they existed mostly in small towns and were concentrated mostly on semipopular music and "sanitated vaudeville." The early lyceums led to certain permanent institutions, such as Lowell Institute in Massachusetts and Brooklyn Institute in New York. Some developed into historical or literary societies, public libraries, or museums.

LYGONIA. A grant, commonly called the Plough Patent, made by the Council for New England, June 26, 1630, of an area forty miles square, west of the Kennebec River in Maine. Settlement by the original grantees failed, and the grant was purchased, Apr. 7, 1643, by Sir Alexander Rigby. George Cleeve was appointed deputy president of the province. The Rigby title was confirmed Mar. 27, 1647, by the Warwick Commission, and thus Sir Ferdinando Gorges was deprived of more than half of his province. Litigation between Gorges' deputy governor and Cleeve was a chief cause of the difficulties of Gorges' government in its formative years, while Cleeve's constant appeals to Massachusetts Bay for aid paved the way for that colony's expansion northward to include jurisdiction over Lygonia in 1658. The king's commissioners of 1664 did not recognize the legality of the Rigby claim, and in 1686 Edward Rigby, Alexander's grandson filed a claim with Massachusetts that was not accepted. In 1691 the new Massachusetts charter put an end to the Province of Lygonia.

LYMAN'S COLONY. *See* **Georgiana.**

LYNCHING. The term derives from a Virginian, Col. Charles Lynch, who presided over the flogging of local criminals and Tory sympathizers during the revolutionary war. Since 1882 (the earliest year for which there is reliable data) lynch mobs have killed over 4,730 persons.

LYON, FORT. Built in Colorado Territory near Bent's New Fort on the Arkansas River. It was named successively Fort Fauntleroy, Fort Wise, and Fort Lyon, the last after the hero of Wilson's Creek. In 1866 the river cut the banks, so that Fort Lyon was moved twenty miles upstream.

LYTTON REPORT (October 1932). After Japan invaded Manchuria in 1931, the League of Nations attempted to halt further hostilities. On Dec. 10, the League appointed American Gen. Frank Ross McCoy to investigate the crisis. The report condemned Japan but recommended that Manchuria become an autonomous state under Chinese sovereignty but in Japanese control. The report was adopted by the League on Feb. 24, 1933. A month later Japan withdrew from the League.

McALLISTER, FORT, CAPTURE OF (Dec. 13, 1864). Fort McAllister, eighteen miles southwest of Savannah, Ga., commanded the mouth of the Ogeechee River and held up Union Gen. William Tecumseh Sherman's "march to the sea" for several days. Union Gen. W. B. Hazen finally effected its capture.

McCARDLE, EX PARTE (1869). Marked the summit of Radical Republican power (*see* Reconstruction) by confirming the supremacy of a legislative majority over the executive and judicial branches of the government. McCardle, a Mississippi editor, had criticized the military commander of Mississippi and Congress. He was jailed and denied benefit of habeas corpus. McCardle endeavored to take advantage of a Radical Republican law providing for an appeal to the Supreme Court.

Alarmed Radicals hastened to restrain the Supreme Court

from declaring the Reconstruction acts unconstitutional. A law was passed stripping the Court of its power of judicial review so far as it concerned the Reconstruction acts. The Supreme Court unanimously decided it had no jurisdiction because of the new restriction and dismissed the case.

McCARRAN-WALTER ACT (1952). The basic, comprehensive immigration law until passage of the Immigration and Nationality Act of 1965. The law, passed over President Harry Truman's veto, retained the national-origin system of the Immigration Act of 1924, under which the United Kingdom, Germany, and Ireland were allotted more than two-thirds of the annual quota of 154,657 persons. The act removed race as a bar to immigration and naturalization, removed discrimination between sexes, gave preference to aliens with needed skills, and provided for more rigorous screening of aliens in order to eliminate security risks and subversives and for broader grounds for the deportation of criminal aliens.

McCARTHY-ARMY HEARINGS (1954). The Permanent Investigations Subcommittee of the Senate Committee on Government Operations, commonly known as the McCarthy Committee, conducted hearings on alleged spying at the army base at Fort Monmouth, N.J.

The hearings were the outgrowth of Wisconsin's Sen. Joseph R. McCarthy's charges that the army was lax in ferreting out Communist spies. The army charged that McCarthy and his subcommittee's chief counsel, Roy M. Cohn, had intervened to obtain special treatment for Private G. David Schine, who, as a good friend of Cohn, had acted as a sometime subcommittee "expert" on Communism. The army charged that, having failed to obtain an officer's commission for Schine, McCarthy and his staff were using the hearings to harass the army. McCarthy and Cohn then charged that the army was, in effect, holding Schine "hostage" in an effort to force them to abandon their investigation.

The hearings soon turned into a shambles. On the very first day (Apr. 22), McCarthy repeatedly interrupted with "points of order" that merely presaged rambling, seemingly irrelevant speeches. The hearings were shown daily on national television, and McCarthy's bulldogged, monotonic interjections became the object of widespread exasperation and derision.

McCarthy made his major blunder late in the hearings. Angered by the cross-examination of Cohn by the army's counsel, Joseph N. Welch, McCarthy blurted out that he had information that a member of Welch's law firm had belonged to a left-wing lawyers' organization. In a short statement redolent of sadness and bitterness, Welch lashed out at McCarthy and his methods, making him appear a vicious bully. McCarthy himself was taken aback by Welch's emotional attack. Moreover, for the first time many Americans gained an insight into the kind of human tragedy McCarthy's "investigations" had caused. From then on, McCarthy was discredited in the eyes of a majority of the television viewers.

After the subcommittee ended its thirty-six days of hearings, it issued four separate reports. The Republican-dominated majority report in effect cleared both McCarthy and the army. The Senate initiated hearings to censure McCarthy for contempt. By a vote of sixty-seven to twenty-two, the Senate "condemned," but did not "censure," McCarthy.

McCONNELSVILLE ORDINANCE. Passed by Citizens of McConnelsville, Ohio, in 1874 for the purpose of restraining the liquor traffic. Taken to the Supreme Court, it was declared constitutional and was adopted in many cities and villages.

McCORMICK REAPER. Although there were earlier patents than the 1834 one of Cyrus Hall McCormick, it was the McCormick reaper that invaded the Middle West, which was ready for an efficient harvester that would make extensive wheat growing possible.

***McCRAY* V. *UNITED STATES,* 195 U.S. 27 (1904).** An act of Congress imposing a prohibitory tax of 10 cents per pound on artificially colored oleomargarine was upheld by the Supreme Court as a valid exercise of the power to lay taxes.

McCREA, JANE, MURDER OF (1777). Jane McCrea of Fort Edward, N.Y., was seized, shot, and scalped by Indians in the service of British Gen. John Burgoyne. Frontiersmen, greatly aroused, helped defeat Burgoyne.

***McCULLOCH* V. *MARYLAND,* 4 Wheaton 316 (1819).** Two questions were involved in the case: first, whether Congress had power under the Constitution to establish a bank and, second, whether Maryland could impose a tax on this bank. A unanimous court upheld the power of Congress to charter a bank as a government agency and denied the power of a state to tax the agency. Chief Justice John Marshall's discussion broadly interpreting the powers of Congress is still a classic statement of implied powers.

McDONALD'S EXPEDITION (1774). Angus McDonald, acting for Lord Dunmore, colonial governor of Virginia, led a ninety-mile expedition of 400 militia against the hostile Shawnee on the Muskingum River in Ohio. Skirmishes with the Indians only led to fresh hostilities in Lord Dunmore's War.

MACDONOUGH'S LAKE CHAMPLAIN FLEET. U.S. naval force in the War of 1812 under the command of Lt. Thomas Macdonough. In 1813 he went into winter quarters at Vergennes, Vt., on Otter Creek. On Apr. 14, 1814, the British fleet appeared off the mouth of Otter Creek, but was driven away by a land battery. Macdonough met the English fleet on Sept. 11, 1814, off Cumberland Head, near Plattsburgh, N.Y., where British and American troops had joined battle. The American and British fleets were roughly equal. The fight was won by Macdonough.

McDOWELL, BATTLE AT (May 8, 1862). The combined Confederate forces of Gen. Thomas J. ("Stonewall") Jackson and Gen. Edward Johnson gained a decisive victory in the engagement at McDowell, Va. Union forces were compelled to retreat toward Franklin.

***MACEDONIAN*.** In 1821, Chilean forces seized $70,400 in silver from the American merchant ship *Macedonian*, asserting that it was Spanish property. Twenty years later the United States demanded repayment. The matter was arbitrated by the king of Belgium, who, in 1863, awarded the owners three-fifths of the amount claimed.

McFADDEN BANKING ACT (Feb. 25, 1927). Set forth the rules by which both national and state banks might maintain home-city and out-of-town branches, changed the restrictions on real estate loans of national banks, and provided indeterminate charters for national and Federal Reserve banks.

McGILLIVRAY INCIDENT (Aug. 7, 1790). Alexander McGillivray signed two treaties with the United States that abrogated the Treaty of Pensacola. McGillivray was commissioned a U.S. brigadier general, at double what the Spanish were paying him. In 1792 the Spanish increased his salary sixfold and he abrogated the U.S. treaties. McGillivray's death in 1793 left both Spanish and U.S. treaties unratified.

McGUFFEY'S READERS. A series of textbooks by William Holmes McGuffey that molded American literary taste and morality from 1836 until the early 20th century. Known as the Eclectic Series, they contained lessons with accompanying pictures and taught principles of religion, morality, and patriotism. They included considerable lore about nature, games and sports, manners, and attitudes toward God, relatives, teachers, companions, unfortunates, and animals. The lessons enforced proverbial wisdom, patriotism, and traditional virtues. By 1920 total sales had reached 122 million copies.

MACHAULT, FORT. Built by the French on the site of Franklin, Pa. (*see* Venango), in 1754. It served as a link in their chain of communications from Lake Erie to the Ohio River. The fort was abandoned in 1759 when communications with Canada were cut in the French and Indian War.

McHENRY, FORT. Built in 1799 on a small island in Baltimore harbor. It was here that during the War of 1812 Francis Scott Key was moved to write "The Star-Spangled Banner" during a British bombardment.

MACHINE, PARTY. In the 19th century party machines controlled by professional politicians arose from the long ballot, the spoils system, the presence of unassimilated subgroups in the larger society, urban expansion, and the convention method of nomination. In return for votes on election day, the machine focused on the personal needs of the minority groups in the community. The precinct and ward leaders provided rent money, fuel, food, and jobs for the needy families and aided the diverse subgroups when they got in trouble with the state. Party functionaries provided sympathy, hospitality, friendship, and social intercourse for the unassimilated. At the apex of the party machine were the city or state bosses. Not all machine bosses ran their organization for selfish motives. Many bosses entered the political arena solely with the idea of public service, but there were those whose political machine was built on the spoils system, corruption, fraud, waste, and graft.

The party machine began to decline in the mid-20th century. The advent of the civil service reduced the sources of patronage; voters became more independent and sophisticated; and direct primaries, the nonpartisan system of elections, voting machines, and strict registration requirements dealt severe blows to the political boss and his machine. In addition, various programs alleviated some of the conditions on which the machine thrived.

MACHINE GUNS. In 1862, Dr. Richard J. Gatling patented a gun with six barrels that rotated around a central axis by a hand crank. Hiram S. Maxim patented the first automatic machine gun in 1884. Powered by recoil energy, it was smaller, lighter, and easier to operate than the Gatling. In 1890, John M. Browning introduced the principle of gas operation, the last basic development in machine-gun design. Browning's guns remained standard equipment for U.S. forces through the Korean War, but in the mid-1950's the Browning .30-caliber gun was replaced by the M-60.

MACHINE TOOLS. Early in the 19th century, British engineers and machinists developed the main categories of modern machine tools: engine lathes equipped with slide rests, boring machines, planers, and shapers, all quickly transferred to America. By the 1840's the demand for machinery in many sectors of the economy was great enough for the manufacture of machine tools to become a specialized activity. In some cases this meant that a firm produced only one type of machine tool with perhaps minor modifications with respect to size, auxiliary attachments, or implements. By 1914 there were over 400 machine-tool manufacturers in the United States.

America's most important contributions to machine-tool design and operation—profile lathes, turret lathes, milling machines, drilling and filing jigs, taps and gauges—were associated with specialized, high-speed machinery devoted to the production of standardized components of complex products. This system of interchangeability of parts requires a high degree of standardization of the final product, as well as the ability to produce individual components with a high degree of precision, so that the expensive processes of fitting can be replaced by the rapid, progressive assembly of parts that readily fit together.

McINTOSH, FORT. Built in 1778 on the Ohio River within the limits of present Beaver, Pa., as a base for a projected expedition against Detroit. From October 1778 to spring

1779 it was the headquarters of the Western Department of the Continental army.

McINTOSH, FORT, TREATIES OF (1785). Agreements whereby the Wyandot, Delaware, Chippewa, and Ottawa tribes ceded much of Ohio and agreed to an exchange of prisoners of war. The Wyandot and Delaware, for goods worth $2,000, deeded to Pennsylvania the lands previously claimed by them within that state. The Indians later repudiated these treaties, and peace was not secured until the Treaty of Greenville of 1795.

MACKENZIE'S TREATY (1831). Kenneth Mackenzie, a director of the American Fur Company, arranged a peace between the warring Blackfoot and Assiniboine. Signed at Fort Union, N. Mex., the treaty pledged the two tribes to perpetual peace and opened a large section of the upper Missouri country to exploitation by the American Fur Company.

MACKEREL FISHERIES. Mackerel supplemented codfish as an important commodity in the profitable trade between New England and the West Indies during the 18th century. To Gloucester, the leading mackerel port after 1840, went the credit for the introduction of the clipper fishing schooner. The adoption about 1850 of the purse seine enabled the mackerel vessels to fish profitably off the New England coast. Fishing vessels also went as far south as Cape Hatteras, N.C., to take mackerel. The fisheries reached their height in 1880–90, after which the abundance of the Atlantic mackerel abruptly declined. With the settlement of the Pacific Coast and Alaska, the Pacific mackerel catch gradually surpassed that of the Atlantic mackerel.

In 1970, 57 million pounds of mackerel, valued at $2 million, were caught by U.S. fishermen; 622,000 pounds of it came from Alaska. (In 1950 the total catch exceeded 165 million pounds.) In 1970 the United States exported only 98,000 pounds (valued at $20,000).

MACKINAC, STRAITS OF, AND MACKINAC ISLAND (formerly the **Straits of Michilimackinac** and **Michilimackinac Island**). Lakes Michigan, Superior, and Huron are connected by the Straits of Mackinac and the St. Marys River. In the middle of the straits is Mackinac Island, once a strategic center of military and commercial operations. The Indian name was Michilimackinac.

French rule was established at Mackinac in the 1660's, and British rule, in 1761. During the American Revolution the British moved their fort from Mackinaw City to Mackinac Island. The United States gained possession of Mackinac by the Treaty of Paris of 1783, but during the War of 1812 the British forced its surrender and held it until 1815.

Mackinac Island then became the center of John Jacob Astor's fur trading business. The advent of the railroad and the decline of the fur trade wrought the doom of Mackinac as a military and commercial center. Since then it has been chiefly a summer resort. The population in 1970 was 517.

MACKINAW BOAT. A light, strongly built, flat-bottomed boat, pointed at both ends, adapted from the Indian Northwest canoe. It was used on the rivers of the interior. Mackinaw boats varied greatly in size; they were commonly propelled by oars and, when conditions permitted, by a sail.

McKINLEY TARIFF (1890). William McKinley, as chairman of the Ways and Means Committee of the House of Representatives, sponsored this strongly protectionist tariff law. It increased tariffs on the items taxed to about 48.4 percent of their value but reduced the number of items on which tariffs were charged (sugar, for example). It provided a reciprocity principle, which allowed the president to increase certain tariffs if countries producing those goods were charging unfair tariffs on American goods.

McLANE-OCAMPO TREATY (1859). This treaty with Mexico granted the United States right of way over the Isthmus of Tehuantepec and provided for reciprocal trade and a loan of $4 million by the United States to Mexico. It was never ratified by the United States.

McLEOD CASE (1840–41). Alexander McLeod, deputy sheriff of Niagara, Upper Canada, was arrested in New York State on charges of arson and murder after his involvement in the destruction of the *Caroline,* an American ship being used by Canadian rebels to bring supplies from New York. The British demanded McLeod's release on the ground that the destruction of the *Caroline* was a public act, but in 1841 he was tried and acquitted in New York. To prevent jurisdictional conflicts in similar cases in the future, a congressional act of 1842 provided for the removal of an accused alien from a state court to a federal court on a writ of habeas corpus.

McLOUGHLIN LAND CLAIM (1829–62). John McLoughlin laid claim in 1829 to the land at the falls of the Willamette River, where he later platted Oregon City. As a nonresident, McLoughlin found his claim contested; much of it was taken away from him but was restored to his heirs by an act of the state legislature in 1862.

McMAHON ACT (1946). The first Atomic Energy Act passed by the U.S. Congress, sponsored by Sen. Brien McMahon of Connecticut. It created the five-man Atomic Energy Commission to conduct atomic research and to hold title to atomic equipment in the United States.

McNAMARA CASE (1910–11). On Oct. 1, 1910, the plant of the *Los Angeles Times* was bombed; twenty persons were killed. Three labor leaders, James B. McNamara, his brother John J. McNamara, and Ortie McManigal, were charged with the crime. McManigal confessed but the brothers pleaded not guilty and became symbols of labor's struggle against capital. Clarence Darrow was their attorney. The trial proceeded slowly and was marked by the arrest of two of Darrow's agents on charges of jury bribing. The brothers confessed to the bombings and were given long sentences. Their confessions were a decided blow to the labor movement.

McNARY-HAUGEN BILL. Legislation effort (1924–28) to create a two-tier system of farm prices: high domestic prices and lower, more competitive prices for exported products. The bill received powerful support from agricultural interests but was vetoed by President Calvin Coolidge.

MACOMB PURCHASE. In 1791 Alexander Macomb contracted for the purchase of 3,635,200 acres of land in the present counties of St. Lawrence, Franklin, Jefferson, Lewis, and Oswego in New York State. A patent issued to Macomb, who, soon becoming financially embarrassed, deeded the tract to William Constable and others.

MACON (Ga.). Fourth largest city in Georgia, with a 1980 population of 121,122. An Indian village was located at the site of modern Macon and was visited as early as 1540 by the Spanish explorer Hernando de Soto. Its central location made the town a valuable trading post. It was established as an American town in the 1820's and a natural railroad city in the late 19th century. The principal activity is the textile business.

MACON'S BILL NO. 2 (May 1, 1810). Enacted to compel Great Britain and France, at war with each other, to stop their illegal seizures of American commercial vessels by banning all trade with those countries until their policies changed. It supplanted the unsuccessful Nonintercourse Act.

MADISON (Wis.). Capital city of Wisconsin, with a 1980 population of 170,382. Madison was founded in 1836 in the center of the region that includes lakes Monona, Mendota, Waubesa, and Kegonsa. The city was the capital of Wisconsin Territory. Madison is in the center of Wisconsin's dairy farming area, and there are important meat-packing and dairy products industries.

MADISON, FORT (sometimes called Fort Bellevue). Built 1808–09 on the west side of the Mississippi, where the city of Fort Madison, Iowa, now stands. Its purpose was to protect the Indian trade (*see* Factory System, Indian). It was attacked during the War of 1812 by Indians supporting the British.

MADISON COUNTY ANTISLAVERY WAR (1859–60). Controversy in southern Kentucky between pro- and antislavery forces. The antislavery Berea School (now Berea College) was founded in 1855. Slaveowners were alarmed over the abolition doctrine preached by John G. Fee and the other founders and by its policy of educating blacks along with whites. An armed mob forced the antislavery families to leave Kentucky.

MADISON'S ISLAND. Name given (1813) by Capt. David Porter to the island of Nuku Hiva in the Marquesas Islands in the South Pacific. Porter, commanding the U.S. frigate *Essex,* erected a fort and formally proclaimed U.S. sovereignty. The United States never ratified annexation, and the Marquesas Islands became a French colony in 1842.

MADISON SQUARE GARDEN. In 1879, William K. Vanderbilt converted Gilmore's Garden on Madison Square in New York City into Madison Square Garden. Vanderbilt turned the exhibition hall into a center for athletic events. Stanford White designed a new Garden for the site in 1890. (It was in the roof garden restaurant of this building that White was murdered by Harry K. Thaw in 1906.) The new Garden housed musical and theatrical performances, horse and dog shows, balls, circuses, public meetings, and athletic events, notably boxing. In 1925 a third Garden was built at Eighth Avenue and Fiftieth Street. It became the world's most famous sports arena. In 1968 a fourth Garden was built atop Pennsylvania Station. The new Garden includes a bowling center, the Felt Forum (a 5,000-seat amphitheater), and a twenty-nine-story office building.

MADRID, TREATY OF (1670). Spain and Great Britain provided for peace between their colonial possessions. By implication, Spain recognized for the first time the legal existence of British colonies in the New World over which it had hitherto asserted a monopoly of sovereignty.

MADRID CONFERENCE (1880). International conference involving Britain, Spain, France, Germany, and the United States on imperialistic rivalry in Morocco. The conference accomplished little, but it was the first time the United States had participated in a European political conference.

MAFIA. *See* **Crime, Organized.**

MAFIA INCIDENT (1890–92). After David C. Hennessey, New Orleans chief of police, was assassinated by a Sicilian secret society, Mafia, nineteen members were indicted, and nine were put on trial. The case made by the state was overwhelming, but none was found guilty. A mass of protest followed and eleven persons were lynched by a mob. Three were Italian subjects, and the Italian government protested and demanded protection for the city's Italian colony. Unsatisfied by the U.S. response, Italy recalled its minister. In 1892, President Benjamin Harrison offered an indemnity of $25,000 to the families of the victims and expressed regrets to Italy for the incident. Diplomatic relations were restored.

MAGAZIN ROYAL. *See* **Niagara, Carrying Place of.**

MAGAZINES. In 1741, America's first two magazines appeared: Andrew Bradford's *American Magazine, or Monthly View* and Benjamin Franklin's *General Magazine and Historical Chronicle.* Neither magazine lasted a year. In the early years, mails were few and slow, and newsstand circulation was so limited as to be nearly useless. Promotion was nearly impossible, and there was virtually no national advertising. Woodcuts or expensive metal engravings were the only possible illustrations.

Among early magazine successes were *Godey's Lady's Book,* the *New York Ledger,* and *Century, Harper's, Scribner's, Atlantic,* and *Forum.* Among the most successful were reprint magazines, based mainly on British reviews.

Littell's Living Age, founded in 1844, was published for nearly a century. The *Literary Digest* lasted until 1936. *Reader's Digest,* originally a reprint magazine, still contains some reprinted material.

A number of factors led to a burgeoning of magazines in the 19th and 20th centuries: printing processes improved; national advertising made large profits possible; and generous mailing privileges for periodicals made distribution cheap and easy. As the reading public became vastly larger, elaborately illustrated popular magazines, with very large circulations justifying much profitable advertising, developed: *Saturday Evening Post, Liberty, Look, Life,* and *Collier's.* Television drew off great numbers of possible readers and advertisers for these mass-circulation magazines; and one by one they disappeared. Only *People* and *TV Guide* could be said to have a mass readership. Otherwise, magazines with a specialized readership prospered. Among these are the *New Yorker, Sports Illustrated,* and *Playboy.* Successful news magazines, such as *Time* and *Newsweek,* continued.

MAGAZINES, CHILDREN'S. The first American juvenile periodical was the *Children's Magazine* (Hartford, 1789). The Sunday-school movement produced the *Youth's Friend and Scholar's Magazine* (Philadelphia, 1823–64), the first of many papers devoted to inculcating religious truth through fiction, verse, and essay. In 1833, *Parley's Magazine* was founded (New York) and eleven years later merged with *Merry's Museum for Boys and Girls* (Boston, 1841–72). The most important children's magazines of the 19th century were *Youth's Companion* (Boston, 1827–1929), *Harper's Young People* (1879–95), *Riverside Magazine* (1867–70), and *Our Young Folks* (Boston, 1865–73) which merged with *St. Nicholas, An Illustrated Magazine for Young Folks,* in 1874. Extolled above all other juvenile periodicals, the monthly *St. Nicholas* (1873–1943) was founded and edited for over thirty years by Mary Mapes Dodge. Among its contributors were Rudyard Kipling; Mark Twain; and Alfred, Lord Tennyson. Among the most successful periodicals of the 20th century were the *American Boy, Youth's Companion, Boys' Life,* the *American Girl, Scholastic, Cricket, Jack and Jill,* and *Sesame Street.*

MAGDALENA BAY RESOLUTION (1912; also known as the Lodge Corollary). Sponsored by Sen. Henry Cabot Lodge and adopted by the Senate, it was aimed at blocking the purchase of a large tract of land in Baja California by a Japanese syndicate. That purchase was deemed a threat to California and the Panama Canal.This was the first time the Monroe Doctrine was applied to an Asiatic power.

MAGEE-GUTIÉRREZ EXPEDITION. *See* **Gutiérrez-Magee Expedition.**

MAGEE-KEARNY EXPEDITION (1820). In 1819 the War Department recognized the importance of the simultaneous movement of troops up the Missouri River toward the Yellowstone River and up the Mississippi to the mouth of the St. Peters (Minnesota) River in case of Indian hostilities (*see* Yellowstone River Expeditions). The army sent a force on July 2, 1820, to lay out a road to St. Peters. After leaving Council Bluffs, Nebr., they traveled twenty-three days and reached St. Peters. They reported this route impracticable and returned to St. Louis by boat (*see* Long's Explorations).

MAGNA CHARTA, or **Magna Carta.** By 1215, England was in the throes of a civil war. King John's blundering foreign policy had alienated many former followers, particularly because of his repeated violations of feudal and common law. An armed revolt by most of John's barons forced his capitulation at Runnymede on June 15, 1215. Here he gave his consent to the Magna Charta. In its essence, the charter simply meant that John, like all other Englishmen, was to be subject to the spirit and letter of the law. His past conduct was condemned; in the future he was to rule in accordance with law and custom. The charter was not a document of human liberties, and until the 17th century the Magna Charta was largely ignored. It remained for the Puritans, lawyers, and members of Parliament of the 17th century, in their contest with the Stuarts, to fashion it into an obstacle to arbitrary government. When the Puritans migrated to the New World, they embedded their ideas in American political philosophy: human rights are not to be destroyed by arbitrary and despotic government; the law of the land is supreme and inviolable; and no individual or government may transcend law.

MAGUAGA, BATTLE AT (Aug. 9, 1812). A U.S. force defeated a British and Indian force at Maguaga, Mich. Fighting with the British was the Shawnee chief Tecumseh.

MAHICAN. *See* **Mohegan and Mahican.**

MAIDEN'S ROCK. A picturesque rocky bluff overhanging Lake Pepin, in Pepin County, Wis. According to Indian legend, a Sioux maiden hurled herself to death from it rather than marry an Indian brave selected by her parents.

MAIL-ORDER HOUSES. Such establishments account for approximately 1 percent of total U.S. retail volume. Most sell specialized lines of merchandise, although the two industry leaders, Sears, Roebuck and Company (founded 1886) and Montgomery Ward (founded 1872), offer much broader lines than even the largest department store. Less than one-third of their volume, however, is accounted for by catalog sales.

The continental rail network and rural free delivery supported the growth of the great mail-order companies. Traditionally, mail-order houses received customer orders by mail, processed them, and dispatched merchandise by parcel post, freight, or express. Present operating methods are characterized by a very large volume of telephone-order buying and selling—and, indeed, catalog-order desks and stores.

MAINE. The most northeasterly of the fifty states was part of Massachusetts from the late 1600's to 1820, when it became the twenty-third state. It has an extremely long and irregular coastline, with numerous bays and inlets, and covers 31,500 square miles.

Maine is believed to have been visited by French, British, and Portuguese explorers in the 1500's, but permanent settlement was undertaken only in 1604 when the French established a small settlement on an island in the St. Croix River that failed after one miserable winter. The English in August 1607 planted a colony on the lower reaches of the Kennebec River, but it too expired. In 1622, Sir Ferdinando Gorges and John Mason received a grant for all lands between the Merrimac and Kennebec rivers. Massachusetts fortified its authority in 1677 by purchasing all claims of the Gorges family. In 1691, William and Mary granted a new charter to Massachusetts that confirmed its title to Maine.

The struggle between England and France for control of North America began on Mount Desert Island in 1613, when the English destroyed a French post. During King George's War in the 1740's and the French and Indian War (1754–63), Maine communities supplied considerable soldiery for the campaigns against the French.

As a part of Massachusetts, Maine was active during the revolutionary war. The Treaty of Paris that ended the war created a boundary dispute between Maine and Canada that was not settled until the conclusion of the Webster-Ashburton Treaty in 1842.

Maine's growth in population after the war was accompanied by a growth of sentiment for statehood. Between 1820 and 1860, Maine's population doubled again, to about 600,000. Most of the population were farmers and lumbermen. The Democrats dominated politics until the mid-1850's, when they were rent asunder by the questions of slavery in the United States and prohibition in Maine. In 1856 the Republican party began a domination of politics that lasted for a century. Since the 1950's however, the state has had an effective two-party system. Maine was the first state to adopt prohibition on a statewide basis (1851) and retained it until the early 1930's.

Amply blessed with many navigable rivers, the state had its needs effectively served by water transportation until after the Civil War. For years Maine was the leading producer of wooden ships in America. Its clippers and downeasters and schooners were constructed in dozens of yards up the rivers and along the coast. As late as 1860, the state had less than 500 miles of railroad. The era of greatest construction was 1865–1900. After the Civil War, textile making became the most important manufacturing activity. After 1900 a decline set in as mills began moving southward.

Maine's pulp and paper industry mushroomed from 1880 to 1910. Soon the pulp and paper industry surpassed textiles as the most important industry, a position it retains. It rests on the solid foundation of the Maine hardwood and softwood forests.

Agriculture, which once featured the small subsistence farms, is now characterized by the large farm, with dairy cattle, poultry, or potatoes. Fishing is relatively unimportant, with lobsters, clams, and herring as the principal products. Tourism is an important industry. The population in 1980 was 1,125,000.

***MAINE,* DESTRUCTION OF THE** (Feb. 15, 1898). In January 1898, the battleship *Maine* was ordered from Key West, Fla., to Havana, Cuba, during that island's revolt against Spanish rule, as an "act of friendly courtesy." There was considerable ill feeling against the United States among the Spaniards, who objected to the presence of the ship. On Feb. 15, two explosions totally destroyed the *Maine.* Two officers and 258 of the crew were killed or died soon afterward. The Spaniards claimed that an internal explosion had been the cause. The Americans claimed that the original cause had been an external explosion that in turn had set off the forward magazines.

News of the disaster stirred up national feeling in the United States, crystallized in the slogan "Remember the *Maine.*" It was a major factor in bringing the United States to a declaration of war against Spain.

A U.S. navy investigation report, published in 1912, stated that a low form of explosive exterior to the ship caused the first explosion. European experts, however, still maintained the theory of an internal explosion. No further evidence has ever been found to solve the mystery.

MAINE BOUNDARY DISPUTE. *See* **Aroostook War; Northeast Boundary; Webster-Ashburton Treaty.**

MAIZE. *See* **Agriculture; Corn.**

MAJORITY RULE. A fundamental American concept, evolved from the principle of the sovereignty of the people. When two candidates are running for an office, the one who receives more than half of the total votes cast shall be elected and his or her policies shall be entitled to a fair trial. Majority rule is limited somewhat by the Constitution. Civil liberties are protected by the fundamental law and cannot be suppressed by a temporary majority. The Constitution itself cannot be amended without the consent of three-fourths of the states. Because of constitutional guarantees of freedom of speech and of the press and other liberties, minority groups in the United States are able to oppose the majority.

MAKAH. Indian tribe occupying the extreme northwestern end of the Olympic Peninsula of the state of Washington, where they still have lands. Their native culture was a southern variation of the rich Northwest Coast development; but the Makah did not achieve the cultural sophistication of the Haida, Tlingit, or Kwakiutl-Nootka.

MAKASSAR STRAIT, BATTLE OF (Jan. 24, 1942). A sortie between a small American force and a large Japanese convoy heading south through Makassar Strait for Balikpapan, Borneo. The American force sank four heavily loaded transports and a patrol boat. It did not prevent the Japanese from swiftly seizing Balikpapan and using it as a base for further advances.

MAKIN RAID (Aug. 17–18, 1942). To divert Japanese attention from embattled Guadalcanal, 200 U.S. Marines landed on Makin Atoll in the Gilbert Islands. They wiped out the Japanese garrison and destroyed installations and supplies before withdrawing the following evening.

MALARIA. A disease characterized by chills and fever that recur at regular intervals, anemia, and an enlarged spleen; it is caused by four species of *Plasmodium,* a protozoan. Long prevalent in Europe and Africa, by 1700 it had become established from South Carolina to New England. Malaria spread into the Mississippi Valley with the American settlers. Generally chronic and debilitating to all ages and often fatal, it placed a heavy burden of ill health on settlers, especially along the waterways that formed the chief routes of commerce.

Malaria was at its height in New England in the 18th century. In the Midwest it reached its peak about 1875. Associated since antiquity with marshes, malaria tended to rise with the initial clearing of land and to fall with cultivation and drainage. The isolation of quinine (from cinchona bark) by French chemists in 1820 made rational therapeutics more practicable.

Around the turn of the century, the role of the mosquito as transmitter was established. Extended antimalaria campaigns began in 1912, particularly in the southern states. In the early 1930's a resurgence of the disease was attacked by drainage and other measures under New Deal relief programs. After World War II the Public Health Service, using DDT, inaugurated a program to eradicate malaria. In 1935 there were about 4,000 malaria deaths in the country, and by 1952 only 25. In the 1980's the United States was free of significant indigenous malaria.

"MALEFACTORS OF GREAT WEALTH." In 1907, President Theodore Roosevelt defended his antitrust policy, blaming the depression (*see* Panic of 1907) partly on "certain malefactors of great wealth."

MALLET BROTHERS EXPLORATIONS (1739–42). The first known traders to cross the Plains from the Missouri River were eight Canadians led by Pierre and Paul Mallet, who explored a route from the Platte River's mouth to Santa Fe. In 1740 they explored the Arkansas River from the Rockies to the Mississippi. They made a second Santa Fe expedition from New Orleans by boat up the Mississippi, Arkansas, and Canadian rivers into central Oklahoma.

MALMÉDY MASSACRE (Dec. 17, 1944). German troops near the Belgian town of Malmédy captured about 100 Americans. They marched the prisoners into a field and systematically shot them. A few feigned death and escaped; eighty-six died. It was the worst single atrocity committed against American troops in Europe during World War II. The German commander and seventy-two others were subsequently tried by an American tribunal. Forty-three were sentenced to death by hanging and the others to imprisonment. The death sentences were commuted, and none of the convicted served a full prison sentence.

MALVERN HILL, BATTLE OF (July 1, 1862). Last of the Seven Days' battles, it ended Union Gen. George B. McClellan's Peninsular campaign. After the Battle of Frayser's Farm, McClellan fell back to Malvern Hill, fourteen miles south of Richmond, Va. Gen. Robert E. Lee launched several attacks against Malvern Hill, and on July 2, McClellan withdrew to his base at Harrison's Landing.

MAMMALOGY. Since Europeans were eager to learn about the curiosities of the New World, explorers and settlers attempted to satisfy the demands for knowledge. William Wood, after living four or five years in Massachusetts, related information about the moose and beaver in his *New Englands Prospect* (1634). William Byrd provided the specimen for the first outstanding contribution to American mammalogy when he sent a female opossum to the Royal Society of London. Progress in describing American mammals was slow during the 18th century. Thomas Jefferson included in his *Notes on the State of Virginia* (1785) tables that compared the weights of European and American species. He also encouraged the successful recovery of mammoth bones by Meriwether Lewis and William Clark and by Charles Willson Peale.

In the 19th century a number of natural history surveys that made useful contributions to mammalogy were written. Some of these were state surveys, of which James E. DeKay's *Zoology of New York* (four volumes, 1842–44) was an outstanding example. The federal government sponsored a series of exploratory expeditions that collected mammalian specimens, but it was with the appointment in 1850 of Spencer F. Baird as assistant secretary of the newly established Smithsonian Institution that descriptive zoology entered a new phase. Baird efficiently organized the zoological representatives for the government's Pacific Railroad surveys, and the specimens and notes from the returning naturalists provided the basis for his careful and lengthy report (1857) on western mammals. It also opened the final phase of the explorative-descriptive period, a phase dominated by museum monographs.

The analysis-management period began with phylogenetic studies, which arose from interest in evolution and paleontology, and with a concern for wildlife management. C. Hart Merriam led both scientific and applied mammalogy in America from the 1890's to the 1920's. His *Mammals of the Adirondacks* (1884) set new standards for regional studies and prepared the way for his appointment as director of the Department of Agriculture's Division of Economic Ornithology and Mammalogy when it was created in 1888. His first priority was to establish the geographical ranges of American mammals. Under his direction, the division (renamed the Bureau of Biological Survey in 1905) studied the economic importance of many species. Merriam became the first president of the American Society of Mammalogists when it was founded in 1919.

MAMMOTH CAVE. In Edmonson County, Ky. Evidences of Indian occupation were found for miles inside its entrance by early explorers. Saltpeter was taken from it to make gunpowder during the War of 1812. The cave and surrounding area were established as a national park in 1936. Total acreage of the park is 51,354.

MANAGED MONEY. Efforts to measure and control the value of money date to the colonial period. Massachusetts, in 1748, adopted a tabular standard made up of an assortment of goods, in specified quantities, to be used as a test of the value of money. All money payments had to be made according to the changes in the value of money as reflected by this goods assortment. Wholesale prices more than doubled during the Civil War, fell by two-thirds between 1865 and 1896, rose moderately until 1913, then more than doubled between 1914 and 1920, and plummeted 40 percent from mid-1920 to mid-1921. Economists who felt there must be some way to improve the situation founded such organizations as the Stable Money League (1921), the National Monetary Association (1922), and the Stable Money Association (1925). None was successful. In the early 1930's, efforts were made to raise prices by manipulating the gold content of the dollar. On Jan. 30, 1934, Congress passed the Gold Reserve Act for that purpose, but the rise did not take place.

In the early 1960's a school of economists, soon known as monetarists, believed that the quantity of money in circulation greatly affected the severity of business cycles and the general price level. Their solution was to increase the money supply by a steady 4 percent a year, the country's annual average rate of economic growth.

Under any money system, central bankers or others in power may to some degree manage the money supply with an economic goal in mind. Since they may do it most easily with irredeemable paper money, that form of money is most often employed.

MANASSAS, BATTLE OF. *See* **Bull Run, First Battle of; Bull Run, Second Battle of.**

MANCHAC. A British trading post established shortly after 1763 at the junction of Bayou Manchac (Iberville River) and the Mississippi. It was captured by the Spanish in 1779.

MANCHESTER (N.H.). Largest city in New Hampshire, with a population of 90,757 in 1980. Manchester's industrial activities include the production of shoes, cotton cloth and clothing products, light machinery, and metal products. The city, located on the Merrimack River, has generous supplies of waterpower.

An early settlement on the site was named Derryville, and in 1807 a canal was opened. It skirted the Amoskeag Falls to permit barges to reach the area from Boston. In 1810 Derryville was renamed after the English textile city.

MANCHURIA AND MANCHUKUO. Russia's economic penetration of Manchuria in the 1890's worried the United States because American exporters fared better there than in China proper and because Russian domination threatened to exclude American goods. From 1901 to 1903, the administration of Theodore Roosevelt quarreled with the Russians in an effort to preserve American opportunities in Manchuria. Japanese military successes there led to control over southern Manchuria, conceded by the Russians in the Treaty of Portsmouth (1905). Roosevelt acquiesced in the parceling of spheres of interest in Manchuria and rejected subsequent Chinese overtures for help in regaining control of the region. The administration of William Howard Taft attempted to internationalize the railroads that were the foundation of the Japanese and Russian spheres. The American plan failed, driving Japan and Russia together.

In various agreements between 1917 and 1922, the United States conceded Japanese economic hegemony. The governments of the Republic of China (1911–49) never exercised more than nominal control over the area.

In 1932, fearing Chinese nationalism there, the Japanese created the puppet state of Manchukuo. The United States refused to concede Japanese dominance over the region. At Yalta (February 1945), Franklin D. Roosevelt secretly agreed to give the Soviet Union Japan's sphere of interest in Manchuria in return for Soviet intervention in the war in Asia. The Red Army entered Manchuria in August 1945 and remained there until April 1946. An agreement between Mao Tse-tung and Joseph Stalin in 1950 led to complete Chinese sovereignty in 1955.

MANDAN, FORT. Built (1804–05) by the expedition of Meriwether Lewis and William Clark at Five Villages, now Stanton, N.Dak. It was an advantageous wintering place because of neighboring Mandan and Hidatsa villages.

MANDAN, HIDATSA, AND ARIKARA. Three Indian tribes of the northern Plains of America that practiced river-bottom maize cultivation along the Missouri River in the general area of North Dakota. The three tribes spoke mutually unintelligible languages. The Arikara appear to have branched off from the Skidi Pawnee, a Caddoan-speaking tribe. Both the Mandan and the Hidatsa spoke Siouan languages.

Although they used the tipi and shared other distinctive elements of the culture of the nomadic bison hunters of the Plains, their use of a complex earth lodge, possibly Pawnee in origin, suggests a trend toward permanent villages. Even so, bundles, the vision quest, ranked clubs or fraternities, the Sun Dance, and the war complex were as much a part of the life of these groups as they were of the life of such other nonagricultural peoples of the area. The three tribes suffered greatly from smallpox, which reduced their population in the mid-19th century.

MANDATES. After World War I, conquered German and Turkish colonies were assigned for administration to individual Allied powers. The United States, not a party to the treaties, took a keen interest in these mandates and insisted on equal rights with the other powers in them. U.S. claims were finally granted by the other powers, and ten treaties were negotiated, securing for the United States all the rights it would have had if it had joined the League of Nations.

MANGAS COLORADAS WARS. A series of Apache hostilities led by Mangas Coloradas ("Red Sleeves"), a chief of the Mimbreño Apache of southwest New Mexico. In 1861, he joined forces with Cochise after the incident at Apache Pass, in which Lt. George N. Bascom had ordered the hanging of Apache hostages. He was wounded in a battle with U.S. troops at Apache Pass on July 15, 1862. He recovered but was taken prisoner in January 1863 and was killed while allegedly trying to escape.

MANGEURS DE LARD (or "pork eaters"). Recruits for the fur trade in Canada, so-called because while en route they were fed on pea soup, bread, and pork, but chiefly on the latter. Bound to a five-years' apprenticeship, they were assigned only the most menial tasks. The term was frequently applied to any newcomer.

MANHATTAN. An island and borough of New York City bounded on the south by New York Bay, on the west by the Hudson River, on the east by the East River, and on the north by the Harlem River and Spuyten Duyvil Creek. The island is 13.5 miles long and 2.25 miles wide (22.6 square miles). It was discovered by Giovanni da Verrazano in 1524 and visited by Henry Hudson in 1609. The name is derived from the Manhattan Indians, who lived on the island. There were white settlers on the island in 1613–14. In 1626 Peter Minuit, an agent of the Dutch West India Company, bought the island from the Canarsie Indians, who had no claim to it, for about $24. Later, other payments had to be made to the Manhattan, the true claimants. New York City spread rapidly over the island in the 19th century. The city was confined to this island alone until Greater New York was created in 1898. (*See also* New York City.)

MANHATTAN PROJECT. Fearful that Germany might produce an atomic bomb before the United States, in 1939 Leo Szilard and some other refugees from Nazi persecution convinced Albert Einstein to use his influence to urge government support from President Franklin D. Roosevelt. This tactic was successful, and by mid-1942, it was obvious that pilot plants—and eventually full-sized factories—would have to be built. Gen. Leslie R. Groves of the U.S. Army Corps of Engineers was given controlling authority. Because much early research was performed at Columbia University in New York, the Engineers' Manhattan District headquarters was initially assigned management of such work, from which came the name "Manhattan Project" for the nationwide efforts. Soon most of the research was consolidated at the University of Chicago. Oak Ridge, Tenn., was the site chosen for separation of the fissionable uranium-235 isotope. Groves proceeded simultaneously on as many fronts as possible. Hence, liquid thermal diffusion, centrifuge, gaseous diffusion, and electromagnetic separation processes were all tried to extract U-235 from U-238. The last two techniques ultimately proved to be the most successful.

In December 1942, Enrico Fermi succeeded in producing and controlling a chain reaction in the pile, or reactor, he built at the University of Chicago. This reactor also furnished the means for a second path to the bomb. Uranium-238, while it does not fission in a reactor, can capture neutrons and ultimately be transformed into a new element, plutonium, not found in nature but highly fissionable. Five gigantic reactors were constructed on the banks of the Columbia River, near Hanford, Wash., to produce plutonium.

In late 1942, Groves placed J. Robert Oppenheimer in charge of a newly created weapons laboratory on an isolated mesa at Los Alamos, N.Mex. Oppenheimer's stature as a leading theoretical physicist encouraged many scientists to work on the project. Relatively little difficulty was encountered in designing a uranium weapon and a test was held at Alamogordo, N.Mex., on July 16, 1945. The first atomic bomb was dropped on Hiroshima, Japan, on Aug. 6, 1945, and the second against Nagasaki, Japan, on Aug. 9, 1945. Japan quickly capitulated.

"MANIFEST DESTINY." Concept of the 1840's and 1850's, suggesting the supposed inevitability of the continued territorial expansion of the United States (*see* Westward Movement). The phrase first referred specifically to the annexation of Texas, but it was quickly utilized in the controversy with Great Britain over Oregon and in the demand for annexations of territory as a result of the Mexican and Spanish-American wars.

MANILA BAY, BATTLE OF (May 1, 1898). Commodore George Dewey with his cruisers, *Olympia* (flagship), *Baltimore, Boston,* and *Raleigh,* and the gunboats *Concord* and *Petrel,* attacked the Spanish squadron at Manila, ten small wretchedly equipped cruisers and gunboats. At about noon the shore batteries were silenced and every Spanish ship, to quote Dewey's report, "was sunk, burned, or deserted." The Spanish suffered 381 casualties, the Americans but nine wounded. Manila surrendered on Aug. 13.

MANILA CONFERENCE (Oct. 24–25, 1966). Held in the Philippines between the United States, represented by President Lyndon B. Johnson, and its allies in the Vietnam War. It reaffirmed American policy in the war in Vietnam.

MANITOULIN ISLANDS. Stretched across northern Lake Huron, they include Cockburn, Drummond, Grand Manitoulin, and Little Manitoulin islands. They were first sighted by French Jesuits about 1640. After the War of 1812 Drummond Island (now part of Michigan) was awarded to the United States and the remainder of the group to Canada. The islands have become popular resorts and fishing grounds.

MANN, FORT (also known as Fort Atkinson). Part of William Gilpin's battalion was quartered there in 1847–48 (*see* Doniphan's Expedition). The exact location in Kansas is in doubt, but one early account located it near the Arkansas River on the route to Santa Fe.

MANN ACT (1910). Aimed at the suppression of the white-slave traffic, the law is an example of federal police legislation for the protection of public morals, based constitutionally upon the commerce power. The Supreme Court held that the act is a proper exercise of the power of Congress to regulate commerce. The Mann Act was reinforced by anti-racketeering laws passed by Congress in 1961 that made interstate travel or transportation for illegal purposes—such as prostitution—illegal.

MANNERS. In colonial New England a hierarchical social structure and a corresponding code of deferential manners were modeled on the society of Puritan England. Morals were equated with religion, and manners with morals. The colonial authorities, backed by church leaders, were harsh with offenders, punishing them in public (pillory, stocks, branding irons, and whips) for disobeying a wide variety of laws regarding dress, scandalmongering, cursing, lying, name-calling, flirting, and making ugly faces. In the South, the gentry set the tone.

After the election of Andrew Jackson to the presidency in 1828, it became necessary to create a democratic code of manners. Some twenty-eight etiquette manuals were published during the 1830's, thirty-six in the 1840's, and thirty-eight more during the 1850's. Americans of all classes in this rapidly changing and egalitarian period were interested in "learning how to behave" correctly. Educational leaders also thought it their duty to inculcate good manners in the classroom; textbook writers obliged with sections on "Politeness" and "Manners at the Table."

Manners were looked upon as a set of rules that stressed truthfulness, sobriety, modesty, temperance, piety, chastity, and fidelity, in the American tradition of democratic values; Old World deferential manners were down-played. After the Civil War, and especially during the Gilded Age, the quest for luxury and the manners of fashion came to the fore. New York became the financial and manners capital of the nation. There was a mushrooming of "high tone" manners, aping the British aristocracy for the most part, but also importing the lighter *ton* of the French. British nannies were imported to impart proper accents to the children of the newly rich.

World War I was a watershed in American manners. After the war, formality was pushed aside. The career of Emily Post was indicative of this trend: she published her *Etiquette, The Blue Book of Social Usage,* in 1922, with the firm desire to preserve the punctilious standards of the Gilded Age. Subsequent editions of the book, however, reflected the more casual mores of the time. This was even more evident in etiquette books published after World War II.

MANORS. Self-sufficient agricultural communities, embracing one or more villages or towns over which seignorial rights and privileges generally obtained. At the time of colonial settlement the manor was the prevailing mode of agricultural life in England. Because the country gentlemen wanted to secure landholdings in the New World the manorial system was established in the proprietary colonies, principally in New York, Maryland, and Carolina.

In New Netherland numerous patroonships, virtually manors, were authorized, but only Rensselaerswyck was successfully established. The early English governors of New York created numerous manors in Westchester, on Long Island, and elsewhere. Their legal and political characteristics were feudal, and confirmed the manorial jurisdiction of Rensselaerswyck. The manorial jurisdiction, however, could not withstand the encroachments of town and county authority, or the opposition of tenants. The chief grievances tenants had against the manor system were insecurity of tenure and perpetual rents. The tenants on the Rensselaerswyck manor agitated against their leasehold estates and perpetual rents, and the controversy was a burning one into the 19th century.

Although the Fundamental Constitutions of Carolina of 1669 set up an aristocratic system of landholding, there is no evidence of any manor actually having been founded. Over a hundred proprietary manors were set up by William Penn for his colony in Pennsylvania but in no case does it appear that manorial jurisdiction was ever exercised.

MANSFIELD, BATTLE OF. *See* **Sabine Crossroads, Battle at.**

MANUEL'S FORT. The first American outpost in present-day Montana, it was built by Manuel Lisa, a fur trader, at the junction of the Yellowstone and Bighorn rivers in 1807. Various trapping expeditions started from this post, including the two ventures of John Colter, who explored Yellowstone Park and first reported the geysers. Hostility of the Blackfoot caused the abandonment of the fort in 1811.

MANUFACTURERS, COLONIAL. *See* **Industries, Colonial.**

MANUFACTURES, RESTRICTION OF COLONIAL. English manufacturers felt that it was imperative to keep the colonies from manufacturing goods that they themselves could produce, and various attempts were made to restrict the development of colonial manufactures. In 1699, at the demand of English woolen manufacturers, a law was passed that forbade the export of wool from one colony to another "or to any other place whatsoever." But any colony could still manufacture woolen goods for consumption within its own borders.

The Hat Act of 1732 provided that no American-made hats could be exported from any colony. The Iron Act of 1750 prohibited the further erection of slitting mills, steel furnaces, and plating mills in the colonies. However, it also encouraged the production of colonial pig iron and bar iron by relaxing the duties when such iron was to be imported into England.

MANUFACTURING. When George Washington became president, the only power-using plants were mills for making flour, lumber, paper, and gunpowder and for grinding plaster. Establishments in the fuel-using industries were limited to charcoal furnaces and forges for working iron; kilns for making lime, tar, and potash; distilleries; brickyards; and a few small glassworks and potteries. During the next quarter of a century, machine spinning and weaving were introduced and nearly 200 cotton mills were erected in New England and the middle states. The use of steam to move machinery became common.

Faced by a scarcity of accumulated funds and entrepreneurial experience, manufacturers adopted corporate organization as a device for assembling capital and economizing management. The corporation has remained the overwhelming mode of organization.

The growth of manufacturing was encouraged by a rapidly

expanding market protected to some degree by tariffs and held together by canals and steam transportation on land and water. The scarcity of labor stimulated the use of power devices. Yankee inventors designed textile machinery that enabled relatively inexperienced operatives to make plain fabrics for common use cheaply and efficiently. Americans developed interchangeable mechanisms, in order to produce goods on a large scale and at low cost. Plain fabrics, hats, footwear, axes and nails, plowshares, and hoes dominated manufacturing output. Pressed glass and porcelain, plated metalwares, lamps, and numerous minor conveniences turned out in quantities by machinery had ceased to be luxuries. Changing fashions increasingly determined consumer demand and the industries that served it. At the same time, growing demands led to the establishment of shops and foundries to build steamboat machinery and locomotives, and improved transportation in turn hastened the spread of industry.

By 1860 the northeastern states were engaged chiefly in mechanical production, the South in growing staple crops such as cotton, and the West in producing and processing other raw materials and provisions. The concentration of manufacturing in the North was a major factor in the outcome of the Civil War.

The end of the war inaugurated a period of high protection during which new branches of manufacture were brought to America from Europe. The discovery of petroleum, the introduction of Bessemer steel, the opening of new mines on Lake Superior and in the South, the growth of inland cities, and a great influx of immigrants turned the nation's energy increasingly toward manufacturing.

Inventions and scientific discoveries multiplied at an accelerated rate. The electric industry arose when the incandescent lamp and alternating current changed illumination and power distribution and substituted electric power for shaft and belt transmission in large plants. Petroleum appeared at the opportune moment to provide lubricants for millions of machine-age bearings and subsequently suggested the development of internal combustion engines, which made oil an indispensable source of power.

By 1890 the United States had surpassed its nearest rivals, England and Germany, in the production of iron and steel and was the leading industrial nation. Between 1869 and 1914 the number of wage earners engaged in manufacturing more than trebled. Meanwhile, the horsepower employed in factories increased nearly tenfold and the gross value of manufactured products rose from $3.4 billion to $24.2 billion.

Only in the 20th century was organized research directed to the discovery of processes and products hitherto unknown. Plastics such as celluloid film led to motion pictures, and the development of synthetic fibers such as rayon greatly changed the textile industry. While the domestic dye industry was largely the result of interrupted trade with Germany in World War I, chemical processes in general were gaining in importance.

Up to 1940 research was largely confined to the electrical, chemical, rubber, and power machinery industries; in other lines innovation came from outside or by chance more than by design. World War II added aircraft and scientific instruments, over 60 percent supported by government orders or grants, to the research-oriented industries. The unusual needs and taxes of World War II increased the pace of diversification. In World War I, the United States had been chiefly a supplier of raw materials and semifinished goods; in World War II it became the chief source of finished military supplies.

Outwardly, the most striking change in United States industry between 1945 and 1980 was its relocation. The movement was away from the Northeast and Middle West to the Sunbelt States by the South and West. Florida, Texas, and California in particular became major manufacturing centers.

The most spectacular industrial developments of the late-20th century were in electronics and aerospace. However, the preeminence that U.S. manufacturers had so long enjoyed was increasingly being undermined by foreign competitors, especially the Japanese.

MANUFACTURING, HOUSEHOLD. During the first century of the United States, most articles of home consumption were made by members of the family. Wool cards, flax hatchels, spinning wheels, hand looms, and dye tubs were in almost every home. The most important household manufactures were textiles and garments. Maple sugar, cheese, cider, soap, candles, shoes, harness, furniture, woodenware, plows, harrows, tools, and nails were other commonly produced items. But the output of local factories and workshops increasingly displayed household products: the total value of family-made goods produced declined from $29 million in 1840 to less than $25 million in 1860.

MANUMISSION. The formal liberation of a slave by means of an instrument of writing, such as a will or a deed of manumission, as prescribed by state law. Personal considerations, religion, the doctrine of natural right, and the schemes for African colonization (*see* American Colonization Society) influenced the slaveowners to free their slaves. Manumission was advocated by the moderate antislavery groups in opposition to the extreme abolitionist program for immediate, unconditional emancipation.

MAPLE SUGAR. The Indians boiled down maple sap into syrup and sugar, usually in bark troughs into which hot stones were dropped. In the late 17th century the English settlers took it up and maple sugar rapidly became an article of food and commerce. On the frontier, where cane sugar and molasses were scarce or unprocurable, the maple tree sweetened the pioneers' food and drink; its sugar was their confection. In the 19th century, less expensive cane sugar replaced it. Maple sugar production is now confined to the Northeast.

MAPPING OF AMERICAN COASTS. In 1500 Juan de la Cosa compiled a large map of the world on which he incorporated all he knew of the Spanish, Portuguese, and English discoveries in America, including those of Amerigo Vespucci and John and Sebastian Cabot. Two years later (1502) the discoveries of Gaspar Corte-Real were outlined on a map drawn by Alberto Cantino. But only four maps are known that were actually printed between 1492 and 1510. The earliest, by Giovanni Contarini (1506), was closely followed in 1507 by a globe and large wall map by Martin Waldseemüller. The globe gores of Waldseemüller were published with a text *(Cosmographiae Introductio)* that suggested for the first time that the New World be called America. The fourth printed map, by Johann Ruysch, appeared in 1508.

Maps by Oronce Fine, whose heart-shaped world was published in 1531, assumed that America was joined to Asia. Others believed that America was a continent beyond which, at some distance, lay the Orient. After Ferdinand Magellan circumnavigated South America in 1520 and Hernando Cortes launched several expeditions in the Pacific Ocean, the western coast of America began to take shape. It was first drawn on a map in 1529, but there was no other good map of the coast until 1544, when a master chart, maintained under the supervision of the Casa de Contraction, was supposed to have added to it all new discoveries as soon as they were made. Many inaccuracies crept into this chart, and many discoverers failed to report their findings. The first authentic map of the coast of California, undated, but based on the discoveries of Cortes in 1535, was followed by a map of the same region by Alonso de Santa Cruz (1542–45).

On his world map of 1538 and his globe of 1541, Gerhardus Mercator separated America from Asia and rejected the Asiatic names commonly used for the New World. With the publication of Mercator's large-scale chart of the world (1569), the science of cartography came into its own, and mariners were able to navigate with a degree of certainty. Mercator's projection, in a modified form, is still in use today.

In the 17th century, maps of the Atlantic coast made the first attempts to lay down the latitudes and longitudes of the region, at the same time adding a great deal of information on the interior of the country. Robert Dudley, an expatriated Englishman, explored the entire West Coast, and his atlas, the *Arcano del Mare,* published in Florence, Italy, in 1646–47, included a precise map of the West Coast.

In the 18th century a survey of the Atlantic coast was sponsored by the British. The charts were published as they were completed and eventually issued as *The Atlantic Neptune* (1774–81). Surveys of the Pacific coast were climaxed by the works of Alexander von Humboldt and Aimé Bonpland. In the 19th century, the mapping of the United States was completed by the Coast Survey (later the Coast and Geodetic Survey). (*See also* Cartography.)

MARAIS DES CYGNES MASSACRE (May 19, 1858). An incident of the Kansas Border War. Charles A. Hamilton, a proslavery settler from Georgia, arrested a number of Free-State men, eleven of whom were shot in a ravine near the Marais des Cygnes River. All were left for dead, though five were only wounded. The shooting, without political significance, was probably an act of revenge.

MARBURY* V. *MADISON, 1 Cranch 137 (1803). A decision of the U.S. Supreme Court. A landmark in U.S. constitutional history, it declared that the Court would declare unconstitutional and void acts of Congress in conflict with the Constitution. By this decision the doctrine of judicial review was firmly established and the position of the judiciary was strengthened in the balance of powers among the legislative, executive, and judicial branches of the government.

The appointments of William Marbury and other Federalists to newly created offices had been made at the last minute by the Federalist administration of John Adams (*see* Midnight Judges). The new president, Thomas Jefferson, and his secretary of state, James Madison, refused to honor the appointments and Marbury sued. The opinion written by Chief Justice John Marshall found that Marbury had a right to his office. The remaining question was whether the Supreme Court could issue the writ of mandamus required to place him in office. The Court answered in the negative, claiming that the law giving the Court that authority went against the Constitution and was therefore void.

MARCH TO THE SEA, SHERMAN'S. *See* **Sherman's March to the Sea.**

MARCY-ELGIN TREATY. *See* **Elgin-Marcy Treaty.**

MARCY'S EXPLORING EXPEDITION (1852). Ordered by the War Department to explore the Red River to its source. Capt. R. B. Marcy was selected to command the expedition. His report, in 1853, disclosed that there were two main branches of the Red River. The valuable lands between were the object of litigation between the United States and Texas in 1896 (*see* Greer County Dispute). Marcy also brought back much valuable scientific information.

MARCY'S MARCH (1857). In the summer of 1857 troops were sent to Utah to control the Mormon problem (*see* Mormon Expedition). The command wintered at Fort Bridger, Wyo. A detachment under Capt. R. B. Marcy was sent to New Mexico for supplies. It marched through deep snow and in bitter cold to Fort Massachusetts, Colo. Marcy's return was delayed, because of information that hostile Mormons planned to intercept, but on June 9, 1858, he reached Fort Bridger.

MARDI GRAS. An elaborate series of street pageants and indoor balls held in New Orleans on Shrove Tuesday, the day before Lent. Mardi Gras is a major tourist attraction in New Orleans, and the balls are elaborate and exclusive.

MARE CLAUSUM. In international law, the principle of the "closed sea" as against *mare liberum,* or a "free sea." The United States has been in favor of the free sea (*see* Freedom of the Seas), though in 1886 it asserted the principle of *mare clausum* in trying to protect its sealing right in Alaskan waters. But America had to surrender the principle; it had invoked the principle of *mare liberum* too often.

MARIA MONK CONTROVERSY. In 1836 the *Awful Disclosures of the Hotel Dieu Nunnery of Montreal,* purporting to be Maria Monk's autobiography, was published. It was actually written by a group of New York clergymen. It was one of the most influential pieces of nativistic propaganda ever printed in the United States. Its stress on priestly immorality aroused a storm of anti-Catholic feeling that persisted even after it was pronounced a fraud.

MARIANA. Territory in Massachusetts between the Salem and Merrimack rivers from the sea to their heads and including Cape Ann. Granted to Capt. John Mason by the New England Council on Mar. 9, 1622, neither Mason nor his heirs could make good their title. By the charter of 1629, it was incorporated into that of the Massachusetts Bay Colony.

"MARIANAS TURKEY SHOOT." *See* **Philippine Sea, Battle of the.**

MARIETTA. First settlement (1788) in the Ohio country, where the Miskingum River empties into the Ohio. It was named in honor of Queen Marie Antoinette of France.

MARIN, EXPEDITION OF (1753). Moving by water from Montreal Capt. Paul Marin established French authority in western Pennsylvania by occupying Presque Isle (now Erie, Pa.), Fort LeBoeuf, and Venango. The expedition alarmed the Indians and precipitated British-American resistance.

MARINE BIOLOGICAL LABORATORY AT WOODS HOLE. Established in 1888, at Woods Hole, Mass., MBL (as it is known) became the summertime center of American biological research. Important research was done in cytology, genetics, developmental biology, and nerve conduction. The teaching program emphasizes invertebrate zoology, marine botany, general physiology, and embryology. There are postdoctoral training programs in neurobiology, fertilization and gamete physiology, and excitable membrane biophysics.

Since 1950, the federal government has been the laboratory's largest single supporter through the National Science Foundation and the National Institutes of Health. In the 1960's MBL added year-round research programs Woods Hole is also the site of the U.S. Fish Commission's laboratories, and the Woods Hole Oceanographic Institution.

MARINE CORPS, UNITED STATES. The U.S. Marine Corps dates its history from Nov. 10, 1775, when the Continental Congress authorized that "two Battalions of Marines be raised." Both the Continental navy and marines were disbanded after the Revolution.

On July 11, 1798, Congress authorized "a Marine Corps." In the Quasi-War with France (1798–1800) the U.S. Marines fought in virtually all sea actions. Next came operations against the Barbary pirates (1801–15), including the march "to the shores of Tripoli."

In the War of 1812 the U.S. Marines' chief service continued to be at sea, but there were neither resources nor opportunities for significant amphibious employment. The next three decades saw operations against the pirates in the Caribbean (1822 to the 1830's), landings in such diverse places as the Falkland Islands (1832) and Sumatra (1831–32), and patrolling off West Africa to suppress the slave trade (1820–61). A marine regiment was improvised for the Seminole War of 1836–42.

In the Mexican War (1846–48) marines executed raids against Frontera, Tampico, and Alvarado (1846–47) and landed with Gen. Winfield Scott at Veracruz (Mar. 9, 1847). A second marine battalion marched with him to Mexico City, coming into prominence in the storming of Chapultepec and the taking of San Cosmé Gate (Sept. 13, 1847). Meanwhile, the Gulf Squadron was conducting successful landings at Alvarado, Tuxpan, Frontera, and up the Tabasco River to San Juan Bautista. In the West, marine landing parties from the Pacific Squadron were repeatedly used in the conquest of California (1846) and against Mexico's west coast ports (1847).

The U.S. Marines were with Commodore Matthew C. Perry when he forced open the doors of Japan to foreign commerce in 1853. A marine detachment from Washington, D.C., captured John Brown at Harpers Ferry, W. Va. (1859).

In the Civil War (1861–65) most service was with the navy, overshadowed by the larger scope and drama of the land campaigns. From 1865 until 1898 there were some thirty-two Marine landings in foreign countries, especially in Latin America.

In the Spanish-American War (1898) a marine battalion seized Guantánamo Bay and accepted the Spanish surrender of Guam and several Puerto Rican ports. A marine regiment was formed for service in the Philippine Insurrection (1899–1904) and later joined the allied relief column sent to Peking in the Boxer Rebellion (1900).

In World War I Marine regiments fought at Belleau Wood, Soissons, St.-Mihiel, Blanc Mont, and in the final Meuse-Argonne offensive (November 1918). After the war, these were large-scale involvement in Nicaragua (1926–33) and China (1926–41).

In World War II, Marine action was most notable in the Pacific. Marines were involved in the defense of Pearl Harbor and the Philippines, and at Guam, Wake, and Midway islands. Beginning with Guadalcanal (August 1942), marine divisions or corps made numerous amphibious assaults. During World War II the Marine Corps reached a peak strength of 485,113.

In the Korean War, marines executed the assault at Inchon and the subsequent recapture of Seoul (September 1950). At the time of the Chinese intervention, the marines were near the Chosin Reservoir in northeastern Korea and fought their way back to Hungnam (December 1950). Two years of trench warfare followed. A brigade-size force was landed in Lebanon (July 1958); and a brigade of marines was used in the Dominican intervention (April 1965).

Marine involvement in Vietnam began in 1954. Ground forces and helicopter units were active there throughout the war. The active Fleet Marine Force is maintained at a minimum of three divisions and three wings, with requisite supporting units. A fourth marine division and wing are contained in the Organized Reserve. Strength of the regular Marine Corps in 1980 was 185,200.

MARION, BATTLE AT (Dec. 18, 1864). Union Gen. George Stoneman, raiding southwestern Virginia from eastern Tennessee, struck the Confederates under John C. Breckinridge at Marion, Va. Stoneman destroyed the salt works there but could gain no decision against Breckinridge.

MARION, FORT. Spanish-built fort at St. Augustine, Fla., known variously as San Juan de Pinos, San Augustine, San Marco, and (by the British) St. Marks. It was finally brought to completion, at enormous cost, in 1756. When the United States acquired Florida in 1819, it was renamed for Gen. Francis Marion.

MARIPOSA LAND GRANT. Originally given to the former Mexican governor Juan Bautista Alvarado, it was for ten leagues, or 44,368 acres. The claim, located within a broad area roughly equivalent to present-day Mariposa County, was purchased by John C. Frémont in 1847, even though there were grave questions as to its validity. Gold was discovered and Frémont pressed his claim to the U.S. Supreme Court, which confirmed it. Frémont's right to the minerals made him rich for a decade. Lacking in business experience, he was taken advantage of and lost ownership of Mariposa. In his later days Frémont lived in poverty. Mariposa itself was subjected to wasteful management. It was said that $20 million in gold was taken from it by 1872, but various costs left little profit.

MARITIME COMMISSION, FEDERAL. Independent regulatory agency, established in 1961 to protect the interests of the public by regulating waterborne shipping in the foreign and domestic offshore commerce of the United States.

MARKETING. *See* **Distribution of Goods and Services.**

MARKETING RESEARCH. The systematic collection and analysis of data to help managers solve the problems they encounter in moving goods and services to market. The range of topics include measuring and forecasting markets, testing the effectiveness of advertising (past or projected), developing new products, forecasting reactions to price changes, selecting and controlling channels of distribution, and organizing marketing staffs. Marketing research has been a major beneficiary of sweeping improvements since the 1920's in statistical methodology, quantitative analysis, and behavioral science, as well as in the use of computers.

MARKETS, PUBLIC. There was a marketplace in Jamestown as early as 1617 and one in New Amsterdam as early as 1647. The sale of meats and vegetables at any other place was illegal. The system was quite general in America in the colonial and early national periods.

"MARK TWAIN." On the old Mississippi River steamboats, the leadmen called the soundings, thus: "quarter twain," indicating 2¼ fathoms; "mark twain," 2 fathoms or 12 feet. "Mark Twain" was made famous as the pen name of Samuel L. Clemens.

MARQUE AND REPRISAL, LETTERS OF. Papers from a belligerent government authorizing privateers to engage in warfare against enemy commerce. The Constitution gives Congress power to "grant Letters of Marque and Reprisal, and make Rules concerning Captures on Land and Water" (Article I, Section 8). During the Revolution, letters of marque were issued by both Congress and state governments to 1,150 vessels, and in the War of 1812 privateers numbering 515 captured about 1,450 prizes. It was practiced only briefly by the South in the Civil War, and in subsequent wars the destruction of enemy commerce has been limited to government-owned vessels.

MARRIAGE. One of the major differences between the British and Spanish colonial settlers is that the former came to America as family units rather than as male adventurers, traders, or priests. From the beginning, marriage and the family has been a central North American institution. The mobility of Americans has made the conjugal family unit far more important than the extended consanguine family characteristic of the settled societies of Europe. Until the Industrial Revolution and the urbanization of America, the conjugal family extended to three generations. By the 1980's, however, the aged tended to live apart and were less likely to be supported by the conjugal unit. Marriage in the 20th century has been marked by fewer children and a rising divorce rate. (*See also* Family.)

MARSHALL CONVENTION. A gathering of the governors of Texas, Louisiana, Mississippi, and Arkansas at Marshall, Tex., in May 1865. It was called by Confederate Gen. Edmund Kirby-Smith for the purpose of obtaining more favorable terms of surrender than had been granted by Gen. Ulysses S. Grant and Gen. William Tecumseh Sherman. It attempted to present terms directly to the federal government but failed.

MARSHALL ISLANDS. A group of coral atolls and reefs located 2,000 nautical miles southwest of Hawaii. The Marshall Islands were granted as a mandate to Japan after World War I by the League of Nations. They were strategically important in World War II, and U.S. efforts to take them focused on Kwajalein atoll, in the center of the Marshalls and headquarters for Japanese defense of the islands. Heavy bombardment began on Jan. 29, 1944, and by Feb. 4 it was taken. The capture of Eniwetok atoll followed on Feb. 21. In 1947 the Marshall Islands became part of the U.S. Trust Territory of the Pacific.

MARSHALL PLAN. Popular name of the European Recovery Program (1948–52), named for Secretary of State George C. Marshall, who proposed it. It was designed to revive the European economy in order to provide political and social conditions under which the nations could survive. Sixteen countries, led by Great Britain and France, established what was to become the Organization of European Economic Cooperation (OEEC), to which West Germany was later admitted. The U.S. Congress in April 1948 enacted legislation for a recovery program that was placed under the control of the Economic Cooperation Administration (ECA). In an effort to restore agricultural and industrial production to prewar levels, create financial stability, promote economic cooperation, and expand exports, the United States in a four-year period appropriated some $12 billion (plus $1.5 million for assistance on credit terms). The combined gross national products of Western Europe rose 25 percent, or 15 percent over prewar levels.

MARTHA'S VINEYARD. Island off the southwestern coast of Cape Cod, Mass., was discovered in 1602 by Bartholomew Gosnold. It was granted to Thomas Mayhew, who planted the first settlement at Edgartown in 1642. The Mayhew family maintained it as a federal outpost until the Revolution put an end to hereditary pretensions. Formerly an important whaling center, in the 20th century Martha's Vineyard became a well-known summer resort.

MARTIAL LAW. The use of military forces to control an area in place of civil authority. President George Washington set the precedent when he dispatched troops to quell the Whiskey Rebellion of 1794 by ordering all rebels to be delivered to civil courts for trial. Thereafter, martial law was rarely invoked. Andrew Jackson declared martial law in New Orleans in the face of imminent British attack in 1814. It was also declared in Indiana in 1864 in the face of Copperhead threats and led to the important Supreme Court decision in *Ex parte Milligan* (1866) protecting civilians from being arbitrarily tried by the military authorities when civil courts are still functioning. Martial law has also been used after natural disasters, as in Wilkes-Barre, Pa., when the Susquehanna River flooded following Hurricane Agnes in June 1972.

Martial law during wartime is more readily declared than in peacetime. It was used in June 1943 to stop a race riot in Detroit. It was also used in Hawaii in the aftermath of the attack on Pearl Harbor.

After the decision in *Brown* v. *Board of Education of Topeka* (1954), the use of martial law accelerated. For example, in Selma, Ala., in 1965 the state National Guard was federalized. In April 1968, after the death of Martin Luther King, Jr., the Riot Act of 1792 was read to the crowds in Washington, D.C., and troops were then employed.

MARTIN-TOLLIVER FEUD (1884–87). In Morehead, Ky., John Martin killed Floyd Tolliver. Martin in turn was slain by Tolliver kinsmen. A vendetta ensued, causing such a state of anarchy that more than half the peaceable citizens of Morehead moved away. Twenty-three men had been killed when, on June 22, 1887, the Tolliver leaders were all killed.

MARTIN* V. *HUNTER'S LESSEE, 1 Wheaton 304 (1816). It established the right of the U.S. Supreme Court to review the decisions of state courts. Congress could confer appellate jurisdiction on the Supreme Court in all cases involving the laws, treaties, and Constitution of the United States.

MARTIN* V. *MOTT, 12 Wheaton 19 (1827). Considering an incident of the War of 1812, the Supreme Court decided that when Congress authorizes the president to call militia against actual or imminent invasion, his decision is "conclusive upon all persons," and calls for prompt obedience.

MARTLING MEN. The Aaron Burr faction of the Democratic-Republican party of New York City, who opposed De Witt Clinton, governor of New York. They took their name from Martling's Tavern, where they met. They were allied with the Tammany Society.

MARY AND JOHN. The ship that sailed from Plymouth, England, on Mar. 20, 1630, and landed on May 30, at Massachusetts Bay, where its passengers founded Dorchester.

MARYLAND. The Proprietary Province of Maryland, named for Queen Henrietta Maria, was granted in 1632 by Charles I to George Calvert, first Baron of Baltimore, a recent convert to the Church of Rome. After his death, his son Cecil received the grant on June 20, 1632. Shortly thereafter a colonizing expedition, under the command of Leonard Calvert, his younger brother, sailed Nov. 22, 1633, from Cowes, Isle of Wight. The two small vessels arrived off the capes of the Chesapeake Bay on Feb. 27, 1634. The first settlement was established at St. Marys City. Although Maryland was founded by Roman Catholics, the Anglican Church was established in 1689 and thereafter, until the Revolution, Catholics could not practice their religion openly.

Maryland established its economy on a money crop, tobacco. A plantation system developed, based on slavery.

Maryland was divided about loyalty to England at the start of the Revolution, but declared its independence by the adoption of the first state constitution in November 1776. After the Revolution, Maryland ceded the land to the central government for what was to become the District of Columbia. (Virginia also gave part of this area just south of the Potomac but this grant was later returned.)

During the War of 1812, Maryland's troops defended Baltimore with the siege of Fort McHenry (1814) and at the Battle of North Point. During the siege of Fort McHenry, Francis Scott Key was a prisoner on a British man-of-war, where he wrote the lyrics to the "Star-Spangled Banner."

During the Civil War, southern Maryland and the eastern shore favored the Confederacy, but a quick takeover of the state by federal troops preserved Maryland for the Union. Marylanders fought on both sides, about 20,000 for the South and about 60,000 for the Union. The major battles of Antietam (or Sharpsburg) and South Mountain (or Boonesboro) were fought on Maryland soil in 1862.

After the Civil War, Maryland converted to a commercial and industrial economy. The Chesapeake and Ohio Canal and the Baltimore and Ohio, the country's first railroad, connected Chesapeake Bay with the Middle West. After 1865 Baltimore became a center of banking and the steel and copper industries. Its port in 1979 was the eighth largest U.S. port in tonnage. Commercial fishing is an important industry.

Maryland cultural and scientific institutions include the Johns Hopkins University and hospital; the Peabody Institute of Music; the Walters Art Gallery; the Shepherd and Pratt Mental Hospital; and the Enoch Pratt Free Library. The U.S.

Naval Academy was founded at Annapolis in 1845. The population in 1980 was 4,216,000.

MARYLAND, INVASION OF (September 1862). Union Gen. George B. McClellan began organizing a force to defend Maryland against Rebel troops concentrating at Frederick, Md. Meantime, Gen. Robert E. Lee detached Gen. Thomas J. ("Stonewall") Jackson to capture Harpers Ferry while Lee led his army westward to an expected junction with Jackson near Hagerstown, Md.

On Sept. 13, McClellan reached Frederick. He hurried troops after Lee. Sharp fights took place at gaps in South Mountain; Lee sent reinforcements, but by nightfall, he directed a retirement toward Sharpsburg, Md. McClellan advanced slowly, diverted by Jackson's movement against Harpers Ferry. As soon as that place surrendered, Jackson hurried to Sharpsburg, leaving A. P. Hill to dispose of captured property and prisoners and then follow promptly.

McClellan reached Sharpsburg on Sept. 16, and his attacks the following day brought on the Battle of Antietam. Lee, outnumbered, held the field, but severe losses and heavy odds made it inadvisable to stay. McClellan did not attack again. On the night of Sept. 18, Lee recrossed the Potomac.

"MARYLAND! MY MARYLAND!" A poem written by James Ryder Randall in April 1861. Set to the music of the old German song "O Tannenbaum," it became one of the marching songs of the Confederate army and later the state song of Maryland.

MASON, FORT. Established by the federal government in Mason County, Tex., in 1851, as frontier protection against the Comanche and Kiowa. There was also a fort of that name in Missouri, and one called Mason's Fort in Pennsylvania.

MASON AND SLIDELL INCIDENT. *See* **Trent Affair.**

MASON BAND. Highwaymen and river pirates led by Samuel Mason who operated in pioneer days at Cave-in-Rock, in Hardin County, Ill.; on the Ohio and Mississippi rivers; and over the Natchez Trace. Mason was killed by two of his men in 1804.

MASON-DIXON LINE. The Pennsylvania boundary with Delaware, Maryland, and West Virginia. It is best known as the symbolic border line between North and South. The Mason and Dixon line was the result of more than a century of dispute between the proprietors of Maryland and Pennsylvania. Finally, in 1760 they reached agreement, and two English surveyors, Charles Mason and Jeremiah Dixon, began the survey of the boundary line in 1763. Completed after four years' work, the boundary line was set at 39°43′17.6″ north latitude. The results were ratified by the crown in 1769. In the meantime, Virginia contested its boundary with Pennsylvania, a dispute that lasted for many years and ended with the extension (1784) of the Mason and Dixon line westward. (*See also* Pennsylvania-Maryland Boundary Dispute; Pennsylvania-Virginia Boundary Dispute.)

MASONRY. *See* **Freemasons.**

MASON TITLE. In 1622, John Mason, former English governor of Newfoundland, received the grant of Mariana in Massachusetts, and, with Sir Ferdinando Gorges, Maine between the Merrimack and Kennebec rivers. In 1629 the Council of New England granted Mason the province of New Hampshire, extending from the Merrimack to the Piscataqua and running inland sixty miles up each river. On Nov. 17 Mason and Gorges were granted Laconia. Mason sent settlers to the Piscataqua. In 1635 the council confirmed Mason, by then its vice-president, in his title to Mariana, New Hampshire, Masonia on the Kennebec, and the south half of the Isles of Shoals. He died soon after.

In 1675 his heirs recovered title, and Samuel Allen bought the title in 1691. From then until the mid-19th century, the long quarrels between the people and government of New Hampshire, the heirs of Mason, and those of Allen were very important in determining the history of the state.

MASSAC, FORT. Built by the French in 1757 in Illinois Country. Originally named Fort Ascension, it was renamed Fort Massiac in 1758. In 1794 the U.S. Army erected a new fort on the site, Fort Massac. It is known principally because George Rogers Clark landed on its site at the outset of his Illinois campaign.

MASSACHUSETTS. Englishmen made the first documented Massachusetts landings: Bartholomew Gosnold around Cape Cod in 1602 and Martin Pring at Plymouth in 1603. French explorer Samuel de Champlain mapped Massachusetts harbors during 1605–06. In 1614 the Dutchman Adriaen Block and the Englishman John Smith charted Cape Cod and Massachusetts Bay.

The first settlement in Massachusetts was made in 1620 by English Pilgrims—Separatists from the Puritan church who had fled persecution to Holland in 1608. On Sept. 16, 1620, thirty-five of these Pilgrims and sixty-seven others—including fourteen servants and artisans and a hired military leader, Myles Standish—set sail in the *Mayflower* from Plymouth, England. Having reached Provincetown in November, they decided to proceed south, and sighting Plymouth on Dec. 11, they chose it for their settlement. During the winter, half of the colonists and crew died, but in the spring the survivors made peace with the Wampanoag, and planted corn, fished, and hunted. In October of 1621 they celebrated their harvest, the first Thanksgiving.

Competitive English merchants built trading bases at Weymouth, Wollaston, and Gloucester; plantations were formed at Medford, Charlestown, Boston, Salem and Gloucester. In 1629 a group of wealthy Puritan merchants secured a royal charter for the Massachusetts Bay Company, and in 1629 and 1630 the first ships reached Boston, carrying Gov. John Winthrop and the Massachusetts Bay Company—the home office complete—together with 800 colonists and horses, cattle, and building supplies. By 1640, 18,000 Bay Company planters populated thirty towns, compared to Plymouth Plantation's nine towns with only 3,000 people. Theocratic intolerance exiled from the Bay Company to neighboring colonies the harshly persecuted Quakers, Baptists, and other dissenters.

The permissiveness toward the Massachusetts Puritans came to an end with the restoration in 1660, and a royal commission was dispatched to New England in 1664. Its clashes with local authority led to the annulment of the Massachusetts Bay Company's charter in 1684 and Massachusetts was placed under the Dominion of New England. But after the Glorious Revolution, King William abolished the Dominion of New England and granted the moderate Massachusetts Province Charter, joining Plymouth, Maine, and the Massachusetts Bay Colony under Gov. William Phips. During much of his governorship Phips was away from Massachusetts, fighting King William's War (1689–97).

Peaceful years followed and nineteen new western Massachusetts towns were founded. Shipbuilding, overseas commerce, and waterpower industries developed a wealthy, moderate, merchant leadership that replaced the theocrats. Economic opportunity for freeholders reduced class distinction. Boston became America's principal seaport.

As maritime competition grew, so did commercial quarrels with the English bureaucracy, resentment of militia mobilization for the Canadian campaigns of King George's War (1745) and the Seven Years' War (1756–63), and outrage at the presence of British regulars. Imperial taxes such as the Stamp Act (1765) brought merchants, small landholders, and debtors into boycotts, riots, and attacks on tax collectors. The Committees of Correspondence and the Sons of Liberty were so effective that the Stamp Act was repealed, but the English initiated the Townshend Acts (1768). The Massachusetts Assembly petitioned other colonies to oppose what they called an English usurpation of power. Riots ensued in Boston, notably the Boston Massacre of 1770. Although the Townshend Acts were substantially repealed, the tax on tea remained, and the Boston Tea Party (1773) precipitated a crisis that resulted in the closing of the port and establishment of military government under Gen. Thomas Gage. Committees of Correspondence of all the colonies sent supply caravans to Massachusetts, and militia, known as the minutemen, were mustered and armed. On Apr. 19, 1775, 400 minutemen from surrounding towns routed three British companies at Concord Bridge, thereby opening the American Revolution. Following the Battle of Bunker Hill (June 17), George Washington arrived to take command of the Massachusetts forces. The British evacuated Boston on Mar. 17, 1776.

Massachusetts was the sixth state to ratify the Constitution (Feb. 6, 1788). Postwar economic depression hit Massachusetts especially hard. England closed its ports to Yankee ships and poured European goods into American harbors. Massachusetts shipmasters found exports embargoed even to the West Indies. Inflation bankrupted farmers and storekeepers and landed them in debtors' prisons. This produced the abortive Shays's Rebellion in 1786. Many pioneer families abandoned Massachusetts and moved westward. But with the opening of the China trade in 1784 the Massachusetts economy began to revive. Bostonian vessels joined other American ships in enormously profitable voyages to China and India, and brought Asian goods directly to Massachusetts warehouses. Profits built shipyards in every river mouth. When the War of 1812 was declared the remnants of the Massachusetts Federalists repudiated "Mr. Madison's War" and occasionally collaborated with the blockading enemy. Despite the disruption of commerce caused by the war, Massachusetts prospered.

After the War of 1812 Massachusetts' East India cotton trade declined by half, but textile manufacturing burgeoned in Fall River, New Bedford, and Lowell. By 1840 Taunton, Brockton, Chelsea, Cambridge, Waltham, Worcester, and Gardner were industrial cities. The Irish potato famine of 1846 brought 50,000 immigrants to work the factories and mills. Yankee products were sent to southern ports, bringing back cotton and hides. In the 1850's enormously profitable domestic trade in supplies for the California gold rush, aboard fast clipper ships, rivaled the earlier China trade. But the advent of steam vessels soon made them uncompetitive.

Massachusetts in the 19th century enjoyed a great literary flowering. Among its leading lights were William Ellery Channing, Daniel Webster, Edward Everett, Richard Henry Dana, William Cullen Bryant, George Bancroft, Jared Sparks, William Hickley Prescott, Nathaniel Hawthorne, Ralph Waldo Emerson, John Greenleaf Whittier, Henry David Thoreau, Louisia May Alcott, James Russell Lowell, Oliver Wendell Holmes, and Henry Wadsworth Longfellow.

Massachusetts was a center of abolitionism in the years preceding the Civil War, particularly under the leadership of William Lloyd Garrison and former President John Quincy Adams. During the Civil War, Massachusetts sent 146,000 men to fight for the Union, of whom 13,942 died.

After the war, Massachusetts prospered. Intense industrial competition from other parts of the country did not unduly disturb the economies of the urban centers and their immediate suburbs. However, the smaller towns languished, their water-powered industries no longer competitive. The state's isolation from raw materials and markets in the depression of the 1930's destroyed its preeminence in textile and shoe manufacture, which moved to the South and West. By 1940 only diversified industries using skilled labor could survive in Massachusetts. These included electronics, machinery, metal fabrication, paper specialties, chemicals, tools, and airplane engines. Service industries—notably finance and insurance—thrived. In the 1970's and 1980's, the state's activities included nuclear physics, chromatography, lasers, solar energy, and computers.

Massachusetts' population increased slightly between 1970 and 1980 (from 5,689,170 to 5,737,037), but most of its cities lost population.

MASSACHUSETTS, FORT (Colo.). Established in 1852, at the foot of Blanca Peak on Ute Creek in the San Luis Valley to protect the settlers on the upper Rio Grande against the Ute Indians. In 1858 the post was moved six miles south and the name changed to Fort Garland.

MASSACHUSETTS, FORT (Mass.). Built in Williamstown in 1744, it was one of the three "Province Forts" for the protection of the Deerfield Valley. In 1746 it was attacked by a party of French and Indians, led by Pierre François, Marquis de Vaudreuil, and its garrison destroyed. It was rebuilt in 1747.

MASSACHUSETTS BALLOT. All voting in New England was by acclamation or by the uplifted hand until 1634, when the ballot was used in electing the governor of Massachusetts, and the practice spread. Kernels of wheat and corn were sometimes used, the wheat for the affirmative and the corn for the negative; in Dedham, in 1643, Indian beans were used, white for the affirmative and black for the negative—hence the term "black ball." The Australian, or secret, ballot was introduced into the United States by Massachusetts in 1878.

MASSACHUSETTS BAY, FRANCHISE IN. In the early colonies, voting was limited to church members, a device deemed necessary if the theocracy was to survive. Only about one-fifth of the adult males had any share in the colony's government. This union of church and state was broken by the annulling of the charter in 1684, but in 1689, the leaders, without authority from England, reestablished the old charter government, but they made a wide extension of suffrage in order to win support for restoring the charter. The new charter of 1691 gave the suffrage to 40-shilling freeholders and to others who had property worth £40 sterling. The state constitution of 1780 contained a similar property qualification, but when a general national movement for a freer suffrage set in, Massachusetts fell into line. (*See* Franchise.)

MASSACHUSETTS BAY COMPANY. The royal charter of 1629 confirmed to a group of merchants and others power to trade and colonize in New England between the Merrimack and the Charles rivers. The group had local powers of self-government, subject to the general government to be established by the council over all New England. The charter gave the general court power to admit new members as a means of limiting the suffrage (*see* Massachusetts Bay, Franchise in) in the colony to those of their own religious faith and in a few years to transform the enterprise from a trading company into a theocracy practically free from outside control. Dissent within the theocracy resulted in the voluntary exile of the group that founded Connecticut and the forced exile of Roger Williams and Anne Hutchinson, founders of Rhode Island towns.

Massachusetts Bay Company remained neutral during the Puritan Revolution in England, but joined with Plymouth, Connecticut, and New Haven in a defensive confederation in 1643 (*see* United Colonies of New England). When the monarchy was restored in 1660, the company recognized its former relationship to the mother country. But it refused to accept many features of England's new colonial policy, especially the Navigation Acts, and gradually incurred the displeasure of the crown. Formal charges were made against the company and the charter withdrawn in 1684, after which the company as a corporation ceased to exist. Its government, however, continued to function without legal status until the establishment of the Dominion of New England in 1686.

MASSACHUSETTS BODY OF LIBERTIES (1641). Code of laws promulgated by the Massachusetts general court and sent to the towns for suggestions. It was to be in force for three years and, if found satisfactory, made perpetual. Based largely on English common law, the code left too much authority to the magistrates. Deputies, at the end of the probation period, replaced the body of liberties with *The Book of the General Lawes and Libertyes* (1648).

MASSACHUSETTS "CIRCULAR LETTER." On Feb. 11, 1768, the Massachusetts House of Representatives, opposing the Townshend Acts of 1767, petitioned George III and drafted a letter describing the petition to the other colonial legislatures. This step toward colonial unity was punished by dissolution of the general court on July 1, 1768.

MASSACHUSETTS GOVERNMENT ACT. Also called the Regulating Act, second of the Coercion Acts, it was passed by Parliament in May 1774, with the intention of quelling disturbances created by the New Englanders protesting the tea tax. The act, in effect, took the executive power from the colonists and removed it to the crown. In Massachusetts it crystalized public opinion in favor of an armed revolt, if need be, to safeguard the liberties of the colony.

MASSIVE RETAILATION DOCTRINE (1954). A foreign policy doctrine in which the United States would resort to nuclear weapons as a deterrent to aggression, primarily directed against the Soviet Union. The doctrine was first articulated by John Foster Dulles in January 1954.

MASS MEDIA. After 1920 radio came into popular favor, and after World War II, television evoked an even greater mass appeal. The term "mass media" was employed to describe them, along with national press. Beginning with the 1960's, the social and political influence and power of the mass media became a matter of national controversy. Important differences in legal status distinguish the various media. Print journalism, thanks to the First Amendment, knows almost no regulation, while radio and television airwave channels, limited in number, are licensed and controlled almost as public utilities.

MASS PRODUCTION. A system of production based on interchangeable parts. The various strands of mass production were brought together by Henry Ford in the manufacture of the Model T automobile in 1903.

The symbol of modern mass production is the moving-belt assembly line. By the 1830's the Cincinnati meat-packing plants were moving carcasses on overhead conveyors. When Ford applied the moving belt principle to the assembly of automobiles, the increase in productivity was immediate and spectacular. The increase resulted only partially from the more minute division of labor and automatic materials handling; in addition, the moving belt was a tool of management, for by means of it the manager could set the pace of work. A good part of the increase in productivity came simply from forcing workers to work faster.

Mass production has been accompanied almost invariably by integration—that is, control by one company of every stage of the productive process from raw materials to the marketing of the finished product. Traditional management was inadequate to the new problems of mass production. Modern management was revolutionarized at the turn of the century by Frederick W. Taylor. He used the stopwatch to analyze and measure work and developed many tools of modern management, including routing, cost accounting, and the organization of management along functional lines. Since World War II the use of systems analysis and the computer has opened a new era.

Mass production requires a market that is both large and capable of absorbing relatively standardized products. The absence of rigid class gradations in America contributes to the uniform mass market required, the luxury trade being small and few being very poor. Mass production in turn tends further to blur class distinctions, at least in consumption. High productivity makes possible high wages, and thus American workers, as consumers, can support the mass-production industries that employ them. Americans are more nearly equal in the consumption of mass-produced products, such as automobiles and home appliances, than in the consumption of craft-produced commodities, such as houses.

In mass-production industries, unions were able to achieve marked rises in wages, especially after World War II. But complaints of dehumanizing working conditions persist. Experiments are underway that look toward replacing the "line" by a "work team" that would set its own pace.

MASS TRANSPORTATION. The movement of large numbers of people from place to place in the urban area—usually to and from their jobs. It is contrasted to "personal" transportation, i.e., the automobile. Mass transportation systems developed along with the growth of cities. The earliest systems involved horse-drawn street cars or vans. Generally, it was found that cars could move more smoothly on rails than over regular street pavements. Some street railways were extended beyond the city limits, employed regular locomotives, and became links in major railroad systems. Others employed electric engines that drew current from overhead wires and became known as "trolley cars." In heavily populated cities, the tracks were often elevated above the streets. Other systems were lowered to keep the rapid transit system out of the way of street traffic. The subways are the most prominent example of running the tracks underground, while in some cities trains were run through open cuts. Once gasoline engines were introduced, bus service began. Trolley systems were generally dismantled, as were some elevated trains.

During the 1970's, many problems in the field of mass transportation surfaced. Equipment was wearing out and replacement costs sky-rocketed. Surface mass transit bogged down in the massive traffic jams caused by the personal automobile.

Although formerly privately owned, virtually all mass transit systems are now publicly owned, typically by an independent agency. The U.S. Department of Transportation has a major responsibility in assisting local governments in planning and developing new systems of mass transportation.

MATAMOROS EXPEDITION (1836). An incident in the Texas Revolution. The provisional government of Texas was divided over a plan to carry the war to Mexico by launching an expedition to seize Matamoros. As the argument raged, the forces gathered to carry on the expedition were left at the frontier, where they were annihilated by the Mexicans. (*See* Goliad, Massacre at).

MATANZAS, FORT, Built in St. Augustine, Fla., by the Spaniards in 1743 as a defense against the British. This coquina structure is maintained by the federal government.

MATCHES. The friction match arrived in New England in the early 1830's. The first American patent was issued to Alonzo D. Phillips of Springfield, Mass., on Oct. 24, 1836, for a match using only phosphorous, chalk, and glue. This patent was sold to Ezekiel Byam, also of Massachusetts, who manufactured the "locofoco."

The major contribution of the United States in match production was in the development of matchmaking machinery. In 1854 William Gates, Jr., and H. J. Harwood patented the first continuous match machine. It later became the standard machine. In 1892 a patent was issued to Joshua Pussey for his book matches, but book matches did not become successful until they were used as an advertising medium.

The alarming development of phossy jaw in workers in American match factories, caused by the inhalation of white phosphorous fumes, prompted Congress in 1910 to levy a 2-cent tax on each box of white phosphorous matches, making their production unprofitable. Since 1913 all matches produced in the United States have been of the nonpoisonous sesquisulfide variety.

MATERNAL AND CHILD HEALTH CARE. Up to about the beginning of the 20th century the mortality rate for infants and children was extremely high. In 1789 about 40 percent of all deaths were among children under five. By 1850 there had been no significant decline in this mortality rate, and although children under one year of age constituted less than 3 percent of the total population, they accounted for 16.8 percent of the deaths. Children from one to four years, inclusive, made up 12.3 percent of the population and accounted for 21.2 percent of the total mortality.

Aside from poor diet, austere treatment, and unhygienic care in the home, disease took a high toll of lives. Gastrointestinal infections produced a high morbidity and mortality rate among infants. Epidemic diseases that particularly affected children were smallpox, scarlet fever, and diphtheria. The inferior state of obstetrical care was also a cause of high material mortality. Puerperal fever was widespread and usually fatal.

The single most important medical contribution to benefit children prior to the modern era was inoculation for small pox, first practiced in the United States in 1721. An improved form of immunization, vaccination with cowpox virus, was introduced in 1800. During the 1850's the first two American hospitals for children were founded in Philadelphia and New York. In 1872 the American Public Health Association was organized, and the following year the AMA formed a section on obstetrics and diseases of women and children. In 1888 the American Pediatric Society was organized.

Of the numerous health problems relating to child care in the late 19th and early 20th centuries, none evoked more concern among physicians and public health officials than dirty and unsafe milk. Only with the acceptance and refinement of the pasteurization process in the first decades of the 20th century was the milk problem solved.

In 1902 the first school nurse in America was appointed in New York City, and by 1911, systems of medical inspection had been adopted by 411 cities. In 1903 Vermont passed a statewide law that required annual eye examination of all schoolchildren. School lunches were first provided in New York City in 1908. In that year New York established its Division of Child Hygiene. It was to set a pattern for city and state health department administrations throughout the country.

The early work of the Federal Children's Bureau, established in 1912, in cooperation with state health departments, and the efforts of medical and welfare organizations resulted in important contributions for the betterment of maternal and child health care. Crippled children also received an attention that had been unknown previously, and work continued to better conditions for the care and education of blind, deaf, and mentally ill children. In 1921 Congress passed the Shepard-Towner Act, which allocated funds to the states for health services for mothers and children. Its important provisions were made part of the Social Security Act of 1935.

Infant mortality continued to decline. In 1906 the infant mortality per 1,000 live births had been 148, but by 1945 it was reduced to 38.3; the maternal mortality rate for 1965, 31.6 deaths per 100,000 live births, was the lowest recorded in the United States to that time. The incidence of poliomyelitis dropped radically after the introduction of the Salk (1955) and the Sabin (1961) vaccines. The widespread use of antibiotics has had an appreciable effect on the infant and maternal health picture.

MATHEMATICAL ASSOCIATION OF AMERICA. *See* **American Mathematical Society.**

MATILDA LAWRENCE CASE (1837). Matilda Lawrence, a slave, left a steamboat at Cincinnati and later claimed her freedom on the ground that she had been brought by her master to free soil. The local court remanded her to slavery, but the issue was ultimately resolved by the Supreme Court in *Dred Scott* v. *Sanford* in 1857.

MAUMEE INDIAN CONVENTION. Conference held in August 1793 by the confederated Indian tribes of the Northwest Territory (Delaware, Wyandot, Miami, and Shawnee). Encouraged by the British, they demanded that the United States give up all the lands of the Northwest Territory. As a result, the army, under Gen. Anthony Wayne, proceeded to carry out its final campaign against these Indians.

MAUREPAS, FORT. Erected by the French in 1699 on the Bay of Biloxi. It was the seat of the first French colony in Louisiana, which was moved to Dauphin Island, near Mobile, in 1702. Fort Maurepas appears to have been occupied until it was destroyed by fire in 1719.

MAURY'S CHARTS. In the autumn of 1847 Matthew Fontaine Maury, then in charge of the Depot of Charts and Instruments of the Navy Department, published his first *Wind and Current Chart of the North Atlantic.* Maury then prepared similar charts for the South Atlantic, North Pacific, South Pacific, and Indian oceans. To explain these charts he issued a pamphlet of ten pages, which grew to 1,257 pages in two quarto volumes, called *Sailing Directions.*

MAUVILLA, BATTLE OF (October 1540). Between the Spanish forces of Hernando de Soto and those of the Indian chief Tuscaluza near the present site of Montgomery, Ala. Mauvilla, a fortified Indian town, was entered by de Soto. A few hours later a Spaniard killed an Indian in a street brawl. In the ensuing fight, Mauvilla was burned, hundreds of its citizens perishing; Tuscaluza committed suicide; and de Soto was seriously wounded. The Spaniards suffered eighty casualties.

MAVERICK. In 1845 Samuel A. Maverick, of San Antonio, Tex., took over 400 head of stock cattle and kept them for eleven years under charge of an irresponsible hand. He ended with fewer cattle than he started with, neighbors having branded the increase. The term "Maverick" came to refer to any unbranded animal. After the Civil War there were hundreds of thousands of maverick cattle in Texas. Mavericking became an occupation that sometimes bordered on, and often led to, theft, though any range man had—and still has—a right to brand any maverick found on his range.

MAXENT, LACLEDE AND COMPANY. A firm established in New Orleans in 1762 maintaining a large-scale commerce with the Indians of the Missouri, which included the Illinois and the Peoria, and all nations residing west of the Mississippi. The company, whose principal partner was Pierre Laclede Liqueste, imported large supplies of goods from Europe and established a post at the present site of St. Louis. The trade established by Laclede extended as far north as St. Peters River (present-day Minnesota River).

MAXIM GUN. Hiram S. Maxim, a native of Maine and later a British subject, invented the first automatic, quick-firing gun in 1884. It used a belt of cartridges, the first model firing more than ten times per second.

MAXWELL LAND GRANT. In northern New Mexico and Colorado, made by the Mexican government on Jan. 11, 1841, to Guadalupe Miranda and Carlos Beaubien. Congress confirmed the title in 1860. Beabien's son-in-law, Lucien Maxwell, eventually acquired 1,714,765 acres. His successors maintained title to this vast estate in four suits before the Supreme Court.

MAY DAY. During the 19th century the first day in May became the traditional family moving day in cities. Since 1890 international Socialist organizations have celebrated it as a world labor holiday, and May Day demonstrations have traditionally emphasized the solidarity of the working classes.

***MAYFLOWER*.** Three-masted, double-decked, bark-rigged merchant ship of 180 tons, with a normal speed of 2.5 miles per hour. In 1620 the *Mayflower* was chartered to take the Pilgrims to America. They left Plymouth harbor on Sept. 16 with 102 passengers and crew. They sighted Cape Cod on Nov. 19, and arrived in what is now the harbor of Provincetown, Cape Cod, Mass., on Nov. 21 and reached the site of Plymouth, Mass., on Dec. 21. The *Mayflower* remained until houses could be built for the new settlement. It sailed for England on Apr. 5, 1621. After 1624 its history is uncertain.

MAYFLOWER COMPACT. An agreement signed on Nov. 11, 1620, by the male passengers on the *Mayflower,* before coming ashore, that they would submit to the will of the majority in whatever regulations of government were agreed upon. Its purpose was to hold in check those who had threatened to strike out for themselves when the Pilgrim leaders decided to land in New England instead of Virginia. The Pilgrims held no patent to settle in New England. The compact established a local government that could maintain order until a patent could be obtained—in effect, a theocracy.

MAYNARD TAPE PRIMER. A waterproofed paper roll of fifty fulminate caps designed by Edward Maynard in 1845 to speed operation of the percussion lock rifle. It was used on many Civil War firearms.

MAYO FOUNDATION. A nonprofit corporation devoted to the conduct and advancement of medical education and research. It was incorporated in 1919 by Dr. William J. Mayo and his brother Dr. Charles H. Mayo, who conveyed all the assets of Mayo Clinic in Rochester, Minn., to the association. Net earnings from the clinic are used to support the foundation's research and teaching programs. The foundation conducts the Mayo Graduate School of Medicine, the Mayo Medical School, and a broad program of medical research.

MAYSVILLE VETO. In 1830 Congress passed a bill authorizing a subscription of stock in the Maysville, Washington, Paris and Lexington Turnpike Road Company. In vetoing the bill President Andrew Jackson pointed out that the project lay entirely within one state (Kentucky) and that it therefore violated the principle that such works, to receive federal aid, had to be national and not local in character.

MAZZEI LETTER (1796). A letter by Thomas Jefferson to Philip Mazzei, an Italian acquaintance. In the letter Jefferson severely criticized Federalist leaders, and certain phrases were interpreted as direct attacks on George Washington. The incident precipitated a permanent rupture between Washington and Jefferson.

MEAT INSPECTION LAWS. Spurred to action by the "embalmed beef" scandal at the time of the Spanish-American War, Congress passed in 1906 the Meat Inspection Act. It gave the secretary of agriculture power to inspect all meat and condemn such products as are "unsound, unhealthful, unwholesome, or otherwise unfit for human food."

MEAT-PACKING. Early meat-packers literally packed cuts of pork and beef into barrels with brine. Meat-packing was essentially a seasonal industry; there was no mechanical refrigeration to aid in keeping the meat from spoiling. Even when salt treatment was used, operations were confined almost entirely to the winter months. The custom was to pack meat through the winter, pile the barrels on the ground outside, and then sell in the spring.

Commercial meat-packing came into existence around 1818 in Cincinnati. By 1850 it was packing 27 percent of the meat products in the West. Chicago, Louisville, and St. Louis soon became rivals. During the Civil War, Chicago reached first rank, but had competition in beef developed in Kansas City, Omaha, Sioux City, and St. Paul. In the 1870's several large packing firms with headquarters at Chicago came to dominate the U.S. meat-packing industry, namely Armour and Company, Swift and Company, and Libby, McNeill and Libby.

Meat-packing subsequently moved farther west with the introduction of efficient motor trucks and the introduction of refrigeration. The big California market surpassed that of the state of New York, and even Chicago closed down its famed stockyards in 1971.

Meat-canning got a considerable boost through the Civil War in providing for the army, and after 1868 Armour and others developed a canned corned beef and roast beef trade. Other companies packed ox and pork tongues and potted meats, chicken, rabbits, ham, and soups.

Corned beef was packed by the Libby company in quadrangular cans that were awkward in shipping, but in 1875 a method was developed for pressing corned beef into tapered tin cans that were easily shipped. A European market was created and the demand for canned corned beef became so great in the United States that it affected the sale of fresh cuts.

Considerable quantities of meat were still smoked (chiefly with hickory wood) in the United States in 1900, when one Chicago firm had in operation forty-three smokehouses, each of which held 60,000 pounds of ham or shoulder or 120,000 pounds of side meat.

The introduction of efficient railroad refrigerator cars soon after 1880 made possible the transportation of fresh meat from as far west as Omaha to New York City without spoilage, and improvements in refrigeration created the possibility of marketing less salty ham and bacon, less heavily smoked meat, and glandular meats throughout the United States and the year round by the start of the century.

MECHANICS' INSTITUTES. Along with lyceums and apprentices' libraries, mechanics' institutes emphasized self-improvement through education in science and its applications. The New York Scientific and Mechanic Institution was established in 1822. Similar institutes quickly followed. Their mission was to provide low-cost technical education to the poor. By midcentury, however, evening lectures tended increasingly to be patronized by the middle classes, who wanted general talks on a miscellany of topics. Furthermore, technical instruction was more effectively carried out in formal classroom situations than by evening lectures. In time, some institutes merged with temperance societies; others were absorbed into the lyceum movement, became a basis for town libraries, were incorporated into new agencies for vocational training, or disappeared for lack of purpose.

MECHANICSVILLE, BATTLE OF (June 26, 1862). Sometimes called the Battle of Beaver Dam Creek. Gen. Robert E. Lee threw 36,000 troops across the Chickahominy toward Gen. Fitz-John Porter's front, east of Mechanicsville, Va. Confederate Gen. Thomas J. ("Stonewall") Jackson, marching from the Shenandoah Valley via Ashland with 18,500 troops, was to envelop the Union flank. Five brigades of A. P. Hill and James Longstreet's divisions of Lee's army assaulted Gen. George A. McCall's division, entrenched behind Beaver Dam Creek, and were severely repulsed. Jackson arrived too late to participate. During the night McCall withdrew and Porter concentrated behind Boatswain's Creek. (*See also* Peninsular Campaign.)

MECKLENBURG DECLARATION OF INDEPENDENCE. Document purportedly adopted by the citizens of Mecklenburg County, N.C., on May 20, 1775, in which they declared themselves independent of England. Most historians agree that the declaration is a "spurious document."

MECKLENBURG RESOLVES. On May 31, 1775, the Mecklenburg County Committee of Safety, meeting at Charlotte, N.C., drew up a set of twenty resolves that suspended all British governmental agencies in the county. It reorganized local government, elected county officials, and provided for nine militia companies held in readiness to execute the commands of the provincial congress. The document stopped short of declaring independence.

MEDAL OF HONOR. *See* **Decorations, Military.**

MEDIATION. *See* **Arbitration; Labor.**

MEDIATION AND CONCILIATION SERVICE, FEDERAL. *See* **Federal Agencies.**

MEDIATION BOARD, NATIONAL. *See* **Federal Agencies.**

MEDICAL EDUCATION. It has been estimated that of the 3,500 physicians in the colonies in 1776, no more than 400 had medical degrees, principally from schools in Edinburgh, London, and Leiden. Medical education in the colonies had scarcely begun. The College of Philadelphia had established the first college of medicine in 1765. King's College (now Columbia University) in New York City established (1767) the second. By 1800, only ten colleges had instituted any kind of medical instruction.

The quality of medical education was not high. The two-term curriculum was conceived as a supplement to, and not a substitute for, the preceptorial, or apprentice, system. The admission requirement was a college degree or its equivalent, including a satisfactory knowledge of Latin, mathematics, and natural and experimental philosophy. Typical requirements were courses in anatomy, materia medica, chemistry, and theory and practice of physic; practical clinical lectures; and one year attending the practice at a hospital. A certificate of apprenticeship and examinations were required before the M.B. was conferred. Then, after three or more years of experience and preparing and defending a thesis in Latin, a candidate was eligible for the M.D. degree. (After 1792 the M.B. degree was abolished.)

Proprietary medical schools, made up of independent self-appointed professors, became prevalent in the early 19th century. In the decades from 1820 to 1850 various state legislatures chartered such independent groups over whom little or no restraint was exercised. Not all proprietary schools had uniformly low standards, but the pressure of competition and the absence of detached governing boards forced standards down. Thus, medical practice was opened to many hundreds of Americans with scant education. By 1837 there were about 2,500 medical students enrolled in thirty-seven schools.

When the American Medical Association (AMA) was founded in 1847, its major goal was to elevate the standards of medical education. Persuasion was its only weapon; nothing substantial was accomplished until after the Civil War. Medical students began going to Europe, especially to German universities and to Vienna, in particular. Returning scholars, some of whom became teachers, started a renaissance in medical education. Progress was slow; even by 1900 little more than 15 percent of 25,000 matriculates in medical schools held a baccalaureate degree, and many students entered medical school with less than a high school diploma.

In 1890 sixty-six medical schools formed the Association of American Medical Colleges (AAMC). Jointly with the AMA's Council on Medical Education and Hospitals (1904), this association became a potent force in shaping the course of medical education. New state medical practice laws were slowly enacted, and medical schools—notably Pennsylvania and Harvard—began making improvements. The most encouraging advance in medical education during the late 19th century was the opening of the Johns Hopkins Hospital (1889) and the Johns Hopkins Medical School (1893). Although under separate boards, they operated essentially as a unit, patterned principally after the German system.

In 1910 a dramatic exposé, the Flexner Report, called attention to the condition of medical education throughout the United States and Canada. It brought to public attention the existence of numerous diploma-mill schools and the large number of mediocre institutions. The AAMC and the council began to classify schools as A, B, or C in quality. States began to reject graduates of class C schools as candidates for certification to practice. Of the 165 medical schools that existed in 1900, fewer than 70 remained within a few years of the publication of the report. By 1929 the A-B-C classification had been dropped, and all schools thereafter were classified as approved, on probation, or not approved. Certain standards came to be common: basic medical training was constituted as two years of preprofessional college education, a four-year graded curriculum, and an approved internship; medical schools maintained a substantial full-time clinical faculty and residency teaching programs.

Facilities were expanded after World War II to accommodate returning American veterans and foreign physicians seeking refresher or residency opportunities. Curricula were frequently upgraded in the light of the information explosion in medical science, initiated in the 1930's. The dramatic acceleration of research in the postwar years was aided by government grants and subsidies through the National Institutes of Health and other federal agencies.

MEDICAL RESEARCH. Early American medical research was sporadic, conducted by individuals, and most often clinically oriented. Important examples are the work of William W. Gerhard on the distinction between typhoid and typhus fevers (1837) and Oliver Wendell Holmes on the contagiousness of puerperal fever (1843); the experimental studies of gastric function by William Beaumont (1833); the introduction of ether anesthesia (1846) through the work of William T. G. Morton and Horace Wells; and the clinical experiments by J. Marion Sims leading to his discovery of a technique for the repair of vesicovaginal fistula (1852).

The first laboratory for experimental physiology in the United States—and one might better say for experimental medicine—was founded in 1871 by Henry P. Bowditch. The influence of German medical research may be seen in the opening of the William Pepper Laboratory of Clinical Medicine in 1894 at Philadelphia, the establishment of laboratories in the medical department at Johns Hopkins in 1905, the organization of the Hygienic Laboratory of the U.S. Public Health Service (1887), and the research laboratories of the New York City Health Department (1892–93).

Widespread public attention was brought to the idea of medical research by showing the great practical benefits in the prevention and treatment of disease that resulted from discoveries in microbiology, nutrition, and experimental medicine. Concurrently a reform of medical education was in the making. Progressive medical schools and hospitals had established pathological, bacteriological, and clinical laboratories. The number of trained researchers was increasing.

The response of private wealth provided the necessary stimulus and example. From 1900 to 1940 the influence of private agencies and funds was stronger than that of the federal government in medical research, owing largely to the impact of those extraordinary organizations established by John D. Rockefeller during the first two decades of the century, particularly the Rockefeller Institute for Medical Research, opened in 1906. Its staff envisioned the need for large-scale support of medical education in relation to research and indicated the major instruments for the achievement of the desired goals. In addition to the establishment of research laboratories, these means included endowment support of research-centered schools of medicine and public health, grants-in-aid for specific research projects, and training for research through fellowships and other means of support. Other privately endowed foundations that provided support for research in medicine and public health are Rockefeller, Carnegie, Duke, Milbank, Commonwealth, and Josiah Macy, Jr.

During and after World War II, the federal government emerged as the major source of support of medical research, especially through the research arm of the U.S. Public Health Service, the National Institutes of Health (NIH). By the mid-1960's the agencies of the U.S. Department of Health, Education, and Welfare provided about 70 percent of the federal funds for medical research. The NIH provided more than three-fifths of the total federal support. In the 1980's a group of solidly established national institutes for medical research existed with impressive intramural programs as well as broad extramural programs for the furtherance and support of research.

MEDICAL SECTS. As the 19th-century demand for health care increased, so did unorthodox systems of medicine. The major groups were the botanical practitioners, the homeopaths, the hydropaths, and the osteopaths. Although some still exist, such groups have become less acceptable to the public and to health professionals.

Samuel Thomson used sweat-producing, emetic, and purgative herbs as well as steam baths and enemas in treating all diseases. He attracted a wide following.

A German physician, Samuel Hahnemann, created a system of treatment based on the belief that drugs would cure if they caused the symptoms of the disease being treated. By 1900 there were twenty-two homeopathic schools, but only a few practitioners were still active in the 1980's.

Water was employed in cure treatments evangelically prescribed by an Austrian layman, Vincent Priessnitz, between 1826 and 1851. Hydropathic colleges, societies, and journals were established. Water-cure establishments appeared throughout the country, and thousands of patients "took the cure." By the late 19th century hydropathy had expanded from a simple treatment to a complex regimen.

Dr. Andrew Taylor Still, the founder of osteopathy, became disillusioned with orthodox remedies and developed a system of medical practice based on the belief that diseases resulted from malalignment of bones, especially those in the spine. By 1910 there were twelve schools of osteopathy, and doctors of osteopathy were eventually licensed in all states. The requirements for education and practice are similar to those of orthodox practice, and the sectarian characteristics of osteopathy have become less and less distinctive.

MEDICAL SOCIETIES. Using the American Medical Association (AMA, 1847) as a model, voluntary medical societies arose during the mid-19th century. They attempted to advance medical knowledge, elevate professional character, and protect the interests of their members. Specialization led to a host of additional societies. A few examples are American Pediatric Society (1888), American Urological Association (1902), American College of Surgeons (1913), American College of Physicians (1915), Aerospace Medical Association (1929), and American Academy of General Practice (1947). As the 20th century unfolded, the individual physician usually belonged to several societies. Membership in the AMA required membership in both a state and a county medical society. By 1972 there were more than 2,500 medical societies in the United States.

MEDICARE. The national program of health insurance for the aged, commonly called Medicare, was enacted in 1965. It finances most of the cost of hospital and nursing-home care for persons over sixty-five years of age through the Social Security system. It also provides voluntary reduced-cost insurance covering doctors' bills.

In 1945 President Harry S. Truman advanced a proposal for health insurance for the entire population, to be financed through Social Security. The American Medical Association, branding that proposal "socialized medicine," led the opposition. Labor groups headed the proponents. Only in 1965 did an act emerge from the Congress, but covering only the elderly.

MEDICINE, FOLK. *See* **Folk Medicine.**

MEDICINE, INDIAN. *See* **Indian Medicine.**

MEDICINE, MILITARY. Military medicine, as a specialty, has focused on the surgical management of mass casualties and on the prevention and treatment of infectious diseases, especially tropical diseases.

Army Medicine. Medical support for an American army began on July 27, 1775, when the Continental Congress established a medical service for Gen. George Washington's army when it was besieging Boston. The organization followed the model of the British army. A hospital corps, providing formal instruction for enlisted men as physicians' assistants, was established in 1887. The army's Nurse Corps was established in 1901, the Dental Corps in 1911, the Veterinary Corps in 1916, and the Sanitary Corps in 1917; the latter became the Medical Service Corps in 1947.

The major military contributions of the surgical disciplines have been in mass casualty management, the evacuation of wounded, and the treatment of battle wounds. Removal of the sick and wounded from the battlefield has always been a part of military operations, and the development of an organized system came about in 1862. The next major advance was the use of airplanes for evacuation of hospitalized patients in World War II and of helicopters as forward tactical air ambulances in the Korean and Vietnamese wars.

Communicable and infectious diseases have always been the major causes of morbidity among troops, and military medicine has made its greatest contributions in this area. Morbidity and mortality data were published beginning in 1840; they were the first national public-health statistics and the beginning of a national approach to public-health epidemiology. In World War I mortality from disease was for the first time less than that from battle wounds, and the application of infectious disease research to military sanitation produced this milestone in the history of war.

The founding in 1893 of the Army Medical School—the first school of public health and preventive medicine in the United States—was the beginning of formal postgraduate education in the basic sciences for army medical officers. Renamed the Walter Reed Army Institute of Research, it honored Walter Reed's work on the transmission of yellow fever in 1900: he and his colleagues, using volunteer test subjects, took only a few months to document mosquito transmission and define the organism as nonbacterial. The institute became the largest tropical medicine research organization in the United States.

Frederick F. Russell developed an American typhoid vaccine in 1909 at the Army Medical School. In 1911 the army was immunized—the first time for an entire army—and typhoid disappeared as a major cause of morbidity and mortality. The introduction of the use of anhydrous chlorine to purify drinking water in 1910 is the basis for present systems of municipal water purification. Army research was also important in the study of the hookworm, beriberi, malaria, typhus, encephalitis, hepatitis, and meningitis.

Navy Medicine. Congressional appropriations on Nov. 2, 1775, provided for surgeons on naval ships, but it was not until 1842 that the Bureau of Medicine and Surgery was established. The navy's Nurse Corps was established in 1903, and its Dental Corps in 1912. A naval laboratory for the production of pure drugs was founded in 1853. The Naval Medical School was established in 1902.

In 1958, navy physicians developed methods for fluid replacement in the treatment of cholera, which became standard procedures. Toxicological research on trace-element effects in the closed environment of submarines produced some of the earliest data now useful for civilian pollution studies.

Aviation Medicine. Aviation medicine began in 1917, when an army research laboratory and the School for Flight Surgeons were established. Louis H. Bauer, the first commandant of the school, wrote the first American textbook of aviation medicine in 1926. A separate Air Force Medical Department was established in 1949. In 1950 the School of Aerospace Medicine began biological research on the effects of space flight, and most of the medical work in the National Aeronautics and Space Administration was done by air force officers. Air force studies of anthropometry, human factors, designs of instruments, displays, and basic work in vibration effects and noise-level tolerance have had widespread application to design.

MEDICINE, OCCUPATIONAL. Attempts to maintain the worker's health and to prevent disease and work-related accidents. Health counseling and health maintenance have evolved as important facets of contemporary occupational medicine, along with psychological testing and industrial psychiatry. As safety engineering has emerged as a key aspect of accident prevention, so environmental engineering has emerged as a concern of occupational medicine.

The first U.S. mutual benefit society, or lodge, was formed by workers in 1793; such lodges strove to make a doctor available to their members. In the early 19th century, labor unions began to concern themselves with safe working conditions, and led by Massachusetts in 1836, the states began to enact laws limiting child labor and women's hours of work.

As the 19th century unfolded, some diseases were diagnosed as occupational. The lung problems among anthracite coal miners, particularly the illness now known as black lung, were described in 1869. Lead colic among lead miners was described in 1884. Safety conditions were considered a national scandal. Railroads, factories, mines, the construction industry, and lumbering all vied for "worst place" in work-connected accidents. Safety inspection and compensation for the results of accidents became public concerns.

The first major industrial medical-care prepayment plan to endure was organized by the Southern Pacific Railroad in 1868. The first company-financed medical department with a full-time staff providing complete medical care for employees and families was established by the Homestake Mining Company of Lead, S.Dak., in 1887.

In the cities, the mutual benefit societies multiplied, 38,000 lodges having been formed by 1867. A high proportion had a lodge doctor, and some built and administered hospitals. The first academic program in industrial medicine was established at Harvard University in 1917. In the following year, the *Journal of Industrial Hygiene* made its appearance; the *Journal of Industrial Medicine* appeared in 1932.

In 1914 the U.S. Public Health Service created a Division of Industrial Hygiene and Sanitation. This grew into the National Institute of Occupational Safety and Health. The formation of state industrial hygiene units was stimulated by the 1935 Social Security Act.

The first state to enact a workmen's compensation law was New York, in 1910, but not until 1955 had all the states enacted such legislation. In 1970 Congress authorized the use of the Social Security system to compensate for industrial diseases by providing work-connected disability payments.

Collective bargaining contracts as sources for medical-care payment grew rapidly after World War II. In 1947 the United Mine Workers of America began services to miners paralyzed from rock falls and to silicotics. It then developed a comprehensive medical care program. By the 1980's, most industrial workers had insurance coverage for hospitalization costs through their places of work.

MEDICINE AND SURGERY. When the United States came into being, there were only about 400 physicians with an earned M.D. degree in the nation. Medical schools were virtually nonexistent, and no regular licensing boards, medical societies, or hospitals existed until the late 18th century. Even by then only a bare beginning had been made in developing a profession of medicine in the United States with requisite educational institutions. (*See* Medical Education.)

Malaria, scurvy, dysentery, and the respiratory diseases of winter were prevalent in New England, the South, and the West. Tuberculosis was, throughout most of the 19th century, the leading cause of death. Sanatoriums built in many healthful mountain retreats were of some help. Against the repeated outbreaks of cholera and yellow fever, physicians were no more effective, but epidemics did spur local and national legislation that led to sanitary improvements.

In the heyday of heroic medicine, the 1810's and 1820's, nature was forced to take a back seat to vigorous dosing with drugs and bleeding with the lancet and by leeches. To the patient already weakened by fever, further insult was brought by blood loss, followed by calomel or castor oil to induce copious diarrhea. The theory was that the disease was caused by a maldistribution of the basic humors of the body—blood, phlegm, yellow bile, and black bile. Purging, bleeding, and blistering would redistribute the humors to their proper place and normal balance.

It would be misleading to assume that the work of the profession was entirely futile. In the first place, as has continued to be the case, many of the physician's therapeutic abilities rested not merely on the use of drugs but also on his skill and art. Second, there were some effective drugs—such as agents as cinchona, opium, and digitalis. By the 1830's, furthermore, important discoveries stemming from the work of Americans also began to appear. The physiological studies of digestion carried out by William Beaumont, published in 1833, captured European praise. In 1837 William W. Gerhard differentiated typhus from typhoid. In 1846, ether anesthesia was announced to the world with immediate acclaim.

American scientific medicine came into its own in the 1890's, and the growing importance of U.S. medicine and surgery in the 20th century may be demonstrated by a variety of yardsticks. Increasingly, discoveries were made in the leading centers of research. Some of those centers were in the medical schools; others were in privately endowed institutes, such as Rockefeller, Sloan-Kettering, and McCormick. The numbers of Nobel prizes awarded to Americans also began to increase as more and more of the influential medical literature originated on the western side of the Atlantic.

The 20th century has seen the increasing specialization of practitioners and the pronounced increase in hospitals and their use. An 1873 survey showed that there were only 149 hospitals for the care of the sick in the entire country, of which only six had been established prior to 1800; by 1973 there were more than 7,000 hospitals with 1.65 million beds. In the 19th century, only the poorer classes generally used hospitals. The upper classes nursed their sick in the home and submitted to surgery on the kitchen table. Postoperative infection rates were actually lower there than in hospitals. Not until the acceptance of Lister's principles of antisepsis in the 1870's and the advent of heat sterilization of operating-room equipment in the 1890's did surgery of the cavities of the body become feasible and safe. (*See* Hospitals.)

Along with changing patterns of medical care have gone changing patterns of disease and a slowly rising life expectancy (*see* Life Expectancy). In 1900 the commonest causes of death were infections, such as tuberculosis, influenza, and dysenteries. By the late 20th century heart disease, cancer, stroke, and accidents accounted for the majority of mortality. The age distribution of the population had changed as well, as the elderly and the very young came to constitute larger percentages. This demographic pattern had implications for medical care because it is precisely these two age groups that require the most physician visits and hospital beds.

MEDICINE CREEK COUNCIL (October 1867). Between the U.S. government and the Kiowa, Comanche, and Apache tribes and parts of the Arapaho and Cheyenne tribes, on Medicine Creek, in South Dakota. The Comanche and Kiowa agreed to relinquish their claims in the Texas Panhandle, and all the Indians accepted removal to new reservations set aside for them. The negotiations did not bring final peace in the Southwest, but went far toward doing so.

"MEDICINE MAN." *See* **Indian Medicine.**

MEDICINE SHOW. About 1830 Gideon Lincecum, a practicing physician, botanist, and entomologist began disseminating the knowledge—some of it secret—that he had learned from a Choctaw medicine man. The stage was prepared for the medicine show and the patent, cure-all medicine sold there. To sell this bottled magic, the showman gave his show free, on town squares or wherever he could find a drawing place for crowds. Often he claimed to be Indian. He employed blackface comedians. Songs and repartee jokes were his stock in trade, and he was an artist at entertaining the crowd while he mixed in praise of the supernal drug.

MEDITERRANEAN FUND. Proposed (1786) by Thomas Jefferson while minister to France. It would have created a single, international fleet to oppose Barbary pirates. The project was too visionary to be realized.

MEEKER MASSACRE (1879). Ute uprising against the arbitrary ways of agent N. S. Meeker of the Ute agency on White River, Colo. On Sept. 10, 1879, one of the Indians assaulted Meeker, and he requested military aid. Maj. T. T. Thornburgh marched with 200 men on Sept. 24 from Fort Fred Steele, Wyo. The Ute ambushed this detachment near Milk River on Sept. 29, killing Thornburgh and nine others. Other Ute attacked the agency, killing Meeker and seven employees, and carrying away three women. Gen. Wesley Merritt relieved Thornburgh's besieged troops on Oct. 5.

MEETINGHOUSE. Used by the Puritans for the church's assembly place; the same place often served for town meetings and other public gatherings. Typically it was a white frame rectangular structure, with end tower topped by a spire. The pulpit dominated the simple interior.

MEIGS, FORT. Built in 1813, on order of Gen. William Henry Harrison, on the south bank of the Maumee River opposite the present town of Maumee, Ohio. From Apr. 28 to May 9, 1813, it was besieged, unsuccessfully, by a force of British, Canadians, and Indians.

MELLON INSTITUTE OF INDUSTRIAL RESEARCH. Founded in 1913 by Andrew Mellon and his brother Richard as a part of the University of Pittsburgh. The institute prospered by providing research facilities for companies that did not have their own. It also subsidized pure research in chemistry. In 1957, an endowment from the Mellon family raised fundamental research to parity with industrial research, and the institute became a center for the training of postdoctoral fellows in science. In 1965 the Mellon Institute was merged into the Carnegie Institute of Technology (founded in 1900) to form Carnegie-Mellon University.

MELTING POT THEORY. Term used to express one theory of the development of American society. It suggests that American culture is a mixture of elements drawn from the different immigrant groups, and the native Indians where they survived. These different groups have actually fused together into a new culture.

Opposing are people who argue for "cultural pluralism." This theory suggests that different cultural patterns and life styles can, and should, exist together in America.

MELUNGEONS (from French *mélange*). Part-Indian people who have long lived in a remote mountain section of Hancock County, Tenn. The Bureau of American Ethnology classes them as an offshoot of the Croatan Indians, but others claim the original stock was Cherokee.

MEMORIAL DAY (last Monday in May). Began in 1868 as Decoration Day, observed on May 30. Its original purpose was to decorate the graves of Union soldiers killed in the Civil War. It has since become the day on which the United States honors the dead of all its wars.

MEMORIAL OF THE PLANTERS AND MERCHANTS OF LOUISIANA (1768). Appeal by citizens of Louisiana to Louis XV of France for support of their revolution against Spain. Louis XV refused to consider taking back the colony. Alexander ("Bloody") O'Reilly, crushed the revolution and established Spanish authority in 1769.

MEMPHIS (Tenn.). City in southwest Tennessee on the east bank of the Mississippi River, on the lowest of the Chickasaw Bluffs. The Chickasaw fixed it as the place where they crossed the Mississippi in their migration from the West. Fort Assumption was built by Jean Baptiste Le Moyne, Sieur de Bienville, on the bluff in 1739 as a base for his campaign against the Chickasaw. In 1795 the Spanish government erected Fort San Fernando, which stood until 1797 (*see* Guion's Expedition). The town was laid out in 1819 and incorporated in 1826. It was in Union hands throughout the Civil War. Rail and river transportation aided in the city's rapid development as a cotton center. But three yellow fever epidemics struck the city in the 1870's, and many fled. By 1900 Memphis was once again a thriving cotton center and the state's largest city. The population in 1980 was 646,356.

MEMPHIS, NAVAL BATTLE AT (June 6, 1862). The Union western flotilla, anchored across the Mississippi two miles above Memphis, was attacked by the Confederate river defense fleet. Three unarmed Union rams ran down past the Rebel flotilla and broke the double Confederate line. The gunboats followed, firing rapidly, and the Rebel fleet was destroyed in seventy minutes. Three Confederate vessels were sunk, four captured, and one escaped. Memphis immediately surrendered to the Union. (*See* Mississippi Squadron.)

MEMPHIS AND CHARLESTON RAILROAD. Begun at Charleston in 1829, by 1845 the road had reached Atlanta. In the same year Memphis was selected as the western terminus. In 1857 the Memphis and Charleston Railroad was completed, thereby breaking the monopoly of New Orleans on the lucrative export trade of the Mississippi Valley.

MENDOZA EXPEDITION (1683). The Jumano Indians of central Texas appealed to the governor of New Mexico for missionaries. In response, Juan Dominguez de Mendoza and Father Nicholás López established a temporary mission on the Colorado River. It was not made permanent.

MENÉNDEZ IN FLORIDA AND GEORGIA. On Aug. 28, 1565, Pedro Menéndez de Avilés arrived at St. Augustine, Fla., with 2,646 persons, for the purposes of colonization. He drove out the French, and the first Jesuit missionaries began their work in Florida. Within two years he had established a line of posts between Tampa Bay and Santa Elena, S.C., and erected forts at Guale in northern Georgia, at Tampa and Charlotte bays on the west coast of the peninsula, and at Biscayne Bay and the St. Lucie Inlet on the east coast. By 1615 more than twenty missions were established in Florida, Georgia, and South Carolina.

MENNONITES. Descendants of an Anabaptist group based on the teachings of Menno Simons. The first Mennonite settlers to come to the New World settled in Pennsylvania in 1683, coming to be known as the Pennsylvania Dutch. Later immigrants settled in the American and Canadian Midwest. Mennonites are generally pacifists who maintain a high degree of community discipline through moderate use of the ban. The Amish, a conservative body of Mennonites founded by Jacob Amman in the 1690's, are particularly notable because they maintain strict customs of dress and advocate separation from the world. In 1978 there were 97,142 members of Mennonite bodies.

"MEN OF THE WESTERN WATERS." People living along the frontiers of the eastern states between 1642 and 1785, referring generally to persons hunting or exploring in the neighborhood of the Ohio and Mississippi rivers.

MENOMINEE IRON RANGE. Situated mainly in the valley of the Menominee River, which lies on the boundary between the upper peninsula of Michigan and northern Wisconsin. Mining dates from the 1870's after the railroads connected the area to the Great Lake ports. Mines were opened at Vulcan, Norway, Iron Mountain, and Iron River, Mich., and at Florence, Wis.

MENTAL HYGIENE MOVEMENT. In 1908 Clifford W. Beers published a bestselling account of his bout with serious mental illness, *A Mind That Found Itself* and founded, first, the Connecticut Society for Mental Hygiene and, in 1909, the National Committee for Mental Hygiene. The committee conducted educational campaigns and recommended reforms in the hospitalization of the mentally ill. It did much to popularize psychiatry in the 1920's. In later years, the mental hygiene movement was associated increasingly with the community psychiatry movement.

MENTAL ILLNESS. American approaches to the care of the mentally ill have generally been derived from European models. By the early 18th century the ancient idea of mental disorder as divine retribution or satanic possession had given way to the view that it was a physical disease of the brain, amenable to treatment by physicians. In general, however, friends, relatives, or town authorities supplied care for "madmen" or "lunatics," often secreted and physically restrained in attics, outhouses, cellars, or shacks. Workhouses and jails frequently also housed the insane, where on rare occasions a physician might visit them. The first hospital in the colonies devoted exclusively to mental patients, now the Eastern State Hospital at Williamsburg, Va., opened in 1773. Lay keepers administered the small asylum with the advice of a physician, who came weekly to see patients and prescribed the conventional contemporary medical therapy—cathartics, emetics, bloodletting, cold and warm showers, and special diets and tonics. The same kinds of therapy were used at the Pennsylvania Hospital by Dr. Benjamin Rush, often called the father of American psychiatry, after he took charge of the mental patients in 1783. He also endeavored to deal with the emotional condition of the mental patients under his care. He tried to establish a kindly, albeit authoritarian, relationship with them and initiated improvements in their living conditions, including opportunity for some sort of occupation.

A system called moral treatment flourished during the early 19th century. It emphasized the emotional needs of patients through the creation of a total therapeutic, benevolent environment, stressing kindness and activity: occupational therapy (especially farming and gardening) was encouraged, and there were recreational programs, such as lectures, lantern-slide showings, and musical concerts. Open hospital practices were variously adopted in the form of open wards, freedom of the grounds, and group activities. New hospitals both state and private, on the moral treatment model opened. There were approximately 26 mental hospitals in the United States by 1849, over 60 by 1866, and 200 by 1900. In 1844 approximately 3.1 percent of the presons estimated to be insane (probably no more than half are so recognized at any time) were in mental hospitals, and by 1900, 24 percent; not until 1940 did the figure rise to 60 percent, most of the patients living in giant state hospitals. The Association of Medical Superintendents of American Institutions for the Insane (later the American Psychiatric Association) was founded in 1844, as was the *American Journal of Insanity* (predecessor of the *American Journal of Psychiatry*). Both helped to spread the idea of moral treatment.

Moral treatment declined after the Civil War. Social resentment against the large immigrant population brought with it a revival of theories of the hereditary and incurable nature of insanity. Concomitantly the germ theory of disease encouraged a reversion to a physiological approach to mental illness. Most hospitals became primarily custodial.

By the turn of the century, a new medical specialist, the neurologist, had begun to dominate psychiatry. A large proportion of the neurologists' patients seemed to be suffering from a supposedly newly discovered disorder, named neurasthenia. It actually resembled the hysteria and hypochondria of old and the conditions called neuroses in the 20th century. The preferred treatment for neurasthenia, which was characterized by weakness, lassitude, tension, and anxiety, was bed rest, nourishing food, and isolation, with a dose of moralizing about self-control. Most were treated by neurologists in their private offices, and thereby was initiated a dual system of dealing with emotional disorders: psychotics within hospitals and neurasthenics (neurotics) in private practice.

Psychoanalysis was first applied to nonpsychotic patients and then tried with psychotics in some hospitals. A trend that began at about the same time was the establishment of the psychopathic hospital as a teaching and research center. The prototype was the Phipps Psychiatric Clinic at Johns Hopkins, which opened in 1913. A new reform movement was launched in 1909 with the founding of the National Committee for Mental Hygiene (*see* Mental Hygiene Movement.)

During the 1930's shock therapy became popular in American mental hospitals—insulin shock, metrazol, and then electroshock, which became in the 1940's the method of choice among nonpsychoanalytically oriented psychiatrists. Another "new" treatment, psychosurgery, came into widespread use, commonly in the form of lobotomy. Lobotomy declined by the 1960's as more effective drugs came into use.

In 1950 the tranquilizer chlorpromazine was synthesized. Thereafter the number of psychopharmacological compounds, especially tranquilizers, and antidepressants, used in the treatment of mental illness proliferated. By the 1980's, psychopharmacology dominated the care of the mentally ill.

Concomitant with the appearance of the new drugs, new psychologically and sociologically oriented approaches to patient care. Among them were milieu therapy, which resembled the moral treatment of a century before, and various behavior modification techniques

Some reformers, recognizing that long-term hospitalization frequently harmed patients, instituted a policy whereby patients were released to halfway houses or other community follow-through programs that monitor the patients progress and supply whatever therapy was required. Severe cutbacks in funds during the late 1970's and early 1980's, however, caused an erosion of the community health programs designed as alternatives to hospital care. The result often was former mental patients left to fend for themselves on the streets.

MERCANTILE AGENCIES. Established after the panic of 1837 to supply credit information to would-be lenders. The first agency, started in 1841, later became R. G. Dun and Company. In 1849 the Bradstreet Company was started. These were the only two general agencies to survive and they were merged into Dun and Bradstreet, Inc., in 1933. It supplies financial and credit ratings and information on concerns in the United States and in many foreign countries.

MERCANTILISM. An economic theory in which a country took measures intended to regulate trade, production, and manufacture. To England the colonies were regarded as chiefly producers of raw materials and markets for goods produced in England. Colonial manufacture for an export trade that competed with that of the home country was discouraged by prohibitive legislation. On the other hand, colonial production of articles needed within the empire was encouraged, and bounties were paid to promote colonial production of such products. The colonial markets were developed by favors instead of compulsion. The usual inducement was export bounties, especially in the case of British manufactures that had foreign competition. Both England and the colonies profited from this 18th-century policy of enlightened mercantilism, and it is difficult to find opposition to the system among revolutionary Americans, so long as measures were purely regulatory and did not levy a tax on the colonists. The system was specifically approved by the First Continental Congress in the Declaration of Rights of Oct. 14, 1774.

MERCER, FORT, ENGAGEMENTS AT (Oct. 22 and Nov. 20, 1777). In the first attack, British Gen. William Howe dispatched 1,200 Hessian troops against the colonial force of 400 at Fort Mercer at Red Bank, N.J.; they were repulsed but attacked again a month later with greater numbers. The fort was then dismantled.

MERCHANT ADVENTURERS. *See* **Adventurers.**

MERCHANT FLEET CORPORATION. *See* **Emergency Fleet Corporation.**

MERCHANT MARINE. The New England colonists took to the sea almost at once. Much of their lumber and fish cargo went to the West Indies to be exchanged for sugar, molasses, or rum; some went along the coast to be exchanged for grain or flour; and some crossed the Atlantic. England's Navigation Laws, aimed at developing a self-sufficient empire, benefited them. (*See* also Mercantilism.) By 1700, Boston ranked third, after London and Bristol, among all English ports in the tonnage of its shipping. By 1730, Philadelphia passed it in commerce, but the New England coast remained the center of shipping activity.

The Revolution brought only a short-lived dislocation of trade. The long Anglo-French wars, starting in 1793, put a premium on the neutral status of American-flag shipping, which could visit ports where the British or French belligerent flags would be vulnerable. The Americans reaped a rich profit. Their registered tonnage tripled from 1790 to 1810, as did combined exports and imports, about 90 percent of which was carried in American bottoms.

After the War of 1812, the U.S. Merchant Marine went through a fairly quiet period. The two principal developments were the rapid expansion of steam navigation and the performance of the transatlantic sailing packets. Robert Fulton's *Clermont* steamed up the Hudson River from New York to Albany and back in 1807. New York quickly utilized the sheltered waters of Long Island Sound as a steam approach to New England, while the ability of steamboats to ascend the Mississippi and its tributaries quickly revolutionized and promoted traffic on western waters. Permanent transatlantic steam navigation dates from 1838, when two British steamships, the *Sirius* and the *Great Western,* arrived at New York on the same day. The American sailing packets from New York to Liverpool, London, and Le Havre had dominated the North Atlantic run since 1818. These square-riggers, sailing on specified dates with passengers, mail, and fine freight, had demonstrated the value of regular line service.

By the 1840's immigration, Britain's repeal of its Corn and Navigation laws, and the discovery of gold in California were combining to bring the American merchant marine to its golden age in the early 1850's, almost equaling Britain's shipping in tonnage and surpassing it in quality.

Oceangoing shipping suffered during the Civil War from Confederate naval raiders. Actually, they caught barely one Union ship in a hundred, but the panic they generated so raised war-risk insurance rates that shippers sought foreign flags that called for no such extra expense. Scores of the finest American square-riggers were consequently transferred to foreign registry and were not permitted to return afterward.

Probably the basic cause of the decline in American oceangoing shipping was the upward surge in the use of steam. The big American square-riggers and the fast but small sailing clippers could not compete.

Congress tried vainly to stimulate American shipping with subsidies for lines to Brazil and the Far East. From 1860 to 1910 the share of U.S. imports and exports carried in American bottoms shrank from 66 percent to 8 percent. With the protected domestic trade, it was a different story. From the 2,974,000 tons of enrolled and licensed shipping in 1860, it had climbed to 6,726,000 tons by 1910.

World War I made the United States suddenly aware of how serious it was to lack shipping flying its own flag. In 1916, Congress established the U.S. Shipping Board, the first body specifically charged with supervision of the merchant marine. The Shipping Board's ambitious shipbuilding program set up numerous new yards, and much of this activity was continued after the war. By 1921 the United States had overtaken Great Britain for first place among the world's merchant fleets; it had some 700 new large steel freighters and 575 smaller ones.

More nearly permanent in national merchant-marine policy, however, was the use of many of the other new freighters on government-supported "essential trade routes" to all parts of the world. At first the new lines were operated directly for the Shipping Board, but as soon as they were on a paying basis, the ships were auctioned off at bargain rates to private operators who would agree to maintain regular service on their lines for a period of years. In 1929 the Jones-White Act provided generous grants to those approved lines that agreed to build new ships.

The depression of the 1930's again threatened U.S. shipping. Congress in 1936 passed the Merchant Marine Act. The Maritime Commission (later the Federal Maritime Board) set policy and the Maritime Administration managed operation. Congress established operating subsidies that went only to lines approved for specific "essential trade routes"; there were usually from a dozen to fifteen such lines on thirty-odd routes from Atlantic, Gulf, or Pacific ports.

During World War II the subsidized merchant marine fully demonstrated its high value, through its adequate ships and operational skill, which did much to provide logistical support for far-flung military operations. Once again the government undertook a tremendous emergency building program, which produced 5,777 vessels, about half of them slow, capacious "Liberty ships."

The foreign services on the essential trade routes continued on a fairly successful basis after the war. Domestic shipping fell off sharply in the coastal and intercoastal trades, in part because of increased competition from railroads and trucks.

In 1970 Congress passed the Merchant Marine Act, which extended and liberalized the 1936 act. It had an immediate quickening effect on merchant shipping; numerous applications for subsidies were made, and plans were laid to build vessels. But the initial exuberance was suddenly dampened when President Richard M. Nixon's 1973 budget slashed the funding of the program $455 million to $275 million.

It was remarked that shipping underwent more drastic changes around 1970 than in any period since the mid-19th century. The jet airplanes virtually drove out regular ocean passenger service. Containerization, with truck bodies, railroad freight cars, and other preloaded containers carried aboard ship were efforts to cut labor costs. Oil tankers increased more than tenfold in size, special ships were developed for natural gas, and bulk carriers were developed to bring iron and other ore from overseas.

MERCHANT MARINE ACTS. *See* **Merchant Marine.**

MERCHANTMEN, ARMED. In the colonial and postrevolutionary periods American shipping interests armed their merchant vessels against piracy and privateering. This self-defense for their merchantmen was linked to freedom of the seas, a condition essential to national economic survival. In 1805 Congress provided that such ships post bond that their ordnance would be used for defense only. During the War of 1812, U.S. armed merchant ships sailed clandestinely in and out of British ports, including the West Indies.

The Declaration of Paris (Apr. 16, 1856) abolished privateering. This action, coupled with the gradual disappearance of piracy, rendered the practice of arming merchantmen virtually obsolete. Nevertheless, in World War I President Woodrow Wilson authorized the arming of U.S. merchant ships in reaction to Germany's unrestricted submarine warfare. During World War II, Congress authorized the use aboard merchant ships of naval armed guards similar to those of World War I.

The convoy routes to Murmansk and to the Mediterranean were among the most dangerous in the history of armed merchantmen. The Allied combat campaigns would never have succeeded without the merchant ship convoys.

MEREDITH CRISIS (Sept. 30–Oct. 10, 1962). James Meredith, a black student, was admitted to the University of Mississippi under federal court order. Attempts to prevent Meredith from attending the university, led by Gov. Ross Barnett, resulted in a riot in which two were killed and federal troops, along with the federalized National Guard, were called up by President John F. Kennedy.

MERIDIAN CAMPAIGN (February 1864). Gen. Ulysses S. Grant sent a force of 20,000 men under Gen. William Tecumseh Sherman to Vicksburg for advance eastward to Meridian, Miss., to destroy Confederate supply depots and railroads. He left Vicksburg on Feb. 3, opposed only by weak Confederate forces. He expected cavalry support, but on Feb. 20 Confederate cavalry under Gen. Nathan B. Forrest stopped that support and Sherman returned to Vicksburg.

MERRILL'S MARAUDERS. A 3,000-man, all-volunteer force, officially the 5307th Provisional Unit, and nicknamed Merrill's Marauders after the field commander, Gen. Frank D. Merrill. Its assignment, in 1943, was to retake north Burma and reopen the land route to China (*see* Burma Road and Ledo Road). Highly mobile, the Marauders were to spearhead short envelopments while Gen. Joseph W. Stilwell's main Chinese columns pushed back the enemy's front.

Entering combat Feb. 24, 1944, the Marauders made an extremely costly five-month, 500-mile trek to take the crucial river town of Myitkyina. Its seige ended successfully Aug. 3 with 123 of the Marauders dead and 8 missing.

***MERRIMAC*, SINKING OF** (June 3, 1898). In the Spanish-American War, an unsuccessful effort to block the harbor entrance at Santiago de Cuba, thereby bottling up a Spanish fleet. Richmond Pearson Hobson with seven men sank the collier *Merrimac* across the narrow entrance; but only two of its sinking charges exploded, and as finally sunk it did not lie athwart the channel or close it effectively. Hobson and his crew were taken prisoner.

MERRIMACK. *See* ***Monitor*** **and** ***Merrimack*****, Battle of.**

MERRYMAN, EX PARTE (1861). A Supreme Court decision in which Chief Justice Roger B. Taney, writing for the majority, ruled that the writ of habeas corpus could be suspended constitutionally only by Congress, not by the president (*see Milligan, Ex Parte*).

MERRY MOUNT (or Mount Wollaston). Site of an Indian trading post, in Quincy, Mass. It was established about 1625 by Thomas Morton, who later erected a Maypole. His practice was to get the Indians drunk before trading with them; and the combination of neglected Indian husbands, liquor, and gunpowder was regarded as a public menace. As a result, Myles Standish was sent in June 1628 to arrest him in the king's name. Morton was sent off to England, from which he returned shortly to set up the Maypole again and resume his practices. Gov. John Endecott cut down the pole again. The Puritans offered to take Morton into the fur-trading monopoly, but he refused because its methods were less profitable. So he was again shipped off to England, where he got revenge by writing his amusing *New English Canaan,* the first of the attacks on the New Englanders.

MESABI IRON RANGE. In northeastern Minnesota, it contained the richest deposit of iron ore in the United States. When its great value became known in the 1890's, there was an unparalleled scramble to enter the land through abuse of the Preemption Act (1841) and the Homestead Act (1862) and for the choicer deposits with the rarer forms of land scrip. John D. Rockefeller acquired some of the greatest deposits. He in turn sold them to Andrew Carnegie, who transferred them to the United States Steel Corporation. More than 2.5 billion tons of ore have been mined from the Mesabi range, but by the middle 1960's the richest of the hematite ore was gone. Only then were the deposits of taconite appreciably valued.

MESA VERDE, PREHISTORIC RUINS OF. The runs in Mesa Verde National Park (52,073 acres) in Colorado represent the most extensive and best preserved of pre-Columbian cliff dwellings. The builders were a race of Indians, supposedly the predecessors of the present Pueblo. The dwellings and temples were composed of stone, clay, and supporting poles. The cliff dwellers flourished in the 11th and 12th centuries, and it is supposed that they were forced to abandon the mesa canyons by a severe drought in 1276.

MESILLA (N. Mex.). An unincorporated town in Dona Ana County, originally situated on the west side of the Rio Grande, but since 1865, because of a change in the river's channel, on the east. In 1861–62, Mesilla was made the capital of a Confederate territory of Arizona.

MESQUITE. A small tree of the Southwest. It can withstand the severest droughts and produce beans, which livestock can exist on, and from which Indians and Mexicans make brew and bread. Its trunks can be used as fence posts and its limbs and roots as fuel.

MESSIAH WAR (1890–91). An outgrowth of the Ghost Dance excitement among the Sioux Indians and the culmination of which was the Battle of Wounded Knee. When troops arrived on Oct. 19, 1890, to quell the disturbance, thousands of Indians fled to the Badlands. Gen. Nelson A. Miles apprehended Chief Sitting Bull, then living on Grand River; the chief was killed, together with six Indian police and eight of his own followers, while resisting arrest. Skirmishing in the Badlands followed, and on Dec. 28 Maj. S. M. Whitside, Seventh Cavalry, discovered the principal band of hostile Indians, under Big Foot, camped on Wounded Knee Creek. Big Foot surrendered, but a massacre of the Indians followed. An estimated 200 to 300 Indians were killed and 29 whites lost their lives. This battle was the only important action. After a few more skirmishes, the overwhelming force under Miles overawed the Sioux and compelled their surrender at Pine Ridge Agency early in January 1891.

METEOROLOGY. The first contributions to scientific meteorology in America were the famous experiments of Benjamin Franklin in the fields of lightning, atmospheric electricity, cyclone theory, and ocean circulation, during the years from 1748 to 1775. In 1821 William Redfield correctly deduced the rotary, progressive nature of the hurricane. Later he published a series of papers leading to the first nearly correct mathematical theory and proof of the "law of storms." James Pollard Espy attempted (in 1828) an explanation of the initial cause and maintenance of the energy of a cyclonic storm on thermodynamic principles. He became world famous because of his "convective" theory of clouds and thunderstorms as well as cyclones. Espy also prepared the first long series of daily analyzed weather charts and was the first official government meteorologist in the United States. Elias Loomis introduced the modern weather chart. He collected observations from all over the eastern and central states and lower Canada and drew colored charts showing the boundaries of clear, cloudy, rainy, and snowy weather. M. F. Maury, a naval officer and founder and director of the U.S. Hydrographic Office in Washington, D.C., pioneered in the compilation of marine charts and sailing directions for all the world's oceans (1847) and an influential textbook on marine meteorology and oceanography (1855).

Joseph Henry's work on magnetism and induction helped to usher in the age of the telegraph, which he was the first to employ (1849) for transmitting weather observations to Washington from observers throughout the United States. As the first secretary of the Smithsonian Institution, Henry collected, analyzed, and posted daily synoptic weather reports and had the data carefully recorded and published for climatological purposes. He also had instruments carefully calibrated and compared with standard instruments of all varieties for atmospheric and solar observations. Henry initiated the study of the light and heat radiated by the sun and received at various places on earth, at sea level, and at high altitudes and the development of instruments capable of measuring solar heat in various areas of the spectrum. The Smithsonian standard instruments have become the basis for worldwide comparisons of instruments and observations.

William Ferrel published his first classical paper on motions in the atmosphere in 1856. It constituted an extremely lucid exposition of the mechanical forces acting on air parcels moving on a rotating earth in the presence of such modifying forces as heating from below in the tropics, cooling in the Arctic, and evaporation and condensation of water vapor. Ferrel is recognized as the father of modern dynamic meteorology and oceanography. The work of L. F. Richardson during the first two decades of the 20th century evolved into the computer models and forecasting method of today, which had ultimately resulted in more successful prediction of disasters, as well as normal, weather phenomena.

METES AND BOUNDS. The ancient system of indicating boundaries of landholdings by reference to natural objects such as trees and stones, as opposed to the modern system based on astronomical lines. The metes and bounds system, which prevails generally in that portion of the country settled before 1785, has caused much uncertainty concerning legal titles and boundaries of holdings.

METHODISTS. In 1771 John Wesley, founder of the Methodist church in England, sent Francis Asbury, who was to become the great apostle of early Methodism, to America. After the revolutionary war, the Methodists completely separated from the Anglican (Episcopal) church. The Christmas Conference, held in Baltimore in 1784, marks the beginning of the Methodist church in America. The conference decided on a form of government by deacons, elders, and superintendents (later bishops); adopted the Book of Discipline, which regulated the life of the church and its members; and elected Thomas Coke and Asbury as its first superintendents.

Methodism entered a period of rapid expansion. The system of circuit riders met the need for clergymen in outlying regions and allowed relatively uneducated men to enter the ministry. The Methodist combination of simplicity, discipline, organization, and lay participation made it the largest Protestant denomination.

The question of slavery, an important issue for churches in both the North and the South, led to the formation of three separate ecclesiastical bodies: the Methodist Episcopal church (1844); the Methodist Episcopal church, South (1844); and the Wesleyan Methodist Connection, a small antislavery church founded in 1843. After the Civil War most black Methodists formed their own denominations.

In the 20th century, Methodism has made some efforts to heal the divisions within its own ranks. In 1939 the Methodist Episcopal church; the Methodist Episcopal church, South; and the Methodist Protestant church merged. In 1968 this church merged with the Evangelical United Brethren to form the United Methodist church.

The principal Methodist groups and their 1980 membership figures are United Methodist church, 9,584,791 members; African Methodist Episcopal church, 1,970,000 members; African Methodist Episcopal Zion church, 1,125,176 members; Christian Methodist Episcopal church, 466,718 members; Evangelical Methodist church, 9,730 members; Free Methodist church of North America, 70,183 members; Primitive Methodist church, U.S.A., 10,222 members; Reformed Methodist Union Episcopal church, 45,000 members; Southern Methodist Church, 11,000 members.

METROPOLITAN STATISTICAL AREAS, STANDARD. *See* **Population.**

MEUSE-ARGONNE OFFENSIVE (Sept. 26–Nov. 11, 1918). The Allied operation that brought World War I to an end. On Sept. 26, 1918, the American First Army initiated its campaign to take Sedan, the strategic hub of German railroad communications. Precipitating heavy combat, the American left deployed via the Argonne forest and the right along the marshes of the Meuse River. The long-standing German defenses were in four lines ten miles deep. Continual rain compounded difficulties of terrain and severely hampered action and supply. The third German line checked the advance on Oct. 3. The results to that date —such as destroying sixteen German divisions—were less than Gen. John J. Pershing had hoped for. However, German generals warned the Reichstag that defeat was inexorably nearing. By Oct. 31 the third German line had been fragmented by the Americans. In the clearing of the deadly

Argonne was the saga of the "Lost Battalion" and the unparalleled exploit of Sgt. Alvin C. York.

All along the western front, the Germans were near exhaustion. On Nov. 1, a renewed attack carried the Americans six miles through the last German line and onto the heights of Barricourt, capture of which compelled the Germans to withdraw west of the Meuse. In retreat and disarray, German troops still fought sharply, but their cause was being rendered militarily chaotic. In the climactic Meuse-Argonne offensive, Pershing deployed twenty-one divisions, comprising some 1.2 million men, of whom one-tenth were casualties in capturing 48,800 prisoners and 1,424 guns.

MEXICAN ASSOCIATION. Organization formed to secure the liberation of Mexico from Spanish rule. Formed in 1805 in New Orleans, it consisted of 300 men interested in establishing American influence in Mexico. Aaron Burr hoped to utilize the Mexican Association in his land conquest conspiracy of 1806; it did in fact back the filibustering expeditions of Francisco Javier Mina and James Long.

MEXICAN BOUNDARY. The Adams-Onís Treaty of 1819 was an attempt to fix a boundary between American and Spanish sovereignties. When Mexico became independent in 1821, it became the basis for the U.S.-Mexican boundary. Various factors—Texas independence, the Mexican War, and conflicting mappings—intervened, however, and the dispute as to the boundary from the Rio Grande to the Colorado under the Treaty of Guadalupe Hidalgo was only ended by the Gadsden Treaty of Dec. 30, 1853, as it went into force on June 30, 1854. The boundary ran from the Gulf of Mexico up the Rio Grande to the southern boundary of New Mexico. The line westward from the Rio Grande ran, as it does now, from 31°47′ north latitude due west one hundred miles, then south to 31°20′ north latitude, and from there along that parallel to 111° west longitude, then going in a straight line to a point on the Colorado River twenty English miles below the junction of the Gila and Colorado, and, finally, up the middle of the Colorado some twenty miles to a point nearly seven miles to the west of the junction of the Gila and Colorado and about ten miles by water below that junction, meeting at that point the boundary from the Colorado to the Pacific. That line of the Gadsden Treaty is now the boundary between Mexico and the states of New Mexico and Arizona, and throughout its entire course from the Rio Grande to the Colorado is well to the south of any possible line under the Treaty of Guadalupe Hidalgo. No change was made by the Gadsden Treaty in the line from the Pacific to the Colorado River (the southern boundary of California).

The boundary between the two countries remains the same, except for the *bancos,* or small tracts of land in the valleys of the rivers that are isolated when the river changes course. One such *banco,* a strip of land known as the Chamizal tract of about 600 acres around El Paso, Tex., and Ciudad Juárez, in Mexico, was the subject of dispute until 1963, when, by the Chamizal Treaty, Mexico received 437 acres and the United States, 133 acres. An artificial riverbed was dug to prevent the Rio Grande from shifting again.

MEXICAN CESSION. *See* **Guadalupe Hidalgo, Treaty of.**

MEXICAN DECREE (Apr. 6, 1830). Sought to save Texas for Mexico by stopping immigration from the United States. Garrisons were sent to Texas to enforce the law, but the Americans already in Texas ignored its provisions and eventually (1836) declared the independence of Texas from Mexico.

MEXICAN GULF PORTS, BLOCKADE OF (1846–48). In the Mexican War. The first success was the capture of Frontera at the mouth of the Tabasco River, on Oct. 23, 1846, by Capt. Matthew Calbraith Perry. On Nov. 14 Commodore David Conner captured Tampico. In March 1847 Veracruz surrendered to Perry and Gen. Winfield Scott. Lt. C. G. Hunter captured Alvarado on Mar. 30, prematurely against orders, and for this was dismissed from the service. Perry proceeded with his squadron of sixteen vessels to Tuspan. On Apr. 18 the town, located five miles above the mouth of the Tuspan River, was captured by ships' barges towed by six small gunboats. Leaving two vessels here, Perry sailed with the rest to Frontera. Ascending the river eighty miles to Tabasco on June 15 and 16, Perry took and held the place. Perry's squadrons cruised up and down the coast until the signing of the Guadalupe Hidalgo Treaty on Feb. 2, 1848.

MEXICAN OIL CONTROVERSY. The expropriation, in 1938, of British and U.S. oil companies. After the U.S. companies, more intransigent than the British, rejected a settlement approved by the highest Mexican labor board, President Lázaro Cárdenas ordered the expropriation of the companies' concessions. The day Mar. 18, 1938, is still celebrated in Mexico as marking "economic independence." The companies claimed their investments and land holdings were worth nearly $500 million, but after long negotiations, a commission agreed in April 1942 that Mexico should pay $24 million to the U.S. companies, and a later settlement was also reached with British companies.

MEXICAN WAR (1846–48). Its immediate cause was U.S. annexation of Texas, which the Mexican government regarded as equivalent to a declaration of war. The American government adopted a conciliatory policy, particularly since it wanted to acquire California and New Mexico from Mexico. President James K. Polk appointed John Slidell as envoy-minister on a secret mission to purchase those territories.

Mexico refused to reopen diplomatic relations. In January 1846, after the Mexican government had refused to receive Slidell, Polk ordered Gen. Zachary Taylor to advance from Corpus Christi, Tex., to the Rio Grande, resulting shortly in conflicts with Mexican troops (*see* Palo Alto, Battle of; Resaca de la Palma, Battle of). On May 11, after arrival of news of the Mexican advance across the Rio Grande and the skirmish with Taylor's troops, Polk submitted to Congress a skillful war message, stating that war existed and that it was begun by Mexico on American soil. He obtained prompt action authorizing a declaration of war.

The military plans included an expedition under Col. Stephen W. Kearny to New Mexico and California, supplemented by an expedition to Chihuahua; an advance across the Rio Grande into Mexico by troops under Taylor to occupy the neighboring provinces; and a possible later campaign of invasion of the Mexican interior from Veracruz.

In these plans Polk was largely influenced by assurances that Antonio López de Santa Anna, then in exile, would cooperate in a peaceful arrangement to cede Mexican territory after the United States put him back in power. The U.S. Navy permitted Santa Anna to pass through Veracruz (*see* Mexican War, Navy in). Having arrived in Mexico, Santa Anna was promptly restored to power, but he made no effort to honor his assurances.

Kearny completed his occupation of New Mexico and California (*see* Doniphan's Expedition; Kearny's March to California). The expedition of Taylor into northern Mexico, reached its climax in February 1847, at Buena Vista. Taylor stubbornly resisted and defeated the attack of Santa Anna's Mexican relief expedition.

Soon thereafter the theater of war shifted to Veracruz, from which the direct route to the Mexican capital seemed to present less difficulty than the northern route. Gen. Winfield Scott was placed in command of the expedition. After the capture of the fortress of Veracruz on Mar. 29, 1847, Scott led his army westward via Jalapa to Pueblo, which he entered on May 15 and from which he began (Aug. 7) his advance to the mountain pass of Cerro Gordo.

In August, after the battles of Contreras and Churubusco, Scott agreed to an armistice as a step toward a diplomatic conference to discuss peace terms—a conference that began on Aug. 27 and closed on Sept. 7 with Mexican rejection of the terms offered. Scott promptly resumed his advance. After hard fighting (Sept. 7–11) at the battles of Molino del Rey and Chapultepec, he captured Mexico City on Sept. 14. Santa Anna was obliged to flee from Mexico.

A peace treaty was completed and signed on Feb. 2, 1848, at Guadalupe Hidalgo. By its terms, Mexico ceded all claims to Texas, and the United States agreed to pay $15 million for New Mexico and California.

MEXICAN WAR, NAVY IN. Because the wide mountainous wastes of northern Mexico constituted a barrier to military invasion of Mexico from the United States, in Washington, D.C., it was decided the main invasion should be made from a naval-supported base at Veracruz, in eastern Mexico.

Meanwhile the Pacific Squadron seized Monterey, San Diego, San Francisco, and other key points on the Pacific, thereby guaranteeing American possession of California. As preparation for Gen. Winfield Scott's invasion from Veracruz, the navy set up an effective blockade (*see* Mexican Gulf Ports, Blockade of).

MEXICAN WAR CLAIMS (1876). Settled by a commission created by the U.S. and Mexican governments. Claims against the United States arose largely from Indian depredations and excesses committed by American soldiers. Those presented against Mexico were largely for the seizure and destruction of property, forced loans, illegal arrests and imprisonments, and murder.

MEXICO, CONFEDERATE MIGRATION TO. After the Civil War an estimated 2,500 Confederate leaders moved to Mexico. Colonies were planted in the provinces of Chihuahua, San Luis Potosí, Jalisco, and Sonora. The best known was the Cordova Valley Colony (*see* Carlotta, Confederate Colony of). Migration to Mexico was encouraged by offering low-priced public lands, free transportation, and toleration for the Protestant churches and schools; but the movement failed for a variety of economic and political reasons. By 1867 most of the adventurers had returned to the United States.

MEXICO, FRENCH IN. In June 1862, a French army, representing the ambitions of Napoleon III, captured Mexico City. A monarchy was declared, to be headed by Ferdinand Maximilian, archduke of Austria, the personal selection of Napoleon III. Maximilian sought to secure recognition by the United States, but it continued to support President Benito Juárez.

During the U.S. Civil War, the United States made mild protests against French intervention, but after the defeat of the South, the United States brought strong pressure on the French. Finally, on Mar. 12, 1867, the last detachment of French soldiers left Mexican soil. The soldiers of Juárez soon captured Maximilian, who was deserted by his Mexican followers. The unfortunate prince was court-martialed and shot on June 19, 1867.

MEXICO, GULF OF. Strategically important since the early Spanish search for a possible water passage through the continental barrier, the Spanish settlement at Havana, Cuba, in 1519, the expedition of Hernando Cortes into the interior from Veracruz, Mexico, and the discovery of gold in Mexico. Later several settlements were planted along the northern coast: a Spanish settlement at Pensacola in 1696, and French settlements at Mobile in 1702 and New Orleans in 1718.

Its subsequent increased importance was especially due to its relations as the receiver of the Mississippi drainage and as the natural commercial outlet of the trans-Allegheny West. American access to the Gulf was secured by the acquisition of Louisiana by purchase in 1803 and by the consequent American claim to the entire Gulf coast from the Perdido on the east to the Rio Grande on the west.

Cuba, which guards the commercial portal water between the Gulf and the Atlantic, was regarded as the strategic key to the Gulf, and therefore to the Mississippi. In the 1850's prominent southern leaders urged the acquisition of Cuba (*see* Ostend Manifesto) as a means of making the Gulf a *mare clausum,* that is, practically an American lake. The commercial and political interests of the United States resulted in the expulsion of Spain (1898) from its last foothold in the Western Hemisphere (*see* Spanish-American War). The Cuban Missile Crisis of 1962 was a latter-day example of U.S. jealousy of its rights in the Gulf.

The Gulf of Mexico continues to be of great economic significance. There are vast oil and gas reserves and great supplies of fish and sulfur. During the 1970's approximately 1 million barrels of oil were being taken from the Gulf daily, and several million tons of sulfur were taken annually.

MEXICO, INDIANS OF. Middle America, in pre-Columbian times, developed a major civilization, comparable to any in such Old World centers as the ancient Near East, India, or China. Agriculture, invented in Middle America at about the same time it was emerging in the fertile crescent of the Near East, spread slowly northward, reaching the Arizona-New Mexico Southwest, the Gulf area, and the riverine systems associated with the Mississippi Valley. Here and there may be found suggestions of Mexican influences among North American tribes—temple mounds, calendars, the new fire rite, and world renewal.

The civilization of Mexico did not spring from one people. The formative phases go back 3,500 years, when distinct cultural systems arose: the Maya, Olmec, Zapotec, Mixtec, and Toltec. The Aztec were viewed as barbarian upstarts. It is known that this group came from the north, conquered, but was assimilated into the existing cultural systems of the Valley of Mexico.

The tendency in the growth of the various states was to build ceremonial centers rather than cities as such. Maize-raising peasant villages clustered about these centers. In such centers, the priests of the Maya, for example, invented a system of writing, developing in this the sole example of New World writing, a script not yet wholly deciphered. Concerned with an agricultural calendar, they evolved systems of higher mathematics, even inventing, quite independently of the Old World, the algebraic concept of zero. Art and architecture were highly developed and diverse.

MEXICO, PUNITIVE EXPEDITION INTO (1916–17). On Mar. 9, 1916, Francisco (Pancho) Villa, with 485 men, crossed the border from Mexico and raided Columbus, N.Mex., killing 18 people. Brig. Gen. John J. Pershing was ordered into the state of Chihuahua in northern Mexico with a force that eventually numbered over 11,000. A long series of diplomatic correspondences ensued. The Mexican government rightly considered the uninvited Pershing force an infringement of its sovereignty, and the United States rightly considered that something must be done to protect American life and property in the absence of Mexican control of the bandits. For a time war seemed imminent and President Woodrow Wilson mobilized the National Guard. Negotiations proved fruitless, but the United States ordered Pershing's force withdrawn in February 1917.

MEXICO, RELATIONS WITH. Boundary problems predominated for thirty years after the United States recognized Mexican independence in 1822. By 1830 some 20,000 Americans had settled in Texas. When Mexico tried to restrict immigration and impose tighter control, the Texans rebelled; they won independence in 1836. U.S. annexation of Texas in 1845 led to war the next year. By the Treaty of Guadalupe Hidalgo (1848), Mexico ceded over a half million square miles to the United States for $18,250,000. In 1853 the United States bought 54,000 square miles of the Mesilla Valley (Gadsden Purchase).

In 1862 Napoleon III dispatched an army to place Archduke Maximilian of Austria on the Mexican throne. The United States, engulfed in the Civil War, was unable to counter France's violation of the Monroe Doctrine until after Appomattox. Then the United States sent troops to the border, and Napoleon withdrew (*see* Mexico, French in).

During the long dictatorship of Porfirio Díaz (1876–1911) relations became increasingly cordial; Díaz welcomed foreign capital, and U.S. investments in mining, land, and manufacturing rose to over a billion dollars, earning huge profits but also arousing resentment among Mexican liberals.

The 1910 revolution produced a generation of conflict between the two nations, culminating in the American occupation of Veracruz in 1914 and in the punitive raids (1916–17) against Francisco (Pancho) Villa.

In 1917 Venustiano Carranza's government promulgated a constitution containing severe restrictions on foreign economic activities, thereby arousing new animosities in the United States. Lázaro Cárdenas's expropriation of major U.S. petroleum holdings in 1938 created a crisis (*see* Mexican Oil Controversy), but a peaceful solution was arranged. A Mexican-American general agreement signed in 1941 settled most outstanding issues. Mexico joined the war against the Axis powers and became a charter member of the United Nations.

After World War II, relations were generally harmonious. Diplomacy assuaged Mexico's ire over treatment of its migrant laborers in the United States and settled the century-old dispute over ownership of the Chamizal district in El Paso.

MEXICO CITY, CAPTURE OF (Sept. 13–14, 1847). The fall of Chapultepec made possible an attack on the western gates of Mexico City. During the night Antonio López de Santa Anna evacuated the city, the citadel surrendering to the Americans at dawn. Gen. Winfield Scott then entered the city.

MIAMI (Fla.). Second largest city in Florida, with a population of 346,931 in 1980. Miami is located on Biscayne Bay in the southeastern section of Florida. It is surrounded by several other cities and towns which together make up one of the largest resort and vacation areas in the nation. Miami Beach, a separate city (population, 96,298 in 1980), is located on a long sandy island between Biscayne Bay and the Atlantic Ocean proper. It is connected to Miami by causeways.

Miami is an important port of entry for airfreight and for seaborne cargoes from Latin America. It is a center of international banking and finance for the Caribbean area and Latin America and is the third largest U.S. clothing maker.

Early efforts to establish a fort on Biscayne Bay by both Spain and the United States were thwarted by the Indians in the vicinity. A few Americans settled in the area during the 1870's and 1880's, planting orange groves and hoping to drain the swampy land. The Florida East Coast Railroad arrived in 1896 and Miami was incorporated.

The boom years of 1920–26 were ended by a combination of business reverses and weather disasters. Bank failures and panic selling of undeveloped land followed. Then in the fall of 1926, the whole area was hit by a massive hurricane.

The years after World War II have been marked by the most substantial growth of the Miami area. Miami has the largest Cuban population in the nation, caused mostly by refugees from the Castro regime in Cuba.

MIAMI, FORT (Ind.). Also called Fort Miamis, at present-day Fort Wayne, Ind., built by the French about 1749. It replaced an older fort of the same name. It was garrisoned by the British under Lt. Robert Butler of Rogers' Rangers. In May 1763, the fort was evacuated, and shortly thereafter it was seized by the Indians in Pontiac's uprising.

MIAMI, FORT (Ohio). At the foot of the Maumee rapids, on the left bank of the Maumee River; built by the British in 1794. The position of the fort, nearly forty miles within American soil, was protested by George Washington and Thomas Jefferson. In 1796, according to Article II of Jay's Treaty, the fort was yielded to the Americans. During the War of 1812 it was retaken by the British.

MIAMI AND ERIE CANAL. *See* **Ohio State Canals.**

MIAMI PURCHASE (1788). In the Old Northwest, extending northward from the Ohio, between the Miami and the Little Miami rivers. Judge John Cleves Symmes, of Morristown, N.J., member of the Continental Congress, was its proprietor. A contract with the Treasury Board granted Symmes and his associates 1 million acres, for which, under the Land Ordinance of 1785, they agreed to pay $1 per acre. Eventually, Symmes could not meet the payments in full, and in 1794 he received a patent for the Miami purchase that covered only 311,682 acres.

The first permanent settlement in the Miami purchase was made on Nov. 18, 1788, at Columbia, at the mouth of the Little Miami. The next settlement, on Dec. 28, 1788, opposite the mouth of the Licking, was given the fanciful name Losantiville, which was changed to Cincinnati. The third settlement, on Feb. 2, 1789, was at North Bend. After the Treaty of Greenville (1795), population spread quickly through the land of the Miami purchase.

MIAMISBURG MOUND. *See* **Adena; Archaeology and Prehistory, North American.**

MIAMI TRAIL. An Indian trail, with several branches, running from the valleys of the Miami and Little Miami rivers of southwestern Ohio to the Cherokee country of the South. It was much used in Indian invasions of Kentucky.

MICHABOUS, GOD OF MICHILIMACKINAC. Also known as Manabozhu and Manitou, he was the greatest deity of the Indians in the area of Mackinac Island, at the junction of lakes Superior, Michigan, and Huron. Mackinac Island was regarded as his home. Ethnologists associate him with the Manitou, a major figure in Algonkin mythology.

MICHIGAN. In 1671 the French, aware of the potential riches from the fur trade of the upper country, claimed the area. In 1701, Detroit, which became the most important French fur-trading center in Michigan, was founded. Michigan remained a great center for the lucrative fur trade throughout the French regime, which ended in 1763.

In 1774, the British attached Michigan to Quebec, but at the close of the Revolution, it was ceded to the United States. But the British retained jurisdiction until 1796. In accordance with the terms of Jay's Treaty, the British withdrew. Michigan then became part of the newly created Northwest Territory. By 1803, Michigan had become a part of Indian Territory. However, in response to the petitions of Detroit residents, Congress authorized the creation of Michigan Territory, which began to function in 1805, with Detroit as the capital. In 1812, Michigan was subject to a second interval of British occupation as the result of the War of 1812. American rule was restored in 1813.

The growth of the territory was closely tied to improved transportation. In 1818 the first steamboat on the Great Lakes made its maiden journey from Buffalo to Detroit. The completion of the Erie Canal in 1825 assured relatively inexpensive water transportation between the East and Detroit. A network of highways radiated out from Detroit into the most fertile counties in the territory. Michigan was admitted to the Union in 1837, and the state grew rapidly. In the 1840's, the vast mineral resources of the upper peninsula were discovered. By 1850 the population was 397,000.

The growth of the state continued after the Civil War. By the beginning of the 20th century, when industrial Michigan really began, agriculture was the leading source of wealth. Lumbering gave rise to great wealth. By the 1920's Detroit was the automotive capital of the nation. The economy of Flint and several other cities also came to be largely dependent on the new industry. Grand Rapids became a major furniture center.

The Great Depression was unusually severe in Michigan. The mining counties of the upper peninsula and the large industrial cities of the lower peninsula had unusually high rates of unemployment. In World War II, Detroit and other cities became great production centers. Michigan plants met staggering industrial goals. All civilian automobile production was terminated. Factories were converted to the manufacture of military items. In the early 1980's, primarily because of the depressed condition of the automotive industry, Michigan faced the worst unemployment market since the 1930's. In 1980 Michigan's population was 9,258,344.

MICHIGAN, LAKE. One of the Great Lakes and the largest lake lying wholly within the United States. It extends 321 miles from north to south. The first known European discoverer was Jean Nicolet in 1634. In the 18th century, Lake Michigan became a highway for explorers and traders; and in the early 19th century, the tide of American settlement began pouring into the area and such thriving cities as Milwaukee, Kenosha, Chicago, and Michigan City were founded. Lake Michigan is now part of the Great Lakes–St. Lawrence Seaway and handles a vast amount of international commerce, particularly in coal, iron ore, limestone, and grain.

MICHIGAN TERRITORIAL ROAD. Laid out in 1830, it ran from Detroit to the mouth of the St. Joseph River and followed approximately the route of the present highway U.S. 12. It was an important route followed by immigrants who settled the southern part of the lower peninsula of Michigan. A stage line over the territorial road was established in 1834.

MICHILIMACKINAC. *See* **Mackinac, Straits of, and Mackinac Island.**

MICMAC. *See* **Abnaki.**

MIDCONTINENT OIL REGION. A vast mineral fuel-producing region situated in the nation's heartland, extending from Nebraska to south Texas and flanked by the Mississippi River and the Rocky Mountains. From earliest times an oil slick on springs and creeks was observed at widely scattered locations. In 1859 subsurface oil was discovered inadvertently in the Cherokee Nation, and thereafter, oil discoveries through digging water wells became a regular occurrence. Prospecting for oil began in the 1880's in Kansas, Indian Territory, and Texas. The production was used as a lubricant, an illuminant (kerosine, coal oil, and rock oil), and medicine.

The premier oil well of the midcontinent region was Spindletop, a dramatic gusher brought in near Beaumont, Tex., on Jan. 10, 1901, which produced 75,000–100,000 barrels a day. The advent of the internal-combustion engine and the concomitant increase in demand for petroleum products led to a sustained flurry of wildcatting (exploration by drilling) throughout the midcontinent region, opening new fields in every state of the region from Nebraska to Louisiana. The oil industry of the midcontinent region has provided a legacy of bonanza wealth and boomtowns reminiscent of the California gold rush in 1848–49. The region's petroleum industry has been a major influence in state and regional economic development, urban evolution, and politics. Around 1945 midcontinent petroleum production peaked and began to level off.

MIDDLE CLASS. Originally referred to the urban craftsmen and the mercantile class in medieval towns and to the position of the class between nobility and peasantry. By the 19th century, the middle class was clearly dominant and had evolved political and economic doctrines, political parties, and life-styles peculiar to itself.

Clear demarcation was generally lacking in the United States, where there is no generally accepted definition of the middle class. Under Communist theory, the middle class, or bourgeoisie, consists of those who own the means of production, such as land, tools, materials, and factories.

MIDDLE-OF-THE-ROAD POPULISTS. In the presidential campaign of 1896, those members of the People's (Populist) party who objected to fusion with either of the older parties. They were unable to prevent the party from accepting the Democratic candidate, William Jennings Bryan, as its candidate for president.

MIDDLE PASSAGE. The trip from Africa to the West Indies, the second leg of the triangular voyage of a slave ship (*see* Triangular Trade). During the passage, the slaves died in large numbers.

MIDDLESEX CANAL. Constructed (1793–1803) between Boston and the Merrimack to bring that river's commerce to Boston without a sea voyage. It was of great economic value in developing New Hampshire, but the railroad made it less valuable, and the last boat passed through in 1852.

MIDEWIWIN, or **Grand Medicine Lodge.** A secret society of medicine men, widespread among the Chippewa. Candidates for membership (either men or women) served an apprenticeship with older mide, and prepared for admission to each of the degrees of the lodge with sweat baths, fasting, ceremonial smoking, and gifts to the mide. The mide possessed an extensive native pharmacopoeia, practiced bloodletting and simple surgery, and used songs and formulas of exorcism. The Midewiwin was the principal means for transmitting legends, songs, and traditional religious lore preserved in pictographs on birch bark. (*See also* Indian Medicine.)

MIDNIGHT JUDGES. Judicial appointments made by John Adams just before he was succeeded in the presidency by Thomas Jefferson. Congress, dominated by Jeffersonians, legislated most of the midnight judges out of their commissions. (*See* Judiciary Act of 1801 and *Marbury* v. *Madison.*)

MIDNIGHT ORDER. Issued in Louisiana on Dec. 5, 1872, by U.S. District Judge E. H. Durell. It cited in contempt the members of a board that had declared the Democratic ticket elected. The order had the effect of making the Republican candidate, W. P. Kellogg, governor of Louisiana.

MIDWAY, BATTLE OF (June 4–6, 1942). A major engagement in the Pacific during World War II. In his resolve to take Midway Island, Japanese Adm. Isoroku Yamamoto drew together one of the most prodigious armadas of modern times—185 warships in all. As the great fleet steamed eastward, U.S. Adm. Chester W. Nimitz stationed his three carriers (*Enterprise, Hornet,* and *Yorktown*) 350 miles northwest of Midway and waited for Yamamoto to make his first tactical move. On June 4 the first wave of enemy aircraft hit Midway and Yamamoto ordered his torpedo-laden reserve aircraft to rearm with bombs for another strike at the island. U.S. dive-bombers struck the Japanese carriers while their flight decks were loaded with fueled aircraft. The *Akagi, Kaga,* and *Soryu* burst into flame. The *Hiryu,* farther to the north, temporarily escaped the holocaust and was able to mount two heavy attacks on the *Yorktown,* forcing its captain to abandon his ship; but he soon retaliated, and by late afternoon the *Hiryu* was burning out of control. All four Japanese carriers finally went down with their planes.

On June 5, Yamamoto accepted the immensity of his losses and canceled the invasion of Midway, but an attack on the retreating Japanese fleet sank the cruiser *Mikuma.* The American naval triumph was flawed when, in the morning of June 7, the *Yorktown* succumbed to its many wounds and the Battle of Midway was over. The U.S. Navy, having inflicted enormous and irreparable damage on a vastly superior fleet, effectively turned the tide of the naval war in the Pacific.

MIDWAY ISLANDS. Located 1,200 miles northwest of Honolulu, they are part of a coral atoll containing two islands (Sand and Eastern), with a total area of about 2 square miles. They were annexed by the United States in 1867. The U.S. navy was given administrative responsibility over the islands in 1903, and they became a station link in the transpacific cable in 1905. They were attacked by the Japanese in World War II (*see* Midway, Battle of).

MIDWINTER INTERNATIONAL EXPOSITION. Exposition held in Golden Gate Park, San Francisco, from Jan. 27 to July 4, 1894. Five American states and nine foreign nations participated officially.

MIER EXPEDITION. An abortive counterexpedition into Mexico ordered by Texas President Sam Houston in November 1842. Only 250 Texas troops crossed into Mexico; they surrendered at Mier on the lower Rio Grande. One-tenth were shot and the others imprisoned near Mexico City.

MIFFLIN, FORT. Originally built as Mud Fort in 1762 on Mud Island, Delaware River, below the mouth of the Schuylkill. The most important of Philadelphia's defenses, it was besieged by the British from Sept. 27 to Nov. 16, 1777, when, razed by gunfire, it was abandoned. After the British evacuation of Philadelphia, it was rebuilt and named for Thomas Mifflin, then governor of Pennsylvania. It was frequently modernized but ceased active use shortly after World War II.

MIGRANT WORKERS. In many branches of agriculture, extra hands are needed in the fields only seasonally, usually at harvesting time. Because of this, migrant workers move from area to area, since harvesting dates vary according to area and crop. Migrant workers have many serious problems. Their children, for example, do not attend school continuously in any one place. Their health needs may go uncared for as they move to catch up with a crop that needs harvesting. Their homes are temporary and often in bad repair. Their special needs and problems were dramatized in California in the 1960's by César Chavez, who successfully organized a union of migrant workers. The need for a number of temporary hands has led in some instances to the importing of illegal immigrant workers from other countries, especially from Mexico.

MIGRATION, GROUP. Settlement of an area by people previously associated with each other who migrated in one body to a new home. The first settlements in the Connecticut Valley were made by the groups that followed Roger Ludlow from the Massachusetts Bay Colony (*see* River Towns of Connecticut). In fact, community migration into new lands previously surveyed was quite typical of the method of early frontier expansion in the New England colonies. The original settlement of Germans and their subsequent migrations in New York were of this type, as were many of the German and Scotch-Irish movements to Pennsylvania.

Various experimental colonies and religious groups migrated westward. The Harmony Society, made up of a sect from southern Germany, settled in western Pennsylvania in 1805 and moved to Indiana ten years later. The Zoarites came to Ohio in 1817 from Württemberg, Germany. In the 1830's a group of ministers in New York's Mohawk Valley drew up a plan for a religious and educational community in the West; the result was the founding of Galesburg and Knox College. The Mennonites nearly always moved in groups.

The Mormons had their origin about 1830 in western New York. In the following decade and a half, they moved consecutively to Kirtland, Ohio; Independence, Mo.; the Far West, north of the Missouri River; Nauvoo, Ill.; and finally to Utah.

MILAN DECREE. *See* **Napoleon's Decrees.**

MILEAGE. Allowance toward the expense of legislators in traveling to and from sessions of their respective bodies. Members of Congress are entitled to one round trip to their district per month while Congress is in session, plus one additional trip to and from Washington, D.C., at the beginning and end of each session. No compensation is allowed for transportation of family or household goods. In the case of state legislators, mileage allowances vary from state to state. Mileage is also commonly provided by law for national and state officials who are required to travel in the performance of their duties, and for jurors and witnesses summoned to testify in courts or before legislative committees.

MILITARY, AFRO-AMERICANS IN THE. Afro-Americans have served in the armed forces during all American wars. It is estimated that some 5,000 black men served in the patriot forces during the revolutionary war, but many more sought and found their freedom behind British lines. At the end of the war the British evacuated 14,000 blacks from the colonies as a reward for their loyalty and service to the British fighting forces.

Afro-Americans fought conspicuously well during the War of 1812. Enlistment of free blacks was specifically provided for by the navy under an act of Mar. 3, 1813, and blacks formed approximately one-sixth of all naval personnel.

In 1820 the army prohibited black recruits, and in 1839 the navy restricted blacks to 5 percent of all naval personnel. Few blacks served in the conflict with Mexico. And at the outset of the Civil War the Union army at first recruited no blacks; it was not until white northern manpower had been drained that blacks appeared in the ranks. In January 1863, as part of the Emancipation Proclamation, President Abraham Lincoln provided for the enlistment of blacks, and by 1865 some 186,000 blacks had worn Union blue. The navy encouraged the enlistment of black sailors. It is estimated that 30,000 blacks, some 25 percent of the Union navy, saw service.

In 1866 Congress established three regular black regiments. They served at remote posts in the West and participated in the subjugation of the Indian tribes.

During the Spanish-American War, four regular and sixteen volunteer black regiments saw service. The volunteer regiments did not see combat, and were used for labor and nursing duty in Cuba and Puerto Rico. After the war the black regular regiments were sent to the Philippines, where they fought against the insurgent forces led by Emilio Aguinaldo. Between 1863 and 1898 thirty-six black soldiers and eight black sailors were awarded the Medal of Honor.

In 1906, the Twenty-fifth Infantry, newly arrived at Brownsville, Tex., was charged with riot and murder during an alleged fray. President Theodore Roosevelt dismissed nearly all the men of the First Battalion without honor. The charges were false, but it was not until 1972 that the army exonerated all those accused. On Aug. 23, 1917, members of a black regiment were involved in a race riot in Houston. Thirteen black soldiers were hanged for murder and mutiny, and forty-one were sentenced to life in prison.

During World War I, 350,000 black soldiers served in the army, but only 40,000 saw combat; the rest were employed as laborers. Of the army's 213 labor battalions, 106 were all-black. Only two black divisions were established.

In World War II black soldiers and sailors, operating in a segregated military force, served largely in quartermaster, engineer, and transport units. This segregated, largely noncombat, status engendered much bitterness among blacks. Not until President Harry S. Truman ordered the racial integration of the armed forces in 1948 did blacks begin to appear in nonsegregated military units. In the 1980's blacks were serving in significant numbers in all branches of the armed forces, occupying all ranks.

MILITARY ACADEMY, UNITED STATES. In 1794, Congress established a School for Artillerists and Engineers at West Point, N.Y., but it was a training school, not a professional one. The establishment of a true military academy awaited the passage of the Act of Mar. 16, 1802, providing for the creation of a corps of engineers consisting of five officers and ten cadets, with a chief of engineers, designated superintendent of a military academy at West Point. The academy existed only on paper until 1812, when Congress provided for a reorganization, authorized a maximum of 250 cadets, and set age and mental requirements for admission that had not previously existed. Maj. Sylvanus Thayer was superintendent for sixteen years (1817–33). He expanded the curriculum and introduced a new system of order, organization, and discipline. The traditional West Point honor system had its origins in Thayer's work.

The U.S. Military Academy was long the only engineering school in the country, and its graduates, working both as civil and military engineers, were largely responsible for planning and directing the building of major canals, roads, and railroads before the Civil War. In that war, West Point graduates dominated the higher positions on both sides.

During the period of 1865–1914 most academy graduates pursued military careers, and in World War I they nearly monopolized the higher ranks, furnishing all commanders of armies and above and about 90 percent of those of corps and divisions. Although this dominance was less in Wold War II, still 70 percent of full generals and 65 percent of all lieutenant generals were graduates of the academy.

After every war there have been extensive changes in organization and curriculum to keep abreast of new developments in military art and technology and, at least to some extent, to adjust to changes in methods and courses in civilian institutions. Women cadets now train alongside men.

MILITARY AID TO THE CIVIL POWERS. The president is the sole judge of the necessity to use federal troops, but state governors can call out the National Guard. The president is empowered to employ troops under Article IV, Section 4, of the Constitution and under the "insurrection" statutes, which allow him to make use of troops to maintain the Constitution, to support federal law enforcement, or to protect interstate commerce and federal property. The president, as commander in chief, also employs troops in humane tasks, such as aiding disaster victims and feeding weather-isolated cattle. In these circumstances, troops work with civil authorities, with or without the benefits of martial law.

Regular troops were sent into the aircraft industry in California in 1940 to break a strike that threatened the national defense; and into Little Rock, Ark., in 1957 when there was doubt that the governor would respond to orders to help desegregate the schools. Troops were called into Detroit in 1967, to the Democratic convention in Chicago in 1968—where the police bore the odium of action—and to many other cities when tensions flared. They were even employed on occasion on college campuses, culminating in the death and wounding of several students at Kent State University, Ohio, in May 1970.

MILITARY COMPANIES, VOLUNTARY. Appeared in considerable numbers in the 1850's. They combined athletic activity with dress parades, competitive drills, and interstate encampments. These companies sometimes received aid from the state, but generally depended on some rich patron and the proceeds from military balls and other entertainments for funds. Most had disbanded before the Civil War began.

MILITARY COMPANY OF ADVENTURERS. *See* **Georgiana.**

MILITARY INTELLIGENCE. *See* **Intelligence, Military and Strategic.**

MILITARY LAW. Regulates the military establishment. For the United States the primary source of military law is legislative enactments of Congress. The amount of legislation and regulation associated with military law has reached huge proportions. It encompasses implementing regulations from the executive branch of the government, and decisions of reviewing courts in the military justice system and federal courts. Military law includes diverse subjects, such as veterans' benefits, retirement, government contract law, the laws of war, civil claims for and against the government, draft law, martial law, international law, military commissions, and courts of inquiry and other fact-finding bodies.

MILITARY ORDER OF THE LOYAL LEGION OF THE U.S.A. Organization established at Philadelphia in 1865 by a group of officers who had served in the Union army during the Civil War. Membership was originally limited to such officers and their eldest male descendants. Membership is now open to all male descendants of Union officers.

MILITARY POLICY. During its early history the United States, relatively safe behind its ocean barriers, maintained a minimum of military forces in peacetime, rapidly expanding them in time of war and just as rapidly demobilizing them at the end of each conflict. World War II brought an end to isolation as the nation assumed a leading role in world affairs. Changed conditions required new military policies stressing the maintenance of adequate forces to protect against attack and to discharge new international responsibilities. The three essential elements of military policy from the beginning were a professional regular army, a militia (*see* Militia), and a navy.

America's emergence as a world power after the Spanish-American War brought some modifications in the old military policy. Both the army and the navy were modernized, and the militia was converted into the National Guard. In the wave of disillusionment after World War I the United States reverted to isolationism and to military policies to match it. All three of the existing elements were cut back and the new one in the military picture—airpower—remained ill-defined and controversial.

Again after World War II the massive military structure was dismantled as hastily and almost as completely as after earlier wars. But in the midst of demobilization, growing tensions with the Soviet Union made clear the necessity for military strength sufficient to guard against Communist encroachments around the globe. Adding to the tensions was a new element for which historic policies provided no guidance, the development by both major powers of nuclear weapons of ever-increasing destructive power.

The central feature of American military policy in the postwar world was the maintenance of a nuclear striking power that would serve to deter any attack on the United States or its principal allies. But the United States had to give consideration to contingencies other than atomic war. Every administration attempted to maintain forces in being or in reserve to deal with a whole spectrum of possible conflicts.

The maintaining of large forces in being required a level of military expenditure undreamed of before World War II and reliance on conscription to maintain military strength. Although President Richard M. Nixon, after 1969, continued the general policies of his predecessors, he started a retrenchment of conventional forces as the United States withdrew from Vietnam, accepted a doctrine of nuclear sufficiency rather than absolute superiority in the face of a great growth in Soviet atomic strength, and ended conscription.

MILITARY ROADS. *See* **Roads, Military.**

MILITARY TRACTS. Land bounties offered in the early national period by the states and the federal government to attract people into the armies or to reward soldiers and officers for their services. Military tracts were set aside in which the warrantee had to locate his land. New York, North Carolina, and Virginia were among the states that set up such tracts. The United States created four military tracts to satisfy the warrants it gave in the revolutionary war and the War of 1812. The first of these was located in central Ohio, adjacent to the Virginia military tract (*see* Virginia Military Reserve in Ohio) and the other three tracts were originally located in Michigan, Illinois, and Arkansas; but when it was reported that the Michigan tract was poorly drained and unsuited to farming, it was abandoned and the Illinois tract was increased to 3.5 million acres and a tract of 500,000 acres was established in Missouri. In these three tracts soldiers of the War of 1812, who received 160 acres each, were required to locate their warrants by lottery.

Most of the recipients refused to move to these tracts to take up their claims. Instead, they sold their warrants to speculators for prices as low as 10 cents an acre. The result was a high percentage of absentee or speculative ownership, a situation that aroused hostility against absentee speculators. Squatters settled upon the absentee-owned lands and flouted all efforts to make them pay rent. Local governments frequently leveled discriminatory taxes on absentee-owned land. Speculators with little capital lost their lands at tax sales; others sooner or later would sell or lease to tenants.

MILITARY WARRANTS. *See* **Land Bounties.**

MILITIA. The militia system is based on the idea that every able-bodied man owes military service to his country. Early American colonists faced Indian attack and famine, and survival dictated that every male colonist be both settler and soldier. The southern colonies made the county the basic unit, each supervised by a lieutenant. In the other states the town was the militia's basic unit.

As the population increased, the entire male population was no longer needed for military campaigns. With the approach of the American Revolution the patriot faction gained control of the militia, which reinforced the Continental army, provided local security, and harassed British detachments. About 164,087, or 41 percent, of the 395,864 troops employed in the formal campaigns were militia.

After the Revolution, attempts were made to make the militia the central focus of the nation's military policy. In 1792, Congress enacted a law (the Militia Act) to the effect that all free, able-bodied, white male citizens between eighteen and forty-five years of age were to be enrolled in the militia by local authorities and that the units were to be organized by the state governors. The law was virtually unenforceable, and annual musters degenerated into drinking brawls in many cases. Generally, militiamen performed poorly in the War of 1812. Many units refused to leave the state or cross the border into Canada. Thereafter the militia idea was slowly abandoned. The militia played no part in the Mexican War, but volunteers units formed an important part of the army. Just before the Civil War those units increased in number, and they provided cadres for units, North and

South, during the war and many partially trained officers.

After the Civil War the volunteer militia units generally adopted the name National Guard. Most of them volunteered for the Spanish-American War. The Dick Act of 1903 in effect transformed the National Guard into a militia. In 1916 it became subject to federal standards of efficiency and federal control, and in 1933 the guard was given the status of a reserve component of the army. In 1956 the regular army took over the basic training of all guardsmen, although when not on active federal service they are under state control.

MILITIA ACT (1792). Because of the growing Indian menace in the Northwest Territory, this act established the principle of universal obligation to military service for all free white male citizens between the ages of eighteen and forty-five. In 1903 the Dick Act repealed this act. (*See* Militia.)

MILLE LACS, BATTLE OF (ca. 1745). As part of their general tribal advance, Lake Superior Chippewa surprised and defeated three Sioux villages at Mille Lacs, Minn. This encounter is sometimes called the Battle of Kathio.

MILLERITES. *See* **Adventist Churches.**

MILLER-TYDINGS ENABLING ACT (1937). An amendment to the Sherman Antitrust Act (1890), it permitted manufacturers of trademarked articles to enter into contracts with retailers for the maintenance of resale prices, thereby exempting interstate fair-trade agreements from the antitrust laws. (*See* Fair Trade Laws.)

MILLIGAN, EX PARTE, 4 Wallace 2 (1866). A Supreme Court case in which the trial and conviction of Lambdin P. Milligan, a civilian, by a military commission in 1864 were invalidated. The Court held that neither the president nor Congress has the power to set up military tribunals except in the actual theater of war, where the civil courts are no longer functioning, and that elsewhere courts-martial have jurisdiction only over persons in the military or naval service of the United States. Later, because the decision seemed to cast doubt upon the legality of the military government established by Congress in former rebellious states, the Court was widely denounced, especially by Radical Republicans.

"MILLIONS FOR DEFENSE, BUT NOT ONE CENT FOR TRIBUTE." Slogan of those who opposed appeasing France (1798) in negotiations to end that country's hostile actions against U.S. shipping. It originated in a toast offered by Robert Goodloe Harper, South Carolina member of the House of Representatives. (*See also* Franco-American Misunderstanding; Naval War with France; XYZ Affair.)

MILL SPRINGS, ENCOUNTER AT (Jan. 19, 1862). Confrontation in Pulaski County, Ky., between about 4,000 Confederates led by George B. Crittenden and an equal number of Union troops under George H. Thomas. With the arrival of about 8,000 reinforcements, the Union troops disastrously defeated the Confederates.

MILL STREAMS. When dams and short canals with locks began to be constructed in the late 18th and early 19th centuries along the navigable rivers of the eastern United States, the fall of the water at the locks was often employed to operate mills and factories. Those early mills had to be actuated directly by a water wheel or turbine, and therefore had to be close to the fall or rapid. Manchester, N.H., Woonsocket and Pawtucket, R.I., Paterson, N.J., and Rochester, N.Y., became important industrial centers because of the mill streams around which they were built.

MILWAUKEE (Wis.). Largest city in Wisconsin, with a population in 1980 of 636,212. It is a leading Great Lakes port and an important manufacturing center. Milwaukee's first settlers were given land titles in 1835. One of these was Solomon Juneau, a French-speaking trader, who was largely responsible for the early growth of the town. Milwaukee attracted many immigrants from Germany after 1848, giving it a strongly German flavor. The German settlers opened breweries, which rapidly established the town's reputation for the manufacture of good beer.

Milwaukee is an important grain market and shipping center as well as a leading city in the production of industrial turbines and electrical equipment. It produces large numbers of shoes and boots. Its harbor became a major seaport when the St. Lawrence Seaway was opened.

MIMS, FORT, MASSACRE AT (Aug. 30, 1813). Attack by a force of about 1,000 Creek on the stockade on Lake Tensaw, near Mobile, Ala. The families of the vicinity had taken refuge in the stockade, which was unprotected. The Creek massacred all but 36 of the fort's 553 inhabitants.

MINA EXPEDITION (1817). Attempt to liberate Mexico by Francisco Xavier Mina, a Spanish exile in the United States. He landed at Soto la Marina, Tamaulipas, in April 1817 and marched into the interior of Mexico. He was captured by the Spanish and executed on Nov. 11, 1817.

MINERALOGY. The main development of mineralogy and geology in the United States took place in the first three decades of the 19th century. The first textbook on mineralogy written in the United States, Parker Cleaveland's *Elementary Treatise on Mineralogy and Geology,* was published in Boston in 1816. The leading figure was Benjamin Silliman, professor of chemistry and natural science at Yale after 1802. Silliman was active as a teacher, editor, and public lecturer, rather than as an investigator. Among his students, Amos Eaton, Charles Upham Shepard, and James Dwight Dana became important in the development of the geological sciences.

The marked growth of the geological sciences in American colleges in the early 19th century was accompanied by the formation of numerous state and local academies, lyceums, and societies concerned with natural history. The *American Journal of Science and Arts,* started by Silliman in 1818, published the bulk of American mineralogical contributions for the next five decades.

Toward the middle of the 19th century courses in analytical chemistry, emphasizing ores, minerals, and agricultural materials, were introduced into many colleges and medical schools. Mineral chemistry and geochemistry developed strongly during the late 1800's, and American work on minerals and rocks was outstanding in those fields. The publications of the U.S. Geological Survey, organized in 1879, and of the state geological surveys carried much descriptive mineralogical and petrographic material. The Mineralogical Society of America was founded in 1919, and the *American Mineralogist* became its journal. Crystallography did not attract much attention in the United States until the early 20th century.

MINERAL PATENT LAW. The mining laws of 1866, 1870, and 1872 adopted the idea of open mineral exploitation of the public lands. A claimant who discovered a mineral lode or a placer—that is, surface deposits of gravels of mineral value, as opposed to lodes or veins of ore—could secure a patent from the United States on the lands covered by his claim. Locations based on discovery of a lode were limited to 1,500 feet by 600 feet, and placer claims, to 20 acres. Under the Mineral Leasing Act of 1920 rights of exploration and production of oil and gas came to be leased, not patented, with royalty paid to the United States as landowner.

MINERAL SPRINGS. Estimated at 10,000 in the United States, several became fashionable resorts and spas. The most famous springs were at Saratoga, N.Y., and White Sulphur Springs, W. Va. They were the scene of famous entertainments, vacations, protracted "cures," political horsetrading, and gambling. (*See also* Resorts and Spas.)

MINE RUN CAMPAIGN (1863). The Union army under Gen. George G. Meade, positioned on the Rapidan River in Virginia, confronted Gen. Robert E. Lee in the forest back of a brook called Mine Run on Nov. 29. The Union advance was detected by Lee and blocked in such force that on the following day the Union army retired across the Rapidan.

MINES, U.S. BUREAU OF. Established in 1910 in response to public demand for a federal program to alleviate coal mine hazards, which caused 2,000 deaths per year. The bureau's activities may be summarized as research aimed at improving health, safety, efficiency, and conservation in mining, mineral processing, and mineral use. By 1930 the bureau had established its role as the principal governmental source of mineral intelligence, and this capability was expanded during World War II. The bureau's *Minerals Yearbook* and *Mineral Facts and Problems* have become worldwide mineral references. The bureau has been called upon for many special defense and civilian studies, including such diverse assignments as the control of civilian use of explosives, and exploration and development of such strategic materials as radium, zirconium, and synthetic liquid fuels. It is the sole U.S. producer of helium.

MINES AND MINING. *See* **Ferrous Metals; Nonferrous Metals;** *and separate articles on the mining of individual metals, such as* **Lead,** *and* **Copper.**

MINESWEEPING. The systematic clearance of mines from an area where they have been planted by submarines, surface ships, or aircraft. Those set off by contact can be swept by a ship towing a serrated wire that cuts the mooring line and thus causes the mine to surface, where it can be destroyed by gunfire. Acoustic mines, which are set off by a built-in hydrophone that amplifies the sound of a ship's engines, are swept by towing a mechanical noisemaker near them. Magnetic mines, which are set off when a magnetic field causes a delicate needle to complete an electrical circuit, are swept by creating such a magnetic field over them with a towed cable in which a pulsating current is maintained. Pressure, or oyster, mines are set off only when a passing ship creates a change in water pressure. Pressure mines, sitting on the bottom, cannot be swept in the conventional sense. However, they are set to sterilize themselves after a certain period, when they become harmless.

After World War I, during which the United States and Great Britain laid the immense North Sea barrage of some 56,000 mines, 230 miles long and from 15 to 35 miles wide, minesweepers spent months clearing mines, with no assurance that all of them had been disposed of.

An estimated 500,000 mines were laid during World War II. In European waters alone, after the war ended, more than 1,900 minesweepers spent a couple of years clearing mines. American minesweepers cleared some 17,000 square miles of water in the Japanese area.

The North Koreans laid influence mines off Korean coasts during the Korean War, and U.S. Air Force planes dropped mines in Haiphong harbor during the Vietnam War. Minesweepers cleared the mines in Korea, and minesweepers and helicopters went into Haiphong later and cleared mines there.

MINGO BOTTOM. A region in Ohio about three miles south of Steubenville, so named for Mingo Indians. In 1782 Mingo Bottom was the rendezvous for the frontiersmen under Col. David Williamson who marched to Gnadenhutten and massacred nearly 100 Christian Indians.

MINIATURIZATION. *See* **Computers.**

MINIÉ BALL. A bullet, invented in 1849 by Capt. Claude Étienne Minié of the French army, that had a deep tapered cavity in the base with a hemispherical iron cup fitted into it. Usable in a muzzle-loading rifle, the Minié ball was used extensively in the Civil War. It greatly expanded the range and accuracy of the rifle.

MINIMUM-WAGE LEGISLATION. In the United States the first state minimum-wage law was passed in 1906 in California and several other states followed suit, but in 1919 and 1921 Nebraska and Texas repealed their enactments. In 1923, in *Adkins* v. *Children's Hospital,* the Supreme Court declared a District of Columbia minimum-wage statute to be unconstitutional. Within the next few years the Supreme Court invalidated several other state laws, basing its rulings on both the Fifth and the Fourteenth Amendments. In the early 1930's several states revived their efforts in the area of minimum-wage legislation. In *West Coast Hotel Company* v. *Par-*

rish (1937), the Supreme Court found state minimum-wage laws constitutional.

The principal federal law affecting wages is the Fair Labor Standards Act of 1938, commonly called the Wages and Hours Law, and amended several times since. It covers those involved in interstate commerce, and was originally planned as an adjunct to the state laws. By the 1980's, however, its amendments made it applicable to a large majority of workers. Originally the Fair Labor Standards Act was aimed at establishing a 40 cents per hour minimum wage; by 1982 the minimum hourly wage was $3.40.

MINING CAMP, LAW OF THE. Extralegal code in the early mining camps of California and Colorado where the United States had not yet established civil government. When miners found a promising spot they quickly formed a mining district, defined its boundaries, passed laws regulating the filing and working of claims, and elected officers, including a sheriff who preserved order. Disputes were settled by the miners court, and usual punishments were hanging, shaving the head, banishment, whipping, and fines. Claims had to be recorded and worked a specified number of days each year. This born-of-necessity law was partially recognized by the United States in its mineral patent law of 1866.

MINING TOWNS. Most of America's mining towns began as boomtowns, and a characteristic the mining towns shared was their rapid growth. Leadville, Colo., started in 1877, grew to a city of 10,000 inhabitants within two years. Nevada City, Calif., was a town that showed phenomenal growth in a few months. Mining towns sometimes achieved permanence, but many of them reverted to ghost towns.

MINISINK INDIAN RAID. Mohawk attack on U.S. troops at Minisink, N.Y., on July 20, 1779. Under Chief Joseph Brant, they won after a hard struggle but lost many men.

MINISINK PATENT. Granted in 1704 by Edward Hyde, Lord Cornbury, to Stephen De Lancey and twenty-three associates, it was a vast tract in Orange and Sullivan counties, N.Y., bounded on the south by Pennsylvania.

MINNEAPOLIS (Minn.). Largest city in Minnesota, with a 1980 population of 370,951. It is one of Minnesota's Twin Cities, sharing its location in partnership with St. Paul. Minneapolis is located at the point where the Minnesota River joins the Mississippi. The area was explored shortly after the Louisiana Purchase by a U.S. Army exploration team headed by Zebulon Pike. In 1819 the Army built Fort Snelling where the city now is. It was the first such post established west of the Mississippi by the Army.

Minneapolis was chartered as a town in 1856 and as a city in 1857. It grew rapidly, using the waterpower from St. Anthony Falls to operate sawmills and flour mills. Those flour milling operations established the city as a major American industrial center. During the 20th century, Minneapolis developed new industries, including precision-tool making and the development of instruments to control temperatures in industrial processes and in homes.

MINNESOTA. The state occupies the Lake Superior highlands, a portion of the prairie plains, and the upper limits of the Mississippi Valley. More than 11,000 lakes are Minnesota's most distinctive feature. Minnesota's waters flow into three great systems: the Mississippi River, Red River of the North, and the Great Lakes–St. Lawrence River system. The Sioux occupied most of Minnesota when the first white men arrived in the mid-17th century. One of these, the Frenchman, Daniel Greysolon, Sieur Duluth, counciled with the Sioux and Chippewa (Ojibwa) and claimed (1679) possession of the area for Louis XIV.

French control of the Northwest was broken by the French and Indian War. In 1763 the French surrendered to the British their extensive dominions in America. But the French had earlier ceded to Spain their claim to lands west of the Mississippi River, which thus did not fall into British hands. Nevertheless, from 1783 until after the War of 1812 the North West Company, a British firm, was in practical control of the Minnesota country, with at least twenty-four posts. The most important were those at Grand Portage, Fond du Lac, and Sandy, Leech, Cass, and Red lakes. After the Louisiana Purchase in 1803 Lt. Zebulon M. Pike was dispatched to explore the upper Mississippi Valley. Pike arrived in the Minnesota country in September 1805.

After the War of 1812, a treaty was negotiated (1815) with the Sioux whereby they accepted the sovereignty of the United States. In 1819 Fort Snelling was established at the junction of the Minnesota and Mississippi rivers (Minneapolis). For a generation it remained the northwesternmost military post in the United States, and around it developed the fur-trading center of the region. By the 1830's, however, the fur trade declined in importance, and in 1842 the American Fur Company went into bankruptcy.

On Mar. 3, 1849, Minnesota Territory was created by the U.S. Congress, and treaties with the Sioux and Chippewa opened up vast areas west of the Mississippi, and an unparalleled rush to the new lands took place. On May 11, 1858, Minnesota became the thirty-second state in the Union.

During the Civil War, Minnesota faced a war within the larger war, one within its own borders. The Sioux, under the leadership of Little Crow pressed the Indian agents for relief from their grievances loss of ancestral lands, dissatisfaction with reservation life, crop failures, starvation, and delay on the part of the government in paying overdue annuities. Their appeals were met with indifference. The murder of five white settlers by four young Sioux on Aug. 17, 1862, provided the fuse that ignited the uprising. Its tragic aftereffects kept the northwestern frontier in a turmoil throughout the Civil War.

Waves of migration after the Civil War diversified Minnesota's population. The largest single immigrant group was German, followed by Norwegians, Swedes, and Danes. During that same period, wheat was king, and it was shipped by rail and boat to markets all over the East and to Europe. The 1880's saw dairy products take a leading position in the state's agricultural economy, and in the north the forests began to be felled under the organized attack of lumber companies. In 1884 the mining of iron ore was begun in the Vermilion Range, and in 1890 and 1891 the much larger deposits of the Mesabi Range were discovered. With the opening of the Cuyuna Range in 1911, Minnesota became the primary U.S. source of iron ore.

Flour milling developed as an adjunct to Minnesota's wheat production, and the raising of livestock increased. As an adjunct to the lumber industry the manufacture of paper became a major industry, particularly in International Falls.

After 1900, Minnesota became an urban, industrial commonwealth. Its industrial power, once closely tied to its varied natural resources—soil, water, timber, and iron—continued to develop, but electronics, adhesives, and abrasives were introduced, adding much diversification.

MINNESOTA MORATORIUM CASE, or *Home Building and Loan Association* v. *Blaisdell et al.*, 290 U.S. 398 (1934). A Supreme Court case in which a Minnesota law giving relief to property owners was upheld. In the Great Depression, many property owners were unable to meet their regular mortgage payments. Minnesota and some other states, passed laws delaying foreclosure. These acts were immediately attacked on constitutional grounds. The Minnesota act was sustained by the U.S. Supreme Court, which held that the emergency justified the state's exercise of power.

MINORITY RIGHTS. Federal and state constitutions guarantee that certain rights such as freedom of speech, association, and the press are particularly sacrosanct to the minority as well as the majority. James Madison argued (*Federalist Papers,* No. 10) that protection against the pressures of a potentially monolithic public opinion may be undergirded by diversity of interests, parties, factions, and sects, or what has since been termed social, economic, and cultural pluralism.

American history has been characterized by an almost constant struggle to protect minority rights against various kinds of encroachments. In 1798, for instance, the Alien and Sedition Acts imposed restrictions on freedom of speech and the press; and the acts were vigorously opposed. As the 19th century progressed, increasing social and economic complexity, expanded use of government regulatory power, and several wars posed new problems and dramatized old ones. Workers, particularly industrial workers, seeking to form unions, were restricted in their attempts to organize labor unions throughout the 19th century, and only in the 1930's were these restrictions somewhat abated. Political minorities were jailed during World War I, investigated by constitutionally and morally questionable methods, particularly in the 1920's and 1950's; often confronted by state statutes making it difficult for minority parties to be listed on the ballot; and punished, not for overt acts, but for allegedly conspiring to organize the Communist party and to teach and advocate the forcible overthrow of the government. During World War II, without trial and solely on the grounds of race, the U.S. government forced thousands of Japanese-Americans to leave their homes and to reside in camps. Afro-Americans were long relegated to racially segregated and inferior schools until in *Brown* v. *Board of Education of Topeka,* (1954), the Supreme Court held that racially segregated schools were inherently unequal; and the civil rights movement of the 1960's sought to secure the rights of racial minorities in public accommodations and other areas. Efforts were also made to buttress the rights of the poor and the aged, of prisoners, gays, and Indians.

MINOR* V. *HAPPERSETT, 21 Wallace 162 (1875). A decision whereby the Supreme Court ruled that women had no constitutional right to vote. Virginia L. Minor, a citizen of Missouri, maintained that the right of suffrage was a privilege of U.S. citizenship. In rejecting this contention, the Supreme Court held that the right of suffrage is not coextensive with citizenship and that the Fourteenth Amendment does not add to the privileges or immunities of citizens of the United States, but merely furnishes an additional guarantee for those in existence.

MINSTREL SHOWS. The first known minstrel troupe appeared in New York City in 1843. By 1857, when the famous Christy Minstrels appeared, the performance had settled into a standard pattern of white performers impersonating blacks. The company had a white interlocutor and two "end men" who bandied jokes with him between vocal solos by others in the circle. There were dances, comic sketches, and acrobatic turns. Minstrelsy was popular through the rest of the century but gradually died out and was practically extinct by 1930.

MINT, FEDERAL. Established in Philadelphia, then the national capital, in 1793. It remained there permanently after other government agencies had been moved to Washington, D.C. Silver coinage began in 1794 and gold coinage in 1795. In 1835 Congress established three branch mints—one at New Orleans and two in the new goldfields, at Charlotte, N.C., and Dahlonega, Ga. The one at New Orleans ceased to coin in 1909 and became an assay office. The other two ceased operations in the 1860's. A branch mint was installed at San Francisco in 1854 and operated until 1955. Another established at Denver in 1862, but no money was made there until 1906. A sixth branch mint at Carson City, Nev., operated between 1870 and 1893. The Bureau of the Mint was created by Congress on Feb. 12, 1873, as a division of the Treasury Department, and supervises the two remaining coinage mints, Denver and Philadelphia; the two assay offices, San Francisco and New York City; and the two bullion depositories, Fort Knox, Ky. (gold), and West Point, N.Y. (silver). The minting of gold coins ceased in 1934.

MINTS, PRIVATE. They frequently appeared in new gold-producing areas when there was a scarcity of U.S. minted coins. Their coins, of original design, circulated freely. In California, in 1849–51, government money was so scarce that several private mints were set up; their coins, though not legal tender, were often accepted as such. A little later, private mints functioned in Oregon, Utah, and Colorado. With the establishment of the U.S. mint at San Francisco in 1854, the need for privately minted coins disappeared.

MINUTEMEN. Popular name for the Massachusetts militia from 1756 through the American Revolution. Other states—Maryland, New Hampshire, and Connecticut—also called their militia minutemen. The famous Massachusetts body developed after the militia was reorganized in 1774 to rid it of Tories. A double system of regiments was established in the province: the regular militia and the minutemen to be ready for any emergency "at a minute's warning." Both regular militia and minutemen fought the British at Concord, and the men the British killed on Lexington green were minutemen. Both minutemen and militia were in the Eight Months Army (*see* Washington's Eight Months Army). The minutemen disappeared in Massachusetts.

MIRAMAR, CONVENTION OF. Signed at Miramar Castle near Trieste on Apr. 10, 1864, by Archduke Ferdinand Maximilian of Austria. Infringing upon the Monroe Doctrine, it was an attempt by Napoleon III to establish a French monarchy in Mexico. (*See* Mexico, French in.)

MIRANDA'S INTRIGUES. Francisco Miranda, a Venezuelan, fled from the Spanish military service to the United States in 1783. He tried to interest high government officials in a plan to emancipate the Spanish Indies by the aid of foreign powers. After war broke out between England and Spain in 1796, he tried to get the American government to enter into an alliance with England and with alleged Spanish-American emissaries for revolutionizing the Indies, but largely because of the reluctance of President John Adams this scheme was frustrated. Miranda managed to recruit a few American troops and made two attempts (1805 and 1806) to liberate Venezuela, but was repulsed by the Spanish. He was captured and imprisoned by the Spanish in 1812.

***MIRANDA* V. *ARIZONA*,** 384 U.S. 436 (1966). A Supreme Court decision in which a five-to-four majority ruled that the prosecution may not use statements obtained by "custodial interrogation" (questioning initiated by law enforcement officers after a person has been taken into custody) unless the person is warned prior to any questioning that he has a right to remain silent and a right to the presence of an attorney. The *Miranda* case was both praised as a civil-liberties landmark and bitterly criticized for unduly restricting law enforcement.

MIRO, FORT. Spanish post established on the Ouachita River in 1785, on the site of present-day Monroe, La. First called Ouachita Post, it was renamed Monroe in 1819.

MISCEGENATION. The first statutes against interracial marriage were enacted in Maryland (1661) and Virginia (1691); Massachusetts, North Carolina, and Pennsylvania soon followed suit. Similar laws were passed in many of the frontier states. It was argued that such laws were designed to preserve racial integrity, but they generally prohibited only interracial marriages involving a white person and a person of another color, not, for example, those between an Indian and a black. As late as 1950 some thirty states still had such laws on their books. In 1967, in *Loving* v. *Virginia*, a unanimous U.S. Supreme Court declared such laws unconstitutional.

MISCHIANZA. An extravagant *fête champêtre* held at the Wharton estate, Walnut Grove, on May 18, 1778, in honor of Sir William Howe, commander of the British forces occupying Philadelphia. The entertainment lasted from four o'clock on the afternoon of May 18 until four o'clock in the morning of the following day.

MISIONES AWARD (1895). The decision ending an Argentine-Brazilian dispute over part of the Misiones Territory between the Iguaçu and Uruguay rivers. The two governments asked President Grover Cleveland to arbitrate, and he upheld Brazil's contentions.

MISSILES, MILITARY. World War II saw the development of missilery by the major participants: the U.S. hand-held bazooka antitank weapon; the artillerylike Soviet Katyusha and U.S. naval barrage rocket; a variety of antiaircraft missiles for air and ground forces; the innovative German V-1 pulse-jet buzz bomb; and the German supersonic, liquid-fuel V-2 ballistic missile with a range of 200 miles, launched by the hundreds against London and Antwerp.

The German V-2 and the American atomic bomb proved the major innovations of World War II, leading directly to the development of strategic missile weapons systems by the 1960's. Lacking a long-range bomber and the atomic bomb in 1947, the Soviet Union immediately gave highest priority to the development of an intercontinental-range missile, nuclear weapons, and long-range jet aircraft. To counter the Soviet missile developments, the United States initiated development of 5,000-mile ICBM's and 1,500-mile intermediate-range ballistic missiles (IRBM's). The first generation of ICBM's (Atlas and Titan 1) and IRBM's (Jupiter, Thor, and nuclear-powered submarine-carried Polaris A1) were quickly followed by subsequent generations. In 1959 Thors were deployed to England and Jupiters to Turkey for NATO. Second-generation ICBM's by the mid-1960's included a solid-propellant and silo-sited Minuteman 1 and 2. In the third generation the Minuteman 3 with MIRV (multiple, independently targeted reentry vehicle) warheads and the submarine-based Polaris A3 (2,500-mile range) were developed. They were followed by the Poseidon (2,500-mile-range MIRV warhead, for an advanced Trident submarine). By 1979 the United States had 1,700 missiles. Development of new MX missiles (land-based mobile missiles) began in the early 1980's; these weapons would supposedly be secure from attack. (*See also* Strategic Arms Limitation Talks.)

MISSIONARY ACTIVITY IN THE PACIFIC. American missionary activity in this area began in 1820 when the American Board of Commissioners for Foreign Missions, founded in 1810 in Massachusetts, sent a party of seventeen led by Hiram Bingham and Asa Thurston to Honolulu to build churches and schools and to heal the sick. American missions were established in Samoa, Micronesia, and, after 1898, the Philippine Islands.

MISSIONARY RIDGE, BATTLE OF (Nov. 25, 1863). Union victory near Knoxville, Tenn. After the successful attack on Confederate Gen. Braxton Bragg's left on Lookout Mountain, Union Gen. George H. Sherman was ordered to turn Bragg's right and sever his communications southward. Bragg's defense was faulty. He had put half his center at the foot of Missionary Ridge, with the other half on the crest of the ridge. His artillery was nearly useless as it could not be sufficiently depressed to sweep the slope of the ridge effectively. The Union troops took the bottom of the ridge and drove the disorganized Confederates from their positions on the top. Before dark the battle was practically over. It only remained for Bragg to withdraw his defeated troops southward to Chickamauga Station and Dalton. A week later Bragg relinquished his command of the Army of Tennessee.

MISSIONARY SOCIETIES, HOME. Voluntary associations, usually under denominational control, for the advancement of religion in needy parts of the United States. In the 18th century missions to the new settlements were sponsored on a small scale by Presbyterian, Baptist, and Congregational associations. A revival of interest in evangelical religion resulted in the establishment of many local missionary societies at the start of the 19th century. Among these were the Missionary Society of Connecticut (1798), the Massachusetts Missionary Society (1799), the Maine Baptist Missionary Association (1804), and the United Domestic Missionary Society of New York (1822). Congregational, Presbyterian, Associate Reformed, and Dutch Reformed churches formed the American Home Missionary Society in 1826.

Throughout most of the 19th century the chief aim of home missionary societies was to send preachers to, and maintain churches on, the western frontier; later more attention was paid to the foreign-born in the cities, and to Afro-Americans. Although concerned primarily with preaching, the home missionary movement has helped in the establishment of many colleges and academies in the West. During the 1930's, many home missionary societies were transformed into social agencies, deemphasizing church programs and intensifying efforts to increase the immigrant's social and economic well-being.

MISSION INDIANS OF CALIFORNIA. Between 1769 and 1823 a chain of twenty-one Franciscan missions was established in California by Father Junípero Serra. The Indians were rounded up by the Spaniards and were concentrated around the missions, to be Christianized and taught agriculture and trades. Soon the tribal names were forgotten, and the Indians came to be known by the names of the missions at which they lived. In 1833, the missions were closed for lack of funds, and the Indians, much reduced in numbers due to epidemics, were turned out to shift for themselves, and for years they drifted around in misery on the margins of the expanding settlements of the whites. Between 1870 and 1907, small parcels of land were purchased for these Indians by the government. The principal surviving groups in southern California are the Diegueño and the Cahuilla.

MISSIONS. *See* **Dominicans; Franciscans; Indian Missions; Jesuit Missions.**

MISSIONS, FOREIGN. American efforts to convert the non-Christian world began in 1810 with the organization of the American Board of Commissioners for Foreign Missions, a society that served the interests of Congregational, Presbyterian, and Reformed churches. Thereafter, separate societies were formed by the other denominations. Bible societies, such as the American Bible Society, undertook the translation of Holy Scripture into the tongues of mission lands. The development of the foreign-missions enterprise was most notable between 1850 and 1930. Reduction in income, unrest in mission lands, opposition from foreign cultures and religions, and a reappraisal by the churches themselves of the gospel in relation to non-Christian faiths have caused a cutback in foreign missions, although many continue to be active.

MISSIONS, FRONTIER. Christians in the older parts of the United States felt that it was their duty to send the gospel to the new settlements in the West. Excessive religious emotionalism (*see* Camp Meetings) and unorthodox creeds, such as Mormonism, were thought to flourish there. Therefore, the various denominations felt it necessary to win adherents and to hold their own constituents in the new settlements.

Missions to the frontiers began early in the 18th century. By the opening of the 19th century the rapidly expanding field led to the organization of many local home missionary societies in New England and New York. These in turn generally grew into or merged with national denominational societies between 1820 and 1835.

MISSIONS OF THE SOUTHWEST. The Spanish mission was meant to be temporary; after the training of the aborigines for citizenship and economic self-dependence, the mission regime was to give way to civil and parochial organization. Along with the mission went the presidio or military guard. The two mutually supporting institutions spearheaded the Spanish advance into the wilderness.

In 1540 Francisco Vásquez de Coronado led his expedition into the Southwest. With him were four Franciscans, whose missionary activities in New Mexico and beyond are the earliest recorded for the Southwest.

The Jesuit order of missionaries began work in Mexico in the 1570's. The Jesuits were active among the Indians of the Sierra Madre, including the Tarahumare, and among the Yaqui and Mayo of lowland Sonora. Meanwhile, Franciscan missionaries were establishing missions among the Pueblo of Arizona and New Mexico.

Numerous missions were established within the limits of present-day New Mexico, Arizona, and Texas. In 1630 they were twenty-five in number, with a Christian population of some 60,000. In 1680 the thirty-three New Mexico missions and the three in Arizona were destroyed in the great Pueblo revolt. With the reconquest of New Mexico in the last decade of the 17th century the missions were restored. The first of the Texas missions was planted among the Jumano of La Junta near present-day Presidio, in 1683; the last foundation, Refugio, on Mission River, was in 1791. The missions of the Southwest declined during the 18th century and, by the Mexican War, were practically nonexistent.

MISSISSINEWA, BATTLE OF (1812). The Miami Indians along the Mississinewa River within the limits of the present Grant County, Ind., were in the service of the British. Gen. William Henry Harrison decided to destroy them, and on Dec. 17 his troops captured and burned an Indian town; three other villages were destroyed shortly thereafter.

MISSISSIPPI. Prior to European exploration, the region was inhabited chiefly by the Chickasaw, Choctaw, Natchez, Biloxi, Tunica, and Pascagoula Indians. Robert Cavelier, Sieur de La Salle, claimed the entire Mississippi Valley for France in 1682. French control of the lower valley was established by the founding of Biloxi by Pierre Lemoyne, Sieur d'Iberville, in 1699. Colonial rivalry led to the French and Indian War (1754–63), which resulted in England's acquisition of French territory east of the Mississippi River, including the southern portion of the present state of Mississippi.

The Mississippi Territory, created on Apr. 7, 1798, included the land area within 32°28′ north latitude on the north, 31° north latitude on the south, the Mississippi River on the west, and the Chattahoochee River on the east. The area between 32°28′ north latitude and the state of Tennessee was added to the Mississippi Territory in 1804. After a revolt in Spanish Florida in 1810 resulted in the establishment of the Republic of West Florida, President James Madison, claiming that area had been a part of the original Louisiana Purchase, declared the Florida republic American territory, and it was incorporated into the Mississippi Territory in 1812 and later divided between Louisiana and Mississippi.

On Dec. 10, 1817, Mississippi was admitted to the Union —a north-south line dividing the territory into the states of Mississippi and Alabama. After a series of Indian cessions (1820, 1830, and 1832) the northern half of the state was opened to white settlement, and Mississippi experienced a massive population increase and economic development. Speculation drove land and slave prices to unrealistic levels. The panic of 1837 caused severe depression and repudiation of the state bonds and drove many residents to seek refuge and fortune in Texas.

During the 1840's and 1850's Mississippi developed an agrarian system based almost exclusively on a one-crop (cotton) economy. By 1860 the state's slave population of 436,631 was larger than its white population of 353,899. Mississippi was the second state to secede, on Jan. 9, 1861, and provided the Confederacy's only president, Jefferson Davis. During the Civil War more than 100 battles and skirmishes were fought in Mississippi, the most important being the Battle of Vicksburg, which fell to a Union siege July 4, 1863.

Mississippi experienced a decade of strife during Reconstruction. Military rule was instituted until a civil government could be established consistent with the Radical Republican program. After five years of confusion and delay Mississippi complied and was readmitted to the Union on Feb. 23, 1870. The prewar power elite, capitalizing on racial prejudice and anxiety, managed to restore itself to power in 1875.

The Redeemers, later called Bourbons, established the iron rule of a one-party system by maintaining the color line in Mississippi politics. Throughout the 1880's, Bourbon favoritism toward railroads and industry was challenged by spokesmen of the small farmers in the white hill counties. In 1890 a new constitution, disfranchising blacks and marking the rise of the "rednecks," reduced political rivalry to the planter-industrial power elite and the small farmers and laborers.

From 1932 until the mid-1950's, Mississippi political campaigns were largely free of racial overtones, although blacks continued to be largely disfranchised. The civil rights movement, however, reactivated race as a major political issue, especially after the Supreme Court's school desegregation decision in 1954. Subsequently, the state's segregated dual-school program was replaced by a unitary system. These changes, along with industrial development and an incipient breakdown in the monolithic party system, inaugurated major readjustments in the state's traditions.

There was large-scale black voter registration in the 1960's, and the presence of thousands of blacks on the voting rolls changed Mississippi politics profoundly. Both a contributing factor to, and a result of, racial and political readjustment after the mid-1950's was the shift from a one-crop cotton economy to a diversified agricultural and industrial system. The percentage of the labor force employed in agriculture dropped from 43 percent in 1950 to 7.3 percent in 1970. In 1980 the population was 2,520,638.

MISSISSIPPI, CONFEDERATE ARMY OF. On Mar. 27, 1862, the Confederate troops under Gen. A. S. Johnston, known as the Army of Kentucky, moved to Corinth, Miss.; they were united with other troops and renamed the Army of Mississippi. At the death of Johnston at Shiloh in Tennessee, Gen. P. G. T. de Beauregard became commander, but was soon succeeded by Gen. Braxton Bragg. After it unsuccessfully invaded Kentucky, the army was reorganized, and on Nov. 20, 1862, it became the Army of Tennessee.

MISSISSIPPI, UNION ARMY OF THE. Constituted in March 1862 under Gen. John Pope to operate against Island No. 10. When Pope was ordered to Virginia, Gen. William S. Rosecrans assumed command. The Army of the Mississippi with that "of the Tennessee," combined under Gen. Ulysses S. Grant, fought Confederate forces at Iuka and Corinth. On Oct. 24, 1862, the Army of the Mississippi became the Thirteenth Army Corps.

MISSISSIPPIAN CULTURES. The prehistoric Mississippian cultures dominated the lower and middle Mississippi Valley from about A.D. 700 to the historic period. Settlements ranged in size from small villages to the city of Cahokia, Ill., with an estimated population of 30,000. Characteristic traits of the cultures are centralized political organization; social stratification; the platform mound-and-plaza complex; and intensive cultivation of corn, beans, and squash. A highly religious cult referred to as the Southern Cult or the Southeastern Ceremonial Complex was an important social institution within most Mississippian cultures. Many features of these Mississippian cultures indicate a Middle American stimulus. But the main impetus of these Mississippian cultures came from indigenous development.

MISSISSIPPI BUBBLE (1720). The disastrous failure of John Law's scheme for exploiting the resources of French Louisiana. Law, a Scot who was a successful banker and financier, organized the Mississippi Company to assume control of Louisiana in 1718. Increasing demand for its stock led to wild speculation that drove the price of shares to high figures, without any sound basis in tangible assets. The anticipated profits were not realized, and soon the scheme revealed itself as a purely speculative venture. In 1720 the company failed, the "bubble" burst, and the stockholders lost their entire investments. Law's connection with the venture ceased, but the company retained control of Louisiana until 1731.

MISSISSIPPI COMPANY OF VIRGINIA. Organized in 1763 by a group including Thomas and Arthur Lee and George Washington to procure a huge tract of land at the junction of the Ohio and Mississippi rivers. It was one of several such enterprises, including the Ohio Company, the Indiana Company, and the Vandalia Company, seeking grants of land. The approach of the American Revolution terminated the hopes of the Mississippi Company, as well as the hopes of the other companies.

MISSISSIPPI DELTAS, BLOCKADE OFF THE. Late in May 1861 the two main ship channels at the mouths of the Mississippi River, Pass à L'Outre and South West Pass, were blockaded by the Union navy. On June 30 the Confederate raider *Sumter* made its famous escape through Pass à L'Outre. Because of the difficulty of blocking all the mouths of the Mississippi and the fact that New Orleans had, in addition to the Delta passes, lateral outlets via Lake Pontchartrain and Barataria Bay, it was impossible for the Union forces to establish an effective blockade. This influenced the decision to attempt the capture of New Orleans itself.

MISSISSIPPI PLAN. Two separate attempts in the South to disfranchise the Afro-American.

The first Mississippi Plan, occurring between the 1870's and the 1890's, refers to the practice by whites of carrying firearms on election day, ostensibly for hunting, but actually as a veiled threat to blacks. Occasionally a gun would "accidentally" go off in the direction of a black near the polls.

The second Mississippi Plan was adopted by the Mississippi constitutional convention of 1890. It required every citizen from twenty-one to sixty to be able to display his poll tax receipt. It also required the would-be voter to be able to read the U.S. Constitution, to understand it when read to him, or to give a reasonable interpretation thereof. Six other southern states adopted similar plans between 1895 and 1910. In 1964 the Twenty-fourth Amendment eliminated the poll tax in federal elections and its use in state elections was later invalidated. Federal legislation passed in 1957, 1960, 1964, and 1965 removed the remainder of the Mississippi Plan.

MISSISSIPPI RIVER. The greatest of the North American rivers has the fifth largest drainage area in the world (1.2 million square miles) and is one of the world's busiest commercial waterways. The river has two main lateral branches —the Ohio River to the east and the Missouri to the west. The length of the Mississippi proper is 2,348 miles, and the waters of its system pass through two Canadian provinces and thirty-one states into the Gulf of Mexico. Its source is Lake Itasca in northwestern Minnesota.

Its discovery is credited to Hernando de Soto, who reached it near the site of Memphis, Tenn., in May 1541. There is no indisputable evidence that another European saw the Mississippi River until 1673, when Louis Jolliet and Father Jacques Marquette paddled their canoes out of the Wisconsin River into the larger stream. They proceeded down the river to a point near the mouth of the Arkansas River, where they turned back. In 1682 Robert Cavelier, Sieur de La Salle, explored the river from the Illinois to its mouth, where on Apr. 9 he took possession of the country for France and named it Louisiana.

In March 1699, two Frenchmen, Pierre Lemoyne, Sieur d'Iberville, and Jean Baptiste Le Moyne, Sieur de Bienville, entered the Mississippi, explored it for some distance, and warned away an English vessel that had arrived on a mission similar to their own (*see* Carolana). The French established themselves first at Biloxi, then on Mobile Bay, and in 1718 they founded New Orleans. Thereafter for nearly a half-century the Mississippi was used and controlled by the French.

At the close of the French and Indian War in 1763 France lost its possessions in the New World, and the Mississippi River became an international boundary. According to the Definitive Treaty of Peace of 1783, the United States was to extend to the Mississippi between Spanish Florida and Canada, and Americans were to have the free navigation of the river (*see* Mississippi River, Free Navigation of).

The Spanish, who controlled the mouth of the river, were not party to the treaty. They imposed duties regarded as prohibitive by the settlers in the Ohio Valley. The West seethed with unrest (*see* Western Separatism). In 1795, in accordance with Pinckney's Treaty with Spain, the river was opened to Americans (*see* Deposit, Right of). In 1800, however, Spain ceded Louisiana back to France (*see* San Ildefonso, Treaty of), and the river was closed once more. The Louisiana Purchase made the Mississippi an American river. Thereafter the Mississippi River served as the great artery of trade and commerce for the whole upper valley (*see* Mississippi Valley). The steamboat *New Orleans* made its historic trip in 1811 from Pittsburgh to New Orleans, and by 1860 more than 1,000 were in service.

During the Civil War the vital importance of the Mississippi to the Confederacy was recognized by both sides, and the struggle for its control was one of the principal aspects of the war (*see* Mississippi River, Opening of the). After the war the railroads diminished the importance of the Mississippi and commercial traffic dwindled. The Mississippi River Commission was established by act of Congress in 1879 to supervise the maintenance and improvement of the river, chiefly by deepening and widening its channels. By 1970 traffic had increased on the river to 230 million tons annually, just slightly less than that on the Great Lakes.

Disastrous floods have made flood control one of the principal concerns of the state and federal governments. Following the flood of 1927 the federal government established a flood control program that, through the construction of 1,870 miles of main stem levees and other measures, has greatly reduced the threat of inundation.

MISSISSIPPI RIVER, FREE NAVIGATION OF. An important issue to inhabitants of the interior Mississippi Valley during the 17th and 18th centuries, when the river was their main highway of commerce and its mouth was owned by a foreign power. France, which then owned Louisiana, gave Great Britain access to the river as part of the settlement at the end of the French and Indian War in 1763. At the same time France ceded Louisiana to Spain. In 1784 Spain closed the river to all foreigners, mainly in the hope of checking the growth of American settlements in the West. The United States sought repeatedly, but in vain, to obtain from Spain treaty recognition of its claim to access. In 1788 Spain undertook a separatist intrigue (*see* Spanish Conspiracy) with the westerners and, in order to promote it, granted them limited privileges of navigation; but they were not satisfied, and by 1794 their threats of violent action had become so menacing that the governments of both the United States and Spain were prodded into renewed activity. Further alarmed by the Jay Treaty of 1794 (by which Britain and the United States renewed their mutual guarantee of free navigation), Spain at last yielded in the Pinckney-Godoy Treaty of San Lorenzo (Oct. 27, 1795). It established the free navigation of the Mississippi by the United States, which also gained the ancillary right of deposit at New Orleans (*see* Deposit, Right of). The question was made moot by the Louisiana Purchase.

MISSISSIPPI RIVER, NAVIGATION ON. Indian craft used on the Mississippi were the bull boat, or coracle, made of buffalo hide stretched on a frame, and the pirogue, or dugout canoe. The French introduced the bateau, which was essentially a large flat-bottomed skiff propelled by oars, and the barge, which was built with keel and ribs and propelled by sails, oars, or cordelle. The Spanish maintained on the river a fleet of galleys, probably large barges or small ships. The Americans introduced the flatboat, or ark, which handled much of the downstream transportation until the Civil War. The keelboat also seems to have been an American adaptation. It was a long, narrow craft built on ribs and keel and propelled by setting poles or cordelle.

The first Mississippi steamboat was the *Orleans* or *New Orleans,* built at Pittsburgh by Nicholas Roosevelt, which entered the Natchez–New Orleans trade in 1811. Steamboats multiplied rapidly after 1820; this necessitated improvements, including dredging of sandbars and clearing river channels. By 1840 steamboat traffic had reached its zenith, but railroads soon began sapping trade from the steamboats. The navigation of the river remains important to carry bulky freight (petroleum, coal, steel), much of it on steel barges, and to check railway rates.

The modern system of improvements for both navigation and flood control date from the establishment of the Mississippi River Commission in 1879. Largely under the direction of army engineers, it has provided vast lines of levees, dams, dikes, cutoffs, reservoirs, spillways, and dredged channels.

MISSISSIPPI RIVER, OPENING OF THE. The strategic importance of the Mississippi River was recognized by both sides in the Civil War. In 1861 the Confederates fortified Columbus, Ky., on the Mississippi; but the Union capture of forts Henry (Feb. 6, 1862) and Donelson (Feb. 16, 1862) led to the evacuation of Columbus. Island No. 10, in the river near the Kentucky-Tennessee boundary, was then fortified by the Confederates, but Union gunboats captured the island on Apr. 7, 1862, and on June 6, 1862, Memphis fell into Union hands, opening the Mississippi as far south as Vicksburg.

Meanwhile, a Union force operating from the Gulf of Mexico captured New Orleans (May 1, 1862) and other river points as far up as Baton Rouge, La. The Confederates now strongly fortified the high bluffs at Port Hudson, twenty-five miles above Baton Rouge, and at Vicksburg, Miss., 200 miles to the north, in an effort to preserve the valuable communication between territories on both sides of the Mississippi.

After a siege of nearly two months Vicksburg surrendered on July 4, 1863. When the news reached Port Hudson, that post also surrendered, on July 9, 1863, since it was no longer of value to the Confederates. This completed the opening of the Mississippi, and the Confederacy was split in two.

MISSISSIPPI SQUADRON. Union naval fleet in service in the Mississippi River during Civil War. The Union Flotilla in the Western Waters by January 1862 consisted of nine iron-clad vessels and three wooden gunboats. Additional ironclads, light-draft steamers, and monitors were added as rapidly as they could be completed. On Oct. 1, 1862, it was rechristened the Mississippi Squadron. An unsuccessful attack on Vicksburg in December was followed by the capture of Arkansas Post, Jan. 11, 1863. Thereafter, the squadron worked in close cooperation with Gen. Ulysses S. Grant in his campaign against Vicksburg. After the fall of Port Hudson, La., July 9, 1863, the only important variation from the monotony of patrol and convoy duty was the Red River campaign, Apr. 8 to May 22, 1864.

***MISSISSIPPI* V. *JOHNSON*, 4 Wallace 475 (1867).** A Supreme Court case in which the governor of Mississippi asked the Court to perpetually enjoin President Andrew Johnson from carrying out the Reconstruction acts passed a few weeks before by the Congress. Speaking for a unanimous Court, Chief Justice Salmon P. Chase denied the petition for lack of jurisdiction, pointing out that the president is the executive department and cannot be restrained by the judiciary.

MISSOURI. A permanent settlement was made west of the Mississippi in present-day Missouri in about 1735, when a small group built a few cabins across from the mouth of the Kaskaskia. Their village was Ste. Genevieve, and it was followed by Pierre Laclede's fur-trading village of St. Louis in 1764. The French villages and fur traders were pawns of European politics. France handed over all of Louisiana to Spain in 1762, and during Spanish rule settlements were made at St. Charles (1769), Carondelet (1767), New Bourbon

(1793), Cape Girardeau (1793), and several other places. In 1780 the British and Indians mounted an unsuccessful attack on St. Louis.

New threats faced the Spanish after the American Revolution. American settlers poured into Missouri. As a result, by 1804 more than half the 10,000 settlers in Missouri were American. American hegemony had been established in 1803 when France sold Louisiana to the United States. After the War of 1812 a mass of immigrants, mainly from the South, crowded the road to Missouri, many bringing slaves. Missouri's population had grown rapidly, from about 10,000 in 1804 and about 20,000 in 1810 to about 66,000 in 1820, just previous to statehood; by 1830 the state's population had reached 140,000, and by midcentury, 682,000.

Economically the state grew rapidly. The staple crops were corn and wheat. After 1820 the Santa Fe trade was an important business for a limited number of Missourians, significant largely because of the silver, furs, and mules that were brought back; large fur companies under the leadership of William H. Ashley, the Chouteaus, and John Jacob Astor were prosperous. Also, because of its location, Missouri was considered the gateway to the West.

The struggle over slavery from 1850 through the Civil War was acute in Missouri. During the 1850's Missouri became a divided state, both political parties splitting over the slave issue. In 1860 and early 1861 Missouri had three elections with four factions contending, but each time the moderates, who were for peace and compromise, won overwhelmingly. The Union armies threw the pro-Confederate state government out early in 1861, for although initial battles at Wilson's Creek and Lexington were favorable to the Confederates, Union strength prevailed. The state suffered from guerrilla warfare for four years; and more than 400 skirmishes were fought on Missouri soil before the end of the war. A provisional state government kept Missouri in the Union.

After the Civil War, Missouri still had close ties with the South, but it looked principally to the West. The railroads were pushed to the state's western boundaries and across the Plains. Farming was productive, and manufacturing supported the immigrant labor that had begun to flow into the state, largely from Germany and Ireland. St. Louis and Kansas City grew into important railroad centers. Growth continued as the cattle and wheat from the Plains flowed in to be converted into beef and flour.

In the 20th century, Missouri's economic development was marked by increasing farm mechanization and expanding industrial production. Politically it continued to be dominated by Democratic machine politics (see Pendergast Machine). In 1945, a new state constitution was adopted which included a nonpartisan plan for electing judges known as the Missouri Plan. By the 1960's, Missouri's inner cities faced decay with increasing suburbanization. In 1980, the population was 4,917,444.

MISSOURI, THREE FORKS OF THE. A picturesque and strategically important spot in Montana, so named because three principal source streams of the Missouri unite there—the Jefferson, the Madison, and the Gallatin. Meriwether Lewis and William Clark camped at the junction in 1805.

MISSOURI BOTANICAL GARDEN. Established in 1840 by Henry Shaw, a merchant, on the grounds of his estate. When Henry Shaw died in 1889, he left the garden with a sizable endowment to the people of St. Louis, and it became the Missouri Botanical Garden. The garden continued to expand and develop, both as a research facility and as a major public attraction. Its scientific program has made significant contributions to the study of botany and is one of the nation's major centers of biosystematic research. In the 1920's a study of tobacco virus done by B. M. Duggar resulted in a breakthrough in modern understanding of viruses.

MISSOURI COMPROMISE (1820–21). First efforts by the U.S. Congress to deal with the extension of slavery into new areas. In 1819 there was an equal number of slave and free states, and when Missouri petitioned for statehood, the House of Representatives passed an amendment to the statehood bill prohibiting the further introduction of slaves into Missouri and providing that all children born of slaves should be free at the age of twenty-five. The amendment was rejected by the Senate. A compromise was effected in 1820 by admitting Maine as a free state and by authorizing Missouri to form a constitution with no restriction on slavery. However, slavery was prohibited in the remainder of the Louisiana Purchase north of 36°30′. Missouri's efforts to exclude free blacks and mulattoes from the state caused a second compromise to be effected in 1821. This stipulated that Missouri would not be admitted until it agreed that nothing in its constitution should be interpreted to abridge the privileges and immunities of citizens of the United States. The pledge was secured. On Aug. 10, 1821, Missouri became a state. In 1854 the Missouri Compromise was repealed (*see* Kansas-Nebraska Act).

MISSOURI FUR COMPANY. *See* **St. Louis Missouri Fur Company.**

MISSOURI-KANSAS-TEXAS RAILROAD. *See* **Railroads; Sketches of Principal Lines.**

MISSOURI PACIFIC RAILROAD. *See* **Railroads; Sketches of Principal Lines.**

MISSOURI RIVER. A major tributary of the Mississippi River and the longest river in the United States (2,466 miles). From its source in southwestern Montana, where the Jefferson, Gallatin, and Madison rivers join together, it winds through one of the most fertile valleys in the world, to its junction with the Mississippi (ten miles north of St. Louis).

The lower Missouri was known to French trappers, traders, and voyageurs in 1705, and in 1720 a Spanish caravan was sent from Santa Fe to the Missouri to drive back the French (*see* Villasur Expedition).

The Missouri was first explored from its mouth to its source by Meriwether Lewis and William Clark (1804–05), and it became the great highway into the West. The first steamboat ever to ascend the river was the *Independence,* which pushed off from St. Louis in 1819. In 1831 Pierre Chouteau succeeded in ascending the Missouri in his steamboat *Yellowstone.* Steamboating on the river reached its peak in the late 1850's and declined following the completion in 1859 of the Hannibal and St. Joseph Railroad.

In 1944 Congress authorized a Missouri River basin project to control flooding of the Missouri, improve navigation, develop hydroelectric power, irrigate over 4.3 million acres in the basin, halt stream pollution, and provide recreation areas. By the 1970's there were seven dams on the Missouri and eighty on its tributaries.

MISSOURI RIVER FUR TRADE. The fur trade was the principal commerce of the early days in the West and the Missouri River and its tributaries constituted one of the three great systems of importance to the fur trader and trapper. Many establishments, variously designated as forts, posts, and houses, were scattered along the Missouri in the wilderness long before the tide of western immigration set in. After the expedition of Pierre Gaultier de Varennes, Sieur de La Vérendrye, in 1738, whose main purpose was one of exploration, came Pierre Menard, fourteen years earlier than Jacques D'Église (1791–95), and then Jean B. Truteau of the Spanish Commercial Company, which erected Truteau's Post in 1794. In 1800 Cedar Post was established in the Sioux country, thirty-five miles below the present site of Pierre, S.Dak. The most important early post was that of the St. Louis Missouri Fur Company. Known as Fort Lisa, it was located in Nebraska, near Council Bluffs, Iowa. The largest and most important of the American Fur Company's forts was Fort Union, in present-day North Dakota.

St. Louis was the greatest center of the fur trade. All the early expeditions were outfitted and started from this point. In 1843 there were 150 fur trading posts, most along the Missouri River. Although the upper reaches of the Missouri were at first walled off by the British and the Blackfoot and Arikara, these obstacles were eventually overcome.

***MISSOURI* V. *HOLLAND*,** 252 U.S. 416 (1920). A Supreme Court case in which it was determined that the treatymaking power extends to a field (i.e., bird migrations) not specifically delegated to the national government. The case rose out of the Migratory Bird Treaty of 1916 with Great Britain.

MITCHELL'S MAP. Published in London in 1755, under the auspices of the Board of Trade by John Mitchell, a Virginian. His map of British and French North America went through more than twenty editions before 1792 and figured in nearly every boundary dispute involving the United States or parts thereof. On it were laid down the first boundaries of the United States following the Treaty of Paris (1783).

MIWOK. Californian Indians spread through the central river valley and to the north of San Francisco Bay. The Miwok were distinguishable by their language, a branch of the Penutian phylum. They depended on acorns for subsistence, made fine basketry, and lived in several hundred small hamlets.

MIXED COMMISSIONS. Instruments of international law composed of members of different nationalities for the purpose of achieving the peaceful settlement of disputes. They include mixed claims commissions, commissions of conciliation, and commissions of inquiry.

Mixed claims commissions arbitrate disputes arising from claims of one state or its nationals against another state regarding damages, debts, boundary questions, and other matters involving claims. Jay's Treaty of 1794 set up such a commission. Following the success of Jay's Treaty, other claims commissions were established. Among them were the Mexican Commission (1868), which disposed of over 2,000 claims; and the U.S.–German Mixed Claims Commission created after World War I to settle war damage claims.

Mixed commissions of conciliation elucidate the facts underlying an international dispute and make nonbinding proposals for settlement. Examples are the "Bryan treaties," concluded by the United States and some American and European states between 1913 and 1915 on the initiative of Secretary of State William Jennings Bryan. Since World War II nearly 200 such commissions have been established.

Mixed commissions of inquiry are similar, but their functions are limited to determining the facts in a controversy.

MOBILE (Ala.). A city in southwest Alabama, located on Mobile Bay. In 1702 Jean Baptiste Le Moyne, Sieur de Bienville, established a fort nearby, but flooding forced the movement of the fort to the present site of Mobile in 1711. It passed to the British in 1763 and to Spain during the American Revolution. The Americans took it in the War of 1812 (*see* Mobile Seized).

During the Civil War, Mobile was one of the most important Confederate ports. It was strongly fortified and was much used by blockade runners until the Battle of Mobile Bay (Aug. 5, 1864) closed the port. After the war, Mobile burgeoned as a major port, exporting lumber, cotton, and naval stores. Mobile is also a major shipbuilding center. The population of the city in 1980 was 200,452.

MOBILE ACT (1804). After the Louisiana Purchase, Spain contended that it owned all territory on the Gulf of Mexico east of the Mississippi. Congress, at President Thomas Jefferson's insistence, passed the Mobile Act, which claimed that area for the United States. The region (eastward from the Mississippi to the Perdido River, and bordering on the Gulf, but not including Mobile) was not actually occupied by the United States until 1810 (*see* West Florida, Annexation of).

MOBILE BAY, BATTLE OF (Aug. 5, 1864). A Union fleet of four monitors and fourteen wooden vessels of war, commanded by Adm. David G. Farragut, forced an entrance into Mobile Bay through a narrow, highly fortified passage. "Damn the torpedoes!" cried Farragut, as his *Hartford* took the lead. His vessels eventually reached the bay, despite the heroic fight put up by the Confederate ironclad *Tennessee.*

MOBILE SEIZED (1813). At the beginning of the War of 1812, Mobile, Ala., was in the possession of Spain. The United States had long coveted the port (*see* Mobile Act) and when the English navy began using it as a base, U.S. forces easily took it. The Spanish protested, but the town passed into the possession of the United States on Apr. 13, 1813 (*see* West Florida, Annexation of).

MOBILIZATION. The process of assembling and organizing troops and matériel for the defense of a nation in time of war or national emergency. It has become a central factor in warfare since the French Revolution and the rise of nationalism. Whereas 18th-century powers relied on regular armies and hired mercenaries to fight limited wars, modern nations have increasingly demanded that every able-bodied citizen respond to mobilization calls.

The mobilization problems experienced in the War of 1812 and the Mexican War (1846–48) continued to plague U.S. military efforts throughout the 19th century. For instance, the militia and volunteer system was never workable.

The Civil War was a total war and thus a modern conflict. Before it ended, various methods of raising troops were resorted to, including calling up the state militias, calling for volunteers, and, most importantly, the draft, implemented by the Conscription Act of 1863.

All the old nightmares of poor mobilization were present in the Spanish-American War (1898), plus some new ones. Only the fact that the war was short and successful helped to ameliorate some of the potentially disastrous problems.

U.S. participation in World War I (1917–18) and World War II (1941–45) introduced speed into the warmaking equation. Although the urgency of mobilization was slightly cushioned by the prior entry of America's allies into both wars, the gigantic scale of mobilization, the increased importance of technology, the total absorption of a sophisticated industrial economy into the war effort, and the huge number of troops all raised mobilization planning to the highest councils of war.

The leading role of the United States in the cold war significantly altered its traditional mobilization techniques. Although never implemented, universal male military training, authorized in principle by the Universal Military Training and Service Act of 1951, was supposed to provide a peacetime pool of manpower that could be drafted in time of national emergency. Until the Korean War (1950–53) the emphasis on air power and nuclear arms allowed the army's strength to slip. Instead of the reserves being called for the Vietnam War, as had been done in the Korean War, forces were raised through increased draft calls. But not calling the reserves was generally considered to have been a mistake, for it gravely weakened the army's strategic reserve.

MOCCASIN. From an Algonkin word for shoe, a foot covering of soft skin, with soft or hard soles. Most American Indian tribes wore moccasins, often decorated with beads and quills. The eastern Indian moccasin had a soft sole and was made by folding a piece of soft tanned skin up over the foot, the seams at the top. The Plains Indians preferred a moccasin with a hard sole. Moccasins were adopted by the whites and universally worn by early traders and trappers.

MODEL CITIES PROGRAM. Part of Lyndon B. Johnson's "Great Society" program, the Demonstration Cities and Metropolitan Area Redevelopment Act (Nov. 3, 1966), funded the rehabilitation of slums and metropolitan-area planning and provided land-development mortgage insurance over a three-year period. The Department of Housing and Urban Development (HUD) was to oversee the program. Sixty-three model cities were chosen to draw up plans, with the emphasis on rehabilitation rather than slum clearance.

MODOC WAR (1872–73). Last of the Indian wars in northern California and southern Oregon. The removal of the Modoc to the Klamath reservation in Oregon in 1864 antagonized them, and one of their younger chiefs, Captain Jack (Kintpuash), led the more aggressive elements back to their former habitat near the Lost River in northern California. A detachment of cavalry tried to return the Modoc to the reservation, and the situation was aggravated when fourteen settlers were killed by the Modoc. The Modoc band consisted of only 75 warriors and about 150 women and children, but they held out in the lava beds that constituted their retreat position for six months against all attempts by troops to dislodge them. The Modoc were finally dislodged only after military operations involving more than 1,000 U.S. soldiers and after dissension had developed among the Modoc themselves. In June 1873 the Modoc left the lava beds and scattered. They were pursued by soldiers and captured, thus ending the war. Captain Jack and three others were tried and hanged; the rest of the band was exiled to Indian Territory.

MODUS VIVENDI. A temporary agreement covering questions that will later be settled by a formal treaty. A notable instance of this use of executive power was Theodore Roosevelt's agreement establishing a financial protectorate over the Dominican Republic.

MOGOLLON (or Western Pueblo). A prehistoric culture developed in southern New Mexico and southeastern Arizona. A distinctive Mogollon tradition appeared about 1000 B.C., when corn, squash, and beans became readily grown. The Mogollon adopted and transmitted many features of Middle American culture at an early date, but their mountain habitat lacked the potential for high agricultural yields that later supported the elaborate ceremonialism characteristic of the Hohokam and the Zuni.

The earliest Mogollon villages and hamlets consisted of from two to about twenty semisubterranean, or pit, houses. Large buildings may have served as community or ceremonial centers. Settlements containing multiroomed pueblo or apartment-type surface dwellings appeared by about A.D. 1000. Some of these settlements grew to large apartments containing well over a hundred rooms. Each community probably remained autonomous and maintained an essentially democratic social organization. Artifacts include wickerwork sandals; ornaments of shell, wood, stone, and bone; string aprons; fur and feather robes; textiles; figurines; pottery; and many tools for collecting and processing food.

MOHAVE. Indian tribe settled along the lower reaches of the Colorado River. The Mohave was the largest of the so-called River Yumans, having a population of about 3,000 in 1680. They spoke Yuman, a subgrouping of a conceptual

Hokan or Hokan-Siouan macrophylum. In the rich alluvial soils of the Colorado the Mohave raised corn but at the same time gathered mesquite beans. Unlike other Californian tribes, the Mohave abandoned basketry in favor of pottery making, a Southwestern trait. They were led by a war chief, who organized formalized battles, virtual games that the tribes of the area carried on among themselves. Religious ceremonials of a group nature were subordinated to dream cycles that formed an integral part of Mohave life: individual dream experiences, either of tribal history and lore or of individual fantasy life were recounted in association with a ritual that suggests a view of reality different from that general among Indians. Mohave contacts with Europeans may have taken place as early as 1540, but they remained essentially free of contact with outsiders, and entered into no treaty with the United States.

MOHAWK AND HUDSON RAILROAD. Opened on Aug. 9, 1831, when the first steam locomotive in New York State, the *De Witt Clinton,* was put into service. The line connected Albany with Schenectady. In 1853 it became part of the New York Central Railroad.

MOHAWK VALLEY. The only natural east-west passage through the Appalachian barrier. From the earliest days of the Dutch period the fur trade moved along this route to Albany. Inevitably there was a clash with the interests of the Iroquois and the French. Both the French and English claimed the Iroquois as subjects. In 1701 the Iroquois signed a treaty (*see* Iroquois Beaver Land Deed) deeding their hunting grounds to the king of England. During the colonial wars the valley settlements suffered cruelly (*see* Schenectady).

A part of the only continuous water route from the Atlantic to the Great Lakes, the valley became the natural route along which highways, railroads, canals, and airports were built. A stream of immigration moved through the valley westward with the opening of the Erie Canal in 1825. The products of midwestern states were carried to eastern markets and eastern goods were sold in the West.

MOHEGAN AND MAHICAN. Two native American tribes speaking differing Algonkin languages but culturally much alike. They are easily confused with each other. The Mohegan were spread through the upper Thames Valley in Connecticut and were often identified with the Pequot. After King Philip's War in 1675, the Mohegan were the dominant Algonkin group in southern New England. Their fame through this period rests largely on their paramount chief, Uncas (*see* Mohegan Case).

The Mahican inhabited the upper Hudson Valley and the area around Lake Champlain. Under pressures from the Mohawk and from Europeans they gradually shifted westward and to the Housatonic in Massachusetts. The Mahican are best known through James Fenimore Cooper's novel *The Last of the Mohicans* (1826).

MOHEGAN CASE. Arose from deeds given in 1640, 1659, and later given by Uncas, Mohegan chief, and his son to the colony of Connecticut. The deeds conveyed virtually the whole Indian country, and the Indians later renounced them. A royal commission set up in 1703 by Queen Anne decided that Connecticut should restore all the lands they had at the time of Uncas' death to the Mohegan. Commissions in 1715, 1738, 1743, and 1773 settled the issue in favor of the colony.

MOHONK, LAKE, CONFERENCE. Held annually between 1883 and 1912 at Lake Mohonk, N.Y., for the purpose of discussing reforms in Indian affairs. It was attended by clergymen, educators, government officials, ethnologists, and other interested persons. The policies recommended by the conference aimed at the assimilation of Indians into the mainstream of American life and were influential in the passage of the Dawes Severalty Act of 1887, which provided for the allotment of tribal land to individual Indians.

MOLASSES ACT (1733). Laid a prohibitive duty on rum, molasses, and sugar imported from foreign colonies into Great Britain's American colonies. The act originated when Barbados led the other British sugar colonies in petitioning Parliament to prohibit the continental colonies from trading with the more fertile foreign West Indies. Smuggling on a large scale minimized the act's effects, but the act probably served as a mildly protective tariff in favor of the British West Indies until its repeal in 1764 by the Sugar Act.

MOLASSES TRADE. The keystone of colonial commerce, supplying as it did a product that enabled the colonists to offset their unfavorable balance of trade with England. Molasses provided a "money cargo" almost as current as cash; but once exported from the British sugar colonies and the foreign West Indies, there was surprisingly little trade in molasses as such. It served as the basis for the triangular trade in which rum sent to Africa brought slaves to the West Indies, where they were exchanged for cash or bills of exchange and more molasses.

In 1704 Parliament confined the exportation of molasses to England or its colonies. In 1733 the Molasses Act unsuccessfully attempted to eliminate trade with the foreign West Indies by prohibitive taxes, and after 1764 the Sugar Acts tried to raise revenue from that trade. Independence freed the thirteen colonies from such restraints, but hampered their trade with the British West Indies. Modifications of the law permitted the direct importation of molasses, but the Navigation Acts continued to limit American shipping until 1830.

MOLECULAR BIOLOGY. In 1926, J. B. Sumner at Cornell University and, from 1930 on, J. H. Northrop at the Rockefeller Institute produced decisive evidence that enzymes were proteins. About a decade later, G. W. Beadle and E. L. Tatum, then at Stanford University, showed from genetic studies on bread molds *(Neurospora)* and bacteria that the action of genes directs the production of enzymes; they summarized their conclusions by the slogan "One gene, one enzyme." By about 1940 it was clear that all enzymes are proteins and that their production is directed by the genes, but the chemical nature of the genes was still obscure.

In 1935, W. M. Stanley, at the Rockefeller Institute, obtained the virus of tobacco mosaic disease as a very large protein molecule. Thenceforth viruses were no longer regarded as mysterious entities, but as defined substances that could be obtained in a pure form. F. C. Bawden and N. W. Pirie in England soon showed that Stanley's virus also contained nucleic acid, a fact of the utmost importance for the development of molecular biology.

An important advance in molecular biology came a few years later at the California Institute of Technology. Max Delbrück, a physicist turned biologist, who had come from Germany, and Salvador Luria, from Italy, showed that bacterial variations were genetically caused. This opened the whole field of bacterial genetics, which was soon to revolutionize all of genetics. Delbrück and his colleagues also made fundamental advances in the study of bacteriophages.

In 1943, Oswald T. Avery at the Rockefeller Institute, with C. M. MacLeod and M. McCarty, announced that the active transforming factor in genetic change was pure DNA. This conclusion was revolutionary, for nearly everyone believed that proteins were the essential genetic material. About 1950, E. Chargaff at Columbia University found a remarkably simple relation for the relative amounts of the various bases in DNA from many different organisms. In 1951, Linus Pauling and R. B. Corey at the California Institute of Technology proposed that the peptide chains of protein molecules could coil into the form of a helix. They also proposed other, more extended, arrangements of amino acids in peptide chains, known as pleated sheets. These structures proved to explain many aspects of the three-dimensional structure of proteins.

In England molecular biologists concluded that DNA was built as a double helix, somewhat like a double spiral staircase, of two polynucleotide chains wound around each other. An enormous amount of new experimental work followed, which fully sustained the fundamental concepts. It was shown that DNA could do more than replicate itself; it could also, in the presence of suitable enzymes and the essential chemical building materials, direct the synthesis of RNA. The RNA then migrates out from the nucleus to the cytoplasm in the outer part of the cell. The RNA in turn was found to direct the synthesis of protein.

The entire genetic code was worked out by 1966. M. Nirenberg at the National Institutes of Health in Bethesda, Md., played a major role in this work, as did S. Ochoa and his collaborators at New York University. H. G. Khorana, a native of India who came to the University of Wisconsin, carried out particularly remarkable chemical syntheses that were essential in unraveling the code.

These discoveries provided an explanation for the simplest kind of genetic mutation—one that results in a change in a single amino acid in a large protein molecule that is otherwise unaltered. Thus, a serious disease—sickle-cell anemia—is caused by an alteration at one single point in the molecule of human hemoglobin, which corresponds to a single base change at one point in human DNA.

Under special circumstances, by means of a suitable enzyme system, RNA can direct the synthesis of a complementary DNA, thus reversing the usual order of events described above, in which DNA furnishes the specific sequence patterns that are transcribed into a complementary RNA. This "reverse transcription" was first reported independently, in 1970, by Howard M. Temin at the University of Wisconsin and by David Baltimore at the Massachusetts Institute of Technology.

MOLINO DEL REY, BATTLE OF (Sept. 8, 1847). During the Mexican War, Gen. Winfield Scott ordered Gen. William J. Worth to storm a stone building at the base of Chapultepec hill, near Mexico City. Heavy casualties resulted, and the "king's mill" did not contain the expected armaments. Although the battle temporarily depressed the army's spirits, later the "mill" provided cover for the assault on Chapultepec.

MOLLY MAGUIRES. A secret and eventually criminal society of Irish labor agitators in the anthracite region of Pennsylvania. From about 1865 until it was broken up in a series of sensational murder trials between 1875 and 1877, it settled labor disputes by intimidation and murder. The name of the society was taken from a group of anti-landlord agitators in the 1840's led by a widow named Molly Maguire.

In 1874 railroad and mine owners hired a Pinkerton detective, James McParlan, to infiltrate the organization. He rose to be secretary of his division. After a particularly outrageous murder in 1875, one assassin was condemned to death. Suspicion arose that a detective was at work and quickly centered on McParlan. Evading one plot to murder him, he continued his pose for some time and then quietly withdrew. The murder prosecutions that followed were based largely on his evidence and shattered the organization forever.

MONEY. Any generally accepted medium of exchange, standard of value, or store of value. The definition has gradually been broadened, so that today money includes demand deposits in commercial banks. Commercial bank time deposits and other assets that can be quickly turned into cash (U.S. Treasury bills and deposits in savings banks and savings and loan associations) are considered "near money."

The Monetary Standard. The monetary standard of the United States is whatever commodity the U.S. Congress designates as the basis of the monetary system. It is the commodity for which all other kinds of money can be exchanged at a fixed ratio. Money that is not redeemable in a specific commodity at a specific rate is fiat money—that is, money backed only by the credit of the issuer.

During the colonial period, many commodities served as money—wampum in New England, beaver skins in the Middle Colonies, and tobacco and many kinds of foodstuffs in the South. Individual colonies issued paper currency.

In 1791 Congress established a bimetallic standard at a ratio of 15 ounces of silver to 1 ounce of gold. By the 1830's, however, silver ceased to circulate, because it was undervalued at the mint; consequently, the country, although legally on a bimetallic standard, was actually on a monometallic gold standard. During the Civil War the right to redeem paper money in specie was suspended. Gold became a commodity that could be bought and sold in a free market, and its value in paper money was no longer fixed but fluctuated from day to day. The suspension lasted until 1879.

Bimetallism officially came to an end when the Coinage Act of 1900 established a monometallic gold standard. A series of executive orders and acts of Congress in 1933 compromised the gold standard by abrogating the right to redeem paper money in gold. The last vestiges of a metallic standard disappeared in the acts of Mar. 3, 1965, and Mar. 18, 1968, which eliminated the gold reserve against Federal Reserve deposits, and the act of July 23, 1965, which ended the coining of silver dollars. All money in the United States came to be fiat money, although U.S. dollars were still accepted internationally on a severely modified gold bullion standard.

Currency. In the colonial period only a small amount of English pounds, shillings, and pence circulated. Most of the money that the colonists used consisted of commodities, non-English (especially Spanish dollars), coins, and paper money. The paper money was of four types: bills of credit or government notes; paper certificates representing deposited coin, bullion, or other commodities; bank notes issued by land banks; and fractional currency (that is, notes in denominations of a shilling or less). Each colony set its own legal value for current coin, and gradually nominal and arbitrary valuations for the current Spanish coins were established, giving rise to an extraordinary confusion of values. The confusion was rendered worse by a multitude of paper-money issues. When the first issue (or "first tenor") depreciated, it was replaced by a "second tenor" and then a "third tenor." The first issue by Massachusetts in 1690 was the first authentic government paper money in history.

During the Revolution, the Continental Congress authorized $241,552,780 of bills of credit between June 22, 1775, and Nov. 29, 1779. In addition, the individual states issued $209,524,776, and there were doubtless other batches of unauthorized issues. The paper money depreciated, slowly at first and then more rapidly. Only a negligible quantity of it was ever redeemed, although the Funding Act of 1790 provided for its redemption for specie (gold and silver) at a ratio of $1 of specie for $100 of Continental currency. The phrase "not worth a Continental" comes from this period.

The Mint Act of 1792 authorized the establishment of a mint to coin (at specified weights) gold eagles ($10 gold pieces), half eagles, and quarter eagles; dollars, of pure silver, half dollars, quarter dollars, dimes, and half dimes; and cents, of copper, and half cents. The system it created did not work. Gold was vastly undervalued, and consequently by the early 1800's, gold coins ceased to circulate. The silver coins disappeared, because they were accepted at face value in Spanish America even though they contained less silver than the Spanish dollar. Furthermore, the market value of the copper in a cent was often higher than 1 cent. In 1806, President Jefferson stopped the minting of silver dollars.

Even if ratios had been correct, gold pieces and silver dollars were too cumbersome to circulate in everyday transactions. What Americans actually used for currency was a hodgepodge of paper money issued by state-chartered commercial banks, by the two United States banks (1791–1811 and 1816–36), and, occasionally, by nonbank corporations.

The gold dollar was devalued in 1834, and Congress further encouraged gold circulation by authorizing the minting of $1 and $20 gold pieces. But the metal in the subsidiary silver coins was worth more as bullion in the open market than its face value as money. Then, in 1853, Congress reduced the silver content of the silver coins.

To help pay for the Civil War, Congress authorized $450 million in paper money, officially known as United States notes but more popularly called greenbacks. This was the first paper money printed by the federal government.

Early in the war the banks and the government stopped redeeming paper money in specie. Eventually $100 in gold commanded $250 in paper. In March 1863, Congress authorized the issue of gold certificates, which were really warehouse receipts, because they were issued in denominations of $20 or more in exchange for gold coin and bullion deposited with the U.S. Treasury. In March 1863, Congress authorized $50 million in fractional paper currency and, in April 1864, changed the coinage weights and ratios.

The National Bank (or Currency) Act of 1863, amended in 1864, established a federally chartered banking system; each national bank was authorized to issue bank notes against federal bonds. In 1866, Congress imposed a 10 percent tax on nonnational bank notes, driving them out of circulation.

In the last quarter of the 19th century, farmers, silver-mine owners, and some businessmen called for the reinstatement of bimetallism. Bankers and other sound-money adherents resisted, and much legislation was passed attempting to reconcile the two opposing views. Eventually, however, the Gold Standard Act of Mar. 14, 1900, ended the silver controversy by adopting a nonmetallic gold standard.

The Federal Reserve Act of December 1913 made additional basic changes in the currency by providing for a Federal Reserve note secured by gold and commercial paper and a Federal Reserve bank note secured by government bonds.

The depression of the 1930's created a new flurry in currency and banking. In April 1933, President Franklin D. Roosevelt recalled gold coin, bullion, and certificates, in effect taking the country off the gold standard. In January 1934 the dollar was devalued from 23.22 grains pure to 13.714 grains. The price of gold was raised from $20.67 to $35 per ounce. In 1935 the issuance of national bank notes ended.

In 1965 the minting of standard silver dollars came to an end, and the silver certificate was also discontinued. In the mid-1970's the currency system consisted of fractional, subsidiary silver and copper currency ($7 billion), a few silver dollars, and $60 billion of paper money issued by Federal Reserve banks. By far the largest part of the money supply was the $200 billion in demand deposits in commercial banks. Thus, the evolution of the American money system has been from bimetallism through a monometallic gold standard to "managed money." The payments mechanism has evolved from a hodgepodge of currencies in the 19th century to a standard flat money. Checks drawn against demand deposits constitute 75 percent of the money supply and cover well over 90 percent of the dollar volume of transactions.

MONHEGAN ISLAND. A small, rocky island, the westernmost of the outlying islands off Penobscot Bay. It is the most prominent landmark on that section of the Maine coast and, as such, was the sailing objective of most of the early voyagers to New England. The island was described by David Ingram in 1569 and was visited by George Weymouth in 1605 and by Capt. John Smith, who spent some time fishing there in 1614. Its present name first appeared in Smith's account. Later he tells us that eighty ships came there to fish between 1614 and 1622, and it became the largest fishing and trading post in New England and the frequent resort of ships from Virginia, Plymouth, and other settlements. Fishing quickly declined and by 1632 Monhegan had become merely a resort for fishermen. The modern settlement of the island dates from 1790.

***MONITOR* AND *MERRIMACK*, BATTLE OF** (Mar. 9, 1862). Stephen Mallory, Confederate secretary of the navy, saw the South's only chance of beating the North at sea in ironclad production. He commissioned thirty-two ironclads, of which fewer than a dozen were ever fully ready.

The Confederates salvaged the U.S.S. *Merrimack*, which had been scuttled in the Union evacuation of Norfolk. They sheathed it with a double layer of 2-inch-thick iron. It was rechristened the C.S.S. *Virginia*, a name that did not gain usage. On Mar. 8, 1862, the *Merrimack* sortied from Norfolk and easily sank the two wooden ships that were protecting the water flanks of the Union position at Newport News. Meanwhile, the Union navy's own ironclad, the *Monitor*, had made a dramatic dash from New York. On Mar. 9 the *Monitor* successfully engaged the *Merrimack* until tide and cumulative damage required it to head for Norfolk.

By naval semantics, both antagonists won: the *Monitor* tactically because it kept the *Merrimack* from destroying the U.S.S. *Minnesota*, which had been its aim; and the *Merrimack* strategically because the Union navy thenceforward stayed out of the Hampton Roads until the *Merrimack* was destroyed by its own crew when the Confederates evacuated Norfolk on May 11, 1862.

MONITORS. Ironclad warships with hulls nearly awash and equipped with revolving gun turrets. The original *Monitor* was completed Mar. 3, 1862. It was towed to Hampton Roads, Va., where it took part in the historic engagement with the *Merrimack* on Mar. 9, 1862. It foundered at sea in a storm off Cape Hatteras, N.C., Dec. 31, 1862. The U.S. government built a number of monitors all patterned on the original, but their performance was disappointing. However, the success of the original *Monitor* gave a worldwide impetus to the adoption of the revolving armored turret. But, it was abandoned speedily because of its various drawbacks.

MONKS MOUND. *See* **Cahokia Mounds; Mounds and Mound Builders.**

MONMOUTH, BATTLE OF (June 28, 1778). The British army, under Sir Henry Clinton, evacuated Philadelphia, June 18, and arrived at Monmouth Courthouse (Freehold, N.J.) on June 26, on its march to New York. George Washington assigned Maj. Gen. Charles Lee to command the advanced corps, then near Englishtown, with orders to attack the British rear. Lee, after long delays, attempted to cut off Clinton's rear guard, but failed. His entire division of over 4,000 men then retreated until halted by Washington. Washington skillfully reformed his lines to meet the enemy, now heavily reinforced. One of the fiercest contests of the war followed. Fought in intense heat and engaging some 10,000 men on each side, the battle ended only with darkness. During the night Clinton's army quietly withdrew. Washington reported his loss at 69 killed, 161 wounded; the Americans buried 249 British on the field. A court-martial sustained charges against Lee of disobeying orders and making an unnecessary retreat.

MONMOUTH PURCHASE. Included the region in present-day New Jersey extending "west from Sandy Point [Sandy Hook] along the coast and up the Raritan River and south for twelve miles from any part of this northern line." The original settlers were Quakers and Baptists from Long Island, N.Y., and Newport, R.I., who established Middletown and Shrewsbury. James Stuart, the Duke of York (later James II), annulled their patent on Nov. 25, 1672, as being in conflict with his prior grant of the territory to John Berkeley and George Carteret.

MONOCACY, BATTLE OF THE (July 9, 1864). A Confederate army of approximately 11,000 men, advancing on Washington, D.C., encountered about 6,000 Union troops strongly posted on the east bank of the Monocacy River, southeast of Frederick, Md. The Union force was routed at heavy cost, and on July 10, the Confederates resumed the march.

MONONGAHELA, BATTLE OF THE (July 9, 1755). Between a British force under Gen. Edward Braddock of Braddock, Pa., and a combined French and Indian force marching from Fort Duquesne. They met at the site of Braddock, Pa. The Indians occupied a commanding hill and forced the British vanguard to retreat, abandoning its guns. The British main body rushed forward hastily, the whole army became an unmanageable huddle, and eventually fled in disorder.

The legend of the cowardice of the troops seems to have less foundation than the charge of incompetence among the officers. Most of the officers, including Gen. Braddock, were killed or wounded, but Lt. Col. George Washington, one of Braddock's aides, was almost miraculously unscathed.

MONONGAHELA RIVER. A tributary of the upper Ohio, it drains the western slopes of the Alleghenies in northern West Virginia, Maryland, and southern Pennsylvania. Its great importance dates from 1750 and 1752 when Christopher Gist explored the region for the Ohio Company, and a path was blazed from the Potomac to the Monongahela.

MONOPOLY. The exclusive control of the output of a good or a service by a single seller. American public policy against monopoly derives in part from early English laws against the practice of purchasing essential commodities to influence their prices and to reap considerable profits from resale. The Anglo-American tradition has frowned on formal or informal agreements to limit output or to raise prices. Public disapproval was manifested in the fact that the parties to the agreement could not enlist the court's assistance in enforcing its terms.

J. P. Morgan built the United States Steel Corporation by acquiring companies that produced more than one-half of all finished steel in the United States in 1901. Similarly, John D. Rockefeller acquired a large number of competing refiners to gain control of nearly 90 percent of the U.S. market for refined petroleum products by the end of the 19th century. Such mergers and the pervasive price-fixing and market-sharing agreements of numerous American enterprises in the 19th century eventually brought about the Sherman Anti-trust Act of 1890 and the Clayton Antitrust Act of 1914.

MONROE, FORTRESS. At Hampton, Va., and commanding the entrance to Chesapeake Bay, one of the principal fortifications on the Atlantic coast. It was completed in 1834. The Confederates made no attempt to capture it, and it remained in Union hands. Gen. George B. McClellan began the Peninsular campaign from it in 1862. Jefferson Davis was confined in Fortress Monroe from 1865 to 1867.

MONROE DOCTRINE. President James Monroe's message to Congress of Dec. 2, 1823, laid down the principle that European governments could establish no new colonies in the Western Hemisphere. The doctrine grew out of Secretary of State John Quincy Adams' response to Russia's attempt to exclude all the Russian vessels from the U.S. northwest coast north of 51°. A second reason for the message lay in the fear that European powers were planning the reconquest of the newly independent Spanish American republics (*see* Latin-American Republics, Recognition of).

While the message was enthusiastically received in the United States, it had little immediate practical influence, and for some time after 1826 Monroe's message remained virtually unnoticed. Minor violations of it occurred in Britain's encroachments in Central America and its acquisition of the Falkland Islands.

The first great revival of interest in the doctrine came in 1845 with the intrigues of Great Britain and France to prevent the annexation of Texas to the United States, the difference of opinion over Oregon between Britain and the United States, and the fear of British purposes in California (*see* Oregon Question). On Dec. 2, 1845, President James K. Polk reiterated the principles of Monroe (*see* Polk Doctrine). Again, as in 1823, the immediate results were not important, but the principle had begun to sink into the American mind. On Apr. 29, 1848, Polk declared that the threat of an English or Spanish protectorate over Yucatán might compel the United States itself to assume control over the region in question. Thus, for the first time, the Monroe principle was made the basis for measures of expansion (*see* "Manifest Destiny"). No action was taken, however.

The Civil War offered to the powers of Europe an excellent opportunity to challenge Monroe's principles. Spain intervened in Santo Domingo, and France established an empire in Mexico (*see* Mexico, French in). While other circumstances contributed to the collapse of Maximilian's empire, there can be no question that two major factors were the diplomatic pressure exerted by the U.S. government in 1865 and French fear of the United States.

The doctrine was cited in the 1880's as reason for forbidding the construction by Europeans of a transisthmian canal (*see* Panama Canal) and as implying that such a canal must be under the exclusive guarantee of the United States. This point of view was accepted by Great Britain in the first Hay-Pauncefote Treaty (Feb. 5, 1900). In 1895 President Grover Cleveland asserted that the doctrine compelled Great Britain to arbitrate a boundary dispute with Venezuela over the limitations of British Guiana. Cleveland's position produced a serious diplomatic crisis, but the moderation displayed by the British government permitted a peaceful solution of the difficulty (*see* Olney Corollary).

The growing nationalism of the United States at the beginning of the 20th century continued to have its effect upon the doctrine. The administration of Theodore Roosevelt, which began with an attitude of great moderation, gradually moved toward the position that the United States must assume a measure of control of the more unruly of the Latin-American states in order to prevent European action against them. In his annual message to Congress in 1904, Roosevelt definitely laid down the doctrine (later called the Roosevelt Corollary to the Monroe Doctrine) that chronic wrongdoing by a Latin-American state might compel American action. The doctrine has figured as justification in the not infrequent interventions in the affairs of Caribbean states (*see* Caribbean Policy).

After World War I, there was increasing resentment against American interference in the affairs of the republics of Latin America (*see* Latin America, U.S. Relations With). Under President Franklin D. Roosevelt pledges against armed intervention were given, and a definite treaty was signed, pledging the signatories not to intervene in the internal and external affairs of one another.

Argentina's policy of neutrality during World War II was a major obstacle to hemispheric unity against the Axis powers. The other nations of the Western Hemisphere adopted the Act of Chapultepec (1945), which broadened the Monroe Doctrine by incorporating the principle that an attack on one country of the hemisphere was to be considered an act of aggression against all the countries of the hemisphere. In 1948 the Organization of American States was established, through which the principles of the Monroe Doctrine could be effected by a system of Pan-Americanism. Despite this emphasis on hemispheric unity, the U.S. fear of Communist infiltration in Latin America led it to take action unilaterally in Guatemala (1954), Cuba (1960–61), and the Dominican Republic (1965) without prior approval or with only very tardy approval by inter-American consultative bodies.

The Monroe Doctrine has never obtained a true international status, and in the United States itself there has been somewhat of a reaction against extreme interpretations of its principles.

MONROE MISSION TO FRANCE (1794–96). James Monroe, a known friend of the French republic, arrived in Paris in August 1794 as American minister. His initial popularity with the French was destroyed when the text of Jay's Treaty with Great Britain became known. Monroe, ignorant of the real character of John Jay's mission, had assured the French government that Jay, in his negotiations with England, had been positively forbidden to weaken the ties between the United States and France. Monroe tried to palliate what seemed to him to be the ill faith of Washington's cabinet. Federalist leaders were able to convince Washington that Monroe's conduct was disloyal to the administration and the president recalled him. Washington's decision was approved by many Americans whose sympathies had been alienated by the bloody excesses of the French Revolution.

MONROE-PINKNEY TREATY (1806). Commercial agreement with Great Britain, intended to replace Jay's Treaty. It was signed by U.S. envoys James Monroe and William Pinkney, but President Thomas Jefferson refused to submit it to the Senate.

MONTANA. The area of Montana came to the United States with the Louisiana Purchase (1803). Early explorers met the major Indian tribes of the region: the Sioux to the east, the Blackfoot and Gros Ventres on the upper Missouri River, the Flathead in the Bitterroot Valley, and the Crow in the Yellowstone Valley. Montana's early growth was linked with the rich fur trade. Prominent were the Missouri Fur Company and the American Fur Company.

A spectacular mining period opened in the 1860's. Emphasis shifted from placer mining to quartz veins and to silver mining in the 1870's and then to Butte's copper and zinc deposits in the 1880's. Failed miners branched out into farming, especially in the Bitterroot and the Gallatin valleys. The Montana area became part of Idaho Territory on Mar. 3, 1863. Continued increase in population led to the organization of Montana Territory on May 26, 1864.

Enormous ranches for both cattle and sheep were built up on the eastern plains. The several homestead acts brought an influx of farmers that eventually led to a balance between stock raising and crop farming. The railroads arrived in the 1880's. Industry grew up around mining, forestry products, and agricultural manufacturing. Montana became a state on Nov. 8, 1889.

The state's most colorful episode was the War of the Copper Kings, at the turn of the century, during which Marcus Daly, William A. Clark, and Frederick A. Heinze used every means, including their great wealth, to promote their mining interests and their political leadership.

Montana's economic growth has been assisted by improvements in agriculture, its major source of income. Petroleum manufacturing and natural gas were developed after 1915. Enormous coal deposits are made available by strip mining. Forests approaching depletion in the 1950's are being placed on a perpetual-yield management basis. Montana's population in 1980 was 786,690, a 13.3 increase over 1970.

MONTDIDIER-NOYON OPERATION (June 9–13, 1918). On June 9, the German army launched an attack on a twenty-mile front west of Soissons, between Montdidier and Noyon. The French launched a counterattack on June 11 that drove the victorious Germans back for three miles. The American First Division at Cantigny came under artillery preparation fire and sustained raids.

MONTE CASSINO. A mountain, 1,674 feet high, about fifty miles north of Naples, and crowned by the famous Benedictine abbey. In World War II, Monte Cassino provided German troops with superb observation over the Allied forces approaching from the south on their way to Rome. The Germans incorporated the hill into their defenses, although they exempted the monastery itself from their fortified positions.

Unable to pass the German defenses, and believing the abbey to be fortified, the Allies on Feb. 15, 1944, destroyed the buildings and their artistic and cultural treasures with an air bombardment by 250 planes. German troops then moved into the abbey and in a fierce battle denied the height to the Allied forces. Not until a powerful spring offensive broke the German defenses did the Allies, on May 18, capture the mountain. The abbey was rebuilt after the war.

MONTEREY. A city on the central coast of California, it was discovered in 1542 by Juan Cabrilla. A settlement was made by Gaspar de Portolá in 1770 and served as the capital of Spanish and Mexican California from 1777 to 1845. Although in the latter year Los Angeles became the seat of civil government, Monterey remained the fiscal and military headquarters, as well as the center of social life. The town was under the U.S. flag for one day, Oct. 19, 1842, when Commodore Thomas ap Catesby Jones seized it in the belief that war existed between Mexico and the United States. Permanent American control came during the Mexican War, with Monterey's surrender, without resistance, to Commodore John D. Sloat on July 7, 1846. Monterey was incorporated in 1850. Monterey has grown in popularity as a resort area. The population in 1980 was 27,558.

MONTERREY, BATTLES OF (Sept. 21–23, 1846). In the Mexican War, Gen. Zachary Taylor's invading army of 6,000 attacked Monterrey (in northeastern Mexico), which was defended by 9,000 men. The city was conquered in three days.

MONTGOMERY (Ala.). Capital city of Alabama since 1846, with a population in 1980 of 178,157. Montgomery was briefly the capital city of the Confederate States of America. Montgomery was established in 1817 on the site of towns long occupied by Alabama Indians. The town became an important shipping and warehousing center for Alabama's cotton raising areas before the Civil War but during the war it was almost completely destroyed. Its modern business activity has developed around the buying and selling of farm produce (more often cattle than cotton in the 1970's), and the manufacture of furniture and cotton fabrics.

MONTGOMERY BUS BOYCOTT (1955–56). Considered the beginning of the modern civil rights movement, the boycott began on Dec. 1, 1955, when Mrs. Rosa Parks, a black seamstress, refused to relinquish her seat on a Montgomery, Ala., city bus to a white man. Mrs. Parks was arrested and fined. Rev. Martin Luther King, Jr., then organized a boycott by Montgomery's black population of all city buses. As a result the bus company lost sixty-five percent of its income. Following a Supreme Court decision of Nov. 13, 1956, the boycott was ended when the bus service began a policy of desegregation.

MONTGOMERY CONVENTION (1861). Assembled at Montgomery, Ala., Feb. 4, to organize the Confederate States of America. Representatives were present from South Carolina, Georgia, Alabama, Mississippi, Florida, and Louisiana. The convention drafted a provisional constitution, then declared itself a provisional legislature, and set up a government. For president and vice-president, the convention selected Jefferson Davis of Mississippi and Alexander H. Stephens of Georgia. The convention sat in Montgomery until May 20, when it adjourned to meet in Richmond on July 20. It added new members as other states seceded and directed the election in November at which a permanent government was elected. With the inauguration of the permanent government (Feb. 22, 1862) it adjourned.

MONTICELLO. The home of Thomas Jefferson, near Charlottesville, Va. Excavation started in 1767–68. Jefferson, as his own architect, built in Italian style, on the model of Andrea Palladio. But after five years in Europe and examination of many buildings, Jefferson greatly altered Monticello. The result was an Italian villa with a Greek portico, a Roman dome, and many colonial features. The home of Jefferson for fifty-six years, on his death the estate passed from his heirs to Uriah Levy. Eventually the estate came under the control of the Thomas Jefferson Memorial Foundation. Jefferson is buried on the grounds.

MONTPELIER (Vt.). Capital city of Vermont, with a population of 8,241 in 1980. It was settled in 1787 and named in honor of French officers from Montpellier, France, who had served in the American Revolution. It became capital in 1805. Most employed residents work for the State government.

MONTREAL, CAPTURE OF (1760). The British victory over the French at Quebec in 1759 was followed by a spirited effort by the French to hold onto their capital city. On May 15, 1760, the English ships appeared below Quebec and the French troops retreated up the river. The English, knowing that Montreal was doomed, prepared at their leisure for the final stroke. On Sept. 8, 1760, the French governor surrendered Montreal, and with it Canada.

MONTREAL, CAPTURE OF (1775). After the fall of St. John's, Newfoundland, Nov. 2, 1775, the main body of the American force under Gen. Richard Montgomery pushed on toward Montreal. Gov. Guy Carleton was in the city, but, as the fortifications were weak and ruinous, he made no attempt to defend it. On Nov. 13 the American troops marched into Montreal without encountering resistance. The city remained in American hands until June 15, 1776.

MONTREAL, WILKINSON'S EXPEDITION AGAINST. In 1813 Gen. James Wilkinson, commander of the northern troops distributed from Champlain to Niagara, N.Y., advanced on Montreal. On Nov. 10 the expedition—about 7,000 men in 300 boats—reached the Long Sault Rapids, still 100 miles from Montreal. It was constantly harried by British troops and gunboats. Further disheartened by wintry weather, sickness, and nonarrival of reinforcements, Wilkinson retreated up the Salmon River. In February 1814 his army withdrew to Plattsburgh (*see* Lacolle Mill, Battle of) and Sackets Harbor, ending this badly mismanaged campaign.

MONUMENTS, NATIONAL. *See* **Parks, National, and National Monuments.**

MOONEY CASE. In 1916 in San Francisco Thomas J. Mooney, a minor labor leader, was one of several persons arrested and tried on the charge of planting a bomb that exploded during a parade, killing ten persons and wounding forty others. Mooney was sentenced to death, but the case was weak and some of the evidence so questionable that the judge who presided at his trial finally became convinced that the trial had been unfair and joined in the long fight to save Mooney. In 1918 President Woodrow Wilson asked Gov. William Stephens of California to commute Mooney's sentence to life imprisonment. Labor and other organizations fought steadily in his behalf, and in 1939, Gov. Culbert L. Olson pardoned and released Mooney.

MOON HOAX. On Aug. 25, 1835, the *New York Sun* announced wonderful new discoveries on the moon. Batlike beings, temples of polished sapphire, and a beautiful inland sea were described and illustrated. The hoax fooled even some Yale professors. It was finally explained as a satire, but it put the *Sun* on the road to prosperity.

MOONIES. *See* **Unification Church.**

MOON LANDING. On July 16, 1969, at Cape Canaveral (then Cape Kennedy), Fla., three astronauts—Neil A. Armstrong, Edwin E. Aldrin, Jr., and Michael Collins—began their voyage toward the first lunar landing. The flight path was so nearly perfect that only one of four planned trajectory corrections had to be made. Early Saturday afternoon (July 19), seventy-six hours after launch, the crew slowed their ship while on the back side of the moon to enter lunar orbit. On Sunday (July 20) Armstrong and Aldrin cut loose from the command module and headed toward the surface of the moon. Dodging a boulder-strewn area the size of a football field, Armstrong set the craft down at 4:17 P.M. (EDT). Six and one-half hours later, after donning a protective suit and life-sustaining backpack, Armstrong climbed down and set foot on lunar soil, saying: "That's one small step for [a] man, one giant leap for mankind." Aldrin soon followed. Half a billion people watched on television as the two astronauts moved about on the lunar surface with its gravity one-sixth that of earth's.

While on the moon's surface, Armstrong and Aldrin raised the American flag, collected 47 pounds of samples, talked with President Richard M. Nixon, and set up scientific equipment that would remain on the moon. After two hours of exploring, they returned to the lunar module and prepared for the return flight. After a smooth flight, their space ship, Apollo 11, splashed down in the Pacific on Thursday (July 24).

MOONSHINE. Originally, smuggled liquor, indicating that it was customarily transported by night. The name "moonshiner" for an illicit distiller in the southern Appalachian area came into popular use in the 19th century. His still was apt to be in a wild place among thickets or rocks, in a gorge or a cave. Illicit whiskey—that is, on which excises have not been paid—has been an issue since the early republic (*see* Whiskey Rebellion). After 1877, armed revenue officers were constantly active in the southern mountains, killings were frequent, and sometimes pitched battles were fought, but the business was never quite eliminated. During the Prohibition era, moonshine came to be made almost everywhere, even in the home. (*See also* Bootlegging.)

MOORE'S CREEK BRIDGE, BATTLE AT (Feb. 27, 1776). A decisive victory of North Carolina Whigs, or Patriots, over North Carolina Loyalists, fought eighteen miles above Wilmington. In the battle, which lasted only three minutes, 1,600 Loyalists were overwhelmed by 1,100 Whigs. It crushed the Loyalists, stimulated the independence movement, and prevented British invasion of the state in 1776.

MORAL MAJORITY. A term used to designate a group of militant conservatives and fundamentalist Christians who united in the late 1970's to support conservative political causes. The Moral Majority as a political organization was brought together by television evangelists such as Jerry Falwell of Virginia and James Robison of Texas. Some have credited it with the defeat of Jimmy Carter by Ronald Reagan in the 1980 presidential election. In the 1980's the moral majority opposed such liberal causes as the Equal Rights Amendment, the Department of Education, school busing, the Panama Canal treaties, homosexual rights, and abortion.

MORALS. From the arrival of colonists until World War I the American moral code was absolutist, puritanical, and individualistic and applied a single standard for all persons. Despite avowals of religious tolerance, a *de facto* Protestant establishment ruled, as in requiring prayer and chapel attendance in schools and colleges. Ascetic Protestant moral standards were applied to all—Catholic, Protestant, Jewish, the unchurched, and the atheists. Moreover, the Protestant ethic was related to the gospel of success: since it was believed that the moral and ascetic individual would become economically successful, economic failure implied immorality.

With the development of the Industrial Revolution new ideas developed, including secular and Christian socialism, the social gospel, and deterministic social science. Within this matrix a new, more collectivist, more political, and more situational and relativist morality emerged. Although no exact dates can be given for the transition, the signs of change extended all the way from the moral indignation over slavery to indignation over the evils of the sweatshop, the assembly line, and capitalism in general—all examples of institutional or situational, rather than purely personal, immorality.

World War I was the great watershed. Puritanical, confident, and success-worshipping Americans who went to war came home to view themselves, in a social context, as the "lost generation." Freudianism, Marxism, and the cultural relativism of social science, combined with the antipuritanical diatribes of H. L. Mencken and the debunking historians, all contributed to the decline of an absolutist and individualistic morality in postwar America. By the 1980's moral relativism, situational rather than principled, and all forms of environmental determinism had come to hold the field, especially among creative and educated groups. Concurrently, there was emerging a conservative countermovement. This was evident in such areas as religion, where evangelical "born again" Christianity was on the rise, and in education, where there was a movement back to a more disciplined, morally centered pedagogy.

MORAL SOCIETIES. The religious upsurge beginning late in the 18th century brought innumerable associations into being whose general intent was expressed by the names of the Society for the Reformation of Morals, organized in 1813, and the New York Moral Reform Society, chartered in 1834. There were dozens of groups printing and distributing moral and religious pamphlets. Antislavery, temperance, antitobacco, and peace societies sprang up.

MORATORIUM, HOOVER. On June 20, 1931, President Herbert Hoover proposed a one-year international postponement of all intergovernmental debts, reparations, and relief debts. He hoped that such action would promote a worldwide restoration of confidence and economic stability. By July 6 the fifteen nations involved had accepted the proposal.

MORAVIAN BRETHREN. Protestant sect tracing its ancestry back to the Hussite movement in 15th-century Bohemia. The first Moravian settlement in America, in Georgia in 1735, was unsuccessful, but enduring settlements were made in Nazareth, Pa., in 1740 and in Salem, N.C., in 1753. The principal Moravian churches are the Moravian Church in America (Northern Province), with 34,424 members in 1981 and the Moravian Church in America (Southern Province), 21,057 members.

MORAVIAN MASSACRE. *See* **Gnadenhutten.**

MORAVIAN TOWN, BATTLE AT. *See* **Thames, Battle of.**

MOREY LETTER. A campaign document in the presidential election of 1880 in which James A. Garfield was purported to have declared himself in favor of "Chinese cheap labor." While it was denounced as a forgery, the suggestion that Garfield might support free immigration has been held responsible for his loss of the electoral votes of California.

MORFIT'S REPORT. President Andrew Jackson sent Henry M. Morfit to Texas in 1836 to obtain information upon which to base a recommendation for or against recognition of Texan independence. Jackson recommended delay.

MORFONTAINE, TREATY OF. *See* **Convention of 1800.**

MORGAN, FORT, SEIZURE OF. *See* **Mobile Bay, Battle of.**

MORGAN-BELMONT AGREEMENT (1895). A contract between the U.S. Treasury Department and the banking houses of J. P. Morgan and August Belmont, American representative of the Rothschilds of Paris. The financiers agreed to buy $62 million worth of government bonds and pay for them in gold, thus replenishing the government's rapidly diminishing gold reserve.

MORGAN'S RAIDS (1862–64). Col. John Hunt Morgan began his Confederate cavalry career as a raider by a spectacular dash into Kentucky from Knoxville, Tenn., in July 1862, destroying quantities of Union arms and supplies with little actual fighting. His most spectacular achievement came in July 1863, when he crossed the Ohio River at Brandenburg, Ky., drove off some Indiana militia, dashed northeastward into Ohio at Harrison, and passed through the suburbs of Cincinnati at night. His dash across southern Ohio ended disastrously in a battle at the ford at Buffington Island but Morgan and 1,200 men escaped, only to be captured at Salineville, Ohio, on July 26. After several months' confinement, Morgan escaped to resume his military career. His raiding activities ended suddenly when he was surprised and killed in eastern Tennessee in September 1864.

MORGAN TRIALS (1827–31). William Morgan of Batavia, N.Y., disappeared in 1826, as he was about to publish a book revealing the secrets of Freemasonry. Several Masons pleaded guilty of conspiracy in abducting Morgan and were given jail sentences and fined; others refused to testify and were imprisoned for contempt. In the subsequent trials, Mason's fate was never determined. The inconclusive trials and the suspicion aroused contributed to the anti-Masonic movement.

MORMON, BOOK OF. According to Mormons, a translation by Joseph Smith of the sacred history of the ancestors of the American Indians who were, at the time the history was written, a white people with inspired prophets similar to those among the Hebrews, from whom it is said they descended. Joseph Smith claimed that this record was delivered to him in the year 1827 by an angel who gave him instructions for translating it. This work is held by the Mormons as equal in authority with the Bible as the word of God.

MORMON BATTALION. U.S. soldiers who served in the war with Mexico (1846–48). They were enlisted from the Mormon camps in Iowa Territory, and were furnished by Brigham Young. The Mormon volunteers marched, under terrible conditions, to California by way of Santa Fe and the Gila River. They reached San Diego, Calif., in January 1847, when the battalion was disbanded; most of the members joined another Mormon outfit under Brigham Young.

MORMON EXPEDITION (1857–58). U.S. army campaign to subdue the Mormons, who were refusing to obey federal laws. President James Buchanan ordered 1,500 artillery troops from Fort Leavenworth, Kans., to Salt Lake City, Utah. Col. Albert Sidney Johnston was designated as commander of the expedition. The lateness of the season and the guerrilla tactics of the Mormons compelled the troops to go into winter camp near Fort Bridger, Wyo. Meanwhile, promises of amnesty by Buchanan, coupled with the threat of federal military intervention, induced Young and his followers to submit, and on June 26, 1858, Johnston's expedition marched into Salt Lake City, Utah, without bloodshed.

MORMON HANDCART COMPANIES. In the immigration of the Mormons to Utah, those with insufficient means to procure horses resorted to the use of handcarts. From Iowa City, Iowa, to Salt Lake Valley, a distance of 1,300 miles they pushed and pulled their carts at an average daily journey of about twenty miles. Travel with handcarts began in 1856 and continued until 1860.

MORMONS. *See* **Latter-Day Saints, Church of Jesus Christ of.**

MORMON TRAIL. The Mormons, after their expulsion from Nauvoo, Ill., in February 1846, took a westerly route along a well-beaten trail, through what is now Iowa, to the Missouri River. By permission of the Omaha Indians, they crossed the Missouri River into Nebraska Territory, where they remained for the winter. In April 1847 they started west, under the leadership of Brigham Young, following the Platte River to Fort Laramie, Wyo. At this point they took the old Oregon Trail, until they reached Fort Bridger in Wyoming. Traveling to the southwest through Echo Canyon to the Weber River, they ascended East Canyon, crossed the Big and Little mountains of the Wasatch Range, and entered the valley of the Great Salt Lake in Utah through Emigration Canyon on July 24, 1847.

MORMON WAR (1844–46). A series of disorders between the Mormon residents of Nauvoo, Ill., and their non-Mormon neighbors. By June 1844 mutual antagonism had reached such a pitch that the Mormon militia was under arms in Nauvoo, while at least 1,500 armed men, bent on the expulsion of the Mormons, had assembled in the county. After Gov. Thomas Ford took personal charge, a peaceful solution appeared possible; but on June 27 the Mormon leader Joseph Smith and his brother Hyrum were murdered. Violence flared again in the fall of 1845 and the militia was called out again. The Mormons promised to leave Illinois the following spring. Anti-Mormons, professing to believe that many intended to remain, moved in force against the city in the fall of 1846. A general engagement, with several casualties, resulted. Peace was patched up and the Mormons hastened their exodus. By mid-December, nearly all had gone.

MORRILL ACT (1862). Act of Congress for the establishment of agricultural and mechanical arts colleges in every state in the Union. States were offered vast grants of land as an endowment for the proposed schools, known as land-grant schools. (*See also* Land Grants for Education.)

MORRIS CANAL AND BANKING COMPANY. Organized in 1824 to build a canal ninety miles across New Jersey from the mouth of the Lehigh River to New York harbor, thus giving a direct water route to the seaboard for Lehigh coal. The canal was completed in 1832. The Morris Company, chartered with banking privileges, was brought into disgrace and ruin by speculators. In 1844 a new canal and banking company was organized. After 1866 the business of the canal declined because of railroad competition. It was leased to the Lehigh Valley Railroad in 1871, was taken over by the state in 1904, and went out of use in 1924.

MORRISTOWN, ENCAMPMENT AT (1776–77, 1779–80). Winter site for the Continental army during the American Revolution. During the first winter, George Washington located the general camp at Lowantica Valley (now Spring Valley), southeast of the town. Two years later (1779–80) the army was encamped at Jockey Hollow, four miles southwest of the general's headquarters at the Jacob Ford Mansion.

MORSE GEOGRAPHIES. Jedediah Morse, the "father of American geography," published the first geography to be published in the United States, *Geography Made Easy.* More than twenty-five editions were published during his lifetime. He wrote four other highly successful geographies.

MORTARS, CIVIL WAR NAVAL. Heavy guns designed to throw shells with a high angle of fire were built at Pittsburgh in 1862 for use by the Union navy in the New Orleans campaign (*see* Mississippi River, Opening of the). Each was mounted on a schooner, and they bombarded forts Jackson and St. Philip, the principal defenses below New Orleans. They were crucial during the siege of Vicksburg the following year; a mortar fleet bombarded the city for forty-two days prior to its surrender, throwing 7,000 shells into it. At the close of the war the navy possessed twenty-six such mortars.

MORTGAGE RELIEF LEGISLATION. During times of widespread financial distress, there has been political pressure to enact debtor relief to avoid foreclosure. Because the law of real property is a function of the states, mortgage relief legislation has also come primarily from the states. The major episodes of mortgage debtor relief followed periods of farm mortgage distress in the late 19th century and between World War I and World War II, especially in the 1930's.

In the 1870's and 1880's and again in the 1920's in the Plains states there was a large-scale overextension of farmer indebtedness, primarily in land mortgages. When farm incomes deteriorated and land values declined in subsequent years, mortgage debt became very burdensome to the borrower. As a result, foreclosure or some other form of distress transfer often occurred. Agitation for debtor relief included demands for inflation of the money supply (such as the Free Silver movement) and for public regulation of business monopolies. Two kinds of mortgage relief legislation emerged: (1) the establishment of statutory periods of redemption that continued after foreclosure sale and (2) the requirement that mortgaged property be sold for fair value.

After 1929, general economic depression—in conjunction with severe drought in some areas—made mortgage distress a national concern. By early 1936, twenty-eight states had passed mortgage relief legislation in one or more of the following forms: (1) moratoria on foreclosures, (2) extensions of redemption periods, and (3) restrictions on the way in which the foreclosed property could by sold.

State mortgage relief legislation met with only limited success, partly because the measures were not enacted until after much of the damage had been done. More important, the problem of mortgage distress was only part of the much larger problem of general economic depression. An attempt at a federal moratorium, the Frazier-Lemke Act of 1934, was declared unconstitutional in 1935, but two years later an amended version was judged constitutional. More effective were the actions of the federal farm-credit agencies in refinancing mortgage loans—actions that benefited lenders by providing welcome liquidity while enabling debtors to escape foreclosure. Similar steps were taken in the field of urban mortgage finance. The prosperity induced by World War II put an effective end to the problem, and widespread mortgage distress did not occur in the postwar period.

MORTIMER, FORT. Built in 1842 on the upper Missouri in what is now North Dakota. It was established by the newly organized Union Fur Company, which hoped to compete with the American Fur Company. After three years of unsuccessful competition the firm sold out to the American Fur Company, and in 1845 Fort Mortimer was abandoned.

MOSBY'S RANGERS. Confederate troops commanded by Col. John S. Mosby. Their main activities consisted of sudden attacks on Union outposts, followed, when pursued, by quick dispersion. To Gen. Philip H. Sheridan, Gen. George A. Custer, and others, Mosby's men were a thorn in the flesh. Efforts to destroy the rangers were provokingly unavailing.

MOSCOW CONFERENCE OF FOREIGN MINISTERS (Oct. 19–30, 1943). Held by U.S. Secretary of State Cordell Hull, British Foreign Secretary Anthony Eden, and Soviet Foreign Minister V. M. Molotov. It issued a four-power declaration (signed also by China) pledging them to set up an international organization for peace. To implement it, the groundwork was laid for the Dumbarton Oaks Conference and the United Nations Conference, San Francisco.

MOSES HIS JUDICIALS. The earliest (1636) compilation of New England legislation, presented to the general court of Massachusetts Bay. It was not of biblical origin, but embodied the trading-company government, the early laws, and the practices of Massachusetts. Although eventually rejected in favor of the Body of Liberties adopted in 1641, it was of influence in other colonies.

MOSQUITO FLEET. A small naval squadron selected by Commodore David Porter in 1823 to wipe out the West Indian pirates. The fleet scoured the coasts of Santo Domingo, Cuba, and part of Yucatán thoroughly over the next few years. By 1829 the fleet had captured about sixty-five pirate craft, virtually destroying their power.

MOSQUITO QUESTION. Mosquito comprised the present east coast of Nicaragua, strategically located for an isthmian canal. In 1844 Britain established a formal protectorate, and American jealousy was aroused. After adoption of the Clayton-Bulwer Treaty (April 1850), the Mosquito question became inseparable from the general Central American question; the United States put a Monroe Doctrine interpretation on the treaty and Britain maintained its right to continue supervision in behalf of the Mosquito Indians there. In 1860 Mosquito was incorporated into Nicaragua.

MOST-FAVORED-NATION PRINCIPLE. In a commercial treaty, an agreement between the two parties that each will extend to the other terms at least as good as those given any third country. In U.S. history, it first appeared in the Treaty of Amity and Commerce with France of 1778 (*see* Franco-American Alliance). It became a standard part of 19th-century treaties, but its application since World War II has been complicated by such regional economic arrangements as the Common Market.

MOTION PICTURES. In 1893 Thomas A. Edison, the "Father of Motion Pictures," received patents for his Kinetograph camera and Kinetoscope viewing apparatus. In 1894 peep-show Kinetoscopes went on public display in New York City, Paris, and London. Screen projection was achieved in 1895 in France by Louis and Auguste Lumière with the Cinématographe; in London by Robert W. Paul with films made by Birt Acres shown in the Bioscope; and in the United States by Thomas Armat, C. Francis Jenkins, Woodville Latham and his sons, Grey and Otway, and others.

The first "movies" were only brief sequences, inserted in a vaudeville show. Before long, personalities of the stage agreed to appear in films. Productions became more elaborate as pictures began to tell a story. Initial production centers in the United States were in, and adjacent to, New York City and in Chicago and Philadelphia. In 1913 the lure of good weather and remoteness called producers west, and Hollywood, Calif., became the American production headquarters while corporate management, financial, and sales departments centered in New York.

Hollywood during the golden age of the silent film, from the days of World War I to the mid-1920's, gave the American film an international flavor and appeal. At a time when many observers felt the silent films were becoming routine, sound became a reality. In 1928 the entire industry shifted to talking pictures, after the great success of *The Jazz Singer,* made by Warner Brothers with Al Jolson, and shown in 1927.

Although there had been experiments with color from the beginning of motion pictures, Technicolor was the first commercially successful process and long remained the standard for color systems. From the time of the release of the record-breaking *Gone With the Wind* in 1939, an increasing proportion of important motion pictures were in color.

Following record attendance during World War II, the American motion picture industry entered a difficult period. It was confronted with intense competition from television. Thereafter production activity at Hollywood studios declined. By 1970 the American industry reached its nadir; five major companies reported a total loss of $500 million. The trend toward merging firms into multicompany conglomerates accelerated, and by the 1980's the major American film companies had either lost their independence through mergers or come under the control of new managements interested in diversification into nonfilm fields. Although the output of feature films had dramatically decreased—as had the number of motion picture theaters—it was still possible for "blockbuster" movies to be enormously profitable.

MOTOR CARRIER ACT (Aug. 9, 1935)**.** This act placed all buses and trucks engaged in interstate commerce under the authority of the Interstate Commerce Commission. The commission was empowered to regulate industry finances and labor, as well as minimum and maximum rates.

MOTOR TRUCK TRANSPORTATION. In the 1890's numerous experimental motor vehicles began to appear throughout the country, and among them were a few motor wagons. During the last three years of the century a few commercial motor vehicles were marketed.

By 1910, improvements in design had begun to make motor trucks economically feasible. Verticle four-cylinder engines began to replace the single-cylinder and double-opposed engines, and planetary transmissions were superseded by sliding gear transmissions, and there was a noticeable trend away from chain drive in favor of several forms of gear drive.

World War I and its aftermath had an immense effect on truck use and development. In 1917, the first long-distance truck shipments were made with trucks hauling military supplies to ports of embarkation. At that time, too, pneumatic tires capable of withstanding heavy truck loads were being developed; the improved tires enabled trucks to double their former speed, an enormous advantage and a practical necessity for intercity trucking. Immediately after the war the good-roads movement began to achieve results, and many previously unpaved highways were surfaced.

Interstate trucking increased steadily during the 1920's and 1930's. Such developments as power-assisted brakes, six-cylinder engines, three-axle trucks, and the use of the semitrailer, adapted to heavier loads, increased 500 percent from 1929 to 1936. Diesel trucks were introduced in the early 1930's, but were not found in significant numbers until the 1950's.

In World War II, trucks served as a mobile assembly line on the home front and were often the decisive factor in the theaters of war. After the war the trucking industry resumed a steady and rapid growth. An important development of the late 1950's and 1960's was "piggybacking," or the long-distance movement of loaded semitrailers on railway flatcars; 1,264,501 semitrailers were loaded on flatcars in 1970. By 1968 there were 75,000 U.S. truck fleets with ten or more units each, and the 1977 truck total of 26,213,000 more than quintupled the 1941 figure.

MOULTRIE, FORT, BATTLE OF (June 28, 1776). Colonial forces at Fort Moultrie, on Sullivan's Island in Charleston harbor, in South Carolina, successfully beat off a British attack. American loss was slight, while that of the British, both in lives and damage to ships, was large. The victory kept the British out of the South for the next two years.

MOUNDS AND MOUND BUILDERS. The numerous ancient artificial structures of earth and stone widely scattered over the eastern United States and the primitive peoples responsible for their construction. The General Mound Area corresponds approximately to the basins of the Mississippi and its tributaries, particularly those to the east, and the Gulf and southeastern seaboard regions.

Conical mounds, reaching up to 70 feet in height, are artificial hillocks of earth, earth and stone, and, occasionally, stone only. They were intended mainly as places of interment and as monuments to the dead. Truncated mounds occur mostly in the lower Mississippi Valley. Most are quadrangular flat-topped pyramids, which served as bases or platforms for sacred and domiciliary structures. These tumuli are sometimes 100 feet high and cover 16 acres of ground. Linear and effigy mounds (so called because they are built in the images of animals, birds, and men) center in southern Wisconsin and adjacent parts of Iowa, Minnesota, and Illinois. The greatest effigy mound is the Serpent Mound, in Adams County, Ohio. This effigy, following the sinuous coils of the serpent, measures 1,330 feet in length. It is supposed that the effigy mounds were adjuncts of the religious observances of their builders.

Defensive earthworks, or fortifications, usually occupy the more or less level tops of isolated hills and consist of walls of earth and stone. The walls were usually fortified by pointed upright stakes or pickets. They are of general occurrence. Geometric enclosures, built by the Hopewell Indians of Ohio, are usually low walls of earth, in the form of circles, squares, octagons, and parallel walls. Occurring singly or in combination, their function apparently was social and ceremonial, rather than defensive.

Shell mounds are accumulations of shells of both marine and fresh-water mollusks, and they occur mainly along the Atlantic tidewater, particularly in Florida, and often are of great extent.

Archaeological investigations have demonstrated that the mound builders were the ancestors of Indian nations living in the same general area at the time of the discovery of America. Explorers of the 16th century found certain tribes in the South using, if not actually building, mounds.

The ages of mounds are established mainly by the radiocarbon dating technique. The shell mounds date from the Archaic period, especially from between 5000 B.C. and 1000 B.C. Earthworks and burial mounds were both constructed from shortly before 1000 B.C. to the historic period. Temple mounds were built beginning about A.D. 700. The mound-building peoples had achieved a considerable degree of advancement: copper was hammered into implements and ornaments; very creditable potteryware was made; and woven fabric of several types was produced.

MOUNTAIN MEADOWS MASSACRE (1857). Occurred in southern Utah in September 1857. Two companies of emigrants on their way to California were attacked by Indians in southern Utah. One company was saved by the help of the Mormon militia and reached the Pacific coast in safety. The other company, numbering 137 persons, was massacred except for seventeen children. John D. Lee, a white farmer who led the Indian attack, was later executed for the crime on the spot where it was committed.

MOUNTAIN MEN. Fur trappers of the Rocky Mountain West. Frenchmen, the most experienced fur gatherers, mingled with Americans and Spaniards at St. Louis in the first decades of the 19th century and made this the great western emporium of the fur trade. Trapping parties and trading company caravans laden with supplies and Indian goods for the mountain trade left from St. Louis.

The mountain man became a recognizable type. The mixed racial strains produced a polyglot jargon known as mountain talk. Mingling with the Indian, he adopted the aborigine's manner of life, his food, clothing, shelter, morals, and frequently his superstitions. With the introduction of the silk hat and the consequent decline in beaver skin prices, the mountain man forsook his traps and began to trade with the Indian. Buffalo robes replaced beaver pelts, and the trading post supplanted the rendezvous. With the coming of emigrant home-seekers and government expeditions, the trapper-trader became scout and guide to lead newcomers over the paths he broke.

MOUNT DESERT. An island off northeastern Maine with an area of about 100 square miles. Jesuit missionaries arrived about 1611 and established a small settlement, which was wiped out in 1613 by a raid of Virginia colonists. The French relinquished claim to the island in 1713, and thereafter it changed hands frequently. In 1762 it was given outright to Sir Francis Bernard in return for services rendered the crown as governor of Massachusetts. In the 19th century it became a summer resort.

MOUNT HOLYOKE COLLEGE. Located in South Hadley, Massachusetts; oldest U.S. college devoted to the education of women. Founded by Mary Lyon, and chartered in 1836. Its first classes were conducted in 1837.

MOUNT HOPE. A hill in the present town of Bristol, R.I. In 1676, in the colony of Plymouth, it was the home of the Wampanoag sachem Metacom (King Philip), the leading spirit in King Philip's War. He was slain at the foot of the hill on Aug. 12, 1676. His spring and "stone seat" are on the east side of the hill.

MOUNT RAINIER NATIONAL PARK. In the state of Washington, includes the 14,410-foot-high Mount Rainier, an extinct volcano covered with glaciers and surrounded by extensive natural forests of Douglas fir and hemlock. The Park was established in 1899.

MOUNT RUSHMORE NATIONAL MEMORIAL. Located in South Dakota, it consists of four gigantic pieces of sculpture carved into the rock face of Mount Rushmore. The four heads represent George Washington, Thomas Jefferson, Abraham Lincoln, and Theodore Roosevelt. The memorial was authorized by Congress in 1925; the work was designed by Gutzon Borglum. Borglum himself did not live to see the completion of the four heads. His son, Lincoln Borglum, carried the work to its conclusion.

MOUNT VERNON. Home of George Washington, situated on the south bank of the Potomac River, near Alexandria, Va. The Washington family acquired title to Mount Vernon in 1690. The central part of the existing house was built about 1743 for Lawrence Washington. When he died in 1752, the property passed to George Washington, his half brother. Here Washington lived the life of a southern planter until the outbreak of the Revolution. At the close of the war he completed his ambitious improvements to the estate. Buildings, gardens, and grounds were developed substantially to their present form and extent during this period. Mount Vernon constitutes one of the best remaining examples of the plantations around which centered the highly developed social and economic life of the South in the 18th century. Washington returned to Mount Vernon at the close of his presidency in 1797. He died on Dec. 14, 1799; he and Martha Washington are interred there in the family vault.

MOUNT VERNON CONFERENCE. *See* **Alexandria Conference.**

MOUNT WASHINGTON, EARLY EXPLORATION OF. In June 1642, Darby Field, accompanied by two Indians, reached the summit of Mount Washington, New Hampshire. In the later colonial period Mount Washington was occasionally ascended by ranging parties, but careful exploration did not take place until after the Revolution. In July 1784 a party that included the clergymen Manasseh Cutler and Jeremy Belknap climbed the mountain and named it.

MOUNT WILSON AND PALOMAR OBSERVATORIES. *See* **Hale Observatories.**

MOURNERS' BENCH. A seat in the open space between pulpit and audience in early revivalist churches. Before it kneeled the repentant seeking salvation.

MOURT'S RELATION. Book printed in London in 1622, a valuable source of information on the Pilgrims' arrival and first months in America. G. Mourt, who signed the preface, is identified as George Morton, who settled in Plymouth in 1623. William Bradford and Edward Winslow generally have been considered the chief authors of the book.

MOVERS. Pioneers who in about 1870 moved into the trans-Missouri region. A canvas-covered farm wagon carried the belongings of the "mover," consisting of a few articles of furniture, cooking utensils, and a scanty supply of farming equipment. Not infrequently the mother drove the team and rode in the wagon while the father and the children drove the loose livestock. Winter movers built a wooden frame on the wagon and kept a stove inside.

MOVIES. *See* **Motion Pictures.**

MOWING MACHINE. As early as 1812 wooden horse-drawn rakes were in use in the East, and in 1856 Cyrenus Wheeler put on the market a two-wheeled mower with a hinged cutter bar that could operate on rough and uneven ground. By 1860 several machines were manufactured that did not differ essentially from the mowers in use today.

MOYNIHAN REPORT. *The Negro Family: The Case for National Action,* by Assistant Secretary of Labor Daniel P. Moynihan, attempted to define the plight of black Americans in 1965. Intended as a prelude to formulating national policy, it provoked a bitter controversy instead, especially concerning the alleged deterioration of the black family.

MRS. O'LEARY'S COW. According to legend the great Chicago fire of Oct. 8–9, 1871, was started when Mrs. O'Leary's family cow upset a lamp. No one really knows how the fire started, and Mrs. O'Leary flatly denied the cow story.

MUCKRAKERS. A group of reformers who, through books and popular magazine articles, laid bare the abuses that had crept into American political, social, and economic life at the beginning of the 20th century. In 1903 Lincoln Steffens' "The Shame of the Cities" and Ida M. Tarbell's "History of the Standard Oil Company" set the pattern. Among the subjects exposed were railroads, banks, the U.S. Senate, food adulteration, traffic in women and children, and fraudulent advertising of patent medicines. Of the novelists, the most important was Upton Sinclair, who, in *The Jungle* (1906), revealed the unsavory conditions in the packing plants of Chicago. President Theodore Roosevelt, thoroughly annoyed with the more sensational of the reformers, likened them to the man with the rake in John Bunyan's *Pilgrim's Progress* who was more interested in the filth on the floor than in a celestial crown, and referred to them as "muckrakers." Despite their detractors, the muckrakers were responsible for much of the progressive legislation of the period.

"MUD MARCH" (January 1863). After his bloody repulse at Fredericksburg, Va., Union Gen. A. E. Burnside planned to move his army across the Rappahannock River and seize positions behind Gen. Robert E. Lee's left flank. His troops marched on Jan. 20, but that night a torrential rain began and continued for days. The whole army was mired down in the mud. Lee scarcely needed to move a soldier; the Union offensive was defeated by the mud. On Jan. 21 Burnside's army returned to Falmouth.

***MUGLER* V. *KANSAS*,** 123 U.S. 623 (1887). A Supreme Court case in which a Kansas prohibition law was declared constitutional. Mugler had argued that since he had invested his money in a brewing business, the law had deprived him of his property without due process of law. The Supreme Court refused to accept this position.

MUGWUMPS. A derisive term applied to those liberal, or independent, Republicans who bolted the party ticket in the presidential campaign of 1884 to support actively the candidacy of Grover Cleveland.

MULCT LAW. A form of local option adopted in Iowa in 1894. Statewide prohibition was amended so that counties could choose to collect an annual mulct tax of $600 to be paid by all persons selling intoxicating liquor. The mulct law was repealed in 1915, and on Jan. 1, 1916, prohibition again went into effect throughout Iowa.

MULE. The mule—hybrid offspring of a jackass and a mare—became important in America in 1785, when George Washington received first an Andalusian jack and jennets from the king of Spain, and, shortly after, a similar Maltese group from the Marquis de Lafayette. By crossing the two breeds Washington secured a mule stock that found ready favor with fellow planters. The mule proved particularly adapted to farm needs. Mules were extensively used in the Civil War in the supply trains, and from that time the "army mule" became proverbial. As mechanization grew, the demand for mules decreased, and there were less than a quarter as many mules in the United States in 1970 as in 1930.

MULE SKINNER. The mule driver flourished during the 1850's and through the 1870's, when millions of tons of freight were being pulled by mules and oxen across the Great Plains. Mules and mule skinners were probably as numerous as oxen and bullwhackers (ox drivers) at that time.

MULLAN TRAIL. Wagon trail of the Pacific Northwest. Built in 1859–60, it was 624 miles long, from the head of navigation of the Missouri River (Fort Benton, Mont.) to Walla Walla, Wash. It was built largely for military purposes, but played an important part in opening the Montana mines.

MULLIGAN LETTERS. Letters written by James G. Blaine during the years 1864–76 to Warren Fisher, Jr., a businessman of Boston, that indicated Blaine had used his official power as speaker of the House of Representatives to promote the fortunes of the Little Rock and Fort Smith Railroad. On June 5, 1876, Blaine read the letters on the floor of the House and his friends claimed they vindicated him. Eight years later, when he was the Republican candidate for the presidency, the letters were published and were probably an important factor in his defeat.

MUNFORDVILLE, CAPTURE OF. Early in the Civil War a Union earthwork was built on a hill near Munfordville, Ky., to guard the important railroad bridge of the Louisville and Nashville Railroad across Green River. In September 1862, the Confederate army under Gen. Braxton Bragg invaded Kentucky and captured it (*see* Kentucky, Invasion of).

MUNICIPAL BANKRUPTCY ACT (May 24, 1934). Defaults on municipal bonds by a large number of cities during the Great Depression led to this act. It permitted local government units to petition the federal courts for the following two years to approve plans for readjusting debt burdens, providing that the holders of 51 percent of the municipal obligations gave their consent.

MUNICIPAL GOVERNMENT. The governmental structure, powers, and processes of incorporated local governments—primarily cities. The powers of U.S. municipal governments derive from the states, who charter municipalities. The governmental structure of U.S. municipalities was adopted from English models introduced in the colonial period. Councillors and aldermen were elected but the mayor was appointed by the colonial governor. Later, the mayor was typically elected also but sometimes chosen by the council.

In the early 20th century, in medium- and small-sized cities, there was a major movement toward council-manager government, with movement in a few cities toward commission government. The major characteristics of council-manager government are a nonpartisan council elected at large, a mayor selected from the council with relatively few formal powers, and a professional manager hired by the council to perform executive and administrative functions. In commission government, executive and legislative functions are merged in the commission, whose members act individually as administrators and collectively as legislators.

MUNICIPAL OWNERSHIP. In the years of greatest public concern, 1898–1913, the term "municipal ownership" was primarily associated with the provision of water, gas, electricity, and transit systems. Also, even in earlier years, cities occasionally operated markets, harbor facilities, and ferries.

During the 19th century cities regularly granted utility franchises to competing promoters. Yet a utility is inherently a monopoly, and by 1900 it was clear that the ethics of competition were not the answer to the problems inherent in monopolies. As a by-product, corrupt deals between utility companies and political bosses and political machines had become the order of the day.

Local leaders, following the example set by Hazen Pingree of Detroit in the early 1890's, took up the reform battle. To many crusaders municipal ownership seemed the only answer—bypassing the corruption, the inordinate profits, the high rates, and the poor service. The trend toward municipally owned waterworks was given some momentum. A few cities took over municipal street lighting, and still fewer, private power plants. In 1912 San Francisco municipalized its trolleys, and in 1919 the first fully municipalized trolley system was completed in Seattle. Under the threat of municipal ownership, corruption by the private utilities was lessened, rates were reduced, service was improved, and yardsticks were provided. Regulation by the states emerged as the answer.

The trend toward municipal ownership of waterworks continued. In 1895, for example, the state of Massachusetts established a metropolitan water district, which gave a central supply source, each community providing its own pipe system. By 1897, 41 of the 50 largest cities had publicly owned systems, as did 100 of the 142 cities with populations between 30,000 and 100,000.

Public ownership of gas and electric plants was quite different. By 1968 only six of the forty-three largest cities operated electric utilities and only three used municipal gas. Priorities granted to publicly owned power plants by federal installations, such as those of the Tennessee Valley Authority and the great dams of the West, gave them some stimulus.

Problems in commuter transport across city boundaries in the largest communities have demonstrated that only the metropolitan area has been adequate to deal with the problems of mass transit. For example, the Washington area public transportation system requires the cooperation of the District of Columbia, the states of Maryland and Virginia, units of local government, and the federal government.

Both public and private rapid-transit systems were facing operating deficits in the 1980's. In 1963 these amounted to only $880,000. By 1973, according to the American Transit Association, their total revenues, which amounted to $1.8 billion, still left a deficit of $681 million.

The most controversial development has been municipally constructed and owned housing. In the depression some subsidized low-rent public housing took place under "local housing authorities." During and after World War II housing shortages were such that the federal government had to subsidize and build houses as a defense measure, utilizing numerous public, private, and nonprofit agencies, including municipalities.

Eventually low-rent housing was explicitly linked with slum clearance and urban renewal. By 1964 under the Great Society programs of Lyndon B. Johnson, this concept evolved into programs that might also include community facilities, transit, and streets. Federal subsidies direct to the local authorities were generous. By 1964 there were 1,454 such projects; of these 60 percent were either under construction or completed. The completed projects were, for the most part, modest ones, as to the size of the city and the funds committed. By 1982 such projects were virtually completed and no new ones contemplated.

MUNICIPAL REFORM. A movement in American local government that has traditionally focused on achieving the goals of honesty in public officials and efficiency and economy in government. The movement became clearly identifiable on a large scale at the close of the 19th century, when the corruption of machine-dominated big cities received publicity in the popular press. Reforms of the electoral system were designed to destroy the power of party machines. Most of the structural reform emphasized the introduction of professional management personnel in the executive branch. The main thrust of this reform has been embodied in the campaign for council-manager government.

The council-manager plan continues to be the main focus of the municipal reform movement in middle-sized cities, which are homogeneous enough to support nonpartisan and at-large electoral reforms but large enough to afford professional executives. In larger cities, the tendency has been toward the concentration of greater power in the mayor, who is generally directly accountable to the electorate.

MUNITIONS. In a strict sense, weapons and ammunition, although broadly it embraces all war matériel. During the American Revolution the colonial militia and Continental forces depended largely on British and European models of muskets and artillery, although some American innovations —especially the Pennsylvania, or Kentucky, rifles—were already apparent. These rifles were far superior in range and accuracy to smooth-bore muskets. The principal artillery pieces of the period were cast-iron, bronze, and brass cannon, taking shot of 4, 9, 12, or 32 pounds, and siege mortars.

The first breech-loading rifle, the Hall, was adopted in 1819, the muzzle-loading musket remained the standard infantry arm until the opening phase of the Civil War.

One of the greatest advantages the Union infantry and cavalry had in the Civil War was in the quality and quantity of their repeating rifles and carbines. The Colt revolving rifle, was introduced in 1858. The fifteen-shot Henry and the seven-shot Spencer—"the seven-forked lightning"—also had a great impact on the war.

Even after the demonstrated success of repeating rifles in the Civil War, the army was slow to modernize. U.S. soldiers were still carrying single-shot Springfields twenty-five years later. In 1890, when a repeating rifle was accepted at last, it was the Danish-designed Krag-Jörgensen magazine rifle, which became the standard shoulder weapon of U.S. forces in the Spanish-American War.

In World War I, the U.S. Army mainly used an adaptation of the British Enfield in the interest of making maximum use of industrial capacity. During World War II and the Korean War, the eight-shot Garand, or M-1, a semiautomatic rifle was standard. In Vietnam the M-16, a lighter rifle that used .22 caliber ammunition, was favored.

Artillery improvements during the Civil War were mostly in the direction of greater size and strength and in the introduction of rifled cannon on a large scale. Some of these guns were of tremendous size and strength. The "Swamp Angel" hurled 200-pound shells more than four miles.

The greatest limitation on artillery, the lack of a good recoil mechanism, was overcome before World War I, the war of artillery par excellence. By far the best recoil system and "recuperators" were those on the French 75-millimeter gun the Allied forces used as their main field artillery weapon. This gun fired a 16-pound shell over a range of three miles at a rate of thirty rounds a minute. Many heavy guns were mounted on railroad cars for long-range bombardment.

Another dominant weapon on the battlefield in World War I was the machine gun, which had its beginning in the multi-barreled Gatling gun of the Civil War. In 1917 the U.S. Army adopted the "best of all machine guns"—the Browning .30-caliber, recoil-operated, belt-fed, water-cooled, heavy weapon fired from a tripod mount. The Browning automatic rifle was a gas-operated, air-cooled, magazine-fed, shoulder weapon, with a cyclic rate of 550 rounds a minute, usually fired from a bipod. It was widely used in World War II.

Other important developments in munitions in World War I were the tank, the airplane, and poison gas. Both the tank and the plane were to be more widely used in World War II, which was fought largely with the improved weapons of World War I. The numbers and effectiveness of tanks and airplanes characterized the military operations of that war. Jet fighter planes came into use by the Korean War, and helicopters were being used for supply and medical evacuation. In Vietnam the jet bomber, the B-52, having a range of over 12,000 miles and carrying a weapons load of 75,000 pounds, was the chief instrument of heavy aerial bombing.

Naval vessels have gone through periods of swift change. Steam power came into use during the Mexican and Civil wars, and the ironclad was introduced during the Civil War. The 1906 British battleship *Dreadnought,* carrying ten 12-inch guns in center-line turrets and having a speed of 21 knots, established a new standard for battleships. This same period saw the conversion from coal to oil and the introduction of the steam turbine for the propulsion of vessels.

The greatest innovation of World War I in naval warfare was the widespread use of the submarine, which in World War II was a major weapon. Development has been continual and spectacular since the advent of nuclear propulsion gave submarines practically unlimited range. In the 1970's about 60 percent of the U.S. attack submarine fleet of over ninety vessels was nuclear-powered.

After World War I the aircraft carrier began to come into prominence. During World War II, battleships were used more for the support of landing operations than for direct ship-to-ship combat. By the end of the war the battleship had given way almost completely to the aircraft carrier. In the post–World War II period nuclear power came into use in the 76,000-ton supercarrier *Enterprise.*

The most spectacular development of all in munitions was the intercontinental ballistic missile with its nuclear warhead. The atomic bomb introduced near the close of World War II had a rating of 20 kilotons; that is, its explosive force was about the equivalent of 20,000 tons of TNT. In 1961 the Soviet Union deployed the SS-7 "Saddler" missile, said to have a warhead with a yield of 5 megatons, the equivalent of 5 million tons of TNT. The U.S. Titan, deployed a year later, was of equal or greater magnitude, but in 1965 the Soviets claimed their SS-9 "Scarp" had a warhead of 20 to 25 megatons. By 1979 the United States had about 7,300 nuclear war heads, while the Soviet Union had 8,100; the combined force of this arsenal could easily destroy both of the superpowers and much of the rest of the world.

***MUNN* V. *ILLINOIS*,** 94 U.S. 113 (1877). A Supreme Court case in which an Illinois regulatory law was upheld. Munn argued that the law, fixing the maximum rates for the storage of grain, constituted a taking of property without due process of law. The Court replied that the warehouse business was "affected with a public interest" and that public control is justified. *(See Wabash, Saint Louis and Pacific Railroad* v. *Illinois.)*

MURCHISON LETTER. *See* **Sackville-West Incident.**

MURDERING TOWN. Probably an Indian encampment in Butler County, Pa. Both George Washington and Christopher Gist mention, in their diaries, passing the place Dec. 27, 1753, on their return from Fort LeBoeuf. Gist named it because an Indian from the encampment fired on him.

MURFREESBORO, BATTLE OF (Dec. 31, 1862–Jan. 2, 1863). Civil War encounter near Nashville, Tenn. After the Battle of Perryville, Gen. Braxton Bragg withdrew his Confederates to Murfreesboro, thirty miles from the Union Army of the Cumberland under Gen. William S. Rosecrans, concentrated at Nashville. Each general aimed to attack on Dec. 31, but Bragg struck first. By nightfall the two nearly equal armies had fought themselves into fatigue, but with the Confederates clearly holding the advantage. On Jan. 2, Bragg sent nearly 10,000 men against the Union rank and broke it, but an insane Union counterattack cracked the assault; sudden artillery concentration shattered it; and the battle stopped. Next day Bragg retreated toward Chattanooga.

MURMANSK. An ice-free Russian port on the Barents Sea. After the revolution took Russia out of World War I, the Allies landed a guard there to protect their stockpiles of military goods. In World War II the "Murmansk run" was the bloodiest of routes for convoys delivering lend-lease supplies to the Soviet Union, whose naval and air forces did not provide adequate protection even in the harbor itself.

MUSCLE SHOALS PROJECT. *See* **Tennessee Valley Authority.**

MUSCLE SHOALS SPECULATION (1783–89). The Muscle Shoals region on the Tennessee River was thought to have great potential value, since it might afford westerners an outlet via Mobile, Ala., at a time when Spain denied them the use of the Mississippi River (*see* Mississippi River, Free Navigation of). Two efforts at colonizing Muscle Shoals (1783–85, 1785–86) were unsuccessful. In 1786 a third attempt was made. It was marked by an intrigue with Spain (*see* Spanish Conspiracy), wherein the new State of Franklin offered to secede from the Union in return for Spanish support of the project. Spain rejected the proposal, but various other schemes were put forward.

MUSEUMS. The earliest learned and historical societies in the United States maintained "cabinets," as museums were often called in the 18th century. The 1769 by-laws of the American Philosophical Society provided for collecting items for such a cabinet.

The Massachusetts Historical Society (founded in 1791) included among its purposes "the collection and preservation of materials for a political and natural history of the United States." Books, manuscripts, and maps predominated in the earliest accessions. As specialized scientific organizations were created during the 19th century, the older societies devoted less attention to natural history collections of objects.

The Peabody Museum of Salem, Mass., is the oldest museum in continuous operation in the United States, by virtue of perpetuating the collections of the East India Marine Society, founded in 1799. It has evolved into an important modern museum, specializing in maritime history, the ethnology of the Pacific islands and Japan, and the natural history of Essex County, Mass.

The federal government's involvement with museums dates from the 1846 act creating the Smithsonian Institution and providing for the formation of a museum of natural history and a gallery of art under its auspices. With the establishment of the American Museum of Natural History (1869) and the Metropolitan Museum of Art (1870) in New York City and of the Museum of Fine Arts (1870) in Boston, the word "museum" replaced "cabinet." During the 20th century establishment of museums of art, history, and science in all parts of the United States accelerated rapidly; the 1975 edition of the *Official Museum Directory* of the American Association of Museums listed 5,225 museums in the United States and Canada and stated that since 1965 six new museums had been founded every seven days.

Late 19th-century museums tended to exhibit objects of the same kind together, whether they were stuffed bears or silver teapots. In the 20th century an attempt was made to place objects in an approximation of their natural setting. While "habitat groups" in natural history museums required work by artists and model-makers, art museums cannibalized ancient buildings to procure structural elements for their "period rooms." The American Wing of the Metropolitan Museum in 1924 brought together architectural elements from widely scattered sources to provide a background for examples of American decorative arts, as did the Henry Francis du Pont Winterthur Museum in 1951 in Winterthur, Del. The restoration of Williamsburg, Va., substantially completed between 1926 and 1941, turned an entire 18th-century town into a museum. Its popularity inspired the foundation of numerous historical museums in which entire villages were re-created. Typical examples are a New England village in Sturbridge, Mass., and a seaport at Mystic, Conn.

MUSIC. During the colonial period, American music was a provincial replica of European patterns. Professional musicians were often assisted by "gentlemen amateurs." From about 1720, informal singing schools were organized in New England to promote group singing, especially of religious songs. These created a demand for books containing the music to be sung. After 1770 several hundred "tunebooks" were published in New England, and during the early 19th century they could also be found in the South and the Midwest. The composers were mostly native-born Americans. They included William Billings, Supply Belcher, Daniel Read, Jeremiah Ingalls, Oliver Holden, and Andrew Law.

After 1800, more secular music by Americans, both vocal and instrumental, began to be published. It was mostly in the form of sheet music, with a prevalence of marches, dances, and sentimental, humorous, patriotic, and topical songs. From about 1820 many pseudo-"Negro" songs began to appear, engendered by the vogue for blackface minstrelsy. The best-known composers of minstrel-show songs were Daniel Decatur Emmett and Stephen Foster. The former is famous as the composer of *Dixie*. The instrumental music of blackface minstrelsy was derived largely from the syncopated banjo tunes of the blacks on the southern plantations. This Afro-American music influenced the style of America's first internationally famous composer, Louis Moreau Gottschalk, a native of Louisiana who studied in France and won celebrity as a pianist who played his own piano pieces based on Creole melodies.

The first American grand opera was William Henry Fry's *Leonora* (1845). Ten years later, George F. Bristow's *Rip Van Winkle* was successfully produced in New York. Both Fry and Bristow composed symphonies, cantatas, and oratorios. Musical societies were also being founded: the Handel and Haydn Society of Boston (1815) and the Musical Fund Society of Philadelphia (1820). The first permanent symphony orchestra was the New York Philharmonic Society (1842). By the end of the century, many other Americans were busily cultivating the traditional forms of European art music, mainly under German influence. Eminent among them was Edward MacDowell, also an excellent pianist, best known for his two piano concertos, his numerous piano pieces, and his *Indian Suite* (1896) for orchestra. He was also the first head (1894–1906) of the music department at Columbia University.

John A. Carpenter was among the first to draw on American popular music, notably in his ballets *Skyscrapers* and *Krazy Kat.* George Gershwin, Marc Blitzstein, Aaron Copland, and Leonard Bernstein, in particular used pop-music elements in their music. Douglas Moore, working in the more traditional vein of grand opera, but on a totally American subject, was very successful with *The Ballad of Baby Doe* (1956). Virgil Thomson shunned realism in *The Mother of Us All* (1947), with a libretto by Gertrude Stein, but packed in a great variety of musical Americana. Undoubtedly the most famous composer of this generation is Copland, who was remarkably successful in writing music that is both personal and unmistakably American. He drew on both jazz elements and American folk music. He has also written much "abstract" or formal music. Roy Harris has striven to express the American spirit in many of his works.

Charles Ives is generally recognized as America's greatest and most original composer. He wrote nearly all of his music between 1894 and 1921, but it was far ahead of its time. His music is full of quotations of American tunes. Of the composers born after 1900, Elliott Carter, John Cage, and Milton Babbitt are among the most influential. Carter produced compositions of great complexity and intellectual depth. Babbitt, with a mathematical background, concentrated on developing the twelve-tone method of Arnold Schoenberg and Anton von Webern. Cage is the antithesis of all that Babbitt and Carter represent. A dedicated iconoclast, he is an advocate of "indeterminacy" and "chance music."

The most original and creative currents in American popular music—ragtime, jazz, blues, rock—came from Afro-American traditions, but both whites and blacks participated in their development. Ragtime has its antecedents in the syncopated banjo tunes played for dancing by black musicians. In the 1890's it emerged as a type of music primarily for piano, with a syncopated melody in the treble (right hand) and a strong regular beat in the bass (left hand). The "classical ragtime" was represented superlatively in such piano "rags" of Scott Joplin as *Maple Leaf Rag* and *The Entertainer.* Joplin was black, but the other outstanding composer of classical piano rags, Joseph Lamb, was white.

The blues are a personal expression of feeling. W. C. Handy's *St. Louis Blues* (1914) became a favorite of jazz musicians and set the pattern for innumerable blues compositions. The early great women blues singers, such as Gertrude ("Ma") Rainey and Bessie Smith, were accompanied by jazz combos during the 1920's. The modern urban blues, featuring big, hard-driving bands, were developed chiefly in Kansas City, Memphis, and Chicago, by such black bluesmen as Bobby Bland and B. B. King. The blues also engendered a percussive piano style called "boogie-woogie." What came to be known as "soul music" developed from a synthesis of blues, jazz, and gospel. Its leading exponents were Ray Charles and Aretha Franklin.

Jazz absorbed both ragtime and blues, as well as gospel hymns, marches, dances, popular songs, and even some classical numbers. Its origins are chiefly associated with New Orleans around the turn of the century. The most influential early jazz pioneer was Joseph ("King") Oliver, who in 1918 went to Chicago, which became the second center of jazz in its early days. During the 1920's, whites and blacks were to vie in developing both the commercial and the creative potential of jazz. Among black jazzmen, Louis Armstrong set new standards for solo improvisation with his creative playing on cornet and trumpet. By the 1930's big bands were the vogue and their music was arranged and written down by musicians with some professional training, such as Fletcher Henderson, Benny Carter, and Duke Ellington, who became an important composer in the jazz idiom. Benny Goodman, a white clarinetist and bandleader, is credited with starting the vogue of "swing" with his nationwide tour in 1934. Jazz has continued to develop dynamically in ever-changing directions. The cool phase of the 1950's was followed by the style known as "hard bop" or "funky," marked by a return to the more primitive roots of jazz.

The music called rock and roll developed from rhythm and blues, a type of urban blues with a strong beat that originally was aimed at black audiences. During the 1950's, elements of pop music and the style known as country and western were fused with rhythm and blues to produce the fast, rocking beat of rock and roll, geared primarily toward the youth market. Prominent among its early practitioners were Bill Haley and the Comets and Elvis Presley, whose background was in country and western but who became the most famous rock and roll singer. Among black performers, none was more influential than Chuck Berry. His music had a great influence on the Beatles, an English quartet. When the latter came to the United States in 1964, they had a tremendous impact. Their unprecedented success stimulated the growth of American bands and launched the era of modern rock.

Bob Dylan started out as an urban folksinger, in the tradition of Woody Guthrie and Pete Seeger, writing his own songs and accompanying himself on the guitar and harmonica. In 1965 he made the transition from folk to rock, adopting the electrified guitar and the basic rock beat. Rather than creating a dichotomy, he helped to create a synthesis known as "folk rock." As a songwriter involved with social-political-moral issues, he became a symbol of protest and alienation.

Politicized folk music came to the fore in the 1930's, largely under the influence of leftist ideology, sung by such singers as Woody Guthrie and Pete Seeger. They were followed in the 1960's by Bob Dylan, Joan Baez, and Guthrie's son, Arlo. This was not traditional folk song, orally transmitted from generation to generation, but rather an adaptation of folk styles to the political issues of an industrialized society.

Country and western music had its origins in the folk music of the southern uplands developed from the heritage of Anglo-Celtic ballads and folksongs. The commercialization of hillbilly music began in the 1920's, largely through the radio and recordings. The first big successes were achieved by the Carter family and by Jimmie Rodgers, famous for his "blue yodel." Rodgers was much influenced by the music of the blacks in his native Mississippi, whose blues he adapted to his own style. Its headquarters were in Nashville, Tenn., from which "The Grand Ole Opry" carried country music across the nation via the radio. By the 1980's country music had become highly varied, and its leading performers achieved a nationwide popularity previously held only by pop artists. Among such stars were Eddie Arnold, Loretta Lynn, Johnny Cash, Willie Nelson, and Dolly Parton.

Beginning with the vogue of European-style operetta as exemplified by the works of Victor Herbert (*The Red Mill,* 1906; *Naughty Marietta,* 1910), the popular musical theater developed a more characteristically American expression in the musical comedy. Following the pioneer entertainer George M. Cohan came Irving Berlin, Jerome Kern, George Gershwin, Cole Porter, and Vincent Youmans, who established the basic type, with a perfunctory plot carried by memorable tunes and an attractive chorus line. With *Show Boat* (1927), Kern broadened the dramatic scope of the popular musical show, particularly in characterization, and pointed the way toward the "musical." Another landmark musical was *Pal Joey* (1940), with music by Richard Rodgers and libretto by Lorenz Hart. After the latter's death, Rodgers teamed with Oscar Hammerstein II to write such famous musicals as *Oklahoma!* (1943), *Carousel* (1945), and *South Pacific* (1949). This vein was continued by Frank Loesser, with *Guys and Dolls* (1950), and by Leonard Bernstein, with *West Side Story* (1957). A high point of this trend was *My Fair Lady* (1956), by Frederick Loewe and Alan Jay Lerner, based on George Bernard Shaw's play *Pygmalion.* In the 1970's and 1980's the field was dominated by the works of Stephen Sondheim (*A Little Night Music; Sweeney Todd*).

MUSKINGUM RIVER CANAL ROUTE. The canal, opened in 1841, connected Zanesville, Ohio, with the Ohio River at Marietta. (*See* Ohio State Canals).

MUSSEL SLOUGH INCIDENT (May 11, 1880). Gun battle near Hanford, Calif., resulting from a long controversy between settlers on railroad lands and the Southern Pacific Company. Seven men died and one was wounded. The settlers opposed the company's asking price for the lands they were farming and unsuccessfully sought help from the courts and President Rutherford B. Hayes. Accompanied by a representative of the Southern Pacific Company, a U.S. marshal attempted to dispossess certain occupants. A crowd of men, some carrying arms, gathered. The marshal, unarmed, counseled restraint, but an unidentified man fired, and a quick blast of shots followed. Tensions relaxed perceptibly after the tragedy. Some settlers purchased lands they had occupied; many did not. The railroad reduced prices by small amounts in some cases.

MUSTANGS. The Spanish raised horses on unfenced ranges. Horse stock strayed from the haciendas; on explorations, horses were lost. The wild increase of these lost and strayed animals were called *mesteños*—mustangs. Their range extended from the plains of Alberta, down the corridor between the Mississippi and the Rocky Mountains, and along the length of the Mesa Central of Mexico. No estimate of the number is possible, but there were millions. Early in the 19th century mustanging began to develop into one of the occupations of the Southwest. Mustangers used various methods to capture the wild horses, but with the development of ranching, mustangs were regarded as a nuisance and killed off. (*See also* Horse.)

MUSTER DAY. Under the militia act of 1792, every able-bodied male between the ages of eighteen and forty-five was a member of the militia. Actual enrollment was accomplished through the annual muster day. After the Civil War muster day was generally neglected.

MUTINY. The most striking example of mutiny in U.S. history is that of the entire Pennsylvania Line, six regiments, which mutinied at Morristown, N.J., on Jan. 2, 1781, and started for Philadelphia to lay their grievances directly before Congress (*see* Pennsylvania Troops, Mutinies of). On Jan. 20, 1781, three New Jersey regiments sought to imitate the Pennsylvania Line. Gen. Robert Howe surrounded the mutineers with infantry and artillery at Ringwood and gave them five minutes to come to time. They yielded; the ringleaders were immediately tried and two of them hanged, whereupon the regiments returned to duty.

In the War of 1812, the Twenty-third Infantry mutinied at Manlius, N.Y.; the Fifth Infantry at Utica; a company of volunteers at Buffalo; and, in 1814, a regiment of Tennessee militia, part of Gen. Andrew Jackson's forces, had a sergeant and five privates condemned to death for inciting mutiny.

A conspicuous maritime case was that on the U.S. brig *Somers* in 1842 when three prisoners were hanged on shipboard as mutineers.

MUTINY ACT OF 1765. A routine parliamentary enactment in most regards but containing a stipulation requiring provincial legislatures to provide barracks, fuel, and certain other necessities for the British troops stationed within their borders. Colonial Whigs feared it was designed to pave the way for a standing army to enforce the Stamp Act. They also viewed it as taxation without representation. New York refused in 1767 to obey it. (*See also* Billeting.)

MUTUAL FUNDS. *See* **Investment Companies.**

"MY COUNTRY, 'TIS OF THEE." Patriotic hymn written in 1832 by Samuel F. Smith. Its melody is based on that of an old German song, the same as that of the British national anthem, "God Save the King (Queen)." Despite strong anti-British feeling in the United States the tune, rechristened "America," became within two or three decades as close to a national anthem as anything in the United States.

MYERS* V. *UNITED STATES 272 U.S. 52(1926). In 1920 President Woodrow Wilson removed Frank S. Myers, a postmaster, without first obtaining the consent of the Senate. Myers challenged the president's right to remove him. He lost, and on appeal the Supreme Court held that officers named by the president were subject to removal at his pleasure, on the basis of the executive power granted in the Constitution.

MYITKYINA, BATTLE OF (May 17–Aug. 3, 1944). Climaxing a ten-month Sino-American campaign in 1943–44 across north Burma, the bitter World War II siege of the railhead and river town of Myitkyina on the Irrawaddy River ended Japan's blockade of China. The siege had the immediate effect of driving away Japanese air power so that American transports could fly a lower-altitude route carrying increased tonnage to China. The costs of the Allied victory were high: the Americans lost 272 killed, 955 wounded, 980 ill; the Chinese, 972 killed, 3,184 wounded, 188 ill. Captured Japanese totaled 187, most of them wounded, while about 600 Japanese made good their escape.

"MY OLD KENTUCKY HOME." Song composed in 1853 by Stephen Foster. It is the state song of Kentucky.

MY LAI MASSACRE (Mar. 16, 1968). An incident during the Vietnam War in which at least 450 Vietnamese civilians, mostly women, children, and old men, were gunned down by U.S. infantrymen in the village of My Lai, South Vietnam. The massacre went unreported in the U.S. press until November 1969, at which time it created a worldwide outcry. The infantry commander, William L. Calley, Jr., was court-martialed on Nov. 24, 1969, and convicted in March 1971, for the premeditated murder of at least twenty-two Vietnamese civilians. A public outcry against Calley's sentencing to life imprisonment caused President Richard Nixon to order Calley returned to his home and placed under house arrest. Calley's sentence was then reduced to twenty years and, after the Supreme Court refused to review the case in 1976, was transferred to parole status.

MYSTICISM. The most famous mystic in early American history was Anne Hutchinson, whose mysticism was evolved from the Puritan emphasis on the Holy Spirit as the means of grace. Her teachings were controversial, and for stating that she believed in immediate revelation, she was exiled from Massachusetts Bay Colony in 1637.

The early Quakers attempted to combine a mystical emphasis on the Inner Light with the organization of English Puritan sects, and these two elements in early Pennsylvania Quakerism frequently pulled in opposite directions. Although Jonathan Edwards was primarily interested in traditional forms of religious experience, many elements in his writings suggest mystical leanings.

Ralph Waldo Emerson was perhaps the most prominent proponent of 19th-century romantic mysticism in America. Building on ideas ultimately derived from German philosophy and—in his later years—from the religions of the East, Emerson evolved a unique American mysticism that stressed the unity of man with all nature.

The popularity of William James's *Varieties of Religious Experience* (1902) also contributed to interest in mysticism. Although James had played down the place of the mystic in the history of religion, many later psychologists believed that mysticism was the fullest form of the religious life, and the topic received a great deal of attention and study.

The Roman Catholic church has always found a place for mysticism, and the mystical experience has continued to be important in many Catholic religious orders. Thomas Merton, a convert to Catholicism, was one of the influential voices for Catholic mysticism in America in the 20th century.

The tradition of Jewish mysticism has been largely represented by Hasidism. Mysticism has always been an important part of American Indian religion, perhaps best exemplified in the Native American Church. Eastern religions, with their strong emphasis on mysticism, won over many adherents in the 1960's and 1970's.

NACOGDOCHES (Tex.). The oldest town in eastern Texas (founded 1779), it was a strategic frontier outpost for Anglo-American immigrants to Texas. It was a center of some revolutionary disturbances, notably the Fredonian Revolt of 1826; and the capital of a political subdivision of Texas. Its inhabitants took a leading part in the Texas revolution in 1836. Its 1980 population was 27,149.

NADER'S RAIDERS. Employees, paid and volunteer, of Ralph Nader, a noted consumer advocate. After 1968 Nader recruited hundreds of college students and young lawyers to investigate various government agencies and private corporations. Operating from Nader's Center for Study of Responsive Law, Washington, D.C., they stimulated important reforms and encouraged the consumer movement.

NAILS, TAX ON (1789). In its first session in 1789 the U.S. Congress levied an import duty of one cent per pound on "nails and spikes," the production of which engaged farmers' families through the winter.

NANTUCKET. An island south of Cape Cod, Mass., it was discovered in 1602 by Bartholomew Gosnold and settled by the English in 1659. Whaling became the major industry, and eventually Nantucket vessels ventured to Asia. Voyages of from four to six years were common. A waterfront fire in 1846, the California gold rush, and the discovery of petroleum contributed to the downfall of Nantucket whaling, always handicapped by an inadequate harbor. In 1869 its last whaling ship cleared port. Since then tourism has become its principal industry.

NAPLES, AMERICAN CLAIMS ON (1809–1842). They arose from seizures of American vessels and cargoes, beginning in 1809, ordered by Joachim Murat, Napoleon I's brother-in-law, as king of Naples. The United States pressed its claims for many years. An agreement was reached in 1836; and by 1842 the last payment was made, the total being $2,049,033.12.

NAPOLEON'S DECREES. Napoleon's economic struggle with Great Britain had the effect of cutting off burgeoning American trade with the Continent and of subjecting American shipping to the British licensing system and, indirectly, to British impressment of seamen. In 1806 Napoleon imposed a paper blockade of the British Isles, and in 1807 he declared lawful prey ships submitting to the British Orders in Council. In retaliation, the Jefferson Administration imposed the Embargo Act of 1807 (*see* Embargo Act).

NARCOTICS TRADE AND LEGISLATION. Extensive use of narcotics in the 19th century can probably be attributed to a reliance on them by the rapidly growing, but poorly trained, medical profession; the lack of laws limiting uses to even broadly defined medical purposes; the increasingly effective marketing of proprietary nostrums without any restraints on claims or contents; and the difficulty of legally controlling unorganized and unlicensed health professions. Between 1905 and 1919, after state controls had been judged ineffective, federal statutes and Supreme Court rulings curbed each of these features of American narcotics distribution.

Largely because of the position of the United States as a victim of foreign production, as early as 1909 Americans sought an international agreement to limit narcotics to strictly medical uses. Worldwide reporting and regulation of opium and coca products gradually evolved after the American-inspired International (or Hague) Opium Convention of 1912, although control sufficient to end the American addiction problem had not yet been attained by the 1980's.

Reducing the number of narcotics addicts after the easy availability of drugs in the 19th century was complicated by constitutional separation of federal and state powers. Federal assumption of traditional states' rights was achieved by the imposition of the taxing prerogative of the national government and by invoking the regulation of interstate commerce. The Harrison Act (1914) made use of both those stratagems in its effort to control the distribution of narcotics. Tax powers were again used to control the use of narcotics in 1937 when the transfer of marijuana from one person to another was prohibitively taxed unless the transferrer was registered with the Treasury Department and paid an annual fee.

Smuggling has remained the focus of attention in the control of narcotics. The amount of drugs smuggled into the country, like the number of drug users or addicts, has been impossible to determine objectively. Estimates have been profoundly affected by political and popular attitudes.

Federal penalties for domestic narcotics violations gradually increased until 1955, when Congress passed both mandatory minimum sentences for many narcotics-related offenses and the death penalty, at the jury's discretion, for some heroin violations. A reaction to severe penalties, particularly to mandatory minimum sentences, set in during the 1960's, caused in part by a rapid rise in drug use—particularly psychedelic substances and cannabis—by middle-class young people, in spite of the harshest penalties. The possession of small quantities of marijuana, for example, was "decriminalized" in a number of states.

Heroin addiction became a major public issue in the mid-1960's, as addiction came to be popularly construed as the cause of a large percentage of both property and violent street crime. Like estimates of the number of addicts, the link between drugs and crime seems to have been heavily influenced, as in the past, by many factors, especially by the desire of both government institutions and the public for simple explanations of fearful and complex social problems. Reliance on therapy or other alternatives to prison for drug abuse did not dramatically reduce the crime rate by the early 1980's. Neither had the widespread use of methadone, as a legal replacement for heroin. Public frustration at this "failure" led to enactment of severe prison penalties in several states, most notably New York, the state having perennially the largest addict population.

NARRAGANSETT BAY. An inlet of the Atlantic Ocean in southeastern Rhode Island, it was visited in 1524 by Giovanni da Verrazano. Dutch explorers and traders recognized the three branches of the bay and called the west passage Sloep Bay (Sloup Bay, Chaloup Bay), the east or middle passage Anker Bay, and the Sakonnet River the Nieuwe River or the Bay van Nassau. English settlers called it Narragansett Bay, after the native Narraganset, who lived on its west shore.

NARRAGANSETT PLANTERS. A group of 17th-century stock and dairy farmers living in the southern portion of the colony of Rhode Island. Their prosperity derived from intercolonial and West Indian trade and slaveholding. Wealth, and the opportunities afforded by the cultural influences of Newport, developed a mode of life unique in the northern colonial countryside, resembling more that of the South.

NARROWS. A strait connecting the upper and lower New York bays and separating Staten Island and Long Island. It was entered by Giovanni da Verrazano in 1524. Its fortifications long provided for an effective defense of New York harbor. In 1964 the Narrows were spanned by the world's longest suspension bridge (4,260 feet), the Verrazano-Narrows Bridge.

NARVÁEZ EXPEDITION (1528–1536). Pánfilo de Narváez, with 600 men and eighty horses, landed at Tampa Bay, Apr. 14, 1528. Marching north along the coast, he lost contact with his ships, and after famine and battles with the Indians, the surviving 247 men managed to follow the Gulf coast on crude flatboats as far as Texas, where the flotilla broke up near Galveston Bay, and Narváez perished in a storm in November 1528. The treasurer of the expedition, Álvar Núñez Cabeza de Vaca, with a few survivors, lived among the coastal Texan Indians for about six years. Then, Cabeza de Vaca and three companions ascended the valley of the Rio Grande, crossed the Sierra Madre ranges, and wandered down through Sonora, to be rescued by Spaniards near Culiacán, only forty miles from the Gulf of California in modern Sinaloa, in March 1536. The account of their journey seems to have been a stimulus in dispatching the expedition of Francisco Vásquez de Coronado in 1540.

NASHOBA. A cooperative or communistic settlement of slaves near Memphis, established in 1825 by Frances Wright, a social reformer from Scotland. She planned a number of such communities to prepare slaves for their freedom. But Wright soon became too ill to continue its management, and those left in charge proved incompetent. Within five years the experiment was completely abandoned.

NASHVILLE (Tenn.). A port city and the capital of Tennessee, it was founded in the winter of 1779–80 as Fort Nashborough. In 1784 the community within the fort was incorporated as the town of Nashville by the North Carolina legislature. The fertility of the Cumberland Basin attracted wealthy investors and speculators, and soon after the arrival of the first steamboat in 1818 Nashville developed into a commercial and manufacturing center. Its population increased from 7,000 in 1830 to 17,000 in 1860. Three of its citizens, Andrew Johnson, Andrew Jackson, and James K. Polk, became president of the United States, and in national politics it wielded an influence out of all proportion to its size.

Nashville, the "Athens of the South," was so strongly Whig that its citizens were able to defeat the secession movement at the Nashville Convention in 1850. Occupied by Union troops in February 1862 without a fight, Nashville suffered less from the war than most important southern cities and made a speedy recovery afterward. By the 20th century it was becoming a manufacturing center as well as a transportation hub. It burgeoned as such after cheap electric power became readily available with the creation of the Tennessee Valley Authority in 1933. Religious publishing is one of its principal industries. It is also the center of the country and western music industry. The population of Nashville in 1980 was 455,651.

NASHVILLE, BATTLE OF (Dec. 15–16, 1864). A dramatic winter conflict in which Union troops moved out of Nashville and fell upon Confederate forces. On the first day the Confederates were pushed back, and on the following day, they were driven in disorderly retreat from the battlefield. It marked the end of the Confederates' Tennessee campaign.

NASHVILLE AND CHATTANOOGA RAILROAD. The first Tennessee railroad to be completed (1854). Designed to extend from Charleston by way of Atlanta to Chattanooga, it assisted in providing the Middle West with an outlet to the southern Atlantic seaboard. It attained considerable military significance during the Civil War. It became part of the Nashville, Chattanooga, and Saint Louis Railroad in 1873.

NASHVILLE CONVENTION (1850). A convention of the slave-holding states assembled at Nashville, Tenn., on June 3, 1850. Nine states were represented, and many of the outstanding political leaders of the South were among its delegates. The convention unanimously adopted twenty-eight resolutions, which affirmed states' rights and the legality of slavery. The resolutions expressed a willingness to extend the Missouri Compromise line to the Pacific. Reassembling six weeks after Congress had adopted the Compromise of 1850, the convention, with a changed and more radical membership, rejected the compromise and called upon the southern states to secede from the Union. The second session of the convention was a fiasco because southern sentiment rapidly crystallized in support of the compromise.

NASSAU, FORT. Built by the Dutch on the Delaware River in 1623, in Gloucester County, N.J. It gave the Dutch fur traders a dominant position in the valley. When Gov. Peter Stuyvesant erected Fort Casimir on the lower Delaware in 1651 to compel the evacuation of the Swedish Fort Elfsborg, to the southeast, he abandoned and destroyed Fort Nassau.

NASSAU PACT (Dec. 18–21, 1962). Made by President John F. Kennedy and Great Britain's Prime Minister Harold Macmillan at Nassau, Bahama Islands. It provided that the two countries, in consultation with other North Atlantic Treaty Organization allies, would cooperate in establishing a multilateral nuclear force. The agreement was undermined by President Charles de Gaulle.

NAST CARTOONS. Thomas Nast's cartoons, appearing in *Harper's Weekly* between 1862 and 1886, not only marked the beginning of the modern political cartoon but were a great force in contemporary politics. His greatest work was in the exposure of political boss William M. Tweed and his cohorts in New York City in 1870. He invented the symbolic Republican elephant and the Democratic donkey and popularized the Tammany tiger, borrowed from a political club emblem.

NATAQUA, PROPOSED TERRITORY OF. A movement of the citizens of Honey Lake Valley, Calif., in 1856, to organize an independent territory. Believing they were too far east to be in California and not liking the government of adjacent Carson County in Utah Territory, they met and adopted laws and regulations for the new territory, but nothing came of the movement.

NATCHEZ (Miss.). Located in southwestern Mississippi. In 1716 Jean Baptiste Le Moyne, Sieur de Bienville, established Fort Rosalie on the site of the present city, on the lowest of the several bluffs on the Mississippi. By 1729 it had become a settlement of 700, but in that year the Natchez, resenting their treatment by the French, destroyed the fort. In 1763 the site came into English possession (*see* Panmure, Fort), and during the Revolution its population, fewer than a hundred and mostly English, was divided into two bitter factions of patriots and Loyalists. After several years of fighting both groups were overpowered by the Spanish, who in turn surrendered the post to the United States in 1798, in compliance with the terms of Pinckney's Treaty of 1795 (*see* Guion's Expedition).

In the first decade of the 19th century the town became a commercial center as the southern terminus of the new road from Nashville, the Natchez Trace. With the increasing production of cotton and the advent of the steamboat on the Mississippi, it was converted from an isolated frontier outpost into a center of planter aristocracy. Following a decline after the Civil War, Natchez regained its economic health in some measure as a shipping point and soon began to capitalize on its natural resources, particularly timber and oil. In the 20th century Natchez gained a reputation as an embodiment of the antebellum South and developed a large tourist industry. The population of Natchez in 1980 was 22,015.

NATCHEZ (Indians). The Muskogean-speaking Natchez constituted the largest and most fully unified of the native tribes of the lower Mississippi in the 17th century. The 18th century saw them driven from their original towns along St. Catherine's Creek in Mississippi as a result of their continuing hostilities with the French and Choctaw. Segments of the Natchez were assimilated by the Creek and Cherokee, and they were settled with their hosts in Oklahoma in the 19th century. Both the culture and the language of the Natchez were destroyed, with the result that the tribe can be said to be extinct.

The uniqueness of Natchez culture lay in its patterns of social and political development, especially in the sociopolitical hierarchy the Natchez created. Their mode of life, village organization, intensive maize cultivation, warfare, and religion relate them closely to other Gulf tribes, but their concepts of hereditary chieftainship and matrilinear nobility have no parallels among American Indians.

NATCHEZ, TREATY OF (May 14, 1790). Between Gov. Manuel Gayoso de Lemos of Mississippi Territory and the Choctaw and Chickasaw nations. It confirmed boundaries of the Natchez District as set originally by the British and the Indians: on the west, the Mississippi; on the east, a line from the Yazoo River, a few miles above Walnut Hills, running south into Florida.

NATCHEZ CAMPAIGN OF 1813. Waged by U.S. forces against the Creek on the eastern frontier of Mississippi Territory. The Indians threatened hostilities early in 1813, and a brigade of volunteers from Natchez country was ordered to Fort Stoddert, on the Tombigbee. Following the Creek attack on Fort Mims on the east bank of the Alabama River thirty-five miles above Mobile, Aug. 30, 1813, the U.S. force was able to destroy the Creek stronghold at the Holy Ground in present Lowndes County, Ala., Dec. 23, 1813 (*see* Creek War).

NATCHEZ TRACE. A road running more than 500 miles from Nashville, Tenn., to Natchez, Miss., on the Mississippi River, roughly following an old Indian trail. In 1801 Gen. James Wilkinson obtained the right of way by treaties with the Chickasaw and Choctaw (*see* Adams, Fort), and in 1806 Congress authorized construction to begin. In a few years it had achieved great economic and military importance.

NATCHITOCHES (La.). It was established on the Red River in 1713–14 and soon became a fortified outpost against neighboring Spanish establishments in Texas. For a century the settlement was a military-commercial center with a cosmopolitan population composed of French, Spanish, Anglo-American, and other elements. During the Franco-Spanish war of 1719 the commandant of Natchitoches drove the Spaniards temporarily from their posts in northeastern Texas, and thereafter Natchitoches figured in inconclusive Franco-Spanish boundary controversies. In 1806, as a U.S. border post, it became the center of military and diplomatic maneuvers culminating in the Neutral Ground Agreement. The town was a military post of some importance at the time of the Texas Revolution (1836) and the Mexican War (1846–48). Natchitoches lost its commercial importance after 1850, when the main channel of the Red River shifted. The population of Natchitoches in 1980 was 16,664.

NATIONAL ACADEMY OF SCIENCES. Established by Congress in 1863, as a private organization to investigate and report on any subject of science or art (technology) whenever called upon by any department of the government. Originally limited by its charter to fifty members, in 1870 that restriction was removed.

The National Research Council was established by the academy in 1916 and in 1950 the National Academy of Sciences and its research council became a single administrative and operating unit, the National Academy of Sciences-National Research Council. Its primary purpose is to promote scientific research, both pure and applied. It draws it membership from scientists, engineers, and other professionals in universities, industry, and government to serve on its several hundred study committees. The home of the National Academy of Sciences is in Washington, D.C.

NATIONAL ADVISORY COMMISSION ON CIVIL DISORDERS. Named by President Lyndon B. Johnson in 1967 and headed by Judge Otto Kerner of Illinois. Its creation followed urban ghetto riots and other instances of racial conflict across the country. The commission issued its findings (known as the Kerner Report) in 1968. This report concluded that America's tradition of white racism was responsible for the riots. The commission deplored the polarization of the nation into two societies, one black and one white, and recommended a massive program of federal spending to correct the inequities produced by centuries of racial discrimination. Although only a few of the commission's recommendations were carried out, the report had appreciable impact upon public opinion and governmental actions.

NATIONAL ADVISORY COMMITTEE FOR AERONAUTICS (NACA). Created by Congress in 1915 "to conduct the scientific study of the problems of flight, with a view to their practical solution." NACA recommendations exercised considerable influence, especially during World War I and World War II. NACA-sponsored research in such innovations as jet propulsion and the excellence of its technical reports earned it an international reputation. World War II prompted NACA's greatest expansion. The Ames Aeronautical Laboratory at Moffett Field, Calif., was founded in 1940, and the Lewis Flight Propulsion Laboratory at Cleveland in 1941. By 1945, NACA had a station for rocket research at Wallops Island, Va., and one for support of the NACA role in the flight test program conducted jointly with the air force and navy at Edwards Air Force Base, Calif. In 1958, NACA emerged as the organizational nucleus of the National Aeronautics and Space Administration.

NATIONAL AERONAUTICS AND SPACE ADMINISTRATION (NASA). On Apr. 2, 1958, President Dwight D. Eisenhower proposed the establishment of a National Aeronautical and Space Agency to absorb the National Advisory Committee for Aeronautics and assume responsibility for all space activities except those with military requirements. The new agency was voted into existence on July 29, 1958, and formally began business on Oct. 1, 1958. Its responsibilities included research as well as developmental, managerial, and flight operations. It had extensive authority for contracting research and development projects. Organizational transfers had to be worked out, most notably the transfer of the famed rocket design team led by Wernher von Braun from the army together with its million-pound-thrust Saturn booster project. But by the end of 1960 NASA was on firm ground, having established two new spaceflight centers (Goddard at Greenbelt, Md., and Marshall at Huntsville, Ala.).

Beginning in September 1959, when it carried out its first successful satellite launching (Vanguard III, which gathered data on earth's magnetic field and the radiation belts first revealed by Explorer I), NASA launched hundreds of instrumented satellites and space probes. During the 1960's a network of satellites launched by NASA for the private Communications Satellite Corporation established a worldwide system of visual and telephonic communication.

Overshadowing all other NASA undertakings was the manned spaceflight program. In November 1958, NASA undertook to place a series of one-man ballistic capsules in earth orbit. Between May 1961 and June 1963, Mercury astronauts successfully flew two suborbital and four orbital missions, extending from three to twenty-two circuits of earth. Late in May 1961, after the Soviet Union's launch of the first manned satellite and a comparatively modest U.S. suborbital launch, President John F. Kennedy set as a national goal a manned landing on the moon "before this decade is out."

For the next few years NASA's budgets continued to grow

—to a peak of $5.25 billion for fiscal year 1965. To carry out Project Gemini, which was to perfect the rendezvous and docking procedures essential to the lunar-orbit mode chosen for the moon mission, and Project Apollo, the moonflight program itself, as well as to carry to completion Project Mercury, NASA moved to create a huge space development aggregation, consisting of the rocket launch facilities at Cape Canaveral, Fla.; the Marshall Space Flight Center in Alabama; a rocket assembly and test plant in southeastern Mississippi; and a new management, crew training, and flight control installation called the Manned Spacecraft Center, near Houston, Tex.

The Gemini program sent twenty astronauts into orbit in two-man spacecraft during 1964–66. Project Apollo, although set back a year by the deaths of three crewmen in a spacecraft fire on the launch pad in January 1967, continued its buildup through earth-orbital and lunar-orbital missions until the Apollo XI mission in July 1969, when two Americans set foot on the moon's surface.

Project Skylab established an American-manned orbital space station in 1973; the development and deployment of a space shuttle system were approved in 1972; and a joint U.S.-Soviet undertaking to rendezvous and dock an American Apollo and a Russian Soyuz spacecraft succeeded in 1975.

NASA's most ambition project of the 1970's was the space shuttle. After ten years of development plagued with difficulties the shuttle Columbia was successfully launched in April 1981, and by July 1982 had made three more test trips and was proclaimed operational. In 1982 NASA's budget was $5.95 billion and the agency was intent on establishing a permanent manned orbital station.

NATIONAL ANTHEM. *See* **"Star-Spangled Banner."**

NATIONAL ASSOCIATION FOR THE ADVANCEMENT OF COLORED PEOPLE (NAACP). The NAACP was founded in 1909–10 by white progressives and black militants led by William English Walling, Mary White Ovington, Oswald Garrison Villard, and W. E. B. Du Bois. Except for Du Bois, who became the association's director of publicity and editor of *Crisis,* its official publication, all of the organization's first national officers were white. At its formation the NAACP adopted a militant program of action demanding equal educational, political, and civil rights for blacks and the enforcement of the Fourteenth and Fifteenth amendments.

The NAACP stressed corrective education, legislation, and litigation. Attorneys for the NAACP won important victories before the U.S. Supreme Court in 1915 (*Guinn* v. *United States*) and 1917 (*Buchanan* v. *Warley*), which struck down the grandfather clause as unconstitutional and nullified Jim Crow housing ordinances in Louisville, Ky. During the 1920's and 1930's, the organization focused its attention on antilynching legislation. Although no federal antilynching bill was passed by Congress, the NAACP's aggressive campaign heightened public awareness of, and opposition to, mob violence against blacks and established the organization as the national spokesman for Afro-Americans.

The NAACP increasingly directed its attention to voting rights, housing, and the desegregation of public education. With Thurgood Marshall as its special legal counsel, the NAACP figured prominently in a series of pro-black Supreme Court decisions that culminated in the landmark case *Brown* v. *Board of Education of Topeka* (May 1954), which declared segregated schools unequal and unconstitutional.

Under its executive secretary, Roy Wilkins, the NAACP was a leading participant in the civil rights movement of the 1960's. Direct actionists, such as the Student Nonviolent Coordinating Committee (SNCC), for a while challenged the organization's hegemony as the country's major civil rights group, but with a 1975 membership of 433,118 and 1,555 branches in all fifty states, the NAACP entered the fourth quarter of the 20th century as the premier active force among black Americans committed to racial integration.

NATIONAL ASSOCIATION OF MANUFACTURERS (NAM). Organized in Cincinnati in 1895, the NAM is composed of manufacturing firms that produce 75 percent of the nation's goods. The association has traditionally espoused an ideology of laissez-faire, antiunion sentiments, and protectionism, which it has disseminated through a vigorous lobby and numerous publications.

NATIONAL BANKING SYSTEM. *See* **Banking.**

NATIONAL BANK NOTES. In 1863 Congress authorized the issuance of national bank notes by national banks. Each national bank was to deposit with the Treasury a specified amount of U.S. bonds and then issue circulating notes, guaranteed by the government, of up to 90 percent of the par value of such deposited bonds.

National bank notes were never a satisfactory currency, the amount in circulation fluctuating more closely with the price of government bonds than with the needs of business. Nevertheless, they constituted the sole U.S. bank note currency until 1914 and remained in circulation after establishment of the Federal Reserve System until 1935, when bonds bearing the circulation privilege were retired by the Treasury.

NATIONAL BUREAU OF ECONOMIC RESEARCH. Founded in 1920, the bureau has sought to maintain a disinterested stance on public issues and makes no policy recommendations. The first set of bureau studies developed a conceptual system for analyzing national income and wealth and presented national income estimates. The national accounts have remained central to the research of the bureau. Its research also deals with current problems of urban economics, health, education, income distribution, and population.

NATIONAL BUREAU OF STANDARDS. Established by Congress in 1901. As custodian of standards, the bureau is authorized to construct when necessary and to maintain the standards of weight and measure, as well as their multiples and subdivisions, required by science, engineering, manufacturing, commerce, and educational institutions; to test and calibrate standard measuring apparatus; to resolve problems in connection with standards; and to determine physical constants and the properties of materials where high accuracy is necessary. It is under the Department of Commerce.

The bureau has developed thousands of new standards of quality, safety, performance, and precision measurement. These standards were fundamental to the development of the radio, radio propagation, automotive technology, aviation, cryogenics, electronics, nuclear physics, and space science. The Bureau of Standards thus became one of the largest institutions for scientific research in the world, with headquarters at Gaithersburg, Md.

NATIONAL COMMITTEE. Each of the major U.S. political parties maintains a national committee with representatives from each state organization. Although formally the governing body of the party, the committee is usually of little significance in its collective capacity; the chairman, named by the presidential candidate, and a small executive committee usually dominate the situation. The members are active and influential, however, in state politics.

NATIONAL CONFERENCE OF CHRISTIANS AND JEWS. Organized in 1928 as a formal meeting place for people concerned about religious freedoms and respect for the religious rights of others. The conference set among its objectives the development of a spirit of brotherhood based on the religious teachings of Christianity and Judaism and the elimination of religious prejudice.

NATIONAL CONGRESS OF AMERICAN INDIANS. An intertribal political action organization founded in 1944 that includes both individual and tribal members. Its political philosophy has been relatively moderate. It has sought primarily to improve the position of Indians within the federal governmental structure.

NATIONAL COUNCIL OF CHURCHES OF CHRIST IN THE UNITED STATES OF AMERICA. An organization of Christian religious groups created in 1950 and comprising over 30 separate sects, representing Anglican (Episcopalian), Protestant, and Eastern Orthodox churches. The council is an instrument for the cooperation of its member churches. Its concerns include Christian life, Christian education, home missions, and foreign missionary activities.

NATIONAL DEBT. *See* **Debt, Public.**

NATIONAL DEFENSE. *See* **Defense, National.**

NATIONAL DEFENSE EDUCATION ACT (1958). First passed to provide direct federal assistance for the improvement of school activities that Congress considered important to the eventual defense of the United States. The act has been extended beyond mathematics and the sciences to include the areas of guidance, library, science, foreign languages, media, and vocational education.

NATIONAL EDUCATION ASSOCIATION (NEA). The largest professional educational organization in the United States. It was created in 1871, growing out of the National Teachers Association. The purpose of the NEA is to promote educational efforts and excellence and to secure teachers' rights. On the federal level it actively lobbies for education legislation, much of which it drafts. On the local level it acts as a bargaining unit. The NEA publishes several journals, bulletins, yearbooks, and research studies. In 1975 it had 50 state and 9,000 local affiliates and a membership of 1.7 million.

NATIONAL EMPLOYMENT SERVICE ACT (June 6, 1933). One of the acts of Franklin D. Roosevelt's New Deal, it sought to minimize the effects of joblessness by authorizing the expansion of the U.S. Employment Service. It authorized a national employment system based on cooperation with states maintaining such services, and required the matching of state appropriations for employment services.

NATIONAL ENVIRONMENTAL POLICY ACT (1969). This act made protection of the environment a matter of national policy by requiring all federal agencies to consider the effects on the environment of all major activities and to include in every recommendation for legislation or other significant actions an environmental impact statement including a written analysis of these effects as well as alternatives to the proposal. The act also established the three-member Council of Environmental Quality to oversee the nation's efforts in dealing with pollution and to make environmental policy recommendations to the president.

NATIONAL GAZETTE. Started in Philadelphia, Oct. 31, 1791, under the patronage of Thomas Jefferson, then secretary of state, who subsidized its editor, Philip Freneau, with the position of translator in the Department of State. It was intended to oppose the Federalist *United States Gazette;* but its attacks on Secretary of the Treasury Alexander Hamilton's policies angered President George Washington, who held Jefferson responsible. It was discontinued shortly after Jefferson's resignation in 1794.

NATIONAL GUARD. The modern counterpart of the militia. The name "National Guard" was first used in 1824 by New York units to honor the Marquis de Lafayette, commander of France's Garde Nationale. The modern National Guard began with the Dick Act of 1903, which divided the militia into the organized militia, or National Guard, and the unorganized militia. The National Defense Act of 1920 established a three-component army: National Guard, organized reserves, and regular army. A 1933 amendment created the National Guard of the United States (NGUS) as a reserve component of the army. Although the composition of this force was identical to that of the state National Guard, it was subject to a call to active duty by the president without his having to go through the governor. In 1947, the Air National Guard was formed.

National Guard units must undergo at least forty-eight drills and fifteen days of field training annually. Aside from being used in wartime, guard units have given aid in times of natural disasters and maintained order during civil disturbances. (*See also* Military Aid to the Civil Powers.)

NATIONAL HOUSING ACT. *See* **Housing Acts.**

NATIONAL INDIAN YOUTH COUNCIL. A political action organization started in 1961 by Indian college students and recent college graduates. The council is more militant than the National Congress of American Indians. It manifests the influence of the civil rights movements of the period of its founding and has used tactics of demonstration and confrontation. It favors the abolition of the Bureau of Indian Affairs.

NATIONAL INDUSTRIAL RECOVERY ACT. *See* **National Recovery Administration.**

NATIONAL INSTITUTE FOR THE PROMOTION OF SCIENCE. Founded in 1840, it reflected the ambitions of its predecessor, the Columbian Institute, and followed the tradition of other philosophical societies in America. Its areas of inquiry ranged over the natural and physical sciences and applied science and agriculture, as well as American history, literature, and the fine arts. Membership was broadly defined, and invitations went to resident politicians, diplomatic representatives, and interested Americans. Its founding coincided with the foundation of the Smithsonian Institution, and it began publishing its *Bulletin* in 1841. It was soon overshadowed by the Smithsonian and other scientific bodies, and by the end of the decade had virtually ceased to exist.

NATIONAL INSTITUTES OF HEALTH (NIH). Originated as the Laboratory of Hygiene and was established at the Marine Hospital, Staten Island, N.Y., in 1887 for research on cholera and other infectious diseases. Its activities continued to widen and in 1948 it was designated the National Institutes of Health. Headquarters are at Bethesda, Md.

An agency of the Department of Health and Human Services, NIH has the mission of improving the health of all Americans. It conducts biomedical research; provides grants to individuals, organizations, and institutions for research, training, and medical education; assists in the improvement and construction of library facilities and resources; and supports programs in biomedical communications. NIH has developed into a great research center consisting of ten institutes (Cancer; Heart and Lung; Allergy and Infectious Diseases; Dental Research; Arthritis, Metabolism, and Digestive Diseases; Neurological Diseases and Stroke; Child Health and Human Development; General Medical Sciences; Eye; and Environmental Health Sciences); four divisions (Computer Research and Technology; Research Grants; Research Resources; and Research Services); the National Library of Medicine; and two centers, the research hospital Clinical Center and the John E. Fogarty International Center.

***NATIONAL INTELLIGENCER*.** A conservative newspaper established by Samuel Harrison Smith in Washington, D.C., Oct. 31, 1800, as the official organ of Thomas Jefferson's Democratic-Republican party. It became a Whig paper during Andrew Jackson's regime but was supplanted by the *Republic* as the Whig organ during Zachary Taylor's presidency. It was returned to favor during Millard Fillmore's administration. The daily edition was merged with the weekly in 1870, moved to New York, and was soon discontinued.

NATIONALIZATION OF U.S. PROPERTY ABROAD. Prior to World War I, few countries ever expropriated the property of aliens, but starting with the Russian Revolution in 1917, expropriations became more commonplace. Often they took the form of vast nationalization programs under which countries took the private property of citizens and aliens alike. Between World War I and World War II, many U.S. nationals, both individuals and corporations, lost their property in this fashion. Whereas some countries compensated the former owners for their losses—Mexico is an example—often such was not the case. Half a century after its revolution, the Soviet Union still had not settled claims.

After the end of World War II, nationalizations became increasingly common. The Communist-bloc countries engaged in such programs, eventually entering into lump-sum settlement agreements, under which compensation averaged well under 50 percent of the value of the claims.

In the 1960's and 1970's numerous nationalizations took place in Latin America. The United States, while acknowledging the right of all countries to nationalize the property of foreigners in the course of making structural changes in their economies, has insisted in all such cases that U.S. claimants be paid appropriate compensation in accordance with international law. An amendment to the Foreign Assistance Act of 1961 stipulated that the United States will suspend foreign aid to countries that do not take steps to provide suitable compensation for the nationalization of U.S. property.

NATIONAL LABOR RELATIONS ACT (NLRA; 1935). The NLRA is the cornerstone of national labor policy. Known initially as the Wagner Act, it guarantees the rights of workers to organize, to bargain collectively with their employers, and to strike (subject to the law). It encourages collective bargaining and provides governmental processes for the selection of employee bargaining representatives. It provided for the establishment of the National Labor Relations Board (NLRB) to administer its provisions. The act outlawed company unions or employer-assisted unions. It prohibited discrimination in employment to encourage or discourage membership in a labor organization but permitted "closed shops" established by collective-bargaining agreements between employers and unions with exclusive bargaining rights. It prohibited employers from discharging or otherwise discriminating against employees who file charges or give testimony under the act. It also made it unlawful for an employer to refuse to bargain collectively with the representative chosen by a majority of employees in a group appropriate for collective bargaining.

The NLRA was amended in 1947 by the Labor Management Relations Act, commonly known as the Taft-Hartley

Act. By it, unions were prohibited from restraining or coercing employees in exercising their rights under the law, refusing to bargain in good faith with an employer when the union is the representative of employees, and engaging in secondary boycotts and certain types of strikes and picketing. Closed shops were outlawed. In 1959 the Landrum-Griffin Act further amended the NLRB. In general it added to those practices forbidden to unions.

The NLRA does not apply to railroads and airlines, which are covered by the Railway Labor Act, or to governmental agencies. Some groups of employees—such as agricultural laborers, domestic employees, and supervisors—are excluded from coverage.

The board is composed of five members appointed by the president subject to approval by the Senate, with each member having a term of five years. The general counsel, whose appointment also must be approved by the Senate, has a term of four years. The board members act primarily as a quasijudicial body in deciding cases on formal records, generally upon review of findings of fact and decisions by its administrative law judges (formerly called trial examiners) in cases of unfair labor practice or upon review of regional director decisions in representation cases. The NLRB has no independent statutory power of enforcement of its orders, but it may seek enforcement in the U.S. courts of appeals.

***NATIONAL LABOR RELATIONS BOARD* V. *JONES AND LAUGHLIN STEEL CORPORATION* 301 U.S. 1(1937).** A Supreme Court decision that upheld the validity of the National Labor Relations Act of 1935. The Court accepted the findings of the National Labor Relations Board that the Jones and Laughlin Corporation was engaged in interstate commerce and that the national government therefore had the constitutional power to regulate it.

NATIONAL MEDIATION BOARD. *See* **Federal Agencies.**

NATIONAL MONETARY COMMISSION. Created in order to determine "what changes are necessary or desirable in the monetary system of the United States or in the laws relating to banking and currency." On Jan. 8, 1912, the commission, composed of nine senators and nine representatives, submitted its report to Congress. The report advocated the establishment of a National Reserve Association with branches to act as a central bank for the United States (*see* Federal Reserve System).

NATIONAL MUSEUM. The National Museum was created as an outgrowth of the Centennial Exposition of 1876 at Philadelphia. A large rambling structure adjoining the Smithsonian Institution in Washington was opened in 1881 as the National Museum. It collected and preserved specimens in all fields of natural and human history, and fostered research and education by scholarly study and publication.

As it grew, it became the depository of collections in many fields, ranging from geology and zoology to anthropology, ethnology, and arts and industries. Indeed, its very multiplication of collections rendered the original unifying entity of the National Museum obsolete and inadequate, and it passed "into disuse" both as a name and as a concept under the museum reorganization of 1968. The director of the National Museum became the director-general of museums, of which there were three main groupings, in natural history, history and technology, and air and space, each housed in its own building in Washington, D.C. Together they virtually eclipse their parent, the Smithsonian Institution, which continues to supervise and integrate them administratively.

NATIONAL ORIGINS QUOTA ACT (1924). The basic U.S. immigration law until it was superseded by the Act of 1965. The National Origins Quota Act limited immigration to 2 percent for each group in the United States, according to the 1890 census, and was to remain in force until 1927, when apportionment of the 1920 census of national origins would serve as the basis for a maximum immigration quota of 150,000 per year. Because of opposition the law did not go into effect until 1929. Because of it reliance on the 1890 census it was seen as discriminatory against Eastern Europeans. The act did not apply to immigrants from the Western Hemisphere.

NATIONAL PARKS AND MONUMENTS. *See* **Parks, National, and National Monuments; Park Service, National, and National Park System.**

NATIONAL RECOVERY ADMINISTRATION. Created by the National Industrial Recovery Act (NIRA) of 1933, a New Deal emergency measure. Aimed at stimulating the economy, the act provided for codes of fair competition, for exemption from antitrust laws, and for the government licensing of business. It guaranteed the right of collective bargaining and stipulated that the codes should set minimum wages and maximum hours.

From its inception through March 1934 the NRA was chiefly engaged in code-making. Industrial councils were authorized to draw up codes of fair competition. Administered by a code authority in each industry, the codes were supposed to stop wasteful competition, effect more orderly pricing and selling policies, and establish better working conditions. Within a year nearly all American industry was codified.

On Feb. 20, 1935, the president recommended to Congress the extension of the NIRA for two years beyond its expiration date of June 1935. On June 14, Congress voted to extend the recovery legislation until Apr. 1, 1936, but repealed the provisions authorizing the president to approve or prescribe codes of fair competition. (On May 27, 1935, in *Schechter Poultry Corporation* v. *United States,* the Supreme Court had invalidated the code-making provisions of the act.) The NRA was terminated on Jan. 1, 1936.

NATIONAL REPUBLICAN PARTY. Political party created by the split in the Jeffersonian Republicans in 1824. John Quincy Adams won the presidency in the House of Representatives, and the opposing elements drew together in support of Andrew Jackson. Both wings continued to call themselves Republicans, but eventually the followers of Adams and Henry Clay were referred to as National Republicans and those of the Jackson faction as Democratic-Republicans. Most of the Federalists remaining on the scene in 1825 gravitated to the National Republicans. Accurately speaking, there were no Whigs and no Democrats until 1834. Then the National Republican party was absorbed by the new and larger Whig party, and Democratic-Republicans took on the name Democrats.

NATIONAL RESOURCES COMMITTEE (NRC). An agency established by executive order in 1934 for the purpose of studying the conservation of natural resources, it replaced the National Planning Board, which had been created in 1933. The NRC was made an independent agency charged with encouraging the creation of state planning boards to carry on the field work. In 1939 the NRC merged with the Federal Employment Stabilization Office to form the National Resources Planning Board, which was abolished in 1943. Its functions were assumed by the Executive office.

NATIONAL RIFLE ASSOCIATION (NRA). Founded in 1871 by National Guard officers in an effort to encourage marksmanship. The main importance of the NRA today lies in its lobbying efforts to prevent strict gun control legislation. The association has gained its greatest political support in small towns and rural areas, especially of the West and South, where hunting is particularly popular. NRA members total more than one million.

NATIONAL ROAD. The section of the Cumberland Road extending westward from Wheeling W. Va. Construction of this western portion was begun from Wheeling toward Zanesville, Ohio, in 1825, following (Ebenezer) Zane's Trace. By 1833 the road was opened to Columbus. The road through Indiana was completed only in 1850 by a state corporation and still later by Illinois. The road went through Vandalia, then the state capital, and eventually reached St. Louis. With the advent of the automobile the National Road became U.S. Route 40.

NATIONAL SCIENCE FOUNDATION (NSF). Created in 1950 to establish science policy for the government as a whole. It would also be the agency charged with funneling federal subsidies to basic research and science education. Under the governance of the twenty-five-member National Science Board, made up of prominent scientists and educators appointed for six-year terms by the president, the NSF has expanded steadily. Although it has had a disproportionate influence in supporting basic research on college campuses, its research budget has always been dwarfed by those of other, related agencies.

NATIONAL SECURITY ACT (1947). The act reorganized the army, navy, and air force (herein made a separate service) into the single National Military Establishment under the Secretary of Defense with cabinet status and established the National Security Council and under it the Central Intelligence Agency (CIA). Amended in 1949, it renamed the National Military Establishment the Department of Defense and created a nonvoting chairmen of the Joint Chiefs of Staff.

NATIONAL SECURITY COUNCIL. A five-member council consisting of the president, vice-president, chief of the National Securities Resources Board, and secretaries of State and Defense, and established by the National Security Act of 1947. The council administers the planning, developing, and coordinating of all functions concerned with the defense of the United States. It has the responsibility of evaluating the aims and commitments of the United States in light of existing or potential war and advises the president on foreign policy decisions and security problems.

NATIONAL TRADES' AND WORKERS' ASSOCIATION. Started in 1910 at Battle Creek, Mich., by C. W. Post to fight trade unions. It advocated arbitration of labor disputes and was against the closed shop, strikes, lockouts, boycotts, and blacklisting. Only a few locals were established. The association ended soon after Post's death in 1914.

***NATIONAL TRIBUNE*.** Soldiers' newspaper founded in 1877, in Washington, D.C. Within seven years, it boasted of a circulation of 112,000 paid subscribers, mostly former Union soldiers (*see* Grand Army of the Republic). Its purpose was to keep them apprised of all pension legislation and urge them to work constantly for more liberal pensions. As the ranks of the veterans thinned out, it became a family newspaper, but in 1926 it resumed its original character in some measure by absorbing the Washington, D.C., continuation of the World War I *Stars and Stripes*.

NATIONAL TRUST FOR HISTORIC PRESERVATION. A private, nonprofit organization chartered by Congress in 1949 to encourage public participation in the preservation of sites, buildings, and objects significant in historical and cultural aspects of America's environment. Its services include counsel and education on preservation and interpretation and administration of historic properties. The trust owns a number of historic properties that are maintained as house museums open to the public. It produces two major publications: *Preservation News,* a monthly newspaper, and *Historic Preservation,* a quarterly color magazine.

NATIONAL UNION ("ARM-IN-ARM") CONVENTION. Held in Philadelphia, Aug. 14–16, 1866. It was an effort by President Andrew Johnson's supporters to unite opposition to the Radical Republicans. Its platform stressed conciliation, equality among the states, and acceptance of the results of the Civil War. Although the convention was widely acclaimed at first, Radical Republican successes in the congressional elections of 1866 demonstrated its failure.

NATIONAL UNION FOR SOCIAL JUSTICE. Organized in 1935 by Charles E. Coughlin, a Roman Catholic priest and popular radio speaker. Units were quickly organized in many states. The union denounced President Franklin D. Roosevelt's New Deal policies and advocated the nationalization of banks and utilities. It disbanded in 1936, but it continued to operate independently in many places. Its weekly magazine, *Social Justice,* continued to publish until 1942, when it was barred from the U.S. mails, because of its anti-Semitic and pro-Nazi statements, under the Espionage Act.

NATIONAL URBAN LEAGUE. Founded (1911) through the consolidation of three earlier black civil rights groups, the National Urban League quickly established itself as the principal agency dealing with the problems of blacks in American cities. It used negotiation, persuasion, education, and investigation to accomplish its economic and social goals: gaining jobs for blacks, attacking the color line in organized labor, sponsoring programs of vocational guidance and job training, and striving for governmental policies of equal employment opportunity. During the Great Depression it lobbied for the inclusion of blacks in federal relief and recovery programs; in the 1940's it pressed for an end to discrimination in defense industries and for the desegregation of the armed forces.

The league trained the first professional black social workers and placed them in community service positions. It works for decent housing, recreational facilities, and health and welfare services. In the 1960's the league embraced direct action and community organization, sponsored leadership training and voter-education projects, helped organize massive demonstrations in support of civil rights and economic justice (the March on Washington of 1963 and the Poor People's Campaign of 1968), and began to concentrate on building ghetto power among blacks. The league had about 50,000 members in 1980.

NATIONAL WAR LABOR BOARD. *See* **War Labor Board.**

NATIONAL WATERWAYS COMMISSION (1909–12). Established by Congress to investigate water transportation and river improvement. The commission of twelve congressmen submitted a preliminary report in 1910 on Great Lakes and inland waterways commerce. It urged continuance of investigations by army engineers and completion of projects under way and opposed improvements not essential to navigation. A final report in 1912 favored the Lake Erie–Ohio River Canal, suggested further study on the Lake Erie–Lake Michigan Canal, opposed the Anacostia-Chesapeake Canal, and urged regulation of all water carriers by the Interstate Commerce Commission.

NATIVE AMERICAN CHURCH. Incorporated in Oklahoma in 1918, the Native American Church has become the principal religion of the Indians living between the Mississippi River and the Rocky Mountains. It is also represented among the Navaho, in the Great Basin, in east-central California, and in southern Canada. An amalgamation compounding some Christian elements with others of Indian derivation, it features as a sacrament the ingestion of the peyote cactus, which may induce hallucinations. Christian elements include the cross, the Trinity, baptism, and modified Christian ethics, theology, and eschatology.

NATIVE AMERICAN PARTY. *See* **American Republican Party.**

NATIVISM. The policy of favoring native inhabitants of a country as against immigrants, particularly those espousing Roman Catholicism. Anti-Catholic sentiment, brought to America by the first English colonists, was fostered by the 18th-century wars with Catholic France and Spain. The Revolution changed the American attitude toward Roman Catholicism, for the liberal spirit of the Declaration of Independence and the French alliance of 1778 both contributed toward a more tolerant spirit.

Anti-Catholic sentiment reappeared in the late 1820's, inspired by mounting Catholic immigration. Protestants, under the influence of the revivalism of Charles G. Finney, quickly rushed to the defense of their religion, and by 1834 intolerance had grown to a point at which the mob destruction of an Ursuline convent at Charlestown, Mass., was condoned rather than condemned. This sign of popular favor resulted in anti-Catholic journals, a flood of anti-Catholic books and pamphlets, and the formation (1836) of the Protestant Reformation Society. But it remained for the New York school controversy of the early 1840's to win over the Protestant middle class. Catholic protests against the reading of the King James Bible in the public schools were misrepresented by propagandists, who claimed that Catholics were opposed to all reading of the Bible. The churches took up the cry against Rome, and nativists organized the anti-Catholic, antiforeign American Republican party. But riots between natives and immigrants in Philadelphia in 1844 turned popular sentiment against the anti-Catholic crusade. Nativistic leaders continued to form anti-Catholic bodies, and these eventually coalesced into the most important of the pre–Civil War societies, the American and Foreign Christian Union.

The heavy immigration from Ireland and Germany so alarmed Americans that political nativism seemed again feasible. The Know-Nothing, or American, party, founded on nativist principles, enjoyed remarkable success in 1854 and 1855. Its brief career was halted as Americans became absorbed in the slavery conflict and forgot their fears of Rome. The Civil War doomed both the Know-Nothing party and the American and Foreign Christian Union.

By the 1880's mounting foreign immigration and unsettled industrial conditions again aimed almost exclusively at the Roman Catholic church. The country was flooded with anti-Catholic documents; newspapers bent on exposing the "errors of Rome" were founded; and a fraudulent document alleged to be a papal bull calling for the massacre of all Protestants was widely circulated. The American Protective Association (1887) pledged its members neither to vote for nor to employ Catholics. Its political failure combined with the interest aroused by the free silver campaign of 1896 to check nativistic agitation. After 1898 there was another brief flurry. New anti-Catholic organizations were formed, the most prominent being the Guardians of Liberty, the Knights of Luther, the Covenanters, and the American Pathfinders. Anti-Catholic newspapers, led by the *Menace,* began to appear, but before this phase of the movement could be translated into politics, World War I intervened.

The next burst of nativistic excitement occurred during the 1920's. The intense nationalism of those years bred antagonism toward immigrants, Communists, and Catholics. The Ku Klux Klan shaped and fostered this prejudice, but its excesses and political corruption brought about its decline. Intolerance had not ended, a fact clearly shown by the presidential campaign of 1928. The presence of Alfred E. Smith, a Catholic, as the Democratic candidate aroused a bitter nativistic propaganda that was important in causing his defeat. The depression of the 1930's and World War II focused attention away from nativism, and the election of a Roman Catholic, John F. Kennedy, to the presidency in 1960 seemed to declare that it was substantially a dead issue.

NATIVISTIC MOVEMENTS, AMERICAN INDIAN. Nativistic movements, variously termed messianic cults, reversion or amalgamation religions, and revitalization movements, have been common among North American Indians. The movements constitute attempts to revive or perpetuate parts of the native culture. Typically, their messianic doctrines have been messages of hope, coming from the Great Spirit or another high deity, promising that if the followers of the prophet conducted themselves properly, there would be a paradise on earth. The conduct called for to bring about these anticipated conditions included return to Indian ways of life and participation in prescribed ritual activities.

The earliest nativistic movement on record in North America started among the Tewa Indians of New Mexico in the late 17th century. It culminated in 1680 when the Pueblo Indians in Arizona and New Mexico rebelled and temporarily expelled the Spaniards from the Southwest. In 1762 the Delaware Prophet appeared in the Lake Erie region, preaching a return to the old customs, and influenced Chief Pontiac to undertake his uprising. Other prophets appeared among the Shawnee, Delaware, Kickapoo, Potawatomi, and Winnebago. A Seneca prophet, Handsome Lake, started a cult among the Iroquois in 1799 that has survived to the present. In southern California in 1801 a nativistic movement spread from the Chumash to the tribes of the interior and the Sierra Nevada. In 1881, Nakaidoklini instigated a nativistic movement among the White Mountain Apache. In the Puget Sound area a Squaxin prophet named John Slocum founded the Indian Shaker religion in 1881, a cult combining Christian elements with Indian-style visions. The Columbia River area was the scene of the Cult of the Dreamers (1884), a movement with strong Roman Catholic overtones.

The most famous of the messianic cults of the North American Indians was that of the Ghost Dance, which began in 1869 when a Paiute of Nevada named Wodziwob began to prophesy supernatural events. A resurgence of the Ghost Dance in 1889, led by another Paiute messiah, named Wovoka, became a more militant movement when it spread into the Plains area, and it came to a climax in 1890 at the Battle of Wounded Knee in South Dakota.

NAT TURNER'S REBELLION (1831). The most significant of a number of slave revolts that occurred in the United States. Nat Turner was a thirty-one-year-old slave, a religious mystic who considered it God's work that he strike against slavery. In Southampton County, Va., on Aug. 21, 1831, Turner and six other slaves killed Turner's owner and the owner's family. They gathered arms and set out to gain support from other slaves. Turner's force grew to about seventy-five slaves, and they killed approximately sixty whites. On Aug. 23, while en route to the county seat at Jerusalem, the blacks were defeated by a large force of white volunteers and trained militia. Turner escaped and attempted unsuccessfully to muster support. He was captured on Oct. 30, sentenced to death, and hanged on Nov. 11. Several of his followers had been hanged earlier. A reign of terror against blacks resulted.

NATURAL BRIDGE OF VIRGINIA. A ninety-foot-high natural arch across Cedar Creek in Rockbridge County, Va. It was included in a grant made by King George III to Thomas Jefferson in 1774. The Jefferson estate sold the property in 1833, and a public highway now crosses the bridge.

NATURAL-GAS INDUSTRY. Until the mid-19th century natural gas was primarily a curiosity. Gas springs had been found near Charleston, W. Va., as early as 1775. In 1796, M. Ambroise and Company, Italian fireworkers in Philadelphia, made the first recorded demonstration of burning natural gas in the United States. It aroused so much interest that, in 1816, Rembrandt Peale put natural gas on display at his famous museum in Baltimore. But perhaps the best-known natural-gas well during these years was in Fredonia, N.Y., discovered in 1824. This spring was used to fuel thirty streetlights in the village and led to the founding in 1858 of the Fredonia Gaslight and Waterworks Company. During the next fifty years scores of natural-gas wells were developed in Ohio and Indiana. By 1900 the value of natural gas produced in the United States amounted to $24 million annually.

Increasing production of petroleum after 1900 boosted available natural gas enormously, since it appeared as a byproduct. In 1920 the total annual value of natural gas produced had reached $196 million, but producers faced serious problems in transporting the gas. Ten years later engineers developed seamless electrically welded pipes that transmitted natural gas cheaply and efficiently, but in the Great Depression, investors were reluctant to develop pipelines.

World War II inaugurated a tremendous boom in natural-gas consumption and production, and after the war investors built thousands of miles of new pipelines from the vast natural-gas fields in the Southwest to all great metropolitan areas. Natural gas quickly displaced coal and fuel oil in residential and commercial buildings because it was more versatile, cheaper, cleaner, more convenient to use, and much easier to transport. By 1970, natural-gas producers supplied more than 42 million individuals and corporations, who paid $11 billion for the product. Between 1950 and 1980 the number of natural-gas wells in the United States almost tripled, totaling about 175,000 in 1980. By then the natural-gas industry had emerged as one of the ten most important in the nation.

This period of growth was accompanied by increasing federal regulation. Between 1914 and 1938, state governments had been the prime regulators of gas production, but their regulations varied greatly and frequently were not enforced. Representatives of the industry as well as conservationists prevailed upon Congress in the New Deal era to extend federal control over the interstate transmission of natural gas. The Natural Gas Act of 1938 placed responsibility for national regulation in the hands of the Federal Power Commission. Between 1942 and 1970 both the Federal Power Commission and the federal courts—in particular, the Supreme Court decision in *Phillips Petroleum Company* v. *Wisconsin* (1954)—extended federal control over virtually all natural gas produced in the United States, but both the Carter and Reagan administrations instituted policies calling for the gradual deregulation of prices. In 1950 the natural-gas industry served 8 million users and had an income of about $1.5 billion; in 1980 it had 47 million consumers and revenues totaling about $48 billion.

NATURALIZATION. The formal and legal adoption of an alien into a political community. Citizenship in the United States is acquired by birth—either in the United States or abroad to American citizens—or by naturalization. The American colonial assemblies exercised a limited right to naturalize individuals and classes of persons. After the Revolution, the states were free to determine their own conditions for citizenship, but the Constitution (Article I, Section 8, Clause 4) provided that Congress alone shall have power "to establish an uniform Rule of Naturalization."

The three principal methods of granting citizenship to aliens are through collective naturalization, judicial naturalization, and derivative naturalization. Collective naturalization entails the simultaneous grant of citizenship to groups of aliens, ordinarily following the acquisition of territory in which they reside. Judicial naturalization, the most widely used and recognized form, entails an individual application by each alien seeking naturalization. Provisions for judicial naturalization have been on the statute books since the First Congress enacted a naturalization law in 1790. Since the First Congress, the process of individual naturalization has been entrusted to the courts. The present statute authorizes the grant of naturalization by naturalization courts, which include all federal district courts and designated state courts.

In order to qualify for naturalization an alien must have been lawfully admitted to the United States for permanent residence and have resided continuously thereafter in the country for five years. The requisite period of residence is reduced for certain special classes, including spouses of American citizens. For many years the naturalization laws excluded blacks and Orientals, but these racial disqualifications were completely eliminated by the McCarran-Walter Act of 1952. The Immigration and Naturalization Service supervises and processes all applications for naturalization. When the applicant has completed the procedure, the court orders the applicant admitted to citizenship, directs that he or she take the oath of allegiance, and issues a certificate of naturalization.

Derivative naturalization, which results from the naturalization of another person, usually a spouse or parent, is an automatic process and, like collective naturalization, does not depend upon the beneficiary's application.

Until 1922 an alien woman acquired derivative U.S. citizenship upon marriage to an American or upon the naturalization of her alien husband; thereafter, a married woman determined her own citizenship. The naturalization laws have always provided for automatic acquisition of derivative citizenship by alien minors upon the naturalization of their parents, although the conditions for it have varied.

NATURAL RESOURCES, CONSERVATION OF. *See* **Conservation.**

NATURAL RIGHTS. Commonly defined as rights that inhere in the individual anterior to the creation of government and are not relinquished upon entrance into civil society. The concept, brought to the American colonies through the writings of John Locke and stated in the New York assembly as early as 1714 by John Mulford, became a part of the revolutionary philosophy. Thomas Paine's conception of popular sovereignty involved the basic notion that rights inhere in the individual, that governments exist only for the further protection of individual rights. This idea was in the mind of Thomas Jefferson when he wrote into the Declaration of Independence that all men "are endowed by their Creator with certain inalienable Rights" and that among these rights are "Life, Liberty, and the pursuit of Happiness."

The first attack on natural rights came in the slavery controversy of the early 19th century. John C. Calhoun believed that government was not a matter of choice but a fundamental necessity to the existence of man; it was therefore fallacious to assume a state of society anterior to the creation of government and from this to attempt to rationalize the formation of political institutions. Not all the defenders of slavery were willing to relinquish the doctrine of natural rights, but those who relied on the doctrine gave it an interpretation that obviated any objection to slaveholding.

Since the Civil War, political theory in the United States has not adhered to the notion of individuality before organization. The dominant view is that natural rights have, at most, ethical significance and no place in political science.

***NAUTILUS*.** A "diving boat," armed with a torpedo, designed and built at Rouen, France, by U.S. engineer Robert Fulton, was launched July 24, 1800. After several successful submersions of it, Fulton submitted his plans for submarine operations against England's navy to Napoleon Bonaparte, who advanced 10,000 francs for repairs and improvements to the *Nautilus*. Although Fulton blew up a French sloop with the *Nautilus* at Brest, Aug. 11, 1801, he dismantled it when Napoleon offered no further encouragement.

NAUVOO, MORMONS AT. In 1839, upon their expulsion from Missouri, the Mormons purchased the embryonic town of Commerce in Hancock County, Ill., changed its name to Nauvoo, and prepared to make it their capital. The city grew rapidly, attracting Mormons from the East and converts from Europe. Its population of about 20,000 in 1845 made it the largest city in Illinois at the time. Nauvoo seemed also to be prosperous, but the prosperity depended principally on money brought to the community by newcomers. By 1845 poverty was widespread, and if the exodus forced by the Mormon War had not taken place, economic collapse probably would have occurred. (*See* Mormon War.)

NAVAHO ("Navajo," according to tribal preference). A southwestern American Indian tribe of the Athapascan language group. Their culture, despite changes in their location and subsistence patterns, remains remarkably intact. Although they reside in the inhospitable San Juan plateau of northern Arizona and New Mexico, spilling over into the extreme south of Utah and Colorado, they constitute the largest contemporary American Indian tribe. The Navaho population was about 145,000 in 1980.

It has been assumed that the Navaho, along with the Apache, gradually made their way southward from northwest Canada and central Alaska and that about 1375–1475 they had migrated into the American Southwest. Their incursions may have been a factor in the abandonment by the Pueblo of their great sites of Mesa Verde, Colo., and Chaco Canyon, N.Mex. The Navaho were heavily influenced by their Pueblo neighbors, and much of their culture is clearly of Pueblo, and especially Hopi, origin.

The Navaho spread out over a vast area, developing small, isolated family plots and moving to new fields as water and wood were available. Ever adept at adopting foreign cultural elements, from the Spanish they acquired domesticated sheep and assumed a mixed farming-pastoral mode. The Navaho thus became the only American Indians to depend on livestock (exclusive of the horse). For weaving, they adopted a loom of European type, but the designs they employ are variations of southwestern elements. Their clothing is Pueblo in origin, but with a Navaho accent, at least for men; women's dress suggests 18th-century Mexico. A brush shelter, reminiscent of the Great Basin, was the rule among them but gave way to the hogan, a rounded, often octagonal dwelling, in the construction of which they relied on brush. Their corn cultivation is Pueblo; their sheep husbandry is Spanish; their hunting and gathering techniques are suggestive of the Basin; and their silver working was learned from the Mexicans.

It is in religion that the Navaho penchant for realigning borrowed cultural elements comes most to the fore. The paraphernalia of their religion is clearly Pueblo: corn pollen, rain symbolism, ritual curing, altars made of multicolored sands, and masks. But while Pueblo religion aimed primarily at fertility and rain, Navaho ritual was directed toward curing and the establishment of communal good through the restoration of the health of the ill. Navaho social organization is based on a network of about sixty maternal clans. It was not until 1923 that the Navaho organized a tribal council.

Always at war with their Pueblo neighbors, the Navaho extended their depredations to white settlers. Treaties of 1846 and 1849 failed to keep the Navaho at peace, and in 1863, Col. Christopher ("Kit") Carson led a punitive expedition against them, destroying their crops and rounding up their sheep; they were carried off into captivity at Bosque Redondo, N.Mex., on the Pecos River, supervised by a garrison at Fort Sumner. Continued resistance by the Navaho—and the great cost to the War Department of enforcing their confinement—led the federal government in 1868 to sign a treaty with them whereby a reservation of nearly 4 million acres was set aside for them in New Mexico and Arizona.

NAVAL ACADEMY, UNITED STATES. Established in 1845 in Annapolis, Md. At that time it offered a five-year course, of which three years were to be spent on board ship in actual service. In 1851 it was reorganized so as to offer a four-year course leading to a bachelor of science degree. During the Civil War, the academy moved to Newport, R.I., and the Annapolis buildings were used as an army hospital.

Throughout its history the Naval Academy has kept uppermost its fundamental mission of educating professional officers rather than technicians. In 1979 the curriculum offered eighteen majors from English to aerospace engineering. The brigade of midshipmen is kept at a strength of approximately 4,500 by a dozen methods of entry, of which congressional appointment supplies the greatest number. Women students were first admitted in 1976.

NAVAL COMPETITION. Begun by the United States when interference with its trade by both Germany and Great Britain caused the enactment of the so-called Plan of 1916. This called for the construction of 168 warships, including 10 battleships and 6 battle cruisers. After World War I, nine major powers abandoned their ambitious plans and proclaimed a moratorium of ten years in building capital ships, except replacements, and accepted a complicated system of parity. Competition thereupon broke out in other types of ships, especially cruisers, destroyers, and submarines.

In the London Naval Treaty of 1930 the number of large cruisers was set at eighteen for the United States, fifteen for Britain, and twelve for Japan. Italy and France refused to ratify the whole treaty and could thus build as many noncapital ships as they wished. As to replacements in capital ships, the five governments agreed to a naval holiday until 1936.

In 1934, Japan announced it would not renew the 1922 treaty or the London Treaty of 1930 when they both expired at the end of 1936. The United States found itself inferior to Japan in small cruisers, destroyers, and submarines and only slightly superior in large cruisers. It thereupon increased its building pace by authorizing increases to treaty strength. At the same time, the United States joined with France and Great Britain in calling for restrictions on all classes of ships. Japan still refused to cooperate, and Congress authorized a 20 percent increase of the navy. The coming of World War II put an end to all international negotiations.

After the war, the chief naval competitor of the United States was the Soviet Union. In the 1950's the well-engineered

Soviet ships in evidence led Westerners to assume the excellence of unseen Soviet submarines. In 1957 the first ship-to-ship missiles appeared on Soviet warships, representing a quantum jump over conventional weapons. The Soviet navy and merchant marine continued unabated expansion into the 1970's.

The U.S. Navy made its own quantum jump. After the 1955 success of the atomic-powered *Nautilus,* the first true submarine able to operate submerged as long as crew and provisions held out, the United States had an unprecedented naval capability. The true submarine received an unprecedented punch with perfection of the Polaris ballistic missile, and in 1959 the nuclear-powered *George Washington* was launched. It boasted a main battery of sixteen atomic-warheaded missiles with a range of over 1,000 miles.

Naval competition became colossally expensive, however, and the navy was reduced from the 812 commissioned vessels of the 1960's to 502 in 1975. In 1975 the nuclear carrier *Nimitz* was completed at a cost of $1 billion with $3 billion more required for the antisubmarine and antimissile vessels with nuclear speeds to defend it in all kinds of weather. Although it was clearly superior to anything the Soviet navy could display, many critics believed that it and the other supercarriers were excessively expensive and perilously vulnerable to missile attack. The U.S. Navy launched its first Trident submarine, *Ohio,* in 1979.

NAVAL HOME. Opened in Philadelphia in 1826 as the Naval Asylum (changed to Naval Home in 1889) to serve jointly as a general hospital and asylum for veteran naval seamen. After 1842, its inmates were encouraged to sign a temperance pledge, thus initiating a movement that resulted in the abolishment of grog in the navy in 1862. In 1976 the Naval Home moved from Philadelphia to Gulfport, Miss., where new facilities could accommodate 600 veterans, double the capacity of the former structure.

NAVAL LIMITATION CONFERENCES. *See* **Fourteen Points; Geneva Three-Power Naval Conference; Great Lakes Disarmament Agreement; Hague Peace Conferences; London Naval Treaty of 1930; London Naval Treaty of 1936; Washington, Naval Treaty of; Washington Conference on the Limitation of Armaments.**

NAVAL OBSERVATORY AND NAUTICAL ALMANAC OFFICE. The U.S. Naval Observatory was founded in 1842 as an outgrowth of the Depot of Charts and Instruments, established in 1830. The depot's function was to test and maintain navigational measuring instruments. Almost from the beginning, however, it was involved in purely astronomical research. Moon culminations, occultations, and eclipses were measured to determine longitude differences.

In 1842, Congress appropriated $25,000 for a permanent building in Washington, D. C. Observations were begun in preparation for a nautical almanac, wind and current charts for improved navigation were published, and the depot was officially recognized as the Naval Observatory. By 1845 the observatory possessed a selection of meridian circles and transit instruments. A 9-inch equatorial telescope was obtained in 1844.

Congress established the Nautical Almanac Office in 1849, and the first volume of the *American Ephemeris and Nautical Almanac,* with tables of predicted positions of astronomical bodies, appeared in 1855. Originally located in Cambridge, Mass., the office moved to Washington, D.C., in 1866 and became part of the Naval Observatory in 1893. The research of the Nautical Almanac Office on the theories of the motions of celestial objects and on the fundamental tables on which the *Almanac* is based appears in a series of volumes entitled *The Astronomical Papers* (first published in 1882). A 26-inch refractor, the largest of its kind at the time, was completed in 1872, and observations commenced in November 1873. It was used by Asaph Hall in the discovery of the two satellites of Mars in 1877. Modernized in 1960, the telescope is still used to photograph double stars.

The observatory's prime function has always been to provide accurate time and the astronomical data necessary for safe navigation at sea, in the air, and in space. A master clock that determines standard time for the United States is maintained at the observatory. Time is determined from observations of the solar system and from the use of atomic clocks.

The staff has also taken part in expeditions to observe eclipses of the sun and transits of planets across the sun. For finer observations the observatory opened a facility at Flagstaff, Ariz., in 1955. A 40-inch reflector for observing comets and minor planets was transferred from Washington and a 61-inch astrometric reflector for measuring the distances of faint stars was installed in 1964.

NAVAL OIL RESERVES. Public lands with petroleum deposits set aside for the use of the navy. They consisted of Naval Petroleum Reserve No. 1 (Elk Hills, Calif.); No. 2 (Buena Vista, Calif.); and No. 3 (Teapot Dome, Wyo.), altogether involving about 50,000 acres of public land. They were set aside in 1912 and 1915 but lay dormant until 1920. In 1921 the Harding administration transferred custody of them from the navy to the Interior Department and, in comparative secrecy, leased the lands to private interests.

A Senate investigation began in 1922, and it eventually discovered that Secretary of the Interior Albert B. Fall had received $100,000 from the president of the company that had leased Elk Hills and had engaged in involved financial dealings with the president of the company that leased Teapot Dome. Through the ensuing litigation the leases were canceled and Fall was convicted on a charge of bribery, but the others were acquitted. (*See also* Elk Hills Oil Scandal; Teapot Dome Oil Scandal.)

NAVAL OPERATIONS, CHIEF OF (CNO). Established in 1915 as an adviser to the secretary of the navy. During World War I some of the secretary's originating authority was delegated to the CNO. Naval officers began a tradition of considering CNO senior. Another top naval officer, CINCUS (acronym for "commander in chief," changed after Pearl Harbor to COMINCH) was, in practice, the commander of the Atlantic, the Pacific, or the Asiatic Fleet. In 1942 the hazy relationship ended when the titles of CNO and COMINCH were merged in the person of Ernest J. King. His successful administration through World War II resulted in the Jan. 12, 1946, general order abolishing COMINCH as such to vest CNO with clear authority and supremacy.

NAVAL ORDNANCE. *See* **Ordnance, Naval.**

NAVAL RESEARCH LABORATORY (NRL). In 1915, Secretary of the Navy Josephus Daniels asked Thomas A. Edison to head the new Naval Consulting Board, which would both initiate and evaluate new weapons for the fleet. Congress appropriated money for a naval laboratory in 1916, but ground was not broken until 1920, in Washington, D.C. The laboratory was commissioned on July 1, 1923.

Early research concentrated on sound and radio. Sonar, in which inaudible high-frequency vibrations are bounced off submerged objects to locate them, was developed by 1935 and put into production by 1938. Radar was proposed in the laboratory as early as 1922; and by 1932, airplanes fifty miles away could be detected by reflected radio waves.

Three important programs instituted after the war concerned upper-atmosphere research (using German V-2 rockets), guided missiles, and nuclear power. By 1971, NRL research was funded at $109 million and divided into four fields: space, oceanography, electronics, and materials.

NAVAL RESERVE. *See* **Navy, United States.**

NAVAL STORES. The resinous products of pines along the southeastern coast of America—tar, resin, pitch, and, to a lesser degree, turpentine—used aboard ships. Tar was used to preserve ropes from decay; pitch of resin was applied to seams in the planking to make them watertight; and turpentine was used in connection with paint. Since they were important in England's colonial commercial policy, the British Board of Trade arranged for a bounty to be paid to colonial producers. The main source of supply was North Carolina and, later, Georgia and northern Florida. The naval importance of these products ended with the coming of steam and of iron and steel hulls.

NAVAL WAR COLLEGE. *See* **Navy, United States.**

NAVAL WAR WITH FRANCE (or the **Quasi-War**). In 1798 the French began to seize and plunder American merchant vessels, and Congress ordered the U.S. fleet to retaliate. George Washington was recalled from retirement and appointed commander in chief of the army. The American navy of only three ships was rapidly enlarged to fifty-five. The first went to sea on May 24, 1798. France placed its reliance on privateers supported by a few frigates and sloops of war.

Action centered in the chief trade areas in the East and West Indies. Aside from numerous actions with privateers, there were only four naval engagements, each an American victory. On Sept. 23, 1800, the United States successfully dislodged the French from the Dutch island of Curaçao. About eighty-five French vessels were captured, and several hundred American merchant vessels were seized. On Sept. 30, 1800, a peace was concluded (*see* Convention of 1800). Claims arising from France's failure to meet its obligations under this treaty helped bring about the purchase of Louisiana. (*See also* French Spoliation Claims.)

NAVIGATION ACT OF 1817. Stating that all cargo between American ports must be carried in ships entirely owned by American citizens, it formed part of the movement toward national self-sufficiency that followed the War of 1812. It was not different in spirit from earlier British and American commercial regulations (*see* Coasting Trade).

NAVIGATION ACTS. They had as an object the protection of British shipping against competition from foreign shippers. No goods could be imported into or exported from any British colony except in English vessels. Other clauses provided that goods from foreign countries could be imported into England only in vessels of the exporting countries or in English ships. The first formal legislation was enacted by Parliament in 1649 and 1651, and was modified in 1660, becoming the basic Navigation Act. This law and others were revised in the final act of 1696.

Another field of legislation related to commodities. Certain important colonial products were enumerated and could be exported from the place of production only to another British colony or to England. With a few exceptions, Asian and European goods could be imported into the colonies only from England. The word "English" referred to the nationality of individuals and not to their place of residence; American colonists were just as much English as their compatriots who resided in London. American shipowners thus gained a practical monopoly of the trade between the continental and West Indian colonies. Residents of Great Britain in turn had a monopoly of the carrying of the heavy enumerated goods from the colonies to the British Isles.

Closely related were the Trade Acts. Most of these were enacted after 1700, and they gradually developed into a complicated system of trade control and encouragement. Colonists were largely limited to buying British manufactures, but an elaborate system of export bounties was provided so that British goods were actually cheaper in the colonies than similar foreign goods. Colonial production of commodities desired in the British markets was similarly encouraged by a variety of measures.

In the main, therefore, the navigation system was mutually profitable to colonies and mother country, even though occasionally colonial industry was discouraged by parliamentary prohibition if it threatened to develop into serious competition with an important home industry.

***NAVIGATOR*.** A handbook for western emigrants, with descriptions of river towns, was launched by Zadok Cramer of Pittsburgh about 1801 and went through twelve editions by 1824. The early editions contained directions for navigating the Ohio River (including the Allegheny and the Monongahela); later editions gave directions for the Mississippi and descriptions of the Missouri and Columbia rivers.

NAVY, CONFEDERATE. Established by act of the Confederate congress on Feb. 21, 1861. As the states composing the Confederacy seceded, they had attempted to create state navies. A few revenue cutters and merchant steamers had been seized and converted into men-of-war. These were turned over to the Confederate navy. Two U.S. shipyards fell to the Confederacy—one when the Gosport Navy Yard at Norfolk, Va., was abandoned and the other when the yard at Pensacola, Fla., was seized. All shipping in the Norfolk yard had been destroyed, but the Confederates raised the hull of the *Merrimack* and converted it into an ironclad ram. Much ordnance was secured from the Norfolk yard. The Pensacola yard was of little value.

The Confederacy had ample naval personnel, as 321 officers resigned from the U.S. Navy and tendered their services. Lack of all necessary facilities, however, and the increasing effectiveness of the Union blockade presented grave obstacles to the building of a Confederate navy. The Confederacy never possessed a mobile fleet, although the ships it secured from the British did much damage to the Union Navy. Those operations gave rise to the *Alabama* Claims against England. Its naval services may be divided into three classes: (1) ships serving in inland waters, both for offense and defense; (2) commissioned cruisers, harrying the commerce of the Union abroad; and (3) privateers. The Confederacy is credited with introducing the ironclad vessel; Confederates also contributed to perfecting the mine.

NAVY, DEPARTMENT OF THE. The unsatisfactory administration of naval affairs by the War Department led Congress to create the Department of the Navy in 1798. Experience during the War of 1812 demonstrated the need for adequate and responsible professional assistants for the secretary, and in 1815 the three-man Board of Navy Commissioners was created. In 1842 an organization of technical bureaus was instituted. These included Navy Yards and Docks; Construction, Equipment, and Repairs; Provisions and Clothing; Ordnance and Hydrography; and Medicine and Surgery. These were altered over the years, and in 1921 the Bureau of Aeronautics was established.

The defect of inadequate professional direction of strategy and the general operations of the fleet was severely felt in all the nation's early wars, and various efforts were made to provide such aid to the secretary. The office of assistant secretary was created permanently in 1890, and in 1898 a temporary board of officers advised the secretary on strategy but had no responsibility or authority respecting fleet operations. In 1900 the secretary appointed a general board of high-ranking officers, which remained in existence as an advisory body without executive functions. The creation by law in 1915 of a chief of naval operations served to rectify many previous administrative defects and to lead to further coordination within the department, the chief having authority commensurate with his great responsibilities as the principal adviser of the secretary and as the person under the secretary having charge of the operations of the fleet.

World War II necessitated minor changes in organization that carried into 1947, when the National Security Act was passed. This act created the Department of Defense, under which the Department of the Navy was subsumed. By the early 1980's the secretary of the navy had three principal assistants: the under secretary, the chief of naval operations, and the commandant of the Marine Corps.

NAVY, UNITED STATES. As colonials, Americans had served in the British navy and aboard merchantmen and had been expert privateers against Britain's foes. In seeking independence, it was natural for them to carry the struggle to sea and to establish their own navy.

The Revolution to the Mexican War. The Continental navy was founded by the Continental Congress on Oct. 13, 1775, to perform duties that privateers shunned. Eleven colonies also had navies that, when totaled, exceeded Continental numbers. Continental captains, including John Paul Jones, John Barry, Lambert Wickes, and Nicholas Biddle, were distinguished from privateers by eagerness to engage warships. Jones gave the navy its battle cry of "I have not yet begun to fight!" in conquering the *Serapis* with *Bonhomme Richard* on Sept. 23, 1779.

During the Revolution, all maritime branches brought in about 800 prizes. The British were further humiliated by the capture of 102 minor men-of-war mounting 2,322 guns, besides 16 privateers with 226 guns. Despite the prowess of the U.S. Navy, it was the French navy that was decisive in the colonists' victory.

American navies vanished in peacetime, but Barbary pirates and warring British and French preyed on U.S. commerce. Consequently, the Navy Department was founded on Apr. 30, 1798, and a buildup was begun. The first man-of-war afloat was the 44-gun frigate *United States.*

In the Naval War with France (1798–1800), the U.S. Navy was greatly expanded through the conversion of merchantmen. Three French warships and eighty-one privateers were captured. Similarly, in the Tripolitan War (1801–05) the navy gave a good account of itself.

By 1805 the officer cadre was firmly established. President Thomas Jefferson turned to gunboat construction to manifest intent to fight only defensively. Construction was halted on eight 74-gun ships. The 176 gunboats that were built proved useless in the War of 1812, while 22 seagoing vessels won glory. The *United States* and the *Constitution* won dazzling victories before preponderant British power closed U.S. ports. Losing 12, the navy captured 15 minor warships and 165 merchantmen. The ubiquitous privateers took an additional 991 merchantmen and 5 small men-of-war. More significant were the victories on inland waters. Capt. Oliver Hazard Perry's victory on Lake Erie (Sept. 10, 1813) settled much of the Canadian boundary. Daniel Todd Patterson's handful of ships was essential to the defense of New Orleans. The war stabilized the U.S. Navy, which was rewarded by a few 74-gun ships of the line.

The Algerian War (1815), suppression of West Indian pirates (1816–29), and antislavery patrols (1820–50) provided training for the Mexican War. Unchallenged in that war, the navy of sixty-three vessels conducted blockade and amphibious operations, the latter exemplified by the landing at Veracruz (Mar. 13, 1847) and the maintenance of the lifeline for Gen. Winfield Scott's triumphal march to Mexico City.

The Civil War to World War I. When the Civil War began, the Union navy had only 8,800 personnel and 42 of 76 vessels ready to close 185 registered harbors in 12,000 miles of indented coastline, exclusive of rivers. The Confederate navy began with 3,000 personnel and 12 sequestered vessels. By war's end, the Union navy had mushroomed to 58,000 sailors in 671 vessels. After Confederate confiscation of some federal ships, the Union lost 109 more. In action, 34 warships were sunk conventionally and 14 by mines, while 16 were captured. The rigors of blockade were witnessed by the loss of 45 men-of-war, including the famous *Monitor.* Confederate figures can only be approximated. Extant official records indicate that the Confederates approximately doubled manpower and commissioned 209 vessels.

The Union navy had three main missions: blockade, army cooperation, and commerce protection. Blockade began by capturing a coaling base at Port Royal, S.C. (Nov. 7, 1861), and ended with the capture of Wilmington, N.C. (Jan. 15, 1865). Altogether, 1,504 blockade runners were captured or destroyed. Cooperating with the army, the navy helped take the Mississippi River, notably by seizing New Orleans (Apr. 25, 1862) and by providing assistance at Vicksburg (Mar. 13–July 4, 1863). Only on the high seas did the Confederate navy conspicuously succeed; 12 Confederate ships took or sank 250 merchantmen.

The U.S. Navy withered in peace until given rationale by the historian Alfred Thayer Mahan, whose writings on sea power (1890–1914) became classics. A small "new navy" of twenty-one modern warcraft was far readier than the Spaniards for the Spanish-American War of 1898, which was distinguished by the easy victory of Commodore George Dewey at Manila (May 1). The navy won national support and began a great expansion, dramatized by the world cruise of the "great white fleet" of sixteen battleships (1907–09).

During World War I, the navy had 497,030 personnel to man 37 battleships and 1,926 lesser vessels. Operations were unglamorous. Since the British after the Battle of Jutland (1916) contained the German navy, the prime mission of the U.S. Navy was offering transport to France for 2,079,880 troops and their supplies. The U-boat was the foe, combated successfully by escort, minefield, and airplane. No American soldier was lost in a France-bound convoy. War losses were minimal for the navy, which lost fewer than 1,300 lives.

Besides the portents of the submarine and airplane, the war had unveiled the amphibious potential that the navy had in the combat readiness and excellence of the marines. With 67,000 men, the U.S. Marine Corps won a place in naval plans.

World War II. Rebounding from the terrible losses at Pearl Harbor, the navy expanded to 3 million men and women serving on 8 battleships, 48 cruisers, 104 aircraft carriers, 349 destroyers, 203 submarines, 2,236 convoy-escort craft, 886 minesweepers, 4,149 large and 79,418 small amphibious craft, 1,531 auxiliaries, and 22,045 other types. Casualties of the navy, marines, and Coast Guard totaled 56,206 dead, 8,967 missing, and 80,259 wounded.

In the war with Germany, the U.S. Navy began as a junior partner to the British navy. Concurrently, the Germans were perfecting submarine tactics, making the Battle of the Atlantic bitter and too often close. In the summer of 1943 the advent of American escort-carrier groups ("hunter-killers") gave defense the decisive edge. Allied forces destroyed 753 of a phenomenal 1,170 U-boats, which sank 197 warships and 2,828 merchantmen.

The liberation of Europe was predicated on reentry onto the Continent, which U.S. amphibious techniques made possible. Beginning with a meager 102 vessels for landings in French Morocco (Nov. 8, 1942), the U.S. Navy multiplied amazingly to 2,489 amphibious craft for the Normandy invasion (June 6, 1944) and lent an equal number to the British.

The U.S. Navy was the major combatant in the Pacific theater of war. The Pacific war can be divided into four stages. Phase one, from Dec. 7, 1941, to June 1942, was defensive. The period had ten naval engagements capped by the Battle of the Coral Sea (May 7–8, 1942), when naval task forces stopped a superior Japanese thrust at southeast New Guinea. The Battle of Midway Island (June 3–6, 1942) was the turning point of the war. Outnumbered American carriers decisively decimated their opposites in the first sea fight by fleets whose ships never sighted each other.

The defensive-offensive period of Midway was a brief phase two, merging with phase three, the offensive-defensive period that committed the marines to the long triumphant fight for Guadalcanal (Aug. 7, 1942–Feb. 9, 1943). The marines drove up the Solomons to join pressure with Gen. Douglas MacArthur's combined forces outflanking the Japanese naval and air bastion of Rabaul on New Britain. About this time, American submarines hit their stride with a deadliness that sank two-thirds of Japanese shipping.

The pure offensive, phase four, opened with the navy thrusting westward into the Marshall Islands. The Battle of the Philippine Sea (June 19–20, 1944) disclosed the fatal deterioration of Japanese carrier aviation when 402 Japanese planes were downed with an American loss of only 17 planes. Saipan, Guam, Tinian, Peleliu, and Ulithi were milestones in the drive, forging a logistic line for naval juncture with the successful forces of MacArthur in a campaign for recapture of the Philippines. On Oct. 20, 1944, MacArthur landed at Leyte Island. The Japanese naval counterattack produced a complex of farflung actions (Oct. 23–26) that crushed Japan as a naval power and left the home islands completely vulnerable. Japan itself became the objective. Marines took Iwo Jima at heavy cost (Feb. 19–Mar. 16, 1945). On Apr. 1, marines and army landed on Okinawa, within easy reach of southern Kyushu. Desperate kamikaze attacks failed to dislodge the supporting fleet, which sustained 5,000 fatalities, 368 damaged ships, and 36 minor vessels lost. When atomic attacks on Hiroshima and Nagasaki ended the war, the navy was preparing for the invasion of Japan.

The Korean and Vietnam Wars. When the Korean War broke out (1950), the navy furnished close air support from carriers and amphibious outflanking as at the port of Inchon. Naval gunfire proved invaluable in preventing free Communist use of the coasts, and the 16-inch guns of the battleships were unexpectedly useful in firing across Communist territory from the seaward rear to knock out positions on reverse slopes of mountains. The navy lost 5 ships and had 87 damaged, while 564 downed aircraft added heavily to the 458 killed or missing and 1,576 wounded.

The U.S. Navy first became involved in Vietnam after the collapse of the French there in 1954, when it evacuated more than 300,000 refugees. In 1955 a small group of advisers helped train South Vietnam's neophyte navy. American warships appeared there in December 1961, with minesweepers helping Vietnamese patrols to find infiltrators among coastal fishing craft. A few months later, destroyer escorts made the same surveillance in the Gulf of Thailand. By the end of 1964, when 23,000 U.S. troops were engaged in operations in South Vietnam, naval commitment had been made. In March 1965, U.S. destroyers started an anti-infiltration patrol-and-search operation that shortly began using conventional warships to maintain radar coverage for directing scores of high-speed miniwarships, both U.S. and Vietnamese. Broadened to include shore bombardment, this inshore blockade continued until the U.S. withdrawal in 1973. After 1966 another naval operation patrolled the numerous outlets of the Mekong River.

The major naval operation of the war began on Aug. 5, 1964, when airplanes from the Seventh Fleet struck targets in North Vietnam. In May 1972, a concentration of six ships conducted the aerial mining of Haiphong and other North Vietnamese harbors. Carrier operations caused the heaviest U.S. naval losses of personnel during the war.

Fleets. The squadron concept that began in the Naval War with France was the basic tactical organization until 1907, when the Atlantic, Pacific, and Asiatic fleets were formed. Within this structure, the force concept grew into the now-familiar task force. In World War II there were eleven fleets with specific geographic areas of operations, except for the Tenth Fleet, which was charged with antisubmarine warfare.

By the early 1980's the Atlantic Fleet maintained the Second and Sixth fleets, the latter in the Mediterranean, while the Pacific Fleet had the Third and Seventh fleets, the latter in Southeast Asian waters. Each great fleet has force subdivisions, such as amphibious, antisubmarine warfare, cruiser-destroyer, hunter-killer, mine, naval air, and submarine.

Ships. The increasing power of cannon about the year 1700 required ships to have a defensive thickness of hull that gradually eliminated the adaptation of merchant vessels for war, except for their use as privateers. The principal types in the sail era were the ship of the line and the frigate. The Civil War witnessed the conversion of civilian vessels, even ferryboats, by the hundreds into gunboats and cruisers. The actual construction during the war was principally of ironclads. Later technology in steel brought into being the familiar battleships, aircraft carriers, cruisers, submarines, and destroyers, obviously built only for combat. Merchantmen continue to be valuable for wartime expansion of fleet auxiliaries, as for supply carriers and tankers.

Traditionally battleships were named after states, carriers after battles or historic ships, cruisers after cities, submarines after sea creatures, and destroyers after naval heroes. There has been some modification of this practice. Names of fleet ballistic-missile submarines may honor outstanding Americans (*Patrick Henry*), as have some carriers since 1955 (*James V. Forrestal*). The torpedo-armed submarines continue bearing the names of sea creatures, but the 688 begun in 1972 was named *Los Angeles*. Increasingly, larger frigates that would once have been called destroyer flotilla leaders honor admirals (*George Dewey*), but the even larger DLGN-37 was laid down in 1972 as the *South Carolina*.

From a 1969 peak of 932 commissioned vessels, of which 481 were combatants, the navy had been shrinking during the 1970's from the combined pressures of soaring costs and federal economizing. The active fleet in the fiscal year 1982 consisted of 448 vessels, including 13 aircraft carriers, 94 surface combatants, and 94 submarines (all except 3 nuclear).

Armament. For several centuries the main battery of line-of-battle warships was artillery, rivaled in World War II by aircraft and in the 1980's by rocketry. The primary cannon of the Continental and U.S. navies were muzzle-loading smoothbore pieces known by weight of shot, from 24-pounders down to 3-pounders. All were extremely inaccurate. The main projectiles were solid spheres slightly less than the diameter of a bore and aimed to pierce a hull. Antipersonnel projectiles were grapeshot and canister—a can filled with musket balls. Antirigging langrage consisted of jagged-edged metal or even broken glass. Very few exploding shells were fired from long guns until reliable, safe fuses appeared in the 1820's. For incendiarism, a shot of lesser caliber could be heated white-hot and loaded against a green-wood core protecting the charge. The carcass was made by suspending a bag of gunpowder within a spherical framework of metal hoops, which was dipped into warmed tar to be shaped into rounded smoothness. Ignited by discharge, a carcass would burn until the gunpowder exploded to spew blazing tar.

By the 1850's there was a whole new generation of larger cannon whose bores were measured in inches. The pair of XI-inch cannon of the *Monitor* fired 168-pound projectiles, and the double-turreted *Miantonomoh* had XV-inch.

By the 1880's the revolution in steel made possible huge masses that could be easily machined; electric motors replaced muscles; and the modern, breech-loading rifle was born, doubling and redoubling in size until it reached the standard 16-inch gun of the battleships. The *New Jersey* hurled one-ton shells twenty miles onto coastal targets in Vietnam. Cannon could be made even larger, but airplanes came to offer a far cheaper means of accurately delivering ordnance at vast ranges far beyond cannon possibilities.

The challenge of the airplane arose during World War I,

but the battleship was believed to be immune. Although in 1936 during the Spanish Civil War the antiquated Republican battleship *Jaime I* was sunk by German bombers, all major navies continued launching battleships. Accurate dive-bombing techniques, pioneered by the U.S. Marines and U.S. Navy, dominated during World War II in the Pacific.

In practical terms, the dive-bomber extended battle ranges to hundreds of miles. The 1944 advent of German rocketry simply spurred postwar development of airborne varieties into the 1972 "smart bombs" used against North Vietnam. Late in World War II, ground-scanning radar made high-level bombing somewhat more accurate, but carpet-bombing —a formation of airplanes salvoing together—remained the best means of hitting a desired target.

Those who expected gigantic missiles to supersede the aircraft carrier, just as the carrier had superseded the battleship, were given pause by the 1945 atomic bombs. Total destruction is implicit both in the fitting of nuclear warheads in an aircraft's air-to-ground missiles for stand-off firing and in the placing of nuclear warheads on ballistic missiles.

Secondary batteries during the Revolution were formed by cannon lighter than the main battery and generally mounted on fore and after castles, and the use of smaller guns to complement a main battery continued into the 20th century. The steel revolution and the development of breech-loading weapons vastly increased rates of fire, while improvements in mounting brought the dual-purpose quick-firing gun that could be aimed horizontally and directly overhead.

The machine guns introduced in the 1880's were comparatively heavy, being intended to sink torpedo boats. Antiaircraft was the primary mission of the .50 Browning, 20mm Oerlikon, and 40mm Bofors used in World War II. Self-propelled torpedoes, first carried aboard tiny speedboats, never fulfilled their threat because they had to be launched at a few hundred yards, necessitating a run-in that afforded an alert man-of-war ample time. By 1900 the speedboat had been replaced by the larger vessel with greater speed originally known as the torpedo-boat destroyer, but the ideal torpedo carrier turned out to be the submarine. As a result, one of a surface ship's best defenses is an antisubmarine torpedo.

Mines, known as "torpedoes" during the Civil War, made a deadly quantum jump from explosion by direct contact to explosion by detonator when the antenna mine was perfected by the Bureau of Ordnance during World War I and made possible the laying of the stupendous North Sea mine barrage that diminished the zest of U-boat operations. World War II brought the magnetic and acoustic mines.

Facilities. The thirteen colonies had a very strong maritime tradition, and easily produced men-of-war for fighting in the Revolution. Construction of naval vessels by private companies has been done ever since. The first navy yard, devoted to the upkeep of ships and some minor shipbuilding, began operations in 1799 within the boundaries of Washington, D.C. Initially engaged in the construction of small gunboats, the Washington Yard soon turned to the production of cannon to such an extent that it became known as the Naval Gun Factory. (It is now a naval museum.) In 1800, yards were established at Portsmouth, N.H., Boston, Mass., and Norfolk, Va., and in 1801 at Philadelphia, Pa., and Brooklyn, N.Y. More than a dozen others were built later; some bases phased out shipbuilding. By World War I, navy yards generally concentrated on repairs, letting private contractors build new vessels, a procedure resumed during World War II.

During World War II, the navy had some 7,200 shore facilities, a figure that was cut back to 800 by 1949 and that has been dwindling ever since in recurrent budget squeezing by the government, compelling the navy to undergo sacrifices (*see* Naval Competition). The transfer of ownership of the Brooklyn Navy Yard to New York City in 1969 was a forecast of the wholesale shutdown in 1973 of 200 facilities.

Since 1830 the navy has led in research and development with the opening in Washington, D.C., of the Naval Observatory and the Hydrographic Office. The gun-testing station built in 1848 on the Potomac River moved its scientific personnel to the present Indian Head, Md., Naval Proving Ground in the 1890's. The Naval Research Laboratory (1923) at Anacostia in Washington, D.C., has evolved into one of the largest centers of applied and pure research, originally paying its way by the 1937 introduction of a practical, seagoing radar. By 1946 the complex of naval research centers required coordination, so the present Office of Naval Research began a systematic study of the basic sciences, including medicine. By the 1980's, there was little in science and technology that remained untouched by the navy.

Naval Reserve. Traditionally, merchant seamen constituted a virtual reserve, epitomized by the volunteers who filled the ships during the Civil War. Massachusetts and some other seaboard states founded state naval militias, but the naval reserve as such was created in 1916. It absorbed the state militias and thereafter expanded. In World War II it provided about 90 percent of naval personnel.

The Act of July 9, 1952, created the present ready, standby, and retired categories, primarily differentiated by liability to recall to active duty. Qualifications are maintained through drills in a broad program of some forty different types of pay and nonpay units, through two-week active-duty-for-training periods, officer schools, correspondence courses, and other ways approved by the chief of naval personnel.

The Student Navy Training Corps was established in 1917 at ninety colleges and universities. This became the basis for normal peacetime procurement of officers and evolved into the present Naval Reserve Officers Training Corps (NROTC) at about sixty colleges and universities in 1980. Selected appointees receive pay throughout the four years of college and concurrently take six hours a week of naval training plus appropriate summer cruises. After graduation, they serve a stipulated time on active duty and then have the option, if recommended, of transferring into the regular navy for a career. For non-NROTC collegiate institutions, there are the Reserve Officer Candidate (ROC) and Naval Aviation Cadet programs. The major means for obtaining the number of junior officers needed annually is the Officer Candidate School at Newport, R.I. Every six weeks a class of college graduates starts the "ninety-day wonder" course. The navy and naval reserve have through such programs the largest percentage of college graduates in the armed services.

During the Vietnam War, service in the naval reserve was very popular, and every unit had long lists of waiting applicants. In the aftermath of the war, the navy commenced an augmentation policy demanding swifter readiness for call-up and more time on active duty.

NAVY YARDS. When piracy by the Barbary states led to the rebirth of the U.S. Navy, building yards were rented in Portsmouth, N.H.; Boston; New York; Philadelphia; Baltimore; and Norfolk, Va., to construct the six frigates authorized in 1794. During the growth of the fleet in the Naval War with France, six navy yards were constructed (1800–01)—Portsmouth, N.H.; Boston (Charlestown); New York (Brooklyn); Philadelphia; Washington, D.C.; Norfolk (Gosport, now Portsmouth, Va.). The yards soon included manufacturing activities, repair shops, and storehouses, as well as shipbuilding. Numerous others were built in the 19th and early 20th centuries. Many were closed after World War II. As of 1975 the active naval shipyards were at Portsmouth, N.H.; Philadelphia; Norfolk; Charleston; Puget Sound; Mare Island; Long Beach; and Pearl Harbor.

NAZARENE, CHURCH OF THE. Formed by the merger of three Pentecostal and Holiness churches in 1907–08. The church generally adheres to the teachings and ecclesiastical structure of late 19th-century Methodism. The Nazarenes believe that regeneration and sanctification are different experiences. They practice faith healing and abstain from the use of tobacco and alcohol. The 1980 membership of the church was 484,276.

NC-4, FLIGHT OF. On May 8, 1919, three Curtis flying boats, with U.S. Navy crews aboard, took off from Rockaway, N.Y., for Plymouth, England, in an attempt to make the first west-to-east crossing of the Atlantic by plane. Four stops were planned, and sixty destroyers patrolled the course to give aid to the 400-horsepower seaplanes. When the squadron approached the Azores, two planes, lost in a fog, were forced down. The NC-1 sank, but its crew was rescued; the NC-3 taxied and drifted 209 miles to Ponta Delgada, Portugal. But the NC-4 reached Portugal safely on May 17 and two weeks later arrived at Plymouth, with complete flying time of 53 hours and 58 minutes.

NEAGLE, IN RE, **135 U.S. (1890).** A case asserting the supremacy of federal law over state law. David Neagle, a deputy U.S. marshal, in the performance of his duties had shot and killed a man. Arrested by California state authorities and charged with murder, Neagle was released by a federal court. His release was upheld by the Supreme Court.

NEAR **V.** ***MINNESOTA*****, 283 U.S. 697 (1931).** Invalidated a Minnesota law that provided for the quashing of "scandalous" periodicals. The *Saturday Press* of Minneapolis and its editor (Near) had been perpetually enjoined from publishing. The Supreme Court declared the statute unconstitutional on the ground that freedom of the press means freedom from prior restraint and that the right to criticize public officials is a fundamental principle of free democratic government.

NEBBIA **V.** ***NEW YORK,*** **291 U.S. 502 (1934).** A U.S. Supreme Court case that upheld a New York State law that regulated the price of milk. The decision greatly expanded the definition of business "affected with a public interest." It helped create the legal basis for the economic planning of the New Deal.

NEBRASKA. The name "Nebraska" derives from the Oto word for the Platte River. Interest in the area dates from the Louisiana Purchase (1803) and the explorations of Meriwether Lewis and William Clark in 1804–06. Manuel Lisa established Fort Lisa (1813–19) as a fur-trading post on the site of the present city of Omaha. Fort Atkinson in the same area served as a military encampment (1818–27). Bellevue, at the southern edge of Omaha, became a permanent trading post in 1819 and remained the nucleus of white settlement. The principal Indian tribes within Nebraska were the Omaha, Oto, Ponca, Missouri, Pawnee, Cheyenne, and Sioux.

In 1844 a Nebraska territorial bill was introduced in Congress. Northerners became interested in the organization of Nebraska Territory to compete with southern routes for the transcontinental railroad. The Nebraska question became embroiled in the controversy over the extension of slavery. Under the Missouri Compromise of 1820, slavery was excluded from the area. The territory was organized under the Kansas-Nebraska Act of 1854 (*see* Kansas-Nebraska Act). Nebraska's area was reduced to approximately its present size by the creation of Colorado and Dakota territories in 1861. The northern boundary was changed from the Niobrara River to 43° north latitude between the Keya Paha and Missouri rivers in 1882.

The first territorial legislature convened at Omaha on Jan. 16, 1855. Territorial politics dealt chiefly with the location of the capital, slavery, the organization of legislative districts, the creation of counties, the disposal of public lands, and the problem of statehood. After Nebraska was admitted to the Union (Mar. 1, 1867), the first session of the state legislature established Lincoln as the capital. A new constitution was adopted in 1875 and remains in effect.

Nebraska's economy, based on agriculture, was, until the development of extensive irrigation in the 1930's, subject to frequent damage from drought. In 1981 it ranked third in the nation in the raising of cattle on farms. The state's limited industry is principally in the processing of agricultural commodities. The population in 1980 was 1,570,006.

NECESSITY, FORT. *See* **Great Meadows.**

NEEDHAM-ARTHUR EXPEDITIONS (1673–74). With the completion in 1646 of Fort Henry (now Petersburg, Va.), there began a generation of western explorations. In one of these, the English explorer James Needham and Gabriel Arthur left the fort in May 1673 and traveled southwestwardly, thereby becoming the first Englishmen reported to have reached the Tennessee country. In 1673 Needham was slain by an Indian guide. Arthur journeyed on to Florida, South Carolina, the Ohio River vicinity, and apparently down the Tennessee River; he was probably the first white man to navigate that stream and to visit the Kentucky country.

***NEELY* V. *HENKEL*,** 180 U.S. 109 (1901). The Supreme Court held that Cuba, although temporarily under a military governor appointed by the American president (as a result of the Spanish-American War), was foreign territory and not in any constitutional sense part of the United States.

NEGATIVE VOICE. After the admission in 1634 of deputies into the General Court of Massachusetts Bay, the assistants claimed a veto, or "negative voice," over the deputies' acts. This issue was resolved in 1644, when the court reconstituted itself a bicameral body of assistants and deputies, each with veto on the other.

"NEGRO PLOT" OF 1741. When widespread fires broke out in New York City in 1741, a hysterical populace attributed them to a plot by blacks supported by the Spanish, who aimed to establish the Roman Catholic church in New York. Despite the lack of evidence, thirty-one blacks and four whites were executed, and seventy transported.

NELSON, FORT. At the Falls of the Ohio in present-day Kentucky, it was named for Gov. Thomas Nelson of Virginia. Built in 1782, Fort Nelson was incorporated in the town of Louisville in 1785.

NELSON-DAVIS QUARREL (1862). Resulted from a severe rebuke received by Gen. Jefferson Columbus Davis from his commanding officer, Gen. William Nelson. On Sept. 29, 1862, Nelson refused to duel with Davis, who then shot and killed Nelson. Davis was indicted but, because of his political influence, was never tried.

NESHAMINY. A creek that flows into the Delaware River three miles north of the Philadelphia city line. In 1777, Gen. George Washington encamped there, before leaving (Aug. 23) to meet the British force at the Battle of Brandywine.

NESTERS AND THE CATTLE INDUSTRY (1867–1886). Beginning in the 1860's open-range cattle grazing from Texas to Montana became the major industry. The cattlemen divided the land into large grazing tracts, some of which they fenced. When farmers, or "nesters," attempted to settle on the range, the cattlemen kept them out by intimidation and actual violence. Congress passed a law in 1885 prohibiting interference with settlers. But of greater potency was the great blizzard of January 1886: range cattle died of freezing and starvation, and most of the cattle barons were financially ruined. Commencing with the spring of 1886, homesteaders, streaming west in covered wagons on a 1,000-mile front, occupied the public domain on the Plains.

NETHERLANDS AWARD (1831). An attempt by King William I of the Netherlands to arbitrate the boundary dispute between Canada and the United States resulting from the War of 1812. The United States refused to accept the award, but the Webster-Ashburton Treaty of 1842, which settled the dispute, was virtually identical to the award.

NEUTRAL GROUND. During the American Revolution, Westchester County, N.Y. (which then included the Bronx), was known as neutral ground because it was not consistently occupied either by the British or by the Americans. After 1806 the region between the Arroyo Hondo, near Natchitoches, La., and the Sabine River, near Nacogdoches, Tex., was also called neutral ground as a result of an agreement between Spain and the United States. In 1830, the Sioux on the north and the Sauk and Fox on the south each ceded twenty miles of land along a line from the Mississippi to the Des Moines River. In this neutral ground, largely in Iowa, the three tribes could hunt but must remain peaceful.

NEUTRALITY. As both a legal status and a political policy, neutrality has figured prominently in American history from 1776 to 1941, but it declined in importance after World War II. Under traditional international law of neutrality, a neutral state has the following duties toward belligerents: (1) impartiality; (2) abstention from assistance to belligerents; (3) prevention of the use of neutral territory as a base for belligerent operations; and (4) acquiescence in belligerent interference with neutral commerce to the extent permitted by international law. The belligerents had corresponding duties toward the neutral.

For the United States, neutrality was a wise policy. George Washington's administration rejected alliance with any foreign power. However, foreign trade was important, and the United States wanted to avoid participation in foreign wars while profiting from them by trade with the belligerents. Neutrality proved precarious, and there were recurring threats of war with Great Britain and the undeclared Naval War with France over neutral rights (1798–1800). During the Napoleonic Wars, Thomas Jefferson attempted to protect American neutral rights through embargoes against belligerents who consistently violated them. These embargoes apparently failed, and there was considerable opposition to them within the United States.

Although the War of 1812 was supposedly fought to protect U.S. neutral rights, the results were inconclusive. The end of the Napoleonic Wars in 1815 left a legacy of generally successful violation of neutral rights by the great maritime powers, Britain and France. The general U.S. policy of neutrality was potentially at variance with the Monroe Doctrine (1823), although the special interest claimed by the principle of European nonintervention in the Western Hemisphere was never brought to a major test.

The American posture as a proponent of neutral rights was altered considerably during the Civil War. Enforcement of the blockade of the Confederacy led to adoption of many of the same practices earlier objected to by the United States. A major issue was raised in the wake of the Civil War in the

Alabama Claims arbitration (1871). The United States sought compensation from Great Britain for losses inflicted on U.S. shipping by Confederate raiders outfitted by the British. Final settlement was more of a political compromise than a legal decision, with the British paying some indemnities.

World War I, the first modern total war, began with the law of neutrality in disarray. The United States attempted to maintain a policy of neutrality and to protect its neutral rights. Both efforts were in vain. Whatever distinctions had been previously possible between combatants and noncombatants were destroyed. The heavy dependence of the Allies on U.S. trade and financial support made U.S. policies inherently unneutral and critically injurious from the German–Central Powers viewpoint. A growing record of infringement of U.S. neutral rights, particularly the German submarine attacks on U.S. shipping, caused public sentiment in the United States to shift from neutrality to the side of the Allies. American reaction against war, power politics, foreign entanglements, and allies who did not repay their war debts contributed to a return to an isolationist policy and to insistence on neutral rights in the interwar period.

The complicated development of U.S. neutrality laws in the 1930's reflected the division between strong isolationist sentiment in Congress and increasing determination in the executive branch to resist aggression. Neutrality acts passed by Congress in 1935, 1936, 1937, and 1939 reflected these differences, as did the uneven record of their enforcement by the administration of Franklin D. Roosevelt.

These differences erupted in the debate over American neutrality from the outbreak of World War II (September 1939) until the Pearl Harbor attack (Dec. 7, 1941). Roosevelt consistently sought liberalization of the U.S. neutrality laws. The concept of neutral impartiality was replaced with that of the arsenal of democracy and open support of Great Britain.

Thus, technological advances in warfare, total-war attacks in an economically interdependent world, and aspirations for collective security against aggressors destroyed the foundations of neutrality as a policy and as a legal status. Since World War II, these forces have continued to preclude a return to traditional neutrality except in Third World nations, which have proclaimed their neutrality in the recurring conflicts and competitions between the superpowers.

NEUTRALITY, PROCLAMATION OF. When news arrived in the United States in April 1793 of the declaration of war by France against Great Britain, and the escalation of the wars of the French Revolution, it was the general disposition of the United States, despite a strong predilection for its old ally France (*see* Franco-American Alliance), to remain neutral. The proclamation of Apr. 22, 1793—a landmark in the history of international law and neutral rights and obligations—enjoined upon citizens of the United States a friendly and impartial conduct and warned them against committing or abetting hostilities against any of the belligerent powers. The policy fixed by the proclamation was carefully carried out, and the executive rules proclaimed to enforce it were soon legislated into the Neutrality Act of June 5, 1794. It set American precedent and law for neutrality.

NEUTRALITY ACT OF 1939. In 1938, impending war in Europe made the United States apprehensive lest the Neutrality Acts of 1935, 1936, and 1937 prevent Great Britain and France from purchasing war matériel from the United States.

The Neutrality Law of 1939 was approved on Nov. 4, after war had broken out in Europe. It was a relaxation of previously self-imposed obligations of neutrality and a deviation from strict juridical neutrality. It was in fact a diplomatic instrument, the purpose of which was to help the Allies win the war without American military involvement.

The act set forth the following: (1) It gave the president and Congress discretion as to which conflicts the law shall apply. (2) It omitted any embargo on war matériel or on anything else (in contrast to the neutrality legislation of 1935–37) but forbade American ships to carry such war matériel. (3) It forbade American ships to go to belligerent ports in Europe or North Africa. (4) It prohibited the arming of American merchant ships. (5) It gave discretionary power to the president to forbid American ships to enter such "combat zones" as he should proclaim. (6) It prohibited American citizens from traveling on belligerent vessels. (7) It allowed American ships to carry all goods except war matériel to belligerent and neutral ports other than in Europe, North Africa, and certain Canadian ports. (8) All goods shipped to European belligerent ports on foreign ships must first have their title transferred from American ownership. (9) It forbade Americans to deal in "bonds, securities, or other obligations" of a belligerent state, but allowed dealing in securities issued previous to the act. (10) Like the previous neutrality legislation, it provided for the licensing of all munitions exports in time of peace or war.

NEUTRALITY ACTS OF 1935, 1936, AND 1937. Represented an effort to strengthen American neutrality in anticipation of another conflict in Europe. The principal provisions of this legislation were (1) prohibition, in time of war between foreign states or of foreign "civil strife," of the export from the United States of war matériel as defined by presidential proclamation, "to any port of such belligerent state, or to any neutral port for transshipment to, or the use of, a belligerent country," with the exception of an American republic at war with a non-American state; (2) prohibition of loans or credits to a belligerent state (with the same exception) by an American national; (3) delegation of discretionary power to the president to forbid exportation on American ships to belligerent countries of articles or materials other than war matériel; (4) establishment of government licensing and control of the munitions industry in time of peace and war; (5) delegation of power to the president to forbid to belligerent submarines or armed merchant ships the use of American neutral ports; and (6) prohibition of the arming of American ships trading to belligerent countries. After the outbreak of war in Europe in September 1939, this legislation was superseded by the Neutrality Act of 1939.

NEUTRAL RIGHTS. In the 18th century there had developed some basic concepts of belligerent and neutral rights in time of war. War engendered rights—primarily concerned with maritime commerce—to prevent nonbelligerents from assisting the enemy. Direct assistance to belligerents through shipment of war matériel could be prevented through blockades, interception, and search and seizure. Neutral rights sought to limit belligerent interference with neutral nations. Among the points most pressed by neutrals were the following: (1) blockades had to be real and effective, not "paper" proclamations; (2) "contraband" had to be limited to matériel closely related to the conduct of war; (3) the right of neutrals to trade among themselves had to be respected.

In effect, neutral rights were defined by Great Britain and France. Despite the attempt by the United States to defend its neutral rights in the undeclared war with France (1798–1800), Thomas Jefferson's embargo of all belligerents (1807–09), and U.S. involvement in the War of 1812, the United States was never able to obtain satisfactory recognition of its rights. When the European nations ended privateering and sought to codify the maritime law of war in the Declaration of Paris in 1856, the United States refused to adhere because of what it regarded as inadequate protection. Despite efforts at the Hague in 1899 and 1907 and in the London Declaration of 1909, an authoritative definition of neutral rights was lacking as World War I began. Thus, U.S. defense of neutral rights in that war was doubly difficult: it ran counter to the necessities of modern total war, which increased with the development of submarine warfare, and it sought legal rights that the United States had never been able to enforce and itself had violated during the Civil War. Nevertheless, it was German violations of neutral rights that brought the United States into the war. Once in the war, the United States adopted Allied policies contrary to traditional neutral rights.

The interwar isolationist movement in the United States revived claims for neutral rights. After war broke out in 1939, President Franklin D. Roosevelt's interventionist policies overrode neutralist sentiments. By the time of the Japanese attack on Pearl Harbor, the United States had engaged in patently unneutral behavior toward Germany. (*See* Neutrality Act of 1939.)

Traditional neutral rights have been virtually eliminated by invocation of preferred status for belligerents engaged in collective security enforcement actions and in collective defense as provided in Article 51 of the UN Charter. More important, modern weaponry and communications have left the neutral no place to hide and few rights to protect.

NEVADA (meaning "snow-covered"). The thirty-sixth state admitted to the Union. Prior to the 19th century, the area's principal inhabitants were members of three Indian tribal groups—the Paiute, Shoshone, and Washo. Mexico laid claim to the territory after a successful revolt against Spain in 1821, but ceded it to the United States in the Treaty of Guadalupe Hidalgo. Two years later, Congress established the territories of Utah and New Mexico as part of the Compromise of 1850, with most of what is now Nevada being a part of the Utah Territory.

The first permanent white settlement was a trading post set up by Mormons in the Carson Valley in 1851, but they removed to the Salt Lake Valley in 1857. A large number of miners were attracted to Virginia City in 1859 with the discovery of silver in the Comstock Lode. Congress created the separate Nevada Territory on Mar. 2, 1861. It became a state on Oct. 31, 1864.

Nevada prospered, and its politics were dominated by the mining interests and the Central Pacific Railroad. With the decline of the Comstock Lode in 1879, many Nevadans turned to cattle and sheep raising. New mineral discoveries in the early 20th century in Tonopah (silver), Goldfield (gold), and Ely (copper) set off a new mining boom. Mineral production fell off after World War I, and in 1931 the legislature legalized gambling, an act that along with the construction of Hoover Dam in 1936 set the stage for a boom in tourism following World War II. The state's population almost quintupled between 1950 and 1980 (from 160,083 to 799,184), with four-fifths of the people residing in the Las Vegas and Reno areas.

NEW ALBION. *See* **Plowden's New Albion.**

NEW AMSTEL. *See* **New Castle.**

NEW AMSTERDAM. Founded in July 1625, when the settlement planted by the Dutch West India Company on Nut (now Governors) Island was transferred to lower Manhattan Island. In 1626, because of Indian troubles, the settlement of Fort Orange (now Albany) was moved to New Amsterdam. (*See* Manhattan.)

New Amsterdam was administered by the director of New Netherland province and his council. Obedience to the orders and laws of the company was expected. The directors were autocratic, and members of the council quarreled with the director and with each other. By 1628, the population of 270 found food was scarce, and housing conditions were little better than at the beginning of the settlement. Despite difficulties, the town continued to grow and make progress. A new fort, girded with stone, was built, and a Dutch Reformed church was begun.

In 1637 the brutal Indian policy of Director Willem Kieft resulted in a war that threatened to wipe out the settlement. Peace was made in 1645, but when Peter Stuyvesant arrived in 1647 to succeed Kieft, he found New Amsterdam in a state of complete demoralization. Street surveyors were appointed to remedy the deplorable conditions of the houses, streets, and fences; and steps were taken to raise money to repair the fort, finish the church, and build a school. In 1653, as a result of much popular agitation, Stuyvesant gave New Amsterdam a burgher government consisting of a schout, two burgomasters, and five schepens. These magistrates eventually exercised almost complete civil jurisdiction.

A census taken in 1656 showed 120 houses and 1,000 inhabitants in the city. As a result of the Dutch Wars, New Amsterdam passed to the English, becoming New York City, in 1664. After the recapture of the colony by the Dutch in 1673, it was called New Orange, and then renamed New York after the restoration of the colony to England in 1674.

NEWARK (N.J.). The largest city in New Jersey, with a 1980 population of 329,248, was founded by Puritans who immigrated from Connecticut in 1666 under the leadership of

Robert Treat. In 1713, Queen Anne granted the town charter. During the Revolution, the town was ravaged by the British troops who followed George Washington's retreating army across New Jersey after its evacuation of Fort Lee in November 1776. The British raided the town several times.

The growth of the city's economy resulted from the construction of the Morris Canal in 1832 and the New Jersey Railroad in 1835 and from a labor force swelled by the large influx of Irish and German immigrants. Newark was incorporated as a city in 1836. It became a leading leather-tanning center. In the post–Civil War period, the city became a diversified industrial and manufacturing center, but leather remained its principal product.

With the construction of a rapid transit system to New York City in 1911, Port Newark in 1915, and Newark Airport in 1928, Newark became a major transportation and shipping center. Airport and seaport expansion was completed in the 1970's. It is also one of the leading insurance centers in the United States. The city's educational complex consists of Essex County College, New Jersey Institute of Technology, New Jersey College of Medicine and Dentistry of Newark, and the Newark Campus of Rutgers University.

A major racial disturbance in 1967 resulted in the death of twenty-six people and the loss of more than $10 million in private property. In 1980, 58 percent of the city's population was black and 19 percent was Hispanic. In July 1970, Kenneth A. Gibson became the first black mayor of Newark.

NEW BEDFORD (Mass.). A seaside city facing Buzzards Bay, with a population of 98,478 (1980). It is the center of a metropolitan area of 169,422. New Bedford is a major fishing port and the home of several textile and machinery companies. It was once the largest whaling port in the world. Its ships made Hawaii a standard calling place and established the first U.S. presence there. In the late 19th century, kerosene replaced whale oil as a lighting fuel, and the city's whaling industry died. New Bedford became an important textile center. The textile industry has declined since the 1930's.

***NEWBERRY* V. *UNITED STATES*,** 256 U.S. 232 (1921). A Supreme Court decision that declared that a party primary was not an essential part of an election and hence did not come under federal law. Truman H. Newberry, in his Senate race against Henry Ford in the Michigan Republican primary of 1920, spent over $100,000, thereby violating federal law. He claimed that he had not known that it was being spent, and the decision allowed him to take his seat. The decision had the effect of giving Southern states a constitutional basis for excluding blacks from voting in primary elections. The decision was overturned in 1944 and in 1953.

NEW BUDA. In 1850 a number of Hungarian exiles began a settlement in Decatur County, Iowa, near the Missouri border, which they named in honor of the Magyar capital of Hungary. The town did not prosper and soon disappeared.

NEWBURGH ADDRESSES. The officers of the Continental Army, long unpaid, suspected, after Yorktown in 1781, that the Congress would be either unable or unwilling to settle their claims before demobilization. Meeting at Newburgh, N.Y., on Mar. 11, 1783, the exasperated officers circulated an eloquent, unsigned address that urged direct action. Gen. George Washington, who was present in camp, denounced the "irregular invitation," and a second anonymous address then appeared, less vehement in tone. Washington advised patience, and his enormous influence calmed the agitation. Maj. John Armstrong, Jr., afterward secretary of war, later admitted (1823) authorship of the two papers.

NEW CAESAREA. Alternate name for New Jersey, given in the original deed of 1664 to territory leased to John Berkeley and Sir George Carteret. "Jersey" is a corruption of Caesar's-ey ("island of Caesar"). The hybrid form, New Caesarea (or sometimes latinized to Nova Caesarea), was rarely used.

NEW CASTLE (Del.). A strategic settlement on the Delaware River founded by the Dutch in 1651 as Fort Casimir. It was captured by the Swedes in 1654, recaptured in 1655, and renamed New Amstel in 1656. The English captured it in 1664. It was renamed New Castle by the representatives of the Duke of York, James Stuart (later James II), whose agents continued to govern it (except for several months in 1673 when the Dutch regained control) until 1682. On Oct. 27, 1682, William Penn first landed on American soil at New Castle and received ownership from the Duke of York's agents. Under the Penn proprietorship New Castle was the seat of the assembly of the Lower Counties, as well as the seat of New Castle County. With the outbreak of the revolutionary war, it became the capital of Delaware. Because of British invasion in 1777, the capital was removed to Dover.

NEW DEAL. The social and economic measures put into effect in the administration of President Franklin D. Roosevelt in 1933–39. They were primarily aimed at relieving the hardships caused by the economic depression that had started in October 1929 and to bring about the recovery of the national economy. In implementing his program Roosevelt had the assistance of Henry Morgenthau, Jr., Henry A. Wallace, secretary of agriculture; Harold L. Ickes, secretary of the interior; and Frances Perkins, secretary of labor. Those on whom Roosevelt leaned for advice who were not members of his official family became known as the "Brain Trust" and included professors, social workers, lawyers, labor leaders, and financiers. Leading members of the group were Raymond Moley; Rexford G. Tugwell; Adolph A. Berle, Jr.; and Harry L. Hopkins.

One of Roosevelt's first acts after inauguration was his declaration (Mar. 6, 1933) of a "bank holiday." In order to halt the collapse of the nation's banking system, he suspended all transactions in the Federal Reserve and other banks and financial associations and embargoed the export of gold, silver, and currency until Mar. 9, when Congress met in special session. On that day the Emergency Banking Relief Act was passed and signed. This gave the president the power to reorganize all insolvent banks and provided the means by which sound banks could reopen their doors without long delay.

On Mar. 12 Roosevelt delivered the first of many radio

"fireside chats" to reassure the country and win support for his policies. The Civilian Conservation Corps (CCC) was established to provide work for men in reclamation projects and in the national parks and forests. The Federal Emergency Relief Administration (FERA) was set up under the direction of Hopkins and authorized to match the sums allotted for the relief of the unemployed by state and local governments with federal funds. The Home Owners' Loan Corporation (HOLC) was authorized to issue bonds to the amount of $3 billion to refinance the mortgages of owners who were about to lose their homes through foreclosure.

The Agricultural Adjustment Administration was empowered to control farm production by paying cash subsidies to farmers who voluntarily curtailed production. The federal government was also authorized to make loans on crops to farmers so that they could hold them for better prices, and to buy surpluses outright. It was hoped that demand would catch up with supply and that farm prices would rise. The president was given the power to inflate the currency by the coinage of silver at a ratio of his own choice, by printing paper money, or by devaluating the gold content of the dollar.

The National Industrial Recovery Act (NIRA) set up the National Recovery Administration (NRA). Under governmental direction, various industries would limit production so as to raise prices. Employees were promised collective bargaining and minimum wages and maximum hours. The Public Works Administration (PWA) was created to provide employment by the construction of public works.

Three measures passed during the "hundred days" of this special session of the Seventy-third Congress belong more to the reform category than to relief or recovery. One was creation of the Tennessee Valley Authority (TVA) to erect dams and power plants, to improve navigation and methods of flood control, to undertake soil conservation and reforestation projects, and to sell electric power and fertilizers.

The Federal Securities Act of May 27 (revised in 1934) regulated the stock market and created the Securities and Exchange Commission (SEC). The Glass-Steagall Banking Act separated investment from commercial banking so that there could no longer be speculation with the depositors' money. It also set up the Federal Deposit Insurance Corporation, by which the government guaranteed bank deposits.

The dollar was stabilized by an executive order of Jan. 31, 1934, which fixed the gold content of the dollar at 59.06 percent of its former value. Title to all gold in the Federal Reserve banks was transferred to the government, which was also buying gold in the world market above the current price.

The Reciprocal Trade Agreement Act was aimed at stimulating foreign commerce. By late 1935 reciprocal trade agreements had been negotiated with fourteen countries and the process continued. Such treaties fitted in with the Good Neighbor policy of the administration, aimed at bringing to an end U.S. intervention in the internal affairs of Latin America.

The Social Security Bill became law in August 1935. A federal tax on employers' payrolls was to be used to build up funds for unemployment insurance. A state that had approved insurance systems could administer up to 90 percent of the payments made within its borders. A tax of 1 percent (raised over the years) was levied on the wages of employees and the payrolls of employers to provide funds for old-age pension insurance. On May 6, 1935, the Works Progress Administration (WPA) was established, with Hopkins as director, to spread employment and increase purchasing power. Among the agencies it established was the Resettlement Administration (RA), the purpose of which was to remove farmers from submarginal to better land and to provide poorly paid workers with "Greenbelt towns" outside cities where they could supplement their salaries by part-time farming. Another was the Rural Electrification Administration (REA), established May 11, which offered low-interest loans to farmers' cooperatives to build power lines with WPA labor in localities where private companies thought investment unjustified. A third was the National Youth Administration (NYA), formed June 26, which aimed at keeping young people at school and out of the labor market. The Federal Theatre Project and Federal Writers' Project provided work for many writers actors, directors, and stage crews.

The Wealth Tax Act was passed on Aug. 30. Taxes on large individual incomes were steeply scaled to 75 percent on those over $5 million. Taxes on estates were increased. Excess-profits taxes on corporations ranged from 6 percent on profits above 10 percent to 12 percent on profits above 15 percent. Income taxes on corporations were graduated from 12.5 percent to 15 percent. The act was regarded by many as a soak-the-rich scheme and a punitive measure by the administration, which had parted company with big business by this time.

The Public Utility Holding Company Act was designed to prevent abuses in that field. It did not require the abolition of utility holding companies but imposed a "death sentence" on those that could not prove their usefulness in five years.

The Wagner-Connery National Labor Relations Act proposed to outlaw employer-dominated unions and assure labor of its right to collective bargaining through representatives chosen by itself. By it the National Labor Relations Board (NLRB) was set up to determine suitable units for collective bargaining, to conduct elections for the choice of labor's representatives, and to prevent interference with such elections.

The constitutionality of much of this innovative legislation became a central issue in 1935. Of the nine justices of the Supreme Court, four were considered to be conservative, three to be liberal, and two were thought to occupy an intermediate position. On Jan. 7 the court decided that section 9c of the NIRA was unconstitutional, a decision that cast in doubt the constitutionality of the whole act. On May 6 the court invalidated the Railroad Retirement Act, which raised the question of the constitutionality of the Social Security Act that was before Congress. On May 27 the Frazier-Lemke Farm Bankruptcy Act was declared unconstitutional, as was the pivotal part of the NIRA. Although efforts were made to rewrite legislation to meet the Supreme Court's objections, the new acts were generally invalidated also. Following his resounding reelection victory, the president sent a proposal to Congress to reorganize the federal judiciary on Feb. 5, 1937. Roosevelt was accused of trying to "pack" the court with judges who favored his legislation, and the plan was defeated;

it was the president's first important defeat at the hands of Congress. In the meantime, the Court was becoming more tractable: it found the Wagner Act valid and declared the Social Security Act constitutional. Thereafter, the Supreme Court posed no threat to New Deal legislation.

Roosevelt's second-term proposals were considerably tamer—and fewer—than those of the first. In general, they were revisions of previous legislation. One important new law was the Fair Labor Standards Act of 1938. It sought an eventual minimum wage of 40 cents an hour and a maximum work week of 40 hours. Time-and-a-half was to be paid for overtime, and labor by children under sixteen was forbidden.

NEW DEAL INDIAN ADMINISTRATION. The Indian Reorganization Act of 1934, also known as the Wheeler-Howard Act, inaugurated a sweeping change in policy in American Indian affairs that has been called the Indian New Deal. It marked a change from the policy of enforced assimilation that had characterized Indian affairs for the preceding half century. The tribes were granted increased self-determination and were given back their constitutional right to religious freedom, which had been taken away by Indian Service officials who had been instructed to stop ceremonial rites that, in their opinion, violated Christian standards. The act halted further allotment of Indian lands and authorized federal appropriations to buy back some lands that had been lost by the tribes. Health and school services were approved. The act was never fully implemented, because of the Great Depression and the outbreak of World War II.

NEW DEPARTURE POLICY. The Democratic party in 1871 accepted the constitutional amendments adopted after the Civil War and sought Liberal Republican cooperation in opposing the Radical Republicans. Eleven state Democratic conventions in the North and West endorsed the New Departure proposal. The policy paved the way for the Democratic–Liberal Republican alliance of the campaign of 1872 and Horace Greeley's endorsement by both groups as candidate for president.

NEW ECHOTA, TREATY OF (signed Dec. 29, 1835). For $5 million and 7 million acres of land, the Cherokee agreed to give up all their territory east of the Mississippi and remove to the West within two years. The treaty was negotiated at New Echota, the Cherokee capital, in northern Georgia. (*See also* Indian Removal.)

NEW ENGLAND. Maine, New Hampshire, Vermont, Massachusetts, Rhode Island, and Connecticut formed a distinct section with a character of its own from the beginning of European settlement in North America. The section is largely cut off from the rest of the continent by the northern spurs of the Appalachian mountain range, and it has no navigable river system to give it access to the hinterland. New England was settled by the strictest of the Puritans. In Massachusetts the government set up was a theocracy that was practically independent of England for a half-century. Connecticut and Rhode Island colonies never had royal governors. Owing to altered conditions in the home country, immigration almost ceased for two centuries after 1640. The poor soil and broken terrain lent itself only to subsistence farming and prevented the development of large estates or staple crops, as well as of slavery. The section became a land of small farms and independent farmers, of fishermen along the coast, and of traders overseas who, lacking furs and staple crops, had to be ingenious in finding ways of making money. There were local differences, but in the period from 1630 to 1830 the New England, or Yankee, character became set. The typical institutions of New England were thus developed almost in isolation—schools, the Congregational church, the town system of government, and the "New England conscience."

NEW ENGLAND, DOMINION OF. Established in June 1686 by the English government for the sake of better administration of its northern American colonies. Edmund Andros was named governor. The dominion included the colonies of Massachusetts, Plymouth, Rhode Island, Connecticut, New Hampshire, Maine; the county of Cornwall (northern Maine); and King's Province (a disputed region in southern New England), which were consolidated into one province. New York and New Jersey were added to the dominion in 1688, making a unit too large for one man to administer well. Andros' autocratic rule was unpopular; upon hearing that James II had abdicated, the colonists rose in revolt against Andros and overthrew him in April 1689.

NEW ENGLAND ANTISLAVERY SOCIETY. Founded at Boston in 1832, later known as the Massachusetts Antislavery Society, it was the first group in America organized on the principle of the immediate abolition of slavery without compensation to slaveholders.

NEW ENGLAND COMPANY (1628–29). The successor to the Dorchester Company, which began settlement of the Massachusetts Bay region. A new group of men interested primarily in making a plantation for religious purposes took over the dying Dorchester plantation, which had originated chiefly as a fishing venture and had failed to establish a strong settlement. The New England Company was an unincorporated, joint-stock venture. The company dispatched a fleet with prospective settlers and supplies and appointed John Endecott governor of the tiny settlement already existing at Naumkeag (later Salem). In 1629 the company secured a royal charter and thereafter was generally known as the Massachusetts Bay Company.

NEW ENGLAND CONFEDERATION. *See* **United Colonies of New England.**

NEW ENGLAND COUNCIL. *See* **Council for New England.**

NEW ENGLAND EMIGRANT AID COMPANY. Organization founded to promote antislavery immigration to Kansas. It was first incorporated by Eli Thayer, Apr. 26, 1854, as the Massachusetts Emigrant Aid Company, its name being changed the following year. A profit-making enterprise, it sent about 2,000 settlers, who founded all the important free-state towns and established mills, hotels, schools, and churches. It was blamed by President Franklin Pierce, Stephen A. Douglas, and the proslavery leaders for all the troubles in Kansas. Its friends believed it had saved Kansas from becoming a slave state. After the Civil War it undertook unsuccessful colonization projects in Oregon and Florida.

NEW ENGLAND PRIMER. First published about 1690, it combined lessons in spelling with a short catechism and versified injunctions to Calvinistic piety. Woodcuts illustrated the alphabet. This eighty-page booklet was for a half century the only elementary textbook in America, and for a century more it held a central place in the education of children.

"NEW ENGLAND WAY." A phrase used to refer to the theocratic practices of the Massachusetts Bay Colony. Intended to prove that "discipline out of the Word" enforced by godly magistrates was possible, Massachusetts considered its churches examples for Puritan reconstruction of the Church of England. It was already a common expression when John Cotton defended its principles in *The Way of the Churches of Christ in New England . . .* (1645), the short title of which was *The New England Way.*

The "New England Way" developed into New England Congregationalism. The church was a body of professed regenerates (the "elect") who subscribed to a "covenant," selected officers, chose and ordained its minister, and was subject to no interchurch organizations. Being "visible saints," they admitted only persons who approved the covenant and whose piety and deportment recommended them to the congregation. They denied separation from the Anglican church; they separated only from its "corruptions," considered themselves true "primitive churches of Christ," and were supremely intolerant of others. Citizenship in the colony depended on church membership.

"NEW ERA" (or **"New Economic Era"**). A term used contemporaneously to describe the period of prosperity just before the Great Depression began in 1929. It was believed that the United States had entered an era of high wages and prices, "easy" credit, and satisfactory profits and that they would continue indefinitely.

NEW FRANCE. The peace with England between 1598 and 1610 made possible the first permanent French establishment in America, at Quebec in 1608. In 1661, Louis XIV assumed direct control of the colony, and it prospered. The Iroquois, who had been dangerous enemies, were subdued, and the boundaries of New France were extended along the Great Lakes and the entire Mississippi Valley.

The revolution of 1688, which placed William III on the English throne, initiated the second Hundred Years' War between France and England. To Old World rivalries the colonies added their own, and the period 1689–1763 witnessed four international wars, in each of which the American colonies participated. The long conflict ended with the surrender of Canada to England (Sept. 8, 1760), while the remainder of New France was divided between England and Spain (*see* Fontainebleau, Treaty of; Paris, Treaty of). New France as a political entity thus ceased to exist, although the French people and culture remained permanently seated in the valley of the St. Lawrence.

NEW FREEDOM. The political and economic philosophy of President Woodrow Wilson at the opening of his first administration in 1913. Wilson's campaign speeches were also published under the title *The New Freedom.* They called for reforms that would restore government to the people. The growth of corporate power, he argued, had rendered obsolete many traditional concepts of American democracy.

NEW FRONTIER. The term used to describe the economic and social programs of the presidency of John F. Kennedy. His administration made innovations at home in economic and defense policies and a manned-flight moon program. Abroad, Kennedy supported the Bay of Pigs invasion of Cuba and the commitment of troops to Vietnam; he also formed the Peace Corps, favored reciprocal trade and the Alliance for Progress, forced the Soviet Union to take its missiles out of Cuba, and signed the nuclear test ban treaty.

NEW GRANADA TREATY. *See* **Bidlack Treaty.**

NEW HAMPSHIRE. The coast of New Hampshire was visited by many fishermen and explorers in the 16th and 17th centuries. In 1622 the Council for New England granted much of Maine and New Hampshire to Sir Ferdinando Gorges and Capt. John Mason and in 1629 regranted to Mason alone an area that he called New Hampshire. Later grants added to the Mason title. Under smaller grants from the council David Thomson settled at Odiorne's Point near Portsmouth in 1623, the first settlement in New Hampshire, and soon after Edward Hilton founded Dover. Massachusetts, objecting to the religious dissenters settling there, assumed control over the region in 1641. Although several Quakers were hanged in 1659–60, there was little other religious persecution in New Hampshire. Farming, lumbering, shipbuilding, fishing, and the fur trade were the chief occupations. No Indian troubles developed until King Philip's War (1675–76), but only one more town was settled by 1675.

In 1679, New Hampshire was created a separate royal province, with a governor and a council chosen by the crown and an elected assembly. It was again ruled by Massachusetts for a time after the fall of Sir Edmund Andros and the Dominion of New England. It became separate permanently in 1692. A long dispute with New York was settled (1777) by the creation of Vermont (*See* New Hampshire Grants).

Immigration was chiefly from Massachusetts and Connecticut, the Scotch-Irish being an important group after 1719. After the Indian wars (1689–1725), the province grew rapidly, but by 1776 its northern half was still unsettled. Portsmouth, the capital, was the only town of size and wealth. The colony's first newspaper, the *New Hampshire Gazette,* was founded in 1756, and Dartmouth College in 1769.

In 1776, the citizens drove out Gov. John Wentworth and created a new government, the first of the colonies to do so.

New Hampshire contributed significantly to the Revolution; scores of privateers sailed from Portsmouth; three ships of the new navy were launched on the Piscataqua; Gen. John Stark won the Battle of Bennington (1777) with local troops; and the New Hampshire regiments did their full share. The Constitution was finally ratified June 21, 1788, making New Hampshire the ninth and decisive state to do so. For some time New Hampshire was Federalist, but a rising Jeffersonian Republican party prevented participation in the Hartford Convention of 1815 and passed the Toleration Act of 1819. A Democratic machine carried New Hampshire for Andrew Jackson and retained control until 1855, while the rest of New England was usually with the opposition. Since then the state has been generally Republican.

In the 19th century cotton mills and other factories were built, notably at Manchester. After 1920 cotton manufacturing declined and was replaced by a more diversified industry. Sheep raising, dairying, and truck farming became important. Lumbering—and the manufacture of paper and other wood products—was still important in the late-1970's, although far less so than at the beginning of the century. Beginning in the mid-1920's a resort and recreation business, especially in winter sports, began to be a major source of revenue. A significant shift occurred in New Hampshire's economy in the 1960's, as the traditional shoemaking, woodworking, and textile industries began to give way to the manufacture of electrical and electronic goods, to insurance and banking, and to other businesses and services. In 1980, New Hampshire ranked forty-second among the states in population, with 920,610 residents.

NEW HAMPSHIRE GRANTS. Early name for what is now Vermont. In 1749, Benning Wentworth, governor of New Hampshire, began granting land in the area in the name of the king of England, and by 1764 a total of 138 townships had been chartered. At that point New York, which also claimed the territory, gained the support of the crown and in 1765 began to charter townships, contending that the prior titles were invalidated. But the settlers, determined to keep their lands, formed a militia to protect them (*see* Green Mountain Boys) and declared themselves (1777) independent of both New Hampshire and New York and entered the Revolution as the separate state of Vermont.

NEW HARMONY SETTLEMENT. Founded in Posey County, Ind., in 1825 by Robert Owen, the English industrialist, on the site of the earlier Harmony Society. Owen attempted to put into practice the theories of socialism and human betterment that he had evolved. The constitution of the community, with a population of about 1,000, provided for absolute equality of property, labor, and opportunity, together with freedom of speech and action. The community attracted notable scientists, educators, and writers. The community as such went out of existence in 1827.

NEW HAVEN COLONY. In 1637, John Davenport, Puritan divine, and Theophilus Eaton, merchant, led a group of Londoners to Massachusetts Bay, to found a commercial settlement, but by 1637 the best harbors of Massachusetts had been occupied. Moreover, they found themselves at odds with Massachusetts Puritans. Therefore, the group decided to settle at Quinnipiac, later known as New Haven.

With additional recruits from Massachusetts, from Wethersfield on the Connecticut River, and from England, the Davenport-Eaton company founded the towns of New Haven, Guilford, Milford, Stamford, Southold on Long Island, and, somewhat later, Branford. Without royal charter, the settlers purchased land from the natives, founded churches, and established a plantation government. At first Guilford and Milford were independent plantations, but Stamford, Southold, and Branford acquired their land from New Haven and always recognized the jurisdiction of the mother town. In 1643, an official colonial government was established. Eaton was governor until his death in 1658. Throughout the existence of the colony, political privileges were restricted to members of Congregational churches.

During its early years, the colony had high hopes of establishing a commercial commonwealth that would extend from the western boundary of Saybrook on the Connecticut River to the Delaware River. Those ambitions brought New Haven into conflict with New Sweden and New Netherland and after the Restoration in England, New Haven merged (1664) with Connecticut in order to protect itself from New York, as New Netherland was by then known.

NEW HOPE CHURCH, BATTLES AT (May 24–28, 1864). While battling his way toward Atlanta, Union Gen. William Tecumseh Sherman attempted to pass to the right of the Confederate army, but Gen. J. E. Johnston, the opposing commander, blocked it in a series of sharp fights in the forests around New Hope Church, Ga. Losses on each side were about 3,000 men.

***NEW IRONSIDES*.** A screw sloop built in Philadelphia in 1861–62. It was 232 feet long, had a speed of 6 knots, and was protected by 4.5 inches of rolled iron armor extending 3 feet below the water line. Sixteen 11-inch Dahlgren smoothbores and two 8-inch Parrott rifles were its chief armament. It took part in all the Union attacks in Charleston harbor in 1863 and was hit many times without damage. It was destroyed by fire in 1866.

NEW JERSEY. Became a historical entity when James, Duke of York, granted (1665) all his lands between the Hudson and Delaware rivers to John, Lord Berkeley, and Sir George Carteret. In 1674, Berkeley sold his interest to a Quaker, John Fenwick, representing Edward Byllynge. Trustees for Byllynge, including William Penn, tried to establish a Quaker colony in West Jersey. Fenwick broke away from the Byllynge group and settled at Salem in November 1675, becoming lord proprietor of his "tenth" of the proprietary lands. The Quintpartite Deed of July 1676 separated New Jersey into east and west, with Carteret as proprietor of East Jersey and Byllynge, William Penn, and two other Quakers as proprietors of West Jersey.

Carteret's lands were sold upon his death in 1682, and the Board of Proprietors of East Jersey was formed in 1684. Both East and West Jersey proprietors wished to end their political control of New Jersey, but the surrender of governmental authority was not accepted by the crown until 1702.

Colonial New Jersey was characterized by ethnic and religious diversity. In East Jersey, Quakers, Baptists, and Congregationalists from New England and Scotch-Irish Presbyterians blended with Dutch settlers from New York. Most people lived in towns with individual landholdings of 100 acres, but the proprietors owned vast tracts of land. West Jersey was a sparsely settled area of large estates owned by English Quakers and Anglicans. Both sections remained agrarian and rural, but commercial farming did develop, and some towns, such as Burlington and Perth Amboy, became points of shipment to New York and Philadelphia. The population of the colony expanded to 120,000 by 1775.

After 1702, the province was ruled by a royal governor, an appointive council, and an assembly. Until 1738 the governor of New York was also governor of New Jersey. By 1763 the New Jersey assembly had gained the initiative in governmental affairs.

By 1774, despite only tepid participation in boycotts and protests over the Stamp Act and Townshend duties, New Jersey was being pushed along toward revolt by the militancy of its larger and more powerful neighbors. With the closing of the port of Boston, the colony formed a provincial congress in May 1775 to assume all power. New Jersey participated in both sessions of the Continental Congress and established a state constitution on July 2, 1776.

Few states suffered as much in the American Revolution. Both British and American armies swept across New Jersey, and Loyalists returned in armed forays and foraging expeditions. The battles of Trenton (Dec. 26, 1776), Monmouth (June 28, 1778), and Springfield (June 23, 1780) helped ensure American independence. At the Constitutional Convention of 1787, New Jersey's William Paterson assumed the role of advocate for the smaller states (*see* New Jersey Plan).

In the Federalist era, industry and transportation began to remold the state. In 1791, Alexander Hamilton helped form the Society for the Establishment of Useful Manufactures, which began operating a cotton mill in the new city of Paterson. Hamilton was also involved in the organization of a similar industrial ventures in New Jersey. From 1800 to 1830, improved roads—notably the Morris Turnpike (1801)—invigorated the state's economy. Steamboats linked New Jersey with New York and Philadelphia. The construction of the Morris Canal (1824–38) and the Delaware and Raritan Canal (1826–38) brought coal and iron to eastern industry. John Stevens completed the Camden and Amboy Railroad in 1834.

By 1860, New Jersey was an urban, industrial state. Such cities as Camden and Hoboken were created by ship and rail facilities, while Newark and Jersey City prospered because of the concentration of industry there. The need for unskilled workers was met by new waves of immigrants. After the 1840's, Germans, Irish, Poles, and other Europeans added to the ethnic and religious diversity of New Jersey. In the 20th century blacks from the South have swelled the urban population. The state has a varied contemporary economic landscape. Its principal industries include tourism, particularly along the Jersey shore; the legalization of gambling in 1978 in Atlantic City made that city one of the nation's major tourist centers. Scientific research, chemical and mineral refining, and insurance are also important. In 1980, with a population of 7,364,158, New Jersey was the second most urbanized state in the nation (89 percent).

NEW JERSEY PLAN. Proposed by William Paterson of New Jersey at the Constitutional Convention in June 1787. Expressing the views of the small faction of states' rights delegates, the plan suggested that the existing Articles of Confederation be simply amended. It called for a one-chamber legislature, in which each state, regardless of size, would have one vote, and it did not provide for a chief executive. Although popular with delegates from smaller states, the plan met prompt defeat.

NEW JERUSALEM, CHURCHES OF THE. The churches of the New Jerusalem follow the teachings of the 18th-century Swedish mystic Emanuel Swedenborg. Their members believe that all of reality is filled with the spirit and that the true nature of reality will be revealed at the second advent when the "New Jerusalem" will be evident to all. In New England, Swedenborg's writings influenced many transcendentalists. The informal organization of the Swedenborgian movement has meant that many of its followers did not join the churches. In the mid-1970's the General Church of the New Jerusalem had more than 2,000 members. Another group, the General Convention, the Swedenborgian Church, had 2,640 members in 1977.

NEWLANDS RECLAMATION ACT (1902). The Reclamation Act of 1902 is usually known as the Newlands Act after its sponsor, Representative Francis Newlands of Nevada. The act stipulated that money received from the sale of public lands be set aside for use in irrigating the dry lands of the United States. Money so invested in irrigation work would be regained by the government through use charges. In this way, a permanent revolving fund was to be set up.

NEW LIGHTS. George Whitefield, an English evangelist, appearing in New England in 1740, gave impetus to a religious movement led by Jonathan Edwards toward the old doctrine of sanctification by faith alone. This became a cult known as the New Lights, which split the religious establishment and brought on the Great Awakening. Connecticut, where the controversy was violent, passed a law in 1742 to restrain the revivalists. Many New Lights leaders, including Edwards, eventually had to leave their parishes.

NEW LONDON, BURNING OF (Sept. 6, 1781). A British fleet from New York landed Gen. Benedict Arnold and about 800 men near New London, Conn. Fort Trumbull was quickly taken and most of the warehouses and residences of the town were burned.

NEW MADRID (Mo.). Founded by a group of Americans under the leadership of George Morgan in 1789, in what was then Spanish Louisiana. Spain hoped to make Louisiana a buffer state between the United States and Mexico by settling it with discontented Americans (*see* Western Separatism). Morgan himself led a party of seventy settlers and numerous Indians in four armed boats into Spanish territory early in 1789 and began to build the town on its present site. He adopted a policy of advanced religious toleration, to the discomfort of the Spanish authorities. Discouraged by the Spanish authorities, Morgan removed himself and left New Madrid administration to the Spanish.

NEW MARKET, BATTLE OF (May 15, 1864). Moving down the Shenandoah Valley from Winchester, Va., Union Gen. Franz Sigel engaged the Confederate forces of Gen. John D. Imboden and Gen. John C. Breckinridge at New Market, Va. The engagement, which resulted in a Confederate victory, afforded Gen. Robert E. Lee the opportunity of concentrating all his resources on the defense of Richmond.

NEW MEXICO. Archaeological discoveries indicate the presence of Sandia and Folsom man in the state more than 10,000 years ago. When the Spanish first arrived in the 16th century, they found some twenty Indian pueblos concentrated along the Rio Grande. Their inhabitants totaled approximately 20,000. The Pueblo civilization, built around the cultivation of corn, was one of the most highly developed of the cultures of native North American Indians.

The Spanish hoped that the area would be as rich in minerals as Mexico, but the expedition in 1540 of Francisco Vásquez de Coronado dashed that dream. Conquest and settlement began in 1598. Franciscan friars converted the Pueblo Indians to Christianity, but many natives resented the intrusion of Hispanic civilization, and in 1680 they drove the white men out in a bloody uprising. The reconquest, led by Diego de Vargas, was accomplished by 1696, and the rest of the Spanish era saw the Pueblo living peacefully with their conquerors. Throughout the 18th century it was the nomadic Apache, Navaho, Ute, and Comanche that threatened both the Spanish and the Pueblo. This native harassment, along with the scarcity of water, led to the concentration of Spanish settlement in the north-central area of the state, along the upper Rio Grande and its tributaries.

Anglo-American intrusion into New Mexico began in the early 19th century with the quest for beaver by the mountain men; was continued with the opening of the Santa Fe trade in 1821; and was increased when the area became part of the United States as a result of the Mexican War. Territorial status was granted in 1850. The nomadic Indians continued to resist this new invasion, which threatened their traditional mode of life. The Navaho were subdued in 1864, the Comanche in 1874, and the last of the Apache in 1886. During the Civil War a Confederate force seized control of much of the territory, but the invaders were driven out by 1862.

After the Civil War the Texas cattle frontier expanded into New Mexico. The coming of the railroads in the 1880's fed an already existing mining boom and brought Anglo-American farmers in large numbers. In 1912 New Mexico became the forty-seventh state. The combination of agriculture and mining has continued; in the early 1980's the state was a leading producer of petroleum, natural gas, and potash and had been the nation's principal producer of uranium since 1950. Cattle ranching continued to be important; and irrigation has greatly increased farm cultivation. World War II and the cold war brought many military installations to New Mexico, notably the nuclear research center at Los Alamos and the White Sands Missile Range. Tourism is also a leading industry because of the state's natural beauty. Its population in 1980 was 1,299,968.

NEW NATIONALISM. The term describing the political philosophy of Theodore Roosevelt that the federal government is the best instrument for advancing progressive democracy. It called for political, social, and industrial reforms, such as government regulation and control of corporations, better working conditions for labor, conservation of natural resources, and a concentration of more power directly in the people. Implied also were the ineffectiveness of the states in dealing with these problems.

NEW NETHERLAND. Dutch province in what is now New York and New Jersey. The Dutch West India Company was organized in 1621, and in 1624 a group of thirty families, mostly Walloons, were sent in the ship *New Netherland.* A few of them remained at the mouth of the Hudson River but the greater part were settled up the river at Fort Orange, where the city of Albany now stands. A fort was also built on Nut (now Governors) Island. In 1625, the settlement on Nut Island was moved to Manhattan Island and called New Amsterdam. A new fort was built. Peter Minuit was appointed director general in 1626 and bought Manhattan from the Indians, paying the value of 60 guilders ($24) in trinkets, thus legalizing the occupation already in effect. In 1626, because of trouble with the Indians, Minuit moved the families at Fort Orange to Manhattan, leaving only a small garrison behind.

The director and his council had great power. Most colonists were bound by contracts to the company. The company had right of first purchase of the produce from farmers, who could sell their farms only to one of the other colonists. Indentured husbandmen, under still more rigid restrictions, worked the company farms. The Reform church was supported, though freedom of conscience was granted.

The first few years showed a moderate profit to the company from trade, but the efforts at colonization proved a loss. In 1629 a new charter provided for the grant of great estates, called patroonships, to such members of the company as should found settlements of fifty persons within four years. The effect of patroonships under the charter has been overemphasized: with the single exception of Rensselaerswyck, they were unsuccessful. In 1638, further to encourage colonization, trade restrictions in the colony were reduced, better provision was offered for transportation of settlers and their goods, and the fur-trade monopoly was discontinued.

In 1637 Willem Kieft was appointed director general. By the summer of 1641 his brutal and unwise Indian policy had created so dangerous a situation that he was constrained to ask the colonists to elect a board to advise with him. The

Indian troubles continued, however, and the board of colonists drew up petitions for needed reforms. Their complaints resulted in the recall of Kieft, and on May 11, 1647, Peter Stuyvesant, his successor, arrived in New Amsterdam. The new director was honorable, active, and conscientious. Despite his autocratic disposition and his hostility to popular demands, he was eventually (1652) instructed by the company to give New Amsterdam a burgher government.

Although Stuyvesant made a sincere attempt to maintain friendly relations with the Indians, he had to fight three Indian wars. The first broke out in 1655 in New Amsterdam and extended to the Esopus settlement, near Kingston, and to Long Island. Five years later there was a serious outbreak at Esopus, which was aggravated when Stuyvesant sent some of the Indian captives to Curaçao as slaves. This incident rankled and the Indians rose again, so it was not until May 1664 that a general peace was signed.

The gradual encroachment of settlers from New England on territory claimed by the Dutch had been a source of trouble since the beginning of the colony. The question of boundaries was finally settled by the Treaty of Hartford in 1650. The last year of the Dutch regime in New Netherland was fraught with grave fear of Indian wars, rebellion, and British invasion. Stuyvesant tried vainly to put the province in a state of defense, but on Aug. 29, 1664, he was forced to surrender to an English fleet, which came to claim the province in the name of James, Duke of York.

NEW ORLEANS (La.). Located between Lake Pontchartrain and the Mississippi River about 100 miles from the Gulf of Mexico, the town was founded in 1718 by the French governor of Louisiana, Jean Baptiste Le Moyne, Sieur de Bienville, and named in honor of the regent of France, the Duc d'Orléans. An unprofitable port, it was transferred to Spain as part of Louisiana Territory west of the Mississippi by the Treaty of Paris of 1763 and then returned to France by the Treaty of San Ildefonso of 1800. In 1803 it was sold to the United States as part of the Louisiana Purchase.

New Orleans was at first a crude frontier town whose chief export was fur. By 1800, however, as a result of the Treaty of Madrid of 1795, New Orleans had become a transshipment point to ocean vessels for flatboats and keelboats, and by 1812, steamboats were traveling the Mississippi. With the defeat of the British in the War of 1812, New Orleans became the Queen City of the South. By 1840 it led the nation in value of exports. It handled much more of exported western produce than all other ports together; the shipping tonnage of its wharves was double that of New York. But the railroads, which its rivals from Mobile to New York began building at midcentury to tap the valley trade, proved its undoing. By 1860 its receipt of western goods had declined to a mere 18 percent of the total volume handled, and its chief economic function became the marketing of cotton and sugar from its hinterland. With the destruction of the local slave economy as a result of the Civil War, the port's profit from that function declined. It was not until World War I that the port began to recover. The development of the petrochemical industry after World War II spurred an economic revival; by 1979 the New Orleans port handled more tons of goods than any other U.S. port. In the rank of urban population New Orleans had declined from third place in 1840 to twenty-second place in 1980, with a population of only 557,482.

New Orleans was frequently smitten by epidemics of yellow fever and cholera and menaced by hurricanes and floods (against which only frail levees protected it). In many ways 19th-century New Orrleans was more a Caribbean than a southern city. Yet its population was cosmopolitan. Many easterners migrated, in search of a quick fortune, and there was a heavy immigration of Irish and Germans. In time they outnumbered the Creoles, who were the descendents of the original French and Spanish settlers.

Because of discoveries of oil and sulfur in Louisiana and in the Gulf of Mexico after World War II, the New Orleans area enjoyed a pronounced industrial boom, but the main economic function of the metropolis remained commercial—the export of most of the grain raised in the Mississippi Valley, for example. It attracts tourists for its annual Mardi Gras festival, the Sugar Bowl football game, and the French Quarter, or Vieux Carré, disparately unique in its Creole architecture and its continuing tradition of jazz, which was born there.

NEW ORLEANS**.** The first steamboat on western waters, built at Pittsburgh by Nicholas J. Roosevelt, under patents held by Robert Fulton and Robert R. Livingston, during 1810–11 (*see* Fulton's Folly). A sidewheeler of between 300 and 400 tons, the *New Orleans* plied the New Orleans–Natchez trade until it sank on July 14, 1814.

NEW ORLEANS, BATTLE OF (Jan. 8, 1815)**.** The War of 1812 did not threaten Louisiana until near its close. In the autumn of 1814 a British fleet of over fifty vessels, carrying 7,500 soldiers under Sir Edward Packenham, appeared in the Gulf of Mexico preparatory to attacking New Orleans, the key to the entire Mississippi Valley. Gen. Andrew Jackson, who commanded the American army in the Southwest, reached New Orleans on Dec. 1, 1814, and immediately began preparations for defense.

Instead of coming up the Mississippi, the superior British navy defeated the small American fleet on Lake Borgne, southwest of the river's mouth; landed troops on its border; and marched them across the swamps to the banks of the Mississippi, a few miles below New Orleans. Jackson had succeeded in assembling a force of between 6,000 and 7,000 troops. In the decisive battle, the British undertook to carry the American position by storm (*see* Chalmette Plantation). So effective was the American defense that the British were repulsed in less than a half-hour, losing over 2,000 men, of whom 289 were killed, including Packenham. The Americans lost only 71, of whom 13 were killed. The British retired to their ships and departed. The battle came two weeks after the war had officially ended (*see* Ghent, Treaty of). It was the only unalloyed American triumph of the war, and it had a tremendous effect upon the political fortunes of Jackson.

NEW ORLEANS, CAPTURE OF (May 1, 1862)**.** In spring 1862 a naval squadron under Union Adm. David G. Farragut, carrying an army commanded by Gen. Benjamin F.

Butler, entered the lower Mississippi. The chief defenses against approach by river to New Orleans were forts Jackson and St. Philip, about sixty miles above the city, between which had been stretched a heavy chain cable. A secondary defense lay beyond it, consisting of fire rafts loaded with pine knots and some armored rams. Farragut succeeded in cutting the chain and passing the forts in the night, and shortly thereafter he appeared before New Orleans. Gen. Mansfield Lovell, with only 3,000 Confederate troops, withdrew northward, and the city fell.

NEW ORLEANS, MARTIAL LAW IN. Reports of the mysterious advance of Aaron Burr and his men down the Mississippi during the fall of 1806 caused much anxiety at New Orleans. Uneasiness was increased when Gen. James Wilkinson and a detachment of troops arrived late in November 1806. Wilkinson imposed martial law and arrested those suspected of being agents or friends of Burr. Wilkinson refused to yield to civil authority (*see* Bollman Case). The panic-stricken city began to throw off this virtual reign of terror only after Wilkinson left for Richmond in May 1807, to testify at the Burr trial.

NEW ORLEANS RIOTS (1873–74). Resulted from the rival gubernatorial claims of Republican W. P. Kellogg, who had federal support, and Democrat John McEnery. The disorders began Mar. 5, 1873, when McEnery's partisans attacked two police stations. They were repulsed with a loss of two killed and several wounded. On Mar. 6, McEnery's supporters in the legislature were arrested and spent some hours in a local jail. Clashes between citizens and Republican officials also occurred elsewhere in Louisiana and were checked by the intervention of U.S. troops. The White League was organized in the spring of 1874 and was responsible for a bloody uprising against Kellogg in New Orleans on Sept. 14, 1874. McEnery took over the state government the following day, but U.S. troops restored Kellogg. The uprising paved the way for the overthrow of the Republican regime in Louisiana three years later (*see* Home Rule in the South, Restoration of).

NEW PLYMOUTH COLONY. Founded by a group of about a hundred English emigrants who came to New England in the *Mayflower* in 1620. The dominant element in this group consisted of religious dissenters who had separated from the Anglican church. Some of these Separatists had come from the Netherlands, where they had been living for more than a decade. Joining with others of their religious persuasion in England, they sailed from Plymouth, England, Sept. 16, 1620. On Dec. 26, after five weeks exploring Cape Cod, the *Mayflower* anchored in the harbor of what came to be Plymouth, Mass. The task of erecting housing was rendered difficult by the lateness of the season, but the local Indians were friendly, a crucial advantage. During the first winter nearly half of the settlers died. By spring there had come a turn for the better, and in a few years the menace of a food shortage was permanently removed.

The capital for the undertaking had been furnished by a group of London merchants, who in 1627 sold their interests to the settlers and withdrew from the venture. From that time on, the planters were the sole stockholders of the corporation. Other villages were established nearby, and the town of Plymouth widened into the colony of New Plymouth.

Although the settlers had no clear right to form a government, they had, before landing, organized themselves into a body politic by entering into a solemn covenant, the Mayflower Compact, that they would make just and equal laws and would yield obedience to the same. Laws were made by the popularly elected General Court, and administrative and certain important judicial functions were performed by the popularly elected governor and the assistants. William Bradford was governor for more than thirty years. New Plymouth was not economically well placed; it was soon overshadowed by Massachusetts Bay and was absorbed by it in 1691.

NEWPORT (R.I.). A city in southeastern Rhode Island on Aquidneck Island, founded in May 1639 by William Coddington, formerly an official in Massachusetts Bay, and John Clarke, a Baptist minister. In Newport was established the second Baptist church in America, and the city subscribed to the same principle of religious freedom that animated the Roger Williams settlement at Providence. Consequently it became a haven for the persecuted; the first Quakers arrived in 1657, and the first Jews in 1658.

Newport was an important colonial seaport: shipbuilding began about 1646, and by the mid-18th century the city was at the height of its commercial glory. During the Revolution the city was held by the British from 1776 to 1779, after which it became the headquarters for America's French allies under the Comte de Rochambeau. The flight of the rich Loyalists during the war led to Newport's economic decline, but about a century later it revived as a summer resort for the rich. Yacht races, including the America's Cup Race, are held off Newport. Newport's population in 1980 was 29,259.

NEWPORT, FRENCH ARMY AT. Forty-four French vessels, bringing a force of 6,000 French soldiers under the command of the Comte de Rochambeau, arrived off Newport, R.I., on July 10, 1780, in support of the American Revolution. Some 600–800 French cavalrymen were sent to Connecticut for the winter, and a part of the infantry was sent to Providence, R.I. On June 10, 1781, the French army left Newport by boat for Providence and thence marched to Yorktown, where it participated in the siege that resulted in the surrender of Gen. Charles Cornwallis and the end of the war.

NEWPORT BARRACKS. Established about 1805 as an arsenal on the Kentucky side of the Licking River, opposite Cincinnati; later used also as a recruit depot. It was menaced during the Civil War in the course of Confederate Gen. Braxton Bragg's invasion of Kentucky in 1862. Later the post was moved several miles inland and renamed Fort Thomas.

NEWPORT NEWS (Va.). A seaport city at the mouth of the James River, with a population of 144,903 in 1980. Together with its neighbor, Hampton, it is the center of a metropolitan area of 363,817 people; it is one of the more rapidly growing metropolitan areas in the country. It is an important commercial and shipbuilding center. The origin of the city's name is in dispute, but "Newport" appears certainly to have been in honor of Christopher Newport, one of the first Englishmen in Virginia in 1607. The city was founded about 1620, but its real growth began in the 19th century. The railroad reached the city in 1882, and four years later, the Newport News Shipbuilding Company was established.

NEW SMYRNA COLONY. During 1767 and 1768 Andrew Turnbull, a Scottish physician, brought some 1,400 persons from Greece, Italy, and Minorca to Florida (then under British rule), to cultivate sugarcane, rice, indigo, cotton, and other crops. The settlement was adjacent to Mosquito Inlet, south of the modern Daytona Beach. After seven or eight years, colonists were to receive tracts of land. New Smyrna lasted until 1776, when the colonists marched to St. Augustine to ask for relief from their indentures. Only 600 by that time remained, and they settled in St. Augustine after they had been released by the governor.

NEW SOUTH. A phrase originally used to designate the post-Reconstruction economic development of the South, particularly the expansion of industry. After Reconstruction, many southerners came to believe that their region's future lay in the development of industry. F. W. Dawson, editor of the *Charleston* (S.C.) *News and Courier,* was an early prophet of this New South concept. He argued that the great significance of the Civil War was the white man's emancipation from slavery and cotton. Another advocate was Henry W. Grady, longtime editor of the *Atlanta Constitution.*

The term "New South" is also commonly applied generally to the South since 1865, just as the term "Old South" describes the antebellum South. Used in this way, the phrase "New South" refers to a South that is changing in every way.

NEWSPAPERS. The history of American newspapers has been a record of infinite variety in editorial leadership and outlook, in effort and application.

Colonial Papers. The earliest colonial newspaper was *Publick Occurrences Both Foreign and Domestick,* which made its first and only appearance in Boston, Mass., on Sept. 25, 1690. It was immediately suppressed. Publisher Benjamin Harris and his printer, Richard Pierce, offended the colonial authorities by not obtaining official permission to publish. Arranged in double columns on three handbill-sized pages, it reported, in a news style anticipating that of modern newspapers, the Thanksgiving plans of "Plimouth" Indians, a suicide, the disappearance of two children, a decline in smallpox, a fire, and other events. The next recorded attempt to establish a publication in the colonies was made by the *Boston News-Letter.* Issue No. 1 covered the week of Apr. 17, 1704. Under various names, it continued to publish until 1776. The *Pennsylvania Gazette,* made famous by Benjamin Franklin, was founded at Philadelphia on Dec. 24, 1728, by Samuel Keimer. It did not prosper, and on Oct. 2, 1729, it was purchased by Franklin and Hugh Meredith. Sole owner after 1732, Franklin turned it into a great success. Franklin's innovations included the first weather report, an editorial column, the first cartoon, and humor. David Hall joined in a partnership in 1748 that lasted until Franklin's retirement in 1766. The last issue was dated Oct. 11, 1815. The outstanding colonial case involving freedom of the press centered around John Peter Zenger and his *New-York Weekly Journal,* the first newspaper to be the organ of a political faction. (*See* Freedom of the Press; Zenger Trial.)

By 1750 there were newspapers in Boston; New York; Philadelphia; Charleston, S.C.; Annapolis, Md.; Williamsburg, Va.; and Newport, R.I. By 1775, on the eve of the Revolution, there were thirty-seven papers in the seaboard colonies. The usual plan for the four-page weekly gazette was to devote the first page to foreign intelligence, the second page to domestic news, the third to local matters, and the back page to advertisements. Other than the Bible and the almanac, the local gazette undoubtedly was the only printed material that entered most colonial homes.

Early Political Papers. Outstanding among patriotic gazettes in the years leading to the Revolution was the *Massachusetts Spy.* Isiah Thomas founded the *Spy* in 1770 in Boston to advance colonial interests. When the British troops took over Boston in 1773, Thomas moved his printing press to Worchester. En route he joined Paul Revere in the historic warning of Apr. 18, 1775, and he himself was a minuteman in the engagements at Lexington and Concord. The May 3, 1775, issue reported the news of those early clashes at arms. The *Spy* became the *Worcester Gazette* in 1781.

After the Revolution, one journal after another enlisted in and led the public debate over political issues. Thus, the Federalist mouthpiece, the *Gazette of the United States,* later known (1804–18) as the *United States Gazette,* edited by John Fenno, espoused the principles of George Washington and John Adams. Secretary of State Thomas Jefferson subsidized the competing *National Gazette,* begun Oct. 31, 1791, at Philadelphia, by appointing its editor, Philip Freneau, translator in the State Department. Freneau's criticisms of Alexander Hamilton brought on complaints from Washington, who held Jefferson responsible. The *National Gazette* ceased publication in 1793, soon after Jefferson's resignation from the secretaryship. In the meantime William Coleman and the *New York Evening Post* became linked to Hamilton, as Noah Webster and the *American Minerva* became associated with John Jay and Rufus King.

Concern late in the 18th century over possible war with France brought on a suspicion of aliens, with the result that the Federalists put through Congress the Alien and Sedition Acts of 1798. Almost immediately the enforcement of these laws was directed against supporters of Jefferson, among them Democratic-Republican newspaper editors. Ten journalists were found guilty, fined, and in several instances jailed for alleged seditious utterances. William Duane was editor of the Philadelphia *Aurora,* the foremost newspaper backing Jefferson. He opposed the restrictions of the Alien and Sedition Acts and in 1799 was arrested. Soon acquitted, he continued his criticism and again was arrested. Following Jefferson's election in 1800 the charges were dropped. Anthony Haswell, editor of the *Vermont Gazette or Freeman's Depository,* issued at Bennington, was among those jailed. His Bennington gazette, the only publication in Vermont at the time, led to his indictment and trial for sedition in 1800. Haswell's imprisonment for two months amounted to political persecution. His $200 fine was returned to his heir by act of Congress in 1844. There were to be other periods with civil liberties under restraint but no time when freedom of the press was so restricted.

Growth of the Press. Independence was followed by a veritable explosion of new journals. Between the peace treaty in 1783 and the year 1800, at least 500 were begun in the original thirteen states. Venturesome printers soon moved west from the seaboard. The first newspaper beyond the Appalachians was the *Pittsburgh Gazette,* issued July 29, 1786, by Joseph Hall and John Scull. Even more daring was Kentuckian John Bradford, a surveyor, who transported a press through the wilderness and on Aug. 11, 1787, founded the *Kentucke Gazette* in Lexington.

In 1791, Robert Ferguson and George Roulstone began publication of the *Knoxville Gazette* in Tennessee. William Maxwell set up the *Centinel of the North-Western Territory* in Cincinnati, in 1793; and in 1804 Elihu Stout moved to Vincennes, in the Indiana Territory and began the *Indiana Gazette.* Joseph Charless started the *Missouri Gazette,* in 1808 in St. Louis. Still another pioneer printer was Matthew Duncan, onetime Kentuckian who began the *Illinois Herald* in May 1814, at Kaskaskia, the first Illinois capital. By 1821 some 250 papers had come into being in the new West. Many were short-lived; most were struggles against odds, but as a whole they helped open up and tame the wilderness. In 1785 two dailies were begun in New York City, and by 1790 the total number of dailies had reached eight. The Sunday newspaper came slowly; the prevailing strictures against work on the Sabbath prevented early acceptance of newspapers for Sunday circulation and reading.

Newspapers left their gazette era behind with the coming of the "penny press." The first one-cent-a-copy venture to succeed was Benjamin H. Day's *New York Sun,* begun in 1833; within two years it boasted the largest daily circulation in the world. The older, well-established, generally dignified dailies sold for six cents, and they were quick to denounce the cut-price upstart as catering to the lower public tastes. Without question the penny press was directed at the common people, but also without question the interests of the common people had gone largely unrecognized in news reporting. Unfortunately, the *Sun* and the other penny newspapers promoted sensationalism to the point of outright faking. They capitalized on street sales, giving rise to the newsboy who ran about the city with newssheets, calling out the headlines.

Experimental war reporting, undertaken in the Mexican War, became a major news activity in the Civil War. Sharing the soldiers' hardships and eluding censors, a network of news gatherers relayed eyewitness dispatches from the battlefronts. For the first time, photography became part of journalism; Mathew B. Brady, in particular, compiled his monumental photographic record of the war and its participants. As interest in the conflict mounted, circulations rose rapidly, with the readers seeking eagerly to learn the latest military developments and the conduct of the government in Washington, D.C.. The southern press supported the Confederacy, and although northern editors generally upheld the Union cause, not a few were opposed to President Abraham Lincoln and some were openly Copperhead.

After the Civil War, the sensationalism introduced by the penny press was revived and extended by the new reliance on advertising. By 1880 advertising met a major part of the costs of publishing a daily—and advertising rates were based on circulation. A consequence was hard-fought competition for both subscribers and street sales. To capture weekend readers, Pulitzer promoted the *New York Sunday World,* with special articles and features including a comic section, first produced in November 1894. Prominent among the comic strips was Richard F. Outcault's "Yellow Kid," a harum-scarum boy in long yellow garb. From that came the term "yellow journalism." In less than a year, William Randolph Hearst, publisher of the *San Francisco Examiner,* entered the New York scene by purchasing the *Morning Journal* and going into headlong conflict with the *World* for circulation. The Cuban problem, the sinking of the *Maine,* and the Spanish-American War were exploited with banner headlines and irresponsible claims and charges.

The Yellow Kid, proved exceedingly popular, and Hearst bid him away from the *World* to the *New York Journal* in 1896. For a time both papers had Yellow Kids. Rudolph Dirks's Katzenjammer Kids, who first appeared in the *Journal* in 1897, set a pattern, as did H. C. ("Bud") Fisher's six-days-a-week "A. Mutt" (later "Mutt and Jeff"), in the *San Francisco Chronicle* beginning in 1907. Other early comic characters included Happy Hooligan, Buster Brown, Foxy Grandpa, Little Jimmy, Hans and Fritz, and Nemo. The power of the comics over circulation was demonstrated when they set styles, gave turns to speech, and affected advertising. Syndicates grew up around the leading comics and bought them away from one another as fortune-making businesses developed from "Jiggs and Maggie," "Andy Gump," "Toonerville Folks," and their contempoaries. As many as 2,500 newspapers used some 250 strips and single panels from some seventy-five agencies. At its peak *Hearst's Comic Weekly: Puck,* distributed by seventeen newspapers, with a total circulation of 5.5 million, ran fifty comics in its thirty-two pages. One syndicate claimed a circulation of more than 50 million.

After World War II the strips generally changed from comics to serial picture stories presenting everything from domestic affairs, ethnic life, military routine, the medical profession, and the conservation of natural resources to high adventure, international intrigue, crime and its detection, and the space age. Whether or not juveniles were harmfully affected by the worst of the strips, as some child psychologists claimed, they continued to be popular, and Popeye, Dick Tracy, L'il Abner, and Little Orphan Annie became part of America's folklore. Nor did the comic strips stop short of politics. Sen. Joseph R. McCarthy was readily recognizable in Walt Kelly's "Pogo," and "Doonesbury" used the White

House as a backdrop and referred by name to the Watergate figures and even went to Vietnam. Although appearing in comic strip format, Gary Trudeau's "Doonesbury" received a Pulitzer Prize for distinguished editorial cartooning in 1975. "Peanuts" by Charles Schulz was the most influential comic strip of the 1970's and early 1980's.

Beginning with William Cullen Bryant (*Evening Post*) and Benjamin H. Day (*Sun*), rivals in New York, the 19th century developed a galaxy of editor-publishers who became national figures. Among these, James Gordon Bennett (*Morning Herald*), Horace Greeley (*Tribune*), Henry J. Raymond (*Daily Times*), Charles A. Dana (*Sun*), Edwin L. Godkin (*Evening Post*), Joseph Pulitzer (*World*), William Randolph Hearst (*Evening Journal*), and Adolph S. Ochs (*Times*) were situated in New York. Others of distinction issued newspapers over the country. They included Samuel Bowles (*Springfield* [Mass.] *Republican,*) Joseph Medill (*Chicago Daily Tribune*), Henry Watterson (*Louisville Courier-Journal*), William B. McCullagh (*St. Louis Globe-Democrat*), William Rockhill Nelson (*Kansas City Evening Star*), Clark Howell (*Atlanta Constitution*), James King (*San Francisco Bulletin*), and Harrison Gray Otis (*Los Angeles Times*).

In the 20th century editors of reputation included the McCormicks and the family of Marshall Field in Chicago and the Binghams in Louisville; Oswald Garrison Villard (*New York Evening Post*), Frank I. Cobb (*New York World*), Gardner Cowles (*Des Moines Register and Tribune*), Victor F. Lawson (*Chicago Daily News*), Lucius W. Nieman (*Milwaukee Journal*), Ernest Greuning (*Portland* [Maine] *Evening News*), Clark McAdams and Oliver K. Bovard (*St. Louis Post-Dispatch*), John S. Knight (*Miami Herald*), Eugene C. Pulliam (*Arizona Republic*), William T. Evjue (*Madison* [Wis.] *Capital Times*), John N. Heiskell (*Arkansas Gazette*), Palmer Hoyt (*Portland Oregonian* and *Denver Post*), Douglas Southall Freeman (*Richmond News Leader*), Josephus and Jonathan Worth Daniels (*Raleigh News and Observer*), Thomas M. Storke (*Santa Barbara* [Calif.] *News-Press*), Ralph McGill (*Atlanta Constitution*), Virginius Dabney (*Richmond Times-Dispatch*), and George B. Dealey (*Dallas Morning News*). Kansas afforded the nation a remarkable pair of small-city editors with broad outlook in William Allen White of the *Emporia Gazette* and Edgar Watson Howe of the *Atchison Daily Globe.*

Although the Hearst-Pulitzer rivalry helped bring on the Spanish-American War, the war itself was so short that the press could do little more than sensationalize developments. Reporter Richard Harding Davis and illustrator Frederic Remington were journalists who rose to national notice. World War I saw the press under heavy censorship and acting largely as a propaganda machine. George Creel's wartime Committee on Public Information produced more than 6,000 anti-German patriotic news releases, widely and dutifully printed in the press. Editors and publishers generally fell in with the wishes of Washington, while the force of law bore against German-language and radical papers. Wartime controls barred two pacifistic Socialist dailies, the *New York Call* and the *Milwaukee Leader,* from the mails.

World War II censorship began with the bombing at Pearl Harbor, and Congress quickly passed the first War Powers Act with the legislative basis for the Office of Censorship. Although war zone dispatches had to be cleared with military censors, most of the censorship was voluntary, self-applied as set out in a "Code of Wartime Practices for the American Press." Several pro-Nazi and Fascist papers were ordered closed. A vast net of war correspondents spread around the globe. In a category by himself was Ernie Pyle, Hoosier reporter, who described in simple, homely, yet graphic, terms the battlefront existence of GI Joe in Africa, Europe, and the Pacific, where Pyle himself was killed.

Censorship plus outright misstatement continued in the cold war years, as evidenced by the slow issuance of full facts concerning the U-2 spy plane episode in 1960, the Bay of Pigs fiasco in 1961, and the Cuban missile crisis in 1962. In the Korean and Vietnam wars, adverse news was not only frowned on officially but occasionally forbidden. Since the war in Vietnam was never formally declared, actual censorship was difficult to apply. Manipulation took its place. Correspondents learned that too often the facts were not as presented in military briefings—for example, shortly before the Tet offensive. The conclusion was inescapable that many of the untruths were deliberate, intended to deceive and, in so doing, to protect diplomatic and military mistakes. Inescapable too was the fact that the press played along far too frequently.

The post–World War I tabloid-sized newspaper had a forerunner in the diminutive *New York Daily Graphic* (1873–89) which specialized in sensational pictures. Three decades passed before Joseph M. Patterson brought out his *New York Illustrated Daily News* (June 26, 1919). It soon had the largest circulation in New York, and twenty years later its distribution was nearly 2 million daily and more than 3 million on Sunday. Enticed by this mass welcome of the *Daily News,* Hearst produced the *New York Daily Mirror* in 1924, and Bernarr Macfadden founded the *Evening Graphic* (1924–32). Cornelius Vanderbilt, Jr., undertook a chain of "clean" tabloids, only to see it collapse in 1926–27. Crime, sex, sports, and comics were the main fare of tabloids; but some, including the *Chicago Sun-Times,* became popular pleaders for policies favorable to masses of city and suburban dwellers.

By the 1980's the *New York Daily News* still enjoyed the nation's record circulation for a general newspaper; but it found itself in serious financial difficulties and locked in an advertising and circulation struggle with another tabloid, the *New York Post.*

Columnists. As the strong editors declined in number and the editorial pages tended toward a more common denominator, a new form of journalistic expression emerged. The byline columnist, with regular offerings of opinion, began with the syndication of Arthur Brisbane and Heywood Broun. Brisbane, who appeared on page 1 of the Hearst press, dealt briefly but positively with almost everything under the sun. Broun, whose far more literary essays decorated the *New York World*'s "opposite editorial page," discussed such heated problems as the Sacco-Vanzetti case, even to the point of being fired by the second generation of Pulitzers.

Although not the most widely read, former *World* editor Walter Lippmann was perhaps most highly esteemed for his thoughtful views, particularly on foreign affairs. Ranging from strongly liberal to equally strongly conservative were a spectrum of opinion shapers, among them Raymond Clapper, Dorothy Thompson, Arthur Krock, Thomas L. Stokes, Marquis W. Childs, Roscoe Drummond, George E. Sokolsky, James J. Kilpatrick, William S. White, Max Lerner, Mike Royko, William F. Buckley, Jack Anderson, and Carl T. Rowan. By the 1980's the *New York Times* shared its editorial columnists, via its wire service, to the extent that James Reston, Tom Wicker, William Safire, Anthony Lewis, and Flora Lewis regularly spoke out far more vigorously than the local editors in whose pages they appeared. Even the humorists Franklin P. Adams, Don Marquis, O. O. McIntyre, Will Rogers, Kin Hubbard, Russell Baker, and Art Buchwald entered the public arena. Sylvia Porter won an appreciative readership for her columns on business, economic, and consumer concerns. Other specialists centered on the military, the family, religion, gardening, sports, and recreation.

Ethnic Press. Newspapers in languages other than English and devoted to diverse social groups appeared in colonial times. Franklin's *Philadelphische Zeitung,* started in 1732 for German immigrants to Pennsylvania, was short-lived, but Christopher Sower's German-language paper, *Zeitung,* launched in 1739, caught on in Germantown, Pa. In St. Louis the *Westliche Post* of Carl Schurz and Emil Preetorius provided immigrant Joseph Pulitzer with his first newspaper job in 1868. In the late 1800's papers in Italian, Polish, Spanish, Yiddish, and other tongues were published in the larger cities. Scandinavians who spread into the Middle West were also served by their own language newspapers. Assimilation of later genrations, along with wars and economic tribulations, undercut foreign-language newspapers until in 1980 only some 200 had survived. The largest circulation, about 125,000, was that of the New York daily *El Diario,* a tabloid in Spanish primarily for emigrants from Puerto Rico.

Freedom's Journal, founded in 1827 in New York, was the first paper written for black people. They began it, so they declared, because "too long others have spoken for us." Frederick Douglass, a former slave, issued the *North Star* in 1847. W. E. B. Du Bois established *The Crisis* in 1910 as the voice of the National Association for the Advancement of Colored People. By the mid-1970's, some 3,000 black-owned and black-conducted papers had been started, but the average life-span was only nine years; survivors in 1982 numbered fewer than 200. The largest black papers and their founding dates are the New York *Amsterdam News,* 1909; *Baltimore Afro-American,* 1892; *Chicago Defender,* 1905; *Pittsburgh Courier,* 1910; *Philadelphia Tribune,* 1884; and the Norfolk *Journal and Guide,* 1911.

American Indian efforts to produce a national paper met with language and distribution difficulties. In the mid-1970's *Wassaja,* with both news and comment, issued monthly from San Francisco's Indian Historical Press. Scattered sheets serving tribes and reservations, some begun in the early 1800's, survived for varying periods. New interest in the native Indian as a minority raised interest in Indian publications.

Chains. The one-man editor-publisher practice of journalism, although persisting in rural areas, followed business trends into partnerships, companies, and corporations with many owners who held shares of stock. Chain ownership and management developed near the end of the 19th century. By 1914 the Scripps-McRae League of Newspapers controlled some thirteen daily publications. In the 1920's the organization became the Scripps-Howard chain, after its new driving force, Roy W. Howard, who extended the enterprise from coast to coast.

William Randolph Hearst was a close second in chain operation. After taking over the *San Francisco Examiner,* he bought the *New York Journal* in 1895 and soon moved into Chicago. By 1951 he owned seventeen dailies and two Sunday papers, to which he supplied national news, editorials, and features. Subsequently the Hearst organization retrenched, and its numbers declined while chain ownership generally expanded. In 1982 the Gannett chain consisted of almost 100 newspapers, the largest number in one ownership. The Knight and Ridder chains merged in 1974 to form Knight-Ridder Newspapers with a national coverage of thirty-five newspapers in sixteen states and a combined circulation of 27 million. Important chains included Chicago Tribune, Cowles, Copley, Lee, Newhouse, and Thomson. Some of the newspapers with the largest circulations were chain owned, among them the *New York Daily News, Philadelphia Inquirer, Detroit Free Press, Chicago Tribune,* and *Los Angeles Times.* Approximately half the dailies were owned by companies or persons that owned other dailies. In nearly half the states more than 50 percent of the newspapers were chain-owned and in Florida the total in chains was 83 percent. Chain newspapers accounted for nearly half of the total circulation in 1960, a proportion stepped up to about two-thirds in less than two decades. A continuation of these trends would place almost all dailies in chain ownership by 1990.

Another trend diversified even major newspaper companies. In 1975 the *New York Times,* for example, had many other business enterprises. These included daily and weekly newspapers in North Carolina and Florida; magazines for the family, golfers, tennis players, and medical circles; television and radio properties; book and music publishing; news and feature services; and teaching materials, filmstrips, a microfilm edition, a large-type weekly, an index service, and newsprint interests. Similarly the Dow Jones Company, publisher of the *Wall Street Journal,* owned and operated *Barron's,* the Ottway group of newspapers, a news service, and a computerized news-retrieval system.

Syndication began before the coming of chains, but the syndicate and chain operation went hand in hand. Hearst, for example, circulated feature material to syndicate subscribers who were not in his chain. The syndicate business grew to vast proportions, providing columnists and comics, religion and recipes, fashions and family counseling, and more in prepackaged daily installments.

Production Methods. Newspaper production changed greatly as mechanical methods supplanted typesetting by hand and hand-fed presses. The steam-powered press was used in 1822, but a decade passed before it was common. The cylinder press, imported in 1824, took a larger sheet of paper. The stereotype was developed in the 1830's, but its adoption awaited the coming in 1861 of the curve-shaped form that could be clamped on rotary-press cylinders. By 1863 newsprint was delivered in rolls instead of cut sheets; in another decade roll-fed presses were common. By 1876 these presses were equipped with folders so that a newspaper of several sections could be printed on as many presses, folded, and assembled for transportation and delivery.

Paper continued to be of the expensive rag manufacture until 1870, when wood-pulp paper began to take its place. From the mid-1840's the telegraph was employed in transmitting news, and it was a factor in reporting the Civil War.

Although few occupations were as laborious as setting type by hand, the hand method was slow to yield to machine methods. Ottmar Mergenthaler, a Baltimore machinist, produced a machine built on the lines of a typewriter. It cast lines from molten metal, automatically spaced, by means of individual matrices assembled via a hand-operated keyboard and returned to a magazine after each use. Mergenthaler's first patent was issued in 1884, and on July 3, 1886, a "linotype" was successfully operated at the *New York Tribune.* Use of the machine spread quickly: 60 were in use in eighteen months, and by 1895 there were 3,100 speeding up typesetting across the country. The speedup proved a boon to afternoon newspapers; and a new era had come to printing.

The linotype fell prey to progress, and by the 1980's many newspaper composing rooms had removed their last "linos," as offset printing and other new techniques took over. Notable developments came, too, in color printing and rotogravure for feature sections, and some newspapers used color in their news and advertising columns. The wire services meantime developed the means by which a single impulse at the starting point caused a step in type production to be taken in the plants of many member newspapers.

The New Journalism. In the late 1960's and into the 1980's unorthodox developments in the press came to be called the "new journalism." The term was used to embrace a wide range of writing—a partially imaginative "nonfiction" as news writing on current events as well as on the "pop culture." The writers included Gay Talese, Tom Wolfe, Lillian Ross, Norman Mailer, Truman Capote, and Jimmy Breslin. Among the new-style papers were the *Maine Times,* Manhattan's *Village Voice,* the *Texas Observer, Cervi's Rocky Mountain Journal,* and the *San Francisco Bay Guardian.* A category of writers known as "advocates" included James F. Ridgeway, Nicholas von Hoffman, Gloria Steinem, Pete Hamill, and Jack Newfield. The term "new journalism" persisted for want of a more exact description. Some of its critics held that it was neither new nor journalism.

Newspaper Rise and Decline. In the half century from 1800 to 1850, the number of dailies increased tenfold, from 24 to 254. Total daily circulation did not quite quadruple; it was 200,000 in 1800 and 758,000 in 1850. Through the 19th century each decade saw increases in the number of dailies, 387 in 1860 with a circulation of 1,478,000 to 574 in 1870 with a circulation of 2,601,000. Technological improvements made larger press runs possible, and as the number of dailies tripled—971 in 1880; 1,610 in 1889; 2,226 in 1899; and peaking at 2,600 in 1909—circulation rose at a faster rate. The circulation figures for those same years were 3,566,000; 8,387,000; 15,102,000; and 24,212,000. By 1920 the number of dailies had declined to 2,324. Circulation continued to rise, reaching 31 million by 1920.

In 1920–30 the number of dailies decreased by about 100. In 1930 there were 2,219 dailies, but the total circulation reached 45,106,000. Under the pressure to combine, the number of dailies dropped in 1941 to 1,857, a decline that continued in the 1940's until the total fell to 1,744. After about 1945 there was a leveling off through the 1950's and 1960's. In the 1970's the number of dailies and the circulation held rather steady. In 1980 there were 1,745 dailies, with a circulation of 62,201,840. A major influence was the rise of television as a means of communication. Where a century earlier, major cities might have had as many as 10 dailies, in 1981 only New York had three general dailies; Philadelphia, Boston, and Los Angeles two each; and Washington, D.C., only one.

The major services for the transmission of news and pictures by wire or radio, the Associated Press and United Press International, were started in 1848 and 1907, respectively. The United Press Association merged with a Hearst wire service, the International News Service, in 1958 to form United Press International.

NEW SWEDEN COLONY. The first permanent settlement in the Delaware River valley and the only Swedish colony in the New World. Established within the boundaries of Wilmington, Del., it was built as Fort Christina in 1638, and in 1640 an expedition arrived with supplies and colonists; other expeditions arrived in 1641 and 1643.

Governor Johan Printz started at once to extend his domain, building small forts on the New Jersey side of the Delaware, near the present site of Philadelphia; at Upland (now Chester, Pa.); and at the mouth of the Schuylkill River. The forests were cleared and farms cultivated; and a village, Christinahamn, was laid out behind Fort Christina. Eventually the colony increased to nearly 400 people. Printz ruled New Sweden with despotic power and was supreme over the whole Delaware Valley. He monopolized the fur trade, driving out the English who came from New Haven and the Dutch who came from New Amsterdam.

In 1654, Printz's successor, Johan Rising, captured the Dutch fort at New Castle, Del., thereby giving Sweden control of the whole valley. This so angered the Dutch in Holland that in 1655 they sent a warship to New Amsterdam, where it was joined by six others. With 300 fighting men Peter Stuyvesant recaptured New Castle and, after a ten-day bloodless siege, Fort Christina. Thus New Sweden disappeared from the map, and a Dutch province took its place.

NEW SWEDEN COMPANY. Established in 1637 for the purpose of trading and planting colonies on the coast of North America from Newfoundland to Florida, this company secured its first foothold on American soil in the present state of Delaware in the year 1638 (*see* New Sweden Colony). The original subscribers were both Swedes and Hollanders; Peter Minuit was chosen director of the expedition. In 1642 the company was reorganized and became entirely Swedish.

NEW THOUGHT MOVEMENT. The name given to a mind-healing movement in the United States. Members look upon Phineas P. Quimby as the movement's founder. The name was first used by the Church of the Higher Life, formed in Boston in 1894, of which some of Quimby's disciples were members. In 1914 the International New Thought Alliance was formed, stressing health, happiness, and success. New Thought groups do not profess to be churches; rather, it is their design to make people efficient within their established patterns of life.

NEWTON, BATTLE OF. *See* **Elmira, Battle of.**

NEW ULM, DEFENSE OF (1862). Citizens of New Ulm, Minn., a town of German immigrants on the Minnesota River, was warned of a Sioux uprising. They hastily barricaded the business section and repulsed a sharp Sioux raid on Aug. 19. Reinforced by volunteer militia, 250 guns faced the main attack on Aug. 23. Against heavy odds, the defenders, after twenty-six had been killed, beat off the Sioux.

"NEW WEST." A term used by historian Frederick Jackson Turner—notably in his 1906 work *Rise of the New West*—and by the school of historians that adopted his view of the importance of the frontier in American history. The term refers to the states to the west of the Allegheny Mountains (Ohio, Indiana, Illinois, Missouri, Kentucky, Tennessee, Alabama, Mississippi, Louisiana) that were rapidly settled after 1815 and became "a dominant force in American life."

NEW YORK. The Provincial Congress of New York on May 27, 1776, declared the right to self-government and on July 9 approved the Declaration of Independence. A convention framed a constitution that the legislature adopted on Apr. 20, 1777. Membership in the upper house (senate) and the governorship became elective, and eligibility to vote for members of the lower house (assembly) was extended to include most white adult males. To vote for governor and senators, one required a 100 freehold, five times greater than that needed to vote for assemblymen.

George Clinton defeated Philip Schuyler, the aristocracy's candidate for governor, and took office in July 1777. Serving six terms (1777–95), he directed the revolutionary militia and harassed the Tories. The flight of many aristocrats weakened the landed class. Clinton championed state sovereignty but failed to prevent the Poughkeepsie Convention from ratifying the federal Constitution on July 26, 1788. Alexander Hamilton and John Jay led the Federalists, the latter serving two terms as governor (1795–1801). The Antifederalists became the Jeffersonian Republicans, later the Democratic party.

The Republican victory of 1800 returned Clinton to the governorship for his last term. Daniel D. Tompkins, Republican governor in 1807–17, was in the forefront of the struggle against the British economic and military warfare that wreaked havoc on New York commerce. The followers of Tompkins and of Sen. Martin Van Buren captured control of the constitutional convention of 1821, which extended male suffrage. The foes of Tompkins and Van Buren rallied around De Witt Clinton who, as canal commissioner and as governor during 1817–22 and 1825–28, promoted the construction of the Erie Canal. The Democrats preached economy, although one branch favored state aid for an enlargement of the Erie Canal, which was authorized in 1835. The Whig party emerged in the 1830's, attracting anti-Masons and the enemies of Andrew Jackson. Antislavery feeling grew, and in 1848 some Democrats formed the Free Soil party, which threw the state and federal elections to the Whigs. The slavery issue also divided the Whigs, who collapsed after the passage of the Kansas-Nebraska Act. Thurlow Weed, Horace Greeley, and William Seward drifted into the newly formed Republican party, which also attracted some Free Soilers.

New York grew spectacularly, winning leadership in population and trade by 1820. Among the contributing factors were the opening up of central and western New York; turnpike and steamboat expansion; and Manhattan's success in capturing the transatlantic, coastal, and interior trades. The completion of the Erie Canal (1825) made transportation cheaper, stimulated urban growth, and encouraged construction of branch canals. The Mohawk and Hudson Railroad in 1831 connected Albany with Schenectady. By 1842 trains ran from Albany to Buffalo over short lines, incorporated in 1853 into the New York Central. Promoters quickly built a network of lines into every section of the state. The factory system—and urbanization—took hold after Pennsylvania coal reached the cities. Wheat cultivation declined, but after 1850 dairying was the most important source of farm income.

In 1861, Gov. Edwin D. Morgan enthusiastically answered President Abraham Lincoln's call for men and supplies, but by July 1863 war weariness and an unfair draft had triggered riots, which Gov. Horatio Seymour, an antidraft Democrat, helped put down. The Civil War had a mixed effect on the economy, in general slowing the rate of growth.

Corruption—typified by Boss William Tweed of Tammany Hall, who dominated New York City politics in the 1860's and 1870's—inspired such reformers as governors Samuel Tilden (1875–76) and Grover Cleveland (1883–85). Governors Theodore Roosevelt (1899–1900) and Charles Evans Hughes (1907–10) headed a distinguished list in the 20th century. Alfred E. Smith reorganized state government during his four terms (1918–20, 1922–28). Gov. Franklin D. Roosevelt carried on Smith's progressivism, passing on the office to Herbert H. Lehman, who, during four terms between 1932 and 1942, regulated public utilities and aided labor. Thomas E. Dewey (1942–54) left three legacies: the New York Thruway; the state university; and the Ives-Quinn Act, the first state law banning discrimination in hiring. Nelson A. Rockefeller in 1958 defeated W. Averell Harriman, a progressive Democratic governor. During his four terms Rockefeller expanded the state university, medical care, and conservation programs. These services and the construction of costly projects—for example, the Albany Mall—increased the debt and required increases in income, sales, and business taxes. Rockefeller resigned his office in 1973, and Lt. Gov. Malcolm Wilson became governor, only to lose to Rep. Hugh Carey in the next election. Carey faced several pressing problems: shrinking state revenues; rising demands by cities and citizens for more aid and services; and the threatened bankruptcy of New York City and the Urban Development Corporation. Carey and legislative leaders were able to patch together measures to rescue New York City, which had to agree to sharper cuts in its employees.

In 1980 New York State residents had a per capita income 8 percent above the national average. New York's leading industries are printing and publishing, apparel, food, chemicals, and primary metals and fabricated metal products, including machinery and transportation equipment. Mineral production was valued at $438 million in 1978. In wholesale and retail trade New York leads the nation; it is also the financial center of the world.

Having reinforced its early population growth by heavy influxes of European immigrants in the late 19th century, of southern blacks after World War I, and of Puerto Ricans after 1940, New York lost its population lead to California in 1963. In 1980 the state's population was 17,557,288. (*See also* New Netherland; New York Colony.)

NEW YORK AND GENESEE COMPANY. A company formed in 1787 for the purpose of obtaining possession of the Indian country in New York State. John Livingston and his partners obtained a 999-year lease for all the Iroquois lands in the state. The Indians denied the legality of the lease because it was not signed by the principal chiefs, and later legislative action nullified the agreement.

NEW YORK CENTRAL RAILROAD. *See* **Railroads, Sketches of Principal Lines.**

NEW YORK, CHICAGO AND ST. LOUIS. *See* **Railroads, Sketches of Principal Lines: Norfolk and Western.**

NEW YORK CITY. Covering 320.38 square miles, the city is divided into five boroughs: Manhattan (New York County), the Bronx (Bronx County), Queens (Queens County), Brooklyn (Kings County), and Staten Island (Richmond County). Its importance has always rested upon the excellence of its ice-free, sheltered harbor and the attendant volume of its commerce. Possessing a shoreline of 578 miles, and served in 1980 by 145 steamship companies and over 50 airlines, it is the premier port of the world.

On Sept. 8, 1664, during the first Anglo-Dutch War, Dutch Gov. Peter Stuyvesant surrendered the city of New Amsterdam to a besieging English squadron commanded by Col. Richard Nicolls, who renamed it New York in honor of James, Duke of York, later James II. Nicolls became the first English governor. In 1673, during the third Anglo-Dutch War, New York was reconquered by the Dutch, but it was returned to England in 1674. At first, the Duke of York, as the new proprietor, permitted a surprisingly liberal and tolerant administration, to insure the gratitude and loyalty of his Dutch subjects and to promote commercial prosperity. On Apr. 27, 1686, Gov. Thomas Dongan granted the first English municipal charter to New York City, adding to earlier municipal prerogatives the right to eminent domain, the right to own and dispose of land, and the right to grant franchises.

The rebellion of 1689–91 led by Jacob Leisler helped to check the increasingly tyrannical policies of James II. Leisler was the *de facto* leader of the colony when Peter de Lanoy became the first popularly elected mayor of the city (1689–1691)—and the last until 1834. It was the controversial Leisler's unjust execution for treason that divided the populace into Leislerians and anti-Leislerians.

Street lights and a night watch appeared in New York in 1697; a serious epidemic of yellow fever broke out in 1702; the public printer William Bradford published the first New York newspaper, the weekly *New York Gazette,* on Oct. 16, 1725; the first stage line ran to Philadelphia in 1730; a fire department was organized in 1731, the year Harlem at the northern end of Manhattan was annexed; and in April 1712 and February 1741 there occurred so-called black insurrections or conspiracies that resulted in harsh reprisals. In 1735, John Peter Zenger, the courageous publisher of the Whiggish *New-York Weekly Journal,* was acquitted of seditious libel against royal Gov. William S. Cosby—a landmark victory for freedom of the press and for American legal interpretation over English common law.

The city was the site of the Stamp Act Congress in 1765, and the Whig leadership drove the colony relentlessly toward revolution, even engaging in clashes with the British soldiery. With the outbreak of hostilities New York was vital to both British and American strategy. Although the province of New York remained in American hands, the city was not so fortunate. Gen. George Washington's army was defeated in the Battle of Long Island (Aug. 25–26, 1776) and on Manhattan Island in the weeks following. The city was occupied by the British military until war's end.

With independence, charters were reinstituted and municipal government restored; the Anglican church was disestablished; and the city began to recover economically. It grew both in population and commercial importance. In the first federal census (1790), New York's population was 33,131. By 1797, New York had moved ahead of Boston and Philadelphia in exports and imports. In population New York by 1830 had outstripped Philadelphia to become the nation's first city and the largest in the hemisphere. The population in that year was 202,589, having risen from 123,706 in 1820.

New York, between 1783 and 1861, faithfully mirrored the developments and issues of the intervening national historical eras. In 1784 the Bank of New York was founded. From 1785 until 1790 the city was the national capital and until 1797 the seat of the state government as well. The city suffered but little ill from the War of 1812 except a few years of decline in maritime activity, profits, and employment owing to a British naval blockade. During the four decades preceding the Civil War the city gained from increasing immigration, banking, exchange and insurance activity, industry, and the growth of the railroads. By virtue of its harbor, the coming of the steamboat, and the importance of the Hudson River and the Erie Canal, New York became a major market and entrepôt between Europe and the American continent.

In 1835 and 1845, much of the city was destroyed by great fires. The gloom of fires, epidemics, slums, and savage partisan politics was relieved by the construction of the Croton water system; the introduction of gas street lamps; the paving of streets; increased educational facilities at all levels; greater attention to charitable needs and social welfare; and increased ferry, rail, and streetcar transportation. In 1860 the population was 814,000.

New York was divided over the issues that led to the Civil War. Once hostilities commenced, however, the city supported the Union. Marring this commitment were the Draft Riots of July 1863, which caused extensive loss of life and property. After the war, New York became the unquestioned symbol of a booming, complex urban enclave and the marketplace of a maturing finance capitalism that had been stimulated by the needs of war. The city had a population of 942,292 in 1870. On Jan. 1, 1898, the present five boroughs were incorporated into the Greater City of New York.

In the early national period the elitist Federalist politics of Alexander Hamilton were dominant, but the Jeffersonian Republicans, led by Aaron Burr locally, gained control. After 1800 government in the city became more representative and democratic, and the city has remained a bastion of the Democratic party. After 1861, New York Democratic politics was dominated by Tammany Hall, a domination that lasted until the fusion mayoralty of Fiorello H. La Guardia in the 1930's. In the 20th century, New York has been the focal point of progressivism, the muckraking movement, and reform. The city strongly supported the New Deal politics of President Franklin Delano Roosevelt, a former governor of New York.

New York has rightly been called the cultural capital of the United States. Its major opera and dance companies, world-famous symphony orchestra, libraries, museums, and theaters make it the center of the arts in the country. As the home of the two largest stock exchanges in the United States and the headquarters of hundreds of banks and corporations, New York is also the major financial center. It is also the center of the publishing, broadcasting, and fashion industries in the United States. Tourism and conventions are other important industries. The United Nations is located in the city.

New York runs one of the largest public education systems in the United States, which includes the multibranched City University of New York (CUNY) and an extensive community college system. Private institutions of higher learning include Columbia, Fordham, Long Island, New York, Yeshiva, Pace, and St. John's universities and Manhattan College. In addition there are several medical schools and research institutions.

New York was faced in the 1970's with the enormous urban problems confronting the other cities in the nation. The city's size intensified the problems. Its population in 1980 was 7,071,030, which included about 1.8 million Afro-Americans and 1.4 million Hispanic-Americans. The shift toward an increased nonwhite population carried divisive overtones in housing, unemployment, welfare, education, and crime. A disastrous financial crisis in 1975 was substantially met by stringent budget cutting.

NEW YORK CITY, CAPTURE OF (July 30, 1673). During the summer of 1673 during the first Anglo-Dutch War, Gov. Francis Lovelace failed to take seriously rumors of a Dutch plan to recapture New York. On July 28 a Dutch fleet of twenty-three ships appeared off Sandy Hook. On July 30 the fleet came within musket shot of Fort James. The fort held out for four hours and then surrendered. The city remained in Dutch hands until the end of the war in 1674.

NEW YORK CITY, PLOT TO BURN. On Nov. 25, 1864, a Confederate attempt was made to burn New York City. Barnum's Museum, the Astor House, and a number of other hotels and theaters were fired with phosphorus and turpentine, but the damage was trifling.

NEW YORK CLEARINGHOUSE. *See* **Clearinghouse, New York.**

NEW YORK COLONY. The year after its addition to the Dominion of New England, 1689, was a time of anxiety, violence, and unrest in the colony of New York (*see* York's, Duke of, Proprietary). The accession of William and Mary to the throne of England resulted in the arrest of Edmund Andros, governor of the dominion. (*see* New England, Dominion of). In New York, Capt. Jacob Leisler seized control of the government. Albany attempted to resist Leisler's authority but was prevented by the burning of Schenectady by the French and Indians in 1690. The following spring, on the arrival of Col. Henry Sloughter, who had been commissioned governor by William and Mary, Leisler and his chief associates were tried for treason; Leisler and Jacob Milbourne, his lieutenant, were executed. Leislerian and anti-Leislerian factions continued to disturb the colony for many years.

Gov. Benjamin Fletcher, who took office in 1692, conciliated the Five Nations and bound them to a renewed alliance with England. This alliance, which had become a cardinal point of British policy in New York, was further strengthened in 1701, during the administration of the Earl of Bellomont, by the action of the Iroquois in conveying to the care of the king of England the western lands they claimed by conquest (*see* Iroquois Beaver Land Deed). An able man, and a friend of the small landowner, the earl's administration was cut short by his death in 1701 (*see* New York State, Land Speculation in).

Edward Hyde, Viscount Cornbury, renewed the policy of making extravagant grants during his governorship, 1702–08. His arrogance and corruption greatly antagonized the assembly, which had been slowly growing in power and importance, and hastened the contest over the power of the purse, which was to agitate the province throughout the remainder of the colonial period. During Queen Anne's War (1702–1713), New York tended to keep neutral. This and the trade between Albany and Montreal were the occasions of bitter complaint from the New England colonies.

The arrival of William Cosby as governor in 1732 witnessed the beginning of a period of violent popular agitation. Smarting under the accusations of maladministration printed in John Peter Zenger's small newspaper, the *New-York Weekly Journal,* Cosby ordered Zenger's arrest. In the trial that followed the principle that truth is the justification for making a public statement was established.

The French continued their encroachments on territory claimed by New York. In 1727 a fort had been built by the British at Oswego to offset the rival French post at Niagara. In 1731 the French occupied Crown Point. Hostilities broke out again in 1744. George Clinton, then governor of New York, was a man of courage and ability, but he possessed little tact. His furious feud with James De Lancey, chief justice of the province, caused a bitter fight over the conduct of the war. As a result the only effective action taken by the colony was through the exertions of Sir William Johnson, who was able to exercise sufficient influence over the Six Nations to keep their friendship (*see* Indian Policy, Colonial).

In 1754, De Lancey, acting head of the provincial government, presided over the Albany Congress, and in the fourth and final war with the French, which followed (*see* French and Indian War), he gave firm support to the king's commanders. In 1759 Jeffrey Amherst, British commander in chief in North America, compelled the French to abandon Ticonderoga and Crown Point, and Niagara was also captured. Until the reduction of Montreal by Amherst in 1760 the western frontier of New York suffered cruelly.

The conviction had been growing in America that taxation should originate only in the colonial assemblies. New York opposed both the Stamp Act and the Townshend Acts. To add to the discontent in New York, the currency bill of 1769 was disallowed (*see* Royal Disallowance). The Sons of Liberty again became active, and in 1770 the disturbances came to a climax in the Battle of Golden Hill. In January 1774 a committee of correspondence was appointed to write to "sister colonies." Local and state revolutionary committees took over the government of the colony. On July 9, 1776, the fourth Provincial Congress of New York approved the Declaration of Independence, and on the following day declared New York a free state (*see* New York State).

"NEW YORK GETS THE NEWS." An expression pertaining to the reaction of patriots in New York City following the Battle of Lexington (Apr. 19, 1775). The news of the battle in Massachusetts threw the city into a state of great excitement. The arsenal was broken open, and about 600 muskets with ammunition were seized and distributed among citizens who formed a voluntary corps. They took possession of the customshouse and the public stores. The government was helpless, and on May 1, a patriot committee assumed control of the city.

NEW YORK, NEW HAVEN AND HARTFORD. *See* **Railroads, Sketches of Principal Lines: Penn Central.**

NEW YORK STATE, LAND SPECULATION IN. Encouraged by the Dutch practice of granting large tracts of land to individuals or associated groups for the promotion of settlement, and continued and extended by the early English governors. From 1690 to 1775 the majority of the prominent men of the colony were involved in some sort of land speculation. Starting with the brief administration of Gov. John Lovelace in 1709, the number of acres to be granted to a single individual was limited. Evasion, however, was common. The governors had come to regard the fees paid for granting patents as a part of their legitimate income. Careless surveys resulted in overlapping claims and litigation. Immigration and settlement were retarded, the settlers preferring the small freeholds offered by other colonies to the landlord-tenant relationship or higher prices in New York. The newly created state government did little, at the conclusion of hostilities in the Revolution, to protect or encourage the small landowner, and speculation continued. In 1786 the claim of Massachusetts to a vast tract east of the present western boundary of New York was settled by giving to Massachusetts the right of first purchase from the Indians and to New York the right of sovereignty to the disputed territory. Much of it ended up in the hands of the Holland Land Company. This pattern of absentee ownership, sometimes foreign, was later to be the cause of considerable disturbance in the six western counties of New York (*see* Antirent War).

NEW YORK UNDER THE DUKE OF YORK. *See* **York's, Duke of, Proprietary.**

NEW YORK WORLD'S FAIRS (1939–40, 1964–65). New York's first international exposition since 1853 (*see* Exhibition of the Industry of All Nations) was opened by President Franklin D. Roosevelt on Apr. 30, 1939. Dedicated to the "building of the world of tomorrow," the fair was constructed on 1,216.5 acres in Flushing Meadow. Tree-lined avenues converged on the focal structures, the 728-foot triangular tapering shaft of the Trylon and the 180-foot-diameter Perisphere. Prototype automobiles hinted at future technological achievements, and television was seen by many for the first time. Sixty-three nations and more than twenty states participated. The first season closed on Oct. 31. The outbreak of World War II precluded the participation of many nations in the fair's second season (May 11–Oct. 27, 1940). Although the fair attracted 44,932,978 visitors, it was a financial failure.

The second fair occupied the same site and was designed to follow its layout. The fair was opened by President Lyndon B. Johnson on Apr. 22, 1964, although all exhibits were not completed. The focal point and symbol, the Unisphere, was a stainless steel open model of the earth. The fair enjoyed the participation of private concerns from sixty-two foreign nations. There were nineteen federal and state pavilions. A replica of a Belgian village, demonstrations of nuclear fusion, the exhibition of Michelangelo's *Pietà,* and a ride across the simulated surface of the moon were featured at the more popular exhibits. The first season closed on Oct. 18. The second season (Apr. 21–Oct. 17, 1965) was highlighted by the visit of Pope Paul VI. The fair closed with a total attendance of 51,607,548—then the greatest on record—and $46 million in defaulted payments to the city of New York and holders of promissory notes.

NEZ PERCÉ WAR (1877). The various bands of the Nez Percé Indians, occupying a large area in the region where Washington, Oregon, and Idaho meet, had been on friendly terms with the whites until the gold rush of 1860 brought swarms of miners and settlers onto their lands. In 1863 some of the chiefs agreed to move to the much smaller Lapwai Reservation in Idaho; but Chief Joseph and his southern Nez Percé refused to leave. Hostilities were precipitated when a few young warriors killed some settlers in revenge for outrages. Troops under Gen. O. O. Howard moved against the Indians, who defeated the soldiers in several battles, notably at White Bird Canyon in Idaho on June 17. Joseph executed a skillful retreat toward Canada; but on Oct. 15, 1877, within thirty miles of the border, he was forced to surrender. With only 300 warriors, Joseph had opposed troops numbering 5,000, traveling more than 1,000 miles in four months with a band that included women and children.

NIAGARA, CARRYING PLACE OF. A portage road fourteen miles in length on the east side of the Niagara River, connecting lakes Ontario and Erie. It was built by the French in 1720 as a detour around Niagara Falls. To protect it, Fort Little Niagara was built in 1751 at the upper landing. The British, realizing its importance, captured it in 1759. Its importance was demonstrated in the relief of Detroit, during Pontiac's War, and in control of the upper lakes until relinquished, under the terms of Jay's Treaty, in 1796 (*see* Border Forts, Evacuation of).

NIAGARA, FORT. Having obtained permission from the Seneca, the French built a stone castle on the eastern shore of the Niagara River at Lake Ontario in 1726, 6.5 miles north of the Niagara Carrying Place. It became the principal guard of the coveted gateway to the rich fur lands in the West. During the French and Indian War the English captured the post on July 25, 1759. It remained a British fortress until 1796, when it was relinquished to the United States (*see* Border Forts, Evacuation of), in accordance with Jay's Treaty. Captured by the British during the War of 1812, it was returned in 1814 under the Treaty of Ghent.

NIAGARA, GREAT INDIAN COUNCIL AT (1764). Between Sir William Johnson, British superintendent of Indian affairs, and deputations from the Ottawa, Huron, Menomini, Chippewa, Iroquois, and others. It convened at Fort Niagara on July 9, with 2,060 Indians assembled—the largest number ever gathered for a peace conference. The Huron and the Seneca, who arrived later, signed treaties ceding land to the British. The other nations made no formal treaties, declaring they had come only to renew their friendship.

NIAGARA CAMPAIGNS. On Oct. 13, 1812, Gen. Stephen Van Rensselaer unsuccessfully attacked the British at Queenston, opposite Fort Niagara on the Niagara River. On May 27, 1813, Col. Winfield Scott, assisted by Commodore Isaac Chauncey's fleet, captured Fort George, adjacent to Queenston, and the British abandoned the entire Niagara frontier to the American troops. The Americans captured Fort Erie, July 3, 1814, defeated the enemy at Chippewa on July 5, and fought the Battle of Lundy's Lane on July 25, with both sides claiming victory.

NIAGARA COMPANY. Formed in 1788 by Col. John Butler, British commissioner of Indian affairs at Niagara, Canada, and six associates. Each held fourteen shares consisting of 20,000 acres each in the Genesee lands. British authorities forced a relinquishment of the major part of the lands.

NIAGARA FALLS. In the Niagara River between lakes Erie and Ontario, composed of the American Falls and the Canadian, or Horseshoe, Falls, separated by Goat Island. It descends 167 feet to the lower river. The first white man to view the cataract was the Recollect friar Louis Hennepin, in 1678.

NIAGARA FALLS, PEACE CONFERENCE AT. *See* **Peace Movement in 1864.**

NIAGARA FALLS POWER. Niagara Falls was seen as an especially attractive source of power for a number of reasons. It was situated near the most highly populated and industrialized center of the country. Its potential capacity was more than 6 million horsepower, and the flowrate was very stable. Thomas Evershed, in 1885 proposed a design that would divert enough water through a tunnel to drive a number of mills located outside the reservation. Construction of the tunnel began in 1890. By 1902 the Niagara power stations were producing one-fifth of the total electrical energy available in the United States. Total capacity of American and Canadian power plants at Niagara Falls reached almost 700,000 horsepower in 1926. Increased transmission voltages, which became standard during the 1920's, enabled Niagara Falls power to be transmitted economically to locations hundreds of miles from the falls and made feasible a superpower zone with interconnected systems throughout the region.

In 1950 the United States and Canada signed the Niagara Diversion Treaty, which protected the scenic value of the falls and equalized the usable flow between the two countries. The generators at Lewiston, N.Y., have a capacity of 1.95 million kilowatts. (*See also* Hydroelectric Power.)

NIAGARA MOVEMENT. A movement organized in 1905 at Niagara Falls, Ontario, Canada, under the leadership of W. E. B. Du Bois and William Monroe Trotter in order to secure full rights for black Americans. It reflected black opposition both to racial discrimination and to the accommodation and gradualism advocated by Booker T. Washington.

Washington's opposition, along with a split between Du Bois and Trotter, weakened the movement. In 1909, Du Bois and other blacks from the Niagara movement joined with white liberals in the formation of the National Association for the Advancement of Colored People (NAACP).

NIBLO'S GARDEN. A 19th-century coffeehouse and theater on lower Broadway in New York City.

NICARAGUA, RELATIONS WITH. Began officially in 1867, when a treaty of amity, navigation, and commerce was signed. Nicaragua, even before then, had extended charters to several private U.S. firms to conduct business there. Several American-sponsored attempts to build a canal failed.

The regime of José Santos Zelaya in Nicaragua (1893–1909) seemed a threat to Central American peace pacts drawn in 1907. The U.S. government showed sympathy for an anti-Zelaya rebellion that began in October 1909, and it refused to recognize Zelaya's successor, José Madriz (1909–10). The United States backed conservative Adolfo Díaz for the presidency (1911–17) and with him concluded arrangements for New York bankers to lend money to Nicaragua and to control Nicaragua's customs collections, national bank, and national railroad until the loans were repaid. When Díaz was threatened in 1912, U.S. marines were sent into the country. The Bryan-Chamorro Treaty, establishing an intimate relationship between the two countries, was ratified in 1916, and the U.S. government chose conservative successors to Díaz in 1917 and 1921. The loans were repaid in 1924, and the token marine force withdrew in August 1925.

A Nicaraguan civil war brought a second landing of U.S. marines in December 1926 and January 1927. The U.S. government secured agreement that Díaz would again serve as president until January 1929 but that his successor should be chosen in free elections supervised by the United States and that the marines would organize and train an efficient constabulary. Under these terms, two liberal generals were elected to the presidency, José María Moncada (1929–33) and Juan Bautista Sacasa (1933–36). Another, Augusto César Sandino, opposed U.S. involvement in the country.

The head of the Nicaraguan constabulary, Anastasio Somoza García, arranged the murder of Sandino in February 1934, the resignation of Sacasa from the presidency in June 1936, and his own election to the presidency in December 1936. With U.S. backing, the Somoza family (father and two sons) continued to rule Nicaragua until 1979, when a civil war led by Sandinist guerrillas forced into exile Gen. Anastasio Somoza-Debayle. A five-member junta seized power and introduced a socialist regime; shortly thereafter, the United States suspended economic aid to Nicaragua, charging that Nicaragua was supplying arms to left-wing Salvadoran guerrillas. In the early 1980's, U.S.-Nicaraguan relations were at the lowest point in decades.

NICARAGUAN CANAL PROJECT. The idea of a waterway along the San Juan River and Lake Nicaragua to connect the Atlantic and Pacific oceans has long been considered since the 18th century. The route was the object of six treaties between the United States and Nicaragua during the 19th century. In 1887 an American corporation undertook survey construction, but political considerations and other factors resulted in the adoption of the Panama route (*see* Panama Canal).

NICKEL. *See* **Nonferrous Metals.**

NICOLET, EXPLORATIONS OF. Jean Nicolet, a native of Cherbourg, France, went to Canada in 1618 and was sent to Allumette Island in the Ottawa River, as an observer of Indian folkways. In 1634, he was dispatched in search of the "People of the Sea," who were surmised to have some connection with Tartary, which Marco Polo had described. Nicolet was thus the first white visitor to Michigan, Wisconsin, and Lake Michigan.

NICOLLS' COMMISSION. In 1664, Charles II named Col. Richard Nicolls, governor of New York, head of a commission to visit New England and to investigate religious, economic, and political conditions. The commissioners offered little hope of a friendly and peaceable settlement of the administration of a colonial policy in New England.

"NIGGER." A term of contempt used in reference to black Americans or to any dark-skinned peoples. During the late 1960's some militant Afro-American leaders of the civil rights movement either stressed the irrelevance of the word in the context of black pride or used its negative implications satirically.

NIGHT RIDERS (or the Silent Brigade). Armed bands of the early 20th century who made war against monopolistic tobacco companies in Kentucky and Tennessee and attacked tobacco farmers who refused to cooperate in the organized effort to break through the abusive control of the trust. Hundreds of farmers who refused to join had their barns burned or crops destroyed.

NILES' WEEKLY REGISTER. A tabloid-size newspaper founded in September 1811 at Baltimore by Hezekiah Niles. In 1837 its name was changed to *Niles' National Register,* which continued in publication until June 1849.

NINE-POWER PACT (1922). Between the United States, Belgium, the British Empire, China, France, Italy, Japan, the Netherlands, and Portugal, concluded at the Washington Naval Conference on Feb. 6. It guaranteed China's territorial integrity and the Open Door principle.

NINETEENTH AMENDMENT (1920). The amendment to the U.S. Constitution, giving women the vote, began at the Seneca Falls Convention of 1848. Following the Civil War, continuous work began for adoption of such an amendment. In 1918, President Woodrow Wilson came out in favor of the amendment, and the next year Congress gave approval. Wisconsin, the first state to ratify, acted June 10, 1919. On Aug. 26, 1920, Tennessee cast the decisive favorable vote.

NINETY-SIX. A village in South Carolina and a British post during the revolutionary war. Besieged by the Americans in May and June 1781. Although the fort withstood the siege, it was too far inland and the British abandoned it.

"NINETY-TWO" AND "FORTY-FIVE." Political catchwords first used together in 1768. "Forty-five" referred to issue number 45 of John Wilkes's newspaper *North Briton,* published in London, Apr. 23, 1763, which involved its publisher in a battle for the freedom of the press. "Ninety-two" was the number of the members of the Massachusetts Assembly who refused, June 30, 1768, to rescind the Massachusetts Circular Letter of Feb. 11, 1768, against the suppression of colonial liberties.

NISQUALLY, FORT, ATTACK ON (May 1849). Located on Puget Sound just north of Fort Vancouver, Fort Nisqually, an agricultural, commercial, and protective center, was unsuccessfully attacked by the Snoquamish, who were angered by the Oregon territorial government. The arrival of two companies of artillery saved the day for the white settlers.

NITRATES. Interest in nitrates stems from the invention of gunpowder, which is composed of about four-fifths potassium nitrate (saltpeter). The settlers at Jamestown were enjoined to collect it, but India remained the chief source. During the Revolution, the colonial governments offered bounties for saltpeter, and some attempted to produce it artificially. Mostly, however, they relied on the French for their supply.

In the first decade of the 19th century, saltpeter was found in large quantities in the caves of Kentucky and Tennessee, was exploited by the Confederate armies. Later, a process was developed to convert sodium nitrate to potassium nitrate, and Chile became the chief source.

As the use of nitrates as fertilizers increased there was intensive competition to develop a process that would convert atmospheric nitrogen to nitrate. The dam at Muscle Shoals, Ala., was built to supply the large quantities of hydroelectric power required for one such process. The most efficient method, however, is the Haber process, which has come to supply most of the world's nitrate requirements.

NIXON, RESIGNATION OF. On Aug. 9, 1974, President Richard M. Nixon resigned the office of president of the United States. He thus became the first president ever to do so. Vice-President Gerald R. Ford assumed the powers of the president.

Nixon's resignation was rooted in the Watergate and other scandals that plagued his second term and eroded the political strength derived from his overwhelming reelection in 1972. Two specific events forced Nixon to resign. In late July 1974 the House Judiciary Committee adopted three articles of impeachment, delineating many specific charges against the president. On July 24, the Supreme Court ruled that he must provide quantities of tapes of White House conversations required in the criminal trials of his former subordinates. The tapes disclosed that Nixon had participated as early as June 23, 1972, in the cover-up of the Watergate burglary. By resigning, Nixon avoided the disgrace implicit in a successful impeachment, and he preserved the pension rights and other perquisites of a former president that would have been lost. On Sept. 8, 1974, President Ford pardoned Nixon.

NOBEL PRIZES. Since their inception in 1901, the prizes have represented international recognition and achievement in the areas of physics, chemistry, physiology or medicine, literature, and peace. (Awards in economics were established in 1969.) During the first decade of the awards, only three prizes were awarded to Americans; among them was the Peace Prize to Theodore Roosevelt in 1906. In the second decade, only four awards were given to Americans. But in later decades the number of prizes claimed by Americans (either born or naturalized citizens) grew remarkably, partly because of the large number of scientists who fled from Europe to the United States during the rise of Nazi Germany.

In all, by 1981 forty-eight U.S. citizens had won (or shared) thirty-two awards in physics. Nineteen prizes had gone to twenty-five Americans in chemistry. The United States won its greatest number of prizes in the area of physiology or medicine, receiving thirty-four prizes among fifty-nine recipients. Only nine writers had won the Nobel Prize in the field of literature. The Peace Prize had been awarded to sixteen Americans, who received or shared fourteen prizes. The prize in economics, awarded by the Central Bank of Sweden, had been won nine times by as many Americans.

NOBILITY, TITLES OF. Although sundry traces of feudalism appear in American colonial law and governmental practice, the Revolution committed the country to a republican system, and the Constitution, in Article I, Sections 9 and 10, prohibits the conferring of titles of nobility by either the United States or the states. Federal officials are likewise forbidden to accept titles from foreign states except with consent of the Congress.

NODDLES ISLAND SKIRMISH. On May 27, 1775, a band of colonials attacked a British marine guard on Noddles Island (now East Boston), killing two guards and wounding two. After firing several buildings and a quantity of hay, the colonials departed.

NOGALES, TREATY OF (Oct. 28, 1793). Pact between Spain and the Creek, Choctaw, Chickasaw, and Cherokee. It validated the Spanish seizure of Walnut Hills, the site of present-day Vicksburg, Miss., where Fort Nogales was erected. The Indians agreed to defend Louisiana and Florida against attack and invoked Spanish assistance in securing boundary settlements with the United States.

NOLAN, EXPEDITIONS OF. At least four expeditions (1792–94, 1794–96, 1797, 1798–1801) into Texas were made by Philip Nolan, a trader and filibuster from Kentucky. Nolan penetrated as far as the Rio Grande in his search for wild horses and skins. In a skirmish near the present Waco, Tex., with a Spanish detachment Nolan was killed, Mar. 21, 1801.

NO MAN'S LAND. *See* **Cimarron, Proposed Territory of.**

NOMINATING SYSTEM. Three chief methods have been devised to nominate candidates for public office in the United States: the caucus system, the convention system, and the direct primary system. Originated early in the 18th century, the caucus system was later adapted to the nomination of governors and other state officers. Members of the legislature belonging to the same party would meet to recommend candidates. The next development was the congressional caucus, wherein members of Congress having the same party affiliation would assemble for the purpose of recommending presidential and vice-presidential candidates. Used first in 1800, the congressional caucus functioned for the last time in the campaign of 1824.

Meanwhile, there was developing in the states the delegate convention system. By 1830 state conventions prevailed everywhere except in the South. Before the system was adapted to the national scene, there was a period of transition from the congressional caucus. In the campaign of 1824, William H. Crawford received the nomination of the Republican congressional caucus, but three of the presidential candidates, John Quincy Adams, Henry Clay, and Andrew Jackson, were nominated more informally by mass meetings, by newspapers, or by state legislative caucuses. In the next campaign, both Adams and Jackson were nominated by similar methods.

In 1831 the Anti-Masonic party, after a preliminary convention held in the previous year, inaugurated the national nominating convention. The National Republicans and the Democrats followed the example, with the result that the national nominating convention became the accepted method of nominating party candidates for the presidency and vice-presidency, while state conventions controlled the selection of candidates for state offices. Party conventions, however, were prone to control by political bosses, and to counteract that tendency, the direct primary system was developed. Originated in Wisconsin in 1903, the primary election system provides for the direct selection of party candidates by popular vote under state supervision. The primary system was adopted in some form in all but five states by 1915 and has been established as the most important nominating method.

NONCONFORMISTS. *See* **Dissenters.**

NONFERROUS METALS. Of the major nonferrous metals —aluminum, copper, lead, zinc, nickel, and tin—all except tin are produced in commercial quantities in the United States.

The first nonferrous metal to be mined and smelted in the United States was lead. English colonists exploited the small deposits along the eastern seaboard, and by 1720 the French had begun to work the Missouri lead mines. The Missouri mines have been in continuous production since 1798.

The opening of the Missouri lead region to American settlers and the discovery of lead in the Wisconsin-Illinois Fever River district occasioned one of the first mineral rushes into the American West by eager miners. By the late 1840's the federal government had abandoned the leasing policy and opened mineral lands to unrestricted exploitation. By 1881 the United States was the leading lead producer in the world. After World War II, domestic production averaged slightly over 1 million tons annually, about 20 percent short of domestic consumption.

Zinc was first put into commercial production toward the end of the 19th century. The opening of the Joplin, Mo., zinc ore district in 1871 provided an easily mined, easily concentrated, and comparatively easily smelted ore. More important, the concurrent huge growth in the galvanizing and munitions industries created an effective demand for zinc metal. By 1917 the United States supplied over 60 percent of the world output. Until World War II the United States continued to be a net exporter of zinc, and only since then has domestic production been insufficient to supply national demand. Most zinc is now used for galvanizing and die-casting.

Copper was being worked by American Indians for fishhooks and ornaments long before Europeans made contact with the Western Hemisphere, but the commercial copper industry in the United States started only in the 1840's. With the discovery of the great western mines, especially at Butte, Mont., in the 1880's the United States became the principal producer of copper in the world—a position it has retained.

The most dramatic development in copper mining and manufacturing occurred early in the 20th century when it was demonstrated that ores containing no more than 1 percent of copper could be profitably developed.

Until the introduction of the electrolytic process in 1886, the price of aluminum had been much too high for industrial uses.

The demand for aluminum accelerated rapidly after World War II and the price made it competitive with other nonferrous metals. In the 1970's the United States produced and consumed 40 percent of the world output.

NONIMPORTATION AGREEMENTS. The American colonies' chief weapon against Great Britain from 1765 to 1775. Nonimportation was first used by New York merchants when they declared that they would order no more British goods until the Stamp Act was repealed—an example quickly followed by the Boston and Philadelphia merchants. British merchants and manufacturers lobbied so vigorously in Parliament that the Stamp Act was repealed.

Many colonial Whigs concluded that they had found a certain defense against the centralizing schemes of British imperialists. With the Townshend duties, Americans again resorted to a boycott of British goods beginning in Boston in 1768. In 1770 the British government repealed all Townshend duties except the tax on tea. This concession proved fatal to the nonimportation agreement. New York merchants, outraged by Newport's flouting of the agreement and suspicious of Boston's good faith opened their port to all British merchandise except tea, which brought about the collapse of the boycott. (*See also* Continental Association.)

NONINTERCOURSE ACT (Mar. 1, 1809). The act designated Great Britain and France as countries with which the United States would hold no commercial relations, but it offered to restore relations with whichever of those nations first withdrew the obnoxious orders and decrees (*see* Napoleon's Decrees; Orders in Council). It was a marked recession from the late embargo, which retained American shipping in home ports, for there was nothing in the Nonintercourse Act of 1809 to prevent a general European trade in which the offender nations might indirectly benefit.

The Nonintercourse Act was itself succeeded in 1810 by Macon's Bill Number 2, which was even milder. Direct commerce with Great Britain and France was reopened, save only that restrictions should be renewed against one nation in the event that the other repealed its offending legislation.

NONINTERVENTION POLICY. In 1936 the United States joined the other American republics in signing a protocol that committed each nation to a policy of nonintervention in the affairs of the other states. This achievement was considerable in view of the fact that the United States had, up to that time, consistently refused to renounce the right of categorical intervention (*see* Intervention.)

NONPARTISAN LEAGUE, NATIONAL. An agrarian political movement formed in North Dakota in 1915. It called for state-owned elevators, mills, and packing plants; state hail insurance; state rural credits; and taxation reform. Assisted by the Equity and Socialist parties, the league won a sweeping victory in the 1916 election: a ticket headed by Lynn J. Frazier captured the primaries of the Republican party and was easily elected. In 1919 the entire league program was enacted into law.

After 1916 the league spread into Minnesota, South Dakota, Montana, Wisconsin, Iowa, Nebraska, Kansas, Colorado, Oklahoma, Idaho, Washington, and Oregon. In each state the program was modified, but state ownership of marketing facilities was the principal point in each platform. In states having large industrial populations, league leaders broadened their program to include the demands of the workingman and were generally able to effect a coalition of farmer-labor forces.

The league began to wane after 1920. Accusations of disloyalty, combined with the cry of socialism, brought the league into disrepute. By 1924 it had almost disappeared; but the left-wing revolt that it had created lived on as the Farmer-Labor party, or as a faction within existing parties.

NONRECOGNITION POLICY. President Woodrow Wilson initiated the practice of refusing to recognize new governments with the regime of Victoriano Huerta in Mexico in 1913 and later the Federico Tinoco government in Costa Rica in 1917 and to that of Álvaro Obregón in 1920 in Mexico. Since then, nonrecognition has often been used to express U.S. displeasure.

NONSENSE, FORT. Popular belief has long connected earthworks at Morristown, N.J., with the second encampment of the American army at Morristown (1779–80). Gen. George Washington, to save his men from the demoralizing effects of camp life, put them to work building a fort never intended for use.

NOOTKA SOUND CONTROVERSY (1789–90). Conflicting British and Spanish claims to the Northwest Coast led to the Spanish seizure of an English expedition to Vancouver Island. Each prepared for war, but on Oct. 28, 1790, Spain conceded (*see* Oregon Controversy).

"NO PEACE BEYOND THE LINE." A phrase that had its origins in the refusal of Spain and Portugal to concede rights to others within the monopolies fixed by the line of demarcation. In the 16th century, diplomats elected to understand that European treaties lost their force in the New World. Beyond these indefinite "lines of amity" hostile acts did not technically break the peace in Europe. By the late 17th century this rule was generally abandoned.

NORFOLK (Va.). Founded in 1682, Norfolk first became a port for the planters of northeastern North Carolina, but in the 18th century, it also became the chief port for the Chesapeake region. During the French Revolution and Napoleonic Wars, it prospered through trade with the West Indies. A decline in the West Indian trade, competition from Baltimore and New York, and failure to secure railroad connections retarded its growth. After the Civil War, Norfolk became the terminus of several railway systems, making it an important exporter of coal, tobacco, and cotton. The city is heavily dependent on its naval yard and other military facilities. The population was 266,979 in 1980.

NORFOLK AND WESTERN. *See* **Railroads, Sketches of Principal Lines.**

"NORMALCY." In a speech in 1920, Sen. Warren G. Harding said, "America's present need is not heroics but healing, not nostrums but normalcy." The word "normalcy" came quickly to signify a return to a high protective tariff, "putting labor in its place," an absence of government interference in private enterprise, and a vigorous nationalistic foreign policy. The slogan was used with great effectiveness by Harding in his successful campaign for the presidency.

NORMANDY INVASION (June 6, 1944). Allied landings in France on D Day, the prelude to the defeat of Nazi Germany in World War II. Known as Operation Overlord, it involved 5,000 ships, the largest armada ever assembled.

Under command of Gen. Dwight D. Eisenhower, with Gen. Bernard L. Montgomery as ground commander, 130,000 American, British, and Canadian troops landed on beaches extending from the mouth of the Orne River near Caen to the base of the Cotentin Peninsula. Another 23,000 landed by parachute and glider. Allied aircraft during the day flew 11,000 sorties. Airborne troops began landing soon after midnight; American seaborne troops at 6:30 A.M.; and, because of local tidal conditions, British and Canadian troops at intervals over the next hour. The bad weather and heavy seas lulled German troops into a false sense of security. Reluctance of staff officers back in Germany to awaken Hitler, for approval to commit reserves delayed a major counterattack against the invasion.

On beaches near Caen, one Canadian and two British divisions made it ashore with relative ease, quickly establishing contact with a British airborne division that had captured bridges over the Orne. By nightfall the troops held beachheads from two to four miles deep.

U.S. troops went ashore at Utah Beach, north of Carentan. Airborne divisions landing behind the beach helped insure success. Another U.S. force landed on Omaha Beach, between Bayeux and Carentan. Sharp bluffs, strong defenses, lack of airborne assistance, and the presence of a powerful German division were catastrophic. But inch by inch the troops forced their way inland, so that when night came the beachhead was approximately a mile deep.

The Germans believed that a second and larger invasion would hit the Pas de Calais and for several weeks held strong forces there that might have been decisive in Normandy. German defense was further deterred by difficulty in shifting reserves, because of bombing of French railroads, disruption of traffic by Allied fighter bombers that had already driven German planes from the skies, and French partisans. By the end of the first week, all Allied beachheads were linked and sixteen divisions had landed; only thirteen German divisions opposed them. By the end of June a million Allied troops were ashore. Of a total of more than 9,000 casualties, approximately one-third were killed.

NORRIDGEWOCK FIGHT (Aug. 23, 1724). The crucial point of Dummer's War. Capt. Jeremiah Moulton, with about eighty men, attacked the stockaded Abnaki town, at the site of Madison, Maine. Between 80 and 100 Indians and a Jesuit missionary were killed.

NORRIS DAM. *See* **Hydroelectric Power.**

NORRIS FARM EXPORT ACT (McNary Act). Sponsored by Sen. George W. Norris and passed on Aug. 24, 1921. It authorized the War Finance Corporation to make advances up to $1 billion to finance agricultural exports.

NORRIS–LA GUARDIA ANTI-INJUNCTION LAW. Passed in 1932, the act forbids issuance of injunctions to sustain antiunion contracts of employment, to prevent ceasing or refusing to perform any work or remain in any relation of employment, or to restrain acts generally constituting component parts of strikes, boycotts, and picketing.

NORSEMEN IN AMERICA. The first Norse voyages to the New World, dated about 986–1020, reached large and inexactly defined areas called Helluland, Markland, and Vinland. The voyages, recorded at least 200 years later in *The Greenlanders' Saga* and *Eirik the Red's Saga,* have some archaeological confirmation. A claim inviting favorable consideration is that Norsemen explored the Canadian littoral. Third and more speculative is the theory of a late immigration, perhaps Norse or Norse-Eskimo, from Greenland into Arctic Canada about 1340.

While Norse acquaintance with North America is acknowledged, its extent is debatable and its duration uncertain. A fixed point is that there were Norsemen at L'Anse aux Meadows about 1000 according to archaeological excavations. Norsemen made many unrecorded but vaguely traceable voyages for at least 350 years thereafter and must at times have wintered away from home; but that they established a single long-lasting colony anywhere in America is not proven. (*See also* Vinland.)

NORTH AFRICAN CAMPAIGN (1942–43). On Nov. 8, 1942, Allied forces under U.S. Gen. Dwight D. Eisenhower landed in French Morocco and Algeria. Allied units tried to take Bizerte and Tunis quickly, but Italian and German troops took a firm hold over northern Tunisia and stopped them. Field Marshal Erwin Rommel's Italo-German army, defeated at El Alamein, was retreating across Libya and at the end of the year would take defensive positions at Mareth, Tunisia, to halt the pursuing British under Gen. Bernard L. Montgomery.

In February 1943 the Axis forces, in the Battle of Kasserine Pass, drove the Americans and French back about fifty miles in southern Tunisia, inflicting severe damage and panic. British Gen. Harold Alexander and U.S. Gen. George S. Patton, Jr., who were put in command, restored confidence. In March, the Allies pushed Rommel's army into the northern corner of Tunisia. The final offensive started on Apr. 22, and Bizerte and Tunis fell on May 7. Arnim surrendered, and the last organized Axis resistance in North Africa ended on May 13.

NORTH AMERICAN LAND COMPANY. Organized in Philadelphia in 1795 by Sen. Robert Morris, John Nicholson, and James Greenleaf to develop and sell 4 million acres in Pennsylvania, Virginia, North Carolina, South Carolina, Georgia, and Kentucky. Repeated attempts to sell stock failed, and in 1797 the company's remaining lands were thrown into the Pennsylvania Property Company.

NORTH ANNA, BATTLE OF (May 23–25, 1864). Failing to break Gen. Robert E. Lee's lines at Spotsylvania, Va., Gen. Ulysses S. Grant moved toward Hanover Courthouse. Lee fortified his army behind the North Anna River at Hanover Junction. There was sharp fighting, but Grant found Lee's position too strong and on May 26 moved by his left toward Hanovertown.

NORTH ATLANTIC TREATY ORGANIZATION (NATO). Founded on Apr. 4, 1949, by Belgium, Canada, Denmark, France, Iceland, Italy, Luxembourg, Netherlands, Norway, Portugal, the United Kingdom, and the United States; Greece, Turkey, Spain, and West Germany joined later. At the close of World War II the United States, the

United Kingdom, France, and the other Western Allies found themselves increasingly in contention with the Soviet Union and its Communists allies. A single defense system was deemed necessary, and a plan was put forward and promptly adopted. The NATO structure consists of a council and a military committee of three commands (Allied Command Europe, Allied Command Atlantic, Allied Command Channel) and the Canadian-U.S. Regional Planning Group.

Beginning in 1965, there was a growing feeling of East-West détente, notably on the bilateral level between individual NATO members and Soviet bloc nations. In spite of temporary setbacks, such as the Soviet invasion of Czechoslovakia (1968), NATO continued the process of adapting its defense machinery, notably in the fields of nuclear planning and policymaking and crisis management. The decision of the French government to withdraw its forces from the integrated NATO commands (1967) necessitated the adaptation of existing structures and their relocation from Paris to Brussels.

Beginning in the late 1960's some people felt that NATO was no longer as necessary as it had been at its inception, because of the apparent decline in the Soviet Union's aggressive and belligerent attitude, the Chinese-Soviet impasse, and the rising cost of weaponry and occupying forces. Furthermore, money and trade differences between NATO members presented problems that caused a reluctance on the part of some members to incur the increasing expense of membership. This attitude was strengthened by a continued discussion and hope of effective arms control.

In the late 1970's and early 1980's, Soviet involvement in Africa, Afghanistan, and Poland led to increased military spending of NATO countries. Amidst growing antinuclear movement, a 1982 NATO summit meeting emphasized the peaceful aims of the alliance and the need for a "genuine détente," while justifying the rearmament programs as necessary defensive measures.

NORTH CAROLINA. The first English colony in America was planted on Roanoke Island in 1585. The settlers soon returned to England, and the second attempt at settlement, in 1587, became known as the Lost Colony. In 1629 Charles I granted Carolana, as it was first called, to Sir Robert Heath, who failed to plant a colony. About the middle of the 17th century, settlers from Virginia began to locate along the Albemarle Sound. In 1663, Charles II granted Carolina to eight lords proprietors, and in 1664 they created two counties—Albemarle and Clarendon (Cape Fear region)—in what is now North Carolina. Efforts to settle Clarendon were soon abandoned, and it was half a century before the Cape Fear country was settled. Until 1711, North Carolina, as the northern portion of Carolina came to be called, was ruled by a deputy governor from Charles Town, although it had its own legislature. In 1712 an independent governor was appointed for North Carolina, and in 1729 it became a royal colony.

North Carolina grew slowly during the proprietary period because of its dangerous coast and other geographical handicaps. Only five towns were founded: Bath (1706), New Bern (1710), Edenton (1712), Beaufort (1715), and Brunswick (1725). From 1729 to 1775, government improved, population increased and spread, agriculture and industry developed, many churches and a few schools were established, and a new and more permanent capital (Edenton) was designated. The lower Cape Fear was settled soon after 1713, and the upper Cape Fear after 1740, largely by Scottish Highlanders. During the next thirty years thousands of Scotch-Irish and Germans moved from Pennsylvania into the Piedmont, and by 1775, settlers had reached the mountains.

North Carolina patriots crushed the Tories at Moores Creek Bridge, Feb. 27, 1776, ending British plans to occupy the South early in the war; and at Halifax, Apr. 12, 1776, they authorized their delegates in the Continental Congress to vote for independence—the first colony to take such action. The Battle at Guilford Courthouse was the most important revolutionary battle in the state.

The state ceded its western lands in 1789, and Tennessee was created therefrom. North Carolina ratified the federal Constitution in 1789, being the penultimate state to accept that document. The University of North Carolina, the first state university in the Union, opened its doors in 1795.

Prior to 1840, North Carolina was one of the most backward states. Unscientific farming, soil exhaustion, lack of manufactures and adequate transportation facilities, commercial dependence on Virginia and South Carolina, emigration, and a planter-controlled government that was unwilling to spend money for internal improvements and education were all contributing factors. The state constitution was revised in 1835, and a more democratic government was created. The Whigs, championing internal improvements, rose to power, and the state enjoyed two decades of progress.

Although North Carolinians held over 300,000 slaves in 1860, Union sentiment was strong, and it was not until May 20, 1861, that the state seceded. It contributed 125,000 men to the southern cause and sustained a fourth of the Confederate losses. Battles were fought at Plymouth, New Bern, Fort Fisher, Bentonville, and elsewhere; and "the last surrender of the Civil War" occurred near Durham. North Carolina was readmitted to the Union in 1868, after it ratified the Fourteenth Amendment and drafted a new state constitution.

Farm tenancy replaced the old plantation economy and tended to increase to such an extent that by the 1930's it became one of the state's greatest social and economic problems. Tobacco and furniture manufacturing became major industries; the textile industry expanded; and railroad construction was revived. As late as 1900, however, North Carolina was still one of the most backward states.

Since 1900, when North Carolina's population was 1,893,-810, the state has become one of the leading agricultural states of the nation, ranking first in tobacco production and high in many other crops as well as in per acre yields. By 1980 the population had increased to 5,874,429.

School desegregation was accomplished in the 1960's with a minimum of difficulty. Increased urbanization; improved means of communication, particularly a network of interstate highways; a number of large trucking firms; the development of deep-water ports at Wilmington and Morehead City; and the growth of industry have altered the rural outlook of the state. The development of Research Triangle Park as a center of industrial and scientific research since 1955 has been a prime factor. Located near Duke University at Durham, North Carolina State University at Raleigh, and the University of North Carolina at Chapel Hill, its facilities have attracted thousands of highly skilled specialists.

NORTH CAROLINA RAILROAD. Built, 1848–56, by the state from Goldsboro to Charlotte (232 miles). By connecting with several roads in eastern North Carolina, it gave the state its first east-west rail connection. In 1895 it became part of the Southern Railway Company system.

NORTH DAKOTA. Formed by a division of Dakota Territory in 1889, the state, 70,665 square miles, is largely a cool, semiarid grassland. The northern region was settled in two booms, the first in 1878–86 and the second in 1898–1915. Four developments were responsible for settlement: a surge of immigration, the development of a gradual-roller milling process for hard spring wheat, the growth of flour milling in Minneapolis, and the building of railroads that tied North Dakota to the Minneapolis market. By 1900, North Dakota had a population of 319,146 and ranked with Minnesota and Kansas as a leading wheat state. The peak of homesteading came in 1906 when original entries were filed on 2,736,460 acres. In 1910, with settlement nearing completion, 71 percent of the population of 577,056 was of foreign stock.

For years North Dakota was a colonial hinterland for the Twin Cities—Minneapolis and St. Paul. Revolting against the exploitation inherent in colonial status, angry farmers joined the Populists in the 1890's. The socialistic Nonpartisan League was the dominant power in state government from 1917 to 1921. In 1919 the legislature established a state-owned bank and a state-owned terminal elevator and flour mill.

In the 1920's and 1930's the agrarian revolt continued. The North Dakota Farmers' Union was organized in 1927. The Farmers' Union secured the passage of an anticorporation farming law in 1932 and stimulated the growth of cooperative grain elevators and oil companies. Drillers discovered oil at Tioga in 1951, the U.S. Corps of Engineers completed Garrison Dam in 1953, and the U.S. Air Force built bases at Grand Forks and Minot in 1956. After reaching a peak in 1930, the population declined to 652,695 in 1980. Although the growing size of farms reduced the rural population, North Dakota has remained essentially rural and farm production the backbone of its economy.

NORTHEAST BOUNDARY. The Definitive Treaty of Peace of 1783 designated the northeastern boundary of the United States, between Maine and New Brunswick, as the St. Croix River to its source, thence a line due north to the highlands dividing the rivers tributary to the St. Lawrence River from those tributaries to the Atlantic, thence along the highlands to the most northwestern head of the Connecticut, down the latter to the forty-fifth parallel and along the parallel to the St. Lawrence (*see* Red Line Map). The controversy over that designation lasted for almost sixty years. In 1841, Secretary of State Daniel Webster and Alexander Baring, Lord Ashburton, the British special minister, negotiated at Washington and agreed to accept as the boundary the upper St. John to the St. Francis, thence a direct southwest line to a point near the southwest branch of the St. John, thence a line via the crest of the hills to the northwest branch (Hall Stream) of the Connecticut River, and west of the Connecticut on the old survey line of the forty-fifth parallel to the St. Lawrence. The Webster-Ashburton Treaty was signed on Aug. 9, 1842.

NORTHERN PACIFIC RAILROAD. *See* **Railroads, Sketches of Principal Lines: Burlington Northern.**

***NORTHERN SECURITIES COMPANY V. UNITED STATES*, 193 U.S. 197 (1904).** A decision of the Supreme Court that upheld the government's contention that the Northern Securities Company, a railroad holding company, had been used as an illegal device for restraining interstate trade and was in violation of the Sherman Antitrust Act. The case began as a contest between John Pierpont Morgan, James J. Hill, and their associates, and Edward H. Harriman and affiliated financial interests for control of the Northern Pacific, Great Northern, Union Pacific, and Chicago, Burlington and Quincy railroads. Out of this contest emerged the Northern Securities Company, which took over all the contestants' stock interests in the Great Northern, Northern Pacific, and Burlington lines—and which the government claimed to be illegal.

NORTHFIELD BANK ROBBERY (Sept. 7, 1876). Eight men, including Frank and Jesse James and the three Younger brothers, rode into Northfield, Minn., to hold up the First National Bank. They killed the teller and engaged in a wild gun battle with citizens, during which two bandits and a bystander were killed. On Sept. 21, posses surrounded four of the gang near Madelia—the James brothers having escaped. The Younger brothers, badly wounded, surrendered.

NORTH SEA MINE BARRAGE. A World War I minefield 230 miles long and from 15 to 35 miles wide, laid by the United States and Great Britain in 1918 between the Orkney Islands and Norway to blockade German submarines. Altogether 70,263 mines were laid, at a cost of $80 million.

NORTHWEST ANGLE. A projection of land extending north of the forty-ninth parallel at the Lake of the Woods on the northern boundary of Minnesota. This area of about 130 square miles, projecting from Manitoba and separated from the rest of Minnesota by a bay of the Lake of the Woods, is the northernmost territory in the United States proper.

NORTHWEST BOUNDARY CONTROVERSY. The Definitive Treaty of Peace of 1783 between the United States and Great Britain provided that the boundary between the United States and British North America should proceed by various streams from the western head of Lake Superior to "the most Northwestern point" of the Lake of the Woods in Minnesota, and thence due west to the Mississippi. The negotiators were using a map drawn in 1755 that did not accurately depict the course of the river. Thus, a serious boundary gap was left. The Convention of 1818 provided that the boundary should proceed from the northwesternmost corner of the Lake of the Woods to the forty-ninth parallel and along that parallel to the Rocky Mountains. Beyond the mountains the western territory and rivers claimed by either party were to be free and open for a term of ten years (extended indefinitely in 1826). The northwest boundary controversy terminated in the Oregon Treaty of 1846 by extending the line of the forty-ninth parallel through to the Pacific Ocean.

NORTH WEST COMPANY. This major fur-trading firm, originating during the Revolution and reorganized in 1783–84, established its posts over much of Canada and the northern United States. Its main line of communication was the canoe route from Montreal to its chief inland depot—Grand Portage before 1804 and Fort William thereafter. Beyond Lake Superior the route to the Pacific was the international boundary waters. Excessive competition with the Hudson's Bay Company led to warfare. In 1821 the two companies merged as the Hudson's Bay Company.

NORTHWEST CONSPIRACY (1863–64). An unrealized Confederate effort to overthrow the governments of Ohio, Indiana, Illinois, and Missouri by using the Sons of Liberty to liberate Confederate prisoners of war in those states.

NORTHWEST ORDINANCES. *See* **Northwest Territory; Ordinances of 1784, 1785, and 1787.**

NORTHWEST PASSAGE. From 1497 to 1800, when it was believed that the riches of the Orient could be reached via a ship route across the northern extremities of North America, a northwest passage was the goal of many explorers. In the 19th century, the search for a water route to the Orient took a more practical bent, a filling-in of geographical and scientific data. Roald Amundsen (1903–06), a Norwegian, was the first to sail from the Atlantic to the Pacific through the Arctic. Of five possible routes through the Canadian Arctic archipelago, only two are practical and only one is deep enough for large ships. Atomic submarines have navigated an under-the-ice route across the North Pole.

NORTHWEST TERRITORY. Comprising the modern states of Ohio, Illinois, Michigan, Indiana, and Wisconsin, it was officially the "Territory Northwest of the River Ohio," as established by Congress on July 13, 1787. Public lands were to be surveyed in townships, each six miles square and divided into thirty-six sections of 640 acres, which would be sold to settlers. The ordinance set aside section sixteen in each township for the support of education. The first legal American settlement was made at Marietta (present-day Ohio), on Apr. 7, 1788. In 1800 the area west of a line north from the mouth of the Kentucky River was set off as Indiana Territory. The diminished Northwest Territory was further decreased in 1803, when Michigan was annexed to Indiana. The Northwest Territory gave place to the state of Ohio on Mar. 1, 1803.

NORUMBEGA. Indian name for the New World north of Florida, appearing on 16th- and 17th-century maps. Samuel de Champlain in 1604 used it for the Penobscot River.

NORWEGIAN CHURCHES. Norwegian-American churches in the 19th century included the Eielsen Synod (1846) and the Norwegian Synod (1853). By 1870, were formed two new bodies, the Norwegian Augustana Synod and the Norwegian-Danish Conference. Hauge's Synod was formed in 1876. The predestination controversy within the Missouri-influenced Norwegian Synod led to the formation in the 1880's of the Anti-Missourian Brotherhood, which assumed leadership in a union movement that created the United Church (1890). Polity and property disputes in the new body produced the Lutheran Free Church (1897). A second offshoot, the Lutheran Brethren, formed in 1900. Negotiations, begun in 1905, brought 98 percent of the Norwegian Lutherans into the Norwegian Lutheran Church of America (1917). Most Norwegian Lutherans belong to one of the three main branches of the Lutheran Church.

NORWEGIAN IMMIGRATION. *See* **Immigration.**

"NOT WORTH A CONTINENTAL." During the revolutionary war the Continental Congress authorized the issuance of bills of credit to the amount of $241,552,780. They depreciated and became a symbol of worthlessness, whence the expression "not worth a continental."

NOVA CAESAREA. *See* **New Caesarea.**

"NO-WIN POLICY." A derogatory term first used in 1950–51 by militant groups who opposed President Harry S. Truman's strategy of limited war in Korea. The term was again used during the Vietnam War by those who opposed the limited military actions of presidents Lyndon B. Johnson and Richard Nixon.

NUCLEAR ENERGY. *See* **Atomic Power Reactors.**

NUCLEAR NONPROLIFERATION TREATY (Mar. 13, 1969). The United States, the Soviet Union, and sixty other nations signed an agreement at the 18-Nation Disarmament Conference in Geneva on July 1, 1968, banning the spread of nuclear weapons. In the treaty the states which had nuclear capabilities pledged not to transfer them to states not processing nuclear weapons and states not processing nuclear weapons pledged not to receive such devices. Ratification of the treaty by Congress was delayed due to the Soviet invasion of Czechoslovakia in August 1968. On Nov. 24, 1969 it was signed by U.S. President Richard Nixon and Soviet President Nikolai V. Podgorny.

NUCLEAR TEST BAN TREATY (Aug. 5, 1963). The United States, Great Britain, and the Soviet Union signed an agreement in Moscow, open for signature to all other nations, calling for the end of nuclear tests in the atmosphere, in space, and underwater. The problem of underground tests was left unmentioned. More than 100 other nations later acceded to the treaty.

NUECES RIVER. Although Texas had never extended west of the Nueces as a Spanish or a Mexican province, the Texas Republic claimed the Rio Grande as its boundary. After annexation, the claim was supported when President James K. Polk sent troops beyond the Nueces and then asked Congress to declare war against Mexico for attacking them because they were on American soil. The Rio Grande became the boundary of Texas by the Treaty of Guadalupe Hidalgo in 1848.

NULLIFICATION. The act by which a state suspends, within its territorial jurisdiction, a federal law. The doctrine of nullification evolved from the theory that the Union represents a compact between sovereign states and that the states are not bound by the acts of the Union when it goes beyond its strict constitutional limits.

The most notable example of nullification occurred when Congress enacted a permanent tariff act in 1832. A South Carolina state convention adopted the Ordinance of Nullification declaring the tariff null and void. President Andrew Jackson denounced nullification as rebellion and treason and asked for passage of a "force act" to enable him to use the army and navy in enforcing the law. However, he also called for measures for reducing the tariff. Both the Force Act and the Compromise Tariff were passed by Congress, but the compromise allowed South Carolina to rescind the Ordinance of Nullification, thereby averting a constitutional crisis. The Supreme Court has denied the power of a state to nullify federal law or policy.

NUMBER 4. Now Charlestown, N.H., Number 4, settled in 1740, was then the most northerly English post in the Connecticut Valley. Attacked frequently by the French and Indians, its fort was of great military importance in protecting Massachusetts.

NUREMBERG TRIALS (1945–49). After World War II, many of the leading figures in German government, military, and economic circles were put on trial by the Allies in Nuremberg, Germany, for crimes against humanity. The idea of prosecution for actions that were inhuman and aggressive was a new one in international affairs. In the first and most important of the thirteen trials, Hermann Goering, who had been Adolf Hitler's first assistant, and twelve others were condemned to death, three were acquitted, and six received jail sentences.

NURSING. American nursing as a profession grew along with the sanitary reforms and scientific progress made by medicine in general in the 19th century. In 1873 four hospitals were operating schools of nursing. By 1893 there were 225 hospital nursing schools, and by 1900, at least 432. The students, almost entirely female, learned from older nurses, matrons, or superintendents, and physicians who volunteered to give lectures or demonstrations. In 1907, Columbia University appointed Mary Adelaide Nutting as the first full-time American professor of nursing.

By 1914 forty-one states had adopted nurse practice acts, thereby establishing state boards of nurse examiners. The graduates of schools approved by these boards were authorized to use the title "Registered Nurse" (RN). Between 1929 and 1937, nursing schools reduced their enrollment, made admission qualifications more rigid, eliminated monthly stipends for hospital services, and discharged students with poor grades. By 1957, 81.9 percent of American nursing schools were under hospital or noncollegiate control. By 1962, 13.8 percent of 31,000 nurse graduates had received baccalaureate degrees—a percentage that continues to rise. In the early 1980's there were over 500 programs in nursing education, including licensed vocational nurses' (LVN) programs.

NUTRITION AND VITAMINS. The original thrust of American interest in nutrition is to be found in W. O. Atwater's compilation of tables published by the Department of Agriculture in 1896. Breaking foods down into percentages of protein, carbohydrates, and fats and indicating caloric values for each food, these tables became basic to the scientific and economic dietetics of the period. Other researchers studied the role of proteins, "essential" amino acids, and unsaturated fatty acids. American scientists also played a prominent role in vitamin research.

The pharmaceutical and chemical industries learned to crystallize and synthesize vitamins: B_6 in 1939, pantothenic acid in 1940, biotin in 1943, and vitamin B_{12} in 1948. A U.S. Census estimate placed the value of the domestic sale of vitamins at $916 million in 1980.

The second consequence of the technological potential in the production of vitamins is the restoration, enrichment, fortification, or supplementation of foods by the addition of vitamins and other dietary essentials. Thirty states have laws requiring enrichment of milk, and in 1974 the National Research Council's Food and Nutrition Board recommended that all foods made of wheat, corn, or rice be enriched with ten named essential nutrients.

Undernutrition and malnutrition persist in American life, and efforts to deal with the problem have existed since the administration of Franklin D. Roosevelt. The school lunch program came into its own under the National School Lunch Act of 1946. A milk program (1954), a school breakfast program (1966), and assistance to day-care centers (1968) were added; and in 1975 it was estimated that 9 million children were involved in the program. Child nutrition programs were severely reduced in 1981.

The food-stamp program (1939) did not become available to every county and city until 1964 but developed into a primary weapon for combating undernutrition and malnutrition. In 1981, when the Reagan Administration began cutting back on the program, a total of 23 million people were covered.

NYE MUNITIONS INVESTIGATIONS (1934–36). A Senate inquiry into the manufacture of arms headed by Sen. Gerald P. Nye. The Senate Munitions Investigating Committee concluded that heavy profits were made by munitions manufacturers during World War I and sought to show, without conclusive evidence, that U.S. entry into the war had been due to the pressure of that industry. Calling the munitions industry "merchants of death," the activities of the committee strengthened isolationist sentiment in the nation and helped create the atmosphere for the neutrality legislation of 1935, 1936, and 1937 (*see* Neutrality Acts of 1935, 1936, and 1937).

OAKLAND (Calif.). The sixth largest city in California, with a population of 339,288 in 1980. It is part of the sixth largest U.S. metropolitan area, for it is associated with San Francisco to make up an area with 3,226,867 people. Located on the east shore of San Francisco Bay, it is linked with San Francisco by the Bay Bridge and by the Bay Area Rapid Transit system. Oakland was established during the Gold Rush of 1849, when it became a supply point for miners working in the mountains east of the town. After the 1906 earthquake, many former residents of San Francisco moved there. Today, Oakland engages in manufacturing, specializing in machinery and shipbuilding, and has docks and supply stations used by the army and navy.

OATHS. *See* **Test Laws**

OATMAN GIRLS. In 1851, Olive Oatman, aged fifteen, and Mary Ann Oatman, aged seven, were taken as captives by western Yavapai in southwestern Arizona. In 1852 the Yavapai traded the girls to the Mohave. Mary Ann died, but Olive lived with the Mohave for four years. In 1856 the Mohave released her.

OATS. First planted in North America about 1600, oats spread throughout the English colonies. Oats can be grown from Alaska to Texas. Long the outstanding feed for horses, oat production declined sharply with the disappearance of horses from American streets and farms. Peak production occurred in 1917 with over 1.5 billion bushels. Production in 1980 was 457,593 million bushels, with Arkansas, Minnesota, Wisconsin, and Oregon the leading producers.

OBERLIN MOVEMENT. An evangelical antislavery movement, it began in 1834 at Lane Theological Seminary in Cincinnati. When the trustees attempted to end the agitation, most of the students transferred to Oberlin College, Ohio. These evangelists converted much of Ohio and the West to abolition.

OBERLIN-WELLINGTON RESCUE CASE. In 1858 a rescue party from Oberlin, Ohio, freed a fugitive slave in the custody of a federal officer, at the village of Wellington. The rescuers were arrested under the Fugitive Slave Act of 1850. From jail they published a newspaper and addressed mass meetings of sympathizers. They were shortly freed.

OBLONG, THE. A narrow strip along the eastern borders of Dutchess, Putnam, and Westchester counties traded to New York by Connecticut in 1731 for a rectangular strip along Long Island Sound. Bickering continued until 1860, when a survey was made that satisfied both states.

OBSERVATORIES, ASTRONOMICAL. During the first fifty years of the new republic, about twenty-five notable observatories were equipped with equatorial refracting telescopes for viewing celestial bodies and with meridian instruments for measuring their positions. The U.S. Naval Observatory, Washington, D.C., established by Congress in 1842, served as the national observatory.

Between the Civil War and World War II observatories proliferated across the United States. They were built on almost every college campus and in the backyards of countless amateur astronomers. As air pollution and the proliferation of electric lights impeded observations in urban areas, observatories were built in more remote areas.

Five times Alvan Clark and Sons of Cambridgeport, Mass., produced refractors larger than any previous ones: 18.5 inches (1863), Dearborn Observatory in Chicago; 26 inches (1872), U.S. Naval Observatory; 30 inches (1883), Pulkovo Observatory, near Leningrad, Russia; 36 inches (1887), Lick Observatory, near San Jose, Calif.; and 40 inches (1897), Yerkes Observatory, at Williams Bay, Wis. (still the largest refractor in use in the early 1980's). A similar series of improvements occurred in the early 20th century, this time with reflectors: 60 inches (1908), Mount Wilson, Calif.; 100 inches (1918), Mount Wilson; and 200 inches (1948), Mount Palomar, Calif.

In the years after World War II, the number of working astronomers vastly increased, and their accomplishments developed dramatically. The range of radiation that astronomers were able to study increased severalfold: radio telescopes "see" the radio waves that reach the earth; rockets carry infrared and ultraviolet detectors above the obscuring atmosphere. Unmanned space missions led to a better understanding of other planets. Contributions were also made by orbiting solar observatories and Skylab.

OCALA PLATFORM. Adopted at a meeting of farmers' organizations at Ocala, Fla., December 1890. It demanded abolition of national banks, a graduated income tax, free and unlimited coinage of silver, establishment of subtreasuries where farmers could borrow money at less than 2 percent interest, and popular election of U.S. senators.

OCCUPATIONS, CHANGES IN. The first reliable estimates of occupation (1820) show farm workers constituting over 70 percent of the population. Each succeeding census has shown a smaller proportion; by 1980, farm workers represented only 3 percent, or fewer than 3 million Americans.

Throughout the 19th century, the developing industrial

sector steadily replaced the farm as the work site. As late as 1900, only about 4 percent of American workers were in professional occupations and about 3 percent were in clerical pursuits; but by 1978 one out of every three employed persons was either a professional or clerical worker.

Through most of the pre–Civil War period, the majority of workers were self-employed. By the early 1980's the vast majority of the labor force worked for wages or salaries. In 1865, about 15 percent of all workers were women. This proportion increased slowly to 20 percent after World War I. Since then, the rate has accelerated, and by 1978, 41 percent of all American workers were women.

OCEANOGRAPHIC SURVEY. The U.S. Coast Survey was founded in 1807 to conduct surveys of coastal waters, but after 1844 it also conducted extensive explorations of ocean tides, currents, and bottom deposits, and participated in research in deep-sea biology. The navy established the Depot of Charts and Instruments in 1830. The depot, in 1854, was separated into the Hydrographic Office and the Naval Observatory, which were given individual status in 1866.

The first oceanographic survey made by the U. S. Navy was of fishing banks off the coast of Massachusetts in 1837. In 1842, Matthew Fontaine Maury laid the foundation for systematic ocean surveying by initiating an extensive uniform system for collecting oceanographic, meteorological, and navigational data. The production of trade-wind charts, thermal charts, whale charts, and storm and rain charts was commenced shortly afterward. Maury himself wrote *The Physical Geography of the Sea* (1855), the basis of modern oceanography.

In 1922 the introduction of a practical sonic depth-finder and the application of photogrammetry to aerial photography marked the beginning of a new era in ocean surveying. After World War II, the U.S.S. *San Pablo* and the U.S.S. *Rehoboth* were employed on oceanographic-acoustic surveying. The National Oceanographic Data Center was established within the Hydrographic Office in 1960. The center was transferred to the National Oceanic and Atmospheric Administration when the latter was established in 1970, as was the National Oceanographic Instrumentation Center, previously a component of the U.S. Naval Oceanographic Office. The Hydrographic Office was redesignated the U.S. Naval Oceanographic Office in July 1962.

OCEANOGRAPHY. Alexander Dallas Bache became superintendent of the Coast Survey in 1843, and under his leadership, it was in the forefront of the exploration of the ocean. Rivaling the survey's efforts were the navy's efforts under Matthew Fontaine Maury, head of the Depot of Charts and Instruments. The depot's investigations reached farther out into the Atlantic because the survey was limited by law until 1959 to U.S. coastal waters.

The exploration of the sea bottom benefited greatly from the invention of a sounder that brought substantial samples back to the surface. Jacob W. Bailey of the U.S. Military Academy, became one of the leading students of marine sediments in the world. In 1847, Louis Agassiz made several Coast Survey cruises along the American coast exploring sea life. By the late 1860's the survey had developed a technique of deep-sea dredging for animals and had mapped the sediments of the east coast. The U.S. Fish Commission established seaside laboratories at Woods Hole, Mass., in 1885. Agassiz's son, Alexander, explored widely in Atlantic and Pacific waters aboard Fish Commission and Coast Survey vessels.

By 1913, when the International Ice Patrol was founded in response to the *Titanic* disaster of 1912, American oceanography—the world's leader until the 1870's—was practically moribund. Leadership in marine science had passed to the British and the Scandinavians.

The *Titanic* sinking and the development of submarines during World War I jointly stimulated research into underwater sound. The result was the greatest American technical advance since the sediment-retrieving sounder: the sonic depthfinder, perfected in the early 1920's. The rebuilding of American marine research began at the same time, led by Alexander Agassiz's students, W. S. Ritter and Charles A. Kofoid, who developed the Scripps Institution in San Diego, and Henry B. Bigelow, who led a long series of cruises to the Gulf of Maine. In 1927 the Rockefeller Foundation began a major effort in oceanography. The result was the founding of the Woods Hole Oceanographic Institution in 1930 and the strengthening of ongoing programs, principally at the University of Washington and the Scripps Institution of Oceanography of the University of California.

World War II brought a considerable expansion of oceanography to meet the demands of submarine and antisubmarine warfare. After 1945 Texas A. & M., Miami, Rhode Island, Columbia, New York, Oregon State, and Johns Hopkins universities began substantial programs of teaching and research. A federal sea grant program, established in 1966, expanded oceanography still further.

OFFICE OF ECONOMIC OPPORTUNITY (OEO). The coordinating agency for the War on Poverty begun by President Lyndon B. Johnson, created by the Economic Opportunity Act of 1964. The act called for a Job Corps; Neighborhood Youth Corps; work training and work study programs; community action programs (dubbed CAP), including Head Start; adult education; loans for the rural poor and small business; work experience programs; and Volunteers in Service to America (VISTA).

From its inception, the OEO came under major congressional attack, and many of the original OEO programs were transferred from OEO to other agencies and departments. Another recurring controversy in OEO concerned the amount of state participation in OEO programs. In the original act, governors were given a veto over proposed work training programs in their states, but in 1965 this provision was modified to allow the OEO director to override a governor's veto. President Richard M. Nixon's 1974 budget contained no funds for OEO, effectively terminating the agency on June 30, 1973. After surviving an additional year on a continuing appropriation, OEO was finally terminated on

Jan. 4, 1975, but a number of its programs were continued through fiscal 1977, and then most of them were transferred to other agencies.

OFFICE OF EMERGENCY PREPAREDNESS. A federal agency established in 1968 as the successor to the Office of Emergency Planning (1962), which itself was the successor to the Office of Civil and Defense Mobilization (1958). This office coordinates planning and control functions on the civil side of war and disaster mobilization, such as the production and stockpiling of critical materials, the maintenance of communications, the relief of stricken areas, and the continuation of government itself.

OFFICE OF MANAGEMENT AND BUDGET (OMB). Established by President Richard M. Nixon in 1971, it superseded the Bureau of the Budget. The OMB works with the Department of the Treasury and the Council of Economic Advisors in formulating government fiscal policy and in coordinating government programs and spending with the economy in general. Once the programs and appropriations of all agencies are evaluated, the OMB prepares the annual budget that the president submits to Congress each January. The director of OMB has cabinet-level status.

OFFICE OF PRICE ADMINISTRATION (OPA). A World War II agency created to set ceiling prices on most commodities and handle rationing of staples.

OFFICE OF SCIENTIFIC RESEARCH AND DEVELOPMENT (OSRD). A civilian agency created by President Franklin D. Roosevelt in 1941 in order to coordinate and facilitate weapons and medical research as part of the national mobilization during World War II. Vannevar Bush, the president of the Carnegie Institution of Washington, D.C., became the director.

OSRD was responsible for the advanced development of radar and the introduction of proximity fuses, the development of mass-production methods for penicillin, the development of DDT, the DUKW, an amphibious vehicle, and initial work on the atomic bomb. It demonstrated the central importance of science and technology to national defense and propelled science into a permanent alliance with the federal government. After 1947, the task of coordinating and supporting scientific research was taken over by other agencies.

OFFICE OF STRATEGIC SERVICES (OSS). A World War II agency charged with centralizing the collection and analysis of strategic information and the planning and performance of special operations, particularly in the realms of espionage and sabotage. Col. William J. ("Wild Bill") Donovan was named director.

The organization of the OSS constantly changed as it grew to an eventual strength of 12,000 personnel drawn from all walks of life, including the military. The office consisted of a headquarters and subordinate offices, and a series of field units in the United States and overseas. The secret intelligence branch dealt with sabotage, spying, demolitions, secret radio communications, and paramilitary functions. The morale operations branch handled propaganda functions. The research and analysis office gathered extensive information on all aspects of the areas in which U.S. forces operated.

The end of the war brought the demise of the OSS, but it was the experience gained by the OSS that laid the foundation for the Central Intelligence Agency, established in 1947.

OFFICERS' RESERVE CORPS. Established in 1916, its primary function has been to provide school-trained officers, educated in leadership and military tactics. The members are assigned to units of the Organized Reserve Corps and to inactive regiments of the regular army. Training includes active duty usually one weekend a month and inactive training consisting of evening and correspondence classes.

The Reserve Officers' Training Corps (ROTC) has been the major means of filling the corps, but in the 1960's and 1970's student opposition to war caused a drop in ROTC enrollment and even the removal of corps units from some colleges. In 1933, the corps consisted of 133,485 officers. By 1970 these figures had dropped to 30,432 army officers and 12,333 air force officers.

OGALLALA (Nebr.). Established on the South Platte River in 1869 as the terminus for one of the important Texas cattle trails (*see* Cattle Drives), it was a station on the new Union Pacific Railroad and became a cow town with a lively reputation. The population in 1980 was 5,638.

OGDEN PURCHASE. In 1826 the Ogden Company purchased from the Iroquois, mainly Seneca, the lands in New York State comprising the reservations of Caneadea, Caughnawaga, Big Tree, Squawkie Hill, Gardeau, and portions of Buffalo Creek, Tonawanda, and Cattaraugus, for the sum of $48,260. In 1838 a majority of the chiefs were prevailed upon to sell their remaining New York reservations to the company for $202,000. Strong opposition to the sale resulted in the Indians retaining their Cattaraugus and Allegheny lands.

OGDENSBURG (N.Y.). An industrial city and port on the St. Lawrence River. In 1749, Father Francois Picquet founded the fortified Indian mission of La Présentation on the site. The British garrisoned the post in 1760, renaming it Fort William Augustus. In 1776 the fort was repaired and remained under British control as Fort Oswegatchie. Permanent settlement was begun under the proprietorship of Col. Samuel Ogden in 1792. In 1813 the British captured the town. Ogdensburg was incorporated as a town in 1818 and chartered as a city in 1868. The city developed into an important port of entry and railroad center with extensive trade in lumber and grain. Its population in 1980 was 12,375.

OGDEN'S HOLE. A rendezvous for fur trappers near the northeast shore of the Great Salt Lake in Utah. It was named after Peter Skene Ogden, a Hudson's Bay Company trapper, as was the present city of Ogden, which stands on the site.

***OGDEN* V. *SAUNDERS*,** 12 Wheaton 213 (1827). A suit in which was upheld the constitutionality of many state bankruptcy laws. It was brought before the U.S. Supreme Court by David Bayard Ogden, who sought a discharge in bankruptcy under New York legislation enacted in 1801. The Court (four to three) upheld the validity of the legislation.

OHIO. The earliest known inhabitants of Ohio were the prehistoric Mound Builders. The Indians inhabiting Ohio in the historic era were their descendants.

La Salle, believed to have been the first white explorer (1669), claimed the whole region for France. By the beginning of the 18th century, both French and British fur traders were moving in and out of the area. The British contested the French claims and established (1747) the Ohio Company to extend Virginia's dominion into Ohio. They built a fort and trading post in 1748 at Pickawillany in the heart of the French trading area. A French expedition to destroy it and other British outposts met with some success, but at the end of the French and Indian War in 1763 the British triumphed. The French gave up all claim to what later became known as the Old Northwest. In 1774, Britain made all of the Ohio country a part of Canada, which became one of the grievances that led to the American Revolution. The Treaty of Paris (1783) ceded the Old Northwest, including Ohio, to the United States. The Ordinance of 1787 created the Northwest Territory, gave full citizenship rights to settlers there, and guaranteed them eventual self-government. Land companies were formed and settlement began. The first permanent white settlement was established at Marietta in 1788. Losantiville (Cincinnati) was founded later the same year. The Ohio Company of Associates, formed in 1786, was the most important of the land companies. The Connecticut Land Company was formed to settle the Western Reserve, and in 1796, Moses Cleaveland, one of its directors, established the first settlement (Cleveland) in the reserve.

With the support of the British, Ohio Indians kept up a relentless guerrilla war. In 1794 a decisive battle was won by the American troops under Gen. Anthony Wayne at Fallen Timbers. Ohio was more or less pacified. In 1800 the western part of the Northwest Territory became the Indiana Territory, and in 1803, Ohio was admitted as the seventeenth state. Chillicothe was the first state capital (the capital was moved permanently to Columbus in 1816).

In the War of 1812 the British invaded northern Ohio but were repulsed, particularly at Fort Meigs (near Toledo). Tecumseh was killed in the Battle of the Thames (1813). His death marked the end of Indian threats in Ohio. The Treaty of Ghent (1814) ended British hopes in the Ohio country.

Ohio entered into its greatest period of growth. Settlements prospered from the rich farmlands. For the first time immigrants began arriving in Ohio directly from Europe. The population of the state, which had reached 581,434 by 1820, almost doubled by 1830. During the 1830's a great transportation building program began. Canals connected the natural waterways. A statewide road system was developed, and the National Road was opened in 1833. The first railroads were built in Ohio in the 1830's, and by midcentury most major cities were connected by rail. The first half of the century had seen Ohio take its place as a major agricultural producer; the second half saw its rise as a commercial and manufacturing center. Cleveland, Youngstown, and Canton became centers of the iron and steel and heavy machinery industries. John D. Rockefeller started the Standard Oil Company at Cleveland. By 1870, Akron was the national center for the rubber industry. Toledo was a glassmaking center, and Cincinnati was one of the great meat-packing centers in the nation.

Between 1869 and 1923 seven native sons of Ohio served as president: Ulysses S. Grant, Rutherford B. Hayes, James A. Garfield, Benjamin Harrison, William McKinley, William Howard Taft, and Warren G. Harding. All were conservative Republicans. A wave of reform hit Ohio in the early 20th century, particularly in local government. Organized labor became politically powerful in the state during the same period.

Ohio prospered during the 1920's but suffered greatly during the Great Depression. There was also much labor strife during that period: the Akron sitdown strikes (1935–37) and the Little Steel Strike (1937) are prominent examples. Ohio labor and industry quickly converted to war production in World War II, and the state prospered as a major producer of war material. This prosperity continued after the war. The opening of the Saint Lawrence Seaway in 1959 made ocean ports of Cleveland and Toledo. In 1980, Ohio had 10,797,419 inhabitants, ranking sixth in the nation.

OHIO, ARMY OF THE. On Nov. 9, 1861, the Union troops in Kentucky were organized as the Army of the Ohio, under Gen. Don Carlos Buell. During 1862 they fought at Shiloh, Tenn. (April), repelled the Confederate invasion of Kentucky (July), and fought at Corinth, Miss. (October). On Oct. 30, 1862, it became the Army of the Cumberland. A new Army of the Ohio was formed, which in 1865 was merged into the Department of the Cumberland.

OHIO, FALLS OF THE. Rapids opposite Louisville, Ky. Flatboats often went down the falls in high water, but steamboat freight and passengers were portaged. A canal was built around the falls in 1830. In 1778, about twenty families settled on Corn Island at the falls, moving to the mainland at Christmas. The name Louisville was adopted presumably because of the Franco-American alliance of the same year. Incorporated as the city of Louisville in 1828. (*See also* Louisville and Portland Canal.)

OHIO, FORKS OF THE. The name given to the junction of the Allegheny and Monongahela rivers, where they form the Ohio River. Historically, the name is often applied to the surrounding country or is used as the equivalent of such names as Fort Duquesne, Fort Pitt, and Pittsburgh. The Ohio Company in 1754 began construction of a rude fort on the point. Before its completion, the French captured it. Until late 1758, as Fort Duquesne, it was under French control. Captured and renamed Pittsburgh and protected by Fort Pitt, it remained under British supervision for more than a decade. (*See* Pittsburgh.)

OHIO AND ERIE CANAL. *See* **Ohio State Canals.**

OHIO COMPANY OF ASSOCIATES. Developed for western settlement by a group of revolutionary war officers from New England. It was organized in Boston in 1786 and a year elapsed before 250 shares had been subscribed and the company was ready to ask Congress for land. By skillful lobbying, the Ohio Company was able to secure 1,781,760 acres on very favorable terms. The tract lay north of the Ohio River. The company later encountered financial difficulties and could not complete its payments. Nevertheless, Congress granted title to 750,000 acres and added 214,285 acres to be paid for with army warrants (*see* Land Bounties) and 100,000 acres to be granted free to actual settlers. The great achievement of the company was the successful beginning of organized settlement north of the Ohio River at Marietta, Ohio, in 1788.

OHIO COMPANY OF VIRGINIA. A partnership organized in 1747 to engage in land speculation west of the Appalachian Mountains. The company petitioned the crown for a grant of 500,000 acres of land in the upper Ohio Valley or elsewhere in the West, 200,000 acres to be granted at once on condition that 200 families be settled on the land within seven years. Early in 1749 the governor of Virginia was directed to make the grant. A road was opened across the mountains, probably in 1752, and in 1753, a settlement was planted in what is now Fayette County, Pa. Early in 1754 the company began, erected a fort at the Forks of the Ohio. The French and Indian War ended the company's activities.

OHIO IDEA. A proposal (1867–68) to redeem Civil War bonds in greenbacks instead of coin. Put forth as an inflationary measure, it was so popular that both political parties in the Middle West were forced to endorse it.

OHIO-MICHIGAN BOUNDARY DISPUTE. Long controversy between Ohio and Michigan Territory over the cape on Maumee Bay in Lake Erie. The dispute reached its climax in the bloodless Toledo War of 1835–36. Congress gave the strip (some 400 square miles) to Ohio but compensated Michigan with statehood and a tract of 9,000 square miles on the Upper Peninsula.

OHIO NATIONAL STAGE COMPANY. Headquartered at Columbus, Ohio, the company operated stagecoaches on the western division of the National Road after its completion to that city in 1833. It had branch lines to all parts of Ohio and western Pennsylvania, and by 1844 had become a near monopoly. The railroads ended its importance in the 1850's.

OHIO RIVER, EARLY DISCOVERY OF. Robert Cavelier, Sieur de La Salle, heard of the "great river" (in the Iroquois tongue, "Ohio"), and became convinced he could descend it to the Gulf of California and perhaps even to China. Leaving Montreal on July 6, 1669, La Salle and twenty men found their way to the marshy country below the falls opposite present-day Louisville, Ky. Whether La Salle abandoned the expedition before it reached the river is a question still raised by historians. News of La Salle's voyage quickly spread. Louis Jolliet's map in 1674 gave the general course of the Ohio as far as the falls, and Jean Baptiste Louis Franquelin's map in 1682 showed that it flowed into the Mississippi River.

According to unverified reports, Abraham Wood, a fur trader at Fort Henry (now Petersburg), between 1654 and 1664, discovered several branches of the Ohio and the Mississippi. If so, he preceded La Salle.

OHIO STATE ANTISLAVERY SOCIETY. Organized in 1835 by abolitionist converts of Theodore D. Weld (*see* Oberlin Movement), the Ohio Society shortly became second only to the New York Society among the state auxiliaries of the American Antislavery Society. By 1848 it had practically merged with the Free Soil party.

OHIO STATE CANALS. In 1825 two major canals were begun in Ohio: the Ohio and Erie from Lake Erie at Cleveland, to the Ohio River at Portsmouth; the Miami and Erie from the Ohio at Cincinnati to Dayton, with a later extension to Lake Erie. By 1832 the 308-mile Ohio and Erie was open. The extension of the Miami and Erie Canal to Toledo and Lake Erie was begun in 1833, but boats did not get through to Toledo until 1843. By the 1850's railroad competition began throttling the canals.

OHIO VALLEY. A natural link between the Appalachians and the Mississippi Valley. In the 17th century there developed a flourishing trade with the Indians. The French established a series of forts in the upper Ohio Valley, and in 1758 the English captured Fort Duquesne at the Forks of the Ohio, rechristening it Fort Pitt, the strategic center of the valley.

"OH! SUSANNA." A minstrel song composed by Stephen Collins Foster in 1848, it became the theme song of the westward migration.

OIL EXCHANGES, EARLY. After the completion of the Drake oil well in 1859 in Titusville, Pa., traders gathered on the streets, in hotels, and in telegraph offices to buy and sell oil. The first organized exchange was established at Titusville in January 1871.

OIL INDUSTRY. *See* **Petroleum Prospecting and Technology.**

OIL SCANDALS. *See* **Elk Hills Oil Scandal; Naval Oil Reserves; Teapot Dome Oil Scandal.**

OISE-AISNE OPERATION (Aug. 18–Nov. 11, 1918). World War I campaign aimed at reducing the Marne salient. After indecisive fighting along the Vesle River two U.S. divisions crossed (Sept. 4) with the general French advance and, against strong opposition, pushed across the watershed toward the Aisne. Before they were relieved, the two divisions had progressed ten kilometers and crossed the Aisne Canal.

Another U.S. division took Juvigny on Aug. 30. On Sept. 2, the division reached the National Road at Terny.

OJIBWA. *See* **Chippewa.**

OKANOGAN, FORT (Wash.). Located on the juncture of the Columbia River and the mouth of the Okanogan River, the fort was built by the Pacific Fur Company in 1811. In 1813 it passed to the North West Company, and in 1821 to the Hudson's Bay Company.

OKEECHOBEE, BATTLE OF (Dec. 25, 1837). The bloodiest engagement of the second Seminole War. Troops under Col. Zachary Taylor met Seminole warriors on the north shore of Lake Okeechobee, Fla. After three hours Taylor, by a flank movement, drove the Indians before him. Twenty-six whites were killed; 112 were wounded. Indian losses were not determined. This conflict proved an important factor in effecting the removal of the Indians from Florida.

OKINAWA. A minor Japanese base during most of World War II, Okinawa became important when U.S. planners decided to seize it as a staging point for their projected invasion of Japan. On Apr. 1, 1945, American forces began a struggle that ended on June 21 with more than 115,000 Japanese defenders vanquished.

Gen. Mitsuru Ushijima, commanding Japan's Thirty-second Army, allowed Gen. Simon Bolivar Buckner's four assault divisions of the U.S. Tenth Army to storm ashore virtually unopposed. Ushijima's troops burrowed into caves and tunnels lying between the beaches and Shuri, the capital. Invading U.S. Army and U.S. Marine Corps attackers eliminated them at heavy cost. Late in May the Japanese retreated to Okinawa's southern tip, where both commanders perished.

Equally bitter was the fighting at sea. Japan's air forces hurled more than 4,000 sorties, many by kamikaze suicide planes, at U.S. and British naval forces. U.S. losses totaled thirty-eight ships of all types sunk and 368 damaged; 4,900 U.S. Navy men died; and U.S. Army and U.S. Marine fatalities numbered 7,900 men.

OKLAHOMA. In the northeast as early as A.D. 500, a village-dwelling people who built the Spiro Mound flourished. In the eastern prairies, the Caddoan occupied village sites after A.D. 1000 and raised various crops, including corn. In the postcontact period, bands of nomadic Osage, Kiowa Apache, and Comanche wandered the western plains. Oklahoma, except for the panhandle, was included in the Louisiana Territory.

Oklahoma became the home of the Five Civilized Tribes. Forced from their homes in the southeast between 1817 and 1842, the Cherokee, Chickasaw, Choctaw, Creek, and Seminole settled in assigned tracts and, by 1856, had established their own autonomous governments. The five tribes adopted slavery and joined the Confederacy during the Civil War. Later the tribes lost half their lands. The federal government relocated Plains Indians, including the Comanche, Cheyenne, Arapaho, Osage, and Pawnee, and eastern tribes, such as the Seneca, Shawnee, and Wyandot, in reservations on these lands in western Oklahoma.

Between 1866 and 1890, white interests in the Indian Territory increased. The movement of vast cattle herds from Texas through Oklahoma encouraged organized use of the rich western grazing lands. Coal discovered in the Choctaw region in 1870 encouraged whites to exploit the territory's mineral wealth, while the construction of some fifteen railroads through Indian lands by 1907 had introduced thousands of whites to the economic potential of these lands. Between 1879 and 1884 attempts were made by organized immigrant groups called boomers to settle on the unassigned lands. Beginning in 1889, much of Indian Territory was opened to white settlers (*see* Oklahoma Openings).

The western part of Indian Territory was made Oklahoma Territory on May 2, 1890, and for seventeen years it was under a territorial government while Indian Territory was governed by the five Indian nations. Pressure developed from the whites for statehood, and between 1889 and 1906 thirty-one bills were introduced for either separate or joint statehood. Congress rejected separate statehood, and on Nov. 16, 1907, the twin territories entered the Union as Oklahoma.

Between 1904 and 1907 Oklahoma experienced a prosperous period in oil production. Wild boomtowns, such as Burbank, flourished, although many had become ghost towns by 1930. The economic depression of the 1930's was extremely serious in the rural areas, and by 1935, 61 percent of the farms in Oklahoma were operated by tenant farmers. Conditions were worsened by the drought of 1934–36; western Oklahoma was part of the Dust Bowl. Many Oklahomans went to Texas or California to become farm laborers, referred to as Okies. In the postwar period, Oklahoma ranked fourth nationally in the production of petroleum, natural gas, and stone. The manufacturing of transportation and farm equipment and clay and glass items, as well as a large cattle industry, gives the state a diversified economy. Of the state's 1980 population of 3,025,266, 67.3 percent was urban.

OKLAHOMA CITY (Okla.). The capital and largest city of Oklahoma, with a population of 403,213 in 1980; it is the center of a metropolitan area of 829,584 people. Oklahoma City began, suddenly, on Apr. 22, 1889. It was located in a part of the Oklahoma Territory that was opened for settlement at noon on that day. By nightfall, about 10,000 settlers were housed in tents within the city limits. Their land claims, established that afternoon, turned the site into a frontier metropolis. It was named state capital in 1910.

During the 1920's, Oklahoma City experienced a great oil boom, the oil providing a basis for private business and public income. Grain elevators and stockyards, cottonseed oil plants, and food processing factories are located in the city.

OKLAHOMA OPENINGS. Opening of former Indian lands in western Oklahoma to white settlement. The first was at high noon, Apr. 22, 1889. This resulted in a "run" in which some 50,000 people took part, each seeking to be the first to settle on one of the 160-acre homestead tracts. In 1901, a parcel of land was distributed by a lottery in which qualified homesteaders were allowed to choose homesteads in the order in which their names were drawn. In 1906 the so-called Big Pasture Lands were auctioned in tracts of 160 acres.

OKLAHOMA SQUATTERS. As early as 1819, white settlers attempted to occupy Indian lands in the southeastern part of Oklahoma, but they were removed by the military. Greer County was entered by settlers soon after 1880, although a presidential proclamation warned them not to occupy it until the question of title had been settled. During 1879–85 so-called boomers sought to settle as squatters on the unassigned lands of central Oklahoma but were removed by U.S. soldiers. Just prior to each of the openings of lands to settlement, a number of people entered on the land before the date set for the opening. These were known as Sooners.

OLD AGE. The number of persons over sixty-five years of age in the United States increased both absolutely and as a proportion of total population during the first three-quarters of the 20th century. In 1900, 3.1 million (about 4 percent of the population) were in this age category; by 1980 the number was estimated at 25.5 million (11.3 percent of the total). The growth in absolute numbers came partly from increased longevity (average life expectancy increased from 47.3 to 73.8 years during the period), partly from high immigration in the early 1900's, and partly from the high birth rates prevailing when that age group was born. The rate of increase of those over sixty-five will continue to rise but then is expected to fall, reaching a minimum in the decade 1990–2000, when the low birth cohorts of the depression decade 1930–40 enter that age group. The increase in the number of persons over sixty-five has had a disruptive effect on the nation's Social Security system (*see* Social Security).

OLD CHILLICOTHE INDIAN TOWN. *See* **Chillicothe.**

OLD COURT–NEW COURT STRUGGLE. A political contest in Kentucky that involved the immunity of the state supreme court (called court of appeals) from legislative control and the finality of its decisions on constitutional questions. Angered at the court of appeals for invalidating laws aimed at easing the hardships of debtors, the state legislature abolished the court, setting up a new court. This act was promptly declared unconstitutional by the "old court," but the new appointees proceeded to organize a "new court." Both courts functioned for two years, but a majority of judges and lawyers adhered to the "old court," and in December 1826 an act was passed repealing the reorganizing act.

OLD DOMINION. When Charles II was restored to the throne in 1660, in response to the loyalty of the Virginia burgesses, he elevated Virginia to the position of a "dominion." Thus, Virginia became known as the Old Dominion.

OLD FIELD SCHOOLS. These schools, quite common in the Southern states before the Civil War, were often established on a field not suitable for farming.

"OLD FUSS AND FEATHERS." Gen. Winfield Scott's nickname. It referred (affectionately or derisively) to the general's love of military pageantry, show uniforms, and meticulousness in military procedure and etiquette.

"OLD HICKORY." Andrew Jackson's nickname, because of his endurance and strength. It was first given him in 1813 by his soldiers during a 500-mile march home from Natchez, Miss., to Nashville, Tenn.

OLD IRONSIDES. *See* ***Constitution.***

OLD NORTH CHURCH. The common name for Christ Church in Boston. Erected in 1723, it was the second Episcopal church to be established in Boston and is the oldest church edifice in the city. It was in the steeple of the Old North Church that two signal lights were hung to indicate to Paul Revere that the British were approaching Lexington on the night of Apr. 18, 1775 (*see* Revere's Ride).

OLD NORTHWEST. Vast area of 248,000 square miles between the Ohio and Mississippi rivers and the Great Lakes. The Definitive Treaty of Peace of 1783 awarded this territory to the United States, and after the different states had ceded their claims (*see* Western Lands), it became a public domain organized as the Northwest Territory.

"OLD OAKEN BUCKET." A poem written by Samuel Woodworth about 1817. It was included in the McGuffey readers and was set to music by Frederick Smith.

"OLD ROUGH AND READY." Gen. Zachary Taylor's nickname. His physical prowess and zeal and the informality of his military attire earned him the sobriquet during the Seminole War in 1841. It was of great service to him as a presidential candidate in 1848.

OLD SOUTH CHURCH. Built in Boston in 1729 to replace the original structure of 1670. Here was held the Boston Massacre town meeting that forced the royal governor to withdraw the British troops from Boston in 1770; and here also was held the Tea Party meeting.

OLD SOUTHWEST. The region lying west of Georgia, South Carolina, and North Carolina and extending to the Mississippi River. After the American Revolution, some feared that this large area would be used to build up the power of the Carolinas and Georgia. Tennessee, Alabama, and Mississippi were formed out of the Old Southwest.

OLEANA. Colony in northern Pennsylvania established in 1852 by the Norwegian violinist Ole Bull, who bought 120,000 acres of land in Potter County and planned a "New Norway." Poor management, unfavorable land and market conditions, and fraud brought about quick collapse.

OLENTANGY, BATTLE OF (June 6, 1782). Near Bucyrus, Ohio, the militia of Col. William Crawford fought off pursuing Indians and British Rangers. This success saved the little army, then commanded by Col. David Williamson in place of Crawford, who had been captured by the Indians.

OLIVE BRANCH PETITION (1775). Sent by the Continental Congress to George III, setting forth the grievances of the colonies. Knowing the king's violent opposition to dealing with the colonies as a united group, each delegate signed the paper as an individual. They made Richard Penn, a staunch Loyalist, their messenger. However, the king refused to see him or to receive the petition.

OLNEY COROLLARY. In 1895, Secretary of State Richard Olney applied the Monroe Doctrine to the Venezuela–British Guiana boundary dispute. He declared the United States to be opposed to the increase by any European power of its possessions in the Americas. Great Britain backed down, and arbitration was reopened.

OLNEY-PAUNCEFOTE TREATY. A general treaty of Anglo-American arbitration drafted in 1896 primarily by Secretary of State Richard Olney and Sir Julian Pauncefote, British ambassador to the United States. Its purpose was to create the mechanisms whereby Anglo-American disputes would be peaceably settled. Parliament promptly ratified the treaty, but the U.S. Senate never ratified it.

OLUSTEE, BATTLE OF (Feb. 20, 1864). Encounter between 5,500 Union troops, under Gen. Truman Seymour, and 5,200 Confederates, under Gen. Joseph Finnegan. It resulted in a Confederate victory and thwarted the Union purpose of gaining possession of the interior of Florida.

OLYMPIA (Wash.). Capital of the state of Washington, with 27,447 people in 1980. First settled in 1846, Olympia soon became the largest settlement in the Puget Sound area. When Washington Territory was established in 1853, Olympia was named as its "temporary" capital and has remained the seat of government since.

OLYMPIC GAMES. The participation of the United States in the Olympic Games is the sole responsibility of the U.S. Olympic Committee (USOC), a private body. It is the policy of the USOC to enter a full complement of athletes in competition in all the sports for which the United States qualifies to participate in both the summer and winter games.

Although the United States has been represented in all sports on the Olympic Games programs, it usually excels in men's track and field, men's and women's swimming and diving, basketball, and rowing. The United States has not traditionally been competitive in cycling, fencing, men's gymnastics, judo, luge (tobogganing), cross-country skiing, and ski jumping or in the team sports of field hockey, team handball (a popular Central European sport), volleyball, and, until 1972, soccer.

It is estimated that at the beginning of a four-year period of preparation for the Olympic Games more than 5 million athletes consider themselves candidates for the fewer than 600 places. Trials are held and invitations are extended to those athletes who have proved themselves in national and international competitions.

In 1980, President Jimmy Carter requested that U.S. athletes not participate in the Moscow Olympics in protest of the Soviet invasion of Afghanistan, and no U.S. teams competed.

OMAHA (Indians). Plains tribe of Indians who inhabited northeastern Nebraska on the Missouri River. They were sedentary and agricultural, tending toward permanent villages and seasonal bison hunts. The Omaha are noted for the complexity of their patrilineal organization. The tribe spoke Siouan and was most closely related to the Ponca, Kansa, and Osage. The Omaha had an estimated population of 2,800 in 1780.

OMAHA (Nebr.). The largest city in Nebraska, with a population of 311,681 in 1980; it was also the center of a metropolitan area of 566,140 people. One of the most important transportation and food-processing centers in the United States, Omaha contains the largest stockyards and meat-packing activities of the country. Omaha became a key railroad town almost overnight in 1865 when the Union Pacific Railroad chose it as the eastern terminus for the first major rail line across the great plains. Earlier it had been an important stopping place for wagons moving westward.

OMNIBUS BILL (1850). It was an attempt at a comprehensive adjustment of territorial questions involving Utah, California, New Mexico, and Texas. Opponents of compromise prevented the adoption of the bill, and it was left to later legislation (*see* Compromise of 1850) to effect its purposes.

OMNIBUS CRIME CONTROL AND SAFE STREETS ACT (June 19, 1968). As the result of a rapid increase in crime during the 1960's, this act was passed to help local governments in dealing with crime. It established the Law Enforcement Assistance Administration (LEAA) in the Justice Department to administer grants to the states for improving local law enforcement operations. The act also permitted wiretapping by all levels of government and attempted to overturn by legislation the liberal trend in defendant protection of the Supreme Court (*see Miranda* v. *Arizona*).

OÑATE'S EXPLORATIONS (1598–1608). The Spanish explorer Juan de Oñate was appointed in 1595 to colonize and govern a new Mexico to be founded on the Rio Grande. He advanced with 400 men and took formal possession near El Paso on Apr. 30, 1598. In the following years he explored and subjugated what are now New Mexico and northeastern Arizona, went as far west as the Gulf of California, and perhaps traveled as far north as Kansas. He was recalled from the governorship in 1608.

ONEIDA COLONY. A radical experiment in social and religious thinking, established in 1848 in Oneida, New York. From literal concepts of perfectionism and Bible communism the colony promulgated economic communism, the rejection of monogamy for complex marriage, birth control, and the eugenic breeding of children. The property of the colony grew to about 600 acres of well-cultivated land, with shoe, tailoring, and machine shops. The group formed a branch colony in Wallingford, Conn. Health was above the average, women held a high place, children were excellently trained, and work was fair and changeable.

In 1879, forced by social pressure from without and the dissatisfaction of the young within, monogamy was adopted, and within a year communism was replaced by joint-stock ownership. In its new form, Oneida continued its commercial success, but as a conventional company. During the 20th century, the Oneida Company was noted for its production of fine silver and stainless steel flatware.

ONION RIVER LAND COMPANY (1773–75). Land speculation venture in what is now Vermont. In 1773 the company bought at least 77,000 acres from claimants under New Hampshire titles, with full knowledge of its disputed title. Ethan Allen, one of the partners, managed the sales and political affairs, and the settlement of Burlington began at once. Success depended on destroying the claims of New York State, and to do this the company resorted to mob violence and the destruction of property, and the use of the Green Mountain Boys, of whom Ethan Allen was colonel. New York outlawed them, but ceased to claim jurisdiction when the Revolution broke out and Vermont became a separate state. The affairs of the company became confused, and the partners benefited little financially.

ONIONS. Onions were first brought to America by the colonists. Wethersfield, Conn., and Barnstable, Mass., soon became noted onion-growing centers. Extensive production of Bermuda onions began soon after 1900 in Texas, California, and Louisiana. By the early 1980's, Texas and California were leading all other states in onion production. In 1980 the United States produced 1.67 million short tons of onions, valued at $346 million.

ONONDAGA, GREAT COUNCIL HOUSE AT. *See* **Iroquois.**

"ONONTIO." The Iroquois name, meaning "great mountain," for the French governors of Canada. It was a translation of the surname of Charles Huault de Montmagny, who became governor of New France in 1636.

ONTARIO, LAKE. The smallest of the five Great Lakes was discovered by Champlain and Brulé in 1615. On early maps the lake appears variously as "Lac St. Louis," "Ontario ou Lac St Louis," and "Lake Ontario or Frontenac." "Ontario" means "high rocks near the water." Fort Frontenac was built in 1673 where the city of Kingston now stands. It was destroyed by the English in 1758. Fort Toronto was built in 1750, where the city of the same name stands today. The lake was the scene of naval or military engagements between 1756 and 1759, and in 1813; and for many generations it was a principal water thoroughfare of the fur trade. Fort Oswego was built in 1727, destroyed by the French in 1756, and rebuilt by the British in 1759 and renamed Fort Ontario. Fort Niagara, built in 1678 by La Salle, was surrendered by the English to the United States in 1796 (*see* Border Forts, Evacuation of).

Lake Ontario became important during the 19th century for the shipping of grain and lumber from the Middle West and Canada, and of coal from Pennsylvania by way of the Welland Canal (first opened in 1829), connecting lakes Erie and Ontario. With the opening of the St. Lawrence Seaway in 1959, shipping through Lake Ontario increased greatly.

"ON TO RICHMOND." On June 28, 1861, an editorial advocating an aggressive military policy entitled "Forward to Richmond" appeared in the *New York Tribune.* Other newspapers took up the phrase, shortening it to "On to Richmond," and it actually influenced federal military policy.

"ON TO WASHINGTON." When the Union army was fleeing from the field after the Battle of Bull Run (July 21, 1861), the cry "On to Washington" was raised among the pursuing Confederate troops. Newspapers throughout the South then took up the phrase and urged it repeatedly.

OPEN COVENANTS, OPENLY ARRIVED AT. The gist of the first of President Woodrow Wilson's Fourteen Points (1918). The proposal reflected the popular slogan "No secret treaties."

OPEN DOOR POLICY. Doctrine of the United States affirming its equal commercial and industrial rights in China. It was formally enunciated by Secretary of State John Hay in 1899 and 1900, but the Open Door policy had already emerged from American expansionism of the mid-19th century. Throughout this early period the United States adapted British commercial policy to its own ends by supporting the notion of free and open competition for trade in international markets, especially the China trade. The increasing commercialization of American agriculture led to a need for greater outlets for American grain and cotton manufactured goods; China was becoming also a potential consumer of the products of American heavy industry, including railroad equipment, and of oil products.

The Open Door formula was stimulated by international rivalry for control of ports, territories, spheres of influence, and economic advantage at the expense of a weak China. It was a time-honored administrative tactic that attempted to strengthen the U.S. position in China by cloaking its claims in the dress of international morality on behalf of China's territorial and political independence while simultaneously protecting the interests of the powers in maintaining the trade and political positions already acquired there.

Hay's Open Door notes to Germany, Russia, and England in 1899, and later to the other powers, are conventionally interpreted as an attempt to bluff them into accepting the American position in China, whereas actually they announced the decision of the United States to press its interests on its own behalf.

The United States attempted to move into Manchuria and China proper via Open Door proposals on behalf of American railroad and banking investment interests in 1909 and 1913. It attempted to protect its stake in China by opposing Japan's 21 Demands on China in 1915, but Japan's ambitions in Manchuria were not to be thwarted.

The Open Door outlook was embedded in the details of the Nine-Power Treaty (1922). By 1931, Japan had effectively negated the Open Door.

OPEN-MARKET OPERATIONS. Process whereby a central bank takes the initiative in the purchase and sale of government securities and other assets, under control of the Federal Reserve System and the twelve Federal Reserve banks. The purpose is to raise or lower money-market rates of interest, thereby exerting control over credit conditions; to facilitate U.S. Treasury financing; and to affect the foreign-exchange value of the dollar.

OPEN-RANGE CATTLE PERIOD. The period of open-range grazing began about 1866. During those years a vast stream of cattle poured north out of Texas to cow towns in Kansas and Nebraska. Mature animals were shipped to market while young steers and breeding animals were driven farther north or west to stock new ranges, the boundaries of each ranchman's pasturelands being determined by unwritten law. Calves were branded so they could be identified at roundups.

Great profits were made in the open-range cattle industry, and cattle companies were formed to take advantage of ranching on the great open ranges of the West.

The year 1885 marks the peak of the open-range cattle industry. By that time most of the range was fully stocked and much of it overstocked. In the terrible winter of 1886–87 hundreds of thousands of cattle died of cold and starvation, and nearly every ranchman on the central and northern Plains faced ruin. The open-range cattle industry never recovered. In addition, the range area was being rapidly settled and enclosed.

OPEN SHOP. *See* **Closed Shop.**

ORANGE, FORT. The Dutch settlement, trading post, and fort on the site of the modern city of Albany, New York. The fort was founded in 1624, but two years later the families settled there were moved back downriver to join the settlement of New Amsterdam. (*See also* Albany.)

ORDER OF AMERICAN KNIGHTS. A Civil War secret order of northern Peace Democrats, or Copperheads. In 1864 the order took the name Sons of Liberty.

ORDER OF THE STAR-SPANGLED BANNER. *See* **American Party.**

ORDERS IN COUNCIL. Executive edicts in Great Britain issued in the name of the king that have the force of law until superseded by acts of Parliament. Two orders in council are of primary interest for their influence upon the United States. Issued on Jan. 7 and Nov. 11, 1807, they were Britain's reply to Napoleon's Berlin Decree, Nov. 21, 1806, imposing a blockade of the British Isles.

The orders of Jan. 7 placed French commerce under a blockade and forbade neutrals to trade from one port to another under Napoleon's jurisdiction. Commercial strangulation of Europe under French control advanced a further step when, by the orders of Nov. 11, it was stipulated that neutral ships, meaning American, might not enter any ports "from which . . . the British flag is excluded." These orders were superseded on Apr. 26, 1809, by a blockade of the Netherlands, France, and Italy; and in June 1812, too late to avert the War of 1812, the orders were actually repealed, a major victory for American diplomacy.

ORDINANCES OF 1784, 1785, and 1787. The establishment of the government of the Confederation was delayed several years over the issue of the disposition of the western lands. Seven states had western land claims, and six had none; and the latter refused to join the Confederation until the former should cede their lands to the new government, to be utilized for the common benefit of all the states. In 1780, New York led the way by giving up all claim to the western lands, whereupon Congress passed a resolution pledging that the lands the states might cede would be erected into new states.

The Ordinance of 1784 provided for an artificial division of the entire West into sixteen districts, each district eligible for statehood upon attaining a population of 20,000.

Next year (May 20, 1785) the ordinance "for ascertaining the mode of disposing of lands in the Western territory" was enacted. It provided a scientific system of surveying and subdividing land. The unit of survey is the township, six miles square.

In March 1786 the Ohio Company of Associates opened negotiations with Congress, which on July 13, 1787, enacted the ordinance for the government of the territory northwest of the Ohio. It provided for a temporary government by agents appointed by Congress; but when the colony numbered 5,000 adult free males, a representative legislature was to be established, and upon the attainment of 60,000 population the territory would be admitted to statehood. The ordinance also provided for the future division of the territory into not less than three nor more than five states; and it contained compacts that established religious freedom, prohibited slavery, and guaranteed the fundamental rights of English liberty and just treatment of the Indians.

ORDNANCE. Originally referred to military firearms, but since about 1890, technical revolutions in weaponry have broadened the meaning of the term, and it now stands for all types of weapons and weapons systems.

Army Ordnance. The manufacture of ordnance has been traditionally a federal concern. In 1794 Congress authorized the establishment of arsenals for the development and manufacture of ordnance at Springfield, Mass., and at Harpers Ferry, Va., and in 1812 created a U.S. Army Ordnance Department to operate them. A major achievement during this period was the introduction of interchangeable parts for mass-produced firearms. Civil War needs sent arsenal and private ordnance production soaring.

Until 1917 the Ordnance Department dominated the army's weapons acquisition process. Between the two world wars the combat arms determined their own needs. On June 16, 1938, the Educational Orders Act authorized the immediate placement of ordnance contracts with civilian firms in order to strengthen outside procurement procedures and ease a future transition to a wartime economy. In World War II, private arms production dwarfed governmental efforts; as ordnance continued to grow more complex, public and private defense production became more integrated.

After 1945 dependence on arsenal production was impractical. Ordnance was increasingly discussed in terms of weapons systems, and the army soon joined the naval and air arms in their dependence on private industry for a great proportion of their ordnance.

Naval Ordnance. Naval ordnance includes all the weapons and their control systems used by naval forces. Until the mid-19th century, U.S. Navy ships were armed with carriage-mounted, muzzle-loading, smooth-bore cannons, principally of iron. At the time of the Civil War, pivot mounts, turrets, rifled guns, and explosive projectiles were beginning to be used. By World War I, directors, rangekeepers (computers), and breechloading steel guns were in use. By World War II, radar, automatic controls, proximity fuses, and bombardment rockets were also added.

Moored mines were used in the Civil War. In World War II, additional sensors were developed (magnetic, pressure, and acoustic). Self-propelled torpedoes were introduced in the late 19th century. Homing torpedoes first appeared in World War II. World War I aircraft were armed with machine guns and crude bombs. Gyroscopic bombsights and aircraft rockets were in use in World War II.

Introduced against Japanese ships in 1945, the first homing missile was the Bat. The first of the navy's long-range ballistic missiles, introduced in 1960, was the submerged-launched, 1,200-mile Polaris. Its successor, Poseidon, has a 2,500-nautical-mile range and was later equipped with multiple warheads. A Trident missile system, with greater range and improved capabilities, was developed in the mid-1970's.

OREGON. This Indian name, possibly of Algonkin origin, was originally applied to the legendary great "River of the West," the Columbia. It appears in print in Jonathan Carver's *Travels Through the Interior Parts of North America* (1788). The region may have been reached by sea by the Spanish Bartolomé Ferrelo in 1543. Capt. James Cook's tremendous profits from sea-otter furs sold in Canton led many British and American traders to the coast. On May 11, 1792, Capt. Robert Gray discovered the "River of the West," which he named the Columbia for his ship.

Thomas Jefferson sent Lewis and Clark, with instructions to find the "River Oregon," which they identified as the Columbia. It was to the Columbia that John Jacob Astor's partners went in 1811 to found Astoria, the first settlement in Oregon, and to develop the fur trade. The Columbia, or Columbia District, was first referred to officially as Oregon in 1822 by John Floyd of Virginia, who introduced a bill to set up the Territory of Oregon.

Under a treaty of 1818 with Great Britain the Northwest was jointly occupied without formation of a government. In 1819 a treaty with Spain set the boundary at 42° and in 1824 and 1825 the Russians relinquished their claims south of 54°40′. Thus, Oregon included British Columbia, Washington, Oregon, Idaho, and parts of Montana and Wyoming. Great Britain claimed all land north of the Columbia River, and American politicians felt that the United States should have all the coast. The militant slogan "Fifty-four Forty or Fight" was used by those advocating the ouster of Great Britain. President James K. Polk negotiated the treaty of 1846, which established the continental boundary as the forty-ninth parallel from the Rockies to Puget Sound, and left Vancouver Island to the British.

Man first arrived in the Oregon region about 10,000 years ago, probably from Asia. The dominant tribe were the Chinook.

About 1830, employees of the old Pacific Fur Company, or freemen, who had not contracted for service with the Hudson's Bay Company, settled as farmers in the Willamette Valley with their Indian families. In 1834 members of the Oregon Methodist Mission settled in the region, followed in 1838 by the Roman Catholic mission. The missions of Marcus Whitman and Henry Spalding were located east of the mountains. Migration of independent settlers began in 1839. Each year saw larger numbers coming over the Oregon Trail to obtain donation land claims, primarily in the fertile Willamette Valley. They guaranteed their squatters rights by organizing a provisional territorial government at Champoeg with the adoption of the Organic Act on July 5, 1843, to meet civil and military needs until the territorial government was established on Mar. 3, 1849. In 1853, Washington Territory was separated from Oregon. Oregon was granted statehood on Feb. 14, 1859, and its present eastern boundary was delineated.

Indians were placed on reservations under a treaty of 1855. Gold rushes of the early 1850's produced the Rogue River War (1855–56), and similar rushes in eastern Oregon during the Civil War and afterward produced wars that resulted in the confinement of the rest of the Indians to reservations. Agriculture is still of major importance, including wheat, food-processing crops, and seeds as well as stock raising. In 1980 Oregon had 2,632,663 people. Lumbering from the start was important. Tourism, metals fabrication, and wood products are Oregon's other major industries. In government, Oregon has contributed innovations, such as the Oregon System, establishing the initiative and referendum in 1902, the gas tax in 1919, and the bottle bill in 1973.

OREGON. At the outbreak of the Spanish-American War, the battleship *Oregon* made a 14,700-mile run, Mar. 19 to May 26, 1898, from the Golden Gate to Key West, Fla. Joining Adm. William T. Sampson's blockading squadron off Cuba, the *Oregon* was able to engage effectively all the Spanish cruisers on July 3. The *Oregon*'s trip gave dramatic evidence of the need for quicker communication by water between the Pacific and the Atlantic.

OREGON LAND FRAUDS. The device of securing state school lands of little value for $1.25 an acre and exchanging them for valuable timberlands was in operation as early as 1890. These frauds were exposed through the investigations of Francis J. Heney and William J. Burns during the administration of President Theodore Roosevelt.

OREGON MEMORIAL OF 1838. Jason Lee, head of the Methodist mission established in Oregon in 1834, went east in 1838, with a petition addressed to Congress. Dated Mar. 16, 1838, the petition asked that the United States take possession of Oregon. The memorial was presented to the Senate on Jan. 28, 1839. Lee urged that protection be extended to the infant colony and that the pioneers be given security in the title to their lands (*see* Oregon Treaty of 1846).

OREGON MISSIONS. Attention was called to the need for Christian work among the Indians of the Pacific Northwest by an appeal made to Gen. William Clark of St. Louis in 1831 by four Flathead Indians, who had journeyed from the Oregon Country seeking religious instructors. The Methodists immediately recommended the establishment of an Oregon mission, and Jason Lee was appointed to head it. Lee established a mission in the Willamette Valley. A year later, Marcus Whitman and Henry H. Spalding began a prosperous mission near what is now Walla Walla, Wash. Lee and Whitman became interested in bringing colonists to Oregon, a policy that their mission boards did not approve. Lee was removed. Whitman and thirteen others were murdered by the Indians in 1847.

Roman Catholic missionaries were also active, and their work was favored by the Hudson's Bay Company as being less likely to interfere with the fur trade.

OREGON PAROCHIAL SCHOOL CASE (*Pierce* v. *Society of the Sisters of the Holy Names of Jesus and Mary,* 268 U.S. 510 [1925]). The Supreme Court invalidated an Oregon statute under which all children would have been required to attend public schools. Aimed at the parochial schools, it was not a compulsory education law or a reasonable regulation of school standards. The statute was an abridgement of liberty under the due process clause of the Fourteenth Amendment.

OREGON QUESTION. By successive treaties the Pacific Northwest was defined until it meant the territory west of the Rocky Mountains, north of 42° and south of 54°40′. The territory was the subject of the conflicting claims of ownership of Spain, Great Britain, the United States, and Russia.

Until the final division of the territory between the United States and Great Britain the Oregon question was the subject of intermittent correspondence between the two governments.

By 1844, popular feeling over Oregon found expression in the political slogan "Fifty-four Forty or Fight," widely used in the campaign in which James K. Polk was elected president. Action followed quickly upon Polk's taking office. On Apr. 27, 1846, Congress authorized him to give Great Britain notice of the termination of the joint occupation treaty. By June 15, 1846, a compromise treaty settled the Oregon question by continuing the boundary east of the Rockies (forty-ninth parallel) to the sea (*see* Oregon Treaty).

OREGON SHORT LINE RAILWAY. A subsidiary of the Union Pacific Railway incorporated in 1881 and completed early in 1882 to run 550 miles from Granger, Wyo., to Huntington, Oreg. It was built to develop the Pacific Northwest and to secure its traffic for the Union Pacific.

OREGON SYSTEM. In 1902, Oregon adopted a state constitutional amendment for direct voter participation in lawmaking. It permits voters to place a law or constitutional amendment before the voters for final action without reference to the legislature. By referendum, a law can be referred to the people for final acceptance or rejection. Other features of the system are the recall, direct primary, presidential preference primary, and state-printed campaign textbooks.

OREGON TRAIL. First traced from the Missouri River to the Columbia River by explorers and fur traders. Knowledge of the trail was current among the traders on the frontier. Guidebooks appeared surprisingly early. The distances on the trail were calculated with a high degree of accuracy.

Independence, Mo., was the most frequent place of departure, and shortly after leaving there the companies commonly organized a government by electing officers and adopting rules of conduct. The emigrants gathered in time to leave in the early spring, so as to take advantage of the fresh pasturage for their animals and to allow all possible time for the long journey.

The wagon traffic on the Oregon Trail during the 1840's and 1850's became so heavy that the road was a clearly defined and deeply rutted way across the country; and generations after the last covered wagon had passed over it hundreds of miles of the trail could still be traced.

OREGON TREATY OF 1846. Fixed the boundary between the United States and British America at the forty-ninth parallel west of the Rocky Mountains except at the western terminus of that line, where it swerved southward around Vancouver Island and out through Juan de Fuca Strait. By the Convention of 1818, the United States and Great Britain had agreed that the country claimed by either west of the Rockies be free and open to the citizens of the two powers (*see* Joint Occupation). Acting under a joint resolution of Congress (Apr. 27, 1846), President James K. Polk transmitted notice for the termination of that treaty. The British foreign minister drafted a treaty that was accepted by Polk and the Senate (June 15, 1846).

ORGANIC LAW. Any fundamental set of rules and principles establishing the organs of government, distributing the powers of government among them, and defining the rights and duties of the government and the people. A second, more restricted use refers to the acts of Congress providing a form of government for the territories.

ORGANIZATION FOR ECONOMIC COOPERATION AND DEVELOPMENT (OECD). It began its existence on Sept. 30, 1961, when it replaced the Organization for European Economic Cooperation (OEEC), organized in 1948 to administer the Marshall Plan. The United States was not a member of OEEC. Its membership in OECD constitutes the first step taken by the United States in economic internationalism. Originally a twenty-nation association, OECD expanded by the addition of four new members by 1981. The purpose of OECD is to foster the free international flow of payments, services, and capital globally, combined with the utilization of human resources and scientific developments.

ORGANIZATION OF AFRO-AMERICAN UNITY. Founded by Malcolm X on Mar. 8, 1964, following his break with the Black Muslims; it was dominated by him until his assassination on Feb. 21, 1965. He and his organization rejected the racist teachings of the Black Muslims but remained devoted to the cause of black liberation. He dominated the Black Muslims from 1954 until his break with Elijah Muhammad in December 1963. The Organization of Afro-American Unity lingered for a few years after Malcom X's death.

ORGANIZATION OF AMERICAN STATES (OAS). Founded at the Ninth International Conference of American States, in Bogotá, Colombia, in March 1948. A charter was adopted formalizing the inter-American system, its key structural features being (1) a council of the OAS to manage the organization's business, (2) subsidiary councils (cultural, economic and social, and juridical), and (3) the Pan-American Union, to function as the general secretariat.

Important meetings and conferences have adopted a declaration against Communist intervention; suspended Cuba from the OAS; issued a declaration on the need for social and economic progress in Latin America; agreed that OAS members can normalize relations with Cuba, and dealt with human rights issues. The OAS has also concerned itself with conflicts between member states.

ORGANIZED LABOR. *See* **Labor.**

ORIENTAL RELIGIONS AND SECTS. Buddhism, the most prominent non-Western faith, is practiced by about 10 percent of Japanese-Americans. The primary form of Buddhism in the United States is the Jodo-Shinshu sect, the most popular in Japan, which was introduced in 1898. In the late 1970's it had a U.S. membership of approximately 60,000, served by eighty religious leaders. Since World War II, Zen Buddhism has grown in popularity among non-Asian Americans. Traced back to the teachings of Bodhidharma in early 6th century, Zen has become secularized in the 20th century. Its basic appeal to Americans lies in its undogmatic and nonmetaphysical character.

Hinduism was introduced by the Swami Vivekananda, who founded the Vedanta Society in 1897, dedicated to the idea of a world religion rooted in Indian concepts. The Self-Realization Fellowship, founded by Paramhansa Yogananda in 1920, has tended to teach a practical form of Hinduism that stresses peace, health, and greater personal powers. It claims to have 200,000 members. In the late 1960's, interest in it was revived by the teachings of Maharishi Mahesh Yogi.

Baha'i, or Bahaism, arose in the 19th century from the teachings of Ali Muhammad, a member of the Shi'ite sect of Islam, who claimed to be a messenger from God. He declared that the laws of Mohammed were abrogated and envisioned a worldwide religion. Bahaism is a syncretistic faith that stresses the inspiration of the founders of all religions and looks toward a worldwide reign of peace, love, and holiness. Doctrinally, its teachings are a philosophical version of the major themes of Judaism, Christianity, and Islam.

American theosophical sects often draw their inspiration from Eastern religions. Organized theosophical groups include the Theosophical Society, the Liberal Catholic Church, the I Am movement, and Rosicrucian societies. All stress the possibility of mystical experience.

ORIGINAL PACKAGE DOCTRINE. First enunciated by the Supreme Court in *Brown* v. *Maryland* (1827), a case challenging a Maryland act of 1821 requiring importers and dealers in foreign goods within the state to take out a $50 license. The Court held that "while remaining the property of the importer, in his warehouse, in the original form or package in which it was imported, a tax upon it is too plainly a duty on imports."

Leisy v. *Hardin,* in which the Supreme Court ruled that Iowa laws could not be applied to interstate freight shipments as long as they remained in the original package, unsold, resulted in the Wilson Original Package Act, to protect the internal police powers of the states. Such shipments were still in interstate commerce and, therefore, under federal jurisdiction. Thus, goods in interstate shipment have not "arrived" for purposes of regulation by the state until they have been delivered into the hands of the consignee, and the original package has been broken. Goods have not arrived for purposes of taxation by the state until they have come permanently at rest within the state and become mingled with the wealth of the state, whether or not the original package has been broken.

ORISKANY, BATTLE OF (Aug. 6, 1777). On Aug. 3, 1777, St. Leger with an army of 1,200 Tories and Indians appeared before Fort Stanwix on the Mohawk River. Gen. Nicholas Herkimer, on Aug. 4, with an army of about 800 men, planned to fall upon St. Leger's rear when Col. Peter Gansevoort, the commanding officer at Fort Stanwix, attacked in front. A detachment of Tories and Indians were sent to ambush the Americans. About two miles west of Oriskany Creek the main body of the Americans entered a ravine. A deadly volley from both sides met them. The main body was thrown into confusion but rallied in one of the bloodiest battles of the

Revolution. The Indians fled and the Tories retreated. Gansevoort and his men captured much-needed supplies and ammunition, and St. Leger retreated to Oswego. (*see* British Campaign of 1777).

ORLEANS, FORT. Built in 1723 on an island in the Missouri River, at the mouth of Grand River, by Étienne Venyard. The French intended to open a trade route to Sante Fe. Orleans was the first fort built on the Missouri.

ORLEANS, TERRITORY OF. Probably first visited by the survivors of Hernando de Soto's expedition in 1543 it was claimed by La Salle for France in 1682. Bienville founded New Orleans in 1718 and made it the capital in 1722. It was sold to the United States in 1803 (*see* Louisiana Purchase). Louisiana was admitted as a state Apr. 30, 1812.

ORNITHOLOGY. During the 16th, 17th, and 18th centuries some travelers, missionaries, and colonists included in their writings minor comments on birds seen, but there were two notable naturalists: Mark Catesby and William Bartram. Alexander Wilson is known as the father of American ornithology for his *American Ornithology* (1808–14). Overlapping Wilson in time was J. J. Audubon, whose *Birds of America* (1827–38) has been called "the greatest monument erected by art to nature."

Spencer F. Baird and Elliott Coues brought order to the nomenclature and classification of the developing science.

In the 1880's an important part of ornithology was collecting specimens; in the latter part of the century these collections began to be consolidated in natural history museums.

In the late 19th century, scientific ornithology was the finding, naming, describing, and classifying of birds. Knowledge of the living bird was considered natural history or popular ornithology. But even while "scientific" ornithology was giving a fairly complete account of American avifauna, inquiring students were beginning to explore distributional, behavioral, and ecological aspects of the living bird in wider concepts of biological theory. A symptom of this change was the founding in 1883 of the American Ornithologists' Union, which published a quarterly journal, *The Auk;* a code of nomenclature; and a checklist of North American birds (several times revised and listing 760 species in its 1957 edition). The union had a membership of 4,000 in 1980.

By the 1930's outlines at least of the life histories of most American birds were known, and from extensive studies of various individual species more general ideas began to emerge on the stimulus for the annual cycle, especially migration; the role of territory; the psychological aspects of behavior, contributing to the development of ethology; and ecological aspects of bird life.

The subspecies concept (leading to the development of trinominal names for recognizable geographical varieties of a species, introduced about 1900) became the raw material for the study of adaptation and of evolution at work.

ORTHODOX CHURCHES. *See* **Eastern Orthodoxy.**

OSAGE. One of the southern Siouan tribes of the western division, found in historical times in Missouri in two principal bands, the Great Osage and the Little Osage. In 1802 nearly half of the Great Osage migrated to the Arkansas River, leaving the remainder on the Osage River in Missouri. By a treaty negotiated in 1808 the Osage ceded all their lands in Missouri and Arkansas, and subsequently were found in Oklahoma. In later treaties, they agreed to remove to Kansas. In 1870 their reservation was established in Osage County, Okla. Their population was estimated at more than 5,000 in 1845; but by 1855, smallpox had reduced it to 3,500. The Osage are among those tribes that have enjoyed large incomes from the production of oil. In the late 1970's they numbered about 6,000.

OSAGE, FORT. Established in September 1808 on the south bank of the Missouri River, nineteen miles east of present-day Kansas City. It was evacuated in June 1813 but reoccupied in 1816. It maintained its importance as the most western outpost of the U.S. government until 1827.

OSAGE HEDGE (or *Maclura*)**.** A thorn-bearing tree, used on the prairies for fences. It produces a pale green fruit from which the tree gets its name—Osage orange. The first nurseries on the treeless prairies raised millions of these "hedge" plants. The thorn on the Osage orange inspired barbed wire.

OSAWATOMIE, BATTLE OF (Aug. 30, 1856)**.** Osawatomie, Kans., was attacked by about 250 proslavery men (supposedly Missourians) and was defended by John Brown with 40 men. The Free State men were soon dislodged from their position along the creek bank and fled, after which the town was sacked.

OSBORN* V. *BANK OF THE UNITED STATES, 9 Wheaton 738 (1824)**.** The jealousies of local banks and the restrictions on credits by the second Bank of the United States in the crisis of 1818 led to the enactment by the Ohio legislature, February 1819, of a tax of $50,000 on each branch of the second bank in the state. The Supreme Court held the law unconstitutional.

OSGOODITES. A New Hampshire religious sect, followers of Jacob Osgood (1777–1844), who left the Freewill Baptists to form a new church in 1812, claiming special powers of prophecy and healing from God. After Osgood's death their number declined, and all were gone by 1890.

OSTEND MANIFESTO. On Apr. 7, 1853, President Franklin Pierce appointed Pierre Soulé minister to Spain with instructions to negotiate for the purchase of Cuba. Soulé failed completely. Soulé, James Buchanan and John Y. Mason met at Ostend, Belgium, in October 1854, signing the notorious manifesto on Oct. 15. In effect, the conferees declared that should Spain refuse to sell and should the United States consider Spain's further possession of Cuba inimical to U.S. domestic interests, forcible seizure would be fully justified.

When the document caused a storm of denunciation, the U.S. disavowed the declaration.

OSTEOPATHY. The general application of manipulative methods based upon recognition of the importance of the structural integrity of the body, and linked with general application of the science of natural immunity, was developed by Andrew T. Still (1828–1917). By 1916 a full four-year course had been established, and by 1980 there were eight U.S. colleges offering the course. The number of practicing osteopaths grew to about 14,000 by 1980. The American Osteopathic Association was organized in 1897.

OSWEGATCHIE, FORT. *See* **Ogdensburg.**

OSWEGO (N.Y.). A city on Lake Ontario, it began as an Indian trading post in 1722, where English and Dutch traders began to assemble and to carry on a thriving trade. In 1726–27, Gov. William Burnet dispatched soldiers and workmen to construct a fort on the west bank of the Oswego River near its mouth. This post was the most important English fortification west of the Hudson.

In 1756 these establishments were destroyed by Louis Joseph de Montcalm. The ruins were later converted into a fortified camp for the British.

In 1759–60 the British rebuilt Fort Ontario, and it again became a base for military operations. It was there on July 24, 1766, that Sir William Johnson met in council the great Ottawa chieftain Pontiac, who signed a peace treaty. Fort Ontario continued as a trading post until 1774, when it was dismantled. In 1777, Oswego served as Lt. Col. Barry St. Leger's base in his operations in the Mohawk Valley.

In the War of 1812, Oswego was a naval base. On May 6, 1814, it was attacked and captured by the British. The settlement was incorporated as a village in 1828 and chartered as a city in 1848.

The completion of the New York State barge system in 1917 brought new prosperity to Oswego. In 1959, with the opening of the St. Lawrence Seaway, Oswego became a major Great Lakes port. The city is a center of hydronuclear electric power for New York State. The population in 1980 was 19,793.

OTSEGO LANDS. A tract of 100,000 acres on the west side of the Susquehanna River and Otsego Lake. The Otsego tract was purchased from the Indians in 1769. William Cooper laid out Cooperstown (1789), built Otsego Hall, and made a fortune from the sale of land to settlers from New England. His son, James Fenimore Cooper, was to romanticize the region in novels and tales of frontier life.

OTTAWA. *See* **Algonquin.**

OUIATENON, FORT. First established by the French in 1720 on the north bank of the Wabash River near present-day Lafayette, Ind. It was a transfer point on the fur-trading route from Fort Miami (Fort Wayne) to Vincennes and Kaskaskia (in southern Illinois). It lost its significance after the revolutionary war and in 1791 was abandoned.

OUR COUNTRY, RIGHT OR WRONG. At a dinner in his honor at Norfolk, Va., Apr. 4, 1816, Capt. Stephen Decatur offered the following toast: "Our country! In her intercourse with foreign nations may she always be in the right and always successful, right or wrong." This toast reflected U.S. nationalism incident to the War of 1812.

OUR FEDERAL UNION! IT MUST BE PRESERVED! President Andrew Jackson's volunteer toast at the Thomas Jefferson anniversary dinner, Apr. 13, 1830, was a rejoinder to speakers for states' rights. These words rallied Unionists and contributed to the successful meeting of the ominous crisis of 1833 (*see* Force Acts).

OUTER SPACE TREATY (Jan. 27, 1967). Signed by the United States, Soviet Union, Great Britain, and fifty-seven other nations, the treaty established general principles for the peaceful exploration of outer space. It banned the employment and testing of weapons in outer space and the establishment of military bases on the moon and other bodies; suspended national claims of soveriegnty in outer space; and established measures for the protection of astronauts.

OVERLAND COMPANIES. Groups who traveled from points east of the Mississippi to the Pacific coast by wagon train, as opposed to those who went by ship around Cape Horn or by the Isthmus of Darien (present-day Isthmus of Panama). The first large overland movement was the "great migration" of 1843 to Oregon, which established the Oregon Trail. The second was the California gold rush of 1849. A company was usually organized by a group of friendly families, and rules were drawn up and accepted before the start of the trek. Usually the most influential man was elected captain; a council of men was sometimes chosen to make policy.

OVERLAND EXPRESS. *See* **Pony Express.**

OVERLAND FREIGHTING. The term "overland freighting" has been applied to the carrying industry on the Overland Trail from points on the Missouri River to the Rocky Mountains or California. As soon as Salt Lake City was founded (1847) and gold discovered in California (1849), a certain amount of hauling began. This was greatly increased during the campaign of Col. Albert S. Johnston against the Mormons (1857) and by the discovery of gold in Colorado in the late 1850's (*see* Pikes Peak Gold Rush). The outfitting towns along the Missouri River (*see* Independence) were the eastern termini of the freighting routes that, for the most part, crossed the Platte Valley or the Kansas Valley to the Rocky Mountains.

Large freighting companies were established to take care of this business. The best known was Russell, Majors and Waddell, which used the towns of Atchison and Leavenworth,

Kans.; St. Joseph, Mo.; and Nebraska City, Nebr., as shipping points. Russell, Majors and Waddell ran twenty-six wagons in a train with an average load of 6,000 pounds each. The train averaged twelve to fifteen miles a day. The time required for a trip from Kansas City to Salt Lake City was about fifty days; the return trip was made in about forty. The freight rate differed with the season and the danger from Indians. The railroad usurped overland freighting.

OVERLAND MAIL AND STAGECOACHES. Monthly government mail services were established from Independence, Mo., to Santa Fe and to Salt Lake City in 1850. Thirty days were allowed for the one-way trip on each line. A similar service was begun between Salt Lake City and Sacramento, Calif., in 1851. Only one team was usually employed for the trip, and no way stations were maintained. Because of these limited facilities, most mail for California went by steamer, via Panama, with a thirty-day schedule from New York to San Francisco.

Proponents of overland mail service advocated a subsidy for the maintenance of stations and changes of teams. They finally pushed their bill through Congress. Under it, the semiweekly Southern, or Butterfield, Overland Mail Company on a twenty-five-day schedule was inaugurated in 1858, via El Paso and Tucson, angering proponents of a central route via Salt Lake City. The postmaster general defended the southern route as the only one feasible for year-round travel. To disprove this, the Pony Express was established on the central route (1860) by William H. Russell and Alexander Majors.

With the outbreak of the Civil War, the overland mail was moved to the central route in Union-controlled territory and was made a daily service (*see* Central Overland California and Pikes Peak Express). Coaches were scheduled to carry letter mail from the Missouri River to California in twenty days, other mail in thirty-five days. Ben Holladay purchased the line and contract in 1862 and extended branches to Oregon and Montana. Wells Fargo purchased Holladay's lines in 1866 and continued operations until the completion of the first transcontinental railroad in 1869 (*see* Union Pacific Railroad).

OVERLAND TRAIL (or Overland Route). A variation of the Oregon Trail, being a short route from the northeastern part of Colorado, near the forks of the Platte River, to Fort Bridger (Wyoming). It was popularized and named in 1862 when Ben Holladay's Overland Stage Line was moved to it from the old emigrant road along the North Platte River. It followed the south bank of the South Platte to Latham, near present-day Greeley, Colo., up the Cache la Poudre River, across the Laramie Plains, over Bridger's Pass (in central Wyoming), and thence west to Fort Bridger. Highways U.S. 30 and Interstate 80 now follow approximately the Overland Trail through western Wyoming.

OVERMAN ACT (May 20, 1918). Congressional criticism of delays of getting troops into action during World War I led President Woodrow Wilson to promote this act giving him almost unlimited power to reorganize, coordinate, and centralize government functions in matters relating to the war.

OVERSEER. The title given the general manager of a large agricultural unit in the antebellum South. It was his duty to maintain discipline, divide the labor, issue all supplies, care for the livestock, keep all tools and buildings in repair, and harvest the crops. The typical overseer was a native southerner, half literate, crude, and mediocre in ability, and often scorned by employer and slaves.

OWEN, FORT. Maj. John Owen built his trading post and stockade on the Bitterroot River, Mont., in 1851, adjacent to the site of St. Mary's Jesuit Mission to the Flathead Indians. In 1874, the post was closed and became dilapidated. It was repaired in 1876 to serve as a refuge for settlers during an Indian outbreak and then allowed to fall into ruin.

OWENITES. *See* **New Harmony Settlement.**

OXEN. Used from the time of the early settlements in America as draft animals and for plowing. Their slowness of pace was counterbalanced by their superiority to the horse in strength and endurance. They were used in logging and in early canal and railroad building. Oxen drew in enormous numbers for freighting in the West. Two large loaded wagons were often hooked together and drawn by six, eight, or ten yoke of oxen. Several rigs were called a "bull train." Oxen were used as late as the 1920's.

OXFORD MOVEMENT (or Tractarian movement). A religious revival that began in 1833 in the Church of England and emphasized the Catholic heritage of the Anglican communion in its doctrine, polity, and worship. In America, where it was commonly called Puseyism, after Edward B. Pusey, canon of Christ Church at Oxford, the movement found congenial soil in the Episcopal church, particularly in the General Seminary in New York City. Opposition by those who believed the movement endangered the protestantism of the church reached considerable proportions, but efforts to obtain a condemnation of Tractarianism by the General Convention of 1844 were unsuccessful. Nonetheless, the movement exercised a permanent influence throughout the Episcopal church both as to the external ceremonial of the liturgy and in a larger emphasis upon sacramental forms.

OYSTER RIVER RAID (July 18, 1694). An Indian war party, recruited in Maine and accompanied by several Frenchmen, surprised the settlement on Oyster River in Dover (New Hampshire). A few houses were successfully defended, but ninety-four persons were killed or captured.

PACIFIC CABLE. *See* **Cables, Atlantic and Pacific.**

PACIFIC COAST, FAKE EXPLORATION OF. The first individuals to attain fame in connection with the Pacific coast were the fakers: authentic persons (with one exception) who claimed exploration without actually going to those places. The earliest was Capt. Lorenzo Ferrer Maldonado, who declared that in 1588 he had voyaged in high latitudes from the Atlantic Ocean through a strait into a large sea and then through another strait that debouched on the western coast of the North American continent. Juan de Fuca, a Greek whose real name was Apostolos Valerianos, stated that in 1592 he had made a voyage along the Pacific coast, during which he had discovered the strait that now bears his name. The most colorful was Adm. Bartholomew de Fonte, created by James Petiver, a London author, in 1708. A letter purportedly written by de Fonte claimed that he had sailed north from Callao, Peru, on Apr. 3, 1640, and discovered a great river. He ascended the river to a lake, then descended a river flowing eastward until he came to the Atlantic Ocean. The letter created a controversy for decades.

PACIFIC FUR COMPANY. Organized by John Jacob Astor in 1810 as the western subsidiary of his American Fur Company. With these companies he hoped to control the American fur market. Astor supplied capital up to $400,000 and was to bear any losses for the first five years. He retained 50 percent of the stock and prorated the remainder among his field partners. The plan of operations centered on the chief depot, Astoria, at the mouth of the Columbia River in Oregon. There was also to be a chain of posts along the Columbia and Missouri river routes. The wreck of two of the ships, unfortunate management in the field, and the War of 1812 resulted in the failure of the Pacific Fur Company.

PACIFIC ISLANDS. *See* **Trust Territory of the Pacific.**

PACIFIC NORTHWEST. A region of the United States comprising the states of Oregon, Washington, and Idaho. The close economic ties and the common historical heritage of the states—all part of Old Oregon—underscore the unity of the region.

PACIFIC RAILROAD. *See* **Railroads, Sketches of Principal Lines: Union Pacific.**

PACIFIC REPUBLIC MOVEMENT. Advocated the separation of the region west of the Rockies into one or more independent states, especially on the eve of secession and during the first year of the Civil War. The first push to create a Pacific coast republic was begun by Oregon Democrats when obliged to submit to the rule of Whig party officials (1849–53) and by the people of California when Congress delayed admission of their state to the Union (1848–50). The Knights of the Golden Circle, a secret organization of southern sympathizers, took an oath to support a Pacific coast republic. It was argued that by the establishment of an independent republic, participation in the strife between North and South could be avoided.

"PACIFICUS" AND "HELVIDIUS." On Apr. 22, 1793, President George Washington issued the proclamation of neutrality designed to keep the United States out of the war between Great Britain and France. The proclamation was defended by Secretary of the Treasury Alexander Hamilton in a series of articles written under the pseudonym "Pacificus" in the *Gazette of the United States* (June 29–July 27, 1793). James Madison, then a member of the House of Representatives, replied to these in a series of letters, in the same paper, as "Helvidius" (Aug. 24–Sept. 18, 1793).

PACIFISM. Four types of pacifism have entered American life and politics: (1) conscientious objection to war, resulting in personal refusal to participate in war or military service; (2) opposition to any violence; (3) a strategy of nonviolent action to overcome specific injustices or to bring about radical change in the social order; and (4) a "positive testimony" to a way of life based on conviction of the power of love to govern human relationships.

Conscientious objection to war was a central doctrine of the "historic peace churches" (Brethren, Mennonites, and Quakers), which held war to be in fundamental contradiction to their faiths. The number of objectors and their actions varied with the moral appeal of each war, reaching a climax of opposition to U.S. military action in Vietnam and Cambodia in the late 1960's. Probably one out of five of those of draft age during this period were exempted from military service because of conscientious objection. During this time, pacifist ranks reached out to most denominations. Also, objections to war from humanitarian or philosophical convictions, rather than religious reasons—the criterion for conscientious objection specified in the Selective Training and Service Act of 1940—were legitimized by a succession of Supreme Court decisions.

The second form of pacifism abjures violence in any form and sees it operating not only in war but also through repressive social institutions. The core of the American antislavery movement was largely pacifist. Social pacifism also infused the struggle for prison reform, the fight against capital punishment, the championing of women's rights, efforts to improve care of the mentally ill and retarded, and the securing of civil rights for all minorities.

Social-reform pacifists were in conflict with those who insisted that effective action demanded violence. They were denounced as softheaded dupes, or lackeys, of the oppressors. To this, pacifism responded with its third pattern—nonviolent direct action. Modeled on Mahatma Gandhi's philosophy of civil disobedience, sit-ins (put to an early test by some unions in the industrial conflicts of the 1930's), marches (which achieved dramatic impact with the "stride toward freedom" from Selma to Montgomery, Ala., of Martin Luther King, Jr.), vigils (usually conducted by smaller groups with a strong religious motif), and boycotts (as notably organized by César E. Chavez, 1965–70, on behalf of grape pickers striking against California growers) became expressions of nonviolent protest. These actions were characterized by extraordinary self-discipline, even when met by violent counteraction.

Two influences combined to generate a fourth type of pacifism. Many conscientious objectors became increasingly troubled by the essentially negative posture of their position, which failed to create conditions for a human community. Second, there was a growing feeling that societies were past reforming and that peace would have to be sought within a small group of kindred souls. Both influences moved toward a definition of pacifism as a total philosophy of life and toward experimentation with human relationships. The first emphasized an outward "testimony" by which the principles of cooperative community could be demonstrated to others. This was the original intent of the Civilian Public Service program, organized voluntarily by the historic peace churches to offer an alternative to military service during World War II. Conscientious objector units worked on conservation and park projects, in fire fighting and disaster relief, in mental health hospitals and schools for retarded children, and as "guinea pigs" for medical research. The effectiveness of this was seriously undermined by Selective Service control and the inescapable consciousness that the testifiers were conscripts, not volunteers. The second approach rejected society in favor of a commune of persons willing to live simply and as independently as possible from the "system."

PACKAGING. Modern packaging began in the late 1890's. Gradually, more and more consumer goods were packed in containers rather than being sent to the retail store in bulk. From 1920 on, packaging of industrial goods increased in importance. Traditionally packaging has been designed to provide protection against waste and loss, identification, attractiveness and salability, light weight, economy of space, saving, low cost, and convenience. Developments since 1950 include composite film structures, shrink packaging, and thermoformed containers, as well as improvements in metal cans, glass and plastic bottles, aerosols, and point-of-sale packages. Consumer trends are encouraging the development of packages that use recycled materials or are recyclable, use child-protective closures, and provide more information.

PACKERS' AGREEMENT (1920). The investigation of the meatpacking industry begun in 1917 by the federal government resulted in the exposure of monopoly and unfair practices. Public opinion forced the larger packers to agree to sell all holdings in public stockyards, stockyard railroads, cold storage warehouses, and terminals; dispose of their interests in all market newspapers; give up the selling of all products unrelated to the meat industry; abandon the use of all transportation facilities for the carrying of any but their own products; and submit to federal injunction forbidding monopoly.

PACKERS AND STOCKYARDS ACT (August 1921). Made it unlawful for packers to manipulate prices, to create monopoly, and to award favors to any person or locality. The regulation of stockyards provided for nondiscriminatory services, reasonable rates, open schedules, and fair charges.

PACKETS, SAILING. The packet, or sailing liner, as distinguished from the "regular trader" and the transient, or tramp, was one of a line of privately owned vessels sailing in regular succession on fixed dates between specified ports. The first transatlantic packet, the Black Ball Line, began monthly service between New York and Liverpool in 1818. By 1822 the Red Star Line, the Blue Swallowtail Line, and doubled Black Ball service made weekly sailings between the two ports, augmented later by the Dramatic Line and "New Line." New York inaugurated similar service with London and Le Havre between 1822 and 1824.

Until 1838 packets conveyed most of the news, cabin passengers, and fine freight. In the next twenty years, with steamships cutting into those lucrative fields, packets carried immigrants. After the 1850's, losing even the steerage trade, they became mere freighters. The last ocean packet sailed in 1881.

The packet principle was successfully extended to coastal runs. By 1826, lines of full-rigged ships were connecting New York with the cotton ports, while lesser lines of brigs or schooners plied other coastal runs.

PACK TRAINS. Organized by trans-Allegheny pioneers. After crops were harvested, a frontier community organized a caravan of packhorses laden with goods for barter—mainly peltry and some ginseng, potash, flax, whiskey, and feed. The string of customarily ten to twenty horses usually followed an old Indian trail. The main Pennsylvania trails were the Kittanning from the Allegheny River down the Juniata Valley, and the Raystown Path from the Ohio to the eastern cities; on the main southerly route Baltimore, the earliest depot, was replaced as trading spread farther west by other Maryland cities—Frederick, Hagerstown, and Cumberland. The pack trains returned with salt, iron, sugar, lead, and urban "luxuries," such as crockery. The widening of the trails to permit wagon passage and the safety of keelboat transportation on the Ohio after 1795 pushed the pack trains into farther frontiers. Pack trains shared the Santa Fe Trail with freighters' wagons, served remote fur-trading and mining posts, and were much used by troops operating against hostile Indians.

PADLOCK INJUNCTION. When the use of the usual processes of the criminal law were insufficient to abate public nuisances, such as gambling or prostitution, the courts issued an order to padlock the premises. Anyone who tampered with the lock was held in contempt of court and punished accordingly. The injunction was used extensively during Prohibition to close premises used for bootlegging. Interpretation of the due process clause of the U.S. Constitution since Prohibition has eliminated padlocking of premises.

PAINTING.

17th Century. American works of this period are basically transplants from the artistic traditions of Europe. The earliest pictures done in America were watercolors and drawings by explorers. The artists recorded the flora and fauna of the New World or made topographical views. French, Spanish, Dutch, and English explorers painted in America. Spanish works date to the early 16th century.

A few painters settled and worked in New England. Probably the first artist by trade to arrive was Augustine Clemens, who emigrated to Boston in 1635. He was trained as a painter in Reading, northwest of London, where a style based on a mixture of traditional late Gothic linear motifs and Dutch baroque realism flourished. Pictures of Boston sitters reveal a wide range of styles and ability. The widely known portraits of John Freake and of Elizabeth Freake with baby Mary may have been done by Samuel Clemens, Augustine's son. Painted in 1674, they boast an inventive combination of naive solutions in drawing and sophisticated composition and design. Several anonymous limners painted the portraits of Abigail Adams; the Gibbs children; and others in Massachusetts.

Toward the end of the century the baroque style emerged more strongly. Thomas Smith, who painted a portrait of President William Ames of Harvard as early as 1680, is the earliest identified painter to use the baroque style. The baroque style emerged earlier in New Amsterdam. The colonists in New Amsterdam came from Holland, where Rembrandt (van Rijn) and Frans Hals were at the height of their careers. The baroque style was not filtered through an intermediate source. As in Boston, many pictures were imported. The first painter to land in New Amsterdam was Evert Duyckinck, in 1638. No pictures by him have been discovered. However, he founded a dynasty of painters in New York that lasted for three generations. By 1700, a school of painters in New York was developing.

18th Century. American painting in the 18th century followed English and continental styles. Even though it imitated European painting, it was imbued with an interest in line, geometry, and direct observation, unlike European work. Before 1727, the most important group of painters was concentrated in the Hudson River valley, sometimes known as patroon painters. Their pictures were generally painted with broken brush strokes, strong colors, and stylized modeling; the compositions often followed English mezzotint prints imported to America. The only patroon artist known by name is Pieter Vanderlyn of Kingston, N.Y.

The best paintings of the period were by Justus Englehardt Kühn and Gustavus Hesselius, who emigrated to the Chesapeake area from Germany and Sweden, respectively. They were trained in the late baroque tradition and brought the elaborate trappings of court painting. Kühn's American subjects were painted in grand gardens and formal settings. Hesselius painted allegorical subjects and Indian chiefs.

With the arrival of Peter Pelham in 1727, American painting changed. Although trained as an engraver in London, Pelham also brought the latest painting techniques to Boston. About this time, Charles Bridges appeared in Virginia, John Watson in New Jersey, and John Smibert in Boston. Smibert was the most significant. The first art exhibition in America was held in his studio in 1730, and after his death in 1751 it became a museum.

The first important native American painter was Robert Feke. Born about 1707, he probably painted as early as 1735. His first major work was the portrait of Isaac Royall and his family done in 1741. In 1742 Feke settled in Newport, and began painting portraits. In 1746 he went to Philadelphia, where he painted many socially prominent Philadelphians. In 1748 he went to Boston, where he produced more than twenty portraits, considered his best work. In 1749 he returned to Philadelphia. Both John Greenwood and Joseph Badger of Boston, who painted as early as the mid-1740's, imitated Feke in their works after 1749. John Hesselius, the son of Gustavus Hesselius, copied many of Feke's works and may have been his student. Thus, Feke may be considered the founder of the American school. English artists came to America, and colonial patrons may have preferred them for a while. The most prominent were John Wollaston and Joseph Blackburn. Wollaston came from London in 1749, and Blackburn arrived in 1754.

Benjamin West and John Singleton Copley, the two most famous American painters of the 18th century, began painting in this period. West was born in Swarthmore, Pa., in 1738, and painted as early as 1747. He progressed under the sponsorship of William Henry of Lancaster, Pa., and his style was influenced by Feke and John Hesselius. By 1759 his portraits reveal the influence of Wollaston. The next year he went to England, where he remained for the rest of his life. In London he became a leading painter and the second president of the Royal Academy of Art. West was a pioneer of all the newest European styles—neoclassicism, history painting, and romanticism.

Copley developed colonial art to its zenith. Copley was born in 1738, probably in Boston. He augmented his early training by copying European prints and studying the work of Blackburn, who came to Boston in 1754. Copley's work until 1765 followed the society portrait format of Feke and Blackburn, but Copley's ability to render objects with intense verisimilitude emerged, culminating in the *Boy With a Squirrel.* Copley incorporated the realism of this work into his society commissions and became increasingly successful, but an ambition to go to England grew. By 1774 the gathering clouds of the Revolution cut into his portrait business, and he decided to travel to Europe; he never returned.

After Copley's departure the most important painter in the colonies was Charles Willson Peale, one of West's first pupils. Peale, who had briefly studied with John Hesselius and visited Copley in Boston, was sent to England in 1765 to study with West while the latter was pursuing his neoclassical style. Peale's first works were influenced by the neoclassical style, but he soon formulated his own style based on aspects of Hogarth and Reynolds. Peale's work often revealed a great interest in nature, and landscapes figure in his portraits.

A long line of artists started painting in America as amateurs, traveled to London to study with West, and returned. John Trumbull and Ralph Earl were from Connecticut. Trumbull first studied painting at Harvard by copying Copley portraits there. He always had a more intellectual approach and became interested in history painting at the suggestion of Thomas Jefferson. Earl was more common; after learning high-style English portrait techniques under West, he returned to Connecticut and changed to a style akin to folk painting.

Gilbert Stuart was the best and most influential pupil of West. He began painting in Newport about 1770 and went to London in 1775. He returned in 1793 and painted many federal leaders, the most famous portraits being those of Washington.

West's school still competed with continental and English artists painting in America—Pierre Charles L'Enfant and Charles Fevret de Saint-Mémin from France, Christian Gullagher from Denmark, and Robert Edge Pine and Edward Savage from England. Francis Guy, John Shaw, and William R. Birch settled in Philadelphia in the 1790's. Their genre, landscape, and marine painting reflected the interests of Trumbull, Earl, and Peale.

Romantic Painting. Although the 19th century saw the fullest expression of romanticism, the 18th century provided the foundation for a change from formalist concepts of rational order to expressions of intuitive impulse. Artists began turning away from the works of man; nature, especially in its wilder aspects, was used as a vehicle for expression. Narrative painting also assumed a romantic character as painters of historical, religious, and genre subjects gave greater emphasis to the drama of the setting.

One of the earliest precursors of the romantic style in America was William Williams, an English adventurer-artist who worked in Philadelphia from 1747 until the Revolution. Many of his conversation-piece portraits contain moody, theatrical backgrounds. Williams' only recognized pupil was West. West's principal American disciples, Copley, Trumbull, and Washington Allston, each turned to historical narrative painting in the romantic mode. Copley's *Watson and the Shark* (1778) reveals West's influence in the direction of forceful romantic realism. Trumbull's most successful efforts were achieved in history painting. Of the three, Allston was most affected by literary values. His career ended with the monumental, never-completed *Belshazzar's Feast,* begun in 1817, which may be considered the terminal effort of West's school. At midcentury the Düsseldorf Academy inspired equally ambitious projects. The central work was Emanuel Leutze's *Washington Crossing the Delaware* (1851), marking a change from romanticism to sentimentality in history painting.

Portraiture also turned from the neoclassical mode to romanticism. Allston's principal pupil, Samuel F. B. Morse, was a prime mover in establishing the romantic poetry of mood. The portrait of his daughter, *The Muse: Susan Walker Morse* (ca. 1835–37), forcefully conveys such emotionalism. The most prolific portrait painter of the period was Thomas Sully, whose large works were charged with dramatic chiaroscuro.

Landscape painting came into prominence in America during the second quarter of the 19th century with a group of New York artists who formed what is loosely known as the Hudson River school. Two of its senior members, Thomas Doughty and Asher B. Durand, were largely self-taught. Doughty's intensely somber and frequently imaginary landscapes epitomize a rustic romanticism. Durand's work, although more sophisticated, offers further example of the school's gentle lyricism. The leader of the school, Thomas Cole, idealized the Hudson River valley landscape and offered interpretations of nature in his paintings that transcend mere description of visual phenomena. His ambitious allegorical fantasies reflect romanticism's preoccupation with the transitoriness of life. His only student, Frederick E. Church, carried landscape painting into a new realm in vast panoramic views of often exotic content. Church was part of a group who developed a new style, luminism. This approach combined a meticulous study of nature with an extremely delicate treatment of atmospheric color; it affected to minimize as much as possible the presence of the artist in the creation of the work. Other notable practitioners were marine painter Fitz Hugh Lane and landscape painters Martin J. Heade, John F. Kensett, and Sanford R. Gifford.

The romantic tradition was strong in the work of American genre painters, especially in the mid-19th century. Literature often furnished the artist with subject matter. The writings of Washington Irving and James Fenimore Cooper gave impetus to the wild visions of John Quidor and Charles Deas. Scenes of everyday life, properly in the genre idiom, were usually portrayed with benign humor. William Sidney Mount devoted his entire career to depicting life in rural Long Island. The western frontier had its own exponent of romantic realism, George C. Bingham. Genre and history mingled in the work of David G. Blythe, whose slightly primitive style often aimed at political satire. George Catlin and Alfred Jacob Miller created an extremely large body of work on the Plains Indians, whom they idealized in styles ranging from romantic realism to fantasy. Seth Eastman was one of the few explorer-artists who was consistently objective in his paintings; yet, even with him, the "noble savage" lingers on.

By the third quarter of the 19th century, fantasy was an important aspect of American romantic tradition. William Rimmer was beset by fears that he externalized in pictures of dreamlike images. The heavily worked paintings of Albert P. Ryder are intensely subjective; yet they possess an enamellike beauty of unusual order. Ralph A. Blakelock concentrated almost exclusively on landscape subjects of a brooding intensity. One of the few painters of fantasy with an academic orientation was Elihu Vedder.

Inevitably realist painters such as Winslow Homer and Thomas Eakins, created certain paintings that partake of the romantic impulse. Poetry of mood is present in large measure; yet the works of the realists and the later impressionists do not aim at generating emotional response from the viewer and true romantic painting ceased to occupy a central place.

Early Naturalism. As early as 1810–20, Charles Willson Peale and his younger brother James were painting landscapes, portraits, and still lifes that were remarkably free of both sentiment and allegory. These were the first endeavors in realistic, yet unidealized, painting and the beginning of a tradition that was to last for half a century.

The portraits of Chester Harding, and many of those by Morse provided uncompromising likenesses without the brilliant surfaces and colorism of the Stuart-Sully tradition and often without their charm. Morse's *Old House of Representatives* (1821–22) and his *View From Apple Hill* (1828–29), despite the idealization of the figures in the latter, are convincing representations; these works place him among the pioneers of naturalism.

Another category of naturalist endeavor was the painting of the flora and fauna as practiced first by Alexander Wilson and later by the better-known John James Audubon.

Genre painting usually derived from European models and included foreign subjects. From the 1830's through the 1850's American subjects and the direct observation of nature were combined. Such a point of view was first manifest in the paintings of rural Long Island in the 1830's by Mount, who portrayed the natural object without reference to allegory, sentiment, or moral commentary.

The genre paintings of Bingham are much more anecdotal than Mount's, and many of his larger canvases are crowded and contrived in comparison. Nevertheless, Bingham was squarely in the naturalist tradition.

American Renaissance. The years 1880–1930 are generally called the American Renaissance because all the arts flourished as never before or since in America. One of these arts was mural decoration. The first great example is that of Constantino Brumidi in the national Capitol. He worked at about the time of the Civil War but had no followers.

Nothing occurred on a grand scale until 1893, with the opening of the World's Columbian Exposition in Chicago. Francis D. Millet was put in charge of the mural work at the fair, and he invited Charles Yardley Turner, Kenyon Cox, Edward Emerson Simmons, William de Leftwich Dodge, to Chicago.

While mural painting flourished for the first time, American easel painting became caught up in European fashion. In the late 19th century, painting turned to a preoccupation with nature in the form of realism and the replacement of the ancient technique of transparent glazes with the use of opaque pigment, called direct painting. The artist painted for himself, not on commission, except for portraits. What had been art of decoration, became a form of self-expression.

Most American painters found their way to Paris. Toward the end of the 1870's the first flood returned and founded the Society of American Artists in New York City to promote naturalism and direct painting. Not long afterward, they won over the National Academy of Design, the nation's chief artistic organization at the time. Eakins is the outstanding example of the artist interpreting nature realistically on the French model.

The most successful expatriates were John Singer Sargent, and James McNeil Whistler.

American easel painters, in accepting the new interpretation of nature and the use of opaque paint, led the American collector to French artists who were more skilled than they.

America succumbed to every artistic fashion coming from Europe. After 1890, influenced by Mary Cassatt, Americans bought French impressionists. An American impressionist school included Cassatt, Childe Hassam, J. Alden Weir, and John H. Twachtman.

A few painters worked independently of European fashion and along traditional lines. Among the older artists were the landscapists Homer, William Trost Richards, and Thomas Moran. Vedder looked to the Italian Renaissance, as did the younger George de Forest Brush.

About 1910 yet another fashion came out of Europe—modern art. Once again foreign artists were the chief beneficiaries of American patronage. The 1920's saw the world of easel painting moving slowly into chaos, with the art museum taking over such artists' organizations as the National Academy of Design and the Pennsylvania Academy of Art.

20th Century. 20th-century American painting can be seen as a series of revolutions against previous styles and approaches. The so-called Ash Can school—which included John Sloan, Maurice B. Prendergast, and Robert Henri—brought forth a revolution in subject rather than in style during the first two decades of the century. From 1910 until about 1915 Stanton Macdonald-Wright and Morgan Russell, dubbing themselves synchromists, produced nonobjective and nearly nonobjective paintings based on the emotive effects of colors. From about 1915 to 1930, Max Weber, John Marin, Joseph Stella, Stuart Davis, and others fragmented and recombined parts of city scenes after the manner of European cubists. During the 1920's Charles Sheeler, Georgia O'Keeffe, and Charles Demuth simplified sometimes to a geometrical core objects pushed starkly up to the frontal plane—a style called precisionism from the dry, linear handling.

In the late 1920's and 1930's there was a reaction against the European-based modernism of the 1920's, and a spirit of isolationism took hold. The regionalists Grant Wood, Thomas Hart Benton, and John Steuart Curry focused on authentically American types. The theme of the city was taken up by Edward Hopper and Charles Burchfield. Ben Shahn, William Gropper, and George Grosz used their posterlike art as a means of social protest.

By the mid-1940's a new wave of modernism, abstract expressionism, had asserted itself in opposition to the naturalism of the 1930's. Painters came from far and wide—Arshile Gorky from Armenia, Willem de Kooning from Holland, Mark Rothko from Russia, Jackson Pollock from Wyoming—to congregate in New York. The presence in New York of such major modernist European émigrés as Piet Mondrian and Salvador Dali encouraged these painters. The German painter Hans Hofmann was an inspiration for the group in the 1940's, as well as a major theoretician of nonobjective painting. The abstract expressionists worked their way through the cubism of Pablo Picasso and the surrealism of Joan Miró to arrive at a variety of nonobjective approaches, which seemed underived and placed a premium on spontaneity of execution. New York became the international center of avant-garde art.

Unassociated with abstract expressionism were the West Coast painter Mark Tobey, whose gossamer-thin, seemingly endless webs of lines were related to the unity preached by his Baha'i faith, and Milton C. Avery, whose flattened landscapes and figures were presented with a childlike directness.

By 1960 abstract expressionism had run its course. Jasper Johns was painting a series of American flags and other recognizable objects, and Robert Rauschenberg was combining silk-screened images with splatters of paint, after the manner of the abstract expressionists. The pop artists Andy Warhol, Roy Lichtenstein, and James Rosenquist did away completely with the gestural, improvisational approach of the abstract expressionists. They worked in the glossy, impersonal format of their subjects—items and images in supermarkets and on billboards. In the late 1960's and increasingly so in the 1970's photorealism was in vogue, with such proponents as Chuck Close, Richard Estes, Alfred Leslie, Philip Pearlstein, and M.C. Escher.

The nonobjective painters of the 1960's, avoided all marks of the manipulation of the paint, as well as the notion of forms existing in some sort of spatial receptacle. Canvases were often left unprimed so that the acrylic paint could seep into the fabric, thus avoiding the sensation of depth. Jules Olitski sprayed his paint onto the canvas in tiny droplets to imitate the look of the atmosphere, and Morris Louis inclined his canvas to let his thinned-out paint flow into vague shapes. In their paintings the color sensation matters; the sorts of psychic innuendoes of abstract expressionism are absent. In the paintings of the hard-edge post-painterly abstractionists, the surfaces are smooth and enamellike, and the colors precisely demarcated. Frank Stella introduced the nonrectilinear canvas, whose shape determined the configurations of the painted surface. A branch of the hard-edge painters, the op (optical) artists, including Richard Anuskiewicz and Victor Vasarely played with a variety of optical illusions.

PAIRING. A practice whereby two members of Congress of opposing parties who plan to be absent agree that, during a specified period, they will refrain from voting in person, but will permit their names to be recorded on opposite sides of each question. It was first used in the House of Representatives in 1824 and was first openly avowed in 1840, but it was not officially recognized in the House rules until 1880. Pairing is also permitted in the Senate and in state legislatures.

PAIUTE. The western Great Basin, an arid desert from southeastern Oregon through southern California, was the homeland of Paiute, of whom there were an estimated 7,500 in 1845. The environment and the mode of subsistence of these peoples precluded any extensive tribal development. Dependent on the gathering of wild seeds and fruits, the small local groupings wandered in areas familiar to them and met with neighboring groups for social activities and marriage.

The Paiute are generally classified on the basis of language. There are two main languages, both branches of Shoshonean, a subdivision of the major Uto-Aztecan phylum. A typical Basin adaptation was achieved especially by the southern Paiute. The northern Paiute were less well defined and spread as a linguistic unit from southeastern Oregon to southeastern California. They were variously identified as Paiute, Mono-Paviotso, and Paviotso and show a gradual fading into the Californian focus. The northern Paiute were first encountered in 1825 by the trader Jedediah Smith. The southern Paiute were described by the Spanish priest Silvestre Vélez de Escalante in 1776. It was a northern Paiute, Wovoka, who in 1889 originated the second Ghost Dance movement. In the early 1980's the northern Paiute numbered about 4,000 and the southern Paiute about 1,800.

PALATINE JURISDICTIONS. The palatine lords in medieval Europe enjoyed within their domains unusual immunities from royal interference. These jurisdictions presented, among other things, a way of governing remote areas, as is suggested by the locations of the three English palatinates of Durham, Cheshire, and Lancashire.

In America the bishopric of Durham is of greatest importance. Although little of the independence of palatine jurisdictions remained by the 17th century, English colonizers undertook to transplant the system to America. The obvious risks assumed by promoters of colonization led to a demand for exceptional rights and powers in controlling their settlements. Where the grant was to a member of the landed classes there was a disposition to follow customary forms and define these powers in terms of feudal prerogatives. Thus, proprietary projects frequently enjoyed jurisdictional rights similar to those of palatine lords. Several grants (notably Maryland in 1632 and Carolina in 1663) even stipulated that the grantees should enjoy an authority equal to that of the bishop of Durham. Such efforts to transfer to America outworn feudal usages led to many problems.

PALATINES. German Protestants from the Rhenish or Lower Palatinate, who in 1708–09, because of war, religious persecution, or famine, went to England to petition for assistance from Queen Anne to settle in America. In July 1709 an abortive attempt was made to settle 794 families in Ireland, and in August of that year a group of 600 were sent to North Carolina. Most were settled in the Hudson Valley, in New York, with the expectation that they would manufacture naval stores. Failing at this, many left for Pennsylvania or New Jersey; and 150 families went to Schoharie, N.Y. On his arrival in 1720, Gov. William Burnet of New York was ordered to move the Palatines to the frontier, and a few settled on the Mohawk near Ilion, in Herkimer County, formerly German Flats.

PALEONTOLOGY. The study of fossil remains. In the 1700's giant fossil teeth led settlers to speculate on the former presence of monstrous beasts. Because of Thomas Jefferson's paleontological interests, the White House had one of the first scientific exhibitions of fossils. During the first quarter of the 19th century, the scientific study of fossils was placed on a firm geologic base by the concepts of stratigraphic succession and correlation. Some of the state geological surveys that were established during the period 1820–50 included paleontology among their published results. The plan for a survey of New York State included the study of fossils. Timothy Conrad was appointed paleontologist of the survey in 1837; he established that the rocks within the state are from the Silurian and Devonian ages. He later did fundamental studies on the younger invertebrates in the coastal plain of the eastern and southern states and was among the first to describe fossils from the Pacific Northwest.

Conrad was succeeded in 1843 by James Hall. Hall's books

have become classics. The second most prolific producer of fossil descriptions, after his contemporary Joachim Barrande, he made the fossils of New York among the best known in the world. In 1878 he was elected president of the First International Geological Congress.

With the Charles Wilkes exploring expedition (1838–42), which employed James Dwight Dana as geologist-paleontologist, the federal government began to assume a role in investigations of natural history and natural resources. During 1840–60, a series of expeditions explored the western territories. In 1879 four separate territorial surveys were combined in the U.S. Geological Survey. Although a few fossils had been described earlier in government documents, F. B. Meek is the first federal paleontologist. He began as Hall's assistant (1852), but eventually went to the Smithsonian Institution, where he was a self-employed paleontologist. Meek was succeeded by C. A. White. By 1900 there were about ten federal paleontologists; the most prominent was C. D. Walcott.

Because the field was so small, one person produced most literature on a large group of fossils. E. O. Ulrich and George H. Girty dominated the study of Lower Paleozoic and Upper Paleozoic rocks, respectively, during the first three decades of the 20th century; T. W. Stanton studied fossils from somewhat younger rocks, and W. H. Dall worked on recent mollusks and allied, relatively young fossils.

The study of fossils is three-fold. Vertebrate fossils have aroused the most interest but have attracted few workers. Invertebrate fossils have received more scientific investigation but less attention; and fossil plants have attracted neither until recently. Plant studies may be divided into two groups. The coal-bearing deposits of eastern North America incorporate impressive fossil floras. J. S. Newberry worked on the plants of Ohio (1869–74); but he is as well known for his work on Paleozoic invertebrates of the West and he was also among the first in the United States to describe fossil fish. The leading paleobotanical specialist was Leo Lesquereux, who wrote *Coal Flora of Pennsylvania* (1879–84). His work was refined and extended by David White of the U.S. Geological Survey. The younger, nonmarine beds of the West also yielded a large number of plants, which were first described by Lesquereux. Lester Ward and Frank Knowlton, both with the Geological Survey, later described these plants and found differences in the age of the beds.

Bones are the best known fossils; and the one particularly associated with North America is the large vertebrate. Just prior to the Civil War vast deposits of extinct mammal remains were found in the Badlands of South Dakota. These were described by Joseph Leidy. His work, completed in 1869, attracted the attention of O. C. Marsh and Edward D. Cope, rivals in pursuit of the big bones. Their feuding, particularly virulent during the 1870's, eventually affected the Geological Survey and was a factor in the resignation of J. W. Powell.

The concept of evolution had essentially no impact on the field of paleontology in America. Louis Agassiz was a leading opponent of Charles Darwin, but eventually he tacitly accepted Darwinian evolution. A few invertebrate paleontologists attempted to find evolutionary principles in the history of certain fossil groups, but generally evolution was ignored. The pursuit of stratigraphic paleontology did not depend on a belief in organic evolution.

For the most part, paleontologists were self-taught. Some learned by working under Hall at Albany. After the Civil War, a number of home-trained paleontologists came from the Cincinnati area, where fossils were prolific. Marsh was the first professor of paleontology in the United States. Not until the 20th century did a few professors give formal training to graduate students.

After World War I a new field opened for paleontology—the study of microfossils, which can be seen only with the aid of a hand lens. One-celled organisms that secrete a calcareous shell were known for many years and had been described as fossils. J. A. Cushman demonstrated that these forms change rapidly through time and can be used to date rocks. Because these small fossils could be recovered from the drill cuttings of oil wells, they found an obvious economic applicability. The years 1920–40 were the era of "the bug picker," and the efflorescence of oil discovery during that time was a result of this work.

The principles of subsurface paleontology developed by the micropaleontologists have been transferred to other groups of still smaller organisms. During the period 1940–60, palynology, the study of spores and pollen, was recognized as a separate subdiscipline. With the development of more sophisticated optical techniques, remains of fossils may be found in the future in virtually every sedimentary rock. The new techniques have been used to push the record of life on earth back. We know that some simple organisms are more than 3 billion years old.

Since World War II, there has been an explosive expansion of the field. The number of paleontologists in the mid-1970's was about 2,000, probably a tenfold increase over the total number for the first 150 years. Although a slow growth in government employment of paleontologists has been compensated for by the interest of oil companies, in the 1970's the majority of the profession were at colleges.

PALMER'S DISCOVERY OF ANTARCTICA. According to the logbook of the sloop *Hero,* Capt. Nathaniel Brown Palmer, an American, discovered the mainland of Antarctica on Nov. 18, 1820, about eighty days before the reputed date of discovery by Capt. John Davis. Palmer made his initial landfall at 63°45′ south latitude and 60°10′ west longitude on that part of the mainland now known as Palmer Peninsula. He explored other parts of the coast going as far as Marguerite Bay, and, with George Powell, discovered the South Orkney Islands in December 1821.

PALMETTO COCKADES. Emblems adopted by the States' Rights party in South Carolina during the nullification controversy in 1832, in which supporters of states' rights tried unsuccessfully to declare the national protective tariff acts of 1828 and 1832 null and void.

PALMITO RANCH, BATTLE OF (May 13, 1865). The last land battle of the Civil War. On May 12, Union Col. Theodore H. Barrett, stationed near the mouth of the Rio Grande in Texas, drove out a small group of Confederates at Palmito Ranch, twelve miles below Brownsville. The following day the southern troops moved back into their former position with reinforcements. Barrett began a retreat. A three-hour running fight began in which Barrett reported a loss in killed and missing of 111 men.

PALO ALTO, BATTLE OF (May 8, 1846). The first battle of the Mexican War. Gen. Zachary Taylor's army of about 2,200 men defeated a Mexican force of nearly three times its number under Gen. Mariano Arista twelve miles northeast of Brownsville, Tex.

PALOMAR OBSERVATORY. *See* **Hale Observatories.**

PAMPHLETEERING. The carrying on of controversy by means of pamphlets, which, because they are inexpensive to produce, provide an easy means of propagating new or unpopular ideas. Sermons, often with a political tinge, were effective as pamphlets in colonial America; and the writings of James Otis, Stephen Hopkins, John Dickinson, and others debated the issue of taxation by Parliament. Leaders of the Revolution wrote many pamphlets to justify their course, and some tracts were issued by the Loyalists. The ablest pamphleteer of the Revolution was Thomas Paine. His *Common Sense* was one of the strongest and most effective arguments for independence, and *The Crisis* papers were a powerful buttress to the morale of the patriot cause.

Issues confronting the new government, and especially the question of the federal Constitution, were freely aired in pamphlets. Multiplication of newspapers in the early national period made pamphlet warfare less common, but religious enthusiasts, reform groups, and propagators of Utopian societies or economic panaceas still found the pamphlet an effective agent. Toward the end of the 19th century, Socialists and Populists used pamphlets to gain converts, and a Free Silverite produced the notorious *Coin's Financial School.* Government propagandists during World War I utilized the pamphlet to sustain morale or refute criticism. Since World War I the pamphlet has been used mostly for information purposes.

PAN-AFRICANISM. Began at the end of the 19th century under the leadership of American and West Indian blacks. It is the belief that, despite linguistic, tribal, or religious differences, Africans are one people whose goal is African unity. Until the end of World War II, the movement was directed mainly against the evils of colonialism.

At the first Pan-African Congress, organized in 1900 by Henry Sylvester-William, a West Indian lawyer, thirty delegates from England, the United States, and the West Indies met in London. The leading figure in this early phase of the movement was W. E. B. Du Bois. At the end of World War I, despite opposition by the U.S. government, Du Bois was able to gather fifty-seven blacks in Paris, including a number of Africans, to appeal to the Peace Conference of Versailles for a code of laws to protect Africans. But the conference was unwilling to extend to Africans the principle of self-determination adopted for Europeans.

Du Bois was still the leading spokesman at the Second Pan-African Congress in 1921, but by then the majority of those attending were from Africa. The third congress, in 1923, and the fourth, in 1927, were even less influential and did little more than keep Pan-Africanism alive.

The Fifth Pan-African Congress, which met in Manchester, England, in 1945, reflected a major change in aim. Two hundred black delegates from all parts of the English-speaking world participated. At the age of seventy-three Du Bois was still the symbolic leader, but active leadership was provided by a group of young energetic Africans, including Jomo Kenyatta of Kenya, Peter Abrahams of South Africa, Nnamdi Azikiwe of Nigeria, and Kwame Nkrumah of the Gold Coast (later Ghana). The main theme was national independence and the strategies for attaining it.

The national movements among various groups of Africans and the successful move to independence, beginning with that of Ghana in 1957, created problems for Pan-Africanism and somewhat altered its direction. Nkrumah, as prime minister of Ghana, defined it as an effort to create a third force in the world to which the industrialized nations would be compelled to give attention and provide assistance. The Organization of African Unity (OAU) was created in 1963 as the instrument for maintaining solidarity and accomplishing this end. But its inability to deal satisfactorily with crisis within Africa limited the effectiveness of this aspect of Pan-Africanism. Furthermore, nationalism within the various black African countries appeared to be a stronger force than Pan-Africanism. After 1968, with the creation of a number of regional economic organizations, the major efforts at international cooperation in Africa began to focus on the economic sphere.

PANAMA, DECLARATION OF. (Oct. 3, 1939). Adopted at Panama City by the Consultative Meeting of Foreign Ministers of the American Republics. To deal with conditions created by the outbreak of war in Europe, sixteen resolutions or sets of resolutions and declarations were adopted, No. XIV, entitled "Declaration of Panama," consisted of a preamble and four declarations: that American waters should be "free from the commission of any hostile act by any non-American belligerent nation; that the republics would attempt to secure compliance with the declaration by the belligerents; that further consultation, if necessary, would be made to "determine upon the measures" to be undertaken "to secure the observance" of the declaration; and that individual or collective patrols by the republics of "the waters adjacent to their coasts" would be made when needed.

PANAMA CANAL. A fifty-one-mile waterway through the Isthmus of Panama, connecting the Atlantic and Pacific oceans. During the last half of the 19th century, U.S. interest in a canal was limited almost exclusively to the Nicaraguan route. In 1849 U.S. private interests obtained an exclusive concession from Nicaragua for construction of a canal there, but the Clayton-Bulwer Treaty of 1850 with Great Britain precluded exclusive construction or control of a canal by either country. Also in 1850, a New York corporation was granted an exclusive concession by New Granada to construct a railroad across the Isthmus of Panama. The railroad, completed in 1855, was an immediate financial success and served as an important factor in subsequent developments.

In 1881, under a concession granted by Colombia in 1878, the French engineer Ferdinand de Lesseps commenced construction of a canal on the Panama route. A substantial amount of excavation had been completed before work was abandoned in 1889, when the French Canal Company went into bankruptcy.

In 1898 the voyage of the U.S.S. *Oregon* around Cape Horn at the outbreak of the Spanish-American War added military necessity to the arguments for construction of a canal. The first Isthmian Canal Commission, appointed in the United States in 1899, submitted a report in 1901 recommending the Nicaraguan route; and in 1901 the United States negotiated the Hay-Pauncefote Treaty with Great Britain permitting U.S. control, operation, and protection of a neutral canal.

In January 1902 the Isthmian Canal Commission recommended construction of a canal on the Panama route if the United States could obtain the assets of the New Panama Canal Company (the name given to the bankrupt French Canal Company after reorganization in 1894) for $40 million and if Colombia would grant perpetual U.S. control over the territory required for the canal. The Spooner Act of June 28, 1902, authorized construction if the commission's conditions were met within a reasonable time. On Jan. 22, 1903, the United States and Colombia signed the Hay-Herrán Treaty meeting the requirements of the Spooner Act, but Colombia refused to ratify the treaty; after the rejection Panama revolted and declared its independence on Nov. 3, 1903. The United States recognized the new government of Panama on Nov. 6; and on Nov. 13, Bunau-Varilla, now Panama's minister to the United States, signed a treaty with the United States providing for the construction and operation of the canal in Panama. The treaty was proclaimed on Feb. 26, 1904.

The treaty granted to the United States in perpetuity the control of a zone of land for a transisthmian canal. Within that zone, Panama granted to the United States all the rights, power, and authority. The United States guaranteed the independence of the Republic of Panama and agreed to pay Panama $10 million in cash and an annuity of $250,000.

The threat to the project posed by tropical diseases was eliminated by the brilliant and energetic program of the health authorities under the direction of Col. William C. Gorgas. The Isthmian Canal Commission was designated to construct the canal, but the exigencies of the work soon required a consolidation of responsibility and authority. As chief engineer (1905–07) and chairman, John F. Stevens is credited with the successful implementation of the first phases of actual construction. After Stevens resigned, the canal was completed under the leadership of Lt. Col. G. W. Goethals (1907–14). In 1906, Congress resolved a bitter controversy by directing the construction of a lock canal rather than a sea-level canal. The canal opened on Aug. 15, 1914.

The canal was operated under the terms of the Panama Canal Act of Aug. 24, 1912, and executive orders. In 1928, Congress authorized the codification of all laws applicable in the Canal Zone and in 1934 enacted the Canal Zone Code.

Even before construction was completed, Panama became dissatisfied with the terms of the 1903 treaty. A treaty signed on Mar. 2, 1936, and ratified in 1939, abrogated provisions of the 1903 treaty guaranteeing the independence of Panama by the United States and requiring Panamanian compliance with sanitary ordinances prescribed by the United States. It increased Panama's annuity to $430,000 and placed certain restrictions on residence, importations, and commercial activities in the Canal Zone.

The 1955 Eisenhower-Remón Treaty further increased Panama's annuity to $1,930,000, provided for the return to Panama of some real estate, withdrew from Panamanian employees living in Panama the privilege of making purchases in Canal Zone stores, granted to Panama the right to tax Panamanians employed in the Canal Zone, provided for equality of opportunity and treatment for Panamanians in Canal Zone employment, and provided for construction of a bridge over the canal at the Pacific entrance. After this treaty, the issues in dispute focused increasingly on demands for recognition of Panama's sovereignty in the Canal Zone. Serious riots along the border occurred in 1959 and 1964.

At the time of the 1964 riots, which resulted in about twenty-four casualties, Panama broke off diplomatic relations with the United States; relations were resumed in April 1964, when negotiations for a new treaty were begun. On July 3, 1967, the treaty negotiators reached agreement on three related treaties: (1) a treaty abrogating the 1903 treaty, recognizing Panamanian sovereignty, and providing for the joint operation of the existing canal until the end of the century, with royalty payments (about $20 million a year) to Panama based on the tonnage of cargo moving through the canal; (2) a treaty granting the United States an option to build a sea-level canal and providing for operation of such a canal by a joint authority for sixty years after its opening or until 2067, whichever is first; and (3) a treaty providing for U.S. military bases in Panama for a period generally coterminous with the periods of operation of any canal by the proposed joint authority. On Aug. 5, 1970, Panama formally rejected the 1967 draft treaties, and negotiations were resumed.

In September 1977 the United States and Panama signed two treaties, which transferred the Canal Zone to Panama's control (it became Colón Free Zone); provided for administration of the canal by a joint U.S.-Panamanian body, the Panama Canal Commission; and stipulated that U.S. military forces would remain in Panama until the year 2000 and would guarantee the canal's neutrality thereafter. Congress ratified both treaties in April 1978.

PANAMA CITY. The capital of Panama since 1903, it was the center from which the exploration and conquest of the Pacific coast of Central and South America were carried on, and a point of transshipment throughout the colonial period. The city was moved to its present location in 1674.

PANAMA CONGRESS. On Dec. 7, 1824, Simón Bolívar sent invitations for a "congress of representatives of the republics, kingdoms, and empires of America" to Colombia, Mexico, Central America, Brazil, the United Provinces of Buenos Aires, and Peru. The United States was eventually invited at the insistence of Colombia and Mexico. Ten meetings were held, at Panama City from June 22 to July 15 1826; but only Colombia, Peru, Mexico, and Central America were represented. The delegates signed a treaty of perpetual union and confederation and a convention providing for a common army and navy.

PANAMA-PACIFIC INTERNATIONAL EXPOSITION (Feb. 4–Dec. 4, 1915). Held in San Francisco, it celebrated the opening of the Panama Canal and the discovery of the Pacific Ocean by Vasco Núñez de Balboa in 1513.

PANAMA RAILROAD. Built by a U.S. company (1849–55) for about $8 million. Until the building of transcontinental railways in the United States, the Panama Railroad carried thousands of passengers on their way from New York to California. Later, the French Panama Canal Company purchased nearly all of the capital stock. These shares were subsequently transferred to the U.S. government in 1902. From 1951 the line was operated by the Panama Canal Company, the U.S. government corporation that operated the Panama Canal; in 1979 the railroad became part of a government-owned system.

PANAMA REVOLUTION. On Aug. 12, 1903, the Colombian senate refused to ratify the Hay-Herrán Treaty authorizing the construction of an interoceanic canal at Panama by the United States. This caused much discontent in Panama, then under Colombian rule, and on Nov. 3 a group of revolutionists seized control of the city and proclaimed the Republic of Panama.

Colombian forces had been sent to Colón, on the opposite side of the isthmus, just before the outbreak, but they were prevented from crossing to Panama by the commander of the U.S.S. *Nashville.* On Nov. 6 the United States recognized the independence of Panama. The revolutionists appointed Bunau-Varilla Panamanian minister at Washington, and on Nov. 18 he signed a treaty with Secretary of State John Hay by which the United States was given the exclusive right to build and control a canal and in return guaranteed Panama's independence (*see* Hay–Bunau-Varilla Treaty).

PANAMA TOLLS QUESTION. A bill enacted late in 1912 to regulate the Panama Canal once it was completed exempted U.S. coastwise vessels from payment of tolls. The British protested, pointing out that the exemption violated the Hay-Pauncefote Treaty of 1901. The American government defended exemption but expressed willingness to arbitrate. Congress repealed the exemption clause, and on June 15, 1914, the president signed the repeal bill.

PAN-AMERICAN CONFERENCES. *See* **Latin America, Relations With.**

PAN-AMERICAN EXPOSITION (1901). Held at Buffalo, N.Y., it witnessed the assassination of President William McKinley after the delivery of his Pan-American speech on Sept. 6, 1901. The fair was designed to show the progress of a century in the New World and to promote commercial and social interests.

PAN-AMERICAN GAMES. A series of contests conducted at four-year intervals for athletes from the American nations. The first games were held in 1951 at Buenos Aires, Argentina. The Pan-American Games are similar to the Olympic Games but include sports such as baseball and women's basketball. Pan-American games have been held at Mexico City (1955), Chicago (1959), São Paulo, Brazil (1963), Winnipeg, Canada (1967), Cali, Colombia (1971), Mexico City (1975), and San Juan, Puerto Rico (1979).

PAN-AMERICAN UNION. An international agency of Western Hemisphere nations with headquarters in Washington, D.C. It was founded on Apr. 14, 1890, as the International Bureau of the American Republics and was renamed in 1910. The union became the permanent secretariat of the Organization of American States (OAS) when it was created by twenty-one republics at Bogotá on Apr. 30, 1948. Under the direction of the OAS Council, it promotes economic, social, juridical, and cultural relations; prepares the programs and regulations of OAS conferences; and serves as the distributor of documents and the custodian of archives of conferences and instruments of ratification of inter-American agreements.

***PANAY* INCIDENT.** On Dec. 12, 1937, Japanese bombers, engaged in war with China, bombed and sank the clearly marked U.S. gunboat *Panay* and three Standard Oil supply ships twenty-seven miles above Nanking on the Yangtze River. The ships were engaged in evacuating American officials from China. Secretary of State Cordell Hull demanded full redress. Japan accepted responsibility, made formal apologies, and promised indemnities, later set at more than $2 million.

PANHANDLE. A long, usually narrow, tract of land appended to the main area of a state.

PANIC OF 1785. Put an end to the business boom following the American Revolution and ushered in a three-year period of hard times. Its causes lay in the overexpansion, extravagance, and debts incurred following the victory at Yorktown; the deflation that accompanied the end of army contracts and privateering; the blow to American manufactures from large imports of British goods; and the lack of adequate credit facilities and a sound circulating medium. The depression was aggravated by the absence of any central mechanism for promoting interstate trade and by state laws interfering with it; by the British refusal to conclude a commercial treaty; and by disorders among debtor groups (*see* Shays's Rebellion).

PANIC OF 1792. The economic prosperity that accompanied the launching of the federal government developed into a speculative boom by late 1791. Schemes for internal improvements; the chartering by state legislatures of inadequately financed banks; and speculation in bank scrip, government securities, and western lands brought a collapse.

PANIC OF 1819. Resulted from a sharp contraction of credit initiated by the second Bank of the United States in seeking to curb speculation in commodities and western lands following the War of 1812. A severe depression, especially in the southern and western states, followed. Many banks suspended specie payments, and the Bank of the United States went through congressional investigation for alleged mismanagement and financial rehabilitation. Manufacturers clamored for more protection, and relief legislation was enacted in several western states. By 1823 the economic picture improved.

PANIC OF 1837. During 1830–36 enormous state debts had piled up from the construction of canals and railroads and in the chartering of new banks. At the same time, many state banks, which after 1833 held deposits of government funds, expanded their credit; land speculation was common; and imports exceeded exports. To check the speculation President Andrew Jackson, on July 11, 1836, issued a specie circular, which required all payments for public lands to be made in specie, thus cramping the operations of the banks financing the western land speculation. On June 23, 1836, Congress passed an act to distribute the surplus revenue in the U.S. Treasury among the states, thereby causing the depository banks to contract their credit. On May 10, 1837, the New York banks suspended specie payment, a move followed by most of the banks. After resumption in 1838, Philadelphia banks suspended specie payments, Oct. 9, 1839, with widespread suspensions in 1842. The depression lasted until 1843 and was most severely felt in the West and the South. The Independent Treasury System was established in 1840 partly as a result of the panic, and the universal distress contributed to the defeat of Martin Van Buren and the return of the Whigs to power that year.

PANIC OF 1857. Followed the boom decade after the Mexican War (1846–48). Speculation and expansion ran riot in railroad construction, manufacturing, the wheat belt, and land; state banking was poorly regulated. The failure of the Ohio Life Insurance Company of Cincinnati in August 1857 pricked the bubble. Unemployment grew, breadlines formed, and ominous signs of social unrest appeared. The depression was most serious in the industrial areas of the East and wheat belt of the West; the cotton belt was less affected. These factors brought overconfidence in the South, an impulse to protection in the East, and a drive for free land in the West.

PANIC OF 1873. Precipitated by the failure of a number of important eastern firms, including Jay Cooke and Company, on Sept. 18. Causes of the panic were worldwide: a series of wars, excessive railroad construction, commercial dislocations caused by the opening of the Suez Canal, speculation, and overexpansion. Others were more peculiar to the United States: currency and credit inflation; governmental waste; overinvestment in railroads, factories, and buildings; and an adverse trade balance.

The depression following the panic proved one of the worst in American history: by 1875 500,000 men were out of work. Wage reductions caused strikes among the coal miners of Pennsylvania and textile operatives of New England and a railroad walkout in 1877 (*see* Railroad Strikes of 1877). In 1878 the depression began to lift, and the following year conditions improved.

PANIC OF 1893. The uneasy state of British security markets in 1890 stopped the flow of foreign capital into American enterprise, and the resale of European-held securities caused a stock market collapse in New York and substantial exports of gold. The panic that seemed inevitable that autumn turned instead to uneasy stagnation as the huge exports of agricultural staples the next two years reestablished gold imports and postponed the crisis. Uncertainty returned in the winter of 1892–93, aided by the well-publicized danger that the country would be forced off the gold standard by the decline in the U.S. Treasury's gold reserve. The National Cordage Company failed in May and touched off a stock market panic. By the end of 1893 about 4,000 banks had collapsed, and there were more than 14,000 commercial failures.

Many of President Grover Cleveland's advisers had been urging him to force repeal of the Silver Purchase Act of 1890. By Oct. 30 it had passed both houses of Congress. In the meantime, imports of gold had stabilized the monetary situation in New York somewhat, but the winter of 1893–94 and the summer following witnessed widespread unemployment, strikes met by violence, and a march on Washington, D.C., by the jobless men of "Coxey's Army." The depression did not lift until the poor European crops of 1897 stimulated American exports and the importation of gold.

PANIC OF 1907. Sometimes called the "rich man's panic," it came as a surprise, although a succession of speculative excesses had preceded it. Bank credit had expanded rapidly between 1897 and 1906, and 1906 also witnessed several profit-dampening reforms, such as the Hepburn Act; the Pure Food and Drug Act; and the New York State insurance reform law. When Henry H. Rogers of Standard Oil had to pay 8 percent interest to float a $20 million bond issue in February 1907, a sharp drop in the stock market took place, the so-called silent panic. The Charles Morse shipping combination collapsed that summer, followed by runs on the Heinze-Morse chain of banks. Runs on the Trust Company of America and several others followed, and there was panic on the stock markets. To halt the panic, Secretary of the Treasury George B. Cortelyou authorized large deposits in several banks. Investment banker J. P. Morgan headed a banking group that used a borrowed emergency fund of nearly $40 million to rescue banks and firms they deemed savable and whose survival was crucial.

Although the panic did not lead to heavy unemployment or to a wave of bankruptcies, or affect agriculture, it seriously damaged the image of the big financiers. Many questioned the desirability of letting one private citizen, Morgan, wield such enormous power in a crisis. On Mar. 30, 1908, Congress passed the Aldrich-Vreeland Currency Act, which provided for the issuance of emergency bank currency in the event of another currency stringency and also created the National Monetary Commission to propose bank reforms. It produced the Aldrich Report of 1911, a major step in setting up the Federal Reserve System in 1913–14. The bank failures also contributed to the establishment in 1910 of the Postal Savings System, created to protect the savings of the poor.

PANIC OF 1920. *See* **Depression of 1920.**

PANIC OF 1929. *See* **Great Depression.**

PANIC OF 1937. *See* **Business Cycles.**

PANICS AND DEPRESSIONS. *See articles on Panics and* **Business Cycles; Depression of 1920; Great Depression.**

PAN-INDIANISM. The Pan-Indian movement represents a growing nationalism among American Indians. The movement incorporates elements from a variety of cultures, but the influence of the Plains culture predominates. The oldest major intertribal organization is the National Congress of American Indians, founded in 1944, which lobbies to advance Indian interests. More militant organizations, the National Indian Youth Council and the American Indian Movement (AIM), were founded in 1961 and 1968. Other organizations include American Indians United, the United Native Americans, and the League of Nations, Pan-Am Indians.

PANMURE, FORT. The former French settlement Fort Rosalie at Natchez, Miss., as renamed after British occupancy in 1764. Bernardo Galvez captured it for Spain in 1779, and the Spanish retained it until 1798, when it was surrendered to the United States in accordance with Pinckney's Treaty. The fort was demolished in 1805.

PANOCHE GRANDE CLAIM. A celebrated land fraud. The land claimed by William McGarrahan, known as the Panoche Grande Rancho, was located in San Benito County, Calif., and included the New Idria Quicksilver Mine, already established by 1854. Based on a pretended land grant that was supposed to have been made to Vicente P. Gomez by the governor of Mexico in 1844, the claim was purchased Dec. 22, 1857, by McGarrahan after squatters had discovered mercury in the area. Because the original Gomez claim was not confirmed after the American conquest of California and because it was denied by the U.S. Supreme Court a number of times, McGarrahan took his case to nearly every Congress during the 1860's, but to no avail. McGarrahan was charged with constant lobbying and malpractice.

PANTON, LESLIE AND COMPANY. Organized in East Florida during the American Revolution by William Panton, Thomas Forbes, and other Loyalists to build up trade and influence with the Creek Indians. Before Pinckney's Treaty, the company helped promote trouble between the Indians and Americans to keep out rivals. After 1795, it confined itself to business and was able to keep most of the trade. The firm and its successor, Forbes and Company, handled most Indian trade until about 1817.

PAOLI, BATTLE OF (Sept. 21, 1777). British Gen. Charles Grey, in an early morning attack, surprised Gen. Anthony Wayne's division of 1,500 men near Paoli Inn, Pa. Under orders from Gen. George Washington to harass the British in order to delay Gen. William Howe's advance on Philadelphia, Wayne maneuvered to join Gen. William Smallwood for a concerted attack. Tory spies had revealed Wayne's position to Grey, and advancing in overwhelming numbers under cover of darkness, the British killed 300 and wounded 70.

PAPAL STATES, DIPLOMATIC SERVICE TO. During 1797–1867 eleven American consuls resident in Rome were accredited to the papal government. Formal diplomatic relations were inaugurated in 1848 with the appointment of Jacob L. Martin as chargé d'affaires; a post that later carried with it the title of minister. The last U.S. minister to the papal states was Rufus King, as the legation was suppressed in 1867 through failure of Congress to continue the appropriation for its support.

PAPER AND PULP INDUSTRY. The first paper mill in the American colonies was established in 1690 at Germantown, near Philadelphia, Pa. A hand mold, a sievelike device, was dipped into a vat of rag fibers in water and then raised. By a "shake," an even layer of wet fibers was deposited on the mold's surface. Removal of the wet mat from the mold and subsequent pressing and drying required two additional men. The three-man team produced about five reams of paper per day.

The establishment of new mills depended on population density both for markets and for adequate rag supplies. By 1810 there were 202 mills in sixteen states. Employment numbered over 2,500. The first machine for making a continuous sheet was installed by Thomas Gilpin in Wilmington, Del., in 1817. Scientific and technical developments between 1828 and 1909 made straw and then wood usable as raw materials.

The 20th century created a forest-based, capital-intensive industry. After World War II, American paper met challenges from plastics and, through "disposables," challenged textiles. Leading the world, U.S. paper production in the late 1970's was over 60 million tons, more than 90 percent of which was domestically consumed. Recycling fiber has received increased attention as a method of conserving resources. Approximately 25.4 percent of all fiber used for papermaking in 1980 was reclaimed.

PAPER MONEY. *See* **Money.**

PARAGUAY EXPEDITION. On Feb. 1, 1855, the U.S.S. *Water Witch* was fired on and the helmsman killed while surveying a channel of the Paraná River, which was claimed by Paraguay. Unable to secure redress, the United States, in December 1858, assembled a squadron of nineteen ships in the Río de la Plata under W. B. Shubrick. Two ships, the *Fulton* and the *Water Witch,* proceeded to Asunción. Shubrick and the U.S. commissioner, James B. Bowlin, easily secured an apology and $10,000 for the family of the helmsman and concluded a treaty that granted free navigation.

PARAPSYCHOLOGY. A term denoting the organized experimental study of purported "psychic" abilities, such as telepathy (the knowledge of human thoughts without sensory communication), clairvoyance (the knowledge of physical objects without sensory aid), psychokinesis (the ability to influence an object physically without contact with it), and precognition (the knowledge of future events).

Organized psychical research came into being in the United States in 1885 with the founding of the American Society for Psychical Research. The most prominent American supporter of psychical research was William James; the three principal leaders of research in its early years were Richard Hodgson, John Hervey Hyslop, and Walter Franklin Prince.

Funds and fellowships for the conduct of psychical research were established at Harvard, Stanford, and Clark in the first two decades of the 20th century, but work there was greatly overshadowed in the early 1930's by Joseph Banks Rhine at Duke University. Rhine ran thousands of tests with students, some of whom achieved striking extra-chance results. The results were published in 1934 in *Extra-Sensory Perception.* A laboratory set up at Duke was for a long time the focus of American parapsychology. Rhine established the *Journal of Parapsychology* in 1937, and in the 1940's he carried his investigations on into psychokinesis and precognition.

By the 1970's research in parapsychology was being pursued at various academic centers, as well as at private foundations.

PARATROOPS. Light infantry, trained and equipped with parachutes, who jump behind enemy lines from aircraft. When used as shock troops, they are dropped within supporting distance of friendly lines to disrupt the enemy's rear area and seize key points. They are usually employed in conjunction with an amphibious landing or a large-scale ground offensive; they are also used as highly mobile reinforcements. As light infantry, they cannot remain in the field long without heavy aerial resupply or contact with ground forces.

Paratroops were first used by the French, on a small scale, during World War I. Between the wars the United States did little to develop an airborne arm, but German success with paratroops early in World War II spurred the formation of five airborne divisions, the 11th, 13th, 17th, 82nd, and 101st. The first jump supported Allied amphibious landings in North Africa; others followed in Sicily, Normandy, southern France, the Netherlands, and Germany. There were two airborne operations during the Korean War and one during the Vietnam War. As of 1975 the army had only one airborne unit, the 82nd Airborne Division; the 101st Airborne is an airmobile unit.

PARCEL POST. The delivery of packages by mail began on Jan. 1, 1913, after years of argument over whether the U.S. Post Office ought to provide such service. Those who argued for it pointed out that the mails reached all parts of the country, while private express services did not. Those opposed argued that the government ought not compete against private companies.

PARDON. *See* **Amnesty.**

PARIS, DECLARATION OF (1856). At the end of the Crimean War (1854–56), Austria, France, Great Britain, Prussia, Russia, Sardinia, and Turkey adopted a declaration that, among other things, outlawed privateering. Invited to adhere to the declaration, Secretary of State William H. Marcy declined because the United States was still a small naval power and unwilling to abandon privateering unless the large naval powers would deny the right of belligerent public warships to capture private property, contraband excepted. Later, during the Civil War, the United States endeavored to accede, in order to outlaw Confederate privateering, but the powers declined.

PARIS, PACT OF. *See* **Kellogg-Briand Pact.**

PARIS, PEACE OF (1783). Following the American Revolution, preliminary articles were signed at Paris between the United States and Great Britain on Nov. 30, 1782, and between the Netherlands and Great Britain on Sept. 2, 1783. On Sept. 3, 1783, three definitive treaties between Great Britain and the United States, France, and Spain were signed.

PARIS, TREATY OF (1763). The result of the British victory in the French and Indian War was an extension of British demands on France to include the cession of all of Canada and the advancement of the boundary of the continental colonies westward to the Mississippi. Both demands, together with the right to navigate the Mississippi, were granted. Cuba, conquered by the British, was returned to Spain, which ceded East and West Florida to Britain. Spain received from France by the Treaty of Fontainebleau (1762) all the territory west of the Mississippi River and New Orleans. France retained only the islands of St. Pierre and Miquelon off the south coast of Newfoundland, together with the privilege of fishing and drying fish along the northern and western coasts of Newfoundland as provided in the Treaty of Utrecht (1713). In the West Indies, Great Britain retained the islands of St. Vincent, Tobago, and Dominica; St. Lucia, Martinique, and Guadeloupe were returned to France.

PARIS, TREATY OF (proclaimed 1899). Terminated the Spanish-American War. Under its terms Spain relinquished all authority over Cuba and ceded Puerto Rico, the Philippine Islands, and Guam, in exchange for $20 million. Hostilities had been suspended Aug. 12, 1898, and on Oct. 1 negotiations opened with the Spanish in Paris. The most difficult question encountered was the disposition of the Philippines and of the $400 million Spanish debt charged against Cuba, which the Spanish wished assumed by either Cuba or the United States. Eventually Spain yielded on both points. The treaty was signed Dec. 10 and ratified by a close vote on Feb. 6, 1899.

PARIS AGREEMENT (1925). An arrangement among Germany's reparations creditors (except the United States) to distribute the annuities paid to them after World War I. The payments had been scaled down from the original reparations bill by the Dawes Plan (1924), after Germany defaulted in 1923. The U.S. share in this distribution was confirmed by the U.S.-German agreement of June 23, 1930.

PARIS CONFERENCES (after World War II). During 1946 two lengthy conferences met at Paris to draft a postwar European settlement. The Council of Foreign Ministers, from the United States, the Soviet Union, Great Britain, and France, met (Apr. 25–May 16, June 15–July 12) to agree on peace treaties for the Axis satellites, Finland, Bulgaria, Romania, Hungary, and Italy. Its agreements were modified by the Paris Peace Conference (July 29–Oct. 15), composed of the twenty-one nations that had fought Germany. Final provisions of the satellite treaties were agreed to at the New York foreign ministers meeting on Nov. 4–Dec. 12.

Another Big Four foreign ministers conference at Paris (May 23–June 20, 1949) dealt with the Big Four's inability to agree on a German peace treaty. The meeting at Paris had been agreed to by the United States, Great Britain, and France in return for Soviet agreement to drop the blockade of Berlin, begun in 1948 in protest against the Western powers' decision to create an independent West Germany. At the conference the West rejected a Soviet plan for German reunification, and the Soviets rejected extension of the new West German constitution to East Germany.

In 1959 the heads of state of the United States, Great Britain, France, and the Soviet Union agreed to hold a summit conference in Paris in May 1960 to discuss a reduction of tensions. Two weeks before its opening, an American reconnaissance aircraft (the U-2) was shot down over the Soviet Union. When President Eisenhower refused to disavow responsibility or apologize for the flight, Khrushchev refused to participate in the conference.

The longest series of negotiations at Paris in which the United States participated (1968–73) was the talks on settlement of the Vietnam War. The United States, the North and South Vietnamese, and the Viet Cong met weekly for four years. In 1969, Henry Kissinger began secret meetings with North Vietnamese politburo member Le Duc Tho. Differences led to a temporary suspension of the talks in December 1972, before the peace settlement of 1973.

PARISH. The unit for ecclesiastical administration, particularly of the Roman Catholic church. It is also the civil or political unit for local administrative purposes in Louisiana, corresponding to the county in other states.

PARITY. A principle in naval defense used as a basis for the limitation of naval armaments adopted at the Washington Conference of 1921–22. As proposed by the American delegation, U.S. superiority in capital-ship tonnage was reduced to equality with the British and to five-thirds of Japan's tonnage; the total tonnage of other types of ships remained unlimited until the London Treaty of 1930 with America's corresponding ratio somewhat reduced. Japan refused to renew the naval limitation treaties on their expiration in 1936, except on a basis of parity in ships, which Britain and America declined.

PARKER'S FORT. Established at the headwaters of the Navasota in Limestone County, Tex., in 1835. In May 1836 the settlement was attacked by 300 Comanche and Caddo. Only one person survived.

PARKS, NATIONAL, AND NATIONAL MONUMENTS. Of the 70.9 million acres (federal land) in the National Park System in 1980, 15.8 million were in forty-eight national parks and 50.2 million in seventy-eight national monuments. National parks can be established only by act of Congress. Most national monuments have been established by presidential proclamation under the Antiquities Act of 1906, which was passed to protect endangered archaeological and scientific sites on federal lands. Whereas the term "monument" is used in Europe principally to describe works of nature and in America most commonly to refer to statues or stone shafts, both meanings are included in the National Park System's usage.

While both national parks and national monuments must possess features that merit commitment to national care, a national park should contain two or more such features, whereas a national monument need not. National parks are relatively spacious; national monuments may be any size. The two largest National Park Service areas in 1980 were national parks in Alaska, Glacier Bay and Katmai. All national parks are categorized as natural, rather than historical, areas except Mesa Verde, Colo. On Dec. 1, 1978, more than 40 million acres in Alaska were added to the National Park System.

PARK SERVICE, NATIONAL, AND NATIONAL PARK SYSTEM. The U.S. Congress established the National Park Service, within the Department of the Interior, in an act signed by President Woodrow Wilson on Aug. 25, 1916. The new agency was to provide central administration of national parks and monuments. Over the years the areas managed by the National Park Service came to include recreational and cultural areas as well as natural wonders and historic monuments and became known informally as the national park system, a name recognized officially by Congress in 1953. Since many of the areas administered by the National Park Service had been set aside as federal preserves before the establishment of the service—the first being Yellowstone National Park in 1872—Congress in 1970 designated 1872 as the date of origin of the National Park System.

The first director of the National Park Service, from 1917 until 1929, was Stephen T. Mather, who acquainted the public with the parks and fought off efforts of private interests to use parklands and waters. He won the support of John D. Rockefeller, Jr., who provided financial aid vital to the acquisition of Acadia, Grand Teton, and Great Smoky Mountains national parks; his son, Laurance S. Rockefeller, contributed the first 5,000 acres of Virgin Islands National Park and additions to Haleakala National Park, Hawaii.

Horace M. Albright, director from 1929 to 1933, expanded the role of the Park Service in the preservation of historic sites. His administrative initiative is also reflected in the fact that he brought the Civilian Conservation Corps into the parks. Arno B. Cammerer, director between 1933 and 1940, added to the National Park System the first rural roadway park, Blue Ridge Parkway, and the first national seashore, Cape Hatteras, N.C. He set up four regional offices and assured massive park improvements.

During World War II the National Park System was not only weakened by a curtailment of funds but also threatened by wartime demands to use the parks for lumbering, mining, grazing, and farming; to whittle down Olympic National Park; and to flood parklands with federal dam waters. The effects of wartime budgetary neglect had become serious when Conrad L. Wirth became director in 1951. Called Mission 66, for its 1966 proposed completion date, his $750-million, ten-year improvement plan produced 100 visitor centers, 575 campgrounds, 12,393 picnic grounds, thousands of miles of roads and trails, and hundreds of other benefits, including 459 historic buildings.

George B. Hartzog, Jr., administered the parks during a record expansion period, from 1964 to 1973. The National Park Service also responded to the urban dweller's needs by creating seven new national parks. Ronald H. Walker, who became director in 1973, while limiting visits to overused areas and fostering safety precautions, stressed the expansion of interpretive services to inform the public about the diversity of the park system and urged public use of lesser-known areas and of parklands within a day's drive of urban centers. In 1980 the National Park System included 333 areas, in every state except Delaware: 126 national parks and monuments and 135 historical areas.

PARLIAMENT, BRITISH. Significant in American history mainly as the embodiment of those rights and liberties possessed under the British constitution by all Englishmen.

Not until the firm establishment of the principle of parliamentary supremacy in England, concurrent with the close of the French and Indian War, did Parliament seriously set itself to the direction of colonial affairs (*see* Colonial Policy, British). It quickly made itself odious to Americans by asserting its authority in regard to colonial taxation and appropriation, which the assemblies had long looked upon as their exclusive domain. Americans felt that Parliament had no right to assume powers that the crown had formerly been unable to make good, and the uncompromising attitude of the ministry of George Grenville concerning the Stamp Act (1765) precipitated a crisis in which colonial opinion stiffened against Parliament. Two years later, the passage of the Townshend Acts widened the breach, and in 1773 the resolution of the prime minister, Frederick, Lord North, to "try the issue [of taxation] in America" led directly to the Revolution.

PAROLE SYSTEM. A phase of penology usually associated with the indeterminate sentence. An offender is released (paroled) from prison upon certain conditions, but remains under supervision of state authorities during the balance of his term. First used in New York State in 1876.

PARSON BROWNLOW'S BOOK. The popular short title of a powerful propaganda book written in 1862 by William G. Brownlow, a Unionist of Tennessee, and entitled *Sketches of the Rise, Progress, and Decline of Secession.*

PARSON'S CAUSE. During the colonial period tobacco was a medium of exchange, and ministers' salaries had been fixed (1748) at 17,200 pounds of tobacco a year. To remedy the distress from fluctuating crops and prices, laws were passed in 1755 and again in 1758 permitting tobacco payments to be commuted in paper money at twopence per pound. As tobacco sold for sixpence a pound, the ministers considered themselves losers and obtained a royal veto in 1759 (*see* Royal Disallowance). In the meantime, ministers' salaries for 1758 had been settled in paper money at the prescribed rate. With the announcement of the veto, ministers started suits for the difference between what they were paid and the value of their tobacco quota at current prices. In Hanover County, Va., the court ruled the act of 1758 was invalid from its passage, but in 1764 the general court of the province held the law good until it was vetoed and left the ministers without any remedy. A general two-penny act was passed in 1769, and the ministers gave up the agitation.

PARTIES, POLITICAL. *See* **Political Parties.**

PARTISAN BANDS. A type of irregular soldiery found mainly in civil war and warfare in defense of invaded territory. Partisan bands resemble guerrillas but are loosely organized and nominally under some constituted government. In the series of wars between the British and French from 1689 to 1763, groups of frontiersmen, in defense of their homesteads, formed irregular military bands, or "rangers," and sometimes made expeditions into the enemy's strongholds. In the American Revolution partisan bands included the Green Mountain Boys in the North and the followers of Col. Andrew Pickens, Lt. Col. Francis Marion, and Col. Thomas Sumter in the South. In the Civil War partisan bands or corps came into existence, of which Mosby's Rangers was the most famous.

PARTY EMBLEMS. *See* **Emblems, Party.**

PARTY GOVERNMENT. Defined as the existence of cohesive political coalitions, programmatic in appeal, and democratically responsive to their electors, party government has never existed in the United States. The British experiment with political parties resulted in policy-oriented and comparatively cohesive groups, characterized by centralized decision-making, clear lines of authority, and even sanctions applicable by a dissatisfied leadership to recalcitrant elected party members. In large part the parliamentary system of government permits the kind of order and appeal to clear issues that a national-level separation of powers superimposed on a federal arrangement of governing units does not.

Although scholarship has shown that there is, in the United States, a greater consensus on issues on the basis of party allegiance than had been realized—especially on social and economic issues—anyone who seeks to assess American parties in relation to such criteria courts disappointment. The major American parties are best understood as loose coalitions of groups that represent an impressively wide variety of interests. One legacy of the Great Depression was the realignment of party appeals along self-consciously economic lines: broadly speaking, those who are better off economically tend to support the Republican party and the less well-to-do, the Democratic.

PASADENA (Calif.). Located northeast of Los Angeles in the San Gabriel Mountains, the city had a population of 119,374 in 1980. Largely residential, it is widely known because of a nearby concentration of scientific and cultural resources: California Institute of Technology, the Henry E. Huntington Library and Art Gallery, and the Mount Wilson Observatory.

PASS CHRISTIAN (Miss.). An early French settlement on the Gulf Coast about sixty miles east of New Orleans. The U.S. flag was hoisted there on Jan. 9, 1811, after the annexation of West Florida, and British and American fleets fought a battle there on Dec. 14, 1814 (*see* Borgne, Battle at Lake). In 1980 the population was 5,014.

PASSES, MOUNTAIN. Early hunters and pioneers found natural outlets through the mountains. In the Appalachians these were generally called "gaps" and in the Rockies "passes."

The most important pass in the Kentucky approach, the Cumberland Gap, which led by way of the Holston and Clinch rivers in eastern Tennessee over and through the mountains and thence along the Kentucky River and its tributaries to the Falls of the Ohio. This was known as Boone's Wilderness Road, and gaps noted by early travelers include Flower Gap, Blue Ridge Gap, and Moccasin Gap, between the north fork of the Holston and Clinch rivers.

On the Virginia road to Pittsburgh was encountered Chester Gap in the Blue Ridge Mountains. On the Forbes Road, running west from Philadelphia to Pittsburgh, Miller's Run Gap was crossed northwest of the present site of Ligonier, in Westmoreland County, Pa.

The river valleys unlocking the southern route to the West were the Gila and the Colorado. The Colorado trail, known as the Spanish Trail, went north from Taos, crossed the Wasatch Mountains and Mojave Desert, and entered California by the Cajon Pass. The Gila route was the shorter trail from Santa Fe, going west across the mountains and, by way of Warner's pass, eventually reaching San Diego.

The Arkansas River route west to Pueblo, Colo., led to three or four different passes—the Williams or Sandy Hill, the Roubideau or Mosca, and the Sangre de Cristo or Music passes. This route crossed the Great Basin of Utah and Nevada and surmounted the Sierra Nevada passes in California. After the eastern escarpment had been scaled, there still remained mountain folds in the Sierra Nevada. The Tehachapi Pass into San Joaquin Valley crossed one such fold.

The central approach to the Rockies was by way of the Platte River. The most important pass in the chain, South Pass, was on this route and was used by many travelers to California (*see* Oregon Trail).

Of all river approaches the Missouri was the most effective and was the route used by Meriwether Lewis and William Clark. Other useful passes of the Northwest were the Nez Percé and Lo Lo through the Bitterroot Mountains on the Montana and Idaho border. The Bozeman Pass offered access from the valley of the Gallatin River to that of the Yellowstone River. For traveling south from Oregon to California the Siskiyou Pass proved useful.

Important passes in the midcontinental region were the Union, crossing the Wind River Mountains in southwestern Wyoming; Cochetope Pass over the San Juan Mountains in southwestern Colorado; and Muddy Pass. Bridger's Pass crossed the divide south of South Pass and saved distance on the California route and so was used by the Pony Express.

PASSPORTS. Issued by local authorities and notaries as well as the secretary of state until 1856 when issuance was confined to the U.S. Department of State. Except for the Civil War period, passports were not required of foreign travelers in the United States until 1918. The requirement was made permanent in 1921.

PATENTS AND U.S. PATENT OFFICE. The American legal and administrative system for issuing letters patent to inventors has attempted since the colonial period to encourage invention and the growth of industry by granting monopolies. The General Court of Massachusetts Bay Colony granted monopolies for stated periods; benefits to inventors or innovators were in the form of monopolies or monetary grants by the colony for each sale of the patented item. Since the Articles of Confederation made no mention of patents, individual states continued the precedent.

In 1790, Congress passed the first patent law. The act provided that petitions for patents would be forwarded to the secretaries of state and war and to the attorney general, that any two members of this patent board could approve a fourteen-year patent, and that the attorney general was to submit the approved patent for the president's signature. When Thomas Jefferson was secretary of state, he played the leading role in this procedure, and his department was the registry for the system. Because of his abhorrence of monopoly, he applied strictly the rule of novelty and usefulness. Only three patents were approved in 1790.

Objections to delays in processing petitions and the narrow interpretation of the 1790 act resulted in passage in 1793 of a new law, providing for termination of the board and an administrative structure for examining petitions. The volume of petitions under the 1793 act caused Secretary of State James Madison to establish in 1802 the Patent Office.

Completely rewritten on July 4, 1836, the new patent law gave the Patent Office responsibility for examining petitions and for ruling on the validity of the claims for an invention, its usefulness, and its workability. The law provided that the fourteen-year monopoly could be extended for an additional seven years if a special board (later, the commissioner of patents) found that the patentee encountered unusual problems in producing and marketing his device. In 1861, Congress withdrew this authority and reserved such grants to itself; to give the patentee additional time for producing and marketing new products, Congress increased the monopoly period to seventeen years.

In 1839, the Patent Office was authorized to disseminate seeds and to collect and publish data of interest to farmers—the predecessor of the Department of Agriculture, established in 1862.

Congress in 1870 added the power to issue trademark patents to the authority under an 1842 act for granting design patents. The 1870 act delegated copyright responsibilities, some of which had been in the Patent Office, to the Library of Congress. It also sanctioned the procedures for adjudicating interferences by establishing the Office of the Examiner of Interferences. The Patent Office was transferred to the Department of the Interior in 1849 and to the Department of Commerce in 1925. A registry office registered applications and assignments of approved patents, published and distributed patent specifications, and organized a scientific and technical library.

PATERSON (N.J.). An industrial city with a population of 137,970 in 1980; together with Passaic and Clifton, it is the core for a metropolitan area of 447,785. Located at the falls of the Passaic River, where a waterfall almost 70 feet high provided power for early factories, Paterson was selected in 1791 as the location for a new industrial town and named after William Paterson, then governor of New Jersey.

Paterson's principal activities have been in thread making; textile dyeing; weaving; and producing laces, ribbons, and synthetic fabrics. From 1840 to about 1910, it was the center of the U.S. silk industry. The industry remained important until the 1940's when raw silk could no longer be secured from the Orient, and when synthetic fibers destroyed the market for pure silk.

PATERSON PLAN. *See* **New Jersey Plan.**

"PATHFINDER." A sobriquet given to John C. Frémont following the publication (1845) of his *Report of the Exploring Expedition to the Rocky Mountains in the Year 1842, and to Oregon and North California in the Years 1843–44.*

PATHFINDER OF THE SEAS. *See* **Maury's Charts.**

PATRIOT WAR (1837–38). The desire to free Canada from British control resulted in the war between Canadian rebels and their American supporters, and the British. Following the failure of three extensive plans in 1838 for widespread contemporaneous attacks along the Canadian border, the movement came completely under the domination of a secret society, the Hunters and Chasers of the Eastern Frontier. International complications were averted as a consequence of the cooperation and vigorous action of the British and American authorities. Congress passed a stronger neutrality act in March 1838, and federal troops were sent to the frontier. The Canadian and British authorities used military and civil measures to prevent retaliatory attacks (*see* Canadian-American Relations). A serious repercussion of the Patriot War was the arrest of the Canadian Alexander McLeod on Nov. 12, 1840, in New York City (*see* Caroline Affair).

PATRONAGE, POLITICAL. Includes all the forms of largesse at the disposal of successful candidates for public office. In the absence of limitations on the officeholder, all public jobs and contracts are dispensed at the discretion of the principal officer of the governmental unit involved. In its most extreme form such political patronage is known as the spoils system. Originally involving only the awarding of jobs, political patronage has come to include the vast range of favors distributed by expanding governmental bureaucracies.

Political patronage was first implemented on a national scale during the administration of President Andrew Jackson (1828–36), and state and local government officeholders were not slow in adopting the system. By 1880, governments were in many cases mere appendages of political machines that grew out of the excesses of the spoils system.

The National Civil Service League, founded in 1881, led a reform movement that succeeded in gaining passage of the Pendleton Act in 1883. It provided for the creation of a civil service commission, for the establishment of open competitive examinations for admission to public employment, and for the protection of classified civil servants from discrimination or removal on account of political or religious beliefs.

By and large, state governments still use the patronage system. According to the National Civil Service League, virtually every state had some sort of merit system by the late 1970's although the number of employees actually hired under merit principles was unknown. City governments have been subjected to public pressure to remove public employment from political patronage. Despite the efforts of reformers, only 75 percent of all American cities had any kind of formal merit system by 1950. Traditionally, counties have been the strongholds of political parties and, as such, are slow to adopt a civil service system. On the local level, however, such as the rural town and the school district, there is either a tradition to maintain or a standard to meet. Patronage exists in the schools, but certain minimum standards must be enforced in order to secure state subsidies. Generally, rural communities are too small and too poor to support an effective personnel program based on merit, and the few positions available are considered patronage for the mayor.

PATRONS OF HUSBANDRY. Founded (1867) as a farmers' lodge by Oliver Hudson Kelley, a Washington, D.C., postal clerk, its purpose was to bring farmers together in local units ("Granges") to learn about improved agricultural methods. It had a secret ritual and admitted both men and women to membership. From it grew the political Granger movement. In 1876 the order reached a membership of 858,050, but by 1880 the collapse of the Granger movement had reduced this figure to 124,420. Thereafter, by abandoning business and politics, the order began a slow and steady growth. (*See also* Granger Movement.)

PATROONS. On June 7, 1629, the directorate of the West India Company granted, and the States General of the Netherlands approved, a charter of freedoms and exemptions; it provided for the grant of great estates, called patroonships, to those members of the company who were able to found settlements of fifty persons within four years after giving notice of their intentions. In 1640 the revised charter reduced the size of future patroonships, but at the close of Dutch rule all but two had been repurchased by the company.

PAULISTS. The Society of Missionary Priests of St. Paul the Apostle, known as the Paulist Fathers, was founded in New York City in 1858 by Father Isaac Thomas Hecker. It was the first U.S. religious society of men in the Roman Catholic church to help men to discover Jesus Christ. Missions to Catholics and lectures for non-Catholics are the special apostolate of the Paulists. Utilizing the written as well as the spoken word, Father Hecker established *The Catholic World* in 1865. The following year he founded the Catholic Publication Society, now known as the Paulist Press.

PAULUS HOOK, SURPRISE OF (Aug. 19, 1779). The British forts on lower Manhattan and at Paulus Hook, N.J., commanded the entrance to the Hudson River. In a bayonet attack at dawn, Maj. Henry Lee, with 200 men, surprised the garrison at Paulus Hook, captured 159 prisoners and regained New Bridge (Hackensack) with the loss of two men.

PAUPERISM. *See* **Poverty and Pauperism.**

PAVING. All the earliest paving in America seems to have been done with cobblestones. The first mention of paving is found in a court record in New Amsterdam in 1655. In Boston, some streets were cobble-paved in the 17th century. In 1832 what is said to have been the first granite or Belgian block pavement in America was laid in New York. That city also introduced wood paving in 1835, laid in hexagonal blocks—said to be a "Russian idea." Later, square blocks were used. In New Orleans, built on soft alluvial soil, many streets were surfaced with thick wooden planks laid crosswise. The first brick street paving was laid in Charleston, W.Va., in 1870. When asphalt was first tried in New York in 1877, it was pronounced a failure; but it shortly afterward became popular, despite its habit of softening and consequent roughening in hot weather. After 1900 it began slowly to be replaced by concrete. By 1980 the surface paving of streets in most major cities was a bituminous mixture from either asphalts or tars.

PAWNEE. When first contacted by Europeans, perhaps as early as 1541 by the expedition of Francisco Vásquez de Coronado, the Pawnee, an American Indian tribe in the Great Plains, lived in the present state of Nebraska. Three main branches or bands spoke a single Caddoan language; a fourth group, the Skidi, spoke a variant dialect. The origins of the Pawnee in the southeast is borne out by their retention of river-bottom agriculture, a trait carried by the Arikara from the Pawnee to the Siouan Mandan and Hidatsa. The Pawnee stressed both the permanent farming village and forays far afield for horses and military honors. They were known for the ceremony of the morning star, a ritual involving human sacrifice for communal good. The Pawnee enjoyed fairly benign relations with Europeans and were often employed as U.S. Army scouts.

PAWNEE ROCK. A pioneer landmark of uplifted sandstone, which has since been largely quarried away, on the old Santa Fe Trail near what is now Pawnee Rock, Kans. It was the scene of tribal warfare between the Pawnee and Cheyenne and furnished cover from which marauding bands of Plains Indians frequently launched attacks on passing wagon trains.

PAWTUCKET (R.I.). Located at Pawtucket Falls, the head of navigation on the Blackstone River, four miles north of Providence. The area was deeded to Roger Williams in 1638, but the first permanent settlement did not begin until 1671. Ironmaking was the only important industry until 1793, the year Samuel Slater installed the first Arkwright machinery for spinning cotton in America at Pawtucket Falls. Chartered as a city in 1885, Pawtucket was a textile manufacturing center until after World War II, when most of the industry moved its factories to the South. The population in 1980 was 71,204.

PAXTON BOYS. During Pontiac's War fifty-seven rangers from Paxton, Pa., killed twenty Conestoga Indians near Lancaster in December 1763. Gov. John Penn's command to bring the culprits to trial was ignored. Aside from the brutality of this event, it is important as evidence of the hatred of the frontiersmen for the eastern domination of the province. Numerous pamphlets were written (one by Benjamin Franklin), and in January 1764, 600 armed "back inhabitants" marched on Philadelphia, intent on destroying their political opponents. Franklin was chiefly responsible for quelling this rebellion. Lazarus Stewart, head of the Paxton Boys, moved with his followers to the Wyoming Valley, an area near present-day Wilkes-Barre, Pa., in 1769. There he engaged in the Pennamite Wars and was killed in the Wyoming massacre of 1778.

PAYNE-ALDRICH TARIFF. *See* **Tariff.**

PAYNE'S LANDING, TREATY OF (May 9, 1832). Made on the Oklawaha River in north central Florida by James Gadsden for the United States, with fifteen Seminole chiefs; it provided for a delegation of Indians to proceed to the West and decide whether land set apart for them there was acceptable. Disputes over this treaty and other problems led to the second Seminole War.

PEABODY FUND. The pioneer U.S. educational foundation was established in 1867 by George Peabody with $1 million. Two years later he added a like sum to encourage and assist general education and teacher training for both whites and blacks in the former Confederacy and West Virginia. Before its dissolution in 1914, it had distributed about $3.65 million.

PEACE COMMISSION OF 1778. The surrender of Gen. John Burgoyne's army at Saratoga on Oct. 17, 1777, inspired the British to propose peace to the colonies, an offer based on repeal of the obnoxious parliamentary legislation since 1763 and a constitutional arrangement of home rule. The government sent to Philadelphia in 1778 a commission headed by Frederick Howard, Earl of Carlisle. The Continental Congress refused to meet with the commission, although the terms that the commission was ready to offer would have been satisfactory before the signing of the Declaration of Independence.

PEACE CONFERENCE AT BUENOS AIRES (Dec. 1–23, 1936). Convened at Buenos Aires to discuss the maintenance of peace in the Western Hemisphere, the conference voted in favor of consulting together and cooperating to settle all threats to American peace from within and without through conciliation and arbitration. In all, seventy acts were approved.

PEACE CONFERENCES. Those international conferences in which the United States has participated in an effort to establish procedures for settling international disputes without resort to the use of force can be divided into four categories: (1) arbitration; (2) efforts to facilitate negotiations between disputants, either through the extension of good offices or through mediation; (3) the establishment of permanent international structures to preserve peace; and (4) direct negotiations with other countries to settle disputes.

The first arbitration agreement in which the United States participated was written into Jay's Treaty of 1794. The Treaty of Ghent of 1814, also with Great Britain, established arbitration boards to handle conflicts over boundaries arising out of the settlement. The most notable 19th-century example was the Treaty of Washington of 1871, in which Great Britain and the United States agreed to submit the *Alabama* claims to arbitration. By the turn of the century considerable sentiment had built up in favor of having the United States sign with other nations bilateral treaties providing for the automatic submission of certain classes of disputes to arbitration. The tendency of arbitration boards to resolve conflicts by splitting the difference between disputants made American diplomats reluctant to employ the procedure for the settlement of significant territorial or financial issues. Disputes involving vital interests were excluded from the arbitration treaties negotiated between 1908 and 1931, and the Senate insisted on the right to reject the use of arbitration in each case. As a result, arbitration was employed only rarely as a means of settling international disputes of minor significance.

The use of mediation in the resolution of international conflicts has not been frequent, but the results obtained have been more significant than those derived from arbitration. The United States accepted Russian mediation in setting up negotiations for settlement of the War of 1812. The United States successfully mediated an end to the struggle between Spain and Chile, Peru, Ecuador, and Bolivia in 1869 but failed in several efforts between 1879 and 1884 to mediate the War of the Pacific. President Theodore Roosevelt successfully mediated the Russo-Japanese War in 1905 and the first Morocco crisis at the Algeciras Conference in 1906. President Woodrow Wilson made several unsuccessful efforts to mediate World War I before the United States entered that struggle. Since World War I most efforts at mediation have been carried out through international organizations rather than through individual countries, although Secretary of State Henry Kissinger had some success in mediating differences between Egypt and Israel following the 1973 Yom Kippur War.

Participation in international organizations has become the principal way in which the United States has sought to establish procedures for maintaining peace. The first significant U.S. participation in such an international conference was at the first Hague Conference (1899). The United States confined its participation to urging the use of arbitration and mediation. The second Hague Conference (1907) produced further refinements in the rules of warfare but resulted in no significant action to prevent war. The United States also participated in a conference of leading maritime powers at London in 1908–09.

World War I greatly increased interest in the possibility of creating an international organization to prevent war. Wilson endorsed this concept in 1916, and following the Allied victory in 1918, he devoted great effort toward the establishment of the League of Nations, whose members were obliged "to respect and preserve as against external aggression the territorial integrity and existing political independence of all Members of the League." Article XVI required members to apply economic and, if necessary, military sanctions against aggressors. Wilson himself did not regard these as ironclad commitments, but because he refused to accept reservations making clear the nonbinding nature of the commitment, the Senate refused to approve U.S. membership.

The United States called the Washington Naval Conference of 1921–22, which imposed limitations on the construction of certain classes of warships, and participated in conferences at Geneva in 1927 and between 1932 and 1934 and at London in 1930, which attempted, generally without success, to extend the disarmament agreements reached at Washington, D.C. Secretary of State Frank B. Kellogg was a prime mover behind the multilateral Kellogg-Briand Pact of 1928, the signatories of which renounced the use of war as an instrument of national policy except in cases of self-defense.

World War II revived interest in an international structure to maintain peace. State Department planners began working, even before the United States entered the war, to create a new international organization to safeguard peace in the postwar period. President Franklin D. Roosevelt and Secretary of State Cordell Hull consulted Congress at every step of this process; the Senate endorsed U.S. membership in the United Nations in July 1945.

In part because the United Nations was not able to deal effectively with conflicts involving the great powers, the United States relied with increasing frequency on direct negotiations with its principal adversary, the Soviet Union, as a means of relaxing international tensions, especially after the Cuban missile crisis of 1962. A similar tendency appeared to be evolving in relations with the People's Republic of China following President Richard M. Nixon's visit to that country in 1972. During the 1970's American diplomats showed less interest in arbitration, mediation, and international organization as mechanisms for the peaceful resolution of disputes between nations than at any other time in the 20th century.

PEACE CORPS. Established by President John F. Kennedy in 1961, the Peace Corps was based on the idea that underdeveloped countries could be helped most when individual Americans with special skills lived and worked with the people and trained them in the use of their own resources. Peace Corps units brought technical assistance to dozens of countries. Teams of corpsmen assigned to individual countries, usually headed by a director, worked at tasks ranging from sanitary engineering through school teaching to child care and nutrition. Volunteers were subjected to an intensive training program, not only in the language of the country in which they would work but in the tasks of physical work and medical assistance that they might be called on to handle.

The Peace Corps was combined with a number of other agencies in 1971 to form a new federal organization known as ACTION. By mid-1974, ACTION had developed three additional programs and was testing several others. During the same period, it had increased its volunteer strength from 22,830 to 127,000. In December 1981, the Peace Corps was separated from ACTION and made an independent agency.

PEACE DEMOCRATS. *See* **Copperheads.**

PEACE MOVEMENT OF 1864. Efforts to end the Civil War in 1864 began in July with negotiations between Horace Greeley of the *New York Tribune* and Confederate commissioners at Niagara Falls, Canada. President Abraham Lincoln's terms were reunion and emancipation. A meeting with the commissioners by Greeley and John Hay, Lincoln's private secretary, showed the impossibility of an agreement. In August an equally futile visit was made by Jeremiah Black, friend of Secretary of War Edwin Stanton, whom he claimed to represent. In Richmond, James F. Jaquess and James R. Gilmore, with Lincoln's permission, interviewed President Jefferson Davis in July, without result. Lincoln's message to Congress in December stipulated a cessation of resistance to the Union as the only basis for peace. Visits to Davis by Francis P. Blair, Sr., in January 1865, led to the abortive Hampton Roads Conference on Feb. 3. Thus ended hope for a negotiated peace.

PEACE MOVEMENTS. Between the American Revolution and World War I, the major American wars were opposed by disparate groups that were unsympathetic to the purposes of a specific war. Opposition to the War of 1812 was centered among conservative Federalists in New England, who flirted with the idea of seceding from the Union in the Hartford Convention of 1814. The Mexican War (1846–48) was opposed most strongly by northern critics of slavery, who attacked the war as a slaveholders' plot to add new land for the expansion of slavery. Opposition to the Civil War was generally of a conservative, often racist, nature, based on opposition to the use of the federal government's power to take action against slavery. Opposition to the Spanish-American War was directed at the decision of President William McKinley's administration to keep the Philippines and suppress the Filipinos by force, an opposition centered among reformers who saw imperialism as contrary to American ideals.

After the outbreak of war in 1914, most of the peace movement came to reconcile itself to the idea of American intervention. New organizations took on the burden of trying to stave off American entry into the war. Once war was declared in April 1917, the nominal peace groups generally gave full support.

In the two decades after the 1918 armistice, a strong disenchantment with the aims and results of World War I was reflected not only in revisionist writings about the war but also in the renewed growth of peace organizations. Disillusionment with war was so widespread that Congress passed a series of neutrality acts in the 1930's aimed at preventing the United States from being drawn into a future war. As war drew nearer the antiwar consensus eroded and the neutrality legislation was circumvented or repealed. Once the United States entered the war officially, American participation received a more nearly unanimous domestic support than in any previous war. Pacifists still refused to accept the war, while preferring the Allied cause to that of Germany and Japan, but many who had espoused absolute pacifism in the 1930's abandoned their position.

The breakup of the wartime alliance and the beginning of the cold war against the Soviet Union in the late 1940's made possible a peacetime draft and increasingly tight alliances with conservative regimes around the world. Critics of the government's stance came to be branded either as subversives or as dupes of world Communism. The outbreak of war in Korea (1950) exacerbated this tendency, and pacifist, as well as radical, groups were reduced to the lowest point of their peacetime influence in at least half a century.

The Korean armistice in 1953 and a general relaxation of tensions in the mid-1950's enabled a peace movement to emerge again in 1957. The issue of nuclear testing was seized upon, both as a symbol of the menace of nuclear war and as an immediate hazard. The National Committee for a Sane Nuclear Policy (SANE) was formed in 1958 by liberals and pacifists. Agitation by this new peace movement contributed to the defeat of President John F. Kennedy's proposals for a far-reaching civil defense program and helped lead to the negotiation of a limited ban on nuclear testing by the United States and the Soviet Union in 1963. The peace movement was not able to slow the steady increase in military appropriations.

The American intervention in Vietnam, which reached major proportions in 1965, elicited a strong and ultimately effective peace movement. The first national demonstrations against the war drew upward of 20,000 young people to Washington, D.C., in April 1965. Half a million persons took part in the spring 1967 antiwar marches in New York City and San Francisco. On college campuses a draft-resistance movement gained momentum. Probably several million persons took part in activities during the antiwar moratorium in October 1969, and on Nov. 15 the largest antiwar demonstration in the nation's history took place in Washington, D.C. In May 1970 hundreds of college campuses were shut down during a nationwide student strike to protest an American invasion of Cambodia. General disillusionment and the growing protest movement led Congress began to pressure the Nixon administration for an end to the war. The administration signed a peace treaty on Vietnam in January 1973.

The early 1980's saw a resurgence of the peace movement, which had begun to spread in Europe several years before. An antinuclear rally in New York in June 1982 was described as the biggest antiwar demonstration ever.

PEACE RESOLUTIONS OF BRITISH PARLIAMENT. Introduced on Feb. 22, 1782, by Gen. Henry Seymour Conway, and passed by the House of Commons on Feb. 28, the resolution prayed that the war in America might no longer be pursued to reduce the inhabitants to obedience by force. On Mar. 4, Conway carried unanimously another motion "that the house will consider as enemies . . . all who shall advise, or . . . attempt, the further prosecution of offensive war for the purpose of reducing the revolted colonies to obedience by force."

"PEACE WITHOUT VICTORY." On Jan. 22, 1917, President Woodrow Wilson stated to the Senate the terms of peace that in his opinion would create "a stable Europe." The peace "must be a peace without victory. . . . Victory would mean peace forced upon the loser, a victor's terms imposed on the vanquished. . . . The right state of mind, the right feeling between nations, is as necessary for a lasting peace as is the just settlement of vexed questions of territory or racial and national allegiance." At that time Wilson was still hoping to mediate between the European powers.

PEACHTREE CREEK, BATTLES ON (July 1864). On the night of July 19, Union Gen. William Tecumseh Sherman's army began crossing Peachtree Creek to move against the Atlanta defenses. Confederate Gen. John Bell Hood planned to attack the Union army as it crossed. The Confederate movement, in late afternoon of July 20, was only partially successful.

During the night of July 21 Hood learned that Sherman's left under Gen. James B. McPherson was exposed and vulnerable. Late at night Confederate Gen. William J. Hardee was ordered to attack McPherson, who was taken by surprise but saved by the fortuitous arrival of the Seventeenth Corps, led by Union Gen. Francis P. Blair, Jr. Sherman was able to reinforce McPherson and halt Hardee. McPherson was killed in the battle, and night closed with Hardee in possession of the field. In this, the bloodiest fight of the Atlanta campaign, Union casualties were 1,600; Confederate, about 2,500.

***PEACOCK-EPERVIER* ENGAGEMENT** (Apr. 29, 1814). The U.S. sloop *Peacock,* commanded by Capt. Lewis Warrington, captured the British brig *Epervier,* commanded by Capt. R. W. Wales, off Cape Canaveral, Fla.

PEA RIDGE, BATTLE OF (Mar. 7–8, 1862). An engagement in northwestern Arkansas near the Missouri state line, also known as the Battle of Elkhorn Tavern. In the struggle for control of the trans-Mississippi, a Confederate army under Maj. Gen. Earl Van Dorn maneuvered against a Union army of about equal strength under Brig. Gen. Samuel R. Curtis. Superior leadership and equipment finally brought victory to the Union army and ended organized fighting in the trans-Mississippi.

***PEARL* CASE.** Shortly after the suppression in 1848 of the underground railroad, the "underground fugitive station" in Washington sent seventy-seven slaves down the Potomac on the schooner *Pearl.* They were apprehended and brought back to Washington. The trial of the fugitives' white "conductors" was published throughout the North, abolitionists making the case a national issue.

PEARL HARBOR. Pearl Harbor naval base on the south coast of Oahu, Hawaiian Islands, six miles west of Honolulu, is large enough to accommodate the entire U.S. fleet. In 1887 the Hawaiian government granted the United States exclusive use of Pearl Harbor as a fueling and naval repair station. In 1908 and 1926 the Navy Department dredged and widened the entrance channel, and in 1919 a huge drydock was completed. It was designated as a naval, military, and airplane base, and all needed facilities were established.

On Saturday, Dec. 6, 1941, many army and navy personnel were on weekend shore leave. At about 3:30 A.M., local mean time, on Dec. 7, a patrolling minesweeper reported the presence of an unidentified midget submarine outside the harbor to the destroyer *Ward,* also on night patrol. No report was made to the commandant until the *Ward* radioed at 6:54 A.M. that it had sunk a submarine, but the information was delayed in reaching the high command; also the harbor gate had not been closed. Virtually the entire U.S. fleet of ninety-four vessels, including eight battleships, was concentrated at Pearl Harbor; the disposition of troops, airplanes, and antiaircraft guns made effective defense nearly impossible.

At 7:55 A.M. on Dec. 7, 1941, the first waves of Japanese bombers attacked airfields and the fleet, particularly the battleships, anchored in the harbor. A second wave came over at 8:50 A.M. Not a single American plane in the area could be got into the air except a fighter squadron at Haleiwa, some miles away, which the Japanese had overlooked. Several of the smaller vessels were able to get into action briefly against Japanese submarines. When the last attacking Japanese planes returned to their carriers at about 9:45 A.M. Pearl Harbor was a smoking shambles. Every American airplane was either destroyed or disabled; the battleships were sunk or disabled; and other naval craft in the harbor had suffered a like fate. Of the personnel in the area, 2,403 were lost; the wounded totaled 1,176. Fortunately, the three carriers of the Pacific fleet were not in the harbor. The next day, Dec. 8, President Roosevelt appeared before Congress and asked for recognition of a state of war. It was granted promptly, with one dissenting vote.

On Dec. 18, 1941, the president appointed a commission under Owen J. Roberts of the U.S. Supreme Court to make an immediate report fixing the responsibility. The report, rendered in January 1942, placed the responsibility and the blame on Rear Adm. H. E. Kimmel and Gen. Walter C. Short, the navy and army commanders at Pearl Harbor.

PEARL RIVER. After the West Florida rebellion (1810), Spain unsuccessfully attempted to make Pearl River in the central part of the present state of Mississippi the eastern limit of American territorial expansion. Congress in 1812 attached West Florida, from the Mississippi to the Pearl, to Louisiana, the area east of the Pearl to Mobile being attached to Mississippi Territory.

PEARY'S POLAR EXPEDITIONS (1891–1909). Robert Edwin Peary was sent in 1891 by the Philadelphia Academy of Natural Sciences to explore northern Greenland. Wintering at McCormick Bay, he started on Apr. 30, 1892, with Eivind Astrup, and crossed the ice cap to Independence Bay on the northeastern coast of the island. The following year he returned to Greenland in the *Falcon.* He repeated the feat in 1895, with H. J. Lee and Matthew Henson.

In 1898 the Peary Arctic Club was organized in New York to finance an expedition under Peary to discover the North Pole. He sailed that year in the *Windward;* wintered at Cape d'Urville; and spent the following year exploring Ellesmere Island. Proceeding along the Greenland coast in 1900, he reached Cape Morris K. Jesup in Hazen Land, now Peary Land, where he struck northward over the ice to latitude 83° 52′. Here he was forced back, but continued eastward along the coast to Wyckoff Island. Two years later he made another attempt, starting this time from Cape Hecla in Grant Land, the northernmost part of Ellesmere Island, only to be stopped by snow at latitude 84°17′.

The Peary Arctic Club was still willing to back Peary and in 1905 sent him out in the specially constructed *Roosevelt* to make another attempt. He wintered at Cape Sheridan, on the northern part of Ellesmere Island, and the following year started northward from Point Moss with Capt. Robert A. Bartlett. In six weeks he reached latitude 87°6′ when open water forced him to turn back. Later in the season he led an expedition westward along the coast to Cape Thomas Hubbard, the northern extremity of Axel Heiberg Island.

Elated at his success the club again sent Peary out in the *Roosevelt* in 1908. Wintering at Cape Sheridan, he gathered a large party in February 1909 at Cape Columbia, on the northern coast of Ellesmere Island, which he divided into detachments that were to precede him, establish caches, and return. At latitude 87°47′ he parted from Bartlett and proceeded with only Matthew Henson and four Eskimos. On Apr. 6, 1909, he reached the North Pole. In 1911, Peary was awarded the rank of rear admiral by Congress.

PECK, FORT. Built in 1867 for the trading firm of Durfee and Peck about 2.5 miles above the Big Dry on the north side of the Missouri River, in Montana. In 1874 the government bought the post and maintained it as an Indian agency until 1879.

PECOS. A town in New Mexico, about thirty miles southeast of Santa Fe, known as Cicuye to the first Spaniards who, under Francisco Vásquez de Coronado, reached it in 1540. Pecos was long the most populous settlement of the Pueblo in New Mexico but was abandoned in 1838.

PECOS TRAIL. *See* **Goodnight-Loving Trail.**

PECULIAR INSTITUTION. A southern euphemism for slavery in general use in the 1830's.

PEDDLERS. When settlements in America were sufficiently advanced to demand surplus commodities, they were transported by backpack, horse, boat, or carriage (*see* Yankee Notions). At times the peddler provided the back settlements with their only outside contact. With improvements in transportation, peddling declined in importance.

***PEGGY STEWART*, BURNING OF.** The *Peggy Stewart* had reached Annapolis by Oct. 14, 1774, with about a ton of tea consigned to Williams and Company. Williams paid the duty on the tea, but permission was not given to land it, even when Williams offered to land it and destroy it. The threatening mob finally allowed the vessel to be run aground on Windmill Point and burned on Oct. 19 (now celebrated in Maryland as "Peggy Stewart Day").

PEJEPSCOT PURCHASE. A tract of land, indefinite in extent, on the Androscoggin River (Maine), purchased Nov. 5, 1714, from the estate of Richard Wharton, by a group of eight proprietors. The proprietors may be credited with the early settlement of Brunswick (incorporated 1717) and Topsham, protected by Fort George, built in 1715. The threat of Indian wars lessened interest in the area from 1720 to 1737, after which the settlements grew rapidly. A dispute with the Kennebec proprietors, who claimed the same land, was settled by compromise in 1766. Other land disputes were settled by legislative action in 1814.

PEKING CONGRESS (October 1900–September 1901). Met to settle the questions arising from the Boxer Rebellion. William W. Rockhill headed the American delegation. By the provisions of the protocol, adopted Sept. 7, 1901, China agreed to punish the officials responsible for the murder of foreigners, allowed the diplomatic corps the right to a fortified legation quarter, and agreed that alien troops might be maintained in China to protect the communication lines running from Peking to the sea. Against the desire of the Americans, China agreed to pay an inflated indemnity of $333 million, of which 7.3 percent was to be paid to the United States.

PEKING TARIFF CONFERENCE. Opened in October 1925 as a result of China's appeal for restoration of its customs autonomy. The U.S. delegation urged tariff autonomy if Chinese *likin* (provincial taxes on goods in transit) were abolished. Civil wars in China forced a two-month recess of the conference, but in March 1926 the U.S. proposals were accepted.

PELAGIC SEALING DISPUTE. The largest seal herd in the world is based on the Pribilof Islands, a small group of U.S.-held islands in the Bering Sea. In the late 19th century the herd was being wiped out; Congress could control killing on the islands but pelagic sealing by Canadian, Russian, Japanese, and other boats threatened to destroy the herd. Secretary of State James G. Blaine's announcement that the United States considered the Bering Sea to be under its control led to serious trouble. A treaty was eventually worked out by which pelagic sealing was sharply limited and the seal herds protected.

PELELIU. One of the southernmost of the Palau Islands, a part of Micronesia that came under Japanese control after World War I. During World War II the islands were an important Japanese defense position. The decision was made in mid-1944 to seize three of the southern Palaus. Resistance did not cease until the end of November, with the death of the last Japanese defenders. The island cost the Americans nearly 2,000 lives, but its value seems doubtful, for airfields in the Palaus could not support the Philippine invasion in the manner expected.

PEMAQUID PAVEMENTS. The unusually extensive stone remains of former constructions seen at Pemaquid Point in Maine until the mid-19th century, when most of them were taken up and used for local buildings. The discovery of a reddish stone native to Florida, called coquina, and coins and weapons of Spanish make, in excavations among these ruins, lent color to the theorv that Pemaquid Point might have been occupied as a fishing base by the Spanish from St. Augustine early in the 16th century.

PEMAQUID POINT. The peninsula on the Maine coast between the Kennebec River region and Penobscot Bay played an important, if shadowy, role in the early history of American colonization. Pavements found there, never satisfactorily explained, give weight to legends of very early occupation by Europeans (*see* Pemaquid Pavements).

There was an Abnaki settlement on Pemaquid Point when George Weymouth landed, June 3, 1605, at New Harbor. Men of the Popham plantation visited the place in 1607. In 1616, Capt. John Smith found a dozen European fishing vessels there. Englishmen were settled permanently at Pemaquid by 1625; Abraham Shurt obtained a grant at Pemaquid in 1631 and built a palisaded post. It was the most vital eastern outpost against the French colonization of Maine. It was granted to the Duke of York in 1664, and was administered as a part of the "County of Cornwall" and the colony of New York under Sir Edmund Andros. It was reclaimed by Massachusetts after the Duke of York became James II. Pemaquid was a key position, heavily fortified, in the Indian wars.

PEMAQUID PROPRIETORS. Claimants to lands at Pemaquid Point on the Maine coast as heirs of Nicholas Davison, who succeeded to the title held under the grant of Feb. 29, 1631, issued by the Council for New England to Robert Aldworth and Giles Elbridge, of 12,000 acres of land plus 100 acres for each colonist. The claim included all of Bristol and parts of Newcastle and Nobleborough (Maine). Other claims, based on Indian deeds, covered much of the same ground. In 1813 the claims under Indian deeds were disallowed, but by agreement the Pemaquid proprietors did not dispossess any settlers, accepting equivalents in unsettled lands elsewhere.

PEMBINA (N. Dak.). A strategic fur trade point for the North West Company in its war with the Hudson's Bay Company and one of the best-known outfitting points for the buffalo hunters. In 1812 the first permanent settlement in North Dakota was made at Pembina by pioneers from Scotland.

PEMBROKE RESOLVES. Drawn up by the citizens of Pembroke, Mass., in 1772 in response to the plea of the Boston committee of correspondence that the New England towns protest against the British ministry's plan of having the Massachusetts judges' salaries paid by the crown.

PEMMICAN. *See* **Agriculture, American Indian.**

PEMMICAN WAR. In 1812 the Hudson's Bay Company established an agricultural colony near Winnipeg, Canada, in the Red River valley, the center of the pemmican-producing area. Pemmican was vital to the rival North West Company, since it was the principal diet of the voyageurs. Miles McDonnell, governor of the Red River settlement, issued a proclamation, Jan. 8, 1814, forbidding the exportation from the colony of pemmican and other supplies. Many acts of violence occurred between the two companies until the British government intervened, and the firms were merged in 1821.

PENDERGAST MACHINE. A Democratic political organization in Kansas City, Mo., founded in 1890 by James Pendergast; when he died in 1911, his brother Thomas took charge. From the time of his appointment to a county judgeship in 1922 until his election to the U.S. Senate in 1934, Harry S. Truman was a beneficiary of the machine, but it is generally agreed that he avoided involvement in the machine's corruption. Pendergast continued to control enough votes to direct state politics, but the machine came to an end when he went to prison for tax fraud in 1939.

PENDLETON ACT (Jan. 16, 1883). The federal government's central civil service law, sponsored by Sen. George H. Pendleton of Ohio. It exempted public officials from political assessments. The Civil Service Commission was reestablished to prepare rules for a limited classified civil service. Competitive examinations were to determine the qualifications of applicants, while appointments were to be apportioned among the states according to population.

PENINSULAR CAMPAIGN (1862). An advance against Richmond, which began on Apr. 4, when Maj. Gen. George B. McClellan got his Union army of 100,000 to attack the Confederate capital by way of the peninsula formed by the York and James rivers. The early Union advance was marked by Confederate resistance behind entrenchments across the peninsula from Yorktown. On Apr. 5, McClellan besieged Yorktown, which was evacuated on May 3. He fought at

Williamsburg on May 5, straddling the Chickahominy River on May 20 and facing a strengthened Confederate force under Gen. Joseph E. Johnston. The first phase of the campaign ended with the indecisive two-day Battle of Fair Oaks (or Battle of Seven Pines), May 31 and June 1. Johnston was wounded on June 1 and Robert E. Lee succeeded to his command. After Fair Oaks came three weeks without fighting, marked by Confederate Gen. J. E. B. Stuart's cavalry raid around the Union army, June 11–13. Lee opened the third phase by attacking the Union right at Mechanicsville on June 26. This began the Seven Days' Battles, during which McClellan changed his base to the James River and retreated, fighting his way to Malvern Hill by July 1. On that night the Union army withdrew and the unsuccessful Union campaign ended.

PENITENT BROTHERS (Los Hermanos Penitentes). A religious organization in New Mexico. The local organizations, often incorporated as *cofradias,* are protected by law. The group's purpose is the celebration, by reenactment, of the Passion of Jesus Christ as observed by medieval Spanish Christians, thus preserving the concept of the expiation of sins through physical suffering. They have been driven to secrecy by the notoriety given the Lenten flagellant exercises.

PENNAMITE AND YANKEE WARS. *See* **Yankee-Pennamite Wars.**

PENN CENTRAL. *See* **Railroads, Sketches of Principal Lines.**

PENN'S DELAWARE TERRITORIES. *See* **Delaware Counties Act of Union; Lower Counties-on-Delaware.**

PENN'S FRAME OF GOVERNMENT. Signed in England and published by William Penn, Apr. 25, 1682, it consisted of twenty-four articles, to which was appended (May 5) the Laws Agreed Upon in England, a bill of rights emphasizing religious liberty. Penn established a governor and council with large governing powers, including the sole power of originating laws, and an assembly limited to approval of laws. Both bodies were to be elected by the freemen, one third of the council and the entire assembly to be chosen annually. The Charter of Privileges of 1701, the work of Penn and the assembly, eliminated the council and gave the assembly complete control over legislation and taxation.

PENN'S HOLY EXPERIMENT. *See* **Holy Experiment.**

PENNSYLVANIA. When settled by Europeans in the early 17th century Pennsylvania was inhabited by some 15,000 Delaware, Susquehanna, and Shawnee Indians. Possession of the territory was disputed by the English, Dutch, and Swedes. Henry Hudson sailing under the Dutch flag had entered the Delaware River on the *Half Moon* in 1609 and Dutch trading posts were subsequently established. In 1637 the Swedes started trade; in 1638 they built Fort Christina, and in 1643, the first permanent settlement and capital within Pennsylvania on Tinicum Island, at the mouth of the Schuylkill River. The Dutch seized New Sweden in 1655, only to lose it to the English in 1664. The territory then was governed under James, Duke of York. Charles II in 1681 made Quaker leader William Penn the governor and proprietor, partly to clear a debt of £16,000 owed Penn's father, Adm. William Penn, and to establish a firmer English control over this key area. Penn made his colony a haven for persecuted Quakers and others under the liberal Frame of Government of 1682 and the Charter of Privileges of 1701. After his death in 1718 the colony was governed briefly by his wife, Hannah Penn; thereafter the proprietorship fell to his sons, John, Richard, and Thomas, and finally to his grandson, John Penn. The Revolution ended the proprietorship in 1776, but political battles had led over the years to a strong colonial assembly.

The liberal government, abundant land, and economic opportunity combined to attract thousands of immigrants. The English Quakers of southeastern Pennsylvania were joined after 1700 by many Germans, who moved into central Pennsylvania, and by 1728 by Scotch-Irish, who moved farther west. Philadelphia grew quickly into the largest city in colonial America and by 1776 was the second largest in the British Empire. Its economy was enriched by agricultural wealth from inland farms, shipbuilding on the Delaware, the charcoal iron industry, the fur trade, and developed commercial leadership. A rich cultural and intellectual life led Philadelphia to be called the Athens of America. The population of Pennsylvania in 1776 was estimated at 275,000.

The Penns had boundary disputes with Maryland, Virginia, and Connecticut because of vague "sea-to-sea" charters. The colonial era also saw Pennsylvania drawn into the war for empire between France and England, as the French sought to occupy the upper Ohio Valley. Forts were built by the French at the present sites of Erie, Waterford, Franklin, and Pittsburgh; the most famous was Fort Duquesne, site of present-day Pittsburgh. English efforts to dislodge the French led to Gen. Edward Braddock's defeat in 1755 but were followed in 1758 by the capture of Fort Duquesne by Gen. John Forbes, who then built Fort Pitt. The conquest of Canada in 1760 ended the French threat, but Pontiac's War threatened western Pennsylvania, which was saved only by Col. Henry Bouquet's relief of beleaguered Fort Pitt in 1763.

The first Continental Congress met in Carpenters' Hall in Philadelphia in 1774, and the second in the Pennsylvania State House (Independence Hall) in 1776; the congress continued to meet there except when Adm. Richard Howe's occupation of 1777–78 forced a withdrawal to Lancaster and York. At the Pennsylvania State House both the Pennsylvania constitution of 1776 and the Declaration of Independence were drawn up. Independence Hall was the seat of the Constitutional Convention (May–September 1787), and Pennsylvania was the second state to ratify the Constitution, on Dec. 12, 1787. Philadelphia was the national capital from 1790 to 1800, when the capital was relocated in Washington, D.C. The state capital was also relocated in the same year, in Lancaster, and thence to Harrisburg in 1812. A new state constitution was adopted in 1790.

After the Revolution the population grew and soon filled

out the frontier. Pennsylvania became a stronghold of Jeffersonian democracy, of which the Whiskey Rebellion against federal excise taxation in western Pennsylvania in 1794 was a manifestation.

The Philadelphia-Lancaster Turnpike, first in the nation, was completed in 1794; many miles of state canals were constructed and linked by the Allegheny Portage Railroad over the Alleghenies in 1835; pioneer railroads were built in the mining regions; and a great growth of commerce and shipbuilding took place. The revolution in industry made Philadelphia a textile center, and the use of anthracite expanded the iron industry. Oil was discovered near Titusville in 1859.

The later years of the 19th century saw a continued growth of industry, with steel replacing iron, notably under the leadership of Andrew Carnegie. The state led in oil production and refining before 1900, as well as in the lumber and leather industries. It was first in anthracite and bituminous coal mining. The development of large-scale industry induced the organization of labor, which had started in Philadelphia much earlier. Labor disorders took place in the 1870's; the famous strike against the Carnegie steel mills at Homestead occurred in 1892 and the great anthracite strike in 1902.

Predominantly Republican in politics after 1870, the state developed an effective two-party system after the 1930's and four times between 1954 and 1978 elected Democratic governors. The Great Depression and a sharp decline in the coal-mining industry, especially anthracite, and steel production created serious economic problems for Pennsylvania. To the decline in anthracite and steel production could be added the increase in population, so that 637,387 people out of Pennsylvania's 11,866,728 were on welfare or relief in 1980.

PENNSYLVANIA, INVASION OF (1863). After the Confederate victory at Chancellorsville, Va., early in May 1863, Gen. Robert E. Lee, decided to divide his army into three corps—Gen. James Longstreet remained in command of the first; generals Richard S. Ewell and A. P. Hill commanded the other two. Meanwhile Lee was developing a plan for future operations. He thought a victory on northern soil essential to Confederate success. The maneuvering of Union Gen. Joseph Hooker out of his positions behind the Rappahannock River was begun on June 3, 1863. By June 12, Hooker had begun to move northward so as to keep between Lee and Washington. On June 23, while the Confederate army was crossing the Potomac River, Confederate Gen. J. E. B. Stuart and his cavalry rode off to harass Hooker's army. Stuart then passed between it and Washington, crossed into Maryland, and rejoined Lee in Pennsylvania on July 2. On June 27, Hooker resigned, and Gen. George G. Meade succeeded him. The Confederate army was moving into Pennsylvania when Lee learned that Meade was in pursuit; on June 29 he ordered a concentration of his scattered army. Stuart's absence deprived Lee of exact knowledge of enemy movements. As a result, Hill's troops, investigating the strength of a Union cavalry force in Gettysburg, inadvertently brought on the three-day battle that ended in Confederate defeat.

On July 4, Lee waited in position for Meade's counterattack, but none was made. After dark the Confederate army began to retreat in driving rain. By July 6 the army was at Hagerstown, Md., drawn up to repel Meade's expected attack, but Meade did not begin pursuit until July 5. Lee moved back slowly to the Potomac at Williamsport, where flood waters compelled another halt. By the time Meade reached a decision to attack, the river had fallen sufficiently to permit Lee's army to cross over into Virginia on July 13–14. Early in August the Confederate army had taken position south of the Rapidan River to protect Richmond. On Aug. 8, Lee, assuming responsibility for the failure, asked President Davis to select someone else to command the army. Davis refused.

PENNSYLVANIA, UNIVERSITY OF. Starting from a 1740 plan for a charity school in Philadelphia, a subsequent plan for a public academy was implemented in 1749, through Benjamin Franklin's *Proposals* and the *Constitutions.* The resulting institution was historic because never before had an institution of higher education been founded on purely secular and civil objectives, without patronage from a religious group, a private sponsor, or a government. Instruction began in 1751; there were 145 pupils. In 1755, a rechartering denominated the school a "College and Academy."

During the years (1749–57) Franklin shepherded the institution, he exemplified the spirit of compromise. Instead of insisting on the utilitarian curriculum that he preferred, he agreed to a major classical emphasis in order to attract important trustees. The first medical school in the colonies (1765) and the first department of botany (1768) were established at the school. The self-perpetuating board of trustees was established in 1749. The Pennsylvania legislature in 1779 confiscated the rights and property of the trustees and changed the corporate title to "Trustees of the University of the State of Pennsylvania," the first designation of any institution as a university in the nation. The rights and property were restored to the "college" in 1789, apparently with the idea that the "university" would function somewhat separately. This anomaly ended in 1791 when the college and university were amalgamated as the University of Pennsylvania, privately controlled and funded.

Little momentum was achieved between 1790 and 1850; the medical school was faltering, and the pioneer law professorship of 1790–91 (the first in the United States) failed (until 1850) to inspire the establishment of a law school. Fortunately, vigor was on the point of resuming, as proved by the addition of the Towne Scientific School (1875), the School of Dentistry (1878), the Wharton School of Business (1881), the Graduate School of Arts and Sciences (1882), and the Veterinary School (1884). Affiliation with the Free Museum of Science and Arts (since 1938, the University Museum) was established in 1887. The Graduate School of Medicine was founded in 1919; the School of Nursing in 1935; and the School of Allied Medical Professions in 1950. The spectrum of academic inquiry was broadened further with the founding of the Moore School of Electrical Engineering in 1923, the College of Liberal Arts for Women in 1933, the Fels Institute of State and Local Government in 1937, and the Annenberg School of Communications in 1959. In 1980 the university had about 18,500 students.

PENNSYLVANIA AND OHIO CANAL. The canal, opened in 1840, ran from the Ohio River near Pittsburgh to Akron, where it connected with the Ohio and Erie Canal. In 1854 the Cleveland and Mahoning Railroad obtained a controlling interest in it, and it soon fell into disuse. By 1874 the canal was closed.

PENNSYLVANIA CANAL SYSTEM. In 1826 the Pennsylvania legislature passed an act for state construction of a waterway from Philadelphia to Pittsburgh (known as the Main Line), and ground was broken at once. From Philadelphia to Columbia along the Susquehanna River a railroad instead of a canal was built and opened in 1834. The canal began at Columbia and followed the Susquehanna and Juniata rivers to Hollidaysburg, from which the Portage Railroad carried the line over the mountains to Johnstown; from there the canal continued to Pittsburgh. Work on several auxiliary canals began in 1828. Leaving the Main Line at the mouth of the Juniata, one of the canals ran up the Susquehanna to Northumberland; one line followed the west branch of the Susquehanna, and the other followed the north branch toward the New York state line. The Delaware Division, following the Delaware River from the mouth of the Lehigh River down to tidewater at Bristol, was in effect a continuation of the Lehigh Canal, privately built, down to the Delaware. Some short branch canals were built; the Monongahela River was improved with locks and dams; and a canal was projected from the Ohio River near Pittsburgh to Lake Erie, of which only 31 miles were built. By 1840 there were 606 miles of canal and 118 miles of railroad in the system, and the expense incurred and authorized then stood at $32 million. On Feb. 1, 1840, Pennsylvania defaulted in the payment of interest on its bonds. The legislature halted construction throughout the whole system. In 1846, the Pennsylvania Railroad was chartered to build a line paralleling the main canal from Philadelphia to Pittsburgh; the canal debt had by 1848 risen to $40 million. The governor was authorized to offer the Main Line for sale. In 1857 the Pennsylvania Railroad bought it for $7.5 million and promptly shut down the Portage Railroad. In 1863–64 it abandoned the west end of the canal, from Johnstown to Pittsburgh. The eastern section was turned over to a subsidiary corporation, the Pennsylvania Canal Company, in 1866. In 1858 the state sold the Delaware, Susquehanna, north branch and west branch divisions to the Sunbury and Erie Railroad. The north branch canal was extended to Athens, Pa., where it connected with the New York State canal system, but the portion of it above Wilkes-Barre was wrecked by a flood in 1865, and the Lehigh Valley Railroad was built on its right of way. In 1871 the Pennsylvania Canal Company operated 358 miles of the old system and carried more than one million tons of freight; thereafter its business declined. In 1889 the eastern fragment of the Main Line was wrecked by a flood and never fully rebuilt. In 1904 the last mile of canal along the Susquehanna was abandoned. The Delaware Division, leased in 1866 by the Lehigh Coal and Navigation Company, continued to operate as long as its sister canal, the Lehigh, functioned. Both ceased operation in 1931.

PENNSYLVANIA-CONNECTICUT BOUNDARY DISPUTE. Originated in the overlapping territorial jurisdictions of the charters granted by Charles II to Connecticut "from sea to sea" (1662) and to William Penn (1681). Connecticut made no effort to give force to its claim until 1774, when it gave official support to the demands of the Susquehanna Company (formed 1753) to the Wyoming Valley in what is now the northeastern portion of Pennsylvania. A year later this territory was made a county under Connecticut jurisdiction, and its inhabitants maintained possession by force of arms in the Pennamite Wars. On Dec. 30, 1782, an interstate commission organized under Article IX of the Articles of Confederation unanimously awarded jurisdiction of the territory in dispute to Pennsylvania. This was the only interstate trial held under the Articles of Confederation, and while the official dispute lasted only from 1775 to 1782, the actual conflict of private titles originated about 1750 and was not finally settled until the first quarter of the 19th century.

PENNSYLVANIA DUTCH. *See* **Pennsylvania Germans.**

PENNSYLVANIA GAZETTE. Samuel Keimer at Philadelphia, Dec. 24, 1728, founded the *Universal Instructor in All Arts and Sciences: and Pennsylvania Gazette.* In 1729, Keimer sold it to Benjamin Franklin and Hugh Meredith, who continued it as the *Pennsylvania Gazette.* Meredith retired in 1732 and Franklin became sole owner. Franklin soon made the *Gazette* the most successful colonial newspaper. He introduced the editorial column, humor, the first weather report, and the first cartoon. On Jan. 12, 1748, he admitted his foreman David Hall to a partnership that continued until 1766, when Franklin retired. Occupation of Philadelphia by the British necessitated issuing the paper at York, Pa., from December 1777 to June 1778. The last issue was Oct. 11, 1815.

PENNSYLVANIA GERMANS. Commonly but erroneously called "Pennsylvania Dutch," they are a distinctive people and should not be confused with the general mass of German-Americans. Among the first settlers entering Pennsylvania under Penn's charter, they increased rapidly after 1727. At the time of the Revolution they composed about a third of the population of the province. Settling in the southeastern part of the colony, they occupied a well-defined geographic area, where they still predominate. This region embraces the counties of Northampton, Lehigh, Berks, Lancaster, Lebanon, and York, and adjacent districts.

PENNSYLVANIA HOSPITAL (Philadelphia). The oldest hospital in the United States. Chartered in 1751, it was founded by Benjamin Franklin and Thomas Bond. The buildings originally erected for it (1755–94), at Eighth and Spruce streets, are still in use. Its records show the admission of many victims of the French and Indian wars. During the Revolution its facilities were used by both the British and Continental armies during their occupation of Philadelphia. The earliest clinical lectures in America were given in its wards by Thomas Bond, and the oldest clinical amphitheater (1804) is still shown.

PENNSYLVANIA-MARYLAND BOUNDARY DISPUTE. Grew out of the ambiguous terms of territorial grants made by the crown to William Penn (1681) and to George Calvert, First Lord Baltimore (1632). Shortly after his arrival in America, Penn held a conference with Charles Calvert, Third Lord Baltimore, but they were unable to agree on boundaries. Thereupon, Penn appealed to the Privy Council. In 1685 an order in council was issued that the region bounded on the east by the Atlantic Ocean and the river and bay of Delaware, and on the west by Chesapeake Bay, should be divided into equal parts by a line drawn from the latitude of Cape Henlopen, on the western side of Delaware Bay, northward to 40° north latitude, the eastern half of which should belong to the king and the western half to Baltimore. From this time on, invasions from Maryland into the Delaware counties were made; Pennsylvania settlers were brought before Maryland courts, their houses burned, and their crops and cattle destroyed or stolen. In 1708 Baltimore petitioned the crown to set aside the order of 1685. Penn countered with another petition and was sustained. Baltimore again petitioned in 1709 but was dismissed, and the order of 1685 was commanded to be put in execution. Actual jurisdiction over the lower counties had been exercised by Pennsylvania since 1693, and on four occasions between 1704 and 1724 the Maryland assembly admitted they were annexed to Pennsylvania. Charles Calvert, Fourth Lord Baltimore, effected an agreement with Penn's widow in 1724, but her death and the infancy of the Pennsylvania proprietors delayed its execution.

The next thirty-five years saw an expensive series of litigations, challenges, and delays. In 1760, Baltimore entered into a final agreement with the Penns, and in 1762 the chancellor ordered it to be executed. Commissioners were again appointed, but the running of the lines was entrusted to two surveyors from England, Charles Mason and Jeremiah Dixon. In 1767, Mason and Dixon finally located at 39°44′ the northern line of Maryland, which has since borne their names.

PENNSYLVANIA PRISON SYSTEM. First developed in Cherry Hill Penitentiary, erected at Philadelphia, 1829–35. Prisoners were confined in large, solitary cells, which flanked corridors that branched out from a central control room. Separate walled exercise yards adjoined the backs of the cells. The inmates spent their years of confinement in solitude, laboring at handicrafts. The system required a minimum of discipline and was widely copied in Europe; but its expense prevented its spread in the United States; it was abandoned in the 1880's.

PENNSYLVANIA RAILROAD. *See* **Railroads, Sketches of Principal Lines: Penn Central.**

PENNSYLVANIA TROOPS, MUTINIES OF. On Jan. 1, 1781, Pennsylvania troops stationed at Morristown, N.J., mutinied. They killed or wounded several officers, and on Jan. 3 started for Philadelphia to place before the Continental Congress demands for back pay, food, clothing, and adjustment of enlistment terms. At Trenton the troops were met by Joseph Reed, president of the Supreme Executive Council of Pennsylvania, who on Jan. 11 secured acceptance of an agreement adjusting their demands. They then returned to Morristown. On June 13, 1783, some Pennsylvania troops in Philadelphia presented a memorial demanding pay due them. Irresolution characterized the reply by Congress, then sitting in Philadelphia. The mutineers made a public demonstration on June 21. Congress, still temporizing, adjourned to Princeton, N.J. The mutineers, hearing of the approach of troops under Gen. Robert Howe, dispersed or surrendered.

PENNSYLVANIA-VIRGINIA BOUNDARY DISPUTE. Originated in the ambiguous terms of the grant of 1681 to William Penn and the claim of Virginia to extend "from sea to sea, west and northwest" over any territory not covered by royal grants. At issue were whether the thirty-ninth or the fortieth parallel was the southern boundary of Pennsylvania and how the western boundary should be drawn. Virginia claimed most of what is now southwestern Pennsylvania. The survey of Charles Mason and Jeremiah Dixon, 1763–67, made it clear that Pennsylvania extended some distance west of the mountains. Early in 1774, John Connolly, acting for Virginia, took possession of Fort Pitt and organized a company of militia in the region; and in 1775 Virginia included the disputed territory in the District of West Augusta and set up a court at Pittsburgh. In 1779, commissioners of the two states agreed to settle the dispute by extending the Mason-Dixon line, which is about a quarter of a degree south of the fortieth parallel, to a point 5° west of the Delaware River and by running the western boundary of Pennsylvania due north from that point.

PENOBSCOT. The peninsula at the mouth of Maine's largest river of the same name was the center of the battleground of the French and the English for the possession of Maine. It was the site of Fort Pentegoet, founded by the French fur trader Claude de Saint-Étienne de la Tour about 1625. The Plymouth Planation established a trading post there about 1626. Sacked by the French in 1631 and captured by them in 1633, it was held by Charles de Menou d'Aulnay (later governor of Acadia) until its recapture by the Puritans in 1654. Returned to the French by the Treaty of Breda (1667), in 1670 it became the seat of Baron Vincent de Castine. Castine and his half-breed son became the leaders of the Indians in King Philip's War. Castine's stronghold at Penobscot did not become completely English until Quebec fell in 1759.

PENOBSCOT EXPEDITION (1779). An attempt by Massachusetts to dislodge the British from Bagaduce (now Castine), on the Penobscot peninsula of Maine, which they had occupied in June 1779. Nineteen armed vessels under Capt. Dudley Saltonstall, together with twenty-four transports carrying about 900 militia under Gen. Solomon Lovell, with Paul Revere as chief of artillery, arrived at Penobscot Bay on July 25. Lovell's men landed, but Saltonstall failed to cooperate. When British naval reinforcements arrived on Aug. 13, Saltonstall hardly attempted a defense and lost nearly all his vessels.

PENOLE. A compound of crushed parched corn, sugar or molasses, and cinnamon, the last optional. Originating in the Spanish Southwest, penole was of great value to early travelers, for a man could live for a month on half a bushel.

PENSACOLA (Fla.). A city on the Gulf of Mexico. The first settlement, soon abandoned, was that of Tristán de Luna y Arellano and 2,000 settlers in 1559. In November 1698, Andrés de Arriola established Fort San Carlos de Austria near the site of Fort Barrancas as a protection against French encroachments. In 1719 Jean Baptiste Le Moyne, Sieur de Bienville, seized the town, only to have it at once recaptured. The French attacked a second time and burned the settlement; but after peace was made, Pensacola was restored to Spain (1723). The Spaniards now made their settlement on Santa Rosa Island, near the entrance to Pensacola Bay, from which a hurricane in 1754 drove them back to the mainland. In 1763 the British obtained Florida, and Pensacola became the government seat of West Florida. The trading house of Panton, Leslie and Company was organized with headquarters at Pensacola. During the Revolution, Pensacola was captured by Bernardo de Gálvez in May 1781. Florida was restored to Spain in 1783 by the Definitive Treaty of Peace, and Pensacola lost its importance. During the War of 1812 the British attempted to use the town as a base of operations, whereupon it was seized by Gen. Andrew Jackson (1814), and the British were expelled. Jackson again occupied Pensacola in 1818, but it was restored to the Spanish. The formal cession of Florida took place in Pensacola on July 17, 1821. Fort Barrancas and the navy yard were surrendered to the Confederates, but Fort Pickens remained in Union hands. Union troops retook the city in 1862.

After the Civil War Pensacola grew in importance as a port, especially for the commercial fishing industry. In 1914 the navy yard was reopened as the U.S. Naval Air Station, with a large aviation school. By 1900 the city's population had risen to 17,747. In 1980 it was 57,619.

PENSACOLA, CONGRESS OF (1765). Held to define boundaries and ensure peace between the Creek Indians and the British.

PENSION ACT, ARREARS OF (Jan. 25, 1879). The act provided that all pensions, old and new, were to commence from the date of discharge. The rates for the period during which arrears of pensions were to be granted were to be the same as those for which the pension was originally allowed. For years this act continued to prove the most burdensome piece of pension legislation in U.S. history.

PENSION PLANS. In the mid-1970's more than 48 million American workers participated in the major private and government retirement programs, exclusive of the federal retirement program, Old-Age, Survivors, Disability, and Health Insurance (OASDHI).

Private pension plans constitute the largest of the major retirement programs (other than OASDHI), having more than 30 million persons on their rolls in 1975, and assets and reserves over $210 billion. They fall into two major groups, those administered by life insurance companies and noninsured plans. Noninsured plans include pension plans administered by trustees, pay-as-you-go plans, and deferred profit-sharing plans. Pension plans insured with life insurance companies in 1975 covered 11.6 million persons and had reserves of $67.4 billion.

Formal retirement plans for private industry were introduced by the American Express Company in 1875 and were soon widely adopted by railroads. By the late 1920's, about 80 percent of all railroad employees had coverage, but only about 10 percent of all American workers in private industry enjoyed this benefit. The establishment of the federal Social Security program in 1935 made the idea of pension planning much more widely applicable. In World War II, contributions to pension plans that conformed to standards prescribed by the Treasury Department were permitted because they were not considered wage or salary increases.

A powerful impetus to the postwar growth of private pension plans came from the trade union drive for inclusion of pensions in contracts. A 1949 Supreme Court decision in the Inland Steel Case required employers to bargain on pensions, and a steel industry fact-finding board held that the industry had an obligation to provide pensions and welfare benefits. The establishment of pension plans in the basic mass-production industries had brought more than 5 million workers within the scope of collectively bargained plans by 1950. The 1950's witnessed rapid expansion of the private pension movement; the rate slackened during the 1960's and 1970's.

In order to increase the protection of private pension plan participants, the Employee Retirement Income Act was enacted by Congress in 1974. Among its major provisions are the establishment of minimum participation standards in regard to age and length of service, the accelerated vesting of benefits for participants after ten to fifteen years of service, and the current funding of normal (annual) costs of pension plans together with the systematic amortization of accumulated unfunded pension liabilities.

PENSIONS, MILITARY AND NAVAL. The United States has granted pensions to participants in all its wars, including Indian wars, and to members of the regular army and navy in peacetime. A separate system for the regular army and navy was established in 1790. These pensions developed independently of the retirement system for regular and lengthy service, which was generally accorded half-pay after a stipulated minimum service. Since World War II even the reserve components of the services have a retirement schedule. Payment for the regular commences on retirement; for the reservist, it is deferred to age sixty-two.

The first service pension law was enacted in 1818, and the first pensions for widows of soldiers of the Revolution were granted in 1836. The first service pension was granted for the War of 1812 in 1871, and for the Mexican War in 1887.

A combination of political factors led to the most generous pension system in the world. An act of 1890 gave a qualified service pension to Civil War veterans who, from any cause, were incapacitated for performing manual labor. In 1904 an administrative order made age above sixty-two years a pensionable disability under this act. Congress recognized this principle in acts of 1907 and 1912. The first Civil War pension for service alone was enacted in 1920. In 1920 a qualified service pension was given to all above sixty-two.

The philosophy of veteran treatment was transformed by World War I and its aftermath. Subsequently the able-bodied veteran shared immediate and substantial benefits with his less fortunate comrades-in-arms. The new policy began during the war with enactments of a liberal life insurance program and a $60 discharge allowance. Thereafter, benefits progressively grew, largely through the efforts of the American Legion, organized (1919) almost simultaneously with the federal Veterans Bureau, created to oversee the traditional caretaking of casualties. Able-bodied veterans were soon lobbying for what was called the Bonus Bill, predicated on $1 per day for domestic service and $1.25 per day for overseas service. Congress passed the bill over President Coolidge's veto. Sums exceeding claims of $50 were paid in life insurance certificates maturing in 1945. An average claim of $400 was worth $1,000 at maturity. In 1931, Congress overrode President Hoover's veto to authorize veteran borrowing from the Treasury of amounts up to 50 percent of their certificates. The next year the Bonus Expeditionary Force marched on Washington, D.C., in a futile effort to force payment. In 1936 President Roosevelt's second veto of a bill for such payment was overridden, and $2.491 billion was disbursed. It was an omen. From the Revolution to 1930 all federal disbursements to veterans totaled about $15 billion, a sum that by 1973 would cover only a year and a half of Veterans Administration (VA) commitments. Established in 1930, the VA expanded rapidly in scope and complexity. By 1981 veterans numbered 30.1 million, 13.3 percent of the citizenry.

Some 60 percent of the VA budget goes to compensation and pensions. In the early 1980's the compensations ranged from $54 (a 10 percent disability) to $1,016 monthly. Some 20 percent of the VA budget goes for medical programs. In 1979 the VA maintained 172 hospitals and 332 other facilities, serving 1,342,000 inpatients.

After World War II, the GI bill of rights gave education or training to nearly 16 million veterans, besides their dependents. The first GI bill was generous, covering up to forty-eight school months all the costs of tuition, fees, and study materials and providing living allowances of a monthly $65–160. The 1972 Vietnam veteran was limited to thirty-six school months and provided with $220–298 per month (by 1980 these benefits had been increased to $342–464). Since 1944 the VA has guaranteed or insured loans for homes, farms, or businesses. In 1979 there were 364,600 loans on the books, 98 percent for homes.

PENSIONS, OLD AGE. *See* **Old Age; Pension Plans; Social Security; Townsend Plan.**

PENTAGON. Located in Arlington, Va., this five-sided (whence its name) structure was the largest office building in the world when it opened in 1943. It houses the Department of Defense.

PENTAGON PAPERS. A forty-seven-volume study of the American involvement in the Vietnam War. Commissioned by Secretary of Defense Robert S. McNamara, it includes internal working papers from the presidential administrations of 1945–68, with analytical commentary by thirty-six military and civilian analysts. While working for the Rand Corporation in 1969 in Santa Monica, Calif., which contributed to the study, Daniel Ellsberg and Anthony J. Russo copied the study and released it to newspapers. In 1971, the *New York Times* and other newspapers published it. After several installments appeared, the Justice Department obtained an injunction barring further publication. However, in *New York Times* v. *United States* (1971), the Supreme Court ruled that the government failed to satisfy the burden of proof necessary to justify prior restraint and had therefore infringed on the First Amendment's guarantees of freedom of the press. Subsequently, Ellsberg and Russo were indicted for espionage, theft, and conspiracy; but in 1973, the courts terminated the case on grounds of gross government misconduct.

PENTECOSTAL CHURCHES. Pentecostalists tend to be conservative on the question of the inspiration of the Bible, to stress the necessity of an emotional conversion, to practice the ministry of healing, and to believe in the experience of the Spirit. The presence of the Spirit may manifest itself in "speaking in tongues" (hence, their name). Pentecostalism appears to have begun in the disputes over the place of "entire sanctification" in 19th-century Methodism. Although John Wesley's doctrine stressed the gradual growth of the Christian toward perfection, many revivalists were teaching the doctrine as if it called for a second experience of the Spirit, following conversion.

While Pentecostalism has spread rapidly and widely in the United States, it has become fragmented into many denominations. The Assemblies of God (founded in 1904) is closest in organization to the principal Protestant denominations, for unlike earlier Pentecostalists, it has a trained ministry and a church structure that combines Congregational and Presbyterian elements. The International Church of the Foursquare Gospel represents another style of the Pentecostal church; founded by evangelist Aimee Semple McPherson in the early 1920's, the church was entirely dominated by her during her lifetime, and after 1944 largely controlled by her son.

In 1981 there were fifteen Pentecostal denominations in the United States, with a combined membership of 2,376,350; the largest was the Assemblies of God (1,064,490 members).

PENTEGOET, FORT. The advanced eastern post of the French in New England, located in what is now Castine,

Maine. Erected about 1625 by Claude de Saint-Étienne de la Tour, a French fur trader, it was seized by a group of Englishmen from the Plymouth Plantation a year later. After the English trading post was sacked in 1631 and then captured in 1633 by the French, Fort Pentegoet remained one of the French strongholds during the French and Indian War.

PEONAGE. Involuntary servitude under which a debtor is forced to make payment to a master by his labor. It differs from slavery, serfdom, and contract labor by both the necessary element of indebtedness and the indefinite term of service. While not wholly confined to blacks, peonage developed in the South after the abolition of slavery. Fines imposed for petty crime were paid by an employer who then exacted work from the sentenced person. In 1910 the Supreme Court declared it to be in violation of the Thirteenth and Fourteenth amendments (*Bailey* v. *Alabama*).

PEOPLE'S PARTY. *See* **Populist Party.**

PEOPLE'S TEMPLE. *See* **Jonestown Massacre.**

PEORIA (Ill.). A city on Peoria Lake and the site of the first permanent French settlement in Illinois Country. Robert Cavelier, Sieur de La Salle, built Fort Crèvecoeur in 1680 near the lake's lower outlet. In 1691–92, Henry de Tonti and François de la Forest erected Fort St. Louis, later named Fort Pimitoui, which probably survived until the transfer of the Illinois Country to Great Britain in 1763. In 1778 a new village was founded on a nearby site. In 1812, Capt. Thomas E. Craig partly burned the French settlement. Fort Clark was built the following year.

American settlement began in the area of Fort Clark in 1819. Its name was changed to Peoria in 1825 when Peoria County was founded. Incorporated as a town in 1835 and chartered as a city in 1845, Peoria's growth was slow until the late 19th century. The city became an important corn trading center and manufacturer of agricultural and earthmoving equipment. A port of entry on the Illinois River and a railroad center, Peoria was Illinois's second largest city from 1880 until the 1950's, when its population declined by 7.7 percent. Peoria's population in 1980 was 124,160.

PEQUOT TRAIL. An Indian route from New London, Conn., across the Pawcatuck River, to Westerly, East Greenwich, and Providence, all in Rhode Island. White settlers early laid out a road along or near the route, which by 1691 was a part of the New York–Boston post road. In the 19th century the trail was paralleled by a turnpike and by the Shore Line of the New Haven Railroad and in the 20th century by a highway.

PEQUOT WAR (1636–37). Prior to any white settlement in Connecticut trouble had developed between Dutch traders and the Pequot. Capt. John Stone, an English trader, and several companions were killed by the Pequot in 1633, as was Capt. John Oldham in 1636, which led to a fruitless attack by a Massachusetts Bay expedition. In April 1637 some Pequot made an attack on Wethersfield that led the general court of the recently settled river towns—Windsor, Hartford, and Wethersfield—on May 1, 1637, to declare war on the Pequot. Ninety men under Capt. John Mason, accompanied by 80 Mohegan under Uncas, made their way downriver to Saybrook. Joined by Capt. John Underhill and 20 Massachusetts men, Mason conferred with the chief, Narraganset Miantonomo, and received further aid. After a two-day march overland, the party surprised and burned (May 26) the Pequot fort near present-day Mystic. Only seven Indians escaped the slaughter. Mason and his men attacked a second Pequot stronghold two miles away the same night. About 300 braves from other Pequot towns started with their families for the Hudson River. They were soon caught in Sasqua swamp, near present-day Southport, Conn. Through the intervention of Thomas Stanton, the women and children were led out of the swamp before the attack was made. The fight on July 13 resulted in the escape of about 60 Pequot and the capture of 180, who were allotted to the Mohegan, Narraganset, and Niantic and absorbed into their tribes. The Pequot ceased to exist as a separate tribe.

PERDICARIS AFFAIR (1904). On May 18, 1904, Ion Perdicaris, a U.S. citizen, and his stepson, Cromwell Varley, a British subject, were abducted near Tangier by the Riffian bandit Ahmed ibn-Muhammed Raisuli. The United States demanded that the Moroccan sultan secure Perdicaris' release and dispatched a warship to Tangier. On June 22, Secretary of State John Hay sent the famous dispatch "Perdicaris alive or Raisuli dead," just as Perdicaris was being released. Hay's dispatch took the country by storm, but State Department doubts about the character of Perdicaris' citizenship were concealed until after President Theodore Roosevelt's election on Nov. 8.

PERDIDO. A river flowing through southwest Alabama to the Gulf of Mexico. The Perdido was the boundary between French Louisiana and Spanish Florida. British East Florida and West Florida were divided at the Apalachicola River in 1763, but since 1783 the Perdido has been the limit of East Florida, now the state of Florida.

PERMANENT COURT OF ARBITRATION (known as the Hague Court of Arbitration). Operates under the Convention for the Pacific Settlement of International Disputes, which dates from the First Hague Peace Conference (1899). The court established was to be "competent for all arbitration cases, unless the parties agree to institute a special Tribunal." Between 1899 and 1932, only twenty-one minor matters were referred to it, and it has not been used since 1932. The United States sought to make it an effective agency by submitting the Pious Fund case to it in 1902, and subsequently the United States agreed to hearings on five more issues.

The reluctance of nations to utilize the court stems from its lack of any compulsory feature requiring states to submit their differences to it and from confusion over its structure and use. Furthermore, the Permanent Court of International Justice, organized in 1921, deprived the tribunal of influence as governments utilized the newer body. The arbitration court heard only four cases after the new agency appeared. Yet the Permanent Court of Arbitration has survived as a functional, if not functioning, agency. The 1980 membership included 74 countries.

PERRY-ELLIOTT CONTROVERSY. At the Battle of Lake Erie (Sept. 10, 1813), Jesse D. Elliott, commander of the *Niagara,* did not move his ship up to support the *Lawrence,* commanded by Oliver Hazard Perry, until the *Lawrence* was practically destroyed. After much private recrimination, Elliott challenged Perry to a duel in 1818, and Perry preferred charges against Elliott for his conduct during the engagement. The charges were pigeonholed, but in 1821, after Perry's death, the controversy was revived. In 1839, when James Fenimore Cooper, in his *History of the Navy of the United States of America,* failed to criticize Elliott, he was violently attacked by friends of Perry, mostly Whigs. Cooper thereupon successfully sued for libel. Later naval historians have tended to criticize Elliott for inaction.

PERRY'S EXPEDITION TO JAPAN. President Millard Fillmore dispatched an expedition to Japan in 1852 under the command of Commodore Matthew Calbraith Perry. It was to arrange for the protection of U.S. seamen and property involved in shipwrecks off the Japanese coast; to obtain permission for U.S. vessels to secure provisions, water, and fuel; and to induce Japan to open up its ports for trade.

Perry's mission was intended to impress upon the Japanese the determination of the United States to enter into treaty relations. Thus, a considerable squadron, first of four war vessels and later of seven, was provided Perry. A first visit was made to the Bay of Yedo (Tokyo) in July 1853. Perry informed the Japanese that he would return the next year for a definite answer to the proposals in a letter from President Fillmore to the emperor; he then withdrew his ships to the China coast and returned in February 1854. On Mar. 31, 1854, the Treaty of Kanagawa, opening Japan to trade and also providing for the care of shipwrecked Americans and for facilities to supply American ships, was signed.

PERRYVILLE, BATTLE OF (Oct. 8, 1862). Confederate Gen. Braxton Bragg's army was drawn up in battle array near Perryville when Union troops under Gen. Don Carlos Buell, marching from Louisville, unexpectedly encountered the Confederate force. A bloody battle followed. The Confederates achieved a tactical success and remained in possession of the battlefield. During the night Bragg withdrew eastward to join Gen. Edmund Kirby-Smith. The following day a retirement southward toward Knoxville, Tenn., was begun.

PERSONAL LIBERTY LAWS. State laws intended to impede the return of fugitive slaves. Slaveowners considered them a gross infringement of rights guaranteed by the U.S. Constitution, and enumerated them among the grievances justifying secession in 1861. The Constitution required that fugitive slaves be delivered to the person having legal claim to them (Article IV, Section II). These general provisions required implementation, and Congress provided it in the first Fugitive Slave Act (Feb. 12, 1793). To safeguard against abuses, such as the seizure of free blacks under perjured testimony or affidavits, Indiana (1824) and Connecticut (1838) provided for jury trials for fugitives, but the bulk of personal liberty laws were adopted after 1842 when the U.S. Supreme Court, in *Prigg* v. *Pennsylvania*, declared that state officials could not be required to enforce the Fugitive Slave Act. Several states responded by forbidding their officers to perform any duties under the 1793 act or to use state jails or prisons for holding fugitive slaves.

After 1850, when the second Fugitive Slave Act, strengthened federal enforcement of Article IV, Section II, the scope of personal liberty laws was greatly enlarged. Rigorous requirements for identification and proof of ownership had to be met, perjury and illegal seizures were heavily penalized, and the use of the jury was in effect a promise that the runaway and those who assisted him would have full measure of "liberty" while the pursuer would encounter equal measure of obstruction.

PERTH AMBOY (N.J.). Settled in 1683–86, the city was the capital (1686–1790) and port of entry of East Jersey. Winning, through the *Hester* case (1700), its contest for commercial independence, Perth Amboy was an important 18th-century slave port and transfer point to the overland stage. The city was occupied by the British in 1776–77. In the early 19th century, Perth Amboy was known as a summer resort. It began to attract heavy industry in the late 1800's and has become an important shipbuilding and oil-refining center, and a major port. The population in 1980 was 38,951.

PET BANKS. When in 1833 the administration of President Andrew Jackson determined to remove governmental deposits from the Bank of the United States, certain state banks, "pet banks," were selected to receive future deposits. By Nov. 1, 1836, there were eighty-nine such banks.

***PETERHOFF* ADMIRALTY CASE.** Elaborated the status of a blockaded river serving both a neutral and a belligerent, and applied the ultimate destination rule to conditional and absolute contraband. The English-owned *Peterhoff* was captured Feb. 25, 1863, en route to Matamoros, Mexico. The Rio Grande offered port facilities to both Matamoros and Brownsville, Tex., then part of the Confederacy. The river mouth was considered within the federal blockade. The U.S. Supreme Court freed the ship and its noncontraband cargo, as the blockade could not preclude free use of the port for goods legally consigned to the neutral city. The seizure of its conditional and absolute contraband was sustained.

PETER PARLEY. The pen name of Samuel G. Goodrich (1793–1860), author of 116 Peter Parley books and 54 others.

PETERSBURG, SIEGE OF (1864–65). Severely repulsed by the Confederate forces of Gen. Robert E. Lee at Cold Harbor (June 3, 1864), Gen. Ulysses S. Grant decided to approach Richmond, Va., from the south, through Petersburg. On June 12, Grant started south and crossed the James River at Wyanoke Neck, June 14–16. His leading corps attacked Petersburg on June 15. After three days of fighting, the federal troops captured the eastern defenses. Lee's army then arrived and repulsed the last assaults.

Grant began siege operations on the eastern front and pushed his left flank southwestward to envelop Petersburg. His first advance, June 21–22, was driven back. The Battle of the Crater, July 30, resulted in another defeat for him. Striking westward, the Union forces, after severe fighting Aug. 18–21 around Globe Tavern, succeeded in cutting the Weldon Railroad. In September, Grant extended his right flank across the James. Grant's capture, Sept. 29, of Fort Harrison, eight miles south of Richmond, compelled Lee to move much of his army north of the James. The Confederates lost further territory on Sept. 30 when Grant's left pushed to within two miles of the Boydton Plank Road, but an attempt to cut this highway was decisively repulsed by Lee on Oct. 27, and field operations virtually ceased during the winter.

His line attenuated, Lee, on Mar. 25, 1865, assaulted Fort Stedman, attempting to penetrate Grant's right and cut his supply railroad. The attack failed, and on Mar. 29, Grant sent Gen. Philip Sheridan, with heavy cavalry and infantry forces, to Dinwiddie Courthouse to destroy the Southside Railroad. Sheridan was defeated on Mar. 31 by Gen. George Edward Pickett's and other divisions, but on Apr. 1 routed Pickett at Five Forks, rendering the railroad indefensible. Lee evacuated Petersburg and Richmond on Apr. 2 and retreated west.

PETITION, RIGHT OF. In the United States it arises from the First Amendment to the Constitution, which provides that "Congress shall make no law respecting . . . the right of the people peaceably to assemble, and to petition the Government for a redress of grievances." Most state constitutions make a similar provision, and the Supreme Court extended the First Amendment right of petition, through the Fourteenth Amendment, to prohibit infringement by a state, in *De Jonge* v. *Oregon* (1937). Originally, peaceful assembly was part of the right to petition. Its independent standing shows both the early importance of petition and the growth of protected expression. Lobbying and bills for private relief are covered. The right has been extended beyond grievances to encompass anything within the jurisdiction of government, including issues of highest national policy. There is no right to action on a petition, only to consideration.

PETITION AND REMONSTRANCE OF NEW NETHERLAND. In order that the colonists of New Netherland might be induced to contribute to the expenses of the government, Peter Stuyvesant in 1647 permitted the election of a board known as the Nine Men. On July 26 and 28, 1649, this board signed two documents of protest to the home government. The petition was a concise statement of the condition of the province, with suggested remedies. The remonstrance was a long essay that gave in more detail the grievances of the petitioners. The autocratic proceedings and personal characters of governors William Kieft and Stuyvesant and their councillors were set forth in forcible terms, questions were raised about the expenditures of public funds, and the administration of justice was severely criticized. A municipal government was requested, the need for more farmers as colonists was stated, and concessions in trading rights asked. Although a new charter with enlarged trading rights was granted by the Amsterdam Chamber of the Dutch West India Company, the arbitrary powers of the governor were confirmed, and Stuyvesant continued his autocratic course until April 1652, when he was instructed by the Amsterdam Chamber to give New Amsterdam a "burgher government."

PETITIONS, ANTISLAVERY. First became a major weapon of abolition agitation in 1836. In that year petitions for legislation against slavery so clogged the congressional schedule that the Democratic majority in the House of Representatives resolved thereafter to table antislavery petitions without any action. This, the first gag rule, was continued in varying forms until 1844. Abolitionists argued that the rule denied them their constitutional right of petition, a contention propounded in Congress by John Quincy Adams. To exploit the issue of the right of petition, the American Anti-Slavery Society initiated a nationwide organization for sending petitions to Congress. The success of the petition campaign led directly to the collapse of the antislavery societies, for the petitioning organization, once it was in operation, neither needed nor desired centralized direction.

PETROCHEMICAL INDUSTRY. Petroleum was long considered a nuisance, but by the 1850's it was recognized that distillation could separate the oil into fractions having various useful properties, notably kerosine. After 1859, when Edwin L. Drake drilled the first commercial well on Oil Creek, at Titusville, Pa., petroleum was no longer a neglected material. The following half-century saw the rise of the petroleum industry, owing largely to the the internal-combustion engine and the resultant wide demand for gasoline. But aside from the adjustment of the distilling process to favor the production of this fraction, and its treatment with sulfuric acid to remove impurities, little attention was given to its chemical character. The most volatile fractions were allowed to escape into the atmosphere; the gasoline and kerosine fractions were collected; and the heavier residue was extracted for greases or tar or was discarded.

The chemical consideration of petroleum began in an effort to maximize gasoline production by cracking the heavier fractions—that is, breaking their molecules, usually by heating them to high temperatures, into smaller fragments, ideally into the compound octane. Studies of the ingredients of petroleum to improve the cracking process gave the industry a better conception of the chemical variety of its raw material, a variety that was further increased by compounds created in the cracking process. In 1926 the industry established a research fund, and some companies established research laboratories, notably the Universal Oil Products Company of Chicago. The petroleum industry began in 1928 to bottle for sale the formerly wasted gases propane and butane and to seek uses for its greases and tars. But not until the 1940's did the industry adopt the practice that had characterized the

German coal industry more than a half-century earlier, the production of pure chemical compounds and their conversion into a wide range of commercial products. The close relationship between petroleum and coal could hardly have been overlooked after the Germans had made artificial gasoline from coal in the 1920's; in the 1940's they made artificial rubber from coal, while Americans were making rubber of petroleum. After World War II the chemical potentialities of petroleum came to be fully exploited, and because of its convenience it replaced other natural raw materials. Rubber, refrigerants, plastics, paints, fibers, detergents, and many other products came to be derived from petroleum.

PETROGRAPHY. The systematic description of rocks began with a technique invented by the Scottish physicist William Nicol, about 1825, for producing polarized light by cutting a crystal of iceland spar (calcite) into a special prism, still known as the Nicol prism. More important was a technique, perfected by Henry C. Sorby in England, and others, about 1840, whereby a slice of rock was ground so thin that light could be transmitted through mineral grains that otherwise appeared opaque. Moreover, the position of adjoining grains was not disturbed, allowing analysis of rock texture. In the 1970's thin-section petrography remained the standard method of rock study. One notable American contribution to petrographic instrumentation was the development of the polarizing plate by Edwin H. Land in the 1930's; by 1947 this synthetic material had largely superseded Nicol prisms in petrographic microscopes. Perfection of reflection microscopes and of polished sections extended petrographic investigations to include opaque ores.

It was principally in Germany that petrography burgeoned in the late 19th century, and American geologists went to Germany for their introduction to this science. The sixth volume of the report of the U.S. Geological Exploration of the Fortieth Parallel, *Microscopical Petrography* (1876), was in fact prepared by Ferdinand Zirkel of Leipzig, one of the two leading petrographers in the world. Subsequent publications of the U.S. Geological Survey, as well as some of the state surveys, were replete with beautifully lithographed plates of distinctive rock types as seen in thin sections. One of the members of the U.S. Geological Survey, George F. Becker recognized that in order to understand rock minerals properly it would be necessary to synthesize them from chemically pure components. This awareness led to the establishment of the Geophysical Laboratory of the Carnegie Institution in 1905, of which Arthur L. Day was first director. Henry S. Washington, a chemist at the Geophysical Laboratory, brought out *The Quantitative Classification of Igneous Rocks* in 1903, a work that had worldwide impact. This was followed in 1917 by *Chemical Analyses of Igneous Rocks,* U.S. Geological Survey Professional Paper 99, perhaps still the largest compendium of chemical analyses of rocks. Meantime, the physicochemical studies of rock-forming minerals at the laboratory were leading to new principles and new interpretations of the origin of rocks, culminating with *The Evolution of the Igneous Rocks* in 1928 by Norman L. Bowen—a publication that has had wide influence.

Until the 1920's, petrographers were concerned chiefly with igneous and metamorphic rocks, for they contained the widest variety of minerals, presented the best-formed crystals, and occurred in the most interesting combinations. Sedimentary rocks, by contrast, appeared relatively uniform and monotonous. Recognition of the economic importance of sediments (especially for their hydrocarbon content) led to an upsurge in sedimentary petrography.

PETROLEUM INDUSTRY. Oil floating on streams in New York was first reported in 1627. After techniques for drilling salt wells were introduced in 1806, oil also appeared, unsought and unwanted. Early colonists used petroleum to caulk ships, and Indians used it as medicine. By the 1830's druggists sold petroleum as a liniment, and in the 1840's several companies sold it as a patent medicine.

One company was the Pennsylvania Rock Oil Company, formed in 1854 by G. A. Bissell and J. G. Eveleth, to exploit an oil spring near Titusville, Pa. They engaged Benjamin Silliman, professor of chemistry at Yale, who in an epochal report of 1855 indicated that petroleum, properly refined, would make a profitable illuminant. The partners hired Edwin L. Drake to develop their property. In April 1859, Drake employed a salt-well driller, "Uncle Billy" Smith, to drill for oil; on Aug. 27, 1859, at a depth of 69.5 feet, oil appeared in the drill-hole. Prospectors rushed to the area as the news spread, and by 1861 they were producing more than 2 million barrels annually.

Techniques for distilling and refining paraffin-type oils from cannel coals and oil shales, developed during the 1850's, were transferred to petroleum refining. Abraham Gesner was the first to market a coal-oil illuminant (in 1856), "kerosine." With the increasing supply of petroleum, coal-oil refiners began using that for raw material, and such processing was well developed by 1862.

In 1865, Samuel Van Syckle successfully pumped crude oil through five miles of 2-inch pipe from the Pithole field in western Pennsylvania to a railroad terminal. Van Syckle's success invited many competitors. In 1865, too, railroad tank cars appeared.

The petroleum industry early exhibited wide fluctuations in price and output, which persisted until the 1930's. New discoveries would attract producers and refiners and output would burgeon and then decline, leaving excess refining capacity and eager producers waiting for the next cycle. After various attempts to stabilize production failed, the Standard Oil Company sought to accomplish the same end by monopolizing the industry. Incorporated in 1870 by John D. Rockefeller and his brother William, the company combined superior efficiency, offers of monopoly profits to competitors who merged with it, and outright threats to increase its market share from 10 percent in 1872 to almost 90 percent by 1880. It could not, however, control entry as new fields opened in Indiana and Ohio in 1882, California in 1893–94, Kansas and Oklahoma in 1906, and along the Texas Gulf in 1901. By 1911, when the U.S. Supreme Court dissolved the combine for violating the Sherman Antitrust Act, the company's market share had fallen to 65 percent. Nonetheless, the industry has traditionally been characterized by large firms: in 1967 the twenty largest oil companies controlled 83 percent of refining capacity in the United States.

Around the turn of the century the industry began to change from producing primarily illuminants to supplying increasing proportions of fuel and motive-energy products. Gasoline grew to become the industry's leading seller, first as an industrial solvent and then as an automotive fuel. From 1919 to 1980, 40–45 percent of the industry's output consisted of automotive gasoline.

The most significant innovations in 20th-century refining techniques involved efforts to increase gasoline yields by cracking—breaking down long hydrocarbon molecules under heat and pressure. Standard Oil Company (Indiana) produced the first commercially cracked gasoline in 1914. Within ten years four other processes were successfully competing with it. Because the patents were widely licensed, cracking spread swiftly: about one-third of all gasoline was cracked by 1929 and one-half by 1939; the figure had increased to about 65 percent or 70 percent by 1975. In 1936–37, higher octane ratings at lower cost became available when Eugene J. Houdry, a French engineer, perfected a commercial method of using chemical catalysts in the cracking process.

The twin pressures of a severely depressed demand (the result of the Great Depression) and unprecedented flush production in Oklahoma and eastern Texas between 1929 and 1932 induced federal and state governments to enact measures, which continued in effect into the 1970's, to conserve crude-oil production. In 1930 the Federal Oil Conservation Board published the federal government's first forecast of demand. Under the short-lived National Recovery Administration's petroleum code of 1933 the Bureau of Mines inaugurated regular monthly forecasts of demand, used by state regulatory commissions to establish production quotas in their states. The major oil-producing states agreed, with the blessing of Congress, to coordinate conservation legislation in the Interstate Oil Compact of 1935. The Connally "Hot Oil" Act of 1935 prohibited interstate shipment of oil produced in violation of state conservation laws.

World War I had placed little strain on the industry until 1917; military requirements did not exceed 15 percent of U.S. crude-oil output. World War II, however, created extraordinary demands that required the rationing of civilian supplies after 1942; in 1945 military procurement equaled one-third of the 1.7 billion barrels of crude oil produced.

From 1945 to 1980 domestic demand nearly quadrupled, while domestic crude-oil production approximately doubled by 1970 and then decreased. American firms, investing in foreign production properties, caused the United States to reverse its historic position in world petroleum markets and become a net importer of oil after 1948. In 1959 the federal government inaugurated a program of oil-import quotas, ostensibly to protect domestic supplies for defense. These quotas were removed in 1973 as the prospects dimmed for obtaining sufficient low-cost foreign oil to supplement costly American crude. In 1970–72 the Organization of Petroleum Exporting Countries, a consortium of nations that produced 35 percent of the world's oil supply, imposed higher taxes on foreign concessions. Simultaneously the growth in demand was accelerated by rising income, heavier and more complicated automobiles, and newly imposed environmental standards. Automobile emission devices, for example, reduced mileage per gallon of gasoline. Clean-air ordinances hastened industry's shift from sulfur-laden coal to fuel oil. The consequent fear of shortage increased pressure on the federal government to grant approval for the development of an estimated 40-billion-barrel untapped reserve in Alaska.

PEYOTE CULT. A religious movement that spread among the reservation Indians of the Plains in the late 19th century. Peyote is a small spineless cactus that grows in the northern half of Mexico and a short distance north of the border in Texas. Sometimes inducing hallucinational visions when ingested, it was used in ceremonies by Indians in pre-Columbian Mexico and is still used by some Mexican tribes, such as the Tarahumare and Huichol. Its first appearance in the United States occurred about 1870, by the Mescalero Apache. Subsequently its use diffused to many of the western tribes. In the southern Plains a cult centering on the use of peyote developed. The eating of peyote was combined with hymn-singing and testimonials, with a fusion of Christian elements and native beliefs. The cult spread rapidly, despite the opposition of authorities; most peyotists are now members of the Native American Church, chartered in Oklahoma in 1918.

"PHANTOM SHIP." As early as 1644 Theophilus Eaton and other merchants of New Haven Colony entrusted the construction of a 100-ton vessel to several feoffees at New Haven. Though "ill built" and "very walt sided," the vessel sailed for England in January 1646, but mysteriously disappeared, a severe blow to the commercial aspirations of the colony. On a June evening in 1648 an apparition of the ship allegedly appeared over New Haven harbor.

PHARMACEUTICAL INDUSTRY. Production of substances for the prevention or treatment of disease began in the colonies as an unspecialized craft when medicinal materials, such as botanical extracts and mineral substances, were often compounded and distributed by physicians of limited training and even by the keepers of general stores. Late in the 18th century and early in the 19th, influenced by changes in medical science, pharmaceutical production and distribution began to emerge as a specialized area of commerce. The first specialized drug houses appeared in Philadelphia. During the early 19th century, leaders of this trade supported the first steps toward the professionalization of pharmacy: the founding in Philadelphia (1821) of a professional organization, the College of Apothecaries (renamed College of Pharmacy in 1822); the beginning of collegiate education in pharmacy; and the founding of the *United States Pharmacopoeia,* an official compendium of medicinal materials.

During the second half of the 19th century the character of production of pharmaceutical preparations changed substantially. Large-scale, specialized, and even mechanized production gradually diminished the importance of compounding in local pharmacies. The rapid growth and dispersion of the population in the last decades of the century stimulated further entry of manufacturers into the field, many of whom were trained pharmacists or physicians who left their professions to produce pharmaceuticals and chemicals for the growing number of local pharmacies. In the late 19th and early 20th centuries many new substances were added to the pharmacopoeia. Leadership in both scientific and commercial development came from Germany, Switzerland, and France. The introduction of aspirin in 1899 indicated the medical and commercial significance of chemical research so characteristic of German industry. Gradually chemists isolated the specific therapeutic agents in many of the traditional botanical materials, and tablets or capsules containing specific agents gradually replaced the old elixirs. In the early 20th century a few American companies, such as G. D. Searle and Parke, Davis and Company, introduced research facilities, but they enjoyed only limited success against the facilities of the larger and more established German and Swiss companies.

The two world wars did much to change the character and role of the American industry. Cut off from the German suppliers, American companies invested increasing sums in research and development. Moreover, American patents held by German firms then became available to American companies. The general character of the pharmacopoeia was changed by new therapeutic approaches that emerged during the first third of the century, including the development of chemicals that specifically attack disease-causing agents without harming the human host; the identification of essential dietary substances; and the identification of hormones. One of the most important new developments, antibiotics, was the product of British research from the late 1920's to the early 1940's, but leading American companies, such as Eli Lilly; Abbott; Upjohn; and Parke, Davis, with the support of the government, introduced commercial production of the first antibiotic, penicillin, during World War II. After the war the leading companies invested heavily in antibiotic research, which helped to place the American industry in a position of international leadership in innovation and sales.

About two dozen corporations came to dominate the industry through their very high investment in scientific research and development, which provided a continual flow of new products, through patent and licensing policies, through substantial investment in sales and promotion of the new products, and through vertical integration and multinational operations. Their profit success brought these leading firms under congressional scrutiny during the late 1950's and the 1960's, when it was alleged that they enjoyed excessive profits in an oligopolistic market structure maintained through certain promotional and licensing practices.

PHARMACY. There are records of an apothecary shop in Boston as early as 1646 but of very few others in all North America in the 17th century. By the end of the 18th century, there were four types of practitioners of pharmacy. There was first the physician, who not only dispensed but also compounded his own medicines. Second, there was the apothecary, the professional pharmacist, who, like his English model, not only compounded and dispensed drugs but also diagnosed and prescribed as well. Third, there was the druggist, later also to be called a pharmacist, who compounded prescriptions in shops whose major concern was in pharmaceutical and related items. Fourth, there was the tradesman, of whom a variety took on a supply of drugs. Moreover, the general store often kept large stocks of medicines, and eventually many evolved into drugstores.

In the 19th century the American drugstore carried a full line of simples (crude drugs); had a prescription counter or section where medicinals and chemicals were compounded and dispensed; had a counter devoted to patent and proprietary medicines and perhaps a separate one devoted to nostrums; and handled a variety of other items, such as confections, perfumes, paints and glass, groceries, spices, and liquor. By the late 1930's the compounding of medicines from chemicals supplied by industrial manufacturers gave way to the dispensing of medications completely prepared by industry. By the 1960's only about 4 percent of all prescriptions required some combination or manipulation of ingredients. The large-scale manufacture of proprietary medicines undermined the professional role of the pharmacist.

Pharmaceutical education began in the United States with the founding of the Philadelphia College of Pharmacy in 1821. Among its contributions was the founding of the *American Journal of Pharmacy* in 1825, the first American serial publication devoted to the scientific and technical aspects of pharmacy. In 1868 the University of Michigan embarked on a full program of scientific training in pharmacy, offering laboratory and practical work as well as lectures, in chemistry, botany, materia medica, and toxicology. Eventually a full-time, day program of two years was developed. The University of Wisconsin followed suit in 1883, and nine years later pioneered in offering a four-year program leading to a bachelor's degree. Eventually the four-year program took hold around the country: the American Association of Colleges of Pharmacy, founded in 1900, adopted a two-year curriculum as a minimum in 1907; a three-year curriculum in 1925, leading to the degree of Ph.G. (Graduate in Pharmacy) or Ph.C. (Pharmaceutical Chemist); a four-year baccalaureate curriculum in 1932; and a five-year curriculum in 1960. The University of Wisconsin was the first to award the Ph.D. in a pharmaceutical specialty, in 1902.

A meeting of representatives of five colleges created the American Pharmaceutical Association in 1852, which serves as the professional organization of pharmacy. For the most part, the economic aspects of pharmacy have been left to the National Association of Retail Druggists, the forerunner of which dates from 1883, and to the state associations, which came into existence after a concerted effort by the American Pharmaceutical Association, begun in 1868.

The first laws providing for the examination and licensing of pharmacists in an American jurisdiction were passed in the Territory of Orleans in 1808. It was only after 1870 that state laws for the examining and licensing of pharmacists began to appear under the pressure of the new state associations. These laws all established state boards of pharmacy, composed of pharmacists, usually having some connection with the state association but technically a governmental agency. The boards examined candidates and usually demanded four years of experience in pharmacy. In the 1930's the requirement of a baccalaureate in pharmacy and a one-year internship became general; later the degree requirement was raised in accord with the five-year program.

Federal legislation pertaining to pharmacy has related to the prevention of the importation of adulterated drugs (going back to 1848); the regulation of the sale of narcotics (first under the Harrison Narcotics Act of 1914); and the concern for purity and proper branding, safety, and efficacy of drugs, under the Pure Food and Drug Act of 1906.

PHELPS-GORHAM PURCHASE. A land acquisition made in April 1788 from Massachusetts by Oliver Phelps and Nathaniel Gorham, consisting of western New York beyond a line beginning eighty-two miles west of the intersection of the Delaware River with the boundary of New York and Pennsylvania and running north through Seneca Lake; a strip of land one mile wide running parallel to the Niagara River was excluded. The rival claims of New York and Massachusetts to the acquired territory were settled in 1786 by the Treaty of Hartford, which gave legal title (in essence, the right of first purchase from the Indians) to Massachusetts and the right of sovereignty to New York. The price agreed to by Phelps and Gorham for this tract was £300,000 Massachusetts currency, to be paid in the depreciated consolidated securities of the state. Difficulties soon arose, for Phelps was able to persuade the Indians to part with only one-third of the land. Unable to make the payments as agreed, Phelps and Gorham were forced in March 1790 to surrender to Massachusetts the two-thirds not yet freed from the Indian rights. This reduced their holdings to two townships, for the previous year they had sold the rest of the remaining third to Robert Morris (*see* Pulteney Purchase). The matter dragged on for years before it was settled.

PHI BETA KAPPA SOCIETY. Founded on Dec. 5, 1776, at William and Mary College, Williamsburg, Va., it was the first undergraduate secret society in the United States. The name was taken from the initial letters of its motto, Φιλοσοφία Βίου Κυβερνήτης ("Philosophy the guide of life"). It became an honor society with members elected on the basis of their class standing. The badge of the society is a golden key. The society had 228 chapters and about 355,000 members in 1980.

PHILADELPHIA (Pa.). The fourth largest city in the United States, with a population of 1,688,210 in 1980. It was one of the first of the 19th-century industrial cities of America. The Swedes planted the first permanent white settlements within the present city boundaries in the 1640's, but the history of Philadelphia begins with William Penn's Pennsylvania charter of 1681; the selection by his surveyors of the site for his principal town and Thomas Holme's application of the famous checkerboard plan to the site; and Penn's arrival in 1682. By the eve of the Revolution, some 28,400 people lived in Philadelphia and the adjacent districts, and the city was the largest in British America. James Logan and Benjamin Franklin and their circles had given the place a considerable cultural eminence as well, represented, for example, by the founding of the American Philosophical Society there in 1743. Philadelphia became an obvious site for intercolonial meetings, and despite much conservatism in the city, the first Continental Congress in 1774 and the second Continental Congress from 1775 through most of the war made Philadelphia a hub of the Revolution. Although Congress departed in 1783, the Constitutional Convention met at the State House in 1787, and the city was the capital of the United States from 1790 to 1800.

The federal period became Philadelphia's golden age: commercial, social, and cultural primacy among American cities as well as political leadership rested with Philadelphia. Indeed, jealousy lest the city overshadow all others in the nation was a factor in keeping the presence of the capital merely temporary. The establishment of the first Bank of the United States there in 1791, following upon Robert Morris' Bank of North America, gave the city a financial preeminence it was to hold until the 1830's. Yet Philadelphia's primacy could not endure. New York had always possessed a better harbor. Once upstate New York began to fill up with settlers, New York could forge ahead in population and commerce, as it did in the early years of the 19th century. Although Pennsylvania built an elaborate combination of canals and railroads west from Philadelphia, the Appalachian Mountains prohibited Philadelphia from matching the advantages of New York's level route to the interior of the continent. By the time the Pennsylvania Railroad established a through line to Pittsburgh in 1854, the commercial superiority of New York was too great.

From the 1830's through the 1860's, the sprawling, bustling modern city emerged; its workers were rapidly transformed from home craftsmen into commuters to factories. The population surged from 111,210 in 1810 to 188,797 in 1830 and to 565,529 in 1860. The Centennial Exposition of 1876, a display principally of new industrial technology, was a climax as well as a celebration; thereafter the generation of business leaders who had guided Philadelphia during its surge of industrialization gave way to a generation that chose to husband its inherited wealth in cautious investments. The political leaders of the city gave the kind of direction that made Lincoln Steffens' describe the city as "corrupt and contented." The Progressive movement came to Philadelphia partially and late. After World War II the 18th-century residential area called Society Hill was revitalized, and much of the old downtown area was reconstructed.

The port of Philadelphia (including the Delaware from Wilmington to Trenton) remained in the mid-1970's second to New York. It was the largest petroleum port, and Philadelphia was the largest petroleum refining center on the East Coast. Major freight yards and rail junctions of the Penn Central and Reading systems maintained the city as a railroad center. Philadelphia remained a diversified manufacturing city of relatively small but numerous factories, including makers of metal products, textiles, food products, and chemicals. As an educational center, Philadelphia had fifteen colleges and universities and six medical schools; there were more than fifty colleges and universities in the area. The Pennsylvania Academy of Fine Arts, founded in 1805 and the oldest art school and art museum in America, by the 20th century was one of several major art galleries, the most notable being the Philadelphia Museum of Art, which opened in 1928. The Philadelphia Orchestra, founded in 1900, remained one of the leading symphony orchestras of the world.

***PHILADELPHIA*, CAPTURE OF THE.** On Oct. 31, 1803, during the Barbary Wars, the frigate *Philadelphia,* commanded by Capt. William Bainbridge, and blockading Tripoli, sailed too near the shore and struck a reef. Efforts to release the frigate proved unavailing, and in the end the ship and its crew of 315 men were captured. This incident prolonged American negotiations with and operations against Tripoli. Stephen Decatur destroyed the captured frigate after the Tripolitans had refloated it. With some eighty men, in the ketch *Intrepid,* Decatur, during the night of Feb. 16, 1804, boarded the *Philadelphia,* cleared it of the enemy, set it afire, and escaped from the harbor.

PHILADELPHIA CORDWAINERS' CASE (1805). In the fall of 1805 the journeymen cordwainers of Philadelphia went on strike to enforce their demands for the wage scale prevailing at New York and Baltimore and for a discontinuance of the rebate of wages for export work. Eight union leaders were then arrested on a charge of criminal conspiracy and tried in the mayor's court of Philadelphia. The court accepted the arguments of Jared Ingersoll for the prosecution and relied upon British authorities, since refuted, to establish the doctrine that "a conspiracy of workmen to raise their wages" was criminal at common law. Despite the efforts of defense counsel Caesar A. Rodney, the defendants were found guilty. The strike was broken, and a precedent was set for the criminal prosecution of labor union activities.

PHILADELPHIA GAS RING. The Republican organization in Philadelphia, under "Boss" James McManes, gained control of the city's gas department in the late 1860's, charged high rates and gave no service, and pocketed the proceeds. The trustees of the gas department, who became known as the "Gas Ring," ultimately controlled state as well as city elections. The organization was defeated in the 1880's by the Committee of One Hundred, a group of independent citizens who successfully prosecuted members of the "ring" and roused the electorate to vote for a reform candidate.

PHILADELPHIA RIOTS (May 6–8 and July 5–8, 1844). Both periods of rioting followed minor clashes between Irish Catholics and native political organizations. Protestants, their antipathies heightened by antipapal propagandists, began systematic attacks on foreigners. During the rioting, Catholic churches were burned, and immigrants' homes were sacked by mobs. A score of persons were killed and nearly 100 wounded.

***PHILANTHROPIST*.** An early antislavery weekly newspaper established by Charles Osborn at Mt. Pleasant, Ohio, in 1817. Osborn sold it in 1818 to Elisha Bates, who continued it for three years as a moral and religious reform advocate. The same title was used for an antislavery newspaper begun at New Richmond, Ohio, in 1836; James G. Birney was its editor. A mob destroyed the press, but the paper was printed for a short time in Warren County. Gamaliel Bailey, associated with Birney, became sole editor in 1837 and continued the paper for several years at Cincinnati.

PHILANTHROPY AND BENEVOLENCE. Puritan leaders, notably John Winthrop and Cotton Mather, urged colonials to recognize God's plan by "doing good." Quakers imbibed this imperative from William Penn. Humanitarianism and revolutionary millenarianism, products of the 18th-century Enlightenment, likewise became parts of the American ethos. Inspired by such motives, colonists pursued philanthropic reputations. John Harvard inaugurated an important mode of giving when he endowed the first Anglo-American college in 1636. Benjamin Franklin helped found not only a school but also a hospital and a library. John Woolman and Anthony Benezet, Quakers, remembered the poor and enslaved.

Stephen Girard, whose benefactions included a college for orphans in Philadelphia, stands out among philanthropists of the new nation. Benjamin Rush established the first free medical clinic in the United States. The organization of the New York Association for Improving the Condition of the Poor in 1841 by Robert M. Hartley and the founding of the Children's Aid Society in New York in 1853 by Charles Loring Brace stemmed from concern about growing poverty. Causes abounded—particularly Dorothea Dix's efforts to improve care of the mentally ill, Samuel Gridley Howe's actions in behalf of the sensorially handicapped, and the abolitionism of William Lloyd Garrison and Frederick Douglass.

The Civil War directed Americans' sympathies to the troops through such private organizations as the U.S. Sanitary Commission, a precursor of the American Red Cross. Northern blacks and whites also manifested concern for the newly freed slaves, from which emerged a joint private-public agency, the Freedmen's Bureau. For the first time on a major scale the federal government helped administer a welfare program for needy Americans.

The Gilded Age produced philanthropists such as Andrew Carnegie. The "stewards of wealth" and their successors endowed American society in the areas of education, art, music, medicine, and science. The Social Gospel and Progressive movements of the turn of the century enlisted citizens in charitable projects. Clara Barton's American Red Cross (1882) and the Charity Organization Movement reflected the desire to bring order to the expanding charity field. Founders of settlement houses—notably Jane Addams, who founded Hull House in Chicago in 1889, and Lillian Wald, who founded the Henry Street Settlement in New York City in 1893—pointed toward social work as a profession.

The 20th century saw a proliferation of charitable agencies and causes. The effort to rationalize giving produced cooperative campaigns, notably the Community Chest and the United Jewish Appeal. Corporations became more philanthropic, and benevolent foundations, such as those of the Rockefeller and Ford families, became a major element in philanthropy. The 20th century also witnessed governmental "charity" in the form of social security; public assistance; and aid to education, the arts, and the sciences.

Coeval with domestic philanthropy has been U.S. philanthropy abroad. Americans have responded to disasters and sought cultural challenges outside the nation. Since the early 19th century, American missionaries have been dispensers of education, medicine, and vocational knowledge and tools. Ad hoc groups have tackled specific crises, such as the Irish potato famine of the 1840's. Permanent organizations have aided victims of famine, war, and other scourges. Important have been the (Quaker) American Friends Service Committee, the Church World Service, the Catholic Relief Services, the (Jewish) Joint Distribution Committee, and CARE (Cooperative for American Remittances Everywhere). Foundations also have been much in evidence, among them the Ford Foundation, the Rockefeller Foundation, and the Near East Foundation.

Congress was first asked to vote relief for foreigners when refugees from the Santo Domingo revolution crowded into the United States in the 1790's. Republicans defeated the measure. In 1812 Congress approved funds for victims of the Venezuelan earthquake, and since then the government has repeatedly made appropriations for disaster victims abroad. Sensitive to the implications of philanthropy abroad, the government has tried at times to control private aid, through the Neutrality Acts of the 1930's and the War Relief Control Board during World War II, and to involve private groups in governmental programs, through, for example, the U.S. Escapee Program of 1954 and the Peace Corps (established in 1961).

Tax exemptions (since 1917) and other devices to encourage benevolence came under congressional scrutiny in 1948, 1952, and 1969, especially with regard to foundations, whose motives have been questioned and programs condemned for being either too radical or too conservative. The private philanthropy funds increased from $9.4 billion in 1960 to $43.3 billion in 1979.

PHILIPPI, SKIRMISH AT (June 3, 1861). Probably the first field action of the Civil War. A Confederate force of about 1,000 under Col. G. A. Porterfield, which had been burning railroad bridges in West Virginia, was surprised and routed at Philippi on a stormy night by Col. B. F. Kelley with a federal command of 3,000. The casualties were few.

PHILIPPINE INSURRECTION (1899–1902). The name most often applied to the Filipino-American War. Spain ceded the Philippine Islands to the United States following the Spanish-American War, by the Treaty of Paris, ratified in 1899. Except for the American force in Manila under Gen. Wesley M. Merritt and his successor, Gen. Elwell S. Otis, the islands were held by Filipino revolutionaries, whose desire for independence clashed with America's imperialistic intentions. Fighting began on Feb. 4, 1899. Otis pursued a cautious policy while awaiting reinforcements. Then, in October, he dispersed the Filipino army in an offensive north of Manila. Emilio Aguinaldo, the Filipino leader, fled into the mountains, and guerrilla warfare ensued.

Despite the efforts of a civilian commission headed by William Howard Taft and the pacification program of the military government under Otis and his successor, Gen. Arthur MacArhtur, guerrillas continued harassing Americans and pro-American Filipinos. President William McKinley's reelection in November 1900 dealt a severe blow to insurgent morale, and MacArthur embarked upon a more forceful pacification program in December. Several thousand guerrillas and their supporters surrendered or were captured between November 1900 and mid-1901. Gen. Frederick S. Funston captured Aguinaldo in March 1901, and the Americans continued making progress in pacification throughout the year. In July Taft and his commission took control of the colonial government from the military; Gen. Adna R. Chaffee replaced MacArthur as military commander in the Philippines. The following year, after the surrender of Gen. Miguel Malvar on Luzon and Gen. Vicente Lucban on Samar, the U.S. secretary of war proclaimed the end of the Philippine Insurrection, but the newly formed Philippine Constabulary fought against recalcitrant guerrillas, bandits, and sporadic uprisings throughout the period of American rule.

PHILIPPINE ISLANDS. An archipelago in the Pacific Ocean lying about 500 miles off the coast of Southeast Asia. Although composed of over 7,000 islands and reefs, its population is confined to eleven islands, the largest of which are Luzon and Mindanao. Predominantly Malay in stock, the population is Christian in its religious allegiance, as a result of the conquest of the islands by Spain in the 16th century.

With the exception of a brief and partial occupation by the British in the 1760's, the Philippines remained a Spanish possession until 1898. In the 19th century a small native professional class, influenced by European doctrines of nationalism and liberalism, began to seek more autonomy, and a brief revolt in the 1870's was succeeded two decades later by the Philippine Revolution. That revolution found its martyr in José Rizal, its organizer in Andres Bonifacio, and its most successful military figure in Emilio Aguinaldo. Although heartened by early victories, Aguinaldo's guerrilla band was faced with a shortage of arms by August 1897 and the prospect of continued Spanish reinforcements. Extracting a large monetary payment and a vague promise of political and religious reforms from the Spanish governor-general, Aguinaldo and the other revolutionary leaders made peace by the Pact of Biacnabato and went into exile.

The promised reforms were forgotten by the Spanish rulers, and in February 1898 guerrilla warfare recommenced in Luzon. The declaration of war against Spain by the United States in April appeared to offer the Filipino revolutionaries the opportunity for military success and independence. Shortly after Commodore George Dewey's naval victory at Manila Bay on May 1, 1898, Aguinaldo returned to the Philippines and with Dewey's encouragement raised a large and motley army that shortly drove the Spanish into the walled city of Manila. Aguinaldo's initial confidence that the United States sought only to offer protection to an independent Philippines was undermined by the arrival of American troops, the arranged capitulation of Manila to the American forces alone, and President William McKinley's decision in October to instruct his commissioners to the Paris peace conference to demand of Spain the cession of the entire archipelago. In December 1898 McKinley issued an executive order claiming American sovereignty throughout the islands. On Feb. 4, 1899, two days before the U.S. Senate confirmed the Treaty of Paris, the Filipino-American War began. The conflict required the expenditure by the United States of $400 million and cost 7,000 American casualties. (*See* Philippine Insurrection.)

Under the auspices of the Republican party the United States made a substantial effort to reconstruct the society and culture of the Filipino people in the years 1900–13. American officials in the islands achieved a measure of success in their determination to Americanize the political, educational, and judicial structures. Under the direction of Secretary of War Elihu Root and the Philippine Government Act of July 2, 1902, the Taft Commission proclaimed the establishment of American-style democratic government as the goal of American policy in the Philippines. In 1907 an elective assembly was instituted, representing the "Christian tribes" of the islands and selected by a restricted suffrage. It served as the lower house of the Philippine national legislature, and the commission became the upper house. The head of the commission, given the title of governor-general, served as chief executive; acts of the legislature could be vetoed by both the governor and the U.S. Congress.

Political tensions arose as the Nacionalista party, pledged to the complete independence of the islands, gradually assumed a dominant position in the assembly. When Woodrow Wilson took office as president in 1913, he appointed as governor-general Francis Burton Harrison, who was sympathetic to the desire of Filipino leaders to shorten the period of tutelage. He accelerated the Filipinization of the civil service and acquiesced in the informal transfer of much of the authority of his office to Filipino department heads. By the Jones Act of 1916 an elective senate replaced the commission as the upper house of the legislature, and suffrage requirements were liberalized. In 1920 Harrison recommended that independence be granted.

Gen. Leonard Wood, appointed by President Warren G. Harding to succeed Harrison in 1921, sought to reassert the U.S. authority in the determination of Philippine social development. The result was a deadlock between the governor-general and the Philippine assembly; a compromise of sorts was reached between Wood's successor, Henry L. Stimson, and the Filipino leaders Manuel Quezon and Sergio Osmeña, but by 1930 it was clear that Filipino demands for self-government would be satisfied only by independence.

The decision to grant independence to the Philippines was in line with the long-term evolution of American Philippine policy. The Tydings-McDuffie Act of March 1934 provided for the complete independence of the islands following a ten-year "commonwealth period." During that period the United States was to maintain its sovereignty over the islands, and certain Filipino exports were to suffer increasing tariff and quota restrictions. The Filipinos formulated and ratified a new constitution in 1935, and in November of that year the Philippine Commonwealth was formally established with Manuel Quezon as its president. Frank Murphy served as American high commissioner.

The commonwealth period, scheduled to end in 1946, was interrupted by the Japanese invasion on Dec. 8, 1941. By May 1942 the entire archipelago was in the hands of the Japanese, who set up a puppet Philippine republic under José P. Laurel. A large majority remained faithful to the Philippine exile government under Osmeña in Washington and assisted the American force under Gen. Douglas MacArthur when it launched an amphibious invasion at Lingayen Gulf in January 1945. The destruction in Manila, where the Japanese fought a last-ditch battle, was but a symbol of the general devastation suffered by the Philippines during the years of occupation and war. When Osmeña returned from Washington, the economy was in a shambles.

The administration of President Harry S. Truman reaffirmed the intention of the United States to assist in the economic rehabilitation of the islands. The Republic of the Philippines came into being July 4, 1946, but congressional legislation respecting future trade relations furnished a source of grievance for the Filipinos. On Apr. 30, 1946, the U.S. Congress concurrently passed the Philippine Rehabilitation Act and the Philippine Trade Act. The former authorized $620 million for the repair of war damages and additional funds for public health and technological training programs if the Philippine legislature accepted the terms of the trade act: Trade between the islands and the United States would be free until 1954, but fixed quotas were established on American products exported to the Philippines. After 1954, Philippine goods would be subject to an annual 5 percent tariff increase until the full rate of 100 percent was reached in 1974. In addition, the Filipinos were required to alter their constitution in order that citizens of the United States would be assured equal rights with citizens of the Philippines in the development of natural resources and the operation of public utilities. Protection of American capital was demanded as the price of rehabilitation aid and limited access to the American market. The Philippine legislature reluctantly agreed.

In March 1947 the United States negotiated with Manuel Roxas, the first president of the Philippine Republic, a military assistance agreement that gave the American army and navy a ninety-nine-year (reduced to twenty-five-year in 1966) lease on twenty-three bases in the Philippines. It also stipulated that the United States would provide arms and technical advice to an expanded Philippine army. During the 1950's, American foreign policy emphasized the strategic importance of the Philippines in a manner unequaled since the days of Commodore Dewey. The Mutual Defense Treaty of 1951 was followed by the inclusion of the Philippines in the Southeast Asia Treaty Organization in 1954 and a succession of military aid missions. American aid was primarily directed toward military assistance programs rather than economic diversification, and the reform programs instituted by Filipino president Ramon Magsaysay lost much of their impetus after his death in a plane crash in 1957. The 1960's saw relatively little progress in such problem areas as tenancy and land monopoly, agricultural inefficiency, retrogressive tax policies, and the dependence of the export sector on the American market.

The Philippines remained in diplomatic alignment with the United States, but many Filipino politicians were urging a more independent stand. Efforts to form an alliance with Malaysia and Indonesia proved ineffectual, but they reflected a determination no longer to serve as a subject ally of the United States. In 1972, facing a secessionist rebellion in Mindanao and rising political opposition from liberal groups in Manila, President Ferdinand Marcos disbanded the Philippine assembly and began to rule by martial law. After some relaxation in the late 1970's, the martial law was lifted in January 1981 and in June of that year Marcos was elected to a new term. During the 1970's President Marcos' government remained friendly toward the United States (a new agreement on U.S. military bases was signed in 1979), but moved in the direction of non-alignment. Diplomatic relations with China were established in 1975 and with the Soviet Union in 1976.

PHILIPPINE SEA, BATTLE OF THE (June 19–20, 1944). The Japanese Mobile Fleet, under Vice Adm. Jisaburo Ozawa, sortied for battle from Tawi Tawi in the Sulu Archipelago on June 13, two days before American marines assaulted Saipan. The main Japanese force of nine carriers and escorting battleships, cruisers, and destroyers rendezvoused east of the Philippine Islands with another battleship force. Adm. Raymond A. Spruance, commander of the Fifth Fleet, off Saipan, mistook this to mean that the Japanese fleet was approaching in two groups. Spruance thus removed his transports 200 miles eastward, formed a gun force of battleships off the west coast of Saipan, and held the fifteen fast carriers of Task Force 58 just west of there to meet the Japanese attack. On June 19, Ozawa's incoming planes were intercepted. The battle lasted most of the day, during which some 300 Japanese planes were shot down and only 30 American planes lost.

Preoccupied with the aerial combat, Vice Adm. Marc A. Mitscher, commander of Task Force 58, could not cruise westward in search of the distant Japanese ships on June 19. Nevertheless, two Japanese heavy carriers sank from damage inflicted during the day by torpedoes from the American submarines, and that night Spruance released Mitscher and his carriers from protecting the beachhead. Ozawa tried to escape westward, but late on June 20 searching American carrier planes sighted his fleet far out in the Philippine Sea. A late afternoon carrier air strike sank one Japanese carrier. To some 475 Japanese aviators lost during the two-day battle, the American fleet lost 130 planes but no ships and only 76 men. The Japanese fleet surrendered control of the Marianas and the central Pacific to the U.S.

PHILIPSE'S PATENT. An enormous tract in Putnam County, N.Y., purchased by Adolphe Philipse from Lambert Dorlandt and Jan Sybrant, who had obtained a license to buy it from the Indians. In 1697, Philipse secured a patent from Gov. Benjamin Fletcher for this tract and some additional land, which was known as Philipse's Highland patent. Both the Highland patent and the manor of Philipsborough in Westchester County were inherited by Frederick Philipse, who on his death divided the Highland patent among his four younger children.

PHILOSOPHY. Because of the brilliance its ministers and magistrates and the intellectual ferment sustained by its churches and colleges, New England first nurtured significant philosophical labors in America. The Puritans articulated and implemented distinctive conceptions of popular sovereignty and natural law matured by 16th-century Calvinists. Reformed or Calvinist doctrines, although rarely expounded in a rigorous philosophical form by 17th-century Puritans, still entailed a substantially well-defined, neo-Augustinian ontology. Such doctrines found philosophical support in the Calvinist apologist Jonathan Edwards, who dominated American philosophy from about 1730 until his death in 1758. At a technical level, his idealism was close to that earlier developed by George Berkeley (himself a two-year resident of Rhode Island) and to that of an American contemporary, Samuel Johnson.

Except to Edwards and his disciples, 18th-century America seemed peculiarly uncongenial to philosophical inquiry. John Adams, Benjamin Franklin, and Thomas Jefferson were fascinated with the physical sciences (natural philosophy) and with traditional issues in political theory, but distrusted metaphysical speculation, remained blind to the most subtle concerns of theology, and unself-consciously revealed rather than rigorously articulated a body of aesthetic and ethical assumptions. Their concern with the sources and economic bases of political authority and with the institutional foundations of public virtue and good citizenship continued into the 19th century. College presidents (usually drawn from the ministry) traditionally taught required courses in moral philosophy or introduced new courses in political economy. Before the Civil War a stream of American ministers and scholars studied in Scottish universities and brought back to America a form of common-sense realism, a philosophic tradition that lasted out the century in many Presbyterian institutions. Secular American philosophers and political economists drew direct inspiration from English utilitarianism.

In New England a diverse group of ministers, scholars, and writers found new philosophical inspiration in German idealism. Some so-called transcendentalists—Frederic Henry Hedge, Theodore Parker, and Octavius Brooks Frothingham—became rather careful students of Immanuel Kant, Johann Fichte, and Georg Hegel. Ralph Waldo Emerson was a sophisticated student of philosophy and thus has an almost Socratic position in American philosophy.

Various schools of idealism flourished in the late 19th century. In St. Louis a circle of lay philosophers spread the glories of Hegel and also launched the *Journal of Speculative Philosophy* (1867–93), the first exclusively philosophical journal in the English language. Lay and academic philosophers cultivated myriad varieties of idealism. The future of American philosophy was most apparent at Cornell University, where the Sage School led the way toward an academic and secular profession. Josiah Royce, at Harvard University, became the very symbol of idealism at its best.

Charles Darwin's *Origin of Species* (1859) invited new conceptions of man, nature, and scientific explanation. The fullest response to these issues came from the American pragmatists. But in the immediate aftermath of the publication of the *Origin of Species* and by request of Darwin, Chauncey Wright, a mathematician and scientist, first showed how the peculiarities of symbolic language provided a naturalistic explanation of man's dominant position in nature. Wright's interest in language, but not his aversion to speculative metaphysics, continued in Charles S. Peirce, who made strikingly original contributions to semantics, symbolic logic, and the philosophy of science. Peirce first matured a pragmatic conception of meaning and an operational conception of scientific method. American followers of Herbert Spencer, notably John Fiske, extrapolated from Darwin a vast, cosmic law of evolution, which had profound implications for society.

William James defies classification. As a Harvard psychologist and philosopher, he responded to, or influenced, almost every philosophical movement of the 20th century. In his *Principles of Psychology* (1890) he broached a new, radical empiricism.

John Dewey was the most systematic, comprehensive, and influential American philosopher. Educated at the University of Vermont and the Johns Hopkins University, he was early captivated by Hegelian idealism; he slowly responded to the naturalistic implications of Darwin's theories and to the challenging psychological theories of James. By 1900 he had espoused a broad, nonmaterialistic form of naturalism, which converted the objective mind of Hegel into the socially developed functions of language and culture. Dewey expanded the methodological insights of Peirce and James and often called his philosophy "instrumentalism."

Dewey, who died in 1952, was, with George Santayana and Alfred North Whitehead, the last of the giants. The age of towering individuals and great systems already seemed at an end. In the 1930's Nazi persecutions drove to America several members of the Vienna circle of logical positivists and some prominent German neo-Marxists, notably Herbert Marcuse. The positivists gained a large following just after World War II and helped stimulate an interest in the philosophy of science. Their iconoclastic attack on speculative philosophy, and the tremendous influence of English analytic philosophy, helped sway many philosophy departments toward specialized, highly technical, largely analytical concerns. Also in the postwar years, European existentialism, already well rooted in theology, had only limited impact on academic philosophers but created great interest among students and in literary circles. In Roman Catholic colleges sophisticated forms of Thomism that had long flourished there received new vigor from such European neo-Thomists as Jacques Maritain. In the 1960's the overweening interest in analytical approaches seemed on the decline, as more philosophers expressed an interest in phenomenology, in traditional metaphysics, and in normative theory. But any such judgment has to be largely impressionistic: American philosophy is much too diverse for easy characterization. But American philosophy was flourishing in the 1970's in both rigor and technical proficiency, although it lacked an earlier breadth of interest and impact on the larger society.

PHOENIX (Ariz.). The capital and largest city of Arizona, with a population of 764,911 in 1980; the center of a metropolitan area including 1,511,552 people. Phoenix is one of America's fastest growing cities; its population between 1950 and 1980 increased more than seven times.

Phoenix is located on the Salt River, one of Arizona's few large streams. The town was established in 1887. Since there was some indication that an ancient Indian village had occupied the site, it was named "Phoenix" after the legendary bird that rises anew from its own ashes. Phoenix became capital of the Territory of Arizona in 1889, after the capital had been shifted back and forth between Prescott and Tucson. When Roosevelt Dam was completed in 1911, Phoenix began to grow rapidly. The dam provided a source of water for irrigating the farmlands of Maricopa County. The farmlands are among the most productive in the country and Phoenix acts as a processing and trading center for them. Cotton gins, and canning and freezing plants operate there. The city also has electronics and aluminum factories.

***PHOENIX*.** The first entirely American-built steamship. It was designed by John Stevens of Hoboken, N.J., in 1806 and was launched Apr. 9, 1808. Robert R. Livingston prevented the vessel from entering waters subject to jurisdiction of New York State (*see* Fulton's Folly). Stevens sent it by sea to the Delaware River to run between Philadelphia and Trenton. Leaving New York, on June 8, 1809, the *Phoenix* reached Philadelphia on June 17, the first steamship to venture upon the open sea.

***PHOENIXIANA*.** A literary work by George Horatio Derby (1823–61), an officer in the U.S. Topographical Engineers who wrote under the pseudonym John Phoenix. The volume, published in 1856, consisted of some thirty short humorous sketches and burlesques of current happenings; all of the vignettes had appeared in California newspapers and magazines between 1850 and 1855.

PHONOGRAPH. On July 30, 1877, Thomas A. Edison filed a provisional specification with the British patent office and on Dec. 24, 1877, applied for a U.S. patent. It was little more than an interesting toy using fragile tinfoil records of little durability. A patent issued in 1886 to Chichester A. Bell and Charles Sumner Tainter for cutting the sound track into wax.

Early phonograph records gave little volume and were not durable. They had to be duplicated either mechanically by pantograph or acoustically. These limitations were overcome by Emile Berliner in a series of patents between 1887 and 1895. The patents covered a wax-coated zinc disk on which the sound waves were cut laterally through the wax to the zinc. The exposed metal was then etched according to the pattern recorded in the wax. This process made a very durable loud-volume record. A matrix or impression made from this original was successfully used to mold duplicates in hard rubber, changed late in 1897 to a shellac composition.

In 1901 a patent issued to Joseph W. Jones for cutting the original records in wax that was subsequently electroplated to allow duplication came as a surprise to Eldridge R. Johnson, who had been making records by the same process, independently devised. After intense legal maneuvering Johnson in 1901 formed the famous Victor Talking Machine Company.

In the 1920's electricity began to be applied with very good effect to problems of the phonograph business that had never been satisfactorily resolved by purely acoustical and mechanical means. The advent of the vacuum tube made amplification easy, and mechanical recording became obsolete. The actual work was accomplished by Joseph P. Maxfield, H. C. Harrison, and associates at the Western Electric Company during 1924, making possible the manufacture of records that could reproduce a much greater range of cycles per second at a much higher volume. These new records led to the creation of the Orthophonic Victrola, the last significant nonelectric phonograph to be produced.

By the 1930's all reproduction from records was electronic, following the trend set by recording techniques of a few years earlier. During World War II, because of a shortage of shellac, a plastic, Vinylite, was substituted. This material made the records unbreakable and greatly reduced surface noise. The weight of the needle was reduced, and a permanent sapphire needle was introduced, whose shape remained constant over a long time and closely conformed to the profile of the record groove, giving better support. This development made possible more closely spaced grooves and a longer playing time for each record. In 1948 the Columbia Record Company introduced microgroove records that made 33 1/3 revolutions per minute.

Electronics, low needle pressure and minimal record wear, very low surface noise, and long playing led to the development of stereophonic recording and playback. By early 1958 stereo made its great leap into the consumer field. The development of quadraphonic sound in the mid-1970's was hailed as a great advance but because the quadraphonic systems had complex electronic requirements, they quickly lost their appeal. Digital recording in the late 1970's was another breakthrough; this high-technology process produces a clearer and more lifelike sound than traditional stereo.

PHOSPHATE INDUSTRY. *See* **Fertilizers.**

PHOTOGRAPHIC INDUSTRY. In 1839 the Frenchman Louis J. M. Daguerre introduced in Paris the first commercial photographic process, the daguerreotype. During the mid-1850's a variety of wet collodion processes replaced the daguerreotype. Owing to the perishability of the photosensitive negative and positive materials, their production remained with the professional photographers. In the early 1880's dry gelatin supplanted wet collodion as the carrier of photosensitive salts on negative glass plates. This technological change permitted centralized factory production of photosensitive materials for the first time.

In 1884 George Eastman sought with William H. Walker, a Rochester cameramaker, to develop an alternative to dry plates. They introduced in 1885 a roll-film system. It consisted of a roll holder that slid into the back of the camera instead of the glass plates, and it employed roll film as the negative replacement for the glass plate. The lack of transparency of the paper film first employed by Eastman and the technical complexity of the later stripping film discouraged professional and amateur photographers from adopting the system. In 1888 Eastman designed a simple-to-operate, highly portable roll-film camera, the Kodak, and provided factory service that included the unloading and reloading of the camera with film and the developing and printing of the pictures. With a successful advertising campaign Eastman revolutionized the industry. During the next decade numerous improvements were introduced, including a Celluloid base for film and daylight-loading film cartridges. The Eastman Kodak Company's tight patent control on the film system and its policy of continuous innovation helped it establish and maintain an almost exclusive position in the market.

As Eastman Kodak grew in size, it acquired, from 1898 to 1908, a number of photographic-paper, plate-camera, and dry-plate companies in the United States and in western Europe. Eastman Kodak held a substantial market share in photographic materials and apparatus both at home and abroad by 1910. In 1912 Eastman established the Eastman Kodak Research Laboratory and appointed as its director the British photochemist C. E. Kenneth Mees.

Early in the 20th century, an American cinematographic industry began to emerge, with innovators in motion picture projection equipment assuming the initial leadership. Large new corporations that integrated production, distribution, and exhibition functions emerged by 1920 as the new leaders of the industry. These included Paramount, Fox, and Loew. The introduction of sound films in the late 1920's altered this structure somewhat as the innovators, Warner and RKO, joined the small group of leaders.

Meanwhile, the growing demand for raw movie film stimulated film production at Eastman Kodak. After 1909 the production of film exceeded the production for still photography. Although the company carefully avoided entry into the professional field, it did introduce home movie equipment with nonflammable film in the early 1920's. From the late 1920's onward the company developed and introduced a series of color processes for motion pictures.

German cameramakers, influenced by cinematography, introduced in the early 1920's small 35-mm cameras. Also, in the late 1920's Ansco, which had faltered since its founding, sold its assets to the I. G. Farben-Industrie and became the American outlet for the research-oriented German photographic industry. With the advent of World War II the U.S. government assumed ownership and operation of the firm, and the government relinquished ownership only in 1965, when the firm became a public corporation, General Aniline and Film (GAF).

In the post–World War II period five developments were of particular importance to the American industry. First, Eastman Kodak successfully introduced and promoted color-print photography. Second, Japan, manufacturer of high-quality miniature cameras, developed a dominant influence in that specialized sector of the American and international market. Third, in 1948 the Polaroid Corporation introduced to the market a new system of photography that produced finished prints direct from the camera. Fourth, Eastman Kodak, in response to the Polaroid challenge, introduced a series of Instamatic camera systems that further simplified negative-positive picture-taking. Fifth, in 1982 Kodak started to market cameras with a 15-exposure film disk cartridge.

PHRENOLOGY. A theory of physiological psychology that posits that the brain is the organ of mind, the brain is a congeries of discrete organs that control different psychological functions, the power of an organ depends on its size, the shape of the skull corresponds to the organs beneath it, and therefore it is possible to discern an individual's character by examining the size and shape of his skull. The study was founded by German physicians Franz J. Gall and Johann K. Spurzheim in the 1790's. The first American phrenologist, Charles Caldwell of Transylvania University, Lexington, Ky., began to lecture on the subject in 1821. Because of the claim that phrenology is an infallible guide to human nature and its improvement, it attracted some of the leading intellectuals and reformers of the 1830's and 1840's. Phrenology reached its height as a respectable scientific movement in the 1840's, before experimental data on physiological psychology undermined its scientific credibility; but it flourished as a popular science and system of divination throughout the 19th century.

PHYSICS. The early American physicists emphasized the accumulation of experimental facts rather than mathematical theorizing, and they made no distinction between abstract and practical research. The archetypical American physicist was Benjamin Franklin, celebrated for his practical lightning rod as well as for his qualitatively speculative and experimental contributions to electrical science.

From the Jacksonian era through the Civil War, American physics became more specialized. The leading physicist of the period was Joseph Henry, who discovered electromagnetic induction. With Henry's support, Alexander Dallas Bache, Franklin's great-grandson and the director of the U.S. Coast Survey, enlarged the scope of the agency to include studies in the geodesy and geophysics of the entire continent. In the 1850's the survey was the largest single employer of physicists in the country.

In the quarter-century after the Civil War, many physicists embraced the new ethic of "pure" science. Between 1865 and 1890 the number of physicists in the United States doubled, to about 150. The profession included Albert A. Michelson, the first American to win the Nobel Prize in physics (1907), who measured the speed of light with unprecedented accuracy and invented the Michelson interferometer during his ether drift experiment in 1881. During the 1880's, Henry A. Rowland won an international reputation for his invention of the Rowland spectral grating and for his painstakingly accurate determinations of the value of the ohm and of the mechanical equivalent of heat. Generally, American physics remained predominantly experimental, with the notable exception of Josiah Willard Gibbs of Yale, an authority in thermodynamics and statistical mechanics.

In 1893 Edward L. Nichols of Cornell University inaugurated the *Physical Review;* six years later Arthur Gordon Webster of Clark University helped found the American Physical Society, which in 1913 assumed publication of the *Review.* After 1900 a rise in electrical engineering enrollments created an increased demand for college teachers of physics. Employment opportunities for physicists rose elsewhere also. General Electric and American Telephone and Telegraph opened industrial research laboratories; and the federal government established the National Bureau of Standards, whose charter permitted it to enter a wide area of physical research.

In the early 20th century of the quantum theory of radiation and the theory of relativity attracted younger scientists. At the University of Chicago, Robert A. Millikan demonstrated that all electrons are identically charged particles (1909) and then more accurately measured the electronic charge (1913). Richard Tolman of the University of Illinois and Gilbert N. Lewis of the Massachusetts Institute of Technology delivered the first American paper on the theory of relativity (1908). By World War I the profession was focusing increasingly on the physics of the quantized atom.

During the war, physicists worked for the military in the development of systems and devices for the detection of submarines and for the location of artillery. Their success bolstered the argument that physics could produce practical and, hence, economically valuable results. Industrial research laboratories hired more physicists in the 1920's, and the funding for physical research rose considerably.

By the end of the 1920's, the United States had more than 2,300 physicists, including the Europeans Paul Epstein, Fritz Zwicky, Samuel Goudsmit, and George Uhlenbeck, who had joined American university faculties. By the early 1930's the American physics profession compared favorably in experimental achievement with its counterparts in Europe. The interest of physicists shifted from the atom to the nucleus and to what were later called elementary particles. In 1932, while conducting research for which they would later win Nobel Prizes, Carl Anderson of the California Institute of Technology identified the positron in cosmic rays, and at the University of California at Berkeley, Ernest O. Lawrence successfully accelerated protons to one million volts of energy with his new cyclotron. Despite the depression, U.S. physicists managed to construct cyclotrons, arguing that the exploration of the nucleus might yield the secret of atomic energy or that the radioactive products of cyclotron bombardment might be medically useful, especially in the treatment of cancer. The profession was further enriched by such refugees from Nazi Europe as Albert Einstein, Hans Bethe, Felix Bloch, Enrico Fermi, Emilio Segrè, and Edward Teller. By the end of the 1930's, the American physics profession led the world in both theoretical and experimental research.

During World War II, physicists, mobilized primarily under the Office of Scientific Research and Development, contributed decisively to the development of microwave radar, the proximity fuze, and solid-fuel rockets. They also worked on the atomic bomb in various laboratories of the

Manhattan Project, notably Los Alamos, N.Mex., which was directed by J. Robert Oppenheimer. After World War II, American physicists became prominent figures in the government's strategic advisory councils. Recognized as indispensable to the national defense and welfare, physics and physicists received massive governmental support in the postwar decades, notably from the National Science Foundation, the Atomic Energy Commission, and the Office of Naval Research. Thus, the profession expanded rapidly, totaling over 30,000 in the mid-1970's. About half of all American physicists were employed in industry, most of the rest in universities and federal laboratories.

Working with highly energetic particle accelerators, American physicists were among the world's leaders in uncovering experimental data about elementary particles. Their achievements included the work of Murray Gell-Mann in particle theory, Julian Schwinger and Richard P. Feynman in quantum electrodynamics, and Tsung Dao Lee and Chen Ning Yang in the nonconservation of parity. American physicists contributed significantly to such other important fields as plasma and low-temperature physics as well as astrophysics and relativity. In applied physics, William Shockley and John Bardeen invented the transistor and Charles H. Townes played a major role in the development of the laser.

PHYSIOLOGY. Physiology and its myriad subbranches have found great favor in health, hygiene, and temperance activities, bringing to large audiences popularized and frequently inaccurate versions of the "correct" functioning of animal and human bodily processes. Physiology as a branch of medicine had a poor following from the colonial era to after the Civil War. The research activities that were conducted were almost exclusively individual enterprises. John Young's digestion experiments at the University of Pennsylvania Medical College in 1803; William Beaumont's study of the digestive process, published in 1833; Silas Weir Mitchell's study of snake venoms (1860); and William J. G. Morton's introduction of ether anesthesia in 1846 are representative of the art prior to 1870. As an academic subject physiology was poorly taught. The courses were almost uniformly didactic in nature with little or no demonstration of physiological principles. The classes of Oliver Wendell Holmes at Harvard (1847–71) and John Call Dalton of the College of Physicians and Surgeons in New York (1855–83) were outstanding exceptions.

The new era in American physiology was preceded by an increase in both the use of textbooks written in America and the number of individual investigators in physiology. Robley Dunglison's *Human Physiology* (1832) went through many editions, and his *New Dictionary of Medical Science and Literature* (1833) became the standard of American medicine. Dalton and Austin Flint, Jr., both contributed textbooks and carried out numerous experiments: Dalton, on bile and liver functions; Flint, on capillary circulation and the physiology of exercise.

The transition of physiology from a superficially treated subject to an experimental science and a field of study of major importance occurred in the 1870's, when scientists trained in the methodologies and philosophies of German and British institutions were engaged by a few U.S. universities and colleges. H. Newell Martin was brought to Johns Hopkins University in 1876 to organize and teach a laboratory-oriented department of biology. Under Martin's direction physiology flourished as a branch of biology and attracted to the field such future eminences as William Henry Howell and Henry Sewall. Howell, who succeeded Martin at Johns Hopkins, conducted extensive research on the circulatory system and was the author of *Textbook of Physiology* (1905).

At Harvard, Henry Pickering Bowditch established the first physiological laboratory in the United States for student use in 1871 and ultimately incorporated physiology into the medical program. Two of his students, Harvey Cushing and Walter B. Cannon, became preeminent in their fields of study, the former in neurophysiology and neurosurgery, the latter in macroscopic physiology and the role of epinephrine (adrenaline) in stress situations. Disciples of Harvard and Johns Hopkins carried the idea of experimental physiology to other schools. Medical schools responded to the changes by converting textbook explications into student-laboratory activities, and after the publication of the 1910 Flexner Report on Medical Education, medical colleges reorganized their curricula. By the mid-1920's virtually all candidates for the M.D. degree were being subjected to an intensive program in physiology.

Contemporary physiology is a powerful discipline in its own right, no longer under the aegis of the medical profession. Nearly 50 percent of the membership of the American Physiological Society (APS), founded 1887, for example, held the Ph.D. degree in 1973; and although approximately half the APS members were employed in medical schools, the remainder taught or conducted research in graduate and undergraduate college programs.

PIAVE RIVER, OPERATIONS ON (October–November 1918). During World War I, in October 1918, the American 332d Infantry Regiment, detached from the 83d Division, made frequent marches, principally for their effect upon Italian morale, behind the Piave River battlefront in Italy. On Oct. 27–28 the regiment assisted Italian forces in establishing bridgeheads on the Piave River, and on Oct. 30, as part of the Italian 31st Division, it joined in the operation that drove the Austrian forces from the Piave to the Tagliamento River.

PICKAWILLANEE. An Indian village near the site of present-day Piqua, Ohio, was founded in 1747 by the Miami, who left their village at the site of Fort Wayne, Ind., desiring British rather than French trade. By 1750 English traders had built storehouses at Pickawillanee. In 1751 Pierre-Jacques de Taffanel, Marquis de La Jonquière, French governor of Canada, sent a party of Indians under French commanders to Pickawillanee to eject the English traders. Although the Ottawa forbade the passage of the expedition through their territory, a small force reached Pickawillanee, killed some of the Miami, and increased the Miami's hostility toward the French. Jonquière's successor, Charles Le Moyne, Baron de Longueuil, feared a general revolt of the Indians, and on June 21, 1752, an expedition of Indians commanded by Charles de Langlade attacked Pickawillanee, destroyed the traders' storehouses, captured several of the English traders (two were sent to France), and killed fourteen Miami. After the Treaty of Logstown (1752), the English influence among the Miami waned, and Pickawillanee was deserted.

PICKENS, FORT. Upon the secession of Florida (Jan. 10, 1861) and the Confederate seizure of forts on the mainland at Pensacola, Lt. Adam J. Slemmer, with forty loyal Union troopers, escaped across Pensacola Bay to Santa Rosa Island and took possession of unoccupied Fort Pickens. Stemmer's handful of men found themselves, in April 1861, short of food and ammunition. A relief expedition, secretly organized by Secretary of State William Henry Seward (*see Powhatan* Incident) and energetically led by Capt. Montgomery C. Meigs and Lt. David D. Porter, reinforced Fort Pickens and saved it from capture. The fort remained an important federal stronghold throughout the war.

PICKETING. The nonviolent competitive tactics of workers in labor disputes with employers have traditionally been limited to the strike, the secondary boycott, and the picket line. To get the person picketed to accede to the aims of the picketers, the tactics of picketing have been to impede deliveries and services; to cause employees to refuse to cross the line to work; to muster consumer sympathy to withhold patronage; and to be a "rallyround" symbol for the picketers and other workers. Picketing has promoted interests other than those of workers, notably in protests against racial discrimination.

PICKETT'S CHARGE (July 3, 1863). More properly the Pickett-Pettigrew charge, it was the culminating event of the Battle of Gettysburg. Having failed on July 1 and 2 to rout the Union forces, Confederate Gen. Robert E. Lee decided to assault their center. For this purpose he designated George Edward Pickett's division; Henry Heth's division, temporarily commanded by J. J. Pettigrew; and two brigades of William Pender's division. After a preliminary bombardment by 125 guns, these troops—forty seven regiments, 15,000 men—were ordered to advance an average of 1,300 yards eastward from Seminary Ridge to a "little clump of trees" on the front of the Second Corps along Cemetery Ridge. The assault was begun at about 2 P.M. It carried the column of attack to the Union position but failed for lack of support when the Union forces closed in from three sides. The Confederates, who were compelled to retreat under heavy fire, lost about 6,000 men.

PIECES OF EIGHT. Spanish silver coins of eight reals (eight bits), first authorized by a law of 1497. Also known as pesos and Spanish dollars, they were minted in enormous quantities and soon became recognized and accepted throughout the commercial world as a reliable medium of exchange. Consequently, Congress, in 1786, adopted the Spanish milled dollar as the basis of the U.S. coinage system.

PIECEWORK. Piecework was common in American industry almost from the first, the amount of work assigned being called a stint or a "stent." It was the only form of incentive wage plan until the rise of industrial management brought the premium differential and task-and-bonus plans into widespread use. The principle upon which all these incentive plans is based is payment for results. A variation of piecework that was in use in American industry during the last half of the 19th century was known as contract work.

PIEDMONT. Geographically, the area of the eastern United States lying at the foot of the easternmost ranges of the Appalachian mountain system; historically, all the territory between these ranges and the fall line on the rivers. "Up-country" and "backcountry" are other terms used to designate the Piedmont region. The Piedmont was settled primarily by small farmers. Socially and economically democratic, Piedmonters were generally at odds with the Tidewater population.

PIEGAN. *See* **Blackfoot.**

PIEGAN WAR (1869–70). By a treaty in 1855 Gen. Isaac I. Stevens, governor of Washington Territory, fixed the hunting grounds of the Blackfoot confederacy—the northern Blackfoot, Blood, and Piegan—north of the Missouri River in Montana. Invasion of this territory by miners and ranchers in 1869 caused the Piegan to make retaliatory raids. Col. E. M. Baker marched against the Piegan on Jan. 6, 1870, striking Chief Red Horn's camp on the Marias River on Jan. 23. Suffering from smallpox, the Indians were unprepared for the attack. Baker's detachment killed 173, including Red Horn and many women and children, with a loss of only one soldier. The attack drew censure from Congress and the press.

PIERRE (S. Dak.). The capital city of South Dakota, with a population of 11,973 in 1980. It has been the capital of the state since 1889. The city was formally incorporated only in 1883, but the site had been important for people moving to the area of the Dakotas for many years before that. In 1913 a lead plate was found in Pierre, dating from 1743, which showed that Sieur de la Vérendrye had visited the area and claimed it for France. The location of Pierre, near the point where the Bad River joins the Missouri, made it an attractive spot for fur-traders who wished to reach beaver traps upstream on the smaller Bad River. Its name is a shortened form of Fort Pierre Chouteau (*see* Pierre, Fort).

PIERRE, FORT. Developed from a small trading post established by Joseph LaFramboise, at the mouth of the Bad River on the west bank of the Missouri in October 1817. The Columbia Fur Company took the business over in 1822 and named the post Fort Tecumseh. In 1828 John Jacob Astor's interests bought the plant, and in 1832 built a new post, named Fort Pierre Chouteau. The "Chouteau" appellation did not become popular and was dropped. In 1855 the federal government bought the plant but dismantled it a year later. The village of Fort Pierre now occupies the area. (*See* Pierre.)

PIERRE'S HOLE, BATTLE OF (July 18, 1832). A trappers' rendezvous, Pierre's Hole was located in the Teton Mountains in eastern Idaho. The battle took place between the Gros Ventres and American fur traders. Apparently the battle started when a trapper killed the Gros Ventres chief in revenge for the murder of his father by the Blackfoot, allies of the Gros Ventres. A false rumor spread through the trappers' ranks that more Blackfoot were attacking their main camp, and so the siege was abandoned.

PIETISM. The name given to the movement in German Protestantism that arose at the end of the 17th century and continued into the 18th century to combat the growing formalism in the Lutheran church. The father of the movement was Philip Jacob Spener, a Lutheran minister in Frankfurt am Main, Germany, who began the formation of *collegia pietatis,* or societies of piety, for the promotion of Bible study and prayer. He stressed Christianity as a way of life rather than as a creed; lay people were urged to take a larger part in the work of the church. In the American colonies the influence of pietism was exerted chiefly through the German Lutherans and the Moravians. Henry M. Mühlenberg was sent to America in 1742 and his leadership among the colonial Lutherans in the formative period served to emphasize that phase of Lutheranism. Count Nikolaus Ludwig von Zinzendorf came in 1741 and set up several Moravian congregations.

"PIG WAR." *See* **San Juan, Seizure of.**

PIKES PEAK. A mountain, altitude 14,110 feet, in the Front Range of the Rocky Mountains in El Paso County, Colorado, was discovered in November 1806 by Lt. Zebulon M. Pike. It was first ascended by Edwin James, J. Verplank, and Z. Wilson of Maj. Stephen H. Long's expedition on July 14, 1820; Long named the peak after James, but popular usage by trappers and others of the name "Pikes Peak" led to an official name change.

PIKES PEAK GOLD RUSH (1858–59). Gold was discovered at Ralston Creek, near present-day Denver, in 1850. Reports of this find led in 1858 to the organization of parties to prospect the region. Placer gold was discovered in Cherry Creek and other tributaries of the South Platte in July 1858. Exaggerated stories of the reputed goldfields circulated in the nation's press during the winter of 1858–59. Inasmuch as Pikes Peak was the best-known landmark, although seventy-five miles from the site of the discoveries, the region was called the Pikes Peak Gold Country, or Cherry Creek Diggings. The meager amount of dust found in 1858 hardly warranted so much excitement. Fortunately, rich gold veins were found in the mountains, the first by John H. Gregory, near present-day Central City, May 6, 1859. It is estimated that 100,000 persons set out for the gold region, that half of them reached the mountains, and that only half of these remained, to found Colorado.

PIKE'S SOUTHWESTERN EXPEDITION (1806–07). Conducted by Lt. Zebulon M. Pike and a small band of U.S. soldiers, it was organized to explore the Arkansas and Red rivers, to gather information about the abutting Spanish territory, and to conciliate the Indian tribes in the newly acquired Louisiana Purchase. Leaving Fort Bellefontaine (near St. Louis) on July 15, 1806, the party traveled to the Pawnee towns in Kansas and then by way of the Arkansas River into Colorado. From here it crossed, in midwinter, the Sangre de Cristo Range to the Conejos, a tributary of the Rio Grande in New Mexico, and built a fort nearby. Learning of Pike's expedition in their territory, Spanish officials sent a detachment of soldiers to bring the men to Santa Fe. From there the Spanish authorities conducted Pike to Chihuahua and then by a circuitous route to the American border at Natchitoches, La., on July 1, 1807. Pike's narrative, *An Account of Expeditions to the Sources of the Mississippi and Through the Western Parts of Louisiana,* published in 1810, afforded his countrymen their first description of the great Southwest.

PIKE'S UPPER MISSISSIPPI EXPEDITION (1805–06). On Aug. 9, 1805, Lt. Zebulon M. Pike left St. Louis with twenty soldiers on a 70-foot keelboat to explore the Mississippi River to its source, conciliate the Indians in the area, assert the authority of the United States over British traders, and procure sites for military posts. Near Little Falls, Minn., Pike built a log fort and traveled for weeks in midwinter by sled and toboggan, ascending to what he thought were the upper reaches of the Mississippi and falsely named Leech Lake as the source of the river. He also met with British traders, urging them to obey the laws of the United States, held councils with the Indians, and made geographical observations. He returned to St. Louis on Apr. 30, 1806.

PILGRIMS. Thirty-five members of an English Separatist church living in Leiden, the Netherlands, who, with sixty-six English sectarians and servants, sailed from Plymouth, England, on Sept. 16, 1620, on the *Mayflower* and founded Plymouth Colony in New England in December.

PILLORY. A device for publicly punishing petty offenders, consisting of a frame with holes in which the head and hands of the standing prisoner were locked.

PILLOW, FORT, "MASSACRE" (Apr. 12, 1864). Fifteen hundred Confederate cavalry under Gen. Nathan B. Forrest attacked Fort Pillow, Tenn., on Apr. 12, 1864. When the Union force refused to submit, the Confederates drove the defenders out of the fort and, despite support of the Union gunboat *New Era,* into the Mississippi River. Forrest took prisoner 168 white and 58 black troops. Surviving Union witnesses testified before federal authorities that on Forrest's orders, Confederates had refused quarter to surrendering soldiers, particularly blacks, and had massacred several hundred.

PILOT KNOB, BATTLE OF (Sept. 27, 1864). When Confederate Gen. Sterling Price and his men—between 12,000 and 15,000 strong—entered Missouri, the only federal force between them and St. Louis was Brig. Gen. Thomas Ewing's command, about 1,000 men, holding Fort Davidson at Pilot Knob. Deciding to capture this stronghold, Price assaulted with two of his three divisions and suffered a bloody repulse, losing possibly 1,500 men. Finding his position untenable, that night Ewing retreated toward Leasburg. Price wasted three days in futile pursuit, permitting St. Louis to be so strongly reinforced that he dared not attack it.

PIMA. The Pima, along with their neighbors and linguistic relatives, the Papago, although characteristically southwestern in their development of an intensive agriculture, used farming methods that suggest backgrounds in the prehistoric Hohokam culture of southern Arizona. The Pima were located in the Salt and Gila river valleys in southern Arizona. The Papago, south of the Pima, inhabited the higher levels away from the rivers. The two tribes spoke closely related languages belonging to the Piman branch of Uto-Aztecan. Both tribes were contacted by the Jesuit missionary Eusebio Francisco Kino in 1681. At that time, it is estimated, there were about 6,000 Papago and 4,000 Pima. The sociocultural differences between the Pima and the Papago were minimal except in general ecological adaptations. The Pima, retaining the riverine focus, dug irrigation canals with wooden tools and became intensive cultivators. The Papago, driven away by the Apache from the rivers to the higher lands, came to depend less on agriculture and more on gathered plants, particularly the mesquite bean. Both groups built round, flat-topped single-family houses in small village communities. Both tribes had a strong sense of identity, the Pima especially having evolved a system of village chiefs and councils. A tribal chief was elected by the villages. Papago villages tended to remain autonomous. Because social changes resulted early from contacts with Europeans, some aspects of Pima-Papago political, social, and religious organization are not wholly clear. Both tribes had harvest festivals in four-year cycles, involving masked figures, a custom shared with other southwestern peoples. The Pima had a summer rain festival, involving the preparation of a wine made from the juice of the giant saguaro cactus. A ceremonial drunkenness was permitted at this time, a custom suggestive of the licensed drinking of pulque in Aztec Mexico: this is the sole appearance of an aboriginal alcoholic drink north of Mexico.

PIMA REVOLT (1751). An uprising by the Upper Pima in northern Sonora in Mexico and southern Arizona. The revolt centered around Luis Oacpicagigua, who aspired to be chief of all the Pima. He planned a revolt to oust the Spaniards from the area, but he had little support among the Pima generally. The revolt began in Saric, in northern Sonora, where Oacpicagigua killed eighteen Spaniards whom he had invited to his house and then attacked the mission of Tubutama. Missionaries were slain at Caborca and Sonoita, and after 100 Spaniards in all had been killed, Oacpicagigua surrendered and was jailed.

PIMITOUI, FORT. Erected in the winter of 1691–92 on the right bank of the Illinois River near the site of Peoria, Ill., by Henry de Tonti and François Dauphin de La Forest. Because it was intended to replace Fort St. Louis it was originally called by that name, but it soon came to be known by the Indian word for the widening of the river near which it was located, now called Peoria Lake. Fort Pimitoui was the nucleus of the first permanent French settlement in the Illinois Country.

PINCKNEY PLAN. A detailed plan of government, containing more than thirty provisions later incorporated in the Constitution, introduced by Charles Pinckney at an early session of the Convention of 1787. The plan has furnished an interesting subject for historical criticism, since the original was not preserved, and the alleged "Pinckney plan," printed many years later as part of the convention record, was obviously of later origin. Its general scope and contents, however, have been deduced from the convention debates.

PINCKNEY'S TREATY (1795). Also called Treaty of San Lorenzo, it was the climax of twelve years of dispute with Spain over the western and southern boundaries of the United States and the navigation of the Mississippi River. The United States contended that its treaty of peace with Great Britain after the Revolution had made the Mississippi River and 31° north latitude its recognized boundaries, and that riparian territorial sovereignty rights upstream gave a "natural right" to free navigation in and out from the ocean, even though the lower reaches of the river were in Spanish possession. The United States and Spain attempted, 1785–86, to reconcile their differences, but the effort failed (*see* Jay-Gardoqui Negotiations). Fearing an Anglo-American alliance to guarantee the free navigation of the Mississippi, Spain met the American demands in a treaty signed by U.S. Minister to Great Britain Thomas Pinckney at San Lorenzo, Oct. 27, 1795. The treaty accepted the boundary claims of the United States (*see* Southern Boundary, Survey of the) at the thirty-first parallel, established commercial relations with Spain, stipulated that Spain would not incite the Indians on its frontier to attack Americans, and provided for the free navigation of the Mississippi by American citizens and Spanish subjects, with a three-year right of deposit at New Orleans, later at some other convenient place in Spanish territory. The treaty also provided for the adjudication by a mixed claims commission of spoliation claims arising over arbitrary captures by Spain of American neutral vessels.

PINE BARREN SPECULATIONS. Perpetrated principally in Montgomery, Washington, and Franklin counties in Georgia, during 1793 and 1794; they rivaled the state's Yazoo sales fraud for notoriety. County officials issued warrants to a small group of speculators calling for more than 17 million acres of land, ten times the area actually in those counties.

PINE BLUFF, BATTLES AT. The first battle at Pine Bluff, Ark., took place on Oct. 25, 1863, during the Union conquest of Arkansas. Confederate Gen. Sterling Price, battling two Union regiments, suffered heavy losses. The second battle at Pine Bluff took place on Feb. 22, 1865; Union cavalry routed a portion of Gen. Edmund Kirby Smith's command.

PINE RIDGE INDIAN WAR. *See* **Messiah War.**

PINE TREE FLAG. A colonial flag of Massachusetts used as early as 1700. The pine tree of Massachusetts was the emblem of New England in general and seems to have been one of the earliest symbols of the union of the thirteen colonies. An evergreen was incorporated into the flags of the American forces from 1775 to 1777 in various ways, often with the motto "An Appeal to Heaven," and the pine tree and this motto were sometimes combined with the rattlesnake flag of the southern colonies with its motto, "Don't Tread on Me."

PINE TREE SHILLING. To secure relief to a certain extent from a great need of currency, Massachusetts established a mint in June 1652. In the following year a crude silver coin was issued. On the obverse was MASATHVSETS IN., between two beaded circles; within the inner circle was a pine tree. On the reverse was NEWENGLAND, AN. DOM., between two beaded circles, and 1652, XII, within the inner one. The Roman numerals indicated the number of pence in a shilling. The mint was closed in 1684.

PINKSTER. The Dutch Pentecost, celebrated in colonial New York and to some extent in Pennsylvania and Maryland, with picnicking, picking "pinkster" flowers (wild azaleas), and neighborly visiting. Forbidden in Albany in 1811, the Pinkster celebration soon disappeared.

PIONEERS. The terms "frontiersmen," "early settlers," and "pioneers" are applied indiscriminately in American history to those who, in any given area, began the transformation of the wilderness and the prairie into a land of homes, farms, and towns. Explorers, fur traders, soldiers, and goldseekers are not classed as pioneers unless they later settled down more or less permanently.

PIONEER STAGE LINE. Began operating in 1851 from Sacramento to Placerville, Calif. In 1857 J. B. Crandall bought an interest in the line, drove an experimental coach over a rough trail through the Sierra Nevada to the Carson Valley, and began operating coaches regularly thereon. In 1860 control passed to Louis McLane (Wells, Fargo and Company's western manager), and from 1861 the Pioneer Stage Line was a link in their Overland Mail route, becoming one of the most famous stage lines of North America. A well-graded, 100-mile macadamized road was built from Carson City, Nev., to Placerville. In 1865 formal announcement was made of the line's passing under Wells Fargo control.

PIOUS FUND CONTROVERSY. The Pious Fund of the Californias was established in the 17th century to maintain and support the Jesuit missions in Upper and Lower California. The Mexican government took over the administration of the fund in the 19th century. When the United States acquired Upper California in 1848, Mexico ceased payment of annuities. In 1875 a complaint was filed by the California bishops with the Permanent Court of Arbitration at The Hague. The appointed arbitrator, Sir Edward Thornton, decided that Mexico would have to pay $904,070.79. Two years later another claim was filed and the missions were awarded $1,420,682.67 in annuities.

PIPE, INDIAN. Pipes of stone, wood, clay, and bone were used among various tribes of the differing culture areas of the present United States. Tubular pipes had a scattered distribution. The more conventional elbow pipe, with stem and bowl, appeared mostly in the Plains and Woodlands; this was the form introduced into Europe in the 16th century. Pipe-smoking rituals were stressed by the Plains and Woodlands peoples, but it must be noted that tobacco and the items associated with it were sacred almost everywhere. A Plains Indian bundle, the wrapped tribal or group fetish, frequently contained a carved pipe bowl of catlinite, along with the reed or wooden stem, the calumet; the latter, carved, incised, and decorated, was often the more important element. In the Woodlands, the eastern Plains, and some of the Gulf area, the calumet might be carried by ambassadors between federated tribes to symbolize states of war and peace, but it might also be employed in an appeal to spiritual beings. The passing of the pipe, solemnly ritualized as it was, became a social adjunct to its intertribal symbolic use.

PIPELINES, EARLY. In order to eliminate the risk, expense, and uncertainty of transporting oil by boat or wagon, Herman Jones proposed in November 1861, at a meeting at Tarr farm on Oil Creek, Pa., the laying of a 4-inch wooden pipe to Oil City. Although the idea met with favor, the state legislature refused to charter the company because of teamster opposition. In 1862 Barrows and Company of Tarr farm began operating the first successful pipeline, conveying oil from the Burning well to their refinery, about 1,000 feet away. Other early experiments with pipelines met with only partial success because of poor quality pipes, leaky lead joints, and faulty pumps. In the fall of 1865 Samuel Van Syckle began trenching and laying a 2-inch wrought-iron pipe from Pithole, Pa., to Miller farm on the Oil Creek Railroad, about five and a quarter miles distant. Just prior to completion of the project, disgruntled teamsters, who saw their occupation threatened, maliciously cut the line in several places. Nevertheless, on Oct. 9, Van Syckle finished his line and made the first test, in which eighty-one barrels of oil were forced through the pipe in one hour. Two weeks later another pipeline was completed from Pithole to Henry's Bend on the Allegheny River. The Van Syckle line proved so successful that a second pipe was laid to Miller farm and began delivering oil on Dec. 8, 1865. Four days later the Pennsylvania Tubing and Transportation Company completed a gravity line from Pithole to Oleopolis, Pa. Aroused over the prospect of the oil trade being diverted to other points, some of the Titusville businessmen organized the Titusville Pipe Company, laid a pipe to Pithole, about nine miles away, and began pumping oil in March 1866. During the same month, Henry Harley and Company laid two pipelines from Bennehoff Run to Shaffer farm on the Oil Creek Railroad, a distance of two miles. During the next few years short pipelines multiplied.

PIQUA, BATTLE OF (Aug. 8, 1780). In retaliation for a raid in early June 1780 by British Capt. Henry Bird and a force made up mainly of Indians, George Rogers Clark led nearly 1,000 frontiersmen up the Little Miami River against the Shawnee towns of Old Chillicothe (near Xenia) and Piqua (near Springfield), both in Ohio. Old Chillicothe was abandoned and burned, and the Indians fled to Piqua, some twelve miles distant. Clark divided his forces in an attempt to surround Piqua, but Col. Benjamin Logan, in command of one of the columns, became entangled in a grassy swamp and accomplished little. Many of the Shawnee fled at Clark's approach, leaving only a few Indians to sustain the American attack. The battle was hardly more than a long drawn-out skirmish, with only seventeen men lost on each side. Clark's men were able to burn the town, fields, and stores.

PIQUA, COUNCIL OF. *See* **Pickawillanee.**

PIRACY. In 1653 Massachusetts made piracy punishable by death; and its governors sometimes sent out armed ships to attack offshore pirates. On the other hand, colonial governors after 1650 granted "privateering" commissions to sea desperadoes and winked at their piracies—a popular procedure then. The Navigation Acts halted all foreign ships from trading in the American colonies and led to colonial smuggling and eventually to piracy. Colonial merchants and settlers bought pirates' stolen goods and thus obtained necessary commodities at a cheap price. New York, Newport, R.I., and Philadelphia were rivals in this trade, with Boston, Virginia, and the Carolinas also buying stolen goods. Richard Coote, Earl of Bellomont, was appointed governor of New York and New England in 1697 with orders to suppress piracy.

The highest number of piracies was committed during 1705–25, and 1721–24 saw a reign of terror on the New England coast. English men-of-war ended this peril, but after the American Revolution piratical attacks on U.S. ships by French "privateers" brought on an undeclared war between France and the United States and led to the creation of the U.S. Navy. Piratical operations of English men-of-war on U.S. coasts and the high seas—including the impressment of American seamen—led to the War of 1812. The period 1805–25 witnessed a resurgence of piracy, which led to the increase of the U.S. Navy suppressing piracy and convoying ships. Over 3,000 instances of piracy were recorded between 1814 and 1824—half of them on U.S. shipping.

Beginning in 1805 the navy was engaged in warring on pirates on the Louisiana and Gulf coasts, which had long been haunted by pirates. The Barataria pirates were driven out in 1814, as well as the Aury-Laffite pirates from Galveston, Texas, in 1817. In 1816–24 the United States faced a perplexing problem in handling the piratical "privateers" of the new Latin-American republics. Congress finally was so angered by these freebooters' depredations that in 1819 an act was passed prescribing the death penalty for piracy. By 1827 piracy had ended on all U.S. coasts.

PISTOLE. A gold coin current in Spain, Italy, and America in the 18th century. Its value varied, but it was commonly worth fifteen English shillings. Its French equivalent was the louis d'or. During the early 18th century Virginians spoke of values in terms of pistoles almost as readily as pounds.

"PIT." The popular name given to the trading floor of any commodity exchange, but most often applied to that of the Board of Trade of the City of Chicago, the largest commodity exchange in the United States. On Apr. 3, 1848, the Chicago Board of Trade was organized "to maintain a Commercial Exchange; to promote uniformity in the customs and usages of merchants; to inculcate principles of justice and equity in trade; to facilitate the speedy adjustment of business disputes; to acquire and disseminate valuable commercial and economic information; and, generally to secure to its members the benefits of cooperation in the furtherance of their legitimate pursuits."

PITHOLE. In 1864 the United States Petroleum Company leased a portion of the Thomas Holmden farm on Pithole Creek, about six miles east of Oil Creek and equidistant from Titusville and Oil City, Pa. The company drilled a well that in January 1865 began flowing at the rate of about 250 barrels of oil a day. The United States well, as it was known, precipitated a stampede to the Holmden farm. Leases sold for fabulous sums; other wells were drilled; and a city called Pithole sprang into existence. In September 1865, the population reached 15,000, and the daily production exceeded 6,000 barrels. Within six months, after the failure of its wells, Pithole became a deserted city.

PITT, FORT. A temporary structure, commonly known as Fort Pitt, was begun in late 1758, after the British forces of Gen. John Forbes routed the French at the confluence of the Monongahela and Allegheny rivers on the present site of Pittsburgh. Named in honor of the British statesman William Pitt the Elder, the fort was completed in January 1759 and stood on the banks of the Monongahela, 200 yards above the site of Fort Duquesne. On Sept. 3, 1759, Gen. John Stanwix personally directed the beginning of the work on a permanent fortification, not completed until the summer of 1761. The British maintained a garrison at Fort Pitt to aid in preserving order among the settlers and Indians until late 1772, when the troops were withdrawn. Only caretakers occupied the fort until January 1774, when John Connolly of Virginia took possession and renamed it Fort Dunmore (*see* Dunmore's War). Capt. John Neville, with a company sent out by the Virginia Provincial Convention, held control from September 1775 to June 1777, relinquishing his command to Gen. Edward Hand of the Continental forces. Except for one short interval, the fort was a base of operations for western campaigns during the Revolution (*see* Broadhead's Allegheny Campaign). Gen. William Irvine repaired the fort in 1782 but thereafter it was permitted to deteriorate.

PITTMAN ACT (Apr. 23, 1918). Provided for the breaking up of not more than 350 million silver dollars and the export of said silver to India and the Orient to benefit the balance of payments of the United States and its allies in World War I. Provision was also made for the issuance of Federal Reserve bank notes to take the place of the silver dollars and certificates withdrawn from circulation and for their subsequent retirement and replacement with silver dollars and certificates through the purchase of silver from domestic producers, at not less than $1 per ounce.

PITTSBURGH (Pa.). A city in southwestern Pennsylvania, situated where the Allegheny and Monongahela rivers form the Ohio. Pittsburgh early earned the sobriquet "Gateway to the West." In 1758, after British Gen. John Forbes and his force came upon the abandoned Fort Duquesne, Forbes renamed the site Pittsbourgh in honor of William Pitt the Elder. From 1759 to 1761 a permanent fort, also named after Pitt, was constructed. Laid out in 1764 by John Campbell, the small trading post became successively a county seat in 1788, borough in 1794, and city in 1816. With the opening of the Mississippi, Pittsburgh began its development as a commercial city. Its manufactures found their way to New Orleans and ultimately to Baltimore and Philadelphia. The impetus given to nascent industry by the demands of westward migration was renewed by the War of 1812. The demand for manufactured products, combined with the relative abundance of certain necessary raw materials, soon made the iron and glass industries of Pittsburgh of national importance. During the Civil War, Pittsburgh iron foundries and mills played an important role in supplying Union armies with cannon and armor plate. The transition from iron to steel was neither long nor difficult, and the city, became the largest steel-producing area in the United States. During World War II Pittsburgh mills produced a third of the steel used in the war effort. After World War II the city began an extensive renovation of the Golden Triangle (the city's business district). Smoke control legislation, first enacted in 1947, extensively reduced the air pollution that had once blighted the city. In 1980 the city's population was 423,938.

PITTSBURGH, INDIAN TREATY AT (1775). The result of a conference of the Indian tribes in that region with commissioners from the Virginia Assembly and Richard Butler, Indian agent for the Indian Department of the Continental Congress. The Delaware, Shawnee, Mingo, Seneca, Wyandot, and Ottawa tribes were restless and uneasy because of Dunmore's War of the previous year. Furthermore, the Shawnee Indians had taken captives and stolen black slaves from Virginians, which the commissioners sought to recover. The commissioners were also anxious to placate the Indians and procure their neutrality in the approaching struggle between Great Britain and the colonies. Chief White Eyes of the Delaware was the spokesman for the Indians; George Morgan, the Indian trader, gave counsel to all; and Butler acted for the Indian Department. The Indians, after receiving promises that the Ohio River boundary would be respected, were satisfied and agreed not to fight in the forthcoming struggle. The Shawnee agreed to return the captives and the stolen slaves, and the Seneca and Delaware engaged to assist them in that duty. The commissioners of Virginia sent letters to white settlers in the region requesting them not to cross the Ohio and to avoid irritating the Indians.

PITTSBURGH GAZETTE (variously the *Pittsburgh Gazette and Manufacturing and Mercantile Advertiser,* the *Pittsburgh Daily Gazette and Advertiser,* the *Pittsburgh Commercial Gazette,* the *Gazette Times,* and the *Pittsburgh Post-Gazette*). Generally considered to have been the first newspaper established west of the Allegheny Mountains. The founders, John Scull and Joseph Hall, printed the first number of the paper on July 29, 1786.

PITTSBURGH RESOLUTIONS (1775). On hearing of the battles at Lexington and Concord in April 1775, a meeting of the Virginia patriots in the vicinity of Pittsburgh was called for May 16. Both a committee of safety for the district of West Augusta, chaired by George Croghan, and a standing committee vested with emergency powers were established. In the resolutions passed at the meeting the patriots expressed their approval of the conduct of the minutemen of Massachusetts as well as their friendship for the Indians.

PITTSBURG LANDING. *See* **Shiloh, Battle of.**

PLACER MINING. A process in which gold or other mineral deposits are found loosely mixed with the sand at the bottom of a stream bed or similar alluvial deposit. It differs from lode mining where the minerals are always found in place. It was placer gold that started the gold rushes to California in 1849, Pikes Peak in 1858, and the Klondike in Canada in 1896. The pure gold is washed from the sand or debris by means of a gold pan. Because of its weight, gold, if present, will gravitate to the bottom of the pan. Here the "colors" (tiny specks) or nuggets of gold are picked out with a tweezer or amalgamated with mercury. Improvements in placer mining, such as the rocker, sluicebox, long tom, hydraulic nozzle, boom dam, or dredge, are all designed to wash more gravel with a given amount of time and labor. The richest placer deposits have been in California and Alaska.

PLAIN, FORT. Built in colonial times near the Mohawk River to protect the farmers near Canajoharie, N.Y., from the Iroquois. It sheltered the settlers from the Onondaga in 1777, and on numerous occasions during the American Revolution provided a rallying point for troop movements up the Schoharie Valley, as well as a refuge for the wounded. The importance of the fort ceased after 1781.

PLAINS, GREAT. *See* **Great Plains.**

PLAINS OF ABRAHAM. *See* **Abraham, Plains of.**

PLANK ROADS. Introduced into the United States from Canada about 1837, they were first constructed in the state of New York and were widely adopted in South Carolina, Illinois, Ohio, and Michigan. Roadways were first well drained, with ditches on either side, then planks, 3 or 4 inches thick and 8 feet long, were laid at right angles to stringers, which were placed lengthwise on the road. For a time plank roads successfully competed with railroads, but were eventually replaced by paved roads.

PLANNED ECONOMY. The theory of a planned economy is that government regulates and controls important elements of the economy in order to achieve certain goals. The theory implies fact-finding to learn what needs must be met; limitation of production to meet those needs; and planning for future needs and for the development of new activities. The theory was embodied to some extent in the New Deal.

PLAN OF 1776. A model set of articles for treaties to be negotiated with foreign powers by the newly independent United States. It was drawn up by a committee composed of John Adams, Benjamin Franklin, John Dickinson, and Robert Morris and was adopted Sept. 17, 1776. The plan remains significant because of its definition of neutral rights.

PLAN OF UNION. An agreement made in 1801 between the Congregational Association of Connecticut and the general assembly of the Presbyterian church to combine their work on the frontier wherever the two bodies came together. The plan provided for the settlement of either a Presbyterian or Congregational minister over mixed congregations and for the settlement of a Presbyterian minister over a Congregational church, and vice versa. It was repudiated by the old-school Presbyterians in 1837 when the Presbyterians were divided into Old and New School bodies and in 1852 by the Congregationalists.

PLANTATIONS. A term applied to the system of planting new settlements. It was first used in connection with the efforts of Sir Humphrey Gilbert and Sir Walter Raleigh to establish colonies in Ireland and the New World. It came to have a special significance in New England, where the Massachusetts Bay Company charter gave the company the right to distribute its lands. Selected leaders received the land for new settlement in trust, they arranged the business details of the planting, they distributed the land, and they organized local government according to instructions given them. Other New England colonies copied it; thus it came to be associated particularly with expansion in Puritan New England.

PLANTATION SYSTEM OF THE SOUTH. In 17th-century England the word "plantation" meant a colony. A company transported the settlers, who were to be laborers, provided the taskmasters, fed and clothed the workers, and received the proceeds of their labor. When Virginia passed to the English crown (1624), it became a commonwealth of independent farms and private plantations based on the company system. The demand for labor was filled by African slaves brought by Dutch traders.

As finally evolved, the system employed large laboring forces (1,000 acres and 100 slaves was considered a highly productive unit), a division of labor, and a routine under the direction of a central authority. While tobacco and rice were important in the evolution of the system, cotton was the greatest force in making it dominant in southern economic life. The plantations were self-sustained communities, with slave quarters, storehouses, smokehouses, barns, tools, livestock, gardens, orchards, and fields. The slaves were usually worked in gangs, although the task system was not uncommon; skilled slaves were employed in their special capacity; and care was taken to keep as large a number of slaves as possible busy throughout the year. In the absence of the owner, the establishment was directed by his agent, usually the overseer.

Climate and soil largely determined the location of the plantation system. The upper South (Maryland, Virginia, Kentucky, North Carolina) produced tobacco; the South Carolina and Georgia tidewater, sea island cotton and rice; the rich bottoms of Louisiana, sugar cane; and the Piedmont region, short staple cotton.

The plantation slave labor system was destroyed by the Civil War. Some plantations operated thereafter on a crop-sharing basis under a centralized authority, for example "Dunleith," in the Yazoo-Mississippi delta. Others operated on a wage-labor basis, but most broke up into small farms, operated by the individual owner, tenant, or sharecropper.

PLASTICS. Natural plastics include horn, hoof, shell, shellac, and certain tars; animal horn, hoof, and tortoiseshell are albumenoids called keratin. From horn, the horners, or hornsmiths, who came to America from England early in the 18th century fabricated combs, buttons, spoons, and other products; their lanthorn windows were converted to glass after 1740. Gutta-percha, a rubberlike product of several trees of Malaysia, was introduced in Europe in 1832, and "gutta-percha" became the generic name for molded plastics, even though they were molded of shellac, rubber, or the pitch-bonded fillers. Shellac preparations, especially shellac-bonded wood flour, became important for molding and laminating and continued in that use until replaced by synthetics after World War II; shellac was the principal material used in phonograph records before the appearance of vinyl.

Nitrocellulose was discovered in Germany in 1845. Its flammability brought it into use as a military propellant, under the name "guncotton." Solutions of nitrocellulose left, on evaporation, a plastic film that was called collodion, used in photography as early as 1851. The compounding of nitrocellulose with other materials, especially camphor, was found to yield a bulkier plastic material. Molded nitrocellulose products were popular but less than satisfactory until technically improved by John W. Hyatt of Albany, N.Y., who introduced injection molding, solvent extrusion (forcing molten plastics through an opening), blow molding (similar to glass blowing), and other fabrication techniques. Hyatt's Celluloid, introduced in 1869, made possible a host of novelties. The Celluloid Manufacturing Company (later Celanese), established in 1871, gave birth to the Hercules Plastics Corporation and the Atlas Powder, Nixon Nitration, and Foster Grant companies.

Bakelite, made from phenol and formaldehyde, is often considered the first truly synthetic plastics material. It takes its name from Leo H. Baekeland, who devoted the years 1902–10 to an attempt to reduce to a usable form the sticky product of certain organic reactions. The resin he succeeded in hardening by heat appeared just in time to serve as an insulating material in the embryonic electrical and automotive industries.

Other new plastics materials appeared with increasing frequency, including new urea resins resembling Bakelite. The process of thermosetting appeared in 1928, acrylics and polyethylene in 1931, vinyl resins in 1933, melamine in 1937, styrene about 1937, Teflon and epoxy in 1938, nylon in 1939, silicones in 1943, polypropylene in 1954, plastic foams (for example, urethane) about 1955, polycarbonate in 1959, and polysulfone in 1965.

By the mid-1970's plastics were proven to be one of the answers to many of the pollution and waste disposal problems. Biodegradable materials had become available, and all plastics could be burned to convert their total energy values into heat. Flame retardant additives eliminated the combustion hazards that were present in the early plastics.

PLATFORM, PARTY. A statement of governmental principle and policy made by a political party to enlist voter support. Some historians have argued that the Virginia and Kentucky Resolutions of 1798–99 constituted the first party platform, but the platform in its modern sense did not appear until the 1830's.

The platform is the responsibility of a committee of the national convention. Opposing platforms have frequently much in common, so the American electorate has long since ceased to attach great importance to the platform.

The student of social and political history cannot disregard party platforms, since they frequently constitute important sources of evidence of popular thought and eventual legislative action. This is especially true of the minor party platforms, such as the Greenback, Populist, and Prohibition parties, with planks that later became bases of important national policies. The Progressive platform of 1912 exercised a decided influence on the domestic policies of both major parties, and various Socialist party platforms influenced President Franklin D. Roosevelt's New Deal legislation and President Lyndon B. Johnson's civil rights legislation.

PLATT AMENDMENT. The basis for Cuban-American relations from 1901 to 1934. Although much of it was drafted by Secretary of War Elihu Root, it became known as the Platt Amendment after Sen. Orville H. Platt of Connecticut, chairman of the Senate committee on Cuban relations. Attached as a rider to the army appropriations bill for the fiscal year ending June 13, 1902, it contained eight articles: (I) Cuba was to make no treaty that would impair its independence; (II) Cuba was not to contract any public debt beyond its ability to meet out of "ordinary revenues"; (III) Cuba was to permit the United States to intervene for the preservation of Cuban independence; (IV) all acts of the United States during the occupation were to be validated; (V) Cuba was to continue the sanitation program started by the United States; (VI) title to the Isle of Pines was to be decided later; (VII) coaling and naval stations chosen by the United States were to be sold or leased; (VIII) the articles were to be embodied in a permanent treaty with the United States.

When the articles were submitted to the Cuban convention with the demand that they be incorporated into the Cuban constitution, a storm of indignation arose. In spite of assurances given by Root that the United States interpreted its right to intervene (Article III) as applying only when Cuban independence was threatened by internal anarchy or foreign attack, the convention continued to balk. Not until the United States threatened to remain in the island did the convention, on June 13, 1901, agree to accept it. On May 22, 1903, the articles were written into a formal treaty. The arrangement aroused increasing bitterness as time went on. While armed intervention was seldom resorted to, except in 1906–09 and again in 1917, there were numerous occasions when the United States exerted pressure. This strengthened the demand for the repeal of the Platt Amendment, to which the United States acceded on May 29, 1934.

PLATTE BRIDGE FIGHT (July 26, 1865). A large body of Sioux, Cheyenne, and Arapaho warriors converged in the hills north of the North Platte River in Colorado, to attack and destroy Platte Bridge, an important link to the West. Troops from the adjacent fort under Lt. Caspar Collins left the post to bring in a wagon train en route from Fort Laramie. Collins and four men were killed, and in a later fight to keep the telegraph lines intact another soldier was killed. The wagon train was wiped out, and twenty men accompanying it were slaughtered. The Indians also suffered heavily.

PLATTE PURCHASE. A tract of almost 2 million acres that extended Missouri's northwest boundary to the Missouri River. It was purchased from the Indians by the federal government in 1836 for $7,500 cash together with specified quantities of merchandise, and annexed to Missouri on Mar. 28, 1837. The region was subsequently divided into six counties: Platte and Buchanan (Dec. 31, 1838), Andrew (Jan. 29, 1841), Holt (Feb. 15, 1841), and Atchison and Nodaway (Feb. 14, 1845).

PLATTE RIVER TRAIL. Owed its importance to South Pass near the southern end of the Wind River Range in southwest Wyoming, then the gateway of the Rockies. The Platte River heads at the pass, and the most direct route from the pass across 780 miles of plains to the Missouri River is down the Platte, which provides water for men and horses. Robert Stuart and six companions, carrying dispatches for the Pacific Fur Company from Astoria in Oregon Territory to St. Louis, traversed the route in 1812–13. Maj. Stephen H. Long's expedition followed it part way to the Rockies in 1819. A brigade of William Henry Ashley's Rocky Mountain Fur Company definitely established the trail in 1825. Branches of the trail, with eastern termini on the Missouri at Westport, Fort Leavenworth, Atchison, and St. Joseph, all converged on the Platte near Grand Island in what is now Nebraska. It was also known as the California Trail, Mormon Trail, and Overland Route. The completion of the Union Pacific Railroad in 1869 ended its importance.

PLATTSBURGH, BATTLE OF (Sept. 11, 1814). An engagement on the western shore of Lake Champlain in New York. Sir George Prevost, governor general of Canada, invaded New York with 14,000 veterans. He was opposed by Gen. Alexander Macomb's 1,500 American regulars and 2,500 militia, who were strongly entrenched south of the Saranac River in the village of Plattsburgh. Macomb's army was supported by a naval squadron of four small ships and ten gunboats under Comdr. Thomas Macdonough. The British invaders were assisted by another flotilla of about the same size commanded by Capt. George Downie.

Prevost planned a joint attack by land and by sea. He goaded Downie into attacking Macdonough, who lay at anchor in Plattsburgh Bay near Cumberland Head. Downie lost his ships and his life in a bloody battle lasting more than two hours. Meanwhile, Prevost failed to fight his way across the Saranac and support Downie. Deprived of naval support, the British army was forced to retreat. Its defeat made peace more certain and cut short British designs of obtaining sole control of the Great Lakes by the Treaty of Ghent.

PLAY PARTY. A form of social diversion formerly very common in the hill region of the South. Young people would assemble to play games that were really a form of folk dancing to the accompaniment of singing.

PLEASANT HILL, BATTLE OF (Apr. 9, 1864). On the night of Apr. 8, following his unsuccessful fight at Sabine Crossroads, La., Union Gen. Nathaniel P. Banks withdrew into strong positions at Pleasant Hill twenty miles away to be ready to unite with the Union fleet in the Red River. Late in the afternoon of Apr. 9, Confederate Gen. Richard Taylor, with 12,000 troops, attacked Banks's 28,000 troops. At first successful, the Confederate exposed right flank was turned and the attack repulsed. The troops were thrown into disorder, part of the line being broken and scattered. The Confederate army retreated in confusion toward Shreveport. Banks did not pursue, but instead withdrew to the Red River.

PLEDGE OF ALLEGIANCE. As part of the celebration to mark the 400th anniversary of the discovery of America, President Benjamin Harrison in 1892 called for patriotic exercises in school. The pledge of allegiance, taken from a children's magazine, the *Youth's Companion,* was first recited by public-school children as they saluted the flag during the National School Celebration held that year. In 1942 Congress made the pledge part of its code for the use of the flag. Authorship of the pledge was claimed by Francis Bellamy, an associate editor of the *Youth's Companion,* in 1923. The original wording was expanded by the National Flag Conference of the American Legion in 1923 and 1924, and the words "under God" were added by Congress in 1954. The text of the pledge is as follows: "I pledge allegiance to the flag of the United States of America and to the Republic for which it stands, one Nation under God, indivisible, with liberty and justice for all."

PLESSY V. FERGUSON, 163 U.S. 537 (1896). Upheld the validity of an 1890 Louisiana statute that required railroads operating in that state to provide "equal but separate accommodations for the white and colored races." For nearly sixty years after the *Plessy* decision the separate-but-equal doctrine enabled states to legislate segregation of races in almost all areas of public activity.

PLOESTI OIL FIELDS, AIR RAIDS ON (1941–44). Refineries located near Ploesti, Romania, provided one-third of the entire oil supply of the Axis. Minor air attacks by the Russians in 1941 were ineffective. The United States lacked the airpower for decisive attacks in 1942, although Liberators en route to China were held in Egypt to bomb Ploesti. Thirteen were dispatched in June 1942, but the distance, small force, high altitude, and adverse weather made the attack ineffective. By mid-1943 the force was available for a one-time attack. Three U.S. Liberator groups based in England joined Maj. Gen. Lewis H. Brereton's two Ninth Air Force groups in Libya. At dawn on Aug. 1, 177 aircraft were airborne on a 2,300-mile mission. Fifty-four aircraft were lost and fifty-five damaged by defending guns, fighters, balloons, and exploding bombs. Refinery production was reduced by about one-half. In April 1944 Maj. Gen. Nathan F. Twining's Fifteenth Air Force struck from Italy, opening a successful high-altitude campaign that continued until Aug. 19.

PLOUGH PATENT. *See* **Lygonia.**

PLOW. *See* **Agricultural Machinery.**

PLOWDEN'S NEW ALBION. The first English colonizing grant of the present New Jersey area, the second in the United States to offer religious liberty; issued June 21, 1634, to nine persons, including Sir Edmund Plowden (1592–1659), soon its sole owner. It was issued by Thomas Wentworth, first Earl of Strafford, lord deputy of Ireland, upon authority from Charles I. Its religious provisions copied those of Maryland: Plowden, of a Shropshire Catholic family, apparently planned New Albion as another Catholic haven.

Plowden, who took upon himself the title Earl Palatine of New Albion, tried four times to settle his province. In the spring of 1648 he sailed to England, reporting at New Amsterdam and to Gov. John Winthrop in Boston his intention to return to America.

In December 1648 *A Description of the Province of New Albion* was published in England with a long foreword signed "Beauchamp Plantagenet." This prospectus fancifully described New Albion; it detailed with considerable accuracy the New Albion charter, Virginia, and Plowden's life; and it reprinted Plowden's colonizing prospectus from 1641, *A Direction for Adventurers to New Albion.* Numerous land suits kept Plowden in England until his death in 1659. No Plowden contested Charles II's grant of these lands to James Stuart, Duke of York, in 1664.

PLUMB PLAN. Glenn E. Plumb, counsel for the organized railway employees, presented a plan for public ownership of railroads to replace the Railway Administration after World War I. Considered in Congress in 1919 as the Sims bill, the plan proposed that railroad properties be purchased at a government-appraised value and be operated by a quasi-public corporation representing the government, operators, and classified employees; and that improvements be financed by federal and local funds, and profits be used to retire the public bonds, reduce rates, and increase railway wages. (*See also* Transportation Act of 1920.)

PLUMMER GANG. Henry Plummer, elected sheriff of Bannack District (now Montana) May 24, 1863, organized a band of fifty outlaws, called the "Innocents," against whom 102 robberies and murders were charged. A vigilance committee, with which Wilbur Fisk Sanders (later senator) was associated, was formed in December 1863 and within six weeks hanged most of the band.

PLYMOUTH, VIRGINIA COMPANY OF (1606–20). One of the two companies incorporated in the first Virginia charter of 1606. In 1605 a group of men representing the City of London and the outports of Bristol, Plymouth, and Exeter petitioned for a charter that would accord them the privilege of planting colonies in America. The rivalry between London and the outports was such that the leaders wished to proceed with the project under separate companies. The charter of 1606 therefore created two companies, the Virginia Company of London, with permission to plant a colony in southern Virginia between 34° and 41° north latitude, to be called the First Colony of Virginia, and the Virginia Company of Plymouth, whose plantation, to be called the Second Colony of Virginia, was to be located to the north between 38° and 45° north latitude, the overlapping area to be considered a neutral zone in which the colonies could not come within one hundred miles of each other.

The Plymouth Company sent out its first expedition in the summer of 1606 to seek a place for a plantation. Unfortunately the vessel was captured by the Spanish near Puerto Rico, and the men carried off as prisoners to Spain, from where a few of them made their way back to Plymouth with difficulty. A second vessel dispatched in the autumn of 1606 reached the coast of Maine in safety, and returned with such glowing accounts that the company sent out two ships in May 1607, the *Gift of God* and the *Mary and John,* carrying settlers. A plantation was begun near the mouth of the Sagadahoc (now Kennebec) River and Fort St. George was built, but it did not prosper. The winter cold, the burning of the storehouse and many dwellings, and the consequent shortage of supplies weakened the interest of the planters, while the death of some of the men, including the governor, George Popham, discouraged the company in England from pushing the enterprise further (*see* Popham Colony). Some of its members continued their interest in the fisheries and sent out several expeditions to fish and trade with the Indians. Profits from these activities were sufficient to convince men like Sir Ferdinando Gorges of the potentialities of the region, and thus to pave the way for the reorganization of the project in 1620 under a new company, the Council for New England.

PLYMOUTH PLANTATION. *See* **New Plymouth Colony.**

PLYMOUTH ROCK. Traditionally (there is no contemporary record) the spot where the Pilgrims disembarked on Dec. 26, 1620, at Plymouth, Mass. It was moved back from its original location (1920) in order to protect and display it.

PLYMOUTH TRADING POST. In 1632 Edward Winslow of Plymouth Colony visited the Connecticut Valley to discover the possibilities of trade. After vain efforts to enlist the cooperation of the Massachusetts Bay Colony in the enterprise, Winslow sent Lt. William Holmes to set up a trading post at the junction of the Farmington River with the Connecticut on Sept. 26, 1633. The trading post soon became the nucleus of the village of Matianuck (renamed Windsor in 1637). Traders and settlers from Massachusetts began to enter the valley the next year and in 1635 located near the post. The Plymouth people soon found themselves crowded out and on May 15, 1637, sold their claims to all except the trading post and a small parcel of land to the Massachusetts settlers (*see* River Towns of Connecticut).

"POCKET." A name given to the southwestern portion of Indiana, embracing ten counties within the area bounded by the Ohio, Wabash, White, and Blue rivers, because of its pendulous geographical relation to the rest of the state. Occasionally the southwesternmost congressional district is so designated.

POCKET VETO. An indirect veto by which a U.S. president negates legislation without affording Congress an opportunity for repassage by an overriding vote. The Constitution (Article I, Section 7) provides that measures presented by Congress to the president within ten days of adjournment (not counting Sundays) and not returned by him before adjournment fail to become law. First employed by President James Madison, the pocket veto has been used by every president since Benjamin Harrison.

POINTE COUPEE. An early French settlement in Louisiana on the west bank of the Mississippi River just below the mouth of Red River. It was an important French post until the end of the French regime in 1762. Many Acadians settled there during the Spanish regime, and its population remained predominantly French.

POINT FOUR. The program announced in President Harry S. Truman's 1949 inaugural address which urged international cooperation to teach self-help to poverty-stricken peoples through provision of technological knowledge and skills and through capital investment. A 1950 appropriation of $35 million introduced U.S. outlays that reached $400 million by 1954. Being vastly inclusive, Point Four necessarily confronted age-old institutions, customs, and vested interests. Yet progress appeared in agriculture, conservation, waterpower, technical skills, and installations. Although the administration of President Dwight D. Eisenhower tended to avoid use of the term, the validity of the Point Four principle continually widened its application. Offers of technical facilities and capital loans and grants to underdeveloped, uncommitted countries became a weapon sharpened by universal use in the cold war.

POINT PLEASANT, BATTLE OF (Oct. 10, 1774). Col. Andrew Lewis with about 1,100 men from the frontier of southwest Virginia marched to join Virginia Gov. John Murray, Earl of Dunmore, on the Ohio River. Arriving at the mouth of the Kanawha River on Oct. 6, they made camp in the point of the two rivers called Point Pleasant. While awaiting the arrival of Col. William Christian with 250 of the rear guard, Lewis' army was attacked early in the morning by a large force of Shawnee, led by Chief Cornstalk. Lewis sent out two divisions under his brother, Col. Charles Lewis, and Col. William Fleming; both officers were soon wounded, the former fatally. The Indians continued fighting until sunset, when they withdrew across the Ohio. The losses on both sides were heavy, the Virginians having more than 80 killed and 140 wounded. The losses of the Indians were about 200 killed. (*See* Dunmore's War.)

POKAGON VILLAGE. The St. Joseph River Potawatomi village was situated in what is now Bertrand Township, Berrien County, in the southwest corner of Michigan. Not far from the site of the old St. Joseph Mission, it became the center of the revived missions of the region when Father Stephen T. Badin was appointed resident missionary in 1830.

POKER. A popular American card game, probably developed from the French card game *poque,* played in French America during the late 18th century and early 19th century. The first known reference to poker in America appears in 1829 in the writings of the British actor Joseph L. Cowell.

POLAR EXPEDITION OF THE *JEANNETTE* (1879–81). Lt. Comdr. George Washington De Long sailed in the Arctic steamer *Jeannette* from San Francisco on July 8, 1879, to the Bering Strait in an attempt to reach the North Pole. De Long sailed through the strait but soon became caught in the ice, drifting northward for twenty-one months and then foundering (June 12, 1881). De Long made his way with three boats to the New Siberian Islands, then tried to reach the Lena River in eastern Siberia. The boats became separated: one was lost; another reached the Lena; the third under De Long reached land, but he and his men all perished from starvation.

POLAR EXPLORATION. Exploration of the polar regions from North America began with the expedition of the 60-ton vessel *Argo* from Philadelphia in 1753 to map the coast of Labrador to the entrance into Hudson Bay. James Eights, a geologist on the Palmer-Pendleton sealing and exploring expedition to antarctic waters in 1829–31, postulated an antarctic continent. The U.S. exploring expedition of 1838–42 under Charles Wilkes mapped the edge of the antarctic continent near the Antarctic Peninsula and for 1,500 miles along the coast of East Antarctica, now called Wilkes Land.

Systematic U.S. exploration of the polar regions began in the 1840's. As head of the U.S. Navy's Depot of Charts and Instruments, Matthew Fontaine Maury sent the first (Edwin Jesse De Haven, 1850–51) and second (Elisha Kent Kane, 1853–55) Grinnell expeditions into the North American Arctic, in which Kane reached 80°40′, and encouraged the Isaac I. Hayes expedition (1860–61), in which Hayes reached 81° 35′. The navy also dispatched an expedition, under John Rodgers and Cadwalader Ringgold (1853–56), to the North Pacific Ocean and into the Arctic Ocean to Wrangel Island.

The Civil War delayed further official polar exploration until the ill-fated U.S.S. *Polaris* expedition under Charles Hall (1871–73) to the northeast coast of Greenland, during which Hall died and crew members suffered a very severe winter. The U.S.S. *Jeannette* under George De Long (1879–81) penetrated the Arctic Ocean through the Bering Strait, was beset in the ice, and for two years drifted west across the top of Siberia to a point near the mouth of the Lena Delta, where it was crushed. During the International Polar Year (1882–83) the Army Signal Office established stations at Point Barrow, Alaska, under P. Henry Ray and in Lady Franklin Bay (Fort Conger), Ellesmere Island, under A. W. Greely, from which extensive explorations and surveys were made of Ellesmere Island and the north coast of Greenland.

From 1885 to 1920 the dominant effort in polar exploration was to attain the North Pole. Most important were the seven successive explorations of Ellesmere Island, northern Greenland, and the adjoining Arctic Ocean by Robert E. Peary (1886–1909) that resulted in his reaching the North Pole on Apr. 6, 1909. Others include Frederick A. Cook's explorations of Ellesmere and Axel Heiberg islands (1907–09); and the Baldwin-Ziegler (1901–02) and the Fiala-Ziegler (1903–05) expeditions to Franz Josef Land in ill-fated attempts to reach the pole. The Jesup North Pacific expedition (1897–1902) and the Harriman Alaska expedition (1899) were privately subsidized scientific explorations, as were the National Geographic Society glaciological surveys of Alaska (1912–19). The Crocker land expedition, led by Donald B. MacMillan (1913–17), explored extensively in northwestern Greenland and Ellesmere Island.

The airplane changed the character and extent of polar explorations between 1919 and 1941. Four U.S. Army Air Service aircraft flew from New York City to Nome, Alaska (1920). The arctic flights included the Roald Amundsen–Lincoln Ellsworth flight in 1925 from Spitsbergen north across the Polar Sea to 88° north latitude; the Donald B. MacMillan–U.S. Navy (Richard E. Byrd) expedition (1925) to northwest Greenland, with flights by Byrd especially into Ellesmere Island; Byrd's flight from Spitsbergen to the North Pole and return in 1926; the George Hubert Wilkins–Carl Ben Eielson flight from Point Barrow, Alaska, across the Arctic Ocean to Spitsbergen in 1928; Wilkins' extensive flights and surveys of the Arctic Ocean north of Canada toward the pole in 1937–38; and Charles A. Lindbergh's survey flight of Greenland in 1931 for an arctic air route. Notable flights to Antarctica included flights by Wilkins in 1928–30 along most of the Antarctic Peninsula; four flights by Ellsworth (1933–39), including his long flight of 1935 from the northern tip of the Antarctic Peninsula to the Ross Ice Shelf beyond Marie Byrd Land; and Byrd's flight from Little America to the South Pole in November 1929. Byrd planned and commanded the first (1928–30) and second (1933–35) Byrd Antarctic expeditions, based at Little America I and II, and the U.S. Antarctic Service (1939–41) expedition, based at Little America III in West Antarctica and Stonington Island in the Antarctic Peninsula.

Terrestrial scientific explorations during the interwar years include those of Louise A. Boyd in the Norwegian and Greenland seas and along the east coast of Greenland (1928–41); the first exploration by a submarine, the *Nautilus,* below the ice of the Arctic Ocean northwest of Spitsbergen, by Wilkins (1931); expeditions to western Greenland made by the University of Michigan under William H. Hobbs (1926–31); and the glaciological and topographic surveys in Alaska of the American Geographical Society (1926–41), led by William Fields and Walter A. Wood, and of the National Geographic Society (1919–41).

During World War II the United States established transarctic air routes; set up air bases and meteorological and other scientific stations; and developed logistic support forces, especially in Alaska, northern Canada, Greenland, and Iceland. Following the war, through about 1956, the United States carried out an accelerated program of polar exploration and scientific investigation. In Antarctica the government launched an all-out program of exploration by the U.S. Navy Antarctic Developments Project (Operation Highjump, 1946–47). The last private expedition to Antarctica was conducted by Finn Ronne as the Ronne Antarctic research expedition (1947–48). It mapped in the Antarctic Peninsula, south into the Weddell Sea, and west around Alexander I Island. These expeditions were followed by the U.S. Navy Second Antarctic Developments Project (Operation Windmill, 1947–48), which mapped the Ross Sea, the coast of West Antarctica, and Wilkes Land. During the austral summer of 1954–55, the icebreaker U.S.S. *Atka* circumnavigated the continent.

In the Arctic the decade after 1945 saw routine scientific flights between Fairbanks and the North Pole; surveys of the Arctic Ocean; the establishment of the U.S. Navy Arctic Research Laboratory at Point Barrow, Alaska; successive penetrations of the Canadian Archipelago by navy task forces in experiments in logistics and tests; exploration for the building of the Distant Early Warning line; and surveys by navy task forces of the coast of northwest Greenland and of Ellesmere Island for bases, which culminated in the building of the giant Thule air base in Greenland.

In 1958 the nuclear submarine *Nautilus* made a 1,830-mile journey under the Arctic icecap. In Antarctica a remarkably high degree of international cooperation and participation has resulted from the Antarctic Treaty (June 21, 1961), signed by twelve governments.

POLICE. The ultimate basis of legal order is the likelihood that laws will be enforced. Police are the repository of these enforcement powers. They are responsible for maintaining the public order; promoting the public health, safety, and morals; and preventing and detecting violations of laws within a political jurisdiction.

The decentralized, local nature of American police agencies reflects their Anglo-Saxon origins. Before the 19th century England and its colonies relied on constables or sheriffs to maintain order, and their offices were outgrowths of still earlier localized systems of maintaining order. The problems of lawlessness and disorder associated with industrialization and urbanization highlighted the inadequacies of these prior systems. Although Boston employed nightwatchmen as early as 1636 and added a daywatch in 1838, the first consolidated city police force in America was created in New York in 1844. Early departments were characterized by political influence, corruption, and inefficiency. Rural areas continued to be served by sheriffs.

Texas established a state police force, the Texas Rangers, in 1835, but most state police forces were not created until the 20th century, partly in response to problems posed by the automobile. While there is no federal police force as such, many police activities are performed by the Federal Bureau of Investigation, established in 1908, and specialized agencies, most of which are within the Department of Justice, the Treasury Department, and the Department of Defense.

POLICE POWERS. The powers encompassed in the general power to govern, often phrased in terms of the power to legislate for the "public health, safety, welfare, and morals." In American constitutional theory the police power is usually conceived as a power of the state (as distinct from the powers of the national government) and thus often called the state police power. Theoretically the powers of the federal government of the United States are enumerated in Article I, Section 8, of the Constitution, but the Tenth Amendment provides that "the powers not delegated to the United States by the Constitution, nor prohibited by it to the States, are reserved to the States respectively, or to the people." The Tenth Amendment is the constitutional basis for the state police power as a reserved power. Article I, Section 10, of the Constitution is an explicit list of limits on state power.

POLICE STRIKE, BOSTON. *See* **Boston Police Strike.**

POLIOMYELITIS (also called infantile paralysis). A disease caused by any of three types of viruses commonly found in the human intestine. Paralysis or death can result if these viruses enter the cells of the central nervous system. The first large polio epidemic in the United States occurred in 1916. The disease achieved national prominence in 1920 when Franklin D. Roosevelt suffered a severe attack. Fund-raising efforts were expanded in 1937 with the formation of the National Foundation for Infantile Paralysis. Using the slogan "The March of Dimes," the foundation was successful in fund-raising campaigns, and large grants were made to scientists and institutions.

In the 1940's and 1950's poliomyelitis was the disease most feared by American parents. Summers were generally regarded as the "polio season," and the closing of swimming pools and other recreational facilities was commonplace. In 1952 more than 21,000 cases of poliomyelitis were reported.

In the 1940's virologists at the Johns Hopkins University discovered that polio is caused by more than one type of virus. It was suspected that there were three such viruses. The typing project, funded by the foundation, started in 1948. One of the virologists engaged was Jonas Salk, then at the University of Pittsburgh. Salk began work on killed-virus vaccines in 1950. A field trial of Salk's vaccines was conducted in 1954. The vaccine for each of the three types was injected separately. About 400,000 children were involved. The results of the trial were made public on Apr. 12, 1955: the vaccines were judged to be safe and about 70 percent effective. The vaccines were licensed two hours after the results were announced.

Research into live-virus vaccines was carried out by Herald R. Cox and Hilary Koprowski at the Lederle Division of the American Cyanamid Company and by Albert Sabin, who was funded by the National Foundation. In 1956 Cox and Koprowski carried out field tests of vaccines for two types of virus in Belfast, Northern Ireland. These tests were judged unsuccessful. Field tests of Sabin's orally administered live-virus vaccine were carried out in the Soviet Union starting in 1957. Vaccines for all three types of virus were tested. These trials were judged completely successful, and the Sabin oral vaccines were licensed in 1960. By the 1970's the Sabin vaccine was used almost exclusively. Since 1965 paralytic poliomyelitis has become a rare disease, but this status can be maintained only by continued vaccination programs.

POLITICAL ASSESSMENTS. A means of gaining funds for political party operations. Generally, the assessment is made against the annual salary paid to a public officeholder or employee and ranges from 1 to 5 percent. Filing fees, which are exacted by parties of persons running in partisan primaries, can be a form of assessment; but the rationale in the case of filing fees is that they tend to prevent cluttering of the ballot by those having little chance of winning. Several state courts have declared filing fees illegal. Holders of public office and public workers are often asked to contribute to party funds by buying reservations to party fund-raising benefits. Technically, such contributions are on a voluntary basis, but subtle pressure can be applied. Little of this type of assessment is obtained at federal levels of employment. Elective federal and state officials are prone to make contributions to party coffers, considering such contributions as evidence of their support of the party that helped to elect them.

Direct political assessment has been outlawed by the Political Activities acts of 1939 and 1940, known as the Hatch acts. Federal civil service rules have forbidden the soliciting or receiving of any "assessment, subscription or contribution" by officers or employees of the federal government. Several states have similar laws preventing the collection of contributions to a party from state and local public employees. Political assessment tends to prevail at state and local levels in the United States because no feasible plan for providing local parties with public funds has been devised. As greater public support of parties through income tax contributions occurs, the need for political assessments should diminish.

POLITICAL CAMPAIGNS. *See* **Campaigns, Political; Campaigns, Presidential.**

POLITICAL PARTIES. The importance and distinctiveness of parties as political organizations spring from their domination of electoral politics. Originally legislative caucuses and elite nominating organizations, the American parties assumed their modern form with the expansion of the male suffrage in the early 19th century, when they became for the first time political organizations with broad support in the electorate and with a network of constituency-based local parties. By the latter half of the century, they had in some cities become instruments by which the new masses of voters wrested control from old patrician and economic elites.

The origin and development of the American political parties stand entirely apart from the U.S. Constitution. The parties have been instruments of the democratization of the Constitution as well as a result of that process, and they transformed the entire process of electing an American president into something approaching a majoritarian decision. From the initial dualism of the Federalists and the Jeffersonians (Democratic-Republicans) the parties realigned in the 1820's into the Whigs, successors to the Federalist traditions, and the Democrats, led by Andrew Jackson; from 1860 on the Democrats and Republicans dominated the American party system (*see* Two-Party System).

The American party system has been marked by considerable decentralization, by nonbureaucratic, skeletal organizations, and by the persistence of only two competitive parties. Largely without formal membership or a career bureaucracy, they have been manned at most levels by only a few functionaries (*see* Political Parties, Organization of). The parties' chief functional trait has been the pragmatic, almost issueless majoritarianism through which they piece together electoral majorities. They have been much less involved in ideology than parties elsewhere. Platforms have revealed only modest differences between the two parties.

The American parties have found their major role as nominators and electors of candidates for public office. They waxed in the 19th century in their ability to confer the party label on candidates, first in party caucuses and then in the more widely consultative conventions that Jacksonian Democracy favored. The quadrennial national conventions at which the parties choose their presidential candidates remain the most important vestige of the parties' unchallenged control of nominations.

Just as the primary ended the party organization's monopoly of nominations, the rise of the new campaign expertise threatens its control of the election campaign. Nonetheless most American officeholders reach office on the ticket of one of the major American parties. Only the American chief executives have overcome fragmented, decentralized party power in the United States: their program and performance become identified with their party, and elections are fought on the executive record.

POLITICAL PARTIES, ORGANIZATION OF. The organization of both the Democratic and Republican parties takes the form of a pyramid of party committees, beginning at the bottom with local ward, city, and county committees, extending through statewide committees, and building to a single national committee at the top. In both parties the national party convention is the highest authority; it defines the powers and the composition of the national committee.

Authority within the parties has always been decentralized. In some states the effective locus of power is the state committees; in others power is further decentralized into autonomous city and county organizations. The national committees of the two parties, both of which date to the years before the Civil War, have never achieved any supremacy in the party organization. The president has customarily subordinated the national committee of his party to his own leadership; in the opposition party the congressional leadership most frequently provides the voice for the national party.

POLITICAL SCANDALS. Scandals come in many forms. Improper handling of government secrets has sometimes erupted into scandal. Edmund Randolph, secretary of state under George Washington, was driven from office for allegedly improper relations with the French. Alger Hiss, in the 1950's, was accused of passing secrets to Communists but went to prison for perjury.

Two sources of temptation to official corruption are the government's possession of extensive properties and the discretionary power of many units of government to award lucrative favors. In 1872 a railroad scandal involving congressmen and other prominent politicians accepting stock in the Crédit Mobilier of America shook the nation. During the administration of Ulysses S. Grant (1869–77), the Whiskey Ring scandal, an extensive tax-evasion scheme; the Belknap scandal, the apparent bribery of the president's personal secretary; and the Black Friday scandal, a conspiracy to corner the gold market, created widespread excitement. The Teapot Dome oil scandal of 1924 resulted in a prison sentence for Secretary of the Interior Albert B. Fall and the resignation of Secretary of the Navy Edwin Denby.

Political scandals often involve personal, not official, acts. Alexander Hamilton's sweeping confession in 1791 of a sordid affair with a Maria Reynolds and the charges that President Andrew Jackson had married Rachel Robards before her divorce became final were major scandals. The refusal of other cabinet wives to accept the wife of Secretary of War John H. Eaton as a social peer resulted in the resignation of Jackson's entire cabinet, with the exception of the postmaster general, in 1831. Dueling provided frequent 19th-century scandals. Disclosures that presidents Grover Cleveland and Warren G. Harding had fathered illegitimate children provided grist for the scandal mill.

The greatest American political scandal came in the 1970's. President Richard M. Nixon was forced to resign after his complicity in covering up the facts after a break-in of Democratic party offices in the Watergate Hotel in Washington, D.C., was revealed.

POLITICAL SCIENCE. By the late 20th century the discipline had evolved through four periods as identified by Albert Somit and Joseph Tanenhaus in the major work on the history of the subject, *The Development of American Political Science: From Burgess to Behavioralism* (1967).

1880–1903. Before 1880 the teaching of political science was almost nonexistent. Not until 1880, when John W. Burgess established the School of Political Science at Columbia University, did political science achieve an independent status with an explicit set of goals. Burgess had been trained in Germany and sought to implement the rigor of his graduate training and the advances of German *Staatswissenschaft* ("political science") in the United States. Under his leadership the Columbia school became the formative institution of the discipline. Theodore Woolsey, Woodrow Wilson, Burgess, Frank J. Goodnow, and A. Lawrence Lowell brought fame and direction to the field with their pioneering works. Columbia began publication of the *Political Science Quarterly* in 1886; Johns Hopkins published the *Johns Hopkins Studies in Historical and Political Science* (1882).

1903–21. With the establishment of the American Political Science Association in 1903, political science formally asserted its independence as a discipline. In 1906 the association began publication of the *American Political Science Review,* the leading professional journal in the discipline. The association's membership rose from 200 to 1,500. An increase in domestically trained Ph.D.'s Americanized the profession, whereas previously the majority of new professionals had earned their degrees at German and French institutions. The second period is significant for the organizational progress made by the discipline; intellectually, the period is less interesting.

1921–45. The intellectual somnolence was abruptly interrupted in 1921 with the publication of Charles E. Merriam's "The Present State of the Study of Politics" in the *American Political Science Review.* Merriam called for a "new science of politics" characterized by the formulation of testable hypotheses (provable by means of precise evidence) to complement the dominant historical-comparative and legalistic approaches. Merriam was joined in his effort by William B. Munro and G. E. G. Catlin—the three being considered the era's leading proponents of the "new science" movement. Opponents of "scientism," most notably William Yandell Elliott, Edward S. Corwin, and Charles A. Beard, questioned the existence of rigorous deterministic laws and the possibility of scientific objectivity by the proponents.

The discipline continued to grow. The association doubled its membership. The number of Ph.D.'s awarded annually increased from thirty-five in 1925 to eighty in 1940; the number of universities granting degrees expanded.

Since 1945. The development of political science after 1945 was dramatic. The association more than trebled in size as a membership of 4,000 in 1946 grew to 15,000 in 1980. Over 500 independent political science departments were in existence. By the mid-1970's more than 300 Ph.D.'s were awarded annually by over seventy-five departments offering doctoral programs. The struggle over behavioralism (the quest for a more scientific study of politics) was of titanic proportions in the last period. The resolution of that conflict was still not clear in the 1970's.

POLITICAL SUBDIVISIONS. Legally defined governmental units that are utilized by a larger unit of government in order to perform its assigned tasks and that, strictly speaking, must be created by the larger unit of government. Some of these subdivisions, such as counties (parishes in Louisiana and boroughs in Alaska), are divisions of the state created primarily for administrative purposes. Others are municipal corporations that perform general governmental functions as agents of the state and as units of local self-government. Still others, towns and townships, are administrative subdivisions of the county that perform services in rural areas. A class of subdivisions known as special districts performs limited special governmental functions as authorized by state law. The 1977 U.S. census of governments found 3,042 counties, 18,862 municipalities, 16,822 townships, and 25,962 special districts.

Public lands in the West were laid out in townships of thirty-six square miles by the federal government. As these lands became states, many midwestern states utilized modified townships as subunits of county government. These units have persisted in spite of frequent challenges.

School districts in 1977 numbered 15,174. Although the locally controlled school is a strong part of the American political tradition, high educational costs and encouragement by state governments have forced large-scale consolidations of these districts since 1955. Between 1962 and 1972 the number of school districts was reduced by 19,504. On the other hand, special districts are increasing rapidly in number, because traditional subdivisions often do not coincide with the areas that need a particular service. Between 1962 and 1977, 7,639 new special districts were formed.

POLITICAL THEORIES. The roots of American political theory are in the modern philosophical doctrine of natural rights and its concomitant, the social contract theory. The main themes and tenets of American political theory have remained constant. The themes are republicanism, constitutionalism, and federalism; the tenets are liberty and equality. The most influential American political theories, until well into the 20th century, were developed and forwarded by men who were active in political life. The principles of liberty and equality pronounced in the Declaration of Independence are the foundation of all later American views. The Declaration says men have, by nature, a perfect equality of unalienable rights and that "among these are Life, Liberty and the Pursuit of Happiness." It goes on to say that "to secure these Rights, Governments are instituted among Men." Implied is the view that the absence of government, or its weakness or ineptitude, is just as great a threat to the enjoyment of natural rights as is tyranny; also implied is an acceptance of the social contract theory.

The Constitution is conceived as setting up a republic that is relatively free of the injustices and inhumanities that a majority, blinded by passion or interest, can inflict on a defenseless minority. Moderation is sought in such a regime, first, by ensuring that all political choices will be made by representative assemblies; second, by establishing a large enough nation to make it unlikely that any merely factious element can be a majority; and, third, by establishing a scheme of intricate devices that reinforce the effects of representation and largeness. One of the devices is bicameralism.

While the "great compromise" at the Constitutional Convention in 1787, which established popular representation in one house and representation by states in the other, served the ends of the American version of federalism, the purpose of bicameralism is to provide by means fully consistent with republican principles a moderating influence on the legislature. Thus, bicameralism in America is an element of the separation of powers, a manifold device meant to curb the potential excesses by republican means.

The second great theme of American political theory is constitutionalism. One of the distinctive features of American constitutional government is judicial review—judgment by the Supreme Court about the constitutional validity of statutes enacted by the Congress—first put into practice in 1803 in *Marbury* v. *Madison.* Each time the Court concludes that an act of Congress is unconstitutional and therefore cannot be enforced, it does so either in the name of some individual liberty guaranteed in the Constitution or in the name of federalism.

The third great theme of American political theory is federalism. Even though the Constitution established a regime that was a mixture of federal and national principles (leaning heavily to the national side), it became the very standard of the new definition of federalism, which, in a nutshell, is the division of powers between the central government and the member states. The Constitution nowhere explicitly grants any powers to the states, but the Tenth Amendment offers the reassurance that the states have whatever power is not given to Congress, not denied to the states by explicit prohibition, and not reserved to the people.

POLITICAL WRITINGS. The first consequential political writing that strictly "belongs" to America is the Mayflower Compact (1620). But the towering documents of America are the Declaration of Independence, written by Thomas Jefferson in 1776, and the Constitution. Prominent among the writings in opposition to the Constitution were those by George Clinton, under the pseudonym "Cato," and those by Richard Henry Lee, called the "Letters of a Federal Farmer." But the most durable arguments were eighty-five articles written in favor of the Constitution by Alexander Hamilton, James Madison, and John Jay for New York newspapers under the pseudonym "Publius." Shortly before the series was completed in the newspapers, the group of eighty-five was published together as a book under the title *The Federalist* (1788). This is the preeminent work in American political thought. Other important works of the period were Thomas Paine's *Common Sense* (1776) and *The Rights of Man* (1792), and a long work by John Adams entitled *A Defence of the Constitutions of Government of the United States of America* (1787–88).

Once the Constitution was adopted, its interpretation became necessary. Important in that respect are Hamilton's financial reports to Congress (1790 and 1791) and Madison's Virginia Resolutions (1798–99) and Jefferson's Kentucky Resolutions (1798). But the chief issue to give rise to political writing was the problem of the Constitution's compromise with slavery, resolved finally by the Civil War, and the concomitant problems of the relation between the states and the

United States. John C. Calhoun's *Disquisition on Government,* completed in 1848, and the magnificent debates between Abraham Lincoln and Stephen A. Douglas in the 1858 campaign for the U.S. Senate in Illinois are leading works. Two speeches of Lincoln must be mentioned: his Gettysburg Address (1863) and his second inaugural address (1865).

Woodrow Wilson's "Peace Without Victory" speech (1917) and his "Fourteen Points" speech (1918) are evidences of American entry into world affairs, as is Franklin D. Roosevelt's "Four Freedoms" speech (1941). The internal companion of the crisis in world affairs was the crisis of the Great Depression. Crises in America have, for good reason, a way of expressing themselves in constitutional terms, and so some of Roosevelt's response to the depression can be seen in his "Fireside Chat" on reorganization of the judiciary (Mar. 9, 1937) and his address on Constitution Day (Sept. 17, 1937). Because so much in America turns on the Constitution, the opinions of U.S. Supreme Court justices in constitutional decisions are among the most important of American political writings: for example, John Marshall's opinion in *Marbury* v. *Madison* (1803; judicial review), *McCulloch* v. *Maryland* (1819; congressional power), and *Gibbons* v. *Ogden* (1824; commerce); Roger B. Taney's and Benjamin R. Curtis' opinions in *Dred Scott* v. *Sandford* (1857; slavery and citizenship); Oliver Wendell Holmes's in *Schenck* v. *United States* (1919; freedom of speech); Felix Frankfurter's and Hugo Black's in *Adamson* v. *California* (1947; rights of the accused); and Earl Warren's in *Brown* v. *Board of Education of Topeka* (1954; equality).

Academic writers played a more prominent role during the 20th century. Admirers of the British parliamentary system have had perhaps the longest influence. The beginning was Wilson's *Congressional Government* (1885), and the high point was reached in the publication of a document by the American Political Science Association in 1950 entitled *Toward a More Responsible Two-Party System: A Report.* Historical determinism and economic determinism never took hold as firmly in the United States as they did in Europe, but a version of those doctrines presented in Charles Beard's *An Economic Interpretation of the Constitution of the United States* (1913) was perhaps the most influential political book in academic circles and, in due course, in public opinion, in the 20th century. Positivism, an intellectual kin of historical determinism, has been more successful in America. A leading exponent is V. O. Key, Jr., in *Politics, Parties and Pressure Groups* (1942). Dominant in the 1950's and 1960's was behavioralism, the root principle of which is that there is a radical and unbridgeable gap between "facts" and "values." The preeminent American critic of behavioralism is Leo Strauss, whose *Natural Right and History* appeared in 1953.

POLK DOCTRINE (Dec. 2, 1845). President James K. Polk's first annual message reaffirmed the Monroe Doctrine but extended its scope and narrowed its boundaries by announcing American determination "that no future European colony or dominion shall, with our consent, be planted or established on any part of the North American continent." He thus added to the idea of noncolonization of unoccupied territory that of "dominion," which has been defined as including acquisition "by voluntary transfer or by conquest of territory already occupied," and emphasized opposition to "any interference." He also restricted the geographical radius of his prohibition to North America. This doctrine, applied in 1848 to discourage Yucatán from voluntarily ceding itself to some European power, was looked upon by Latin-American nations as a limitation upon their sovereignty.

POLLOCK'S AID TO THE REVOLUTION. With the opening of hostilities between the American colonies and Great Britain, the supply of gunpowder and arms heretofore purchased by the colonists in England and the West Indies was cut off. An agent sent by the governor of Virginia to New Orleans (1776) procured 10,000 pounds of powder through the mediation of Oliver Pollock with Luis de Unzaga y Amezaga, the Spanish governor. George Rogers Clark, after the capture of Kaskaskia (July 4, 1778), turned to Pollock for assistance as he had been directed to do by Virginia Gov. Patrick Henry. Arms, powder, blankets, sugar, coffee, and other supplies forwarded by Pollock enabled Clark to gain and hold possession of the Illinois Country. Serving also as commercial agent for the Continental Congress, Pollock continued to forward similar cargoes of goods procured from Spanish creditors for the use of the American army in the East. By July 1779 Pollock's credit was exhausted and he was forced to mortgage his landholdings and dispose of his slaves. By the close of the war, he had advanced for the American cause his entire property amounting to $100,000 and an additional $200,000 that he had borrowed. This amount surpasses the contribution of any other person.

***POLLOCK* V. *FARMERS LOAN AND TRUST COMPANY*, 157 U.S. 429 (1895).** A case in which the Supreme Court ruled that the income tax provision of the Gorman-Wilson tariff (1894) was unconstitutional on the ground that it was a direct tax and hence subject to the requirement of apportionment among the states according to population. In a prior hearing, only the tax on real estate income had been declared unconstitutional and the Court had divided evenly, four to four, regarding other forms of income. On a rehearing, the Court decided five to four against the income tax on personal property, owing to the fact that one justice, evidently David J. Brewer, now reversed himself to oppose the income tax, and another, Howell E. Jackson, who had not participated in the earlier hearing, voted with the minority. This decision inspired a popular attack on "judicial usurpation," resulting in the Democratic income tax plank of 1896 and leading ultimately to the passage of the Sixteenth Amendment (1913).

POLL TAX. A tax levied on each person within a particular class (for example, adult male) rather than on his property or income is called a poll, head, or capitation tax. Poll taxes were employed in all the American colonies. Poll taxes continued to be levied by most states through the 19th century and well into the 20th. In 1923 thirty-eight states permitted or required the collection of poll taxes. For many years states (five states as late as 1962) used the poll tax as a means of discouraging blacks from registering to vote by making the payment of the tax a prerequisite to the exercise of the right to vote. In 1964 the Twenty-fourth Amendment to the Constitution was ratified, nullifying all state laws requiring payment of a poll tax as a condition to vote in federal elections. Because the amendment made no mention of purely state elections, a few states continued the levy as a prerequisite for voting in state elections until 1966, when the Supreme Court, in *Harper* v. *Virginia Board of Elections,* ruled that it violates the Fourteenth Amendment.

***POLLY* ADMIRALTY CASE** (1802). Partly as a means of diverting enemy colonial commerce through British ports, and partly as a means of ingratiating the neutral United States, then on the verge of hostilities with France, British orders in council of Jan. 25,, 1798, allowed neutral vessels to carry the produce of any island or settlement of France, Holland, or Spain direct to a British port or to a port of their own country. This permitted the development of an American entrepôt traffic of West Indian goods to European ports after Americanization in the United States. In the case of the *Polly,* tried by British admiralty courts in 1802 (during the interim of peace), it was decided that this circuitous voyage (via the United States and Americanization of French colonial goods) to French enemy ports, was not a violation of the Rule of the War of 1756. (*See also Essex.*)

POLYGAMY. Polygamous living has been a custom practiced by certain sects and minorities, the most important of these in the United States being the Mormons and the Oneida Perfectionists. In the antebellum South, slaves were encouraged or permitted to mate according to the wishes of their owners, sometimes polygamously. Polygamous living is practiced by many persons secretly, or with the knowledge of limited circles of acquaintances; it is distinguished from prostitution in that it involves continuity of relationship, with affection and responsibility toward the extra mate. Toleration has varied from time to time and from place to place. (*See* Latter-day Saints, Church of Jesus Christ of; Oneida Colony.)

POMEROY CIRCULAR. A pronouncement of Salmon P. Chase for the presidency was issued in January 1864 by a national executive committee of Radical Republicans over the signature of its chairman, Sen. Samuel C. Pomeroy. Distributed secretly at first, it was publicized through the *National Intelligencer,* Feb. 22. Unconditional Union men, believing President Abraham Lincoln's reelection undesirable and impossible, found that Chase, then secretary of the Treasury in Lincoln's cabinet, combined those qualities necessary for a more vigorous prosecution of the war. In explaining the circular to the Senate in March, Pomeroy asserted that the committee, without consulting Chase, had drafted him as their candidate. Meanwhile, the Chase boom had collapsed with the declaration of Ohio Unionists for Lincoln.

PONCE DE LEÓN'S DISCOVERY OF FLORIDA (1513). In 1512 Juan Ponce de León secured a royal grant, with the title of *adelantado,* to conquer the island of Bimini to the north of Cuba where the fountain of youth presumably was located. Sailing from Puerto Rico on Mar. 3, 1513, he sighted the mainland on Mar. 27, and on Apr. 2 landed just north of the present site of St. Augustine. The region was named Florida in honor of the Easter season. Returning to Spain in 1514, he received a grant to colonize the islands of Florida and Bimini. In 1521 he undertook a second expedition from Puerto Rico to Florida. Reaching the peninsula on the western coast, he and his party were attacked by Indians, and in a battle he was severely wounded. The expedition returned to Havana, Cuba, where Ponce de León died.

PONTCHARTRAIN, LAKE. In southeastern Louisiana, five miles north of New Orleans, was named by Pierre Lemoyne, Sieur d'Iberville, in 1699 in honor of Louis de Phélypeaux, Comte de Pontchartrain, French minister of marine. The lake is about 40 miles long and covers about 600 square miles. It was connected to New Orleans by canal in 1795, by railroad in 1831, and by ship canal in 1921. The Bonnet Carre spillway, completed in 1935 to protect New Orleans from Mississippi River floods, connects lake and river thirty-five miles above the city. The lake is crossed by two causeways twenty-three miles long, which form the longest bridge in the world. Lake Pontchartrain formed a link in the British inside passage to the Mississippi, 1763–83, and in the later overland route to the north and east.

PONTCHARTRAIN DU DÉTROIT, FORT. Established by Antoine de la Mothe Cadillac on July 24, 1701. Around it grew up the city of Detroit. Frequently enlarged, and with various changes of name (Fort Lernoult, Fort Shelby, Detroit), it served for 125 years.

PONTIAC'S WAR (1763–64). An uprising of Indians in 1763 after the end of the French and Indian War, in opposition to British expansion in the Great Lakes area. The leader was an Ottawa chief named Pontiac, who had long been hostile to the English and had fought against them at Gen. Edward Braddock's defeat in 1755.

Most of the Indians of the Great Lakes area had been on better terms with the French than with the English, and they were outraged when the British commander, Gen. Jeffrey Amherst, banned the credit and gifts that the Indians had been accustomed to receiving from the French.

Pontiac, following the teachings of the Delaware Prophet, attempted to forge unity among the Indians of the area; he succeeded in convincing the Delaware, Shawnee, Chippewa, Miami, Potawatomi, Seneca, Kickapoo, and others that they should join him. In the spring of 1763 he convened a council of the Indian allies at the mouth of the Ecorse River, a few miles from Detroit; and at the end of May 1763, the aroused warriors attacked every British fort in the area, taking eight out of ten of them and killing the garrisons. The main fortifications, Fort Pitt and Detroit, were, however, successfully defended. Because of the central location and military importance of Detroit, Pontiac himself directed the attack on it. He had planned a surprise attack; but the post commander, Maj. Henry Gladwin, was warned in advance, and the gates were closed. Pontiac laid siege to the fort, a tactic that was without precedent in Indian military history, and continued to besiege it until November. Realizing that he could expect no assistance from the French and suffering defection of his Indian allies, Pontiac retreated to the Maumee River. Col. John Bradstreet entered Detroit with troops on Aug. 26, 1764, and prevented a renewal of the siege; but a formal peace was not concluded until July 24, 1766. Pontiac was unsuccessful in arousing the tribes along the Mississippi River to another effort, and in 1769 he was killed by an Illinois Indian.

PONTOTOC, TREATY OF (Oct. 20, 1832). Negotiated by Gen. John Coffee, U.S. commissioner, with the Chickasaw at their council house in what is now Pontotoc County, northeast Mississippi. The treaty provided for the cession of Chickasaw lands (6,283,804 acres) in northeastern Mississippi and the removal of the tribe west of the Mississippi, thereby extinguishing the last Indian titles to lands in the state (*see* Indian Removal). The United States promised the Indians the proceeds from the sales of the lands.

PONY EXPRESS. In September 1857 a contract was granted to John Butterfield and his Overland Mail Company for the overland mail to California, which began operation one year later over a circuitous southern route. The shortest time made on this route was twenty-two days. Many Californians, including Sen. William M. Gwin, believed that a central route was entirely feasible. Gwin, early in 1860, induced William H. Russell, of the freighting firm of Russell, Majors and Waddell, to demonstrate the practicability of a central route by establishing a pony express (*see* Central Overland California and Pikes Peak Express).

Starting at St. Joseph, Mo., the route followed the well-known Oregon-California trail by way of Fort Kearny and Scottsbluff (Nebraska), Fort Laramie, South Pass, and Fort Bridger (Wyoming), and Salt Lake City. From there the trail went around the southern end of the Great Salt Lake, by way of Fort Churchill, Carson City (both in Nevada), and Placerville (California) to Sacramento. Stations were built at intervals of about fifteen miles. Fleet, wiry, Indian ponies were purchased; and lightweight riders were hired. On Apr. 3, 1860, the service was inaugurated. It was like a giant relay, in which about seventy-five ponies participated in each direction. At each station the riders were given two minutes in which to transfer the saddlebags to fresh ponies and be on their way again. After riding a certain distance, one rider would hand the mail over to another, and so on, until the destination was reached. During the eighteen months of the operation of the pony express only one trip was missed. The service was weekly at first and later semiweekly. When the telegraph lines were joined on Oct. 24, 1861, all need for the pony express was eliminated. Russell, Majors and Waddell was virtually ruined by the experiment.

POOLS, RAILROAD. Agreements between railroads to divide competitive business are called pools. Equalization was made either by dividing traffic or by dividing income. Since traffic pools limited the right of the shipper to route his own business, money pools were more common. The cattle eveners' pool, formed in 1875 to equalize traffic in livestock between Chicago and New York, was an example of the traffic type. The Chicago-Omaha pool, dividing business among three railroads, dated from 1870. Pooling agreements, common from 1870 to 1887, were outlawed by the Interstate Commerce Act of 1887. They were succeeded by rate agreements, at least one of which, the Buffalo Grain Pool, was practically a pooling agreement. Rate agreements were held to violate the Sherman Antitrust Act of 1890 in *United States* v. *Trans-Missouri Freight Association* (1897). In the Transportation Act of 1920 pooling agreements were legalized when approved by the Interstate Commerce Commission.

POOR, CARE OF. *See* **Poverty and Pauperism.**

POOR PEOPLE'S CAMPAIGN (1968). A march on Washington, D.C., designed by the late Rev. Martin Luther King to dramatize the plight of 30 million Americans living below the poverty line. Marchers began to arrive in May and set up an encampment in a meadow by the Potomac called "Resurrection City." Divided in leadership with the death of King, and exploited by its militant elements, the marchers dispersed in June.

POOR RICHARD'S ALMANAC (1732–96). Published in Philadelphia by Benjamin Franklin, it contained, in addition to the usual almanac information, maxims, saws, and pithy sayings written by Franklin. Each edition saw an increase in sales until 10,000 copies were printed annually, approximately one for every hundred people in the colonies. It eventually became the second most popular book in the American colonies, the Bible being first. It is probable that Franklin ceased to write for the almanac after 1748, when he began to devote most of his time and energy to public affairs, although he continued as its editor and publisher. In 1757, after editing the 1758 edition, he disposed of the almanac, which continued to appear until 1796. In 1758 Franklin collected the best of his writings from *Poor Richard's Almanac* in *Father Abraham's Speech,* more commonly known as *The Way to Wealth.* (*See also* Almanacs.)

POOR WHITES. A term applied, frequently in scorn, to the lowest social class of white people in the South. Before the Civil War most early writers and travelers were interested only in the aristocracy and slaves and tended to dismiss almost all others as "poor whites." After the Civil War the term took on a more elastic meaning as the rapid spread of sharecropping and farm tenancy engulfed even many of the formerly independent yeomanry in poverty. During the almost continuous agricultural depression that ran from the 1870's through the 1930's great numbers of southerners found themselves vulnerable to derision as "poor whites."

POPE-McGILL FARM ACT (also known as the Agricultural Adjustment Act of 1938). Title I added amendments to the Soil Conservation and Domestic Allotment Act of 1936. Title II authorized the secretary of agriculture to complain to the Interstate Commerce Commission concerning freight rates on farm products and to set up four regional laboratories to find new uses for agricultural products. The Federal Surplus Commodities Corporation continued until June 30, 1942, when the Agricultural Marketing Service assumed many of its functions. Title II authorized the secretary of agriculture, under prescribed conditions, to proclaim national marketing quotas for tobacco, corn, wheat, cotton, and rice. Title IV had to do with "Cotton Pool Participation Trust Certificates," while Title V created the Federal Crop Insurance Corporation with a capital of $100 million within the Department of Agriculture to insure wheat crops.

"POP-GUN" BILLS. Tariff measures passed by the Democratic House of Representatives after the elections of 1890. Although blocked in the Senate, the "pop-gun" bills were effective in focusing attention on the defects in the McKinley Tariff of 1890 and creating issues for the campaign of 1892. The term arose when the Republicans contemptuously referred to the measures as "pop guns."

POPHAM COLONY. The first attempt by England to colonize the New England coast. On May 31, 1607, the Plymouth Company of Virginia sent out about 120 colonists on two ships, the *Mary and John* and the *Gift of God.* George Popham, nephew of Sir John Popham, chief justice of England and sponsor of the venture, was president and Raleigh Gilbert was admiral. These men sailed south along the Maine coast to Seguin Island and then landed at the mouth of the Kennebec River in August 1607. They built a fort, which they named St. George, a storehouse, fifty dwellings, and a church. The settlers began the construction of a ship, *Virginia of Sagadahoc,* the first ship built by Englishmen in North America. They explored the river up to Merrymeeting Bay, the Androscoggin River to the Pejepscot River, Casco Bay on the coast to the west, and eastward to Pemaquid Point. They made friends with the Indians and traded with them. But things went wrong; quarrels arose, and all but forty-five men had to be shipped home when the second ship left in December. On top of that came a savage Maine winter. Popham died on Feb. 5, 1608. In the summer of 1608, ships brought news of the deaths in England of Sir John Popham and Gilbert's brother, Sir John Gilbert, who left him an inheritance of property. In September the remaining settlers went home.

POPULAR SOVEREIGNTY. The right of the people to rule. "Squatter sovereignty" literally means the right of people living anywhere without a government to form a body politic and practice self-government. When the theory that the people of a federal territory had the right to determine the slavery question for themselves was first enunciated, it was dubbed "squatter sovereignty" by its opponents. The term is often used as the equivalent of popular sovereignty.

Lewis Cass, senator from Michigan and later secretary of state, in 1847, made the first clear statement of the principle. Sen. Stephen A. Douglas of Illinois made the Kansas-Nebraska Act a popular sovereignty measure.

POPULATION, GROWTH AND MOVEMENTS OF. The area now comprising the United States was virtually empty in 1650; yet it is somewhat startling to realize that during the 330-year period to 1980 its exogenous population increased more than 4,000-fold. This works out to an average annual rate of growth of 2.6 percent, a figure well above the rate of increase in the 1970's of the world's less-developed regions. From 52,000 people in 1650, the population of the United States had grown to over 226 million by 1980. Most of the growth came from the excess of births over deaths, which is estimated to have been nearly 3 percent per year at the beginning of the 19th century.

In the decade 1840–50 net immigration passed the 1 million mark, mounting to its maximum of 6.3 million from 1900 to 1910. During the Great Depression decade there was a net outward movement, but after that the total rose to almost 4 million in the 1960's. The gains through immigration were more than cancelled by the falling rates of natural increase, which dropped systematically from about 1830 to 1930, giving the United States one of the world's early and most sustained declines in natural increase.

It is estimated that in the 1820's there were about 55 births a year per 1,000 population. By 1935–39 the number had fallen below 19. Then came wartime and postwar rebound, culminating in the "population explosion" of the 1950's, with a rate of nearly 25 per 1,000. It was followed by a sharp decline in the 1960's and the early 1970's, reaching 15 per 1,000 population in 1974; by 1980 the birth rate slightly increased to 16.2 per 1,000.

The rapid rate of growth in the early years was apparently also fostered by a favorable death rate for the time. Nothing very precise can be said about it because, without registration, deaths are more difficult to estimate than births. The death registration was not started until 1900; and the death rate for the total population dropped from 16.2 per 1,000 during 1900–05 to 8.9 in 1980. The rate for the nonwhite population was substantially higher than that for the white until 1969, but then fell below it. This does not mean that the nonwhite population is healthier than the white: the death rate gives the number of deaths per 1,000 population; the nonwhites, having higher birth rates, are more heavily loaded with young people for whom the risks of death are relatively low. (*See also* Life Expectancy.)

The varying rates of accretion by birth and migration, and depletion by death, have left their marks on the age composition of the population. The falling proportion of females in the childbearing years is both consequence and cause of falling birth rates, and the higher proportions in the nonwhite than in the white population account in part for the higher birth rates of the nonwhites. Most pronounced of all is the rise of the old-age population. Between 1890 and 1980 the proportion of the population aged 65 and over more than doubled for males and increased more than 3.5 times for females. These changes are reflected in the changing average age. The median age for the whites rose from 22.5 years in 1890 to 31.3 in 1980. For the blacks it rose from 17.8 years in 1890 to 24.9 in 1980.

The most dramatic change in the nation's pattern of settlement is in the shift from the country to the city. At the first U.S. census in 1790 about 95 percent of the population lived in rural areas. By 1980 this proportion was down to 26.3 percent and, because of the ease of transportation, many of those who lived in the country worked in the city. The largest single factor underlying this change is the dramatic increase in the productivity of agriculture per man. In the early days of the Republic it probably took about 75 percent of the labor force to produce the nation's food and fiber. In 1980 only 2.7 percent of the total was engaged in agriculture. The drift to major metropolitan areas is shown by the increase of Standard Metropolitan Statistical Areas (SMSAs), which include all counties having a city of 50,000 or more population and the counties of urbanized character contiguous to them. By 1980 these areas contained 75 percent of the population. It is to be noted, however, that a larger proportion of this metropolitan population lived outside the central cities than lived inside.

POPULISM. It grew out of an agrarian movement of protest in the 1890's against some of the consequences of industrialization, reached its greatest intensity in the depression crisis following the panic of 1893, and lost its driving force just when success seemed imminent, during the presidential election of 1896. The Populist movement thus met defeat even before the candidates of 1896 entered the climactic stage of the campaign; and William McKinley's convincing triumph over Bryan removed whatever consolation the Populists might have salvaged from the election. Farm organizations gained considerable political influence as pressure groups in the 20th century, but the hope of building a national party on agrarian principles had disappeared.

POPULIST PARTY. Organized during July 1892, at a convention held in Omaha, Nebr. It grew out of a number of smaller previous organizations, which had sprung up among American farmers. These included the Farmers' Alliance, the Grangers, and the Greenback party's remnants.

During the 1880's and early 1890's, farm prices were very low and deflation was affecting American business. Many farm families faced the possible loss of their farms by foreclosure. Farmers generally believed that railroad companies were cheating them by charging high rates for small freight loads, and by favoring the bigger companies, the "trusts."

A number of farm leaders became leaders in the Populist party. They included some of the most colorful figures in American politics, people like Jerry Simpson, who, when he accused his opponent of being a "silk stocking" candidate, was immediately nicknamed "Sockless Jerry." Another colorful Populist was Mary Elizabeth Lease of Kansas, a powerful speaker who advised her farmer audiences to raise "less corn and more Hell" if they wanted lawmakers to pay attention to them. Populists included Negro farm organizations, members of the Knights of Labor, and the Southern Alliance.

In 1892, the new party entered the presidential race by nominating James B. Weaver. Weaver scored about a million popular votes, and he took the electoral votes of Colorado, Idaho, Kansas and Nevada, plus one electoral vote each in North Dakota and Oregon. The electoral vote of other states stayed in Democratic hands by rather small margins. Populist strength showed up in Alabama, Georgia, North Carolina, Texas, South Carolina, and Nebraska. The 1892 election returned Populist supporters to the House of Representatives and to the U.S. Senate.

Populist ideas were eventually taken over by the larger parties. These proposals included: (1) Free and unlimited coinage of silver with 16 ounces of silver valued as one ounce of gold. (2) A graduated income tax, with higher rates to be charged on large incomes than the rate charged on lower incomes. (3) Direct election of U.S. senators by the people, rather than indirect election by state legislatures. (4) Government ownership and management of railroads and the wire communications systems—the telephone and telegraph. (5) Recovery of the land granted the railroads, and its use for other public purposes. (6) A system of sub-treasuries, and federally owned grain elevators in which farmers could deposit their crops when prices were low.

The Populists tried to develop an alliance with all workmen but city dwellers thought of Populists as unreliable and even dangerous. However, by 1896, the Populists were so strong that there was danger that one of the major parties would break up as people moved out of it and became Populists. When William Jennings Bryan was nominated for president by the Democrats, his campaign was pitched toward free and unlimited coinage of silver. The Populists, meeting in a separate convention, had to make up their minds to accept Bryan or put another candidate in the field who would split the "silver vote" and insure a Republican victory. The Populists decided to nominate Bryan, although they named their own vice-presidential candidate. As the Democrats continued to take over many Populist positions as their own, the Populist party slipped from its position of influence. It continued until 1904 but was no longer significant as a vote-getting organization. (*See also* Granger Movement, Greenback Party, Knights of Labor.)

PORCUPINE'S GAZETTE (Mar. 4, 1797–Oct. 26, 1799). A daily and triweekly newspaper published at Philadelphia by William Cobbett ("Peter Porcupine"), a vituperative British journalist who advocated alliance with England and war against France and freely attacked many prominent citizens. Loss of a libel suit for $5,000, instituted by Dr. Benjamin Rush during the yellow fever epidemic, caused its failure.

"PORK BARREL." A familiar term in American politics, generally applied to local projects and improvements for which appropriations are obtained by legislators for the benefit of their constituents. The phrase probably originated in the pre–Civil War practice on southern plantations of distributing salt pork to the slaves from large barrels. The term is generally used, especially by journalists and reformers, in a derogatory sense, condemning such projects as a waste.

PORTAGES AND WATER ROUTES. In colonial days, travel by water was subject to interruption, either by rapids, shallows, or falls in a river, or at points where the transit from one river system to another must be made. At such places, boat and cargo had to be carried around the obstruction or across the intervening land. The term "portage" signifies both the act of transporting a boat and its cargo overland and the place where such a land carriage is necessary. At places where the volume of travel was considerable, either Indians or some white trader frequently maintained horses or oxen and carts for hauling boats across the portage.

The French, securing a foothold at the mouth of the St. Lawrence River, found themselves on a waterway that offered ready access to the interior. By the Richelieu River–Lake Champlain route they might pass southward to the Hudson River, while numerous tributaries of the Ottawa and the St. Lawrence rivers pointed the way to Hudson Bay.

The Ottawa River route to the upper Great Lakes was opened by the French explorer Samuel de Champlain, 1615–16. From Lake Erie the Ohio River might be reached by numerous routes. From Lake Superior one might pass by numerous river and portage routes to Hudson Bay, to the Mississippi River system, or to the great river systems that drain the vast interior plain of Canada into the Arctic Ocean. From Lake Michigan many routes led to the Mississippi system, the best-known portages being the Fox-Wisconsin at Portage, Wis.; the Chicago-Illinois at Chicago (*see* Chicago Portage); and the St. Joseph–Kankakee at South Bend, Ind. (*see* St. Joseph, Fort); while from the St. Joseph, access was open to the Wabash and the Ohio rivers. With the Mississippi system once gained, the entire heart of the continent from the Arctic to the Gulf of Mexico and westward to the Rockies lay open to the traveler. At places where a break in transportation occurred (Niagara, Erie, Fort Wayne, Chicago, for example), forts were frequently placed and the foundations of future cities laid.

PORT AUTHORITIES. Quasi-public, tax-free organizations. Port authorities as a rule cannot levy taxes, but derive income from tolls, largely from bridges and tunnels, and rentals from airports, heliports, and marine and bus terminals. They can also borrow money, secured by tax-free bonds. The port authority is relatively free from political interference. Its operating head is usually an executive director, who is controlled by a board of commissioners of which he may be a member. The Port Authority of New York and New Jersey (*see following article*) is the oldest in the United States.

Many other port cities have established port authorities with varying degrees of power and coverage, as in Boston, Baltimore, Savannah, Mobile, Toledo, San Francisco, Los Angeles, Pensacola, and Norfolk. In some cases the port authority is a state-controlled unit, as in Maine, North Carolina, New Hampshire, Virginia, South Carolina, Georgia, Alabama, and Puerto Rico, but the jurisdiction of these port authorities is usually restricted.

PORT AUTHORITY OF NEW YORK AND NEW JERSEY. A self-supporting, interstate corporate organization of New York and New Jersey, created in 1921 with a view to solving the problems caused by the artificial New York–New Jersey boundary line down the middle of the Hudson River. The Port Authority is permitted "to purchase, construct, lease and/or operate any terminal or transportation facility" and "to make charges for the use thereof." Its sphere of jurisdiction extends over a twenty-five-mile radius from the Battery, the southern extremity of Manhattan.

Among the facilities built, owned, and operated by the Port Authority are the Goethals Bridge between Staten Island and Elizabeth, N.J. (opened 1928), the George Washington Bridge (1925–31), the Bayonne Bridge (1928–31), Lincoln Tunnel (first tube completed 1937; second, 1945; third, 1957), Port Authority Bus Terminal (1949–50; addition, 1975–81), and the George Washington Bridge Bus Station (opened 1963). Facilities built and operated by the Port Authority but owned by the city of New York include the New York City Passenger Ship Terminal (completed 1974). The Port Authority also operates the following facilities: Port Authority Trans-Hudson (PATH) System, Journal Square Transportation Center, the Holland Tunnel, Outerbridge Crossing, four airports (John F. Kennedy, LaGuardia, Newark, and Teterboro), two heliports (Port Authority–Downtown and Port Authority–West 30th Street), seven marine terminals, two truck terminals (Newark and New York City), the World Trade Center, and eight trade development offices (London, Tokyo, Zurich, and five in the United States). The Port Authority's net operating revenues in 1980 were $210.4 million; total assets on Dec. 31, 1974, were more than $4 billion.

PORTER CASE. Gen. Fitz-John Porter was considered one of the ablest Union generals and was one of Gen. George B. McClellan's most intimate friends. On Nov. 27, 1862, he was arraigned before a court-martial in Washington, D.C., and charged with disobeying the orders of Gen. John Pope during the second Battle of Bull Run (Aug. 29–30, 1862). On June 21, 1863, Porter was found guilty and "forever disqualified from holding any office of trust or profit under the government of the United States." This verdict was the cause of much controversy until twenty-three years later when a bill was passed by Congress and signed by President Grover Cleveland that restored Porter to the U.S. Army on Aug. 7, 1886, with the rank of colonel. It has been charged that Porter was used as a scapegoat by the Radical Republicans and other enemies of McClellan.

PORT GIBSON, BATTLE AT (May 1, 1863). Union Gen. John A. McClernand's van of Gen. Ulysses S. Grant's flank movement on Vicksburg, Miss., struck Gen. J. S. Bowen's outnumbered Confederates on a divided road ten miles from Bruinsburg and four miles from Port Gibson. Dual attacks were checked in bitter fighting, until McClernand's last reserve hit the southern flank while Grant personally directed reinforcements from James B. McPherson's corps against the northern flank. Bowen's brigades got away to Grand Gulf, north of Port Gibson.

PORT HUDSON, SIEGE OF (March–July 1863). Following the Battle of Baton Rouge, Aug. 5, 1862, Confederate Gen. John C. Breckinridge occupied the high bluff at Port Hudson, twenty-five miles to the north, which was strongly fortified during the next few months to protect Confederate supplies coming down the Red River. Union Adm. David G.

Farragut attacked Port Hudson on Mar. 14, 1863, in an attempt to join Gen. Ulysses S. Grant before his attack on Vicksburg, Miss., but only two gunboats succeeded in passing the fortifications. While Grant invested Vicksburg, Gen. Nathaniel P. Banks besieged Port Hudson for six weeks. The fall of Vicksburg rendered Port Hudson useless to the Confederates, and on July 9, 1863, Gen. Frank Gardner surrendered this last Confederate stronghold on the Mississippi.

PORTLAND (Maine). The largest city in the state, with a population of 61,572 in 1980; the center of a metropolitan area that included 183,457 people. The location on a narrow peninsula that juts into Casco Bay provides ideal anchorages for oceangoing ships. The city is the closest U.S. seaport to Europe and is an important port of entry for oil and other products. It has many factories which process Maine wood products and paper, as well as food-packing houses.

The earliest settlements by Englishmen on the site of Portland date from 1623. They were abandoned, however, and later trading posts were established in 1628 and in the 1630's. In 1675, a town on the site (called Falmouth) had several hundred residents. This early Falmouth was wiped out in an Indian war but was resettled in 1716 under the lead of Samuel Moody. The city prospered, but the start of the American Revolution brought a new disaster. The Falmouth residents were strongly anti-British. The British bombarded and burned the place, but it was rebuilt.

Portland took its present name in 1786. Its shipbuilding and dock facilities grew, and it became a railroad center as lines connected it with Boston and other New England cities. Portland was the first capital of Maine, remaining as the center of government from 1820 to 1832. (Augusta was then designated the capital because it was more centrally located in the state.) Portland's growth continued until July 4, 1866, when the city suffered one of the greatest fires in east-coast city history, although no lives were lost. Portland turned into a tent city for a time, but was rebuilt with new street patterns.

During the 20th century, Portland has served as an important center for the export of Canadian products. The city is connected by pipeline to Montreal. The University of Maine has established a campus in Portland.

PORTLAND (Oreg.). The largest city in the state, with a population of 366,383 in 1980; the center of a metropolitan area that included 1,007,130 people. The city is located on both banks of the Willamette River, where that river joins the Columbia. It is an important seaport although it is located 90 miles up the Columbia River from the Pacific Ocean.

Portland's first residents established themselves on the site around 1845. They were New Englanders who had moved to Oregon. They settled an argument over naming their new town by tossing a coin. The winner of the toss, who was a settler from Portland, Maine, named the settlement after his home town. Portland grew slowly in its early years, but began a rapid period of growth after the Civil War.

Exports of Oregon products through Portland began in earnest in the 1870's and 1880's, when wheat, lumber, and fruits from the interior were brought to Portland. When the water power of the Willamette and Columbia rivers was harnessed to drive electric generators, Portland was in an ideal position to become a manufacturing center since large supplies of electricity were at close hand. This advantage was developed during World War II, when the city became the home of one of the most important aluminum factories in the United States.

Portland prides itself as the "Rose City." Its climate and soil are so well suited to rose culture that practically every house in the city has some rose bushes. Although the University of Oregon is located in Eugene, the University's Medical and Dental Schools are in Portland. Portland is the home of several other colleges, including the University of Portland, Portland State College, and Reed College.

PORT REPUBLIC, BATTLE OF (June 9, 1862). After his defeat of Union Gen. John C. Frémont at Cross Keys, near Harrisonburg, Va., Confederate Gen. Thomas J. ("Stonewall") Jackson hurried to Port Republic and destroyed the bridge across the Shenandoah River there, thus dividing Frémont's force. On the following day, Jackson defeated the two Union brigades south of the river, numerically much inferior to his own force (*see* Jackson's Valley Campaign).

PORT ROYAL (Nova Scotia). At the site of present-day Annapolis Royal on the southern shore of the Annapolis Basin, Nova Scotia, it was the most important outpost of the French in Acadia against colonial New England. The earliest settlement of the name was begun in 1605 by Pierre du Guast, Sieur de Monts, deserted in 1608, reoccupied in 1610, and destroyed by Capt. Samuel Argall from Virginia in 1613, but rebuilt by French settlers. The Huguenot Claude de la Tour brought some Scottish settlers to Acadia in 1630 in behalf of Sir William Alexander, to whom James I of England had granted the region in 1621 (reconfirmed by Charles I in 1625), calling it Nova Scotia. Charles de Menou d'Aulnay obtained control in 1636, moved the fort to the site of the present town in 1643, and began a long rivalry with La Tour's son Charles, who, as governor of the French fort St. Louis at St. John, controlled much of the trade. On d'Aulnay's death in 1650, La Tour had possession until the place was captured by a New England expedition under Maj. Robert Sedgwick in 1654. Returned to the French in 1670, Port Royal in 1684 became the seat of their government in Acadia. It was the center from which they attacked New England shipping and the scene of much illicit trade with New Englanders. Captured by Sir William Phips in 1690, it was restored to the French by the Treaty of Ryswick in 1697. Several times threatened with attack from Boston, the town was finally taken by a great expedition in 1710 under Col. Francis Nicholson and Col. Samuel Vetch (*see* Queen Anne's War). Acadia was ceded to England by the Treaty of Utrecht. England's hold was precarious after the French built Louisburg on Cape Breton Island in 1713. Twice attacked and several times threatened in King George's War, Annapolis Royal (as it was called by the English) lost its strategic importance and also its position as seat of the government with the building of Halifax by the English in 1749.

PORT ROYAL (S.C.). A town on Port Royal Island in southeastern South Carolina. The French diplomat, soldier, and Huguenot leader Jean (Jan) Ribault in May 1562 settled twenty-eight or thirty Frenchmen, almost all Huguenots, on Parris Island where they constructed a fort, named Charlesfort after Charles IX of France, about three miles from the modern town of Port Royal. They named the harbor containing the island Port Royal from its size.

Ribault returned to France for reinforcements, and the settlers, soon discouraged, mutinied, killing their commander; then constructed a tiny vessel and set sail for France. To prevent further trespass in the region, the Spanish built St. Augustine to the south in 1565 and destroyed the French Fort Caroline, built in 1564 on the St. Johns River. Spain then built Fort San Felipe on the site of Port Royal in 1566, introduced farmers and missionaries, and explored the interior as far as the North Carolina mountains and eastern Alabama. Indians expelled the Spaniards and burned their fort in 1576, but in 1577 Spain built Fort San Marcos near the same spot. Sir Francis Drake's burning of St. Augustine in 1586 forced Spain's abandonment that year of Port Royal. The English who under the authority of the Lords Proprietors of Carolina settled South Carolina in 1670 landed at Port Royal, but in a few days moved to the site of Charleston to eliminate the danger of attack by the Spanish. In 1684 fifty-one Scotch Covenanters settled at Port Royal but were driven off by Spaniards in 1686.

The modern town of Port Royal was the center of a major cotton-growing region in the first half of the 19th century. The town was captured Nov. 7, 1861, by a Union fleet, and after the Civil War, Port Royal became mainly a fishing village and resort. The 1980 population was 2,977.

PORTSMOUTH (Va.). A city just west of Norfolk, with a population of 104,577 in 1980; together with Norfolk and Virginia Beach, it is the center of a metropolitan area which includes 799,853 people. Despite its name, the Norfolk Navy Yard is located in Portsmouth and is its largest industry and employer. Other installations include one of the largest naval hospitals and a museum of American naval history.

Portsmouth was built on the site of an Indian village, beginning in 1664. The navy yard was established there as a result of actions during the American Revolution. A Scottish shipbuilder had constructed a boatyard next to Portsmouth before the Revolution began. During the fighting, he remained loyal to England, so his yard plus his other property were confiscated. The "Gosport" shipyard became a Virginia state navy yard and was a major target for British invading forces through the Revolution. The navy yard and town were the scene of heavy fighting during the War of 1812. During the Civil War, the port and navy yard changed hands twice.

PORTSMOUTH, TREATY OF (Sept. 5, 1905). Brought to a close the Russo-Japanese War and gave formal sanction to Japan's supplanting of Russian interests and political influence in Korea and southern Manchuria. It represented Japan's first forward step in territorial expansion on the Asiatic mainland. From the opening of the peace negotiations Russia had agreed to cede the special rights the czarist government held in southern Manchuria, but the conference almost broke up over Japan's demand for the further cession of the island of Sakhalin, north of Japan in the Sea of Okhotsk, and payment of an indemnity. At this point President Theodore Roosevelt, whose earlier intercession had been instrumental in bringing about the conference and for its being held in Portsmouth, N.H., again intervened, bringing such pressure as he could on the Russian and Japanese governments in favor of peace. As a result, Russia agreed to cede the southern half of Sakhalin while refusing to pay any indemnity, and Japan accepted these terms. Roosevelt was widely hailed for his contribution to peace and won the Nobel Peace Prize in 1906, but bitter resentment was created in Japan.

POSSESSIONS, INSULAR. *See* **Insular Possessions.**

POSTAL SERVICE, UNITED STATES. The first proposals for establishment of a post office in America seem to have come from New England in 1638. The general court of Massachusetts in 1639 established Richard Fairbanks' house in Boston as "the place appointed for all letters" to and from overseas. The first intercolonial post was established by Gov. Francis Lovelace of New York in 1673, when monthly trips to Boston were inaugurated. In 1692 the crown issued a grant to Thomas Neale to set up and maintain a post office in the colonies for the term of twenty-one years.

In 1711 the British Parliament reorganized the postal system in all its dominions, including the colonies, and in 1730 Alexander Spotswood, a former governor of Virginia, was named postmaster general. Spotswood's most notable appointment was that of Benjamin Franklin as deputy postmaster at Philadelphia in 1737. In 1753 the crown appointed Franklin and William Hunter of Virginia joint postmasters general for the colonies. During his tenure as a colonial postal official Franklin effected many improvements: he surveyed new postal routes and established overnight delivery between Philadelphia and New York. In 1755 he established a direct packet line from England to New York and, later, to Charleston, S.C.

On May 29, 1775, the newly formed Continental Congress appointed a committee headed by Franklin to set up a postal system independent of the crown, and in July, Congress established such a system with Franklin as its first postmaster general.

Although the Articles of Confederation contained a clause establishing a federal post office, it was not until Oct. 18, 1782, that the Congress passed "An Ordinance for Regulating the Post-Office of the United States of America." When the Constitution went into effect in 1789, establishment of "Post Offices and post Roads" was called for under Article I, Section 8. There were about seventy-five post offices in the thirteen states and 2,400 miles of post roads to serve a population of 3 million (*see also* Post Roads). Legislation in 1789 and 1794 established the post office as a permanent part of the federal government. Before the close of Washington's second term in office, the number of post offices, the number of miles of post road, and the amount of postal revenues had quintupled.

The Post Office Act of 1792 had set postage rates ranging from 6 cents for a single-page letter going as far as 30 miles to 25 cents for one going over 450 miles. The act had also established postal policy, three important facets of which were the following: (1) the post office must be self-supporting; (2) it must use any profit to extend services; and (3) Congress, not the postmaster general, must establish the nation's post roads. At one point Congress actually became involved in constructing post roads, but President James Monroe put a stop to the practice.

In 1794 the first letter carriers appeared in the cities. They were not paid salaries; instead, they collected 2 cents for each letter they delivered, in addition to postage. Joseph Habersham, postmaster general from 1795 to 1801, instituted government-owned coach service between Philadelphia and New York in 1799. By 1813 steamboats had become an important means of transporting the mail. In that year all steamship lines were declared post routes; in 1838 the railroads were also declared post routes. An 1845 law created the contractor system—the hiring of private, or star route, contractors to carry the mail between post offices. (*See* Pony Express.)

From the Jackson years to the eve of the Civil War, the postal service showed a phenomenal growth. Postage stamps made their appearance in the United States shortly after their use was adopted in England in 1840. The first stamps in the United States were used by private expresses and local deliveries. Congress enacted a law on Mar. 3, 1847, authorizing the use of adhesive postage stamps in America for the first time. Put on sale in New York City on July 1, the first stamps were printed by private manufacturers until July 1, 1894, when the printing was transferred to the Bureau of Engraving and Printing. In 1869 the first stamps printed in two colors were issued, a novelty not repeated until 1901. The first commemorative series—featuring Christopher Columbus and the discovery of America—appeared in 1893, and the first airmail stamp (24 cents) was issued in 1918.

During the Civil War the Confederacy established its own postal system, patterned after the U.S. Post Office. Operation of the Confederate postal system was hampered almost from its inception on June 1, 1861. It was difficult to send and receive foreign mail because of the blockading of southern ports by the Union fleet. Another problem was stamps. The first Confederate government postage stamp was issued more than four months after the postal service went into business. It was difficult to find competent printing firms and even more difficult to procure adequate materials for printing.

Originally the post office was subordinate to the Treasury Department, but on Mar. 9, 1829, President Andrew Jackson named William T. Barry postmaster general, the first postmaster general to become a member of a president's cabinet. The postal system became the chief patronage-dispensing agency of the political party in power, which led to many abuses in the century that followed. On Feb. 5, 1969, Postmaster General Winton M. Blount announced that patronage would be removed from the Post Office Department and that no more employees would be appointed with political recommendation. Blount staffed the Post Office Department with executives from business and industry and began a massive introduction of business management techniques.

On Aug. 12, 1970, President Nixon signed the Postal Reorganization Act, which took effect on July 1, 1971. The act created an independent government agency, removing the postmaster general from the president's cabinet and effectively eliminating politics and politicians from the management of postal affairs. It was expected that the Postal Service would become self-supporting by the mid-1980's, but despite increases in postal rates, the agency has been beset by growing financial problems.

POSTAL TELEGRAPH COMPANY. Organized June 21, 1881, with Elisha Gray's harmonic telegraph and a new patented wire as its chief assets. In 1883 John W. Mackay became interested and was elected president. The company was placed in receivership in 1884 and reorganized in 1886 as the Postal Telegraph Cable Company. Through Mackay's business genius it rapidly extended its lines and became the major rival to Western Union. In 1928 it became a part of the International Telephone and Telegraph Corporation, although retaining its own corporate identity.

POST ROADS. The earliest colonial mail carrying, between New York and Boston, and later, between New York and Albany, in the late 17th century, traced routes that became great highways and are still known as the post roads. The Continental Congress began creating post roads during the revolutionary war. To designate a highway as a post road gave the government the monopoly of carrying mail over it; on other roads, anybody might carry it. At first the mail was conveyed on horseback; later it was carried in stagecoaches. But as late as 1825 Postmaster General John McLean reported that "the intelligence of more than half the Nation is conveyed on horseback." In early days horseback travelers often sought the company of the post rider for guidance and protection; later, the mail coach was an important passenger carrier as well. In 1787 connecting stretches of road reaching as far north as Portsmouth and Concord, N.H., as far south as Augusta, Ga., and as far west as Pittsburgh were declared post roads, as were others in the more settled area between; but many of the new routes were not expected to be self-supporting, and so were let out to contractors. Between 1790 and 1829 successive acts of Congress increased the post road mileage from 1,875 to 114,780. Steamboat captains carried many letters in the early days and collected the fees for them, until in 1823 all navigable waters were declared to be post roads, which checked the practice. Private letter-carrying companies after 1842 did much house-to-house mail business in the larger cities; but the postmaster general circumvented them in 1860 by declaring all the streets of New York, Boston, and Philadelphia to be post roads.

POSTS, ARMY SUPPLY. Before the development of modern transportation the War Department found it difficult to provision army posts, many of which were located at great distances from settled communities. To offset high shipping costs, the government advertised its contracts yearly in papers throughout the country, for in that way it hoped to reach some bidder close to a post who would probably submit a reasonable offer. Consequently, merchants everywhere had an opportunity to bid for the privilege of supplying needed items. Not all contracts went to merchants, but they obtained a large percentage because they acquired considerable farm produce in barter for goods; they were familiar with the problem of transporting supplies; and they knew the best markets in which to purchase articles unobtainable locally.

POTASH (potassium carbonate). Together with soda (sodium carbonate) potash has been used from the dawn of history in bleaching textiles and making glass and soap. Soda was principally obtained by leaching the ashes of sea plants, and potash from the ashes of land plants. They were more or less interchangeable, and were only vaguely differentiated before the mid-18th century.

With the advent of gunpowder at the end of the Middle Ages potash found a new use, in the manufacture of saltpeter (in converting calcium nitrate into potassium nitrate), and this was not a use for which soda could be substituted. Potash production was urged on the first settlers to Virginia, where the first factory, established in 1608, was a "glass house," and the first cargo to England included potash. England obtained most of its potash from Russia, but a potash crisis about 1750 led Parliament to remit the duty and the Society of Arts of London to offer premiums for the production of potash in America. In the two decades after 1761 they distributed about £900 and fourteen gold medals for this purpose.

Potash-making became a major U.S. industry. Thomas Jefferson listed potash as the sixth most important export in 1792. After about 1820 New England was replaced by New York as the most important source; by 1840 the center was in Ohio. Potash production was always a by-product industry, following from the need to clear land.

By 1850 potash had become popular as a fertilizer, while forests available for indiscriminate burning were becoming increasingly rare. After 1861 the United States joined most of the rest of the world in dependency on German potash; when World War I cut off this source of supply, frantic efforts produced some domestic potash, notably from some western saline lakes, especially Searles Lake, in the Mojave Desert of California. The wartime urgency directed attention to reports of potash salts having been brought up in drilling for oil. By following these clues, large deposits were found near Carlsbad, N.Mex. After 1931 a number of mines there supplied about 90 percent of the domestic requirement of potash, most of the remainder coming from Searles Lake; 95 percent of this was used in fertilizer.

POTATOES. The so-called Irish potato, a native of the Andes, was introduced into England in the 16th century. A ship is known to have carried potatoes from England to Bermuda in 1613, and in 1621 the governor of Bermuda sent to Gov. Francis Wyatt of Virginia two large chests filled with plants and fruits then unknown to the latter colony, among them potatoes. It seems that their cultivation did not spread widely until a party of Scotch-Irish immigrants brought potatoes with them to Rockingham County, N.H., in 1719. Aroostook, the northernmost county of Maine, began extensive potato growing; Aroostook housewives are said to have been the first, or among the first, to make starch for their white garments by soaking potato pulp in water and then drying it. Eventually Aroostook produced 90 percent of the nation's potato starch. The use of this starch declined greatly in the 20th century, and industrial alcohol appeared as a new means of saving the culls and the surplus.

Sweet potatoes (botanically, wholly unrelated to the Irish tuber) were being cultivated by the American Indians before Columbus. Because of the fact that they could be best grown in the South, and because they give an enormous yield (200 to 400 bushels per acre), they became a favorite vegetable in that section, while remaining unknown to the table in large areas of the North.

By 1980 annual U.S. production of Irish potatoes had reached 301 million hundredweight; production of sweet potatoes in the same year totaled over 14 million hundredweight.

POTOMAC, ARMY OF. The demoralization of the Union forces after the first Battle of Bull Run (July 21, 1861) left Washington, D.C., in an undefended state. Immediately after congressional authorization for the acceptance of volunteers, the Division of the Potomac was created (July 25, 1861), and two days later Gen. George B. McClellan was placed in command. The immediate purpose was to guard the approaches to the Potomac River and thus to protect Washington. The army participated in the Peninsular Campaign, the Seven Days' Battles (June 26–July 2, 1862), at Antietam (Sept. 17, 1862), at Gettysburg, and in the surrender of Robert E. Lee. McClellan was replaced as its commender by Gen. Henry W. Halleck in 1862, who was succeeded by Gen. Ambrose E. Burnside, Gen. Joseph Hooker (1863), Gen. George C. Meade (1863), and Gen. Ullyses S. Grant (1864).

POTOMAC COMPANY. Organized in 1785 with the idea that it would eventually achieve a waterway connection between the Potomac and Ohio rivers. George Washington was one of the incorporators and was elected president. Work was begun that summer on a short canal with locks around the Great Falls of the Potomac, near the present site of Washington, D.C.—the first corporate improvement of navigation for public use in America. This canal was not completed until 1802. By 1808 there were four more short canals between Washington and a point above Harpers Ferry, the longest one 3,814 yards in length. The project was not a paying one, and when the Chesapeake and Ohio Canal Company was organized, the Potomac Company willingly surrendered its charter and rights to the new corporation in 1828.

POTOMAC RIVER. Drains the western slopes of the central Allegheny Mountains of West Virginia into the Chesapeake Bay. Two main streams, the North Branch and the South Branch, and several minor streams unite to form the upper Potomac. A freshwater river for 287 miles, the Potomac below Washington, D.C., is a tidal estuary.

Spaniards probably reached the Potomac estuary before 1570. Capt. John Smith visited, described, and mapped it in 1608. Capt. Samuel Argall, deputy governor of Virginia, and others sailed its waters in the next decade. In the late 1620's Virginia traders frequented its waters and shores. Probably agents of George Calvert before 1632 explored the upper Potomac. After the founding of Maryland in 1634, the Potomac was the early passageway of the colony. In following decades its southern shores were gradually settled by Virginians. But owing to the falls above Washington, D.C., and at Harpers Ferry the upper Potomac was long unimportant. About 1740 Thomas Cresap, militant Marylander, settled at Oldtown (also called Shawanese Oldtown) above the junction of the South Branch and the Potomac, in western Maryland. Slowly the Potomac Valley became a pathway to the Ohio Valley, utilized by the Ohio Company of Virginia, by George Washington, and by Gen. Edward Braddock. Over this route traveled the first settlers to the Monongahela country.

POTSDAM CONFERENCE (July 17–Aug. 2, 1945). The last meeting during World War II of the three allied chiefs of state—President Harry S. Truman, Prime Minister Winston Churchill, and Marshal Joseph Stalin. Germany, but not Japan, had already surrendered. Truman, Churchill (who was replaced during the conference by the new prime minister, Clement Attlee), and Stalin fixed terms of German occupation and reparations and replaced the European Advisory Commission (set up at the Moscow Conference of Foreign Ministers in October 1943) with the Council of Foreign Ministers of the United States, Great Britain, France, and Russia, charged with preparing peace terms for Italy, Romania, Bulgaria, Austria, Hungary, and Finland. Since Russia had not yet declared war on Japan, the Potsdam Declaration (July 26, 1945) was signed by the United States and Great Britain only. The declaration called for Japan to surrender but gave assurances that it would be treated humanely.

POTTAWATOMIE MASSACRE. The murder by free-state men of five proslavery settlers near Dutch Henry's Crossing at Pottawatomie Creek, Franklin County, Kans., on the night of May 24–25, 1856 (*see* Border War). The principal facts became known almost immediately. John Brown, four of his sons, and three others were accused of the murders; warrants were issued, but only one arrest was made (that of James Townsley). But the case never went to trial.

POTTERY. In 1611 "4 potters of earth" were listed among tradesmen being sent to Virginia, and archaeologists have found evidence in Jamestown of pottery made locally by about 1630. In Massachusetts potters began work at Salem in 1635. For nearly two centuries thereafter American pottery remained at a folk level.

Small potteries in the 17th and 18th centuries furnished a local market with lead-glazed red earthenware made from the same native clay as bricks. Red clay was fairly common throughout the colonies, and redware was made from New Hampshire to Georgia.

The arrival of German potters in the 18th century profoundly influenced the character of earthenware in the middle Atlantic colonies and in the interior regions of the South. Germanic pottery was often decorated with multicolored slips, and its designs were scratched through a coating of slip to reveal the red body. The almost simultaneous beginning in the 1720's of the manufacture of blue-decorated, salt-glazed stoneware in Philadelphia and New York established a Rhenish-derived tradition that spread through the Northeast and Midwest after the Revolution. Stoneware differed from redware by being fired to a much higher temperature and only once. In Virginia the "Poor Potter of Yorktown" made English-style stoneware before 1740. Elsewhere in the South ash-glazed and salt-glazed stoneware was fashioned in rural potteries during the 19th and 20th centuries.

Attempts to make "delftware" in New Jersey in 1688; porcelain in Savannah, Ga., in 1736; and Staffordshire-type "queensware" in Charleston, S.C., in 1771 met with little success. However, one of the Charleston queensware potters taught his art to the Wachovia Moravians, who then produced it successfully in an unusual cultural adoption. In Philadelphia, Bonnin and Morris briefly made English-type soft-paste porcelain in 1771–73, to be followed in 1827 by William Ellis Tucker's French-style porcelain.

An influx of British potters after 1825 led to factory production of molded stoneware and Rockingham, Parian, and porcelain ware. In 1828 David Henderson and J. Henderson bought the Jersey Porcelain and Earthenware Company (founded in 1825 in Jersey City) and began making the first pressed earthenware in molds in America. After David Henderson's death in 1845 his workmen drifted to other potting centers, such as Bennington, Vt.; Trenton, Woodbridge, and South Amboy, N.J.; and East Liverpool, Ohio.

Jersey City potters also migrated, first to Woodbridge, then South Amboy, and finally Trenton. Salamander Works was located in Woodbridge from 1836 until the 1850's. It was operated by two Frenchmen, Michel Lefoulon and Henri De Casse. The Congress Pottery and the Swan Hill Pottery in South Amboy were making the same type of ware the potters had made in Jersey City. In Trenton there had been a succession of redware potteries since colonial times, that of J. McCully surviving into the 1850's. By 1863 there were ten potteries in Trenton, and in 1881 of the thirty-eight firms in New Jersey, thirty-five of them were in Trenton.

The other potting center in the United States was in East Liverpool, Ohio, on the Ohio River, where pottery development began in the 1850's and has continued to the present. The same names—William Bloor, John Goodwin, Henry Speeler, James Taylor, and Moses Callear—appeared both in East Liverpool and in Trenton, indicating that the distance from one end of Pennsylvania to the other was no obstacle to the industry even in the 19th century.

In the 1970's, East Liverpool and Trenton continued to be important producers of dinnerware, sanitary ware, and giftware. To these traditional items have been added sophisticated 20th-century technical objects, such as ceramic armor, heat shields on spacecraft, and the magnets that hold refrigerator doors closed.

POULTRY CASE. *See Schechter Poultry Corporation* v. *United States.*

POULTRY INDUSTRY. Poultry includes chickens, turkeys, ducks, geese, and guinea fowl, but chickens represent about 95 percent of all the poultry raised in the United States. A great deal of poultry is now raised in large farm complexes which produce marketable chickens (generally broilers) for freezing and sale over a large area of the country. Nevertheless, poultry farmers are concerned also with providing fresh poultry and fresh eggs to nearby urban markets. The leading states in chicken production in 1980 were California, Georgia, Arkansas, Pennsylvania, and Indiana; and in broiler production Arkansas, Georgia, Alabama, North Carolina, and Mississippi. Minnesota, North Carolina, and California were the principal producers of turkeys. Egg production in 1980 accounted for about $3.3 billion in sales.

POVERTY AND PAUPERISM. Colonial poor laws followed English precedents in assigning responsibility for financing and distributing poor relief to the local authorities. As a general rule, relief was reserved for persons who by birth or by a year or more of residence had established legal settlement in the town or county where assistance was sought. The overthrow of English rule brought little change to the system.

By about 1825 four methods of public assistance were in operation: outdoor relief, that is, assistance to the needy in their own homes; auctioning individual paupers to the lowest bidder; contracting with a private individual to care for a group of paupers; or maintaining all the paupers in a town or county poorhouse. Welfare reformers urged that institutional care in strictly supervised almshouses be substituted for other methods of public relief, since the rigor and discipline of institutional life would reform the inmates and deter impostors from seeking to live at public expense. In practice, almshouses proved to be not reformatories but custodial institutions for the aged, infant, infirm, and handicapped poor. Later in the century numerous efforts were made to put private charity on a businesslike basis. The movement culminated in the 1870's and 1880's with the establishment of charity organization societies, forerunners of family service agencies.

The acknowledged intent of 19th-century welfare reform was to stimulate self-support by making public assistance difficult to obtain and unpleasant to receive. This negative approach was accompanied by positive efforts to prevent pauperism by broadening economic and educational opportunities for the population, such as the Homestead Act of 1862; free, public, tax-supported schools; and state educational institutions for the deaf, blind, and mentally retarded.

Better provision for needy children was an essential step toward breaking the cycle of dependency. Nearly all reformers agreed on the unsuitability of conglomerate almshouses for child rearing and advocated removal of children from poorhouses to environments better suited to their development as responsible citizens. Another course that was advocated was to provide a surviving parent—most often a widowed mother—with an allowance so that she could maintain her children in their own home under her care. This was the method endorsed by the first White House Conference on the Care of Dependent Children, held in 1909, which opposed the breakup of homes solely because of poverty.

The conference recommended that mothers' aid be financed by private charity rather than by public funds, but the mothers' pension laws adopted in forty-five states in the twenty years after 1911 authorized payments from money raised by taxation. The laws were permissive rather than mandatory and were so administered that only mothers deemed "fit" and "proper" received aid. Nevertheless, by the 1920's almost as many dependent children were being cared for in their own homes as in institutions, and many more than in foster homes. This revolutionary change was expanded under the Social Security Act of 1935.

Even before 1929 it became apparent to many that the want and insecurity of the poor were attributable less to personal failings of the sufferers than to inequality in the distribution of wealth and income and the haphazard operation of the economic machine. The experience of the Great Depression embedded these convictions in the consciousness of a large segment of the American people. The depression shattered the myth that private charity could tide over the deserving poor in bad times. It also required state and federal governments to become much more involved in welfare activities than ever before. Between 1930 and 1933 states joined local governments in efforts to deal with unemployment relief. When President Franklin D. Roosevelt took office, the federal government was already lending states and cities funds that provided 80 percent of all aid to the unemployed. After 1933 federal agencies made emergency grants to states and municipalities for cash and work relief. Beginning in 1935 the Works Progress Administration (WPA), the New Deal's major relief program, provided jobs for an average of 2 million persons a month for six years.

The Social Security Act of 1935 sought to provide a long-term answer to problems of economic insecurity. It included a national system of old-age insurance financed by contributions from employers and employees; state-administered unemployment insurance financed by a federal payroll tax; grants-in-aid to states for federally approved, but state-administered, programs for maternal and child health; aid to the blind; aid to the aged not eligible for federal old-age insurance; and aid to dependent children.

Numerous reforms strengthened the position of organized workers and installed built-in stabilizers in the economy. Prosperity during and after World War II encouraged the belief that expanding productivity would solve the problems of poverty and dependency. In the late 1950's, however, pockets of poverty were discovered in such areas as Appalachia, and government reports called attention to a "low income population" immune to the benefits of economic growth.

In 1959, 40 million Americans, constituting 22 percent of the population, lived in "poverty" as defined by the federal government. By 1980 according to federal agencies, the number of persons living in poverty had declined to about 25 million, or 11.6 percent of the total population. The federal poverty index used to distinguish the poor from the nonpoor was the minimum income (periodically adjusted) deemed necessary for an individual or a family of specified size to obtain a subsistence level of food and other essential goods and services. In 1979 the poverty line was set at $3,689 for an individual and $7,412 for a "nonfarm" family of four. The population living in poverty was composed mainly of children under sixteen years of age, persons sixty-five years of age or over, and women aged sixteen to sixty-four; 66 percent of the poverty population was white, 31 percent black.

President Johnson, in signing the Economic Opportunity Act of 1964, launched his administration's war on poverty; the act focused on disadvantaged youth and provided training to equip them for work; it also incorporated programs to encourage involvement of the poor, organized and assisted by federally paid advocates, in efforts for community betterment.

Despite the officially recorded decline in poverty, welfare rolls and expenditures increased steeply in the 1960's and 1970's. By 1980 the nation's welfare rolls exceeded 15 million persons, over 11 million of whom were aided through the aid to families with dependent children (AFDC) program. It has been widely predicted that President Reagan's budget cuts in the early 1980's would result in increased poverty.

POVERTY POINT. A site in Louisiana, peculiarly representative of an Archaic-stage prehistoric culture that once existed in the area. In addition to typical Archaic stone projectile points, grooved stone axes, adzes, celts, tubular pipes, and steatite and sandstone vessels, the site also contains some of the most impressive aboriginal earthworks and mounds in North America, constructed between 1300 and 200 B.C.

POWDER RIVER CAMPAIGN. *See* **Sioux Wars.**

POWELL CASE (1967). Adam Clayton Powell, a veteran member of the U.S. House of Representatives, was denied membership in the House on the grounds of alleged misconduct before his reelection in 1966. Reelected in a special election in April 1967, Powell chose to challenge the House's decision in U.S. courts. At issue was the question whether the House could deny membership on any grounds other than those stipulated in the Constitution, namely, age, citizenship, and residence. In 1969 in *Powell* v. *McCormack* the Supreme Court ruled in his favor, declaring that the House had exceeded its constitutional authority.

POWELL'S EXPLORATIONS (1869, 1871–72). John Wesley Powell, professor of geology at the Illinois State Normal University, led two major expeditions down the Colorado River. For the first expedition in 1869, Powell organized a company of eleven men, and in May, aboard four boats, they entered the Colorado at the Green River, in western Wyoming. The expedition explored the length of the Green and Colorado rivers to the mouth of the Virgin River, in southeastern Nevada. The party did not emerge until Aug. 29, after a journey of 900 miles. Powell reported the expedition to Congress, which in 1870 appropriated funds for the exploration of adjacent rivers and territories. The second expedition (1871–72) included such eminent geologists as Grove Karl Gilbert and Clarence Dutton and the archaeologist William H. Holmes. The collaboration of these men did much to formulate the basic principles of structural geology. As a result of the expedition's success, Powell was named director of the Survey of the Rocky Mountain Region in 1877. Two years later all local surveys were merged in the U.S. Geological Survey, and Powell was made chief of this bureau in 1881. Among Powell's publications of these explorations are *The Exploration of the Colorado River of the West* (1875) and *The Geology of the Eastern Portion of the Uinta Mountains* (1876).

POWELL'S VALLEY. The most westerly of the long narrow valleys in southwestern Virginia and northeastern Tennessee. It leads directly to Cumberland Gap. In 1750 Thomas Walker explored the valley (*see* Loyal Land Company), and one of his party, Ambrose Powell, cut his name on a tree, hence the name. The first cabin in the valley was built in 1768 by Joseph Martin. There Daniel Boone's party was turned back, in 1773, from Kentucky after the Indians had killed his son and others. Through Powell's Valley passed the land route to Kentucky and the Wilderness Road. It was traversed by thousands of caravans.

POWER COMMISSION, FEDERAL. *See* **Federal Agencies.**

POWERS, SEPARATION OF. One of the fundamental constitutional principles under which governmental powers are vested in three different branches of government: the legislative, the executive, and the judicial. While the idea of separation of powers may be traced back to Aristotle, it was Charles de Secondat, Baron de Montesquieu, who first formulated it as a doctrine for safeguarding liberty in his *Spirit of Laws* (*L'Esprit des Lois,* 1748). A similar idea was expressed by Sir William Blackstone in his *Commentaries on the Laws of England* (1765–69). These writings were well known to the Founding Fathers. In the tenth resolve of the Declaration of Rights adopted by the First Continental Congress in 1774, the importance of the principle of separation of powers was clearly recognized. When the original state constitutions were drafted during the period of the Revolution, considerable attention was given to the application of the principle. By the time of the framing of the U.S. Constitution in 1787, the doctrine was accepted without question by the national leaders. Yet it was not written directly into the Constitution. Rather, it was incorporated in it through the "distributing clauses," as the opening statements of the first three articles of the Constitution are called.

POWHATAN CONFEDERACY. A 17th-century chiefdom among the Algonkin-speaking Indians of the Virginia coastal plain. Chief Powhatan (properly the name of his principal village) inherited dominion over seven local groups. Thereafter he extended his sway north and south on the tidewater plain and across Chesapeake Bay to its eastern shore, until it embraced some thirty tributary groups, having an estimated population of 9,000. The center of Powhatan's domain lay on the James, Pamunkey, and Mattaponi rivers. Farmers who supplemented their agricultural produce through fishing, hunting, and gathering, they dwelt in villages that were often fortified; the largest had over 200 inhabitants.

The early settlers were dependent for sustenance on the purchase or seizure of Indian foodstuffs, and during the "starving time" in 1609 some were lodged with the Indians. Powhatan was treated by the English as minor, barbaric royalty, and the marriage of his daughter Pocahontas to John Rolfe was instrumental in concluding peace between him and the English. With the death of Powhatan in 1618, power passed by turns to Opechancanough, who in 1622 led his people into sudden war against the colonists. The colonists launched merciless reprisals until 1631. In 1644 the aged chieftain essayed a last, desperate campaign that ended in his defeat and death. Thereafter, the Virginia colony, in an early form of indirect rule, incorporated the chiefdom in subordinate status. In the last official act of the Tributary chiefs, as they were by then known, a delegation participated in the Treaty of Albany (1722) with the Iroquois.

***POWHATAN* INCIDENT** (April 1861). President Abraham Lincoln determined not to give up the two remaining federal forts in southern territory—Fort Sumter at Charleston, S.C., and Fort Pickens at Pensacola, Fla. Relief expeditions were ordered to the forts and sailed from New York on Apr. 8. Meanwhile, Secretary of State William H. Seward, in an attempt to maintain his supremacy in Lincoln's cabinet, secretly ordered the warship *Powhatan* to Fort Pickens instead of Fort Sumter, and secured Lincoln's signature to the order. Controversy arose between Seward and Secretary of the Navy Gideon Welles over the Pickens relief expedition, and Lincoln ordered the *Powhatan* on Apr. 5 to join the expedition to Sumter. Seward telegraphed David Dixon Porter, commander of the *Powhatan,* over his own signature, but the ship was already on its way to Fort Pickens when the telegram was received. Porter declined to obey the order over Seward's name, stating that the presidential order took precedence. The Pickens expedition was successful, but without the *Powhatan*'s firepower, the relief of Sumter failed.

POWNALL, FORT (Maine). Named after Gov. Thomas Pownall of Massachusetts Bay, who was largely responsible for its erection in 1759. This fort, situated on the Penobscot River near what is now Fort Point, was one of the most defensible strongholds occupied by the British during the French and Indian War.

POWWOW. A word drawn from an Algonkin stem referring to magical ritual, it appears first in Massachusetts in 1624, used in this sense. By 1812 the meaning in English had changed, and the word was used to designate any gathering of American Indians, whether ceremonial or social.

PRAGMATISM. A worldwide philosophic movement that was most important in the United States in the late 19th and early 20th centuries. Pragmatism arose as the most sophisticated attempt to reconcile science and religion in the wake of the widespread scholarly acceptance of Darwinian biology. The pragmatists argued that the truth of an idea lay primarily in its ability satisfactorily to orient individuals to the world of which they were a part, but also in its consistency with other ideas and its aesthetic appeal; ideas were plans of action and would be deemed true if action in accordance with them "worked" in the long run. One center, at the University of Chicago, was led by John Dewey, who later taught at Columbia, and included James H. Tufts, George Herbert Mead, and Addison W. Moore. The other center, with its nucleus at Harvard University, included Charles S. Peirce, William James, Josiah Royce, and Clarence Lewis.

PRAIRIE. A geographical region in the United States whose eastern border is an irregular line running southeast through Minnesota, Wisconsin, and western Indiana and then extending southwest through Illinois, Missouri, Oklahoma, and Texas. Its western boundary merges into the Great Plains. The prairie is a vast area of grassland.

PRAIRIE DOGS. Burrowing rodents that infested the Plains in immense numbers. Since they lived underground in large colonies, threw up craters of earth at the surface of their burrows (excluding rain), and lived on grass, they destroyed vast areas of good grazing land. Cattlemen considered them pests for this reason and also because horses often broke their legs by stepping in their holes. Farmers and ranchers have greatly reduced the number of prairie dogs mainly by poisoning. Protected colonies can be found in South Dakota, Wyoming, Oklahoma, and Texas.

PRAIRIE DU CHIEN (Wis.). Originally a French settlement commanding the western end of the Fox-Wisconsin Waterway from the Great Lakes to the Mississippi River. The site was first visited in 1673 by Louis Jolliet and Jacques Marquette. About 1685 Nicolas Perrot, a French officer, built Fort St.-Nicolas. In the 18th century the place acquired its name from a Fox Indian chief named Alim (meaning "dog," whom the French called Le Chien). The settlement of French traders and voyageurs began about the middle of the 18th century. After the cession in 1763 of all this region to the British by the Treaty of Paris, their traders mingled with the French, and during the expansion of the fur trade Prairie du Chien became an important mart. During the American Revolution a small fort was built by the British at Prairie du Chien, from which a raid was undertaken against the Spanish and Americans at St. Louis and Cahokia, in southwestern Illinois. This fort was burned to prevent it from falling into the hands of the Americans and Spanish, who made a retaliatory raid. In 1781 three French-Canadian settlers of Prairie du Chien purchased the site from the Indians. By the end of the century it contained about 100 houses.

On the outbreak of the War of 1812 all Americans were driven from the region, and the British enrolled the Indians in their forces. In 1814 Gen. William Clark came up the river from St. Louis and built Fort Shelby at Prairie du Chien, raising the first American flag in what is now Wisconsin. The British sent an expedition from the Straits of Mackinac to dislodge the Americans. The Americans were defeated, and Fort Shelby became Fort McKay.

After the Treaty of Ghent (1814) Prairie du Chien was occupied permanently by the Americans. Fort Crawford was built in 1816 and American traders and settlers flocked thither. In 1817 the first priest came up the river, and about the same time the first school was begun. In 1818 the town became the seat of Crawford County.

Prairie du Chien became a steamboat port in the 19th century, the first steamboat going up the river in 1823, and in 1857 the railroad from Milwaukee entered the city. After the Civil War, the development of a variety of industries—the manufacture of fertilizer, cement, woolens, and building fixtures and butter production—led to the granting of a city charter in 1872. The city has remained small, its population in 1980 being only 5,859.

PRAIRIE DU CHIEN, INDIAN TREATY AT (Aug. 19, 1825). The two great tribes of Chippewa and Sioux had been enemies for over a century and had drawn neighboring tribes into the feud. In 1824 a deputation to Washington, D.C., requested the federal government to set up boundaries between the tribal lands. The treaty of 1825 was called for that purpose. Gen. William Clark of St. Louis and Gov. Lewis Cass of the Michigan Territory were the American commissioners. More than 1,000 tribal chiefs assembled. The Philadelphia artist, J. O. Lewis, was present, and painted many chiefs from life. The treaty contained no cession of land. Boundaries were established, which the several tribes agreed to respect. The parties to the treaty were Sioux, Chippewa, Sauk and Fox, Potawatomi, Winnebago, and Iowa.

PRAIRIE FIRES. In the autumn a stroke of lightning, a match carelessly dropped, sparks from a locomotive, or the burning wads from the discharge of a shotgun were enough to start a blazing fire that moved across the prairie with the speed of the wind. Sometimes entire settlements were devastated. So intense was the heat from a prairie fire in South Dakota in 1871 that the wall of fire leaped across the Vermillion and James rivers. The settlers in Wells County, N.Dak., in the 1880's observed that prairie fires starting far to the north would burn six weeks or more. Very little could be accomplished fighting a head fire, but side fires could be put out. It was the unwritten law that at the first word of warning every able-bodied man was to appear with fire-fighting equipment to help extinguish the blaze. When the prairies were settled and the land broken, prairie fires disappeared.

PRAIRIE GROVE, BATTLE AT (Dec. 7, 1862). Also known as the Battle of Fayetteville or Battle of Illinois Creek. After the Confederate defeat at Corinth, Miss., Confederate Gen. John Pemberton ordered Gen. Theophilus Holmes to send Thomas Hindman's Arkansas troops to Vicksburg, Miss. Resentful, Hindman planned to attack the Union forces under Gen. James Blunt before leaving the state. Learning that Gen. Francis Herron was coming up to reinforce Blunt at Prairie Grove, Ark., Hindman decided to destroy Herron first and then engage Blunt. Confederate Gen. John Marmaduke's cavalry was successful against Herron, but when Hindman advanced his infantry, instead of attacking he went into a defensive position. This tactic allowed Blunt to join Herron, and with superior numbers they forced Hindman to retreat in defeat to Van Buren, Ark.

PRAIRIE SCHOONER. A large wagon used for long-distance travel and freight transport in the 19th century. Originally, the wagon was made with the sides of the box sloping outward. Arching wooden bows supported a canvas cover. Seen in the distance, the vehicle so resembled a ship at sea as to suggest the name. The descendant of the old Conestoga wagon, it was first brought into common use in the Santa Fe trade after 1821; it was later used by settlers. The prairie schooner was usually drawn by three to six yoke of oxen or by four to six mules.

PREEMPTION. The right of first purchase, a significant aspect of U.S. land law in the 19th century. In U.S. early land policy, settlement was restricted to surveyed areas, and the surveys were not made far in advance of demand (*see* Public Lands, Survey of). Inevitably, settlers pushed farther into the unsurveyed territory. Since all lands when first brought on the market were put up at auction, the threat of a government sale hung over squatters (*see* Public Land Sales).

The squatters early pressured Congress to grant them the right of preempting their claims in advance of the land sale, so the settlers would not be obliged to bid for their land against speculators. Congress granted preemption rights to sixteen special groups from 1801 to 1830, and between 1830 and 1840, it gave preemption rights on five occasions to all squatters on surveyed lands. In 1841 a general law was passed, which gave the preemption right for up to 160 acres to any squatter who was then located on or in the future might settle on surveyed public lands. This act, although a victory for the West, by no means satisfied the settlers on the frontier. It applied to neither Indian reservations nor unsurveyed lands; it did not provide for free grants to actual settlers; and it retained the minimum price of $1.25 per acre.

The 1841 law remained in effect for fifty years, but became subject to serious abuses. In areas where the size of a squatter's claim to public land was limited, predatory interests found it possible to acquire large tracts by employing "floaters" to preempt land for them. False swearing, bribery of the land officers, laxity of supervision, and general western approval of such practices made evasion of the law easy. In 1891, when sentiment against the monopolization of the public lands had become sufficiently aroused, the preemption law was repealed. (*See also* Homestead Movement.)

PREFERENTIAL VOTING. A method of voting under which the voter expresses a first choice, second choice, and sometimes third and further choices among the candidates nominated. It is frequently used as a substitute for primary elections. It is one feature of the Hare system of proportional representation and is also used in several different forms for majority elections of individual officials.

PREPAREDNESS. The name of a campaign to strengthen U.S. military forces after the outbreak of World War I in Europe. Early leaders in the movement were Theodore Roosevelt and Gen. Leonard Wood; both men favored some form of universal military service. During 1914 and 1915, two organizations came into being that thereafter played a great part in the preparedness campaign: the National Security League and the League to Enforce Peace. Initially, the Wilson administration was decidedly cool to the preparedness agitation. As time passed the president apparently decided that preparedness was a logical corollary to his policy of attempting to compel the combatants to respect American rights.

PRESBYTERIANISM. The name of the Presbyterian church is derived from its government by a hierarchy of church courts composed of both teaching (clerical) and ruling (lay) elders, or presbyters. Doctrinally, Presbyterian churches are part of the Reformed tradition founded by John Calvin in the 16th century. Their most widely accepted standard is the Westminster Confession of Faith, drafted in 1646. The theology, influenced chiefly by the Puritan tradition, stresses the role of the divine decrees, the use of the covenant system, the identification of the Lord's Day with the Christian sabbath, and the subjective operation of grace.

Francis Mekamie, called the founder of American Presbyterianism, organized the Presbytery of Philadelphia in 1706. By 1716 the church was large enough to form itself into a synod representing four presbyteries and thirty ministers. A conflict between New England and Scotch-Irish clergymen concerned the terms of subscription to the Westminster standard; it was settled by a compromise in 1729 that adopted a looser form of subscription. The church was also active in the Great Awakening. The center of Presbyterian evangelical Calvinism was the Log College, established by William Tennent. Its graduates were active revivalists and tended to form their own ecclesiastical party. Gilbert Tennent, the son of William, was the leader of the small revival that swept the middle colonies in the 1730's and was later a leading supporter of the evangelistic tours of George Whitefield. As the revival grew, so did tension between the two parties in the church. In 1741 Gilbert Tennent preached the so-called Nottingham sermon, "The Danger of an Unconverted Ministry," which heralded the coming division of the church into the Synod at New York, or New Side, and the Synod of Philadelphia, or Old Side. A reconciliation occurred only after the New Side made diplomatic advances to the Old Side pastors. But the controversy lay just beneath the surface, and the theological issues raised by evangelicalism were to contribute to the later Old School–New School schism.

Although the spread of Presbyterianism was initially hampered by its insistence on a learned ministry, its high standards enabled it to become the educator of the West. Presbyterians were the great college founders of the region and, in the period before the Civil War, exercised the greatest cultural influence on that emerging society. In 1801 the Presbyterians joined the Congregationalists in the Plan of Union, to promote a joint endeavor in the West. Although the abrogation of the Plan of Union in 1837 and the division of the church into New School and Old School groups were ostensibly over theological issues, it appears that the question of race was a hidden item on the agenda of the southern delegations. The New School Presbyterians were unable to maintain unity after 1857, when the small number of southern evangelicals withdrew. The Old School remained united until hostilities actually began. After the Civil War, Old School and New School factions in both the North and South reunited, leaving the main division in Presbyterianism on regional lines.

Since the Civil War the Presbyterian churches have been troubled by theological controversies. The most serious was the fundamentalist-modernist controversy in the early part of the 20th century. Since the 1960's the Presbyterian church, at least in the North, has moved toward greater theological comprehensiveness. Following the merger of the Presbyterian Church in the United States of America and the United Presbyterian Church of North America in 1958, the new church began examining its confessional standards. The result of its deliberations was the adoption of the Book of Confessions, which added to the traditional Westminster standard such traditional symbols as the Apostles Scots Confession of 1560 and such modern statements of faith as the Barmen Declaration (1934) and the Confession of 1967. Although some lay groups protested the new position, it seemed to be firmly established in the mid-1970's. In 1980 there were eight principal Presbyterian denominations in the United States, with a combined membership of 3,615,742. The largest was the United Presbyterian Church in the U.S.A. (2,520,367 members).

PRESERVATION MOVEMENT. The historic-preservation movement in the United States began in 1850 when New York State became the first agency to preserve officially a historic house as a museum: the Hasbrouck House, George Washington's headquarters at Newburgh, N.Y. Although there was national enthusiasm to memorialize the first president, Congress rejected three proposals that the U.S. government acquire Mount Vernon, Washington's estate in Virginia. In 1858 a private group, the Mount Vernon Ladies' Association of the Union, rescued the estate.

The first federally purchased historic house was the Custis-Lee Mansion in Arlington, Va., bought in 1883. The first federal park tract protected for historic value was Casa Grande, an excavated pueblo in Arizona that was acquired by authorization of Congress in 1889.

The passage of the Antiquities Act in 1906 authorized the president to declare as national monuments historic landmarks, historic and prehistoric structures, and other objects of historic or scientific value located on lands owned or controlled by the government. The Historic Sites Act of 1935 declared it a national policy to preserve for public use historic sites, buildings, and objects of national significance. The National Trust for Historic Preservation of 1949 authorized the establishment of a nonprofit, educational corporation to further the purpose of the Historic Sites Act.

The National Historic Preservation Act of 1966 acknowledged that governmental and nongovernmental preservation programs up to that time were inadequate to preserve the national heritage, and stated that although the major preservation burdens were borne by the private sector, the federal government should accelerate its activities and give maximum encouragement to the National Trust for Historic Preservation and to local and state governmental efforts. The preservation program of the National Park Service was strengthened. Also, the National Register for Historic Places —which lists districts, sites, buildings, structures, and objects of local, regional, state, and national significance—was expanded. The act also authorized grants to the states for 50 percent of the cost of preparing statewide historic-preservation plans and historic-site surveys and gave assistance to preservation projects.

Since 1850 historic preservation has developed from a pastime to a national movement. The National Trust sets national standards and provides direction for its members and the general public. In 1980 it had about 165,000 members.

PRESIDENT. A forty-four-gun American frigate, under the command of John Rodgers, it fired the first shot of the War of 1812, in a chase of the *Belvidera.* After being blockaded in New York for a year, the *President,* under Stephen Decatur, attempted to escape to sea on Jan. 14, 1815, but was overtaken, first by the British frigate *Endymion,* which it finally crippled, and then by the frigates *Tenedos* and *Pomone.* Surrounded by superior forces, Decatur, himself twice wounded, surrendered. The *President* was taken to Spithead, England, but never saw service under the British flag.

PRESIDENT. The highest office of the nation, created by the U.S. Constitution. The Constitution vests the executive power in the president and charges him to take care that the laws are faithfully executed. He is also commander in chief of the armed forces. Some of his constitutional powers, such as the veto, pertain to the legislative process. Much of a president's authority is delegated to him by statute. In almost every instance of national emergency—a devastating depression, a major war—presidents have exceeded their constitutional and legal powers, and such actions have generally been legitimized through public approval.

The presidency is an evolving, rather than a static, institution, and it now differs significantly from what was envisioned for it by its founders. Among the factors that have influenced its development are the following: (1) democratization of the means of nominating and electing the chief executive, lending substance to the claim that he is the only official elected by all the people; (2) ambiguity in the constitutional phrases defining presidential power and duties; (3) expansion in the role of the government, and the consequent creation of a vast bureaucracy under the president; (4) recurring periods of emergency and peril, during which the executive power seems to thrive and expand; and (5) the rise of the United States as a major world power and the preoccupation with foreign policy in the political arena.

President	Party	Inauguration	Vice-president	
George Washington	Federalist	1789	John Adams	(1789–97)
John Adams	Federalist	1797	Thomas Jefferson	(1797–1801)
Thomas Jefferson	Democratic-Republican	1801	Aaron Burr	(1801–05)
			George Clinton	(1805–1809)
James Madison	Democratic-Republican	1809	George Clinton	(1809–12)
			Elbridge Gerry	(1813–14)
James Monroe	Democratic-Republican	1817	Daniel D. Tompkins	(1817–25)
John Quincy Adams	Democratic-Republican	1825	John C. Calhoun	(1825–29)
Andrew Jackson	Democratic	1829	John C. Calhoun	(1829–32)
			Martin Van Buren	(1833–37)
Martin Van Buren	Democratic	1837	Richard M. Johnson	(1837–41)
William Henry Harrison	Whig	1841	John Tyler	(1841)
John Tyler[1]	Whig	1841		
James K. Polk	Democratic	1845	George M. Dallas	(1845–49)
Zachary Taylor	Whig	1849	Millard Fillmore	(1849–50)
Millard Fillmore[1]	Whig	1850		
Franklin Pierce	Democratic	1853	William R. King	(1853)
James Buchanan	Democratic	1857	John C. Breckinridge	(1857–61)
Abraham Lincoln	Republican	1861	Hannibal Hamlin	(1861–65)
			Andrew Johnson	(1865)
Andrew Johnson[1]	Union	1865		
Ulysses S. Grant	Republican	1869	Schuyler Colfax	(1869–73)
			Henry Wilson	(1873–75)

President	Party	Inauguration	Vice-president	
Rutherford B. Hayes	Republican	1877	William A. Wheeler	(1877–81)
James A. Garfield	Republican	1881	Chester A. Arthur	(1881)
Chester A. Arthur[1]	Republican	1881		
Grover Cleveland	Democratic	1885	Thomas A. Hendricks	(1885)
Benjamin Harrison	Republican	1889	Levi P. Morton	(1889–93)
Grover Cleveland	Democratic	1893	Adlai E. Stevenson	(1893–97)
William McKinley	Republican	1897	Garret A. Hobart	(1897–99)
			Theodore Roosevelt	(1901)
Theodore Roosevelt[1]	Republican	1901	Charles W. Fairbanks	(1905–09)
William Howard Taft	Republican	1909	James S. Sherman	(1909–12)
Woodrow Wilson	Democratic	1913	Thomas R. Marshall	(1913–21)
Warren G. Harding	Republican	1921	Calvin Coolidge	(1921–23)
Calvin Coolidge[1]	Republican	1923	Charles G. Dawes	(1925–29)
Herbert Hoover	Republican	1929	Charles Curtis	(1929–33)
Franklin D. Roosevelt	Democratic	1933	John N. Garner	(1933–41)
			Henry A. Wallace	(1941–45)
			Harry S. Truman	(1945)
Harry S. Truman[1]	Democratic	1945	Alben W. Barkley	(1949–53)
Dwight D. Eisenhower	Republican	1953	Richard M. Nixon	(1953–61)
John F. Kennedy	Democratic	1961	Lyndon B. Johnson	(1961–63)
Lyndon B. Johnson[1]	Democratic	1963	Hubert H. Humphrey	(1965–69)
Richard M. Nixon	Republican	1969	Spiro T. Agnew	(1969–73)
			Gerald R. Ford	(1973–74)
Gerald R. Ford[2]	Republican	1974	Nelson A. Rockefeller	(1974–77)
James E. Carter	Democratic	1977	Walter Mondale	(1977–81)
Ronald Reagan	Republican	1981	George Bush	(1981–)

[1]Vice-presidents who succeeded to the presidency upon the death of an incumbent president.
[2]Vice-president who succeeded to the presidency upon the resignation of a president.

The office of president is also subject to the influence of personality. Throughout history a number of broad presidential types have emerged. One is a literalist president, who functions in close obedience to the letter of the Constitution and the traditional separation of powers. At the other end of the continuum is a strong president. Such a president views his powers with a maximum liberality and, in the process of using them, frequently incites constitutional controversies; he establishes new precedents and breaks old ones. Most modern commentators suggest that national demands and expectations push a president more and more to adopt the strong role.

PRESIDENT, WAR POWERS OF. *See* **War Powers of the President.**

PRESIDENTIAL DISABILITY. Article II, Section 1, of the Constitution provides that if the president is unable to discharge the powers and duties of his office, they shall devolve on the vice-president. A number of presidents have been disabled for periods of time (James A. Garfield, Woodrow Wilson, Dwight D. Eisenhower). There were no prescribed procedures for establishing such inability or for determining when it had ceased—and without such procedures a vice-president might be reluctant to take action for fear he would be viewed as a usurper and provoke a constitutional crisis. But some presidents reached informal understandings with their vice-presidents on this issue. In 1967 the Twenty-fifth Amendment was adopted to deal, at least in part, with this problem. Disability extends not only to physical illness but also to mental illness or to a president who is missing or captured by an enemy. The determination of such disability can be made either by the president himself or by the vice-president acting with a majority of the cabinet or some "other body as Congress may by law provide." In such cases the vice-president is to serve as acting president. The end of such disability can be determined by the president or by Congress.

PRESIDENTIAL ELECTIONS. *See* **Campaigns, Presidential; Election of the President; Electoral College.**

PRESIDENTIAL EXEMPTION FROM SUBPOENA. Thomas Cooper, scientist and political philosopher, criticized acts of President John Adams and was tried for violation of the sedition act in 1800. Cooper asked the court to issue a subpoena for Adams so that he could prove the truth of the allegedly seditious statements. Justice Samuel Chase declared the attempt to subpoena him an improper and indecent act. During the trial of Aaron Burr in 1807, Chief Justice John Marshall declared that the president was subject to subpoena because no distinction was made as to persons subject to such compulsory processes of the Court. Marshall issued the subpoena, but President Thomas Jefferson flatly refused to appear. There was no way of forcing his appearance, and a precedent was established to the effect that the president could not be subpoenaed into court against his will. In 1974 the Supreme Court faced the issue of whether or not President Richard M. Nixon could be compelled by a subpoena *duces tecum* to produce for use in a criminal case the tape-recorded conversations that ultimately played such an important role in his downfall (*see* Nixon, Resignation of; Watergate). The Court, in *United States* v. *Nixon,* 418 U.S. 683 (1974), decided that the president could, under this particular set of facts, be subpoenaed.

PRESIDENTIAL MESSAGES. Article II, Section 3, of the Constitution charges the president to give Congress information on the state of the Union, and tradition has dictated that he do so annually. The Budget and Accounting Act of 1921 imposes on the president the duty of presenting an annual executive budget to Congress, and the Full Employment Act of 1946 requires an annual economic report.

PRESIDENTIAL SUCCESSION. Article II, Section 1, of the U.S. Constitution provides for the succession of the vice-president to the presidency of the United States in case of the death or resignation of the president or his removal from office. Before ratification of the Twenty-fifth Amendment in 1967, there was no clearly defined constitutional line of succession if the vice-president should succeed to the presidency and then die, but Congress, in 1947, had provided by law for such an eventuality by establishing a line of succession. The speaker of the House of Representatives was placed next in line after the vice-president; next came the president pro tempore of the Senate; and then the members of the cabinet, beginning with the secretary of state. An earlier act (1886) had placed the members of the cabinet in line after the vice-president.

The Twenty-fifth Amendment provides a means of filling the vice-presidential post in case of a vacancy: the president nominates a vice-president, subject to confirmation by Congress (majority vote in both chambers). If so confirmed, the new vice-president would then be eligible for succession to the presidency. This amendment was first used in 1973 upon the resignation of Spiro Agnew.

The Twentieth Amendment, ratified in 1933, deals with another possible problem: if the president-elect dies or fails to qualify for office by the date of the inauguration, the vice-president-elect shall act as president. Furthermore, if neither the president-elect nor the vice-president-elect qualifies, Congress is empowered to declare who shall act as president.

PRESIDENTIAL TITLE. The title for the new chief executive of the United States was the subject of some controversy at the Constitutional Convention of 1787. The contest over titles was continued into the First Congress. A Senate committee, after deciding that the ambassadorial "his excellency" was too paltry for the ruler of a young republic, urged that the chief executive be addressed as "His Highness, the President of the United States of America and Protector of their Liberties," and it is stated that this was the title George Washington preferred. The more republican House of Representatives remained obdurate, and the Senate was "desirous of preserving harmony with the House of Representatives" and agreed that "the present address be 'To the President of the United States,' without addition of title."

PRESIDIO. A Spanish institution established primarily to hold the frontiers of Spain's territory in America against foreign aggressors and to protect the missions. Presidios were forts or posts where soldiers lived with their families, cultivating the surrounding land.

PRESQUE ISLE, FORT. Constructed on the shore of Lake Erie at the site of present-day Erie, Pa., under the French command of Capt. Pierre Paul Marin, in 1753. After the French abandoned Fort Presque Isle on Aug. 13, 1759, the British utilized it as a frontier outpost. During the general Indian uprising of 1763 (*see* Pontiac's War), the Indians captured the fort on June 22 and burned it. A U.S. fortification, designated as Presque Isle, was erected nearby in the summer of 1795.

PRESS, FREEDOM OF THE. *See* **Freedom of the Press.**

PRESS GANG. The British government never devised an orderly procedure for impressment, or conscription, for naval service. In practice, captains of short-handed men-of-war sent armed details to scour English waterfronts or board merchantmen to exercise direct and immediate conscription. Their use in colonial ports was a minor cause of the American Revolution; it was a major cause of the War of 1812.

PRESSING TO DEATH. According to English judicial practice, if a person accused of a felony contumaciously refused to plead either guilty or not guilty and so blocked a trial, weights might be placed on the person's chest until a plea was entered. The practice was rare in the American colonies, the only recorded instance of it being the case of Giles Corey, who was accused of witchcraft in Salem in 1692.

PRESSURE GROUPS. Organized interests that seek to persuade governmental officials to adopt policies favorable to the group's goals. Most political goals of pressure groups are relatively narrow—for example, the American Petroleum Institute's pressure for oil depletion deductions on taxes. Groups do pursue policies that mix collective benefits for large segments of society with selective benefits for the pressure group. Since their activities have negative implications in a democracy, pressure groups frequently try to minimize their visibility by using soft-sell tactics, by claiming to protect the public interest, and by obscuring interest continuity through reliance on *ad hoc* groups for different issues. About half of the national associations are business groups, and most of the remainder are professional, farm, and employee associations. Groups formed primarily for political purposes, including the Americans for Democratic Action, the Liberty Lobby, and the League of Women Voters, are much fewer in number than associations based on an economic interest.

PRIBILOF ISLANDS. Islands in the Bering Sea, were first visited in 1786 by the Russian explorer Gerasim Pribylov. The islands were ceded to the United States by Russia in 1867. As the summer breeding grounds of the largest known herd of seals they became the subject of a controversy between the United States and other nations slaughtering the seals for their fur. In 1869 the U.S. Congress passed a law restricting the sealing. An American cutter seized Canadian vessels engaged in pelagic sealing in 1886. The British government vigorously protested, and an arbitration tribunal decided (in 1893) against the United States. The dispute was finally settled in 1911 by the North Pacific Sealing Convention between Great Britain, Russia, Japan, and the United States.

PRICE CONTROLS. Aside from Congress fixing the price of gold and silver, the federal government took little action between 1775 and 1917. New England drafted schedules at price conventions in 1776–78, but Connecticut alone put them into effect. Enforcement proved impossible.

In World War I the War Industries Board imposed selective controls effectively and accumulated administrative experience. In 1942–45 the Office of Price Administration approached complete regulation of all prices and rents. Many orders began with a "freeze" (seller's prior maximum price) to be replaced later by "flat" pricing (uniform ceilings for comparable sellers). Practically all prices zoomed upward after the lid was lifted in 1946. Several states then assumed rent controls.

The Office of Price Stabilization imposed milder regulations during the Korean War. The persistence of creeping inflation during the late 1960's prompted the administration of Lyndon B. Johnson to establish guidelines on wage increases and pressure large concerns against raising prices. President Richard M. Nixon established the Cost of Living Council, the Price Commission, and the Pay Board, attacking the problem at strategic points, but avoiding enforcement of the World War II variety.

PRICE IN MISSOURI (1861–64). Sterling Price was elected on Feb. 18, 1861, as a Unionist, to the Missouri convention. The convention, of which Price became president, was to determine Missouri's attitude toward secession. Union Capt. Nathaniel Lyon's capture of Camp Jackson, in St. Louis, on May 10, 1861, drove Price into the secessionists' camp, and many Missourians followed him. Price, put in command of the Missouri State Guard by Jackson, met Lyon at Wilson's Creek, near Springfield, on Aug. 10, 1861. Lyon was killed, and Price went north and captured Lexington on Sept. 20. Price and 5,000 of his men officially joined the Confederacy on Mar. 6, 1862. Subsequently, he returned to Arkansas and was engaged in the Red River campaign of 1864 and at Jenkins Ferry. Later that year he made his famous raid into Missouri. Entering from the southeast with 12,000 men on Sept. 19, he went north to Pilot Knob and then toward Jefferson City, but could not capture the capital. He then swung west toward Independence and destroyed the railroads, bridges, and telegraph lines behind him. He was caught between Curtis' and Gen. Alfred Pleasanton's armies at Westport, now Kansas City, and his army was nearly destroyed. Price managed to escape into Arkansas with 6,000 men.

PRICE MAINTENANCE. Agreements on price maintenance can be of two types. In horizontal price maintenance producers or merchants handling a particular good agree among themselves to set a standard price. In vertical price maintenance a producer agrees with his retailers not to allow prices to fall below a minimum level. Both forms of price-fixing have been viewed unfavorably through much of American history, and each was forbidden by the Sherman Antitrust Act of 1890.

Small retailers began to solicit government support for vertical price maintenance in the early 20th century. Large, vertically integrated merchandising companies, and high-volume discount houses were undermining the traditional market structure. Because of their size these firms could operate on a smaller profit margin, underselling lower-volume merchants. A 1911 Supreme Court ruling effectively ended any possibility of price maintenance in interstate commerce.

In the Robinson-Patman Act of 1936 small merchants were successful in obtaining federal sanctions against price discrimination. Although this act reduced the competitive advantage of chain stores, it did not keep them from cutting prices in retail sales. In 1937 the Miller-Tydings Enabling Amendment modified the Sherman act, removing restrictions on vertical price agreements. All but three of the states quickly enacted fair-trade laws that allowed manufacturers to set minimum retail prices.

Although price maintenance laws are widespread, they apparently have had little impact on the economics of retail merchandising. In the 1950's the federal courts exempted mail-order houses located in non-fair-trade states from these laws. Except for particular items—such as liquor—in which the government takes a special interest, the laws were being widely circumvented in the 1970's.

PRICES. Ratios of exchange, usually for money, in sales of commodities, services, securities, land, and anything else of value. Price trends reflect the relative rates of growth in commodity output and the money supply. Upward trends favor debtors (including governments) at the expense of creditors, and conversely. Those with fixed incomes suffer when prices rise and benefit when they fall. American prices show four secular trends: downward in 1607–1720, upward in 1721–1814, downward in 1814–96, and upward after 1896.

The decline before 1720 ran counter to the European price level, which rose until around 1680. Tobacco, the Chesapeake staple, depreciated sharply soon after settlement; yet production kept expanding. Some growers turned to wheat and other crops. Indian corn, New England's original staple, gradually went down in price. Other grains, wool, fish, and meats behaved similarly. These declines, caused by expansion of population and production, were probably moderated by successive devaluations of colonial shillings.

Distinct local price patterns developed during the 18th century. The New England price trough occurred in 1721, after some revival in 1710–20. With expanding currency, particularly in the 1740's, Boston wheat appreciated over 600 percent to a peak in 1749, and silver rose from 12 to 60 shillings an ounce. This unique inflation collapsed in 1750 when Massachusetts Bay reverted to hard money, redeeming many notes with silver from England. Another boom occurred in 1756–63, but quotations receded well before 1775.

The middle colonies' grains settled to a fraction of a penny a pound about 1721, as did flour. Production evidently continued ahead of the market (mostly Lisbon and the West Indies). Paper money began to appear on a conservative basis (Benjamin Franklin printed New Jersey's). Prices stopped falling, but made no great advance until 1748–49. Virtually all colonies began expanding note issues in 1755. Philadelphia and New York price quotations (in domestic currency) held upward trends until the Revolution, measuring overall about 25 percent over 1750 and 60 percent over 1720.

The Revolution brought third-degree inflation, influencing American opinion for generations. Wartime prices rose at various rates in the same or different markets. British occupation brought hard money into some localities. Philadelphia imported goods rose rapidly in 1777–78, domestic goods, in 1779–80. The maximum hard-money quotations on Boston wheat (1782) measured some 50 percent above prewar. A New York index peaked at 318 during 1779–80, also implying a currency far more valuable than continentals.

In 1784–1861 commodities were so favored in speculation that newspapers carried prices-current with commendable regularity. Monthly index numbers, and quotations on many commodities, are available for Boston, New York, Philadelphia, Charleston, New Orleans, Cincinnati, and San Francisco for part or all of the period. The Hoover-Taylor annual index combines local series to show average price behavior. Comprehensive farm prices have been assembled for Vermont after 1790 and Virginia after 1800.

A notable deflation occurred in the 1780's. Reaction against soft currencies, continued growth of production, and abeyance of capital imports brought an acute money shortage. Although Charleston enjoyed a rice boom in 1786, prices elsewhere settled near the prewar level until 1788–89. Commerce and finance approached a standstill.

The establishment of the federal government and several eastern banks, including the first Bank of the United States, and outbreak of war in Europe turned markets sharply upward. They continued to improve until 1814, following short cycles with such troughs as the ones in 1802–03 and 1808. The 1814 peak was a high point in price history. A postwar boom then took place in commodities and western lands, culminating in panics, depression, and a deflation centering in 1821.

The nation next experienced two tides, 1821–43 and 1843–62, marked by inflation over twelve to fifteen years and deflation thereafter. Immigration, exports of cotton and foodstuffs, international movements of capital and specie, public land sales, and construction were all factors. Twin peaks occurred in 1836–39 and 1855–57, followed by deep troughs in 1842–43 and 1860–62. The first tide featured credit and notes of state banks and the second Bank of the United States. The second saw California prices rise to two lofty peaks in 1849–52 when gold output temporarily outran commodity imports.

Over the years 1800–61 a noteworthy increase of farm prices accompanied the decline of freight rates to seaboard markets. The steady improvement of farmers' purchasing power was enhanced further by general declines in the prices of goods brought into the interior. This caused a remarkable appreciation in real estate in the interior.

The Civil War dispersed regional prices into three groups reflecting currencies and economic conditions. The North and Far West experienced second-degree inflations, and the Confederacy a third-degree inflation. Most commodities, such as metals and fibers and their derivatives, followed a conventional inflation pattern. However, heavy production and the disruption of normal trade caused foods and farm products to remain unusually cheap in 1861–62, until military demands and the circulation of U.S. notes began taking effect. They dropped again in 1863.

The Confederacy's regional index reflected the heavy dependence on paper currency to finance the war. Import prices quickly outran export prices, and different markets inflated to various degrees. In late 1864 goods were nearly twice as high in besieged Richmond as elsewhere. A wage index lagged far behind.

From 1865 to 1896 U.S. and world prices receded remarkably, reaching a record low. The contraction periods of four-year cycles occasionally outlasted the expansions. Evidently production outran money supply, and the velocity of circulation was declining. A definitely upward trend characterized 1896–1914, commonly attributed to important gold discoveries in Alaska and South Africa.

The United States suffered much less inflation than Europe during World War I. The wholesale level remained around 100 until 1916 but then rapidly advanced to 164 by April 1917 (base year, 1913). It was held to 195 at the armistice; but a postwar boom carried the index to 240 early in 1920. After a sharp deflation in 1921 it leveled off for most of the 1920's at 40 percent above 1913. Some felt price stability had finally been attained. Agricultural prices were much below others, whereas securities underwent a boom culminating in the crash in the New York stock market in October 1929.

The Great Depression developed in stages, spreading over much of the world. The Bureau of Labor Statistics (BLS) wholesale index subsided 10–20 percent each year until 1933, touching bottom at 85 (on the base 1913). Agricultural products and raw materials dropped most because heavy output faced severe competition in world markets. Manufacturers' prices resisted reduction. Some, such as the prices of Ford automobiles, increased to reflect quality improvements, but prices were eventually cut in most lines, such as radios and electric appliances, regardless of improvements in quality. Federal and state governments tried various approaches to "reflate" prices, some involving radical departures from past policy. By 1937 the BLS index had regained the 1930 level (124), but it suffered a relapse in 1938–39.

U.S. prices rebounded in the national defense epoch (1940–41), reaching 142 as the nation entered World War II. Under a crash program including price controls, rationing, priorities, and savings bonds, the BLS wholesale index was held to 152 during hostilities. Vigorous inflation broke out when controls were removed.

The 1973 U.S. price level was low compared with past levels in the United States and with 1973 levels abroad; it took fewer U.S. labor hours to earn a steak or an automobile than labor hours anywhere else. Nevertheless, the inflation that began in 1933 and was continuing in the late 1970's meant great hardship to pensioners and others with relatively fixed incomes, and deprived long-range creditors of an untold amount of purchasing power.

***PRIGG* V. *COMMONWEALTH OF PENNSYLVANIA*,** 16 Peters 539 (1842). Edward Prigg was indicted for kidnapping in the York County court under a Pennsylvania statute of 1826 prohibiting forcible seizure of fugitive slaves. Judgment for the commonwealth was affirmed by the Supreme Court of Pennsylvania in 1840. The state of Maryland then petitioned the U.S. Supreme Court for a writ of error. The Court declared the Pennsylvania statute unconstitutional because the federal Fugitive Slave Act of 1793 superseded all state legislation on the subject. In consequence, a number of northern states passed so-called personal liberty laws, prohibiting state officials from cooperating with persons seeking to capture and return fugitive slaves.

PRIMARY, DIRECT. The most widely used system in the 20th century for nominating candidates of a political party for elective office is the direct primary. Potential candidates of a given party for an office must obtain a designated minimum number of signatures of party members to allow their names to be printed on the ballots. Those candidates are then voted on by all the members of the given party in the election district on a prescribed date. The winners of the direct primary for each office for each political party are allowed to represent their respective parties in the general election. Before the early 1900's nominations were made by the congressional and legislative caucuses' declaring nominees or by delegate conventions. Democrats in Crawford County, Pa., first used the system on Sept. 9, 1842; the Republicans started to use the "Crawford County system" in 1860.

Two types of direct primaries exist: closed and open. A closed primary, used by almost all states, is a direct primary in which evidence of party membership is required. An open primary is a direct primary in which no party membership test is given, no record of the voter's choice of party ballot made, and no challenge made as to party affiliation.

PRIMARY, RUNOFF. A second direct primary, held shortly after the first primary, between the two candidates having the largest vote if neither has a majority.

PRIMARY, WHITE. One of several means used by white southern politicians in the first half of the 20th century to control black political power (*see* Suffrage, Afro-American). By preventing blacks from voting in Democratic primaries, southern whites effectively disfranchised them, since primaries are more important than general elections in one-party states. By midcentury the white primary was legally abolished in all states.

PRIMOGENITURE. Legally, primogeniture connotes the right of the eldest son to inherit the estate of a parent to the exclusion of all other heirs. Primogeniture existed in all of the original thirteen colonies. The movement for free and equitable inheritance was fostered by the American Revolution. Stimulated by the democratic philosophy of Thomas Jefferson, the Virginia assembly attacked primogeniture and in 1785 abolished it. Georgia and North Carolina had done the same in 1777 and 1784, respectively. The other states followed this lead, although it was not until 1798 that Rhode Island abolished primogeniture..

PRINCE GEORGE, FORT. Built in November 1753 by Gov. James Glen of South Carolina. It was placed on the eastern side of the Keowee River, opposite the Cherokee town of Keowee. It withstood successfully the Cherokee attacks of 1759–61.

PRINCETON, BATTLE OF (Jan. 3, 1777). Leaving three regiments at Princeton, N.J., British Gen. Charles Cornwallis arrived at the Delaware River near sunset on Jan. 2, 1777, to avenge George Washington's defeat of the Hessians at Trenton. Cornwallis found Washington's army of 5,000 men occupying a precarious position along Assunpink Creek. Cornwallis decided to "bag him" in the morning. Advised by Gen. Arthur St. Clair, Washington executed a brilliant military maneuver. At midnight, leaving his campfires burning, he quietly withdrew the main body of his army along an unpicketed road and gained the British rear. Approaching Princeton at about daybreak, the Americans encountered a force under Col. Charles Mawhood just leaving the village to join Cornwallis. Gen. Hugh Mercer's brigade engaged Mawhood's troops at close range but was driven back after bayonet fighting. Rallied by Washington and joined by new arrivals, the patriots, with deadly rifle fire, drove the enemy from the field and village and infused new life and hope into a cause that appeared all but lost.

***PRINCETON*, EXPLOSION ON THE** (Feb. 28, 1844). The *Princeton,* the first warship driven by a screw propeller, carried a 12-inch gun, the "Peacemaker," the largest gun yet forged for the American navy. While a party of about 200 government officials, including President John Tyler, was cruising down the Potomac aboard the *Princeton,* the gun was fired to entertain the company. It burst and killed several persons, including Secretary of State Abel P. Upshur and Secretary of the Navy Thomas W. Gilmer.

PRINCETON UNIVERSITY. Founded in 1746 as the College of New Jersey, Princeton was the fourth college established in the American British colonies. The first president was the Rev. Jonathan Dickinson; the first classes were held at his home in Elizabeth, N.J. On his death the institution was transferred to Newark, and the Rev. Aaron Burr became the second president. In 1756 the college was moved to the town of Princeton.

In the 19th century, under the presidency of James McCosh, the faculty was strengthened; graduate studies were introduced; and the School of Science, the predecessor of the School of Engineering and Applied Science, was established. Woodrow Wilson, who took office as president of the university in 1902, six years after the college was named Princeton University, recruited many younger faculty members to staff the preceptorial method of instruction.

Further growth in facilities and curriculum took place under presidents John G. Hibben (1912–32) and Harold W. Dodds (1933–57); during Dodds's administration the Woodrow Wilson School of Public and International Affairs was established, the Firestone Library erected, and the James Forrestal Campus acquired. The presidency of Robert F. Goheen (1957–72) witnessed the expansion of the Woodrow Wilson School to embrace professional training for public service and the admission of women students. In 1972 William G. Bowen became the seventeenth president of Princeton. In the spring of 1981 the university had 810 faculty members and 5,931 students.

PRINCIPIO COMPANY. A bloom forge, built in Maryland in 1715 at the head of Chesapeake Bay, was the origin of the Principio Iron Works. In 1718 the first quantity of bar iron exported from the colonies to England was made at this forge. Principio furnace went into operation in 1724. In 1780, when Maryland confiscated British property within the state, the existence of the company came to an end.

PRINTERS, TRAMP. A class of itinerant printers in the 19th century; most were farm boys indentured in the shops of rural weeklies who fled to larger towns overcrowded with printers.

PRINTER'S DEVIL. When printing was first introduced in the 15th century, it was associated with black magic. Printers consequently dubbed their young helpers, blackened with ink, "devils." In America the chore boy or youngest apprentice was called the printer's devil.

PRINTING. In the British settlements of North America the earliest press began work at Cambridge, Mass., in 1639. Evidently the first thing printed was "The Oath of a Free-man," a single sheet. The mechanisms and operations of the Cambridge press are best understood by reference to Joseph Moxon's *Mechanick Exercises on the Whole Art of Printing* (1682–84). The first imported printing machine was a "common press" of the cumbrous timber and metal construction generally used in Europe. American manufacture did not begin until 1769 when Isaac Doolittle, a clockmaker of New Haven, Conn., built a press for William Goddard of Philadelphia. Around 1800, Adam Ramage, a Scotsman, began to manufacture in Philadelphia the presses that bore his name. All of these presses were operated by a hand lever that applied pressure to the platen by a central screw, held in a framework of wood. In 1816 George Clymer made his Columbian press, which substituted direct leverage for the screw; and Otis Tuft used a toggle joint in place of the screw. The latter brought out the Washington handpress but sold the patent in 1825 to R. Hoe and Company. Before midcentury the great majority of well-done books and magazines were printed on the power-propelled bed-and-platen Adams press. Immediately following this was the development of the cylinder press, the letterpress printers' standby for the next hundred years.

Letter Cutting and Typefounding. By Moxon's time, the art of letter cutting and all that went into the making of punches, molds, and matrices were jealously guarded craft secrets. For 200 years the types of the New World printers had been imported from Europe. In 1769 Abel Buell of Killingworth, Conn., embarked on the business of typefounding. Better types were made at Germantown, Pa., by Jacob Bay and Justus Fox during the War for Independence. From this point the future of type manufacture was firmly taken over by John Baine, Archibald Binny, and James Ronaldson. Their Philadelphia typefoundry began operations in 1796.

Mechanical Typecasting, Punch Cutting, Typesetting. William Church, a Vermonter who worked in England, in 1822 patented a machine for casting and composing type on workable principles. David Bruce, in 1838, patented the pivotal typecaster, wherein a pump forced the fluid metal into the mold and matrix and produced better types at a much cheaper rate; from about 1840 this machine came into general use among typefounders. The New York house of James Connor first made electrotype matrices for types in 1845. Despite the commercial advantage of the electrotype offerings, printers preferred the durability and sharpness of types from steel punches engraved and matrices struck in solid metal. Linn Boyd Benton of Milwaukee in 1884 patented a pantograph punch-cutting machine that took the individual drawing and engraving of each letter out of the hands of the craftsmen.

Ottmar Mergenthaler of Baltimore had found the major obstacle to completing his Linotype was the lack of punches in the great quantities required to produce the vast numbers of matrices needed for his machine, which was in fact a self-contained type-foundry. More than 6,000 Mergenthaler Linotypes were in service before the century closed. Another hot-metal composing machine, the Monotype, was under development by Tolbert Lanston and J. S. Bancroft at the same time. Unlike the Mergenthaler Linotype, which set a line at a time and then cast it, the Monotype encoded copy as punched tape and set accordingly in a separate casting machine as individual characters.

Before the middle of the 20th century, other means of achieving similar purposes much more speedily and cheaply were developing. They were often based on seemingly unrelated experiments in the fields of lithography and offset printing, photography and color processes, and techniques of automation and electronics.

PRINTMAKING. About 1670 John Foster, Boston's first printer, cut on wood and printed a stark memorial portrait of the Rev. Richard Mather. A few professional printmakers came to the colonies from London. Notable among them was the mezzotint engraver Peter Pelham. His fourteen mezzotint portraits engraved in Boston between 1728 and 1751, are the most important series of 18th-century American prints.

Philadelphia and later New York were to preempt Boston's early leadership in the graphic arts. The small views of Philadelphia engraved on copper by William Birch and Thomas Birch, published in Philadelphia in 1800, and the engravings by Alexander Lawson of Alexander Wilson's studies of birds, illustrating Wilson's *American Ornithology* (Philadelphia, 1808–14), were the most ambitious printmaking enterprises in the young American cities. Forty years later, in Philadelphia John James Audubon in the 1840's issued his great lithographed series *Viviparous Quadrupeds of North America.* In New York Alexander Anderson produced 6,000 prints before his death in 1870; more important was his introduction of the skills that made wood engraving a 19th-century industry, for many years the medium of American book and magazine illustration. The New York firm of Currier and Ives, beginning in the 1840's, produced on a vast scale, lithographed, hand-colored scenes for a mass audience.

Many 20th-century American artists have explored printmaking. John Sloan's etchings, John Marin's etchings, George W. Bellows' lithographs, the etchings and lithographs of Reginald Marsh, and the etchings of Edward Hopper are landmarks of American art before World War II. In the decades after 1945, the earlier tradition of small black-and-white prints gave way to larger works and to a preference for color. The silk-screen prints of Ben Shahn, the woodcuts of Antonio Frasconi, Leonard Baskin, and Carol Summers, and the lithographs and etchings of Jasper Johns are among many American prints of outstanding quality made in these years.

PRISON CAMPS, CONFEDERATE. *See* **Andersonville; Castle Thunder; Confederate Prisons.**

PRISON CAMPS, UNION. Most captured Confederate soldiers were released on parole in the first year of the Civil War, but captured officers and civilian prisoners were confined in forts and other structures adapted temporarily as prisons. Lt. Col. William Hoffman was appointed the commissary general of prisoners on Oct. 7, 1861. He constructed a central depot for 1,200 inmates on Johnson's Island in Lake Erie to consolidate the prisoners, but the capture of 14,000 Confederates at Fort Donelson (Feb. 15–16, 1862) rendered the depot inadequate. After the establishment of an agreement to exchange prisoners in June 1862, the number of inmates declined from 19,423 to 1,286, enabling Hoffman to close most of the camps and to consolidate the captives at Johnson's Island; Alton, Ill.; and Camp Chase, Ohio. When difficulties concerning prisoner exchange arose in early 1863, the number of inmates increased, closed camps were reactivated, and conditions deteriorated. To consolidate and regulate facilities Hoffman established large permanent prisons at Fort Delaware, Del., Rock Island, Ill., Point Lookout, Md., and Elmira, N.Y. Starting in February 1865, when the Union prisons held over 65,000 inmates, the federal government began to return large numbers of soldiers to the Confederacy.

PRISONERS, EXCHANGE OF. *See* **Exchange of Prisoners.**

PRISONS AND PRISON REFORM. Rarely used before the 19th century, imprisonment became between 1820 and 1900 the focus of criminal policy. Largely as the result of the efforts of the Quakers a cell block in the Walnut Street jail in Philadelphia was opened in 1790 as the penitentiary for the commonwealth, the first such institution in the United States.

By 1823 two competing models of prisons had emerged in the United States. The penitentiary system established by the Quakers was designed to save the offender through reflection and penitence. The competing system was represented by a prison constructed at Auburn, N.Y. The objective of the Auburn system was to produce obedient citizens. Prisoners were to be housed under conditions of stern discipline and employed in a system of congregate labor. The Auburn system was to become predominant.

Before the Civil War industrial prisons that produced substantial quantities of goods were established in many states. After the war both business and labor protested the competition of prisonmade goods. Prisons became increasingly overcrowded and costs of new construction were prohibitive. Moreover, it appeared to many observers that the function of the prison as a place of reform had been forgotten.

At that point a significant new era in prison reform began. Enoch C. Wines, corresponding secretary of the Prison Association of New York, used his post to advance many proposals for the improvement of prison conditions. Largely on Wines's initiative a congress on prison reform was convened at Cincinnati, Ohio, in October 1870. The declaration of the congress emphasized the responsibility of society for the reformation of criminals and noted that education, religion, and industrial training are valuable aids in such an undertaking; that discipline should build the self-respect of each prisoner; and that prison systems should be centrally controlled to assure a stable, nonpolitical administration.

Despite the optimism of the reformers of the late 19th century, American prisons changed little until the 1930's. Prison reform once more became a major object of study with the appointment by President Herbert Hoover in 1929 of the first federally sponsored study group, the National Commission on Law Observance and Enforcement. It was during this period, also, that the recognition that all prisoners did not require confinement in maximum security cages led to the development of institutions of lesser custody.

During the late 1950's and early 1960's changes in prison programs were influenced by the work of the Joint Commission on Mental Health and Illness, which began in 1955. Congress authorized the use of work release, study release, emergency furloughs, and community treatment centers (halfway houses) for adult federal offenders in 1965. Similar statutes were enacted in more than half the states within the next ten years.

A significant development has been the intervention of the courts since about 1965 in matters relating to postconviction rights of offenders, disciplinary matters, administrative interrogations and investigations, the adequacy of physical facilities, medical treatment, administrative liability, and rehabilitation. The introduction of new concepts of fairness in the administration of prisons may well be the most significant development that took place in the history of these institutions.

The failure of the prison during the last fifty years to demonstrate its ability to rehabilitate offenders has led to a debate about the future of imprisonment. The position that appears to have the strongest support is that while prisons should be used primarily for the purposes of punishment and deterrence, there is a need not only to maintain but to expand existing institutional programs. These, it is agreed, should be made available on a "non-coercive, facilitative" basis and that a prisoner's release from the institution should in no way depend on the extent to which he has become involved in them.

PRISON SHIPS. Used by both the Americans and the British during the Revolution for confining naval prisoners. The former maintained such ships at Boston and at New London, Conn., and the latter at Halifax, Nova Scotia; at Antigua, British West Indies; and at Wallabout Bay, Brooklyn. It has been estimated that some 11,500 men died on these ships.

PRIVATEERS AND PRIVATEERING. The participation of privately armed American colonists in the wars of England did not begin until King William's War (1689–97). In King George's War (1744–48) privateering began to assume the proportions of a major maritime business, and it is said that during the French and Indian War (1754–63) 11,000 Americans were engaged in such operations.

During the Revolution, most colonies issued letters of marque and reprisal, and the Continental Congress sanctioned privateering: 1,151 American privateers captured about 600 British vessels. Although the operations of the privateers had been financially profitable and an invaluable aid to the navy, the U.S. government soon joined the movement in Europe to abolish privateering. It reversed its position in 1798 in the face of the arrogant depredations of armed vessels sailing under republican France (*see* Franco-American Misunderstanding). Before the close of hostilities in 1801, upward of 1,000 vessels had been armed. In the War of 1812, 515 letters of marque and reprisal were issued, under which 1,345 British vessels are known to have been taken.

The United States, with its naval superiority, did not find it expedient to issue letters of marque and reprisal during the Mexican War (1846–48). The United States declined to accede to the Declaration of Paris (1856), outlawing privateering among the principal world powers, but when the Confederate States of America issued letters of marque, President Abraham Lincoln endeavored to treat the Confederate privateers as pirates. The United States' attempt at privateering in 1863 proved abortive, and privateering ended with the downfall of the Confederacy.

PRIVILEGE IN COLONIAL GOVERNMENTS. Rights and exemptions claimed by colonial legislatures in imitation of the British House of Commons. The five privileges usually petitioned for by the speaker of the house in London—freedom from arrest, freedom from molestation, freedom of speech, access to the crown, and favorable construction on all official acts of the house—had become practically universal in the colonies outside New England in the 18th century. Privilege was further expanded by extension to servants of members, officers of the house, and people who had given evidence. Privilege gradually extended to also include the rights to settle disputed elections, control members, and punish outsiders who abused individual members or insulted the house itself. Parliament disapproved of the independent position colonial assemblies achieved by claims to privilege.

PRIVILEGES AND IMMUNITIES OF CITIZENS. Article IV, Section 2, guarantees that citizens of each state shall be entitled to all privileges and immunities of citizens in the several states. The first authoritative definition of privileges and immunities was given by Justice Bushrod Washington on circuit in *Corfield* v. *Coryell* (1823); the privileges and immunities protected, he said, were those "which are, in their nature, fundamental; which belong, of right, to the citizens of all free governments."

The second privileges and immunities clause, in the Fourteenth Amendment, forbids states to make or enforce any law abridging the privileges and immunities of citizens of the United States. It was one of three standards written into the post–Civil War amendment for the purpose of, but not limited to, protecting the rights of the newly freed blacks.

PRIVY COUNCIL. A body of advisers to the English crown. In the 17th century, the council filled a place roughly corresponding to that now occupied by the cabinet. The council contained all of the ministers of state. New colonies fell under the special care of the council. This body heard appeals from colonial courts, and colonial laws were referred to it for approval or veto (*see* Royal Disallowance).

PRIZE CASES, CIVIL WAR. After the firing on Fort Sumter, Lincoln, by executive proclamations (in April and May 1861), virtually declared war, called for volunteers, enlarged the regular army, suspended the writ of habeas corpus, and blockaded various southern ports. Not until July did Congress, meeting in special session, retroactively legalize these executive measures. In 1863 the Supreme Court held, in a narrow five-to-four decision, that Lincoln's blockade by executive proclamation was constitutional and that civil war had "legally" existed between April and July 1861, even though Congress did not recognize a state of war until July 13. (*See also Amy Warwick* Admiralty Case.)

PRIZE COURTS. Although operating under the rules of international law, prize courts are national instrumentalities. Their function is to pass on the validity and disposition of prizes, a term referring to the seizure of a ship and/or its cargo by the maritime forces of a belligerent, not its land forces. According to the U.S. Prize Act of 1941, the seizure of aircraft may also fall under the jurisdiction of prize courts. Whether the broad principles of judicial prize doctrine can be adopted to capture by aircraft remained a subject of legal argument in the mid-1970's. In the United States, jurisdiction in prize matters belongs to the federal district courts, with the right of appeal to the circuit court of appeals and ultimately the Supreme Court.

PRIZEFIGHTING. The sport was introduced in America by visiting British sailors in the early 19th century. Wagers were sometimes enormous; entire plantations sometimes changed hands. One slave, Tom Molineaux, earned his freedom by winning a huge bet for his master. Molineaux then went to England and had two epic bouts with the English champion Tom Cribb.

John L. Sullivan, son of Irish immigrants, did much to make the sport popular in the last part of the 19th century. His fight in New Orleans on Sept. 7, 1892, against James J. Corbett, also of Irish descent, caused intense interest all over America. In a startling upset, Corbett won by a knockout. Corbett lost the title in 1897 to "Ruby" Robert Fitzsimmons, the lightest man to hold the championship. Two years later Fitzsimmons was knocked out by the powerful James J. Jeffries.

The sport's golden age was from 1910 to 1930. After John A. (Jack) Johnson, a black from Galveston, Tex., wrested the world's heavyweight title from Tommy Burns in 1908, a wide search was made in America for a "white hope"—a Caucasian who could beat Johnson. In 1910, after Johnson soundly defeated Jeffries—far from his prime—riots erupted in many American cities. In 1915, in Havana, Cuba, Johnson was knocked out by Jess Willard, who was in turn defeated by William Harrison (Jack) Dempsey in 1919. The outstanding promoter of the era was George Lewis (Tex) Rickard. Dempsey's two fights with James Joseph (Gene) Tunney (1926, 1927), promoted by Rickard, excited the nation as no sports events had up to that time. Tunney won both contests.

After Tunney retired in 1928, interest in the sport lagged until Joe Louis (Joseph Louis Barrow) captured the heavyweight title from the "Cinderella Man," James J. Braddock, in June 1937. Louis' previous knockout by the German Max Schmeling in 1936 was an astounding upset. Their second bout, in 1938, having political overtones, was an emotional as well as an athletic event. A determined Louis knocked out the German in the first round in Madison Square Garden, New York City. "Jersey Joe" Walcott took the crown from Louis in 1951, and Rocky Marciano (Rocco Marchegiano) beat Walcott in 1952. Marciano retired in 1955 without having lost a fight. The most controversial fighter of the 1960's and early 1970's was Cassius Clay, later known as Muhammad Ali. Ali won the championship in 1964 from Sonny Liston, but was deprived of his title and his license to box for refusing to serve in the army. (He had unsuccessfully asked to be exempt from service because of his adherence to the Black Muslim faith.) His license, but not the title, was restored in 1970.

PRIZE MONEY. The Continental Congress adopted the European practice of justifying low naval pay by splitting with captains and crews the proceeds from captured enemy vessels sold by prize courts. Privateers, which were privately owned, received all the proceeds from a sale. In raiding British commerce during the Revolution, more than 1,000 privateers took about 600 prizes sold for the then great total of $18 million.

Although Congress declined to authorize privateers for the Quasi-War with France (1798–1800), enterprising captains succeeded in stoutly defending themselves to the extent of taking fourteen French armed cruisers. Meanwhile, forty-nine men-of-war of the new U.S. Navy made ninety-five captures on the basis of the 1798 prize law.

The war against commerce-poor Tripoli (1801–05) found Congress ultimately considering $100,000 for the survivors or heirs of Stephen Decatur and his seventy volunteers who in the *Intrepid* audaciously retook and blew up the unfortunate U.S. frigate *Philadelphia.*

In the War of 1812, 492 American privateers took 1,344 prizes, most of them in 1814 during the last six months of the war. U.S. naval vessels, while nowhere near as successful as the privateers, made some spectacular captures. Typical combat awards were $50,000 voted to Isaac Hull and the crew of the 44-gun *Constitution* for the 38-gun *Guerrière* and $25,000 to Jacob Jones and the 18-gun *Wasp* over the equal H.M.S. *Frolic.*

Although the Confederacy had only a minor portion of the prewar U.S. merchant marine, blockading was lucrative for the Union navy. Foreigners gambled for huge profits to be made running the blockade.

In the growth of the navy, requiring assignment of able officers to shore duties, it became manifest that resultant denial of opportunities for prize money at sea was unjust. Thus, in 1898, Congress voted $2 million for navywide distribution, and in 1900 it abolished the prize law and enacted a reasonable pay scale.

PROCLAMATION MONEY. Coin valued according to a proclamation of Queen Anne issued on June 18, 1704, and in effect until 1775. The various colonial valuations of Spanish pieces of eight, the most common coins in the American colonies, were superseded by a uniform fixed valuation of six shillings. This attempt to unify the silver currency of the colonies failed.

PROCLAMATION OF 1763. A document issued by the British government regulating the settlement of land in North

America. Parts of the territory in America acquired through the Treaty of Paris were organized as the provinces of Quebec, East Florida, West Florida, and Grenada. The most significant part of the proclamation was that aimed at conciliating the Indians. The governors of the provinces and colonies were forbidden to grant lands "beyond the Heads or Sources of any of the Rivers which fall into the Atlantic Ocean from the West and North West." Settlement upon the Indian lands was prohibited, and settlers already on such lands were commanded "forthwith to remove themselves." Furthermore, private purchases of land from the Indians were forbidden; those that had been made in the Indian reservation were voided; and future purchases were to be made officially, by the governor of the colony involved, for the crown alone. Indian traders were to be licensed and to give security to observe such regulations as might be promulgated. Settlers, however, disregarding the proclamations, swarmed over the mountains, and their encroachments were one of the causes of Pontiac's War.

PROCLAMATIONS. Official or general notices to the public. Such notices are issued by American political executives either in connection with the conduct of government or for ceremonial purposes. Proclamations related to governmental conduct include those always issued by the president or the governor when an emergency situation requires the establishment of martial law, as in the case of Abraham Lincoln's Proclamation of 1861. Ceremonial proclamations may be issued in connection with the observance of legal holidays.

PRODUCTIVITY, CONCEPT OF. The term "productivity" usually denotes the ratio of economic output to any or all associated inputs, in real terms. Only when output is related to all associated tangible inputs in total-productivity measures is the net saving of real costs, and thus the effect of technological innovations and other factors increasing productive efficiency, indicated. Partial-productivity ratios of output to one input-class, such as labor (usually measured as output per man-hour), reflect substitutions among factors, as well as changes in productive efficiency. Measurement of output per man-hour in major industries and sectors of the United States was made a regular part of federal government statistical programs in 1940 under the Bureau of Labor Statistics in the U.S. Department of Labor.

PROFITEERING. Popularized during World War I, the term "profiteering" refers to the making of unconscionable profits. Profiteering has appeared especially in times of economic stress and widespread shortages. For example, when President Grover Cleveland turned to J. P. Morgan for aid in coping with the panic of 1893, Morgan provided the necessary assistance but made a profit of $7.5 million on the deal. (*See also* Revolutionary War, Profiteering in.)

PROFIT SHARING. Annual bonuses, or plans to distribute a percentage of profits to all workers, appeared in the United States shortly after the Civil War. These plans were largely confined to medium-size companies and never became widespread. An allied movement, particularly popular in the 1920's, was the purchase of stock in the company by employees. Management offered easy payments and often a price lower than the current market figure. It was hoped that the plan would reduce labor turnover and give workers a stronger interest in company welfare.

PROGRESS AND POVERTY **(1880).** The magnum opus of American economist Henry George (1839–97) and the bible of his Single Tax movement. He advocated the destruction of land monopoly by shifting all taxes from labor and its products to land.

PROGRESSIVE MOVEMENT. A reform effort of the first two decades of the 20th century. It had supporters in both major political parties and pursued a number of goals, ranging from prohibition and woman's suffrage to antitrust legislation, industrial regulation, tax reform, and workmen's compensation. In 1912 some of the people committed to those goals formed an important third party.

PROGRESSIVE PARTY (or Bull Moose Party). The party's origins can be traced to Theodore Roosevelt's presidency, 1901–09. Roosevelt's proposals for the regulation of transportation and industry, tax reform, labor laws, and social welfare legislation helped to shape a loose coalition of Republican senators and representatives, mostly from the Midwest, who were eager to make their party an instrument of reform.

The progressive ranks included senators Robert M. La Follette of Wisconsin, and William E. Borah of Idaho, and Rep. George W. Norris of Nebraska. By 1910 the Republican party suffered at the polls; the Democrats gained control of the House for the first time in eighteen years. In the wake of the election Republican insurgents formed the National Progressive Republican League on Jan. 21, 1911. Ostensibly created to advocate progressive principles, the league was widely regarded as a device for La Follette to wrest the Republican nomination from Taft in 1912.

Roosevelt announced late in February 1912 that his "hat was in the ring." Most of La Follette's backers immediately declared their support for the former president. There followed a bitter series of battles for delegates to the Republican National Convention, scheduled to meet June 18, 1912, in Chicago. Roosevelt, backed by many of the rank and file but by few party professionals, determined to abandon his lifelong Republicanism and form a new party. Roosevelt called for the first Progressive National Convention to meet in Chicago on Aug. 5, 1912.

That convention adopted a remarkably advanced platform. Condemning what it called "the unholy alliance between corrupt business and corrupt politics," the platform called for the adoption of primary elections; the short ballot; initiative, referendum, and recall measures; the direct election of U.S. senators; and woman suffrage. It advocated federal legislation establishing minimum standards of industrial safety and health; minimum wages for women; the eight-hour day in many industries; medical, old-age, and unemployment insurance; stronger regulation of interstate business; a tariff commission; public ownership of natural resources; graduated income and inheritance taxes; improved educational services for immigrants; and government supervision of securities markets. It endorsed collective bargaining, the establishment of industrial research laboratories, government-business cooperation to extend foreign commerce, the creation of a department of labor, and the prohibition of child labor. It strongly opposed the power of the courts to nullify social and economic legislation.

Roosevelt finished second in the national balloting, with 4.1 million popular and 88 electoral votes. But at the state and local levels, the party did less well. It was able to field full slates in only fifteen states. In 1913 it could count only one governor, two senators, sixteen representatives, and 250 local elected officials. The elections of 1914 produced more disasters for the party. When in June 1916, in Chicago, Roosevelt declined the Progressive nomination, the national committee agreed to endorse the Republican candidate, Charles Evans Hughes. Most Progressives thereupon rejoined the party they had left in 1912. A die-hard contingent persevered until April 1917, when in a final convention in St. Louis it merged with the Prohibition party.

PROGRESSIVE PARTY (1947–52). Established in 1947 and expiring shortly after the 1952 national elections, the Progressive party claimed that it was the true heir to the philosophy of Franklin D. Roosevelt and condemned the administration of Harry S. Truman. The party opposed the administration's loyalty-security program, called for bolder civil rights and welfare measures, charged that the large military budgets fostered bellicosity, blamed the administration in large measure for the cold war, and offered a policy of accommodation with the Soviet Union. In 1948 the party selected as its candidate Henry A. Wallace, formerly vice-president under Roosevelt. The party won 1,157,172 votes, or 2.4 percent of the popular vote, most of it from New York City and Los Angeles. The crushing defeat, growing anticommunism in America, and renewed charges of Communist domination soon weakened the party. In 1952 the party ran Vincent W. Hallinan, an attorney, and received 140,023 votes.

PROHIBITION. The campaign against the manufacture and sale of alcoholic beverages. Three periods of legislative activity are apparent. First, between 1846 and 1855, following the lead of Maine, thirteen states passed prohibition laws. Within a decade nine of these measures had been either repealed or declared unconstitutional. After Kansas, in 1880, had written prohibition into its constitution, there was a revival of the temperance movement, stimulated by the persistent efforts of the Prohibition party (1869), the Woman's Christian Temperance Union (1874), and, most powerful of all, the Anti-Saloon League (1893). Again results were impermanent, for by 1905 only Kansas, Maine, Nebraska, and North Dakota were prohibition states. On the eve of the U.S. entrance into World War I, there were prohibition laws in twenty-six states.

By December 1917, both the Senate and the House of Representatives had approved a resolution to add an amendment to the Constitution prohibiting the "manufacture, sale or transportation" of intoxicating beverages. Within thirteen months ratification by the legislatures of three-quarters of the states had been secured, and a year later the Eighteenth Amendment went into effect.

The opponents of Prohibition soon directed their attack against the efforts of governmental agents to enforce the law. They insisted that corruption was rampant in federal and state enforcement units and that disrespect for all law was becoming a characteristic of those who flouted the liquor laws with impunity. Popular disgust over the failure of enforcement grew so steadily that the Democratic National Convention in 1932 demanded repeal of the Eighteenth Amendment. The Democratic landslide in the November elections persuaded Congress that the time for action had come. In the short session (Feb. 20, 1933) a resolution was approved providing for an amendment to accomplish repeal. Submitted to conventions in the several states, the Twenty-first Amendment was ratified in less than a year.

PROHIBITION PARTY. Oldest of the third parties in the United States, organized in 1869 after nearly three-quarters of a century of temperance agitation had failed to influence the platforms of the major parties. The campaign of 1872 marked its initial appearance in national politics. Nine states were represented at its first national convention in Columbus, Ohio, Feb. 22, 1872. James Black of Pennsylvania was nominated for president. Candidates have appeared in every presidential campaign since 1872 but have never won any electoral votes. The peak of the party's popular support was reached in 1892 when its candidate for president, John Bidwell, received 271,000 votes (*see* Presidential Campaigns: Campaign of 1896).

PROJECT MERCURY. The first series of manned space flights operated by the United States. The Mercury spacecraft were manned by individual astronauts.

PROMONTORY POINT (Utah). The site of the completion, on May 10, 1869, of the first transcontinental railroad. President Leland Stanford of the Central Pacific Railroad, using a silver sledgehammer, drove the last golden spike into a polished California laurel tie.

PROPAGANDA. Any form of controlled communication for the purpose of influencing the opinions, emotions, attitudes, or behavior of an intended audience. Although the distinctions are frequently unclear or indefinite, there are differences between propaganda and associated uses of communication to inform or instruct. The content of propaganda may be true or false, real or fabricated. The consistent distinction is in whether the communication is sponsored to influence or is prepared and disseminated to contribute to entertainment or general knowledge.

America has employed propaganda in each of its wars. In the Revolution news-sheets and pamphlets were used to carry the speeches and writings of leaders who sought to build a willingness to go to war. The Declaration of Independence, used to unify the colonists and justify the Revolution, stands as an example of highly effective propaganda. The increased communications capabilities effected by the time of the Civil War made it possible for each side in that conflict to conduct active propaganda, making appeals designed to strengthen its cause and weaken the opponent. The Emancipation Proclamation (1863) was a masterful propaganda stroke, for once the war became characterized as a crusade against slavery, it became very difficult for any European government to support the Confederacy.

The experiences gained during World War II and in the subsequent occupation of Germany and Japan caused the United States to provide continuing policies and capabilities to conduct communications with foreign audiences. In 1953 the United States Information Agency (USIA) was established to help achieve U.S. foreign policy objectives by influencing public attitudes in other nations, and to advise other agencies on the implications of foreign opinion for present and contemplated U.S. policies, programs, and official statements. The USIA operates four media services: broadcasting (Voice of America), the Information Center Service, the Motion Picture and Television Service, and the Press and Publications Service.

PROPERTY. The most important division of property is that between real and personal. Real property consists of land and things permanently attached to land. Personal property consists of all other property that is capable of ownership. Another classification divides property into corporeal and incorporeal. The former term refers to tangibles, such as land, livestock, implements, furniture, automobiles, and the like; the latter refers to intangibles, such as contract rights, franchises, claims against others, notes, stocks, bonds, and insurance policies. Corporeal personal property is also known as chattels or goods. In the eyes of the law, property consists of legal relations between a person called the owner and other people. The owner's legal rights constitute his property.

The feudal system of land tenures in England was based on the theory that all land was owned by the king, who allotted it among his lords; they in turn parceled out its use among the villeins, who tilled the land. The rights of the lords to such services were gradually reduced by statutes, until a more or less absolute ownership (called free and common socage) was created. This was the type of land ownership that was transplanted to America. There are important limitations on ownership of land; no type of ownership can be said to be absolute. Owners may not use land in such a way as to create public nuisances or injure their neighbors, property may be taken for taxes and is subject to execution for the payment of debts, it is liable to escheat (reversion to the state) if a deceased owner has no will or heirs, and it is subject to the power of eminent domain and to curtailment under the police power. The subjection of both real and personal property to the police power is of growing importance. Many businesses formerly classed as private are now subject to such governmental supervision as the public interest deems. Although state and federal legislative power to curtail the use of private property is limited by the due process clauses of the Fifth and Fourteenth amendments to the U.S. Constitution, court decisions indicate that this protection is less absolute than formerly.

PROPERTY INSURANCE. *See* **Insurance.**

PROPERTY QUALIFICATIONS. The rationale behind property qualifications was that only property owners possessed "stock" in the state, which was regarded as a corporation. Almost all states had property requirements for voting at the time of the American Revolution. In the early 19th century the newly admitted western states had few property requirements for voting, and the eastern states tended to reduce the requirements. By the time of the Civil War virtually all property requirements for voting had been eliminated. The Twenty-fourth Amendment effectively outlawed property qualifications for voting in federal elections by abolishing all poll or other taxes as requirements for voting. This prohibition was extended to state elections by a 1966 Supreme Court decision. A 1973 Supreme Court decision permitted states to limit voting to property owners in "special" districts.

PROPHET DANCE. A cult movement that arose among the Indian tribes of the Plateau area of the Pacific Northwest before the end of the 18th century. Although it may have had its roots in native beliefs about death and rebirth, the cult appears to have been indirectly influenced by Europeans. The Prophet Dance emphasized beliefs in the impending destruction of the world and its subsequent renewal, concomitant with the return of the dead Indians.

PROPHET'S TOWN. In 1808, on the west bank of the Wabash River just below the mouth of the Tippecanoe River (in present-day Tippecanoe County, Ind.), Tenskwatawa, an orator and reformer known as the Shawnee Prophet and brother of Tecumseh, established his headquarters. Groups of northwestern tribesmen, dissatisfied with white encroachments on their land, gathered at Prophet's Town to plan a concerted resistance. After the Battle of Tippecanoe in 1811, the Shawnee Prophet abandoned the town.

PROPORTIONAL REPRESENTATION. An electoral device, the intent of which is to make a representative body a faithful image of its electorate. Ideally, the system gives legislative voting strength proportionate to the electoral strength of every shade of societal opinion. The use of proportional representation in the United States has been rare. It has been tried by several cities, notably Cincinnati; Boulder, Colo.; and New York. In the late 1960's the system was adopted by the Democratic party for selecting delegates to the Democratic National Convention. Opponents contend that the system vitiates democracy on the interparty and intraparty levels.

PROPRIETARY AGENT. A business representative of the proprietor of an American colony. Many proprietors found it necessary to employ agents to attend to colonial business both in London and in America. Proprietors frequently acted as their own agents in London. Agents handled the survey and sale of lands, the collection of proprietary revenue, and the management of estates.

PROPRIETARY PROVINCES. The proprietorship succeeded the trading company as a device employed to build England's colonial empire (*see* Colonial Policy, British). The proprietary province was virtually a feudal jurisdiction in which, with specified exemptions, the lord proprietor exercised sovereign powers. He could appoint all officials; create courts, hear appeals, and pardon offenders; make laws and issue decrees; raise and command a militia; and establish churches, ports, and towns. The charters of Maryland and Pennsylvania contained the important limitation requiring the proprietor to make laws by and with the consent of the freemen. These provinces were, thus, feudal only in name. The proprietors were forced to accede to the insistent demands of the people and to yield to them political privileges and powers (*see* Colonial Assemblies). The land of the proprietary province, however, constituted a great private domain. The proprietor granted it to settlers on his own terms. He could mortgage it for debt, as William Penn did. New provinces could come into existence by subgrants. Estates could be transferred into new hands by purchase.

The royal grant of Maryland to Cecilius Calvert, Lord Baltimore, in 1632, was of the feudal, or proprietary, type. Seven years later, Sir Ferdinando Gorges received a royal charter for Maine, also of the feudal or proprietary type. In 1664 the king granted what came to be known as New York, New Jersey, and Delaware, to the Duke of York as a proprietary. By the charters of 1663 and 1665 a group of eight men received the broad area of Carolina, in which two colonies came into existence under one board. The proprietary continued until 1729, when the owners sold their proprietary rights to the king, with the exception of the Granville Grant. Pennsylvania, founded under a charter issued to William Penn in 1681, was the last of the proprietary colonies.

PROSPECTORS. Persons who explore for minerals. For many 19th-century prospectors the hope of one day striking it rich was a lifelong preoccupation; and most prospectors were not placer miners by trade. The 19th-century prospectors' explorations accelerated the settlement of the West. By the mid-20th century prospecting in the United States was being done, for the most part, by representatives of giant corporations, who relied heavily on geological research and sophisticated detection equipment.

PROSTITUTION. Until the last part of the 19th century Americans ignored prostitution, regarding it as a crime only when it became an offense to public decency. In most areas of America during the colonial and early national periods prostitution was a more or less irregular occupation for a few women. By the middle of the 19th century the growth of the industrial cities and the opening of the western frontier had led to an increase in prostitution, which by general agreement was concentrated in segregated or red-light districts.

The reluctance of law enforcement officials to move against the tolerated houses was overcome by the Iowa Injunction and Abatement Law of 1909, which was widely copied by other states. Under this law any taxpayer might institute an action in equity against property used for prostitution. The U.S. government also entered the field with laws against procuring and transporting women across state borders for immoral purposes (federal Mann Act or White Slave Traffic Act of 1910). The army's decision in World War I to inspect the soldiers for venereal disease rather than prostitutes also proved a boost in the campaign against tolerated houses. By the 1920's legally tolerated districts had mostly disappeared.

After World War II, when effective cures for venereal disease had been developed, legal attitudes toward prostitution began to be questioned again. The American Law Institute and the American Civil Liberties Union have urged that sexual activities between consenting adults not be subject to criminal penalties. Instead they would return to the earlier common-law regulation of prostitution. In the mid-1970's several states were considering action in this area; but only in Nevada is prostitution legally tolerated on a county-by-county basis.

PROTECTION. *See* **Tariff.**

PROTECTIVE WAR CLAIMS ASSOCIATION. Began operations in 1863 in New York and Philadelphia under the sponsorship of the U.S. Sanitary Commission, to assist in settling claims of soldiers, sailors, and their relatives and to prevent imposture, fraud, and false claims.

PROTECTORATE. An arrangement by which a major power assumes the right to "protect"—actually to govern—another area of the world. Some protectorates have been sought voluntarily by the protected nation. Many have been forced on the protected group by the larger nation. The League of Nations and the United Nations have granted large countries the authority to manage the affairs of smaller ones until they are prepared for full international activity. The Trust Territory of the Pacific is not called a protectorate, but it has been in effect a U.S. protectorate.

PROTRACTED MEETING. A religious convocation especially common during the 19th century in the rural districts of the South and West. Although often similar in nature to a revival meeting, a protracted meeting was nevertheless somewhat different, since its purpose was not only to create a rebirth of religious fervor and swell the ranks of church members but also to provide the religious people of a community with spiritual sustenance and social contacts. It usually lasted two or three weeks, closing only when attendance and interest began to lag.

PROVIDENCE (R.I.). The capital and largest city in Rhode Island, with a population of 156,804 in 1980; the center of metropolitan area that included 917,962 people and took in a cluster of smaller cities. Providence is an important seaport, transportation center, and manufacturing city. Its location, facing Narragansett Bay, provides it with an excellent, well-protected harbor.

Providence is a distribution point for oil and other imported products. Its manufacturing activities range from silverware to clothing, including many forms of metal working and machinery building. It is the home of several institutions of higher education, including Brown University (and its college for women, Pembroke College), Rhode Island College, Rhode Island School of Design, and Providence College.

Providence was established by Roger Williams in 1636 (*see* Providence Plantations). Many Providence-based ships were involved in the slave trade; rum manufactured in the city was used as one element in that trade. Ships out of Providence became prominent in the trade to India and China after the American Revolution, and the city then began its rise as a manufacturing center. Rubber manufacturing became important in the late 19th century and continues to be a major employer (along with plastics manufacturing) in the 20th century.

PROVIDENCE, DIVINE. *See* **Divine Providences.**

PROVIDENCE ISLAND COMPANY (1630–1641). Incorporated for the purpose of colonizing the islands of Providence, Henrietta, and Association in the Caribbean, because they offered opportunities for illicit trade and buccaneering in the nearby Spanish colonies. Although profit was the promoters' objective, they were also interested in founding a colony for Puritans. From the outset the undertaking failed to prosper. After 1635 the company expanded its program by attempting to colonize on the mainland of Central America. Since its leaders in England were by then no longer in sympathy with the Puritans in Massachusetts, they tried to divert to Providence Island English Puritans planning to go to New England; they even attempted to transplant to the islands New England Puritans.

PROVIDENCE PLANTATIONS. The original name for the first settlement in Rhode Island, made by Roger Williams in June 1636, after he fled from Massachusetts to escape religious persecution. Williams bought a large tract of land from the Narragansett Indians, and in 1638 he joined with twelve other settlers in forming a land company. A covenant was drawn up in 1637 providing for majority rule "only in civill things," thus permitting religious liberty. Under the parliamentary charter of 1644, Providence was joined with Newport and Portsmouth as the Incorporation of Providence Plantations in the Narragansett Bay in New England. "Providence Plantations" still remains as part of the official title of the state of Rhode Island.

PROVINCETOWN PLAYERS. The most distinguished American little theater group first produced plays in 1915 in Provincetown, Mass. Its discovery of Eugene O'Neill and its production during two summers of numerous successful dramas prompted it to establish the Playwrights' Theater in New York City's Greenwich Village. Although the Provincetown Players was essentially a cooperative, the dominant and adventurous George Cram Cook was its leader. Its great days ended in 1922, when the success of *The Emperor Jones* took O'Neill's plays to Broadway.

PROVINCIAL CONGRESSES. The extralegal, or revolutionary, assemblies that sprang up in most of the colonies in the early stages of the American Revolution. The provincial congresses or conventions were generated by or through the local committees that flourished in every colony (*see* Committees of Correspondence; Committees of Safety). In some instances the colonial assembly was the promoting agency. In Massachusetts, for instance, the assembly merely transformed itself into a provincial congress. Virginia pursued a similar course.

The earliest revolutionary assemblies were called together primarily for the purpose of choosing delegates to the proposed Continental Congress, which convened in September 1774. The next group of assemblies met to select delegates to the Second Continental Congress, which opened in May 1775. The Second Continental Congress, in its turn, further promoted the provincial congresses by tentatively advising certain of them (New Hampshire, South Carolina, and Virginia) to set up their own governments; on May 10, 1776, the Continental Congress urged all provincial congresses to do so.

First called as advisory rather than as lawmaking bodies, the provincial congresses had already severed virtually every tie to British authority, and, presumably acting as representatives of the sovereign people, they had gradually taken over the functions of government, either directly or through committees of safety of their own creation. It remained only for each colony to definitely set up its own system of government.

PRUDHOMME BLUFFS (Écores Prudhomme, also known as the Third Chickasaw Bluffs). A strategic point located on the Mississippi River about 150 miles below the mouth of the Ohio; it was the site of a fort erected by the French explorer Robert Cavelier, Sieur de La Salle, in 1682, and of a new Spanish fort occupied shortly before 1795.

PRUSSIA, TREATIES WITH. In 1785 the United States made a treaty with Prussia that embodied the principles of the Plan of 1776 plus additional principles of the so-called Plan of 1784. The latter provided for preemption rather than confiscation of defined contraband and, in case of war between the two treaty parties, for considerate treatment of enemy aliens and their property within each enemy's domains. The treaty was renewed with some alterations in 1799 and 1828 and continued until World War I.

PSYCHOLOGICAL WARFARE. Official agencies to organize this effort were not designated until the Allied and Axis powers did so during World War I. The U.S. Committee on Public Information (Creel Committee) marked the United States's foray into formal propaganda activities; and in quite a different application, the propaganda section of the American Expeditionary Forces staff headquarters represented the first official U.S. experiment in the military use of psywar.

Psywar is not a substitute for military operations but a complement; it is divided into two broad categories. Strategic psywar usually targets the enemy in its entirety—troops, civilians, and enemy-occupied areas. Tactical psywar usually supports localized combat operations by fostering uncertainty and creating dissension.

Psywar activities were resumed in World War II. Hastily improvised propaganda agencies jealously fought over spheres of interest and mission assignments. It was only when the Office of War Information (OWI) and the Office of Strategic Services (OSS) were formed and their respective functions later redefined that this infighting ceased. Leaflets were by far the most prevalent means of delivery, but loudspeaker and radio broadcasts were also employed.

PSYCHOLOGY. In the first part of the 19th century teachers of moral philosophy courses in colleges spent much time on psychological problems. Most teachers followed the Scottish school of commonsense philosophers, who held that in addition to sensations, inherent moral sense informed a person's mind. Faculty psychology later added the idea that a human mind has the faculties of intellection, feeling, and willing. Each teacher made his own synthesis of faculty and commonsense psychologies.

As the 19th century progressed, philosophical writers and teachers incorporated other European ideas. Particularly influential were the works of association psychologists, such as John Stuart Mill and Herbert Spencer, and the neurophysiologists, who were providing a nervous system correlate for the association of ideas. In the mid-19th century, phrenology provided an important model for a scientific psychology. By the later part of the century, philosophers increasingly were called upon to discuss the physiological basis of thinking. In 1887 religious philosopher George Trumbull Ladd of Yale published the first American textbook of psychology that incorporated the experimental work that was making Germany the fountainhead of what was coming to be called "the new psychology."

A number of Americans studied the new psychology in Germany. Typically the new psychologist presented a trained subject with a sensory stimulus and then recorded what the subject reported was going on in his own mind. By 1874 William James, who had specialized in the teaching of psychology at Harvard, had a few instruments for classroom purposes; but the first formal experimental laboratory in the United States was established by G. Stanley Hall at Johns Hopkins in 1883. Because the development of psychology coincided with the expansion of the American university, graduate school, and scientific laboratory, the discipline was able to establish itself rapidly; by early in the 20th century it had largely separated itself from philosophy departments. In 1887 Hall set up the *American Journal of Psychology,* and in 1894 James McKeen Cattell and J. Mark Baldwin issued the *Psychological Review.* The American Psychological Association was founded in 1892, and by 1899 it had 127 members.

Initially American psychology followed a two-volume textbook published in 1890 by James and acclaimed all over the world. James eclectically surveyed the literature of his day, including neurophysiological, experimental, and philosophical works. He also discussed the general biological setting and such areas as emotion, instinct, and hypnotism that were not strictly experimental. He introduced the concept of the stream of consciousness and emphasized an adaptive, action-oriented view of man.

By the time of World War I, American psychologists were emphasizing viewpoints that differentiated their own discipline from their counterparts overseas. One emphasis was individual differences, pioneered especially by Cattell, who used tests to measure such differentiations. Another was functionalism, the emphasis on the growing, adaptive organism. In 1898 Edward L. Thorndike pioneered experimentation in animal psychology in the area of learning and so began both the use of animal experiments and an interest in mental adaptability (soon known as learning theory). In 1913 John B. Watson of Johns Hopkins introduced behaviorism, an emphasis on performance rather than conscious thought, and experiment under scientifically controlled conditions; thus, he made animal studies the model for human psychology.

The great opportunity to apply psychology came with World War I, when the armed services utilized psychologists in a number of capacities but most notably to apply newly introduced intelligence tests to all army recruits. Mental tests of all sorts created a large market for psychological services thereafter, and the profession grew very rapidly. By 1930 there were 1,100 members of the American Psychological Association. Clearly also, by the interwar years American psychologists dominated the discipline in almost every field throughout the world.

Animal psychology, particularly the inference that animal reactions reveal patterns of human behavior, was an American hallmark of psychology; and the special field that dominated the best efforts was learning theory. But American efforts also proliferated in the applied and clinical fields, especially with mental tests and the influx of psychoanalysts into the United States in the 1930's. A special new interest of the pre–World War II era was personality theory, which combined clinical with genetic and learning viewpoints.

During World War II, psychologists again made themselves useful. An ambitious group centered at Yale determined to bring psychologists into American life as much as possible, largely by expanding the work of clinical and applied psychologists. The group obtained training subsidies from the National Institute of Mental Health, and in the 1950's and 1960's expanded the profession dramatically. In 1980 there were about 50,000 members of the American Psychological Association. Neobehaviorism and learning theory were supplemented as central fields by a renewed interest in cognitive processes, while genetic, abnormal, and social psychology all flourished.

"PUBLIC BE DAMNED." On Oct. 8, 1882, as a New York Central Railroad train bearing W. H. Vanderbilt, president of the railroad, was approaching Chicago, two newspaper reporters boarded the train and interviewed Vanderbilt. In the course of the interview, Vanderbilt replied to a question about "the public benefit," "The public be damned," adding that the public's only interest in the railroads was to get as much as possible out of them for the least cost.

PUBLIC CREDIT ACT (Aug. 4, 1790). A federal statute enacted after Alexander Hamilton's "First Report on the Public Credit" of Jan. 14, 1790. The act provided for the payment of the government's obligations at par with interest (except that Continental currency was to be redeemed at 100 to 1 in specie); the assumption of state debts for services or supplies during the Revolution; and the authorization of loans to meet these obligations.

PUBLIC DEBT. *See* **Debt, Public.**

PUBLIC DOMAIN. The public domain is distinguished from national domain and acquired land. National domain arises from political jurisdiction; acquired land is either bought or received as gifts. The first portion of the public domain or public land was created by cessions of their western land claims by seven of the original thirteen states. Between 1802 and 1898 huge additions to the national domain and the public domain were made through the Louisiana Purchase, the Florida Purchase, the annexation of Texas, and the huge purchase from Mexico in 1848, the Gadsden Purchase, the purchase of Alaska, and the annexation of Hawaii.

From the outset there were two views concerning the policy that should govern the disposal of the public lands. The first, sponsored by Alexander Hamilton, was that the government's need for money to retire its revolutionary war debt and to meet its expenses required it to pledge the public domain for the payment of that debt and to extract from it the greatest possible income. The other view, held by Thomas Jefferson, was that farmer-owners with a stake in the land made the most responsible citizens and that the public lands should be easily accessible to them at little cost. Hamilton's view prevailed for a time. The basic established price was not very high, but to frontiersmen lacking capital or credit it was more than they could raise. Their solution was to squat on public land. Squatters protected themselves through claim associations, and in 1841 sustained a major victory with the adoption of the Distribution-Preemption Act.

In 1862 the West gained its major triumph in the Homestead Act, which made public lands free to settlers who would live on and improve tracts of up to 160 acres for five years. Unfortunately, a substantial portion of the best arable lands had already been alienated through sale to speculators, grants to states, and direct grants to corporations. Grants to states and railroads alone amounted to well over 300 million acres. Individual speculators and land companies invested heavily in land during boom periods, 1816–19, 1833–37, and 1853–57.

Farmers in the High Plains, where a portion of the land had to be left fallow each year, needed up to 320 acres for the extensive cultivation that was necessary. Congress met this difficulty by increasing the quantity that farmmakers could acquire by enacting the Timber Culture Act of 1873, the Desert Land Act of 1877, and the Timber and Stone Act of 1878. Combined with the Preemption and Homestead acts, these measures permitted individuals to acquire up to 1,120 acres in the semiarid High Plains and in the intermountain and desert regions.

Conservationists determined to retain a portion of the land in public ownership: an amendment to the General Revision Act of 1891 authorized the president to withdraw from public entry forest lands on which organized management policies could be introduced. Under President Theodore Roosevelt's leadership gross withdrawals were pushed to nearly 160 million acres. The Reclamation Act (Newlands Act) of 1902 provided that the income from the sale of public lands be used for construction of high dams on western rivers. The government gave an enormous boon to the development of the eleven far western states; but the provisions of the act that were designed to make small farmers the major beneficiaries have been frustrated, and instead large individual and corporate owners have derived the greatest returns.

In 1916 the National Park Service was created to administer areas of superlative natural beauty that were being set aside from the public lands as permanent reserves—Yosemite, Yellowstone, Hot Springs, Glacier, Sequoia, Mount Rainier, Grand Canyon, and Crater Lake.

Rapid and unscientific exploitation of mineral lands by destructive and wasteful practices induced Roosevelt to order the withdrawal of 66 million acres suspected of being underlain with valuable coal deposits and a smaller acreage of suspected oil-bearing land. In 1920 the Mineral Leasing Act provided some control over the exploitation of these withdrawn lands for the first time and allocated 37.5 percent of the proceeds from leasing to the states in which the lands were located and 57.5 percent to reclamation projects; the remaining 5 percent went for schools. The last important withdrawal of public lands from entry was made in 1934. The harmful effects of overgrazing on the ranges of the West had become so evident that even the livestock industry was persuaded to accept federal control.

By the early 1980's there were 186 million acres in the national forests, 26 million acres of which were acquired land bought for watershed protection and other conservation objectives. Best known of the public lands are the 66 million acres in the national parks and national monuments. Of the original 1.23 billion acres in the fifty states, the public domain comprised 762 million acres in 1981.

PUBLIC HEALTH. American colonies during the 17th century took community action to try to control certain diseases, to prevent famine, and to take care of sanitary problems. Port cities established quarantine stations to guard against infected ships; travelers along the roads were inspected at ferry landings or tollhouses; pesthouses were established to isolate infected persons; and sometimes houses and goods were fumigated.

The great population increase and national growth of the 19th century brought a corresponding expansion of public health activities and organizations. Before midcentury, cities had to take over and expand water and sewer systems; to provide for garbage removal; to inspect slum housing, factories, and schools; to build public dispensaries and hospitals;

to inaugurate public vaccination programs; and to foster health education.

Only after the Civil War, with the founding of the American Public Health Association in 1872, was a real basis established for scientific sanitary and health work. During the 1870's, as earlier, public hygienists paid most of their attention to cleansing the environment. Increasingly boards of health became impatient with their general sanitary activities and in the decades after 1885 focused instead on the laboratory diagnosis of disease, on the control of specific infected individuals, and on the development of immunizing agents.

Before the last quarter of the 19th century the federal government played a relatively small role in public health. The first federal civilian agency with broad public health responsibilities was the National Board of Health, created in 1879 with high hopes, but it faded after 1883 because of political squabbling. The Marine Hospital Service, which went back to 1798, acquired federal quarantine functions in the early 1890's. Then, in a series of reorganizations, expansions, and changes of name over the next twenty years, it gradually evolved into the U.S. Public Health Service. By 1910 the service's scientific activities included the regulation of serums and toxins, the conduct of field epidemiological investigations, and the carrying out of laboratory research.

Continuing expansion of public health work in the 20th century was supplemented by private health agencies that sprang up to help educate the public, foster research, and promote legislation. Departments and schools of public health were established after 1910, beginning with those at the Massachusetts Institute of Technology, Harvard, and Johns Hopkins.

In the early 20th century many health officials thought their new knowledge and methods would soon eradicate the infectious diseases and turn the United States into a sanitary utopia. While such diseases as typhoid fever, diphtheria, and scarlet fever did decline greatly, other events, such as the influenza pandemic of 1918–19, pointed up the great difficulties that remained. As concepts of the role of government have gradually changed over the years, so the early 20th-century rejection of health insurance has been slowly undergoing modification, to the point where a comprehensive system of state medicine does not seem to be far off. (*See also* Hygiene.)

PUBLICITY ACTS. In order to restrict stock inflation and overcapitalization and the sale of bogus securities, Congress passed the Publicity Acts of 1903 and 1909, often referred to as the federal Blue Sky laws. These acts, the initial ones in the regulation and control of securities, have been reinforced by similar measures in the states and by the Federal Securities Act (1933) and the Securities Exchange Act (1934).

PUBLICITY AND CORRUPT-PRACTICES LAWS. Publicity laws are an integral part of corrupt-practices legislation; the latter term refers to the regulation of money in the political process. Federal provisions controlling political finance are principally contained in the Federal Election Campaign Act (FECA) of 1972, which was revised in 1974, 1976, and 1979. Federal law requires comprehensive disclosure of candidate and committee receipts and expenditures. Federal law limits amounts contributed by individuals and groups and by candidates to their own campaigns, and it limits amounts that can be spent by, or on behalf of, candidates for federal office. This law is a notable improvement over corresponding provisions of the predecessor Federal Corrupt Practices Act, which was in effect from 1910 until 1972. Federal law requires candidates to file periodic reports, before and after election, disclosing all receipts and expenditures, itemizing full information to identify each person contributing in excess of $250 and each lender or endorser of a loan, and all transfers of funds between committees. The bipartisan Federal Election Commission receives the reports and administers the law.

Major restrictions in the 1974 and 1979 amendments limit contributions to $1,000 per individual for each primary, runoff, or general election, with an aggregate contribution limit of $25,000 to all federal candidates annually; to $5,000 per organization, political committee, and national and state party organizations for each election, but no aggregate limit on the amount organizations can contribute in an election or on the amount organizations can contribute to party organizations supporting federal candidates; to $50,000 for president, $35,000 for U.S. senators, and $25,000 for representatives by candidates and their immediate families.

The national party is allowed to spend $10,000 per candidate in House general elections; $20,000 or 2 cents per eligible voter, whichever is greater, for each candidate in Senate general elections; and 2 cents per voter in presidential general elections. These expenditures are in addition to each candidate's individual spending limit. Fund-raising costs of up to 20 per cent of the candidate spending limit are allowed as an average above the limit.

PUBLIC LAND COMMISSIONS. Established by the U.S. government on four occasions to review federal land policies and to make recommendations for their improvement or redirection. The first of these was authorized by Congress in 1879, when widespread abuse of the settlement laws existed. Recommendations for change included abolition of the unnecessary receivers' office in each land district, better salaries for the staff of the General Land Office, classification of the public lands, sale of the grazing lands, and exchange of lands between the railroads and the government to block areas for more effective management. Congress was not moved to action, although some of the reforms were adopted in 1889–91, by which time the best of the arable land had gone into private ownership.

In 1903 President Theodore Roosevelt appointed the second commission, which recommended the repeal of the Timber and Stone Act of 1878, as had the first commission. It also urged the appraisal of timber and other lands before they were sold; the establishment of grazing districts to be administered by the Department of Agriculture, with fees to be charged for use of the public ranges for grazing; the repeal of the lieu land feature of the Forest Management Act of 1897; and additional safeguards in the Homestead Act of 1862 and

Desert Land Act of 1877. Congress was not receptive, although the lieu land provision was repealed and the forest reserves were transferred from the Department of the Interior to the Agriculture Department's Bureau of Forestry under Pinchot.

President Herbert Hoover proposed to convey the remaining public lands not subject to controlled use by a government agency to the western states. In response to his request, Congress authorized the appointment of the third commission, known as the Committee on the Conservation and Administration of the Public Domain. The committee recommended that the public lands, minus mineral rights, be turned over to the states in the hope that they would establish grazing control but that if they did not, the United States should undertake to do so in the recalcitrant states. It also recommended a procedure to eliminate those portions of the national forests it was not deemed desirable to retain. No action was taken.

The fourth commission came into existence in 1964, the Public Land Law Review Commission. Again, failing to recognize that the public lands belong to the nation and that people of all states are deeply concerned about their management, the commission was strongly slanted toward the western viewpoint. Its final report, *One Third of the Nation's Land,* contained homilies about planning for future needs and multiple use but placed emphasis on giving commercial interests more leeway in utilizing and acquiring ownership of the public lands, although requiring that they pay more for those privileges. Conservationists long accustomed to regarding the National Forest Service as the best administrative agency dealing with land matters were troubled by the proposal to consolidate it with the Bureau of Land Management. Environmentalists feared that the commission's failure to recommend the repeal of the Mining Act of 1872, which had been responsible for some of the most serious errors of the past in land administration, showed a marked insensitivity to public attitudes.

PUBLIC LANDS. *See* **Public Domain.**

PUBLIC LANDS, FENCING OF. The range cattle industry was based on the use of the public domain for grazing purposes. There was no serious objection to this practice as long as the range remained open and the country was not wanted by settlers. After the invention of barbed wire during the 1870's, complaints began to pour into the General Land Office that illegal enclosures of public land were being made. By this means land companies were able to control large ranges and keep other cattlemen out. Settlers were also demanding access to the land, and fence-cutters' wars were frequent occurrences. Congressional legislation and a presidential proclamation in 1885 ordered the removal of the fences, but it was not until 1889 that any progress was made in eliminating the illegal fencing of public land.

PUBLIC LANDS, SURVEY OF. The first settlers measured out lands on the basis of "metes and bounds," the shape of a tract being determined by natural features. The colonies began a system of surveys for outlining towns. Massachusetts attempted to lay them out in six-mile-square tracts. Connecticut likewise attempted a five-mile-square town, and the square town, or township, was, in a small way, attempted in South Carolina.

The present rectangular survey was adopted as a feature of the Land Ordinance of 1785. It provides for the survey of all public land into townships six miles square (*see* Seven Ranges, Survey of). The townships are numbered running north and south from certain east-west baselines (*see* Geographer's Line). A township is divided into thirty-six sections, each a mile square. This survey system applies, with a few local exceptions, to all states of the Union except the thirteen original states and Vermont, Maine, Kentucky, Tennessee, West Virginia, Hawaii, and Texas.

PUBLIC LAND SALES. It was the practice of the United States after the Indian title to land had been surrendered and the land surveyed and divided into townships to offer the sections at public auction. The minimum price was $2.00 an acre until 1820 and $1.25 an acre thereafter. Credit was allowed before 1820, but later the successful bidder had to pay the full cash price on the day of sale. The sales reached their peak in 1836, when 25 million acres were sold and the receipts constituted nearly one-half of the total revenue of the government. Some of the buying was by petty speculators, but more was bought by eastern capitalist speculators and land companies. Anxiety about their claims led squatters to organize claim associations to prevent competitive bidding and provide a form of registration of boundaries before the county organization and title registration had been established. In a few instances prices were bid to absurd levels, as in potential cotton districts of Mississippi and Alabama, but it was usual to forfeit the contracts without making any payment; then at the next sale the lands could go for the minimum price. Worker demands for "lands for the landless" led the government to slow down the public offering of land at auction in the late 1850's and after 1862 leave most public land open only to entry by settlers under the preemption and homestead laws.

PUBLIC LAND STATES. The thirty "sovereign" commonwealths created by the United States out of territory (1) ceded by the older states (Ohio, Indiana, Illinois, Michigan, Wisconsin, Alabama, and Mississippi); (2) acquired by purchase (Florida, Alaska, and all the states west of the Mississippi River except Texas, Oregon, Washington, and Idaho); or (3) acquired from England by the Oregon Treaty of 1846 (Washington, Oregon, and Idaho). Within these thirty public land states there were 35 million acres in land claims given by predecessor governments and reservations established by Virginia and Connecticut that never became part of the public lands of the United States.

PUBLIC OPINION. A term that has been in common usage in the United States since the late 18th century. In its earliest usage the "public" in "public opinion" was equated with the landholders or propertyowners in whom the franchise was vested. Public opinion is commonly associated with concepts integral to democracy and consequently receives very close attention. Majority rule, consent of the governed, and representative government can hardly be discussed without reference to it.

Public opinion research burgeoned after 1935. Both American and world associations for public opinion research came into being. The Gallup Poll, originated by George H. Gallup in the 1930's, became the prototype of public opinion polling around the world, as many other widely known polling organizations were developed, mostly in the decade 1935–45: the Harris Poll, the Opinion Research Corporation, and the National Opinion Research Center.

PUBLIC OWNERSHIP. In the first half of the 19th century, the only important federal ownership was in the first and second Bank of the United States, chartered in 1791 and 1816 for twenty-year periods. The government subscribed to one-fifth of the capital of both banks and appointed their directors. Although the banks did provide some central banking functions, they were essentially private. Some states have established banks, flour mills, and housing programs and have offered loans to farmers. Others have only miscellaneous holdings.

Most government ownership has been on the federal level. The Congress was authorized under the Constitution to establish a post office and a mint, to build post roads, and to provide for the common defense. Federal ownership was limited to those areas throughout the 19th century. In 1904 the federal government reentered the field of corporate enterprise when it purchased the Panama Railroad Company, which was part of the Canal Zone. Under the Shipping Act of 1916 the U.S. Shipping Board was authorized to form one or more corporations to purchase, construct, equip, maintain, and operate merchant vessels. At the beginning of World War I the Shipping Board formed the Emergency Fleet Corporation.

In addition to transportation, public ownership has been most notable in the light and power industry. In 1925 less than 4 percent of all electric power for public use was produced in publicly owned and operated plants; in 1960 the figure was closer to 20 percent. The beginnings of public power on a large scale date to World War I, but it was the Tennessee Valley Act of 1933 that created a broad program for flood control, navigational aids, power production, and reforestation. The Tennessee Valley Authority (TVA) brought electricity to the region, fostered rapid industrialization, and supplied energy for the atomic energy plants at Oak Ridge and at Paducah, Ky.

There was also a great expansion in the lending operations of the national government. In 1916 the twelve federal farm banks were set up, and these continued to operate in the mid-1970's. The largest loan agency, the Reconstruction Finance Corporation (RFC), was a product of the Great Depression. It began operations in July 1932 to rescue foundering businesses by granting temporary loans. Gradually the powers of the RFC were broadened. In 1933 it was permitted to subscribe to preferred stock in sound banks; and in 1939 it was allowed to assist in the financing of wartime agencies to make loans to new industries that could not obtain funds from commercial banks. It was liquidated in 1953.

While the total of federal assets continued to grow, the bulk of the assets was not in areas that competed directly with private business in the early 1980's. Federal facilities accounted for about 20 percent of all public construction in the United States, but they were mostly in water resources, power generation, space facilities, research complexes, defense establishments, office buildings, and museums.

PUBLIC REVENUE. *See* **Revenue, Public.**

PUBLIC UTILITIES. Standing between the privately owned competitive firms and government departments or bureaus public utilities are for the most part profit-oriented, privately owned firms. Since public ownership is shunned and competition is considered to be an inadequate regulator, government regulation replaces control through market processes.

Among the industries that have at one time or another been classified as public utilities are (1) industries providing transportation (common carriers—railroads, bus lines, trucking companies, pipelines); (2) industries providing services incidental to transportation (stockyards, warehouses, elevators, docks, terminals); (3) industries providing services facilitating communication (telegraph, telephone, radio and television broadcasting); (4) industries furnishing facilities that provide power, light, heat, and refrigeration; and (5) industries furnishing facilities that provide water and sanitation.

The early corporations in America were chartered by special legislative acts. Along with each grant of special privilege went the understanding that the corporation so chartered was to serve the public interest. And what the state gave the state could take away in the event of unsatisfactory performance. Even before the Dartmouth College decision this approach had been successfully protested by the owners of property used in the provision of public utility services, on the very grounds validated by the Dartmouth College case: a corporation charter was not a revocable gift, but instead a contract for services, revocable only by mutual agreement. The Dartmouth College decision did not end the use of regulation by charter. State legislators simply built additional restrictions and controls into the charter itself and supplemented them by the passage of control statutes and the establishment of investigatory commissions. But in the face of rapidly changing economic circumstances, this proved to be an awkward, hit-or-miss procedure. An alternative arrangement, the "mixed corporation," whereby state governments provided part of the capital and secured some degree of control, also proved not to be viable.

As the 19th century wore on, the practice of regulating by charter fell into disfavor. The distinction between public utilities and other industries narrowed. That the distinction was a vital one became manifest after the Civil War. Users of railroad services often found themselves confronted with exorbitant, discriminatory demands by sole providers of what had by then become a vitally necessary service. The result was the passage of state laws, in the Midwest and elsewhere, setting limits on railroad rates and limiting the ability of railroads to discriminate between customers. Opposition to the practice of legislative control was intense, but it received a sharp setback in 1877 when the U.S. Supreme Court (*Munn v. Illinois*) laid down the dictum that when property was devoted to a public calling, it was subject to public control.

The rudiments of federal control of the railroads came into being in 1887, in the form of the Interstate Commerce Act, which established the Interstate Commerce Commission (ICC) to administer the act. Federal regulation was established in principle, but effective regulation in practice proved to be far more difficult to institute. During the first decade of the 20th century the federal legislature extended the jurisdiction of the commission to telephone, telegraph, and cable companies. As other public utilities developed, they were placed under the jurisdiction of specialized federal commissions, such as the Federal Power Commission and Civil Aeronautics Board.

State governments moved in the direction of establishing strong commissions that could provide continuous supervision of the intrastate public utilities and permit the setting of general standards of control. In general the public utility commissions fixed rates that would justify reasonably adequate service and facilities, by administrative order on the basis of the common law.

By the end of the 1920's the secure role of the public utilities was reflected in the vigorous movement of public utility securities in the booming stock market. Later this hard-won consensus largely evaporated. The comprehensive regulation of virtually all industries during the New Deal period, during World War II, and in the price control era of the early 1970's served to blur the distinction between ordinary competitive firms and public utility companies. But perhaps of greatest importance was the conviction that the regulatory process was not working. By the mid-1970's some tentative moves had been made in the direction of recognizing that one public utility industry cannot be singled out for control without taking into account repercussions on other regulated industries. In 1978 airlines were deregulated and in 1979 trucking and railroad regulation was substantially reduced.

PUBLIC UTILITY HOLDING COMPANY ACT. *See* **Wheeler-Rayburn Act.**

PUBLIC WORKS ADMINISTRATION (PWA). A government agency created in 1933 by the National Industrial Recovery Act. It continued with changes in organization until 1943, when it was absorbed into a different federal agency. It provided work for the unemployed by carrying on major public projects: slum clearance, dam-building for flood control, land conservation, highway and airport construction, and the construction of public buildings.

PUEBLO. The Pueblo Indians of Arizona and New Mexico share an essentially uniform culture and society, but their languages include four major linguistic families.

Spanish knowledge of the Pueblo dates from 1539, when Marcos de Niza reported on the fabled Seven Cities of Cíbola. Spanish contacts with the Rio Grande Pueblo and occasional visits to the western Hopi and Zuni continued until missionary and military pressures instigated the Pueblo Revolt of 1680–96. The Pueblo were centered in Arizona and New Mexico by 1700, and although influenced by the Spanish, they tended to retain their aboriginal theocratic organization. Nominally Christian, the Pueblo have effected a syncretism of aboriginal modes and Roman Catholic elements. The Spanish-built churches were eclipsed by the presence of the kiva, the semisubterranean ritual chamber where the agricultural fetishes continue to be kept.

Archaeologists trace the beginnings of the Pueblo to the so-called Basket Maker horizon, a desert focus of incipient desert agriculture two millennia old. The great period of the Pueblo, from A.D. 1000 to 1300, was marked by population concentration in Mesa Verde, Chaco Canyon, and other prehistoric monuments. These were marked by multistoried buildings of coursed stone and adobe. The great sites were abandoned because of drought.

Some differences in societal structure appear between the western and eastern Pueblo. Hopi and Zuni in the west strongly stress matrilineal kinship, having elaborate clan organizations based on affiliation through the female line. In the east there is paternal development with dual divisions of village society, the so-called moiety organizations.

***PUEBLO* INCIDENT** (Jan. 23, 1968). Twenty miles from Wonsan, North Korea, four North Korean patrol craft ordered the U.S.S. *Pueblo* to heave to. When it failed to do so, the vessels brought it under fire. Engaged in the collection of electronic intelligence, the *Pueblo* did not resist, and it was seized. According to U.S. sources, the ship was in international waters. North Korea charged that it was an "armed spy boat" in the territorial waters of North Korea. The U.S. government gained release of the crew eleven months later by signing an apology, which it simultaneously repudiated. The ship remained in North Korea.

PUEBLO REVOLT (1680–96). In New Mexico, a revolt was engineered by Popé, a Tewa Indian of San Juan Pueblo, who in 1675 had been flogged by the Spaniards for practicing Pueblo religious rites. Popé preached a return to Indian ways, plus the driving out of the Spaniards. All the Pueblo north of Isleta, N.Mex., participated. In a concerted uprising the Indians destroyed all the missions and killed about 400 Spaniards. The rest of the Spaniards fled south to El Paso. Attempts at reconquest by the Spaniards were unsuccessful prior to 1692, by which time the brief unity of the Pueblo had been shattered by internal dissension.

PUERTO RICO. The island of Puerto Rico is the smallest and most easterly of the Greater Antilles, which form the broken northern boundary of the Caribbean Sea. Discovered by Christopher Columbus on his second voyage in 1493, the island was colonized in 1508 by Juan Ponce de León. The scarce gold deposits and the sparse Indian population were both soon exhausted by the Spaniards, who retained the island principally as a key defense outpost. After the Spanish-American War, the United States retained Puerto Rico as its first colony in the tropics. Substantial private investments were made in the establishment of large agricultural corporations dedicated to sugarcane.

The islanders, although largely of Spanish stock, with African and some Indian admixtures, accepted the change of sovereignty with favor, expecting it would bring them a more democratic form of government. Although they were granted American citizenship in 1917, it was not until 1947 that they were given the right to elect their own governor. The first elected Puerto Rican governor was Luis Muñoz Marín. With the permission of the U.S. government and the approval of the people of Puerto Rico, he created the Commonwealth of Puerto Rico. Established by a constitutional convention in 1952, under it local autonomy is restricted only by the U.S. Constitution and laws of Congress that specifically mention Puerto Rico. Puerto Rico elects a nonvoting resident commissioner to Congress. The existing relationship with the United States was approved by more than 60 percent of those voting in a plebiscite in 1967. A sizable minority, 38.9 percent of those voting, expressed support for eventual statehood for Puerto Rico. A small group in favor of independence, estimated at roughly 10 percent of the population, boycotted the plebiscite.

For the first fifty years under American control Puerto Rico was primarily a producer of agricultural products, such as sugar, pineapples, coffee, and tobacco. Although Puerto Rico lies within the customs barrier of the United States, federal tax laws, including income and excise taxes, do not apply to the island. An industrial development program known as Operation Bootstrap was so successful in bringing industrial enterprises to the island that by 1957 the contribution of the industrial sector of the economy surpassed that of the agricultural sector. In the 1970's tourism was making an important contribution to the island economy, and Puerto Rico had an important potential source of income in the form of untapped minerals, such as copper, nickel, and some iron. With a population density of about 900 persons per square mile in 1975, Puerto Rico has been the source of a migration of about a million people to the United States. (*See also* Foraker Act; Jones Act.)

PUGET SOUND. An arm of the Pacific Ocean located in northwestern Washington. The British expedition under Capt. George Vancouver was the first to explore Puget Sound (1792). The sound itself was named for one of Vancouver's officers, Lt. Peter Puget. Important ports have developed along the shores of Puget Sound, and the establishment in 1891 of the Puget Sound Naval Shipyard at Bremerton created an immense ship construction industry.

PUJO COMMITTEE. In February 1912 the House of Representatives passed a resolution directing its Committee on Banking and Currency to ascertain whether there existed "a money trust." A subcommittee headed by Rep. Arsène Pujo of Louisiana conducted hearings, at which J. P. Morgan, George F. Baker, and other financiers testified. The committee issued a majority report declaring that existing banking and credit practices resulted in a "vast and growing concentration of control of money and credit in the hands of a comparatively few men." This disclosure led eventually to the passage of the Federal Reserve Act (1913) and the Clayton Antitrust Act (1914).

PULASKI, FORT. Named for Casimir Pulaski, Polish military commander in the American Revolution; located on Cockspur Island in Savannah harbor, commanding both channels of the Savannah River. Construction began in 1829 and was completed in 1847. Georgia state troops seized Fort Pulaski in January 1861, but on Apr. 11, 1862, it was recaptured and held by Union forces for the remainder of the Civil War. The fort was designated Fort Pulaski National Monument in 1924.

PULLMAN COMPANY. *See* **Pullmans; Pullman Strike; Railroads, Sketches of Principal Lines.**

PULLMANS. The railroad sleeping cars that popularized long-distance rail travel. New York cabinetmaker George M. Pullman arrived in Chicago during 1855 to improve poor sleeping car conditions. At Bloomington, Ill., in 1858, Pullman remodeled two Chicago and Alton coaches into sleeping cars, each of which contained ten sleeping sections, two washrooms, and a linen locker. Although this venture proved unprofitable, Pullman in 1864 created a more elaborate car. The "Pioneer," as it was called, was enlarged in height and width and contained a folding upper berth, sliding seats, artistically decorated furnishings, special car springs, and better lighting, heating, and ventilation. In 1867 the Pullman Palace Car Company was incorporated, with a capitalization of $1 million.

PULLMAN STRIKE (1894). As a result of the panic of 1893, the Pullman Palace Car Company, which manufactured sleeping cars, lowered the wages of its employees an average of 25 percent. No reduction was made in the rentals and fees charged employees in the company town at Pullman, just south of Chicago. About 4,000 disgruntled employees joined Eugene V. Debs's American Railway Union in the spring of 1894. On May 11, 1894, about 2,500 Pullman employees quit work and forced the closing of the shops. The company refused to bargain with the union, although Pullman officials expressed readiness to deal with employees individually. The local strike soon developed into a general railroad strike.

Federal judges William A. Woods and Peter S. Grosscup issued a "blanket injunction," prohibiting all interference with trains. The injunction was defied, and violence was resorted to by the strikers. Thereupon, President Grover Cleveland ordered federal troops into Chicago on July 4. Following their arrival, there was much mob violence and destruction of railroad property. By July 13 some trains were running under military guard, and a few days later the strike was broken.

PULP. *See* **Paper and Pulp Industry.**

PULTENEY PURCHASE (1791). The residue of the Phelps-Gorham Purchase (from Massachusetts), comprised over 1 million acres in western New York. These "Genesee lands" were purchased for £75,000 from William Franklin, Robert Morris' London agent, by a group calling itself the Pulteney Associates. Charles Williamson, the group's first American agent, laid out Bath, N.Y., in 1793. The last transaction of the Pulteney Associates was recorded in December 1926.

PUMP-PRIMING. Government spending during a recessionary period, in an attempt to stimulate private spending and the expansion of business and industry. Economic pump-priming was begun in 1932 under President Herbert Hoover, when the Reconstruction Finance Corporation was created to make loans to banks, railroads, and other industries. President Franklin D. Roosevelt became convinced by the fall of 1933 that pump-priming was necessary to achieve economic recovery. Thereafter, through the Reconstruction Finance Corporation, the work-relief agencies, the Public Works Administration, and other organizations, billions of dollars were used for priming the pump. The recession of 1937 caused the Roosevelt administration to again resort to extensive pump-priming in 1938.

In the post–World War II period, pump-priming has become an unquestioned function of government economic policy. Some government programs, such as unemployment insurance, automatically act as pump-primers, since government expenditures must increase as people lose jobs during a recession. Since the 1960's, putting more disposable income into the economy by cutting taxes has come to be a widely accepted economic policy.

PUNISHMENT, CRUEL AND UNUSUAL. Prohibition of "cruel and unusual punishments" was included in a number of the original state constitutions of the revolutionary period. When a national Bill of Rights was adopted in 1791, the guarantee was included in the Eighth Amendment to prevent excesses by the government such as had been common in 17th-century England.

In the 1960's the issue of whether capital punishment was "cruel and unusual" became prominent. In 1972 the U.S. Supreme Court, in *Furman* v. *Georgia,* did strike down all capital punishment statutes, but only on the grounds that the death sentence was being administered arbitrarily. In the wake of the decision several states enacted laws that mandated capital punishment for certain crimes, removing any discretion judges or juries had in handing down the sentence. By 1981, thirty-six states had capital punishment.

PUNISHMENTS, COLONIAL. Although punishments in colonial America were generally harsh, the New England colonies and the Quaker colonies of Pennsylvania and West Jersey had a more humane set of criminal penalties than prevailed in New York and the South. In West Jersey only treason and murder were capital offenses, and in Pennsylvania murder alone was punishable by death. Imprisonment at hard labor was prescribed in most cases for noncapital crimes, but by 1700 the Quakers had abandoned their early humane theories with regard to punishment.

In Massachusetts barbarous or inhumane tortures were forbidden almost from the beginning. However, the Puritan code leaned in the direction of exemplary and humiliating punishments, such as the ducking stool for the scold, the stocks for the vagrant, the letter "A" sewn on the garment for the adulterer, and the branding iron for the burglar; drunkards were required to sit astride a wooden horse with an empty pitcher in one hand. Hanging was the normal method of capital punishment, and it was by this method, not by burning, that persons convicted of witchcraft in New England were executed.

In New York and the South two tendencies stand out conspicuously—the extreme severity of the penalties prescribed and the almost exclusive employment of fines or some form of corporal punishment. Whipping, branding, mutilations, confinement in the stock or pillory, and ducking were among the most prevalent forms of corporal punishment. At times whippings were carried to excess. (The New Englanders observed the Mosaic law setting thirty-nine stripes as the maximum penalty.) In addition to hanging, burning and quartering were also employed in New York and the South as means of capital punishment. Many of the blacks convicted in the "Negro Plot" of 1741 were burned at the stake. Others were sent to a penal colony, a method also used in New England for dealing with captive Indians in wartime. Treason was punished by dismembering the body of the executed person and disposing of the parts in various communities.

Both in New England and in the South mutilation was not uncommon. In the South, for contempt of court, an ear might be cut off or a tongue pierced with a hot iron. In Virginia an ear might be nailed to the pillory and then cut off to punish a slave for running away. For slander, in Virginia, the tongue might be bored through with an awl.

PURCHASING POWER. *See* **Money.**

PURE FOOD AND DRUG MOVEMENT. The American colonies, enacted local laws to fight adulteration of bread, butter, and beer and to strive for honest and proper weighing, packing, and storing of various foods. Toward the middle of the 19th century, states and municipalities expanded laws striving to protect milk, meat, and other susceptible foods. By 1900 most states had enacted general food laws, but few of them were effective.

The first federal law in the field, passed in 1848, forbade the importation of adulterated and spurious drugs. During the quarter of a century after 1880, more than a hundred food and drug bills were introduced into Congress, which enacted special laws concerning tea, oleomargarine, filled cheese, mixed flour, renovated butter, meat exports, and opium imports. A general law, with broad provisions covering all foods and drugs, was passed in 1888 for the District of Columbia.

Most food producers favored national regulation. At the turn of the century a revitalized American Medical Association became a powerful lobbying force in behalf of a law.

The Pure Food and Drugs Act of 1906 forbade interstate and foreign commerce in adulterated and misbranded food and drugs. Drugs had either to abide by standards of purity and quality listed in the *United States Pharmacopoeia* or the *National Formulary* or to meet individual standards chosen by their manufacturers and stated on labels. Food standards were not provided, but the law prohibited the adulteration of food by the removal of valuable constituents, the substitution of ingredients so as to reduce quality, the addition of deleterious ingredients, the concealment of damage, and the use of spoiled animal or vegetable products. Making false or misleading label statements regarding a food or drug constituted misbranding. The courts in general gave the law a liberal interpretation, treating convicted violators leniently, with light fines and almost no imprisonments.

In 1933 a strong consumer-oriented measure went to the Congress from the Food and Drug Administration (FDA)—the new name adopted for the Bureau of Chemistry in 1927. The affected industries found great fault with it. A five-year period of attritional compromise began. Despite the compromises, the Food, Drug, and Cosmetic Act of 1938 greatly strengthened consumer protection. It increased penalties and added a new legal weapon, the injunction. The FDA was empowered to establish food standards that had the effect of law. Cosmetics and therapeutic devices came under regulation for the first time. False labeling was extended to now include not only erroneous positive statements but also the failure to include adequate warnings. New drugs could not be marketed until their manufacturers had convinced the FDA of their safety.

This "new drug" provision furnished a precedent for one of the major regulatory developments occurring after 1938, the trend toward preventive law. Congress enacted laws requiring proof of safety prior to marketing for pesticides (1954), food additives (1958), and color additives (1960). Laws forbade the marketing of insulin and antibiotics until the FDA had tested and certified each batch. An important new step, premarketing proof of drug efficacy, was added in 1962.

Besides acquiring new duties within its traditional areas of control, the FDA constantly acquired new tasks by act of Congress. Modest controls over household containers of caustic poisons (1927) were expanded (1960) and extended to flammable fabrics (1953, 1967), products emitting radiation (1969), and toys (1969). In 1972 the FDA was given responsibility for regulating biological products, such as vaccines, which the Public Health Service had controlled since 1902.

Critics found fault with the FDA's organization and procedures, particularly shortcomings of scientific competence. Congress, while giving the FDA more money and new tasks, also markedly increased the degree and continuity of oversight. A new wave of critics came with the ecological crisis. Environment-minded consumers condemned the FDA's policies as industry-oriented, as not severe enough in their definitions of hazards to health. Such dissatisfaction led to a broad consumer-product safety law, passed in 1972, which gave to the new Consumer Product Safety Commission regulatory authority over consumer products not traditionally within the FDA's purview.

Meat inspection under the Department of Agriculture was expanded to cover other than red meats. Dangerous drugs, such as barbiturates, amphetamines, and LSD, which might be abused, became subject to special regulation by the FDA under a 1965 law. In 1968 the FDA's Bureau of Drug Abuse Control was fused with the Bureau of Narcotics to form the Bureau of Narcotics and Dangerous Drugs in the Department of Justice. In 1973 the name of this bureau was changed to the Drug Enforcement Administration.

PURITANS AND PURITANISM. The terms "Puritans" and "Puritanism" originated in England in the 1560's, when they were used to describe the people who wished to reform the Church of England and strove to "purify" it of what they considered the remnants of Roman Catholicism. Puritans were men of intense piety, who took literally and seriously the doctrines of original sin and salvation by faith; they believed that true Christians should obey the will of God as expressed in divine revelation, and they condemned the Church of England because they found its order impious and anti-Christian. After 1603 their opposition to the church became allied with the parliamentary opposition to the royal prerogative; in the 1640's Puritans and Parliamentarians united in open warfare against Charles I. Puritanism was thus a movement of religious protest connected with the struggle of a rising capitalist middle class against the absolutist state. It proved incapable of maintaining unity within its own ranks and split into myriad sects and opinions. A small congregation of these extremists fled to America and established the Plymouth colony in 1620, although the major contribution of Puritanism to America was made through the settlement established by the Massachusetts Bay Company in 1630. Within the next decade some 20,000 persons came to Massachusetts and Connecticut and there built a society and a church in strict accordance with Puritan ideals. Ruled by vigorous leaders, these colonies were able to perpetuate and to institutionalize Puritanism in America long after the English movement had sunk into confusion.

PURPLE HEART, ORDER OF THE. *See* **Decorations, Military.**

PUT-IN BAY NAVAL BATTLE. *See* **Erie, Lake, Battle of.**

QUAKER HILL, BATTLE AT. *See* **Sullivan in Rhode Island.**

QUAKERS. Members of the Society of Friends, first came to America after Quakerism emerged from the Puritan Revolution in England. The society was founded by George Fox, who began preaching in 1647, as a democratic, apostolic Christian sect, and since it had no place for priest or presbyter, it seemed to threaten church and government alike. Fox's doctrine that God's Inner Light illuminates the heart of every man and woman converted many; Ann Austin and Mary Fisher carried the message to Barbados in 1655 and thence to Boston in 1656. There the Puritan authorities imprisoned them, burned their Quaker books, and finally shipped them back to Barbados. Zealous Quaker missionaries, continuing to invade the Massachusetts Bay Colony, suffered fines, flogging, banishment, and even hanging. In Rhode Island, on the other hand, leading families embraced the new faith and established the "yearly meeting" for worship and church business at Newport in 1661.

Continuing persecution at home prompted an increasing emigration of British Quakers to the New World. Settlements in West Jersey preceded the "Holy Experiment" that William Penn, convert to Quakerism, undertook in 1681 in Pennsylvania. The Pennsylvania Friends organized a yearly meeting in 1681, which became the most influential in America; other yearly meetings took form in Maryland (1672), New York (1695), and North Carolina (1698); subordinate quarterly meetings were established, with monthly meetings the basic congregational units of the society. Friends met for worship to wait upon the Lord, maintaining a silence broken only by occasional sermons and prayers by men and women who felt the Spirit move them. They renounced ritual and the outward sacraments and eschewed music and art.

As persecution almost ceased after the British Toleration Act of 1689, quietism rather than active proselytism became the rule. Friends perfected their organization as a "peculiar people" and punished by disownment breaches of the discipline, such as marrying out of the society. They withdrew from politics after the mid-18th century, primarily because of the conflict between their pacifism and the military necessities of the French and Indian War and the American Revolution.

The evangelical movement that splintered 19th-century American Protestantism also brought schism to the Society of Friends. The Great Separation of 1827–28, beginning in Philadelphia, produced Orthodox and Hicksite groups, the former evangelical and the latter more Unitarian in tendency. The Hicksites avoided further separations and united in the biennial General Conference in 1902. But among the Orthodox, evangelicalism produced schism after schism, beginning with a small Wilburite, or Conservative, separation in New England in 1845. The Philadelphia yearly meeting forestalled further division by ceasing to correspond with other Orthodox bodies in 1857 and by refusing to join the Orthodox Five Years Meeting, which began to take form in 1887.

Theological differences diminished in the 20th century among Friends in the eastern United States and Canada, who largely followed the older Quaker practice of unprogrammed, nonpastoral worship. On the other hand, the fundamentalist-modernist controversy gave fresh life to evangelical fervor in some western Orthodox meetings. Oregon withdrew from the Five Years Meeting in 1926—after 1965 called Friends United Meeting—as did Kansas in 1937; and in 1966 they both joined Ohio and Rocky Mountain yearly meetings in forming the Evangelical Friends Alliance.

Quakers had attacked the slave trade and slavery in the 18th and 19th centuries and made notable contributions in the fields of Indian relations, prison reform, education, woman's rights, temperance, and the care of the insane, and their modern descendants sought to apply Quaker principles to the problems of war and social maladjustment. The American Friends Service Committee, organized in 1917 to enable Friends to substitute noncombatant relief work for military service, united all Quaker groups in promoting their peace testimony. The committee's pioneering in crisis situations in the United States and abroad brought them and their English counterpart, the Friends Service Council, the Nobel Peace Prize in 1947.

Friends opposed the Vietnam War from the beginning and highlighted their peaceful campaign against the war by attempting to bring relief to suffering civilians on both sides. As in World War II some went to prison rather than have anything to do with the Selective Service System, while others accepted alternative service under civilian auspices. The five major Quaker groups in North America had 131,000 members in the early 1980's.

QUANTRILL'S RAID (Aug. 21, 1863). William Clarke Quantrill, at the head of a band of 448 Missouri guerrillas, raided Lawrence, Kans., in the early dawn. The town was taken completely by surprise and was undefended; the raiders scattered over the town, killing, burning, and plundering indiscriminately. The known dead numbered more than 150. Withdrawing at the approach of federal troops, the guerrillas, although pursued, were able to reach Missouri with few losses (*see* Border War).

QUARTERING. *See* **Billeting.**

QUARTERING ACTS. The first quartering act was passed in March 1765 for a two-year term; it required the colonies to provide barracks for British troops. A second act, 1766, provided for quartering troops in inns and uninhabited buildings. The Quartering Act of June 2, 1774, one of the Coercion Acts, was passed by Parliament to permit effective action by the British troops sent to Boston after the Tea Party in 1773. It provided that when there were no barracks where troops were required, the authorities must provide quarters for them on the spot; if they failed to do so, the governor might compel the use of occupied buildings. (*See also* Billeting.)

QUASI-JUDICIAL AGENCIES. Administrative bodies that, although different in character and function from courts, adjudicate while engaging in public administration. The Interstate Commerce Commission (created in 1887) is the most striking example. Franklin D. Roosevelt's presidency (1933–45) marked a growing awareness of the agencies' revolutionary role within the American legal setup and the beginning of persistent attempts to curb such agencies. Compromise was achieved in the 1946 Administrative Procedure Act prescribing uniform procedures for agency hearings, greater publicity for administrative regulations, broader judicial review, and separation of prosecutorial and decisional functions through an increase in the independence of hearing examiners.

QUASI-WAR. *See* **Naval War With France.**

QUEBEC, CAPTURE OF. In 1759 British Gen. James Wolfe was ordered to capture Quebec. Sailing from Louisburg in May, he landed on the Île d'Orléans below Quebec and made many abortive attempts against the city. The

French under Marquis Louis Joseph de Montcalm defended the north bank of the St. Lawrence from the city to the Montmorency River. On July 31 Wolfe aimed an unsuccessful stroke by land and water at the Montmorency end. Attacks in August were also unsuccessful.

On Sept. 3, Wolfe secretly moved 3,000 soldiers to the ships upstream. On the night of Sept. 12, he effected a surprise landing near the city and made it possible for about 5,000 troops, rowed over from the south shore and brought downstream by the ships, to land safely and climb to the heights of the Plains of Abraham by six in the morning.

Montcalm thus had to assemble and fight for the possession of Quebec. Wolfe was killed on the field, and Montcalm was mortally wounded. Wolfe's successor entrenched and closed in, and the surrender of Quebec on Sept. 18 made inevitable British hegemony in Canada.

QUEBEC, PHIPS'S ATTACK ON (1690). In retaliation for French depredations, the New England colonies and New York formed an expedition to capture Canada for England. On Aug. 9 Sir William Phips sailed from Massachusetts with thirty ships, 2,000 men, and provisions for four months, bound for Quebec. When the English fleet appeared before Quebec on Oct. 16, the fortress was garrisoned by 2,700 men. The English landing party was repulsed, and Phips within a week sailed for home.

QUEBEC ACT (May 20, 1774). One of the Intolerable Acts, passed by Parliament to pacify the French-Canadians by granting free exercise of the Roman Catholic religion and reestablishing French civil law in Quebec. The boundaries of Quebec were extended to the Ohio River and to the Mississippi. The interior was thereby closed and the hopes of colonial land speculators were blasted. Colonial propagandists used the act to widen the breach between Great Britain and colonies.

QUEBEC CONFERENCES (1943–44). During World War II, two important conferences were held in Quebec, Canada. The first, Aug. 11–24, 1943, brought President Franklin D. Roosevelt and British Prime Minister Winston Churchill together. They and their military staffs agreed on the general plan for an invasion of Normandy, a "Second Front" against Hitler's Germany. They also set up a special command in southeastern Asia under Adm. Lord Louis Mountbatten. A second conference was held Sept. 11–16, 1944. This dealt with postwar settlements with the Germans and Japanese.

QUEEN ANNE'S WAR (1702–13). American counterpart of the War of the Spanish Succession fought in Europe. In America the war was fought in the West Indies and on the Carolina and New England frontiers. After some indecisive battles between the English and French, military activity in the West Indies was restricted to privateering, from which English colonial trade suffered. In December 1702 South Carolinians destroyed the town of Spanish St. Augustine.

New England bore the brunt of the war against the French in Canada. Until 1709 neither New York nor England rendered material assistance. English settlements became victims of French and Indian raids. With British support, colonial troops took Port Royal in October 1710, marking the fall of Acadia to Great Britain.

In 1711, peace negotiations began in Europe. In October 1712, American colonial governors received a royal proclamation of an armistice, and on Apr. 11, 1713, Queen Anne's War was concluded by the Treaty of Utrecht.

QUEENSTON HEIGHTS, BATTLE OF (Oct. 13, 1812). Arose out of the attempt of American Maj. Gen. Stephen Van Rensselaer to invade Canada across the Niagara River. The advanced units of the American force (about 3,100 men) established themselves upon the steep escarpment overlooking Queenston, Ontario, and defeated attempts of the British to dislodge them. The British commander, Maj. Gen. Isaac Brock, was killed. Later in the day British Maj. Gen. Roger Sheaffe and about 1,000 men captured the whole force that had crossed the Niagara.

QUIDS. Adapted from *tertium quid* ("third something"), the term "quid" was used in the early 19th century to refer to a member of a third political party or faction composed of disaffected Jeffersonian (or Democratic) Republicans who attracted Federalist support with varying success.

QUINTEROS BAY EPISODE (Aug. 20, 1891). One factor that caused anti-U.S. feeling among rebel Chilean forces known as Congressionalists, following the overthrow of President Balmaceda. The Valparaíso press charged that a U.S. ship captain broke neutrality laws when, after observing the landing of rebel forces at Quinteros Bay, he was said to have reported it to the Balmaceda government. Investigations failed to show any impropriety in the captain's actions, but the Congressionalists attacked American sailors from the U.S.S. *Baltimore* in Valparaíso in October.

QUITRENTS. As it was transplanted from England to the American colonies, the quitrent was a feudal due payable by freeholders to the proprietaries to whom the land had been granted. Later, it became a crown revenue in the royal colonies. The annual amount of the quitrent was nominal, varying from two to four shillings per 100 acres, with occasionally one pence per acre. After the outbreak of the American Revolution the assemblies summarily ended these feudal dues upon the land.

QUIVIRA. *See* **Coronado's Expedition; Gran Quivira.**

***QUO WARRANTO*.** A writ to determine the right to the use or exercise of a franchise, public office, or liberty. Used to initiate proceedings for the forfeiture of the Massachusetts Bay charter in 1684. The writ has given way to the speedier "information in the nature of a *quo warranto*." Generally, *quo warranto* proceedings are not employed if other legal remedies are available; since about 1775, they have been civil in character.

QUOTA SYSTEM. There were no numerical restrictions on immigration into the United States until 1921, when a law was passed, purportedly temporary, specifying that annual immigration from any country outside the Western Hemisphere and Asia was limited to 3 percent of those born in that country who resided in the United States in 1910. The Immigration Act of 1924 allocated quotas for each country outside the Western Hemisphere. The quotas were fixed on a "national origins" basis, related to the national origins of the U.S. population in 1929, with a maximum total allocation of approximately 150,000. In 1965, new legislation was adopted establishing a total annual allocation of 170,000 for all countries outside the Western Hemisphere. Since 1965 visas have been allocated under the Eastern Hemisphere quota on a first-come, first-served basis. The 1965 act also established an annual allocation of 120,000 for immigrants from the Western Hemisphere. Amendments in 1976 made admission procedures for both hemispheres equal—with a seven-category preference system, a 20,000 people per-country limit, and an overall limit of 270,000 people per year. A bill in 1980 tripled refugee admissions from 17,400 to 50,000 per year, and allowed the president to admit more refugees in emergencies.

RABAUL, AIR CAMPAIGN AGAINST (1943–44). In August 1943 the Allies decided to neutralize and bypass the key Japanese base of Rabaul, on New Britain, leaving its ultimate reduction to air attacks. By fall Allied advances in New Guinea and in the Solomons had all but isolated Rabaul. Allied air power struck with increasing intensity at the enemy base. By March 1944, the nearly 100,000 Japanese troops still defending Rabaul were isolated and impotent.

RACE RELATIONS. In complex societies such as the United States, race relations involve behavior between large categories of human beings classified on the basis of observable physical traits, particularly skin color.

The Colonial Period. Race relations in America began when the first Europeans labeled the diverse indigenous ethnic groups "Indians"; when groups forcibly brought from Africa became "Negroes"; and when Europeans conceived of themselves as "Whites." Until 1871, treaties were signed with Indian "nations"; whites infiltrated their territories; conflict and war ensued; and the Indians were driven from their territory in violation of treaties.

In 1619 the first blacks arrived in the English colonies, probably as indentured servants. Between 1660 and 1770 black chattel slavery was institutionalized into the legal system. English culture was forcibly imposed on diverse black ethnic groups, eliminating most of their African heritage.

1783–1900. White Americans increased their migration into Indian territories to the west and into the Spanish empire (and after 1821, Mexico). The policy toward Indians before the Civil War was the removal of Indians to then unwanted territories west of the Mississippi River. Numerous conflicts took place as Indians resisted invasion of their territories and their placement on reservations. With the defeat of the Apache in 1886, the Indian wars came to an end; the Indian population of 1 million had been reduced to about 200,000 and was forced into impoverishment on reservations. Under the General Allotment Act (Dawes Severalty Act) of 1887, Indians were to be transformed into individualistic and responsible farmers on family-owned plots.

By 1804 all the northern states had either eliminated slavery or passed laws for its gradual abolition. But the humanitarian motives behind the antislavery laws were not sufficient to prevent severe discrimination and segregation on the 10 percent of the black population that resided in the North.

In the South slavery became more profitable and more widespread after the invention of the cotton gin in 1793, and the number of black slaves reached 3,953,760 by 1860. After the Civil War, blacks improved their economic status as a whole, engaged in civil rights efforts to enforce new antidiscrimination laws, and became politically active. However, with each depression in the later 19th century blacks lost their hard-won gains, were deserted by liberals, and saw a number of rights eliminated or curtailed by the Supreme Court. With the passage of numerous state and local ordinances dealing with segregation, the disfranchisement of the black voter, and the economic relegation of blacks to the lowest menial occupations, the apartheid system was complete until after World War II. In the North blacks could vote and segregation was never formalized into the legal code; but *de facto* segregation and a disproportionate placement in the less desirable occupations were still a social reality.

After the Mexican War in 1848, half of Mexico was annexed to the United States, and the estimated 150,000 Mexicans in the territory became a minority as Americans inundated the area. Most Mexicans were reduced to landless menial labor by 1900. Those of Spanish and of Indian-Spanish, or mestizo, descent were lumped together by Americans and viewed as a single, distinct, and inferior race—a view intensified by the entrance of over 700,000 immigrants from rural Mexico between 1900 and 1930.

During the same period Asian immigrants arrived to meet demands of an expanding economy. They met increasing resistance by white workers and West Coast legislatures. The peak decades for the Chinese immigration were 1861–90 (249,213) and 1891–1920 (239,576) for the Japanese. The Chinese were discriminated against by the constitution of California; were forced to pay discriminatory taxes and fees; and were subjected to numerous acts of violence. By arriving in a more stable period, the Japanese avoided this "frontier" situation but were excluded from white unions and denied ownership of land by a number of western states. Further Asian immigration was almost terminated by congressional acts in 1902 and 1924.

1900–45. By the 20th century almost all nonwhites were in the lowest occupation and income categories in the United States and were attempting to accommodate themselves to this status within segregated areas—barrios, ghettoes, reservations. The great majority of whites justified this condition on the ground that nonwhites were biologically inferior. A number of major incidents of racial conflict occurred. A major racist policy of the federal government was the internment of 110,000 Japanese living on the West Coast in 1942.

1945–75. A number of nonwhite organizations sought changes in American race relations. The government and the courts, largely reacting to these groups, ended the legality of segregation and discrimination in schools, public accommodations, the armed forces, housing, employment practices, eligibility for union membership, and marriage and voting laws. The federal government in March 1961 began a program of affirmative action in hiring minorities and committed itself to promoting Indian self-determination within the reservation framework (1969).

Most overt forms of discrimination had been eliminated by the mid-1970's. Changes in dominance and social distance were accompanied by white resistance at the local level, leading to considerable racial conflict into the 1970's.

The major developments in the 1970's were the increased efforts by federal agencies to enforce civil rights laws of the 1960's; a greater implementation of affirmative-action programs; an increased number of black Americans in government positions; and the resistance in numerous communities to busing to achieve racial integration in the public schools.

RACE RIOTS. If slave revolts are excluded, there were relatively few such riots prior to the 1960's, considering the prevalence of racism and racial discrimination. The most serious race riots were between Irish and other whites in Boston in 1837, between blacks and whites in Philadelphia in 1838, between Chinese and whites in San Francisco in 1877, between Italians and other whites in New Orleans in 1891. In the 20th century riots took place between blacks and whites in East St. Louis in 1917, Chicago in 1919, and Detroit and Harlem in New York City in 1943.

In the 1960's the most serious widespread series of race riots in the history of the United States occurred as part of a more general period of racial disturbance, which involved demonstrations by civil rights activists against segregation and discrimination. Over 250 disturbances occurred during the period, more than 50 of which are considered full-fledged riots. These arose largely from the minority group's striking out against racial oppression. Characteristically, a local incident or an event in some other area (as was the case with the assassination of Martin Luther King, Jr., in 1968, when violence erupted in 125 cities) led to the gathering of a crowd, which turned into mobs that set fires, looted stores, and fought with police. Whereas earlier race riots were characterized by white violence against blacks or other minorities, the 1960 riots were largely characterized by black violence against property. In both periods the vast majority of the casualties were blacks. Major riots of the period occurred in Birmingham, Ala., in 1963; New York in 1964; Watts in Los Angeles in 1965; and Chicago in 1966. In 1967 alone Tampa, Fla.; Cincinnati; Atlanta; Newark, Plainfield, and New Brunswick, N.J.; and Detroit all experienced riots.

The widespread disorders of the 1960's led President Lyndon B. Johnson to establish a National Advisory Commission on Civil Disorders on July 29, 1967. The report reviewed the history of the riots, examined the causes, and made recommendations. It identified white racism as the main cause.

RACING. *See* **Automobile; Horse Racing; Yacht Racing.**

RADAR. Acronym for "radio detection and ranging," a method of locating distant targets by measurements made on electromagnetic radiation reflected from them. Regular brief bursts of ultrashort radio waves are beamed toward the target by a scanning antenna. The resulting echoes are then displayed on a cathode-ray tube by means of a scanning signal synchronized with the antenna, so that a map of the entire area being scanned is created. In other versions continuous waves are used; in some, only moving targets are detected (for example, in police sets used to detect speeding vehicles).

Radar goes back to observations, in the 1920's, of the unintentional perturbations caused by obstacles moving in a radio field. As World War II approached, government (mainly military) laboratories in several countries became concerned with locating unseen enemy ships and aircraft. The nation that made the greatest progress before the outbreak of the war was Great Britain. By the time of the air Battle of Britain, the system was fully operational and is credited with swinging the balance in the defenders' favor.

American military developments had started in the early 1930's at the Naval Research Laboratory under R. M. Page and at the army's Signal Corps laboratories under W. D. Hershberger. By the time the United States was drawn into the war, radar had been installed on several capital warships and in a number of critical shore installations. Great Britain continued making improvements and sent a delegation to the United States in an effort to enroll U.S. industry in the war effort. British and U.S. radar developments were combined, and the resulting equipment was largely interchangeable between the forces of the two nations.

RADICAL REPUBLICANS. The determined antislavery wing of the Republican party during the first twenty years of its existence, beginning in the mid-1850's. When the Civil War broke out, the radicals insisted on its vigorous prosecution. The radicals' emphasis on speedy emancipation often brought them into conflict with Lincoln. They criticized his failure to oust conservative cabinet members and demanded that he abolish servitude.

In the controversy about Reconstruction the radicals were the main proponents of the protection of black rights in the South. Instrumental in the passage of the Wade-Davis Bill (1864), which would have freed all remaining slaves and set forth a stringent plan of reconstruction, they mercilessly denounced Lincoln when he vetoed it. He later cooperated with them in effecting the passage of the Thirteenth Amendment.

The radical Republicans at first welcomed President Andrew Johnson's accession. But when he insisted on his mild plan of Reconstruction, the radicals induced the moderates to cooperate in passing various measures for the protection of the blacks: the Fourteenth Amendment, the Freedmen's Bureau, and the civil rights acts. The group was also responsible for the inauguration of radical Reconstruction, and provided the impetus for Johnson's impeachment.

Their influence gradually waned, although they enabled the party to pass the Fifteenth Amendment, implement Reconstruction, and enact enforcement bills as well as one last civil rights measure. But the weakening of the reform spirit, the death and retirement of leading radicals, and the emergence of new issues contributed to their decline.

RADICAL RIGHT. Sociopolitical movements and parties that constitute a conservative backlash in response to supposed threats against the values and interests of their supporters. Such backlashes usually stem from rapid social or economic change. The protesting groups seek to maintain or narrow lines of power and privilege.

Threats to the religious values of the most traditional evangelical groups gave rise in the late 1790's and again in the late 1820's to efforts to eliminate what they considered to be irreligious elements and liberal forces: the Illuminati and the Masons (*see* Anti-Masonic Movements.) For the next century the most important source of rightist backlash in politics was anti-Catholicism.

The same deep streak of anti-Catholic feeling was seized on by the Native Americans of the 1840's, the Know-Nothings of the 1850's, the American Protective Association of the 1890's, and the multimillion-member Ku Klux Klan of the 1920's.

The 1930's witnessed many extremist movements. The most potent on the right was that led by a Catholic priest, Charles E. Coughlin, which was anti-Semitic and increasingly pro-Fascist.

After World War II the anti-Catholicism and anti-Semitism of the radical right were supplanted by concern with the supposed threats of Communists and blacks. The most prominent movement of the early 1950's followed the line of Sen. Joseph R. McCarthy's investigations into alleged Communist infiltration of the government and policy-controlling institutions. The largest and most important rightist movement linked to racial concerns was manifested in the presidential campaigns of Gov. George Wallace of Alabama from 1964 to 1972. (*See also* Moral Majority.)

RADICALS AND RADICALISM. In pre–Civil War America many of the utopian community experiments could be described as radical. The Workies, a political party organized in 1829, was radical, as were William Lloyd Garrison and other abolitionists. The abolitionist movement was sometimes described as having conservative, moderate, and radical wings; the label Radical Republican came to be attached to certain leaders (*see* Radical Republicans).

Radicalism in politics from 1865 to World War I was centrally associated with proposals to alter fundamentally the "capitalist" economic and social system. Radicals demanded far-reaching changes in property relations, distribution of wealth and income, or the status of labor. The Knights of Labor were originally thought of as radical, as were the Greenback Labor party, the Free Silver men, the Single Taxers of Henry George, and many leaders of the so-called Populist revolt. There were several types of so-called agrarian radicals. There were the Socialist Labor party, established in 1877, and the American Socialist party, founded in 1901. The anarchists should also be mentioned, and their leaders, Emma Goldman and Alexander Berkman. American syndicalism was represented by the Industrial Workers of the World, founded in 1905, which until the end of World War I symbolized for many all that was iniquitous in radicalism.

After World War I, much radicalism came to be concentrated in the so-called Communist movement and its "front" groups. During the 1950's "Communist radicals" became the targets of Sen. Joseph McCarthy's campaigns, and "McCarthyism" became a kind of shorthand for "antiradicalism."

During the 1960's many leaders and movements appeared that were called radical either by themselves or by their critics. Students for a Democratic Society (SDS) was one such group, with its criticism both of the Old Left (the Marxists) and of orthodox American politics. The student protest movement and the civil rights movement were described as being radical. The peace movement of the 1960's, which concentrated on ending the Vietnam War, produced a number of leaders who were seen by others as radical. It is highly characteristic of the American experience that many proposals that at one time were described as radical should later be adopted as public policy; for example, federal income taxes, collective bargaining, and Social Security.

RADIO. As early as 1876 experimental "concerts" were transmitted by Alexander Graham Bell from Paris to Brantford, Ontario, Canada. The following two decades witnessed considerable experimental work relating to conveying concerts and entertainments over wire line.

Guglielmo Marconi's investigations and those of other radio-telegraph pioneers were concerned primarily with the transmission of Morse Code intelligence via radio. The person most responsible for initiating a viable system of radiotelephony was Reginald Fessenden, who developed the high frequency alternator and whose radio-telephone transmissions from Brant Rock, Mass., in November and December 1906 provided crucial tests for the new technology. Lee De Forest proceeded similarly but employed the modulated high frequency arc as the transmission device.

By 1914 the triode vacuum tube, a De Forest invention, led to outstanding improvements in radio technology. De Forest and Edwin H. Armstrong designed further circuit innovations to make the tube practical for radio receivers and transmitters. In 1915 the Bell System conducted tests in transatlantic radiotelephony employing the antenna of Navy Station NAA, Arlington, Va.

The period 1915–20 saw a rapid increase in experimentation by radiotelephone enthusiasts. Although the Radio Act of 1912 provided only marginal regulation, the Department of Commerce issued Special Land Station designations to many amateurs and to college experimental stations.

In 1919 the Radio Corporation of America (RCA) was formed to preserve U.S. initiatives in the wireless field. It absorbed the Marconi Wireless Telegraph Company of

America and entered into manufacturing agreements with the Westinghouse Electric Corporation and the General Electric Company.

News and entertainment broadcasting as an industry originated with the transmission of the returns of the Harding-Cox presidential election over station KDKA, Pittsburgh, on Nov. 2, 1920. The first broadcasting stations were assigned to either 360 or 400 meters (833 or 750 kilocycles per second [kHz]), but the Department of Commerce was faced with critical regulatory problems under the Radio Act of 1912, which did not envision such rapid growth. Out of four major industry-government conferences held under the aegis of Secretary of Commerce Herbert Hoover arose the modern AM (amplitude modulation) broadcast structure, covering the band of frequencies from 550 to 1600 kHz.

During 1920–30 certain unique problems developed. The expansion of the medium was limited in that only so many broadcast stations could be assigned within the allowable spectrum space without serious interstation interference. The 700-odd stations in existence by 1927 seemed the maximum that could be tolerated. On Feb. 23, 1927, President Calvin Coolidge signed the Radio Act of 1927, creating the five-member Federal Radio Commission to regulate radio communication.

Owing to the rapid growth of telecommunications, President Franklin D. Roosevelt recommended that a single agency be created to cover all the new developments in electronics, and Congress passed the Communications Act of 1934, which established the Federal Communications Commission (FCC).

The design of directive antenna arrays for broadcast stations greatly extended the capability of the AM spectrum. A system capacity in excess of 4,500 stations arose by 1980. Owing largely to the efforts of Armstrong, frequency modulation (FM) was introduced. It freed the system of static and allowed efficient use of the higher frequency spectrum to permit wide-range high-fidelity broadcasting. AM interests could not envision any significant improvement in service by changing to FM. Television was "just around the corner," and RCA chose to put its research and development task force to work on that. A victory for Armstrong was the adoption of FM for the television sound channel, under FCC regulations, adopted for the commercial introduction of television, July 1, 1941.

The spectacular rise of FM broadcasting after 1960 can be traced to several developments in sound engineering technology. In 1947 Harry Olson of RCA proved that a type of distortion termed harmonic must be extremely low in electronic reproducers for the listener to enjoy high-fidelity broadcasting. In 1957–58 came stereophonic recordings and, experimentally, several stereo broadcast systems. By 1961 stereo FM was in commercial service. For the first time in 1979 more people listened to FM than to AM stations.

RADIO ASTRONOMY. *See* **Astronomy.**

RADIOCARBON DATING. Measurement of the age of dead matter by comparing the radiocarbon content with that in living matter. It was discovered at the University of Chicago in the 1940's. In 1960 Willard F. Libby was awarded the Nobel Prize in Chemistry for his development of the radiocarbon dating method.

Radiocarbon, or radioactive carbon (C-14), is produced by cosmic rays in the atmosphere and is assimilated only by living beings. At death the assimilation process stops, and thereafter the immutable radioactive loss through decay is no longer compensated by the intake of food. The law of radioactive decay is that a given fraction is always lost in a given time. The half-life of radiocarbon, 5,730 years, is the time for 50 percent loss. Thus, 5,730 years after a tree has fallen, it will have half the radiocarbon content of a living tree. The discovery of the radiocarbon dating method has given a much firmer base to archaeology and anthropology.

RADISSON'S *VOYAGES* (1669). Pierre Esprit Radisson was mistakenly thought to have been one of two traders sent by New France in 1654 to establish trade with the western tribes scattered by the Iroquois. His brother-in-law, Médard Chouart, Sieur de Groseilliers, does appear to have been one of the traders, who traveled around Lake Huron and Lake Michigan.

Its chief value lies in its descriptions of Indians before they were influenced by white men. They learned from the Indians of an easy route for fur trading from Hudson Bay to the great beaver country northwest of Lake Superior, and of the supposed Northwest Passage in that area. These ideas led them to seek financial aid to explore the possibilities of Hudson Bay for trade and for a route to Asia. In England they succeeded. The Hudson's Bay Company was founded on May 2, 1670, after Groseilliers' return from a successful trip to Hudson Bay in 1668 and 1669.

RAFTING, EARLY. Before the Civil War, chiefly on the rivers of the Mississippi Valley, rafts with crude lean-tos were used as transportation downstream by the poorer immigrants. They were steered by long sweeps.

RAIL FENCES. For many years following the first settlement in America, rail fences were common. Pine, oak, and chestnut were favorite woods for rails, the tree trunks being cut into 11-foot lengths about 4 or 5 inches thick.

RAILROAD ADMINISTRATION, U.S. In December 1917 President Woodrow Wilson established the Railroad Administration to control and operate all rail transport for the duration of World War I. Terminal companies, an express company, and certain coastal and inland waterways and piers were included, but not street cars, interurban lines, or industrial railroads. In general, personnel and administrative machinery were retained, under the direct charge of a federal manager, usually an officer of the corporation. Unified terminals were organized, locomotives and freight cars were standardized, and the purchasing of equipment and supplies was centralized. In March 1920 the railroads were returned to private management.

RAILROAD BROTHERHOODS. The traditional pattern of union organization in the railroad industry has been along multiple craft-union lines. In 1980 there were about fifteen separate unions representing the approximately 540,000 railway workers of the nation. Historically, the unions have been divided into the operating employees, involved in the physical movement of trains, and nonoperating employees.

The five major brotherhoods (the "Big Five") have been the operating unions: locomotive engineers (founded in 1863), railroad conductors (1868), locomotive firemen and enginemen (1873), railway trainmen (1883), and switchmen (1894). Four of the operating brotherhoods merged on July 1, 1969, into the United Transportation Union. With only the locomotive engineers remaining aloof, the new union represented about 87 percent of the operating employees.

RAILROAD CONSPIRACY (1849–50). Directed against the Michigan Central Railroad, by persons angered by disputes over rights of way, location of stations, and killing of cattle by locomotives. The conspirators stoned and shot at trains, destroyed culverts, removed rails, and burned stations. Twelve were given prison sentences ranging from five to ten years.

RAILROAD CONVENTIONS. Phenomena of the early years of railroad promotion. They were held before the railroads were built rather than after, and were composed of railway builders and public-spirited citizens. The most notable were the Pacific Railroad conventions in St. Louis and Memphis, October 1849, and in Philadelphia, April 1850, held to demonstrate popular demand for federal aid for a railroad to the Pacific coast, to formulate a plan of financing it, and to assert claims for the eastern terminus. Congress gave their resolutions scant courtesy.

RAILROAD LAND GRANTS. *See* **Land Grants for Railways.**

RAILROAD MEDIATION ACTS. The federal government tried in the 1890's to devise machinery to avoid railroad strikes and assure uninterrupted transportation service without denying the rights of workers to organize. In the Erdman Act of 1898 and the Newlands Act of 1913 Congress created mediation procedures, and in the Adamson Act of 1916 it established the eight-hour day on the railroads. The Transportation Act of 1920 founded the Railroad Labor Board. After the board failed to prevent the shopmen's strike of 1922, Congress passed the Railway Labor Act of 1926. As amended in 1934, it continues to be the basic legislation in the field.

RAILROAD POOLS. *See* **Pools, Railroad.**

RAILROAD RATE LAW. Attempts to regulate railroad rates by law began at the state level. The Granger laws of the 1870's were passed by the states in response to demands by farmers for lower rates on agricultural products from the Midwest to the eastern seaboard and by midwestern river towns that rates be based on mileage. The Supreme Court in *Munn* v. *Illinois* (1877) declared for the right of states to fix interstate rates so long as the federal government did not act. The decision in *Wabash, Saint Louis and Pacific Railroad Company* v. *Illinois* (1886) reversed *Munn,* and Congress passed the Interstate Commerce Act of 1887.

The fatal weakness of the act was that it prohibited pooling, an anomaly that led experts to predict correctly that the only other antidote to rate chaos—consolidation of the railroads into a few systems—would be adopted.

While the Elkins Act of 1903 enhanced the powers of the Interstate Commerce Commission (ICC) to deal with rebates as criminal acts, it was the overloading of the American railroad system after 1898 that effectively killed rate cutting. The Hepburn Act of 1906 gave the ICC power to fix specific maximum rates and broadened its jurisdiction. The Hepburn Act was overshadowed by the Mann-Elkins Act of 1910, which enabled the ICC effectively to freeze rates at 1890's levels. When the government took over the railroad system in December 1917, the ICC was as far from developing a criterion of "reasonableness" of rates as ever. The U.S. Railroad Administration raised rates by almost 60 percent, returning them to about the level of the 1890's in real dollars. Meanwhile, in the *Shreveport* case (1914) the Supreme Court had completed the reversal of the *Munn* decision by giving the ICC power to set intrastate rates.

Neither the power to pool revenues nor the encouragement of consolidation, both features of the Transportation Act of 1920, was germane to postwar regulatory problems. By 1933 the emergence of competition by trucks had become the problem. Despite acts passed in 1940 and 1958 in favor of a balanced transportation system, both the ICC and lawmakers shrank from lowering rates, and the Supreme Court failed consistently to enunciate a rule of ratemaking based on cost. As a result the railroads lost most of their profitable, high-class freight and came to be operated at a fraction of capacity.

RAILROAD RATE WARS. In the competitive struggle for traffic, freight rates and passenger fares were cut by rival railroads and steamship lines. Railroad competition became particularly severe when, after 1869, the trunk line railroads, especially the Pennsylvania Railroad and the New York Central, reached the large cities of the Middle West. Recurrent rate wars caused freight rates and passenger fares to fall to absurdly low prices. The excesses resulted in sharp fluctuations in rates and bankruptcy of many railroads. In 1874 the Baltimore and Ohio Railroad was extended to Chicago, and the Grand Trunk Railroad was opened to Milwaukee. The following two years witnessed one of the most disastrous railroad rate wars in history, between the Baltimore and Ohio, Erie, Grand Trunk, New York Central, and Pennsylvania railroads. This ruthless competition led to a temporary truce and a traffic-sharing arrangement in 1877.

Competition among railroads serving the northern Atlantic ports resulted in rate wars among the railroads and between the railroads and the Erie Canal. Competition among southern railroads was intensified as several railroads reached inland points, such as Atlanta. Severe competition occurred between railroads and water carriers at principal ports on the Atlantic Ocean, Gulf of Mexico, Mississippi River, and Ohio River. In the West rate wars resulted from the multiplication of railroads and the struggle between the railroads and steamboat lines for freight at important traffic centers.

Railroad rate wars led to the demand for federal regulation. Congress in 1887 established the Interstate Commerce Commission.

RAILROAD REBATES. *See* **Rebates, Railroad.**

RAILROAD RETIREMENT ACTS. A railroad retirement act was approved by President Franklin D. Roosevelt, June 27, 1934. Retirement allowances were provided for certain categories of employees, two-thirds of the cost to be borne by employers and the balance by the employees. In March 1935 the U.S. Supreme Court, in *Railroad Retirement Board* v. *Alton Railroad Company,* declared the act unconstitutional. New legislation was promptly introduced, and two bills were passed the following August but were challenged. Conferences of railroad managements and the employee organizations were begun. In May 1937 new legislation approved by both parties was introduced in Congress and carried with little opposition (Railroad Retirement Act of 1937).

RAILROAD RETIREMENT BOARD. *See* **Federal Agencies.**

RAILROAD RETIREMENT BOARD* V. *ALTON RAILROAD COMPANY, 295 U.S. 330 (1935). A case in which the Supreme Court invalidated the Railroad Pension Act of 1934. The majority opinion declared the act contrary to the due process clause of the Fifth Amendment because of a long series of arbitrary impositions on the carriers and, furthermore, because "the pension plan thus imposed is in no proper sense a regulation of the activity of interstate transportation."

RAILROADS. The earliest railroads in the United States were short wooden tramways connecting mines or quarries with nearby streams, upon which horses could draw heavier loads than on roads. The idea of the railroad as it came to be was first expounded by Col. John Stevens of Hoboken, N.J., who in 1812 published his *Documents Tending to Prove the Superior Advantages of Rail-Ways and Steam Carriages Over Canal Navigation.* He secured a charter from New Jersey authorizing a railroad across the state, but was unable to enlist the capital. The first chartered railroad in the United States was the Granite Railway of Massachusetts, a three-mile line built in 1826, which used horses to haul stone. The first common carrier of passengers and freight, the Baltimore and Ohio, was chartered by Maryland on Feb. 28, 1827. The first passengers were carried in January 1830 in single cars drawn by horses.

Stevens had built a tiny steam locomotive that ran on a circular track on his estate in 1825. The *Stourbridge Lion,* imported from England by the Delaware and Hudson Canal and Railroad, proved to be too heavy for the track. In August 1830 the Baltimore and Ohio experimented with the diminutive *Tom Thumb,* built and operated by Peter Cooper. The essential elements of the modern railroad were first combined on the South Carolina Canal and Rail Road Company (later included in the Southern Railway system) when, on Dec. 25, 1830, it inaugurated scheduled service on the first six miles of its line out of Charleston with the steam locomotive *Best Friend,* the first to pull a train of cars on the American continent.

Railroads opened for operation by steam power in the early 1830's included the Mohawk and Hudson; the Camden and Amboy; the Philadelphia, Germantown and Norristown; and the railroad connecting New Orleans with Lake Pontchartrain.

By 1835 railroads ran from Boston to Lowell, to Worcester, and to Providence. The Baltimore and Ohio had built a branch to Washington, D.C., and had pushed its main line westward to the Blue Ridge. Several New York businessmen started the New York and Erie, headed westward for Lake Erie.

1840–60. By 1840, 2,800 miles of railroad were in operation in the United States, with mileage in every seacoast state, Kentucky, Ohio, Indiana, Michigan, and Illinois. In the second decade mileage more than trebled, reaching 9,000 miles. Lines had been opened in Vermont and Wisconsin, and missing links had been supplied, so that by 1850 it was possible to travel between Boston and Buffalo, with numerous changes of cars, and between Boston and Wilmington, N.C., with occasional gaps covered by steamboat. By 1850, also, there had been developed a standard American-type locomotive, with a four-wheel swivel leading truck and four driving wheels, coupled.

In the 1850's mileage again more than trebled, as the ambitious efforts to reach the West were fulfilled. New York was connected with the Great Lakes, both by the Erie Railroad and by way of Albany and the New York Central. Philadelphia established an all-rail connection with Pittsburgh, and Baltimore reached the Ohio at Wheeling.

Other lines were being built across the more open and level country of the Middle West. Chicago was entered from the East in 1852 almost simultaneously by the Michigan Central and the Michigan Southern. Lines were building west from Chicago—the Galena and Chicago Union (later the Chicago and North Western), which brought the first locomotive to the future rail center on a Great Lakes sailing vessel, and the Chicago and Rock Island, which reached the Mississippi River in 1854.

But before the rails reached the great river from the East, railroads had started from the west bank. The first locomotive beyond the Mississippi ran on Dec. 9, 1852, on the Pacific Railroad of Missouri (later the Missouri Pacific) from St. Louis five miles westward. In 1856 the Iron Horse crossed the Mississippi on the first railroad bridge, that of the Rock Island line, later called the Chicago, Rock Island and Pacific. Before the end of the decade, the railroad had reached the Missouri on the Hannibal and St. Joseph. For the most part these routes had been built as separate local lines, lacking physical connections without which through movement of freight and passengers was impossible. One road built as a unit was the Illinois Central, connecting East Dubuque and Cairo. The line of more than 700 miles was completed in 1857.

During the years the policy was in effect (1850–71) federal land grants were made to aid in the building of less than 10 percent of the railroad mileage of the United States, by which some 131 million of the approximately 1.4 billion acres of public lands owned in 1850 were transferred to private ownership. In return for the grants the railroads carried government freight, mail, and troops at reduced rates until 1946, when the arrangement was ended by act of Congress.

1861–65. With the coming of the Civil War, the building of new railroads was slowed down somewhat, but the existing railroads were called upon to play essential roles in the struggle. More than two-thirds of the 1861 mileage and an even greater proportion of railroad transportation capacity lay in the states that adhered to the Union.

1865–1916. There had been agitation for a transcontinental railroad since 1848 at least, and during the 1850's the topographical engineers of the army had explored five routes. Ultimately railroads were built on all those routes. A railroad between the Missouri River and California was undertaken by the Union Pacific, building westward from Omaha, and by the Central Pacific (later part of the Southern Pacific), building eastward from Sacramento, Calif. On May 10, 1869, the construction crews met and joined tracks at Promontory, Utah. The second transcontinental connection was supplied in 1881 when the Atchison, Topeka and Santa Fe, building westward, met the Southern Pacific, building eastward, at Deming, N.Mex.

The first route to reach the Pacific Northwest was opened in 1883 by the Northern Pacific. A second route was opened a year later when the Oregon Short Line, built from a junction with the Union Pacific, joined tracks with the Oregon Railway and Navigation Company (both later part of the Union Pacific system).

The 1880's recorded the greatest growth in railway mileage, with an average of more than 7,000 miles of new line built each year. By the end of the decade the conversion from iron to steel rail was largely completed. The same decade also saw the standardization of track gauge, of car couplers, of train brakes, and of time, all essential steps toward a continent-wide commerce by rail.

In 1886 the U.S. Supreme Court held, in *Wabash, Saint Louis and Pacific Railroad Company* v. *Illinois,* that Congress had exclusive jurisdiction over interstate commerce and that a state could not regulate even the intrastate portion of an interstate movement. This led to the creation of the Interstate Commerce Commission (ICC).

1917–41. In April 1917, the United States entered World War I, and on Dec. 26, 1917, President Woodrow Wilson issued his proclamation taking over the railroads for operation by the government, to start Jan. 1, 1918.

Congress voted to return the railroads to private operation and set up the terms in the Transportation Act of 1920. Among the changes in government policy was recognition of a measure of responsibility for financial results, found in the direction to the ICC to fix rates at such a level as would enable the railroads, as a whole or in groups, to earn a fair return on the value of the properties devoted to public service.

Mileage of all tracks, including additional main tracks, passing tracks, sidings, and yards reached its maximum of 430,000 miles in 1930. At about this time, wooden cars virtually disappeared. The steam locomotive became more powerful and more efficient. The diesel locomotive was introduced. Passenger car air conditioning was introduced in 1929, and the first all air-conditioned train was operated in 1931. Streamlining was added to passenger train service, beginning in 1934. Passenger train speeds were increased, and overnight merchandise freight service for distances of more than 400 miles was inaugurated. Centralized traffic control and train operation by signal indication multiplied the capacity of single-track lines and even made it possible to take up trackage that was no longer required.

1942–60. The combined effect of these and other improvements in plant, methods, and organization was such that the railroads, continuing under private operation, were able to meet all transportation demands during World War II. In May 1946, President Truman, acting under his war powers, seized the railroads as a means of dealing with a nationwide strike by the engineers and trainmen. Similar seizures took place in 1948 and 1950, the latter lasting nearly two years. In 1951 Congress amended the 1934 Railway Labor Act by removing the prohibition against compulsory union membership, thereby permitting the establishment of the union shop by negotiation. Throughout the postwar years the railroads carried forward a program of capital improvements. The most striking and significant change was the displacement of the steam locomotive by the diesel-electric.

1961–80. In this period, American railroads achieved some technical gains, but in other areas they suffered losses. Total mileage declined from 216,000 miles in 1961 to 163,000 miles in 1979. Total operating revenues for the industry climbed from $9.2 billion in 1961 to an all-time high of about $25.7 billion in 1979, much of the increase caused by inflation. Freight revenue increased from 84 to 93 percent of the total. While freight carloading declined because of larger cars, there was a significant increase in total ton-mileage, and the 916 billion ton-miles reached in 1979 was a record high. However, the railroads' share of total intercity commercial freight was still declining, dropping from 43 percent in 1961 to about 36 percent in 1979. The discontinuance of hundreds of passenger trains and the growing popularity of jet air travel caused an even greater decline. The 12 billion passenger-miles in 1979 was only about 50 percent of the 1961 figure, and the railroads' share of all passenger traffic declined from 26 percent in 1961 to less than 5 percent in 1979 most of it urban commuter traffic.

Passenger service dropped off sharply between 1960 and 1979; the average mileage per passenger declined from 65 to 24. Early in 1969 a government-sponsored project for high-speed passenger service was started with Metroliner service between New York City and Washington, D.C. In May 1971 most railroad passenger service was taken over by the federally sponsored National Railroad Passenger Corporation, soon to be known as Amtrak. Amtrak provided passenger service consisting of about 1,300 trains a week, running over 20,000 miles of track on twenty-two different railroads, and serving 340 American cities. The financial support provided by the government assured at least some continuing rail passenger service for the immediate future.

A major development was the trend toward merger or consolidation: in the late 1950's there were 116 Class I railroads operating in the nation, and by 1979 there were just 40. Extensive operational savings were projected and claimed for nearly every proposed railroad merger, and often such economies were realized, when the consolidation was orderly and well planned.

Most railroad managers still believed their industry to be overregulated. Nor did they feel that any significant improvement came with the establishment, in 1966, of the new Department of Transportation. When the newly merged Penn Central went into bankruptcy in 1970, Congress did pass legislation that provided some indirect financial support. In some quarters a renewed consideration of possible nationalization of the nation's railways was favored. An effort to avoid nationalization led to the establishment in 1976 of the private, but federally financed Consolidated Rail Corporation (Conrail), which took over six bankrupt railroads in the Northeast and Midwest. Despite that the industry continued to be beset by declining profits and soaring costs. In order to avert a still deeper crisis President Jimmy Carter proposed deregulation of railroads in 1979; the final bill was passed the following year.

RAILROADS, SKETCHES OF PRINCIPAL LINES

Atchison, Topeka and Santa Fe. Chartered in 1859 to connect Atchison and Topeka, Kans., it expanded rapidly. It was a pioneer in the use of diesel locomotives, especially in freight service. The system of just under 13,000 miles made the Santa Fe first in mileage in the middle decades of the 20th century.

Atlantic and Pacific. Land grant railroad chartered on July 27, 1866, to run along the thirty-first parallel from Springfield, Mo., to Needles, Calif. Railroad building had reached Vinita, Indian Territory, when the panic of 1873 ended operations. In 1876 the company was reorganized as part of the St. Louis and San Francisco. Four years later the Atchison, Topeka and Santa Fe bought a half interest.

Boston and Maine. The first of the 111 companies absorbed into it was the Boston and Lowell, chartered in 1830. The name "Boston and Maine" dates from 1835. In 1980 the railroad operated 1,393 miles of line in Massachusetts, New Hampshire, Maine, Vermont, and New York.

Burlington Northern. In 1970 the ICC approved the merger of the Chicago, Burlington and Quincy, the Great Northern, and the Northern Pacific into the Burlington Northern. In 1980 Burlington Northern acquired St. Louis–St. Francisco. The combined trackage of 27,361 miles in 1980 made it the longest in the nation.

Chicago, Burlington and Quincy. The original unit of the Burlington system was the Aurora Branch Railroad, a 12-mile line chartered in Illinois in 1849. It expanded through amalgamation into a system that in the early 1970's extended from Chicago and St. Louis to Minneapolis–St. Paul and thence to Montana, Wyoming, Colorado, and the Gulf coast of Texas. The Burlington pioneered in the development of streamline passenger equipment with the first Zephyr in 1934.

Great Northern. The original line was the Saint Paul and Pacific, which started in 1862 to build northward and westward from St. Paul. The transcontinental line was opened in 1893. In the early 1970's the company operated 8,200 miles of road, extending from Minneapolis–St. Paul and the head of the Great Lakes to Vancouver, British Columbia; Seattle; and Portland, Oreg.

Northern Pacific. The first of the northern transcontinental lines was chartered by an act of Congress signed by President Abraham Lincoln on July 2, 1864. Construction to connect the head of the Great Lakes with Portland, Oreg., was started in 1870 and completed in 1883. In the early 1970's the company operated 6,700 miles of line, extending from Minneapolis–Saint Paul and Duluth-Superior, on Lake Superior, to Seattle and Tacoma, Wash., and Portland.

Saint Louis–San Francisco. The Saint Louis–San Francisco, started in 1866, was planned to run from Springfield, Ill., to the Pacific coast; but its point of origin was changed to St. Louis, and it never reached the California city. It developed 4,800 miles, from St. Louis and Kansas City, Mo., to Oklahoma and northern Texas, on the southwest, and to Florida, on the southeast. The "Frisco" is one of the few systems to operate in both the West and the Southeast.

Central of Georgia. Chartered in 1833 as the Central Railroad and Banking Company of Georgia to build a railroad from Savannah to Macon. Operated 2,000 miles of line in Georgia, Alabama, and Tennessee in the early 1980's. It should not be confused with the Georgia Railroad between Augusta and Atlanta, built and owned by the Georgia Railroad and Banking Company, also incorporated in 1833, and operated under lease after 1882.

Chesapeake and Ohio. The 22-mile Louisa Railroad, chartered in Virginia in 1837, had grown into the 4,800-mile Chesapeake and Ohio system by the early 1980's, extending from Hampton Roads, Va., and Washington, D.C., to Louisville, Ky., Chicago, the Straits of Mackinac, and the western shore of Lake Michigan (by car ferry). Between 1960 and 1963 it took over the larger Baltimore and Ohio.

Baltimore and Ohio. Chartered in 1827, the Baltimore and Ohio was built to Wheeling on the Ohio River by late 1852. Later it expanded to Philadelphia and New York City and to St. Louis and Chicago, extending its mileage to 5,500.

Chicago and North Western. Chartered in 1848, the Galena and Chicago Union was the first railroad to serve Chicago. It became the Chicago and North Western in 1859. Eight years later it was the first line to reach the Missouri River at Omaha, where it connected with the Union Pacific. It acquired the Chicago Great Western in 1968, thus extending its system to 10,700 miles (8,786 in 1980).

Chicago, Milwaukee, Saint Paul and Pacific. Its earliest "ancestor" was chartered in 1847 to build a line across Wisconsin to the Mississippi. By 1900 the Chicago, Milwaukee and Saint Paul operated between the Great Lakes and the Missouri River. Between 1905 and 1909 the line was extended to the Pacific coast. In 1921 the line was extended into Indiana. The Milwaukee operated about 6,800 miles in 1980.

Chicago, Rock Island and Pacific. Incorporated in 1847 to build from Rock Island to LaSalle, Ill., but built from Chicago under an amended charter, this was the first railroad to bridge the Mississippi, in 1856. It operated about 7,000 miles of line in the 1970's, extending from Chicago, St. Louis, and Memphis on the east, to Minneapolis–St. Paul on the north, Colorado and New Mexico on the west, and the Texas and the Louisiana Gulf coast on the south. In the late 1970's the company filed for bankruptcy.

Delaware and Hudson. The original company, the Delaware and Hudson Canal Company, chartered in 1823, built a canal and a railroad to bring out coal from Carbondale, Pa., to Rondout, N.Y., on the Hudson River. On this line, in 1829, the first steam locomotive on an American railroad made its first, and only, run. The canal was abandoned in 1898. The system, extending through upstate New York to Montreal, Quebec, Canada, was built up to over 1,700 miles by 1980.

Denver and Rio Grande Western. Chartered in 1870 by Denver interests; a narrow-gauge line that reached southern and western Colorado and extended to Salt Lake City. By 1890 main lines had been converted to standard gauge. Consolidation with the Denver and Salt Lake shortened the distance between terminals by 175 miles. In the early 1980's the road operated about 1,850 miles, of which some was narrow gauge.

Erie Lackawanna. A 2,900-mile road formed in 1960 out of the Delaware, Lackawanna and Western and the Erie. In 1976 the company, after it had filed for bankruptcy, became part of Consolidated Rail Corporation (Conrail).

Delaware, Lackawanna and Western. Chartered in 1851 to build an outlet for the coal of the Lackawanna Valley, the Liggitt's Gap Railroad was extended west to Buffalo, north to Lake Ontario, and east to New York via Hoboken, N.J., becoming the Delaware, Lackawanna and Western.

Erie. Chartered as the New York and Erie, in 1832, to build from Piermont, N.Y., on the Hudson, to Dunkirk, on Lake Erie, the Erie completed a 6-foot-gauge track in 1851. After a reorganization in 1941, it began a career of solid success. Before merging in 1960, the Erie operated 2,300 miles, extending from New York City to Buffalo, Cleveland, and Chicago.

Florida East Coast. The work of Henry M. Flagler. Acquiring the railroad in 1885, he steadily pushed it southward from St. Augustine, reaching Miami in 1896. The overseas extension, built across the Florida keys and stretches of open sea, reached Key West in 1912. In 1935 the extension suffered severe hurricane damage and was abandoned as a railroad, to become the overseas highway to Key West. In 1980 the railroad operated 870 miles.

Grand Trunk Western. A subsidiary of the Canadian National Railways, the Grand Trunk Western was built from Port Huron and Detroit across Michigan, Indiana, and Illinois, reaching Chicago in 1881, and then extended to Milwaukee, via cross-lake car ferry. The tunnel under the St. Clair River was completed in 1891. In 1980 the Grand Trunk Western operated 929 miles. Other Canadian National subsidiaries in the United States include the Grand Trunk to Portland, Maine (1853), and the Central Vermont (1899).

Hannibal and Saint Joseph. A Missouri railway line, incorporated in 1847. Work began in 1851, completed in 1859. It was enormously important during the next two or three years. St. Joseph was the starting point for the Pony Express and the nearest railroad terminus during the Pikes Peak gold rush, for which the railroad carried the mails.

Illinois Central Gulf. A 8,366-mile-line, the result of the 1972 merger of the Gulf, Mobile and Ohio and the Illinois Central.

Gulf, Mobile and Ohio. Dates from 1940, when the corporation was formed by the consolidation of the Gulf, Mobile and Northern with the Mobile and Ohio, which built a through line from Mobile, Ala., to St. Louis. In 1947 the firm absorbed the Alton, originally the Chicago and Alton, which dated from 1847. At the time of its merger it had a 2,700-mile system extending from Chicago and Kansas City, Mo., to Mobile and New Orleans.

Illinois Central. Incorporated in 1851, it was still operating in the early 1970's under its original charter, which called for a 705-mile railroad in Illinois. Along with the Mobile and Ohio, the Illinois Central received the first railroad land grant provided by the federal government. After the Civil War a southern line to the Gulf was acquired. At the time of the 1972 merger the Illinois Central operated a 6,700-mile system in fourteen states, extending from Chicago west to the Missouri River and south to New Orleans and Birmingham, Ala.

Lehigh Valley. Originally chartered as the Delaware, Lehigh, Schuylkill and Susquehanna to haul coal from Mauch Chunk, Pa., the Lehigh Valley adopted its present name in 1853. The line expanded to 925 miles, reaching the Niagara frontier on the west and New York on the east. The company went bankrupt and in 1976 became part of Conrail (Consolidated Rail Corporation).

Louisville and Nashville. Chartered in 1850, the Louisville and Nashville completed its line in 1859. The railroad by 1980 had created a 6,570-mile system from Chicago, Cincinnati, and St. Louis to Memphis, Atlanta, and New Orleans. The oldest existing part was between Lexington and Frankfort, Ky., chartered in 1830, opened for traffic in 1834, and acquired by the Louisville and Nashville in 1881.

Missouri, Kansas and Texas. The Union Pacific, Southern Branch, chartered in 1865, was the first of several short roads to make up the Missouri, Kansas and Texas, organized in 1870. A line from Junction City, Kans., was built to the southern border of Kansas by 1870, and to Texas by 1872. Expansion created a system of 2,175 miles (1980) from St. Louis and Kansas City, Mo., to San Antonio and Houston.

Missouri Pacific. The Pacific Railroad of Missouri, the earliest part of the Missouri Pacific, was chartered on July 4, 1851, to build a line of 5.5-foot gauge from St. Louis to the West Coast. The first locomotive west of the Mississippi ran on this road in December 1852. In 1978 the company acquired the Texas and Pacific. The road expanded from St. Louis, Memphis, and New Orleans to Omaha; Pueblo, Colo.; Laredo, Tex.; and the Gulf coast; over 11,500 miles in 1980.

Texas and Pacific. Chartered in 1871, the Texas and Pacific took over the barely started projects of the Southern Pacific (not related to the later company of that name), formed in 1856; the Memphis, El Paso and Pacific, also formed in 1856; and the Southern Transcontinental, organized in 1870. From northeast Texas, at Marshall and Texarkana, lines were built westward toward El Paso and eastward to New Orleans. In 1882, at Sierra Blanca, Tex., the Texas and Pacific met the crews of the Galveston, Harrisburg and San Antonio, building the Southern Pacific line eastward. Joint trackage was arranged, effecting an entrance into El Paso for the Texas and Pacific. The line to New Orleans was completed in 1882. In the early 1970's the company operated 2,100 miles of line.

Norfolk and Western. The City Point Railway, a 9-mile line between Petersburg, Va., and the James River, chartered in 1836, is the oldest part of the Norfolk and Western. It grew into the Southside Railroad which stretched across southern Virginia from tidewater to Tennessee and with extensions westward into the coal fields, and became the basis of the Norfolk and Western. The railroad grew to 2,700 miles with the addition of the Virginian in 1959. In 1964 two other roads, the Nickel Plate and the Wabash, were added, creating a system of 7,448 miles by 1980.

New York, Chicago and Saint Louis. The Nickel Plate Road, as the New York, Chicago and Saint Louis is usually called, was opened between Buffalo and Chicago in 1882; the last spike, at Bellevue, Ohio, was nickel plated. Control soon passed to the New York Central. In 1916 control was sold to the Van Sweringen brothers. They added the Lake Erie and Western and the Toledo, Peoria and Western; subsequently the Wheeling and Lake Erie was added. In the early 1970's the system operated 2,200 miles, extending from Buffalo and Wheeling to Chicago and Peoria, Ill., and St. Louis.

Wabash. The Northern Cross, 12 miles long, built in 1838, was the first railroad in Illinois and the earliest part of the Wabash. It became a system of nearly 3,000 miles, stretching from Buffalo and Toledo to St. Louis, Kansas City, Mo., Omaha, and Des Moines. The Ann Arbor Railroad, with car ferries across Lake Michigan, extended the system.

Penn Central. The Pennsylvania New York Central Transportation Company was created in 1968 out of the New York Central, the Pennsylvania, and the New York, New Haven and Hartford. The problems facing the 21,000-mile Penn Central forced it into bankruptcy in 1970. Congress provided some indirect financial aid, but after nearly three years of receivership the Penn Central was still operating hundreds of miles of excess track that produced very little profitable traffic. In 1976 Penn Central became part of Conrail.

New York Central. The Mohawk and Hudson, the oldest of the many companies that made up the New York Central, was incorporated in 1826 and ran its first train in 1831. The Hudson River Railroad was added to the New York Central (organized in 1853) in 1869, to be followed by the Lake Shore and Michigan Southern, the Michigan Central, the Big Four, the Boston and Albany, the West Shore, the Toledo and Ohio Central, and others, including the separately operated Pittsburgh and Lake Erie. The system grew to more than 10,000 miles, extending from Montreal, Boston, and New York to the Straits of Mackinac, Chicago, and St. Louis.

New York, New Haven and Hartford. Earliest of the approximately 125 companies that made up the New York, New Haven and Hartford was the Boston and Providence, chartered in 1831 and in operation by 1834. The Hartford and New Haven, incorporated in 1833, connected New Haven with Springfield, Mass., by 1844, the year in which a railroad was chartered to connect New Haven with New York. This line, providing the first all-rail service between Boston and New York via Springfield, was opened in 1848. The Shore Line, between New Haven and Providence, was leased in 1870. The New York, New Haven and Hartford thus came to operate 1,800 miles. Between 1907 and 1914 the railroad installed the first railroad electrification using high-voltage alternating-current transmission.

Pennsylvania. Long known as the "standard" railroad, because of the high quality of its property and operation, and its unbroken record of dividend payments. It was chartered in 1846 to build a line between Harrisburg and Pittsburgh. The line was expanded to a system of 10,000 miles, eastward to Philadelphia, New York, Washington, D.C., and Norfolk, Va., and westward to Chicago and St. Louis. The oldest segment of the system was the pioneer Camden and Amboy, chartered by New Jersey in 1830 and completed in 1834.

Pullman Company. George M. Pullman built his first sleeping cars (rebuilt coaches of the Chicago and Alton) in 1858. His first completely Pullman-built car was finished in 1864. By the end of the century the name "Pullman" was synonymous with the sleeping-car business, although the company also manufactured passenger and freight cars. An antitrust suit required the enterprise to divest itself of either the car-manufacturing or the car-operating business. In 1947 the latter was taken over by fifty-seven railroads.

Reading. The Reading Company, which operated 1,200 miles of line in Pennsylvania, New York, and Delaware in the early 1970's, was a successor to the Philadelphia and Reading Railroad, incorporated in 1833, although parts had been built by still earlier companies. On one of these predecessor lines, the Philadelphia, Germantown and Norristown, *Old Ironsides,* the first locomotive built by Matthias Baldwin, ran in 1832. In the 1970's the Reading owned a majority of the stock of the Jersey Central Lines. In the early 1970's the company went bankrupt and in 1976 it became part of Conrail.

Saint Louis–Southwestern. The "Cotton Belt" started as the Tyler Tap Railroad, chartered in 1871, to connect Tyler, Tex., to a main-line railroad. It expanded to 1,500 miles, connecting St. Louis and Memphis with Fort Worth, Dallas, and Waco, Tex. The present name dates from 1891.

Seaboard Coast Line. In 1967 the Atlantic Coast Line and the Seaboard Air Line merged to form the Seaboard Coast Line; mileage in 1980 was 8,771.

Atlantic Coast Line. The Richmond and Petersburg was chartered in 1836 to connect those Virginia cities. The Atlantic Coast Line was created out of that line and dozens of other southern railways, including lines serving the Carolinas, Georgia, Alabama, and Florida. It became the Atlantic Coast Line in 1900, when the parent company absorbed its southern connections. In the early 1970's the railroad operated 5,600 miles of line and had substantial interests in the Louisville and Nashville, the Clinchfield, and other roads.

Seaboard Air Line. The name was first applied in 1889 to a loose operating association of a half a dozen separate connecting railroads in Virginia and the Carolinas. The oldest was the Portsmouth and Roanoke, chartered in 1832, built from Portsmouth, Va., to Weldon, N.C. In 1900 the railroads were consolidated and grew into a system of 4,000 miles extending from Norfolk and Richmond to both coasts of Florida.

Soo Line (Minneapolis, Saint Paul and Sault Sainte Marie). Chartered in 1873 by businessmen of Minneapolis to build a line eastward to the Canadian border at Sault Ste. Marie, the Soo Line reached the sault in 1887. It had also extended westward, finally connecting with the Canadian Pacific at Portal, N.Dak. After 1909 the Soo Line operated the Wisconsin Central, effecting an entrance into Chicago. The 4,450-mile system (1980) became a separately operated subsidiary of the Canadian Pacific in the 1940's.

Southern Pacific. Its beginnings were in Louisiana, Texas, and California. In Louisiana the New Orleans, Opelousas and Great Western Railroad was chartered in 1850 to build from New Orleans westward. In the same year, in Texas, the Buffalo Bayou, Brazos and Colorado was chartered; it was in operation by 1852. The Sacramento Valley Railroad also started in 1852. The Central Pacific, incorporated in California in 1861, undertook the task of building a railroad eastward over the Sierra Nevada and, in 1862, was selected to build the western leg of the first transcontinental route. The Southern Pacific, incorporated in California in 1865, built south and east, to become part of the second transcontinental route. The interests of the Central Pacific and the Southern Pacific were closely linked as early as 1870. In 1934 the twelve companies making up the Southern Pacific interests in Texas and Louisiana were consolidated into the Texas and New Orleans Railroad. In 1980 the Southern Pacific Transportation Company operated more than 13,000 miles of line.

Southern Railway. The Southern Railway was formed in 1894, when the purchasers of the Richmond and Danville were authorized to acquire the East Tennessee, Virginia and Georgia, and other lines, among them the pioneer South Carolina Railroad. The system came to include the separately operated Cincinnati, New Orleans and Texas Pacific; Alabama Great Southern; New Orleans and Northeastern; Georgia, Southern and Florida; and Carolina and Northwestern railroads. A total mileage of over 10,000 in 1980 extended from Washington, D.C., Cincinnati, and St. Louis to New Orleans, Mobile, and Florida.

Union Pacific. The Union Pacific was incorporated in 1862, to build westward from the Missouri River to meet the Central Pacific of California, building eastward. To the 1,000 miles of the original main line, the company added the Kansas Pacific; Denver Pacific; Oregon Short Line; Oregon-Washington Railway and Navigation Company; San Pedro, Los Angeles and Salt Lake; and others. In 1980 it operated 9,266 miles of line, from Council Bluffs, Iowa, Omaha, Nebr., St. Joseph, Mo., and Kansas City, Mo., to Portland, Oreg., Seattle and Spokane, Wash., and Los Angeles.

Western Pacific. The latest of the transcontinental connections was the Western Pacific, organized in 1903 and opened between Salt Lake City and Oakland–San Francisco, Calif., in 1909. A branch line connecting with the Great Northern, opened in 1931, added a north-south route to the original east-west line. Total mileage, including the subsidiary Sacramento Northern, was 1,435 in 1980.

RAILROADS IN THE CIVIL WAR. Northern railroad building westward into the Ohio and Mississippi valleys had insured the adherence of these sections to the Union. Southern construction was mainly east and west between the Atlantic seaboard and the Mississippi River, and from Richmond to the Carolinas and Georgia. For military purposes perhaps the most important lines were those from the Gulf states to Richmond via Chattanooga enabling shipment of supplies and munitions to Virginia and the transfer of troops on interior lines.

On Jan. 31, 1862, President Lincoln was authorized "to take possession of [certain] railroad and telegraph lines." On Feb. 11, 1862, a military director and superintendent of railroads were appointed. Although government work practically monopolized the transportation system of the Confederacy, it was not until February 1865 that authorization was given to take over the southern railroads. Of a total mileage of 31,256 in the United States in 1861, less than 30 percent, or 9,283 miles, was in the Confederate states, soon reduced by Union captures to about 6,000 miles. In general the northern railroads were better built, better equipped, and better run. Inability of the Confederate government, at first, to appreciate the proper use of railroads and later states' rights opposition to government control and operation of the roads as an auxiliary to southern defense were in no small measure responsible for the final collapse of the Confederacy.

RAILROAD STRIKE OF 1877. On July 17, 1877, after a new 10 percent wage reduction, trainmen halted freight cars of the Baltimore and Ohio Railroad at Martinsburg, W.Va. When the local militia proved sympathetic, President Rutherford B. Hayes sent federal soldiers. Sympathetic strikes in other cities brought further news of rioting. The precedent of federal troops in industrial disputes became an active one, and the states strengthened their policing activities.

RAILROAD STRIKES OF 1886. During 1884–85, the Knights of Labor succeeded in winning four of the five major railroad strikes, but Jay Gould secretly prepared to break the power of the order. When the Texas and Pacific Railroad office at Marshall, Tex., discharged its union foreman, a general strike was ordered for Mar. 1, 1886. Under Martin Irons, 900 men struck, tying up 5,000 miles of railway in the central states. Gould would neither arbitrate unless the workers returned to work nor would he reinstate discharged strikers. The strike collapsed on May 3. This defeat discredited industrial unionism and the Knights of Labor, assuring the subsequent victory of the craft unions.

RAILROAD SURVEYS, GOVERNMENT. Interest in a railroad to the Pacific coast became keen and widespread after the Mexican cession of 1848. The question of the best route became the subject of a great deal of discussion. In 1853 Congress added the sum of $150,000 to an army appropriation bill to defray the expenses of surveying feasible routes. Five routes were surveyed. The surveys themselves did not bring agreement as to a route. When the Pacific Railroad Bill was adopted in 1862, the central route from the western border of Iowa to the California-Nevada line was chosen.

RAILS. The earliest steam railroads used wooden "strap" rails, with flat strips of bar iron secured to the upper surface. Because they were light and because of the danger of the strap rails coming loose, heavy rolled iron rails were imported from England. The rolling of heavy iron rails in the United States was begun in 1844 at the Mount Savage Rolling Mill in Maryland. Rails of the inverted U, or Evans, type and of the T type—designed in 1830 by Robert L. Stevens—were manufactured.

The U.S. manufacture of Bessemer steel rails did not begin until 1867. The greater uniformity, strength, and hardness gave them excellent wearing qualities. By 1912 open-hearth steel rails had surpassed Bessemer rails. The use of rail welded into strips up to one-half mile in length did not become common in the United States until the 1950's.

"RAIL SPLITTER." A nickname for Lincoln; originated in the Illinois State Republican Convention at Decatur, May 9, 1860, when Richard J. Oglesby and John Hanks marched into the hall with two fence rails placarded, "Abraham Lincoln, The Rail Candidate for President in 1860."

RAILWAY ADMINISTRATION ACT. *See* **Railroad Administration, U.S.**

RAILWAY LABOR ACTS. *See* **Railroad Mediation Acts.**

RAILWAYS, ELECTRIC. Thomas Davenport of Vermont in 1836 and Robert Davidson of Scotland in 1838 devised electrically propelled cars using voltaic batteries. Sir William Siemens and Johann Halske's third-rail electric railway appeared in 1879. Stephen D. Field and Thomas A. Edison exhibited an electric locomotive in 1883, and Charles J. Van Depoele demonstrated in 1883 a car taking power from a wire laid in a trough. Short electric street railways were built in Providence and Kansas City in 1884. By 1890 there were 1,200 miles of electric street railway in the United States, and by 1895, 10,863 miles. In 1896–97 Chicago elevated lines began to be electrically operated, followed in 1901 by New York and Boston. The Chicago, Milwaukee and St. Paul's 645-mile electrification through the Western Mountains (constructed 1914–18) was an epochal achievement. (*See also* Interurban Electric Lines; Subways.)

RAILWAY SHOPMEN'S STRIKE. The Railway Employees Department of the American Federation of Labor, representing 400,000 members, struck July 1, 1922, protesting unfavorable decisions of the Federal Labor Board (*see* Railroad Mediation Acts) and the unpunished violations of the Transportation Act by the carriers. A settlement was effected largely in favor of the carriers by the Baltimore Agreement on Oct. 27.

RAINES LAW. A New York State liquor tax law of 1896, devised by John Raines, Republican state senator, which prohibited Sunday and all-night sales by the retail liquor trade, but exempted hotels. The number of hotels increased rapidly, especially in New York City, where many became resorts of prostitution, known as "Raines Law hotels."

RAINFALL. *See* **Droughts.**

RAINMAKING ON THE GREAT PLAINS. A tree-planting plan was based on the principle that trees would serve as windbreaks and retard evaporation on the leeward side; another plan involved constructing ponds to increase humidity. High explosives were also given trials by the U.S. Department of Agriculture. Prayer was offered in the drier states at camp meetings and revivals held in the summer, when drought was most threatening. In the 1940's attempts to induce increased rainfall by means of seeding clouds with silver iodide or salt failed.

RAISIN RIVER MASSACRE (Jan. 22, 1813). Following surrender of Detroit to the British in August 1812, the Americans raised two new armies to recover the post. Gen. James Winchester encamped at Maumee Rapids (above Toledo), facing British Gen. Henry A. Proctor at Amherstburg on the Detroit River. On Jan. 14, 1813, Winchester sent 650 Kentuckians to recover Frenchtown (modern Monroe), at the mouth of the Raisin River, from a British-Indian force; he then led 300 more to the support of his force. Proctor advanced from Amherstburg and at dawn, Jan. 22, assailed the American army. A frightful massacre followed, the Americans suffering a loss of some 900 killed or taken prisoner. The affair stirred American opinion deeply and "Remember the River Raisin" became a rallying cry.

RALEIGH (N.C.). Identified and constructed as the state capital under acts of the North Carolina legislature in 1792, and named in honor of Sir Walter Raleigh. Its population in 1980 was 149,771. It is a manufacturing and commercial center with factories for electronic, metal, and lumber products and with several food-processing plants. Raleigh is also an important cultural and research center; North Carolina State University is located there, as are several other colleges. The first nuclear research reactor used for exclusively peaceful purposes was constructed in Raleigh for use at North Carolina State.

RALEIGH CONFERENCE OF SOUTHERN GOVERNORS (Oct. 13, 1856). Called by Virginia Gov. Henry A. Wise—a proslavery Democrat largely responsible for James Buchanan's nomination for the presidency in 1856—to formulate a policy in the event that the Republican, antislavery candidate, John C. Frémont, was elected. Only the governors of Virginia, North Carolina, and South Carolina attended, and they were unable to adopt a program.

RALEIGH LETTER (Apr. 17, 1844). Written by Henry Clay, Whig presidential candidate, to explain his opposition to the proposed annexation of Texas, condemning it as both inexpedient and dishonorable, which displeased many southern voters and contributed to his defeat.

RALEIGH'S LOST COLONY. The group usually designated as the Lost Colony cleared from Plymouth, England, on May 8, 1587, and reached Roanoke Island in the Albermarle region of North Carolina (then Virginia) on July 22. On Aug. 18, Ellinor (or Elyoner) White Dare, daughter of Gov. John White, gave birth to a daughter, Virginia, the first English child born in America. On Aug. 27 White reluctantly sailed to England for supplies; he was not able to come back to Roanoke Island until August 1590. He discovered no trace of the colony except the letters "C R O" carved on a tree and the word "CROATOAN" cut on the doorpost of the palisade. It has usually been assumed that the colonists went to the friendly Croatoans to the south but it has also been suggested that they were victims of the Spanish. Settlers at Jamestown after 1607 were told by Indians that some of the colonists from Roanoke Island, apparently trying to make their way to Chesapeake Bay, were caught between two warring bodies of Indians not far from their destination and slaughtered. Rumors circulated in Virginia that a few had escaped and were held by Indians to engage in metalwork, but attempts to find them failed.

RALEIGH'S PATENT AND FIRST COLONY. On Mar. 25, 1584, Queen Elizabeth renewed Sir Humphrey Gilbert's patent of 1578 in the name of Gilbert's half-brother, Walter Raleigh (*see* Gilbert's Patent). On Apr. 27 Raleigh sent out an expedition led by Philip Amadas and Arthur Barlowe. They entered Albemarle Sound in July and a few days later landed at Roanoke Island. After two months' exploring and trading with the Indians, they returned to England. Elizabeth named the new land "Virginia" and knighted Raleigh.

In April 1585 Raleigh sent out a colony of 108 men, with Ralph Lane as governor and Sir Richard Grenville in command of the fleet; they landed at Roanoke Island on July 27. About a month later, Grenville returned to England. Lane built a fort and dwelling houses. War with the Indians broke out in the spring of 1586; Lane won an easy victory, but unrest and distress continued to increase. When Sir Francis Drake's fleet appeared and offered to take the colony back to England, Lane consented. About two weeks later, Grenville arrived with supplies; he soon returned to England, but left fifteen men on Roanoke Island. When the next Raleigh colony (*see* Raleigh's Lost Colony) arrived at Roanoke in July 1587, they found only the bones of one of the men Grenville had left and the fort and houses in ruins.

RALEIGH TAVERN (Williamsburg, Va.). Twice, in 1769 and 1774, the house of burgesses, dissolved by the governor, met in rebellious session at this hostelry. Tradition has it that Phi Beta Kappa was organized in Raleigh Tavern in 1776. In 1859 it was destroyed by fire. The present building came into being as part of the Williamsburg restoration.

RALSTON'S RING. A group of San Francisco financiers headed by William C. Ralston that, in the early 1860's, sought to capitalize the profits of the Comstock Lode in Nevada. The ring organized the Bank of California in 1864 and supported efforts to build a tunnel to mine the lode. In the early 1870's, as president of the bank, Ralston engaged in unwarranted speculation with the bank's funds; the panic of 1873 almost overthrew the ring and the bank, but both survived until a second crash in 1875.

RAMBOUILLET DECREE. *See* **Napoleon's Decrees.**

RAMS, CONFEDERATE. The distinguishing feature of the rams built by the Confederate forces was a massively constructed bow carrying an iron beak or ram; the novelty of their design was the armor-plated casemate constructed amidship to house the artillery, with sides sloped to cause the enemy's cannonballs and projectiles to ricochet. The *Virginia,* first and most famous of this type, was constructed on the salvaged hull of the U.S. frigate *Merrimack.*

RANCH. An extent of land on which cattle, sheep, or horses are raised and pastured. In the United States most ranching is carried out west of the Mississippi River. Ranches vary greatly in size, although several thousand acres are generally required to qualify a unit as a ranch. The King Ranch in Texas is the largest in the country, comprising about 1 million acres. Traditionally, ranches were family-run affairs, but the modern ranch is as often owned by a corporation.

RANCHOS DEL REY (royal ranches). Established under the Spanish regime in California during the 18th century at San Diego, San Francisco, and Monterey. In 1800 they possessed 18,000 head of sheep. After the secularization of the California missions (1825) the *ranchos* passed into private hands.

RANDOLPH, FORT (W.Va.). Originally Fort Blair, built by the British at Point Pleasant, near the junction of the Ohio and Kanawha rivers, it was abandoned in 1774 and was destroyed at the beginning of the revolutionary war in 1775. The Americans rebuilt it early in 1776, naming it Fort Randolph. The fort withstood an attack by Indians in 1778.

RANDOLPH PLAN. *See* **Virginia Plan.**

RANDOLPH'S COMMISSION. In 1676 Edward Randolph was commissioned to carry to Massachusetts Bay Colony the king's orders concerning the boundary disputes with Robert Mason and the heirs of Sir Ferdinando Gorges. Randolph was also to make a complete investigation concerning colonies. He made a comprehensive report, adverse as far as Massachusetts was concerned; most serious of all offenses listed were the flagrant breaches of the Navigation Acts and the denial of parliamentary legislative authority over the colony. Randolph's report was chiefly responsible for the reopening of the fifty-year-old question as to the legal position of the Massachusetts Bay Company, which ended in the annulment of the charter in 1684.

RANGE CATTLE INDUSTRY. *See* **Open-Range Cattle Period.**

RANGER-DRAKE **ENGAGEMENT** (Apr. 24, 1778). The Continental sloop *Ranger,* Capt. John Paul Jones commanding, sighted the British ship *Drake* anchored at Carrickfergus, Ireland, there expressly to capture Jones. Waiting until it came within close range, Jones raked the *Drake,* until it called for quarter.

RANGERS. Specially trained infantry capable of acting in small groups to make rapid attacks into enemy territory and withdraw without major engagement. Rangers are traced back before the American Revolution, when groups of specialized infantry were used by the British to cope with the French and Indians, notably Rogers' Rangers.

Rangers fought in the War of 1812, in the Black Hawk War, and in the Mexican War. In the Civil War many units of both the North and South adopted the name; Col. John S. Mosby's Rangers and Gen. Alfred H. Terry's Texas Rangers are the best known.

Rangers were not used again until World War II, when six ranger battalions were organized and saw action in Africa, Europe, and the Pacific. After the invasion of Korea, sixteen ranger companies were organized, seven of them fighting in Korea. In 1951 it was decided that ranger-trained personnel would be better utilized if they were spread among standard infantry units.

RAPPAHANNOCK STATION, BATTLE AT (Nov. 7, 1863). Union Gen. George G. Meade's army, following Gen. Robert E. Lee after the latter's abortive Bristoe campaign, reached Rappahannock Station, Va., where Gen. Harry T. Hays's Confederate division was found holding two formidable redoubts on the north bank of the Rappahannock River. Meade ordered an attack; the Union troops assaulted, capturing two brigades. Next day other Union troops turned Lee's right, and he retired behind the Rapidan River.

RAPPIST COMMUNITY. *See* **Harmony Society.**

RATE BASE. *See* **Public Utilities.**

RATON PASS. Through the Raton Mountains, on the Colorado–New Mexico boundary, just north of Raton, N.Mex. During the 18th and 19th centuries it was an important gateway between the upper Arkansas basin and eastern New Mexico.

RATTLESNAKE FLAG. A yellow field bearing a coiled rattlesnake and the motto "Don't Tread on Me," used during the French and Indian War (1754–63) as a colonial symbol. It was presented to the Continental Congress by Col. Christopher Gadsden of South Carolina and unofficially adopted by Capt. Esek Hopkins as a commodore's flag.

RATTLETRAP. *See* **Willing Expedition.**

RAYMOND, BATTLE OF (May 12, 1863). Having crossed the Mississippi River below Vicksburg and captured Port Gibson, Gen. Ulysses S. Grant's army moved to cut the railroad between Vicksburg and Jackson. His right corps, that of Gen. James B. McPherson, advanced toward Jackson, where it encountered Confederate Gen. John Gregg's brigade deployed across the road at Raymond. Union Gen. John A. Logan's division drove Gregg toward Jackson. Next day McPherson reached Clinton, on the railroad.

RAYSTOWN PATH. Named for Raystown (now Bedford, Pa.). It led from near Carlisle, Pa., in the Susquehanna Valley to Shannopin's Town (now within Pittsburgh) and Logstown, eighteen miles below Pittsburgh. Much of it today parallels closely the Lincoln Highway west from Chambersburg to Pittsburgh.

RAZORBACK HOGS. Half-wild mongrel descendants of domestic hogs, once common all over the South. Derived from European importation, many were as fierce as wild boars; hunting them was a great sport.

REACTORS. *See* **Atomic Power Reactors.**

READING RAILROAD. *See* **Railroads, Sketches of Principal Lines.**

READJUSTER MOVEMENT. In Virginia Rev. John E. Massey, Col. Frank G. Ruffin, and others contended that the massive state debt, funded in 1871, ought to be readjusted so that it could be met without ruin to farmer taxpayers or the neglect of public schools and charities. Gen. William Mahone, seeking the Democratic gubernatorial nomination, endorsed the idea in 1877, and in 1879 organized the Readjuster party. Winning the legislature in 1879, and gaining the governorship in 1881 with William E. Cameron as their candidate, the new party scaled the debt by the Riddleberger Bill of 1882, enacted laws in the economic and social interest of the masses, and apportioned the offices among its leaders.

REAPER. *See* **Agricultural Machinery; McCormick Reaper.**

REAPPORTIONMENT, CONGRESSIONAL. *See* **Apportionment.**

REBATES, RAILROAD. Special low rates that a railroad carrier charged its favored customers; the practice developed in the mid-1850's and continued because of the spectacular railroad rate wars. The outstanding recipient of railroad rebates was the Standard Oil Company, and much of its early success may be traced to the advantages it enjoyed in the way of rate concessions.

The Interstate Commerce Act (1887) prohibited rate discrimination and established a fine of $5,000 for each violation, and two years later violation was made a penitentiary offense. Under the Elkins Act (1903) any departure from a printed rate was considered an offense. At the same time, the penalty of imprisonment was dropped, the maximum fine raised to $20,000, and the law applied to shippers who received rebates as well as to carriers who granted them. The Hepburn Act (1906) restored the penalty of imprisonment and subjected the receiver of a rebate to a fine equal to three times the rebates received during the preceding six years.

REBELLION, RIGHT OF. According to the theory of John Locke, government powers are fiduciary, and the right of revolution exists when a government abuses or ill-uses this authority or oppresses its people. It was largely on this basis that the American patriots justified their rebellion against Great Britain and the leaders of the Confederate States of America justified their secession from the Union.

REBELLIONS. *See* **Insurrections, Domestic.**

REBEL YELL. The description given by Union soldiers and the general public to the high-pitched shout used by the Confederates in the Civil War.

RECALL. An electoral process for determining whether or not the voters wish to retain a public official in public office before his term comes to an end. It can be invoked through a special election upon the filing of a petition signed by a stipulated number of qualified electors who seek a ballot determination of the issue.

Originally provided for in the Los Angeles city charter (1903) and in the Oregon state constitution (1908), the concept of the recall found wide acceptance among the electoral reform proposals of early 20th-century American progressivism. By 1980 recall provisions were incorporated into the constitutions of fourteen states; elective judicial officials were exempted constitutionally from recall in six. The recall has rarely been invoked on a statewide basis.

RECESSION OF 1937. In August 1937 a decline set in that was as rapid as the recovery of 1933 had been, resulting in a 27 percent reduction of business activity by the end of the year. A further sharp decline in activity occurred in the first six months of 1938, after which activity turned sharply upward to the end of the year. Although this recession was unusually severe, no panic ensued either in the stock market or in business.

RECIPROCAL TRADE AGREEMENTS. The Trade Agreements Act (June 12, 1934) delegated to the president the power to make foreign-trade agreements with other nations on the basis of a mutual reduction of duties. The act limited reduction to 50 percent of the rates of duty existing then and stipulated that commodities could not be transferred between the dutiable and free lists. The power to negotiate was renewed for either two or three years periodically until 1962. Each trade agreement was to incorporate the principle of "unconditional most-favored-nation treatment," to avoid a great multiplicity of rates.

The United States usually proceeded by making direct concessions only to so-called chief suppliers—namely, countries that were, or probably would become, the main source, or a major source, of supply of the commodity under discussion. It used its bargaining power by granting concessions in return for openings to foreign markets. Between 1934 and 1947 the United States made separate trade agreements with twenty-nine countries.

American authorities in 1945 made proposals for the expansion of world trade and employment. Twenty-three separate countries then conducted tariff negotiations bilaterally on a product-by-product basis, with each country negotiating its concessions on each import commodity with the principal supplier of that commodity. The various bilateral understandings were combined to form the General Agreement on Tariffs and Trade (GATT), signed in Geneva on Oct. 30, 1947 (*see* General Agreement on Trade and Tariffs).

With the expiration of the eleventh renewal of the Reciprocal Trade Agreements Act, Congress passed the Trade Expansion Act of 1962, by which the president was authorized, through trade agreements with foreign countries, to reduce any duty by 50 percent of the rate in effect on July 1, 1962. The president was empowered to reduce tariffs on industrial products by more than 50 percent, or to eliminate them completely when the United States and the Common Market together accounted for 80 percent or more of the world export value; he could also reduce the duty by more than 50 percent or eliminate it on an agricultural commodity. President Lyndon B. Johnson pushed through a new round of tariff bargaining that culminated in a multilateral trade negotiation known as the Kennedy Round. The agreement reached on June 30, 1967, reduced tariff duties an average of about 35 percent on some 60,000 items representing an estimated $40 billion in world trade.

RECIPROCITY. *See* **Reciprocal Trade Agreements; Tariff.**

RECLAMATION. Federal assistance in the reclamation of arid lands by means of irrigation began when Congress enacted the Desert Land Act of 1877; although 10 million acres passed from government ownership under the provisions of the act, widespread fraud limited its effectiveness. Somewhat more positive were the results of the Carey Act of 1894, under which 1,067,635 acres were reclaimed.

The Reclamation Act of 1902 authorized the secretary of the interior to construct irrigation works in the sixteen western states and to pay for them from a revolving reclamation fund accumulated from the sales of public lands in those states (*see* Newlands Reclamation Act). Ethan Allen Hitchcock, secretary of the interior, promptly created the Reclamation Service, and within one year had authorized the construction of three projects—the Newlands in Nevada, the Salt River in Arizona, and the Uncompahgre in Colorado.

On June 20, 1923, the Reclamation Service was renamed the Bureau of Reclamation. By 1978 the bureau and its predecessor had built 309 storage dams and dikes, which provided water for over 9 million acres, producing over $4 billion worth of crops a year, and had constructed forty-nine hydroelectric power plants.

RECOGNITION, POLICY OF. The U.S. Constitution is silent on the matter of recognition of new states and new governments and thus gives no indication which organ of government is charged with that responsibility. In practice, the executive has discharged that function, and it has been generally accepted that the power of the president to recognize any country is absolute. Recognition may be conditional, but once granted, it is not normally withdrawn. Severance of diplomatic relations does not necessarily affect recognition. The mere entry into relations with a new state or government does not imply recognition if there is no intent.

The criteria for recognition were established by Secretary of State Thomas Jefferson in 1792: if a new government possessed the machinery of state, if it governed with the assent of a majority of the people, and if it met with no substantial resistance, American recognition followed; recognition was not a moral act and did not imply approval. One additional criterion is the new state's or new government's capacity and willingness to carry out its international obligations. The refusal of the United States to recognize the Soviet Union (1917–33), the People's Republic of China (1949–1978), and Fidel Castro's regime in Cuba constitutes a clear departure from America's traditional recognition policy.

RECOLLECTS. *See* **Franciscans.**

RECONSTRUCTION. According to the Crittenden-Johnson Resolutions of July 1861, the object of the war was to restore the Union with "all the dignity, equality, and rights of the several States unimpaired." Congress refused to reaffirm its policy; President Abraham Lincoln viewed the process of wartime reconstruction as a weapon to detach southerners from their allegiance to the Confederacy and thus shorten the war. Consequently, on Dec. 8, 1863, he issued a proclamation of amnesty that promised full pardon to all but a select group of disloyal citizens (*see* Reconstruction, Lincoln's Plan of). The president's plan encountered resistance in Congress.

With the end of war the problem of Reconstruction became more acute. If the seceded states were to be restored without any conditions, local whites would soon reestablish Democratic rule, but many doubted the feasibility of enfranchising newly liberated slaves. Lincoln's successor, Andrew Johnson, was wholly out of sympathy with black suffrage.

Johnson's plan, published on May 29, 1865, called for the speedy restoration of southern governments based on the (white) electorate of 1860. High Confederate officials and all those owning property valued at more than $20,000 were excluded from his offer of amnesty, but they were eligible for individual pardons. Appointing provisional governors who were to call constitutional conventions, Johnson expected the restored states to ratify the Thirteenth Amendment abolishing slavery, nullify the secession ordinances, and repudiate the Confederate debt. In operation the president's plan revealed that little had changed in the South. Not one of the states enfranchised even literate blacks; some balked at nullifying the secession ordinances; others hesitated or failed to repudiate the Confederate debt; and Mississippi refused to ratify the Thirteenth Amendment. When Congress met in December, it refused to admit any of the representatives from the seceded states. All matters pertaining to the restoration of the South were to be referred to the newly created Joint Committee of Fifteen on Reconstruction.

Congress then developed a Reconstruction plan of its own: the Fourteenth Amendment. Moderate in tone, it neither conferred suffrage on the blacks nor exacted heavy penalties from the whites. Clearly defining American citizenship, it made blacks part of the body politic, sought to protect them from state interference, and provided for reduced representation for states disfranchising prospective voters. Johnson was wholly opposed to the measure. Believing the amendment subversive of the Constitution and of white supremacy, he used his influence to procure its defeat in the southern states, an effort that succeeded everywhere except in Tennessee, which was admitted on July 24, 1866. Congress proceeded to shackle him by restricting his powers of removal (Tenure of Office Act) and of military control ("Command of the Army" Act). In addition, it passed a series of measures that inaugurated the congressional or "radical" phase of Reconstruction (*see* Reconstruction Acts). The president refused to concede defeat, and his intransigence resulted in a complete break with Congress (*see* Impeachment Trial of Andrew Johnson).

During 1867 and 1868 radical Reconstruction had been gradually initiated. The electorate ratified the new charters in all but three states—Mississippi, Texas, and Virginia. Accordingly, in the summer of 1868 the compliant states were readmitted and the Fourteenth Amendment declared in force. Because Georgia later excluded blacks from its legislature and because Mississippi, Texas, and Virginia, for various local reasons, did not ratify their constitutions on time, those four states were subjected to additional requirements. These included the ratification of the Fifteenth Amendment, prohibiting the denial of suffrage on account of race. After complying with the new demands, these states too were restored to their places in the Union in 1870, and the amendment was added to the Constitution.

The end of Reconstruction came at different times in the several states. In some cases terror instigated by the Ku Klux Klan and its successors overthrew Republican administrations; in others, conservatives regained control by more conventional means. By 1876 Republican administrations survived only in Florida, Louisiana, and South Carolina. For a time blacks continued to vote, although in decreasing numbers, but by the turn of the century they had been almost eliminated from southern politics.

RECONSTRUCTION, LINCOLN'S PLAN OF. In his proclamation of Dec. 8, 1863, President Abraham Lincoln offered pardon, with certain exceptions, to those southerners who would take an oath to support the U.S. Constitution and abide by federal laws and proclamations concerning slaves. When oath-takers equal in number to one-tenth of the state's voters in 1860 should "reestablish" a government in a seceded commonwealth, Lincoln promised executive recognition to such government without commitment as to congressional recognition. Both the plan and the whole southern policy of Lincoln were denounced as far too lenient.

RECONSTRUCTION ACTS. A series of laws designed to carry out the congressional program of Reconstruction. The first act (Mar. 2, 1867) divided all southern states except Tennessee into five military districts to be commanded by general officers. Conventions chosen by universal male suffrage were to frame constitutions, which would have to be accepted by the electorate; then, after ratifying the Fourteenth Amendment, the southern states would be deemed ready for readmission to the Union.

When southerners refused to take steps to call conventions, a supplementary act (Mar. 23, 1867) provided that the commanding generals initiate the voting process. A second supplementary act (July 19, 1867) declared that the state governments were strictly subordinate to the military commanders, broadly defined the disfranchising clauses, and spelled out the generals' right to remove state officers. After the conservatives in Alabama had defeated the radical state constitution by registering but not voting, a third supplementary act (Mar. 11, 1868) enabled a majority of the actual voters, rather than of the registrants, to ratify.

RECONSTRUCTION AND THE CHURCHES. Most of the major northern churches had entered the South during the war, having won the consent of the War Department to take over church buildings abandoned by southern ministers. At the close of the war they looked upon the South as a new mission field, and new organizations were formed to carry on work in the South, especially among the freedmen. Numerous northern ministers found employment in the Freedmen's Bureau, and some became involved in carpetbag and Afro-American politics. The former slaves were gathered into independent congregations all over the South, a great majority being Methodists and Baptists; Afro-American churches were used by unscrupulous carpetbag and black politicians to gain control of the black ballot. Generally speaking, the black ministers were the first recognized leaders of the freedmen.

RECONSTRUCTION FINANCE CORPORATION (RFC). President Herbert Hoover recommended, and Congress created, the RFC on Jan. 22, 1932, to make loans not only to banks but also to insurance companies and railroads and, by the Emergency Relief and Construction Act of July 21, 1932, to states and to farmers. The immediate aim was to restore faith in financial institutions generally, prevent ruinous liquidation, and revive the economy through the restoration of credit. During World War II, through the Defense Plant Corporation, a subsidiary, the RFC invested some $7 billion in various defense-related industries. On July 30, 1953, President Dwight D. Eisenhower signed a bill ending the Reconstruction Finance Corporation. It had loaned out $12 billion, of which all but $800 million was repaid. Its successor was the Small Business Administration.

RECOVERY, FORT (Ohio). Built in what is now west central Ohio near the Indiana line in December 1793 by a detachment of Gen. Anthony Wayne's army on the site of Gen. Arthur St. Clair's defeat, Nov. 4, 1791, by the Indians along the Wabash and Maumee rivers; one of the soldiers' first duties was to inter the bones of the 600 slain on the field two years earlier. It had little importance except as a supply base and as an identification point for the Indian boundary delineated in the Treaty of Greenville (Aug. 3, 1795); a small village grew up around the site of the fort.

RECOVERY ADMINISTRATION, NATIONAL. *See* **New Deal.**

RECRUITMENT. The U.S. armed services have depended for the greatest number of their troops on recruitment by voluntary enlistment. Because the given strength of the armed forces has generally been limited by law, recruitment has occasionally been suspended for brief periods.

During the Mexican War (1846–48) the only recruitment was of mounted ranger companies to protect the outlying districts of the new Republic of Texas. During the Civil War (1861–65), Union recruitment involved, in many instances, the paying of recruits a sum of money for joining (many people collected the money and then paid others only a small portion of it to take their places on the rolls). Much of the armies on both sides consisted of volunteer forces.

Recruiting for all branches of the armed forces proceeds in about the same manner, although methods have changed greatly over the years. The armed forces initiated a great number of training programs for recruits and offered many specialized technical courses. Job opportunities proved a greater attraction in the midst of the depressed economic conditions of the 1970's than appeals to patriotism.

RED CLOUD'S WAR. *See* **Sioux Wars.**

RED CROSS, AMERICAN. Founded May 21, 1881, by Clara Barton to provide care to ill and wounded soldiers in wartime. Disaster relief became a major program of the Red Cross in the United States.

Between 1906 and 1914 the Red Cross established its first aid, public health nursing, and water safety training programs. During World War I, it set up and staffed fifty-eight base hospitals and forty-seven ambulance companies overseas to care for the wounded. The Junior Red Cross (later Red Cross Youth Service Programs) was organized in 1917. Extensive civilian war relief activities were carried on overseas.

After the war Red Cross safety training, home care of the sick, accident prevention, and nutrition education gained in popularity. In World War II the Red Cross carried on civilian relief operations in sixty countries; recruited registered nurses for military duty, and trained nurse's aides to care for civilian patients; and established worldwide welfare and recreation programs to serve U.S. troops. The first nationwide blood program was organized, and more than 13 million units of blood were collected for the armed forces from volunteer donors. In 1948 the Red Cross established a program to provide blood and its components to civilians without charge. A member of the international League of Red Cross Societies, which it helped to found in 1919, the American Red Cross was cooperating with 122 other societies.

REDEMPTIONERS. White immigrants who, in return for their passage to America from Europe, sold their services for two to seven years. Upon arrival in port, captains of vessels having redemptioners aboard advertised in newspapers the sale of their services to persons who should advance the cost of their passage.

RED LEGS. So called because of their red leggings, these were members of a secret military society organized in Kansas in 1862 by George W. Hoyt. Their predatory activities rivaled those of Missouri guerrillas; and they served as federal scouts in border conflicts.

RED LINE MAP. In 1782, Benjamin Franklin marked the boundary of the United States for the reference of Charles Gravier, Comte de Vergennes, French foreign minister, in a "strong red line" on a copy of John Mitchell's *Map of British and French Dominions in North America.* This copy has never since been located in the French archives. In 1932 a transcript of the map, red line and all, was discovered in the Spanish archives.

RED RIVER BOUNDARY DISPUTE. *See* **Greer County Dispute.**

RED RIVER CAMPAIGN (1864). Union Gen. Henry W. Halleck ordered an invasion of the great cotton-growing sections of Louisiana, Arkansas, and Texas, under the command of Gen. Nathaniel P. Banks. By the middle of March a Union fleet and Banks's army had taken Fort DeRussy (Mar. 14) and occupied Alexandria (Mar. 16), there to await the arrival of reinforcements from the Mississippi River. The retreating Confederate troops under Gen. Richard Taylor, receiving reinforcements as they retired, halted at Mansfield, south of Shreveport. On Apr. 8 Taylor sustained Banks's attack; the Union forces were defeated and driven back in confusion (*see* Sabine Crossroads, Battle at). The next day Taylor's troops advanced against Banks's army at Pleasant Hill, southeast of Mansfield, and in their turn were repulsed. During the night the Union army retreated to Alexandria.

When the threat of Banks's advance was removed, Confederate Gen. Edmund Kirby-Smith, at Shreveport, undertook both to pursue Banks and to crush Union Gen. Frederick Steele. He attacked at Jenkins Ferry, Ark., on the Saline River, on Apr. 30; Steele retreated to Little Rock. Kirby-Smith then turned southward to join Taylor for a final blow against Banks. He was too late. Banks had reembarked and started on his way back to the Mississippi, where the troops were dispersed. The defeat of Banks's expedition ended important operations in the trans-Mississippi. The Confederate forces held out until May 26, 1865, when Kirby-Smith surrendered.

RED RIVER CART TRAFFIC. The Red River cart was a two-wheeled vehicle developed from a primitive cart used at Pembina, N. Dak. in 1801; it had wheels made from sections of tree trunks, some 3 feet in diameter, was made entirely of wood, carried a maximum load of 1,000 pounds, and was drawn by an ox or Indian pony with a rude harness of rawhide. The traffic began as early as 1822. A train of Red River carts a mile in length was not at all infrequent. The carts were loaded at Fort Garry (Winnipeg) or Pembina with buffalo robes, pemmican, dried meat, and furs. Two trips during the season was the limit, since the carts were unable to travel more than twenty miles a day.

The Red River cart trails most used were on the west side of the river, their location being dependent on the season. Streams were crossed, where necessary, by the use of hastily improvised rafts. On the east side of the Red River the trail ran southeast to Fort Snelling. Later the trails crossed the Mississippi River at Sauk Rapids and reached St. Paul.

RED RIVER INDIAN WAR (1874–75). As a result of the Treaty of Medicine Lodge, in October 1867, the Comanche, Kiowa, and Kataka were put on a reservation about the Wichita Mountains and the Arapaho and Cheyenne on another farther north (both within western Oklahoma). The Indians, however, again and again slipped away to raid the borders of Kansas, Colorado, New Mexico, and Texas. During the summer of 1874, both cavalry and infantry advanced against the Indians who were encamped along the Red River, its tributaries, and the canyons of the Staked Plain (Llano Estacado) in west Texas and southeastern New Mexico. More than fourteen pitched battles were fought before the Indians returned to their reservations.

RED RIVER OF THE NORTH. This river forms the boundary between Minnesota and North Dakota and flows through Manitoba, Canada, into Lake Winnipeg. It was discovered by Pierre Gaultier de Varennes, Sieur de La Vérendrye, French explorer and fur trader, in 1733; by the middle of the century it was the center of a profitable fur trade. American fur traders did not push into the Red River country until after the War of 1812. In the 1840's American and British traders fought hard for the trade of the country; but by the middle of the century American farmers were advancing into the region. During the decades of the 1870's, 1880's, and 1890's, thousands of settlers—mostly northern Europeans and eastern Americans—poured into the Red River valley. Before the close of the century, the Red River country ranked first among the wheat-producing regions of North America.

RED RIVER POST. French encroachments into Texas after 1685 aroused the Spaniards to establish missions and military posts in the region. In 1691 Don Domingo de Teran, governor of Coahuila (Mexico) and Texas, established a post among the Caddo on the Red River, near the northwestern corner of modern Louisiana; the post was abandoned in 1693.

RED RIVER RAFT. Logs and other debris blocked the channel of the Red River of the South for a distance of 180 miles above Coushatta Bayou, stopping steamboat navigation at Natchitoches, La. Capt. Henry Miller Shreve, between 1833 and 1839, entirely removed the raft, leaving the river navigable for more than 1,000 miles. Shreveport, named in honor of Shreve, arose as the commercial center of the region thus opened to settlement. Total congressional appropriations for that project approximated $1 million.

RED SHIRTS. Bands of armed horsemen who overthrew Radical Republican rule in South Carolina. Beginning in 1870, whites, without official sanction, organized themselves in groups for protection against the black militia, and, as the political campaign of 1876 got under way, they converted white sentiment to a policy of no compromise with the Radical Republicans by bloody work at the Hamburg Riot of July 8. Within two months of that event a Garibaldian uniform was adopted, and thousands of red-shirted whites rode about encouraging the Wade Hampton canvass for governor, disturbing Radical Republican meetings, and terrorizing blacks. There were 290 companies composed of 14,350 men. By intimidation the Red Shirts secured a majority for Hampton in the November election and forced the flight of Radical Republican officeholders when the federal troops were withdrawn from the state in April 1877.

REDSTONE OLD FORT. The pioneers' name for a Mound Builder entrenchment at the confluence of Dunlap's Creek with the Monongahela River in southwestern Pennsylvania. Fort Burd was erected at the site in 1759 by Col. James Burd of the Pennsylvania militia. In 1785 the site was rechristened Brownsville.

REED RULES. Adopted by the House of Representatives on Feb. 14, 1890, they were Speaker of the House Thomas B. Reed's rules for more efficient procedure in that body. They permitted the suppression of dilatory tactics, substituted a "present" for a "voting" quorum, reduced the size of the Committee of the Whole, and provided changes in the order of business. They greatly increased the power of the speaker; twenty years later the rules were considerably modified in this particular. (*See also* Cannonism.)

REED TREATY (also known as the U.S. Treaty of Tientsin; June 18, 1858). Following the defeat of China in the Anglo-French War (1857–58), the Treaties of Tientsin opened up eleven more treaty ports to foreign trade and residence and provided for extraterritorial protection of foreign nationals traveling and trading throughout all China. The British Treaty of Tientsin further stipulated the right of a diplomatic representative to appear at Peking; the toleration of the Christian religion, missionaries, and converts; and fixed tariff charges. Despite the fact that the United States had remained neutral during the war, William B. Reed, the American minister, simultaneously negotiated a treaty securing for U.S. citizens equality of treatment extended to other foreigners.

REFERENDUM. A referendum generally involves the submission of a public-policy measure or question directly to the people at a formal election for their approval or disapproval. The Massachusetts constitution of 1780 is usually credited with introducing the use of statewide constitutional referenda. The statewide legislative referendum came somewhat later. Major impetus for legislatures to submit measures to the voters came with the Progressive movement. By 1975 provision for the use of the legislative referendum could be found in the constitutions of at least twelve states. Twenty-three states permitted a citizen-initiated legislative referendum on the filing of a petition (containing a specified number of signatures) with the secretary of state.

REFORESTATION. Artificial regeneration of forests by tree planting dates back to the colonial period in the United States, but general and successful reforestation did not occur until the 20th century. In 1905 the Forest Service began a program of reforesting the national forests, and by 1914 nearly 10,000 acres a year were being reforested. The Clarke-

McNary Act of 1924 provided federal subsidies for tree planting and nursery establishment. Establishment of the Civilian Conservation Corps (CCC) in 1933 made a rapid increase in tree planting possible, but by 1945 annual reforesting again covered less than 140,000 acres.

After World War II, efforts expanded slowly but steadily. In 1960 more than 2.1 million acres were reforested. When the soil bank program ended, reforesting dropped to about 1.4 million acres a year during the period 1962–67; the trend then reversed itself, and reforestation covered nearly 2 million acres in 1973.

REFORMATORIES. Institutions designed primarily for youthful offenders of the law, originating in part in the experience of the United States in the operation of its first prisons (*see* Prisons and Prison Reform). Initially, the child-saving institutions, the houses of refuge for juvenile offenders, were designated as reformatory in character. In 1876 a new institutional program was established at Elmira, N.Y., at what was to become the first reformatory for young men. The program included elementary education for illiterates, designated library hours, lectures by faculty of Elmira College, and vocational training.

Despite the enthusiasm of the reformers and the construction of many reformatories designed on the Elmira model, the reformatory system did not produce the results expected. Some of its innovations, however, were to have a profound impact on correctional reforms introduced in the 20th century. Many types of prisoners who in the latter part of the 19th century would have served their sentences in walled prisons may now be found in smaller, more open facilities, which are believed to provide a better climate for delivery of correctional services.

REFORMED CHURCHES. The American representatives of Dutch Calvinism. Their first American congregation was the Collegiate Church in New York City, established in 1628. The church was divided by the Great Awakening over the issue of evangelism and its relationship to the church in the Netherlands; it declared itself independent in 1819. In 1822 the Christian Reformed Church left the parent body. The principal Reformed denominations in 1980 were the Christian Reformed Church, 213,995 members; Reformed Church in America, 211,000; Hungarian Reform Church in America, 10,500; Protestant Reformed Churches in America, 4,040; and Reformed Church in the United States, 3,790.

REFRIGERATION. Several types of refrigeration machine were developed in the 19th century. The cooling effect of expanding air was used by John Gorrie, a Florida physician who was concerned with relieving the sufferings of malaria victims in the southern summer climate. In Gorrie's machine water was injected into a cylinder in which air was compressed by a steam engine. This cooled the air. The air was allowed to expand in contact with coils containing brine, which was then used to freeze water. Gorrie's machine was scarcely used, but his 1851 patent was a model for others.

More important were "absorption" machines. The first important example was developed in France, by Ferdinand Carré, about 1858: a vessel containing a solution of ammonia in water was connected by a tube to a second vessel; when the former was heated and the latter cooled (by immersing it in cold water), the ammonia was evaporated from the first vessel and condensed in the second; heating was then terminated and the ammonia allowed to reevaporate, producing a refrigerating effect on the surface of the second (ammonia-containing) chamber. Such a "machine" was inexpensive, simple, and well suited for use in isolated areas. One of them, the Crosley "Icyball," was manufactured in large numbers in the United States in the 1930's.

These machines were ultimately replaced by the vapor compression machine, in which a volatile fluid is circulated while being alternately condensed (with the evolution of heat) and evaporated (with the absorption of heat). This is the principle of the modern refrigeration machine. Oliver Evans, an American mechanic, had proposed in 1805 to use ether in such a machine, and in 1834 Jacob Perkins, an American living in London, actually built one. Improved versions were developed and were manufactured from the 1850's.

Ammonia replaced the ethers in a few machines from the 1860's and became the most common refrigerating fluid by 1900. In 1930 Thomas Midgley, Jr., announced his success with the compound dichlorodifluoromethane. Under the commercial name Freon 12, it became the most widely used refrigerant. (*See also* Food Preservation.)

REFUGEE TRACT. Established by the Act of Feb. 18, 1801, this narrow strip of 103,527 acres extending forty-two miles eastward from the Scioto River at Columbus, Ohio, was set aside for Canadians who had aided the American Revolution and had become refugees.

REGICIDES. When the justices who condemned Charles I were exempted from amnesty at the Restoration, three of them, variously called the Colonels, the Judges, or the Regicides, escaped to New England with royal agents in pursuit. Lt. Gen. Edward Whalley, a cousin of Oliver Cromwell, and Maj. Gen. William Goffe, Whalley's son-in-law, arrived in Boston on July 26, 1660. After much moving about to elude the agents, in October 1664 they took refuge in Hadley, Mass.; Whalley died there late in 1674 or 1675. Goffe moved to Hartford, where he died in 1679. The third regicide was John Dixwell, who escaped to Germany in 1660 and appeared at Hadley in February 1665. At New Haven, under the name of James Davids, he was twice married and lived quietly until his death on Mar. 18, 1689.

REGISTRATION OF VOTERS. The first voter registration law was enacted in Massachusetts in 1800. Most large cities initiated registration laws between 1850 and 1900, but election fraud was common. Since 1900 reform legislation has made registration laws more effective.

To register, the voter appears before county or city election officials during a set period and establishes his or her right to vote. Once the person is registered, his or her name appears on registration lists and is checked off when he or she votes. In 1970 Congress passed a voting rights act that replaced the confusing pattern of state residency requirements with a uniform national law for presidential elections. Nationwide approximately 75 percent of those eligible to vote are registered.

REGULATING ACT. *See* **Massachusetts Government Act.**

REGULATORS. Irregular armed combinations, organized in numerous southern communities after the Civil War to obstruct the welfare activities of the Freedmen's Bureau. These vigilantes, known also as "Black-Horse Cavalry" and "Jayhawkers" in Georgia and Louisiana, generally rode at night, in disguise, employing arson, murder, and mutilation to terrorize the freedmen and prevent the exercise of their rights to make labor contracts and to migrate.

REGULATORS OF NORTH CAROLINA. The struggle of the settlers in the 18th-century backcountries of North Carolina against the oppressive administration of the laws by corrupt officials, and excessive fees charged by them and by attorneys, began in 1764 in Anson, Orange, and Granville counties. In the spring of 1768 the protesters organized what they termed the "Regulation," centered in Orange County. The new governor, William Tryon, in July and August 1768 assembled at Hillsboro a body of militia to suppress a threatened uprising; the agitation subsided.

The second phase of the Regulation covered the years 1769–71 and took the form of driving local justices from the bench and threatening violence. Energetic preparations were made for a military expedition to Orange County, and there resulted the Battle of Alamance (May 16, 1771) between about 1,000 militia and 2,000 Regulators, which ended in disaster for the latter.

REGULATORS OF SOUTH CAROLINA. Irregular and sporadic organizations of backcountry settlers formed 1767–69 for the purpose of breaking up bands of horse thieves that had established a reign of terror. With the creation of courts in the interior of the province, the movement came to an end.

RELIEF. In colonial America local governments provided relief for the needy. Under the prevailing system, called outdoor relief, individuals were farmed out to the lowest bidder or a contract was given for the care of all paupers in a local community. Direct aid, when given, was in kind—that is, in goods or food, not cash. The able-bodied were expected to work for the aid provided. In the 18th century county governments assisted in the care of the needy. In the 19th century the number of almshouses, county poor farms, and state institutions for the insane, blind, and crippled grew. Inefficiency and graft in the giving of contracts to operate county and state institutions were fairly common, and the inmates were often cruelly treated.

The Great Depression had a tremendous impact on the philosophy and the practice of providing relief or giving public assistance. President Herbert Hoover established the President's Emergency Relief Organization and later the President's Emergency Employment Committee; the first stimulated relief activity, while the second stressed work relief for the able-bodied.

In 1932 Congress created the Reconstruction Finance Corporation, which was authorized to lend $300 million in relief funds directly to the states. In the spring of 1933 President Franklin D. Roosevelt initiated the nation's first direct federal relief program with the establishment of the Federal Emergency Relief Administration (FERA). In the early fall of 1933 Roosevelt launched the Civil Works Administration (CWA). Local officials initiated most projects. There were over 4 million on CWA rolls in early February 1934; most workers repaired roads and schools, laid sewer pipes, and built small airports. Operating concurrently with the FERA and the CWA were the Civilian Conservation Corps (CCC) and the Public Works Administration (PWA). (*See* separate articles.)

The FERA remained in existence through 1935, providing relief funds for the sick, the crippled, dependent mothers and their children, and the elderly. The Federal Surplus Relief Corporation provided means for the distribution of large amounts of surplus foods to the needy. Work relief projects were set up for women and white-collar workers, and efforts were made to upgrade the skills of workers. The Social Security Act of 1935 provided for unemployment compensation for a set number of weeks; old-age assistance payments for millions of Americans aged sixty-five and over; and economic aid for the blind, the crippled, and dependent mothers and children. In 1935 the Roosevelt administration, by an act of Congress, launched the Works Progress Administration (WPA). The WPA provided work for over 5 million Americans between July 1935 and December 1938. (*See* Works Progress Administration.)

Principal changes and advancements in public assistance after World War II include aid to the permanently and totally disabled (1950); federal financial participation in vendor payments for medical care (1950); medical assistance for the aged (1960); extension of aid to families of dependent children (AFDC) to include, at the option of the state, children of the unemployed (1961); increased federal sharing in the cost of providing social services and establishing improved programs of rehabilitation, self-support, and self-care (1962); replacement of medical assistance for the aged by a broader program of medical assistance for the medically needy (1965); work-study grants for needy college students (1965); emphasis on work by the able-bodied as a component in public assistance by the inclusion of mothers as eligible for training and education for employment (1965); and the provision of work experience and training programs for employable adults (1965 and 1967). By 1969 these programs and others were providing aid to more than 10.2 million persons at an annual cost in excess of $10.6 billion in federal and state funds. In 1981 President Ronald Reagan presented his "New Federalism" plan, which proposed to shift more responsibility for relief programs to individual states; by mid-1982 the plan was still being debated.

RELIEF ACT OF 1821. When the credit system was abolished by the Land Act of 1820, delinquent land purchasers owed the government more than $21 million. In order to aid settlers in completing their payments, Congress passed a relief act (Mar. 2, 1821) remitting accrued interest, offering a liberal discount for prompt payment, granting a further extension of time, and permitting purchasers to cancel their debt by relinquishing a portion of their land.

RELIGION. When the Anglicans arrived in America, they envisioned the new land in terms of the traditional parish system, in which a settled minister represented both civil and religious order. But almost as soon as the colony of Virginia was founded, the settlers began to devise their own pattern of church life; by means of the vestry system, the leading laymen were able to control both the tenure and the salary of the local clergy.

The Glorious Revolution in England (1688) resulted in a number of new Anglican establishments: Maryland (1702), South Carolina (1706), and North Carolina (1715). The establishment in New York (1693) provided for an orthodox clergyman in each parish but did not specify denomination. When disestablishment came after the American Revolution, the Broad Church tradition of the South combined with the High Church tradition of New England to produce a church that was democratic in its government and yet preserved the values of an episcopal organization. (*See* Episcopal Church.)

The New England Puritans, with the exception of the Plymouth settlers, were nonseparating Congregationalists. The local parishes were independent congregations that owed cooperation to each other. Each member of a church was to have had an experience of conversion; all the residents of the area were expected to attend services and live Christian lives. (*See* Congregational Churches; Puritans and Puritanism.)

Puritanism generated dissent, and the problem of religious diversity was the center of many disputes. In the first generation, Anne Hutchinson shocked the Massachusetts Bay Colony with her emphasis on the indwelling of the Holy Spirit and was banished. Roger Williams, perhaps the region's greatest heretic, challenged the union of church and state on biblical grounds and, following his expulsion from Massachusetts, went to Rhode Island, where he founded a colony based on complete religious toleration.

The Middle Colonies experienced the religious diversity that was to become the national norm. Pennsylvania was established by William Penn as a colony of refuge for the Society of Friends, and the proprietor encouraged immigration by any group that desired to come. The Mennonites established themselves in the southern part of the colony; other German groups who came were the Church of the Brethren and the Moravian Brethren. Lutheran and Presbyterian churches were first organized in America in the Middle Colonies (*see* Lutheran Churches; Presbyterianism).

The Great Awakening (*ca.* 1739–44), an explosion of the revivalist impulse, was not confined to any particular denomination or region (*see* Great Awakening). It influenced the development of the nation in a variety of ways. It brought the colonists together as no earlier event had done and created a feeling of intercolonial solidarity. Its radical emphasis on the individual and the sanctity of his own experience contributed to the emerging sense of democracy that was to sustain the Revolution.

The crisis of the Revolution led American religion to reorganize itself along denominational lines similar to those in colonial Pennsylvania. Although the last vestige of establishment was not removed until 1833, when Massachusetts disestablished Congregationalism, the denominational system was fully operative by 1800. The Revolution increased the visibility of rational religion and revealed a lack of vitality in the churches.

The second Great Awakening in the East was a relatively mild renewal movement. The western clergyman Charles G. Finney, the first great urban revivalist, introduced an element of the older enthusiasm in the 1820's. (*See also* Evangelism, Evangelicalism, and Revivalism)

Western revivalism generated a number of peculiarly American denominations. Western New York, known as the "burned over district" because of its revivalistic fervor, produced two influential movements: the Latter-Day Saints (Mormons), and Adventism, which survives in a number of denominations. Farther south the western revival generated an interest in restorationism, or the belief that the apostolic pattern of Christianity could be recreated; the Christian Churches, or Disciples of Christ, institutionalized this thrust. Based on the circuit rider or traveling preacher, Methodism spread a revivalist theology that stressed the possibility of a holy life—entire sanctification or holiness—and each man's responsibility before God (*see* Methodists).

The voluntary societies were the second response to the postrevolutionary crisis of faith. Often called the righteous empire, various societies sought to reform morals, to raise money for domestic and foreign missions, to work with the urban poor, to end or modify slavery, and to distribute Bibles and tracts. It was a setback for American ecumenism when the denominations asserted their authority in many of the spheres that had been served by the societies, especially foreign and domestic missions.

Although revivalism was the most influential element in early 19th-century religion in the United States, it was not unopposed. On the religious left, the Unitarians broke away from Congregationalism to advocate a theology based on the Enlightenment. Unitarianism generated its own radicals: the transcendentalists.

From the right, a stricter confessional movement sought to return Presbyterianism to the Westminster Standard of 1646; this theology, which drew heavily on Scottish common-sense philosophy, legitimized Presbyterian withdrawal from the voluntary societies and was a source of later fundamentalism.

By 1850 immigration had made the Roman Catholic church the largest single religious body in America. Immigration also changed the direction of American Lutheranism: many immigrants formed their own synods, and their confessional heritage contributed to the weaning of Lutheranism from its earlier participation in the Evangelical consensus.

The Civil War marked a turning point in American religious history. Before the conflict the churches were divided over the issue of slavery, and many denominations split, notably the Baptists and Methodists (1844–45). After the war the religious development of the north and the south followed separate paths. After the war blacks organized their own churches, free from white domination, and continued the development of their own religious practices. (*See* Afro-American Church.)

After the Civil War the churches were confronted with the questions raised by modern scientific, evolutionary, and historical thinking. While many Americans continued to think in the older Evangelical pattern, other Christians sought new expressions of Christian faith. Building on the older evangelicalism and the new liberalism, the Social Gospel was recovered. (*See* Social Gospel.)

The publication of the Fundamentals (1910–13), a series of conservative tracts, heralded the beginning of the fundamentalist-modernist controversy. The controversy faded into the background with the advent of the Great Depression, but it remained an undercurrent in Protestant life. In the 1970's fundamentalist churches, separated from the major denominations, were the fastest-growing segment of American Protestantism.

The late 19th and early 20th centuries saw an increase in the number of Jews in the United States. American Judaism has been a dynamic movement in its Reformed, Conservative, and Orthodox branches and has established a religious community second only to that in Israel (*see* Judaism).

The most significant religious movement since World War I has been the quest for Christian unity. The first institutional expression of this search was the Federal Council of Churches of Christ (1908). It was succeeded in 1950 by the National Council of Churches, which includes interdenominational agencies for missions and education. The search for unity also found expression in the merger of many denominations. The United Lutheran Church was formed in 1918 and the American Lutheran Church in 1930; the Methodists ended their North-South schism in 1939. On a more adventuresome level, the Congregational Christian and the Evangelical and Reformed churches, both the product of earlier mergers, joined in 1957 to form the United Church of Christ. The Consultation on Church Unity (COCU), convened in 1962, attempted to unite nine major denominations.

Despite a superficial religious revival in the 1950's, religion steadily lost influence in the United States after World War I. The participation of the churches in public questions alienated many: the Left felt that the churches were too slow to act, while the Right resented the direction the churches took. In addition, the rise of the so-called "civil religion," an amorphous blend of American religiosity and patriotism, displaced traditional religion for some.

RELIGIOUS LIBERTY. At the time of the establishment of the American colonies, everywhere, with the possible exception of Holland, unity of religion was considered essential to the unity of the state. The American colonies became the first place in the world where complete religious liberty was actually tried in a political state. When Roger Williams established Rhode Island the principle was there put into operation. A majority of the colonies were begun as proprietary grants; in order to attract settlers to buy and settle the land, persecuted religious groups from almost every country in western Europe were invited to come to these colonies. Another factor creating an environment in America favorable to religious liberty was the fact that, by the end of the colonial period, a great majority of the population throughout the colonies was unchurched, and unchurched people generally are opposed to granting special privileges to any one religious body; the political leaders who led in the movement to separate church and state, such as James Madison and Thomas Jefferson, were nonchurch members.

Although there were no direct religious issues involved in the revolutionary war, the disturbed political and social situation that it created, together with the necessity for the formation of new governments, gave opportunity for the new principle, religious liberty, to be incorporated in the new constitutions as they were adopted. Thus, the new state and federal constitutions simply took over, in this respect, what already was to a large degree in practical operation.

RELIGIOUS THOUGHT AND WRITINGS. Most American theologians in the colonial period were influenced by the Reformed (Calvinist) tradition as it had been interpreted by a succession of pastor-theologians connected with the University of Cambridge; it was a practical theology, emphasizing religious experience and Scripture. Cotton Mather was America's first great theological mind. In works dealing with church history (*Magnalia Christi Americana,* 1702), ethics (*Bonifacius,* or *Essays to Do Good,* 1710), and science (*The Christian Philosopher,* 1721), he sought to show the harmony between traditional faith and the emerging Enlightenment.

Jonathan Edwards attempted to justify the Evangelical Calvinism of the Great Awakening with categories drawn from John Locke. In *A Treatise Concerning Religious Affections* (1746) religious emotions were the building blocks of a faith that sought to express itself in love. He attempted to refute the "rational religion," or Arminianism, that was threatening Calvinism in *Freedom of the Will* (1754), *The Great Christian Doctrine of Original Sin Defended* (1758), and *The Nature of True Virtue* (1765). Edwards inspired America's first theological school, the New England theology.

The second Great Awakening did not produce a theological harvest comparable to that of the earlier revival. Charles G. Finney, in his *Lectures on Systematic Theology* (1846–47), stressed the power of man to cooperate with the divine will, the religious value of democracy, and the possibility of avoiding willful sin (perfectionism).

Two reactions against the dominant revivalist theology of the 19th century should be noted. Unitarianism, which initially drew its inspiration from the Enlightenment, gradually broadened into transcendentalism: Ralph Waldo Emerson challenged the young clergymen of Harvard in his "Divinity School Address" (1838) to experience the divine within nature and themselves; Theodore Parker, in his sermon "The Transient and Permanent in Christianity" (1841), denied the supernatural and urged Christians to move beyond Christ and stand for the truths He had taught.

Although the Mercersberg theologians Philip Schaff and John W. Nevin articulated an orthodox theology based on romantic motifs, the more stringent conservatism of Charles Hodge was more influential. His *Systematic Theology* (1871–75) was based as much on the Scottish Enlightenment as it was on the Reformed tradition; Princeton conservatism, as his school was called, contributed to Presbyterian resistance to interdenominational cooperation and was one of the sources of later fundamentalism.

During the post–Civil War period theologians began to struggle with the issues raised by modern science and historical criticism. George A. Gordon, Theodore T. Munger, and Newman Smyth, pastor-theologians, were able to aid many in reconciling science and religion. William Newton Clarke, a Baptist professor at Colgate Seminary, built both on their work and on the work of German theologians in his *Outline of Christian Theology* (1898), which was the first comprehensive statement of American liberalism.

Industrialization raised theological, as well as practical, questions. Although many of the themes of the Social Gospel movement had appeared earlier, the movement did not become influential until the publication of *The Christian Way* by Washington Gladden in 1877; basically the Social Gospel stressed the need for a Christian business ethic to replace laissez-faire capitalism. Its greatest proponent was Walter Rauschenbusch. In his major works, *Christianity and the Social Crisis* (1907) and *A Theology for the Social Gospel* (1917), he argued for a realistic understanding of social evil in contrast to the sentimental view of many of his co-workers. These new directions evoked a conservative reaction. J. Gresham Machen was the most militant defender of the old orthodoxy; in his *Christianity and Liberalism* (1923) and *The Virgin Birth of Christ* (1930) he charged the liberals with teaching a new religion.

The period following the Great Depression saw a general repudiation of the most optimistic aspects of liberalism. American theologians turned to existentialism and the Reformation for guidance; two brothers, Reinhold and H. Richard Niebuhr, were the most sophisticated theologians of this movement, called realism or neo-orthodoxy. H. Richard Niebuhr, in his great theological history, *The Kingdom of God in America* (1937), argued that the doctrine of the divine sovereignty is at the heart of American theology. His mature views are most characteristically expressed in *The Meaning of Revelation* (1941), which maintained that the church could find itself only as a confessing community. Reinhold Niebuhr directed his attention to a revision of the Social Gospel in *Moral Man and Immoral Society* (1932) and in *The Nature and Destiny of Man* (1941–43), which stressed the depths of human sinfulness on both individual and corporate levels.

Neo-orthodoxy was not unopposed, and many liberals continued to develop their own paradigms. Henry Nelson Wieman, a religious naturalist at the University of Chicago, developed his own distinctive position based on his understanding of the good; his best-known works are *Religious Experience and Scientific Method* (1926), *Methods of Religious Living* (1929), and the *Source of Human Good* (1949). The neo-orthodox consensus began to weaken in the later 1950's when the questions raised by the older liberalism reoccupied center stage. In many ways, Gabriel Vahanian's *Death of God: The Culture of Our Post-Christian Era* (1961) set the stage for a decade of debate. Despite the optimism of such neo-Social Gospel works as Harvey Cox's *Secular City* (1965), theologians seemed unable to find either traditional or innovative ways to deal with a mounting sense of social crisis.

RELOCATION PROGRAM, JAPANESE-AMERICAN. *See* **Japanese-American Relocation.**

RELOCATION PROGRAM, VOLUNTARY. Started in 1952 for the resettlement of reservation Indians in selected urban areas, with government assistance. They were assisted in moving to such cities as Chicago, Los Angeles, Oakland, and Denver with money for transportation and moving costs; once in the cities they were aided in finding employment and housing. In 1962 the name of the program was changed to the Employment Assistance Program, and it was expanded to include job placement on or near the reservations. By the mid-1970's more than 100,000 Indians had been resettled in thirteen cities, although at least a third of them moved back to the reservations.

REMAGEN (Germany). Site of a railroad bridge across the Rhine that American troops captured in World War II. Contingents of Combat Command B, Ninth Armored Division, arrived on Mar. 7, 1945, as the troops drew near, the Germans set off demolitions designed to destroy the bridge, but when the smoke cleared, it still stood. Infantrymen raced across under heavy fire and a bridgehead was established which served to attract German reserves and thus facilitate Rhine crossings at other points. With planes, artillery, and rockets, the Germans tried without success to destroy the bridge. On Mar. 17, as American engineers worked to repair damage, the bridge nevertheless collapsed, but by that time a number of tactical bridges were in place.

"REMEMBER THE ALAMO." Battle cry in which the bitterness of the Texans over the massacres by Mexican forces at the Alamo in San Antonio (Mar. 6, 1836) and at Goliad (Mar. 27) found expression.

"REMEMBER THE *MAINE*." A popular slogan current just before and during the Spanish-American War (1898). Popular opinion, led by such "yellow" journals as the *New York Journal* and *New York World,* held Spain responsible for the destruction of the battleship *Maine* in Havana harbor on Feb. 15, 1898.

REMOVAL, EXECUTIVE POWER OF. The power to effect removals is the logical complement of the appointive power of chief executives. The First Congress, in legislation establishing executive departments, gave recognition to the proposition advanced by James Madison that the president's power of removal is inherent in the general grant of executive power and in the duty to "take care that the laws be faithfully executed." Congress imposed drastic limits on the removal power in the Tenure of Office Act of 1867, which provided that all executive officers appointed by the president and confirmed by the Senate could not be removed without senatorial consent. President Andrew Johnson's removal of Secretary of War Edwin McMasters Stanton led to the filing of impeachment charges by the House of Representatives. The courts did not pass on the constitutionality of the Tenure of Office Act prior to its repeal in 1887.

The Supreme Court, in *Myers* v. *United States* (1926), upheld President Woodrow Wilson's 1920 removal of Postmaster Frank S. Myers of Portland, Oreg., in violation of a rider to an 1876 appropriation bill, and held invalid any congressional limitation of the president's power to remove any of his appointees. In *Humphrey's Executor* v. *United States* (1935) the Court confined the scope of the *Myers* case to include only "all purely executive officers." The doctrine of the *Humphrey* case has generally prevailed. However, in *Morgan* v. *Tennessee Valley Authority* (1940), *certiorari denied* (1941), the U.S. Court of Appeals upheld removal of a Tennessee Valley Authority director; it held that statutory language limiting removal to specific causes did not deny the president the power of summary removal as part of his duty to execute the laws.

REMOVAL ACT OF 1830. Enacted by a close vote on May 28, it authorized the president to cause territory west of the Mississippi to be divided into districts suitable for exchange with Indians living within any state or territory of the United States for lands there claimed and occupied by them, and authorized the president to make such exchange.

REMOVAL OF DEPOSITS. As early as Sept. 19, 1832, the *Washington Globe* began hinting that the veto of the bill rechartering the second Bank of the United States would be followed by the removal of the government deposits from the institution and their placement in state banks. In July 1833 Amos Kendall was sent to arrange with various state banks to receive the deposits. President Andrew Jackson assumed responsibility for the removal policy. Secretary of the Treasury William J. Duane refused to order the removal and was dismissed (Sept. 23); he was replaced by Roger B. Taney, who carried out the president's program. Later, both Jackson and Taney were censured by the Senate for their parts in the episode.

RENDEZVOUS. *See* **Trappers' Rendezvous.**

RENEGOTIATION BOARD. *See* **Federal Agencies.**

RENO (Nev.). Major city in western Nevada, with a population of 100,756 in 1980. It was the center for a county-wide metropolitan region of 193,870 people. Reno was founded in 1868, named after a Civil War leader, Gen. Jesse Reno. It prospered as a trading center for mining districts of western Nevada, but its reputation comes from its very active divorce court. Nevada divorces are granted to residents of at least six weeks standing.

The city is a major resort, being close to Pyramid Lake and to a popular ski center. Its economic activities are tied to the mines and irrigated farms. The University of Nevada is located in Reno. Its mining museum and library are centers of information for mining engineering for the entire country.

RENO, FORT (Okla.). A post established in Indian Territory in 1874, near the present town of El Reno. In 1876 it was named in honor of Gen. Jesse Reno. It was garrisoned continuously until 1908, when it became a remount depot.

RENO, FORT (Wyo.). Fort Connor, a stockade built on Powder River in 1865, was enlarged in 1866 and named Fort Reno, for Gen. Jesse Reno. It was abandoned in 1868, but was temporarily reestablished in 1876.

REORGANIZED CHURCH OF JESUS CHRIST OF LATTER-DAY SAINTS. Claims to be the continuation of and successor to the Church of Jesus Christ of Latter-Day Saints, organized by Joseph Smith, Jr., on Apr. 6, 1830, at Fayette, N.Y. (*see* Latter-Day Saints, Church of Jesus Christ of). After Smith and his brother Hyrum were killed by a mob in Carthage, Ill., June 27, 1844, many factions were formed. One, including Joseph Smith III, Smith's eldest son, and other members of Smith's family, finally formed a new group in 1852, still under the name of the Church of Jesus Christ of Latter-Day Saints. In October 1869, for legal reasons, the word "Reorganized" was added. Independence, Mo., was named as the central place for the establishment of the church. The members of the reorganized church reject the name Mormon because of the association of the name in the popular mind with doctrines and practices that they have always repudiated.

REPARATION COMMISSION (1920–30). Directed by the Treaty of Versailles to estimate damage done by Germany to Allied civilians and their property during World War I and to formulate methods of collecting assessments. In June 1920 the Supreme Council decided that Germany should pay at least 3 billion gold marks for thirty-five years, not to exceed 269 billion marks. The commission reported to the Supreme Council in April 1921 that damages amounted to 132 billion marks and recommended annual payments of 2 billion marks and 26 percent of German exports, with a cash payment of 1 billion marks by Sept. 1. Economic and monetary chaos in Germany coupled with resentment at the reparations scheme brought a Franco-Belgian force into the Ruhr. By the time of complete collapse of the German mark in 1923, there had been paid in cash, commodities, and services an amount estimated by the commission at approximately 10.5 billion gold marks and by the Germans at something over 42 billion marks.

In 1922 Secretary of State Charles E. Hughes had suggested that the whole issue be taken out of politics and adjusted on economic principles, and intimated that American experts might help. Accordingly, a committee with Charles G. Dawes as chairman worked out a plan to go into effect on Sept. 1, 1924, with a sliding scale of annuities in cash and kind, together with suggestions how revenues should be raised and payments distributed. The plan worked fairly well, providing for payment of nearly 10 billion marks to the creditors and allowing stabilization of German currency and an upward trend in German economic life. Desire of the creditor powers to arrange a definitive settlement and to have turned into marketable bonds Germany's future obligations brought a second committee of experts. The conference, under Owen D. Young, in the spring of 1929 produced a plan that, somewhat modified by the Reparation Commission, arranged for annuities running until 1988 and aggregating with interest 121 billion marks. On May 17, 1930, the Young Plan went into operation and the Reparation Commission ceased operations. In barely two years, however, payments stopped with the moratorium proposed by President Herbert Hoover, effective June 30, 1931, after a sum of 2.871 billion marks had been paid. Thenceforward reparations were suspended regardless of the Lausanne Agreement (July 9, 1932), which attempted to replace the Young Plan.

REPARATIONS. Payments that one nation is forced to make to another in order to repair damages done, ordinarily during wartime. Following World War I and World War II, reparations payments were required of Germany and its allies for damage done during the wars. (*See* Reparation Commission.)

REPEATING. A corrupt election practice in which persons cast ballots in more than one precinct or vote under different names more than once in the same precinct. It has disappeared with the adoption of adequate registration laws.

REPRESENTATION. The democracy of the modern world has generally been representative democracy. A representative is someone who will be held responsible by those for whom he acts, who must account for his actions.

A representative, said Thomas Hobbes, is a man who acts in the name of another, who has been given authority to act by that other, so that whatever the representative does is considered the act of the represented. Edmund Burke thought of a representative essentially as representing, not individuals, but the large, stable interests that constitute the national interest. The duty of each representative is to determine the good of the whole, and the selfish wishes of parts of the nation or the wills of individual voters are irrelevant. John Stuart Mill said that what distinguishes a representative assembly is its accurate correspondence to the larger population for which it stands.

REPRESENTATIVE GOVERNMENT. Government that represents all the people, giving effect to their opinions and interests, not imposing on them the opinions and interests of their rulers. Representative government emerged in the 17th century and had come to be virtually universal by the mid-20th century in the sense that most governments claimed to be representative. Representative government in its present form is democratic government. According to the modern theory, democratic government deals with its problems most competently and protects the liberties of the people most effectively when assemblies are composed of representatives of the citizenry rather than of the citizens themselves en masse. Alexander Hamilton, James Madison, and John Jay, the authors of *The Federalist* (1788) hoped and intended that the representatives of the American people would "refine and enlarge" the views of their constituents and be governed not by temporary and partial considerations, but by the true interests of the country.

REPRESENTATIVES, HOUSE OF. *See* **Congress, United States.**

REPRISAL, LETTERS OF. *See* **Marque and Reprisal, Letters of.**

REPTILES. *See* **Herpetology.**

REPUBLIC. Government in which politics is a public affair and not the personal prerogative of a single ruler. According to this interpretation "republic" is synonymous with "representative democracy." (*See* Representative Government.)

REPUBLICAN PARTY. The Republican name was first adopted at a meeting in Ripon, Wis., on Feb. 28, 1854, and the first convention of a Republican state party was held at Jackson, Mich., on July 6, 1854. The sentiments of the new party were agrarian and radical. Opposition to the slavocracy was coupled with support for railroads, free homesteads, and the opening of the West by free labor. Support for the protective tariff was added in an appeal to the manufacturing (as opposed to the plantation) interest.

The 1856 Republican National Convention nominated John C. Frémont of California for the presidency. Frémont was defeated, but he established the organizational base of the new party. Winning every free state in 1860, Abraham Lincoln could not deter the southern secessionists.

After Lincoln's assassination, Radical Republicans in Congress asserted party leadership. Republicans demonstrated their sectional nature by nominating former Union soldiers—Ulysses S. Grant, Rutherford B. Hayes, James A. Garfield, Benjamin Harrison, and William McKinley—and Republicans occupied the White House for all but eight of the thirty-two years following Lincoln's first election.

McKinley's election in 1896 established the Republicans as the normal majority party, representing industrial progress, northern farmers, middle-class respectability, eastern urban labor, and even college presidents. McKinley was assassinated during his second term, and Theodore Roosevelt became president and made the Republicans also the party of conservation and reform. Only a feud between Roosevelt and his successor, William Howard Taft, brought about the Democratic victory that installed Woodrow Wilson in the White House in 1913.

Warren G. Harding and Calvin Coolidge personified the Whig tradition. Herbert Hoover's defeat for a second term by Franklin D. Roosevelt was followed by the stunning defeat of Alfred M. Landon, the Kansas Progressive, in 1936. The

Republicans were cast in a long-term minority role.

As the New Deal added organized labor, urban minorities, and intellectuals to the base of the South, the Republicans came to be regarded as the party of eastern big business and midwestern farmers. Conservative Republicans predominated in Congress, while presidential nominations were controlled by the eastern, liberal, internationalist wing. Dwight D. Eisenhower's popularity made inroads even into southern Democratic allegiances, but little of his popularity was transferred to the Republican party. "Ike" had a Republican Congress for only two of his eight years as president. His vice-president, Richard M. Nixon, lost narrowly to John F. Kennedy in 1960. Four years later, Republican delegates from the South and West repudiated the eastern leadership by nominating Barry Goldwater, an avowed conservative. Goldwater carried only his native Arizona and five states of the Deep South against Lyndon B. Johnson.

In 1968 Nixon claimed a moderate position and beat Hubert H. Humphrey. In 1972 Nixon defeated Sen. George McGovern in a historic personal landslide, but offered little support to other Republican candidates, and the Democrats retained control of Congress.

Beginning in 1973, press exposures, congressional investigations, and court proceedings revealed the complicity of Nixon administration officials in the Watergate burglary. Tainted by an unrelated Maryland scandal, Vice-President Spiro T. Agnew resigned in October 1973. Nixon appointed House Minority Leader Gerald R. Ford to replace Agnew. When Nixon was forced by a Supreme Court decision to release tape recordings that proved he had known of his leading aides' involvement in Watergate, he resigned (August 1974) rather than face impeachment proceedings. Gerald Ford's accession to the presidency was greeted with relief because of his apparent honesty and plain-spokenness. But this image was immediately tarnished when he pardoned Richard Nixon.

In 1976 Ford was narrowly defeated by Jimmy Carter, but the Republicans scored a major election victory four years later when the conservative Ronald Reagan became president and Senate came to be dominated by Republicans for the first time since the early 1950's.

REPUBLICANS, JEFFERSONIAN, or **Democratic-Republicans.** The first opposition party under the new national government. In the first two congresses the Federalist party aroused the hostility of members who disliked the funding system, the revenue acts, the first Bank of the United States, and the tendency to create a powerful national authority by liberal construction of the Constitution. The frank reliance of the Federalists on "the wise and good and rich," their liking for forms and ceremonies that smacked of the aristocratic, and particularly their horror of the French Revolution, tended to make the opposition the party of the common man and gave it its title of "Republican."

Thomas Jefferson supplied the necessary leadership and philosophy for the party. Organization spread throughout the country, and the Democratic Clubs played an important part. Jefferson won the presidency in 1800, carried out mild reforms and innovations, and was reelected four years later. With the election of James Madison to the presidency in 1808, there ensued twenty years when the Democratic-Republican party was in reality a collection of sectional and personal factions. There was a gradual broadening of the suffrage, an increasing democratizing of local life, a perceptible emphasis on humanitarian reform, and, after the War of 1812, the development of a nationalist spirit. With the election of Andrew Jackson in 1828, a new and more logical alignment of "National" and "Democratic" Republicans evolved a few years later into the Whig and Democratic parties respectively.

REPUDIATION OF PUBLIC DEBT. To the extent that a nation allows its currency to depreciate in value and pays its domestic and international borrowings in that currency, it is also repudiating part of its public debt. Since March 1933 individuals have not had the right to demand gold coin for paper dollars, and on Aug. 15, 1971, President Richard M. Nixon informed foreign central banks and treasuries, who did have that right, that they had lost it too. Between 1940 and 1980 the dollar lost about 80 percent of its buying power. Between 1939 and 1952 the dollar depreciated at an annual rate of 5 percent a year on the average and lost half its buying power.

REPUDIATION OF STATE DEBTS. In the 1830's various American states incurred heavy debts in the construction of canals and railroads and the creation of banks. By 1839 the public indebtedness of American states amounted to $170 million. Between 1841 and 1842 eight states and one territory defaulted on their interest payments (*see* State Debts.)

The second attack of state repudiation came with the funding of state debts incurred during Reconstruction. These bonds were issued by governments not representative of the southern states. Foreign investors were warned not to purchase them. The forced repudiation of the Confederate war debts by the Fourteenth Amendment strengthened the southerner's opposition to payment, especially since a large proportion of these securities were held by the "conquerors of the north." The ravages of the Civil War, misrule of the Reconstruction period, and hard times following the panic of 1873 increased the burdens of the southern people; but in no case were debts scaled or repudiated until it was impossible to discharge them.

RESACA DE LA PALMA, BATTLE OF (May 9, 1846). The day following Gen. Zachary Taylor's minor triumph at Palo Alto, Texas, the Mexican army under Mariano Arista fell back five miles to the Resaca de Guerrero. After fierce hand-to-hand combat, the Mexican left gave way. Arista's army crumbled under the American assault. Taylor's men pursued the Mexicans to the Rio Grande. Mexican losses were 547 killed, wounded, or missing. American losses were 33 killed, 89 wounded. Taylor wrote his report at the Resaca de la Palma, which gave the battle its name.

RESERVATIONS, INDIAN. *See* **Indian Reservations.**

RESERVATION SYSTEM, TERMINATION OF. In 1953 the House of Representatives provided for a speedy end to federal supervision of Indians of five states and seven other tribes. Termination laws were enacted for the Menomini of Wisconsin, the Klamath of Oregon, and a few other small groups, despite intense opposition by the Indians. The effects of the laws were disastrous, and many members of the tribes were soon on public assistance. President John F. Kennedy in 1961 halted further termination.

RESERVED POWERS OF STATES. The Tenth Amendment states, "The powers not delegated to the United States by the Constitution, nor prohibited by it to the States, are reserved to the States respectively, or to the people." The powers prohibited to the states by the Constitution are found principally in Article I, Section 10, and in the Fourteenth, Fifteenth, Nineteenth, Twenty-fourth, and Twenty-sixth amendments (*See* Constitution of the United States.) But all remaining powers of government are theirs.

The Supreme Court of the United States is the final arbiter in case of conflict between a state and the national government over the right to exercise a governmental power. On occasion, as in the Child Labor Cases, the Court has declared acts of Congress invalid because they invaded the reserved powers of the states.

RESERVED POWERS OF THE PEOPLE. The Tenth Amendment reserves all powers not granted to the United States by the Constitution, nor prohibited by it to the states, to the states respectively or the people. The people referred to were the people of the several states, not the people of the United States. The phrase "to the people" is a recognition of the right of the people to create and alter their state governments at will.

Bills of rights to protect the citizen of the state from his state government are found in every state constitution (*see* Bills of Rights, State). In many states the people have reserved to themselves the power to propose new laws through the initiative or to require the submission to popular vote of laws passed by the legislature through the referendum.

RESERVE OFFICERS' TRAINING CORPS. As World War I raged in Europe the National Defense Act of 1916 provided for the establishment of the Reserve Officers' Training Corps (ROTC). Fully trained college graduates were assured commissions in an Officers' Reserve Corps that would become available for active duty in a major war. The navy began similar training in 1925. Military training in secondary schools in the Junior Reserve Officers' Training Corps, begun on a sizable scale by the 1890's, also flourished after World War I. At the outset of World War II the army's college units furnished more than 100,000 officers, and 7,000 served with the navy and Marine Corps.

After 1945 the air force joined the army and navy in reviving campus military training. The primary objective of college military training changed from reserve to active duty service; the bulk of military graduates after 1953 were required to serve two years or more of active duty. From 1961 through the conflict in Southeast Asia, almost all college military graduates were called to active duty. The unpopularity of the Vietnam War led to widespread and sometimes violent opposition to military training on civilian campuses. Some colleges abandoned military activity altogether, and most of them discontinued compulsory training. In 1980 the enrollment was 257,000.

RESETTLEMENT ADMINISTRATION. Before 1933 agricultural economists had urged the adoption of certain controls in land use and the retirement from cultivation of badly eroded and submarginal lands. The conservation-minded New Deal undertook to retire submarginal land. The Resettlement Administration was created in May 1935 to administer the program, resettle the displaced farmers, and help tenants become homeowners. In 1937 the Resettlement Administration was transferred to the Department of Agriculture, where it became the Farm Security Administration.

RESIDENCY REQUIREMENTS FOR VOTING. Early in the history of the United States it was established that only residents of a given jurisdiction might vote in its elections. Until 1970 typical requirements called for one year of residence in the state, six months in the county, and thirty days in the precinct. Because of the growing mobility of the population, such restrictions barred from the polls millions of otherwise qualified voters. Congress responded in 1970 with legislation that fixed thirty days as the maximum durational residence requirement for voting in presidential elections. In 1972 the Supreme Court indicated that a thirty-day requirement for voting in state and local elections was adequate.

RESOLUTIONS, LEGISLATIVE. Three classes of resolutions are used by Congress. The simplest is one by which one house deals with its own affairs. Concurrent resolutions involve action by both houses; they are without force and effect beyond the confines of the Capitol. They may be used to express an opinion or purpose of Congress. Most often, they are used to make corrections in bills passed by both houses, or to fix a time for adjournment, for example.

Joint resolutions must be approved by both houses and the chief executive, who may also veto them, with the exception of joint resolutions proposing amendments to the Constitution, which are not submitted to the president. Joint resolutions have the force and effect of law; they are ordinarily used for minor legislative purposes, but they have also been employed for important foreign policy actions.

RESORTS AND SPAS. An interest in mineral springs began in the American colonies in the 17th century. Following the French and Indian War the springs became as much a vogue in America as they were in England, both because of their therapeutic promise and because they had become a "fashionable indulgence." Stafford Springs, Conn., Berkeley Warm Springs, Va., and many others conceded preeminence to Saratoga Springs, N.Y., in the 19th century.

The seashore also offered some hope to the sick, but the attraction was more often recreational. By mid-19th century the Atlantic coast (and to a lesser extent, the Gulf coast) was dotted with resorts. Long Branch and Cape May, N.J., catering to the gentry from New York, Philadelphia, and the South, lost their fashionable position at the end of the century to Newport, R.I., the most exclusive resort of them all. In the late 1800's Atlantic City, N.J., had begun to flourish; by the 1950's it boasted 1,200 hotels and 12 million visitors a year.

A third type of resort—the "mountain" house—attracted easterners, and the late 19th century saw the white Mountains, the Berkshires, the Adirondacks, and much of the Appalachian chain studded with resort hotels, some very large and very fashionable.

In the settlement of the American West, hotels and sanitariums, catering especially to the tubercular and asthmatic, played a significant role in the growth of such cities as Denver and Colorado Springs, Colo.; San Diego, Pasadena, Los Angeles, and Santa Barbara, Calif.; Phoenix and Tucson, Ariz.; and San Antonio and El Paso, Tex. But by the 1890's bitter experience and new medical knowledge brought disillusionment. Florida, too, had had an appeal to health seekers going back to antebellum days, but its buildup as a winter resort was the work of entrepreneurs who mixed railroading and the hotel business.

It was not until the Olympic Winter Games of 1932 at Lake Placid, N.Y., that American interest in skiing began to skyrocket. Ski resorts first became popular in northern New York and New England. The introduction of uphill transportation—the first rope tow was built at Woodstock, Vt., in 1933—turned skiing into a downhill sport. Colorado was not far behind in developing ski resort areas. In Idaho the Union Pacific Railroad created Sun Valley in 1936.

"RESTOOK WAR." *See* **Aroostook War.**

RESTRAINING ACTS. *See* **Coercion Acts.**

RESTRAINT OF TRADE. The 20th-century importance of the legal doctrine relating to restraint of trade stems from its statutory recognition by the antitrust laws of the United States. The federal courts were obliged to clarify restraint of trade concepts in dealing with section 1 of the Sherman Antitrust Act (1890), which declared every contract, combination, or conspiracy in restraint of trade or commerce to be illegal. Judge William Howard Taft, in *United States* v. *Addyston Pipe and Steel Company* (1898), divided restraints in to those ancillary or subordinate to the main purpose of the agreement and those nonancillary, constituting its core, and held that ancillary restraints alone were to be assessed for reasonableness, depending on their impact on third parties or on the public, while those deemed nonancillary were judged unlawful per se. Using a different approach in *Standard Oil Company of New Jersey* v. *United States* (1911), Chief Justice Edward D. White applied the test of reasonableness to all restraints, taking the view that only an unreasonable agreement constituted a restraint under the law. In practice courts continued to find agreements directly restricting market competition both unreasonable and illegal.

The general terms of the Sherman Act were supplemented by subsequent legislation that sought to deal more specifically with abuses in restraint of trade. The Clayton Antitrust Act (1914) declared price discrimination illegal when it undermined competition, and outlawed other restraints, such as tying and exclusive dealing arrangements. The Federal Trade Commission Act of 1914 established a commission with the responsibility of maintaining fair competition and the power to bring charges of illegality. The Robinson-Patman Act (1936) expanded the area of illegal price actions. Although "the rule of reason" remained residual to court interpretation, a trend initiated by the Clayton Act toward holding specific restraints illegal per se has continued.

Subsequently the definition of combinations in restraint of trade was extended, and the search for factual proof of market effects was sharpened. In *American Tobacco Company* v. *United States* (1946), the court moved against oligopoly by accepting evidence of parallel price movement as proof of conspiracy in restraint of trade. The Clayton Antitrust Act phrase "may be to lessen competition" has been construed as bringing the future market effects of restraints within the purview of the law; most frequently invoked in merger actions, this broader interpretation brought the courts to consider market foreclosure and the elimination of potential competition to be restraints of trade. The Celler-Kefauver Act of 1950 established the first significant preventive antitrust measure designed to treat monopolistic restraints in their "incipiency."

Union activity was at first considered subject to the restraint of trade clause of the Sherman Act, and injunctions were issued against strikes as early as 1893. The public reaction to the Supreme Court's ruling in *Loewe* v. *Lawler* (1908) led Congress to pass the labor exemption provisions of the Clayton Act but the widespread use of injunctions in labor disputes was not effectively limited until the Norris-La Guardia Act in 1932.

RESUMPTION ACT (Jan. 14, 1875)**.** The Resumption Act provided for the replacement, "as rapidly as practicable," of Civil War fractional currency by silver coins. Provision was also made for reducing the greenback total to $300 million. Most important of all, the secretary of the Treasury was directed to "redeem, in coin" legal-tender notes presented for redemption on and after Jan. 1, 1879. The inflationists in 1878 succeeded in securing the enactment of a measure stopping the destruction of greenbacks when the total outstanding was $346,681,000.

RETALIATION IN INTERNATIONAL LAW. Retaliation is a nonamicable action short of war taken by one state against another in response to conduct that the retaliating state considers injurious or unfriendly. The retaliation is generally in kind when in response to a legal act, such as discrimination in tariffs or legislation against aliens; such action is called retortion. Reprisal, on the other hand, is a retaliatory action that seeks redress for an illegal act, such as confiscation or seizure of property, or injury to citizens of the retaliating state. Several forms are withdrawal or severance of diplomatic relations, display of force, pacific blockade, embargo, nonintercourse, bombardment, or seizure and occupation of property. Retaliation takes place in wartime, too, by the belligerents who respond to the introduction by the enemy of measures deemed illegal.

REUNION (Tex.). A French colony near Dallas, established under the leadership of Victor Prosper Considérant in April 1855, by French Socialists who were followers of Charles Fourier. Attempts were made to organize colonies in Houston, Tex., and at Uvalde, Tex., but, like Reunion, they were never successful. The population reached 300; the colony continued until 1867, when it was disbanded.

REVENUE, PUBLIC. Before 1913 customs duties and proceeds from the sale of public lands constituted the major part of the revenue of the federal government; thereafter, taxes on the income of individuals and corporations became the dominant source. Excise taxes on the sale of selected commodities—notably alcohol, tobacco, and automobiles—provide an important, but lesser, source of revenue.

State governments, in contrast, have generally depended most heavily on sales taxes, although most have adopted personal and/or corporate income taxes. Cities, counties, and other local governments raise the bulk of their income from the traditional taxes on property values.

REVENUE SHARING. A system by which tax moneys collected at one government level are shared with government agencies operating at a more restricted or lower level. In 1972 revenue sharing between the United States and local governments was instituted under a formula worked out by Congress; the idea was advanced by President Richard M. Nixon, and was enacted after several years of debate.

REVERE'S RIDE. Paul Revere, a Boston silversmith and a messenger of the Massachusetts Committee of Safety, had foreseen an attempt by the British troops in Boston to seize the military stores collected in Concord, and had arranged to signal a warning to the Whigs in Charlestown. In the late evening of Apr. 18, 1775, he was told that the British were about to begin their march to Concord, and he signaled the fact by two lanterns hung by a friend from the tower of the Old North Church in Boston. Borrowing a horse in Charlestown, he started for Concord via Medford, alarming the country as he went. About midnight he arrived in Lexington, and roused John Hancock and Samuel Adams. Joined by William Dawes and Samuel Prescott, Revere then set forward with his news, only to be intercepted by a patrol of British officers. Prescott leaped a fence and escaped, carrying the alarm to Lincoln and Concord; Dawes fled back toward Lexington; but Revere was taken. Assuring his captors that the country was roused against them, he so alarmed them that they set him free. He returned to Lexington, helped to save Hancock's papers, and saw the first shot fired on the green.

REVIVALS. *See* **Evangelism, Evangelicalism, and Revivalism.**

REVOLUTION, AMERICAN. The conditions that made many, perhaps most, Americans receptive to the idea of independence included (1) a system of imperial regulation that subordinated the colonial polity to the administrative direction of officials in London; (2) a web of economic controls, generally designated as the mercantile system, that restricted colonial trade, manufacturing, and fiscal policy by parliamentary legislation; (3) the laxity of enforcement of both the political and the economic controls, permitting the colonies to develop, in effect, a wide degree of autonomy; (4) the conceptualization in the American mind during the years of "salutary neglect" of the rights to self-government as arising from the intrinsic character of the British constitution and from those natural laws that the European Enlightenment professed to be the normative feature of the political world; and (5) the series of British measures designed to reassert the primacy of imperial over colonial interests.

English Mercantilism. Historians writing in the century following independence were wont to attribute primary responsibility for the Revolution to the British mercantile system—specifically, the cluster of regulatory acts passed by Parliament between 1660 and 1696 (*see* Navigation Acts). Originally intended to bar the Dutch from the imperial carrying trade, the laws created heavy and increasing trade deficits in the colonies and an imbalance of payments in Britain's favor. There is little evidence, however, that these deficits were major causes of colonial complaint. Further, they were offset by colonial profits earned in trade with southern Europe and the West Indies, funds brought to America by immigrants, and expenditures by the British government for the defense and administration of the colonies.

On the other hand, neither the benefits nor the burdens of English mercantilism were evenly distributed within the colonies. The merchants of New England and the Middle Colonies were often able to meet their trade balances with Great Britain only by illicit trade with the West Indies, and smuggling everywhere eased somewhat the burdens of lawful observance of the Navigation Acts. Southern planters traded so exclusively with the mother country and were so dependent on its credits that they found themselves saddled, by 1776, with a huge debt.

Old Colonial System. Although the crown after 1625 asserted its jurisdiction over all the colonies, it developed no overall administration for them. In 1696 a new body, the Board of Trade, was established to handle colonial affairs. Not until 1768 was a secretary of state for American affairs created as a separate cabinet post. A host of other officials assisted in administering the empire, but the linchpin of empire was the royal governor, who sat in all the colonies except Connecticut and Rhode Island, where by charter right the governor was elected. The governor possessed in theory all the majesty of the crown itself within the colony over which he held sway.

But practice did not comport with theory. In America the governor's extensive prerogatives were effectively weakened by the rising power of the assemblies, controlled by local elites, who by 1776 dominated the political, social, and economic life of their colonies. By 1776 the assemblies not only possessed fiscal power but, through it, controlled the appointment of local officials whose salaries they determined. As early as 1670 one chief executive complained that the assembly's fiscal powers had "left his Majesty but a small share of the Sovereignty." The shortcomings of imperial administration in the colonies were paralleled by weaknesses in the machinery of government in London.

Crisis of Empire. The need for a less "slovenly and chaotic" system of governance was evident in the late 1740's, as governors deluged the Board of Trade with complaints about the intractability of their assemblies. The outbreak of the French and Indian War (or the Great War for Empire) in 1754 temporarily halted the campaign to reduce the autonomy of the colonies, but the war itself emphasized the need for the effort. As a matter of equity no less than of financial necessity, the colonies were to be required to share the new burdens of empire. Thus came into being the Quartering Act (1765), the Currency Act (1764), the Stamp Act (1765), the Revenue Act (1764) and the Townshend Acts (1767).

The efforts at tightening the reins of imperial administration could scarcely have come at a less opportune time in America. Flushed with the victory over the French, the colonists saw themselves as the saviors of the British Empire in America. The removal of the enemy in Canada decreased their military dependence on England, and their heightened sense of independence and self-confidence led them to expect a more important, not less important, role in the empire.

As they argued their case, the colonists came to formulate a well-rounded constitutional theory representing an American consensus: The British constitution fixed the powers of Parliament and protected the liberties of the citizen; such a constitution could not be changed by the stroke of a pen; the powers of Parliament were limited; and those powers were specifically limited with regard to the American colonies by their immutable right to legislate for themselves in matters of internal concern. The crown denied Americans rights that Englishmen at home possessed.

The heavy emphasis that Americans placed on constitutional forms of protest bespoke the essential conservatism of the colonial leadership. But the protesters were not unwilling to employ more forcible means of expression to achieve their ends. These other "necessary ingredients" in the American opposition were economic coercion by the boycott of British imports; mob violence, such as the intimidation of stamp distributors; and outright defiance of the law, including the refusal to do business with stamped documents.

The furious American protests took British officialdom by surprise. In the face of the colonial onslaught, Parliament retreated: it repealed the Stamp Act in 1766 and the Townshend Acts in 1770; and it modified the Proclamation of 1763 so as to permit gradual movement of settlers and fur traders to the West. The retreat was prompted by the damage done to British economic interests by the colonial boycotts. On the issue of its right to tax the colonies, Parliament did not retreat at all.

Between 1770 and 1773, incidents in the colonies maintained and even escalated the mutual suspicions already generated (*see* Battle of Golden Hill; Boston Massacre; *Gaspée,* Burning of the; Wilkes Fund Dispute). In Massachusetts such radicals as Samuel Adams used each anniversary of the Boston Massacre to remind Bostonians of the need for eternal vigilance to prevent the utter extinction of American liberties by British armies.

Disclaiming independence, the colonists came to conceive of the empire as a divided sovereignty. Their reluctant acceptance of the idea of separation from the British Empire was given emotional support by the conviction that Britain had lost its ancient virtue, corrupted its constitution, and abandoned the liberties of its citizens. John Locke's familiar compact theory of government provided theoretical justification for the last resort of a free people whose liberties were infringed by an arbitrary government: dissolution of the original compact.

By 1776, Americans possessed the machinery for revolution as well as the ideology. At the local level, militants had organized groups called Sons of Liberty to carry on the agitation against the Stamp Act. A system of committees of correspondence was initiated by the Virginia legislature in 1773. Other colonial assemblies took up the idea, and a network of official legislative committees was soon in existence to concert uniform efforts against British measures. In 1773 Great Britain unwittingly put the system to the test by the enactment of the Tea Act, a blunder of the most momentous consequence (*see* Tea, Duty on). Tea "parties" in a number of colonies destroyed the company's product before it could be distributed. When Parliament in 1774 punished Massachusetts by a series of acts (*see* Intolerable Acts) that included the suspension of the province's charter of government and the closing of the port of Boston, the intercolonial apparatus of committees of correspondence went into action. Relief supplies were sent from everywhere to the beleaguered city, and a congress of the colonies convened in Philadelphia on Sept. 5, 1774.

The issue debated in Philadelphia at the Continental Congress was not the East India Company's monopoly, or even the tea tax, but the larger issue of the rights of the colonies and their constitutional relationship with Great Britain. The Declaration of Rights reaffirmed the colonists' right to "a free and exclusive power of legislation in their several provincial legislatures." By the meeting of the Second Continental Congress on May 10, 1775, hostilities had already commenced. Blood had been shed at Lexington and Concord on Apr. 19, and in all the colonies militia units were being organized and armed. With the appointment on June 15 of George Washington to command an American army, the Revolution had begun, but its objectives were not yet clearly defined.

Conciliation or Independence. Many conservatives clung to the hope that friends of America in Great Britain would bring about a change in the ministry and thereby end colonial grievances. These hopes were shattered by the failure of every plan of accommodation that emanated from Britain before 1776. Sentiment for independence was increasingly aired in the press and was given its clearest expression in Thomas Paine's pamphlet *Common Sense,* which appeared in January 1776. Paine reassured Americans that they need not fear the separation from Englishmen abroad: they were indeed a different people, not Britons transplanted but new men in a new world. A substantial minority of Americans declined to opt for independence (*see* Loyalists).

Declaration of Independence. In the Declaration of Independence, adopted on July 4, 1776, the colonists voiced their aspirations for the future as well as their rejection of the past. The Declaration's lengthy indictment of George III and its detailed enumeration of colonial grievances were history; the almost incidental preamble, expounding the principles of equality and popular government, was prophecy. It is unlikely that the conservative signers of the document fully recognized its revolutionary implications.

Diplomacy. Although the Declaration of Independence represented America's rejection of the Old World, the Revolution was from its inception pursued in an international context. One purpose of the Declaration was to enlist the sympathetic ear of "a candid world" and to state the causes of separation in such a way as to ensure the "decent respect" of the "opinions of mankind." Few Americans believed that they could fight a successful war without aid from abroad.

The Franco-American Alliance 1778 reflected the colonies' desperate need for men, money, arms, and recognition; France, in turn, found the alliance a useful tool in its long-range diplomatic struggle to reduce the power of Great Britain. France had begun sending supplies to the colonies secretly even before independence was declared, and unofficially from 1776 to 1778, but it required the American victory at Saratoga in October 1777 Great Britain's peace overtures on the basis of home rule within the empire (*see* Peace Commission of 1778) to convince the French that an open and official alliance could be risked. A commercial treaty assured each signatory of "most favored treatment" in its trade with the other; a political compact united the two countries in the war against Britain, each agreeing not to make peace without the consent of the other.

The French liaison was enormously useful to the colonists. On the negative side, the entry of Spain into the war in 1779 as an ally of France confused the objectives of the conflict, for Spain was interested in recapturing Gibraltar from Britain and was assured of French assistance, thus linking the American cause to Spain's European interests. The French alliance proved even more embarrassing to the new United States when it sought in the years after the Revolution to pursue an independent diplomatic course.

That the alliance with France was a mixed blessing was made evident during the peace negotiations with Great Britain. Technically, the American peace commissioners—Benjamin Franklin, John Adams, and John Jay—were barred from undertaking negotiations without the consent of the French ally; the boldness of America's "militia" diplomats in negotiating a treaty and then presenting it as a *fait accompli* to their French ally was rewarded by extraordinarily favorable terms. By the Definitive Treaty of Peace, to which France ultimately acceded, the United States secured recognition, all of the trans-Appalachian West to the Mississippi River, and the liberty of fishing off the Newfoundland banks. In return the United States promised to place no lawful impediments in the way of the collection of private British prewar debts in the United States and to recommend to the states the restoration of confiscated Loyalist property.

Results of the Revolution. The American Revolution overflowed its narrow banks and produced consequences greater than intended. The war disrupted existing social institutions, enlarged the body politic, and established new standards by which to measure social progress. The suspicion of power and privilege and the assumption that men had "a common and an equal right to liberty, to property, and to safety; to justice, government, laws, religion, and freedom" became the yardsticks by which institutions in the new republic were tested, immediately and in the distant future.

REVOLUTION, FINANCING OF THE. One of the most difficult tasks that faced the Continental Congress was raising money to finance the revolutionary war. Following hostilities at Bunker Hill (June 17, 1775) an issue of $2 million in bills of credit was voted, based on the credit of the states; Congress continued until Nov. 29, 1779, to emit paper money to the amount of $241,552,380, to be redeemed by the states. Depreciation set in shortly, and by March 1780, in spite of legal-tender laws and an attempt to fix prices, the value of continental currency in silver had fallen to forty to one; prices rose to unheard of heights; while excessive speculation and counterfeiting demoralized the whole financial structure of the struggling colonies. Other means used to obtain funds included domestic and foreign loans; lotteries; and prize money received from the sale of captured enemy vessels. Domestic loans were offered for sale from time to time at high rates of interest. Certificates of purchasing agents were used extensively in payment for supplies to be used by the army, and Alexander Hamilton estimated in 1790 that they were outstanding to the amount of $16,708,000. Foreign loans secured from France, Spain, and Holland through the influence of Benjamin Franklin and John Adams proved invaluable: French loans from 1777 to 1783 amounted to $6,352,500; Spanish loans, to $174,017; and Dutch loans, to $1,304,000.

On Feb. 20, 1781, Robert Morris was appointed by Congress to the new Office of Superintendent of Finance. He brought some order out of the existing chaos, but was hampered by continued state refusal to levy taxes, and by inadequate financial provisions of the Articles of Confederation. It remained for the new Constitution and the financial genius of Hamilton (*see* Assumption and Funding of Revolutionary War Debts) to place the United States on a firm national and international credit basis.

REVOLUTION, PROFITEERING IN THE. Many merchants took advantage of the colonies' straits during the crisis. Fortunes were made overnight from speculation in commodities: profiteers bought all available goods, held them until prices rose, and then sold for profits of double or more. Both the national and state governments tried, through taxation, embargo, and price-fixing, to halt the profiteering, but they were too weak to enforce regulations.

REVOLUTION, RIGHT OF. *See* **Rebellion, Right of.**

REVOLUTIONARY COMMITTEES. The American Revolution was fomented by committees and, in great measure, conducted by committees. First were the committees of correspondence, so called because they were chiefly engaged in gathering information and propagandizing their doctrines by means of the quill. There followed the committees of safety, whose function was to keep the revolutionary spirit alive and assist in its formulation. In some instances these colonial committees were instrumental in establishing provincial congresses; they were also the chief agencies either directly or through the provincial congresses, in calling together a convention of colonial committees, the First Continental Congress (September 1774). The Continental Congress had to do much of its work through committees of its own members; and such were the importance and the permanence of the tasks devolving upon some of these committees that they came to be called "standing committees."

REVOLUTIONARY WAR (1775–83). Fought over a huge area, from Canada to Florida, from the Atlantic to the Mississippi, it marked the first time in modern history that a colonial people had fought a successful revolutionary war for their freedom and independence. The war began in Massachusetts, where British troops had been stationed for some time. Gen. Thomas Gage, on orders from London to take action, sent troops through Lexington to Concord to seize provincial military stores. American armed resistance on Apr. 19, 1775, was followed by the arrival outside Boston of an army of New England militia, which fought the king's regulars in the bloody Battle of Bunker Hill on June 17. The Continental Congress, then meeting at Philadelphia, adopted the New England forces—the nucleus of the U.S. Continental Army, as it was known after Congress declared independence on July 2, 1776. George Washington was named commander in chief.

In 1776 the major scenes of action shifted to the middle states after British Gen. William Howe, Gage's successor, evacuated Boston. British strategy called for dividing the colonies along the Lake Champlain–Hudson River waterway. An army under Gen. Guy Carleton, governor of Quebec, threw a small American invasionary force out of Canada and proceeded southward in order to link up with Howe on the Hudson, from which point the two commanders were to overwhelm New England. A temporary setback at the hands of a tiny American fleet on Lake Champlain and the lateness of the season resulted in Carleton's return to Canada. Howe was unable to carry out all of his part of the scheme, for it took the general and his brother Adm. Richard Howe from August until November to clear Gen. Washington from New York City and its environs. Washington was an aggressive fighter. After escaping through New Jersey and over the Delaware River, he struck back at the unsuspecting British already settled in winter quarters, picking off their garrisons at Trenton on Dec. 26, 1776, and at Princeton on Jan. 3, 1777. Despite the greatest British military effort in history to that time—the sending of more than 30,000 soldiers and more than 40 percent of the Royal Navy to America—the campaign of 1776 had failed to throttle the rebellion.

The following year once more saw operations conducted by two British armies. The Canadian-based army under Gen. John Burgoyne had no assurances of help from Howe as it pressed down the Lake Champlain–Hudson River trough. Howe, after much indecision, decided to leave Sir Henry Clinton with a garrison force at New York City and lead the bulk of his army by sea in a move against Philadelphia. Burgoyne managed to take Fort Ticonderoga on July 5, 1777, but his overconfidence and the dense wilderness of upper New York led to his downfall. Initially, he lost valuable days by proceeding at a leisurely pace, giving the Americans time to destroy his road southward. Eventually he advanced to rugged Bemis Heights, near Saratoga, N.Y., where Gen. Horatio Gates's American northern army was securely dug in. In two major battles, on Sept. 19 and Oct. 7, Burgoyne lost heavily in men; he surrendered at Saratoga on Oct. 17.

Howe, meanwhile, pursued a strategy that made little sense: he landed at the head of the Chesapeake, more than fifty miles from Philadelphia, which Washington raced southward to defend. At Brandywine Creek, Washington, on Sept. 11, failed to halt Howe in several hours of fighting; soon after the British general entered Philadelphia, Washington assaulted Howe's advance base at Germantown, Pa., on Oct. 4, but the Americans were again driven off.

The year 1778 was a transitional period in the war. The American forces not only survived the cruel winter at Valley Forge but emerged a more formidable threat than ever, owing to the labors of Prussian drillmaster Baron Friedrich Wilhelm von Steuben and to increasing aid from France (*see* Franco-American Alliance of 1778). The Howe brothers resigned their American positions, and Clinton became the military commander. His orders were to evacuate his army from Philadelphia, concentrate his forces at New York City, and send several thousand men to help cope with French threats in the West Indies. Clinton made good his withdrawal, although at Monmouth Courthouse in New Jersey he was overtaken on June 28 and fought to a standstill by Washington, who then also moved northward and spent the next three years watching the British from outside New York City.

Just as the war in the North was indecisive, so too the conflict in the West saw neither side gaining the upper hand. George Rogers Clark in 1778 eased the pressure on the new settlements in Kentucky and Tennessee by taking several British-controlled villages in the Illinois Country and capturing the hated Col. Henry Hamilton, the so-called "hair-buyer." But neither Clark nor American commanders at Fort Pitt (Pittsburgh) were strong enough to destroy the anchor points of British power in the interior, Detroit and Niagara.

The South was long neglected except for a half-hearted British naval stab at Charleston, S.C., in 1776; it became after 1778 the principal area of operations and the scene of the war's climax. Unable to win in the North, British strategists believed that the thinly settled South, with a reputedly Loyalist-leaning majority, could be easily overrun; and Washington could not come to the assistance of southern rebels as long as Clinton maintained a strong detachment at New York. From 1778 to 1781 the southern campaign was a catalog of American reversals. Georgia fell in 1779; South Carolina, in

1780. Two American armies were erased in the latter state—at Charleston in May, when besieged Gen. Benjamin Lincoln surrendered the American southern army, and at Camden in August, when Gates was crushed by Gen. Charles Cornwallis, whom Clinton had placed in command in the South. And yet, under Gen. Nathanael Greene, still another southern force took the field. Although suffering the loss of two strong detachments in encounters at King's Mountain on Oct. 7, 1780, and Cowpens on Jan. 17, 1781, Cornwallis pursued Greene into North Carolina, where, after a bloody contest at Guilford Courthouse on Mar. 15, the British army limped eastward and then northward to the Virginia coast. Greene returned southward and brilliantly cut off every British post save Charleston and Savannah, Ga. Meanwhile, Cornwallis united with a British raiding party in Virginia and soon dug in at Yorktown, where he was vulnerable to a land and sea blockade. Franco-American army and navy operations proved decisive: joined in Rhode Island by French troops under the command of Jean Baptiste Donatien de Vimeur, Comte de Rochambeau, Washington raced southward and prepared to open siege operations before Yorktown on Sept. 28, while a French fleet from the West Indies under Comte François Joseph de Grasse sealed off a sea escape. Cornwallis capitulated on Oct. 19. (*See also articles on individual battles.*)

REVOLUTIONARY WAR, AMERICAN ARMY IN THE. The American army of the Revolution stemmed from the various local minutemen, alarm companies, and volunteers who had sprung to arms to meet the British expedition against Lexington and Concord and pursued the redcoats back to Boston on Apr. 19, 1775. Many of these men remained to besiege the city, and they were joined by volunteers from other New England colonies in the weeks that followed, but there was no overall command and no definite enlistments. Finally the Massachusetts Provincial Congress sent an urgent appeal to the Continental Congress in Philadelphia asking it to adopt the new army and provide direction. The Congress responded. On June 14 it authorized the raising of ten companies of riflemen in Virginia, Maryland, and Pennsylvania as the nucleus of a new national army, and on June 15 it appointed George Washington commander in chief. By July 3 Washington had arrived in Cambridge, Mass., to take command, and a few weeks later the rifle regiments joined him. His plan of organization called for a Continental army of twenty-six regiments or battalions of infantry with a strength of 728 men each, one regiment of riflemen, and one of artillery, for a total of 20,372 men. Each of the infantry regiments was to consist of eight companies of 86 men, 4 officers, and 8 regimental staff officers. All were to be enlisted until the end of 1776 and responsible only to the Continental Congress. The effective date for the new organization was to be Jan. 1, 1776, but when that day arrived, arrangements were far from complete. By March, when the spring campaign began, only 9,170 men had joined the ranks, and Washington had to rely on help from local militia units in order to obtain an adequate operating force.

Congress authorized additional regiments. The rifle and artillery regiments became a corps and a brigade, respectively. Cavalry, light infantry, and artificer regiments were added, as well as special mixed units called legions. Before the end of the war, Congress had authorized eighty-eight battalions totaling 80,000 men, but the quota was never met. Some of the regiments were never raised; others were always under strength. The actual number of men under arms varied, but the best estimates indicate that the usual number was about 10,000. To muster an adequate force, Washington had to rely on state regiments and on local militia organizations called out for short-term emergencies; almost all major actions and campaigns were fought with a mixture of these troops, even after 1776 when Congress began to recruit soldiers for longer periods—usually three years or the duration of the war.

REVOLUTIONARY WAR, BRITISH ARMY IN THE. In April 1775 the British army numbered only about 32,000 men, of whom 6,991 were in America. By March 1782, through recruiting, impressment, and the hiring of German regiments, the total had risen to 113,000 effectives, including 8,756 in the West Indies and 46,000 in North America; of the latter, two-thirds were Germans or American provincials.

In all about 2,000 British officers served in America during the war. Commonly they were promoted gratis to fill vacancies caused by death, or else, with permission, they bought commissions from previous holders and could sell out at any time; in 1783 most of those still serving reverted to the reserve on half pay for life. A few were members of Parliament, a dozen were baronets, and at least seventy-eight were peers or sons of peers. By contrast, private soldiers represented strictly nonpolitical Britain. Those serving in 1775 had largely enlisted for life or according to regimental contract; others, later, for three years or until the "rebellion" ended, at the crown's option. Voluntary enlistment was stimulated by bounties; by acceptance of Roman Catholics, previously excluded; by the creation of dozens of new regiments; and by pardoning of convicts on condition of enlistment. Press acts of May 1778 and February 1779 provided for conscripting the unemployed poor—but not voters—for service of five years or the duration of war. Difficulties of recruitment and transport made conservation of men the paramount concern; major engagements had to be avoided, and no commander dared exploit an advantage if he would thereby diminish compactness and facilitate desertion.

REVOLUTIONARY WAR, CONTINENTAL NAVY IN THE. In October 1775 the Continental Congress appointed a committee charged with founding a modest navy; originally called the Naval Committee and then the Marine Committee, in 1779 it became the Board of Admiralty. Effective colonial naval power had actually commenced with the initiative of Gen. George Washington. As the commander besieging Boston in the spring of 1775, he commissioned six schooners and a brigantine for a tiny naval force.

The first of the twenty-seven men-of-war of the Continental navy were converted from merchant vessels at Philadelphia. Esek Hopkins was the first commodore to go to sea, aboard the *Alfred,* carrying thirty guns, and leading the *Columbus, Andrew Doria, Cabot, Providence, Hornet, Wasp,* and *Fly.*

Congress next employed the navy as bearers of American products to French and Dutch ports in the West Indies to be exchanged for military supplies. At the same time, Continental cruisers strove to slow the buildup of the king's strength on the American coast. The coast of Britain was not immune: Lambert Wickes, in the *Reprisal,* took or sank eighteen British vessels in Irish waters in 1776.

The British response was more than mere augmentation of the blockade: it was a thrust in the autumn of 1777 at the supposed heart of the rebellion, Philadelphia. The loss of the city cost the Continental navy its main base, three new frigates, and six smaller units. Most of the sizable Pennsylvania navy was also wiped out. (Only Delaware and New Jersey lacked a state navy.)

The open advent of France into the war probably averted the extinction of the Continental navy. In July 1778, when the Brest fleet sailed for New York, British ships-of-the-line had to concentrate to offer formal battle. French regularization of supplies abated the securing of munitions via the West Indies, and the navy could embark on offensives.

REVOLUTIONARY WAR, FOREIGN VOLUNTEERS IN. The ideal of human liberty actuating the colonies in 1776 found response in the hearts of many Europeans, especially in France. The first secret aid ships of Pierre Augustin Caron de Beaumarchais landed about thirty volunteers in March and April 1777 at Portsmouth, Va. Marie Joseph du Motier, Marquis de Lafayette, and his eleven officers, arrived in July. More than half of these men were rejected by Congress and had their expenses paid back to France.

Among the most notable of those commissioned were Charles Armand, Marquis de la Rouërie; Pierre Charles l'Enfant, later designer of the national capital; Philippe Tronson du Coudray; Thaddeus Kosciusko, a Lithuanian, who arrived in 1776 and built the fortifications at West Point; Louis Lebegue DuPortail, who fortified Valley Forge; and Casimir Pulaski, a Polish count. Only two of Lafayette's officers were retained by Congress: Johann Kalb (Baron de Kalb), and the latter's aide Paul Dubuisson. The last secret aid volunteers to arrive came in December 1777, sent by Beaumarchais: among them were Baron Friedrich von Steuben and his interpreter, Pierre Étienne Du Ponceau.

REVOLUTIONARY WAR, LOYALIST TROOPS IN THE. In America loyal subjects were fleeing to British posts, ready for revenge and exerting a moral claim on the royal bounty; at no time between the Battle of Bunker Hill and peace in 1783 were refugees not recruited. At times, especially 1780–82, Loyalists under arms may have exceeded patriot troops.

New York and New England provided scores of officers, midshipmen, and seamen for the Royal Navy. From New York between 6,000 and 16,000 Loyalists went out in privateers. The regular army attracted Loyalist refugees, but the term of enlistment was long, the supply of free commissions was limited, and indigent refugees could not buy commissions. Temporary provincial regiments were created, therefore, specifically for Loyalists, who would serve only in America or in the West Indies; they ranked just below the regulars, but ahead of the militia, in command and privileges. Provincial regiments were chronically undermanned; about sixty-eight corps were started; many were disbanded and their manpower reconstituted; only half a dozen attained full strength. Before peace came, however, about 19,000 had served as provincials.

The provincials were not the only Loyalists in land service. Between 10,000 and 20,000 royal militiamen enrolled and chose their own officers during British occupations in Georgia, the Carolinas, New York, and Maine; heavily dependent on the army, those in the South experienced the bitterest fighting of the war. Elsewhere, notably in Pennsylvania, Loyalist guerrillas seriously annoyed the patriots, although they were not of major help to the British.

REVOLUTION OF 1800. The election of 1800, which established Thomas Jefferson's Republican party in control of both the presidency and the Congress, is sometimes called the Revolution of 1800; it marked the end of Federalist party power and the beginning of a much more democratic approach to government.

REVOLUTION OF 1828. The election of 1828 is often regarded as a "revolution" because it brought the Jacksonian Democrats to power. Andrew Jackson and his supporters stood for a more popular type of democracy than had been practiced before his election. (*See* Jacksonian Democracy.)

REVOLUTION OF 1910. In 1910 a move within Congress curbed the power of the Speaker of the House, "Uncle" Joseph Cannon, who had for a long time acted like a dictator, deciding bills to be considered, committee assignments, and the procedures of the House. This "revolution" restored power and dignity to the individual members.

RHEA LETTER. On Jan. 6, 1818, Gen. Andrew Jackson wrote to President James Monroe, offering to conquer the Floridas if approval was signified "through any channel (say Mr. J. Rhea)." Monroe, ill at the time, left the passage unread. Subsequently, Jackson received a letter from Rep. John Rhea of Tennessee, which he construed as giving Monroe's sanction to the plan; on this basis Jackson claimed Monroe's authorization for his campaign in Florida, despite the president's denial (*see* Arbuthnot and Ambrister, Case of).

RHODE ISLAND. Smallest in size of the United States (approximately forty-eight miles long and thirty-seven miles wide), Rhode Island was founded in 1636 by colonists who accompanied Roger Williams to Providence after his banishment from Massachusetts. The exiles agreed that their government applied "only in civill things"; they thus set a precedent for the separation of church and state and for religious freedom. Others fled Massachusetts under the leadership of William Coddington and John Clarke and settled Portsmouth (1638), on the island of Aquidneck in Narragansett Bay—after 1644 known as Rhode Island, because of Giovanni da Verrazano's 1524 description of it as resembling the isle of Rhodes. Dissatisfaction in Portsmouth prompted Coddington to found Newport (1639). The fourth original settlement is associated with Samuel Gorton, a religious mystic, who was banished from Plymouth, Mass., and later founded Warwick (1648). Each of the plantations purchased their lands from the Indians. The union of these settlements started in 1644, when Williams went to England and obtained a parliamentary charter. The first legislature met on May 19, 1647. In 1663 Clarke obtained a new royal charter that gave Rhode Island virtual autonomy; it remained in force until 1842.

Although farming was the principal occupation, the carrying trade, re-exports, and the slave trade were vital to the colonial economy. In the 19th century the hinterland surrounding Providence became the most heavily industrialized and densely populated region of the nation. The first successful cotton factory was established in 1790 at Pawtucket Falls; before the Civil War, Rhode Island cotton manufacturing was among the most important industries in the country, employing nearly 16,000 people and producing over $20 million in cotton goods. The state also became a leader in the silver and costume jewelry industries.

The royal charter of 1663 took no account of the size or wealth of a town in distributing representation in the general assembly, disfranchised the mass of industrial workers who did not own land, and failed to provide a bill of rights or to guarantee an independent judiciary. The struggle for constitutional changes resulted in the bloodless Dorr War of 1842. Concessions by the incumbent government in 1843 led to partial reforms in representation and voting. In 1935 the complete reorganization of the state government was achieved.

Since World War II, Rhode Island has adjusted to its latest economic and social transformation by less concentration of employment in textiles and by economic diversification, especially reliance on small, technologically innovative industries, particularly electronics; tourism; expansion of government and military employment; small dairy, fishing, and poultry businesses; and a large and successful program of urban renewal. The state's population in 1980 was 947,154.

RHODE ISLAND, COLONIAL CHARTERS OF. Roger Williams secured the first Rhode Island charter in March 1644 from a parliamentary commission headed by Robert Rich, Earl of Warwick. It provided for an elected president, assistants, and general court and guaranteed liberty of conscience. The restoration of Charles II in 1660 made necessary a royal charter, which was secured July 8, 1663, by John Clarke. It provided for an elected governor, deputy-governor, assistants, and general assembly. Separation of church and state was maintained; suffrage was left to colonial control.

RHODE ISLAND IN THE DUTCH WAR OF 1653. The council of state having authorized the colony to take warlike action against the Dutch, the Rhode Island assembly in May 1653 issued privateer commissions to John Underhill, William Dyer, and Edward Hull, and subsequently to Thomas Baxter and to the vessel *Debora.* Rhode Island was the only New England colony actively to engage against the Dutch in this war.

RHODES SCHOLARSHIPS. Established by the will of Cecil J. Rhodes, South African statesman and financier, to provide appointments for study in the University of Oxford to students drawn from eighteen countries. Thirty-two students from the United States are selected annually. U.S. candidates should be unmarried citizens between the ages of eighteen and twenty-four, with at least junior standing in a recognized degree-granting university or college. Appointments are for a period of two years in the first instance, with the possibility of renewal for a third. The stipend is calculated to cover all tuition expenses and to provide a living allowance.

RHYOLITE (Nev.). Chief town of the Bullfrog Mining District, in southern Nye County, during the active period, 1904–14. Mining decline was followed by abandonment of the railroad in 1914, leaving Rhyolite a ghost town.

RIBBON FARMS. Name given by the American settlers at Detroit and elsewhere to the narrow riverfront farms of French feudal origin. A typical farm might be one or more arpents (192.24 English feet) wide and either 40 or 80 arpents (1.5 to 3 miles) deep.

RICE, FORT (N.Dak.). Established July 11, 1864; the military reservation at this point was authorized on Sept. 2, 1864. Situated on the west bank of the Missouri River, ten miles north of the mouth of the Cannonball River, the fort was named for Henry M. Rice, first U.S. senator from Minnesota. The fort was first occupied by Gen. Alfred Sully in his operations against the Dakota Indians (1864–65); it was abandoned in 1878, and the garrison was transferred to Fort Lincoln. The military reservation was vacated in 1884.

RICE-CAMPBELL DEBATES (Nov. 15–Dec. 2, 1843). Nathan Lewis Rice, an Old-School Presbyterian, and Alexander Campbell, a founder of the Disciples of Christ, debated in Lexington, Ky., before large crowds; Henry Clay was moderator. The propositions debated were the nature, purpose, and regulation of baptism and its relation to church creeds. The debates fixed public attention on the Disciples of Christ as a denomination, consolidated their doctrines of primitive Christianity around the ordinance of baptism, clarified the differences between them and the Presbyterians and Baptists, and emphasized the Disciples' plea for Christian union.

RICE CULTURE AND TRADE. Before 1860 the growing of rice on American soil was confined largely to the banks of the slow-moving creeks, inlets, and rivers located along the Atlantic coastline from Virginia to Florida. The Carolina coast, especially the Charleston area, was the scene of the earliest attempts at rice culture during the last decade of the 17th century. By the early 18th century rice had become a major export crop. By 1840 other areas—such as Georgetown and Beaufort, S.C., Wilmington, N.C., and the entire hundred-mile seacoast of Georgia—offered competition to

Charleston. After the Civil War, the bulk of American rice came to be produced in the prairie regions of Texas, Arkansas, and Louisiana.

During the colonial period the bulk of the crop was then sent to the West Indies and Europe. In the 19th century 20 percent of the harvest was marketed in the West Indies; 5 percent, directly to Europe; and the remainder to commerce centers in the North for domestic consumption or transshipment to Europe.

"RICH, AND GOOD AND WISE." *See* **"Wise, and Good and Rich."**

RICHELIEU RIVER. A Canadian river flowing northward from Lake Champlain into the St. Lawrence River; discovered by Samuel de Champlain in 1609. It was first known to the French as the Rivière des Iroquois. Afterward it was the recognized thoroughfare, in peace and war, between New England and New France. The Chambly canal, 11.8 miles long and with nine locks, enabled the Richelieu River to remain an important shipping route between Montreal and New York City.

RICHMOND (Va.). Soon after Jamestown was founded (May 1607) Capt. Christopher Newport led an expedition up the James River to the fall line and erected a cross dedicated to James I on the future site of Richmond. The general assembly granted an act of incorporation in 1742. The continuing westward shift of population together with the town's strategic location at the head of navigation made Richmond a commercial center of growing importance.

As the Revolution approached, considerations of security led many to regard Richmond rather than Williamsburg as the proper political center of Virginia. The convention of 1775 was held there, and in 1779 Richmond became the capital of the new state. Within a generation after the war, Richmond was the social, cultural, and economic hub of the state. In 1860, with a population nearing 40,000, Richmond was the terminus for five railroads and was ranked thirteenth in manufacturing among American cities.

In May 1861 the capital of the Confederate states was moved from Montgomery, Ala., to Richmond. It was closely beleaguered in 1862 but was relieved by Gen. Robert E. Lee's offensive in the Seven Days' Battle. Two years later federal forces under Gen. Ulysses S. Grant began a long siege that ended with the fall of Richmond on Apr. 2, 1865. Postwar recovery was relatively rapid, thanks largely to the vitality of the tobacco industry, which also would later help to soften the effects of the Great Depression. Richmond's population in 1980 was 219,214.

RICHMOND, BATTLE OF (Aug. 29–31, 1862). Confederate Brig. Gen. Edmund Kirby-Smith, with some 16,000 troops, invaded Kentucky in the direction of Lexington. His first skirmish with Union troops occurred on Aug. 29 near Rogersville, south of Richmond, Ky. Here the Confederates were repulsed, but the next day Kirby-Smith drove the raw Union force of about 7,000 men, under Maj. Gen. William Nelson and Brig. Gen. Mahlon D. Manson, through the streets of Richmond. The Union troops made two or three desperate attempts to stop the enemy but were defeated.

RICHMOND, BURNING AND EVACUATION OF (April 1865). On Sunday, Apr. 2, Union forces captured the outer works around Petersburg, Va. On notice from Gen. Robert E. Lee, Confederate President Jefferson Davis and his cabinet left Richmond. By military order of the Confederates, bridges and warehouses, along with shipping, were fired; once started, the fire, driven by high winds, spread to the business district. The burning and evacuation of Richmond signalized the overthrow of the Confederacy.

RICHMOND, CAMPAIGN AGAINST (1864–65). The campaign against Richmond began early in May 1864 when Gen. Ulysses S. Grant crossed the Rapidan River and entered the Wilderness, a defense forest in northeastern Orange and northwestern Spotsylvania counties, in command of an army of 122,000 men. Gen. Robert E. Lee's army, a much smaller force, contested Grant's for eleven months. A furious two-day struggle (May 5–6) in the Battle of the Wilderness was followed by a flanking march to Spotsylvania Courthouse, eleven miles southwest of Fredericksburg, where another indecisive conflict took place (May 8–21). Another move to his left by Grant brought the two armies together on the North Anna River (May 23–25), but Grant declined battle and, by a flanking march, reached Cold Harbor, where on June 3 his troops were devastated in direct attack on Confederate entrenchments. Stalled north of the James River, Grant crossed the river late in June and sought to force the Confederates out of Richmond by cutting its railway connections with the lower Confederacy. Failures before Petersburg in June and in the Battle of the Crater on July 30 reduced operations to a nine-months siege of Petersburg. By the following spring it was necessary for Lee's army to evacuate Petersburg and abandon further defense of Richmond, Apr. 2, 1865. Lee's troops were surrounded at Appomattox and compelled to surrender on Apr. 9.

RICHMOND JUNTO. A group headed by Thomas Ritchie, editor and publisher (1804–45) of the *Richmond Enquirer,* that controlled Virginia Democratic politics for more than a quarter century. Strongly states' rights in tone, the junto played a large part in defeating Martin Van Buren for the Democratic presidential nomination in 1844.

RICH MOUNTAIN, BATTLE OF (July 11, 1861). Planning to seize western Virginia for the Confederacy, Gen. Robert S. Garnett fortified the roads to Wheeling and Parkersburg at Laurel Mountain and Rich Mountain. Union Gen. George B. McClellan, advancing from Grafton, held the Confederates while Gen. William S. Rosecrans led a column around the left of those on Rich Mountain and cut off the Confederate retreat. Confederate Lt. Col. John Pegram, commanding there, surrendered. Garnett was killed.

RICKERT RICE MILLS, INC.* V. *FONTENOT, 297 U.S. 110 (1936). A case in which the Supreme Court invalidated a statute amendatory to the Agricultural Adjustment Act of

1933. The statute of 1935 had attempted to clarify the provisions of the original enactment. Funds impounded during the proceedings were returned to the Rickert Rice Mills and companion complainants, but the Court refused to discuss the procedure of recovering money previously paid under the unconstitutional processing tax provisions.

RIDERS, LEGISLATIVE. Sections or clauses not germane to the subject matter of a bill that are added by amendment before passage, with the expectation that the sentiment favorable to the bill will be sufficient to sweep the whole enactment through the final vote and secure executive approval. Riders are most commonly used in the federal government and in connection with appropriation acts.

RIDGEFIELD, BATTLE OF (Apr. 27, 1777). On Apr. 25 a detachment of British troops, under the command of William Tryon, disembarked at Compo Point (present Westport, Conn.) and marched rapidly inland to Danbury, Conn. The next day they burned the supplies stored there. Retreating by way of Ridgefield on Apr. 27, they were followed by Maj. Gen. David Wooster with 200 men and attacked twice; on the second attack, just outside Ridgefield, Wooster was mortally wounded. At Ridgefield the retreating British found the way blocked by generals Gold Selleck Silliman and Benedict Arnold with 500 Connecticut militia. After a frontal attack, which failed, Tryon ordered an attack on the left flank; Arnold was unhorsed and the barricade forced.

RIDGELY, FORT (Minn.). The sale of their Minnesota lands by the Sioux, under the Treaty of Traverse des Sioux (July 23, 1851), and the concentration of these Indians on small upper Minnesota River reservations brought about the establishment of Fort Ridgely, Apr. 29, 1853, on the north bank of that river in Nicollet County. On Aug. 20 and 22, 1862, it was successfully defended against powerful Sioux attacks (*see* Sioux Uprising in Minnesota). The post became obsolete and was abandoned on May 22, 1867.

RIFLE. The process of rifling gun barrels is accomplished by cutting spiral grooves from the breech to the muzzle, inside the gun barrel; the grooves cause the ball to spin when leaving the barrel and impart stability to the projectile. In America, German gunsmiths working in Pennsylvania and other Middle Atlantic states modified the short, large-caliber, German "Jaeger" rifle into the long, graceful, and accurate American rifle. During the American Revolution these uniquely American weapons were often referred to as "long rifles"; the term "Kentucky rifle" was probably not used until the end of the War of 1812. Later the name "Pennsylvania rifle" came into limited usage to denote the place of manufacture of the majority of the weapons.

The first official U.S. Army rifle was the model of 1803, produced at the federal arsenal at Harpers Ferry, Va., and used by special rifle regiments. The musket continued to dominate the battlefield until the introduction of the U.S. rifle-musket, Model 1855, which fired the lead hollow-base Minié bullet.

During the Civil War many types of breech-loading rifles and carbines were developed. Some early breechloaders, such as the Henry and Spencer rifles, used metallic cartridges with a self-contained, rim-fire primer, which eliminated the need for a separate priming cap. Muzzle-loading rifle-muskets were later converted to breechloaders firing a rim-fire cartridge; a modification of this conversion resulted in the adoption of the U.S. Rifle, Model 1873. This simple and dependable single-shot rifle became the first U.S. martial arm to utilize the center fire primer in the cartridge. The Krag-Jörgensen rifle, an excellent five-shot, bolt-action rifle, was based on a Danish design and was known officially as the U.S. Rifle, Model 1892. The U.S. Rifle, Model 1903, based on the Mauser bolt-action principle, was adopted to replace the Krag rifle and was the standard arm of the U.S. armed forces until World War II, when it was replaced by the semiautomatic M1 Garand rifle. The dependable, eight-shot Garand rifle was replaced in 1957 by the M14 rifle, 7.62-mm caliber, to comply with standards set up by the North Atlantic Treaty Organization. The M14 was based on the Garand, but was fitted with a twenty-round detachable magazine and a selector switch for fully automatic fire; it was replaced with the experimental AR-15 rifle, officially adopted under the designation of U.S. Rifle M16 A1 in 1967.

RIFLE, RECOILLESS. A lightweight, air-cooled, manually operated, breech-loading, single-shot, direct-fire weapon used primarily for defense against tanks and secondarily against fortifications and personnel; it was first developed by the German army in World War II. The rifle remains motionless when fired.

RIGHT OF SEARCH. *See* **Visit and Search.**

RIGHT OF WAY LAW OF 1852. All railroad, plank road, and turnpike companies chartered by the public-land states before 1862 were given a right of way of 100 feet through the public lands, with station sites and the right to take timber and stone from adjoining lands for construction purposes. In 1855 the act was amended to make it apply to the territories.

RIGHTS OF ENGLISHMEN. Henry Care's *English Liberties, or the Free-born Subject's Inheritance* was reprinted at Boston (1721), and British liberties came to be defined in terms of laws that stood above both king and Parliament, and of which the colonists could not therefore be deprived. Applied to the relations between the home government and the colonies after 1761, the colonists claimed the right of Englishmen to be taxed only in case they were represented (*see* Taxation Without Representation).

RIGHTS OF MAN. A defense of the French Revolution written by Thomas Paine in reply to Edmund Burke's *Reflections on the Revolution in France* (1790). The work, dedicated to George Washington, appeared in two parts (1791, 1792); its circulation was very great. To Paine the rights of man were indefeasible. Only when it could be said in any country that its people were happy might that country boast of its constitution and government. (*See also* Natural Rights.)

RIGHTS OF THE BRITISH COLONIES ASSERTED AND PROVED. A tract written by James Otis (1764) that denied the authority of Parliament to tax the colonies, drawing analogy between the colonies and Ireland. It favored representation in Parliament for the colonies, and declared that acts against natural equity or the British constitution were void.

RIGHT-TO-WORK LAWS. During the 1940's and 1950's many states passed labor laws designed to limit the power of labor unions, which had worked out contracts with many companies requiring workers to join unions or lose their jobs. The "right-to-work" laws provide that no worker may be forced to join a union as a condition of his employment.

RILEY, FORT (Kans.). Named for Maj. Gen. Bennet Riley; located on the north bank of the Kansas River, just east of the mouth of the Republican River, in Geary County. Built in 1853, it soon became important in frontier defense. Its troops helped to protect emigrants and the overland mail during the Civil War. A school of instruction for cavalry and light artillery was located at Fort Riley on Mar. 14, 1892. In 1917 it was converted to a U.S. Army staging and training center; by 1981 it occupied 56,000 acres.

RINGGOLD GAP, BATTLE OF (Nov. 27, 1863). After their defeat on Missionary Ridge, the Confederate Army of Tennessee retreated southward into northwestern Georgia. Gen. Ulysses S. Grant sent Union Gen. Joseph Hooker in pursuit (*see* Chattanooga Campaign). Confederate Gen. Patrick R. Cleburne, in command of the rear guard, halted at Ringgold Gap to insure the safe withdrawal of the army and trains. Hooker attacked repeatedly but was repulsed. After dark, Cleburne withdrew, and Hooker's pursuit ended.

RINGGOLD-RODGERS EXPLORING EXPEDITION (North Pacific Exploring and Surveying Expedition). Consisted of five naval vessels under Comdr. Cadwalader Ringgold; sailed from Norfolk, Va., in June 1853. It surveyed in the western Pacific from Tasmania northward to Herald Island in the Arctic Ocean. When the ships reached China in 1854, Ringgold fell ill, and the expedition was turned over to Comdr. John Rodgers. The expedition continued, surveying the Hawaiian and Society islands and the coast of Japan. It reached the Arctic Ocean in August 1855, some vessels continuing work until 1859.

RINGS, POLITICAL. Groups of persons, usually headed by a political boss, organized to control a city, county, or state, and primarily interested in deriving large personal profit. Political rings have been found as far back as colonial days, but particularly in the late 19th century.

William Marcy Tweed did the most to bring political rings into the limelight. The famous political ring that bears his name was organized in 1869 and composed of Tweed, Mayor A. Oakey ("O.K.") Hall, Comptroller Richard ("Slippery Dick") Connolly, and Peter B. ("Brains") Sweeny.

The Philadelphia Gas Ring actually exerted greater political influence but indulged in less peculation. The Tweed Ring came to grief within three years of its founding, but the Gas Ring wielded great political power from 1865 until 1887.

"Colonel" Edward Butler built a political ring in St. Louis in the 1890's. This ring disposed of valuable franchises to the highest bribers. About 1900 the "genial doctor," A. A. Ames, constructed a ring around the Minneapolis Police Department, which preyed upon thieves, gamblers, and other crooks. The "Curly Boss" Abraham Ruef and members of the San Francisco Board of Supervisors sold numerous official favors to public utilities until his trial for bribery, conviction, and imprisonment in 1911. (*See also* Bosses and Bossism, Political.)

RIO DE JANEIRO CONFERENCE (Aug. 15–Sept. 2, 1947). A meeting of nineteen American republics (Nicaragua and Ecuador did not take part) in line with the long-standing U.S. practice of encouraging cooperation among the twenty-one republics. The participating countries signed the Inter-American Treaty of Reciprocal Assistance (Sept. 2, 1947), also known as the Pact of Rio. It became the duty of each member to assist in meeting an armed attack by a country against an American country, pending action by the United Nations; or if an American country were threatened by a situation not involving an armed attack by another country (for example, a revolution), the members would immediately meet to decide on what measures should be taken.

RIO GRANDE. North American river, 1,300 miles of which form the boundary separating the United States and Mexico. The Rio Grande—known in Mexico as the Río Bravo del Norte—is 1,885 miles long. The Treaty of Guadalupe Hidalgo (1848) recognized the river as an international border.

Seasonal flooding causes the Rio Grande to change its course from time to time. The International Boundary Commission was established by Mexico and the United States to settle disputes arising from such changes (*see* Mexico, Relations with). The Rio Grande is not important as a trade route —it is navigable only for a short distance from its mouth—but its waters have been important for irrigation in the arid Southwest from prehistoric times. Cooperation between the two countries has resulted in various irrigation and flood-control projects, the most spectacular being the vast Amistad Dam (1969) at Del Rio, Tex.

RIO GRANDE, ENGLISH COLONY ON THE. From 1832 to 1834 John Charles Beales (an Englishman), with other empresarios, secured grants from the Mexican state of Coahuila-Texas embracing much of present western Texas and eastern New Mexico. Most of the other empresarios left their interests to Beales. Not having money to promote the venture, he organized in New York a joint-stock company.

The site selected was on Las Moras Creek, about six miles above its confluence with the Rio Grande. Here, on Mar. 16, 1834, a small town was built and named Dolores in honor of Beales's wife. The colony was doomed to failure, so when Santa Anna crossed the Rio Grande in 1836 to suppress the Texas Revolution, the colonists started in ox-drawn wagons for Matamoros. All but two women and three children were massacred by Comanche. The two women were ransomed several months later by the Comancheros (New Mexican traders), and the children died in captivity.

RIO GRANDE, SIBLEY'S OPERATIONS ON THE (1861–62). In June 1861 Maj. Henry H. Sibley received permission from the Confederacy to drive the Union soldiers from New Mexico. A regiment was raised at San Antonio and marched to Fort Bliss, near El Paso. From here Sibley, now a general, moved up the Rio Grande toward Fort Craig, where Union Col. Edward R. Canby made his headquarters. On Feb. 21, 1862, in the Battle of Valverde, Canby was driven across the river into the fort. Sibley took Albuquerque without a fight. Desperate for provisions, Sibley continued on toward Santa Fe. He was met, Mar. 28, by Union Col. John P. Slough, from Fort Union, and at Glorieta, Sibley was stopped. He began his retreat back down the Rio Grande. Caught between Canby and Slough, he made a 100-mile circuit around Fort Craig through the pathless mountains. Forced to abandon his wagons, he was soon without food, water, and supplies. On July 6, 1862, he crossed back into Texas. He had lost over 500 men, killed, dead from disease, or prisoners, and the Union forces still held New Mexico.

RIO PACT. *See* **Rio de Janeiro Conference.**

RIPLEY, FORT. A one-company army post, first called Fort Gaines, established Apr. 13, 1849, on the west bank of the Mississippi near the Crow Wing River, in what is now central Minnesota. Built to control the Winnebago Long Prairie Reservation. Chippewa unrest in August 1862 brought an increased garrison. The fort was abandoned about 1877.

RIPPER LEGISLATION. Acts of state legislatures whereby local (usually city) officials of one party are turned out of office and replaced with political opponents. Legislatures can forego frontal attacks on undesired employees by cutting an agency's budget drastically and thereby forcing the layoff of staff. This is known as "riffing," from RIF (reduction in force). Civil service commissions that enforce the merit system have been starved into impotence to hide patronage firings and hirings. Compulsory retirement ages can be manipulated to trigger early departures and open new slots for the majority party.

RIP RAPS CONTRACT SCANDAL. In 1818, under Secretary of War John C. Calhoun, a contract was made with Elijah Mix to strengthen the fortification on the Rip Raps, a small island on the Virginia coast. Calhoun's enemies associated him and his chief clerk, Maj. Christopher Van Deventer, a brother-in-law of Mix, with scandals growing out of this contract, and forced its cancellation in 1822. In 1827 a committee of the House of Representatives exonerated Calhoun, but ordered Van Deventer dismissed.

RIP VAN WINKLE. The story of the ne'er-do-well Rip Van Winkle, who wandered off with his dog and gun into the Catskill Mountains, slept for twenty years, and returned only to find what his creator, Washington Irving, calls "the dilapidations of time," appeared in *The Sketch Book of Geoffrey Crayon, Gent.* (serialized 1819–20).

RIVER AND HARBOR IMPROVEMENTS. The First Congress enacted legislation for "the establishment and support of the Lighthouses, Beacons, Buoys, and Public Piers"; and in 1790 states began levying tonnage duties for deepening harbors and removing sunken vessels. The founding of the U.S. Military Academy at West Point, N.Y., in 1802 made possible a technically competent corps of engineers within the army.

Presidential vetoes, based on constitutional scruples, curbed the will of Congress for a time and left the initiative largely to the states. The General Survey Act of Apr. 30 authorized planning for roads and canals "of national importance in a commercial or military point of view" and empowered the president to employ army engineers in this work. An appropriation act of May 24 provided $75,000 for navigation improvements on the Ohio and Mississippi rivers.

Between 1824 and 1831, the War Department Board of Engineers for Internal Improvements outlined a comprehensive plan. With federal subsidies and technical aid from army engineers, states and chartered companies soon began construction of important canals. The U.S. Army Corps of Engineers launched a nationwide endeavor that has continued to this day. Snagging on the Mississippi, opening up the log-choked Red River, deepening the Ohio, preserving St. Louis as a river port, and clearing harbors all along the Atlantic and Gulf coasts were among its early activities. In 1857 the Corps of Engineers introduced the seagoing hopper dredge at Charleston, S.C. The corps also entered the field of lighthouse construction.

During the last third of the 19th century, the Corps of Engineers expended nearly $333 million on rivers and harbors. The corps established a permanent, nationwide system staffed by military and civilian engineers. Meanwhile, Congress created special organizations: the Mississippi River Commission (1879); the Missouri River Commission (1884–1902); the office of the supervisor, New York harbor (1888); and the California Debris Commission (1893). Among major projects were improvement of the Mississippi by wing dams, revetments, and levees and construction of the Eads Jetties that opened the river's South Pass to ocean traffic; canalization of the Ohio; a ship channel to connect the Great Lakes between Buffalo, N.Y., Chicago, and Duluth, Minn.; erection of Tillamook (Oregon) and Stannard Rock (Michigan) lighthouses; and the Muscle Shoals Canal in the Tennessee River and the "Soo" locks at Sault Ste. Marie, Mich. Virtually every major harbor was improved for shipping.

By the turn of the century, a trend toward comprehensive planning and multiple-purpose projects was discernible. In 1902 Congress created the Board of Engineers for Rivers and Harbors. The Intracoastal Waterway, authorized in 1909, was to connect all ports from Boston to the Rio Grande. The act of Mar. 3, 1909, that created the National Waterways Commission directed the chief of engineers to aim for multipurpose projects. Hence, the way was open to marry navigation improvement with hydropower development and flood protection. In 1917 flood control work on the Mississippi was formally recognized as a national responsibility. The corps also undertook such work on the Sacramento River in California and began construction of their first multipurpose dam at Muscle Shoals, Ala.

In 1927 Congress instructed the army to make a comprehensive survey of the multiple-use potentialities of the nation's rivers. This survey furnished basic guides for many valuable public works projects. At the same time, federal programs for flood control expanded. In 1936 nationwide flood-control activities became a function of the corps. From this time forward, goals steadily widened to encompass water supply, recreation, fish and wildlife conservation, pollution abatement, and flood plain management.

Authorization of the Pick-Sloan Plan for the Missouri River Basin launched the nation's first postwar attempt at comprehensive basin development. Constructed under the plan was a series of dams and reservoirs, the largest being Garrison in North Dakota and Oahe, Big Bend, Fort Randall, and Gavins Point in South Dakota; extensive systems of levees and floodwalls; and a 9-foot channel upstream on the Missouri to Sioux City, Iowa. Similar developments followed in the Columbia River and Arkansas River basins. Other projects of special importance were construction of the St. Lawrence Seaway, recanalization of the Ohio, and modernization of the Black Warrior–Tombigbee Waterway in Alabama. (*See also* Engineers, Corps of).

RIVERMEN OF THE OHIO. When white immigrants began to push into the Ohio Valley, larger and more substantial craft than canoes were needed for ever-increasing numbers of people, household and kitchen furnishings, and livestock. This led to flatboats and keelboats and numerous modifications. The operators were known as rivermen, of whom Mike Fink and others were notorious. Such rivermen gave place to the rousters, gamblers, and bullies of the passenger packets of Ohio River navigation.

RIVER NAVIGATION. The native Americans' means of navigating American rivers was by bullboats (coracles), bark canoes, and pirogues; and the whites added to these bateaux, keelboats, and barges. Where the nature of the river permitted, sailing craft were utilized.

Boatbuilding was among the earliest activities of the colonists, especially in New England and New Amsterdam and on Delaware Bay. Flatboats (arks or Kentucky boats) were built at the headwaters of eastern and western rivers for the transportation of produce, coal, cattle, and immigrants.

Regular packet boats were rare in the keelboat age on the western rivers, but in the East they existed on the Hudson and Delaware. The Spanish maintained a fleet of galleys on the Mississippi for military purposes, and the United States built a number of gunboats during the Revolution and the following years. Gunboats and keelboats were used against the Indians on the western rivers as late as the War of 1812, and thereafter steamboats took their place.

Robert Fulton's *Clermont* was launched on the Hudson in 1807, and a battle royal was soon initiated between river and coastwise steamboats and sailing packets, with the former destined to eventual victory. Fulton's boats were built with deep hulls, and it was not until Henry Shreve's *Washington* was launched in 1816, with its boilers on the deck, that a craft was found suitable for western river navigation.

By 1850 the railroads had begun to sap the trade from the steamboats and canals. The tremendous volume of transport needed during the Civil War gave the steamboats a new lease on life. Barges came into general use for carrying heavy goods and were towed by steamboats. During this second great age of the steamboat, lines of packets were formed and schedules became more honored by observance. By the 1880's, however, the competition of the railroads parallel to the rivers was rapidly displacing steamboats.

RIVERS. *See articles under specific name of river.*

RIVERS IN AMERICAN DIPLOMACY. The Mississippi Question was one of the first major diplomatic issues. Spain denied that the United States (after 1783) extended to that river, at least below the Ohio River, and refused to admit any right of the citizens of the United States to free navigation of the stream through Spanish territory. Spain's distresses in Europe impelled it in 1795 to concede the imperfect American claims in Pinckney's Treaty. Spain in 1802 revoked the right of deposit established in this treaty, and the consequent alarm of American western citizens, who feared French control of the river, led to the procurement of all Louisiana.

The Rio Grande was claimed, somewhat expansively, by the Republic of Texas as its boundary with Mexico (*see* Mexico, Relations with). The Columbia River played an epochal part in the Pacific Northwest (*see* Oregon Question). The British government contended that the Columbia River from its intersection with 49° north latitude to the sea was the boundary of British North America, but in the Oregon Treaty of 1846 it accepted the line of 49° to the sea, with the provision that British subjects trading with the Hudson's Bay Company were to enjoy the free navigation of the river.

RIVER TOWNS OF CONNECTICUT. Windsor, Hartford, and Wethersfield, together with Springfield until it was discovered that it lay in Massachusetts. The settlement of these towns represented a group migration from the Massachusetts Bay Colony, from the summer of 1635 through 1636. Practically the whole town of Dorchester removed to Windsor; Newtown (Cambridge) removed to Hartford; and Watertown removed to Wethersfield.

A group of Puritan "lords and gentlemen" in England put forth a claim through a deed or patent allegedly derived from Robert Rich, Earl of Warwick (*see* Connecticut, Old Patent of), and in the summer of 1635 sent over John Winthrop as governor, with orders to build a fort at Saybrook. The settlers made no objection to the fort but ejected a party that attempted to take up land where Windsor was to be founded.

Possession of the land was followed by a federated form of government under a general court, the first meeting of which, on Apr. 26, 1636, was presided over by Roger Ludlow, the leader of the migration. The river towns evolved into the commonwealth of Connecticut.

***RIVINGTON'S GAZETTE*.** Published in New York City from 1773 to 1783; one of the more important colonial newspapers. James Rivington named his paper *Rivington's New-*

York Gazetteer; or the Connecticut, New Jersey, Hudson's River, and Quebec Weekly Advertiser, but this was soon shortened. It strongly favored the Tories during the Revolution. Armed patriots destroyed Rivington's press in November 1775 and forced suspension of the paper until October 1777, when it was revived under the patronage of the king's government. The *Gazette* was useful to the English. Rivington remained in New York City after the war, trying to continue publication, but the last issue printed was Dec. 31, 1783. Thereafter he continued business only as a bookseller.

ROAD IMPROVEMENT MOVEMENT. The first national legislation to improve roads, the Federal Aid Road Act, was passed in 1916. Initially, road construction funds came from poll taxes, general property taxes, and bond issues. Automobile license fees and gasoline taxes eventually came to supply the bulk of funds. By act of Congress, 1921, the federal government began giving, through the U.S. Bureau of Public Roads, financial assistance to states for construction of highways. By 1937 more than $1 billion had been distributed. The Interstate Highway Act of 1956 authorized construction of a 42,500-mile nationwide network of limited-access highways. By 1981 over 40,000 miles had been completed.

ROADS. As early as 1639 the Massachusetts Bay Colony court ordered that roads be laid out. The New England township system also specified the construction of roads. Even the Virginia statutes at large for the period 1619–60 stated that highways should be laid out. But little was done toward actual improvement in overland transportation.

The inauguration of stagecoach passenger and mail service and the introduction of the Conestoga wagon freight business during the 18th century provided the necessary inducement for road improvements. Land companies also had their effect on early road building; under the auspices of the Ohio and Transylvania companies the first trails were blazed into the Old Northwest and Kentucky. In March 1775, under the direction of the Transylvania Company, Daniel Boone and his party left the Watauga to cut a wagon trail into Kentucky (the Wilderness Road).

The new U.S. government took steps toward the construction of roads under federal auspices. In the Enabling Act of 1802 provision was made for an East-West road that, when extended, was destined to become the National (or Cumberland) Road.

Early roads, except for some in the larger cities, were generally dirt roads. On occasion little more was done than to clear a roadway. Corduroy roads made of logs laid transversely or plank roads were sometimes employed, but such roads presented a very rough surface, did not last long, and were rarely well maintained. During 1792–94 the Philadelphia and Lancaster Turn Pike Company constructed a sixty-six-mile macadamized toll road.

The immense flow of vehicles over the Lancaster Turnpike demonstrated the volume of traffic that would accompany well-built roads through populous areas. In 1806 the decision was reached to expand the Cumberland Road into a national toll road from the Atlantic Ocean to St. Louis, and construction was begun two years later. It never got beyond Vandalia, Ill., which it reached in 1852. As far as Terre Haute, Ind., the road was superbly built, but from that point westward it remained a dirt road. Ultimately the National Road was completely abandoned by Congress and was ceded to the states through which it passed.

With the discovery of gold in California in 1848 migration westward took on greater magnitude. Before long, some trails were converted into passable roadways, and as early as the autumn of 1849 teamsters, using horses, mules, or oxen, were able to haul supplies to some of the mining towns, although the routes were far from smooth.

Shortly after the settlers and miners came to the Pacific coast they began to clamor for an immediate, safe, and practical overland route to serve until a railroad could be built. In 1857 the Overland California Mail Bill became law. This measure empowered the postmaster general to provide a liberal subsidy to a firm that he might select "for the conveyance of the entire letter mail from . . . the Mississippi River . . . to San Francisco." The route became known as the Butterfield, or Southern Overland, route. In 1860 this stage road was extended northward from San Francisco to Portland, Oreg. The outbreak of the Civil War necessitated switching into northern territory, and thereafter it followed in a general way the old Oregon-California Trail.

With the advent of the automobile after 1900, interest increased in view of the inadequacy of state and county roads. As late as 1908 there was not a single mile of concrete highway and only 650 miles of macadam. In 1912 a plan was proposed for the construction of a direct transcontinental road to be called the Lincoln Highway. This enterprise was not completed until 1930, but it marked the beginning of widespread federal and state aid for highway construction. (*See* Road Improvement Movement.)

By the late 1960's serious questions were being raised about the national devotion to highways. Accelerated highway building seemed to increase rather than relieve congestion. Annual highway fatalities moved above the 50,000 mark in the 1970's. The automobile was recognized as the primary source of air pollution, and by the mid-1970's a more balanced approach to transport planning was being counseled. The highway bill of 1978 earmarked almost 30 percent of transportation funding for mass transit programs.

ROADS, MILITARY. From the colonial period to the beginning of the 20th century, many notable achievements were made in the construction of military roads: the Braddock Road, cut through the wilderness to Fort Duquesne in 1755; George Rogers Clark's road to Kaskaskia and Vincennes, built in 1778 and 1779; the long stretches of corduroy road laid by the engineer battalion in the Civil War; the blazing of jungle trails in the Philippines during the insurrection of 1899–1902; and the road constructed in 1916 by engineers of the punitive expedition to Mexico, which made possible the first motorized movement by an army.

The first conflict to require substantial hard-surfaced roads, World War I witnessed the debut of army engineer units trained especially for roadbuilding. In World War II, U.S. Army engineers completed more than 10,000 miles of road in the southwest Pacific area alone. The Ledo Road, linking India with China, and the Alcan, or Alaska, Highway, stretching across northwestern Canada and southeastern Alaska, rank among the greatest military roads of all times. The largest engineering project undertaken by the U.S. armed forces in a foreign country involved reconstruction of highways in the Republic of Vietnam.

ROAD SURVEY BILL. *See* **Survey Act of 1824.**

ROAD WORKING DAYS. Until the development of modern highways, rural Americans often paid road taxes by working on road construction jobs. Road working days were usually fixed when farm work was not pressing and were more often occasions for socializing than for hard work.

ROANOKE, SETTLEMENT AT. *See* **Raleigh's Patent and First Colony; Raleigh's Lost Colony.**

ROANOKE ISLAND, CAPTURE OF. On Feb. 8, 1862, Union Gen. A. E. Burnside overran the weakly fortified Confederate positions on Roanoke Island, N.C. The capture enabled Union troops to occupy Elizabeth City.

ROBBER BARONS. Widely used to describe big businessmen of the late 19th century. It implies that entrepreneurial policies and practices were characterized by a ruthless and unscrupulous drive for monopoly and economic power. "Robber barons" became a permanent part of the historian's vocabulary in 1934 in Matthew Josephson's *The Robber Barons: The Great American Capitalists, 1861–1901.* After World War II historians and economists attempted to evaluate the late-19th-century businessman in a more objective way. Rather than concentrate on the destructive characteristics of the moguls, the revisionists examined their creative contributions.

ROBINSON, FORT. Located on White River at the Red Cloud agency in Nebraska; built by the army in 1874 and used, for the most part, to maintain order among the Sioux warriors recently settled on the Red Cloud agency.

ROBINSON-PATMAN ACT (Federal Anti-Price Discrimination Act). Passed by Congress in 1936 primarily to protect independent merchants against the preferential wholesale prices of chain stores. The act, sponsored by Sen. Joseph T. Robinson and Rep. Wright Patman, prohibited discrimination in price or terms of sale between purchases of commodities of like grade or quality, prohibited questionable brokerage or advertising allowances, and attempted to prevent unreasonably low prices to destroy competition.

ROCHESTER (N.Y.). Important center for precision instrument design and optical work; third largest city in New York. In 1980 its population totaled 241,741 and it was the center for a metropolitan area of 970,313 people. Located on both sides of the Genesee River, near Lake Ontario. A small French fort stood on the site in the early 18th century, and a few people settled in the area later in the century. The modern town dates from about 1812, when it was established under the leadership of Nathaniel Rochester. It became a village in 1817, and was incorporated as a city in 1834.

The chief influence on the growth of Rochester was the Erie Canal, which went through it. Rochester tailoring companies are nationally famous for men's suits and overcoats. George Eastman made his city a photographic capital.

Rochester's educational center includes the University of Rochester, the Eastman School of Music, and a number of other colleges. Cultural resources include a widely respected symphony orchestra, and the leading U.S. museum collection of photographs and photographic materials.

ROCHESTER RAPPINGS. Spiritual manifestations reported by Margaret and Kate Fox, who claimed that rappings on walls and furniture had occurred at their home in Hydesville, N.Y., in 1848 and at their sister's home in Rochester in 1849. Credence given to these claims marked the beginning of spiritualism in the United States. The sisters subsequently confessed to faking.

ROCKEFELLER FOUNDATION. Established by John D. Rockefeller and chartered on May 14, 1913, in New York State, "to promote the well-being of mankind throughout the world." By the end of 1981 the foundation had paid out close to $1.54 billion.

During its first fifteen years the foundation devoted itself almost entirely to public health and the medical sciences. By 1929 the work of the foundation included support of the natural sciences, the social sciences, and the arts and humanities.

About 1952 the foundation began to reduce the support of science and scholarship in the West to help the developing world. Pioneering programs in agriculture, initiated in Mexico in 1943, led to greater production of food crops in many countries. These as well as population stabilization efforts and strengthening of selected universities to serve the needs of their regions, were being continued in the 1970's with a greater emphasis on their economic and social consequences.

ROCKEFELLER UNIVERSITY. Founded in 1901 by John D. Rockefeller as the Rockefeller Institute for Medical Research. Simon Flexner was elected director in 1902. In 1904 temporary laboratories were set up in New York City. Soon the institute acquired the site overlooking the East River. The first permanent buildings were dedicated in 1906. Flexner regarded investigation of disease as the institute's central purpose. He was succeeded in 1935 by Herbert Spencer Gasser, and under his direction greater emphasis was placed on study of the cell.

A special committee chaired by Detlev W. Bronk recommended that the institute include graduate education. A reorganization was effected, and Bronk was named the first president of the institute. In 1954 it became part of the University of the State of New York, with authority to grant the degrees of doctor of philosophy and doctor of medical science. The name "The Rockefeller University" was adopted in 1965.

ROCKETS. Hale 16-pound rockets were adopted by the U.S. Army in the 1840's. Rockets were adapted to whaling in the mid-1850's and also were used for signal flares and shore-to-ship lifeline rescue. On Nov. 9, 1918, Robert H. Goddard of Clark University demonstrated a small solid-fuel rocket, the genesis of the hand-held antitank "bazooka." Goddard tested the world's first liquid-fuel rocket (gasoline and liquid oxygen) at Auburn, Mass., on Mar. 16, 1926.

The German V-2 liquid-fuel ballistic rocket was a major innovation during World War II. German engineers with their designs of V-2 rockets were transferred to the United States in 1945. The Soviet Union began intensive rocket development in 1947. By 1954 the feasibility of thermonuclear warheads and Soviet rocket progress had created a crisis, and President Eisenhower approved an urgent ICBM development program. In 1955 he also approved the first U.S. space satellite program. On Oct. 4, 1957, the Soviet Sputnik I, the first man-made earth satellite, was launched. It triggered a race in space achievement.

In the 1960's thousands of silo-sited or nuclear-submarine-based missiles as well as observation satellites and tactical missiles became a reality. The civilian National Aeronautics and Space Administration (NASA) undertook, after Oct. 1, 1958, the development of rocket carriers for space missions. After the Soviet Union placed the first man in earth orbit in 1961, President John F. Kennedy called for a manned lunar landing by 1970. The Apollo program was started, and the Apollo 8 crew were the first men to fly around the moon (Christmas eve, 1968); the first men landed on the moon in July 1969. By the early 1980's planetary probes had been launched towards Mars, Jupiter, Venus, Mercury, and Saturn. The first reusable manned spacecraft, which completed its first trip into orbit in April 1981.

ROCK ISLAND BRIDGE CASE (1857). A suit for damages that grew out of the collision, in 1856, of the steamer *Effie Afton* with the newly erected railroad bridge connecting Rock Island, Ill., and Davenport, Iowa. The jury failed to reach a verdict.

ROCKY MOUNTAIN FUR COMPANY. A partnership of fur traders established in 1822. It opened up the wealthiest fur sections of the West. It was the first to depend primarily on directly trapping beaver rather than by trading with Indians. The company was dissolved in 1834.

ROCKY MOUNTAINS. A vast mountain system that extends from northern Mexico to northwest Alaska, for more than 3,000 miles, and forms the continental divide. Spanish pioneers in Mexico were the first white men to see the Rocky Mountains. Francisco Vásquez de Coronado, in 1540, was the first to see the U.S. Rockies. The presence of precious metals induced the earliest exploration and first settlements, by Spaniards in the southern portion. Trappers and traders became the mountain men, the real trailblazers of the central Rockies. Their pack trains and wagons broke the practicable trails into and over the mountains.

The original French claim to the drainage area of the Mississippi River indicated the crest of the Rockies as the western boundary of the Louisiana Purchase (1803). Meriwether Lewis and William Clark, in the Northwest (1804–06), and Zebulon M. Pike, in the Southwest (1806–07), led the first official expeditions into the Rocky Mountains. Gold discoveries during the 1850's and 1860's led to permanent settlement in the Rockies. The federal government has established four national parks in the Rocky Mountain region.

RODEOS (roundups). Cattle and horses on the open range drifted over vast areas, necessitating periodic roundups. During the 1870's and 1880's as many as 200 to 300 riders would gather. Cattle would be rounded up for shipping to market, calves would be branded, and strays returned to their proper ranges. The roundups brought together socially men leading isolated lives, and they eventually became festivals of a kind. Buffalo Bill's Wild West Show proved the popular interest in a dramatization of the skills involved in roundup (or rodeo) work. Around 1900 Booger Red and other cowpunchers put on bronco-riding exhibitions and charged admission. In 1908 the Millers of Oklahoma put their 101 Ranch exhibition on the road. Rodeos now draw millions of spectators annually to watch steer and bronco riding, wild-cow milking, bulldogging, and calf-roping.

RODNEY'S RIDE. After Richard Henry Lee's resolution for independence was debated in the Continental Congress on July 1, 1776, a preliminary vote was taken. One of Delaware's delegates, Thomas McKean, voted for the resolution; George Read voted against it; Cæsar Rodney was absent on official business in Delaware. McKean sent a messenger to Rodney urging him to hurry to Philadelphia. Rodney mounted a fleet horse and, changing horses at intervals, covered some eighty miles by the morning of July 2. He arrived in Philadelphia in time to join McKean in casting Delaware's vote for independence when the formal vote of Congress was taken.

RODRÍGUEZ-CHAMUSCADO EXPEDITION. In 1580, Augustin Rodríguez, a Franciscan lay brother, obtained permission to cross the Rio Grande and found a mission among the Pueblo. Two Franciscan priests, Francisco López and Juan de Santa Maria, joined him, accompanied by nine soldiers and sixteen Mexican Indian converts under Francisco Sánchez Chamuscado. Leaving Santa Bárbara (Chihuahua) on June 5, 1581, they entered a region near present-day Bernalillo (N.Mex.). The friars visited Indian towns, while Chamuscado led his men westward. Juan de Santa Maria was murdered by hostile Indians. Chamuscado ordered a return to Mexico, leaving the friars without military protection. Rodríguez and López were soon after killed by Indians.

ROGERENES (Rogerene Baptists or Rogerene Quakers). A nonconformist sect founded about 1675–77 by John Rogers. Among the Rogerenes' beliefs, based on a literal interpretation of the New Testament, were separation of church and state, nonviolence, baptism of believers only, no medical care for the sick, and no observance of a special Sabbath. However, until about 1705 they did observe a seventh-day Sabbath on Saturday, working on Sunday. This and other practices brought upon them fines, whippings, imprisonment, and confiscation of property by Connecticut authorities. Their retaliation consisted of entering churches of their persecutors and making protests. Under the Connecticut constitution of 1818, separation of church and state (and thus religious liberty) was established. Because their purpose was realized and because of westward emigration, the sect dwindled in influence and numbers.

ROGERS' RANGERS. The most colorful corps in the British-American army during the French and Indian War, commanded by Maj. Robert Rogers. The 600 frontiersmen conducted scores of raids. On Jan. 21, 1757, the rangers escaped extermination by a superior French force between Crown Point and Ticonderoga, N.Y. At the Battle of Snowshoes, on Mar. 13, 1758, Rogers lost 130 of his 180 men. In 1760 Rogers journeyed to Detroit, where he received the surrender of the French posts.

ROMAN CATHOLIC CHURCH. *See* **Catholicism.**

ROORBACK. Any defamatory falsehood or forgery published for political effect. Originated in the presidential campaign of 1844, when, to injure the candidacy of James K. Polk, the *Ithaca* (N.Y.) *Chronicle* published a defamatory falsehood said to be from Baron von Roorback's *Tour Through the Western and Southern States in 1836.*

ROOSEVELT COROLLARY. A policy of action by the United States in certain unstable Latin-American republics to forestall intervention by European creditor nations. Such action was allegedly a responsibility derived from the Monroe Doctrine. The corollary to the doctrine was first set forth by President Theodore Roosevelt in May 1904. In 1905 the corollary was invoked to justify U.S. establishment of customs control over the Dominican Republic. Financial controls and interventions during the administrations of William Howard Taft and Woodrow Wilson were based on it.

ROOT ARBITRATION TREATIES. A series of twenty-five bilateral pacts concluded in 1908 and 1909 while Elihu Root was U.S. secretary of state. The pacts remained the chief bipartite nonaggression treaties to which the United States was a signatory until 1928. In general, the Root treaties obligated the parties to arbitrate differences of a legal nature and those relating to the interpretation of a treaty. They generally provided that controversies should be submitted to a tribunal of the Permanent Court of Arbitration.

"ROOT, HOG OR DIE." An expression originating in the mid-19th century or earlier, based on the hog's habit of digging for food. It means "Work or starve."

ROOT MISSION TO RUSSIA. In April 1917 President Woodrow Wilson appointed a mission to go to Russia, chiefly to ascertain whether Russia's active participation in World War I could be continued after the March revolution. The mission was headed by Elihu Root. It concluded that the most effective action the United States could take was to spend a large sum on propaganda to offset the strenuous German efforts to stimulate Russian peace sentiment. The mission's recommendations were practically ignored.

ROOT-TAKAHIRA AGREEMENT (Nov. 30, 1908). U.S. Secretary of State Elihu Root and the Japanese ambassador, Baron Kogoro Takahira, declared the wish of the two governments to develop their commerce in the Pacific; their intention to defend the Open Door policy and the independence and integrity of China; their resolve to respect each other's territorial possessions in the Pacific; and their willingness to communicate with each other if these principles were threatened.

ROSALIE, FORT. Erected by the French under Jean Baptiste Le Moyne, Sieur de Bienville, in 1716, on the site of present-day Natchez, Miss. In 1722 it became the administrative center of the civil and military district of Natchez. The original fort was destroyed by the Indians during the Natchez massacre in 1729, but a new fort was constructed soon thereafter. It remained an important French post until 1763. In 1764 British troops occupied and repaired the fort, which was renamed Fort Panmure.

ROSEBUD INDIAN RESERVATION. Established in 1890 in southwestern South Dakota. Home of the Brulé Sioux. In the 1970's it became a center of activity of the American Indian Movement. The reservation's population in 1972 was 7,488.

ROSE INTRIGUE. An 1808 conspiracy involving British minister Sir George Rose and some New England Federalists. Strong pro-British sentiment had developed in New England as a result of President Thomas Jefferson's embargo on British goods and his Francophile tendencies. Rose entered into an intrigue with Timothy Pickering and the Essex Junto to secure repeal of the embargo and to ensure peaceful relations between the United States and Great Britain. The embargo remained in effect until March 1809.

ROSENBERG CASE. On Apr. 5, 1951, Julius Rosenberg and his wife Ethel were sentenced to death for furnishing vital information on the atomic bomb to Soviet agents. Evidence was supplied by Ethel Rosenberg's brother, David Greenglass, who was himself sentenced to fifteen years' imprisonment. Morton Sobel was sentenced to thirty years. Despite worldwide appeals to President Eisenhower to commute their sentences, the Rosenbergs were executed at Sing Sing Prison on June 19, 1953. Controversy continues over the case.

ROSS, FORT. A Russian trading post established in 1812 on the Pacific Coast, about fifty miles north of present San Francisco. The post was not a success, although it remained in Russian hands for nearly thirty years. In 1841, the post was sold to John Sutter.

ROSS, IN RE, 140 U.S. 453 (1891). A case in which the Supreme Court clearly stated three principles related to imperial growth: the United States has jurisdiction over aliens on U.S. ships in foreign waters; the United States may exercise extraterritorial rights under treaty provisions; and constitutional guarantees do not extend beyond U.S. shores.

ROTARY INTERNATIONAL. An organization of service clubs, made up of business and professional men. Each Rotary club is a separate unit, bound together by an international affiliation of clubs. Rotary received its name from its early practice of rotating the meeting-place from one man's business to another. The organization was founded in Chicago by Paul P. Harris in 1905.

ROTATION IN OFFICE. The theory of public employment that maintains short terms of office and frequent changes in personnel are desirable. It is based on the premise that long continuance in office leads incumbents to become arrogant and unmindful of their obligations as public servants.

ROUGH RIDERS. Officially the First U.S. Cavalry Volunteers. It was recruited for the Spanish-American War. Leonard Wood, of the Army Medical Corps, left his post as White House physician to accept the colonelcy; Theodore Roosevelt became lieutenant colonel. The Rough Riders had a brief training period at San Antonio in the spring of 1898 and then entrained for Tampa, Fla. There the horses were abandoned, and in the chaos of embarkation, only slightly more than half the regiment left Florida. The fragment that did reach Cuba lived up to its advance publicity. From Las Guásimas to San Juan Hill, the Rough Riders' attacks were often unconventional but usually successful.

ROUNDUP. *See* **Rodeos.**

ROUSE'S POINT BOUNDARY CONTROVERSY. A dispute between the United States and Great Britain over the New York–Canadian border. The Proclamation of 1763 set the forty-fifth parallel as the boundary. A survey in 1766 determined where the line should run. Gov. William Tryon of New York had it surveyed in 1771–74. The Definitive Treaty of Peace, 1783, retained the forty-fifth parallel as the United States–Canadian boundary between the Connecticut and St. Lawrence rivers. A new survey made in 1818–19 found that the true parallel was far south of Tryon's line. The Webster-Ashburton Treaty, 1842, retained the line of 1774.

ROUSSEAU'S RAID (July 10–22, 1864). To assist Union Gen. William Tecumseh Sherman's advance to Atlanta, Gen. L. H. Rousseau assembled 2,500 cavalry and destroyed the West Point and Montgomery Railroad in Alabama from a point opposite Tuskegee to Opelika.

ROYAL COLONIES. Except for Connecticut and Rhode Island, the thirteen colonies began as chartered, or proprietary, provinces—and the other two shortly came to be chartered as well. Governmental problems eventually caused most proprietors to surrender their charters to the crown. The new form of government was known as a royal province, and it began first in Virginia in 1624. At the Revolution only Connecticut, Maryland, Pennsylvania, and Rhode Island retained the earlier forms of government.

No legal limitations stood between the king and the people. The king was represented by a royal governor appointed and removable at will, whose authority rested upon a commission and a set of instructions. The governor was assisted by a council of twelve, appointed by the crown.

Each colony had an elected assembly that had complete control over lawmaking, taxation, and public revenues (subject to royal veto). Most royal govenors were dependent upon the assembly for financial support. This opened the way for popular control of government by the assemblies, and by 1764 the royal provinces were, essentially, self-governing commonwealths. By act of Parliament in 1767 the royal governors and other civil officers were made independent of the assemblies.

Judges were appointed by the crown, usually for life terms. After 1760 they could be removed by the crown just as governors could, and under the act of 1767 they were no longer paid by the assemblies.

ROYAL DISALLOWANCE. The Privy Council had the power to approve or disallow colonial legislation. By 1730 this power applied to all colonies except Connecticut and Rhode Island. Although only a very small percentage of colonial laws were disallowed, the practice when used helped to tighten the mercantilist vise on the colonies.

RUBBER INDUSTRY. The first record of rubber in the United States is a patent for gum elastic varnish for footwear issued to Jacob F. Hummel in 1813. By 1833 America's pioneering rubber factory had been established at Roxbury, Mass. By 1840 the infant industry had experienced a speculative boom and a disastrous collapse. The primary cause for the loss of confidence was the fact that rubber products had not proved reliable (they softened in the heat and stiffened in the cold).

The basic technical problem of early rubber manufacture was solved by Charles Goodyear's discovery in 1839, at Woburn, Mass., of the vulcanization process, which gives rubber a durable quality. The "elastic metal" would soon prove indispensable to the automobile industry. Long before the end of the 19th century, America's consumption of raw rubber had grown twentyfold. Wherever elastic, shock-absorbing, water-resistant, insulating, and air- and steamtight properties were required, vulcanized rubber was used. Most of the raw rubber came from Brazil.

Between 1849 and 1900 the industry's output of manufactured goods—chiefly footwear, mechanicals (for use with machinery), proofed and elastic goods, surgical goods, bicycle tires, and toys—increased from $3 million to $53 million. By the eve of World War I production had come to be dominated by the "Big Four": Goodyear Tire and Rubber Company, United States Rubber Company, B. F. Goodrich Company, and Firestone Tire and Rubber Company. A fifth giant was added to the "Big Four" in 1915 when the General Tire and Rubber Corporation was formed at Akron. Partly to be close to the carriage-making industry, the center of rubber manufacture had shifted from New England to Akron, Ohio.

The most dramatic phase of the industry's growth followed the introduction of the internal combustion engine, cheap petroleum, and the pneumatic tire. Between 1900 and 1920, consumption of raw rubber increased tenfold. By 1940 the United States was consuming 726,000 tons out of a world total of 1,243,000 tons of crude rubber.

The industry began a search for rubber substitutes in the 1920's. A few hundred tons a year of synthetic rubber were produced. As Japan seized the rubber lands of Southeast Asia during World War II, U.S. production of synthetic rubber was increased a hundredfold. About three-fourths of America's needs were being met by synthetic rubber. By 1979, of a world output of 9.3 million metric tons, the United States produced about 30 percent. That year, the United States had consumed only 732,000 metric tons of a world output of approximately 3.9 million tons of natural rubber.

RUBÍ'S TOUR. The Marqués de Rubí was commissioned to inspect the northern military posts of New Spain. During 1766–68, he traversed the northern border, from Texas to Sonora, and found it subject to chronic Indian attack. Rubí suggested a realignment of the presidios, abandonment of Louisiana border posts, and an exterminatory war against the eastern Apache. Most of his recommendations were adopted in 1772.

RUFFNER PAMPHLET. An 1847 publication that included the antislavery address before the Franklin Literary Society given by Henry Ruffner, president of Washington College, in Lexington, Va. Ruffner contended that slavery retarded the industrial and commercial development of the South.

RULE OF REASON. A judicial principle applicable to the interpretation of legislation whose purpose and intent are open to serious question. Application has been largely restricted to interpretation of the Sherman Antitrust Act of 1890. The Supreme Court in 1911 enunciated the rule of reason and used it to conclude that the statutory prohibition of "all combinations in restraint of trade" actually meant "all unreasonable combinations in restraint of trade."

RULE OF THE WAR OF 1756. In 1756, while France and Great Britain were at war, the French opened their colonial trade to the neutral Dutch. Great Britain notified the Netherlands that Great Britain would not allow neutrals to engage in time of war in a trade from which they were excluded in time of peace (the Rule of the War of 1756).

During the Napoleonic Wars, the neutral United States endeavored to circumvent the rule by taking French colonial goods to American ports and reexporting them as American goods. In the case of the *Polly* in 1802 it was held that this circuitous voyage did not constitute a violation of the rule. In the case of the *Essex* (1805) the British prize courts decided that payment of drawbacks on colonial goods reexported by way of neutral countries nullified the neutralization of those goods and subjected them to capture.

RULES OF THE HOUSE. The Constitution gives the House of Representatives the right to make its own rules, which are adopted anew by each Congress, usually with few or no changes. Legislative reorganization acts such as those of 1946 and 1970 made extensive changes. The 1970 act allowed radio and television coverage of committee hearings, required that committee roll-call votes be made public, and strengthened the rights of the minority party. The 1936 compilation of the House rules and precedents filled eleven volumes and was still being used in the mid-1970's.

RULES OF WAR. *See* **War, Laws of.**

RUMBOUT'S PATENT. A tract of 85,000 acres in Dutchess County near present-day Fishkill, N.Y. License to purchase from the Indians was given to Francis Rumbout and Gulian Verplanck by Gov. Thomas Dongan in 1682.

"RUM, ROMANISM AND REBELLION." *See* **Burchard Incident.**

RUM ROW. Soon after the beginning of Prohibition in 1919, liquor began to be smuggled into the United States by sea. In the South, rumrunners operated directly from the West Indies; but farther north large vessels waited outside the three-mile jurisdictional limit for smaller, faster boats to transship the cargo and make a run for shore. This chain of loitering vessels came to be known as Rum Row.

RUMSEY'S STEAMBOAT. On Dec. 3, 1787, James Rumsey exhibited at Shepherdstown (then in Virginia, now in West Virginia) a boat propelled by water forced out through the stern by a pump operated by a steam engine. The boat moved against the current at the rate of three miles per hour. Being without funds for further experiments, Rumsey went to Philadelphia, where the Rumseian Society was formed. In May 1788 it provided funds for him to go to England to carry on his steamboat experiments. He died Dec. 20, 1792, a few days before public trial of his boat. The following February his boat made a successful trip on the Thames at four knots. In 1785 Rumsey had invented a watertube boiler of the type employed in the 20th century.

RUM TRADE. Began in the New England colonies in the 17th century. Since the lumber and fishing industries of New England were unable to find large enough markets in England, the colonies were forced to seek a market in the West Indies. There, lumber and fish were paid for by molasses. The manufacture of rum from the molasses became one of the earliest of the New England industries. In 1731, 1.25 million gallons of rum were manufactured in Boston from molasses.

The Yankee traders saw that the most pressing need of the

island planters was for slaves. Adventurous New England sea captains became familiar with the African Gold Coast, engaging in triangular trade: molasses to New England, rum to Africa, slaves to the West Indies.

These northern colonies soon came into conflict with Great Britain. Yankee traders found it more profitable to deal with the French, Dutch, and Spanish islands than with the English. In France, legislation forebade importation of rum from its colonies, so most of the molasses supply of the French islands was available to the Yankees. The British Parliament attempted, through the Molasses Act of 1733, to limit this trade by imposing high duties on non-British molasses imported into New England. Smuggling reached an enormous scale.

In 1763 the conflict over molasses imports reached crisis proportions, largely because of the war between Great Britain and France. Parliament passed the Sugar Act and attempted to enforce it by the use of the British navy, customs commissioners, and writs of assistance, actions that are recognized as causes of the American Revolution.

RUNIC INSCRIPTIONS. *See* **Kensington Stone; Norsemen in America.**

RURAL DEVELOPMENT. President Theodore Roosevelt appointed the Country Life Commission in 1908 to report on country life. When the report was submitted to Congress in 1909, the president stressed the failure of country life to satisfy the "higher social and intellectual aspirations of country people." This and superior urban business opportunities were contributing to movement to the cities.

Congress expressed concern about the "overbalance of population in industrial centers" in the National Industrial Recovery Act of June 16, 1933, which authorized $25 million to bring about a better balance. The balance of farm to nonfarm population in rural areas began to shift after 1940. By 1980 farm people constituted slightly more than 10 percent of rural population. As a result, during the 1960's and 1970's government programs shifted emphasis from individual farmers to rural communities.

In 1954, President Eisenhower asked that particular attention be given to low-income farmers. A report was prepared on the development of agriculture's human resources. The report recommended improving prospects in part-time farming and nonfarm work, increasing training in trades and industrial skills, improving the health of poor farm families, and encouraging decentralization of the defense industry to provide more jobs in rural areas.

The Economic Opportunity Act of 1964 provided for a job corps, community action programs, and loans to low-income rural families. The 1965 Housing and Urban Development Act authorized the Farmers Home Administration to make loans for purchase of previously occupied homes and farms or for improvements in farm buildings. The rural development program was limited by substantial cuts in funds for domestic programs during 1964 and 1965.

Congress, in the Agricultural Act of 1970, committed itself to achieving a sound balance between rural and urban America and to giving the highest priority to the revitalization and development of rural areas. Funding was substantially increased.

The Rural Development Act of 1972 expanded the basic statutory missions of the Department of Agriculture to include rural development and empowered the secretary of agriculture to coordinate the rural development work. The act established, for the first time, a framework for the organization of a comprehensive program of rural development, but by the mid-1970's, neither adequate leadership nor funds had been provided to fully implement the law. A subsequent bill, the Rural Development Policy and Coordination Act of 1979, provided for the formulation of an overall rural development strategy by September 1982.

RURAL ELECTRIFICATION ADMINISTRATION. *See* **New Deal.**

RURAL FREE DELIVERY (RFD). A service designed to bring mail directly to rural people; initiated in 1896. Rep. Thomas E. Watson of Georgia was the author of the first free rural delivery legislation, enacted in 1893 and providing $10,000 for an experiment. Although Watson's bill was enacted in 1893, service was not started until 1896 because of the opposition of Postmaster General Wilson S. Bissell. Postmaster General William L. Wilson, who had succeeded Bissell, decided to experiment. Eighty-two pioneer routes were started by spring 1897, scattered through twenty-eight states and the territory of Arizona. In testing the cost, Wilson laid the pioneer routes in areas having a sparse population and no roads as well as in more favorable areas. He estimated that extending the service nationally would cost between $40 million and $50 million.

After Wilson left office, Perry S. Heath, the first assistant postmaster general, and August W. Machen, superintendent of free delivery, began active promotion of RFD. Securing an appropriation of $150,000 in 1898, they announced that any group of farmers wanting a mail route need only petition their congressman for it. Congressmen were overwhelmed with petitions they could not resist. In 1902 there were not more than 8,000 routes. Three years later there were 32,000. In 1981 there were 36,635 rural routes extending 2.3 million miles.

RURAL HEALTH. Since public health prior to the 20th century was conceived largely in terms of epidemic diseases, the health of the rural population of America, which faced neither large-scale sanitary problems nor major epidemics, received little consideration until municipalities began promoting health activities beyond their boundaries for their own protection. In the late 19th century New York City secured the passage of state laws requiring residents and communities in the Croton watershed to make adequate provision for sewage disposal. The city also began sending its milk inspectors out to farms and dairies.

At about the same time state health departments were set

up. Although responsible for the state as a whole, their chief concern was with towns and incorporated areas.

The Rockefeller Foundation in 1910 allocated $1 million to eradicate hookworm in the rural South. County health departments began springing up throughout the region. Meanwhile, the U.S. Public Health Service became interested in pellagra and typhoid fever, plaguing many rural areas. The Public Health Service played an important role in building county health units.

The Social Security Act in 1935 opened up a new era in public health. Relatively large sums of money were made available for grants-in-aid to promote health work at state and local levels. By 1942 about 75 percent of the American population was served by health agencies. The majority of the remaining 25 percent lived in small communities and rural areas. By 1959 the mortality rates and life-expectancy statistics showed virtually no difference between the general level of health in urban and rural areas. By the early 1980's rural isolation had disappeared in large measure; most of the rural population no longer lived on farms.

RURAL LIFE, CHANGES IN. Rural life meant farm life in colonial America, and for more than a hundred years after the Declaration of Independence. The first settlers were forced into a subsistence level of farming, but their food problems were solved within a few years through the adoption of Indian practices and European methods. By the mid-1600's farming methods and farm life were generally fixed.

The self-sufficient farm family in the North produced its own food, clothing, house furnishings, and farm implements, and most of its other needs. Water usually had to be hauled by hand from a spring or well. Women were responsible for the gardens, and many had to help in the fields. Fireplaces were used for heating and cooking, and chimney flues were the chief source of ventilation in the winter. There was no indoor plumbing, only outdoor privies. Added to the back-breaking drudgery were the isolation and lack of adequate communication and social life. After the home, the rural school and church played the largest social role. The school year was frequently limited to four or five months. Families were close knit; in addition to the common sharing of work, the limited social life was shared.

Farm life in the South differed from the North because of the development of staple cash crops, large plantations, and slave labor. The plantation system dominated the economy, and the planters dominated the colonial governments. Yet the small farmers far outnumbered the planters, and their economy was largely one of self-sufficiency. Living in a spacious house and served by slaves, the planter did not depend on the community for his social life or the education of his children. His slaves lived in cabins with lean-to roofs.

After the Civil War many of the plantations were broken up, but the planters who retained their old estates and newcomers devised a new labor system that gave the former slave no more economic security than he had had in slavery. The sharecropper was hired before the spring planting season to grow cotton or tobacco. The whole crop was taken by the landlord, who assessed its value, deducted what the cropper owed him from his share, and paid for the remainder, if any.

The rise of manufacturing with its resulting concentration of population in towns and cities after 1820, providing a market for farmers, brought about important changes. With cash for their crops, farmers could buy clothes, tools, and furniture they had formerly made. Sons and daughters began migrating to mill towns. Those who remained behind began developing a taste for urban standards of living. By 1900 the movement of farm people to towns and cities led to the fear that rural culture would be lost. (*See* Rural Development.)

Commercialization of agriculture contributed to improvement of rural life. Organizations such as the National Grange and the National Farmers' Alliance and Industrial Union and agricultural fairs improved agriculture and expanded social life and education of farm people. The nationwide organization of the Federal-State Cooperative Extension Service (1914), with country agricultural agents and 4-H clubs, contributed to social life and education.

In the 1930's many new government programs were instituted that, with modifications, remained in effect in the 1970's—price support and adjustment, rehabilitation and development, and rural electrification. The widespread extension of rural electrification after 1935 made it possible for the farm family to enjoy many of the conveniences of the city and to automate some farm operations. The great wartime demand for food and the doubling of farm prices led to the adoption of many technological improvements that revolutionized agricultural production. The result of this increase in the efficiency of farm production was a great decline in the farm population.

Some rural residents not engaged in farming supply goods, services, machinery, feed, fuel, fertilizer, financing, or labor to farmers. Others perform activities related to farming but generally no longer done on farms, such as hatching chickens, making butter and cheese, and slaughtering poultry and meat animals.

Rural residents receive less than their national share of income, health services, education, and government services for the disadvantaged. In the late 1970's the incidence of poverty in most rural counties, those not in commuting distance of urban employment centers, was almost double that in nonrural counties.

RURAL POST ROADS ACT (1916). Passed to provide aid to states by the federal government in the construction of rural post roads. The measure carried an appropriation of $5 million, to be increased annually until, for the fifth year, the amount available would be $25 million. (*See also* Rural Free Delivery.)

RUSH-BAGOT AGREEMENT. *See* **Great Lakes Disarmament Agreement.**

RUSSELL, MAJORS, AND WADDELL. William H. Russell of Missouri and Alexander Majors of Kentucky formed a partnership on Dec. 28, 1854, and procured a contract for carrying government supplies from Fort Leavenworth, Kans., to the Plains and mountain army posts, using about

350 wagons. They took in another partner, William B. Waddell, and in 1858 carried 16 million pounds of government freight and used 4,000 men, 3,500 wagons, 1,000 mules, and 40,000 oxen. They later absorbed the Leavenworth and Pikes Peak Express and Hockaday and Liggett's stage line, reorganized as the Central Overland California and Pikes Peak Express. In 1860–61 they operated the Pony Express. Their losses were so heavy that they were forced out of business.

RUSSELL SAGE FOUNDATION. One of America's oldest general-purpose foundations, established in 1907 by Margaret Olivia Sage (Mrs. Russell Sage) for the improvement of social and living conditions in the United States. She provided a principal of $10 million and later added another $5 million. In its early years the foundation sought to investigate the causes of adverse social conditions. It helped effect change in child welfare, working conditions for women, education, and social work. In later years the foundation funded social science research relating to policy formation in social change, law, education, human resources, mass media, and biology.

RUSSIA, U.S. RELATIONS WITH. Ever-shifting European alliances found Russia a British ally during the American Revolution, although Russia did not send troops to aid England. Catherine II promised to withhold recognition so long as England considered the Americans rebels. Russia did not extend diplomatic recognition to the newly formed American nation. In the interim, a backdoor diplomacy existed from December 1780, when Francis Dana was sent to Russia. While the American minister's mission was unsuccessful insofar as recognition was concerned, his efforts brought an increase in Russo-American trade.

When the Franco-Russian alliance (1807) brought war with England, Alexander I formally recognized the United States (1809). Russia's expression of friendship was as much tied to its aims in North America as to problems with England. The czar's ukase of 1821 warning all foreign vessels to stay outside 100 miles of the Pacific coast north of the fifty-first parallel and Russia's claim of exclusive trading right in the North Pacific that proved to be most significant. American warnings culminated in the Monroe Doctrine (1823), indirectly aimed at Russia. A treaty was signed (Apr. 17, 1824) limiting Russian influence to north of 54°40′.

Russia refused to be drawn into European schemes to meddle in the American Civil War. Hints of a willingness to sell Alaska were eagerly accepted and the agreement was signed on Mar. 30, 1867.

After the Boxer Rebellion in China, Russia continued to occupy Manchuria; in the ensuing war the United States sided with Japan. At the Portsmouth (N.H.) Conference, Theodore Roosevelt hammered out an agreement (Sept. 5, 1905) unfavorable to Russia.

With the fall of the Romanov dynasty in 1917, the United States saw its entry into World War I as a struggle against autocracy. The provisional government that replaced the czarist regime was immediately recognized and $325 million was allocated to help Russia stay in the fight. The weakness of the government and increased German pressure on the battlefield set the stage for the Bolshevik seizure of power.

The Bolsheviks announced a "decree for peace," declaring the U.S. role in the war as nothing more than a means of exploiting the American arms industry. The desire of the Allies to keep Russia in the war was paramount, and little could be done to stop the propaganda except to withhold acceptance of the Soviet government. This led to the situation of Allied embassies in a state none of them recognized. The signing of the Treaty of Brest-Litovsk (Mar. 3, 1918) with Germany set into motion reactions felt around the world.

In 1933 the realization of the potential of the Russian market, a new American administration, and a more Western-oriented Soviet foreign policy finally brought American recognition (Nov. 16). By the end of 1939 the Soviet agreements with Nazi Germany, the attack on Finland, and the seizure of the Baltic states again strained relations. There were hopes in 1940 that the Soviet Union would break away from Germany, but the signing of the Russo-Japanese Neutrality Pact (Apr. 13, 1941) and the Soviet rejection of U.S. warnings of an imminent German invasion negated any hope of improving relations at the moment.

When Germany invaded the Soviet Union on June 22, 1941, the United States gave support on a cash-and-carry basis. By the end of the war, $9.5 billion in aid had been furnished. Stalin received Franklin D. Roosevelt's assurances that a second front would be opened in France before the end of 1942. By August it had become obvious that the promise could not be kept, and Winston Churchill's explanation of the facts to Stalin laid seeds of distrust of Western intentions that have remained to this day.

The creation of the United Nations saw the United States and the Soviet Union seated as permanent members of the Security Council. In drafting the UN Charter, the Soviet Union sponsored a position of unanimity on all decisions. This position has brought the two nations into a number of confrontations.

Stalin's reiteration in February 1946 that war was inevitable so long as capitalism existed left little doubt that a state of ideological warfare existed. Conferences in Europe did settle most of the issues relating to the former Axis powers, but the Soviet Union established its own recovery program in Eastern Europe. In effect, the result was the formulation of two spheres separated by "an iron curtain."

The next decade saw the failure of the Soviet attempt to blockade Berlin (1948), the creation of the North Atlantic Treaty Organization (NATO, 1949), and the belated counter-coalition, the Warsaw Pact (1955). In 1950 the attack on South Korea led the United States into armed conflict with Soviet-supported powers. Even so, it was Soviet initiatives in 1951 that helped bring about an armistice in 1953. A period of lessening tension followed Stalin's death (Mar. 5, 1953) that culminated in Nikita S. Khrushchev's visit to the United States in September 1959. The spirit of the Camp David summit meeting was destroyed eight months later when the Soviet Union shot down an American U-2 spyplane (May 1, 1960) near Sverdlovsk in central Russia. When Khrushchev demanded an apology from the United States, President Dwight D. Eisenhower refused and the summit conference just beginning in Paris to settle the Berlin question collapsed. The Vienna conference (June 1961) between Khrushchev and President John F. Kennedy also failed to reach agreement on Berlin. In retaliation, the Communists cut off east-west access in the city by constructing the Berlin Wall. Although this led to a confrontation, it did not reach the magnitude of the Cuban missile crisis. (*See* Cuban Missile Crisis.)

The following year (Aug. 5, 1963) a nuclear test ban treaty was signed and much of the antagonism of the preceding decade abated. Since 1963 the Soviet Union and the United States have taken a number of steps toward rapprochement. The signing of the Strategic Arms Limitation Treaty in 1972 and the Helsinki agreement on European security and cooperation in 1975 seemed to augur well for the future of U.S.-Soviet ties, but in the late 1970's the relations between the two superpowers began to worsen and by 1982 had reached a new nadir. It was the result of harsh Soviet treatment of dissidents, Soviet invasion of Afghanistan in 1979 and an indirect involvement in Africa and Central America, suspension of U.S. grain sales to the Soviet Union in January 1980 (lifted in April 1981), and crackdown on the Polish independent trade unions in December 1981. (*See also* Cold War.)

RUSSIAN-AMERICAN COMPANY. *See* **Russian Claims.**

RUSSIAN CLAIMS. The creation of the Russian-American Company in 1799, with Aleksandr A. Baranov as manager, was the first occasion for Russia to define its claims to North American lands. These extended from the fifty-fifth parallel to the Bering Strait. The problem of securing supplies for the Alaskan establishments caused the Russians to look toward the Spanish settlements far to the South. Finally, it was decided to plant a colony on the California coast above the Spanish settlements. Fort Ross, begun in 1809 at Bodega Bay in what is now Marin County, was intended as a supply station for meat and grain. In 1841 the Fort Ross settlement was abandoned.

In 1821, on renewing the charter of the company, the Russian government declared its authority would extend as far down the coast as 51° north latitude. Great Britain and the United States succeeded in limiting Russia's exclusive claim to the southern line of 54°40′ north latitude. The British-Russian treaty of 1825 also delimited the Russian claims from the coast inland, thus establishing the basis for the boundary of Alaska as granted by Russia to the United States in 1867.

RUSSIAN FLEETS, VISIT OF. In September 1863, during the Civil War, six Russian warships arrived at New York and, in October, six more warships anchored off San Francisco. The northern states warmly welcomed both fleets, believing that they came as possible allies. On Apr. 25, 1864, both fleets were ordered home; they had not come as northern allies, but, fearing war with Great Britain and probable blockade, had been ordered to neutral ports.

RUSSIAN RECOGNITION. *See* **Soviet Union, Recognition of.**

RUSTLERS. *See* **Cattle Rustlers.**

RUSTLER WAR. A conflict centering in Johnson County, Wyo. Finding it impossible to stop cattle stealing or to secure convictions in the local courts, cattlemen brought in a group of hired gunmen from Texas in April 1892 and organized an expedition to hunt down and kill some seventy men who they claimed were known to be cattle thieves. The expedition first visited the K. C. Ranch, where two alleged thieves were killed. The cattlemen soon met resistance and took refuge in the T A Ranch, where they were besieged for three days by a force of some 200 men. President Benjamin Harrison sent U.S. troops from Fort McKinney to the scene. The cattlemen gladly surrendered; they were delivered over to the civil courts for trial, but were eventually acquitted. (*See also* Cattle Associations.)

RUTGERS UNIVERSITY. Chartered as Queens College in 1766; began operations in New Brunswick, N.J., in 1771. It owed its origin to the Dutch Reformed church, with which it remained affiliated for nearly a century. In 1825 its name was changed to Rutgers College to honor a benefactor, Col. Henry Rutgers of New York City. It became the land-grant college of New Jersey in 1864; in 1945 it achieved legal recognition as the state university, and in 1956 management was vested in a board of governors, a majority of whose members were state appointees. A Newark campus was established in 1946 and a Camden campus in 1952.

***RUTGERS* V. *WADDINGTON*.** *See* **Trespass Act.**

RYSWICK, PEACE OF (Sept. 30, 1697). This treaty ended King William's War between the English and French and the Iroquois and French. By its provisions all conquests made during the war were to be mutually restored. The ownership of the lands lying around Hudson Bay was to be decided by an Anglo-French joint commission; such a commission met in 1699 but failed to reach a decision.

SABBATH-DAY HOUSES. Small buildings where members of a congregation who had come from a distance would take refuge between the morning and afternoon church services. Common in colonial New England; revived in the West where, at least in Texas, they lasted into the 20th century.

SABINE CROSSROADS, BATTLE AT (Apr. 8, 1864). During his raid up the Red River Valley in Louisiana, in the spring of 1864, Union Gen. Nathaniel P. Banks marched overland toward Shreveport. He was met and defeated by Confederate forces under Gen. Richard Taylor in the Battle of Sabine Crossroads, about forty miles south of Shreveport.

SABINE RIVER BOUNDARY. *See* **Louisiana Purchase, Boundaries of; Neutral Ground.**

SABLE ISLAND (Canada). About 150 miles east of Halifax, Nova Scotia; of interest to colonial New Englanders and

Acadians as a place to obtain walrus, seal, wild horses, and black foxes. Attempts to make settlements there failed.

SABOTAGE. A term that first came into general use in the United States early in the 20th century, borrowed from the syndicalist movement of southern Europe and introduced by the Industrial Workers of the World (IWW) to describe one phase of its fundamental strategy of direct action. Sabotage tactics represented a means of harassing the avowed class enemy—capitalist employers—without forgoing wages.

The practice of sabotage involves injury, in some way, of the employer's property, as by surreptitiously mixing a little sand in lubricating oil; the aim is invariably vexation and pecuniary loss to the employer. The general terrorist strategy of the IWW made little appeal to American labor.

SACCO-VANZETTI CASE. Nicola Sacco, a skilled shoeworker, and Bartolomeo Vanzetti, a fish peddler, were arrested on May 5, 1920, for a payroll holdup and murder in South Braintree, Mass.; a jury, sitting under Judge Webster Thayer, found the men guilty on July 14, 1921. Complex motions relating to old and new evidence, and to the conduct of the trial, were argued before Thayer, the Massachusetts supreme court, and a special advisory commission serving the governor; the accused were executed on Aug. 23, 1927.

Throughout the trial the men were disadvantaged by their declared philosophical anarchism, their status as unassimilated alien workers, and the general "Red baiting" atmosphere of the times. Scholarly legal opinion overwhelmingly holds that the case is an extremely serious instance of failure in the administration of justice. A proclamation by the governor of Massachusetts in 1977 stated that Sacco and Vanzetti had not been treated justly.

SACHEM. The native federation of the Iroquois rooted its political organization in a council of fifty sachems, who represented their respective tribes in deliberations of "peace." The sachem offices were named, and to some degree ranked, and passed to the office-holder through the female line. The component tribes of the Iroquois league were allowed varying numbers of sachems: the Onondaga, although smallest in numbers, had fourteen sachems; the Mohawk and Oneida, nine each; the Cayuga, ten; and the Seneca, eight. The great council deliberated on all external affairs affecting the tribes.

Among the various Algonkin-speakers of New England, chieftainships were designated as sachemships if a federation was involved, both as a result of Iroquois influence and as a defense against the imperialistic Iriquois. First used in England about 1625 in the sense of any Indian chief, the term was adopted to refer to the ranked officialdom of the Tammany Hall organization in New York City.

SACKETS HARBOR, OPERATIONS AT. In the War of 1812 the importance of naval control of Lake Ontario made the Sackets Harbor naval base, in northern New York, a hive of shipbuilding activity. The base survived two British attacks, the first, July 19, 1812, being limited to an ineffective two-hour naval bombardment. The second, May 27–29, 1813, was a combined operation by Commodore James Lucas Yeo's squadron and more than 1,000 British regulars and Indians under Gen. George Prevost.

SACKVILLE, FORT. *See* **Knox, Fort (Ind.).**

SACKVILLE-WEST INCIDENT. In September 1888 Lord Lionel Sackville-West, the British minister at Washington, D.C., received a letter saying that the writer was a naturalized Englishman who desired advice as to how he should vote. The letter was actually written by George Osgoodby, a fruit grower and a Republican. The minister replied that he thought the incumbent, President Grover Cleveland, more friendly to England than Benjamin Harrison. The Republicans published the correspondence, expecting that the incident would turn the Irish vote away from Cleveland. Sackville-West's explanations only made matters worse, and he was dismissed by Cleveland.

SACO BAY, SETTLEMENT OF. In 1630 Richard Vines, by a grant made by the Council for New England (Feb. 23, 1629) to John Oldham and himself, began a settlement on the south side of the Saco River, in southwestern Maine; in 1631 Thomas Lewis and Richard Bonython, by a grant of the same date, began a settlement north of the river. Farther east Thomas Cammock, in 1633, took possession of 1,500 acres granted Nov. 1, 1631; and beyond that was the land granted to Robert Trelawney and Moses Goodyear (Dec. 1, 1631), of which John Winter took possession in 1632. Andrew Alger, who came with his brother Arthur and Winter, settled Dunstan (the village of Scarboro), claiming under Indian deed. All the Saco Bay settlements were abandoned during King Philip's War in 1675.

SACRAMENTO (Calif.). Located at the point where the American River enters the Sacramento River. John Sutter established his "fort" there in 1839; the gold rush to the area boomed the population. In 1854 Sacramento was made the state capital. It was the original base of the men who built the Central Pacific Railroad, and it became the principal repair center for the Southern Pacific Railroad. The city is connected with San Francisco Bay by the Sacramento River, and by a "Deepwater Ship Canal"; the riverfront has levees and docks from which local products are shipped. Sacramento is the center of a large fruit-growing district, and has an important meat-packing industry. Two air bases are nearby. Population in 1980 was 275,741.

SACRAMENTO, BATTLE OF (Feb. 28, 1847). During the Mexican War, the Mexicans under Gen. José A. Heredia erected fortifications on the Sacramento River. Although superior in number, they were routed with heavy losses by Col. Alexander W. Doniphan's Missouri mounted volunteers.

SADDLEBAG BANKS. Under the free bank laws passed by middle western states in 1851–53, anyone purchasing state bonds up to a given amount might start a bank and issue notes in a commensurate sum. Smart promoters "organized" many such banks, giving as their location remote, unknown (sometimes imaginary) hamlets, the object being to keep the notes in circulation and make it difficult for any noteholder to collect their face value from the "bank of issue."

SADDLES. Saddles have been of three principal types: (1) the English saddle—a flat tree with low pommel and cantle, introduced into America during the early colonial period; (2) the army saddle—first fully developed during the Civil War and, in its initial form (the McClellan), an English tree modified by heightening pommel and cantle, dishing the seat, and lengthening the stirrup leathers; and (3) the stock saddle —interchangeably termed "cowboy," "cow," "Mexican," "western," and "range" saddle.

SAFETY FIRST MOVEMENT. Massachusetts pioneered, in 1877, in the establishment of factory safeguards and, in 1886, in the reporting of accidents. Voluntary efforts of leading corporations, particularly those of the steel industry in 1907, accelerated the efforts to reduce accidents. The greatest incentive came with the passage of thirty workmen's compensation laws, 1910–15. The Iron and Steel Engineers' Association in 1913 organized the National Safety Council, which carries on research in the development and standardization of safety methods and devices.

SAFETY FUND SYSTEM. A plan incorporated in the Safety Fund Act (1829) for the mutual insurance of the debts of New York State banks. Each bank incorporated in the state was required to contribute each year to the safety fund an amount equal to one-half of 1 percent of its capital stock, until such contributions aggregated 3 percent of its capital stock. Whenever a bank failed, after its assets had been fully utilized, this fund was to be used in settlement of its debts. Should this safety fund be drained by a succession of bank failures, the state comptroller was empowered to levy on the banks for additional contributions. As experience accumulated, the need became clear for giving the holders of the notes of a defunct bank priority in the distribution of its assets.

SAGADAHOC. The alternative ancient Indian name for the Kennebec region and river in Maine, especially that stretch of the river from Merrymeeting Bay south to the Atlantic Ocean. (*See also* Kennebec River Settlements.)

SAGE PLAINS. California-bound emigrants turning south at Fort Boise, Idaho, to the Malheur and Pitt rivers, encountered the Sage Plains on the way to Sacramento. After 1844 it was given the name of Death Route.

SAG HARBOR (N.Y.). A village at the eastern end of Long Island, one of the leading whaling ports up to the mid-19th century. During the Revolution it was, for a time, used by the British as a depot for military stores. In the spring of 1777 the Americans, angered by the destruction of Danbury, Conn., raided Sag Harbor: Lt. Col. Return Jonathan Meigs with 234 men in whale boats crossed Long Island Sound from Connecticut on May 23, destroyed the military supplies, and took ninety prisoners. The last whaling ship sailed out of the harbor in 1871. Sag Harbor then developed as a yachting and resort community.

SAGINAW, FORT (Mich.). In 1822 soldiers from Fort Howard on the Fox River in Wisconsin, led by Maj. Daniel Baker, established Fort Saginaw on the west bank of the Saginaw River. After an epidemic of fever the following summer, the fort was abandoned. A small community around the abandoned fort became the city of Saginaw.

***SAGINAW*'S GIG, CRUISE OF THE.** Undertaken to rescue the officers and seamen of the U.S.S. *Saginaw,* wrecked by a reef near Ocean Island in the mid-Pacific on Oct. 29, 1870. A party of five men volunteered to navigate the ship's gig to Honolulu and secure relief; they left Ocean Island on Nov. 18 and arrived on Dec. 19 off the island of Kauai, one of the Hawaiian group. They had lost their oars in a storm, and in attempting to land without them they upset the gig; Coxswain William Halford alone survived to reach the shore with the commander's dispatches. The Hawaiian government immediately sent a steamer, the *Kilauea,* with supplies to rescue the men left on Ocean Island. The *Saginaw*'s gig is now permanently on display at the U.S. Naval Academy.

SAGINAW TREATY (Sept. 24, 1819). Gov. Lewis Cass of the Michigan Territory negotiated a treaty with the Chippewa at Saginaw, in which a large land cession, located chiefly in Michigan Territory, was obtained from the tribe. Sixteen reservations were established for the tribe within the lands ceded. The United States agreed to pay annually $1,000 in silver; to convert all previously promised annuities into payments in silver; and to aid the Indians in agriculture, in return for the privilege of building roads through their country.

SAILOR'S CREEK, BATTLES AT (Apr. 6, 1865). After the Battle of Five Forks, Gen. Robert E. Lee abandoned Petersburg and Richmond, Va., eluded Union Gen. George Meade at Jetersville, and fled westward. Near Sailor's Creek, Union pursuers overtook Gen. John Brown Gordon, Gen. Richard H. Anderson, and Gen. Richard Stoddert Ewell, protecting the trains. Union Gen. Andrew A. Humphreys' II Corps drove Gordon toward the Appomattox River. Union Gen. Philip H. Sheridan's cavalry corps struck from the south and demolished Anderson on the road from Rice's Station. In the center at Sailor's Creek, Union Gen. Horatio G. Wright's VI Corps charged Ewell's ridge position, outflanking left and rear from the northeast as Sheridan sent cavalry against its right. Ewell surrendered. Anderson's and Gordon's reduced commands escaped toward Appomattox.

SAILORS' SNUG HARBOR. A home for retired seamen on Staten Island, N.Y., created by the estate of Robert R. Randall, a New York merchant, in 1801; its beginning was delayed by litigation until 1831. Randall's farm in mid-Manhattan was the nucleus of the trust, and ground rents from the land have made it one of the world's wealthiest charities. Sailors' Snug Harbor moved in 1976 to a new facility, which accommodates 120 retired mariners, at Sea Level, N.C.

ST. ALBANS RAID (Oct. 19, 1864). A raid into Vermont from Canada, led by Confederate Lt. Bennett H. Young, with about thirty men not in uniform, in retaliation for the depredations of Union Gen. Philip H. Sheridan in Virginia (*see* Shenandoah Campaign). Three banks were looted of over $200,000, but an attempt to burn the town failed; one citizen was killed. The raiders escaped into Canada.

ST. ANTHONY, FALLS OF. A waterfall in the Mississippi River in Minneapolis, named after St. Anthony of Padua by Father Louis Hennepin, the first white man known to arrive there (1680). Attracted by their water power, settlements grew up on either side of the falls, St. Anthony and Minneapolis, beginning in 1837 and uniting under the latter name in 1872. Lumber and flour industries were developed. Threatened with destruction in 1869, the falls were saved with emergency cofferdams; later a great dike and apron preserved the falls permanently.

ST. ANTOINE, FORT. A French military post built (1686) by Nicholas Perrot on the southeast shore of Lake Pepin and named for Antoine Le Febvre de La Barre, governor of New France. There, in May 1689, Perrot staged a ceremony of annexation in which he took possession for France of the upper Mississippi and the Sioux country. The fort was abandoned in 1690.

ST. AUGUSTINE (Fla.). The oldest settlement in North America, founded by Pedro Menéndez de Avilés in September 1565 near the site of Juan Ponce de León's landing in 1513. Menéndez hoped to make St. Augustine the center of an ambitious expansion, but it remained the garrisoned settlement, generally poor and needy, from which radiated mission enterprise to the south, west, and north. As the colonial rivalry of England and Spain developed, it was attacked by British corsairs and by expeditions from the southern colonies. It was defended by Castillo de San Marcos (Fort Marion), begun in 1672 and completed in 1756.

When Florida was ceded to the British in 1763 St. Augustine was the government seat of East Florida, and it remained so after restoration to Spain in 1783. It was one of three Spanish forts in East Florida when the United States acquired the region (*see* Adams-Onís Treaty).

During early territorial days, St. Augustine was connected with Pensacola by the new national road and developed a reputation as the leading winter resort, a position it held until the opening of south Florida. During the 1820's the orange industry became important, but the great freeze of 1835 and the purple scale sent the groves farther south; the second Seminole War (1835–43) frightened away many settlers; and between 1830 and 1839 the population dropped nearly 50 percent. In 1937 historical restoration was begun, and the city once again became a popular resort area. The city's population in 1980 was 11,985.

SAINT-CASTIN'S TRADING HOUSE. Situated at the French fort at Pentegoet, the present town of Castine, Maine. Jean-Vincent d'Abbadie de Saint-Castin, gentleman adventurer, came to the Penobscot Bay region about 1667 and amassed a fortune in trade, particularly after Fort Pentegoet came into his hands (1676). The seizure of his trading house in 1688 by New England Gov. Edmund Andros was believed by the people of New England to have been the cause of King William's War (1689).

ST. CHARLES, FORT (Minn.). Established in 1732 by Pierre Gaultier de Varennes, Sieur de La Vérendrye, on the southern shore of the Northwest Angle inlet of the Lake of the Woods, it served as a base for explorations of the Northwest; it was used for more than two decades.

ST. CLAIR, FORT (Ohio). A stockade for storage purposes, built by American troops (1791–92) during the expeditions against the northwestern Indians, a mile north of the present village of Eaton. It constituted a lesser link in the chain of communications erected between Fort Washington (Cincinnati), built 1789, and the Lake Erie region.

SAINT CLAIR'S DEFEAT (Nov. 4, 1791). To subdue the Indians on the Ohio frontier, President George Washington obtained from Congress authority to raise an army of 3,000 men and appointed Arthur Saint Clair, governor of the Northwest Territory, to command it.

Plans were made to have the army in readiness at Fort Washington (Cincinnati) by July 10, but October had arrived before as many as 2,000 men could be assembled, and their quality was deplorable; the supplies provided were poor; the commissary department was both corrupt and incompetent; and the commander was sick and incapable. The army stumbled northward through the Ohio wilderness; about sunrise of Nov. 4 it was furiously assailed in its camp at present-day Fort Recovery, and after two hours the survivors fled to Fort Jefferson, twenty-two miles away.

ST. CROIX. A river forming the southern section of the Maine–New Brunswick boundary. After the extinction of the short-lived St. Croix Island settlement, the precise location of the St. Croix River was lost sight of; two sizable rivers, known locally as the Schoodiac and the Magaguadavic, were alternately claimed by 17th- and 18th-century mapmakers as the true St. Croix. The British and American negotiators of the preliminary articles of the Definitive Treaty of Peace (1783) used John Mitchell's map of North America (1755), which designates the Magaguadavic as the St. Croix, and the treaty placed the boundary of the United States and Canada at that river. After the treaty was ratified, the two governments disputed the identity of the St. Croix. Some 2 million acres of coastal land were involved. By Jay's Treaty of 1794 the identity of the true St. Croix River was left to a mixed commission, which in 1798 fixed on the Schoodiac.

ST. CROIX SETTLEMENT. In March 1604 Pierre du Guast, Sieur de Monts, sailed with two vessels to Acadia to establish a fur-trading monopoly and settlements. With Samuel de Champlain and more than 100 settlers, de Monts "entered a river almost half a league in breadth at its mouth" and came to an island, which he and Champlain named St. Croix Island. During the winter, scurvy developed among the settlers, and thirty-five perished; the survivors moved in the summer of 1605 to Port Royal (now Annapolis Royal, Nova Scotia). While de Monts returned to France, Champlain explored the Atlantic coast. Two years later the remaining settlers returned to France, and their buildings were completely destroyed in 1613 by the English from Virginia.

SAINT-DENIS' EXPEDITION. In 1714 Louis Juchereau de Saint-Denis led a French expedition from the present Natchitoches, La., into Spanish Texas, which resulted in establishing a profitable trade between the French post of Natchitoches, of which he was commandant 1722–44, and the Spanish territory to the southwest.

STE. GENEVIEVE LEAD MINING DISTRICT. The exclusive right of lead mining and fur trading in the Missouri area was given to financier John Law of the Company of the Indies, who commissioned Philip Renault in 1723 as director general of mining operations. A rapid development followed, and lead was carried to Kaskaskia (Ill.) to be shipped down the Mississippi. By 1735 Ste. Genevieve was established above Kaskaskia in what is now eastern Missouri and became the shipping point for the lead mining district of the hills a few miles to its west. With the building of a railroad connecting the "lead belt" with St. Louis, Ste. Genevieve lost its lead shipping industry; Flat River became the most important of a number of mining towns in St. François County, one of the greatest lead-producing areas in the world. (*See also* Lead Industry.)

ST. FRANCIS, ROGERS' EXPEDITION AGAINST. Having been driven from their New England lands by the British, the Indians of the St. Francis mission village in Quebec (mostly Abnaki) made several retaliatory raids into New England during the early years of the French and Indian War. Because of attacks against Gen. Jeffrey Amherst's army at Crown Point, Maj. Robert Rogers left Crown Point on Sept. 13, 1759, with seventeen whaleboats and a force of rangers. They arrived in Missisquoi Bay, at the northern end of Lake Champlain, on Sept. 23, hid the boats, and set off through the forest for St. Francis. On Sept. 25 the boats were discovered and burned by the French and Indians. On Oct. 5 the detachment sighted St. Francis; and at dawn on Oct. 6 Rogers attacked, burning the town, killing 200 Indians, releasing 5 whites who had been held captive, and keeping 5 Indian children as prisoners. An hour after the attack he commenced his homeward trip. On Oct. 14, near Lake Memphremagog, the detachment ran short of food; Rogers divided his force into small companies, so that they might live off the country, and ordered them to rendezvous at the mouth of the Ammonoosuc. On Oct. 16 one of the companies was ambushed by French and Indians and destroyed. Several days later Rogers arrived at the mouth of the lower Ammonoosuc to find that Amherst had sent provisions as requested, but that they had been taken away a few hours before his arrival. He built a raft and on Oct. 27 set off down the Connecticut to get supplies for his starving men; on Oct. 31 he arrived at the fort at Number 4 (Charlestown, N.H.). He returned at once to the mouth of the Ammonoosuc with food for the survivors of the expedition. Of the 142 men who attacked St. Francis, 93 returned.

ST. FRANÇOIS XAVIER, FORT. *See* **Green Bay.**

ST. GERMAIN-EN-LAYE, TREATY OF (Mar. 29, 1632). The general settlement between England and France that followed the Treaty of Susa (1629). Its American section provided for the return by England to France of all places occupied by England in New France, Acadia, and Canada.

ST. IGNACE MISSION. Father Claude Dablon, superior of the Jesuit missions of the Upper Lakes, began on Mackinac Island in the winter of 1670–71 a mission named for St. Ignatius. In the spring of 1671 Father Jacques Marquette arrived with his Huron flock from the upper end of Lake Superior; the mission was soon, very probably in 1672, being conducted on the mainland promontory north of the Straits of Mackinac with Father Marquette in charge. There, surrounded by a fort, a French village, a village of Huron, and one of the Ottawa, it was maintained until 1706. Reopened about 1712, it was moved, probably in 1741, to a site on the mainland south of the island, where Jesuits were in charge until 1765.

ST. JOHN, FORT (La.). Also called Fort St. Jean, Fort San Juan, and Spanish Fort; built by France on Lake Pontchartrain, to protect New Orleans from the rear. It was occasionally garrisoned by Spaniards between 1776 and 1803; held by American troops during the British attack on New Orleans in 1814–15; occupied by Confederate forces at the outbreak of the Civil War; and since abandoned.

ST. JOHNS, SIEGE OF (1775). The newly fortified position of St. Johns, on the Richelieu River in Quebec, was the first important obstacle encountered in the American invasion of Canada in 1775. After two initial movements made against it by Gen. Philip Schuyler had failed, the post was invested on Sept. 17 and bombardment began on Sept. 25. On Nov. 2, the commander of the fort signed a capitulation providing for the surrender of his force with the honors of war to Gen. Richard Montgomery (who had replaced Schuyler on Sept. 13). With this surrender, the way to Montreal and Quebec was open.

ST. JOSEPH (Mo.). City on the Missouri River, founded by Joseph Robidoux as a trading post called Blacksnake Hills in 1826. The town was platted in 1843 and incorporated in 1845; the city was incorporated in 1851. Economic growth, particularly in grain and livestock, was stimulated by the outfitting of Oregon and California immigrants and furnishing of supplies to military posts. In 1859 the Hannibal and Saint Joseph Railroad was completed; in 1860 St. Joseph became the eastern terminus of the Pony Express. The construction of stockyards, the completion of the Missouri River bridge, and the extension of the railroad accelerated St. Joseph's growth as a grain and cattle mart. By the 20th century it was a major transportation terminus; meat-packing, flour milling, and cereal manufacture became important industries. The population had reached 76,691 by 1980.

ST. JOSEPH, FORT (Mich.). Near present-day Niles; one of the earliest centers of French activity in the Great Lakes area. Precise dates for the establishment of both the fort and St. Joseph Mission are unknown; it is known that Father Claude Jean Allouez labored and died (1689) at the mission. The fort was garrisoned by French soldiers from about 1700 to 1760; a British troop then took it over, but it was destroyed in 1763 during Pontiac's War. In July and August 1779 a British force occupied it for several weeks; in December 1780 a band of raiders from Cahokia (Illinois) plundered it. In January 1781 the Spanish governor at St. Louis dispatched a small army against Fort St. Joseph; the fort was occupied on Feb. 12, and for twenty-four hours the flag of Spain flew over it. The Spanish army then retired.

ST. LAWRENCE RIVER. The largest river in North America, it was explored by Jacques Cartier in 1535 as far as the island of Montreal, Cartier having discovered the Gulf of St. Lawrence in his voyage of the previous year. With its tributary, the Ottawa River, and with the Great Lakes, it formed the main water thoroughfare from the sea to the interior of the continent during the 17th and 18th centuries.

During the 19th century shipping developed on the Great Lakes; canals were built and channels deepened in the connecting rivers and the St. Lawrence; and grain and other commodities were brought down to Montreal from both the Canadian and American West for shipment to Europe and elsewhere. Ocean vessels of limited draft made their way up from the sea through the St. Lawrence and the Great Lakes. (*See also* St. Lawrence Seaway.)

ST. LAWRENCE SEAWAY (1959). Stretching 2,342 miles from Lake Superior to the Atlantic, the St. Lawrence Seaway opens the industrial and agricultural heart of North America to deep-draft ocean vessels via three series of locks, at Sault Ste. Marie, at the Welland Canal, and at the head of the St. Lawrence River. The waterway accommodates vessels 730 feet long, with a 76-foot beam and a draft of 26 feet.

The Wiley-Dondero Act of 1954 authorized the St. Lawrence Seaway Development Corporation to construct that part of the seaway in the United States, and construction began under agreement with Canada. The seaway is operated by entities of two governments—each with authority to negotiate with the other; its operating expenses are met from tolls assessed on shippers.

ST.-LÔ (France). A town of about 10,000 people during World War II, and the capital of the Department of Manche in Normandy, St.-Lô marked the culminating act of the Battle of the Hedgerows and the opening event of American troops breaking out of Normandy. Gen. Omar N. Bradley's First U.S. Army started the battle in the Cotentin peninsula on July 4, 1944, and closed it on July 18 with the capture of St.-Lô. Bradley, on July 25, launched Operation Cobra with the support of heavy bombers and broke the German defenses in Normandy.

ST. LOUIS (Mo.). Founded on the west bank of the Mississippi River Feb. 15, 1764, by Pierre Laclède Ligueste. St. Louis early became the center of the fur trade and the starting point of most expeditions and trails into the western country. Soon after the purchase of Louisiana from France by the United States in 1803, the town was overrun by a large number of speculative New Englanders, who launched a very considerable boom. In course of time a new town grew up beside the old one.

In 1808 St. Louis was incorporated as a town, and in 1822 it was chartered as a city. A new city charter in 1876 separated the city from St. Louis County; the city is still independent from any of the Missouri counties.

With the advent of the steamboat St. Louis rose very rapidly in both population and wealth. Iron, lead, and zinc from nearby mines; bituminous coal from across the river; farm and garden products from rich valleys nearby; hemp, cotton, and sugar from the South—all contributed to make St. Louis the great river capital of the West and, with the coming of the railroads in the 1850's, the second largest railroad center of the United States.

The Louisiana Purchase Exposition, held in St. Louis in 1904, highlighted the city's rapid industrial expansion. Although slowed by the depression of the 1930's, the expansion was revived during World War II, particularly in aircraft production. Other major manufacturers include chemicals, electrical equipment, and iron and steel products.

St. Louis is also a noted cultural center, housing one of the oldest symphony orchestras in the nation, the Missouri Botanical Garden, the St. Louis Municipal Theater, and many institutions of higher learning. The city's population in 1980 was 453,085.

ST. LOUIS, BRITISH ATTACK ON (May 26, 1780). Instructions had been received by British Gen. Frederick Haldimand, governor of Canada, to reduce the Spanish and Illinois posts. In consequence he organized a force of about 1,200 for a surprise attack on St. Louis. The garrison had some warning the previous day that they would be attacked, and the village was successfully defended by 50 soldiers and 280 townsmen, with a loss of 104 men. The attackers were so badly demoralized and delayed that the whole expedition collapsed and the British menace from the West was entirely removed.

ST. LOUIS, FORT (Ill.). Intended as the principal defense of the colony established by Robert Cavelier, Sieur de La Salle. It was built on Starved Rock in the winter of 1682–83 by La Salle and Henry de Tonti. Nine years later it was abandoned in favor of Fort Pimitoui (now Peoria), but Tonti and others used it intermittently for a decade.

ST. LOUIS, FORT (Tex.). At first, a temporary fort built by Robert Cavelier, Sieur de La Salle, in 1685 near the shore of Matagorda Bay and the mouth of a river that he called La Vaca (since identified as Garcitas Creek) to house his colony of more than 180 persons; later, it was moved five or six miles up the river where a permanent fort was built. La Salle set out from Fort St. Louis on his three futile attempts between 1685 and 1687 to reach the Mississippi. Sickness, accidents, and desertions reduced the number of colonists until there were only about thirty left in 1687; most of those remaining were massacred by Indians early in 1689. Alonso de León, governor of Coahuila, found the ruins of the fort; in 1690 he burned the buildings that remained.

SAINT LOUIS MISSOURI FUR COMPANY. This company, not to be confused with the Missouri Fur Company, was formally organized through articles of copartnership dated Mar. 7, 1809, to launch hunting and trading expeditions on the upper Missouri River and tributaries for a term of three years.

The first expedition left St. Louis in June 1809 with 172 men and nine barges loaded with goods worth $4,269; the main party reached the Bighorn River about Nov. 1, where they built a trading post. A profitable trading and trapping campaign ensued, but two of the partners suffered severe losses through treachery of the Blackfoot: many of the men were killed and all of their horses, guns, traps, and furs were taken (*see* Manuel's Fort). The company was reorganized Jan. 14, 1812; the capital was fixed at $50,000 and the time limitation at 1818. An expedition with two barges, leaving in May 1812, yielded a profit of $9,000. Fort Manuel and probably Fort Lisa were established on this expedition. The company was dissolved Jan. 17, 1814.

The Missouri Fur Company was a partnership formed by Manuel Lisa and Theodore Hunt in July 1814. For this company Lisa conducted expeditions up the Missouri River from 1814 to 1817. This company expired by limitation in July 1817, and another Missouri Fur Company was organized by Lisa in April 1819. Their principal establishment was at Fort Lisa. Lisa died in 1820, but the firm continued in business until about 1830.

SAINT LOUIS–SAN FRANCISCO. *See* **Railroads, Sketches of Principal Lines.**

SAINT LOUIS–SOUTHWESTERN. *See* **Railroads, Sketches of Principal Lines.**

ST. LOUIS WORLD'S FAIR. *See* **Louisiana Purchase Exposition.**

ST. MARKS, FORT (Fla.). Located on Apalachee Bay; was fortified by the English early in the 18th century and served also as a trading post. When the Treaty of Paris (1763) fixed the western boundary of British Florida at the Apalachicola River, British troops occupied St. Marks. By the Definitive Treaty of Peace (1783) it was transferred to Spain, a British trading firm being permitted to remain. During the Civil War it was used by the Confederates as a blockade-running and saltmaking center. The fort was destroyed by a Union naval raiding party in 1862, but was rebuilt. The salt works were destroyed in 1864.

ST. MARTIN'S STOMACH. When Alexis St. Martin, a young French-Canadian voyageur, was wounded accidentally in the stomach by a gunshot on Mackinac Island, June 6, 1822, he was cared for by William Beaumont, the post surgeon. The patient recovered, but the hole in his stomach would not close; a fold of the stomach's coats filled the orifice, forming a lid that could be pushed aside by a finger.

In May 1825 Beaumont began testing the time required to digest particular foods by introducing pieces tied to threads into the stomach and withdrawing them at intervals. His observations and conclusions, published in *Experiments and Observations on the Gastric Juice and the Physiology of Digestion* (1833), have been called the "greatest contribution ever made to the knowledge of gastric digestion." St. Martin became the father of seventeen children, farmed a little, "hired" out his stomach to at least one other physician for experiments, and exhibited himself to the public. He died in 1880.

ST. MARYS (Md.). The first settlement in Maryland; founded Mar. 27, 1634, on the north bank of the Potomac River not far from its mouth. Capital of Maryland until 1694, and later renamed St. Marys City. The village rapidly declined during the 18th century until little remained of it.

ST. MARYS, TREATY OF (June 16, 1820). Negotiated with the Chippewa by Lewis Cass, territorial governor of Michigan. The Indians ceded to the United States a four-mile-square tract at the Sault (present-day Sault Ste. Marie) on which Fort Brady was erected (1822).

ST. MARYS FALLS SHIP CANAL. *See* **Sault Ste. Marie Canals.**

ST.-MIHIEL, OPERATIONS AT (Sept. 12–16, 1918). The front between the Moselle River and the Argonne Forest in France having been selected as the field for American operations against German forces after the successful Aisne-Marne offensive, the American First Army was organized Aug. 10 and immediately began gathering its troops between the Moselle and Verdun. Marshal Ferdinand Foch and Gen. John J. Pershing planned that this army should direct its first blow against the German salient at St.-Mihiel. Nine American divisions (550,000 men) and four French divisions (70,000) were assembled under Pershing's command. Seven American divisions were placed on the south face of the salient, two American and two French divisions on the west face, and two French divisions around its tip. The Germans held this front with nine divisions (about 60,000 men). On the morning of Sept. 12, after a violent artillery bombardment, the First Army advanced into the salient. By Sept. 16 the salient was entirely obliterated. The Americans suffered 7,000 casualties.

ST. PAUL (Minn.). State capital, and one of the Twin Cities (*see separate article*). Built on a series of terraces above the

Mississippi River, just downstream from the junction of the Mississippi and the Minnesota. In 1680 Father Louis Hennepin visited the area; many other French explorers, fur traders, and missionaries passed through it from time to time, but there were no permanent settlements. After the Louisiana Purchase, a U.S. Army exploration party was led up the Mississippi by Zebulon Pike (1805–06). Pike arranged with the local Sioux for permission to build a fort (within the present limits of Minneapolis); the fort, later named Fort Snelling, was built in the 1820's. A French-Canadian nicknamed "Pig's Eye" Parrant, who had made a nuisance of himself at the fort, was ordered off the base and settled at the site of St. Paul. Father Lucien Galtier, a missionary, built a church which he named after St. Paul (1841), and the settlement then came to be known as St. Paul's Landing. In 1849 it was incorporated as a town, and named capital of the new Territory of Minnesota; it was incorporated as a city in 1854.

As the capital, the city attracted lawyers and others concerned with government. In 1882 a stockyard was established. During the 20th century St. Paul has remained an important commercial and shipping center; it is also home to a major automobile assembly factory, and to the Minnesota Mining and Manufacturing Company (3-M). The population in 1980 was 270,230.

ST. PETERSBURG (Fla.). A city on the west shore of Tampa Bay, with a population of 236,893 in 1980. Located on Pinella Peninsula, a narrow strip of land, and separated from the Gulf of Mexico by a number of low-lying sandy islands. Its original land transportation connection was a railroad built in 1888; the railroad builder, Peter Demens, named the terminal after his home town in Russia. During the middle years of the 20th century, causeways were built to connect the city with the offshore islands, and a bridge across Tampa Bay links it to the city of Tampa. Substantially a resort and retirement city, St. Petersburg has a national reputation as the "Sunshine City," for it averages 300 days per year of sunshine.

ST. PHILIP, FORT, SURRENDER OF. *See* **Mississippi River, Opening of the.**

ST. STEPHENS (Ala.). Begun about 1789 as a fortification on the site of a former French post at the head of navigation on the Tombigbee River by the Spaniards after their conquest of West Florida; found to be on the American side of the demarcation line of 1798 (*see* Southern Boundary, Survey of the), and surrendered to Lt. John McClary in 1799. St. Stephens survived as a town and became the seat of the government trading house established by Joseph Chambers in 1803.

ST.-VITH (Belgium). A town where for six days during World War II American troops denied critical roads to German forces attacking in the Battle of the Bulge (Dec. 16–21, 1944). Although the Germans took the town late on Dec. 21, the defenders held nearby for another day until authorized to withdraw. The Americans lost 6,000 of 22,000 men, plus 8,000 captured.

SAIPAN (June 15–July 9, 1944). Measuring about fourteen miles by five miles, Saipan is the northernmost of the southern Mariana Islands. In June 1944, when it was invaded by American forces, it was the most heavily fortified of the entire Marianas chain. Overall command of the operation was given to Adm. Chester W. Nimitz. After two days of intense preliminary bombardment by naval guns and aircraft, two marine divisions landed at dawn on June 15 on the eastern coast of the island and by nightfall had established a defensible beachhead. By July 9 the northernmost point of the island was declared secured. Total American casualties came to an estimated 14,111 killed and wounded, while almost the entire Japanese garrison of about 30,000 men was wiped out. The inner defense line of the Japanese empire had been cracked; Premier Hideki Tojo and his entire war cabinet resigned forthwith; and the American forces were at last within bombing range of the enemy homeland.

SALARIES. *See* **Wages and Salaries.**

SALARY GRAB. The popular name for a congressional act for boosting specified federal salaries. It was originally designed to benefit the president only; as finally passed (Mar. 3, 1873), the bill provided increases of salary for the president, the chief justice, the vice-president, cabinet members, associate justices, the speaker of the House, and senators and representatives. A last-minute amendment made the advance for the members of Congress retroactive. Coming when Congress was in disfavor because of scandals, the "salary grab" and the "back pay steal" became issues in all the elections of that year. Consequently, most congressmen, for political or other reasons, either refused to accept the increase or, having received it, returned it to the U.S. Treasury or donated it to charity. In January 1874 the Forty-third Congress repealed the legislation except for those provisions affecting the salaries of the president and the justices.

SALEM (Mass.). In 1626 Roger Conant and a few settlers of the defunct Dorchester Company moved up from Cape Ann and built some huts on the peninsula of Salem. On Sept. 6, 1628, John Endecott and the colonists sent out by the Massachusetts Bay Company in the ship *Abigail* reached Salem with a copy of the charter that superseded the rights of the Dorchester Company. Hugh Peter was instrumental in starting the fisheries through which a valuable trade with Spain, Portugal, and the West Indies was built up. Salem was incorporated as a town in 1630.

In 1692 a wave of witchcraft hysteria, which had spread all over Europe, reached Salem, and an outburst of accusations occurred, chiefly at Salem Village (now Danvers). Those accused of witchcraft were tried in Salem, and nineteen persons were hanged (*see* Witchcraft).

The capital of Massachusetts was twice transferred to Salem: under Gov. William Burnet in 1728 and under Gov. Thomas Gage in 1774. The first armed resistance to the British troops occurred at the North Bridge on Feb. 26, 1775. By the second quarter of the 19th century, Salem had lost much of its shipping to the larger ports of Boston and New York.

Since then the economy has been based on such diverse industries as the manufacture of shoes and other leather goods, textiles, and games and the tourist industry. Salem's population in 1980 was 38,220.

SALEM (Ore.). Capital city of Oregon; located on the Willamette River. The first white settlement on the site was made by Jason Lee, a Methodist missionary, who arrived in June 1840. The town of Salem was laid out in a survey in 1854, with a square grid of streets which provided for very broad avenues throughout the town. Salem is an important food packing and processing center for fruits and vegetables raised in the Willamette valley. Population in 1980 was 89,233.

SALERNO (Italy). A seaport where Anglo-American forces in World War II came ashore against German opposition on Sept. 9, 1943, the morning after the Italian government announced its surrender to the Allies. Lt. Gen. Mark W. Clark's Fifth U.S. Army made the amphibious landings with three divisions, a relatively small force. The defense was so effective that a German counterattack on Sept. 13–14 came close to reaching the beaches and splitting the British and American components at the Sele River. The arrival of Allied follow-up units, intensified air strikes, and increased naval gunfire support turned the tide. On Sept. 20, German forces started withdrawing slowly to the north; on Oct. 1 Allied troops entered Naples.

SALESMAN, TRAVELING. *See* **Traveling Salesmen.**

SALES TAXES. These consist of two types: excise taxes and general sales taxes. The excise tax is placed on specified commodities and may be at specific rates or on an ad valorem basis. The general sales tax can be a manufacturers' excise tax; a retail sales tax paid by consumers; a "gross income" tax applied to sales of goods and provision of services; or a "gross sales" tax applied to all sales of manufacturers and merchants. The sales tax in its modern form was first adopted by West Virginia in a gross sales tax in 1921. During the 1930's many states adopted the sales tax as a replacement for the general property tax that had been their chief source of income. The adoption of sales taxation slowed somewhat during the 1940's but became more popular in the post–World War II period. In 1980 forty-five states and the District of Columbia levied a sales tax in some form.

SALK VACCINE. *See* **Poliomyelitis.**

SALMON FALLS, ATTACK ON (Mar. 18, 1690). Louis de Buade, Comte de Frontenac, governor of New France, sent out three expeditions against English settlements in the winter of 1690. The smallest, of about fifty men, half French and half Abnaki, reached Salmon Falls, N.H., after a journey of two months from Three Rivers, Quebec. At daybreak they attacked the fortified house and two stockades, completely surprising the settlers and finding no opposition. The buildings and nearby farms were burned, and at least thirty persons were killed; fifty-four were made prisoners. A force from Portsmouth, N.H., caught up with the raiders but was repulsed.

SALMON FISHERIES. Salmon along the northern New England coast had been fished out by 1850. On the Pacific coast six varieties of salmon had been taken by the American Indians before the arrival of Europeans. In the 1820's the Hudson's Bay Company failed to develop an English market for barreled salmon from the Columbia River but did create a modest trade with California, South America, and Hawaii. Extensive development of the West Coast industry began in 1864, when William, John, and George Hume and Andrew S. Hapgood, all from Maine, built a salmon cannery on the Sacramento River; in 1866 they moved to the Columbia River. The salmon business spread to the coastal rivers, to the Puget Sound, to British Columbia, and, before 1890, to Alaska. After 1890 Alaska became the dominant producer. Since 1918, with wide seasonal fluctuations, the production trend has been downward.

Attempts to regulate fishing periods and to establish hatcheries had begun by the 1880's. Competition between American and Canadian fishermen for Fraser River fish brought about the establishment of the International Pacific Salmon Fisheries Commission in May 1930. High-seas salmon fishing by the Japanese led to friction and the North Pacific Fisheries Convention of 1953 (signed by Canada, Japan, and the United States), but many issues still were not resolved by the early 1980's.

SALOONS. Establishments that sold alcoholic beverages; from 1870–1900 one could be found on nearly any corner. The standard drinks were straight corn or rye whiskey and beer; fancier drinks were on display but seldom sold. The free lunch consisted of salty foods to stimulate thirst. The saloon's alliance with gambling and prostitution contributed to its downfall.

SALT. Common salt (sodium chloride) can be obtained through the evaporation of seawater or of inland brine springs, or mined as rock salt. The British colonies in America were well situated for the production of sea salt (there were saltworks at the Jamestown and Plymouth colonies), but they were largely importers of salt from England or from the West Indies.

Interior America possessed many brine springs, known as "licks" because wild animals congregated around them to lick the salt deposits. Most salt-producing lands were reserved to the states, which leased them to private producers. Salt production from brine began on the Scioto River in Jackson County, Ohio, before 1800, and when the state was organized in 1803 the area was set aside as a state reservation. But as salt proved to be plentiful the interests of governments waned. Salt became plentiful in consequence of the discovery of rich sources at great depths. In the Kanawha country, near present-day Charleston, W. Va., in 1806–08, strong brine found at 98 feet made Kanawha a leading salt-producing region. In 1883 salt production began at Wyoming County, N.Y., from a deep well that had been made in search of oil.

Rock salt had been found and was produced at various places in New York from 1886. The first discovery of deep rock salt in the United States is thought to have been made in 1841 near Abingdon, Va. Deep salt strata can either be mined or, often more economically, made sources of brine by adding water. Since the 1850's one of the most important sources of salt in the United States has been the tidelands of San Francisco Bay.

The artificial soda (sodium carbonate) industry came to the United States in 1882, and by 1900 consumed about half of the salt used in the country. By 1957 nearly 80 percent of the salt consumed in the United States went to the chemical industry. The primary uses of sodium are in the manufacture of caustic soda (sodium hydroxide); in the process for producing aluminum; and in the plastics and detergents industries. By the 1970's over half the salt used in the United States was converted to chlorine (and sodium), the chlorine ultimately being converted into the chlorinated hydrocarbons used in plastics, solvents, automotive fluids, and pesticides. Despite the growing chemical industry, its share of American salt had dropped by 1974 to 63 percent, because of the salting of highways for snow and ice removal. American salt production in 1979 was 45.8 million short tons.

SALT LAKE CITY (Utah). Capital and largest city of Utah, located on the Jordan River thirteen miles east of the Great Salt Lake. Founded by Brigham Young and his Mormon followers in 1847. It was originally laid out in ten-acre squares with streets 132 feet wide after the plan of the City of Zion prepared in 1833 by Joseph Smith, and was called Great Salt Lake City until 1868. It has been the headquarters of the Church of Jesus Christ of Latter-Day Saints (Mormons) since its founding; it was entirely Mormon in population until the Utah War of 1857–58. For a brief period Salt Lake City was the capital of the State of Deseret, and in 1856 it became the capital of Utah Territory; in 1896 it became the state capital. Industries include oil refining, food processing, and the manufacture of textiles and electronic equipment. The population in 1980 was 163,033.

"SALT RIVER" (or "up Salt River"). A term used to describe political defeat. During the presidential campaign of 1832 Henry Clay, as the candidate against President Andrew Jackson, hired a boatman to row him up the Ohio River to Louisville, where he was to make a speech; but the boatman, said to be a Jackson man, rowed Clay, by mistake or by design, up the Salt River (a Kentucky branch of the Ohio) instead, and Clay failed to reach Louisville in time for his speech. His defeat for the presidency brought later derisive references to this incident.

SALT SPRINGS TRACT. A tract of 24,000 acres of land along the Mahoning River, near Niles, Ohio, granted (1788) by Connecticut (*see* Western Reserve) to Gen. Samuel H. Parsons. Parsons visited his lands but, returning home in 1789, was drowned. At first the Parsons claim was disregarded by the Connecticut Land Company, but later parts of two townships were given to his heirs. The springs were never developed commercially.

SALT WAR (1877). A disturbance in El Paso County, Texas, over the free use of the salt lakes east of San Elizario, a town on the Rio Grande. The salt question became involved in politics, and a feud developed between Louis Cardis, backed by the Mexicans, and Charles H. Howard, supported by the Americans. Howard killed Cardis, and the bitter feeling that followed culminated in a riot at San Elizario, in which Howard and two others were slain by a mob of Mexicans.

SALVATION ARMY. An evangelistic organization created in 1865 by William Booth, a former Methodist, to work among the poor of London. The present military format dates from the publication of *The Orders and Regulations for the Salvation Army* in 1878. Booth became known as General Booth. The uniforms were adopted in the early 1880's. A branch of the army was formed in the United States in 1880 and received leadership from Evangeline Cory Booth, the general's daughter, 1904–34. The group has been noted for the vigor of its preaching, its energetic use of music, and its crusades on behalf of the poor and oppressed. The U.S. membership in 1980 was 414,659.

SALZBURGERS IN GEORGIA. In 1734 a group of seventy-eight Protestants, who had been driven out of Salzburg, Austria, by the bishop of Salzburg, landed in the new colony of Georgia. They were settled by James Oglethorpe up the Savannah River at a place that they called Ebenezer; they later moved to a more convenient spot on the river itself, bringing the name Ebenezer with them.

SAM HOUSTON, FORT (Tex.). U.S. Army post located in San Antonio, Tex., originally the mission of San Antonio de Valero. Known as the Alamo, the mission was secularized in 1794 and became a Spanish military post; from 1848 it was used as an American troop garrison. Construction of a permanent post began in the late 1870's, and in 1890 it was redesignated Fort Sam Houston to honor the leader and hero of the Texas Revolution. Fort Sam Houston is now the home of the Fourth Army and the Brooke Army Medical Center.

SAMOA, AMERICAN. After several abortive efforts to settle its fate, the United States, Germany, and England agreed in 1899 to divide the islands of the Samoa group at the 171st meridian, with Germany acquiring the islands of Western Samoa (which eventually became an independent state) and with the United States acquiring the six eastern islands, thereafter known as American Samoa. In 1900 and 1904, respectively, the principal chiefs of Tutuila and the three Manua islands, the major islands of the American Samoa group, voluntarily ceded their islands to the United States; in 1925 a seventh island, Swains Island, was acquired. The seven principal islands that constitute American Samoa have a total land area of seventy-six square miles. The seat of government is on the island of Tutuila, which has 80 percent of the population and 55 percent of the land, and where the port of Pago Pago is located.

American Samoa was first administered by the U.S. Navy. Administration was transferred to the Department of the

Interior by executive order in 1951, and governors of Samoa have since been civilians, appointed by the secretary of the interior. In 1960 the interior secretary, under authorization from the president, approved a constitution that had been drafted by a constitutional convention elected by the Samoans. It grants extensive legislative authority to a bicameral legislature; the lower house is popularly elected and the upper house is composed largely of Samoan chiefs. The judicial branch includes the High Court of American Samoa and lesser courts. There is no appeal to the U.S. federal judicial system.

The Samoan population, numbering about 32,000 in 1980, is largely Polynesian. Although increasingly westernized, the Samoans continued to cling to a strong local clan system, the matai system. They are nationals but generally not citizens of the United States. The processing of fish, caught by foreign fishing fleets, and, increasingly, tourism represent Samoa's principal economic activities.

SAMPLERS. Originally, a means of keeping samples of stitches used in embroidering household linens before books of patterns existed. What is believed to be the earliest example of a sampler in the United States (now in the Essex Institute, Salem, Mass.) was worked by Anne Gower in 1610 and brought by her to America. Not infrequently the creation of children as young as age five, American samplers excel in originality, inventiveness, and decorative quality.

SAMPSON-SCHLEY CONTROVERSY. When the Battle of Santiago began (July 3, 1898) Adm. William T. Sampson in his flagship *New York* was seven miles to the east, in distant signal range but unable to participate effectively against the Spanish ships fleeing the Cuban harbor. Sampson had signaled that the other ships should disregard the movement of the flagship, but did not turn over command to Commodore Winfield S. Schley, second in command; however, Schley—actually Sampson's senior in rank—received popular credit for the victory. The resultant controversy raged bitterly in press and Congress, halted promotion of both officers, and raised criticism of Schley's conduct earlier in the campaign. In 1901 a court of inquiry requested by Schley found against him. Upon final appeal, President Theodore Roosevelt declared Santiago "a captains' battle," in which "technically Sampson commanded" and movements followed standing orders.

SAM SLICK. A literary character created by Thomas Chandler Haliburton (1796–1865), a Canadian humorist who achieved his fame as a portrayer of the New England Yankee. In several volumes of sketches Haliburton carried Sam Slick, a Yankee clock peddler, through numerous adventures.

SAN ANTONIO (Tex.). Founded in 1718 by a Spanish military expedition that established a mission and presidio; the families of the soldiers formed the nucleus of a village, or civil settlement. In 1731 the village was reinforced by a small colony from the Canary Islands. The settlement became the civil and military capital of Texas during the Spanish-Mexican regime. During the Texas Revolution, it was first captured from its strong Mexican garrison by siege (December 1835) and later recaptured by Gen. Antonio López de Santa Anna in the tragic assault on the Alamo (March 1836), only to be regained by the Texans as a result of their victory at San Jacinto (April 1836). During 1842 it was twice occupied by Mexican raiders, and was the scene of desperate fighting in which a considerable proportion of the Comanche leaders who had assembled for a council to discuss terms of peace were massacred. Soon after the annexation of Texas by the United States in 1845, San Antonio became the chief military post in a line of forts established to guard the southern and western frontiers. The population of San Antonio in 1980 was 785,410.

SAN ANTONIO MISSIONS. Lying in and near San Antonio, Tex., these were founded by the Spanish Franciscans 1718–31 and formed the center of activity in Texas during the 18th century. San Antonio de Valero in San Antonio, the present much-visited Alamo, is the oldest. Best known of the other four missions along the San Antonio River are Purísima Concepción and, the most beautiful of all, San José, which was founded in 1720 by Antonio Margil.

SANBORN CONTRACTS. President Ulysses S. Grant's secretary of the Treasury, W. A. Richardson, in collusion with Rep. Benjamin F. Butler of Massachusetts, gave to John D. Sanborn of Boston contracts to collect large sums of overdue federal internal revenue taxes. Since little effort had been made to secure payment, Sanborn easily collected $427,000 at a commission of 50 percent. On May 4, 1874, the House Ways and Means Committee exposed the fraud. The committee privately asked Grant to remove Richardson from the cabinet. Butler was defeated for reelection.

SAND CREEK MASSACRE (Nov. 29, 1864). Colorado militiamen descended upon an encampment of Southern Cheyenne at Sand Creek, thirty miles northeast of Fort Lyon in southeastern Colorado Territory, killing about a third of a band of 500, most of whom were women and children. The chief of the Cheyenne, Black Kettle, had tried to keep peace with the whites, but there had been a number of incidents and clashes between white gold miners and the Indians. Chief Black Kettle, having been guaranteed safe conduct after a conference with the governor, had brought his band to Sand Creek and had placed them under the protection of the fort. The wanton massacre was a cause of further Indian warfare in the Plains.

SAN DIEGO (Calif.). A seaport located about twelve miles from the Mexican border. It was named San Diego de Alcalá de Henares, after a Spanish monk, in 1602. A presidio was founded in 1769 by Gaspar de Portolá, governor of Baja (Lower) California; a military post until 1835, it occupied the site known today as Old Town. The town was practically extinct when California became a state (1850). The present metropolis, three miles below Old Town, was founded in 1867 by Alonzo E. Horton, a merchant prospector of San Francisco. San Diego was incorporated in 1872, and its favorable climate drew many settlers. The population and real estate values boomed after the arrival of the Santa Fe Railway in 1884. The rapid growth of the city led to the development in the 20th century of the aerospace, electronics, and shipbuilding industries; it is also headquarters for the Eleventh Naval District and home of a number of army, navy, and Coast Guard installations. Balboa Park, center of the city's cultural activities, also houses the San Diego Zoo, one of the largest in the world. The city's population in 1980 was 875,504.

SANDUSKY (from the Huron *Otsaandosti,* meaning "cool water"). Name applied to the river, bay, and Indian villages in northern Ohio. The Wyandot (Huron) from Detroit occupied the region by 1740 and permitted English traders to erect a post on the northern side of the bay in 1745. The French displaced the English and built "Fort Sandoski" (1751), but soon evacuated it. Both Lower Sandusky (Fremont) and Upper Sandusky were important Indian centers during the American Revolution. By the Treaty of Greenville the former became a government military reservation, two miles square. In 1816 an act of Congress created the town of Croghansville in the reservation; later they were united and became Lower Sandusky, which was renamed Fremont. The present city of Sandusky on the bay was settled in 1817.

SANDWICH ISLANDS. *See* **Hawaii.**

SANDY CREEK, BATTLE OF (May 30, 1814). Driven into Sandy Creek, on the New York shore of Lake Ontario, while transporting guns and cables from Oswego to Sackets Harbor, U.S. Capt. Melancthon Woolsey ordered 120 riflemen to wait in ambush for six pursuing British boats. The riflemen captured all the boats, inflicting a loss of 18 killed, 40 wounded, and about 130 captured; one American was wounded.

SAN FELIPE-CORREO **AFFAIR.** The *Correo de Méjico,* a Mexican revenue cutter, on Sept. 1, 1835, attempted to capture the *San Felipe,* which was allegedly laden with munitions for the coming Texan revolt. The Texans but attacked and captured the cutter, thus stirring Mexico City to punitive action that committed the Texans to war.

SAN FRANCISCO (Calif.). In 1769 during the course of Spain's settlement of Upper (Alta) California, Gaspar de Portolá discovered San Francisco Bay, and in 1776 Spain occupied the peninsula site of the present city. The mission San Francisco de Asís was dedicated on Oct. 9. Three miles away, the small trading settlement of Yerba Buena (changed to San Francisco in 1848) grew up on the beach, beginning in 1835. In the early 19th century New England whalers used the bay as a provisioning and refitting station, and American traders largely dominated Yerba Buena, except for a short period of control by the Hudson's Bay Company. Capt. John B. Montgomery of the U.S. Navy established American rule on July 9, 1846, during the Mexican War.

With the discovery of gold on the American River in 1848, San Francisco mushroomed from about 900 people to a town of at least 10,000 by September 1849. In 1850 it was incorporated as a city. Politics largely continued to be corrupt until 1906, when a sweeping graft investigation, halted temporarily by the great earthquake and fire of that year, brought about the victory of a reform party.

Threatened in the 1870's by a severe financial crash, the city's position was assured by the completion of the transcontinental railroad in 1869 and the Panama Canal in 1914.

During the 20th century San Francisco became the financial capital of the West. It also became an important cultural center; its War Memorial Opera House (1934) was the first major opera house in the United States to be municipally built and owned. Important innovations in public transportation include the cable cars, first installed in 1873, the San Francisco-Oakland Bay Bridge (1936), the Golden Gate Bridge (1937), and the Bay Area Rapid Transit (BART) system (opened 1972). In 1980 the city's population was 678,974.

SAN FRANCISCO DE LOS TEJAS. The first Spanish mission established in eastern Texas, founded in 1690 west of the Neches River, near the present Weches. Pestilence and Indian hostility led to its abandonment in 1693. In 1716 it was refounded farther inland near the present Alto, where it was called San Francisco de los Neches. Three years later it was again abandoned, and in 1721 it was reestablished. It was moved in 1730 and refounded the next year at San Antonio, under the name of San Francisco de la Espada.

SAN FRANCISCO EARTHQUAKE (April 1906). The first and heaviest shocks came early on the morning of Apr. 18 and were followed by minor tremors for the next three days. Serious damage was produced in an area about 450 miles long and 50 miles wide. In San Francisco, buildings crumbled, streets on filled ground buckled, and gas and water mains ruptured. Fire raged through the central business and residential districts for three days before being controlled; some 497 city blocks were razed, or about one-third of the city. Dynamite and artillery were used to check the holocaust. There were about 700 deaths, and some 250,000 homeless refugees.

SAN GABRIEL, BATTLE OF (Jan. 8–9, 1847). A conflict between about 600 American soldiers, sailors, and volunteers, commanded by Commodore Robert F. Stockton and Gen. Stephen W. Kearny, and 500 Mexicans under Col. José María Flores, Andrés Pico, and José Antonio Carrillo, at Paso de Bartolo on the San Gabriel River, a little north of present-day Whittier, Calif. The Mexicans were dislodged from their position on Jan. 8, after about two hours of fighting. As the American forces continued their advance toward Los Angeles the next day, the Mexicans attacked them on both flanks, near the Los Angeles River. This action, known also as the Battle of La Mesa, resulted in the retreat of Flores' command. On Jan. 10 the Americans reoccupied Los Angeles, and three days later the remnants of the Mexican forces surrendered at Rancho Cahuenga.

SANGRE DE CRISTO GRANT. In 1844 the Mexican government deeded to Narcisco Beaubien and Stephen Louis Lee a parcel of 1,038,195 acres in the San Luis Valley of southern Colorado and northern New Mexico, including the main waters of the Costilla, Trinchera, and Culebra rivers and extending from the Rio Grande on the west to the summit of the Sangre de Cristo range on the east. Beaubien and Lee died in New Mexico in the Taos massacre of 1847; the former's claim passed to his father, Carlos, who purchased Lee's share from his estate for $100. The Sangre de Cristo became American territory after the Mexican War (1848), and in 1860 Congress confirmed the original charter. In 1864, after Carlos Beaubien's death, William Gilpin, Colorado's first territorial governor, and some associates purchased the grant. It was later divided and developed.

SAN ILDEFONSO, TREATY OF. A secret treaty, executed in preliminary form Oct. 1, 1800, and made effective Oct. 15, 1802, by which Spain retroceded Louisiana to France in return for the newly created Italian kingdom of Etruria. Rumors of the pending transfer rekindled President Thomas Jefferson's interest in the Mississippi Valley (*see* Louisiana Purchase).

SANITARY COMMISSION, UNITED STATES. Created by the federal government in June 1861 under the presidency of Rev. Henry W. Bellows, who had been active in organizing war-relief work. Its purpose was to assist in the care of sick and wounded soldiers and their dependent families during the Civil War. It was supported mainly by private contributions. (*See also* Christian Commission.) The commission employed as many as 500 agents. Its work included field and hospital medical inspection, field ambulance and hospital service, and hospital cars and steamers; it also maintained feeding stations and soldiers' lodges.

SANITATION, ENVIRONMENTAL. As the colonial settlements grew, their sanitary problems intensified. Despite a series of ordinances prohibiting the practice, drainage ditches, canals, docks, gutters, and vacant lots continued to be repositories for garbage, offal, carrion, rubbish, and human waste products. Municipal authorities began assuming some responsibility for street cleaning and sewage removal, but their efforts rarely achieved more than temporary success. The first tentative steps in the direction of sewer systems arose from the offensive condition of the drainage ditches and canals. In despair, local residents began demanding that these ditches be covered. In 1703 a "Common Sewer" was constructed along Broad Street in New York City. In the succeeding years New York and other towns gradually built more of these sewers; they were originally meant to be conduits for draining surface water, but so much sewage flowed into the gutters that they were in actuality sewers, pouring their contents into the adjacent bodies of water.

By the 1790's Boston, Philadelphia, New York, and other cities were developing elementary water systems. Wooden pipes and primitive steam engines supplied water to the homes of the well-to-do, and occasional hydrants appeared in the poorer neighborhoods. Unfortunately the water sources were often polluted, and the frequent loss of pressure combined with leaking pipe connections led to contamination.

In the 19th century industrialization and urbanization crowded the working poor into squalid warrens and created an ideal environment for Asiatic cholera and other enteric disorders. During the first half of the century temporary health boards emerged, which occasionally initiated massive sanitary programs that involved removing garbage and dead animals from the streets and lots, emptying privies and cesspools, and draining the many stagnant pools. But the sheer size of the garbage and human waste problems made the fight for a cleaner environment a losing battle.

Agitation for sanitary reform resulted in the formation of the Louisiana State Board of Health and a series of national sanitary conventions in the 1850's, but the Civil War cut these short. During the later years of the 19th century, water systems were improved and extended, sewer systems began replacing the haphazard construction of individual conduits, street paving improved drainage and facilitated the collection of garbage and rubbish, and technological improvements eliminated many of the former nuisances.

By the advent of the 20th century, the old fears of miasmas and sewer gas were replaced by equally grave apprehensions about germs. Environmental sanitation benefited from the rising standard of living that brought higher standards of personal and public hygiene. Technology solved the problem of safe water supplies through the introduction of rapid sand filtration and chlorination and made possible effective sewer systems in the major cities; it facilitated garbage collection and street cleaning and brought profound changes in the food-processing industry. (*See also* Public Health.)

SAN JACINTO, BATTLE OF (Apr. 21, 1836). On Mar. 11, 1836, five days after the defeat at the Alamo, Gen. Sam Houston took command of 374 men at Gonzales and two days later began his retreat from Mexican Gen. Antonio López de Santa Anna's advance; Houston's band was the sole body under arms in the republic. On Apr. 20, with about 800 men, Houston intercepted Santa Anna, with about 900 troops, at a ferry over the San Jacinto River. Houston waited for the men under Gen. Martín Perfecto de Cos to join Santa Anna the following morning; then, cutting down a bridge protecting his own as well as the Mexicans' avenue of retreat, Houston formed up under a screen of trees and attacked. Santa Anna's surprise was complete, and organized resistance ended within twenty minutes. The rest was slaughter. Texan losses were 16 killed, 24 wounded including Houston. Santa Anna, a prisoner, signed armistice terms under which the other divisions of his army immediately evacuated Texas.

SAN JOSE (Calif.). San Jose was established as Pueblo de San Jose de Guadalupe in 1777, the first *pueblo* (municipal government) founded by the Spaniards in California. It is the commercial and manufacturing center for a very rich fruit-growing region; in recent years factories for making electronic equipment, assembling cars and trucks, and making farm machinery have been added. The population has grown rapidly in recent decades, to a 1980 total of 636,550.

SAN JUAN (P.R.). Capital and largest city of Puerto Rico, with a 1980 population of 535,000, San Juan was first settled in 1521 by Spaniards under the leadership of Juan Ponce de Leon. It is located on an excellent natural harbor on the north coast of the island. The harbor was an important naval base for the Spaniards, and the city was the scene of battles with the Dutch, English, and French in its colonial period. San Juan harbor and airfield handle most of Puerto Rico's foreign and mainland traffic.

SAN JUAN COUNTRY. Located in southwestern Colorado; includes rich ranching land, the Mesa Verde National Park, and the gold and silver mines around Creede, Durango, Ouray, Rico, Silverton, and Telluride. After discovery of rich ore in the San Juan Mountains (1870–71) the region flourished until the silver collapse in 1893, although mining for gold and other minerals has continued.

SAN JUAN HILL AND EL CANEY, BATTLES OF (July 1, 1898). After the withdrawal of Spanish outposts from Las Guásimas, Cuba, the key points defending Santiago de Cuba against U.S. Gen. William Shafter's advance, June 1898, were along a line from San Juan Hill northeast to El Caney. On July 1 the Americans attacked along the entire line. Gen. Henry Lawton's division, on the right, carried El Caney. One division and Col. Theodore Roosevelt's dismounted Rough Riders captured San Juan. This placed the American army in control of high ground overlooking Santiago and in position to isolate the city. Adm. Pascual Cervera y Topete sought safety, July 3, in a dash to the open sea; he and the Spanish fleet were overwhelmed by the superior firepower of the U.S. Navy, which had been blockading the harbor. Santiago surrendered on July 17.

SAN JUAN ISLAND, SEIZURE OF (July 1859). San Juan Island, important for its position midway in the Juan de Fuca Strait, became the object of rivalry between American settlers in Washington Territory and the Hudson's Bay Company, with headquarters at Victoria, British Columbia. The alleged shooting of a pig by an American and his threatened removal to Victoria for trial provided the necessary "incident": within a month 500 American soldiers invaded the island and two British warships took up a menacing position. The American and British governments temporarily settled the dispute in March 1860 by arranging for joint occupation, which continued until 1872, when William I of Germany arbitrated the matter and settled the boundary line through the Haro Strait, thus giving San Juan Island to the United States.

SAN LORENZO, TREATY OF. *See* **Pinckney's Treaty.**

SAN MARCO, FORT. *See* **Marion, Fort.**

SAN PASQUAL, BATTLE OF (Dec. 6, 1846). Eighty mounted Mexicans, under the command of Capt. Andrés Pico, attempted to halt the advance of Gen. Stephen Kearny's 160 U.S. cavalrymen coming from Santa Fe, N.M., at San Pasqual, forty miles northeast of San Diego, Calif. Kearny had been reinforced by forty men from San Diego, but the Mexicans broke through their lines. Pico received no reinforcements and had to give way, so that Kearny, with the aid of 200 marines, reached San Diego safely on Dec. 12.

SAN SALVADOR. *See* **Watlings Island.**

SANTA ELENA. *See* **Port Royal.**

SANTA FE (N.M.). Abandoning their first settlement in New Mexico, on the Rio Chama, the Spaniards selected for their capital a more suitable site twenty-five miles to the southeast and in 1609 founded the present city of Santa Fe. The town suffered severely during the Pueblo revolt (1680) when it was abandoned by the Spaniards, not to be recovered until 1692. During the first half of the 18th century Santa Fe was the objective of Mexican traders from Chihuahua and of French traders from the Mississippi Valley. Gen. Stephen W. Kearny occupied the city in 1846 and suppressed the revolt that broke out the next year. Santa Fe remained the capital when Congress organized New Mexico into a territory (1850) and made it a state (1912). The second oldest European settlement in the United States, Santa Fe has become a cultural center of the Southwest. Without major industries, it depends on tourism for its economic well-being. In 1980 its population was 48,899.

SANTA FE RAILROAD. *See* **Railroads, Sketches of Principal Lines: Atchison, Topeka and Santa Fe.**

SANTA FE TRAIL. An important commerce route from 1821 to 1880. The greater extent of its 780 miles from Missouri to Santa Fe, N.M., lay across the Plains and avoided the rivers, so that wagons could easily traverse it; it was later extended south from Santa Fe for an additional thousand miles through El Paso to the Mexican towns of Chihuahua and Durango. Prior to the opening of the trail, the city of Santa Fe was supplied with goods brought by mule at great expense from the Mexican seaport of Veracruz over a roundabout path, the last 500 miles of which were infested with Apache. First to arrive was William Becknell of Arrow Rock, Mo., who reached Santa Fe on Nov. 16, 1821. There was no well-defined Santa Fe Trail prior to Becknell's journey. Becknell started from Franklin, Mo., followed the prairie divide between the tributaries of the Kansas and Arkansas rivers to the Great Bend of the Arkansas, then followed the Arkansas almost to the mountains before turning south to New Mexico. The Missouri River terminus was first Franklin, then Independence, and finally Westport (now Kansas City). At the western end the trail turned south to Santa Fe from the Arkansas by three different ways: the Taos Trail diverged from the Arkansas at the Huerfano River, in what is now south central Colorado; a middle course branched from the Arkansas west of the mouth of Purgatory River to cross Raton Pass on the present Colorado–New Mexico border; the shortest and in later times the most-traveled route was the Cimarron Cutoff, leaving the Arkansas near the present city of Cimarron, Kan. (this crossing varied), and proceeding southwest across the Cimarron Valley. Federal mail service by stagecoach was instituted in 1849. Completion of the last section of the Atchison, Topeka and Santa Fe Railroad in 1880 ended the importance of the wagon road.

SANTA MARIA. The flagship of Christopher Columbus' fleet of three vessels that reached the New World on Oct. 12, 1492 (*see* America, Discovery and Early Exploration of). Two months later it ran aground off the coast of Hispaniola. From the wreckage Columbus erected a fort at La Navidad.

SANTA ROSA ISLAND, BATTLE ON (Oct. 8–9, 1861). On Jan. 10, 1861, Union troops were withdrawn from Pensacola, Fla., to Fort Pickens on Santa Rosa Island in the Gulf of Mexico, leaving the navy yard and mainland forts to the Confederates. In April reinforcements reached Pickens, and in June volunteer forces arrived (*see Powhatan* Incident). By midsummer Pensacola was blockaded. In September Union soldiers burned the dry docks and the schooner *Judah*. The Confederates retaliated by a night attack (Oct. 8–9) on Santa Rosa; they surprised and burned the Union camp, driving the troops to the fort, and at daylight withdrew to the mainland. Both sides claimed victory.

SANTEE CANAL. Connecting the head of navigation on the Cooper River with the Santee River in South Carolina, this was a work of private enterprise, built 1792–1800. Intended to cheapen the transportation of foodstuffs from the interior of the state to the low-country plantations, the enterprise was never a financial success; it was abandoned about 1858.

SANTIAGO, BLOCKADE AND BATTLE OF. Ten days after four armored cruisers commanded by Spanish Adm. Pascual Cervera y Topete arrived at the harbor of Santiago de Cuba on May 19, 1898, they were blockaded by Adm. William T. Sampson and Commodore Winfield S. Schley with four battleships and two armored cruisers. On the morning of July 3 Cervera dashed out to avoid being caught in a trap by the army encircling the city (*see* San Juan Hill and El Caney, Battles of). The blockaders quickly closed in, and destroyed the Spanish fleet. The greater Spanish loss, about 400 killed, as compared with one American killed and one seriously wounded, was due primarily to the American rapidfire guns, which drove the gunners from their stations. The victory removed all chance of Spanish naval resistance in the Western Hemisphere. A controversy arose as to who should receive the chief credit for the victory (*see* Sampson-Schley Controversy).

SANTIAGO DE CHILE INTER-AMERICAN CONGRESS (Mar. 25–May 3, 1923). The fifth Inter-American Congress was held at Santiago, Chile. Mexico, unrecognized by the United States, was absent. Peru, at odds with Chile over the Tacna-Arica dispute, did not attend, nor did Bolivia. The principal achievements of the conference were the adoption of the Gondra Convention (a multilateral cooling-off device for the preservation of peace) and a projected reform of the Pan-American Union at Washington, D.C.

SANTO DOMINGO. *See* **Dominican Republic.**

SANTO DOMINGO, SECRET MISSION TO (May–June 1846). Soon after the Republic of Santo Domingo separated from Haiti in 1844, it became necessary for Secretary of State James Buchanan to investigate its social stability and resources, preliminary to according recognition. Two navy lieutenants, David D. Porter and William E. Hunt, accomplished the work: Porter traveled through the little-known interior of the island while Hunt in the brig *Porpoise* surveyed its coast. The reports being favorable, friendly relations between the two countries were shortly established.

SARATOGA, SURRENDER AT (Oct. 17, 1777). After his defeat at the second Battle of Freeman's Farm (Oct. 7), British Gen. John Burgoyne with his 4,500 exhausted men slowly retreated northward. He neglected to crush a detachment of 1,300 Continental militia posted to block his retreat, but instead took up a strong position near Old Saratoga (now Schuylerville, N.Y.). The American forces under Gen. Horatio Gates now consisted of about 5,000 regulars and more than 12,000 militia. Burgoyne could not decide what to do; while he hesitated, Gates surrounded his position. Burgoyne finally asked for terms on Oct. 13. Gates at first demanded an unconditional surrender but on Oct. 15 accepted Burgoyne's "convention," which provided that the British troops should be returned to England on condition that they would take no further part in the war (*see* Convention Army). Burgoyne, having heard that Sir Henry Clinton had captured the Continental forts near West Point (*see* Highlands of the Hudson) and was sending an expedition against Albany, now tried to delay the surrender, but on the afternoon of Oct. 16 he accepted the inevitable, and the formal laying down of arms took place on the next day. This event marked the turning point of the American Revolution, since France now decided to enter the war as an ally of the Americans.

SARATOGA SPRINGS (N.Y.). A city in east central New York, west of the Hudson River, with more than 100 natural mineral springs. In the summer of 1767 Sir William Johnson, suffering from a wound received in the French and Indian War, was taken by the Mohawk to bathe in the healing waters of High Rock Spring. In 1789 Gideon Putnam, called the founder of Saratoga Springs, settled in the area; in 1802 he began construction of the Grand Union Hotel. Other hotels were built, and the popularity of the springs increased rapidly. Incorporated as a village in 1826, Saratoga was declared to be a "resort of wealth, intelligence and fashion—a political observatory." During the 1860's Civil War profiteers discovered Saratoga Springs: drilling was started on six new springs; several new hotels were opened; and the first horse races were run at the Travers track. In 1863 the Saratoga Association for the Improvement of the Breed of Horses was organized; its annual races continue to draw large crowds. Throughout the last quarter of the 19th century, Saratoga Springs was the most fashionable spa in the United States. Commercial bottling of the waters nearly depleted the springs, but the state intervened. In 1909 New York State acquired the property and in 1916 the springs were placed in the charge of a conservation commission. In 1980 the city had 23,906 inhabitants.

SATELLITES. *See* **Communication Satellites; Space Exploration.**

SAUGUS FURNACE. Erected on Saugus Creek near Lynn, Mass., in 1646 by British and colonial proprietors to smelt bog ores found in the vicinity. This furnace, with a capacity of 7 or 8 tons a week, cast cannon and hollow ware directly from the ore as well as pig iron. The enterprise was not very profitable but operated intermittently for more than 100 years until neighboring ore and timber were exhausted. (*See also* Bog Iron Mining; Iron and Steel Industry.)

SAUK PRAIRIE. A large and fertile prairie that stretches along the Wisconsin River, rimmed by the bluffs of the Baraboo Range, in Sauk County, Wis. On this prairie the Sauk settled about the middle of the 18th century, after having been driven from the shores of Green Bay by the French. The first British officer in Wisconsin, who occupied Fort Edward Augustus at Green Bay, 1761–63, made a treaty of alliance with the Sauk chiefs. In 1777 Capt. Charles Michel de Langlade, of the British Indian department, sent his nephew, Charles Gautier de Verville, to arouse the Wisconsin Indians for auxiliaries in Canada to assist in repelling the American invasion. Gautier arrived at Sauk Prairie in May 1778, only to find that he had been preceded by a messenger from the tribes of the eastern United States, to engage the western Indians to come to the support of Gen. George Washington's army. At the same time a Spanish messenger from St. Louis arrived bidding for the Sauk trade and alliance. Gautier succeeded in securing a number of Sauk for Langlade's party; but the tribe began moving to the Mississippi near the mouth of Rock River, in what is now northwest Illinois, in order to approach the Spanish and the Americans of the Illinois settlements, which were captured by George Rogers Clark in July 1778.

SAULT STE. MARIE (Mich.). Located on the south bank of the St. Marys River, at the falls (*see* Sault Sainte Marie Canals). First settled by Father Jacques Marquette in 1668 (*see* Sault Sainte Marie Mission and Trading Post). Incorporated in 1887. An important railway and shipping center, and site of numerous industries. Connected by an international bridge with the city of Sault Ste. Marie, Canada. Population in 1980 was 14,448.

SAULT STE. MARIE, GREAT PAGEANT AT (June 14, 1671). Jean Talon, Canada's "great intendant," annexed the unknown "country of the West" to the French crown by proclamation, by staging, through his agent, Simon François Daumont, Sieur de St. Lusson, a dramatic ceremony at Sault Ste. Marie. St. Lusson's *prise de possession* ignored standing Spanish and English claims to the territory.

SAULT STE. MARIE CANALS, or **Soo Canals.** Two U.S. canals and one Canadian canal, connecting Lake Superior with Lake Huron. The first U.S. canal (1855) is an artificial waterway on the St. Marys River and was originally known as the St. Marys Falls Ship Canal. In 1797 the North West Company of Montreal constructed a small canal and lock on the north shore of the rapids of St. Marys River, where the water of Lake Superior descends to the level of Lake Huron. An American canal was projected by Michigan in 1837, and was ready for use in June 1855. Tolls were charged, but they were inadequate. In 1881 the state ceded the canal to the United States, which abolished tolls and assumed maintenance and control. The U.S. Army Corps of Engineers operates the canals and has enlarged both the canals and locks. The largest lock, the Davis Lock, is 1,350 feet long. A new lock was built on the site of the earlier Poe Lock in the early 1960's after the opening of the St. Lawrence Seaway.

SAULT STE. MARIE MISSION AND TRADING POST. The sault or rapids of the St. Marys River, which discharges the waters of Lake Superior into Lake Huron, were a favorite rendezvous in colonial days for Indians and traders. The designation Sault Ste. Marie (St. Marys Falls) originated with the Jesuit missionaries. The first white man to reach the sault appears to have been Étienne Brulé sometime during 1621–23. In 1668 Father Jacques Marquette opened a mission post on the south (American) side of the rapids, around which grew the earliest settlement of whites in Michigan. As a trading center and crossroads the settlement began early to decline, owing partly to the enterprise of the Hudson's Bay Company to the north; later, the North West Company, and afterward the American Fur Company, maintained important posts at the sault. The mission declined toward the end of the 17th century.

SAVAGE'S STATION, BATTLE AT (June 29, 1862). Union Gen. George B. McClellan, having abandoned his base on the Pamunkey River in Virginia (*see* Stuart's Ride), left Gen. Edwin V. Sumner's and Gen. William B. Franklin's corps to guard a temporary issue depot at Savage's Station while the rest of the army retreated across White Oak Swamp. Confederate Gen. John B. Magruder pursued and attacked the Union forces during the afternoon. Sumner repulsed Magruder's attacks; after destroying vast quantities of supplies, the Union troops retired after nightfall.

SAVANNAH (Ga.). Located on a plateau overlooking the Savannah River, eighteen miles from the Atlantic Ocean, it was settled in 1733 under the leadership of Gen. James E. Oglethorpe as the first community in the Georgia colony and was Georgia's capital until 1786. At the end of the colonial period Savannah had fewer than 500 houses and was surrounded by a pine forest, but luxuriant rice fields and savannas stretched northward and eastward from the town. A promising export trade in rice, indigo, lumber, potash, and skins had begun. The royal governor was forced to flee in 1776, but he returned and restored British authority there in 1779; the British remained in possession until July 11, 1783.

Incorporated as a city in 1789, Savannah was the first planned city in the United States; its original ground plan featured broad streets in checkerboard design and numerous public squares. Serious yellow fever epidemics occurred in 1820, 1854, and 1876. Cholera swept the city in 1834. Savannah fell to Gen. William Tecumseh Sherman in December 1864. The years 1880–1900 saw economic recovery and some growth.

In the early 20th century Savannah became one of the world's largest cotton and naval stores markets. At mid-century these activities had declined, but manufactures included sugar, lumber, fertilizer, paint, roofing, steel products, and gypsum materials. Savannah's fisheries also remained important. The population in 1980 was 141,634.

SAVANNAH. The first ship to cross the Atlantic Ocean propelled or aided by steam. Built in New York as a 300-ton sailing ship with auxiliary steam power; bought by a shipping company in Savannah, Ga., whence it sailed for Liverpool on May 24, 1819, arriving on June 20.

SAVANNAH, SIEGE OF (September 1779)**.** Comte Jean Baptiste Hector d'Estaing with about 4,500 soldiers, joined by Benjamin Lincoln with about 2,100 Americans, sought to wrest Savannah from the British, who had about 2,500 defenders. After a siege of three weeks, on Oct. 9 a general assault was made that resulted in a disastrous failure; more than 1,000 of the attacking forces were killed. Lack of coordination between the French and Americans was held responsible for the defeat.

SAVANNAH, SIEGE OF (December 1864)**.** On Dec. 10, Union Gen. William Tecumseh Sherman began to invest Savannah (*see* Sherman's March to the Sea). A skillful Confederate defense at Honey Hill kept the railroad open to Charleston, S.C. But Fort McAllister, eighteen miles to the southwest and commanding the southern water approach, was captured, and connection was established with the Union supply fleet. Greatly outnumbered, Gen. William J. Hardee, the Confederate commander, after a brief defense on the night of Dec. 20, withdrew into South Carolina (*see* Carolinas, Sherman's March Through the).

SAVINGS AND LOAN ASSOCIATIONS. The first of these was the Oxford Provident Building Association, founded in 1831 in a suburb of Philadelphia. Early associations were simply cooperative clubs, usually created by working-class people of limited resources to build themselves homes. Gradually they became more formal, opened offices, and sought members who did not plan to build. They were usually called building and loan associations, but they were also known as cooperative banks in New England and as homestead associations in Louisiana. Lenders and borrowers both are voting members of these mutual organizations. Persons placing savings with them are shareholders, not depositors, and receive dividends, not interest.

The Home Owners Loan Act of June 13, 1933, provided for the first time for nationally chartered federal savings and loan associations. These had to belong to the Federal Home Loan Bank System, but state associations might also become members. The Home Loan Bank Board also directs the Federal Savings and Loan Insurance Corporation, created by law of June 27, 1934, to insure savings accounts. State member associations are not obliged to belong to it, although most large ones do. Associations normally invest about 80 to 85 percent of their funds in mortgages; during the 1950's and 1960's they supplied between 22 and 38 percent a year of all monies lent to finance nonfarm homes.

SAVINGS BANKS. *See* **Banks, Savings.**

SAVINGS BONDS. After the discontinuation of "liberty loans"—U.S. Treasury bonds sold to the public in small denominations during World War I—no similar offering was made by the federal government until 1935. Between March 1935 and April 1941, $3.95 billion worth of "baby bonds" were issued in denominations of from $25 to $1,000; these were taken off the market on Apr. 30, 1941, and the following day the first of the defense savings bonds, in the same denominations and bearing the same 2.9 percent interest, were issued. In December, when the United States entered World War II, defense savings bonds became known as war savings bonds. After the war they were once again known as defense bonds; after the Korean War they were simply called savings bonds.

Savings stamps, introduced during World War I, were revived in a different form in April 1941. They were sold in denominations of from 10 cents to $5. They bore no interest, but could be exchanged for bonds in units of $18.75—the price of a bond redeemable at maturity for $25. The stamp program was discontinued in 1970.

SAWMILLS. By 1634 a sawmill was in operation on the Piscataqua River (between the present states of Maine and New Hampshire); by 1706 there were seventy. A primitive type had a single sash saw pulled downward by a waterwheel and upward by an elastic pole, but more usually the saw was moved both up and down by waterpower.

Shortly before 1810 Oliver Evans' wood-burning high-pressure steam engines began to be installed in sawmills, making it possible to manufacture lumber where waterpower was not available. Circular saws, introduced about the middle of the 19th century, increased mill capacity, but turned too much of the log into sawdust. Band saws are now used extensively because they are faster, create less sawdust and more usable wood with their narrower kerf, or cut, and can handle logs of the largest size.

Giant sawmills developed for the most part in the great forest regions west of the Appalachians: in the white-pine belt of the Great Lakes Basin, in the yellow-pine area of the South, and in the fir and redwood forests of the Pacific Northwest. (*See also* Lumber Industry.)

SAYBROOK, or **Old Saybrook** (Conn.)**.** Located on Long Island Sound and the west bank of the Connecticut River. On July 7, 1635, John Winthrop, Jr., was appointed "governor of the river Connecticut" for one year; he arrived in Boston on Oct. 6 and sent out a party of about twenty men, who began the settlement of Saybrook on Nov. 24, on land claimed by the Dutch, who had settled there in 1623. Winthrop reached Saybrook in late spring of 1636. George Fenwick, now one of the patentees, became a magistrate of the Connecticut colony and on Dec. 5, 1644, sold the fort and land at Saybrook to Connecticut. Saybrook has remained a small residential community and was incorporated as a town in 1854. In 1980 its population was 9,287.

SAYBROOK PLATFORM. A revision of the ecclesiastical polity of the colony of Connecticut, drawn up by a synod meeting at the call of the legislature in Saybrook, Sept. 9, 1708. Its chief feature was an accentuation of the principle of "consociation," or rule by councils, away from the independency of early Congregationalism: the churches were organized into county associations ruled by a council of ministers and lay delegates, which was given extensive disciplinary powers over erring congregations and supervision over the choice of new pastors; county associations then sent delegates to an annual assembly that regulated the whole colony, making the church practically a form of presbyterianism.

SCAB. A term of opprobrium applied to one who takes the job of a union worker during a strike. It was used in 1806 at a trial in Philadelphia of eight workingmen for intimidation of nonunion men (*see* Philadelphia Cordwainers' Case).

SCALAWAG. The term of opprobrium applied by conservative southerners to native whites who joined with the freedmen and the carpetbaggers in support of Republican policies during Radical Reconstruction. The word, originally used to describe runty or diseased cattle, came to be a synonym in the antebellum period for a "mean fellow, a scape grace," and acquired its political connotations after the war. Comprising approximately 20 percent of the white electorate, they often provided the crucial margin of victory for the Republicans.

SCALPING. The Indians of the North American Plains, Great Lakes, the Eastern Woodlands, and the Gulf stressed war as a major social institution. All took scalps in the course of warfare, although how the scalp was taken and handled reflected various local customs. Natives of California, the Plateau, and segments of the Northwest Coast practiced scalping, although it began to fade in the latter area, where, as among the Tlingit, head trophies appeared. Scalping was not known to the Eskimo. The Pueblo Indians kept enemy scalps, usually those of Navaho and Apache, in the ceremonial chambers, "feeding" them corn pollen in solemn fertility rituals. The variations in custom were extensive: scalps might be braided together, as among some Plains tribes; stretched on frames and painted, as among the Pueblo; or, as with the South American Guaycurú, used as drinking vessels.

SCANDINAVIAN IMMIGRATION. *See* **Immigration.**

***SCHECHTER POULTRY CORPORATION* V. *UNITED STATES*,** 295 U.S. 495 (1935). Also known as the "Sick Chicken Case." Led to a unanimous Supreme Court decision that declared the National Industrial Recovery Act (NIRA) of June 16, 1933, unconstitutional. The case, and that of *United States* v. *Schechter,* arose out of alleged violations of the Code of Fair Competition for the Live Poultry Industry of metropolitan New York, which had been established by the NIRA. While granting that Congress had authority to regulate not only interstate commerce but also those intrastate activities that directly affected such commerce, the Court insisted that codes could not regulate activities that only indirectly affected commerce among the states.

***SCHENCK* V. *UNITED STATES*,** 249 U.S. 47 (1919). A unanimous Supreme Court decision that upheld the Espionage Act of 1917. The act was used to prosecute Charles T. Schenck, secretary of the Socialist party, who circulated leaflets encouraging resistance to the draft. The Supreme Court sustained the act. In his opinion Justice Oliver Wendell Holmes made his famous statement that absolute freedom of speech may be curtailed if "the words used . . . create a clear and present danger" of substantive evils.

SCHENECTADY (N.Y.). City in eastern New York; founded in 1661 when Arent Van Curler and eighteen associates purchased from the Mohawk a tract on the Mohawk River, thirteen miles northwest of Fort Orange. Although its location on the Mohawk pointed to its growth as a trading center, Schenectady (because of the Dutch West India Company's monopoly) was forbidden to engage in the fur trade and so developed first as an agricultural community. In 1690 a party of French regulars and Indians attacked Schenectady and burned it to the ground. The village was rebuilt and slowly continued to grow. It became the center of a prosperous farming community. In the 19th century Schenectady became known as the Gateway to the West. Schenectady's location on the Erie Canal added to the city's importance as a transshipment point. The demand for locomotives led to a large locomotive works in 1848. This and the large plant established by the General Electric Company in 1892 were largely responsible for Schenectady's spectacular growth. The city had a population of 67,972 in 1980.

SCHLOSSER, FORT, ATTACK ON (July 5, 1813). A British detail under Lt. Col. Thomas Clark crossed the Niagara River in three boats, arriving at Fort Schlosser, on the east bank of the Niagara River in New York, a little after daybreak. They captured and removed to Canada arms, ammunition, equipment, provisions, two bateaux, and a gunboat. As they were embarking with the booty, about fifteen men came to the beach and fired shots, but there were no casualties.

SCHOENBRUNN. "Beautiful spring" was a mission of the Moravian Brethren established by David Zeisberger and Delaware Indians in 1772 near present-day New Philadelphia, Ohio. John Heckewelder and others joined him, and several missions were organized along the Tuscarawas River for Christian Delaware and Mohican from Pennsylvania. During the Revolution the inhabitants, who were pacifists, were forced to move to Lichtenau, Ohio. In 1779 a new Schoenbrunn was set up across the river, but it was destroyed in 1782, during bloody struggles between Indians and white frontiersmen. Schoenbrunn Village State Memorial, a restoration to its original appearance, was established in 1923.

SCHOMBURGK LINE. A survey made from 1841 to 1843 by Sir Robert Hermann Schomburgk, English-German geographer, to establish a boundary between British Guiana and Venezuela. Venezuela repudiated the survey, and the boundary remained in question until President Grover Cleveland in 1895 forced the parties to submit to arbitration. Negotiations were concluded in 1899.

SCHOOL, DISTRICT. A small country school organized to serve a particular neighborhood rather than a whole township. Most New England towns contained several villages as well as a wide farm population. The original town school was supported in whole or in part by a town tax. Eventually the divided school evolved, in which the school went for a portion of the year to a village. When these short school terms were made permanent, the school district was formed. This was made legal in Massachusetts in 1789. The district school system of the early 19th century made possible a school system controlled and supported by the public that patronized it. The system after the middle of the 19th century was modified in most western states when the township system or the county system or both were superimposed on the district system. By the close of the 19th century, good roads made possible the consolidated school, which has gradually replaced the one-room, ungraded district school throughout most of the country.

SCHOOLBOOKS, EARLY. In colonial America, catechisms and the Bible were the most commonly used books of elementary instruction, although a few small texts and hornbooks of English origin were imported. Various primers were adapted to American schools, but among Calvinists and Lutherans *The New-England Primer* (1690) was preeminent until 1800. Thomas Dilworth's *New Guide to the English Tongue* (1740) dominated spelling and reading instruction until Noah Webster's revolutionary born and flamingly patriotic *A Grammatical Institute of the English Language,* which comprised a speller (1783), a grammar (1784), and a reader (1785). With Webster's dictionaries, published in 1806 and 1828, it standardized spelling and pronunciation in America. English composition as a separate subject was introduced in the 1840's, but it was not until 1851 that the first textbook, G. P. Quackenbos' *First Lessons in Composition,* was published. History texts tended to stress political and military events and extol American representative democracy. Although books of reading selections varied little in type, two series became especially popular: Samuel Griswold Goodrich's *Peter Parley* series of books for children, and William Holmes McGuffey's *Eclectic Readers* (1836). In general it may be said that the contents of textbooks remained haphazard in choice and arrangement until about 1825, when the principles of Johann Heinrich Pestalozzi redirected educational activity toward observation, investigation, and discussion and away from memorization and rote recitation. (*See* Education.)

SCHOOL LANDS. When Congress created new states out of the public domain it reserved to itself the management and disposal of the public land within their boundaries. Chief among the government's means of disposal of these lands were land grants to the states to aid in the development of elementary schools.

Ohio was the first state in which the land grant policy was put into practice (1803). Some states held the lands and proceeds from them as trustees for the townships, while others turned them over to the townships. Local management generally led to careless administration and reckless use of funds derived from the sale. State management frequently played into the hands of large speculator groups. The more common procedure was to require that the school funds be invested in state bonds paying 6 percent interest. The lands did aid materially in making elementary schools possible in communities with an insufficient tax base.

Management of school lands in the newer states of the Far West was more successful, partly because Congress attempted to prescribe more fully the conditions under which the lands should be sold and partly because the states were more prudent in their administration.

SCHOOLS, PRIVATE. Private, nonpublic, or independent schools do not receive governmental support and are not under direct governmental control. Some are religious, some secular, while others are operated for profit.

Private instruction was available in Boston by 1630, even before public schools. Several noteworthy secondary private schools were the Collegiate School of New York (1638), the oldest private day school in America; the Roxbury (Mass.) Latin School (1645); the Hopkins Grammar School (New Haven, Conn., 1660); and the William Penn Charter School (Philadelphia, 1689).

During the 18th century, private schools pioneered in teaching modern and practical subjects. Open evenings, they provided opportunities for advanced education and economic mobility: the Dummer (1763), Phillips Andover (1778), Phillips Exeter (1778), and Deerfield (1799) academies. The Zion Parnassus Academy (1785) in North Carolina also prepared teachers. Religious schools were opened by the Quakers, Episcopalians, and Lutherans. Jews opened a school in New York City (1731), and Roman Catholic schools were under way later in the 18th century. The Free (later Public) School Society operated private schools (1806–53) that were taken over by the New York City Board of Education. Other developments were the growth of Presbyterian parochial schools and the spread of the Catholic parochial school system (1884); the establishment of private normal schools; the opening of Round Hill (1823), A. Bronson Alcott's Temple (1834), and John Dewey's Laboratory (1896) schools, all noted for progressive ideas and practices; the first kindergarten (1856); female academies and seminaries; and the Gilman Country Day School, Baltimore (1897).

Parochial schools experienced financial difficult after 1945, partially as a result of judicial bans on public support. In 1980 slightly over 5 million pupils (kindergarten to grade 12) were in nonpublic schools out of a total pupil population of 46,-921,000. The largest group attended Roman Catholic schools, which numbered 9,686 with a total enrollment of 3,163,759.

SCHOOLS, PUBLIC. *See* **Education.**

SCHOOLTEACHERS, EARLY. Teachers were scarce in early colonial days. The simple rudiments were taught at home; women sometimes taught their own and neighbors' children, or older girls conducted dame schools. The colonial schoolmaster seldom received as much as a third of the sum paid a pastor. Preachers conducted parish or grammar schools (*see* Latin Schools); young college graduates taught school while preparing for professional careers; indentured servants earned their freedom by teaching; and other men and women dedicated their lives to education.

Girls were generally excluded from colonial public schools; but private schools made progress in educating women. After the Revolution girls were admitted to a few academies, but in the main received advanced education at such schools as Sarah Pierce's at Litchfield, Conn. (1792). Some graduates were pioneers in establishing women's colleges. With the founding of normal schools, open to women and chiefly concerned at first with the training of elementary-school teachers, women replaced men as teachers in the lower schools.

SCHOONER. A sailing vessel that originated at Gloucester, Mass., in 1713–14. It is a fore-and-aft-rigged craft, originally small (50 to 100 tons), with two masts, designed for coastwise trade, but developed in the 1880's and 1890's into vessels of 2,000 to 3,000 tons, having four, five, and even six masts. Only one seven-master was attempted (1901–02). The use of schooners declined gradually, beginning in the mid-1800's with the advent of steam-powered vessels.

SCHUYLER, FORT. *See* **Stanwix, Fort.**

SCHWENKFELDERS. Followers of Kaspar Schwenkfeld, a 16th-century German religious reformer. Persecuted as sectarians, they emigrated to Pennsylvania in 1734. In 1980 there were five churches with 2,763 members; headquarters are at Pennsburg, Pa.

SCIENCE, POPULARIZATION OF. In the decades 1820–50, the nascent American scientific community was professionalizing itself. The professional status of scientists was threatened afterward primarily by the evolution controversy, during which many popularizations of Charles Darwin's theory of evolution were written to protect the scientists' independence. While modernists were persuaded, fundamentalists were not.

In the 1920's a group of scientific leaders attempted to convince the public and industrialists that financial support would bring economic progress and preserve democracy. They aided Edward Wyllis Scripps, the newspaper magnate, and Edwin E. Slosson, a chemist and journalist, in founding the Science Service in 1921. This agency provided authenticated news about science, published school periodicals, and broadcast radio programs about science.

The atomic scientists' movement originated in 1944 at the Metallurgical Laboratory at the University of Chicago, part of the Manhattan Project to build the atomic bomb. The scientists campaigned to educate the federal government on the dangers of secret, military-controlled, domestic atomic research and on the necessity of internationally controlled atomic weapons. Their efforts led to creation of the civilian Atomic Energy Commission in 1946. Many of the scientists also acted to secure federal patronage of basic scientific research. Scientists lobbied from 1945 to 1950 to obtain the National Science Foundation (created in 1950).

SCIENTIFIC AMERICAN. A magazine of popular science which owed its early success to the great appeal applied science had for 19th-century Americans. Rufus Porter designed the first issue (Aug. 28, 1845) as a family newspaper. Instead of politics, he interspersed poetry, religion, and news curiosities amidst advancements in the mechanic arts. Within the first year Porter sold his interests to Alfred E. Beach and Orson D. Munn. Under the name Munn and Company, Beach and Munn dropped poetry and religion, altered the format, and introduced prize schemes to increase circulation, which by 1853 had reached 30,000. They also opened a patent agency. Inventors who employed the company's services were rewarded by publication of their invention in *Scientific American.* The *Scientific American Supplement,* initiated in 1876 to provide more technical and special information, was the first step in the transformation of *Scientific American* from a mechanics' newspaper into a magazine of popular science. The patent agency was separated from the publishing company in the 1890's, and in 1921 the *Supplement* was dropped while the paper was made into a monthly magazine, with feature articles by outside specialists. In 1947 Munn and Company sold the magazine to the newly formed Scientific American Publishing Company. Under the editorship of Gerard Piel, *Scientific American* was broadened to encompass the physical, biological, and social sciences—basic and applied—and was glamorized by charts and photographs. It found wide acceptance and by 1980 had a monthly circulation of 712,900 copies.

SCIENTIFIC EDUCATION. Viewed first as an ally of religion, science came to be valued in the early 19th century in utilitarian terms. Mechanics' institutes, academies, and military schools brought the rudiments of science and engineering to a wide audience. The lyceum movement popularized science for the public. Natural philosophy was supplemented in some of the newer colleges with applied science courses. The U.S. Military Academy at West Point (after 1816) and Rensselaer Polytechnic Institute (founded 1824) began to produce a small but important cadre of professional engineers. Scientific schools, still primarily engineering, were established at Harvard (1847) and Yale (1860).

The expansion of scientific education after the Civil War was given special impetus by the Morrill Act (1862), which established the land-grant colleges, and the beginning of graduate education. By the late 1970's federal support had created seventy-two land-grant institutions devoted to the application of science to national needs. The graduate school, heralded by Johns Hopkins University (founded 1876), began the transformation of the American university into a research institution.

The phenomenal growth of scientific education in the 20th century resulted from the increasing demands of a technological society, expansion of college enrollments, and, most important, a public policy that led to large-scale support for research and training. Federal support was channeled to universities through the National Science Foundation, the Atomic Energy Commission, the Department of Defense, the National Institutes of Health, and the National Aeronautics and Space Administration. Most of the research funds went to science and eingineering.

SCIENTIFIC MANAGEMENT. A term adopted in 1911 to identify the system of manufacturing management developed and promoted by Frederick Winslow Taylor of Philadelphia. The original term is still used to describe the whole movement in the 20th century toward systematic coordination and control of machines, materials, and workers in manufacturing operations. Subdisciplines, such as time and motion study, production planning, and inventory control, were included in Taylor's doctrine; later elaborations have included statistical quality control, operations research, and systems analysis. Taylor's particular system included the rationalization of both machines and people. It grew out of many years of investigations and experiments pursued by Taylor successively in the works of the Midvale Steel Company and the Bethlehem Steel Company. In addition to its early effects on industrial productivity, the Taylor system triggered a remarkable popular "efficiency" craze that by 1912 reached into schools, churches, and homes. Dozens of articles in large-circulation magazines brought to a wide audience the notion that efficiency was in itself a positive good.

SCIENTIFIC PERIODICALS. At first, colonial Americans found European journals, especially the Royal Society's *Philosophical Transactions,* adequate for publication of their scientific work, but eventually American science expanded to the point where it could sustain journals of its own. The *Transactions of the American Philosophical Society* (1769–) constituted the first long-lived periodical that devoted a large part of its contents to science. In 1780 the American Academy began its *Memoirs,* and in 1787 the New York Regents started its *Reports.* Many agricultural magazines and some physicians' journals, such as the *Medical Repository* (1797–1824) in New York, also accepted original scientific papers.

The earliest periodical in the United States devoted exclusively to science was Dr. Archibald Bruce's *American Mineralogical Journal* (1810–14), a one-volume venture of four annual issues that terminated with its editor's death. More important was the establishment of the *American Journal of Science* (1818–). American scientific societies founded before the Civil War began printing proceedings, reports, memoirs, journals, transactions, and bulletins soon after their establishment. Especially noteworthy were the Academy of Natural Sciences of Philadelphia (founded 1812), the Lyceum of Natural History of New York City (1817; later the New York Academy of Sciences), the Franklin Institute (1824) in Philadelphia, the Albany Institute (1824), the Boston Society of Natural History (1830; merged eventually into the city Museum of Science), the Association of American Geologists (1840; the American Association for the Advancement of Science from 1848), the Smithsonian Institution (1846), and the Chicago and the St. Louis academies of science (both 1856). Medical and agricultural journals expanded to embrace trade and business journals before subsiding in the face of increasing specialization. The growth of scientific periodicals was curbed somewhat by the appearance of another agent active in scientific publication—the government. The reports of state geological and natural history surveys were usually published with public money as separate monographs, and the results of federal surveys of the trans-Mississippi West appeared in documents that were part of the federal executive or congressional series.

Scientific literature in the 19th century increased enough to warrant the founding of the *Annual of Scientific Discovery* (1850–71), the first sustained American journal devoted to abstracting scientific material published elsewhere. The antebellum era also saw the beginning of a few specialized periodicals: the *Mining Magazine* (1853–61) of New York, the *American Entomological Society Proceedings* (1861– ; title changed in 1867 to *American Entomological Society Transactions*), the *American Journal of Conchology* (1865–71), and the *American Ethnological Society Transactions* (1845–53). However, long-lived specialized journals required a national professional society for editorial and financial backing. These organizations began mostly in the 1880's and 1890's, and with them began the enormous proliferation of scientific journals that still marked publishing in the 1970's. Journals of national scope were established in anthropology, economics, and sociology. *Scientific American* (1845–) and *Popular Science Monthly* (1872–) aimed more at the general public. These magazines were financed as commercial ventures.

SCIENTIFIC SOCIETIES. Emerged concomitant with an increasing interest in science in the 17th century. Americans recognized the relationship between scientific advance and the creation of such organizations. Highly visible and self-selecting European societies served as models for the Americans. Nearly a century passed after Increase Mather's short-lived Boston Philosophical Society (1683) before two ongoing groups, the American Philosophical Society (1743) in Philadelphia and the American Academy of Arts and Sciences (1780) in Boston, were founded.

Like their predecessors, these groups were dedicated to a broad understanding of natural philosophy. Later groups stressed the natural sciences, such as the Academy of Natural Sciences of Philadelphia (1812), the Lyceum of Natural History of New York City (1817; later the New York Academy of Sciences), and the Boston Society of Natural History

(1830). By the 1840's limited effectiveness and local constraints led to efforts to found a national scientific organization. The specialized and highly integrated Association of American Geologists and Naturalists (AAGN), founded in 1840, was the first. In 1848 the AAGN became the multidisciplinary American Association for the Advancement of Science (AAAS). Its leadership included geologists, physicists, mathematicians, and biologists. The AAAS through the 1850's was the only forum for discussing mutual concerns for the growing number of scientific practitioners. The sectional meetings of the AAAS inadvertently led to the development of specialized professional societies. The young organizations tended to reflect academic disciplines as well as the traditional technical and scientific arts. In fact, applied fields, such as engineering, had groups that slightly predated the new societies. Established gradually, the new specialized societies in such areas as physics, chemistry, and geology, as well as in economics and anthropology, were part of national science by the turn of the century.

National groups sought to renew their public identity (the AAAS assumed publication of *Science,* for example) while they continued to advocate governmental support for science (especially the National Academy of Sciences, founded in 1863). The AAAS began a policy of affiliating specialized societies. In 1916 the National Research Council, formed by the National Academy of Sciences, supervised manpower and fund allocation. After the war the council continued to offer recommendations and attempted to balance support for basic research and applied projects. The American Council of Learned Societies (1919) and the Social Science Research Council (1923) similarly coordinated diverse but parallel professional groups. Other such groups were established after World War II.

The professionalization of science was made possible through institutions—especially scientific societies—that created a sense of common respect, a vehicle for united action, a group capable of enforcing ethical and procedural standards, and a concern for the public awareness of, and support for, science. (*See also* Scientific Periodicals.)

SCIOTO COMPANY. A speculative land-buying syndicate organized to purchase territory in the Ohio Valley. It was established in July 1787 when the Rev. Manasseh Cutler, attempting to purchase 1.5 million acres of land for the Ohio Company, was approached by New York speculators who offered Cutler enough money for a down payment on his land if he would secure for them, concealing their names, an option from Congress on the great tract of land north and west of the Ohio Company's proposed purchase. New York and Massachusetts speculators divided the thirty shares among themselves. Joel Barlow was sent to France as their agent, and with William Playfair, an unscrupulous Englishman, organized the Compagnie de Scioto to sell the Scioto lands. Although sales were active at first, the French company presently collapsed. The financial panic of 1792 swept away the fortunes of the leading American partners, and the Scioto Company defaulted on its contract with the government. Thus the 500 or more Frenchmen who had purchased what they thought were deeds to land owned by the company had in fact acquired only options to buy the homesites. Congress, recognizing their plight, awarded them land elsewhere in Ohio.

SCIOTO GAZETTE. A newspaper established in Chillicothe, Ohio, by Nathaniel Willis on Apr. 25, 1800. That year it absorbed *Freeman's Journal,* successor to the *Centinel of the North-Western Territory,* first newspaper in the Old Northwest. Published continuously with little change of name, the *Scioto Gazette* was originally Democratic-Republican, later Whig, and eventually Republican. The last edition was published in December 1939; on Jan. 2, 1940, it became the *Chillicothe Gazette.*

SCIOTO TRAIL. Frontier route that followed the Sandusky and Scioto valleys almost due south from Sandusky Bay to the Ohio River through Kentucky to Cumberland Gap, in Tennessee. A branch ran southeast from the Scioto River along the divide west of the Hocking River to the mouth of the Great Kanawha River, which it followed into Virginia. The main trail was used for the fur trade, as a warpath, and during the American Revolution for raids in Kentucky by Ohio tribes. Part of the trail near Cumberland Gap (Warriors' Path) was used for Daniel Boone's Wilderness Road.

SCOPES TRIAL. The fundamentalist movement led to the passage of laws in Tennessee forbidding the teaching of the theory of evolution. In 1925, a high school teacher, John Thomas Scopes, was tried for violating the state's "monkey law" (the Butler Act of Mar. 21, 1925). Scopes and three friends decided to test the law's constitutionality.

The Monkey Trial aroused enormous interest. William Jennings Bryan, political leader and ardent fundamentalist, served as a volunteer lawyer for the prosecution, while Scopes had as defenders several eminent attorneys, including Clarence S. Darrow. Judge John T. Raulston tried to run a fair and orderly trial in the circus atmosphere that sprang up.

The defense attacked the law on three main constitutional grounds: first, that it violated the First and Fourteenth amendments to the Constitution by writing into the law a religious doctrine; second, that it was unreasonable in that it forbade the teaching of a well-established fact of nature; and third, that it was vague, because it did not say whether it meant "teach" in the sense of "set forth" or "explain" or in the sense of "advocate" or "recommend." They brought to Dayton a dozen scientists to testify to the evidence for evolution. The prosecution, however, had their testimony excluded as irrelevant. Darrow hinted that he wanted a guilty verdict to make possible an appeal. The jury obliged, and Scopes was fined $100. When the case was appealed, the Tennessee Supreme Court set aside the verdict because the judge had committed a legal blunder in levying the fine.

SCOTCH-IRISH. A people, in the American colonies and the United States, emanating from the Scottish Protestants who were transplanted to Ulster, Ireland, chiefly during the 17th century, and from their descendants. The migrations from Scotland to Ulster, begun during the years from 1607 to 1609 under the sponsorship of James I. By the close of the 17th century, adverse economic conditions and political and religious disabilities arose, creating in them a desire to leave Ireland. Consequently, thousands of these people emigrated to America.

The Scotch-Irish began to arrive in the middle of the 17th century and continued to settle in small numbers until about 1715. This influx was greatly accelerated after 1717 because of worsening conditions in Ulster. As many as 10,000 reputedly arrived in Pennsylvania within a single year. Various studies indicate that in 1790 probably 6 percent of the U.S. population were Scotch-Irish or of Scotch-Irish extraction. On their arrival in America, they tended to penetrate to the frontiers. While they may now be found in every state in the Union, they settled in greater numbers in Tennessee, Kentucky, Missouri, Ohio, Indiana, and Illinois.

SCOTT, FORT. On the Marmaton River in Bourbon County, Kans.; established in 1842 as an intermediate post on the military road from Fort Leavenworth, Kans., to Fort Gibson, Okla. Fort Scott, named for Gen. Winfield Scott, was abandoned as a post during 1853–54. In 1855 the federal government sold the fort's substantial frame buildings at public auction to some settlers, and shortly thereafter the present city of Fort Scott came into existence. The city, with a population of 8,893 in 1980, is located in an agricultural area and is a center of dairy farming. Coal, gas, oil, and limestone are among its natural resources.

SCOTT-PILLOW QUARREL. Maj. Gen. Gideon J. Pillow commanded Gen. Winfield Scott's Third Division in the Mexican War. In 1847, after the Battle of Contreras and the Battle of Chapultepec, Pillow claimed undeserved credit for the victories. Scott asked that the report be revised, which was done, but not to Scott's satisfaction. Then Pillow published in the *New Orleans Delta* an anonymous and vainglorious account of his military prowess. Arrested for insubordination and disrespect, in 1848 Pillow appeared before the same court that, on the basis of Pillow's appeal of Scott's charges, was investigating Scott's conduct. Both were exonerated, but Pillow was discredited by the army.

SCOTTSBORO CASE. In April 1931 in Scottsboro, Ala., eight of nine black teenagers were sentenced to death for allegedly raping two white women. (The ninth was sentenced to life imprisonment.) From 1931 to 1937, during a series of appeals and new trials, the case grew to an international cause célèbre as the International Labor Defense (ILD) and the Communist Party of the U.S.A. spearheaded efforts to free the "Scottsboro boys." Each successful appeal was followed by retrial and reconviction. Finally, in 1937, defense attorney Samuel Leibowitz and the nonpartisan Scottsboro Defense Committee arranged a compromise whereby four of the nine were released and the remaining five were given sentences ranging from twenty years to life. Four of the five defendants were released on parole from 1943 to 1950. The fifth escaped in 1948. In 1966 Judge James Edwin Horton revealed theretofore confidential information that conclusively proved the innocence of the nine defendants.

SCOUTING ON THE PLAINS. Fur trappers and hunters who penetrated the West before the advent of civilization acquired a remarkable knowledge of the geography and Indian tribes of the country that fitted them to be scouts and guides in the later military campaigns on the Plains. Kit Carson, Jim Bridger, Bill Williams, Charlie Reynolds, Billy Comstock, and Sharp Grover were former fur trappers, while others, including Billy Dixon and William F. ("Buffalo Bill") Cody, were buffalo hunters.

Nevertheless, the army would have been seriously handicapped had it not been for friendly Indian scouts. Osage, Pawnee, Tonkawa, Delaware, Seminole, Shoshone, Crow, Arikara, Cheyenne, and Sioux did scouting, trailing, and fighting for the army in the 19th century.

In the Southwest, friendly Apache, Mohave, Papago, and other Indian scouts actually bore the brunt of many campaigns against hostile Apache, notably in the Geronimo wars of 1881–83 and 1885–86.

SCRANTON (Pa.). City in northeastern Pennsylvania, with a population of 88,117 in 1980. Located in the Lackawanna River valley, near the nation's largest known deposit of anthracite coal. Scranton was economically depressed in the mid-20th century when the use of anthracite coal declined. The city then developed the "Scranton Plan," community construction of buildings that could be leased to companies which would do business in the area. In the 1970's industrial companies turned out products ranging from plastic appliances to television parts.

SCRIPPS INSTITUTION OF OCEANOGRAPHY. In the early 1890's William E. Ritter of the University of California conceived the project of a systematic biological survey of the Pacific Ocean adjacent to the California coast. Explorations culminated in 1900 in a permanent seaside station at San Pedro. The site was shifted in 1903 to San Diego. The Marine Biological Association of San Diego was organized to found and endow the San Diego Marine Biological Institution. The present site in northern La Jolla was acquired in 1907, and Ritter became the first permanent resident director in 1909. In 1912 the institution became the Scripps Institution for Biological Research of the University of California. Gifts from newspaper publisher Edward W. Scripps and especially his sister Ellen remained the chief source of support until World War II. In 1925 the institution was renamed the Scripps Institution of Oceanography. Subsequent directors emphasized physical oceanography, research cruises, and a deep-sea drilling project. The Scripps Institution became the nucleus of the San Diego campus of the university, first opened to undergraduates in 1964.

SCULPTURE. The beginnings of American sculpture are found in 17th-century gravestones of New England. Increased wealth of the 18th century brought about a demand for fine wood carving for elegant Chippendale furniture and elaborate decorative architectural carving. The Skillins family of Boston and Samuel McIntire of Salem excelled, as did William Rush of Philadelphia. They also carved handsome figureheads for ships.

After the revolutionary war Americans turned to foreign sculptors to produce marble images of their great men. The neoclassic sculpture of the Frenchman Jean-Antoine Houdon influenced several generations of American sculptors. By the second quarter of the 19th century America had produced its own native school of sculptors, led by Horatio Greenough, Hiram Powers, and Thomas Crawford, all of whom went to live in Italy. Countless Americans visited Greenough in Florence to have busts made of themselves. Crawford later created the sculptures for the pediment of the Senate wing of the U.S. Capitol (1855) in his studio in Rome.

Henry Kirke Brown also went to Italy, but in 1846 returned to America, rejecting Italianate neoclassicism for naturalism. With Brown the age of bronze sculpture began in America. Clark Mills, former plasterer with no formal training in sculpture, created a tour de force in bronze equestrian statuary: the *Andrew Jackson* (1848–53, Washington, D.C.). Two other talented sculptors of the period were Erastus Dow Palmer and John Rogers.

Another generation followed the first to Italy—William Wetmore Story created heroic marble figures. Most acclaimed was *Cleopatra* (1858, Metropolitan Museum of Art). From Baltimore William Rinehart came to Rome in 1858 where he, too, created marble images of antique subjects and naturalistic portraits of prominent Americans. Randolph Rogers epitomized romantic neoclassicism in his statue of *Nydia, The Blind Girl of Pompeii* (1859, Metropolitan Museum of Art).

Bronze portrait statuary was created in large amounts, particularly by John Quincy Adams Ward. His *Henry Ward Beecher* (1891, Brooklyn, N.Y.) and *President James A. Garfield* (1887, Washington, D.C.) possess the unromanticized, undramatic naturalism then in vogue. Ward was one of the founders of the National Sculpture Society.

With the rise of Augustus Saint-Gaudens and Daniel Chester French the aesthetics of naturalism was revitalized. Italy was largely rejected, and the new style came out of the École des Beaux Arts in Paris. At the World's Columbian Exposition (Chicago, 1893), Saint-Gaudens, French, and others collaborated with numerous architects to give the exposition that neobaroque exuberance that characterizes the Beaux Arts style. Saint-Gaudens and French dominated this golden age. French's career began auspiciously with the bronze *Minuteman* (1874, Concord, Mass.) and closed half a century later with his marble, seated *Abraham Lincoln* (1922), part of the Lincoln Memorial in Washington, D.C.

In the years preceding World War I the conservatives, represented by the academic tradition and the advocates of the eclectic Beaux Arts style, entrenched themselves against the aesthetic assault of the modern movement. Paul Manship and Paul Jennewein represented a compromise that drew on the past but incorporated some abstraction.

After World War II American sculpture moved dramatically toward abstract and nonobjective form. David Smith introduced welded metal, and Alexander Calder developed mobiles and stabiles; both men were greatly influenced by constructivism. Others owed more to abstract expressionism: Seymour Lipton, Herbert Ferber, and Theodore J. Roszak.

The 1960's and 1970's brought American sculpture into a direct confrontation with reality as it incorporated everyday objects into its art—as in George Segal's *Girl in Doorway* (1965) and Marisol's *Women With Dog* (1964). "Junk sculpture," or assembled discarded objects, is represented by Louise Nevelson and Richard Stankiewicz, while "light sculptures"—using neon and fluorescent tubes—have been created by Dan Flavin and Chryssa. Another modern sculptural form is the monumental outdoor "land art" or "earthworks"; among the artists who created these sculptures are Michael Heizer, Robert Smithson, Walter de Maria, and Richard Lerra.

SCURVY. One of the earliest references to scurvy, a deficiency disease caused by a lack of vitamin C (ascorbic acid) in the diet, occurred in 1631 when John Winthrop, writing to his wife in England who was preparing to join him in Massachusetts, cautioned her: "Remember to bringe juice of lemons to sea with thee, for thee and thy company to eate with your meate as sauce." Scurvy continued to flourish even though the simple remedy for its control was known. The first in the United States to describe night blindness (1842) as one of the symptoms of scurvy was Edward Coale. Modern methods of food preservation and distribution and improved eating habits have made a diet rich in vitamin C, and scurvy has ceased to be a major American public health problem.

SEABOARD AIR LINE RAILROAD. *See* **Seaboard Coast Line.**

SEABOARD COAST LINE. *See* **Railroads, Sketches of Principal Lines.**

SEA FENCIBLES. The first organization of the U.S. Army charged exclusively with coast defense. By an act of Congress on July 26, 1813, ten separate companies were organized to be employed "as well on land as on water for the defense of the ports and harbors." Their most notable service was at the defense of Fort McHenry, Sept. 13, 1814, which also included the Baltimore Fencibles, one of several volunteer companies of the same class of troops. The Sea Fencibles were discharged on June 15, 1815.

SEALERS, TOWN. Officers chosen by the New England town meeting for annual terms to test and certify the accuracy of weights, scales, and measures.

SEALING. Began in the North Atlantic in connection with whaling early in the 17th century and developed into a separate occupation late in the 18th century. Hunting of the small hair seal became an important commercial activity in the late 18th and early 19th centuries. Their numbers, as a result of reckless exploitation, have steadily declined. In 1970 Canada and Norway, prompted by public outcries over the killing of baby "whitecoat" seals, agreed to restrict the killing of seals off Newfoundland and Labrador, as of 1971. The seals of Antarctic waters, mainly the southern elephant and South American fur seal, were nearly exterminated during the 19th century but began to recover when regulations were introduced in 1881. In 1972 twelve nations signed a treaty giving complete protection to some varieties of seals and restricting the killing of others.

American sealing interests have centered largely on the northern fur seal herd of the Pribilof Islands—Saint Paul and Saint George—in the Bering Sea. The seal being migratory, the Pribilofs contain the rookeries to which the herd returns from far south every spring. There the young are born and grow strong enough to endure the winter migration, which takes them to the latitudes of California and Mexico. It was not until 1786 that its breeding grounds were discovered. Thereafter the ruthless slaughter by Russian fur traders of Alaska threatened the complete destruction of the herd, but it was saved when the killing began to be restricted by the Russian-American Company by 1835. When the United States bought Alaska in 1867 the herd numbered about 3 million.

A serious threat was the rapid rise, beginning in the 1880's, of pelagic, or deep-sea, sealers. Land killing could be regulated; but because several different nationalities—Americans, Canadians, Mexicans, Russians, and Japanese—preyed upon the herd at sea, saving even a remnant of the herd became a grave problem. In 1886 the United States seized several Canadian pelagic vessels, but in 1893 an arbitration tribunal at Paris required that damages be paid owners of the vessels. Although the tribunal imposed some regulations on pelagic sealing, it seemed as if the herd would become extinct. In 1911, a treaty was signed by Great Britain, Russia, Japan, and the United States outlawing pelagic sealing and in 1941, by the United States and Canada continuing the ban. A 1957 pact signed by the United States, Canada, Japan, and the Soviet Union extended the prohibition.

SEAL OF THE CONFEDERATE STATES OF AMERICA. The official embossed emblem of the Confederacy, commissioned by the Confederate congress and decreed to depict Thomas Crawford's equestrian statue of George Washington in Richmond, Va., with the date Feb. 22, 1862 (Jefferson Davis' inauguration day), and the motto *Deo Vindice.* The seal was cut in solid silver by Joseph Shepherd Wyon of London. It reached Richmond in September 1864 but was never affixed to any document. The seal was lost during the war, but was recovered and is now displayed in Richmond's Museum of the Confederacy.

SEAL OF THE UNITED STATES (the **Great Seal**). The official embossed emblem that validates a U.S. government document. Work on the design of a seal was begun by a committee appointed by the Continental Congress on July 4, 1776. It took Congress six years more to obtain a satisfactory design. The obverse of the seal finally adopted was a depiction of the American eagle, and the pyramid and the Eternal Eye of God, symbols of the Freemasons, was selected for the reverse. The Great Seal is pictured on the U.S. one-dollar bill. The seal is kept by the secretary of state and is affixed to such documents as foreign treaties and presidential proclamations on the signed order of the president and, since an executive order in 1952, on certain other documents without a presidential warrant. Although recut six times for various reasons, the appearance of the Great Seal is still precisely as decreed by the Continental Congress on June 20, 1782.

SEAMEN'S ACT OF 1915. Also known as the **Furuseth Act** because it embodied reforms advocated by Andrew Furuseth and as the **La Follette Seaman's Act** because of strong support from Sen. Robert M. La Follette. Approved Mar. 4, 1915, it applied to crews of vessels registered in the United States and to those of foreign countries in United States ports. It was designed to improve living and working conditions, attract American citizens to the sea, and provide greater safety. Among its more important provisions were those abolishing imprisonment for desertion; reducing penalties for disobedience and for neglecting to join or quitting a vessel; regulating hours of work; fixing minimum scale and quality of food; regulating wages; and requiring 75 percent of the members of each ship department to understand the language spoken by the officers.

SEA OTTER TRADE. Europeans and Americans first came to the North Pacific coast of America in the late 18th century in pursuit of sea otter skins from the Aleutian Islands to Baja (Lower) California. In China the furs were exchanged at good profit for prized Oriental goods. Russia and Spain were the pioneer nations to engage in the trade. The great fur rush to the Northwest coast was caused by published accounts of Capt. James Cook's last Pacific voyage, 1776–79. English and American vessels led the drive, but within a decade the former had practically withdrawn. In the early 19th century American and Russian traders entered the California sea otter fields, where they poached throughout the Spanish period. After 1821 the liberal policy of Mexico stimulated the California trade, and many Americans became Mexican citizens in order to participate in the business. The sea otter trade came to an end when ruthless hunting, intensified by firearms, had nearly exterminated the animals. At the beginning of the 20th century the sea otter was so rare that its pelts were the most valuable of all furs. A treaty signed in 1910 by the United States, Great Britain, Russia, and Japan banned the hunting of sea otter, but it was thought to be too late until the 1930's, when several sea otter colonies were discovered in the Aleutians and along the California coast.

SEA POWER. Sea power rests on profits from domestic industry, enhanced by overseas trade; sustaining a strong military fleet for use not in warfare but in securing and maintaining significant trading ports; and avoiding war whenever possible. When forced into war, prudent sea power adheres to three priorities: protect the home base; keep the fleet relatively strong; and use the fleet only for inducing the enemy to peace.

For a full century after 1815 the small U.S. fleet supported worldwide ocean trade and fisheries. By 1914 the United States was the preeminent non-European naval power. Adm. Alfred Thayer Mahan's theory that naval power and control of the seas are decisive in international politics was widely accepted throughout the world.

After World War I no nation has adhered consistently to classic uses of sea power. As a Pacific naval power the United States followed the classic rules of sea power during World War II. Operating from close-supporting mobile sea bases, elements from all U.S. armed forces advanced amphibiously along the island approaches to Japan. Yet when the United States intervened in Vietnam, it foresook transpacific sea-based operations and relied almost totally on land-based forces.

SEARCH, RIGHT OF. *See* **Search and Seizure, Unreasonable; Visit and Search.**

SEARCH AND SEIZURE, UNREASONABLE. The American colonists' hostility to general warrants and writs of assistance is reflected in the Fourth Amendment to the U.S. Constitution, which prohibits "unreasonable searches and seizures" and requires that warrants be issued upon "probable cause, supported by oath or affirmation, and particularly describing the place to be searched, and the person or things to be seized." Unless exceptional circumstances exist, such as the need to act swiftly to prevent the destruction of evidence, an officer must obtain a search warrant, a written authorization by a judicial officer. An arrest may be made without a warrant, even though it is practicable to obtain one. "Incident to the arrest," the person may be searched without a warrant, as may the area "within his immediate control," in order to protect the officer against hidden weapons or to prevent destruction of evidence. In the 1968 stop-and-frisk cases, the Supreme Court held that an officer who lacks adequate grounds to make an arrest or search may nevertheless briefly detain a person in a public place and conduct a carefully limited search of the outer clothing to discover weapons.

The U.S. Supreme Court, in *Mapp* v. *Ohio* (1961), held that the Fourth Amendment is enforceable against the states and requires the exclusion of illegally seized evidence in state, as well as federal, prosecutions. By the late 1970's, however, the continued vitality of this doctrine, known as the "exclusionary rule," appeared to be in serious jeopardy. In *Rakas* v. *Illinois* (1978) the scope of the exclusionary role was severely limited.

SEATTLE (Wash.). Largest city in the state of Washington, with 493,846 residents in 1980. Seattle is located on the eastern shore of Puget Sound, on Elliot Bay. Its east side faces Lake Washington, a long and large body of fresh water.

The first settlement by white men was at Alki Point in 1851. The settlement grew slowly until the 1860's. At one time, it was nearly overrun and destroyed by Indians, but was saved by the guns of a U.S. Navy sloop-of-war. The town was named "Seattle" in honor of a friendly Indian chief. Seattle's importance as a seaport for lumber grew rapidly after the Civil War. Its location made it ideal for ship traffic to and from Alaska. When overland rail connections with the east were completed in the 1890's, Seattle's importance as a shipping and transportation center was established for good.

A major fishing fleet is based at Puget Sound, and shipbuilding is carried on both on the Sound and on Lake Washington. It is an aircraft-building center, and a key link in transportation for the northwestern states. Firms are engaged in lumber handling and metal work, and the state of Washington's banking and insurance industries have headquarters there. The University of Washington is located in the city, as are Seattle University and Seattle-Pacific College.

SEATTLE WORLD'S FAIR (1962). Opened on Apr. 21. Set on a 74-acre site linked by a 1.2-mile monorail to the main business district of Seattle, Century 21, as it was officially known, was dominated by the 600-foot "space needle" and featured twenty national and eighty-three commercial exhibitions. Financed largely by public capital, the exposition drew 9,609,969 paying visitors and closed on Oct. 21.

SECEDED STATES, CONGRESSIONAL REPRESENTATION OF. With the exception of five representatives from the northwestern counties of Virginia, none of the states that seceded from the Union during the Civil War was represented in the House of Representatives after May 1861. Two senators, elected by the loyal part of the Virginia legislature, were admitted by the Senate in July 1861. Andrew Johnson, however, was the only regularly elected senator from one of the seceded states (Tennessee) who retained his seat in the Senate. He continued until he was appointed military governor of Tennessee in March 1862.

SECESSION, ORDINANCE OF. The enactment in legal form by which eleven southern states withdrew from the Union in 1860–61. According to the compact theory of union, sovereign states had entered the partnership by ratifying the Constitution of the United States. Secession, therefore, was achieved by a repeal of the act of ratification. This was accomplished in each state by a convention.

SECESSION, RIGHT OF. The southern states of the American Union were advancing no new theory when they appealed to and exercised the right of secession in 1860–61. The right of a people to establish, alter, or abolish their government and to institute a new one if their safety and happiness demanded it was a fundamental principle of the American Revolution (*see* Declaration of Independence).

The first serious threat of secession came in 1798 when the Democratic-Republicans, smarting under Federalist legislation, talked of separation. John L. Taylor, a prominent North Carolina judge, openly advocated secession, but the more moderate views of Thomas Jefferson prevailed. After Jefferson's presidential victory in 1801 the New England Federalists sought a remedy against Democratic domination. The purchase of Louisiana further antagonized the Federalists, and the Essex Junto planned a new confederacy composed of

New England and New York. Alexander Hamilton blocked their efforts. The disgruntled Federalists of New England resorted to treasonable action in opposing "Mr. Madison's war," and in 1814 met secretly in the Hartford Convention. No doubt their object was dissolution of the Union and formation of a New England confederacy if their program of constitutional reform failed. Fortunately the peace treaty prevented action.

The next rumblings were heard in the southern states. Threats of separation were made over the Missouri question (*see* Missouri Compromise) and the Indian controversy (*see Cherokee Nation* v. *Georgia*), and the tariff issue brought these threats to the very threshold of action. South Carolina nullified the tariff acts of 1828 and 1832 and signified its intention of seceding if the federal government attempted coercion (*see* Nullification).

Slavery in the territories caused both North and South to threaten to secede. John Quincy Adams thought the free states would secede if Texas were annexed, and the southern leaders threatened separation if slavery were excluded from the Mexican cession. This controversy culminated in the Nashville Convention of 1850 and state conventions in several southern states. These conventions reluctantly accepted the Compromise of 1850 and secession was halted.

The threat of secession was the last resort of the minority to protect its interests under the Constitution, and was constantly present from the Revolution to the Civil War.

SECESSION OF SOUTHERN STATES. On Abraham Lincoln's election to the presidency, the governor of South Carolina, William H. Gist, recommended and the legislature called a state convention, which met on Dec. 20, 1860. By a unanimous vote the convention passed an ordinance dissolving "the union now subsisting between South Carolina and other States." The convention issued a Declaration of Immediate Causes, expressing the states' rights view of the Union, and appointed commissioners to other southern states and to Washington, D.C. Overriding minorities, six other states by conventions passed ordinances of secession early in 1861: Mississippi, Florida, Alabama, Georgia, Louisiana, and Texas, thus completing the secession of the lower South.

President James Buchanan, believing secession unconstitutional but considering himself without authority to coerce, and anxious not to give the upper South cause for secession, was determined not to risk war by an overt act in protecting federal property and sustaining the operation of federal laws. The South Carolina commissioners, sent to negotiate with Buchanan for the peaceful division of property and debts, demanded that Maj. Robert Anderson, then occupying Fort Sumter in Charleston harbor, evacuate that post. This he refused to do. Meanwhile Congress was sifting compromise proposals.

With compromise failing and Buchanan taking a firmer attitude as he became less hopeful of peace and union (he sent the *Star of the West* to reinforce Sumter), representatives from the seceded states met at Montgomery on Feb. 4, 1861, to organize a new nation. Peaceful secession seemed remote after Lincoln's fateful decision to relieve Fort Sumter, the firing on the fort on Apr. 12, and Lincoln's call for volunteers three days later. This practical state of war compelled the states of the upper South to make a reluctant choice between the Confederacy and the Union.

By May 20 Virginia, Arkansas, Tennessee, and North Carolina had also seceded. Opposition to secession in Virginia led to formation of a separate state. The border slave states of Kentucky, Maryland, Delaware and Missouri did not secede, and Kentucky's attempted neutrality failed.

SECRET PROTOCOL OF 1917. During the conversations preceding the signing of the Lansing-Ishii Agreement of Nov. 2, 1917, Secretary of State Robert Lansing had striven to include the following statement: "The Governments of the United States and Japan will not take advantage of the present conditions to seek special rights or privileges in China which would abridge the rights of subjects or citizens of other friendly states." This was precisely what the Japanese negotiator did not wish to accept. With the express approval of President Woodrow Wilson, this formula was relegated to a secret protocol signed on Oct. 31. But the language of the secret protocol sounds more like an epitaph for the formula than a confirmation of it: "Upon careful examination of the question, it was agreed that the clause above quoted being superfluous in the relations of the two Governments and liable to create erroneous impressions in the minds of the public, should be eliminated from the declaration. It was, however, well understood that the principle enunciated in the clause which was thus suppressed was in perfect accord with the declared policy of the two Governments in regard to China." The protocol was kept secret until 1935.

SECRET SERVICE, UNITED STATES. Created on July 5, 1865, as a bureau of the Department of the Treasury, to suppress rampant counterfeiting. It was hoped that the adoption of a national currency in 1863 would resolve the problem. But it, too, was soon counterfeited extensively.

In addition to the suppression of counterfeiting, the Secret Service was often requested to conduct investigations later assigned to other government agencies. These included mail frauds, bank and train robberies, bounty claims, illicit traffic in whiskey, Ku Klux Klan activities, and counterespionage. The Secret Service continues to suppress forgery and fraudulent negotiation or redemption of government checks, bonds, and other obligations or securities of the United States.

The Secret Service has greatly expanded. After the assassination of President William McKinley in 1901, it was assigned to protect President Theodore Roosevelt, although legislation authorizing presidential protection by the Secret Service was not enacted until 1906. Between 1913 and 1971 such protection was extended to other public personages. On Mar. 19, 1970, President Richard M. Nixon established the Executive Protective Service, a uniformed division of the Secret Service. This increased the former White House Police Force. The Executive Protective Service protects the White House and foreign missions in the metropolitan area of the District of Columbia.

SECRET SOCIETIES. Organized, in most instances, for the social and moral welfare of members and to promote good fellowship and patriotism, they have also done a great amount of charitable and educational work. Freemasonry, the ritual and philosophy of which have influenced many similar organizations, was introduced from Great Britain about 1730; the Independent Order of Oddfellows was brought over from the same country in 1819. A roster of indigenous societies would be encyclopedic. A few well-known ones are the Knights of Pythias, founded in 1864; the Benevolent and Protective Order of Elks, 1868; the Knights of Columbus, 1882; and the Loyal Order of Moose, 1888.

For a decade following 1826 there was a strong popular prejudice against secret orders. While directed primarily against the Masons, this prejudice was even directed against college fraternities. The movement soon subsided; and ritual and secrecy were effectively used to promote a wide variety of causes—temperance, liquor control, agricultural improvement, life insurance, and the betterment of the underprivileged. Local societies occasionally showed vigilante proclivities.

The subversive and revolutionary secret society, so common in Europe, has had an unfruitful field in America, although the prerevolutionary Sons of Liberty, the Knights of the Golden Circle during the Civil War, and the Molly Maguires in the post–Civil War period are somewhat analogous. Antiforeign and anti-Catholic prejudice produced the secret Know-Nothing party in the 1850's, and seventy years later the revived Ku Klux Klan.

SECTIONALISM. The spirit of sectionalism and its manifestations have been present throughout American history, and every major region has strongly espoused its sectional interests. The Constitutional Convention bogged down over the question of the economic interests of the South. Although less cohesive than the South, the middle states expressed concern for the protection of their grain exports. New England sectionalism appeared during the War of 1812, when citizens of that region generally criticized "Mr. Madison's war." Pioneers who drove the frontier westward quickly developed loyalties to their new regions, advancing their economic and political interests.

During the first half of the 19th century the United States consisted of three large and rather ill-defined regions: the North (the area north of the Ohio River and the Mason-Dixon Line); the South; and the West (the large area west of the Appalachian Mountains). The history of the United States from 1800 to 1865 is largely the history of the relationship of those three regions.

Northerners and southerners generally believed that the western lands should be sold to the highest bidder, gaining revenue for the U.S. Treasury. Westerners were not yet advocating that the land be given away (as they did after the Civil War), but they did favor charging settlers only a minimum amount. Trade between North and West was advanced when better transportation facilities were developed, and both sections' economies improved. When states and private enterprise did not provide enough means of transportation between the regions, northerners and westerners demanded that the national government construct additional internal improvements. The South objected to national money being spent on such projects. As the North developed more industry it demanded a protective tariff; the South remained primarily an agricultural region, trading cotton and tobacco in European and world markets, and it preferred low tariff rates. The West was divided on the tariff: the Northwest favored a high tariff, while the Southwest desired low rates. The tariff dispute brought a crisis in 1832, when South Caroiina nullified a tariff law passed by Congress. A compromise resolved the disagreement.

The question of expansion of slavery into the western territories overshadowed all other sectional concerns in the twenty years prior to the Civil War. Northerners hoped to prohibit the spread of slavery, while southerners believed they had the right to take their slaves wherever they migrated. The annexation of Texas, the Wilmot Proviso, the Mexican War, and the admission of California as a state all became primarily sectional issues. The Civil War was the ultimate consequence of extreme sectionalism, but sectionalism did not die at Appomattox.

After Reconstruction the development of the Solid South, the relegation of the freed black to a position of inferiority, and the status of the South as an economic appendage of the North were all manifestations of sectional differences. By mid-20th century the Solid South was breaking up. The southern economy prospered, the South's standard of living rose, and southerners had increased purchasing power. All these factors combined to diminish sectionalism in the South, although it continued to be a political and economic factor between rural and urban areas around the nation.

SECURITIES AND EXCHANGE COMMISSION. The Securities and Exchange Commission was created by statute in 1934, absorbing certain functions that the Securities Act of 1933 had assigned to the Federal Trade Commission. The task of this agency is to protect the public and investors against malpractices in securities markets. Those who offer securities for sale must disclose pertinent information for investors before their offering can be registered with the commission as required by law. The commission also registers and supervises national exchanges, brokers, investment companies, and investment counselors; investigates malpractices; maintains surveillance over the transactions of public utility holding companies; and advises courts in bankruptcy proceedings. Its sanctions include the withholding and revocation of registration and the initiation of prosecution.

SEDGWICK, FORT. Established in northeast Colorado by the U.S. Army in 1864 at the junction of Lodge Pole Creek with the South Platte River to maintain control over the Sioux, Cheyenne, and Arapaho during the Civil War. It was abandoned in 1871.

SEDITION ACTS. The first national sedition act was passed by the Federalist-dominated Congress of 1798, and was intended to halt Democratic-Republican attacks on the government and to ferret out pro-French sympathizers in case of war with France. The second sedition act, passed during World War I, was aimed at subversives, such as pacifists or "Bolsheviks" who interfered with the war effort.

The Sedition Act of 1798 reestablished the English common law on seditious libel, but with important changes. It accepted jury determination of sedition and allowed truth to be considered in defense. The act expired in 1801, and during President Thomas Jefferson's tenure all persons convicted under the act were pardoned; Congress voted to repay all fines. The act was generally assumed to be unconstitutional, and in 1964 the Supreme Court flatly declared it inconsistent with the First Amendment.

The Sedition Act of 1918 made it a felony to interfere in the war effort; to insult the government, the Constitution, or the armed forces; and "by word or act [to] support or favor the cause of the German Empire or its allies in the present war, or by word or act [to] oppose the cause of the United States." The most vital difference between this act and that of 1798 was the emphasis in 1918 on criticism of the government and its symbols as opposed to the listing of individual officers in the 1798 act. The national hysteria produced by the war ran its course by the early 1920's, and the Sedition Act was repealed in 1921. Similar acts passed by the states resulted in litigation reaching the Supreme Court, and the Court began extending the strictures of the First Amendment to the states.

Although the Alien Registration Act of 1940, better known as the Smith Act, is not called a sedition act, it had that as a major purpose. The Smith Act prohibits advocacy of forceful overthrow of the government and makes it a crime to belong to an organization subsequently found to be guilty of advocating forceful removal of the government.

SEGREGATION. Attempts by the majority to separate and keep apart from themselves minority groups such as Afro-Americans, Indians, immigrants, and Mexican-Americans. During the colonial period and early years of the United States, white Americans generally kept themselves apart from the Indians. Segregation of the white and black races was a recognized element in the pre–Civil War slave system; and after slavery was abolished, white southerners were determined to continue racial separation. Several southern states passed laws forbidding blacks to ride in first-class passenger railway cars, and numerous local ordinances requiring racial segregation in most public facilities followed. These laws stimulated Congress to pass the Civil Rights Act of 1875, to assure equal accommodations in public conveyances, inns, theaters, and other places of public entertainment. In 1883 the Supreme Court ruled this act unconstitutional. The Interstate Commerce Commission ruled that railroads must provide equal facilities for both races. Even though facilities were never equal, the Supreme Court upheld a separate-but-equal transportation law in the *Plessy* v. *Ferguson* (1896) decision. The separate-but-equal concept spread to other areas, particularly education, and it went without successful challenge for nearly sixty years. In the meantime, southern city governments and state legislatures adopted ordinances prohibiting certain activities by blacks. Unwritten laws, regulations, customs, traditions, and practices restricting the freedom of blacks in all parts of the country also developed. In the North and West during the time of slavery, discriminatory practices were not uncommon. As the black population in the North and West grew after the abolition of slavery, restrictions increased. This was especially true during and after World War I, when great numbers of southern blacks moved northward and westward in search of economic opportunity. Some states passed statutes prohibiting intermarriage. Separate schools were often permitted and sometimes required. *De facto* segregation occurred in residential housing; as a result, blacks crowded into the ghettos of the cities. During World War II, blacks were helping the nation fight a war to free the world's enslaved peoples, and they demanded that segregation throughout the United States be abolished (*see* Integration).

SEIGNIORAGE. Originally, a small profit beyond charges for actual mint expenses. In 1792 the U.S. Congress established "free coinage"—the minting of unlimited quantities of coins from gold and silver sold to the Treasury free of seigniorage. The reaction of the prosilver forces to the drastic fall in the price of silver in the late 19th century brought about the more modern meaning, in which advocates of increased silver coinage defined the very wide gap between the face value of silver dollars and the legislated price of silver as seigniorage. They implied that the government, too, profited from increased silver coinage, since it was able to buy a dollar's worth of goods and services with silver that cost only 50 cents or so.

SELDEN PATENT. The first and most bitterly contested of all automobile patents. The original application for a patent on a vehicle propelled by an internal combustion engine was filed in 1879 by George B. Selden, but was kept pending while Selden attempted to interest capital in his ideas, and the patent was not issued until 1895. The rights were eventually brought into the possession of the Electric Vehicle Company. In 1900 this concern began a vigorous enforcement of its patent rights by filing suit against the Winton Motor Carriage Company. The case dragged along for three years, only to be abandoned when Winton and nine other companies organized the Association of Licensed Automobile Manufacturers and agreed to pay royalties.

Henry Ford refused to take part, and in 1903 an infringement suit was filed against him. The case was spun out for eight years. A principal argument of the defense was that the Selden patent contemplated use of the Brayton two-cycle motor (invented by George Brayton in 1872 and improved by Selden), and not the Otto four-cycle engine then being used in practically all cars. The lower court upheld the claim of infringement, but the court of appeals, which ruled in Ford's favor (1911), stated that the patent was not being infringed by manufacture of vehicles using the Otto-type motor.

SELECTIVE SERVICE ACT. *See* **Draft.**

SELECTIVE SERVICE SYSTEM. *See* **Draft.**

SELECTMEN. Executive officers chosen, since earliest times, at town meetings in all New England states except Rhode Island. The usual number has been three, although five to nine are chosen in some large communities. Annual election has been the prevailing rule, with terms of three years. Their functions are determined by state law and usually involve preparation of the warrant for annual or special meetings, supervision of local highways, valuation and assessment of property, election control, issuance of licenses, and poor relief. Earlier they were also vested with police and educational functions.

SELF-SERVICE STORES. Self-service is a retailing method whereby the labor of the customer in selecting goods is substituted for that of a store clerk. Often self-service includes the customer bringing the goods to a checkout stand or cashier's booth, where payment is made and purchases are packaged. Although self-service was used to some degree in country stores during the 19th century, its significant use was first noted in southern California grocery stores in 1912. The man frequently cited as the originator of self-service grocery stores is Clarence Saunders, who established a chain of Piggly Wiggly Stores in Memphis, Tenn., in 1916. Saunders had 2,700 stores in forty-one states by 1928.

Initially the major chains ignored this new marketing concept, but in 1936–37 the Great Atlantic and Pacific Tea Company (A&P) and some other large chains began converting to supermarkets. Following the success of self-service in food stores, the practice was adopted by many kinds of stores. F. W. Woolworth began self-service operations in 1952. By the 1960's general merchandise firms, such as S. S. Kresge, and drug companies, such as Walgreen, were converting existing stores to self-service and all their new stores used this marketing innovation. Department store firms such as R. H. Macy and Company and Gimbel Brothers had at least converted their budget basement departments to self-service.

SEMICONDUCTORS. *See* **Computers.**

SEMINOLE. One of the Five Civilized Tribes, living chiefly in Florida and Oklahoma in the 20th century. Originally of Muskhogean stock and spoke Muskogee or Hitchiti. In the early 18th century they were associated with the Lower Creek on the Chattahoochee River in Georgia, but they began to move into Florida after 1700. By 1775 they had become known as the Seminole -"separatist" or "wild people." Their numbers were later augmented by Upper Creek, conquered tribes, and fugitive black slaves. Although the Seminole were town dwellers, they derived their living from farming, supplemented by hunting and trading; they developed a complex social organization in which military prowess played a major role.

The end of the Revolution brought the Seminole into conflict with Georgia over runaway slaves. During the War of 1812 Seminole raids on the Georgia border and retaliatory expeditions from the United States culminated in the first Seminole War (1816–18) and Andrew Jackson's punitive expedition in 1818. The acquisition of Florida by the United States brought the Seminole under American control.

A major part of the tribe resisted the treaties of Camp Moultrie (1823), Payne's Landing (1832), and Fort Gibson (1833), in which chiefs agreed to move from Florida to a reserve in the West. Eventually attacks escalated into the second Seminole War (1835–42). After that war most hostile Seminole were moved to Creek lands west of the Mississippi.

The Seminole Treaty of 1866 provided for a new reservation of 200,000 acres (now Seminole County, Okla.) and a grant of $235,362. In 1901 the Seminole became U.S. citizens, and by 1902 land allotments had been made to all Seminole citizens. Tribal government was extinguished in 1906. Oil production began on a large scale in 1923 and 1924. In 1967 a federal claims court upheld a 1964 verdict of the Indian Claims Commission that the Seminole had been illegally deprived of some 32 million acres in Florida, paving the way for compensation. By 1980 there were some 4,000 Seminole living in Oklahoma and Florida.

SEMINOLE WARS. In 1816 there was no united confederation of Indians in Florida, only the Mikasuki, Seminole, and some splinter groups. Neamathla, chief of the Mikasuki at Fowltown staged raids into the United States, causing a force under Col. David Twiggs to be sent from Fort Scott. The resulting battle on Nov. 21, 1817, opened the first Seminole War (1817–18). In March 1918 Maj. Gen Andrew Jackson reached Fort Scott, built up his force, and followed the Indians eastward toward the Suwannee River, destroying their villages. By April he had broken all Indian resistance west of the Suwannee.

In 1821 Florida was transferred to the United States by Spain. In 1830 Congress passed the Indian Removal Act, to transplant all the eastern Indians somewhere west of the Mississippi. This Act brought on the second Seminole War (1835–42). Osceola, the guiding spirit of resistance to removal, directed the murder of an Indian agent, and the massacre of two companies, and rapidly devastated northeastern Florida. Maj. Gen. Thomas S. Jesup was the pivotal figure in the war. He had scant respect for Indians and abandoned the conventions of "civilized" war, seizing Osceola under a flag of truce in 1837. By the time Jesup was relieved in 1838 about 100 Indians had been killed and 2,900 captured. During the next four years leadership on both sides changed frequently. By 1842 there were no more than 300 Seminole left in Florida, and the government ended its attempts to force them to leave. The Indians formally agreed to confine themselves to the area south of Pease Creek and west of Lake Okeechobee.

When Florida became a state in 1845, it sought to expel the Seminole completely. Military patrols and survey parties vandalized property deep in Indian country, including that belonging to the foremost Seminole leader, Billy Bowlegs. Bowlegs fought back and the third Seminole War (1855–58) was under way. There were perhaps 360 Seminole in Florida, 120 of them warriors. Forces under Brig. Gen. William S. Harney, a hardened Indian fighter, finally brought the chiefs to a conference at Fort Myers in 1858. There 165 persons, including Bowlegs, surrendered and were shipped west. Later

75 more migrated. This left roughly 125 Florida Seminole, who were allowed to remain in their homeland.

SENATE. *See* **Congress, United States.**

SENATE CLOTURE RULE. *See* **Cloture.**

SENATE CONFIRMATION. *See* **Confirmation by the Senate.**

SENATORIAL COURTESY. *See* **Courtesy of the Senate.**

SENATORS, ELECTION OF. Until 1866 the state legislatures determined their own procedure for electing U.S. senators, in some cases the chambers voting separately, in others in joint session. Frequent deadlocks and other unsatisfactory conditions led Congress in that year to prescribe a uniform procedure, under which both branches first voted separately by roll call and in case of disagreement were required to meet in joint session and continue voting daily until a candidate secured a majority. In the meantime there was a growing demand for popular election. By use of the direct primary for nominating senatorial candidates and exaction of pledges from state legislators to support the popular choice, the old system of election was being rapidly nullified when, in 1913, it was formally transferred to the electorate by the Seventeenth Amendment.

SENECA. *See* **Iroquois.**

SENECA FALLS CONVENTION. The first modern woman's rights convention, called by Lucretia Mott and Elizabeth Cady Stanton, was held in the Wesleyan Methodist Church at Seneca Falls, N.Y., July 19–20, 1848. Stanton read a "Declaration of Sentiments," listing many discriminations existing against women, and the convention adopted eleven resolutions, one of them calling for woman suffrage. This convention launched the organized modern woman's rights movement.

SENIORITY SYSTEM. Seniority is the status or importance gained by a person because of his length of service. Seniority often determines the order in which employees are dropped when business slackens. Promotions in some businesses and in many government operations depend on seniority. In the armed forces, seniority in rank often determines which of several officers holding the same rank will command a unit. In the U.S. Senate and House of Representatives members of the majority party with the longest service tend to get the chairmanship of important committees regardless of their ability. The Senate adopted a seniority system in 1847; the House, in 1910.

SEPARATION OF CHURCH AND STATE. A principle of American government which requires that religious and political activities must be conducted independently of each other. The first clause of the first Amendment to the U.S. Constitution was devoted to the separation of church and state: "Congress shall make no law respecting an establishment of religion, or prohibiting the free exercise thereof."

Most states have constitutional provisions written in exactly the same terms as those found in the Bill of Rights, while some have even more restrictive language. There have been many constitutional law cases in which arguments over the nature of "establishment" were the key issue. U.S. Supreme Court decisions have forbidden such practices as requiring common prayer in public schools or requiring cadets at the nation's military academies to attend chapel services.

SEPARATION OF POWERS. *See* **Powers, Separation of.**

SEPARATIST MOVEMENT. *See* **Western Separatism.**

SEPARATISTS (Independents). Radical Puritans who, in the late 16th century, advocated thoroughgoing reform within the Church of England. In the main, Separatists proposed a congregational or independent form of church polity, wherein each church was to be autonomous, founded upon a formal covenant, electing its own officers and restricting the membership to "visible saints." Separation was held a major offense by the regular Puritans as well as by Anglicans and royal authorities; yet the Puritans who settled Massachusetts Bay in 1620 already believed that Congregationalism rather than Presbyterianism was the polity of the New Testament, and when founding churches at Salem and Boston, 1629 and 1630, sought advice from the Separatists at Plymouth. In England during the 1640's the minority wing of the Puritan party maintained Congregationalism and were known as Independents, but the multitude of sects that arose out of the disorders of the time also took unto themselves the title of Independents, so that the term came to be a vague designation for opponents of Presbyterianism. Orthodox New England Puritans, although practicing a Congregational discipline, always denied that they were either Separatists or Independents.

***SEQUOIA*.** A genus of coniferous trees, comprising the species *Sequoia sempervirens* (the redwood) and *Sequoia gigantea* (the big tree). Both species average 275 feet in height, with trunks from 15 to 35 feet in diameter. They are the largest of all American forest trees. The redwood is found in the Pacific Coast region, from California to Oregon; the big tree is known only on the west slope of the Sierra Nevada in California. They probably first became known to the white man in 1833, when Capt. Joseph Walker's expedition sighted them.

SEQUOIA NATIONAL PARK. An area of some 385,000 acres in the Sierra Nevadas of eastern California. The park was created on Sept. 25, 1890, to protect the groves of *sequoia gigantea* (big tree), which are among the largest and oldest of living things. Within the park are Mt. Whitney, Kern River Canyon, and the Great Western Divide.

SEQUOYAH, PROPOSED STATE OF. Consideration of a state to include the lands of the Indian Territory was precipitated by Congress setting Mar. 4, 1906, as the date on which governments of the Five Civilized Tribes were to end. Although there was some support for joint statehood with Oklahoma Territory, a number of influential Indians were opposed. Conventions were held at Eufaula on Nov. 28, 1902, and May 21, 1903, at which Indians of the Five Tribes expressed their opposition to a single state encompassing Indian and Oklahoma territories. A conference of Creek was held at Muskogee on July 14, 1905, at which further opposition to joint statehood was given voice. On Aug. 21, at a convention attended by 182 Indian and white delegates, it was decided that a constitution would be drafted for—and Congress be requested to admit—the Indian Territory as a separate state with the name Sequoyah. A constitution was submitted on Sept. 8 and ratified by the people of Indian Territory, but Congress refused to consider admission of Sequoyah to the Union. The movement's leaders became leaders of the Oklahoma constitutional convention the following year.

SEQUOYA'S SYLLABARY. The Cherokee alphabet, developed early in the 19th century by Sequoya, a half-breed Cherokee also known as George Gist. Using symbols adapted from English, Greek, and Hebrew letters, Sequoya's syllabary consists of eighty-six characters. He submitted it to the leaders of the Cherokee nation in 1821, who approved it.

SESQUICENTENNIAL INTERNATIONAL EXPOSITION. Held in League Island Park and environs, Philadelphia, from June 1 to Dec. 1, 1926. It was designed to celebrate 150 years of American independence. Two notable features were the reproduction of High Street, Philadelphia's main street of 1776, and the Pennsylvania State Building. Sixteen foreign nations participated in the exposition, the total cost of which was almost $19 million.

SETTLEMENT WORK. *See* **Social Settlements.**

SEVEN CITIES OF CIBOLA. *See* **Cibola.**

SEVEN DAYS' BATTLES (June 25–July 1, 1862). Succession of battles in which Gen. Robert E. Lee's army forced that under Union Gen. George B. McClellan to abandon its threatening position east of Richmond and retreat to the James River.

McClellan had pushed his right wing under Gen. Fitz-John Porter northward across the Chickahominy River, hoping that Gen. Irvin McDowell's corps would join it from Fredericksburg. Aware that Porter was separated from McClellan, Lee ordered Gen. Thomas J. ("Stonewall") Jackson to fall on Porter's right and rear. Lee, crossing the Chickahominy north of Richmond, would assail Porter in front.

Skirmishing took place on June 25. Lee attacked at Mechanicsville (June 26) but, since Jackson had not arrived, he was repulsed. Porter withdrew to Gaines' Mill, where on June 27 the Confederate forces drove him across the Chickahominy. The Union base on the Pamunkey River was transferred by water to Harrison's Landing on the James. On June 29 McClellan's troops repulsed attacks at Savage's Station. Discovering that his adversary was retiring on the James, Lee hurried columns to Frayser's Farm. Here his assaults on June 30 failed to interrupt McClellan's retreat. McClellan, continuing his retirement, occupied Malvern Hill, where on July 1 Lee's final attack suffered decisive repulse. McClellan then fortified his army at Harrison's Landing. Casualties over the seven days of fighting were heavy.

"SEVEN PILLARS." The seven men who entered into the covenant founding the first church at New Haven colony, Aug. 22, 1639. They were John Davenport, the minister; Theophilus Eaton, a wealthy merchant; Robert Newman; Mathew Gilbert; Thomas Fugill; John Ponderson; and Jeremy Dixon.

SEVEN PINES. *See* **Fair Oaks, Battle of.**

SEVEN RANGES SURVEY. The first surveys under the Ordinance of 1785—the Seven Ranges—were made south of the Geographer's Line (*see* Public Lands, Survey of). Not for fifteen years were lines run north of this base. The survey was begun Sept. 23, 1785. But hostile Indians, disease, bad weather, and other hazards interposed such obstacles that only four ranges were surveyed along the outside lines of the townships by Feb. 21, 1787. The ranges were placed on sale later in the year. Because section lines had not been surveyed but merely marked on township plats, difficulties developed, particularly where the windings of the Ohio River were little known. The Seven Ranges formed a triangle with a western boundary ninety-one miles in length, a northern one of forty-two miles, and the Ohio River as the third side.

SEVENTEENTH AMENDMENT. Demand for the popular election of U.S. senators appeared in the 1830's, but the prestige and general effectiveness of the upper chamber were such that little headway was made until after the Civil War. Recurrent cases of buying election from venal legislatures and other unsatisfactory features gave tremendous impetus to the movement. A proposed amendment to the Constitution, making direct election possible, passed the House several times, but it was not until 1912 that the Senate finally accepted the inevitable. Ratification followed, and the amendment became effective May 31, 1913.

SEVENTH-DAY ADVENTISTS. *See* **Adventist Churches.**

SEVEN YEARS WAR. *See* **French and Indian War.**

SEVERN, BATTLE OF THE (Mar. 25, 1655). An engagement between Puritan settlers of Providence (present-day Annapolis) in Maryland, and the forces of the colony's Protestant governor, William Stone. About 125 men fought on each side, the Puritans assisted by two armed ships in the Severn River. Both parties lost about fifty men, but Stone was defeated and taken prisoner and four of his men were executed. For three years the Puritans practically controlled the colony.

"SEWARD'S FOLLY." *See* **Alaska.**

SEWING MACHINE. The sewing machine evolved as a mid-19th-century American invention. Elias Howe, Jr., usually credited as the inventor, was not the first patentee of an American sewing machine. John J. Greenough, Benjamin W. Bean, and several others patented ideas in the early 1840's, before Howe was granted the first patent for the two-thread, lockstitch sewing machine in 1846. Howe's machine met little success in America at the time. Taking his machine to England, Howe finally sold the patent rights in that country to William Thomas. On his return home he found that John Bachelder had patented a continuous-feed, vertical-needle machine in 1849; Isaac M. Singer had used earlier ideas with his heart-shaped cam to move the needle and received a patent in 1851; and A. B. Wilson patented the stationary rotary bobbin in 1852 and the four-motion feed in 1854; but no single manufacturer could make a practical machine without being sued for infringement of patent by another. In 1856 Orlando B. Potter, lawyer and president of the Grover and Baker Sewing Machine Company, suggested pooling the patents. This was accomplished, but each company maintained itself separately, and there was competition in the manufacturing and improving of the various machines. The four members of the "Sewing-Machine combination" were Elias Howe, Jr.; Wheeler and Wilson Manufacturing Company; I. M. Singer and Company; and Grover and Baker Sewing Machine Company. The combination remained active until 1877, when all the major patents expired.

The sewing machine was the first widely advertised consumer product. Foreign competition began to invade the field in the 20th century. Ingenious sewing machines continue to be produced, including those that "sew" without thread, but most of the machines produced in the United States are highly specialized manufacturing machines.

SEXUAL ATTITUDES. In general the first American settlers, for the most part members of puritanical sects, were more hostile to sex, particularly outside marriage, than their European contemporaries. The New England settlers tried to base their sex code on the Bible, until it was realized that some sexual transgressions, such as rape, were not punished in the Bible. They then enacted much more restrictive codes, which tended to make sexual transgressions, including fornication, criminal as well as religious offenses. Court records indicate that there were probably more indictments for illicit sexual relations in 17th-century Massachusetts than for crimes against property.

For a brief time adultery and bestiality received the death penalty. Animals involved were destroyed. Later, capital punishment tended to be replaced by whipping, branding, and special clothes or symbols. In the southern colonies fornication was punished by fine or whipping as well as public penance in a church. Adultery received a double penalty. There were numerous laws against miscegenation. One colonial custom that has received considerable attention is bundling. (*See* Bundling.)

In the 18th century sexual crimes declined as respect for privacy grew and as the general traditions of English common law on sexual activities were incorporated into American law. During the 19th century the more or less free and open acceptance of sex, which encouraged widespread discussion of sex and dissemination of birth control information, ran into a countercurrent based on new and supposedly scientific assumptions about sex, many of which later proved to be erroneous. The chief exponent of these ideas was an 18th-century Swiss physician, Simon-André Tissot. He believed that sexual activity caused blood to rush to the brain, thereby starving the nerves and increasing the likelihood of insanity. His association of masturbation with insanity became a major theme in American ideas about sex in the 19th century. Benjamin Rush introduced similar ideas to America, and they were advocated by a number of medical practitioners until well into the 20th century. Particularly influential in this respect was the American reformer Sylvester Graham. Such stern moralizing resulted in a growing hostility and fear of any sexual activity that did not result in procreation. This undercurrent of fear toward open sexuality contributed greatly to antipornography and antiprostitution campaigns in the last part of the 19th century.

Since 1900 there has been a long line of American investigators into sex. Notable among them was Alfred C. Kinsey at the University of Indiana, and one of the more influential was that run by William H. Masters and Virginia E. Johnson at St. Louis. Ultimately research into sexual processes undermined the erroneous ideas of Tissot and Graham.

Tied in with the 19th-century aversion to sex was the fear of venereal disease. Fears of venereal diseases declined only with the advent of safe medical cures. By the end of World War I, the new findings about sex were being disseminated to a wider audience. As contraceptives became more effective and widespread and as abortions became legally available in the 1970's, women were able to express their own sexuality more freely than before. The new openness about sex has also led to the gay rights movement, in which both male and female homosexuals publicly opposed discrimination.

SEYBERT, FORT, MASSACRE AT (Apr. 28, 1758). During the French and Indian War defenses were built by Col. George Washington in and about the South Branch of the Potomac River. Indians led by Killbuck, a Delaware chieftain also known as Gelelemend, attacked Fort Seybert (in present-day Pendleton County, W.Va.), murdered seventeen of its occupants, and carried others into captivity.

SHACKAMAXON, TREATY OF. Traditionally known as the Great Treaty; much doubt still remains about its details. There is no doubt that William Penn met the Delaware in 1682 at Shackamaxon (now Kensington), the chief village of the Delaware, and entered into negotiations with them for friendly relations. On June 23, 1683, several agreements were signed with the Indian chiefs granting to Penn and his heirs land in southeastern Pennsylvania (present-day Bucks County). The leading representative of the Indians was Tamanen (Tammany). No valid reason exists for rejecting the traditional story of Penn's meeting the Indians seated under a large elm. Penn described the seating arrangements of a meeting with the Indians in a letter to the Free Society of Traders in England written on Aug. 16, 1683.

SHADES OF DEATH. The name given the densely wooded northern part of the Great Swamp lying some twelve miles southeast of Wilkes-Barre, Pa., toward Easton, and shown on maps before 1778. It acquired added significance from being the refuge of many survivors fleeing from the Wyoming massacre (1778).

SHADRACH FUGITIVE SLAVE CASE. While being held for examination under the Fugitive Slave Act in 1851, a slave named Shadrach was allowed to walk out of a federal court in Boston and escape into Canada. The incident added to the growing controversy between antislavery and proslavery forces.

SHAKER RELIGION, INDIAN. A nativistic cult started by John Slocum, a Squaxin Indian of Puget Sound, in 1881. Slocum was believed to have died and to have been resurrected twice. He claimed that he had been to heaven and had returned to preach a new doctrine, much of which he had actually learned from white missionaries. Slocum preached that God had told him to tell the Indians to give up their evil ways, including drinking alcohol, and be absolutely nonviolent. The religion manifests Roman Catholic and Presbyterian doctrine combined with old Indian religions, and features ringing of bells and nervous twitchings of the body, interpreted as a sign of spiritual power. The cult spread to other Indians of the Northwest and California and is still active.

SHAKERS. Members of the United Society of Believers in Christ's Second Coming, a movement founded by Ann Lee Standerin, or Stanley, on the basis of revelations to her that the Second Coming would be in the form of a woman and that she was that woman. She and her followers moved from England to the New World in 1774 and established themselves at what was to become Watervliet, N.Y., in 1776, with a communal rule of life. Their practice of celibacy was related to their millennial beliefs: there was no need to procreate, since the end was near. They were distinctive in their adherence to spiritualism and the important place they gave to seances in their worship. The name Shaker came from a ritual form of dancing that often became quite frenzied. The Shakers reached their largest membership (6,000) before the Civil War and have declined continually since that time. By 1981 only a few Shakers were left. Most people know of the sect through its furniture, which was classical in its functional simplicity.

SHALAM, LAND OF. A communistic, agrarian, humanitarian, and vegetarian colony established on about 1,000 acres of irrigated land near Doña Ana, N.M., by Andrew M. Howland, a Boston philanthropist, under the influence of John B. Newbrough, a religious mystic who had written *Oahspe: A New Bible* (1882). The colony, incorporated in 1885 under the name First Church of the Tae, was composed mainly of orphan children. It was a financial failure, and broke up in 1901.

SHANTY TOWNS. These first appeared during the lag in reemployment after World War I (*see* Depression of 1920), rising on dump heaps or wastelands within or at the edges of large industrial cities. Single men who had fitted into an economy of abundance as transient workers built crude homes of any free material available, such as boxes, waste lumber, and tin cans.

SHARECROPPER. A farm tenant who pays rent with a portion (usually half) of the crop he raises. Although sharecropping had largely disappeared by the 1970's, it was once prevalent in the South. A product of Reconstruction, its primary purpose was to establish a stable, low-cost work force that would replace slave labor. Working usually under close supervision, the sharecropper often lacked title to his harvest, a factor that distinguished him from a share tenant. At harvest, the landlord established the crop's worth, subtracted what was owed him, and remitted the remainder to the tenant.

SHARE-THE-WEALTH MOVEMENTS. At the lowest point of the Great Depression, a prophecy of impending doom, and a promise of potential utopia, together with the distress of the unemployed, the insecurity of the middle class, and the plight of the aged, formed the common basis of appeal for the mass organizations that sprang into existence in the South and West between 1933 and 1936. Among those declaring their purpose to be the redistribution of wealth were Francis E. Townsend's plan, Louisiana Sen. Huey P. Long's Share-Our-Wealth Clubs, the National Union for Social Justice party, and Upton Sinclair's End Poverty in California (EPIC). All, except the EPIC, depended fundamentally on a core of inflationist doctrine. Mingling utopianism with religious zeal, they adopted such new techniques as national radio hookups, skilled publicity methods of pressure politics, huge "conventions" characterized by frenzied emotionalism, and blind trust in spectacular individual leaders.

SHARPSBURG. *See* **Antietam, Battle of.**

SHARPSHOOTER. The term for a highly skilled marksman, from the German *Scharfschütze* (in use as early as 1802 in Austria). When the Sharps breechloading rifle was introduced (1857), troops armed with this weapon were called sharpshooters. In the Civil War two volunteer regiments of sharpshooters were raised (1861) for the Union army, differing from other volunteer units in being made up of companies drawn from several states with federally appointed officers. In 1884 sharpshooter became a grade of qualification for rifle practice in the army. Since 1907, army and navy rifle qualification standards rank sharpshooters above marksmen and below expert riflemen.

SHARPS RIFLE. One of the earliest successful breechloaders, invented by Christian Sharps about 1848. It was manufactured at Hartford, Conn., by the Robbins, Kendall and Lawrence Company until 1856, and then by the Sharps Rifle Company, also at Hartford. The Sharps rifle first attracted wide attention during the Kansas Border War (1855–56), when some 900 of them, often called "Beecher's Bibles," were used by the Free-State party. These rifles probably saved Lawrence, Kan., from attack during the Wakarusa War (1855) and were undoubtedly a factor in provoking the proslavery men to acts of violence. Later they were used by James Montgomery, leader of the free-state men, in the border war and by John Brown at Harpers Ferry. The Sharps rifle was used by the Union army during the Civil War. It had a high reputation for range and accuracy.

SHAWMUT. The Indian name of the peninsula on which the town of Boston was planted. The name fell into disuse very early, long before urban growth effaced the three hills (Tremont) and the narrow isthmus which joined it to the mainland at the south.

SHAWNEE. A southern tribe of the Algonquin, first recognized as inhabiting the Cumberland basin in what is now Tennessee with an outlying colony on the Savannah River in South Carolina. The latter group was the first to abandon its southern hunting grounds, in a migration (*ca.* 1677–1707) caused by friction with the nearby Catawba who were favored by the whites. Their new homes were in the valleys of the Susquehanna and Delaware rivers, but congestion soon caused them to move to the upper Ohio Valley (*see* Shawnee and Delaware Migration). The Shawnee on the Cumberland began retreating north as the result of friction with the Cherokee and Chickasaw about 1710 and merged with their brethren from the east in a group of villages on the Ohio River.

The Shawnee were the spearhead of resistance to advancing settlement in the frontier warfare of 1755–95, supporting and being supported first by the French and then by the English. By 1795 their homes were in the valley of the upper Miami, and the Treaty of Greenville of that year forced them to retreat to Indiana. The loss of British support, as the result of the War of 1812, hastened the rapid dispersion of the Shawnee. The main body (over 1,000) is now incorporated with the Cherokee in Oklahoma.

SHAWNEE AND DELAWARE MIGRATION. A move to the Ohio Valley from the Susquehanna and Delaware river valleys (*ca.* 1720–53) caused by the encroachment of whites; by such aggravations as the Walking Purchase of 1737, in which the Delaware were forced to relinquish about 1,200 square miles in eastern Pennsylvania; by the decline of hunting and knowledge of better hunting grounds in the West; by the probability that the Iroquois would not be able to keep them out of the new grounds; and by encouragement from both French and English traders.

SHAWNEE PROPHET. Founder of a nativistic religion strongly influential among the Indians of the Great Lakes region in the early 19th century. The prophet, Tenskwatawa ("The Open Door"), was the brother of the Shawnee chief Tecumseh. His doctrine was similar to that of the earlier Delaware Prophet; it predicted the return of aboriginal conditions through supernatural means. The prophet advocated a reform ethic: Indians were to abandon alcohol, cease intermarrying with whites, and live peacefully with one another. His vision in 1805 inspired Tecumseh to attempt to unify the Indians to halt the white invaders. On Nov. 7, 1811, during an absence of Tecumseh, the prophet led an unsuccessful attack on Gov. William Henry Harrison's troops at Tippecanoe (*see* Tippecanoe, Battle of).

SHAWOMET. Land in eastern Rhode Island, purchased (1642) from the Indians by Samuel Gorton, a contentious religious leader, and his followers. A controversy arose over ownership of the land with the Indians and with Massachusetts Bay, and that colony sent an armed force that captured the settlement in September 1643 and took Gorton and others prisoner to Boston. On his release in March 1644, Gorton returned to Narragansett Bay, obtained from the Narragansett an act of submission to the king, and took this to England, where his rights to Shawomet were upheld and Massachusetts Bay was forced to withdraw. After returning to Shawomet (May 1648), Gorton renamed the settlement Warwick in honor of the Earl of Warwick, who had given him a letter of safe conduct. (*See also* Gortonites.)

SHAW'S EXPEDITION. In his reminiscences, Col. John Shaw claimed that in the spring of 1809, with two companions, he left Cape Girardeau, Mo., and reached the neighborhood of the Colorado mountains in one of the earliest attempts to reach New Mexico from Missouri. It is not certain that he intended to reach Santa Fe, and the inaccuracy of his statements in some instances throws doubt on others. There is no contemporary evidence to support his contention.

SHAYS' REBELLION (August 1786–February 1787). The outstanding manifestation of the discontent widespread throughout New England during the economic depression following the Revolution. Many small property holders in Massachusetts were losing their possessions through seizures for overdue debts and delinquent taxes; many faced imprisonment for debt. Town meetings and county conventions petitioned for lightening of taxes; sought suspension, abolition, or reform of certain courts and revision of the state constitution; and especially urged the issue of paper money. Lacking, in many cases, property qualifications for voting, the malcontents, beginning at Northampton, Aug. 29, resorted to massed efforts to intimidate and close the courts to prevent action against debtors. Fearful they might be indicted for treason or sedition by the state supreme court at Springfield, in late September they appeared there in armed force. Daniel Shays, a local officeholder, emerged as leader, demanding that the court refrain from indictments and otherwise restrict its business. A clash with neighborhood militia under Maj. Gen. William Shepard was avoided when both bands agreed to disperse. The court adjourned.

In January the insurgents returned to Springfield for supplies from the Confederation arsenal there. Shepard's forces repulsed the Shaysites' attack on the arsenal (Jan. 25); Gen. Benjamin Lincoln's men dispersed a nearby insurgent force under Luke Day. Lincoln surprised and captured most of the remaining insurgents early in February, and the rebellion soon collapsed. Shays escaped to Vermont and eventually was pardoned. James Bowdoin, governor during the insurrection, was defeated at the next election; reforms in line with the Shaysites' demands were soon made, and amnesty granted with few exceptions.

SHEEP RAISING. Sheep were introduced into Virginia (1609) and Massachusetts (1629) by the English, into New York (1625) by the Dutch, and into New Jersey (1634) by the Swedes. These animals were unimproved. In colonial times sheep were raised to supply wool for homespun clothing; the number of sheep remained relatively few and the quality and quantity of the wool poor.

The first merinos were imported in 1801–02 from France and from Spain. With the passage of the Embargo Act (1807), native mills increased, wool prices skyrocketed, and the demand for fine-wool sheep became insatiable; a merino craze followed. After 1815 British woolen imports again depressed the industry. The growth of the factory system and the tariff of 1828 revived it. In the 1830's, 60 percent of American sheep were in New England and the middle Atlantic states. After 1840 the center of sheep raising shifted westward; by 1850 it was in the Ohio Valley.

The Civil War produced a second merino craze. Sheep raising continued to expand west to the Rocky Mountains and Pacific Coast states. By 1935, 60 percent of all the sheep in the United States were in the western states. The total number of sheep raised throughout the country reached a peak that same year of 51.8 million. By 1980 the number of sheep had declined to 12.7 million, of which only about half were raised in the western states.

SHEEP WARS. Range battles fought in the American West between cattle and sheep ranchers. Although some of the confrontations were undoubtedly caused by disputes over land and water rights, the main cause was that the grazing habits of sheep destroyed the range, sometimes making the lands unusable to cattle herds for months, and sheep polluted watering places used by cattle.

After passage of the Homestead Act of 1862, the free prairie range, upon which the cattlemen depended, rapidly diminished. By 1875 clashes between cattlemen and sheepmen were regular occurrences along the New Mexico–Texas boundary. Some range controversies ended in bloodshed. In Colorado, Nevada, Idaho, Wyoming, and Montana many men were killed in the bitter wars, along with thousands of sheep. The sheep wars subsided only when the disputed areas were occupied by landowners and with the fencing of the open range.

SHEFFIELD SCIENTIFIC SCHOOL. At Yale College in 1846 unsalaried professorships in agricultural and practical chemistry were created through the efforts of John Pitkin Norton (appointed to the agricultural chemistry professorship) and Benjamin Silliman, Jr. (appointed to the practical chemistry professorship). The School of Applied Chemistry was opened in 1847 in a house for which Norton and Silliman paid $150 to Yale, equipped largely at their own expense. Joseph E. Sheffield, wealthy railroad builder and philanthropist, became the principal benefactor of the school, his gifts ultimately amounting to $1.1 million. Renamed the Yale Scientific School in 1854, when it was combined with the School of Engineering established in 1852, it became the Sheffield Scientific School in 1861, with a separate board of trustees established in 1871.

In 1852 Yale offered the bachelor of philosophy degree to students of the Scientific School; in 1861 the doctor of philosophy degree was granted, the first Ph.D. in America. In 1863 the Scientific School became the Connecticut beneficiary under the U.S. land grant act (Morrill Act, 1862). In 1860 a general course was established for undergraduates that omitted classical studies. In 1870 the school instituted a program in biological science preparatory to medical studies, in addition to offering specific programs for teachers of science; explorers; scientific investigators; chemists; and others. The school returned to its original status as a graduate department in 1945.

SHELBY'S MEXICAN EXPEDITION (1865). After the downfall of the Confederacy, Gen. Joseph O. Shelby, a southern cavalry commander, called on his men to follow him into Mexico rather than surrender. There the men voted to enlist in the army of Emperor Maximilian, then precariously maintaining his throne. With 1,000 men, including many Confederate notables, Shelby crossed the Rio Grande to Piedras Negras from Eagle Pass, Tex., burying the Confederate flag in the river on July 4, 1865. The expedition began fighting its way across northern Mexico toward Monterrey, impeded by guerrillas supporting Benito Juárez, the Mexican Republican leader who was fighting Maximilian. At Monterrey, the expedition broke up into several parts, going to Canada, British Honduras, the Mexican state of Sonora, or joining the French army in Mexico. Shelby, with the remnant of his men, marched to Mexico City. Maximilian refused the offer of Shelby's sword, fearing the displeasure of the United States, and the Confederates attempted to establish a colony on land given them by the Empress Carlota. After the overthrow of Maximilian (1867) the colony broke up.

***SHENANDOAH*.** Last armed cruiser to carry the Confederate flag and, next to the *Alabama*, the most destructive to Union shipping. Originally an Indiaman named the *Sea King*, it was purchased in England in September 1864, sailed to Madeira, reequipped, and renamed. The *Shenandoah* captured nearly forty prizes valued at about $1.4 million. After the war the British government transferred the cruiser to the United States, by whom it was sold to the sultan of Zanzibar. Later it was lost at sea. (*See also* Alabama Claims.)

SHENANDOAH CAMPAIGN (1864). Coincident with Gen. Ulysses S. Grant's advance (*see* Wilderness, Battles of the), Union forces in western Virginia, under Gen. Franz Sigel, moved eastward to clear the Shenandoah Valley and cut Gen. Robert E. Lee's supply communications. After engagements at Cloyd's Mountain (May 9), New Market (May 15), and Piedmont (June 5), the Union columns under Gen. David Hunter, Sigel's successor, were united for an advance on Lynchburg. To meet this threat, Lee detached Gen. Jubal A. Early's corps with instructions to defeat Hunter, move down the valley into Maryland, and threaten Washington, D.C. Early drove Hunter into the mountains, crossed the Potomac, defeated Union Gen. Lew Wallace at Monocacy, Md., on July 4–5, and on July 11 halted before the defenses of Washington. Too weak to do more than threaten, he withdrew into the valley; late in July he again crossed into Maryland, destroyed vast supplies, burned Chambersburg, Pa. (July 30), and then safely withdrew. Alarmed by Early's successes, Grant consolidated all Union troops in the valley under Gen. Philip H. Sheridan. A month of maneuvers followed. On Sept. 19 Sheridan, with a three-to-one superiority, defeated Early at Opequon and at Fisher's Hill. On Oct. 19 Early attacked during Sheridan's absence and was at first successful (*see* Cedar Creek, Battle of), but was again defeated, and retreated up the valley. By mid-December 1864 both Early and Sheridan had been recalled to Virginia.

SHENANDOAH HUNTING PATH. *See* **Virginia Path.**

SHENANDOAH VALLEY. That part of the great valley between the Allegheny and the Blue Ridge mountains extending from the Potomac River at Harpers Ferry south to the watershed of the James River a few miles southwest of Lexington, Va. The lower valley, extending from the Potomac forty miles south, was settled chiefly by English immigrants from tidewater Virginia; the middle, from near Strasburg to the vicinity of Harrisonburg, was settled almost wholly by Germans; and the upper, from Harrisonburg to the waters of the James, originally more wooded than the middle and lower valley, was the part chosen by the Scotch-Irish immigrants, most of whom came from Pennsylvania.

SHERIDAN'S RIDE. During the Shenandoah campaign of 1864, Confederate Gen. Jubal A. Early attacked Union Gen. Philip H. Sheridan's army at dawn on Oct. 19 along Cedar Creek, near Strasburg, Va. Two Union corps, awakened from sleep, were quickly thrown into panic. Other troops rallied and resisted the Confederate advance, but were slowly forced back. Sheridan, returning from Washington, D.C., had stopped at Winchester on the night of the 18th; awakened by the distant sound of artillery firing, he left for the front and soon began to meet the routed commands, who told him that all was lost. He reached the battlefield about 10:30 A.M., and his presence quickly restored confidence. By midafternoon the Confederates were in retreat.

SHERIDAN-WARREN CONTROVERSY. Union Gen. Philip H. Sheridan was dissatisfied with Gen. Gouverneur K. Warren's handling of his troops at the Battle of Five Forks (Apr. 1, 1865); in spite of conflicting orders, Warren won a valuable victory, but Sheridan relieved him of his command. Warren made repeated requests for a board of inquiry, but it was not until 1879 that one was ordered. Warren was fully exonerated, the court criticizing the manner of his relief.

SHERMAN ANTITRUST ACT (July 2, 1890). The first federal law directed against industrial combination and monopoly (*see* Antitrust Laws). Fortuitously associated with the name of Sen. John Sherman of Ohio, its prime authors were the leading Republican members of the Senate Judiciary Committee—George F. Edmunds of Vermont and George F. Hoar of Massachusetts. The key provision of the act was incorporated in the first of its eight sections: "Every contract, combination in the form of trust or otherwise, or conspiracy, in restraint of trade or commerce among the several states, or with foreign nations, is hereby declared to be illegal." (*See also* Restraint of Trade.)

The only successful prosecutions under the Sherman Act in the 1890's were those waged against labor unions. The presidency of Theodore Roosevelt witnessed an effort to revive the act as an instrument of federal regulation of big business, but the effort was largely unsuccessful. With the administration of Woodrow Wilson, the Clayton and Federal Trade Commission acts were passed (1914); later presidents used primarily these instruments and the cease-and-desist orders of the regulatory commissions. Since the administration of Franklin D. Roosevelt and the New Deal, the Sherman Antitrust Act has played only a comparatively minor role. Although insufficient to the task assigned, the act was noteworthy as a pioneer measure in the field of federal regulatory legislation.

SHERMAN SILVER PURCHASE ACT (July 14, 1890). A compromise bill (*see* Free Silver) named for Sen. John Sherman of Ohio. The act provided for the issuance of legal tender notes sufficient to pay for 4.5 million ounces of silver bullion each month at the prevailing market price; enough silver dollars were to be coined from the bullion purchased to redeem all the outstanding Treasury notes issued in this manner. The notes were made full legal tender except where otherwise expressly stipulated in the contract, and were made redeemable on demand in either gold or silver coin at the discretion of the secretary of the Treasury, although the act went on to declare it to be "the established policy of the United States to maintain the two metals on a parity with each other upon the present legal ratio or such ratio as may be established by law." The Sherman Act increased the circulation of redeemable paper currency in the form of Treasury notes by $156 million, and it accentuated the drain on the government's gold reserves by requiring the Treasury notes to be redeemed in gold as long as the Treasury had gold in its possession. The act was repealed in the autumn of 1893. (*See also* Panic of 1893.)

SHERMAN'S MARCH TO THE SEA. Against Gen. Ulysses S. Grant's judgment, Gen. William Tecumseh Sherman conceived the plan of marching across Georgia from Atlanta to Savannah in order to destroy the food supplies of a region on which Gen. Robert E. Lee largely depended and to break the will of the people to continue the war. On Nov. 15, 1864, he burned Atlanta, preparatory to setting out on his march the next day. With four army corps and 5,000 cavalrymen, in all numbering 62,000 men, he pointed his course toward Milledgeville, then the state capital, Sandersville, Louisville, Millen, and Savannah. The army was spread out sufficiently to cover a course sixty miles wide through the state. Cutting all communications, Sherman lived off the country through which he marched. His regularly organized raiding parties ranged widely. Within a week the left wing reached Milledgeville, but not in time to capture the fleeing state officials. On Dec. 10 the army drove in the pickets before Savannah and, after a ten-day siege, forced the Confederates to flee across the Savannah River into South Carolina. Union troops occupied Savannah on Dec. 21, and Sherman sent a message to President Abraham Lincoln giving him the city for a Christmas present. Sherman estimated that he had inflicted damages amounting to $100 million—four-fifths of which was "simple waste and destruction."

SHILOH, BATTLE OF (Apr. 6–7, 1862). Gen. Ulysses S. Grant's capture of Fort Henry (Feb. 6) in northwestern Tennessee and Fort Donelson (Feb. 15–16) twelve miles away opened the Cumberland and Tennessee rivers to Union water traffic and pierced the center of the Confederate far-flung defensive line. Union Gen. Don Carlos Buell was able to occupy Nashville with the Army of the Ohio, and Gen. Henry W. Halleck on Mar. 1 could order Gen. Charles F. Smith with 30,000 troops of the Army of the Tennessee by water to concentrate at Shiloh (or Pittsburg Landing) twenty-five miles north of the Confederates under Gen. Albert S. Johnston at Corinth, Miss. Grant arrived and assumed command on Mar. 16. Buell's 25,000 troops were to join by marching overland from Nashville preparatory to a vigorous combined thrust southward.

On Apr. 3 Johnston moved out of Corinth, 50,000 strong, to strike Grant's force before the junction could be effected. On Apr. 6, after an undetected slow massed march, Johnston made a surprise attack early in the morning against the unfortified Union position. Vigorous attacks drove in Grant's outlying units, shattered the hastily formed lines in all-day fighting, which was costly for both sides, and pushed the Union troops against the river.

Grant, absent when Johnston struck, hurried to the scene, approved arrangements that Gen. James B. McPherson had made in his stead, coordinated the defense, concentrated rear units, and—Buell arriving by night—counterattacked next morning. The Confederates were disrupted and confused by their own violent attacks and the death of Johnston. Grant's stroke, with the fresh troops of Buell and Gen. Lew Wallace, aided by portions of Gen. William Tecumseh Sherman's and Gen. John A. McClernand's commands, swept them from the field toward Corinth.

SHIMONOSEKI EXPEDITION (1864). The opening up of Japan to foreign intercourse and particularly the treaties of 1858 with foreign powers, made in the name of the shogun, aroused the opposition of the Japanese nobles who capitalized on popular hostility to foreigners as a means of overthrowing the shogun. The lord of the Choshiu clan, whose holdings were near the Shimonoseki Strait, fired on French, Dutch, and American ships in the strait in June and July. The U.S.S. *Wyoming,* in Yokohama, sailed to Shimonoseki Strait and sank two of the Choshiu craft; British ships bombarded the city of Kagoshima. U.S. Secretary of State William H. Seward permitted a small American chartered steamer to take part with British, Dutch, and French warships in a punitive bombardment of Shimonoseki in September. An indemnity of $3 million was extracted from Japan, but the United States returned its share ($750,000) in 1883.

SHINPLASTERS. A term applied in the United States at various times to privately issued fractional paper currencies or to those issued by other than the regularly constituted authorities, and, less frequently, to all fractional paper money. The term originated during the Revolution. Since the establishment of the federal government it seems likely that the three or four years prior to the passage of the Coinage Act of 1853, when much of the fractional silver disappeared from circulation, and in 1862, before the postage stamp currency and fractional paper notes were used, represent the two instances in which shinplasters circulated most widely.

SHIPBUILDING. One of the leading industries before the American Revolution, especially in New England. The English Navigation Acts, which prohibited the carrying of goods between England and the colonies in foreign ships, classified colonial-built ships as English built. With an abundant supply of oak and pine growing almost to the water's edge, a vessel could be built in America for about 30 percent less than in England; on the eve of the Revolution a third of the vessels in British registry were American built. The next boom came between the mid-1840's and the mid-1850's, the so-called Golden Age of American shipbuilding. For those ready to pay the price, excellent crack packets and clippers could be built on New York's East River or around Boston harbor. Good substantial cargo carriers could be built more cheaply along the Maine coast, particularly at Bath, Casco Bay, and the central coast.

An entirely new picture emerged after the Civil War. With Britain turning out compound-engine freighters in large quantities, American square-riggers were gradually squeezed out of most of the deep-sea trades, except for Maine's excellent Down Easters. Cheaper coal and iron were available to foreign shipbuilders; the American merchant marine declined; and the government failed to build up its navy for a period of twenty years after the Civil War. The shipbuilding industry could not overcome these handicaps until World War I, the beginning of an extraordinary period of shipbuilding activity. However, there was little demand for new tonnage after the boom ended. Naval construction was reduced by the international disarmaments agreements in the 1920's, and in 1929 amounted to only 128,976 tons, the lowest since 1830.

In World War II the navy spent $19 billion, building everything from landing craft up to superdreadnoughts and carriers; the Maritime Commission spent $13 billion constructing 5,777 ships. The end of the war brought another shipbuilding slump. In 1956 only two freighters and six tankers were under construction. The postwar construction, however, did produce some distinctive new types of ships: the liner *United States* (1952) established a record as the fastest afloat. The use of nuclear power was initiated by the submarine *Nautilus;* nuclear reactors also powered the giant carrier *Enterprise* and the passenger liner *Savannah.* The Merchant Marine Act of 1970 came as a blessing to the dwindling industry, although the act's programs were later cut back in budget reducing moves.

SHIPPING, OCEAN. A peculiarity of ocean shipping has been its international nature: the ships of one maritime nation have differed little from those of another. From early colonial times to about 1870 there was little change in the ordinary cargo ships. The conventional major carrier in those early years was the three-masted square-rigged ship, or bark. Smaller vessels were also used: two-masted square-rigged brigs for runs to the Mediterranean or the West Indies and still smaller fore- and aft-rigged schooners or sloops for coastal and other short runs. An important innovation was the creation in 1818 of the American Black Ball Line, sailing on fixed schedules between New York City and Liverpool with passengers, mail, and fine freight, but still using conventional ships. This new line pattern, highly profitable, expanded, but chiefly from New York.

In 1838 regular transatlantic service by steam-driven ships began, but ordinary cargoes still continued to go by square-riggers, now somewhat larger. A quiet revolution occurred about 1870 with the compound engine, which, by using the steam twice (and later three or four times), cut costs, so that a freighter could profitably carry such heavy cargoes as grain, coal, and sugar. These new freighters gradually drove the square-riggers from their older runs.

By the 1920's the oil tanker was a prominent part of ocean shipping, and the older type of freighters became known as dry cargo ships. The U.S. World War II emergency program produced numerous 16,000-ton T-2 tankers, which became the standard for a while. Many tankers were owned by the major oil companies, and because of high American crew wages, many were registered in the merchant marines of Panama and Liberia.

An important innovation of the 1960's was the introduction of containerization. The previous cargo ships had had open holds into which longshoremen loaded the individual bags, boxes, and bales that made up a cargo. Shippers remedied this by assembling the cargo beforehand and sending it aboard in a single container. One early step was the so-called "sea train," where loaded freight cars could be run aboard on tracks and run off at the other end. Later came other "roll on-roll off" devices for the same purpose. Then came big metal containers; a large ship might have a thousand of them hoisted aboard. To save more time, the LASH (lighter-aboard-ship) system was inaugurated, whereby scores of self-operating little lighters could be hoisted over the side to run into port while the mother ship kept on without loss of time.

The most dramatic innovation during the 1960's was the vastly increased tonnage of tankers and bulk carriers. About 1970 the designation "very large crude carrier" (VLCC) was applied to ships of 150,000 tons or more; by the autumn of 1972 six ships measuring more than 250,000 tons were under construction and one of nearly 500,000 tons was planned.

One serious consideration in the increased tanker size was the matter of finding where to land the oil; few ports could provide the necessary draft. Offshore loading into pipe facilities seemed one answer. Coastal communities, moreover, were concerned with the danger of oil spills, especially after a number of serious accidents had shown what extensive damage could result.

SHIPPING ACT OF 1916. This act created the U.S. Shipping Board *(see below).* In time of emergency the transfer of American-flag ships to foreign registry or ownership was restricted and the president was given power to conscript vessels. Various practices, including deferred rebates, were declared unfair and prohibited to ocean common carriers. (*See also* Emergency Fleet Corporation.)

SHIPPING BOARD, UNITED STATES. Created by the Shipping Act of 1916, it controlled the Emergency (later Merchant) Fleet Corporation, established in 1917, and carried out merchant marine policy. It was superseded in 1933 by the U.S. Shipping Board Bureau of the Department of Commerce. (*See also* Merchant Marine.)

SHIPS OF THE LINE (or **Line-of-Battle Ships).** The 18th- and early 19th-century counterparts of modern first-class battleships, ships fit to engage the most formidable enemy ships in battle line. As planned for the U.S. Navy, they were about 190 feet long, of about 2,600 tons displacement, and mounted at least 74 guns on three decks. The first, the *America,* was launched at Portsmouth, N.H., Nov. 5, 1782, and was given to the French. In 1813 Congress authorized four more: the *New Orleans,* which was never launched; the *Franklin;* the *Washington;* and the *Independence.* In 1816 Congress authorized nine ships of the line; two were never completed. None of these ships was ever engaged in battle. The introduction of steam, explosive shells, and armor plate rendered them obsolete before they could be used in actual warfare.

SHIRT-SLEEVE DIPLOMACY. Concerning a note written by Secretary of State Walter Q. Gresham in 1895 to the British government during the seal fisheries controversy, a British editor, alleging its crudeness and tactlessness, remarked caustically that the secretary would appear to have written it in his shirt sleeves. Many Americans professed to accept the British editor's quip as a compliment, as picturing a diplomacy less verbose and franker and more honest than the old sort.

SHIVAREE. Derived from the French *charivari,* meaning mock music made on pots and pans, this designated in rural America, particularly in the Middle West, the custom of serenading newly wedded couples with a variety of noisemaking devices, the object being to exact a "treat." Refusal to serve the serenaders with refreshments resulted in some form of hazing. In New England the custom was referred to as a serenade or callathump.

SHOE MANUFACTURING. *See* **Boot and Shoe Manufacturing.**

SHOOTING MATCH. An event especially popular in the backwoods of the South in the early 19th century. The prize was at times a turkey or a cow. For a cow valued at $20, contestants paid the owner 25 cents a shot; eighty shots were to be purchased, and any entrant could buy any number. The best shot took the hide and tallow; second and third best shots, a hindquarter each, and so on. It was likely to be an all-day festival, women quilting and providing food, and everybody dancing through the night.

SHOP COMMITTEE. Part of the intensified efforts of employers shortly before and during World War I to allay labor unrest and reduce industrial friction. The distinctive feature of the shop committee was joint representation of employers and employees on a single body; jurisdiction was generally limited to one establishment, and powers to the settlement of grievances. The War Labor Board secured the establishment of shop committees in over 600 plants. During the 1920's the committees were either abandoned or transformed into employee-representation plans or company unions.

"SHOT HEARD ROUND THE WORLD." A line from Ralph Waldo Emerson's *Concord Hymn,* written for the dedication (1837) of the monument at Concord Bridge in Massachusetts. The line is also carved on the base of Daniel Chester French's statue *The Minute Man of Concord* (1875). The first stanza of the *Concord Hymn* is as follows:

By the rude bridge that arched the flood,
Their flag to April's breeze unfurled,
Here once the embattled farmers stood,
And fired the shot heard round the world.

SHOWBOATS. William Chapman, an English actor, had a small floating theater built at Pittsburgh in 1828 and toured the Ohio and Mississippi rivers until his death in 1839; his widow then managed the boat until 1847, when she sold it. Other showboats appeared on the Ohio–Mississippi river system before the Civil War, including two circus craft. Meanwhile, Henry Butler had in 1836 placed a boat on the Erie Canal system—by day a "museum" with a few stuffed animals and wax figures, by night a theater. A fleet of three boats on the Pennsylvania canals, lashed alongside each other at night with the sides removed, became a vaudeville auditorium. The Civil War damaged the showboat business, but it revived again in the 1870's. W. P. Newman's Great American Water Circus, which carried forty horses and fourteen parade wagons, appeared on the Ohio in 1901; two barges side by side with hulls filled with earth and a canvas top overhead, supplied the ring. In 1925 there were fourteen showboats on the midwestern rivers and one touring Chesapeake Bay and the North Carolina sounds. The last showboat to tour on a regular basis in the United States was the *Golden Rod* (1943).

SHREVEPORT (La.). Shreveport was named in honor of Major Henry Miller Shreve, who invented steam-powered rams to tear a channel through an enormous mass of driftwood that had blocked the Red River to all transportation for many years before 1833 (*see* Red River Raft). The city became capital of the Confederate state of Louisiana in 1863. It was the last state capital in the Confederacy to surrender to Union forces. Until the 20th century, Shreveport was a cotton-trading town. Located in the center of a major petroleum and natural-gas producing area, it now processes and ships these materials. In addition, the city has furniture and paper-making factories. Its location on the Red River provides water transportation routes downstream to the Mississippi and the Gulf of Mexico, and upstream to Arkansas and Texas. The population in 1980 was 205,815.

SHREVEPORT RATE CASE (or *Houston, E. and W. T. R. Company* v. *United States*), 234 U.S. 342 (1914). The case grew out of a complaint by jobbing interests of Shreveport, La., against the authority of the Texas Railroad Commission to fix rates on freight shipments wholly within the state of Texas, where rates were lower than those on comparable shipments between Louisiana and Texas. In 1911 the Railway Commission of Louisiana placed the complaint before the Interstate Commerce Commission, which decided against the discriminatory rates. The case was appealed to the federal courts, and in a momentous decision the Supreme Court held that Congress through such an agency as the Interstate Commerce Commission may step in and override rates prescribed by a state within its borders, if such rates impose an "undue burden" on interstate commerce as a whole, or if they unduly discriminate.

SIBERIAN EXPEDITION (1918–20). The invasion and occupation of eastern Siberia by Allied forces. Its main purpose was to keep Siberia out of German hands; its immediate purpose was to rescue the Czechoslovak Legion, a unit of nationalist Czechs that had been formed to fight the Germans and had attached itself to the Russian army. The legion found itself isolated in Russia after the collapse of the czarist government. However, when Japanese and British troops landed at Vladivostok on Apr. 9, 1918, President Woodrow Wilson protested strongly. The Bolshevik government had granted the Czechoslovak Legion the use of the Trans-Siberian railroad in its effort to reach Vladivostok. When collisions with the Bolshevik forces resulted, Wilson reluctantly allowed U.S. troops to help rescue the Czechs and to restrain the Japanese. The Czechs complicated the issue by deciding to fight actively with the anti-Bolshevik White Army forces. Meanwhile, Maj. Gen. William S. Graves sailed from San Francisco with a contingent on Sept. 2, 1918, to join the U.S. infantry regiments from the Philippines; with a force of about 10,000, including experienced railroad men, he assumed responsibility for the Trans-Siberian east of Lake Baikal. The skirmishes that took place, resulting in the deaths of thirty-six U.S. soldiers, were against Russian bandits for the most part, rather than against either czarist or Bolshevik forces. Finally, the Czechs bought peace with the Bolsheviks and were allowed to resume evacuation from Russia. In January 1920 Graves was ordered to recall his men to Vladivostok; in April the last Americans sailed for home.

SIBLEY EXPEDITION TO DAKOTA. *See* **Dakota Expeditions of Sibley and Sully.**

SIBLEY EXPEDITION TO THE RIO GRANDE. *See* **Rio Grande, Sibley's Operations on.**

SICILIAN CAMPAIGN. In accordance with a decision made at the Casablanca Conference (January 1943), combined British and American ground, naval, and air forces under Lt. Gen. Dwight D. Eisenhower invaded Sicily on July 10, 1943, and conquered the island in thirty-eight days. Lt. Gen. Bernard L. Montgomery's British Eighth Army, including Canadian troops, landed on the eastern coast of Sicily; Lt. Gen. George S. Patton's Seventh U.S. Army came ashore on the southern coast. They were opposed by 200,000 Italian troops, plus 30,000 Germans. With a beachhead well in hand, Montgomery advanced through Syracuse and Augusta to Catania, in order to seize Messina. Patton was to protect his flank, but obtained permission to extend westward toward Palermo; on July 22 he took the city. Montgomery was halted before Catania by a strong defensive line anchored on Mount Etna.

Suspicious of eventual Italian capitulation, Adolf Hitler began to favor evacuating Sicily in order to avoid having his forces trapped on the island. The German commander in Sicily began to take control of the fighting, and by August the Axis effort in the northeastern corner of Sicily became a distinct delaying action designed to preserve conditions for an orderly withdrawal to the mainland.

Patton received permission, on July 25, to advance on Messina. Thus began a contest between Montgomery and Patton to take Messina first. Patton launched three small amphibious end runs to help his forces forward; Montgomery, after taking Catania on Aug. 5, instituted a single amphibious operation. On Aug. 8, Hitler decided to evacuate Sicily; the meticulously planned withdrawal started Aug. 11. On Aug. 17, Patton entered Messina, and the campaign ended.

SIC SEMPER TYRANNIS **("Thus always to tyrants").** The motto of Virginia since 1776, recommended by George Mason, its probable originator. When President Abraham Lincoln was fatally shot on Apr. 14, 1865, in Ford's Theater, his assassin, John Wilkes Booth, shouted "*Sic semper tyrannis!* The South is avenged!"

SIDELING HILL. A ridge rising to an elevation of 2,195 feet, approximately seventeen miles west of Fort Loudon, Pa.; site of an attack by the Black Boys in March 1765 on a convoy of eastern goods, including ammunition and liquor, on its way to the Indian country beyond Fort Pitt. Incensed at a series of Indian raids during and after Pontiac's War (1763) and convinced that the much-needed supplies would precipitate another period of raiding, the people of the Conococheague Valley determined to prevent the delivery of the goods, particularly arms that might be used against them. Col. James Smith collected ten members of the Black Boys, a vigilante group, and ambushed the pack train on Sideling Hill; the attackers burned those goods they did not take.

SIEGFRIED LINE. Name given by Allied troops to fortifications erected before World War II along Germany's western frontier; the name probably was derived either from a German defensive position of World War I, the *Siegfriedstellung,* or from the Siegfried legend. Known to the Germans as the Westwall, it was begun in 1938 as a short belt of fortifications in the Saar region opposite France's Maginot Line, but later was extended to the Swiss and Dutch frontiers and was a band approximately three miles deep of more than 3,000 mutually supporting concrete pillboxes, troop shelters, and command posts. Where no natural antitank obstacles existed, a belt of pyramidal concrete projections called "dragon's teeth" barred access across the terrain. The line contributed to German success in bluffing France and Great Britain at Munich in 1938. The line was neglected following German victory over France in 1940, but as Allied armies approached in September 1944, Adolf Hitler decreed that it be held. The U.S. V Corps opposite the Belgian Ardennes and the VII Corps south of Aachen quickly penetrated, only to be contained by German reserves. A penetration in October north of Aachen precipitated no deep advance, so that not until early spring of 1945, after German strength had been dissipated in the Battle of the Bulge, was the line pierced along its full length.

SIGNAL CORPS, U.S. ARMY. Created by Congress on June 21, 1860; for over a century the term "Signal Corps" (and, for a time, "Signal Service") referred to both a separate unit within the War Department (and its successor, the Department of the Army) and the units having primary responsibility for army signal communications. The corps first used Albert James Myer's wigwag system of visual signaling, but in 1862 it introduced the Beardslee magnetoelectric tactical telegraph machine, leading to a conflict with the U.S. Military Telegraph. The Military Telegraph ended with the Civil War, and, as the years passed, the corps became responsible for army photography; established a pigeon service; and adapted to its uses the conventional electric telegraph, heliograph, and telephone, as well as radio, radar, and the communications satellite. From 1870 to 1891 the corps provided the United States with its first national weather service, which in 1891 became the Weather Bureau, and from 1908 to 1918 directed the army's first aeronautical program using heavier-than-air craft. A series of changes (1962–74) has eliminated the Signal Corps as a bureau, but the Signal Corps continues as an indispensable branch of the army.

SIGN LANGUAGE. A method of gesture communication in general use among Indians of the Great Plains area, developed because of the nomadic existence of the interior tribes that frequently met other tribes with alien tongues. Largely manual, it became so universal that a Blackfoot from the Canadian border could exchange ideas with a Comanche.

SILHOUETTES. Black profile portraits cut out of paper or painted on cards, used as wall decorations during the first half-century of the republic.

SILK CULTURE AND MANUFACTURE. Efforts at silkworm raising, most prolonged in Georgia in the 18th century and in Connecticut during the early national period, failed mainly because the amounts and levels of skill required in silkworm breeding and cocoon reeling were underestimated. Silk growing was generally abandoned after the Chinese mulberry tree *(Morus multicaulis)* craze of the 1830's collapsed.

Small mills that manufactured sewing silk, ribbons, and trimmings from imported raw silk appeared in New England after 1810. Silk throwing (yarn making) reached the factory stage by the 1840's, centered in Philadelphia, New York City, and the Connecticut River valley. The invention of the sewing machine increased demand for sewing silks after 1850. Following the Civil War major growth was spurred by the imposition of luxury tariffs on imported silk products (1861, 1864) and the completion of a direct transpacific and transcontinental route (1869). Simultaneously the industry relocated to northern New Jersey, which offered cheap female labor and proximity to New York markets. Power-loom silk weaving after 1870 brought the factory production of broad goods. Pressures from New Jersey labor unions persuaded the silk throwers and spinners to move in search of cheap labor to the mining towns of Pennsylvania in the 1880's; weaving mills followed. By the 1920's Pennsylvania and New Jersey contained three-quarters of the nation's silk industry. Annual raw silk imports rose from $3 million in 1870 to $427 million in 1929. After 1900 the demand for hosiery yarns became particularly important. Increased production of synthetic fibers after the 1930's and the interruption of silk imports from Japan and China during World War II shrank the industry. Its annual raw-silk consumption fell from a peak of 81 million pounds in 1930 to 1 million in 1980.

SILL, FORT (Okla.). A military reservation and site of the U.S. Army Artillery and Guided Missile Center and School. It was established as Camp Wichita on Jan. 8, 1869, near the foot of the Wichita Mountains in what is now Comanche County by Gen. Philip H. Sheridan and was renamed Fort Sill on July 2, honoring Brig. Gen. Joshua W. Sill, U.S. Army Volunteers. During the Indian Wars it was a center for negotiations with a number of tribes and a base for numerous campaigns. The School of Fire for Field Artillery was established there in 1911. Also established there was the School of Musketry, forerunner of the Infantry School, Fort Benning, Ga., and, after World War II, the Army Aviation School, subsequently moved to Fort Rucker, Ala. During World War I, Camp Doniphan was located on the reservation.

SILVER, PEWTER, AND OTHER METALWORK.

Silver. The terms "goldsmith" and "silversmith" were synonymous in England and America during the 17th and 18th centuries, and silversmiths worked in both metals. England's apprenticeship system, established by the Worshipful Company of Goldsmiths of the City of London, was transported to the colonies, where apprentices served from the age of fourteen to the age of twenty-one. City ordinances in Boston (1660) and New York City (1675) set down that no person could open shop who was not of age and had not served a full seven-year apprenticeship.

Working silver began with melted coins assayed to the sterling standard (925 parts silver to which 75 parts of copper were added for hardness). Baltimore (*ca.* 1814–29) was the only city to make this standard law after much petitioning had failed in other cities. American marks were usually the maker's initials; by 1725 the surname alone or full name was also used. In the 19th century the place of origin was sometimes added. From 1820 to 1860 American silver was usually marked "coin" or "pure silver coin" (900 parts pure), but after 1860 the common mark was "sterling." The Stamping Act of 1906 made sterling the measure of purity in American silver.

Most of the procedures in making silver objects were changed by the wide availability of sheet silver by the 1790's. Stamped borders and moldings were manufactured by 1810, and by 1860 the process was almost totally industrialized and specialization was born. Centers of the craft were Boston, Philadelphia, and New York City in the 17th and 18th centuries and later Baltimore and Providence. The emphasis was primarily utilitarian in both domestic and religious pieces. American silver designs were distinctive parallels of English precedents. Although less ostentatious, they were always of fine quality, as in the exemplary pieces by Paul Revere and Jacob Hurd of Boston, Myer Myers of New York City, and Joseph Richardson, Sr., of Philadelphia. These standards were maintained in the 19th century by the works of Obadiah Rich of Boston; the Forbes of New York City; Fletcher and Gardiner, and Chaudron and Rasch of Philadelphia; and Samuel Kirk of Baltimore. Later 19th-century firms producing fine examples of the art were Tiffany, Gorham, Whiting, and Kirk.

Pewter. In the 18th century most tableware was either wooden or pewter. There are fewer examples of prerevolutionary pewter than of silver, however, due to England's embargo on unwrought pewter and to the innate softness of the metal. Pewter making began as early as 1630 in the Massachusetts Bay area. Makers were almost wholly dependent on damaged or discarded English pieces; the quality of the metal was high, if not always the workmanship. Originally the metal was tin-based, with varying amounts of lead added, but the English guilds later permitted the use of several alloys in pewter making.

Itinerant pewterers were common, and even isolated villages had at least one spoon molder and mender. Major cities for artisans were Hartford, Philadelphia, and New York City. Noteworthy pewterers were John Bassett of New York City and Samuel Danforth of Hartford; more than five generations of Danforths and their trainees were prolific from prerevolutionary times to the end of the britannia period (ca. 1860's).

Styles of American pewterware were not as ornate or diverse as those of European origin. Aside from tableware and serving pieces, other objects included baby bottles, candlesticks, inkstands, furniture hardware, and communion flagons.

Manufacturing methods began to displace the American pewterer and his casting techniques by the second decade of the 19th century. Pewter's softness was at last surpassed by britannia metal, also known as white metal, which did not have to be annealed, did not work-harden, contained no lead, and would polish to a sheen comparable to that of silver. Britannia's use in the United States dates from 1814 in Salem, Mass., but it was not until the second quarter of the 19th century that stamping and spinning methods, new tools, and the ready availability of raw materials made britannia successful enough to compete with silver. However, britannia had fallen from fashion by the late 1860's because of the advent in 1845 of electroplating, a process of electrolysis whereby a thin film of silver is affixed to a base metal, which made silverware available to the middle class.

Other Metals. There are only cursory 18th-century accounts of work in iron, brass, and copper. Tradesmen in these metals included coppersmiths, braziers, founders, blacksmiths, gunsmiths, and whitesmiths, who produced items for domestic and agricultural use and for other trades and industries of the age. Existing pieces are numerous, but marked examples are rare; attributions to American craftsmanship are usually made on stylistic grounds. Much of the work in these fields was imported, and English rule rigidly controlled colonial manufacture. Workshops were quietly operated in outpost areas. After the Revolution, crafts flourished until the Industrial Revolution took its toll. (*See also* Copper Industry; Iron and Steel Industry.)

SILVER AS MONEY. *See* **Bimetallism; Bland-Allison Act; Free Silver; Money; Pittman Act; Sherman Silver Purchase Act; Silver Legislation; Trade Dollar.**

SILVER DEMOCRATS. A term used at various times after 1878 to refer to those members of the Democratic party who were active advocates of free coinage of silver at the 16 to 1 ratio. More general use of the term followed the inauguration of President Grover Cleveland in 1893 and his calling of a special session of Congress to repeal the Sherman Silver Purchase Act of 1890; this repeal split the party wide open, with Silver Democrats in opposition to the administration. The national convention of July 1896 was a test of strength between the administration and the Silver Democrats. Their complete victory at the convention made the Silver Democrats the regulars beyond question, and the term tended to fall into disuse, encouraged also by the decline of free coinage as a political issue. Nevertheless, the platform of 1900 was a Silver Democratic document, and only in 1904 was free coinage repudiated by the party's candidate, Alton B. Parker.

SILVER DOLLAR. *See* **Money.**

SILVER GRAYS. Name given to a conservative minority of New York's Whig party in 1850. Approving of the conciliatory policies of President Millard Fillmore, the faction bolted the party's state convention of 1850 when the radical antislavery attitude of Sen. William H. Seward was endorsed. The faction was called the Silver Grays because of the color of the hair of Francis Granger, one of the bolters. A few weeks later they called a convention of their own.

SILVER LEAGUE. A term applied to various pro-silver propaganda organizations of the late 19th century. More precisely, it referred to the American Bimetallic League (organized 1892), the most active agitator of the silver cause. In 1895 it consolidated with its principal competitor, the National Bimetallic Union; the new organization, the American Bimetallic Union, was exceedingly active in 1896 in spreading the free-coinage doctrine and in attempting to bring about a union of all silver factions in national politics.

SILVER LEGISLATION. It was the intention of the founders of the nation to establish a monetary system in which both gold and silver were legal tender; but the system was a failure, since the free-market value of silver was higher than its monetary value. The establishment by Congress of subsidiary silver coinage in 1853 confirmed this situation legally, but accidentally left the silver dollar as a standard coin, although the market value of silver continued to make its coinage impossible. In a revision of the statutes in 1873 the unknown piece was dropped (*see* Crime of 1873).

In 1873 the world market ratio of silver to gold fell below 16 to 1 for the first time in history, and a movement developed, promoted by the silver interests and embraced by agrarian and proinflation elements, for the restoration of bimetallism. In the 1870's, 1890's, and 1930's, the efforts of this pressure group almost achieved bimetallism and succeeded in extracting legislation giving a cash subsidy to the producers of silver. For example, the Bland-Allison Act of 1878 required the U.S. Treasury to buy $2–4 million worth of silver a month. The Sherman Silver Purchase Act of 1890 (repealed at the insistence of President Grover Cleveland in 1893) mandated Treasury purchases of 4.5 million ounces of silver a month.

The Silver Purchase Act of 1934 followed an unprecedented decline in the price of silver. It provided for the nationalization of domestic stocks of silver and for the purchase of silver by the Treasury until the price should reach $1.2929 per ounce or the value of the amount held should equal one-third of the value of the government's gold holdings. The immediate effect of the legislation was a speculative rise in the market price of silver to 81 cents an ounce, which destroyed the currency systems of China and Mexico.

In 1939 the president's powers to debase the gold standard and buy silver were renewed, and Congress was allowed to set the price for domestic silver. In World War II a shortage of silver developed, and the price rose rapidly. In 1943 the Green Act provided that U.S. industries might buy silver from the Treasury at the price originally paid for it, and large amounts of silver, all of which was returned, were lent to U.S. allies.

In the 1960's, when strong industrial demand for silver created another worldwide shortage, the metal was virtually eliminated from the U.S. monetary system. The Silver Purchase Act was repealed in 1963. Under the Coinage Act of 1965, silver was eliminated from two subsidiary coins (the quarter and dime) and its content in the half-dollar was reduced from 90 percent to 40 percent. By another act of Congress, U.S. Treasury certificates could no longer be redeemed in silver after June 28, 1968. (*See also* Bimetallism.)

SILVER PROSPECTING AND MINING. The Spanish had worked small silver mines during their occupation of New Mexico, California, and Texas. Small amounts of silver also were recovered by mining in New Hampshire after 1828 and in Virginia and Tennessee after 1832. Large-scale silver mining had its beginning in Nevada after 1859, when prospectors staked the Ophir, or Comstock, lode; they were looking for gold, but their bonanza mine yielded more silver than gold. The Comstock ores were so rich that within two decades more than $300 million worth of silver and gold had been extracted.

The pattern of goldseekers finding silver was repeated in the years that followed. At Georgetown, Colo., a gold placer camp developed as the center of a silver-producing district after the opening of the Belmont lode in 1864. The gold camp of Oro City, Colo., was almost a ghost town when ores of carbonate of lead with a rich silver content were discovered in 1877 and the greatest of Colorado silver cities, Leadville, was born.

The prosperity of the silver mining industry during the 19th century was intimately related to the currency policy of the federal government, particularly after the demonetization of silver in 1873. During the quarter of a century that followed, the huge quantities of silver produced depressed the price, already reduced by demonetization. With the repeal of the Sherman Silver Purchase Act in 1893, the market fell to levels so low that many mines suspended operations.

The industry recovered sufficiently to make the years 1911–18 the peak years in volume of production; an annual average of 69,735,000 fine ounces of silver were produced. Then continuing low prices for silver and high production costs limited activity in mining. In 1980 the United States produced 38.1 million fine ounces of silver; most of it from mines in Idaho, Arizona, Montana, and Colorado.

SILVER PURCHASE ACT. *See* **Silver Legislation.**

SILVER REPUBLICAN PARTY. An organization formed by the delegates who bolted the Republican convention of 1896 after its adoption of the gold plank, which advocated gold only, rather than gold and silver, as the basis of the U.S. monetary system. The Silver Republicans later endorsed the Democratic presidential candidate, William Jennings Bryan. In the West the Silver Republicans formed state organizations, which usually fused with the Democrats or Populists in local politics. In 1900 the party met in its first and only national convention. In March 1901 the party's members in Congress joined in an address urging all supporters to unite with the Democratic party.

SINGING SCHOOLS. Found in every part of the United States at some time, these were especially common in the rural districts of the South and West in the 19th century. A singing school was usually conducted by an itinerant teacher who collected a small fee from each student; a session continued from two to four weeks, with a meeting held each evening. Each evening was spent in group singing interspersed from time to time with instruction from the teacher.

SINGLE TAX. A levy proposed by Henry George in his *Progress and Poverty* (1879): in place of all other taxes George advocated a single tax that would appropriate for government use all of the economic rent on land. More than a mere fiscal device, this was set forth as a vehicle for social reform. The program had but limited acceptance despite vigorous attempts to promote it.

SINGLETON PEACE PLAN. In the winter and spring of 1865, James Washington Singleton, a native of Virginia, was the bearer of confidential messages between President Abraham Lincoln and Confederate authorities. These messages dealt at first with the achievement of peace and later with the return of the South to the Union. Singleton's mission was ended by Lincoln's death.

SINKING FUND, NATIONAL. Secretary of the Treasury Alexander Hamilton insisted that creation of public debt should be accompanied by means of extinguishment. Under the Funding Act of 1790, Congress established a sinking fund administered by high government officers; it was supplied by surplus revenue from customs duties and $2 million of borrowed money. Hamilton checked the panic of 1792 by purchasing securities at market rate, below par, for the sinking fund. The sinking fund was reorganized in 1802; a definite annual appropriation, $8 million, was used to retire maturing bonds and buy in the market; the obligations acquired were destroyed, not retained at interest as in Hamilton's scheme. The years 1801–12 brought America prosperity, and large appropriations were made to the sinking fund.

The decade 1848–57 boomed as a result of Mexican War expenditures, railroad expansion, gold discoveries, and increased imports. To return surpluses to circulation, Congress authorized the purchase of bonds in the market above par. In spite of a sharply rising debt during the Civil War, Congress ordered a 1 percent repurchase, an empty gesture while heavy deficits persisted. In the prosperous 1920's appropriations to the sinking fund grew from $261 to $388 million. The Great Depression ushered in an era of deficit spending, prolonged by World War II and the Korean and Vietnam wars. Instead of being subjected to statutory reduction, the public debt constantly increased; the debt ceiling was regularly raised by Congress, and refunding was systematized.

SINO-JAPANESE WAR. The conflict between China and Japan in 1894–95 concerned the United States only indirectly: a treaty with Korea pledged the United States to exert its good offices in the event of a dispute with foreign powers, and efforts were consequently made to induce Japan and China to withdraw their troops from Korea. The United States rejected British overtures for foreign intervention to avert the war, but was instrumental in bringing Japan and China together for the final peace negotiations.

SIOUX. *See* **Dakota.**

SIOUX-CHIPPEWA WAR. For nearly two centuries prior to 1858, the Sioux and the Chippewa battled for control of the northern Wisconsin and Minnesota hunting grounds, as the latter tribe moved slowly westward along the Great Lakes. With firearms from French traders, the Chippewa defeated a Sioux-Fox alliance near Saint Croix Falls, Wis., then destroyed the Sioux villages at Sandy Lake and Mille Lacs, Minn. The withdrawal of the Sioux to southern Minnesota and their receipt of firearms after 1750 produced a territorial stalemate, and the intertribal war became a series of retaliatory raids punctuated by truces. The government vainly laid down a boundary line between the two in 1825.

The establishment of the Indian agency at Fort Snelling in 1819 drew the Chippewa deep into Sioux territory, and conflicts were inevitable. In 1827 Sioux treacherously murdered Chippewa just outside the fort. The battles of Rum River and Stillwater in 1839 resulted from a Chippewa ambush, and the Lake Pokegama Sioux raid of 1841 produced the Kaposia battle of 1842. The sharp fight near Shakopee, Minn., May 27, 1858, closed the series of ambushes with a final stalemate.

As a consequence of Chippewa pressure, the Sioux began to move westward into the Plains in large numbers, abandoning their villages and farms. With the departure of the Sioux the Chippewa came to control the territory around the headwaters of the Mississippi River; the Santee (or Eastern) Sioux, however, remained around the Minnesota River south of the present Minneapolis–St. Paul area, and were successful in opposing further Chippewa inroads into their territory.

SIOUX CLAIMS COMMISSION. Following the Minnesota Sioux uprising, Congress (Feb. 16, 1863) abrogated all Minnesota Sioux treaties; declared forfeit their lands and annuities; appropriated $200,000 from such funds for damages to whites; and established a claims commission, which, after hearings, awarded 2,635 claimants $1,370,374, an amount duly paid by appropriation.

SIOUX COUNCIL (July 27–Aug. 3, 1889). During the 1880's pressure on the federal government for the reduction of the so-called Great Sioux Reservation, an area roughly extending from Nebraska's northern line to the 46th parallel and from the Missouri River to 104 degrees west longitude, led to several attempts to negotiate with the Sioux. A law was passed by Congress on Mar. 2, 1889, setting aside certain areas for six reservation groups in Dakota Territory and opening the balance for sale to whites at $1.25 per acre, the amounts received to be credited to Indian funds. The law required the consent of three-fourths of the adult male Sioux. A three-man commission, after visiting several of the smaller agencies concerned, began its most important council at Standing Rock, on July 27. John Grass, chief spokesman for the Standing Rock Sioux, objected to the government's failure to observe the Treaty of Laramie (1868), particularly in respect to payments, schools, and so forth, and was dissatisfied with the low price offered for the land. In successive sessions the commissioners, by minor concessions, met the objections. Indian agent James McLaughlin in secret conferences finally persuaded Grass and Chief Gall to accept the act, and the formal signing followed on Aug. 3. The compensation for the land sold was estimated at upward of $7 million.

SIOUX TREATIES. Negotiations and treaties with the Sioux covered a period of some eighty-five years (1805–89) and a geographical area extending from Fort Snelling (Minn.) and Portage des Sioux (Mo.) on the Mississippi to Fort Laramie (Wyo.). On Sept. 23, 1805, Lt. Zebulon M. Pike, at Pike's Island (Minn.), purchased from the Minnesota Sioux for $2,000 in goods a tract roughly nine miles square at the mouth of the Minnesota River for a military post (later Fort Snelling). Between 1815 and 1817 a series of peace agreements acknowledging the sovereignty of the United States were negotiated at Portage des Sioux and St. Louis with various Siouan tribes.

The extension of fur trading operations up the Missouri River and the movement of troops up that stream (*see* Yellowstone River Expeditions) produced friction with the Sioux and other tribes; in 1825, several treaties, such as that of Fort Lookout (S.D.), provided for peaceful relations and the admission of traders to the country. The same year witnessed the great treaty council of Prairie du Chien (Wis.), where the Sioux and other warring tribes, under governmental supervision, agreed upon mutual boundary lines and the maintenance of intertribal peace. The treaty of July 15, 1830, negotiated also at Prairie du Chien, was concerned with peace measures between the Sauk and Fox and the Minnesota Sioux and allied groups, and attempted to set up a block of neutral territory between tribal enemies.

By the Treaty of Washington (Sept. 29, 1837) the Sioux began the sale of their Minnesota lands and the assignment of treaty funds to settle debts to traders; by the time the agreements of Traverse des Sioux and Mendota (1851) and Washington (1858) had been completed, they retained only a ten-mile-wide strip in that state. The great treaties of Fort Laramie in 1868 attempted to end the Indian wars by setting up a vast Sioux reserve west of the Missouri River and promising certain annuities and payments; the Indians were to withdraw opposition to the building of railroads through their country.

The act of Mar. 3, 1871 (*see* Indian Policy, National), prohibited further treatymaking with Indian tribes, but in order to secure Indian acceptance of laws applicable to them, periodic councils for ratification were held, of which those in the summer of 1889 with the Sioux are typical (*see* Sioux

Council). The Indians in these assemblies acted as individuals, not as agents for semi-independent tribal entities.

SIOUX UPRISING IN MINNESOTA (1862). Following the cession of nearly 1 million acres of their land, the Santee Sioux in 1862 were crowded onto a reservation along the upper Minnesota River without any hunting areas. In July about 5,000 starving Indians assembled at the Upper Agency at Yellow Medicine, Minn., to receive the government's annual payment of $72,000 for their lands. The gold shipment did not arrive on Aug. 1 as expected, and anger mounted when the Indian agent at the Lower Agency at Redwood refused to give the Indians food from the government's stores. On Aug. 17 four young Sioux murdered five settlers near Acton, Minn., and on the following day the Sioux rose in full force and attacked the Redwood agency, killing twenty white men. For two weeks Sioux raiding bands swept through southwestern Minnesota. Despite the loss of twenty-four soldiers ambushed at the Redwood Ferry on Aug. 18, government troops successfully defended Fort Ridgely and New Ulm (Aug. 19–26) against Little Crow's warriors, permitting the movement up from Fort Snelling of about 1,400 troops under Col. Henry H. Sibley. The soldiers' victory at Wood Lake on Sept. 23, following their Birch Coulee triumph on Sept. 2–3, crushed the uprising. Thirty-eight Sioux were executed at Mankato on Dec. 26. More than 800 settlers had been killed.

SIOUX WARS. The first clash between the Sioux and American troops occurred in 1854, near Fort Laramie, Wyo., when Lt. J. L. Grattan and eighteen men were killed. In retaliation, Gen. W. S. Harney in 1855 attacked a camp of Brulé Sioux near Ash Hollow, Neb., and killed about a hundred. With the beginning of the Civil War, regular army troops were replaced by state and territorial militiamen in attempting to keep the Indians peaceful. After the uprising of 1862 (*see* Sioux Uprising in Minnesota) some of the dispersed Sioux sought refuge in Canada, while others joined the Teton Sioux in the plains of South Dakota. The Teton were not generally hostile to the whites until 1865, when they joined with the Arapaho and Cheyenne in attacking emigrants on the Bozeman Trail to the Montana goldfields. In 1865 the Teton under Chief Red Cloud defeated an army unit at the Upper Platte Bridge.

With the end of the Civil War, regular federal troops were rushed to the Plains in an attempt at pacification, but the Sioux were aroused by the government's intention to erect forts along the Bozeman Trail. Red Cloud's War (1866–67) followed. In 1868 the government agreed to abandon the trail and forts and Red Cloud signed a treaty of peace at Fort Laramie.

The treaty had guaranteed the Sioux possession in perpetuity of the Black Hills, but in 1874 there was a rush of gold prospectors into the area. The consequence was the Black Hills War (1876) in which Gen. George Armstrong Custer and his troops were killed at the Battle of the Little Bighorn on June 25. The Sioux separated after the battle: Gen. George Crook defeated American Horse's band at Slim Buttes on Sept. 9; Sitting Bull was pursued to Canada by Gen. Nelson A. Miles; Crazy Horse and his Oglala fought on until they were induced by hunger to surrender (Jan. 7, 1877). Relative peace then prevailed until the final Sioux uprising, sometimes called the Messiah War, which attended the religious excitement of the Ghost Dance in 1890. On Dec. 15 Chief Sitting Bull was killed by Indian police who had been sent to arrest him, and the pacification of the Sioux was completed on Dec. 29 with the massacre of some 300 Sioux at the so-called Battle of Wounded Knee.

SIT-DOWN STRIKES. *See* **Strikes.**

SIT-INS. During the 1960's numerous protest groups used a "sit-in" tactic to dramatize their protests or positions on public questions. Government offices, schools, and places of business were often occupied in civil rights "sit-ins."

SIX NATIONS. *See* **Iroquois.**

SIX-SHOOTER. *See* **Colt Six-Shooter.**

SIXTEENTH AMENDMENT. The amendment to the U.S. Constitution authorizing Congress to impose a federal income tax. In 1908 the Democratic platform endorsed such an amendment, and it was widely supported by the progressive wing of the Republican party. President William Howard Taft eventually recommended submission of an amendment to the states, and the necessary resolution passed both houses of Congress by overwhelming majorities in July 1909. The necessary ratifications were forthcoming, and the amendment was declared effective Feb. 25, 1913.

SIXTEEN TO ONE. *See* **Bimetallism.**

SKIING. In 1856 the Norwegian John ("Snowshoe") Thompson drew attention to skiing when he began carrying the mail over the Sierra Nevada on skis: he covered ninety miles in three days and returned in two days. California gold miners took up ski racing in the 1860's, plunging downhill at speeds reportedly over 80 miles per hour. The first ski club in the United States was organized at La Porte, Calif., in 1867. In the 1880's and 1890's the Norwegian rage for ski jumping spread to America.

Skiing became popular among college students shortly after organization of the Dartmouth Outing Club in 1909. In the 1920's Dartmouth imported Austrian ski coaches, and in 1925 slalom was introduced at the Dartmouth winter carnival. In 1929 the first American ski school opened at Franconia, N.H. With the development of the ski lift in the 1930's, alpine skiing prevailed. The first rope tow in the United States was installed at Woodstock, Vt., in 1934. The 1932 Winter Olympics, held at Lake Placid, N.Y., were broadcast on radio, stoking the ski fever in the United States. The Sun Valley, Idaho, resort was opened in 1936. By the decade's end skiing had been transformed from a collegiate pastime into almost a mass movement.

During World War II many of America's best skiers joined the Eighty-seventh Mountain Infantry Regiment; the regiment was expanded into the Tenth Mountain Division, which saw action in Italy. In the 1940's and 1950's elaborate release bindings superseded cables; metal skis, developed by Howard Head of Baltimore, superseded wooden skis; packed, groomed slopes replaced powdery fields, and in some places, snow was artificially made. At the same time ski racing became a popular spectator sport. In 1960, Squaw Valley, Calif., was host to the Winter Olympics, where ski racing was televised live for the first time in America. In 1961 the first U.S. professional ski race took place.

In the early 1960's the commercialization of skiing led some people, many of them disenchanted alpine skiers, to take up ski touring, or cross-country skiing, through the woods and fields, first in New England college towns, and by the late 1960's across the country. In the mid-1970's, alpine skiers, estimated at between 2 million and 4 million, and alpine resort developers found themselves increasingly at odds with environmentalists over the future of the mountains.

SKINNERS. *See* **Cowboys and Skinners.**

SKYJACKING. *See* **Hijacking, Aerial.**

SKYSCRAPERS. *See* **Architecture.**

SLADE'S GIRLS. Young women sent west as teachers in the middle of the 19th century by the Board of National Popular Education. This organization was founded in 1847 under home missionary impulses; by 1857 it had sent more than 400 women from New England and New York to western states and territories.

SLAUGHTERHOUSE CASES, 16 Wallace 36 (1873). Considered as the Supreme Court's first interpretation of the due process clause of the Fourteenth Amendment. In 1869 the carpetbag legislature of Louisiana granted a monopoly of the slaughtering business within New Orleans to a single corporation, thereby depriving some 1,000 persons of their occupation. This monopoly was challenged in the courts mainly as a violation of the Fourteenth Amendment, particularly with reference to the privileges and immunities clause, the denial by the state of equal protection of the laws, and a deprivation of property under the due process clause. Justice Samuel Miller declared that the "one pervading purpose" of the Fourteenth Amendment was protection of the newly freed slaves and not transferring the control over the entire domain of civil rights from the states to the federal government; this was in flagrant violation of the intent of the Radical Republican framers of the amendment, who had desired to bring about federal protection of corporations and other businesses from discriminatory state legislation, as well as to achieve social guarantees for blacks.

SLAVE INSURRECTIONS. Until well into the 20th century, historians tended to picture insurrections among slaves as seldom occurring in the United States. However, insurrection was more frequent than earlier historians had acknowledged. For example, of a total of 1,418 slave convictions, in the state of Virginia in the period 1780–1864, 91 were for insurrection and 346 for murder; when this is added to the several recorded examples of plots and revolts in the state in the 17th and early 18th centuries, the record for that state alone is impressive.

The first slave revolt in territory that became the United States took place in 1526 in a Spanish settlement near the mouth of the Pee Dee River in what is now South Carolina, when several slaves rebelled and fled to live with Indians of the area. The most serious insurrections in the British colonies occurred in New York and in South Carolina. In 1712 a slave conspiracy in New York City led to the death of nine whites and the wounding of five or six others. Six of the rebels killed themselves to avoid capture; of those taken into custody twenty-one were executed in a variety of ways. In 1739 in Cato's Revolt at Stono, S.C., near Charleston, blacks seized guns and ammunition and fought the militia before being defeated; approximately twenty-five whites and fifty blacks were killed. In 1741 a conspiracy among slaves and white servants in New York City led to the execution of thirty-one blacks and four whites.

The successful slave revolt in Haiti during the French Revolution led to a series of plots in the South. Others followed up to the Civil War (*see* Gabriel's Insurrection; Nat Turner's Rebellion; Vesey Rebellion). Each uprising brought a new crop of repressive laws.

SLAVE REPRESENTATION. *See* **Compromises of the U.S. Constitution.**

SLAVERY. In August 1619 a Dutch frigate sold twenty black captives to settlers in Jamestown, Va.; it is not certain whether these black bondsmen were indentured servants or slaves. By the year 1640 some blacks in Virginia were being held in perpetual bondage as *de facto* slaves and some of their children had inherited the same obligation, while others remained contracted servants or had been set free by their masters. By the 1660's Virginia had enacted a series of laws giving statutory recognition to the institution of slavery.

By the end of the 17th century slavery had gained legal recognition throughout British America, but had taken firmer root along the southern seaboard in the middle Atlantic and New England settlements. Each region passed in the course of the 18th century elaborate slave codes to regulate slave activity and to protect white society against black uprisings: slaves were denied the right to marry, own property, bear arms, or defend themselves against assault. So that baptized slaves and children fathered by white men could not escape enslavement, colonial legislatures ruled that conversion to Christianity had no effect upon a person's condition, bond or free, and that status was determined by the race of the mother. The slave population grew from 20,000 in 1700 to 500,000 by the time of the American Revolution. South Carolina had a slave population in 1765 of 90,000 out of a total population of 130,000.

Strong abolitionist impulses inspired by the Quakers, the libertarian ideals of the war for independence, black freedom petitions, and the marginal importance of slavery to the

North's economy produced a number of state court decisions and laws gradually abolishing slavery in New England and the middle Atlantic states.

To hold together the newly formed republic, the framers of the U.S. Constitution agreed at the Constitutional Convention (September 1787) to several compromises favorable to southern interests: the Constitution included a provision by which, for purposes of congressional apportionment, a slave was to be counted as three-fifths of a person; an extension of the slave trade until 1808; and a fugitive slave clause, which ensured the return of runaway slaves to their masters. But the passage by Congress in 1787 of the Northwest Ordinance, which prevented the expansion of slavery into the midwestern territories, and the closing in 1808 of the African slave trade greatly restricted the future development of American slavery and deeply affected its character. However, the institution had become by the late 1780's a viable economic system so intricately woven into the social fabric of southern life that black emancipation was never seriously considered.

After the 1808 prohibition, cotton planters were forced to turn to the domestic slave trade then being developed by states in the upper South, such as Virginia and Maryland, which had an excess supply of slaves; during the four decades preceding the Civil War, this trade accounted for the transfer of about 200,000 slaves from the soil-exhausted Chesapeake Bay region to the alluvial Black Belt area. Despite its volume, the domestic slave trade failed to supply the number of slaves needed on the extensive cotton fields. Since Congress could not be persuaded to reopen the trade with Africa, the planters had no choice but to increase their slave force by natural reproduction; the growth of the slave population from 750,000 in 1790 to over 4 million in 1860 was attributable almost entirely to natural reproduction. Almost half a million slaves were employed in nonagricultural pursuits in the cities, towns, and labor camps of the antebellum South, but the farm or plantation remained the slave's typical environment. The bulk of the slave population was owned by a distinctly small segment of southern society.

By the 1830's, virtually all opposition among southern whites to the institution of slavery had disappeared. Headed by George Fitzhugh, the proslavery ideologue of Virginia, southern apologists popularized arguments that slavery was a positive good, divinely ordained, and that blacks were inherently inferior to whites. Yet, absolute control of slave activity was never achieved. "Day-to-day resistance," expressed in malingering, work slowdowns, sabotage, arson, self-mutilation, and the feigning of illness or incompetence, was the common opposition to the slave system. Thousands of slaves tried to secure their freedom by fleeing from the South, and many succeeded with the assistance of free blacks working as "agents" for the "Underground Railroad." The most dramatic, but also rarest, form of slave protest was open rebellion (*see* Slave Insurrections).

Southern politicians, led by John C. Calhoun of South Carolina, upheld the principle of states' rights in Congress and sought to maintain a balance in the Senate between free and slave states (*see* Slave States). Senators Stephen A. Douglas of Illinois and Henry Clay of Kentucky produced an omnibus bill, the Compromise of 1850, which temporarily settled the dispute and succeeded in preventing the threatened secession of the South from the Union, but tempers inflamed by the passage of the stringent Fugitive Slave Act (1850), Harriet Beecher Stowe's novel *Uncle Tom's Cabin* (1852), the Kansas-Nebraska Act and conflict of 1854, and the Dred Scott Supreme Court decision of 1857 brought the nation to the brink of war. When white abolitionist John Brown and his interracial band attacked the federal arsenal at Harpers Ferry, Va. (now West Virginia), in 1859 to incite a general slave insurrection and Republican Abraham Lincoln of Illinois was elected president in 1860, most whites in the South were convinced that the only way to preserve southern civilization was to secede from the Union (*see* Secession of Southern States; Civil War).

When Lincoln dispatched federal troops to repress the rebels, he had no intention of freeing the slaves; his sole aim was restoration of the Union. Military expediency and growing moral concern soon transformed the conflict into a crusade to free the slaves as well as to save the Union. Abolitionists and Radical Republicans gradually convinced Congress and much of the general public of the need to abolish slavery. In the spring and summer of 1862, Lincoln signed legislation abolishing slavery in the District of Columbia, banning slavery in the territories, and freeing slaves who escaped to northern lines. These actions were followed in the fall by decisions to authorize the enlistment of black volunteers into the army and to issue a preliminary emancipation proclamation.

By the terms of the preliminary announcement, issued by Lincoln in September 1862, all slaves in those states still in rebellion on Jan. 1, 1863, would be freed. Slaves in the loyal border states and in areas occupied by Union forces were excluded from the ruling; had the Confederates surrendered within a period of 100 days, the South might have been able, under the provisions of Lincoln's proclamation, to retain its slaves. The Confederacy refused to surrender, forcing the president to issue the Emancipation Proclamation on its scheduled date (*See* Emancipation Proclamation.) The document left in bondage some 800,000 slaves in the border states and in areas controlled by the federal government. They were not freed until the adoption in December 1865 of the Thirteenth Amendment, which formally brought to an end nearly 250 years of black slavery in America. (*See also* Antislavery.)

SLAVERY, INDIAN. Evidence indicates that few Indian tribes within the area of the United States made slaves of people of their own race. A mild form of slavery apparently existed among several tribes in the Pacific Northwest; elsewhere it was the general practice to adopt prisoners of war into membership in the tribe. Black slaves were held by some southern Indians, notably among the Five Civilized Tribes. Having come into possession of runaway southern slaves, these slaveholders took their slaves with them when they were removed to the region of the present state of Oklahoma (*see* Indian Removal). During the Civil War large portions of these tribes allied themselves with the southern Confederacy, partly because of their slaveholding. After the war this slavery was abolished, not only by the Thirteenth Amendment but also by specific clauses in treaties made in 1866 with the Five Civilized Tribes.

SLAVES, FUGITIVE. *See* **Fugitive Slave Acts.**

SLAVES, INDIAN. The selling of captive American Indians into slavery was inaugurated by early Spanish explorers in the New World and was continued by later Europeans. Carolina was early made a hunting ground by the Spaniards for Indian slaves, who were sent to Cuba. The English settlers of South Carolina during the Indian wars before and after 1675 practiced on a large scale the enslavement of Indians for whom they found a steady and profitable market in the West Indies. In New England during the Pequot War of 1636–37 and King Philip's War of 1675–76, captive Indians were sold into slavery, the males shipped to the West Indies and the females scattered among the white settlers. The French destroyed the Natchez villages in 1730 and sold 450 captive Indians into slavery in Santo Domingo. The last-known survival of the custom was in Alabama during the enforced Indian removals of 1836, when a number of Creek were held in servitude.

SLAVE SHIPS. The earliest slave ships were converted merchantmen; later, special vessels were built, based on troop transports and equipped with air scuttles, ports, and open gratings. The first definitely authenticated American ship to carry slaves was the *Desire,* sailing out of Salem, Mass., in 1638. Many of these vessels were heavily armed both for self-defense and for highjacking other slavers. Many slavers rigged a shelf in the middle of the hold called a "slave deck," which extended 6 feet from each side to hold additional slaves. Sometimes a second slave deck was also used, leaving only 20 inches of headroom, so that the slaves were unable even to sit upright during the entire voyage. When the slave trade was made illegal in 1808, traders turned to fast ships to outrun the British frigates guarding the African coast. Every consideration was sacrificed for speed, and the accommodations for the slaves were even worse than on earlier vessels. The last American slaver was probably the *Huntress* of New York, which landed a cargo of slaves in Cuba in 1864.

SLAVE STATES. Those states where slaveholding was sanctioned by law. This was all the states in 1776. Under the influence of the American Revolution, slavery disappeared north of Delaware and Maryland. Pennsylvania moved against it in 1780, Massachusetts in 1783, and Connecticut and Rhode Island in 1784. New York (1785) and New Jersey (1786) passed acts that were followed by more effective legislation in 1799 and 1804. The Northwest Ordinance (1787) prohibited the establishment of slavery in that territory. However, the Compromise of 1820 was worked out to define the territory from which slave states might develop, and by 1845 nine new slave states had entered the Union. On the eve of the Civil War the slave states were Alabama, Arkansas, Delaware, Florida, Georgia, Kentucky, Louisiana, Maryland, Mississippi, Missouri, North Carolina, South Carolina, Tennessee, Texas, and Virginia.

SLAVE TRADE. African slaves were first brought to the New World shortly after its discovery by Christopher Columbus (there are records of them in Haiti in 1501), but the slave trade proper began in 1517, when Charles V of Spain issued the Asiento, a contract giving the holder a monopoly on importing slaves to the Spanish dominions. For the next two centuries the Asiento was to be a much coveted prize in European wars and treaties.

Portugal claimed the west coast of Africa as a result of expeditions sent out by Prince Henry the Navigator and at first controlled the export of slaves. Portugal's hegemony was soon challenged by French, Dutch, Swedish, Danish, Prussian, and English slavers, but Portugal managed to retain control of the area south of the Bight of Benin. The Bight of Benin provided so many slaves that it became known as the Slave Coast.

Slavery was a recognized institution in Africa; some of the tribes particularly associated with the trade were the Mandingo, Ashanti, Yoruba, Ewe, and Ibo. The local kings sold their surplus slaves, as well as criminals, debtors, and prisoners of war, to the European traders. In times of famine, parents often sold their children. These sources did not meet the constantly growing demand, and soon slave-catching raids were organized by the coastal tribes.

England, as the outstanding sea power, gradually came to control the trade. The first black slaves were landed in Jamestown, Va., in 1619. After slavery was abolished in the northern colonies, the New England colonies continued to take an active part in the slave trade itself, providing ships and crews and selling the slaves south of the Mason-Dixon Line. The trade expanded rapidly after 1650; by 1750, 100,000 slaves a year were arriving. By the 18th century, the actual slave catching was done mainly by such warlike inland tribes as the Ashanti and the Dahomey, with the coastal tribes acting as middlemen.

In 1713 the Treaty of Utrecht gave England the Asiento and a virtual monopoly of the trade north of the equator. The American colonies developed triangular trade in the mid-18th century: a captain would load up with trade goods and rum and sail to Africa, where the goods would be exchanged for slaves; he would then land his slaves in the West Indies and take on a cargo of molasses, which he would transport to New England to be made into rum. The base of the triangle, the run across the middle of the Atlantic, became known as the Middle Passage.

At first slavers attempted to make some provisions for the welfare of their human cargo, such as "loose packing" (not overcrowding the slaves). Later most slavers became convinced that it was more profitable to pack slaves into every available square foot of space and make a run for it ("tight packing"); with good winds the voyage could be made with little loss of life in two months, but with contrary winds most of the human cargo would be lost. (*See* Slave Ships.)

By the end of the 18th century there began to be strong moral opposition to the slave trade, although many considered it an economic necessity and the only method of providing manpower. Great Britain abolished the trade in 1807, and the United States did the same in 1808; the other European and South American countries gradually followed suit. However, the trade continued to increase despite the prohibition.

Slavers were declared pirates by both the United States and Great Britain under the treaty of 1820. In 1839 the Equipment Clause was passed, authorizing a frigate's captain to seize a ship if it was obviously fitted out as a slaver with slave decks, large amounts of extra water casks, shackles, and grilled hatches. The Webster-Ashburton Treaty of 1842 provided for American warships to cruise along the coast with the British vessels, but few American frigates were ever sent, and most of those did not take their duty seriously.

With the abolition of slavery in the United States and the end of the Civil War, the trade largely came to an end. A few cargoes were probably run to Brazil in the 1870's and possibly even in the early 1880's, but to all intents and purposes, the trade was finished. In 1867 the slaving squadron was withdrawn.

Some 15 million blacks were exported from Africa during the 300 years of the slave trade. For Africans, it was a disaster. It bled dry great sections of the continent, leaving communities so weak that they could not harvest crops; encouraged local wars; and discouraged development of the continent's resources, because the trade was so profitable nothing else could compete with it.

SLAVOCRACY. In its broader sense, this refers to the persons or interests in the antebellum South representing slavery and using their influence to preserve and expand that institution; the slavocracy was successful in securing the recognition of slavery in the Constitution, in continuing the slave trade for some years, and in adding nine slave states to the Union by 1845. In its more restricted sense, the term "slavocracy" was used in the North during the 1850's to designate a group of southern expansionists supposedly plotting to extend the area of American slavery into the territories and possibly to Mexico, Cuba, and Central America.

SLEEPING CARS. *See* **Pullmans.**

SLEEPY HOLLOW. A valley through which flows the Pocantico River, about three-quarters of a mile north of Tarrytown, N.Y.; famous for its old Dutch church (1699) and for its association with the writings of Washington Irving. Romantic memories of Sleepy Hollow recur in Irving's essays and attain their most complete expression in "The Legend of Sleepy Hollow," originally published in *The Sketch Book* (Dec. 29, 1819).

SLIDELL'S MISSION TO MEXICO. John Slidell, a Democratic congressman from Louisiana, was sent to Mexico by President James K. Polk in November 1845 to secure a boundary adjustment. He was authorized to commit the U.S. government to pay liberal bonuses in return for relinquishment by Mexico of claims to certain territory. Notwithstanding previous pledges, the Mexican government did not receive Slidell officially. After the formal rejection of his proposal (Dec. 21, 1845) Slidell withdrew to Jalapa, where he remained until April 1846, fulfilling the auxiliary purpose of his mission, to act as an observer, and striving "to place [the United States] in the strongest moral position before our own people and the world by exhausting every means of conciliation." Failure of the mission presaged war.

SLIM BUTTES, BATTLE OF (Sept. 9, 1876). After the Sioux victory at the Battle of Little Bighorn (June 25–26), troops under Gen. George Crook and other commanders pursued the Indians. Crook finally abandoned pursuit and marched for the Black Hills settlements; at Grand River a party of 150 cavalrymen was sent ahead for supplies, and twenty miles south, at Slim Buttes, they discovered a Sioux village containing 100 warriors under American Horse. At daybreak on Sept. 9 the cavalrymen rushed the village and captured it. Crook brought up the main body of troops by noon, and American Horse, mortally wounded, surrendered. Crazy Horse, arriving tardily with a large force, attacked but was repulsed.

SLOCUM, GENERAL. See **Disasters.**

SLOOP. A naval vessel, generally square-rigged and three-masted and carrying all its guns on the open spar deck. In the War of 1812 U.S. sloops such as the *Wasp* won many famous actions. More heavily armed wooden-screw sloops, such as the *Hartford,* saw action in the Civil War.

SLUMS. Seriously blighted residential districts that contribute to the social disorganization of their inhabitants. The slow-growing cities in the American colonies escaped the blighting effects of slums until their increased size in some cases made the primitive sanitary facilities unwholesome; but it was not until 1832, when the ravages of cholera exacted a heavy toll among the inhabitants of congested urban districts, that New York, Philadelphia, and Boston recognized the existence there of wretched slums. In New York the draft riots of 1863 revealed the extent of alienation that had developed in the slums. As a result the Citizens' Association appointed a council of hygiene and public health, which conducted an investigation that prompted the adoption of the first tenement house law in 1867.

The rapid influx of poor Irish and German immigrants in the 1840's and 1850's inundated the older districts of most cities. Many substantial old houses and some warehouses were hastily converted into multiple residences with minimal sanitary facilities, and flimsy annexes were added. When the early housing codes in New York City endeavored to preserve some open space and, later, to ban dark rooms, the builders added additional floors and provided airshafts that carried foul odors and sounds into every apartment; solid rows of new five- and six-story tenements extended over wide districts and attracted only the poorest residents. Each fresh invasion deteriorated the housing stock. A federal survey in 1893 found the worst slum districts largely concentrated in New York and Chicago, but later studies found them widely present in most older cities of the Northeast.

The sudden drop in the tide of immigrants during World War I brought a sharp decline in the density of many old ethnic districts; but World War I stimulated a movement of blacks from the South that continued until the 1960's. The settlement of these blacks in old immigrant districts spurred the migration of former residents to the outskirts and suburbs, creating inner-city black ghettos that added the new dimension of prejudice to the problems of the slums. The pressure for federal action mounted, spurring an expansion of the public housing program. Unfortunately the demolition of old tenements had the effect of scattering their inhabitants. Efforts to locate the new projects in outlying wards met stiff neighborhood resistance; the result was a concentration of the low-cost units in high-rise blocks that in some cities exceeded the worst densities of the old slums. The introduction of new model-city participatory programs for the redevelopment of blighted districts offered federal assistance for their rejuvenation; these proved insufficient, however. Frustrated by the limited accomplishments, the federal government terminated the model-city projects and merged its subsidies in a block-grant system that turned responsibility for the fate of the slums back to the cities.

SMALL BUSINESS ADMINISTRATION. *See* **Federal Agencies.**

SMALLPOX. In its classic form, an acute, highly contagious disease with an average fatality rate for untreated cases of about one in five; survivors are often permanently disfigured or disabled. Brought to the Americas by explorers and settlers, it destroyed many Indian tribes and became epidemic several times in the British colonies in the 1600's. To prevent the introduction and spread of the disease, the New England colonies created an elaborate system of quarantine and isolation during the 18th century.

Inoculation produced a comparatively mild case of smallpox and conferred lifelong immunity. Cotton Mather persuaded Dr. Zabdiel Boylston to try it in Boston in 1721; a violent controversy ensued. Statistics showed, however, that the case fatality rate for inoculated smallpox was much lower than for natural smallpox and inoculation became widely accepted. Inoculation entailed some risk, and, if unregulated, could expose the community to the hazard of contagion. Several colonies passed laws prohibiting inoculation except during epidemics or in isolated hospitals, and were thus able to avoid smallpox altogether for years; in the Middle Colonies, by contrast, inoculation was freely allowed.

In 1798 the English physician Edward Jenner introduced vaccination—that is, the inoculation of cowpox, using techniques virtually identical to those used for the inoculation of smallpox (now known also as variolation). It was an immeasurable advance. Soon after Jenner's announcement several physicians sought to import vaccine, and vaccine institutes were organized to treat the poor free, the first under James Smith in Baltimore in 1802. Vaccination was not universal in the 19th century. Preservation of live vaccine virus was difficult, and the vaccine sometimes became contaminated. The introduction of animal vaccine produced in calves in 1870 and of glycerinated lymph somewhat later helped to obviate these difficulties. As health departments began urging compulsory vaccination, especially after the pandemic of 1870–75, antivaccination societies were founded. As a result, the United States, of the twenty-six countries reporting smallpox morbidity to the League of Nations in 1921–30, had the highest attack rate of any nation except India. The use of vaccination increased substantially during the 1930's and World War II, and the incidence of smallpox diminished dramatically. In 1967 the World Health Organization (WHO) began a program of intense surveillance and vaccination aimed at eradicating the disease. By 1980 the world was considered free of smallpox, and vaccination was discontinued.

SMELTERS. Smelting is a method of separating gold, silver, and other metals from their ores with heat intense enough to melt the ores. A Spanish law required a government smelter to be established in every mining district in the New World and required all miners to bring their gold and lead-silver to a government furnace; ruins of crude smelters have been found in southern California. In 1750 coal was first used as a fuel for smelting; beginning in 1830, anthracite coal was used. Colorado's gold sulfide ores defied recovery until a professor of chemistry built the Boston and Colorado smelter at Blackhawk (1867). Its successor, built at Argo (near Denver) in 1878, began the smelting of copper ores in reverberatory furnaces; until 1900 the Argo smelter was the only one to smelt gold and silver ores to matte exclusively in reverberatories. A major change in smelter design in the late 1800's was the introduction of much larger furnaces.

Cutthroat competition between the smelters led to combination. On Apr. 4, 1899, the American Smelting and Refining Company brought together eighteen of the country's largest smelting companies. In 1901 the firm of Meyer Guggenheim and his sons, the largest of the independents, joined the trust under terms that ensured them control of American Smelting.

SMITH, FORT (Ark.). Established (1817) by Maj. Stephen H. Long on what is now the Arkansas-Oklahoma border, at the confluence of the Arkansas and Poteau rivers; named for Col. Thomas A. Smith. Founded to protect frontier settlements from Indian attacks, by the 1840's the fort became a significant point for pioneers bound for Santa Fe. It was also an important border post during the Civil War.

SMITH, FORT, COUNCIL OF (September 1865). A peace council of federal commissioners and representatives of the Five Civilized Tribes and other smaller tribes of Indian Territory that had allied themselves with the Confederacy during the Civil War. The Indians were told that by joining the Confederacy they had made themselves liable to a forfeiture of all the rights guaranteed them in former treaties. The various tribes then signed an agreement formally establishing peace and amity with the United States and further agreed to send commissioners to Washington, D.C., the following year to negotiate new treaties.

SMITH, FORT C.F. (Mont.). Named for Gen. Charles Ferguson Smith; established (1866) by Lt. Col. N. C. Kinney at the Bighorn River crossing of the Bozeman Trail. During most of its existence, the fort was besieged by hostile Sioux (*see* Sioux Wars). On Aug. 1, 1867, Indians attacked haymakers and their soldier escort in a meadow three miles northeast of the fort (*see* Wagon Box Fight). By agreement with the Sioux, the fort was abandoned in August 1868.

SMITH ACT (June 28, 1940). This act provides for the registration and fingerprinting of aliens living in the United States and declares it unlawful to advocate or teach the forceful overthrow of any government in the United States or to belong to any group advocating or teaching such action. The act has been strongly criticized on the ground that it interferes with freedom of speech. In *Dennis* v. *United States,* concerning the conviction of eleven Communists under the act, the Supreme Court in 1951 upheld its constitutionality. In 1957, in *Yates* v. *United States,* the Court held that the teaching or advocacy of the overthrow of the U.S. government that was not accompanied by any subversive action was constitutionally protected free speech.

SMITH EXPLORATIONS (1822–31). Jedediah Strong Smith, fur trader and explorer, joined William Henry Ashley's expedition in 1822 to establish the Rocky Mountain Fur Company. The expedition began at St. Louis and ascended the Missouri River. In 1824 Smith headed the first party of Americans to travel through South Pass (Wyoming). In 1826 he led a party from the Great Salt Lake in Utah to southern California—the first Americans to reach the Spanish settlements by an overland route (*see* Cajon Pass). In 1827 he and two companions returned to the Great Salt Lake by the central route; shortly afterward he set out again for California. In 1827–28 he traveled up the Pacific coast, opening up a new route to Fort Vancouver on the Columbia River. Smith lost all but three of his men by massacre on the Umpqua River in Oregon. In 1829 he explored the Snake River country, and the following year he returned overland to St. Louis. In the spring of 1831 he set out with a wagon train for Santa Fe, N.M., and while seeking water for his party was killed by the Comanche.

SMITH-HUGHES ACT (1917). This act created the Federal Board for Vocational Education for the promotion of training in agriculture, trades and industries, commerce, and home economics in the secondary schools, and provided funds to prepare teachers of vocational subjects. Funded by federal grants-in-aid to be matched by state or local contributions, the act required that state boards submit their plans to the board for approval, thus providing for greater federal control in aid to education.

SMITH-LEVER ACT (1914). This provided for an elaborate system of agricultural extension work conducted through a field force of specialists with the assistance of federal grants-in-aid based on equal state contributions. Students not attending college received instructions in agriculture and home economics from county agents and thus enjoyed indirectly the benefits of the agricultural colleges and experimental stations.

SMITHSONIAN INSTITUTION. Chartered by Congress (1846) pursuant to the will of the Englishman James Smithson (1765–1829), who bequeathed his fortune (about $550,000) to "the United States of America, to found at Washington, under the name of the Smithsonian Institution, an Establishment for the increase and diffusion of knowledge among men." The Smithsonian derives its support both from appropriations from Congress and from private endowments; it is considered an independent establishment in the role of a ward of the U.S. government, the trustee. It is governed by a board of regents made up of the vice-president and chief justice of the United States (ex officio) and three U.S. senators, three representatives, and six citizens named by Congress. The regents elect one of their number as chancellor and choose a secretary, who is the executive officer, or director, of the institution. The institution over the years has assembled under its wings a group of museums and art galleries and other branches that have made it perhaps the largest museum and cultural complex in the world.

The following bureaus and agencies are under the Smithsonian's administration (located in Washington unless otherwise noted): The National Museum of Natural History, which with the National Museum of History and Technology constitutes the National Museum; the Smithsonian Astrophysical Observatory (1890), in Cambridge, Mass.; the National Zoological Park (1889); the National Collection of Fine Arts (1846) and the National Portrait Gallery (1962), which have, since 1968, jointly occupied the renovated Old Patent Office Building; the Freer Gallery of Art (1923), a center for the study of Oriental art; the Radiation Biology Laboratory (established in 1929 as the Division of Radiation and Organisms), in Rockville, Md.; the Smithsonian Tropical Research Institute (1940) on Barro Colorado Island, Panama; and the National Air and Space Museum. The International Exchange Service was initiated in 1850 to facilitate the international exchange of scientific and other scholarly publications; the Science Information Exchange, Inc., under the aegis of the Smithsonian since 1954, is a center for prepublication information about research that is planned or in progress in the United States and in some other countries. Several additional adjuncts of the Smithsonian Institution include the Cooper-Hewitt Museum of Decorative Arts and Design (1967), in New York City; the Joseph H. Hirshhorn Museum and Sculpture Garden (1974); and the Center for the Study of Man (1968). There are also three agencies technically under the aegis of the Smithsonian but administered by separate boards of trustees: the National Gallery of Art (1941); the John F. Kennedy Center for the Performing Arts (1971); and the Woodrow Wilson International Center for Scholars (1968).

The Smithsonian museums contain dozens of exhibit halls and vast study collections. The institution is equally famous for its worldwide exploration programs. The first Smithsonian publication, *Ancient Monuments of the Mississippi Valley,* was issued in 1848, and since that time thousands of books, pamphlets, catalogs, bulletins, and periodicals have appeared. Since 1970, in conjunction with a subsidiary organization, the Smithsonian Associates, the institution has published a popular magazine, *Smithsonian.*

SMOKY HILL TRAIL. A route from the Missouri Valley to Denver that came into importance with the Pikes Peak gold rush in the late 1850's. About 600 miles long, it led westward up the Kansas (Kaw) River and the Smoky Hill fork to its source, thence westerly to and along Big Sandy Creek, and down Cherry Creek to its mouth at Denver. A party of goldseekers broke the trail in the fall of 1858; it soon acquired the nickname "Starvation Trail." The Butterfield Overland Dispatch was established on the trail in 1865 and later competed with Holladay's Overland Mail, established in 1866. The stage service was displaced when the Kansas Pacific Railroad completed its track from Kansas City, Mo., to Denver in 1870. Highways U.S. 40 and Interstate 70 now follow rather closely the old trail.

SMOOT-HAWLEY TARIFF. *See* **Tariff.**

SMUGGLING, COLONIAL. Parliament was surprisingly negligent in providing for the enforcement of the Navigation Acts: not until 1673 were officials appointed to enforce them, and they didn't have the powers granted customs officers in England until 1696. Accounts of tobacco packed in flour barrels and foreign wine masquerading as New England rum, the connivance of officials, forgery of certificates, and tarring and feathering of informers all show that violations occurred. The bulk of the trade with Europe was legitimate. Violations of the Molasses Act (1733) were a different matter: the amount of rum produced in the northern colonies demonstrates that a flourishing illicit trade existed with the Dutch, French, and Spanish West Indies. The fact that the European clauses of the laws were reasonably well enforced left the colonists with an unfavorable balance of trade in the Old World. After the Molasses Act, illicit trade with the non-British West Indies was an economic necessity. The treasonable aspect of such trade with the French colonies during the French and Indian War (1754–63) aroused British resentment, and subsequent attempts to restrain the trade such as the American Revenue Act of 1764 (the Sugar Act) awakened active opposition in the colonies. The new duties in America imposed by such measures as the Townshend Acts (1767) and the decreased drawbacks on goods that the colonists were obliged to acquire in England either tended to increase smuggling or added economic grievances to political irritation. The Tea Act of 1773, by which the East India Company was granted the right to sell its tea directly to its agents in the colonies, aroused smugglers, whose profits were threatened by the company's lower-priced legally imported tea, and angered law-abiding colonial tea merchants, who were also undersold by the company. Smuggling was thus a part of the ferment leading to the American Revolution.

SNAGBOATS. Twin-hull steamboats designed especially for use in removing snags from western rivers. Operating during low water, the heavy iron-plated beam connecting the two hulls, below the water line, was run under the snag to loosen it from its moorings, after which it was hauled aboard and disposed of. Snag losses mounted to $1,362,500 between 1822 and 1827.

SNAKE RIVER. Formerly the Lewis, a 1,038-mile stream that rises in Shoshone Lake in Yellowstone National Park in northwest Wyoming, loops about southwestern Idaho, forms part of the Idaho-Oregon and the Idaho-Washington boundaries, and cuts across southeast Washington to empty into the Columbia River. Meriwether Lewis and William Clark followed the Snake from the mouth of the Clearwater in Idaho to the Columbia in 1805. The Rocky Mountain Fur Company and the Hudson's Bay Company competed up and down the stream through the early 19th century. From Fort Hall, Idaho, the Oregon Trail paralleled the river closely for some 400 miles. In the 20th century irrigation canals and hydroelectric power projects were established along the Snake.

SNAP CONVENTION (1892). A New York state convention called by supporters of Sen. David B. Hill for president on Feb. 22 to control the election of delegates to the Chicago Democratic national convention; it was nicknamed the "Snap Convention" because it was held at an unusually early date. To oppose the Hill delegation, the "Anti-Snappers" called a convention and sent a protesting delegation to Chicago.

SNELLING, FORT (Minn.). Established (1819) by Col. Henry Leavenworth as part of a general plan of frontier defense. Its site at the junction of the Mississippi and Minnesota rivers, was selected in 1805 by Lt. Zebulon M. Pike. It was first called Fort St. Anthony, but in 1825 its name was changed to Fort Snelling in honor of Col. Josiah Snelling, who had become commandant in 1820 and had erected permanent buildings and fortifications. The fort was headquarters for the Indian agency; it also served to protect the headquarters of the American Fur Company, located across the Minnesota River at Mendota. It lost its importance when other northeastern forts were established and was abandoned in 1858, but was reoccupied in 1861. A museum of Minnesota history was later established in the Round Tower of the fort, the oldest structure still standing (1976) in the state.

SNOWSHOES. Snowshoes, known in both the Old World and the New World, seem to have reached their highest form of development among the Indians of Canada and the northern United States. The French traders and immigrants adopted them, as did the trappers and traders in New England and the North Atlantic states.

SNUG HARBOR. *See* **Sailors' Snug Harbor.**

SOAP AND DETERGENT INDUSTRY. Traditionally soap has been manufactured from alkali (lye) and animal fats (tallow), although vegetable products such as palm oil and coconut oil can be substituted for the tallow. Soapmaking began in America during the earliest colonial days. Tallow came as a by-product of slaughtering animals for meat, or from whaling; farmers produced alkali as a by-product of clearing their land, and until the 19th century wood ashes served as the major source of lye; soapmaking remained widely dispersed, and no large producers emerged. But by the eve of the American Revolution the colonies had developed a minor export market; in 1770 they sent more than 86,000 pounds of soap worth £2,165 to the West Indies.

The growth of cities and the textile industry in the early 19th century stimulated the rise of soapmaking firms. By 1840 Cincinnati had become the leading soapmaking city. A major change in soap manufacture occurred in the 1840's with the substitution of soda ash, a lye made through a chemical process, for lye made from wood ashes. Factories remained small. Almost all soapmakers also produced tallow candles, which for many was the major business. The firms made soap in enormous slabs, and these were sold to grocers, who sliced the product like cheese for individual consumers; there were no brands.

Between the end of the Civil War and 1900 the market for candles diminished sharply, and soapmakers discontinued that business; at the same time competition rose. Many soapmakers began to brand their products and to introduce new varieties of toilet soap made with exotic ingredients. Advertising, at first modest but constantly growing, became the major innovation, and proved amazingly effective. The soap industry pioneered in radio advertising, particularly by developing daytime serial dramas ("soap operas"). In 1966 three out of the top five television advertisers were soapmakers.

By the late 1920's three firms had come to dominate the industry: Colgate-Palmolive-Peet, incorporated in 1928 in New York State (founded by William Colgate in 1807); Lever Brothers, an English company that developed a full line of heavily advertised soaps in the 19th century and in 1897 and 1899 purchased factories in Boston and Philadelphia; and Procter and Gamble, established in Cincinnati in 1837. The 1930's marked the start of a revolution: synthetic detergent—not a soap, but a chemical synthesis that substituted fatty alcohols for animal fats. Detergents are superior to soap in certain industrial processes (the making of textile finishes, for example); they work better in hard water; and they eliminate the soap curd responsible for bathtub rings. By 1980 detergents had almost eliminated soap from the laundry market, but toilet soap remained unchallenged by detergents.

SOCIAL COMPACT. *See* **Compact Theory.**

SOCIAL DEMOCRATIC PARTY. The Social Democracy of America as an organization was formed at Chicago (June 1897) of sections of the American Railway Union, the Socialist Labor party clubs, and various religious and trade-union groups. In June 1898, during the Social Democracy's first national convention, a group of thirty-three delegates who were committed to political activism formed the Social Democratic party of America. Later that year the Social Democrats were able to send two members to the Massachusetts legislature and to elect the mayor of Haverhill, Mass.; during the presidential election of 1900 their candidate, Eugene V. Debs, polled 87,814 votes. The subsequent fusion (1901) of anti-De Leonites from the Socialist Labor party and the Social Democratic party led to a new party designation, the Socialist party of America.

SOCIAL GOSPEL. A late 19th- and early 20th-century American Protestant reform movement attempting to apply the principles of Christianity to social and economic problems. Among the early leaders in the movement were Washington Gladden, Richard Theodore Ely, Charles Monroe Sheldon, Walter Rauschenbusch, and Shailer Mathews. Their advocacy of abolition of child labor, a shorter work week, improved factory conditions, and a living wage for all workers, as well as prison reform and changes in the free-enterprise system, led to the establishment of social-service agencies and the adoption of liberal social programs.

SOCIALIST LABOR PARTY. Out of several American branches of the Socialist First International (1864) emerged the Social Democratic Workingmen's Party of North America (1874), which in 1877 was transformed into the Socialist Labor party. Extensive industrial dissatisfaction stimulated its growth. Daniel De Leon, who had been associated with the Knights of Labor and with Edward Bellamy's Nationalist movement, became editor (1892) of the Socialist Labor party weekly, *The People,* and until his death in 1914 was the party's leading publicist. Among the central ideas of the party have been its emphasis on industrial unionism as against craft unionism, its advocacy of militant political action and the strike, and its insistence on party discipline. Its ideology has been Marxist throughout.

In its early days the Socialist Labor party seemed to show much promise in terms of numbers and electoral strength, but factional struggles and the formation of the ideologically less rigid Socialist party of America (1901) weakened it. Although it nominated a candidate for the presidency of the United States in every election from 1892 until 1968, its vote remained small.

SOCIALIST MOVEMENT. Socialism advocates that the major instruments of production, distribution, and exchange should be owned and administered by society for the welfare of all rather than for the benefit of a few. There have been many schools of Socialist thought, differing in strategy and in interpretation of ultimate goals.

In America the Socialist movement began during the early part of the 19th century, when communitarian experiements such as Brook Farm (1841) and the Oneida Colony (1848) were established. After the Civil War the influence of Marxian socialism began to be felt in the United States. The hard times of the 1870's and 1880's stimulated the development of the movement. In 1877 the Socialist Labor party was established. Edward Bellamy's followers in the Nationalist movement a decade later were fundamentally Socialist, and many Populists had somewhat the same point of view. In 1897 the Social Democracy of America was launched by Eugene V. Debs; out of it emerged the Social Democratic party in 1898—which, with other groups, established the Socialist party of America in 1901. (*See* Socialist Party of America.) The party began to disintegrate after the Bolshevik revolution in Russia in 1917. Dissidents formed the Communist party and the Communist Labor party; in 1920 another splinter group established the Proletarian party. By the 1950's the formal

Socialist movement in the United States had been reduced greatly. The Socialist party ceased to run candidates for the presidency after 1956. Although other groups called Socialist continued to exist and to nominate candidates, their electoral strength was small: in the 1968 presidential election the Socialist Labor party won 52,588 votes and the Socialist Workers party (Trotskyite), only 41,300.

SOCIALIST PARTY OF AMERICA. Formed in July 1901 by a union of the Social Democratic party and a wing of the Socialist Labor party, the Socialist party gave to American radicalism a unique era of organizational unity; only the tiny Socialist Labor party and, later, the Industrial Workers of the World remained outside. The party incorporated surviving elements of western populism and was also well entrenched in the labor movement. In 1912, the high point of their electoral success, Eugene V. Debs, running for the U.S. presidency, gained 6 percent of the vote, and some 1,200 Socialists were elected to public office, including seventy-nine mayors.

The party in 1913 cast out the syndicalist wing led by William D. Haywood, the one group not committed to political action. World War I severely tested the Socialist movement. Unlike its western European counterparts the American party adhered to the stand of the Second International against war. Wartime persecution hurt the movement: Debs and many others went to prison; vigilante action and the barring of Socialist literature from the mails weakened outlying bodies, especially in the western states. But the party made a strong showing in wartime elections.

The Bolshevik revolution in Russia (1917) was the turning point. The American party leaders did not think that the United States was ripe for revolution, nor were they willing to reconstitute the party along Leninist lines. With the left wing about to take over, the established leadership in May 1919 suddenly expelled seven foreign-language federations and the entire Michigan party and invalidated the elections to the national executive committee. Not only was American radicalism permanently split between Communists and Socialists, but the latter had lost their authenticity as a movement of radical action. By 1928 Socialist membership was not a tenth of the 1919 level, and the party had evolved into an essentially reformist movement whose appeal was largely to the urban middle class. After 1956 the Socialist party ceased to nominate presidential candidates and increasingly viewed itself as an educational rather than a political force. In 1972 the Social Democratic Federation, a moderate wing that had split away in 1936, was reunited with the Socialist party; at the end of 1972 the name was changed to Social Democrats USA.

SOCIAL LEGISLATION. Until the 1930's the protection of the living standards of citizens threatened by unemployment, sickness, disability, accident, old age, and other circumstances was largely left to private, religious, and charitable institutions in the United States, or to state and local authorities. The general welfare clause of Article I, Section 8, of the Constitution was interpreted narrowly by the federal government, which did little for social welfare. In the 19th century various states built workhouses and almshouses, following such examples as New York's County Poor House Act of 1824. In 1863 Massachusetts created a unified state board of charities. Other states followed suit, and in the late 19th century the Charity Organization Society became a national lobby for social legislation: housing and tenement laws, prison reforms, health laws, and protection of child labor. The indigent blind were first aided by Indiana state law in 1840, and first given annual pensions by Ohio in 1898. The first state school for the feebleminded was established in Boston in 1848. Only for the deaf did the federal arm intervene: in 1864 Congress funded the Columbia Institute for the Deaf and Dumb (now Gallaudet College) in Washington, D.C. Congress created the Children's Bureau in 1912, and the Maternity and Infancy Act of 1921 led many states to found child welfare divisions. Most states protected child and women's labor by 1930, though with great local variations.

The two chief periods of federal social legislation were the 1930's and 1960's. The Social Security Act of 1935, part of the New Deal, is the keystone of the modern American welfare state (*see* Social Security). The act has been amended many times (significantly in 1965) and its scope and coverage broadened. Federal measures—the Coal Mines and Safety Act of 1969 and the Occupational Safety and Health Act of 1970—extended coverage to occupational diseases and took notice of the demand for relaxation of work controls over youths and women.

Social legislation of the late 1940's, 1950's, and 1960's dealt with housing, education, and civil rights; the War on Poverty of the 1960's; and social security extensions for medical protection in 1965 (*see* Medicare). Local authorities were given federal funds to buy up slum property and build housing under the Housing Act of 1949, but the true beginning of urban renewal came with the Housing Act of 1954. Housing acts of 1961 and 1962 tried to take into account the wishes of that part of the population most in need of improved housing. In 1965 President Lyndon B. Johnson succeeded in achieving cabinet status for the new, unified Department of Housing and Urban Development. The next year the Demonstration Cities Act aimed to steer policy away from mere slum clearance to rehabilitation of existing structures (*see* Model Cities Program) and rent supplements were designed to scatter poor families in better-class housing.

The population boom brought pressure for federal aid to education, in the National Defense Education Act of 1958 and the Elementary and Secondary Education Act of 1965. Modeled largely on New Deal ideas, Johnson's Economic Opportunity Act of 1964 offered youth programs (the Job Corps and college work-study programs); small business loans; the VISTA program; and a controversial plan for the participation of the underprivileged in antipoverty activities. Community action programs (CAP) were funded to fight local poverty through local groups, such as neighborhood councils. The Headstart program encouraged school boards to begin training preschool children. Politics, and fear that the poor would become a political force, led to the abandonment of most participatory schemes.

In the 1960's public assistance rolls grew enormously, and the public welfare system became bureaucratic and complex. Simpler methods of countering poverty were offered, such as the negative income tax and the guaranteed income plan. During President Nixon's administration some responsibility for public relief and assistance was shifted from the federal government to the states and local communities (through revenue sharing and block grants), but it was not until President Ronald Reagan took office that a major overhaul of the federal social programs began. The budget reconciliation bill of July 1981 cut a number of welfare programs such as Aid to Families with Dependent Children, food stamps, school lunches, day care funding, and subsidized housing. President Reagan's "New Federalism" plan also intended to give the states much greater responsibility for welfare programs; the plan was still debated by the end of 1982.

SOCIAL SECURITY. The social security system in the United States began Aug. 14, 1935, when the Social Security Act was signed by President Franklin D. Roosevelt. The basic program of this act was contained in Title II, which authorized a "basic floor of protection against loss of income" through a compulsory government system of insurance that provides benefits related to wage loss. Title II was amended in 1939 to extend benefits to survivors upon the death of the wage earner and to certain dependents. In 1954 coverage was extended to farm operators and most farm and domestic workers, and in 1956 to most of the self-employed and to the armed forces. Further amendment in 1956 extended coverage to totally disabled workers fifty years of age and over, and, in 1958, to their dependents. By 1982 almost all the gainfully employed were covered. The benefit formula in Title II has been amended from time to time to provide larger benefits; automatic cost-of-living increases were initiated in 1972. As benefit costs have risen, successive social security tax adjustments have been made to meet them. In 1981 the employer-employee tax rate for the cash benefit was set at 6.65 percent each (9.30 percent for the self-employed) of the first $29,700 of covered earnings.

Titles I and III of the original Social Security Act provided for federal grants to the states to help finance public assistance for the needy aged, families with dependent children, the blind, and, beginning in 1950, the permanently and totally disabled. These are "needs test" programs, sometimes called "welfare," for people who do not qualify for social security (social insurance) or whose payments under that program have been too small to provide benefits adequate to meet basic needs. Amendments in 1972 transferred, as of Jan. 1, 1974, the administration of the adult categories of public assistance (the aged, blind, and disabled) from the states to the federal government and guaranteed a minimum monthly income to those with no other income. The minimum Social Security benefit was eliminated in 1981.

Title IV of the original act provided federal grants for child welfare services, maternal and child health services, and services for crippled children, but the health provisions were greatly enlarged by the amendments passed in 1965 (*see* Medicare).

The administration of the Social Security system was originally placed under the direction of the bipartisan Social Security Board. Subsequent reorganizations eliminated the board, established the Social Security Administration in its place, and placed it under the Department of Health, Education, and Welfare (which became the Department of Health and Human Services in 1980). Unemployment insurance, originally under the board, was transferred to the Department of Labor. In the late 1970's and early 1980's the Social Security funds were being rapidly depleted because of economic recession, and in April 1982 the trustees of the fund warned that the system could go bankrupt by 1983.

SOCIAL SETTLEMENTS. Neighborhood social-service centers established to aid urban dwellers. In 1886 Stanton Coit and Charles B. Stover, following the example of Toynbee Hall, London (1884), established the first American settlement house, the Neighborhood Guild (later University Settlement) in New York City. Many others followed: College Settlement, New York, 1889; Hull House, Chicago, 1889; East Side House, New York, 1891; Northwesetern University Settlement, 1891; South End House, Boston, 1892; Henry Street Settlement, New York, 1893. Economic distress brought a rapid increase in the number of settlements established after 1893. After World War I there was a decline in the number of houses founded, as government and private agencies assumed much of the work of the settlements. The Young Men's Christian Association and other national agencies carried on similar work. The mid-1970's saw a resurgence in the founding of settlement houses.

SOCIAL WORK. The profession of social work in the United States developed early in the 20th century among persons employed in local and state charitable organizations. By World War I paid workers were displacing wealthy volunteers in many agencies. Professional associations emphasized communication between members, ethics, quality in education and performance, research and writing, and improved working conditions. Six such organizations merged in 1955 to form the National Association of Social Workers (NASW).

Social work education started in New York City in 1898 with an agency-sponsored summer school. Collegiate auspices (Simmons College and Harvard) were achieved in Boston in 1904, and by 1930 two-year graduate programs were becoming standard. In 1980 eighty-seven universities in the United States offered masters degrees and twenty-one offered doctoral degrees in social work.

Emphasis in the profession has always been divided between effecting "retail" individual social adjustments and "wholesale" solutions through institutional change. In the post-World War II era the National Mental Health Act financed a sharp increase in the psychiatric aspect of social work. Notable early leaders of social work include Mary Richmond (1861–1928), Jane Addams (1860–1935), Richard Cabot (1868–1939), and Harry Hopkins (1890–1946). The influential magazine *The Survey,* until its demise in 1952, was a principal interpreter of social work concerns.

SOCIETY FOR THE PREVENTION OF CRUELTY TO ANIMALS. *See* **Animal Protective Societies.**

SOCIETY FOR THE PREVENTION OF CRUELTY TO CHILDREN. In April 1874 the American Society for the

Prevention of Cruelty to Animals rescued and obtained the protection of the state for Mary Ellen Wilson, a mistreated child. In April 1875 the first child protective agency, the New York Society for the Prevention of Cruelty to Children, was incorporated. During the ensuing quarter century more than 150 similar societies were formed across the country. Upon receipt of a complaint alleging child neglect or abuse, the child protective agency investigates and offers indicated services to correct unwholesome home conditions and, in appropriate situations, secures protection of the child by legal proceedings.

SOCIETY FOR THE PROPAGATION OF THE GOSPEL IN FOREIGN PARTS (sometimes called the Venerable Society). Founded in 1701 to conduct the foreign mission work of the Anglican church overseas. Between 1702 and 1785, when it withdrew from the mission field in the United States, it assisted 202 central stations, sent out 309 ordained missionaries, and distributed thousands of Bibles and other religious works. In many colonies the first schools and the first libraries were founded by the society. The society is still engaged in missionary activity in various parts of the world.

SOCIETY OF CINCINNATI. *See* **Cincinnati, Society of the.**

SOCIETY OF COLONIAL WARS. Composed of a General Society and constituent state societies (thirty in 1980); established in 1892 to perpetuate the memory of events of colonial history from the settlement of Jamestown, Va. (1607), to the Battle of Lexington (1775), by membership, preservation of records, commemorations, and memorials. Membership (4,250 in 1980) is open to male lineal descendants of men who assisted in the establishment, defense, and preservation of the American colonies.

SODA FOUNTAINS. Apparatus for generating and dispensing soda waters, developed following a demand created when a Philadelphia perfumer began to serve soda water with fruit juices soon after 1800. In about 1858 the marble fountain was invented and patented in Massachusetts. An American soda fountain was exhibited in Paris in 1867. In 1874 the proprietor of a soda fountain in Philadelphia combined ice cream and soda water to "invent" the ice cream soda. In 1970 more than half of the approximately 50,000 drugstores in the United States had soda fountains.

SOD HOUSE. A dwelling made of dirt, constructed by settlers on the Great Plains in the 19th century in areas where timber and stone were not available. The Plains Indians had long made their permanent winter homes from sod. In many counties 90 percent of the people at one time or another lived in sod houses. Some of the sod houses were built half above ground and half underground, with the lower part made of bare earth.

SOFT DRINK INDUSTRY. Early in the 1800's carbonated soda water was introduced from Europe, where it had long been prized for the medicinal properties of the soda (sodium carbonate) in the liquid. By the 1820's equipment for producing and dispensing carbonated soda water had been installed in apothecary shops throughout the country.

During the 1830's the soda was eliminated from carbonated soda water—the result being a drink taken for refreshment rather than for medicinal purposes. The demand for plain carbonated water—which kept the name "soda water"—was considerably intensified a few years later by the addition of various flavorings, sometimes blended with cream, to the drinks sold by the apothecaries.

The possibility of selling flavored carbonated drinks in bottles early attracted the attention of American businessmen. In 1899 the industry produced nearly 39 million cases of bottled drinks (12 bottles per capita), worth $23 million. The growth of the bottling industry was comparatively slow during the 19th century, until a series of innovations greatly increased the efficiency of bottling operations. The final step toward complete automation came with the introduction of the bottle conveyor belt during the 1920's. During the 20th century companies such as Coca-Cola, Pepsi-Cola, Hires, and Dr. Pepper—organized originally to supply local markets with their concentrated syrups—began franchising bottlers throughout the country to produce and distribute the finished drinks. Growing competition at the national (and international) level led these companies to adopt vigorous advertising and marketing programs.

SOFT MONEY. The opposite of hard money, which is based on specie. The term originated about 1876 when the Greenback party was formed by debtor farmers and others who sought to raise agricultural prices by means of an inflated currency; they thought that the currency should be a government paper one, not redeemable in specie, but convertible on demand into federal interest-bearing notes that would serve as legal tender for the payment of debts and taxes. (*See also* Greenback Party.)

SOIL BANK PROGRAM. Designed as a means of persuading farmers to turn over part of their land for conservation purposes during set periods of time, the soil bank idea was advanced during President Dwight D. Eisenhower's administration, and was managed by the Agricultural Stabilization and Conservation Service. Farmers signed government contracts in which they agreed to keep some of their land out of agricultural production, and to institute soil conservation practices on that land in return for government subsidies. The purpose was twofold: farm output was restricted by withdrawing some land from production, and soil conservation practices could lead to greatly enriched soil. (*See also* Agriculture.)

SOIL CONSERVATION. *See* **Agriculture.**

"SOLD DOWN THE RIVER." This refers to the punishment meted out to unruly slaves in the border slave states in antebellum days: the belief was prevalent that labor on Louisiana sugar plantations and the great cotton estates of the lower South was exceedingly severe, and the mere threat of being "sold down the river" usually changed the conduct of unruly slaves.

SOLDIERS AND SAILORS CONVENTIONS (1866). Political gatherings held during the political campaign waged by President Andrew Johnson and his conservative supporters against the Radical Republicans as they sought to influence the outcome of fall elections. Attempting to show themselves as national in scope, Johnson and his supporters met at the National Union Convention in Philadelphia, on Aug. 14. At a second meeting (Sept. 17), conservative federal veterans urged support of the president's policies of conciliation and immediate restoration of the seceded states to the Union.

The Radicals countered by calling northern and southern supporters of congressional Reconstruction policies to a gathering at Philadelphia on Sept. 3. A second group, mostly former military men, met at Pittsburgh in the Soldiers and Sailors Convention (Sept. 25); Gen. Jacob Dolson Cox, of Ohio, was permanent president. The convention's resolutions endorsed the Fourteenth Amendment as "wise, prudent, and just" and denounced the Johnson policies.

SOLDIERS' HOMES. The United States Naval Home, in Philadelphia, Pa., was the first home for disabled veterans, authorized in 1811 but not completed and occupied until 1831. In the mid-1970's the home had a capacity of approximately 350. The U.S. Soldiers' and Airmens' Home, in Washington, D.C., with a capacity of approximately 3,000, was authorized in 1851. Accommodations are available for women veterans. The National Home for Disabled Volunteer Soldiers—an agency to provide a place of residence, complete medical treatment, and hospital care—was created by Congress by an act of Mar. 3, 1865, as amended by an act of Mar. 21, 1866. The first home under its auspices was established at Augusta, Maine; by 1930 ten more branches had been established, bringing the total capacity to approximately 25,000. In 1923 accommodations were provided for women veterans. By 1980 additional domiciliary care had been provided for by the Veterans Administration at sixteen field stations for approximately 8,000 patients.

SOLID SOUTH. A term used to refer to the political domination of the southern states by southern Democrats after the Reconstruction era. A one-party system developed when Republicans proved to be weak in numbers and power and when blacks were wholly or partially disfranchised. From 1877 until 1976 Democratic candidates won more than 90 percent of all elections in the southern states.

In the 1950's southern blacks began to vote in increasing numbers. Furthermore, the conservative southern Democrats began to acknowledge that their political philosophy was closer to mainstream Republicanism. In 1972 President Richard M. Nixon won the electoral votes of all eleven southern states in an unprecedented reversal of history. By 1973 state Republican parties were viable competitors in Tennessee, Virginia, and Florida, and conditions were such that Republicanism was likely to grow in strength in the remaining southern states. In 1980 all southern states except Georgia voted for the Republican candidate Ronald Reagan.

SOMERS ISLES. *See* **Bermuda Islands.**

***SOMERS* MUTINY** (1842). The U.S. brig *Somers* was en route from Africa to New York when, on Nov. 26, the purser's steward reported to Comdr. A. S. Mackenzie that Acting-Midshipman Philip Spencer had asked him to aid in seizing the ship, murdering the officers, and turning pirate. Spencer and two seamen named as accomplices were held prisoner, and a court of inquiry adjudged them guilty. Mackenzie caused them to be hanged on Dec. 1. Subsequently Mackenzie was tried by court-martial for his act, but was acquitted.

SOMERS' VOYAGE TO VIRGINIA (1609). The Virginia Company placed Sir George Somers in command of the largest expedition yet attempted for purposes of English settlement in America. Somers sailed from Plymouth on June 2, with a possible total of 800 prospective colonists. Seven weeks out of port, the *Sea Adventure,* carrying Somers, Sir Thomas Gates, and Capt. Christopher Newport, was separated from its consorts in a severe storm. It foundered off Bermuda on July 28, but all passengers were saved. In two small vessels Somers eventually brought his company to Jamestown, arriving on May 24, 1610; the remainder of the fleet had reached Virginia the preceding summer. The settlement of Bermuda by a group of Virginia adventurers (1612) was a direct outgrowth of Somers' experiences there.

SOMME OFFENSIVE (Aug. 8–Nov. 11, 1918). The first Americans to serve on the western front in World War I were some 2,500 medics and engineers with the British in the Battle of Cambrai, which started in the Somme River area in northern France on Nov. 20, 1917. These detachments were still present for the second Battle of the Somme commencing on Mar. 21, 1918, the first of five efforts by the Germans to win the war before the American Expeditionary Forces were ready. The 131st Infantry of the Thirty-third National Guard Division from Illinois fought under Gen. Sir Henry Rawlinson, helping capture Hamel on July 4, losing nearly 1,000 at Chipilly Ridge and Gressaire Wood on Aug. 9, pressing on to help take Etinchem Spur on Aug. 13.

As the British planned their share of French Gen. Ferdinand Foch's grand offensive, Gen. John J. Pershing lent Rawlinson the Second Corps of George W. Read. Read's corps entered the British line east of Péronne. In Rawlinson's attack of Sept. 29, the corps broke through the Hindenburg Line at the Bellicourt Canal Tunnel. Alternating attacks with the Australian corps of Sir John Monash, Oct. 9–21, Read's divisions captured Bancourt-le-Grand, Premont, and Vaux-Andigny; crossed the Selle River; took Ribeauville, Mazinghien, and Rejet-de-Beaulieu; and nearly reached the Sambre River—a hard-fought advance of eleven and a half miles, costing 3,414 killed and 14,526 wounded.

SONS OF LIBERTY (American Revolution). Radical organizations formed in the American colonies after Parliament's passage of the Stamp Act in 1765. New York and Boston had two of the largest and most active Sons of Liberty chapters. Members circulated patriotic petitions, tarred and feathered violators of patriotic decrees, intimidated British officials and their families, and stimulated a consciousness of colonial grievances by propaganda. Upon discovering that British authorities were unable to suppress them, the Sons of Liberty issued semiofficial decrees of authority and impudently summoned royal officials to "liberty trees" to explain their conduct to the people.

SONS OF LIBERTY (Civil War). A secret organization of Copperheads, strongest in the Northwest, was formed in 1864 by the reorganization of the Order of American Knights, with C. L. Vallandigham of Ohio, then in exile in Canada, as supreme commander. The 300,000 members were sworn to oppose unconstitutional acts of the federal government and to support states' rights principles. They opposed the draft and discouraged enlistments. (*See also* Northwest Conspiracy.) Six members of the organization were arrested and tried for treason at Indianapolis in September and October 1864; three were condemned to death but never executed.

SONS OF THE AMERICAN REVOLUTION, NATIONAL SOCIETY OF THE. The Sons of Revolutionary Sires was organized in San Francisco in 1875; in 1889 it combined with certain members of the Society of the Sons of the Revolution to organize in New York City the Sons of the American Revolution (incorporated in 1906). Membership (21,477 in 1980) is restricted to lineal descendants of those who saw actual military or naval service during the revolutionary war.

SONS OF THE REVOLUTION, GENERAL SOCIETY OF THE. Organized in New York City in 1876, and reorganized in 1883, its membership (6,600 in 1980) consists of male lineal descendants of those who actively participated in procuring American independence during the revolutionary war. The society became active in preserving and marking historic spots, especially in the vicinity of New York City. The New York City Chapter, an autonomous state society, has its headquarters in Fraunces Tavern.

SONS OF THE SOUTH (sometimes called Blue Lodges, Social Bands, or Friends Society). A secret society formed in 1854 and devoted to making Kansas a slave state. Bands of members, mostly Missourians, encouraged southern emigration to Kansas, protected proslavery settlers there, and in numerous other ways (some illegal and violent) tried to counteract efforts to make Kansas a free state.

SOO CANAL. *See* **Sault Ste. Marie Canals.**

SOO LINE. *See* **Railroads, Sketches of Principal Lines.**

SOONERS. Persons who illegally entered certain lands in the Indian Territory prior to the date set by the U.S. government for the opening of the lands to settlement. The term was first used in connection with the settlement of the so-called Oklahoma Lands in 1889.

SORGHUM. In the 1840's sorghum seeds were imported from Liberia and grown in the United States, with a view to manufacturing sugar commercially from the plant's juice; however, it yielded only uncrystallizable glucose syrup. During the Civil War, with southern molasses unavailable in the North, sorghum became a popular product in the upper Mississippi Valley. Great quantities were used as a substitute for sugar on the prairie frontier.

SOUND DUES. By "immemorial prescription" Denmark claimed the right to collect dues on ships passing through the Sound, between Denmark and Sweden. American vessels paid the dues until 1854, when Secretary of State William L. Marcy informed Denmark that the United States intended to stop paying. Denmark, in 1855, invited an international congress to meet in Copenhagen to discuss the problem; the United States refused to send delegates. In February 1856 the congress decided to replace the dues with a one-time payment to Denmark of 35 million rix-dollars, the amount each nation was to pay being based on its proportion of the total trade through the Sound. The United States agreed by treaty (1857) to pay its share, 717,829 rix-dollars ($393,011). Denmark agreed to maintain lighthouses, buoys, and other improvements.

SOUTH, ANTEBELLUM. Southern civilization had its inception in the 1607 settlement of Englishmen at Jamestown, Va., and modified English traditions and institutions continued to dominate southern society into the late 20th century; of the South's white population in 1860—about 60 percent of the total—no less than two-thirds was of English stock. The London (later, Virginia) Company initiated what was originally intended to be a trading factory at Jamestown, but trade with the native Indians proved unprofitable and attention turned after 1619 to the production of tobacco. Entrepreneurial tobacco plantation agriculture began an independent development in Virginia and Maryland in the early 17th century; the rice and indigo plantations of South Carolina and the sugar plantations of Louisiana were African and/or West Indian transplants in the early 18th century. The tobacco, rice, indigo, and sugar plantations were territorially delimited; they did not undergo any significant westward expansion. Following the invention of the cotton gin in 1793 and the surging demand for raw cotton in England incident to the Industrial Revolution, it was the cotton planters who mobilized the tremendous energy necessary to cross southern state boundaries, and by 1860 they had carried the institution of the plantation all the way to eastern Texas.

In the course of bringing land into new, and presumably higher, economic uses, the plantation became a political institution, a little state or subdivision of the state, within which a monopoly of authority was exercised by the planter. By virtue of his authority he pursued a sort of military agriculture, employing a hierarchically ordered, regimented labor, imported and distributed as a utility. The concept of race was elaborated into a set of symbols and dogmas to set the races apart and keep both the mixed and the unmixed portions of the nonwhite population within the ranks of the laboring caste. It thus became a political idea.

The southern region in the larger world community and the individual plantation in the forest were highly isolated, and the resultant culture was a product of isolation. Its literature emphasized manners and chivalry and was generally romantic. On the eve of the Civil War the South was still overwhelmingly rural, and its towns and small cities were gracious plantation capitals.

There was little place for free public schools until near the end of the pre–Civil War period, but academies were fairly numerous, as were state and denominational colleges. These educational institutions, as well as military schools, functioned within the plantation system to indoctrinate and to support it. The county developed as a primary social, as well as governmental, unit, with the plantation often functioning as an informal, but effective, subdivision. The states, too, came under control of planter oligarchies. All lived under the laws sponsored by plantation interests.

SOUTH AMERICA, U.S. RELATIONS WITH. *See* **Latin America U.S. Relations With.**

SOUTHAMPTON (Long Island, N.Y.). The oldest English town in New York, was settled in 1640. The original inhabitants came from Lynn, Mass. The settlers, under the leadership of Edward Howell, received title to the land from the Earl of Sterling, who had been granted Long Island in 1635 by Charles I, and from the local Indian tribes. Southampton's early connections were almost wholly with Connecticut, but after the English conquest of New Amsterdam, it took its place in the proprietary colony of the Duke of York. Located on the south shore of Long Island, the village of Southampton has developed into a summer resort. Its population in 1970 was 4,904.

SOUTHAMPTON INSURRECTION. *See* **Nat Turner's Rebellion.**

SOUTH CAROLINA. In 1526 Vásquez de Ayllón led an expedition of Spaniards from Hispaniola to San Miguel de Gualdape on Winyah Bay. Jean Ribault tried to plant a colony of French Huguenots at Port Royal in 1562. The English, under charters of 1663 and 1665, began the continuous settlement of South Carolina at Albemarle Point on the Ashley River in April 1670. The Fundamental Constitutions of 1669 were never adopted by the colonists, since the feudal system they provided for was unsuited to the wilderness. In 1706 an act established the Church of England. Rice, produced by the labor of black slaves, became the first great staple. In December 1719 the proprietary government was overthrown.

The reorganization of the government under royal authority by Gov. Robert Johnson (1730–35) and the successful growing of indigo by Eliza Lucas Pinckney (1744) ushered in years of prosperity. Fear of the Indians was removed by Col. James Grant's victory over the Cherokee at the Battle of Etchohih (June 10, 1761); fear of the Spaniards, by the cessation of Florida to England in the Treaty of Paris (1763). It was the merchants and planters who engineered the revolutionary activity in South Carolina. After the last royal governor had fled (Sept. 15, 1775), the patriots, led by Christopher Gadsden, Henry Laurens, and John Rutledge, meeting in the provincial congress, drew up a temporary constitution on Mar. 26, 1776, and a more permanent one on Mar. 19, 1778, which disestablished the Anglican church. After the British took Charleston on May 12, 1780, the backcountry held the British at bay until Gen. Nathanael Greene's Continental army could drive the British army back upon its last base at Charleston. The low-country elite recognized the backcountry's contribution to the winning of the Revolution by consenting in 1786 to the removal of the capital from Charleston to Columbia and in 1790 to a new constitution that established two sets of state officials, one in Charleston and one in Columbia. With the sudden expansion of cotton production after 1793, any chance for the elimination of slavery disappeared as the institution spread with cotton rapidly into the backcountry. The backcountry and low-country sections moved in 1803 to reopen the slave trade, which had been cut off in 1787, and agreed in 1808 by an amendment to the state constitution to divide equally the representation in the general assembly.

The U.S. Congress brought an end to the foreign slave trade on Jan. 1, 1808, and President Thomas Jefferson's embargo struck a mortal blow at foreign commerce; with this economic disruption, the merchant class quickly declined in influence. Those who opposed slavery, particularly the Quakers, began to move to the Old Northwest. A law of 1820 made it almost impossible to free slaves. The threats of slave insurrections in Charleston (1822) and in Georgetown (1829) and the rapid decline in the price of cotton during that decade placed the state on the defensive. John C. Calhoun's *Exposition* of 1828 and the Ordinance of Nullification of Nov. 24, 1832, declaring void the tariffs of 1828 and 1832, were the first protective gestures; the Ordinance of Secession of Dec. 20, 1860, was thought to be the ultimate protection. The Civil War, which began at Fort Sumter on Apr. 12, 1861, ended disastrously with the burning of Columbia on Feb. 17, 1865. The state signaled its contrition by ratifying the Thirteenth Amendment on Nov. 13, 1865, but balked at accepting the Fourteenth Amendment until July 9, 1868. The new constitution of 1868 provided for more democratic forms of government, black suffrage, and free public education; but the constitution of 1895 drove blacks from the polls. From 1902, when the last black left his seat in the state legislature, until 1970, when blacks reappeared in that body, a segregated society existed.

South Carolina's economy took on renewed life only with the advent of World War II. The new prosperity rested on the presence of army, air, and naval installations; the rapid industrialization of the state; and the redevelopment of the port of Charleston. The textile industry, which antedated the Civil War, remained the major industry, while good water supplies and untapped labor reserves induced many blue-chip companies to open plants in small towns throughout the state. The population of South Carolina in 1980 was 3,119,208.

SOUTH CAROLINA, PROPOSED NOBILITY IN. The Fundamental Constitutions of Carolina (1669) reserved two-fifths of the land for a hereditary nobility, whose estates were to be inalienable and indivisible. Some proprietors of the colony established estates, and twenty-six landgraves and thirteen caciques also acquired estates and seats in the governor's council. These proprietary efforts to transfer English feudal law and practice to America produced a half-century of conflict, until South Carolina became a royal colony in 1719.

SOUTH CAROLINA, SPANISH EXPEDITIONS AGAINST. French attempts to gain a foothold along the southern Atlantic coast prompted Spain to capture Fort Caroline (Florida) and to found St. Augustine in 1565. In the same year Spaniards from Cuba burned the abandoned Charlesfort at Parris Island (*see* Port Royal). British settlement of South Carolina began in 1670. In August of that year Spanish vessels from St. Augustine appeared before Charleston but retired without attacking. South Carolinians began trading with the Spanish Indians, and in 1686 the Spanish, in retaliation, destroyed Stuart's Town, near Port Royal, and raided to the north. Spanish Indians, retaliating for attacks in 1702 on St. Augustine and on the Tallahassee region, were crushed by South Carolina traders and Indians. In 1706 a Franco-Spanish naval attack on Charleston failed disastrously. Forces from St. Augustine, seeking to avenge a Georgia–South Carolina attack on Florida in 1740, were defeated in 1742 at Bloody Marsh, Ga. The Spanish then abandoned their planned attack on South Carolina.

SOUTH CAROLINA, STATE BANK OF. A commercial, state-owned institution (1812–68) located in Charleston, with branches in Columbia, Camden, and Abbeville. The state deposited its funds in the bank, accepted its notes, and limited its debt-contracting power. The bank made loans to the state without interest, managed the state's debt, and from its profits retired a large part of that debt. James H. Hammond, who became state governor in 1842, charged the bank with favoritism and with possessing dangerous power, and succeeded in imposing charter revisions beneficial to the state.

SOUTH CAROLINA CANAL. *See* **Santee Canal.**

SOUTH CAROLINA INTERSTATE AND WEST INDIAN EXPOSITION (Dec. 1, 1901–June 1, 1902). Held at Charleston; designed to promote closer commercial relations between the United States and the seventy principal West Indian islands. The exposition covered 160 acres, with 20 acres of midway attractions. There was a display of West Indian resources and products, but emphasis was upon American manufactures and exports.

SOUTH CAROLINA RAILROAD. The South Carolina Canal and Railroad Company, organized in 1827, constructed a railroad line from Charleston to Hamburg (across the Savannah River from Augusta, Ga.); completed in October 1833, the line was 136 miles long. In 1843 the company merged with the Louisville, Cincinnati and Charleston Railroad Company to form the South Carolina Railroad Company. In 1848 a branch of thirty-seven miles was constructed from Kingville, on the Branchville-Columbia line, to Camden. In 1878 the company was forced into bankruptcy and sold to a group of New York entrepreneurs; the new company was known as the South Carolina Railway Company. In 1894 the railroad was again sold as a result of bankruptcy and became the South Carolina and Georgia Railroad Company. In 1899 the Southern Railway Company acquired control of the firm, and in the early 1980's it was still providing freight service on the three lines.

SOUTH DAKOTA. The southern half of what was Dakota Territory. The southeastern part of the present state is corn belt, and the northeastern, lake country. West of the Missouri River is the land of the cattleman and the wheat rancher. On the extreme western edge of the state are the Black Hills. The state received its name from the Dakota Sioux who inhabited all sections of it by the mid-18th century; their descendants are located on nine reservations. All the state west of the Missouri River was part of the great Sioux reservation created by the Treaty of 1868, later broken up by cessions in 1877 and 1889 and by the heavy influx of white settlers engendered by the Dawes General Allotment Act of 1887.

South Dakota, which was admitted to the Union as a state on Nov. 2, 1889, is predominantly agricultural in its economy and outlook. In the west the gold mining industry has receded until only one major mine, the Homestake at Lead, remains; it is the largest operating gold mine in the Western Hemisphere and a product of the great Black Hills gold rush of 1876. Numerous ethnic groups make up the state's population: predominant are the Norwegians, Germans, and Russians who came in the late 19th century; there are also concentrations of Czechs, Irish, Finns, and French. The state was one of the leaders in the Populist movement in the 1880's and 1890's and in state socialism during the Progressive era. The Democratic party subsequently made severe inroads into Republican control, and a two-party system emerged. In 1980 South Dakota had a population of 690,178.

SOUTHEAST ASIA TREATY ORGANIZATION (SEATO). Formed by a treaty signed on Sept. 8, 1954, at Manila, by the United States, Great Britain, France, Australia, New Zealand, the Philippines, Pakistan, and Thailand, with headquarters at Bangkok. Cambodia, Laos, and the Republic of Vietnam, protocol states, were represented by observers. The treaty called for collective action to resist armed attacks and to counter subversion from without against the territorial integrity and the political stability of any of the eight member nations; the provisions were consistent with those of the United Nations. The signators also subscribed to the Pacific Charter, a statement of ideals and intentions. SEATO activities were concerned not only with defense against subversion and aggression from outside but also with the promotion of social, economic, and cultural developments among its member nations. France and Pakistan gradually reduced their activities as members of SEATO; on Nov. 8, 1972, Pakistan announced its decision to withdraw, and the withdrawal became effective one year later. In 1977 SEATO was dissolved.

SOUTHERN BOUNDARY, SURVEY OF THE. On Mar. 29, 1798, surveying was begun on the border between the southern United States and the Spanish colonies of East Florida and West Florida. Participating in the project were Andrew Ellicott, U.S. commissioner; Thomas Freeman, surveyor (soon suspended by Ellicott); and Stephen Minor and Sir William Dunbar, Spanish commissioners. The line surveyed extended from the Mississippi River eastward along the thirty-first parallel to its intersection with the Chattahoochee River (*see* Dunbar's Line), followed that river southward to its junction with the Flint, and then ran southeast directly to the head of Saint Marys River and down that stream to the Atlantic Ocean (*see* Pinckney's Treaty). The work was laborious and frequently interrupted, and took over two years to complete.

SOUTHERN CAMPAIGNS OF THE AMERICAN REVOLUTION. A vigorous effort by the British, who had suffered setbacks in the North, to stamp out rebellion in the Carolinas and Georgia. On Dec. 26, 1779, Sir Henry Clinton and Gen. Charles Cornwallis sailed from New York with 8,000 men, landing at Savannah. They surrounded the forces under Gen. Benjamin Lincoln in Charleston and compelled his surrender on May 12, 1780; the only American regiment not in Charleston was destroyed at Waxhaw Creek on May 29. Partisan leaders such as Thomas Sumter, Francis Marion, and Andrew Pickens then raised troops of patriots and engaged in guerrilla warfare. Gen. George Washington sent 2,000 men under Gen. Johann Kalb to the aid of South Carolina; Kalb was superseded by Horatio Gates, who lost most of his army at the Battle of Camden (Aug. 16), and again the Carolinas seemed conquered. Cornwallis detached Maj. Patrick Ferguson with 1,200 men to recruit in the highlands, but this force was annihilated at Kings Mountain on Oct. 7, and another detachment was destroyed at the Battle of Cowpens (Jan. 17, 1781). Nathanael Greene succeeded Gates in December 1780; with Gen. Daniel Morgan's aid, he lured Cornwallis into North Carolina and dealt him a crippling blow at Guilford Courthouse on Mar. 15, 1781. The British commander retired to Wilmington, N.C., and then marched into Virginia. Benedict Arnold had been sent into Virginia with 1,600 British troops by Sir Henry Clinton, but initiated no major actions. Greene returned to South Carolina, and although he theoretically lost engagements at Hobkirk's Hill (Apr. 25), Ninety-Six (May 22–June 19), and Eutaw Springs (Sept. 8), he so weakened the British forces that by Dec. 10, 1781, he had won his objective and driven the only remaining British army in the Deep South into a state of siege at Charleston. Meanwhile, Cornwallis had been cornered by a joint American-French force, and surrendered at Yorktown, Va., on Oct. 19, 1781.

SOUTHERN CHRISTIAN LEADERSHIP CONFERENCE (SCLC). An outgrowth of the Montgomery (Ala.) Improvement Association (founded 1955). The SCLC, based in Atlanta, was formed in 1957 as a "non-sectarian coordinating agency" for "nonviolent direct mass action," the first major civil rights organization to originate in the South. It was an umbrella of loosely affiliated organizations, mostly of black Baptist churches, that sought "full civil rights and total integration of the Negro into American life." SCLC's principal force was symbolic, especially through its president, Martin Luther King, Jr.

SOUTHERN COMMERCIAL CONVENTIONS. Convocations in the third quarter of the 19th century intended to promote the economic development of the South; most notable were the sessions of the so-called Southern Commercial Convention, which met successively at Baltimore, Memphis, Charleston, New Orleans, Richmond, Savannah, Knoxville, Montgomery, and Vicksburg between December 1852 and May 1859.

The South was not keeping pace with the North in population, manufacturing, railroad building, shipping, and other lines of economic development. In addition, the superior population and wealth of the free states were giving them an advantage in the struggle over slavery. The convention examined a wide variety of proposed remedies. As time went by and the convention failed to produce tangible results, the sessions came to be dominated by the secessionists of the lower South, who contended that the Union was an obstacle to southern economic development. The net result of the gatherings was the promotion of southern sectionalism.

SOUTHERN CULT (or Southeastern ceremonial complex). Associated mainly with prehistoric Mississippian cultures in the Eastern Woodlands between about A.D. 900 and the historic period. The series of rituals, objects, and iconographic elements integrated into the ceremonial complex was a blend of indigenous and Middle American religious themes connected with the harvest and renewal.

Major cult centers were established at a number of Mississippian towns, including Moundville (Alabama), Etowah (Georgia), and Spiro (Oklahoma). The ceremonial complex has often been considered a cult connected with death and death symbols; however, it may have served primarily as an integrating institution during the development and spread of the Mississippian cultures. It seems certain human sacrifice was an integral part of cult activities.

SOUTHERN EXPOSITION. First opened at Louisville, Ky., in the summer of 1883; revived each year through 1887. The principal exhibit covered fifteen acres. After the first year the educational exhibits disappeared, and industry and amusement dominated the exposition.

SOUTHERN LITERARY MESSENGER. A magazine devoted especially to literature and the fine arts, published at Richmond, Va., 1834–64. Its most famous editor was Edgar Allan Poe. The magazine usually reflected the views of the southern slave-owner. From January 1846 through October 1847, while Benjamin Blake Minor was editor and proprietor, it was known by the more ambitious title *Southern and Western Literary Messenger and Review.*

SOUTHERN OVERLAND MAIL (also known as the **Butterfield Overland Mail**). First land mail route from the East to California. A congressional act (Mar. 3, 1857) provided for a semiweekly service on a twenty-five-day schedule. The route ran from St. Louis and Memphis to San Francisco by way of Fort Smith, Ark., El Paso, Tex., and Tucson, Ariz. John Butterfield, W. G. Fargo, and others were the contractors. Service began Sept. 15, 1858, with four-horse coaches; the passenger fare was $100 to $200 each way. The schedule was successfully maintained until the outbreak of the Civil War, when the line was moved to a more northerly route (*see* Overland Mail and Stagecoaches).

SOUTHERN PACIFIC RAILROAD. *See* **Railroads, Sketches of Principal Lines.**

SOUTHERN RAILROAD ROUTE. A southern route of travel from New Mexico to California via the Gila River was well known prior to the Mexican War; during the war, when Gen. Stephen W. Kearny made his expedition (1846) from Leavenworth, Kans., to San Diego, Calif., he reported that the southern travel route was also suitable for a railroad line. Kearny was accompanied by Lt. W. H. Emory, whose notes and sketches were the basis for the proposal. The Gadsden Purchase (1853) guaranteed a right-of-way entirely within the United States. Also in 1853, Congress appropriated $150,000 for Pacific railway surveys, one of which was made soon thereafter over the southern approach; surveying east of El Paso was done by Capt. John Pope, and surveying farther west was conducted by Lt. John G. Parke.

SOUTHERN RAILWAY. *See* **Railroads, Sketches of Principal Lines.**

SOUTHERN RIGHTS MOVEMENT. Although as old as the Union itself, the antebellum movement for southern rights is particularly associated with aggressive efforts during the late 1840's and the 1850's to solidify the South for the protection of its interests, particularly slavery. Influenced by John C. Calhoun, southern congressmen in Washington issued addresses to the southern people in 1848 and 1850, urging "unity among ourselves"; and various southern legislatures resolved to act with unity of purpose. Southern commercial conventions worked for economic independence, while certain politicians were interested in a sectional political party. William L. Yancey organized the League of United Southerners in 1858. Among the lesser lights was a group who had always advocated a southern Confederacy. This group became the nucleus of the movement for southern independence after the election of Abraham Lincoln in 1860.

SOUTHERN UNIONISTS. Of the fifteen slave states at the time of the Civil War, the border states of Missouri, Kentucky, Virginia, Maryland, and Delaware were the greatest strongholds of unionism: if war came they saw themselves as the battlefield; and they had economic and social connections with both north and south. All except Virginia were able to prevent secession, and that part of Virginia joining free territory broke away and formed the state of West Virginia. In the Confederacy itself there were many people who remained loyal to the Union. They lived mostly in the mountains or in the pine barrens and other less fertile regions. East Tennessee was the outstanding storm center. Fundamental love for country, opposition to the leadership of the slaveholders, and dislike of conscription and Confederate revenue measures combined to make people Unionists. Almost 300,000 southerners fought in the Union armies.

SOUTH IMPROVEMENT COMPANY. Utilized by John D. Rockefeller and associates in an attempt (1871–72) to secure a monopoly of the petroleum industry by exclusive rebates from railroads serving the oil-producing region of Pennsylvania. Resistance from producers, public indignation, and annulment of the firm's charter defeated the scheme.

SOUTHOLD (Long Island, N.Y.). Purchased and settled by migrants from the New Haven colony in the summer of 1640. Southold became part of Connecticut on Oct. 9, 1662, when a charter uniting New Haven with the older Connecticut colony was promulgated. But Southold was forced to submit to the Duke of York's less libertarian government in 1665.

SOUTH PASS. Most celebrated of the passes in the Rocky Mountains; through it ran the great emigrant trail to Oregon and California. Located in Wyoming at the southern end of the Wind River Mountains; the approach to the pass is very gradual. Discovery was made in 1824 by Thomas Fitzpatrick, a fur trader. Capt. Benjamin L. E. Bonneville first took wagons over the pass in 1832, and a few years later it became the mountain gateway on the Oregon Trail.

SOUTH PLATTE ROUTE. A branch of the Oregon (or Overland) Trail. Leaving the main trail at Julesburg, Colo., the branch route followed the right bank of the South Platte River to Denver. An important stage and freight route, it was attacked by Cheyenne in 1865. Julesburg was looted and burned, and ranches up and down the river were destroyed; traffic on the South Platte route was suspended for a considerable period.

SOUTH SEA EXPEDITION. *See* **Wilkes Exploring Expedition.**

SOUTHWEST. Roughly the southwestern quarter of the United States. So considered, it includes Oklahoma, Texas, New Mexico, Arizona, the southern half of California, and the southern portions of Kansas and Colorado. With the exception of most of Kansas and Oklahoma, which formed part of the Louisiana Purchase, all of the Southwest was part of the possessions of Spain, and later of Mexico, well into the 19th century.

SOUTHWEST, OLD. First applied to the region of present Tennessee and Kentucky, but later extended to include Alabama and Mississippi and sometimes even Louisiana and Arkansas. In colonial times it came within the limits of Virginia, North Carolina, South Carolina, and Georgia. The Proclamation of 1763 reserved the Old Southwest "under the sovereignty, protection, and dominance of the king" and forbade further land grants west of the Appalachians by colonial governments. Colonial adventurers and land speculators paid little attention to this proclamation. In 1769 emigrants, mostly from Virginia, established a settlement along the Watauga River, the first in what is now Tennessee. In 1774, Richard Henderson was instrumental in organizing the Louisa Company (Transylvania Company), which established a settlement at Boonesborough in a region later part of Kentucky. Near the end of the Revolution, Nashborough (Nashville) in the Cumberland Valley of Tennessee was founded. Virginia stamped out the Henderson venture, but other settlements led to the state of Kentucky in 1792. Watauga grew into the state of Franklin, which North Carolina suppressed, but the settlements, with those in the Nashborough region, developed into Tennessee, admitted to the Union in 1796. After the treaty of peace in 1783, fixing the western limits of the United States at the Mississippi, a movement sprang up to force the states with western lands to cede them to the central government. Virginia refused to cede the Kentucky region but later gave it permission to become a state; North Carolina in 1789 gave up the Tennessee region; South Carolina ceded its dubious claim to a twelve-mile-wide strip south of Tennessee; but Georgia refused to make terms that Congress would accept, and Spain declared all lands south of 32°28′ its own. To add to the complication, powerful tribes of Indians held actual control of most of the region. In 1795 Georgia sought profit from the confusion by selling most of it to four Yazoo companies. The first federal control over any part of the Old Southwest came with the organization of the Southwest Territory in 1790.

SOUTHWEST BOUNDARY. *See* **Adams-Onís Treaty; Louisiana Purchase, Boundaries of; Mexican Boundary.**

SOUTHWESTERN OIL FIELDS. Large-scale production of petroleum in the southwestern states—including Arkansas, Louisiana, Kansas, Oklahoma, Texas, and New Mexico —is essentially a 20th-century phenomenon. Between 1859 and 1900 the major domestic sources of crude oil in the United States were in the Northeast—in New York, Pennsylvania, Ohio, and West Virginia. Most of their flow was refined into kerosine. But during the 20th century the center of American oil production shifted to the Southwest, to the midcontinent fields, and the Gulf area, as technological changes created major new national markets for gasoline, fuel oil, and natural gas.

In the two decades before World War I, Kansas, Oklahoma, and Texas first became important producers. Exploitation of southwestern oil fields was undertaken by independent producers as well as major integrated oil corporations.

Between World War I and World War II the Southwest firmly established itself as the major oil-producing region in the United States. In the 1920's, oil drillers uncovered great new reserves in Oklahoma, Texas, and Louisiana and made notable finds in Arkansas, Kansas, and New Mexico. Discovery of vast reserves from 1927 to 1935 plunged the already ailing industry—beset by the world depression—into economic chaos. Only World War II revitalized southwestern oil production, which increased output significantly to supply war needs.

During the three decades after World War II the southwestern oil fields almost doubled their production. At the same time, natural gas, a by-product, became a major new form of energy. Texas retained its position as the greatest oil-producing state; Louisiana emerged as a close rival, while Kansas, Oklahoma, Arkansas, and New Mexico continued to provide smaller, but significant, sources of supply. A major new development was extensive offshore drilling in the Gulf of Mexico, which came to supply an increasing percentage of total national production.

Exploitation of the southwestern oil fields was accompanied by considerable government regulation. A prime goal has been conservation of oil and stabilization of production and prices. In 1935, the southwestern states formed the Interstate Oil Compact composed of a representative from each oil-producing state to coordinate their respective policies. During the next four decades the Interstate Oil Compact Commission did much to stabilize production and decrease waste.

SOUTHWEST FUR COMPANY. John Jacob Astor, chief proprietor of the American Fur Company and the Pacific Fur Company, organized the Southwest Fur Company, which in 1811 bought out the British-owned Michilimackinac (Mackinaw) Company at Mackinac; this was to give Astor control of the fur trade of the Great Lakes and the upper Mississippi, for his associates agreed to sell their stock in the Southwest Company to him in five years. Unfortunately his partners were British directors of the North West Company of Canada. In the War of 1812 the North West's traders occupied the trading forts of the Southwest Fur Company. After the war Astor dissolved the company, regained its scattered properties, merged them with the American Fur Company as its northern department, and placed an American, Ramsay Crooks, in command.

SOUTHWEST POINT. Promontory located where the Clinch and Holston rivers form the Tennessee. It was crossed by the Cumberland Road and was the western outpost of the state of Franklin, organized briefly in the 1780's in the Tennessee region, then part of North Carolina. The settlement of Kingston, now part of the Knoxville metropolitan area, was established at Southwest Point. In 1792 U.S. troops were stationed there to protect settlers on the road to Nashville and in the surrounding territory. The land, formally ceded by the Cherokee in the Tellico treaty, Oct. 27, 1805, was tentatively designated as the state capital.

SOUTHWEST TERRITORY. Set up in 1790 and officially denominated the "Territory of the United States, south of the River Ohio." It consisted of the future state of Tennessee, and in theory a strip that South Carolina had ceded and, the Georgia western lands. The government was bound by conditions set by North Carolina in its cession of 1789. William Blount served as governor and superintendent of Indian affairs. When Tennessee became a state in 1796, the territorial government fell into abeyance. It was reinstated in 1798, when the Mississippi Territory was established.

SOVEREIGNS OF INDUSTRY. A cooperative movement in the 1870's concerned with distribution of the necessities of life. It grew out of the Patrons of Husbandry and at one time numbered 40,000 members. It maintained cooperative stores and absorbed some trade unions. The organization declined after 1875.

SOVEREIGNTY, DOCTRINE OF. A legal concept that attempts to explain the final location and source of political authority. Sovereignty may be defined as that supreme authority which is externally independent and internally paramount, and a sovereign nation as a political community without a political superior. Sovereignty is usually considered to be indivisible, but the administration or use of sovereign powers may be delegated to various subordinates. In accordance with this theory, sovereignty lies in the people of the United States, who have created a national government and delegated to it certain sovereign powers. (*See also* Popular Sovereignty; State Sovereignty.)

SOVIET UNION, RECOGNITION OF. On Nov. 7, 1917, the government of Aleksandr F. Kerenski in Russia was overthrown by the Bolsheviks who, the following February, annulled all state debts. Because of this and negative reaction to Communist propaganda in the United States, administrations until 1933 refused to recognize the Soviet government. President Franklin D. Roosevelt, believing that recognition would stimulate trade, invited the Soviet Union to discuss the matter. As a result, he accorded recognition on Nov. 16, 1933.

SOW CASE (1643–44). A Massachusetts lawsuit that had far-reaching consequences. The case arose out of a controversy between a poor woman, Sherman, and a well-to-do shopkeeper, Keayne, over the ownership of a sow. Lower courts decided in favor of Keayne, but Sherman appealed to the General Court, or legislature. The majority of assistants, or magistrates, supported Keayne; the deputies supported Sherman. Although up to that time the assistants and deputies had sat in one body, the case resulted in division of the General Court into two houses.

SPACE EXPLORATION. The direct collection of information from outside the earth's atmosphere began on Oct. 4, 1957. *Sputnik*—a Russian-built artificial satellite—was launched into orbit around the earth. A full-scale U.S. effort to develop satellites and spacecraft was begun following *Sputnik.* A "space race" developed between the two powers. Other nations joined space exploration and by 1980 nine countries, in addition to the United States and Soviet Union, had launched space vehicles.

The fear that nations might fight each other in outer space led to a Space Treaty, signed in 1967 by the United States, the Soviet Union, Great Britain, and a number of other powers, in which it was agreed not to use outer space as a setting for nuclear weaponry.

During the joint Apollo-Soyuz mission in 1975 the U.S. and Soviet spacecrafts successfully docked in space, but further cooperative undertakings were gradually abandoned because of the worsening U.S.–Soviet relations.

Several satellites have been put in orbit to gather information about the atmosphere or the solar system. These assist in weather forecasting and tracking serious storms. Others have carried plants and animals into orbit and reported on the effects of radiation or weightlessness upon them. The very first U.S. scientific satellite, Explorer I, confirmed that the earth is surrounded by two "belts" of radiation. There are also satellites gathering data for high-energy astrophysics (quasars, pulsars, black holes), measuring continental drift motions, studying the sun, and exploring interplanetary space.

Satellites in the Transit series are used as artificial guideposts for navigation by ships and aircraft. The communications satellites (some of which can transmit televised events to all parts of the world) include ATS, Intelsat, Marisat, Relay, Syncom, Telstar, and Westar.

A number of satellites in orbit were fired by the military forces of different countries. These are presumed to be used to gather information ("intelligence") about other countries.

Space probes are "shots" by unmanned spacecraft, intended to examine the conditions around the moon, planets, or other heavenly bodies. The Russian Zond-3 went into orbit around the moon in 1965 and relayed photographic information about the surface on the far side of the moon. The U.S. probe, Mariner IV, photographed the surface of the planet Mars in 1964, and Mariner VII sent back photographs of the surface of Mars in great detail in 1969. The Pioneer series of interplanetary spacecraft explored Jupiter (1973 and 1974), Venus (1978), and Saturn (1979); in 1986 Pioneer 10 is expected to be the first man-made object to leave the solar system. Two Viking spacecrafts landed on Mars in 1976. For more than three years one of the probes searched for life on the planet, but the results were negative. The two Voyagers explored Jupiter in 1979 and Saturn in 1980 and 1981. Among the early accomplishments of manned missions were the development of systems for docking space vehicles and the development of systems by which men could move and work outside the space vehicle.

The U.S. manned space program included:

Project Mercury. This program had its start in 1961, a rocket shot of an individual astronaut (Alan B. Shepard, Jr.). The first American to fly a Mercury capsule in orbit was John Glenn (Feb. 20, 1962). Mercury flights used one pilot, and gave six men experience in space flights. The longest Mercury mission was 22 orbits.

Project Gemini. The Gemini flights involved two pilots each, and were intended to refine space technology and teamwork. The first American to leave a spacecraft in flight was Edward H. White, who took a "space walk" on June 4, 1965. Nine subsequent Gemini missions included rendezvous in space, docking with orbiting rockets, and further space walks.

Project Apollo. The Apollo missions were designed to place a man on the moon. Apollo flights carried a crew of three, and a three-part spacecraft. The "Command Module" carried the crew and returned it to the earth, with any moon rocks or other materials gathered. The "Service Module" carried fuel and rockets for power during the mission, and was attached to the Command Module until the end of the mission. The "Lunar Module," or "LEM," was detached from the Apollo, and made the actual descent to the surface of the moon. It carried its own rockets, so that it could launch itself from the surface of the moon to the Command Module, which remained in orbit around the moon. The LEM was then cut loose to crash on the moon's surface and determine facts about the moon's composition.

The first four Apollo flights included the first manned test of Apollo, TV transmissions from space, and orbiting the moon. In July 1969, Astronauts Neil A. Armstrong and Edwin E. Aldrin made the first lunar landing, while Michael Collins operated the Command Module in orbit around the moon. Millions of people on earth viewed the operation on television. Five subsequent landings took place by 1973 and involved use of the Lunar Rover vehicle on the moon's surface and the collection of moon materials. The last Apollo mission was the rendezvous with the Soviet Soyuz in 1975.

Skylab Project (1973–74) placed a flying laboratory in orbit around the earth at an altitude of about 270 miles. Skylab was equipped with advanced scientific instruments with which to observe the sun and other space objects from outside earth's atmosphere. Three missions visited the station, the third spending a record time of 84 days there. In 1979 Skylab crashed on parts of Australia and the Indian Ocean. The development of the space shuttle, a reusable spacecraft, was beset with troubles from the beginning (in the early 1970's); the worst moment was the death of two technicians at a countdown rehearsal in March 1981. But the space shuttle Columbia finally took off on April 12, 1981, and landed safely two days later on a desert in California. By July 1982 three more test flights had taken place and Columbia became operational.

SPANISH-AMERICAN RELATIONS. Relations between the United States and Spain were marked by mutual antagonism until the end of the 19th century. The sense of rivalry between Protestant Britain and Catholic Spain was extended to the New World as Britain established dominion over what Spain considered its monopoly. When the American colonists sought independence, Spain was desirous of using the event to strike at England and recover territories lost by the Treaty of Utrecht (1713) and the Peace of Paris (1763), but anxious about the effect the American Revolution would have on its colonies. Spain did not promptly recognize American independence; and even though it granted loans and subsidies to the rebels, Spain's military efforts were principally aimed at recovering Florida and its Mediterranean island possessions.

The issues between Spain and the new republic included boundaries, relations with the Indians, navigation of the Mississippi, and trade. Commissions sent to Spain to settle the issues were unsuccessful. What changed the situation was the French Revolution and Spain's change of ally from Britain to France. The desire of Spain to protect itself better across the seas made it yield on the litigated points. In Pinckney's Treaty (Oct. 27, 1795) (Treaty of San Lorenzo), Spain recognized the thirty-first parallel as the boundary to the south, free navigation of the Mississippi by U.S. citizens, and the privilege of deposit. The principle of neutral rights was affirmed, and each side agreed to restrain the Indians within its borders from attacking the territory of the other.

Pinckney's Treaty and the fact that Louisiana Province proved to be a heavy burden led to Spain's retrocession of Louisiana to France (1800). France then sold Louisiana to the United States in 1803. Soon the purchase of Louisiana led to boundary disputes. The United States contended that the Rio Grande was the western boundary, thus including Texas in the purchase, and that the Perdido River was the eastern boundary, thus including a sizable part of West Florida. Spain disputed both claims. President Thomas Jefferson took the first step of inducing Congress to pass the Mobile Act on Feb. 24, 1804. He then sent James Monroe to assist Charles Pinckney in Madrid to secure recognition of the title of the United States to West Florida and the cession of East Florida. The United States would either renounce its pecuniary claims against Spain or buy the Floridas directly. Continued Spanish spoliations on American neutral shipping brought Spain and the United States close to war.

During the Spanish civil war after 1808 the United States suspended diplomatic relations with Spain; Spanish authority was gravely weakened in the New World in this period.

Secretary of State John Quincy Adams and the Spanish minister, Luis de Onís, began talks on the Louisiana boundaries late in 1817: the United States would withdraw pecuniary claims against Spain in exchange for the Floridas. On the western side of Louisiana, the boundary line was drawn largely along the west banks of the Sabine, Red, and Arkansas rivers; thence north to the forty-second parallel; and westward all the way to the Pacific Ocean (*see* Adams-Onís Treaty). Signed on Feb. 22, 1819, the treaty was not fully ratified until 1821, in part because of Spanish attempts to secure a pledge from the U.S. government not to assist the rebellious Latin-American colonies. The United States granted recognition to the new Latin-American republics in March 1822, and the Monroe Doctrine was proclaimed in December 1823.

Cuba was next. The desirability of acquiring Cuba became part of the idea of Manifest Destiny. Attempts to acquire Cuba by purchase or other means culminated in the sensational Ostend Manifesto of 1854. The Civil War diverted American attention from Cuba, but interest was rekindled during the Cuban wars of independence. The first, in 1868–78, was the more prolonged and sanguinary, but it came at a time when Americans were weary after the Civil War and national attention was turned inward. Fighting erupted anew in Cuba in 1895. This time the United States was prepared for pursuing an adventurous foreign policy. Spain's procrastination with the Cuban problem and the hardships caused by the militarily and strategically logical "reconcentration" policy introduced by the Spanish commander Gen. Valeriano Weyler provided grist for the interventionist mill. The last straws were the leak of private correspondence of the Spanish minister, Dupuy de Lôme (Feb. 9, 1898), and the sinking of the *Maine* in Havana harbor on Feb. 15, 1898. President William McKinley submitted the Cuban question to Congress on Apr. 11, 1898. On Apr. 19 a joint declaration of Congress included the independence of Cuba as part of the ultimatum to Spain; when this was not accepted, Congress, on Apr. 25, declared a state of war to have been in existence since Apr. 21. The Spanish-American War lasted only three months. By the Treaty of Paris of Dec. 10, 1898, the United States obtained Puerto Rico, Guam, and the Philippines and established a protectorate over Cuba. The loss did not long embitter Spanish-American relations.

When the Spanish civil war broke out in 1936, the United States applied the new neutrality legislation, depriving the legitimate Spanish republican government of the right to purchase arms and ammunition. On Apr. 1, 1939, the United States recognized the regime of Francisco Franco. During World War II the Allies were able to keep wavering Spain neutral. At the end of the war, the United States led in the effort to deny Spain's admission to the United Nations and to recall the chiefs of diplomatic missions from Madrid, as well as to encourage the establishment of a democratic regime in Spain. During the Korean War, when questions of security overrode those of ideology, full diplomatic relations were resumed with Spain (November 1950). More far-reaching was the signing of the Pact of Madrid on Sept. 26, 1953, which allowed the United States to build air and naval bases in Spain for ten years. In 1963 and again in 1975 the agreement was renewed. Although the economic and military aid given to Spain had been reduced, the latter was able to change the nature of the pact to a quasi-alliance. After Franco's death in 1975 Spain reestablished democracy; relations with the United States continued without any significant changes. A new defense pact was signed in 1982, permitting the United States to maintain its bases on Spanish soil, but restricting some of the operations.

SPANISH-AMERICAN WAR (1898). The sinking of the battleship *Maine* in Havana harbor on Feb. 15 provided a dramatic motive for the Spanish-American War, but underlying causes included U.S. economic interests and genuine concern over Spanish misrule. Rebellion in Cuba had erupted violently in 1895, and although by 1897 a more liberal Spanish government had adopted a conciliatory attitude, U.S. public opinion would not be placated by anything short of full independence for Cuba.

The *Maine* had been sent to Havana ostensibly on a courtesy visit but actually as protection for American citizens. Madrid agreed to arbitrate but would not promise independence for Cuba. On Apr. 11, President William McKinley asked Congress for authority to intervene. Congress, on Apr. 19, passed a resolution declaring Cuba independent, demanding withdrawal of Spanish forces, directing the use of armed force to put the resolution into effect, and pledging that the United States would not annex Cuba. On Apr. 25 Congress declared that a state of war had existed since Apr. 21.

The North Atlantic Squadron, concentrated at Key West, Fla., was ordered on Apr. 22 to blockade Cuba. The squadron, commanded by Rear Adm. William T. Sampson, consisted of five modern battleships and two armored cruisers. The Spanish home fleet under Adm. Pascual Cervera had sortied from Cadiz on Apr. 8, and although he had only four cruisers and two destroyers, the approach of this "armada" provoked near panic along the U.S. East Coast, causing Sampson to detach a flying squadron under Commodore Winfield Scott Schley to intercept Cervera.

Initial U.S. strategy was to blockade Cuba while the insurgents continued the fight against the Spanish, with the expectation of an eventual occupation of Cuba by an American army. At the war's beginning, the strength of the U.S. Regular Army under Maj. Gen. Nelson A. Miles was only 26,000. The mobilization act of Apr. 22 provided for a wartime army of 125,000 volunteers (later 200,000) and an increase in the regular army to 65,000. Thousands of volunteers and recruits converged on ill-prepared southern camps.

In the Western Pacific, Commodore George Dewey had been alerted to prepare his Asiatic Squadron for operations in the Philippines. On Apr. 27 Dewey sailed from Hong Kong with four light cruisers, two gunboats, and a revenue cutter. Dewey entered Manila Bay in the early morning hours on May 1. Rear Adm. Patricio Montojo had one modern light cruiser and six small antiquated ships, with protection of Manila's shore batteries. Dewey shot Montojo's squadron out of the water, but had insufficient strength to land and capture Manila itself.

At the end of July some 15,000 men under Maj. Gen. Wesley Merritt had reached the Philippines. En route, the escort cruiser *Charleston* had stopped at Guam and accepted the surrender of the island from the Spanish governor, who had not heard of the war. Dewey and Merritt themselves did not hear immediately of the peace protocol, and on Aug. 13 an assault against Manila was made. The Spanish surrendered after token resistance.

In the Atlantic, Cervera managed to slip into Santiago on Cuba's southeast coast. Schley took station off Santiago and was joined by Sampson. To support these operations a marine battalion seized nearby Guantánamo. Sampson, reluctant to enter the harbor because of mines and land batteries, asked for U.S. Army help. Maj. Gen. William R. Shafter, at Tampa, Fla., received orders to embark his V Corps. By June 20 he was standing outside Santiago. Sampson wanted Shafter to reduce the harbor defenses; Shafter was insistent that the city be taken first and decided on a landing at Daiquiri, east of Santiago. On June 22, after a heavy shelling of the beach area, the V Corps began going ashore. The Spanish did nothing to interfere. Once ashore, Shafter was joined by insurgent leader Calixto Garcia and about 5,000 revolutionaries.

Between Daiquiri and Santiago were the San Juan heights. In the battles of San Juan Hill and El Caney, the Americans won the ridge line; the Spanish withdrew to an inner defense line. (*See* San Juan Hill and El Caney, Battles of.)

Shafter asked Sampson to come into Santiago Bay and attack the city, but for Sampson there was still the matter of the harbor defenses. He took his flagship eastward on July 3 to meet with Shafter, and while they argued, Cervera inadvertently resolved the impasse by coming out of the port on orders of the Spanish captain general. His squadron was annihilated by Schley, and on July 16 the Spaniards signed terms of unconditional surrender.

On July 21 Miles sailed from Guantánamo to Puerto Rico. He landed near Ponce on July 25 and against virtually no opposition began a march to San Juan, which was interrupted on Aug. 12 by the signing of a peace protocol.

The peace treaty signed in Paris on Dec. 10, 1898, established Cuba as an independent state, ceded Puerto Rico and Guam to the United States, and provided for the payment of $20 million to Spain for the Philippines.

SPANISH-AMERICAN WAR, NAVY IN. The Spanish-American War lasted only about ninety days, yet it marked the generally successful combat trial of the then new American navy. The main combat areas of the war were Spanish possessions in the Philippines and Caribbean. In both theaters American naval ascendancy was first established, to assure sea control before undertaking amphibious and military operations. (*See* Spanish-American War.) There were many important naval lessons learned in the war. The necessity for overseas bases for logistic support became evident. The war also added strong impetus to the growing demand for an American navy second to none.

SPANISH CAPTURE OF BRITISH POSTS (1779–81). The final stage in Spain's participation in the American Revolution. Between 1776 and 1779 Spain had secretly supported the war against Great Britain, in order to weaken its imperial rival. Money and war materials were sent through intermediary merchants, and American privateers with prizes were protected in Spanish ports. On June 21, 1779, Spain formally joined France in hostilities against Great Britain. It did not, however, explicitly guarantee the independence of the United States.

Spain's military operations were conducted along the Anglo-Spanish frontier on the Mississippi River and the Gulf of Mexico. Under Bernardo de Gálvez, governor of Louisiana, the posts at Fort Manchac, Baton Rouge, and Natchez were easily taken from the British late in 1779. Fort Charlotte (Mobile) was captured Mar. 17, 1780, and Fort George (Pensacola) surrendered May 9, 1781, after a long naval siege combined with a land attack. Thus Spain restored its control of East Florida and West Florida, although its claim of control also of navigation on the Mississippi was not upheld in the Definitive Treaty of Peace of 1783.

SPANISH CONSPIRACY. Intrigues between Spain and Americans living in what was then the western United States; they began in 1786 and continued for a score of years thereafter. The main purpose of Spain was to defend Louisiana and Florida by promoting the secession of the West from the United States. The Spanish employed bribery, manipulated commerce on the Mississippi River, and exploited sectional antagonism between East and West.

The first intrigue, a short-lived one begun in 1786 by Diego de Gardoqui (Spanish minister to the United States) and James White (a prominent North Carolina landowner), was related to the Muscle Shoals speculation, in which leaders of the breakaway state of Franklin attempted to settle the Muscle Shoals (Ala.) region. The central figure in the Spanish intrigues, however, was James Wilkinson, and their focal point was in Kentucky. In 1786 great indignation was aroused in the West by the decision of Congress not to press the United States' claim to the free navigation of the Mississippi; and in 1787 Wilkinson went to New Orleans to try his hand at direct negotiation with the Spanish officials of Louisiana. He won some commercial privileges for the western people and more for himself, took an oath of allegiance to the Spanish crown, and became the principal agent of Spain in its secessionist intrigue; he was awarded a pension of $2,000 a year (later $4,000), paid to him for many years after he became an officer in the U.S. Army (1791). The existence of the conspiracy was widely suspected almost from the beginning; partial revelations were made in the 1790's; and many details were exposed in 1806 by the *Western World* (a Kentucky newspaper) and in 1809 by Daniel Clark's *Proofs of the Corruption of . . . Wilkinson.* Nevertheless, full legal proof was lacking. The exposure did, however, put an end to the conspiracy, which had become a farce.

SPANISH DOLLAR. First coined in 1728 to replace the old piece of eight; circulated throughout the commercial world and became accepted as a reliable medium of exchange. It served as the metallic basis of the monetary system of the British colonies prior to the Revolution. Congress adopted it in 1786 as the basis of the U.S. coinage system.

SPANISH-INDIAN RELATIONS (1783–1803). During 1782–83, Spain formulated a plan to handle its dealings with Indians east of the Mississippi through Lt. Gov. Gilbert Antoine de Saint Maxent, who was also to monopolize the Indian trade. Direct trade between Louisiana and France was permitted by a cedula of Jan. 22, 1782, but Maxent failed to fulfill his contract. Louisiana Gov. Esteban Miró had to buy gifts for the Creek who attended the "congress" in Pensacola at which Miró negotiated the treaty of May 31–June 1, 1784. The Creek accepted Spanish protection and promised to deal only with Spanish traders. Their chief, Alexander McGillivray, became Spanish commissary. At Mobile in July the Choctaw and Chickasaw similarly came under Spanish protection.

Through McGillivray's influence Panton, Leslie and Company obtained the Creek trade through Pensacola, with the privilege of importing goods from England. The company was given the Mobile trade in 1788, and was one of the mainstays of Spanish-Indian policy. Without consulting his protectors, McGillivray sent the Creek against the Georgians in 1786. Miró nevertheless supplied guns and ammunition until stopped in 1787 by Spain. Munitions were furnished again in 1789 to offset the influence of the British-backed adventurer William Augustus Bowles, who attempted to drive the Spanish out of Florida. Insufficient support from Spain, however, was a major factor in causing McGillivray to agree to the Treaty of New York in 1790, in which he declared allegiance to the United States. Miró's successor, Francisco Luis Hector, Baron de Carondelet, won McGillivray back as a Spanish ally in 1792; McGillivray died the next year.

Meanwhile, Carondelet was working to create a confederation of southern Indians and to establish Spanish domination west of the Alleghenies. His subordinate, Manuel Gayoso de Lemos, built a fort at Nogales (Walnut Hills) in 1792, and in October 1793, Gayoso negotiated the Treaty of Nogales, establishing the Indian confederation. The next year Fort Confederation was built on the Tombigbee River, and Fort San Fernando was erected at Chickasaw Bluffs in 1795. Carondelet was then stopped by the Treaty of San Lorenzo (or Pinckney's Treaty) in 1795. Early in 1798 all Spanish garrisons retired below the thirty-first parallel.

Spain and the United States had scarcely resolved their differences when Bowles, returning in 1799, threw the Lower Creek into confusion. Through the cooperation of both nations he was captured in 1803.

SPANISH-MISSOURI FUR COMPANY. Organized May 5, 1794, as the "Spanish Commercial Company for the Exploration of the Country West of the Misuri." Jacques Clamorgan was the chief director. The Spanish government granted the company exclusive trading rights along the upper Missouri above the Ponca Indian villages, and the firm sent three expeditions up the river in 1794 and 1795. The first two were commanded by Jean Baptiste Truteau and the third by James Mackay. The company was not successful; Clamorgan, Loisel and Company apparently took over the business.

SPANISH POSTS ON THE MISSISSIPPI, SURRENDER OF. *See* **Guion's Expedition; Southern Boundary, Survey of the.**

SPANISH SUCCESSION, WAR OF THE. *See* **Queen Anne's War.**

SPANISH SUPPLIES FROM NEW ORLEANS (1776–79). When armed hostilities between Great Britain and the American colonies began in 1775, trade between Britain and the colonies was suspended, and British fleets blockaded Atlantic ports to prevent American importation from foreign countries. The colonists turned to the Spanish-controlled port of New Orleans as a source of supplies. The Spanish government was nevertheless careful to avoid war with Britain. However, through the influence of Oliver Pollock, an American trader and financier in New Orleans, agents were permitted to purchase guns, gunpowder, blankets, and medicines, especially quinine. The supplies were rowed up the Mississippi in boats carrying the Spanish flag. The chief obstacle was the lack of colonial funds to purchase supplies. Pollock went bankrupt when the revolutionary governments concerned were tardy in repaying advances made by him in their behalf. When France joined the United States in the war against Britain in 1778, American dependence on the New Orleans trade ended.

SPANISH TRAIL. An overland route between Santa Fe, N.Mex., and Los Angeles. It dates from 1775–76, during Spanish control of the Southwest. Two Franciscan monks first traversed most of the trail, Father Francisco Garcés in 1775–76, and Father Silvestre Velez de Escalante in 1776. Jedediah Smith, an American trader and explorer, came up the western half of the trail, but the first American to cover its full length was William Wolfskill, who led a company of trappers over it in 1830–31. Afterward, annual expeditions of traders used the trail. The trail was later an important immigrant route, and the Mountain Meadows massacre took place on it in 1857.

SPARS. *See* **Women in the Military Services.**

SPEAKEASY. An illicit or unlicensed establishment dispensing alcoholic beverages. The speakeasy reached its heyday during the Prohibition era (1919–33).

SPEAKER OF THE HOUSE OF REPRESENTATIVES. The speakership of the U.S. House of Representatives is the first officer named in the U.S. Constitution. There is no requirement that the speaker be a House member, or even an American citizen, but in 1789 the House chose a member, Frederick A. C. Muhlenberg, as its first speaker, and the tradition of choosing from its membership has continued. The speakership has come to be regarded as second only in power and importance to the presidency, standing behind the vice-president in succession to the presidency. His first duty is to preside over the House of Representatives. He interprets the rules of the House, and his rulings can be overturned by a majority of the House. He preserves order, enforces the rules, refers bills and resolutions to the appropriate committees, and prevents dilatory tactics from paralyzing House action. He chooses the member who will preside as chairman of the Committee of the Whole, where the House conducts much of its important business. He serves as liaison to the president.

Until the early 20th century, the speakership was a highly partisan office, used by the majority to work its will. The tradition then developed of a scrupulously fair presiding officer, but in his role as leader of his political party in the House, there is no pretense of nonpartisanship. The speaker has great influence in placing his party's members on committees. (Until the House internal revolution in 1910, the speaker for years had named all committee chairmen and appointed all committee members for both majority and minority parties.) The speaker is also influential in determining which bills the House will consider.

SPECIE CIRCULAR. In pursuance of President Andrew Jackson's policy of making specie the chief form of money in circulation, several circulars were issued by the Treasury Department. The first, Nov. 5, 1834, ordered collectors of customs and receivers of public money not to accept, after Jan. 1, 1835, any form of money not described in a congressional resolution of Apr. 30, 1816. The order was designed specifically to exclude drafts of branches of the Bank of the United States. On Apr. 6, 1835, a circular directed collectors and receivers to accept, after March 1836, only gold and silver for payments less than $10. The specie circular of July 11, 1836, addressed to the receivers of public money and to the deposit ("pet") banks for U.S. government funds, directed that, after Aug. 15, 1836, nothing but gold or silver should be accepted as payment for public land. Until Dec. 15, however, "actual settlers or *bona fide* residents in the State" could use paper money in paying for up to 320 acres of government land. By curbing land speculation, the specie circular of 1836 probably hastened the panic of 1837.

SPECIE PAYMENTS. Under a system of specie payments it is required by law or custom that fiduciary money, usually in the form of bank notes or government paper money issues, be redeemed at par and upon request of the issuing bank or the Treasury in metallic coin. The maintenance of specie payments in the United States was difficult from the outset. Alexander Hamilton had recommended in 1791, and Congress adopted in 1792, a bimetallic standard of value, under which the dollar was defined in terms of both silver and gold (*see* Bimetallism). Essentially, after 1834 and until 1934, the dominant standard of value in the United States was gold coin.

A difficulty in maintaining specie payments during the 19th century was America's usually unfavorable balance of trade. The tendency for specie to be exported in payment for goods was exacerbated in times of war and economic crisis. Also, until 1864, when the National Banking System was established, it was difficult to control the paper bank-note issues of the state-chartered banks. In wartime, moreover, the federal government was forced to meet its needs for revenue through issue of irredeemable paper money. In 1814–15, specie payments were suspended by most banks and by the U.S. Treasury in some sections of the country. Coin payments were resumed in February 1817. Another great credit expansion fostered by the second Bank of the United States culminated in the panic of 1819 and a severe depression during which most banks in the South and West refused to pay specie.

Solid economic development and feverish speculation in land led to the panic of 1837 and a nationwide suspension of specie payments. The cessation of European investment was followed by large exports of specie. Partial resumption was achieved prematurely in 1838. Continuing outflows of metallic coin brought another suspension in 1839. Finally specie payments resumed in 1842.

The cycle repeated itself in the 1850's. Railroad and industrial expansion was fueled by heavy investment. State bank-note issues increased and speculation was prevalent. In 1857 capital imports from Europe slackened and the flow of California gold decreased. Money became tight. A panic in New York City spread to the rest of the country. Specie payments were suspended, but resumed six months later.

The departure from gold payments by the banks and the government on Dec. 30, 1861, was forced by domestic hoarding and export of specie as the domestic military situation deteriorated. In February 1862 the government began issuing U.S. notes, better known as "greenbacks." These notes were legal tender and by 1865 had been issued to the amount of $431 million. While the issuance had not caused the suspension of specie payments, the failure of Secretary of the Treasury Hugh McCulloch's contraction program after the Civil War made resumption very difficult. On Jan. 14, 1875, Congress passed the Resumption Act, which provided that coin payments be resumed on Jan. 1, 1879.

Despite the Free Silver agitation of the late 19th century, the United States adhered to the gold standard. The defeat of William Jennings Bryan in 1896 effectively squelched the silver movement, and the Gold Standard Act of 1900 legally placed the nation's money on the monometallic basis.

Difficulties in maintaining gold payments were encountered in 1893 and 1907. The basic problem was the maintenance of an adequate reserve of gold for redemption. The panic of 1907 was caused by unsound bank investments. A deviation from the gold standard occurred shortly after the United States entered World War I. On Sept. 7 and Oct. 12, 1917, President Woodrow Wilson placed an embargo on exports of coin and bullion. These restrictions were removed in June 1919.

The economic cataclysm of the 1930's marked the end of a legitimately defined specie standard of value. The 1929 stock market crash was followed by more than 5,000 bank failures. Gold began to be hoarded, and the specie basis of the system was further threatened by gold exports. In the two weeks preceding the inauguration of President Franklin D. Roosevelt on Mar. 4, 1933, the Federal Reserve banks lost more than $400 million in gold. Several states had already declared banking "holidays" when Roosevelt, on Mar. 6, issued an executive order closing all banks for four days. By the end of March most banks had been allowed to reopen, but specie payments were not resumed. In April 1933 the break with the gold standard was made complete. No person or institution was permitted to hold gold or gold certificates. An embargo was placed on all international transactions in gold except under license issued by the secretary of the Treasury. On June 5, Congress declared void the "gold clause" in government bonds and private obligations. The dollar was stabilized by the Gold Reserve Act and a presidential order in January 1934. Secretary Henry Morgenthau announced the Treasury's willingness to buy and sell gold at the new rate of $35 per ounce.

Operating under a favorable balance of payments, the United States amassed a gold reserve of more than $24 billion in 1949. After that time, deficits in the international balance reduced the gold stock to about $10 billion by 1971. The continuing deterioration of the balance of payments and the threat to the gold stock impelled President Richard Nixon on Aug. 15, 1971, to order that the Treasury cease all purchases and sales of gold. By the early 1980's the dollar was not maintained at any fixed value in terms of gold; in 1982 a special commission rejected a return to the gold standard.

SPECIFIC DUTIES. *See* **Duties, Ad Valorem and Specific.**

SPELLING BEE (Spelling Match). A teaching device employed in American schools. During the 19th century, students competed for the honor of best speller in the class. By the 1840's middle western communities held spelling matches as part of an evening's entertainment, and popularity spread to the West. The National Spelling Bee, conducted by Scripps-Howard Newspapers and other newspapers since 1939, was instituted by the Louisville (Ky.) *Courier-Journal* in 1925.

SPENCER RIFLE. A self-loading, repeating weapon patented by Christopher M. Spencer in 1860 and adopted by the U.S. Army. It was the first widely used magazine repeater. Many Civil War officers declared the rifle the best weapon of its time. Eight Spencer patents were obtained during 1860–73.

SPERMACETI TRUST. Formed to monopolize the manufacture and sale in America of candles made from sperm whale oil. Production in America began in Rhode Island about 1750. In 1761 Richard Cranch and Company proposed the formation of a "union," or trust, for all the colonies and enlisted most manufacturers. The nine members of the United Company of Spermaceti Candlers, most of them located in New England, agreed on a maximum buying price for whale "head-matter," on commissions for factors, and on selling prices for candles, and the members pledged to prevent any increase in competition. They also began to build up a whaling fleet. The sperm-candlemaking process had been a trade secret, but by 1772 Nantucket Islanders had learned it. The spread of knowledge of the manufacturing process and the founding of other factories broke the power of the trust.

SPIES. Only once has America ever entered a war with adequate espionage service in operation: the Revolution. Months before the Battle of Lexington (April 1775), Paul Revere and a group of patriots had begun to keep British Gen. Thomas Gage's troops under observation. This group kept patriot leaders continually informed and gave early warning of the march to Lexington and Concord. Unfortunately, it failed to detect the leading British secret agent, who was performing similar services for Gage—Benjamin Church, a member of the Massachusetts Provincial Congress.

Unfortunately, the espionage service of Revere's group covered only parts of New England and was allowed to lapse. When Washington had been driven to Harlem by the British and the need for spies became pressing, Washington sent out Nathan Hale—a brave and devoted man, but completely untrained. Hale was carrying incriminating papers on his person when he was captured and executed by the British in September 1776. After this tragedy, Washington set up an intelligence network in Manhattan, New Jersey, and Long Island, which did admirable service throughout the rest of the war.

As the Civil War approached, the federal government again neglected to prepare an espionage system in advance. In the meantime, Capt. Thomas Jordan, a Virginian on duty in the War Department, set up a ring of Confederate spies in Washington, D.C., which he handed over to Rose O'Neal Greenhow. Her lax security soon destroyed the ring, but not before it had supplied Union Gen. Irvin McDowell's exact marching orders for Bull Run. The first Union efforts at espionage in 1861 were mainly failures, but as the war continued Union intelligence became very skillful. Elizabeth Van Lew, a Union loyalist living in Richmond, began spying and built up a large network in Richmond, which was later taken into the much larger system directed by Gen. George Henry Sharpe for Gen. Ulysses S. Grant's forces.

"Sheridan's Scouts," commanded by Union Maj. H. H. Young, kept its men continually in the Confederate ranks and even in Gen. Jubal A. Early's headquarters. Union Gen. G. M. Dodge operated a network of nearly 100 secret agents throughout the Confederacy during most of the war.

A modern military intelligence division had been organized some years before World War I, and the navy had created the Office of Naval Intelligence. These were largely devoted to analyses of "overt" information from attachés and published sources. Before the war was over, however, there was a large and effective spy system in Europe.

As World War II approached, the armed forces began to enlarge their intelligence services, mainly by calling in specially qualified reserve officers. A new espionage service was organized, but it was obvious that operations would have to be larger than ever before. President Franklin D. Roosevelt set up the Office of Strategic Services (OSS). The OSS made some serious blunders, but it did a great deal of useful espionage and sabotage. Its successor, the Central Intelligence Agency (CIA), has since continued its work on a permanent basis. The control of German sabotage attempts was much improved over that of World War I, and numerous German spies and saboteurs were captured and executed by the military authorities.

The successor of OSS, the Central Intelligence Agency (CIA), was created in 1947. During the cold war period intelligence activities mushroomed and by the 1970's at least nine U.S. government entities were gathering intelligence information (CIA, the Defense Intelligence Agency, State Department, intelligence sections of the Army, Navy, and Air Force, the National Security Agency, the Atomic Energy Commission, and the FBI); the CIA was by far the most important of them.

SPIRIT LAKE MASSACRE. During 1856 cabins were built by white settlers at Okoboji lakes and one at Spirit Lake, in the state of Iowa. The winter of 1856–57 was bitterly cold, and Indians and settlers alike suffered. On Mar. 7, 1857, a small band of Sioux under Inkpaduta attacked the cabins. Thirty-two men, women, and children were killed and four women were taken captive. After an unsuccessful attack on Springfield, Minn., Inkpaduta fled westward. Two of the women were killed; one was released through the mediation of friendly Indians; and one (who wrote a harrowing account of her experience) was finally ransomed.

SPIRIT OF ST. LOUIS. *See* **Lindbergh's Atlantic Flight.**

***SPIRIT OF '76*.** A painting by Archibald M. Willard, a carriage painter in Wellington, Ohio. The original sketch, made in 1874 or 1875, was intended only as a humorous presentation of a Fourth of July celebration and was entitled *Yankee Doodle.* The patriotic spirit prior to the centennial celebration at Philadelphia was responsible for the change to the final, serious painting. The painting, of heroic size, was purchased by Col. Devereux in 1880 and presented to his native town of Marblehead, Mass., where it now hangs in the town hall.

SPOILS SYSTEM. "To the victor belong the spoils of the enemy" is the motto of the spoilsmen, proclaimed in 1832 by Sen. William L. Marcy of New York. In essence, the spoils system is an arrangement in which loyalty and service to a political party is the primary criterion for appointment to public office. Following an election, incumbent officeholders are summarily removed and replaced by those faithful to the victorious party. These dismissals are defended by the premise that rotation in office is an integral part of the democratic process.

President George Washington appointed people on the basis of loyalty to the Federalist party; John Adams made appointments on leaving office, including John Marshall's appointment as chief justice of the Supreme Court; and Thomas Jefferson replaced many Federalists with Democratic-Republicans. Andrew Jackson developed and justified the spoils system. Jackson was the first to articulate, legitimize, and establish it in the American political context. Despite all the publicity he gave to the spoils system, Jackson actually removed very few officeholders. During his tenure of office (1829–36) only one-tenth to one-third of all federal officeholders were replaced.

The spoils system grew by leaps and bounds after the Jacksonian era. Each successive administration engaged in wholesale removals of political opponents in favor of loyal supporters. Abraham Lincoln removed over 75 percent of the incumbent officeholders he inherited from his predecessors. It was not until the assassination of President James A. Garfield in 1881 by a demented officeseeker who blamed the president for his rejection that efforts to reform the system met with any success. In 1883 Congress enacted the Pendleton Act, which created the Civil Service Commission and a merit system for appointments to lower federal offices. Since then, successive presidents have, with few exceptions, extended the Civil Service classification list, so that by the 1970's more than 90 percent of all nonelective federal positions were included. Eligibility for these offices is determined by competitive examinations.

SPOKANE. Second largest city in the state of Washington, with a population of 171,300 in 1980; the center of a metropolitan area which included 341,058 people. Spokane is located in eastern Washington, chief city in an area nicknamed the "Inland Empire." The earliest settlement was a British trading post called Spokane House, founded in 1810 by the North West Company. An American-owned trading post was built in 1812 by John Jacob Astor's Pacific Fur Company to rival the British post. The original trading posts disappeared after 1846, when the British had to withdraw. The modern city of Spokane dates from 1872.

Spokane is the home of an important aluminum plant, operating with electric power generated from the Spokane River. It is also a center for food processing.

SPOKANE HOUSE. Trading post built by the North West Company, a British fur-trading company, in 1810–11 at Spokane Falls, about ten miles north of present-day Spokane, Wash. The center of the Columbia, Kootenay, and Flathead rivers fur trade, it was later taken over by the Hudson's Bay Company. It was abandoned in 1826.

SPOLIATION CLAIMS. *See* **French Spoliation Claims.**

SPORTS. *See individual articles on* **Baseball, Basketball, Golf, Football, Hockey, Horse Racing, Olympic Games, Prizefighting, Skiing, Tennis, Yacht Racing.**

SPOTSWOOD'S EXPEDITION. *See* **Knights of the Golden Horseshoe.**

SPOTSWOOD'S IRON FURNACES. Erected by Gov. Alexander Spotswood of Virginia soon after 1716 at Germanna on an extensive land grant about twenty miles above the falls of the Rappahannock River. The original enterprise was a charcoal-fired smelting furnace that cast sow (or pig) iron from rock ores. Spotswood later built an air furnace at Massaponax, and also had an interest in a third smelting furnace at Fredericksville, a now extinct town. Shortly after the Revolution records of the ironworks cease.

SPOTSYLVANIA COURTHOUSE, BATTLE OF (May 8–21, 1864). Gen. Ulysses S. Grant's southward march from the Wilderness in Virginia was stopped northwest of Spotsylvania Courthouse by the Confederate army. The Confederates were reinforced until they were entrenched along a front four miles long reaching to Spotsylvania Courthouse. The Union army captured a salient occupied by the Confederates. The opposing armies engaged in hand-to-hand combat on May 9. About midnight the Confederates retired to an inner line. Thereafter for some days Grant gradually withdrew his right and pushed his left southward, and on May 20 he marched toward Hanover Courthouse. At the North Anna River, however, Lee again blocked him. Grant's losses at Spotsylvania were 17,000; Lee's, 8,000.

***SPRINGBOK* ADMIRALTY CASE.** Elaborated the doctrine of continuous voyage. The *Springbok,* English owned both as to vessel and cargo, was captured by a Union cruiser on June 29, 1862. The neutral port of Nassau was its destination. The American admiralty courts held that the merchandise was intended for immediate transshipment through the Union blockade. The courts further held that the *Springbok* should be released but the cargo confiscated. The British Foreign Office accepted this decision. Its principle was often invoked against American cargoes (1914–17) intended for Germany via a neutral port.

***SPRINGER* V. *UNITED STATES*,** 102 U.S. 586 (1881). A case in which the Supreme Court unanimously upheld the validity of a federal income tax. It declared that direct taxes, within the meaning of the Constitution, were capitation and real estate taxes. An income tax was not a direct tax, the Court held, and could therefore be levied on individuals without apportionment among the several states.

SPRINGFIELD (Ill.). Capital city of Illinois, with a population of 99,637 in 1980; the center of a metropolitan area that included 186,104 people. Springfield is the government center of the state, and a market town for part of the richest farmland in the United States. There are also several important manufacturing facilities.

Springfield's first permanent residents arrived in the year Illinois became a state, 1818. The original capital was at Kaskaskia, too far from the center of the state for continued use. Vandalia, the second capital, was also far from the center. In 1837 the legislature made the new permanent capital at Springfield.

SPRINGFIELD (Mass.). A large industrial city located on the Connecticut river, with a population of 152,319 in 1980. Springfield and its vicinity make up one of the oldest manufacturing centers in Massachusetts, specializing in radio equipment, firearms, paper, and chemicals.

Springfield was founded in 1636 when the original Connecticut River towns were set up by pioneers from Massachusetts Bay. Springfield was within the land granted to the Massachusetts Bay Colony, and it was incorporated as a Massachusetts town in 1641. The town was destroyed during King Philip's War in 1675, but it was soon rebuilt, since the waterpower of the river was a valuable resource. During Shays' Rebellion in 1786 the Springfield arsenal was a major objective of the rebels. The city developed during the 19th century as one of the many Massachusetts mill towns, emphasizing cotton textile making.

SPRINGFIELD (Mo.). Third largest city in Missouri, with a population of 133,116 in 1980 and center of a metropolitan area of 207,830. It is located in southwestern Missouri among the Ozark Mountains, in an area of dairy farming, poultry farms, and feeder farms for cattle. The city includes plants where milk and meat are processed, and factories for the production of clothing and steel products.

Springfield was first settled in 1829. It was a stopping place on the "Butterfield Stage" line for coaches and wagons headed toward Texas and California. During the Civil War, it was an important crossroads town. Confederate forces occupied it after the battle of Wilson's Creek from 1861 through February 1862; from then until the end of the war, Union forces controlled it.

SPRINGFIELD, BATTLE OF (June 23, 1780). When Sir Henry Clinton, British commander in New York, heard rumors of mutiny in George Washington's army at Morristown, N.J., he invaded New Jersey with over 5,000 men. At Springfield, Maj. Gen. Nathanael Greene, with 1,000 troops, contested Clinton's advance. So vigorous was Greene's defense of the bridge before that town that Clinton proceeded no farther and, after burning the village, returned to Staten Island.

SPRING HILL, ENGAGEMENT AT (Nov. 29, 1864). On Nov. 28 forces of Confederate Gen. John B. Hood and Union Gen. John Schofield faced each other at Columbia, Tenn. During the night Hood moved northward to get across Schofield's line of retreat. Gen. James Wilson, commanding Schofield's cavalry, reported Hood's movement and urged a prompt retreat, but Schofield delayed. Hood's troops gained position about Spring Hill, on the line of retreat. After dark on Nov. 29, Schofield's troops marched within earshot of Hood's army. For some reason no attack was ordered. By daylight Schofield had passed safely northward.

SPRING WELLS, TREATY OF (Sept. 8, 1815). Made near Detroit, between the United States and seven Indian tribes of the Northwest. With the Chippewa, Ottawa, and Potawatomi the treaty restored prewar relations, specified by the Treaty of Ghent (ending the War of 1812); with the Seneca, Delaware, Miami, and Shawnee, the new pact confirmed a treaty made at Greenville, Ohio, the preceding year, and granted amnesty for Indian misdeeds since that time.

"*SPURLOS VERSENKT*." A German phrase used by Count Luxburg, the German chargé d'affaires at Buenos Aires, Argentina, in telegrams of May 19 and July 9, 1917, to Berlin. Luxburg advised that Argentine ships be spared by German submarines or else "sunk without a trace being left." These telegrams were made public in the United States on Sept. 8, 1917, and in consequence the count was expelled by the Argentine government.

"SQUARE DEAL." Used with political significance by President Theodore Roosevelt. He first used the phrase in Kansas while on a tour of the western states as he explained the principles to be embodied in the platform of the Progressive party. The "square deal" included Roosevelt's ideals of citizenship, the dignity of labor, nobility of parenthood, great wealth, success, and the essence of Christian character. Later it was applied to industry.

SQUATTER SOVEREIGNTY. *See* **Popular Sovereignty.**

SQUATTERS' SOCIETIES. *See* **Claim Associations.**

SQUAW CAMPAIGN (February 1778). Gen. Edward Hand, sent by Gen. George Washington to defend the western frontier, ordered out the militia of Westmoreland County, Pa., to seize some military stores at Sandusky (now northern Ohio). The troops, hindered by wet weather from reaching their objective, fell on two small camps of Indians composed mainly of Delaware women and children. One or two squaws were killed and two captured, later sent back to their tribe. The expedition proved a failure.

SQUIER TREATY (Sept. 3, 1849). Signed by Ephraim George Squier, diplomatic agent of President Zachary Taylor, with Nicaragua. It gave the United States exclusive rights to a transisthmian canal route through Nicaragua. It was discarded in favor of the Clayton-Bulwer Treaty (1850) with England. (*See also* Panama Canal.)

"SQUIRREL HUNTERS." A southern Ohio militia hastily gathered in 1862 when Cincinnati was in imminent danger of attack by Confederate troops (*see* Kentucky, Invasion of). Gov. David Tod asked men to bring their own arms. The response was largely from men accustomed to squirrel hunting.

STABILIZATION FUND. *See* **Gold Standard.**

***STAFFORD* V. *WALLACE*,** 258 U.S. 495 (1922). The Packers and Stockyards Act of 1921 gave to the secretary of agriculture the authority to regulate operations of livestock dealers and commission men. In a case that T. F. Stafford and others brought against Secretary of Agriculture Henry C. Wallace, the act was challenged on the ground that such businesses were not in interstate commerce, but were purely local. In the decision handed down by the Supreme Court on May 1, 1922, Chief Justice William Howard Taft declared that such regulation was a proper exercise of federal power under the Constitution.

STAGE, FISHING. A high wooden platform built on the shore for drying fish. The term is also used for the place on which the land operations—cleaning, curing, and oil extraction—connected with fishing were carried on.

STAGECOACH LINES OF THE SOUTHWEST. The California gold discovery of 1848 made necessary transcontinental stagecoach lines. In the summer of 1849 stage service was provided between Independence, Mo., and Santa Fe, N.Mex.; and two years later another was instituted between Independence and Salt Lake City. Coaches over the central route made monthly runs. But a more satisfactory service was provided in 1857 between San Antonio, Tex., and San Diego, Calif., via the Gila Trail when semimonthly coaches were used. Within the next decade thousands of miles of stage lines were in use (*see* Southern Overland Mail).

STAGECOACH ROBBERIES. Occurred throughout America, but the dramatic character of western holdups, together with the large amounts of booty secured, make them more important. Of these the California robberies stand out because of the movement of gold ore. The first robbery of importance was in 1852. In fifteen years of operation ending in 1869 Wells, Fargo and Company suffered 313 stage robberies. A second era of stage holdups followed the discovery of gold in the Black Hills of South Dakota.

STAGECOACH TRAVEL. The first successful stagecoach lines in America were established in the northern colonies in the two decades before the Revolution, most of them running from Boston, New York, and Philadelphia. No stagecoaches ran south of Annapolis in colonial times. These lines were aided financially when, in 1785, Congress first provided for the carrying of mail by stagecoach. The U.S. Post Office frequently gave financial assistance to proprietors who established lines through new territory. Rapid development of stagecoach facilities west of the Alleghenies did not take place until the Jacksonian era when Post Office subsidies increased greatly. The mileage of mail stage lines tripled between 1828 and 1838. After railroads invaded the heaviest routes of travel the stage lines became extensions of advancing railheads or feeders from fertile tributary areas. In mountainous regions they lingered, serving isolated valleys and villages until the coming of the motor bus.

STAKED PLAIN (Llano Estacado). The high level part of northwest Texas and eastern New Mexico that lies above the Cap Rock escarpment, bounded on the north by the Canadian River and on the west by the Mescalero Ridge. Francisco Vásquez de Coronado led the first expedition of white men across it (1541). It was so named, perhaps, by an expedition which drove stakes by which to retrace its route, or after the numerous stalks of the yucca plant, suggesting a "plain of stakes." The Comanche occupied the region until about 1880. The plain thereafter became cattle country, and later a dry farming and oil and natural-gas producing region.

STALWARTS. Certain conservative Republican leaders led by Sen. Roscoe Conkling of New York who opposed the southern policy and the civil-service reform program of Rutherford B. Hayes's administration and dubbed his adherents "Halfbreeds." After Conkling's retirement in the 1880's the designation passed out of use.

STAMP ACT (1765). In addition to the support of a colonial military force, increased sums were necessary to maintain British naval supremacy. The British ministry decided to levy a parliamentary tax on the colonies. The first step was the Sugar Act of 1764. The old severe duties on colonial trade with the foreign West Indies were reduced in the hope that it would yield some revenue. This was held to be less than the colonial share, and Sir George Grenville, chancellor of the Exchequer, proposed a stamp tax on the colonies. For a year he gave the colonies an opportunity to suggest other means. They protested strongly against a stamp act but suggested nothing more than taxation by the colonial assemblies as of old. And so Parliament passed the Stamp Act of 1765. The use of stamps was required on all legal and commercial papers, pamphlets, newspapers, almanacs, cards, and dice. Parliament, in harmony with the rule not to receive petitions against revenue bills, did not heed the colonial protests. Even the colonial agents failed to understand the colonial temper. News of the Stamp Act blew up a colonial storm, and violent colonial opposition finally nullified the act in 1766.

STAMP ACT CONGRESS (1765). As a result of the Stamp Act the House of Representatives of Massachusetts issued in June a call to all colonies to send delegates to New York City. Nine colonies responded, and twenty-seven delegates met from Oct. 7 to Oct. 25. They framed resolutions of colonial rights and grievances and petitioned king and Parliament to repeal the objectionable legislation.

STAMP ACT RIOT (Nov. 1, 1765). The day the Stamp Act went into effect, the Sons of Liberty erected a sham gallows in New York City and hung there effigies of Lt. Gov. Cadwallader Colden, marched to Fort George where the stamps were being kept and taunted the soldiers, seized the lieutenant governor's coach and burned it, and broke into another British official's house and gutted it.

STAMPEDES. The most hazardous event of roundups and cattle drives. The frantic flight that the rancheros called *estampida* was especially characteristic of longhorns. A herd peacefully bedded down might, with the instantaneity of forked lightning, thunder away in headlong flight. The only way to check it was to circle the leaders and thus swing the mass into a "mill."

STANDARD OIL COMPANY. An Ohio corporation incorporated on Jan. 10, 1870, with a capital of $1 million. It took the place of the previous firm of Rockefeller, Andrews and Flagler (formed 1867), whose refineries in Cleveland were probably the largest in the world at that time. Standard Oil early in 1872 swallowed practically all rival refineries in the Cleveland area. Between 1872 and 1879 it bought pipelines and refineries in New York, Kentucky, and Pennsylvania. By 1879 Standard Oil controlled from 90 to 95 percent of the refining capacity of the United States, immense pipeline and storage-tank systems, and powerful marketing organizations at home and abroad. Under John D. Rockefeller's leadership it was the first company in the world to organize the oil industry. There were thirty-seven stockholders, of whom Rockefeller, with 8,894 shares, held nearly three times as much as any other man. Standard Oil of Ohio was the nucleus of an almost nationwide industrial organization, the richest and most powerful in the country. On Jan. 2, 1882, the Standard Oil Trust Agreement set up the first trust in the sense of a monopoly in American history. All stock and properties were transferred to a board of nine trustees, consisting of the principal owners and managers, with Rockefeller as head. The total of the trust certificates was $70 million, considerably less than the actual value of the properties. This lasted until 1892, when, as the result of a decree by the Ohio courts, the Standard Oil Trust dissolved, and the separate establishments and plants were reorganized into twenty constituent companies. But by informal arrangement, unity of action was maintained until they were gathered into a holding company (Standard Oil of New Jersey) in 1899. In 1911 a decree of the U.S. Supreme Court forced a more complete dissolution.

***STANDARD OIL COMPANY OF NEW JERSEY* V. *UNITED STATES*,** 221 U.S. 1 (1911). Originated in 1906 when the federal government filed a suit against more than seventy corporations and individuals, alleging that they were violating the Sherman Antitrust Act of 1890. In 1909 the U.S. Circuit Court for the Eastern District of Missouri upheld the charge. The court's decree held that the combining of the stocks of various companies in the hands of the Standard Oil Company of New Jersey in 1899 constituted "a combination in restraint of trade and also an attempt to monopolize and a monopolization under Sec. 2 of the Antitrust Act." The New Jersey corporation was forbidden to control thirty-seven subsidiary companies or to vote their stock. On May 15, 1911, the decree was upheld by the Supreme Court.

STANDARDS, NATIONAL BUREAU OF. *See* **National Bureau of Standards.**

STANDARDS OF LIVING. Most often measured by per capita national income, although some scholars prefer the related measure, per capita consumption of goods and services. On the basis of per capita income, the American standard of living has been among the highest in the world since the early 18th century. Between 1840 and 1980 per capita income, after allowance for price changes, increased almost ninefold.

Standards of living have varied from region to region. Incomes of families in the Midwest and especially the South have tended to be lower than those of families in the Northeast and Far West. This reflects the concentration of farming, traditionally a low-income industry, in the former regions. Regional differences, after widening between the middle and end of the 19th century (because of the Civil War), have narrowed drastically in the 20th century, the result of industrialization of the Midwest and South and the relative improvement in agricultural incomes. The distribution of income by size has been roughly the same as in most Western European nations for which data are available. Just before the Civil War the richest 5 percent of U.S. families probably had about eight times as much income as the remaining 95 percent. After the 1920's the degree of inequality diminished somewhat, the rich losing and the poor gaining. By the 1950's the richest 5 percent had about five times the income per family of the remaining 95 percent. From then to the mid-1970's the distribution was rather stable, those in the middle-income groups gaining slightly at the expense of both rich and poor. In the late 1970's and early 1980's the higher income families became more numerous, mainly because of a large increase in women's employment.

STANDARD TIME. *See* **Railroads.**

STANDING ORDER. Until the end of the 18th century, New England was dominated by a close association of the clergy, the magistrates, and the well-to-do, which controlled political, economic, social, and intellectual life. This control rested on popular acceptance and was so firmly established as to win the name of the Standing Order.

"STANDPATTERS." Came into political parlance in connection with the cleavage in the Republican party during

President William Howard Taft's administration. The insurgent Republicans, styling themselves "progressives," called the conservatives "standpatters" and denounced them as satisfied with the present social order, as being against reform, and as devoted to the vested interests.

STANSBURY EXPLORATION (1849–50). Led by Capt. Howard Stansbury of the U.S. Army; had for its object a survey of the Great Salt Lake valley, an inspection of the Mormon colony, and an examination of a new route through the mountains. These were all accomplished in the face of difficulties and described in Stansbury's illustrated report (1852) and atlases.

STANTON, FORT. Established by the U.S. Army in Lincoln County, N.Mex., in 1856 to hold the Apache in check. In 1871 the Mescalero Apache were placed on a reservation in the southeastern part of the county. The fort was abandoned in 1896.

STANWIX, FORT. In 1758 the old fort at the Oneida (upstate New York) carrying place, destroyed in 1756, was rebuilt and named Stanwix after its builder, Gen. John Stanwix. Its strategic location between the upper Mohawk River and Wood Creek made it an important point of defense and a center of Indian trade. The fort was used by Sir William Johnson, superintendent of Indian affairs, as the site of a meeting in November 1768 at which the Iroquois signed the first Treaty of Fort Stanwix. The fort was allowed to fall into disrepair. It was rebuilt and called Fort Schuyler in honor of Gen. Philip J. Schuyler. It was there that in 1777 British Gen. Barry St. Leger was held back on his way to Albany by soldiers under Gen. Benedict Arnold. After being severely damaged by fire and flood in 1781, the fort was rebuilt, renamed Fort Stanwix, and in 1784 used for negotiation of the second Treaty of Fort Stanwix. The present city of Rome was founded on the site of the fort.

STANWIX, FORT, TREATY OF (1768). The proclamation of 1763, establishing the Appalachians as the dividing line between white settlements and Indian lands, was only temporary, and London officials sought a more tenable line of demarcation. In early 1768 two Indian superintendents, Sir William Johnson and John Stuart, received instructions to proceed with negotiations. Johnson met with the Iroquois and their allies at Fort Stanwix in October and November 1768. Ostensibly on their own initiative, but probably at Johnson's urging, the Iroquois ceded far more land than the British government had sought to obtain. Within the area of the cession certain land speculators received a direct grant of land, known as Indiana and previously claimed by Virginia. The inclusion of the area between the Kanawha and Tennessee rivers, clearly beneficial to Virginia land interests, was undoubtedly an attempt to gain the acquiescence of that colony in the Indiana grant. By accepting so large a cession, Johnson had violated his instructions, and the Board of Trade condemned his actions in April 1769.

STANWIX, FORT, TREATY OF (1784). The Iroquois had been weakened by the revolutionary war, and their leaders recognized the futility of further resistance to white advance. Consequently at Fort Stanwix on Oct. 22, 1784, they ceded a small tract of land in western New York, and all that part of Pennsylvania north and west of the Indian boundary line established by the 1768 Treaty of Fort Stanwix (about one-fourth of the state). They also relinquished their claim to land west of the Ohio River.

***STARE DECISIS*.** The principle of deciding judicial controversies and cases on the basis of precedent. In American and British legal circles, adherence to precedent is frequently cited as an attribute ensuring stability not only in the legal system but in the political system as well. Both the cross-cultural and the Anglo-American assumptions concerning the significance and impact of adherence to *stare decisis* have been subjected to serious logical and empirical challenges.

***STAR OF THE WEST*.** An unarmed merchant vessel that President James Buchanan, influenced by Unionist cabinet members, secretly dispatched on Jan. 5, 1861, to reinforce Fort Sumter, S.C. Reaching Charleston harbor on Jan. 9, the vessel was fired on by batteries on Morris Island and Fort Moultrie. The *Star of the West* withdrew. It was captured by Confederate forces on Apr. 20, 1861.

STAR ROUTE FRAUDS. Star routes were roads where mail was carried, under private contracts. Extensive frauds in the Post Office Department caused great financial losses to the government. Congressional investigations, special agents, Pinkerton detectives, and attorneys brought about more than twenty-five indictments. Trials in 1882 and 1883 proved frauds on ninety-three routes, but no convictions resulted. The government was defrauded of about $4 million.

STARS, FALLING OF THE (Nov. 12–13, 1833). A meteor shower, visible over a large portion of the United States, occurs every November and peaks every 133 years. During the "falling of the stars" in November 1833, the meteors descended as numerous as snowflakes. At Niagara Falls a luminous table appeared above the falls emitting streams of fire; at Fort Leavenworth, Kans., soldiers could read ordinary print at night. Many religious people interpreted the phenomenon as the end of the world. The meteor shower of November 1966 occurred at dawn and was visible only in the West.

STARS AND BARS. *See* **Confederate Flag.**

STARS AND STRIPES. *See* **Flag of the United States.**

"STAR-SPANGLED BANNER." Inspired by the British attack on Fort McHenry in the War of 1812. Francis Scott Key, a young Baltimore lawyer, had gone to the British to seek the release of a prominent physician. Because of plans for the attack, Key was detained on ship in the harbor the night of Sept. 13–14, 1814, watching the British bombard the fort. When dawn disclosed the American flag still flying,

Key's emotions were so stirred that he wrote the words of the "Star-Spangled Banner." He adapted them to a popular drinking song, "To Anacreon in Heaven." The original version was printed as a handbill the next day; a week later it appeared in a Baltimore newspaper. The song soon became in fact the national anthem, but it was not until 1931 that Congress officially recognized it as such. The actual "star-spangled banner" that flew over Fort McHenry is on display in the Smithsonian Institution.

STARVED ROCK. Rises abruptly 140 feet above the river on the south side of the Illinois River nearly opposite the town of Utica, Ill., in Starved Rock State Park. Three sides of the rock, the top surface of which approximates an acre, are almost sheer; on the fourth side the ascent is difficult. Near the rock Louis Jolliet and Jacques Marquette found the Great Village of the Illinois in 1673; on it Robert Cavelier, Sieur de La Salle, and Henry de Tonti erected Fort St. Louis in 1682–83. Known to French explorers simply as *le rocher,* Starved Rock received its present name from a tradition that a band of Illinois Indians was besieged on its summit and starved into submission.

STARVING TIME. The food shortage at Jamestown in the winter of 1609–10. There was a similar shortage of food at Plymouth in the spring of 1622. The Jamestown starving time was relieved by the arrival of a ship from England, that at Plymouth by the arrival of a fishing vessel via Virginia.

STATE, DEPARTMENT OF. U.S. foreign relations were handled under the Articles of Confederation by Congress until the creation of a department of foreign affairs and the office of secretary for foreign affairs in 1781. The cabinet-level Department of Foreign Affairs was created on July 27, 1789. Because of the need to provide for the administration of "home affairs," Congress on Sept. 15, 1789, changed the name of the Department of Foreign Affairs to the Department of State and changed the title of secretary for foreign affairs to secretary of state. Until the establishment of the Department of the Interior in 1849, and even afterward in some respects, the secretary of state handled both foreign and home affairs, including the Patent Office and the censuses. By the 1980's the secretary of state administered a large department of government, acted as principal adviser to the president on foreign affairs, and handled many on-site diplomatic negotiations personally. The secretary of state is the senior member of the president's cabinet and was first in the presidential succession after the vice-president until 1947, when the speaker of the House was added to the succession.

Thomas Jefferson, the first secretary of state, had a staff of five clerks; two U.S. diplomatic agents were stationed abroad, and only four foreign governments had representatives in the United States. By the time of the expansion of the U.S. role in world affairs toward the end of the 19th century, the State Department had begun to take on more suitable dimensions. Even so, in 1938 there were still only 766 Foreign Service officers (as compared with 3,379 in 1968). In 1981 the State Department employed 23,439 people.

Until the landmark Rogers (Foreign Service) Act of May 24, 1924, there were no formal and specific requirements for entry into the U.S. Foreign Service at each level, nor did the service have any real organizational structure. The Rogers Act amalgamated consular and diplomatic personnel and established a system of written and oral qualifying examinations. As a consequence of these reforms (and later modifications, such as the Foreign Service Act of 1946) a true career service came into being.

The foreign services of the Commerce and Agriculture departments and the Bureau of Mines were merged into the U.S. Foreign Service in 1939 and 1943, respectively. But the Treasury Department kept its separate foreign service, and in 1954 the Department of Agriculture created a new foreign agricultural service, with more than sixty foreign posts. By the early 1960's only 7,200 of the 30,000 U.S. federal civilian employees abroad worked for the State Department. For this reason President John F. Kennedy on May 29, 1961, issued an order that the chief of a diplomatic mission abroad was in charge of the whole mission, a position reaffirmed by President Richard M. Nixon on Sept. 18, 1969. Thus foreign affairs personnel abroad came, in principle, under the Department of State.

Coordination at home between the State Department and other agencies involved in foreign affairs was also a problem of considerable magnitude. One of the major reasons for the establishment (and later refinements) of the National Security Council (NSC) under the president was to ensure a unified foreign policy formulation and implementation.

As the Department of State grew in size the problem of coordination within it (as compared with other agencies) also grew. In 1870 the department had only sixteen separate units; by 1948, 113; and the problem has continued to grow. The number of top management employees also increased. In addition, there were special missions to the United Nations, Organization of American States, North Atlantic Treaty Organization, Organization for Economic Cooperation and Development, International Atomic Energy Agency, European Office of the United Nations, and European Communities.

STATE BANKING. *See* **Banking.**

STATE BANK OF INDIANA. Created in 1834 as a federation of banks under control of a central board at Indianapolis. The board had power to fix the rate of dividend, make inspections, control issues, and order receiverships. Each of the ten branches originally established was mutually liable for the debts of the whole system, and a minimum fund was required to be reserved from profits as a surplus. The state owned one-half of the stock and elected the president and some members of the board. The State Bank of Indiana was one of the few successful state banks of the period. By limitation of its charter it went into a two-year liquidation period in 1857 and expired in 1859. It had withstood the panics of 1837 and 1857, paid high dividends, and turned over to the common-school fund several million dollars.

STATE BANK OF SOUTH CAROLINA. *See* **South Carolina, State Bank of.**

STATE BOUNDARY DISPUTES. *See* **Boundary Disputes Between the States.**

STATE CHAIRMAN. The individual serving as the executive director of a political party on a statewide level, usually elected by the state central or state executive committee. In a few states the chairman is elected in the party primary, by the party candidates, or by the state convention. The chairman's duties are fund raising, organizing and administering the party, helping in the selection and nomination of candidates, and preparing the party for elections.

STATE CONSTITUTIONS. In the American federal union each of the states has operated at all times under a written constitution of its own. Several of the earliest constitutions were hastily drawn and soon replaced, but others served for years with only minor changes. The Massachusetts constitution of 1780, although extensively revised, still remains in force, the oldest in America. It was the first to be framed by a convention elected for that purpose and referred to the voters for their approval. In all other states the first revolutionary constitutions were the work of provincial congresses or assemblies. Pennsylvania's was the most radical. It created a plural executive, a unicameral legislature, and a council of censors to investigate the government every seven years. Maryland's was probably the most conservative, if only for the high property qualifications it set for officeholders.

Only nineteen states, as of 1981, still operated under the constitution with which they entered the Union, and even these were extensively revised. Three states have constitutions that date back to the 18th century—Massachusetts (1780), New Hampshire (1784), and Vermont (1793). Nearly half, twenty-one, were adopted between 1860 and 1899, when new constitutions had to be framed both for the new western territories and the states of the defeated Confederacy. Unlike the federal constitution, all but a few abound with references to the Deity. In every state the legislative, executive, and judicial powers are vested in separate and distinct departments, and the legislature is effectively barred from exercising sweeping power either by detailed restriction on its use or by an equally expansive guarantee of personal rights. The doctrine of popular sovereignty is implied in every state constitution. In most states the constitution has become so detailed and rigid as to require frequent change. In every state, amendments or revisions may be proposed either by the legislature or by an elective convention called for that purpose. Specific amendments are usually proposed by the legislature or the voters; more thoroughgoing revision, by constitutional conventions or commissions.

STATE DEBTS. *See* **Debts, State.**

STATE EMBLEMS, NICKNAMES, MOTTOS, AND SONGS. Must be adopted officially by action of the legislative bodies of the respective states to which they belong. Travel guides and almanacs usually list the state birds, flowers, trees, nicknames, mottos, and songs; some states have also adopted state gems, animals, fish, and so on.

STATE FAIRS. The state fair has its roots in Europe, where market fairs have been popular for centuries. It was not until the early 19th century that formal agricultural shows and fairs were held in America (*see* County Fairs).

Most fairs and farming societies fell on hard times from 1825 to 1840, but with assistance from state governments, America's fairs returned, this time to stay. The first annual state fair was held in Syracuse, N.Y., in 1841. Many of the early state fairs traveled to the farmers, changing sites from year to year. By 1900 most state fairs had fixed locations and permanent facilities, usually near urban centers.

STATE GOVERNMENT. The Declaration of Independence proclaimed each and all of the colonies to be "free and independent states," wedded by a mutual pledge of lives, fortunes, and sacred honor in "support of this Declaration." The Second Continental Congress asked each state to prepare a new constitution. Connecticut and Rhode Island simply erased provisions about their allegiance to the king from their colonial charters and used them as state constitutions. The new constitutions adopted by the other eleven states made few obvious changes in the lives of their people. Where necessary, they democratized electoral procedures and established permanent representative assemblies. Many states gave their legislative assemblies power to select both governors and judges, thereby canceling the ideal of balancing the powers of the various branches of government. (*See also* State Constitutions.)

Most important in the general transformation of state government has been the ascendance of executive authority over state legislatures. Drafters of early state constitutions, still reacting against the primary role of colonial governors as agents of the king, provided for the dominance of state government by legislatures. The strong legislature–weak governor tradition lasted well into the 19th century, before some efforts were made to cut back on legislative powers. Early in the 20th century, a movement began to strengthen the executive powers of governors. This trend responded to the abuse of power recorded in many state legislatures, to their growing ineffectiveness, and to the need for streamlining governmental processes. The adoption of various forms of civil service to staff state administrations transferred much power from patronage to professionalism, although in some cases it has led to more, instead of less, bureaucracy. Other reforms that have promoted better state government have been extensive revisions of state constitutions, including revitalization of many governmental processes, and new fluency in interstate and municipality-state relations. (*See also* Interstate Compacts.)

States continued to expand their spheres of influence, becoming every year more involved in almost all functions and services performed for American citizens—not only in such traditional fields as education, highway construction, and social welfare but in vital new areas like mental health, environmental protection, population control and dispersal, and land-use planning.

STATE GOVERNMENTS, COUNCIL OF THE. *See* **Council for New England.**

STATE LAWS, UNIFORM. In the 18th and 19th centuries the exercise of state sovereignty resulted in the development of separate and often conflicting state legal systems. A valid divorce in one state, for example, was occasionally a nullity in another. Toward the end of the 19th century such factors as improved transportation and increased commerce persuaded lawmakers that it would be desirable to make some laws uniform throughout the states. In 1892, state representatives first met at what was to become the annual National Conference of Commissioners on Uniform State Laws. They faced two monumental tasks; to draft legislation acceptable to themselves as representatives and to convince at least some of the state legislatures that the particular uniform act was wise state policy. It is not surprising that no uniform act has met with unanimous success.

The Negotiable Instruments Act and its successor, the Uniform Commercial Code (UCC), have been the most significant of the uniform acts. As of 1981, the UCC was law in all states except Louisiana, and its provisions were the legal framework of most business dealings in the United States. There were over 150 uniform acts, some of which were not adopted by any states. For example, conflicting laws governing marriage and divorce still allowed for "unknowing bigamists." Since 1892 the conference has convened every year except 1945. Through its president it makes a yearly report to the American Bar Association, which in turn passes on the efficacy of new acts and provisions. The commissioners, generally three from each state, are appointed by the respective governors, who over the years have made a practice of selecting leading lawyers, judges, and law professors.

STATE-MAKING PROCESS. The original thirteen states had all been colonies of Great Britain, and following their successful war for independence, they formed the original United States of America. The Constitution of the United States went into effect in 1789 after its ratification by conventions in eleven of the states; North Carolina and Rhode Island followed suit soon after. Vermont was admitted into the Union in 1791 by act of Congress. Kentucky, originally a part of Virginia, was formed into a county of that state in 1776; Virginia consented to the creation of a new state in 1789, and Kentucky was admitted as a state in 1792. North Carolina originally included the territory comprising what is now Tennessee, which it transferred to the Union in 1784; Tennessee was admitted as a state in 1796. All these creations of states and admissions to the Union were authorized by acts of Congress. Texas was an independent nation from 1836 to 1845, after winning its independence from Mexico. It was annexed to the Union by joint resolution of Congress in 1845. Hawaii had also been an independent nation, but before becoming a state it had functioned as an incorporated territory for many years. Maine separated from Massachusetts in 1820, and in 1863 during the Civil War, West Virginia separated from Virginia. The remainder of the states were carved out of the public lands that came to the United States as the result of various cessions and annexations.

The famous Northwest Ordinance, or Ordinance for the Government of the Territory of the United States Northwest of the River Ohio, was passed on July 13, 1787. This ordinance was the basis upon which all public lands and foreign possessions of the United States were administered during the succeeding century. (*See* Ordinances of 1784, 1785, and 1787; Territorial Governments.) Ohio, the first state to be founded under the Northwest Ordinance, was admitted to the Union in 1803. As soon as an organized territory had maintained self-government and had grown in population enough to justify its admission as a state, Congress passed a specific act under which the people of the territory could choose delegates to a territorial constitutional convention. The constitution was then submitted to the people of the territory for their ratification and was generally accepted by them. The prospective state next applied to Congress for admission to full status in the Union. Congress usually passed the necessary enabling act; after acceptance by the people and government of the territory, a new state was then formally admitted into the Union. Each new state acquired complete equality with all the other states.

The Northwest Ordinance forever prohibited slavery within territories soon to be organized. Congress refused to admit Utah to the Union until Utah included in its constitution a provision prohibiting polygamy, then practiced by the Mormons. Utah complied and was admitted in 1896. Alaska was another special case: because of its vast area, sparse population, difficult climate and topography, Indian and Eskimo problems, and past history of federal subsidies, the Alaska Statehood Act and the accompanying Alaska Omnibus Act made unique and detailed provisions for continuing federal rights and responsibilities in this state, unparalleled in the others.

STATEN ISLAND PEACE CONFERENCE (Sept. 11, 1776). In May 1776, Gen. William Howe and Adm. Richard Howe had been appointed peace commissioners by King George III. After the Battle of Long Island the Howes sent Congress a proposal that an informal peace conference be held. On Sept. 6, Congress appointed Benjamin Franklin, John Adams, and Edmund Rutledge to confer with Lord William Howe. The meeting took place on Staten Island and, although cordial, was fruitless. Howe's demand for a revocation of the Declaration of Independence as a necessary preliminary to negotiations for peace left no further grounds for discussion.

STATES, RELATIONS BETWEEN THE. The U.S. Constitution provides the basic principles governing relations between the states, subject ultimately to judicial and political interpretation. Article IV, Section 1, provides, "Full Faith and Credit shall be given in each State to the public Acts, Records, and judicial proceedings of every other State." Article IV, Section 2, provides for citizens to be entitled to "all Privileges and Immunities of Citizens in the several States." It aims at protecting individuals from unequal application of the law regardless of state of origin; it also provides for interstate extradition of fugitives from the justice of another state. The privileges and immunities clause is subject to much judicial interpretation.

The clause that has given rise to the most interesting body of interstate relations is Article I, Section 10, which prohibits a state from entering "into any Treaty, Alliance, or Confederation" and prevents any "Agreement or Compact with another State" without consent of Congress. (*See* Interstate Compacts.) Regulation, planning, conservation, and sharing services have all been effectively implemented through compacts, sometimes with as few as two states (the Arkansas River Compact Administration) and sometimes embracing nearly all. Although it has been suggested that at least in one case, the Southern Regional Education Board, the purpose of a compact had questionable initial motives (perpetuating segregation in higher education), the compact has ended by allowing member states to take advantage of educational specialties each has had to offer students from the other states.

Other forms of "federalism without Washington" have included the cooperative adoption of uniform laws through the National Conference of Commissioners on Uniform State Laws. The umbrella organization, the Council of State Governments, was organized in 1935 for interstate cooperation. However, elective and administrative officials of the various states convened as early as 1878, at the National Convention of Insurance Commissioners. Many more such organizations come into being each year to exchange experiences, draft uniform or model state legislation, resolve jurisdictional disputes, or even agree on proposed legislation that Congress may be asked to enact "governing" them with their consent.

STATE SOVEREIGNTY. The part the states should play in the American political system was the subject of prolonged debate in the Convention of 1787, only many men failed to understand that two jurisdictions largely coordinate could work toward a similar end; they feared lest the surrender of a portion of the power wielded by the states would end in the destruction of personal liberty. Finally, a compromise was reached whereby the states were secured against encroachment by the national government through their equal representation in the Senate (*see* Connecticut Compromise). The problem of sovereignty remained unresolved when the government under the Constitution was inaugurated in 1789. Until the 1830's and 1840's, when the theory of John C. Calhoun became influential, the characteristic American doctrine was that in the United States the sovereignty had been divided without the destruction of its life principle.

Calhoun, in insisting that sovereignty in the United States is indivisible, returned to the issues debated in the federal convention. He declared that the Constitution of the United States was ordained and established by the people of the several states, acting as so many sovereign political communities, and not by the people of the United States, acting as one people, though within the states. The influence of Calhoun is without question; his political theories became the dogma of the states' rights party and found expression in the constitution of the Confederate States. The nationalist theory of the Union was defended by Daniel Webster, who insisted that the Constitution is an agreement among individuals to form a national government. The controversy remained for the Civil War to settle. (*See also* States' Rights.)

STATES' RIGHTS. Advocates of the principle of states' rights believe that considerable governmental authority should be located in the separate and collective states of the United States. The concept of states' rights arose as an extension of colonial rights. At the Constitutional Convention (1787) states' rights proponents pressed to include their ideas in the Constitution, but there was also the desire for a strong national government, with minimal power residing with the states. In 1791 the Tenth Amendment was added to the Constitution, which spelled out the states' rights doctrine: "The powers not delegated to the United States by the Constitution, nor prohibited by it to the States, are reserved to the States respectively, or to the people." The Kentucky and Virginia Resolutions (1798), which protested acts passed by the national Congress, were manifestations of states' rights, as was the Hartford Convention of 1814, called by New Englanders who disagreed with President James Madison's wartime policies.

The South is the section of the country most often associated with the doctrine. In the first half of the 19th century, when disputes arose over the tariff, public land policies, and the like, southern leaders used arguments based on states' rights in their attempts to protect their economic interests. Overriding all the other disputes was the question of the extension of slavery into the American territories. The Civil War established the supremacy of the national government and relegated the states to lesser political and economic positions. In the first half of the 20th century, southern politicians continued to speak about states' rights, but this was often nothing more than oratory to please southern voters.

After midcentury, when the power, size, and authority of the national government became greater and more complex, politicians who talked about states' rights often found they had more receptive audiences. Controversies over the administration of welfare programs and other social services gave states' rights advocates issues they could exploit. More important, the cry for states' rights was often a thinly disguised but firm stand against racial integration. (*See also* Federal-State Relations.)

STATES' RIGHTS DEMOCRATS (Dixiecrats). A number of southern Democrats split from the national organization during the 1948 presidential campaign, organized as the States' Rights Democrats, and cast their votes for J. Strom Thurmond of South Carolina in opposition to the regular Democratic presidential candidate, President Harry S. Truman. Thurmond won the electoral votes of Alabama, Louisiana, Mississippi, and South Carolina, plus one of the electoral votes of Tennessee. The seceding group did not continue as a separate party beyond the 1948 election.

STATES' RIGHTS IN THE CONFEDERACY. The doctrine of states' rights was productive of disastrous results when applied by extremists to the Confederate government during the Civil War. Conscription was attacked as unconstitutional and its operation impeded even after favorable decisions by the courts. The army was crippled by the insistence on the right of states to appoint officers, and by the policy of some states of withholding men and arms from the Confederate government and themselves maintaining troops. On similar grounds the states' rights faction opposed suspension of the writ of habeas corpus; the impressment of supplies for the army was broken down; and laws were repealed that had given the government a monopoly in foreign trade by means of which it had exported cotton and brought in war supplies through the blockade.

STATUE OF LIBERTY (properly, *Liberty Enlightening the World*). Located on Liberty (formerly Bedloe's) Island in New York Harbor; conceived by the French sculptor Frédéric August Bartholdi as a gift to the United States from the people of France. The colossal copper figure was shipped in sections in 1885 and unveiled on Oct. 28, 1886.

***STATUTES AT LARGE, UNITED STATES*.** A chronological publication of the laws enacted in each session of Congress since 1789. This series is cited as "Stat.," with the volume number preceding and the page number following. These volumes also contained presidential executive orders until the *Federal Register* began publication (1936), and included treaties until the publication *Treaties and Other International Agreements* began (1950). The *Statutes at Large* is legal evidence of the laws passed by Congress. The *United States Code* updates the laws in force by subject.

STATUTES OF LIMITATIONS. All of the states of the United States have statutes limiting the time within which a person having a cause for court action is permitted to bring suit for the recovery of his rights. As time passes, witnesses die, papers are destroyed, and the conditions of transactions are forgotten. Such laws prevent the enforcement of stale claims that might earlier have been successfully defended.

STATUTORY LAW. As distinguished from constitutional law and the common law, that law which is laid down by a legislature. The U.S. Congress and state legislatures enact statutes either by bill or by joint resolution, and these make up the statutory law. Federal statutes take precedence over state statutes, and state statutes are superior to the common law. Statutory law is inferior to constitutional law; courts exercise the power of judicial review when they declare statutes unconstitutional. Statutory law is codified under titles describing the areas of action to which they pertain. The federal code and the various state codes are also issued in "annotated codes," which reflect the decisions of the courts regarding the statutes and are published by either public authorities or private sources. Enforcement of statutory law lies with the administrative branch of the government.

STAY AND VALUATION ACTS. As a result of the panic of 1819, many citizens of the new western states were unable to meet their obligations. Foreclosures and forced sales at ruinous prices became common, and the states of Illinois, Missouri, Kentucky, and Tennessee adopted stay and valuation laws. A stay law provided for a moratorium or extension of time for meeting a debt obligation. The extensions ranged from three to thirty months. The stay law usually applied an unpleasant alternative to the case of a creditor who would not agree to the valuation laws, which provided for the appointing of a local board to set a fair value on property offered in satisfaction of debt, usually a price much above that which would be secured at forced sale. If the creditor would not accept this overvalued property in satisfaction of his debt, he was forced to defer collection for the duration of the period provided by the accompanying stay law. The state courts declared both varieties of relief laws unconstitutional. (*See* Old Court—New Court Struggle.)

STEAMBOATING ON WESTERN WATERS. Inaugurated by the *New Orleans* in 1811; the first steamboat navigated the Missouri in 1819, the Tennessee in 1821, the upper Mississippi in 1823, and the Illinois in 1828. Before the Civil War, more than forty tributaries of the Mississippi system had been navigated by steamboat. By 1846 there were 1,190 steamboats on western waters and fully 10,126,160 tons of freight valued at $432,621,240 were transported annually, nearly double the U.S. foreign commerce. Pittsburgh, Cincinnati, and Louisville were great Ohio ports, while New Orleans dominated the lower Mississippi.

STEAMBOAT MONOPOLIES. The successful trip of Robert Fulton's *Clermont* from New York to Albany in 1807 secured for his company a monopoly on the Hudson for twenty years: others who desired to operate steamboats were required to secure a license from the Fulton company. Such monopolies were granted by states on a number of rivers, but led to disputes. The controversy between New York and New Jersey over control of navigation on the Hudson River reached the U.S. Supreme Court; in the case of *Gibbons* v. *Ogden* (1824), the decision of Chief Justice John Marshall destroyed all monopolistic rights enjoyed by the Fulton company. This decision determined the outcome in all pending steamship monopoly cases.

STEAMBOAT RACING. Although editorials denounced the practice as dangerous, fast boats were popular with travelers and shippers. Moreover, few explosions occurred while boats were racing, for engineers were more alert. Many races were against time, captains endeavoring to break records between ports. By 1840 the average speed was about six miles per hour upstream, and ten to twelve miles per hour downstream; fast boats could average better than ten miles per hour upstream. In 1815 the *Enterprise* churned from New Orleans to Louisville in twenty-five days; by 1853 the *Eclipse* had reduced this time to four days, nine hours, and thirty minutes. Racing reached its zenith in 1870 when the *Robert E. Lee* raced from New Orleans to St. Louis in three days, eighteen hours, and fourteen minutes, defeating the *Natchez* by over three hours; more than $1 million in bets is said to have changed hands.

STEAMBOATS. Practical steamboat experiments began with the double-acting engine in 1782. The most successful inventor was John Fitch, who established regular steamboat service between Philadelphia and New Jersey in 1790; however, successful commercial navigation is usually dated from the voyage of Fulton's *Clermont* in 1807. The first steamboat on western waters, the *New Orleans,* was built from Fulton-Livingston patents in 1811. In 1813 Daniel French launched the 25-ton *Comet,* a stern-wheeler featuring vibrating cylinders. The *New Orleans* and *Comet* served as models until 1816, when Henry M. Shreve built his second steamboat, the 403-ton *Washington.* Shreve contributed three ideas to the *Washington:* he placed the machinery and cabin on the main deck; used horizontal cylinders with vibrations to the pitmans; and employed a double high-pressure engine. He also introduced the second deck, which became standard on all western steamboats thereafter. Thereafter, steamboats increased in tonnage; they boasted ornate cabins and private staterooms, bars and barber shops, bands and orchestras, and steam whistles and calliopes. Steam was used to work the capstan, handle the spars, or swing the stage. An auxiliary engine, or doctor, pumped water into the boiler. Coal gradually replaced wood. Spacious decks with promenades were built high above the main deck—the texas (for the crew) and the pilot house being placed high above all. In 1878 the third *J. M. White,* built at Louisville, was 325 feet long, with a 50-foot beam and an 11.5-foot hold. The main cabin was 260 feet long, and it could carry 8,500 bales of cotton.

STEAM POWER AND ENGINES. The first useful steam engine was developed in England by Thomas Newcomen and was put into operation by 1712. In 1755 the first steam engine began operation in the American colonies, at a copper mine in Belleville, N.J. The Newcomen engines were large, expensive, and cumbersome; except for draining valuable mines or providing water for large cities, they were not economically attractive in America. After the improvements made by James Watt beginning in 1764, it occurred to many that the steam engine might be applied to propelling boats. (*See* Steamboats.)

In 1802 Oliver Evans of Philadelphia became the first American to make steam engines for the general market; he was followed by James Smallman in 1804, and with the addition of Daniel Large and others, that city soon became the center of engine building. New York City became another center of engine manufacture. During the War of 1812 the building and use of engines spread to the western states. The first engine built in Pittsburgh was completed in 1811; the first engine shop in Kentucky was opened in Louisville in 1816. Work in Cincinnati, Ohio, began soon afterward, and by 1826 that city had five steam-engine factories. This western activity was brought about in part by the widespread use of steamboats on the western waters, the demand for engines on southern sugar plantations, and the easy accessibility of iron and coal around Pittsburgh.

By 1838 steam power was widely accepted all over the United States. The steam engine had a profound effect on the nature of cities. Formerly centers only of trade, culture, and government, they now became centers of manufacturing and, consequently, the home of a large class of factory operatives.

As the first machine necessarily made of iron, the steam engine had a critical influence on the development of the iron industry. In addition, rolling mills began to multiply only when boiler plate came into demand from engine builders; these boiler-plate makers in turn became the first to construct iron boats. The harnessing of steam engines to railroad locomotion increased the demand for rails as well as engines. The demand for coal, both for iron furnaces and steam boilers, was also greatly stimulated.

In the 20th century steam power has remained of primary importance only in the generation of electricity in power plants, although its potential use in automobiles periodically receives attention.

STEDMAN, FORT, ASSAULT ON (Mar. 25, 1865). South of the Appomattox River in Virginia, John B. Gordon's corps held the left of the Confederate defenses before Petersburg. In his front the Union army's Fort Stedman was 200 yards distant. Strongly reinforced, Gordon assaulted the works before dawn with about 11,000 men. The garrison was surprised and the fort captured easily, but further advance was smothered by the fire of adjacent Union batteries.

STEEL. *See* **Iron and Steel Industry.**

STEELE'S BAYOU EXPEDITION (Mar. 14–27, 1863). During Gen. Ulysses S. Grant's advance on Vicksburg, Miss., flanking expeditions were set afoot to get into the rear of the city. One of these was an effort by Gen. William Tecumseh Sherman and Adm. David D. Porter with gunboats to reach the Sunflower and Yazoo rivers by way of Steele's Bayou, which flows into the Mississippi a few miles above the Yazoo. Falling streams and Confederate obstructions foiled the movement.

STEEL STRIKES. Before the 1935 National Labor Relations Act, with its provision for certification elections, the union-recognition issue in the basic steel industry was resolved not by ballot but by brute force. The Homestead strike of 1892 was followed by other landmark violent strikes, in 1901, 1909, and 1919. In 1919 the U.S. Steel Corporation defeated a massive organizing attempt by twenty-four unions led by the American Federation of Labor (AFL). After driving out the Amalgamated Iron and Steel Workers in 1909, U.S. Steel maintained an open-shop policy until the recognition of the Steel Workers' Organizing Committee of the Congress of Industrial Organizations (CIO) in the John L. Lewis-Myron C. Taylor discussions of 1937. The rest of the steel companies, known collectively as "Little Steel," delayed recognition of the union in 1937 by defeating the steelworkers in the last of the violent and bitter struggles.

Free collective bargaining between the Steelworkers Union and the industry essentially began in 1946. In 1946–59 the union had the contractual right to strike ten times and struck five. Most of the strikes lasted about one month (1946, 1949, 1956); the 1952 strike lasted two months, and the 1959 strike went on for more than three. These were all peaceful strikes in which the companies made no attempt to operate the mills; when the union struck it shut down the industry and typically brought some form of government intervention in what were regarded as national emergency situations. The 1952 strike created a constitutional crisis in which the Supreme Court ruled that President Harry S. Truman's seizure of the mills was unconstitutional. The 116-day 1959 strike was ended by the Supreme Court. After 1959 crisis bargaining gave way to joint study under the auspices of the Human Relations Committee; subcommittees worked constructively on many issues until political upheaval in the union in 1965 ended formal joint study. The period of 1959–1977 was without major strikes. From August till November 1977 about 15,000 steelworkers struck in Minnesota and Michigan, demanding production bonuses.

STEERING COMMITTEES. Committees frequently found in legislatures and generally concerned with such matters as the scheduling of legislation. In the U.S. Congress they are party committees, and may be involved in the formulation of party tactics and positions for particular bills. In the Senate, such committees were established in the late 19th century, and each prepared a legislative schedule when its party was the majority party. In the late 1940's both parties assigned the scheduling duties to their newly created policy committees; the Republican steering committee was displaced, but the Democrats reconstituted their steering committee as a committee on committees, responsible for assigning party members to the standing committees. In the House, steering committees were established in the 20th century to assist the leaders in the formulation of strategy. In 1949 the Republican Steering Committee was renamed the Policy Committee. The Democratic committee has met only infrequently and has had no great impact on party decisions; in 1975 it assumed the committee-assignment function formerly exercised by the Democratic members of the Ways and Means Committee and attempted to play a more active role.

STEPHENSON, FORT, DEFENSE OF (Aug. 1–2, 1813). When British Gen. Henry A. Proctor failed to dislodge Gen. William Henry Harrison from Fort Meigs on the Maumee River, he withdrew down the Maumee and then proceeded up the Sandusky River to Fort Stephenson (now Fremont, Ohio). Maj. George Croghan, the commander, with about 160 men and one cannon, resisted the assaults of some 1,200 British and Indians equipped with light artillery, inflicting heavy losses on them while his own losses were one killed and seven wounded. Proctor withdrew on Aug. 3 and made no further attempt to invade Ohio.

STERLING IRON WORKS. One of the oldest iron and steel producing plants in the United States; located in the Ramapo Mountains at Sterlington, N.Y. It dates from 1738, when Cornelius Board built the first furnace. Purchased in 1740 by Henry Townsend, it remained in that family until 1864 when the Sterling Iron and Railway Company acquired it. The superiority of Sterling iron made it the preferred source of munitions during the Revolution.

STEUBEN, FORT (Ohio). Built on the present site of Steubenville as a fortification against the Indians; its immediate purpose was protection for the surveyors of the Seven Ranges. Begun in 1786 by Col. John Francis Hamtramck, it was completed the next year and was garrisoned by U.S. troops, 1786–87. It consisted of four blockhouses set diagonally on the corners with lines of pickets forming the sides. Apparently it burned to the ground in 1790.

STEVENS' INDIAN TREATIES. Gov. Isaac I. Stevens of Washington Territory was also superintendent of Indian affairs for his territory. Between Nov. 29, 1854, and Dec. 21, 1855, he negotiated a number of important treaties with the Indian tribes north of the Columbia River and west of the Cascade Mountains, largely in cooperation with Joel Palmer, the superintendent of Indian affairs for Oregon. The general policy for the treaties (following the one worked out by Palmer in Oregon) was to concentrate the Indians on a few reservations, pay for their lands with useful goods, and instruct them in farming. The Medicine Creek Treaty (Dec. 26, 1854), with the Puget Sound tribes, accepted the reservation policy. In 1855 three treaties with the Canoe of the sound region were signed.

The great council for the interior opened in the Walla Walla Valley in May 1855; the treaty was proclaimed June 12, 1855. The outbreak of Indian wars and friction between the Indian agents and federal military officers delayed ratification of the Walla Walla treaties by the federal government until Mar. 8, 1859.

STEVENS' RAILROAD SURVEY. Isaac I. Stevens of Massachusetts was appointed governor of the newly created Washington Territory and given the added duties of superintendent of Indian affairs for the Pacific Northwest and director of the survey to find a northern railway route to the Pacific coast. Capt. George B. McClellan was assigned to assist in the active direction of the survey. Stevens' personal command, while on the overland trip to the coast, explored the passes in the Rocky and Bitterroot mountains. The location of a suitable pass into the Puget Sound region (across the Cascades) proved the most difficult problem of the survey. A. W. Tinkham received orders at Walla Walla to attempt passage of the Snoqualmie Pass, and with the aid of two Indian guides made the trip through it and discovered grades practicable for a railway. McClellan contested the practicability of the route discovered by Tinkham, but it was accepted by Stevens.

STILLWATER, BATTLE OF. *See* **Freeman's Farm, Battles of.**

STILLWATER CONVENTION (1848). When Wisconsin was admitted to the Union in 1848, a large part of what is now eastern Minnesota was excluded from the new state. A demand for a territorial government by the people of this unorganized area led to a public meeting on Aug. 4, and a convention on Aug. 26, both at Stillwater. Sixty-one delegates signed memorials to Congress and to the president recommending the "early organization of the Territory of Minnesota." In October, acting on the assumption that the territory of Wisconsin was still in existence, the people of the excluded area elected Henry H. Sibley as delegate to Congress, and in January 1849 he was seated. Congress authorized the creation of Minnesota Territory that same year.

STIMSON DOCTRINE. Secretary of State Henry L. Stimson issued diplomatic notes to China and Japan (Jan. 7, 1932) stating that the United States would not recognize any changes in territory or other privileges brought about by use of armed force. This "Stimson Doctrine" was approved by President Herbert Hoover and became an important part of American foreign policy; it was based on the Kellogg-Briand Pact (1928), which bound the signatory countries not to use war as a means of gaining national objectives.

STOCK EXCHANGES. *See* **Exchanges.**

STOCKS. A device for punishing petty offenders, consisting of a frame in which the culprit's hands, or hands and feet, were confined while he was kept in a sitting posture. They were required by law in some of the American colonies. When the offense was one that displeased the public, the onlookers adjusted the punishment by throwing things at the culprit, by pulling the stool from beneath him, or by tipping him over backwards so that he hung head down.

STOCK TICKER. A printing telegraph system by which records of stock transactions are sent from an exchange as they occur and are printed at once on a tape at each place where a ticker is located. It was introduced into the New York Stock Exchange in 1867; its speed was subsequently improved by Thomas Edison. In 1964 a ticker printing 900 characters a minute and able to record the transactions of 10 million shares per day came into use. Further improvements include the reproduction of the tape on a screen and the joining of the ticker to a computer (1965).

STOCKTON (Calif.). An inland seaport city, located in the San Joaquin Valley 88 miles from San Francisco Bay, Stockton was a supply base for the gold-seekers in the mountains to the east and did not develop significantly until after construction (1928) of a deep-water channel (32 feet deep) connecting it to the bay. Its chief industrial activities include food packing and freezing, wine-making, and the shipping of agricultural products from the surrounding valley. Population in 1980 was 149,779.

STOCKTON-KEARNY QUARREL. On July 23, 1846, Commodore Robert F. Stockton relieved Commodore John D. Sloat as commander of the U.S. naval force fighting the Mexicans on the Pacific coast. Stockton aggressively extended Sloat's conquest to the south. When Gen. Stephen W. Kearny, under orders to take possession of California and to set up a temporary civil government, arrived at San Diego in December, he found Stockton unwilling to relinquish his command. Strained relations existed until the middle of January 1847, when Stockton passed the governorship over to John C. Frémont, who was in turn succeeded by Kearny early in March.

STOCKYARDS. By the outbreak of the Civil War, livestock had become one of the chief freight items of the western railroads. At the various western termini the early stockyards were either private or were owned and operated by the railroads. As the traffic increased, need for a consolidated yard became clear to all. On Dec. 25, 1865, the Union Stock Yards were opened in Chicago. Under a charter granted by the Illinois legislature, a company known as the Union Stockyard and Transit Company was formed with a capital of $1 million; the railroads running into Chicago took most of the stock. As the trade in western cattle grew, yards were opened in Kansas City (1871), St. Louis (1872), Cincinnati (1874), Omaha (1884), and St. Paul and Denver (1886). (*See also* Livestock Industry; Meat-Packing.)

STODDERT, FORT (Ala.). A stockaded work constructed July 1799 near the junction of the Alabama and Tombigbee rivers, about fifty miles above Mobile; named for the first secretary of the navy, Benjamin Stoddert. It became a thriving settlement and military post, as well as a port of entry, the seat of a court of admiralty, and the revenue headquarters of the district of Mobile. The fort acted as a check on ambitious frontiersmen anxious to take Spanish Mobile (*see* Kemper Raid). The first newspaper within the present limits of Alabama was published at the fort. With the taking of Mobile in the War of 1812, Fort Stoddert lost its importance and was abandoned.

STONE FLEETS. Small sailing vessels loaded with stone, which the Navy Department chased in northern ports during the Civil War and sank at the entrances of southern harbors in the hope of closing the channels to blockade runners. Three were sunk in Ocracoke Inlet, N.C., Nov. 18, 1861; sixteen in the main entrance to Charleston harbor, Dec. 20, 1861; and twenty in Maffitt's Channel, another entrance to Charleston harbor, Jan. 26, 1862. The work accomplished nothing since marine worms ate away the ships' timbers and the stones sank in the mud.

STONE RIVER, BATTLE OF. *See* **Murfreesboro, Battle of.**

***STONEWALL*.** A Confederate ironclad ram, built in France, sold to Denmark, and purchased from that country by Confederate agents. Under the command of Capt. Thomas J. Page, the *Stonewall* sailed from Copenhagen (Jan. 7, 1865) to Cuba. After the war, it was delivered to the United States and subsequently sold to Japan.

STONEY CREEK, BATTLE OF (June 6, 1813). Gen. John Chandler and William H. Winder, with about 1,400 Americans, encamped on June 5 at Stoney Creek at the western end of Lake Ontario, near the British camp at Burlington Heights. The following morning, British Gen. John Vincent, with about 700 British regulars, attacked the Americans. Heavy casualties were suffered on both sides; both American commanders, eighteen other officers, and eighty men, as well as ordnance, were captured. The American army withdrew (*see* Niagara Campaigns).

STONINGTON, BOMBARDMENT OF (Aug. 9–12, 1814). Four British vessels, detached from the squadron blockading

New London, Conn., appeared off the borough of Stonington, Conn., and gave warning of one hour for the removal of noncombatants before bombarding the town. Although the attack continued at intervals for three days, no buildings were destroyed, no persons were killed, and few were wounded. The citizens, assisted by the local militia, prevented any attempt to make a landing. The action was probably intended as a preliminary to a British attack on New London.

STONY POINT, CAPTURE OF (July 16, 1779). Stony Point, a rocky peninsula on the west bank of the Hudson River, was connected with Verplancks Point on the east shore by Kings Ferry, a link between two main roads leading from New England to Pennsylvania. On May 31, 1779, the British occupied the two points and began to fortify them. Gen. George Washington decided that a surprise attack on Stony Point was practicable and chose Gen. Anthony Wayne and the American Light Infantry, about 1,300 men, for the attack, which took place at midnight. While a small detachment in the center fired noisily, two silent columns with bayonets swarmed over the fortifications to kill and wound 123 men and to take more than 540 prisoners. Although Washington abandoned the works on July 18, the expedition had done much for morale.

STORE BOATS. Each year from about 1800 to the time of the Civil War numerous flatboats, fitted out as store or trading boats with shelves and counters, descended the Ohio and Tennessee rivers with the spring floods. They held large stocks of groceries, liquors, dry goods, and hardware. They carried a calico flag to indicate their character and responded to a hail from dwellers on the banks, or tied up near a plantation or hamlet too small to afford a store and announced their arrival by a blast on a tin horn.

STORES, GENERAL. In their heyday general stores quickly followed peddlers into newly occupied regions. To survive in the limited markets, storekeepers sold and bartered great varieties of merchandise to customers, marketed crops taken in trade, operated local post offices, provided credit and elementary banking services, and served as social agents. From colonial times through much of the 19th century they constituted the typical retail unit; but in 1977 they made up less than 50,000 of the 1,855,068 retail units in the United States.

***STOURBRIDGE LION*.** The first steam locomotive to run on a track in America. The Delaware and Hudson Canal Company built a railroad line between its mines at Carbondale, Pa., and its canal terminus at Honesdale, Pa. The 9-horsepower *Stourbridge Lion,* built in England, was tested at Honesdale on Aug. 8, 1829. It weighed 7 tons, whereas the company had specified only 3. The first trip was its last; it was discarded as being too heavy for any bridge.

STRANGITE KINGDOM. After the death (June 1844) of Joseph Smith, founder and prophet of Mormonism, a struggle over the vacant succession ensued. Among the aspiring prophets was James J. Strang. With the aid of "angelic visitations," Strang developed the holy city of Voree, near modern Burlington, Wis., in the years 1844–49, and attracted a considerable following of Mormons scattered throughout the country. Strang's attention was then diverted to the Beaver Islands in Lake Michigan, where in 1849 the city of St. James was founded as his new holy city. A year later the Kingdom of God on Earth was formally proclaimed, with Strang as God's vice-regent who should establish his rule in this world. Strang for six years dominated his several thousand subjects. At length he was murdered by disgruntled conspirators (June 1856), and his followers were driven into exile by a frontier mob. A tiny body of zealots remained faithful to the Strangite faith.

STRATEGIC ARMS LIMITATION TALKS (SALT). In 1968 President Lyndon B. Johnson and Leonid I. Brezhnev, Soviet Communist party chairman, agreed to open the Strategic Arms Limitation Talks. For political and military reasons, however, opening of the talks was postponed until November 1969. The official delegates met in Helsinki, and later in Vienna; but the real negotiations were carried on in secret meetings between presidential assistant Henry A. Kissinger and Soviet ambassador Anatoly Dobrynin, culminating in the SALT I agreement hammered out at the Moscow summit of 1972. SALT I limited each side to two ABM sites, outlawed mobile land missiles, prohibited interference with spy satellites, and restricted the number of strategic missiles each country could have.

SALT I lacked controls on manned bombers and on multiple warheads. At the Vladivostok summit of 1974, President Gerald R. Ford announced that he and Brezhnev had already reached a tentative SALT II agreement limiting all strategic weapons. They promised to restrict their arsenals to 2,400 strategic missiles each, 1,320 of which could have multiple warheads.

When President Carter assumed office in 1977 the U.S.-Soviet relations had cooled off. Nevertheless, U.S.-Soviet negotiations continued and in June 1979 President Carter and the Soviet President Leonid Brezhnev signed the SALT II treaty in Vienna. It was immediately attacked in the United States, the harshest critic being Senator Henry Jackson, who charged Carter with "appeasement." The debate about SALT II continued without any results until January 1980 when President Carter, in view of recent Soviet invasion of Afghanistan, asked Congress to delay the consideration of the treaty.

STRATFORD HALL. In Westmoreland County, Va., about a mile from the Potomac River; built by Thomas Lee in the 1720's. Home of the Lees until 1822. In 1929 it was acquired by the Robert E. Lee Foundation and restored.

***STRAUDER* V. *WEST VIRGINIA*, 100 U.S. 303 (1880).** A case in which the Supreme Court declared that a West Virginia statute restricting jury service to whites violated the Fourteenth Amendment. The Court also upheld the Civil Rights Act (1866) provision for removal of cases to the federal courts when equal rights were denied in state courts.

STRAWBERRY BANK (N.H.). David Thomson's settlement on the Piscataqua River (*see* New Hampshire) was taken over in 1630 by the Laconia Company. Capt. John Mason secured in 1631 more colonists who moved the settlement to the west bank of the upper harbor and named it for the many wild strawberries growing there. The company failed in 1634, leaving Mason to work alone until his death in 1635. The slowly growing Strawberry Bank formed its own government and elected Francis Williams governor, until 1641; it then placed itself under Massachusetts. In 1653 it changed its name to Portsmouth.

STREET RAILWAYS. The first street railway in America was laid on Bowery and Fourth Avenue, from Prince Street to Murray Hill, New York City, in 1832–33. It was a financial failure, and not until 1836 was another car line attempted, this one in Boston. Between 1850 and 1855, six new lines were built in various cities. In 1856 the modern type of streetcar rail was designed for a Philadelphia line. In 1855–60 thirty new lines were built; in 1860–80 eighty more came into being; by 1890 there were 769 such railways.

Beginning in the 1870's, steam cars were tried in some cities, but they were highly objectionable. The cable car next became the most popular form of rapid transit. The first such line was completed in San Francisco in 1873; during the next fifteen years most of the larger cities had one or more cable lines, but they were very costly. Electric cars, introduced between 1880 and 1890, rapidly superseded all other systems (*see* Railways, Electric). By 1920 street railways in most places were losing money heavily; fares were raised, but this only increased competition. After 1930 the railway lines began to be replaced by motor buses.

STRICT CONSTRUCTION. Those who favor strict construction believe that no government agency (president, Congress, or court) should extend the meaning of any part of the Constitution beyond its literal meaning. The argument over interpretation of the Constitution led to the development of the first major political parties in the United States; the Federalists, who believed that the federal government ought to be able to interpret its powers widely or "loosely," opposed the Jeffersonian Republicans, who wanted strict limits set on the powers of the federal government.

STRIKES. Organized work stoppages by employees, which may be classified by purpose: the organization strike, pressuring the employer to recognize the union as the collective voice of the employees; the economic strike, designed to improve economic returns to the workers through higher wages or fewer hours; the sympathy strike, bringing pressure on an employer, government body, or group of consumers to grant the demands of a group of workers other than the strikers. In the sitdown strike the strikers occupy the work premises to assure that no substitute workers are brought in. The jurisdictional strike is intended to persuade an employer to recognize and deal with the strikers in preference to another group of organized workers; the wildcat strike is a work stoppage in violation of an existing collective agreement prohibiting strikes between the parent union and the employer; the grievance strike protests an alleged failure of the employer to carry out the terms of the agreement or to settle a dispute not covered by the "prohibition to strike" clause of the contract.

Most early strikes in the United States did not involve a labor union or organization. The workers merely got together on a temporary basis to present their demands or to take joint action to protect their interests. Early court rulings declared strikes to be illegal (*see* Philadelphia Cordwainers' Case). The case of *Commonwealth* v. *Hunt* (1842) was considered by many to be the first break in the early judicial rulings: the court ruled that it was not unlawful for laborers to go on strike to gain a closed shop; illegality would depend on the means used. Labor organizations were not yet free to strike; the injunction was used against them. (*See* Injunctions.) In 1921 it became evident that the courts believed a common-law right to strike existed that they were obligated to protect. The Norris-La Guardia Act of 1932 forbade the use of injunctions in labor disputes and repudiated antiunion (yellow-dog) contracts as a basis for equal and equitable rights. Section IV of this act protected the right to strike by specifying actions that were not subject to injunctions.

The Strikebreakers Act (June 24, 1936) made it a felony to transport strikebreakers in interstate commerce. In *National Labor Relations Board* v. *Fan Steel Corporation* (1939) it was ruled that sit-down strikes were illegal. The National Labor Relations Board devised the theory that employees who strike for purely economic reasons may be replaced, but that those whose strike is caused or prolonged by unfair labor practices on the part of the employer may not be replaced or discharged. Some contracts provide for legal strikes despite the existence of a labor agreement. (*See also* Labor; National Labor Relations Act; Taft-Hartley Act.)

STRIP MINING. A technique for extracting minerals from the surface of the earth, used extensively for coal, copper ore, and iron ore. The soil and other material lying above the mineral is first stripped away; power shovels or similar tools are then used to scoop up the mineral. Strip mining is much less expensive than most other types of mining, and far less dangerous for miners. On the other hand, it usually leaves lasting scars on the earth's surface.

STUART'S RIDE (1862). As Gen. Robert E. Lee prepared to resist Union Gen. George B. McClellan's attempt to capture Richmond (*see* Seven Days' Battles), it was necessary to know the exact position of the Union right (*see* Jackson's Valley Campaign). On June 13 Confederate Gen. J. E. B. Stuart's cavalry accomplished this. Then, Stuart decided to ride around McClellan's army, since such a movement would be unexpected. On June 14 Stuart was behind McClellan; on June 15 the cavalry rode into Richmond with 165 prisoners. McClellan changed his supply base to the James River.

STUDENT NONVIOLENT COORDINATING COMMITTEE (SNCC). Founded April 1960 to coordinate the southern black college-student nonviolent direct-action protests against lunch-counter segregation that had arisen earlier in the year. With the dropping of the color bar at many dining facilities, SNCC changed from a committee coordinating campus-based groups to a staff organization that initiated its own projects in local communities and played a central role in the desegregation and voter registration campaigns that followed in the Deep South. Disillusioned, by 1966 they adopted an ideology of black separatism and revolutionary violence, which led to the ultimate disappearance of the organization.

STUDENTS FOR A DEMOCRATIC SOCIETY (SDS). The main organizational expression of the campus-based radical movement known as the New Left in the 1960's, SDS originated as the student department of the League for Industrial Democracy, a mildly social-democratic educational service. Under the leadership of Tom Hayden and Al Haber of the University of Michigan, SDS in 1962 issued the "Port Huron Statement," a sixty-four-page document that proclaimed independence from traditional radical and liberal formulas and that became a manifesto for student activists of the new generation. SDS sponsored the first national demonstration against the Vietnam war (April 1965); from then on its growth was rapid. By the end of the decade, SDS at the national level was an avowedly revolutionary organization. At many schools, notably at Columbia University in 1968, SDS chapters led disruptive protests against university ties with the military and other issues.

At its annual convention in June 1969, SDS split into two groups, one (led by members of the Progressive Labor party) advocating a worker-student alliance and the other (led in part by people who later formed the "Weather Underground") placing main emphasis on support for Third World and black revolutionaries. In 1970 SDS factions went underground.

STUMP SPEAKERS. Campaigning among the scattered settlements of the backwoods, the successful candidate for town, county, or state office, mounting a stump in a clearing, stressed the things that would appeal to his farmer, woodsman, village-storekeeper hearers. Thus was the pattern set for all later appeals to the rural vote; and stumping lasted into the 20th century, using the private train and the automobile equipped with loudspeakers.

***STURGES* V. *CROWNINSHIELD*,** 4 Wheaton 122 (1819). Ruling on the constitutionality of a New York State bankruptcy law, the Supreme Court maintained that state bankruptcy laws were permitted since congressional legislation was lacking. The Court concluded that the power of Congress to enact "uniform laws on the subject of bankruptcies" was supreme but not exclusive until Congress, by legislation, makes it so and that the obligation of contracts lies in the law that makes the contract binding at the time it is made, and provides the remedy in case of breach; but the New York law was declared invalid because it applied retroactively.

SUBLETTE'S CUTOFF. A dry branch of the Oregon Trail between South Pass and Bear River, Wyo., fifty-three miles shorter than the better-watered Fort Bridger route. Part of the cutoff was used in 1832 for pack mules by William L. Sublette, fur man and congressional aspirant. It was also called Meek's, Greenwood's, or Hedspeth's cutoff.

SUBMARINES. The first operating submarine was tested by the Dutch inventor Cornelis Drebbel (1620–24). The first submarine used in combat was built in 1775 by David Bushnell, a Yale student; a one-man wooden craft, it failed in its submerged attack on the British ship *Eagle* in New York harbor (1776). Robert Fulton built the *Nautilus* (1801) of wood covered by iron plates; although successful in submerged tests against wooden ships, it failed to interest any government. In the Civil War the Confederacy undertook the construction of various submarines. The first submarine to sink a ship was the hand-powered *Hunley,* made of boiler plate and manned by a crew of nine (*see following article*).

Modern undersea craft in America evolved from the pioneering work of John P. Holland and Simon Lake. Holland built six submarines (1875–97). His most famous craft, the 53-foot *Holland,* was built at his own expense and became the U.S. Navy's first submarine; it was launched in 1897 and accepted by the navy in 1900. Lake's company built twenty-seven submarines for the United States, with the first completed in 1911. The first German vessel, the 139-foot U-1, was completed in 1905. At the outset of World War I there were submarines in the fleets of all the major navies; the standard submarine was about 200 feet long and displaced several hundred tons on the surface. In World War II, two developments—radar and the snorkel (breathing tubes enabling submarines to draw in air for their diesels and crew from just under the surface)—had a major impact on submarine combat.

The world's first nuclear-powered submarine, the U.S.S. *Nautilus,* was launched in 1954. With a 3,000-ton displacement and 320 feet long, it cruised 60,000 miles on its initial fuel and traversed the Arctic Ocean under the ice cap, crossing the North Pole on Aug. 3, 1958.

The majority of U.S. nuclear submarines are primarily intended to destroy enemy submarines; the remainder are the fleet ballistic-missile submarines armed with strategic Polaris or Poseidon missiles for use against cities and other fixed, land targets. In the early 1980's the United States had about eighty attack submarines and forty ballistic-missile submarines.

SUBMARINES AND TORPEDOES, CIVIL WAR. The Confederacy employed the only real submarine in combat during the Civil War when the *Hunley,* a hand-propelled ironclad vessel with a spar explosive attached to its bow, attacked the Union corvette *Housatonic* in Charleston harbor, S.C., in February 1864. Both vessels sank. The Union built one submarine, the *Alligator,* which sank while under tow off Cape Hatteras, N.C.

Torpedoes—now called mines—were used principally by the Confederacy to protect its rivers and harbors. Although the first Union ironclad, the *Cairo,* was sunk by a mine in December 1862 inland on the Yazoo River in Mississippi, mine warfare was employed mainly along the coast. Mines were normally anchored to streambeds and detonated on contact or were fired manually or electronically from land. Cigar-shaped ironclad rams equipped with a spar torpedo (mine), of a class of semisubmersibles known as Davids, and other mine-equipped boats never seriously threatened the Union blockade. Nets and log booms placed around Union ships and anchorages, coupled with the use of picket boats farther out, effectively countered the offensive mines.

SUBSIDIES. The United States has been exceedingly liberal in granting subsidies to various commercial enterprises, despite frequent doubts concerning constitutionality. Throughout U.S. history, state and privately owned transportation improvements have been freely subsidized. In the 19th century Congress subsidized canals and railroads with both funds and land grants.

Mail subsidies to the merchant marine were generously granted during 1845–58, 1864–77, 1891, and after World War I. Between 1926 and 1933, $87 million in mail subsidies were given to various air transport companies. In the 19th century many newspapers were largely financed by government advertising, and a change in administration often meant loss of patronage. Cheap postage rates on fourth-class matter have also served as a subsidy to newspapers and periodicals.

The establishment in 1932 of the Reconstruction Finance Corporation and in 1933 of the Public Works Administration marked a new era in government subsidies. Not only were loans made to banks, railroads, and industrial corporations at low rates, but outright grants were offered to state and local governments for improvements. Tariffs, although not strictly speaking subsidies, have the same effect; they artificially increase the income of producers of protected goods.

SUBSISTENCE HOMESTEADS. Played an important role in the earlier stages of the nation's industrialization, since workers frequently supplemented their wages by cultivating small plots of land to supply the food required by their families. The practice declined with increasing urbanization. In 1933 the National Industrial Recovery Act provided $25 million "to aid in the redistribution of the overbalance of population in industrial centers by establishing subsistence homesteads." The Federal Subsistence Homestead Corporation built communities of homes located on tracts of one to five tillable acres, offering them at low rentals to the eligible unemployed. The program was terminated in 1942.

SUBSTITUTES, CIVIL WAR. No conscription in the North during the Civil War was absolute. There was always the opportunity for the drafted man to hire a substitute. This was first allowed in the militia draft of 1862. The Conscription Act of Mar. 3, 1863, legalized this method of draft evasion. Until the act of Feb. 24, 1864, the conscript could choose between hiring a substitute or paying $300 as commutation of service. Thereafter, substitution alone was permitted, except for conscientious objectors. Exemption by substitution extended until the next draft, when the principal again became liable. At once prices of substitutes rose far above $300. Legal draft evasion became the prerogative of only the unusually well-to-do. The Confederacy also allowed a limited substitution system.

SUBTREASURIES. After President Andrew Jackson had the government's deposits removed from the second Bank of the United States, they were placed in so-called "pet banks." This did not prove satisfactory, and an act, approved July 4, 1840, set up an independent treasury. Subtreasuries were established at New York, Philadelphia, Charleston, New Orleans, St. Louis, and Boston; and later at Chicago, San Francisco, and Cincinnati. The Federal Reserve Act of 1913 provided that the Federal Reserve banks might act as fiscal agents for the government. This made the subtreasuries unnecessary. The last one was abolished Feb. 10, 1921.

SUBURBAN GROWTH. "Suburban growth" describes both the radial expansion of one or more clusters at an urban site and the integration of previously distinct settlements into a unified economic and social system. Even in the 1970's small towns in the Northeast, protected from adjacent cities by substantial open spaces, were being suburbanized in much the same way as the Plymouth Colony was suburbanized by Boston in the 17th century and Brooklyn by New York City in the 19th century.

The older pattern has been reversed in the largest cities in the nation. They are denser at their centers and more capital-intensive in their land use than small cities. As a result, only in their outer rings do they usually allow for the spacious single-family dwellings. Through the 19th and into the 20th century most of these cities were able to consolidate their outer rings into unified political units. After about 1920, large city annexation was sharply reduced as the suburban areas became more politically organized.

SUBVERSION. Subversive activities of totalitarian inspiration aroused congressional concern in the 1930's and led to the creation of the Special Committee on Un-American Activities in 1938, which in 1945 became a standing committee of the House of Representatives.

In 1946 defected Soviet code clerk Igor Gouzenko revealed the existence of widespread Soviet espionage in Canada and led indirectly to the arrest and conviction of Klaus Fuchs, Julius and Ethel Rosenberg, and others. The following year, alarmed at the extent of Communist penetration of government and its cold war implications, the administration of Harry S. Truman promulgated Executive Order 9835 to screen government employees for subversive connections.

Testimony before the House Committee on Un-American Activities in 1948 by confessed former Soviet espionage agents Elizabeth Bentley and Whittaker Chambers revealed extensive policy and espionage penetration of the federal government at high echelons. Of the fifty or so persons named as spies or contacts, a majority took the Fifth Amendment.

Public fear of Communist activities reached its high-water mark in the late 1940's and early 1950's. Sen. Joseph R.

McCarthy became chairman of the Senate Committee on Government Operations (*see* McCarthy-Army Hearings). The McCarthy affair brought congressional probes of Communism into a disrepute from which they never fully recovered.

SUBVERSIVE ACTIVITIES CONTROL BOARD. *See* **Federal Agencies.**

SUBWAYS. Street congestion in the larger American cities was becoming intolerable in the late 19th century. Elevated railroads in New York, Chicago, and Boston were unsatisfactory because of noise, unsightliness, and depreciation of adjacent property values. Between 1895 and 1900 Boston removed 1.7 miles of trolley-car tracks from crowded streets and placed them underground.

By 1900, when New York City's first contract for a subway was let, a billion passengers a year were riding crowded, slow streetcars. The first subway line was opened by the Interborough Rapid Transit Company on Broadway in 1904. By 1930 the Interborough operated 224 miles of subway and 139 miles of elevated line. The Brooklyn Rapid Transit Corporation developed a network of lines in Brooklyn and entered Manhattan by three tunnels under the East River, the last completed in 1924. The Hudson and Manhattan Tubes, completed in 1911, connected Manhattan with Jersey City, Hoboken, and Newark, N.J. In 1940 the New York subway system was unified under the Board of Transportation, which became the New York City Transit Authority in 1953. In 1981 it operated about 230 miles of subway routes.

Philadelphia opened its first subway in 1907. After 1920 Newark, St. Louis, and Los Angeles placed short sections of their surface-car lines underground. Between 1938 and 1943 a short subway was built in Chicago to supplement the elevated lines. The Bay Area Rapid Transit (BART) system in the San Francisco area, opened in 1973–74, comprises 75 miles of line, of which 16 are in tunnels under the city. In 1976 the first stage of a comprehensive metropolitan transit system, 4.5 miles of subway, was completed in Washington, D.C.; by 1981 about 40 miles and 44 stations had been opened.

SUEZ CRISIS (October-November 1956). In July 1956, following Egypt's trade agreement with the Soviet Union, the United States and Great Britain withdrew an offer to aid in the construction of the Aswan High Dam on the Nile River. Egypt retaliated by nationalizing the Universal Suez Canal Company, an international corporation that long had operated the Suez Canal. Britain and France, dependent on oil supplies brought through the canal, proposed that the United States endorse their employment of military force to recover control of the canal. U.S. Secretary of State John Foster Dulles emphatically refused. The crisis came to a head on Oct. 29 when Israel, fearing further raids by Egypt, invaded the Gaza Strip and the Sinai peninsula, inflicting a stinging defeat on the Egyptian forces. The Israeli military operation was followed two days later by preconcerted British and French attacks on Egypt. The United States, backed by the Soviet Union, was instrumental in a call by the United Nations for an immediate cease-fire. This was arranged (Nov. 2) and an international peace force was dispatched to the Near East, where it remained until May 1967.

"SUFFERING TRADERS." A group of men trading to the western Indian tribes who lost horses, goods, and in some instances their lives to Indians on foray during Pontiac's War (1763). Their sufferings were set forth as a basis for compensation in the form of a land grant at the Treaty of Fort Stanwix in 1768.

SUFFOLK, OPERATIONS AT (1863). In February 1863 Confederate Gen. James Longstreet's corps was detached from Gen. Robert E. Lee's army to the vicinity of Petersburg, Va. Longstreet went with two divisions into southeastern Virginia to collect forage and provisions. He became involved in a fruitless siege of Union headquarters at Suffolk (April).

SUFFOLK BANKING SYSTEM. In 1818 the Suffolk Bank in Boston agreed to redeem the notes of any New England bank at par if the issuing bank would keep with it a permanent deposit of $2,000 or upward and deposit sufficient funds to redeem any of its notes that might reach Boston through the ordinary channels of trade. Country bankers were enraged, for the plan threatened to reduce note circulation and the profit of their banks. But the Suffolk Bank persisted and by 1824 other Boston banks joined. Specie redemption so elevated the standing of all New England bank notes that they gradually were accepted at par throughout the country. This specie plan was incorporated into the National Bank Act of 1863.

SUFFOLK RESOLVES (Sept. 9, 1774). The best-known meeting held in Massachusetts in 1774 to protest the Coercion Acts was that of delegates from Boston and other towns in Suffolk County, held at Dedham on Sept. 6 and adjourned to Milton on Sept. 9. Joseph Warren presented the resolves, which refused obedience to the acts, or to officials created under them; urged weekly militia musters, nonpayment of taxes, and nonintercourse with Great Britain; and suggested a provincial congress meet at Concord in October. The resolves were passed unanimously and endorsed by the Continental Congress on Sept. 17.

SUFFRAGE. *See* **Franchise; Voting; Woman's Rights Movement.**

SUFFRAGE, AFRO-AMERICAN. Voting requirements and access to suffrage were written into state constitutions or passed by state legislatures during the Revolution. In some cases free blacks were excluded; in others they were not. By 1840 over 90 percent of the free blacks lived in states that excluded them from or put limitations on suffrage.

After the Thirteenth Amendment (1865) had ended slavery, the Fourteenth Amendment sought to nationalize citizenship and remove it from the caprice of states. It made blacks citizens of the United States and the state in which they lived, prohibited the enforcement by states of laws that would abridge the privileges of citizens, and required each state to provide equal protection of the law for all. To establish voting firmly as a right, the Fifteenth Amendment (1870) provides that "the right of citizens of the United States to vote shall not be denied or abridged by the United States or by any State on account of race, color, or previous condition of servitude."

Blacks voted in numbers throughout the South during Reconstruction and the years immediately following. However, legal and extralegal efforts to destroy their political influence began immediately. Secret societies of southern whites—the Ku Klux Klan was the most powerful—used threats and violence to discourage blacks from voting. Southern states used several methods of disfranchisement—gerrymandering, complicated registration and voting procedures, state constitutional changes, poll taxes, and literacy tests, and property-ownership requirements (*see also* Grandfather Clause).

Improvement took place after 1914 mainly through the Supreme Court, the movement by blacks to states having no official limitation on suffrage, and federal legislation to protect voting rights. The Supreme Court declared unconstitutional the grandfather clause, voided white primaries, and struck down gerrymandering efforts. The Twenty-fourth Amendment, adopted in 1964, prohibited use of the poll tax as a requirement for voting in federal elections. The Supreme Court invalidated the poll tax as a requirement for voting in state elections in 1966. Further action was still needed to insure voting rights for blacks in the South. The alternative to which blacks turned in the 1950's and 1960's was protest demonstrations..

Even after the passage of the Civil Rights Act of 1964, which was intended to eliminate existing loopholes in the area of voting, southern officials found ways to prevent blacks from voting. Their actions led to further demonstrations by blacks. Reaction to white violence stimulated the drive that led to passage of the Voting Rights Act of 1965. The new law suspended literacy tests and other devices in states and counties that used them and in which less than 50 percent of those of voting age had voted in 1964. It also authorized sending federal registrars to areas where local officials refused to obey the law.

SUFFRAGE, COLONIAL. Voting qualifications were fixed by each colony, and in many the requirements were changed during the colonial period. The generally accepted philosophy was the English concept that only those with "a stake in society" should vote. American practice generally mirrored English theory, each colony establishing some property qualification for voting. Many colonies had alternatives to landholding as a suffrage qualification, usually the possession of other property but sometimes mere taxpaying.

Limitations of race, sex, age, and residence were more often the result of custom than of law. Generally, Jews and Roman Catholics were barred, usually by their inability to take the English test oaths with regard to the Anglican church. Maryland and New York specifically barred Catholics by statute, and New York excluded Jews by law in 1737. These prohibitions were not always enforced. Jews appear on New York City voting lists in 1768 and 1769, and Catholics voted in Virginia in 1741 and 1751. Women were excluded by statute only in four colonies, but there is rare evidence that any ever voted anywhere. The age qualification was almost universally twenty-one. Pennsylvania's two-year residence requirement was the most stringent. Slaves and indentured servants were denied the franchise, and in the Carolinas, Georgia, and Virginia, freed blacks as well. Indians did vote at times in Massachusetts.

SUFFRAGE, EXCLUSION FROM THE. It is generally estimated that because of state property and taxpaying qualifications, fewer than one-fourth of all white adult males were eligible to vote in 1787–89. States had largely abandoned the property qualifications for voting by 1850. The Fifteenth Amendment, ratified in 1870, forbade denial of the right to vote "on account of race, color, or previous condition of servitude." The Nineteenth Amendment (1920) prohibited denial of the right to vote on account of sex. The poll tax was outlawed for federal elections by the Twenty-fourth Amendment (1964) and for state elections by a Supreme Court decision (1966). The Twenty-sixth Amendment (1971) lowered the age limit for federal and state voting to eighteen. Obstacles to Afro-American suffrage were progressively eliminated by Supreme Court decisions (1944, 1965) and by federal legislation, notably the Voting Rights Act of 1965. Lengthy local residential qualifications were declared unconstitutional by the Supreme Court in 1972. Unequal voting power resulting from malapportionment was held unconstitutional in Court decisions beginning in 1962. By 1972 all persons over eighteen, of whatever sex, color, or race, were legally entitled to vote.

SUFFRAGE, WOMAN. *See* **Woman's Suffrage.**

SUGAR ACTS. In 1764 George Grenville, chancellor of the Exchequer, enacted a new sugar act, by which he undertook to end the smuggling trade in foreign molasses and at the same time secure a revenue (*see* Molasses Act). The duty on foreign molasses was lowered from six to three pence a gallon, the duties on foreign refined sugar were raised, and an increased export bounty on British refined sugar bound for the colonies was granted. The net result was to give the British sugar planters an effective monopoly of the American sugar market; smuggling of foreign sugar became unprofitable; and the old illicit trade in foreign molasses was disturbed. There were violent protests at first; two years later the duty was lowered to one penny a gallon, applied alike to foreign and British imports, and the protests came to an end. At this lower rate it was an important revenue producer.

Other phases of the Sugar Act of 1764 were far more irritating: a new duty on wine imported from Madeira; and new bonding regulations compelling ship masters to give bond, even when loaded with nonenumerated goods (*see* Enumerated Commodities). Bond had to be given before any article enumerated or nonenumerated was put on board. Any ship caught with any article on board before bond covering that article had been given was subject to confiscation.

SUGARCANE. Brought to the New World by Christopher Columbus; first cultivated successfully in Louisiana around the mid–18th century. Although efforts to make sugar from the cane juice succeeded in Louisiana and Florida, until the 1790's cane was cultivated mainly for syrup and rum. As a result of a protective tariff, the introduction of cold-resistant cane varieties, the adoption of steam power for grinding cane, and notable advances in the processes of clarification and evaporation of cane juice, the growth of the cane sugar industry was impressive prior to the Civil War. Although cane was grown for syrup mainly on small farms in the South, only on the large plantations in south Louisiana and Texas was a successful sugar industry established. Although sugar production in Texas ended in the 1920's, a thriving industry emerged in Florida. When Puerto Rico and Hawaii were acquired by the United States in 1898, sugar culture was already well established in both areas.

SUGAR HOUSE PRISONS. There were several sugar refineries commonly called sugar houses in New York City when the American Revolution began. These sturdy brick and stone buildings were used by the British as prisons. Shocking narratives were prevalent of cruelty and privations in these prisons.

SUGAR INDUSTRY. In colonial America sugar was made from maple sap for household use and local trading. Major improvements were made in the manufacture of sugar, including the introduction in the 1820's of steam power for crushing cane and the invention in the 1840's of a multiple-effect system for evaporating cane juice, which replaced the open kettle boilers and revolutionized sugar manufacture.

Prior to 1861, most Louisiana cane sugar was shipped to cities throughout the Mississippi Valley and the East Coast, and much of it was consumed in the form of raw sugar. Refiners in eastern cities imported raw sugar from the West Indies and produced a dry, white sugar.

In the 20th century further improvements occurred in sugar culture and manufacture (*see* Sugarcane). In the late 19th and early 20th centuries, the cultivation of sugar beets spread from the Great Lakes to California, and in both cane and beet processing, large expensive central mills dominated the manufacture of sugar. By the 1960's the refining branch of the sugar industry was dominated by large corporations and was concentrated in coastal cities.

SUGAR ISLANDS. Popular name in colonial times for the sugar-producing islands of the West Indies, not including the Greater Antilles.

SUGAR TRUST. First applied to a combination of owners of sugar refineries effected in 1887, which was held to be illegal by the New York Court of Appeals. The term thereafter applied to the American Sugar Refining Company, organized in 1891 under the laws of New Jersey. With merely a change in name and in technical legal form, the practical management remained the same. By March 1892 the trust had obtained a practical monopoly of the business of refining and selling sugar. The combination was prosecuted by the Department of Justice as a combination in restraint of interstate commerce, prohibited by the Sherman Antitrust Act of 1890, but the Supreme Court in 1895 held that the primary business of the American Sugar Refining Company was manufacturing, not commerce; and that the act did not prohibit combinations of manufacturers.

SULFUR INDUSTRY. *See* **Chemical Industry.**

SULLIVAN-CLINTON CAMPAIGN (1779). Planned by Gen. George Washington in an effort to curb the attacks of the Indians and Tories on the frontiers of New York and Pennsylvania. Originally planned in 1778 as a westward movement along the Mohawk River, the main drive was shifted in 1779 to the Susquehanna River. The command was given to Gen. John Sullivan. In order to hold the eastern tribes of the Iroquois in check, Gen. James Clinton, who was in charge of the New York wing of the army, sent Col. Goose Van Schaick in April to make a surprise attack on the Onondaga. The major force of the campaign was mobilized in Easton, Pa. On June 18 Sullivan with about 2,500 men moved toward Wyoming, Pa. On Aug. 11 the army reached Tioga, and the following day the greater part of the troops was pushed forward to attack the Indian town of Chemung. The Indians fled and ambushed part of the men, killing six. Sullivan fell back to Tioga, where Fort Sullivan was built for supplies. On Aug. 22 he was joined by Clinton, with 1,500 men, who had proceeded southwestward from Canajoharie on the Mohawk, destroying the Indian villages on the upper Susquehanna. On Aug. 26 Sullivan moved his whole force toward the territory of the Cayugua and Seneca. At Newtown, near the present city of Elmira, N.Y., the Indians and Tories made their only stand and were driven from the field. From Newtown the army pushed forward to old Genesee Castle. Forty Indian villages were burned and 160,000 bushels of corn destroyed. Failing to make a junction with Col. Daniel Brodhead, Sullivan returned to Easton.

SULLIVAN IN RHODE ISLAND (1778). Because of expected reinforcement by a French fleet under Comte Jean Baptiste d'Estaing, with 4,000 soldiers, Brig. Gen. John Sullivan planned a joint attack on the British at Newport, R.I. D'Estaing arrived off Newport early in August. A British squadron appeared, and D'Estaing decided to attack it, but a furious gale damaged his ships and sent him to Boston for repairs. Lacking d'Estaing's support, Sullivan withdrew, and the British pursued. On Aug. 29, a spirited fight took place, the Battle of Rhode Island, or Battle of Quaker Hill. All British attacks were repelled, but news of coming British reinforcements caused Sullivan to cross to Tiverton on the mainland. The British returned to Newport.

SULLY, FORT. Built by Gen. Alfred Sully in 1863 as a station for the army in the war against the Sioux. It was first located three miles below Pierre, S.Dak., but in 1866 was relocated twenty-eight miles above Pierre where forage was more abundant. It was abandoned in 1891.

SULLY'S EXPEDITIONS. *See* **Dakota Expeditions of Sibley and Sully.**

SUMMER RESORTS. *See* **Resorts and Spas.**

SUMMIT CONFERENCES. Summit meetings involving the United States since World War II have been of two types, one held between adversaries and the other among allies, and at two levels, between chiefs of government and between foreign ministers. Summitry serves several purposes. A summit gathering can signal major changes in the relationships between the participants, as did Dwight D. Eisenhower's 1955 meeting with the Soviet leaders or Richard M. Nixon's 1972 journeys to Peking and Moscow. A second aim is to resolve major conflicting interests. Thus, Nixon and the Soviet leaders signed an arms control agreement. A third objective is for the leaders to take one another's measure. John F. Kennedy met Nikita S. Khrushchev in Vienna in 1961 to caution him not to confuse American restraint with a lack of will to uphold vital interests and therefore precipitate a confrontation through miscalculating. Summit meetings of allies usually intend to strengthen the alliance and solve disagreements; an example is the annual summit of leaders of seven industrial nations, which was initiated in 1975.

SUMNER, FORT. A military post on the Pecos River in east central New Mexico, established in 1862, near Bosque Redondo, a reservation where 8,000 Navaho and 400 Mescalero Apache were held as prisoners of war. Regular troops had been withdrawn from New Mexico because of the Civil War, and the Navaho had increased their raids on the Rio Grande settlements. Kit Carson and his militiamen pursued a strategy of killing Navaho sheep and destroying crops until starving Navaho began to straggle in to Fort Defiance to surrender. Eventually 8,000 of them made the "Long Walk" of 300 miles to detention at Fort Sumner. In 1868, after signing a treaty, the Navaho were permitted to return to a new reservation in their homeland in northeastern New Mexico and adjacent Arizona, and Fort Sumner was abandoned.

SUMNER'S EXPEDITION (1857). Depredations by the Cheyenne in Kansas and Nebraska caused Col. Edwin V. Sumner to march against them from Fort Leavenworth with six companies of cavalry and three of infantry. On July 29 the cavalry encountered 400 warriors on Solomon Fork of the Kansas River. A pitched battle ensued, with Sumner losing eight men, killed or wounded. Leaving one company, which built Fort Floyd, to protect the wounded and sick, he fruitlessly pursued the Indians. Marching 1,000 miles, the soldiers returned to Fort Kearny in August, many barefooted or destitute of clothing.

SUMPTUARY LAWS AND TAXES, COLONIAL. "Sumptuary laws" usually refer to legal attempts to regulate food, clothing, morals, amusements, church attendance, and Sabbath observance. There were sumptuary laws in all of the colonies. The laws against wearing gold decorations, lace, silks, and similar materials when one's station in life did not warrant such expensive clothing were confined mostly to the 17th century and were not peculiar to New England. In 1621 directions were sent to Virginia limiting the right to wear such apparel to members of the council. Laws against sex immorality were similar in all the colonies, although in the South they were directed particularly against relations of whites with blacks.

SUMTER, FORT. Situated on a sandbar at the mouth of the harbor of Charleston, S.C., and commanding the sea approach to the city. On the night of Dec. 26, 1860, following the passage of the Ordinance of Secession (Dec. 20) by South Carolina, Maj. Robert Anderson, in command of the Union forces at Charleston, removed his garrison from Fort Moultrie, on Sullivan's Island, to Fort Sumter. Upon assuming the office of president in March 1861, Abraham Lincoln dispatched a fleet to relieve the fort. With this fleet momentarily expected at Charleston, Gen. Pierre G. T. Beauregard, in command of the Confederate forces, offered Anderson a final opportunity to evacuate. This was not accepted, and at 4:30 on the morning of Friday, Apr. 12, the Confederate batteries opened fire on Fort Sumter. On Apr. 13, after a bombardment of thirty-four hours, Anderson surrendered; the Civil War had begun.

On Apr. 7, 1863, Fort Sumter, garrisoned by Confederates, was attacked by a Union fleet of nine ironclads. This engagement inflicted one of the greatest defeats in U.S. naval history, and inaugurated the era of the modern steel navy.

In August 1863 the great siege of Fort Sumter, by combined Union naval and land forces, began and lasted for 567 days. Fort Sumter was never surrendered by the Confederates. On Feb. 17, 1865, when the approach of Gen. William Tecumseh Sherman's army of 70,000 made the evacuation of the whole Charleston sector inevitable, the fort was closed and abandoned.

SUN COMPASS. A nonmagnetic instrument that indicates direction by using the path of the sun as a reference line. The Ordinance of 1785 provided for a rectangular system of land survey based on astronomical lines. William A. Burt of Michigan, a surveyor, convinced that the magnetic needle could not be relied upon for accuracy, invented the sun compass (patented 1836).

SUN DANCE. One of the great communal rituals among the Plains Indians. Although the ceremonies were most often initiated by an individual, generally in the name of a relative or associate killed in battle, the more pervasive purpose of the rites was to restore order in the world, to effect for the benefit of the group the continuation of life, the world, and the human enterprise. Among the major features of the Sun Dance were a specially obtained central dance pole, a characteristic lodge, elements of self-torture by the dancers, the lowering of sexual restrictions, altars, priestly figures, and vows of revenge against enemies. At the dance, held in series of four-day cycles, four being a sacred number, dancers might skewer the flesh of their back to cords and allow themselves to be suspended from the central pole.

SUNDAY SCHOOLS. The Sunday school was formed in the American colonies solely to give religious instruction. Francis Asbury organized what was probably the first Sunday school in America, in Hanover County, Va., in 1786. Four years later the American Methodists officially adopted the Sunday school. In December 1790 Bishop William White of the Protestant Episcopal church formed a Sunday school in Philadelphia; and in January 1791 he and others of Philadelphia organized the First Day Society (Sunday School Society), an interdenominational body and the first of its kind. Sunday schools then began to appear in numerous places. The early Sunday school movement was largely interdenominational. In 1817 the American Sunday School Union was organized in Philadelphia. In 1824 the union began the publication of its *Sunday School Magazine,* the beginning of a vast Sunday school literature. In 1903 the Religious Education Association was formed to raise the teaching standards of Sunday schools.

SUPERIOR, LAKE. Largest of the Great Lakes and the largest body of fresh water in the world; probably discovered by Étienne Brulé about 1622. During the 17th and early 18th centuries French explorers investigated the various shores, founded missions, and built trading posts and forts. In the days of the fur trade three canoe routes were used from Lake Superior to the West, by way of Grand Portage, the Kaministikwia River, and the St. Louis River at Fond du Lac; and important posts were maintained at Sault Ste. Marie and Grand Portage, the latter being removed in 1801 by the North West Company to Fort William, at the mouth of the Kaministikwia. The search for copper mines led to the building of the first sailing ship on Lake Superior in 1737.

In the 19th and 20th centuries Lake Superior became the center of an important mining region, which includes the Sudbury district (copper, nickel) in southern Ontario and the Mesabi Range (iron) in Minnesota. To provide access to the lower Great Lakes, a ship canal was built (completed 1855) along the St. Marys River. A number of industrial, manufacturing, and port cities were established on the lake, including Duluth, Minn.; Superior, Wis.; and Sault Ste. Marie.

SUPERMARKET. *See* **Self-Service Stores.**

SUPPLY, CAMP. A post established on the Canadian River in present northwest Oklahoma by Gen. Alfred Sully in November 1868. From this point Gen. George A. Custer began his Washita campaign of 1868, and it was important in the Indian war of 1874–75. It was abandoned about 1895.

SUPREME COURT. Created by the Judiciary Act of 1789; originally consisted of a chief justice and five associate justices. Congress has varied the size of the Court, but since 1869 the Court has included a chief justice and eight associate justices. All justices are appointed by the president, subject to confirmation by the Senate. It is unusual for the Senate to refuse to confirm a presidential nomination. Political considerations are usually important factors in the nomination and confirmation process. The appointee's philosophy is invariably a subject of extensive inquiry and debate in the Senate Judiciary Committee and on the floor of the Senate.

The justices hold office for life and can be removed from office only by impeachment, which requires a two-thirds vote of the Senate. No Supreme Court justice has ever been impeached. The first black justice, Thurgood Marshall, was appointed in 1967 and the first woman justice, Sandra Day O'Connor, began to serve in 1981.

Six justices constitute a quorum. The regular term begins on the first Monday in October and generally ends the following June. In unusual circumstances the Court may hold a special term during the summer recess.

The Court disposes of a large number of cases each year. For example, in the 1980 term 5,144 cases were filed, 4,357 cases were disposed of, oral argument was heard in 154 cases, and 123 opinions were written. The Supreme Court's main business is to review appeals from the lower federal courts and from the state courts in cases arising under the federal Constitution, an act of Congress, or a treaty of the United States. Having the power of judicial review, the Court may declare federal and state statutes to be unenforceable if found to be in conflict with the Constitution. Since the great power-limiting clauses of the Constitution, such as the due process and equal protection guaranties, are phrased in very broad and generous language, the Court has much room in which to maneuver. It has also had the responsibility of drawing the lines between individual liberties and permissible social controls.

SUPREME COURT PACKING BILLS. Congressional measures designed to alter the composition of the Supreme Court to correct alleged judicial errors or to secure desired decisions. They characteristically have taken the form of changes in the number of justices.

The Judiciary Act of 1789 fixed the number of justices at six; this number was successively altered to five in 1801; six in 1802; seven in 1807; nine in 1837; ten in 1863; seven in 1866; and to nine in 1869, where it still stood in the 1970's despite the effort in 1937 of President Franklin D. Roosevelt to increase the number to as many as fifteen. Some of these alterations were attempts to reduce the work load of the Court or to render it more efficient rather than to pack it.

The Judiciary Act of 1801 was an attempt to pack the federal judicial system rather than the Court itself. Having lost the election of 1800 to the Republicans, the Federalists moved to entrench themselves in the federal courts. This attempt to pack the Court with Federalists was thwarted by the Democratic-Republicans, who on Mar. 8, 1802, repealed the judiciary act of the previous year.

During the Civil War period, another packing bill was enacted. In July 1866 Congress reduced the size of the Court (then composed of ten members) to seven to prevent President Andrew Johnson from appointing justices who might overrule the Radical Reconstruction program over which

Congress and the new president were at loggerheads. In April 1869, the number was increased to nine.

The most important court-packing bill in American history was rejected by Congress. This measure was the one proposed by Roosevelt. Angered by a series of decisions that had emasculated his New Deal, he submitted a plan to Congress on Feb. 5, 1937. Among other provisions, the plan authorized the president to appoint an additional justice for each one who, having reached the age of seventy, failed to retire. The total number of Supreme Court justices was not to exceed fifteen. After some five months of intensive congressional and public debate, the Senate rejected the president's proposal.

SURGERY. *See* **Medicine and Surgery.**

SURROGATE'S COURT (court of probate). A county court having jurisdiction over the settlement of the estates of deceased persons. It receives wills for probate, issues letters of administration, supervises the management of the property, hears and allows claims against the estate, and decrees distribution in accordance with the probated will or, if no will, the laws of inheritance. In many states such a court also has jurisdiction over guardianships of minors, insane persons, habitual drunkards, and spendthrifts.

SURTAX. An additional tax paid on the same "tax base" as an original tax. It may take the form of a flat percentage imposed on the price of some product already taxed. Income surtaxes may be added in the income tax as originally computed or in the form of an extra percentage of the tax.

SURVEY ACT OF 1824. Interest in national internal improvements increased after Secretary of the Treasury Albert Gallatin's Report on Roads, Canals, Harbors, and Rivers (1808). After two bills were vetoed by Presidents James Madison and James Monroe, Rep. Henry Clay introduced the General Survey Act in 1824, passed by Congress and approved by Monroe. The act authorized the president, with the aid of army engineers, to conduct surveys of such canal and turnpike routes as would serve an important national interest.

SURVEY SYSTEM, NATIONAL. *See* **Public Lands, Survey of.**

SUSAN CONSTANT. Flagship of the three vessels conveying the founders of the first successful English settlement in the New World; sailed down the Thames for Virginia on Dec. 20, 1606. The ship and its consorts, the *Godspeed* and *Discovery,* were under the command of Christopher Newport. Arriving at Chesapeake Bay, the ships landed, Apr. 26, 1607, at the cape named Henry. After sailing well up the Powhatan (James) River to have better protection against Spaniards, the colonists established themselves at a site which they named James-Forte or Jamestowne (May 14, 1607).

SUSQUEHANNA COMPANY. A merging of a number of smaller groups of Connecticut farmers who organized at Windham, Conn., in 1753 for the purpose of settling on lands in Wyoming Valley, in northeastern Pennsylvania, basing their claim on the Connecticut Charter of 1662. The company leaders engaged John Lydius to effect a purchase of lands from the Six Nations, and this was done at the Albany Congress in 1754. The Susquehanna Company merged with the first and second Delaware companies, started a settlement at Wyoming in 1762 (wiped out by Indians in 1763), sent Eliphalet Dyer to London in 1764 to obtain a charter for a separate colony, and, after the Treaty of Fort Stanwix (1768), established the town of Wilkes-Barre.

SUSQUEHANNA SETTLERS. Sent from Connecticut into the valley of the Susquehanna River in Pennsylvania by the Susquehanna Company. The French and Indian War made any further effort at settlement unwise until 1762. (*See* Susquehanna Company.)

***SUSSEX* CASE.** On Mar. 24, 1916, the English channel steamer *Sussex* was attacked by a German submarine. Eighty persons were killed or injured, two of the latter being Americans. The United States stated that unless Germany "should immediately declare and effect an abandonment of its present methods of submarine warfare against passenger and freight-carrying vessels," the United States would sever diplomatic relations with Germany. The German government gave the necessary assurances, but with the qualification that Great Britain abandon the blockade of Germany. The United States refused to accept the German qualification. When Germany renewed submarine warfare on Feb. 1, 1917, the United States severed relations (Feb. 3).

SUTLER MERCHANT. A feature of army life until after the Civil War. Because army posts frequently were located at considerable distances from towns, some arrangement had to be made to furnish troops with simple luxuries and wants to supplement regular army rations. Consequently, a civilian was given a contract to keep a store at each army post. The post council determined his stock, regulated prices, and sometimes claimed a small part of his profit.

SUTRO TUNNEL. Adolph Sutro, operator of an ore stamp mill at Virginia City, Nev., conceived the idea of a tunnel into the side of Mount Davidson to intercept all the mines on the Comstock silver lode, drain them of water and gases, and make ore removal easier. Ground was broken in 1869. Unable to obtain funds in America, Sutro found backers in England. The tunnel broke through into the Savage Mine July 8, 1878, but by that time the best days of the Comstock lode were over. The tunnel property was sold in 1889 to satisfy the English investors' bond mortgage.

SUTTER'S FORT. Built in 1841 on the site of what is now Sacramento, Calif. Near this stronghold, on land belonging to Capt. John Augustus Sutter, gold was discovered on Jan. 24, 1848. Following the discovery of gold in California, squatters dispossessed Sutter. By 1852 Sutter was bankrupt.

SWAMP ANGEL. An 8-inch Parrott gun used by Union soldiers in the siege of Charleston, S.C., in 1863. It was mounted on a battery constructed on piles driven into the swamp. After firing thirty-six shots, it burst on Aug. 23.

SWAMP FIGHT. *See* **Great Swamp Fight.**

SWAMPLANDS. The public land states contained great areas of swamp and overflowed lands that were neglected by the early settlers, who could not drain them. By the Swamp Land Act of 1850, 70 million acres passed into the possession of the states.

"SWANEE RIVER." The popular title given in America to Stephen Collins Foster's "Old Folks at Home" (published 1851).

SWEATSHOP. An undesirable work environment characterized by job insecurity, low wages, long hours, and poor, often unhealthful, working conditions. Historically, the garment trades and cigar manufacturing in the years 1880–1910 provide outstanding examples of sweated trades.

SWEDEN, NEW. *See* **New Sweden Colony.**

SWEDENBORGIANISM. *See* **New Jerusalem, Churches of the.**

SWEDISH IMMIGRATION. *See* **Immigration.**

SWEEPING RESOLUTION (Ohio General Assembly, January 1810). Declared vacant all judgeships and other state offices filled by appointment by the assembly for seven-year terms on the ground that all such terms began with statehood in 1803 and had expired. The purpose was to fill the judgeships with men amenable to the will of the legislature. The principle of the resolution was repealed in 1812.

***SWIFT* V. *TYSON*,** 16 Peters 1 (1842). In *Swift* v. *Tyson* the rule was established that in matters of commercial law where the federal court deemed a uniform rule preferable to separate state rules, it might give its own interpretation of the common law. On the basis of this decision a considerable body of common law of commercial relations developed. The rule was reversed in *Erie Railroad* v. *Tompkins* in April 1938.

"SWING ROUND THE CIRCLE." A tour that President Andrew Johnson made to Chicago (Aug. 28–Sept. 15, 1866) to participate in laying the cornerstone of a monument to Stephen A. Douglas and to bring his moderate views on Reconstruction before the people.

SWISS SETTLERS. *See* **Immigration: The German Wave.**

SYCAMORE SHOALS, TREATY OF (1775). Negotiations began on Mar. 14, 1775, between Judge Richard Henderson, representing North Carolina (Transylvania Company), and Chief Attakullaculla of the Cherokee, at Sycamore Shoals on the Watauga River. On Mar. 17 a treaty was signed that conveyed to the members of the Transylvania Company the vast domain lying between the Kentucky River and the south watershed of the Cumberland River—about 17 million acres. The recited consideration was £2,000. A smaller tract was conveyed by a separate instrument called the Path Deed.

SYMMES PURCHASE. *See* **Miami Purchase.**

SYNDICALISM (revolutionary industrial unionism). In the United States syndicalism has been identified with the Industrial Workers of the World (IWW), founded in 1905. The IWW supported the creation of strong, centralized unions and was opposed to action through the existing government. The aim of the syndicalists was the establishment of a producers' cooperative commonwealth, in which industries would be socially owned, but managed by *syndicats* or labor unions. Syndicalists emphasized the class struggle, were opposed to militarism, imperialism, and patriotism, and advocated direct action, mainly sabotage and the general strike. Antisyndicalist laws in several states developed from the fact that the movement sought the abolition of political government, tended to condone violence, and was uncompromisingly militant. The syndicalist movement waned after World War I.

SYNOD OF DORT. An assembly of delegates from the principal Reformed or Calvinistic churches of the Netherlands, Germany, Switzerland, and England, was held at Dort (Dordrecht) during 1618–19. The synod condemned the doctrine of free will propounded in Holland during the previous two decades. It published five canons, declaring the approved Calvinist positions concerning innate depravity, irresistible grace, election, reprobation, and the perseverance of the saints. These canons thereafter furnished the standard of orthodoxy for Congregational and Presbyterian churches.

SYRACUSE (N.Y.). Fifth largest city in New York State, with a population of 170,105 in 1980. The city is an industrial center located on a site long used by Onondaga Indians before white men reached the region. It is built over and near important salt deposits, which provided the Iroquois tribes with the means of preserving meat. The earliest industry of the modern city was also based on salt. Syracuse received its city charter in 1825.

TABERNACLE, MORMON. A large turtle-shaped auditorium in Salt Lake City, built between 1863 and 1867. It is noted for its acoustic properties and the fact that the massive roof is a lattice truss held together by wooden pegs and strips of rawhide. It rests on forty-four red sandstone piers. The auditorium seats 8,000 and the general conferences of the Mormon church are held in it.

TABLOIDS. *See* **Newspapers.**

TACNA-ARICA CONTROVERSY. Under the Treaty of Ancón (1833), which ended the Chile-Peru War, Chile was to hold Tacna and Arica for ten years, after which a plebiscite was to determine the disposition of these formerly Peruvian provinces. The terms of the plebiscite repeatedly brought the two powers to the verge of war until they agreed in 1922 to arbitration by the president of the United States. In 1925 President Calvin Coolidge decided that the plebiscite should be held under the direction of a commission representing the two countries and the United States but in June 1926 the United States and Peru decided to terminate the plebiscitary proceedings, on the ground that the Chilean authorities had made a free vote impossible. At the suggestion of Secretary of State Frank B. Kellogg diplomatic relations between Chile and Peru were resumed in 1928. The following year a proposal made by President Herbert Hoover was accepted whereby Chile returned Tacna to Peru but retained Arica, paying a $6 million indemnity.

TACOMA (Wash.). Third largest city in the state of Washington, with a population of 158,501 in 1980; the center of a metropolitan area which included 482,692 people. Tacoma is a seaport and a manufacturing city. Its port facilities on Puget Sound have been important for shipping lumber products. The city is close to a major U.S. Army base (Fort Lewis) and acts as a supply center for troops based there, in addition to its market activities for surrounding farms, paper mills, and electric parts manufacturers.

TAFIA. A low-grade rum, originating principally in Louisiana and the West Indies, which served as a staple of trade and a medium of exchange between the Indians and the French and Spanish in the Mississippi Valley and the Floridas.

TAFT COMMISSION (second Philippine Commission). Supervised the transfer from military to civil government in the Philippine Islands. The commission of five assumed legislative authority on Sept. 1, 1900. The president of the commission, William Howard Taft, became civil governor on July 4, 1901. The commission organized the administrative services and passed laws concerning health, education, agriculture, and public works. On Sept. 1, 1901, three Filipinos were also appointed to the commission, and each American member became an executive department head. In 1907 the commission became the upper house of the Philippine legislature.

TAFT-HARTLEY ACT (Labor-Management Relations Act). Enacted on Aug. 22, 1947. Sponsored by Sen. Robert A. Taft and Rep. Fred Hartley, it amended the National Labor Relations Act of 1935 (Wagner Act) in reaction to the unregulated growth of organized labor and certain alleged abuses of power by some labor leaders. The Wagner Act gave employees the right to organize and bargain collectively free from employer interference. In 1937 the Supreme Court declared the act constitutional.

Whereas the preamble of the Wagner Act limited the blame for labor disputes obstructing commerce to employers, the Taft-Hartley Act extended the blame to the conduct of unions. The definition of unfair labor practices by employers was tightened. The freedom of unions in the exercise of economic pressure was limited by six unfair union labor practices. Other major changes consisted of allowing the employees the right to reject organization; the closed shop agreement was outlawed; state right-to-work laws were given precedence over the Taft-Hartley provision for union shops by majority vote of the workers; unions were prohibited for the first time from engaging in secondary strikes; unions could be sued as entities; political contributions and expenditures of unions were restricted; internal union affairs were regulated and reports were required to be filed; no benefits were accorded any labor organization unless the union officers filed affidavits showing that they were free from Communist party affiliation or belief; and the power of "discretionary injunction" was restored to the courts. The act remained unchanged until passage of the Landrum-Griffin Act in 1959.

TAFT-KATSURA MEMORANDUM (July 29, 1905). An "agreed memorandum" between Secretary of War William Howard Taft and Prime Minister Taro Katsura of Japan. The memorandum invoked Japanese-American cooperation "for the maintenance of peace in the Far East." Thus it expressed an approval by the Roosevelt administration of Japanese suzerainty over Korea and a disapproval by Japan of "any aggressive designs whatever on the Philippines." This agreement remained secret until 1925.

TAFT-ROOSEVELT SPLIT. At the outset of the administration of Republican President William Howard Taft (1909) political observers in Washington, D.C., noted adverse criticism of the president by men who had been closely associated with Theodore Roosevelt's reform policies. Within a year, in both House and Senate, the Republican party was seriously divided. Gradually the general issue was drawn between those who supported Taft, backed by the party machine in both Senate and House and most of the states, and those who were known as Insurgents, led by Sen. Robert M. La Follette. On Aug. 31, 1910, in Kansas, Roosevelt delivered his "New Nationalism" speech, interpreted as an attack on Taft's conservatism. In the congressional and state elections the Republicans suffered general defeat. The following year the Insurgents organized the Republican-Progressive League, and in 1912 the Progressive-Republicans selected La Follette to contest in the primaries with Taft for the presidential nomination. La Follette's failure led seven Republican state governors to urge Roosevelt to permit the use of his name in the preconvention canvass. Regular party leaders, including many former friends of Roosevelt, kept control of the national convention and renominated Taft. Roosevelt bolted, organized the Progressive party, and became that party's candidate for the presidency. Roosevelt and Taft were both defeated by the Democratic candidate, Woodrow Wilson.

TALISHATCHEE, BATTLE OF. *See* **Creek War.**

TALLADEGA, BATTLE OF. *See* **Creek War.**

TALLAHASSEE (Fla.). Capital city of Florida, with a population of 82,548 in 1980. Tallahassee has two major universities: Florida State University and Florida Agricultural and Mechanical University. The city is an important shipping and marketing center for a large region of pine forests and farms.

Tallahassee had been a sort of capital for the Apalache Indians before Spanish explorers reached the area. The city is inland from the Gulf of Mexico, but it served as a collection and shipment center for cotton and other products in the 19th century. During the Civil War, it was defended in small-scale battles against Union forces sent from the Gulf coast. The last Confederate victory in the eastern part of the country was won in defense of Tallahassee (Mar. 6, 1865).

TALLMADGE AMENDMENT. A bill proposed on Feb. 13, 1819, by Rep. James Tallmadge of New York to amend Missouri enabling legislation by forbidding further introduction of slavery into Missouri and declaring that children born of slaves after admission of the state should be free upon reaching the age of twenty-five. The House adopted the amendment but the Senate rejected it. The Missouri Compromise (1820) settled the issue.

TALL STORIES. Comic folktales characterized by grotesque exaggeration. The tall story has flourished in the United States and is thoroughly characteristic of the popular psychology that resulted from the rapid expansion of the country in the 19th century. The subjects of the tall stories, or tall tales, were things with which the tellers were familiar: weather, fauna, topography, and adventure. Plainsmen told of seeing prairie dogs 20 feet in the air digging madly to get back to the ground. In the southern highlands astounding tales arose, such as that of David Crockett, who used to save powder by killing raccoons with his hideous grin. Other characters who were subjects of tall stories were Tony Beaver, a West Virginia lumberman; Paul Bunyan, a northern lumberman, with his blue ox, Babe; Mike Fink, king of the Keelboatmen; Freebold Freeboldsen; Kemp Morgan; and Pecos Bill.

TAMMANY HALL. Patterned after the prerevolutionary Sons of Saint Tammany, named for Tamanend, a legendary Delaware chief, the Society of Saint Tammany was founded in May 1789 by William Mooney as a patriotic, fraternal society with an elaborate Indian ritual. The society became identified with Thomas Jefferson's Democratic-Republican party. Tammany joined the Aaron Burr faction in New York City, which opposed the faction headed by De Witt Clinton. The Federalist members resigned from the society and Tammany lost all pretense of nonpartisanship. As the city grew, so did the opportunities for aggrandizement in the form of franchises, contracts, and patronage for Tammany supporters. The venality of the board of aldermen—most of them Tammany men—in the 1850's earned them the title of the Forty Thieves. Upon the election of Fernando Wood as mayor in 1854, city hall became and remained a Tammany fiefdom until the advent of Fiorello La Guardia in 1933. With the elevation of William Marcy Tweed to grand sachem of the Tammany Society in 1863, the fraternal organization was subsumed by the political. Tammany became the prototype of the corrupt city machine. The corruption of the Tweed Ring was all pervasive. (*See* Tweed Ring.) "Honest" John Kelly turned Tammany into an efficient, autocratic organization that for several generations dominated New York City politics. Kelly's successor was Richard Croker, somewhat more in the Tweed mold. In 1932 Mayor James J. Walker was brought up on corruption charges before Gov. Franklin D. Roosevelt and resigned. In retaliation the Tammany leaders refused to support Roosevelt's bid for the Democratic nomination for president. As a result, the Roosevelt faction funneled federal patronage to New York City through the reform mayor, La Guardia (a nominal Republican). Carmine G. De Sapio briefly revived Tammany Hall in the 1950's, but lost control of his district to reformers in 1961. Shortly thereafter the New York County Democratic Committee dropped the name Tammany.

TAMMANY SOCIETIES. Organizations patterned after the New York and Philadelphia Tammany societies appeared in several states about 1810. Rhode Island politics were controlled by a local Tammany society in 1810–11; an Ohio society played an active part in the factional struggles of Republicans in 1810–12.

TAMPA (Fla.). A city located on Tampa Bay in western Florida, with a population of 271,523 in 1980. Tampa is a seaport, and one of the leading industrial and commercial cities of the Gulf Coast area. Large quantities of Florida's phosphate rock are shipped for eventual use as fertilizer in American and foreign farm areas. It is a major center in the orange juice canning business, and one of the world's greatest cigar-making cities.

Tampa Bay was the landing area of Hernando De Soto in his 1539 expedition; however, the Spaniards were unable to establish a town on the site because of Indian opposition. A garrison of U.S. troops was installed in Fort Brooke on the bay in 1824, and an American town developed around the fort. Tampa Bay was used as a base by Confederate blockade runners and then by Union naval vessels during the Civil War. It served as one of the chief supply bases for U.S. forces during the Spanish-American War. Tampa developed rapidly after its first railroad reached the city in 1884.

TAMPICO AFFAIR. *See* **Veracruz Incident.**

TAOS (N.Mex.). Officially Don Fernando de Taos; a town and resort on the Rio Grande about seventy miles from Santa Fe. Within three miles of one another stand Taos Pueblo, one of the oldest existing pueblos in the United States, and Ranchos de Taos, a Spanish town built before 1680. The pueblo was discovered in 1540 by some of Francisco Vásquez de Coronado's men; Juan de Oñate's expedition arrived there in 1598 and gave it its present name. Spaniards came as missionaries early in the 17th century. With Taos as headquarters, the Indian leader Popé planned and carried out in 1680–82 a general revolt against Spanish rule (*see* Pueblo Revolt). After 1822 Americans made Taos the center of a very active fur trade. At the turn of the 20th century Taos developed as an art colony. The population in 1980 was 3,369.

TAOS TRAIL. The route of the Taos Trail varied considerably; roughly it ran north from Taos, crossed the Sangre de

Cristo Range at La Veta Pass, and followed the Huerfano River to the Arkansas. It served as a road for Spaniards and later for American fur trappers.

TAPPAN PATENT. A tract of wild land located at Tappan, N.Y., on the west side of the Hudson; purchased (July 1, 1682) from the Indians, with the permission of the governor of New Jersey, by a group of Dutch farmers residing on Manhattan Island. In 1683 some of the shareholders settled on the land. The following year a boundary dispute arose between New York and New Jersey, and New York ordered the settlers to prove their title. On Mar. 17, 1687, a patent was issued by Gov. Thomas Dongan to the subscribers; in 1704 the land was legally apportioned.

TAR. Made in the American colonies as a by-product of land clearing and as a regular industry, both to supply local shipyards and for export. In 1705, moved by a desire to lessen the navy's dependence on Sweden for naval stores, Parliament established bounties upon those imported from the colonies including one of £4 sterling per ton on tar. Annual shipments of pitch and tar from the colonies to Great Britain increased from less than 1,000 barrels to more than 82,000 barrels. The commercial manufacture of tar expanded, especially in North Carolina, and during the era of wooden ships it remained important. In the 20th century most of the tar produced was distilled to yield carbolic oil, naphtha, and other crude products.

TAR AND FEATHERS. Pouring molten tar over the body and covering it with feathers was an official punishment in England as early as the 12th century. It was never legal in the United States, but was always a mob demonstration. A number of Loyalists were tarred and feathered at the beginning of the revolutionary war. The practice vanished in the late 19th century.

TARASCON, BERTHOUD AND COMPANY. Louis A. Tarascon, John A. Tarascon, and James Berthoud fled from France during the French Revolution. They settled in Ship pingport on the Ohio (which became a part of Louisville, Ky.), and engaged in milling and other commercial activities.

TARAWA (Nov. 20–24, 1943). As the opening blow in the American offensive through the central Pacific, U.S. Marines under the command of Maj. Gen. Julian C. Smith began landing on Betio, an islet in the Tarawa atoll, on the morning of Nov. 20. Tarawa, part of the Gilbert Islands, had been occupied by the Japanese early in the war. Despite heavy preassault bombardment, the 4,500 defenders fought back stubbornly from strong defenses. Moreover, many assault craft grounded on a reef, and the marines had to wade 400–500 yards to the beach through devastating Japanese fire. By nightfall 5,000 Americans had landed, but over 1,500 were killed or wounded. A final Japanese counterattack was defeated on the night of Nov. 22–23, and the last defenders were eliminated on the 24th.

TARIFF. A duty levied on goods coming into the ports of a nation from foreign sources (called a specific duty if levied at so much per article or unit of weight or measure; called ad valorem if levied at so much per dollar value). Tariffs may be either for raising revenue or for protecting the domestic economy. A policy of absolutely unhampered economic intercourse is described as free trade (*see* Free Trade). As a practice and as a philosophy of the national government, levying import duties was born with the Constitution, while the stipulation was clearly made that exports should not be subject to duties.

The Democratic party, since the beginning of the nation, has traditionally sponsored low tariff rates. Whether the rates have been high or low, revenue has been an important aspect of the U.S. tariff. Money for the maintenance of the government until 1860 was derived overwhelmingly from the customs dues. From 1868 until the end of the first decade of the 20th century the tariff, thoroughly protectionist, was still the greatest single contributor of revenue.

Tariff Commissions. *The Revenue Commissions.* Section 19 of the Internal Revenue Act of Mar. 3, 1865, authorized the secretary of the Treasury to appoint a commission of three persons to "inquire and report" on how much money should be raised by taxation to meet the needs of the government, the sources from which it should be drawn, and the "best and most efficient mode of raising the same." The commission was neither impartial nor nonpolitical, with two protectionists and one representative of Western agrarian, Democratic, and other minority interests. A new tariff bill was put before the House on June 25, 1866. In July leaders of the hopelessly entangled Congress substituted for the commission the new Office of Special Commissioner of the Revenue. The office came to an end on June 30, 1870.

Tariff Commission of 1882. In December 1881 President Chester A. Arthur, confronted with domestic and foreign economic disturbances and plagued with a Treasury surplus of $100 million, recommended a tariff commission. The report of the commission as submitted to Congress cited facts to show that some of the high rates were injurious to the interests supposed to be benefited. Reductions in the general tariff were recommended. No basic changes were made, and the Democrats, when they returned to power in the House in December 1883 let the commission die.

Tariff Board. President William Howard Taft created the Tariff Board, which made studies of discriminatory practices on the part of foreign states and investigated American industries in relation to cost of production, duties demanded, and duties already exacted. But the board's life was short. The Democrats, suspecting anything Republican as protectionist, refused in 1912 to make appropriations for its continuance.

Tariff Commission of 1916. President Wilson in 1916 appointed what is often referred to as the first nonpartisan tariff commission. The work of the commission was first used in the preparation of the incongruous Fordney-McCumber tariff of 1922. That legislation not only continued the commission but also increased its powers. The president was authorized to raise or lower duties by not more than 50 percent of the ad valorem rate on articles that threatened to capture American markets because of a higher cost of production. Although it was obvious that Europe could pay its huge debt to the United States only through the shipments of goods, the Tariff Commission under the Smoot-Hawley tariff continued its cost investigations.

Tariff Powers of the President. The president has become a powerful factor both in shaping and in applying the tariff. The authority necessary to carry out the reciprocity provisions of the tariffs of 1890 and 1897 was carefully circumscribed, but in 1909 the president was given rather broad powers in the Payne-Aldrich bill. These powers were further enlarged in 1922, when, in the Fordney-McCumber Tariff Act he was delegated the right to raise or lower established duties by 50 percent without further reference to Congress.

Tariff of 1789. Controversy over tariff for revenue only and tariff for protection began with the First Congress. A bill of 1789, presented by James Madison as a simple means of raising money, emerged as a partially protective measure. Several states were able to impose ad valorem duties in defense of leading articles of manufacture in the new nation. On Dec. 5, 1791, Secretary of the Treasury Hamilton submitted his brilliant Report on Manufactures, but his pleas for further protection were ignored. Congress did make many changes by increasing duties on special items and by enlarging the free list of raw materials, but the general level remained much the same.

Tariff of 1816. The bill passed in April 1816 marks the beginning of tariff for protection. Cotton and woolen goods and pig iron and hammered and rolled bars were especially favored. Estimates of the general average rate of protection have varied from 30 percent to 45 percent. The argument for higher rates continued. The South was becoming a bitter enemy of a tariff system that seemed to benefit only manufacturers. Growers of foodstuffs and hemp, flax, and wool in western Pennsylvania, Ohio, Indiana, Illinois, Kentucky, and Missouri joined the middle Atlantic states in a protectionist alliance and in 1824 passed a new tariff that not only raised the rates of 1816 substantially but also placed duties on such untaxed products as lead, glass, hemp, silk, linens, and cutlery.

"Tariff of Abominations." The woolen manufacturers especially were dissatisfied with tariff of 1824. In 1827 the deciding vote of Vice-President Calhoun alone defeated a bill that would have raised the ad valorem duty on woolen cloth to about 70 percent. In that same year delegates from more than half the states, in a meeting at Harrisburg, Pa., spoke out dramatically for general tariff increases. The tariff issue had become not only sectional but partisan as well. Jackson supporters are charged with constructing a tariff in such a way that its anticipated defeat would isolate New England but bring enough support in New York, Pennsylvania, and the West—with the vote of the South—to elect the general. The measure was pushed through Congress in 1828.

Cottons, woolens, iron, hemp, flax, wool, molasses, sailcloth, and whatever else could be protected was protected in the new bill. The tax on raw wool, molasses, and sailcloth irked the New Englanders, but enough of them voted for the measure to pass it. Nobody was pleased; the phrase "tariff of abominations" was bandied about everywhere and in the South became a rallying point for nullificationists.

Compromise Tariff of 1833. Henry Clay pushed through Congress in 1832 a bill that removed most of the objectionable features of the "abominations" tariff and lowered general duties slightly below those of 1824. But in November 1832 South Carolina declared the act (as well as its predecessor) null and void. Jackson asked Congress for a force act authorizing the use of military power.

Clay and Calhoun worked out a compromise plan. They revised the tariff and passed the force bill on Mar. 1, 1833. To please the South they enlarged the free list and stipulated that all rates above 20 percent should be lowered to that level by June 30, 1842. To placate the protectionists they provided for gradual reduction of one-tenth every two years until 1840 (the remaining six-tenths was to be removed in the last six months). The compromise tariff was replaced by a measure that reversed temporarily the downward trend of duties. Because financial and business conditions had improved, the trend turned downward again in the Walker Act of 1846, and further reductions were made in 1857.

Morrill Tariffs. The first of the Morrill tariffs, enacted Mar. 2, 1861, was precipitated by the panic of 1857. Succeeding acts in 1862 and 1865 raised the rates to undreamed-of heights. Revenue was not completely forgotten, but the need to assuage American manufacturers upon whose products heavy internal revenue taxes had been levied was far more important. The end of the Civil War and a growing Treasury surplus soon brought repeal of most of the internal revenue levies. The Morrill tariffs, however, remained basically undisturbed until 1890, when they were raised.

McKinley Tariff of 1890. The Republicans chose to regard the election of Benjamin Harrison to the presidency in 1888 as a mandate for higher tariffs. Rep. William McKinley's bill, pushed through the House by Speaker Thomas B. Reed, was reshaped in the Senate. Taxes on tobacco and alcohol were reduced, but the tariff duties were raised appreciably. Bounties were given sugar growers, and for the first time a reciprocity provision was included.

Wilson-Gorman Tariff of 1894. Success seemed within reach of the tariff-reform Democrats, but hopes of reductions soon faded. The Harrison administration had stripped the Treasury of its surplus, a paralyzing panic fell on the country, and Cleveland split his party into bitter factions by his determined repeal of the Sherman Silver Purchase Act. The bill that William L. Wilson introduced in the House in 1894 fell in the Senate into the hands of Arthur P. Gorman of Maryland, a protectionist Democrat, and was completely reshaped; 634 amendments were added. Cleveland let the Wilson-Gorman bill become a law without his signature.

Dingley and Payne-Aldrich Tariffs. After victory in 1896, the Republicans pushed through the House the bill that Nelson W. Dingley introduced in March 1897. After 872 amendments and two months in the Senate, the bill emerged from Congress with the highest duties ever passed. By 1908, pressure for reduction had become so great that even the Republicans seemed to promise downward revision.

The moderate House bill that Sereno E. Payne submitted early in 1909 was quickly passed. Nelson W. Aldrich reshaped it in the Senate; 847 amendments were made, almost wholly in the interest of higher duties. The tariff remained protectionist.

Underwood Tariff of 1913. In tariff philosophy President Wilson represented not only the majority of his party but also intellectuals, who had long been questioning protectionist practice. Soon after Rep. Oscar W. Underwood of Alabama revealed his tariff proposals to the special Congress in 1913, the lobbyists flocked into Washington. The president struck out in a biting condemnation and the "third house" departed. Approved by the Senate with few changes, the measure became effective in October, providing the first real and consistent reductions since the tariffs of 1846 and 1857. Rates averaged roughly 26 percent; some had not been lower since the first tariff. Unfortunately the low duties never had a chance to prove themselves because of World War I.

Fordney-McCumber and Smoot-Hawley Tariffs. Pulling the nation out of its economic difficulties by increasing protection after World War I was attempted by an emergency tariff of 1921 designed to soothe the discontented farmers and check some beginning imports from Europe. But it was the bill introduced in the House by Joseph W. Fordney and taken up in the Senate by Porter J. McCumber that sought to withdraw the nation from the economic world. The farmers were again promised impossible prosperity by levying duties on products already in overabundance at home. The rates in general were the highest in American history, and a flexible provision by which the president could revise rates up or down by 50 percent ensured maintenance of the equal-cost-of-production principle. Conditions did not improve materially, and the only answer was more protection. The Smoot-Hawley Act of June 1930 set a new record in restrictive legislation. European nations passed retaliatory laws. The depression grew worse, war-debt payments from Europe ceased, and world economy ground to a standstill.

Tariffs by Reciprocity Agreements. Sen. Cordell Hull of Tennessee became secretary of state under President Franklin D. Roosevelt and in 1934, by authority of the Reciprocal Trade Agreements Act of that year, inaugurated a series of executive agreements with foreign nations by which he in part freed trade not only for the United States but, also, by applying the most-favored-nation clause principle, for other nations as well. But World War II, with its appalling destruction, soon swept over Europe and Asia. Old nations and new needed everything but had no money with which to buy, and the United States, surfeited with goods, had no place to sell. In the United States it was obvious also that Europe, the major prewar market of the United States, must be restored. Thus the Marshall Plan, the Point Four program, and various other restorative measures were instituted.

In the United States tariff had already ceased to be a strictly domestic and political issue. Foreign considerations had become a major factor in the formulation of tariff policy. It was obvious that a free world economy required an international mechanism for payments. A conference at Bretton Woods in New Hampshire in 1944 set up the basic machinery for a world monetary system. The two significant units were the International Monetary Fund (IMF) and the International Bank for Reconstruction—known simply as the World Bank.

Economic restoration after World War II rested heavily on American money and on international reform in tariff duties. The General Agreement on Tariffs and Trade (GATT), formulated by many nations in Geneva in 1947 and devoted in large part to the reduction of tariffs and the abolition of trade discriminations, was firmly established by January 1948. The United States, largely ignoring the International Trade Organization (ITO), actively participated in the work of GATT from the beginning. Although tariff reform in the nation was still governed by the Trade Agreements Act of 1934 and its many extensions (eleven by 1958), significant reductions in U.S. duties were made in the immediate postwar years. Reformers provided safeguards against injuries to industries through "peril point" judgments and "escape clause" decisions. A peril point judgment was the rate of duty judged to be the minimum that would not injure the particular industry involved. Escape clause decisions provided for relief from injuries after rate reductions had been agreed on.

1960–72. Although an undercurrent of bitterness was apparent, the 1960's opened on an expanding economy. The Democrats had won the presidency under John F. Kennedy in 1960; and ministers were preparing for a session in Geneva to set up ground rules for the coming meeting of GATT. But the last extension of the Reciprocal Trade Agreements Act of 1934 was to expire in June 1962, and a new law was needed if the dream of the reformers was to be achieved.

In the legislation he proposed, Kennedy sought power not only to make tariff revisions at home but also to bargain with authority abroad. Foreign imports, he argued, could do little damage to the United States because of its tremendous industrial potential.

A bill was enacted as the Trade Expansion Act in late summer 1962. The president was given permission to make across-the-board tariff cuts of 50 percent or more on a most-favored-nation basis, to include agricultural items, and to reduce tariff levies up to 100 percent on a few items. Tariffs of 5 percent of less could be entirely eliminated, as could duties on certain tropical products. He was required to insert terminal dates on all items negotiated, consult the Tariff Commission and the departments concerned, and withhold most-favored-nation status from any country dominated by Communism. He was directed to reserve any article from negotiation that was protected under the escape clause and any products included in the act's national security amendment, as, for instance, petroleum.

The general meeting of GATT, called the Kennedy Round, convened at Geneva on May 16, 1964. For nearly four years the GATT delegates argued over reducing international tariff barriers equitably. The achievements were substantial. The United States won its initial argument over the method of reducing rates. The escape clause was appreciably modified as the government for individual plants—not a complete industry—assumed responsibility for training and otherwise aiding workers who had lost their jobs and also for reestablishing the displaced industrialist. Tariff reductions were, in view of the enormity of opposing factors, remarkable. The average rate arrived at was slightly more than 35 percent; 66 percent of the imports of the industrialized countries—except meat, cereal, and dairy products—were either freed of duty or subject to 50 percent or more reduction. On the other hand little was done concerning tariffs on such items as iron and steel, textiles, clothing, and fuel. Most nations were disappointed, but the agreement was signed on Jan. 30, 1967.

While the delegates from the United States were urging free international trade at Geneva, many at home were pressing hard for a return to a protective tariff. Americans were angered by European grumbling about NATO and the IMF. The European countries were working together; Canada refused to join any group; the countries of Latin America were in the developing stage; and it appeared the United States might be standing alone. In addition the balance of trade had swung heavily against the United States in the late 1950's.

By 1970 the protectionist movement had achieved its greatest intensity since the days of the Great Depression. Industrialists were thoroughly convinced that the escape clause as modified in the 1962 Trade Expansion Act was no friend of the manufacturers and that the Tariff Commission and other agencies concerned were interested only in economic philosophy.

Congress, urged by many groups at home and irked by French and Japanese protective actions abroad, was by late 1970 pushing hard toward restrictive legislation. On June 29, 1971, the cry went up, "Stop the flow of imports!" "Save American jobs!" The Burke-Hartke Act, which provided that the nation should, in effect, return to the tariff rates of the Smoot-Hawley law of 1930, was passed. Foreign reaction to the Burke-Hartke Act was quick and uncompromising. Some European countries placed immediate restrictions on American goods; and in November at a meeting of 102 nations, a common and biting retaliation was agreed on. Pressure for repeal of the Burke-Hartke Act soon appeared in the United States, and was backed by many groups, including labor. On Dec. 24, 1971, Congress repealed the act. At the beginning of 1972 world leaders were speaking out for freer international trade. But inflation, sweeping over Europe and Japan, further threatened unity. Even some of the leaders of the movement to liberate world commerce had faltered. Rep. Wilbur D. Mills, chairman of the powerful House Ways and Means Committee, wavering in his long-time devotion to free trade, declared that he would support higher tariffs and import quotas unless "some other countries mended their ways."

The U.S. administrations of the late 1970's and early 1980's generally advocated a free trade policy, despite calls from American manufacturers for import restrictions. President Ford's limits on specialty-steel imports seemed to indicate that the country was moving toward protectionism, but one of the first decisions Jimmy Carter took as a president was to reject shoe-import curbs (mainly from Taiwan and South Korea). President Reagan had also strong free-trade views. His policy statement on U.S. foreign trade, released in July 1981, declared that "import restrictions, subsidies to domestic industries and other market-distorting measures should be avoided." This approach was strongly criticized by labor representatives who charged that lack of trade barriers meant loss of jobs for Americans.

TARIFF BOARD. *See* **Tariff.**

TARIFF COMMISSIONS. *See* **Tariff.**

"TARIFF FOR REVENUE ONLY." *See* **Tariff.**

"TARIFF OF ABOMINATIONS." *See* **Tariff.**

TARPLEY LETTER (July 9, 1849). Hoping to prevent submission or secession of the South, Sen. John C. Calhoun wrote Collin S. Tarpley, urging that Mississippi call all those who desired to save the Union and southern institutions to meet and issue an address on southern grievances. The Nashville Convention resulted.

TASK FORCE 58 (1944–45). In World War II the Pacific Fleet of the U.S. Navy was divided into the Third and Fifth (or Central Pacific Force) fleets, of which the fast carriers became (January 1944) Task Force 58 (TF 58). This system, which enabled ships to be transferred between commands with a minimum of administrative detail, became the basis for postwar naval organization afloat. It included up to sixteen "fast" (33 knots) aircraft carriers. Designed originally to seek out and destroy the Japanese fleet and naval air forces, the carriers did so in 1944 at the battles of the Philippine Sea and of Leyte Gulf; and as a defensive covering and air support for the amphibious forces in 1943–44, they participated in the captures of the Gilbert, Marshall, New Guinea, Mariana, Palau, and Philippine islands and in the neutralization of Truk. During 1945 they supported the landings at Iwo Jima and Okinawa.

TAVERNS. The colonial tavern or inn served as a political headquarters and village club; a stopping place for travelers; and a place of refreshment. In Pennsylvania the word "inn" predominated, but "tavern" was generally preferred in New England; in Virginia and many parts of the South a hostelry was apt to be called an ordinary. U.S. friendship with France during the American Revolution caused the gradual introduction of the word "hotel," and "tavern" came to be applied to a mere drinking place.

TAXATION. The imposition of compulsory contributions on the subjects of a government for meeting all or part of the expenditures of that government.

Colonial Period. The government expenditures of the colonies were relatively simple and limited. The taxing systems varied in the three main sections of the country. The New England colonies favored a poll (capitation or head) tax; a tax on the gross produce of the land, which was finally developed into a general property tax; and a faculty tax (an arbitrary tax on the assumed income or earnings of laborers, artisans, and tradesmen). The southern colonies, dominated by large landowners, preferred import and export duties, supplemented at times by the poll tax. The middle Atlantic colonies evolved a mixed system of import duties, excises on beverages, and property taxes. In all the proprietary colonies, except New Netherland, quitrents (very light annual feudal payments on all grants of land) were imposed, but were resisted by the colonists. The local colonial governments maintained themselves by fees, fines, and compulsory contributions of services; by voluntary monetary contributions early in colonial history; and by taxes on real and personal property throughout the rest of the colonial period.

Until the end of the French and Indian War (1763) England never attempted to collect much revenue from the colonies. In 1765 Parliament passed the Stamp Act, which, contrary to precedent, was an internal tax imposed from without; the resentment against this tax, and against the 1764 sugar tax, led the colonists to oppose all forms of taxation by England on the principle of "no taxation without representation." Parliament in 1767 revived its tax policy and imposed import duties on certain commodities through the Townshend Acts; a strong colonial nonimportation movement caused Parliament in 1770 to repeal all these duties, except that on tea.

Revolution and Confederation Period. In 1775 the Continental Congress authorized an army and navy, a committee for foreign affairs, the supervision of the frontier Indians, and the administration of the post office. Although heavy war taxes might have been desirable, the colonies had not granted to the Continental Congress the power to levy taxes; requisitions on the colonies could not be imposed by force by any central authority and were little honored. Consequently, Congress depended for its revenue mainly on the issuance of paper money and on domestic and foreign loans. The colonial or state governments had the power to levy taxes: the New England states, New Jersey, and Maryland used this power to cover their expenses, to retire their own early currency issues, and to raise part of their contributions to the Continental government; New York, Pennsylvania, and the southern states made no attempt to levy direct taxes.

The Articles of Confederation (1781) did not confer upon the Congress the right to levy taxes, but did empower it to contract debts and to apportion the sums needed to cover its expenses among the states in proportion to the value of the land, buildings, and improvements thereon within each state. The taxes for paying that proportion were to be levied by the legislatures of the several states; however, the states proved indifferent. Efforts in 1781–82 to secure approval for a Confederation land tax, a poll tax, and a liquor excise were fruitless.

1789–1865. The framers of the new constitution of 1787 strengthened the national government by empowering Congress "To lay and collect Taxes, Duties, Imposts and Excises, to pay the Debts and provide for the common Defence and general Welfare of the United States" (Article I, Section 8). (*See also* General Welfare Clause.) But certain limitations were imposed: all duties, imposts, and excises were to be (geographically) uniform throughout the United States; direct taxes were to be laid in proportion to the population; no duties were to be imposed by Congress on articles exported from any state. On the other hand, no export or import duties were to be imposed by any state without the consent of Congress. Direct taxes were understood to be taxes on land and poll taxes—an interpretation sanctioned by U.S. Supreme Court decisions (1796–1881). The first use by Congress of its tax powers was in the passage of the tariff act of July 4, 1789. (*See also* Tariff.) The American people were by their past political experience hostile to internal taxation, but when the early customs duties failed to produce adequate revenue, Congress established an internal revenue system. From 1791 to 1802 Congress experimented with excise taxes on all distilled spirits (1791); on carriages, the sale of certain liquors, snuff manufacture, sugar refining, and auction sales (1794); and with stamp duties on legal transactions, including a duty on receipts for legacies and probates of wills—the first step in the development of the federal inheritance tax (1797). The first direct tax was imposed in 1798 on all dwelling houses, lands, and slaves between twelve and fifty.

The unpopularity of the 1791 tax led to the Whiskey Rebellion in 1794 and to the 1802 abolition of the Federalist system of excise duties and direct taxes, with the exception of the salt tax (eliminated in 1807). For revenue President Thomas Jefferson relied on customs receipts, land sales, and the postal services. The War of 1812 forced Congress to adopt new internal taxes: direct taxes on houses, lands, and slaves were enacted in 1813, 1815, and 1816 for some $12 million and apportioned among the states on the basis of the 1810 census. Congress also enacted duties on liquor licenses, auction sales, carriages, refined sugar, distilled spirits, and other articles. But these duties and the direct taxes were repealed late in 1817 in response to popular pressure.

Congress passed a series of internal revenue bills between 1861 and 1865 that revived the direct tax, introduced the first national income tax and genuine national inheritance tax, and restored excise taxes on spirituous and malt liquors, tobacco, and carriages. It also developed many new excise taxes, on manufactured goods (especially luxuries); the gross receipts of transportation and insurance companies; the circulation, deposits, and capital of banks; stamps on legal documents and instruments of evidence; and licenses for carrying on certain trades, professions, and businesses. The principle of progressive income taxation was embodied in both the 1862 and 1864 internal revenue acts, as was the important administrative device of tapping revenue at the source. During the Civil War the Congress of the Confederate States of America passed a direct tax; an income tax; a property tax on naval stores, agricultural products, and all kinds of money and currency on hand and on deposit; a tax on profits from any business; and a license tax.

These taxes were insufficient, and the Confederacy resorted to issuing bonds and paper money.

1866–1913. Internal revenue taxes were gradually repealed between 1866 and 1883, after which the only commodities taxed were liquor and tobacco. Political pressure led first to the reduction of the income tax in 1867 and 1870 and then to its expiration in 1872. The taxes on legacies and successions were repealed in 1870. In 1894 Congress passed a 2 percent tax on all personal and corporate income over $4,000, including gifts and inheritances, but the Supreme Court in 1895 (*Pollock* v. *Farmers' Loan and Trust Company*) declared that the tax on rents or income from property was a direct tax, had to be apportioned among the states according to population, and was unconstitutional unless so apportioned.

The Spanish-American War in 1898 forced Congress to nearly double the tobacco and beer taxes, to adopt special stamp and occupation taxes, and to impose a tax on legacies and distributive shares of personal property, graduated both according to the degree of relationship and the amount of the estate. (*See also* Inheritance Tax Laws.)

The Progressive movement had as a major objective the passage of a federal income tax law. To prevent the passage of such a law, conservative Republicans put through Congress in 1909 the first federal corporation tax since the Civil War, a 1 percent tax on the net income above $5,000 of every corporation organized for profit. The Supreme Court decided that the 1909 tax was not a direct tax but an excise. In 1913 the Sixteenth Amendment was adopted, with its explicit grant of power to Congress to levy income taxes without apportionment among the states. This sanctioned the 1913 federal income tax law with a progressive rate scale that had as its maximum a 7 percent tax on personal net income over $500,000, as well as a 1 percent tax on corporate net income.

1914–40. Congress passed four major revenue acts between October 1914 and February 1919 that greatly increased the rates of the corporation and personal income taxes and added a special tax on munitions manufacturers, an estate tax, an excess profits tax, a war profits tax, transportation taxes, and a wide variety of new excise taxes on goods and services, mainly luxuries and amusements. The duties on fermented liquors, wines, and tobacco were raised. The principle of progression was applied to the corporation, estate, personal income, excess profits, and war profits taxes so as to increase the burden on high incomes and large fortunes. The tax on personal incomes rose to 77 percent on income over $1 million. A tax was imposed on undistributed corporation profits, but it proved ineffectual and was repealed in 1918. Two factors that reduced the war revenue from taxes were the sharp drop in imports and customs duties that followed the outbreak of war in Europe and the loss in revenue caused by state and federal prohibition laws passed between 1914 and 1918.

After World War I Congress gradually repealed the special war taxes, notably the excess profits tax, and made sharp reductions in corporate and personal income, as well as estate, tax rates. A federal gift tax was introduced in 1924 to counteract widespread avoidance of federal estate taxes; it was repealed in 1926, and permanently restored in 1932.

The 1929 depression forced Congress and President Herbert Hoover into raising the corporate and personal income tax rates; doubling the estate tax rates; reenacting the gift tax; and imposing numerous manufacturers excise taxes and sales taxes on gasoline, luxury, and sporting articles, and special taxes on bank checks, bond transfers, and telephone, telegraph, and radio messages. With the inauguration of President Franklin D. Roosevelt in 1933 and the institution of his New Deal, tax laws were passed to prevent an unjust concentration of wealth and economic power and to induce business to adopt certain recovery policies. In 1933 Congress enacted a corporation excess profits tax, a capital stock tax, and an increase in the gasoline tax. In 1934–35 the surtax rates on personal income and the rates of the estate and gift taxes were increased, and a tax was imposed on the undistributed net income of personal holding companies. In 1935 the corporate income tax and the excess profits tax were made higher, on a progressive scale, and the Social Security Act established old-age insurance for qualified workers through payroll taxes on both employers and employees and unemployment insurance through a payroll tax on employers. (*See also* Social Security.) In 1936 a graduated undistributed corporate income or profits tax was levied in order to induce corporations to distribute their earnings to their stockholders (repealed in 1939). The corporate income tax was increased in 1938 and 1939.

1940–81. Six important revenue bills between June 1940 and May 1944 raised progressively the rates on personal income to a maximum of 94 percent on income over $200,000, while lowering the exemption to $500 per person, whether married, single, or dependent; thus the number of persons paying income taxes rose from 4 million in 1939 to 42.7 million in 1945. Heavy excises were enacted on commodities needed for military purposes in order to limit their consumption by civilians. To prevent war profiteering, drastic increases in corporate and excess profits taxes were enacted. The excess profits tax, reintroduced in 1940, rose to a gross rate of 95 percent. The combined normal and surtax corporation tax rate was raised from 19 percent in 1940 to 40 percent by 1942. Substantial revenue was obtained from the excise taxes on distilled spirits, wines, fermented malt liquors, tobacco, transportation of persons and property, telephone and telegraph messages, theater admissions, and manufactures. The rates of the estate and gift taxes were greatly increased in 1941.

In September 1945 Congress began easing the tax capital-reconversion burdens of American businesses through the 1945 Tax Adjustment Act. In November Congress passed the Reconversion Tax Act, which repealed the capital stock tax and the excess profits tax, the latter effective at the end of 1945. Corporate and personal income tax rates were moderately reduced. In 1948 Congress made large reductions in the personal income, estate, and gift taxes. Husbands and wives were allowed to divide their incomes on joint income tax forms and thereby reduce their taxes.

The trend to lower taxes was halted by the outbreak of the Korean War in June 1950. In three revenue bills (1950–51) Congress raised personal and corporation income taxes to World War II levels or higher; reimposed an excess profits tax; and increased excise taxes above World War II rates. In 1954, one year after the Korean War ended, Congress repealed the excess profits tax and enacted a comprehensive downward revision of the income tax. The excise taxes affecting motorists were increased to aid in financing the highways.

President Lyndon B. Johnson pushed through Congress in 1964 a bill providing $11.5 billion in income tax reductions for the calendar years 1964 and 1965. The rate scale for individual income taxes was reduced from a range of 20–91 percent to 14–70 percent; for corporations the combined normal and surtax rate was reduced from 52 to 48 percent. In June 1965 Congress scaled down the excise taxes that still remained from the Korean War to all but a few major taxes levied for sumptuary and regulatory reasons and as user charges. In 1966 Congress enacted a Tax Adjustment Act that provided for withholding personal income taxes at graduated rates ranging up to 30 percent instead of at a flat rate of 14 percent. A surtax on individual and corporate income taxes was enacted in 1968 and scheduled to expire on June 30, 1969; it was later extended at 10 percent through Dec. 31, 1969, and then at 5 percent for the first six months of 1970. The Tax Reform Act of 1969 was the most widespread tax reform measure in the history of American tax legislation. It included stricter rules on the creation and operation of private charitable foundations; the elimination of a long-standing 25 percent ceiling on long-term capital gains for those with such gains in excess of $50,000 a year; and the imposition of a minimum tax of 10 percent on "tax preference" (tax-free) income in excess of $30,000 a year. Substantial tax-relief measures in the act included a four-step increase in the deduction for personal dependency from $600 in 1969 to $750 in 1973; a new minimum standard deduction set at $1,100 for 1970; and a gradual increase in the standard deduction for taxpayers (not itemizing their tax returns) to 15 percent, with a $2,000 ceiling, in 1973. Significant federal tax changes embodied in the Revenue Act of 1971 included a 7 percent investment tax credit, a repeal of the 7 percent automobile excise tax, and an increase in the personal income tax exemption for 1972.

The next wide-ranging tax revision bill was adopted, after numerous compromises, in 1976. This Tax Reform Act limited tax shelter investments; raised standard personal deduction to 16 percent of adjusted gross income, with a ceiling of $2,400; simplified tax forms; restricted various business deductions, such as using home for business; increased taxes on very high incomes; and made changes in taxation of foreign income. The Revenue Act of 1978 signaled a change in the tax legislation trend: in contrast with the bills of the previous decade, which usually favored lower-income groups and limited some "loopholes," the 1978 bill cut taxes for the wealthy. The taxes on capital gains, the largest loophole used by the rich, were substantially reduced (60 percent, instead of 50, could be excluded from ordinary taxation), and the corporate tax rate was lowered from 30 to 28 percent.

Large tax cuts were part of Ronald Reagan's presidential campaign platform, and although the final Economy Recovery Tax Act (August 1981) reflected numerous concessions, it was nevertheless a revolutionary measure. Substantially reducing both individual and business taxes, the bill was expected to save taxpayers $749 billion over the following five years—and thus spur economic growth. The major provisions included a 5 percent individual tax cut in October 1981 and 10 percent cuts in July 1982 and July 1983; reduction of the top tax rate on investment from 70 to 50 percent; reduction of the capital gains tax from 28 to 20 percent; accelerated depreciation of business assets; and gradual reduction of estate and gift taxes. The standard deduction in 1981 was $2,300 and the non-taxable income was $3,300.

State and Municipal Taxation. State taxation in the United States in 1774–89 followed the sectional pattern established before the American Revolution. In 1789 the states gave up the use of export, impost, and tonnage duties. During the 19th century state taxation was restricted mainly to general property tax, although some states introduced special bank taxes, insurance company taxes, general corporation taxes, and inheritance taxes. As late as 1902 the general property tax furnished 52 percent of the revenue of the states. Corporation and personal income taxes became increasingly important after 1911; and after 1920 gasoline taxes became another leading source of revenue. By 1940 property taxes supplied only one-sixteenth of state tax revenue. Since the 1930's the chief state taxes, in addition to the corporation and individual income taxes, have been the general sales tax, the gasoline tax, and the payroll tax for unemployment insurance; revenue has also been produced by specific taxes on the retail sale of tobacco products and alcoholic beverages, and by inheritance and estate taxes.

By 1900 the general property tax used by counties, municipalities, and other local governing authorities as their principal source of revenue had become a selective tax on real estate and business personalty (that is, equipment and inventory). As the cost of local government increased with the accelerated growth of cities, the consequent shift from low to high rates in the general property tax led to severe criticism of the undervaluation of real property and inadequate assessment of personal property. Improvements in tax administration and the establishment of local boards of review and equalization were accompanied by an increase in the practice of dividing certain state-collected taxes between state and local governments; several states ceased to tax property and left that source of revenue to local units of government. Increasingly after World War II, local governments began imposing payroll, income, sales, gasoline, automobile, and other taxes; nevertheless, the property tax in the 1970's accounted for most of all local revenue. As inflation in the 1970's became more burdensome to state and local taxpayers, Congress, in October 1972, inaugurated its revenue-sharing program. The State and Local Assistance Act of 1972 specified the distribution of $5.3 billion for the calendar year 1972; a third of the funds were to go to the states and two-thirds to the local governments. The revenue sharing program was extended in

1976 and again in 1980. (*See also* Revenue Sharing.)

Increasing property taxes led to a "taxpayer's revolt" in 1978 when California voters approved Proposition 13, which cut property taxes in the state by 57 percent. Other states followed the example by putting limits on property taxes. In the early 1980's state legislation tended to increase sales and excise taxes and decrease personal income taxes.

Taxation in Territories and Possessions. In the so-called Insular Cases of 1901 the U.S. Supreme Court drew a distinction between "incorporated" and "unincorporated" territories: in the case of incorporated territories, the entire Constitution and the laws and treaties of the United States apply, including those constitutional provisions and statutes relating to federal taxation; in the case of unincorporated territories, Congress, subject to Supreme Court rulings, has almost unlimited power of legislation. In either case, the citizens of the territories have been subject to federal taxation without representation in Congress.

On the subject of local taxation the national government has permitted a considerable measure of local autonomy, even in the unincorporated territories. Congress has limited the imposition of federal income and estate taxes on U.S. citizens who are bona fide residents of the unincorporated territories. The detailed rules are to be found in the U.S. Internal Revenue Code.

TAXATION NO TYRANNY. Title of a political pamphlet written by Samuel Johnson, probably at the instigation of the British ministry, in 1775. A reply to the declaration of the Second Continental Congress setting forth their reasons for taking up arms, its object was to justify the repressive measures against the colonies. The tone of the pamphlet contributed to ending all hopes of compromise.

TAXATION WITHOUT REPRESENTATION. This became an issue in the American colonies when Charles Townshend (1767) sought to impose, and enforce, taxes on the colonies. The colonists agreed with Charles Pratt, Earl of Camden, and with William Pitt, Earl of Chatham, that in the matter of internal taxation they were free from parliamentary control. External taxes for the regulation of colonial trade could be levied by Parliament but only with the consent of the colonies. The real grievance of the colonists lay in the defective system of parliamentary representation, which permitted the manipulation of the "rotten boroughs" to insure a continuous standing majority in support of the ministers. At first the representation was held to be one of land but was later shifted to the assertion that in Parliament all British subjects find a virtual representation. The theory of virtual representation was attacked in England and was wholly rejected in the colonies, where it appeared irreconcilable with the dogma that government derives its just powers from the consent of the governed. The colonists insisted that representation was achieved only through an assembly of men actually elected by the persons they were intended to represent.

TAX COURT OF THE UNITED STATES. Created in 1924 as an agency of the executive branch of the government, with power to hear appeals from rulings under the Revenue Act of 1924, it has been changed several times since then. In 1969 it was established as a "court of record" within the judicial branch of the federal government. The U.S. Tax Court has the power to settle cases concerning deficiencies or overpayments in income, excess profits, estate, gift, and holding company taxes; its decisions, in most instances, can be appealed to a U.S. Court of Appeals.

TAX IN KIND, CONFEDERATE (1863–65). A 10 percent levy in the general tax law of 1863 on agricultural products. Collected by the quartermaster in the form of produce or, until March 1865, in currency, it furnished most of the army's food after September 1863. It was the first heavy tax on small farmers.

TAYLOR SYSTEM. *See* **Scientific Management.**

TEA, DUTY ON. Tea coming to Colonial America was subject to British import and excise or inland duties. The import duties were practically fixed at 11.67 percent; the inland duties varied from four shillings in 1723 to one shilling plus 25 percent ad valorem in 1745. In 1748 a rebate of the inland duty was given on tea exported to the colonies or to Ireland, and in 1767 the Tea Act provided a rebate of the import duty as well as the inland duties, so that tea left England duty free. Also in 1767 the Revenue Act levied an American duty of three pence per pound collectible at the American ports. The changes made in 1767 lowered the cost of tea in America and resulted at first in increased exports, in spite of a campaign against the use of tea and an attempted boycott against its importation. In 1773 a change was made in the law by which the East India Company was permitted to export tea directly to America and set up wholesale markets in the colonies. These changes eliminated the middlemen and created a monopoly, precipitating agitation in America (*see* Boston Tea Party; Tea Parties).

TEACHERS COLLEGES. *See* **Education.**

TEACHERS' LOYALTY OATH. Since 1863 nearly two-thirds of the state legislatures have enacted compulsory loyalty oaths for teachers. Almost all require an affirmation to uphold federal and state constitutions; some prohibit membership in subversive groups and the teaching of subversive doctrines, and others ask for sweeping disclaimers of past beliefs and associations. The years following World War II, early in the cold war period, produced a bumper crop of such oaths. In *Pierce* v. *Society of the Sisters of the Holy Name* (1925), the U.S. Supreme Court held that a state could require a teacher to be "of patriotic disposition"; subsequently the Court has struck down some loyalty oaths for being so all-encompassing as to infringe on First Amendment rights.

TEA GROWING IN THE SOUTH. Trials at Middleton Barony, S.C., in 1800 by the French botanist François André Michaux, and later by agents of the federal government, proved that tea could be grown in the warmer regions of the South but did not lead to its propagation commercially. After

1890 chemist Charles Upham Shepard, Jr., established a tea farm at Summerville, S.C. When Congress in 1898 imposed a protective duty, an extensive development of tea farms in the Summerville area was planned; these plans were halted when the duty was repealed five years later. Efforts in 1909 to reenact the tax failed, and the Summerville project was abandoned.

TEA PARTIES. Name given to several prerevolutionary episodes protesting the British taxation of tea. The first (Dec. 16, 1773) was held at Boston (*see* Boston Tea Party). Previously, citizens of New York had persuaded consignees to refuse to receive any tea, and the first cargo at that port (April 1774) was turned back; a consignment discovered on board another vessel was, after the Boston precedent, thrown into the river. At Portsmouth, N.H., and Philadelphia tea ships were turned away. At Annapolis, Md., citizens forced the owner of an offending vessel, the *Peggy Stewart,* to put it to the torch. Edenton, N.C., held the Ladies' Tea Party, at which the women of the neighborhood passed resolutions against the use of tea.

TEAPOT DOME OIL SCANDAL. In 1921, by an executive order, President Warren G. Harding transferred control of the naval oil reserves at Elk Hills, Calif., and Teapot Dome, Wyo., from the Department of the Navy to the Department of the Interior. The following year Secretary of the Interior Albert B. Fall leased, without competitive bidding, the Teapot Dome fields to Harry F. Sinclair, president of the Mammoth Oil Company, and the Elk Hills fields to Edward L. Doheny, a personal friend. In 1923 Sen. Thomas J. Walsh of Montana led a Senate investigation of the leases and found that in 1921 Doheny had lent Fall $100,000 (without interest) and that shortly after Fall's retirement as secretary of the interior (March 1923) Sinclair had loaned Fall $25,000. Fall was convicted of accepting bribes; Sinclair and Doheny were acquitted of bribery charges.

TECHNOCRACY MOVEMENT (1932–33). An ephemeral effort to arouse support for a politico-industrial organization of society based on advanced technology. First used by William Henry Smyth, an inventor and social reformer, in 1919, the term "technocracy" was revived by Howard Scott, an engineer, during the Great Depression. Scott proposed that technologists, or technocrats, direct a new society in which "energy certificates" would replace money and in which each citizen would have an annual income in exchange for a minimum amount of work.

TECUMSEH, CRUSADE OF (about 1806–13). The American government acquired most of modern Ohio from the Indians by the Treaty of Greenville (1795) while it recognized their ownership of the remainder of the Old Northwest. Before long, fresh cessions of land were demanded and obtained, and the Indian was debauched and his means of existence destroyed by his contact with the white race.

These conditions evoked the remarkable crusade of Tecumseh and his brother, the Shawnee Prophet, to rescue their people from impending doom. Sweeping social and religious reforms were instituted, including abstinence from liquor, community of property, and adherence to the native way of life. To stay the white advance, Tecumseh sought to organize a tribal confederacy and to establish the principle that the land was the common property of all the tribes, to be alienated only by their common consent. (*See also* Shawnee Prophet.)

TECUMSEH, FORT. *See* **Pierre, Fort.**

TEHERAN CONFERENCE (Nov. 28–Dec. 1, 1943). The first war conference attended by President Franklin D. Roosevelt, Prime Minister Winston Churchill, and Marshal Joseph Stalin, it was convened because of the evident need to coordinate Western military plans with those of the Soviet Union. The three leaders made important military decisions regarding a second front in Europe and discussed the boundaries of Poland and the future of Germany. Stalin also renewed his pledge to help in the fight against Japan after Germany's defeat. A separate protocol was signed by the Big Three promising to maintain Iran's independence.

TELEGRAPH. The requisite technical elements of the telegraph became available by the mid-1830's; its potential social utility was soon perceived by a number of men, including Samuel Morse, a professor of art at New York University (NYU). Important contributions to the development of a successful system were made by Morse's associates Leonard D. Gale, a chemist, and Alfred Vail, an engineer. A major innovation (generally attributed to Vail) was the introduction of the "Morse Code," a bisignal code that has since evolved into the pulse code system used in digital computers and space telemetry systems. Morse and his associates conducted a public demonstration of their new communications system in 1838, but their first intercity line (a forty-mile line between Washington, D.C., and Baltimore) was not completed until 1844.

When Congress declined to develop the telegraph as a national public utility, Morse and his associates organized the Magnetic Telegraph Company (1845). The next decade was marked by expansion and the creation of many small competing telegraph companies. By 1852 the United States had about 15,000 miles of telegraph lines. The Western Union Company, which eventually established an effective national monopoly of the industry, was organized in 1856; the first transcontinental line was completed in 1861. The first transatlantic telegraph cable became operational in 1858; it failed, but final success was achieved in 1866 (*see* Cables, Atlantic and Pacific).

World attention was first directed to the military implications of the telegraph by its use in the American Civil War to control not only the movement of troops and supplies but also field tactics. Postwar innovations were mainly directed toward increasing the information-handling capacity of telegraph lines by multiplexing techniques.

TELEGRAPHERS' STRIKE (1883). On July 16, the Brotherhood of Telegraphers of the United States and Canada approached the larger companies of the 200 then in business, demanding an eight-hour day, seven-hour night, equal pay for men and women, a general wage increase of 15 percent, and extra pay for Sunday work. The companies refused to accept the terms, and at noon on July 19 the strike began. However, solidarity was lacking and many remained at work, keeping up a partial service, while the companies were filling the strikers' places with new employees. On Aug. 15 the brotherhood capitulated.

TELEPHONE. The technical feasibility of an electromagnetic telephone appears to have been recognized by several inventors by the early 1870's. The most famous of these inventors was Alexander Graham Bell, whose telephone patent led to the organization of the largest industrial corporation in the world. Bell and his assistant, Thomas A. Watson, achieved the first successful transmission of articulate speech in March 1876, and Bell gave the first public demonstration at the Philadelphia Centennial Exposition later the same year. The Bell Telephone Company, which eventually became the American Telephone and Telegraph Company, was organized in 1877.

In the preelectronic phase of technical development that lasted until the eve of World War I important innovations included the carbon transmitter, central switchboards, multicircuit cables, hard-drawn copper wire, loading coils, and the four-parameter transmission theory. An experimental line between Boston and New York City was first completed in 1884 using hard-drawn copper wire. The introduction of loading coils during the first decade of the 20th century made feasible a 2,000-mile circuit without amplifiers. The Bell Company maintained an effective monopoly of the industry in the United States until the expiration of Bell's patents in the 1890's; most smaller companies were finally absorbed or went out of business.

The introduction of electronic vacuum-tube amplifiers in 1912 enabled the first transcontinental conversation by wire in 1915. The first transatlantic radio telephone conversation using vacuum-tube techniques was achieved by Bell System engineers the same year. The advent of radio-electronic methods enabled the completion of a worldwide telephone system during the 1920's; the capacity of wire circuits was also greatly increased during the interwar years with the use of wave filters, negative feedback amplifiers, and wide-band coaxial transmission lines. Another significant development during the 1920's was the introduction of automatic dialing in larger cities using electromechanical switches.

The third major phase in the evolution of the telephone was stimulated by the introduction in 1948 of solid-state amplifiers and switching circuits and the application of microwave techniques similar to those used in radar systems during World War II. Microwave links capable of carrying television as well as numerous telephone channels were introduced by the Bell System in 1946. Similar techniques were used in the design of the first international communications earth satellite, Telstar (1962). In 1981 the U.S. and international communication satellites included the Intelsat, Marisat, Relay, Syncom, and Westar series.

Advances in communications technology in the 1970's led to International Direct Distance Dialing, beginnings of visual telephone service, and the use of telephone networks for data processing. Research has also begun on the laser-powered fiber optics system for transmission of local calls, and on electronic telephones. By 1980 the telephone had become an inseparable part of American life: 96 percent of households had a telephone, as compared with 62 percent in 1950.

TELEPHONE CASES. Shortly after Alexander Graham Bell was granted a patent on the telephone in 1876 other inventors who had been working on the idea came to light. The Western Union Telegraph Company organized a subsidiary corporation, which took over Amos E. Dolbear's telephone inventions, Thomas A. Edison's transmitter, and other devices and began manufacturing and installing telephones. The Bell Telephone Company brought suit, and on Nov. 10, 1879, the Western Union forces capitulated. Other inventors and pseudo inventors sprang up, and during a quarter century the holders of the Bell patent had to battle through more than 600 lawsuits. Daniel Drawbaugh, an obscure Pennsylvania mechanic who claimed to have had a workable instrument by 1866, came nearest to defeating them: the Supreme Court sustained Bell's claim in 1887 by a vote of four to three. The government itself sought from 1887 to 1897 to annul the patent, but failed.

TELEVISION. In 1873 the telegraph engineer Willoughby Smith noted that the electrical resistance of selenium changed when exposed to light. Various possibilities of converting photographic images into an electrical impulse equivalent were soon explored, particularly in France and England, but the basic problem was unresolved until 1884, when Paul G. Nipkow of Germany designed a scanning disc with the potential for sequentially transmitting individual segments of the picture. The advent of vacuum-tube amplifiers and practical phototubes by 1920 made a commercial system feasible.

In the period 1925–30 both John Logie Baird of England and Charles Francis Jenkins of the United States developed scanning disc systems to the point of quasicommercial application. The Jenkins Laboratories of Washington, D.C., began operation of station W3XK in 1928. By 1931 some two dozen stations employing low-definition scanning (30–60 lines) were in service.

Work on the optical-electrical conversion (camera) tube was done principally by Philo Taylor Farnsworth, an independent inventor, and Vladimir K. Zworykin, working first at Westinghouse and later with Radio Corporation of America (RCA). In 1923 Zworykin applied for a patent on an all-electronic scanning system; his camera device, the iconoscope, had certain intrinsic advantages in terms of image intensification and predominated in the experimental research of the late 1930's. Farnsworth's image dissector tube, electron-multiplier, and other contributions in electronic circuit design were crucial to the technology. Electronic methods sometimes incorporated mechanical scanners at the transmission end; but by 1938 the all-electronic era had begun. By the summer of 1939 the National Broadcasting Company provided extensive programming over station W2XBS New York.

In December 1939 the Federal Communications Commission (FCC) tentatively adopted rules to permit a sponsored program service in which fees collected supported further experimental work; conflicts arose, however, and the industry was compelled to examine all aspects of the new technology through the National Television Systems Committee (NTSC). Full commercial program service was authorized by the FCC on July 1, 1941. The engineering standard of 525 picture lines, 30 frames per second, was officially adopted.

Color television originated with the work of Herbert Eugene Ives of Bell Telephone Laboratories in the late 1920's. Baird in England had some success by 1938 with rotating color discs and a cathode ray tube; Peter Carl Goldmark of CBS Laboratories achieved the most notable success in the United States with a high definition color system by 1940. Program transmissions were extended in 1945 employing developmental UHF (ultrahigh frequency) stations in New York City. By 1950 the CBS system (termed "field-sequential") was of sufficient quality to offer serious consideration for commercial adoption; the main drawback was the use of a rotating color wheel and noncompatibility with the monochrome service. The successful development of an all-electronic system by RCA led to a revised set of standards formulated by the NTSC. The NTSC system was authorized for broadcasting in 1953, but more than a decade elapsed before improvements in electron-optics and circuit design made color receivers attractive enough for large-scale purchase by the general public.

The television industry expanded spectacularly from six television stations in 1946 to 1,031 stations in 1981. In the 1970's the fastest growing segment was cable television, which transmits television signals by means of cables; last restrictions on the number of signals a cable system might carry were removed in 1980. With almost 80 million sets in the country and an average viewing time of thirty hours per week, television represents a major, if not the major, influence on contemporary Americans.

TELLER AMENDMENT (Apr. 19, 1898). A disclaimer on the part of the United States of any intention "to exercise sovereignty, jurisdiction or control" over the island of Cuba when it should have been freed from Spanish rule. It was proposed in the Senate by Henry M. Teller of Colorado as an amendment to the joint resolution declaring Cuba independent and authorizing intervention.

TEMPERANCE MOVEMENT. The first temperance society in America was formed in 1808 at Moreau, Saratoga County, N.Y., by Billy J. Clark, a physician who had been impressed by Benjamin Rush's *An Inquiry Into the Effects of Spirituous Liquors on the Human Mind and Body* (first published in 1784). Lyman Beecher, pastor at East Hampton, N.Y., was inspired by Rush's essay to preach a series of sermons in 1810 against the current drinking customs. At Litchfield, Conn., the following year, Beecher persuaded political and ecclesiastical leaders of the "standing order" to organize; from this agitation came the Connecticut Society for the Reformation of Morals (May 19, 1813). Meanwhile, the Massachusetts clergy, supported by Federalist politicians, had organized their campaign against intemperance (February 1813) under the leadership of Jedidiah Morse and Jeremiah Evarts. Auxiliary societies were soon formed in New England and New York.

In 1825 Lyman Beecher again stirred his parishioners with powerful sermons, which were printed and widely distributed. On Feb. 13, 1826, sixteen clergy and laymen in Boston signed the constitution of the American Society for the Promotion of Temperance. Using a system of state, county, and local auxiliaries, the Boston society soon claimed to be national. By 1834 there were auxiliaries in every state, approximately 5,000 locals, and 1 million pledge signers. Two years later there were eleven weekly and monthly journals devoted solely to temperance. In 1836, at the annual convention of the American Temperance Union (ATU), sponsored by the American Temperance Society, the delegates by a narrow majority adopted a total abstinence pledge. The Washington Temperance Society in 1841 began to stage "experience meetings"; the emotionalism of such meetings was contagious, and the most successful temperance lecturer of the day, John B. Gough, soon utilized it in winning converts.

Beneath the surface the temperance movement had been slowly converted into a campaign for prohibition. A few leaders had long been eager to direct the force of law against the liquor traffic and had denounced the licensing of retail dealers in intoxicants. (*See* Prohibition; Prohibition Party.) The Twenty-first Amendment (1933) repealed Prohibition. Thereafter the temperance movement waned, local option was put into effect in a number of states, and by 1966 no statewide prohibition law existed in the United States.

TEMPORARY NATIONAL ECONOMIC COMMITTEE (TNEC). A joint executive-legislative body authorized by Congress in 1938 in response to recommendations submitted by President Franklin D. Roosevelt for curbing monopolies and the concentration of economic power. Under the chairmanship of Joseph C. O'Mahoney, TNEC conducted public hearings from December 1938 to April 1940 to determine the effects of monopoly on prices, wages, profits, and other aspects of the national economy. Several antitrust suits were initiated by its investigations.

TENANT FARMER. *See* **Agriculture.**

TENEMENTS. Legally defined as multiple dwellings, buildings in which more than three families live independently under one roof. Unlike apartment houses, they became notorious for their degraded condition in the major cities of the eastern seaboard, the South, and the Midwest.

In 1867 the first Tenement House Law, establishing minimum standards for room size, ventilation, and sanitation, was passed in New York City. The second Tenement House Law, an amendment of the one of 1867, was passed in 1879, requiring that tenements henceforth constructed occupy not more than 60 percent of the lot. A competition held in the same year resulted in the notorious "dumbbell" tenement, so called because the plans called for a dumbbell-shaped building. In 1899 Ernest Flagg designed the first fireproof tenement.

In 1900 the Charity Organization Society held a competition that resulted in the "new law" tenement, which supplanted the "dumbbell" plan. (*See also* Slums.)

TEN-FORTIES. Gold bonds issued during the Civil War that were redeemable after ten years and payable after forty years. Authorized by Congress (Mar. 3, 1864) to allow greater freedom in financing the Civil War, their low 5 percent interest made them unpopular.

TENNESSEE. In 1540 the Spanish explorer Hernando de Soto visited the southeastern part of what is now Tennessee. In 1673 Father Jacques Marquette and Louis Jolliet laid claim to the entire Mississippi Valley in the name of France; in the same year James Needham and Gabriel Arthur penetrated into upper East Tennessee and laid the foundation for a British claim to the area. English fur traders from South Carolina established a profitable business with the Cherokee and Creek. Meanwhile the French, exploring eastward from the Mississippi River, waged war against the Chickasaw of West Tennessee, and attempted to entice the Cherokee of East Tennessee away from their allegiance to the British. In 1756 the British began building Fort Loudoun on the Little Tennessee River (near present-day Vonore) to provide protection for the Cherokee from the French. The fort was besieged by the Cherokee in retaliation for English atrocities and was captured in 1760, bringing to a virtual end South Carolina's efforts to establish permanent settlements in the Tennessee area. The next efforts were from Virginia. As early as 1750 Thomas Walker passed through and named the Cumberland Gap and Cumberland Mountains; in 1768 Thomas Hutchins surveyed the Cumberland River from its mouth to Middle Tennessee.

The first permanent white settler, William Bean, built his cabin near the Watauga River in 1768. He was soon joined by other settlers who in 1772 drew up a compact of government called the Watauga Association. In 1776 the settlers petitioned the colony of North Carolina to extend its jurisdiction over their area, and the following year North Carolina created Washington County with boundaries that included all of present-day Tennessee. The success of the Wataugans created widespread interest among land speculators. Judge Richard Henderson's Transylvania Company purchased 20 million acres of land in Kentucky and Tennessee from the Cherokee; settlement of the Middle Tennessee portion followed in 1779–80. Although British troops did not operate in the sparsely settled Tennessee area during the revolutionary war, the colonists were busy defending against Indians who remained loyal to Great Britain. (*See also* Kings Mountain, Battle of.)

In 1789, following an unsuccessful attempt by the East Tennesseans to establish a separate state of Franklin, North Carolina ceded its western lands to the federal government. Congress then organized the Territory South of the River Ohio, and in 1796 made Tennessee the nation's sixteenth state. Land open for settlement was increased substantially in 1818 when all of West Tennessee was acquired from the Chickasaw. By 1830 Tennessee was the seventh ranking state in population. It remained, however, a predominantly agricultural state of small to medium farms, a minority of which had slaves. Corn was the dominant crop, with cotton important in the south central and southwestern counties and tobacco important in the north central area. There was little industry except the mining and smelting of iron. Tennessee earned the nickname the "Volunteer State" in the War of 1812, enhanced that reputation in the Mexican War, and contributed more fighting men than any other state during the Civil War. Tennessee's heavy enlistments in both the Union and Confederate armies reflected the sharply divided loyalties of its people over the issues of slavery and secession. The state was last to leave the Union (June 8, 1861) and first to return (July 24, 1866), and had more battles fought on its soil than any state except Virginia.

During the years following the Civil War the state began to industrialize. Coal, iron, and copper were successfully mined in the southeastern portion, and railroads were constructed. Distilleries, grist and woolen mills, and furniture factories used the products of the state's farms. Following World War I Tennessee emerged as an important industrial state. A network of dams for hydroelectric power, navigation, and flood control, built on the Tennessee River by the Tennessee Valley Authority and on the Cumberland River by the U.S. Corps of Engineers, made this development possible. Agriculture continued to be significant, but cotton declined in importance, and beef and dairy cattle became the biggest source of farm income. Small farms were consolidated as people moved to the cities and towns. Chemicals, food products, and textiles, as well as mining and smelting, provided the industrial base for a diversified economy. TVA power was also crucial in the location of the Atomic Power Laboratories at Oak Ridge. Lakes along the Tennessee and Cumberland rivers helped generate recreational income from tourism, fishing, and boating. From a population of 77,262 in 1795, Tennessee's population had increased to 3,835,078 in 1980.

TENNESSEE. A Confederate ram, fitted out and commissioned at Mobile, Ala., on Feb. 16, 1864. As the flagship of Adm. Franklin Buchanan's squadron, it engaged in a prolonged engagement with Adm. David G. Farragut's fleet at the entrance to Mobile Bay on Aug. 5, 1864, when it was captured.

TENNESSEE, ARMY OF (Confederate). The designation given, Nov. 20, 1862, by Gen. Braxton Bragg to the reorganized Army of Mississippi. Soon afterward it fought at Stone's River, Tenn., and later engaged in a summer campaign in middle Tennessee (*see* Tullahoma Campaign). Reinforced by troops from Virginia, it achieved a brilliant victory at Chickamauga (September 1863). The siege of Chattanooga followed, to be ended by defeat and withdrawal into Georgia (*see* Ringgold Gap, Battle of). Bragg was replaced by Gen. William J. Hardee and then by Gen. Joseph E. Johnston, who opposed Gen. William Tecumseh Sherman's advance to Atlanta. Because of his failure to defeat Sherman, Johnston was replaced by Gen. John B. Hood (*see* Davis-Johnston Controversy). Severe fighting followed and Hood was forced out of Atlanta. Concentrating his army, Hood marched northward into Tennessee (*see* Hood's Tennessee Campaign). Defeated at Franklin and at Nashville, the army retired into Mississippi. Gen. Richard Taylor replaced Hood. Later the army was transferred eastward to aid in opposing Sherman (*see* Carolinas, Sherman's March Through the) and was included in Johnston's surrender. (*See also* Bentonville, Battle of.)

TENNESSEE, ARMY OF THE (Union). Composed largely of Middle West regiments, it was constituted from the forces gathered by Gen. Ulysses S. Grant after his capture of Fort Donelson, Tenn. With the Army of the Ohio, it fought at Shiloh (April 1862). Later it was transferred to Memphis and from there began the movement that culminated in the capture of Vicksburg, Miss. Under Gen. William Tecumseh Sherman the army was moved in November 1863 to Chattanooga to reinforce the Army of the Cumberland. When Sherman began his Atlanta campaign, Gen. J. B. McPherson commanded the army; he was killed in battle, and was replaced first by Gen. John A. Logan and then by Gen. Oliver O. Howard. The army constituted the right wing in Sherman's march to the sea. It was present at the siege of Savannah and on the northward march through the Carolinas, and participated in the operations culminating in Confederate Gen. Joseph E. Johnston's surrender. On May 24, 1865, still commanded by Howard, it marched in the Grand Review in Washington, D.C., after which it was demobilized.

TENNESSEE BOND CASES, 114 U.S. 663 (1885)**.** Part of an unsuccessful attempt by certain holders of Tennessee bonds, who were constitutionally prevented from bringing suit against the state to obtain payment, to enforce a lien in their own behalf. The state had taken the lien on the property of the railroad companies to which the bonds had been issued under the operation of a system of loans instituted in 1852. The Supreme Court decided that although the lien had been executed, the state was at the outset, and remained, the sole debtor bound by the bonds. The decision made certain the acceptance by the bondholders of a settlement arranged by the legislature in 1883, refunding the debt at fifty cents on the dollar.

TENNESSEE CENTENNIAL EXPOSITION (May 1–Oct. 31, 1897)**.** Held at Nashville to celebrate the centennial of the state's admission into the Union, it cost approximately $1.2 million and extended over 200 acres. There were exhibits from other states and foreign nations, but the emphasis was on Tennessee and its mines, agriculture, and manufactures. The principal feature was an allegedly exact reproduction of the Parthenon in Athens.

TENNESSEE RIVER. Formed by the confluence near Knoxville, Tenn., of the Holston River, which rises in southwest Virginia, and the French Broad River, which has its source in western North Carolina. Called for a time the Cherokee River, it was used extensively by Indians on war and hunting expeditions. The Tennessee Valley played an important part in the Anglo-French rivalry for the control of the Old Southwest; and the river was an important route for migration. Use of the river for navigation was handicapped by the presence of serious obstructions, especially the Muscle and Colbert shoals at the "Great Bend" in northern Alabama. In the 20th century emphasis shifted to power production and flood control, and the construction during World War I of the Wilson Dam and nitrate plants at the Muscle Shoals initiated a nationwide controversy over the question of public or private ownership and operation of power facilities. Under the Tennessee Valley Authority the river has been made into a chain of reservoirs, or lakes, held back by nine major dams. A canal designed to connect the Tennessee River with the Gulf of Mexico via the Tombigee River was planned for completion in the 1980's.

TENNESSEE VALLEY AUTHORITY (TVA)**.** A government-owned dam and nitrate-producing facility at Muscle Shoals, on the Tennessee River in northwestern Alabama, completed too late to produce the intended munitions for World War I, became the seedling of an audacious experiment in river valley development—the Tennessee Valley Authority. Nebraska Sen. George W. Norris hoped to build more dams and bring public control to the Tennessee River; almost singlehandedly he held the dam in government ownership until 1933 when, prodded by President Franklin D. Roosevelt, Congress enacted the Tennessee Valley Act. The Tennessee drains a seven-state area of 40,000 square miles, where 52 inches of annual rainfall often brought damaging floods. Roosevelt and the first directors of the TVA—Chairman Arthur E. Morgan, David Lilienthal, and Harcourt A. Morgan—envisioned a publicly owned corporation, nationally financed, which would harness the floods and draw electric power from the torrent. The TVA was also to be a regional planning authority, with a wide mandate for such undertakings as economic development, recreation, reforestation, and the production of fertilizer.

Private utilities fought TVA power policies in the courts, and there were internal feuds, but by 1941 the authority was operating eleven dams with six more under construction and was selling low-cost electric power to 500,000 consumers in six states. TVA technicians developed a concentrated phosphate fertilizer well adapted to the soils of the area, and 25,000 demonstration farms instructed local citizens in scientific farming. During World War II, 70 percent of TVA power went to defense industries, chief among them the Oak Ridge atomic project. In 1981 it was estimated that $2,118 million in flood damages had been averted by the authority's dams since 1936; freight traffic on the Tennessee, which had been 1 million tons in 1933, had increased to 32 million tons in 1981; and power revenues came to $2,525 million, of which TVA returned $106 million to the U.S. Treasury. About 2.8 million residential, commercial, and industrial consumers used TVA power in 1981.

TENNIS (more properly, Lawn Tennis)**.** A derivative of the ancient game of court tennis. Maj. Walter Clopton Wingfield demonstrated a game he called "Sphairistike," or lawn tennis, in Wales in December 1873. Wingfield's game, played on a court shaped like an hourglass, was brought to the United

States by way of Bermuda in 1874, and was first played at the Staten Island Cricket and Baseball Club (New York City). The first tennis tournament in the United States was held at Nahant (Mass.) in 1876 on a Wingfield hourglass court, using Wingfield's scoring method—the 15-point game of racquets. The next year, at the first Wimbledon (England) championship, the present scoring system of 15, 30, 40, games and sets—used for centuries in court tennis—became official. The first official tennis championship in the United States was held in 1881 at the Newport Casino in Rhode Island under the auspices of the U.S. National Lawn Tennis Association, or USNLTA (the "National" was dropped in 1920, the "Lawn" in 1975). Richard D. Sears of Boston won the first championship, a feat that he repeated annually through 1887.

At first tennis was confined almost entirely to the Northeast, including the Ivy colleges. But the Cincinnati Tennis Club opened in 1880, and the game spread south to Atlanta, and New Orleans, where the first southern championship was held in 1886. The Scarlet Ribbon Club in Chicago was authorized in 1887 by the USNLTA to conduct a western tournament. The California Lawn Tennis Club was organized in San Francisco in 1884, and was allotted the Pacific coast sectional championship by the USNLTA in 1889. The national doubles championships were awarded in 1893 to Chicago. The first Davis Cup matches, between the United States and the British Isles, were held in 1900 at the Longwood Cricket Club in Brookline, Mass. In 1900 there were only forty-four clubs in the United States; by 1908 there were 115, and championships were held in all but three states.

Amateurism became a problem for administrators of the USLTA in the 1920's. In 1925 a new "player-writer" rule forbade players from writing current reports on tournaments in which they competed. Amateur tennis went into high gear following World War II in the promotion of the junior development program. The Tennis Educational Foundation was organized by Lawrence A. Baker in 1951, and sectional foundations and tennis-patrons groups also provided funds. Physical education instructors in the schools were trained to teach tennis, and an inner-city program was begun to work with underprivileged youths.

In 1968 the whole structure of the game was reshaped. Open tournaments, advocated by the British in a revolt, were sanctioned by the ILTF, permitting amateurs to compete against professionals. New promoters and commercial sponsors came into the game, and the schedule of tournaments was revised and enlarged. The World Championship of Tennis (WCT) contracted the services of almost all the top-ranking male players and dispatched them on tours across the United States and abroad, many of which were televised. More and more matches were televised after James H. Van Alen of Newport devised the "sudden death" tiebreaker, making it possible to control the length of matches. The new scoring was introduced at Forest Hills in 1970, the year after Richard ("Pancho") Gonzales and Charles Pasarell played a match at Wimbledon that required 112 games and lasted 5 hours and twelve minutes. The prize money available for professional players greatly increased and in 1980 the top players were earning over half a million dollars.

"TENNIS CABINET." Journalistic description of a group of friends with whom Theodore Roosevelt rode, walked, and played tennis during his presidency (1901–09). Official matters were often informally discussed, and the president admitted seeking advice from this trusted circle, which included Gen. Leonard Wood, Gen. Thomas H. Barry, Robert Bacon, James Garfield, and Gifford Pinchot.

TENOR, OLD AND NEW. Old and new issues of paper money. In colonial times paper money was issued without much provision for redemption; when it depreciated a new tenor would be made, and the old tenor was redeemed at a discount in the new tenor.

TENURE OF OFFICE ACT (Mar. 2, 1867). Passed over President Andrew Johnson's veto, it was designed to restrict Johnson's appointing and removing power. The Senate's consent was required for removals in all cases in which its consent was necessary for appointment. After considerable debate a proviso was inserted that cabinet members should hold office during, and for one month after, the term of the president who made the appointment, subject to removal only with the Senate's consent. Violation of the act was made a high misdemeanor. When Johnson attempted to remove Secretary of War Edwin M. Stanton the Radical Republican Congress proceeded with its long-laid plans for the impeachment and trial of the president; but as Stanton was not a Johnson appointee, the act could not be applied to him. Sections of the act were repealed early in Ulysses S. Grant's first administration; the rest of the act was repealed in 1887.

TEPEE. *See* **Architecture: American Indian.**

TERRITORIAL GOVERNMENTS. Congress enacted the Northwest Ordinance of 1787 for the region north of the Ohio River and westward to the Mississippi; under its terms the territories could look forward to eventual statehood. As modified by congressional enactments after 1789, the ordinance became the general model for the handling of all the territories that ultimately achieved statehood. A three-stage development was provided for. In the initial stage the president, with the consent of the Senate, appointed a territorial governor, a secretary, and three judges. The governor served as head of the militia and superintendent of Indian affairs; he was authorized to establish townships and counties, appoint their officials, and, in conjunction with the judges, adopt laws for the territory. The second stage began when the territory, or any division of it, attained an adult male population of at least 5,000: the inhabitants were then entitled to set up a legislature consisting of a house of representatives elected for two years, a council appointed by the president for five years, and a nonvoting delegate to Congress elected by the house and council. The governor enjoyed authority to convene or dissolve the legislature and was also permitted an absolute veto over legislative enactments. Finally, when the total population reached 60,000, the territory could petition Congress for admission to the Union. (*See* State-making Process.)

The governments established for the Southwest, Mississippi, and Indiana territories in 1790, 1798, and 1800, respectively, followed closely the pattern described above. The Minnesota Territory (1849) served as the prototype for later territorial organizations: the governor, secretary, and judges were appointed for four years; members of the council and the congressional delegate were chosen by the local electorate for two-year terms. The governor shared appointive power with the council, and a two-thirds vote of the legislature could override his veto. The legislature was empowered to apportion itself, fix qualifications for suffrage, and organize judicial districts. Most local officials were elected. Legislative and gubernatorial acts were subject to the approval of Congress. Judicial power was placed in supreme, district, probate, and justice-of-the-peace courts.

With the acquisition of Hawaii (1898) and the possessions resulting from the Spanish-American War the question was posed: Does the Constitution follow the flag? That is, were the natives of these overseas possessions entitled to all of the rights and privileges guaranteed to the inhabitants of the continental United States by the Constitution? The Supreme Court in the Insular Cases of 1901 distinguished between incorporated and unincorporated territories (*see* Insular Cases). For the incorporated territories, Congress was bound by all the constitutional limitations not obviously inapplicable; for the unincorporated territories, Congress was bound to observe only the "fundamental" guarantees embodied in the Constitution. It was eventually determined by the Supreme Court that such guarantees as trial by jury and indictment by grand juries were not among the fundamental rights guaranteed to inhabitants of unincorporated territories, although the majority of the provisions of the Bill of Rights were applicable. No territory of the United States remains in the incorporated category. The Virgin Islands, Guam, and American Samoa are examples of unincorporated territories. Puerto Rico was designated a commonwealth in 1952; the term describes a high degree of local autonomy, under a constitution drafted and adopted by the residents, pursuant to congressional enabling legislation that the residents themselves had approved earlier by referendum. (*See also* Insular Possessions, *and articles on individual territories.*)

TERRITORIAL WATERS. A belt of coastal waters subject to territorial jurisdiction of littoral states but open to innocent passage of foreign ships. A limit of one marine league (three miles) from the coast was accepted by many countries, including the United States, until the mid-20th century; others claimed from four to twelve miles, and two United Nations conferences (1958) failed to secure international agreement. A third conference on the law of the sea (1973–75) also failed. The U.S. limit in the early 1980's was three nautical miles (which equals 3.6 statute miles).

TERRITORIES OF THE UNITED STATES. Those dependencies and possessions over which the United States exercises jurisdiction. The force of the Northwest Ordinance of 1787 set the precedent that territorial status was a step on the path to statehood, during which time residents of the territories maintained their citizenship and their protections under the Constitution. Alaska and Hawaii, admitted in 1959, were the last of the territories to become states. For the Spanish possessions ceded to the United States in 1898, the peace treaty did not include the promise of citizenship found in earlier treaties of annexation. Subject only to the limitations of the Constitution, Congress was free to determine the political status and civil rights of the inhabitants. (*See* Insular Cases; Territorial Governments.) Congress uniformly chose to treat its new acquisitions as unincorporated territories. Puerto Rico, organized as a commonwealth (1952), enjoys the maximum degree of autonomy accorded to any of the territories. (*See also* Guam; Insular Possessions; Panama Canal; Puerto Rico; Samoa, American; Trust Territory of the Pacific; Virgin Islands of the United States.)

TERRY'S TEXAS RANGERS. Popular name for a unit of ten companies of volunteer horsemen mustered into the Confederate army as the Eighth Texas Cavalry. Commissioned to "recruit a regiment of skilled horsemen for immediate service," B. F. Terry and Thomas S. Lubbock promptly enrolled at Houston 1,000 men, many of whom were former Texas Rangers. In November 1861 they joined Gen. Albert S. Johnston's force at Bowling Green, Ky. Although Terry was killed in their first engagement at Woodsonville, Ky., his name clung to the organization. Terry's Texas Rangers rendered valuable service at Shiloh, in the campaigns around Murfreesboro, Chattanooga, Atlanta, and Knoxville, and in their last engagement, at Bentonville, N.C. (1865).

TERTIUM QUIDS. *See* **Quids.**

TEST LAWS. The Civil War and Reconstruction eras witnessed an attempt by the national government to establish criteria of loyalty. Both Abraham Lincoln and Andrew Johnson considered loyalty oaths and disloyalty proceedings to be an integral part of war and reconstruction policy. The "ironclad oath" was the result of a statute passed by Congress July 2, 1862, which called on every federal officeholder to swear that he had "never voluntarily borne arms against the United States" or given any aid to those so doing. Congress in 1864 broadened the scope of the oath to include its own membership, which would effectively bar returning reconstructed state delegations; on Jan. 24, 1865, the oath was extended to lawyers practicing in federal courts.

Under Johnson the issue of loyalty oaths became critical to Radical Republican policy (*see* Reconstruction Acts). The new Missouri state constitution prescribed the test oath not only for lawyers but also for clergymen, teachers, candidates for office, and voters. Various constitutional challenges were raised to the oaths, and in 1866 the Supreme Court heard the cases of *Cummings* v. *Missouri* and *Ex Parte Garland,* the first a challenge to the state law and the latter a challenge to the federal test-oath act of 1865. On Jan. 14, 1867, by two five-to-four decisions, the Supreme Court invalidated the test oath of 1865 on the grounds that the oath provision was a bill of attainder and an *ex post facto* law since it punished for acts not punishable at the time committed. The test oath itself was modified in 1868 for national legislators, who now had only to swear to future loyalty. In 1871 Congress further modified the oath for all former Confederates to a promise of future loyalty. Finally, in 1884 Congress repealed the test-oath statutes.

TEXAN EMIGRATION AND LAND COMPANY. Also known as the Peters' Colony Company, it introduced 2,205 families into north central Texas between 1841 and 1848. Organized by W.S. Peters and associates of Louisville, Ky., and Cincinnati, Ohio, the company entered into contract with the Republic of Texas on Nov. 9, 1841 (modified July 26, 1842, and Jan. 20, 1843). In distributing free land—one section (640 acres) to each head of a household and one-half section to each unmarried man—the company was to be allowed to retain alternate sections of land for its own benefit; however, other immigrants moved into the same 16,000 square miles of land assigned to the company and claimed homesteads by preemption. Conflicts waxed after annexation, leading to two armed raids by settlers (1848 and 1852) on company headquarters at Stewartsville. Land title claims were quieted after Gov. Peter H. Bell called the fourth legislature into special session in 1853: a law was passed granting each settler rights prior to those of the company on land actually occupied as a homestead; the company was compensated in part with a tract of unoccupied land in west Texas.

TEXAN-SANTA FE EXPEDITIONS. After Spain established Santa Fe and San Antonio as centers of New Mexico and Texas, respectively, joining the two areas was an enduring frontier objective. Small parties led by Pedro Vial and José Mares traveled across the intervening plains country (1786–89), and in 1808 Capt. Francisco Amangual led 200 men from San Antonio to Santa Fe, but these efforts did not effect a satisfactory communication. The Texan–Santa Fe expedition of 1841 was occasioned by Texas' claim of New Mexican territory and President Mirabeau B. Lamar's desire to divert the regular Santa Fe trade to Texas. Gen. Hugh McLeod commanded a force of 321 men, which was harassed by the Kiowa and was eventually captured in sections by New Mexican troops. The captured Texans were subjected to many indignities en route to Mexico City, and became the subject of a heated diplomatic controversy. Most of the prisoners were released in April 1842.

TEXAS. Spanish interest in Texas dates from the mapping of the Gulf of Mexico by Alonso Alvárez de Pineda in 1519. In 1528–36 Álvar Núñez Cabeza de Vaca and in 1540–44 Francisco Vásquez de Coronado explored much of western Texas; survivors of Hernando de Soto's expedition entered east Texas. Reports stressing Indian hostility and the arid nature of the land discouraged permanent settlement north of the Rio Grande. The Spanish title to Texas remained uncontested until 1684, when French colonists and soldiers commanded by Robert Cavelier, Sieur de La Salle, erected Fort Saint Louis in the vicinity of Matagorda Bay. As a response to the French intrusion, Alonso de León established three missions in east Texas; continuing border struggles across the Sabine River led to the creation of additional missions and presidios (forts). Spain founded San Antonio in 1718 as its principal military garrison.

In 1810 Father Miguel Hidalgo y Costilla proclaimed Mexico's independence from Spain. In the ensuing struggle, Texas became a battleground and a number of filibustering expeditions were launched from New Orleans. American colonization of Texas began in 1821 under the leadership of Moses Austin, who was awarded a permit by Spanish authorities at San Antonio to settle 300 families in Texas (the contract was later honored by the National Congress of Mexico after independence was won); the provisions of the agreement were carried out by Austin's son Stephen.

One of the main irritants of the American pioneers was the question of slavery. Stephen Austin had assured his colonists that slavery had obtained legal recognition from Mexico, with the stipulation that children born to slaves in Texas would be emancipated at the age of fourteen; but the institution was placed in jeopardy again and again. However, the colonists' specific grievances were lack of trial by jury, the use of Spanish as the official language in legal and commercial transactions, and burdensome customs regulations. Some of the colonists believed that outstanding differences could be resolved if Texas were granted separate statehood, but a more radical faction, led by Sam Houston, looked to complete autonomy and eventual annexation by the United States. When Antonio López de Santa Anna seized dictatorial authority in 1834 and called for additional troops to invade Texas, a military conflict became inevitable. The first clash of the Texas Revolution took place at Gonzales on Oct. 2, 1835. Encouraged by the relative ease of their triumph, the Texan "Army of the People" moved quickly to capture Goliad; in December, San Antonio was occupied after the Mexican garrison capitulated. In late February 1836 the main contingent of Santa Anna's army reached San Antonio, where the Texas defenders were encamped in the Alamo (*see* Alamo, siege of the). Campaigning along the coast, Gen. José Urrea forced the surrender of Col. James Fannin at Goliad (*see* Goliad, Massacre at). News of the fall of the Alamo reached Gen. Houston at Gonzales. Mustering a band of early colonists to Texas and some American volunteers, Houston retreated to the Brazos River, casually pursued by an overconfident Santa Anna. The decisive battle of the campaign was fought at San Jacinto on Apr. 21, 1836; the Texans vanquished the Mexican army and imprisoned its leader (*see* San Jacinto, Battle of). In return for his life Santa Anna recognized the independence of Texas.

During the early stages of the war, Texas had been governed by a "Consultation." When Mexican liberals failed to support the goal of separate statehood, a convention was called that promulgated a declaration of independence (Mar. 2, 1836). A constitution for an independent Texas was also written, with the stipulation that it would not become legally binding until ratified by the people, and the Republic of Texas was born. Sam Houston was elected president in September 1836. The United States became the first nation to commence diplomatic relations with Texas. Annexation talks were tentatively begun. In accordance with the constitution of the republic, Houston could not immediately succeed himself as president, and Mirabeau B. Lamar was elected in 1838. When Mexico refused to meet with peace commissioners sent to Veracruz, the president launched an unsuccessful military expedition to Santa Fe in order to assert the Texan claim to the Rio Grande as its western boundary. Houston was reelected in 1841 and insisted on a posture of peace toward Mexico. The capstone of his administration was the successful conclusion of the annexation negotiations. The state officially joined the Union on Dec. 29, 1845.

Texans soon found themselves involved in another conflict with Mexico. Although it had consented to annexation, Mexico insisted that the boundary of the United States was at the Nueces rather than the Rio Grande (*see* Mexican War). A victorious peace was dictated to Mexico in 1848 by the Treaty of Guadalupe Hidalgo, and the Rio Grande was certified as the boundary by both countries. During the war, Col. Stephen Kearny occupied Santa Fe and established the Territory of New Mexico. This gave rise to an acrimonious boundary dispute since Texas claimed the Rio Grande to its source, thence north on the meridian to the 42nd parallel, thereby including parts of New Mexico as well as the future states of Kansas, Oklahoma, Colorado, and Wyoming. The dispute had national consequences because it involved lands north of 36°30′ and was related to the divisive question of slavery in the territories. Texas was willing to compromise if some settlement of its outstanding indebtedness could be realized; the debt, of approximately $10 million, was assumed by the United States as compensation for a reduction in the state's boundary claims.

In the 1850's, loyalty to the Union or secession became the dominant issue in Texas politics. The majority of Texans viewed the election of Abraham Lincoln as a threat to their slave property and to states' rights. A popular convention endorsed secession, the people ratified it, and Texas officially joined the Confederacy on Mar. 2, 1861. There was little fighting within Texas, which served principally as a conduit for supplies from Mexico. The most spectacular engagement was at Sabine Pass on Sept. 18, 1863, where fewer than fifty men frustrated a Union plan to land 5,000 troops along the Gulf coast. The last battle of the Civil War was fought at Palmetto Ranch, near Brownsville, and led to the final surrender of Confederate troops under Gen. Edmund Kirby-Smith.

By 1866 local elections were held and a constitution written. However, the Reconstruction Act of 1867 declared all prior governments illegal and resulted in the adoption of a new constitution in 1869. The Republican party controlled the elections of 1869. Legislative inexperience was primarily responsible for the passage of many questionable statutes, particularly concerning taxation; financial irregularities increased. By 1874 Texas politics was again under local management when a Democrat, Richard Coke, was chosen governor.

The post-Reconstruction era spawned an economic boom. Internal railroad construction, made possible by state land bonuses, increased appreciably. By the mid-1870's nearly every major city in Texas had passenger and freight service, and attention turned to interstate and transcontinental railroads. Texas increased its production and became the leading cotton-growing state in the Union. The cattle industry also made great strides. The piney woods area of east Texas continued to sustain the lumber industry. In the Rio Grande Valley citrus fruit production became increasingly important. But it was the discovery of oil at Corsicana in 1895 and Spindletop, near Beaumont, in 1901 that revolutionized the state and the national economy. The Texas Company (now Texaco), Gulf Oil Company, and Humble Oil Company (now Exxon) all had their beginnings in the Texas oil fields.

The state has maintained its rate of economic growth and vitality in the 20th century. Construction of a ship channel linking Houston, the U.S. petrochemical center, to the Gulf of Mexico and the advent of the space age combined to make the city one of the fastest-growing in the nation; Houston also became a medical and research center of international fame. Dallas continued to lead in finance, marketing, and insurance activities. The rate of employment in Texas was consistently above the national average. The 1970's witnessed a spectacular economic and demographic growth. While in 1970 Texas ranked thirty-second among U.S. states in per capita income, its rank changed to twentieth in 1980. During the same period the population increased by about 27 percent, to 14,228,383.

TEXAS AND PACIFIC RAILWAY. *See* **Railroads, Sketches of Principal Lines.**

TEXAS CENTENNIAL CENTRAL EXPOSITION. Held at Dallas from June 6 to Nov. 29, 1936, and June 12 to Oct. 31, 1937; largest of the celebrations held to mark the centennial of Texan independence. It cost $25 million; occupied 200 acres in State Fair Park; and attracted almost 13 million visitors. Fifty buildings housed exhibits on the American scene; the principal feature was the "Cavalcade of Texas," a historical spectacle of Texan history.

TEXAS NAVY. Mexico's President Santa Anna was advised against castigation of the rebellious Texans until a Mexican Gulf fleet had been completed paralleling Santa Anna's military advance. But Santa Anna would not wait. In the meantime the Texans, with four small armed ships, were able to seize control of the Gulf. By 1837 Mexico had acquired supremacy on the Gulf, and Texas suffered a partial blockade. In 1838 France blockaded Mexico and destroyed its fleet. Alarmed by French withdrawal in 1839, President Mirabeau B. Lamar committed Texas to a naval program. By 1840 the fleet consisted of an eleven-gun steamer, a twenty-two-gun flagship, and five men-of-war, which Lamar sent to strengthen the negotiations of James Treat. Had Treat followed instructions and traded on the presence of the fleet, he might have been successful. The collapse of the Treat negotiations caused Lamar to enter into a *de facto* alliance with the state of Yucatán, then fighting for independence from the Mexican union. The squadron, under Commodore Edwin W. Moore, captured Tabasco. As late as spring 1843 it fought engagements off Campeche with new Mexican steam warships built and commanded by the British. After annexation, the fleet became the property of the U.S. government.

TEXAS PUBLIC LANDS. By the treaty of annexation between the Republic of Texas and the United States, approved by Congress Mar. 1, 1845, it was stipulated that the state of Texas was to retain control of its 167 million acres of public lands. These lands have since been disposed of; only widely scattered scraps remain.

TEXAS RANGERS. As early as 1826 Texas colonists had from "20 to 30 Rangers in service" against Indians. For years the Texas Rangers were loosely and impermanently organized minutemen. About 1840 a definite corps developed. It ranged out mostly from San Antonio against Indians and Mexicans and made the six-shooter the weapon of the horseback West. During the Mexican War the rangers achieved fame. In the 1870's they brought law and order to the Rio Grande border. In 1935 the Texas Rangers were merged with the state highway patrol.

***TEXAS* V. *WHITE*,** 7 Wallace 700 (1869). An attempt by the Reconstruction governor of Texas to prevent payment on federal bonds disposed of by the secessionist state government in payment of supplies for the Confederacy. The Supreme Court acknowledged the governor's competence to sue on the ground that Texas was now, and had never ceased to be, a member of "an indestructible Union"; hence the ordinance of secession was void. The Court denied the power of the secessionist government to dispose of state property for purposes of rebellion. The decision was overruled in 1885.

TEXIAN. A variant of the word "Texan" that was popular during the ten years of the Republic of Texas.

TEXTILES. Technology. All the technological elements of the European handicraft textile trades came to America with the colonists for the preparation of wool, cotton, and linen yarn, and for weaving and finishing woolen cloth. All operations, apart from fulling, could be performed in the home.

Fortuitously, the American Revolution coincided with Britain's industrialization. Between the revolutionary war and the War of 1812 the immigration of British artisans and the promotion of the American interest in manufacturing brought the new British industrial techniques of manufacturing textiles to the United States. In defiance of British prohibitory laws, the essential components of the new cotton processing system crossed the Atlantic as whole machines, parts, plans, or mental images. The elements of the new woolen manufacturing system were smuggled out of Britain. This period also witnessed the invention by Americans of the cotton gin, by Eli Whitney (1794); the rotary cloth shear, by Samuel G. Dorr (1792); and card clothing machines, by Amos Whittemore (1797) and Pliny Earle (1803).

By the 1830's the factory system, utilizing the new powered machinery, emerged as the dominant organizational form in the cotton and woolen industries. During the initial period of industrialization, 1814–40, a variety of significant innovations appeared. Inventions important for cotton manufacturing were the railway drawing head, by William B. Leonard (1833); roving speeders, by George Danforth (1824) and Gilbert Brewster (1829); the roving frame differential gear, by Asa Arnold (1823); cap spinning, by Charles Danforth (1828); ring spinning, which raised spindle speeds from 3,000 to 6,000 revolutions per minute, by John Thorp (1828); self-acting loom temples, by Ira Draper (1816); the dobby head for fancy powerloom weaving, by William Crompton (1837); and stop motions for the warping frame, by Paul Moody (1816), and for the drawing frame, by Samuel Batchelder (1832). The use of self-acting cotton mules, some from England, spread in the 1830's and 1840's. In woolen manufacturing, John Goulding's condenser (1826), the woolen power loom (1820's), and Crompton's dobby head effected the greatest savings.

Orders for equipment brought a period of relative technological stagnation between the 1840's and about 1870, when immigration, the Civil War, and the westward movement stimulated the demand for textiles. Apart from George Wellman's self-stripping card (1853) and the popularization of ring frames, improvements in cotton machinery came from England: fly frames and a highly productive slasher. In the woolen industry the Apperly intermediate card feed, also from England, and self-acting winding devices for spinning jacks were introduced in the 1860's. In weaving, Crompton increased fancy broadloom speeds to eight-five picks per minute (1857) and Lucius J. Knowles invented a more rugged head motion and the open-shed principle (1863). Use of the rotary fulling mill, claimed by American and British patentees, spread in the 1840's. Probably the most significant innovations were Erastus B. Bigelow's jacquard power loom for weaving Brussels carpets (1846–48) and Elias Howe's sewing machine (1846).

After 1870 inventive effort was directed toward labor-saving improvements. High speeds, simple designs, hard-wearing construction, large capacity, automatic feeding and control, and further mechanization of manual tasks were introduced. The most spectacular results occurred in the cotton industry. In cards, higher capacities were complemented by the perfected self-clearing action of the revolving flat card, imported from England in 1885. With the rise of the competitive southern cotton industry in the 1880's, the northern mills turned to the manufacture of finer goods. To make these, Heilmann-type combers, invented in 1845, were brought from Europe. American combers culminated in the Whitin model of 1904–05, which outpaced European models in simplicity, speed, and capacity.

But spinning and weaving underwent the most farreaching changes. Buying up spindle patents and manufacturing the best of them, George Draper and Sons of Hopedale, Mass., created a revolution in ring spinning. Francis J. Rabbeth's spindle (1878) raised spindle speeds up to 10,000 revolutions per minute. They spelled extinction for the cotton mule.

The automatic loom, developed by a group of Draper engineers (1888–94), incorporated James H. Northrop's bobbin changer, a self-threading shuttle, a weft feeler, and Charles F. Roper's warp stop motion. The automatic loom could weave indefinitely.

Capital-intensive trends continued in other branches of the textile industry. William C. Bramwell's automatic card feed

(1876) and the belated adoption (1870's) of the English automatic mule stood out in woolen manufacturing. Higher throwing speeds and the automatic loom (about 1916) gained the largest labor savings for the silk industry. The perfection of the automatic, seamless, circular knitting machine by J. L. Branson and E. R. Branson (1899) and others gave an enormous fillip to the hosiery trade.

The rise of modern science transformed the nature of textile innovation. The succession of synthetic dyes discovered after 1856 reduced labor costs, widened color ranges, improved color consistency, and encouraged better fabric designs. Synthetic fibers presented more profound changes. Viscose rayon and acetate, pioneered in Europe and commercially manufactured in America after 1910 and 1918, respectively, had begun to challenge the supremacy of the natural fibers by the 1930's. The discovery of polymer fibers, beginning with nylon, developed 1928–38 by Wallace H. Carothers of E. I. Du Pont de Nemours and Company, eventually made it possible to program a fiber with particular chemical and physical properties for specific uses.

In traditional yarn and cloth manufacturing, labor-saving innovations continued. Fernando Casablancas' long draft roving and spinning heads (1913) were adopted in the U.S. cotton industry in the 1930's. The continuous spinning principle was at last applied to wool in Durrell O. Pease's woolen ring spinning frame (1888–95), developed by the Whitin Machine Works (1928–31). It completely ousted the woolen mule in the 1940's and 1950's.

Technical developments in the 1950's and 1960's included nonweaving techniques for making carpets and disposable clothing and breakspinning in which twist is inserted without package rotation. In traditional processing, labor and capital savings were pursued through electronic and mechanical automation, greater capacities, and higher speeds.

Industry. Cotton textile manufacture was the first American industry to make the transition from a handicraft to the factory system and to develop the automated technology necessary for large-volume production. By 1900 the textile industry was probably the nation's largest single employer of industrial labor and producer of machine-made goods. The first phase of the textile industry's development took place in the 1790's, when Samuel Slater introduced the automated carding and spinning machinery that Richard Arkwright and Jedediah Strutt had recently developed in England. Backed by Rhode Island mercantile capital, Slater organized in southern New England a number of small, power-driven spinning factories. The second phase of the industry's development began during the War of 1812, when a group of Boston merchants led by Francis Cabot Lowell and Nathan Appleton entered the industry with their large financial resources. To Slater's preparatory machinery they added components necessary for the application of power and automation to textile manufacturing processes. Between 1820 and 1830 they organized a number of large and very profitable factories at Waltham and Lowell, Mass. The Lowell industrial pattern was repeated in numerous New England towns between 1830 and 1850.

The promotional pattern developed at Lowell had serious implications for the industry's future. The industry thus continued to expand at a furious rate in good times and bad, and capacity increased without regard to market demand. When the South began to industrialize after the Civil War, it was able to import from New England the technology and equipment necessary to build a large textile industry rapidly. By 1950 the industry had largely moved to the Southeast.

THAMES, BATTLE OF THE (Oct. 5, 1813). During the War of 1812 the surrender of Detroit and Michigan Territory gave the British control of practically all the region tributary to the upper Great Lakes. Thereafter the American objective was to recover, the British to retain, Detroit and the Northwest; the two leaders were British Gen. Henry A. Procter and American Gen. William Henry Harrison. Harrison established Fort Meigs (above Toledo), which Procter twice attacked. Meanwhile Capt. Oliver Hazard Perry won the Battle of Lake Erie. Loss of naval control rendered Procter's position untenable, and he sought to retire to Lake Ontario, while Harrison, convoyed by Perry's fleet, hotly pursued. The race ended when Procter was brought to bay a few miles east of Thamesville. Harrison's strength was overwhelming and there could be but one issue to the battle. The battles of Lake Erie and the Thames restored the American dominance in the Northwest.

THANKSGIVING DAY. After the first harvest of the Plymouth, Mass., colonists in 1621, Gov. William Bradford appointed a day of thanksgiving and prayer. Another in 1623 celebrated rain after a drought. After 1630 an annual thanksgiving came to be observed after harvest, and other New England colonies took up the practice. The Continental Congress recommended days of thanksgiving, and in 1784 it decreed a special one for the return of peace. President George Washington proclaimed one on Nov. 26, 1789, at the setting up of the new government, and another in 1795 for general benefits. President James Madison in 1815 again asked the nation to give thanks for peace. By 1830 New York had adopted the day as an annual custom, and other northern states followed. In the South the custom was adopted by Virginia in 1855 and thereafter by the other southern states. President Abraham Lincoln in 1863 made a national proclamation, fixing the fourth Thursday in November. After many changes and disagreements Congress enacted a resolution in 1941 setting the fourth Thursday of November as Thanksgiving.

THEATER. The first known performance in the English colonies, an amateur production of a playlet called *Ye Bare and Ye Cubb,* was presented in Virginia in 1665. Productions by students took place at Harvard (1690) and at William and Mary (1702), and between 1700 and 1750 strolling amateurs were seen at Williamsburg, Va., New York City, Philadelphia, and other major towns. But not until 1752 did the first important professional actors, a company led by Lewis Hallam, appear in the colonies.

The Hallam troupe, a family operation, arrived in September 1752 in Williamsburg and in the next three years performed there and in New York, Philadelphia, and Charleston, S.C. In 1755 the troupe sailed for Jamaica, where a theater operation under David Douglass was already established. The next year Hallam died, and in 1758 his widow married Douglass, who took over the company. Douglass established the first fairly substantial permanent theater buildings in the colonies, among them the Southwark Theatre in Philadelphia (1766) and the John Street Theatre in New York (1767). In 1775, after the Continental Congress banned all "exhibitions of shews, plays, and other expensive diversions and entertainments," Douglass left permanently for Jamaica. The prohibition was more honored in the breach, and the Revolution marked a return to amateur performance.

After the war, Douglass' troupe soon returned to America, competing with other new companies. By the 1790's there were four principal professional circuits in the East, centered at Charleston, Philadelphia, New York, and Boston. The theatrical fare offered consisted mostly of English plays, although an increasing number of Americans were writing plays: Royall Tyler, author of *The Contrast* (1787), the best-known early American play; the painter and theater manager William Dunlap; and John Howard Payne, the first American to achieve international recognition as a playwright.

West of the Alleghenies, professional performance conditions remained primitive. Troupes toured by flatboat or wagon, setting up whenever and wherever there was a chance of attracting a profitable crowd, carrying only the few simple sets and equipment necessary to turn any convenient room into a crude theater. By the late 1830's showboats brought theater to major river towns. Among the pioneer professional companies in the West were those of James H. Caldwell, Noah Miller Ludlow, and Solomon Franklin Smith.

Gradually, a small group of talented and imaginative native actors developed, among them Edwin Forrest, the first American actor to gain international fame. Forrest popularized an "American" school of acting, a highly athletic performance style. Much of Forrest's success came in new American plays, a number of them built around native themes or characters. From the 1830's to the Civil War era the romantic Indian play provided a staple of American entertainment.

Also popular toward the middle of the century were plays featuring the so-called "Yankee," a simple and often naive figure, invariably earnest, stout-hearted, and patriotic, first seen in the character of Jonathan in Tyler's *The Contrast.* Between 1830 and 1850 dozens of tailor-made Yankee plays appeared. If the Yankee stood for rural values and standards, urban life was represented by the figure of the volunteer fireman. The fireboy appeared initially as the diamond-in-the-rough Mose the Bowery Bhoy in Benjamin A. Baker's *A Glance at New York in 1848* (1848), the first of many city lowlife comedies in vogue until the 1860's.

Immensely popular at mid-century was the minstrel show, a uniquely American form of variety performance that featured white entertainers in blackface presenting songs, jokes, dances, and comedy sketches. The professional minstrel troupes flourished from about 1850 to 1870. Also in demand were burlesques, in which well-known plays, novels, events, and personalities were parodied in light musical productions. Among the best-known were those created by John Brougham and George W. L. Fox. Fox also helped to popularize pantomime in the United States.

Professional theater troupes reached the Far West spurred by the appearance of gold in California in 1848, the discovery of the Comstock lode in 1859, and other major mining strikes. Troupes in the West were also fostered by the Mormons, who after 1865 sponsored a resident professional company in Salt Lake City, Utah. In 1869 the first transcontinental railroad opened the entire West to touring companies.

The number of resident stock companies in America gradually increased; there were about fifty on the eve of the Civil War. Among the best was the company formed in 1853 at the Arch Street Theatre in Philadelphia by John Drew and Louisa Lane Drew, founders of the Drew-Barrymore theatrical dynasty. Although the stock company remained the major producing organization in most urban areas, its form was altered by new developments. Companies relied less on producing many plays in rotation, choosing instead to limit the number and give each a relatively long run. By the last quarter of the century local repertory had been almost totally destroyed by the long-run concept and the touring company. As railroad connections improved, "combination" companies —packages made up of a long-running play or plays, a star, and a company of supporting players—began to appear more frequently. Gradually local stock companies could perform in their own theaters only when those theaters were not occupied by combination productions. By 1900 there was scarcely a resident stock company left.

As the touring show replaced the stock company, critical booking problems developed. This led to the increased use of booking agents and, in 1896, to the so-called "Theatrical Syndicate," which offered managers a full season of first-class road shows on the understanding that the managers book only through the syndicate. Uncooperative managers and producers were often forced out of business, and stars who refused to appear in syndicate shows often found it impossible to obtain any theater in which to perform. The syndicate was opposed by a number of powerful figures in the American theater, among them the Shubert brothers, Sam S., Lee, and Jacob J. Setting up a rival operation, the Shuberts gradually wrested more and more control from the syndicate until, by 1916, it was no longer an effective force in the theater.

The 19th-century theater witnessed a growth of interest in both realism and spectacle. By the last third of the century, elaborate machinery was being developed at major theaters to handle an increasingly complex and detailed stagecraft and one that relied more heavily on the three-dimensional box setting. Realism and spectacle presented difficult staging problems for touring companies, which were often forced to work in theaters outfitted only with traditional stage machinery, much of it of doubtful quality.

By the last quarter of the century a number of professional playwrights had emerged, including Steele MacKaye, Bronson Howard, Bartley Campbell, and Augustus Thomas. Among the most notable were William Clyde Fitch; the playwright-actor William Gillette, best known for his Civil War melodrama *Secret Service* (1895) and his adaptation from the stories of Sir Arthur Conan Doyle, *Sherlock Holmes* (1899); and James A. Herne, author of the important realistic drama *Margaret Fleming* (1890). The farces of Charles H. Hoyt and Edward Harrigan were an important contribution to the stage of the day, as the plays of George M. Cohan were in the first years of the new century. The burlesque tradition moved farther in the direction of the musical variety show, which it was to become in the 20th century. Vaudeville, which had developed out of the earlier male-only variety shows, had become a vital force and remained so until the 1930's. The Yiddish Theater in New York, at a low ebb around the turn of the century, was shortly to begin a period of great creativity and prosperity under such figures as Maurice Schwartz and Rudolph Schildkraut.

Gradually, the work of European playwrights, directors, and stage designers began to make its influence felt in the United States. The plays of Henrik Ibsen and George Bernard Shaw were produced in America, and by World War I American audiences had seen Dublin's Abbey Theatre (1911), Sergei Diaghilev's Ballets Russes (1916), and Jacques Copeau's company (1917), as well as Max Reinhardt's starkly designed production of *Sumurun* (1912). Other European experiments in stage and costume design—generally referred to collectively as the "new stagecraft"—were brought to the United States in the work of Joseph Urban, the Viennese designer.

Among the most important influences from Europe was the so-called "independent theater" movement. The result in the United States was a number of "little theaters" that drew their inspiration from the independent theater tradition. Among the best known were the Neighborhood Playhouse and the Washington Square Players, established in New York in 1915, and the Provincetown Players, founded at Provincetown, Mass., the same year and relocated in New York in 1916. The Washington Square Players became the Theatre Guild in 1918 and, under the leadership of director Philip Moeller and Lee Simonson, presented a number of excellent plays.

Ironically, the Great Depression produced some of America's most interesting theater work. An active workers' theater movement, which led to the production of many Socialist protest plays, had begun to develop as early as the mid-1920's. In 1933 the Theatre Union was formed in New York to coordinate workers' theater groups around the country. By 1937 the Theatre Union had failed, and by the beginning of World War II workers' theater had largely disappeared. Meanwhile the Federal Theatre Project was established in 1935. Out of the Federal Theatre came the experimental Mercury Theatre, founded in 1937 by Orson Welles and John Houseman.

In 1923–24 Konstantin Stanislavski's Moscow Art Theatre toured the United States. Two of the actors, Richard Boleslavski and Maria Ouspenskaya, remained in America and from 1923 to 1930 ran the American Laboratory Theatre, which first popularized the Stanislavski System of actor training in America. In 1930 former students were influential in founding the Group Theatre, modeled on Stanislavski's organization. The Actors Studio, founded by Strasberg, Crawford, and Kazan in 1947, became the home of the Stanislavski System in America. The Playwrights' Company, founded in 1938, continued to be a force until 1960.

Between World War I and World War II the United States began to produce playwrights of international reputation: Maxwell Anderson, Sidney Howard, Robert E. Sherwood, Philip Barry, Elmer Rice, S. N. Behrman, Thornton Wilder, Clifford Odets, and Lillian Hellman. Perhaps America's most important playwright was Eugene O'Neill.

The years after World War II witnessed the development of a number of other new playwrights, notably Tennessee Williams and Arthur Miller. In the 1960's, Broadway produced Neil Simon and Edward Albee. In the same period the American musical comedy was developed to a high level in such work as *Oklahoma!* (1943), by Oscar Hammerstein II and Richard Rodgers, and the musicals of Alan Jay Lerner and Frederick Loewe. Other important musical comedies were by Jules Styne and Leonard Bernstein, and Arthur Laurents.

In spite of such capable work, Broadway theater offerings continued to decline in both number and quality, the victims of rising ticket prices and growing competition from television. The postwar era was marked, however, by a flurry of regional theater activity. Interest in regional theater continued throughout the 1970's. Many of the summer stock companies founded during the postwar period have succeeded, and light summer theater entertainment is available throughout the country.

The problems that beset the New York theater in the 1950's led to the growth of the off-Broadway movement, which featured low-budget, often experimental productions of plays that could not get a hearing on Broadway. Important off-Broadway organizations included the Circle in the Square, founded in 1951 by José Quintero and Theodore Mann, and the Phoenix Theatre, founded in 1953 by Norris Houghton and T. Edward Hambleton.

The Living Theatre (1948), directed by Julian Beck and Judith Malina, began as an off-Broadway troupe, then became part of the later off-off-Broadway movement. Centering around experimental performance, off-off Broadway attained international importance through several play-producing organizations. The same period produced a number of experimental theater companies, which depended less on the work of playwrights than on productions created out of group exercises and improvisation. Along with the Living Theatre, other important companies working in this way included Joseph Chaikin's Open Theater and Richard Schechner's Performance Group. In the 1960's and 1970's much interest was generated by the Ontological-Hysteric Theater (1968–1977), an experimental group directed by Richard Foreman.

By the late 1970's and early 1980's, Broadway theater had become more and more oriented toward entertainment, with showy musicals, many of them revivals, overshadowing drama and even comedy. Despite increasing ticket prices, the attendance soared to about 10 million people per year.

THEOCRACY IN NEW ENGLAND. Usually applied to the political regime set up by the founders of the Massachusetts Bay and New Haven colonies. The leaders deliberately intended to create a "Bible Commonwealth," a society in which the fundamental law would be the revealed Word of God, and God would be regarded as the supreme legislator. Consequently the political theory assumed that the colonies were based on the Bible and that all specific laws must be required to show biblical warrant.

THEOLOGY. *See* **Religious Thought and Writings.**

THEOSOPHY. Defined by its expounders as a religion-philosophy-science brought to America by "messengers of the guardians and preservers of the ancient Wisdom-Religion of the East." Its founder was an eccentric Russian noblewoman, Helena P. Blavatsky. After extensive travels in the Far East, where she claimed to have received instruction from "Sages of the Orient," she came to New York City (July 7, 1873) and two years later, with William Q. Judge, Henry Steel Olcott, and fifteen others, formed the Theosophical Society. The purpose was to further a universal brotherhood of humanity without distinction of race, color, sex, caste, or creed; to further the study of the ancient scriptures and teachings, such as Brahmanical, Buddhist, and Zoroastrian; and to investigate the "unexplained laws of Nature" and the psychic and spiritual powers latent in man. It accepts the miracles of Jesus but denies their supernatural character, holding that they were accomplished through natural laws. In the early 1980's there were 6,000 members of theosophical societies, known as lodges, in the United States.

THIRD PARTIES. Although the fortunes of the various third (or "minor") political parties have waxed and waned, there have been few periods since the middle of the 19th century in which the American party system has been without them. Diverse both in origin and goals, third parties have been largely noncompetitive within the American two-party system.

Some of the American third parties have been marked by overriding commitments to issues, such as the antislavery Liberty and Free Soil parties of the 1840's and 1850's, the agrarian protest parties of the post–Civil War period (Greenback and Populist parties), and the Socialist parties of the 20th century. While these parties have rejected to varying degrees the electoral competitiveness of the major parties, some have been electoral such as parties in the more conventional sense, the National Progressive ("Bull Moose") party of 1912 and the Dixiecrat party of 1948.

In organizational form, too, American third parties have been diverse. A good many have been small organizations with national memberships but with little or no state or local apparatus. Others have developed the layers of party committees found in the major parties. Still others, such as George Wallace's American Independent party in the 1960's and 1970's, have largely been national movements centering around a single person and maintaining only those local organizations necessary to achieve access to the ballot in the states. Some third parties have had virtually no organization.

The electoral effect and importance of the third parties have not been great. Since the formation of a stable two-party system around the time of the Civil War, no third party has won a presidential election. Only the National Progressive Party of 1912, with Theodore Roosevelt as its candidate, came in second. Only four other third parties have even carried a state in a presidential election: the Populists in 1892, the Progressives in 1924, the Dixiecrats in 1948, and the American Independents in 1968. Many of the third parties by the middle of the 20th century found it increasingly difficult both to get on the ballots of the states and to muster the resources for a campaign.

Some third parties have enjoyed at least short periods of electoral success in some states and localities. Some have controlled local offices for varying periods of time; the Socialist party held many mayorships before World War I. In 1968 and afterward, the predominantly black National Democratic party of Alabama elected a number of local officials. The Nonpartisan League controlled the North Dakota governorship and legislature from World War I into the 1920's, and its offshoot, the Farmer-Labor party of Minnesota, controlled that state's governorship and showed substantial strength in the legislature throughout the 1930's. Other local parties captured one of the two major parties in the primary and ran its candidates under that party's label; the Wisconsin Progressives so operated within the Republican party until the 1930's.

THIRD-TERM DOCTRINE. The Constitutional Convention of 1787 made no explicit determination that the president was eligible for reelection, but that step was generally presumed to be permissible without limitation on the number of terms. In the New York ratifying convention, a proposed ban on a third term was defeated. The doctrine that the president should be limited to two terms received its original impetus from George Washington for reasons that were personal rather than political. In 1796, Washington, because of age and poor health, eagerly desired retirement. Thomas Jefferson was the first president to assert the third-term doctrine on political grounds. Jefferson wanted to safeguard the two-term limit with an amendment. His successors James Madison and James Monroe fortified the doctrine by serving only two terms each. Andrew Jackson also relinquished the presidency after a second term. For a century the doctrine was favored by the fact that between the presidencies of Jackson and Franklin D. Roosevelt, there were only four chief executives—Ulysses S. Grant, Grover Cleveland, Theodore Roosevelt, and Calvin Coolidge—who were in a position to tamper with it. During World War II the doctrine was finally overcome when Franklin D. Roosevelt was elected to not only a third but a fourth term. Doubtless the pressures of war prompted the doctrine's defeat. But the defeat was only temporary. In 1951 the Twenty-second Amendment was adopted, a sweeping incorporation of the third-term doctrine into the Constitution.

THIRTEENTH AMENDMENT. One of the so-called Civil War amendments, the amendment abolished slavery. Before the war, Congress had adopted a resolution for an amendment that would deny it the power to abolish slavery in any state. But as the war progressed both the president and Congress became convinced that the federal government must assume power over slavery. By the Confiscation Acts of 1861–62, slaves of disloyal owners were subject to forfeiture to the national government and could thereby be freed. The Emancipation Proclamation, Jan. 1, 1863, as a war measure, declared free the slaves in the parts of the Confederacy still unconquered. At the end of the war existing laws and proclamations left the slaves of loyal owners untouched and did not apply to the whole of the slave-owning region; they provided for freeing the slaves, but did not abolish slavery. An amendment to the U.S. Constitution was required to clarify the legal issues. In its final form the resolution was reported to the Senate by Lyman Trumbull of Illinois, chairman of the Judiciary Committee. The resolution passed the Senate, Apr. 8, 1864, by a vote of 38 to 6. In the House it failed at first to secure the necessary two-thirds vote, but passed later, 119 to 56, with 8 representatives not voting (Jan. 31, 1865). Ratification by the former seceded states was required as part of President Andrew Johnson's Reconstruction program, and eight of these states were counted officially in the three-fourths of the states necessary to ratification on Dec. 18, 1865.

THOMAS AMENDMENT (1933). The popular term for Title III of the Agricultural Adjustment Act of May 12, 1933. It gave the president power, directly or through the secretary of the Treasury, to inflate the currency by (a) making agreements with the Federal Reserve Board and Federal Reserve banks for the latter to buy up to $3 billion of government securities, (b) issuing $3 billion in U.S. notes, (c) devaluing the dollar up to 50 percent and/or reestablishing bimetallism, and (d) receiving war debt payments in silver at 50 cents an ounce up to $200 million.

THOMAS AMENDMENT OF 1820. *See* **Missouri Compromise.**

"THOUSAND DAYS." A term sometimes used to designate the period of President John F. Kennedy's administration from Jan. 20, 1961 to Nov. 22, 1963.

THREE-FIFTHS COMPROMISE. *See* **Compromises of the U.S. Constitution; Constitution of the United States.**

THREE-MILE ISLAND. On March 28, 1979, an operating nuclear power reactor at Three Mile Island in the Susquehanna River near Harrisburg, Pa., was shut down due to a series of mishaps. A hydrogen bubble had formed in the overheated reactor, causing fear of a core meltdown or the possibility of a hydrogen explosion. During the subsequent three days panic spread among the nearby population, with many fleeing the area. Although the worst did not occur, it was the worst nuclear accident to date in the nation.

THREE-MILE LIMIT. *See* **Territorial Waters.**

THREE NOTCH ROAD. So-called from the manner of marking the trees along its course, a pioneer road of Mississippi connecting Natchez with St. Stephens, on the lower Tombigbee. It was first marked after the Choctaw cession of 1805 and formed part of the northern boundary of that cession.

THREE RIVERS, BATTLE OF (June 8, 1776). A force of about 2,000 men under Brig. Gen. William Thompson attempted to surprise the British garrison at Three Rivers, in Quebec, Canada. The Americans were misled by a guide and their attack delayed, while the garrison, commanded by Brig. Gen. Simon Fraser, was much stronger than they had believed and was supported by ships on the Saint Lawrence River. The attack was a failure.

THREE SAINTS BAY. Site of the first permanent European settlement in Alaska on the south shore of the island of Kodiak. Gregory Ivanovich Shelekhov, a Russian fur trader, set up permanent headquarters there in 1784 because it was near the Aleutian Islands fur areas.

THRESHING MACHINE. The colonial farmer brought to the task of threshing the same primitive methods used from ancient times. Three processes were involved: threshing, or shelling the kernels from the head with the flail; raking off the straw, leaving the grain and the chaff; and winnowing, separating the chaff from the grain, by throwing the grain in the air, allowing the wind to blow away the chaff. The credit for developing a complete thresher for accomplishing all three processes goes to Andrew Meikle of Scotland, who in 1788 patented a thresher, in 1789 added a separator, and in 1800 added a fanning mill. This machine could not be operated by hand. Until the application of the steam engine, the only solution was horse power. Then, in the early 1820's, Jacob Pope put on the market a cheap hand-operated thresher. The first American machine to combine the three operations was built by John and Hiram Pitts of Winthrop, Maine. In 1840 John Pitts had established a factory at Albany, which was later moved to Buffalo. Hiram Pitts in 1847 began manufacturing threshers in Alton, Ill., moving to Chicago in 1851. Up to the late 1870's the horse continued to be the source of power. Then, in the Far West, where wheat was grown on a large scale, the steam tractor came into general use. Here too the thresher was attached to the harvester, making a single unit, the combine.

THRIFT STAMPS. To increase savings in the United States during World War I and obtain money for war expenses the government created thrift stamps and war savings certificates. Thrift stamps were about the size of postage stamps and cost twenty-five cents but bore no interest. The purchaser was given a card containing spaces for sixteen stamps. A card filled, with a value of $4.00, could be exchanged for a war savings stamp (certificate).

TICONDEROGA, CAPTURE OF (1775). The immediate object of capturing the British post of Ticonderoga was not only to take the dilapidated fort, but also to obtain cannon for the siege of Boston. The Hartford Committee of Correspondence raised more than fifty men and £300 and urged the Green Mountain Boys to take part. It was decided that Ethan Allen should command, and the rendezvous was set for Hand's Cove on the eastern shore of Lake Champlain. Meanwhile, Col. Benedict Arnold had been commissioned by the Massachusetts Committee of Safety to raise 400 men, and with a single servant he arrived at Hand's Cove to claim command. It was finally agreed that Allen and Arnold should enter the fort side by side at the head of the column. Early in the morning of May 10, Allen, Arnold, and eighty-three men crossed the lake in two boats. After a harangue by Allen, the expedition passed through the ruined walls and without bloodshed subdued the sleepy garrison, consisting of Capt. William Delaplace, Lt. Jocelyn Feltham, and forty-three men.

TICONDEROGA, FORT. Begun in October 1755 by the Marquis de Lotbinière as an outpost for Fort St. Frédéric, the fort was named Carillon by the French. It commanded the route between lakes Champlain and George and was called Ticonderoga by the English. The fort has been restored.

TICONDEROGA, OPERATIONS AT (1758–59). In 1758 British Gen. James Abercromby, with more than 15,000 men, attacked Louis Joseph, Marquis de Montcalm, the French commander, who had only 3,600 men. Montcalm decided to build and defend a strong abatis to the northwest of the fort. When Gen. George Augustus Howe, Abercromby's second in command, was killed, the soul went out of the expedition. Abercromby, ignoring his artillery, tried to take the impregnable French position by storm and lost 1,944 men as against 377 lost by the French. He retreated in a panic.

The next summer Sir Jeffrey Amherst led another army against Ticonderoga. He had 11,000 men, and the French, about 3,500. So thoroughly did Amherst prepare his siege that on July 26, 1759, the French blew up the fort and retreated.

TICONDEROGA, TAKING OF. In 1777 the British moved to recapture Fort Ticonderoga, N.Y., occupied by Americans since 1775. British Gen. John Burgoyne's 9,000 men were opposed by Gen. Arthur Saint Clair's 2,500. The British dragged cannon up Sugar Hill (Mount Defiance), which commanded the fort from the southwest. Mount Independence to the southeast was connected with Ticonderoga by a bridge of boats. Shortly after midnight on July 6, Saint Clair retreated across the bridge, leaving the fort to the British.

TIDELANDS. Lands lying under the sea beyond the low-water limit of the tide but considered within the territorial waters of a nation. The U.S. Constitution does not specify whether ownership of these lands rests with the federal government or with the individual states. The states generally proceeded as if they were the owners. The value of the tidelands was heightened when it became known that vast deposits of oil and natural gas lay within their limits. The first producing offshore oil well was completed in 1938 in the Gulf of Mexico one mile off the Louisiana coast; in 1947 the second well was brought in off the coast of Terrebonne Parish, also in Louisiana. In that same year the Supreme Court ruled *(United States* v. *California)* that all tidelands were owned by the federal government. The issue became important in the 1952 presidential campaign. The Republican candidate, Dwight D. Eisenhower, pledged legislation that would restore the tidelands to the states. In 1953 two acts were passed that fulfilled his promise. The Submerged Lands Act extended state ownership to 3 miles from their actual coastline except for Florida and Texas, where ownership was extended to 10.5 miles. The Outer Continental Shelf Lands Act gave the United States paramount rights from the point where state ownership leaves off to where international waters begin. Numerous lawsuits were initiated, and state taxes and leasing fees were put in escrow, pending final resolution. The issue was finally decided on May 31, 1960, when the Supreme Court ruled that Mississippi, Alabama, and Louisiana owned the rights to the offshore lands for 3.5 miles, and Texas and Florida rights were ruled as extending 3 leagues, or approximately 10.5 miles. Although the other Gulf states objected to what was considered preferential treatment to Florida and Texas, no new legislation resulted, and in 1963 the U.S. Justice Department settled the last of the tidelands controversies; it ruled that the 1953 act gave control to the states of islands near the shore that were created after the states had been admitted to the Union.

TIDE MILLS. Mills erected in the flat tidal coast country, where other waterpower was not available. A dike was built across the mouth of a marsh or inlet so the tide could enter and fill the reservoir thus formed. The water was retained until the receding ocean left a head sufficient to turn an undershot waterwheel for a few hours. Such mills were in operation in eastern Massachusetts as early as 1650.

TIDEWATER. That part of the Atlantic coastal plain lying east of the points in rivers reached by oceanic tides. Merchants and shippers in the towns and planters growing tobacco, rice, indigo, and cotton dominated the tidewater population. First to settle and the earliest to be established economically, socially, and politically, the inhabitants of the tidewater regions secured control of the government. But the later population, composed largely of small farmers, which moved beyond into the piedmont region, found this tidewater domination of government both unfair and injurious. Sometimes, as in Bacon's Rebellion of 1676 in Virginia, the Paxton riots of 1764 in Pennsylvania, and the Regulator movement of 1768–71 in North Carolina, the conflict resulted in open warfare.

TIGRE ISLAND. The acquisition of California in 1848 was an immediate stimulus to U.S. and British rivalry for isthmian advantages, from Tehuantepec, Mexico, to Panama. Tigre Island, located in the Gulf of Fonseca, off the coast of Honduras, was a pawn in the game. Great Britain illegally seized the island. The United States countered by getting a cession treaty of questionable validity from Honduras. The issue was liquidated in the self-denying clauses of the Clayton-Bulwer Treaty of 1850.

TILLMANISM. A South Carolina aspect of the agrarian movement inaugurated by Benjamin R. Tillman in 1885. In letters to the *Charleston News and Courier* he expressed the grievances of the white rural population against the dominant forces of the post-Reconstruction period in that strongly southern commonwealth. He accused the merchants of extortionate charges for advances to farmers; the oligarchy under former Gov. Wade Hampton of greed and of failure to be progressive; the state college of improper expenditure of federal appropriations for agricultural education; and the Afro-American of trying to recover his Reconstruction privileges. His formula for success was effective appeal to the prejudices of the majority against the minority. In 1890, after arousing unparalleled enthusiasm for himself and his measures by a canvass of the state, Tillman became governor. Officeholders were supplanted by Tillman partisans; black suffrage was destroyed, and the white masses gained greater political power; colleges were founded for vocational education of white boys and girls; corporations were forced to pay a greater share of taxation; and a state liquor monopoly was established.

TIMBER CULTURE ACT (1873). Principal deterrents to settlement in the Plains country were absence of timber, insufficient rainfall, hot winds, and dust storms. A weather hypothesis of the 1870's was that growing timber tempered the climate and increased humidity and perhaps rainfall. Residents of the Plains country urged the government to encourage tree planting. Congress passed the Timber Culture Act, according to which 160 acres could be entered by settlers who would set out 40 acres to trees. Ten million acres were donated, but much fraud was involved and little permanent tree growth resulted. Widespread abuse of the act led to its repeal in 1891.

TIMBERLANDS. *See* **Lumber Industry.**

TIME, STANDARD. *See* **Railroads.**

"TIMES THAT TRY MEN'S SOULS." Short title of the first of twelve essays published during the American Revolution by Thomas Paine. The first was written in 1776. The essays, collected under the title *The Crisis,* were intended to bolster the morale of the American people.

TIME TABLE CONVENTIONS. *See* **American Railway Association.**

TIN CAN. The earliest tin cans were laboriously made and sealed by hand. Two of the most important improvements in their manufacture were the drop press invented by Allen Taylor in 1847 and the combination press invented by Henry Evans a few years later. The lock seamer was invented in 1869 and the automatic soldering of can ends in 1876. The first completely automatic canmaking machinery was put into operation in 1885 in Baltimore. The manufacture of aluminum cans began in 1958. Aluminum is less expensive than tin; aluminum cans weigh less than tin, thereby reducing shipping costs. By the 1970's tin cans, aluminum cans, and cans combining both metals were all being produced.

TINIAN (July 24–Aug. 1, 1944). The invasion of Tinian by American forces in World War II was a natural sequel to the capture of Saipan, another of the Mariana Islands about three miles south of Saipan. To take advantage of field artillery based on Saipan, landing beaches on northern Tinian were chosen for amphibious assault. On July 24, the Marines landed and pushed rapidly inland. The landing was preceded by several days' bombardment by ships, field artillery, carrier-based aircraft, and aircraft based on Saipan. Tactical surprise was achieved, since the Japanese had concentrated defenses against beaches to the south. The Marines quickly overran the island. Tinian was declared secured on Aug. 1. Tinian was then developed into the major U.S. Air Force base for the strategic bombardment of Japan.

TIN PAN ALLEY. A phrase probably coined early in the 1900's, describing the theatrical section of Broadway in New York City, where the popular song publishers were located, initially the area around Twenty-eighth Street and Sixth Avenue. The term suggests the tinny quality of the cheap, overabused pianos in the song publishers' offices. The term became applied to the industry at large.

TINTYPE. A distinctively American style of photograph, made by the wet process on black japanned metal; patented by Hamilton L. Smith of Gambier, Ohio, in 1856. Originally introduced as the melainotype and the ferrotype.

TINWARE PEDDLERS. In 1738 two brothers, Irish tinsmiths named Edward and William Pattison, settled in Berlin, Conn. Because tinplate was scarce they began to import tinplate from England. The plate was shaped into vessels and sold from door to door. When the local demand had been met they carried their wares to nearby settlements. Others soon entered the business. With a cart or wagon loaded with tin vessels the peddlers would start in the autumn on an expedition into the southern states or wherever they could find settlements. After the close of the War of 1812 as many as 10,000 boxes of tinplate a year were made into tinware in the village. By 1820 the peddler began to add other items to his stock; other methods of distribution had become more efficient; and the tinware peddler disappeared.

TIPPECANOE, BATTLE OF (Nov. 7, 1811). The opposition of Tecumseh to the steady advance of European settlers in the Northwest produced a situation that could be resolved only by military might. In the summer of 1811 the Indian leader, after renewing his demands on Gen. William Henry Harrison, governor of the Indiana Territory, at Vincennes, departed to rally tribes of the Southwest to the confederacy he was organizing. Harrison decided to strike first. The Indian capital of Prophetstown was on Tippecanoe Creek, 150 miles north of Vincennes; and Harrison began his northward advance on Sept. 26 with 1,000 soldiers. Most of October was spent constructing Fort Harrison at Terre Haute, about sixty-five miles from Vincennes, to serve as an advance base. On Oct. 28 the march resumed, and a week later the army was within striking distance of Prophetstown. Harrison yielded to belated appeals for a conference. He encamped on an elevated site a mile from the village. Although mutual promises were exchanged that no hostilities would be indulged in before the morrow, warriors were stirred to a frenzy by Tecumseh's brother, known as the Prophet. Shortly before dawn (Nov. 7) they stormed the still-sleeping camp. The soldiers sprang to action, and the battle raged until daylight, when a series of charges drove the warriors from the field. Harrison razed the Indian town on Nov. 8 and began the retreat to distant Fort Harrison.

"TIPPECANOE AND TYLER TOO!" The campaign slogan of the Whigs in 1840, when William Henry Harrison, the hero of the Battle of Tippecanoe, and John Tyler were their candidates for the presidency and vice-presidency, respectively.

***TITANIC*, SINKING OF THE** (Apr. 14, 1912). The largest ship in existence at the time, the White Star liner *Titanic*, bound for New York on its maiden voyage with 2,223 persons aboard, struck a partly submerged iceberg in the North Atlantic at 11:40 P.M. It sank 2 hours and 40 minutes later, with the loss of 832 passengers and 685 of the crew. The liner *Californian* was only a few miles distant, but its operator was asleep and its instruments silent. The eastbound liner *Carpathia*, fifty-six miles distant, caught the *Titanic*'s distress signal, sped to the scene, picked up over 700 survivors, and returned to New York.

TITHES, SOUTHERN AGRICULTURAL. An expedient of the Confederate congress for securing subsistence for its armies. Taxes collected in the depreciated currency of the times did not bring in enough revenue; the levy in kind was adopted on Apr. 24, 1863, to tap resources of Confederate farms. It was reasoned that one-tenth of the products of a population of 7 or 8 million would support armies less than one-tenth as numerous. Complaints because of alleged class distinctions led to modification, but it was an important factor in the survival of the southern armies.

TITHINGMEN. Town officers of colonial New England charged with getting out church attendance and maintaining decorous conduct on the Sabbath.

TITLES OF NOBILITY. *See* **Nobility, Titles of.**

TLINGIT. *See* **Haida.**

TOBACCO AND NARCOTICS, AMERICAN INDIAN. The smoking of hemp and some other drugs was known in Eurasia before 1492. But the world at large is indebted to the American Indians for the domestication of tobacco. Christopher Columbus' crew observed the natives of Hispaniola smoking cigars, and by 1559 Portugal and Spain imported tobacco leaves for their alleged medical properties. By 1600 tobacco was raised widely in Europe despite initial adverse reactions from both church and state, and it continued to spread across Asia.

Tobacco appears wild in the tropics and in desert areas. Its spread and hybridization by man, the fact that it was smoked in many forms, eaten, chewed, sniffed, and drunk, and employed ceremonially, socially, and individually are all features suggestive of considerable antiquity. The tropical forests of South America have been regarded by some as the point of origin of tobacco domestication. But the narcotic properties of tobacco may have been discovered several times in the course of American Indian cultural development.

The distribution of the uses of tobacco varies. Tropical South America and the Antilles had the cigar, Mexico and the Pueblo region knew corn-husk cigarettes, while pipes appear all over. In the West, tobacco was eaten with lime, a practice common in California, the Great Basin, and southeastern Alaska. In the Great Lakes region the association of the pipe with peace deliberations gave rise to the American "peace pipe" concept. In southern California some Indian tribes drank a mixture of tobacco and datura, the jimsonweed or toloache, both vision-inducing drugs.

Several hallucinogenic drugs were known to native North America. In addition to the jimsonweed of the Southwest, peyote is perhaps the best known. *Lophophora williamsii*, the cactus that produces color visions and hallucinations when ingested, spread from Mexico to the Southwest in the 18th century. In the 20th century peyote became associated with the revivalistic Native American Church.

Most native American narcotics, including tobacco, appear to have been evolved by the farmers of Middle America. Hallucinogenic mushrooms and peyote were Mexican discoveries that spread to the north. The Pima and Papago of Arizona made wine from the saguaro cactus, the only verifiable instance of North American alcohol. The persimmon wine of the Virginia tribes may be aboriginal but is authenticated with difficulty. It is eminently clear that when the native cultures of North America sought release in drugs, they most often depended on tobacco.

TOBACCO AS MONEY. Because of the scarcity of metallic money, Virginia, Maryland, and North Carolina used tobacco as currency throughout most of the colonial period. In 1619 the Virginia legislature "rated" tobacco at "three shillings the best and the second sort at 18d. in the pound," and a statute of 1642 made tobacco a legal tender. Maryland began to use tobacco for money soon after its founding. In 1715 the North Carolina legislature fixed the price of tobacco at 10 shillings per hundredweight. North Carolina used tobacco as money until the Revolution.

Overproduction of tobacco led to sharp fluctuations in its market price, although the price was theoretically fixed. There was also a tendency to pay debts in inferior tobacco, in spite of inspection laws. It was also found to be impracticable to transfer large quantities of tobacco from hand to hand. Accordingly in 1727 Virginia adopted "tobacco notes," certificates issued by official inspectors of government warehouses. Apparently Maryland made little use of tobacco notes.

TOBACCO CONTRACT. After the exemption from customs duties allowed by the charters of the Virginia Company and the Bermuda Company had terminated in 1619, it proved difficult to secure satisfactory terms for the importation of colonial tobacco into England. Sir Edwin Sandys, whose followers controlled both companies, negotiated with the government in 1622 a contract giving the companies a joint monopoly of all tobacco importations. The terms were none too favorable. An appeal to the Privy Council set aside the contract in March 1623. The struggle brought a signal victory to Sandys' opponents in the offer in April of terms more favorable than any since 1619, and led directly to a petition for a royal investigation. The contract contributed to the dissolution of the Virginia Company of London in 1624.

TOBACCO COOPERATIVES. *See* **Cooperatives, Tobacco.**

TOBACCO INDUSTRY. John Rolfe's experiments in 1612 to develop a tobacco to replace the indigenous variety soon produced a major exportable staple for Virginia, Maryland, and North Carolina. The exportation of over 100 million pounds annually to England by the eve of the Revolution is evidence of its economic significance. The tobacco industry had regained its prewar productivity by 1790, when about 78 percent of the crop was exported.

The decline and later end of tobacco production in postrevolutionary tidewater Virginia was accompanied by a comparable expansion into the piedmont district of Virginia and North Carolina and into South Carolina and Georgia by the early 1790's. By 1800 tobacco was emerging as a staple in Kentucky and Tennessee. During the next half century Florida, Louisiana, Missouri, Ohio, Arkansas, Indiana, Pennsylvania, New York, Connecticut, and Massachusetts began to produce tobacco commercially. Southern Wisconsin joined on the eve of the Civil War. In the late 19th and early 20th centuries, northern Wisconsin, Minnesota, South Carolina, Georgia, and Alabama became tobacco-producing states.

Another significant development in the 19th century was the gradual differentiation of tobacco into several types. This resulted principally from the spread of the culture to new and different soil compositions, hybridization, and the development of three distinct curing methods (flue, darkfired, and air). Changes in the popular method of consuming tobacco and the increase in consumption also had a profound effect on the development of various tobaccos. At the end of the colonial period all American tobacco tended to be classified as one type and was smoked in clay pipes or ground up and used as snuff. During the first half of the 19th century chewing became the chief method of consuming tobacco.

In the antebellum period cigar consumption grew large enough to cause farmers in New England, New York, and Pennsylvania to try their hand at growing Cuban tobacco. Chewing-tobacco consumption peaked and began its decline by the 1890's; cigar consumption continued to rise until 1907, and the production of cigar tobacco spread to Wisconsin, Florida, and Georgia.

Long before chewing and cigar consumption reached their peak of consumption, Americans returned to pipe smoking in large numbers and added the cigarette habit. The smoking fad, aided by the perfection of American cigarette-manufacturing machines in the 1870's, rejuvenated the bright-tobacco industry in the southern states. By 1921 the cigarette had become the chief means of consuming tobacco in the United States and made the bright tobacco of the southern states the world's leading tobacco crop. In 1980 cigarettes accounted for 86 percent of the tobacco consumed in the United States.

TOBACCO WAREHOUSES. Authorized by the Grand Assembly meeting at Jamestown, Va., Feb. 1, 1632. Each planter was required to store all of his crop (except some for family use), not to exceed 1,500 stalks, in one of five designated warehouses. Inspectors burned the unsalable and repacked for London the marketable tobacco. This good quality tobacco was produced in the back settlements, the upper Chesapeake Bay, and between the James and Potomac rivers. By 1730 Virginia and Maryland had warehouses every fourteen miles. By 1833 tobacco warehouses dotted the Mississippi.

TODD'S TAVERN, ACTION AT (May 7, 1864). As Gen. Ulysses S. Grant's army moved to the left at the close of the Battles of the Wilderness in Virginia, Gen. Philip H. Sheridan's cavalry defeated Confederate Gen. J. E. B. Stuart's cavalry at Todd's Tavern on the Brock Road, and drove it almost to Spotsylvania Courthouse, five miles distant.

TOHOPEKA, BATTLE AT. *See* **Horseshoe Bend, Battle of.**

"TOKYO EXPRESS." The highspeed Japanese convoys of troop-carrying destroyers and cruisers that delivered reinforcements by night to Guadalcanal from August 1942 through January 1943.

TOLEDO (Ohio). Large industrial city in northwestern Ohio, with a population of 354,635 in 1980. Toledo is important both as an industrial center and as a port; it is located at the western end of Lake Erie, at the mouth of the Maumee River. Its port is one of the busiest on the Great Lakes, for it handles soft coal, petroleum, iron ore, cement, and food products from the Ohio-Indiana agricultural region. Among Toledo's own manufactures, glass ranks high. A major automobile plant is located in the city, and several important plants manufacture such items as weighing scales and spark plugs.

The Maumee is the largest river emptying into the Great Lakes and has been a major avenue for business and freight since the days of Indian control. The so-called "Toledo War" took place in 1835 and 1836, when Michigan Territory was applying for statehood. Michigan argued that the boundary lines of Ohio had been set too far north when Ohio entered the Union. The Toledo War almost reached the shooting stage. U.S. government officials settled the matter by awarding Michigan the "Upper Peninsula" in place of its claim to Toledo and the mouth of the Maumee. A few months later Toledo became incorporated.

Toledo's growth was due to the construction of the Wabash and Erie Canal in 1843. This water route used the Maumee River for a good stretch of its length, and connected Lake Erie with the Wabash River in northern Indiana. Even though canal traffic fell off rapidly when railroads became available, Toledo continued to prosper.

TOLEDO WAR. *See* **Toledo (Ohio).**

TOLERATION ACTS. Among the many codes, charters, laws, concessions, and proposals in the colonial period to assure full freedom of worship, three acts were especially important. The Toleration Act of 1649 guided the policy of the Maryland proprietors except for the period 1654–58. In Connecticut the Toleration Act of 1708 provided freedom of worship but gave no release from paying rates to the established church. However, in 1727–29 Quakers, Baptists, and Episcopalians were exempted. In all the colonies the dissenters were a growing majority. In Virginia and Maryland dissenters were granted the benefits of the English Toleration Act of 1689.

TOLL BRIDGES AND ROADS, PRIVATE. Developed out of the desire to improve land transportation with a minimum burden on public treasuries. These were commonly owned by private corporations and operated for profit. State and colonial governments determined toll rates and generally provided for reversion to the public at the end of a stated number of years or on provision of a reasonable return to their proprietors. Sarah Knight wrote of crossing toll bridges on a journey from Boston to New York in 1704. The first wave of toll bridge construction began about 1730 in the northern colonies. The second wave of bridge building arrived with the turnpikes, about 1800. Turnpike companies, which took over most of the existing highways and constructed many new ones, generally provided necessary small bridges without special toll charges. But many bridge companies were formed to build spans over the more important rivers. Most roads had become free and public by 1850. The same is true of toll bridges, although some were situated favorably enough to warrant continued private ownership. Those that did not become free were those that defied duplication because they were expensive and because of engineering difficulties. Many toll bridges built in the late 19th century and throughout the 20th century were financed by local or state governments.

TOLLS EXEMPTION ACT (Aug. 24, 1912). In anticipation of the opening of the Panama Canal, Congress exempted American vessels in coastwise traffic from the payment of tolls. The Hay-Pauncefote Treaty of 1901 had provided that the canal should be free to ships of all nations. President Woodrow Wilson, on Mar. 5, 1914, made an eloquent plea for repeal. The act was repealed a few weeks later. Congress, however, expressly denied any relinquishment of the right to grant exemptions to coastwise shipping.

TOMAHAWK. Small ax used mainly by Indians instead of warclubs. The early tomahawks made by the English and French had wide chopping blades and a kind of hook at the top. Later, French traders introduced one with a pointed blade, obviously a weapon. By 1700 metal tomahawks with wooden handles were the preferred hand weapons of the Algonkin- and Iroquois-speaking Indians.

TOMAHAWK CLAIMS. By blazing, or marking, of trees that encompassed the lands they desired, frontiersmen often asserted irregular claims or "rights" before these lands were surveyed or settled, especially between the Ohio and Muskingum rivers after Pontiac's War (1763). Colonial land laws sometimes admitted these claims; the national land system gave them no legal recognition.

TOMBIGBEE VALLEY. The northeast counties of Mississippi and most of west Alabama drain through the Tombigbee Valley, which played an important part in the early history of the Old Southwest. It was the site of the French Fort Tombecbee in 1735 for expeditions against the Chickasaw; location of the Battle of Ackia in 1736; and was explored by the British in 1771 to promote commercial relations with the Choctaw. After the Revolution settlers came down the valley, and in 1821 steamboats began to ascend the Tombigbee River. Lands watered by the streams produced large quantities of cotton. Napoleon built the short-lived colony of Demopolis at the junction of the Black Warrior and Tombigbee rivers. The valley embraces much of the lands claimed by the Choctaw prior to the treaty of 1765 with the British.

TOMBSTONE (Ariz.). A former silver-mining town located in the San Pedro River Valley. Ed Schieffelen discovered a large silver deposit there about 1878. Production of silver on a large scale began in 1880. During the next twenty years the district yielded about $40 million in silver and $3 million in gold. Tombstone attained notoriety because of its extravagant social life; its numerous gunmen; and the violent feuds among the miners, gamblers, and outlaws. In the 1890's the mines began to be flooded with underground water and were nearly all abandoned by 1911. Tombstone declined steadily in population (1,632 in 1980) as the mining interests of Arizona shifted from silver to copper. Landmarks include the O.K. Corral, where a gunfight took place between the Earps and the Clantons, and Boot Hill, where many notorious men are buried.

TOMS BROOK, BATTLE AT (Oct. 9, 1864). After the Battle of Winchester, Va., Gen. Philip H. Sheridan pursued Confederate Gen. Jubal A. Early to Mount Jackson, east of the Shenandoah Mountains, and then withdrew north to Strasburg. Early's cavalry following, Sheridan ordered his own cavalry to attack. The Confederates formed behind Toms Brook; they were routed, fleeing twenty-six miles through Woodstock to Mount Jackson and losing their artillery and trains.

***TOM THUMB*.** A locomotive built by Peter Cooper for use on the new Baltimore and Ohio Railroad, which at the beginning used horses as motive power. In its test in 1830 the engine, on a double track line out of Baltimore, raced against a car drawn by a horse. It would have won had not a pulley belt slipped off.

TONDEE TAVERN. Constructed in Savannah by Peter Tondee a few years before the Revolution, it became the "Cradle of Liberty" in Georgia. Practically all the early meetings to oppose the king's authority took place there, and the revolutionary state government made the Tondee Tavern longroom its legislative chamber. When the independent state government returned to Savannah in 1782 it first met at Tondee's.

TONKIN GULF NAVAL EPISODE. *See* **Tonkin Gulf Resolution.**

TONKIN GULF RESOLUTION (Aug. 7, 1964). Two attacks by North Vietnamese torpedo boats on U.S. destroyers, the *Maddox* and the *Turner Joy,* (Aug. 2 and 4, 1964) in the Gulf of Tonkin and retaliation by U.S. carrier planes, led to a congressional resolution. On the grounds that these attacks on U.S. destroyers represented a "systematic campaign of aggression by North Vietnam against South Vietnam," Congress jointly resolved to support President Lyndon B. Johnson's determination "to take all necessary measures to repel any armed attack against the forces of the United States." The Tonkin Gulf Resolution precipitated a vast increase in America's military involvement in South Vietnam. National disillusionment over the Vietnam War led to the resolution's repeal on Jan. 13, 1971.

TONNAGE ACT (1789). The second law passed by Congress under the Constitution taxed foreign ships five to eight times per ton more than the six cents per ton levied on American vessels. A more severe discrimination virtually closed the coasting trade and fisheries to foreign-owned ships. Between 1815 and 1830 this policy of encouraging the merchant marine by discrimination was generally abandoned.

TONQUIN. A ship of the expedition that established Astoria (Oregon) in 1811. After landing its cargo, the vessel proceeded northward on a trading voyage, was attacked by Indians, who killed most of the crew, and was finally destroyed by an explosion of gunpowder in the hold.

TONTINE PLAN. Named after a Neapolitan banker, Lorenzo Tonti, the plan combined both lottery and old-age security features in the United States during the late 18th century. A group of persons would hold real estate with the understanding that it, or the amount for which it sold, would ultimately be divided among certain surviving members. This plan became extensively applied to life insurance policies after 1868. The tontine policies received no dividends for a specified period, and in the event of a lapse the policyholder received nothing. The plan eventually developed into the less drastic "deferred dividend" plan, which, in turn, was weakened by the insurance investigation of 1905 and the regulatory legislation that followed.

"TOO PROUD TO FIGHT." In Philadelphia on May 10, 1915, three days after the sinking of the *Lusitania,* President Woodrow Wilson spoke to some newly naturalized citizens. The phrase "too proud to fight" was caught up by critics, especially in England, but it revealed the president's mind and probably helps to explain why he did not make the sinking of the *Lusitania* a cause for war.

TOPEKA (Kans.). Capital city of Kansas, with a population of 115,266 in 1980, located at the site of a very old Indian village on the Kansas River. The city is on both sides of the river, including the old-time ferry terminals that made Topeka an important crossing point.

The modern city dates from 1854, when a group of railroad promoters decided that it would be a good site for a rail terminal. The railroad eventually was built—the Atchison, Topeka, and Santa Fe. Topeka was selected as the state capital by the first official state government, elected in 1861.

Topeka is an important marketing town and a center for warehouses and grain elevators. It is also the home of the Menninger Foundation, one of America's leading institutions for the treatment and study of psychiatric and nervous disorders.

TOPEKA MOVEMENT AND CONSTITUTION. The movement for statehood launched by free-state Kansans in opposition to the proslavery territorial government was inaugurated in 1855, directed by an executive committee headed by James H. Lane. A "people's" assembly at Topeka, Sept. 19, called an election for members of a constitutional convention on Oct. 9. Fifty-one delegates were chosen but only thirty-seven signed the constitution. The convention was held Oct. 23 to Nov. 12. The constitution was not unlike other organic acts in its provisions for the forms and functions of government. Sections in the bill of rights prohibited slavery and declared invalid indentures of blacks executed in other states. The service of free blacks in the militia was prohibited, but the fundamental question of admitting them to Kansas was referred to the voters along with the constitution and a general banking law. On Dec. 15 the instrument was ratified, 1,731 to 46; the banking law was approved; and a provision to exclude free blacks was adopted by a majority of nearly three to one. State officials were chosen. Lane was dispatched to Congress to petition for admission. On Mar. 4, 1856, the legislature assembled at Topeka and elected U.S. senators. The House of Representatives passed a bill July 3, 1856, to admit Kansas under the Topeka constitution; but five days later the Senate substituted its own measure authorizing a constitutional convention. Practically, the movement terminated with the senatorial rejection, although subsequent sessions of the legislature convened, the last on Mar. 4, 1858.

TORDESILLAS, TREATY OF (June 7, 1494). The discovery of America by Christopher Columbus raised a question about the claims of Spain and Portugal. Pope Alexander VI, a Spaniard, settled the dispute by a series of papal bulls in 1493 that awarded to Spain exclusive dominion over all new lands west and south of a line to be drawn from the North Pole to the South Pole, 100 leagues west of the Azores and

Cape Verde Islands. All lands to the east and south of the line were to go to Portugal. The kings of Portugal and Spain subsequently agreed by the treaty to shift the demarcation line to a point 370 leagues west of the Cape Verde Islands.

TORIES. *See* **Loyalists.**

TORNADOES. Violent cyclonic storms that occur in connection with severe thunderstorms. A typical tornado appears as a funnel cloud hanging from the base of a cumulonimbus cloud, but the funnel may be obscured by low clouds or walls of heavy rain or may be so broad or short that it does not seem to have the typical shape. Wherever the vortex touches the ground it usually destroys everything in its path. Tornadoes may occur singly, over a path less than a mile wide, but sometimes ravage an area 200 miles or more in length. On Feb. 19, 1884, a swarm of sixty tornadoes struck the Gulf states and left over 400 dead. The thirty-seven Palm Sunday (Apr. 11, 1965) tornadoes struck six states (Indiana, Illinois, Michigan, Wisconsin, Iowa, and Ohio), killed 271 persons, and inflicted $300 million in property damage. From noon on Apr. 3, 1974, to noon on Apr. 4, 148 tornadoes devastated parts of thirteen states (Illinois, Indiana, Michigan, Ohio, Kentucky, Tennessee, West Virginia, Virginia, North Carolina, South Carolina, Georgia, Alabama, and Mississippi). (*See also* Disasters: Storms and Floods.)

TORONTO. *See* **York, Capture and Destruction of.**

TORPEDO WARFARE. The direct ancestor of the modern torpedo was the self-propelled, or "automobile," torpedo developed in the 1860's by Robert Whitehead, an Englishman in the employ of the Austrian navy. The Whitehead torpedo was a cigarshaped weapon that carried an explosive charge in its nose. It was powered by a small reciprocating engine and could be set to run at a predetermined depth. By the 1870's the automobile torpedo had been adopted by all the major navies. By the eve of World War I the effective range of the torpedo was just under 7,000 yards, and its top speed was over 40 knots. The 21-inch torpedo, the largest then in general use, had a bursting charge of 700 pounds of explosive.

Until about 1900 the principal carrier of the torpedo was the torpedo boat. The first U.S. torpedo boat was completed in 1890; it had a maximum speed of 23 knots and an armament of three 6-pounders and three 18-inch torpedo tubes on a displacement of 116 tons. Beginning in the 1890's the major powers began to develop the torpedo boat destroyer, or simply "destroyer," a large, faster torpedo vessel with a gun armament heavy enough to outfight a torpedo boat. By the outbreak of World War I the destroyer, now about 1,000 tons, had largely usurped the function of the torpedo boat.

The warship destined to make most effective use of the torpedo was the submarine. During World War I German submarines came close to winning the war for the Central Powers. Between the wars the torpedo-carrying airplane, or torpedo plane, added a new dimension. In World War II this weapon played a prominent part in naval operations. Japanese torpedo planes helped cripple the American fleet at Pearl Harbor.

In World War II the submarine proved even more formidable than in World War I. Tonnage losses to German U-boats rose into the millions before the Allies were finally able to win the long Battle of the Atlantic. In the Pacific, American submarines devastated the Japanese merchant marine and accounted for 28 percent of all Japanese naval shipping sunk in the war.

TORRENS SYSTEM. Provides for the registration of titles to land instead of deeds or conveyances of land. Title searches are made by the government instead of by private abstractors and attorneys, and when the title is registered it is insured. Thereafter no title search is necessary and the heavy expense for abstracts under the old system of deed registration is ended. The system was first introduced in America in 1895, and in the 1970's was used by twenty states. It has failed to make greater headway because of the high initial cost of title registration.

TORREYS' TRADING POST. Established in 1843 by the Torrey brothers, George Barnard, and others eight miles southeast of present Waco, Tex. Many Indian councils were held there, for it was the main point of contact between the Texas Republic government and the Indians. It lost its importance after Barnard's Trading Post was established in 1849.

TOTEM POLES. *See* **Architecture: American Indian.**

TOULOUSE, FORT. An important fortified French trading post on the Coosa River near Wetumpka, Ala., built by Jean Baptiste Le Moyne, Sieur de Bienville, in 1714. After the territory was ceded to the English in 1763, the post was abandoned. It was rechristened Fort Jackson during the Creek Wars. There Andrew Jackson signed the treaty of peace with the Creek, Aug. 9, 1814.

TOURISM AND TOURIST INDUSTRY. Business activities associated with traveling, sight-seeing and vacations. Many businesses depend on tourist trade, and tourist-related activities are a major economic resource in several parts of the country. Transportation companies, hotels or motels, food and guide businesses, all depend heavily on tourists. In 1977 the tourist industry accounted for 5.76 million jobs, and $171.4 billion.

TOWBOATING. The deficiencies of railroad transportation during World War I led to the Transportation Act of 1920, section 500 declaring it to be the policy of Congress to promote water transportation in connection with the commerce of the United States. Out of this act sprang the Inland Waterways Corporation (1924) and its Federal Barge Line. The completion of the 9-foot channel of the Ohio River in 1929 was followed by similar improvements on the Mississippi and its tributaries, and the Gulf Intra-Coastal Canals by the U.S. Army Engineers. Private capital followed with heavy investments in towboats (tugboats) and barges.

Towboat power soared from 600 to 2,400 horsepower before World War II. The shift from steam to diesel engines cut crews from twenty to thirteen. By 1945 fully 50 percent of the towboats were diesel; by 1955, 97 percent were diesel. Meanwhile the paddlewheel had given way to the propeller, the still popular twin propeller, and the triple propeller by the 1960's. During this decade the towboats of the Federal Barge Line could boast four propellers turned by 9,000 horsepower. A new dimension was attained in 1974 with the 10,500-horsepower triple-screw, capable of handling 40 barges with a capacity of 50,000 tons. By the late 1970's there were a dozen 10,500-horsepower towboats built or being built for the Mississippi.

Of about 350 million tons transported by some 3,000 towboats in the mid-1970's, almost one third were coal and lignite destined largely for generating plants. Crude petroleum, gasoline, distillate and residual fuel, grain, sand, gravel, and crushed rock were the other commodities.

TOWN. *See* **Local Government; Town Government.**

TOWN GOVERNMENT. A form of local government unique to New England. Towns were formed in colonial New England based on the relatively small geographic area served by a church. These units gradually assumed many of the civil functions normally associated with municipalities. With the formation of state governments in New England, towns were also used to perform functions that elsewhere were assigned to counties and townships. Some towns are referred to as "plantations" in Maine and as "locations" in New Hampshire.

The fundamental political characteristic of town government is its devotion to direct democracy. In the traditional form, the legislative body is the town meeting, which consists of all qualified voters, who meet to choose officials and set basic policy. The town meeting is held annually and follows a published agenda. In addition to its power to hold elections and pass ordinances, the meeting is responsible for levying taxes and incurring indebtedness.

Traditionally a board of selectmen of three to nine members has been designated as the principal administrative agency of the town. The selectmen carry on the business of the town between annual meetings and make necessary decisions to implement policies established by the meeting. The town clerk, treasurer, assessor, road commissioner, overseer of the poor, constable, and school committee may be elected by the meeting. The burdens of day-to-day administration fall most heavily on the clerk.

TOWN MEETINGS. *See* **Town Government.**

TOWNSEND PLAN (Old-Age Revolving Pension). Announced on Jan. 1, 1934, by its originator, Francis E. Townsend, it speedily enrolled millions of supporters in one of the most astonishing social movements of the period. In a bill endorsed by Townsend, the plan provided that every person sixty years of age or over who was a citizen of the United States and had been for at least five years should receive from the U.S. Treasury an annuity "not exceeding $200 per month," provided he should "not engage in any gainful pursuit," and should spend within the United States all of each month's annuity during the month it was received or five days thereafter. The $20 billion a year necessary in financing it was to be raised by a "duty of 2 per centum upon the gross dollar value of each transaction done within the United States." Congress repeatedly rejected bills putting forth the Townsend Plan, mainly because it was condemned by economists. The movement died out during the period of economic recovery in the late 1930's.

TOWNSHEND ACTS (June-July 1767). Four acts imposed on the American colonists by Parliament; named for Charles Townshend, chancellor of the Exchequer and head of the British government at the time they were enacted.

The first act suspended the New York assembly from further legislative activities until it complied with the provisions of the Quartering Act of 1765, which required colonies to supply British troops with barracks or other shelter; straw for bedding; cooking utensils; firewood for cooking and heating purposes; and a ratio of rum, cider, or vinegar to combat scurvy.

The second act was the Revenue Act. It levied import duties payable at American ports on white and red lead, painters' colors, various kinds of paper, glass, and three pence a pound on tea. All were legally importable only from Great Britain. The revenue was to go first to the cost of collection, then to support an independent civil establishment in America—that is, judges, governors, and other crown employees.

The new taxes were to be collected by a Board of Customs Commissioners, established by the third Townshend Act. The board was stationed at Boston and was given complete control over all customs in America. Costs of this new costly establishment were to be paid out of the revenue and out of seizures.

The fourth act, passed on July 2, repealed the inland duties on tea in England and permitted it to be exported to the colonies free of all British taxes.

TOWNSHIP SYSTEM. As provided for in the Ordinance of 1785, an adaptation of a system of local governmental units involving a system of land survey, ownership, and settlement. The words "town" and "township" have been, and still are, much confused. In parts of New England a town is a subdivision of a county. In other parts the county subdivision is called a township, as is the case over a large part of the country. American townships are, with a few exceptions, six miles square, divided into thirty-six miles-square sections.

TOWSON, FORT. First called Cantonment Towson; a frontier military post established about 1823 in the Indian country on the Red River, in the southeastern part of the present state of Oklahoma. It was named for Col. Nathan Towson, paymaster general of the army. Soon it was connected by military roads with Natchitoches, Fort Leavenworth, and other frontier posts, but it appears to have been abandoned after the annexation of Texas in 1845.

TRACE. *See* **Buffalo Trails.**

TRACTS. Extensive essays, political, religious, and social tracts were prevalent from the 17th century to the Civil War.

They were often controversial, espousing the cause of a certain sect or political party, such as Thomas Paine's *Common Sense* and *The Crisis,* 1776. Some were used as a means of personal attack or were aimed at social reform. Tracts reappeared as propaganda literature during World War I.

TRADE, BOARDS OF. *See* **Chambers of Commerce.**

TRADE, DOMESTIC. Inland commerce was extremely limited during the formative years of the colonies. But the colonies were a ready market envisioned as sources of supply for the mother country. Westward over the deer and buffalo trails flowed items prized by the Indians, and furs and skins obtained from the Indians were transported east. But basic needs alone soon ceased to be the only concern of colonial traders. Artisans in the cities along the Atlantic coast began to challenge English workmen in the production of luxuries.

Colonial trade not only brought controversy with the mother country but also created hostilities between the colonies. The Revolution only intensified the domestic disputes. Since national power was lacking under the Articles of Confederation, the states set up tax barriers against incoming goods or sought to monopolize waterways. No other action in the history of domestic trade has equaled in significance the stipulations in the Constitution that the exchange of goods and services among the states must be open and free and that this exchange is the concern of the national government.

The most important impetus to domestic trade was the revolution in transportation. The steamboat brought to maturity the expanding market along the southward-flowing rivers west of the Appalachians. Wagons laden with merchandise had long rolled over the mountains to the headwaters of the Ohio. From Pittsburgh and the tributaries of the Ohio hundreds of boats, gathering products and sometimes distributing goods, floated southward to New Orleans. Goods moved to eastern coastal cities or to foreign markets. The completion of the Erie Canal in 1825 opened the isolated market of the Great Lakes to tràde. Soon live animals, seeds, plants, furniture and other manufactured goods were moving westward on the canal from Albany to Buffalo and then along Lake Erie to Cleveland or Toledo, or up through Lake Huron and down Lake Michigan to Chicago. Grains from northern Ohio, Indiana, and Illinois poured into the lake ports. It was the railroads, however, that made both local and sectional markets effective. Beginning in Baltimore in 1828, they spread rapidly north and south and inland to the mountains. In the 1840's tracks began to parallel the Erie Canal across New York, and in the 1850's the New York Central, the Erie, the Pennsylvania, and the Baltimore and Ohio tapped the West. The entire Atlantic coast as far south as Baltimore turned slowly to manufacturing. Many ports lost business and Chicago rose to commercial grandeur with the growth of the railroads.

The age of steel profoundly shifted U.S. economic centers after the Civil War. The rich ore at the farther reaches of Lake Superior superimposed on the agricultural Middle West a great industrial empire along the lakes and eastward to Pittsburgh, on the edge of the bituminous coal fields.

The first transcontinental railroad (1869) and others beyond the Mississippi were soon bringing copper, lead, and other metals from the Rockies. Long trains of ice-cooled cars began to carry fruits and vegetables from the Pacific coast to eastern cities. Refrigerated cars fanned out from the packing houses of Chicago, carrying fresh meat, especially beef, to the butcher shops of the nation.

By 1900 goods for personal consumption had begun a steady gain in domestic commerce, and the appearance of the automobile and the truck after World War I did much to destroy the country store, although mail-order houses continued to flourish. Trucks increased both in number and size; and the trains lost relative to this more facile vehicle. Powerful towboats, pushing huge barges of oil, crushed stone, building materials, and similar products on inland rivers returned the waterways to economic importance. The airplane achieved some significance in freight transportation of special goods.

The decade of the 1960's was a period of rapid growth but also a period of foreign controversy and domestic uncertainty in trade. The full impact of the economic revolution following World War II became evident. Markets were disturbed as products from the free world displaced traditional American goods: especially steel, compact automobiles, textiles of man-made fibers, footwear, and electronic goods.

The 1970's opened with much promise and some fears. The value of sales in the various products groups had maintained their rapid growth in most areas. But a part of the seeming trade prosperity was merely inflation, and the investment of American capital abroad had cost 500,000 jobs in the United States. A gasoline shortage occurred in October 1973, when the oil-producing countries of the Middle East placed an embargo on further shipments of crude oil. Many gas stations closed on Saturdays and Sundays. On Jan. 2, 1974, President Nixon signed into law a measure setting a maximum 55-mile-per-hour speed limit on the highways. Inflation ate away at the value of the dollar, and each year the dollar's purchasing power declined. Prime interest rates by midyear 1974 had reached 12 percent, unemployment on a national basis was pressing beyond 6 percent, and even the most optimistic admitted that a recession unequaled in some ways since the 1930's had hit the nation.

Trade in 1975 declined drastically in many areas. Construction ceased in many places, and automobile plants and dealers' yards were filled with unsold cars. Factory rebates by car manufacturers and discounts by condominium owners on luxury apartments did not attract many buyers. In spite of surpluses, prices, contrary to traditional economic behavior, continued to rise. Unemployment in January 1975 reached 8.2 percent, the highest in sixteen years, and industrial production fell an alarming 3.6 percent.

By the end of September 1975 the recession had basically spent itself, but its residue of high prices, unemployment, and discontent in the marketplace made the recovery unreal to many. Before December, however, it was clear to the economic analysts that the rate of inflation had slowed, that the unemployment situation had improved, and that production had made a slow start upward.

In the late 1970's the economy recovered for a short period, but by the end of the decade and in the early 1980's the economic conditions reached alarming dimensions: the inflation was 11.3 and 13.5 percent in 1979 and 1980, respectively; the prime interest rate climbed to 21.5 percent in late 1980; and the unemployment rate was over 10 percent in the fall of 1982, with manufacturing, agriculture, and construction suffering most. The number of retail trade failures rose from 2,889 in 1978 to 3,183 in 1979, and 4,910 in 1980, and sales declined by 3.4 percent from 1979 to 1980.

TRADE, FOREIGN. The United States throughout its history has been relatively self-sufficient; yet foreign trade has, since the colonial period, been a dominant factor in the growth of the nation. The colonies were founded basically for the purpose of commerce.

Colonial Period. Foreign trade was primarily in outgoing raw materials and incoming manufactured goods during the colonial period. Simple economic necessity had turned the colonists to agriculture. Dictated by climatic and soil conditions and other factors, production in each section determined the course of its commerce. The trade of colonies south of Pennsylvania was chiefly with England. Ships called at the wharves of plantations along the rivers of Maryland and Virginia for tobacco and the next year returned with goods ordered from London and other cities. Furs, skins, naval stores, and tobacco made up early cargoes from the Carolinas, but after 1700 rice gained the lead. Before the middle of the century indigo had become a profitable crop.

Grain, flour, meat, and fish were the major products of Pennsylvania and New Jersey and the colonies to the north. Yet shipment of these materials to England endangered long-established interests of Englishmen at home. Although small amounts of naval stores, iron, ship timbers, furs, whale oil and whalebone, oak and pine plank, and staves, barrels, and hoops went off to London, other markets had to be sought in order to obtain means of paying for the large amounts of goods bought in England. The search for sales brought what is often referred to as the triangular trade, with southern Europe, Africa, and the West Indies. For example, rum was exchanged in Africa for slaves, and the slaves in turn sold in the West Indies for specie or for more molasses for New England rum distilleries. These islands, in fact, provided an inexhaustible market for fish, meat, foodstuffs, and live animals, as well as pearl ash, potash, cut-out houses, lumber, and finished parts for making containers for sugar, rum, and molasses. Corn, wheat, flour, bread, and vegetables found their greatest outlet in the islands.

1776–1814. Although the Revolution did not destroy American trade, even with the British, the former colonies obviously lost their preferred position in the world of commerce and also the protection of the powerful empire fleet. British trade regulations of 1783 and 1786–87 closed the ports of the West Indies to the ships of the new nation and protected others by heavy tonnage duties. Varying tariffs in the ports and hostile action and counteraction among the states kept commerce in perpetual uncertainty and prevented retaliation against European discriminations, but trade went on either in traditional channels or in new markets. In May 1785 the *Empress of China,* from Canton, returned to New York, and in August the *Pallas,* manned by lascars, put into Baltimore with its cargo of tea, china, silks, satins, gauzes, velvets, umbrellas, paper hangings, and similar items from the Orient. Means were found for evading the restrictions in the West Indies, and enough luxuries were brought in from England to disturb the already uncertain economic situation.

Shipping interests in the new Congress secured legislation favoring American-owned ships. The tonnage registered for foreign trade increased in 1789–1810 from 123,893 to 981,000, and imports and exports in American bottoms jumped roughly from 20 percent to 90 percent. Even the smallest towns sent out cargoes of lumber, horses, hay, grain, and other products wanted in the West Indies. The China trade increased. But there were difficulties. The British and the French were hostile in the West Indies; treaty privileges were sparingly and grudgingly given everywhere. The Barbary pirates preyed on the ships of the young nation, and England began impressment.

The Napoleonic Wars turned production forces to military goods, drove merchant ships from the seas, and pushed prices upward rapidly. Although many ships were seized, American merchant captains and the nation prospered until President Thomas Jefferson, seeking to maintain peace, induced Congress in 1807 to pass the Embargo Act. Exports and imports fell. Repeal of the embargo brought some revival, but other restrictions and the war against England drove exports and imports down even more. Domestic economy and foreign trade had been dealt a severe blow; both recovered quickly, however, when at the end of the war all restrictions on tonnage and on goods based on nationality of ship were repealed on a reciprocity basis.

1815–1860. Foreign trade in the years between 1815 and 1860 moved generally upward. Agricultural products made up most exports. Cotton led all the rest. The West Indies and South America took large amounts of grain and flour, and English demands increased steadily after the repeal of the corn laws in 1846. Tobacco, rice, meat, and meat products, as well as lumber, naval stores, barrels and kegs, staves, and hoops moved out in large quantities. Cottons, woolens, silks, iron, cutlery, china, and a miscellany of other items made up the bulk of the incoming cargoes.

1860–1940. As the nation became increasingly industrialized between the Civil War and World War II, domestic production and domestic trade were its basic concerns. (*See* Trade, Domestic.) The percentage of foreign trade carried in American bottoms decreased greatly. That did not mean, however, any lessening in total ocean commerce. The value of exports and imports combined rose markedly. Cotton, wheat, flour, and other farm products continued to move out in ever larger amounts, but it was obvious that agriculture was losing out to manufactured goods. Europe was becoming less important in American foreign trade. Shipments to and from Asia, Oceania, Africa, Canada, and Latin America were growing rapidly. Cotton, wheat, petroleum, tobacco, metals, and a great variety of manufactured goods flowed out from ports on the Atlantic, the Gulf, and the Pacific. The return flow was made up of tropical foods and materials, coffee, sugar, wool, rubber, silk, paper and paper stock, and a growing amount of raw materials. Two world wars and a depression completed the revolution.

World War I restored temporarily the supremacy of Europe as a consumer of American agricultural products. But new goods also made up large portions of the cargoes—chemicals, explosives, firearms, special woods for airplane propellers, barbed wire, and other needs of fighting forces. The value of exports and imports more than doubled during the war. But neither the trade of the war years nor that of the 1920's was normal. The huge purchases of the Allies were based on government credits in the United States. The economic structure fell apart in 1929. Prices declined sharply everywhere; world credit and world finance broke down; foreign exchange transactions were curtailed or taken over completely by government in many places; and the principal powers sought to maintain themselves by hiding behind high tariffs, trade licenses, and fixed quotas. The climax was reached in the Smoot-Hawley Tariff of 1930, which brought retaliatory restrictions from other nations. Foreign trade of the nation dropped to $2.9 billion in 1932. The slow climb upward to $6.6 billion in 1940 was in part the result of reciprocity agreements rather than trade restrictions as essentials in commercial revival.

1941–1960. In the war years 1941–45 more than $50 billion in goods went out of American ports, and $17 billion came in. But about $32.9 billion of the exports were lend-lease war materials to fighting allies and no payment was expected. The whole international economic structure was, in fact, undergoing a basic revolution.

During the war a great army of women had joined the working force in the United States as new production plants sprang up. Thousands of men and women moved off the farm to the busy industrial cities. By the end of the war production facilities had roughly doubled; the nature of the outpouring products had changed astoundingly.

Fearful of communism and convinced that hunger must be eliminated if traditional nations were to be reestablished and if new ones were to be created on the principle of freedom of choice, the United States initiated (1947) the Marshall Plan, which provided $12 billion in aid for the economic recovery of Europe. On Apr. 3, 1948, President Harry S. Truman signed the European Recovery Act, which gave out at least $17 billion over a four-year period. Machinery for regulating international monetary and trade relations had already been established by the end of the 1940's (*see* Tariff).

The 1950's were years of growth and adjustments from a basically nationalistic thinking concerning tariffs and trade to a basically international philosophy of freedom of world commerce from deadening restrictions. The free trade movement gained remarkable headway. In 1957 the European Economic Community (EEC), generally known as the Common Market, was formed; three years later the European Free Trade Association was established. With the United States and Canada, the groupings came to be called the Atlantic Community.

1961–81. But not all was harmony in the new economic community. The mercantilists quarreled with the tariff reformers everywhere, and in the United States there was opposition to shifting control of tariff rates from Congress to an international body. The decade of the 1960's was at times a period of bitter controversy (*see* Tariff).

The foreign trade of the United States had undergone profound changes. The great surpluses that had marked U.S. world commerce from the 1870's began in the 1950's a decline that reached significant proportions in the 1960's. The great steel empire of Andrew Carnegie and Henry Clay Frick was crumbling because of new mills and less costly labor in other countries. Freighters put into ports on the Atlantic, the Pacific, and the Gulf and even traveled down the Saint Lawrence Seaway to Cleveland, Detroit, and Chicago to unload finished industrial goods. Between 1960 and 1967 finished goods in U.S. imports increased 150 percent.

Steel, automobiles, textiles, and electronic goods led the new imports. Competing steelmaking plants, although new, were not appreciably more efficient than those of the United States. Basically the steel problem was too much steel.

The automobile industry was turned topsy-turvy also. In 1968 the number of imported cars rose to 1.5 million; in 1980 it increased to about 3 million, with almost 2 million cars from Japan. Textile and footwear manufacturers, too, protested the loss of markets because of competing goods from other countries, especially Japan. Electronic and telecommunications goods in foreign trade added appreciably to the deficit in the United States. Between 1965 and 1980 such imports, by value, mostly from Japan, increased at the annual rate of 175 percent.

American foreign trade was involved not only in the complex industrial world but also in the even more complex monetary world. The annual unfavorable balance of payments, sometimes of several billion dollars, made it difficult for the nation to pay its bills. The merchandise exchange was with few exceptions favorable to the United States until the mid-1970's; but by 1980 it had reached minus $25 billion. Military commitments in Europe and elsewhere, the Vietnam War, heavy expenditures of U.S. tourists abroad, shipping charges, and a host of other payments left the nation each year through the 1960's and the 1970's heavily indebted.

Through the 1960's U.S. imports grew twice as fast as exports, and the small trade surplus fell each year far short of meeting the persistent foreign debt. Dollar claims piled up in Europe. The impending crunch came in August 1971, when higher interest rates in the United States, rumors of revaluations, and a growing American deficit, swelled by strikes and threatened strikes, poured a flood of unwanted dollars into Europe. Speculators, corporations, commercial banks, and other holders, protecting themselves from changes in currency values, began to scurry out from under their surplus dollars. They returned to the United States $4 billion in the second week of August. On Aug. 15 President Richard M. Nixon closed the door on gold redemptions and levied a 10 percent surtax on dutiable imports. Despite many fears that the action might disrupt the monetary world, the situation cleared appreciably.

By February 1972 the monetary situation had begun to deteriorate rapidly. Europe began to enact currency controls. The pound had fallen drastically, and the dollar had come again under heavy pressure. American foreign trade throughout the year remained the largest in the world, but exports made no appreciable gains on imports. The surtax, soon removed, had not lessened appreciably the amount of goods coming into American ports. Tariff walls had come down, but other barriers had gone up.

The dollar, devalued again in February 1973 and further deteriorated through the succeeding currency float, continued to decline relative to the currencies of the Common Market and Japan. A gasoline shortage developed with the oil embargo of October 1973, and by the early months of 1974 the economic situation was recognized as a full-blown depression, with further unemployment but no end to inflation. In the late 1970's the dollar continued to fall against other currencies and imports were increasing at a faster rate than exports. Because of rising unemployment American labor leaders were calling for protectionist measures against some imports, such as cars from Japan and shoes from Taiwan and South Korea, but both President Carter and President Reagan were staunch supporters of free trade.

TRADE, FREE. *See* **Free Trade.**

TRADE ACTS. *See* **Navigation Acts.**

TRADE AGREEMENTS. *See* **Reciprocal Trade Agreements.**

TRADE AND PLANTATION, BOARD OF. *See* **Board of Trade and Plantations.**

TRADE ASSOCIATIONS. Common among a wide variety of industrial, financial, and commercial firms. Usually made up of enterprises engaged in one line of business, trade associations appeared in large numbers for the first time in the late 19th century. The associations developed in industries as diverse as sugar refining, steel making, and textile production. Producers sought to eliminate cutthroat competition. There were attempts to set prices, limit production, allot quotas, and provide penalties for those who exceeded their quotas and rebates to those who did not meet their prescribed sales. The need for cartels declined at the turn of the century.

In the 20th century, nevertheless, the number of trade associations continued to grow as they took on new functions. Periods of rapid growth occurred as a result of World War I, the "cooperative-competition" and "open-price" movements of the 1920's, and the National Recovery Administration. Trade associations sought to help their members by distributing information about the industry's prices; attempting to standardize products; promoting the industry's products; bargaining with unions; training employees; instructing members in improved methods of production, management, and accounting; providing industrial cost analyses; and seeking to control unfair methods of competition.

TRADE COMMISSION, FEDERAL. *See* **Federal Agencies.**

TRADE DOLLAR. A special type of silver dollar, weighing 420 grains instead of the standard 412.5 grains, was created by the currency law of 1873, ostensibly to encourage trade with China, but more probably to provide a market for domestic silver producers (*see* Crime of 1873). Another provision in the law made all silver coins legal tender to five dollars. The total coinage was 36 million. The bulk went to China, but at least 6 million were forced into circulation in this country. Coinage of the trade dollar was stopped in 1878 and redemption was authorized in 1887.

TRADE EXPANSION ACT (Oct. 11, 1962). This act gave the president the power to cut tariffs up to 50 percent below the 1962 level or raise them 50 percent above the 1934 level within the subsequent five years. It also removed tariffs on products in which the United States and Western Europe accounted for 80 percent of world trade.

TRADEMARKS. Used by some makers of merchandise, particularly in fields requiring special skill or artistic merit. The mark might be either a signature or some distinctive symbol or label. As early as 1791 a Boston manufacturer petitioned Congress for the right to register his trademark and have it protected against imitation. The first federal act permitting trademark registration was passed in 1870. Registrations averaged less than 1,000 a year for the first ten years, and never reached 2,000 in any one year until 1902. The act of 1905 made registration of a trademark *prima facie* evidence of ownership. In 1906 more than 10,000 marks were registered.

TRADE UNIONS. *See* **Labor.**

TRADE WITH THE ENEMY ACTS. Restriction of trade with the enemy as a means of economic coercion and domestic conservation took place during the French and Indian War (1756–63), the Franco-American "misunderstanding" of 1798–1800, the War of 1812, and by both belligerents during the Civil War, although during most conflicts embargoes were often evaded and indirect trade developed through neutral ports. Imports of war materials from the enemy country were sometimes opportunistically permitted.

During World War I extensive measures were taken to prevent enemy trading and to enforce the Allied blockade of Germany. They included the Trading With the Enemy Act of Oct. 6, 1917. Such trade was carefully defined, almost completely prohibited, and severely penalized. The War Trade Board licensed importers and exporters, the Federal Trade Commission reviewed enemy-alien applications for patents, and the Treasury regulated insurance companies with enemy-alien connections. At the outset of World War II Congress renewed and enlarged presidential power to seize any property belonging to an enemy or its ally.

After 1950 the Trading With the Enemy Act was extended to additional situations. After the Korean "emergency" of 1950 ceased, the embargo against China and North Korea became part of the cold war arsenal. In 1963 trading with Cuba was proscribed, and in 1964, North Vietnam.

In 1969 President Richard Nixon opened the door to trade with China, and by 1975 there was a steady trade in nonrestricted goods between China and the United States. Although in the late 1970's trade with the Communist bloc remained restricted, it seemed likely that in the future the Trading With the Enemy Act would apply only to "hot war" adversaries.

TRADING COMPANIES. Played an important part in the early settlement of America. Six incorporated British companies established settlements: the Virginia Company (1606), the London and Bristol Company (1610), the Council for New England (1620), the Bermuda Company (1622), the Massachusetts Bay Company (1629), and the Old Providence Company (1630). Their settlements were at Jamestown, Sagadahoc, Newfoundland, Bermuda, Salem, and Old Providence, respectively. The Dutch used a similar organization to plant their settlement in New Netherland at New Amsterdam. The Hudson's Bay Company was a trading but not a colonizing company.

Companies were of two types. One was the joint-stock company that was legally incorporated by the crown under the great seal by a royal charter. Stock was sold to whoever would buy, and the stockholder's liability was limited to his investment. The charter gave the company title to a specific territory, granted a legal monopoly to trade in that region, and empowered the company to exercise extensive governmental powers over any settlements that might be made.

Another type of trading company was less formal and was called "Associates." It was somewhat like a partnership but had limited liability for the members. Such companies were not fully incorporated, and their territorial grants came from some legally incorporated company. This device was largely used in the settlement of Virginia by the London Company. Regions were settled by groups of men called Associates who, in return for a title to a specified tract of land, agreed to transport a certain number of settlers to a given area and establish them within a limited time.

TRADING POSTS, FRONTIER. From the establishment of Jamestown (1607) until the end of Indian treatymaking (1871), traders and trading posts were important factors in border relations. By 1774 Albany and Oswego, N.Y., were major trade centers for the Iroquois and other northwestern tribes. Indians would exchange their furs for guns, ammunition, hatchets, knives, kettles, and blankets. During colonial rivalries, Spain and France also had their strategic trading posts. After American independence, President George Washington proposed, and Congress inaugurated (1796), the setting up of government factories and trading posts, and every border fort became a trade center. Opposition by individual traders led to abandonment of the policy in 1822. Shortly after American occupation of the Louisiana Territory (1804), trading posts were established throughout the trans-Mississippi West. Saint Louis was the center for supplying traders and posts within the Pacific Northwest and Midwest, and New Orleans the Southwest. (*See* articles on forts under individual names.)

TRAIL DRIVERS. Cowboys who moved cattle from a home range to a distant market or another range. The typical herd consisted of about 2,500 head of cattle. The typical outfit consisted of a boss, who might or might not be the owner; from ten to fifteen hands, each of whom had a string of from five to ten horses; a horse wrangler who drove and herded the cow horses; and a cook. The men drove and grazed the cattle most of the day, herding them by relays at night. Ten or twelve miles was considered a good day's drive. (*See also* Cattle Drives.)

TRAIL OF TEARS. Name given by the Cherokee to the forced journey in 1838 from their lands in Georgia through Kentucky, Illinois, and Missouri to Oklahoma, based on the signing by a minority of the Cherokee leaders of the Treaty of New Echota in 1835, under the terms of which the Cherokee were to surrender their lands and move west of the Mississippi. They were sent on the long journey in detachments of about 1,000 each. The journey was made mostly on foot, under military escort, beginning in October and November. Some 4,000 Cherokee perished.

TRAILS. *See* **Buffalo Trails.**

TRAINING DAY IN NEW ENGLAND. The day for drilling the local militia. On training day all able-bodied men, with the exception of a few professionals, such as ministers, magistrates, town herdsmen, and millers, met to elect officers, drill, and converse. In 1649 the General Court defined the purposes of the day as drilling and fortification. At first captains were required to train the companies every week; in 1636 eight days in every year were ordered; in 1660 the number was reduced to six; in 1679 to four. Because the militia organization was an integral part of the community life, the whole town began to gather on training day. By the end of the century the day had become the occasion for a sort of bazaar.

TRAIN ROBBERIES. The first train robbery in America on record was that of an Adams Express car on the New York, New Haven and Hartford Railroad, which was rifled of $700,000 between New York and New Haven in 1866. That same year the first train holdup by the four Reno brothers occurred in southern Indiana. After one of the Reno brothers was arrested in 1867, the remainder of the gang staged a number of bold bank and train robberies in southern Indiana and Illinois in 1868. The Farringtons operated in 1870 in Kentucky and Tennessee; and Jack Davis of Nevada started operations at Truckee by robbing an express car of $41,000. The year 1870 marked the height of train robberies, East and West. The Jesse James gang began to operate in 1873 near Council Bluffs, Iowa. For nine years they terrorized the Middle West. Only after Jesse was shot and his brother Frank retired did trainmen breathe more freely. Sam Bass in Texas, the Dalton boys in Oklahoma, and Sontag and Evans in California are other robbers with well-known records. After 1900 the number of holdups declined conspicuously.

TRANS-APPALACHIA. That part of North America lying west of the Appalachian Mountains. Used mainly in reference to late colonial and early national history, it refers particularly to the region drained by the Ohio River and thus includes Kentucky, Tennessee, and parts of the Old Northwest.

TRANSCENDENTALISM. A philosophical term developed by the German philosopher Immanuel Kant that embodies those aspects of man's nature transcending, or independent of, experience. It became the inspiration of a liberal social and cultural renaissance in New England during 1830–45 and received its chief American expression in Ralph Waldo Emerson's individualistic doctrine of self-reliance. Experiments in "plain living and high thinking" like Brook Farm and Fruitlands attracted the exponents of a new self-culture; and social utopians, from vegetarian enthusiasts to abolitionists, found a congenial atmosphere within the movement.

TRANS-MISSISSIPPI EXPOSITION. Held at Omaha, Nebr., from June 1 to Oct. 31, 1898, devoted to the products, industries, and culture of states west of the Mississippi. There were twelve principal buildings, 2,613,408 visitors, and $1,-924,078 in receipts. It was unsuccessfully reopened the following year as the Greater American Exposition.

TRANSPORTATION, DEPARTMENT OF. On Mar. 2, 1966, President Lyndon B. Johnson, in a message to Congress, proposed a department of transportation that would include all principal executive transport functions together with certain safety and administrative functions of the regulatory agencies. The proposal precipitated sharp controversy in Congress. The amended bill was signed into law on Oct. 15, 1966. On Apr. 1, 1967, the department was activated by executive order. Under the department's auspices were placed the Federal Aviation Administration, the Bureau of Public Roads, the Coast Guard, the Alaska Railway, the Saint Lawrence Seaway Development Corporation, the Great Lakes Pilotage Administration, the safety functions of the regulatory agencies (to be administered by the bill), administration of the 1966 automobile acts (Highway Safety Act and National Traffic and Motor Vehicle Act), and the high-speed surface transportation program. In addition the department was given responsibility for transport research and the development of a national transportation policy. Urban transport responsibilities were added at a later date.

TRANSPORTATION ACT OF 1920 (Esch-Cummins Act). The U.S. government took over and ran the railroads from Dec. 26, 1917, until Mar. 1, 1920. The roads were obliged to carry a heavy volume of traffic, without much attention to replacements or maintenance. The roads were in a deplorable condition when, after a little more than two years, they were returned to private operation. The act of Feb. 28, 1920, was the result. The bill of Sen. Albert B. Cummins in the Senate and the bill of Rep. John Jacob Esch in the House resulted in a compromise. The act became effective on Mar. 1, a little more than three months after President Woodrow Wilson's proclamation of Dec. 24, 1919, providing for return of the railroads to private operation. Consolidations were authorized, a six-month guarantee period was established, and extensive loans were authorized. Arbitration without power of enforcement was provided, and provision was made for voluntary adjustment boards to settle labor disputes. These provisions were to be enforced by the Railroad Labor Board, consisting of nine members and having national jurisdiction.

TRANSPORTATION AND AGRICULTURE. *See* **Agriculture.**

TRANSPORTATION AND TRAVEL. Most of the early American colonists lived near rivers, inlets, and bays adjoining the Atlantic, and water provided their means of travel and transportation. Numerous types of sailing vessels carried men and cargoes to the West Indies and neighboring coastal points. Farmers living above seaports moved their produce in flatboats, "fall boats," and rafts along the rivers.

At first all land travel was done on foot or horseback. Vehicles were scarce during the first century of colonization. Although private coaches appeared in Boston as early as 1685, by 1697 no more than thirty carts and other wheeled contrivances were in use in Philadelphia. The first two American wheeled vehicles were the chair, a two-wheeled two-passenger cart drawn by one horse, and the chaise, which had a leather top and was swung on leather braces. They were followed by the curricle, chariot, and stagecoach.

By the close of the colonial period a network of dirt and corduroy roads existed throughout the northern and central colonies. The first regular stage line, established on Mar. 8, 1759, used a springless Jersey wagon. By the Revolution coach travel was available in all the colonies at moderate fare.

The Conestoga wagon partly solved the problem of overland freight. The Conestoga was developed in Pennsylvania; its chief characteristics were its large canoe-shaped bottom, where goods could ride at sharp angles, its sturdy running gear, and its great capacity, which required four to twelve horses to pull it. Some wagon owners made freighting a business, and farmers found a new way to bring their goods to the nearest port.

One of the most striking changes following independence was the rapid growth and westward march of the American people. The migration to the West was accompanied by a persistent demand for the improvement of transportation. It was met by the construction of the National, or Cumberland, Road; state and privately owned turnpikes; a network of canals; and the discovery, survey, and popularization of trails extending from the Middle West to New Mexico, Utah, California, and the Pacific Northwest. By 1817 a regular stagecoach service had been established on the National Road. To a smaller degree activity could be observed on the main road that followed the Shenandoah Valley through the Cumberland Gap. Once across the mountains this traffic took to water to reach Indiana, Illinois, and Missouri.

The opening of the Erie Canal brought thousands of emigrants into the northern portions of the Old Northwest and provided a direct commercial artery between New York City and the Northwest. Canalboats, which resembled Mississippi and Ohio River keelboats and barges, contained a superstructure, or cabin, that provided very meager accommodations for passengers and crew.

During and immediately after the revolutionary war James Rumsey and John Fitch experimented in steamboat building, but not until the launching of Robert Fulton's *Clermont* in 1807 were steamboats commercially successful. By 1820 steamboat companies operated on practically all the navigable rivers and lakes between the Atlantic coast and the Mississippi River. During the 1850's over 1,000 steamboats navigated the Mississippi. By World War I steamboats had almost disappeared from the rivers, but a revival of river traffic began in the 1920's in the form of modern barge transport for freight.

The reason for the decline in river transportation was the railroad, which could not only crisscross the land between watercourses but could parallel the water routes and bring new standards of speed and convenience. In Baltimore on July 4, 1828, America's first railroad line designed to be a public carrier was started. Known as the Baltimore and Ohio, by 1852 it extended from Chesapeake Bay to the Ohio River at Wheeling. At about the same time other lines were built. At the outbreak of the Civil War there were 30,000 miles of railroads.

In the Far West the stagecoach business achieved gigantic proportions with the establishment in 1858–61 of a semiweekly passenger and mail service over a 3,600-mile stage road between Saint Louis and Portland, Oreg., via El Paso and San Francisco.

The express business first became important on the Pacific coast. Since the government mail service was inadequate, express companies—the most important of which were the Adams and the Wells Fargo—were organized to carry the mails and small parcels. Their duties soon included the transportation of gold dust from the mines to designated depositories and the issuing of bills of exchange. By 1860 there were over 264 companies in California, and scores more in other parts of the Far West. The Pony Express was organized in 1860 to carry mails across the Plains and over the mountains between Saint Joseph, Mo., and Sacramento, Calif.

The Far West regarded the stagecoach and the Pony Express as merely stopgaps until the transcontinental railroads could be completed. On July 1, 1862, President Abraham Lincoln signed the act providing for the construction of the Union Pacific-Central Pacific Railroad. On May 10, 1869, at Promontory, Utah, Leland Stanford, president of the Central Pacific, drove in the spike that bound the East and West.

The invention of the internal combustion engine in the last quarter of the 19th century paved the way for automobile, bus, truck, and airplane transportation and the ultimate conversion of railroad power from steam to diesel. Although the use of motor vehicles began in the 1890's, the improvement of highways did not get under way on a major scale until after World War I. But more than a decade was to pass before the extent of the national commitment to highway transport became apparent. Until that time the country experienced a great flowering of the interurban electric railway—primarily for passenger traffic but incidentally for freight. Most interurban railway building occurred between 1900 and 1908.

With the advent of long-distance truck and bus operations, it became apparent that motor vehicles would serve primarily not as a feeder of the railroad system but would become a competitor of considerable importance. By 1935 the threat was regarded by Congress as sufficiently serious to warrant the extension of federal regulation to interstate transportation by bus and truck. The development of motor transport freed light industry from dependence on fixed rail locations. Meanwhile, the auto and the bus bid fair to complete the demise of the local passenger train except for commuter service in a few of the larger cities.

In the 1920's the federal government revived its interest in the improvement of inland and coastal waterways. A resurgence of inland water transport followed—not, however, on the old pattern, but as a highly efficient barge industry moving bulk commodities. By the 1950's barge transport had become the fastest growing method of freight transport. The Saint Lawrence Seaway, opened in 1959, gave the United States a "fourth seacoast" and considerably transformed the commerce of the Great Lakes region.

Both world wars stimulated the technological development of transportation, especially aviation. The U.S. Post Office established a transcontinental airmail service in the early 1920's using war-surplus planes. Contract service with commercial carriers began after 1925, and efforts were made to encourage the development of passenger and express traffic. Within a decade a network of services joined all principal points, but widespread public acceptance of air travel was not achieved until after World War II.

Heavy public investment in highways, airports, and waterways laid the ground for continued expansion of the nonrail forms of transport. Railroads, confined to private sources of capital, continually fell behind in the application of available technology. Although rail freight traffic continued to grow, and an all-time record of 927 billion ton-miles was set in 1979, the rate of growth was modest.

In an increasingly affluent society, travel expanded rapidly and was indulged in by a growing proportion of the population. Air transport became the major means of intercity commercial passenger transport, with the number of passengers increasing from 62 million in 1960 to 297 million in 1980. But the nation was not prepared to allow rail passenger service to disappear entirely. In May 1971 a skeleton passenger service was taken over by Amtrak, a semipublic corporation. A bright spot in rail passenger service was the introduction of the Metroliner between New York and Washington, D.C., which reversed the downtrend in rail travel in that corridor and was the only Amtrak service that covered its operating costs.

In the 1960's and 1970's growing concern about the quality of the environment confronted transport with new problems. The automobile was recognized as the number one source of air pollution. Application of emission control devices increased gasoline consumption at the very time that serious fuel shortages were developing. Superhighways were attacked for their effects on the landscape and the disruption that they generated in urban communities. New airports in some major metropolitan areas were successfully opposed at the site selection stage.

TRANSYLVANIA COMPANY. An unincorporated association composed, at its largest, of nine influential citizens of North Carolina. It was organized in 1774 to invest in vacant, unpatented wild lands, within the chartered limits of North Carolina and Virginia. In the fall of 1774 Capt. Nathaniel Hart paid a visit to the Overhill Cherokee at their Otari towns to negotiate for the lease or purchase of an immense tract of land between the Kentucky and Cumberland rivers. At the beginning of 1775 new articles of copartnership were entered into to define the terms of the joint venture more clearly. The Transylvania partners took what purported to be an absolute conveyance of the millions of acres in question from the chiefs of the Cherokee. The peculiar proprietary tenure had a system of quitrents, by which this vast domain was to be held and disposed of. There was an abortive attempt to form a provisional government and enact emergency measures for the infant colony at Boonesborough in May 1775. The attempted purchase from the Indians was publicly denounced by the governors of the two states involved and the scheme was invalidated. In 1778 Virginia granted the company 200,000 acres at the mouth of the Green River in Kentucky and in 1783 North Carolina granted it an equal amount in Powell's Valley, in east Tennessee.

TRAPPERS' RENDEZVOUS. The Rocky Mountain Fur Company of William H. Ashley relied on itinerant parties equipped to trap rather than trade. This method of doing business necessitated annual gatherings of the itinerant parties, at which time pack outfits from St. Louis delivered equipment, supplies, trade goods—and liquor—and picked up the product of the trappers' work. Indians came to these meetings to participate in the trade. These notable fairs in the wilderness became known as annual rendezvous. The first one, a mild affair on the Sweetwater River in Wyoming in 1824, was held for the convenience of scattered parties who had trapped the Wind River country in 1823–24. In the summer of 1825, Ashley assembled his parties, joined by a Hudson's Bay Company group, on Henry's Fork of the Green River. The next year, Ashley met with his company at a site near the present Ogden, Utah. There he disposed of his interests in the Rocky Mountain Fur Company to some of his associates who continued with the rendezvous method until the 1840's.

TRAPPERS' TRAIL. *See* **Cherokee Trail.**

TRAPPING. Until the middle of the 19th century trapping of animals was a prime factor in the process of westward movement, for professional trappers and traders not only developed a source of wealth for a growing nation but, more importantly, they explored the rivers, blazed trails through unmapped forests, brought hostile Indians under control, made known the agricultural values of the wilderness, and extended American holdings to the Pacific Ocean.

The upper Missouri trapper of 1830 was a composite picture of the many types that had dared the wilderness through 200 years of westward progress. With him he took a method that had its beginnings in the Indian trade on the Saint Lawrence and Potomac rivers and a paraphernalia that sprang from roots deep in the countries of Europe. Many of his items of equipment and objects of trade had not changed in two centuries of use in America. In following his profession, the trapper of the upper Missouri traveled with a company of companions who were employed by one of the established trading firms of Saint Louis or who worked out of that city as free and independent trappers.

Beaver no longer constitutes the chief item in the American fur trade, and Saint Louis has competition from the raw fur dealers in Chicago, New York, Saint Paul, and other large centers of fur trade. Trapping in the United States in the 1970's brought largest returns in muskrat, fox, nutria, lynx, opossum, and raccoon, and the volume of business was far greater than it had ever been during the days of the mountain man. (*See also* Fur Trade.)

TRAVEL. *See* **Transportation and Travel.**

TRAVELING SALESMEN. Representatives of business firms who travel through assigned territories to solicit orders for future deliveries of their employers' goods and services. They seek orders from other business firms and public institutions and usually sell from samples or descriptions of their products rather than carry goods for immediate delivery. Traveling salesmen were virtually nonexistent before the mid-19th century. After 1840 manufacturers began to take the initiative and send salesmen in search of customers. Many states and municipalities, acting at the behest of their local wholesalers, imposed costly licensing requirements on traveling salesmen entering their jurisdictions. These barriers proved ineffective and eventually were declared unconstitutional. The U.S. Census reported 7,262 traveling salesmen in 1870 and 223,732 in 1930, but these figures may represent only one-half to one-third of the true numbers. No more recent data were available in the mid-1970's, but the number of salesmen had undoubtedly increased after 1930.

TRAVERSE DES SIOUX, TREATY OF (July 23, 1851). Signed at Traverse des Sioux, by which the Upper Sioux ceded to the United States all their lands in Iowa and Minnesota east of a line following the western bank of the Red River through Lake Traverse, and from there southwesterly to the Big Sioux River and along the western bank of that river to the Iowa line. The chief consideration to the Indians was an annual interest payment of $68,000 for fifty years, $40,000 in cash. The reservation assigned them extended along the upper Minnesota River, ten miles wide on either side. Later, on Aug. 5, the Lower Sioux ceded the same lands in a treaty at Mendota. These treaties, ratified at Washington, D.C., on June 23, 1852, with amendments later accepted by the Indians, were proclaimed by President Millard Fillmore on Feb. 24, 1853. Dissatisfaction of the Indians with the treaties and their nonfulfillment culminated in the Sioux War of 1862.

TRAVOIS. A device used chiefly by the Plains Indians. It consisted of poles lashed on the back of a horse so that the ends dragged behind. Usually in moving camp the teepee poles were used as the poles; the teepee cover, food, luggage, and even people rode on the dragging ends. Sometimes specially constructed travois, consisting of two springy poles and a litter, were used to transport children or the elderly. Dogs often dragged small travois.

TREASON. The U.S. Constitution restrictively defines treason against the United States and denies Congress authority to enlarge the constitutional definition. State constitutions contain similar limiting definitions of treason against a state. By these definitions treason "shall consist only in adhering to . . . Enemies" of the nation or state, "giving them Aid and Comfort," or "in levying War against" the nation or state. Enemies are only those opponents against whom the nation has formally declared war. Aid and comfort can be any form of benefit, in fact, tendered to the enemy. The federal and state constitutions require that government prove that a defendant has committed an overt act in pursuing his treasonable intention and that the act be proved by "the testimony of two witnesses to the same overt act, or on confession in open court."

TREASON TRIALS. Between 1795 and 1960 there were some fifty charges of treason against the United States that produced reported court opinions. There were only two reported trials for treason against a state. Few treason trials grew out of the American Revolution against crown sympathizers or out of the Civil War against supporters of the Confederacy. The Revolution involved bitter domestic conflict, but the new states dealt with disaffected persons mainly by property confiscation and summary administrative or court-martial proceedings. The scale of the Civil War barred wholesale treason prosecutions.

In four instances treason trials bore a political tinge in circumstances short of civil war: (1) convictions in the Pennsylvania Whiskey Rebellion (1795) and house tax riot cases, or Fries's Rebellion (1800); presidential pardons released the defendants; (2) prosecution of Aaron Burr for levying war to separate the West from the United States (1807); Chief Justice John Marshall directed dismissal for want of proof of a sufficient overt act; (3) conviction by the Rhode Island court of Thomas Wilson Dorr for an armed effort to install an extralegal government (1844); imprisoned, Dorr was pardoned (1845); and (4) conviction and execution of John Brown by Virginia (1859) for armed insurrection "to free slaves."

There was also strong political color in abortive treason prosecutions against Mormon leaders by Missouri (1838) and Illinois (1844). U.S. indictments for Mormon activity to resist federal troops in Utah in 1856–57 probably involved true levying of war; presidential pardon nullified the charges. Likewise political were Pennsylvania indictments for treason by levying war in 1892 against Homestead strike leaders; under severe criticism, the prosecutions were dropped.

Treason trials incident to World War I and World War II, however, produced no abuse of the charge to suppress proper political activity. The only significant treason prosecutions were for aiding spies of an enemy country.

TREASURY, UNITED STATES. The U.S. Treasury was created by act of Congress on Sept. 2, 1789. Alexander Hamilton, the first secretary of the Treasury, besides collecting and disbursing the public revenue, made the Treasury a prime agency for promoting the economic development of the country. Since the depression of the 1930's, the regulatory functions of the Treasury have been articulated and elaborated.

The four basic responsibilities of the Treasury are (1) to frame and recommend financial, tax, and fiscal measures; (2) to serve as financial agent for the U.S. government; (3) to enforce certain laws; and (4) to manufacture coins and currency. The Treasury formerly also included the postal service, the Coast Guard, the Bureau of Narcotics, and the parent agencies of the departments of the Interior, Commerce, and Labor. Other wide and varied powers and duties have gradually devolved on the Treasury. Besides his domestic concerns, including management of the public debt, the secretary of the Treasury represents the United States in foreign financial organizations.

More than 80 percent of the Treasury's annual appropriation and 90 percent of the personnel are assigned to revenue collection. Principal internal sources are individual and corporation income taxes; excise, estate, and gift taxes; and employment taxes under the Social Security system.

The Department also includes the Customs Bureau, the Office of the Comptroller of the Currency, the Bureau of Engraving and Printing, the Mint, the Secret Service, the Bureau of Alcohol, Tobacco, and Firearms, and the Office of Management.

TREASURY NOTES. *See* **Money.**

TREAT MISSION. James Treat, a native of New York, was appointed by the Republic of Texas as a confidential agent in 1839 to negotiate peace with Mexico. Recognition of Texas independence and of the Rio Grande boundary were the primary objectives. Texas was willing to pay $5 million for the liquidation of all Mexican claims. Treat reached Mexico City and obtained a hearing from the Council of State, but the Mexican Congress refused to negotiate and his mission failed.

TREATIES, COMMERCIAL. Bilateral or multilateral international agreements dealing with matters of trade, navigation, taxation, exchange controls, and the treatment of nationals (individuals or corporations) of one country in the territory of the treaty partners with regard to business activities. Other subjects may range from the admission of civil aircraft to the registration of trademarks and copyrights. Between the two world wars, commercial treaties covered "friendship, commerce, and consular rights." Since World War II they have been concerned with "friendship, commerce, and navigation." Commercial treaties are instruments of foreign economic policy of a country; their major objective is to enhance the economic position of states and their nationals in the world and thereby strengthen their political power in international affairs.

In the United States commercial treaties may be either formal accords requiring consent of the Senate or executive agreements; the latter can be concluded by the president without the approval of the Senate, either as a consequence of his constitutional power to conduct foreign affairs or by special authorization of Congress. The first commercial treaty of the United States was the Treaty of Amity and Commerce with France in 1778. (*See also* Most-Favored-Nation Principle; Tariff; Trade, Domestic; Trade, Foreign.)

TREATIES, MOST-FAVORED-NATION. *See* **Most-Favored-Nation Principle.**

TREATIES, NEGOTIATION AND RATIFICATION OF. The U.S. Constitution states: "He [the president] shall have Power, by and with the Advice and Consent of the Senate, to make Treaties, provided two thirds of the Senators present concur." The founding fathers envisaged the making of treaties as a composite function of the two branches, a joint effort operating on the whole process from negotiation to ratification. From the beginning, things turned out differently.

There are five distinct stages in the making of a treaty. The first is negotiation, when the president appoints the negotiator, prepares the instructions, and signs the draft of the treaty. In the second stage, the treaty is sent to the Senate for its "advice and consent." Four courses are open to the senators: consent, reject, block by tabling, or consent with reservations or amendments. If the Senate consents, the president then proceeds to the third stage, ratifying the treaty (although he need not), after which he proceeds to exchange ratifications with the cosignatory nation, the fourth stage, and finally proclaims it the law of the land. If the Senate refuses its consent to the treaty, the president cannot proceed to ratification; if the Senate attaches reservations or amendments to the treaty, the president may accept or reject them.

A threat to the Senate's role is the practice of presidents entering into international agreements by executive action alone. Such executive agreements are not authorized by the Constitution but neither are they forbidden. They do not have the force of law but are, generally, binding on the courts while they are in effect for the duration of the administration that made them.

It should be noted that the treaty power is exclusively federal. The Constitution provides that "No State shall enter into any Treaty, Alliance, or Confederation" nor "without the Consent of Congress . . . enter into any Agreement or Compact with another state, or with a foreign Power."

TREATIES WITH FOREIGN NATIONS. In international usage the term "treaty" has the generic sense of "international agreement." Rights and obligations, or status, arise under international law irrespective of the form or designation of an agreement. But in constitutional usage, treaties are sometimes distinguished from less formal agreements. The Constitution of the United States distinguishes treaties from other agreements and compacts in several ways.

The first way is that only the federal government can conclude a "Treaty, Alliance, or Confederation"; states can make an "Agreement or Compact" with other states or with foreign powers but only with consent of the Congress.

The second way is that treaties are negotiated and ratified by the president, but he must obtain the advice and consent of the Senate, two-thirds of the senators present concurring. Advice and consent came to be confined only to ratification.

The third way that the Constitution distinguishes treaties from "agreements and compacts" is that treaties made under authority of the United States are stated to be part of the supreme law of the land (with the Constitution and statutes "made in pursuance thereof"), which judges in every state are bound to enforce.

Fifteen treaties were concluded prior to the Constitution of 1789, using procedures made difficult by political decentralization. They were negotiated by commissioners appointed and instructed by the Continental Congress and ratified by the Congress. Technically the assent of all thirteen colonies was required until ratification of the Articles of Confederation in 1781, and thereafter of nine. Despite difficulties the pre-Constitution Congress concluded the Treaty of Paris (1783) ending the revolutionary war; arrangements for refinancing debts to France (1782, 1783); commercial treaties with the Netherlands (1782), Sweden (1783), and Prussia (1785); the Treaty of Peace and Friendship with Morocco (1786); and a consular convention with France (1788).

At first treatymaking under the Constitution was concerned mainly with avoiding entanglement in the Napoleonic Wars and consolidating the territorial position of the new republic (*see* Jay's Treaty; Barbary Wars; Pinckney's Treaty; Adams-Onís Treaty; Ghent, Treaty of; Convention of 1818 with England). Thereafter attention turned to the westward movement that rounded out the continental domain and to external trade (*see* Webster-Ashburton Treaty; Guadalupe Hidalgo, Treaty of; Gadsden Purchase.) Russia ceded Alaska to the United States by a treaty in 1867. (*See also* Clayton-Bulwer Treaty; Hay-Pauncefote Treaties; Hay-Herrán Treaty; Paris, Treaty of (1898); Platt Amendment.) A treaty with Panama in 1903 granted the United States the Canal Zone in perpetual leasehold; a 1978 treaty returned the zone to Panama.

Commercial relations with an ever-expanding group of states led to numerous regulatory conventions. Early treaties of commerce and navigation arranged tariff concessions reciprocally; rights of merchant ships in foreign waters; and definition of consular functions in relation to nationals, national vessels, and exports. Growth in the 20th century of corporate enterprise in foreign countries led to provisions for protection and regulation of it. Since World War II there has been emphasis on aid for reconstruction, military assistance, and financial and technical assistance for development. This has led to numerous treaties, followed by executive agreements elaborating detailed applications of programs authorized in treaties or basic statutes. Similarly, many conventions have elaborated principles of reciprocal trade agreements acts, later of the General Agreement on Tariffs and Trade (1948), and of the Chicago Air Convention (1944) regulating international air transport.

Commercial relations have increased violations of the rights of nationals, producing international claims sponsored by governments. Consequently many conventions have been concluded creating commissions to hear one or a series of claims (*see* Treaty of Washington; Pelagic Sealing Dispute; Permanent Court of Arbitration; Hague Peace Conferences; Root Arbitration Treaties). The United States also made arbitral commitments under the United Nations Charter (1945) and the General Treaty of Inter-American Arbitration (1929).

There are early cases of extradition by the United States of fugitives from justice without treaty; this is no longer permitted (*see* Jay's Treaty; Webster-Ashburton Treaty). The United States is a party to the multilateral Montevideo Convention on Extradition (1933), which has helped to unify practice among Western Hemisphere states.

Beginning with the Red Cross Convention of 1854, the United States has concluded multilateral treaties, but these totaled only seventy before 1914, nearly half the products of the Hague Conferences, which condified international law regulating warfare and created the Permanent Court of Arbitration; the Central American Peace Conference of 1907, and several Pan-American conferences. Others regulated or created agencies to regulate weights and measures, submarine cables, exchange of documents, protection of industrial and literary property, sanitation and public health, wireless telegraphy, salvage, the African slave trade, white slavery, and safety at sea. There was one important political convention, the General Act of the Algeciras Conference (1906). The United States rejected the League of Nations Covenant and the Statute of the Permanent Court of International Justice, then initiated the Kellogg-Briand Pact (1928) for renunciation of aggressive war, and ratified the Charter of the United Nations and the Statute of the International Court of Justice (1945). It has participated in formation of the Organization of American States (1948), with consultative and security functions, and in many Pan-American agreements for economic and cultural cooperation. Beginning in 1947 it constructed a network of defensive alliances, including the North Atlantic Treaty Organization (1947) and the Southeast Asia Treaty Organization (1954). In the 1970's efforts to slow down the nuclear arms race led to the Strategic Arms Limitation Treaties with the Soviet Union (1972 and 1979; the latter treaty was not ratified).

TREDEGAR IRON WORKS. The Tredegar rolling mill, privately built at Richmond, Va., in 1836, was first operated by the Tredegar Iron Company, Jan. 2, 1838. Joseph Reid Anderson saved it from failing in 1841. In 1843 he leased the works and in 1848 bought them. By 1860 he manufactured for a national market nearly every type of iron, including 1,200 cannon for the U.S. government. Tredegar iron, because of its great tensile strength, ranked as one of the three leading charcoal irons. Until 1863 it constituted the Confederate government's only source for cannon other than by capture. Reincorporated after the war as the Tredegar Company, with Anderson as president, it led in rebuilding the new South.

TREE PLANTING ON THE PLAINS. The first settlers entering Kansas and Nebraska in 1854 found that the number of trees diminished as they advanced westward, until on the High Plains no timber existed except in scanty fringes beside watercourses. Desire for beauty, shade, windbreak, and fuel induced the pioneers to set out groves. Sen. Phineas W. Hitchcock of Nebraska introduced the Timber Culture Bill (1873) providing that a settler on public domain could acquire title to 160 acres by planting 40 acres to trees. The next year the requirement was reduced to 16 acres and two years of successful tree growth. Beginning in 1934 the federal government engaged in wholesale tree planting in selected localities scattered from the 25-inch rainfall line west to the Rocky Mountains.

TREE-RING DATING (dendrochronology). A method of dating by the study of the differences and sequences of the annual rings of trees. The rings of trees of the same species can vary in thickness according to the amount of rainfall, and excessively wet and dry seasons can be identified by wide and narrow rings, respectively. The method was developed by Andrew E. Douglass, an Arizona astronomer, about 1914, to date ruins in New Mexico and Arizona.

TRELAWNEY PLANTATION (Richmond's Island, Me.). Typical of early fishing and trading posts along the New England coast. Title was based on a grant by the Council for New England to Robert Trelawney and Moses Goodyear, merchants of Plymouth, England, in 1631. In addition to fishing, there was trade with Indians and white settlers. Agriculture was carried on, and pigs, goats, and cattle were raised. In 1648, after the death of Trelawney (1644) and of John Winter, who directed the plantation (1645), Robert Jordan, an Anglican minister and Winter's son-in-law, was awarded the plantation as security for a claim that Winter's estate had on the proprietor. Trelawney's minor heirs never had a hearing, and their intermittent efforts (1677 to 1758) to recover were unsuccessful.

TRENCHES IN AMERICAN WARFARE. Not until the Revolution did opposing forces face each other in the field and begin to use hasty field entrenchments. The Battle of Bunker Hill was the first case; a flimsy entrenchment was built, on Gen. Israel Putnam's theory that "an American soldier is not afraid for his head, but terribly afraid for his legs; cover these, and he will fight all day." Gen. George Washington used trenches continually and freely. Trenches were little used in the War of 1812 and the Mexican War. At the beginning of the Civil War the soldiers of both sides resented work on trenches. The Battle of Chancellorsville, Va., was a trench battle, and thereafter both sides acquired great skill and ingenuity. The ultimate development in trenches was at Petersburg, Va., in 1864–65. The trenches dug there were the forerunners of those dug in 1914–18 in France. Parallel lines of trenches were created, each side holding them with the minimum force and keeping the maximum force free for maneuver against the exposed flanks. The foxhole, a more temporary shelter, largely replaced the trench in World War II and the Korean War. In the Vietnam War the bunker afforded some protection against artillery.

***TRENT* AFFAIR.** Involved the disputed doctrine of the freedom of the seas during the Civil War. In August 1861 the Confederate government selected as diplomats James Murray Mason of Virginia for London and John Slidell of Louisiana for Paris. The commissioners successfully ran the blockade to Havana, Cuba, where they took passage, Nov. 7, 1861, on the *Trent,* a British ship. The next day, without instructions, Union Capt. Charles Wilkes stopped the *Trent,* searched the vessel, arrested the commissioners and their secretaries, and removed them to his ship.

A demand for war spread through the British Isles. Lord John Russell drafted a demand for an apology and for the immediate release of Mason and Slidell. If this demand were not met, the British minister at Washington, D.C., was to come home. At the same time the British government rushed 8,000 troops to the defense of Canada and forbade temporarily the exportation of arms and ammunition.

President Abraham Lincoln, fortunately, was cautious, and Secretary of State William H. Seward soon realized that the alternative to surrendering the commissioners was war with England. Seward "cheerfully liberated" them. He said Wilkes had erred in not bringing the ship into port for adjudication and had violated American established policy of freedom of the seas.

TRENTON (N.J.). Capital city of New Jersey, with a population of 92,124, according to the 1980 census. It is also an industrial city, with specialized manufacturing plants producing steel wire and cable, machinery, chemical products, pottery and chinaware.

Trenton was established on the banks of the Delaware River at the first line of waterfalls on the river. This was the "head of navigation," and the city began its modern business activities as a service town where riverboats had to stop. Stagecoach lines, then canal and rail lines, linked this natural crossroads location with important cities. (*See also* Trenton, Battle of.)

TRENTON, BATTLE OF (Dec. 26, 1776). Following Gen. George Washington's evacuation of New Jersey, British Gen. William Howe had established two unsupported cantonments of 1,500 Hessians each, at Bordentown and Trenton. To Washington, facing the dissolution of his army and sure the enemy only awaited the freezing of the Delaware River to seize Philadelphia, the exposed posts offered an opportunity. On Christmas night, with 2,500 troops, he crossed the Delaware at McKonkey's Ferry, eight miles above Trenton. Delayed by floating ice and a storm of sleet and snow, his two columns, under his command and that of Gen. John Sullivan, reached the village at 8 A.M. The Hessians, who, as Washigngton had foreseen, had spent Christmas night celebrating, were completely surprised. The Americans fired from houses and cellars and from behind trees and fences, while their artillery raked the two main streets of the town. In the battle, lasting scarcely forty minutes, the Hessians lost 30 killed (including Rall) and 1,000 taken prisoner, while the patriots had only two officers and two privates wounded. The victory was a turning point in the Revolution.

TRENTON DECREE. Beginning in 1757, both Pennsylvania and Connecticut claimed part of Pennsylvania lying between the forty-first and forty-second parallels. Intermittent civil war was waged between settlers. Pennsylvania appealed to Congress, empowered under the Articles of Confederation to arbitrate jurisdictional disputes between states. A court of commissions, meeting at Trenton, N.J., rendered a unanimous decision on Dec. 20, 1782, which supported Pennsylvania's claim.

TRESPASS ACT (1783). An act contrary to the provisions of the Definitive Treaty of Peace; passed in New York at the insistence of Gov. George Clinton. Primarily designed to benefit the owners of real estate in or about New York City whose property had been occupied by the British during the Revolution, it permitted the owners of such real estate to sue to recover rents and damages.

TREVETT* V. *WEEDEN (1786). A decision rendered by Judge David Howell of Rhode Island, frequently cited as a precedent for the doctrine of judicial review laid down by Chief Justice John Marshall in *Marbury* v. *Madison* (1803). Acts of the legislature provided heavy fines for those refusing to accept the state's depreciated paper currency at par. John Weeden, a butcher, was acquitted on the ground that the acts were unconstitutional and void.

TREVILIAN STATION, BATTLE AT (June 11–12, 1864). Union Gen. Philip H. Sheridan, commanding 10,300 cavalry, left the Pamunkey River in Virginia on June 7 under orders to destroy the Virginia Central Railroad and join Gen. David Hunter at Charlottesville. Confederate Gen. Wade Hampton, with 5,000 horsemen, intercepted Sheridan at Trevilian Station on June 11. Union Gen. Alfred T. A. Torbert's division, attacking Hampton's right, was struck in the rear by Fitzhugh Lee's division. Union Gen. George A. Custer's brigade was driven back, but recovered its ground. During the night Hampton retired one mile. Sheridan attacked again the next day; but, unable to make progress or reach Charlottesville, he retired to the York River.

TRIANGLE FIRE (Mar. 25, 1911). The Triangle Shirtwaist Company, occupying the three top floors of a ten-story loft building in New York City, suffered a disastrous fire in which an estimated 147 lives, mostly women and girls working there, were lost. The cause of the fire was unknown. It was found that little provision had been made for fighting fire; that there was only one narrow fire escape; that some of the exit doors were habitually kept locked; and that stairway entrances were cluttered. The disaster led to sweeping reforms in building and factory laws, especially precautions against fire.

TRIANGULAR TRADE. The English colonies north of Maryland did not, from their beginnings, have great staple products readily exportable directly to England in exchange for European goods. As they were unable or forbidden by law to manufacture their needs in the colonies, they were forced to balance their trade by engaging in complex trading enterprises, to dispose of diversified surpluses in non-English markets in order to provide purchasing power in England. One means was the triangular trade, sometimes called the "three-cornered," or "roundabout," trade.

In its simplest form, near the mid-18th century, its three corners were, in sequence, a port in the northern colonies (most commonly Boston or Newport, R.I.), the Gold Coast of Africa, and a port in the West Indies (often Kingston, Jamaica). Roots of the triangular trade extended into early Massachusetts commerce, although the trade itself did not flourish until after 1700. In the 1640's New England sales of fish and lumber in Spain and concurrent commerce with the West Indies must have suggested the roundabout trade; and in the 1650's New England vessels engaged directly in the African slave trade. Meanwhile, New England trade with the sugar colonies reached enormous proportions, and the uses of rum in the Indian trade and in the fisheries came to be widely recognized.

TRIBAL COURTS, INDIAN. *See* **Indian Tribal Courts.**

TRIBUTE. To avert the loss of commercial vessels and the enslavement of American seamen, the United States for many years followed the example of other Christian powers in dealing with the piratical governments of Morocco, Algiers, Tunis, and Tripoli. These Barbary governments regarded the Mediterranean as their private property, and demanded that other nations pay them a fixed annuity or give them many valuable presents for safe transit. (*See* Barbary Wars.)

TRIPARTITE AGREEMENT. An international monetary agreement entered into by France, England, and the United States on Sept. 25, 1936, to stabilize their currencies at home and in the exchange. Following suspension of the gold standard by England in 1931 and the United States in 1933, a serious disequilibrium developed between their currencies and those of the gold bloc countries, particularly France. As devaluation had raised import prices and lowered export prices in England and America, the gold bloc countries would eventually have to devaluate unless international stabilization was agreed on by leading monetary powers. The franc was devalued practically simultaneously with the announcement of the Tripartite Agreement. By this informal, relative, and provisional agreement the three powers were pledged to refrain from competitive depreciation and to attempt to maintain currencies at existing levels.

TRIPOLI, WAR WITH. *See* **Barbary Wars.**

TRIST MISSION. As the Mexican War drew to a close, Nicholas P. Trist, chief clerk of the Department of State, was designated to negotiate the peace, but was recalled when the administration decided on harsher terms than the instructions given Trist. He nevertheless remained in Mexico, where on Feb. 2, 1848, he was the sole American negotiator of the Treaty of Guadalupe Hidalgo.

TROUP AND CLARK PARTIES. The two factions in Georgia state politics after the disappearance of the Federalists. They reached their greatest virulence 1819–25, during which time George M. Troup and John Clark, who gave their names to the parties, were each elected governor twice. Although differing little in principles, the Troup party tended to represent the aristocratic states'-rights tradition and the Clark party the frontier nationalistic group.

***TRUAX* V. *CORRIGAN*, 257 U.S. 312 (1921).** A case in which the Supreme Court held unconstitutional the antiinjunction law of Arizona (1913). Conspiracy and illegal picketing and boycott by strikers were alleged; the majority opinion held that the action of the strikers was coercive, a violation of the plaintiff's right of property, and a denial of free access of employees, owners, and customers to the place of business. The Court held that the Arizona law deprived the owner of property without due process of law and was invalid under the Fourteenth Amendment.

TRUCKING INDUSTRY. The modern trucking industry developed with the highway network and the automobile industry in the 20th century; earlier, most long-distance freight had been handled by railroad. The trucking lines have historical connections with the freight wagon lines that hauled goods overland between cities before the development of railroads. The Teamsters Union, which includes unionized truck drivers, is one of the most powerful unions in the United States.

Trucks have taken an increasing portion of the inter-city freight carried within the United States since World War II; the industry had grown to handle over 20% by 1960, and has retained that share of the freight market. So much freight was moved by truck that many railroads began to offer their own trucking services, carrying loaded trailer trucks on flat cars between cities. This "piggy-back" system permitted truck drivers to move the trailers to and from the trains at the point of departure and the destination, while the long-distance runs were hauled without drivers and crews by the railroad.

TRUMAN ASSASSINATION ATTEMPT (Nov. 1, 1950). Two Puerto Rican Nationalists, Oscar Collazo and Griselio Torresola, attempted to assassinate President Harry S. Truman at Blair House in Washington, D.C. Torresola was killed instantly in the attempt. Collazo was captured and tried and sentenced to death for the killing of a guard. On July 24, 1952, Truman commuted the sentence to life imprisonment.

TRUMAN DOCTRINE. On Mar. 12, 1947, President Harry S. Truman asked Congress for $400 million for the defense of Greece and Turkey from the pressure of Soviet communism. On May 15, Congress, although the country was officially at peace, voted the money, thus sanctioning a radical departure from the traditional policy of "nonentanglement" in European affairs. Truman declared it to be a general principle of American policy "to help free peoples to maintain . . . their national integrity against aggressive movements that seek to impose upon them totalitarian [Communist] regimes."

"TRUST-BUSTING." A term that originated during the administration of Theodore Roosevelt, marking the turn from apathetic enforcement of the Sherman Antitrust Act of 1890 to energetic prosecution of lawbreakers in big business.

TRUSTS. A term so broadly used that a precise definition is impossible; generally it refers to an industrial monopoly, although banking combines have been known as money trusts, public utilities have been called power trusts, and railroad companies and labor organizations have been prosecuted under the federal antitrust laws (*see* Antitrust Laws). On the other hand, local monopolies are not trusts. It is the attempt, or the ability, to set prices in a national market, or even a large portion of it, that makes a concern a trust.

National monopolies first became apparent in American industry after the Civil War as cheaper transportation widened markets. The first trust was the Standard Oil Company, founded in 1879 and renamed the Standard Oil Trust in 1882. The stockholders in numerous refining, pipeline, and other companies assigned their stock to a board of nine trustees at a stipulated price and received trust certificates; the trustees had legal and voting rights in the stocks; and the stockholders received the profits. This system was soon copied by other industries: the American Cotton Oil Trust was set up in 1884, the National Linseed Oil Trust in 1885, and the Distillers and Cattle Feeders Trust, known as the whiskey trust, in 1887.

Public agitation over these giant organizations led to the testing of their legality in state courts, which decided that entering into such agreements was beyond a corporation's powers (*see also* Sherman Antitrust Act). Between 1891 and 1897 only fifty combinations capitalized at $1 million or more were formed, most of them of the property-holding type. But antitrust legislation was not effective for long. In addition, a satisfactory substitute for the trustee device was found when New Jersey in 1889 and 1893, and then other states, authorized corporations receiving charters from them to hold stock in other corporations, a right not previously enjoyed. The security holding company, which this made possible, differed from the trustee system in that ownership was substituted for trusteeship. New trusts were formed in rapid succession. The census of 1900 showed 185 industrial combinations, seventy-three of them capitalized at $10 million or more, turning out 14 percent of the industrial products of the nation; 1901 witnessed the founding of the billion-dollar U.S. Steel Corporation; and by 1904 there were 318 trusts that controlled 20 percent of the manufacturing capital of the country. The so-called rich man's panic of 1907 brought the movement to a close.

The trust-busting movement began with the Supreme Court decision of Mar. 14, 1904, against the Northern Securities Company. Suits were brought against forty-four trusts and combinations during President Theodore Roosevelt's administration and against ninety more under President William Howard Taft. In 1914 the Clayton Antitrust and Federal Trade Commission acts attempted to restore free competition in trade and industry.

The public subsequently became less hostile toward trusts. The Webb-Pomerene Act (1918) and the Merchant Marine Act (1920) permitted American concerns to combine to some extent in their foreign business. The merger became the chief method of combination because the Clayton Act virtually forbade large-scale commercial combination by stock purchase. However, public utility empires still used the holding company device. During the prosperous 1920's businesses in the same line were permitted increasingly to compare recent statistical information; basing point systems grew in popularity; and in 1933 a joint sales agency, including producers of 75 percent of the coal output, was judged not contrary to the antitrust laws. During the administration of President Franklin D. Roosevelt, under the National Industrial Recovery Act of 1933, trade associations and other industrial groups were permitted to control prices and to determine production and were encouraged to draw up codes of fair competition; they were promised that any action taken in compliance with an approved code would not subject them to prosecution under the antitrust laws. The Federal Trade Commission was to enforce these codes. Within the first month over 400 codes were filed, and many were too hastily approved; code groups were permitted many liberties forbidden under the antitrust laws, especially the soft coal, petroleum, lumber, and cleaning and dyeing businesses. The Supreme Court's decision in *Schechter Poultry Company* v. *United States* (May 1935) brought this experiment in industrial self-government to an end.

In World War II, the government suspended prosecution of the trusts and encouraged cooperation among industries in the interest of efficiency. The Office of Price Administration found this concentration of economic power useful in effecting price controls. About 1946 the Antitrust Division began investigations of 122 companies. One of Antitrust's greatest victories was the Supreme Court's order in 1948 to the Cement Institute to abandon its basing-point system, for the decision obliged some twenty-five other industries, among them steel, to give up their basing-point systems as well.

By 1950 a few corporations had incomes greater than that of any state or city government in the country. In 1950 the Celler-Kefauver Act forbade a company to acquire all or part of the assets of another if the consequence would be to reduce competition. Nevertheless, between 1950 and 1969 some 17, 000 mergers took place. During the 1960's many of the mergers were conglomerates that Antitrust at first believed could not be shown to lessen competition. But after about 1969 the Federal Trade Commission increased its attack on mergers, even of the general sort. In 1980 the hundred largest industrial corporations had combined assets of $784 billion.

TRUST TERRITORY OF THE PACIFIC. The Pacific Trust Territory comprises about 2,000 islands in the Mariana, Caroline, and Marshall groups. Their land mass totals only 700 square miles, but they are located over an ocean area of 3 million square miles. About 100 of the islands are inhabited, with a population of approximately 130,000 in 1970. The people of the Trust Territory are Micronesians, descendants of migrants who came from Asia perhaps 3,500 years ago. They are diverse in terms of language, culture, and level of sophistication; nine mutually unintelligible languages, with various dialects, are spoken.

Spain ruled these islands for two centuries, until other European powers vied for their control in the 19th century. By 1900 they were part of the German empire and, as such, were seized by Japan early in World War I. Japanese rule continued, legitimated by a League of Nations mandate in 1920, until the islands were captured, seriatim, by U.S. forces in World War II. In 1947 the United States placed the islands under the trusteeship system of the United Nations, and the Trust Territory of the Pacific Islands, with the United States as administering authority, was born.

The U.S. Congress has provided that civil administration of the Trust Territory shall be vested in whatever agency the president may choose. Until July 1, 1951, that agency was the Department of the Navy, but administration was then transferred to the Department of the Interior. With the seat of government in Saipan, in the Marianas, the Trust Territory's government is headed by a high commissioner appointed by the president. The bicameral, popularly elected Congress of Micronesia has broad lawmaking authority. The judicial system is headed by a high court, whose judges are appointed by the secretary of the interior. Each of the six districts of the Trust Territory has also been provided with a governmental structure: the Marianas, Yap, Palau, Truk, Ponape, and the Marshalls.

Although the Trust Territory is administered by the United States, it is not a U.S. territory, since the United States claims no sovereignty over it. Negotiations looking toward a new political status for the Trust Territory commenced in the late 1960's. In 1976 the Northern Mariana Islands became a commonwealth of the United States; the other Trust Territory islands have been negotiating a free association arrangement.

TRUTH-IN-LENDING ACT (May 29, 1968). This act required that manufacturers disclose to consumers information about credit transactions in terms of the annual rate calculated under specified procedures.

TRYON'S LINE. William Tryon, as royal governor of North Carolina, in pursuance of agreements made with the Cherokee (Oct. 20, 1765, and June 13, 1767), had a line run between North Carolina and the Cherokee hunting grounds in the summer of 1767, as a part of the line referred to in the Proclamation of 1763. Three commissioners ran the line from the Reedy River, where the North Carolina-South Carolina line terminated, to the top of Tryon Mountain of the Blue Ridge Mountains; from there it followed a straight course to Chiswell's Mines (present Austinville, Va.) on the New River. Tryon then forbade anyone to buy land from the Indians or to issue grants beyond and within a strip one mile east of the line.

TSIMSHIAN. *See* **Haida.**

TUBAC (Ariz.). The first settlement founded by Spaniards in Arizona, it lies about twenty miles north of the Mexican border, on the Santa Cruz River. Visited by missionaries as early as 1691, the site was probably not permanently occupied by whites before 1750. A rebellion of the Pima in the following year led to the establishment of a Spanish military presidio at Tubac in 1752, chiefly for the protection of the Jesuit missions of San Cayetano del Tumacácori (founded 1697) and San Xavier del Bac. The presidio was moved from Tubac to Tucson in 1776, but small Spanish, Pima, and Mexican garrisons were stationed there for varying periods after 1784, until the time of the Mexican War (1846).

TUBERCULOSIS. Called also phthisis or consumption, tuberculosis was one of the great killer diseases throughout much of American history. Its incidence began rising in the 18th century and reached a peak in America around the mid-19th century. The two most common forms of therapy were shutting the patient in a closed room away from all drafts (and fresh air), or else urging him to seek a warmer climate. The Southwest became the mecca for "lungers," as tubercular patients were often known.

In 1882 Robert Koch announced the discovery of tubercle bacillus *(Mycobacterium tuberculosis).* Meanwhile, the incidence of tuberculosis was beginning to decline. The death rate from tuberculosis in leading American cities was in excess of 400 per 100,000 population during the early years of the 19th century; by 1900 the estimated rate was down to about 200. The American pioneer in the field of tuberculosis sanatoriums was Edward L. Trudeau, who in 1884 opened a small sanatorium at Saranac Lake, N.Y., modeled on one of the European establishments. In 1894 he established a laboratory devoted to the study of tuberculosis. Within a few years the emphasis in tubercular therapy came to be placed upon rest, fresh air, and a sound diet. The New York City Health Department in 1889 commissioned three consultants to investigate tuberculosis; the resulting report clearly stated that the disease was communicable and preventable. As it became clear that tuberculosis was a communicable disorder and that physicians were not cooperating, the department passed an ordinance (1897) making case reporting compulsory. Other city and state health departments soon established similar programs. This large-scale attack brought a sharp reduction in the national tuberculosis death rate.

TUCSON (Ariz.). Founded in 1776 by Spanish settlers who moved to the area from Mexico, it was the northernmost town established in Arizona, and was provided with walls to help defend it from marauding Apache. Tucson had a long history of battles and defenses, but was surrendered without a shot to U.S. forces during the Mexican War. The peace treaty ending the Mexican War added Tucson to the United States. During 1862, the city was controlled by Confederate forces until it was captured by Californians and held by them for the Union. It was capital of Arizona Territory for ten years (1867–77), and remained an important center for southern Arizona after the government moved to Prescott and then to Phoenix. Arizona's cattle industry centers on Tucson and it is a key railroad and highway point. It is also the site of the University of Arizona and the location for a number of astronomical studies. Population in 1980 was 330,537.

TUGBOAT. *See* **Towboating.**

TULE LAKE, BATTLES OF (1873). Sieges during the Modoc War, in the lava beds south of Tule Lake on the California-Oregon boundary. The first attempt to dislodge the Modoc was made by Lt. Col. Frank Wheaton on Jan. 16–17, without success. After Maj. Gen. E. R. S. Canby was killed during peace negotiations on Apr. 11, fighting continued in the lava beds until Apr. 20 with Col. Jefferson Davis in command. A major attack was made by Col. Alvan C. Gillem, Apr. 15–17, after which the Indians fled to another part of the lava beds.

TULLAHOMA CAMPAIGN (June–August 1863). After the Battle of Murfreesboro at the beginning of the year, Confederate Gen. Braxton Bragg retired southward to Tullahoma, in middle Tennessee; Union Gen. William Rosecrans occupied Murfreesboro. As soon as the weather and roads permitted, Rosecrans, on June 24, moved to maneuver Bragg out of Tennessee and to occupy Chattanooga. By July 3, with only minor engagements at Liberty and Hoover gaps, Rosecrans had forced Bragg to the vicinity of Chattanooga. These successes, coinciding with Confederate defeats at Gettysburg and Vicksburg, marked the turning point of the war; except for the "barren" victory at Chickamauga, the Confederate Army of Tennessee thenceforward fought on the defensive.

TULSA (Okla.). Tulsa citizens called their city "Oil Capital of the World" in the earlier years of the 20th century, and oil is still a very important part of the city's work. It was a tiny town before oil was discovered in the vicinity in 1901, but the population grew rapidly as oil workers and supply companies moved in; it was incorporated as a city in 1902. By 1907, it had grown large enough to establish the University of Tulsa. Company headquarters, banks, pipeline terminals, and refineries were put up in the city to handle the oil industry's needs. One of the most important trade magazines in the industry was published at Tulsa. World War II introduced another important industry—aircraft building and repair. Other factories in the city produce steel products, chemicals based on petroleum, and electrical equipment. It is the inland terminal of the Arkansas River Project, which provided a waterway nine feet deep all the way to the Gulf of Mexico and turned Tulsa into an important port in the late 1960's. The 1980 population was 360,919.

TUNIS. *See* **Barbary Wars.**

TUNNELS. The earliest transportation tunnels in the United States were built for canals, the first being constructed in 1818–21 to carry the Schuylkill Canal through a hill at Pottsville, Pa., followed by the tunnel of the Union Canal at Lebanon, Pa. (1825–27). The first U.S. railway tunnel was probably that of the New York and Harlem Railroad at Ninety-first Street in New York City (1837).

The beginning of modern methods came with the digging of the railroad tunnel through Hoosac Mountain, Mass. (1854–76), which was initially carried on by hammer drilling, hand shoveling, and hand setting of black-powder charges; in 1866 Charles Burleigh introduced the first successful pneumatic drill, and the newly invented nitroglycerin was first used to shatter the rock. For tunneling through soft ground the tunnel-driving shield, patented in 1818 by British engineer Marc Isambard Brunel, was introduced in the United States by Alfred Ely Beach in New York City (1869–70).

The safest and most economical method of tunneling—the trench method—was first used in the Detroit River Tunnel of the Michigan Central Railroad (1906–10): cylindrical concrete sections with sealed ends were poured on land, towed to position, sunk into a trench previously dredged in the riverbed, and covered with gravel. The longest tunnel built by this method is the subaqueous portion of the Chesapeake Bay Bridge and Tunnel (1960–64). The pioneer automotive tube was the Clifford M. Holland Tunnel under the Hudson River at New York City (1920–27). The complete mechanization of rock tunneling was finally achieved in 1952 by means of the mechanical mole.

TUPELO, BATTLE AT (July 14, 1864). Union Gen. A.J. Smith, with 14,000 troops near Memphis, Tenn., undertook to prevent Confederate Gen. Nathan Bedford Forrest, with 12,000 men, from interrupting Gen. William Tecumseh Sherman's rail communications in Tennessee (*see* Atlanta Campaign). Smith marched southward and on July 14 sent Gen. Benjamin H. Grierson's cavalry division to Tupelo, Miss., to destroy the Mobile and Ohio Railroad. Following with his two infantry divisions, Smith was attacked by Forrest one mile west of Tupelo. The Confederates were defeated in four assaults.

TURBINE. A rotating machine that takes energy from a stream of fluid passing through it to produce mechanical energy. Steam and gas turbines employ rotating blades attached to a horizontal rotating shaft; water turbines usually have a vertical shaft to permit water to flow downward through inlet gates into a rotating impeller wheel. In the United States, beginning around 1850, water turbines began to replace breast and overshot waterwheels. Much of this progress is attributable to James B. Francis, who developed an axial-flow water-turbine design that bears his name. In 1880 Lester A. Pelton patented a turbine for use with high-level water supplies, such as are available in the western United States. Sir Charles A. Parsons in England, Carl G. P. De Laval in Sweden, C. E. A. Rateau in France, and Charles G. Curtis in the United States were some of the men associated with the early development of the steam turbine. De Laval is credited with having effectively developed the simple turbine involving nozzles working on a single blade row. In 1884 Parsons developed the reaction turbine that bears his name. Rateau in the early 1890's developed the multistage arrangement known as pressure compounding. Curtis invented velocity compounding, an arrangement employing two blade rows that are placed on the same rotating element with turning vanes between the rows, making it possible to take the kinetic energy out of the steam jet in two steps; he combined his invention with the developments of other inventors to make a turbine (patented 1896) similar to those now in use. Gas turbines did not assume commercial significance until the mid-1940's, when their suitability for aircraft became evident.

"TURF AND TWIG." A somewhat primitive ceremony used in England down to and during the time of the early American settlements, as a tangible and visible part of the "livery of seizin." The turf and twig ceremony of transfer was used in several American colonies, including Pennsylvania, Delaware, and Maine. The ceremony consisted of delivery of a turf with a twig upon it.

TURNER'S, NAT, REBELLION. *See* **Nat Turner's Rebellion.**

TURNPIKES. *See* **Lancaster Pike; National Road; Roads; Toll Bridges and Roads, Private.**

TURPENTINE TRADE. *See* **Naval Stores.**

TUSCARORA WAR (1711–13). The lower Tuscarora of eastern North Carolina, led by Chief Hencock, were moved to attack their white neighbors by the vicious practices of white traders and because of their alarm at settlers' encroachments on their hunting grounds. A sudden massacre (September 1711) almost overwhelmed the white colony. Col. John Barnwell of South Carolina led a relief expedition of about 50 whites and more than 350 Indian allies; his campaign (January–April 1712) weakened the enemy, but ended in a poorly observed truce. A second South Carolina expedition, commanded by Col. James Moore, consisted of 33 whites and almost 1,000 Indians. The main body of the enemy took refuge in Fort Nohoroco, near present-day Snow Hill, N.C. A three-day engagement (March 1713) resulted in Tuscarora acceptance of a treaty of peace. Most of the Tuscarora trekked northward and joined their kindred; thereafter the Five Nations were known as the Six Nations.

TUSKEGEE INSTITUTE. In 1881 Lewis Adams, a mechanic and former slave, and George W. Campbell, a banker and former slaveowner, both of Tuskegee, Ala., saw the need for the education of black youth in Macon County and secured a charter, which appropriated $2,000 annually for teachers' salaries, from the state legislature. Booker T. Washington was chosen to head the school, and the coeducational Tuskegee Normal and Industrial Institute was established by an act of the Alabama general assembly. Tuskegee Institute is now a small university offering undergraduate degrees in arts and sciences, applied sciences, education, engineering, nursing, and veterinary medicine—and work at the master's level in each area except nursing. Enrollment, predominantly undergraduate, was 3,721 in 1981. Physical facilities include 4,925 acres of land and 159 buildings.

TVA. *See* **Tennessee Valley Authority.**

TWEED RING. Led by William Marcy Tweed, New York State senator and political boss, it robbed the New York City treasury of a minimum of $30 million in the thirty months ending July 31, 1871. Matthew J. O'Rourke, a journalist who, while county bookkeeper, exposed the frauds, reckoned $200 million as the total stealings of the ring and the lesser Tweed rings from Jan. 1, 1865, to July 31, 1871; this included fraudulent bond issues, the sale of franchises, tax reductions, and other official favors.

In New York City Tweed was sovereign: he controlled the police, the district attorney, the courts, and most of the newspapers; a Democrat, he silenced the Republican party by putting scores of its leaders on the payroll. The ring's recklessness and the magnitude of its thefts shoved the city to the verge of bankruptcy and led to the ring's undoing. Three of the ring judges, George G. Barnard, John H. McCunn, and Albert Cardozo, were impeached. Tweed, reputedly worth $12 million at the peak of his power, made a partial confession. He died in Ludlow Street jail on Apr. 12, 1878.

TWELFTH AMENDMENT (proclaimed Sept. 25, 1804). The U.S. Constitution originally provided that "the Person having the greatest Number of Votes shall be the President, if such Number be a Majority of the whole Number of Electors appointed; . . . after the Choice of the President, the person having the greatest Number of Votes of the Electors shall be the Vice-President." It soon became evident that this arrangement was not satisfactory: the almost inevitable result was a lack of harmony between the president and vice-president; in case of the death of the president, a change of party control in the middle of the four-year term could result, without any mandate from the people.

In 1800 an acute situation developed. Thomas Jefferson and Aaron Burr not only received the largest number of votes, but the same number; it was, therefore, necessary for the House of Representatives to break the tie (*see* Jefferson-Burr Election Dispute). Steps were promptly taken to prevent the recurrence of such a situation.

The Twelfth Amendment instructed electors to cast separate ballots for president and vice-president; having passed the Senate on Dec. 2, 1803, it was proposed to the states by Congress on Dec. 9, following its passage by the House. Formal notice of ratification was made in time for its provisions to be effective in the presidential election of 1804.

TWELVE-MILE LIMIT. *See* **Territorial Waters.**

TWENTIETH AMENDMENT. *See* **Lame-Duck Amendment.**

TWENTY-ONE GUN SALUTE. British naval tradition originally recognized seven guns as the British national salute; regulations provided that ships should fire but seven guns, but that forts could fire three shots for every shot afloat because powder was easier to keep ashore than on shipboard. When gunpowder was improved the sea salute was made equal to the shore salute. The British proposed that the United States should return their salutes "gun for gun"; accordingly the United States adopted the twenty-one gun salute and the gun for gun return on Aug. 18, 1875.

TWENTY-FIRST AMENDMENT (proclaimed Dec. 5, 1933). Provided for repeal of the Eighteenth Amendment; proposed by Congress in February 1933, and ratified by the thirty-sixth state within ten months. It apparently permits states to levy an import tax on alcoholic beverages, operative against goods produced in other states, thereby modifying the provision of Article I of the Constitution prohibiting state imposts or the barring of importation altogether.

TWENTY-SECOND AMENDMENT (Feb. 26, 1951). Sent to the states by Congress on Mar. 21, 1947, this amendment provides that "No person shall be elected to the office of the President more than twice." It was the result of agitation following President Franklin D. Roosevelt's running for and being elected to a third and a fourth term. A qualifying clause prevented President Harry S. Truman, who as vice-president became president upon the death of Roosevelt (Apr. 12, 1945), from running for reelection more than once.

TWENTY-THIRD AMENDMENT (Mar. 29, 1961). Proposed by Congress on June 17, 1960, the amendment grants the right to vote in federal elections for three electors for president and vice-president to residents of the District of Columbia. The District had previously not had national voting rights.

TWENTY-FOURTH AMENDMENT (proclaimed Feb. 4, 1964). Eliminated poll taxes in federal elections; five states still required payment of poll taxes prior to passage of the amendment. (*See also* Poll Tax.)

TWENTY-FIFTH AMENDMENT (Feb. 10, 1967). Proposed in 1965, this deals with the troublesome problem of presidential disability and succession. Sections 3 and 4 set forth in detail what is to be done in the event that the president himself feels he is "unable to discharge the powers and duties of his office" or "Whenever the Vice-President and a majority of either the principal officers of the executive department or of such other body as Congress may by law provide . . . [find] that the President is unable to discharge the powers and duties of his office." Section 2 provides that "Whenever there is a vacancy in the office of the Vice-President, the President shall nominate a Vice-President who shall take office upon confirmation by a majority vote of both Houses of Congress." Spiro T. Agnew resigned as vice-president in October 1973, and the following month Rep. Gerald R. Ford was nominated and confirmed as vice-president. When Ford succeeded Richard M. Nixon to the presidency, following Nixon's resignation (August 1974), and when Nelson A. Rockefeller was nominated by Ford and confirmed as vice-president, the United States for the first time in its history had an unelected president and vice-president.

TWENTY-SIXTH AMENDMENT (June 30, 1971). This amendment gives eighteen-year-olds the constitutional right to vote in both federal and state elections, a direct outcome of the political activism of young citizens in the 1960's. Congress had already lowered the voting age to eighteen in the Voting Rights Act of 1970, but the Supreme Court held that the law was constitutional and enforceable only in federal elections.

TWIN CITIES. Saint Paul and Minneapolis, Minn., situated at the head of navigation on the Mississippi River. They have become the financial, cultural, and educational center of a wide region. (*See* Minneapolis; Saint Paul.)

"TWISTING THE BRITISH LION'S TAIL." A phrase that first began to appear in print about 1885, although it had been popular since the end of the revolutionary war. Orators, particularly Irish politicians and others desirous of winning the Irish vote, boasted that the United States had whipped England twice, and could and would do it again on any provocation.

TWO-PARTY SYSTEM. Throughout most of its history, the American party system has been dominated by two major, competitive parties, beginning with the Federalists and the Antifederalists in the 1790's. Since the Civil War the same two parties—the Democratic and Republican—have constituted the two-party system, and all American presidents and almost all members of Congress have been either Democrats or Republicans. While the two-party system has long characterized national politics, it has not invariably marked the politics of the states. The incidence of statewide one-partyism has declined in the 20th century, but the Democrats maintained a one-party supremacy in the states of the Deep South from the Reconstruction period into the 1960's and in some cases into the 1970's. Some states have had three-party systems for short periods of time; Wisconsin, North Dakota, and Minnesota all included a party from the Progressive movement in their party systems in the 1930's and 1940's. (*See also* Political Parties.)

TWO PENNY ACT (1755). Enacted by the Virginia assembly in anticipation of a shortage in the tobacco crop, it permitted payment, over a ten-month period, of obligations due in tobacco at a commutation rate of two pence per pound. In 1758 a similar act of one-year's duration was passed. The clergy of the established church, whose salaries were fixed in terms of tobacco, raised the principal objection (*see* Parson's Cause).

TWO-THIRDS RULE. At the Democratic convention in Baltimore in May 1832, the committee on rules reported the following resolution: "Resolved, that each state be entitled in the nomination to be made of a candidate for the vice-presidency, to a number of votes equal to the number to which they will be entitled in the electoral colleges, under the new apportionment, in voting for President and Vice-President; and that two thirds of the whole number of the votes in the convention shall be necessary to constitute a choice." This rule was followed by all Democratic conventions in making nominations until the convention at Philadelphia in June 1936, when the rule was abolished and a majority vote substituted.

TYDINGS-McDUFFIE ACT (Mar. 24, 1934). In January 1933 Congress passed the Hawes-Cutting Act providing for the independence of the Philippine Islands after twelve years and for trade relations with the United States effective ten years after the inauguration of the authorized commonwealth government; because of tariff and immigration provisions this act was rejected by the Philippine legislature. The Tydings-McDuffie Act eliminated certain objectionable provisions of the Hawes-Cutting Act and was passed and ratified by the Philippine legislature on May 1, 1934. In order to cushion the economic effects of this act and to facilitate independence on July 4, 1946, the Philippine Economic Adjustment Act was passed in 1939.

TYPEWRITER. The first U.S. patent for a writing machine was issued to William A. Burt of Detroit in 1829 for his "Typographer." This was an indicator-type machine using printers' type arranged on a swinging sector; operation was slow but effective. Giuseppe Ravazza in Italy in 1855, William Francis in the United States in 1857, and Peter Mitterofer in Austria in 1866 used individual keys for each character and typebars pivoted around an arc so that all printed at the common center. The first really successful machine used the same general arrangement of bars pivoted around an arc; the inventor was Christopher Latham Sholes of Milwaukee, who acquired two patents in 1868, and by 1872 had developed what is essentially the modern key arrangement. In 1873 E. Remington and Sons, arms manufacturers of Ilion, N.Y., redesigned the component parts, adapting them to more economical manufacture. The first examples, completed in 1874 and priced at $125, typed only capital letters. By 1878 Lucien S. Crandall had perfected the means for shifting the cylinder, or platen, and Byron A. Brooks had developed multicharacter typebars. Type-wheel machines were developed in order to avoid the specifics of patents that had already been granted, the Hammond and the Blickensderfer being the most widely accepted. It was not until 1908 that Remington adopted a visible writing machine, in which the carriage need not be lifted up in order to read the written line. The Underwood typewriter appeared about 1895 and came to be considered the standard machine. The early 20th century saw the universal acceptance of visible writing, a uniform keyboard, and the scaling down of size to create portable machines. Several electric machines were introduced, the most successful being made by Blickensderfer in Stamford, Conn., prior to 1909. Electric typewriters achieved popularity following the introduction of a motor-driven variety by Electromatic Typewriters, Inc., of Rochester, N.Y., in 1930. In the machine introduced in 1961 by International Business Machines Corporation (IBM) the type is on a swiveling ball-shaped shuttle on a light carriage that travels inside the framework of the machine.

U-BOATS. *See* **Submarines.**

U-2 INCIDENT (1960). On May 5, the Soviet Union announced that an American U-2 (Lockheed high-altitude) plane used for reconnaissance missions had been shot down on May 1 twelve hundred miles inside the Soviet Union. On May 7, Premier Nikita Khrushev announced that the pilot, Francis Gary Powers, was alive and had confessed to being a spy for the CIA. As a result, Secretary of State Christian Herter announced that the United States had engaged in extensive aerial surveillance over the Soviet Union since 1956, and President Dwight D. Eisenhower acknowledged that he had authorized the flights. At the opening of the Four-Power Summit Conference in Paris on May 16, Khrushchev demanded that the United States renounce all flights over the Soviet Union. As a result of the U.S. refusal to do so, the meeting broke up on May 17. Powers was tried by the Soviet Union, found guilty, and sentenced to ten years imprisonment. He was released on Feb. 10, 1962, in exchange for the U.S. convicted Soviet spy Rudolf Abel.

UINTAH, FORT (Utah). A fur-trading post built by Antoine Robidoux on the banks of the Uinta River above the mouth of the Duchesne (1831). John C. Frémont passed it in 1844 and recorded later that the fort had been attacked by the Utah and the entire garrison killed.

"UNCLE SAM." Nickname of the U.S. government. First used during the War of 1812, it was applied somewhat derisively to customhouse officers and to soldiers by those opposed to the war. The name is also identified with Samuel Wilson of Troy, N.Y. (1766–1854), known as "Uncle Sam" Wilson, who supplied barrels of beef to the government; in 1961 Congress recognized Wilson as a namesake for America's symbol.

UNCLE TOM'S CABIN; OR, LIFE AMONG THE LOWLY. A novel by Harriet Beecher Stowe, published serially in the *Washington National Era* (June 5, 1851–Apr. 1, 1852) and in book form (Mar. 20, 1852). Mrs. Stowe, acquainted with the bitter criticism of the Fugitive Slave Law of 1850 in New England and determined to write an account of slavery as she had known it in Cincinnati, intended to condemn the system, not the slaveholder; although based on fact, the book was not an accurate picture of the system. Three hundred thousand copies were sold the first year and more than one million by 1860; produced on the stage, it reached millions who never read the book. Most potent of all accounts of slavery, it lighted a torch in the North and was a contributing cause of the Civil War.

UNCOMPAHGRE (Colo.). A cantonment or agency located on the Uncompahgre River to supervise the Ute collected there. An uprising of the Ute (1879), partly because of pressure from the settlers for lands, resulted in the establishment of Fort Crawford (1880) on the west bank of the river, about eight miles south of the present town of Montrose; it was abandoned in 1890.

"UNCONDITIONAL SURRENDER." The most popular of several nicknames bestowed on Gen. Ulysses S. Grant after the capture of Fort Donelson, Tenn. (1862). The Confederate commander, Simon B. Buckner, proposed an armistice to discuss terms; Grant replied that no armistice would be accepted, but only "unconditional surrender."

UNDERGROUND RAILROAD. The name used by both the abolitionists and the defenders of slavery to describe the informal network of sympathetic northerners that helped guide fugitive slaves through the free states to Canada in the years before the Civil War. Although George Washington had reported systematic efforts by Quakers to aid slaves as early as the 1780's, it was not until the 1830's that the idea of a deep-laid abolitionist scheme spread, and the term "Underground Railroad" gained currency. Abolitionists who took pride in the work of the "Liberty Line" counted its activities among the most important weapons in the war on slavery. In the postwar years the coordinated efforts of Quaker, Covenanter, and Methodist "conductors," secretly operating at night, to transport slaves from "station" to "station" along an intricate maze of routes through the northern states became a standard part of the romance of antebellum America.

UNDERWATER DEMOLITION TEAMS (UDTs). The assault by U.S. Marines at Tarawa Island in the western Pacific (November 1943) demonstrated the absolute need for a sure method of detecting and then destroying underwater obstructions and mines close to shore, where minesweepers could not go. The U.S. Navy then organized intensively trained volunteer officers and men into teams of expert swimming scouts, whose duties were the reconnaissance of the seaward approaches to landing beaches; the location, improvement, and marking of usable channels for landing craft; and the demolition of both natural and artificial obstacles. UDTs were "first in" at Kwajalein, Saipan, Tinian, Guam, Peleliu, Anguar, Leyte, Lingayen, Luzon, Borneo, Iwo Jima, and Okinawa in the Pacific, 1944–45. In the European theater, UDTs combined with U.S. Army beach clearance personnel at Normandy and in southern France in 1944. During the Korean War UDTs prepared the way for the amphibious Inchon landing (September 1950) and cooperated with special U.S. Marine Corps raider units striking far inland. In the Vietnam War special volunteer units recruited from UDTs called SEALs (Sea-Air-Land approaches) made intelligence forays and commando raids into Vietcong-held territory in South Vietnam.

UNDERWOOD TARIFF. *See* **Tariff.**

UNEMPLOYMENT. The United States has suffered throughout its history from a wide variety of causes of unemployment as it moved from a predominantly agricultural to an industrial society. Disguised unemployment showed itself most vividly during the depression of the 1930's when industrial workers returned to their farm families as a refuge and helped in the chores. In 1936 John Maynard Keynes challenged the historic explanation of unemployment by the classical economists, who denied the existence of involuntary unemployment. Keynes was able to demonstrate that the private enterprise system could find equilibrium at a wide variety of points of unemployment and that full employment was only a special case of equilibrium that would only be attained as the result of deliberate economic policies pursued by the government.

The New Deal under President Franklin D. Roosevelt confined itself to measures to alleviate the pain of unemployment rather than implementing policies designed to change the dynamics of the labor market. In 1946 the Full Employment Act made full employment a matter of national policy. Implementation of the act meant that a great deal more had to be known about the nature of the demand and supply for labor. Since 1940 the U.S. Census Bureau has made monthly sample surveys of the labor force, so that data are now much more accurate.

The unemployment rate for persons under the age of twenty-five is generally higher than the rate for others, because they have not had the opportunity to acquire skills and they suffer the lowest seniority under union contracts. Men over forty and especially past the age of fifty-five find it more difficult to obtain reemployment than do younger men. And blacks suffer a disproportionately high rate of unemployment because of continuing discrimination and their historic concentration in southern agriculture. Certain industries have more than their share of unemployment. There may be a long-run declining demand for labor, as in agriculture; seasonality, as in the garment industry; or some other basic irregularity in their operations, as in commercial construction.

Women are a particularly volatile element in the labor market. By the 1970's it was increasingly usual for both members of the family to seek work to attain an income to accord with rapidly rising aspirations.

There has been much dispute over the definition of full employment. In an expanding, dynamic economy some people will leave one job to seek a better one elsewhere; during the post-World War II days the figure for this phenomenon was assessed to be 2 percent. Many European countries showed unemployment figures below 2 percent during the post-World War II years, and during World War II the United States fell below this figure. However, by 1970 the figure rose to 4 percent, as the agricultural revolution of the late 1940's and the 1950's resulted in the migration of many unskilled agricultural workers, including blacks and poor whites from Appalachia, into the major cities. It was public policy in the 1970's to attack this problem by a two-pronged strategy: the development of manpower programs to train the unskilled in a skill for which a labor market demand was anticipated, and the manipulation of the economy by fiscal and monetary measures to increase demand. During 1975–76 the U.S. unemployment figures remained at 8 percent without provoking much protest. In 1978 Congress passed the Humphrey-Hawkins Act, with a commitment to 4 percent unemployment by 1983, but a recessionary economy led to an increasing unemployment rate. It climbed over 10 percent in late 1982, which was the highest rate since 1941.

Robert Solow of the Massachusetts Institute of Technology, responding to the question of whether or not automation was causing unemployment, noted that despite all the talk about the accelerated pace of technology, productivity between 1947 and 1964 continued to increase a constant 3.2 percent a year. He claimed that automation is unrelated to unemployment; the critical question is whether the economy is operating at capacity. A new kind of unemployment—bipolar unemployment—has appeared in the United States. It affects those at the bottom of the educational ladder and those at the top. The problem of the uneducated and untrained is self-evident. Those at the top of the educational ladder find themselves obsolete overnight when defense and space exploration programs are contracted suddenly.

UNEMPLOYMENT INSURANCE. Monetary benefits paid by the states to unemployed workers established under the authority of the Social Security Act of 1935. State plans vary among themselves in the amount of benefits, duration of benefits, administrative procedures, and eligibility requirements.

UNICAMERAL LEGISLATURES. A legislature consisting of a single representative house. With the exception of New Hampshire and South Carolina, the original colonies were governed by unicameral assemblies. The early charters called for a governor assisted by a council of counselors appointed by the crown, the proprietor, or the proprietary council, on the governor's recommendation. The council, drawn usually from the landed gentry or merchant class, acted as an advisory cabinet for the governor, as a legislative chamber, and as a court of last resort. Deputies were added to the council as representatives of local interests, or freemen. Stages in the transition from governor's council to senate and then to separate houses included the introduction of the representative system; the desire of the counselors to sit separately because the peoples' representatives eventually outnumbered them; and the gradual separation of executive and judicial authority from the council, thus making it primarily a legislative body. When state governments were formulated during the revolutionary period, only Pennsylvania and Georgia adopted the unicameral legislative form. Georgia adopted bicameralism in 1789, after twelve years, and Pennsylvania in 1790, after fourteen years. Vermont provided for a unicameral legislature when it became an independent state in 1777—fourteen years before being admitted to the Union—and retained it until 1836. A revival of interest in the unicameral form occurred during the period 1910–20. Although only Nebraska adopted the one-house legislature in 1934, the proposal received serious consideration in several states. Interest in unicameralism was revived yet again after the Supreme Court decision in *Reynolds* v. *Sims* (1964), which ruled that both houses must be apportioned on the basis of population.

UNIFICATION CHURCH. A religious cult founded by the Rev. Sun Myung Moon in Korea in 1954, it began U.S. missionary operations in 1973. Starting with a few hundred followers, he built a U.S. membership of 10,000 in three years. Criticism of Moon's methods of conversion and his widespread business interests created widespread antagonism to the cult. His followers, popularly called "Moonies," were often found in public places selling wares made by the organization. In the 1980's, following a federal case brought against Moon for tax evasion, the cult declined in numbers.

UNIFORM CODE OF MILITARY JUSTICE. The basic federal statute governing the U.S. military justice system. The principal objective of the military justice system is to deter conduct prejudicial to good order and discipline. The need to govern the young army and fledgling navy spurred the colonies to adopt the familiar British system of military justice.

Articles of War. The British Articles of War of 1765 contained a special section on military justice, adopted intact by the Provisional Congress of Massachusetts on Apr. 5, 1775. On June 14 the second Continental Congress resolved to raise a military force; a committee composed of George Washington, Philip Schuyler, Silas Deane, Thomas Cushing, and Joseph Hewes proposed a code of sixty-nine articles based on the British Articles of War of 1765 and the Massachusetts articles. On June 30, 1775, this first American code was adopted by the Continental Congress. A new committee revised the 1775 code and recast its articles so that they would more closely parallel the British Articles of War; the Continental Congress approved the revised Articles of War on Sept. 20, 1776, which remained in force (with one major revision in 1786) until 1806. On Apr. 10, 1806, a new code of 101 articles superseded the old code and remained in force for more than sixty years. The Articles of War of 1874 lasted with few modifications until Mar. 1, 1917, when the Articles of War of 1916 became effective. Following the induction of approximately 4 million men into the army during World War I, pressure was brought to bear to improve the code. On Feb. 4, 1921, the Articles of War of 1920 became effective, and remained in force throughout World War II. A surge of criticism of military justice followed the war. In 1948 the Articles of War were amended and became effective on Feb. 1, 1949; their intent was to make army courts-martial procedure similar to civilian trial procedure.

Articles for the Government of the Navy. On Nov. 28, 1775, the Continental Congress enacted the Rules for the Regulation of the Navy of the United Colonies. These rules set forth only a few offenses and their punishments, and provided further that all other offenses committed on board ship should be punished "according to the laws and customs in such cases at sea." The inclusion of custom followed the pattern of British naval law of that period; as the U.S. Navy developed its own values and traditions, custom became less and less applicable. Congress made six statutory changes to naval law between 1775 and 1862, but the pressures of the Civil War emphasized the problem of administering law that was partially statutory and partially customary. As a result, Congress enacted the twenty-five Articles for the Government of the Navy in 1862; these were revised on numerous occasions and expanded to seventy articles by 1950.

The Uniform Code. Following World War II, the navy recommended revision of all the Articles for the Government of the Navy with one exception. In the meantime, the army reform bill of 1948 had been enacted, and there was a pervasive opinion in Congress that the basic laws governing all the U.S. armed forces should be uniform.

The Uniform Code of Military Justice, 140 articles, was passed by Congress in April 1950, and became effective May 31, 1951. This model law closely aligned military justice procedure with civilian procedures and contained major innovations in trial procedures and accused rights. Congress did not include a detailed account of how the code was to be implemented; it delegated to the president the authority to establish the rules of evidence and the procedures before courts-martial. In 1951 President Harry S. Truman issued, under his signature, the Manual for Courts-Martial, which is the basic directive implementing the Uniform Code of Military Justice. In 1968 Congress made significant changes in the Uniform Code of Military Justice, having made minor revisions in 1963. The changes again reflected the application of civilian concepts of jurisprudence to the military justice system.

UNION, FORT (N.Mex.). Established (1851) north of the present Watrous, Mora County, by Col. E. V. Sumner to help protect the inhabitants of the region from hostile Ute and Apache. It was one of the most important military establishments in the Southwest, frequently serving as headquarters of the Department of New Mexico. During the Civil War the Confederates attempted to capture it (*see* Rio Grande, Sibley's Operations on). Evacuated by the army in 1891, the post gradually fell into ruin.

UNION, FORT (N.Dak.). Built on the northerly side of the Missouri River, just above the mouth of the Yellowstone, by Kenneth McKenzie for the American Fur Company, it was the most important fort of the company. The enclosure was about 60 feet north of the river bank, the fort proper having a front of 220 feet and depth of 240 feet. The fort was built for trading with the Assiniboine and as a central depot to the scattered outposts, from which unification it derived its name. It was in use before it was completed. On Feb. 3, 1832, a fire destroyed the west quadrangle; the fort was completed in 1834 and continued in existence until 1867, when it was bought by the United States, torn down, and the materials used to complete Fort Buford about two miles down the Missouri. Fort Union was never Fort Floyd, as some writers have supposed: these forts were coexistent in 1830 as shown by a letter of McKenzie, dated Fort Union, May 5, 1830. The ruins of Fort Union were designated a national historic site in 1954.

UNION OR LOYAL LEAGUES. *See* **Loyal Leagues.**

UNION CANAL. A canal connecting the Schuylkill and Susquehanna rivers in Pennsylvania was suggested by William Penn in 1690; in 1762 the course was surveyed from Reading to Middletown, but the canal was not completed until 1828. It was enlarged in 1850, but it never prospered thereafter, and was abandoned in 1885.

UNION COLONY. Organized in New York City in December 1869 by Nathan C. Meeker, agricultural editor of the *New York Tribune,* in order to plant a settlement in Colorado. Within four months there were about 450 members, all characterized by high moral standards that included abstinence from alcohol. In the Cache la Poudre Valley north of Denver the town of Greeley was established in 1870, named for Horace Greeley, editor of the *Tribune.* In return for fees that varied from $50 to $200, members received farming land and the right to buy lots in the colony town. The success of this semicooperative venture stimulated similar undertakings. Greeley was incorporated as a city in 1885.

UNION DEMOCRATS. A coalition of conservatives during the Civil War who supported the war aims of the conservative Republicans to preserve the federal union and not interfere with slavery. The party was vigorously supported by such representative Democrats as Sen. Stephen A. Douglas and Gov. John Brough in the North, and by minorities of Democrats in the South. In the election of 1864 a Union Democrat, Andrew Johnson, ran for vice-president as President Abraham Lincoln's running mate.

UNION LABOR PARTY. Organized at Cincinnati (Feb. 22, 1887) in an attempt to unite the remnants of the Greenback Labor party with wage earners made articulate by the industrial conflicts of the period. Alson J. Streeter of Illinois, presidential nominee in 1888, received only 147,000 votes, the bulk of which came from the agricultural South and West.

UNION NAVY. The Union navy, numbering 42 active ships at the outset of the Civil War and expanding to some 700 at the peak of the conflict, gave the North overwhelming advantages in mobility and flexibility and enabled the Union to maintain a blockade of more than 3,000 miles of Confederate coastline from Virginia to Texas. The blockade sealed off southern ports and denied the South free access to Europe and the West Indies, while the markets of the world remained open to the North; it also discouraged direct foreign intervention in the war. In combined operations with the Union army —particularly at Hatteras Inlet (Aug. 29, 1861) and Port Royal, S.C. (Nov. 7, 1861), and at Wilmington, N.C. (Jan. 13–15, 1865)—the Union navy seized strategic locations on the Confederate coast, thus depriving the South of blockade-running havens and providing the North with base facilities and coaling stations.

On western waters, shallow-draft Union gunboats carried out a series of decisive riverine operations that ultimately divided the South along the Mississippi River. After the capture of New Orleans (Apr. 25, 1862) by a fleet under Flag Officer David G. Farragut, Union naval forces steaming up the Mississippi and forces fighting their way downstream converged on Vicksburg, Miss. (*see* Vicksburg in the Civil War).

UNION PACIFIC RAILROAD. *See* **Railroads, Sketches of Principal Lines.**

UNION PARTY. After the Union defeat at the first Battle of Bull Run (July 21, 1861), many leaders urged that all Union men, regardless of party, stand together for the preservation of the Union. Consequently a Union party ticket, pledged to the prosecution of the war, appeared in most of the important state elections in the fall of 1861, representing a coalition of Republicans and Union, or War, Democrats.

UNION PRISONS. *See* **Prison Camps, Union.**

UNION RIGHTS PARTY (properly the Union and Southern Rights party or, later, the Constitutional Union party). Organized largely under Whig leadership in Georgia in 1850 following the enactment of the Compromise of 1850, which precipitated a secession movement among some of the Southern Rights forces. The party undertook to control the state convention called by Gov. George W. Towns; its success and its program were revealed in the Georgia Platform adopted by that convention. The Union Rights party continued through the state elections of 1851. Similar movements existed in Mississippi and Alabama and there was talk of organizing a National Union party.

UNIONS, LABOR. *See* **Labor.**

UNION SENTIMENT IN BORDER STATES. Strong nationalist feeling had been expressed in the compromises sponsored by Henry Clay and others, and in the winter of 1860–61 the border states urged schemes of compromise and conciliation. After the outbreak of war a large majority of the people of Maryland, western Virginia, and Missouri rallied to the Union cause, and by September Kentucky ceased to be neutral. Unionist sentiment was strongest in the cities and in communities accessible to railroads and navigable rivers. Although much harassed by Confederate raids and guerrilla bands, the order states contributed heavily in men to the Union armies.

UNION SENTIMENT IN THE SOUTH. At the very beginning of the Civil War the Confederacy had within its borders a number of citizens who thought their first allegiance was to the old Union, particularly in the mountainous parts of Virginia, North Carolina, Tennessee, Georgia, and Alabama. These Unionists constantly increased their numbers as the war progressed. After passage of the conscription, impressment, and tax-in-kind laws, a large number of previously loyal Confederates acted in concert with the Unionists. Throughout most of the southern states the Unionists organized themselves into secret peace societies: the Peace and Constitutional Society in Arkansas; the Peace Society in Alabama, Georgia, Mississippi, and probably Florida; and the Heroes of America in North Carolina, east Tennessee, and southwest Virginia. Their main objectives were to provide mutual protection; to render aid to the Union troops; and to weaken the Confederate forces.

UNION SHOP. A factory, or place of business, in which the contract between the owners (or management) and the labor union representing the workers requires every employee to become a member of the union. Union shop agreements do not limit employment opportunities only to union members: anyone may secure a job in a union shop, but non-union workers must join the union within a certain fixed period of time (normally thirty days).

UNITARIANS. *See* **Congregational Churches.**

UNITED AMERICANS, ORDER OF. A nativistic benevolent association formed in New York in 1844, it quickly attained national membership, which was limited to American laborers. Members were promised old-age benefits, but the society was principally an agency to disseminate anti-Catholic and antiforeign propaganda. Its secret methods and elaborate ritual were copied by the Know-Nothing party.

UNITED COLONIES OF NEW ENGLAND (or New England Confederation). Founded May 19, 1643, in Boston, it consisted of the four colonies of Massachusetts, Plymouth, Connecticut, and New Haven; Rhode Island and Maine were excluded because of their political and religious uncongeniality. It gradually evolved from complex motives, chief of which was defense. The colonists also had in mind the well-being of their state religion and the spread of the gospel according to its doctrines; and there were such intercolonial problems as control of runaway servants and prisoners. The government consisted of a board of eight commissioners, two from each member colony. A vote of six was necessary to make action legal; if six could not agree, the business in question was then to be referred to the general courts of the four constituent colonies. The commissioners were to meet annually and oftener if necessary; they had power to make ordinances concerning general matters of a civil nature and to act as arbitrators in the settlement of conflicts between members or with foreign countries or colonies. In case of war, the burden of expense and of soldiers was to be born in proportion to the size of the male population between the ages of sixteen and sixty. It lost influence after Connecticut's absorption of New Haven in 1662, but continued to exist until the annulment of the Massachusetts charter in 1684.

UNITED CONFEDERATE VETERANS (UCV). Organized at New Orleans June 10, 1889, by fifty-two delegates representing nine Confederate veterans' organizations. Its military type of command was elaborated at Chattanooga in 1890, with authority over the Trans-Mississippi and East of Mississippi departments. In 1894 the latter was reorganized as the departments of the Army of Northern Virginia and the Army of Tennessee; the Division of the Northwest was added at a later date. The basic constitution and bylaws were adopted at Houston in 1895. During 1892–99 the UCV waged throughout the South a successful campaign against the use of public school textbooks that appeared deficient in patriotism and historical impartiality. The UCV reached its zenith about 1907, when 12,000 members paraded past 200,000 viewers in Richmond. The last reunion was held at Norfolk, Va., on May 30, 1951.

UNITED DAUGHTERS OF THE CONFEDERACY (UDC). A patriotic and service society organized in Nashville, Tenn., Sept. 10, 1894. Membership in the early 1980's numbered approximately 35,000, with some 1,000 local groups. Eligible for membership are female lineal or collateral descendants of persons who served honorably in the army, navy, or civil service of the Confederate States of America or gave material aid to that cause.

UNITED EMPIRE LOYALISTS. The name applied to those inhabitants of the thirteen colonies who remained loyal to the British crown at the time of the Revolution, and particularly to those who migrated to what is now Canada (*see* Loyalists).

UNITED MINE WORKERS OF AMERICA (UMWA). An industrial union representing workers in the bituminous and anthracite coal fields of the United States and Canada, founded in 1890. It grew rapidly under the leadership of John Mitchell before World War I and had a membership of over 500,000 by 1920, when John L. Lewis became its president. The industry depression and anti-unionism of the 1920's lowered membership by 1930 to less than 100,000. Lewis rebuilt the UMWA into one of the most effective but imperially governed unions in the country. He then took the lead in industry mechanization, which reduced the UMWA's membership by more than two-thirds but improved wages and the competitive position of the industry. The tenure of President W. A. Boyle (1960–72) was less successful. Arnold Miller's presidency (1972–79) was marked by factionalism, wildcat strikes, and instability. Upon his retirement Miller was succeeded by Sam M. Church, who in turn lost in the 1982 elections to Richard L. Trumka. By 1982 the UMWA had 160,000 active members, about 32,000 of them on layoffs.

UNITED NATIONS (UN). The United Nations is an international organization established in 1945. Its mission is to keep peace among nations, and to contribute to the improvement of living conditions in the world as a means of keeping peace. The UN Charter is regarded as a "multilateral" treaty of the United States, binding on American policies and activities. The name "United Nations" began to be used as early as 1942 to designate the countries that were at war against the Axis powers (Germany, Italy, Japan and their associates). The "United Nations Declaration" was issued on January 1, 1942. A conference at Bretton Woods, N.H. in July 1944, dealt with methods of international economic cooperation after the war. Another conference, held at Dumbarton Oaks near Washington, D.C., from August to October 1944, was concerned with the details of the postwar system. To supply immediate aid to the peoples and countries which might be freed from the grip of enemy forces in the last phases of World War II, the "United Nations Relief and Rehabilitation Administration" (UNRRA) was set up. UNRRA worked from 1943 to 1947 distributing millions of dollars worth of food and equipment in countries that had been damaged by Axis invasion during the war. The drafting of a final charter for the United Nations was accomplished at San Francisco, Calif., Apr. 25–June 26, 1945. All the countries at war with the Axis were represented at this Conference.

United Nations Charter. The Charter, agreed to by the delegates of fifty nations, made it clear that the UN was *not* a new sovereign power. Article I of the Charter stated that the organization was based on the equality of the sovereign nations that were its members. The nations did not give up either their independence or their power to direct their own affairs.

The Charter called for a number of organizations within the UN. The chief organs are:

The General Assembly. The General Assembly includes every member nation. Each nation has one vote on any General Assembly question, but there is a provision that requires "important" questions to be decided by a two-thirds vote of the General Assembly, if the Assembly agrees (by a majority vote) that a question is important.

The General Assembly meets once a year, but it may be called into special sessions in case of emergency. Its chief task is to recommend ways for the member nations to preserve peace. It can recommend solutions to international problems, but these are not necessarily binding. It has the power to admit or suspend member nations, and its decisions can overrule those of any other organ of the UN.

The Security Council. The Security Council was originally set up with eleven members, but the number was expanded to fifteen in 1965. There are five permanent members, each with veto power over decisions of the Council: the United States, the Union of Soviet Socialist Republics, the United Kingdom (Great Britain), France, and China. The ten nonpermanent members are elected from among the other nations by the General Assembly for two-year terms, which are set so that five are replaced each year. There is an informal agreement as to how these ten seats are divided: five are held by African or Asian countries; two by Latin American countries; one by an eastern European state; and two by countries in western Europe or elsewhere in the world. The Security Council is in continuous session, with meetings at least every two weeks. Its task is to handle threats to world peace at once as they arise: to investigate disputes between nations, and to take action against aggressors when one country has been identified as the "aggressor" in a dispute. It can call on the armed forces of UN members to stop any aggressive action. It has direct supervision of the International Atomic Energy Agency.

The Economic and Social Council. This is the UN agency through which engineering, agricultural, medical, and many specialized agencies operate—units such as the World Health Organization, the International Labor Organization, the International Bank for Reconstruction and Development, UNESCO (The United Nations Educational, Scientific, and Cultural Organization), and UNICEF. The fifty-four members of the Economic and Social Council are elected by the General Assembly for three-year terms.

The Trusteeship Council. Trusteeship implies that the major country which holds a trusteeship over an undeveloped country has an obligation to bring the subject people up to full independence with speed and with security. The Trusteeship Council has been very active in encouraging the independence of many small nations in the world, which have become self-governing and are now members of the UN itself.

The International Court of Justice. This organization continues the work begun by the World Courts before World War II. It is the "judicial branch" of the United Nations and is in session in The Hague, the Dutch city where the World Court used to sit. All members of the UN are automatically members of the International Court of Justice and may bring cases to it; however, there is no requirement that nations must submit cases or disputes to it. The International Court's charter provides that no nation in the world may supply more than one judge to the fifteen-man bench of the Court.

The Secretariat. The everyday work of the United Nations is done by the Secretariat. The Secretary-General heads the Secretariat, and is the chief executive officer for the United Nations. The Secretariat has always been located in the United States; since 1950, it has been housed on the east side of Manhattan, in the heart of New York City. The ground on which the UN buildings are erected is officially United Nations territory.

United Nations Operations. The UN recognizes five official languages—English, Russian, French, Spanish, and Chinese. All official business must be recorded in all the languages, and it is possible for visitors to listen to simultaneous translations of debates and arguments being conducted in the Security Council or the General Assembly. The UN has been involved in every major international dispute or problem since its formation in 1945. The United States has been a leading member in the United Nations since its founding and has contributed a majority of the funds used by its various agencies. By 1981 UN membership had grown to 154 countries.

UNITED NATIONS CONFERENCE (San Francisco, Apr. 25–June 26, 1945). Attended by fifty countries, forty-six of them signatories of the United Nations Declaration, in order to put into final form the proposals for an international peace organization that were drafted at the Dumbarton Oaks Conference in 1944. The rift between East and West, indications of which had already appeared, made itself felt during the conference. Three main points of contention developed, with respect to each of which the United States and the Soviet Union took opposing stands: the disposition of dependent peoples; regional collective security arrangements; and the use of the veto in the Security Council. After some acrimony these controversies were resolved, and the United Nations Charter was unanimously approved on June 26, 1945.

UNITED NATIONS DECLARATION (Jan. 1, 1942). Soon after Japan's attack on Pearl Harbor (Dec. 7, 1941), Prime Minister Winston Churchill hastened to Washington, D.C., and with President Franklin D. Roosevelt announced a "Declaration by United Nations," open to all nations, to constitute a military alliance against "Hitlerism." The declaration was initially signed by the United States, the United Kingdom, the Soviet Union, China, Australia, Belgium, Canada, Costa Rica, Cuba, Czechoslovakia, the Dominican Republic, El Salvador, Greece, Guatemala, Haiti, Honduras, India, Luxembourg, the Netherlands, New Zealand, Nicaragua, Norway, Panama, Poland, South Africa, and Yugoslavia. Later signers were Brazil, Chile, Colombia, Ecuador, Egypt, Ethiopia, France, Iceland, Iran, Iraq, Liberia, Mexico, Paraguay, Peru, the Philippines, Saudi Arabia, Turkey, Uruguay, and Venezuela. The declaration reads, in part:

The Governments signatory hereto,

Having subscribed to . . . the Atlantic Charter . . . *Declare:*

(1) Each government pledges itself to employ its full resources, military or economic, against those members of the Tripartite Pact and its adherents with which such government is at war.

(2) Each Government pledges itself to co-operate with the Governments signatory hereto and not to make a separate armistice or peace with the enemies.

The foregoing declaration may be adhered to by other nations as which are, or which may be, rendering material assistance and contributions in the struggle for victory over Hitlerism.

UNITED NATIVE AMERICANS. A Pan-Indian organization started in the San Francisco Bay area in 1968 under the leadership of Lehman Brightman, a Sioux. Activist in nature, it condemns the whole structure of Indian affairs. Membership in 1980 was 12,000.

UNITED PRESS INTERNATIONAL (UPI). A worldwide news gathering and distributing agency, formed May 16, 1958, by the merger of the United Press Associations (1907) of Edward Wyllis Scripps and the International News Service (1909) of William Randolph Hearst. (The United Press, a news organization of the early 1880's set up in opposition to the Associated Press [AP], had no connection with the United Press Associations.) During the 1970's, UPI had approximately 1,200 newspaper clients in the United States and a like number abroad for a total of about 2,400 in the world. Its radio and television subscribers in the United States were about 3,600, and elsewhere in the world some 600. The subscribers also included magazines, periodicals, and specialized publications.

UNITED SERVICE ORGANIZATION (USO). Organized in 1940 to provide entertainment and other services to military personnel in the United States. USO centers and canteens were set up near major military and naval bases. The organization did valuable work during World War II and has continued its activities at home and abroad to the present time.

***UNITED STATES*.** A 44-gun frigate designed by Joshua Humphreys of Philadelphia and launched on May 10, 1797, the first vessel of the U.S. Navy. During the Quasi-War with France (1798–1800) it took seven prizes; in 1800 it carried the peace commissioners to Europe. In the War of 1812, under Capt. Stephen Decatur, Jr., it captured the British 38-gun *Macedonian.* During 1815–18 under various commanders, the *United States* aided in keeping the Barbary powers subdued and thereafter saw service on many foreign stations. On Apr. 21, 1861, it was burned at the Norfolk Navy Yard to prevent its falling into the hands of the Confederate troops.

UNITED STATES, BANK OF THE. *See* **Bank of the United States.**

UNITED STATES CODE*.** *See* ***Code, United States.

UNITED STATES OF AMERICA. First used officially as a name for the thirteen colonies in the Declaration of Independence.

Among the forms used in 1775 were "all the English colonies on this continent" (the fast-day proclamation of June 12) and "associated colonies" (committee report, June 19). In official documents thereafter, the name was usually the "United Colonies of America," or "of North America" (more often the latter), and frequently with "twelve" or "thirteen," as the case might be, prefixed, sometimes also preceded by the word "English." As the idea of independence grew, writers more and more employed the term "states." The term was accordingly used in the Virginia Resolutions of May 15, 1776. From the Declaration of Independence the name "United States of America" was taken over into the Articles of Confederation (1777) and then into the Constitution (1787).

For a brief period the name the "United States of North America" was used. In the treaty with France (Feb. 6, 1778) the name is set down as "the thirteen United States of North America." On May 19, 1778, Congress adopted "the Stile of the Treaties of Paris," but on July 11 that action was rescinded and the word "North" dropped.

UNITED STATES STEEL CORPORATION. Formed in 1901 by combining ten corporations active in iron and steel making, land ownership with mineral rights, and railroading. The largest owners of the prior companies included Andrew Carnegie, Henry Clay Frick, and Elbert Gary. J. Pierpont Morgan was the banker who financed the merger. The corporation is one of the largest factors in the world's steel production.

***UNITED STATES* V. *BUTLER*.** *See* **Hoosac Mills Case.**

***UNITED STATES* V. *CLARK*,** 31 Federal Reporter 710 (1887). A federal circuit court in Michigan asserted that by enlistment a soldier surrenders his liberty, waives some civil rights, and subjects himself to the Uniform Code of Military Justice. The Supreme Court (*In Re Grimley,* 137 U.S. 147) in 1890 adopted this view, holding that "enlistment changes the status."

***UNITED STATES* V. *CRUIKSHANK*,** 92 U.S. 542 (1876). In considering the 1870 Ku Klux Klan Act provision forbidding interference with constitutional rights, the Supreme Court held that the Constitution does not grant the rights of assembling peaceably and bearing arms; it merely forbids Congress to infringe upon them. The Fourteenth Amendment's due process and equal protection clauses guarantee the citizen against encroachment by the states, but not against encroachment by another citizen.

***UNITED STATES* V. *E. C. KNIGHT COMPANY*,** 156 U.S. 1 (1895). The first Supreme Court case involving the Sherman Antitrust Act (1890), which forbade combinations restraining interstate commerce. The American Sugar Refining Company purchased four independent concerns, giving it control of 98 percent of the country's output. The Court held that the acquisition of refineries and the business of sugar manufacturing within a state bore no direct relation to interstate commerce, and hence were not in violation of the act. The decision stimulated the formation of trusts.

***UNITED STATES* V. *HARRIS*,** 106 U.S. 629 (1883). The Supreme Court held unconstitutional the 1871 Ku Klux Klan Act provision that penalized conspiracy to deprive any person of equal protection of the laws. It was broader than the Thirteenth Amendment warranted, and neither the Fourteenth Amendment nor Fifteenth Amendment authorized Congress to legislate directly upon the acts of private persons.

***UNITED STATES* V. *LANZA*,** 260 U.S. 377 (1922). Decisions in Ohio (1847, 1850) and Illinois (1852) had indicated that concurrent jurisdiction by federal and state systems over counterfeiting and fugitive slave offenses might be enforced by either without violating the Fifth Amendment's double jeopardy clause. The Eighteenth Amendment in 1919 gave Congress concurrent powers with the states over enforcing Prohibition. Federal courts in Alabama, Connecticut, New Hampshire, North Dakota, Ohio, and New York had upheld the right of federal agents to try offenders already tried in state courts. In the Lanza case, tried in the state of Washington, that right was denied. On appeal to the Supreme Court, Chief Justice William Howard Taft held that a second trial might be had, saying: "The defendants committed two different offenses by the same act, the offense against the State and a different offense against the United States," and denied the double jeopardy plea.

***UNITED STATES* V. *LEE*,** 106 U.S. 196 (1882). In 1857, upon the death of George Washington Parke Custis, his Arlington estate passed to his daughter, Mary Lee, wife of Robert E. Lee. During the Civil War the estate was seized by the United States for delinquent taxes, offered for sale, and bid on by an army officer, who wished to turn it into a national cemetery and military post. After the death of Mrs. Lee, her son Custis brought an action to eject the superintendent of Arlington Cemetery on the grounds of trespass. The Supreme Court held that the United States was not in lawful possession of the estate. The matter was settled by the government's paying for possession.

***UNITED STATES* V. *REESE*,** 92 U.S. 214 (1876). A case in which the Supreme Court declared that the Fifteenth Amendment authorized Congress to prevent denial of the franchise only because of race, color, or previous condition of servitude. Therefore parts of the 1870 Ku Klux Klan Act, which provided punishment for obstructing citizens from voting, were unconstitutional because they were not limited to this type of discrimination.

***UNITED STATES* V. *TEXAS*,** 143 U.S. 621 (1892). By act of Congress, May 2, 1890, the attorney general was instructed to enter suit in the Supreme Court to decide the true boundary between United States territory and Texas. Texas demurred on the grounds of no jurisdiction because of the particular wording of the act authorizing the suit. The demurrer was overruled and the Court assumed jurisdiction.

***UNITED STATES* V. *TRANS-MISSOURI FREIGHT ASSOCIATION*,** 166 U.S. 290 (1897). Eighteen western railroads attempted to fix freight rates by mutual agreement. The government brought suit to dissolve the association on the grounds that it violated the Sherman Antitrust Act. The Supreme Court held that the Sherman Act did apply to railroads and that it prohibited all contracts in restraint of interstate or foreign commerce, not merely those in which the restraint was unreasonable.

***UNITED STATES* V. *WONG KIM ARK*,** 169 U.S. 649 (1898). An important interpretation of the clause in the Fourteenth Amendment declaring that "all persons born or naturalized in the United States and subject to the jurisdiction thereof, are citizens of the United States and of the State wherein they reside." Wong Kim Ark was an American-born Chinese laborer, whose parents were ineligible for citizenship under the naturalization laws. On his return to this country from a visit to China an attempt was made to debar him from entry under the Chinese Exclusion Acts. Claiming that his birth in San Francisco conferred citizenship, Wong Kim Ark secured a writ of habeas corpus, and the Supreme Court upheld his contention. The principle laid down in this decision also served to protect Orientals born in this country against discriminatory state legislation.

"UNITED WE STAND, DIVIDED WE FALL." A favorite toast, in varying forms, of political orators from Benjamin Franklin to Abraham Lincoln, and the motto of Kentucky (1792). It gained currency after John Dickinson's "Liberty Song" was published (July 18, 1768) in the *Boston Gazette.*

UNIT RULE. A practice formerly observed by the Democratic party at its national conventions, in which the entire vote of a state delegation must be cast as a unit for the candidate preferred by a majority of that delegation. It enjoyed official sanction, but convention rules did not mandate its use. The 1968 Democratic convention voted to release all delegates from the unit rule constraint. The Republican party has never given official status to the unit rule, and its use at Republican conventions has been infrequent.

UNIVERSITIES, STATE. The revolutionary constitutions of Pennsylvania and North Carolina (1776) provided for "one or more universities." Georgia chartered the first state university in 1785, but instruction in its original Franklin College only dated from 1801, and the first degrees were granted in 1804. The University of North Carolina, chartered in 1789, began instruction in 1795. The principle of the Northwest Ordinance of 1787 that "schools and the means of education shall forever be encouraged" and the consequent allotment of land for educational purposes, underlay the founding of state universities north of the Ohio River and west of the Mississippi River: Ohio University (1804), at Athens, and Miami University (1809), at Oxford, Ohio, were the first chartered state institutions in the Northwest area. By 1861 there were twenty-one state universities. The Morrill Act (1862) provided land grants to the states for the establishment of colleges; the second Morrill Act (1890) furnished funds to the land-grant institutions; and the Hatch Experiment Station Act (1887) provided money for agricultural and scientific research.

After 1945 many states—California and New York for example—expanded and unified the control of their institutions of higher education. State universities have played a significant role in teacher preparation, other professional education, scientific and technological research, scholarly publication, and the expansion and equalization of educational opportunity. Some, like Michigan State University, have been active in aiding (chiefly through government contracts) higher education in developing countries.

UNKNOWN SOLDIER, TOMB OF THE. In Arlington National Cemetery, near Washington, D.C.; dedicated in 1921 as a memorial to all American soldiers and sailors who lost their lives in World War I. In 1958 two other nameless soldiers, one to represent members of the armed forces lost in World War II and one to represent those who died in the Korean War, were also buried in the tomb, which was renamed the Tomb of the Unknowns. In 1973 Congress authorized plans to add a burial place for an unidentified casualty of the Vietnam War.

UNREASONABLE SEARCH AND SEIZURE. *See* **Search and Seizure, Unreasonable.**

UNWRITTEN CONSTITUTION. Tradition and customs related to the U.S. Constitution are often referred to as the "unwritten Constitution." For example, it is traditional for the President to arrange for Senators of his party to approve people whom he appoints to major government positions. This "Senatorial courtesy" is part of the unwritten Constitution; it has no specific legal or constitutional authority.

UPPER AND LOWER LAKES. The French, who first explored the Great Lakes, reached them via the St. Lawrence River, Ottawa River, and Lake Nipissing route to Georgian

Bay (Samuel de Champlain, 1615). From there they extended their explorations to lakes Huron, Michigan, and Superior; the adjoining country was known as the Upper Country, and the three lakes as the Upper Lakes. Direct access from Lower Canada, via the Upper St. Lawrence River to Lake Ontario and Lake Erie, was gained only in the 18th century; the name Lower Lakes came to be employed to distinguish lakes Erie and Ontario from the remaining, or Upper, Great Lakes. The terms have been loosely used at different times; thus, in negotiating the Rush-Bagot Agreement (*see* Great Lakes Disarmament Agreement), Lake Erie was included among the Upper Lakes.

UPPER PENINSULA OF MICHIGAN. A geographically distinct region added to Michigan (1837) as compensation for the so-called Toledo Strip ceded by Michigan to Ohio as part of the settlement of their long-standing boundary dispute. (*See* Ohio-Michigan Boundary Dispute.)

UPPER SANDUSKY (Ohio). A village on the Sandusky River and the seat of Wyandot County; referred to as Sandusky until the mid-19th century. It became a headquarters of the Wyandot during the American Revolution. The Wyandot villages, located in the "Sandusky Plains," a nearly treeless prairie, served as a base of operations for British-Indian forays and a center to which captives and plunder were brought; the Wyandot remained under British influence until Gen. Anthony Wayne's victory at the Battle of Fallen Timbers (1794). Gen. William Henry Harrison erected Fort Ferree at Sandusky during the War of 1812. Indian treaties in 1817–18 reserved a considerable part of present-day Wyandot County and a portion of Crawford County for the Wyandot and Delaware; in 1842 the last reservation was ceded to the United States and opened for white settlement. In 1843 the federal government laid out the present town, calling it Upper Sandusky, on a tract of 619.47 acres; it includes the site of the last Wyandot village. In 1980 the population was 5,967.

URBAN RENEWAL. The sum of the processes of building, clearing, rebuilding, modernizing, and renovating, by which cities are rebuilt. The term first came into general use in the 1950's, succeeding "urban redevelopment."

During the 1930's the federal government sponsored public housing projects to clear slums and replace them with housing for low-income families. Other federal agencies holding foreclosed mortgages experimented with programs of neighborhood rehabilitation to improve the value of deteriorating properties. During the years 1940–45 these experiments were reviewed and reformulated and were expressed in the urban redevelopment title of the Wagner-Ellender-Taft bill, the first comprehensive piece of national housing legislation, finally enacted as the Housing Act of 1949. Under that legislation the federal government offered loans to local governments to enable them to plan for, acquire, and clear slum areas for urban redevelopment; install needed public improvements; and sell the resulting sites to private or public agencies for the ultimate planned reconstruction. Under amendments enacted in 1954 greater emphasis was given to renovation and rehabilitation of areas as opposed to clearance and reconstruction, and the term "urban renewal" was substituted for "urban redevelopment."

With the assistance provided by the Housing Act, 1,100 municipalities in the United States had undertaken 2,800 urban renewal projects involving federal-grant contracts of $10 billion by the early 1970's. Involving residential, commercial, civic, and industrial land uses, the projects included 200,000 acres of urban land, 80,000 of which were marked for clearance. Overall, the projects completed and committed by 1972 involved the relocation of 530,000 people, the provision of new homes for 630,000, and the rehabilitation of 149,000 structures containing 300,000 dwelling units. Under the Housing Act of 1975 all federal aids for community development were lumped into a block grant composition in which every city shares. Despite the large number of publicly sponsored projects, private renewal is considerably greater in volume and area, although no systematic records are available to compare its relative impact.

URSULINE CONVENT BURNED (Aug. 11, 1834). The Ursuline convent school established in Charlestown, Mass. (near Boston), in 1820 attracted little attention until the early 1830's when members of the Protestant clergy, the Boston press, and a self-proclaimed "escaped nun," Rebecca Theresa Reed, began spreading tales of its immorality and proselytizing efforts. In 1834 a member of the order, Elizabeth Harrison, temporarily deranged, fled to the home of her brother. She later returned voluntarily but rumors that she was being forcibly detained brought a mob together; the sisters and pupils were driven out, and the convent burned.

URSULINES. The first Roman Catholic teaching order for women, founded in Italy in 1535. On Sept. 13, 1726, the French order of Ursulines (established in 1612) signed a contract with the Company of the Indies to send a group to New Orleans to take charge of the hospital there and to establish a school for girls. With Marie Tranchepain de St. Augustin as mother superior, the group arrived in 1727. In 1770 they were relieved of their duties in connection with the hospital, but their convent and school for girls is still in existence. In the 1970's there were about 1,500 Ursulines in the United States.

USEFUL MANUFACTURES, SOCIETY FOR ESTABLISHING. Founded in 1791 by Alexander Hamilton to show America the way to independence of European manufactures by establishing a center of great factories. A perpetual charter granted by the New Jersey legislature exempted the society from county and township taxes and authorized it to engage freely in manufacturing and selling, acquire real estate, improve rivers, dig canals, collect tolls on improvements, and incorporate a municipality to be called Paterson. Seven hundred acres were purchased (May 1792) from Dutch farmers for $8,320 at the Great Falls of the Passaic River, where a small cotton factory was built. In 1794 dissatisfaction among the workers led to the closing of the mill, the first lockout in American history. After 1796, when manufacturing was abandoned because of financial reverses, the society's chief business was leasing sites and furnishing water and electric power and capital to other manufacturing enterprises. The city of Paterson tried for more than a century to break the society's charter and to terminate its tax immunity; in 1945 the city acquired the society's properties for $450,000 and the society was dissolved by its board of governors.

UTAH. The first Europeans arrived in what is now Utah (named for the Ute Indians) from Santa Fe, most likely in the 17th century. The expedition of Francisco Atanasio Domínguez and Silvestre Velez de Escalante in 1776 was the first fully recorded trip. Between 1811 and 1840 mountain men hunted in Utah, from the north (Astorians and British of the Hudson's Bay Company), from the east (Americans in the employ of William H. Ashley and Andrew Henry), and from the southeast out of Taos and Santa Fe. Between 1841 and 1846 government explorers and emigrants crossed Utah. Although some mountain men had built forts as supply stations and rendezvous points for trappers in the region (Fort Uintah, 1837; Fort Davy Crockett, 1837; Fort Bridger, 1843; Fort Buenaventura, 1846), permanent settlement was begun by the Mormons. Expelled from their homes in Nauvoo, Ill., in 1846, the Mormons fled west; the vanguard, led by Brigham Young, entered Salt Lake Valley July 24, 1847. From 1847 to 1868 about 68,000 immigrants from the United States, Great Britain, and northern Europe followed the Mormon Trail into Utah. With Salt Lake Valley as a center, settlements were established in other major valleys. Little difficulty arose between Indians and new settlers, partly because of a Mormon policy of benevolence and peaceful coexistence. In time the expansion of the white settlement and federal removal of the Indians to reservations in the 1860's resulted in the Black Hawk War, 1865–68. In March 1849 the Mormons set up the provisional state of Deseret and petitioned Congress to accept that government, but the petition was denied and the territory of Utah was created by an act of Sept. 9, 1850. Brigham Young was appointed the first governor.

A few non-Mormons came to Utah in the 1850's and 1860's. Upon completion of the first transcontinental railroad at Promontory Summit in northwestern Utah (May 10, 1869) the non-Mormon influence increased rapidly in railroading, mining, business, and politics. Conflicts between Mormons and non-Mormons, led by federal territorial appointees, were waged over Mormon policies with regard to Indian relations, economics, political parties, the courts, militia, education, immigration, and polygamy. Utah was occupied by federal troops in 1857–61 by the Utah expedition under Albert Sidney Johnston, sent to suppress an alleged rebellion, and in 1863 by California volunteers under Patrick E. Connor, sent to guard overland routes and communications. The federal crusade against the Mormons took the form of judicial actions against Mormon polygamists found in violation of federal legislation enacted to meet the Mormon "problem"; test cases taken to the U.S. Supreme Court proved fruitless for the Mormons, and Utah was admitted into the Union, Jan. 4, 1896.

Utah's pioneer character persisted into the 1930's, modified by the gradual coming of electricity and the automobile. Economic development was stimulated by World War I, but agriculture and mining declined, beginning in the early 1920's. Major changes during and after World War II included rapid increases in population and expansion in business, industry, and education, with a heavy reliance on federal spending and defense industries. Utah's 1980 population was 1,461,037, about 68.5 percent of which was Mormon.

UTE. Some 4,500 Ute Indians occupied central and western Colorado and all of what is now eastern Utah in 1845. The Ute were bound together by commonality of language, culture, and ecological adaptation. Theirs was a traditional Basin-type gathering culture until at least the late 18th century, when they began to obtain horses, adopted the tipi and a modification of the Sun Dance, and generally began to conform to the culture of the Plains. A chief named Taiwi was successful in effecting a Ute federation, but by 1849 the Ute bands began to sign treaties with the United States.

UTOPIAS AND UTOPIANISM. In 1516 Sir Thomas More, English scholar, lawyer and saint, published a story in Latin commonly known by a short form of the original title —*Utopia.* (He invented this word by combining two Greek words which mean "nowhere.") Utopia was supposed to be an ideal country where the people lived under perfect conditions; in describing it, More was able to criticize many aspects of life in England at that time and suggest reforms. Ever since, "Utopia" and "Utopian" have been used to describe any ideal attempt to reform society which does not take human defects and failings into account. Attempts to establish Utopian communities have met with little success.

UTRECHT, TREATY OF (Apr. 11, 1713). Concluded Queen Anne's War. France restored to Great Britain the Hudson Strait and Bay within boundaries to be defined by commissioners, and the English Hudson's Bay Company was to be indemnified for losses incurred through French action in times of peace. France also conceded to Great Britain the island of Saint Christopher, Acadia, and Newfoundland and its adjacent islands, but retained Cape Breton Island and the islands of the Saint Lawrence River. French fishermen retained the right of drying fish, caught off Newfoundland, on shores between Cape Bonavista and Point Riche. Frenchmen in newly acquired British territory might exercise the Roman Catholic religion so far as British laws allowed. France acknowledged British sovereignty over the Five Nations of Iroquois, and each party agreed not to interfere with Indians under the other's influence. For its part Spain pledged (July 13, 1713) that no portion of Spanish America would ever be transferred to any foreign power.

VALCOUR ISLAND, BATTLE OF (Oct. 11, 1776). Benedict Arnold with fifteen hastily constructed vessels, mounting about eighty guns and manned by 700 inexperienced men, mostly soldiers, disputed control of Lake Champlain with Sir Guy Carleton, who commanded twenty-five vessels, about ninety guns, and 700 experienced sailors. Defeated in a seven-hour battle at Valcour Island, N.Y., Arnold slipped past the

British at night and for two days kept up a running fight. He lost ten ships and nine-tenths of his men, but his resistance had delayed British invasion for another year. Carleton withdrew and dispersed his forces into winter quarters in Canada.

VALLANDIGHAM INCIDENT. Clement L. Vallandigham of Dayton, Ohio, a Copperhead leader and former congressman, was arrested on charges of treason on May 5, 1863. Vallandigham had denounced the war, violating Gen. Burnside's order which prohibited expressions of sympathy for the enemy. A court-martial found him guilty of attempting to undermine the government and sentenced him to imprisonment for the duration of the war. President Lincoln commuted the sentence to banishment to the Confederacy. Vallandigham left the South for Canada. In February 1864 Vallandigham appealed to the U.S. Supreme Court for revision of the sentence. The Court declared its authority did not extend to a military commission. Vallandigham returned to the United States in June and took part in a political campaign for governor of Ohio. To avoid a backlash from his supporters, he was not reimprisoned, even though his banishment required his detention in case of return.

VALLEY CAMPAIGN, JACKSON'S. *See* **Jackson's Valley Campaign.**

VALLEY FORGE. Encampment ground for the Continental army from Dec. 19, 1777, until June 19, 1778; situated on the west bank of the Schuylkill River, in Chester County, Pa., about twenty-five miles northwest of Philadelphia.

After the Americans had been defeated at Brandywine, Paoli, and Germantown and after the British had occupied Philadelphia (then the national capital), Gen. George Washington led 11,000 regular troops to Valley Forge from Whitemarsh to take up winter quarters. Washington's plans were well drawn and his staff efficient, but negligence and mismanagement on the part of others, particularly the commissary department and the transport service, almost destroyed the Continental army during the encampment. An early winter, with heavy snows and abnormally freezing weather, prevented the delivery of regular supplies. A January thaw brought mud so deep that hundreds of army wagons had to be abandoned. The neglect of the army by the Continental Congress and the failure of the commissary officers to forward food, clothing, and supplies by the most available routes increased the sufferings of the men. Many soldiers deserted. Camp fever—probably typhus—and smallpox were epidemic, and medical supplies were lacking. About 2,500 men died.

VALVERDE, BATTLE OF (Feb. 21, 1862). Confederate troops invaded New Mexico, and in February 1862 Brig. Gen. Henry H. Sibley, with about 2,500 men, attacked Fort Craig, where most of the army of the territory was assembled under Col. E. R. S. Canby, joined by New Mexico volunteers and a company from Colorado Territory, total troops numbering 3,810. Sibley attempted to cross the Rio Grande at Valverde but was opposed. Canby then withdrew to the fort, but declined to surrender. Sibley advanced to Albuquerque and Santa Fe. Subsequent fighting at Apache Canyon and Glorieta resulted in the defeat of Sibley and his retreat.

VANCOUVER, FORT. Located on the north bank of the Columbia River, about 100 miles from its mouth (site of present-day Vancouver, Wash.); the western headquarters of the Hudson's Bay Company from 1825 to 1845. The fort replaced Fort George as chief western post of the company.

Fort Vancouver's first location was almost a mile from the river; but in 1829 the fort was rebuilt on the banks. The declining importance of fur trading in the region, combined with fear of unfriendly relations with incoming American settlers, led the company to transfer its principal western post to Victoria on Vancouver Island in 1845. Old Fort Vancouver and its lands were purchased by the U.S. government in 1848.

VANCOUVER'S EXPLORATION. To carry out the terms of the Nootka Sound Convention of 1790, settling a Spanish-British dispute over fur trading on the island now named Vancouver, Capt. George Vancouver was sent by Great Britain to meet the Spanish commissioner at the island. He sailed from England in January 1791, with instructions to survey the American Pacific shoreline from 30° to 60° north latitude, especially to see whether there were interlocking river systems for communication into the interior.

Vancouver reached the coast off California on Apr. 17, 1792. He skirted the northern California and southern Oregon coast rather far out. He observed the mouth of the Columbia River but mistook its true nature. Farther north he explored Juan de Fuca Strait and Puget Sound. Vancouver made fairly accurate charts of the coast from California, including the lower hundred miles of the Columbia River, recently discovered by the British explorer Capt. Robert Gray.

VANDALIA COLONY. A project for a settlement on the Ohio River, sponsored in the early 1770's by the Grand Ohio Company (Walpole Company). Although the colony never materialized, the movement typified many land speculation schemes in England and America in the 18th century.

The plan had its origin in a grant of land known as "Indiana," part of the Treaty of Fort Stanwix, Nov. 3, 1768, made by the Six Nations to a group of Pennsylvania traders to reimburse them for losses sustained in Pontiac's War. Samuel Wharton and William Trent, agents of the Indiana Company, proceeded to England in 1769 to seek royal confirmation. When it was not immediately forthcoming, a company in London petitioned the crown for a considerably larger grant of 2,400,000 acres. This group was reorganized on Dec. 27, 1769, as the Grand Ohio Company. It then petitioned to purchase a vast tract of some 20 million acres bounded on the northwest by the Ohio River.

The plan contemplated establishment of a new colony, Vandalia, with a separate royal government and with ownership vested in the proprietors of the Grand Ohio Company. The project encountered strong opposition from influential British quarters and from rival speculative interests in Virginia that claimed almost the same territory. The outbreak of hostilities in America in 1775 ended all hope of success.

VANDERBILT CUP RACE. *See* **Yacht Racing.**

***VANHORNE'S LESSEE* V. *DORRANCE*,** 2 Dallas 303 (1795). One of the earliest cases in which a federal court asserted the right to disregard a state law held to be in conflict with the state constitution. Justice William Paterson instructed a federal circuit court jury to consider a Pennsylvania law divesting one person of property and vesting it in another as unconstitutional and void.

VAN NESS CONVENTION (Feb. 17, 1834). Negotiated at Madrid, by Cornelius P. Van Ness and José de Heredia; settled American claims against Spain subsequent to 1819, arising principally from irregular seizures of American property in Spanish operations against its rebellious colonies. After unsuccessfully pressing claims for $2.5 million for a decade, the United States accepted $600,000 in 5 percent perpetual Spanish bonds, with mutual cancellation of claims. The bonds were finally redeemed in cash by Spain in 1907.

VAN ZANDT, FREE STATE OF. A northeastern Texas county created from Henderson County on Mar. 20, 1848, named for Isaac Van Zandt, a prominent diplomat of the Republic of Texas. The origin of the term "Free State" is uncertain and has become a part of folklore.

VARE CASE. In 1926 William S. Vare, leader of the Philadelphia Republican organization, won the Pennsylvania primaries for the U.S. Senate nomination. A Senate investigation of campaign expenditures resulted in refusal to accept Vare's election after he had defeated the Democratic nominee in the general election. The verdict was reached on the grounds that corrupt practices and exorbitant expenditures had been employed in obtaining the nomination, despite the fact that Vare's major competitor had spent at least twice as much.

VAUDEVILLE. Live variety shows, extremely popular in the United States in the second half of the 19th and early 20th century. Singing, dancing, and acrobatic acts were seen in small concert halls in the early 19th century. They became known as "variety," and by 1860 there were theaters in all the larger cities. Many noted legitimate actors first appeared in variety. Late in the 19th century the French word *vaudeville* came into use. B. F. Keith, F. F. Proctor, Marcus Loew, Alexander Pantages, and the firm Sullivan and Considine and Orpheum operated large vaudeville circuits. But between 1910 and 1930 motion pictures supplanted stage shows, and after 1930 vaudeville acts were rarely seen.

***VEAZIE BANK* V. *FENNO*,** 8 Wallace 533 (1869). In 1866 Congress imposed a 10 percent tax on notes issued by state banks to drive them out of circulation. In 1869 the Supreme Court upheld the constitutionality of the enactment on the ground that this destructive use of the taxing power was for an object clearly within the constitutional powers of Congress —to regulate the currency of the nation.

VENANGO. Site at the junction of French Creek and the Allegheny River in northwestern Pennsylvania. Long inhabited by Indians, the site first appears in records in connection with the establishment of a fur-trading post by John Frazer. In the struggle between the French and English, Venango became important. A French expedition drove out Frazer in 1753. Fort Machault was erected on the site in 1754. Much enlarged in 1758, it was abandoned and burned by the French at the time of the British attack on Niagara (July 1759). Fort Venango, built by the British in 1760, was destroyed by the Indians in 1763. After the revolutionary war, Fort Venango was replaced by Fort Franklin, which for a decade remained a haven for frontier settlers threatened by Indians.

VENEZUELA, BLOCKADE OF. In 1902 the German, British, and Italian governments decided to compel Venezuelan President Cipriano Castro to settle claims for defaulted debts and for injuries suffered by their nationals during years of internal disorder in Venezuela. A formal blockade of Venezuela was established by the three powers in December 1902; several Venezuelan gunboats were seized; and fortifications were bombarded. Within a few days Venezuela made a proposal for arbitration, supported by the United States. The claims involved were settled either by direct bilateral agreements or by the decisions of mixed commissions.

VENEZUELA, PERRY'S MISSION TO (1819). During the Spanish-American revolution, Secretary of State John Quincy Adams ordered Capt. Oliver Hazard Perry to Venezuela and Argentina to explain to rebel leaders the U.S. policy of neutrality in the revolution and to protest hostile acts by rebel agents and privateers. Perry interviewed revolutionary leader Simón Bolívar but died before completing his mission.

VENEZUELA BOUNDARY CONTROVERSY. When Great Britain annexed the territory of British Guiana in 1814, there was no definite western boundary. In 1840 a British agent, Robert Schomburgk, surveyed a line west of the British settlements, which the British government adopted. Venezuela made a counterclaim covering two-thirds of the British colony. In 1876 the United States began to urge a settlement by arbitration. The British refused any plan that did not guarantee the continuance under their flag of all British settlements. In 1885–86 the British authorities suddenly extended their claims to include some 30,000 square miles to the west of the Schomburgk line, a region where gold was reported. The Venezuelan government protested and broke off diplomatic relations. The United States then began to exert increasing pressure for a settlement by arbitration. Finally, in July 1895, Secretary of State Richard Olney demanded a settlement, under the authority conferred upon the United States by the Monroe Doctrine. Lord Salisbury, the British prime minister and foreign secretary, disputed this interpretation of the doctrine and reiterated the British refusal to accept unrestricted arbitration. President Grover Cleveland then asked Congress for authority to appoint a commission to determine and maintain the legal boundary. Salisbury offered to discuss the boundary problem with Olney, the latter acting as the representative of Venezuela. No progress was made until Olney suggested that settlements in existence for sixty years be guaranteed. After reducing sixty years to fifty, Salisbury accepted this solution, and a treaty was signed in 1897. Olney's provision enabled the arbitrators, in 1899, to award to Venezuela the land "grabbed" in 1885–86, the rest of the boundary following approximately the Schomburgk line.

VENGEANCE-CONSTELLATION* FIGHT.** *See* ***Constellation-Vengeance **Encounter.**

VERACRUZ, SIEGE AND CAPTURE OF. *See* **Mexican War.**

VERACRUZ INCIDENT. When Victoriano Huerta seized the Mexican presidency in 1913, the United States refused to recognize him. Early in 1914, when Tampico was under martial law, some U.S. marines were arrested but were quickly released and apologies made. Adm. Henry T. Mayo insisted that a twenty-one gun salute to the American flag be fired. When the salute was not forthcoming, Pres. Woodrow Wilson ordered a fleet to Veracruz. Troops were landed on Apr. 21 and, aided by bombardment, they took the city. Continued American political pressure forced Huerta out in July.

VERMONT. Became an independent republic in 1777 as a result of its position on the frontier of New England and New York, and on the Canadian border. The first state to be admitted to the Union after the original thirteen (1791), it exemplified the emerging American colonial policy of bringing new territory into organic unity with existing states on an equal basis.

At the outbreak of the Revolution there were perhaps 10,000 inhabitants of the woods between the Connecticut River and the Hudson-Champlain waterway, an area that legally belonged to New York by a royal grant of 1664, confirmed in 1764. The British instructed New York, however, to confirm grants from New Hampshire Gov. Benning Wentworth to bona fide settlers. All semblance of local New York government in the Connecticut Valley collapsed after its court was closed at Westminster in March 1774. The revolutionary war ended New York's chances to reclaim Vermont.

But the Republic of Vermont (1777) was pro tem, as most inhabitants wanted statehood within the Union and Champlain Valley interests sought free trade via the Saint Lawrence River. Congress would not consider Vermont demands until the larger questions of money, debts, trade, and western lands were settled. Lt. Gov. Frederick Haldimand offered self-government within the empire and discontinued the 1778–80 raids up the Otter Valley and across the mountains. The peace treaty of 1783, by confirming the 1763 Canadian boundary at 45° north latitude, established Vermont as American.

Vermont met its expenses by selling confiscated Tory lands. Expansion by admitting New Hampshire and New York towns to the republic failed. Compromise finally ended the land controversy; Vermont paid $30,000 to satisfy New York claims and was admitted to the Union on Mar. 4, 1791. Heavy migration from southern New England (1781–1810) and a high birthrate added nearly 200,000 people to the population between the Revolution and the War of 1812.

The small state needed a large United States to give its citizens opportunity in the railroad age. Its economy for over a century depended on versatility, ingenuity, patent monopolies, cheap labor, and nearness to seaboard cities. From its farms came wool, then butter and cheese, and later milk; from its quarries, marble, granite, and slate; from its forests, timber, pulp, and processed hardwoods; and from its shops, tools, machines, scales, organs, and textiles. Its rail connections provided an alternate bridge via Montreal in the competing transcontinental systems.

Nostalgia for rural America led vacationers to the state's accessible hills and lakes. Tourist consciousness and institutional camps date from the 1890's; the good-roads movement lagged until the 1927 flood required reconstruction of the highway system. After World War II millions of dollars were invested in ski resorts and after 1958 in interstate highways.

VERRAZZANO-NARROWS BRIDGE. This bridge across the Narrows of New York harbor was opened to traffic in November 1964. It had to be high enough to clear the tallest ships likely to enter the harbor, so it was constructed from high ground on the Brooklyn and Staten Island sides of the Narrows. It reaches a height of 228 feet, and its length, 4,260 feet, makes it the longest suspension bridge in the world. It was named in honor of Giovanni da Verrazzano, the Italian sea captain who explored the coastal area of present New York for the King of France in 1524.

VERSAILLES, TREATY OF. The peace treaty between the Allies and Germany at the end of World War I, signed on June 28, 1919, by the United States, Great Britain, France, Italy, Japan, and twenty-three other Allied and Associated Powers, and Germany. It had fifteen parts comprising 440 articles. Part I was the convenant of the League of Nations. Part II defined the boundaries of Germany in Europe. In Part III Germany consented to the abrogation of the neutrality of Belgium and Luxembourg and to the exclusion of the latter from the German Customs Union. Germany acknowledged the independence of Austria; accepted demilitarization of the Rhineland and a zone extending 50 kilometers east of the Rhine; and ceded to France the coal mines of the Saar. Part IV deprived Germany of its overseas possessions. Part V provided for the disarmament of Germany, "in order to render possible the initiation of a general limitation of the armaments of all nations." Part VI dealt with prisoners of war and graves. In Part VII, Wilhelm II, the former kaiser, was indicted for "a supreme offense against international morality and the sanctity of treaties," and he was to be tried by the five principal Allied Powers. (The trial never took place because the Netherlands, to which he fled after the war, refused to extradite him.) Germany also promised to deliver any of its nationals who might be accused by the Allies of having violated the laws and customs of war.

Part VIII dealt with reparation: "The Allied and Associated Governments affirm and Germany accepts the responsibility of Germany and her allies for causing all the loss and damage to which the Allied and Associated Governments and their nationals have been subjected as a consequence of the war imposed on them by the aggression of Germany and her allies." The purpose of this article was to establish the legal liability of Germany for reparation, to which it had agreed in the armistice of Nov. 11, 1918." Part IX contained financial clauses. Part X dealt with tariffs, business contracts, and the like. Part XI gave the Allies the right of unimpeded aerial navigation over Germany. In Part XII, which dealt with ports, waterways, and railways, international control of the Rhine, Oder, and Elbe rivers was established. The Kiel Canal was opened to all nations. Part XIII established the International Labor Office as an autonomous branch of the League of Nations.

Part XIV provided for guarantees. The Allies were to occupy the Rhineland and its bridgeheads for fifteen years, although certain zones were to be evacuated at the end of five years and others at the end of ten. Article 430 empowered the Allies to reoccupy the region at any time if Germany defaulted on reparation payments. Germany was to pay the cost of the armies of occupation. Part XV dealt with miscellaneous items.

The harshness of the treaty, which both injured German pride and impeded Germany's economic recovery, is considered by many historians to have helped cause Adolf Hitler's rise to power and World War II. The treaty was promptly ratified by Germany but more slowly by the Allied Powers. It came into force on Jan. 10, 1920, without having been ratified by the United States, and it was rejected by the U.S. Senate on Mar. 19, 1920. The war between the United States and Germany was formally ended in 1921 by the Treaty of Berlin.

VESEY REBELLION. A plot by South Carolina blacks in 1821–22 to annihilate the white population of Charleston. The leader was Denmark Vesey, who had been brought to Charleston in 1783. In 1800 he purchased his freedom. The fact that his children, born of a slave mother, were the property of her master aroused his resentment. Sometime around Christmas 1821 the rebellion plot took form. The participants, said by some to include 2,000–3,000 slaves, planned to seize arms and ammunition stored in the city and massacre the white population. The plot was betrayed to the authorities, and Vesey and other principal conspirators were arrested, tried, and executed.

VETERANS ADMINISTRATION. The U.S. government agency that handles matters of disability compensation, pensions, home and educational loan benefits, medical care, and housing for American war veterans; established on July 3, 1930. Offices for veterans' affairs prior to 1930 originated in the common colonial practice of supporting those disabled in the defense of the colony. A federal veterans' pension provision was administered by the secretary of war under the supervision of Congress from 1776 to 1819, when the program passed entirely to the War Department. In 1849 it moved to the Interior Department, where it remained until 1930 as the Bureau of Pensions. The Veterans Administration assumed the functions of the Bureau of Pensions; the National Home for Disabled Volunteer Soldiers (1866), with branches around the country; and the Veterans Bureau (1921).

VETERANS DAY. A federal legal holiday, observed on the fourth Monday in October. The holiday was moved by Act of Congress in 1971. The holiday had been observed on November 11, commemorating the end of World War I. "Armistice Day" was changed to "Veterans Day" after World War II, and the day became a day of tribute to all veterans of American wars.

VETERANS' ORGANIZATIONS. Have flourished in the United States since the revolutionary war, and have provided honorably discharged former servicemen agencies through which they could commemorate their participation in American wars and assist disabled veterans or their widows and children. The first veterans' association in the United States was the Society of the Cincinnati, founded in 1783 by Gen. Henry Knox and close friends. The society brought together Continental army officers, usually those supporting strong central government and a standing army. Veterans of the Civil War started the Grand Army of the Republic (GAR) in 1866, based on state organizations that sent delegates to annual GAR national encampments. The GAR died with its last member in 1956.

Of the national veterans' organizations existing in the early 1980's, the American Legion (1919) remains the largest with 2.6 million members. It is organized into autonomous local posts and county, district, and state jurisdictions, all subordinate to a national commander. The legion maintains headquarters in Indianapolis, Ind., and publishes the *American Legion Magazine.* The Veterans of Foreign Wars (VFW) is similarly organized. It was founded in 1899. The VFW is headquartered at Kansas City, Mo., and publishes the *V.F.W. Magazine.* In 1982 the VFW had almost 2 million members.

The Disabled American Veterans (DAV) was begun at Cincinnati, Ohio, in 1919 by disabled veterans of World War I. The American Veterans of World War II, Korea, and Vietnam (AMVETS) was started in 1944 as the American Veterans of World War II, consolidating several smaller existing groups. In 1982 it had 200,000 members. Smaller, informal groups based on service with a specific unit or in a certain theater of war brought the total of American veterans' groups in 1982 to over 100.

VETERINARY MEDICINE. The first American work that included a discussion of animal disease was the anonymous *Husband-man's Guide* (Boston, 1710). Few serious outbreaks of animal disease in America were recorded before 1750, one of the first being "horse catarrh" (equine influenza) in 1699.

America's first veterinary surgeon was John Haslam, a graduate of the Veterinary College of London, who came to New York in 1803. He was ahead of his time, as was James Carver, who graduated from the London school in 1815, and whose ill-fated *Farrier's Magazine* (1818) was the first veterinary periodical publication (two issues) in America.

In 1807 the eminent physician Benjamin Rush strongly advocated the establishment of a school of veterinary medicine at the University of Pennsylvania, but this did not materialize until 1884. The Boston Veterinary Institute was opened in 1855 by George H. Dadd, a British medical man. The school had only six graduates when it closed in 1858, and Dadd became better known for two books, *The American Cattle Doctor* (1850) and *The Modern Horse Doctor* (1854). Dadd was an early advocate of rational medical treatment and humane surgery, including the use of general anesthesia. He was also founder and editor of the *American Veterinary Journal* (1851–52; 1855–59). The first veterinary journal to have real impact was the *American Veterinary Review* (1875). In 1915 the *Review* was purchased by the American Veterinary Medical Association and renamed the *Journal of the American Veterinary Medical Association.*

Organized veterinary medicine had its shaky beginnings in Philadelphia in 1854 when Robert Jennings, a nongraduate practitioner, was instrumental in founding the American Veterinary Association. This was superseded in 1863 when a separate group founded the U.S. Veterinary Medical Association (USVMA) in New York. In 1898 it changed its name to the American Veterinary Medical Association.

The veterinary educational system in the United States had its inception as a series of two dozen proprietary schools, which until 1927 had about 11,000 graduates. Following the ill-fated attempt in Boston and another in Philadelphia, the New York College of Veterinary Surgeons (1857–99) was the first viable school, but it was overshadowed by the American Veterinary College (New York, 1875–98). Most successful were the schools in Chicago (1883–1920) and Kansas City (1891–1918), with about 4,400 graduates.

The first of the university schools were established at Iowa State University (1879) and the University of Pennsylvania (1884). By 1918 nine additional schools had been established at land grant universities. Increasing demand for veterinary services after World War II resulted by 1975 in a school at Tuskegee Institute and eight at land grant institutions.

About 1860 large-scale animal disease began to be a problem throughout the United States and in part was responsible for the formation of the U.S. Department of Agriculture in 1862, and of its Bureau of Animal Industry (BAI) in 1884. The Morrill Land Grant Act of 1862 accelerated the establishment of agricultural colleges, the first of which had been Michigan State (1855), and most of the twenty-two in existence by 1867 offered instruction in veterinary science. After World War II employment opportunities for veterinarians broadened greatly, and many graduates entered such areas as public health, laboratory animal medicine, zoo animal practice, medical research, radiology, ophthalmology, and equine practice.

VETO, ROYAL, OF COLONIAL ACTS. *See* **Royal Disallowance.**

VETO POWER OF THE PRESIDENT. The veto power of the president is one of his two constitutionally authorized instruments of legislative leadership, the complementary tool being the authority to send messages to Congress proposing legislation. Within ten weekdays of the submission of a measure to him, the president may either sign it into law; disapprove it, returning it to the house of origin with his signature; or do nothing, in which case the bill becomes law without his signature. If Congress adjourns within the ten weekdays, however, presidential failure to act kills the bill (pocket veto). If the president exercises his veto, Congress may pass the bill over the veto by a two-thirds vote in each house. All bills and joint resolutions are submitted to the president for approval or disapproval, with the exception of joint resolutions proposing constitutional amendments.

The framers of the Constitution apparently conceived of the presidential veto as one of the checks and balances designed to prevent legislative encroachments on the executive branch. It was employed sparingly by the first seven presidents. Andrew Jackson changed the nature of the veto power by using it to impose his policy views on Congress. Since that time presidents have used the veto as a means of shaping legislation. Until 1865 nine presidents had vetoed only thirty-six bills, with Jackson accounting for twelve. The veto has subsequently been used by all presidents except James A. Garfield.

VIAL'S ROAD. Traced by Pedro Vial and two companions from New Mexico to St. Louis in 1792. Indians robbed them, and although they left Santa Fe in May, they did not reach St. Louis until October. The Spanish governor intended to use the road for trading with the French at Saint Louis, but the pathfinding venture was never followed up.

VICE-PRESIDENCY. The office of vice-president was established by the Constitution to provide a successor if the president should die, resign, or otherwise be unable to perform the duties of his office. In addition the vice-president was to be the presiding officer of the U.S. Senate, voting in case of a tie. Other functions performed by recent vice-presidents include ceremonial duties (often as a stand-in for the president), such as dedicating buildings and visiting foreign countries. Executive assignments, such as membership on various councils and commissions, have increased. Besides presiding over the Senate, some occupants of the office have attempted to exert behind-the-scenes influence in support of the president's legislative programs.

The office has a mixed historical record. In the early history of the republic it was held by such distinguished public figures as John Adams and Thomas Jefferson. In the 19th century it faded into obscurity. There was an occasional flurry of interest in the office, particularly when a president died, but it was usually short-lived. By 1975 eight vice-presidents had succeeded to the office on the death of the president, four of them in the 20th century; and one, Gerald R.

Ford, had been appointed vice-president when the incumbent resigned and succeeded to the presidency when the president resigned.

Recent presidents have made conscious effort to give additional duties to the vice-president. Indeed, by the 1970's the office appeared to be achieving a status whereby the incumbent is one of the likely presidential nominees when the president does not run. Vice-presidential candidates are selected at the national party conventions. By custom, such a decision is made by the presidential candidate, who usually chooses someone who can bring support to the ticket from important electoral groups. A vice-presidential candidate runs in tandem with the presidential candidate, so, at least since the ratification of the Twelfth Amendment (1804), both winners will be of the same political party. The Twenty-fifth Amendment (1967) provides that if the office of vice-president becomes vacant, the president may nominate a successor, subject to confirmation by both houses of Congress by majority vote. (*See list of Vice-Presidents under President*.)

VICK ESTATE. A tract of land owned by Newitt Vick until his death in 1819, it included the site of Vicksburg, Miss. Vick's male heirs sold their interests to Seargent S. Prentiss. Female heirs established their claim to the estate in a U.S. Supreme Court decision in 1845.

VICKSBURG (Miss.). A city on the high eastern bank of the Mississippi River, just below the mouth of the Yazoo River. Near the site of the present-day city the French built Fort St. Pierre in 1719; the Spanish built Fort Nogales in 1791. River traders later called the site Walnut Hills, and after the area came under British rule, Fort Nogales became Fort McHenry. Permanent settlement began with Newitt Vick, a Virginia Methodist preacher, who established a mission in 1814. Five years later, Vick set aside 200 acres for a town site. Settlers incorporated the town in 1825. Vicksburg prospered following the opening of the Mississippi-Yazoo Delta for settlement and after the removal of the Choctaw by treaties. The delta was extremely fertile cotton country, and Vicksburg began to rival Natchez as Mississippi's center of wealth and political power. Vicksburg's location made it strategically important during the Civil War (*see* Vicksburg in the Civil War). The decline of steamboating after the Civil War reduced the city's importance. In the 20th century, harbor improvements and construction of a bridge across the Mississippi again made Vicksburg a major transport center. The city's population in 1980 was 25,434.

VICKSBURG IN THE CIVIL WAR. Until after the fall of New Orleans to Union forces in April 1862, Vicksburg, Miss., was practically undefended by the Confederate army. By May, Vicksburg's importance as an obstacle to Union control of the Mississippi River had become evident, and Confederate Gen. Mansfield Lovell ordered rapid construction of fortifications. In November Gen. Ulysses S. Grant began his campaign against Vicksburg, moving south from Memphis through northern Mississippi. The advancing forces were beaten at Chickasaw Bluffs on Dec. 27–29. Four subsequent unsuccessful attempts to reach Vicksburg culminated in the burning of the Union supply depot at Holly Springs, Miss. Grant decided to abandon his base at Memphis, move down the west bank of the Mississippi, recross the river below Vicksburg, and try to capture the city from the east. The plan was successful. Gen. John C. Pemberton, unexpectedly finding Grant's army to his east, sent only a small force to oppose it. Within three weeks Vicksburg was in a state of siege. Aided by bombardment from the river fleet, Grant assaulted the Vicksburg lines. Each attack was repulsed with heavy loss. Dwindling food and ammunition supplies, mounting casualties, sickness, and the impossibility of reinforcement or relief finally induced Pemberton to surrender on July 4, 1863. For the rest of the war, Vicksburg was a Union base of operations.

VICKSBURG RIOTS. White citizens of Vicksburg and Warren County (Miss.) had organized to oppose the policies and actions of the Reconstruction state government. When federal authorities refused requests by state officials for U.S. troops, disturbances began (Dec. 7, 1874). Two whites and twenty-nine blacks were killed in the riots.

VICTORY LOAN OF 1919. A bond issue intended to help pay the costs of World War I. The act provided for the issue of two series of three-to-four year 4.75 percent and 3.75 percent convertible gold notes; the total amount of the issue, dated May 29, 1919, was $4.5 billion. Bearer notes were issued from $50 to $10,000, registered notes from $50 to $100,000. The maturity date was May 20, 1923, but both series were callable for redemption in whole or in part on June 15 or Dec. 15, 1922, on four months' notice.

VIETNAM WAR (1957–1975). Began as a Communist insurgency supported by North Vietnam, and later involved direct North Vietnamese intervention supported by the Soviet Union and the People's Republic of China. The United States fought in conjunction with South Vietnam, with assistance from the Republic of Korea (South Korea), Australia, New Zealand, Thailand, and the Philippines. There were 45,943 U.S. battle deaths, the fourth most costly American war in terms of loss of life. The Vietnam War followed the Indochina War of 1946–54 in which France sought to reestablish colonial control. American involvement began in mid-1950 when President Harry S. Truman invoked the Mutual Defense Assistance Act of 1949 to provide aid to French forces.

Through the Geneva Accords of 1954, ending the Indochina War, Vietnam was divided by the Demilitarized Zone (DMZ) at the seventeenth parallel. The division in effect created two nations: a Communist north (Democratic Republic of Vietnam) and a non-Communist south (Republic of Vietnam). (*See also* Geneva Accords of 1954.) Following the accords, the United States through the Military Assistance Advisory Group (MAAG), Indochina, aided the South Vietnam government of President Ngo Dinh Diem under the Southeast Asia Treaty Organization (SEATO). Upon French withdrawal in 1956, the United States doubled its forces to about 684, maintaining that the additions conformed with limitations of the Geneva Accords in that they replaced French advisers. Beginning in 1957, Communist guerrillas (Vietcong, or VC) opened a terrorist revolt, which intensified as 65,000 Communists infiltrated from North Vietnam. The first two American deaths occurred in July 1959.

By mid-1961 President John F. Kennedy increased U.S. advisers to 16,000 and, the next year, to 23,000. American helicopter companies supported the ARVN (Army of the Republic of Vietnam). A joint headquarters, Military Assistance Command, Vietnam (MACV), replaced the MAAG.

Yet the insurgency continued to increase. Diem's assassination during a *coup d' état* on Nov. 1, 1963, led to a succession of unstable governments. U.S. casualties increased. After two incidents in August 1964 involving U.S. destroyers and North Vietnamese patrol boats in the Gulf of Tonkin, American planes raided North Vietnam and Congress authorized President Lyndon B. Johnson to "repel any armed attack against the forces of the United States and to repel further aggression." That resolution served as a legal basis for subsequent increases in U.S. commitment.

Slow to use the authority, Johnson authorized only limited covert operations by South Vietnamese in North Vietnam and U.S. bombing of North Vietnamese supply routes in Laos, known collectively as the Ho Chi Minh Trail. When in February 1965 the VC killed thirty-one Americans, Johnson sanctioned retaliatory air strikes against North Vietnam. Soon afterward he sanctioned a sustained but carefully controlled aerial campaign beginning on Mar. 2.

When several North Vietnamese regiments were detected within South Vietnam, the MACV commander, Gen. William C. Westmoreland, requested U.S. troops to protect American installations. In June, B-52 strategic bombers began raiding VC bases within South Vietnam, and the 173rd Airborne Brigade made the first American ground offensive.

Johnson on July 28 announced deployments that by the end of 1965 brought U.S. strength to 180,000 and by 1969 reached a peak of 543,400. A stable government meanwhile emerged in Saigon under Nguyen Van Thieu. MACV constructed or expanded ports at six sites, erected fortified camps, built depots, paved thousands of miles of roads, and created extensive airfields. Buying time for the logistical effort, Westmoreland employed early arriving combat units as fire brigades against major threats. The most notable success was in the Central Highlands. In the Battle of the Ia Drang Valley, the first U.S. airmobile unit, the First Cavalry Division, used helicopters expeditiously and drove a decimated North Vietnamese division into Cambodia.

That the enemy could retire with impunity into Cambodia and use the port of Sihanoukville to offset the U.S. Navy's sealing of the South Vietnamese coast was frustrating; but Johnson forbade cross-border operations except for bombing of the Ho Chi Minh Trail. This dictated for Westmoreland a strategic defensive aimed at enemy attrition. Some American units pursued large enemy formations and penetrated VC logistical bases; others worked with the ARVN to protect villages against local guerrillas.

In some ways a primitive war, it nevertheless involved sophisticated weapons and equipment and constant ingenuity to root the enemy from jungle and verdant rice paddies. Fighting sometimes inevitably produced civilian casualties, as a result both of enemy terrorism and on one occasion, at My Lai in 1968, of a serious lapse of discipline in a U.S. unit.

In early 1967 North Vietnamese buildup within the DMZ prompted reinforcement of U.S. Marines in the north; and later that year North Vietnamese forays across Cambodian and Laotian frontiers produced sharp clashes and the siege of a marine base at Khe Sanh. These moves concealed a covert buildup around South Vietnam's cities. On Jan. 30–31, 1968, during the Tet (lunar new year) holidays, 84,000 Communists attacked seventy-four towns and cities. Although the ARVN cleared most localities quickly, fighting in Saigon and Hue was protracted. Controlling Hue for almost a month, the enemy executed 3,000 civilians. Despite 32,000 dead, the offensive produced no lasting Communist military advantage, but it made a sharp psychological impact on American public opinion, feeding already strident demands for withdrawal. Although North Vietnam agreed to negotiate after Johnson halted most bombing of the north, the negotiations, opening in Paris in May, were unproductive for a long time.

The enemy's heavy losses made possible gradual American withdrawal. A program to upgrade the ARVN began in 1969 with the administration of President Richard M. Nixon, and the first American units withdrew that summer. Nixon gained some time when North Vietnamese leader Ho Chi Minh died on Sept. 3, 1969, and by American and South Vietnamese operations in April–May 1970 to eliminate enemy sanctuaries in Cambodia and by an ARVN raid in February 1971 on the Ho Chi Minh Trail. When North Vietnam during Easter 1972 attacked, only a residual American ground force remained, but the U.S. Air Force and U.S. Navy provided critical support. The offensive scored sharp initial gains, but the ARVN rebounded creditably. Nixon reacted by sealing the port of Haiphong and again bombing North Vietnam.

North Vietnam finally entered meaningful negotiations. Nixon's special adviser, Henry A. Kissinger, and North Vietnamese representative Le Duc Tho conducted months of secret discussions ending in a cease-fire effective Jan. 28, 1973. Under the agreement, prisoners of war were returned, American troops withdrew, and a four-nation commission supervised the truce. The Communists retained control of the northern province, large tracts of sparsely populated mountain regions, and some enclaves in populated areas.

Because of the continued presence of North Vietnamese troops within South Vietnam, the position of the South Vietnamese was precarious, particularly after American military intervention was eliminated when Congress prohibited funds for all American combat action in Southeast Asia after Aug. 15, 1973. Through 1973–74 the North Vietnamese, in violation of the cease-fire agreement, massed more men and supplies inside South Vietnam and in January 1975 launched a major attack that ended in the capture of Phuoc Long province. Then they opened an offensive in the Central Highlands and extended it to the northern provinces. The South Vietnamese attempted to withdraw and concentrate on the defense of the southern third of the country and of coastal enclaves in the north and center, but the withdrawal quickly turned into a rout. Successively the country's major cities fell.

With the imminent collapse of South Vietnam, President Thieu on Apr. 21 resigned in favor of his vice-president, who in turn resigned on Apr. 28 in favor of Gen. Duong van Minh, who was committed to negotiate with the Communists. The Minh government surrendered on Apr. 30, 1975, whereupon North Vietnamese and VC troops entered Saigon only hours after the U.S. completed an emergency airlift of embassy personnel and thousands of South Vietnamese.

It was the longest American war and in terms of money ($138.9 billion) only World War II cost more. In addition to U.S. combat deaths, 1,333 men were missing and 10,298 dead of noncombat causes. The Communists lost at least 937,000 dead. The Communists gained control not only of South Vietnam but also of neighboring Cambodia and Laos.

VIEUX CARRÉ ("Old Square"). The old French and Spanish section of New Orleans, bounded by the Mississippi River on the southeast, Rampart Street on the northwest, Canal Street on the southwest, and Esplanade Avenue on the northeast. It is a popular tourist attraction.

VIGILANTES. Members of citizens' committees set up in western communities to maintain order before law courts were organized and peace officers were elected. Since protection could not be had from state and county governments, leading citizens sought, by mass action, to drive desperadoes from their midst. One of the most successful was the San Francisco Vigilance Committee, set up in 1851. Among the thousands who flooded into California following the discovery of gold in January 1848 were many outlaws. The vigilantes began summary executions of outlaw leaders, and other outlaws scattered throughout the West.

Many Rocky Mountain communities took up the vigilante movement. In some instances action was little more than that of a mob; in others it was deliberate and well planned. Groups were formed by Missourians, and in Colorado and Montana (1854–64).

Much effective vigilance committee work was done in Texas, New Mexico, and Kansas after the Civil War. The work of the committee at Fort Griffin, Tex., is best known.

VIKINGS. *See* **Norsemen in America; Vinland.**

VILLA RAID AT COLUMBUS (Mar. 9, 1916). Mexican outlaw raids against U.S. nationals and their property on both sides of the border culminated on the night of Mar. 8–9, 1916, in Pancho Villa's raid on Columbus, N. Mex. Units of the cavalry stationed at Columbus drove the Mexicans back across the border. The raid was directly responsible for U.S. Gen. John J. Pershing's punitive expedition into Mexico.

VILLASUR EXPEDITION (1720). Don Pedro de Villasur left Santa Fe with forty-two soldiers and sixty Indian allies for a reconnaissance of the French thrust from the east into Spanish territory. On Aug. 13 the party was attacked and routed by a band of Pawnee, allies of the French, on the south side of the North Platte River (in the vicinity of present-day North Platte, Nebr.). Forty-four members of Villasur's party were killed, including Villasur himself.

VILLERE'S PLANTATION, BATTLE AT (1814). After defeating the inferior American fleet on Lake Borgne, La., the British landed and marched through the swamps to Villere's plantation on the eastern bank of the Mississippi River, a few miles below New Orleans. At the plantation U.S. Gen. Andrew Jackson attacked and repulsed the British forces on the foggy night of Dec. 23. After the engagement the British retired until the decisive Battle of New Orleans (won by the Americans) on Jan. 8, 1815.

VINCENNES (Ind.). The French government began early in the 18th century to erect a chain of fortified posts in the New World. An Indian village on the east bank of the Wabash River, 150 miles above its mouth, was selected as a suitable site and around this post a permanent settlement grew up; fur traders probably made this important Indian village their headquarters as early as 1700. François Marie Bissot, Sieur de Vincennes, was stationed at the post in 1736, and it came to be named after him. From the Indians the Vincennes settlers received a large tract of land on both sides of the Wabash River. Five thousand acres of this grant were designated as common fields and enclosed with pickets. Adjoining the village were the narrow, ribbonlike strips of land, from one-half to a mile long and from ten to forty rods wide, common to French settlements, which were plowed, sowed, and reaped according to rules agreed upon in the public assembly made up of all males of military age.

The British took Vincennes from the French in 1777. Americans under George Rogers Clark captured the post, lost it, and ultimately recaptured it in 1779. Subsequently, immigrants from Kentucky and Virginia with land warrants for service in the Revolution began coming to Vincennes. In 1790, Knox County, the first organized government in Indiana, was formed, with Vincennes as the county seat. Ten years later the Indiana Territory, which included practically all of the Northwest Territory, excluding Ohio, was created by an act of Congress. In 1813 the capital was relocated at Corydon because of its more central situation within Indiana Territory. Vincennes continued to be an important trading center.

VINCENNES, FRENCH DEFECTION AT (1797). An incident fomented by local intrigues against the United States by British and Spanish sympathizers and stimulated by a ten-year accumulation of complaints against U.S. governance. Some of the defection's leaders, men of means, held slaves, which the Northwest Ordinance of 1787 prohibited; provisions of the Land Act of 1796 also caused dissatisfaction. Winthrop Sargent, acting governor of the Northwest Territory, personally adjusted many of the land claims of French settlers, extended civil rights and privileges previously withheld or denied, and made delayed appointments of civil and militia officers, thus averting serious trouble.

VINCENNES, TREATY OF (June 7, 1803). William Henry Harrison, governor of the newly created Indiana Territory, was instructed by the federal government to gain title to Indian lands in the area. After a preliminary conference in the fall of 1802, Harrison succeeded in getting a formal treaty signed at Fort Wayne. This document provided for the cession by nine tribes (the Shawnee, Potawatomi, Miami, Wea, Eel River, Delaware, Piankashaw, Kaskaskia, and Kickapoo) of a tract of land around Vincennes extending along the Wabash River for about twenty-five miles north from the mouth of the White River, and extending from twelve miles west of the Wabash to seventy-two miles east of that river. By a supplementary treaty signed at Vincennes (Aug. 7, 1803) several tracts were ceded for way stations from Clarksville to Kaskaskia via Vincennes.

VINDICATION OF THE BRITISH COLONIES. A tract by James Otis (1765) defending the colonies against British policy. Specifically repudiating any thought of independence on the part of the colonists, Otis insisted on their possession of the rights of Englishmen, particularly that of self-taxation.

VINLAND. The name used by medieval Scandinavian historians and saga writers to denote the southernmost area on the Atlantic coast of North America visited by Norse mariners about A.D. 1000. The first sighting is attributed to the Icelander Bjarni Herjolfsson about 986, the first landing to Leif Ericson a few years later, and the first attempt at colonization to Thorfinn Karlsefni.

Saga tradition speaks of three lands west or southwest of Greenland, named by their explorers after a quality of the region: Helluland (Flatstoneland), Markland (Woodland), and Vinland (Wineland). The most northerly, Helluland, is commonly identified with the southern portion of Baffin Island; there has also been an increasing acceptance of Markland as the coast of Labrador south of the medieval treeline and of Vinland as the area beginning in northern Newfoundland and extending a variably defined distance southward. Discovery of Norse remains at L'Anse aux Meadows in northern Newfoundland in the early 1960's and some admittedly disputable cartographical evidence appear to confirm this; but other localities have been advanced, from Hudson Bay to well south of Virginia. (*See also* Kensington Stone; Norsemen in America.)

VIRGINIA. The first permanent English settlement was established on a peninsula of the James River on May 24, 1607, under a charter granted by James I to the London Company. The stockade village, called Jamestown in honor of the king, was unfortunately located in a grassy swamp with great swarms of malaria-bearing mosquitos and little fresh water or tillable soil. The London Company was bankrupt by 1624; James I revoked the company's charter, and thereafter the colony came under the direct administration of the crown.

After the establishment of royal administration the colony enjoyed greater stability and growth. However, the real catalyst in the eventual prosperity of Virginia was the discovery that tobacco could be grown for a profit and that black slaves could be exploited to the advantage of the spreading tobacco agriculture; this produced an economic, social, and political organism dominated by the planter aristocracy.

Under the London Company the colony was administered by an appointed governor and council, with an elected assembly called the House of Burgesses (added in 1619). After royal authority was established, the governor and council were appointed by the king, while the burgesses were elected by the qualified citizenry. During the second half of the 17th century the council and the burgesses gradually developed into a two-house legislature known as the General Assembly. A property qualification for voting and officeholding somewhat restricted the electorate, but the House of Burgesses was fairly representative of the farmers and planters of the tidewater region. Once a home-grown elite was firmly entrenched in power in the tidewater, political and social affairs were stable during the first half of the 18th century.

In 1699 Williamsburg became the capital of the province; Richmond was laid out on land owned by William Byrd II in 1737 and became the seat of government in 1779. Nurtured by the College of William and Mary, the General Assembly, and the town's several law offices and taverns, the Williamsburg environment spawned a generation of political leaders of unusual ability and intellect. The chief port of the province was Norfolk, which had achieved a population of 6,000 by the eve of the Revolution. During the 18th century the population of Virginia grew from an estimated 72,000 to over 807,000; at the end of the century slaves constituted about 42 percent of the population.

The state was a major scene of battle during the latter stages of the war for independence; the final surrender of British forces took place at Yorktown on October 19, 1781. Virginians dominated the presidency until 1824. Agriculture remained the chief occupation after the founding of the nation. Tobacco remained an important staple in the southside, but increasingly wheat, other grains, and garden crops were planted in the tidewater and lower piedmont. Richmond became one of the nation's important flour-milling centers. Cattle raising and orchard cultivation were important in the Shenandoah Valley and the Blue Ridge foothills. A slight decline in slavery attended the changing pattern of agriculture. Slaves composed 40 percent of the population of Virginia in 1810, but only 33 percent by 1850.

By the early national period the free white population of the tramontane region outnumbered that of eastern Virginia, but the General Assembly remained under the control of tidewater and piedmont interests. In 1816 a convention of westerners met in Staunton to call for reapportionment, suffrage expansion, and constitutional reform. The increasing numbers of workers in the iron foundries and textile mills of Wheeling found difficulty in meeting the property qualification for voting and resented the fact that the slaveholders in the east refused to recognize western interests. Western appeals for internal improvements were frequently ignored.

In 1829 a convention was held in Richmond to revise the state constitution. Small concessions were granted to the western part of the state in slightly increased representation in the General Assembly, but full white manhood suffrage was denied. A broad discussion of slavery occupied the General Assembly session of 1831–32; in addition to defeating gradual emancipation, the assembly imposed a more rigid slave code.

The state became the scene of almost continuous warfare between 1861 and 1865. About 170,000 Virginians served in the Confederate Army. Extensive areas of the state and major cities were largely destroyed. Lee surrendered his forces to Ulysses S. Grant at Appomattox Courthouse on Apr. 9, 1865. Earlier, on June 20, 1863, the fifty western counties of the Old Dominion were admitted to the Union as the state of West Virginia; the state thus lost nearly 35 percent of its land area and about 25 percent of its population.

As a result of the Civil War nearly 500,000 Virginia slaves were emancipated, and the state had to accept the provisions of the Reconstruction Acts of 1867 in order to regain statehood. Conditions for readmission included the writing of a new state constitution providing for universal suffrage, a free public school system and other welfare measures, and a system of local democracy based on the New England township model. In October 1867 a convention met in Richmond. Twenty-five of the delegates were black. The resulting constitution was approved by the new electorate on July 6, 1869; in January 1870 Virginia returned to the Union.

A fever of railroad speculation and fraud swept the state during the 1870's and 1880's, and a real estate boom and bust in the Shenandoah Valley and southwestern regions dashed many hopes for quick riches. However, considerable growth did occur. In the 1880's the state was disturbed by a political insurgency called the Readjuster movement. At issue was the state's burdensome debt, which maintained taxes at a high level and almost destroyed the new public school system (*see* Readjuster Movement). White control over the electorate was accomplished by the Democratic machine in 1902 with the promulgation of a new frame of government, which set forth a literacy test and a poll tax as requisites for voting. The electorate was reduced by 50 percent, and after 1904 only a small number of blacks continued to exercise the franchise.

The issue of school integration brought profound changes. A campaign of massive resistance opposed implementation of the 1954 Supreme Court ruling in *Brown* v. *Board of Education of Topeka.* Rather than comply with court-ordered integration, Gov. J. Linsey Almond, Jr., closed public schools. White students attended hastily prepared private academies, while black children were without schools for five years. At length the impetus behind massive resistance died down, as adverse publicity drove prospective investors from the state and parents tired of the uncertainty in the schools.

Virginia's economic prosperity in the 20th century was based more on industry and government than on traditional agriculture. The export of coal through Hampton Roads, the chemical industries in Richmond, Hopewell, and Roanoke, textile mills in Danville, and furniture manufacturing in the southwest are of particular note. Stimulated by the expansion of U.S. Navy facilities during World War II, shipbuilding became a multimillion dollar business in Newport News and Portsmouth. Government is the second largest source of employment in Virginia, with the Department of Defense in Arlington, the Marine Corps base at Quantico, the Norfolk Naval Base, and the National Aeronautics and Space Administration at Langley providing jobs for thousands of people. Tourism had developed into a billion-dollar-a-year enterprise by 1970. In agriculture, the most significant changes came in the development of increasing numbers of dairy farms in the northern part of the state and of truck farms on the eastern shore. The population of Virginia more than doubled between 1900 and 1980, growing from 1,854,000 to over 5,346,279.

***VIRGINIA*.** The first steamboat to navigate the upper Mississippi River above the Des Moines Rapids, it reached Fort Snelling in southeastern Minnesota, May 10, 1823, twenty days out of St. Louis. Built at Wheeling (then part of Virginia) in 1819, the 109-ton stern-wheeler sank after it was snagged below St. Louis in the fall of 1823.

VIRGINIA, ARMY OF. Constituted June 26, 1862, it consisted of the corps of Union generals John C. Frémont, Nathaniel P. Banks, and Irvin McDowell, with Gen. John Pope as commander. Pope was ordered to drive Gen. Robert E. Lee out of Richmond (*see* Seven Days' Battles). The Confederate army marched northward to oppose Pope. Union Gen. George B. McClellan's Army of the Potomac was ordered to Pope's aid. The combined Union armies were defeated in the second Bull Run campaign (Aug. 29–30, 1862) and retreated into Washington, D.C. Pope was relieved, and the Army of Virginia was broken up and dispersed.

VIRGINIA, ARMY OF NORTHERN. On June 1, 1862, after the wounding of Gen. Joseph E. Johnston (*see* Fair Oaks, Battle of), Confederate President Jefferson Davis placed Robert E. Lee in command of the Confederate army and officially designated it the Army of Northern Virginia. Thereafter, this most famous of Confederate armies was commanded by Lee and became one of the most effective fighting weapons ever constituted. Gen. Thomas J. ("Stonewall") Jackson's foot cavalry, Gen. James Longstreet and Gen. Ambrose P. Hill's fighters, Gen. J. E. B. Stuart's horse, and the batteries of Maj. John Pelham and Col. W. J. Pegram were among its personnel. Originally organized in divisional form, after the second Battle of Bull Run (Aug. 29–30, 1862) it was divided into two corps under Longstreet and Jackson. Following Jackson's death (May 10, 1863) after Chancellorsville, Va. (May 2–4, 1863), it was reorganized into three corps under Longstreet, Gen. Richard S. Ewell, and Hill. Its effective battle strength was at a maximum in the Seven Days' Battles (June 26–July 2, 1862), when it exceeded 90,000; from that time on, its strength steadily declined until at Appomattox, only 8,000 men were in line.

VIRGINIA, UNIVERSITY OF. Founded by Thomas Jefferson at Charlottesville; chartered in 1819. Developed from an academy charter of 1803, its buildings were started in 1817, and eight schools were opened in 1825. Jefferson, also the architect, spoke of his connection with its foundation as one of the three achievements of his life by which he wished to be remembered. The university was administered by a chairman of the faculty until 1904, when Edward A. Alderman became the first president. The university's specific contributions to American education have been the secularization of scientific thought; the installation in 1842, along lines suggested by Jefferson in 1818, of student self-government; and the establishment of an elective system of study. In 1944

Mary Washington College for women, established in 1908 at Fredericksburg, was consolidated with the University of Virginia.

VIRGINIA AND KENTUCKY RESOLUTIONS (passed by the legislature of Virginia, Dec. 24, 1798, and of Kentucky, Nov. 16, 1798, and Nov. 22, 1799). The Kentucky resolutions were written by Thomas Jefferson, and the Virginia one by James Madison. The immediate occasion was to protest against the passage of the Alien and Sedition Acts (1798) by the Federalist administration. Both sets of resolutions took the position that the federal government was one of limited and delegated powers only, but there was the further question as to who should judge whether the central government was overstepping its rightful powers. Jefferson stated that the federal government could not be the final judge of its own powers, and that the states—perhaps even one state—should be. Madison's words were less emphatic, but all three resolutions can easily be made to appear as advocating the doctrines of state sovereignty, nullification, and secession as those doctrines were later developed. In 1828 when John C. Calhoun was preaching his versions of state sovereignty and nullification, Madison pointed out that the Union was a constitutional one, not a mere league, and that his Virginia resolution of 1798 could not be considered as affording a basis for Calhoun's interpretation.

The resolutions, as passed, were forwarded for comment to the legislatures of the other states, which proved cool to the suggestions made, and in a number of cases replied that states could not decide on the constitutionality of federal laws because that power belonged to the judiciary (where, in the course of U.S. development, it was finally to be lodged). The resolutions were used to buttress the doctrines of states' rights.

VIRGINIA CAPES, BATTLE OF (Sept. 5–9, 1781). Of itself, the naval battle of the Virginia Capes was trifling, but its grand result was the sealing of British Gen. Charles Cornwallis and his troops into the trap of Yorktown, Va., leading to the surrender that established American independence. In late July 1781 Adm. François Joseph Paul de Grasse in Haiti studied the requests from Gen. George Washington and his French ally Gen. Jean Baptiste de Vimeur, Comte de Rochambeau, for cooperation. De Grasse reached the Virginia Capes on Aug. 30 and anchored in Lynnhaven Bay inside Cape Henry. Landing his regiments for temporary control by Marie Joseph du Motier, Marquis de Lafayette, he sent shallow-draft vessels up the bay to fetch the soldiers of Washington and Rochambeau. Thus, the French fleet was undermanned and at anchor on Sept. 5 when British Adm. Thomas Graves and nineteen ships appeared. The alarmed French made emergency haste to get under way, their efforts hindered by a headwind on which the British rode in ease. However, slow obedience spoiled the opportunity for crushing the disordered French. Graves had to shift to a seaward southerly course, shorten sail, and let the French sortie. There ensued four days of inconclusive clashes. Neither side lost a ship, but French gunners aimed at British rigging, gradually crippling enough Britons in sail power so that de Grasse could at last get free and return to the Chesapeake where reinforcement from Newport, under Adm. Louis de Barras, awaited him. When Graves reapproached the capes on Sept. 12, the assemblage of thirty-six alert French ships was nearly double his nineteen, and he made for his base at New York. Cornwallis saw himself deserted, lost hope, and surrendered.

VIRGINIA CITY (Nev.). The largest and most famous of Nevada's early mining towns came into existence in 1859. By 1861, when Congress organized Nevada Territory, it was a town of importance with a population of more than 3,000. It was incorporated as a city in 1864 and by the 1870's its population had grown to about 30,000. The city declined in the 1880's when the ores of the great Comstock mining region failed. Disincorporated, Virginia City was eventually abandoned, becoming a ghost town; some buildings were preserved or restored, making it a popular tourist attraction.

VIRGINIA COMPANY OF LONDON. One name for the commercial enterprise that was established in 1606 and that governed the colony of Virginia (1609–24). The Society of Adventurers (that is, investors) to trade in Virginia was organized by letters patent dated Apr. 10, 1606, and issued to Sir Thomas Gates, Sir George Somers, and others. The document specified that there were to be two colonies, called "the first Colony" and "the second Colony" (*see* Plymouth, Virginia Company of). The "first Colony" included "any place upon the said coast of Virginia or America" between 34° and 41° north latitude; the "second Colony" was to be between 38° and 45° north latitude; neither group of colonists was to "plant" itself within 100 miles of the other. Each colony was to be governed ultimately by a council in London and in day-to-day matters by a local council responsible to the body in London. The king retained authority over affairs in Virginia by making the governing council in England responsible to himself.

In 1609 a "Second Charter" was granted to the company, converting it into a corporation. The entrepreneurs, with Sir Thomas Smith as treasurer, became distinctly proprietary, retaining commercial responsibilities and also assuming governmental functions in place of the king. Another charter (1612) strengthened the authority of the company, making it overlord of a proprietary province. In 1619 the Virginia Company adopted "Orders and Constitutions," intended to ensure legality of action.

Between 1619 and 1622 factions developed in the company as a result of the administration of Samuel Argall, deputy governor of the colony, who exploited the lands and trade of the company for himself and his friends. This exploitation led to the formation of an administration under the Earl of Southampton, Lord Cavendish, Sir Edwin Sandys, John Ferrar, and Nicholas Ferrar. Also, political difficulties arose. On Apr. 17, 1623, a committee headed by Lord Cavendish was summoned before the Privy Council to defend the company against the "grievances of Planters and Adventurers." Judgment against the Virginia Company was rendered on May 24, 1624, and it was thereby dissolved.

VIRGINIA DECLARATION OF RIGHTS (June 12, 1776). Formulated by George Mason and adopted by the Virginia Convention, preceding by seventeen days the adoption of the constitution that made Virginia an independent state. It furnished a model for similar declarations in other state constitutions and also for the Bill of Rights.

VIRGINIA DYNASTY. A term applied to the succession of Virginia presidents, especially 1801–25.

VIRGINIA EXILES. A score or more prominent Philadelphia Quakers who were exiled to Winchester, Va., for seven months in 1777–78. Accused of showing "a disposition inimical to the cause of America" during the Revolution, they were banished without a hearing. Undoubtedly some of the group were British sympathizers, but nearly all were conscientious objectors to all war and revolution.

VIRGINIA INDIAN COMPANY. In order to delimit French activities in the West, Gov. Francis Nicholson throughout the 1690's urged the creation of a strong trading concern, but not until the project was taken over by Gov. Alexander Spotswood did it bear fruit. Authorized by provincial statute in 1714, the Virginia Indian Company was given exclusive control over traffic with the Indians. The organization supplied tributary tribes, reopened trade with the Catawba and Cherokee, and sponsored the discovery (1716) of a passage through the Blue Ridge Mountains at or near Swift Run Gap. The act creating the corporation was disallowed by the English Privy Council in 1717 on the ground that the enterprise constituted a monopoly.

VIRGINIA MILITARY RESERVE IN OHIO. In ceding its land claims north of the Ohio (*see* Western Lands), Virginia reserved the district between the Little Miami and Scioto rivers for its revolutionary war veterans of the Continental establishment, in case sufficient good lands could not be found for them in Kentucky. Grants were found necessary north of the Ohio, the first survey being made in 1787. Land warrants were issued by the state; the patent was issued by the federal government upon proper certification. Many war veterans assigned their warrants to speculators, who came to control large tracts. The Virginia legislature, Dec. 6, 1852, released all further claims on such lands. Total grants on military bounties in the region amounted to 4,334,800 acres. Ungranted lands (76,735.44 acres) were turned over to the state of Ohio in 1871 and given by the state to the Ohio Agricultural and Mechanical College (later Ohio State University).

***VIRGINIAN RAILWAY COMPANY* V. *SYSTEM FEDERATION NO. 40*,** 300 U.S. 515 (1937). The Railway Labor Act (1926, amended 1934) required a carrier in labor disputes to treat with the agent certified by the National Mediation Board as the proper bargaining representative of its employees. The carrier argued that this was compulsory bargaining, depriving it of liberty and property without due process of law; furthermore, the employees concerned were engaged solely in intrastate commerce. The Supreme Court held that the act compelled only the preliminary steps to agreement and not agreement itself, which was not inconsistent with the Fifth Amendment.

***VIRGINIA OF SAGADAHOCK*.** A 30-ton pinnace built in 1607 in the short-lived Popham Colony on the banks of the Kennebec River in Maine, the first ship built by Englishmen in North America. The ship was named in honor of "Virginia," the name Englishmen gave all the Atlantic coast at the time, and "Sagadahock" from the Indian name of the river.

VIRGINIA PATH. The route taken by hunting parties of Indians through Virginia from the Potomac River to the Carolinas. Entering Virginia in present-day Loudoun County approximately at the mouth of the Monocacy River (Md.), the path ran east of the Blue Ridge Mountains and ended at the island of the Occaneechees in the Roanoke River below the junction of the Dan and Staunton rivers.

VIRGINIA PLAN. A strongly nationalistic plan for the new government, proposed to the Constitutional Convention (1787) by Edmund Randolph of Virginia, its fifteen resolutions were adopted as the basis for further deliberations. It provided for a bicameral legislature, the lower house to be elected by the people of the several states on a proportional basis and the upper house to be elected by the lower out of nominations submitted by the state legislatures. Congress was to elect an executive officer and a judiciary; a portion of the latter, sitting with the executive, was to constitute a "council of revision," with an absolute veto over all legislation. The plan also proposed to endow Congress with the power to disallow state laws "contravening" the articles of Union, and to use force against any state derelict in its obligations to the Union.

VIRGINIA RESOLUTIONS (1847). The first official state pronouncement against the Wilmot Proviso (1846), it served as a model for other southern protests, and thereafter became the symbol of Virginia's stand on congressional interference with slavery in the territories. The resolutions pledged resistance "at all hazards" to the enforcement of the proviso.

VIRGINIA RESOLVES (May 16, 1769). The first American protests against the Townshend Acts of 1767 and the treatment of Massachusetts for resenting these acts. Prepared by George Mason and introduced by George Washington in the House of Burgesses, they besought the king to quiet the minds of Virginians and avert from them threatened dangers to their lives and liberties. Adoption of the resolves led to similar adoptions by the other colonial assemblies.

***VIRGINIA* V. *TRANSYLVANIA COMPANY*.** In the 1770's the Transylvania Company met with determined opposition on the part of a considerable portion of the settlers who claimed that the land company was asking exorbitant prices for lands. A petition of grievances was sent to the legislature of Virginia. George Rogers Clark called a meeting of the settlers (June 6, 1776); it resulted in Clark and the lawyer Gabriel Jones being sent to a constitutional convention at Williamsburg, to which Richard Henderson had presented a memorial for the recognition of his company's claims. On July 4, 1776, the convention appointed commissioners to take proof in behalf of Virginia. A session of the general assembly, following the adjournment of the convention, organized Kentucky County—an assertion of jurisdiction as against the Transylvania government. The final decision of the general assembly (Nov. 4, 1778) was that the Transylvania title was void. A consolation grant of 200,000 acres was awarded.

***VIRGINIA* V. *WEST VIRGINIA*.** When Congress admitted West Virginia to the Union (1863), its constitution contained provision for assumption of an "equitable" portion of the undivided state's debt. After futile attempts at adjustment through commissions, West Virginia became neglectful and Virginia gave to creditors certificates representing what it declared to be West Virginia's obligation to them. This arrangement having proved unsatisfactory, Virginia, by acts of 1894 and 1900, took steps that resulted in its bringing suit in the U.S. Supreme Court in 1906. In 1915 the Court decreed that West Virginia should pay $12,393,929 to certificate holders in final settlement. In 1918 the Court asserted its power to enforce its decision but postponed further action in the belief that West Virginia would now discharge its plain duty, whereupon West Virginia paid.

VIRGIN ISLANDS OF THE UNITED STATES. Located forty miles east of Puerto Rico, in the Caribbean Sea; their total area is 133 square miles, including sixty-eight islands, of which St. Croix, St. Thomas, and St. John are the largest. The population in 1980 was 95,000. Before becoming U.S. possessions the three major islands were owned by Denmark, officially after 1754. President Abraham Lincoln began negotiations for their purchase, but the U.S. Senate refused to ratify the final treaty in 1870. Unsuccessful attempts at purchase in 1893 and 1902 were attributable to Danish reluctance. World War I raised the possibility that a victorious Germany would demand the islands and threaten the hegemony of the United States in the Caribbean; a purchase treaty was signed on Aug. 4, 1916, followed quickly by Danish and U.S. congressional ratification. The price paid was $25 million. The transfer became official on Mar. 31, 1917.

The inhabitants were made U.S. citizens in 1927. Administration was carried out by the U.S. Department of the Navy until 1931, when its duties were assumed by the Department of the Interior. Limited internal self-government has existed since the passage of the Organic Act of 1936. The territorial governor, previously appointed by the U.S. president, was first elected by direct popular vote in 1970. By the Revised Organic Act of 1954 legislative power—subject to the governor's veto—is vested in a unicameral legislature of fifteen popularly elected senators. The judicial system is part of the U.S. federal judiciary, with a U.S. district judge as its highest officer. Economically the islands depend on tourism and agriculture; sugarcane is the principal crop and sugar and rum the principal exports. Farming and clerical work are the main occupations.

***VIRGINIUS* AFFAIR** (1873). News reached the United States on Nov. 5 that the *Virginius*, a ship of American registry engaged in carrying arms to Cuban rebels, had been captured (Oct. 31) by a Spanish gunboat in British waters near Jamaica; on Nov. 12 confirmation arrived that Capt. Joseph Fry of the *Virginius* and fifty-three crew members and passengers had been executed as pirates by the governor of Santiago. The case against Spain was thus extremely serious, but the registration papers had been fraudulently obtained and the vessel's actual owners were members of a Cuban revolutionary committee in New York. Secretary of State Hamilton Fish drafted a virtual ultimatum. Transferring the negotiations to Washington, D.C., Fish and the Spanish minister achieved a compromise. The attack on the *Virginius* was an injury, and the *Virginius* and its survivors must be restored to the United States. The *Virginius* was surrendered on Dec. 16, but foundered before reaching port. The survivors were surrendered to U.S. authorities Dec. 18 at Santiago. Spain also paid an $80,000 indemnity.

VISIBLE ADMIXTURE LAW (1859). Enacted by the Ohio General Assembly, it provided that all persons having "a distinct and visible admixture of African blood" should be denied the franchise. Persons more than half white had previously been regarded as eligible to vote under the term "white" in the state constitution, but Democrats charged that voters of mixed blood had decided the state election of 1857. A Republican state supreme court in February 1860 declared the act unconstitutional.

VISIT AND SEARCH. A procedure whereby a naval vessel of a belligerent stops a foreign vessel on the high seas, sends a boat to examine the latter's papers to determine the character of its cargo and passengers, and searches the vessel to allay suspicions of unlawful behavior. Neutral merchant vessels may be visited and searched on the high seas on the suspicion of assisting the enemy through the transport of contraband goods, the breaking of blockade, or other unneutral acts. Visitation was originally carried out at the place of meeting at sea, but after World War II it became accepted as legitimate to divert a neutral merchant vessel to the home port of the warship conducting the visitation if search at sea was considered either impossible or impractical. If evidence of unlawful behavior exists, the belligerent state may bring the vessel before its prize courts and claim it as a prize of war after legal condemnation. If the suspicions are unfounded, the owners of the neutral vessel are entitled to compensation. During peacetime a vessel may be visited and searched by a warship if it is suspected of engaging in piracy, in slave trade, or committing other international crimes.

VISTA. *See* **Volunteers in Service to America.**

VITAL STATISTICS. While the word "statistics" did not come into use until the 1790's and the word "demography" about a half-century later, Americans from the first were concerned with demographic problems and used statistics in manifold ways—administratively, polemically, and scientifically—to deal with them. In almost every colony some early provision was made, through either parish registers or government register offices, for keeping records of births or baptisms, marriages, and deaths or burials. Population enumerations were carried out relatively frequently before 1790 in New York and Rhode Island, and rarely in Massachusetts and Virginia. Statistics of diseases and accidents began to appear first in the diaries of clergymen, planters, and other literate men, but after 1700 the establishment of colonial newspapers provided a medium for publication of bills of mortality.

During the course of the 19th century, statistics played a central role in illuminating such demographic matters as the spread of slavery, mass immigration from Europe, and the decline of the Indians. The decennial federal census, launched in 1790, broadened the scope of its demographic inquiries several times during the next century. The states and local communities remained, throughout the century, the fundamental loci of the collection and use of vital statistics. Statistics on the perishing heathen, drunkenness and prostitution, poverty and crime, and insanity helped bring various reform movements to public attention. More significant were the permanent programs for compiling health statistics. By 1800 several of the larger eastern cities were regularly recording deaths, and sometimes births, for public health purposes; this reporting was frequently expanded during epidemics of yellow fever or cholera. During the 1840's and 1850's legislatures began to provide for statewide systems of vital statistics registration. By the Civil War vital statistics were being published regularly and widely in medical journals, but even more in the reports of hospitals, asylums, health departments, and registration offices of many of the older cities and states, where they provided concrete and convincing bases for public health action. The compilation of these reports gradually became a specialized function, and those engaged in it began achieving professionalism before 1900. The American Statistical Association was established in 1839; texts on vital statistics were available by 1890, and around this time instruction in the subject began to be offered in medical schools.

One of the sophisticated applications of vital statistics, actuarial science, began in the United States late in the colonial period. A handful of small, church-run annuities societies were established beginning in 1759. Actuarial work was considerably accelerated beginning in the 1830's with the establishment of commercial life insurance firms. Following this, several Americans produced important actuarial studies, some before the Civil War.

Mechanization of vital statistics processing started in the 1880's with John Shaw Billings' use of the Hollerith tabulating machine to handle census data, and spread rapidly. At about the same time, a significant improvement was effected by the creation of the national death registration area (followed by birth and marriage registration areas); an innovation of Billings, this device brought about uniform registration procedures and standards for the entire country. Even so, it was not until 1933 that a truly national comparability of vital statistics became possible.

VITAMINS. *See* **Nutrition and Vitamins.**

VOICE OF AMERICA. A broadcasting service that came into being Feb. 24, 1942, to combat enemy propaganda and explain to the world America's wartime goals. It was continued after World War II as an integral part of an information program on the United States and its policies. Since 1953 it has been a part of the U.S. Information Agency.

VOLSTEAD ACT. The Eighteenth Amendment (ratified Jan. 29, 1919) needed a law to enforce it, and therefore the National Prohibition Act, introduced by Rep. Andrew J. Volstead (Minn.), was passed by Congress in October 1919. It was vetoed by President Woodrow Wilson (Oct. 27), but repassed by the House the same day and by the Senate the following day. It construed intoxicating liquor as that containing more than 0.5 percent alcohol by volume. It fixed penalties for liquor sales; provided for injunctions against hotels, restaurants, and other establishments found to be selling liquor; contained a search and seizure clause; and continued the taxation of alcoholic beverages.

VOLUNTEERS. Volunteers for military service were used during the Revolution and the Indian wars of the late 1700's and played a small part in the War of 1812. Some military operations in the Mexican War (1846–48) and in the Philippines (1898–99) were carried out by volunteer forces, and volunteers comprised the bulk of the forces of both the Union and Confederate sides of the Civil War. Permanent state militia units tended to put military training on a volunteer basis, and until World War I, individuals volunteered for national military service through the state quota system.

With the passage of the Selective Service Act of 1917, volunteer forces began to diminish, although never really dropping out of existence. With the passage of the National Defense Act of 1920 all state volunteers, serving in what came to be called the National Gaurd, were required to take dual oaths, to the state and federal governments, and were then subject to federal military call whenever necessary. The state militias and National Guard kept up the supply of volunteers, but in the national military service the numbers severely lessened. The furor during the Vietnam War over the draft reawakened interest in building an all-volunteer army, and in 1973 the Selective Service System was abolished. In 1980, President Carter reinstituted draft registration for eventual emergency. Meanwhile, the armed forces remained voluntary. As an incentive, volunteers now choose their branch of service and the course of study to follow while fulfilling military obligations.

VOLUNTEERS IN SERVICE TO AMERICA (VISTA). Established as a sort of domestic Peace Corps in 1965, it is an organization of volunteers who work among poor Americans and in U.S. areas which have few public services. VISTA was one of the agencies combined in 1971 into ACTION, a government agency supervising and coordinating foreign and domestic aid programs.

VOTER. *See* **Franchise.**

VOTERS, REGISTRATION OF. *See* **Registration of Voters.**

VOTING. *See* **Ballot; Franchise; Voting Machine.**

VOTING, EDUCATIONAL TESTS FOR. *See* **Literacy Test.**

VOTING BEHAVIOR. As individuals, American voters tend to exhibit a pattern of regular support for one of the two major parties; once identification is established, that attachment is not easily changed. Although less visible since the 1960's, strong patterns of voting regularity have existed for geographical sections of the country in presidential elections. The most obvious example was the support for more than 100 years of southern voters for Democratic presidential candidates: from 1860 until 1968 a majority of the eleven states of the Confederacy supported all Democratic presidential candidates, although the "solid South" began to break up with the 1948 election (in the 1968 and 1972 presidential elections the Democratic presidential candidates failed to carry a single southern state). Parts of New England and the Great Plains have been dependable areas for the Republican party; between 1860 and 1972 Vermont supported only one Democratic presidential candidate—Lyndon B. Johnson in 1964.

In congressional, gubernatorial, and state legislative voting Democratic solidarity persisted in the southern states; in the mid-1970's Louisiana, Alabama, Mississippi, South Carolina, Texas, Georgia, and Arkansas were still classified as Democratic one-party states. Six New England and midwestern states—Vermont, South Dakota, Maine, New Hampshire, Kansas, and North Dakota—were classified as modified one-party Republican states in which only a few Democrats have been elected to office since the Civil War. Even in competitive states regular patterns of one-party voting have existed in certain geographical locations. In Illinois, Indiana, and Ohio, for example, voting patterns have persisted since the Civil War in which certain counties regularly support either Democratic or Republican candidates. Residents of New York City have supported every Democratic presidential candidate since Thomas Jefferson. Voting regularity also can be identified according to such factors as religion, economic interests, and race.

VOTING MACHINE. A complex mechanical and electrical interlocking device used for registering and automatically counting votes.The voting machine was invented in Paris in 1849; in the United States Thomas A. Edison patented a machine in 1869. In 1892 the first voting machine used in an official election in the United States was used in Lockport, N.Y. In 1896 the U.S. Voting Machine Company of Jamestown, N.Y., was founded, and in 1925 it and other producers were consolidated into the Automatic Voting Machine Company; the Shoup Voting Machine Company entered the field early in the 1930's. The Seiscor Voting Machine was invented in 1961; the Coleman Vote Tally System, using fluorescent ink for marking combined with data processing for counting, was introduced in 1962; the Coyle Electronic (1959) and Harris Votomatic (1964) voting machines used cards punched by voters, which were then counted at data-processing centers.

VOTING RIGHTS ACT OF 1965. This act provided (1) for the suspension of literacy tests as a qualification to vote in state and local elections; (2) for the appointment by the U.S. attorney general of federal examiners to supervise voter registration in states and subdivisions where literacy tests were in force Nov. 1, 1964, "and where fewer than 50% of voting age residents were registered to vote on that date or actually voted in the 1964 Presidential election"; (3) for the authorization of federal courts to suspend tests used "with the effect" of discriminating, in voting rights suits brought by the U.S. attorney general; (4) for the guarantee of a citizen's right to vote in spite of an inability to read or write English if he had completed a sixth-grade education conducted in another language in a school under the American flag; (5) for approval by the U.S. attorney general of new voting laws enacted in states or subdivisions where voter qualification laws had been nullified; (6) for a prohibition "against the lifting of a suspension of tests and devices for five years after the entry of a federal court finding that a state or political subdivision had discriminated against voters"; (7) for review by a three-judge federal district court in Washington, D.C., to determine registration compliance and an ending of the federal examiners' role in a locality; (8) for subsequent lawsuits to enjoin a new law in an area whose voter qualification laws had been nullified; (9) for the end of poll taxes in state and local elections; and (10) for criminal penalties for "officials who denied any qualified voter the right to vote," including participation in party primaries, caucuses, and conventions.

The 1965 act was extended by Congress for five years in 1970 and amended to include (1) an extension from five to ten years of the period during which an affected area must abstain from using literacy or other qualifying tests; (2) the basing of the automatic "trigger formula" (where fewer than 50 percent of the eligible residents were registered to vote) on 1968 presidential voting; (3) the suspension of literacy tests until Aug. 6, 1975; (4) a thirty-day residency requirement for voting in presidential elections (applied to state and local elections but subsequently amended by the Court to allow a fifty-day period); and (5) a voting age of eighteen for all elections. (*See also* Franchise: Nationalizing the Suffrage.)

VOYAGEURS (or *engagés*). Men employed by fur traders—especially by the North West, the American, and the Hudson's Bay companies—to paddle their canoes and perform other menial tasks connected with the securing of furs and the maintenance of posts in the interior. From the mid-17th century until the third quarter of the 19th century these men formed a rather distinct class with distinct dress, customs, methods of building houses in the interior, vocabulary, and repertoire of songs. Their great service to their continent was the exploring of its rivers and lakes, the naming of these and other topographical features, and the establishment of many settlements.

Voyageurs were generally categorized: (1) according to

experience, the pork eaters *(mangeurs de lard)* and the winterers; and (2) according to skill, the guides, middlemen, and end men *(bouts)*. The pork eaters were the novices; the winterers had spent at least one winter in the interior. The guides were the men capable of directing the course of a brigade of canoes; the middlemen *(milieux)* sat in the middle of the canoe and merely propelled it in unison without attempting to guide its course, which was governed by the *bouts* (the two men who stood in the prow and stern respectively); the *bouts* were divided into the *avant*, positioned in the prow, and the steersman *(gouvernail)* in the stern.

WABASH, ST. LOUIS AND PACIFIC RAILROAD* V. *ILLINOIS **(1866).** The U.S. Supreme Court ruled that no state could impose regulations on rates charged in interstate commerce. Illinois, following the Grangers, had attempted to prevent the railroad from charging high rates for short hauls.

WABASH AND ERIE CANAL. A waterway originally planned to follow the Maumee and Wabash rivers from Lake Erie to the Ohio River, agreed upon by the states of Ohio and Indiana in 1829 (*see* Indiana State Canals). State lands were sold in Indiana to raise money; $200,000 was borrowed; and in 1832 excavation began. Ohio was to build eastward from the Indiana line, but delayed action for several years. By 1841 the canal was in operation only from Fort Wayne to Logansport, Ind., and the state was nearly bankrupt. In 1843 Ohio completed the eastern section of the canal, and in 1844 the fastest canal packet service in the country was operating between Toledo, Fort Wayne, and Lafayette. The canal was opened to Terre Haute in 1849; but flood damage and the competition of railroads built parallel to its course foreshadowed its end. In 1856 it reached Evansville on the Ohio River, 452 miles from Toledo, making it the longest canal in the United States—but it was already dying. The portion below Terre Haute was closed in 1860, and the last short stretch near Lafayette was abandoned in 1875.

WABASH LAND COMPANY. *See* **Illinois and Wabash Company.**

WABASH RAILROAD. *See* **Railroads, Sketches of Principal Lines: Norfolk and Western.**

WABASH TOWNS, EXPEDITIONS AGAINST (May and August 1791). Indians operating from their towns on the Wabash and Eel rivers in northern Indiana, encouraged by Gen. Josiah Harmar's defeat in October 1790, constantly raided across the Ohio River into Kentucky. Accordingly, in the spring of 1791 Gen. Charles Scott was authorized to lead an expedition against the Kickapoo Eel River villages. He destroyed towns and crops and took prisoners. In August Col. James Wilkinson led an equally destructive expedition against the Indians in the vicinity of L'Angville (present Logansport). These expeditions infuriated the Indians, who eagerly joined the expedition that accomplished Gen. Arthur St. Clair's defeat (Nov. 4) near present-day Fort Wayne.

WACHOVIA. *See* **Bethabara.**

***WACHUSETT* AFFAIR.** On Oct. 7, 1864, the U.S.S. *Wachusett* captured the Confederate cruiser *Florida* in the Brazilian port of Bahia, despite the attempted interference of Brazilian naval forces. The *Florida* was taken to Hampton Roads, Va., where it later sank. At the demand of the Brazilian government, the *Wachusett*'s commander was court-martialed; the American consul at Bahia, implicated in the affair, was dismissed; and the crew of the *Florida* was released.

WAC, WAF. *See* **Women in the Military Services.**

WADE-DAVIS BILL. Passed by Congress July 2, 1864, and pocket-vetoed by President Abraham Lincoln on July 4, this bill provided that the government of a seceded state could be reorganized only after a majority of the white male citizens had taken the oath of allegiance to the United States and a constitution acceptable to the president and Congress was adopted. Rep. Henry W. Davis of Maryland and Sen. Benjamin F. Wade of Ohio, sponsors of the bill, believed along with other Radical Republicans that Reconstruction was the prerogative of Congress rather than of the president.

WADSWORTH AGREEMENT (May 25, 1923). An executive agreement signed between the United States and the principal powers allied against Germany in World War I, it provided that the net cost ($255,544,810.53) of the American Army of Occupation in the Rhineland should be paid out of Allied reparation cash receipts from Germany in twelve annual installments. Germany defaulted after the collapse of reparations in 1932.

WAGE AND PRICE CONTROLS. The U.S. government has at times imposed legal limits on wages, and on the prices of certain goods or services. During World War I, controls were clamped on rents, and an effort was made to hold other prices and wages in line. The U.S. Supreme Court agreed in a 1921 case that the federal government had the power to set maximum rents, as well as the power to set rates for public utilities such as electricity or gas. During World War II the Office of Price Administration (OPA) was created by Act of Congress (1942) and continued to work until 1946; this organization set maximum prices for goods and provided for the rationing of scarce civilian goods to the public. At the same time, wages were stabilized by a Wage Stabilization Board. Rents were also controlled, and continued under federal rule for a short time after the war. In some states and cities, rent controls continued for many years. Wage and price controls were imposed again (1951–53) during the Korean War.

Peacetime wage and price controls have been made possible by many acts of Congress, but these were "standby" powers for the President to use only in case of emergency. During the 1960's presidents John F. Kennedy and Lyndon B. Johnson used "guidelines" for the guidance of labor and large business companies on prices or wages. The guidelines were intended to prevent agreements that would push prices too high, too fast, and result in inflation. Compliance with guidelines, however, was not enforced by law, and some companies and unions chose not to cooperate. In August 1971, President Richard Nixon surprised business and labor by suddenly using his powers to "freeze" wages and prices for a 90-day period. This was followed by the creation of a board to review applications for price and wage increases, before such increases would be permitted. President Carter set up wage-price guidelines in the late 1970's; but since their acceptance was voluntary, they proved ineffective.

WAGES AND HOURS OF LABOR, REGULATION OF. The principal legislation aimed at regulating wages and hours was the Fair Labor Standards Act of 1938, passed after the wage and hour codes under the National Industrial Recovery Act were invalidated by the U.S. Supreme Court in 1935 (*Schechter* v. *United States*). The 1938 law was limited to fixing a minimum rate only. In 1981 the minimum wage was $3.35 per hour, lower than the rates actually being paid in most fields. In setting a maximum standard of forty hours per week and eight hours per day, beyond which time-and-a-half pay is required, the 1938 law established a standard that was still close to the prevailing practice in 1975. Only for employees in big-city offices and in a few fields were standard work-hour schedules currently below these levels.

At the beginning of the 19th century the number of work hours ranged upward from twelve hours a day, six days a week. Public agitation in the 1820's eventually led to a new norm of ten hours a day and sixty hours a week in most industries. After the Civil War, the eight-hour day became the focus of a national movement, and recurring efforts were made to pass federal and state laws limiting hours of work for all classes of labor. Employers vigorously resisted these efforts, and during the 19th century the courts struck down many of these laws on the grounds that they abridged freedom-to-contract rights. The first enforceable law limiting hours of work for women and children was enacted in Massachusetts in 1879.

The legal regulation of hours of labor for men followed a different course because of stronger court resistance. One widely used approach was to enact state and federal statutes limiting men's hours in specified industries, such as mining, railroads, and buses; in 1916 Congress passed the Adamson Act, which provided for the eight-hour day for operating railroad employees with time-and-a-half for overtime. Court approval for general hours legislation was secured in 1917 when the Supreme Court upheld an Oregon law establishing ten hours for most men in mills, factories, or manufacturing establishments (*Bunting* v. *Oregon*).

Government efforts to establish minimum wage standards traditionally centered on protecting women and children. These efforts were brought to a halt in 1923, when the Supreme Court ruled that such legislation deprived individuals of their freedom to contract (*Adkins* v. *Children's Hospital*). In 1937 the Supreme Court upheld the authority of the states to enact such legislation (*West Coast Hotel Company* v. *Parrish*), and in 1941 it upheld the national minimum wage law as a valid exercise of the federal power to regulate interstate commerce (*United States* v. *F. W. Darby Lumber Company*).

WAGES AND SALARIES. Wages are payments for work done on a per-piece or a time-rated basis, for which an hour is generally the basic unit. In contrast, salary rates are usually stated on a monthly basis with all months treated as if they were of equal length and contained an equal number of workdays. Salary payments are usually made monthly, and wage payments are usually made each week or each two weeks. It is often important in the case of wages to distinguish the rate from the actual earnings resulting from the rate and the time (number of units) involved, especially in seasonal businesses. The variable relationship between wage rates and actual wages received (worker earnings) is documented in the early 19th-century record of America's leading industry of that day, cotton textile manufacturing, where the workers' annual earnings had a greater fluctuation than their average daily earnings or their hourly wage rates. Between 1825 and 1860 the maximum length of the workday (April) changed from 13.52 to 11.17 hours; the minimum workday (December) fell from 12.30 to 11.00 hours.

Beginning in the 1960's inequitable wage and salary payments were offered as evidence of sexual or racial job discrimination. Little attention seems to have been given to the possibility that discrimination may have been practiced through the classification of more desirable jobs as salaried. Data of the New England cotton textile industry show only small variations in the ratio of male-female earnings in a comparison of predominantly male- and female-staffed departments over a ninety-year period, 1.04 for 1825–34 to 1.12 for 1905–14. The differing lengths of the pay periods for salaried and wage workers also reflect in some measure the degree of the worker's replaceability. Those least skilled and most easily replaced usually held jobs having the shortest pay and termination periods.

Probably the most persistent long-run change in the character of wages and salaries resulted from the conversion of payments "in kind" to payments in money. In the U.S. economy this change took place largely through the replacement of farming with employment in manufacturing and the services. Wage payments in kind also generally signified the existence of a significant personal bond between the employer and the employee. The long-run substitution of money payments for payments in kind also led to the increasing importance of distinguishing money wages from real wages. It is extremely difficult to measure with confidence, and draw satisfactory conclusions from, the long-run trends in real worker earnings; comparisons involving different time periods and price deflators of necessity juxtapose unlike groups of obtainable consumer commodities, unlike jobs performed, and personal incomes that contained unlike portions derived from wages or salaries.

WAGES-HOUR ACT. *See* **Fair Labor Standards Act.**

WAGNER ACT. *See* **National Labor Relations Act.**

WAGNER BATTERY, SIEGE OF (July 10–Sept. 6, 1863). Wagner Battery, originally known as "Neck Battery," was first built as an openwork on the south end of Morris

Island, 2,600 yards from Fort Sumter—part of the defenses of Charleston, S.C. It was never completely armed; yet, for fifty-eight days men and artillery beat off the combined efforts of Union land and naval forces, finally succumbing to Gen. Quincy A. Gillmore.

WAGNER-CROSSER RAILROAD RETIREMENT ACT. *See* **Railroad Retirement Act.**

WAGNER-STEAGALL ACT. *See* **Housing Acts.**

WAGON BOX FIGHT (Aug. 2, 1867). Sioux under Red Cloud attacked a woodcutting detail under Capt. James Powell near Fort Phil Kearny, Wyo. Thirty-two men retreated to a corral built of wagon boxes, from which they repulsed all attacks of the Sioux; seven men were killed. Powell estimated the Indian loss at 180 killed and wounded.

WAGONERS OF THE ALLEGHENIES. Transported merchandise from eastern ports to western entrepôts, returning with farm products; they rose to prominence 1810–20, before competition from the railroads. Their chief routes were the Pennsylvania Road (*see* Forbes Road) from Philadelphia to Pittsburgh and the Cumberland Road from Baltimore to Wheeling.

WAGON MANUFACTURE. In the 19th century, wagons were the products of local handcraftsmen who worked in small shops. Since wagons required iron components, shops often had smiths making and attaching iron fittings. Machine-made wheels were made by specialists, and malleable iron castings eliminated much work. By the early 1900's mechanization and specialization had reduced prices of wagons and were carried over into the automobile industry.

WAGON TRAIN CHARGE (Nov. 8, 1874). Leading a cavalry detachment from Gen. Nelson A. Miles' Indian Territory expedition, Lt. Frank D. Baldwin routed Grey Beard's camp at McClellan's Creek on the Staked Plain (Llano Estacado) of Texas, recapturing two children.

WAGON TRAINS. For protection and efficiency, traders and emigrants of the trans-Mississippi West before 1880 often gathered their wagons into trains. William L. Sublette, partner in the Rocky Mountain Fur Company, conducted a ten-wagon, mule-drawn train over the Oregon Trail to Wind River (Wyo.) between Apr. 10 and July 16, 1830, arriving back at St. Louis on Oct. 10. Capt. Benjamin L. E. Bonneville's fur-trading expedition probably took the first wagons through South Pass, in July 1832. In 1843 the "cow column" Oregon emigrant party of 1,000 brought nearly 120 wagons to the Columbia River. Joseph B. Chiles guided three wagons to California. The Stevens-Murphy-Townsend 50-person-party, in October–December of 1844, was the first to bring wagons from Missouri and through the Sierras by the California Trail, Donner Lake, and Truckee Pass; it was guided by Caleb Greenwood. William Becknell took three wagons to Santa Fe in May–July 1822; the first wagon trail from Santa Fe to southern California was marked during the Mexican War by Lt. Col. Philip St. George Cooke with his Mormon Battalion (Oct. 19, 1846–Jan. 29, 1847), by way of Guadalupe Pass, the Gila River, and Colorado Desert to San Diego. From January–June 1849, 5,516 wagons passed Fort Kearny on the Platte River, bound for California or the Columbia Valley. In 1865, 30–50 canvas-topped wagons, each bearing 4,000–7,000 pounds, drawn by five or six yoke of oxen, made up an ordinary train; others were five miles long.

With the Union Pacific–Central Pacific tramontane railway line (completed May 1869) wagon trains decreased in size. Stagecoach lines, the conquest of the Rocky Mountain and Great Plains Indians, and the far western railways built in the 1880's limited wagon trains to freighting heavy goods.

WAGON YARD. Common throughout the prairie West from 1870–1900; consisted of a square enclosed by sheds divided into stalls. One side had a grocery, feed store, and gate. Travelers cooked, ate, and slept in the camp house.

WAKARUSA WAR (Nov. 26–Dec. 7, 1855). After the murder of an antislavery settler 1,200 proslavery Missourians and Kansans assembled at Franklin on the Wakarusa River for an attack on Lawrence. Charles Robinson and James H. Lane prepared to defend the town against attack. Territorial Gov. Wilson Shannon signed a "treaty" with Lane and Robinson, conferred with proslavery leaders, and secured their reluctant acquiescence. Both parties then disbanded.

WAKE, DEFENSE OF (Dec. 8–23, 1941). Wake, a mid-Pacific atoll flanking Japanese Marshall and Mariana islands, was garrisoned by 449 marines and 68 unarmed naval personnel. Its ground defenses consisted of six 5-inch guns, twelve 3-inch antiaircraft guns, machine guns, and the marines' individual weapons. Besides its artillery, manned by the First Defense Battalion, Wake had a marine fighting squadron (VMF-211) with twelve Grumman F4F-3 fighters. The administrative base commander was navy Comd. Winfield Scott Cunningham; the defense commander was marine Maj. James P. S. Devereux. Since Wake had no radar a Japanese air onslaught destroyed seven Grummans and hit an eighth. Cannibalization and maintenance enabled VMF-211 to keep two to four fighters airborne daily against succeeding attacks through Dec. 22, when the last defending planes were shot down. Marine fighters and flak destroyed 21 Japanese aircraft and 51 others sustained damage. Wake fell on Dec. 23, after landings commanded by Rear Adm. Sadamichi Kajioka that cost the attackers two destroyers and 300 casualties in ground fighting. Eighty-one marines were killed or wounded.

WAKEFIELD. Plantation on the Potomac, in Westmoreland County, Va. George Washington was born there (1732). Bought by Augustine Washington in 1718, it adjoined lands of his grandfather, John Washington. The house burned to the ground in 1779 and was not rebuilt. The government erected a monument there in 1896. In 1923 the Wakefield National Memorial Association was organized by Mrs. H. L. Rust to build a duplicate of the birth house, to restore the graveyard holding five generations of Washingtons, and to recreate the original estate. In 1930 the federal government took over the property, now named the George Washington Birthplace National Monument. The rebuilt mansion was completed in 1931.

WALDEN. A pond near Concord, Mass. In 1854, Henry David Thoreau published eighteen essays in *Walden: or Life in the Woods,* describing his solitary life in a cabin on the shore of Walden Pond. The essays are notable for their philosophical individualism and their observations of nature.

WALDENSES. Heretical Protestant sect; originated by Peter Waldo of Lyons, France, in the 12th century. In 1893 a colony led by Matteo Prochett and Charles A. Tron purchased 5,000 acres in the North Carolina foothills, founding the town of Valdese. The settlement operated at first on a communal basis that was soon abandoned. They then developed a wine industry, hosiery mills, cotton mills, lumber plants, a bakery, and a macaroni factory.

WALDO PATENT. Embraced land from Muscongus Bay to the Penobscot River in the district of Maine. Included in the grant of James I to the Council for New England in 1620, it was transferred in 1629 to John Beauchamp and Thomas Leaverett. In 1719, the Ten Proprietors and the Twenty Associates joined the partnership, developing resources and hastening settlement. In 1729 Col. David Dunbar, the king's surveyor, challenged the rights of the associates; they granted (1731) Gen. Samuel Waldo one-half of the claim for defending their title. Waldo, returning to America, settled the land, establishing iron and lime manufactures. He increased his share to 500,000 acres and set it off in 1732 by a deed of partition. At Waldo's death in 1759 the patent fell to his children. After the Revolution four-fifths were purchased by Gen. Henry Knox. When he died (1806) the patent was divided among his creditors and broken up into small lots for sale.

WALKER EXPEDITION (1833–34). The first American trapping expedition to cross the Sierra Nevada into California. Capt. Benjamin L. E. Bonneville dispatched sixty men, under Joseph R. Walker, from Green River (Wyo.), July 24, 1833, to trap and explore between Great Salt Lake and the Pacific. Walker led his expedition down the Humboldt River to the Carson Sink and Walker Lake in western Nevada, then over the Sierra Nevada to the present Yosemite National Park. He discovered the California Big Tree (*see* Sequoia). The party also discovered the Yosemite or Hetch Hetchy valleys. Descending to the San Joaquin Valley, Walker continued to the coast. In February 1834, the party started back east, crossing the Sierras through a gap since known as Walker Pass. Walker reached Carson Sink, then rejoined Bonneville on the Bear River (Utah).

WALKER'S FILIBUSTERING EXPEDITIONS (1853–60). In 1853 William Walker, with a small force, landed in Lower California, which he proclaimed an independent republic, naming himself its president. Shortly thereafter he "annexed" neighboring Sonora. Interference of the U.S. government with the shipment of supplies soon brought this venture to an end. In 1855 Walker accepted the invitation of a revolutionary faction in Nicaragua to bring an armed force into that country. Shortly after his arrival he obtained the cooperation of the Accessory Transit Company, an American corporation, and with its aid he captured the city of Granada. Walker became commander in chief of the army. The new government was recognized by the United States in May 1856; and, in July, Walker, had himself chosen president. At that juncture he took sides against Cornelius Vanderbilt in a struggle within the transit company for its control. Vanderbilt sent agents to aid a coalition of Central American states in preventing recruits and supplies from reaching the filibusters. Cut off from all aid, Walker surrendered on May 1, 1857. to Comdr. Charles H. Davis of the U.S. Navy.

Walker made two more attempts to establish himself in Central America. In November 1857 he landed with an armed force near Greytown, Nicaragua, but he was promptly arrested by Commodore Hiram Paulding. His last attempt, in 1860, was frustrated by Capt. Norvell Salmon of the British navy, who arrested Walker on the coast of Honduras as he was making his way into Nicaragua and surrendered him to the Honduran authorities. Walker was condemned to death by a court-martial and died on Sept. 12, 1860.

WALKING DELEGATE. Important in trade unionism; either as an organizer or business agent. As an organizer, he persuades workers to join the union and demand standard wages, hours, and employment conditions. As an agent, he safeguards agreements and adjusts grievances.

WALKING PURCHASE. In 1683 the Delaware Indians deeded to William Penn a tract "as far as a man can go in a day and a half"—forty miles as walked by Penn. In 1737, the Delaware agreed to a new release of this tract. Thomas Penn employed experts, one of whom, starting near Wrightstown meetinghouse, reached the Poconos, 66 miles away. The land thus included portions of the present Bucks and Carbon counties, nine-tenths of Northampton, and a fourth of Monroe and Pike counties.

***WALK-IN-THE-WATER*.** The first steamboat to navigate the upper Great Lakes. Built by Noah Brown and named after an Indian chief, it was launched on May 28, 1818, at the Black Rock shipyard at the mouth of Scajaquada Creek (now Buffalo, N.Y.). On Aug. 23 it left port on its first voyage and stayed in service until wrecked off Buffalo on Nov. 1, 1821.

WALLACE, FORT. Built in September 1865 at the junction of Pond Creek and Smoky Hill River, south of the present town of Wallace (Kans.). Named for Gen. William H. L. Wallace, it was important during the building of the Union Pacific Railroad and the Cheyenne raids, but was abandoned in 1882.

WALLA WALLA SETTLEMENTS. Began in 1818 with an Indian trading post, Fort Nez Perce, on the bank of the Columbia River at its junction with the Walla Walla. Waiilatpu, the mission of Marcus Whitman built 20 miles upriver in October 1843, was the next white settlement. It was destroyed when the Cayuse killed Whitman, his wife, and twelve others in 1847. A new settlement nearby, known as Whitman or French Town, was inhabited by Catholic French-Canadians and half-breeds.

A few whites had settled in the Walla Walla Valley by 1855, at the time of the Indian uprising in eastern Washington (*see* Yakima Indian Wars), but were ordered out by the U.S. Indian agent. He also forced Fort Nez Perce to be abandoned at the same time. A new Fort Walla Walla, a U.S. military post, was erected in November 1856 on the site of the present city of Walla Walla. By 1859, with the end of the Yakima Indian Wars, the valley had 2,000 white settlers. In 1862 Walla Walla was incorporated, and Wallula at the mouth of Walla Walla River was laid out as a town. A connecting railroad was completed in the 1870's.

WALLOONS. French-speaking people of Celtic stock in northeast France (present-day Belgium) who became Protestant during the Reformation. Many, exiled to Holland, England, and Germany, emigrated to America in the 1620's, becoming the first colonizing settlers in New Netherland.

WALL STREET. A stockade across lower Manhattan Island, built in 1653; over the years it became the synonym for the financial interests of the United States. After the Revolution, Wall Street was the location of New York's principal merchants, of the Tontine Coffee House (an early type of life insurance association), and of Federal Hall, where President George Washington gave his inaugural address and the first Congress held its meetings. When the New York Stock Exchange was formalized in 1817, it was on Wall Street. A century later expanding business forced it to Broad Street. Other exchanges for coffee, cotton, produce, and metals were attracted to the neighborhood, as well as banks, insurance companies, shipping agencies, and corporations.

WALL STREET EXPLOSION (Sept. 16, 1920). Occurred across from the headquarters of the J. P. Morgan Company on Wall Street near the corner of Broad Street, New York City. It was believed to have been caused by a bomb carried in a one-horse wagon seen near the spot by witnesses. Horse and wagon were destroyed, and forty persons were killed.

WALNUT HILLS. *See* **Nogales, Treaty of; Vicksburg.**

WALPOLE GRANT. *See* **Grand Ohio Company; Vandalia Colony.**

WALSH-HEALY ACT (June 30, 1936). Established standards for work on federal contracts involving a purchase of supplies exceeding $10,000. The contractor must pay prevailing wages; establish a 40-hour week; employ no male under 16 or female under 18; and use no convict labor. Contractors must be manufacturers of, or regular dealers in, the materials and supplies purchased by the government.

WAMPUM. Strings of beads and shells, used to recount events, messages, treaties, or rituals. Among the Algonkin tribes, wampum was the badge of chiefly rank. The Iroquois borrowed the idea. In New Netherland it was used as a medium for exchange.

WANDERER. A ship owned by Charles A. I. Lamar and other southerners interested in reopening the African slave trade, it landed a cargo of 450 blacks near Brunswick, Ga., in December 1858. The ship was seized and sold by federal authorities, but the owners escaped punishment and the blacks were sold in Georgia and Mississippi.

WANGHIA, TREATY OF (July 3, 1844). The first Sino-American treaty; negotiated between Caleb Cushing and Commissioner Extraordinary Tsi-yeng, representative of the emperor of China. It insured extraterritorial legal rights for Americans living in China, opened five Chinese ports to U.S. merchants, and gave the United States most-favored-nation treatment. (*See* China, U.S. Relations With.)

WAPPINGER CONFEDERACY. A confederation of nine Algonkin-speaking tribes occupying the east bank of the Hudson from Poughkeepsie to Manhattan, as well as the territory extending to the Connecticut River valley. A war with Dutch settlers killed 1,600 Indians from 1640–1645. As they gradually dwindled in number, they sold their lands to the whites, and the survivors joined the Mahican and Nanticoke. They were finally merged with the Delaware.

WAR, ARTICLES OF. *See* **Uniform Code of Military Justice.**

WAR, DECLARATION OF. The Constitution places the power to declare war in the legislative branch. Modern apologists for presidential authority invoke Article I, Section 8, "Congress shall have Power . . . to declare War," as a partial basis for presidential power to initiate wars or military actions. Early Supreme Court decisions supported congressional authority. *Talbot* v. *Seeman* (1801) held that Congress's power to make war embraced specifying its dimensions. The president's obligation to observe the limitations imposed by Congress was laid down in *Little* v. *Barreme* (1804). (*See* War Powers of the President.)

WAR, LAWS OF. A branch of international law that regulates the instruments and methods of warfare. The laws cover the commencement of hostilities, their conduct, and the relations between belligerents and neutrals and consist of customary and treaty rules, national codes, and draft rules.

The Crimean War, the U.S. Civil War, and the Franco-Prussian War led to a strong movement for the codification of the laws of war. The Declaration of Paris of 1856 outlawed privateering and established clearer rules on blockades and the rights of neutral shippers. The Geneva Convention of

1864 addressed the treatment of the sick and wounded, and the 1868 Declaration of Saint Petersburg restricted small explosive and incendiary projectiles. The regulations issued at the Hague Conference (1899) led to rules signed by the United States and others. The 1907 Hague Conference codified the laws and customs of war on land and sea, set forth the duties and rights of neutrals, and dealt with the legalities of the commencement of hostilities.

World War I halted further codification of the laws of war. In the peace conferences of 1919–20 and before World War II legislative efforts focused on preventing war and amending existing laws rather than on codification. Legists revived the doctrine of the illegality of war. The Hague Conference of 1922 (not ratified by the United States) failed to restrict aerial warfare. The 1925 Geneva Protocol, which the United States ratified in 1974, outlawed chemical, gas, and bacteriological warfare. The Geneva conventions of 1929 and 1949, which the United States had ratified earlier, covered the treatment of the sick and wounded and the status of noncombatants. The Washington Disarmament Conference of 1922 and the 1936 London Protocol sought to regulate the use of submarines against merchant ships. These attempts to encompass new weapons and practices of war were incomplete and fell behind technological advances. Some felt atomic weaponry made useless codes on the treatment of the sick, wounded, and captured or the immunity of open cities.

Appended to the London Agreement of 1945, the Nuremberg Charter empowered a tribunal to prosecute crimes against peace, war crimes, and crimes against humanity (genocide and the treatment of civilians). This was reaffirmed in 1946 in United Nations Resolution 95. The United States recognized the offenses enumerated at Nuremberg and condemned genocide in principle, but it did not ratify the Genocide Convention of 1949, on the grounds that it infringed on the constitutional rights of individual nations.

Vietnam raised additional controversy over the legality of U.S. involvement, since war was not declared; the legal definition of the war (civil, guerrilla or national); the applicability of the laws of war; adherence to the laws and conventions of war; and the tactics (U.S. firepower and bombing, defoliants, and the damage to noncombatant areas).

WAR AMENDMENTS. The Thirteenth, Fourteenth, and Fifteenth amendments to the Constitution, certified as adopted on Dec. 18, 1865, July 20, 1868, and Mar. 30, 1870, respectively. They guarantee rights and privileges to Afro-Americans: freedom (the Thirteenth Amendment); citizenship (Fourteenth); and the vote (Fifteenth).

WAR AND ORDNANCE, BOARD OF. Authorized by the Continental Congress, June 12, 1776, to assume administrative control of the army. Five members of Congress and a paid secretary controlled supplies and munitions; supervised the raising, equipping, and dispatching of troops; kept a register of officers; and recorded accounts of the condition and disposition of troops. On Oct. 17, 1777, the board was reduced to three members, none a member of Congress. On Oct. 29, 1778, two members of Congress were added; on Feb. 7, 1781, a department of war was authorized; and on Oct. 30, 1781, Gen. Benjamin Lincoln was appointed secretary. The Board of War theoretically ceased to exist. Lincoln resigned Nov. 29, 1783. No successor was appointed, until Gen. Henry Knox was named, Mar. 8, 1785.

WAR BONNET CREEK, FIGHT ON (July 17, 1876). The Fifth Cavalry, under Col. Wesley Merritt, at War Bonnet Creek (now Hat Creek at Montrose, Nebr.), intercepted Cheyenne fleeing from the Red Cloud Agency, Camp Robinson, and prevented them from joining Sitting Bull. William F. Cody ("Buffalo Bill") opened the fight by killing Yellow Hand (Hay-o-wei, or Yellow Hair). The Indians were driven back to the reservation.

WAR CRIMES TRIALS (Nov. 1945–Oct. 1946). At Nuremberg, Germany, surviving Nazi leaders were tried before an international tribunal as war criminals charged with violating international law, waging aggressive warfare, and committing "crimes against humanity." Nineteen of twenty-two high officials were found guilty. Twelve, including Hermann Göring, Joachim von Ribbentrop, and Artur von Seyss-Inquart, were sentenced to death. Eight were eventually hanged. Comparable trials of Japanese leaders held at Tokyo, from May 1946 to November 1948, had similar results.

WAR DEMOCRATS. The Democratic wing in the North that supported the Union during the Civil War.

WAR DEPARTMENT. Civilian agency created in 1789 to administer the army. After the War of 1812 Secretary of War John C. Calhoun reorganized the department into bureaus, with a commanding field general. Bureau chiefs advised the secretary and commanded troops. Congress regulated the bureaus. In 1903 Secretary Elihu Root appointed a general staff. His successor, William Howard Taft, returned to the secretary–bureau chief alliance, subordinating the chief of staff to the adjutant general. In 1911 Secretary Henry L. Stimson and Maj. Gen. Leonard Wood, his chief of staff, sought to organize the army along modern lines. The bureau chiefs and Congress struck back in the National Defense Act (1916), reducing the size and functions of the general staff.

During World War I, Secretary Newton D. Baker reorganized the army's supply system and practically wiped out the bureaus. They regained their former independence after the war. The chiefs of staff gained authority over them by 1939, when Gen. George C. Marshall assumed that office. Marshall created the Army Ground Forces; the Army Air Forces; and the Army Service Forces, for administrative and logistical operations. The Operations Division acted as Marshall's general planning staff.

Under the National Security Act of 1947, amended in 1949, the War Department became the Department of the Army within the Department of Defense and the secretary of the army an operating manager for the new secretary of defense.

WARD LEADER. A ward, precinct, or assembly district official elected or appointed to maximize voter turnout in support of his party's candidates. Nonelectoral functions include maintaining the party cadre between elections and aiding citizens seeking governmental action.

***WARE V. HYLTON*, 3 Dallas 199 (1797).** The question was whether a Virginia statute sequestering prewar debts owed to the British or allowing payment in depreciated currency took precedence over a treaty with Great Britain. The U.S. Supreme Court ruled that a national treaty stood above state law.

WAR FINANCE CORPORATION. Created by Congress on Apr. 5, 1918, to facilitate the extension of credit to vital war industries, through loans to financial institutions. In six months it advanced $71,387,222. After World War I the corporation's charter was greatly expanded. In 1919 it financed agricultural exports, and in 1921 initiated nationwide loan agencies for agricultural and livestock industries. The Agricultural Credits Act (1923) terminated the corporation.

WAR HAWKS. Term applied to members of the Twelfth Congress (1811–13) who advocated the War of 1812. Their leaders, chiefly from regions least affected by British interference with "free trade and sailors' rights," saw concrete advantages in war. Northwesterners held the British responsible for their Indian troubles and expected to drive the British from Canada. Southerners planned to wrest Florida from Spain, England's ally.

WAR INDUSTRIES BOARD. Agency formed in 1917 to mobilize industry, fix prices, and raise the volume of munitions. It was terminated by executive order on Jan. 1, 1919.

WAR LABOR BOARD (1918–19). Created by President Woodrow Wilson on Apr. 8, 1918, to secure voluntary, peaceful arbitration of industrial disputes. The board's decisions depended on cooperation by employers and employees and on public opinion. It's principles included abandonment of strikes and lockouts, the right of collective bargaining, adjustment by conciliation and mediation, maximum production, determination of wages and hours in accordance with prevailing local standards, and the right to a living wage.

WAR OF 1812. Provoked by Great Britain's maritime policy in its war with Napoleon and by its overfriendly relations with the Indian tribes of the Northwest. The war was facilitated by the desire of the West and South to secure possession of Canada and Florida.

Neither England nor France paid much heed to the rights of neutrals. Napoleon sought to exclude neutral ships from all trade with Great Britain; the British forbade neutral ships to trade with France or with French dependencies except after touching at English ports. U.S. ships, by conforming to the demands of one nation, were subject to confiscation by the other. Great Britain also "impressed" from U.S. ships deserters from the Royal Navy or other British subjects liable to naval service. U.S. citizens were frequently victims.

In 1807, when the *Leopard* fired on the U.S.S. *Chesapeake* and removed three U.S. citizens, Congress passed the Embargo Act (1807) forbidding the departure from U.S. ports of all vessels not engaged in coastwise trade. The embargo proved more injurious to the United States than to France and England, and was repealed (March 1809); the subsequent Nonintercourse Act forbade trade with the offending powers. Macon's Bill No. 2 (May 1810) reopened trade, but promised that if either England or France revoked its measures, nonintercourse would be revived against the other.

Napoleon persuaded President James Madison to reinstitute nonintercourse against Great Britain (November 1810). When Britain refused to modify its policy, Madison recommended that Congress prepare for hostilities (Nov. 5, 1811).

To the Twelfth Congress, British crimes were not confined to the high seas. The West had grievances not felt along the seaboard (*see* War Hawks). In Ohio and the Indiana, Illinois, and Michigan territories, Indians, led by Shawnee chief Tecumseh, seemed disposed to unite against further encroachments on their lands. Sympathetic British agents in Canada sent Tecumseh arms; the British were also thought to be inciting the Indians. When an army under Gen. William Henry Harrison, governor of Indiana Territory, suffered severe losses in an Indian attack near Tippecanoe (Nov. 7, 1811), the Northwest held the British responsible and demanded their expulsion from Canada. This demand was balanced by a southwestern and southern demand for East and West Florida, Spanish provinces coveted for their strategic position, navigable rivers, and the harborage they gave to Indians and runaway slaves. The United States had long claimed a portion of West Florida as part of the Louisiana Purchase, and had begun absorbing it piecemeal (*see* Baton Rouge, Seizure of). Spain's alliance with Great Britain offered an excuse for seizing both provinces.

On June 4, 1812, the House declared war; the Senate approved on June 17; and Madison on June 18. Congressional trifling, few and ill-trained troops, military incompetence, and defective strategy led to early defeats. In the first year Gen. William Hull surrendered at Detroit (Aug. 16), generals Stephen Van Rensselaer and Alexander Smyth failed on the Niagara River (*see* Niagara Campaigns), as did Gen. Henry Dearborn at Lake Champlain (November). The next year saw the recovery of Detroit and a British defeat at the Thames (Oct. 5) by Harrison, but closed with Gen. James Wilkinson's failure against Montreal (Nov. 11), the capture of Fort Niagara (Dec. 18), and the burning of Buffalo, N.Y., by the British (Dec. 29–30). By the summer of 1814, British veterans were present in such force that U.S. troops hoped only to hold their own. Hard fighting at Chippewa (July 5, 1814), Lundy's Lane (July 25), and Fort Erie (Aug. 2–Sept. 1) demonstrated U.S. prowess but conquered no territory.

Meanwhile, a British army burned Washington, D.C. (Aug. 24–25), but failed to take Baltimore (Sept. 12–14). Troops advancing from Montreal reached Plattsburgh, N.Y., on Lake Champlain, but retreated when the accompanying fleet was destroyed (*see* Macdonough's Lake Champlain

Fleet). At New Orleans on Jan. 8, 1815 (two weeks after the signing of the peace treaty), Gen. Andrew Jackson inflicted on British Gen. Edward Pakenham the most crushing defeat of the war.

The Sioux of the Mississippi Valley, who traded with the English, favored them. The Sioux of the Missouri Valley favored the Americans. The Yanktonai, ranging from Big Stone Lake to the Missouri River, supported the English. In 1811 Capt. William Clark, western commissioner of Indian affairs, sent Manuel Lisa to the upper Missouri to build a post; it was ready in October 1812.

On Mar. 10, 1813, the united tribes burned the fort, killing fifteen. Lisa escaped with the remnants of his men and wares, and at Cedar Island, below the present Pierre, N.D., established a camp for the Missouri Sioux.

Victories on Lake Erie (September 1813) and Lake Champlain (September 1814) led to U.S. control of those waterways, but the British tightened its blockade on the coast.

In November 1812, the British instructed Adm. John B. Warren to blockade the Chesapeake and Delaware bays. The blockade extended to New York, Charleston, Port Royal, S.C., Savannah, and the mouth of the Mississippi in the spring of 1813; Long Island Sound in November 1813; and the entire eastern seaboard in May 1814.

The British maintained at least ten ships and many frigates and sloops. Only rarely did a U.S. vessel get through, and trade nearly ceased. Only Georgia, by way of Spanish Florida, and New England, up to the summer of 1814, could export. Exports from Virginia fell from $4.8 million in 1811 to $17,581 in 1814. New York and Philadelphia suffered too. The war ruined farmers and forced the suspension of specie payments by all banks south of New England by the early fall of 1814. Imports also declined, save through the favored New England ports; revenue from import duties, more than $13 million in 1811, were less than $6 million in 1814, and from the ports south of New England fell near zero.

U.S. and British peace commissioners met at Ghent in the summer of 1814. The British accepted the peace *status quo ante bellum* as to territory. Britain's right to navigate the Mississippi and the U.S. right to inshore fishing on British North American coasts lapsed. The Treaty of Ghent, signed Dec. 24, 1814, was ratified unanimously by the Senate.

WAR ON POVERTY. Begun in 1964 as a key to President Lyndon B. Johnson's "Great Society," the program aimed to reduce national poverty through government aid programs.

WAR OPPOSITION ORGANIZATIONS. *See* **Peace Movements.**

WAR POWERS ACT. *See* **War Powers of the President.**

WAR POWERS OF THE PRESIDENT. The president can initiate and wage wars; for authority he relies on his constitutional designation as commander in chief, his obligation to faithfully execute the law, and the "executive power" vested in his office. Congress is empowered to declare war, but presidents have often committed the armed forces to conflict. Only five of eleven wars have been declared by Congress: the War of 1812, the Mexican War, the Spanish-American War, and the two world wars.

Nuclear weapons establish the president as chief field commander. He alone decides when to use them, as Harry S. Truman did against Japan. In the 1962 Cuban missile crisis, John F. Kennedy, after imposing a blockade, was kept apprised of the whereabouts of approaching Soviet vessels and personally gave the order to board them.

The power to wage war gives the president many choices. He can direct military campaigns, as Abraham Lincoln did in the Civil War; reduce or terminate hostilities, as Lyndon B. Johnson did in North Vietnam in 1968; or launch major policies as Franklin D. Roosevelt did to dispatch economic and military aid to the Allies in World War II.

The Vietnam War led to the War Powers Act (1973), which requires the president to report emergency military action to Congress within 48 hours. Combat action must end in 60 days, unless Congress authorizes the commitment. The deadline can be extended for 30 days. Congress can order immediate removal of the forces by adopting a resolution not subject to presidential veto.

WAR PRIZES. *See* **Prize Cases, Civil War; Prize Courts; Prize Money.**

WARREN, FORT FRANCIS E. Established in 1867 in Cheyenne, Wyo., to protect the Union Pacific Railway against attacks from the Cheyenne, Nez Perce, and Sioux. Originally named after Gen. David A. Russell, the fort's name was changed in 1929 to honor Francis E. Warren, U.S. senator from Wyoming.

WARREN COMMISSION. Appointed on Nov. 29, 1963, by President Lyndon B. Johnson to report on the assassination of President John F. Kennedy. Chief Justice Earl Warren headed it. Other members were Sen. Richard B. Russell of Georgia; Sen. John Sherman Cooper of Kentucky; Rep. Hale Boggs of Louisiana; Rep. Gerald R. Ford of Michigan; Allen W. Dulles, former director of the Central Intelligence Agency (CIA); and John J. McCloy, former president of the World Bank and adviser to Kennedy. The commission and its staff reviewed reports by the Federal Bureau of Investigation (FBI) and other agencies, and weighed the testimony of witnesses. Its report of Sept. 24, 1964, concluded that Lee Harvey Oswald acted alone, that Jack Ruby alone murdered Oswald, and that neither was part of a conspiracy. The commission investigated myths and rumors concerning the number, origin, and direction of the shots; the number of assassins; and the possible connections between Oswald and the FBI, the CIA, and the Soviet and Cuban governments. It criticized the FBI and the Secret Service for inadequately protecting the president and poorly coordinating their information. Published as *Report of the President's Commission on the Assassination of President John F. Kennedy,* it aroused great controversy.

WARREN'S TRADING POSTS. Abel Warren established at least three trading posts on the Red River between present-day Texas and Oklahoma. The first, established in 1836, was in Fannin County, Texas; the second, maintained from 1837 to 1848, was near Walnut Creek, in the present Love County, Okla.; and the third (established 1848) was maintained for a while near Cache Creek, in the present Cotton County, Okla.

WARRIORS PATH, GREAT. The war road between the Shawnee and Wyandot of the Ohio country and the Catawba and Cherokee of western North Carolina ran along what is now eastern Kentucky, past the upper Blue Licks (Licking River) and the Red River branch of the Kentucky River to the Cumberland Gap. It passed down Powell Valley and crossed the Clinch and Holston rivers. There it divided, going east to the Catawba towns, and west across the Nolichuckey and the French Broad rivers to the Overhill Cherokee towns. The path was mentioned in 1750 by Thomas Walker in his western explorations (*see* Loyal Land Company).

WARS AND CAMPAIGNS, INDIAN. Indian wars and campaigns before the Civil War cannot be grouped conveniently. After the war they fall into three classifications: wars of the Great Plains, the Southwest, and the Northwest. Important wars and campaigns are as follows:

1790–95 Northwestern Indian War (Ohio)
1811–13 Northwestern Indian War (Indiana)
1812 Seminole War (Florida)
1813 Peoria War (Illinois)
1813–14 Creek War (Georgia, Alabama, Mississippi, Tennessee)
1817–18 Seminole War (Florida, Georgia)
1823 Arikara and Blackfoot War (Missouri River region, Dakota Territory)
1832 Black Hawk War (Illinois, Wisconsin)
1835–42 Seminole War (Florida, Georgia, Alabama)
1836–37 Creek War (Georgia, Alabama)
1836–37 Sabine, or Southwestern, War (Louisiana)
1847–50 Cayuse War (Oregon)
1849–61 Campaigns against the Navaho, Comanche, Cheyenne, Lipan, and Kickapoo (Texas, New Mexico)
1850–53 Utah Indian War
1851–52 California Indian War
1851–56 Rogue River War against the Yakima, Klikitat, Klamath, and Salmon River tribes (Oregon, Washington)
1855–56 Campaign against the Sioux, Cheyenne, and Arapaho
1855–58 Seminole War (Florida)
1857 Campaign against the Sioux (Minnesota, Iowa)
1858 Campaign against the Northern Indians (Washington Territory)
1858 Campaign against the Spokane, Coeur d'Alene, and Paloo (Washington Territory)
1858 Campaign against the Navaho (New Mexico)
1858–59 Campaign against the Wichita (Indian Territory)
1861–90 Apache Wars, including campaigns against Victorio and Geronimo
1862–67 Sioux War (Minnesota, Dakota Territory)
1863–70 Campaigns against the Cheyenne, Arapaho, Kiowa, and Comanche (Kansas, Colorado, Indian Territory)
1865–68 Northwestern Indian War (Oregon, Idaho, California, Nevada)
1867–81 Campaigns against the Lipan, Kiowa, Kickapoo, and Comanche
1872–73 Modoc War (Oregon)
1874–75 Campaigns against the Cheyenne, Arapaho, Kiowa, Comanche, and Sioux (Kansas, Colorado, Texas, New Mexico, Indian Territory)
1874–79 Campaigns against the Sioux and Cheyenne (Wyoming, Nebraska, Dakotas, Nevada, Montana, Indian Territory, Kansas)
1877 Nez Perce War (Utah)
1878 Bannock War—Bannock, Paiute, Shoshone (Idaho, Washington, and Wyoming territories)
1878 Campaign against the Ute (Colorado)
1879 Campaign against the Sheepeater (Idaho)
1879–80 Campaigns against the Ute (Colorado, Utah)
1890–91 Sioux Campaign (South Dakota)
1895 Campaign against the Bannock
1898 Campaign against the Chippewa (Leech Lake, Minn.)

WARSHIPS.

Sailing Warships. On Oct. 13, 1775, the Continental Congress had two merchantmen converted to warships. Frigates, brigs, sloops, and schooners were also constructed or bought, giving the Continental Navy a total of 340. After independence, the United States sold them all. In 1794, Barbary pirates caused the building of six frigates. In 1798–1800, during the Quasi-War with France, the U.S. frigate *Constellation,* commanded by Commodore Thomas Truxtun, defeated the *Insurgente* (Feb. 9, 1799) and the *Vengeance* (Feb. 1–2, 1800). In the Barbary Wars, 1801–05 and 1815, U.S. ships won again. In the War of 1812 the U.S. *Constitution* (Capt. Isaac Hull) defeated the *Guerrière* (Aug. 19, 1812) and the *United States* (Commodore Stephen Decatur) defeated the *Macedonian* (Oct. 25, 1812). Changes in technology caused the demise of sailing warships. In 1817 the navy listed 110 sailing ships and one steamer; in 1845, when the Mexican War began, 67 sailing ships and 9 steamers. After the Civil War, only 109 of 681 ships were sail. By the 1870's the era of the sailing warships was over.

Steam and Nuclear Warships. The first steam warship, the *Demologos,* was designed by Robert Fulton in the War of 1812. Then came the frigate *Fulton,* launched in 1837. Naval experts were skeptical about steamers. The large paddle wheels seemed vulnerable and limited space for broadside batteries. When the screw propeller replaced the paddle wheel the frigate *Princeton,* launched in 1843, was fitted with the new device. By the Civil War the United States had 20 wooden, screw-propelled men-of-war. The battle between the ironclads C.S.S. *Virginia* (actually the captured Union *Merrimack*) and the U.S.S. *Monitor* at Hampton Roads in 1862 was the first between armored ships and between two powered only by steam. During 1860–90 armor improved in quality, guns increased in power, mines became more reliable, and the self-propelled torpedo was perfected.

After 1865 the U.S. navy consisted of old wooden cruisers and obsolete monitors. Congress appropriated money for new warships in 1883, when the modern steel cruisers *Atlanta, Boston,* and *Chicago,* and a dispatch boat, the *Dolphin,* formed the nucleus of the "New Navy."

By the Spanish-American War (1898) the United States had four battleships, three other armored ships, and over 20 cruisers, gunboats, and torpedo boats. The war increased the number of battleships to 16, but all were made obsolete by the new British *Dreadnought.* It was faster, larger, and carried guns of the largest caliber. The first U.S. all-big-gun ships, the *South Carolina* and *Michigan,* were completed in 1910.

Other ships were the heavy cruiser, developed during World War I, a fast, lightly armored ship of 10,000 tons, with 8-inch guns, used for scouting, patrolling, and raiding commerce; the light cruiser, smaller and mounted with 6-inch guns; and the destroyer, 1,000 to 2,000 tons, with torpedoes and 4- or 5-inch guns, invaluable against submarines.

Between the two world wars came the aircraft carrier; its chief weapons were bombers that took off and landed from its deck. In World War II aircraft carriers facilitated battles between fleets hundreds of miles apart. The first nuclear submarine was the U.S.S. *Nautilus*, built in 1954. Nuclear power made warships faster, more reliable, and free of their bases. In the 1960's the U.S.S. *Enterprise,* a carrier, the *Long Beach,* a cruiser, and the *Bainbridge,* a destroyer, were completed. In the 1950's, missiles replaced guns on large ships. A typical warship of the 1970's carried antisubmarine and antiaircraft missiles in addition to, or instead of, guns.

Battleships. During the Revolution ordinary ships were converted to warships. But increases in the size and power of cannon necessitated the thickening of a warship's hull, raising its cost steeply. Only a nation could afford warships, so converted merchantmen were used for privateering or raiding. By 1900 "battleship" had its present meaning and was sometimes listed as a "capital ship." After 1928 capital ships included aircraft carriers. The United States had only ten modern vessels by World War II. All had 16-inch main batteries. Six of the vessels displaced 35,000 tons: the 1940–41 *North Carolina, Washington, Alabama, Indiana, Massachusetts,* and *South Dakota;* four others displaced 45,000 tons: *Iowa, Missouri, New Jersey,* and *Wisconsin.* After World War II, some served during the Korean and Vietnam wars.

Cruisers. During the era of wooden ships, cruisers sailed along trade routes to attack or defend merchantmen. Ships of the line (the largest ships) sometimes served as cruisers, but more often frigates and smaller men-of-war were used. With steam, horizontal shellfire, and armor, classifications were jumbled. Unarmored ships became popular for defense, and cruisers evolved into warships rated just below the battleship.

The first U.S. cruisers by type were designed in 1882: the 4,500-ton *Chicago* and the 3,000-ton *Atlanta* and *Boston.* At 14 knots, the *Chicago,* with an 8-inch rifled main battery, and the others, with 6-inch main batteries, could overtake merchantmen and evade battleships. The *Chicago,* a prototype of the heavy cruiser, was classed "CA." Later CAs kept 8-inch guns, adding belt armor, gun turrets, and control positions. The light cruiser (CL) had 5- or 6-inch guns and equivalent armor.

Naval architects sought more speed: the 1889 *Charleston* made 19 knots, the 1904 *Charleston* 22, and the 1942 *Rochester* 33. The 1889 *Charleston* was 3,730 tons and the 1904 9,700. World War I classes were 14,000 tons. In World War II the 8-inch guns of America's 32 heavy cruisers were used in shore bombardments. They used their secondary batteries for antiaircraft fire, as did the 42 light cruisers. The *Atlanta* and *Juneau* (five-inch, 38-gun light cruisers) were designed as antiaircraft vessels. In 1973 heavy cruisers were the largest gunships in commission.

Destroyers. With the invention by Robert Whitehead of England of a self-propelled torpedo in 1868 came speedboats capable of using them. By 1884 Russia had 138, Britain 130, and France 107. In the United States, Congress authorized the *Ericsson,* completed in 1897; it had three 18-inch torpedo tubes, four 1-pounder quick firers, a crew of 22, and could do 24 knots. Its hull was 150 feet by 15.5 feet, drawing 4 feet 9 inches and displacing 120 tons. The 1900 *Decatur* had two 18-inch tubes, two 3-inch guns, and a crew of 73 doing 28 knots in a hull 250 feet long, 24 feet wide, and drawing 6.5 feet, displacing 450 tons. A second *Decatur,* used during World War II, had four 18-inch tubes, four 4-inch and two 3-inch guns, and 126 men, did 36 knots, was 314 feet long, and weighed 1,190 tons. The 1956 *Decatur* had additional armament for antisubmarine attack, three 5-inch and four 3-inch guns, and 311 men, did 33 official knots, and displaced 3,800 tons. Experimentation in the 1970's with hydrofoils, "surface effects," and "captured air bubbles" and possibilities of speeds in excess of 100 knots did not alter the destroyers' multiple roles. The United States had 267 destroyers in World War I and none were lost. Of the 459 destroyers used in World War II, 71 were lost, plus 11 of 498 destroyer escorts.

Frigates. Frigates repeated signals from the flagship, towed disabled ships, and rescued survivors. A heavy frigate carried 38 to 44 long guns, usually 18- or 24-pounders. It had up to 12 short-range guns, called carronades, which fired up to 68-pounder shot; their range was under 300 yards. A light frigate had from 24 to 36 long guns, 12- or 18-pounders. The first U.S. frigates were sturdier than Britian's and were heavily armed.

"Patrol frigate" designates convoy escorts larger than destroyer escorts. The 100 built during World War II had a 17,000-mile-range at 11 knots.

In 1975 an American frigate had the displacement of a World War II light cruiser, might be nuclear powered, and was armed with missiles.

WAR TRADE BOARD. Created by President Woodrow Wilson, Oct. 12, 1917. Control over imports and exports was vested in the agency. Its board had representatives of the

State, Treasury, Agriculture, and Commerce departments, and of the food administrator and the chairman of the U.S. Shipping Board, with Vance C. McCormick as the chairman. The duties and functions of the board were transferred to the Department of State on July 1, 1919.

WARWICK. *See* **Shawomet.**

WARWICK COMMISSION. Established 1643 to control colonial affairs after the Puritan Revolution in England; headed by Robert Rich, Earl of Warwick, governor in chief and lord high admiral of the colonies. Despite extensive powers, it interfered little with the colonies, ignoring most disputes. It granted Rhode Island a charter (Mar. 24, 1644). In 1649, the Commonwealth in England revoked its powers.

WARWICK PATENT. *See* **Connecticut, Old Patent of.**

WASHAKIE, FORT. An army post (1869–1909) maintained for the protection of the Shoshone on the Wild River reservation near Lander, Wyo. It was called Camp Augur in 1869, Camp Brown in 1870, and in 1878 Fort Washakie, after the Shoshone chief.

WASHINGTON, D.C. In 1791 President George Washington chose land on the peninsula formed by the Potomac and the Anacostia rivers for the Federal City.

Pierre Charles L'Enfant designed broad avenues radiating from public buildings, and monuments. Pennsylvania Avenue connected the Capitol and the president's house, and there was a 400-foot-wide avenue (later the Mall) between the Capitol and a planned equestrian statue of Washington (the site of the Washington Monument). L'Enfant objected to the commissioners' public sale of city lots, and was dismissed in 1792. His plan was imperfectly followed, and for decades the city was a blend of large public buildings, broad dusty avenues, and empty fields with private constructions. Nevertheless, by 1800 building had progressed far enough to allow the government to move there from Philadelphia.

The city charter of 1802 stated that citizens could elect a council; the council chose the mayor. During 1820–1871 the mayor was elected. The Constitution empowered Congress "to exercise exclusive Legislation" over the District of Columbia; its citizens had no federal vote (*see* District of Columbia). A nonvoting delegate was elected to Congress from 1871–1874; the city had a governor, council, and boards of health and public works appointed by the president after conflicts with Congress and post–Civil War urban problems led to federal control. In 1874 Congress established a commission form of government. Under the Organic Act (1878) three presidentially appointed commissioners, along with boards and federal agencies, governed the city under the District Committees of the Senate and House. The Board of Trade (founded in 1889) furthered civic progress but blocked reforms.

In 1967 Congress instituted a "mayor-commissioner," a deputy, and a nine-member council appointed by the president. Congress in 1970 again allowed a delegate to Congress, still without voting power. In 1973 Congress allowed Washington to elect its own mayor, a 13-member council, and neighborhood councils. The council had legislative authority, subject to congressional veto, and Congress kept budget approval.

Washington's real estate was usurped by streets, public buildings, and monuments. A transient population of congressmen and government officials caused further problems, especially in the 19th century. The population grew rapidly from 61,122 in 1860 to 131,700 in 1870; to 437,571 by 1920; and to 802,178 in 1950. After 1950 government agencies and research and development firms moved to Maryland and Virginia. The metropolitan population was 2,861,123 in 1970, but in the city it dropped to 756,510.

In 1860, 18 percent of the city was black. After the Emancipation Proclamation of 1863 (district slaves were freed in 1862) the black population grew. The city could not handle it and did not enforce laws against discrimination. Many whites welcomed the loss of home rule in 1871 since it nullified black suffrage. The black community, one-third of the population until 1950, developed its own culture, aided by Howard University, founded in 1867 as a biracial institution. In 1934, the Alley Dwelling Authority began effective slum clearance, halted by World War II. The District of Columbia Redevelopment Act (1945) continued the effort. Discrimination in government hiring abated in the 1930's and after World War II. The Fair Housing Ordinance was passed for Washington in 1962. Nearly 70 percent of the population was black in 1967, as were the mayor and five of the nine members of the District Council.

"Boss" Alexander R. Shepherd, appointed territorial governor by President Ulysses S. Grant in 1873, built adequate water and sewer facilities, paved streets, and planted trees at a huge cost. The McMillan Commission (1901), led by Michigan Sen. James McMillan and including C. F. McKim, Augustus Saint-Gaudens, and Frederick Law Olmsted, provided guidelines for development continued by the Fine Arts Commission (1910) and the National Capital Park and Planning Commission (1926). In 1926 Congress launched projects including the Federal Triangle. Important buildings are the Washington Monument (completed 1884), the Lincoln Memorial (1922), the Jefferson Memorial (1943), the Smithsonian Institution (1846), the National Gallery of Art (1941), the Kennedy Center for the Performing Arts (1971), the Capitol (begun 1793; dome completed 1863), and the White House (begun 1792).

Washington, D.C., houses the headquarters of professional, trade, and labor organizations; government agencies and research facilities are there. It is also the site of protests and demonstrations, such as Coxey's Army of unemployed workers from Ohio in 1894, the Poor People's Campaign and Resurrection City of 1968, and demonstrations during the Vietnam War.

WASHINGTON, D.C., BURNING OF (Aug. 24–25, 1814). Authorized by British Vice Adm. Alexander Cochrane as a response to depredations in Canada, and to demoralize the U.S. government during the War of 1812. British regulars routed militia at Bladensburg, Md., Aug. 24. That evening, they invaded Washington. Troops burned the Capitol, the

White House, and the Treasury, reducing to ruins the departments of state and war, private dwellings, two ropewalks, a tavern, printing establishments, and naval structures and supplies.

WASHINGTON, FORT (N.Y.). Built during the Revolution, at the upper end of Manhattan Island, to guard the Hudson. On Nov. 16, 1776, it surrendered to the British.

WASHINGTON, FORT (Ohio). Built in 1789 at Cincinnati, to protect settlements; the base for expeditions against the Indians around the Wabash and the Maumee. After Gen. Anthony Wayne defeated the Indians at the Battle of Fallen Timbers, Aug. 20, 1794, the importance of Fort Washington declined. It was abandoned in 1804.

WASHINGTON, STATE OF. The region was probably first seen by explorers Juan Pérez in 1774 and Bruno Heceta in 1775. In 1778 James Cook reached Nootka Sound. In 1792 Robert Gray, a Boston sea captain and trader, discovered the Columbia River and the English explorer George Vancouver mapped Puget Sound and related waters. In 1792–93 Alexander Mackenzie of the North West Fur Company led an expedition to the Pacific across what is now British Columbia. Meriwether Lewis and William Clark in 1803–06 went from St. Louis to the Columbia and back. David Thompson, explorer, geographer, and trader for the North West Company, built a trading post on the Spokane River in 1810. John Jacob Astor's Pacific Fur Company established Astoria on the lower Columbia in 1811; in 1813 the post was sold to the North West Company, which in 1821 combined with the Hudson's Bay Company. The Hudson's Bay Company established the Columbia District, which dominated the fur trade and exploited lumber, fish, and farming resources.

After 1818 Great Britain and the United States held Oregon Country jointly. In 1846, the Oregon Treaty set the U.S. boundary between Vancouver Island and the mainland. Missionaries came in the 1830's, and in the early 1840's settlers organized a government in the Willamette Valley. Congress in 1848 created the Oregon Territory. In 1853 Washington Territory was created. Ten years later, Washington obtained its present boundaries. In the 1850's sawmills were built around Puget Sound for lumber, piling, and ship timber. Mining rushes increased the population, but development was slowed by Indian troubles in 1856–59. Forests, which made Washington the leading U.S. lumber producer for 40 years in the 20th century, salmon runs in the Columbia River, and the minerals and extensive grasslands brought settlers in the 1860's and 1870's. Others came in the 1870's and 1880's to the wheatlands around Walla Walla and in the Palouse country. The population grew with the completion of the Northern Pacific Railroad in 1883: in 1880 it was 75,116; in 1890, 357,222. The Grand Coulee Dam (completed 1942) provided hydroelectric power and water for the Columbia basin. Wheat, fruit, and dairy products continue to represent the major farm production.

In 1889 Washington was admitted to the Union by the Omnibus Bill, which also admitted North Dakota, South Dakota, and Montana. The first forty years of statehood saw the adoption of such progressive measures as the direct primary (1907), woman's suffrage (1910), workmen's compensation (1911), and the initiative, referendum, and recall (1913). The Industrial Workers of the World (IWW) enlisted support in the logging camps and the harvest fields and played a part in the unsuccessful Seattle General Strike of 1919.

Extensive shipbuilding during World War I, the rise of the Boeing Company as a manufacturer of airplanes, extensive dam building on the Columbia for hydroelectric power, and construction by the federal government of the Hanford Atomic Works during World War II were the major economic developments of the 20th century. The population in 1980 was 4,130,163.

WASHINGTON, TREATY OF (May 8, 1871). The amicable settlement of the Alabama Claims and other differences between the United States and Great Britain.

In January 1871, London financier John Rose and Secretary of State Hamilton Fish made arrangements with the British minister, Sir Edward Thornton, for submission to a joint high commission of the questions of the Alabama Claims, the rights of American fishermen in Canadian waters, and the water boundary between British Columbia and the state of Washington. The treaty made explicit the impropriety of vessels constructed, equipped, and armed as the *Alabama* had been and dealt with the use of neutral territory by belligerent vessels.

WASHINGTON AND LEE UNIVERSITY. Founded at Lexington, Va., (1749) as Augusta Academy, it was called Liberty Hall in 1776 and chartered as Liberty Hall Academy in 1782. After George Washington's gift of shares in the James River Company it was changed to Washington Academy (1798) and to Washington College in 1813. Robert E. Lee became president in 1865, and one year after his death (1870), it became Washington and Lee University.

WASHINGTON BENEVOLENT SOCIETY. Founded in New York in 1808 to strengthen the Federalist party, it spread into New England. It was charged with corrupting elections by gifts or intimidation, was discredited by its disloyal criticism of James Madison's administration, and later disappeared.

WASHINGTON DISTRICT. In 1775, the settlers in the Tennessee country on the Watauga and Nolichuckey rivers organized a committee of safety. They assumed for their region the name of Washington District—the first territorial division in America to be named for Gen. George Washington. In July 1776, the inhabitants sent a petition to North Carolina asking to be placed under its protection. On Aug. 22, the petition was granted and the western settlers were granted a county form of government.

WASHINGTON ELM. The tree under which George Washington took command of the U.S. army on July 3, 1775, on Cambridge Common in Massachusetts. It fell in 1924.

WASHINGTON MONUMENT. Erected in Washington, D.C., to honor George Washington, on the Mall between the

Capitol and the Lincoln Memorial. Designed by Robert Mills, it was completed in 1884. At 555 feet, 5 1/8 inches, it was long the highest masonry structure in the world. Elevators within the shaft rise to 500 feet. Congress granted the site in 1848; in 1860, the structure reached 156 feet, then stopped for lack of funds. Work resumed in 1876. The aluminum capstone was set in place on Dec. 6, 1884, and the monument opened to the public in 1888.

WASHINGTON NAVAL CONFERENCE (1921–22). Called by the United States to deal with the arms race and security in the Pacific. The major treaties drafted and signed were: the Four-Power Treaty, in which the United States, Great Britain, France, and Japan promised to respect each others' possessions in the Pacific; another Big Four treaty, in which each country agreed to consult the others in the event of aggression by another power; the Five-Power Naval Treaty, which put a ten-year holiday on ship construction and fixed the ratio of ship tonnage between the Big Four and Italy; and the Nine-Power Treaty, in which all of the conference participants (the Big Four, Italy, Portugal, China, Belgium, and the Netherlands) affirmed the Open Door principle for China and agreed to respect its independence. A fifth treaty restricted submarine use during war and outlawed poison gases. Other treaties dealt with Chinese sovereignty and U.S. and Japanese cable rights in the Pacific.

WASHINGTON PEACE CONVENTION. *See* **Border Slave State Convention.**

WASHINGTON'S EIGHT MONTHS ARMY. Organized after the battles of Lexington and Concord (Apr. 18–19, 1775). Massachusetts asked the other New England colonies to help create an army of 30,000, but it never exceeded 20, 000. It fought at Bunker Hill, and on July 2, George Washington took command. The army blockaded Boston and detachments manned the navy. Enlistments expired on Dec. 31 and Washington reenlisted the troops.

WASHINGTON'S FAREWELL ADDRESS (first published on Sept. 19, 1796). Set forth George Washington's reasons for not running for a third term as president. It also presents his belief in a strong union; states the principles of domestic contentment and foreign respect; and justifies his neutrality toward France and England.

WASHINGTON'S MISSION TO THE FRENCH. *See* **LeBoeuf, Fort, Washington's Mission to.**

WASHINGTON'S WESTERN LANDS. George Washington owned 45,000 acres, more than half of it in present-day West Virginia. Four tracts were along the Ohio River, at Round Bottom, at Washington Bottom, at present-day Ravenswood, and at Millwood. Three tracts in southwest Pennsylvania totaled 4,695 acres. He also had 5,000 acres on Rough Creek, Ky., and 3,051 on the Little Miami River near Cincinnati. Most of this acreage came from the French and Indian War, the rest from purchases of claims. The lands were sold by his heirs.

WASHITA, SHERIDAN'S OPERATIONS ON THE (1868–69). In August 1868 Cheyenne, Comanche, and Kiowa killed or captured 124 settlers in Kansas, Colorado, and Texas. Lt. Gen. Philip H. Sheridan garrisoned Fort Cobb on the Washita River, ordering Gen. Alfred Sully to establish Camp Supply north on Beaver Creek. From there Gen. George A. Custer marched on the Cheyenne of Black Kettle on the Washita, Nov. 27, killing 103 and capturing 51, with a loss of 35 killed or wounded. On Dec. 25 Maj. A. W. Evans defeated a Comanche-Kiowa band at Soldier Spring, south of the Wichita Mountains. In 1869, after Sheridan established Fort Sill, on Cache Creek, completing a line of posts, Custer and Gen. Eugene A. Carr crushed the Cheyenne.

***WASP*.** Two warships used in the War of 1812. The first, commanded by Master Commandant Jacob Jones, on Oct. 18, 1812, 500 miles east of the Chesapeake Capes, captured England's *Frolic,* commanded by Capt. Thomas Whinyates. The Americans suffered five casualties, the British ninety. Both vessels were damaged. The British *Poictiers* captured the *Wasp,* taking it to Bermuda.

The second *Wasp,* commanded by Johnston Blakely, sailed from Portsmouth, N.H., on May 1, 1814. Off the English Channel, it raked the British *Reindeer* on June 28, 1814. Twenty-five British were killed, and forty-two wounded; the U.S. loss was five killed and twenty-one wounded. On Sept. 1, Blakely destroyed the British *Avon,* commanded by James Arbuthnot. The *Avon* lost nine killed and thirty-three wounded; the *Wasp,* two killed and one wounded. The *Wasp* then captured the *Atlanta* off the Madeiras and disappeared.

WATAUGA SETTLEMENT AND ASSOCIATION. In 1768 bordermen in Virginia and North Carolina ventured into Tennessee, disregarding the Cherokee claim. In 1769 William Bean of Pittsylvania County, Va., settled on the Watauga; another settlement was established nearby by James Robertson. The gap between them was filled by immigrants. In 1772 the settlers formed the Watauga Association. In 1775 the Brown settlement, on the Nolichuckey, joined this government. Wataugans joined the Holston settlement in the campaign of 1774 against the Indians on the Ohio and fought in the Battle of Point Pleasant.

"WATCHFUL WAITING." Coined to describe President Woodrow Wilson's policy toward Mexico from 1913 to 1917.

WATERBURY (Conn.). A city on the Naugatuck River, it had a population of 103,266 in 1980. It was established as Mattatuck plantation in 1677, and incorporated as Waterbury in 1686. In the 18th century it was notable for its clock manufacture. Since the early 19th century it has been an important center for brass manufacture.

WATERGATE. The scandals of Richard M. Nixon's presidency. News accounts, in June 1971, of secret U.S. bombings in Cambodia led to wiretaps of reporters and staff aides. In June 1971 the *New York Times* published the Pentagon Papers, a confidential Defense Department study of Vietnam. This led to the "Plumbers" unit, led by E. Howard Hunt, Jr., a former agent of the Central Intelligence Agency (CIA), and G. Gordon Liddy. To secure information on Daniel Ellsberg, who had released the Pentagon Papers, Hunt and others broke into the office of his psychiatrist, in September 1971, and photographed documents. During the 1972 primaries, the Plumbers espionage sabotaged Democrats Sen. Edmund S. Muskie, Sen. George McGovern, and Sen. Hubert H. Humphrey, and the Democratic National Committee's headquarters in the Watergate complex.

Liddy, Hunt, former CIA operative James W. McCord, Jr., and a six-man group led by Bernard L. Barker, on the night of May 27, 1972, taped doors to the Democratic headquarters, tapped telephones, took documents, photographed others, and monitored the bugs while attempting to break into McGovern's headquarters. On June 17, a security guard at the complex noticed that doors had been taped open and removed the tape. When he later returned and found the doors retaped, he summoned Washington police. The burglars, including McCord, were arrested. E. Howard Hunt's White House number was found on the person of two of the burglars, the first indication of White House involvement.

A cover-up began immediately. On Aug. 29, Nixon declared that his counsel John W. Dean III had concluded that "no one in the White House staff" was "involved." The five burglars and two associates (Hunt and Liddy) were convicted (Jan. 30, 1973) in the U.S. District Court. On Mar. 23, Judge John J. Sirica released a letter in which McCord stated that higher-ups were involved. Nixon professed ignorance but his claims were challenged by his own conduct, investigations by the Senate Watergate committee (chaired by Sen. Sam Ervin), studies by the House Judiciary Committee, and tapes of White House conversations.

On Apr. 30, 1973, Nixon accepted "responsibility" for the Watergate events but denied any prior knowledge of a cover-up. White House aides and Justice Department officials resigned and were indicted, convicted (including Mitchell, Dean, H. R. Haldeman, and John D. Ehrlichman), and imprisoned. Nixon was named an unindicted coconspirator. Probing by Special Watergate Prosecutor Archibald Cox led to his firing. His successor, Leon Jaworski, was denied requests for evidence. Impeachment charges asserted that Nixon had obstructed justice and failed to uphold the law. On Aug. 9, 1974, he resigned. His successor, Gerald R. Ford, on Sept. 8, 1974, pardoned him.

WATER HOLES. Drinking places in the arid sections of the West. Some show paintings and other indications that they were sites of Indian religious veneration.

WATER LAW. Important west of the ninety-eighth meridian, where irrigation was necessary for crops and streams. Old English law giving the owner of the banks of a river unrestricted use of the water passing through his property was modified.

WATERPOWER. A common and useful method of generating waterpower was a paddlewheel near a waterfall. The water was diverted into a ditch and conveyed to the waterwheel located beside or beneath the mill. River systems, particularly along the Atlantic coast, provided waterpower. It was brought increasingly into use from about 1820, to the needs of an emerging industrialism. By 1840 there were well over 50,000 gristmills and sawmills in the United States; one-half of them could be found in the Middle Atlantic states and New England. Waterpower complexes, the largest of which were found on the Merrimack and Connecticut rivers in New England, provided the power base of some of the country's largest industrial centers. The turbine, developed by the French engineer Benoît Fourneyron (1827), was improved in the United States by Uriah A. Boyden, in 1844, and James B. Francis, in 1851. The "impulse" turbine, used in small steep streams, was also developed in the United States.

Marked advances in the efficiency of steam engines and boilers in the late 19th century narrowed the cost advantage long enjoyed by waterpower; and steam power provided the dependability and flexibility in supply that waterpower lacked. By 1870 steam power passed waterpower capacity in manufacturing. The success of the Niagara hydroelectric power project of the early 1890's marked the beginning of a new age in the history of waterpower. Based on the electrical transmission of energy, hydroelectric power bore little significant relation to the traditional direct-drive waterpower in which each establishment, small or large, had its own power plant, most establishments leasing the use of the water by which its wheels were driven. After 1900 hydroelectric power was produced in plants of enormous capacity and distributed over long distances by high-tension power lines. (*See also* Hydroelectric Power.)

WATER POWER ACT (June 10, 1920). Established a Federal Power Commission consisting of the secretaries of War, Interior, and Agriculture, with an executive secretary directly responsible for its administration. The commission was empowered to issue licenses, limited to fifty years, for the construction of power facilities on U.S. water reserves on public lands and navigable streams; it was also authorized to regulate rates and security issues of licensees.

WATER SUPPLY AND CONSERVATION. In the colonial period there were experiments such as the Boston Water-Works Company of 1652 and the system built by the Moravians at Bethlehem, Pa., in 1754. In 1774 New York City commissioned Christopher Colles to construct a waterworks system utilizing a steam engine. Until the 1790's, most cities depended on water drawn from public pumps, wells, and rainwater. In order to obtain the copious quantities of water necessary to flush the streets, the city councils of Philadelphia, New York, and Baltimore all authorized the building of public waterworks in 1798 and 1799. Philadelphia carried through its project, but New York and Baltimore encountered so many difficulties that they turned the problem over to private water companies. In Philadelphia, Benjamin Latrobe's Centre Square Water Works opened on Jan. 27, 1801. The system, which depended on two steam engines, did not supply enough water for the rapidly growing city. A new system was built under the supervision of Frederick Graff. The Fairmount Water Works (1822) relied on a dam built across the Schuylkill River and on waterwheels that pumped the water into a large reservoir on Fairmount Hill, from which it ran by gravity under the city streets. New York used horse power and later a steam engine to pump water into a reservoir on Chambers Street in November 1799, but did not obtain an adequate supply of water until 1842, with the opening of the Croton Aqueduct.

By 1860 there were still seventy-nine privately owned waterworks in the United States as compared with fifty-seven publicly owned ones, but the movement toward municipal systems was particularly characteristic of the larger cities. Even publicly owned systems found it difficult to provide for future needs. Not only did the cities grow rapidly in population, but new domestic and industrial uses for water placed unanticipated demands on sources of supply. Although New York City extended its system by building reservoirs in the Catskill Mountains (1917) and at the headwaters of the Delaware River (1955), it suffered from recurrent water crises. New York's use of the Delaware River encountered strong opposition from Philadelphia and those New Jersey cities that also drew from this source. In 1961 the United States Congress established the Delaware River Commission to apportion the river's flow among the rival claimants (New York, New Jersey, Delaware, and Pennsylvania).

The water needs of arid southern California were even more voracious. In 1913 Los Angeles began to use water drawn from the Owens River in the eastern Sierras, 233 miles away; in 1941 this supply had to be augmented by the 392-mile Colorado River Aqueduct. Subsequently the city had to tap still other sources.

In the 1880's, contaminated drinking water caused typhoid epidemics in Chicago, Cleveland, Newark, N.J., and Lowell, Mass. The cities had been discharging their untreated sewage into lakes and streams. Some cities abandoned the polluted sources and built new reservoirs in protected watersheds; others extended their intakes far out into the lakes. Most cities found it necessary to filter the water or to treat it chemically.

Both the problem of pollution and the problem of adequate supply caused growing concern during the 1960's and 1970's. There were significant experiments in preparing drinking water by desalination of seawater at Coalinga, Calif. (1959), and Freeport, Tex. (1965). In 1965 Congress passed the Water Quality Act to curbe pollution of streams and lakes. In 1972 Congress passed the Clean Water Act, authorizing federal aid to eliminate industrial waste and sewage from streams and lakes. In 1972 President Richard Nixon and Prime Minister Pierre Trudeau of Canada signed the Great Lakes Water Quality Agreement, providing for a joint effort to end pollution of the Great Lakes, on which many cities depended for drinking water. The Safe Drinking Water Act in 1974 authorized the Environmental Protection Agency to establish national standards for drinking water.

WATERWAYS, INLAND. The U.S. system of inland waterways of 27,000 miles of navigable rivers and canals bears approximately 15 percent of the total intercity freight movements.

In the colonial period, ships sailed the coastal and tidewater streams. Waterways also provided routes for pioneers. Virginians and Marylanders used the James and Potomac rivers, Pennsylvanians the Susquehanna, and New Englanders and New Yorkers the Connecticut and the Hudson-Mohawk. After Robert Fulton introduced the steamboat in 1807, its use spread throughout the nation, especially on the western rivers. The War of 1812 demonstrated the need for improved transportation, and many canals were built. By 1850, there were 4,000 miles of canals in the United States.

The railroad, introduced in 1830, had better speed, directness, and continuity of service, and by 1900 dominated transportation. A reemergence of the waterways occurred early in the 20th century, the result of government development of waterways for flood control, irrigation, power production, recreation, and navigation; the development of submarines and their threat to oceanborne commerce; improved maritime technology; and the economy of water transportation. The 1908 report of the Inland Waterways Commission and traffic on the railroads showed the need for waterways. The government chartered the Inland Waterways Corporation in 1924 to operate a barge line on the Mississippi. The diesel-powered tugboat, special-purpose barges and tankers, and all-weather, 24-hour navigational systems led to traffic to the waterways. Twentieth-century projects include the Atlantic Intracoastal and Gulf Intracoastal waterways; protected channels; the recanalization of the Ohio River; and the development of both the Columbia River and the Saint Lawrence Seaway (opened in 1959).

WATERWAYS TREATY (Jan. 11, 1909). Negotiated by Elihu Root and James Bryce, it provided for an international commission for Canadian–U.S. disputes. It limits the diversion of water on each side of Niagara Falls; provides for use of boundary waters; and guarantees navigation of Lake Michigan and all canals connecting boundary waters.

WATLINGS ISLAND (now **San Salvador**). An island eighteen miles long, in the Bahamas, in the British West Indies, 220 miles northeast of Cuba. On Oct. 12, 1492, Christopher Columbus probably landed there.

WATTS RIOTS. *See* **Race Riots.**

WAUHATCHIE, BATTLE OF (Oct. 28–29, 1863). Fought at the foot of Lookout Mountain during Ulysses S. Grant's advance on Chattanooga. Joseph Hooker's Union division under Gen. John W. Geary was attacked by a Confederate force under Col. John Bratton. Hooker ordered Oliver Otis Howard's corps to reinforce Geary. Bratton withdrew, thus saving the Union supply line from Nashville. The Union loss was 420, Confederate, 356.

WAVES. *See* **Women in the Military Services.**

WAWAYANDA PATENT. Granted Mar. 5, 1703, to John Bridges and eleven associates by the governor of New York and New Jersey, Edward Hyde, Lord Cornbury; confirmed by Queen Anne. It consisted of 150,000 acres in Orange

County, N.Y., bounded on the east by the Highlands of the Hudson, on the north by the division line between Orange and Ulster counties, and on the south by the division line between New York and New Jersey.

WAXHAW. Village in South Carolina on the Catawba River, on and near Waxhaw Creek, extending into North Carolina. Andrew Jackson was born near the border line in South Carolina on Mar. 15, 1767. Waxhaw Settlement was the site of the revolutionary war Battle of Hanging Rock.

WAXHAW, BATTLE OF (May 29, 1780). Col. Abraham Buford, with 380 Virginia troops, was marching to Charleston; hearing of its fall, he retreated northward. Col. Banastre Tarleton overtook him with 300 cavalry at Waxhaw, near North Carolina. The British killed 113, wounded 150 and took 53 prisoners. Buford and other men escaped. The British loss was 20.

WAX PORTRAITS. Patience Lovell Wright made wax portraits of George Washington and Benjamin Franklin. Itinerant modelers like Johan Christian Rauschner and George M. Miller made miniatures in varicolored wax, often jeweled, of local worthies. Robert Ball Hughes of Boston used white wax, Giuseppi Volaperta made reliefs of three presidents in red, and Reuben Moulthorpe of Connecticut molded heads in the round and made wax works.

WAYNE, FORT. Built by Gen. Anthony Wayne at the junction of the St. Joseph and St. Marys rivers, in present-day Indiana, in 1794. The Indian treaties of 1803 and 1809 were negotiated there by Gov. William Henry Harrison of Indiana Territory. In August 1812 Indians under British influence besieged the fort but Harrison relieved it on Sept. 12. It was abandoned as a military post on Apr. 19, 1819.

WAYNE, FORT, TREATY OF (Sept. 30, 1809). Concluded by William Henry Harrison, then governor of Indiana Territory, with the Delaware, Potawatomi, Miami, and Eel River tribes, it ceded to the United States 2.5 million acres on the upper Wabash River. It aroused opposition among the Indians, and helped decide them against the United States in the War of 1812.

WAYNE CAMPAIGN (1792–95). Gen. Anthony Wayne organized an army northwest of the Ohio River; in 1793 he advanced to Fort Washington (present-day Cincinnati), then north to Greenville, and sent a detachment to build Fort Recovery. On June 30, 1794, 2,000 Indians assaulted it and were defeated. Wayne continued north. At the junction of the Glaize and the Maumee rivers he built Fort Defiance. On Aug. 15, he pursued the Indians down the Maumee, and on Aug. 20 defeated them. At the British Fort Miami Wayne destroyed Indian and British property, marched up the Maumee to the Wabash Portage, and built a fort. He returned to Greenville, awaiting the Indian peace offer. The Treaty of Greenville (1795) gave southern and eastern Ohio to the United States, recognized Indian claims in the Northwest, and gave them sites for forts together with free passage of the rivers and portages.

WAYNE-WILKINSON QUARREL. Gen. James Wilkinson resented not being appointed commander of the western army of Anthony Wayne's Indian campaign in 1792–95. The two men criticized each other and the army split into factions. Finally each preferred charges against the other. When Wayne died (1796), they were forgotten.

WAYS AND MEANS, COMMITTEE ON. Established in the House of Representatives (1795) and made a standing committee in 1802. It has jurisdiction over all revenue measures and has been at the center of struggles over reciprocal trade, Social Security, medicare, and revenue sharing.

WCTU. *See* **Woman's Christian Temperance Union.**

"WE ARE COMING, FATHER ABRAHAM, THREE HUNDRED THOUSAND MORE." One of the most popular Civil War songs, written by the Quaker abolitionist James Sloan Gibbons. It appeared in the *New York Evening Post* after President Abraham Lincoln's call on July 2, 1862, for 300,000 volunteers after Gen. George B. McClellan's defeat at Richmond.

"WEATHERMEN." *See* **Students for a Democratic Society.**

WEATHER SERVICE, NATIONAL. Established in 1870 under the Army Signal Service. The Department of Agriculture took it over in 1891, the Department of Commerce in 1940, and the National Oceanographic and Atmospheric Administration in 1970. Original duties included storm warnings, forecasts, and other services. River-flood warnings were greatly improved in the 1930's with the unit hydrograph. In the 1890's fruit growers received special warnings by telephone or telegraph. The hurricane service, developed before World War I, was decentralized in 1935, and modernized with the rawinsonde and tracking by aircraft, radar, and space satellites. In 1950 the bureau established a unit for tornadoes, floods, and blizzards. After 1914 it issued forest fire advisories. Arctic and Atlantic Ocean observation networks opened after World War II. The Air Commerce Act (1926) provided hourly observations and frequent forecasts at airports. Air-mass analysis, the radiosonde (1937), and two-way radio improved service.

Teletype (developed in the 1920's), wirephoto weather maps (1934), and facsimile transmission of weather maps (1950's) enhanced communications. Upper-air readings progressed from balloons and kites to pilot balloons and airplane observations before the radiosonde. Rain gauges were developed, as were the ceilometer, the telepsychrometer, the recording river-flood gauge, radar (after 1945), and the space satellite (1960). General forecasts were made by district centers in the 1890's; they were revised four times daily starting in 1939 and prepared for zones within states in the 1940's; weekly forecasts were issued during 1908–40; the five-day forecast appeared in 1940 and was released twice a week until 1970. The 30-day outlook began 1948. Research now includes evaporation, pollution, cloud seeding, radioactivity, solar radiation, and computers.

WEBB EXPORT ACT (Apr. 10, 1918). Freed exporters from antitrust laws, permitting combinations in selling agencies. In 1924 the Federal Trade Commission ruled that Webb associations could limit themselves to price fixing and allotting export orders.

WEBB-KENYON ACT (Mar. 1, 1913). Prohibited the transportation in interstate commerce of liquor. It was vetoed by President William Howard Taft, who said it delegated federal power to the states. It was repassed, and upheld by the Supreme Court (*Clark Distilling Company* v. *Western Railway Company,* 242 U.S. 311 [1917]). The law was later included in the Twenty-first Amendment to the Constitution, repealing Prohibition.

WEBSTER-ASHBURTON TREATY (1842). Settled dispute over the northeastern boundary (Maine and New Brunswick) between England and the United States. The boundary was also fixed at the head of the Connecticut River, at the north end of Lake Champlain, in the Detroit River, and at the head of Lake Superior. It included an extradition article, and one providing for free navigation of the St. John River. The United States was assured against interference with its ships.

WEBSTER-FAIRBANK TRIALS (1844–45). Calvin Fairbank and Delia A. Webster abducted the slaves Lewis Hayden and family from Lexington, Ky., to an Underground Railroad station at Hopkins, Ohio, in September 1844. Webster served two years in a penitentiary, while Fairbank was pardoned Aug. 23, 1849, after serving five years.

WEBSTER-HAYNE DEBATE (January 1830). One of the most significant constitutional debates ever held in Congress, covering public lands, tariff, slavery, local patriotism, sectionalism, the Constitution, and the Union. Samuel A. Foote of Connecticut introduced a Senate resolution (Dec. 29, 1829) to restrict the sale of public lands. Thomas Hart Benton of Missouri attacked it and called upon the South to protect the West. Robert Y. Hayne of South Carolina denounced the East, claiming the federal government threatened the states' independence. Daniel Webster of Massachusetts debated Hayne, showing the fallacy of twenty-four separate states interpreting the Constitution.

WEBSTER-PARKMAN MURDER CASE. John White Webster, a professor at Harvard College and lecturer at the medical school, was convicted of murdering Dr. George Parkman, benefactor of the school and prominent citizen of Boston, and hanged on Aug. 30, 1850. Webster's confession, adverse publicity, suppression of evidence, and the harshness of Judge Samuel Shaw have since been questioned.

WEBSTER'S BLUE-BACKED SPELLER. Popular name of Noah Webster's *Elementary Spelling Book,* published since 1783. The first edition appeared as *A Grammatical Institute of the English Language, Part I: A New and Accurate Standard of Pronunciation.* In 1788 it became *The American Spelling Book.* It appeared after 1843 as *The Pictorial Elementary Spelling Book.* Nearly 100 million copies have been printed.

WEBSTER'S DICTIONARY. *See* **Dictionaries.**

WEEHAWKEN. Township in northeastern New Jersey, on the Hudson River opposite New York City, just north of Hoboken. A dueling ground was located there. Alexander Hamilton and Aaron Burr (July 11, 1804), John B. Church (1799), Philip Hamilton, Alexander's son (1801), De Witt Clinton (1802), and Commodore Oliver Hazard Perry (1818) all fought there.

WEEKS ACT (1911). Sponsored by Rep. John W. Weeks of Massachusetts and approved by President William Howard Taft, it authorized interstate compacts to conserve forests and water; grants to states to prevent forest fires on watersheds of navigable waters; acquisition of land to protect watersheds, to be held as national forest land; and grants to states of proceeds from national forests within their boundaries.

"WE HAVE MET THE ENEMY, AND THEY ARE OURS." On defeating the British fleet under Robert H. Barclay in the Battle of Lake Erie, Sept. 10, 1813, Oliver Hazard Perry, commander of the U.S. fleet, dispatched the famous message to Maj. Gen. William Henry Harrison, commander of the western army at Seneca, Ohio.

WELCOME. A 300-ton vessel, Robert Greenway, Master, that sailed from Deal, England, on Sept. 1, 1682, with William Penn and a party of 100. They landed at New Castle, Pa., in October. One-third of the passengers died of smallpox on the voyage.

WELFARE SERVICES. Aid provided under the Social Security Administration, by public or private pension and retirement systems, by health and educational organizations, and through unemployment insurance and workmen's compensation. Church groups and private agencies also provide help for the sick, disabled, very old or very young, lonely, or economically dependent.

In the colonial period social welfare depended on the church and private gifts. "Poor laws" were passed in every colony. After the Revolution, state law provided orphan asylums. The public school system began with special schools for poor children. Public hospitals, homes for the aged or orphans, "county farms," and "poorhouses" appeared in the early 19th century. The Freedmen's Bureau, set up in 1865, supplied food and help to blacks freed from slavery. Federal aid went to seamen in the merchant marine, war veterans, and Indians on reservations.

The start of the 20th century saw state and workmen's

compensation, which insured workers in case of injury on the job. Some states tried to set the earliest age and maximum hours that children could work. The federal Bureau of Mines (started in 1910) dealt with the health and working conditions of miners. New Deal legislation, from 1933 to 1940, set up social welfare systems supported by the federal government. The Social Security Act provided insurance against unemployment, and allowances for retired workers, widows, and children of deceased workers. The government gave work relief to the unemployed, and granted money for better housing and hospital facilities. The Department of Health, Education, and Welfare, created with cabinet rank in 1953, was charged with handling federal assistance programs set up to help state and local governments provide welfare payments. Federal assistance was greatly extended in the 1960's. In 1965, "Medicare" provisions to assist the sick were passed by Congress and signed by President Lyndon B. Johnson and the Department of Housing and Urban Development was created. Welfare payments, including aid to dependent children, the aged, blind, and disabled and unemployment compensation, amounted to over $143 billion in 1970, over half paid by the federal government.

WELLS, FARGO AND COMPANY. Organized in 1852, it installed ocean service between New York and San Francisco via Panama, and operated all over the Pacific coast. In ten years it was the chief letter-carrier to mining camps; carried millions more in gold, silver, and bullion than any other agency; and took over the Pony Express. Its operations extended to western Canada, Alaska, Mexico, the West Indies, Central America, Hawaii, China, and Japan. Wells, Fargo merged with the American Railway Express Company in 1918, but continued to function for more than 30 years on 14,000 miles of railway in Mexico and in Cuba. As a subsidiary of American Express, it became an armored-car service.

WEST, AMERICAN. The acquisition of the West began in 1763 after the French and Indian War, when France ceded Canada and the Old Northwest to Britain. After the American Revolution the size of the nation was almost doubled by the Louisiana Purchase.

The first frontier was the Piedmont and the Connecticut Valley; then came the tramontane frontier, the Ohio Valley and the Kentucky grasslands, the Great American Desert and beyond to Oregon, to Pikes Peak and California.

Except for the Mormons, Americans moved west as individuals or as families rather than as communities. They followed roads and trails marked by explorers, hunters, and fur traders. The first homes were small, rough, and quickly constructed. Dense forests and herds of wild animals were a handicap to homesteaders lured west by land speculators. Indians also suffered. Reservations brought them into central settlements; they were scattered again when inadequate landholdings were allocated to families, along with whites who purchased surplus lands.

The Congress of the Confederation drew up basic charters concerning the West. The Ordinance of 1785 provided for the survey and sale of western lands; the Northwest Ordinance (1787) established a government for the region and encouraged education; the Preemption Act (1841) safeguarded the land rights of frontiersmen; the Homestead Act (1862) offered free land.

***WEST COAST HOTEL COMPANY* V. *PARRISH*,** 300 U.S. 379 (1937). U.S. Supreme Court decision involving the constitutional validity of a Washington State commission that fixed minimum wages for women. The question: Was minimum-wage legislation an infringement of the due process clause of the Fourteenth Amendment of the Constitution? Chief Justice Charles Evans Hughes, speaking for the Court, held that although both parties were of full age and competent to contract, the state could interfere where the parties were not equal in bargaining power, or where public health required that the weaker party be protected.

WESTERN, FORT. Built in 1754 on the Kennebec River (now Augusta, Maine) to protect traders and promote trade with Indians.

WESTERN BOUNDARIES (1783–98). The Definitive Treaty of Peace of 1783 with Great Britain laid down the northern boundary (since rectified and delineated) as far as the Lake of the Woods in present-day Minnesota. From the Lake of the Woods it continued west to the Mississippi; then went down to 31° north latitude, east to the Chattahoochee; followed it to the Flint, on what is now the southwest border of Georgia; then to the St. Marys, which forms part of the southeast border of Georgia; and down the Atlantic.

England refused to evacuate strategic frontier posts within U.S. territory at Michilimackinac, Detroit, Niagara, Oswego, Oswegatchie, Pointe au fer, and Dutchman's Point (*see* Border Forts, Evacuation of). They wanted to preserve the Canadian fur trade, which reached far south into U.S. territory, and retain Indian allies. In the Southwest, Spain kept posts at Memphis, Vicksburg, Natchez, Fort St. Stephens, and Fort Confederation on the Tombigbee River in what is now Alabama. During 1783–89, the government could not cope with these questions. The federal government inaugurated by President George Washington under the Constitution, aided by European wars, allowed the United States to redeem territory. The Northwest was evacuated in 1796 according to the terms of Jay's Treaty (1794) with England, and the Southwest freed of Spanish troops in 1798, as a result of the execution of Pinckney's Treaty (1795).

The line due west from the Lake of the Woods to the Mississippi proved geographically impossible because its source is 150 miles south. This left a boundary gap. It disappeared in the Convention of 1818 with Great Britain, which provided for a line drawn from the northwesternmost point of the Lake of the Woods to the forty-ninth parallel, to continue west to the "Stony Mountains."

WESTERN DESIGN. Plan of the English Protector, Oliver Cromwell, to usurp Spain in the Caribbean. A military force under Adm. William Penn and Gen. Robert Venables reached Barbados in 1655 and sailed to Santo Domingo (Hispaniola). 7,000 men attacked the city but were repulsed. The expedition then took Jamaica. Penn sailed for England, leaving Adm. William Goodsonn in command. In the next year Goodsonn sacked and burned Santa Marta. The new colony of Jamaica failed to induce immigration from the British Isles or New England and was reinforced by prisoners and deportees from Great Britain and Ireland.

***WESTERN ENGINEER*.** The first steamboat to ascend the Missouri River to Council Bluffs (above Omaha), in 1820.

WESTERN EXPLORATION. In 1804 President Thomas Jefferson sent Meriwether Lewis and William Clark up the Missouri River to seek a water route to the Pacific; to counsel with the Indians and summon certain important chiefs to Washington, D.C.; and to observe the land and its resources. They left St. Louis, wintered with the Mandan in present North Dakota, and crossed the Rockies to the mouth of the Columbia. Zebulon Montgomery Pike in 1805–06 examined the upper Mississippi and in 1806–07 explored the region drained by the Red and Arkansas rivers. He crossed the Rio Grande and was detained by the Spanish. During the next three decades there were studies of the Ouachita and lower Red rivers, and Stephen H. Long in 1820 went into Colorado and along the Arkansas and Canadian rivers. Naturalists John Bradbury, Thomas Nuttall, and David Douglas were also developing an interest in the West.

The fur trade advanced geographical knowledge. The Hudson's Bay Company and the American Fur Company penetrated new areas; Manuel Lisa and Pierre Chouteau dominated trade on the upper Missouri; the Astorians went to the mouth of the Columbia in 1811–12; Joseph R. Walker and Jedediah S. Smith ranged between the Wasatch Mountains and the Sierra Nevada, and went to the Pacific coast.

John Charles Frémont, an officer in the Corps of Topographical Engineers, traveled in 1842 to South Pass and the Wind River Range in present Wyoming. In 1843–44 he went to the Great Salt Lake, the Dalles of the Columbia, central Oregon, western Nevada, across the Sierra Nevada, and California. Naval captain Charles Wilkes went to the South Pacific, the Antarctic, and the Pacific Northwest.

The Department of War in 1853 authorized the survey of continental rail routes. Topographers, botanists, geologists, and zoologists produced the *Pacific Railroad Reports* between 1855 and 1860. Between 1867 and 1879, surveys were conducted by Clarence King, George M. Wheeler, Ferdinand V. Hayden, and John Wesley Powell, sponsored by the Department of War and the Department of the Interior. Their scientific corps published still definitive data and maps. The U.S. Geological Survey (1879) marked the end of the age of exploration.

WESTERN FEDERATION OF MINERS. Labor union of miners and smelters in the Rocky Mountain states. Organized in 1893, it was affiliated with the American Federation of Labor (AFL), but broke away because of its conservative policies. The Western Federation called for the Cripple Creek, Colo., strike of 1894, the strike at Leadville, Colo., in 1896, and others in the Coeur d'Alene district, in Idaho, in 1896 and 1897. The federation joined the Industrial Workers of the World in 1905 but seceded in 1907 and rejoined the AFL in 1911. In 1916 it became the International Union of Mine, Mill, and Smelter Workers.

WESTERN MERCHANTS AND THE INDIAN TRADE. Large concerns dominated the Indian trade, but small storekeepers did much business too. Government agents with the Indian tribes often disliked fur-company traders, and sometimes diverted purchases to storekeepers. The removal of tribes west of the Mississippi during the administration of President Andrew Jackson (*see* Indian Removal) led to the supplying of rations to emigrants.

WESTERN PACIFIC. *See* **Railroads, Sketches of Principal Lines.**

WESTERN RESERVE. Part of northeastern Ohio on the south shore of Lake Erie, once belonging to Connecticut; an irregular quadrilateral—with Conneaut, Youngstown, Willard, and Port Clinton at the corners. The charter that the Connecticut river towns obtained from King Charles II in 1662 fixed the colony's boundaries north and south by parallels extending westward to the Pacific. The king granted parts to the Duke of York and to Adm. William Penn; King James had already given Virginia all the land included in Connecticut's boundaries beyond Pennsylvania.

In 1786 Connecticut ceded all its western lands except for the Western Reserve. In 1792, 500,000 acres were assigned to towns along Long Island Sound as compensation for losses during the Revolution. In 1795 the rest of the Western Reserve was sold to thirty-five Connecticut landowners. Moses Cleaveland in 1796 supervised a survey and other preparations for settlement. In 1800 Connecticut and the United States arranged for the Western Reserve to be attached to the Ohio Territory. Gov. Arthur St. Clair named it Trumbull County and organized a local government. With the Erie Canal (completed 1825), the population grew, and Trumbull County was redivided into many counties.

WESTERN RESERVE, RELIGION IN (1795–1837). Its early religion was conservative toward revivalism and radical in theology. The Congregational Association of Connecticut and the Presbyterian church sent missionaries from Connecticut and Massachusetts, but Presbyterians eventually claimed most of the churches. Unitarianism made slight headway, but Arminianism developed under Charles G. Finney among the Oberlin Association (1836). New School Arminianism was responsible for the excision of the Western Reserve Synod (1837) from the Presbyterian church. With immigration from western Pennsylvania came Methodists and Baptists. Mormonism was established at Kirtland in 1831, and Universalism, Spiritualism, Shakerism, and Adventism soon appeared.

WESTERN SEA, SEARCH FOR THE. Attempts to find a way across the continent to the Pacific Ocean led to the exploration of many lakes and rivers. The French explorer La Vérendrye went from Lake Superior to the Lake of the

Woods, and from there to Lake Winnipeg and the Saskatchewan River in what is now south-central Canada. Alexander Henry and Peter Pond, in the late 18th century and the beginning of the 19th, ascended both branches of the Saskatchewan to their sources in the Canadian Rocky Mountains and discovered and explored the Athabasca River, Lake Athabasca, and Peace River. Alexander Mackenzie, by way of the Peace, the Fraser, the Blackwater, and the Bella Coola rivers, reached the Pacific in July 1793. Lewis and Clark ascended the Missouri in 1804 and reached the Columbia in 1805. Simon Fraser descended the river that bears his name to the sea in 1808. David Thompson spent 1807–1811 surveying the Columbia and the Kootenay rivers.

WESTERN SEPARATISM. New commonwealths in Kentucky and Tennessee labored under disputed boundaries, uncertain land titles, inefficient and insufficient military and judicial protection, remoteness from the seat of government, and eastern control of legislatures. The West interpreted progress in terms of land values, population, and accessible commercial outlets. Eastern markets were too remote. Resentment grew against Spanish officials who restricted trade privileges and navigation of the Mississippi. News of John Jay's proposed compromise treaty (*see* Jay-Gardoqui Negotiations) in 1786 nearly led to insurrection. Intrigue and negotiation with Spain (*see* Spanish Conspiracy), with France (*see* Genêt Mission), and with England (*see* Blount Conspiracy), leading to possible separation, followed in the Kentucky and Tennessee districts. Calmer judgment prevailed, for Kentucky entered the Union in 1792 and Tennessee joined in 1796. With Jay's Treaty (signed 1794) and Pinckney's Treaty (1795) western discontent ended.

WESTERN UNION TELEGRAPH COMPANY. Grew out of the New York and Mississippi Valley Printing Telegraph Company, organized in 1851 by Hiram Sibley and Samuel L. Seldon of Rochester, N.Y., to use Royal Earl House's recently invented printing telegraph. Reorganized as Western Union in 1856, it absorbed smaller companies idly, and by 1860 reached from the Atlantic to the Mississippi, and from the Great Lakes to the Ohio. By 1861 it was the first transcontinental telegraph line. By 1900 it had a million miles of telegraph lines and two international cables. During the 1960's and 1970's, Western Union became involved in satellite communications, computer systems, hotel reservation and money-order services, and teleprinters.

WEST FLORIDA. *See* **Florida.**

WEST FLORIDA, ANNEXATION OF (1810–11). In 1810 inhabitants of West Florida near the Mississippi revolted against Spain, and requested annexation to the United States (*see* Mobile Act). President James Madison asserted the right to West Florida by virtue of the Louisiana Purchase (1803) and ordered the territorial governor of Orleans, William C. C. Claiborne, to extend authority over the district.

WEST FLORIDA CONTROVERSY. The area from the Mississippi to the Perdido river on the Gulf of Mexico was included in Spain's claims from 1492 on, but from 1699 to 1763 France occupied it as part of Louisiana. Great Britain held it from 1763 (*see* Paris, Treaty of) until the Definitive Treaty of Peace of 1783. After 1803 the United States claimed it as part of the Louisiana Purchase. Spain refuted the claim, but could not defend it. Congress, by the Mobile Act (1804), authorized the president to assume control. U.S. frontiersmen rebelled against Spain in 1810, whereupon the United States seized a portion included in Louisiana in 1812 (*see* West Florida, Annexation of). The rest was added to Mississippi Territory in 1813 (*see* Mobile Seized). U.S. troops under Andrew Jackson occupied it in 1814. Spain relinquished all claim in the Adams-Onís Treaty of 1819.

WEST INDIA TRADE. Colonial commerce with the West Indies was known as the triangular trade. Colonial ships with soap, candles, buttons, provisions, sheep and hogs, lumber, horses, and rum sailed to the coast of Africa for slaves; in the West Indies ports, the slaves were traded for sugar and molasses, distilled into New England rum sent to New York and Pennsylvania. Rum traffic and the slave trade supported shipowners, farmers, artisans, shipbuilders, sailmakers, cordwainers, metal workers, shipmasters and crews, lumbermen, fishermen, sugar planters and African tribes.

WEST INDIES, DANISH. *See* **Virgin Islands of the United States.**

WEST JERSEY. In 1674 Edward Byllynge, a Quaker, purchased Lord John Berkeley's interest in New Jersey. John Fenwick managed the property for a share in it. Byllynge later sold his rights to Daniel Coxe, a non-Quaker, who became chief proprietor of West Jersey. By the Quintipartite Deed (1676) a line running from Little Egg Harbor to the Delaware River at the forty-first parallel divided the province. Sir George Carteret received East Jersey, and Quakers West Jersey. In 1675 Fenwick founded a colony at Salem. In 1675, Burlington was founded on the Delaware River; it became the chief port and capital. In 1693 Coxe sold his proprieties to the West Jersey Society, which governed the province until its surrender to the crown in 1702.

WEST JERSEY CONCESSIONS (also known as the "Laws, Concessions and Agreements"). Provisions for the colonization and government of West Jersey. The work of William Penn, they were approved and signed by 151 emigrants and issued by the proprietors in March 1677. The land was subdivided into ten equal parts subdivided into tenths; grants were made to settlers subject only to the annual quitrent. Government rested on a bill of rights including absolute religious freedom, public trial by jury, right of petition, freedom from arbitrary arrest or imprisonment for debt, and equal taxation by representatives. The province was governed by the concessions until 1702.

WESTMINSTER, TREATY OF (Feb. 19, 1674), a treaty of peace between the Netherlands and Britain, providing for the return of the colony of New Netherland to England and renewing the Treaty of Breda of 1667.

WESTMINSTER CONFESSION OF FAITH. The doctrinal formula prepared by the Westminster Assembly of Divines (1643–49) and the strongest statement of Calvinistic doctrine. At once adopted by the Church of Scotland, it has been modified in the interest of a more liberal position. The American Congregationalists incorporated the confession in their Cambridge Platform (1648), with the exception of that part which deals with polity and discipline. The Synod of Philadelphia (1729) adopted the confession and since that time it has remained the doctrinal basis of American Presbyterianism.

WESTON'S SETTLEMENT (1622–23). Thomas Weston, the English merchant who had been active in helping finance the Pilgrims to found Plymouth in 1620, became alienated from that enterprise and attempted to establish a separate settlement and rival trading center. His colonists, under the leadership of Andrew Weston, landed at Plymouth in June 1622, where they remained for some time as unwelcome guests of the Pilgrims. They moved on to Wessagusset, now Weymouth, to begin a plantation of their own. Lacking effective leadership and the strong motivation of the Pilgrims, they abandoned the plantation in 1623.

WESTO WAR (1680). The Westo Indians along the Savannah River, allies of the Spanish, rose up against the encroaching English settlements of South Carolina. They were quickly crushed by the end of the year. As a result, the Spanish authorities withdrew from their northernmost missions.

WEST POINT (N.Y.). The site of the U.S. Military Academy (founded 1802). It is also the site of remains of two military posts, forts Clinton and Putnam, built by the Continental army during the Revolution.

The swift collapse of the Hudson River defenses in October 1777 impressed on the Continentals the need for a proper defense. The provincial congress of New York initiated a new survey of the Highlands of the Hudson, with the result that West Point was chosen as the site of the citadel for a strong system of defenses. The original plans were those of French engineer Lt. Col. Louis de La Radiere. In their execution, a brigade under Gen. Samuel H. Parsons began breaking ground on Jan. 20, 1778. In spite of extreme suffering among the men, the construction of gun emplacements at the river's edge and of a stone fortress at the nose of the peninsula, Fort Arnold (later, Clinton) was pressed vigorously. In March 1778 Tadeusz Kosciuszko took over the construction work. Washington made his headquarters there for the four months following July 28, 1779. In April of the previous year a great 60-ton chain had been stretched across the river to Constitution Island, closing it to navigation (*see* Hudson River Chain). Protective water batteries on both sides effectively barred the channel. On the first ridge west of the plateau, forts Webb, Wyllys, and Putnam protected the land approaches. These in turn were covered by four redoubts on a ridge lying west and south. The seizure of West Point was always present in the British plans of campaign after 1777, but it was never threatened.

A corps of invalids (veterans) created by act of Congress, June 20, 1777, was transferred four years later to West Point, with the intention of using them as a cadre for the instruction of candidates for commissions. The germ of the idea that ultimately produced the U.S. Military Academy existed in that plan. In June 1784 Congress reduced the army to eighty men, of which fifty-five were detailed to guard stores at West Point. When domestic violence and foreign embroilments later forced Congress to increase the army, West Point became the garrison station of a corps of artillerists and engineers. In 1802 Congress established the U.S. Military Academy at West Point.

WESTPORT. A town, located on the Missouri River, now a residential district of Kansas City, Mo. In 1831 the Rev. Isaac McCoy, a Baptist missionary, purchased the land. John C. McCoy, his son, established a store on the land to trade with Indians and settlers and in 1833 laid out the town of Westport. Other trading houses were soon established. Westport's Indian trade eventually extended to the Rocky Mountains. During the late 1840's and early 1850's, together with Kansas City, Westport superseded Independence as an outfitting and starting point for traders, trappers, emigrants, and explorers following the Santa Fe and Oregon trails. During the Civil War its trade decreased. After that conflict, the town declined. It was annexed to Kansas City in 1899.

WESTPORT, BATTLE OF (Oct. 23, 1864). A battle in Gen. Sterling Price's third invasion of Missouri during the Civil War. Price, with 9,000 men of the Confederate army of the trans-Mississippi, was opposed by Gen. Alfred Pleasanton with 6,500 men and Gen. Samuel R. Curtis with 15,000 men. Gen. John S. Marmaduke's Confederate division fought unsuccessfully against Pleasanton's army at the Big Blue, while Curtis' troops slowly forced back the rest of Price's army from the valley of Brush Creek, facing Westport, Mo. By evening the Confederates were in full retreat. Losses on both sides totaled about 1,000 dead and severely wounded.

WEST'S STEAMBOAT. In 1794, at Lexington, Ky., Edward West, a Virginia emigrant, exhibited his steamboat. A miniature boat, the engine lacked a flywheel or a counterbalance of any kind. In order to overcome the inertia of dead center, the pistons were equipped with brackets, which came in contact with springs that kept the engine in motion. On July 6, 1802, West secured a patent for his steamboat, but it never got beyond the experimental stage.

WESTSYLVANIA. A proposed fourteenth state to be established between the Allegheny Mountains and the Ohio River, and extending from the Iroquois boundary line of 1768 (about Kittanning, Pa.) to a line drawn from the mouth of the Scioto River to the Cumberland Gap. A movement for a meeting of the settlers to consider the project in June 1776 probably never materialized. By Aug. 1, a petition was in circulation in the region requesting the establishment of a new state. The Continental Congress refused to act upon the petition.

WEST VIRGINIA. Entered the Union as a state in 1863. Prior to that year it was part of Virginia. Between about 1731 and the French and Indian War (1754–63), several thousand settlers, chiefly of German, Scotch-Irish, and English stock, entered the eastern panhandle. After Iroquois and Cherokee claims to trans-Allegheny West Virginia were extinguished in 1768, settlers began to occupy the Monongahela, Greenbrier, Kanawha, and Ohio valleys.

Early in the 19th century significant differences developed between eastern and western Virginia. Despite eastern efforts to appease the west by legislation favorable to internal improvements and free public schools and by sharing political advantages, differences between the two sections had become deep-seated. In 1861, when Virginia adopted its ordinance of secession, counties in the northwestern part of the state set up the Restored Government, which remained loyal to the Union; its capital was Wheeling, and Francis H. Pierpont was elected governor. The following year the Restored Government, safely behind Union lines, consented to the formation of the state of West Virginia. Congress gave its approval, President Abraham Lincoln reluctantly signed the statehood bill, and West Virginia entered the Union on June 20, 1863. Since 1885 the state capital has been Charleston.

With abundant resources, West Virginia made striking industrial advances during its first half-century of statehood. From 1909 to 1924 West Virginia was first in the production of natural gas; its production of oil peaked in 1900, and of lumber in 1909. But the state's economic lifeblood was the coal industry, which grew steadily until 1947, when 173,653,816 tons were mined. World War I provided the impetus for giant chemical industries in the Kanawha and Ohio valleys and for the steel industry in the northern panhandle. This industrial growth was fostered and accompanied by the construction of railroads and river improvements and by an influx of laborers. After World War II the state suffered severe population losses, partly the result of technological unemployment caused by mechanization of the coal mines and an increase in surface mining. The total population dropped from 2,005,553 in 1950 to 1,744,237 in 1970. In 1980 the population had increased to 1,949,644.

WESTWARD MOVEMENT. The movement of people that resulted in the settlement of America. In general usage, the westward movement is considered to have begun with the first expansion from Atlantic tidewater settlements into the interior. In most respects the movement lost its typical characteristics around the end of the 19th century, when there could no longer be said to be a frontier line.

Westward movement began in 1635, when a group of Massachusetts Bay colonists, led by Roger Ludlow, moved westward into the Connecticut Valley (*see* River Towns of Connecticut). King Philip's War (1675–76) temporarily checked expansion, and during the series of struggles between the French and the English the New England frontier settlements suffered from frequent Indian raids (*see* Colonial Wars). By 1754 the New England frontier had been extended well into Vermont, New Hampshire, and Maine.

The settlement of interior New York was long delayed, especially because of the unenlightened land policy of the colony. The only notable activity before the French and Indian War (1754–63) was that of German immigrants, fleeing from the Palatinate. Beginning in 1710 they settled on both banks of the Hudson River near Saugerties. A few years later some of these Germans made homes for themselves along the Schoharie River; and still later (1723–24) others went far up the Mohawk River and established the settlement known as the German Flats (opposite the present town of Herkimer).

In Pennsylvania religious toleration, liberal land policy, and widespread advertising of that colony attracted a host of immigrants who rapidly moved into the interior. By 1750 the frontier settlements extended along the foot of the mountains from Easton southwestward to the Maryland line.

South of Pennsylvania, frontier expansion was the achievement of two streams of settlers: one that pushed westward from the tidewater regions, and the other that flowed southward from Pennsylvania. Virginia was well occupied as far west as the fall line by 1700. During the first quarter of the 18th century the country between the fall line and the Blue Ridge Mountains was settled. The Shenandoah Valley received some settlers from eastern Virginia, but its settlement was accomplished mainly by Germans and Scotch-Irish moving southward from Pennsylvania between 1730 and 1750. The occupation of the piedmont and mountain regions in the Carolinas came a little later and in about the same manner, with Scotch-Irish, Germans, and others from the North pioneering the way in the upland backcountry.

Thus, by 1750 settlements extended far into the interior of New England; there were agricultural outposts up the Mohawk in New York; from Pennsylvania southward settlers were living close up against the Appalachian barrier; and there were scattered cabins on westward-flowing streams. There the advance was halted by the French and Indian War.

No sooner had Fort Duquesne and the other western posts of France been captured in 1758 and 1759 than the westward march was resumed, and the frontier crossed the mountains in complete disregard of the royal Proclamation of 1763. By Braddock's Road settlers from Maryland and Virginia moved inland as far as the Forks of the Ohio, where they were joined by others coming across Pennsylvania by Forbes Road. In Virginia, the Carolinas, and Georgia cabins appeared farther up the streams and even in Powell's Valley and on such westward-flowing rivers as the Cheat, the Holston, the Clinch, and the French Broad. About 1769, pioneers from Virginia began to settle along the Watauga River, in what is now northeastern Tennessee. Before the beginning of the revolutionary war numerous settlements were made in West Florida. By this time also settlements had been established in central Kentucky around Boonesborough.

The close of the revolutionary war was followed by a great outpouring of people, principally from Virginia and North Carolina, into central Kentucky and Tennessee. Across the Ohio River there also appeared the vanguard of the stream of emigrants who soon transformed that region into a land of homes, farms, and towns. The principal effects of the westward movement down to 1810 were seen in Ohio, Kentucky, and Tennessee. The decade following the War of 1812 saw the entire frontier moved westward. So many settlers poured into the Old Southwest that Mississippi and Alabama were admitted into the Union before the close of the decade. The movement into the Old Northwest resulted in the creation of the states of Indiana and Illinois. Across the Mississippi the influx of settlers set the stage for the struggle over the admission of Missouri (*see* Missouri Compromise). By 1830 settlers were moving into the territories of Michigan and Arkansas, and there were probably 20,000 Americans in Texas, which still belonged to Mexico. During the 1830's the movement to Michigan and Arkansas, especially to the former, reached such large proportions that two new states were admitted. Illinois nearly trebled in population, and two new territories (Wisconsin and Iowa) were created. The 1840's were notable years in the westward movement. Not only was the frontier expansion into Wisconsin and Iowa vigorous, but settlements appeared on the Pacific coast. Early in that decade there began the movement of pioneers over the long Oregon Trail to the Pacific Northwest. In 1846 and 1847 the Mormons made their hegira from Nauvoo, Ill., to Utah. At the close of the decade came the rush to the gold fields in California.

During the 1850's migration to Oregon, California, and Texas continued unabated. New converts swelled the population of the Mormons in Utah, and the Territory of New Mexico attracted thousands of settlers. The struggle for Kansas brought streams of zealous emigrants from the North and the South into that territory. The population of the eight states of the upper Mississippi Valley increased by more than 3.35 million, or more than 167 percent. The Civil War checked the westward movement. And yet, even during those troubled years, there was a surprisingly large migration to the gold and silver discoveries in Colorado, Nevada, Oregon, Idaho, and Montana. After the war large numbers of southern sympathizers left their homes for the West.

It was during the decades of the 1870's and the 1880's that the Great Plains—the last American frontier—received the greatest number of westward-moving settlers. By 1890 Kansas and Nebraska were populous states, and the newly admitted states of North Dakota and South Dakota had substantial populations. Just at the close of the decade of the 1880's there was a dramatic rush of settlers to Oklahoma. With the closing decade of the 19th century the story of the westward movement in America may well close. The farmers' frontier had advanced into some part of almost every section and region, and the pioneer phase of the occupation of the land within continental boundaries of the United States, excluding Alaska, was finished.

WETHERSFIELD. *See* **River Towns of Connecticut.**

WHALEBACKS. Steamships with convex upper decks (resembling in shape the backs of whales), first constructed in the 1880's at Duluth, Minn., by Alexander McDougall. They were designed to maximize the amount of hold space available for carrying bulk cargoes.

WHALING. In the 18th and 19th centuries the whaling industry provided oil for lamps and spermaceti for candles. Whaling was pursued by some of the earliest settlers of southeastern Massachusetts and Long Island. Nantucket became one of the great whaling centers of the world. Important fishery grounds were Davis Strait (between Greenland and Canada), the Gulf of St. Lawrence, and the Strait of Belle Isle (separating Newfoundland Island from the Canadian mainland). Between 1770 and 1775 the industry expanded to an extent previously unparalleled. At the outbreak of the Revolution colonial ships had ventured south of the equator. The war seriously crippled American whaling. Hundreds of Nantucket seamen emigrated from New England to sail under the French or British flags. The Pacific fishery grew rapidly and, after the War of 1812, Pacific whaling was almost an American monopoly for nearly one hundred years. New Bedford, Mass., became the foremost whaling port of its day. The Arctic Ocean whaling grounds were discovered in 1846, when an American ship drifted in a dense fog northward through the Bering Strait. Proximity to the new grounds and the advent of steam whalers (1879–80) made San Francisco a major whaling port. The long four- or five-year voyages of the 1840's and 1850's from Atlantic ports were reduced to voyages of less than one year's duration out of San Francisco. Whaling ended in the first decade of the 20th century because of the discovery of petroleum, the development of electricity, and the scarcity of whales.

WHEAT. Introduced by the first colonists, wheat early became the major cash crop. In colonial times its culture became concentrated in the middle colonies. In the mid-18th century, wheat culture spread to the tidewater of Maryland and Virginia. As the frontier crossed the Appalachian Mountains, so did wheat raising. By 1840 Ohio was the premier wheat-producing state, but twenty years later Illinois took the lead; it retained the lead for three decades, until it was overtaken by Minnesota in 1889. Leadership moved with the farming frontier onto the Great Plains in the first years of the 20th century. In 1909 North Dakota lead, followed by Kansas, but between 1919 and 1975 the order was reversed, except in 1934 and 1954, when Oklahoma and then Montana moved into second place.

The majority of eastern farmers preferred soft winter wheat, such as Mediterranean (introduced in 1819), but the Great Plains farmers found those varieties ill-adapted to that area. Hard red spring wheats, such as Red Fife and bluestem, proved more suited to the northern Plains, while Turkey, a hard red winter wheat introduced into central Kansas by Mennonites, became popular on the southern Plains. Early maturing Marquis was introduced from Canada in 1912, and by 1929 it was planted on 87 percent of the hard spring wheat acreage. It proved susceptible to the black stem rust and after 1934 lost favor to Thatcher and in the late 1960's to Chris and Fortuna. On the southern Plains, Tenmarq, released by the Kansas Agricultural Experiment Station in 1932, superseded Turkey and was in turn replaced by Pawnee and later by Triumph and Scout. In the 1960's the wheatgrowers of the Columbia Valley began to favor a new short-stemmed soft white winter wheat, known as Gaines.

Wheat until the early national period was sown by broadcasting, reaped by sickles, and threshed by flails. In rapid succession in the 19th century, sowing with drills replaced broadcasting, cradles took the place of sickles, and the cradles in turn were replaced by reapers and binders. Steam-powered threshing machines superseded flails. In the 1930's the small combine combined reaping and threshing into one operation.

The marketing of wheat went through parallel changes. Initially the harvest was sacked, shipped, and stored in warehouses, but after the Civil War wheat began to flow first to the country elevators and from there to terminal elevators, from which it was sold through grain exchanges.

Since colonial times wheat growers have produced a surplus for export. Expansion of acreage during World War I and contraction of demand overseas after its termination created an accumulation of surpluses that could not be marketed. The resulting low prices prompted growers to seek government support of prices, first through the McNary-Haugen bills, which failed to become law, and later through the Agricultural Adjustment Act of 1933. Increasing production, which reached a billion bushels in 1944, permitted an expansion of wheat and flour exports as part of the nation's foreign assistance programs. In fiscal year 1966, exports amounted to 858,657,000 bushels, of which 571,154,000 were disposed of as food aid. A disastrous drought in the Soviet Union in 1972 led to the sale of 388,489,000 bushels to that country in one year and the conclusion in 1975 of an agreement to supply the Soviets with breadstuffs over a five-year period.

WHEELER COMPROMISE (1876). An agreement between two antagonistic political factions in Louisiana. The accord was reached under a congressional investigating committee headed by Republican Rep. William A. Wheeler. It stipulated that the Republican Reconstruction governor, William Kellogg, whose 1872 election was disputed, should complete his term and that twelve Democratic members of the state legislature, all of whom had been excluded by the Kellogg faction, should be reinstated. A caucus of the Louisiana Conservative (Democratic) party ratified the agreement, and the state legislature accepted it.

WHEELER-HOWARD ACT (June 18, 1934). The act gave tribes on reservations the right to adopt, by a majority vote, a constitution for local self-government; alternatively, if one-third of the reservation petitioned for a charter of incorporation, the secretary of the interior could issue one to become effective on approval by the Indians at a special election. The act also provided that Indians who qualified for administrative positions maintained by the Indian Office were to receive preference. Up to $250,000 was authorized to be spent annually to educate young Indians. To encourage economic development, $250,000 annually was authorized to pay for organizing Indian chartered corporations. A revolving fund of $10 million was established to make loans to such corporations. To develop and enlarge tribal lands, the act prohibited future allotments in severalty, provided that surplus lands previously available for sale were to be restored to tribal ownership, and authorized up to $2 million a year to enlarge the tribal land holdings.

WHEELING (W. Va.). Located on the Ohio River, the site of Wheeling was first settled in 1769 by Ebenezer Zane. Five years later Fort Fincastle was built; in the revolutionary war the post was renamed Fort Henry, for Patrick Henry. Fort Henry was attacked by Indians on Sept. 1, 1777, and again by a British and Indian force on Sept. 10, 1782. After the Revolution a village grew up about the fort. In 1795 this village was first organized as a town; it was chartered as a city in 1806 and incorporated in 1836. With the coming of the steamboat in 1811 and the completion of the Cumberland Road to the Ohio River in 1818, Wheeling grew rapidly. In 1853 the Baltimore and Ohio Railroad reached Wheeling. On May 13, 1861, the first Wheeling Convention, at which delegates from twenty-six western Virginia counties voted against secession from the Union, convened. Wheeling was the seat of the Virginia Restored Government from June 19, 1861, to June 20, 1863, when it became the first capital of West Virginia. On Apr. 1, 1870, the capital was moved to Charleston, but on May 23, 1875, it was returned to Wheeling, where it remained until 1885, when it was returned to Charleston.

Wheeling is an industrial city. It was long an important shipbuilding and wagonmaking center. It is a center as well for the match-manufacturing, tobacco, glass, tableware, packing, and brewing industries. The city's population in 1980 was 43,070.

WHEELING BRIDGE CASE. A lawsuit initiated in 1849 that grew out of the efforts of Pittsburgh to prevent the construction of a suspension bridge over the Ohio River at Wheeling, then part of Virginia, on the grounds that the bridge would interfere with navigation. The Supreme Court sustained the contentions of Pittsburgh, but they were nullified by an act of Congress.

WHIG PARTY. A major political party formed in the early 1830's to challenge the policies of the Democratic party under Andrew Jackson. The party's leaders were mainly representatives of the vested property interests. The term "Whig" was used in 1832 by the antitariff leaders of South Carolina, but it soon came to be applied to all that found themselves opposed to the Jacksonian Democratic party. Jackson's war on the Bank of the United States; his promotion in 1836 of Martin Van Buren as his successor in the presidency; and former National Republicans and the remnants of the Anti-Masonic party added to the opposition party. Whig candidate William Henry Harrison's successful "log cabin" campaign for the presidency in 1840 gave the party important strength in the backcountry. The Whig success of 1840 made it the temporarily dominant party. Clay promptly laid down a nationalistic program, to which the majority of the party rallied, despite the insistence of John Tyler (who became president when Harrison died shortly after his inauguration) on continuing Whig traditions of the 1830's. Read out of the party, Tyler watched in dismay the acceptance of the Clay formula. The issues of the annexation of Texas and of the extension of slavery in time proved a menace to the solidarity of the party. The election of 1844, in which Democrat James Polk defeated Clay, showed that the Whigs had lost the support of expansionist forces. The conservative property interests of leading Whigs made them opponents of the Mexican War and of expansion. While some of the northern Whigs were antislavery people (Conscience Whigs), other party supporters were sufficiently proslavery to be labeled "Cotton Whigs." In the sectional disputes of 1850–51, southern Whigs were prominent among the forces that fought secession (*see* Compromise of 1850). By 1852 sectional allegiance had become so strong that the party began to disintegrate.

WHIP, PARTY. Party leader in both the Senate and the House of Representatives. In the House the party whip ranks immediately below the speaker and majority leader (if in the minority party, he is second behind the minority leader); in the Senate he is second in his party hierarchy behind the majority (or minority) leader. His duties are to make sure that members are in the chamber during crucial votes; to forecast how members will vote; to persuade all members to support the party leadership; to alert party leaders to shifting congressional opinions; and to distribute information on pending amendments or bills. Party whips were first employed in the U.S. Congress in 1899.

WHIPPING POST. *See* **Flogging.**

WHIPPLE'S EXPEDITION (1853–56). An army survey of the West ordered by Congress to locate a route for a railroad to the Pacific Ocean. Lt. Amiel W. Whipple traced the thirty-fifth parallel beginning at Fort Smith on the Arkansas River in July 1853. Crossing Oklahoma and the panhandle, he reached Albuquerque in November. From there he crossed the Sierra Madre and the Sierra Nevada and reached Los Angeles in the spring of 1854.

WHISKEY. In the late 17th century western Pennsylvania became a center of rye-whiskey making. Maryland began producing liquor about the same time. Whiskey became the leading spirituous drink outside of New England, where rum remained the favorite drink. Kentuckians discovered that whiskey could be produced from Indian corn, and this eventually became America's leading spirituous product, exceeding in volume the rye whiskeys of Maryland and Pennsylvania. In 1792 there were 2,579 small distilleries in the United States. Enormous distilling plants grew up in Kentucky, manufacturing sour mash, sweet mash, Bourbon—so called from the Kentucky county of that name—and a small percentage of rye. Ohio and Illinois also developed large distilling industries. During 1901–1919 there were withdrawn from bonded warehouses after payment of tax a yearly average of 60 million gallons of whiskey. The Prohibition era (1919–33) destroyed many long-established companies whose distilleries, if reopened at all after the repeal of the law, were in many cases under other ownership. In 1935 Kentucky produced 197 million gallons of whiskey. Producing a relatively low 104 million gallons in 1955, whiskey distillers in the United States put out 160 million gallons in 1970. By 1972 production had fallen again, to 126 million gallons.

WHISKEY REBELLION (1794). In the 1790's the failure to open the Mississippi River to navigation, the dilatory conduct of the Indian wars, the speculative prices of land, ill-paid militia duty, scarcity of specie, and the creation of a salaried official class accented western grievances. The excise law of 1791, which taxed whiskey—the chief transportable and barterable western product—furnished a convenient peg on which to hang these grievances. In May and June 1794 Congress passed a measure making offenses against the excise law cognizable in state courts. While the bill was in Congress the U.S. District Court of Pennsylvania issued a series of processes returnable to Philadelphia. A federal marshal was attacked in Allegheny County while serving a process, and on July 17 several hundred men, led by members of a local "Democratic society," attacked and burned the home of the regional inspector of the excise. At the same time they used stolen letters in stirring up the people to attack Pittsburgh. A muster of the southwestern militia was called at Braddock's Field for Aug. 1. The militia march on Pittsburgh on Aug. 2 was carried through without violence. Nevertheless, on Aug. 7 President George Washington issued a proclamation ordering the disaffected westerners to their homes and calling up the militia. On Aug. 14–15 delegates from the Monongahela Valley met at Parkinson's Ferry, but were prevented from drastic measures by moderates. A committee appointed by Washington met with a western committee and arranged that the sentiment of the people of the western counties concerning submission be taken on Sept. 11. The vote was unsatisfactory, and Washington set in motion the militia army under Secretary of the Treasury Alexander Hamilton. The western counties were occupied during November, and more than a score of prisoners were sent to Philadelphia. All of them were acquitted or pardoned.

WHISKEY RING. A group of western distillers and public officials in the Internal Revenue Service who formed a conspiracy to evade the whiskey tax. Benjamin H. Bristow, secretary of the Treasury in President Ulysses S. Grant's cabinet, procured the indictment (May 10, 1875) of more than 230 persons and the conviction of 110, including 4 government officials. During the course of the litigation allegations were made that the illegal abatements of taxes were to raise funds for the Republican party and that the improprieties involved not only Grant's private secretary, Gen. Orville E. Babcock (indicted Dec. 9), but in a measure the president himself.

WHISKEY TOWNS. Grew up around saloons established just outside the borders of Indian lands or other areas where the sale of liquor was prohibited. In most of these the sale of whiskey was the chief business.

WHISPERING CAMPAIGNS. A political term involving the spreading of slanderous rumors and accusations by word of mouth against a political opponent. The term first appeared in print about 1920, during the whispering campaign against Warren G. Harding by the Democrats.

WHISTLE STOP. Small towns, or crossroads, where passenger trains would not regularly make a stop. If someone wanted to board the train at such a place, a special signal would be shown and the engineer would acknowledge it by blowing the locomotive whistle; notice that the train was going to stop and let passengers off was also given by whistle. American political candidates campaigning usually traveled by rail. To reach the people in the small towns and country districts, a candidate for office would have the train halted at "whistle stops."

WHITE CAPS. An antiblack, night-riding organization in south central Mississippi, around 1900. Centered chiefly in Lincoln County, they were broken up by prosecution during Gov. James K. Vardaman's administration (1904–08).

WHITE CITIZENS COUNCILS. Organized in the southern states to obstruct the implementation of the U.S. Supreme Court's desegregation decision of 1954 (*Brown* v. *Board of Education of Topeka*). Originating in Mississippi, the councils advocated white supremacy and resorted to economic pressure against local advocates of desegregation.

WHITEHALL, TREATY OF (1686). Provided for the cessation of hostilities in America between Great Britain and France and a mutual abstention from illicit commerce. Its most significant provision was the clause embodying the principle of the "two spheres": armed clashes in America were not to be considered as causes of war between France and Great Britain in Europe, and a European conflict between them was not to be considered a cause for war in America. The treaty was supplemented by the appointment of commissioners, in 1687, to adjust the Anglo-French disputes in America and to arrange a boundary between their respective possessions there. The work of the commissioners came to naught by reason of the English Revolution of 1688.

WHITE HOUSE. The residence of every president of the United States since John Adams became its first occupant on Nov. 1, 1800. The selection of a site for the president's house was made by President George Washington and Maj. Pierre Charles L'Enfant, the French planner of the city of Washington. In 1792 the commissioners of the federal city drew up a competition for the design of a house for the president. The winning design was the creation of James Hoban, an Irish-born architect who modeled his entry after Leinster House in Dublin, Ireland. In Jefferson's time (1807) the east and west terraces were added to the mansion; in 1824 the South Portico was completed, and in 1829 the North Portico. The terraces were the work of the architect Benjamin Latrobe, and the two porticoes incorporated the designs of both Latrobe and Hoban. In 1948 a balcony was added to the South Portico at the request of President Harry S. Truman. The West Wing of the White House, which contains the offices of the president and his staff, was built in 1902 as a temporary office building. It expanded over the years until it was double its original size. The East Wing was completed during World War II (1942) to provide further office space.

WHITE HOUSE OF THE CONFEDERACY. A Greek revival mansion in Richmond, Va. Designed by Robert Mills and built in 1818, it was bought by the city of Richmond on June 11, 1861; it was furnished and presented to Confederate President Jefferson Davis. When he refused the gift, the Confederate government rented it. As the executive mansion, it was occupied by Davis until he was forced to leave it on Apr. 2, 1865. On Apr. 3, 1865, the Union commander, Godfrey Weitzel, made the mansion his headquarters. After the federal government returned it in 1870, the city used it as a public school. On June 12, 1894, the city deeded it to the Confederate Memorial Literary Society. It is now the home of the Museum of the Confederacy.

WHITE LEAGUE. Organized in Louisiana in 1874, it first appeared at Opelousas in April and then spread rapidly throughout the state. Except for the New Orleans League, it consisted of political clubs with little or no connections between the different units. Its object was to protect the white race and eliminate from public office the Republicans. There was no serious clash between it and the state authorities until the uprising in New Orleans on Sept. 14. Having attained its object when the radical state government was overthrown, the league declined and, after 1877, disappeared.

WHITEMARSH (Pa.). A township adjacent to Philadelphia on the northwest, it was the site of Gen. George Washington's encampment from Nov. 2 until Dec. 11, 1777. According to tradition, on Dec. 2 Lydia Darragh, a nurse, overheard British officers plan an attack on Washington's Whitemarsh encampment. On Dec. 4 she met one of Washington's officers and told him the British plans. The troops at Whitemarsh successfully withstood the attack, Dec. 5–7.

WHITE OAK SWAMP, BATTLE AT (June 30, 1862). Union Gen. George B. McClellan's cattle herd and train of 3,600 wagons passed White Oak Swamp (Virginia) on June 29 (*see* Seven Days' Battles). Union Gen. William B. Franklin's corps remained behind to guard the crossing. Gen. Thomas J. ("Stonewall") Jackson was in pursuit and shelled the Union troops vigorously but did not attempt to cross the swamp. Gen. Robert E. Lee's attacks at Frayser's Farm having meanwhile been repulsed, Franklin that night retired safely to Malvern Hill.

WHITE PLAINS, BATTLE OF (Oct. 28, 1776). Gen. George Washington's troops had taken up a strong position across the roads leading up the Hudson River from New York to New England. Strongly entrenched on the high ground northwest and northeast of the village of White Plains, he waited for British Gen. William Howe's next move. Avoiding a direct attack on Washington's front, Howe sent a detachment to gain Chatterton Hill, a rocky eminence near White Plains. But the British were forestalled by Gen. Alexander McDougall, who gained the hill and held it until British reinforcements forced a retreat. The British suffered about 300 casualties, the Americans more than 200.

WHITES, POOR. *See* **Poor Whites.**

"WHITE SQUADRON." A group of ships so called because they were painted white, comprised the first modern American steel vessels *(Atlanta, Boston, Chicago,* and *Dolphin)* to be completed (1887–88) after the naval decay following the Civil War.

"WHITEWASH." Meaning to free from debt through bankruptcy, it was a common expression in the English colonies. It was applied politically by 1800, the *Philadelphia Aurora* (July 2, 1800) referring to a "whitewash" for President John Adams. This adaptation, meaning to give misconduct an appearance of good character through superficial examination, was common by 1839.

WHITE WOMAN OF THE GENESEE. A name applied to Mary Jemison, who, at age fourteen, was captured by the Iroquois in 1758. She was adopted by a Seneca family living on the Ohio River, and two years later married a Delaware named Sheninjee. In 1762 she and her family moved to the banks of the Genesee River in New York State; her husband died the same year. Three years later she married a Seneca warrior. Aided by her husband and eight children she raised a large herd of cattle on a tribal grant of land. Her title to the land was confirmed by New York State in 1817, and in the same year she became a naturalized citizen. In 1831 Mary Jemison moved to the Buffalo Creek Reservation.

WHITMAN MASSACRE (Nov. 29, 1847). Growing trouble between Marcus Whitman and the Cayuse to whom he ministered as a missionary doctor at Waiilatpu (near the present city of Walla Walla, Wash.) led to an attack that resulted in the death of Whitman, his wife, and twelve others. Until ransomed by the Hudson's Bay Company fifty-three women and children were held captive by the Indians. Distrust by the Indians had been aroused by the increasing numbers of settlers and Whitman's apparent greater success in treating the diseases of the whites than of the Indians.

WHITMAN MISSION. *See* **Walla Walla Settlements.**

WICHITA (Kans.). A city on the Arkansas River, started as a trading post established by James R. Mead for the Wichita in 1864. It became a settlers' village and cowboy trading town on the Chisholm Trail in 1868. In 1870 the trading post was incorporated as a town and in 1871 as a city. When the railroads passed the new city by, the boosters laid their own track twenty-six miles north to Newton, Kans., in 1872 and connected with the Santa Fe Railroad. This made Wichita the railhead of the Texas cattle drive. The development of natural resources of the area, the growth of agriculture in the surrounding region, and the development of industry led to Wichita's prosperity during the 20th century. Aircraft construction and oil recovery and refining are two major industries. In 1980 the city had a population of 279,272.

WICKERSHAM COMMISSION (officially the National Commission on Law Observance and Enforcement). Appointed by President Herbert Hoover in May 1929, with George W. Wickersham as chairman. The findings were published in 1931. The most widely discussed was that on Prohibition. Others covered methods of dealing with juvenile delinquency, the cost of law enforcement, interrogation of criminal suspects, lawless practices in law enforcement, and the belief that criminals were mostly foreign born.

WICKIUP. *See* **Architecture: American Indian.**

WIDE-AWAKES. An antiforeign, anti-Catholic organization that flourished around 1850 (*see* Nativism). In the presidential campaign of 1860, Republican marching clubs under this name arose everywhere.

WIGWAM. An Algonkin word meaning "dwelling." Wickiup is a variant of the same term. The wigwam in New England was a dome-shaped structure or a similar elongated form, covered with bark, mats, or thatch. Later, the term was applied to structures more correctly designated tepees.

"WIGWAM." The name given to the headquarters of Tammany societies, so called because of the pseudo-Indian organization of the society. The name was first used by the Tammany Hall organization in New York City.

WILDCAT BANKS. State-chartered banks in the 1830's and 1840's, so-called because of their remote locations. These banks often borrowed enough gold to show the state inspectors, so that their charters could be granted. They then returned the borrowed gold and printed banknotes in great quantities. These pieces of paper currency were circulated, usually at less than face value, among people who could be persuaded to take them. Wildcat banks often loaned large sums, in banknotes, to speculators in public land or other ventures. In the panics of 1818, 1837, 1841, and 1847, many of the wildcat banks went out of business. (*See* Banking.)

WILDCAT MONEY. Currency issued by wildcat banks. They created a confusion in the currency and gave point to Secretary of the Treasury Salmon P. Chase's demand for a national bank currency (*see* Banking).

WILDCAT OIL DRILLING. Hardly had Edwin L. Drake completed his oil well on Oil Creek, Pa., in 1859, than others seeking similar good fortune set to drilling nearby with spring poles. The wildcatter hazarded his all and often that of his supporters on discovering oil in the most unexpected places. The early oil companies depended on such prospectors.

WILDERNESS, BATTLES OF THE (May 5–7, 1864). On May 4, 1864, Gen. Ulysses S. Grant's army was across the Rapidan River in Virginia, preparing to attack Gen. Robert E. Lee's forces. Instead of attacking the Union troops in the act of crossing, Lee preferred to engage Grant in the Wilderness, a heavily wooded and tangled region, where the Union two-to-one superiority in numbers and artillery would be somewhat neutralized. Grant directed his main movement at Lee's right, hoping to get clear of the Wilderness before effective resistance could be offered. Lee moved rapidly to check this attempt. Road divergence separated his two wings; Confederate Gen. James Longstreet, expected to support either wing, was late in arriving. On May 5 Grant attacked. Confederate generals Richard S. Ewell on the left and Ambrose P. Hill both held firm. Night ended the fighting. The next day Grant resumed his attack. Hill's troops were driven in confusion. Lee personally rode among the fleeing men to rally them. Longstreet's tardy command arrived and struck with suddenness and fury, driving Grant's men back. Ewell, on Lee's left, repulsed all attacks. On May 7 the two armies faced each other from behind hasty breastworks. Once the fighting began, the brush caught fire and many wounded were burned to death. Perceiving the uselessness of again assaulting Lee's lines, Grant decided to move by the flank toward Richmond, thus forcing Lee to come and meet him at Spotsylvania Courthouse.

WILDERNESS ROAD. A road from eastern Virginia through the mountain pass known as Cumberland Gap, to the interior of Kentucky and thence to the Ohio and beyond. A rudimentary route already existed when, in March 1775, Daniel Boone and a party of about thirty woodsmen undertook to clear and mark out a trail at the instance of the Transylvania Company. Its total length was close to 300 miles. After Kentucky had become a state, renewed efforts to grade, widen, and reinforce the road were put forth. For more than half a century after Boone, the Wilderness Road was a principal avenue for the movement of immigrants and others to and from the early West. Today it is part of U.S. Route 25.

WILDLIFE PRESERVATION. The first game law, for the protection of deer, was passed by the town of Newport in 1639. Other colonies followed suit, and after independence state and local communities continued to pass laws regulating the taking of game, fish, and birds. The contradictory maze of early state, county, and local ordinances, with no machinery for centralized enforcement, provided typically for a closed season and fines for offenders—part of which (usually half) went to the informer and the rest to the treasury. These laws were almost universally ineffective. During the last two decades of the 19th century the game enforcement machinery was dramatically improved on the state level. Agencies grew in size, complexity, and centralization. An important innovation, widely adopted, was a North Dakota law of 1895 requiring a hunting license, which for the first time provided a steady and dependable source of revenue. By 1904 most states had some kind of fish and game agency. The federal government took an important step in 1900 with the passage of the Lacey Act, which made it illegal to ship game killed in violation of state law across state lines.

The concept of refuges was crucial in the growth of concern for the wild habitat. It began with the creation of Yellowstone National Park in 1872. Later parks followed this pattern, and on Aug. 25, 1916, the National Park Service, a regulatory agency with power to formulate a park wildlife policy, was established. Meanwhile, the Bureau of Biological Survey had already acquired regulatory powers, along with the beginnings of a domain. Created by Congress in 1885 by a small appropriation for research in the Department of Agriculture, it was charged in 1900 with enforcement of the Lacey Act. An act of 1913 placed migratory and insectivorous birds under federal authority, and the 1916 treaty with Great Britain for the protection of migratory birds in the United States and Canada expanded this power to regulate. In 1903 the first wildlife sanctuary outside the park system, Pelican Island, off the east coast of Florida, was placed under its jurisdiction. The Biological Survey, which merged with the Bureau of Fisheries in 1940 to become the Fish and Wildlife Service, eventually presided over a vast network of such refuges—in 1971, a total of 29,284,761 acres in 329 areas. The final ingredient in the emergence of a diversified federal refuge system was the creation of breeding sanctuaries for game in the national forest reserves. After the concept of a refuge system, the doctrine of the Forest Service was the most important element in the development of a wildlife policy (*see* Forestry). Finally there was the emergence of the profession of wildlife management. In 1934 the Biological Survey set up research and training programs at ten land grant universities. From this beginning wildlife management grew to full professional status, and by the 1970's training through the doctorate was available in many universities.

The growth of a public wildlife policy was partly a response to pressures from organized groups. The Boone and Crockett Club, formed in 1887, worked for game laws on the state level, watched over the development of Yellowstone as a game preserve, lobbied for the creation of more parks, and rallied support for bison protection. Other organizations and clubs—such as the Sierra Club, the New York Audubon Society, the American Game Conference (later North American Wildlife Conference), and the American Ornithological Union (which was mainly responsible for the creation of the first refuge at Pelican Island)—formed an expanding interlocking wildlife lobby on the national and state levels.

WILD RICE (*Zizania aquatica*). Native to North America, it conditioned to a great degree the life of certain Indian tribes in the so-called wild-rice district—Wisconsin and a part of eastern Minnesota. Among the Indians who were largely dependent on it for their food supply were the Chippewa, the eastern Sioux, and the Menomini.

WILD WEST SHOW. An entertainment featuring exhibitions typical of the life of cowboy, Indian, and soldier. The first was the "Wild West, Rocky Mountain and Prairie Exhibition" of William F. Cody ("Buffalo Bill") and W. F. Carver, opening at Omaha, Nebr., May 17, 1883. It was reorganized in 1884 by Cody, Bogardus, and Nate Salsbury. Buffalo Bill's Wild West toured Europe in 1887, 1889–92, and 1902–07. At the Chicago World's Fair in 1893 the "Congress of Rough Riders of the World" was featured. Pawnee Bill's own Wild West show achieved great success after 1890, and for nineteen years it toured the United States, Canada, and (in 1894) Europe. Buffalo Bill merged with Pawnee Bill in 1909 and with the Sells-Floto circus in 1913. Financial troubles were attributed to motion-picture competition. The rodeo is a closely related form of entertainment.

WILKES EXPLORING EXPEDITION (1838–42). Officially the U.S. Exploring Expedition, it was authorized by Congress in 1836 to investigate the great holes that Capt. John Cleves Symmes believed lay at the poles of the earth, and which he believed hollow and habitable. Organized without guiding precedent by Jeremiah N. Reynolds and Capt. Thomas ap Catesby Jones, the expedition floundered during two years of strife. Gray and Jones finally resigned in disgust, Reynolds was shouldered aside, and the enterprise was placed under the jurisdiction of Secretary of War Joel Roberts Poinsett. After a succession of his seniors had refused it, Lt. Charles Wilkes accepted the command. A fleet of six ships sailed from Hampton Roads, Va., in August 1838. In the course of the four years' cruise, most of it in the Pacific, it charted and surveyed upward of 200 islands, the Northwest coast, and San Francisco Bay, and coasted the Antarctic continent for 1,500 miles. It returned with collections in natural history, unprecedented in magnitude, that were housed in the U.S. National Museum, the U.S. Herbarium, and the U.S. Botanic Garden. The building set up for making the observations, which served as base for those made at sea, became the U.S. Naval Observatory.

WILKES FUND DISPUTE. A fund of £17,000 was raised in Europe and America to pay the debts of and defend John Wilkes, English political figure and writer, charged with libeling King George III in 1863. The South Carolina House of Commons voted £1,500 for the fund in 1769. The crown denied its right to do this, the commons defended it, and the controversy continued until the beginning of the Revolution.

WILKINSON, FORT. Named for Gen. James Wilkinson and situated on the Oconee River near Milledgeville, Ga., it was constructed about 1797. On June 16, 1802, Wilkinson negotiated a treaty with the Creek as initial fulfillment of the Georgia Compact; soon afterward troops were withdrawn from the fort.

WILLAMETTE VALLEY SETTLEMENTS. About 1830 French-Canadian employees of the Hudson's Bay Company took up farms on the French Prairie, the region within the great bend of the Willamette River below Salem (Oreg.). They were followed by Methodist missionaries led by Jason Lee in 1834. By 1841, there were settled in the lower Willamette Valley nine missionary, sixty-five American, and sixty-one French-Canadian families. On May 3, 1843, the American settlers in the valley elected officers, and on July 5 adopted a constitution, thus setting up a provisional government. The following year the French-Canadians joined this government, and in 1845 it was expanded to include the officials of the Hudson's Bay Company. The overland immigration to the Willamette Valley began in 1841. By the end of 1845 the population of the valley numbered about 6,000. The Donation Land Law (1850), which gave each married settler in Oregon 640 acres of land, speeded up settlement.

WILLIAM AND MARY, COLLEGE OF. Chartered by William III and Mary II on Feb. 8, 1693. William and Mary's first president was Rev. James Blair. The first college building was erected in 1695; it was rebuilt and enlarged after a fire in 1705. Redesigned after fires in 1859 and 1862, it was restored to its 18th-century appearance in 1928–30. Many of the students of the early college were leaders in the Revolution, including Thomas Jefferson, James Monroe, Richard Bland, Peyton Randolph, Edmund Randolph, and Benjamin Harrison. In 1776 the Phi Beta Kappa Society was organized. Schools of medicine, law, and modern languages were established in 1779. The college was closed briefly in 1781, when it was occupied by the British; during the Civil War; and again from 1881 until 1888 for lack of funds. In 1888 a state grant enabled the college to reopen to educate male teachers; and in 1906 the property of the college was deeded to the Commonwealth of Virginia. The college became coeducational in 1918. Branches that opened during the 1920's in Richmond and Norfolk became, in 1962, Virginia's state-supported urban universities, Virginia Commonwealth University and Old Dominion University, respectively. In 1967, William and Mary was redesignated a university.

WILLIAM AND MARY, FORT. The leading radicals of Portsmouth, N.H., were warned by Paul Revere on Dec. 13, 1774, that Gen. Thomas Gage might take over the military stores at Fort William and Mary, located on New Castle, an island at the mouth of the harbor. Several hundred men under John Langdon and Pierse Long crossed over the next day, received the brief fire of the garrison of six without harm, seized the fort, and removed about 100 barrels of powder. On Dec. 15 Gen. John Sullivan with another party took the muskets and some of the cannon; further action was blocked by the arrival of a naval vessel.

WILLIAM HENRY, FORT, MASSACRE AT (Aug. 10, 1757). Marquis Louis Joseph de Montcalm, the French commander, with an army numbering 8,000, including 2,000 Algonkin allies, laid siege to the British Fort William Henry at the head of Lake George, N.Y., early in August. Fewer than 2,500 men defended the post. They were forced to surrender on Aug. 9, although Montcalm agreed to give the garrison safe-conduct to Fort Edward. But the Indians began a general massacre. Montcalm and his chief officers were able to restrain the Indians only with the greatest difficulty. Although some accounts put the number massacred as high as 1,500, the best evidence shows that only about 50 were killed.

WILLIAMSBURG (Va.). A city in southeastern Virginia, located on the peninsula between the York and James rivers, had its origins in a central section of Middle Plantation, a palisaded outpost established between the James and York in 1633. The town received its present name in 1699 in honor of William III, at which time it became the capital of the colony of Virginia. From 1699 to 1779 Williamsburg remained the economic, educational, religious, and social, as well as the governmental, center of the colony. It was the scene of much political activity in the period preceding the

American Revolution, and toward the end of that struggle it was occupied in turn by British and American forces. Owing to the desire for a more central capital, the seat of government was removed to Richmond in 1779. Until the 20th century, except for intervals during the Civil and World wars, Williamsburg remained a quiet county seat and college town. During the Battle of Williamsburg in 1862, Union troops occupied the town and remained there until 1865. In 1926 William A. R. Goodwin, twice rector of historic Bruton Parish Church, persuaded John D. Rockefeller, Jr., to sponsor the preservation and restoration of scores of 18th-century buildings because of Williamsburg's important contributions to the independence movement. Architects came to study the old buildings, researchers sought records and other documents, and archaeologists studied the earth layer by layer.

The Raleigh Tavern was opened to the public in 1932, followed in 1934 by the Governor's Palace and the capital. By 1980 more than thirty buildings were open on regular schedules. Costumed hosts and hostesses interpret the history and the lives and times of the colonial inhabitants. Craftsmen demonstrate a score of colonial trades. The city's population in 1970 was 9,069.

WILLIAMSBURG, BATTLE OF (May 5, 1862). An incident in the retreat of the Confederates under Gen. Joseph E. Johnston from Yorktown, Va., to the Chickahominy River, and their pursuit by the Union forces under Gen. George B. McClellan. On the outskirts of Williamsburg, Va., swampy terrain and strong redoubts commanding the roads brought pursuit to a halt on May 4. Determined attacks on these defenses on May 5 constituted the battle. Union losses in the battle were 2,239; Confederate losses were not much smaller.

WILLIAMSON PURCHASE. *See* **Pulteney Purchase.**

***WILLIAMS* V. *MISSISSIPPI*,** 170 U.S. 213 (1898). A test by Henry Williams, a black, of Mississippi's constitution of 1890 and code of 1892, which required a literacy test. Williams claimed that the franchise provisions denied blacks equal protection of the law guaranteed by the Fourteenth Amendment. The Supreme Court decided (Apr. 25, 1898) that mere possibility of discrimination was not grounds for invalidating the provisions.

***WILLING*.** A large Mississippi River ship, armed with cannon and manned by forty-six men, which George Rogers Clark sent from Kaskaskia (Ill.) to Vincennes (Ind.) in 1779 to cooperate in the reduction of the latter fort. It arrived too late to participate in the assault (*see* Clark's Northwest Campaign).

WILLING EXPEDITION (1778–79). Sanctioned by the Commerce Committee of the Continental Congress and commanded by James Willing of Philadelphia, its purpose was to despoil British property and trade on the lower Mississippi River. Willing, with a party of about thirty men, left Fort Pitt on Jan. 10, 1778, in an armed boat, the *Rattletrap,* and arrived in Natchez on Feb. 19, intimidating British subjects and seizing their property on the way. With the cooperation of volunteers from New Orleans, including Oliver Pollock and his nephew, Thomas Pollock, Willing continued to attack the settlers in British Florida. His men returned by way of the Mississippi, but Willing sailed for Philadelphia later in the year, only to be captured by the British.

WILLS CREEK POST. *See* **Cumberland, Fort.**

WILMINGTON (Del.). The largest city in Delaware, with a population of 70,193 according to the 1980 census. The city is headquarters of the largest chemical company in the United States. E. I. DuPont de Nemours has been operating in and near Wilmington since 1802, when the company's founder opened his first gunpowder mill there. The site of Wilmington, facing the Delaware River where two smaller streams enter it, was the location of a Swedish trading post and fort (Fort Christina) as early as 1638. The name Wilmington was given the place by William Penn, proprietor of the Delaware area, in honor of an English friend, the Earl of Wilmington. The water power of Brandywine Creek and of the Christina River helped attract light industry. The modern city is the result of the activities of the DuPont company, which has turned it into a major industrial center. Many other industries have been located in the area in order to profit from its good transportation systems and from closeness to the source of DuPont chemical products. Chemical manufacturing companies, auto assembly plants, paper manufacturers, and iron and steel mills are in the Wilmington area. It is the world center for production of vulcanized rubber.

WILMINGTON RIOT (Nov. 9, 1898). A meeting of whites was held at Wilmington, N.C., to protest black rule; most of the city offices were held by blacks, who outnumbered the whites 17,000 to 8,000. It was demanded that the editor of the Afro-American newspaper remove himself and his press by 7 o'clock the next morning. When this demand was not met, 600 armed whites destroyed the printing material, and the building "took fire" and burned to the ground. A race riot followed, and some ten blacks were killed and three whites wounded. All of the city officials resigned and were succeeded by white Democrats.

WILMOT PROVISO (1846). Soon after the Mexican War began, President James K. Polk requested $2 million from Congress with which to negotiate peace, it being understood that territory would be acquired from Mexico. On Aug. 8, a bill to appropriate the sum was moved in the House of Representatives. David Wilmot, a Democrat from Pennsylvania, proposed "neither slavery nor involuntary servitude shall ever exist in any part of said territory" as an amendment to the bill. This amendment became known as the Wilmot Proviso. It precipitated a bitter debate over the question of slavery in the territories. An effort was made in the House to amend the proviso by limiting its application to the region north of the Missouri Compromise line, but this was defeated. The appropriation bill carrying the Wilmot Proviso was then passed by the House by a vote of eighty-seven to sixty-four. The bill as amended was then sent to the Senate; but the Senate adjourned before a vote was taken. In the next Congress, a bill to appropriate $3 million for peace negotiations was introduced in the House, and Wilmot again moved his proviso. The bill as amended was carried in the House, Feb. 15, 1847, by a vote of 115 to 106. The Senate refused to consider the amended bill, but passed one of its own appropriating the desired sum. After bitter debate the House concurred in the Senate bill, and the $3 million became available to Polk without Wilmot's conditions.

WILSON-GORMAN TARIFF ACT. *See* **Tariff.**

WILSON'S CREEK, BATTLE OF (Aug. 10, 1861). A battle in Missouri between Union troops under Gen. Nathaniel Lyon and the Missouri State Guard under Confederate Gen. Sterling Price, cooperating with Confederates from Arkansas under Gen. Ben McCulloch. Lyon had 5,400 men, and Price and McCulloch had nearly 11,000. Lyon attacked the combined force at Wilson's Creek, Mo., ten miles southwest of Springfield. He sent Gen. Franz Sigel to make a flank attack, but McCulloch defeated him, and both armies turned on Lyon. At the critical moment Lyon was killed. The Union army retreated east toward Rolla. Total casualties were 2,544.

WINCHESTER, BATTLE OF (May 25, 1862). The disaster to Union Gen. John R. Kenly's forces at Front Royal, Va., placed the command of Gen. Nathaniel P. Banks at Strasburg, consisting of some 10,000 Union troops and sixteen guns, in peril from Confederate forces operating in the Shenandoah Valley under Gen. Thomas J. ("Stonewall") Jackson and Gen. Richard S. Ewell. Banks delayed starting for Winchester until he was all but outflanked. With Jackson striking at his flank and rear and Ewell striving to intercept him, he finally reached Winchester on May 24. There he was attacked by Ewell, soon reinforced by Jackson, their combined troops and guns double his own. Against these odds Banks retreated beyond Winchester, where the Confederates, unable to break his columns, allowed him to proceed unmolested to the Potomac River.

WINCHESTER, BATTLE OF (Sept. 19, 1864). On Aug. 7, 1864, Union Gen. Philip H. Sheridan was placed in command of all troops in the Shenandoah Valley, and was directed to halt the offensive operations of Confederate Gen. Jubal A. Early and to drive the Confederates from the valley (*see* Shenandoah Campaign). With reinforcements from Gen. Ulysses S. Grant's army, Sheridan forced Early up the valley; and when the latter was also reinforced, Sheridan withdrew northward. Early, following in pursuit, divided his force about the same time that his reinforcements were recalled by Gen. Robert E. Lee (*see* Petersburg, Siege of). Sheridan with superior force attacked the Confederates and forced them back. Reinforced by concentrating detachments, Early halted, attacked, and drove the Union troops back. He then took position behind Opequon Creek at Winchester. Sheridan, again reinforced, counterattacked on Sept. 19, 1864. After severe fighting, the Confederate left was turned, and Early's troops were forced back in some confusion. After dark the Confederate army retired southward.

WINDMILLS. Windmills did not become a feature of American life until after the Civil War, and then in the West. The occupation of lands beyond the belt of regular rain, springs, streams, and shallow underground water tapped by hand-dug wells made windmills a necessity. Well-drilling machinery and practical mills made them a possibility. Popularized in the 1870's, they came to dot the prairie states.

WINDSOR. *See* **River Towns of Connecticut.**

WINE AND WINEMAKING. In 1619 the Virginia Company brought to the colony some experienced French vineyardists to grow grapes and start manufacturing wine. The experiment failed. Although some wine was produced throughout the colonial period, little was sold commercially. The earliest successful commercial winery in the United States was established near Cincinnati, Ohio, by Nicholas Longworth. After numerous failures trying to naturalize imported European vines, he succeeded in making good marketable wine from native Catawba grapes. By the mid-1850's the production of his vineyards, together with that of other nearby vintners, made Ohio the leading wine state, with a total 1859 production of some 568,000 gallons. Within a decade California became the nation's top producer of wines. Originally introduced into Baja California by Spanish missionaries at the end of the 17th century, vines of the European *Vitis vinifera* spread from there to California proper. Agoston Haraszthy de Mokcsa, a Hungarian nobleman, and other vineyardists were responsible for introducing hundreds of premium European grape varieties to California, the only state that had both suitable soil and climate for their successful cultivation. In the 1870's the industry was nearly destroyed by an infestation of phylloxera, devastating plant lice. National prohibition, beginning in 1919, dealt California vintners an even more shattering blow; repeal in 1933 brought a new surge of production, but it required almost two decades for the industry to reestablish itself. By 1970 California accounted for some 85 percent of the nation's total wine production. Winemaking also was an important business in several eastern states, of which New York was the leader.

WINNEBAGO. A tribe of Indians, originally located in east central Wisconsin from Green Bay westward to the Wisconsin River and southward to the Fox River. Known from roughly 1671, when they were nearly destroyed in a war with the Illinois, their population of that date is estimated at 3,800. The tribe spoke a Siouan language fairly closely related to Oto and Iowa. Pushed west of the Mississippi by governmental decree in 1825 and 1832, the Winnebago settled in sections of Iowa and Minnesota. During the Civil War, white settlers, alarmed at the Dakota outbreak of 1862, forced the removal of many to Dakota Territory, and some continued southward to settle with the Omaha in Nebraska. Others managed to retain their Wisconsin and Iowa holdings.

WINNEBAGO, FORT. The third military post built in Wisconsin after the American occupation. It stood at the portage of the Fox-Wisconsin waterway. After the uprising in 1827, known as the Winnebago War, Maj. David E. Twiggs of the U.S. First Infantry was sent in 1828 to begin this post. During the Black Hawk War of 1832 Fort Winnebago was a center for supplies. The garrison was maintained until 1845.

WINNEBAGO WAR (1827). The Winnebago resentment of the coming of settlers to southwestern Wisconsin led to the uprising. The vigorous measures of Michigan Territory Gov. Lewis Cass and of the army snuffed out the war before it really got started.

WINONA SPEECH (Sept. 17, 1909). President William Howard Taft made a tour of the Middle West in order to defend his policies. At Winona, Minn., Taft defended the Payne-Aldrich Bill as the best tariff ever passed. The furor created by this defense of the tariff overshadowed the constructive features of the speech and widened the breach between Insurgents and Standpatters in the Republican party.

WINSTON-SALEM (N.C.). A city in the north-central part of North Carolina, with a population of 131,885, according to the 1980 census. Winston-Salem was formed in 1913 by the combination of two much older towns. Salem had been established in 1753 by a group of Moravian settlers who migrated to the area. The Moravians were committed to preach Christianity to the Indians and were confirmed religious pacifists. They emphasized handcrafts and community spirit in their town. Since 1950, Old Salem has been restored as a historic area. The town of Winston, largely devoted to trade and a traffic center, was established in 1849; it developed as an industrial town. Winston-Salem is one of the largest tobacco processing and cigarette manufacturing centers in the world. In addition to its tobacco factories, the city has many small- and medium-sized industrial plants.

WIRELESS TELEGRAPHY. *See* **Radio.**

WISCONSIN. The French were the first Europeans in the area; Jean Nicolet, sent by Samuel de Champlain, stepped ashore probably near Green Bay in 1634. A French missionary, Father Claude Jean Allouez, was in the region by 1665. Green Bay was the strategic entrance to the Fox-Wisconsin rivers waterway that carried Louis Jolliet and Jacques Marquette to the Mississippi River in 1673. This passage was vital to the Montreal-based fur traders until the War of 1812. Pierre Esprit Radisson and Médart Chouart, Sieur de Groseilliers, were the first traders to follow in expeditions into Lake Superior (1654 and 1660). Their difficulties with the French government resulted in the founding of the Hudson's Bay Company in 1670. Nicolas Perrot represented French imperial policy and the trade from 1668 until 1696, when traders were ordered from the interior. He built posts on the upper Mississippi and took formal possession for France in 1689.

The Indians of the Wisconsin country were an important military resource of the French in the long series of wars (1689–1763) in which France lost Canada to the British. Charles Michel de Langlade, whose family held trading rights at Green Bay, played a critical role in the rout of Gen. Edward Braddock's army in 1755. Typical of the French-Canadians in the fur trade, Langlade transferred his allegiance to the British after 1763. Years of French trade and missionary activity had resulted in scant settlement in Wisconsin. The small British garrison posted to Green Bay left almost immediately with Pontiac's War in 1763, and none returned. The fur trade was carried on much as before except for the competition of Scotsmen who moved in on the Montreal traders. The American Revolution disrupted the trade. Although the Wisconsin Indians sided with the British, the military and diplomatic skills of George Rogers Clark, aided by the French and Spanish in the interior, kept them largely neutralized.

The generous boundaries granted by the British in 1783 made the Wisconsin country American in name but not in fact. The British retained the right of access to the trade and navigation rights on the Mississippi. Wisconsin was the westernmost part of the Northwest Territory, coming under the Ordinance of 1787. It was successively a part of Indiana Territory (1800), Illinois Territory (1809), and Michigan Territory (1818). The Montreal traders had little interference from the Americans in Wisconsin until 1816, when a law was passed excluding foreigners from the fur trade. The War of 1812 was an unqualified American disaster in Wisconsin. Expeditions from St. Louis sent in 1814 to establish a fort at Prairie du Chien were repulsed. The victory of Commodore Oliver Hazard Perry in September 1813 on Lake Erie had already made British success west of there temporary. Wisconsin was confirmed to American ownership by the Treaty of Ghent in 1814.

A mining rush to the Galena lead district brought Americans in large numbers to southwestern Wisconsin after 1822. Encounters with the Winnebago led to incidents and cession of the lead region in 1829. Other Indian land cessions followed: Ottawa, Potawatomi, Chippewa, Menomini, and Sioux between 1829 and 1848, well in advance of settlement. Much of the Black Hawk War (1832) was fought in Wisconsin. Settlement along the Lake Michigan shore began seriously in the 1830's. It was in part agricultural and in part a feverish growth of towns at the sites of present-day Milwaukee, Racine, and Kenosha, all happening about the same time Chicago was being settled. Early settlement on the lake was primarily Yankee in origin. The lead miners, although largely from border states, were southerners in culture and politics. Wisconsin Territory was created in 1836. The Organic Act establishing the territory became the model for most of the trans-Mississippi territories. Statehood was achieved on May 29, 1848. Settlement was rapid after 1836. By 1850 the population had grown to 305,000.

Wisconsin was a leading wheat producer in the decade of the Civil War. Diminishing returns from wheat led to a painful adjustment to dairying, livestock, and specialized cash crops, beginning in the 1870's. Dairy sciences brought the University of Wisconsin at Madison to prominence. Aside from flour milling, the principal industry was lumbering, based on the extensive pinelands of the northern half of the state. By 1900 this resource was near exhaustion, and Minneapolis and Duluth had captured the wheat trade and milling. Since the state was blessed with abundant waterpower, lumber and flour milling capital turned to papermaking. Milwaukee and southeastern Wisconsin cities used the Great Lakes to offset a lack of coal, oil, and developed ores to bring the resources and a skilled labor force together. Heavy machinery, machine tools, foundries, electrical machinery, agricultural implements, beer, automobiles and trucks, aluminum ware, and light gasoline engines are familiar Wisconsin products. The population was 4,705,335 in 1980.

***WISCONSIN ET AL.* V. *ILLINOIS AND CHICAGO SANITARY DISTRICT*.** *See* **Chicago Sanitary District Case.**

WISCONSIN IDEA. The cooperation between the experts at the University of Wisconsin and the administration of the state under the Progressive party. The reforms advocated by the Progressives in the early 20th century, under the leadership of Robert M. La Follette, Sr., were embodied for the most part in commissions; the aid of university specialists was often invoked.

WISCONSIN PORTAGE. *See* **Fox-Wisconsin Waterway.**

***WISCONSIN RAILROAD COMMISSION* V. *CHICAGO, BURLINGTON AND QUINCY RAILROAD COMPANY*,** 257 U.S. 563 (1922). Congress, by the provisions of the Transportation Act of 1920, undertook to guarantee to the railways "a fair return upon a fair valuation." Previously, the Wisconsin Railroad Commission had entered into an agreement with the defendant railroad, by which intrastate transportation of persons was to be provided at the rate of 2 cents a mile; after the passage of the federal act, the state commission sought to compel the continuance of the agreement. The railway contended that at such a rate, it could not earn the fair return contemplated in the law. The Supreme Court accepted this view and emphasized the fact that the Interstate Commerce Commission, under the Transportation Act of 1920, had valid power and the duty to raise the level of intrastate rates.

"WISE, AND GOOD AND RICH." The Federalists, with their distrust of democracy and the common man, laid great stress on aristocratic and propertied influence in government. John Adams, writing before the adoption of the Constitution, spoke of "the rich, the well-born, and the able." Alexander Hamilton took notice of the phrase in *The Federalist.* Fisher Ames of Massachusetts, one of the ablest leaders of the Federalist party, gave the expression perhaps its best-known form in 1802.

WISE, FORT. *See* **Lyon, Fort.**

WISTAR PARTIES. Organized in Philadelphia in 1818 as an outgrowth of the Saturday evening salons at the home of Dr. Caspar Wistar, where members of the American Philosophical Society (APS) entertained distinguished scientists, diplomats, and travelers until they acquired their own headquarters (Philosophical Hall). After Wistar's death in 1818 the Wistar Association was formed; it is made up of APS members (twenty-four) and headed by a dean. The Annual Wistar Party, the organization's major event, is held each November at Philosophical Hall.

WITCHCRAFT. The belief in witchcraft came to America with the colonists. Margaret Jones was executed for witchcraft in Boston in 1648. Soon after, Mary Parsons of Springfield, Mass., was indicted for witchcraft. Other accusations occurred at scattered points in New England and the other colonies. In February 1692 in Salem Village (now Danvers), a group of young women and girls, who had been amusing themselves during the long winter listening to the lurid tales of Tituba, an old slave, showed signs of hysteria. They presently began to accuse persons of bewitching them. A powerful and inflammatory sermon was preached at the village by a visiting clergyman against the machinations of the devil. The civil magistrates entered the case. A special court to try the cases was appointed by the governor, and between May and September 1692 several hundred persons were arrested; nineteen were hanged and many imprisoned.

While a few later cases of witchcraft occurred in Virginia in 1706, in North Carolina in 1712, and perhaps in Rhode Island in 1728, this outbreak at Salem Village practically ended prosecutions for witchcraft in America.

"WITCH-HUNT." An expression used to characterize the post–World War II obsession with Communist conspiracies. Under pressure from conservatives in and out of Congress, President Harry S. Truman issued Executive Order 9835 on Mar. 12, 1947, setting up a federal loyalty program. This was followed by the establishment of similar loyalty programs at the state and local level. The dangers posed by the real threat of Soviet power and the goading of Republicans who accused Truman and the Democrats of being "soft on communism" led to the sensational trial of the Communist party leadership. Indicted under the Smith Act of 1940, eleven Communists were charged with conspiracy. The federal government again moved to block the internal threat of communism by passing the Internal Security Act of 1950, usually known as the McCarran Act. Of more immediate impact were Sen. Joseph R. McCarthy's attempts to take over the loyalty program at all levels. Beginning in 1950, McCarthy claimed to have a list of fifty-seven known Communists who were still working in the State Department. Following up the technique of naming names and figures but producing little substantial evidence, McCarthy accused a large number of individuals of being Communists or Communist sympathizers. The most publicized case arising from the witch-hunt of the 1950's was the confrontation between Alger Hiss and Whittaker Chambers, the revelation of the "pumpkin papers," and Hiss's subsequent conviction on perjury charges. Another cause célèbre, the trial of Ethel and Julius Rosenberg, ended with the execution of the Rosenbergs in 1953.

WITHLACOOCHEE RIVER, BATTLES AT (Dec. 31, 1835; Feb. 27–Mar. 6, 1836). Practically the first engagement of the second Seminole War occurred near Fort Drane in north central Florida when Gen. Duncan L. Clinch fought the Seminole under Osceola and Alligator at a Withlacoochee River ford on Dec. 31, 1835. Two months later, Gen. Edmund P. Gaines, returning to Fort Brooke, met Osceola's force of 1,500 Indians and blacks and was held up at the river ford from Feb. 27 to Mar. 6. (*See also* Seminole Wars.)

"WITH MALICE TOWARD NONE, WITH CHARITY FOR ALL." The opening phrases of the last sentence of President Abraham Lincoln's second inaugural address.

WOLFF PACKING COMPANY V. COURT OF INDUSTRIAL RELATIONS, **262 U.S. 522 (1923).** Following serious labor disorders in 1920 the Kansas legislature passed an act declaring that the manufacture of food and clothing, mining, public utilities, and transportation were businesses affected with a public interest. An industrial court was empowered to fix wages and labor conditions whenever the public peace or health was endangered. In 1923 a unanimous decision of the U.S. Supreme Court dealt the Kansas industrial court a deathblow by declaring the fixing of wages in a packing plant a deprivation of property and a denial of the freedom of contract guaranteed by the Fourteenth Amendment.

WOMAN'S CHRISTIAN TEMPERANCE UNION. Originated in the Woman's Temperance Crusade, which started in Fredonia, N.Y., and Hillsboro, Ohio, in December 1873. The spirit of the crusade spread, and saloons were closed in many towns across several states. But Crusade women met in Chautauqua, N.Y., and issued a call for a national convention of temperance women to be held in Cleveland on Nov. 18–20, 1874. Delegates from seventeen states answered the call, and the National Woman's Christian Temperance Union (WCTU) was founded with Annie Wittenmyer as the first president. Every state soon had a WCTU organization, and the impact of these organizations began to be felt in public affairs. They campaigned for state legislation requiring scientific temperance instruction in the public schools, which was accomplished by 1902. Many of the victories over the liquor traffic, including national prohibition, are attributable to voters who had learned in school the evil effects of alcoholic beverages. The foresighted leaders of the WCTU, under the guidance of Frances Elizabeth C. Willard, established a wide-ranging program of reform, including woman suffrage, equal rights, child welfare, better home standards, prison reforms, moral education, purity standards, international arbitration, and world peace. It has also continually waged a major fight against the liquor traffic, narcotics and tobacco, child labor, juvenile delinquency, prostitution, and gambling. By 1975 it had organizations in more than seventy nations and approximately 250,000 members in the United States. The World's Woman's Christian Temperance Union was tentatively organized in 1883 with Margaret Lucas Bright of England as presiding officer. Miss Willard was elected the first president at the first world convention held in Boston in 1891.

WOMAN'S PARTY, NATIONAL. Inspired by English suffragettes, Alice Paul led a group of women out of the National American Woman Suffrage Association in 1914 to form the Congressional Union, renamed the National Woman's Party in 1916. Its purpose was to put pressure on the Democratic party to secure the right of women to the suffrage. From July 14 to Oct. 6, 1917, it picketed in Washington, D.C. Mobs attacked the women and destroyed their banners without interference from the police. Although the demonstrations were peaceful, many women were jailed and drew attention to their campaign through hunger strikes. This period was climaxed by the attempted burning in effigy of President Woodrow Wilson on New Year's Day, 1917. Wilson did give official support to the Nineteenth Amendment, which was the object of the women's campaign, and eventually persuaded the one senator whose vote was needed to pass it (1920). Subsequently the activities of the Woman's Party were oriented toward passage of further legislation to end discrimination against women.

WOMAN'S RIGHTS MOVEMENT. Women who were active in the fight against the crown organized to spur the boycott of British goods. During this time, prominent women, such as Abigail Adams, wrote and spoke privately about the need for the male leaders of the struggle for independence to rectify the inferior position of women. But only in the 19th century, when large numbers of women left their homes to assume factory and teaching jobs, did they begin to act politically in their own behalf. Early organizers for woman's rights began by working with black women who had escaped slavery; others organized against inhumane conditions in the factories. The women who first spoke in public on questions of slavery and female abuse were viciously attacked, and women who organized schools in the early 1800's were harassed incessantly. Several who attended an antislavery convention in London were refused seats. While in London they laid plans to launch a movement for woman's rights in the United States. In 1848, they called a public convention at Seneca Falls, N.Y., to discuss the status of women. At this convention a declaration written by Elizabeth Cady Stanton, Lucretia Mott, and others laid the groundwork for a series of meetings and new associations.

After the Civil War, an alliance between the temperance campaign and the movement for suffrage began to replace the earlier alliance between abolitionists and feminists. A split in the movement developed in 1869, rival publications were launched, and women divided on many issues. One group attacked organized religion openly and worked with immigrant groups who were organizing unions in industry. Another nominated Victoria Woodhull, an advocate of free love and socialism, for president of the United States in 1872. After the turn of the century the Woman's Christian Temperance Union, the Young Women's Christian Association, and hundreds of other women's clubs centered mainly in the Midwest joined in a federation to secure the vote for women, and their more radical sisters joined with them in national organization toward that end. Black women's clubs, organized mainly around problems of health and the proliferation of prostitution in the cities, also joined the federation.

Women secured the vote only after a long struggle and

after another split in the movement occurred between women who wanted to work legally state by state and women who organized ongoing militant actions in the nation's capital (*see* Woman's Party, National). Most feminists who advocated and fought for workers' control of the mines and factories never committed themselves to suffrage, but less revolutionary professional and middle-class women who worked with poor women organizing settlement houses in the cities did gain much support for suffrage from working-class women.

After securing the vote through ratification of the Nineteenth Amendment in 1920, gaining improved working conditions in factories, and bettering the legal status of women in marriage and divorce, women retired temporarily from organized activity pertaining to woman's rights. During World War II, women again assumed new work roles and new prerogatives by joining in the war effort, but when the war was over they were encouraged to return to domestic careers. Political apathy in the 1950's was followed by a rebirth of feminist activity in the 1960's. Women united to demand the legalization of abortion, the allocation of public monies for child care, the freedom to pursue new life-styles, and more information on the history of women. They began to publish their own newspapers and journals and to reach out to apolitical women through the establishment of small discussion groups. Other groups, such as the National Organization for Women (NOW), organized in 1966, and the Caucus of Labor Union Women (CLUW), formed in 1973, joined the struggle at other levels, pushing for a series of legislative measures to equalize the opportunities for men and women. A debate centered around the drive to secure passage of the Equal Rights Amendment, which would help professional women by eliminating restrictions imposed on the advancement of women at work. Women eventually united in support of the amendment, but it was defeated in 1982. Many states, however, passed individual equal rights amendments.

WOMAN'S SUFFRAGE. Under English rule a few colonies, notably New York, permitted women of property to "vote their estates"; but with independence such suffrage was taken away, except in the case of New Jersey. That state, by its constitution of 1776, gave qualified "inhabitants" the right to vote; but, owing to irregularities in the elections, suffrage was limited in 1807 to free white men. Woman suffrage was included in the program adopted at the Seneca Falls Convention in 1848. Efforts to secure the vote for women in connection with the enfranchisement of the Afro-American by the Fourteenth and Fifteenth amendments failed, and in 1869 a split over policy in the recently formed American Equal Rights Association somewhat weakened the reform movement. The resulting American Woman Suffrage Association, led by Lucy Stone and Julia Ward Howe, and the National Woman Suffrage Association, championed by Elizabeth Cady Stanton and Susan B. Anthony, reunited twenty-one years later as the National American Woman Suffrage Association. Although bitterly opposed, the suffragists widened their influence through intensive lobbying.

Gradually some states gave women limited suffrage, usually for municipal elections. In 1869, when Wyoming organized as a territory it gave women the vote; when admitted as a state in 1890 the right was retained. In 1893 Colorado gave women the suffrage; in 1896, Utah and Idaho; in 1910, Washington State; in 1911, California; in 1912, Arizona, Kansas, and Oregon; in 1913, Alaska Territory; and, the same year, Illinois, by statute, gave them presidential and municipal suffrage; in 1914 Nevada and Montana granted them full suffrage; and in 1917, impelled by changes produced by World War I, New York granted women the suffrage.

Led by Alice Paul and Lucy Burns, in 1913, radical suffragettes began to bring pressure on President Woodrow Wilson's administration to secure passage of a proposed amendment to the U.S. Constitution by using militant methods, which the National American Woman Suffrage Association disapproved. Consequently the radicals reorganized separately as the Congressional Union. Later, as the National Woman's party, they continued their militant tactics. In January 1918 Wilson came out for the amendment, which passed Congress the next year, and was ratified in time for the national election of 1920 (*see* Nineteenth Amendment).

WOMEN IN THE MILITARY SERVICES. The extensive employment of women with full military status was a direct outgrowth of the manpower crisis of World War II. The idea had its genesis with the creation of the Army Nurse Corps in 1901, followed by the Navy Nurse Corps in 1908. During World War I the navy enlisted some 11,000 women (known as "Yeomanettes") to do clerical work, and the Marine Corps enlisted 300 "Marinettes." This practice ended with the war. Only the nurse corps survived the postwar period.

During World War II, with its enormous demands for manpower, the country turned to this largely untapped resource of qualified volunteers. Following a precedent set by the British, the U.S. Army on May 14, 1942, established the Women's Army Auxiliary Corps (WAAC), forerunner of the Women's Army Corps (WAC, September 1943). The navy followed suit with the WAVES (Women Accepted for Voluntary Emergency Service) on July 30, 1942, the Marine Corps with Women Marines (WMs) on Feb. 13, 1943, and the Coast Guard with the SPARs (taking the name from the Coast Guard motto "Semper Paratus; Always Ready") on Nov. 23, 1942. This was the first time that women were employed on a relatively large scale by the armed forces of the United States. Some 300,000 women joined the officer and enlisted ranks during this period. Also during World War II, the Army Air Forces, which became the U.S. Air Force in 1947, employed women pilots to ferry aircraft and perform other noncombat flying duties. Known as WASPs (Women Airforce Service Pilots), this group was a paramilitary organization—its members wore uniforms but were actually civilians under contract to the army.

In 1947 women were first granted permanent military status. In that year both the Army and Navy Nurse Corps were made permanent and the Army Women's Medical Specialist Corps was established. On June 12 of the following year Congress enacted the Women's Armed Services Integration Act, which provided permanent status for women serving in the army, navy, and Marine Corps and integrated women into the newly created air force. Although the air force did not designate women as a separate group or corps, they became known by the acronym "WAF" (Women in the Air Force). The Air Force Nurse Corps and Medical Specialist Corps were established in 1949. Subsequently, the nurse corps and medical specialist corps ceased to be all-female organizations.

On Nov. 8, 1967, a bill was passed to remove certain legal limitations on strengths (2 percent of the authorized strength of each service) and promotions of women in the armed forces. This law expanded the utilization and promotion of women, especially to general and flag officer rank. The first women to be promoted to brigadier general in the army were Anna Mae Hayes and Elizabeth P. Hoisington (1970); in the air force, Jeanne M. Holm (1971) and E. Ann Hoefly (1972). The first female navy rear admiral was Alene B. Duerk (1972). The first woman major general was Holm (1973).

WOODEN INDIAN. All through the 19th century the gaudily painted effigy of an Indian carved from wood, sometimes with tomahawk uplifted and sometimes peacefully proffering a bundle of cigars to the passerby, was a familiar figure beside the doors of tobacco shops in America. The first small images of this sort were seen in England in the 17th century.

WOOD LAKE, BATTLE OF (Sept. 23, 1862). Foragers from Col. Henry H. Sibley's camp near Wood Lake, in southwest Minnesota, on the morning of Sept. 23 stumbled on Little Crow's warriors, lying in ambush to attack the main army. Quickly reinforced, Sibley's men decisively defeated the Sioux, with white losses of forty-one killed and wounded.

WOODLAND TRADITION. A general term applied to advanced Archaic and Formative cultures that made cord-marked and fabric-marked pottery, constructed burial mounds and earthworks, and cultivated some domesticated plants in native eastern North America. Cord-marked and fabric-marked pottery is the diagnostic trait of the tradition, for domesticates and earthen structures are associated with other cultural traditions too. The tradition has been divided into Early (1000–300 B.C.), Middle (300 B.C.–A.D. 700), and Late (A.D. 700–1700) periods. The Woodland Tradition originated in the general Great Lakes area by about 1000 B.C. and climaxed during the Early and Middle periods in the Adena (1100 B.C.–A.D. 200) and Hopewell (300 B.C.–A.D. 250) cultures. After A.D. 700, the emergence of Mississippian cultures with new ceramic and artifact traditions greatly decreased the areal extent of Woodland Tradition cultures.

WOODSTOCK MUSIC FESTIVAL (Aug. 16, 1969). Three hundred thousand rock fans attended a rock music festival near Bethel, N.Y., to listen to performances by such popular artists as Joan Baez, Ravi Shankar, Jimi Hendrix, and the Jefferson Airplane. Despite rain, traffic jams, and water shortages, the good nature of the mostly youthful participants created a mystique that gained national attention. The festival's name soon became a term used to define an entire generation—the Woodstock Generation.

WOODWARD PLAN. *See* **Detroit, Woodward Plan of.**

WOOL GROWING AND MANUFACTURE. Sheep raising was introduced into the Atlantic colonies in the 17th century. Household manufacture of wool was widespread; cards, spinning wheels, and looms were standard equipment in many homes. Sheep were unimproved, the wool coarse, and the homespun rude but serviceable. Itinerant weavers were numerous, and weaving shops were to be found in towns, although woolen goods were still imported from England by those colonials who could afford them. English policy was aimed at discouraging the growth in the colonies of wool manufacture. The Revolution spurred efforts to expand both wool growing and manufacture. Between the Revolution and the Civil War, the character of the wool industry changed substantially. The introduction early in the 19th century of many Spanish merinos enabled growers to provide a fine wool suitable to the needs of an expanding manufacture. By the mid-19th century modifications in the breed had produced an American merino that had a heavier fleece. Wool production moved westward. In 1860 Ohio, Michigan, and California were among the five leading wool-producing states. Despite the increase in flocks, raw or manufactured foreign wool accounted for most of that fiber consumed in the United States. Household manufacture steadily declined with the Industrial Revolution. Although the manufacture of wool was widely diffused, the great bulk of it was located in southern New England and in the middle Atlantic states. The Civil War brought to both growers and manufacturers an unprecedented demand and prosperity. With cotton in short supply in the North, civilian demand for woolens increased as military needs skyrocketed. The war's end found farms and factories with enlarged productive capacities and the government with a huge surplus of clothing.

Wool growing has long been of diminishing importance in the U.S. economy. Stock sheep numbered 51 million in 1884 and only 15 million in 1973, and since 1961 the number has declined annually. For most of the 20th century the sale of sheep has been the chief source of income from sheep raising. Although sheep are raised in all the states, about three-quarters of the stock sheep in 1973 were in South Dakota, Texas, and the Far West. The development of man-made fibers has reduced the mill consumption of scoured wool per capita, and by 1971 it was only nine-tenths of a pound. In the Wool Act of 1954 Congress sought by means of price support to encourage the annual production of about 300 million pounds of shorn wool, but the goal had not been reached as of the mid-1970's. Imports of raw wool regularly exceeded the domestic clip.

Since 1865 U.S. wool manufacture has undergone many vicissitudes. An outstanding development during the fifty years after 1865 was the rise of the worsted industry over the carded wool industry. The growth of the ready-to-wear clothing industry changed marketing methods. The average size of wool manufacturing plants increased, while the number declined sharply. Most of the small, scattered, local mills ceased production. Since World War II the south Atlantic states became major producers, and by the 1970's their mills were consuming more wool than those of New England.

In 1864 the National Association of Wool Manufacturers was formed, and in 1865 the National Woolgrowers' Association was established. They formed an alliance that, representing both agricultural and manufacturing interests, bore fruit in high duties on imports of both wool and woolens. During the making of the Payne-Aldrich tariff (1909) and the years of debate that followed, Schedule K became the most publicized tariff schedule in U.S. history. Japan became the leading exporter of woven wool fabrics to the United States during the 1960's and 1970's. American exports represented a small part of U.S. mill output. In 1971 President Richard M. Nixon negotiated agreements with Japan, Taiwan, South Korea, and Hong Kong limiting their exports of the manufactures of wool and man-made fibers to the United States. The greatest threat to American wool manufacture in the 20th century was the competition of man-made fibers.

WOOLLY HEADS. A term of derision applied in various regions after the late 1840's to northerners, usually Whigs, of antislavery propensities who presumably championed the rights of the Afro-Americans. It was often a synonym for Conscience Whigs.

WORCESTER (Mass.). An industrial city with a population of 161,799, according to the 1980 census.

Worcester's first settlement dates from 1682, but the settlement was abandoned in 1702 because of Indian warfare. Resettled in 1713, it grew into a permanent town. During 1791, the Worcester court decided that a black slave should be granted freedom under the State Bill of Rights, which declared that men are born "free and equal." The town grew rapidly after 1828 when the Blackstone Canal connected it with Providence, Rhode Island. The canal provided an outlet for Worcester's textile mills, and the builders of the canal, largely Irish immigrants, provided permanent residents to work in the mills. Worcester has a mixed industrial output, including a large number of different machine and metal products. It is also the home of the American Antiquarian Society. Among Worcester's educational institutions, Clark University played an important part in American cultural history; it sponsored American appearances by the European psychoanalyst Dr. Sigmund Freud, and it served as an academic base for Dr. Robert Goddard, the American expert on rocket propulsion.

***WORCESTER* V. *GEORGIA*,** 6 Peters 515 (1832). A decision of the U.S. Supreme Court handed down in the controversy between Georgia and the Cherokee, in which Chief Justice John Marshall held that the Cherokee were a nation under the protection of the United States and free from the jurisdiction of Georgia. The case arose over the arrest of Samuel A. Worcester and ten other missionaries for having violated a Georgia law forbidding white men to reside in the Cherokee country without first taking an oath of allegiance to the state and securing a permit. *(See also Cherokee Nation* v. *Georgia.)*

WORKINGMEN'S PARTY. A political organization organized in Philadelphia in 1828 that agitated for protection of mechanics from the competition of prison contract labor and for free public education. The party was established the following year in New York City. Under the leadership of Fanny Wright and her young protégé, Robert Dale Owen, the movement spread rapidly, and a demand for universal education was added to the party platform. In 1830 Erastus Root, speaker of the New York State Assembly, packed the local and state conventions of the "Workies" with his own men and secured his nomination by them for governor of New York. This nomination was denounced by Owen and Wright, and another convention of bona fide delegates of the Workingmen's party met and named their own candidate. Nevertheless, the heyday of the party's influence was passing.

WORKMEN'S COMPENSATION. *See* **Employers' Liability Laws.**

WORKS PROGRESS ADMINISTRATION (WPA). President Franklin D. Roosevelt established the Works Progress Administration (WPA) by executive order on May 6, 1935, to organize "light" public works projects for those workers not employed by the "heavy" public works agencies, primarily the Public Works Administration (PWA) and the Tennessee Valley Authority (TVA). As it turned out, the WPA became the government's major public works effort under director Harry L. Hopkins (1935–39). In 1939 the WPA was renamed Works Projects Administration. The WPA set up divisions in every state, sought local sponsors for the work, and began approving an impressive range of projects. Where people had useful skills, the WPA was eager to preserve them. Discovering that artists, musicians, and writers were hit hard by the Great Depression, the WPA organized projects to utilize their talents. The Federal Theatre Proejct, headed by Hallie Flanagan, reached an audience estimated at 30 million people. The Federal Arts Project employed artists to decorate public buildings with murals. The Federal Writers' Project turned out city, state, and territorial guides; regional and geographic studies; and histories of America's ethnic groups. WPA funds were used to pay unemployed dentists for repairing teeth, nurses for making home visits, taxidermists for stuffing birds, and biologists for planting oysters. But the main thrust of WPA projects was directed toward offering employment to semiskilled and unskilled citizens. This meant a major effort in the construction of public facilities. The WPA built 1,634 new school buildings, 105 airports, 3,000 tennis courts, 3,300 storage dams, 103 golf courses, and 5,800 mobile libraries. By 1941 the agency had spent $11.3 billion to provide work for 8 million. On June 30, 1943, with wartime production absorbing most of the unemployed, Roosevelt gave WPA its "honorable discharge," and in three months the agency mailed its last checks.

WORLD COURT. *See* **International Court of Justice.**

WORLD ECONOMIC CONFERENCE (1933). Projected with President Herbert C. Hoover's endorsement and provided with an agenda largely perfected in conferences between Roosevelt and foreign delegations visiting him at Washington, D.C., in May 1933, the conference met at London on June 10. The European nations proposed immediate agreement on currency stabilization under a gold standard. The United States had proposed first to effect tariff reduction; it refused to renounce freedom to devalue the dollar, insisting that its purchasing power, not its gold content, needed stabilizing. The conference adjourned July 28, a failure.

WORLD'S COLUMBIAN EXPOSITION (May 1–Oct. 30, 1893). Celebrating the 400th anniversary of the discovery of America by Christopher Columbus, it was held in Chicago at Jackson Park. The exposition cost more than $20 million; forty-six foreign nations and nearly all the American states officially participated; admissions totaled 27.5 million.

The most significant influence of the exposition was its great effect on American architecture. A group of 150 buildings, designed by such architects as Louis H. Sullivan, Richard M. Hunt, Stanford White, and Charles F. McKim, embodied the new classicism of the American Renaissance.

WORLD'S FAIRS. *See under name of world's fair, as in* **New York World's Fairs** *or* **Seattle World's Fair.**

WORLD'S INDUSTRIAL AND COTTON CENTENNIAL EXPOSITION (1884). Opened in New Orleans on Dec. 1. The $2 million exposition celebrated the centenary of the export of six bags of cotton from the United States.

WORLD WAR I (1914–18). When the June 1914 assassination of the heir to the Austro-Hungarian throne at Sarajevo (now part of Yugoslavia) propelled the European powers into war, President Woodrow Wilson urged Americans to remain "impartial in thought as well as action." Americans tried to conform until early 1915, when a German submarine sank the British liner *Lusitania,* with a loss of 1,198 lives, including 128 Americans. In March 1916, a submarine sank the French channel steamer *Sussex* with further loss of American lives.

Wilson was so disturbed by the submarine threat and the carnage in Europe that he advocated limited increases in American armed forces. In May 1916 Congress passed the National Defense Act, which projected ultimately an army of 223,000 and a National Guard of 450,000 and gave the president power to place defense orders and force industry to comply.

Germany's military leaders persuaded Kaiser Wilhelm II that France and Britain could be crushed by unrestricted submarine warfare before the United States could make its weight felt. On Jan. 31, 1917, Germany informed all neutrals that U-boats would sink all vessels, neutral and Allied alike, without warning. Wilson broke diplomatic relations with Germany, although he still hoped to avoid war. He demurred even when Britain on Feb. 23 revealed the contents of an intercepted telegram from the German foreign secretary, Arthur Zimmerman, to the German minister in Mexico proposing an alliance of Germany, Mexico, and Japan against the United States. In return, Mexico was to regain the territory of Texas, New Mexico, and Arizona. Wilson's only move was to ask Congress for authority to arm merchant ships; blocked by a filibuster, he had to proceed under an old law.

In the next few weeks submarines sank four American ships at a cost of fifteen American lives. Wilson on Apr. 2 asked Congress for a declaration of war, which was signed on Apr. 6.

As the United States entered the war, Allied fortunes were approaching the nadir. Russian military units riven by revolutionary cells had begun to collapse, opening the way for the Bolsheviks to seize power and sue for peace. Mutiny spread through fifty-four French divisions, and the Battle of Passchendaele resulted in 245,000 British casualties. Before an Austrian offensive—the Battle of Caporetto—the Italian army lost 305,000 men. Yet the most serious crisis of all was at sea, where in February alone submarines had sunk 781,000 tons of shipping. Only the U.S. Navy was in a position to provide immediate help. The convoy system, protected by warships, reduced losses sharply and ended the crisis.

The U.S. Army numbered only 307,000 men. Maj. Gen. John J. Pershing headed an advance contingent of the American Expeditionary Forces to Paris on July 4. He participated in a ceremony at the tomb of the Marquis de Lafayette, where Lt. Col. C. E. Stanton—not Pershing—uttered the words "Lafayette, we are here." Meanwhile, on May 18, 1917, Congress passed the Selective Service Act. Of close to 4 million who eventually served, 2.8 million were drafted.

When the transportation system by autumn of 1917 appeared about to collapse, the U.S. Treasury took charge of all railroads. The powers of the U.S. Shipping Board, created in 1916, were expanded in 1917, and by the end of the war its Emergency Fleet Corporation had built up a fleet of 10 million tons. But not until 1918 was the National War Labor Board created to coordinate labor. The efforts of the Committee on Public Information to influence public opinion, begun in April 1917, were soon reinforced by the Espionage Act of 1917 and, later, by the Sedition Act of 1918, which sharply curtailed public expression of opinion. Stung by congressional criticism of delays in getting troops into action, Wilson promoted the Overman Act, passed on May 20, 1918, giving him almost unlimited power to reorganize, coordinate, and centralize governmental functions. About two-thirds of war expenses, including loans to the Allies, were met by bond issues widely oversubscribed.

Only the Springfield rifle was available in appreciable numbers, and its production could be augmented by plants that had been filling Allied orders for the British Lee-Enfield rifle. All American troops reaching France in 1917 had to use Allied weapons, although new and excellent U.S. Browning models became available in volume by mid-1918. Of some 2,250 artillery pieces used by U.S. forces, only 100 were of American manufacture. A small U.S. tank corps had to use French tanks throughout, and American aviators had to fly Allied planes.

Soon after reaching France, Pershing recommended sending 1 million men by the end of 1918. The army reached a strength of 3.7 million in 62 divisions, 42 of which went overseas. Pershing resisted strong pressures from the British and French to feed the ill-trained, inexperienced American soldiers into Allied divisions as replacements so that their strength could be quickly brought to bear. Not until the end of May were American forces to participate actively in the fighting. The first major American action was in Lorraine. The Germans took the village of Siecheprey but lost it to U.S. counterattack. The Germans left behind 160 dead but took 135 prisoners and inflicted 634 casualties. The first American offensive, May 28, captured the village of Cantigny and held it against powerful counterattacks. The Americans lost 1,607 men, including 199 killed.

Through the spring of 1918 the Germans launched a series of powerful offensives. Attacking on May 27, the Germans scored a quick success and in three days reached the Marne River at Château-Thierry, less than fifty miles from Paris. The Third Division and the Second Division threw back every German thrust, and on June 6 the Second Division counterattacked through Belleau Wood. It was a costly American debut—9,777 casualties, including 1,811 dead—but the moral effect on both sides was great.

Pershing meanwhile pressed his case for a separate American force. Marshal Ferdinand Foch designated a sector in Lorraine facing a salient near Saint-Mihiel. With Pershing as commander, headquarters of the U.S. First Army opened on Aug. 10. As Foch prepared a general offensive, the First Army attacked. The Germans had begun to withdraw before the preliminary bombardment began, so that success was swift.

As part of the general offensive, the First Army attacked on Sept. 26 northward along the west bank of the Meuse River through the Argonne Forest in the direction of Sedan. It was the greatest battle fought by American troops to that time—1.25 million participated, incurring 120,000 casualties.

The overall German position was becoming desperate, and on Oct. 4 the German chancellor cabled Wilson, asking for an armistice in keeping with the Fourteen Points that Wilson had proposed early in the year. The British and French objected on the basis that the Germans should be given no quarter, and Wilson rejected the request. The kaiser meanwhile had begun to listen to the voices of a disillusioned people, the noise of riots in the streets, and the rumblings of Marxist revolution. The kaiser sent delegates to France to discuss armistice terms. On Nov. 9 he abdicated and fled into exile. The fighting ended at 11 A.M., Nov. 11, 1918.

More than 8.5 million men died in the war among total casualties of 37.5 million. American casualties were 320,710.

WORLD WAR I, U.S. RELIEF IN. With the exception of the Commission for Relief in Belgium (1914), the period of mass relief occurred after the armistice, when government finance, cash sales, and benevolence poured millions of tons of supplies into Central and Eastern Europe, where 200 million people were in need. Benevolence, through the American Relief Administration alone, amounted to $134 million after the armistice, and total supplies to more than $1 billion. About $6 billion worth of American food and other supplies was sent to Europe during 1914–23. U.S. government subsidies and loans for supplies amounted to $624 million during the armistice, and $81 million in reconstruction and relief of the Russian famine.

The American Relief Administration (ARA) was created early in 1919 to administer a congressional appropriation of $100 million for European relief, to be partially repaid by the countries aided. Herbert Hoover, U.S. food administrator, was appointed director-general of relief. Eighty percent of the supplies came from the United States. The original U.S. appropriation excluded enemy countries, but their condition was such that special finance was immediately found and $282 million worth of supplies went to Germany and $98 million to Austria. The ARA instituted child feeding, transported or allocated food for private agencies, and transmitted $6 million in cash from individuals or groups in the United States to Europe. At liquidation of the armistice program on June 30, 1919, the ARA had delivered 1,728,000 metric tons of supplies at an operating cost of 53/100 of one percent of sales value, and returned $84 million of the congressional appropriation to the U.S. Treasury in foreign government obligations. The American Red Cross spent overseas 56 cents on each dollar collected during 1914–19, and some $200 million altogether in Europe during 1914–23.

The American Friends Service Committee (Quakers) was organized after U.S. entry into the war, but American Quakers had previously worked with British Quakers in war relief. The American Friends' greatest achievement was child feeding in Germany, 1919–22, where they distributed $9 million worth of relief, about $6 million allocated by the ARA or European Relief Council. The Friends raised more than $1 million from German-Americans. They were also active in Poland, Austria, Serbia, Yugoslavia, and Russia.

The Jewish Joint Distribution Committee was formed in November 1919 to distribute relief funds for American Jewish societies, and by the end of 1926 had spent $69 million abroad. They distributed through other organizations until 1920 and worked closely with the ARA through 1923, sending a vast number of food packages and bulk sales to Poland, Austria, and Russia. In 1920 the Jewish Distribution Committee began its own medical work and reconstruction, and in 1921, refugee and child care, repatriation, and cultural work in twelve European countries besides Palestine. Near East Relief derived from a committee organized in 1919 for Armenian-Syrian relief. The ARA, Red Cross, and others made large allotments to Near East Relief, which during 1919–23 distributed some $28 million in supplies—$16 million from government credits and the rest from benevolence.

The Young Men's Christian Association and the Young Women's Christian Association gave large amounts of relief to all European countries. The Federal Council of Churches, Knights of Columbus, and National Catholic Welfare Council were members of the European Relief Council, and the Rockefeller Foundation, Laura Spelman Rockefeller Memorial, and Commonwealth Fund made large gifts to the ARA.

WORLD WAR I PEACE CONFERENCE (Jan. 18, 1919–June 28, 1919). This, the Treaty of Versailles, named after its place of signing, was followed by treaties with Austria, Bulgaria, Hungary, and Turkey, all similar to the treaty with Germany. Peace negotiations had begun in October 1918, when Germany proposed to Woodrow Wilson a peace conference based on the president's Fourteen Points and on subsequent elaborations and clarifications. Wilson had little difficulty in accepting the German offer, but Great Britain protested against the doctrine of freedom of the seas and France wanted an "elucidation" that Germany would pay war damages. Nevertheless, with these two specific exceptions, the Fourteen Points became a framework within which the negotiators at Paris sought to effect peace.

WORLD WAR I WAR DEBTS. During and immediately after World War I, America's cobelligerents borrowed some $10.350 billion from the U.S. Treasury; $7,077 billion represented cash loans extended prior to the armistice; $2.533 billion was advanced to finance reconstruction after the armistice; postarmistice relief supplies and liquidated war stocks amounted to an additional $740 million. Total foreign indebtedness, including interest due before funding of the original demand obligations but excluding loans to Czarist Russia, came to $11.577 billion. In turn, the U.S. government borrowed from its own citizens, for the most part through Liberty Bonds paying 5 percent interest. Woodrow Wilson agreed to grant the debtor nations a three-year postponement of interest payments. Eventually debtors would be required to make good the loans. Otherwise, the burden would have to be borne by the American taxpayer.

In February 1922 Congress created the World War Foreign Debt Commission to seek funding arrangements providing for amortization of principal within twenty-five years and an interest rate of not less than 4.25 percent. Disregarding this limitation on its mandate, the commission managed to reach agreement with thirteen European debtor nations before its five-year term expired. The settlements all provided for repayment of principal over a sixty-two-year period. The interest rate, determined in each case according to capacity to pay, varied from an average of 3.3 percent for Great Britain to 0.4 percent for Italy. Nevertheless, the governments of the four principal debtor nations—Great Britain, France, Italy, and Belgium—believed that the debts should have been canceled altogether. They settled most unwillingly. In 1931 the Hoover Moratorium provided for temporary cessation of all intergovernmental transfers to cope with the international banking crisis that accompanied the depression. After the moratorium expired, the debtors found various excuses not to resume payment on a regular basis. By 1934 every European nation except Finland had defaulted. Congress expressed its displeasure in April 1934 by passing the Johnson Debt Default Act, effectively prohibiting defaulting governments from further borrowing in American markets for several years.

WORLD WARS, PROPAGANDA IN THE. *See* **Propaganda; Psychological Warfare.**

WORLD WAR II. By 1939 isolationism was no longer gospel. Militarist-dominated Japan was by then clearly embarked on the conquest and domination of eastern Asia. Germany was recognized as a danger to the United States, to its neighbors, and to humanity at large. The National Socialists (Nazis) rearmed the nation, reentered the Rhineland (March 1936), forced a union with Austria (March 1938), seized Czechoslovakia with false promises (October 1938–March 1939), made a nonaggression pact with Russia to protect its eastern frontier (Aug. 23, 1939), and then overran Poland (Sept. 1–Oct. 6, 1939), bringing France and Great Britain into the war in consequence of their pledge to maintain Polish independence. In May 1940 a power thrust swept German troops forward through France, drove British forces back across the English Channel (June 4), and compelled France to surrender (June 22). An attack on England, aimed to deny use of Britain as a springboard for reconquest of the Continent, failed in the air and did not materialize on land. Open breach of the nonaggression treaty was followed by a German invasion of Russia in June 1941.

Meanwhile, Japan had been fortifying Pacific islands and encroaching on China, starting open war at Peking in 1937.

The United States opposed Japanese expansion diplomatically by every means short of war, and military staff planning began as early as 1938 to consider that a two-ocean war was bound to come and to calculate that the issues in the Orient would have to be largely decided in Europe. It would be America's safest course in the long run, it was felt, to maintain the integrity of the Western Hemisphere by preventing the defeat of the British Commonwealth, and it was felt that America's eventual western defense line must run from Alaska through Hawaii to Panama.

Rearmament started at home, developing and producing new weapons and new planes, and speeding up motorization of U.S. land forces. The Uranium Committee was created in 1939, the National Defense Research Committee in 1940, and the Office of Scientific Research and Development in 1941 to develop radar and antisubmarine devices. Formation of the Council of National Defense to coordinate industry, finance, transportation, and labor in the event of open war, showed a high-level realization of the seriousness of impending events. Prior to America's formal entry into war, the United States assisted France and Britain by shipping tanks and weapons and by furnishing much material to help equip the British Home Guard. The United States turned over naval destroyers to Britain to hold down the submarine menace, and itself patrolled large areas of the Atlantic Ocean against the German U-boats, with which U.S. ships were involved in shooting incidents. The United States also took over rights and responsibilities at defense bases on British possessions bordering the Atlantic.

In 1940 the invasions of Norway, Denmark, Holland, Belgium, Luxembourg, and France triggered American actions. Military expansion began in earnest.

The Selective Service and Training Act of Sept. 16, 1940, instituted peacetime conscription for the first time in U.S. history, registering 16 million men in a month. Also it brought the National Guard into active federal service to ready it for combat. In July 1940 the Export Embargo Act, which was to be used as a war measure, was passed, followed by the Lend-Lease Act of March 1941 to help prospective allies and others in need of aid. U.S. military leaders strongly preferred to avoid war with Japan. In November 1940 Adm. Harold R. Stark and Gen. George C. Marshall jointly declared that America's major course of action for the time being would therefore be: (a) to rearm; (b) to avoid provoking attack; and (c) to restrict Pacific actions so as to permit major offensive action in the Atlantic theater. In August 1941 Roosevelt and Prime Minister Winston Churchill met at Argentia, Newfoundland, and formulated war plans. For the first time in U.S. history the country was militarily allied before war came. At this meeting was established the Atlantic Charter. In September 1941, the draft act was extended, by a single vote in Congress, and the full training, reorganization, and augmentation of U.S. forces began.

Organization, Preparation, and Strategy. On Dec. 7, 1941, a sneak attack by Japanese carrier-based planes severely crippled the U.S. fleet at Pearl Harbor, dooming American forces in the Philippines. Japan was now free to expand into Southeast Asia and the East Indies toward Australia. The very next day Congress declared war on Japan, and on Dec. 11 met declarations from Italy and Germany—allied to Japan by treaties. Before the month of December was out, Churchill was in Washington, and within weeks there was created the Combined Chiefs of Staff.

Almost instantly on the declaration of war, under the first War Powers Act, there began a reorganization and expansion of the army and the navy, including the National Guard, already in federal service. Cavalry units were transformed into armored forces. New types of troops were formed: mountain units, armored divisions, and airborne divisions. The old square infantry divisions were altered to the new triangular division pattern for greater mobility and increased firepower. New activities were created for psychological warfare, and for civil affairs and military government in territories to be liberated or captured. The air force also underwent a great expansion. Notable was the creation and shipment to England of high-level, precision daylight bombing units. Increasingly the bombing disrupted German factories and rail lines, weakening the entire economy of Germany.

The War Department was completely reorganized in March 1942. Combat branch chiefs were abolished and new broader agencies took over—the air forces, the ground forces, and the services of supply. A new and important operations division was created for strategic planning. The air forces were separated from the army and were represented coequally in staff meetings.

Quickly there came from Congress the first War Powers Act, the second War Powers Act, the Emergency Price Control Act, with its Office of Price Administration, the War Production Board, the National War Labor Board, the Office of War Information, and the Office of Economic Stabilization. Items such as coffee, sugar, meat, butter, and canned goods were rationed for civilians, as were also heating fuels and gasoline. Rent control was established. Two-thirds of the planes of civilian airlines were taken over by the air force. Travel was subject to priorities for war purposes. There was also voluntary censorship of newspapers, under only general guidance from Washington.

It was recognized and accepted that, as Stimson said, "in wartime the demands of the Army enter into every aspect of national life." Local draft boards had great leeway in drawing up standards of exemption and deferment and at first favored agriculture over industry; but soon controls were established according to national needs. By 1945 the United States had engaged more than 16 million men under arms and still improved its economy. It has been calculated that at one time it took half the total resources of the nation in materials and labor to support U.S. forces and to help U.S. allies.

Vitally important was the protection of the delivery of troops and munitions across the Pacific and Atlantic. German submarines were active against all transatlantic shipping and along the eastern coast of the United States. The challenge was met by air and sea action against enemy underwater craft, and by the construction of two great pipelines to bring oil overland to the eastern seaboard. The grand strategy was to defeat Germany while containing Japan.

Campaign in the Pacific. After the strike at Pearl Harbor, the Japanese overran the Philippines, Guam, and Wake. Japan then easily seized Attu and Kiska in the Aleutian Islands in early June 1942. It continued to attract U.S. attention and some troops toward Alaska until its forces were withdrawn in March 1943.

Gen. Douglas MacArthur had been pulled out of the Philippines and sent to Australia. With great skill, MacArthur used American and Australian forces to check Japanese inroads in New Guinea at Port Moresby and land and sea forces to push the Japanese back from spot to spot to take the villages of Buna and Sananada, although not until January 1943. To block a hostile thrust against MacArthur's communications through New Zealand, troops landed in the Solomon Islands, where they took Guadalcanal by February 1943. The push north continued to Bougainville in November 1943 and Green Islands in February 1944, isolating many Japanese stations in the Solomons. MacArthur then leapfroged ground units along the northern coast of New Guinea and west to Morotai by September 1944, employing to the full the new capabilities of modern planes and using amphibious assaults to capture Japanese airfields.

Previously and almost concurrently, the navy with marine and army troops was successfully hitting the Marshall Islands at Eniwetok and Kwajalein, the Gilberts at Makin and Tarawa, and—turning north—the Marianas at Guam and Saipan in June and July 1944, largely bypassing Truk and the Carolines, and leaving them to be mopped up at leisure. To assist the army's move on the Philippines, the navy and marines also struck westward at the Palau Islands in September 1944, and had them in hand within a month. American control of the approaches to the Philippines was now assured. Two years earlier, in the Coral Sea and also in the open spaces near Midway, in May and June 1942, respectively, the U.S. Navy had severely crippled the Japanese fleet. Air and submarine strikes closer in had a serious weakening effect. It was the result of these efforts, equally with the army advance in the New Guinea area, that enabled MacArthur's forces, supported by Adm. William F. Halsey and the Third Fleet, to return in October 1944 to the Philippines on the island of Leyte. Their initial success was endangered by a final, major Japanese naval effort near Leyte, which was countered by a

U.S. naval thrust that wiped out much of the Japanese fleet. Army progress was thereafter steady. Manila and Corregidor fell in February 1945, Mindanao in March.

American land and sea forces were now in position to drive north directly toward Japan itself. Marines had landed on Iwo Jima on Feb. 19 and invaded Okinawa on Apr. 1, both within good flying distance of the main islands. The Japanese navy and air force were so depleted that in July 1945 the U.S. fleet was steaming off the coast of Japan and bombarding almost with impunity.

It had been initially expected that the United States would need the China mainland as a base for an attack on Japan. Japan had dug into Burma and imperiled India. Gen. Joseph W. Stilwell had been sent: (a) to command American forces in China; (b) to serve Chiang Kai-shek as chief of staff; and (c) anomalously, to serve under the British commander of the Burma-India theater of operations. Efforts to reinforce the Chinese against the Japanese on the Asian mainland had not been fully successful. Japanese thrusts forced Stilwell out of China and Burma in disastrous retreat. But the sea and land successes by the spring of 1945 made it possible to think of an actual invasion of Japan without using China. Several factors made for greater and swifter successes than had been planned: (a) employing the fleet as a set of floating air bases, as well as for holding the sea lanes open; (b) the U.S. submarine service's sinking of more than 200 enemy combat vessels and more than 1,100 merchant ships; (c) MacArthur's leapfrogging tactics, letting many advanced Japanese bases simply die on the vine; (d) the air force's bombing ahead of the advancing troops.

Such results had demonstrated great skill in the coordination of air power with land and sea power. The Japanese had foolishly challenged the manpower and the industrial power of the United States, and had been defeated by only that portion of American resources that could be spared for the Pacific area. In spite of the crippling of the U.S. Navy at Pearl Harbor, the United States was simply too strong to be beaten, even though it was fighting another war across the Atlantic.

Campaigns in Africa and Italy. In Europe the United States furnished materials to Britain, air bombardment units, and a small but steadily growing number of ground troops. Also, planes and tanks were sent to bolster the defense of Egypt, threatened by German successes in the Western Desert. Special facilities were set up in the Persian Gulf to furnish tanks and trucks through Iran to the Soviet Union.

Pressures, notably from Russian leaders, early began building for an invasion of the European mainland. There not being sufficient buildup in England for a major attack across the Channel in 1942—even for a small preliminary beachhead—Allied troops invaded northwest Africa from Casablanca to Oran and Algiers on Nov. 8, 1942. After the long coastal strip had been seized and the temporarily resisting French brought to the side of the Allies, the Anglo-American forces pushed east. Air, army, and armor attacks and counterattacks, notably in February 1943 at the Kasserine Pass, ended with the Allied conquest of Tunisia and a great German surrender at Tunis, Bizerte, and Cape Bon on May 12–13, 1943. The operation was conducted with Gen. Dwight D. Eisenhower in command, using a mixed Anglo-American staff. Shortly before this, at their conference in Casablanca in late January, Roosevelt and Churchill called for the "unconditional surrender" of the Axis powers. It would be a war to the finish.

The next step was an Anglo-American invasion of Sicily, beginning July 9, 1943, using large-scale parachute drops and perfected beach-landing skills. On Sept. 3 Italy proper was invaded. Five days later Italy surrendered, but the Germans occupied Rome and took control of the Italian government. After a long check midway up the boot of Italy on a line through Cassino, a dangerous landing was made at Anzio, Jan. 22, 1944. Fierce German counterattacks there were stopped, and a following breakthrough carried U.S. forces past Rome, which fell June 4, 1944, and the next month to the line of Florence and the Arno River, the British on the east and the Americans on the west. Thereafter, Italy ceased to be the scene of major strategic efforts; troops were diverted to support the Normandy invasion by a landing in southern France.

Campaigns in France, Germany, and the Low Countries. For the principal invasion of France, an inter-Allied planning staff had been created in March 1943 in London. In May the first tentative attack date was set—early May of the following year—for what was called Operation Overlord. That same summer some U.S. troops from the Mediterranean theater began to be withdrawn and shipped to England. There was a one-month delay in the target date for the invasion of France, to secure more landing craft and more troops to make a broader beach base for the initial thrust. Finally, after a day's further delay owing to bad weather conditions, on June 6, 1944, the greatest amphibious invasion in history was launched across the English Channel, involving more than 5,300 ships and landing craft. It was on the Normandy coast, from the Cherbourg peninsula to the mouth of the Orne, that the landings were made at selected beaches, the Second British Army and the First Canadian Army on the east and the American First Army on the west. All ground forces were under the command of British Gen. Bernard L. Montgomery, with Eisenhower as Supreme Allied Commander. The landing force was assisted and protected by costly but successful landing by parachute and glider of 12,000 British and American troops.

The steady stream of men and materials was seriously interrupted only once, when a four-day storm prevented beach debarkations. By that time, there were over 600,000 Allied troops ashore. By June 27 Cherbourg had fallen; and the U.S. forces had a seaport and were ready to spin about and head south.

The Germans had been reinforcing their positions, although badly hampered by aerial bombardments of road and rail lines and convoys in motion. There followed a month of almost pedestrian fighting. Then, late in July, the American infantry and tanks pierced the enemy line near Saint-Lô and swung rapidly to the southwest toward Coutances, capturing outflanked German troops.

The Germans reacted to this penetration by finally drawing their reserve Fifteenth Army out of the Calais area, where it had been held by the threat of a second landing. They struck directly west across the American front. This effort was blocked by Bradley's forces; the British pushed slowly but inexorably southwards; the American First and Third armies mostly abandoned the drive in Brittany and Brest and raced eastwards toward Paris. At the same time they circled northeast around Falaise, vast numbers of Germans were killed or captured. German resistance in northern France crumbled. On Aug. 25 Paris fell with scarcely a battle.

The German withdrawal was generally successful. In spite of the enormous American support buildup on the Normandy beaches, in spite of emergency supply by airplane, and in spite of immobilizing some units to use their trucks to carry food, ammunition, and gasoline to the most forward units, forward supply was seriously lacking to U.S. forces.

A landing was made in southern France on Aug. 15, 1944, by a Franco-American force. It swept up the Rhone Valley, made contact with the previously exposed right flank of the racing American Third Army, and then turned east and northeast to extend the front of the U.S. forces. By September, a German army in southwest France had surrendered. Also by September the general American eastward advance was checked, largely because the U.S. forces had run ahead too fast for their supplies. German units halted the major Allied offensive (Sept. 17–25) to capture the Rhine bridges at Arnhem. But France was almost completely liberated from German occupation.

The overall strategic idea was to make the final major Allied effort over the Rhine north of Cologne and through the relatively open country north of the Ruhr. Aachen fell in October. Applying pressure on their left, the Americans thinned their center. There the Germans struck hard on Dec. 16 in the wooded and hilly Ardennes, in a final bid with a newly trained and reorganized force. The Americans swung their Third Army south near Bastogne in southeast Belgium, and received reserves from the British. At the peak of the German penetration—not far from the Meuse River—leading German units, out of gasoline, were captured. On the U.S. side, losses had been serious; but by Jan. 1, every lost tank and artillery piece had been replaced from the American supply pipeline. Germany, like Japan, could not match the weight of U.S. industrial support. In bitter January weather, the Germans stubbornly resisted, but the Battle of the Bulge was their final major effort. They had used up their last major resources and had failed.

From bases in Britain and from bases successively in North Africa and Italy, American bombers had struck at the heart of the German economy. By large-scale air raids, a decisive proportion of German oil production was knocked out. Except for a short campaign in December 1944, German planes had ceased to be a threat. German flying bombs (V-1) and rockets (V-2) continued to blast Britain until their installations were overrun in late March 1945, but they had no effect on ground operations or on air superiority as a whole.

In February 1945 the American armies struck out into the Palatinate and pushed the German forces back across the Rhine. The enemy destroyed bridges as they retreated—all but one. On Mar. 7 a unit of the U.S. First Army approached the great railway bridge at Remagen, downstream from Koblenz, found it intact, dashed over it, and tore the fuses from demolition charges. Plans had not existed for a crossing here, but the opportunity was promptly exploited. Troops were moved over the bridge for several days until it collapsed from damage, but by then pontoon bridges were in place. The U.S. east bank holdings were slowly expanded against sharp German resistance.

The northern crossing of the Rhine was effected on Mar. 22, 1945.

Germany had now practically collapsed. The British on the American left raced toward Hamburg and the Baltic. The U.S. First Army pressed through to Leipzig (Apr. 20), and met the Russians on Apr. 25, 1945, at Torgau on the Elbe River, which had been established by the Yalta Conference as part of the boundary with the Russians. The U.S. Third Army dashed toward Bavaria to prevent possible German retreat to a last stand in the south. The southernmost flank of the American forces swung southwards toward Austria at Linz and toward Italy at the Brenner Pass. The U.S. Seventh Army on May 4 met the Fifth Army at the Brenner Pass, coming up out of Italy where German resistance had likewise collapsed. Germany asked for peace and signed it at Allied headquarters at Rheims on May 7, 1945.

Surrender of Japan. Progress in the Pacific theater by this time had been substantial. U.S. ships and planes dominated sea and air close to Japan. Protracted cleanup operations against now-isolated Japanese island garrisons were coming to a close. American planes were bombing Tokyo regularly. A single raid on that city on Mar. 9, 1945, had devastated 16 square miles, killed 80,000 persons, and left 1.5 million people homeless. But the Japanese were still unwilling to surrender. Approved by Roosevelt, scientists working under military direction had devised a bomb based on atomic fission. A demand was made upon Japan on July 26 for surrender, threatening with repeated warnings the destruction of eleven Japanese cities in turn. The Japanese rulers scorned the threats. Then President Harry S. Truman gave his consent for the use of the atomic bomb, and on Aug. 6 Hiroshima was hit, with 75,000 people killed. There were more warnings, but still no surrender. On Aug. 9 Nagasaki was bombed. Two square miles were wiped out and 39,000 people killed. Five days later, on Aug. 14, the Japanese agreed to surrender. The official instrument of surrender was signed on Sept. 2, 1945, on board the battleship *Missouri* in Tokyo Bay.

WORLD WAR II, NAVY IN. *See* **Navy, U.S.**

WORMLEY CONFERENCE (1877). The name grew out of the fact that the conference was held at Wormley's Hotel in Washington, D.C. This conference resulted in the Wormley Agreement that the Democrats would permit the counting of the electoral votes that would make Rutherford B. Hayes president of the United States, and that in return the Republicans would withdraw federal troops from the southern states, thus consenting to the overthrow of the carpetbag governments in these states.

WOUNDED KNEE, BATTLE OF (Dec. 29, 1890)**.** The last important clash of Indians with U.S. troops, at Wounded Knee, S.D., was a massacre, rather than a battle, during the Messiah War. Chief Sitting Bull had been killed on Dec. 15, 1890, by Indian police sent to arrest him. Some of Sitting Bull's followers then came into the Standing Rock Agency in southern North Dakota to surrender, while others fled west to join Chief Big Foot, a leader in the Ghost Dance religion, whose band had been augmented by other Sioux caught up in the wave of enthusiasm for the cult. They numbered 120 men and 230 women and children. On Dec. 29, when the Indians were being disarmed, a shot was fired—it is uncertain by whom. The cavalrymen opened fire with rifles and Hotchkiss guns, which poured two-pound explosive shells among the Indians, killing about 300 Indians. The casualties of the soldiers were 29 dead and 33 wounded. Wounded Knee, which ended the resistance of the Indians on the western Plains to white settlement, was the final fight between Indians and the U.S. Army.

WRITS OF ASSISTANCE. Search warrants issued to the customs officers by the superior courts of the various colonies. First issued in Massachusetts in 1751, neither the issue nor the use of such writs seems to have excited controversy until 1761, when new writs were applied for as the old ones were expiring. There was some delay but the writs were issued (1762) after instructions had been received from England supporting their legality. That closed the controversy in Massachusetts. The Townshend Revenue Act (1767) authorized writs of assistance, but did not specify form. A form was prepared similar to the one that had been granted in Massachusetts. Every customs officer in America was sent a copy of the desired writ and directed to request the attorney general of his colony to secure such writs from the superior court. There was delay in most of the courts, and the issue dragged through 1768 to 1772. This resulted in a direct refusal by the courts of Connecticut, Rhode Island, New York, New Jersey, Pennsylvania, Maryland, Virginia, and North Carolina, although the judges offered to issue writs in particular cases. In some cases the refusals stated that the forms presented to the judges were novel and unconstitutional. Finally in 1772 the customs officers reported that they had secured writs in East Florida, West Florida, South Carolina, Bahama, Bermuda, New Hampshire, Nova Scotia, and Quebec. It was the raising of the issue that made writs a common grievance as stated in the Declaration of Independence. (*See also* Unreasonable Searches and Seizures.)

WYANDOTTE CONSTITUTION (1859)**.** The constitution under which Kansas became a state was drafted at Wyandotte (now Kansas City, Kans.) by the first territorial convention in which Republicans and Democrats participated (July 5–29) and was adopted by popular vote on Oct. 4. It prohibited slavery, and reduced Kansas to its present boundaries. (*See also* Lecompton Constitution.)

WYOMING. Means in Indian "at the end of the plains." Before 1865, occupancy of the area had been limited to Indians (Oglala and Brulé Sioux, Arapaho, Cheyenne, Crow, and Shoshone), some mountain men, and some soldiers. Congress created Wyoming Territory in 1868 and made Wyoming the forty-fourth state, with the same boundaries as the territory, in 1890. Westward progress of Union Pacific railroad construction prompted formation of the territory from parts taken from the Dakota, Idaho, and Utah territories. Several settlements sprang up along the railroad in southern Wyoming—Cheyenne, Laramie, Rawlins, Rock Springs, Green River, and Evanston. For many years Wyoming appeared to be a "thoroughfare rather than a destination," as people poured through South Pass in covered wagons and, later, eighty miles south, in Union Pacific trains. Not more than 10 percent of the 9,118 persons counted in the census of 1870 were still living in the territory in 1880, although the population had doubled in the decade. Thereafter, the open-range cattle industry provided permanent economic activity.

Slow growth has generally characterized the territory and state of Wyoming. The people have earned their livelihood by grazing cattle and sheep; producing oil and coal; working for the Union Pacific; catering to tourists, trout fishermen, and hunters of wild game (mule deer, antelope, elk, moose, and bear); and, since World War II, mining trona and uranium. National forests, which cover one-seventh of the state, and two national parks (Yellowstone and Grand Teton) have played major roles in the important tourist industry.

Because Wyoming has ranked among the five leading oil states since 1960, not a few men have become immensely wealthy from oil discoveries, but most of the people have found it necessary to work hard merely to survive. Feeling dependent on protective tariffs and preferring conservative solutions for their problems, the majority of Wyoming voters have been affiliated with the Republican party. Without any silver and with only a few rebellious dirt farmers among them, they stayed on the fringes of the Populist movement in the 1890's. Likewise they avoided the mainstream of progressivism that followed populism in the early 20th century. Republicans have usually dominated all three branches of the state government. Democrats did control the legislature in 1935 and 1937, and they have shared control on other occasions. In 1980, the population was 470,816.

WYOMING MASSACRE, or the **Battle of Wyoming** (July 3, 1778)**.** A battle in eastern Pennsylvania between Butler's Rangers, commanded by the Loyalist Maj. John Butler, and the Connecticut settlers in the Wyoming Valley, under Col. Zebulon Butler. The able-bodied men of the settlement were with Gen. George Washington's army, but Zebulon Butler, home on furlough, gathered the families in Forty Fort on June 30 after learning of the British approach. On July 3, Butler led the small garrison of about 300, the majority of whom were boys and old men, against a force four times their number. The thin line held, then, overwhelmed by the Indians, broke into confusion. The wounded were slain on the spot or killed later. Barely sixty people escaped to surrender on July 4.

WYOMING VALLEY, SETTLEMENT OF. According to Connecticut's charter of 1662, its territory reached across the continent in a narrow strip from Narragansett Bay to the Pacific Ocean. But Charles II granted part of the same area to the Duke of York in 1664, and still another part to William Penn in 1681 (*see* Pennsylvania). In the early 1750's the Connecticut general assembly received several petitions from persons who wished to settle within Connecticut's charter limits (*see* Connecticut's Western Lands). In 1753 the Susquehanna Company was formed, at Windham, Conn., to buy land, colonize, and evangelize the Indians. The section chosen, called Wyoming Valley, is located on the Susquehanna River, within present Pennsylvania. In 1754 the company purchased a large tract from the Six Nations, and in the same year the general assembly gave approval to the plan for settlement. The French and Indian War (1754–63), together with the intervention of Pennsylvania and Sir William Johnson, superintendent of Indian affairs, interfered with settlement until 1762, when the first settlers were sent out. The Indians drove them out in October 1763, and no further attempt at settlement was made until 1769, when more than 100 settlers, led by Maj. John Durkee, arrived. There followed many years of strife, called the Pennamite War (*see* Yankee-Pennamite Wars). The entire group of settlements was officially set up as the town of Westmoreland in Litchfield County, in 1774, and two years later, declared to be a separate county of Connecticut. One of the last acts of the Pennsylvania proprietary government was the unsuccessful invasion of the valley in December 1775. The Wyoming Valley settlers supplied many men for the Continental army during the revolutionary war. This so depleted the number of able-bodied men at Wyoming that there was very little protection against Indians and Tories (*see* Wyoming Massacre). In December 1782 five impartial commissioners, appointed by Congress to settle the land title controversy by arbitration, decided in favor of Pennsylvania. The settlers who held land through the Susquehanna Company were loath to be dispossessed. Finally, the Pennsylvania legislature passed the Compromise Act of 1799, by which Pennsylvania claimants in the Wyoming Valley were paid off and titles in the seventeen Connecticut townships established before 1782 were confirmed to the Connecticut settlers on payment to Pennsylvania of a certain sum per acre.

XYZ AFFAIR (1797–98). Incensed at the negotiation by the United States of Jay's Treaty with Great Britain (1794), France issued decrees against American shipping and refused to receive Charles Cotesworth Pinckney, the American minister. President John Adams held to a pacific course and sent a mission to Paris composed of Pickney, John Marshall, and Elbridge Gerry. The American ministers arrived on Oct. 4, 1797, just after their supporters in the French legislature had been destroyed by a coup d'état. The Directory's armies were victorious in Italy and the Rhineland, and Charles Maurice de Talleyrand-Périgord, the new foreign minister, thought he could take advantage of the bitter feud between Federalists and Democratic-Republicans in the United States. Talleyrand received the envoys unofficially on Oct. 8 and stated they would have an audience with the Directory as soon as a report could be prepared on American affairs. Weeks of official silence ensued. Meanwhile, three unofficial agents of the foreign minister—later referred to in dispatches as X, Y, and Z—called on the Americans suggesting a gratuity of $250,000 for Talleyrand, a loan to France, and an indemnity for Adams' criticism of France in a speech to Congress. The ministers were willing to consider a payment to Talleyrand after a treaty had been signed, and they even proposed that one of them return to confer with Adams regarding a loan, provided the Directory would cease its attacks on American shipping and negotiate with the two ministers who remained. Not even these concessions could secure the reception of the ministers by the Directory.

The publication of its ministers' dispatches by the American government created a stir. The incident was given a mysterious quality by the substitution of the letters X, Y, and Z for the names of Talleyrand's agents. The Federalists made political capital of the situation, and Congress abrogated the treaties of 1778, suspended commercial relations with France, authorized the seizure of armed French vessels, and strengthened the nation's naval and military forces. Talleyrand, thoroughly alarmed, sought to prevent a declaration of war. The policy he and Adams then pursued led to the Convention of Sept. 30, 1800.

YACHT RACING. The sport gained its formal start in the saloon of John C. Stevens' sloop *Gimcrack* on July 30, 1844, where nine gentlemen met to form the New York Yacht Club under Commodore Stevens. In 1851 George Steers designed the *America* on pilot schooner lines for Stevens and a syndicate of New York Yacht Club members with the understanding that if the *America* could not beat any other yacht, regardless of size, at home or abroad, the syndicate need not accept it. It was sailed across the Atlantic to challenge Britain's fastest. The cup it won is still called the America's Cup. By 1975 American yachts had defended it successfully twenty-one times. The most persistent challenger was Sir Thomas Lipton, who tried five times with successive yachts named *Shamrock* to "lift the mug." In 1934 Thomas O. M. Sopwith in the *Endeavour* came closest to winning but lost to Harold S. Vanderbilt's *Rainbow* with Sherman Hoyt at the wheel. At first the cup races were sailed in schooners and then later in sloops over 100 feet long with towering topmasts and huge jackyard topsails. In 1931 the J-Class boats were introduced, the biggest and fastest of which was Vanderbilt's *Ranger,* built for the 1937 series to defeat Sopwith's *Endeavour II.* Since World War II the America's Cup races have been sailed in 12-meter (44-foot) yachts.

Ocean Racing. After *America*'s trip abroad, a number of wealthy yacht owners campaigned overseas. Characteristic of this period was the ocean race of December 1866, in which the *Henrietta* beat the *Fleetwing* and the *Vesta* from Sandy Hook, N.J., to Cowes, England, in under fourteen days, for a purse of $90,000. The climax of big boat racing came in 1905 when Kaiser Wilhelm II sponsored a race from Sandy Hook, N.J., to the Lizard peninsula in England, in which the

185-foot, three-masted schooner *Atlantic* defeated ten others. The *Atlantic* set a record that still stood in 1975—twelve days, four hours, and one minute. In 1906 Thomas Fleming Day, editor of *Rudder,* promoted a race from New York City to Bermuda in small boats manned by amateurs and commanded by their owners. The *Tamerlane* led the way to a series of Bermuda races in the same tradition. Except for a hiatus during wars, the Bermuda race has been sailed in even years and attracts fleets of over 175 starters. The record passage was sailed by the *Ondine* in four hours short of three days.

In 1928 a significant ocean race was run from New York City to Santander, Spain. The small class was won by the *Niña,* designed by W. Starling Burgess to the handicap rule then in use. Since then, the rules have become increasingly complex and designers increasingly ingenious in devising fast boats with low ratings. One of the leaders in this design competition was Sparkman and Stevens of New York, whose *Dorade, Stormy Weather, Mustang,* and *Finisterre* set and held many records. The Cruising Club of America, cosponsor of the Bermuda race, developed a measurement rule in America and the Royal Ocean Racing Club developed one in Britain. After ten years of compromise, the two clubs in 1970 brought out the International Offshore Rule (IOR), which has been progressively revised. Almost every year American yachts start in the Fastnet race, the Honolulu race, the Sydney-Hobart race, the Admiral's Cup race, or one of the many special transoceanic contests run under the IOR.

Class Racing. Before 1850 time allowances, when used at all, were figured against tonnages, calculated by the same formula used for commercial vessels. The British then adopted Thames Measurement (TM), which encouraged deep and narrow yachts. This was superseded in 1887 by the Dixon Kemp Rule and in 1906 by the International Rule, under which yachts are grouped in classes such as 6-meters, 8-meters, and 12-meters. Each class is governed by a formula that allows some variation within the rule but is supposed to produce yachts that can race on an even basis. Under this rule the America's Cup races are sailed in 12-meters. After the development of the Star boats in 1911, a movement grew in America around the concept of a one-design class. Each yacht was to be exactly like every other yacht in the class, built to the same molds and rigged to identical specifications. Nathanael G. Herreshoff was one of the leaders in this movement, but other designers followed. In 1974 there were at least 256 different one-design classes under 40 feet long.

Olympic Racing. The hottest competition in one-designs comes in the Olympic races. The oldest Olympic class still racing in the 1970's was the Star, first used in Olympic competition in 1932 and won by the United States in 1932, 1948, 1956, and 1968. The Dragons were introduced in 1948, won in 1968 by the United States. Finns and 5.5's superseded 6-meters. The 5.5's were dominated by the United States in 1952 and 1960. The Flying Dutchman class, small, delicate, and highly tuned, has never been won by Americans, but H. ("Buddy") Melges of the United States won the Soling class in 1972.

YADKIN RIVER SETTLEMENTS. The Yadkin River valley of North Carolina was settled after 1740, although Henry McCulloh received an extensive grant of land in that region in 1737. In 1745 Arthur Dobbs and John Selwyn bought 400,000 acres from the McCulloh estate, and the following year a few families moved to the west of the Yadkin. About 1750 a few Germans settled along the Yadkin, and in 1753 Moravians from Bethlehem, Pa., planted the Wachovia Colony and founded three towns—Betharaba, Bethania, and Salem. From that date to the outbreak of the American Revolution, thousands of Scotch-Irish and Germans moved to the valley.

YAKIMA INDIAN WARS (1855–58). The Yakima, in alliance with the Klikitat, started a war with settlers in 1855 under the chieftain Kamaiakan, of the Yakima. In August 1855 parties of prospectors passing through Yakima country were attacked. When the Indian agent A. J. Bolon went alone to confer with Kamaiakan, he was killed. A small detachment of regulars under Maj. Granville O. Haller left the Dalles to arrest the murderers but was forced to retreat. All regulars from the western posts were put into the field, and companies of volunteers were called from Oregon and Washington. Regulars under Maj. Gabriel J. Rains and volunteers under J. W. Nesmith jointly invaded the Yakima country during November–December 1855. Although there was no decisive engagement, they swept the Indians from the country. At the same time, Col. James K. Kelly conducted a campaign in the Walla Walla Valley. There he became involved in a winter campaign, which ended, for the regulars, after a four-day battle in early December. The Indians were driven across the Snake River, but the poorly equipped and poorly provisioned volunteers endured a severe winter in the Indian country. The war had many outcroppings in widely separated regions. The regular army was aroused from its indifferent handling of the war by a defeat suffered under Col. Edward J. Steptoe in the Spokane country in May 1858. The military authorities then recognized the seriousness of the situation and pushed the war rigorously. Col. George Wright, in charge of the campaign in the Spokane country, broke the power of the Indians and forced them to submission in the early fall of 1858.

YALE BAND. The name given to the group of seven students from the Theological Department of Yale College who on Feb. 21, 1829, signed an agreement expressing their readiness to go to the state of Illinois to establish a seminary of learning. As a result of their labors Illinois College was established at Jacksonville in 1829, and numerous Presbyterian and Congregational churches were formed.

YALE UNIVERSITY. Founded in October 1701. Classes were first taught at Killingworth, now Clinton, Conn., in the house of the first rector, the Rev. Abraham Pierson. After Pierson's death in 1707, the college moved to Saybrook, and in 1716 to New Haven. Two years later, Elihu Yale sent nine bales of East India goods, which, when sold, brought the college £562 12s; and the institution, in gratitude, took his name. The Anglo-Irish philosopher George Berkeley (later bishop of Cloyne) gave the college his farm in Rhode Island and a collection of valuable books in 1731–33. The first brick building, Connecticut Hall (still standing), was built in 1752; the first professorship, a chair in divinity, was established in 1755; others in mathematics, physics, and astronomy were added in 1771. In 1975 the university comprised twelve schools: Yale College (1701); School of Medicine (1810); Divinity School (1822); Law School (1824); Graduate School (1847); School of Art (1865); School of Music (1894); School of Forestry and Environmental Studies (1900); School of Architecture (1913); School of Nursing (1923); School of Drama (1955); and School of Organization and Management (1975). Yale had the first gallery of fine arts among American colleges (1832) and also conferred the first degree of doctor of philosophy (1861). Its Sheffield Scientific School was established in 1858. The *Yale Literary Magazine* (1836) is the oldest monthly magazine in the United States; the *Yale Daily News* (1878) is the oldest college daily paper. In 1975 Yale was a university of about 9,400 students, of whom 4,900 were enrolled in the undergraduate school, which became coeducational in 1969. Women were first permitted to enroll in the Yale Graduate School in 1892 for the Ph.D. degree.

YALTA CONFERENCE (Feb. 4–11, 1945). President Franklin D. Roosevelt, British Prime Minister Winston Churchill, and Soviet Marshal Joseph Stalin met at Yalta, at a turning point of World War II, when the imminent collapse of Germany made it necessary to make plans for administering Europe. After amicable discussions Roosevelt, Churchill, and Stalin announced publicly on Feb. 11 agreement on the occupation of Germany by the United States, Great Britain, the Soviet Union, and France in four separate zones; a conference of the signatories of the United Nations Declaration to open at San Francisco Apr. 25, 1945, for the purpose of establishing a world peace organization; a (then secret) big-power voting formula in the new organization; an eastern boundary of Poland mainly following the Curzon Line (which gave the Soviet Union about one-third of prewar Poland), for which Poland was to be compensated by unspecified German territory in the north and west, and a new, freely elected, democratic Polish government; and freely elected democratic governments for other liberated European nations. A supplementary secret agreement provided for Soviet entry into the war with Japan in two or three months after Germany surrendered, and in return British and American acceptance of the status quo of Outer Mongolia; restoration to the Soviet Union of its position in Manchuria before the Russo-Japanese War (1904–05), with safeguarding of Soviet interests in Dairen, Port Arthur, and the Manchurian railways; and the cession to the Soviet Union of the Kurile Islands and the southern half of Sakhalin Island.

YAMASEE WAR (1715–16). The Indians of southeastern South Carolina were becoming increasingly incensed about encroachments on their land. At dawn, Apr. 15, 1715, possibly urged on by Spaniards, they killed about ninety traders and their families in the vicinity of Port Royal. Subsequently Yamasee bands raided plantations. Most of the Indian nations between Saint Augustine and Cape Fear, and some in the interior, allied themselves with the Yamasee. Aided by supplies from New England and a few troops from North Carolina and Virginia, South Carolina gradually gained the upper hand; in the autumn the Yamasee were driven far southward into Florida. Although a peace was signed in January 1716, the Lower Creek remained openly hostile and migrated westward to obtain protection of the French at Mobile.

YANKEE. A privateer brig from Bristol, R.I., with eighteen guns and 120 officers and men. During the War of 1812, it cruised off Halifax, Nova Scotia, and in the south Atlantic and took eighteen prizes worth nearly $1 million. In two later voyages under Elisha Snow the *Yankee* cruised off Ireland and in the Atlantic with success, one prize (the *San Jose Indiano*) netting $500,000. In six voyages it captured British ships worth $5 million.

"YANKEE DOODLE." A popular American national air or march. The origin of the tune, like that of the words, is uncertain. It is supposed to have been introduced to the colonies by an English fife major of the Grenadier Guards about 1750, played in a Philadelphia ballad opera in 1767, and played by English bands in America as early as 1768. The words probably originated after 1764 and it is likely that they were embodied in their present form about 1775.

YANKEE NOTIONS. After 1700, a large number of small articles—such as brooms, pots, pans, tongs, roasting ovens, brass and copper utensils, clocks, spinning wheels, wooden bowls, and plates—were made in New England during the winter months when farming was impossible. As soon as roads were passable in the spring, peddlers would set out with one-horse carts full of these articles for the far South or for the western frontiers. The fame of these small wares, or Yankee notions, thus spread throughout the country.

YANKEE-PENNAMITE WARS (1769–72, 1775, and 1784). Settlers under Connecticut titles and under Pennsylvania titles disputed their claims by force. In 1769 the Pennsylvanians dispossessed Maj. John Durkee from the blockhouse and fort at Wilkes-Barre. The next spring the Connecticut settlers, led by Lazarus Stewart and his Paxton Boys, recaptured the fort. In 1771 Stewart, or one of his party, killed an attacking Pennamite, and the leader of the Paxton Boys fled to Connecticut. By the summer of 1772 the Connecticut people had gained permanent possession of the region, and peaceful settlement began. There was a threat of renewal of the war in December 1775, when a sheriff in Northumberland County led a militia troop against the Wyoming settlements, but he was repulsed. In 1784 the second so-called Pennamite-Yankee War broke out when local authorities of Pennsylvania, acting in close cooperation with Pennsylvania claimants, dispossessed those holding Connecticut titles. (*See* Wyoming Valley, Settlement of.)

YAP MANDATE. When the mandates system was established at the end of World War I, Japan was given the mandate over former German possessions in the Pacific lying north of the equator. This included the Marshall, Mariana (Ladrone), and Caroline islands. Among the last group was the small island of Yap, in which the United States was interested because of its proximity to Guam and the Philippines and its position as the connecting link for cable communication to and from the Far East. Although agreeing to a Japanese mandate over these islands, President Woodrow Wilson had reservations against the inclusion of Yap, desiring instead that it be put under special international control, and formal protest was made against this feature of the mandate to Japan, to the other principal Allied powers, and to the League of Nations Council. The controversy was settled during the Washington Conference on the Limitation of Armaments (1922), when the United States formally agreed to the terms of the Japanese mandate, including expressly the island of Yap, and obtained from Japan complete equality with respect to the cables.

YAZOO-CHATTAHOOCHEE LINE. Running between the rivers named was the northern limit of British West Florida by Order in Council, March 1764. Important as a factor in Spain's boundary dispute with the United States, 1783–95, which was settled by Pinckney's Treaty, it became the first northern boundary of Mississippi Territory in 1798.

YAZOO FRAUD (1795). Georgia legislature enacted a law selling 35 million acres of its western lands, comprising the present states of Alabama and Mississippi, to four land companies for $500,000. The sale was a corrupt bargain. Nearly all the Georgia legislators who voted for the law had been bribed by agents of the land companies. It soon became a public scandal, in part because of the efforts of James Jackson, a prominent Georgia politician who resigned his seat in the U.S. Senate to campaign for the repeal of the 1795 law. Jackson accomplished this objective in 1796, when a newly elected Georgia legislature revoked the sale. Georgia's repeal of the corrupt sale effectively denied the 35 million acres to the speculators, but the Yazoo fraud became a national political and legal issue for nearly twenty years.

YAZOO PASS EXPEDITION (Feb. 6–Apr. 12, 1863). Failing in their frontal attack on Vicksburg, Miss., during the Civil War, the Union forces sought to turn Vicksburg's right flank. Opposite the Union base at Helena, Ark., the levee was blasted, and an amphibious expedition composed of six gunboats and transports with 800 troops set out across the flooded upper Yazoo Delta, hoping to reach the high ground east of the Yazoo River. After extricating themselves from frequent log jams in the old pass and chopping their way through overhanging branches along the Coldwater and the Tallahatchie, the troops were blocked just short of their objective by an improvised Confederate battery behind cotton bales, which the Confederates called Fort Pemberton. Gen. Ulysses S. Grant hastily dispatched a force to save them from capture, while Adm. David D. Porter and Gen. William Tecumseh Sherman launched a much larger expedition into the waterways of the lower Yazoo Delta as a diversion. (*See also* Vicksburg in the Civil War.)

YELLOW CREEK MASSACRE. *See* **Cresap's War.**

"YELLOW-DOG" CONTRACT. An agreement signed by a worker in which he promises not to join a union while working for a company. Such agreements, often called ironclad documents in the late 19th century, were first used during the period of labor unrest of the 1870's. Companies used these agreements to prevent unions from securing a base in their firms. But there were those inside and outside the labor movement who wanted to protect the right of a worker to join a union, and by the 1890's fifteen states had enacted laws that prohibited "yellow-dog" contracts. In addition, Congress passed the Erdman Act in 1898, which outlawed the "yellow-dog" contract as a condition of employment on the railroads. But the U.S. Supreme Court in 1908 (*Adair* v. *United States)* declared unconstitutional the Erdman Act provisions dealing with the "yellow-dog" contract, while in 1915 (*Coppage* v. *Kansas)* it voided a similar state law. As unions attempted to expand in the 20th century, use of the "yellow-dog" contract increased. In the Norris–La Guardia Anti-injunction Act passed in 1932, Congress declared that "yellow-dog" contracts were in conflict with public policy. After the passage of the Wagner Act in 1935, the National Labor Relations Board ruled that an employer was engaging in an unfair labor practice if he demanded that workers sign such an agreement.

YELLOW FEVER. In *The History of New England* (1647) by John Winthrop, the first reference is found to yellow fever in America. The effort of the Massachusetts court on that occasion to exclude from Massachusetts the crew and the cargo of the ship that had brought the fever (Barbados distemper) from the West Indies to America was the colonies' initial enforcement of quarantine. British ships that had sailed from Boston in an unsuccessful effort to capture Martinique brought back an epidemic of yellow fever in 1694, and subsequently, despite its endemic focus on the African coast, yellow fever emerged as a peculiarly American disease ("the American plague"). It spread through America as the African slave trade increased and proliferated. The worst American epidemic of yellow fever occurred in 1793, in Philadelphia.

In 1900 the U.S. Army Yellow Fever Commission, with Walter Reed, James Carroll, Jesse W. Lazear, and Aristides Agramonte, was sent to track the pestilence in Cuba. The group, working with the aid of Carlos J. Finlay, demonstrated Finlay's theory that the infection is transmitted by the bite of the female *Aëdes aegypti* mosquito. William Crawford Gorgas, chief sanitary officer of the Panama Canal Commission from 1904 until 1913, eliminated the mosquito in the region of the canal and made possible the building of the Panama Canal. The last epidemic of yellow fever in the United States occurred in New Orleans in 1905. Vaccines against the disease were developed in the early 1940's and are required of anyone traveling to a hazardous area.

YELLOW JOURNALISM. A term applied to sensationalism in news presentation, first used in the 1880's. Advertising paid a large share of the publishing costs, and since space rates were based on distribution, there was constant pressure to increase the number of subscribers. After his purchase of the *New York World* in 1883, Joseph Pulitzer used high-pressure methods to accomplish this end. One of his innovations was a Sunday edition, carrying special articles and comic strips. One of the strips featured a character called the "Yellow Kid," and from this character the name "yellow journalism" was derived.

YELLOW PERIL. A racial epithet fashionable in Europe and America in the late 19th and 20th century. Its historical roots can be traced to the persistent theme in Western culture that the barbarian hordes of Asia, a yellow race, were always on the point of invading and destroying Christendom and Western civilization. The specifics of the yellow peril mania are evident in the Chinese Exclusion Acts, passed between 1880 and 1904; and they received strong currency in treaties and enactments with Japan, especially the treaty of 1894, and also after the Russo-Japanese War in the Immigration Act of 1907 as well as the Gentlemen's Agreement in the same year. United States treaties with Japan in 1911 and 1913 contributed to the yellow peril idea, as did Woodrow Wilson at Versailles (1919) when he refused to support a social equality clause on behalf of Japan in the postwar settlement. The yellow peril fear peaked in 1924 when Congress ended the Gentlemen's Agreement by excluding all Asian aliens from U.S. citizenship.

***YELLOWSTONE*.** The first steamboat to navigate the upper Missouri River, between Omaha, Nebr., and Fort Union, Mont., was built at Louisville, Ky., for the American Fur Company. In 1831 it reached Fort Tecumseh (Pierre, S.D.) after a difficult trip.

YELLOWSTONE NATIONAL PARK. The world's first national park, Yellowstone is 3,468 square miles (2,219,823 acres) of scenic grandeur in Wyoming, Montana, and Idaho. Its establishment by act of Congress, signed Mar. 1, 1872, by President Ulysses S. Grant, marked the start of the national-park movement. Yellowstone was still the country's largest national park in 1975. Its 3,000 hot springs and 200 geysers, including the popular Old Faithful, are the world's largest concentration of thermal features. Its wildlife include grizzly and black bears, elk, bighorn mountain sheep, moose, antelope, coyotes, occasional wolves and mountain lions, the country's only continuously wild herd of buffalo, and the once nearly extinct trumpeter swan and 240 other species of birdlife. The park was administered by the U.S. Army from 1886 to 1918. Visits in 1975 totaled 2,246,132.

YELLOWSTONE RIVER EXPEDITIONS (1819–25). Secretary of war John C. Calhoun planned to overawe British fur traders and the Indians of the upper Missouri. Five steamboats were commissioned to ascend the Missouri, and to carry the expedition of 1,100 men commanded by Gen. Henry Atkinson. Unfortunately the steamboats were unsuited for Missouri navigation. Two turned back at the start; only one reached Council Bluffs, in what is now Iowa, halfway to the Yellowstone, and only after voyaging the entire summer of 1819.

Continued Indian attacks on fur traders resulted in a second expedition in 1825 with 476 men under Atkinson, accompanied by Benjamin O'Fallon, Indian agent. Among subordinate officers were Henry Leavenworth, Stephen W. Kearny, and Bennett C. Riley, western soldiers whose names are perpetuated in forts Leavenworth, Riley, and Kearny. Atkinson's party traveled in eight keelboats, arrived at the Yellowstone in August, and returned the same season. This show of force enabled O'Fallon and Atkinson to conclude treaties with fifteen tribes.

YELLOW TAVERN, BATTLE AT (May 11, 1864). As Union forces pressed southward during the last phase of the Civil War, Gen. Philip H. Sheridan left Gen. Ulysses S. Grant's army near Spotsylvania, Va., on May 9, 1864, and rode for Richmond via Beaver Dam Station. He had under his command the divisions of Gen. David Gregg; Gen. James Wilson; and Gen. Alfred Torbert, the latter division commanded by Gen. Wesley Merritt because of Torbert's illness —a total of 10,000 horsemen. Pursuing with 5,000 cavalry, Confederate Gen. J. E. B. Stuart headed off Sheridan's force at Yellow Tavern, six miles north of Richmond. Stuart placed Gen. Lunsford L. Lomax's brigade on his left and Gen. Williams C. Wickham's on his right. They were attacked by Merritt and later by Wilson and Gregg. Lomax's line was broken, and there Stuart was mortally wounded.

YERBA BUENA. *See* **San Francisco.**

YORK (Pa.). A city in southeastern Pennsylvania, was the capital of the United States from Sept. 30, 1777, to June 27, 1778. As the British, under Gen. William Howe, occupied Philadelphia, Congress deemed it wise to move west of the Susquehanna River. During this period John Hancock resigned the presidency of Congress, and Henry Laurens succeeded him; the Articles of Confederation were drawn up; Gen. John Burgoyne surrendered at Saratoga; and Baron Friedrich Wilhelm von Steuben joined the American forces.

YORK, ATTACK ON (1692). Led by Madokawando, 150 Abnaki warriors attacked the frontier town of York, Maine, on Jan. 25, 1692. Of a total population of 500, about 50 were killed, and about 80 were made captives.

YORK, CAPTURE AND DESTRUCTION OF (1813). After the commencement of the War of 1812, Commodore Isaac Chauncey's fleet, with a force under Gen. Zebulon M. Pike, sailed from Sackets Harbor, N.Y., on Apr. 25 to attack York (now Toronto), Ontario. The Americans landed on Apr. 27. The riflemen under Maj. Benjamin Forsyth were the first ashore and advanced to attack the enemy, 700 regulars under Gen. Roger H. Sheaffe. The main body of troops led by Pike forced the British to retreat. The Americans captured one of the batteries and were a short distance from the main works when a powder magazine was exploded, killing about a hundred Americans and forty of the enemy. Pike was mortally wounded. Sheaffe and his regulars retreated toward Kingston. The remaining defenders capitulated. After destroying many military stores the Americans evacuated the post on May 8 and soon it was reoccupied by the British. The American forces under Chauncey and Col. Winfield Scott recaptured the fort without opposition on July 30.

YORK'S, DUKE OF, PROPRIETARY. King Charles II decided to conquer New Netherland and to bestow it on his brother James Stuart, Duke of York. After purchasing the claims of the heirs of Sir William Alexander, Earl of Stirling, to Long Island and northern Maine, the king conveyed to the duke in March 1664, several months before the conquest of New Netherland, a proprietary stretching from the Connecticut River to the Delaware River and Delaware Bay, including Martha's Vineyard, Nantucket, and Long Island and the part of Maine between the St. Croix and the Pemaquid. The duke's charter made him lord proprietor with complete authority to rule his province. All legislative, executive, and judicial power was vested in him, subject only to appeal to the king. He delegated his authority to governors, whom he carefully instructed about policy. Regions preponderantly English were governed by laws of neighboring colonies, drawn up in a code called the Duke's Laws. Although he at first denied petitions for representation, he later instructed his governor, Sir Edmund Andros, to call an assembly, which met for a few sessions in 1683–85 and adopted the Charter of Liberties.

Even before the conquest of New Netherland, the duke leased to his friends John, Lord Berkeley of Stratton, and Sir George Carteret the rich farmlands of the Jerseys. In 1664 another piece was to go to Connecticut, whose charter of 1662 overlapped the duke's grant. Long Island was also included in both grants. The commission headed by Col. Richard Nicolls assigned Long Island to New York in 1667 but surrendered to Connecticut the lands west of the Connecticut River to within twenty miles of the Hudson. When the duke's province was restored to him in 1674, after the conquest of the Dutch, he instructed Andros to assume jurisdiction over western Connecticut. Connecticut refused to recognize these claims until 1687, when Connecticut was incorporated into the Dominion of New England.

The duke's possessions on the west bank of Delaware Bay were given to William Penn in 1682. In 1682 York executed two leases, one for New Castle and the land within a radius of twelve miles and the other for the land to the south as far as Cape Henlopen. These lands were not included in his charter, but from the time of the conquest of New Netherland, he considered himself possessor by right of conquest of all lands taken from the Dutch. The duke made an effort to obtain a royal grant, and received one on Mar. 22, 1683. Doubt as to its validity prompted the duke, after his accession to the throne as James II in 1685, to plan to grant Penn a royal charter, but he was prevented by his abdication in 1688. The last sizable outlying section of the duke's proprietary to go was Pemaquid, which, as the County of Cornwall, was added to the Dominion of New England in June 1686.

YORKTOWN (Va.). The land along York River was patented by Nicholas Marteau (or Martiau), a Walloon, soon after his first appearance in Virginia in 1621. York County, then called Charles River County (the name was changed in 1642), was one of the eight original shires of Virginia, set up in 1634. In 1691 Benjamin Reade, a grandson of Marteau, sold the colony fifty acres of his ancestral tract, on which a port was to be located, for 10,000 pounds of tobacco. The town thus founded quickly became the county seat, and in 1697 a courthouse was built there. The first customhouse in America was built in Yorktown in 1706. Yorktown's prosperity as a port was destroyed by the revolutionary war, though it gained a permanent place in history as the site of Gen. Charles Cornwallis' surrender in October 1781, ending the war. Strategically located, it was besieged by Union Gen. George B. McClellan during the Peninsular Campaign of the Civil War, in 1862, and evacuated by the Confederates. In the 20th century Yorktown's original prosperity revived somewhat through nearby naval establishments and tourism.

YORKTOWN CAMPAIGN (Aug. 30–Oct. 19, 1781). The decisive fighting that won independence for the thirteen colonies at Yorktown, Va. The campaign was sired by the frustrations British Gen. Charles Cornwallis experienced in his 1780–81 southern campaign. Unable to defeat American Gen. Nathanael Greene, Cornwallis looked for greater success in Virginia, where 4,200 men had been sent from New York by the British commander in chief, Gen. Henry Clinton. Commanded by Gen. William Phillips and Benedict Arnold, the British were carefully watched by 1,500 Americans under Marie Joseph du Motier, Marquis de Lafayette.

Cornwallis marched from Wilmington, N.C., with 1,500 veterans of his southern venture. Reaching Petersburg, Va., on May 20, he took command of troops demoralized by the death of Phillips on May 13. Dismissing Arnold and inspirited by more fresh troops from New York, giving him 7,200 men altogether, Cornwallis moved against Lafayette's slender force. Lafayette adeptly disengaged, retreating toward oncoming Gen. Anthony Wayne and 1,000 Pennsylvania Continentals; Wayne and Lafayette met on June 10 near the Rapidan River as Gen. Friedrich Wilhelm von Steuben approached with 450 recruits. The increase of Lafayette's forces to 3,200 men sapped the offensive spirit of Cornwallis, who swerved toward the James River and was followed by an emboldened Lafayette. At Jamestown a skirmish checked Lafayette on July 6.

Meanwhile, Clinton, with 16,700 men at New York, thought himself menaced by Gen. George Washington's 8,500 troops, augmented by 4,756 French regulars commanded by Jean Baptiste de Rochambeau. By repeated orders Clinton told Cornwallis to hasten 3,000 troops by sea to New York. Cornwallis began looking for a harbor suitable for embarkation. Cornwallis on July 26 selected Yorktown and then quickly commenced earthworks to hold Lafayette's 4,760 men at bay until the British fleet could arrive. On Aug. 21

Washington detached twelve of his battalions under Gen. William Heath to watch Clinton and then slipped away so adroitly that the allied army was two weeks gone before Clinton realized it. After touching Chesapeake Bay's Head of Elk and Annapolis, the allies were assisted by light vessels from de Grasse in concentrating with Lafayette to start a formal siege of Yorktown on Sept. 28. The French portion, bolstered by three regiments from their Caribbean garrison plus some marines from their fleet, put in line 7,800 regulars. Washington had 5,640 Continentals and 3,200 Virginia militia. The allied total was about 17,000.

Early in September, de Grasse and his fleet had won what became a vast strategic victory in the Battle of the Virginia Capes. Unmenaced by the British fleet, Washington and Rochambeau husbanded men by careful, time-consuming siegework. After opening the first parallel on Oct. 6, the allies made their way inward to within 300 yards of the British earthworks by Oct. 11. The second parallel was close enough for a charge. A night attack led by Col. Alexander Hamilton on Oct. 14 pushed in the British left that had been strongly set above the York River. Unless the British fleet could intervene, the end was inevitable. Cornwallis, erroneously thinking himself abandoned, opened surrender negotiations on Oct. 17. Two days later (Oct. 19) the British troops at Yorktown formally surrendered.

YOSEMITE NATIONAL PARK. Located in the California High Sierra country and consisting of 1,189 square miles (760,917 acres). Capt. Joe Walker's trappers discovered much of the area around Yosemite in 1833, but there is no record of a white man entering Yosemite Valley until William Penn Abrams, a millwright, did so in 1849. State volunteers, under Maj. James D. Savage, explored and named the hidden vale in 1851. In 1864 President Abraham Lincoln signed an act of Congress granting Yosemite Valley and the Mariposa Grove of giant sequoia trees to California on condition that the areas be held for public use. In 1890 Congress authorized Yosemite National Park—about 2 million acres surrounding the Yosemite Valley state park. In 1905 California ceded Yosemite Valley to federal control, and boundary changes eventually reduced the park to its present size. From 1891 to 1916 the park was administered by the U.S. Army. From 1901 to 1913 Yosemite was the center of a bitter conservation controversy over San Francisco's building of a dam on the Tuolumne River for water and power.

"YOUNG AMERICA." A phrase generic to the period 1840–1852, designating anything that exhibited the youthful spirit of energy and enterprise characteristic of the times. Historically, it was a concept related to ideas of capitalistic progress and romantic individualism. Also an aggressively nationalistic term, it combined democratic universalism with the notion of manifest destiny espoused by elements in the Democratic party. Intermingling with these sources was political Young Americanism, beginning with Edwin de Leon, influenced by younger party leaders and by George Henry Evans, and culminating in the Young America Democratic faction (1851–56). The latter sought to revitalize its party by uniting all sections on a platform of free trade, foreign markets, a subsidized merchant marine, annexation southward, and the encouragement of republican movements abroad.

YOUNG MEN'S AND YOUNG WOMEN'S HEBREW ASSOCIATIONS (YM-YWHA). The first Young Men's Hebrew Association (YMHA), organized in 1854 in Baltimore, Md., was an outgrowth of Jewish literary societies. The facilities of early YMHAs consisted mainly of reading rooms. Immediately after the Civil War, YMHAs began to develop rapidly, especially in the South and Midwest. When Jewish immigrants from eastern Europe came to America in unprecedented numbers between 1881 and 1910, the YMHAs offered classes in citizenship and English. The first Young Women's Hebrew Association (YWHA) was established in New York City in 1888. They grew rapidly, but gradually the YWHA joined with the YMHA to form the YM-YWHA. After two abortive attempts to organize nationally, the Council of Young Men's Hebrew and Kindred Associations was organized on Nov. 2, 1913. During World War I, YMHAs rallied their resources around the Jewish Welfare Board, which had been set up to serve Jewish personnel in the U.S. armed forces. In 1921 the council merged with the Jewish Welfare Board, which has since acted both as the national arm of the YM-YWHAs and as the agency for service to Jewish military personnel. After World War II the YM-YWHAs broadened their character to become Jewish community centers. In the mid-1970's more than 400 YM-YWHAs served over 1 million American Jews.

YOUNG MEN'S CHRISTIAN ASSOCIATION (YMCA). The first YMCA in the United States was formed in Boston in 1851 by T. V. Sullivan, following the plan of a society organized in London in 1844 by George Williams. Forty more units were organized in the United States within the next three years, and an international convention was held at Buffalo, N.Y., in 1854. Thereafter, annual conventions took place until the Civil War disrupted the movement. After the war a period of rapid growth ensued and buildings that served both as residential hotels and as religious, cultural, and recreational centers were built in many cities. During World War I the YMCA handled nine-tenths of the welfare work among the American forces in Europe. During the five years following the war, it gave educational assistance to more than 100,000 former servicemen studying in schools and colleges. In World War II the YMCA was one of the six organizations that founded the United Service Organizations (USO). Religious and other services to prisoners of war were provided under the auspices of the World Alliance of YMCAs in both world wars. By 1974 there were 8.7 million registered constituents—36 percent of them women and girls —in 1,842 member associations across the United States. Such long-standing programs for youth and adults as water safety and other physical education enrolled 4.5 million persons in 1974. The Y-Indian Guides and Princesses, for fathers and sons, mothers and daughters, had increased their membership to 510,000.

YOUNG PLAN. The popular name of a plan recommended by a committee of experts, in its report of June 7, 1929, for the final settlement of the German reparations due as a result of World War I. This plan was largely adopted by the governments concerned. Its popular name was derived from the fact that Owen D. Young, one of the American experts, was elected chairman of the committee. The Young Plan set forth a schedule of annuity payments by Germany that, it was thought, would be within the capacity of that country to pay and established the machinery for transferring such payments in the form of the Bank for International Settlements. In 1932 over 90 percent of the reparations that were to have been paid under the Young plan were canceled.

YOUNGSTOWN (Ohio). An industrial city with a population of 115,436 according to the 1980 census. The Mahoning River runs through the city, and is lined on both banks with steel mills and steel-working factories. Youngstown ranks fourth among all American steel and pig-iron producing cities, and also includes electrical and metal machine shops and a large rubber factory. Youngstown was first settled in 1797 by a party of pioneers headed by John Young on land bought from the Connecticut Land Company. It was part of the Western Reserve of Connecticut. Iron was produced as early as the 1820's, but the first genuine steel mill at Youngstown was not built until 1892. The city grew substantially during the 20th century, as demand for steel increased. Youngstown lost population during the 1950's and 1960's. Partly because of the declining city population, and partly because of problems in getting school tax rates approved by the taxpayers in 1968, Youngstown became the first major American city to close down its public schools for part of the academic year.

YOUNG WOMEN'S CHRISTIAN ASSOCIATION OF THE UNITED STATES OF AMERICA (YWCA). First established in Great Britain in 1855, the YWCA reached the United States in 1858. The National Board of the YWCA of the U.S.A. was formed in 1906. Its headquarters are in New York City. Active in both World War I and World War II, in 1941 the YWCA of the U.S.A. became one of six national organizations that organized the United Service Organizations (USO). By 1975 YWCA programs were offered in 6,400 locations, including more than 400 community associations, 200 campus YWCAs, and 200 registered YWCAs. Members and program participants totaled 2.45 million. The multifaceted YWCA is aimed at helping to develop the full potential of the women it serves—most of whom are between the ages of twelve and thirty-five. The YWCAs provide residential halls, classes, athletic programs, recreational facilities, and lectures and forums on subjects of interest to women.

YOUTH ADMINISTRATION, NATIONAL (NYA). Established by executive order on June 26, 1935, as a division of the Works Progress Administration (WPA). It remained under WPA jurisdiction until 1939, when it was housed under the Federal Security Agency until its dissolution in September 1943. Roosevelt established the NYA to devise useful work for some of the estimated 2.8 million young people who were on relief in 1935. NYA activities took two directions: the student work program for youths in school (elementary to graduate) and out-of-school employment for the needy unemployed between the ages of sixteen and twenty-four.

YOUTH MOVEMENTS. The largest manifestations of student activism in the period before World War I were settlement-house work and support for Christian missionary endeavors. More than 12,000 volunteers, most of them college students, were working in settlement houses in lower-class urban neighborhoods. The Student Volunteer Movement, founded in 1886 as an offshoot of the Young Men's Christian Association, was primarily concerned with sponsoring and recruiting young people for missionary work. During the early 20th century the most dynamic political organization active on campuses was the Intercollegiate Socialist Society (ISS), founded in 1905 and later renamed the League for Industrial Democracy. The ISS had about 1,300 undergraduate members before World War I. Campuses first became prominent centers of radical activity in the 1930's, with the main focus on foreign policy. Communist party members and sympathizers played an important role, especially through the American Student Union (1935–40), formed through a merger of the Communist-led National Student League (1932–36) and the student affiliate of the social-democratic League for Industrial Democracy. An estimated 500,000 students took part in demonstrations or rallies against war in 1936. A large number of students took the Oxford Pledge, promising refusal to fight in a war if the United States became involved. The only important student group in the 1950's was the National Student Association (NSA), established in 1946, which soon came to depend on covert funding from the Central Intelligence Agency; subsidies were given in the belief that the NSA, which was fairly liberal, could be a credible front for the U.S. government in dealing with foreign student groups.

The long period of quietude was broken in the winter and spring of 1960 when students at black colleges in the South held sit-ins at whites-only lunch counters demanding the right to equal service. The Student Nonviolent Coordinating Committee (SNCC) was founded at this time by representatives of student protest groups across the South. These demonstrations stimulated support activities by sympathetic students on predominantly white northern campuses. In five years SNCC became an organization of full-time field workers challenging racial discrimination. During part of the early 1960's the flourishing concern, especially on northern campuses, with issues of war and peace was reflected mainly in opposition to nuclear testing. The Student Peace Union (founded 1959) reached its peak of activity in 1961–62, with about 2,000 members. Another theme of student activism was voiced in the free speech movement at the University of California, Berkeley, in the fall of 1964, in which participants criticized the modern state university as being factorylike in its operation and purposes. By the mid-1960's, the campus-based movement known as the New Left had emerged. Growing out of the civil rights movement and the free speech movement, it was greatly stimulated by the escalation of the Vietnam War in 1965. The New Left, which had as its main organizational vehicle the Students for a Democratic Society (SDS), was unique among American radical movements in that it centered on young people. SDS broke off its nominal affiliation with the social-democratic League for Industrial Democracy in 1965 and did not affiliate with any other political group. The New Left placed major emphasis on racial oppression at home and on alleged American imperialism abroad, rather than on class issues. It also assumed the trappings of a rebellious youth culture. It was the main political current on campuses in the late 1960's. Even though SDS disintegrated in 1969, spontaneous campus protest remained strong through the 1969–70 school year. The American invasion of Cambodia in 1970 (coupled with the killing of four Kent State University students by the Ohio National Guard) touched off the greatest wave of campus protests in American history, and hundreds of colleges were closed by protesting students or worried administrators.

YPRES-LYS OPERATION (Aug. 19–Nov. 11, 1918). In July 1918 the American Twenty-seventh Division, under Gen. John F. O'Ryan, and the American Thirtieth Division, under Gen. Edward M. Lewis, were placed in line with the British Second Army, near Ypres (or Ieper), Belgium. Following a British attack, the American divisions from Aug. 31 until Sept. 2 advanced some 2,000 yards, capturing Lankhof Farm and Voormezeele and occupying Vierstraat Ridge and parts of Mont Kemmel and Wytschaete Ridge. In October the Thirty-seventh Division, under Gen. Charles S. Farnsworth, and the Ninety-first Division, under Gen. William H. Johnston, were withdrawn from the American First Army and sent to reinforce the French Sixth Army, advancing toward Brussels. From Oct. 30 to Nov. 4 the Thirty-seventh Division, attacking east, cleared Cruyshautem Ridge and crossed the Scheldt River at Eyne and Heurne. On its right the Ninety-first Division flanked and captured Spitaals-Bosschen and took Audenarde. Returning to line Nov. 9, the Ninety-first crossed the Scheldt, and both divisions had progressed some distance east of it by Nov. 11. Each division suffered about 1,600 casualties in the Belgian operations.

YUCATÁN. In 1848 a revolt of the Maya threatened the upper class in Yucatán. As the state government was at odds with the central government of Mexico, it appealed for help to the United States, Great Britain, and Spain, offering sovereignty over Yucatán to any power that might respond. In April 1848, President James K. Polk asked Congress authority to send help and stated that the United States could not consent to the transfer of Yucatán to any European power. This declaration against a transfer of territory even by voluntary action of its inhabitants involved a new interpretation of the Monroe Doctrine, which has been referred to as the Polk Doctrine. Neither Great Britain nor Spain showed any inclination to accept the annexation proposal. The Maya revolt was eventually suppressed.

YUKON. A river that rises in British Columbia, flows northwest through Yukon Territory, and then across Alaska. In 1842 the Russian Lavrenti Alekseev Zagoshkin explored part of the river. In 1850 Robert Campbell of the Hudson's Bay Company descended the river from Fort Selkirk to Fort Yukon, proving the identity of the Yukon. In 1866 Robert Kennecott surveyed a route for the Western Union Telegraph Company. In 1873 gold seekers began to arrive. The Klondike gold rush in 1896 and later gold rushes influenced conditions in the Yukon region. In 1898 the U.S. Geodetic Survey mapped the delta of the Yukon. Although the Yukon River is used for salmon fishing and for hydroelectric power, it was still largely undeveloped in the 1970's.

YUMA, FORT. From the late 18th century the Yuma operated a crude ferry service at the confluence of the Colorado and Gila rivers, for travelers between California and Sonora and Santa Fe. After the Treaty of Guadalupe Hidalgo between the United States and Mexico in 1848, U.S. boundary surveyors and their military escort camped on the California side at this Indian ferry, and in 1849 John Glanton and other Americans are said to have seized the ferry from the Indians and operated it for emigrants. The hostile conduct of the Yuma toward the ferrymen and westbound emigrants led to the establishment of a permanent military camp on the California side. On Nov. 27, 1850, Maj. Samuel P. Heintzelman, in charge of U.S. troops brought from San Diego, named the new post Camp Independence, but in March 1851 the name became Camp Yuma. Abandoned in December 1851, it was reoccupied on Feb. 22, 1852, as Fort Yuma. Fort Yuma flourished as a station on early stagecoach lines beginning in 1857. The lands included in the military reservation of Fort Yuma lay at first partly in California, partly in Arizona; this was changed on June 22, 1874, when the land on the Arizona side was given to the Department of the Interior. The fort, on the California side, was turned over to the same department on June 9, 1884, for use as an Indian school.

YUROK. A native American culture in northwestern California and adjacent coastal Oregon. The area had several tribal groups speaking different and unrelated languages but with similar life modes. These included the Yurok and Wiyot, Algonkin-speakers; the Karok, speaking Hokan; and the Hupa and Tolowa, Athapascan-speaking tribes. These tribes lived as small population enclaves along the beaches and in the valleys fronting the northwestern California coast. Culturally, the groups may be classed as basically Californian, possessing the strong sense of separatism characteristic of the area, as well as acorn dependence and basketry elaboration. On the other hand, unlike tribes in the rest of California, the Yurok and their neighbors were influenced by the rich culture of the Northwest Coast. Modified plank houses and salmon dependence suggest regions farther north, as do a dependence and emphasis on wealth.

ZANE'S TRACE AND GRANTS. In 1796 Congress authorized President George Washington to contract with Ebenezer Zane to build a trace through Ohio. This was first a bridle path from the Ohio River at Wheeling to Limestone (later Maysville), Ky. The path east of Zanesville later was developed into the National Road. For locating and building the trace, Congress gave Zane the privilege of locating military warrants on three sections of land amounting to 1,920 acres. The first of these was at the Muskingum River, the second at the Hocking River, and the third at the Scioto River.

ZARAH, FORT. Built in September 1864 by Gen. S. R. Curtis on the left bank of Walnut Creek, about four miles east of the present town of Great Bend, Kans. Its purpose was to furnish the army with a base for operations against hostile Kiowa and Comanche. It was abandoned in 1869.

ZENGER TRIAL. William Cosby, colonial governor of New York, provoked an opposition party. This group established John Peter Zenger as printer of the *New York Weekly Journal,* first published Nov. 5, 1733. Strictures published in this paper led the governor to have Zenger arrested. His cause became that of the people, and when the governor arbitrarily debarred his New York counsel, his case was taken by Andrew Hamilton of Philadelphia. It was tried Aug. 4, 1735. The printer was charged with seditious libel. Hamilton admitted the publication, but denied that it was a libel unless false and sought to prove the truth of the statements. The court held that the fact of publication was sufficient to convict and excluded the truth from evidence. Hamilton made an eloquent appeal to the jury to judge both the law and the fact, and the verdict was "not guilty." Zenger was released. It set a precedent against judicial tyranny in libel suits.

ZIMMERMAN TELEGRAM (1917). German submarine action during World War I resulted in U.S. severance of diplomatic relations with Germany on Feb. 3, 1917. On Feb. 24 the British delivered to the U.S. ambassador in London an intercepted German telegram, dated Jan. 19, declaring that unrestricted submarine warfare would begin on Feb. 1. The note, sent by German Foreign Secretary Arthur Zimmerman to the German minister in Mexico, expressed the fear that the United States would not remain neutral and directed the minister to arrange an alliance between Mexico and Germany and to urge Japan to switch to the German side. Mexico was to attack the United States on its southwestern border and recover Texas, New Mexico, and Arizona. The publication of the note on Mar. 1 was an important factor in the declaration of war against Germany.

ZINC. *See* **Nonferrous Metals.**

ZION NATIONAL PARK. Established in 1919, in an area of southwestern Utah. Its central feature is Zion Canyon, a deep gorge in which many layers of rock have been exposed. Zion National Park is also notable for unusual rock formations, some of which are brilliantly colored.

ZOAR SOCIETY. Organized by 225 German Separatists who emigrated from Württemberg in 1817 under the leadership of Joseph Michael Baumler. They founded Zoar, in Tuscarawas County, Ohio, in that year, and in 1819 they formed the Separatists Society of Zoar. All property was communally owned, and the farms, shops, and factories were managed by regularly elected trustees. The society attained its greatest prosperity in the 1850's. It was dissolved in 1898.

ZOLLVEREIN TREATY, WHEATON'S (1844). Henry Wheaton, chargé d'affaires and minister to Prussia, 1835–46, labored for eight years to negotiate a commercial reciprocity treaty between the United States and the German Zollverein, or economic union, composed of Prussia and eighteen German inland states. After all the members of the Zollverein assented to the treaty, it was signed on Mar. 25. The Committee on Foreign Relations of the U.S. Senate reported, June 14, against ratification, and the treaty was rejected.

ZONING ORDINANCES. Regulate the uses to which property may be put, the height and bulk of structures, the area of a lot that may be occupied, and the density of population on the lot. Zoning regulations are uniform within a district but vary from one district to the next. A typical zoning ordinance also contains provisions for special-use permits, administrative variances and adjustments in case of hardship, and the continuation and elimination of existing nonconforming uses. The first comprehensive zoning ordinance was adopted in New York City in 1916. Stimulated by the publication in 1924 of a standard zoning enabling act by the U.S. Department of Commerce and the rapid adoption of state enabling authority throughout the country, zoning spread quickly. While some early zoning was attempted through eminent domain, zoning ordinances have been adopted under the police power. Their basic constitutionality was sustained in numerous cases, notably the landmark decision in 1926 of the U.S. Supreme Court in *Village of Euclid* v. *Ambler Realty Company* (272 U.S. 365).

ZOOLOGICAL PARKS. The Philadelphia Zoological Garden, opened July 1, 1874, has been called America's first zoo. The Lincoln Park Zoological Gardens (Chicago) and the Cincinnati Zoo opened the following year. Since many zoos began as local parks housing a few native animals, it is impossible to assign a definite establishment date for many zoos.

From their start in the United States, zoos consisted of animals in barred and fenced cages. In 1907 at Stellingen, Germany, Karl Hagenbeck constructed a zoo featuring spacious enclosures in which animals were confined by hidden moats. The St. Louis Zoological Park incorporated many such exhibits into its construction (1921). The Detroit Zoological Park (opened Aug. 1, 1928) and the Chicago Zoological Park, or Brookfield Zoo (July 1, 1934), were constructed entirely along the lines of these new concepts. The Works Progress Administration helped greatly in the construction and expansion of U.S. zoos during the Great Depression. On Oct. 8, 1924, the American Association of Zoological Parks and Aquariums (AAZPA) was established.

New approaches to the exhibition of animals constantly appear. The Arizona-Sonora Desert Museum at Tucson, Ariz., presents an in-depth view of all facets of the Sonora Desert region. The Sedgwick County Zoo in Wichita, Kans., is largely devoted to ecological themes with an ethological interpretation. The New York Zoological Park (Bronx Zoo), established in 1899, opened World of Darkness (1969) and

World of Birds (1972), which explain the factors affecting the lives of nocturnal animals and birds, respectively.

ZOUAVES. A corps of the French army first raised in Algeria in 1831 exclusively from the tribe of that name. Their unusual drill and uniform were popularized in the United States by Col. Elmer E. Ellsworth. In the Civil War Ellsworth's First New York Fire Zouaves (Eleventh New York Infantry) attracted much attention, but it was mustered out a year after the death of its colonel in 1861. The Zouave idea was soon abandoned.

ZUNI. A tribe of village-dwelling Indians in New Mexico. They were discovered in 1539 by Marcos de Niza, a Franciscan friar, and his guide Estevan. A story was current in Mexico that seven cities, rich in gold, lay in a country to the north, called Cibola. Seven Zuni towns were found by the Marcos party, but Estevan, leading the advance, was killed, whereupon Marcos turned back. The next year Francisco Vasquez de Coronado led an army into the country, which found no difficulty in capturing the Zuni towns. The Spanish exercised intermittent control over them. In 1680 the Zuni numbered 2,500, occupying three villages instead of seven, and by the 20th century they occupied only a single village. The Zuni, like the Hopi, are a strongly matrilineal society, the individual acquiring clan membership through his mother. The Zuni stress the element of the secret society, initiated by males acting as priests to carry on the ceremonies to bring the rain so necessary to an agricultural system in a desert.

ZWAANENDAEL COLONY, or **Swaanendael** ("Valley of Swans"). Founded on the west shore of Delaware Bay near present Lewes, Del., in 1631. Samuel Godyn, Samuel Blommaert, and Kiliaen Van Rensselaer obtained privileges from the Dutch West India Company for the establishment of this colony and secured the services of David De Vries, an experienced navigator, by making him a partner. Capt. Pieter Heyes landed at Lewes Creek in the spring of 1631 in the ship *Walvis ("Whale")* with twenty-eight men and supplies. In the fall, a palisaded building called Fort Optlandt was erected. While De Vries was making preparations to sail to the Delaware River in the spring of 1632, news was received that all in the settlement had been massacred by Indians.